Official Guide to
Bed & Break[...]
Guest Accommodat[...]

There's something different
around every corner

England

English Tourism Council

The English Tourism Council

The English Tourism Council is the national body for English Tourism and is funded by the Department for Culture, Media and Sport. Its role is to support the business of tourism and to drive forward a long-term vision for the industry. It will do this by working to improve the quality of England's tourism experience - for example, by working to increase standards in accommodation and service quality across the industry - to strengthen competitiveness and to encourage the wise growth of tourism. The ETC is a strategic body brokering partnerships, setting standards, developing policy, providing research and forecasts, and championing issues at the highest level.

Cover Pictures:
Front Cover: Lavenham Great House, Lavenham, Suffolk
Back Cover: (from top) Rowanfield Country Guest House, Ambleside, Cumbria
Burbush Farm, Burley, Hampshire
Bettmans Oast, Biddenden, Kent

Photo Credits:
Cumbria - Cumbria Tourist Board
Northumbria - Northumbria Tourist Board, Graeme Peacock, Mike Kipling, Colin Cuthbert and Michael Busselle
North West - North West Tourist Board, Cheshire County Council, Lancashire County Council, Marketing Manchester
Yorkshire - Yorkshire Tourist Board
Heart of England - Heart of England Tourist Board

East of England - East of England Tourist Board Collection
South West - South West Tourism
South of England - Southern Tourist Board, Peter Titmuss, Chris Cove-Smith and Iris Buckley
South East England - South East England Tourist Board, Chris Parker and Iris Buckley

Published by: The English Tourism Council, Thames Tower, Black's Road, Hammersmith, London W6 9EL.
ISBN 0 86143 226 6
Publishing Manager: Michael Dewing
Technical Manager: Marita Sen
Compilation & Production: Guide Associates, London
Design: Jackson Lowe Marketing, Lewes, East Sussex
Typesetting: Tradespools Ltd, Somerset and Jackson Lowe Marketing, Lewes
Maps: © Maps In Minutes™ (1999)
Printing and Binding: Acorn Web Offset Ltd, Normanton, West Yorkshire
Advertisement Sales: Jackson Lowe Marketing, 23 Cliffe High Street, Lewes, East Sussex BN7 2AH. (01273) 487487
© English Tourism Council (except where stated)

Where to Stay in England 2001
Contents

WELCOME TO WHERE TO STAY
How to find your way around the guide including colour maps

PLACES TO STAY AND THINGS TO DO
Accommodation entries, places to visit, regional tourist board contact details and travel to the area

FURTHER INFORMATION
Detailed information on accommodation ratings, guidance on how to book, events and more

KEY TO SYMBOLS
A key to symbols can be found on the inside back cover.
Keep it open for easy reference.

A Warm
Welcome

Welcome to our 26th edition – it's so easy to use, and packed with information.

For short breaks, family holidays, touring holidays or business stop-overs *Where to Stay* is all you need. This guide contains over 10,000 places to stay in a wide choice of locations at prices to suit all budgets.

You'll also find
- ideas about what to do while you're away
- advice and information on booking your accommodation
- colour location maps
- local Tourist Information Centre telephone numbers
- information on events throughout the country

How to use
The Guide

The guide is divided into the 10 English Regional Tourist Board regions (these are shown on page 13). Within these sections you will find a brief introduction to the area, contact details for the Regional Tourist Board, information about places to visit during your stay, and clear information entries on accommodation within the region. Accommodation is listed alphabetically in order of place name. If you would like to know more about the city, town or village in which you wish to stay, you will find brief descriptions at the end of each regional section. Or you can contact the local Tourist Information Centre - the telephone number can be found next to the town name on the accommodation entry pages.

Finding your
Accommodation

Whether you know exactly where you want to stay or only have an idea of the area you wish to visit, it couldn't be easier to find accommodation to suit you in *Where to Stay* You can find your accommodation in several ways:

BY PLACE

if you know the town or village look in the comprehensive town index at the back.

BY AREA

if you know the area look at the full colour maps starting on page 16. All the places in black offer accommodation featured in this guide.

BY REGION

if you know which part of England look in the relevant regional section. These are colour coded at the top of each page. A map showing the regions can be found on page 13.

BY COUNTY

if you know which English county look at the county listing on page 14 to find the region it is in.

Exclusive accommodation listings

Where to Stay is the only guide to contain details of ALL guest accommodation which has been quality assessed by the English Tourism Council, giving you the widest choice of accommodation.

Types of Accommodation

Guest accommodation is featured in this guide which includes Guest Houses, Small Hotels, Bed and Breakfast, Farmhouses and Inns.

Within each entry you will find a brief description of each property and facilities available.

(We publish a separate guide for hotel accommodation).

Accommodation
Ratings & Awards

Ratings and awards are an indication of quality which help you find the most suitable accommodation to meet your needs and expectations. You'll find several in this guide:

DIAMOND RATINGS FOR QUALITY

The English Tourism Council's quality assurance scheme awards **One to Five Diamonds** giving you reliable information about the quality of the accommodation you can expect. (See opposite). You'll find something to suit all budgets and tastes.

SPECIAL AWARDS FOR EXCELLENCE

Gold and Silver Awards - Part of the English Tourism Council scheme, Gold and Silver Awards are given to establishments achieving the highest levels of quality within their Diamond rating. So if you're looking for somewhere special, turn to page 9 for a list of Gold Award holders which have an entry in the regional sections of this guide. Silver award holders are too numerous to list, but they are clearly indicated in the accommodation entries.

The annual **England for Excellence awards** are the Oscar's of the tourism industry. Details of nominees and winners for 2000 can be found on page 12.

NATIONAL ACCESSIBLE SCHEME FOR SPECIAL NEEDS

Establishments which have a **National Accessible rating** provide access and facilities for wheelchair users and people who have difficulty walking. Turn to page 10 and 11 for further details.

How do we arrive at a Diamond rating?

The English Tourism Council has more than 50 trained assessors throughout England who visit properties annually, generally staying overnight as an anonymous guest. They award ratings based on the overall experience of their stay, and there are strict guidelines to ensure every property is assessed to the same criteria. High standards of housekeeping are a major requirement; heating, lighting, comfort and convenience are also part of the assessment.

THE ASSESSOR'S ROLE - GUEST, ASSESSOR AND ADVISOR

An assessor books their accommodation as a 'normal' guest. He or she will take into account all aspects of the visiting experience, from how the telephone enquiry is dealt with to the quality of the service and facilities on offer.

During their stay the assessor will try to experience as many things as possible including the quality of food, the knowledge of staff and services available. They will even check under the bed!

After paying the bill the assessor reveals who they are and asks to look round the rest of the establishment. The assessor will then advise the proprietor of the Diamond rating they have awarded, discussing the reasons why, as well as suggesting areas for improvement.

So you can see it's a very thorough process to ensure that when you book accommodation with a particular Diamond rating you can be confident it will meet your expectations. **After all, meeting customer expectations is what makes happy guests.**

Ratings you can trust

When you're looking for a place to stay, you need a rating system you can trust. The English Tourism Council's ratings give a clear guide to what to expect, in an easy-to-understand form. Properties are visited annually by trained, impartial assessors, so you can have the confidence that your accommodation has been thoroughly checked and rated for quality before you make your booking.

DIAMOND RATINGS

Ratings are awarded from One to Five Diamonds. The more Diamonds, the higher the quality and the greater the range of facilities and level of service provided. The brief explanations of the Diamond ratings outlined here show what is included at each rating level (note that each rating also includes what is provided at a lower Diamond rating).

♦　　　　Clean and comfortable accommodation offering as a minimum, a full cooked or continental breakfast. Other meals, if provided, will be freshly prepared. Towels are provided and heating and hot water will be available as reasonable times. An acceptable overall level of quality and helpful service.

♦♦　　　A higher level of quality and comfort, with greater emphasis on guest care in all areas.

♦♦♦　　A very good overall level of quality in areas such as comfortable bedrooms, well maintained, practical decor, the choice of items at breakfast, customer care and all-round comfort. Where other meals are provided these will be freshly cooked from good quality ingredients.

♦♦♦♦　A very good level of quality in all areas. Customer care showing very good attention to your needs.

♦♦♦♦♦ An excellent overall level of quality - for example, ample space with a degree of luxury, a high quality bed and furniture, excellent interior design and customer care which anticipates your needs. Breakfast offering a wide choice of high quality fresh ingredients. Where other meals are provided these will feature fresh, seasonal, and often local ingredients.

Gold and Silver Awards

Look out, too, for the English Tourism Council's Gold and Silver Awards, given to establishments which not only achieve the overall levels of quality within their Diamond rating, but also reach the highest levels of quality in specific areas identified by guests as being really important to them. They reflect the quality of comfort and cleanliness you'll find in bedrooms and bathrooms as well as the quality of service you'll enjoy throughout your stay.

Accommodation
Entries explained

Each accommodation entry contains detailed information to help you decide if it is right for you. This information has been provided by the proprietors themselves, and our aim has been to ensure that it is as objective and factual as possible. To the left of the establishment name you will find the Diamond rating and quality award, if appropriate.

At-a-glance symbols at the end of each entry give you additional information on services and facilities - a key can be found on the back cover flap. Keep this open to refer to as you read.

A sample entry is shown below.

Look out for Welcome Host, a nationally recognised customer care initiative, sponsored in England by the English Tourism Council. Establishments with the Welcome Host symbol [⚜] have shown their commitment to courtesy and service and aim to provide high standards of service and a warm welcome for all visitors.

Sample Entry

BATH Map ref 2B2

◆◆◆◆
BRETHERTON HOUSE
17 Easton Road, Bath BA21 3LN
T: (01225) 000222
F: (01225) 000222
E: bretherton@bath.co.uk

Silver Award

Bedrooms: 3 double, 2 single
Bathrooms: 5 en-suite

Lunch available
EM 1830 (LO 2100)
Parking for 6
CC: Mastercard, Access, Delta

B&B per night:
S £20.00-£35.00
D £30.00-£45.00

HB per person:
DY £30.00-£50.00

OPEN All year round

Elegant and peaceful house with beautiful garden. Spacious and very comfortable. All rooms en-suite; home cooking. Convenient for city centre.

1   Town or village with map reference

2   Diamond rating and quality award (where applicable)

3   Establishment name, address and contact details

4   Accommodation details, including credit cards accepted

5   National Accessible Scheme rating (where applicable)

6   Prices per night for bed & breakfast (B&B) staying in a single (S) or double (D) room. The double room price is for two people. Half board (HB) prices are shown as a daily rate (DY) per person and include room, breakfast and dinner

7   Accommodation description

8   Months open

9   At-a-glance symbols (key on back cover flap)

Gold
Award Establishments

Establishments featured in the regional sections of this Where to Stay guide, which have achieved a Gold Award for an exceptionally high standard of quality, are listed on this page. Please use the Town Index at the back of the guide to find the page numbers for their full entry.

Silver Awards also represent high standards of quality and there are many establishments within this guide which have achieved this. Gold and Silver Awards are clearly indicated in the accommodation entries.

For further information about Gold and Silver Awards, please see page 7.

The Pictures:
1 Glencot House, Wookey Hole, Somerset;
2 Hooke Hall, Uckfield, East Sussex;
3 Tregea Hotel, Padstow, Cornwall.

Avonside Cottage, Warwick, Warwickshire
Blounts Court Farm, Devizes, Wiltshire
Bokiddick Farm, Bodmin, Cornwall
Boxbush Barn, Westbury-on-Severn, Gloucestershire
Broomshaw Hill Farm, Haltwhistle, Northumberland
Burbush Farm, Burley, Hampshire
Burhill Farm, Broadway, Worcestershire
Burr Bank, Cropton, North Yorkshire
Chalon House, Richmond, Greater London
Cloud High, Barnard Castle, Durham
The Cottage, Bishop's Stortford, Hertfordshire
Cotteswold House, Bibury, Gloucestershire
Efford Cottage, Lymington, Hampshire
Glencot House, Wookey Hole, Somerset
Hazel Bank Country House, Borrowdale, Cumbria
High Buston Hall, Alnmouth, Northumberland
Hill House Farm, Ely, Cambridgeshire
Hooke Hall, Uckfield, East Sussex
Knottside Farm, Pateley Bridge, North Yorkshire
Leighton House, Bath, Bath & North East Somerset
Magnolia House, Canterbury, Kent
Hotel Number Sixteen, London
Number Twenty Eight, Ludlow, Shropshire
The Nurse's Cottage, Sway, Hampshire
The Old Tump House, Blakeney, Gloucestershire
Omnia Somnia, Ashbourne, Derbyshire
Peacock House, Beetley, Norfolk
Pinnacle Point, Eastbourne, East Sussex
The Paddock, Leominster, Herefordshire
Ravenscourt Manor, Ludlow, Shropshire
The Ringlestone Inn & Farmhouse Hotel, Maidstone, Kent
Ryegate House, Stoke-by-Nayland, Suffolk
Seaham Guest House, Weymouth, Dorset
Tavern House, Tetbury, Gloucestershire
Thanington Hotel, Canterbury, Kent
Thatch Lodge Hotel, Lyme Regis, Dorset
The Three Lions, Fordingbridge, Hampshire
Tregea Hotel, Padstow, Cornwall
Villa Magdala Hotel, Bath, Bath & North East Somerset
Willowfield Country Guesthouse, Church Stretton, Shropshire

National
Accessible Scheme

The English Tourism Council and National and Regional Tourist Boards throughout Britain assess all types of places to stay, on holiday or business, that provide accessible accommodation for wheelchair users and others who may have difficulty walking.

Accommodation establishments taking part in the National Accessible Scheme, and which appear in the regional sections of this guide are listed opposite. Use the Town Index at the back to find the page numbers for their full entries.

The Tourist Boards recognise three categories of accessibility:

 CATEGORY 1   Accessible to all wheelchair users including those travelling independently.

 CATEGORY 2   Accessible to a wheelchair user with assistance.

 CATEGORY 3   Accessible to a wheelchair user able to walk short distances
and up at least three steps.

If you have additional needs or special requirements of any kind, we strongly recommend that you make sure these can be met by your chosen establishment before you confirm your booking.

The criteria the English Tourism Council and National and Regional Tourist Boards have adopted do not necessarily conform to British Standards or to Building Regulations. They reflect what the Boards understand to be acceptable to meet the practical needs of wheelchair users.

The National Accessible Scheme forms part of the Tourism for All Campaign that is being promoted by the English Tourism Council and National and Regional Tourist Boards. Additional help and guidance on finding suitable holiday accommodation for those with special needs can be obtained from:

Holiday Care,
2nd Floor, Imperial Buildings,
Victoria Road,
Horley, Surrey RH6 7PZ

Tel: (01293) 774535
Fax: (01293) 784647
Minicom: (01293) 776943

CATEGORY 1

- Bath, Bath & North East Somerset
  - Carfax Hotel
- Crookham, Northumberland
  - The Coach House at Crookham
- Ely, Cambridgeshire - Rosendale Lodge
- Hinckley, Leicestershire
  - Woodside Farm Guesthouse
- Kettlewell, North Yorkshire - High Fold
- Telford, Shropshire - Old Rectory
- Wilmslow, Cheshire - Dean Bank Hotel
- Woodbridge, Suffolk - Grove House

 CATEGORY 2

- Castle Donington, Leicestershire
  - Donington Park Farmhouse Hotel
- Southport, Merseyside - Sandy Brook Farm

CATEGORY 3

- Ambleside, Cumbria - Borrans Park Hotel
- Arundel, West Sussex - Mill Lane House
- Ashburton, Devon - New Cott Farm
- Bakewell, Derbyshire - Tannery House
- Boscastle, Cornwall - The Old Coach House
- Bridgnorth, Shropshire - Bulls Head Inn
- Carlisle, Cumbria - Newfield Grange Hotel
- Colyton, Devon - Smallicombe Farm
- Cressbrook, Derbyshire - Cressbrook Hall
- Dorking, Surrey - Bulmer Farm
- Durham - St Aidan's College
- Earls Colne, Essex - Riverside Lodge
- Fareham, Hampshire - Avenue House Hotel
- Frome, Somerset - Fourwinds Guest House
- Heathfield, East Sussex - Spicers Bed & Breakfast
- Henley-on-Thames, Oxfordshire - Holmwood
- Henstridge, Somerset - Fountain Inn Motel
- Ingleton, North Yorkshire - Riverside Lodge
- Kirkbymoorside, North Yorkshire - The Cornmill
- Lenham, Kent - The Dog & Bear Hotel

- Lower Whitley, Cheshire - Tall Trees Lodge
- Northallerton, North Yorkshire
  - Lovesome Hill Farm
- Norwich, Norfolk - Elm Farm Country House
- Oxford, Oxfordshire - Acorn Guest House
- Redcar, Tees Valley - Falcon Hotel
- Runswick Bay, North Yorkshire
  - Ellerby Hotel
- Salisbury, Wiltshire - Byways House
- Sarre, Kent
  - Crown Inn (The Famous Cherry Brandy House)
- Skegness, Lincolnshire
  - Chatsworth Hotel
  - Saxby Hotel
- Skipton, North Yorkshire - Craven Heifer Inn
- Stratford-upon-Avon, Warwickshire
  - Church Farm
- Sway, Hampshire - The Nurse's Cottage
- Weston-super-Mare, North Somerset
  - Moorlands Country Guesthouse
- Whitley Bay, Tyne & Wear - Marlborough Hotel
- Winchester, Hampshire - Shawlands

*(The information contained on these pages
was correct at the time of going to press.)*

The England for Excellence
Awards 2000

LA CREME DE LA CREME

If you are looking for somewhere truly outstanding, then why not
try one of the establishments listed below. Having proved their
mettle at a regional level, each one has made it through to the
semi-finals of the 2000 England for Excellence Awards. Run by the
English Tourism Council in association with the Regional Tourist
Boards, these highly competitive annual awards reward only the very
best in English tourism. So if somewhere has made it through to the
short-list, you can be sure that they really are the bees knees.

ENGLAND FOR
EXCELLENCE
AWARDS 2000

Sponsored by:

Bessiestown Farm, Longtown, Carlisle SILVER	Tel: 01228 577219
Bodkin Lodge, Market Rasen, Lincolnshire WINNER	Tel: 01673 858249
Burr Bank, Pickering, North Yorkshire	Tel: 01751 417777
Efford Cottage, Everton Lymington, Hampshire	Tel: 01590 642315
Grove Thorpe, Brockdish, Diss SILVER	Tel: 01379 668305
Hatpins, Bosham, West Sussex	Tel: 01243 572444
Number Sixteen, 16 Sumner Place, London	Tel: 020 7589 5232
Swing Cottage Guest House, Littleborough, Lancashire	Tel: 01706 379094
The Old Manse, Chatton, Alnwick	Tel: 01668 215343
Victoria Lodge, Lynton, Devon	Tel: 01598 753203

Regional
Tourist Board areas

This *Where to Stay* guide is divided into 10 regional sections as shown on the map below. To identify each regional section and its page number, please refer to the key below. The county index overleaf indicates in which regional section you will find a particular county.

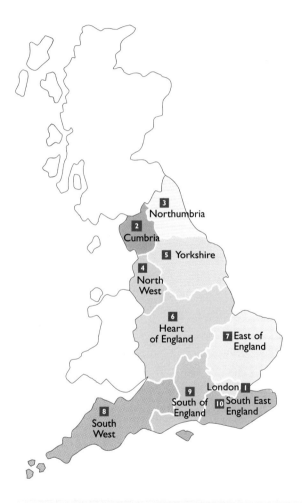

Key to Map	page
1 London	29
2 Cumbria	57
3 Northumbria	97
4 North West	121
5 Yorkshire	141
6 Heart of England	193
7 East of England	283
8 South West	329
9 South of England	413
10 South East England	461

Each of the ten English regions shown here has a Regional Tourist Board which can give you information about things to see or do locally. Contact details are given both at the beginning and end of each regional section.

LOCATION MAPS

Colour location maps showing all the cities, towns and villages with accommodation in the regional sections of this guide can be found on pages 16-28. Turn to the Town Index at the back of this guide for the page number on which you can find the relevant accommodation.

In which region is
the county I wish to visit?

COUNTY/UNITARY AUTHORITY	REGION
Bath & North East Somerset	South West
Bedfordshire	East of England
Berkshire	South of England
Bristol	South West
Buckinghamshire	South of England
Cambridgeshire	East of England
Cheshire	North West
Cornwall	South West
Cumbria	Cumbria
Derbyshire	Heart of England
Devon	South West
Dorset (Eastern)	South of England
Dorset (Western)	South West
Durham	Northumbria
East Riding of Yorkshire	Yorkshire
East Sussex	South East England
Essex	East of England
Gloucestershire	Heart of England
Greater London	London
Greater Manchester	North West
Hampshire	South of England
Herefordshire	Heart of England
Hertfordshire	East of England
Isle of Wight	South of England
Isles of Scilly	South West
Kent	South East England
Lancashire	North West
Leicestershire	Heart of England
Lincolnshire	Heart of England
Merseyside	North West
Norfolk	East of England
North East Lincolnshire	Yorkshire
North Lincolnshire	Yorkshire
North Somerset	South West
North Yorkshire	Yorkshire
Northamptonshire	Heart of England
Northumberland	Northumbria
Nottinghamshire	Heart of England
Oxfordshire	South of England
Rutland	Heart of England
Shropshire	Heart of England
Somerset	South West
South Gloucestershire	South West
South Yorkshire	Yorkshire
Staffordshire	Heart of England
Suffolk	East of England
Surrey	South East England
Tees Valley	Northumbria
Tyne & Wear	Northumbria
Warwickshire	Heart of England
West Midlands	Heart of England
West Sussex	South East England
West Yorkshire	Yorkshire
Wiltshire	South West
Worcestershire	Heart of England
York	Yorkshire

Making a Booking

Please remember that changes may occur after the guide is printed. When you have found a suitable place to stay we advise you to contact the establishment to check availability, and also to confirm prices and any specific facilities which may be important to you. Further advice on how to make a booking can be found at the back of this guide, together with information about deposits and cancellations. When you have made your booking, if you have time, it is advisable to confirm it in writing.

MAP 1

Location
Maps

Every place name featured in the regional accommodation sections of this Where to Stay guide has a map reference to help you locate it on the maps which follow. For example, to find Colchester, Essex, which has 'Map ref 3B2', turn to Map 3 and refer to grid square B2.

All place names appearing in the regional sections are shown in black type on the maps. This enables you to find other places in your chosen area which may have suitable accommodation - the Town Index (at the back of this guide) gives page numbers.

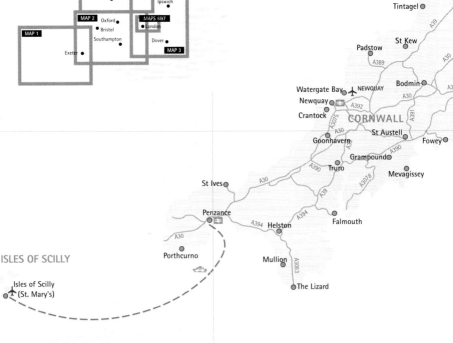

MAP 1

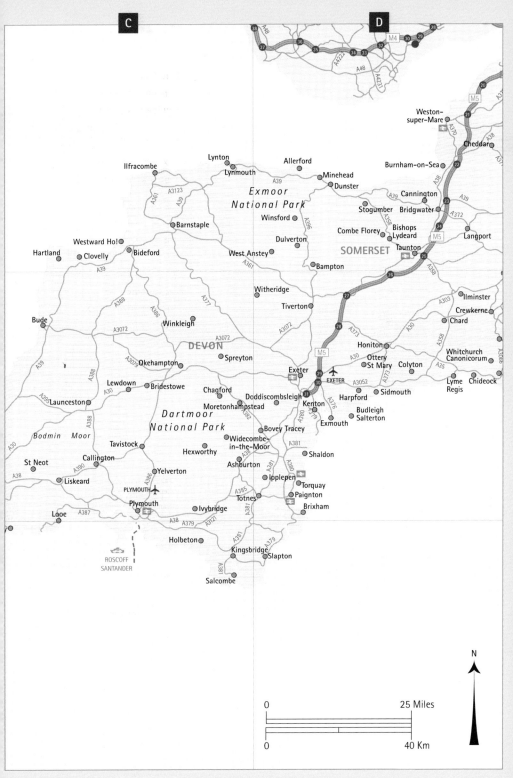

All place names in black offer accommodation in this guide.

MAP 2

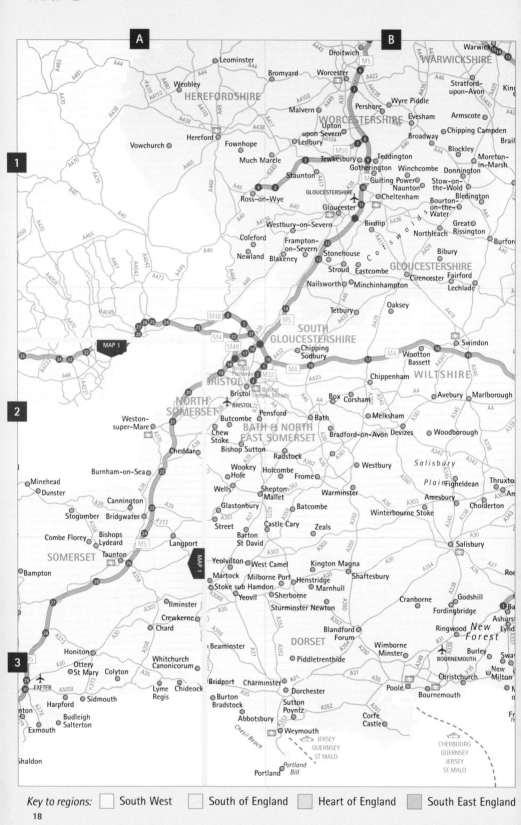

Key to regions: ☐ South West ☐ South of England ☐ Heart of England ☐ South East England

18

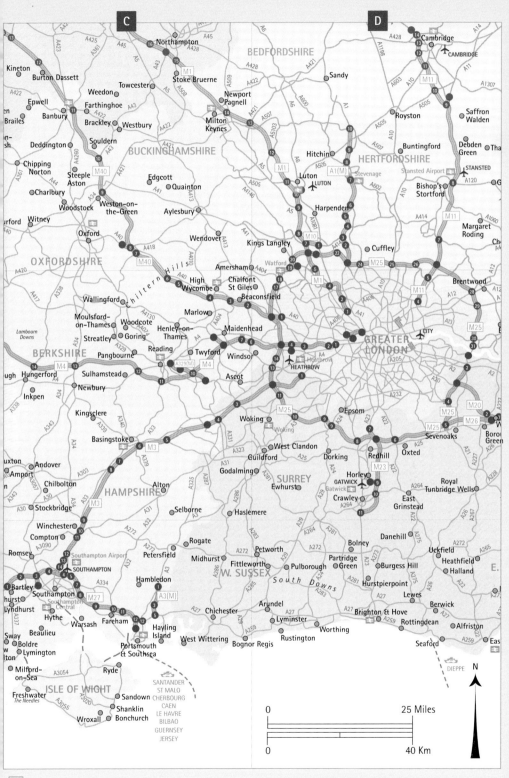

MAP 2

East of England   *All place names in black offer accommodation in this guide.*

MAP 3

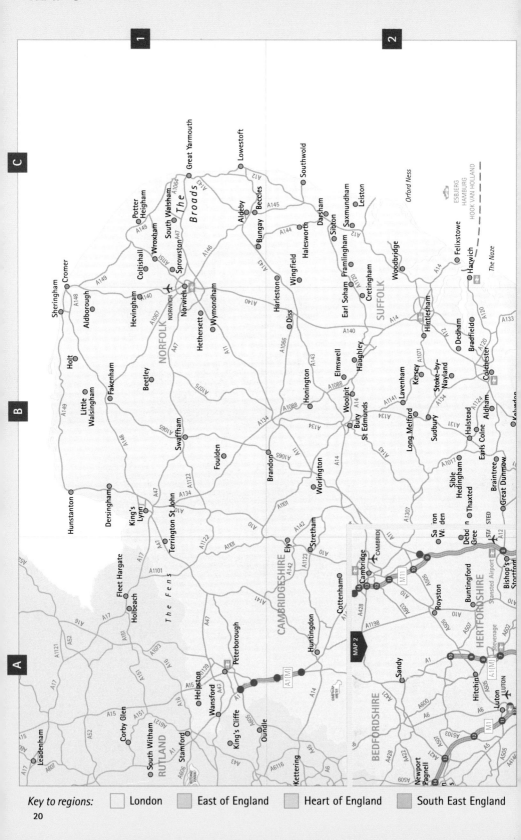

20

Key to regions: ▢ London ▢ East of England ▢ Heart of England ▢ South East England

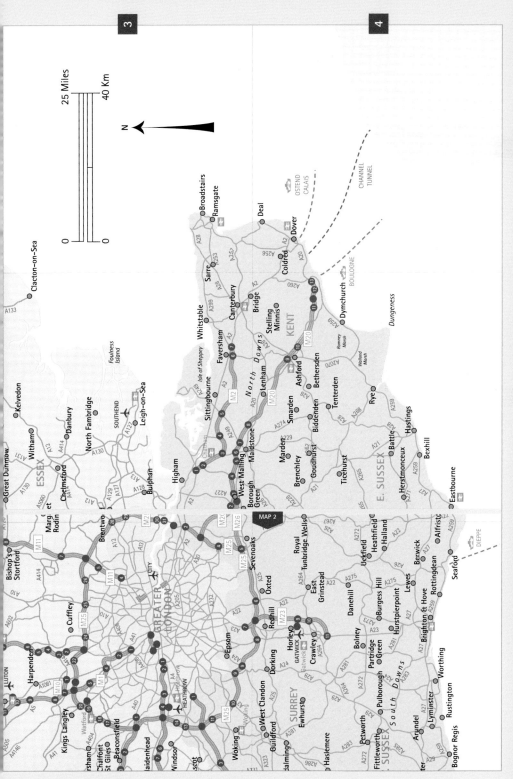

MAP 3

25 Miles

40 Km

N

Broadstairs
Ramsgate
Deal
Dover
CHANNEL TUNNEL
OSTEND
CALAIS
BOULOGNE
Dymchurch
Dungeness

Clacton-on-Sea
A133

Sarre
A28
A26
A253
A257
A256
Coldred
A2
A20
A260
A259

Whitstable
Faversham
Canterbury
A299
A2
Bridge
Stelling Minnis
KENT
A20
M20
Ashford
Bethersden
Romney Marsh
Walland Marsh

Foulness Island

Kelvedon
Danbury
North Fambridge
Leigh-on-Sea
SOUTHEND
A127

Great Dunmow
Witham
ESSEX
A131
A12
A414
Chelmsford
A130
A1060
A414
A129
A128
A13
A127
Bulphan

Higham
Sittingbourne
Isle of Sheppey
Maidstone
West Malling
Borough Green
Lenham
Smarden
Marden
Brenchley
Goudhurst
Biddenden
Tenterden
Ticehurst
Rye
A259
Hastings
Battle
Bexhill
Herstmonceux
Eastbourne
E. SUSSEX
M2
M20
A249
A20
A274
A229
A262
A21
A265
A28
A268
A259
A2070
A271

Bishop's Stortford
M11
A414
A10
Cuffley
M25
A602

Marg
Rodin
Brentwo
A12
A2
M25
Sevenoaks
Oxted
Royal Tunbridge Wells
East Grinstead
Uckfield
Heathfield
Halland
Berwick
Alfriston
Seaford
DIEPPE
MAP 2
M26
A264
A22
A275
A26
A272
A27
A259

CITY
GREATER LONDON
A205
A20
A21
Epsom
Redhill
Horley
GATWICK
Crawley
Dorking
M23
Bolney
Partridge Green
Danehill
Burgess Hill
Hurstpierpoint
Lewes
Rottingdean
Brighton & Hove
Worthing
A23
A272
A273
A281
A264
A275
A27

LUTON
Harpenden
A1081
M1
Kings Langley
Watford
Beaconsfield
Maidenhead
Windsor
scot
HEATHROW
West Clandon
Woking
Guildford
Ewhurst
Haslemere
Petworth
Fittleworth
Pulborough
South Downs
SURREY
W. SUSSEX
Arundel
Lyminster
Rustington
Bognor Regis
A24
A25
A3
M25
A281
A283
A29
A272
A286
A284
A27
A259

A5
A4146
A41
A405
A404

All place names in black offer accommodation in this guide.

21

MAP 4

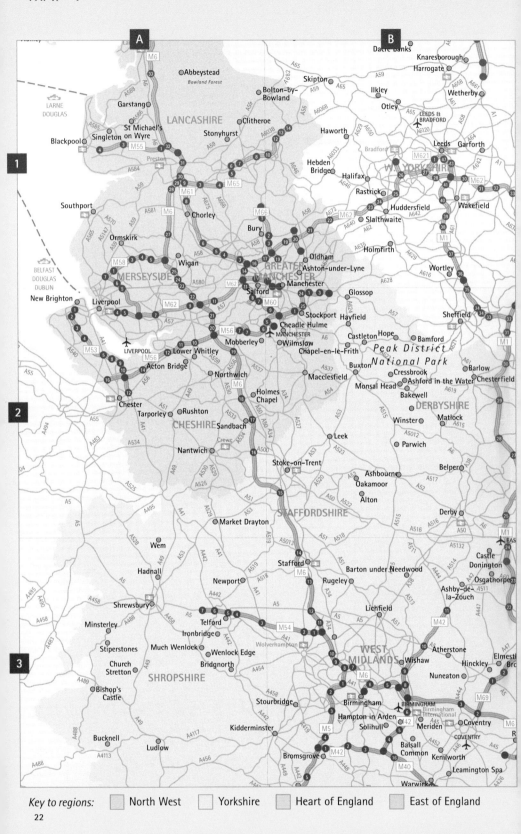

Key to regions: North West | Yorkshire | Heart of England | East of England

MAP 4

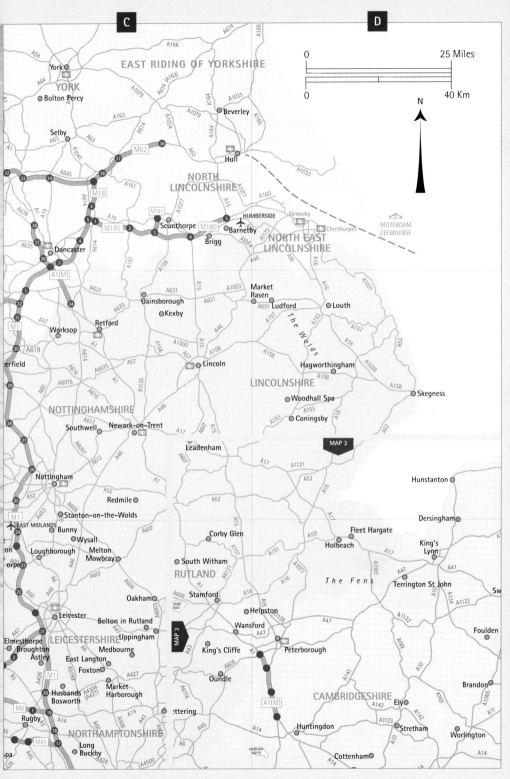

All place names in black offer accommodation in this guide.

MAP 5

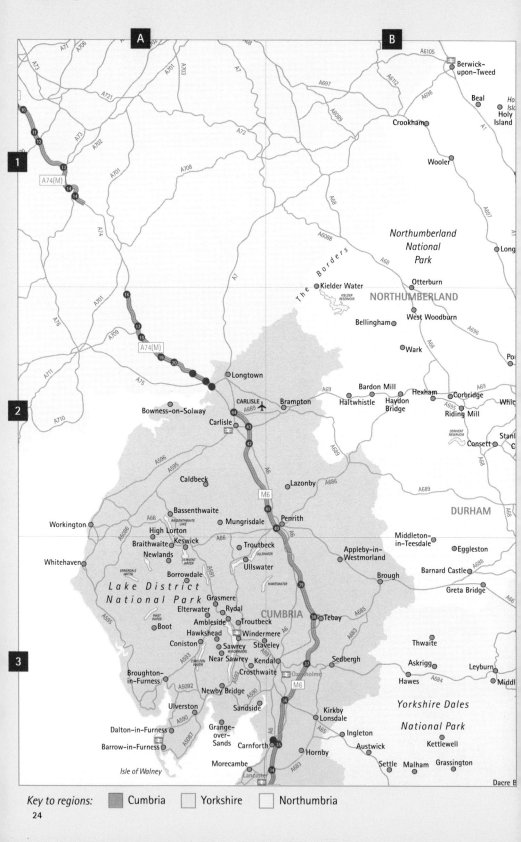

A   **B**

1

2

3

A74(M)

A74(M)

Berwick-upon-Tweed
Beal
Holy Island
Holy Island
Crookham
Wooler
Long

Northumberland National Park

Kielder Water
KIELDER RESERVOIR
NORTHUMBERLAND
Otterburn
West Woodburn
Bellingham
Wark
Po

The Borders

Longtown
Bowness-on-Solway
CARLISLE
Brampton
Bardon Mill
Hexham
Corbridge
Whic
Carlisle
Haltwhistle
Haydon Bridge
Riding Mill
DERWENT RESERVOIR
Stanl
Consett
C

A74(M)

Caldbeck
Lazonby
M6
DURHAM

Workington
Bassenthwaite
BASSENTHWAITE LAKE
Mungrisdale
Penrith
Middleton-in-Teesdale
Eggleston
High Lorton
Braithwaite
Keswick
Troutbeck
Appleby-in-Westmorland
Barnard Castle
Newlands
DERWENT WATER
Whitehaven
ULLSWATER
Ullswater
Brough
Greta Bridge
Borrowdale
ENNERDALE WATER
HAWESWATER
A66

Lake District National Park
Grasmere
Elterwater
Rydal
CUMBRIA
Tebay
Thwaite
Boot
WAST WATER
Ambleside
Troutbeck
Hawkshead
Windermere
Askrigg
Leyburn
Coniston
CONISTON WATER
Sawrey
Staveley
Sedbergh
Hawes
Middl
Near Sawrey
Kendal
WINDERMERE
Crosthwaite
Oxenholme
Broughton-in-Furness
M6
Yorkshire Dales
Newby Bridge
Kirkby Lonsdale
National Park
Ulverston
Sandside
Dalton-in-Furness
Grange-over-Sands
Ingleton
Kettlewell
Barrow-in-Furness
Carnforth
Hornby
Austwick
Settle
Malham
Grassington
Isle of Walney
Morecambe
Lancaster
Dacre B

Key to regions: Cumbria   Yorkshire   Northumbria

24

MAP 5

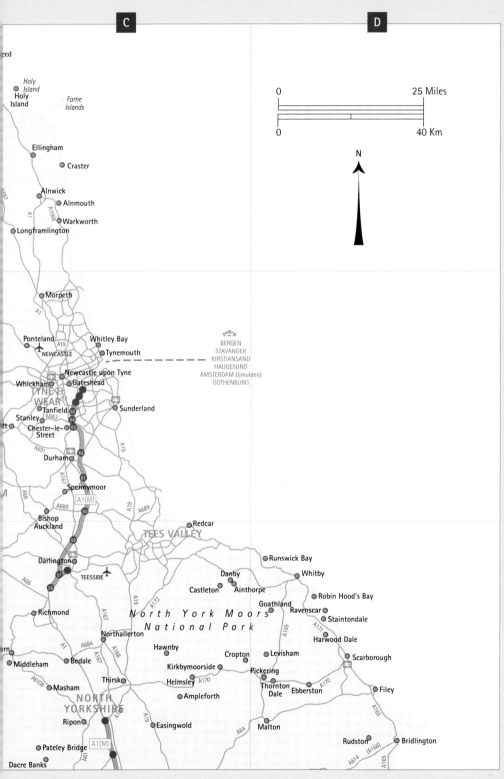

C **D**

0   25 Miles

0   40 Km

N

eed

Holy
Island
Holy
Island   Farne
Islands

Ellingham

Craster

Alnwick
Alnmouth
Warkworth
Longframlington

Morpeth

A1

Ponteland   Whitley Bay
A19
NEWCASTLE   Tynemouth

Whickham Newcastle upon Tyne
Gateshead

TYNE &
WEAR

Tanfield 65
Stanley   A963 64   Sunderland
Chester-le- 63
Street

A691   A19

Durham 62

A167 61

Spennymoor
A1(M)
A689   A689
A68 60

Bishop
Auckland   Redcar

TEES VALLEY
59

Darlington

A66 57   TEESSIDE   Runswick Bay
56   Danby   Whitby
       Castleton   Ainthorpe
         Goathland   Robin Hood's Bay
Richmond   A19   A172   *North York Moors*   Ravenscar   Staintondale
A167   *National Park*   A169
Northallerton   A171   Harwood Dale
A1   A684   A168   Hawnby   Cropton   Levisham   Scarborough
rn   Middleham   Bedale   A167   Kirkbymoorside   Pickering
A6108   Thirsk   Helmsley A170   Thornton   Ebberston   Filey
Masham   Ampleforth   Dale   A170   A165
NORTH
YORKSHIRE
Ripon   A19   Easingwold   A64   Malton
Pateley Bridge   A1(M)   Rudston   A166   Bridlington
Dacre Banks   A61   A614   A165

BERGEN
STAVANGER
KIRSTIANSAND
HAUGESUND
AMSTERDAM (Ijmulden)
GOTHENBURG

All place names in black offer accommodation in this guide.

MAP 6

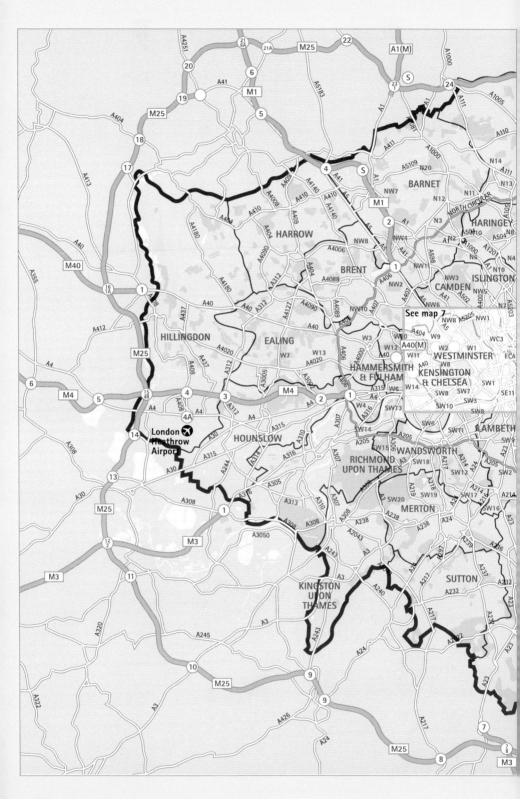

MAP 6

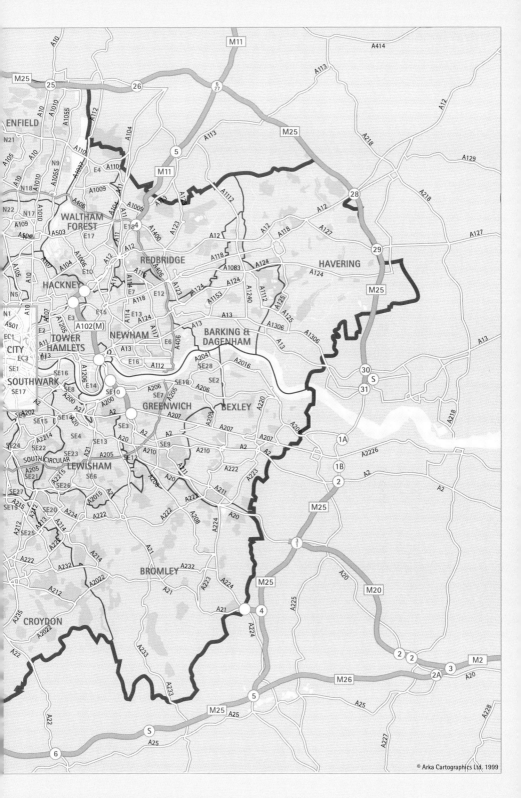

© Arka Cartographics Ltd. 1999

MAP 7

Central London

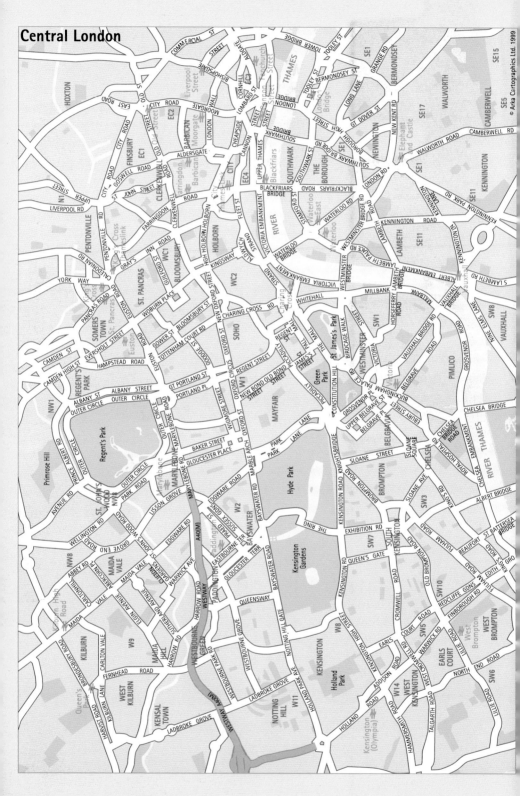

© Arka Cartographics Ltd. 1999

London

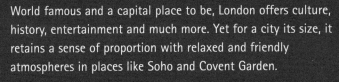

World famous and a capital place to be, London offers culture, history, entertainment and much more. Yet for a city its size, it retains a sense of proportion with relaxed and friendly atmospheres in places like Soho and Covent Garden.

Shoppers can spend, spend, spend in swanky Knightsbridge, or save, save, save at the Petticoat Lane, Brick Lane and Portobello markets. And for eating out, London is an explosion of tastes – traditional, international, and exotic. The outskirts of the city have their attractions, too, such as the Royal Observatory in Greenwich, and the botanical gardens at Kew.

For the perfect overview, book a flight on the world's highest observation wheel, 'The London Eye', open daily.

*Greater London,
comprising the
32 London Boroughs*

FOR MORE INFORMATION CONTACT:
London Tourist Board
6th floor, Glen House, Stag Place,
London SW1E 5LT
Telephone enquiries – see Visitorcall on page 34
Internet: www.LondonTown.com

The Pictures:
1 Piccadilly Circus;
2 Tower Bridge;
3 The maze at Hampton Court;
4 Canary Wharf.

Where to Go in London - see pages 30-32
Where to Stay in London - see pages 35-56

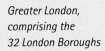

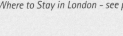

Whilst in
LONDON ...

You will find hundreds of interesting places to visit during your stay, just some of which are listed in these pages.

Contact any Tourist Information Centre in and around London for more ideas on days out.

Chessington World of Adventures

Leatherhead Road, Chessington KT9 2NE
Tel: (01372) 729560
Dr Chessington, creator of the World of Adventures, has invented thrilling rides and attractions for all the family, with crazy entertainers and rare animals in themed lands.

Design Museum

Shad Thames, London SE1 2YD
Tel: (020) 7403 6933
One of London's most inspiring attractions, concerned solely with the products, technologies and buildings of the 20th and 21st centuries.

Hampton Court Palace

Hampton Court, East Molesey KT8 9AU
Tel: (020) 8781 9500
The oldest Tudor palace in England with many attractions including the Tudor kitchens, tennis courts, maze, State Apartments and King's Apartments.

HMS Belfast

Morgan's Lane, Tooley Street, London SE1 2JH
Tel: (020) 7940 6300
World War II cruiser weighing 11,500 tonnes, now a floating naval museum with nine decks to explore. Many naval exhibitions also on show.

Kensington Palace State Apartments

Kensington Gardens, London W8 4PX
Tel: (020) 7937 7079
Furniture and ceiling paintings from the Stuart-Hanoverian periods, rooms from the Victorian era and works of art from the Royal Collection. Also Royal Ceremonial Dress Collection.

Kew Gardens (Royal Botanic Gardens)

Kew, Richmond TW9 3AB
Tel: (020) 8940 1171
Three hundred acres containing living collections of over 40,000 varieties of plants. Seven spectacular glasshouses, two art galleries, Japanese and rock garden.

London Aquarium

Riverside Building, London SE1 7PB
Tel: (020) 7967 8000
Dive down deep beneath the Thames and submerge yourself in one of Europe's largest displays of aquatic life.

London Dungeon

Tooley Street, London SE1 2SZ
Tel: 0891 600 0666
The world's first medieval horror museum. Now featuring two major shows, 'The Jack the Ripper Experience' and 'The Judgement Day Ride'.

London Eye
Jubilee Gardens, South Bank, London SE1
Tel: 0870 5000 600
At 135 metres (443ft) high, this is the world's highest observation wheel. It provides a 30-minute slow-moving flight over London.

London Planetarium
Marylebone Road, London NW1 5LR
Tel: (020) 7935 6861
Visitors can experience a virtual reality trip through space and wander through the interactive Space Zones before the show.

London Transport Museum
Covent Garden Piazza, London WC2E 7BB
Tel: (020) 7379 6344
The history of transport for everyone, from spectacular vehicles, special exhibitions, actors and guided tours to film shows, gallery talks and children's craft workshops.

London Zoo
Regent's Park, London NW1 4RY
Tel: (020) 7722 3333
One of the world's most famous zoos and home to over 600 species. Including the new 'Web of Life' exhibition, and a full daily events programme.

Madame Tussaud's
Marylebone Road, London NW1 5LR
Tel: (020) 7935 6861
World-famous collection of wax figures in themed settings which include The Garden Party, 200 Years, Superstars, The Grand Hall, The Chamber of Horrors and The Spirit of London.

Museum of London
London Wall, London EC2Y 5HN
Tel: (020) 7600 3699
Discover over 2,000 years of the capital's history, from prehistoric to modern times. Regular temporary exhibitions and lunchtime lecture programmes.

National Gallery
Trafalgar Square, London WC2N 5DN
Tel: (020) 7747 2885
Gallery displaying Western European paintings from about 1260-1900. Includes work by Botticelli, Leonardo da Vinci, Rembrandt, Gainsborough, Turner, Renoir, Cezanne.

National Maritime Museum
Romney Road, London SE10 9NF
Tel: (020) 8858 4422
This national museum explains Britain's worldwide influence through its explorers, traders, migrants and naval power. Features on ship models, costume and ecology of the sea.

National Portrait Gallery
St Martin's Place, London WC2H 0HE
Tel: (020) 7306 0055
Permanent collection of portraits of famous men and women from the Middle Ages to the present day. Usually free, but a charge may be made for some exhibitions.

Natural History Museum
Cromwell Road, London SW7 5BD
Tel: (020) 7942 5000
One of the most popular museums in the world and one of London's finest landmarks, it houses the natural wonders of the world.

Rock Circus
Piccadilly Circus, London W1V 9LA
Tel: (020) 7734 7203
Madame Tussaud's new Rock Circus features special audio, visual and animatronic effects, plus wax figures of the pop world's biggest names of past and present.

Royal Air Force Museum
Grahame Park Way, Hendon, London NW9 5LL
Tel: (020) 8205 2266
Britain's National Museum of Aviation features over 70 full-sized aircraft, Flight Simulator, 'Touch and Try' Jet Provost Trainer and Eurofighter 2000 Theatre.

The Pictures:
1 Harrods;
2 Big Ben;
3 The Whitechapel at the Tower of London;
4 Trafalgar Square;
5 Battersea Park Pagoda;
6 Hays Galleria;
7 China Town;
8 Richmond Lock.

Royal Observatory Greenwich

Greenwich Park, London SE10 9NF
Tel: (020) 8858 4422
Museum of time and space, and site of the Greenwich Meridian. Working telescopes and planetarium, timeball, Wren's Octagon Room and intricate clocks and computer simulations.

St Paul's Cathedral

St Paul's Churchyard, London EC4M 8AD
Tel: (020) 7236 4128
Wren's famous cathedral church of the diocese of London incorporating the Crypt, Ambulatory and Whispering Gallery.

Science Museum

Exhibition Road, London SW7 2DD
Tel: (020) 7942 4454
See, touch and experience the major scientific advances of the past 300 years. The world's finest collections in the history of science, technology and medicine.

Shakespeare's Globe Theatre Tours and Exhibition

New Globe Walk, Bankside, London SE1 9DT
Tel: (020) 7902 1500
Against the historical background of Elizabethan Bankside — the City of London's playground in Shakespeare's time — the exhibition focuses on actors, architecture and audiences.

Tate Modern

Bankside Power Station, Sumner Street, London SE1
Tel: (020) 7401 5081
Home of the Tate Gallery of Modern Art with displays of 20thC art ranging from Andy Warhol to Rachel Whiteread and Henri Matisse to Henry Moore.

Tower Bridge Experience

Tower Bridge, London SE1 2UP
Tel: (020) 7403 3761
Exhibition explaining the history of the bridge and how it operates. Original steam-powered engines on view. Panoramic views from fully-glazed walkways. Gift shop.

Tower of London

Tower Hill, London EC3N 4AB
Tel: (020) 7709 0765
Home of the 'Beefeaters' and ravens, the building spans 900 years of British history. On display are the nation's Crown Jewels, regalia and armoury robes.

Victoria and Albert Museum

Cromwell Road, London SW7 2RL
Tel: (020) 7942 2000
The V&A holds one of the world's largest and most diverse collections of the decorative arts, dating from 3000BC to the present day.

Vinopolis, City of Wine

Bank End, London SE1 9BU
Tel: (020) 7645 3700
Vinopolis offers all the pleasures of wine under one roof. The Wine Odyssey tour includes free tastings from over 200 wines. Four restaurants on site.

Westminster Abbey

Parliament Square, London SW1P 3PA
Tel: (020) 7222 5152
One of Britain's finest Gothic buildings. Scene of the coronation, marriage and burial of British monarchs. Includes nave and cloisters, Royal Chapels and Undercroft Museum.

The Pictures:
1 Guards at Buckingham Palace;
2 St Paul's Cathedral;
3 Tower Bridge at night;
4 Eros in Piccadilly Circus;
5 River Thames at night.

Find out more about
LONDON ...

A free information pack about holidays and attractions in London available on written request from:

LONDON TOURIST BOARD AND CONVENTION BUREAU
6th Floor, Glen House, Stag Place, London SW1E 5LT.

TOURIST INFORMATION CENTRES

POINT OF ARRIVAL
● **Heathrow Terminals 1, 2, 3 Underground Station Concourse,** Heathrow Airport, TW6 2JA.
Open: Daily 0800-1800; 1 Jun-30 Sep, Mon-Sat 0800-1900, Sun 0800-1800.
● **Liverpool Street Underground Station,** EC2M 7PN.
Open: Daily 0800-1800; 1 Jun-30 Sep, Mon-Sat 0800-1900, Sun 0800-1800.
● **Victoria Station Forecourt,** SW1V 1JU.
Open: 1 Jun-30 Sep, Mon-Sat 0800-2100, Sun 0800-1800; 1 Oct-Easter, daily 0800-1800; Easter-31 May, Mon-Sat 0800-2000, Sun 0800-1800.
● **Waterloo International Terminal**
Arrivals Hall, London SE1 7LT. *Open: Daily 0830-2230.*

INNER LONDON
● **Britain Visitor Centre**
1 Regent Street, Piccadilly Circus, SW1Y 4XT.
Open: Mon 0930-1830, Tue-Fri 0900-1830, Sat & Sun 1000-1600; Jun-Oct, Sat 0900-1700.
● **Greenwich Tourist Information Centre**
Pepys House, 2 Cutty Sark Gardens SE10 9LW.
Tel: 0870 608 2000; Fax: (020) 8853 4607.
Open: Daily 1000-1700; 1 Jul-31 Aug, daily 1000-2000.
● **Lewisham Tourist Information Centre**
Lewisham Library,
199-201 Lewisham High Street, SE13 6LG.
Tel: (020) 8297 8317.
Open: Mon 1000-1700, Tue-Fri 0900-1700, Sat 1000-1600.
● **Southwark Information Centre**
London Bridge, 6 Tooley Street, SE1 2SY.
Tel: (020) 7403 8299.
Open: Easter-31 Oct, Mon-Sat 1000-1800, Sun 1030-1730; 1 Nov-Easter, Mon-Sat 1000-1600, Sun 1100-1600.

● **Tower Hamlets Tourist Information Centre**
18 Lamb Street, E1 6EA.
Fax: (020) 7375 2539.
Open: Mon, Tues, Thur & Fri 0930-1330,1430-1630, 0930-1300; Sun 1130-1430.

OUTER LONDON
● **Bexley Hall Place Visitor Centre**
Bourne Road, Bexley, Kent DA5 1PQ.
Tel: (01322) 558676; Fax: (01322) 522921.
Open: Mon-Sat 1000-1630, Sun 1400-1730.
● **Croydon Tourist Information Centre**
Katharine Street, Croydon CR9 1ET.
Tel: (020) 8253 1009; Fax: (020) 8253 1008.
Open: Mon-Wed 0900-1800, Thu 0930-1800, Fri 0900-1800, Sat 0900-1700, Sun 1400-1700.
● **Harrow Tourist Information Centre**
Civic Centre, Station Road, Harrow HA1 2XF.
Tel: (020) 8424 1103; Fax: (020) 8424 1134.
Open: Mon-Fri 0900-1700.
● **Hillingdon Tourist Information Centre**
Central Library, 14 High Street, Uxbridge UB8 1HD.
Tel: (01895) 250706; Fax: (01895) 239794.
Open: Mon, Tue & Thu 0930-2000, Wed 0930-1730, Fri 1000-1730, Sat 0930-1600.
● **Hounslow Tourist Information Centre**
24 The Treaty Centre,
Hounslow High Street, Hounslow TW3 1ES.
Tel: (020) 8583 2929; Fax: (020) 8583 4714.
Open: Mon, Wed, Fri & Sat 0930-1730, Tue & Thu 0930-2000.
● **Kingston Tourist Information Centre**
Market House, Market Place,
Kingston upon Thames KT1 1JS.
Tel: (020) 8547 5592; Fax: (020) 8547 5594.
Open: Mon-Fri 1000-1700, Sat 0900-1600.
● **Richmond Tourist Information Centre**
Old Town Hall, Whittaker Avenue, Richmond TW9 1TP.
Tel: (020) 8940 9125; Fax: (020) 8940 6899.
Open: Mon-Sat 1000-1700; Easter Sunday-end Sep, Sun 1030-1330.

- **Swanley Tourist Information Centre**
London Road, BR8 7AE.
Tel: (01322) 614660.
Open: Mon-Thu 0930-1730, Fri 0930-1800, Sat 0900-1600.
- **Twickenham Tourist Information Centre**
The Atrium, Civic Centre, York Street, Twickenham,
Middlesex TW1 3BZ.
Tel: (020) 8891 7272.
Open: Mon-Thu 0900-1715; Fri 0900-1700.

VISITORCALL

The London Tourist Board and Convention Bureau's
'Phone Guide to London' operates 24 hours a day.
To access a full range of information call 09064 123456.
To access specific lines dial 09064 123 followed by:

What's on this week	– 400
What's on next 3 months	– 401
Rock and pop concerts	– 422
Visitor attractions	– 480
Where to take children	– 424
Museums and galleries	– 429
Palaces (including Buckingham Palace)	– 481
Current exhibitions	– 403
Changing the Guard	– 411
West End shows	– 416
Eating out	– 485
London line 2000:	**09064 663344**

Calls cost 60p per minute at all times (as at
June 2000). To order a Visitorcall card please
call (020) 7971 0026.

ARTSLINE

London's information and advice service for disabled
people on arts and entertainment. Call (020) 7388 2227.

HOTEL ACCOMMODATION SERVICE

Accommodation reservations can be made throughout
London. Call the London Tourist Board's Telephone
Accommodation Service on (020) 7932 2020 with your
requirements and Mastercard/Visa/Switch details.

Reservations on arrival are handled at the Tourist
Information Centres at Victoria Station, Heathrow
Underground, Liverpool Street Station, Waterloo
International and Heathrow Terminal 3. Go to any of
them on the day when you need accommodation. A
communication charge and a refundable deposit are
payable when making a reservation.

WHICH PART OF LONDON?

The majority of tourist accommodation is situated in
the central parts of London and is therefore very
convenient for most of the city's attractions and
night life.

However, there are many hotels in outer London which
provide other advantages, such as easier parking. In the
'Where to Stay' pages which follow, you will find
accommodation listed under INNER LONDON (covering
the E1 to W14 London Postal Area) and OUTER
LONDON (covering the remainder of Greater London).
Colour maps 6 and 7 at the front of the guide show
place names and London
Postal Area codes and will
help you to locate
accommodation in your
chosen area of London.

The Pictures:
1 Buckingham Palace;
2 Big Ben and the Houses of
   Parliament;
3 Westminster Abbey.

Getting to
LONDON ...

BY ROAD: Major trunk roads into London include: A1, M1, A5, A10, A11, M11, A13, A2,
M2, A23, A3, M3, A4, M4, A40, M40, A41, M25 (London orbital).
London Transport is responsible for running London's bus services and the underground
rail network. (020) 7222 1234 (24 hour telephone service; calls answered in rotation).

BY RAIL: Main rail termini:
Victoria/Waterloo/Charing Cross - serving the South/South East;
King's Cross - serving the North East; Euston - serving the North West/Midlands;
Liverpool Street - serving the East; Paddington - serving the Thames Valley/West.

FINDING ACCOMMODATION
IS AS EASY AS *1 2 3*

Where to Stay makes it quick and easy to find a place to stay.
There are several ways to use this guide.

1 Town Index
The town index, starting on page 748, lists all the places with
accommodation featured in the regional sections. The index
gives a page number where you can find full accommodation
and contact details.

2 Colour Maps
All the place names in black on the colour maps at the front
have an entry in the regional sections. Refer to the town index
for the page number where you will find one or more
establishments offering accommodation in your chosen
town or village.

3 Accommodation listing
Contact details for **all** English Tourism Council assessed
accommodation throughout England, together with their
national Star rating is given in the listing section of this guide.
Establishments with a full entry in the regional sections are
shown in blue. Look in the town index for the page number on
which their full entry appears.

London

If you are looking for accommodation in a particular establishment in London and you know its name, this index will give you the page number of the full entry in the guide.

Where to stay in

LONDON

Accommodation entries in this region are listed under Inner London (covering the postcode areas E1 to W14) and Outer London (covering the remainder of Greater London) - please refer to the colour location maps 6 and 7 at the front of this guide.

If you want to look up a particular establishment, use the index on the previous pages which will give you the page number.

At-a-glance symbols at the end of each accommodation entry give useful information about services and facilities. A key to symbols can be found inside the back cover flap. Keep this open for easy reference.

A complete listing of all English Tourism Council assessed guest accommodation appears at the back of this guide.

INNER LONDON
LONDON E4

◆◆◆◆
Silver Award

AUCKLANDS
25 Eglington Road,
North Chingford, London, E4 7AN
T: (020) 8529 1140
F: (020) 8529 9288

Bedrooms: 1 double,
1 twin
Bathrooms: 1 public

Lunch available
EM 1700 (LO 2300)

B&B per night:
S Min £35.00
D Min £70.00

OPEN All year round

Comfortable Edwardian period family home with exclusive facilities in quiet suburb, easy access to City. Solar-heated swimming pool in landscaped garden. Gourmet meals on request.

LONDON E7

◆

FOREST VIEW HOTEL
227 Romford Road, Forest Gate,
London, E7 9HL
T: (020) 8534 4844
F: (020) 8534 8959

Bedrooms: 8 single,
5 double, 2 twin, 2 triple,
3 family rooms
Bathrooms: 4 en suite,
3 private, 3 public

EM 1830 (LO 2100)
Parking for 15
CC: Barclaycard, Delta,
Eurocard, JCB, Maestro,
Mastercard, Solo, Switch,
Visa, Visa Electron

B&B per night:
S £35.00–£35.00
D £50.00–£59.00

HB per person:
DY £42.00–£49.00

OPEN All year round

Catering for business and tourist clientele. En suite rooms with tea/coffee making, direct-dial telephone and TV. Full English breakfast. Warm and friendly atmosphere.

NB **IMPORTANT NOTE** Information on accommodation listed in this guide has been supplied by the proprietors. As changes may occur you are advised to check details at the time of booking.

LONDON E7 continued

♦ **GRANGEWOOD LODGE HOTEL**

104 Clova Road, Forest Gate,
London, E7 9AF
T: (020) 8534 0637 & 8503 0941
F: (020) 8503 0941

Bedrooms: 9 single,
2 double, 3 twin, 1 triple,
2 family rooms
Bathrooms: 2 en suite,
4 public

Parking for 2
CC: Barclaycard,
Mastercard, Switch, Visa

B&B per night:
S £21.00–£24.00
D £34.00–£45.00

OPEN All year round

Comfortable budget accommodation in a quiet road. Pleasant garden. Easy access to central London, Docklands and M11. 12 minutes to Liverpool Street station.

LONDON N1

♦♦♦ **KANDARA GUEST HOUSE**

68 Ockendon Road, London,
N1 3NW
T: (020) 7226 5721 & 7226
3379 (answerphone)
F: (020) 7226 3379
E: admin@kandara.co.uk
I: www.kandara.co.uk

Bedrooms: 4 single,
2 double, 1 twin, 4 triple
Bathrooms: 5 public

CC: Barclaycard, Delta,
Eurocard, Mastercard,
Visa

B&B per night:
S £39.00–£47.00
D £51.00–£59.00

OPEN All year round

Small family-run guesthouse near the Angel, Islington. Free street parking and good public transport to West End and City.

LONDON N4

♦♦ **COSTELLO PALACE HOTEL**

374 Seven Sisters Road,
Finsbury Park, London, N4 2PG
T: (020) 8802 6551
F: (020) 8802 9461

Bedrooms: 3 single,
17 double, 20 twin,
4 triple
Bathrooms: 44 en suite

Parking for 35
CC: Barclaycard, Delta,
Mastercard, Solo, Switch,
Visa, Visa Electron

B&B per night:
S £45.00–£50.00
D £60.00–£65.00

OPEN All year round

Ideally situated for all amenities, exhibition centres, bus and underground. Bedrooms are attractively decorated with en suite facilities, direct-dial telephone, Sky TV, tea and coffee facilities.

LONDON N7

♦♦ **FIVE KINGS GUEST HOUSE**

59 Anson Road, Tufnell Park,
London, N7 0AR
T: (020) 7607 3996 & 7607 6466
F: (020) 7609 5554

Bedrooms: 6 single,
3 double, 3 twin, 2 triple,
2 family rooms
Bathrooms: 11 en suite,
3 public

CC: Amex, Barclaycard,
Eurocard, Mastercard,
Visa

B&B per night:
S £24.00–£30.00
D £38.00–£45.00

OPEN All year round

Privately-run guesthouse in a quiet residential area. 15 minutes to central London and convenient for London Zoo and most tourist attractions. Unrestricted parking in road.

LONDON N8

♦♦ **HOMESTEAD**

141 Ferme Park Road, Crouch End,
London, N8 9SG
T: (020) 8347 8768
F: (020) 8348 2256

Bedrooms: 1 double,
2 twin, 3 triple, 2 family
rooms
Bathrooms: 3 en suite,
4 private, 1 private
shower

CC: Barclaycard, Delta,
Eurocard, Maestro,
Mastercard, Switch, Visa

B&B per night:
S £25.00–£30.00
D £44.00–£48.00

OPEN All year round

Victorian terraced house, built in 1880, situated in Crouch End. Many local amenities including 41 restaurants. Within 7 miles central London, public transport accessible 24 hours.

♦♦♦ **WHITE LODGE HOTEL**

1 Church Lane, Hornsey, London,
N8 7BU
T: (020) 8348 9765
F: (020) 8340 7851

Bedrooms: 7 single,
3 double, 3 twin,
3 family rooms
Bathrooms: 8 en suite,
3 public

EM 1800 (LO 1900)
CC: Barclaycard, Eurocard,
Mastercard, Visa

B&B per night:
S £28.00–£30.00
D £38.00–£46.00

OPEN All year round

Small, friendly, family hotel offering personal service. Easy access to all transport, for sightseeing and business trips.

LONDON N16

ROSE HOTEL
♦♦

69-71 Stoke Newington Road,
London, N16 8AD
T: (020) 7254 5990 & 7923 0483
F: (020) 7923 0483
E: rosehotel@easicom.com

Bedrooms: 2 single,
12 double, 3 twin,
1 family room
Bathrooms: 3 public,
16 private showers

EM 1830 (LO 2100)
CC: Amex, Barclaycard,
Delta, Mastercard, Switch,
Visa, Visa Electron

B&B per night:
S £35.00–£40.00
D £45.00–£55.00

HB per person:
DY £40.00–£55.00

OPEN All year round

Family-run hotel within easy reach of the City and West End. Good access to public transport.

LONDON N22

PANE RESIDENCE
♦♦

154 Boundary Road, Wood Green,
London, N22 6AE
T: (020) 8889 3735

Bedrooms: 1 single,
2 twin
Bathrooms: 1 public

Parking for 2
CC: Eurocard

B&B per night:
S £22.00–£24.00
D £32.00–£36.00

OPEN All year round

In a pleasant location 6 minutes' walk from Turnpike Lane underground station and near Alexandra Palace. Kitchen facilities available.

LONDON NW3

DILLONS HOTEL
♦

21 Belsize Park, Hampstead,
London, NW3 4DU
T: (020) 7794 3360
F: (020) 7431 7900
E: desk@dillonshotel.demon.co.uk
I: www.dillonshotel.demon.co.uk

Bedrooms: 2 single,
3 double, 4 twin, 2 triple,
2 family rooms
Bathrooms: 7 en suite,
3 public

CC: Barclaycard, Delta,
Eurocard, JCB,
Mastercard, Solo, Switch,
Visa, Visa Electron

B&B per night:
S £30.00–£40.00
D £44.00–£54.00

OPEN All year round

Victorian stucco-fronted house, convenient for central London and just 6 minutes from either Swiss Cottage or Belsize Park tube stations. Most rooms have private shower/wc.

LONDON NW6

CAVENDISH GUEST HOUSE
♦♦♦♦

24 Cavendish Road, London,
NW6 7XP
T: (020) 8451 3249 (Answerphone)
F: (020) 8451 3249

Bedrooms: 2 single,
1 double, 1 twin, 2 triple
Bathrooms: 2 en suite,
2 public

Parking for 4

B&B per night:
S £30.00–£45.00
D £54.00–£57.00

OPEN All year round

In a quiet residential street, 5 minutes' walk from Kilburn underground station, 15 minutes' travelling time to the West End. Easy access to Wembley Stadium, Heathrow, Gatwick.

LONDON SE3

THE GROVERS
♦♦♦

96 Merriman Road, London,
SE3 8RZ
T: (020) 8488 7719 &
07713 226393 (Mobile)
F: (020) 8488 7719

Bedrooms: 1 single,
1 double, 1 twin
Bathrooms: 1 public

Parking for 3

B&B per night:
S £27.50–£27.50
D £55.00–£55.00

OPEN All year round

Family house in a residential road with 3 letting rooms and off-street parking. Close to local shops, pub, restaurant and buses. Use of garden.

AT-A-GLANCE SYMBOLS

Symbols at the end of each accommodation entry give useful information about services and facilities. A key to symbols can be found inside the back cover flap. Keep this open for easy reference.

◆◆◆◆

NUMBER NINE BLACKHEATH

9 Charlton Road, Blackheath, London, SE3 7EU
T: (020) 8858 4175 & 07957 361997
F: (020) 8858 4175
E: no9limited@hotmail.com
I: www.numbernineblackheath.com

A family-run Victorian guesthouse, recently refurbished. Blackheath and Greenwich within 15 minutes' walk. Central London 25 minutes by public transport. Bathrobes and security boxes in all rooms. All major credit cards accepted.

Bedrooms: 4 twin,	Parking for 4
1 family room	CC: Amex, Barclaycard,
Bathrooms: 2 public	Delta, Eurocard, JCB,
	Mastercard, Solo, Switch,
	Visa, Visa Electron

B&B per night:
S Min £50.00
D Min £70.00

HB per person:
DY Min £70.00

OPEN All year round

LONDON SE6

◆◆◆

THORNSBEACH

122 Bargery Road, Catford, London, SE6 2LR
T: (020) 8695 6544 & 8244 5554
F: (020) 8695 9577
E: helen@thornsbeach.co.uk
I: www.thornsbeach.co.uk

Bedrooms: 1 single,
1 double
Bathrooms: 1 en suite,
1 public

CC: Barclaycard, Delta,
Eurocard, JCB, Maestro,
Mastercard, Solo, Switch,
Visa, Visa Electron

B&B per night:
S £25.00–£29.00
D £55.00–£63.00

OPEN All year round

Spacious, comfortable Edwardian house within conservation area. Substantial organic breakfasts. Ample parking. Five minutes' walk to cinema and shops. Convenient for City, West End, Lewisham and Kent.

LONDON SE9

◆◆

MEADOW CROFT LODGE

96-98 Southwood Road,
New Eltham, London, SE9 3QS
T: (020) 8859 1488
F: (020) 8850 8054

Bedrooms: 4 single,
3 double, 9 twin,
1 family room
Bathrooms: 1 private,
4 public, 9 private
showers

Parking for 9
CC: Amex, Barclaycard,
Mastercard, Visa

B&B per night:
S £22.00–£28.00
D £43.00–£49.00

OPEN All year round

Between A2 and A20, near New Eltham station with easy access to London. Warm and friendly atmosphere. TV in rooms. British Tourist Authority London B&B award 1990.

◆◆

WESTON HOUSE

8 Eltham Green, Eltham, London,
SE9 5LB
T: (020) 8850 5191
F: (020) 8850 0030

Bedrooms: 3 single,
2 double, 3 twin, 1 triple,
1 family room
Bathrooms: 4 en suite,
1 public, 4 private
showers

Parking for 6
CC: Barclaycard, Delta,
Eurocard, Mastercard,
Solo, Switch, Visa, Visa
Electron

B&B per night:
S £35.00–£40.00
D £45.00–£50.00

OPEN All year round

Victorian hotel with modern comforts in Eltham Green conservation area, close to Maritime Greenwich and Millennium Dome. 20 minutes from central London, convenient for A2, M20, A205.

LONDON SE12

◆◆

KINGSLAND HOUSE

45 Southbrook Road, Lee, London,
SE12 8LJ
T: (020) 8318 4788

Bedrooms: 3 twin
Bathrooms: 2 public

B&B per night:
S £27.50–£27.50
D £50.00–£50.00

OPEN All year round

Detached house in conservation area, close to Blackheath/Greenwich and with easy access to City/West End. Off A205 South Circular, 8 minutes' walk from Lee station.

CONFIRM YOUR BOOKING
You are advised to confirm your booking in writing.

LONDON SE13

◆ **13 WELLMEADOW ROAD**
Hither Green, London, SE13 6SY
T: (020) 8697 1398

Bedrooms: 1 single,
3 twin, 1 triple
Bathrooms: 2 public

EM 1900 (LO 2030)
Parking for 2

B&B per night:
S £21.00–£21.00
D Min £34.00

HB per person:
DY £23.00–£23.00

OPEN All year round

Family home: 3 minutes BR station (London 20 minutes); 3 minutes South Circular; 6 minutes A2 motorway (Dover 1 hour).

LONDON SE18

Rating
Applied For

DOVER HOUSE
155 Shooters Hill, London,
SE18 3HP
T: (020) 8856 9892
F: (020) 8856 9892

Bedrooms: 1 single,
2 twin, 1 triple
Bathrooms: 2 public

Parking for 3

B&B per night:
S £25.00–£30.00
D £40.00–£60.00

OPEN All year round

A large Victorian, semi-detached family house in the heart of the millennium Greenwich Village. Just 8 miles from the centre of London.

LONDON SE27

◆ **THE WHITE HOUSE**
242 Norwood Road, West Norwood,
London, SE27 9AW
T: (020) 8670 4149 & 8761 8892
F: (020) 8670 6440
E: dmark@globalnet.co.uk
I: memberstripod/twhgh

Bedrooms: 2 single,
1 family room
Bathrooms: 3 en suite,
1 public

Parking for 3

B&B per night:
S £19.00–£20.00
D £30.00–£31.00

OPEN All year round

Listed Georgian house with forecourt parking, on main road. Buses and trains to the city and 15 minutes by train to Wimbledon. Close to Crystal Palace National Sports Centre.

LONDON SW1

◆◆ **AIRWAYS HOTEL NATIONLODGE**
29-31 St George's Drive, Victoria,
London, SW1V 4DG
T: (020) 7834 0205 & 7834 3567
F: (020) 7932 0007
E: sales@airways-hotel.com
I: www.airways-hotel.com

Bedrooms: 9 single,
9 double, 11 twin,
5 triple, 5 family rooms
Bathrooms: 39 en suite,
1 public

CC: Amex, Barclaycard,
Delta, Diners, JCB,
Maestro, Mastercard,
Solo, Switch, Visa, Visa
Electron

B&B per night:
S £49.00–£59.00
D £59.00–£79.00

OPEN All year round

Within walking distance of Buckingham Palace and Westminster Abbey. Convenient for Harrods and theatreland. Friendly personal service. Full English breakfast.

◆◆ **CARLTON HOTEL**
90 Belgrave Road, Victoria, London,
SW1V 2BJ
T: (020) 7976 6634 & 7932 0913
F: (020) 7821 8020
E: cityhotelcarlton@btconnect.com
I: home.btconnect.com/
cityhotelcarlton

Bedrooms: 4 single,
5 double, 2 twin, 6 triple
Bathrooms: 11 en suite,
1 public, 1 private
shower

CC: Amex, Barclaycard,
Delta, Diners, Eurocard,
Mastercard, Solo, Switch,
Visa

B&B per night:
S £45.00–£54.00
D £54.00–£64.00

OPEN All year round

Small, friendly B&B near Victoria station and within walking distance of famous landmarks such as Buckingham Palace, Trafalgar Square, Piccadilly Circus. A lot to offer at a moderate all-inclusive rate.

◆◆ **CASWELL HOTEL**
25 Gloucester Street, London,
SW1V 2DB
T: (020) 7834 6345
E: manager@hotellondon.co.uk
I: www.hotellondon.co.uk

Bedrooms: 2 single,
7 double, 4 twin, 2 triple,
2 family rooms
Bathrooms: 7 en suite,
5 public

CC: Barclaycard, Delta,
Eurocard, JCB,
Mastercard, Solo, Switch,
Visa, Visa Electron

B&B per night:
S £36.00–£62.00
D £44.00–£75.00

OPEN All year round

Pleasant, family-run hotel, near Victoria coach and rail stations, yet in a quiet location.

RATING All accommodation in this guide has been rated, or is awaiting a rating, by a trained English Tourism Council assessor.

LONDON SW1 continued

◆◆ DOVER HOTEL

44 Belgrave Road, London, SW1V 1RG	Bedrooms: 4 single, 13 double, 7 twin,	CC: Amex, Barclaycard, Delta, Diners, Eurocard,	B&B per night: **S £40.00–£55.00**
T: (020) 7821 9085	5 triple, 4 family rooms	JCB, Maestro, Mastercard,	**D £50.00–£70.00**
F: (020) 7834 6425	Bathrooms: 29 en suite,	Switch, Visa, Visa Electron	
E: dover@rooms.demon.co.uk	2 public, 4 private		OPEN All year round
I: www.rooms.demon.co.uk	showers		

Friendly bed and breakfast hotel within minutes of Victoria station and Gatwick Express. Most rooms with satellite TV, shower/WC, telephone, hairdryer. Very competitive prices.

◆◆◆ MELITA HOUSE HOTEL

35 Charlwood Street, Victoria, London, SW1V 2DU	Bedrooms: 4 single, 10 double, 2 twin,	CC: Amex, Barclaycard, Delta, Eurocard, JCB,	B&B per night: **S £55.00–£70.00**
T: (020) 7828 0471 & 7834 1387	3 triple, 3 family rooms	Maestro, Mastercard,	**D £80.00–£90.00**
F: (020) 7932 0988	Bathrooms: 22 en suite,	Solo, Switch, Visa, Visa	
E: reserve@melita.co.uk	1 public	Electron	OPEN All year round
I: www.melita.co.uk			

Elegant, family-run hotel in excellent location close to Victoria station. Rooms have extensive modern facilities. Warm, friendly welcome, full English breakfast included.

◆ STANLEY HOUSE HOTEL

19-21 Belgrave Road, London, SW1V 1RB
T: (020) 7834 5042 & 7834 7292
F: (020) 7834 8439
E: cmahotel@aol.com
I: www.affordablehotel.com

B&B per night:
S £42.00–£52.00
D £52.00–£62.00

OPEN All year round

In elegant Belgravia, only a few minutes' walk from Victoria station and with easy access to West End. All rooms en suite, with colour TV, direct-dial telephone, hairdryer. Friendly, relaxing atmosphere at affordable rates.	Bedrooms: 4 single, 23 double, 7 twin, 5 triple, 5 family rooms Bathrooms: 44 en suite, 8 public	CC: Amex, Barclaycard, Delta, Diners, Mastercard, Switch, Visa

◆◆◆◆ WINDERMERE HOTEL

142-144 Warwick Way, Victoria, London, SW1V 4JE
T: (020) 7834 5163 & 7834 5480
F: (020) 7630 8831
E: windermere@compuserve.com
I: www.windermere-hotel.co.uk

B&B per night:
S £67.00–£88.00
D £84.00–£136.00

OPEN All year round

BTA Trophy winner. Small, friendly hotel with well-equipped bedrooms and a cosy lounge. English breakfast and dinner are served in the elegant licensed restaurant.	Bedrooms: 4 single, 10 double, 5 twin, 1 triple, 2 family rooms Bathrooms: 20 en suite, 2 public	EM 1730 (LO 2230) CC: Amex, Barclaycard, Delta, Eurocard, JCB, Mastercard, Switch, Visa

LONDON SW5

◆◆ HOTEL EARLS COURT

28 Warwick Road, Earls Court, London, SW5 9UD	Bedrooms: 6 single, 4 double, 2 twin, 5 triple	CC: Amex, Barclaycard, Diners, Eurocard, JCB,	B&B per night: **S £30.00–£49.00**
T: (020) 7373 7079 & 7373 0302	Bathrooms: 6 private,	Mastercard, Visa	**D £49.00–£60.00**
F: (020) 7912 0582	4 public, 3 private		
E: hotel.earlscourt@virgin.net	showers		OPEN All year round
I: freespace.virgin.net/ hotel.earlscourt/index.htm			

A friendly, clean and comfortable, centrally located bed and breakfast, opposite Earl's Court Exhibition Hall and 50 yards from Earl's Court underground station (Warwick Road exit)

♦♦♦

A gem of a hotel in a beautiful big city. The decor, art and colour will cheer you up the moment you arrive. All rooms are individually styled, ranging from 4-poster Victorian room to dungeon room. Rooms also have safes and ISDN ports for laptops.

KENSINGTON INTERNATIONAL HOTEL

4 Templeton Place, London, SW5 9LZ
T: (020) 7370 4333
F: (020) 7244 7873
E: hotel@kensington-international-hotel.co.uk
I: www.kensington-international-hotel.co.uk

Bedrooms: 15 single, 17 double, 23 twin, 2 triple, 1 family room
Bathrooms: 58 en suite

EM 1800 (LO 2300)
CC: Amex, Barclaycard, Delta, Diners, Eurocard, JCB, Maestro, Mastercard, Solo, Switch, Visa, Visa Electron

B&B per night:
S £80.00–£100.00
D £100.00–£120.00

OPEN All year round

 16 ⚬

♦♦

LORD JIM HOTEL

23-25 Penywern Road, London, SW5 9TT
T: (020) 7370 6071 &
07957 167081
F: (020) 7373 8919
E: taher_tayeb@compuserve.com
I: www.lord-jim-hotel.co.uk

Bedrooms: 8 single, 6 double, 5 twin, 9 triple, 7 family rooms
Bathrooms: 11 en suite, 6 public, 3 private showers

CC: Amex, Barclaycard, Delta, Diners, Eurocard, Maestro, Mastercard, Solo, Switch, Visa Electron

B&B per night:
S £30.00–£48.00
D £45.00–£59.00

OPEN All year round

Budget-priced, well-serviced bed and breakfast, ideally situated for Earl's Court and Olympia exhibition halls. Convenient for museums, city, and Heathrow and Gatwick airports (via Victoria).

USE YOUR *i*s

There are more than 550 Tourist Information Centres throughout England offering friendly help with accommodation and holiday ideas as well as suggestions of places to visit and things to do. You'll find TIC addresses in the local Phone Book.

♦♦

MERLYN COURT HOTEL
2 Barkston Gardens, London, SW5 0EN
T: (020) 7370 1640
F: (020) 7370 4986
E: london@merlyncourt.demon.co.uk
I: www.smoothhound.co.uk/hotels/merlyn.html

B&B per night:
S £35.00–£60.00
D £50.00–£75.00

OPEN All year round

Well-established, family-run, good value hotel in quiet Edwardian square, close to Earl's Court and Olympia. Direct underground link to Heathrow, the West End and rail stations. Car park nearby.

Bedrooms: 4 single, 4 double, 4 twin, 2 triple, 3 family rooms
Bathrooms: 11 en suite, 6 public, 1 private shower

CC: Barclaycard, Delta, Eurocard, JCB, Mastercard, Switch, Visa

---

♦♦

OLIVER PLAZA HOTEL
33 Trebovir Road, Earl's Court, London, SW5 9NF
T: (020) 7373 7183
F: (020) 7244 6021
E: oliverplaza@capricornhotels.co.uk
I: www.capricornhotels.co.uk

Bedrooms: 3 single, 13 double, 14 twin, 3 triple, 5 family rooms
Bathrooms: 38 en suite

Parking for 4
CC: Amex, Barclaycard, Delta, Diners, Eurocard, JCB, Maestro, Mastercard, Solo, Switch, Visa, Visa Electron

B&B per night:
S £40.00–£45.00
D £40.00–£65.00

OPEN All year round

Friendly hotel with emphasis on efficiency of service and comfort for guests. Fully refurbished in 1999. Good access to public transport and shopping facilities.

♦♦
Ad p15

RAMSEES HOTEL
32-36 Hogarth Road, Earl's Court, London, SW5 0PU
T: (020) 7370 1445
F: (020) 7244 6835
E: ramsees@rasool.demon.co.uk
I: www.ramseeshotel.com

B&B per night:
S £33.00–£40.00
D £45.00–£52.00

OPEN All year round

Our friendly staff are here to make your stay comfortable. Ideally located in fashionable Kensington, close to the heart of the city. One minutes' walk Earl's Court station, making major shopping areas of Knightsbridge, Oxford Street and tourist attractions of Buckingham Palace, Tower of London and museums within easy reach.

Bedrooms: 13 single, 22 double, 11 twin, 15 triple
Bathrooms: 47 en suite, 13 public, 8 private showers

CC: Amex, Barclaycard, Delta, Diners, Eurocard, JCB, Maestro, Mastercard, Solo, Switch, Visa, Visa Electron

---

♦♦
Ad p15

RASOOL COURT HOTEL
19-21 Penywern Road, Earl's Court, London, SW5 9TT
T: (020) 7373 8900 & 7373 4893
F: (020) 7244 6835
E: rasool@rasool.demon.co.uk
I: www.rasoolcourthotel.com

B&B per night:
S £36.00–£42.00
D £48.00–£54.00

OPEN All year round

Family-run hotel ideally located in fashionable Kensington, within one minutes' walk of Earl's Court station which makes the shopping areas of Knightsbridge, Oxford Street and tourist attractions of Buckingham Palace, the Tower of London and museums with easy reach. The immediate area has a variety of restaurants and shops for your convenience.

Bedrooms: 25 single, 16 double, 8 twin, 8 triple
Bathrooms: 35 en suite, 4 public, 12 private showers

CC: Amex, Barclaycard, Delta, Diners, Eurocard, JCB, Maestro, Mastercard, Solo, Switch, Visa, Visa Electron

◆
Ad p43

WINDSOR HOUSE

12 Penywern Road, London, SW5 9ST
T: (020) 7373 9087
F: (020) 7385 2417

B&B per night:
S £23.00–£42.00
D £38.00–£64.00

OPEN All year round

Central London. Friendly, family-run bed and breakfast. Beautiful Victorian building. Excellent budget standard. Spacious, comfortable rooms. Ideal for double/family rooms (3,4,5). Children – the more the merrier! Use of new hotel kitchen for preparing own teas/meals. Super garden. NCP parking.

Bedrooms: 2 single, 4 double, 4 twin, 1 triple, 8 family rooms
Bathrooms: 10 en suite, 6 public, 8 private showers

◆◆

YORK HOUSE HOTEL

27-28 Philbeach Gardens, London, SW5 9EA
T: (020) 7373 7519 & 7373 7579
F: (020) 7370 4641
E: yorkhh@aol.com

Bedrooms: 16 single, 3 double, 3 twin, 2 triple, 3 family rooms
Bathrooms: 3 en suite, 7 public

CC: Amex, Barclaycard, Delta, Diners, Eurocard, JCB, Mastercard, Solo, Switch, Visa, Visa Electron

B&B per night:
S £33.00–£47.00
D £54.00–£73.00

OPEN All year round

Conveniently located in Kensington close to Earl's Court and Olympia exhibition centres and the West End. Underground direct to Heathrow Airport.

◆◆◆◆

FIVE SUMNER PLACE HOTEL

5 Sumner Place, South Kensington, London, SW7 3EE
T: (020) 7584 7586
F: (020) 7823 9962
E: reservations@sumnerplace.com
I: www.sumnerplace.com

B&B per night:
S £85.00–£99.00
D £141.00–£152.00

OPEN All year round

Awarded "best small hotel". In South Kensington, one of the most stylish and sought-after locations in London, the hotel brings the charm and elegance of a former age to the 20thC. Ideally placed for visiting the sights. This family-owned and run hotel offers excellent service and personal attention.

Bedrooms: 3 single, 5 double, 5 twin
Bathrooms: 13 en suite, 1 public

CC: Amex, Barclaycard, Eurocard, JCB, Mastercard, Switch, Visa

---

◆◆◆◆◆
Gold
Award

HOTEL NUMBER SIXTEEN

16 Sumner Place, London, SW7 3EG
T: (020) 7589 5232
F: (020) 7584 8615
E: reservations@numbersixteenhotel.co.uk
I: www.numbersixteenhotel.co.uk

Bedrooms: 9 single, 23 double, 4 triple
Bathrooms: 32 en suite, 2 private

CC: Amex, Barclaycard, Delta, Diners, Eurocard, Mastercard, Switch, Visa

B&B per night:
S £100.00–£140.00
D £175.00–£200.00

OPEN All year round

With atmosphere of a comfortable townhouse in very attractive street. Secluded award-winning gardens. Winner of the Spencer Trophy.

WELCOME HOST This is a nationally recognised customer care programme which aims to promote the highest standards of service and a warm welcome. Establishments taking part in this initiative are indicated by the ⚘ symbol.

LONDON SW14

◆◆◆ **106**
106 East Sheen Avenue, London,
SW14 8AU
T: (020) 8255 1900
F: (020) 8876 8084
E: rpratt@easynet.co.uk

Bedrooms: 2 single,
1 twin
Bathrooms: 1 public

B&B per night:
S £30.00–£35.00
D £50.00–£50.00

OPEN All year round

Warm welcome in elegant Edwardian house. Near Richmond Park yet 30 minutes central London. Many repeat bookings.

◆◆◆ **THE PLOUGH INN**
42 Christchurch Road, East Sheen,
London, SW14 7AF
T: (020) 8876 7833 & 8876 4533
F: (020) 8392 8801
E: ploughthe@hotmail.com

Bedrooms: 1 single,
3 double, 3 twin, 1 triple
Bathrooms: 8 en suite

Lunch available
EM 1930 (LO 2130)
Parking for 4
CC: Amex, Barclaycard,
Delta, Eurocard,
Mastercard, Solo, Switch,
Visa, Visa Electron

B&B per night:
S £60.00–£65.00
D £80.00–£90.00

HB per person:
DY £70.00–£75.00

OPEN All year round

Delightful old pub, part 16thC, next to Richmond Park. En suite accommodation, traditional ales, home-cooked food.

LONDON SW18

◆◆◆ **THE BREWERS INN**
147 East Hill, Wandsworth, London,
SW18 2QB
T: (020) 8874 4128
F: (020) 8877 1953
I: www.youngs.co.uk

Bedrooms: 4 single,
9 double, 3 twin
Bathrooms: 16 en suite

Lunch available
EM 1800 (LO 2200)
Parking for 10
CC: Amex, Barclaycard,
Delta, Diners, Mastercard,
Switch, Visa

B&B per night:
S £58.00–£78.00
D £68.00–£88.00

OPEN All year round

Sixteen en suite bedrooms, all with air conditioning. Large bar and bistro, a la carte restaurant. Patio garden and car park. Excellent full English breakfast included.

◆◆◆ **GROSVENOR ARMS**
204 Garratt Lane, Wandsworth,
London, SW18 4ED
T: (020) 8874 2709
F: (020) 8874 0813

Bedrooms: 3 twin,
1 triple
Bathrooms: 3 public

Lunch available
EM 1830 (LO 1930)
CC: Barclaycard, Delta,
Mastercard, Switch, Visa

B&B per night:
S £35.00–£40.00
D £40.00–£48.00

OPEN All year round

Well-maintained 3-storey pub, over 100 years old, with a large garden. Spacious and comfortable, family-run by Maureen and Jim. Convenient for city centre.

LONDON W1

◆◆

LINCOLN HOUSE HOTEL
33 Gloucester Place, London, W1H 3PD
T: (020) 7486 7630
F: (020) 7486 0166
E: reservations@lincoln-house-hotel.co.uk
I: www.lincoln-house-hotel.co.uk

B&B per night:
S £65.00–£69.00
D £85.00–£89.00

OPEN All year round

Built in the days of King George III, this hotel offers Georgian charms and character. En suite rooms with modern comforts. Competitively priced. Located in the heart of London's West End, next to Oxford Street and most famous shopping attractions, close to theatreland. Ideal for business and leisure.

Bedrooms: 6 single,
8 double, 4 twin, 3 triple,
1 family room
Bathrooms: 20 en suite,
2 private, 1 public

CC: Amex, Barclaycard,
Delta, Diners, Eurocard,
JCB, Mastercard, Solo,
Switch, Visa, Visa Electron

WHERE TO STAY
Please mention this guide when making your booking.

◆◆ **MARBLE ARCH INN**
49-50 Upper Berkeley Street,
Marble Arch, London, W1H 7PN
T: (020) 7723 7888
F: (020) 7723 6060
E: marble@rooms.demon.co.uk
I: www.rooms.demon.co.uk

Bedrooms: 2 single,
8 double, 9 twin, 6 triple,
4 family rooms
Bathrooms: 25 en suite,
2 public, 4 private
showers

CC: Amex, Barclaycard,
Delta, Diners, Eurocard,
JCB, Maestro, Mastercard,
Solo, Switch, Visa, Visa
Electron

B&B per night:
S £30.00–£60.00
D £40.00–£70.00

OPEN All year round

Friendly bed and breakfast hotel within minutes of Hyde Park, Oxford Street, Heathrow Express. Most rooms with satellite TV, shower/WC, telephone, hairdryer. Very competitive prices.

◆◆ **ALBRO HOUSE HOTEL**
155 Sussex Gardens, London,
W2 2RY
T: (020) 7724 2931 & 7706 8153
F: (020) 7262 2278

Bedrooms: 2 single,
6 double, 6 twin, 1 triple,
3 family rooms
Bathrooms: 16 en suite,
1 public

Parking for 1
CC: Barclaycard, Eurocard,
Mastercard, Visa

B&B per night:
S £40.00–£56.00
D £56.00–£72.00

OPEN All year round

Ideally located in pleasant area near public transport. Nice rooms, all en suite. English breakfast. Languages spoken. Friendly and safe. Some parking available.

◆◆◆  **ALLANDALE HOTEL**
3 Devonshire Terrace, Lancaster Gate,
London, W2 3DN
T: (020) 7723 8311 & 7723 7807
F: (020) 7723 8311
E: info@allandalehotel.co.uk
I: www.allandalehotel.co.uk

B&B per night:
S £45.00–£50.00
D £60.00–£65.00

HB per person:
DY £34.00–£35.00

OPEN All year round

Quietly situated, family-run hotel. All bedrooms have private shower, toilet and TV. Full English breakfast. Close to 2 underground stations, Lancaster Gate and Paddington. Stroll in Hyde Park or take a bus to Oxford Street, West End theatres, museums and art galleries. Saturday Portobello antiques, Sunday Bayswater Road open air art.

Bedrooms: 2 single,
8 double, 5 twin, 2 triple,
3 family rooms
Bathrooms: 18 en suite,
1 public

CC: Amex, Barclaycard,
Delta, Diners, Eurocard,
JCB, Mastercard, Visa,
Visa Electron

◆◆  **BARRY HOUSE HOTEL**
12 Sussex Place, London, W2 2TP
T: (020) 7723 7340 & 7723 0994
F: (020) 7723 9775
E: bh-hotel@bigfoot.com
I: www.hotel.uk.com/barryhouse

B&B per night:
S £37.00–£50.00
D Min £75.00

OPEN All year round

We believe in family-like care. Comfortable en suite rooms with TV, telephone and hospitality tray. Located close to Hyde Park, the West End, Paddington Station and many tourist attractions. We offer tourist information, sightseeing and tours arranged, theatre tickets and taxis booked.

Bedrooms: 4 single,
4 double, 7 twin, 2 triple,
1 family room
Bathrooms: 14 en suite,
2 public, 1 private
shower

CC: Amex, Barclaycard,
Delta, Diners, Eurocard,
JCB, Mastercard, Solo,
Switch, Visa

 CREDIT CARD BOOKINGS If you book by telephone and are asked for your credit card number it is advisable to check the proprietor's policy should you cancel your reservation.

LONDON W2 continued

CLASSIC HOTEL
◆◆

92 Sussex Gardens, Hyde Park,
London, W2 1UH
T: (020) 7706 7776
F: (020) 7706 8136
E: bookings@classic-hotel.com
I: www.classic-hotel.com

Bedrooms: 2 single,
3 double, 4 twin, 3 triple,
1 family room
Bathrooms: 13 en suite

Parking for 2
CC: Amex, Barclaycard,
Delta, Diners, Eurocard,
JCB, Maestro, Mastercard,
Solo, Switch, Visa, Visa
Electron

B&B per night:
S £45.00–£52.00
D £60.00–£76.00

OPEN All year round

Rooms with private shower and toilet, colour TV, fridge. Parking facility. Ideal for business, shopping, leisure. Close to Paddington mainline and underground station.

EUROPA HOUSE HOTEL
◆◆

151 Sussex Gardens, London,
W2 2RY
T: (020) 7723 7343 & 7402 1923
F: (020) 7224 9331
E: europahouse@enterprise.net
I: www.europahousehotel.com

Bedrooms: 3 single,
3 double, 6 twin, 4 triple,
2 family rooms
Bathrooms: 18 en suite,
1 public

Parking for 1
CC: Amex, Barclaycard,
Delta, Diners, Eurocard,
Mastercard, Switch, Visa,
Visa Electron

B&B per night:
S £42.00–£52.00
D £60.00–£70.00

OPEN All year round

Close to Hyde Park and convenient for Heathrow/Paddington rail link. All rooms with en suite facilities, tea and coffee making facilities, colour TV. English breakfast included.

HYDE PARK ROOMS HOTEL
◆

137 Sussex Gardens, Hyde Park,
London, W2 2RX
T: (020) 7723 0225 & 7723 0965

Bedrooms: 5 single,
6 double, 2 twin, 2 triple,
1 family room
Bathrooms: 6 en suite,
2 public

Parking for 1
CC: Amex, Barclaycard,
Diners, Mastercard, Visa

B&B per night:
S £30.00–£40.00
D £45.00–£60.00

OPEN All year round

Small centrally located private hotel with personal service. Clean, comfortable and friendly. Within walking distance of Hyde Park and Kensington Gardens. Car parking available.

KENSINGTON GARDENS HOTEL
◆◆◆

9 Kensington Gardens Square,
London, W2 4BH
T: (020) 7221 7790
F: (020) 7792 8612
E: kensingtongardenshotel@
phoenixhotel.co.uk
I: www.kensingtongardenshotel.co.
uk

Bedrooms: 8 single,
5 double, 2 twin, 2 triple
Bathrooms: 13 en suite,
4 private showers

Lunch available
EM 1900 (LO 2300)
CC: Amex, Barclaycard,
Delta, Diners, Eurocard,
Mastercard, Solo, Switch,
Visa, Visa Electron

B&B per night:
S £53.00–£62.00
D £79.00–£89.00

OPEN All year round

Beautifully refurbished Victorian building, centrally situated close to Bayswater and Queensway underground station. Easy access to airports and British Rail stations.

LANCASTER COURT HOTEL
◆◆

202-204 Sussex Gardens,
Hyde Park, London, W2 3UA
T: (020) 7402 8438 & 7402 6369
F: (020) 7706 3794
E: lch300999@compuserve.com
I: www.lancaster-court-hotel.co.uk/

Bedrooms: 13 single,
10 double, 7 twin,
7 triple, 5 family rooms
Bathrooms: 24 en suite,
2 public, 14 private
showers

Parking for 10
CC: Amex, Barclaycard,
Delta, Diners, Eurocard,
JCB, Mastercard, Solo,
Switch, Visa, Visa Electron

B&B per night:
S £35.00–£55.00
D £55.00–£85.00

OPEN All year round

Two minutes from Lancaster Gate and Paddington tube. Rooms tastefully decorated. Oxford Street, Harrods and theatres all nearby. Friendly and courteous service. Apply for special midweek and weekend offers.

MANOR COURT HOTEL
◆

7 Clanricarde Gardens, London,
W2 4JJ
T: (020) 7727 5407 & 7792 3361
F: (020) 7229 2875

Bedrooms: 5 single,
5 double, 4 twin, 5 triple,
1 family room
Bathrooms: 6 en suite,
3 private, 4 public,
7 private showers

CC: Amex, Delta, Diners,
Eurocard, JCB, Maestro,
Mastercard, Solo, Switch,
Visa, Visa Electron

B&B per night:
S £35.00–£50.00
D £50.00–£65.00

OPEN All year round

Family-run bed and breakfast hotel within walking distance of Hyde Park and Kensington Gardens. Near Notting Hill Gate underground and Airbus stop. All rooms have colour TV and telephone.

◆◆ **OLYMPIC HOUSE HOTEL**

138-140 Sussex Gardens, London, W2 1UB	Bedrooms: 9 single, 1 double, 11 twin, 9 triple, 6 family rooms	Parking for 4 CC: Amex, Barclaycard, Mastercard, Switch, Visa	B&B per night: **S £45.00–£55.00** **D £60.00–£72.00**
T: (020) 7723 5935 F: (020) 7224 8144 E: olympichousehotel@btinternet.com	Bathrooms: 30 en suite, 2 public, 3 private showers		OPEN All year round

Small, centrally-located, privately-run hotel. Offers both comfort and personal service in warm and friendly atmosphere. All rooms have shower, WC, hairdryer, telephone, radio, colour TV and satellite.

◆◆◆ **RHODES HOUSE HOTEL**

195 Sussex Gardens, London, W2 2RJ	Bedrooms: 3 single, 3 double, 3 twin, 5 triple, 4 family rooms	CC: Barclaycard, Eurocard, JCB, Maestro, Mastercard, Solo, Switch, Visa, Visa Electron	B&B per night: **S £55.00–£70.00** **D £65.00–£85.00**
T: (020) 7262 5617 & 7262 0537 F: (020) 7723 4054 E: chris@rhodeshotel.com I: www.rhodeshotel.com	Bathrooms: 18 en suite		OPEN All year round

Rooms with private facilities, air-conditioning, satellite TV, telephone, refrigerator, hairdryer, tea/coffee-making facilities. Friendly atmosphere. Families especially welcome. Excellent transport for sightseeing and shopping.

RUDDIMANS HOTEL

160-162 Sussex Gardens, London, W2 1UD

T: (020) 7723 1026

F: (020) 7262 2983

E: reserve@ruddimanshotel.co.uk

I: www.ruddimanshotel.co.uk

B&B per night:
S £34.00–£46.00
D £52.00–£62.00

OPEN All year round

Welcome to a warm, friendly, hospitable yet novel atmosphere in the heart of London, second to none. If you are looking for something slightly different, for example a buffet breakfast consisting of English and continental delights all included in the price of your stay, then why not give us a call?	Bedrooms: 8 single, 13 double, 6 twin, 11 triple, 3 family rooms Bathrooms: 33 en suite, 2 public	Parking for 4 CC: Amex, Barclaycard, Delta, JCB, Maestro, Mastercard, Solo, Switch, Visa

ST DAVID'S AND NORFOLK COURT HOTEL

16 Norfolk Square, Hyde Park, London, W2 1RS	Bedrooms: 19 single, 17 double, 10 twin, 22 triple, 6 family rooms	CC: Amex, Barclaycard, Delta, Diners, Eurocard, JCB, Maestro, Mastercard,	B&B per night: **S £49.00–£54.00** **D £59.00–£74.00**
T: (020) 7723 3856 & 7723 4963 F: (020) 7402 9061	Bathrooms: 37 en suite, 14 public, 6 private showers	Solo, Switch, Visa, Visa Electron	OPEN All year round

Small, friendly hotel in front of a quiet garden square. Central location, economical prices. Reckons to serve the "best English breakfast" in London.

◆◆ **ABBEY LODGE HOTEL**

51 Grange Park, Ealing, London, W5 3PR	Bedrooms: 10 single, 2 double, 1 twin, 2 triple, 1 family room	CC: Barclaycard, Delta, Diners, Eurocard, Mastercard, Switch, Visa	B&B per night: **S £39.00–£45.00** **D £49.00–£57.00**
T: (020) 8567 7914 F: (020) 8579 5350 E: enquiries@londonlodgehotels.com I: smoothhound.co.uk/hotels/abbeylo1.html	Bathrooms: 16 en suite		OPEN All year round

All rooms en suite, with colour TV, tea/coffee making facilities and radio alarm clocks. Very close to 3 underground lines. Midway central London and Heathrow.

LONDON W5 continued

◆◆◆ GRANGE LODGE HOTEL

48-50 Grange Road, Ealing, London, W5 5BX
T: (020) 8567 1049
F: (020) 8579 5350
E: enquiries@londonlodgehotels.com
I: www.smoothhound.co.uk/hotels/gran.html

Bedrooms: 8 single, 2 double, 2 twin, 2 triple
Bathrooms: 9 en suite, 2 public

Parking for 8
CC: Barclaycard, Delta, Diners, Eurocard, Mastercard, Switch, Visa

B&B per night:
S £30.00–£45.00
D £45.00–£57.00

OPEN All year round

Quiet, comfortable hotel, close to 3 underground stations. Midway central London and Heathrow. Colour TV, tea/coffee-making facilities, radio/alarm, most rooms en suite.

LONDON W6

◆◆

HOTEL ORLANDO

83 Shepherds Bush Road, Hammersmith, London, W6 7LR
T: (020) 7603 4890
F: (020) 7603 4890

B&B per night:
S £35.00–£40.00
D £44.00–£52.00

OPEN All year round

Family-run business for the last 22 years. Situated near Hammersmith tube station, ideal for easy connection to central London. Newly decorated and all rooms have en suite facilities and colour TV. Homely welcome from Italian proprietor.

Bedrooms: 4 single, 1 double, 5 twin, 2 triple, 2 family rooms
Bathrooms: 14 en suite

CC: Amex, Delta, Eurocard, Mastercard, Solo, Switch, Visa, Visa Electron

LONDON W8

◆◆◆

HOTEL ATLAS-APOLLO

18-30 Lexham Gardens, London, W8 5JE
T: (020) 7835 1155 & 7835 1133
F: (020) 7370 4853
E: reservations@atlas-apollo.com
I: www.atlas-apollo.com

B&B per night:
S £75.00–£85.00
D £90.00–£100.00

OPEN All year round

Friendly, long established hotel, situated close to Earl's Court and Olympia exhibition centres and the shopping areas of Knightsbridge and Kensington High Street. Spacious, well-furnished bedrooms all with colour TV, direct-dial telephone and en suite bathroom.

Bedrooms: 28 single, 7 double, 44 twin, 14 triple
Bathrooms: 93 en suite

CC: Amex, Barclaycard, Delta, Eurocard, JCB, Mastercard, Switch, Visa, Visa Electron

◆◆ CLEARLAKE HOTEL

18-19 Prince of Wales Terrace, Kensington, London, W8 5PQ
T: (020) 7937 3274
F: (020) 7376 0604
E: clearlake@talk21.com

Bedrooms: 2 single, 5 double, 1 twin, 6 family rooms
Bathrooms: 14 en suite

CC: Amex, Barclaycard, Diners, Mastercard, Visa

B&B per night:
S £40.00–£55.00
D £50.00–£75.00

OPEN All year round

Comfortable rooms in a hotel in a quiet cul-de-sac, with view of Hyde Park. Self-catering apartments also available. Close to shops and transport.

ACCESSIBILITY

Look for the 🔲🔲🔲 symbols which indicate accessibility for wheelchair users. A list of establishments is at the front of this guide.

LONDON W14

◆◆◆◆

AVONMORE HOTEL
66 Avonmore Road, Kensington, London, W14 8RS
T: (020) 7603 3121 & 7603 4296
F: (020) 7603 4035
E: avonmore.hotel@dial.pipex.com
I: www.avonmore.hotel.dial.pipex.com

B&B per night:
S £60.00–£85.00
D £85.00–£95.00

OPEN All year round

Award-winning, privately owned and run hotel with friendly atmosphere. Refurbished to highest standards, with all in-room facilities. Ideally situated for sights of London and Olympia and Earl's Court exhibition centres. Excellent value for money.

Bedrooms: 1 single, 2 double, 3 twin, 3 triple; suites available
Bathrooms: 7 en suite, 1 public

CC: Amex, Barclaycard, Delta, Diners, Eurocard, JCB, Mastercard, Switch, Visa

LONDON WC1

◆

ARRAN HOUSE HOTEL
77 Gower Street, London, WC1E 6HJ
T: (020) 7636 2186 & 7637 1140
F: (020) 7436 5328
E: arran@dircon.co.uk
I: www.proteusweb.com/arran

Bedrooms: 6 single, 6 double, 4 twin, 10 triple, 2 family rooms
Bathrooms: 5 en suite, 5 private, 5 public, 4 private showers

Parking for 2
CC: Barclaycard, Delta, Eurocard, Mastercard, Solo, Switch, Visa, Visa Electron

B&B per night:
S £45.00–£55.00
D £55.00–£75.00

OPEN All year round

Small, comfortable, family-run bed and breakfast hotel in central London, convenient for theatres, shopping and public transport.

◆◆◆

CRESCENT HOTEL
49-50 Cartwright Gardens, Bloomsbury, London, WC1H 9EL
T: (020) 7387 1515
F: (020) 7383 2054
E: general.enquiries@ crescenthoteloflondon.com
I: www.crescenthoteloflondon.com

Bedrooms: 12 single, 2 double, 3 twin, 7 triple, 3 family rooms
Bathrooms: 18 en suite, 4 public, 3 private showers

CC: Barclaycard, Delta, Eurocard, Mastercard, Visa

B&B per night:
S £43.00–£70.00
D £80.00–£82.00

OPEN All year round

Refurbished, family-run hotel in quiet Georgian crescent, with private gardens and tennis courts. All rooms have colour TV, tea/coffee tray and direct-dial telephone, most en suite.

◆

GOWER HOUSE HOTEL
57 Gower Street, London, WC1E 6HJ
T: (020) 7636 4685
F: (020) 7636 4685

Bedrooms: 4 single, 2 double, 6 twin, 3 triple, 1 family room
Bathrooms: 3 en suite, 3 public

CC: Barclaycard, Eurocard, JCB, Mastercard, Switch, Visa

B&B per night:
S £40.00–£42.00
D £50.00–£52.00

OPEN All year round

Friendly bed and breakfast hotel within easy walking distance of the British Museum, shops, theatres and restaurants. Near Goodge Street underground station.

◆◆

GUILFORD HOUSE HOTEL
6 Guilford Street, London, WC1N 1DR
T: (020) 7430 2504
F: (020) 7430 0721
E: guilford-hotel@lineone.net
I: www.guilfordhotel.co.uk

Bedrooms: 3 single, 2 double, 1 twin, 5 triple, 1 family room
Bathrooms: 5 public

Parking for 3
CC: Amex, Barclaycard, Delta, Diners, Mastercard, Switch, Visa, Visa Electron

B&B per night:
S £30.00–£39.00
D £45.00–£54.00

OPEN All year round

Centrally located bed and breakfast, walking distance to British Museum, Trafalgar Square, Piccadilly Circus, Oxford Street, Theatreland and West End. Easy access to public transport.

HALF BOARD PRICES Half board prices are given per person, but in some cases these may be based on double/twin occupancy.

LONDON WC1 continued

ST ATHANS HOTEL
20 Tavistock Place, Russell Square, London, WC1H 9RE
T: (020) 7837 9140 & 7837 9627
F: (020) 7833 8352

Bedrooms: 14 single, 13 double, 15 twin, 1 triple, 5 family rooms
Bathrooms: 8 en suite, 15 public

CC: Amex, Barclaycard, Diners, Eurocard, JCB, Mastercard, Visa

B&B per night:
S £30.00–£40.00
D £40.00–£50.00

OPEN All year round

Simple, small but clean family-run hotel offering bed and breakfast.

LONDON WC2

ROYAL ADELPHI HOTEL
21 Villiers Street, London, WC2N 6ND
T: (020) 7930 8764
F: (020) 7930 8735
E: info@royaladelphi.co.uk
I: www.royaladelphi.co.uk

Bedrooms: 20 single, 12 double, 13 twin, 2 triple
Bathrooms: 34 en suite, 4 public

Lunch available
EM 1800 (LO 2300)
CC: Amex, Barclaycard, Delta, Diners, Eurocard, Maestro, Mastercard, Switch, Visa, Visa Electron

B&B per night:
S £50.00–£70.00
D £70.00–£95.00

OPEN All year round

Centrally located and ideal for theatreland, near Embankment and Charing Cross underground. All rooms with colour TV, hairdryer, tea/coffee facilities. Most rooms have private bathrooms.

OUTER LONDON
BROMLEY

GLENDEVON HOUSE HOTEL
80 Southborough Road, Bickley, Bromley, BR1 2EN
T: (020) 8467 2183
F: (020) 8295 0701

Bedrooms: 2 single, 3 double, 2 twin, 3 triple
Bathrooms: 10 en suite

EM 1900 (LO 2000)
Parking for 7
CC: Barclaycard, Mastercard, Switch, Visa

B&B per night:
S £34.00–£39.95
D Min £50.50

HB per person:
DY £52.00–£64.00

OPEN All year round

Family-run hotel with all rooms en suite, tea/coffee, TV, telephone, car park, catering for business travellers and tourists. Convenient base for Bromley, London and Kent.

CROYDON *Tourist Information Centre Tel: (020) 8253 1009*

ALPHA GUEST HOUSE
99 Brigstock Road, Thornton Heath, Surrey CR7 7JL
T: (020) 8684 4811 & 8665 0032
F: (020) 8405 0302

Bedrooms: 5 single, 1 double, 4 twin, 1 triple
Bathrooms: 6 en suite, 2 public

Parking for 5

B&B per night:
S £25.00–£35.00
D £40.00–£50.00

HB per person:
DY £25.00–£30.00

OPEN All year round

Modern, family-run residence in ideal location near Croydon (20 minutes from Victoria station). Tea and coffee-making facilities, satellite TV, free parking and varied breakfasts.

CROYDON HOTEL
112 Lower Addiscombe Road, Croydon, CR0 6AD
T: (020) 8656 7233
F: (020) 8655 0211

Bedrooms: 1 single, 2 double, 3 twin, 2 triple
Bathrooms: 6 en suite, 1 public

Parking for 4
CC: Barclaycard, Delta, Eurocard, Mastercard, Visa

B&B per night:
S £35.00–£50.00
D £55.00–£65.00

OPEN All year round

Close to central Croydon (route A222) and 10 minutes' walk from East Croydon station. Opposite shops and restaurants. Frequent direct trains to Victoria and Gatwick Airport.

STOCKS
51 Selcroft Road, Purley, Surrey CR8 1AJ
T: (020) 8660 3054
F: (020) 8660 3054

Bedrooms: 1 double, 2 twin
Bathrooms: 2 en suite, 1 public

Parking for 3

B&B per night:
S £25.00–£25.00
D £46.00–£50.00

OPEN All year round

Central London 20 minutes by train. Convenient for M25, M23 and Gatwick Airport. Within walking distance of Purley station.

IDEAS For ideas on places to visit refer to the introduction at the beginning of this section.

◆◆◆ **HINDES HOTEL**

8 Hindes Road, Harrow, Middlesex HA1 1SJ	Bedrooms: 4 single, 4 double, 6 twin	EM 1700 (LO 1900) Parking for 20
T: (020) 8427 7468 (Reservations)	Bathrooms: 7 en suite, 2 public	CC: Amex, Barclaycard, Delta, Diners, Eurocard, JCB, Maestro, Mastercard, Solo, Switch, Visa, Visa Electron
F: (020) 8424 0673		

B&B per night:
S Min £39.00
D Min £50.00

OPEN All year round

Homely owner-run bed and breakfast hotel near the M1. West End 15 minutes by underground. Convenient for Wembley Stadium complex.

See under Hounslow

◆◆◆◆

ASHDOWNE HOUSE

9 Pownall Gardens, Hounslow, Middlesex TW3 1YW

T: (020) 8572 0008
F: (020) 8570 1939
E: mail@ashdownehouse.com
I: www.ashdownehouse.com

B&B per night:
S £60.00–£65.00
D £69.50–£79.00

OPEN All year round

Very comfortable Victorian house with elegant rooms, all en suite and non-smoking. Walking distance of the high street and Hounslow Central underground station (for access to central London and Heathrow Airport). Hampton Court Palace, Kew Gardens, Twickenham rugby ground and Syon Park are easily reached by car or bus.

Bedrooms: 2 single, 3 double, 2 twin	Parking for 4
Bathrooms: 7 en suite	CC: Barclaycard, Delta, Mastercard, Visa

◆◆◆

SHALIMAR HOTEL

215-221 Staines Road, Hounslow, Middlesex TW3 3JJ

T: (020) 8572 2816 & 0500 238239 (Free call)
F: (020) 8569 6789

B&B per night:
S Max £55.00
D Max £65.00

OPEN All year round

Located in centre of Hounslow, close to underground, M4, M25, M3 and 3 miles from Heathrow. Fantastic shopping centre within walking distance. En suite rooms, colour TV, tea/coffee bar. Beautiful illuminated large lawn and garden. TV lounge and bar.

Bedrooms: 14 single, 7 double, 14 twin, 5 triple	Parking for 10
Bathrooms: 30 en suite, 10 private showers	CC: Amex, Barclaycard, Delta, Diners, Eurocard, JCB, Maestro, Mastercard, Solo, Switch, Visa, Visa Electron

◆◆ **SKYLARK BED & BREAKFAST**

297 Bath Road, Hounslow, Middlesex TW3 3DB	Bedrooms: 8 single, 8 double, 2 twin, 1 triple, 1 family room	Parking for 8 CC: Amex, Barclaycard, Eurocard, Mastercard, Visa
T: (020) 8577 8455		
F: (020) 8577 8741	Bathrooms: 11 en suite, 1 private, 8 private showers	

B&B per night:
S £50.00–£50.00
D £65.00–£65.00

OPEN All year round

Skylark Bed & Breakfast is 100 yards from Hounslow West underground station and 3 miles from Heathrow Airport. All rooms are en suite.

SYMBOLS The symbols in each entry give information about services and facilities. A key to these symbols appears at the back of this guide.

PURLEY

♦♦♦ FOXLEY MOUNT

44 Foxley Lane, Purley, Surrey
CR8 3EE
T: (020) 8660 9751
F: (020) 8660 9751

Bedrooms: 1 single,
1 twin, 1 triple
Bathrooms: 1 public

Parking for 3

B&B per night:
S Max £25.00
D Max £40.00

OPEN All year round

Large Edwardian house, family-run bed and breakfast. Walking distance to Purley station. Twenty minutes to Gatwick or central London by train.

RICHMOND *Tourist Information Centre Tel: (020) 8940 9125*

♦♦♦♦♦
Gold
Award

CHALON HOUSE

8 Spring Terrace, Paradise Road, Richmond,
Surrey TW9 1LW
T: (020) 8332 1121
F: (020) 8332 1131
E: virgilioz@aol.com

B&B per night:
D £70.00-£90.00

OPEN Feb-Nov

Listed Georgian townhouse. Quality en suite bedrooms with big comfortable beds and breakfast tailored to your taste. 5-minute walk to Richmond station and 7 miles to central London. Picnic in Kew Gardens or relax at one of the many traditional pubs along the Thames.

Bedrooms: 1 double,
2 twin
Bathrooms: 3 en suite

EM 2000
Parking for 3

♦♦♦

HOBART HALL HOTEL

43-47 Petersham Road, Richmond, Surrey
TW10 6UL
T: (020) 8940 0435 (Answerphone) & 8940
1702
F: (020) 8332 2996
E: hobarthall@aol.com

B&B per night:
S £40.00-£60.00
D £55.00-£85.00

OPEN All year round

Built circa 1690 with 1752 additions. Past tenants include the Earl of Buckinghamshire, the Hon Henry Hobart and the Duke of Clarence (King William IV). Situated on the banks of the River Thames, but also in the historic town of Richmond, guests have the best of both worlds, with modern accommodation.

Bedrooms: 7 single,
5 double, 3 twin, 4 triple
Bathrooms: 15 en suite,
3 private, 3 public

Lunch available
Parking for 17
CC: Amex, Barclaycard,
Diners, Eurocard,
Mastercard, Switch, Visa

♦♦♦ QUINNS HOTEL

48 Sheen Road, Richmond, Surrey
TW9 1AW
T: (020) 8940 5444
F: (020) 8940 1828
I: www.quinnshotel.com

Bedrooms: 6 single,
24 double, 7 twin,
1 family room
Bathrooms: 23 en suite,
6 public

Parking for 14
CC: Amex, Barclaycard,
Delta, Diners, JCB,
Mastercard, Solo, Switch,
Visa

B&B per night:
S £40.00-£80.00
D £60.00-£95.00

OPEN All year round

Ideally located for business or pleasure, within easy reach of central London, airports and local places of interest.

♦♦♦ RICHMOND PARK HOTEL

3 Petersham Road, Richmond,
Surrey TW10 6UH
T: (020) 8948 4666
F: (020) 8940 7376
E: richmdpk@globalnet.co.uk

Bedrooms: 2 single,
18 double, 2 twin
Bathrooms: 22 en suite

CC: Amex, Delta,
Eurocard, Mastercard,
Solo, Switch, Visa

B&B per night:
S £69.00-£79.00
D £90.00-£110.00

OPEN All year round

Privately-owned hotel in the heart of Richmond. All rooms en suite with direct-dial telephone, colour TV, radio and tea/coffee-making facilities.

RICHMOND continued

◆◆◆ RIVERSIDE HOTEL

23 Petersham Road, Richmond,
Surrey TW10 6UH
T: (020) 8940 1339
F: (020) 8948 0967
E: riversidehotel@yahoo.com
I: www.smoothhound.co.uk/hotels/
riversid.html

Bedrooms: 6 single,
10 double, 2 twin,
2 triple
Bathrooms: 20 en suite

Parking for 2
CC: Amex, Barclaycard,
Delta, Mastercard, Switch,
Visa

B&B per night:
S £60.00–£65.00
D £80.00–£85.00

OPEN All year round

Elegant Victorian townhouse overlooking the Thames in Richmond town centre. The rooms are en suite and offer satellite TV and tea/coffee facilities.

TWICKENHAM *Tourist Information Centre Tel: (020) 8891 7272*

◆◆◆ 3 WALDEGRAVE GARDENS

Strawberry Hill, Twickenham,
TW1 4PQ
T: (020) 8892 3523

Bedrooms: 2 double,
1 twin
Bathrooms: 2 public

B&B per night:
S £20.00–£40.00
D Min £40.00

OPEN All year round

Large house with garden, close to Strawberry Hill station and 30 minutes by train to Waterloo.

UPMINSTER

◆◆◆ CORNER FARM

Corner Farm, Fen Lane,
North Ockendon, Upminster, Essex
RM14 3RB
T: (01708) 851310
F: (01708) 852025
E: corner.farm@virgin.net

Bedrooms: 2 single,
2 twin
Bathrooms: 1 en suite,
1 public

Parking for 10
CC: Barclaycard, Eurocard,
Mastercard, Visa

B&B per night:
S £25.00–£28.00
D £35.00–£37.50

OPEN All year round

Attractive detached bungalow in rural setting. Breakfast served in farmhouse conservatory (30 metres). No public transport. Friendly atmosphere. Parking. No smoking, children under 14 or pets.

WELLING

◆◆◆◆ DE + DEES B & B

91 Welling Way, Welling, Kent
DA16 2RW
T: (020) 8319 1592
F: (020) 8319 1592

Bedrooms: 1 single,
1 double, 1 triple
Bathrooms: 1 public

EM 1830
Parking for 5

B&B per night:
S £20.00–£25.00
D Min £40.00

OPEN All year round

Homely family B&B, 3 minutes' walk from station – 20 minutes by train to London. Free transport to and from station. TV and tea/coffee facilities in bedrooms.

WEMBLEY

◆ AARON (WEMBLEY PARK) HOTEL

8 Forty Lane, Wembley, Middlesex HA9 9EB
T: (020) 8904 6329 & 8908 5711
F: (020) 8385 0472
E: susmil@susmil.freeserve.co.uk
I: aaronhotel.com

B&B per night:
S £29.00–£49.00
D £59.00–£79.00

OPEN All year round

We are a small, family-run hotel which has just been refurbished. Within easy reach of Wembley Park station and Wembley Stadium, Arena and Conference Centre. Easily accessible from A406 (North Circular Road), M1 and A1. West End of London is approximately 20 minutes away.

Bedrooms: 3 single,
1 twin, 4 triple, 2 family
rooms
Bathrooms: 9 en suite,
1 private, 1 public

Lunch available
EM 1800 (LO 2000)
Parking for 14
CC: Amex, Barclaycard,
Delta, Diners, JCB,
Maestro, Mastercard,
Solo, Switch, Visa, Visa
Electron

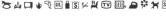

PRICES

Please check prices and other details at the time of booking.

LONDON

WEMBLEY continued

◆◆◆ ADELPHI HOTEL

4 Forty Lane, Wembley, Middlesex HA9 9EB T: (020) 8904 5629 F: (020) 8908 5314 E: adel@dial.pipex.com I: www.hoteladelphi.co.uk	Bedrooms: 4 single, 4 double, 3 twin, 1 triple, 1 family room Bathrooms: 9 en suite, 2 public	EM 2000 (LO 2100) Parking for 12 CC: Amex, Barclaycard, Delta, Diners, Eurocard, JCB, Mastercard, Solo, Switch, Visa, Visa Electron	B&B per night: S £38.00–£45.00 D £48.00–£58.00 OPEN All year round

Close to Wembley Stadium and Wembley Park underground, 15 minutes from West End. Attractive decor. TV lounge, tea/coffee in rooms.

◆◆◆ ARENA HOTEL

6 Forty Lane, Wembley, Middlesex HA9 9EB T: (020) 8908 0670 & 8904 0019 F: (020) 8908 2007 E: enquiry@arenahotel.fsnet.co.uk I: www.arena-hotel.co.uk	Bedrooms: 2 single, 2 double, 3 twin, 3 triple, 3 family rooms Bathrooms: 13 en suite, 1 public	Parking for 15 CC: Amex, Barclaycard, Delta, Diners, Eurocard, JCB, Maestro, Mastercard, Solo, Switch, Visa, Visa Electron	B&B per night: S £45.00–£49.00 D £55.00–£59.00 OPEN All year round

All rooms en suite, with satellite TV, tea/coffee making facilities and direct-dial telephone. Ideally situated, with Wembley Stadium complex only 1 mile away.

◆◆◆ ELM HOTEL

1-7 Elm Road, Wembley, Middlesex HA9 7JA T: (020) 8902 1764 F: (020) 8903 8365 E: elm.hotel@virgin.net I: www.elmhotel.co.uk	Bedrooms: 7 single, 7 double, 11 twin, 6 triple, 3 family rooms Bathrooms: 30 en suite, 1 public	Parking for 7 CC: Amex, Delta, Eurocard, Mastercard, Solo, Switch, Visa, Visa Electron	B&B per night: S Max £48.00 D Max £65.00 OPEN All year round

Ten minutes' walk (1200 yards) from Wembley Stadium, Conference Centre, and Arena, 150 yards from Wembley Central station, underground and mainline station.

WORCESTER PARK

◆◆◆ THE GRAYE HOUSE

24 The Glebe, Worcester Park, Surrey KT4 7PF T: (020) 8330 1277 & 07710 376494 E: graye.house@virgin.net I: www.smoothhound.co.uk	Bedrooms: 1 double, 1 twin Bathrooms: 2 en suite	Parking for 3	B&B per night: S £30.00–£35.00 D £45.00–£60.00 OPEN All year round

A modern, comfortable townhouse, which serves as a family home. Rooms are en suite. Close to stations and amenities. Annexe with 4 larger rooms also available.

QUALITY ASSURANCE SCHEME

For an explanation of the quality and facilities represented by the Diamonds please refer to the front of this guide. A more detailed explanation can be found in the information pages at the back.

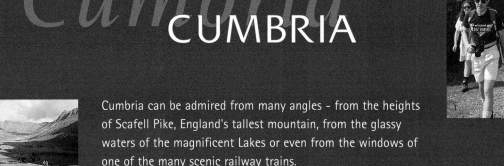

CUMBRIA

Cumbria can be admired from many angles - from the heights of Scafell Pike, England's tallest mountain, from the glassy waters of the magnificent Lakes or even from the windows of one of the many scenic railway trains.

The Lake District is also Beatrix Potter country and you can visit her charming house at Hilltop near Sawrey. Or take a leisurely cruise across Lakes Windermere or Coniston. Cumbria's coastline boasts superb sands. And if you yearn for the bustle of city life, head for historic Carlisle.

Fell racing attracts competitors from all over the world. It's a sprint to the top of a fell (or peak) and is nearly as exhausting to watch as to run!

The county of Cumbria

FOR MORE INFORMATION CONTACT:
Cumbria Tourist Board
Ashleigh, Holly Road, Windermere,
Cumbria LA23 2AQ
Tel: (015394) 44444
Fax: (015394) 44041
Email: mail@cumbria-tourist-board.co.uk
Internet: www.gocumbria.co.uk

The Pictures:
1 Walking at Wasdale;
2 Great Langdale;
3 Ullswater;
4 Derwentwater.

Where to Go in Cumbria - see pages 58-61
Where to Stay in Cumbria - see pages 62-94

Whilst in
CUMBRIA ...

You will find hundreds of interesting places to visit during your stay, just some of which are listed in these pages.

Contact any Tourist Information Centre in the region for more ideas on days out in Cumbria.

Appleby Castle

Appleby-in-Westmorland, Cumbria CA16 6XH
Tel: (017683) 51402
A beautiful castle with breathtaking views, steeped in history. The Great Hall is a must for anyone to see.

Aquarium of the Lakes

Newby Bridge, Ulverston, Cumbria LA12 8AS
Tel: (015395) 30153
Discover the UK's largest collection of freshwater fish in Britain's award-winning freshwater aquarium. Meet mischievous otters, diving ducks, sharks and rays.

Brantwood, Home of John Ruskin

Coniston, Cumbria LA21 8AD
Tel: (015394) 41396
Superb lake and mountain views. Works by Ruskin and contemporaries, memorabilia. Ruskin watercolours. Craft and picture gallery, gardens.

Brockhole Visitor Centre

National Park Authority, Windermere,
Cumbria LA23 1LJ
Tel: (015394) 46601
Interactive exhibitions, audio-visual show, shop, gardens, grounds, adventure playground, dry-stone walling area, trails, events and croquet. Cafe with home cooked food.

Cars of the Stars Motor Museum

Keswick, Cumbria CA12 5LS
Tel: (017687) 73757
Features TV and film vehicles including the Batmobile, Chitty Chitty Bang Bang, the James Bond collection, Herbie, FAB 1 plus many other famous cars and motorcycles.

The Dock Museum

Barrow-in-Furness, Cumbria LA14 2PW
Tel: (01229) 894444
The museum, which straddles a Victorian graving dock, presents the story of steel shipbuilding for which Barrow is famous. Interactive displays and nautical adventure playground.

Dove Cottage and Wordsworth Museum

Town End, Grasmere, Cumbria LA22 9SH
Tel: (015394) 35544
Wordsworth's home from 1799-1808. Poet's possessions, museum with manuscripts, farmhouse reconstruction, paintings and drawings. Special events throughout the year.

Eden Ostrich World

Langwathby, Penrith, Cumbria CA10 1LW
Tel: (01768) 881771
Working farm with lots of farm animals, some of them rare breeds. Covered and outdoor play areas, picnic areas, tearoom and craft shop.

Furness Abbey

Barrow-in-Furness, Cumbria LA13 0TJ
Tel: (01229) 823420
Ruins of a 12thC Cistercian abbey, the second wealthiest in England. Extensive remains include transepts, choir and west tower of church, canopied seats and arches.

Graythwaite Hall Gardens

Newby Bridge, Ulverston, Cumbria LA12 8BA
Tel: (015395) 31248
Rhododendrons, azaleas and flowering shrubs. Laid out by T Mawson, 1888-1890.

Heron Corn Mill and Museum of Papermaking

Waterhouse Mills, Beetha, Milnthorpe,
Cumbria LA7 7AR
Tel: (015395) 65027
Restored working corn mill featuring 4.9-metre (14ft) high breastshot waterwheel. The museum shows paper making both historic and modern with artefacts, displays and diagrams.

Hill Top

Near Sawrey, Ambleside, Cumbria LA22 0LF
Tel: (015394) 36269
Beatrix Potter wrote many of her popular Peter Rabbit stories and other books in this charming little house. It still contains her own china and furniture.

K Village Heritage Centre

Netherfield, Kendal, Cumbria LA9 7DA
Tel: (01539) 732363
Heritage centre within the 'K' Village where visitors can follow numbered exhibits detailing the history of K Shoes in Kendal and the Lake District since 1842.

Lakeland Motor Museum

Holker Hall, Cark in Cartmel,
Grange-over-Sands, Cumbria LA11 7PL
Tel: (015395) 58509
Over 10,000 exhibits including rare motoring automobilia. A 1930s garage recreation and the Campbell Legend Bluebird Exhibition.

Lakeland Sheep and Wool Centre

Cockermouth, Cumbria CA13 0QX
Tel: (01900) 822673
An all-weather attraction with live sheep shows including working dog demonstrations. Also large screen and other exhibitions on the area. Gift shop and cafe.

Lakeside and Haverthwaite Railway

Haverthwaite Station, Ulverston, Cumbria LA12 8AL
Tel: (015395) 31594
Standard gauge steam railway operating a daily seasonal service through the beautiful Leven Valley. Steam and diesel locomotives on display.

Levens Hall

Levens, Kendal, Cumbria LA8 0PD
Tel: (015395) 60321
Elizabethan mansion incorporating a pele tower. Famous topiary garden laid out in 1694, steam collection and plant centre. Shop, play area, picnic area.

Linton Tweeds

Shaddon Mills, Shaddon Gate, Carlisle, Cumbria CA2 5TZ
Tel: (01228) 527569
Centre shows history of weaving in Carlisle up to Linton's today. Visitors can try weaving and other hands-on activities.

Lowther Leisure and Wildlife Park

Hackthorpe, Penrith, Cumbria CA10 2HG
Tel: (01931) 712523
Attractions include exotic birds and animals, rides, miniature railway, boating lake, play areas, adventure fort, Tarzan trail, international circus and a puppet theatre.

Muncaster Castle, Gardens and Owl Centre

Ravenglass, Cumbria CA18 1RQ
Tel: (01229) 717614
The most beautifully situated Owl Centre in the world. See the birds fly, picnic in the gardens and visit the Pennington family home.

The Pictures:
1 Buttermere;
2 Carlisle Castle;
3 Watendlath Bridge;
4 Derwentwater;
5 Green Gable;
6 Kirkstile Inn.

Tullie House Museum and Art Gallery

Carlisle, Cumbria CA3 8TP
Tel: (01228) 534781
Major tourist complex housing museum, art gallery, education facility, lecture theatre, shops, herb garden restaurant and terrace bars.

Ravenglass and Eskdale Railway

Ravenglass, Cumbria CA18 1SW
Tel: (01229) 717171
England's oldest narrow-gauge railway runs for 11km (7 miles) through glorious scenery to the foot of England's highest hills. Most trains are steam hauled.

Ullswater Steamers

Kendal, Cumbria LA9 4QD
Tel: (017684) 82229
Relax and enjoy beautiful Ullswater combining a cruise with a visit to other local attractions. All boats have bar and toilet facilities.

Senhouse Roman Museum

The Battery Sea, Brows, Maryport, Cumbria CA15 6JD
Tel: (01900) 816168
Once the headquarters of Hadrian's Coastal Defence system. The UK's largest group of Roman altar stones and inscriptions from one site. Roman military equipment, stunning sculpture.

Windermere Steamboat Museum

Bowness-on-Windermere, Cumbria LA23 1BN
Tel: (015394) 45565
A wealth of interest and information about life on bygone Windermere. Regular steam launch trips, vintage vessels and classic motorboats. Model boat pond and lakeside picnic area.

Sizergh Castle

Kendal, Cumbria LA8 8AE
Tel: (015395) 60070
Strickland family home for 750 years, now National Trust owned. With 14thC pele tower, 15thC great hall, 16thC wings. Stuart connections. Rock garden, rose garden, daffodils.

The World of Beatrix Potter

Bowness-on-Windermere, Cumbria LA23 3BX
Tel: (015394) 88444
The life and works of Beatrix Potter presented on a 9-screen video-wall. Beautiful three dimensional scenes bring her stories to life.

South Lakes Wild Animal Park

Dalton-in-Furness, Cumbria LA15 8JR
Tel: (01229) 466086
Wild zoo park in over 17 acres of grounds. Over 120 species of animals from all around the world. Large waterfowl ponds, miniature railway, cafe.

Townend

Troutbeck, Windermere, Cumbria LA23 1LB
Tel: (015394) 32628
Typical Lakeland statesman farmer's house c1626. All original interiors, carved woodwork and domestic implements from the family who lived there for over three centuries.

Trotters World of Animals

Coalbeck Farm, Bassenthwaite, Cumbria CA12 4RE
Tel: (017687) 76239
Farm park with collection of rare and interesting farm animals, poultry and baby animals, reptile house and bird of prey centre.

The Pictures:
1 Shoreline, Derwantwater;
2 Windermere Steamer;
3 Maryport;
4 Brundholme Wood;
5 Lake Windermere;
6 Cycling at Coniston;
7 Holker Hall, Grange-over-Sands;
8 Muncaster Castle;
9 Loughrigg.

Find out more about
CUMBRIA ...

Further information about holidays and attractions in Cumbria is available from:

CUMBRIA TOURIST BOARD

Ashleigh, Holly Road, Windermere, Cumbria LA23 2AQ.

Tel: (015394) 44444

Fax: (015394) 44041

Email: mail@cumbria-tourist-board.co.uk
Internet: www.gocumbria.co.uk

The following publications are available from Cumbria Tourist Board:

Cumbria Tourist Board Holiday Guide (free)
Tel: 08705 133059

Events Listings (free)

Cumbria The Lake District Touring Map
including tourist information and touring caravan and camping parks £3.95
Laminated Poster - £4.50

Getting to
CUMBRIA ...

BY ROAD: The M1/M6/M25/M40 provide a link with London and the South East and the M5/M6 provide access from the South West. The M62/M6 link Hull and Manchester with the region. Approximate journey time from London is 5 hours, from Manchester 2 hours.

BY RAIL: From London (Euston) to Oxenholme (Kendal) takes approximately 3 hours 30 minutes. From Oxenholme (connecting station for all main line trains) to Windermere takes approximately 20 minutes. From Carlisle to Barrow-in-Furness via the coastal route, with stops at many of the towns in between, takes approximately 2 hours. Trains from Edinburgh to Carlisle take 1 hour 45 minutes. The historic Settle-Carlisle line also runs through the county bringing passengers from Yorkshire via the Eden Valley.

www.travelcumbria.co.uk

Where to stay in

CUMBRIA

Accommodation entries in this region are listed in alphabetical order of place name, and then in alphabetical order of establishment.

Map references refer to the colour location maps at the front of this guide. The first number indicates the map to use; the letter and number which follow refer to the grid reference on the map.

At-a-glance symbols at the end of each accommodation entry give useful information about services and facilities. A key to symbols can be found inside the back cover flap. Keep this open for easy reference.

A brief description of the towns and villages offering accommodation in the entries which follow, can be found at the end of this section.

A complete listing of all English Tourism Council assessed guest accommodation appears at the back of this guide.

AMBLESIDE, Cumbria Map ref 5A3 *Tourist Information Centre Tel: (015394) 32582*

◆◆◆◆
Silver
Award

BORRANS PARK HOTEL
Borrans Road, Ambleside, LA22 0EN
T: (015394) 33454
F: (015394) 33003
E: info@borranspark.co.uk
I: www.borranspark.co.uk

B&B per night:
S £60.00–£90.00
D £70.00–£90.00

HB per person:
DY £55.00–£65.00

OPEN All year round

Peacefully situated on the outskirts of Ambleside in the heart of Lakeland, just a short stroll from the shores of Lake Windermere. Enjoy a candlelit dinner featuring award-winning traditional home cooking and a memorable sweet trolley. Extensive wine list, log fire and 4-poster bedrooms with private spa baths.

Bedrooms: 9 double, 3 twin
Bathrooms: 12 en suite

EM 1900 (LO 1800)
Parking for 20
CC: Barclaycard, Delta, Eurocard, JCB, Maestro, Mastercard, Solo, Switch, Visa, Visa Electron

---

◆◆◆

CLAREMONT HOUSE
Compston Road, Ambleside, LA22 9DJ
T: (015394) 33448
F: (015394) 33448
E: olwenm@supanet.com

Bedrooms: 1 single, 4 double, 1 twin, 1 triple
Bathrooms: 6 en suite, 1 public

CC: Amex, Barclaycard, Delta, Diners, Eurocard, JCB, Maestro, Mastercard, Solo, Switch, Visa, Visa Electron

B&B per night:
S £17.00–£27.50
D £34.00–£55.00

OPEN All year round

All rooms have colour TV, tea/coffee-making facilities and most have en suite facilities. Cycles secured at night.

◆◆◆◆

COMPSTON HOUSE HOTEL

Compston Road, Ambleside, LA22 9DJ
T: (015394) 32305
F: (015394) 32652
E: compston@globalnet.co.uk
I: www.compstonhouse.co.uk

B&B per night:
S £20.00–£25.00
D £40.00–£70.00

OPEN All year round

Compston House is an American-style hotel, where your hosts Sue and Jerry Virtes from New York welcome you with warm hospitality. Enjoy complimentary use of a local leisure club. You also have the choice of a full English breakfast or full American breakfast (with pancakes). Non-smoking. Free parking.

Bedrooms: 1 single, 7 double, 1 twin
Bathrooms: 9 en suite

CC: Barclaycard, Delta, JCB, Mastercard, Solo, Switch, Visa

▲⅓12 🏠🍴💻↓🍷🛎️⑤✕🍴▥◪✳️✕🐾🏧 SP T

◆◆◆◆

ELDER GROVE

Lake Road, Ambleside, LA22 0DB
T: (015394) 32504
F: (015394) 32504

Bedrooms: 2 single, 6 double, 1 twin, 1 triple
Bathrooms: 10 en suite

Parking for 10
CC: Barclaycard, Delta, Eurocard, JCB, Mastercard, Solo, Switch, Visa, Visa Electron

B&B per night:
S £24.00–£34.00
D £48.00–£68.00

OPEN All year round

Enjoy quality accommodation and service in our Victorian house. Pretty bedrooms with private bathrooms, relaxing bar and lounge, hearty Cumbrian breakfast, car park. Non-smoking.

▲⅓🏠🍴💻↓🍷🛎️⑤✕🍴📺▥◪🏧🏧 SP T ◉

◆◆◆

FERN COTTAGE

6 Waterhead Terrace, Ambleside, LA22 0HA
T: (015394) 33007

Bedrooms: 2 double, 1 twin
Bathrooms: 1 public

B&B per night:
S £18.00–£20.00
D £30.00–£34.00

OPEN All year round

Homely Lakeland-stone cottage on edge of village. Two minutes to head of Lake Windermere and steamer pier. Friendly atmosphere, hearty breakfast. Non-smoking.

▲⅓4 💻↓Ⓤↆ✕🍴📺▥🏧 SP

◆◆◆◆

GLENSIDE

Old Lake Road, Ambleside, LA22 0DP
T: (015394) 32635

Bedrooms: 1 single, 2 double, 1 twin
Bathrooms: 2 public

Parking for 3

B&B per night:
S £16.00–£18.00
D £32.00–£36.00

OPEN Feb–Nov

18thC farmhouse with old world charm, offering high standard of accommodation. Ideally situated between village and lake. Private parking, non-smoking, walks from the door.

▲⅓5 💻↓Ⓤↆ⑤✕🍴📺▥✳️✕🏧 SC T

REGIONAL TOURIST BOARD The ▲ symbol in an establishment entry indicates that it is a Regional Tourist Board member.

Grey Friar Lodge Country House Hotel

Clappersgate, Ambleside, Cumbria LA22 9NE
Tel & Fax: (015394) 33158
E-mail: greyfriar@veen.freeserve.co.uk • Web: www.cumbria-hotels.co.uk

A warm welcome awaits visitors to Pamela & David Veen's country house. This delightful former vicarage enjoys magnificent views of the Brathay River and fells. The house is tastefully furnished with antiques and bric a brac. Most en-suite bedrooms have antique or four-poster beds. Good traditional cooking is enjoyed by all.

Open February - December

- 8 Bedrooms (7 en-suite)
- Parking facilities • Fully licensed
- We operate a no-smoking policy
- All major credit cards accepted
- Set evening menu available

SILVER AWARD

Single	£36.50-£60.00	Half-board	£41.50-£50.50
Double	£53.00-£85.00	Evening meal	£18.50

AMBLESIDE continued

GREY FRIAR LODGE COUNTRY HOUSE HOTEL

Clappersgate, Ambleside, LA22 9NE
T: (015394) 33158
F: (015394) 33158
E: greyfriar@veen.freeserve.co.uk
I: www.cumbria-hotels.co.uk

B&B per night:
S £36.00–£60.00
D £53.00–£85.00

HB per person:
DY £54.50–£59.50

OPEN Feb–Dec

A warm welcome awaits visitors to Pamela and David Veen's country house. This delightful former vicarage enjoys magnificent views of the Brathay River and fells. The house is tastefully furnished with antiques and bric-a-brac. Most en suite bedrooms have antique or 4-poster beds. Good traditional cooking is enjoyed by all.

Bedrooms: 7 double,
1 twin
Bathrooms: 7 en suite,
1 private

EM 1900 (LO 1930)
Parking for 12
CC: Barclaycard, Delta, Eurocard, JCB, Mastercard, Solo, Switch, Visa, Visa Electron

Δ12 ▦ ▢ ↻ ⓢ ⌿ ⏰ 🖳 ◪ ✳ ✗ 🚲 SP

◆◆◆
HILLSDALE

Church Street, Ambleside, LA22 0BT
T: (015394) 33174
E: gstaley@hillsdale.freeserve.co.uk
I: www.hillsdale.freeserve.co.uk

Bedrooms: 1 single,
5 double, 1 twin, 1 triple
Bathrooms: 4 en suite,
1 public, 2 private showers

B&B per night:
S £17.00–£25.00
D £34.00–£50.00

OPEN All year round

Family-run hotel in centre of village. Generous English/vegetarian breakfast. Good value for money. Ideal base for walks, eating out, pubs etc.

Δ ▦ ▢ ↻ UL ⓢ ⌿ 🖳 ◪ 🚲 T

◆◆◆
LATTENDALES

Compston Road, Ambleside,
LA22 9DJ
T: (015394) 32368
E: admin@latts.freeserve.co.uk
I: www.latts.freeserve.co.uk

Bedrooms: 2 single,
4 double
Bathrooms: 4 en suite,
1 public

EM 1830 (LO 1700)

B&B per night:
S £18.00–£20.00
D £36.00–£50.00

OPEN All year round

Traditional Lakeland home in the heart of Ambleside. Central for walking or touring, comfortable en suite accommodation with full English/vegetarian breakfast. Discount for multiple nights.

Δ8 ▢ ↻ ⓢ ⌿ ⏰ 🖳 ◪ ✗ 🚲 SP T

◆◆◆
LYNDHURST HOTEL

Wansfell Road, Ambleside,
LA22 0EG
T: (015394) 32421
F: (015394) 32421
E: lyndhurst@amblesidehotels.co.uk
I: www.amblesidehotels.co.uk

Bedrooms: 5 double,
1 twin
Bathrooms: 6 en suite

EM 1830 (LO 1830)
Parking for 9

B&B per night:
S Max £30.00
D £40.00–£55.00

HB per person:
DY £36.00–£43.00

OPEN All year round

Small, attractive Lakeland-stone hotel with private car park. Quietly situated for town and lake. Pretty rooms, delicious food – a delightful experience.

Δ ▦ ▢ ↻ ⓢ ⏰ 🖳 ◪ ✳ ✗ 🚲 SC 🚲 SP T

USE YOUR *i*s

There are more than 550 Tourist Information Centres throughout England offering friendly help with accommodation and holiday ideas as well as suggestions of places to visit and things to do. You'll find TIC addresses in the local Phone Book.

◆◆◆◆◆
Silver
Award

ROWANFIELD COUNTRY GUESTHOUSE
Kirkstone Road, Ambleside, LA22 9ET
T: (015394) 33686
F: (015394) 31569
E: email@rowanfield.com
I: www.rowanfield.com

Idyllic, quiet countryside setting, central Lakeland. Rowanfield enjoys breathtaking lake and mountain views. A beautiful period house with Laura Ashley style decor. All bedrooms en suite with powerful showers, some have baths, queen and king beds. Fabulous food created by chef patron. Dinner available certain weeks of the year. Superior breakfasts.

Bedrooms: 5 double, 1 twin, 1 triple
Bathrooms: 7 en suite

Parking for 8
CC: Barclaycard, Delta, Maestro, Mastercard, Solo, Switch, Visa, Visa Electron

B&B per night:
S £52.00–£65.00
D £62.00–£90.00

HB per person:
DY £55.00–£68.00

OPEN Mar–Dec

THE RYSDALE HOTEL
Rothay Road, Ambleside, LA22 0EE
T: (015394) 32140 & 33999
F: (015394) 33999

Bedrooms: 4 single, 3 double, 1 twin, 1 triple
Bathrooms: 6 en suite, 2 public

Parking for 2

Family-run hotel with magnificent views over park and fells. Good food, licensed bar. Friendly, personal service. Ideal walking base. No smoking.

B&B per night:
S £19.00–£27.00
D £44.00–£60.00

OPEN Feb–Dec

THORNEYFIELD GUEST HOUSE
Compston Road, Ambleside, LA22 9DJ
T: (015394) 32464
F: (015394) 32464
E: info@thorneyfield.co.uk
I: www.thorneyfield.co.uk

Bedrooms: 1 single, 3 double, 1 triple, 2 family rooms
Bathrooms: 5 en suite, 2 private

CC: Barclaycard, Delta, Diners, JCB, Mastercard, Solo, Switch, Visa

Elegant family-run guesthouse in village centre, with friendly and helpful service. Close to park, miniature golf, tennis, Lakes and fells. Large family rooms available.

B&B per night:
S £18.00–£25.00
D £36.00–£50.00

OPEN Feb–Dec

TOCK HOW FARM
High Wray, Ambleside, LA22 0JF
T: (015394) 36106
F: (015394) 36106

Bedrooms: 1 double, 1 family room
Bathrooms: 1 public

Parking for 3

300-acre family-run farm, overlooking Blelham Tarn with spectacular views of surrounding fells. Breakfast a speciality.

B&B per night:
S £28.00–£32.00
D £40.00–£48.00

OPEN All year round

ASBY GRANGE FARM
Great Asby, Appleby-in-Westmorland, CA16 6HF
T: (017683) 52881

Bedrooms: 2 double
Bathrooms: 1 public

EM 1800 (LO 2000)
Parking for 4

300-acre mixed farm. 18thC farmhouse in beautiful and peaceful countryside, 5 miles south of Appleby. Ideal for touring Lakes and Yorkshire Dales. Convenient for M6.

B&B per night:
D £32.00–£34.00

OPEN Apr–Oct

BONGATE HOUSE
Appleby-in-Westmorland, CA16 6UE
T: (017683) 51245 & 51423
E: bongatehse@aol.com

Bedrooms: 1 single, 3 double, 2 twin, 1 triple, 1 family room
Bathrooms: 5 en suite, 1 public

EM 1900 (LO 1800)
Parking for 10

Family-run Georgian guesthouse within easy walking distance of small market town centre. Large garden. Relaxed, friendly atmosphere and lovely breakfasts.

B&B per night:
S £19.50–£19.50
D £39.00–£44.00

OPEN Mar–Oct

APPLEBY-IN-WESTMORLAND continued

Silver Award

BRIDGE END FARM

Kirkby Thore, Penrith, CA10 1UZ
T: (017683) 61362

Bedrooms: 2 double, 1 twin
Bathrooms: 2 en suite, 1 private

EM 1800 (LO 1930)
Parking for 3

B&B per night:
S £23.00–£25.00
D £44.00–£46.00

HB per person:
DY £32.00–£35.00

OPEN All year round

Delightful 18thC farmhouse on dairy farm in Eden Valley. Lovely, spacious bedrooms, furnished with antiques. Delicious home-made breakfast and dinners. You will never forget Yvonne's sticky toffee pudding.

BARROW-IN-FURNESS, Cumbria Map ref 5A3 *Tourist Information Centre Tel: (01229) 894784*

ARLINGTON HOUSE HOTEL AND RESTAURANT

200-202 Abbey Road, Barrow-in-Furness, LA14 5LD
T: (01229) 831976
F: (01229) 870990

Bedrooms: 2 double, 6 twin
Bathrooms: 8 en suite

EM 1930 (LO 2045)
Parking for 20
CC: Amex, Barclaycard, Eurocard, Mastercard, Visa

B&B per night:
S £60.00–£70.00
D £80.00–£90.00

OPEN All year round

Relaxed hotel with an elegant restaurant. In the town, yet not far away from the Lakes and sea.

BASSENTHWAITE LAKE, Cumbria Map ref 5A2

Ad p15

LAKESIDE

Dubwath, Bassenthwaite Lake, Cockermouth, CA13 9YD
T: (017687) 76358

B&B per night:
S £25.00–£29.00
D £54.00–£62.00

OPEN All year round

Elegant Edwardian double-fronted house with oak floors and panelled entrance hall, standing in its own garden overlooking Bassenthwaite Lake. All rooms en suite with tea-making facilities and TV. Private car park and parking in grounds.

Bedrooms: 5 double, 2 twin, 1 triple
Bathrooms: 7 en suite, 1 private

EM 1900 (LO 1000)
Parking for 8

BOOT, Cumbria Map ref 5A3

THE BURNMOOR INN

Boot, Holmrook, CA19 1TG
T: (019467) 23224
F: (019467) 23337
E: enquiries@burnmoor.co.uk
I: www.burnmoor.co.uk

Bedrooms: 1 single, 3 double, 3 twin, 2 triple
Bathrooms: 9 en suite

Lunch available
EM (LO 2100)
Parking for 30
CC: Barclaycard, Delta, Eurocard, JCB, Maestro, Mastercard, Solo, Switch, Visa, Visa Electron

B&B per night:
S £27.00–£30.00
D £54.00–£60.00

HB per person:
DY £36.00–£47.50

OPEN All year round

Warm 400-year-old inn. En suite comfort, good food in bar and restaurant (served all day). Open all year, resident proprietors Harry and Paddington Berger.

TOWN INDEX

This can be found at the back of the guide. If you know where you want to stay, the index will give you the page number listing accommodation in your chosen town, city or village.

◆◆◆◆
Silver
Award

GREENBANK COUNTRY HOUSE HOTEL

Borrowdale, Keswick, CA12 5UY
T: (017687) 77215
F: (017687) 77215

B&B per night:
S £28.00–£34.00
D £56.00–£68.00

HB per person:
DY £42.00–£48.00

OPEN Feb–Dec

A refurbished Victorian country house, Greenbank is the friendliest hotel in the Lake District. It stands in an acre of garden high up on the wooded slopes in the heart of Borrowdale. Superb walking and touring area. En suite bedrooms, log fires, restaurant licence. Excellent home-cooked food from local produce.

Bedrooms: 1 single,
5 double, 2 twin, 1 triple
Bathrooms: 9 en suite

EM 1900 (LO 1700)
Parking for 15
CC: Barclaycard, Delta,
Maestro, Mastercard,
Switch, Visa

◆◆◆◆◆
Gold
Award

HAZEL BANK COUNTRY HOUSE

Rosthwaite, Keswick, CA12 5XB
T: (017687) 77248
F: (017678) 77373
E: enquiries@hazelbankhotel.demon.co.uk
I: www.hazelbankhotel.demon.co.uk

HB per person:
DY £43.00–£59.50

OPEN All year round

Exquisite, historic, Victorian country house in outstanding position set in 4-acre grounds. Peaceful, idyllic location with superb views of central Lakeland Fells. Beautifully appointed. Bedrooms all en suite. Excellent cuisine using local produce. Puddings and sauces a speciality, vegetarians welcome. An ideal base for walking. Non-smokers only.

Bedrooms: 5 double,
4 twin; suite available
Bathrooms: 9 en suite

EM 1900 (LO 1900)
Parking for 12
CC: Barclaycard, Delta,
Eurocard, JCB,
Mastercard, Switch, Visa

◆◆◆◆

WALLSEND

The Old Rectory, Church Lane, Bowness-on-Solway, Carlisle, CA7 5AF
T: (016973) 51055 & 614224
F: (016973) 52180
E: wallsend@btinternet.com

B&B per night:
S £20.00–£22.00
D £40.00–£44.00

HB per person:
DY £28.00–£30.00

OPEN All year round

Peaceful old rectory located in own wooded grounds at end of Hadrian's Wall in Solway AONB. All rooms en suite. Picturesque village on Solway Firth with local pub/restaurant 150 yards away. Easy access to/from historic city of Carlisle, North Lakes and Scotland. Ideal for walkers, cyclists and just "getting away". Warm welcome and relaxing atmosphere.

Bedrooms: 1 single,
2 double, 1 triple
Bathrooms: 4 en suite

EM 1830 (LO 2000)
Parking for 6

QUALITY ASSURANCE SCHEME

Diamond ratings and awards were correct at the time of going to press but are subject to change. Please check at the time of booking.

BRAITHWAITE, Cumbria Map ref 5A3

◆◆◆ **COLEDALE INN**

Braithwaite, Keswick, CA12 5TN
T: (017687) 78272

Bedrooms: 1 single,
6 double, 1 twin, 3 triple,
1 family room
Bathrooms: 12 en suite

Lunch available
EM 1830 (LO 2100)
Parking for 15
CC: Barclaycard, Delta,
Eurocard, Mastercard,
Switch, Visa

B&B per night:
S £17.00–£25.00
D £44.00–£60.00

OPEN All year round

Victorian country house hotel and Georgian inn, in a peaceful hillside position away from traffic, with superb mountain views. Families and pets welcome.

BRAMPTON, Cumbria Map ref 5B2

◆◆◆ **BLACKSMITHS ARMS HOTEL**

Talkin Village, Brampton, CA8 1LE
T: (016977) 3452
F: (016977) 3396

Bedrooms: 3 double,
2 twin
Bathrooms: 5 en suite

Lunch available
EM 1830 (LO 2100)
Parking for 10
CC: Amex, Barclaycard,
Delta, Eurocard, Maestro,
Mastercard, Solo, Switch,
Visa, Visa Electron

B&B per night:
S £30.00–£30.00
D £45.00–£45.00

OPEN All year round

Country inn in scenic countryside half a mile from Talkin Tarn. Walking, golf, pony trekking, sailing, windsurfing, fishing, Hadrian's Wall and Lake District within easy reach.

◆◆◆

WALTON HIGH RIGG

Walton, Brampton, CA8 2AZ
T: (016977) 2117 (Answerphone available)

B&B per night:
S £18.00–£22.00
D £32.00–£40.00

HB per person:
DY £26.00–£30.00

OPEN All year round

202-acre mixed farm. 18thC Listed farmhouse on roadside, 1 mile from Walton and Roman Wall, 3.5 miles from Brampton. Family-run with pedigree cattle and sheep, farm trail to waterfall. Friendly atmosphere, delicious food. Good stopover or holiday base. Ideal centre for walking, fishing, golf and horse-riding.

Bedrooms: 1 family
room
Bathrooms: 1 private,
2 public

EM 1800
Parking for 4

BROUGH, Cumbria Map ref 5B3

◆◆◆ **RIVER VIEW**

Brough, Kirkby Stephen, CA17 4BZ
T: (017683) 41894
F: (017683) 41894
E: riverviewbb@talk21.com

Bedrooms: 1 single,
1 double, 1 triple
Bathrooms: 1 en suite,
1 public

Parking for 3

B&B per night:
S £18.00–£20.00
D £34.00–£40.00

OPEN All year round

Converted barn overlooking river in quiet location near village centre. Clean, comfortable family home. Ideal for visiting dales and Lakes. Convenient north/south stopover.

BROUGHTON-IN-FURNESS, Cumbria Map ref 5A3

◆◆◆ **BROOM HILL**

New Street, Broughton-in-Furness,
LA20 6JD
T: (01229) 716358 &
07966 129439 (New mobile no)
F: (01229) 716358

Bedrooms: 3 double
Bathrooms: 2 en·suite,
1 private

Parking for 7

B&B per night:
S £23.00–£23.00
D £46.00–£46.00

OPEN Mar-Oct

Beautiful Georgian country mansion with secluded grounds and magnificent views, yet within walking distance of the centre of this unspoilt village.

QUALITY ASSURANCE SCHEME

Diamond ratings and awards are explained at the back of this guide.

CALDBECK, Cumbria Map ref 5A2

◆◆◆ **THE BRIARS**
Friar Row, Caldbeck, Wigton,
CA7 8DS
T: (016974) 78633

Bedrooms: 1 single,
1 double, 1 twin
Bathrooms: 1 private,
1 public

Parking for 3

B&B per night:
S £19.00–£21.00
D £38.00–£42.00

OPEN All year round

140-acre mixed farm. In lovely village of Caldbeck overlooking Caldbeck Fells. Ideal for touring Lakes and Scottish Borders. Right on Cumbria Way route.

◆◆◆◆

SWALEDALE WATCH
Whelpo, Caldbeck, Wigton, CA7 8HQ
T: (016974) 78409
F: (016974) 78409
I: nan.savage@talk21.com

B&B per night:
S £20.00–£24.00
D £36.00–£42.00

HB per person:
DY £30.00–£36.00

OPEN All year round

A working farm outside picturesque Caldbeck. Enjoy great comfort, excellent food and a warm welcome amidst peaceful unspoilt countryside. Central for touring, walking or discovering the rolling northern fells. A memorable walk into Caldbeck is through "The Howk", a limestone gorge. Relax "at home" with open fires – your happiness is our priority.

Bedrooms: 2 double,
2 triple
Bathrooms: 4 en suite

EM 1900 (LO 1400)
Parking for 10

CARLISLE, Cumbria Map ref 5A2 *Tourist Information Centre Tel: (01228) 625600*

◆◆◆◆ **CORNERWAYS GUEST HOUSE**
107 Warwick Road, Carlisle,
CA1 1EA
T: (01228) 521733

Bedrooms: 4 single,
1 double, 3 twin, 1 triple,
1 family room
Bathrooms: 3 en suite,
2 public

Parking for 6

B&B per night:
S £16.00–£18.00
D £28.00–£36.00

OPEN All year round

Five minutes to rail and bus stations and city centre. M6 exit 43. Colour TV, central heating in all bedrooms. Tea and coffee facilities. Lounge, payphone.

◆◆◆ **NEWFIELD GRANGE HOTEL**
Newfield Drive, Kingstown, Carlisle,
CA3 0AF
T: (01228) 819926 & 07930 278214
F: (01228) 546323
E: bb@newfield53.freeserve.co.uk
I: www.newfield53.freeserve.co.uk

Bedrooms: 2 single,
5 double, 5 twin, 2 triple
Bathrooms: 14 en suite

EM 1800 (LO 1930)
Parking for 20
CC: Amex, Barclaycard,
Delta, Eurocard,
Mastercard, Switch, Visa

B&B per night:
S £35.00–£40.00
D £45.00–£50.00

OPEN All year round

Peaceful, quiet place to stay away from the noise of passing traffic yet within easy reach of the M6. Standing in its own grounds. Non-smoking establishment.

◆◆◆ **WARREN GUESTHOUSE**
368 Warwick Road, Carlisle,
CA1 2RU
T: (01228) 33663 & 512916
F: (01228) 33663

Bedrooms: 3 double,
1 twin, 2 triple
Bathrooms: 6 en suite

Lunch available
EM 1800 (LO 2000)
Parking for 6

B&B per night:
S £20.00–£25.00
D Min £40.00

OPEN All year round

Very comfortable, friendly guesthouse close to Hadrian's Wall, a good base for Scotland and the Lake District. Full fire certificate. Outstanding chamberpot collection.

TOWN INDEX
This can be found at the back of this guide. If you know where you want to stay, the index will give you the page number listing accommodation in your chosen town, city or village.

CONISTON, Cumbria Map ref 5A3

◆◆

CROWN HOTEL
Coniston, LA21 8EA
T: (015394) 41243
F: (015394) 41804
E: enntiidus@crownhotel

B&B per night:
S £30.00–£60.00

HB per person:
DY £35.00–£45.00

OPEN All year round

The Crown Hotel has been completely refurbished to a very high standard to ensure the comfort of all our guests. Enjoy the delights of Coniston and the lake where Donald Campbell attempted to break the world water speed record.

Bedrooms: 6 double, 4 twin, 1 triple, 1 family room
Bathrooms: 12 en suite

Lunch available
EM 1900 (LO 2100)
Parking for 30
CC: Amex, Barclaycard, Delta, Diners, JCB, Maestro, Mastercard, Solo, Switch, Visa, Visa Electron

---

◆◆

SHEPHERDS VILLA
Tilberthwaite Avenue, Coniston, LA21 8EE
T: (015394) 41337

Bedrooms: 6 double, 3 twin, 1 family room
Bathrooms: 3 en suite, 2 private, 2 public

Parking for 10
CC: Barclaycard, Delta, Eurocard, JCB, Maestro, Mastercard, Solo, Switch, Visa, Visa Electron

B&B per night:
S £18.00–£23.00
D £36.00–£46.00

OPEN All year round

A friendly, comfortable family-run guesthouse, offering spacious accommodation in a quiet spot on the edge of the village. Ideal touring and walking base.

◆◆◆

THWAITE COTTAGE
Waterhead, Coniston, LA21 8AJ
T: (015394) 41367
E: m@thwaitcot.freeserve.co.uk
I: www.thwaitcot.freeserve.co.uk

B&B per night:
D £42.00–£48.00

OPEN All year round

Beautiful 17thC cottage with oak beams and log fires in secluded wooded garden within walking distance of lake and village. Three charming bedrooms either en suite or with private bathrooms. Perfect base for a walking holiday. Membership of Langdale Leisure Club included in room rates – in case it rains. Non-smoking.

Bedrooms: 2 double, 1 twin
Bathrooms: 1 en suite, 2 private

Parking for 3

◆◆◆

WILSON ARMS
Torver, Coniston, LA21 8BB
T: (015394) 41237
F: (015394) 41590

B&B per night:
S £27.00–£30.00
D £50.00–£54.00

OPEN All year round

In the small village of Torver, 2.5 miles from Coniston. Ideal walking area. Well stocked bar, log fire on cooler days. Good central location for touring the Lakes. Meals prepared with local fresh produce. Surrounded by beautiful fells.

Bedrooms: 4 double, 1 twin, 1 triple, 1 family room
Bathrooms: 6 en suite, 1 private

Lunch available
EM 1800 (LO 2100)
Parking for 15
CC: Barclaycard, Delta, Diners, Mastercard, Switch, Visa

CROSTHWAITE, Cumbria Map ref 5A3

◆◆◆◆ **CROSTHWAITE HOUSE**
Crosthwaite, Kendal, LA8 8BP
T: (015395) 68264
F: (015395) 68264
E: crosthwaite.house@kencomp.
net

Bedrooms: 1 single,
3 double, 2 twin
Bathrooms: 6 en suite

EM 1900 (LO 1900)
Parking for 10

B&B per night:
S £22.00–£25.00
D £44.00–£50.00

HB per person:
DY £37.00–£40.00

OPEN Feb–Nov

Mid-18thC building with unspoilt views of the Lyth and Winster valleys, 5 miles from Bowness and Kendal. Family atmosphere and home cooking. Self-catering cottages also available.

◆◆◆ **THE PUNCH BOWL INN**
Crosthwaite, Kendal, LA8 8HR
T: (015395) 68237
F: (015395) 68875
E: enquiries@punchbowl.fsnet.co.
uk
I: www.punchbowl.fsnet.co.uk

Bedrooms: 3 double
Bathrooms: 3 en suite

Lunch available
EM 1800 (LO 2100)
Parking for 25
CC: Barclaycard, Delta,
Eurocard, Maestro,
Mastercard, Switch, Visa

B&B per night:
S £37.50–£40.00
D £55.00–£60.00

HB per person:
DY £50.00–£60.00

OPEN Jan–Oct, Dec

Coaching inn with 3 double bedrooms, all with private facilities. Adjacent to Crosthwaite Church in the Lyth Valley, 5 miles from Windermere and Kendal.

DALTON-IN-FURNESS, Cumbria Map ref 5A3

◆◆ **BLACK DOG INN**
Holmes Green, Broughton Road,
Dalton-in-Furness, LA15 8JP
T: (01229) 462561 &
07931 751282 (Mobile)
F: (01229) 468036
E: jack@blackdoginn.freeserve.co.
uk

Bedrooms: 2 double
Bathrooms: 2 en suite

Lunch available
EM 1700 (LO 2030)
Parking for 30
CC: Barclaycard,
Mastercard, Switch, Visa

B&B per night:
S £22.50–£30.00
D £35.00–£45.00

HB per person:
DY £27.50–£35.00

OPEN All year round

Old coaching inn, situated in rural surroundings, with log fires, cask ales and home-cooked food. Local Camra Pub of the Year 1998 and 1999.

ELTERWATER, Cumbria Map ref 5A3

◆◆◆◆

ELTERWATER PARK
Skelwith Bridge, Ambleside, LA22 9NP
T: (015394) 32227
F: (015394) 31768
E: enquiries@elterwater.com
I: www.elterwater.com

B&B per night:
D £56.00–£70.00

HB per person:
DY £43.00–£50.00

OPEN Feb–Dec

Lovely stone-built house. Fell views from all rooms, walks from the house, lake access. Excellent cuisine, elegant decor with antiques. At gateway to Langdale, Elterwater village 1.5 miles. Personal attention.

Bedrooms: 3 double,
1 twin
Bathrooms: 4 en suite

EM 1900 (LO 2000)
Parking for 7
CC: Barclaycard,
Mastercard, Visa

GRANGE-OVER-SANDS, Cumbria Map ref 5A3 *Tourist Information Centre Tel: (015395) 34026*

◆◆◆ **CORNER BEECH**
Kents Bank Road, Grange-over-
Sands, LA11 7DP
T: (015395) 33088 (Answerphone)
F: (015395) 35288
E: freda.lightfoot@cornerbeech.
ndirect.co.uk
I: www.cornerbeech.ndirect.co.uk

Bedrooms: 1 double,
2 twin, 2 family rooms
Bathrooms: 5 en suite,
1 public

EM 1830 (LO 1700)
CC: Barclaycard, Delta,
JCB, Mastercard, Solo,
Switch, Visa, Visa Electron

B&B per night:
S £25.00–£30.00
D £45.00–£55.00

HB per person:
DY £33.00–£38.50

OPEN Mar–Nov

Elegant Edwardian house overlooking Morecambe Bay close to the promenade. Spacious, centrally heated en suite rooms. Restaurant/bar and separate lounge. Home cooking.

MAP REFERENCES
Map references apply to the colour maps at the front of this guide.

GRANGE-OVER-SANDS continued

◆◆◆◆

ELTON HOTEL
Windermere Road, Grange-over-Sands,
LA11 6EQ
T: (015395) 32838

B&B per night:
S £25.00–£29.00
D £40.00–£48.00

HB per person:
DY £31.00–£35.00

OPEN Mar–Dec

Our superior rooms have all the little extras to make them "home from home", with the emphasis on clean and comfortable. Good home cooking a speciality. Two minutes on level to all amenities. Ground floor rooms. Ideal location for touring Lakes. Come and enjoy a warm welcome from Ian and Christine.

Bedrooms: 4 double,
2 twin, 1 family room
Bathrooms: 5 en suite,
2 private showers

EM 2100

◆◆◆◆

MAYFIELDS
3 Mayfield Terrace,
Kents Bank Road, Grange-over-
Sands, LA11 7DW
T: (015395) 34730
I: www.accommodata.co.uk/
010699.htm

Bedrooms: 1 single,
1 double, 1 twin
Bathrooms: 2 en suite,
1 public, 1 private
shower

Lunch available
EM 1830
Parking for 3

B&B per night:
S Max £23.00
D Max £50.00

HB per person:
DY £35.00–£37.00

OPEN All year round

Victorian terraced townhouse, tastefully furnished and equipped to a high standard. In a pleasant position on fringe of town close to promenade and open countryside.

◆◆◆

SOMERSET HOUSE
Kents Bank Road, Grange-over-
Sands, LA11 7EY
T: (015395) 32631

Bedrooms: 3 single,
2 double, 3 triple
Bathrooms: 1 public,
4 private showers

Lunch available
EM 1830

B&B per night:
S £18.00–£22.00
D £34.00–£40.00

HB per person:
DY £25.00–£32.00

OPEN All year round

Enjoy our small privately-run hotel and relax. Lovely home-cooked meals. Near shops, lakes and beautiful homes and estates. Ideal area for walkers.

GRASMERE, Cumbria Map ref 5A3

◆◆◆◆

ASH COTTAGE GUEST HOUSE
Red Lion Square, Grasmere,
Ambleside, LA22 9SP
T: (015394) 35224

Bedrooms: 1 single,
3 double, 3 twin, 1 triple
Bathrooms: 8 en suite

EM 1845 (LO 1915)
Parking for 9

B&B per night:
S £25.00–£30.00
D £46.00–£60.00

HB per person:
DY £36.00–£42.00

OPEN All year round

Detached guesthouse with comfortable en suite bedrooms, personal attention and fine home cooking. Licensed. Pleasant award-winning garden. Private parking.

◆◆◆

HOW FOOT LODGE
Town End, Grasmere, LA22 9SQ
T: (015394) 35366

Bedrooms: 4 double,
2 twin
Bathrooms: 6 en suite

Parking for 6
CC: Barclaycard, Delta,
Mastercard, Switch, Visa

B&B per night:
S £33.00–£35.00
D £44.00–£52.00

OPEN Feb–Dec

Beautiful Victorian house in peaceful surroundings. Spacious rooms with lovely views. Ideal base for walking and exploring the Lake District.

CHECK THE MAPS
The colour maps at the front of this guide show all the cities, towns and villages for which you will find accommodation entries.
Refer to the town index to find the page on which they are listed.

◆◆◆◆

REDMAYNE COTTAGE
Grasmere, Ambleside, LA22 9QY
T: (015394) 35635 & 07977 596133

B&B per night:
D £44.00–£54.00

OPEN Feb–Nov

From its superb elevated private situation Redmayne Cottage enjoys breathtaking panoramic views of the lake and mountains. Convenient for Grasmere village amenities. Completing the picture, spacious luxury en suite double bedrooms have colour TV, hospitality tray and many thoughtful extras. Exclusively for non-smokers. Regret no children or pets. Private enclosed parking.

Bedrooms: 3 double
Bathrooms: 3 en suite

Parking for 3

◆◆◆

TRAVELLERS REST
Grasmere, Ambleside, LA22 9RR
T: (015394) 35604 (Enquiries) &
0500 600725 (Reservations)
I: www.lakelandsheart.demon.co.uk

B&B per night:
S £20.00–£40.00
D £40.00–£80.00

HB per person:
DY £37.00–£60.00

OPEN All year round

Located on the edge of Grasmere village, this 16thC former coaching inn is renowned for its food and hospitality. Cosy and welcoming, with real fires in winter, beer gardens surrounded by stunning views for summer days. Ideal base for exploring the Lake District.

Bedrooms: 5 double, 3 twin
Bathrooms: 8 en suite

Lunch available
EM 1900 (LO 2130)
Parking for 45
CC: Barclaycard, Delta, Mastercard, Switch, Visa

◆◆◆◆

WOODLAND CRAG GUEST HOUSE
How Head Lane, Grasmere,
Ambleside, LA22 9SG
T: (015394) 35351 (Answerphone)
F: (015394) 35351

Bedrooms: 2 single, 2 double, 1 twin
Bathrooms: 3 en suite, 1 public

Parking for 5

B&B per night:
S £25.00–£30.00
D £50.00–£60.00

OPEN All year round

Charming Victorian Lakeland-stone house with lake and fell views. Beautiful walks radiate from here. Peacefully situated in landscaped grounds on edge of village. No smoking, please.

◆◆◆◆
Silver
Award

BETTY FOLD COUNTRY HOUSE
Hawkshead Hill, Ambleside, LA22 0PS
T: (015394) 36611

B&B per night:
D £50.00–£60.00

HB per person:
DY £38.00–£43.00

OPEN Mar–Nov

This unique, spacious, award-winning house has an elevated position with fine views from all rooms. Noted for its peaceful, friendly atmosphere. Set in 3 acres of natural garden, rich in wildlife. Ideally located for walking, touring and outdoor pursuits. Excellent food, freshly prepared from traditional recipes.

Bedrooms: 2 double, 1 twin
Bathrooms: 3 en suite

EM 1900 (LO 0900)
Parking for 10

◆◆◆◆
Silver
Award

BORWICK LODGE

Outgate, Ambleside, LA22 0PU
T: (015394) 36332
F: (015394) 36332
E: borwicklodge@talk21.com
I: www.smoothhound.co.uk/hotels/
borwickl.html

B&B per night:
S £45.00–£65.00
D £50.00–£80.00

OPEN Mar–Dec

A leafy driveway entices you to a rather special 17thC country house with panoramic lake and mountain views, quietly secluded in the heart of the Lakes. Beautiful en suite bedrooms include special occasions and romantic breaks with king-size 4-poster beds. Rosemary and Colin Haskell welcome you to this most beautiful corner of England. Totally non-smoking.

Bedrooms: 5 double,
1 family room
Bathrooms: 6 en suite

Parking for 8

◆◆◆◆

THE SUN INN

Main Street, Hawkshead, Ambleside,
LA22 0NT
T: (015394) 36236 & 36353
F: (015394) 36155
E: thesuninn@hawkshead98.freeserve.
co.uk
I: www.suninn.co.uk

B&B per night:
S £35.00–£45.00
D £64.00–£80.00

HB per person:
DY £44.00–£50.00

OPEN All year round

17thC coaching inn situated in the delightful unspoilt village of Hawkshead, surrounded by the most beautiful countryside. We have 8 bedrooms (all en suite, 2 with 4-poster beds) individually furnished to make the best of the traditional oak beams and Lakeland stone walls. The area is very popular with walkers, cyclists and tourists.

Bedrooms: 6 double,
2 twin
Bathrooms: 8 en suite

Lunch available
EM 1800 (LO 2130)
Parking for 8
CC: Barclaycard, Delta,
Mastercard, Solo, Switch,
Visa

◆◆◆◆

YEWFIELD VEGETARIAN GUEST HOUSE

Yewfield, Hawkshead, Ambleside, LA22 0PR
T: (015394) 36765
F: (015394) 36765
E: derek.yewfield@btinternet.com
I: www.yewfield.co.uk

B&B per night:
S £25.00–£32.00
D £40.00–£74.00

OPEN Feb–Nov

A peaceful and quiet retreat in the heart of the Lakes, perfect for lovely walking holidays, an impressive Gothic vegetarian guesthouse set in its own 26-acre organic gardens and grounds. All rooms individually appointed to a very high standard with en suite bath and shower. Completely non-smoking.

Bedrooms: 2 double,
1 twin
Bathrooms: 3 en suite

Parking for 10

MAP REFERENCES
The map references refer to the colour maps at the front of this guide. The first figure is the map number; the letter and figure which follow indicate the grid reference on the map.

HIGH LORTON, Cumbria Map ref 5A3

SWINSIDE END FARM

Scales, High Lorton, Cockermouth,
CA13 9UA
T: (01900) 85134

Bedrooms: 2 double,
1 twin
Bathrooms: 1 en suite,
1 public, 2 private
showers

B&B per night:
S Min £18.00
D Min £36.00

OPEN All year round

300-acre mixed farm. A working farm in Lorton Valley. Four miles from Cockermouth and 7 miles from Keswick.

KENDAL, Cumbria Map ref 5B3 *Tourist Information Centre Tel: (01539) 725758*

GATESIDE FARM

Windermere Road, Kendal, LA9 5SE
T: (01539) 722036
F: (01539) 722036
E: gatesidefarm@aol.com

B&B per night:
S £22.00–£25.00
D £36.00–£46.00

HB per person:
DY £27.50–£45.50

OPEN All year round

16thC farmhouse on traditional Lakeland working farm, 2 miles north of Kendal on A591 and easily accessible from M6, junction 36. All bedrooms have colour TV, tea/coffee-making facilities, some are en suite. Good home-cooked breakfasts, evening meals on request. Lovely walks (maps provided). Short or weekly stays welcome.

Bedrooms: 3 double,
1 twin, 1 family room
Bathrooms: 2 en suite,
2 public

EM (LO 1700)
Parking for 7

HILLSIDE GUEST HOUSE

4 Beast Banks, Kendal, LA9 4JW
T: (01539) 722836

Bedrooms: 2 single,
3 double, 1 twin
Bathrooms: 4 en suite,
1 public

Parking for 2

B&B per night:
S £18.00–£21.00
D £36.00–£42.00

OPEN Apr–Oct

Small elegant Victorian guesthouse near shops and town facilities, convenient for the Lakes, Yorkshire Dales and Morecambe Bay. En suite and appointed to a very high standard.

KENDAL ARMS AND HOTEL

72 Milnthorpe Road, Kendal, LA9 5HG
T: (01539) 720956
F: (01539) 724851

B&B per night:
S £25.00–£50.00
D £50.00–£60.00

HB per person:
DY Min £35.00

OPEN All year round

Traditional family inn with hotel lodge. En suite rooms, satellite TV. Quality food, real ales, children's playground, large function suite.

Bedrooms: 3 double,
5 twin
Bathrooms: 8 en suite

Lunch available
EM 1730 (LO 2100)
Parking for 50
CC: Barclaycard, Delta,
Eurocard, Mastercard,
Switch, Visa

MILLERS BECK

Stainton, Kendal, LA8 0DU
T: (015395) 60877

Bedrooms: 2 double,
1 twin
Bathrooms: 3 en suite,
1 public

EM 1900 (LO 1930)
Parking for 4

B&B per night:
S Min £25.00
D £46.00–£50.00

OPEN Mar–Dec

Converted former cornmill on 3 levels. Large residents' lounge and 2 gallery sitting areas. Comfortable open dining area. Self-catering suites available. Warm welcome.

CUMBRIA

◆◆◆◆ ACORN HOUSE HOTEL
Silver
Award

Ambleside Road, Keswick, CA12 4DL
T: (017687) 72553
F: (017687) 75332
E: enq@acornhouse.demon.co.uk
I: www.smoothound.co.uk/hotels/
acornhse.html

Bedrooms: 6 double,
1 twin, 3 triple
Bathrooms: 9 en suite,
1 private

Parking for 10
CC: Barclaycard, Delta,
Eurocard, Mastercard,
Switch, Visa

B&B per night:
S £28.00–£35.00
D £50.00–£66.00

OPEN Feb–Nov

Elegant Georgian house set in colourful garden. All bedrooms tastefully furnished, some 4-poster beds. Cleanliness guaranteed. Close to town centre. Good off-street parking. Strictly no smoking.

◆◆◆ THE ANCHORAGE
14 Ambleside Road, Keswick,
CA12 4DL
T: (017687) 72813

Bedrooms: 1 single,
3 double, 2 triple
Bathrooms: 6 en suite,
1 public

EM 1830 (LO 1500)
Parking for 7

B&B per night:
S £20.00–£23.00
D £40.00–£46.00

HB per person:
DY £31.00–£33.00

OPEN All year round

Comfortable house, serving good home cooking, with owners who make every effort to please.

◆◆◆◆ ANWORTH HOUSE
27 Eskin Street, Keswick, CA12 4DQ
T: (017687) 72923

Bedrooms: 3 double,
1 twin, 1 family room
Bathrooms: 5 en suite

CC: Barclaycard, Eurocard,
JCB, Maestro, Mastercard,
Solo, Switch, Visa, Visa
Electron

B&B per night:
S £25.00–£25.00
D £44.00–£52.00

OPEN All year round

Quiet location, yet ideally situated for town centre and walking. Small, friendly guesthouse offering tastefully furnished, comfortable en suite accommodation, a relaxed atmosphere and good food.

◆◆◆◆ AVONDALE GUEST HOUSE
20 Southey Street, Keswick,
CA12 4EF
T: (017687) 72735
F: (017687) 75431
I: www.smoothhound.co.uk/hotels/
available/html

Bedrooms: 1 single,
4 double, 1 twin
Bathrooms: 6 en suite

CC: Amex, Barclaycard,
Delta, Eurocard, JCB,
Mastercard, Visa

B&B per night:
S £21.00–£22.50
D £42.00–£45.00

OPEN All year round

High quality, comfortable guesthouse with well-appointed en suite rooms. Close to town centre, theatre, lakes and parks. Non-smokers only, please.

◆◆◆◆ BADGERS WOOD
30 Stanger Street, Keswick,
CA12 5JU
T: (017687) 72621
F: (017687) 72621
E: enquiries@badgers-wood.co.uk
I: www.badgers-wood.co.uk

Bedrooms: 1 single,
3 double, 1 twin, 1 triple
Bathrooms: 4 en suite,
1 public

B&B per night:
S £17.50–£17.50
D £35.00–£44.00

OPEN Mar–Dec

Spacious, comfortable Victorian house. All bedrooms have mountain views, most have own toilet. Quiet, elevated location, close to town centre.

◆◆◆ BECKSTONES FARM GUEST HOUSE
Thornthwaite, Keswick, CA12 5SQ
T: (017687) 78510
E: beckstones@lineone.net
I: website.lineone.net/~beckstones

Bedrooms: 4 double,
1 twin, 1 triple
Bathrooms: 6 en suite

Parking for 8

B&B per night:
S £25.00–£27.00
D £43.00–£50.00

OPEN All year round

Quality en suite B&B in converted Georgian farmhouse. Lounge. Magnificent mountain views. Keswick 10 minutes' drive. Bassenthwaite Lake 10 minutes' walk. Bar meals 3 minutes' walk.

COLOUR MAPS Colour maps at the front of this guide pinpoint all places under which you will find accommodation listed.

KESWICK continued

◆◆◆ BONSHAW GUEST HOUSE

20 Eskin Street, Keswick, CA12 4DG
T: (017687) 73084

Bedrooms: 3 single,
3 double, 1 twin
Bathrooms: 4 en suite,
1 public

EM 1800 (LO 1600)
Parking for 6
CC: Barclaycard, Delta,
Eurocard, Mastercard,
Switch, Visa

B&B per night:
S £15.00–£21.50
D £30.00–£43.00

HB per person:
DY £25.00–£31.50

OPEN All year round

Small, friendly, comfortable guesthouse, providing good home cooking. Convenient for town centre and all amenities. En suite rooms available. Private car park. Non-smoking.

◆◆◆◆ EDWARDENE HOTEL

26 Southey Street, Keswick,
CA12 4EF
T: (017687) 73586
F: (017687) 73824
E: haveabreak@edwardenehotel.
fsnet.co.uk
I: www.edwardenehotel.co.uk

Bedrooms: 2 single,
6 double, 2 twin,
1 family room
Bathrooms: 11 en suite

Lunch available
EM 1830 (LO 1930)
CC: Amex, Barclaycard,
Delta, Mastercard, Solo,
Switch, Visa, Visa Electron

B&B per night:
S £27.00–£27.00
D £54.00–£54.00

HB per person:
DY £38.00–£40.00

OPEN All year round

Family-run hotel, superb Victorian slate building in heart of Keswick. Two lounges with TV, all en suite. Home cooking, hearty breakfasts, dinner available, relaxed atmosphere.

◆◆◆◆◆ THE GRANGE COUNTRY HOUSE HOTEL

Silver Award

Manor Brow, Ambleside Road,
Keswick, CA12 4BA
T: (017687) 72500
E: sagem02458@talk21.com

Bedrooms: 7 double,
3 twin
Bathrooms: 10 en suite,
1 public

EM 1900 (LO 2030)
Parking for 13
CC: Barclaycard, Delta,
Mastercard, Visa

B&B per night:
D £63.50–£79.50

HB per person:
DY £49.75–£57.75

OPEN Mar–Nov

A building of charm, fully restored and refurbished with many antiques. Quiet, overlooking Keswick with panoramic mountain views. Log fires, freshly-prepared food, lovely bedrooms and good company.

◆◆◆ HEDGEHOG HILL GUESTHOUSE

18 Blencathra Street, Keswick,
CA12 4HP
T: (017687) 74386
E: hedhil@fsbdial.co.uk

Bedrooms: 2 single,
4 double
Bathrooms: 4 en suite,
1 public

B&B per night:
S £17.50–£18.50
D £42.00–£48.00

OPEN All year round

Friendly Victorian guesthouse near town centre and lake. Lovely views, comfortable en suite rooms, freshly cooked breakfast with choice, vegetarian options.

◆◆◆

LINNETT HILL
4 Penrith Road, Keswick, CA12 4HF
T: (017687) 73109

B&B per night:
S £26.00–£26.00
D £48.00–£50.00

OPEN All year round

Georgian house built in 1812. Overlooks Fitz Park and the River Greta. View of Skiddaw and Latrigg. Close to Keswick's market square and short level walk to the shores of Derwentwater. All rooms en suite with colour TV, hairdryer and tea/coffee-making facilities. Large car park and secure cycle storage.

Bedrooms: 1 single,
7 double, 2 twin
Bathrooms: 10 en suite

Parking for 12
CC: Barclaycard, Delta,
Maestro, Mastercard,
Solo, Switch, Visa, Visa
Electron

◆◆◆ LITTLETOWN FARM

Newlands, Keswick, CA12 5TU
T: (017687) 78353

Bedrooms: 1 single,
4 double, 2 twin, 1 triple,
1 family room
Bathrooms: 6 en suite,
2 public

EM 1900
Parking for 10
CC: Barclaycard,
Mastercard, Visa

B&B per night:
S £28.00–£32.00
D £56.00–£64.00

HB per person:
DY £40.00–£44.00

OPEN Feb–Nov

150-acre mixed farm. In the beautiful, unspoilt Newlands Valley. Comfortable residents' lounge, dining room and cosy bar. Traditional 4-course dinner 6 nights a week.

◆◆◆◆

LYNWOOD HOUSE
35 Helvellyn Street, Keswick, CA12 4EP
T: (017687) 72398
F: (017687) 74090
E: lynwoodho@aol.com

B&B per night:
S £18.00–£18.50
D £33.00–£41.00

OPEN All year round

Situated in a quiet, residential area, our family-run Victorian guesthouse is a 5-minute stroll from Keswick town centre. Each room has TV and tea/coffee facilities, while a comfortable lounge with extensive collection of books is available for your relaxation. Breakfast menu options include traditional, vegetarian and organic dishes.

Bedrooms: 1 single,
2 double, 1 triple
Bathrooms: 1 en suite,
1 public

◆◆◆◆

THE PADDOCK
Wordsworth Street, Keswick,
CA12 4HU
T: (017687) 72510

Bedrooms: 5 double,
1 family room
Bathrooms: 5 en suite,
1 private

Parking for 5

B&B per night:
D £38.00–£42.00

OPEN All year round

Guesthouse offering comfortable en suite accommodation and good food. Within easy walking distance of the town centre, Fitz Park and Derwentwater. Parking. Non-smoking.

◆◆◆◆

RAVENSWORTH HOTEL
29 Station Street, Keswick, CA12 5HH
T: (017687) 72476
F: (017687) 75287
E: info@ravensworth-hotel.co.uk
I: www.ravensworth-hotel.co.uk

B&B per night:
S £25.00–£36.50
D £48.00–£55.00

OPEN All year round

Non-smoking, family-run, award-winning licensed hotel, decorated to a high standard. All rooms are en suite with radio/alarm, colour TV and beverage tray. After a hearty breakfast the Ravensworth makes an ideal base for exploring the Lakes before relaxing in our splendid lounge or "Herdwick" bar.

Bedrooms: 5 double,
3 twin
Bathrooms: 6 en suite,
2 private

Parking for 5
CC: Barclaycard, Delta,
JCB, Mastercard, Solo,
Switch, Visa, Visa Electron

◆◆◆

RICHMOND HOUSE
37-39 Eskin Street, Keswick,
CA12 4DG
T: (017687) 73965
E: richmondhouse@easycom.com

Bedrooms: 2 single,
6 double, 1 twin,
1 family room
Bathrooms: 9 en suite,
1 private

EM 1900 (LO 1700)
CC: Amex, Barclaycard,
Eurocard, Mastercard,
Visa

B&B per night:
S £18.00–£24.00
D £36.00–£43.00

HB per person:
DY £30.00–£35.00

OPEN All year round

Family-run guesthouse, home-from-home, easy walking distance to town centre and lake. Vegetarians catered for. Non-smokers only, please.

IMPORTANT NOTE Information on accommodation listed in this guide has been supplied by the proprietors. As changes may occur you are advised to check details at the time of booking.

◆◆◆◆

RICKERBY GRANGE

Portinscale, Keswick, CA12 5RH
T: (017687) 72344
F: (017687) 75588
E: val@ricor.demon.co.uk
I: www.ricor.demon.co.uk

B&B per night:
S £28.00–£30.00
D £56.00–£60.00

HB per person:
DY £41.00–£43.00

OPEN All year round

Detached country hotel in its own gardens, quietly situated in the pretty village of Portinscale, three-quarters of a mile from Keswick. Easy access to all parts of the Lakes. Comfort and good service, a cosy bar, elegant restaurant, imaginative cooking, comfortable lounge all there for your enjoyment. Ground floor rooms available.

Bedrooms: 2 single, 7 double, 1 twin, 3 triple
Bathrooms: 11 en suite, 1 public, 1 private shower

EM 1900 (LO 1930)
Parking for 14

◆◆◆

SANDON GUESTHOUSE

13 Southey Street, Keswick, CA12 4EG
T: (017687) 73648

Bedrooms: 2 single, 2 double, 1 twin, 1 triple
Bathrooms: 4 en suite, 1 public

EM 1800 (LO 1830)

B&B per night:
S £16.00–£17.00
D £38.00–£40.00

HB per person:
DY £26.00–£30.00

OPEN All year round

Charming Lakeland-stone Victorian guesthouse, conveniently situated for town, theatre or lake. Friendly, comfortable accommodation. Ideal base for walking or cycling holidays. Superb English breakfast.

◆◆◆

SEYMOUR HOUSE

36 Lake Road, Keswick, CA12 5DQ
T: (017687) 72764 &
0800 0566401 (freefone) & 07721 957899 (mobile)
F: (017687) 71289
E: andy042195@aol.com
I: www.seymour-house.com

B&B per night:
S £25.00–£45.00
D £42.00–£60.00

HB per person:
DY £33.50–£37.50

OPEN All year round

This is the place to stay. A warm welcome is assured every visit, breakfast is great, the rooms comfortable and the location hard to beat – quiet, yet in the heart of the town, close to Derwentwater "queen of the Lakes". Talk Andy into cooking dinner and you're in for a treat.

Bedrooms: 1 single, 3 twin, 6 family rooms
Bathrooms: 4 en suite, 3 public

Lunch available
EM 1830
Parking for 5
CC: Barclaycard, Delta, Diners, Eurocard, JCB, Mastercard, Solo, Switch, Visa, Visa Electron

---

◆◆◆◆

SHEMARA GUEST HOUSE

27 Bank Street, Keswick, CA12 5JZ
T: (017687) 73936

B&B per night:
S £25.00–£25.00
D £39.00–£50.00

OPEN All year round

A warm welcome awaits you at our quiet, friendly guesthouse, close to the town centre. All rooms have colour TV, tea/coffee trays, central heating, mountain views and are furnished to a high standard. Some private parking. Excellent Cumberland or continental breakfast. Non-smoking establishment.

Bedrooms: 5 double, 1 twin, 1 triple
Bathrooms: 7 en suite

Parking for 5
CC: Barclaycard, Delta, JCB, Mastercard, Solo, Switch, Visa, Visa Electron

KESWICK continued

◆◆◆◆ SUNNYSIDE GUEST HOUSE

25 Southey Street, Keswick, CA12 4EF	Bedrooms: 1 single, 4 double, 1 twin, 1 triple	Parking for 8
T: (017687) 72446	Bathrooms: 5 en suite, 2 private, 2 public	
F: (017687) 74447		
E: raynewton@survey.u-net.com		
I: www.survey.u-net.com		

B&B per night:
S £24.00–£24.00
D £38.00–£48.00

OPEN All year round

Comfortable Victorian house, 5 en suite, 2 standard rooms, all with colour TV and tea/coffee-making facilities. Relaxing guest lounge. Central location, parking for 8 cars.

◆◆◆ SWINSIDE INN

Newlands, Keswick, CA12 5UE	Bedrooms: 4 double,	Lunch available
T: (017687) 78253 & 78285	1 twin, 1 family room	EM 1800 (LO 2100)
F: (017687) 78253	Bathrooms: 4 en suite,	Parking for 40
E: theswinsideinn@btinternet.com	1 public	CC: Barclaycard, Delta,
I: www.kesnet.co.uk		JCB, Mastercard, Solo,
		Switch, Visa

B&B per night:
D £40.00–£52.00

OPEN All year round

Situated amidst stunning views and great walks. 500 year-old inn, log fires, spacious en suite and standard rooms, excellent food and ales. Drying room and parking.

◆◆◆ WATENDLATH GUEST HOUSE

15 Acorn Street, Keswick, CA12 4EA	Bedrooms: 4 double,
T: (017687) 74165	1 twin
	Bathrooms: 2 en suite,
	1 public

B&B per night:
D £36.00–£42.00

OPEN Jan–Nov

Within easy walking distance of the lake, hills and town centre. We offer a warm and friendly welcome and traditional English breakfast.

KIRKBY LONSDALE, Cumbria Map ref 5B3 *Tourist Information Centre Tel: (015242) 71437*

◆◆ THE COPPER KETTLE

3-5 Market Street, Kirkby Lonsdale, Carnforth, Lancashire LA6 2AU	Bedrooms: 2 double, 1 twin, 1 triple	Lunch available
T: (015242) 71714	Bathrooms: 3 en suite,	EM 1800 (LO 2100)
F: (015242) 71714	3 public	CC: Amex, Barclaycard, Delta, Diners, Eurocard, JCB, Maestro, Mastercard, Solo, Switch, Visa, Visa Electron

B&B per night:
S £22.00–£27.00
D £35.00–£41.00

HB per person:
DY £27.00–£30.00

OPEN All year round

Part of an old manor house, built in 1610, on the border between the Yorkshire Dales and the Lakes.

LAZONBY, Cumbria Map ref 5B2

◆◆◆◆ HARLEA

Lazonby, Penrith, CA10 1BX	Bedrooms: 2 double,	Parking for 4
T: (01768) 897055	1 twin	
E: harlea.eden@ukgateway.net	Bathrooms: 2 en suite, 1 private	

B&B per night:
S £23.00–£25.00
D £39.00–£42.00

OPEN All year round

Well appointed early Victorian former coach house. Offering superb accommodation with comfort and style. Breathtaking views of Pennines, overlooking Settle Line.

LONGTOWN, Cumbria Map ref 5A2

◆◆◆◆ BRIAR LEA HOUSE

Brampton Road, Longtown, Carlisle, CA6 5TN	Bedrooms: 2 double, 1 twin	EM Parking for 14
T: (01228) 791538	Bathrooms: 3 en suite	
F: (01228) 791538		

B&B per night:
S £25.00–£30.00
D £39.00–£50.00

HB per person:
DY £28.50–£34.00

OPEN All year round

Secluded, substantial country house set in 1.25 acres of grounds. Easy access M6, A74, A7, Carlisle, North Lakes and Scotland await.

CONFIRM YOUR BOOKING
You are advised to confirm your booking in writing.

MUNGRISDALE, Cumbria Map ref 5A2

◆◆◆

NEAR HOWE HOTEL
Mungrisdale, Penrith, CA11 0SH
T: (017687) 79678
F: (017687) 79678

B&B per night:
S £23.00–£23.00
D £38.00–£46.00

HB per person:
DY £29.00–£33.00

OPEN Mar–Nov

Farmhouse in quiet surroundings within easy reach of all lakes. Good walking. Homely hotel offering good home-cooked food and bar. Ideal stopover for trips to Scotland.

Bedrooms: 3 double, 1 twin, 2 triple, 1 family room
Bathrooms: 5 en suite, 1 public

EM 1700 (LO 1700)
Parking for 10

NEAR SAWREY, Cumbria Map ref 5A3

◆◆◆

BEECHMOUNT COUNTRY HOUSE
Near Sawrey, Ambleside, LA22 0JZ
T: (015394) 36356
I: www.beechmountcountryhouse.co.uk

Bedrooms: 2 double, 1 triple
Bathrooms: 2 en suite, 1 public

Parking for 4

B&B per night:
S £25.00–£30.00
D £44.00–£44.00

OPEN All year round

Spacious country house in Beatrix Potter's village, with its old world inn. Lovely rooms, superb lake and country views. Fabulous breakfast including vegetarian. Excellent value.

◆◆◆◆

LAKEFIELD
Near Sawrey, Ambleside, LA22 0JZ
T: (015394) 36635 (Answerphone)
F: (015394) 36635

B&B per night:
S £29.00–£40.00
D £50.00–£58.00

OPEN All year round

A warm welcome awaits at our modern bungalow overlooking Esthwaite Water, offering a high standard of comfort in en suite bedrooms with colour TV, tea/coffee-making facilities. Central heating, delicious hearty breakfasts. Ample parking, secure cycle store. An ideal location for fell and valley walks. Exclusively non-smoking.

Bedrooms: 1 double, 1 twin
Bathrooms: 2 en suite

Parking for 2

◆◆◆

TOWER BANK ARMS
Near Sawrey, Ambleside, LA22 0LF
T: (015394) 36334
F: (015394) 36334

Bedrooms: 2 double, 1 twin
Bathrooms: 3 en suite

Lunch available
EM 1830 (LO 2100)
Parking for 8
CC: Amex, Barclaycard, Delta, JCB, Mastercard, Solo, Switch, Visa, Visa Electron

B&B per night:
S Min £37.00
D Min £52.00

OPEN All year round

Next door to Hill Top, the former home of Beatrix Potter. It features in the tale of Jemima Puddleduck.

NEWBY BRIDGE, Cumbria Map ref 5A3

◆◆◆◆

LOW GRAYTHWAITE HALL
Graythwaite, Newby Bridge, LA12 8AZ
T: (015395) 31676
F: (015395) 31948

Bedrooms: 1 double, 1 twin, 1 family room; suite available
Bathrooms: 2 en suite, 1 private

Parking for 15

B&B per night:
S £25.00–£30.00
D £45.00–£50.00

OPEN Mar–Dec

Grade II Listed building known locally as Statesman's House. Full of lovely old panelling, open log fires and a wealth of antiques and paintings.

CUMBRIA

NEWLANDS, Cumbria Map ref 5A3

◆◆ LOW SKELGILL
Newlands, Keswick, CA12 5UE
T: (017687) 78453

Bedrooms: 2 double, 1 twin
Bathrooms: 1 public

Parking for 4

B&B per night:
S £17.00–£17.00
D £32.00–£34.00

OPEN Mar–Oct

60-acre hill farm. Small traditional working sheep farm at the foot of Catbells in the peaceful Newlands Valley. Wonderful walking area. Homely comfortable accommodation. Meals available at local inns.

PENRITH, Cumbria Map ref 5B2 *Tourist Information Centre Tel: (01768) 867466*

◆◆◆ ALBANY HOUSE
5 Portland Place, Penrith, CA11 7QN
T: (01768) 863072
F: (01768) 863072
I: www.albanyhouse.com.uk

Bedrooms: 1 double, 3 triple, 1 family room
Bathrooms: 2 en suite, 2 public

Parking for 1

B&B per night:
D £36.00–£52.00

OPEN All year round

Large Victorian terraced house run by proprietress and providing good facilities. Ideal for Lake District and stopover to or from Scotland. Children welcome, special diets on request.

◆◆◆ BLUE SWALLOW GUESTHOUSE
11 Victoria Road, Penrith, CA11 8HR
T: (01768) 866335

Bedrooms: 2 twin, 2 triple, 1 family room
Bathrooms: 3 en suite, 1 public

Parking for 3

B&B per night:
S £22.00–£26.00
D £36.00–£40.00

OPEN All year round

Family-run, mid-Victorian townhouse, comfortable and well-appointed throughout. Situated in Eden Valley, 5 minutes from Lakeland. Hearty breakfast and cleanliness assured.

◆◆◆◆ HORNBY HALL COUNTRY GUEST HOUSE
Hornby Hall, Brougham, Penrith, CA10 2AR
T: (01768) 891114
F: (01768) 891114

Bedrooms: 1 single, 2 double, 4 twin
Bathrooms: 3 en suite, 2 private, 1 public

EM 1900 (LO 2100)
Parking for 10
CC: Barclaycard, Delta, Eurocard, Mastercard, Switch, Visa

B&B per night:
S £28.00–£43.00
D £58.00–£70.00

HB per person:
DY £45.00–£52.00

OPEN All year round

16thC farmhouse with original dining hall. Fishing on Eamont available. Easy reach of Lakes and Yorkshire Dales. Home-cooked local produce.

◆◆◆◆
Silver Award

ROUNDTHORN COUNTRY HOUSE
Beacon Edge, Penrith, CA11 8SJ
T: (01768) 863952
F: (01768) 864100
E: enquiries@roundthorn.co.uk
I: www.roundthorn.co.uk

B&B per night:
S £33.75–£45.00
D £48.00–£65.00

OPEN All year round

Grade II Listed Georgian mansion, set in landscaped grounds, from which there are panoramic views of the Eden Valley, Pennines and Lakeland fells. All rooms are en suite and have TV and tea/coffee-making facilities. The house is fully licensed and rates include a hearty Cumbrian breakfast.

Bedrooms: 8 double, 2 triple
Bathrooms: 10 en suite

Parking for 70
CC: Amex, Barclaycard, Delta, Diners, Eurocard, JCB, Maestro, Mastercard, Solo, Switch, Visa, Visa Electron

---

WELCOME HOST This is a nationally recognised customer care programme which aims to promote the highest standards of service and a warm welcome. Establishments taking part in this initiative are indicated by the ⊛ symbol.

♦♦♦

WOODLAND HOUSE HOTEL

Wordsworth Street, Penrith, CA11 7QY
T: (01768) 864177
F: (01768) 890152
E: ivordavies@woodlandhouse.co.uk
I: www.woodlandhouse.co.uk

B&B per night:
S £29.50–£37.00
D Max £48.00

OPEN All year round

Elegant and spacious Victorian house, situated in a quiet residential street, just 5 minutes' walk from Penrith centre. It is at the foot of Beacon Hill, the top of which provides panoramic views of the Pennines and Lake District. Library of books and maps for walkers and nature lovers.

Bedrooms: 3 single, 2 double, 2 twin, 1 triple
Bathrooms: 7 en suite, 1 private

EM 1845 (LO 1430)
Parking for 6
CC: Barclaycard, Delta, Mastercard, Switch, Visa

♦

NAB COTTAGE GUEST HOUSE

Nab Cottage, Rydal, Ambleside, LA22 9SD
T: (01539) 435311
F: (01539) 435493
E: ell@nab.dial.lakesnet.co.uk
I: www.lakesnet.net/homepages/ell/nab

B&B per night:
S £20.00–£25.00
D £40.00–£50.00

HB per person:
DY £32.00–£37.00

OPEN All year round

Grade II Listed 16thC cottage overlooking Rydal Water. Former home of Thomas de Quincey with many literary associations. Friendly service, informal atmosphere, home-made bread, log fires, great walking, lake views. Somewhere to let go.....

Bedrooms: 1 single, 3 double, 2 twin, 1 triple
Bathrooms: 3 en suite, 1 public

EM 1900
Parking for 12

♦♦♦

KINGFISHER HOUSE AND RESTAURANT
Sandside, Milnthorpe, LA7 7HW
T: (015395) 63909
F: (015395) 64022
E: kingfisherest@tinyworld.co.uk

Bedrooms: 1 single, 2 double, 1 twin, 1 triple
Bathrooms: 5 en suite

Lunch available
EM 1830 (LO 2030)
Parking for 22
CC: Barclaycard, Delta, Eurocard, JCB, Maestro, Mastercard, Solo, Switch, Visa, Visa Electron

B&B per night:
S Min £30.00
D Min £48.00

OPEN Feb–Dec

Comfortable accommodation with beautiful views over Kent Estuary and Lakeland hills. Ideal for bird-watching, ramblers and golf enthusiasts. Excellent food available in our restaurant.

♦♦♦♦

BUCKLE YEAT GUEST HOUSE
Sawrey, Ambleside, LA22 0LF
T: (015394) 36446 & 36538
F: (015394) 36446
E: info@buckle-yeat.co.uk
I: www.buckle-yeat.co.uk

Bedrooms: 1 single, 4 double, 2 twin
Bathrooms: 6 en suite, 1 private

Parking for 9
CC: Amex, Barclaycard, Delta, JCB, Maestro, Mastercard, Solo, Switch, Visa, Visa Electron

B&B per night:
S £25.00–£27.00
D £50.00–£54.00

OPEN All year round

17thC oak-beamed cottage, famous for its connections with Beatrix Potter, provides a warm, friendly and centrally located base and excellent value for money.

CREDIT CARD BOOKINGS If you book by telephone and are asked for your credit card number it is advisable to check the proprietor's policy should you cancel your reservation.

SAWREY HOUSE COUNTRY HOTEL

Silver Award

Near Sawrey, Ambleside, LA22 0LF
T: (015394) 36387
F: (015394) 36010
E: enquiries@sawrey-house.com
I: www.sawrey-house.com

Bedrooms: 1 single,
5 double, 4 twin, 1 triple
Bathrooms: 11 en suite

EM 1930 (LO 2000)
Parking for 20
CC: Barclaycard, Delta,
Mastercard, Visa

B&B per night:
S £45.00–£65.00
D £90.00–£112.00

HB per person:
DY £60.00–£70.00

OPEN Feb–Nov
& Christmas

Warm, friendly atmosphere. Quality bedrooms, many with lake views, good food, log fire. Hotel overlooks Esthwaite Waters, magnificent views. Two red rosettes for food.

WEST VALE COUNTRY HOUSE

Far Sawrey, Hawkshead, Ambleside,
LA22 0LQ
T: (015394) 42817
F: (015394) 88214

Bedrooms: 3 double,
2 triple, 1 family room
Bathrooms: 6 en suite,
1 public

EM 1900 (LO 1600)
Parking for 8
CC: Barclaycard, Delta,
JCB, Mastercard, Solo,
Switch, Visa, Visa Electron

B&B per night:
S £28.00–£29.00
D £50.00–£52.00

HB per person:
DY £35.00–£38.00

OPEN Mar–Oct

A warm welcome awaits you at this peaceful family-run guesthouse, with home cooking, log fire and fine views.

SEDBERGH, Cumbria Map ref 5B3

ASH HINING FARM

Howgill, Sedbergh, LA10 5HU
T: (015396) 20957
F: (015396) 20957

Bedrooms: 1 double,
1 twin
Bathrooms: 1 public

EM 1800 (LO 1830)
Parking for 4

B&B per night:
S £20.00–£22.00
D £36.00–£40.00

OPEN Feb–Nov

Beef breeding farm situated in the Howgill Fells and with panoramic views. Five miles M6, 20 miles Windermere. Ideal for walking or touring. Excellent home cooking.

DALESMAN COUNTRY INN

Main Street, Sedbergh, LA10 5BN
T: (015396) 21183
F: (015396) 21311
I: www.infotel.co.uk

Bedrooms: 1 single,
1 twin, 4 triple, 1 family
room
Bathrooms: 7 en suite

Lunch available
EM 1800 (LO 2130)
Parking for 13
CC: Barclaycard, Delta,
Eurocard, JCB, Maestro,
Mastercard, Solo, Switch,
Visa, Visa Electron

B&B per night:
S £25.00–£30.00
D £50.00–£60.00

OPEN All year round

On entering Sedbergh from the M6 the Dalesman is the first inn on the left. 17thC but recently refurbished by local craftsmen. 10% discount on weekly bookings. Winter breaks available.

STAVELEY, Cumbria Map ref 5A3

TARN HOUSE

18 Danes Road, Staveley, Kendal,
LA8 9PW
T: (01539) 821656 (Answerphone)
& 07771 516156 (Mobile)

Bedrooms: 2 double,
1 twin
Bathrooms: 1 public

Parking for 3

B&B per night:
S £22.00–£22.00
D £34.00–£34.00

OPEN Feb–Nov
& Christmas

Comfortable accommodation with a homely atmosphere and ideal for touring the Lake District.

TEBAY, Cumbria Map ref 5B3

PRIMROSE COTTAGE

Orton Road, Tebay, Penrith,
CA10 3TL
T: (015396) 24791 &
07778 520930 (Mobile)

Bedrooms: 2 double,
1 twin
Bathrooms: 1 en suite,
2 private

Parking for 6

B&B per night:
S £25.00–£30.00
D £38.00–£40.00

HB per person:
DY £30.00–£35.00

OPEN All year round

Close to M6, junction 38. Overnight stops/short breaks. North Lakes and Yorkshire Dales nearby. Excellent facilities include 4-poster bed, jacuzzi bath. Also self-catering ground floor flat.

RATING All accommodation in this guide has been rated, or is awaiting a rating, by a trained English Tourism Council assessor.

TROUTBECK, Cumbria Map ref 5A2

◆◆◆ **GILL HEAD FARM**
Troutbeck, Penrith, CA11 0ST
T: (01768) 779652
F: (01768) 779130
E: gillhead@talk21.com
I: www.gillheadfarm.co.uk

Bedrooms: 3 double, 2 twin
Bathrooms: 5 en suite

EM 1830
Parking for 8

B&B per night:
S £20.00–£20.00
D £40.00–£40.00

HB per person:
DY £28.00–£28.00

OPEN All year round

Beautiful 17thC farmhouse, on a working hill farm, offering quality en suite accommodation in Lake District National Park. Delicious home cooking, log fires and in a central location for touring beautiful lakes.

TROUTBECK, Cumbria Map ref 5A3

◆◆◆◆ **HIGH FOLD FARM**
Troutbeck, Windermere, LA23 1PG
T: (015394) 32200
F: (015394) 34970

Bedrooms: 2 double, 2 triple, 1 family room
Bathrooms: 3 en suite, 1 public

Parking for 6

B&B per night:
S £25.00–£30.00
D £40.00–£50.00

OPEN All year round

Unbeatable views over the Troutbeck Valley. Well furnished, comfortable accommodation of the highest standard. Excellent breakfasts. An ideal centre for walkers and for touring Lakeland.

ULLSWATER, Cumbria Map ref 5A3

◆◆◆

KNOTTS MILL COUNTRY LODGE
Watermillock, Penrith, CA11 0JN
T: (017684) 86699
E: knottsmill@cwcom.net
I: www.knottsmill.cwc.net

B&B per night:
S £25.00–£37.50
D £40.00–£60.00

HB per person:
DY £37.00–£44.95

OPEN All year round

A country lodge offering quality serviced accommodation and delicious home-cooked food. In private grounds set in magnificent scenery around Ullswater with stunning views of the surrounding hills. Ideal for walking, touring, bird-watching and sailing. Relaxed welcoming atmosphere in a peaceful setting, yet only 10 minutes from the M6.

Bedrooms: 2 double, 2 twin, 2 triple, 2 family rooms
Bathrooms: 8 en suite

EM 1830 (LO 1930)
Parking for 10

◆◆◆

LAND ENDS
Ullswater, Penrith, CA11 0NB
T: (017684) 86438
F: (017684) 86959

B&B per night:
S £31.50–£33.50
D £56.00–£60.00

OPEN All year round

One mile from Ullswater, Land Ends is a haven of peace and quiet. Our traditional farmhouse has been tastefully renovated providing 9 en suite bedrooms, cosy lounge and bar. In 7 acres of grounds, gardens and ponds with red squirrels, owls, ducks and wonderful birdlife, this is the perfect place to relax.

Bedrooms: 3 single, 4 double, 2 twin
Bathrooms: 9 en suite

Parking for 15

WHERE TO STAY
Please mention this guide when making your booking.

CUMBRIA

♦♦♦
MOSS CRAG
Eagle Road, Glenridding, Penrith, CA11 0PA
T: (017684) 82500 & 0789 9777419 (BT transfer when absent)
F: (017684) 82500
E: mosscrag@talk21.com

B&B per night:
S £30.00–£35.00
D £41.00–£57.00

HB per person:
DY £37.00–£45.00

OPEN Jan–Nov

Small, friendly family-run guesthouse overlooking Glenridding Beck, and close to Ullswater shore. Individually tastefully decorated rooms await your arrival. All rooms have TV, hospitality tray, etc. A good wholesome breakfast will start your day, whether walking, climbing, fishing, sailing or just touring the area.

Bedrooms: 4 double, 2 twin
Bathrooms: 4 en suite, 1 public

Lunch available
EM 1930 (LO 1930)
Parking for 9
CC: Delta, JCB, Mastercard, Solo, Switch, Visa, Visa Electron

---

♦♦♦
TYMPARON HALL
Newbiggin, Stainton, Penrith, CA11 0HS
T: (017684) 83236
F: (017684) 83236
E: margaret@peeearson.freeserve.co.uk
I: www.peeearson.freeserve.co.uk

Spacious and very comfortable 18thC manor-house. Colourful summer garden. Lake Ullswater 10 minute drive. Excellent home cooking. En suite available.

Bedrooms: 2 double, 1 twin
Bathrooms: 3 en suite

EM 1830 (LO 1430)

B&B per night:
S £25.00–£35.00
D £46.00–£50.00

HB per person:
DY £35.00–£37.00

OPEN All year round

♦♦♦
ULLSWATER HOUSE
Pooley Bridge, Penrith, CA10 2NN
T: (017684) 86259

Centrally situated in Pooley Bridge. The well appointed rooms are quiet, and each has a fridge containing alcoholic and soft drinks.

Bedrooms: 3 double, 1 twin
Bathrooms: 4 en suite

EM 1900 (LO 1900)
Parking for 4

B&B per night:
S £21.00–£28.00
D £42.00–£42.00

HB per person:
DY £32.00–£53.00

OPEN All year round

ULVERSTON, Cumbria Map ref 5A3 *Tourist Information Centre Tel: (01229) 587120*

♦♦♦♦
VIRGINIA HOUSE HOTEL
24 Queen Street, Ulverston, LA12 7AF
T: (01229) 584844
F: (01229) 588565
E: virginia@ulverstonhotels.co.uk
I: www.ulverstonhotels.co.uk

Elegant Georgian townhouse situated in the town centre. Grade II Listed building.

Bedrooms: 3 single, 3 double, 1 twin
Bathrooms: 7 en suite

CC: Amex, Delta, Diners, JCB, Maestro, Mastercard, Solo, Switch, Visa, Visa Electron

B&B per night:
S £25.00–£35.00
D £50.00–£56.00

OPEN All year round

WHITEHAVEN, Cumbria Map ref 5A3 *Tourist Information Centre Tel: (01946) 852939*

♦♦♦♦
CORKICKLE GUEST HOUSE
1 Corkickle, Whitehaven, CA28 8AA
T: (01946) 692073
F: (01946) 692073
E: corkickle@tinyworld.co.uk

Elegant Georgian townhouse close to town centre, offering high standards of comfort. Ideal base for business or leisure visitors.

Bedrooms: 2 single, 3 double, 1 twin
Bathrooms: 4 en suite, 2 private, 1 public

EM 1900
Parking for 2

B&B per night:
S £22.50–£35.00
D £45.00–£50.00

OPEN All year round

HALF BOARD PRICES Half board prices are given per person, but in some cases these may be based on double/twin occupancy.

WINDERMERE, Cumbria Map ref 5A3 *Tourist Information Centre Tel: (015394) 46499*

◆◆◆◆ **THE ARCHWAY**

13 College Road, Windermere, LA23 1BU	Bedrooms: 2 double, 1 twin, 1 triple	EM 1845	B&B per night:
T: (015394) 45613 (Answerphone) & 45328	Bathrooms: 4 en suite	Parking for 1	**S £25.00–£40.00**
F: (015394) 45328		CC: Delta, Eurocard, JCB, Maestro, Mastercard,	**D £50.00–£65.00**
E: archway@btinternet.com		Solo, Switch, Visa, Visa Electron	HB per person:
I: www.lakedistrictguesthouses.co.uk			**DY £39.00–£46.00**

OPEN All year round

Impeccable Victorian guesthouse with a breakfast well worth getting up for. Good food and comfort the priority. Easy access to Lakes, ideal for touring. Non-smoking.

◆◆◆◆ **ASHLEIGH GUEST HOUSE**

11 College Road, Windermere, LA23 1BU	Bedrooms: 1 single, 3 double, 1 triple	Parking for 1	B&B per night: **S £25.00–£35.00**
T: (015394) 42292 & 07940 598634 (Mobile)	Bathrooms: 5 en suite		**D £42.00–£55.00**
F: (015394) 42292			OPEN All year round

Beautiful, comfortable Victorian home with stunning mountain views. Breakfast choice. Quiet central location. Non-smoking. All rooms en suite with colour TV.

◆◆◆◆◆
Silver Award

THE BEAUMONT

Holly Road, Windermere, LA23 2AF

T: (015394) 47075

F: (015394) 47075

E: thebeaumonthotel@btinternnet.com

I: www.lakesbeaumont.co.uk

B&B per night:
S £36.00–£40.00
D £60.00–£100.00

OPEN Feb–Dec

The Beaumont is an elegant Victorian villa occupying an enviable position for all amenities of Windermere/Bowness and is an ideal base from which to explore Lakeland. The highest standards prevail and the lovely en suite bedrooms are immaculate. We provide all modern comforts, superb breakfasts, genuine hospitality, excellent value. Private car park.

Bedrooms: 1 single, 7 double, 1 twin, 1 triple	Parking for 10
Bathrooms: 10 en suite	CC: Barclaycard, JCB, Mastercard, Switch, Visa, Visa Electron

---

◆◆◆ **BECKMEAD HOUSE**

5 Park Avenue, Windermere, LA23 2AR	Bedrooms: 1 single, 2 double, 1 twin, 1 family room	B&B per night: **S £15.50–£20.00**
T: (015394) 42757	Bathrooms: 1 en suite, 1 private, 1 public,	**D £31.00–£50.00**
F: (015394) 42757	2 private showers	OPEN All year round

Delightful stone-built Victorian house with reputation for high standards, comfort and friendliness. Delicious breakfasts. Convenient for lake, shops, restaurants and golf-course.

◆◆ **BOWFELL COTTAGE**

Middle Entrance Drive, Storrs Park, Bowness-on-Windermere,	Bedrooms: 1 double, 1 twin, 1 triple	EM 1800 (LO 2000)	B&B per night: **S £20.00–£25.00**
Windermere, LA23 3JY	Bathrooms: 1 en suite, 1 public	Parking for 6	**D £37.00–£45.00**
T: (015394) 44835			HB per person: **DY £30.00–£34.00**

Cottage in a delightful setting, about 1 mile south of Bowness just off the A5074, offering traditional Lakeland hospitality. Secluded parking in own grounds.

OPEN All year round

IDEAS For ideas on places to visit refer to the introduction at the beginning of this section.

◆◆◆ **BROOK HOUSE**
30 Ellerthwaite Road, Windermere,
LA23 2AH
T: (015394) 44932

Bedrooms: 1 single,
4 double, 1 twin
Bathrooms: 3 en suite,
3 private showers

Parking for 7

B&B per night:
S £17.00–£20.00
D £35.00–£50.00

OPEN All year round

This immaculately kept guesthouse, in a quiet part of Windermere, offers en suite facilities,
tea/coffee making, private car park, good food, warm personal welcome.

◆◆◆ **COLLEGE HOUSE**
15 College Road, Windermere,
LA23 1BU
T: (015394) 45767
E: clghse@aol.com
I: www.college-house.com

Bedrooms: 2 double,
1 twin
Bathrooms: 3 en suite

Parking for 3

B&B per night:
S £21.00–£31.00
D £32.00–£52.00

OPEN All year round

Warm, comfortable, Victorian family house. En suite rooms with gorgeous mountain
views. Nice garden. Quiet location. Close to village centre. Private parking. Non-smoking.

◆◆◆◆

THE FAIRFIELD
Brantfell Road, Bowness-on-Windermere,
Windermere, LA23 3AE
T: (015394) 46565
F: (015394) 46565
E: Ray&barb@the-fairfield.co.uk
I: www.the-fairfield.co.uk

B&B per night:
S £25.00–£32.00
D £50.00–£64.00

OPEN Feb–Nov

Small, friendly, family-run, 200-
year-old Lakeland guesthouse for
non-smokers. Set in a peaceful
garden environment, close to
Bowness village and lake shore.
Well-appointed and tastefully
furnished bedrooms all with TV,
hairdryers, welcome tray,etc.
Breakfasts are a speciality. Leisure
club facilities nearby. Genuine
hospitality and a warm welcome.

Bedrooms: 1 single,
5 double, 1 twin, 1 triple,
1 family room
Bathrooms: 8 en suite,
1 private, 1 public

Parking for 14
CC: Barclaycard, Delta,
Mastercard, Switch, Visa

◆◆◆ **FIRGARTH**
Ambleside Road, Windermere,
LA23 1EU
T: (015394) 46974
F: (015394) 42384

Bedrooms: 1 single,
3 double, 3 triple,
1 family room
Bathrooms: 8 en suite

Parking for 8
CC: Amex, Barclaycard,
Delta, Diners, Eurocard,
JCB, Mastercard, Solo,
Switch, Visa, Visa Electron

B&B per night:
S £17.50–£24.00
D £35.00–£42.00

OPEN All year round

Elegant Victorian country house offering good breakfast, friendly atmosphere, private
parking, close to lake viewpoint. Ideally situated for touring all areas of Lakeland. Tours
arranged.

◆◆◆◆ **HILTON HOUSE**
New Road, Windermere, LA23 2EE
T: (015394) 43934
F: (015394) 43934

Bedrooms: 1 single,
4 double, 1 triple,
1 family room
Bathrooms: 7 en suite

Parking for 10

B&B per night:
S £22.00–£30.00
D £40.00–£60.00

OPEN All year round

Detached Lakeland residence in woodland setting. Colour TV, hospitality trays, excellent
food. Guest satisfaction is our aim. Large garden, private car park. Non-smoking.

ACCESSIBILITY
Look for the 🔲🔲🔲 symbols which indicate accessibility for
wheelchair users. A list of establishments is at the front of this guide.

♦♦♦

HOLLY LODGE

6 College Road, Windermere, LA23 1BX
T: (015394) 43873
F: (015394) 43873

B&B per night:
S £19.00–£27.00
D £38.00–£54.00

OPEN All year round

Traditional Lakeland family-run guesthouse in a quiet location close to shops, restaurants, buses and trains. Friendly atmosphere. Good English breakfast with varied menu. Each bedroom individually furbished, with refreshment tray. Separate lounge with open fire. Advice is readily available to make your stay with us memorable.

Bedrooms: 1 single,
5 double, 2 twin, 2 triple,
1 family room
Bathrooms: 6 en suite,
2 public

Parking for 7

♦♦♦

HOLMLEA

Kendal Road, Bowness-on-Windermere, Windermere, LA23 3EW
T: (015394) 42597

Bedrooms: 2 single,
3 double, 1 twin
Bathrooms: 4 en suite,
1 public

Parking for 7

B&B per night:
S £18.00–£28.00
D £36.00–£56.00

OPEN All year round

Four minutes' walk from lake and local amenities. Free access to nearby leisure club. Colour TV, tea/coffee facilities. A warm welcome awaits.

♦♦♦♦

IVY BANK

Holly Road, Windermere, LA23 2AF
T: (015394) 42601 & 07808 516245
E: ivybank@clara.co.uk
I: www.ivybank.clara.co.uk

B&B per night:
S £20.00–£30.00
D £36.00–£50.00

OPEN All year round

Pretty Victorian stone-built family home in a quiet central location. All bedrooms are en suite, attractively decorated and comfortably furnished. Informal atmosphere and substantial choice for breakfast. There are several beautiful view points within 30 minutes' walk. Private car park and storage for cycles. Free use of local leisure club.

Bedrooms: 3 double,
1 twin, 1 triple
Bathrooms: 5 en suite

Parking for 8
CC: Barclaycard, Delta,
Eurocard, Mastercard,
Visa

♦♦♦♦♦

Silver
Award

LAKESHORE HOUSE

Ecclerigg, Windermere, LA23 1LJ
T: (015394) 33202
F: (015394) 33213
E: lakeshore@lakedistrict.uk.com
I: www.lakedistrict.uk.com

B&B per night:
S £75.00–£112.50
D £130.00–£170.00

OPEN All year round

Fine lodgings in a haven of peace and tranquillity for the discerning on the shores of Lake Windermere. Unsurpassed comfort in glorious surroundings – with simply the best view in England. Highest standard bed/breakfast with own private access. Breakfast is served in Lakeshore's 45ft long, carpeted conservatory/pool.

Bedrooms: 2 double,
1 twin
Bathrooms: 3 en suite,
1 public

Parking for 6
CC: JCB, Maestro,
Mastercard, Solo, Switch,
Visa, Visa Electron

WINDERMERE continued

◆◆◆ LANGDALE VIEW GUEST HOUSE

114 Craig Walk, Off Helm Road, Bowness-on-Windermere, Windermere, LA23 3AX T: (015394) 44076	Bedrooms: 1 single, 3 double, 1 twin Bathrooms: 4 en suite, 1 private	EM 1800 (LO 1600) Parking for 6

Quiet Christian guesthouse with home cooking. Silver setting. En suite rooms, some with views. Non-smoking. Friendly atmosphere, private parking. Will collect from station.

B&B per night:
S £19.00–£29.00
D £37.00–£58.00

HB per person:
DY £34.00–£44.00

OPEN All year round

◆◆◆◆ LAUREL COTTAGE

St Martin's Square, Kendal Road, Bowness-on-Windermere, Windermere, LA23 3EF
T: (015394) 45594
F: (015394) 45594
E: enquiries@laurelcottage-bnb.co.uk
I: laurelcottage-bnb.co.uk

Charming early 17thC cottage with garden, located minutes from Lake Windermere. Close by are shops, pubs, restaurants and bistros to suit every taste. Whilst the cottage retains many original features, we continue to give all our guests the comforts of the present.

Bedrooms: 2 single, 8 double, 1 twin, 2 triple Bathrooms: 11 en suite, 1 public	Parking for 8

B&B per night:
S £22.00–£26.00
D £46.00–£68.00

OPEN All year round

◆◆◆ LINDISFARNE

Sunny Bank Road, Windermere, LA23 2EN T: (015394) 46295 & 07711 329540 (Mobile) F: (015394) 45310 E: lindisfarne@zoom.co.uk	Bedrooms: 2 double, 1 twin, 1 family room Bathrooms: 2 en suite, 2 private	EM 1800 (LO 2000) Parking for 4

Traditional detached Lakeland stone house, ideally situated in quiet area, close to lake, shops and scenic walks. Varied breakfasts, friendly and flexible hours.

B&B per night:
S £20.00–£25.00
D £34.00–£45.00

HB per person:
DY £27.00–£32.50

OPEN All year round

◆◆◆ LINGWOOD

Birkett Hill, Bowness-on- Windermere, LA23 3EZ T: (015394) 44680 F: (015394) 48154 E: enquiries@ lingwood-guesthouse.co.uk I: www.lingwood-guesthouse.co.uk	Bedrooms: 3 double, 2 triple, 1 family room Bathrooms: 4 en suite, 2 private, 1 public	Parking for 6 CC: Barclaycard, Delta, JCB, Mastercard, Solo, Switch, Visa, Visa Electron

A warm welcome awaits you at this family-run guesthouse. En suite rooms. Ideal for walking and lake use. Special rates for 3-day breaks.

B&B per night:
S £19.00–£30.00
D £38.00–£56.00

OPEN All year round

◆◆◆ OAKWORTH

11 Upper Oak Street, Windermere, LA23 2LB T: (015394) 42782 F: (015394) 42265	Bedrooms: 1 double, 1 triple, 1 family room Bathrooms: 2 en suite, 1 public	Parking for 2

Small guesthouse in quiet road close to bus and rail staion. Single, double, family/twin rooms with TV, tea/coffee. Parking. Tours arranged.

B&B per night:
S £14.00–£22.00
D £30.00–£50.00

OPEN All year round

QUALITY ASSURANCE SCHEME

Diamond ratings and awards were correct at the time of going to press but are subject to change. Please check at the time of booking.

◆◆◆◆

Lakeland-stone detached guesthouse built in 1873 as the home for a prosperous corn merchant. Ideally situated on edge of Windermere village, facing Library Gardens. All bedrooms have en suite or private facilities. Extensive full English breakfast with alternatives. Private parking. Convenient for buses and trains. A warm welcome assured.

RAYRIGG VILLA GUEST HOUSE
Ellerthwaite Square, Windermere, LA23 1DP
T: (015394) 88342
E: rayriggvilla@nascr.net
I: www.smoothhound.co.uk/hotels/rayrigg.html

Bedrooms: 5 double, 1 twin, 1 family room
Bathrooms: 5 en suite, 2 private

Parking for 7
CC: Barclaycard, Delta, JCB, Mastercard, Solo, Switch, Visa, Visa Electron

B&B per night:
D £40.00–£60.00

OPEN All year round

◆◆◆

A traditional Lakeland stone guesthouse situated in a quiet, yet central location, by the side of Mylne Beck as it flows into Lake Windermere. Excellent breakfasts. All rooms have colour TV and tea/coffee-making facilities. Double, twin and family accommodation in comfortably furnished en suite bedrooms. Private car parking.

ROCKLEA
Brookside, Lake Road, Windermere, LA23 2BX
T: (015394) 45326
F: (015394) 45326
I: www.rocklea.co.uk

Bedrooms: 2 single, 3 double, 1 twin, 1 triple
Bathrooms: 7 en suite

Parking for 4
CC: Amex, Barclaycard, Delta, Diners, Eurocard, JCB, Mastercard, Switch, Visa

B&B per night:
S £19.00–£28.00
D £38.00–£56.00

OPEN All year round

◆◆◆

Traditional Lakeland guesthouse. Large enough to offer variety and choice, but small enough to provide informal, friendly service. Comfortable en suite rooms. Ideally situated midway between Bowness and Windermere villages, 10 minutes' walk from lake. Chef/proprietor cooks fabulous breakfasts/dinners using fresh local produce. Parking. Free use nearby luxury leisure facilities.

ST JOHN'S LODGE
Lake Road, Windermere, LA23 2EQ
T: (015394) 43078
F: (015394) 88054
E: mail@st-johns-lodge.co.uk
I: www.st-johns-lodge.co.uk

Bedrooms: 2 single, 8 double, 1 twin, 2 triple, 1 family room
Bathrooms: 12 en suite, 2 private

EM 1900 (LO 1700)
Parking for 11
CC: Barclaycard, Delta, Eurocard, JCB, Mastercard, Solo, Switch, Visa, Visa Electron

B&B per night:
S £19.00–£28.00
D £38.00–£56.00

HB per person:
DY £32.00–£42.00

OPEN All year round

TOWN INDEX
This can be found at the back of this guide. If you know where you want to stay, the index will give you the page number listing accommodation in your chosen town, city or village.

◆◆◆◆

STORRS GATE HOUSE
Longtail Hill, Bowness-on-Windermere,
Windermere, LA23 3JD
T: (015394) 43272
E: enquiries@storrsgatehouse.co.uk
I: www.storrsgatehouse.co.uk

B&B per night:
D £46.00–£60.00

HB per person:
DY £37.00–£44.00

OPEN All year round

Delightful, quality country guesthouse in secluded gardens, minutes from the lake, where you can relax and enjoy warm, friendly hospitality all year round. All rooms en suite or private facilities, with colour TV and tea/coffee. Delicious home cooking using local produce. Log fires, ample parking. Exclusively non-smoking. Brochure with pleasure.

Bedrooms: 3 double, 1 twin
Bathrooms: 3 en suite, 1 private

EM 1900
Parking for 8
CC: Barclaycard, Delta, JCB, Mastercard, Solo, Switch, Visa, Visa Electron

♠ 🐾 10 🏠 ☐ 👇 ⑤ ⌇ ♨ TV ▥, 🍴 ✳ ✈ 🚲 ⚓ SP 🎋

◆◆◆

SUNNY-BEC
Thornbarrow Road, Windermere, LA23 2EN
T: (015394) 42103

Bedrooms: 2 double, 1 twin, 1 triple
Bathrooms: 3 en suite, 1 public

Parking for 5
CC: Barclaycard, Delta, Mastercard, Switch, Visa

B&B per night:
D £40.00–£56.00

OPEN All year round

Spacious, detached Lakeland guesthouse, a short walk from the lake and shops. Quiet, with a friendly atmosphere. Gardens with barbecue and stream.

🐾 3 🔥 🍴 🖼 ☐ 👇 ⌇ UL 🔒 ⑤ ⌇ ▥, 🍴 ✳ ⚓ SP T

◆◆◆◆

TARN RIGG
Thornbarrow Road, Windermere, LA23 2DG
T: (015394) 43690
E: stay@tarn-rigg.co.uk
I: www.tarn-rigg.co.uk

B&B per night:
S £25.00–£30.00
D £50.00–£60.00

OPEN All year round

Welcome to the Lake District. Built in 1903, Tarn Rigg is situated in an ideal position midway between Windermere and Bowness. Panoramic Langdale Pike views. Quiet, convenient location, ample parking, beautiful 0.75 acre grounds. Spacious en suite rooms with excellent modern facilities. Rooms with lake views available.

Bedrooms: 1 double, 2 twin, 2 triple
Bathrooms: 5 en suite

Parking for 10
CC: Amex, Barclaycard, Delta, Diners, Eurocard, JCB, Maestro, Mastercard, Switch, Visa

♠ 🐾 📞 🖼 ☐ 👇 ⌇ UL 🔒 ⑤ ⌇ ▥, 🍴 ✳ ⚓ SC ⚓ SP

◆◆◆

THORNBANK HOUSE
4 Thornbarrow Road, Windermere, LA23 2EW
T: (015394) 43724
F: (015394) 43724

B&B per night:
S £25.00–£35.00
D £42.00–£55.00

HB per person:
DY £32.00–£36.00

OPEN Feb–Nov

Warm and friendly family-run guesthouse, ideally located between Windermere and the lake. Good home cooking. Ample car parking. Use of local leisure facilities. Residential licence. All bedrooms en suite and non-smoking. De luxe and 4-poster room available at a small supplement. Children welcome.

Bedrooms: 4 double, 1 triple, 1 family room
Bathrooms: 6 en suite

EM 1900 (LO 1900)
Parking for 7
CC: Amex, Barclaycard, Delta, JCB, Mastercard, Solo, Switch, Visa

♠ 🐾 🔥 🏠 🖼 ☐ 👇 ⌇ 🔒 ⑤ ⌇ ♨ TV ▥, 🍴 ▶ ✳ ✈ 🚲 SC SP T

◆◆

UPPER OAKMERE

3 Upper Oak Street, Windermere,
LA23 2LB
T: (015394) 45649 & 07798 806732

Bedrooms: 3 double,
1 twin, 1 triple
Bathrooms: 2 en suite,
1 public

Lunch available
EM 1730 (LO 1830)
Parking for 2

B&B per night:
S £11.00–£16.00
D £20.00–£36.00

Ideal location, 100 yards from main High Street. Friendly atmosphere, home cooking. Single people/party bookings. Open all year. Pets welcome.

HB per person:
DY £16.00–£22.95

OPEN All year round

◆◆◆◆

VILLA LODGE GUEST HOUSE

25 Cross Street, Windermere, LA23 1AE
T: (015394) 43318
F: (015394) 43318
E: rooneym@btconnect.com
I: www.villa-lodge.co.uk

B&B per night:
S £23.00–£45.00
D £46.00–£90.00

HB per person:
DY £35.00–£60.00

OPEN All year round

Traditional Lakeland guesthouse in an elevated setting in Windermere. All bedrooms en suite, 4-poster bed for that special occasion. Excellent home cooking, evening meal optional extra. Residential licence. Two minutes from rail and bus station. Private car park. Pets welcome by arrangement.

Bedrooms: 2 single,
5 double, 1 twin
Bathrooms: 8 en suite

EM 1900
Parking for 8
CC: Barclaycard, Delta,
Mastercard, Solo, Switch,
Visa

◆◆◆

VIRGINIA COTTAGE

1 and 2 Crown Villas, Kendal Road,
Bowness-on-Windermere,
Windermere, LA23 3EJ
T: (015394) 44891 & 44855
F: (015394) 44891
E: paul-des@virginia-cottage.
freeserve.co.uk

Bedrooms: 1 single,
8 double, 1 triple,
1 family room
Bathrooms: 9 en suite,
2 private, 2 public

Parking for 9

B&B per night:
S £19.00–£32.00
D £36.00–£72.00

OPEN All year round

Situated in heart of Bowness. Our rooms are spacious and well appointed offering all the comforts of home and more! Hearty welcome and breakfast assured.

◆◆◆◆

WESTWOOD HOUSE

4 Ellerthwaite Road, Windermere,
LA23 2AH
T: (015394) 43514

Bedrooms: 5 double
Bathrooms: 5 en suite

Parking for 4

B&B per night:
S £20.00–£25.00
D £35.00–£40.00

Small, family-run guesthouse in a pleasant central location overlooking the library and small park. All rooms decorated to a high standard.

OPEN All year round

◆◆◆

YORKSHIRE HOUSE

1 Upper Oak Street, Windermere, LA23 2LB
T: (015394) 44689
E: applethwaitehouse@btinternet.com
I: www.btinternet.com/
~applethwaitehouse

B&B per night:
S £16.00–£40.00
D £32.00–£50.00

OPEN All year round

We offer you a warm welcome and a hearty breakfast in our family-run guesthouse. Clean, comfortable rooms with colour TV and complimentary hot drinks. Situated in a quiet cul-del-sac just minutes from the village centre. Garage for cycle storage. Families, vegetarians and pets all most welcome.

Bedrooms: 2 double,
1 triple, 2 family rooms
Bathrooms: 3 en suite,
1 public

CC: Delta, Diners,
Mastercard, Solo, Switch,
Visa, Visa Electron

♦♦♦ **MORVEN GUEST HOUSE**

Siddick Road, Siddick, Workington, CA14 1LE	Bedrooms: 2 single, 1 double, 3 twin	Lunch available EM 1800 (LO 1900)	B&B per night: S £26.00–£28.00
T: (01900) 602118 & 602002	Bathrooms: 6 en suite	Parking for 20	D £40.00–£46.00
F: (01900) 602118			

Detached house north-west of town. Ideal base for western Lakes and coast. Start of C2C cycleway. Car park, cycle storage.

OPEN All year round

COUNTRY CODE

Always follow the Country Code
Enjoy the countryside and respect
its life and work Guard against
all risk of fire Fasten all gates
 Keep your dogs under close control
 Keep to public paths across
farmland Use gates and stiles to
cross fences, hedges and walls
Leave livestock, crops and machinery
alone Take your litter home
Help to keep all water clean
Protect wildlife, plants and trees
Take special care on country roads
Make no unnecessary noise

A brief guide to the main Towns and Villages offering accommodation in CUMBRIA

A AMBLESIDE, CUMBRIA - Market town situated at the head of Lake Windermere and surrounded by fells. The historic town centre is now a conservation area and the country around Ambleside is rich in historic and literary associations. Good centre for touring, walking and climbing.

- **APPLEBY-IN-WESTMORLAND, CUMBRIA** - Former county town of Westmorland, at the foot of the Pennines in the Eden Valley. The castle was rebuilt in the 17th C, except for its Norman keep, ditches and ramparts. It now houses a Rare Breeds Survival Trust Centre. Good centre for exploring the Eden Valley.

B BARROW-IN-FURNESS, CUMBRIA - On the Furness Peninsula in Morecambe Bay, an industrial and commercial centre with sandy beaches and nature reserves on Walney Island. Ruins of 12th C Cistercian Furness Abbey. The Dock Museum tells the story of the area and Forum 28 houses a modern theatre and arts centre.

- **BASSENTHWAITE LAKE, CUMBRIA** - The northernmost and only true "lake" in the Lake District. Visited annually by many species of migratory birds.

- **BORROWDALE, CUMBRIA** - Stretching south of Derwentwater to Seathwaite in the heart of the Lake District, the valley is walled by high fellsides. It can justly claim to be the most scenically impressive valley in the Lake District. Excellent centre for walking and climbing.

- **BRAITHWAITE, CUMBRIA** - Braithwaite nestles at the foot of the Whinlatter Pass and has a magnificent backdrop of the mountains forming the Coledale Horseshoe.

- **BRAMPTON, CUMBRIA** - Excellent centre for exploring Hadrian's Wall. Wednesday is market day around the Moot Hall in this delightful .sandstone-built town. Wall plaque marks the site of Bonnie Prince Charlie and his Jacobite army headquarters whilst they laid siege to Carlisle Castle in 1745.

- **BROUGH, CUMBRIA** - Village lying at the foot of Stainmore on the site of a Roman fort. Remains of a medieval castle restored in the 17th C.

- **BROUGHTON-IN-FURNESS, CUMBRIA** - Old market village whose historic charter to hold fairs is still proclaimed every year on the first day of August in the market square. Good centre for touring the pretty Duddon Valley.

C CALDBECK, CUMBRIA - Quaint limestone village lying on the northern fringe of the Lake District National Park. John Peel, the famous huntsman who is immortalised in song, is buried in the churchyard. The fells surrounding Caldbeck were once heavily mined, being rich in lead, copper and barytes.

- **CARLISLE, CUMBRIA** - Cumbria's only city is rich in history. Attractions include the small red sandstone cathedral and 900-year-old castle with magnificent view from the keep. Award-winning Tullie House Museum and Art Gallery brings 2,000 years of Border history dramatically to life. Excellent centre for shopping.

- **CONISTON, CUMBRIA** - The 803m fell Coniston Old Man dominates the skyline to the east of this village at the northern end of Coniston Water. Arthur Ransome set his "Swallows and Amazons" stories here. Coniston's most famous resident was John Ruskin, whose home, Brantwood, is open to the public. Good centre for walking.

- **CROSTHWAITE, CUMBRIA** - Small village in the picturesque Lyth Valley off the A5074.

D DALTON-IN-FURNESS, CUMBRIA - Conveniently located between Ulverston and Barrow. There exists the remains of a 14th C tower in the main street of the village.

E ELTERWATER, CUMBRIA - Attractive village at the foot of Great Langdale with a small village green as its focal point. Elterwater, one of the smallest lakes in the Lake District, was named by the Norsemen as "Swan Lake" and swans still frequent the lake.

G GRANGE-OVER-SANDS, CUMBRIA - Set on the beautiful Cartmel Peninsula, this tranquil resort, known as Lakeland's Riviera, overlooks Morecambe Bay. Pleasant seafront walks and beautiful gardens. The bay attracts many species of wading birds.

- **GRASMERE, CUMBRIA** - Described by William Wordsworth as "the loveliest spot that man hath ever found", this village, famous for its gingerbread, is in a beautiful setting overlooked by Helm Grag. Wordsworth lived at Dove Cottage. The cottage and museum are open to the public.

H HAWKSHEAD, CUMBRIA - Lying near Esthwaite Water, this village has great charm and character. Its small squares are linked by flagged or cobbled alleys and the main square is dominated by the market house, or Shambles, where the butchers had their stalls in days gone by.

- **HIGH LORTON, CUMBRIA** - On the B5292 between Keswick and Cockermouth. Spectacular views from nearby Whinlatter Pass down this predominantly farming valley.

K KENDAL, CUMBRIA - The "Auld Grey Town" lies in the valley of the River Kent with a backcloth of limestone fells. Situated just outside the Lake District National Park, it is a good centre for touring the Lakes and surrounding country. Ruined castle, reputed birthplace of Catherine Parr.

- **KESWICK, CUMBRIA** - Beautifully positioned town beside Derwentwater and below the mountains of Skiddaw and Blencathra. Excellent base for walking, climbing, watersports and touring. Motor-launches operate on Derwentwater and motor boats, rowing boats and canoes can be hired.

- **KIRKBY LONSDALE, CUMBRIA** - Charming old town of narrow streets and Georgian buildings, set in the superb scenery of the Lune Valley. The Devil's Bridge over the River Lune is probably 13th C.

L LAZONBY, CUMBRIA - Busy, working village of stone cottages, set beside the River Eden amid sweeping pastoral landscape. Good fishing available.

- **LONGTOWN, CUMBRIA** - Perfect base from which to explore the magnificent Borderlands, lying adjacent to the site of the Battle of Solway Moss fought in 1542 between the English and the Scots. Handsome bridge and England's largest sheep market.

M MUNGRISDALE, CUMBRIA - Set in an unspoilt valley, this hamlet has a simple, white church with a 3-decker pulpit and box pews.

N NEAR SAWREY, CUMBRIA - Lies near Esthwaite water. Famous for Hill Top Farm, home of Beatrix Potter, now owned by the National Trust and open to the public.

- **NEWBY BRIDGE, CUMBRIA** - At the southern end of Windermere on the River Leven, this village has an unusual stone bridge with arches of unequal size. The Lakeside and Haverthwaite Railway has a stop here, and steamer cruises on Lake Windermere leave from nearby Lakeside.

P PENRITH, CUMBRIA - Ancient and historic market town, the northern gateway to the Lake District. Penrith Castle was built as a defence against the Scots. Its ruins, open to the public, stand in the public park. High above the town is the Penrith Beacon, made famous by William Wordsworth.

R RYDAL, CUMBRIA - Small hamlet next to Rydal Water, a small, beautiful lake sheltered by Rydal Fell. Once the home of William Wordsworth, Rydal Mount is open to the public. It is a good centre for walking and touring.

S SANDSIDE, CUMBRIA - On the extensive sands of the Kent Estuary between Miththorpe and Amside. Magnificent views across the bay. Immediately behind the village lie the remains of the dismantled railway and station and behind this the old quarry face dominates the landscape.

- **SAWREY, CUMBRIA** - Far Sawrey and Near Sawrey lie near Esthwaite Water. Both villages are small but Near Sawrey is famous for Hill Top Farm, home of Beatrix Potter, now owned by the National Trust and open to the public.

- **SEDBERGH, CUMBRIA** - This busy market town set below the Howgill Fells is an excellent centre for walkers and touring the Dales and Howgills. The noted boys' school was founded in 1525.

- **STAVELEY, CUMBRIA** - Large village built in slate, set between Kendal and Windermere at the entrance to the lovely Kentmere Valley.

- **T** **TEBAY, CUMBRIA** - Village lying amongst high fells at the north end of the Lune Gorge.

- **TROUTBECK, PENRITH, CUMBRIA** - On the Penrith to Keswick road, Troutbeck was the site of a series of Roman camps. The village now hosts a busy weekly sheep market.

- **TROUTBECK, WINDERMERE, CUMBRIA** - Most of the houses in this picturesque village are 17th C, some retain their spinning galleries and oak-mullioned windows. At the south end of the village is Townend, owned by the National Trust and open to the public, an excellently preserved example of a yeoman farmer's or statesman's house.

- **U** **ULLSWATER, CUMBRIA** - This beautiful lake, which is over 7 miles long, runs from Glenridding to Pooley Bridge. Lofty peaks ranging around the lake make an impressive background. A steamer service operates along the lake between Pooley Bridge, Howtown and Glenridding in the summer.

- **ULVERSTON, CUMBRIA** - Market town lying between green fells and the sea. There is a replica of the Eddystone lighthouse on the Hoad which is a monument to Sir John Barrow, founder of the Royal Geographical Society. Birthplace of Stan Laurel, of Laurel and Hardy.

- **W** **WHITEHAVEN, CUMBRIA** - Historic Georgian port on the west coast. The town was developed in the 17th C and many fine buildings have been preserved. The Beacon Heritage Centre includes a Meteorological Office Weather Gallery. Start or finishing point of Coast to Coast, Whitehaven to Sunderland, cycleway.

- **WINDERMERE, CUMBRIA** - Once a tiny hamlet before the introduction of the railway in 1847, now adjoins Bowness which is on the lakeside. Centre for sailing and boating. A good way to see the lake is a trip on a passenger steamer. Steamboat Museum has a fine collection of old boats.

- **WORKINGTON, CUMBRIA** - A deep-water port on the west Cumbrian coast. There are the ruins of the 14th C Workington Hall, where Mary Queen of Scots stayed in 1568.

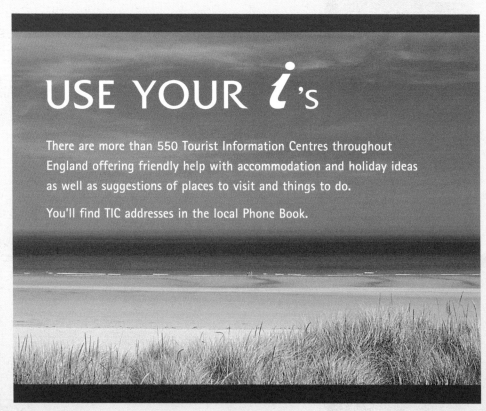

USE YOUR *i*'s

There are more than 550 Tourist Information Centres throughout England offering friendly help with accommodation and holiday ideas as well as suggestions of places to visit and things to do.

You'll find TIC addresses in the local Phone Book.

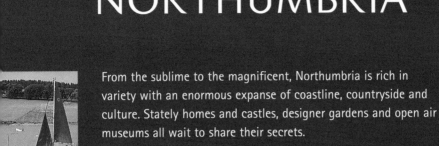

NORTHUMBRIA

From the sublime to the magnificent, Northumbria is rich in variety with an enormous expanse of coastline, countryside and culture. Stately homes and castles, designer gardens and open air museums all wait to share their secrets.

Discover Durham with its imposing Cathedral where the Venerable Bede, England's first historian, is buried. And from the beautiful fishing village of Seahouses, nature lovers will enjoy the boat trip around the Farne Islands to see eider duck, puffins and grey seals.

On the last Saturday in June the week long medieval Alnwick Fair begins. Be sure to catch unique events such as dwyle flonking - hitting your opponent with a beer-soaked rag on a stick!

The counties of
County Durham, Northumberland,
Tees Valley & Tyne & Wear

FOR MORE INFORMATION CONTACT:
Northumbria Tourist Board
Aykley Heads, Durham DH1 5UX
Tel: (0191) 375 3000
Fax: (0191) 386 0899
Internet: www.ntb.org.uk

Where to Go in Northumbria - see pages 98-101
Where to Stay in Northumbria - see pages 102-118

The Pictures:
1 Hadrian's Wall, Northumberland;
2 Kielder Water, Northumberland;
3 Washington Old Hall,
   Tyne & Wear;
4 Durham Cathedral.

Whilst in
NORTHUMBRIA ooo

You will find hundreds of interesting places to visit during your stay, just some of which are listed in these pages.

Contact any Tourist Information Centre in the region for more ideas on days out in Northumbria.

Auckland Castle

Bishop Auckland, County Durham DL14 7NR
Tel: (01388) 601627
Principal country residence of the Bishops of Durham since Norman times. The chapel and staterooms are open to the public.

Bamburgh Castle

Bamburgh, Northumberland NE69 7DF
Tel: (01668) 214515
Magnificent coastal castle completely restored in 1900. Collections of china, porcelain, furniture, paintings, arms and armour.

Bede's World

Jarrow, Tyne & Wear NE32 3DY
Tel: (0191) 489 2106
Discover the exciting world of the Venerable Bede, early medieval Europe's greatest scholar. Church, monastic site, museum with exhibitions and recreated Anglo-Saxon farm.

Belsay Hall, Castle and Gardens

Belsay, Newcastle upon Tyne NE20 0DX
Tel: (01661) 881636
House of the Middleton family for 600 years in 30 acres of landscaped gardens and winter garden. 14thC castle, ruined 17thC manor house and neo-classical hall.

Captain Cook Birthplace Museum

Marton, Middlesbrough, Cleveland TS7 6AS
Tel: (01642) 311211
Early life and voyages of Captain Cook and the countries he visited. Temporary exhibitions.

Cragside House, Gardens and Grounds

Rothbury, Morpeth, Northumberland NE65 7PX
Tel: (01669) 620333
House built 1864-1884 for the first Lord Armstrong, a Tyneside industrialist. Cragside was the first house to be lit by electricity generated by water power.

Discovery Museum

Blandford Square, Newcastle upon Tyne NE1 4JA
Tel: (0191) 232 6789
Discovery Museum offers a wide variety of experiences for all the family to enjoy. Visit the Science Factory, Great City, Fashion Works and maritime history.

Dunstanburgh Castle

Craster, Alnwick, Northumberland NE66 3TT
Tel: (01665) 576231
Romantic ruins of extensive 14thC castle in dramatic coastal situation on 30-metre (100ft) cliffs. Built by Thomas, Earl of Lancaster. Remains include gatehouse and curtain wall.

Durham Castle

Palace Green, Durham DH1 3RW
Tel: (0191) 374 3863
Castle founded in 1072, Norman chapel dating from 1080. Kitchens and great hall dated 1499 and 1284 respectively. Fine example of motte-and-bailey castle.

Gisborough Priory

Guisborough, Cleveland TS14 6HG
Tel: (01287) 633801

Remains of a priory founded by Robert de Brus in AD1119 for Augustinian canons in the grounds of Gisborough Hall. Main arch and window of east wall virtually intact.

Hall Hill Farm

Lanchester, Durham DH7 0TA
Tel: (01388) 730300

Family fun set in attractive countryside. See and touch the animals at close quarters. Farm trailer ride, riverside walk, teashop and play area.

Hartlepool Historic Quay

Hartlepool, Cleveland TS24 0XZ
Tel: (01429) 860006

An exciting reconstruction of a seaport of the 1800s with buildings and a lively quayside.

Housesteads Roman Fort

Haydon Bridge, Hadrian's Wall, Hexham, Northumberland NE47 6NN
Tel: (01434) 344363

Best preserved and most impressive of the Roman forts. Vercovicium was a 5-acre fort for an extensive 800 civil settlement. Only example of a Roman hospital.

Josephine and John Bowes Museum

Barnard Castle, Durham DL12 8NP
Tel: (01833) 690606

French-style chateau housing art collections of national importance plus archaeology of south west Durham.

Killhope, the North of England Lead Mining Museum

Cowshill, St John's Chapel, County Durham DL13 1AR
Tel: (01388) 537505

Most complete lead mining site in Great Britain. Mine tours available, 10-metre (34ft) diameter waterwheel, reconstruction of Victorian machinery, miners lodging and woodland walks.

Life Interactive World

Times Square, Newcastle upon Tyne NE1 4EP
Tel: (0191) 261 6006

This remarkable visitor experience is at the heart of the International Centre for Life, a £58 million landmark Millennium project.

Lindisfarne Castle

Holy Island, Berwick-upon-Tweed, Northumberland TD15 2SH
Tel: (01289) 389244

Fort converted into a private home for Edward Hudson by the architect Sir Edwin Lutyens in 1903.

National Glass Centre

Sunderland, Tyne & Wear SR6 0GL
Tel: (0191) 515 5555

A large gallery presenting the best in contemporary and historical glass. Master craftspeople demonstrate glass-making techniques. Classes and workshops available.

Natures World at the Botanic Centre

Acklam, Middlesbrough, Tees Valley TS5 7YN
Tel: (01642) 594895

Demonstration gardens, wildlife pond, gold medal-winning white garden, environmental exhibition hall, shop, tearoom and river Tees model.

Newcastle Cathedral

Church of St Nicholas, Newcastle upon Tyne NE1 1PF
Tel: (0191) 232 1939

13thC and 14thC church, added to in 18thC-20thC. Famous lantern tower, pre-reformation font and font cover, 15thC stained-glass roundel in the side chapel.

The Pictures:
1 The Angel of the North, Gateshead;
2 Boulby Cliff, Cleveland;
3 Tynemouth Priory and Castle, Tyne & Wear;
4 Dustanburgh, Northumberland;
5 Alnwick, Northumberland;
6 Beamish, County Durham;
7 Bridges over the Tyne, Newcastle;
8 Bamburgh, Northumberland.

8

The North of England Open Air Museum

Beamish, County Durham DH9 0RG
Tel: (01207) 231811
Visit the town, colliery village, farm, railway station, Pockerley Manor and 1825 railway, recreating life in the North East in the early 1800s and 1900s.

Otter Trust's North Pennines Reserve

Vale House Farm, Bowes, County Durham DL12 9RH
Tel: (01833) 628339
A branch of the famous Otter Trust. Visitors can see Asian and British otters, red and fallow deer and several rare breeds of farm animals in this 230-acre wildlife reserve.

Raby Castle

Staindrop, County Durham DL2 3AY
Tel: (01833) 660202
Medieval castle in 200-acre park. Includes a 600-year-old kitchen, carriage collection, walled gardens and deer park. Home of Lord Barnard's family for over 370 years.

Sea Life Aquarium

Long Sands, Tynemouth, Tyne & Wear NE30 4JF
Tel: (0191) 257 6100
More than 30 hi-tech displays provide encounters with dozens of sea creatures. Journey beneath the North Sea and discover thousands of amazing creatures.

South Shields Museum and Art Gallery

Ocean Road, South Shields, Tyne & Wear NE33 2JA
Tel: (0191) 456 8740
Galleries of Catherine Cookson memorabilia and local history. Also an exciting programme of exhibitions and events.

Thomas Bewick Birthplace Museum

Cherryburn, Mickley, Northumberland NE43 7DB
Tel: (01661) 843276
Birthplace cottage (1700) and farmyard. Printing house using original printing blocks. Introductory exhibition of the life, work and countryside.

Wallington House, Walled Garden and Grounds

Wallington Cambo, Morpeth,
Northumberland NE61 4AR
Tel: (01670) 774283
Built in 1688 on the site of an earlier medieval castle and altered in the 1740s. Interior has plasterwork, porcelain, furniture, pictures, needlework and a dolls house. Walled garden.

Washington Old Hall

Washington, Tyne & Wear NE38 7LE
Tel: (0191) 416 6879
The home of George Washington's ancestors, from 1183-1288, remaining in the family until 1613. The manor, from which the family took its name, was restored in 1936.

Wet 'N Wild

Royal Quays, North Shields NE29 6DA
Tel: (0191) 296 1333
Tropical indoor water park. A fun water playground providing the wildest and wettest indoor rapid experience. Whirlpools, slides and meandering lazy river.

Wildfowl and Wetlands Trust

Washington, Tyne & Wear NE38 8LE
Tel: (0191) 416 5454
Collection of 1,250 wildfowl of 108 varieties. Viewing gallery, picnic areas, hides and winter wild bird feeding station, flamingos and wild grey heron. Food available.

The Pictures:
1. Freeborough Hill, Cleveland;
2. Roseberry Topping, Northumberland;
3. Cragside Estate, nr. Rothbury, Northumberland;
4. Alnwick Castle, Northumberland;
5. Bamburgh, Northumberland.

Find out more about
NORTHUMBRIA ...

Further information about holidays and
attractions in Northumbria is available from:

NORTHUMBRIA TOURIST BOARD
Aykley Heads, Durham DH1 5UX.
Tel: (0191) 375 3000
Fax: (0191) 386 0899
Internet: www.ntb.org.uk

The following publications are available free from the
Northumbria Tourist Board, unless otherwise stated:

Northumbria 2001

information on the region, including hotels, bed and
breakfast and self-catering accommodation, caravan
and camping parks, attractions, shopping, eating and
drinking

North of England Bed & Breakfast Map

value for money bed and breakfast accommodation in
Northumbria and Yorkshire

Going Places

information on where to go, what to see and what to
do. Combined with the award-winning Powerpass
promotion which offers 2-for-1 entry into many of the
region's top attractions

Group Travel Directory

guide designed specifically for group organisers,
detailing group accommodation providers, places to
visit, suggested itineraries, coaching information and
events

Educational Visits

information to help plan educational visits within the
region. Uncover a wide variety of places to visit with
unique learning opportunities

Discover Northumbria on two wheels

information on cycling in the region including an order
form allowing the reader to order maps/leaflets from a
central ordering point

Freedom

caravan and camping guide to the North of England.
Available from Freedom Holidays, tel: 01202 252179

Getting to
NORTHUMBRIA ...

BY ROAD: The north/south routes on the A1 and A19 thread the region as does the
A68. East/west routes like the A66 and A69 easily link with the western side of the
country. Within Northumbria you will find fast, modern interconnecting roads between
all the main centres, a vast network of scenic, traffic-free country roads to make
motoring a pleasure and frequent local bus services operating to all towns and villages.

BY RAIL: London to Edinburgh InterCity service stops at Darlington, Durham,
Newcastle and Berwick upon Tweed. 26 trains daily make the journey between
London and Newcastle in just under 3 hours. The London to Middlesbrough journey
takes 3 hours. Birmingham to Darlington 3 hours 15 minutes. Bristol to Durham
5 hours and Sheffield to Newcastle just over 2 hours. Direct services operate to
Newcastle from Liverpool, Manchester, Glasgow, Stranraer and Carlisle. Regional
services to areas of scenic beauty operate frequently, allowing the traveller easy
access. The Tyne & Wear Metro makes it possible to travel to many destinations
within the Tyneside area, such as Gateshead, South Shields, Whitley Bay and
Newcastle International Airport, in minutes.

Where to stay in
NORTHUMBRIA

Accommodation entries in this region are listed in alphabetical order of place name, and then in alphabetical order of establishment.

Map references refer to the colour location maps at the front of this guide. The first number indicates the map to use; the letter and number which follow refer to the grid reference on the map.

At-a-glance symbols at the end of each accommodation entry give useful information about services and facilities. A key to symbols can be found inside the back cover flap. Keep this open for easy reference.

A brief description of the towns and villages offering accommodation in the entries which follow, can be found at the end of this section.

A complete listing of all English Tourism Council assessed guest accommodation appears at the back of this guide.

ALNMOUTH, Northumberland Map ref 5C1

♦♦♦♦
Gold
Award

Elegant Listed Georgian house with commanding coastal views. Comfortable and stylish with antique furnishings. Relaxed atmosphere, warm hospitality and peaceful village setting.

HIGH BUSTON HALL
High Buston, Alnmouth, Alnwick, NE66 3QH
T: (01665) 830606 &
07050 041774 (Mobile (Mr Atherton))
F: (01665) 830707
E: highbuston@aol.com
I: members.aol.com/highbuston

Bedrooms: 3 double   EM
Bathrooms: 2 en suite,   Parking for 9
1 private

B&B per night:
S £45.00–£45.00
D £75.00–£75.00

OPEN All year round

CHECK THE MAPS
The colour maps at the front of this guide show all the cities, towns and villages for which you will find accommodation entries. Refer to the town index to find the page on which they are listed.

◆◆◆

HOPE AND ANCHOR HOTEL

44 Northumberland Street, Alnmouth, Alnwick, NE66 2RA
T: (01665) 830363
E: alan@hope-and-anchor.demon.co.uk

B&B per night:
S £24.00–£30.00
D £46.00–£62.00

HB per person:
DY £36.00–£45.00

OPEN All year round

Charming old English hotel, set in historic coastal village. Oak-beamed bar, cosy fire, comfortable dining room, terraced patio garden. En suite and standard bedrooms, with easy chairs, wash hand basin, colour TV, tea/coffee/biscuits. We are proud of our reputation for cleanliness, good food, comfort and hospitality.

Bedrooms: 2 double,
1 twin, 2 triple
Bathrooms: 4 en suite

Lunch available
EM 1900 (LO 2030)

ALNWICK, Northumberland Map ref 5C1 *Tourist Information Centre Tel: (01665) 510665*

◆◆◆

EAST CAWLEDGE PARK FARM
Alnwick, NE66 2HB
T: (01665) 606670 & 605705
F: (01665) 605963

Bedrooms: 1 double,
1 twin
Bathrooms: 1 public

Parking for 4

B&B per night:
S Min £20.00
D Min £40.00

OPEN All year round

A farmhouse with lovely walks through woods and river. An old railway line leads to little village with country pub (Lesbury). Short walk to historic town of Alnwick.

◆◆◆◆
Silver Award

NORFOLK
41 Blakelaw Road, Alnwick, NE66 1BA
T: (01665) 602892
I: www.norfolk.ntb.org.uk

Bedrooms: 1 double,
1 twin
Bathrooms: 2 en suite

EM 1800
Parking for 2

B&B per night:
S Min £20.50
D Min £41.00

HB per person:
DY Min £31.00

OPEN Apr–Oct

Detached house, quiet area. Tastefully furnished, comfort assured. En suite. Guests' sitting room, separate dining room. Traditional home-cooked 4-course evening meals. No smoking.

◆◆◆

ROCK MIDSTEAD FARM HOUSE

Rock Midstead, Rock, Alnwick, NE66 2TH
T: (01665) 579225
E: ian@rockmidstead.freeserve.co.uk

B&B per night:
S £18.00–£36.00
D £36.00–£52.00

HB per person:
DY £30.50–£48.50

OPEN All year round

Comfortable, spacious farmhouse set in peaceful organic dairy farm, with extensive views of surrounding countryside. Ideal for walking or cycling. Excellent home cooking, fresh-baked bread daily, afternoon tea on the lawn. Log fires. En suite rooms with colour TV and radio. Perfect base for exploring coastline, castles, hills and historic houses.

Bedrooms: 2 double,
1 twin
Bathrooms: 2 en suite,
1 private

Lunch available
EM 1800 (LO 2100)
Parking for 5

BARDON MILL, Northumberland Map ref 5B2

◆◆◆◆

CARRSGATE EAST
Bardon Mill, Hexham, NE47 7EX
T: (01434) 344376 (Answerphone available) & 07710 981533 (Mobile)
F: (01434) 344011
E: lesley@armstrongrl.freeserve.co.uk

Bedrooms: 2 double
Bathrooms: 2 en suite

Parking for 6

B&B per night:
S £20.00–£25.00
D £38.00–£50.00

OPEN Mar–Nov

Enjoy relaxing surroundings, well-appointed rooms and great views, in this comfortable 17thC home. Ideal base for exploring south west Northumbria.

BARNARD CASTLE, Durham Map ref 5B3 *Tourist Information Centre Tel: (01833) 690909 or 630272*

◆◆◆◆
Gold
Award

CLOUD HIGH

Eggleston, Barnard Castle, County Durham DL12 0AU
T: (01833) 650644
F: (01833) 650644

B&B per night:
S Min £30.00
D £46.00–£50.00

OPEN Mar–Nov

Idyllically situated at 1,000ft in peaceful countryside, Cloud High commands magnificent unrivalled views of Teesdale and surrounding dales. Here the emphasis is on comfort, quality and relaxation with every amenity in the lovely en suite bedrooms and private lounge. Breakfasts are our speciality with a choice of traditional or interesting alternatives.

Bedrooms: 2 double, 1 twin
Bathrooms: 3 en suite

Parking for 4

🅰 📺 ⌷ ♨ ✆ 🛈 ⑤ ⟡ 🅟 📺 🏠 🚗 ✻ ✕ 🚲 🅣

◆◆◆

OLD WELL INN

21 The Bank, Barnard Castle,
County Durham DL12 8PH
T: (01833) 690130
F: (01833) 690140
E: reservations@oldwellinn.co.uk
I: www.oldwellinn.co.uk

B&B per night:
S £48.00–£58.00
D £60.00–£70.00

OPEN All year round

Recommended by The Times, Sunday Telegraph and featured on BBC "Holidays Out", The Old Well, a 17thC coaching inn, boasts 10 spacious, tastefully decorated en suite bedrooms along with refreshingly varied menus. Surrounded by antique shops, outstanding scenery and castles, and offering value for money. Special weekend breaks throughout the year.

Bedrooms: 6 double, 2 twin, 2 triple
Bathrooms: 10 en suite

Lunch available
EM 1800 (LO 2130)
CC: Amex, Barclaycard, Delta, Eurocard, Mastercard, Solo, Switch, Visa, Visa Electron

🅰 🚏 🚲 ✆ ⌷ ♨ ⑤ ⟡ 🅟 🏠 ☕ 🍴 ✻ 🚲 🆂🅲 🚭 🆂🅿 🏠 🅣 ⊚

BEAL, Northumberland Map ref 5B1

◆◆◆

BROCK MILL FARMHOUSE

Brock Mill, Beal, Berwick-upon-Tweed, TD15 2PB
T: (01289) 381283 & 07889 099517
F: (01289) 381283

Bedrooms: 1 single, 1 double, 1 triple
Bathrooms: 2 public

B&B per night:
S £16.00–£20.00
D £32.00–£40.00

OPEN Feb–Nov

220-acre mixed farm. Peaceful farmhouse, ideal for touring and golf, situated just off Holy Island road. Spacious, comfortable rooms. Private lounge/dining room. Walled garden.

🅰 🚏 📺 ⌷ ♨ 🆄🅻 🛈 ⑤ ⟡ 🅟 📺 🏠 ☕ ✻ ✕ 🚲 🆂🅿 🅣

BELLINGHAM, Northumberland Map ref 5B2 *Tourist Information Centre Tel: (01434) 220616*

◆◆◆◆

LYNDALE GUEST HOUSE AND HOLIDAY COTTAGE

Off The Square, Bellingham, Hexham, NE48 2AW
T: (01434) 220361 &
03778 925479 (Mobile)
F: (01434) 220361
E: lyndale.SmoothHound@chelsolfdemon.co.uk
I: www.SmoothHound.co.uk/hotels/lyndale.html

Bedrooms: 2 double, 1 twin
Bathrooms: 2 en suite, 1 private, 1 public

EM 1800 (LO 1900)
Parking for 6
CC: Barclaycard, Delta, Eurocard, JCB, Mastercard, Visa

B&B per night:
S £25.00–£35.00
D £46.00–£50.00

HB per person:
DY £35.50–£37.50

OPEN All year round

Close to Hadrian's Wall, Kielder Water, Borders and Pennine Way. Relax in the walled garden or sun lounge. Excellent dinners/good breakfasts. Walking, biking, watersports, golf.

🅰 🚏 🚲 🚏 📺 ⌷ ♨ 🆄🅻 🛈 ⑤ ⟡ 🅟 📺 ◐ ⟡ 🏠 🍴6 ☕ 🍴 ✻ ✕ 🚲 🆂🅲 🆂🅿 🅣 ⊚

◆◆◆ **LADYTHORNE HOUSE**

Cheswick, Berwick-upon-Tweed, TD15 2RW	Bedrooms: 1 single, 1 double, 2 twin, 2 triple	Parking for 8
T: (01289) 387382	Bathrooms: 3 public	

F: (01289) 387073 (telephone above number first)
E: parkerbankb@ladythorne.freeserve.co.uk

B&B per night:
S £14.50–£17.00
D £29.00–£34.00

OPEN All year round

Grade II Listed Georgian house dated 1721. Magnificent views of the countryside, close to unspoilt beaches. Large garden, families welcome. Meals available within 5 minutes' drive.

◆◆◆◆

THE OLD VICARAGE GUEST HOUSE

24 Church Road, Tweedmouth, Berwick-upon-Tweed, TD15 2AN
T: (01289) 306909

B&B per night:
S £26.00–£18.00
D £32.00–£52.00

OPEN All year round

Set in a peaceful location only 10 minutes' walk from the town centre and beautiful beaches. Spacious bedrooms are tastefully decorated with many thoughtful extras. An outstanding breakfast served in our elegant dining room will ensure a perfect start to your day. We look forward to welcoming you.

Bedrooms: 1 single, 4 double, 1 twin, 1 triple
Bathrooms: 4 en suite, 1 public

Parking for 4

◆◆◆◆

ROB ROY

Dock Road, Tweedmouth, Berwick-upon-Tweed, TD15 2BQ
T: (01289) 306428
I: www.secretkingdom.com/rob/roy.htm

B&B per night:
S Min £27.00
D Min £46.00

OPEN All year round

Stone-built pub with cosy bar and log fire. One mile to Berwick centre from our riverside location. Our restaurant and bar menus offer choice local seafood, lobster, oysters, scallops. Visit Northumbria's beautiful coastline and castles, walk the Cheviots or the beautiful Tweed Valley. Or just enjoy Rob Roy hospitality.

Bedrooms: 1 double, 1 twin
Bathrooms: 2 en suite

Lunch available
EM 1900 (LO 2130)
CC: Amex, Barclaycard, Delta, Diners, JCB, Mastercard, Switch, Visa, Visa Electron

---

◆◆◆ **FIVE GABLES GUEST HOUSE**

Five Gables, Binchester, Bishop Auckland, County Durham DL14 8AT	Bedrooms: 1 single, 1 double, 1 triple	EM 1900
	Bathrooms: 3 en suite	Parking for 3

T: (01388) 608204
F: (01388) 663092
E: book.in@fivegables.co.uk
I: www.fivegables.co.uk

B&B per night:
S £25.00–£27.50
D £42.00–£45.00

HB per person:
DY £37.00–£39.50

OPEN All year round

3 miles from Bishop Auckland, 15 minutes from Durham. Victorian house in country. Self-catering cottage available.

SYMBOLS The symbols in each entry give information about services and facilities. A key to these symbols appears at the back of this guide.

CHESTER-LE-STREET, Durham Map ref 5C2

◆◆◆◆ **HOLLYCROFT**

11 The Parade, Chester-le-Street, County Durham DH3 3LR	Bedrooms: 1 double, 1 twin	Parking for 3
T: (0191) 388 7088 & 07932 675069 (Mobile)	Bathrooms: 2 en suite, 1 public	
E: cutter@hollycroft11.freeserve. co.uk		

B&B per night:
S £25.00–£25.00
D £42.00–£42.00

OPEN All year round

Traditional townhouse ideally located for Durham County's riverside cricket ground, A1(M), Beamish Museum, Durham City, Newcastle and MetroCentre.

CONSETT, Durham Map ref 5B2

◆◆◆

BEE COTTAGE FARM
Castleside, Consett, County Durham
DH8 9HW
T: (01207) 508224 (Answerphone available)

B&B per night:
S £28.00–£35.00
D £44.00–£70.00

HB per person:
DY £42.50–£49.50

OPEN All year round

Working farm set in peaceful surroundings. Quiet, pleasant walks, unspoilt views. Ideally situated for Beamish Museum, Durham Cathedral, Hadrian's Wall or an overnight break in a long journey. Some ground floor rooms. Tea room open Easter – October 1-6 pm. Evening meals availble. No smoking and dogs by arrangement. You will be made very welcome.

Bedrooms: 1 single, 3 double, 4 twin, 1 triple, 3 family rooms; suites available	Lunch available EM 1900 (LO 2000) Parking for 20
Bathrooms: 5 en suite, 2 public	

CORBRIDGE, Northumberland Map ref 5B2

◆◆◆◆ **FELLCROFT**

Station Road, Corbridge, NE45 5AY	Bedrooms: 1 twin, 1 triple	EM 1830 (LO 2200) Parking for 3
T: (01434) 632384	Bathrooms: 1 en suite, 1 private	

B&B per night:
S £20.00–£22.00
D £33.00–£35.00

OPEN All year round

Well-appointed stone-built Edwardian house with full private facilities. Quiet road in country setting, half a mile south of market square. Non-smokers only, please.

CRASTER, Northumberland Map ref 5C1

◆◆◆

COTTAGE INN
Dunstan Village, Craster, Alnwick,
NE66 3SZ
T: (01665) 576658
F: (01665) 576788

B&B per night:
S Max £35.00
D Max £63.00

HB per person:
DY Max £45.00

OPEN All year round

Family-run inn half a mile from the sea. All rooms are ground floor and have garden view. Noted for excellent food. Situated in an Area of Outstanding Natural Beauty. Many places of interest to visit, as well as golf, riding and fishing in the vicinity.

Bedrooms: 2 double, 8 twin	Lunch available EM 1800 (LO 2130)
Bathrooms: 10 en suite	Parking for 60 CC: Barclaycard, Delta, Mastercard, Switch, Visa

CHECK THE MAPS
The colour maps at the front of this guide show all the cities, towns and villages for which you will find accommodation entries.
Refer to the town index to find the page on which they are listed.

CROOKHAM, Northumberland Map ref 5B1

◆◆◆◆ **THE COACH HOUSE AT CROOKHAM**

Cornhill-on-Tweed, TD12 4TD	Bedrooms: 2 single,	EM 1930 (LO 1930)	B&B per night:
T: (01890) 820293	2 double, 5 twin	Parking for 12	S £23.00–£39.00
F: (01890) 820284	Bathrooms: 6 en suite,	CC: Mastercard, Visa	D £46.00–£78.00
E: thecoachouse@englandmail.	1 private, 2 public		
com			HB per person:
I: www.secretkingdom.com/coach/			DY £40.50–£56.50
house.htm			
			OPEN Apr–Oct

Spacious rooms, arranged around a courtyard, in rolling country near the Scottish border. Home-cooked, quality fresh food. Rooms specially equipped for disabled guests.

DARLINGTON, Durham Map ref 5C3 *Tourist Information Centre Tel: (01325) 388666*

◆ **ABERLADY GUEST HOUSE**

51 Corporation Road, Darlington,	Bedrooms: 2 single,	Parking for 2	B&B per night:
County Durham DL3 6AD	3 twin, 2 triple		S £14.00–£17.50
T: (01325) 461449 & 07970 379939	Bathrooms: 2 public		D £28.00–£28.00

Large Victorian house near town centre. Short walking distance to Railway Museum. Within easy reach of 4 golf courses and leisure centre.

OPEN All year round

DURHAM, Durham Map ref 5C2 *Tourist Information Centre Tel: (0191) 384 3720*

◆◆◆ **60 ALBERT STREET**

Western Hill, Durham, DH1 4RJ	Bedrooms: 1 single,	Parking for 2	B&B per night:
T: (0191) 386 0608 &	1 double, 1 twin, 1 triple	CC: Barclaycard, Delta,	S £20.00–£26.00
07930 369429 (Mobile)	Bathrooms: 2 en suite,	Eurocard, JCB,	D £44.00–£52.00
E: laura@sixtyalbertstreet.co.uk	1 public	Mastercard, Solo, Switch,	
I: www.sixtyalbertstreet.co.uk		Visa, Visa Electron	OPEN All year round

Elegantly restored Victorian townhouse situated in quiet conservation area near railway station. Five minutes' walk to central market square, cathedral, shops and restaurants. Private parking.

◆◆◆ **BAY HORSE INN**

Brandon Village, Durham, DH7 8ST	Bedrooms: 3 double,	Lunch available	B&B per night:
T: (0191) 378 0498	6 twin, 1 family room	EM 1900 (LO 2200)	S £35.00–£40.00
	Bathrooms: 10 en suite	Parking for 25	D £45.00–£50.00
		CC: Amex, Barclaycard,	
		Delta, Mastercard, Solo,	OPEN All year round
		Switch, Visa, Visa Electron	

Ten stone-built chalets 3 miles from Durham city centre. All have shower, toilet, TV, tea and coffee facilities and telephone. Ample car parking.

◆◆◆ **CASTLE VIEW GUEST HOUSE**

4 Crossgate, Durham, DH1 4PS	Bedrooms: 1 single,	CC: Barclaycard, Delta,	B&B per night:
T: (0191) 386 8852	3 double, 2 twin	JCB, Mastercard, Solo,	S £40.00–£40.00
F: (0191) 386 8852	Bathrooms: 6 en suite	Switch, Visa, Visa Electron	D £55.00–£55.00
E: castle_view@hotmail.com			
			OPEN All year round

250-year-old, Listed building in the heart of the old city, with woodland and riverside walks and a magnificent view of the cathedral and castle.

◆◆◆ **CASTLEDENE**

37 Nevilledale Terrace, Durham,	Bedrooms: 2 twin	Parking for 3	B&B per night:
DH1 4QG	Bathrooms: 1 public		S Max £25.00
T: (0191) 384 8386 &			D Max £40.00
07710 425921 (Mobile)			
F: (0191) 384 8386			OPEN All year round
E: lornabyrne@tinyworld.co.uk			

Edwardian end-of-terrace house half a mile west of the market place. Within walking distance of the riverside, cathedral and castle.

PRICES
Please check prices and other details at the time of booking.

DURHAM continued

Rating Applied For	**CATHEDRAL VIEW GUEST HOUSE** 212 Gilesgate, Durham, Co Durham DH1 1QN T: (0191) 386 9566 F: (0191) 386 9566 E: cathedralview@hotmail.com	Bedrooms: 3 double, 2 twin, 1 triple Bathrooms: 6 en suite	CC: Barclaycard, Mastercard, Visa	B&B per night: S £42.00–£42.00 D £52.00–£52.00 OPEN All year round

Grade II Listed townhouse in the heart of city. All rooms en suite, furnished to highest standard. Views of cathedral and castle. Quality and hospitality assured.

◆◆◆	**COLLINGWOOD COLLEGE CUMBRIAN WING** South Road, Durham, DH1 3LT T: (0191) 374 4568 F: (0191) 374 4595 E: collingwood_college. conference@durham.ac.uk	Bedrooms: 194 single, 16 twin Bathrooms: 210 en suite	Lunch available EM 1800 (LO 1900) Parking for 130 CC: Barclaycard, Delta, Mastercard, Switch, Visa	B&B per night: S £30.00–£30.00 D £49.00–£49.00 HB per person: DY Min £36.95 OPEN Jan, Mar–Apr, Jul–Sep, Dec

Nestling amongst unspoilt greenery, this is one of Durham's newest colleges and has an unrivalled reputation for service and hospitality, ensuring that guests will be eager to return.

◆◆◆

THE GILESGATE MOOR HOTEL

Teasdale Terrace, Gilesgate, Durham,
Co Durham DH1 2RN
T: (0191) 386 6453
F: (0191) 386 6453

B&B per night:
S £18.00–£25.00
D £36.00–£45.00

HB per person:
DY £23.00–£30.00

OPEN All year round

Comfortable family-run inn on the outskirts of Durham City. The accommodation throughout is finished to the highest standard and offers an ideal base for exploring Durham City and the surrounding area. We guarantee a warm, friendly welcome and high standards of service throughout your stay.	Bedrooms: 3 twin, 1 family room Bathrooms: 2 en suite, 1 public	Lunch available Parking for 7 CC: Barclaycard, Mastercard, Visa

---

◆◆	**REDHILLS HOTEL** Redhills Lane, Crossgate Moor, Durham, DH1 4AW T: (0191) 386 4331 F: (0191) 386 9612	Bedrooms: 5 single, 1 double Bathrooms: 2 public	Lunch available EM 1900 (LO 2200) Parking for 80 CC: Amex, Barclaycard, Delta, Mastercard, Switch, Visa	B&B per night: S £28.00–£34.00 D £34.00–£40.00 HB per person: DY £34.00–£40.00 OPEN All year round

Small, friendly hotel with well appointed bedrooms and personal service, only 2 minutes from Durham city centre.

◆◆◆	**ST AIDAN'S COLLEGE** University of Durham, Windmill Hill, Durham, DH1 3LJ T: (0191) 374 3269 F: (0191) 374 4749 E: a.davis.conf@durham.ac.uk I: www.st-aidans.org.uk	Bedrooms: 72 single, 24 twin Bathrooms: 96 en suite, 4 public	Lunch available EM 1800 (LO 2000) Parking for 80 CC: Barclaycard, Delta, Eurocard, JCB, Mastercard, Switch, Visa, Visa Electron	B&B per night: S £30.00–£32.00 D £52.00–£55.00 HB per person: DY £42.00–£44.00 OPEN Jan, Mar–Apr, Jul–Sep

Set in landscaped gardens, overlooking one of the most visually attractive cities in Britain, Durham. Ideal base to visit Northumbria. Adjacent golf course, free tennis.

 REGIONAL TOURIST BOARD The ⋀ symbol in an establishment entry indicates that it is a Regional Tourist Board member.

DURHAM continued

◆◆ **ST CHAD'S COLLEGE**
18 North Bailey, Durham, DH1 3RH
T: (0191) 374 3364
F: (0191) 374 3309
E: St-Chads.www@durham.ac.uk
I: www.dur.ac.uk/StChads

Bedrooms: 63 single,
31 twin
Bathrooms: 16 en suite,
33 public, 5 private
showers

Lunch available
EM (LO 1730)

B&B per night:
S £20.00–£26.00
D £36.00–£47.00

OPEN Apr, Jul–Sep,
Dec

In the heart of historic Durham, adjacent to the castle and cathedral, designated a World Heritage site. Comfortable and convenient accommodation, friendly service.

Ⓜ ⛷ ⚒ ♿ 🛈 Ⓢ ⚲ 🅿 📺 ◑ 🖥 🖨 🍴100 ☎ ❄ ✈ ⌂ Ⓣ

◆◆ **TREVELYAN COLLEGE (MACAULAY WING)**
Elvet Hill Road, Durham, DH1 3LN
T: (0191) 374 3765 & 374 3768
F: (0191) 374 3789
E: trev.coll@durham.ac.uk
I: www.dur.ac.uk/~dtr0www

Bedrooms: 253 single,
27 twin
Bathrooms: 50 en suite,
47 public

Lunch available
EM 1800 (LO 1930)
Parking for 100
CC: Barclaycard, Delta,
Mastercard, Switch, Visa

B&B per night:
S £20.00–£30.00
D £36.00–£54.00

HB per person:
DY £30.25–£40.25

OPEN Jan, Mar–Apr,
Jul–Oct, Dec

Set in parkland within easy walking distance of Durham City. Air-conditioned Cloister Bar, TV lounges, tennis court, ample parking. Standard and en suite rooms available.

Ⓜ ⛷ ⚒ ♿ 🛈 Ⓢ 🅿 📺 🖥 🍴300 ☎ ❄ ✈ ⌂ Ⓣ ◎

EGGLESTON, Durham Map ref 5B3

◆◆◆

MOORCOCK INN
Hill Top, Gordon Bank, Eggleston,
Barnard Castle, County Durham DL12 0AU
T: (01833) 650395
F: (01833) 650052

B&B per night:
S £20.00–£25.00
D £32.00–£37.00

OPEN All year round

Country inn with scenic views over Teesdale. Ideal walking country. Cosy en suite bedrooms, open log fire in lounge bar. Over 50 malt whiskies and a selection of real ales. Excellent home-cooked food using local produce. Our speciality is Teesdale lamb and locally produced beef and pork. Also, extensive fish menu.

Bedrooms: 2 single,
5 double
Bathrooms: 4 en suite,
1 public

Lunch available
EM 1900 (LO 2100)
Parking for 50
CC: Barclaycard, Delta,
JCB, Mastercard, Solo,
Switch, Visa, Visa Electron

Ⓜ ⛷ 📺 🖥 ♿ 🛈 Ⓢ ⚲ 📺 🖥 🍴90 ☎ ♉ ⛽ Ⓢ🅲 ↘ Ⓢ🅿

ELLINGHAM, Northumberland Map ref 5C1

◆◆◆ **PACK HORSE INN**
Ellingham, Chathill, NE67 5HA
T: (01665) 589292 &
07050 189333 (Mobile)
F: (01665) 589053
E: graham.simpson@farmline.com
I: www.thepackhorseinn.co.uk

Bedrooms: 2 double,
3 twin
Bathrooms: 5 en suite

Lunch available
EM 1800 (LO 2100)
Parking for 20
CC: Barclaycard, Delta,
JCB, Mastercard, Solo,
Switch, Visa

B&B per night:
S £15.00–£25.00
D £20.00–£45.00

OPEN All year round

Stone-built inn set in beautiful countryside. Comfortable rooms, all en suite. Excellent food served. Self-catering cottage also available.

Ⓜ ⛷ 📺 🖥 ☎ 🛈 Ⓢ ⚲ 📺 🖥 ♿ ☎ ♉ ↟ ✓ ❄ ⛽ Ⓢ🅲 ↘ Ⓢ🅿 ⌂ ◎

GATESHEAD, Tyne and Wear Map ref 5C2 *Tourist Information Centre Tel: (0191) 477 3478*

◆◆◆ **SHAFTESBURY GUEST HOUSE**
245 Prince Consort Road,
Gateshead, Tyne and Wear NE8 4DT
T: (0191) 478 2544
F: (0191) 478 2544

Bedrooms: 2 single,
6 twin, 2 triple
Bathrooms: 2 en suite,
3 public

Parking for 12

B&B per night:
S £22.00–£32.00
D £32.00–£42.00

OPEN All year round

Charming, family-run guesthouse. Ideal for MetroCentre, Newcastle City/Arena, Gateshead Stadium. Opposite Gateshead leisure centre. A1 north, A167 Gateshead (south). A1 south, A184 Gateshead.

Ⓜ ⛷ 📺 ☎ Ⓢ ⚲ 🖥 ♿ Ⓢ🅲 Ⓢ🅿 ⌂ Ⓣ

QUALITY ASSURANCE SCHEME
Diamond ratings and awards are explained at the back of this guide.

GRETA BRIDGE, Durham Map ref 5B3

Silver Award

THE COACH HOUSE
Greta Bridge, Barnard Castle,
County Durham DL12 9SD
T: (01833) 627201
F: (01833) 627201
E: info@coachhousegreta.co.uk
I: www.coachhousegreta.co.uk

Bedrooms: 2 twin,
1 family room
Bathrooms: 1 en suite,
1 private

EM 1930
CC: Barclaycard, Delta,
JCB, Mastercard, Solo,
Switch, Visa, Visa Electron

B&B per night:
S £45.00–£45.00
D £64.00–£64.00

HB per person:
DY £52.00–£52.00

OPEN All year round

Former coaching inn on the River Greta, ideally situated for the dales and lakes. Extremely comfortably furnished, charming garden and lovely walks.

HALTWHISTLE, Northumberland Map ref 5B2 *Tourist Information Centre Tel: (01434) 322002*

Silver Award

ASHCROFT
Lantys Lonnen, Haltwhistle, NE49 0DA
T: (01434) 320213
F: (01434) 320213

B&B per night:
S £25.00–£30.00
D £48.00–£55.00

OPEN All year round

Elegantly furnished former vicarage in beautiful terraced gardens with private parking. Warm welcome and extensive breakfast choice. Non-smoking. Conveniently situated on the southern edge of town, yet only 100m from town facilities. The perfect base to explore Hadrian's Wall and surrounding area. Colour brochure available.

Bedrooms: 1 single,
2 double, 3 twin,
1 family room
Bathrooms: 7 en suite

CC: Barclaycard, Eurocard,
Mastercard, Visa

Gold Award

BROOMSHAW HILL FARM
Willia Road, Haltwhistle, NE49 9NP
T: (01434) 320866 & 0771 483 5828 (Mobile)
F: (01434) 320866
E: broomshaw@msn.com
I: www.broomshawhill.ntb.org.uk

B&B per night:
D £44.00–£47.00

OPEN Mar–Oct

Original 18thC farmhouse, enlarged and modernised to high standards, whilst retaining its original features. The house stands on the side of a valley on the conjunction of a bridleway and footpath, both leading to Hadrian's Wall. Close to all major Roman sites. Town amenities less than three quarters of a mile.

Bedrooms: 2 double,
1 twin
Bathrooms: 2 en suite,
1 private

Parking for 8

HALL MEADOWS
Main Street, Haltwhistle, NE49 0AZ
T: (01434) 321021

Bedrooms: 1 single,
1 double, 1 twin
Bathrooms: 1 public

Parking for 3

B&B per night:
S £17.00–£18.00
D £34.00–£36.00

OPEN All year round

Built in 1888, a large family house with pleasant garden in the centre of town. Ideally placed for Hadrian's Wall and close to bus and rail.

OAKY KNOWE FARM
Haltwhistle, NE49 0NB
T: (01434) 320648
F: (01434) 320648

Bedrooms: 2 triple
Bathrooms: 1 private,
2 public

EM 1700 (LO 1530)
Parking for 8

B&B per night:
S £20.00–£25.00
D £35.00–£40.00

OPEN All year round

300-acre livestock farm. Overlooking the Tyne Valley, within walking distance of Haltwhistle and the Roman Wall, this comfortable farmhouse offers friendly family holidays.

HALTWHISTLE continued

◆◆◆◆ **THE OLD SCHOOL HOUSE**

Fair Hill, Haltwhistle, NE49 9EE
T: (01434) 322595
F: (01434) 322595
E: vera@oshouse.freeserve.co.uk
I: www.oshouse.freeserve.co.uk

Bedrooms: 2 double,
1 twin
Bathrooms: 1 en suite,
2 private

Parking for 6

B&B per night:
D £36.00–£42.00

OPEN All year round

Stone-built house. Quiet location, yet convenient for town. Clean, comfortable bedrooms. Hadrian's Wall on doorstep. Brillant breakfasts (no need for lunch!). Warm welcome guaranteed.

HAYDON BRIDGE, Northumberland Map ref 5B2

◆◆◆ **HADRIAN LODGE**

Hindshield Moss, North Road,
Haydon Bridge, Hexham, NE47 6NF
T: (01434) 688688
F: (01434) 684867
E: hadrianlodge@hadrianswall.co.uk
I: www.hadrianswall.co.uk

Bedrooms: 1 single,
3 double, 1 twin,
3 family rooms
Bathrooms: 5 en suite,
3 public

Lunch available
EM 1800 (LO 2100)
Parking for 25
CC: Amex, Barclaycard,
Mastercard, Switch, Visa

B&B per night:
S £19.50–£28.00
D £38.00–£55.00

HB per person:
DY £24.50–£33.00

OPEN Mar–Oct

Idyllic rural location, overlooking lakes (fishing available), near Housesteads Roman Fort and Hadrian's Wall. Cosy residents' bar, delicious home-cooked meals. Warm welcome. Write/ring for brochure.

HEXHAM, Northumberland Map ref 5B2 *Tourist Information Centre Tel: (01434) 605225*

◆◆◆

ANICK GRANGE
Hexham, NE46 4LP
T: (01434) 603807

B&B per night:
S £17.50–£20.00
D £35.00–£40.00

OPEN Apr–Sep

Charming 17thC farmhouse on a 363-acre mixed farm. Spacious, comfortable rooms with all facilities, a pretty garden and a warm atmosphere. Wonderful open views. One mile from Hexham. Explore Hadrian's Wall and the beautiful North Pennines, both only 20 minutes' drive away.

Bedrooms: 1 single,
1 twin, 1 triple
Bathrooms: 1 en suite,
1 public

Parking for 4

◆◆◆ **THE BEECHES**

40 Leazes Park, Hexham, NE46 3AY
T: (01434) 605900

Bedrooms: 1 single,
2 twin
Bathrooms: 1 en suite,
1 public

EM 1830 (LO 2000)
Parking for 1

B&B per night:
S £20.00–£20.00
D £40.00–£50.00

OPEN All year round

Situated in interesting garden, with balcony to enjoy Hexham views. Evening meal by arrangement.

COUNTRY CODE Always follow the Country Code ✿ Enjoy the countryside and respect its life and work ✿ Guard against all risk of fire ✿ Fasten all gates ✿ Keep your dogs under close control ✿ Keep to public paths across farmland ✿ Use gates and stiles to cross fences, hedges and walls ✿ Leave livestock, crops and machinery alone ✿ Take your litter home ✿ Help to keep all water clean ✿ Protect wildlife, plants and trees ✿ Take special care on country roads ✿ Make no unnecessary noise

◆◆◆

DUKESFIELD HALL FARM

Steel, Hexham, NE46 1SH
T: (01434) 673634
E: cath@dukesfield.netlineuk.net

B&B per night:
D £40.00–£40.00

OPEN All year round

Charming Grade II Listed farmhouse set in 300 acres, 5 miles south of Hexham and ideally situated for walking, cycling, touring or just relaxing. Charming en suite bedrooms and a delightful guest lounge, with a friendly atmosphere. Local country pub 1.5 miles.

Bedrooms: 1 double, 1 twin
Bathrooms: 2 en suite

Parking for 4

◆◆◆

ROSE AND CROWN INN

Main Street, Slaley, Hexham, NE47 0AA
T: (01434) 673263
F: (01434) 673305

Bedrooms: 1 single, 2 twin
Bathrooms: 3 en suite

Lunch available
EM 1830 (LO 2200)
Parking for 32
CC: Amex, Barclaycard, Delta, Eurocard, JCB, Mastercard, Solo, Switch, Visa

B&B per night:
S £27.50–£32.50
D £45.00–£50.00

OPEN All year round

Warm, friendly, family-run business with good wholesome home cooking and a la carte restaurant. All bedrooms en suite in this 200-year-old Listed village freehouse in Slaley.

HOLY ISLAND, Northumberland Map ref 5B1

◆◆◆

BRITANNIA

Britannia House, Holy Island, Berwick-upon-Tweed, TD15 2RX
T: (01289) 389218

Bedrooms: 1 double, 1 twin, 1 triple
Bathrooms: 1 en suite, 1 public

Parking for 4

B&B per night:
S £22.00–£22.00
D £38.00–£38.00

OPEN Mar–Nov

Comfortable, friendly bed and breakfast in centre of Holy Island. Tea-making facilities in all rooms. TV lounge. En suite available.

KIELDER WATER, Northumberland Map ref 5B2

◆◆◆◆

THE PHEASANT INN (BY KIELDER WATER)

Stannersburn, Falstone, Hexham, NE48 1DD
T: (01434) 240382
F: (01434) 240382
E: thepheasantinn@kielderwater.demon.co.uk

B&B per night:
S £30.00–£40.00
D £50.00–£64.00

HB per person:
DY £30.00–£40.00

OPEN All year round

Charming 16thC inn, rertaining its character while providing comfortable, modern en suite accommodation. Features include stone walls and low-beamed ceilings in the bars, antique artefacts and open fires. Emphasis on traditional home cooking, using fresh vegetables, served in bar or dining room. Sunday roasts are renowned for their quality.

Bedrooms: 4 double, 3 twin, 1 family room
Bathrooms: 8 en suite

Lunch available
EM 1900 (LO 2100)
Parking for 30
CC: Barclaycard, Delta, Eurocard, JCB, Mastercard, Switch, Visa

---

MAP REFERENCES
The map references refer to the colour maps at the front of this guide. The first figure is the map number; the letter and figure which follow indicate the grid reference on the map.

LONGFRAMLINGTON, Northumberland Map ref 5C1

◆◆◆◆ BESOM BYRE

Longframlington, Morpeth,
NE65 8EN
T: (01665) 570136 (Answerphone)
F: (01665) 570136

Bedrooms: 1 twin,
1 triple
Bathrooms: 2 en suite

EM 1800 (LO 2000)
Parking for 3

B&B per night:
S £19.50–£19.50
D £39.00–£39.00

HB per person:
DY £27.00–£27.00

OPEN All year round

A converted stone barn. Each en suite room has patio doors to beautiful 1-acre garden overlooking fields and hills.

MIDDLETON-IN-TEESDALE, Durham Map ref 5B3 *Tourist Information Centre Tel: (01833) 641001*

◆◆◆ BELVEDERE HOUSE

54 Market Place, Middleton-in-
Teesdale, Barnard Castle,
County Durham DL12 0QH
T: (01833) 640884
F: (01833) 640884
E: infobelvedere@thecoachhouse.
net
I: www.thecoachhouse.net

Bedrooms: 2 double,
1 twin
Bathrooms: 3 en suite

Parking for 3

B&B per night:
S £17.00–£17.00
D £32.00–£32.00

OPEN All year round

18thC house, centrally situated in dales village. Enjoy a warm welcome and great breakfast. Explore Teesdale's beautiful countryside and places of historic interest. Magnificent waterfalls.

◆◆◆ BLUEBELL HOUSE

Market Place, Middleton-in-
Teesdale, Barnard Castle,
County Durham DL12 0QG
T: (01833) 640584

Bedrooms: 2 double,
1 twin
Bathrooms: 2 en suite,
1 private

Parking for 4

B&B per night:
S £21.00–£25.00
D £32.00–£34.00

OPEN All year round

Quiet, comfortable rooms at the rear of the house, all with private shower and WC and tea/coffee facilities. Guest TV lounge. Reduced double/twin rates for longer stays.

◆◆◆ MARKETPLACE GUEST HOUSE

16 Market Place, Middleton-in-
Teesdale, Barnard Castle,
County Durham DL12 0QG
T: (01833) 640300

Bedrooms: 2 double,
1 twin
Bathrooms: 3 en suite

Parking for 2

B&B per night:
S £21.00–£21.00
D £38.00–£38.00

OPEN All year round

Friendly guesthouse, recently refurbished. Situated in centre of the village, close to all amenities. All rooms en suite.

MORPETH, Northumberland Map ref 5C2 *Tourist Information Centre Tel: (01670) 511323*

◆◆◆

COTTAGE VIEW GUEST HOUSE

6 Staithes Lane, Morpeth, NE61 1TD
T: (01670) 518550
F: (01670) 510840
E: cottageview.morpeth@virgin.net
I: www.cottageview.co.uk

B&B per night:
S £20.00–£29.50
D £30.00–£39.50

HB per person:
DY £27.45–£36.95

OPEN All year round

Centrally situated licensed family-run guesthouse, most rooms en suite, all with remote control TV and tea/coffee facilities. Meals in the Cottage Restaurant. Two TV lounges, one with Sky. Night porter, private car park. Fax, E-mail and photocopying facilities. Football package deals. Group bookings welcome.

Bedrooms: 15 double,
5 twin, 1 triple, 4 family
rooms
Bathrooms: 19 en suite,
2 public

EM 1600 (LO 2100)
Parking for 16
CC: Barclaycard, Delta,
Diners, Eurocard,
Mastercard, Switch, Visa

PRICES

Please check prices and other details at the time of booking.

113

NEWCASTLE UPON TYNE, Tyne and Wear Map ref 5C2 *Tourist Information Centre Tel: (0191) 277 8000 Or 214 4422 (located in airport)*

♦♦♦

DENE HOTEL
38-42 Grosvenor Road, Jesmond,
Newcastle upon Tyne, NE2 2RP
T: (0191) 281 1502
F: (0191) 281 8110

B&B per night:
S £34.50–£39.50
D £57.50–£59.50

OPEN All year round

Close to city centre with excellent shopping, leisure facilities and nightlife. Centrally based for touring the beautiful Northumbria countryside with its host of historic heritage.

Bedrooms: 4 single,
7 double, 5 twin, 4 triple
Bathrooms: 18 en suite,
2 public, 2 private
showers

Lunch available
EM 1830 (LO 2030)
Parking for 17
CC: Amex, Barclaycard,
Delta, Diners, Mastercard,
Solo, Switch, Visa

♦♦

ELDON HOTEL
24 Akenside Terrace, Jesmond,
Newcastle upon Tyne, NE2 1TN
T: (0191) 281 2562
F: (0191) 213 0546
E: enquiries@acornproperties.
freeserve.co.uk

Bedrooms: 5 single,
3 double, 1 triple,
4 family rooms
Bathrooms: 6 en suite,
3 public

EM 1700 (LO 2100)
Parking for 7
CC: Barclaycard, Delta,
Mastercard, Visa

B&B per night:
S £20.00–£30.00
D £35.00–£50.00

HB per person:
DY £25.00–£30.00

Clean, quiet, small privately-owned hotel within walking distance of the city centre, and 2 minutes' walk from Jesmond metro. On-site parking.

OPEN All year round

♦♦♦♦

THE KEELMAN'S LODGE
Grange Road, Newburn,
Newcastle upon Tyne, NE15 8NL
T: (0191) 267 1689 (9am-11pm every day)
& 267 0772
F: (0191) 499 0041
E: admin@petersen-stainless.co.uk
I: www.petersen-stainless.co.uk

B&B per night:
S Max £39.00
D Max £55.00

OPEN All year round

Purpose-built stone lodge in riverside country park. Close to A1, A69, railway stations and airport. Ideal base for exploring Hadrian's Wall, Holy Island and Tyne Valley. Local pursuits include cycling, walking, fishing, golf. Big Lamp Brewery and pub adjacent with children's playground. Quality accommodation highly rated by previous customers.

Bedrooms: 6 triple
Bathrooms: 6 en suite

Lunch available
EM 1700 (LO 2100)
Parking for 6
CC: Amex, Barclaycard,
Delta, Eurocard,
Mastercard, Switch, Visa

OTTERBURN, Northumberland Map ref 5B1 *Tourist Information Centre Tel: (01830) 520093*

♦♦♦

BUTTERCHURN GUEST HOUSE
Main Street, Otterburn, NE19 1NP
T: (01830) 520585
F: (01830) 520874
E: keith@butterchurn.freeserve.co.
uk
I: www.butterchurn.freeserve.co.uk

Bedrooms: 2 double,
2 twin, 3 triple
Bathrooms: 7 en suite

Parking for 11
CC: Barclaycard, Delta,
Mastercard, Visa

B&B per night:
S £20.00–£25.00
D £40.00–£40.00

OPEN All year round

In village centre, on the River Rede. Central for Roman Wall and Kielder Water. Within easy reach of Northumberland coast. All rooms en suite.

IMPORTANT NOTE Information on accommodation listed in this guide has been supplied by the proprietors. As changes may occur you are advised to check details at the time of booking.

PONTELAND, Northumberland Map ref 5C2

◆◆◆◆

HAZEL COTTAGE
Eachwick, Dalton, Newcastle upon Tyne,
NE18 0BE
T: (01661) 852415
F: (01661) 854797
E: hazelcottage@eachwick.fsbusiness.co.uk

B&B per night:
S £25.00–£25.00
D £40.00–£40.00

HB per person:
DY Min £33.00

OPEN All year round

A warm welcome awaits you in our comfortable, traditional Northumbrian farmhouse, set in a lovely, tranquil rural area. Delightful en suite bedrooms with TV, tea-making facilities and everything for your comfort. Freshly prepared evening meals and splendid breakfasts. Newcastle, Hexham, Hadrian's wall, Metrocentre within easy reach. Non-smoking.

Bedrooms: 1 double,
1 twin
Bathrooms: 2 en suite

EM 1900 (LO 1830)
Parking for 4

REDCAR, Tees Valley Map ref 5C3 *Tourist Information Centre Tel: (01642) 471921*

◆◆◆

FALCON HOTEL
13 Station Road, Redcar, Cleveland
TS10 1AH
T: (01642) 484300

Bedrooms: 8 single,
2 double, 6 twin,
3 family rooms
Bathrooms: 12 en suite,
3 public

EM 1700 (LO 1900)

B&B per night:
S £16.00–£25.00
D £27.00–£35.00

HB per person:
DY £22.50–£31.50

OPEN All year round

Licensed hotel in centre of town with recent extension of en suite twins and singles. Within easy reach of the Cleveland Hills.

RIDING MILL, Northumberland Map ref 5B2

◆◆◆◆

LOW FOTHERLEY FARMHOUSE BED AND BREAKFAST
Riding Mill, NE44 6BB
T: (01434) 682277
F: (01434) 682277
E: hugh@lowfotherley.fsnet.co.uk
I: www.westfarm.freeserve.co.uk

B&B per night:
S £20.00–£25.00
D £40.00–£50.00

OPEN All year round

Imposing Victorian farmhouse on a working farm in the Northumberland countryside. On the A68, close to the market towns of Hexham, Corbridge and to Hadrian's Wall. Recently refurbished and decorated to a high standard. We offer warm, spacious and comfortable bedrooms. Families are very welcome.

Bedrooms: 1 double,
1 family room
Bathrooms: 1 en suite,
1 private

SPENNYMOOR, Durham Map ref 5C2

◆◆◆

THE GABLES
10 South View, Middlestone Moor,
Spennymoor, County Durham
DL16 7DF
T: (01388) 817544
E: thegablesghouse@aol.com

Bedrooms: 2 double,
4 twin
Bathrooms: 3 en suite,
1 public

EM 1845 (LO 1900)
Parking for 7
CC: Mastercard, Visa

B&B per night:
S £20.00–£36.00
D £38.00–£55.00

OPEN All year round

Spacious Victorian detached house in quiet residential area. 7 miles from Durham city centre. Ground floor en suite rooms available. Car park. Substantial breakfast. Dogs welcome.

 COLOUR MAPS Colour maps at the front of this guide pinpoint all places under which you will find accommodation listed.

SPENNYMOOR continued

◆◆◆◆ IDSLEY HOUSE

4 Green Lane, Spennymoor, Bishop Auckland, County Durham DL16 6HD T: (01388) 814237	Bedrooms: 1 single, 1 double, 2 twin, 1 triple Bathrooms: 4 en suite, 1 private	EM (LO 1900) Parking for 8 CC: Amex, Barclaycard, Delta, Eurocard, JCB, Mastercard, Switch, Visa

B&B per night:
S £32.00–£35.00
D £48.00–£48.00

OPEN All year round

Detached Victorian residence in quiet area at junction of A167/A688, opposite council offices. Just 8 minutes south of Durham City. Tastefully furnished, spacious bedrooms, safe parking on premises.

STANLEY, Durham Map ref 5C2

◆◆◆ BUSHBLADES FARM

Harperley, Stanley, County Durham DH9 9UA T: (01207) 232722	Bedrooms: 2 double, 1 twin Bathrooms: 1 en suite, 1 public	Parking for 6

B&B per night:
S £20.00–£25.00
D £34.00–£39.00

OPEN All year round

60-acre livestock farm. Comfortable Georgian farmhouse, in rural setting. Within easy reach of Durham City, Beamish Museum, A1M, MetroCentre and Roman Wall.

◆◆◆ HARPERLEY HOTEL

Harperley, Stanley, County Durham DH9 9TY T: (01207) 234011 F: (01207) 232325 E: harperley-hotel@supernet.com	Bedrooms: 2 single, 3 double Bathrooms: 5 en suite	Lunch available EM 1930 (LO 2115) Parking for 200 CC: Amex, Barclaycard, Delta, JCB, Mastercard, Solo, Switch, Visa

B&B per night:
S £35.00–£35.00
D £45.00–£45.00

OPEN All year round

Converted granary on the outskirts of Stanley, in the country park area close to the old watermill. Recently refurbished to a high standard.

SUNDERLAND, Tyne and Wear Map ref 5C2 *Tourist Information Centre Tel: (0191) 553 2000 or 553 2001 or 553 2002*

◆◆ ACORN GUEST HOUSE

10 Mowbray Road, Hendon, Sunderland, SR2 8EN T: (0191) 514 2170	Bedrooms: 1 double, 6 twin, 1 family room Bathrooms: 4 public	EM 1700 (LO 1900)

B&B per night:
S £18.00–£25.00
D £34.00–£48.00

HB per person:
DY £17.00–£25.00

OPEN All year round

Victorian property situated near city centre, Mowbray Park, local amenities. Our rooms have central heating, TV, hand-basins, shaver points, tea/coffee making facilities. Secure parking.

TANFIELD, Durham Map ref 5C2

◆◆◆ TANFIELD GARDEN LODGE

Tanfield Lane, Tanfield, Stanley, County Durham DH9 9QF T: (01207) 282821 & 0797 039 8890 (Mobile) F: (01207) 282821	Bedrooms: 3 double, 1 twin, 1 triple Bathrooms: 3 en suite, 1 public	Parking for 8

B&B per night:
S £28.00–£32.00
D £38.00–£43.00

OPEN All year round

Guesthouse in private grounds offering first-class accommodation. Close to Beamish Museum and MetroCentre. Also within easy reach of Durham and Newcastle. Private parking.

TYNEMOUTH, Tyne and Wear Map ref 5C2

◆◆◆◆ MARTINEAU GUEST HOUSE

57 Front Street, Tynemouth, North Shields, Tyne and Wear NE30 4BX T: (0191) 296 0746 (Answerphone) E: martineau.house@ukgateway.net I: www.martineau-house.co.uk	Bedrooms: 1 double, 1 twin Bathrooms: 2 en suite	CC: Barclaycard, Mastercard

B&B per night:
S £35.00–£45.00
D £45.00–£50.00

OPEN All year round

18thC Georgian townhouse situated in the heart of Tynemouth village, offering panoramic views of the Priory, River Tyne and village life.

WARK, Northumberland Map ref 5B2

◆◆◆

BATTLESTEADS HOTEL
Wark, Hexham, NE48 3LS
T: (01434) 230209
F: (01434) 230730
E: info@battlesteads-hotel.co.uk
I: www.Battlesteads-Hotel.co.uk

B&B per night:
S £30.00–£35.00
D £60.00–£70.00

HB per person:
DY £43.00–£48.00

OPEN All year round

18thC inn, formerly a farmhouse, in the heart of rural Northumberland, close to the Roman Wall and Kielder Water. An ideal centre for exploring Border country and for relaxing, walking, cycling or horse-riding. Collection and delivery service operated for walkers and cyclists.

Bedrooms: 1 single,
4 double, 3 twin,
2 family rooms
Bathrooms: 10 en suite

Lunch available
EM 1830 (LO 2130)
Parking for 50
CC: Amex, Barclaycard,
Delta, Eurocard,
Mastercard, Solo, Switch,
Visa

WARKWORTH, Northumberland Map ref 5C1

◆◆◆◆

BECK 'N' CALL
Birling West Cottage, Warkworth, Morpeth,
NE65 0XS
T: (01665) 711653
E: beck-n-call@lineone.net
I: website.lineone.net/~beck-n-call/

B&B per night:
D £37.00–£41.00

OPEN All year round

Beck 'N' Call is an outstanding traditional country cottage (over 200 years old) where guests receive a warm welcome. Set in large terraced gardens with a stream, it is within 5 minutes' walk of the village, river walks, and the most beautiful sandy beach and dunes.

Bedrooms: 2 double,
1 triple
Bathrooms: 2 en suite,
1 private

Parking for 4

WEST WOODBURN, Northumberland Map ref 5B2

◆◆◆◆

PLEVNA HOUSE
West Woodburn, Hexham,
NE48 2RA
T: (01434) 270369 &
07703 778323 (Mobile)
F: (01434) 270369
E: plevnaho@aol.com
I: www.plevnahouse.ntb.org.uk

Bedrooms: 2 double
Bathrooms: 2 en suite

EM 1800 (LO 2030)
Parking for 4

B&B per night:
S £25.00–£25.00
D £36.00–£40.00

HB per person:
DY £48.00–£52.00

OPEN Mar–Oct

Old country house and garden. Central for Borders, Hadrian's Wall, Kielder, coast and the National Trust's Wallington and Cragside. Comfort, relaxation and a warm welcome assured.

WHICKHAM, Tyne and Wear Map ref 5C2

◆◆◆◆

EAST BYERMOOR GUEST HOUSE
Fellside Road, Whickham,
Newcastle upon Tyne, NE16 5BD
T: (01207) 272687
F: (01207) 272145
E: eastbyermoor-gh.arbon@virgin.
net

Bedrooms: 4 double,
2 twin
Bathrooms: 5 en suite,
1 private

EM 1800 (LO 2130)
Parking for 13
CC: Barclaycard, Delta,
Eurocard, JCB,
Mastercard, Solo, Switch,
Visa, Visa Electron

B&B per night:
S £25.00–£25.00
D £50.00–£50.00

OPEN All year round

Former farmhouse (approximately 200 years old) in open countryside. Near Gateshead MetroCentre, Newcastle, Durham and Sunderland. Rural but convenient.

CONFIRM YOUR BOOKING
You are advised to confirm your booking in writing.

WHITLEY BAY, Tyne and Wear Map ref 5C2 *Tourist Information Centre Tel: (0191) 200 8535*

♦♦♦♦ **MARLBOROUGH HOTEL**

20-21 East Parade, The Promenade, Whitley Bay, Tyne and Wear NE26 1AP T: (0191) 251 3628 F: (0191) 252 5033 E: marlborough.hotel@virgin.net I: freespace.virgin.net/marlborough. hotel/	Bedrooms: 6 single, 3 double, 4 twin, 2 triple, 1 family room Bathrooms: 13 en suite, 2 public	EM 1830 (LO 1930) Parking for 7 CC: Amex, Barclaycard, Delta, Mastercard, Solo, Switch, Visa	B&B per night: S £22.00–£38.00 D £45.00–£60.00 HB per person: DY £33.95–£49.95 OPEN All year round

Seaside hotel with fine sea views. Comfortable, modern accommodation with friendly service. Close to MetroCentre and ferry terminal.

WOOLER, Northumberland Map ref 5B1

♦♦ **LORETO GUEST HOUSE**

1 Ryecroft Way, Wooler, NE71 6BW T: (01668) 281 350	Bedrooms: 1 single, 2 double, 2 twin, 1 family room Bathrooms: 6 en suite	EM 1800 (LO 1830) Parking for 12	B&B per night: D £37.00–£38.00 HB per person: DY £25.00–£26.00 OPEN All year round

Family-run early Georgian house in spacious grounds, in lovely Cheviot village. Central for touring and walking and close to coastline. All home cooking, all rooms en suite.

USE YOUR *i*s

There are more than 550 Tourist Information Centres throughout England offering friendly help with accommodation and holiday ideas as well as suggestions of places to visit and things to do. There may well be a centre in your home town which can help you before you set out. You'll find addresses in the local Phone Book.

A brief guide to the main Towns and Villages offering accommodation in
NORTHUMBRIA

ALNMOUTH, NORTHUMBERLAND -
Quiet village with pleasant old buildings, at the mouth of the River Aln where extensive dunes and sands stretch along Alnmouth Bay. 18th C granaries, some converted to dwellings, still stand.

ALNWICK, NORTHUMBERLAND -
Ancient and historic market town, entered through the Hotspur Tower, an original gate in the town walls. The medieval castle, the second biggest in England and still the seat of the Dukes of Northumberland, was restored from ruin in the 18th C.

BARDON MILL, NORTHUMBERLAND -
Small hamlet midway between Haydon Bridge and Haltwhistle, within walking distance of Vindolanda, an excavated Roman settlement, and near the best stretches of Hadrian's Wall.

BARNARD CASTLE, DURHAM - High over the Tees, a thriving market town with a busy market square. Bernard Baliol's 12th C castle (now ruins) stands nearby. The Bowes Museum, housed in a grand 19th C French chateau, holds fine paintings and furniture. Nearby are some magnificent buildings.

BEAL, NORTHUMBERLAND - Tiny hamlet with an inn at the junction of the A1 which leads on to the causeway to Holy Island. Some farmhouses and buildings are dated 1674.

BELLINGHAM, NORTHUMBERLAND -
Set in the beautiful valley of the North Tyne close to the Kielder Forest, Kielder Water and lonely moorland below the Cheviots. The church has an ancient stone wagon roof fortified in the 18th C with buttresses.

BERWICK–UPON–TWEED, NORTHUMBERLAND - Guarding the mouth of the Tweed, England's northernmost town with the best 16th C city walls in Europe. The handsome Guildhall and barracks date from the 18th C. Three bridges cross to Tweedmouth, the oldest built in 1634.

BISHOP AUCKLAND, DURHAM -
Busy market town on the bank of the River Wear. The Bishop's Palace, a castellated Norman manor house altered in the 18th C, stands in beautiful gardens. Entered from the market square by a handsome 18th C gatehouse, the park is a peaceful retreat of trees and streams.

CHESTER-LE-STREET, DURHAM -
Originally a Roman military site, town with modern commerce and light industry on the River Wear. The ancient church replaced a wooden sanctuary which sheltered the remains of St Cuthbert for 113 years. The Anker's house beside the church is now a museum. Home of Durham County Cricket Club.

CONSETT, DURHAM - Former steel town on the edge of rolling moors. Modern development includes the shopping centre and a handsome Roman Catholic church, designed by a local architect. To the west, the Derwent Reservoir provides water sports and pleasant walks.

CORBRIDGE, NORTHUMBERLAND -
Small town on the River Tyne. Close by are extensive remains of the Roman military town Corstopitum, with a museum housing important discoveries from excavations. The town itself is attractive with shady trees, a 17th C bridge and interesting old buildings, notably a 14th C vicarage.

CRASTER, NORTHUMBERLAND -
Small fishing village with a fine northward view of Dunstanburgh Castle. Fishing cobles in the tiny harbour, stone cottages at the water's edge and a kippering shed where Craster's famous delicacy is produced give the village its unspoilt charm.

CROOKHAM, NORTHUMBERLAND -
Pretty hamlet taking its name from the winding course of the River Till which flows in the shape of a shepherd's crook. Three castles - Etal, Duddo and Ford - can be seen, and nearby the restored Heatherslaw Mill is of great interest.

DARLINGTON, DURHAM - Largest town in County Durham, standing on the River Skerne and home of the earliest passenger railway which first ran to Stockton in 1825. Now the home of a railway museum. Originally a prosperous market town occupying the site of an Anglo-Saxon settlement, it still holds an open market.

DURHAM, DURHAM - Ancient city with its Norman castle and cathedral, now a World Heritage site, set on a bluff high over the Wear. A market and university town and regional centre, spreading beyond the market-place on both banks of the river.

EGGLESTON, DURHAM - Small village between Barnard Castle and Middleton-in-Teesdale on the edge of the moors. Once a smelting centre for the North Pennines lead industry but no trace of it remains today.

GATESHEAD, TYNE AND WEAR -
Facing Newcastle across the Tyne, a busy industrial centre which grew rapidly early in the 20th century. Now it is a town of glass, steel and concrete buildings. Home of Europe's largest indoor shopping and leisure complex, the Metro Centre.

HALTWHISTLE, NORTHUMBERLAND -
Small market town with interesting 12th C church, old inns and blacksmith's smithy. North of the town are several important sites and interpretation centres of Hadrian's Wall. Ideal centre for archaeology, outdoor activity or touring holidays.

HAYDON BRIDGE, NORTHUMBERLAND -
Small town on the banks of the South Tyne with an ancient church, built of stone from sites along the Roman Wall just north. Ideally situated for exploring Hadrian's Wall and the Border country.

MAP REFERENCES
Map references apply to the colour maps at the front of this guide.

USE YOUR *i*s
There are more than 550 Tourist Information Centres throughout England offering friendly help with accommodation and holiday ideas as well as suggestions of places to visit and things to do. You'll find TIC addresses in the local Phone Book.

HEXHAM, NORTHUMBERLAND - Old coaching and market town near Hadrian's Wall. Since pre-Norman times a weekly market has been held in the centre with its market-place and abbey park, and the richly-furnished 12th C abbey church has a superb Anglo-Saxon crypt.

HOLY ISLAND, NORTHUMBERLAND - Still an idyllic retreat, tiny island and fishing village and cradle of northern Christianity. It is approached from the mainland at low water by a causeway. The clifftop castle (National Trust) was restored by Sir Edwin Lutyens.

K KIELDER WATER, NORTHUMBERLAND - A magnificent man-made lake, the largest in Northern Europe, with over 27 miles of shoreline. On the edge of the Northumberland National Park and near the Scottish border, Kielder can be explored by car, on foot or by ferry.

L LONGFRAMLINGTON, NORTHUMBERLAND - Pleasant village with an interesting church of the Transitional style. On Hall Hill are the remains of a camp with triple entrenchment. Brinkburn Priory is nearby.

M MIDDLETON-IN-TEESDALE, DURHAM - Small stone town of hillside terraces overlooking the river, developed by the London Lead Company in the 18th C. Five miles up-river is the spectacular 70-ft waterfall, High Force.

MORPETH, NORTHUMBERLAND - Market town on the River Wansbeck. There are charming gardens and parks, among them Carlisle Park which lies close to the ancient remains of Morpeth Castle. The chantry building houses the Northumbrian Craft Centre and the bagpipe museum.

N NEWCASTLE UPON TYNE, TYNE AND WEAR - Commercial and cultural centre of the North East, with a large indoor shopping centre, Quayside market, museums and theatres which offer an annual 6 week season by the Royal Shakespeare Company. Norman castle keep, medieval alleys, old Guildhall.

O OTTERBURN, NORTHUMBERLAND - Small village set at the meeting of the River Rede with Otter Burn, the site of the Battle of Otterburn in 1388. A peaceful tradition continues in the sale of Otterburn tweeds in this beautiful region, which is ideal for exploring the Border country and the Cheviots.

R REDCAR, TEES VALLEY - Lively holiday resort near Teesside with broad sandy beaches, a fine racecourse, a large indoor funfair at Coatham and other seaside amusements. Britain's oldest existing lifeboat can be seen at the Zetland Museum.

S SPENNYMOOR, DURHAM - Booming coal and iron town from the 18th C until early in the 20th century when traditional industry gave way to lighter manufacturing and trading estates were built. On the moors south of the town there are fine views of the Wear Valley.

STANLEY, DURHAM - Small town on the site of a Roman cattle camp. At the Beamish North of England Open Air Museum numerous set-pieces and displays recreate industrial and social conditions prevalent during the area's past.

SUNDERLAND, TYNE AND WEAR - Ancient coal and shipbuilding port on Wearside, with important glassworks since the 17th C, although glassmaking here dates back more than 1,000 years.

TYNEMOUTH, TYNE AND WEAR - At the mouth of the Tyne, old Tyneside resort adjoining North Shields with its fish quay and market. The pier is overlooked by the gaunt ruins of a Benedictine priory and a castle. Splendid sands, amusement centre and park.

W WARK, NORTHUMBERLAND - Set in the beautiful North Tyne Valley amid the Northumbrian fells, old village just above the meeting of Warks Burn with the North Tyne. Grey stone houses surround the green with its shady chestnut trees and an iron bridge spans the stream. The mound of a Norman castle occupies the river bank.

WARKWORTH, NORTHUMBERLAND - A pretty village overlooked by its medieval castle. A 14th C fortified bridge across the wooded Coquet gives a superb view of 18th C terraces climbing to the castle. Upstream is a curious 14th C Hermitage and in the market square is the Norman church of St Lawrence.

WEST WOODBURN, NORTHUMBERLAND Small hamlet on the River Rede in rolling moorland country.

WHITLEY BAY, TYNE AND WEAR - Traditional seaside resort with long beaches of sand and rock and many pools to explore. St Mary's lighthouse is open to the public.

WOOLER, NORTHUMBERLAND - Old grey-stone town, market-place for foresters and hill farmers, set at the edge of the north-east Cheviots. This makes a good base for excursions to Northumberland's loveliest coastline, or for angling and walking in the Borderlands.

AT-A-GLANCE SYMBOLS

Symbols at the end of each accommodation entry give useful information about services and facilities. A key to symbols can be found inside the back cover flap. Keep this open for easy reference.

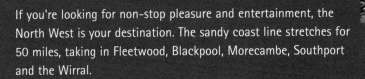

NORTH WEST

If you're looking for non-stop pleasure and entertainment, the North West is your destination. The sandy coast line stretches for 50 miles, taking in Fleetwood, Blackpool, Morecambe, Southport and the Wirral.

Blackpool offers superlative rides and dazzling shows. Town lovers will be spoilt for choice with Lancaster, Chester, Liverpool and Manchester all excellent for shopping, history, culture and nightlife. And when it's time for some peace and quiet, head for beautiful Lune Valley and the Forest of Bowland.

The annual Lancashire food festival in early March is an excellent opportunity to taste local delicacies, including Lancashire Hotpot and Black Pudding.

The counties of
Cheshire, Greater Manchester, Lancashire,
Merseyside and the High Peak District of
Derbyshire

FOR MORE INFORMATION CONTACT:
North West Tourist Board
Swan House, Swan Meadow Road,
Wigan Pier, Wigan WN3 5BB
Tel: (01942) 821222
Fax: (01942) 820002
Internet: www.visitnorthwest.com

The Pictures:
1 Blackpool Pleasure Beach;
2 Knowsley Safari Park,
   Merseyside;
3 Japanese Garden, Tatton Park.

Where to Go in the North West - see pages 122-125
Where to Stay in the North West - see pages 126-139

Whilst in the
NORTH WEST ...

You will find hundreds of interesting places to visit during your stay, just some of which are listed in these pages.

Contact any Tourist Information Centre in the region for more ideas on days out in the North West.

Arley Hall and Gardens

Arley, Northwich, Cheshire CW9 6NA
Tel: (01565) 777353
Early Victorian building set in 12 acres of magnificent gardens. 15thC tithe barn and a unique collection of watercolours of the area.

Astley Hall Museum and Art Gallery

Astley Park, Chorley, Lancashire PR7 1NP
Tel: (01257) 515555
Dates from 1580 with subsequent additions. Unique collections of furniture including a fine Elizabethan bed and the famous Shovel Board Table.

The Beatles Story

Albert Dock, Liverpool, Merseyside L3 4AA
Tel: (0151) 709 1963
Liverpool's award-winning visitor attraction with a replica of the original Cavern Club. Available for private parties.

Beeston Castle

Beeston, Tarporley, Cheshire CW6 9TX
Tel: (01829) 260464
A ruined 13thC castle situated on top of the Peckforton Hills, with views of the surrounding countryside. Exhibitions are held featuring the castle's history.

Blackpool Sea Life Centre

The Promenade, Blackpool, Lancashire FY1 5AA
Tel: (01253) 622445
Tropical sharks up to 2.5m (8ft) in length housed in a 100,000-gallon water display, with an underwater walkway. The new 'Lost City of Atlantis' is back.

Blackpool Tower

The Promenade, Blackpool, Lancashire FY1 4BJ
Tel: (01253) 622242
Inside the Tower you will find the Tower Ballroom, a circus, entertainment for the children, the Tower Top Ride and Undersea World.

Boat Museum

Ellesmere Port, Cheshire CH5 4FW
Tel: (0151) 355 5017
Over 50 historic craft, the largest floating collection in the world. Restored buildings, traditional cottages, workshops, steam engines, boat trips, shop and cafe.

CATALYST: The Museum of the Chemical Industry

Widnes, Cheshire WA8 0DF
Tel: (0151) 420 1121
Catalyst is the award-winning family day out where science and technology come alive.

Chester Zoo

Upton-by-Chester, Cheshire CH2 1LH
Tel: (01244) 380280
One of Europe's leading conservation zoos with over 5,000 animals in spacious and natural enclosures. Now featuring the new 'Twilight Zone'.

Croxteth Hall and Country Park

Liverpool, Merseyside L12 0HB
Tel: (0151) 228 5311
An Edwardian stately home set in 500 acres of countryside (woodlands and pasture), featuring a Victorian walled garden and animal collection.

Dunham Massey Hall Park and Garden

Altrincham, Cheshire WA14 4SJ
Tel: (0161) 941 1025
An 18thC mansion in a 250-acre wooded deer park. Over 30 rooms open to the public. Collections of furniture, paintings and silver. Restaurant and shop.

East Lancashire Railway

Bury, Greater Manchester BL9 0EY
Tel: (0161) 764 7790
Thirteen kilometres (8 miles) of preserved railway operated principally by steam. Traction Transport Museum close by.

Frontierland Western Theme Park

Promenade, Morecambe, Lancashire LA4 4DG
Tel: (01524) 410024
Over 40 thrilling rides and attractions including the Texas Tornado, Polo Tower, Perculator and Stampede rollercoaster. The indoor Fun House complex features live shows in summer.

Gawsworth Hall

Gawsworth, Macclesfield, Cheshire SK11 9RN
Tel: (01260) 223456
Beautiful Tudor half-timbered manor-house with tilting ground. Pictures, sculpture and furniture on display. Open-air theatre.

Granada Studios

Water Street, Manchester M60 9EA
Tel: (0161) 832 9090
Europe's only major television theme park, providing a unique insight into the fascinating world behind the television screen.

Jodrell Bank Science Centre, Planetarium and Arboretum

Lower Withington, Macclesfield, Cheshire SK11 9DL
Tel: (01477) 571339
Exhibition and interactive exhibits on astronomy, space, energy and the environment. Planetarium and the world-famous Lovell telescope, plus a 35-acre arboretum.

Knowsley Safari Park

Prescot, Merseyside L34 4AN
Tel: (0151) 430 9009
An 8km (5 mile) safari through 500 acres of rolling countryside. See the world's wildest animals roaming free. Picnic area, shops, cafeteria.

Lady Lever Art Gallery

Port Sunlight Village, Higher Bebington, Wirral CH62 5EQ
Tel: (0151) 478 4136
The first Lord Leverhulme's magnificent collection of British paintings dated 1750-1900. British furniture, Wedgwood pottery and oriental porcelain.

Lancaster Castle

Shire Hall, Castle Parade, Lancaster, Lancashire LA1 1YJ
Tel: (01524) 64998
Shire Hall has a collection of coats of arms, a crown court, a grand jury room, a 'drop room' and dungeons. External tour of the castle.

Lyme Park

Disley, Stockport, Greater Manchester SK12 2NX
Tel: (01663) 762023
A National Trust country estate set in 1,377 acres of moorland, woodland and park. This magnificent house has 17 acres of historic gardens.

The Pictures:
1   Little Moreton, Congleton, Cheshire;
2   Bridgewater Hall, Manchester;
3   Peckforton, Cheshire;
4   Blackpool Beach;
5   Rural Cheshire, Marbury;
6   Liverpool Football Club Stadium.

123

Macclesfield Silk Museum
The Heritage Centre, Macclesfield, Cheshire SK11 6UT
Tel: (01625) 613210
*Tells the story of the silk industry in Macclesfield.
Features textiles, garments, models and room settings.*

Merseyside Maritime Museum
Albert Dock, Liverpool, Merseyside L3 4AQ
Tel: (0151) 478 4499
*Set in the heart of Liverpool's historic waterfront. The
museum holds craft demonstrations, working displays
and permanent galleries.*

The Museum of Science & Industry in Manchester
Castlefield, Manchester M3 4FP
Tel: (0161) 832 2244
*Based in the world's oldest passenger railway station
with working exhibits which bring the past to life. The
galleries will amaze, amuse and entertain.*

Norton Priory Museum and Gardens
Runcorn, Cheshire WA7 1SX
Tel: (01928) 569895
*Medieval priory remains, purpose-built museum,
St Christopher's statue, sculpture trail and award-
winning walled garden, all set in 39 acres of beautiful
gardens.*

Rufford Old Hall
Rufford, Ormskirk, Lancashire L40 1SG
Tel: (01704) 821254
*One of the finest 16thC buildings in Lancashire with a
magnificent hall, particularly noted for its immense
moveable screen.*

Southport Zoo and Conservation Park
Princes Park, Southport, Merseyside PR8 1RX
Tel: (01704) 538102
*Lion, snow leopards, chimpanzees, monkeys, penguins,
giant tortoise, reptile house, aquarium and much more.
Snack bar, gift shop, picnic area.*

Tate Gallery, Liverpool
Albert Dock, Liverpool, Merseyside L3 4BB
Tel: (0151) 702 7400
*The National Collection of Modern Art is housed here in
a converted warehouse.*

Tatton Park
Knutsford, Cheshire WA16 6QN
Tel: (01625) 534400
*Historic mansion with a 50-acre garden, traditional
working farm, medieval manor-house and a 2,000 acre
deer park. Sailing and outdoor centre, and an adventure
playground.*

Wigan Pier
Wallgate, Wigan, Lancashire WN3 4EF
Tel: (01942) 323666
*Wigan Pier combines interaction with displays and
reconstructions plus the Wigan Pier Theatre Company.
Facilities include shops and a cafe.*

Wildfowl and Wetland Trust
Martin Mere, Burscough, Lancashire L40 0TA
Tel: (01704) 895181
*A 376-acre wild area, 20-acre lake and 45 acres of
gardens. Rare and exotic ducks, geese, swans and
flamingoes. Pantry, gift shop, art/craft gallery.*

Find out more about the
NORTH WEST ₒₒₒ

Further information about holidays and attractions
in the North West is available from:

NORTH WEST TOURIST BOARD

Swan House, Swan Meadow Road, Wigan Pier, Wigan WN3 5BB.

Tel: (01942) 821222

Fax: (01942) 820002

Internet: www.visitnorthwest.com

The following publications are available free from the North West Tourist Board:

Best of the North West

a guide to information on the region including hotels, self-catering establishments, caravan and camping parks. Also includes attractions, major events, shops and restaurants

Discovery Map

a non-accommodation guide, A1 folded to A4 map including list of visitor attractions, what to see and where to go

Bed and Breakfast Map

forming part of a family of maps for England, this guide provides information on bed and breakfast establishments in the North West region

Freedom

forming part of a family of publications about caravan and camping parks in the north of England

Stay on a Farm

a guide to farm accommodation in the north of England

Group Travel Planner

a guide to choosing the right accommodation, attraction or venue for group organisers

Venues

a 6-monthly newsletter about conference venues in the North West region

Schools Out

a 6-monthly newsletter aimed at schools providing information about where to go and what to see

The Pictures:
1 Healey Dell, Rochdale;
2 Pavilion Gardens, Buxton;
3 Bridgewater Canal, Manchester;
4 Lytham, Lancashire;
5 The Rows, Chester;
6 Barca Cafe Bar, Manchester;
7 Albert Dock, Liverpool.

Getting to the
NORTH WEST ...

BY ROAD:
Motorways intersect within the region which has the best road network in the country. Travelling north or south use the M6 and east or west the M62.

BY RAIL:
Most North West coastal resorts are connected to InterCity routes with trains from many parts of the country and there are through trains to major cities and towns.

Where to stay in the

NORTH WEST

Accommodation entries in this region are listed in alphabetical order of place name, and then in alphabetical order of establishment.

Map references refer to the colour location maps at the front of this guide. The first number indicates the map to use; the letter and number which follow refer to the grid reference on the map.

At-a-glance symbols at the end of each accommodation entry give useful information about services and facilities. A key to symbols can be found inside the back cover flap. Keep this open for easy reference.

A brief description of the towns and villages offering accommodation in the entries which follow, can be found at the end of this section.

A complete listing of all English Tourism Council assessed guest accommodation appears at the back of this guide.

ABBEYSTEAD, Lancashire Map ref 4A1

◆◆◆

Stone-built farmhouse set in peaceful countryside with glorious views of the Bowland Fells, yet only 3.5 miles from junction 33 of M6 and 5 miles from Lancaster University. Set in extensive gardens on the edge of the Forest of Bowland, ideal base for Lakes, dales and historic Lancaster.

GREENBANK FARMHOUSE

Abbeystead, Lancaster, LA2 9BA
T: (01524) 792063
E: tait@greenbankfarmhouse.freeserve.co.uk
I: www.greenbankfarmhouse.co.uk

Bedrooms: 1 double, 2 twin
Bathrooms: 2 en suite, 1 public

Parking for 6

B&B per night:
S £20.00–£25.00
D £34.00–£38.00

OPEN All year round

WELCOME HOST This is a nationally recognised customer care programme which aims to promote the highest standards of service and a warm welcome. Establishments taking part in this initiative are indicated by the ⬡ symbol.

ACTON BRIDGE, Cheshire Map ref 4A2

◆◆◆◆

MANOR FARM
Cliff Road, Acton Bridge, Northwich, CW8 3QP
T: (01606) 853181
F: (01606) 853181

B&B per night:
S £22.00–£25.00
D £44.00–£48.00

OPEN All year round

Peaceful, elegantly furnished country house. Open views from all rooms. Situated down long private drive, above wooded banks of the River Weaver. Large garden provides access to private path through woodland into the picturesque valley. In central Cheshire, ideal location for business or pleasure, convenient for Chester, Merseyside and motorways.

Bedrooms: 1 single, 2 twin
Bathrooms: 1 en suite, 2 private

Parking for 14

ASHTON-UNDER-LYNE, Greater Manchester Map ref 4B1 *Tourist Information Centre Tel: (0161) 343 4343*

◆◆◆

LYNWOOD HOTEL
3 Richmond Street, Ashton-under-Lyne, Lancashire OL6 7TX
T: (0161) 330 5358
F: (0161) 330 5358

Bedrooms: 2 single, 2 twin
Bathrooms: 2 en suite, 1 public

Parking for 4

B&B per night:
S £20.00–£29.00
D £40.00–£44.00

OPEN All year round

Small, comfortable, family-run hotel in quiet position. Convenient for motorways, G-Mex, the Arena Velodrome. 20 minutes to Manchester Airport. A warm welcome.

BLACKPOOL, Lancashire Map ref 4A1 *Tourist Information Centre Tel: (01253) 478222*

◆◆◆

ARNCLIFFE HOTEL
24 Osborne Road, Blackpool, FY4 1HJ
T: (01253) 345209 &
07802 438907 (Mobile (Ansafone))
F: (01253) 345209
E: arncliffehotel@talk21.com

B&B per night:
S £13.00–£25.00
D £26.00–£50.00

HB per person:
DY £20.00–£32.00

OPEN Mar–Dec

Small, homely, family-run hotel, built in the same year as the famous Tower. Situated in the South Shore, 1 minute from the Promenade, Pleasure Beach and Sandcastle leisure complex. Catering for couples and families. Cleanliness and good home cooking assured: "Heartbeat" award for last 6 years. Major credit cards accepted.

Bedrooms: 1 single, 5 double, 1 twin, 1 family room
Bathrooms: 5 en suite, 1 public

EM 1700 (LO 1300)
CC: Barclaycard, Delta, Mastercard, Visa

◆◆◆

BEVERLEY HOTEL
25 Dean Street, Blackpool, Lancashire FY4 1AU
T: (01253) 344426

Bedrooms: 1 single, 5 double, 1 twin, 2 triple, 2 family rooms
Bathrooms: 11 en suite

EM 1700
CC: Amex, Barclaycard, Delta, Diners, Eurocard, JCB, Mastercard, Solo, Switch, Visa

B&B per night:
S Min £18.00
D Min £34.00

OPEN All year round

Licensed family-run hotel, with good home-cooked food. All rooms en suite. Adjacent promenade, Pleasure Beach and swimming complex, with local shopping facilities nearby.

CREDIT CARD BOOKINGS If you book by telephone and are asked for your credit card number it is advisable to check the proprietor's policy should you cancel your reservation.

BLACKPOOL continued

♦♦♦♦

COLLINGWOOD HOTEL
8-10 Holmfield Road, North Shore,
Blackpool, Lancashire FY2 9SL
T: (01253) 352929
F: (01253) 352929
E: enquiries@collingwoodhotel.co.uk
I: www.collingwoodhotel.co.uk

B&B per night:
S £19.00–£26.00
D £38.00–£52.00

HB per person:
DY £24.00–£32.00

OPEN All year round

Family supervised hotel, established for 24 years, in a select area just off Queens Promenade, near Gynn Gardens. Decorated and furnished to the highest standard with all the comforts of a modern hotel. Fine restaurant with plenty of choice. A warm and friendly welcome assured. Excellence is our standard. Private car park.

Bedrooms: 2 single,
8 double, 3 twin, 3 triple,
1 family room
Bathrooms: 17 en suite

EM
Parking for 11
CC: Amex, Barclaycard,
Delta, Diners, Mastercard,
Switch, Visa

♦♦♦♦

CROYDON HOTEL
12 Empress Drive, Blackpool, FY2 9SE
T: (01253) 352497

B&B per night:
S £18.00–£26.00
D £36.00–£52.00

HB per person:
DY £22.00–£30.00

OPEN Apr–Oct

The Croydon is a small, warm and friendly family-run hotel. All rooms equipped with private shower and toilet, colour TV and tea-making facilities. Private car park. Resident owners Keith and Mary Staniland winners of award for best steak and kidney pies in the UK.

Bedrooms: 2 single,
5 double, 1 twin, 2 triple
Bathrooms: 10 en suite

EM 1700 (LO 1700)
Parking for 8

♦♦

HURSTMERE HOTEL
5 Alexandra Road, Blackpool,
FY1 6BU
T: (01253) 345843
F: (01253) 347188

Bedrooms: 5 double,
1 twin, 2 triple, 4 family
rooms
Bathrooms: 12 en suite,
1 public

EM 1700 (LO 1700)
Parking for 6

B&B per night:
D £36.00–£48.00

HB per person:
DY £24.00–£30.00

OPEN Mar–Nov

Ideally situated between Central and South Piers. Close to Promenade, within easy reach of all amenities. All rooms en suite. Bar, pool table and disco.

♦♦♦

MAY–DENE LICENSED HOTEL
10 Dean Street, Blackpool, FY4 1AU
T: (01253) 343464
F: (01253) 401424

Bedrooms: 5 double,
1 twin, 1 triple, 3 family
rooms
Bathrooms: 7 en suite,
1 private, 2 public

EM 1700 (LO 1730)
Parking for 9
CC: Amex, Barclaycard,
Delta, Diners, Mastercard,
Switch, Visa

B&B per night:
S £25.00–£60.00
D £40.00–£60.00

HB per person:
DY £27.00–£40.00

OPEN All year round

In a sun-trap area close to South Promenade, Sandcastle, Pleasure Beach, markets and pier. Clean and friendly. Good food prepared by C&G qualified cooks.

♦♦♦

PENRHYN HOTEL
38 King Edward Avenue, Blackpool,
Lancashire FY2 9TA
T: (01253) 352762
E: ericpenrhyn@talk21.com

Bedrooms: 4 double,
1 twin, 2 triple
Bathrooms: 7 en suite

Lunch available
EM 1700 (LO 1800)
Parking for 2

B&B per night:
S £16.00–£19.00
D £38.00–£22.00

HB per person:
DY Min £24.00

OPEN All year round

Small family-run hotel with a big welcome. Comfortable, attractive bedrooms, all en suite, home cooking. Situated close to Queens Promenade, Gynn Gardens and golf course.

SUNNYSIDE HOTEL

◆◆◆

36 King Edward Avenue, North Shore,
Blackpool, Lancashire FY2 9TA
T: (01253) 352031
E: stuart@sunnysidehotel.com
I: www.sunnysidehotel.com

B&B per night:
S £17.50–£23.50
D £30.00–£45.00

HB per person:
DY £20.00–£27.50

OPEN All year round

Small hotel, BIG welcome, situated adjacent to promenade in a select, quiet area of North Shore yet near the town centre attractions. South-facing sun lounge, bar lounge, spacious dining area with varied menu to suit your needs. All bedrooms are en suite. Unrestricted street parking, and private parking for 4 by arrangement.

Bedrooms: 1 single,
3 double, 2 triple/twin,
2 family rooms
Bathrooms: 8 en suite

EM 1700 (LO 1700)

ඊ3 ▤ ▯ ♦ ⌲ Ⓢ ⋈ ⓉⓋ ▥ ❀ ✗ ⋈ SC SP ◉

WINDSOR HOTEL

◆◆◆

53 Dean Street, Blackpool, FY4 1BP
T: (01253) 400232
F: (01253) 346886
E: reservations@windsorhotel.co.uk
I: www.windsorhotel.co.uk

B&B per night:
S £20.00–£28.00
D £40.00–£56.00

HB per person:
DY £27.00–£35.00

OPEN All year round

Fully refurbished for the discerning guest. All rooms en suite with direct-dial computer lines, colour TV. Good home cooking caters for customers' individual needs. Well stocked bar with daily newspapers. Close to promenade, entertainment. Car parking. You are assured of a warm, personal reception from resident proprietors.

Bedrooms: 1 single,
5 double, 4 twin, 2 triple
Bathrooms: 12 en suite

EM 1700 (LO 1900)
Parking for 11
CC: Amex, Barclaycard,
Delta, Eurocard, JCB,
Maestro, Mastercard,
Solo, Switch, Visa, Visa
Electron

ඊ ⌂ ☎ ▤ ▯ ♦ ⌲ ▮ Ⓢ ⋋ ⋈ ⓉⓋ ▥ ▰ SC ⋋ SP Ⓣ

◆◆◆

WINDSOR PARK HOTEL

96 Queens Promenade, Blackpool,
FY2 9NS
T: (01253) 357025

Bedrooms: 1 single,
8 double, 1 twin, 1 triple
Bathrooms: 11 en suite

EM 1730 (LO 1900)
Parking for 7
CC: Delta, Mastercard,
Visa

B&B per night:
S £17.00–£20.00
D £34.00–£40.00

HB per person:
DY £22.00–£25.00

OPEN Apr–Oct
& Christmas

Hotel overlooking the Irish Sea. All bedrooms have en suite facilities. Full central heating, licensed bar, car park.

ඊ ▤ ▯ ♦ ▮ Ⓢ ⋋ ⋈ ⓉⓋ ▥ ▰ ✗ ⋈ ⋋ ◉

◆◆◆

COPY NOOK HOTEL

Bolton-by-Bowland, Clitheroe,
BB7 4NL
T: (01200) 447205
F: (01200) 447004
E: copynookhotel@btinternet.com
I: www.copynookhotel.com

Bedrooms: 1 single,
2 double, 2 twin,
1 family room
Bathrooms: 6 en suite

Lunch available
EM 1900 (LO 2130)
Parking for 80
CC: Amex, Barclaycard,
Delta, Eurocard, JCB,
Maestro, Mastercard,
Solo, Switch, Visa, Visa
Electron

B&B per night:
S Max £40.00
D Max £60.00

OPEN All year round

Traditional country inn, set in rural countryside. All the charm and atmosphere of yesteryear combined with the modern comforts of today. Only 3 minutes from A59.

ඊ ☎ ▯ ♦ ⌲ ▮ ⋋ ▥ ▰ ▮50 ♦ ∪ ↙ ✗ ▰

RATING All accommodation in this guide has been rated, or is awaiting a rating, by a trained English Tourism Council assessor.

◆◆◆

ROSTREVOR HOTEL AND BISTRO

148 Manchester Road, Bury, Lancashire
BL9 0TL
T: (0161) 764 3944
F: (0161) 764 8266
E: enquiries@rostrevor.co.uk
I: www.rostrevorhotel.co.uk

B&B per night:
S £30.00–£37.50
D £44.00–£50.00

HB per person:
DY £26.00–£29.00

OPEN All year round

Small, family-run hotel, overlooking open parkland, 10 minutes' walk town centre, Bury's famous markets, leisure centre and steam railway. The Rostrevor is a well established business and tourist hotel, offering quiet, comfortable accommodation with feature fireplaces and decorative plasterwork, plus homely atmosphere and northern hospitality. Special weekend rates.

Bedrooms: 5 single,	EM 1800 (LO 2000)
5 double, 4 twin	Parking for 14
Bathrooms: 14 en suite	CC: Amex, Barclaycard,
	Delta, Diners, JCB,
	Mastercard, Switch, Visa

🅰🐕🏠🍴🖵📶🛈🆂🏨📺🛏️.🖪🍵12 ✂ 🆂 🌿 🆂🅿 🏤 🆃

◆◆◆

LONGLANDS HOTEL

Tewitfield, Carnforth, LA6 1JH
T: (01524) 781256
F: (01524) 69393

B&B per night:
S £22.50–£25.00
D £45.00–£50.00

OPEN All year round

Old world coaching inn, on the A6070 half a mile from M6 exit 35. Convenient for the Lakes, Yorkshire Dales, the seaside resort of Morecambe and historic Lancaster. Regular live entertainment. Bar snacks and a la carte restaurant. All bedrooms en suite. A warm welcome guaranteed.

Bedrooms: 2 single,	Lunch available
1 double, 2 twin, 1 triple	EM 1730 (LO 2130)
Bathrooms: 6 en suite	Parking for 175
	CC: Barclaycard, Delta,
	Mastercard, Solo, Switch,
	Visa, Visa Electron

🅰🐕🖵📶🛈🆂📺🛏️.🖪🔍☝👣✿🚐🆂🌿🆂🅿🆃

◆◆◆

SPRING COTTAGE GUEST HOUSE

60 Hulme Hall Road,
Cheadle Hulme, Stockport, Cheshire
SK8 6JZ
T: (0161) 485 1037

Bedrooms: 1 single,	Parking for 6
3 twin	CC: Barclaycard, Delta,
Bathrooms: 2 en suite,	Mastercard, Solo, Switch,
1 public	Visa, Visa Electron

B&B per night:
S Max £22.00
D Max £41.00

OPEN All year round

Beautifully furnished Victorian house, in historic part of Cheadle Hulme. Convenient for airport, rail station and variety of local restaurants.

🐕♿🖵📶🛈🆄🅻🛏️.🖪✿🚐🆂🅿

◆◆

ABBOTSFORD COURT HOTEL

17 Victoria Road, Chester, CH2 2AX
T: (01244) 390898
F: (01244) 390898
E: abbotsford_court_hotel@
hotmail.com

Bedrooms: 2 single,	EM
4 double, 2 twin,	Parking for 6
2 family rooms	
Bathrooms: 9 en suite,	
1 public	

B&B per night:
S £24.00–£35.00
D £44.00–£50.00

HB per person:
DY £34.00–£45.00

OPEN All year round

The centrally located Abbotsford Court offers you a warm and friendly welcome, with good food and service in comfortable surroundings. Near bus and railway stations. Within 5 minutes' walk of the city centre.

🅰🐕♿🏠🍴🖵📶🛈🆂🕎🆐🛏️.🖪🐾🆂🆃

WHERE TO STAY

Please mention this guide when making your booking.

CHESTER continued

◆◆◆ **CHEYNEY LODGE HOTEL**
77-79 Cheyney Road, Chester,
CH1 4BS
T: (01244) 381925

Bedrooms: 1 single,
4 double, 2 twin, 1 triple
Bathrooms: 8 en suite

Lunch available
EM 1800 (LO 2000)
Parking for 12
CC: Barclaycard, Delta,
Maestro, Mastercard,
Switch, Visa

B&B per night:
S £24.00–£30.00
D £39.00–£44.00

HB per person:
DY £29.45–£32.95

OPEN All year round

Small, friendly hotel of unusual design, featuring indoor garden and fish pond. 10 minutes' walk from city centre and on main bus route. Personally supervised, emphasis on good food.

🅰 ⌂ ♿ ⌿ ☎ ▤ ⬜ 🛁 ⓘ S Ⓜ 🎔 🖂 ✕ SP T

◆◆◆◆ **GOLBORNE MANOR**
Platts Lane, Hatton Heath, Chester,
CH3 9AN
T: (01829) 770310 & 07774 695268
F: (01829) 770370
E: ann.ikin@golbornemanor.co.uk

Bedrooms: 1 double,
1 twin, 1 triple
Bathrooms: 3 en suite,
1 public

Parking for 8

B&B per night:
S £28.00–£35.00
D £58.00–£68.00

OPEN All year round

19thC manor-house renovated to a high standard, set in 3.5 acres. Lovely rural setting with fine views. Five miles south of Chester, off A41 Whitchurch road, turning right just after DP Motors. Ample parking.

🅰 ⌂ ▤ ⬜ ♿ ⊕ UL ⓘ S ✂ 🎔 ▥ 🖂 ⟟ 🔦 Ⓤ ⟟ ✽ ✕ 🚗 🐾 T

◆◆◆◆

GROVE HOUSE
Holme Street, Tarvin, Chester, CH3 8EQ
T: (01829) 740893
F: (01829) 741769

B&B per night:
S £25.00–£38.00
D £56.00–£60.00

OPEN All year round

Warm welcome in relaxing environment. Spacious, comfortable rooms, attractive garden. Ample parking. Within easy reach of Chester (4 miles) and major North West and North Wales tourist attractions. NWTB Place to Stay Award 1996 and 1997. Closed Christmas and New Year.

Bedrooms: 1 single,
1 double, 1 twin
Bathrooms: 2 en suite,
1 private

Parking for 8

⌂ 12 ▤ ⬜ ♿ ⊕ UL ⓘ S ✂ TV ▥ 🖂 Ⓤ ⟟ ✽ ✕ 🚗

◆◆◆◆
Silver
Award

MITCHELLS OF CHESTER GUEST HOUSE
28 Hough Green, Chester, CH4 8JQ
T: (01244) 679004
F: (01244) 659567
E: mitoches@dialstart.net

Bedrooms: 1 single,
2 double, 2 twin,
1 family room
Bathrooms: 6 en suite,
1 public

Parking for 5
CC: Delta, Mastercard,
Visa

B&B per night:
S £30.00–£38.00
D £48.00–£60.00

OPEN All year round

Tastefully restored, elegant Victorian residence, with steeply pitched slated roofs, sweeping staircase, antique furniture in tall rooms with moulded cornices. Compact landscaped gardens. Close city centre.

🅰 ⌂ ♿ ⬜ ⊕ UL S ✂ 🎔 TV ▥ 🖂 ✽ 🚗 SC SP 🐾 T

◆◆◆ **RECORDER HOTEL**
19 City Walls, Chester, CH1 1SB
T: (01244) 326580
F: (01244) 401674
E: ebbs@compuserve.com
I: www.ourworld.compuserve.com/
homepages/ebbs

Bedrooms: 1 single,
5 double, 4 triple,
1 family room
Bathrooms: 11 en suite

Parking for 6
CC: Amex, Barclaycard,
Delta, Mastercard, Solo,
Switch, Visa, Visa Electron

B&B per night:
S £35.00–£45.00
D £49.00–£70.00

OPEN All year round

Centrally-situated Grade II Listed building on the walls of Chester overlooking the river. En suite rooms with TV and coffee-making facilities.

🅰 ⌂ ♿ ☎ ⬜ ⊕ UL ✂ ▥ 🖂 ✕ 🚗 T

HALF BOARD PRICES Half board prices are given per person, but in some cases these may be based on double/twin occupancy.

CHORLEY, Lancashire Map ref 4A1

◆◆◆◆

PARR HALL FARM

Parr Lane, Eccleston, Chorley, PR7 5SL
T: (01257) 451917
F: (01257) 453749
E: parrhall@talk21.com

B&B per night:
S £25.00–£35.00
D £40.00–£50.00

OPEN All year round

Georgian farmhouse built in 1721 and tastefully restored. Quiet rural location within easy walking distance of good public houses and restaurants and village amenities. Conveniently situated for Lancashire coast and countryside, Lake District and Yorkshire Dales. Manchester Airport 45 minutes, junction 27 (M6) 5 miles north on B5250.

Bedrooms: 1 single, 2 double, 1 twin
Bathrooms: 4 en suite

Parking for 20
CC: Delta, Mastercard, Visa

CLITHEROE, Lancashire Map ref 4A1 *Tourist Information Centre Tel: (01200) 425566*

◆◆◆◆

RAKEFOOT FARM

Chaigley, Clitheroe, BB7 3LY
T: (01995) 61332 &
07889 279063 (Mobile)

Bedrooms: 3 double, 2 twin, 3 family rooms
Bathrooms: 6 en suite, 2 private

Parking for 12

B&B per night:
S £17.00–£25.00
D £34.00–£40.00

HB per person:
DY £29.00–£37.00

OPEN All year round

Working family farm. 17thC farmhouse and traditional stone barn conversion, between Clitheroe and Chipping. Panoramic views in Forset of Bowland. Home cooking. Also self-catering cottages.

◆◆◆

SELBORNE GUEST HOUSE

Back Commons, Kirkmoor Road,
Clitheroe, BB7 2DX
T: (01200) 423571 & 422236
F: (01200) 423571
E: judithv.barnes@lineone.net

Bedrooms: 2 double, 1 twin
Bathrooms: 3 en suite

EM 1900 (LO 1800)
Parking for 6

B&B per night:
S £20.00–£22.50
D £37.00–£40.00

HB per person:
DY £30.00–£35.00

OPEN All year round

Detached house on quiet lane giving peace and tranquillity but within walking distance of the town, bus and rail interchange. Private parking. Open all year.

GARSTANG, Lancashire Map ref 4A1 *Tourist Information Centre Tel: (01995) 602125*

◆◆◆

WOODACRE HALL FARM

Scorton, Preston, PR3 1BN
T: (01995) 602253 (Answerphone)
F: (01995) 602253

Bedrooms: 2 double
Bathrooms: 1 en suite, 1 private

Parking for 4

B&B per night:
S £20.00–£22.00
D £36.00–£40.00

HB per person:
DY £26.00–£28.00

OPEN Mar–Nov

150-acre dairy and livestock farm. Built in the late 1600s, the former home of the 4th Duke of Hamilton, written about in A Hewitson's book "Northward", chapter XIII.

HOLMES CHAPEL, Cheshire Map ref 4A2

◆◆◆◆

PADGATE GUEST HOUSE

Twemlow Lane, Cranage,
Middlewich, CW4 8EX
T: (01477) 534291
F: (01477) 544726

Bedrooms: 1 single, 1 double, 1 twin
Bathrooms: 1 en suite, 2 public

EM 1900 (LO 2000)
Parking for 5

B&B per night:
S Min £20.00
D Min £44.00

OPEN All year round

Quiet country location 2 miles from junction 18 of M6, 17 miles from Manchester Airport. First class accommodation, excellent home cooking and warm welcome assured.

ACCESSIBILITY

Look for the ⬚ ⬚ ⬚ symbols which indicate accessibility for wheelchair users. A list of establishments is at the front of this guide.

HORNBY, Lancashire Map ref 5B3

CASTLE HOTEL
Main Street, Hornby, Lancaster, LA2 8JT
T: (015242) 21204
F: (015242) 22258

B&B per night:
S £25.00–£40.00
D £40.00–£60.00

HB per person:
DY £65.00–£80.00

OPEN All year round

Grade II Listed stone hotel dating from 1680. Located in Area of Outstanding Natural Beauty in the Lune Valley within easy reach of Lake District and Yorkshire Dales. Spacious bars, fine restaurant, elegant bedrooms, ballroom and function rooms. Discreet service and exceptional food ensure a memorable visit.

Bedrooms: 8 double, 2 twin, 1 triple, 1 family room
Bathrooms: 8 en suite, 2 public

Lunch available
EM 1830 (LO 2100)
Parking for 30
CC: Barclaycard, Delta, JCB, Mastercard, Solo, Switch, Visa, Visa Electron

LIVERPOOL, Merseyside Map ref 4A2 *Tourist Information Centre Tel: 0906 680 6886 (premium rate)*

◆◆ **ANTRIM HOTEL**
73 Mount Pleasant, Liverpool, L3 5TB
T: (0151) 709 5239 & 709 9212
F: (0151) 709 7169
E: antrimhotel@ukbusiness.com

Bedrooms: 8 single, 2 double, 8 twin, 2 family rooms
Bathrooms: 7 en suite, 1 public, 9 private showers

EM 1800 (LO 2000)
Parking for 2
CC: Amex, Barclaycard, Delta, Diners, Eurocard, Maestro, Mastercard, Solo, Switch, Visa, Visa Electron

B&B per night:
S £32.00–£42.00
D £42.00–£57.00

OPEN All year round

Friendly, family-run city centre hotel, convenient for shops, rail and bus stations, Albert Dock and all major tourist attractions. Twenty minutes from the airport.

◆◆ **HOLME LEIGH GUEST HOUSE**
93 Woodcroft Road, Wavertree, Liverpool, L15 2HG
T: (0151) 734 2216 & 427 9806
F: (0151) 291 9877
E: bridges01@cableinetco.uk

Bedrooms: 4 single, 1 double, 5 twin
Bathrooms: 6 en suite, 1 public

CC: Amex, Barclaycard, Mastercard, Switch, Visa

B&B per night:
S £16.50–£22.00
D £29.95–£39.95

OPEN All year round

Victorian red brick 3-storey corner dwelling and fashion shop, facing on to Lawrence Road. Just 2.5 miles from city centre, 2 miles from M62.

◆ **LORD NELSON**
Lord Nelson Street, Liverpool, L3 5PD
T: (0151) 709 4362
F: (0151) 707 1321

Bedrooms: 26 single, 12 double, 17 twin, 2 triple, 1 family room
Bathrooms: 29 en suite, 6 public

EM 1730 (LO 2100)
CC: Amex, Barclaycard, JCB, Mastercard, Solo, Switch, Visa, Visa Electron

B&B per night:
S £23.00–£27.00
D £38.00–£44.00

OPEN All year round

Fully licensed city-centre hotel adjacent to Lime Street Station, main shopping centre and entertainments. Ideal for business and tourism. Bar food available in the evenings.

LOWER WHITLEY, Cheshire Map ref 4A2

◆◆◆ **TALL TREES LODGE**

Tarporley Road, Lower Whitley, Warrington, WA4 4EZ
T: (01928) 790824 & 715117
F: (01928) 791330
E: booking@talltreeslodge.co.uk
I: www.talltreeslodge.co.uk

Bedrooms: 13 double, 1 twin, 6 triple
Bathrooms: 20 en suite

Parking for 40
CC: Amex, Barclaycard, Delta, Maestro, Mastercard, Solo, Switch, Visa, Visa Electron

B&B per night:
D £35.00–£39.95

OPEN All year round

2.5 miles south of junction 10 of the M56. Take A49 towards Whitchurch. Little Chef and BP garage on site. A warm welcome awaits you.

IDEAS For ideas on places to visit refer to the introduction at the beginning of this section.

♦♦♦ **MOORHAYES HOUSE HOTEL**

27 Manchester Road, Tytherington, Macclesfield, SK10 2JJ T: (01625) 433228 F: (01625) 429878 E: helen@moorhayeshouse.freeserve.co.uk	Bedrooms: 2 single, 5 double, 1 twin, 1 triple Bathrooms: 7 en suite, 1 public	Parking for 14 CC: Barclaycard, Delta, Eurocard, JCB, Maestro, Mastercard, Solo, Switch, Visa, Visa Electron	B&B per night: S £28.00–£40.00 D £42.00–£55.00 OPEN All year round

Warm welcome, comfortable house with gardens and parking. Half a mile from town centre. Hearty breakfasts. Most rooms en suite with tea/coffee, TV and telephone.

♦♦♦

SANDPIT FARM
Messuage Lane, Marton, Macclesfield, SK11 9HS
T: (01260) 224254

B&B per night:
S £20.00–£22.50
D £40.00–£45.00

OPEN All year round

110-acre arable farm. Comfortable, oak-beamed house. 1 double and 1 twin room are en suite, other twin room has adjacent bathroom. Convenient for stately homes and National Trust properties. Easy access to Peak District, Chester and Manchester Airport. 4 miles north of Congleton, 1 mile west of A34.	Bedrooms: 1 single, 1 double, 2 twin Bathrooms: 2 en suite, 1 private, 1 public	Parking for 4

♦♦♦ **REMBRANDT HOTEL**

33 Sackville Street, Manchester, M1 3LZ T: (0161) 236 1311 & 236 2435 F: (0161) 236 4257 E: rembrandthotel@aol.com I: www.therembrandthotel.co.uk	Bedrooms: 15 double, 3 twin, 1 triple, 1 family room Bathrooms: 15 en suite, 2 public	Lunch available EM 1700 (LO 2000) CC: Amex, Barclaycard, Delta, Diners, JCB, Maestro, Mastercard, Switch, Visa	B&B per night: S £40.00–£50.00 D £45.00–£55.00 OPEN All year round

Small, friendly hotel in city centre, adjacent to main coach station and near main railway station. In the vibrant gay village.

See under Cheadle Hulme, Manchester, Mobberley, Salford, Stockport, Wilmslow

♦♦♦♦
Silver
Award

THE HINTON
Town Lane, Mobberley, Knutsford, WA16 7HH
T: (01565) 873484
F: (01565) 873484

B&B per night:
S £38.00–£44.00
D £50.00–£58.00

OPEN All year round

Award-winning bed and breakfast for both business and private guests. Within easy reach of M6, M56, Manchester Airport and InterCity rail network. Ideal touring base, on the B5085 between Knutsford and Wilmslow. Beautifully appointed rooms with many extras. All good home cooking.	Bedrooms: 2 single, 1 double, 1 twin, 1 triple Bathrooms: 5 en suite	EM 1800 (LO 1900) Parking for 10 CC: Amex, Barclaycard, Diners, Mastercard, Visa

SYMBOLS The symbols in each entry give information about services and facilities. A key to these symbols appears at the back of this guide.

MORECAMBE, Lancashire Map ref 5A3 *Tourist Information Centre Tel: (01524) 582808 or 582809*

◆◆ **SUNNYSIDE HOTEL**
8 Thornton Road, Morecambe,
LA4 5PB
T: (01524) 418363

Bedrooms: 7 double,
2 twin
Bathrooms: 3 en suite,
2 public

EM 1730 (LO 1830)

B&B per night:
S £15.00–£17.00
D £30.00–£34.00

HB per person:
DY £21.00–£23.00

OPEN All year round

Situated 80 yards from the Promenade and offering good food and friendly atmosphere. Comfort and cleanliness assured.

NANTWICH, Cheshire Map ref 4A2 *Tourist Information Centre Tel: (01270) 610983*

◆◆◆◆ **HENHULL HALL**
Welshmans Lane, Nantwich,
CW5 6AD
T: (01270) 624158 &
07774 885305 (Mobile)
F: (01270) 624158
E: philip.percival@virgin.net

Bedrooms: 1 double,
1 twin
Bathrooms: 1 en suite,
1 private

Parking for 4

B&B per night:
S Min £25.00
D Min £50.00

OPEN All year round

Spacious beautifully appointed farmhouse on the edge of historic town of Nantwich and bordering the Shropshire Union Canal. Garden setting amidst working farm. Central for Chester, Potteries, M6.

NEW BRIGHTON, Merseyside Map ref 4A2

◆◆◆ **SHERWOOD GUEST HOUSE**
55 Wellington Road, New Brighton,
Wirral, CH45 2ND
T: (0151) 639 5198

Bedrooms: 1 single,
3 twin, 2 triple
Bathrooms: 3 en suite,
1 public

EM 1800 (LO 1900)

B&B per night:
S £15.00–£20.00
D £30.00–£35.00

HB per person:
DY £20.00–£28.00

OPEN All year round

Family guesthouse facing promenade and Irish Sea. Close to station and M53. Ideal centre for Chester, North Wales, Lakes and Liverpool (15 minutes).

NORTHWICH, Cheshire Map ref 4A2 *Tourist Information Centre Tel: (01606) 353534*

◆◆◆ **PARK DALE GUEST HOUSE**
140 Middlewich Road, Rudheath,
Northwich, CW9 7DS
T: (01606) 45228
F: (01606) 331770

Bedrooms: 3 single,
2 twin, 1 triple
Bathrooms: 3 en suite,
1 public

Lunch available
EM 1730 (LO 1930)
Parking for 7

B&B per night:
S Min £20.00
D Min £40.00

HB per person:
DY Min £26.00

OPEN All year round

Warm and friendly accommodation within easy reach of town centre and the tourist attractions of the north west. Convenient for motorway links and Manchester Airport.

OLDHAM, Greater Manchester Map ref 4B1 *Tourist Information Centre Tel: (0161) 627 1024*

◆◆◆ **GLOBE FARM GUEST HOUSE**
Huddersfield Road, Standedge,
Delph, Oldham, OL3 5LU
T: (01457) 873040
F: (01457) 873040
I: www.smoothhound.co.uk/hotels/
globef.html

Bedrooms: 4 single,
5 double, 4 twin,
1 family room
Bathrooms: 14 en suite

EM 1830
Parking for 30
CC: Barclaycard, Delta,
JCB, Maestro, Mastercard,
Solo, Switch, Visa, Visa
Electron

B&B per night:
S Min £25.00
D Min £39.50

HB per person:
DY £28.00–£33.25

OPEN All year round

18-acre mixed farm. Quarter of a mile from the Pennine Way and high walking country. 14 en suite bedrooms, and small campsite. Large car park.

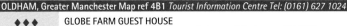

QUALITY ASSURANCE SCHEME
Diamond ratings and awards were correct at the time of going to press but are subject to change. Please check at the time of booking.

ORMSKIRK, Lancashire Map ref 4A1

♦♦♦♦

THE MEADOWS
New Sutch Farm, Sutch Lane, Ormskirk,
L40 4BU
T: (01704) 894048

B&B per night:
S £19.50–£19.50
D £35.00–£35.00

OPEN All year round

Lovely 17thC farmhouse situated down a private country lane. Relaxed and friendly atmosphere. Three pretty en suite ground floor bedrooms with all home comforts. Both lounge and dining room overlook beautiful gardens. Enjoy a hearty breakfast whilst listening to the birdsong. Welcome pot of tea. M6, 15 minutes, A59, 5 minutes.

Bedrooms: 1 single,
2 double
Bathrooms: 2 en suite,
1 private

Parking for 8

RIBBLE VALLEY

See under Clitheroe

RUSHTON, Cheshire Map ref 4A2

♦♦♦

HILL HOUSE FARM BED AND BREAKFAST
The Hall Lane, Rushton, Tarporley,
CW6 9AU
T: (01829) 732238 (Answerphone) &
07973 284863 (Mobile)
F: (01829) 733929

B&B per night:
S £25.00–£35.00
D £40.00–£50.00

OPEN All year round

Hill House Farm ia a Victorian former farmhouse situated in the middle of beautiful Cheshire countryside, offering quality accommodation with comfortable bedrooms. All private or en suite. Full English breakfast a speciality. Ideal base for Oulton Park, Beeston Castle, Nantwich and the City of Chester.

Bedrooms: 1 double,
1 twin, 1 triple
Bathrooms: 2 en suite,
1 private

Parking for 10

ST MICHAEL'S ON WYRE, Lancashire Map ref 4A1

♦♦♦

COMPTON HOUSE
Garstang Road,
St Michael's on Wyre, Preston,
PR3 0TE
T: (01995) 679378
F: (01995) 679378
E: djones@compton-hs.freeserve.
co.uk
I: www.in-uk.com/compton

Bedrooms: 1 double,
2 twin
Bathrooms: 3 en suite

Parking for 6

B&B per night:
S £25.00–£30.00
D £40.00–£40.00

OPEN All year round

Well-furnished country house in own grounds in a picturesque village, near M6 and 40 minutes from Lake District. Fishing in the Wyre. "Best-Kept Guesthouse" award 1995 and 1996.

SALFORD, Greater Manchester Map ref 4B1 *Tourist Information Centre Tel: (0161) 848 8601*

♦♦♦

HAZELDEAN HOTEL
467 Bury New Road, Kersal Bar,
Salford, Lancashire M7 3NE
T: (0161) 792 6667 & 792 2079
F: (0161) 792 6668

Bedrooms: 9 single,
5 double, 5 twin, 2 triple
Bathrooms: 20 en suite,
1 private

EM 1900 (LO 2100)
Parking for 23
CC: Amex, Barclaycard,
Delta, Diners, Mastercard,
Switch, Visa

B&B per night:
S £35.00–£42.00
D £47.00–£53.00

HB per person:
DY £37.00–£52.00

OPEN All year round

Renovated Victorian mansion in residential area of Salford. Two miles exit 17 M62, 2.5 miles city centre on A56. Fully stocked bar, beautiful garden. Restaurant, TV lounge.

SALFORD continued

♦ **WHITE LODGE PRIVATE HOTEL**
87-89 Great Cheetham Street West,
Broughton, Salford,
Greater Manchester M7 2JA
T: (0161) 792 3047

Bedrooms: 3 single,
3 double, 3 twin
Bathrooms: 2 public

Parking for 6

B&B per night:
S Min £20.00
D £34.00–£36.00

OPEN All year round

Small, family-run hotel, close to city centre amenities and sporting facilities.

SANDBACH, Cheshire Map ref 4A2

♦♦♦♦ **MOSS COTTAGE FARM**
Hassall Road, Winterley, Sandbach,
CW11 4RU
T: (01270) 583018

Bedrooms: 1 single,
1 double, 1 twin
Bathrooms: 1 en suite,
1 public

EM 1700 (LO 1900)
Parking for 10

B&B per night:
S Min £20.00
D Min £45.00

OPEN All year round

Beamed farmhouse in quiet location just off A534, close junction 17 of M6. 1 double en suite. All rooms have TV, tea-making. Evening meals available.

SINGLETON, Lancashire Map ref 4A1

♦♦ **OLD CASTLE FARM**
Garstang Road, Singleton,
Blackpool, FY6 8ND
T: (01253) 883839
F: (01253) 883839

Bedrooms: 1 twin,
1 triple, 1 family room
Bathrooms: 1 public

Parking for 20

B&B per night:
S Min £18.00
D Min £36.00

OPEN Apr–Oct

Take junction 3 off M55, follow Fleetwood sign to first traffic lights. Turn right, travel 200 yards on A586 to bungalow on the right.

SOUTHPORT, Merseyside Map ref 4A1 *Tourist Information Centre Tel: (01704) 533333*

♦♦♦♦ **AMBASSADOR PRIVATE HOTEL**
13 Bath Street, Southport, PR9 0DP
T: (01704) 543998
F: (01704) 536269

Bedrooms: 4 double,
2 twin, 2 triple
Bathrooms: 8 en suite,
2 public

EM 1800 (LO 1900)
Parking for 6
CC: Barclaycard,
Mastercard, Visa

B&B per night:
S £25.00–£36.00
D £50.00–£50.00

HB per person:
DY £35.00–£46.00

OPEN All year round

Delightful small quality hotel with residential licence, 200 yards from promenade, conference facilities, Lord Street and gardens. All bedrooms en suite.

♦♦♦ **LEICESTER HOTEL**
24 Leicester Street, Southport,
PR9 0EZ
T: (01704) 530049
F: (01704) 530049
E: leicester.hotel@mail.cybase.co.uk

Bedrooms: 2 single,
3 double, 3 twin
Bathrooms: 3 en suite,
2 public

EM 1800
Parking for 8
CC: Diners, Eurocard,
Mastercard, Visa

B&B per night:
S £18.00–£25.00
D £35.00–£40.00

OPEN All year round

Family-run hotel with personal attention, clean and comfortable, close to all amenities. Car park. Licensed bar. TV in all rooms. En suite available.

♦♦♦ **SANDY BROOK FARM**

52 Wyke Cop Road, Scarisbrick,
Southport, PR8 5LR
T: (01704) 880337
F: (01704) 880337

Bedrooms: 1 single,
1 double, 2 twin, 1 triple,
1 family room
Bathrooms: 6 en suite

Parking for 9

B&B per night:
S £20.00–£20.00
D £34.00–£34.00

OPEN All year round

27-acre arable farm. Comfortable accommodation in converted farm buildings in rural area of Scarisbrick, 3.5 miles from Southport. Special facilities for disabled guests.

TOWN INDEX

This can be found at the back of this guide. If you know where you want to stay, the index will give you the page number listing accommodation in your chosen town, city or village.

STOCKPORT, Greater Manchester Map ref 4B2 *Tourist Information Centre Tel: (0161) 474 4444*

◆◆◆

NEEDHAMS FARM
Uplands Road, Werneth Low,
Gee Cross, Hyde, Cheshire
SK14 3AG
T: (0161) 368 4610
F: (0161) 367 9106
E: charlotte@needhamsfarm.
demon.co.uk
I: www.needhamsfarm.co.uk

Bedrooms: 2 single,
3 double, 1 twin, 1 triple
Bathrooms: 6 en suite,
1 private

EM 1900 (LO 2130)
Parking for 12
CC: Mastercard, Visa

B&B per night:
S £20.00–£22.00
D £34.00–£36.00

HB per person:
DY £27.00–£29.00

OPEN All year round

30-acre beef farm. 500-year-old farmhouse with exposed beams and open fire in bar/ dining room. Excellent views. Well placed for Manchester city and airport.

STONYHURST, Lancashire Map ref 4A1

◆◆◆◆
Silver
Award

ALDEN COTTAGE
Kemple End, Birdy Brow, Stonyhurst,
Clitheroe, Lancashire BB7 9QY
T: (01254) 826468
E: carpenter@aldencottage.f9.co.uk

B&B per night:
S £23.00–£26.00
D £45.00–£50.00

OPEN All year round

Quality accommodation in an Area of Outstanding Natural Beauty overlooking the Ribble and Hodder Valleys. Charmingly furnished rooms with all modern comforts, fresh flowers, etc. Private facilities include jacuzzi bath. Ribble Valley Design and Conservation Award winner.

Bedrooms: 2 double,
1 twin
Bathrooms: 1 en suite,
1 private, 1 public,
1 private shower

Parking for 6

TARPORLEY, Cheshire Map ref 4A2

◆◆◆

FORESTERS ARMS
92 High Street, Tarporley, CW6 0AX
T: (01829) 733151
F: (01829) 730020

Bedrooms: 1 double,
2 twin
Bathrooms: 1 en suite,
2 public, 1 private
shower

Lunch available
EM 1800 (LO 2030)
Parking for 30
CC: Amex, Barclaycard,
Delta, Eurocard, JCB,
Maestro, Mastercard,
Solo, Switch, Visa, Visa
Electron

B&B per night:
S £24.50–£30.00
D £36.00–£45.00

HB per person:
DY £29.50–£35.00

OPEN All year round

Country public house, on the edge of the village of Tarporley, offering a homely and friendly service. Weekly rates negotiable.

WIGAN, Greater Manchester Map ref 4A1 *Tourist Information Centre Tel: (01942) 825677*

◆◆◆

WILDEN
11a Miles Lane, Shevington, Wigan,
Lancashire WN6 8EB
T: (01257) 251516 (Answerphone
available) & 07798 935373 (Mobile)
F: (01257) 255622
E: wildenass@aol.com

Bedrooms: 2 double,
1 twin
Bathrooms: 1 en suite,
1 public

CC: Barclaycard, Delta,
Mastercard, Switch, Visa

B&B per night:
S £20.00–£25.00
D £35.00–£40.00

HB per person:
DY £25.00–£30.00

OPEN All year round

U-shaped bungalow in a secluded location, set in just under half an acre of land. Comfortable accommodation, finished to a very high standard. Off-road parking, landscaped gardens.

WILMSLOW, Cheshire Map ref 4B2

◆◆◆

DEAN BANK HOTEL
Adlington Road, Wilmslow, SK9 2BT
T: (01625) 524268
F: (01625) 549715

Bedrooms: 1 single,
5 double, 6 twin, 5 triple
Bathrooms: 17 en suite

Lunch available
EM 1700 (LO 1930)
Parking for 24
CC: Amex, Barclaycard,
Mastercard, Visa

B&B per night:
S £35.00–£39.50
D £45.00–£52.00

HB per person:
DY £31.95–£48.95

OPEN All year round

Family-run, countryside hotel in a peaceful setting, ideal for leisure breaks, long or short stay business accommodation and Manchester Airport. Home-cooked evening meals.

MARIGOLD HOUSE

◆◆◆◆

132 Knutsford Road, Wilmslow, SK9 6JH
T: (01625) 584414 & 07778 509565

Bedrooms: 1 double, 2 twin
Bathrooms: 3 en suite

Parking for 4

B&B per night:
S £30.00–£35.00
D £40.00–£45.00

OPEN All year round

18thC period house with oak beams, flagged floors and antique furnishings. Log fires in winter. Private sitting room and dining room. Courtesy car to airport.

WIRRAL, Merseyside

See under New Brighton

COUNTRY CODE
Always follow the Country Code ✿
Enjoy the countryside and respect
its life and work ✿ Guard against
all risk of fire ✿ Fasten all gates
✿ Keep your dogs under close control
✿ Keep to public paths across
farmland ✿ Use gates and stiles to
cross fences, hedges and walls ✿
Leave livestock, crops and machinery
alone ✿ Take your litter home ✿
Help to keep all water clean ✿
Protect wildlife, plants and trees ✿
Take special care on country roads ✿
Make no unnecessary noise ✿

A brief guide to the main Towns and Villages offering accommodation in the
NORTH WEST

A ACTON BRIDGE, CHESHIRE - Village with old farmsteads and cottages on a picturesque section of the River Weaver. Riverside walks pass the great Dutton Viaduct on the former Grand Junction Railway and shipping locks on the Weaver Navigation Canal.

• **ASHTON-UNDER-LYNE, GREATER MANCHESTER** - The largest town in the borough of Tameside, with excellent access to central Manchester and to the foothills of Pennines. Famous for its 700-year-old market and the confluence of 3 canals at Portland Basin. The Church of St Michael and All Angels has a spectacular window.

B BLACKPOOL - Britain's largest fun resort, with Blackpool Pleasure Beach, 3 piers and the famous Tower. Host to the spectacular autumn illuminations.

• **BOLTON-BY-BOWLAND, LANCASHIRE** - Village near the Ribble Valley with 2 greens, one with stump of 13th C market cross and stocks. Whitewashed and greystone cottages.

• **BURY, GREATER MANCHESTER** - Famous for its black puddings, huge open market and East Lancashire Steam Railway, birthplace of Sir Robert Peel, founder of the police force and Prime Minister. Bury Art Gallery has an important collection of Turner and Constable paintings.

C CARNFORTH, LANCASHIRE - Carnforth station was the setting for the film "Brief Encounter". Nearby are Borwick Hall, an Elizabethan manor house, and Leighton Hall which has good paintings and Gillow furniture and is open to the public.

• **CHEADLE HULME, GREATER MANCHESTER** - Residential area near Manchester with some older buildings dating from 19th C once occupied by merchants and industrialists from surrounding towns. Several fine timber-framed houses, shopping centre and easy access to Manchester Airport.

• **CHESTER, CHESHIRE** - Roman and medieval walled city rich in treasures. Black and white buildings are a hallmark, including 'The Rows' - two-tier shopping galleries. 900-year-old cathedral and the famousChester Zoo.

• **CHORLEY, LANCASHIRE** - Set between the Pennine moors and the Lancashire Plain, Chorley has been an important town since medieval times, with its covered markets. The rich heritage includes Astley Hall and Park, Hoghton Tower, Rivington Country Park and the Leeds-Liverpool Canal.

• **CLITHEROE, LANCASHIRE** - Ancient market town with a 800-year-old castle keep and a wide range of award-winning shops. Good base for touring Ribble Valley, Trough of Bowland and Pennine moorland. Country market on Tuesdays and Saturdays.

G GARSTANG, LANCASHIRE - Market town. The gateway to the fells, it stands on the Lancaster Canal and is a popular cruising centre. Close by are the remains of Greenhalgh Castle (no public access) and the Bleasdale Circle. Discovery Centre shows history of Over Wyre and Bowland fringe areas.

H HOLMES CHAPEL, CHESHIRE - Village with some interesting 18th C buildings and St Luke's Church encased in brick hiding the 15th C original.

L LIVERPOOL, MERSEYSIDE - Vibrant city which became prominent in the 18th C as a result of its sugar, spice and tobacco trade with the Americas. Today the historic waterfront is a major attraction. Home to the Beatles, the Grand National, two 20th C cathedrals and many museums and galleries.

M MACCLESFIELD, CHESHIRE - Cobbled streets and quaint old buildings stand side by side with modern shops and three markets. Centuries of association with the silk industry; museums feature working exhibits and social history. Stunning views of the Peak District National Park.

• **MANCHESTER, GREATER MANCHESTER** The Gateway to the North, offering one of Britain's largest selections of arts venues and theatre productions, a wide range of chain stores and specialist shops, a legendary, lively nightlife, spectacular architecture and a plethora of eating and drinking places.

• **MORECAMBE, LANCASHIRE** - Famous for its shrimps, Morecambe is a traditional resort on a wide bay with entertainments, spacious beaches, and seafront illuminations. Bubbles Leisure Park, Frontierland and other attractions nearby. Stunning views across the bay.

N NANTWICH, CHESHIRE - Old market town on the River Weaver made prosperous in Roman times by salt springs. Fire destroyed the town in1583 and many buildings were rebuilt in Elizabethan style. Churche's Mansion (open to the public) survived the fire.

• **NEW BRIGHTON, MERSEYSIDE** - This resort on the Mersey Estuary has 7 miles of coastline, with fishing off the sea wall and pleasant walks along the promenade. Attractions include New Palace Amusements, Floral Pavilion Theatre, ten pin bowling and good sports facilities.

• **NORTHWICH, CHESHIRE** - An important salt-producing town since Roman times, Northwich has been replanned with a modern shopping centre and a number of black and white buildings. Unique Anderton boat-lift on northern outskirts of town.

O OLDHAM, GREATER MANCHESTER - The magnificent mill buildings which made Oldham one of the world's leading cotton-spinning towns still dominate the landscape. Ideally situated on the edge of the Peak District, it is now a centre of culture, sport and shopping. Good art gallery.

• **ORMSKIRK, LANCASHIRE** - Market town with interesting parish church of St Peter and St Paul containing bells brought from nearby Burscough Priory after its dissolution; half-timbered medieval manor houses, museum of Lancashire folk life and Martin Mere Wildfowl and Wetlands Centre.

S ST MICHAEL'S ON WYRE, LANCASHIRE Village near Blackpool with interesting 13th C church of St Michael containing medieval stained glass window depicting sheep shearing, and clock tower bell made in 1548.

• **SALFORD, GREATER MANCHESTER** - Industrial city close to Manchester with Roman Catholic cathedral and university. Lowry often painted Salford's industrial architecture and much of his work is in the local art gallery. Salford Quays provide a backdrop to pubs, walkways and a large cinema complex.

• **SANDBACH, CHESHIRE** - Small Cheshire town, originally important for salt production. Contains narrow, winding streets, timbered houses and a cobbled market-place. Town square has 2 Anglo-Saxon crosses to commemorate the conversion to Christianity of the King of Mercia's son.

• **SINGLETON, LANCASHIRE** - Ancient parish dating from 1175, mentioned in Domesday Book. Chapel and day school dating back to 1865. Mainly rural area to the north of St Anne's.

• **SOUTHPORT, MERSEYSIDE** - Delightful Victorian resort noted for gardens, sandy beaches and 6 golf-courses, particularly Royal Birkdale. Attractions include the Atkinson Art Gallery, Southport Railway Centre, Pleasureland and the annual Southport Flower Show. Excellent shopping, particularly in Lord Street's elegant boulevard.

• **STOCKPORT, GREATER MANCHESTER** - Once an important cotton-spinning and manufacturing centre, Stockport has an impressive railway viaduct, a shopping precinct built over the River Mersey and a new leisure complex. Lyme Hall and Vernon Park Museum nearby.

T TARPORLEY, CHESHIRE - Old town with gabled houses and medieval church of St Helen containing monuments to the Done family, a historic name in this area. Spectacular ruins of 13th C Beeston Castle nearby.

W WIGAN, GREATER MANCHESTER - Wigan is an ancient settlement which received a royal charter in 1246. Famous for its pier distinguished in Orwell's "Road to Wigan Pier". The pier has now been developed as a major tourist attraction.

• **WILMSLOW, CHESHIRE** - Nestling in the valleys of the Rivers Bollin and Dane, Wilmslow retains an intimate village atmosphere. Easy-to-reach attractions include Quarry Bank Mill at Styal. Lindow Man was discovered on a nearby common.

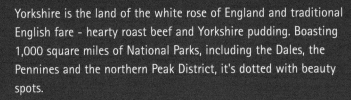

YORKSHIRE

Yorkshire is the land of the white rose of England and traditional English fare - hearty roast beef and Yorkshire pudding. Boasting 1,000 square miles of National Parks, including the Dales, the Pennines and the northern Peak District, it's dotted with beauty spots.

Abbeys and castles, quiet country lanes and inns, coastline, museums, designer shopping, and café society, Yorkshire's got it all. Cruise the network of historic canals, and discover the industrial past at the National Coal Mining Museum in Wakefield, or Grimsby's National Fishing Heritage Centre.

The Egton Bridge Old Gooseberry Show on the first Tuesday in August is something different. It includes a competition to find the heaviest gooseberry.

The counties of North, South, East and West Yorkshire and Northern Lincolnshire

FOR MORE INFORMATION CONTACT:

Yorkshire Tourist Board
312 Tadcaster Road, York YO24 1GS
Tel: (01904) 707070 (24-hour brochure line)
Fax: (01904) 701414
Email: info@ytb.org.uk
Internet: www.yorkshirevisitor.com

The Pictures:
1 Hull Fair;
2 Castle Howard, North Yorkshire;
3 Spurn Lighthouse, Holderness.

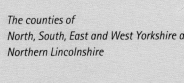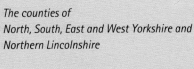

Where to Go in Yorkshire - see pages 142-145
Where to Stay in Yorkshire - see pages 146-189

Whilst in
YORKSHIRE ...

You will find hundreds of interesting places to visit during your stay, just some of which are listed in these pages.

Contact any Tourist Information Centre in the region for more ideas on days out in Yorkshire.

Bolton Abbey Estate

Bolton Abbey, Skipton, North Yorkshire BD23 6EX
Tel: (01756) 710533
Ruins of a 12thC priory in a park setting by the river Wharfe. Tearooms, nature trails, fishing, fell-walking and picturesque countryside.

Cusworth Hall Museum of South Yorkshire Life

Cusworth Hall, Doncaster, South Yorkshire DN5 7TU
Tel: (01302) 782342
Georgian mansion in landscaped park containing Museum of South Yorkshire Life. Special educational facilities.

Deep Sea Experience Centre

Cleethorpes, North East Lincolnshire DN35 8SE
Tel: (01472) 290220
Touch the rays, watch the sharks being fed and see fish from coastal waters. Dine in the famous Shark Bite Restaurant or stroll around Davy Jones' gift shop.

Elsham Hall Country & Wildlife Park

Elsham, Brigg, North Lincolnshire DN20 0QZ
Tel: (01652) 688698
Trout and carp lakes, wild butterfly garden walkway, animal farm, pets' corner, adventure playground, new falconry centre, craft centre, art gallery and shop.

Eureka! The Museum for Children

Discovery Road, Halifax, West Yorkshire HX1 2NE
Tel: (01422) 330069
Eureka! is the first museum of its kind designed especially for children up to the age of 12 with over 400 hands-on exhibits.

Flamingo Land Theme Park, Zoo and Holiday Village

Kirby, Malton, North Yorkshire YO17 6UX
Tel: (01653) 668287
One-price family funpark with over 100 attractions and 8 shows. Europe's largest privately-owned zoo and its only triple looping coaster!

Fountains Abbey and Studley Royal

Studley Park, Ripon, North Yorkshire HG4 3DY
Tel: (01765) 608888
Largest monastic ruin in Britain, founded by Cistercian monks in 1132. Landscaped garden laid between 1720-1740 with lake, formal water garden, temples and deer park.

Helmsley Castle

Helmsley, York YO62 5AB
Tel: (01439) 770442
The great ruined keep dominates the town. Other remains include a 16thC domestic range with original panelling and plasterwork. Spectacular earthwork defences.

Jorvik Viking Centre

Coppergate, York YO1 9WT
Tel: (01904) 643211
Travel back in time in a 'time car' to a recreation of Viking York. See excavated remains of Viking houses and a display of objects found.

Last of the Summer Wine Exhibition (Compo's House)

30 Huddersfield Road, Holmfirth, Huddersfield HD6 1JS
Tel: (01484) 681408
Collection of photographs and memorabilia connected with the television series 'Last of the Summer Wine'.

Leeds City Art Gallery

The Headrow, Leeds LS1 3AA
Tel: (0113) 247 8248
British paintings, sculptures, prints and drawings of the 19thC and 20thC. Henry Moore gallery with permanent collection of 20thC sculpture.

Life Force - The National Millennium Faith Experience

St Peter's House, 8 Petergate, Bradford BD1 1DN
Tel: (01274) 224540
A unique interactive experience exploring the faiths and beliefs of different cultures, and how they have influenced some of Bradford's famous people, including the Bronte sisters. Exciting restaurant serving international cuisine.

Lightwater Valley Theme Park

North Stainley, Ripon, North Yorkshire HG4 3HT
Tel: (01765) 635321
Set in 175 acres of parkland, Lightwater Valley features a number of white-knuckle rides and children's rides along with shopping malls, a restaurant and picnic areas.

Mother Shipton's Cave & the Petrifying Well

High Bridge, Knaresborough, North Yorkshire HG5 8DD
Tel: (01423) 864600
The oldest tourist attractions in Britain, opened in 1630. Cave, well, museum, playground and 12 acres of riverside grounds.

The Pictures:
1 North Yorkshire Moors, Westerdale;
2 Countryside near Grimsby;
3 Keighley and Worth Valley Railway;
4 Felixkirk, North Yorkshire Moors;
5 The Humber Bridge;
6 Victoria Quarter, Leeds;
7 Nora Batty's Cottage, Holmfirth;
8 Skidby Windmill.

National Fishing Heritage Centre

Alexandra Dock, Grimsby,
North East Lincolnshire DN31 1UZ
Tel: (01472) 323345
A journey of discovery, experience the reality of life on a deep-sea trawler. Interactive games and displays. Children's area.

National Museum of Photography, Film & Television

Bradford, West Yorkshire BD1 1NQ
Tel: (01274) 202030
This fascinating and innovative museum houses the three types of media that have transformed the 20thC. Includes galleries dedicated to digital imaging, news, light and magic.

National Railway Museum

Leeman Road, York YO26 4XJ
Tel: (01904) 621261
From rocket to Eurostar, from giants of the steam age to a miniature railway ride – discover it all in a fun-packed family day.

Newby Hall & Gardens

Ripon, Yorkshire HG4 5AE
Tel: (01423) 322583
Late 17thC house with additions. Exceptional interior by Robert Adam. Classical sculpture, Gobelins tapestries, 25 acres of gardens, miniature railway and children's adventure garden.

North Yorkshire Moors Railway

Pickering, North Yorkshire YO18 7AJ
Tel: (01751) 472508
Evening and Sunday lunchtime dining service trains offer a unique and nostalgic experience with a wonderful selection of menus to suit all tastes.

Nunnington Hall

Nunnington, York YO62 5UY
Tel: (01439) 748283
Large 17thC manor house situated on the banks of the river Rye. Hall, bedrooms, nursery, maid's room (haunted) and Carlisle collection of miniature rooms. National Trust shop.

Piece Hall

Halifax, West Yorkshire HX1 1RE
Tel: (01422) 358087
Built in 1779 and restored in 1976, this Grade I Listed building forms a unique and striking monument to the wealth and importance of the wool trade.

Pleasure Island Family Theme Park

Kings Road, Cleethorpes,
North East Lincolnshire DN35 0PL
Tel: (01472) 211511
The east coast's biggest fun day out, with over 50 rides and attractions. Whatever the weather, fun is guaranteed. Interactive play area, undercover attractions and shows from around the world.

Ripley Castle

Ripley, Harrogate, North Yorkshire HG3 3AY
Te: (01423) 770152
Home to the Ingilby family for over 26 generations. Set in the heart of a delightful estate with Victorian walled gardens, deer park and pleasure grounds.

Ryedale Folk Museum

Hutton-le-Hole, York YO62 6UA
Tel: (01751) 417367
Reconstructed local buildings including cruck-framed long houses, Elizabethan manor house, furnished cottages, craftsmen's tools, household and agricultural implements.

Sea Life Centre

Scalby Mills, Scarborough, North Yorkshire YO12 6RP
Tel: (01723) 376125
Meet creatures that live in and around the oceans of the British Isles, ranging from starfish and crabs to rays and seals.

Sheffield Botanical Gardens

Clarkehouse Road, Sheffield S10 2LN
Tel: (0114) 250 0500
Extensive gardens with over 5,500 species of plants. Landscape by Robert Marnock, famous 19thC landscape designer.

Skipton Castle

Skipton, North Yorkshire BD23 1AQ
Tel: (01756) 792442
One of the most complete and well-preserved medieval castles in England. Civil War royalist stronghold.

Wensleydale Cheese Visitor Centre

Gayle Lane, Hawes, North Yorkshire DL8 3RN
Tel: (01969) 667664
Museum, video and interpretation area, plus viewing gallery. Handmade Wensleydale cheese, licensed restaurant, specialist cheese shop, farm animals in a natural environment.

Wigfield Farm

Worsbrough Bridge, Barnsley, South Yorkshire S70 5NQ
Tel: (01226) 733702
Open working farm with rare and commercial breeds of farm animals including pigs, cattle, sheep, goats, donkeys, ponies, small animals, snakes and other reptiles.

York Minster

Deangate, York YO1 7HH
Tel: (01904) 557200
The largest medieval Gothic cathedral in England. Museum of Saxon and Norman remains. Chapter house. Unrivalled views from the tower.

Find out more about
YORKSHIRE ₒₒₒ

Further information about holidays and attractions in the Yorkshire region is available from:

YORKSHIRE TOURIST BOARD
312 Tadcaster Road, York YO24 1GS.
Tel: (01904) 707070 (24-hour brochure line)
Fax: (01904) 701414
Email: info@ytb.org.uk
Internet: www.yorkshirevisitor.com

The following publications are available free from the Yorkshire Tourist Board:

Yorkshire Visitor Guide 2001
information on the region, including hotels, self-catering, caravan and camping parks. Also attractions, shops, restaurants and major events

Yorkshire – A Great Day Out
non-accommodation A5 guide listing where to go, what to see and where to eat, the list goes on! Including map

Bed & Breakfast Touring Map
forming part of a 'family' of maps covering England, this guide provides information on bed and breakfast establishments in the Yorkshire and Northumbria regions

What's On
listing of events. Published three times a year

Stay on a Farm in the North of England
farm holiday accommodation in the North of England

Freedom
caravan and camping guide to the North of England

Group Operators' Guide 2001
a guide to choosing the right venue for travel trade and group organisers including hotels, attractions and unusual venues

Conference and Venue Guide 2001
a full-colour, comprehensive guide to conference facilities in the region

The Pictures:
1 North Yorkshire Moors, Railway
   Steam Train;
2 Worsbrough Mill Museum,
   South Yorkshire;
3 York Minster;
4 Thixendale in the Wolds,
   East Yorkshire;
5 The beach at Bridlington,
   East Riding of Yorkshire;
6 Low Petergate and Minster
   Towers, York;
7 The Mills at Luddenden;
8 Flamborough, East Riding
   of Yorkshire.

Getting to
YORKSHIRE ...

BY ROAD: Motorways: M1, M62, M606, M621, M18, M180, M181, A1(M). Trunk roads: A1, A19, A57, A58, A59, A61, A62, A63, A64, A65, A66.

BY RAIL: InterCity services to Bradford, Doncaster, Harrogate, Kingston upon Hull, Leeds, Sheffield, Wakefield and York. Frequent regional railway services city centre to city centre including Manchester Airport service to Scarborough, York and Leeds.

Where to stay in

YORKSHIRE

Accommodation entries in this region are listed in alphabetical order of place name, and then in alphabetical order of establishment.

Map references refer to the colour location maps at the front of this guide. The first number indicates the map to use; the letter and number which follow refer to the grid reference on the map.

At-a-glance symbols at the end of each accommodation entry give useful information about services and facilities. A key to symbols can be found inside the back cover flap. Keep this open for easy reference.

A brief description of the towns and villages offering accommodation in the entries which follow, can be found at the end of this section.

A complete listing of all English Tourism Council assessed guest accommodation appears at the back of this guide.

AINTHORPE, North Yorkshire Map ref 5C3

◆◆◆◆

THE FOX & HOUNDS INN

45 Brook Lane, Ainthorpe, Whitby,
North Yorkshire YO21 2LD
T: (01287) 660218
F: (01287) 660030
E: ajbfox@globalnet.co.uk

Bedrooms: 4 twin
Bathrooms: 4 en suite

Lunch available
EM 1800 (LO 2130)
Parking for 20
CC: Barclaycard, Diners,
Mastercard, Visa, Visa
Electron

B&B per night:
S £33.00–£35.00
D £56.00–£60.00

OPEN All year round

16thC former coaching inn, now a high quality residential country inn and restaurant. Set amidst the beautiful North York Moors National Park.

AT-A-GLANCE SYMBOLS

Symbols at the end of each accommodation entry give useful information about services and facilities. A key to symbols can be found inside the back cover flap. Keep this open for easy reference.

AMPLEFORTH, North Yorkshire Map ref 5C3

◆◆◆◆◆
Silver
Award

SHALLOWDALE HOUSE

West End, Ampleforth, York, YO62 4DY
T: (01439) 788325
F: (01439) 788885

B&B per night:
S £44.00–£55.00
D £64.00–£80.00

HB per person:
DY £52.00–£60.00

OPEN All year round

Elegant, modern country house, with impressive hillside garden, on the southern edge of the North York Moors National Park (20 miles from York). Wonderful views from every room. Thoughtfully prepared freshly-cooked food, and a quiet and relaxing ambience created by enthusiastic and dedicated proprietors. Reductions for 3 nights or more.

Bedrooms: 2 double, 1 twin
Bathrooms: 2 en suite, 1 private

EM 1930 (LO 1200)
Parking for 3
CC: Barclaycard, Delta, Mastercard, Visa

ASKRIGG, North Yorkshire Map ref 5B3

◆◆◆

HOME FARM

Stalling Busk, Askrigg, Leyburn,
North Yorkshire DL8 3DH
T: (01969) 650360

B&B per night:
D Max £38.00

HB per person:
DY Max £30.00

OPEN All year round

Situated amidst breathtaking scenery overlooking Semerwater Lake in Wensleydale. The 17thC beamed farmhouse with log fires is beautifully furnished with antiques, brass beds patchwork quilts, etc. Bed and breakfast with optional evening meal. Traditional cooking and home-made bread are the order of the day. Licensed.

Bedrooms: 3 double
Bathrooms: 2 public

EM 1930 (LO 1800)
Parking for 4

◆◆◆◆
Silver
Award

STONEY END

Worton, Leyburn, North Yorkshire DL8 3ET
T: (01969) 650652
F: (01969) 650077
E: stoneyendholidays@btinternet.com
I: www.wensleydale.org/links/
stoneyendfrm.htm

B&B per night:
D £25.00–£27.50

OPEN All year round

Stoney End ia a Grade II Listed building dating back to the 17thC which originally provided a barn for the neighbouring farmhouse. Converted in 1990, it is now a family home full of interest and character which we are happy to share with our guests.

Bedrooms: 2 double
Bathrooms: 1 en suite, 1 private

Parking for 6
CC: Barclaycard, Mastercard, Visa

CHECK THE MAPS

The colour maps at the front of this guide show all the cities, towns and villages for which you will find accommodation entries.
Refer to the town index to find the page on which they are listed.

AUSTWICK, North Yorkshire Map ref 5B3

◆◆◆◆ **WOODVIEW GUEST HOUSE**

The Green, Austwick, Lancaster,
LA2 8BB
T: (015242) 51268

Bedrooms: 3 double,
1 twin, 1 triple, 1 family
room
Bathrooms: 6 en suite

EM 1800 (LO 1930)
Parking for 6
CC: Barclaycard, Delta,
Eurocard, Mastercard,
Switch, Visa

B&B per night:
S £35.00–£40.00
D £50.00–£60.00

OPEN All year round

One of the oldest (c1700) farmhouses in Austwick, an elegant Grade II Listed building on The Green. All rooms en suite. Packed lunch available. Welcome drink on arrival.

BARNETBY, North Lincolnshire Map ref 4C1

◆◆◆◆ **REGINALD HOUSE**

27 Queens Road, Barnetby,
North Lincolnshire DN38 6JH
T: (01652) 688566
F: (01652) 688510

Bedrooms: 1 double,
1 twin
Bathrooms: 2 en suite

EM
Parking for 4

B&B per night:
S £20.00–£25.00
D £35.00–£40.00

OPEN All year round

Quiet, family-run guesthouse in Barnetby Village. 5 minutes M180 and railway station, 3 miles Humberside Airport. Near Grimsby, Scunthorpe and Hull.

BEDALE, North Yorkshire Map ref 5C3

◆◆◆◆

THE CASTLE ARMS INN

Snape, Bedale, North Yorkshire DL8 2TB
T: (01677) 470270
F: (01677) 470837
E: castlearms@aol.com

B&B per night:
S £45.00–£45.00
D £59.00–£59.00

HB per person:
DY £39.00–£45.00

OPEN All year round

A family-run 14thC inn which has been completely refurbished. Nine en suite twin/double bedrooms have been added, all furnished to an exceptioanl standard and including TV and tea/coffee-making facilities. A warm welcome awaits you, with open fires, traditional ales and real home cooking.

Bedrooms: 3 double,
6 twin
Bathrooms: 9 en suite

Lunch available
EM 1830 (LO 2100)
Parking for 15
CC: Barclaycard, Delta,
Eurocard, JCB, Maestro,
Mastercard, Solo, Switch,
Visa, Visa Electron

◆◆◆◆◆ **ELMFIELD COUNTRY HOUSE**

Arrathorne, Bedale, North Yorkshire
DL8 1NE
T: (01677) 450558
F: (01677) 450557
E: stay@elmfieldhouse.freeserve.
co.uk

Bedrooms: 4 double,
3 twin, 2 triple
Bathrooms: 9 en suite

EM 1830
Parking for 25
CC: Barclaycard, Delta,
Eurocard, Mastercard,
Switch, Visa

B&B per night:
S Min £35.00
D £50.00–£55.00

HB per person:
DY £37.00–£47.00

OPEN All year round

Country house in own grounds with special emphasis on standards and home cooking. All rooms en suite. Bar, games room, solarium. Ample secure parking.

BEVERLEY, East Riding of Yorkshire Map ref 4C1 *Tourist Information Centre Tel: (01482) 867430*

◆◆◆ **EASTGATE GUEST HOUSE**

7 Eastgate, Beverley,
East Riding of Yorkshire HU17 0DR
T: (01482) 868464
F: (01482) 871899

Bedrooms: 5 single,
6 double, 2 twin, 3 triple
Bathrooms: 7 en suite,
3 public

B&B per night:
S £24.00–£34.00
D £38.00–£46.00

OPEN All year round

Family-run Victorian guesthouse, established and run by the same proprietor for 29 years. Close to town centre, Beverley Minster, Museum of Army Transport and railway station.

MAP REFERENCES The map references refer to the colour maps at the front of this guide. The first figure is the map number; the letter and figure which follow indicate the grid reference on the map.

BOLTON PERCY, North Yorkshire Map ref 4C1

♦♦♦♦ GLEBE FARM
Bolton Percy, York, North Yorkshire
YO23 7AL
T: (01904) 744228

Bedrooms: 1 twin
Bathrooms: 1 en suite

Parking for 2

B&B per night:
S £22.00–£24.00
D £44.00–£48.00

OPEN Apr–Nov

225-acre mixed farm. Excellent accommodation in self-contained en suite annexe on family-run farm. Conservatory, garden, ample parking.

BRIDLINGTON, East Riding of Yorkshire Map ref 5D3 *Tourist Information Centre Tel: (01262) 673474*

♦♦♦♦

BAY COURT HOTEL
35a Sands Lane, Bridlington,
East Riding of Yorkshire YO15 2JG
T: (01262) 676288

B&B per night:
S £25.00–£25.00
D £50.00–£56.00

HB per person:
DY £34.00–£37.00

OPEN Mar–Oct

Small, high quality, non-smoking licensed hotel, 50 yards from quiet North Beach, offering tasteful accommodation, delicious food, wide choice of wines and a friendly welcome. Comfortable lounge and south-facing sun patio enable you to enjoy peaceful sea views. Convenient for cliff walks, moors, Wolds villages, stately homes, beaches and coves – or just relaxing!

Bedrooms: 2 single,
3 double, 2 twin
Bathrooms: 5 en suite,
2 private

Lunch available
EM 1800 (LO 1900)
Parking for 5
CC: Mastercard, Visa

♦♦♦

BOSVILLE ARMS COUNTRY HOTEL
High Street, Rudston, Driffield,
East Yorkshire YO25 4UB
T: (01262) 420259
F: (01262) 420259
E: hogan@bosville.freeserve.co.uk

B&B per night:
S £29.95–£29.95
D £49.50–£57.50

HB per person:
DY £36.95–£44.95

OPEN All year round

Family-run country motel with village pub and quality restaurant. All rooms en suite. Located in beautiful historic Wolds village, only minutes from coast and golf courses. Art breaks with resident artist available. Quality accommodation, good food and fine ale, in a friendly country environment.

Bedrooms: 3 twin,
3 family rooms
Bathrooms: 6 en suite

Lunch available
EM 1900 (LO 2130)
Parking for 30
CC: Delta, Mastercard,
Switch, Visa

Rating Applied For

THE FERNS HOTEL
Main Street, Carnaby, Bridlington,
North Humberside YO16 4UJ
T: (01262) 678961
F: (01262) 400712
E: theferns.hotel@virgin.net

Bedrooms: 4 single,
5 double, 2 twin
Bathrooms: 11 en suite

Lunch available
EM 1800 (LO 2130)
Parking for 80
CC: Barclaycard, Delta,
Mastercard, Solo, Switch,
Visa

B&B per night:
S Min £39.25
D Min £59.75

OPEN All year round

Family-run hotel with a bias towards health and fitness. Gym, indoor pool, sauna, solarium, steam room and spa bath are all included with your stay.

NB IMPORTANT NOTE Information on accommodation listed in this guide has been supplied by the proprietors. As changes may occur you are advised to check details at the time of booking.

BRIDLINGTON continued

◆◆◆ **THE WHITE ROSE**

123 Cardigan Road, Bridlington,
East Riding of Yorkshire YO15 3LP
T: (01262) 673245 &
07860 159208 (Mobile)

Bedrooms: 2 double,
2 twin, 1 triple
Bathrooms: 4 en suite,
1 private shower

Lunch available
EM 1730 (LO 2100)
Parking for 2
CC: Barclaycard,
Mastercard, Visa

B&B per night:
S £22.00–£25.00
D £40.00–£44.00

HB per person:
DY £27.00–£29.00

OPEN All year round

Personal attention with warm, friendly hospitality and emphasis on food. No hidden extras. Near the South Beach, spa and harbour. Special pensioners' weeks at discount prices.

BRIGG, North Lincolnshire Map ref 4C1

◆◆◆ **HOLCOMBE GUEST HOUSE**

34 Victoria Road, Barnetby,
North Lincolnshire DN38 6JR
T: 07850 764002
F: (01652) 680841
E: holcombe.house@virgin.net
I: holcombeguesthouse.co.uk

Bedrooms: 7 single,
2 twin, 2 triple
Bathrooms: 3 en suite,
1 private, 6 public,
1 private shower

EM 1900 (LO 2000)
Parking for 9
CC: Mastercard, Switch,
Visa

B&B per night:
S £20.00–£27.50
D £32.50–£40.00

HB per person:
DY £22.50–£33.50

OPEN All year round

Pleasant, homely accommodation in centre of Barnetby village. 5 minutes M180 and railway station, 3 miles Humberside Airport, 15-30 minutes from Grimsby, Scunthorpe and Hull.

CASTLETON, North Yorkshire Map ref 5C3

◆◆◆

THE ESKDALE INN

Station Road, Castleton, Whitby,
North Yorkshire YO21 2EU
T: (01287) 660234

B&B per night:
S £22.00–£29.00
D £40.00–£48.00

HB per person:
DY £27.00–£39.00

OPEN All year round

Family-run inn set in the North York Moors National Park just yards from the River Esk and Esk Valley Railway. An ideal base for exploring the beautiful surrounding countryside. Two cosy bars, poolroom and beer garden. Offering comfortable accommodation, with both bedrooms en suite. Home-cooked bar meals and Sunday lunches.

Bedrooms: 2 double
Bathrooms: 2 en suite

Lunch available
EM 1800 (LO 1900)
Parking for 30
CC: Switch

CROPTON, North Yorkshire Map ref 5C3

◆◆◆◆◆
**Gold
Award**

BURR BANK

Cropton, Pickering, North Yorkshire
YO18 8HL
T: (01751) 417777 & 0776 884
2233 (Mobile)
F: (01751) 417789
E: bandb@burrbank.com
I: www.burrbank.com

Bedrooms: 2 double,
1 twin
Bathrooms: 3 en suite

EM 1900 (LO 1900)
Parking for 10

B&B per night:
S £27.00–£27.00
D £54.00–£54.00

HB per person:
DY £43.00–£43.00

OPEN All year round

Winner YTB "Guest Accommodation of the Year" 2000. Home cooking, personal attention, comfortable, quiet and spacious. 80 acres. Close to York, coast, moors, dales.

WELCOME HOST This is a nationally recognised customer care programme which aims to promote the highest standards of service and a warm welcome. Establishments taking part in this initiative are indicated by the ⊛ symbol.

CROPTON continued

◆◆◆◆
Silver
Award

HIGH FARM

Cropton, Pickering, North Yorkshire
YO18 8HL
T: (01751) 417461

B&B per night:
S £24.99–£24.99
D £40.00–£40.00

OPEN All year round

Relax in the friendly atmosphere of this elegant Victorian farmhouse surrounded by beautiful gardens, on the edge of quiet, unspoilt village and overlooking North York Moors National Park. Peaceful base for walkers, nature/garden lovers. Steam railway and Castle Howard nearby. Village inn has own brewery. A warm welcome awaits.

Bedrooms: 3 double
Bathrooms: 3 en suite

Parking for 10

DACRE BANKS, North Yorkshire Map ref 4B1

◆◆◆◆

THE ROYAL OAK INN

Oak Lane, Dacre Banks, Harrogate,
North Yorkshire HG3 4EN
T: (01423) 780200
F: (01423) 781748
E: royaloakdacre@scock@virgin.net

B&B per night:
S £30.00–£35.00
D £50.00–£50.00

OPEN All year round

This 18thC inn is an ideal centre for walking and fishing in the Yorkshire Dales. Well-appointed bedrooms and a separate dining room. Fresh home-cooked food served every day. Fresh fish and local beers a speciality, various diets catered for. Garden overlooking Nidderdale. Outdoor seating area with a boules piste.

Bedrooms: 1 double,
2 twin
Bathrooms: 3 en suite

Lunch available
EM 1830 (LO 2100)
Parking for 15
CC: Barclaycard, Delta,
Eurocard, Mastercard,
Solo, Switch, Visa, Visa
Electron

DANBY, North Yorkshire Map ref 5C3

◆◆◆
ROWANTREE FARM
Ainthorpe, Whitby, North Yorkshire
YO21 2LE
T: (01287) 660396
E: krbsatindall@aol.com

Bedrooms: 1 twin,
1 family room
Bathrooms: 1 public

EM 1830 (LO 1200)
Parking for 6

B&B per night:
S Min £17.00
D Min £34.00

HB per person:
DY Min £25.00

OPEN All year round

120-acre mixed farm on the outskirts of Danby village. Panoramic moorland views and ample car parking facilities. Home cooking. Ideal walking country.

◆◆◆
SYCAMORE HOUSE
Danby Dale, Danby, Whitby,
North Yorkshire YO21 2NW
T: (01287) 660125 (Answerphone)
& 07403 714676 (Mobile)
F: (01287) 669122
E: sycamore.danby@btinternet.
com

Bedrooms: 1 double,
1 twin, 1 triple
Bathrooms: 1 en suite,
1 public

EM 1800 (LO 2000)
Parking for 6

B&B per night:
S £20.00–£20.00
D £40.00–£40.00

HB per person:
DY £32.00–£32.00

OPEN All year round

A comfortable 17thC stone-built home offering modern facilities and conveniences. Stunning views reinforce the welcome that awaits you. Please contact us for a brochure.

PRICES
Please check prices and other details at the time of booking.

DONCASTER, South Yorkshire Map ref 4C1 *Tourist Information Centre Tel: (01302) 734309*

♦♦♦♦ LOW FARM

The Green, Clayton, Doncaster, South Yorkshire DN5 7DB
T: (01977) 648433 (Answerphone available) & 640472 (Fax/phone/answerphone)
F: (01977) 640472
E: bar@lowfarm.freeserve.co.uk
I: www.lowfarm.freeserve.co.uk

Bedrooms: 1 single, 4 double, 2 twin
Bathrooms: 3 en suite, 1 private

Parking for 13

B&B per night:
S £20.00–£28.00
D £40.00–£56.00

OPEN All year round

Restored 17thC farmhouse and restored barns in rural village with 10 other working farms. In conservation village in South Yorkshire, within easy reach of Doncaster.

EASINGWOLD, North Yorkshire Map ref 5C3

♦♦♦♦ DIMPLE WELLS

Thormanby, York, YO61 4NL
T: (01845) 501068
F: (01845) 501068

Bedrooms: 1 double, 1 twin
Bathrooms: 2 en suite

Parking for 4

B&B per night:
S £25.00–£27.50
D £50.00–£55.00

OPEN All year round

Quality home from home. En suite rooms, Aga-cooked breakfasts. Located in Herriot Country, in extensive grounds against the backdrop of White Horse of Kilburn.

EBBERSTON, North Yorkshire Map ref 5D3

♦♦♦ FOXHOLM HOTEL

Ebberston, Scarborough, North Yorkshire YO13 9NJ
T: (01723) 859550 & 07977 141656 (Mobile)
F: (01723) 859550
E: kay@foxholm.freeserve.co.uk
I: www.foxholm.freeserve.co.uk

Bedrooms: 2 double, 2 twin
Bathrooms: 4 en suite, 1 public

Lunch available
EM 1900 (LO 2100)
Parking for 20
CC: Delta, Mastercard, Visa

B&B per night:
S £30.50–£32.50
D £51.00–£55.00

OPEN All year round

Small, personally-run, fully licensed country hotel in rural setting. Ground-floor en suite rooms overlooking peaceful gardens.

♦♦♦ GIVENDALE HEAD FARM

Ebberston, Scarborough, North Yorkshire YO13 9PU
T: (01723) 859383
F: (01723) 859383
E: sue.gwilliam@talk21.com
I: www.visityorkshire.com

Bedrooms: 2 double
Bathrooms: 1 en suite, 1 public

Parking for 4

B&B per night:
S £18.00–£20.00
D £36.00–£40.00

OPEN All year round

180-acre mixed farm. Family-run, offering a quiet location and lovely views. Dalby Forest is on doorstep. Ideal base for touring, walking and mountain biking .

FILEY, North Yorkshire Map ref 5D3

♦♦♦ SEAFIELD HOTEL

9-11 Rutland Street, Filey, North Yorkshire YO14 9JA
T: (01723) 513715

Bedrooms: 2 single, 4 double, 4 triple, 5 family rooms
Bathrooms: 14 en suite, 1 public

EM 1800 (LO 1600)
Parking for 7
CC: Barclaycard, Delta, Mastercard, Visa

B&B per night:
S £19.00–£21.00
D £38.00–£42.00

HB per person:
DY £25.00–£27.00

OPEN All year round

Small, friendly and comfortable hotel in the centre of Filey, close to the beach and all amenities. Car park. Family rooms.

GARFORTH, West Yorkshire Map ref 4B1

♦♦♦ MYRTLE HOUSE

31 Wakefield Road, Garforth, Leeds, LS25 1AN
T: (0113) 286 6445

Bedrooms: 1 single, 1 double, 1 twin, 3 triple
Bathrooms: 3 public

B&B per night:
S £18.00–£20.00
D £36.00–£40.00

OPEN All year round

Spacious Victorian terraced house between M62 and A1 (M1, junction 47). All rooms have tea and coffee making facilities, TV, vanity basins and central heating.

REGIONAL TOURIST BOARD The ⋔ symbol in an establishment entry indicates that it is a Regional Tourist Board member.

GOATHLAND, North Yorkshire Map ref 5D3

♦♦♦ **FAIRHAVEN COUNTRY HOTEL**

The Common, Goathland, Whitby,
North Yorkshire YO22 5AN
T: (01947) 896361

Bedrooms: 2 single,
2 double, 2 twin, 2 triple,
1 family room
Bathrooms: 4 en suite,
3 public

EM 1900 (LO 1730)
Parking for 10
CC: Barclaycard, Delta,
Eurocard, JCB,
Mastercard, Solo, Switch,
Visa, Visa Electron

B&B per night:
S £22.00–£34.00
D £44.00–£54.00

HB per person:
DY £35.75–£47.75

OPEN All year round

*Edwardian country house with superb moorland views in the centre of Goathland village.
Warm hospitality and fine food in a relaxed atmosphere.*

♦♦♦

HEATHERDENE HOTEL

The Common, Goathland, Whitby,
North Yorkshire YO22 5AN
T: (01947) 896334 (Answerphone available)
F: (01947) 896334
E: smtco@globalnet.co.uk
I: www.touristnetuk.com/ne/heatherdene

B&B per night:
S £30.00–£35.00
D £50.00–£70.00

HB per person:
DY £39.00–£49.00

OPEN All year round

*Heatherdene is a licensed hotel
situated in Goathland. Formerly a
vicarage, the accommodation is
spacious and comfortable with
magnificent views. Home cooking
and a warm welcome are
Heatherdene specialities. An ideal
base for exploring the national park.
The North Yorkshire Moors Railway is
only a short walk from the hotel.*

Bedrooms: 2 single,
2 double, 1 twin, 1 triple
Bathrooms: 5 en suite,
1 private shower

Lunch available
EM 1800 (LO 1900)
Parking for 12
CC: Barclaycard, Delta,
Eurocard, JCB, Maestro,
Mastercard, Solo, Switch,
Visa, Visa Electron

GRASSINGTON, North Yorkshire Map ref 5B3

♦♦♦ **CLARENDON HOTEL**

Hebden, Grassington, Skipton,
North Yorkshire BD23 5DE
T: (01756) 752446
E: clarhotel@aol.com
I: www.daelnet/information/
clarendonhotel.

Bedrooms: 2 double,
1 twin
Bathrooms: 3 en suite

Lunch available
EM 1830 (LO 2100)
Parking for 30
CC: Barclaycard, Delta,
JCB, Mastercard, Solo,
Switch, Visa

B&B per night:
S £35.00–£35.00
D £46.00–£50.00

OPEN All year round

*Yorkshire Dales village inn serving good food and ales. Personal supervision at all times.
Steaks and fish dishes are specialities. Seven nights for the price of six.*

♦♦♦ **FORESTERS ARMS HOTEL**

20 Main Street, Grassington,
Skipton, North Yorkshire BD23 5AA
T: (01756) 752349
F: (01756) 753633
E: phil&rita@theforesters.
freeserve.co.uk

Bedrooms: 4 double,
1 twin, 2 triple
Bathrooms: 7 en suite,
1 public

Lunch available
EM 1800 (LO 2030)
Parking for 2
CC: Barclaycard, Delta,
Mastercard, Solo, Switch,
Visa

B&B per night:
S £25.00–£35.00
D £50.00–£70.00

OPEN All year round

*Formerly an old coaching inn, situated in picturesque village, serving lunch and evening
meals. Hand-pulled ales and en suite accommodation.*

♦♦♦ **GRANGE COTTAGE**

Linton, Skipton, North Yorkshire
BD23 5HH
T: (01756) 752527

Bedrooms: 1 double,
1 twin
Bathrooms: 1 public,
1 private shower

Parking for 4

B&B per night:
S £25.00–£25.00
D £44.00–£45.00

OPEN Mar–Oct

*Stone-built cottage with open fires and warm hospitality. In a quiet backwater of a
picture postcard village, perfect for hiking and car touring in the dales.*

QUALITY ASSURANCE SCHEME

Diamond ratings and awards are explained at the back of this guide.

GRASSINGTON continued

◆◆◆◆

LONG ASHES INN
Long Ashes Park, Threshfield, Skipton,
North Yorkshire BD23 5PN
T: (01756) 752434
F: (01756) 752937
E: info@longashesinn.co.uk
I: www.longashesinn.co.uk

B&B per night:
S £47.50–£47.50
D £75.00–£75.00

HB per person:
DY £50.00–£60.00

OPEN All year round

Charming old dales inn set in the heart of picturesque Wharfedale. Wide range of hand-pulled ales and freshly prepared food. Beautifully appointed en suite accommodation, with TV and tea/coffee making facilities. Perfect for exploring the dales. Heated indoor pool, sauna, squash court adjacent, for use by residents.

Bedrooms: 3 double,
1 twin, 1 family room;
suite available
Bathrooms: 5 en suite

Lunch available
EM 1830 (LO 2130)
Parking for 60
CC: Barclaycard, Delta,
Eurocard, Mastercard,
Solo, Switch, Visa, Visa
Electron

◆◆◆

NEW LAITHE HOUSE
Wood Lane, Grassington, Skipton,
North Yorkshire BD23 5LU
T: (01756) 752764 (Answerphone available)
E: enquiries@newlaithehouse.co.uk
I: www.newlaithehouse.co.uk

Bedrooms: 3 double,
2 twin, 1 triple
Bathrooms: 4 en suite,
1 private, 1 private
shower

Parking for 8

B&B per night:
D £46.00–£54.00

OPEN All year round

Situated in a quiet location. An ideal base for walking or fishing and for visiting the many historic towns in North and West Yorkshire.

HALIFAX, West Yorkshire Map ref 4B1 *Tourist Information Centre Tel: (01422) 368725*

◆◆◆

THE ELMS
Keighley Road, Illingworth, Halifax,
West Yorkshire HX2 8HT
T: (01422) 244430
I: sylvia@theelms.f9.co.uk

Bedrooms: 2 single,
1 double, 1 triple
Bathrooms: 3 en suite,
1 private

EM 1800 (LO 2000)
Parking for 14

B&B per night:
S £21.00–£23.00
D £40.00–£44.00

HB per person:
DY £31.00–£36.00

OPEN All year round

Victorian residence with gardens and original ornate ceilings, within 3 miles of Halifax. Traditional Yorkshire family welcome. Sorry, no late night keys after 1am.

HARROGATE, North Yorkshire Map ref 4B1 *Tourist Information Centre Tel: (01423) 537300*

◆◆◆

ALAMAH
88 Kings Road, Harrogate,
North Yorkshire HG1 5JX
T: (01423) 502187
F: (01423) 566175

Bedrooms: 2 single,
2 double, 2 twin,
1 family room
Bathrooms: 6 en suite,
1 private shower

Parking for 8
CC: Delta, Eurocard,
Mastercard, Visa

B&B per night:
S £27.00–£32.00
D £50.00–£52.00

OPEN All year round

Comfortable rooms, personal attention, friendly atmosphere and full English breakfast. 300 metres from town centre, 150 metres from Exhibition Centre. Garages/parking.

◆◆◆◆

THE ALEXANDER
88 Franklin Road, Harrogate,
North Yorkshire HG1 5EN
T: (01423) 503348
F: (01423) 540230

Bedrooms: 2 single,
2 double, 3 triple
Bathrooms: 5 en suite,
1 public

Parking for 2

B&B per night:
S £25.00–£27.00
D £48.00–£50.00

OPEN All year round

Friendly, family-run elegant Victorian guesthouse with some en suite facilities. Ideal for conference centre and Harrogate town. Good touring centre for dales. Non-smokers only, please.

MAP REFERENCES
Map references apply to the colour maps at the front of this guide.

HARROGATE continued

ANRO
♦♦♦

90 Kings Road, Harrogate,
North Yorkshire HG1 5JX
T: (01423) 503087
F: (01423) 561719
E: anro@joyner.fsnet.co.uk
I: www.smoothhound.co.uk/hotels/
anro.html

Bedrooms: 3 single,
1 double, 2 twin,
1 family room
Bathrooms: 4 en suite,
1 public

EM 1815 (LO 1630)
CC: Delta, Eurocard,
Mastercard, Visa

B&B per night:
S Min £23.00
D Min £46.00

HB per person:
DY Min £37.00

OPEN All year round

Comfortable refurnished bedrooms, friendly personal service. Central position, 2 minutes from the conference centre and near Valley Gardens, town, bus, rail stations. Ideal for dales. Home cooking.

ASHBROOKE HOUSE HOTEL
♦♦♦♦

140 Valley Drive, Harrogate,
North Yorkshire HG2 0JS
T: (01423) 564478
F: (01423) 564478
E: ashbrooke@harrogate.com
I: www.harrogate.com/ashbrooke

Bedrooms: 3 single,
2 double, 1 twin, 1 triple
Bathrooms: 4 en suite,
1 private, 2 public,
1 private shower

CC: Barclaycard, Delta,
Eurocard, Mastercard,
Visa

B&B per night:
S £28.00–£35.00
D £52.00–£52.00

OPEN All year round

Elegant Edwardian townhouse hotel, close to town, conference centre and countryside, offering quality accommodation. Children and pets most welcome.

♦♦♦♦

ASHLEY HOUSE HOTEL
36-40 Franklin Road, Harrogate,
North Yorkshire HG1 5EE
T: (01423) 507474
F: (01423) 560858
E: ron@ashleyhousehotel.com
I: www.ashleyhousehotel.com

B&B per night:
S £37.50–£70.00
D £55.00–£80.00

HB per person:
DY £42.50–£62.00

OPEN All year round

Close to the town centre, Ashley House is a friendly hotel aiming to give you a memorable stay and value for money. Delightful bar with extensive collection of whiskies. Excellent restaurants within walking distance. Tour the Yorkshire Dales and Moors from our convenient location in this lovely spa town.

Bedrooms: 5 single,
6 double, 7 twin
Bathrooms: 18 en suite

EM 1800 (LO 1930)
Parking for 6
CC: Amex, Barclaycard,
Delta, Diners, Eurocard,
Mastercard, Solo, Switch,
Visa

ASTON HOTEL
♦♦♦

7-9 Franklin Mount, Harrogate,
North Yorkshire HG1 5EJ
T: (01423) 564262
F: (01423) 505542
E: astonhotel@btinternet.com

Bedrooms: 2 single,
7 double, 4 twin, 1 triple,
1 family room
Bathrooms: 15 en suite

Lunch available
EM 1800 (LO 2000)
Parking for 6
CC: Eurocard, Mastercard,
Solo, Switch, Visa, Visa
Electron

B&B per night:
S £25.00–£49.50
D £55.00–£95.00

OPEN All year round

Comfortably furnished, quiet, medium-sized, privately-owned, licensed hotel. Three minutes' walk from Harrogate Conference Centre, exhibition and town centres.

CAVENDISH HOTEL
♦♦♦♦

3 Valley Drive, Harrogate,
North Yorkshire HG2 0JJ
T: (01423) 509637

Bedrooms: 3 single,
4 double, 2 twin
Bathrooms: 9 en suite

CC: Barclaycard, Delta,
Eurocard, Mastercard,
Visa

B&B per night:
S £35.00–£50.00
D £55.00–£65.00

OPEN All year round

Overlooking the beautiful Valley Gardens in a quiet location yet close to conference centre and extensive shopping area. Ideal for business or pleasure.

CREDIT CARD BOOKINGS If you book by telephone and are asked for your credit card number it is advisable to check the proprietor's policy should you cancel your reservation.

HARROGATE continued

♦♦♦ ETON HOUSE

3 Eton Terrace, Knaresborough Road, Harrogate, North Yorkshire HG2 7SU	Bedrooms: 1 single, 1 double, 2 triple, 3 family rooms	Parking for 10
T: (01423) 886850	Bathrooms: 4 en suite, 2 public	
F: (01423) 886850		

B&B per night:
S £20.00–£40.00
D £45.00–£50.00

OPEN Feb–Nov

Still here after 20 years, this homely guesthouse with spacious comfortable en suite rooms, all with TV and tea/coffee facilities. Situated on A59 on the edge of the Stray and close to town.

🖥 ❄ 🍴 UL S ✂ ♨ TV ▥ T

♦♦♦♦ GARDEN HOUSE HOTEL

14 Harlow Moor Drive, Harrogate, North Yorkshire HG2 0JX	Bedrooms: 3 single, 2 double, 2 twin	EM 1900 (LO 1200)
T: (01423) 503059	Bathrooms: 5 en suite, 2 private showers	CC: Barclaycard, Mastercard, Visa
F: (01423) 503059		
E: gardenhouse@hotels.harrogate.com		
I: www.harrogate.com/gardenhouse		

B&B per night:
S Min £24.00
D Min £52.00

HB per person:
DY Min £41.00

OPEN All year round

Small, family-run, Victorian hotel overlooking Valley Gardens, in a quiet location with unrestricted parking.

🅰 🖥 2 🖳 ❄ 🍴 S ♨ ▥ ✈ T ⊛

♦♦♦ HOLLINS HOUSE

17 Hollins Road, Harrogate, North Yorkshire HG1 2JF	Bedrooms: 1 single, 1 double, 3 twin	CC: Barclaycard, Delta, Eurocard, Mastercard, Switch, Visa
T: (01423) 503646 (Answerphone available)	Bathrooms: 3 en suite, 1 public	
F: (01423) 503646		

B&B per night:
S £26.00–£26.00
D Min £46.00

OPEN All year round

Non-smoking establishment offering quiet, clean accommodation in warm, friendly, family-run Victorian house. Excellent food. Close to shops, leisure facilities and restaurants.

🅰 🖥 5 ❄ 🍴 UL S ✂ ▥ ☀ ✈ 🐾 T

♦♦♦ SCOTIA HOUSE HOTEL

66-68 Kings Road, Harrogate, North Yorkshire HG1 5JR	Bedrooms: 6 single, 3 double, 5 twin, 1 triple	EM 1830 (LO 1930) Parking for 6
T: (01423) 504361	Bathrooms: 12 en suite, 1 public	CC: Amex, Barclaycard, Delta, Eurocard, Mastercard, Solo, Switch, Visa, Visa Electron
F: (01423) 526578		
E: info@scotiahotel.harrogate.net		
I: www.scotiahotel.harrogate.net		

B&B per night:
S £29.00–£34.00
D £60.00–£64.00

OPEN All year round

Award-winning, warm, friendly hotel opposite conference centre and close to town and amenities. Individually styled bedrooms offering colour TV, telephone, beverage tray, modem point etc.

🅰 🖥 7 📺 🛎 ☎ ❄ 🍴 S ✂ ♨ TV ▥ ☂ ➤ T

♦♦♦♦

VALLEY HOTEL

93-95 Valley Drive, Harrogate,
North Yorkshire HG2 0JP
T: (01423) 504868
F: (01423) 531940
E: valley@harrogate.com
I: www.harrogate.com/valley

B&B per night:
S £35.00–£45.00
D £55.00–£65.00

OPEN All year round

Hotel overlooking Valley Gardens, offering a warm welcome both to tourists and business people. All rooms with bathrooms. Lounge bar. Lift to all floors. Internet access/e-mail facilities available. Free permits for on-street parking.	Bedrooms: 4 single, 3 double, 5 twin, 2 triple, 2 family rooms	Parking for 3
	Bathrooms: 16 en suite	CC: Amex, Barclaycard, Delta, Diners, Eurocard, Mastercard, Solo, Switch, Visa

🅰 🖥 ☎ 📺 ❄ 🍴 S ✂ ♨ ⊞ ▥ ☂ SP T

COLOUR MAPS Colour maps at the front of this guide pinpoint all places under which you will find accommodation listed.

HARWOOD DALE, North Yorkshire Map ref 5D3

◆◆◆◆
Silver Award

HARDWICK HOUSE
Harwood Dale, Scarborough,
North Yorkshire YO13 0LA
T: (01723) 870682
F: (01723) 871416
E: hardwick@globalnet.co.uk

Bedrooms: 1 double,
1 triple, 1 family room
Bathrooms: 3 en suite

Parking for 5

B&B per night:
S £30.00–£30.00
D £50.00–£50.00

OPEN All year round

En suite accommodation, equipped to the very highest standard, set in spectacular, unspoilt open countryside. Only 4 miles from the coast.

HAWES, North Yorkshire Map ref 5B3

◆◆◆

EBOR GUEST HOUSE
Burtersett Road, Hawes,
North Yorkshire DL8 3NT
T: (01969) 667337
F: (01969) 667337
E: eborhouse@freeserve.co.uk

Bedrooms: 2 double,
1 twin
Bathrooms: 2 en suite,
1 public

Parking for 5

B&B per night:
D £34.00–£40.00

OPEN All year round

Small, family-run guesthouse, double-glazed and centrally-heated throughout. Walkers are particularly welcome. Centrally located for touring the dales.

◆◆◆

WHITE HART INN
Main Street, Hawes,
North Yorkshire DL8 3QL
T: (01969) 667259
F: (01969) 667259
E: gordon@white-hart.totalserve.co.uk
I: www.wensleydale.org

Bedrooms: 1 single,
4 double, 2 twin
Bathrooms: 2 public

Lunch available
EM 1900 (LO 2100)
Parking for 7
CC: Barclaycard, Delta,
Diners, Eurocard,
Mastercard, Switch, Visa,
Visa Electron

B&B per night:
S £22.00–£25.00
D £42.00–£42.00

OPEN All year round

17thC coaching inn with a friendly welcome, offering traditional fare. Open fires, Yorkshire ales. Central for exploring the dales.

HAWNBY, North Yorkshire Map ref 5C3

◆◆◆

THE HAWNBY HOTEL
Hawnby, York, YO62 5QS
T: (01439) 798202 (Answerphone 1600-1900)
F: (01439) 798344
E: info@hawnbyhotel.co.uk
I: www.hawnbyhotel.co.uk

B&B per night:
S Min £45.00
D Min £60.00

HB per person:
DY £45.00–£55.00

OPEN All year round

The Hawnby Hotel is situated in an unspoilt village in the heart of the North Yorkshire Moors National Park, offering spectacular views from its hilltop location. Six exceptional en suite bedrooms. 25-seat "Mexborough" restaurant offering home-made English fare. Cosy country pub soaking up the village atmosphere, both past and present. A peaceful relaxing break at any time of year.

Bedrooms: 2 double,
4 twin
Bathrooms: 6 en suite

Lunch available
EM 1800 (LO 2100)
Parking for 8
CC: Barclaycard, Delta,
JCB, Mastercard, Solo,
Switch, Visa, Visa Electron

HAWORTH, West Yorkshire Map ref 4B1 *Tourist Information Centre Tel: (01535) 642329*

◆◆◆

THE APOTHECARY GUEST HOUSE
86 Main Street, Haworth, Keighley,
West Yorkshire BD22 8DA
T: (01535) 643642
F: (01535) 643642
E: apot@sisley86.freeserve.co.uk
I: www.sisley86.freeserve.co.uk

Bedrooms: 1 single,
4 double, 1 twin, 1 triple
Bathrooms: 6 en suite,
1 private

Parking for 7
CC: Mastercard, Visa

B&B per night:
S £19.00–£25.00
D £38.00–£42.00

OPEN All year round

At the top of Haworth Main Street opposite the famous Bronte church, 1 minute from the Parsonage and moors. Ten minutes' walk from steam railway.

HAWORTH continued

◆◆ BRONTE HOTEL

Lees Lane, Haworth, Keighley,
West Yorkshire BD22 8RA
T: (01535) 644112
F: (01535) 646725

Bedrooms: 3 single,
3 double, 2 twin, 3 triple
Bathrooms: 8 en suite,
1 public

Lunch available
EM 1900 (LO 2130)
Parking for 55
CC: Amex, Barclaycard,
Mastercard, Switch, Visa

B&B per night:
S £20.00–£35.00
D £42.00–£50.00

OPEN All year round

On the edge of the moors, 5 minutes' walk from the station and 15 minutes' walk to the Parsonage, the former home of the Brontes.

◆◆◆ EBOR HOUSE

Lees Lane, Haworth, Keighley,
West Yorkshire BD22 8RA
T: (01535) 645869

Bedrooms: 3 twin
Bathrooms: 1 en suite,
1 public

Parking for 2

B&B per night:
S £17.00–£17.00
D £32.00–£34.00

OPEN All year round

Yorkshire stone-built house of character, conveniently placed for the main tourist attractions of Haworth, including the Worth Valley Railway and Bronte Parsonage and Museum.

HEBDEN BRIDGE, West Yorkshire Map ref 4B1 Tourist Information Centre Tel: (01422) 843831

◆◆◆ ROBIN HOOD INN

Pecket Well, Hebden Bridge,
West Yorkshire HX7 8QR
T: (01422) 842593 &
07979 854338 (Mobile)
F: (01422) 844938
E: enquires@therobinhoodinn.co.
uk

Bedrooms: 2 double,
1 twin, 1 family room
Bathrooms: 1 en suite,
1 public

Lunch available
EM 1700 (LO 2130)
Parking for 28
CC: Visa

B&B per night:
S £18.50–£27.50
D £37.50–£44.00

HB per person:
DY £27.50–£33.50

OPEN All year round

Traditional inn on the edge of Calderdale and Pennine Way, Bronte Country, Hardcastle Crags. Near Hebden Bridge. Real ale and home-made food.

HELMSLEY, North Yorkshire Map ref 5C3

◆◆◆◆

LASKILL FARM

Hawnby, York, YO62 5NB
T: (01439) 798268
F: (01439) 798268
E: suesmith@laskillfarm.fsnet.co.uk

B&B per night:
S £28.50–£30.00
D £57.00–£60.00

OPEN All year round

700-acre mixed farm, peaceful setting within North York Moors National Park. Ideal for stately homes and walking. Natural spring water. Peace and tranquillity, idyllic surroundings, every comfort. York 45 minutes. Laskill Farm has earned its reputation from attention to detail, friendly, personal service and, most of all, value for money. Recommended on "Holiday" programme.

Bedrooms: 1 single,
3 double, 2 twin
Bathrooms: 5 en suite,
1 private

EM 1900
Parking for 10
CC: Barclaycard,
Mastercard, Switch, Visa,
Visa Electron

HOLMFIRTH, West Yorkshire Map ref 4B1 Tourist Information Centre Tel: (01484) 222444

◆ THE OLD BRIDGE BAKERY

15 Victoria Street, Holmfirth,
Huddersfield, HD7 1DF
T: (01484) 685807

Bedrooms: 2 single,
1 double, 1 triple
Bathrooms: 4 en suite

Lunch available
Parking for 2

B&B per night:
S £17.50–£20.00
D £35.00–£40.00

OPEN All year round

Located in the centre of Holmfirth, a traditional bakery/sandwich bar/shop business, with 4 cosy well-decorated bedrooms, all with en suite facilities.

CONFIRM YOUR BOOKING

You are advised to confirm your booking in writing.

HOLMFIRTH continued

◆◆◆ 29 WOODHEAD ROAD

Holmfirth, Huddersfield, HD7 1JU	Bedrooms: 1 twin	Parking for 2
T: (01484) 683962 (Answerphone available)	Bathrooms: 1 private	

200-year-old family home, 5 minutes' walk from Holmfirth. Tea and coffee available at any time. Good walking area and pleasant countryside.

B&B per night:
S £17.00–£17.00
D £34.00–£34.00

OPEN All year round

HUDDERSFIELD, West Yorkshire Map ref 4B1 *Tourist Information Centre Tel: (01484) 223200*

◆◆◆ ASHFIELD HOTEL

93 New North Road, Huddersfield,	Bedrooms: 8 single,	EM 1830 (LO 2000)
HD1 5ND	5 double, 2 twin, 5 triple	Parking for 20
T: (01484) 425916	Bathrooms: 8 en suite,	CC: Amex, Barclaycard,
F: (01484) 425916	3 public, 3 private	Delta, Diners, Eurocard,
E: ashfieldhotel@excite.co.uk	showers	Mastercard, Switch, Visa
I: www.smoothhound.co.uk/hotels/		
ashfieldhotel.html		

Family-run licensed hotel with emphasis on home-cooked food and friendly service. Half a mile from town centre and within 2 miles of M62.

B&B per night:
S £22.00–£28.00
D £36.00–£50.00

HB per person:
DY £28.00–£34.00

OPEN All year round

◆◆◆ THE MALLOWS GUEST HOUSE

55 Spring Street, Springwood,	Bedrooms: 1 single,	Parking for 3
Huddersfield, West Yorkshire	1 double, 4 twin	
HD1 4AZ	Bathrooms: 3 en suite,	
T: (01484) 544684	1 public	

An elegant, impeccably maintained Listed building with tastefully furnished, spacious bedrooms. Close to town centre, 1.5 miles from M62.

B&B per night:
S £19.50–£29.50
D £35.00–£40.00

OPEN All year round

◆◆◆◆ WOODS END

46 Inglewood Ave, Birkby,	Bedrooms: 1 double,	Parking for 2
Huddersfield, HD2 2DS	1 twin	
T: (01484) 513580 & 07710 691151	Bathrooms: 1 public	
F: (01484) 513580		

Modern, Yorkshire stone, detached 5-bedroomed house, quiet cul-de-sac location. Five minutes to Huddersfield and to the M62. Tastefully furnished to a high quality.

B&B per night:
S Min £20.00
D £40.00–£50.00

OPEN All year round

HULL, Kingston upon Hull Map ref 4C1 *Tourist Information Centre Tel: (01482) 223559 (Paragon Street) or 702118 (King George Dock)*

◆◆◆◆ CONWAY-ROSEBERRY HOTEL

86 Marlborough Avenue, Hull,	Bedrooms: 1 single,	CC: Barclaycard,
HU5 3JT	2 double, 1 twin	Mastercard, Visa
T: (01482) 445256 &	Bathrooms: 2 en suite,	
07909 517328 (Mobile)	1 public, 2 private	
F: (01482) 445256	showers	

Comfortable guesthouse in quiet conservation area. Emphasis on good food, cleanliness and service, in a friendly atmosphere.

B&B per night:
S £19.00–£30.00
D £34.00–£42.00

OPEN All year round

◆◆◆ THE EARLSMERE HOTEL

76-78 Sunnybank,	Bedrooms: 2 single,	CC: Barclaycard,
Off Spring Bank West, Hull,	1 double, 6 twin	Mastercard, Visa
HU3 1LQ	Bathrooms: 9 en suite,	
T: (01482) 341977	1 public	
F: (01482) 473714		
E: hotel7678.freeserve.co.uk		

Small family-run hotel in a quiet area overlooking the private grounds of Hymers College. Local buses 50 metres from door, city centre 1 mile, Humberside Airport 25 minutes' drive.

B&B per night:
S £19.00–£28.00
D £30.00–£40.00

OPEN All year round

ACCESSIBILITY

Look for the ♿ 🦽 🚶 symbols which indicate accessibility for wheelchair users. A list of establishments is at the front of this guide.

HULL continued

◆◆◆ THE OLD ENGLISH GENTLEMAN

22 Worship Street, Hull, HU2 8BG	Bedrooms: 1 single,	Lunch available
T: (01482) 324659	1 double, 2 twin	EM 1700 (LO 2000)
	Bathrooms: 2 public	Parking for 10
		CC: Mastercard, Visa

B&B per night:
S £22.00–£25.00
D £32.00–£38.00

HB per person:
DY £26.50–£29.50

OPEN All year round

Traditional character pub, photographs adorn the walls of past visiting theatrical performers. Good value, home-cooked food. Friendly atmosphere, good standard accommodation.

ILKLEY, West Yorkshire Map ref 4B1 *Tourist Information Centre Tel: (01943) 602319*

◆◆◆◆

COW & CALF

Hangingstone Road, Ilkley, West Yorkshire
LS29 8BT
T: (01943) 607335
F: (01943) 604712
I: www.cowandcalf.co.uk

B&B per night:
S £45.00–£45.00
D £55.00–£55.00

OPEN All year round

This most accommodating inn stands on top of Ilkley Moor, having superb gardens and commanding unrivalled views over Wharfedale and the famous Cow and Calf Rocks. With real log fires and the best quality food served all day, every day, you are assured of the best in Yorkshire hospitality.	Bedrooms: 4 single, 10 double, 2 twin Bathrooms: 16 en suite	Lunch available EM (LO 2130) Parking for 50 CC: Barclaycard, Delta, Mastercard, Solo, Switch, Visa, Visa Electron

◆◆◆◆

GROVE HOTEL

66 The Grove, Ilkley, West Yorkshire
LS29 9PA
T: (01943) 600298
F: 0870 706 5587
E: info@grovehotel.org
I: www.grovehotel.org

B&B per night:
S £42.00–£45.00
D £59.00–£64.00

OPEN All year round

This very well cared for, friendly hotel offers thoughtfully equipped bedrooms together with a cosy lounge and small bar. Breakfast is served in the bright dining room. The hotel is convenient for several local restaurants and shops. An excellent base for exploring the Yorkshire Dales, Ilkley, Haworth and Bronte Country.	Bedrooms: 2 double, 2 twin, 2 triple Bathrooms: 6 en suite, 1 public	Parking for 5 CC: Amex, Barclaycard, Delta, Diners, Eurocard, JCB, Mastercard, Switch, Visa, Visa Electron

◆◆◆◆ ONE TIVOLI PLACE

Ilkley, West Yorkshire LS29 8SU	Bedrooms: 2 double,	EM 1900 (LO 2100)
T: (01943) 600328 & 07860 293193	1 twin	CC: Barclaycard,
F: (01943) 600320	Bathrooms: 3 en suite	Mastercard, Switch, Visa
E: tivolipl@aol.com		

B&B per night:
S £30.00–£30.00
D £50.00–£50.00

HB per person:
DY Min £35.00

OPEN All year round

Warm, friendly guesthouse with en suite facilities offering a high standard of accommodation and excellent home cooking.

◆◆ ROBERT'S FAMILY BED AND BREAKFAST

63 Skipton Road, Ilkley,	Bedrooms: 2 double,	Parking for 5
West Yorkshire LS29 9HF	1 twin	CC: Barclaycard, Delta,
T: (01943) 817542	Bathrooms: 2 en suite,	Eurocard, Mastercard,
E: roberts.petra@tauc21.com	1 public	Visa

B&B per night:
S £30.00–£30.00
D £36.00–£40.00

OPEN All year round

Pleasant, detached house with garden. Near Yorkshire Dales and within easy reach of motorway connections, airport and other towns and cities in the region.

ILKLEY continued

SUMMERHILL GUEST HOUSE

24 Crossbeck Road, Ilkley,
West Yorkshire LS29 9JN
T: (01943) 607067

Bedrooms: 2 single,
1 double, 2 twin
Bathrooms: 1 en suite,
1 public

Parking for 5

B&B per night:
S £17.50–£23.50
D £35.00–£46.00

OPEN All year round

Elegant Victorian villa with beautiful garden opening on to Ilkley Moor. Quiet position, lovely views, private parking. Easy walking distance to town.

♦♦♦

INGLETON, North Yorkshire Map ref 5B3

♦♦♦♦

FERNCLIFFE COUNTRY GUEST HOUSE

55 Main Street, Ingleton, Carnforth,
North Yorkshire LA6 3HJ
T: (015242) 42405 (Answerphone)
E: ferncliffe@hotmail.com

B&B per night:
S £29.00–£29.00
D £46.00–£46.00

OPEN Feb–Oct

Ferncliffe is a Victorian, dales-style, detached house on the edge of Ingleton. A warm welcome is assured from your hosts Susan and Peter Ring. An ideal base to explore the Yorkshire Dales and South Lakes area. The comfortable rooms are en suite, with beverage tray and colour TV.

Bedrooms: 1 double,
4 twin
Bathrooms: 5 en suite

EM 1830 (LO 1930)
Parking for 5
CC: Delta, Mastercard,
Visa

♦♦♦♦

INGLEBOROUGH VIEW

Main Street, Ingleton, Carnforth,
North Yorkshire LA6 3HH
T: (015242) 41523
I: www.ingleton.co.uk/stayat/
ingleboroughview/index.htm

Bedrooms: 3 double,
1 family room
Bathrooms: 2 en suite,
2 private

Parking for 5

B&B per night:
S £25.00–£30.00
D £40.00–£44.00

OPEN All year round

Attractive Victorian house with picturesque riverside location. All rooms have superb views. Highly recommended for food, comfort and hospitality. Ideally situated for local walks/touring dales.

♦♦♦♦

PINES COUNTRY HOUSE

Ingleton, Carnforth, Lancashire
LA6 3HN
T: (015242) 41252
F: (015242) 41252
E: pineshotel@aol.com
I: www.yorkshirenet.co.uk/stayat/
thepines

Bedrooms: 4 double,
2 twin, 1 triple
Bathrooms: 7 en suite

Lunch available
EM 1900 (LO 2000)
Parking for 14
CC: Barclaycard,
Mastercard, Visa

B&B per night:
D £50.00–£50.00

HB per person:
DY £38.00–£41.00

OPEN Feb–Nov

Splendid Victorian country house, excellent rooms, food and view. Licensed, sauna, car park. Beautiful conservatory dining room. Brochure sent with pleasure.

♦♦♦

RIVERSIDE LODGE

24 Main Street, Ingleton, Carnforth,
Lancashire LA6 3HJ
T: (015242) 41359
E: manuel@telinco.co.uk
I: www.telinco.co.uk/riversidelodge

Bedrooms: 5 double,
3 twin
Bathrooms: 8 en suite,
1 public

Parking for 8
CC: Barclaycard, Delta,
Mastercard, Visa

B&B per night:
S £26.00–£37.00
D £46.00–£46.00

OPEN All year round

Elegant detached Victorian house, with conservatory, set in the Yorkshire Dales. Pets welcome. Sauna, games room, river access, pleasant gardens.

QUALITY ASSURANCE SCHEME

Diamond ratings and awards were correct at the time of going to press but are subject to change. Please check at the time of booking.

INGLETON continued

♦♦♦ **SPRINGFIELD COUNTRY HOUSE HOTEL**

Main Street, Ingleton, Carnforth,
Lancashire LA6 3HJ
T: (015242) 41280
F: (015242) 41280
I: www.destination-england.co.uk.
springfield

Bedrooms: 3 double,
1 twin, 1 family room
Bathrooms: 5 en suite,
1 public

EM 1830 (LO 1700)
Parking for 12
CC: Amex, Barclaycard,
Delta, Diners, Eurocard,
Mastercard, Visa

B&B per night:
S £23.00–£24.00
D £46.00–£48.00

HB per person:
DY £34.00–£35.00

OPEN All year round

Detached Victorian villa in its own grounds with patios and garden down to river. Home-grown vegetables, home cooking. Private fishing, car park. Pets welcome.

KETTLEWELL, North Yorkshire Map ref 5B3

♦♦♦♦♦
Silver
Award

HIGH FOLD

Kettlewell, Skipton, North Yorkshire
BD23 5RJ
T: (01756) 760390
F: (01756) 760390
E: deborah@highfold.fsnet.co.uk
I: www.highfold.co.uk

B&B per night:
S Min £37.00
D Min £60.00

OPEN All year round

A delightful 17thC converted barn in the picturesque village of Kettlewell, ideal base for touring, walking or cycling. The accommodation is eclectically elegant, enhanced by beamed ceilings, stone features and a collection of antiques. Three beautifully furnished en suite rooms with garden or valley views. You can enjoy breakfast, made with local produce, overlooking the famous Dalesway.

Bedrooms: 3 double
Bathrooms: 3 en suite

Parking for 7

KIRKBYMOORSIDE, North Yorkshire Map ref 5C3

♦♦♦♦

THE CORNMILL

Kirby Mills, Kirkbymoorside, York,
North Yorkshire YO62 6NP
T: (01751) 432000
F: (01751) 432300
E: cornmill@kirbymills.demon.co.uk
I: www.kirbymills.demon.co.uk

B&B per night:
S £35.00–£42.50
D £50.00–£65.00

HB per person:
DY £45.00–£52.50

OPEN Apr–Oct

Converted 18thC watermill and Victorian farmhouse providing luxury bed and breakfast accommodation on the River Dove. Bedrooms (some with 4-posters and one for wheelchairs), lounge, bar, wood-burning stove and bootroom are in the farmhouse. Sumptuous breakfasts and pre-booked group dinners are served in the mill, with viewing panel in the floor.

Bedrooms: 3 double,
2 twin
Bathrooms: 5 en suite

EM 1900
Parking for 10
CC: Barclaycard,
Mastercard, Visa

♦♦♦♦ **HIGH BLAKEY HOUSE**

Blakey Ridge, Kirkbymoorside, York,
YO62 7LQ
T: (01751) 417186 (Answerphone)
E: highblakey.house@virgin.net
I: www.freespace.virgin.net/
highblakey-house

Bedrooms: 1 double,
2 triple
Bathrooms: 1 en suite,
1 public

Parking for 3

B&B per night:
S £24.00–£28.00
D £48.00–£56.00

OPEN All year round

Where major walks meet stunning views of Farndale and Rosedale. North Yorkshire Moors attractions all around. Historic Lion Inn opposite. Peace, comfort and a warm welcome.

KNARESBOROUGH, North Yorkshire Map ref 4B1

◆◆◆ EBOR MOUNT

18 York Place, Knaresborough,
North Yorkshire HG5 0AA
T: (01423) 863315
F: (01423) 863315

Bedrooms: 1 single,
4 double, 1 twin, 2 triple
Bathrooms: 8 en suite,
1 public

Parking for 8
CC: Barclaycard, Delta,
Eurocard, Mastercard,
Switch, Visa, Visa Electron

B&B per night:
S £19.00–£22.00
D £38.00–£44.00

OPEN Jan–Nov

Charming 18thC townhouse with private car park, providing bed and breakfast accommodation in recently refurbished rooms. Ideal touring centre.

◆◆◆◆ HOLLY CORNER

3 Coverdale Drive, High Bond End,
Knaresborough, North Yorkshire
HG5 9BW
T: (01423) 864204
F: (01423) 864204
I: www.knaresborough.co.uk/
guest-accom/

Bedrooms: 1 single,
1 double; suite available
Bathrooms: 2 private,
2 public

Parking for 1

B&B per night:
S £26.00–£32.00
D £45.00–£52.00

OPEN All year round

Tudor-style house in quiet, private street on town outskirts. Friendly B&B. Personal service guaranteed. Easy access town, Dales, A1(M). No smoking. Parking. Plants/preserves for sale.

◆◆◆◆ NEWTON HOUSE HOTEL

5-7 York Place, Knaresborough,
North Yorkshire HG5 0AD
T: (01423) 863539
F: (01423) 869748
E: newton@knaresborough.co.uk
I: www.harrogate.com/newton

Bedrooms: 1 single,
6 double, 3 twin, 2 triple
Bathrooms: 11 en suite,
1 private

EM 1830 (LO 1930)
Parking for 10
CC: Barclaycard, Delta,
Eurocard, JCB,
Mastercard, Switch, Visa,
Visa Electron

B&B per night:
S £35.00–£55.00
D £55.00–£70.00

HB per person:
DY £43.00–£53.50

OPEN Jan, Mar–Dec

Charming, family-run, 17thC former coaching inn, 2 minutes' walk from the market square, castle and river. Spacious and comfortable accommodation. Ideal Harrogate, York, Dales.

◆◆◆

WATERGATE LODGE

Watergate Haven, Ripley Road,
Knaresborough, North Yorkshire HG5 9BU
T: (01423) 864627
F: (01423) 861087
E: watergate.haven@virgin.net
I: business.virgin.net/watergate.haven

B&B per night:
S £29.50–£29.50
D £49.50–£49.50

OPEN All year round

Comfortable en suite bedrooms, ideal for business or holidays. Tastefully appointed with many personal touches. Spectacular setting with woodland walks to River Nidd, Knaresborough and the Nidd Gorge, an Area of Outstanding Natural Beauty. Good travel links to all areas. Many nearby attractions. Convenient for Harrogate, York and the Yorkshire Dales.

Bedrooms: 2 double,
1 twin, 1 triple
Bathrooms: 4 en suite

Parking for 12

LEEDS, West Yorkshire Map ref 4B1 *Tourist Information Centre Tel: (0113) 242 5242 or 246 8122*

◆◆◆ AINTREE HOTEL

38 Cardigan Road, Headingley,
Leeds, LS6 3AG
T: (0113) 275 8290 & 275 7053
F: (0113) 275 8290

Bedrooms: 5 single,
4 double, 2 twin
Bathrooms: 6 en suite,
2 public

EM
Parking for 8
CC: Barclaycard, Eurocard,
Mastercard, Switch, Visa

B&B per night:
S £24.00–£31.00
D £41.00–£45.00

HB per person:
DY £34.50–£41.50

OPEN All year round

Small, comfortable licensed family hotel in tree-lined road, overlooking Headingley Cricket Ground. Close to university, public transport and shopping centre, 1.5 miles from city centre.

RATING All accommodation in this guide has been rated, or is awaiting a rating, by a trained English Tourism Council assessor.

LEEDS continued

◆◆◆ **AVALON GUEST HOUSE**

132 Woodsley Road, Leeds, LS2 9LZ	Bedrooms: 4 single,	Parking for 10
T: (0113) 243 2545	2 double, 3 twin,	CC: Delta, Mastercard,
	1 family room	Switch, Visa
	Bathrooms: 5 en suite,	
	2 public	

B&B per night:
S £25.00–£36.00
D £36.00–£50.00

HB per person:
DY Min £25.00

OPEN All year round

Superbly decorated Victorian establishment close to the university, Leeds General Infirmary and less than 1 mile from the city centre.

◆◆◆ **BROOMHURST HOTEL**

12 Chapel Lane, Off Cardigan Road,	Bedrooms: 8 single,	EM 1800 (LO 2100)
Headingley, Leeds, LS6 3BW	4 double, 2 twin, 2 triple,	Parking for 15
T: (0113) 278 6836 & 278 5764	2 family rooms	CC: Barclaycard, Eurocard,
F: (0113) 230 7099	Bathrooms: 14 en suite,	Mastercard, Switch, Visa
	3 public	

B&B per night:
S £25.00–£31.00
D £36.00–£45.00

HB per person:
DY £35.50–£41.50

OPEN All year round

Small, comfortable hotel in a quiet, pleasantly wooded conservation area, 1.5 miles from the city centre. Convenient for Yorkshire County Cricket Ground and university. Warm welcome.

◆◆◆ **GLENGARTH HOTEL**

162 Woodsley Road, Leeds, LS2 9LZ	Bedrooms: 9 single,	Lunch available
T: (0113) 245 7940	2 double, 3 twin, 1 triple	EM 1900 (LO 2100)
F: (0113) 216 8033	Bathrooms: 8 en suite,	Parking for 8
	3 public	CC: Barclaycard,
		Mastercard, Switch, Visa

B&B per night:
S £25.00–£40.00
D £36.00–£50.00

HB per person:
DY £25.00–£40.00

OPEN All year round

Attractive, family-run Victorian hotel close to university, city hospital and Park Lane College, within a mile of city centre. Easy access to M1 and M62.

◆◆◆◆

PINEWOOD HOTEL

78 Potternewton Lane, Leeds, LS7 3LW
T: (0113) 262 2561 & 0800 096
7463 (Freephone)

B&B per night:
S Min £37.00
D Min £46.00

HB per person:
DY Max £49.00

OPEN All year round

An attractively decorated and well-furnished hotel, with many extras. A warm welcome in a small hotel of distinction. Convenient for shopping, theatre, visiting the famous Yorkshire Dales and moors. Special weekend rates. Closed Christmas and New Year. At first roundabout leaving Leeds centre, turn right and hotel is 600 yards on left.

Bedrooms: 5 single,	EM 1830 (LO 1000)
3 double, 2 twin	CC: Amex, Barclaycard,
Bathrooms: 10 en suite	Delta, Eurocard,
	Mastercard, Visa

◆◆◆ **ST MICHAEL'S TOWER HOTEL**

5 St Michael's Villas, Cardigan Road,	Bedrooms: 7 single,	EM 1830 (LO 2000)
Headingley, Leeds, LS6 3AF	7 double, 7 twin, 1 triple,	Parking for 20
T: (0113) 275 5557 & 275 6039	1 family room	CC: Barclaycard, Delta,
F: (0113) 230 7491	Bathrooms: 12 en suite,	Eurocard, Mastercard,
	4 public	Switch, Visa

B&B per night:
S £23.00–£31.00
D £36.00–£45.00

HB per person:
DY £43.50–£41.50

OPEN All year round

Comfortable, licensed hotel, 1.5 miles from city centre and close to Headingley Cricket Ground and university. Easy access to Yorkshire countryside. Warm welcome from friendly staff.

LEEDS/BRADFORD AIRPORT

See under Leeds, Otley

WHERE TO STAY
Please mention this guide when making your booking.

♦♦♦♦♦

THE MOORLANDS

Levisham, Pickering, North Yorkshire
YO18 7NL
T: (01751) 460229 (Answerphone available)
F: (01751) 460470
E: ronaldoleonardo@aol.com
I: www.smoothhound.co.uk/hotels/moorlands.html

Elegant Victorian country house, set in 4 acres of garden and woodland with superb views. Spacious and very comfortable. Ideal base for exploring the North York Moors, coast and York. A warm welcome awaits. Stabling available.

Bedrooms: 2 single, 4 double, 1 twin
Bathrooms: 7 en suite

Parking for 10

B&B per night:
S £35.00–£40.00
D £80.00–£100.00

OPEN Mar–Nov

♦♦♦

HAYLOFT SUITE

Foal Barn, Spennithorne, Leyburn, North Yorkshire DL8 5PR
T: (01969) 622580

Bedrooms: 1 double, 1 twin; suite available
Bathrooms: 2 private

Parking for 1

B&B per night:
S £25.00–£30.00
D £50.00–£60.00

OPEN All year round

200-year-old barn. Private suite exclusive to 1 party. Beams, log fire. Warm welcome, peace and comfort. Garden courtyard.

♦♦♦♦♦
Silver
Award

PARK GATE HOUSE

Constable Burton, Leyburn, North Yorkshire DL8 2RG
T: (01677) 450466
E: parkgatehouse@freenet.co.uk

18th C house of character and charm, conveniently situated in Lower Wensleydale. Attractively furnished to a high standard with low oak beams, inglenook fireplace and cottage gardens. Each bedroom is decorated in country style with pretty fabrics and old pine furniture. Private facilities, TV and refreshment tray.

Bedrooms: 3 double, 1 twin
Bathrooms: 3 en suite, 1 private

EM 1900 (LO 2000)
Parking for 6
CC: Barclaycard, Mastercard, Visa

B&B per night:
S £33.00–£38.00
D £55.00–£65.00

HB per person:
DY £40.00–£45.00

OPEN All year round

♦♦♦

BECK HALL GUEST HOUSE

Malham, Skipton, North Yorkshire BD23 4DJ
T: (01729) 830332

Bedrooms: 1 single, 9 double, 2 twin, 2 triple
Bathrooms: 10 en suite, 1 private, 1 public

Lunch available
EM 1900
Parking for 30
CC: Barclaycard, Delta, JCB, Maestro, Mastercard, Solo, Switch, Visa, Visa Electron

B&B per night:
S £23.00–£30.00
D £36.00–£52.00

HB per person:
DY £25.00–£33.00

OPEN All year round

Family-run guesthouse set in a spacious riverside garden. Homely atmosphere, 4-poster beds, log fires, large car park.

TOWN INDEX

This can be found at the back of this guide. If you know where you want to stay, the index will give you the page number listing accommodation in your chosen town, city or village.

MALTON, North Yorkshire Map ref 5D3 *Tourist Information Centre Tel: (01653) 600048*

♦♦♦ **THE GEORGE HOTEL**

19 Yorkersgate, Malton,
North Yorkshire YO17 7AA
T: (01653) 692884 & 07768 344337
F: (01653) 698674

Bedrooms: 4 double,
1 twin, 3 triple, 1 family
room; suite available
Bathrooms: 9 en suite

Lunch available
EM 1830 (LO 2100)
Parking for 12
CC: Barclaycard, Delta,
Maestro, Mastercard,
Solo, Switch, Visa, Visa
Electron

B&B per night:
S £32.00–£32.00
D £48.00–£48.00

OPEN All year round

Family-run hotel, dating from 16thC, now totally refurbished. In town centre location with own car park. Families welcome. Great food served both lunchtimes and evenings.

MASHAM, North Yorkshire Map ref 5C3

♦♦♦♦ **LIMETREE FARM**

Hutts Lane, Grewelthorpe, Ripon,
North Yorkshire HG4 3DA
T: (01765) 658450

Bedrooms: 2 double,
1 twin
Bathrooms: 2 en suite,
1 private

Parking for 10

B&B per night:
S £28.00–£30.00
D £45.00–£50.00

HB per person:
DY £35.00–£38.00

OPEN All year round

60-acre mixed farm. Small farm nature reserve. Open fires, beams, oak panelling, exposed stonework and antique furniture. Private facilities all rooms. Colour brochure.

MIDDLEHAM, North Yorkshire Map ref 5C3

♦♦♦ **THE PRIORY**

West End, Middleham, Leyburn,
North Yorkshire DL8 4QG
T: (01969) 623279

Bedrooms: 1 single,
2 double, 3 twin, 1 triple,
1 family room
Bathrooms: 4 en suite,
1 private, 2 public

EM (LO 1830)
Parking for 5

B&B per night:
S £25.00–£29.00
D £44.00–£50.00

HB per person:
DY £35.00–£42.00

OPEN Mar–Oct

Friendly, family-run Georgian property opposite Richard III castle. Local amenities and ideal centre for walking, golfing and touring in surrounding beautiful dales countryside. Brochure.

NORTHALLERTON, North Yorkshire Map ref 5C3 *Tourist Information Centre Tel: (01609) 776864*

♦♦♦ **ALVERTON GUEST HOUSE**

26 South Parade, Northallerton,
North Yorkshire DL7 8SG
T: (01609) 776207
F: (01609) 776207

Bedrooms: 2 single,
1 double, 1 twin, 1 triple
Bathrooms: 3 en suite,
1 public

EM 1830 (LO 1700)
Parking for 5

B&B per night:
S £19.50–£25.00
D Min £39.95

OPEN All year round

Family-run guesthouse convenient for county town facilities and ideal for touring the dales, moors and coastal areas.

♦♦♦♦

LOVESOME HILL FARM
Lovesome Hill, Northallerton,
North Yorkshire DL6 2PB
T: (01609) 772311

B&B per night:
S £20.00–£30.00
D £40.00–£60.00

OPEN Mar–Oct

Come and experience life on our working farm. Relax in our individually furnished en suite granary rooms, of which two are on the ground floor. For the romantic, our Gate Cottage, with antique half-tester bed, corner bath and own patio, is a must. Home-made biscuits and tea on arrival. "You'll love it".

Bedrooms: 1 single,
3 double, 1 triple,
1 family room
Bathrooms: 6 en suite

EM 1900
Parking for 10

HALF BOARD PRICES Half board prices are given per person, but in some cases these may be based on double/twin occupancy.

OTLEY, West Yorkshire Map ref 4B1 *Tourist Information Centre Tel: (0113) 247 7707*

◆◆

PADDOCK HILL

Norwood, Otley, West Yorkshire
LS21 2QU
T: (01943) 465977 (Answerphone available)

Bedrooms: 2 single,
1 double, 1 twin
Bathrooms: 1 public,
1 private shower

Parking for 3

B&B per night:
S £15.00–£16.00
D £30.00–£36.00

OPEN All year round

Converted farmhouse on B6451. Open fires, lovely views; quiet, rural setting. Convenient for "Emmerdale" and "Heartbeat" country and for the dales. Leeds 16 miles, York 28 miles.

PATELEY BRIDGE, North Yorkshire Map ref 5C3

◆◆◆◆◆
Gold
Award

KNOTTSIDE FARM

The Knott, Pateley Bridge, Harrogate,
North Yorkshire HG3 5DQ
T: (01423) 712927
F: (01423) 712927

B&B per night:
S £40.00–£40.00
D £50.00–£56.00

HB per person:
DY £42.00–£45.00

OPEN All year round

This elegant, beautifully furnished, comfortable 17thC country house has superb views overlooking Nidderdale and is within easy reach of York, Harrogate, dales and moors. Nigel is Cordon Bleu trained – cooking is the love of his life and he responds to all dietary needs. A perfect spot for a relaxing break.

Bedrooms: 2 double
Bathrooms: 1 en suite,
1 private

EM 1900 (LO 2000)
Parking for 4

PICKERING, North Yorkshire Map ref 5D3 *Tourist Information Centre Tel: (01751) 473791*

◆◆◆

BARKER STAKES FARM

Lendales Lane, Pickering, North Yorkshire
YO18 8EE
T: (01751) 476759

B&B per night:
D £40.00–£45.00

HB per person:
DY Min £30.00

OPEN All year round

Comfortable accommodation in a 17thC farmhouse in the peaceful Vale of Pickering. Large, tranquil garden, private river fishing. Excellent walking area, close to North York Moors, steam railway, York and Heritage Coast. Warm Yorkshire welcome assured, hearty farmhouse breakfasts with home-made bread. Evening meals by prior arrangement.

Bedrooms: 2 double
Bathrooms: 1 public

Parking for 4

◆◆◆◆
Silver
Award

EDEN HOUSE

120 Eastgate, Pickering,
North Yorkshire YO18 7DW
T: (01751) 472289 & 476066
F: (01751) 476066
E: edenhouse@breathemail.net
I: www.edenhousebandb.co.uk

Bedrooms: 2 double,
1 twin
Bathrooms: 3 en suite

EM 1830 (LO 1900)
Parking for 4

B&B per night:
S £25.00–£30.00
D £42.00–£46.00

HB per person:
DY £36.00–£40.00

OPEN All year round

Highest quality accommodation and food with service to match. Large gardens, private car parking. First choice when visiting this beautiful area.

CHECK THE MAPS

The colour maps at the front of this guide show all the cities, towns and villages for which you will find accommodation entries.
Refer to the town index to find the page on which they are listed.

PICKERING continued

THE OLD MANSE GUEST HOUSE

Middleton Road, Pickering,
North Yorkshire YO18 8AL
T: (01751) 476484
F: (01751) 477124
E: valerie-a-gardner@talk21.com

Bedrooms: 1 single,
4 double, 1 twin, 2 triple
Bathrooms: 8 en suite

Parking for 8

B&B per night:
S £21.00–£25.00
D £42.00–£48.00

HB per person:
DY £36.00–£38.00

OPEN All year round

Fine Edwardian house in 1 acre of garden/orchard. A short walk to the steam railway and town centre.

RASTRICK, West Yorkshire Map ref 4B1

◆◆◆◆◆
Silver
Award

ELDER LEA HOUSE

Clough Lane, Rastrick, Brighouse,
West Yorkshire HD6 3QH
T: (01484) 717832 (Answerphone) &
07721 046131 (Mobile)
F: (01484) 717832
E: pinetrees@gallery 2a.freeserve.co.uk

A warm welcome awaits you on arrival at our elegant Victorian home, beautifully furnished and set in delightful gardens. Comfortable and attractive en suite bedrooms. Delicious home-cooked breakfasts. Freshly-made toasted sandwiches available throughout the evening in guest lounge. Ideal for touring or business. Close to motorways, Pennines and Summer Wine Country.

Bedrooms: 2 double
Bathrooms: 2 en suite

EM 1800 (LO 1900)
Parking for 7

B&B per night:
S £35.00–£40.00
D £55.00–£55.00

HB per person:
DY £45.00–£50.00

OPEN All year round

RAVENSCAR, North Yorkshire Map ref 5D3

◆◆◆

BIDE-A-WHILE

3 Loring Road, Ravenscar,
Scarborough, North Yorkshire
YO13 0LY
T: (01723) 870643

Bedrooms: 2 double,
1 family room
Bathrooms: 3 en suite

Lunch available
EM 1700 (LO 1830)
Parking for 6

B&B per night:
S £20.00–£23.00
D £37.00–£43.00

HB per person:
DY £25.00–£29.50

OPEN All year round

Small guesthouse offering clean, comfortable accommodation in a homely atmosphere. Home cooking with fresh produce. Sea views from all rooms. Edge of North York Moors.

◆◆◆◆

CLIFF HOUSE

Ravenscar, Scarborough, North Yorkshire
YO13 0LX
T: (01723) 870889
E: hodgson@cliffhouse.fsbusiness.co.uk
I: www.smoothhound.co.uk/hotels/
cliffhouse.html

Cliff House commands a unique position, providing breathtaking sea views. Ideally placed for coastal and country walks. Newly-appointed rooms, excellent food wih unusual breakfast choices. The area will appeal to nature lovers, geologists, artists, fossil hunters and photographers. Peace and tranquillity rule in "the town that never was".

Bedrooms: 1 double,
1 twin
Bathrooms: 2 en suite

EM 1900

B&B per night:
D £40.00–£50.00

HB per person:
DY £28.00–£35.00

OPEN All year round

IDEAS For ideas on places to visit refer to the introduction at the beginning of this section.

RAVENSCAR continued

◆◆◆

Georgian country house, reputedly a former smugglers' haunt, with panoramic views over national park and sea. In open countryside with wonderful walks in every direction. Ideal country holiday area – located at southern end of Robin Hood's Bay. Whitby, Scarborough and "Heartbeat" Country within easy reach. Self-catering cottage also available.

SMUGGLERS ROCK COUNTRY HOUSE

Ravenscar, Scarborough, North Yorkshire
YO13 0ER
T: (01723) 870044
F: (01723) 870044
E: info@smugglersrock.co.uk
I: www.smugglersrock.co.uk

Bedrooms: 1 single, 3 double, 1 twin, 2 triple, 1 family room
Bathrooms: 8 en suite

EM 1830 (LO 1630)
Parking for 12

B&B per night:
S £26.00–£28.00
D £46.00–£50.00

HB per person:
DY £35.00–£40.00

OPEN All year round

RICHMOND, North Yorkshire Map ref 5C3 *Tourist Information Centre Tel: (01748) 850252*

◆◆◆

HOLMEDALE
Dalton, Richmond, North Yorkshire
DL11 7HX
T: (01833) 621236
F: (01833) 621236

Bedrooms: 1 double, 1 twin
Bathrooms: 1 en suite, 1 public

EM 1800 (LO 1200)
Parking for 2

B&B per night:
S Min £18.00
D Min £36.00

HB per person:
DY Min £26.00

OPEN All year round

A warm welcome awaits in our Georgian house in a quiet village, midway between Richmond and Barnard Castle. Ideal for the Yorkshire and Durham dales.

RIPON, North Yorkshire Map ref 5C3

◆◆◆

THE COOPERS
36 College Road, Ripon,
North Yorkshire HG4 2HA
T: (01765) 603708 (Answerphone available)
E: joe_cooper74@hotmail.com

Bedrooms: 1 single, 2 triple; suite available
Bathrooms: 1 en suite, 1 public

Parking for 3

B&B per night:
S £18.00–£19.00
D £32.00–£38.00

OPEN All year round

Spacious, comfortable Victorian house in quiet area. En suite facilities available. Special rates for children. Cyclists welcome (storage for bicycles). Take-away meals acceptable in rooms.

◆◆◆◆◆
Silver
Award

Rambling 16thC farmhouse, full of character and charm, in glorious countryside near Fountains Abbey. Welcoming, spacious and offering superb quality and comfort. En suite bedrooms, 2 on ground floor, have large, comfortable beds, warm towels, colour TV, hairdryer and refreshments tray. Delicious breakfasts! Pretty walled garden. Safe car parking.

MALLARD GRANGE

Aldfield, Ripon, North Yorkshire HG4 3BE
T: (01765) 620242 (Long rings please)

Bedrooms: 2 double, 2 twin
Bathrooms: 4 en suite

Parking for 4

B&B per night:
D £46.00–£50.00

OPEN All year round

SYMBOLS The symbols in each entry give information about services and facilities. A key to these symbols appears at the back of this guide.

RIPON continued

◆◆◆ MOOR END FARM

Knaresborough Road, Littlethorpe,
Ripon, North Yorkshire HG4 3LU
T: (01765) 677419
E: pspensley@ukonline.co.uk
I: www.yorkshirebandb.co.uk

Bedrooms: 2 double,
1 twin
Bathrooms: 2 en suite,
1 private

Parking for 7
CC: Visa

B&B per night:
S £28.00–£32.00
D £37.00–£47.00

OPEN All year round

Relax in the friendly, peaceful atmosphere of this Victorian farmhouse. Well furnished and decorated. Delicious breakfast. Pleasant garden. Safe parking. Excellent meals found locally. Non-smoking.

ROBIN HOOD'S BAY, North Yorkshire Map ref 5D3

◆◆◆◆

FLASK INN TRAVEL LODGE

Robin Hoods Bay, Fylingdales, Whitby,
North Yorkshire YO22 4QH
T: (01947) 880692 & 880592
F: (01947) 880592
E: flaskinn@aol.com

B&B per night:
S £28.00–£28.00
D £40.00–£40.00

OPEN All year round

Newly-opened small country lodge adjoining the Flask Inn. Ideally situated between Scarborough and Whitby on the A171, within easy reach of all major tourist attractions. All rooms are ground floor, centrally heated, en suite and include colour TV and tea/coffee facilities.

Bedrooms: 1 single,
2 double, 2 twin,
1 family room
Bathrooms: 6 en suite

Lunch available
EM 1900 (LO 2100)
Parking for 20
CC: Barclaycard, Delta,
Eurocard, Maestro,
Mastercard, Solo, Switch,
Visa, Visa Electron

RUDSTON, East Riding of Yorkshire Map ref 5D3

◆◆◆ EASTGATE FARM COTTAGE

Rudston, Driffield,
East Riding of Yorkshire YO25 0UX
T: (01262) 420150 (Answerphone available) & 07710 161897 (Mobile)
F: (01262) 420150
E: ebrudston@aol.com
I: www.eastgatefarmcottage.com

Bedrooms: 1 single,
2 double; suite available
Bathrooms: 1 en suite,
2 private

EM 1900 (LO 2100)
Parking for 10

B&B per night:
S £20.00–£26.00
D £36.00–£40.00

HB per person:
DY £36.00–£44.00

OPEN All year round

Delightful 18thC cottage with friendly atmosphere. Centrally heated, en suite bedrooms. Aga cooking available. Sea, freshwater fishing, pony trekking and picturesque walks within 1 mile.

RUNSWICK BAY, North Yorkshire Map ref 5D3

◆◆◆◆ CLIFFEMOUNT HOTEL

Runswick Bay, Saltburn-by-the-
Sea, Cleveland TS13 5HU
T: (01947) 840103
F: (01947) 841025
E: cliffemount@runswickbay.fsnet.
co.uk
I: www.cliffemounthotel.co.uk

Bedrooms: 1 single,
10 double, 2 twin
Bathrooms: 12 en suite,
1 private

Lunch available
EM 1900 (LO 2130)
Parking for 30
CC: Barclaycard, Delta,
Eurocard, Maestro,
Mastercard, Solo, Switch,
Visa, Visa Electron

B&B per night:
S £28.50–£46.00
D £57.00–£77.50

HB per person:
DY £42.00–£65.00

OPEN All year round

Relaxing hotel on the clifftop with panoramic views of Runswick Bay. 9 miles north of Whitby. Noted for cuisine.

◆◆◆◆ ELLERBY HOTEL

Silver
Award

Ellerby, Saltburn-by-the-Sea,
Cleveland TS13 5LP
T: (01947) 840342
F: (01947) 841221
E: ellerbyhotel@yahoo.co.uk
I: www.smoothhound.co.uk/hotels/
ellerby.html

Bedrooms: 5 double,
4 triple
Bathrooms: 9 en suite

Lunch available
EM 1900 (LO 2200)
Parking for 60
CC: Barclaycard, Delta,
Maestro, Mastercard,
Solo, Switch, Visa, Visa
Electron

B&B per night:
S £40.00–£45.00
D £60.00–£67.00

OPEN All year round

Residential country inn within the North York Moors National Park, 9 miles north of Whitby, 1 mile inland from Runswick Bay.

SCARBOROUGH, North Yorkshire Map ref 5D3 *Tourist Information Centre Tel: (01723) 373333*

◆◆◆ EXCELSIOR PRIVATE HOTEL

1 Marlborough Street, Scarborough,
North Yorkshire YO12 7HG
T: (01723) 360716

Bedrooms: 2 single,
4 double, 2 triple
Bathrooms: 6 en suite,
1 public

EM 1730

B&B per night:
S £20.00–£25.00
D £40.00–£50.00

HB per person:
DY £25.00–£30.00

OPEN Apr–Oct

Totally non-smoking North Bay seafront Victorian residence with magnificent sea view. Traditional home-cooked fresh produce. Dinner B & B weekly £150-£160, over 60s £140-£150.

◆◆◆ PARMELIA HOTEL

17 West Street, Southcliff,
Scarborough, North Yorkshire
YO11 2QN
T: (01723) 361914
E: parmeliahotel@btinternet.com

Bedrooms: 2 single,
6 double, 2 twin, 4 triple
Bathrooms: 11 en suite,
1 private, 1 public

EM 1800 (LO 1845)

B&B per night:
S £19.50–£24.50
D £39.00–£45.00

HB per person:
DY £29.50–£34.50

OPEN Mar–Nov

Spacious, licensed hotel with emphasis on comfort, quality and home cooking. On the South Cliff near the Esplanade Gardens, the cliff lift to the Spa and the beach.

SCUNTHORPE, North Lincolnshire Map ref 4C1

◆◆◆ BEVERLEY HOTEL

55 Old Brumby Street, Scunthorpe,
North Lincolnshire DN16 2AJ
T: (01724) 282212
F: (01724) 2/0422

Bedrooms: 5 single,
3 double, 5 twin, 2 triple
Bathrooms: 15 en suite

Lunch available
EM 1830 (LO 1930)
Parking for 15
CC: Delta, Mastercard,
Switch, Visa

B&B per night:
S £38.50–£42.00
D £48.50–£52.00

OPEN All year round

In the pleasant, quiet residential district of Old Brumby off the A18, close to Scunthorpe town centre.

SELBY, North Yorkshire Map ref 4C1 *Tourist Information Centre Tel: (01757) 703263*

◆◆ HAZELDENE GUEST HOUSE

34 Brook Street, Doncaster Road,
Selby, North Yorkshire YO8 4AR
T: (01757) 704809
F: (01757) 709300
E: hazeldene@breathemail.net
I: www.smoothhound.co.uk/hotels/
hazel.html

Bedrooms: 2 single,
3 double, 3 twin
Bathrooms: 3 en suite,
2 public

Parking for 6
CC: Mastercard, Visa

B&B per night:
S £30.00–£32.00
D £42.00–£45.00

OPEN All year round

A popular choice period house B&B in a market town location 12 miles south of York. On the A19, with easy access to the A1 and M62.

SETTLE, North Yorkshire Map ref 5B3 *Tourist Information Centre Tel: (01729) 825192*

◆◆◆◆ ARBUTUS GUEST HOUSE

Riverside, Clapham, North Yorkshire
LA2 8DS
T: (015242) 51240
F: (015242) 51197
E: david@arbutus.co.uk
I: www.arbutus.co.uk

Bedrooms: 1 single,
1 double, 2 twin, 2 triple
Bathrooms: 5 en suite,
1 public

Lunch available
EM 1830 (LO 1200)
Parking for 8

B&B per night:
S £20.00–£26.00
D £49.00–£52.00

HB per person:
DY £35.50–£41.50

OPEN All year round

Situated in the heart of the beautiful village of Clapham. Country guesthouse offering traditional home cooking and a friendly atmosphere. Ideal for touring, walking and relaxing.

◆◆◆ MAYPOLE INN

Maypole Green, Main Street,
Long Preston, Skipton,
North Yorkshire BD23 4PH
T: (01729) 840219
E: landlord@maypole.co.uk
I: www.maypole.co.uk

Bedrooms: 1 single,
2 double, 1 twin, 1 triple,
1 family room
Bathrooms: 6 en suite

Lunch available
EM 1830 (LO 2100)
Parking for 30
CC: Barclaycard, Delta,
Mastercard, Solo, Switch,
Visa, Visa Electron

B&B per night:
S Min £29.00
D Min £47.00

OPEN All year round

17thC inn, with open fires, on village green. Many attractive walks in surrounding dales. Four miles from Settle. Winter breaks.

◆◆◆

WHITEFRIARS COUNTRY GUEST HOUSE

Church Street, Settle, North Yorkshire
BD24 9JD
T: (01729) 823753
I: www.whitefriars-settle.co.uk

B&B per night:
S Min £18.50
D £37.00–£46.00

HB per person:
DY £30.50–£35.00

OPEN All year round

17thC family home standing in three-quarters of an acre of secluded gardens, 50 yards from the town's central market place. This delightful guesthouse offers traditional, pleasantly furnished accommodation. Two lounges together with a beamed dining-room, where good home cooking is served. The house is fully no smoking.

Bedrooms: 1 single, 3 double, 3 twin, 1 triple, 1 family room
Bathrooms: 5 en suite, 1 private, 1 public

EM 1900 (LO 2000)
Parking for 9

SHEFFIELD, South Yorkshire Map ref 4B2 *Tourist Information Centre Tel: (0114) 273 4671 or 221 1900*

◆◆◆

ETRURIA HOUSE HOTEL
91 Crookes Road, Broomhill, Sheffield, South Yorkshire S10 5BD
T: (0114) 266 2241 & 267 0853
F: (0114) 267 0853
E: etruria@waitrose.com

Bedrooms: 4 single, 3 double, 2 twin, 1 triple
Bathrooms: 6 en suite, 2 public

Parking for 10
CC: Barclaycard, Mastercard, Visa

B&B per night:
S £28.00–£38.00
D £42.00–£52.00

OPEN All year round

Small family-run hotel, giving personal service. Five minutes from the city centre/hospitals/universities. Peak District easily accessible. Weekend rates.

◆◆◆◆

HOLME LANE FARM PRIVATE HOTEL
38 Halifax Road, Grenoside, Sheffield, S35 8PB
T: (0114) 246 8858
F: (0114) 246 8858

Bedrooms: 4 single, 1 double, 2 twin
Bathrooms: 7 en suite

Parking for 10
CC: Eurocard, Mastercard, Visa

B&B per night:
S £28.00–£28.00
D £48.00–£48.00

OPEN All year round

15-acre arable farm. Converted barn and cottage on A61, 3 miles from motorway and Sheffield. Near Meadowhall Shopping Centre and a short run from the Peak District.

◆◆

PEACE GUEST HOUSE
92 Brocco Bank, Sheffield, S11 8RS
T: (0114) 268 5110 & 267 0760

Bedrooms: 3 single, 1 double, 2 twin, 1 family room
Bathrooms: 1 en suite, 2 public, 2 private showers

EM 1700 (LO 1900)
Parking for 6
CC: Barclaycard, Mastercard, Visa

B&B per night:
S Min £25.00
D Min £35.00

OPEN All year round

Adjacent to Encliffe Park, convenient for university, hospitals and Peak District Route. One mile from city centre. All rooms colour TV, some en suite.

QUALITY ASSURANCE SCHEME

For an explanation of the quality and facilities represented by the Diamonds please refer to the front of this guide. A more detailed explanation can be found in the information pages at the back.

◆◆◆

CRAVEN HEIFER INN

Grassington Road, Skipton, North Yorkshire BD23 3LA

T: (01756) 792521 & 07767 476077
F: (01756) 794442
E: philandlynn@cravenheifer.co.uk
I: www.cravenheifer.co.uk

B&B per night:
S £45.00–£45.00
D £45.00–£45.00

OPEN All year round

Traditional country inn, serving cask ale and excellent home-cooked food, all day every day. Bar food or enjoy a meal in our restaurant overlooking the Yorkshire Dales. Excellent car parking. Most rooms ground floor. Non-smoking restaurant. Non-smoking rooms available. Prices shown are per room (max 2 people) including buffet breakfast.

| Bedrooms: 1 single, 12 double, 3 twin, 2 triple, 2 family rooms | Lunch available EM (LO 2100) Parking for 78 |
| Bathrooms: 17 en suite, 2 public | CC: Barclaycard, Delta, Mastercard, Solo, Switch, Visa, Visa Electron |

◆◆◆◆

NAPIER'S RESTAURANT

Chapel Hill, Skipton,
North Yorkshire BD23 1NL
T: (01756) 799688
F: (01756) 798111
I: www.restaurant-skipton.co.uk

| Bedrooms: 1 single, 2 double, 2 twin | Lunch available EM 1900 (LO 2145) Parking for 25 |
| Bathrooms: 5 en suite | CC: Amex, Barclaycard, Delta, Eurocard, Maestro, Mastercard, Solo, Switch, Visa, Visa Electron |

B&B per night:
S £55.00–£55.00
D £67.00–£67.00

HB per person:
DY £64.00–£64.00

OPEN All year round

Napier's dates back to the 18thC. Originally a large farmhouse, but now offering luxury accommodation in a picturesque corner of the historic centre of Skipton.

◆◆◆◆

HEY LEYS FARM

Marsden Lane, Cop Hill, Slaithwaite,
Huddersfield, HD7 5XA
T: (01484) 845404 &
07803 744499 (Mobile)
F: (01484) 843188

| Bedrooms: 1 double, 1 twin | EM 1800 (LO 1900) Parking for 10 |
| Bathrooms: 1 en suite, 1 public | |

B&B per night:
S £20.00–£25.00
D £40.00–£50.00

HB per person:
DY £35.00–£40.00

OPEN All year round

14-acre equestrian farm. Beautifully restored 17thC farmhouse. Panoramic views over moorland. Log fires, comfortable, warm and welcoming. Heart of the South Pennines. Evening meal by arrangement.

◆◆◆◆

WELLINGTON LODGE

Staintondale, Scarborough,
North Yorkshire YO13 0EL
T: (01723) 871234
F: (01723) 871234
E: info@llamatreks.co.uk
I: www.llamatreks.co.uk

B&B per night:
D £44.00–£44.00

OPEN All year round

Magnificent views of the Heritage Coast, nestled twixt sea and moor in the North York Moors National Park, we are ideally placed for walking, touring or even llama trekking. Wellington Lodge has stylishly decorated en suite rooms, offers warm hospitality, tea and home-made cakes on arrival and tasty breakfasts served in the sun lounge.

| Bedrooms: 2 double | EM 1830 (LO 1830) |
| Bathrooms: 2 en suite | Parking for 2 CC: Amex, JCB, Maestro, Mastercard, Solo, Switch, Visa, Visa Electron |

PRICES

Please check prices and other details at the time of booking.

THIRSK, North Yorkshire Map ref 5C3

FOURWAYS GUEST HOUSE

◆◆

Town End, Thirsk, North Yorkshire YO7 1PY	Bedrooms: 3 single, 2 double, 2 twin, 1 family room	Lunch available EM 1830 (LO 1930) Parking for 10
T: (01845) 522601	Bathrooms: 7 en suite, 1 public	CC: Barclaycard, Delta, Eurocard, Mastercard, Visa
F: (01845) 522131		
E: fairways@nyorks.fsbusiness.co.uk		

BtB per night:
S £17.00–£19.00
D £34.00–£38.00

OPEN All year round

Guesthouse close to town centre, 2 minutes' walk from the surgery of famous vet and author James Herriot. Centrally located for touring North Yorkshire Moors and Yorkshire Dales.

LABURNUM HOUSE

◆◆◆◆

31 Topcliffe Road, Thirsk, North Yorkshire YO7 1RX	Bedrooms: 2 double, 1 twin	Parking for 3
T: (01845) 524120	Bathrooms: 2 en suite, 1 private	

BtB per night:
D £40.00–£44.00

OPEN Mar–Oct

Spacious, comfortable detached house on the edge of town, overlooking Hambleton Hills and playing fields. Furnished with antiques and traditional furniture. Prices for single on application.

LAVENDER HOUSE

◆◆◆

27 Kirkgate, Thirsk, North Yorkshire YO7 1PL	Bedrooms: 1 single, 2 triple	Parking for 3
T: (01845) 522224 (Answerphone)	Bathrooms: 2 public	

BtB per night:
S £17.00–£17.00
D £34.00–£34.00

OPEN All year round

Let us offer you a warm welcome to Lavender House. We are next to the World of James Herriot and close to the market square.

PLUMP BANK

◆◆◆◆

Felixkirk Road, Thirsk, North Yorkshire YO7 2EW	Bedrooms: 1 double, 1 twin	Parking for 6
T: (01845) 522406	Bathrooms: 2 en suite	

BtB per night:
S Max £22.00
D Max £40.00

OPEN Mar–Sep

From Thirsk take the A170 Scarborough road. After 1 mile turn left for Felixkirk and Boltby and house is on the left after 100 yards.

TOWN PASTURE FARM

◆◆◆

Boltby, Thirsk, North Yorkshire YO7 2DY	Bedrooms: 1 twin, 1 triple	EM Parking for 4
T: (01845) 537298	Bathrooms: 2 en suite	

BtB per night:
S £19.50–£20.00
D Min £39.00

OPEN All year round

180-acre mixed farm. Farmhouse with views of the Hambleton Hills, in picturesque Boltby village within the boundary of the North York Moors National Park.

THORNTON DALE, North Yorkshire Map ref 5D3

THE BUCK HOTEL

◆◆◆

Chestnut Avenue, Thornton Dale, Pickering, North Yorkshire YO18 7RW	Bedrooms: 2 double, 1 twin, 1 family room	Lunch available EM 1900 (LO 2100) Parking for 17
T: (01751) 474212	Bathrooms: 4 en suite	
F: (01751) 474212		

BtB per night:
S £26.00–£26.00
D £42.00–£42.00

OPEN All year round

In the beautiful village of Thornton Dale, a comfortable family-run hotel with excellent en suite accommodation. Village inn atmosphere. Quality food. Open all year.

TANGALWOOD

◆◆◆

Roxby Road, Thornton Dale, Pickering, North Yorkshire YO18 7SX	Bedrooms: 1 double, 1 twin	Parking for 3
T: (01751) 474688	Bathrooms: 1 en suite, 1 private	

BtB per night:
S £20.00–£25.00
D £32.00–£38.00

OPEN Apr–Sep

Large detached house situated in a quiet part of this picturesque village. Clean and comfortable. A warm welcome and good food provided.

THWAITE, North Yorkshire Map ref 5B3

◆◆◆ **KEARTON COUNTRY HOTEL**

Thwaite, Richmond, North Yorkshire
DL11 6DR
T: (01748) 886277
F: (01748) 886590
E: jdanton@aol.com

Bedrooms: 1 single,
5 double, 1 twin, 5 triple,
1 family room
Bathrooms: 8 en suite,
5 private showers

Lunch available
EM 1830
Parking for 40
CC: Barclaycard, Delta,
JCB, Mastercard, Switch,
Visa

B&B per night:
S £24.00–£26.00
D £48.00–£52.00

HB per person:
DY £29.00–£32.00

OPEN Mar–Dec

Situated in the charming village of Thwaite in Swaledale and within easy reach of York, the Lake District, Herriot Country and the Yorkshire Dales.

WAKEFIELD, West Yorkshire Map ref 4B1 *Tourist Information Centre Tel: (01924) 305000 or 305001*

◆◆◆

HEATH HOUSE

Chancery Road, Ossett, West Yorkshire
WF5 9RZ
T: (01924) 260654 & 273098
F: (01924) 260654
E: bookings@heath-house.co.uk
I: www.heath-house.co.uk

B&B per night:
S £23.00–£30.00
D £38.00–£45.00

OPEN All year round

Set in spacious gardens, a warm welcome awaits you at Heath House. Our family home for over half a century, we take great pleasure in sharing it with our guests. Ideally situated 1.5 miles west of junction 40 M1 on the A638. Leeds, Bradford, Wakefield and Dewsbury easily accessible.

Bedrooms: 1 single,
1 double, 2 twin
Bathrooms: 3 en suite,
1 public

Parking for 9
CC: Amex, Barclaycard,
Delta, Mastercard, Visa

WETHERBY, West Yorkshire Map ref 4B1 *Tourist Information Centre Tel: (0113) 2477251*

◆◆ **PROSPECT HOUSE**

8 Caxton Street, Wetherby,
West Yorkshire LS22 6RU
T: (0113) 247 7251

Bedrooms: 1 single,
3 double, 2 twin
Bathrooms: 4 en suite,
1 public

Parking for 6

B&B per night:
S £23.00–£46.00
D £46.00–£50.00

OPEN All year round

Established 40 years. En suite rooms available. Near York, Harrogate, Dales, Herriot Country. Midway London/Edinburgh. Restaurants nearby. Pets welcome.

WHITBY, North Yorkshire Map ref 5D3 *Tourist Information Centre Tel: (01947) 602674*

◆◆◆◆ **GLENDALE GUEST HOUSE**

16 Crescent Avenue, Whitby,
North Yorkshire YO21 3ED
T: (01947) 604242

Bedrooms: 1 single,
5 double
Bathrooms: 5 en suite,
2 public

EM 1600 (LO 1730)
Parking for 6

B&B per night:
S £18.00–£18.00
D £46.00–£48.00

HB per person:
DY £33.00–£34.00

OPEN Mar–Nov

Family-run Victorian guesthouse. On the West Cliff, offering good food and cleanliness. Rooms are attractively decorated and have excellent facilities. Private parking, pets welcome.

◆◆◆ **PARTRIDGE NEST FARM**

Sleights, Whitby, North Yorkshire
YO22 5ES
T: (01947) 810450 & 811412
F: (01947) 811413
E: pnfarm@aol.com
I: www.tmis.uk.com/partridge-nest/

Bedrooms: 2 family
rooms
Bathrooms: 1 public

Parking for 20

B&B per night:
S Max £18.00
D Max £32.00

OPEN All year round

Farmhouse B&B with 2 double rooms with unbeatable views and informal, friendly, relaxed atmosphere. Farm is also a working equestrian centre.

WHITBY continued

◆◆◆◆

SEACLIFFE HOTEL

12 North Promenade, West Cliff, Whitby,
North Yorkshire YO21 3JX
T: (01947) 603139 & 08000 191747
F: (01947) 603139
E: julie@seacliffe.fsnet.co.uk
I: www.seacliffe.co.uk

B&B per night:
S £39.50–£49.50
D £65.00–£71.00

OPEN All year round

Whitby's premier family hotel overlooking the sea. All rooms en suite – wine and dine in our candlelit a la carte restaurant. Local seafood a speciality. Golf course nearby. Tee-off times may be booked through the hotel.

Bedrooms: 1 single, 13 double, 2 twin, 3 triple, 1 family room	EM 1800 (LO 2045) Parking for 8	CC: Amex, Barclaycard, Delta, Diners, Mastercard,
Bathrooms: 20 en suite, 1 public		Solo, Switch, Visa

WORTLEY, South Yorkshire Map ref 4B1

◆◆

WORTLEY HALL LTD

Wortley, Sheffield, South Yorkshire
S35 7DB
T: (0114) 288 2100 & 288 5750
F: (0114) 283 0695
E: wortley.hall@virgin.net

Bedrooms: 7 single, 12 double, 25 twin, 6 triple, 4 family rooms	Lunch available EM 1900 (LO 2130) Parking for 100	
Bathrooms: 24 en suite, 22 public	CC: Barclaycard, Delta, Mastercard, Switch, Visa, Visa Electron	

B&B per night:
S £19.00–£26.50
D £38.00–£53.00

HB per person:
DY £26.00–£33.50

OPEN All year round

An 18thC country mansion set within 26 acres of formal gardens and woodland. Listed building.

YORK, North Yorkshire Map ref 4C1 *Tourist Information Centre Tel: (01904) 621756 or 554488*

◆◆◆◆
Silver
Award

THE ACER HOTEL

52 Scarcroft Hill, York, YO24 1DE
T: (01904) 653839
F: (01904) 677017
E: info@acerhotel.co.uk
I: www.acerhotel.co.uk

B&B per night:
S £35.00–£40.00
D £50.00–£60.00

OPEN All year round

Elegant, award-winning hotel, tastefully restored to a high standard. Superior en suite accommodation is provided in a relaxed and pleasant atmosphere. Beautiful 4-poster room. Special occasion requests for champagne, flowers and chocolates catered for. A substantial 4-course breakfast is offered. Ten minutes' walk to attractions and railway station.

Bedrooms: 2 double, 1 family room	CC: Barclaycard, Delta, Eurocard, Mastercard, Visa
Bathrooms: 3 en suite	

◆◆◆

ALDWARK GUEST HOUSE

30 St Saviourgate, Aldwark, York,
YO1 8NN
T: (01904) 627781

Bedrooms: 1 double, 1 twin, 1 triple, 1 family room
Bathrooms: 3 en suite, 1 private shower

B&B per night:
S £25.00–£30.00
D £40.00–£50.00

OPEN All year round

City-centre guesthouse, close to the Minster and all amenities, offering en suite rooms and a warm, friendly atmosphere. Listed building 1702.

MAP REFERENCES The map references refer to the colour maps at the front of this guide. The first figure is the map number; the letter and figure which follow indicate the grid reference on the map.

♦♦♦

ALFREDA GUEST HOUSE

61 Heslington Lane, Fulford, York,
YO10 4HN
T: (01904) 631698
F: (01904) 411215

B&B per night:
S £25.00–£45.00
D £40.00–£60.00

OPEN All year round

Edwardian residence in large grounds. Car park with security lighting and camera. En suite rooms with colour TV, radio, direct dial telephone, tea/coffee facilities. Double glazing, CH. Close to Fulford golf and 15 minutes York University.

Bedrooms: 4 double, 2 twin, 2 triple, 2 family rooms
Bathrooms: 10 en suite

Parking for 21
CC: Amex, Barclaycard, Eurocard, Mastercard, Switch, Visa

♦♦♦♦

ASCOT HOUSE

80 East Parade, York, YO31 7YH
T: (01904) 426826
F: (01904) 431077
E: j&k@ascot-house-york.demon.co.uk
I: www.smoothhound.co.uk/hotels/ascothou.html

B&B per night:
S £20.00–£24.00
D £40.00–£48.00

OPEN All year round

A family-run, 15-bedroomed Victorian villa, built in 1869, with en suite rooms of character and many 4-poster or canopy beds. Delicious traditional English breakfasts. Fifteen minutes' walk to city centre, Jorvik Viking Museum or York Minster. Residential licence and residents' lounge, sauna, private enclosed car park.

Bedrooms: 1 single, 8 double, 3 twin, 2 triple, 1 family room
Bathrooms: 12 en suite, 1 private, 1 public

Parking for 12
CC: Barclaycard, Delta, Diners, Eurocard, JCB, Maestro, Mastercard, Solo, Switch, Visa, Visa Electron

---

♦♦♦♦

ASHBOURNE HOUSE
139 Fulford Road, York, YO10 4HG
T: (01904) 639912
F: (01904) 631332
E: ashbourneh@aol.com

Bedrooms: 3 double, 2 twin, 2 family rooms
Bathrooms: 6 en suite, 1 private

Parking for 7
CC: Amex, Barclaycard, Diners, Eurocard, Mastercard, Visa

B&B per night:
S £34.00–£40.00
D £40.00–£60.00

OPEN All year round

Charming, comfortable, family-owned and run licensed private hotel. On main route into York from the south and within walking distance of city centre.

♦♦♦

ASTLEY HOUSE

123 Clifton, York, YO30 6BL
T: (01904) 634745 & 621327
F: (01904) 621327
E: astley123@aol.com
I: members@aol.com/astley1223/astley.html

B&B per night:
S £25.00–£50.00
D £50.00–£64.00

OPEN All year round

Superb accommodation, centrally situated. 10 minutes' walk from York Minster. All en suite, satellite TV, 4-poster, hearty English breakfasts. Car parking. Bargain midweek breaks.

Bedrooms: 8 double, 1 twin, 3 triple
Bathrooms: 12 en suite

Parking for 6
CC: Barclaycard, Delta, Mastercard, Solo, Switch, Visa

QUALITY ASSURANCE SCHEME
Diamond ratings and awards are explained at the back of this guide.

♦♦♦ **THE BAR CONVENT ENTERPRISES LTD**
17 Blossom Street, York, YO24 1AQ
T: (01904) 643238 & 629359
F: (01904) 631792
E: info@bar-convent.org.uk
I: www.bar-convent.org.uk

Bedrooms: 8 single,
1 double, 6 twin
Bathrooms: 1 en suite,
5 public

Lunch available
EM 1830

B&B per night:
S £21.00–£23.00
D £40.00–£42.00

HB per person:
DY £33.50–£35.50

OPEN Feb–Dec

The oldest Catholic convent in the UK, housed in a Georgian building dating from 1767. Museum and cafe.

♦♦♦

BARRINGTON HOUSE
15 Nunthorpe Avenue, Scarcroft Road,
York, YO23 1PF
T: (01904) 634539

B&B per night:
S £18.00–£25.00
D £36.00–£50.00

OPEN All year round

Beautiful Edwardian guesthouse in quiet cul-de-sac. Ten minutes' walk from city centre and all York's attractions. Near station, racecourse and theatres. All en suite and hearty breakfasts. Parking on street. From A64 take York west A1036. Approximately 2 miles, turn right into Scarcroft Road, 2nd right into Nunthorpe Avenue.

Bedrooms: 1 single,
2 double, 1 twin, 1 triple,
2 family rooms
Bathrooms: 7 en suite

CC: Barclaycard, Delta,
Eurocard, Mastercard,
Switch, Visa, Visa Electron

♦♦♦ **BEDFORD HOTEL**
108-110 Bootham, York, YO30 7DG
T: (01904) 624412
F: (01904) 632851

Bedrooms: 2 single,
8 double, 2 twin, 4 triple,
1 family room
Bathrooms: 17 en suite

EM 1830

CC: Amex, Barclaycard,
Delta, Diners, Eurocard,
Mastercard, Solo, Switch,
Visa, Visa Electron

B&B per night:
S £35.00–£43.00
D £50.00–£66.00

HB per person:
DY £35.00–£43.00

OPEN All year round

Family-run, licensed hotel. Five minutes' walk along historic Bootham to the famous York Minster and city centre.

♦♦♦ **BLAKENEY HOTEL**
180 Stockton Lane, York, YO31 1ES
T: (01904) 422786
F: (01904) 422786
E: reception@blakeneyhtlyork.
abelgratis.co.uk
I: www.blakeneyhtlyork.abelgratis.
co.uk

Bedrooms: 3 single,
4 double, 5 twin,
6 family rooms
Bathrooms: 9 en suite,
1 private, 3 public

Lunch available
EM 1830 (LO 1930)
Parking for 12
CC: Amex, Barclaycard,
Delta, Eurocard,
Mastercard, Visa

B&B per night:
S £25.00–£30.00
D £45.00–£55.00

OPEN All year round

Comfortable, family-run, licensed hotel. Quiet residential area within easy reach of the city centre and attractions. Evening meals available, en suite facilities. Car park.

USE YOUR *i*s
There are more than 550 Tourist Information Centres throughout England offering friendly help with accommodation and holiday ideas as well as suggestions of places to visit and things to do. You'll find TIC addresses in the local Phone Book.

♦♦♦

BLUE BRIDGE HOTEL

Fishergate, York, YO10 4AP
T: (01904) 621193
F: (01904) 671571
E: book@bluebridgehotel.co.uk
I: www.bluebridgehotel.co.uk

B&B per night:
S £40.00–£45.00
D £55.00–£60.00

HB per person:
DY £37.00–£60.00

OPEN All year round

Located a short stroll from the town centre along the banks of York's beautiful River Ouse. With free parking, the hotel offers an ideal location to enjoy this historic city. Rooms are traditionally furnished with the usual trimmings. New for 2000 are Craig's restaurant, offering incredible choice and value, public cellar bar and residents' lounge bar.

Bedrooms: 2 single, 6 double, 2 twin, 5 triple
Bathrooms: 13 en suite, 1 public

EM 1830 (LO 2100)
Parking for 20
CC: Barclaycard, Delta, Eurocard, JCB, Maestro, Mastercard, Solo, Switch, Visa, Visa Electron

---

♦♦♦

BOOTHAM GUEST HOUSE

56 Bootham Crescent, York, North Yorkshire YO30 7AH
T: (01904) 672123
F: (01904) 672123
E: boothamguesthouse@btinternet.com

Bedrooms: 2 single, 3 double, 1 twin, 1 triple
Bathrooms: 5 en suite, 1 public

Parking for 4
CC: Barclaycard, Mastercard, Visa

B&B per night:
S £20.00–£30.00
D £40.00–£50.00

OPEN All year round

Family-run guesthouse in a quiet crescent off the main thoroughfare. Only a few minutes' walk from the city centre and Minster.

♦♦♦

BOWEN HOUSE

4 Gladstone Street, Huntington Road, York, YO31 8RF
T: (01904) 636881
F: (01904) 338700
E: info@bowenhouse.co.uk
I: www.bowenhouse.co.uk

B&B per night:
S £23.00–£28.00
D £37.00–£48.00

OPEN All year round

Small, family-run, Victorian guesthouse, with period furnishings throughout, where excellent breakfasts are cooked to order, using free-range eggs. The private car park has security lighting. York Minster and the city centre are within a 10-minute walk. The whole house is of a non-smoking standard.

Bedrooms: 1 single, 2 double, 1 twin, 1 family room
Bathrooms: 2 en suite, 1 public, 1 private shower

Parking for 4
CC: Mastercard, Visa

♦♦♦

BUTTERWORTH WELGARTH HOUSE

Wetherby Road, Rufforth, York, YO23 3QB
T: (01904) 738592 & 738595
F: (01904) 738595

Bedrooms: 1 single, 4 double, 2 twin
Bathrooms: 6 en suite, 1 private

Parking for 10
CC: Delta, Mastercard, Visa

B&B per night:
S £18.50–£25.00
D £37.00–£50.00

OPEN Feb–Dec

Comfort and friendliness assured at this attractive country guesthouse, 3 miles from York. Ideal touring base for Yorkshire Dales and convenient for park and ride.

♦♦♦

CARLTON HOUSE HOTEL

134 The Mount, York, YO24 1AS
T: (01904) 622265
F: (01904) 637157
E: etb@carltonhouse.co.uk
I: www.carltonhouse.co.uk

Bedrooms: 1 single, 6 double, 5 triple, 1 family room
Bathrooms: 13 en suite, 1 public

Parking for 7

B&B per night:
S £30.00–£30.00
D £54.00–£54.00

OPEN All year round

Hotel in Georgian terraced home, family-run for 50 years. Just outside city walls, close to all attractions and amenities.

◆◆◆

CAVALIER HOTEL
39 Monkgate, York, YO31 7PB
T: (01904) 636615
F: (01904) 636615
E: julia@cavalierhotel.fsnet.co.uk
I: www.cavalierhotel.co.uk

B&B per night:
S £30.00–£49.50
D £50.00–£65.00

OPEN All year round

Georgian family-run hotel close to the city centre, only yards from the ancient Bar Walls, minster and many of York's famous historic landmarks.

Bedrooms: 2 single, 4 double, 2 twin, 2 family rooms
Bathrooms: 7 en suite, 3 public

Parking for 6
CC: Barclaycard, Delta, Maestro, Mastercard, Solo, Switch, Visa, Visa Electron

---

◆◆◆◆

CITY GUEST HOUSE
68 Monkgate, York, YO31 7PF
T: (01904) 622483
E: info@cityguesthouse.co.uk
I: www.cityguesthouse.co.uk

Bedrooms: 1 single, 5 double, 1 twin
Bathrooms: 6 en suite, 1 private

Parking for 6
CC: Delta, Mastercard, Visa

B&B per night:
S £25.00–£35.00
D £46.00–£58.00

OPEN All year round

Small, friendly, family-run guesthouse in attractive Victorian townhouse. Five minutes' walk to York Minster, close to attractions. Private parking. Cosy en suite rooms. Restaurants nearby. Non-smoking.

◆◆◆

CLARENCE GARDENS HOTEL
Haxby Road, York, YO31 8JS
T: (01904) 624252
F: (01904) 671293

B&B per night:
S £30.00–£40.00
D £45.00–£60.00

HB per person:
DY £32.50–£42.50

OPEN All year round

Just 10 minutes' walk to the historic and beautiful city of York. This 18-bedroom hotel offers all en suite rooms, licensed bar, restaurant, telephones in all rooms, large car park with adjacent bowling green and children's park.

Bedrooms: 1 single, 4 double, 8 twin, 1 triple, 4 family rooms
Bathrooms: 18 en suite

EM 1900 (LO 2015)
Parking for 60
CC: Amex, Barclaycard, Delta, Mastercard, Switch, Visa

◆◆◆◆

CLAXTON HALL COTTAGE
Malton Road, York, YO60 7RE
T: (01904) 468697
E: claxcott@aol.com
I: www.members.aol.com/claxcott

B&B per night:
S £20.00–£27.50
D £40.00–£55.00

HB per person:
DY £29.50–£37.00

OPEN All year round

Carol and Martin welcome you to their peaceful 18thC cottage set in 1 acre gardens with panoramic views. Beams and log fires. Romantic candlelit dinners a speciality (available on request). Home-baked cake on arrival. Castle Howard 6 miles, York 4 miles. Easy access to moors, dales and coast.

Bedrooms: 2 double, 1 twin
Bathrooms: 1 en suite, 1 public

EM 1900 (LO 2000)
Parking for 12

NB **IMPORTANT NOTE** Information on accommodation listed in this guide has been supplied by the proprietors. As changes may occur you are advised to check details at the time of booking.

COOK'S GUEST HOUSE

◆◆◆

120 Bishopthorpe Road, York,
YO23 1JX
T: (01904) 652519 &
07946 577247 (Mobile)
F: (01904) 652519

Bedrooms: 1 double,
1 family room
Bathrooms: 2 en suite

CC: Visa

B&B per night:
D £40.00–£48.00

OPEN All year round

Featured on TV's "This Morning", small, friendly and comfortable guesthouse with unique decor. 10 minutes' walk to city, railway station and racecourse.

CORNMILL LODGE, VEGETARIAN BED AND BREAKFAST

◆◆◆

120 Haxby Road, York, YO31 8JP
T: (01904) 620566
E: cornmill@aol.com
I: members.aol.com/cornmil/hi.htm

Bedrooms: 1 single,
1 double, 1 twin, 1 triple
Bathrooms: 3 en suite,
1 private shower

Parking for 4
CC: Eurocard, Mastercard,
Visa

B&B per night:
S £20.00–£25.00
D £40.00–£50.00

OPEN All year round

Well-appointed guesthouse only 12 minutes' walk from York Minster. Most rooms en suite. No smoking. Car park. Launderette nearby. Friendly welcome. Vegetarian/vegan catering.

CROOK LODGE

◆◆◆◆

26 St Mary's, Bootham, York,
YO30 7DD
T: (01904) 655614
F: (01904) 655614

Bedrooms: 5 double,
2 twin
Bathrooms: 7 en suite

Parking for 8

B&B per night:
S £35.00–£58.00
D £50.00–£58.00

OPEN Feb–Dec

Early Victorian residence 450 yards from city centre. Bedrooms all en suite with colour TV, radio. Private car park. Special breaks, dinner, bed and breakfast. No smoking, no children.

CUMBRIA HOUSE

◆◆◆

2 Vyner Street, Haxby Road, York,
YO31 8HS
T: (01904) 636817 & 0771 278
0004 (Mobile)
E: reservation@cumbriahouse.
freeserve.co.uk
I: www.cumbriahouse.freeserve.co.
uk

Bedrooms: 1 single,
3 double, 1 triple,
1 family room
Bathrooms: 2 en suite,
2 public

Parking for 5
CC: Barclaycard,
Mastercard, Visa

B&B per night:
S £18.00–£22.00
D £36.00–£44.00

OPEN All year round

Family-run guesthouse, 12 minutes' walk from York Minster. En suites available. Easily located from ring road. Private car park. Brochure.

◆◆◆◆

CURZON LODGE AND STABLE COTTAGES

23 Tadcaster Road, Dringhouses, York,
North Yorkshire YO24 1QG
T: (01904) 703157
F: (01904) 703157
I: www.smoothhound.co.uk/hotels/curzon.
html

B&B per night:
S £42.00–£55.00
D £59.00–£79.00

OPEN All year round

Charming 17thC Listed house and former stables in a conservation area overlooking York racecourse. Ten comfortable en suite rooms, some with 4-poster or brass beds. Country antiques, books, prints, fresh flowers and complimentary sherry lend traditional ambience. Delicious breakfasts. Warm relaxed atmosphere with restaurants a minute's walk. Entirely non-smoking. Parking in grounds.

Bedrooms: 1 single,
4 double, 3 twin, 1 triple,
1 family room
Bathrooms: 10 en suite

Parking for 16
CC: Barclaycard, Delta,
Eurocard, JCB,
Mastercard, Solo, Switch,
Visa, Visa Electron

MAP REFERENCES
Map references apply to the colour maps at the front of this guide.

◆◆◆ **FAIRTHORNE**
356 Strensall Road, Earswick, York, YO32 9SW
T: (01904) 768609
F: (01904) 768609

Bedrooms: 1 double, 1 triple
Bathrooms: 2 en suite

Parking for 6

B&B per night:
S £18.00–£20.00
D £32.00–£32.00

OPEN All year round

Detached dormer bungalow with spacious gardens, 4 miles from York city centre. Family-run guesthouse with private car parking and en suite.

◆◆◆

FARTHINGS HOTEL
5 Nunthorpe Avenue, York, YO23 1PF
T: (01904) 653545
F: (01904) 628355
E: farthings@york181.fsbusiness.co.uk

B&B per night:
S £25.00–£35.00
D £40.00–£55.00

OPEN All year round

Welcoming family-run Victorian guesthouse in quiet location, 10/15 minutes' stroll from city centre. Selection of quality rooms, including en suite, all with colour TV and tea/coffee-making facilities. All rooms non-smoking. Breakfast freshly cooked to order. On-street parking.

Bedrooms: 1 single, 6 double, 1 twin, 2 triple
Bathrooms: 6 en suite, 2 public

CC: Barclaycard, Delta, Eurocard, Mastercard, Solo, Switch, Visa

---

◆◆◆ **FOSS BANK GUEST HOUSE**
16 Huntington Road, York, YO31 8RB
T: (01904) 635548

Bedrooms: 2 single, 3 double, 1 twin
Bathrooms: 2 en suite, 4 private showers

Parking for 5

B&B per night:
S £18.00–£20.00
D £36.00–£42.00

OPEN Feb–Dec

Small Victorian family-run guesthouse, comfortable and friendly, on the north-east side of the city. 5 minutes' walk from the city wall. Non-smoking throughout.

◆◆◆◆
Silver
Award

FOUR SEASONS HOTEL
7 St Peter's Grove, Bootham, York, North Yorkshire YO30 6AQ
T: (01904) 622621
F: (01904) 620976
E: roe@fourseasons.netlineuk.net
I: www.fourseasons_hotel.co.uk

B&B per night:
D £56.00–£63.00

OPEN Feb–Dec

Elegant Victorian hotel, ideally situated in a peaceful cul-de-sac only 7 minutes' stroll from the minster and York's many other historic attractions. Accommodation is in beautifully appointed and tastefully furnished en suite bedrooms, all fully equipped. Four-course English breakfast, cosy lounge, residential licence and private car parking.

Bedrooms: 2 double, 1 twin, 1 triple, 1 family room
Bathrooms: 5 en suite

Parking for 8
CC: Delta, Mastercard, Solo, Switch, Visa, Visa Electron

WELCOME HOST This is a nationally recognised customer care programme which aims to promote the highest standards of service and a warm welcome. Establishments taking part in this initiative are indicated by the ⊕ symbol.

♦♦♦

GREENSIDE

124 Clifton, York, YO30 6BQ
T: (01904) 623631
F: (01904) 623631

B&B per night:
S Min £18.00
D Min £30.00

HB per person:
DY Min £27.50

OPEN All year round

Charming, detached, conservation owner-run guesthouse, fronting on to Clifton Green. Ideally situated, 10 minutes' walk from the city walls and all York's attractions. Offers many facilities, including an enclosed locked car park. All types of ground/first floor bedrooms are available in a warm homely atmosphere.

Bedrooms: 1 single,
3 double, 2 twin, 2 triple
Bathrooms: 3 en suite,
2 public

EM 1800 (LO 1800)
Parking for 6

♦♦♦♦

THE HAZELWOOD

24-25 Portland Street, York, YO31 7EH
T: (01904) 626548
F: (01904) 628032
E: Reservations@thehazelwoodyork.com
I: www.thehazelwoodyork.com

B&B per night:
S £35.00–£70.00
D £63.00–£85.00

OPEN All year round

In the very heart of York, only 400 yards from York Minster yet in an extremely quiet location and with private car park. Enjoy the relaxed atmosphere of our elegant Victorian townhouse providing high quality accommodation in individually designed en suite bedrooms. Wide choice of delicious breakfasts including vegetarian. Completely non-smoking.

Bedrooms: 1 single,
7 double, 4 twin, 2 triple
Bathrooms: 14 en suite

Parking for 11
CC: Barclaycard, Delta,
Eurocard, JCB,
Mastercard, Solo, Switch,
Visa, Visa Electron

♦♦♦

HILLCREST GUEST HOUSE

110 Bishopthorpe Road, York, YO23 1JX
T: (01904) 653160
F: (01904) 656168
E: hillcrest@accommodation.gbr.fm
I: www.accommodation.gbr.fm

B&B per night:
S £19.00–£27.00
D £34.00–£52.00

OPEN All year round

Spaciously, elegant Victorian townhouse 10 minutes' walk from city centre and racecourse. Next to Rowantree Park. Private car park. Highly complimented, generous breakfast selection. Special diets catered for. En suite ground floor room available. Enjoy comfort, cleanliness and personal attention in a relaxed and homely atmosphere. Bargain breaks, November – March. Non-smoking.

Bedrooms: 3 single,
5 double, 2 twin, 1 triple,
2 family rooms
Bathrooms: 7 en suite,
3 public

EM 1800 (LO 1500)
Parking for 8
CC: Barclaycard, Delta,
Eurocard, Mastercard,
Visa

COLOUR MAPS Colour maps at the front of this guide pinpoint all places under which you will find accommodation listed.

◆◆◆

HOLLY LODGE

206 Fulford Road, York, YO10 4DD
T: (01904) 646005
I: www.thehollylodge.co.uk

B&B per night:
S £48.00–£68.00
D £48.00–£68.00

OPEN All year round

Beautifully appointed Georgian Grade II building where you are assured of a warm welcome. 10 minutes' riverside stroll to centre, conveniently located for all York's attractions including Barbican and university. All rooms individually furnished, each overlooking garden or terrace. On-site parking, easy to find. Booking recommended.

Bedrooms: 3 double, 1 twin, 1 family room
Bathrooms: 5 en suite

Parking for 8
CC: Delta, Mastercard, Visa

◆◆◆◆

HOLMWOOD HOUSE HOTEL

114 Holgate Road, York, YO24 4BB
T: (01904) 626183
F: (01904) 670899
E: holmwood.house@dial.pipex.com
I: www.holmwoodhousehotel.co.uk

B&B per night:
S £50.00–£75.00
D £65.00–£90.00

OPEN All year round

Elegant Victorian house with a secure car park. Carefully restored and furnished with antiques. Five minutes' walk from the city walls, 10 minutes' walk from the station. Two family suites available.

Bedrooms: 10 double, 3 twin, 1 triple
Bathrooms: 14 en suite

Parking for 9
CC: Barclaycard, Delta, Mastercard, Solo, Switch, Visa

◆◆◆

LINDEN LODGE

6 Nunthorpe Avenue, Scarcroft Road, York, YO23 1PF
T: (01904) 620107
F: (01904) 620985

B&B per night:
S £22.50–£26.00
D £45.00–£52.00

OPEN All year round

Linden Lodge is a friendly, licensed hotel, with a warm welcome. All rooms have remote control colour TV, welcome tray and hairdryer. Choice of singles, twins, doubles and family rooms, en suite or standard. Situated 10 minutes' walk from city centre, railway station and racecourse. Unrestricted parking.

Bedrooms: 2 single, 7 double, 2 twin, 2 family rooms
Bathrooms: 9 en suite, 1 public

CC: Amex, Barclaycard, Delta, Eurocard, JCB, Maestro, Mastercard, Solo, Switch, Visa, Visa Electron

---

CREDIT CARD BOOKINGS If you book by telephone and are asked for your credit card number it is advisable to check the proprietor's policy should you cancel your reservation.

◆◆◆◆

THE MANOR COUNTRY HOUSE

Acaster Malbis, York, YO23 2UL

T: (01904) 706723
F: (01904) 706723
E: manorhouse@selcom.co.uk
I: www.manorhse.co.uk

B&B per night:
S £38.00–£55.00
D £54.00–£70.00

OPEN All year round

Family-run manor set in 5 acres of beautiful mature grounds around private fishing lake. Enjoy riverside walks. Close to the racecourse and only 10 minutes by car from city centre. Local riverbus to York (Easter to October). Within easy reach of the dales, moors, stately homes and splendid coastline.

Bedrooms: 1 single, 4 double, 2 twin, 3 triple
Bathrooms: 10 en suite

Parking for 15
CC: Barclaycard, Delta, Eurocard, Mastercard, Visa

◆◆

MARTIN'S GUEST HOUSE

5 Longfield Terrace, York, YO30 7DJ
T: (01904) 634551 (Answerphone)
F: (01904) 634551
I: www.smoothhound.co.uk.hotels/martins.html

Bedrooms: 1 single, 3 double, 1 triple
Bathrooms: 2 en suite, 1 public

Parking for 3
CC: Eurocard, Mastercard, Visa

B&B per night:
S £17.00–£18.00
D £36.00–£44.00

OPEN All year round

A charming, lovingly-restored Edwardian townhouse in the heart of historic York. Free parking. Within walking distance of all major attractions.

◆◆◆

MIDWAY HOUSE

145 Fulford Road, York, YO10 4HG

T: (01904) 659272
F: (01904) 659272
E: midwayhouse@btinternet.com
I: www.s-h-systems.co.uk/hotels/midway.html

B&B per night:
S £22.00–£42.00
D £36.00–£62.00

OPEN All year round

Elegant 1897 late-Victorian detached villa, totally non-smoking. Spacious, en suite bedrooms., 4-poster and ground floor rooms available. We are close to the city centre and university and have a spacious on-site car park for 14 cars. Excellent full English breakfast served in a friendly and informal atmosphere.

Bedrooms: 1 single, 8 double, 1 twin, 2 triple
Bathrooms: 10 en suite, 1 public

Parking for 14
CC: Mastercard, Visa

◆◆◆

MONKGATE GUEST HOUSE

65 Monkgate, York, YO31 7PA
T: (01904) 655947
E: jmb@monkgate.swinternet.co.uk

Bedrooms: 2 single, 3 double, 2 twin, 2 family rooms
Bathrooms: 2 en suite, 1 private, 2 public

Parking for 6

B&B per night:
S £19.00–£25.00
D £50.00–£54.00

OPEN All year round

Georgian cottages, tastefully renovated to retain original character, cosy and rambling. Very easy walk to York Minster and city attractions. Private parking. Non-smoking. Families welcome.

ACCESSIBILITY

Look for the 🏠🏠🏠 symbols which indicate accessibility for wheelchair users. A list of establishments is at the front of this guide.

◆◆◆ **MOORGARTH GUEST HOUSE**
158 Fulford Road, York, YO10 4DA
T: (01904) 636768 (Answerphone available)
F: (01904) 636768
E: moorgarth@fsbdial.co.uk
I: www.avaweb.co.uk/moorgarth.york.html

Bedrooms: 1 single, 4 double, 2 twin, 1 triple, 1 family room
Bathrooms: 8 en suite, 1 private

Parking for 5
CC: Amex, Barclaycard, Delta, Maestro, Mastercard, Solo, Switch, Visa, Visa Electron

B&B per night:
S £19.00–£23.00
D £38.00–£46.00

OPEN All year round

Victorian townhouse with a warm, friendly atmosphere, near all tourist attractions and 10 minutes' walk from the city centre. All rooms en suite. Car parking available.

◆◆◆

OAKLANDS GUEST HOUSE
351 Strensall Road, Old Earswick, York, YO32 9SW
T: (01904) 768443 (Answerphone available)
E: mavmo@oaklands5.fsnet.co.uk
I: www.business.thisisyork.co.uk/oaklands/

B&B per night:
S £18.00–£26.00
D £36.00–£42.00

OPEN All year round

A very warm welcome awaits you at our attractive and comfortable home set in open countryside, yet only 3 miles north of York. Within very close reach of the A1237 York ring road, the A64 and A19, giving ready access to the moors, coast and dales and many other great attractions.

Bedrooms: 1 double, 1 twin, 1 triple
Bathrooms: 2 en suite, 1 public

Parking for 7

◆◆◆ **ORILLIA HOUSE**
89 The Village, Stockton-on-the-Forest, York, YO32 9UP
T: (01904) 400600
F: (01904) 400101
E: orillia@globalnet.co.uk

Bedrooms: 4 double, 1 twin, 2 triple
Bathrooms: 7 en suite

Parking for 10
CC: Barclaycard, Mastercard, Visa

B&B per night:
S £24.00–£26.00

OPEN All year round

A warm welcome awaits you in this 300-year-old house of charm and character, opposite church. Three miles north east of York.

◆◆◆

PRIORY HOTEL & GARTH RESTAURANT
126-128 Fulford Road, York, YO10 4BE
T: (01904) 625280
F: (01904) 637330
E: reservations@priory-hotelyork.co.uk
I: www.priory-hotelyork.co.uk

B&B per night:
S £40.00–£55.00
D £55.00–£80.00

HB per person:
DY £40.00–£45.00

OPEN All year round

A Victorian-style family-run hotel, only a few minutes' walk to city centre. The university, and racecourse are only 1.5 miles, the McArthur Glen Centre and Golf Course 2 miles. Pam's Bar and Garth Restaurant. Ample parking. Please send for brochure.

Bedrooms: 1 single, 6 double, 3 twin, 2 triple, 4 family rooms
Bathrooms: 16 en suite

EM 1830 (LO 2130)
Parking for 24
CC: Amex, Barclaycard, Delta, Diners, Mastercard, Switch, Visa

---

◆◆◆ **QUEEN ANNE'S GUEST HOUSE**
24 Queen Anne's Road, Bootham, York, YO30 7AA
T: (01904) 629389
F: (01904) 619529
E: info@queenannes.fsnet.co.uk
I: www.s-h-systems.co.uk/hotels/queenann

Bedrooms: 1 single, 4 double, 1 twin, 1 family room
Bathrooms: 5 en suite, 1 public

Parking for 3
CC: Mastercard, Visa

B&B per night:
S £16.00–£18.00
D £36.00–£42.00

OPEN All year round

Spick and span. Warm and friendly. Five minutes' walk to city centre. All rooms with TV, tea and coffee, most en suite. Hearty English breakfast.

◆◆◆

ROMLEY GUEST HOUSE

2 Millfield Road, Scarcroft Road, York,
YO23 1NQ
T: (01904) 652822
E: info@romleyhouse.co.uk
I: www.romleyhouse.co.uk

B&B per night:
S £18.00–£21.00
D £36.00–£52.00

OPEN All year round

Family-run guesthouse, few minutes'
walk form city centre and all
attractions, offers happy
atmosphere, hearty breakfast, home
comforts. All rooms are well
appointed (en suite available) with
colour TV, clock radio alarms, tea/
coffee-making facilities. Comfortable
residents' lounge with licensed bar.

Bedrooms: 1 single,
2 double, 1 twin, 1 triple,
1 family room
Bathrooms: 2 en suite,
1 public, 1 private
shower

Parking for 1
CC: Delta, Eurocard,
Mastercard, Visa

◆◆◆

ST DENY'S HOTEL

51 St Denys Road, York, YO1 9QD
T: (01904) 622207 & 646776
F: (01904) 624800
E: info@stdenyshotel.co.uk
I: www.stdenyshotel.co.uk

B&B per night:
S £35.00–£50.00
D £45.00–£80.00

OPEN All year round

A warm welcome awaits you at St
Deny's. City centre location within
the walls of historic York, with on-
site parking. Newly refurbished
licensed bar. Corporate accounts and
group bookings welcome. With the
Jorvik Viking Centre 2 minutes' walk
away, we offer the ideal base from
which to explore this beautiful city.

Bedrooms: 2 single,
5 double, 3 twin, 3 triple
Bathrooms: 13 en suite

Parking for 9
CC: Barclaycard, Eurocard,
JCB, Maestro, Mastercard,
Solo, Switch, Visa, Visa
Electron

◆◆◆

ST PAUL'S HOTEL

120 Holgate Road, York, YO24 4BB
T: (01904) 611514
E: normfran@supernet.com

Bedrooms: 1 single,
1 double, 2 triple,
2 family rooms
Bathrooms: 6 en suite

EM
Parking for 8

B&B per night:
S Min £25.00
D Min £50.00

OPEN All year round

Close to York's many attractions, this small, family-run hotel has a warm atmosphere and
serves a hearty breakfast. Come as a guest and leave as a friend.

◆◆◆

SAXON HOUSE HOTEL

Fishergate, 71-73 Fulford Road,
York, YO10 4BD
T: (01904) 622106
F: (01904) 633764
E: saxon@househotel.freeserve.co.
uk
I: www.saxonhousehotel.co.uk

Bedrooms: 2 single,
8 double, 2 triple,
2 family rooms
Bathrooms: 14 en suite

Parking for 16
CC: Barclaycard, Delta,
Mastercard, Switch, Visa

B&B per night:
S £30.00–£46.00
D £48.00–£65.00

OPEN All year round

Victorian hotel offering a friendly welcome and personal service. Close to all city-centre
attractions, golf course, race course, university, Barbican leisure centre and Designer
Outlet.

QUALITY ASSURANCE SCHEME

Diamond ratings and awards were correct at the time of going to press but
are subject to change. Please check at the time of booking.

◆◆◆ SKELTON GRANGE FARMHOUSE

Orchard View, Skelton, York,
YO30 1XQ
T: (01904) 470780
F: (01904) 470229
E: info@skelton-farm.co.uk
I: www.skelton-farm.co.uk

Bedrooms: 1 single,
2 double, 1 twin,
1 family room
Bathrooms: 5 en suite

EM
Parking for 6
CC: Barclaycard,
Mastercard, Solo, Switch,
Visa, Visa Electron

B&B per night:
S £25.00–£35.00
D £40.00–£50.00

OPEN All year round

Welcoming 17thC farmhouse offers quiet, rural comforts and stylish en suite rooms, 2.5 miles from York. Gardens, private parking. Traditional pubs and restaurants nearby.

◆◆◆

Anne and Dave offer a warm and friendly welcome to their very well-appointed guesthouse. Excellently situated for all of York's attractions, just 10 minutes' walk to city centre and racecourse. All rooms have tea/coffee, colour TV, radio/alarms and fridge. Parking facilities available.

SOUTHLAND'S GUEST HOUSE

69 Nunmill Street, South Bank, York,
YO23 1NT
T: (01904) 631203
I: www.southlandsguesthouse.freeserve.
co.uk/

Bedrooms: 2 double,
1 twin, 2 triple
Bathrooms: 4 en suite,
2 public

Parking for 4
CC: Barclaycard, Delta,
Eurocard, Mastercard,
Visa

B&B per night:
D £38.00–£46.00

HB per person:
DY £19.00–£25.00

OPEN All year round

◆◆◆ TREE TOPS

21 St Mary's, Bootham, York,
YO30 7DD
T: (01904) 658053
F: (01904) 658053
E: treetops.guesthouse@virgin.net.
co.uk

Bedrooms: 1 single,
6 double, 1 twin
Bathrooms: 7 en suite,
1 private

Parking for 7
CC: Mastercard, Visa

B&B per night:
S £29.00–£29.00
D £50.00–£54.00

OPEN All year round

Elegant Victorian guesthouse, 5 minutes' walk from York Minster, river and city centre. En suite and standard rooms, all with colour TV and hospitality trays. No smoking, please.

◆◆◆ TYBURN HOUSE

11 Albemarle Road, The Mount,
York, YO23 1EN
T: (01904) 655069
F: (01904) 655069
E: york@tyburnhotel.freeserve.co.
uk

Bedrooms: 2 single,
3 double, 3 twin, 3 triple,
2 family rooms
Bathrooms: 12 en suite,
1 private

B&B per night:
S £27.00–£35.00
D £54.00–£70.00

OPEN Mar–Oct

Family-owned and run guesthouse overlooking the racecourse. In a quiet and beautiful area, close to the city centre and railway station.

◆◆◆ WARRENS GUEST HOUSE

30 Scarcroft Road, York, YO23 1NF
T: (01904) 643139
F: (01904) 658297
I: www.warrens.ndo.co.uk

Bedrooms: 2 double,
1 twin, 3 triple
Bathrooms: 6 en suite

Parking for 8
CC: Mastercard, Visa

B&B per night:
S Min £35.00
D £45.00–£60.00

OPEN Mar–Nov

Victorian townhouse approximately 350 yards city walls. Well furnished en suite rooms, residents' lounge. Choice of breakfast in the conservatory. Private floodlit car park. CCTV.

TOWN INDEX

This can be found at the back of this guide. If you know where you want to stay, the index will give you the page number listing accommodation in your chosen town, city or village.

♦♦♦

WESTGATE HOTEL
132 The Mount, York, YO24 1AS
T: (01904) 653303
F: (01904) 635717
E: westgateyork@gofornet.co.uk
I: www.smoothhound.co.uk/hotels/
westgate.html

Elegant Georgian townhouse situated on the level, 5 minutes' walk from city walls at Micklegate Bar. Town centre, railway station and racecourse are 10 minutes' walk away. Full English breakfast, diets catered for. All rooms with shower en suite, tea/coffee facilities, colour TV. Car parking.

Bedrooms: 2 single,
2 double, 2 triple,
2 family rooms
Bathrooms: 10 en suite

Parking for 4
CC: Delta, Eurocard,
Mastercard, Solo, Switch,
Visa, Visa Electron

B&B per night:
S £27.00–£30.00
D £50.00–£56.00

OPEN All year round

♦♦♦

YORK LODGE GUEST HOUSE
64 Bootham Crescent, Bootham,
York, YO30 7AH
T: (01904) 654289 &
07860 449460 (Mobile)
F: (01904) 488803
E: moore.york@virgin.net

Family-run guesthouse, within 10 minutes' walk of city centre attractions, offering a warm, friendly and relaxing stay.

Bedrooms: 1 single,
3 double, 2 twin, 1 triple,
1 family room
Bathrooms: 4 en suite,
2 public

Parking for 3
CC: Barclaycard,
Mastercard, Visa

B&B per night:
S £20.00–£24.00
D £40.00–£48.00

OPEN All year round

AT-A-GLANCE SYMBOLS
Symbols at the end of each accommodation entry give useful information about services and facilities. A key to symbols can be found inside the back cover flap. Keep this open for easy reference.

YORKSHIRE

A brief guide to the main Towns and Villages
offering accommodation in **YORKSHIRE**

AMPLEFORTH, NORTH YORKSHIRE -
Stone-built village in Hambleton Hills. Famous for its abbey and college, a Benedictine public school, founded in 1802, of which Cardinal Hume was once abbot. Romanesque-style church by Sir Giles Scott, completed in 1961 just after his death.

ASKRIGG, NORTH YORKSHIRE -
The name of this dales village means "ash tree ridge". It is centred on a steep main street of high, narrow 3-storey houses and thrived on cotton and later wool in 18th C. Once famous for its clock making.

AUSTWICK, NORTH YORKSHIRE -
Picturesque, peaceful dales village with pleasant cottages, a green, an old cross and an Elizabethan Hall.

AYSGARTH, NORTH YORKSHIRE - Famous for its beautiful Falls - a series of 3 cascades extending for half a mile on the River Ure in Wensleydale. There is a coach and carriage museum at Yore Mill and a National Park Centre. A single-arched Elizabethan bridge spans the River Ure.

BEDALE, NORTH YORKSHIRE - Ancient church of St Gregory and Georgian Bedale Hall occupy commanding positions over this market town situated in good hunting country. The hall, which contains interesting architectural features including great ballroom and flying-type staircase, now houses a library and museum.

BEVERLEY, EAST RIDING OF YORKSHIRE -
Beverley's most famous landmark is its beautiful medieval Minster dating from 1220, with Percy family tomb. Many attractive squares and streets, notably Wednesday and Saturday Market and North Bar Gateway. Famous racecourse. Market cross dates from 1714.

BOLTON PERCY, NORTH YORKSHIRE -
Secluded village of limestone with red-brick buildings. Exceptional 15th C parish church contains medieval stained glass and monument to Fairfaxes. 15th C half-timbered gatehouses with carved timber-work.

BRIDLINGTON, NORTH YORKSHIRE -
Lively seaside resort with long sandy beaches, Leisure World and busy harbour with fishing trips in cobles. Priory church of St Mary whose Bayle Gate is now a museum. Mementoes of flying pioneer, Amy Johnson, in Sewerby Hall. Harbour Museum and Aquarium.

BRIGG, NORTH YORKSHIRE - Small town at an ancient crossing of the River Ancholme, granted a weekly Thursday market and annual horsefair by Henry III in 1235. Once a manufacturing town for agricultural implements.

CASTLETON, DERBYSHIRE - Large village in a spectacular Peak District setting with ruined Peveril Castle and 4 great show caverns, where the Blue John stone and lead were mined. One cavern offers a mile-long underground boat journey.

CROPTON, NORTH YORKSHIRE -
Moorland village at the top of a high ridge with stone houses, some of cruck construction, a Victorian church and the remains of a 12th C moated castle. Cropton Forest and Cropton Brewery nearby.

DANBY, NORTH YORKSHIRE - Eskdale village 12 miles west of Whitby. Visit the Moors Centre at Danby Lodge, a former shooting lodge in 13 acres of grounds including woodland and riverside meadow. Remains of medieval Danby Castle.

DONCASTER, SOUTH YORKSHIRE -
Ancient Roman town famous for its heavy industries, butterscotch and racecourse (St Leger), also centre of agricultural area. Attractions include 18th C Mansion House, Cusworth Hall Museum, Doncaster Museum, St George's Church, The Dome and Doncaster Leisure Park.

EASINGWOLD, NORTH YORKSHIRE -
Market town of charm and character with a cobbled square and many fine Georgian buildings.

EBBERSTON, NORTH YORKSHIRE -
Picturesque village with a Norman church and hall, overlooking the Vale of Pickering.

FILEY, NORTH YORKSHIRE - Resort with elegant Regency buildings along the front and 6 miles of sandy beaches bounded by natural breakwater, Filey Brigg. Starting point of the Cleveland Way. St Oswald's church, overlooking a ravine, belonged to Augustinian canons until the Dissolution.

GARFORTH, WEST YORKSHIRE - Town 7 miles east of Leeds, between Temple Newsam Estate and Lotherton Hall. Old coal mining district of Leeds.

GOATHLAND, NORTH YORKSHIRE -
Spacious village with several large greens grazed by sheep, an ideal centre for walking the North York Moors. Nearby are several waterfalls, among them Mallyan Spout. Plough Monday celebrations held in January. Location for filming of TV "Heartbeat" series.

GRASSINGTON, NORTH YORKSHIRE -
Tourists visit this former lead-mining village to see its "smiddy", antique and craft shops and Upper Wharfedale Museum of country trades. Popular with fishermen and walkers. Cobbled market square, numerous prehistoric sites. Grassington Feast in October. National Park Centre.

HALIFAX, WEST YORKSHIRE - Founded on the cloth trade, and famous for its building society, textiles, carpets and toffee. Most notable landmark is Piece Hall where wool merchants traded, now restored to house shops, museums and art gallery. Home also to Eureka! The Museum for Children.

HARROGATE, NORTH YORKSHIRE - Major conference, exhibition and shopping centre, renowned for its spa heritage and award-winning floral displays, spacious parks and gardens. Famous for antiques, toffee, fine shopping and excellent tea shops, also its Royal Pump Rooms and Baths. Annual Great Yorkshire Show in July.

HARWOOD DALE, NORTH YORKSHIRE -
A relatively undiscovered, idyllic corner of the North York Moors between Captain Cook and Herriot country. On the fringe of Dalby Forest and the Cleveland Way, it is ideal for walkers and sightseeing. The dale is easily accessible from the A171.

HAWES, NORTH YORKSHIRE -
The capital of Upper Wensleydale on the famous Pennine Way, Yorkshire's highest market town and renowned for great cheeses. Popular with walkers. Dales National Park Information Centre and Folk Museum. Nearby is spectacular Hardraw Force waterfall.

HAWORTH, WEST YORKSHIRE - Famous since 1820 as home of the Bronte family. The Parsonage is now a Bronte Museum where furniture and possessions of the family are displayed. Moors and Bronte waterfalls nearby and steam trains on the Keighley and Worth Valley Railway pass through.

HEBDEN BRIDGE, WEST YORKSHIRE -
Originally a small town on packhorse route, Hebden Bridge grew into a booming mill town in 18th C with rows of "up-and-down" houses of several storeys built against hillsides. Ancient "pace-egg play" custom held on Good Friday.

HELMSLEY, NORTH YORKSHIRE -
Delightful small market town with red roofs, warm stone buildings and cobbled market square, on the River Rye at the entrance to Ryedale and the North York Moors. Remains of 12th C castle, several inns and All Saints' Church.

HOLMFIRTH, WEST YORKSHIRE - Village on the edge of the Peak District National Park, famous as the location for the filming of the TV series "Last of the Summer Wine".

HUDDERSFIELD, WEST YORKSHIRE -
Founded on wool and cloth, has a famous choral society. Town centre redeveloped, but several good Victorian buildings remain, including railway station, St Peter's Church, Tolson Memorial Museum, art gallery and nearby Colne Valley Museum.

HULL - Busy seaport with a modern city centre and excellent shopping facilities. Maritime traditions in the town, docks museum, and the home of William Wilberforce, the slavery abolitionist, whose house is now a museum. The Humber Bridge is 5 miles west.

ILKLEY, WEST YORKSHIRE - Former spa with an elegant shopping centre and famous for its ballad. The 16th C manor house, now a museum, displays local prehistoric and Roman relics. Popular walk leads up Heber's Ghyll to Ilkley Moor, with the mysterious Swastika Stone and White Wells, 18th C plunge baths.

- **INGLETON, NORTH YORKSHIRE** - Thriving tourist centre for fell-walkers, climbers and pot-holers. Popular walks up beautiful Twiss Valley to Ingleborough Summit, Whernside, White Scar Caves and waterfalls.

K KETTLEWELL, NORTH YORKSHIRE - Set in the spectacular scenery of the Yorkshire Dales National Park in Wharfedale, this former market town is a convenient stopping place for climbers and walkers. Dramatic rock formation of Kilnsey Crag is 3 miles south.

- **KIRKBYMOORSIDE, NORTH YORKSHIRE** - Attractive market town with remains of Norman castle. Good centre for exploring moors. Nearby are wild daffodils of Farndale.

- **KNARESBOROUGH, NORTH YORKSHIRE** - Picturesque market town on the River Nidd. The 14th C keep is the best-preserved part of John of Gaunt's castle, and the manor house with its chequerboard walls was presented by James I to his son Charles as a fishing lodge. Prophetess Mother Shipton's cave. Boating on river.

L LEEDS, WEST YORKSHIRE - Large city with excellent modern shopping centre and splendid Victorian architecture. Museums and galleries including Temple Newsam House (the Hampton Court of the North), Tetley's Brewery Wharf and the Royal Armouries Museum; also home of Opera North.

- **LEVISHAM, NORTH YORKSHIRE** - Small, pretty North York Moors village at the edge of Newtondale, a deep natural gorge which runs south from the moors to Pickering, 5 miles away, and through which runs the moorland steam railway. Ideal base for exploring this scenic area and the East Coast.

- **LEYBURN, NORTH YORKSHIRE** - Attractive dales market town where Mary Queen of Scots was reputedly captured after her escape from Bolton Castle. Fine views over Wensleydale from nearby.

M MALHAM, NORTH YORKSHIRE - Hamlet of stone cottages amid magnificent rugged limestone scenery in the Yorkshire Dales National Park. Malham Cove is a curving, sheer white cliff 240 ft high. Malham Tarn, one of Yorkshire's few natural lakes, belongs to the National Trust. National Park Centre.

- **MALTON, NORTH YORKSHIRE** - Thriving farming town on the River Derwent with large livestock market. Famous for racehorse training. The local museum has Roman remains and the Eden Camp Modern History Theme Museum transports visitors back to wartime Britain. Castle Howard within easy reach.

- **MASHAM, NORTH YORKSHIRE** - Famous market town on the River Ure, with a large market square. St Mary's Church has Norman tower and 13th C spire. Theakston's "Old Peculier" ale is brewed here, also home of the Black Sheep Brewery. Druids Temple, a replica of Stonehenge.

- **MIDDLEHAM, NORTH YORKSHIRE** - Town famous for racehorse training, with cobbled squares and houses of local stone. Norman castle, once principal residence of Warwick the Kingmaker and later Richard III. Ancient stronghold of the Neville family was taken over by the Crown after the Battle of Barnet in 1471.

N NORTHALLERTON, NORTH YORKSHIRE - Formerly a staging post on coaching route to the North and later a railway town. Today a lively market town and administrative capital of North Yorkshire. Parish church of All Saints dates from 1200. Dickens stayed at The Fleece.

O OTLEY, WEST YORKSHIRE - Charming market and small manufacturing town in Lower Wharfedale, the birthplace of Thomas Chippendale, painted by Turner. Old inns, medieval 5-arched bridge, local history museum, maypole, historic All Saints' Church. Beautiful countryside. Annual carnival.

P PATELEY BRIDGE, NORTH YORKSHIRE - Market town at centre of Upper Nidderdale. Flax and linen industries once flourished in this remote and beautiful setting. Remains of Bronze Age settlements and disused lead mines.

- **PICKERING, NORTH YORKSHIRE** - Market town and tourist centre on edge of North York Moors. Parish church has complete set of 15th C wall paintings depicting lives of saints. Part of 12th C castle still stands. Beck Isle Museum. The North York Moors Railway begins here.

R RAVENSCAR, NORTH YORKSHIRE - Splendidly-positioned small coastal resort with magnificent views over Robin Hood's Bay. Its Old Peak is the end of the famous Lyke Wake Walk or "corpse way".

- **RICHMOND, NORTH YORKSHIRE** - Market town on edge of Swaledale with 11th C castle, Georgian and Victorian buildings surrounding cobbled market-place. Green Howards' Museum is in the former Holy Trinity Church. Attractions include the Georgian Theatre, restored Theatre Royal, Richmondshire Museum, Easby Abbey.

- **RIPON, NORTH YORKSHIRE** - Ancient city with impressive cathedral containing Saxon crypt which houses church treasures from all over Yorkshire. Charter granted in 886 by Alfred the Great. "Setting the Watch" tradition kept nightly by horn-blower in Market Square. Fountains Abbey nearby.

- **ROBIN HOOD'S BAY, NORTH YORKSHIRE** - Picturesque village of red-roofed cottages with main street running from clifftop down ravine to seashore, a magnet for artists. Scene of much smuggling and shipwrecks in 18th C. Robin Hood reputed to have escaped to continent by boat from here.

- **RUNSWICK BAY, NORTH YORKSHIRE** - Holiday and fishing village.

S SCARBOROUGH, NORTH YORKSHIRE - Large, popular East Coast seaside resort, formerly a spa town. Beautiful gardens and two splendid sandy beaches. Castle ruins date from 1100; fine Georgian and Victorian houses. Scarborough Millennium depicts 1,000 years of town's history. Sea Life Centre.

- **SCUNTHORPE, LINCOLNSHIRE** - Consisted of 5 small villages until 1860 when extensive ironstone beds were discovered. Today an industrial "garden town" with some interesting modern buildings. Nearby Normanby Hall contains fine examples of Regency furniture.

- **SELBY, NORTH YORKSHIRE** - Small market town on the River Ouse, believed to be birthplace of Henry I, with a magnificent abbey containing much fine Norman and Early English architecture.

- **SETTLE, NORTH YORKSHIRE** - Town of narrow streets and Georgian houses in an area of great limestone hills and crags. Panoramic view from Castleberg Crag which stands 300 ft above town.

- **SHEFFIELD** - Local iron ore and coal gave Sheffield its prosperous steel and cutlery industries. The modern city centre has many interesting buildings - cathedral, Cutlers' Hall, Crucible Theatre, Graves and Mappin Art Galleries. Meadowhall Shopping Centre nearby.

- **SKIPTON, NORTH YORKSHIRE** - Pleasant market town at gateway to dales, with farming community atmosphere, a Palladian Town Hall, parish church and fully roofed castle at the top of the High Street. The Clifford family motto, "Desoramis" is sculpted in huge letters on the parapet over the castle gateway.

- **STAINTONDALE, NORTH YORKSHIRE** - Moors village north-west of Scarborough with shire horse farm and visitor centre.

T THIRSK, NORTH YORKSHIRE - Thriving market town with cobbled square surrounded by old shops and inns. St Mary's Church is probably the best example of Perpendicular work in Yorkshire. House of Thomas Lord - founder of Lord's Cricket Ground - is now a folk museum.

- **THORNTON DALE, NORTH YORKSHIRE** - Picturesque village with Thorntondale Beck, traversed by tiny stone footbridges at the edge of pretty cottage gardens.

- **THWAITE, NORTH YORKSHIRE** - Quiet village, ideal for walking the fells of Great Shunner, Kisdon, High Seat, Rogan's Seat and Lovely Seat.

W WAKEFIELD, WEST YORKSHIRE - Thriving city with cathedral church of All Saints boasting 247-ft spire. Old Bridge, a 9-arched structure, has fine medieval chantry chapels of St Mary's. Georgian architecture and good shopping centre (The Ridings). National Coal Mining Museum for England nearby.

- **WETHERBY, WEST YORKSHIRE** - Prosperous market town on the River Wharfe, noted for horse-racing.

- **WHITBY, NORTH YORKSHIRE** - Holiday town with narrow streets and steep alleys at the mouth of the River Esk. Captain James Cook, the famous navigator, lived in Grape Lane. 199 steps lead to St Mary's Church and St Hilda's Abbey overlooking harbour. Dracula connections. Gothic weekend every April.

Y YORK - Ancient walled city nearly 2,000 years old, containing many well-preserved medieval buildings. Its Minster has over 100 stained glass windows and is the largest Gothic cathedral in England. Attractions include Castle Museum, National Railway Museum, Jorvik Viking Centre and York Dungeon.

Ratings you can trust

English Tourism Council

GUEST
ACCOMMODATION

When you're looking for a place to stay, you need a rating system you can trust. The **English Tourism Council's** ratings are your clear guide to what to expect, in an easy-to-understand form. Properties are visited annually by our trained impartial assessors, so you can have confidence that your accommodation has been thoroughly checked and rated for quality before you make a booking.

Using a simple One to Five Diamond rating, the system puts great emphasis on quality and is based on research which shows exactly what consumers are looking for when choosing accommodation.

"Guest Accommodation" covers a wide variety of serviced accommodation for which England is renowned, including guesthouses, bed and breakfasts, inns and farmhouses. Establishments are rated from One to Five Diamonds. The same minimum requirement for facilities and services applies to all Guest Accommodation from One to Five Diamonds. Progressively higher levels of quality and customer care must be provided for each of the One to Five Diamond ratings. The rating reflects the unique character of Guest Accommodation, and covers areas such as cleanliness, service and hospitality, bedrooms, bathrooms and food quality.

Look out, too, for the English Tourism Council's Gold and Silver Awards, which are awarded to those establishments which not only achieve the overall quality required for their Diamond rating, but also reach the highest levels of quality in those specific areas which guests identify as being really important for them. They will reflect the quality of comfort and cleanliness you'll find in the bedrooms and bathrooms and the quality of service you'll enjoy throughout your stay.

The ratings are your sign of quality assurance, giving you the confidence to book the accommodation that meets your expectations.

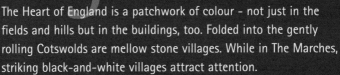

HEART OF ENGLAND

Heart of England

The Heart of England is a patchwork of colour - not just in the fields and hills but in the buildings, too. Folded into the gently rolling Cotswolds are mellow stone villages. While in The Marches, striking black-and-white villages attract attention.

The cosmopolitan cities of Birmingham and Coventry rub shoulders with classic spa and market towns. And the lively university city of Nottingham is filled with cinemas, wine bars, restaurants and clubs. This is Shakespeare country and it's also home to Althorp House, the resting place of Princess Diana.

If you happen to be in the Staffordshire village of Wetton, be sure to time your visit for the annual World Toe-Wrestling Championships in June!

The counties of
Derbyshire, Gloucestershire,
Herefordshire, Leicestershire, Lincolnshire
Northamptonshire, Nottinghamshire,
Rutland, Shropshire, Staffordshire,
Warwickshire, Worcestershire
and West Midlands

FOR MORE INFORMATION CONTACT:
Heart of England Tourist Board
Larkhill Road, Worcester WR5 2EZ
Tel: (01905) 761100
Fax: (01905) 763450

The Pictures:
1 Darwin Statue, Shrewsbury;
2 Anne Hathaway's Cottage,
   Warwickshire;
3 Warwick Castle.

Where to Go in the Heart of England - see pages 194–198
Where to Stay in the Heart of England - see pages 199–276

Whilst in the
HEART OF ENGLAND ...

You will find hundreds of interesting places to visit during your stay, just some of which are listed in these pages.

Contact any Tourist Information Centre in the region for more ideas on days out in the Heart of England.

Acton Scott Historic Working Farm
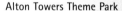

Acton Scott Church, Stretton, Warwickshire SY6 6QN
Tel: (01694) 781306
Demonstrates farming and rural life in south Shropshire at the close of the 19thC.

Alton Towers Theme Park

Alton, Stoke-on-Trent, Staffordshire ST10 4DB
Tel: 0870 5204060
Theme Park with over 125 rides and attractions including Oblivion, Nemesis, Haunted House, Runaway Mine Train, Congo River Rapids, Log Flume and many children's rides.

The American Adventure

Ilkeston, Derbyshire DE7 5SX
Tel: (01773) 531521
The American Adventure has action and entertainment for all ages. The Missile white-knuckle rollercoaster, Europe's tallest skycoaster and the world's wettest log flume.

Belton House, Park and Gardens

Belton, Grantham, Lincolnshire NG32 2LS
Tel: (01476) 566116
The crowning achievement of restoration country house architecture, built in 1685-1688 for Sir John Brownlow with alterations by James Wyatt in 1777.

Belvoir Castle

Belvoir, Grantham, Lincolnshire NG32 1PD
Tel: (01476) 870262
The present castle is the fourth to be built on this site and dates from 1816. Art treasures include works by Poussin, Rubens, Holbein and Reynolds. Queen's Royal Lancers display.

Birmingham Botanical Gardens and Glasshouses

Edgbaston, Birmingham, West Midlands B15 3TR
Tel: (0121) 454 1860
Fifteen acres of ornamental gardens and glasshouses. Widest range of plants in the Midlands from tropical rainforest to arid desert. Aviaries with exotic birds, child's play area.

Black Country Living Museum

Dudley, West Midlands DY1 4SQ
Tel: (0121) 557 9643
One of Britain's best open-air museums. Wander around original shops and houses, ride on fair attractions and take a look down a mine.

Museum of British Road Transport

Coventry, West Midlands CV1 1PN
Tel: (024) 7683 2425
Two hundred cars and commercial vehicles, 200 cycles and 75 motorcycles from the 19thC to date, plus the 'Thrust 2' land speed story.

Butlins Family Entertainment Resort

Roman Bank, Skegness, Lincolnshire PE25 1NJ
Tel: (01754) 762311
New skyline pavilion, toyland, sub tropical waterworld, tenpin bowling and entertainment's centre. Live shows.

Cadbury World

Bournville, Birmingham, West Midlands B30 2LD
Tel: (0121) 451 4180
The story of Cadbury's chocolate. Includes chocolate-making demonstration and childrens attractions.

Chatsworth House and Garden

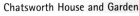

Bakewell, Derbyshire DE45 1PP
Tel: (01246) 582204

Built in 1687-1707 with a collection of fine pictures, books, drawings and furniture. Garden laid out by 'Capability' Brown with fountains, cascades, a farmyard and playground.

Cotswold Farm Park

Guiting Power, Cheltenham, Gloucestershire GL54 5UG
Tel: (01451) 850307

Collection of rare breeds of British farm animals. Pets' corner, adventure playground, farm trail, picnic area, gift shop and cafe. Lambing and other seasonal farming displays.

Drayton Manor Family Theme Park

Tamworth, Staffordshire B78 3TW
Tel: (01827) 287979

A major theme park and zoo, with 100 rides and attractions. Set in 250 acres of countryside with lakes, nature trail, farmyard, restaurants and bars.

The Heights of Abraham Cable Cars, Caverns and Country Park

Matlock Bath, Matlock, Derbyshire DE4 3PD
Tel: (01629) 582365

A spectacular cable car ride takes you to the summit where there are a wide variety of attractions for young and old alike. Gift shop and coffee shop.

Ironbridge Gorge Museum

Ironbridge, Telford, Shropshire TF8 7AW
Tel: (01952) 433522

World's first cast-iron bridge. Museum of the River Visitor Centre, Tar Tunnel, Jackfield Tile Museum, Coalport China Museum, Rosehill House, Blists Hill Museum and Museum of Iron.

Lincoln Castle

Castle Hill, Lincoln, Lincolnshire LN1 3AA
Tel: (01522) 511068

A medieval castle including towers and ramparts with a Magna Carta exhibition, a prison chapel experience, reconstructed Westgate and popular events throughout the summer.

Midland Railway Centre

Butterley Station, Ripley, Derbyshire DE5 3QZ
Tel: (01773) 747674

Over 50 locomotives and over 100 items of historic rolling stock of Midland and LMS origin with a steam-hauled passenger service, a museum site, country and farm park.

National Sea Life Centre

Brindleyplace, Birmingham, West Midlands B1 2HL
Tel: (0121) 633 4700

Over 55 fascinating displays. The opportunity to come face-to-face with hundreds of sea creatures, from sharks to shrimps.

The National Tramway Museum

Crich, Matlock, Derbyshire DE4 5DP
Tel: (01773) 852565

A collection of over 70 trams from Britain and overseas dating from 1873-1957. Tram rides on a 1.6 km (1-mile) route, a period street scene, depots, a power station, workshops and exhibition.

The Pictures:
1 Rockingham Castle, Northamptonshire;
2 Chatsworth House, Derbyshire;
3 South Shropshire Hills;
4 New Place, Stratford-upon-Avon;
5 Brindley Place, Birmingham;
6 Robin Hood Statue, Nottingham;
7 Alderton, Gloucestershire;
8 Rutland Water.

Severn Valley Railway

Bewdley, Worcestershire DY12 1BG
Tel: (01299) 403816
Preserved standard gauge steam railway running 2.6 km (16 miles) between Kidderminster, Bewdley and Bridgnorth. Collection of locomotives and passenger coaches.

Shakespeare's Birthplace

Stratford-upon-Avon, Warwickshire CV37 6QW
Tel: (01789) 204016
The world famous house where William Shakespeare was born in 1564 and where he grew up. See the highly acclaimed exhibition 'Shakespeare's World'.

Nottingham Industrial Museum

Wollaton Park, Nottingham, Nottinghamshire NG8 2AE
Tel: (0115) 915 3910
An 18thC stables presenting the history of Nottingham's industries: printing, pharmacy, hosiery and lace. There is also a Victorian beam engine, a horse gin and transport.

Ye Olde Pork Pie Shoppe and the Sausage Shop

Melton Mowbray. Leicestershire LE13 1NW
Tel: (01664) 562341
Oldest and only remaining pork pie bakery producing authentic Melton Mowbray pork pies. Learn why Melton Mowbray became the original home to the pork pie industry. Demonstrations and tastings. Adjacent Dickinson & Morris Sausage Shop.

Peak District Mining Museum

Matlock Bath, Matlock, Derbyshire DE4 3NR
Tel: (01629) 583834
Explore 3,500 years of lead mining history with displays, hands-on exhibits and climbing shafts. Go underground and learn to pan for gold. Plus 'Hazards of Mining' display.

Rugby School Museum

Little Church Street, Rugby, Warwickshire CV21 3AW
Tel: (01788) 556109
Rugby School Museum tells the story of the school, scene of Tom Brown's Schooldays, and contains the earlier memorabilia of the game invented on the school close.

The Shrewsbury Quest

Abbey Foregate, Shrewsbury, Shropshire SY2 6AH
Tel: (01743) 243324
Twelfth-century medieval visitor attraction. Solve mysteries, create illuminated manuscripts, play medieval games and relax in the unique herb gardens. Gift shop and cafe.

Shugborough Estate

Shugborough, Milford, Staffordshire ST17 0XB
Tel: (01889) 881388
Eighteenth-century mansion house with fine collection of furniture. Gardens and park contain beautiful neo-classical monuments.

Skegness Natureland Seal Sanctuary

The Promenade, Skegnes, Lincolnshire PE25 1DB
Tel: (01754) 764345
Collection of performing seals, baby seals, penguins, aquarium, crocodiles, snakes, terrapins, scorpions, tropical birds, butterflies (May-October) and pets.

Snibston Discovery Park

Coalville, Leicester, Leicestershire LE67 3LN
Tel: (01530) 510851
An all-weather and award-winning science and industrial heritage museum.

Spode Visitor Centre

Spode, Stoke-on-Trent, Staffordshire ST4 1BX
Tel: (01782) 744011
Visitors are shown the various processes in the making of bone china. Samples can be bought at the Spode Shop.

The Tales of Robin Hood

Maid Marian Way, Nottingham NG1 6GF
Tel: (0115) 948 3284
Join the world's greatest medieval adventure. Ride through the magical green wood and play the Silver Arrow game, in the search for Robin Hood.

Three Choirs Vineyards

Baldwins Farm, Newent, Gloucestershire GL18 1LS
Tel: (01531) 890223
Internationally award-winning wines are available for tasting and for sale. Winery gallery shows you how wine is made. Restaurant with magnificent views of the vines. Peaceful ponds, plus vineyard walks.

Twycross Zoo

Twycross, Atherstone, Warwickshire CV9 3PX
Tel: (01827) 880250
Gorillas, orang-utans, chimpanzees, a modern gibbon complex, elephants, lions, giraffes, a reptile house, pets' corner and rides.

Walsall Arboretum

Lichfield Street, Walsall, West Midlands
Tel: (01922) 653148
Picturesque Victorian park with over 79 acres of gardens, lakes and parkland.

Warwick Castle

Warwick CV34 4QU
Tel: (01926) 406600
Set in 60 acres of grounds. State rooms, armoury, dungeon, torture chamber, clock tower. A Royal Weekend Party 1898, and Kingmaker — a preparation for battle attractions.

Wedgwood Visitor Centre

Barlaston, Stoke-on-Trent, Staffordshire ST12 9ES
Tel: (01782) 204141
The visitor centre is located in the Wedgwood factory which lies within a 500 acre country estate. You can see potters and decorators at work. Also museum and shop

The Wildfowl and Wetlands Trust

Slimbridge, Gloucester, Gloucestershire GL2 7BT
Tel: (01453) 890333
Tropical house, hides, heated observatory, exhibits, children's playground and pond zone. Shop and restaurant.

Worcester Cathedral

10A College Green, Worcester, Worcestershire WR1 2LH
Tel: (01905) 611002
Norman crypt and chapter house, King John's Tomb, Prince Arthur's Chantry, medieval cloisters and buildings. Touch and hearing control, visually impaired facilities available.

The Pictures:
1 Symonds Yat, Wye Valley;
2 Fords Hospital, Coventry;
3 Alford Craft Market, Lincolnshire;
4 Shrewsbury Castle;
5 River Avon and Warwick Castle, Warwick;
6 Stratford-upon-Avon;
7 Nr. Chapel-en-le-Frith, Peak District;
8 Lamport Hall, Northamptonshire.

HEART OF ENGLAND

Find out more about the
HEART OF ENGLAND ...

Further information about holidays and attractions
in the Heart of England is available from:

HEART OF ENGLAND TOURIST BOARD
Larkhill Road, Worcester WR5 2EZ.

Tel: (01905) 761100
Fax: (01905) 763450

The following publications are available free from the Heart of England Tourist Board:

Bed & Breakfast Touring Map including Caravan and Camping

Escape & Explore

Events list

Great Places to Visit

Activity Holidays in the Heart of England

Food & Drink

The Pictures:
1 Packwood House, Warwickshire;
2 Black Country Museum, Dudley;
3 Ye Olde Trip to Jerusalem Inn,
   Nottingham;
4 Mary Arden's house, Wilmcote;
5 Burghley Horse Trials, Stamford.

Getting to the
HEART OF ENGLAND ...

BY ROAD: Britain's main motorways (M1/M6/M5) meet in the Heart of England; the
M40 links with the M42 south of Birmingham while the M4 provides fast access from
London to the south of the region. These road links ensure that the Heart of England is
more accessible by road than any other region in the UK.

BY RAIL: The Heart of England lies at the centre of the country's rail network. There
are direct trains from London and other major cities to many towns and cities within
the region.

Where to stay in the
HEART OF ENGLAND

Accommodation entries in this region are listed in alphabetical order of place name, and then in alphabetical order of establishment. As West Oxfordshire and Cherwell are promoted in both Heart of England and South of England, places in these areas with accommodation are listed in this section. See South of England for full West Oxfordshire and Cherwell entries.

Map references refer to the colour location maps at the front of this guide. The first number indicates the map to use; the letter and number which follow refer to the grid reference on the map.

At-a-glance symbols at the end of each accommodation entry give useful information about services and facilities. A key to symbols can be found inside the back cover flap. Keep this open for easy reference.

A brief description of the towns and villages offering accommodation in the entries which follow, can be found at the end of this section.

A complete listing of all English Tourism Council assessed guest accommodation appears at the back of this guide.

ALTON, Staffordshire Map ref 4B2

♦♦♦♦

BRADLEY ELMS FARM
Threapwood, Cheadle, Stoke-on-Trent, ST10 4RA
T: (01538) 750202
F: (01538) 753135

Bedrooms: 3 double, 3 twin, 2 triple, 1 family room
Bathrooms: 9 en suite, 1 public

EM 1830 (LO 2000)
Parking for 10

B&B per night:
D £40.00–£46.00

OPEN Jan–Oct

Well-appointed farm accommodation providing a comfortable and relaxing atmosphere for that well-earned break. 3 miles from Alton Towers, close to Potteries and Peak District National Park.

 🅰🛏🖥🖵💧📶🆂🅺🍴🕐🏧🛏🍽10 ❄🐕🚲 Ⓣ

♦♦♦

BULLS HEAD INN
High Street, Alton, ST10 4AQ
T: (01538) 702307
F: (01538) 702065
E: janet@alton.freeserve.co.uk
I: www.thebullsheadinn.co.uk

Bedrooms: 3 double, 1 twin, 2 family rooms
Bathrooms: 5 en suite, 1 public

Lunch available
EM 1830 (LO 2130)
Parking for 15
CC: Barclaycard, Delta, Mastercard, Switch, Visa

B&B per night:
S £30.00–£35.00
D £50.00–£55.00

OPEN All year round

In the village of Alton close to Alton Towers, an 18thC inn with real ale and home cooking.

🅰🛏🖥🖵💧🍷🆎🍴🖵🛏🚲 SP 🎱 Ⓣ

CHECK THE MAPS
The colour maps at the front of this guide show all the cities, towns and villages for which you will find accommodation entries.
Refer to the town index to find the page on which they are listed.

ALTON continued

◆◆◆◆

FIELDS FARM

Chapel Lane, Threapwood, Alton, Stoke-on-Trent, Staffs ST10 4QZ
T: (01538) 752721 & 07850 310381
F: (01538) 757404

B&B per night:
S Min £22.00
D £33.00–£40.00

HB per person:
DY £24.00–£32.00

OPEN All year round

Traditional farmhouse hospitality and comfort in picturesque Churnet Valley, 10 minutes from Alton Towers. Near Peak Park and within easy reach of Potteries and many stately homes. Stabling available. Ideal for walking, cycling, riding and fishing. Dogs by arrangement. Proprietor Pat Massey.

Bedrooms: 2 double, 1 twin
Bathrooms: 2 en suite, 1 private

Parking for 6

◆◆◆

HILLSIDE FARM

Alton Road, Denstone, Uttoxeter, ST14 5HG
T: (01889) 590760

Bedrooms: 1 double, 1 triple, 2 family rooms
Bathrooms: 1 en suite, 1 private, 1 public

Parking for 7

B&B per night:
S £18.00–£22.00
D £34.00–£38.00

OPEN Mar–Nov

Victorian farmhouse with extensive views to the Weaver Hills and Churnet Valley. Situated 2 miles south of Alton Towers on B5032.

ARMSCOTE, Warwickshire Map ref 2B1

◆◆◆◆
Silver
Award

WILLOW CORNER

Armscote, Stratford-upon-Avon, CV37 8DE
T: (01608) 682391 (Answerphone) &
0780 371 0149 (Mobile)
E: 113610.3511@compuserve.com
I: www.shakespeare-country.co.uk

B&B per night:
D £50.00–£56.00

OPEN All year round

This 300-year-old thatched cottage retains many original features, including low-beamed ceilings and magnificent inglenook. Once the village smithy, situated in a peaceful Jacobean hamlet. En suite bedrooms, hospitality tray, TV, hairdryer. Delicious breakfasts with home-made produce. A stroll away is the village inn. Easy access Stratford, Warwick and the Cotswolds.

Bedrooms: 2 double, 1 twin
Bathrooms: 3 en suite

Parking for 3

CHECK THE MAPS

The colour maps at the front of this guide show all the cities, towns and villages for which you will find accommodation entries. Refer to the town index to find the page on which they are listed.

◆◆◆

THE BLACK HORSE INN
Main Road, Hulland Ward, Ashbourne,
DE6 3EE
T: (01335) 370206
F: (01335) 370206

B&B per night:
S £38.00–£44.00
D £55.00–£65.00

OPEN All year round

Dating from the 1690s and personally run by owners. Four-poster en suite accommodation. Home-cooked food, vegetarian options, traditional Sunday carvery. Guest beers, bar games, beer garden. Set in Derbyshire Dales on edge of Peak District National Park, 4 miles Ashbourne. Ideal for Carsington Water, Alton Towers, Chatsworth and Dovedale.

Bedrooms: 4 double
Bathrooms: 4 en suite

Lunch available
EM 1800 (LO 2200)
Parking for 75
CC: Barclaycard, Delta, Eurocard, JCB, Mastercard, Solo, Switch, Visa

◆◆◆

COMPTON HOUSE
27-31 Compton, Ashbourne,
DE6 1BX
T: (01335) 343100
F: (01335) 348100
E: jane@comptonhouse.co.uk
I: www.comptonhouse.co.uk

Bedrooms: 3 double,
2 triple
Bathrooms: 3 en suite,
1 private

Parking for 6
CC: Amex, Barclaycard, Delta, Eurocard, JCB, Mastercard, Solo, Switch, Visa, Visa Electron

B&B per night:
S £21.00–£25.00
D £40.00–£45.00

HB per person:
DY £30.00–£37.00

OPEN All year round

Originally 3 terraced cottages, now converted into one friendly house, just within the town centre and with all the comforts to make your stay enjoyable.

◆◆◆◆

CROSS FARM
Main Road, Ellastone, Ashbourne, DE6 2GZ
T: (01335) 324668

B&B per night:
S £20.00–£22.00
D £34.00–£38.00

OPEN All year round

Stone farmhouse, approximately 150 years old, with large family and two double/twin bedrooms which are en suite with tea/coffee-making facilities and television. Good breakfasts served. Village location with pleasant walks nearby, pub within walking distance. Local attractions include Alton Towers (4 miles), Derbyshire Dales, Potteries. Reductions for children. Winter breaks available.

Bedrooms: 2 double,
1 twin, 1 family room
Bathrooms: 4 en suite

Parking for 6

◆◆◆◆

DOVE HOUSE
Bridge Hill, Mayfield, Ashbourne,
DE6 2HN
T: (01335) 343329

Bedrooms: 1 twin
Bathrooms: 1 en suite

Parking for 1

B&B per night:
S £25.00–£28.00
D £38.00–£40.00

OPEN All year round

Large, detached Victorian house with conservatory and garden. Guest sitting room. One mile from Ashbourne, ideal location for access to Peak District and Alton Towers.

QUALITY ASSURANCE SCHEME
Diamond ratings and awards were correct at the time of going to press but are subject to change. Please check at the time of booking.

ASHBOURNE continued

◆◆◆◆◆
Gold
Award

OMNIA SOMNIA

The Coach House, The Firs, Ashbourne, DE6 1HF
T: (01335) 300145
F: (01335) 300958
E: omnia.somnia@talk21.com

B&B per night:
S £45.00–£50.00
D £65.00–£75.00

HB per person:
DY Min £52.50

OPEN All year round

A winner of many awards, a unique combination of undiluted luxury, unexpected delights and intricate detail. Enjoy the experience enhanced by silver cutlery, white linen, crystal glass and fine china in sensational surroundings. Your expectations, whatever they are, will be exceeded. Three very special, very different rooms await your discovery.

Bedrooms: 3 double; suite available
Bathrooms: 3 en suite

EM 1900 (LO 2000)
Parking for 4
CC: Amex, Delta, JCB, Mastercard, Solo, Switch, Visa

◆◆◆

OVERFIELD FARM

Tissington, Ashbourne, DE6 1RA
T: (01335) 390285

Bedrooms: 1 double, 1 twin
Bathrooms: 1 en suite, 1 public

Parking for 2

B&B per night:
D £40.00–£45.00

OPEN All year round

A working farm in the picturesque village of Tissington, 3 miles from Ashbourne. This delightful farmhouse enjoys a sunny south-facing position with splendid views. Private entrance and key.

◆◆◆◆

THORPE COTTAGE

Thorpe, Ashbourne, DE6 2AW
T: (01335) 350466 &
04411 217475 (Mobile)
F: (01335) 350217

B&B per night:
S £18.00–£20.00
D £36.00–£56.00

OPEN All year round

Grade II limestone cottage, newly refurbished with antiques. Situated at the edge of conservation village, within walking distance of Dovedale. Welcoming, attentive hospitality. Splendid fireside breakfast with the now rapidly becoming famous freshly-made muffins! Also separate self-contained cottage with 4-poster bed. Self-catering or bed and breakfast. Short breaks.

Bedrooms: 1 single, 2 double, 1 twin, 2 family rooms
Bathrooms: 2 en suite, 2 private, 1 public

Parking for 8

COUNTRY CODE Always follow the Country Code ✿ Enjoy the countryside and respect its life and work ✿ Guard against all risk of fire ✿ Fasten all gates ✿ Keep your dogs under close control ✿ Keep to public paths across farmland ✿ Use gates and stiles to cross fences, hedges and walls ✿ Leave livestock, crops and machinery alone ✿ Take your litter home ✿ Help to keep all water clean ✿ Protect wildlife, plants and trees ✿ Take special care on country roads ✿ Make no unnecessary noise

ASHBOURNE continued

◆◆◆◆

THE WHEELHOUSE
Belper Road, Hulland Ward, Ashbourne, DE6 3EE
T: (01335) 370953

B&B per night:
D £40.00–£40.00

OPEN Mar–Nov

18thC former public house, midway between Ashbourne and Belper. Easy access to Carsington, Peak District, Chatsworth and Alton Towers. Renowned for excellent breakfast. Quality is our keynote. Comfortable beds, high standard of cleanliness, residents' lounge. Highly praised garden. Country pubs nearby, serving meals. Remembered, and revisited, by many.

Bedrooms: 1 double, 1 twin
Bathrooms: 2 private

Parking for 4

ॐ2 ▣ ♿ ⑤ ⅍ ♨ ⊙ ◑ ⬚ �"SP

ASHBY-DE-LA-ZOUCH, Leicestershire Map ref 4B3 *Tourist Information Centre Tel: (01530) 411767*

◆◆◆◆

MEASHAM HOUSE FARM
Gallows Lane, Measham, Swadlincote, Derbyshire DE12 7HD
T: (01530) 270465
F: (01530) 270465

Bedrooms: 2 twin, 1 triple
Bathrooms: 3 en suite, 1 public

Parking for 10

B&B per night:
S £22.00–£22.00
D £44.00–£44.00

OPEN All year round

500-acre mixed farm. 200-year-old Grade II Listed Georgian farmhouse. 2 miles from A42 junction 12, 8 miles from M1 junction 22.

Ⓜ ॐ ❏ ♿ ☜ ⑩ ▮ ⑤ ⅍ ♨ ⊙ ⬚ ⌂ ∪ ✳ �" 🏠 Ⓣ

ASHFORD IN THE WATER, Derbyshire Map ref 4B2

◆◆◆◆
Silver
Award

GRITSTONE HOUSE
Greaves Lane, Ashford in the Water, Bakewell, DE45 1QH
T: (01629) 813563
F: (01629) 813563

Bedrooms: 2 double, 1 twin
Bathrooms: 1 en suite, 1 public

B&B per night:
D £45.00–£50.00

OPEN All year round

Charming 18thC Georgian house offering friendly service and accommodation designed with comfort and style in mind. Ideal centre for exploring the Peak District's scenery.

Ⓜ ▣ ❏ ♿ ☜ ⑩ ⑤ ⅍ ♨ ⊙ ⬚ ⌂ ✕ �" 🏠 Ⓣ

ATHERSTONE, Warwickshire Map ref 4B3

Rating
Applied For

MYTHE FARM BED & BREAKFAST
Pinwall Lane, Sheepy Magna, Atherstone, CV9 3PF
T: (01827) 712367 &
07710 643143 (Mobile)
E: bosworth/advertising@connectfree.co.uk

B&B per night:
S £25.00–£30.00
D £40.00–£40.00

OPEN All year round

Elegant Regency farmhouse, with spacious interior and attractive bedrooms. Set in attractive countryside in the heart of the Midlands, within 20 miles of Birmingham, Leicester and Coventry and close to Hinkley, Tamworth, Nuneaton and Atherstone. Beautiful riverside walks with interesting things to see on this working farm. A warm welcome guaranteed.

Bedrooms: 1 twin, 2 triple
Bathrooms: 3 private, 1 public

Parking for 10

Ⓜ ॐ2 ⚶ ▣ ❏ ♿ ☜ ⑩ ▮ ⅍ ♨ ⊙ ⬚ ♪ ✳ SP 🏠 Ⓣ ◉

CONFIRM YOUR BOOKING
You are advised to confirm your booking in writing.

BAKEWELL, Derbyshire Map ref 4B2 *Tourist Information Centre Tel: (01629) 813227*

◆◆◆ **CASTLE CLIFFE**

Monsal Head, Bakewell, DE45 1NL
T: (01629) 640258
F: (01629) 640258

Bedrooms: 2 double,
1 twin, 2 family rooms
Bathrooms: 5 en suite,
1 public

Parking for 15
CC: Barclaycard, Delta,
Mastercard, Switch, Visa

B&B per night:
S £30.00–£36.00
D £45.00–£55.00

OPEN All year round
(closed Christmas)

Victorian stone house overlooking beautiful Monsal Dale. Noted for its friendly atmosphere, hearty breakfasts, log fires and exceptional views. Choice of dinner venues within walking distance.

🅰🐄🖵💧🕯Ⓢ🍴🐾📺🖥🖫🍽15♨🌸🚲SPⓉ🌐

◆◆◆◆ **EASTHORPE**

Buxton Road, Bakewell, DE45 1DA
T: (01629) 814929 (Answerphone)

Bedrooms: 1 double,
1 triple
Bathrooms: 2 en suite

Parking for 1

B&B per night:
D £40.00–£48.00

OPEN All year round

A welcome awaits you at this family-run house 200 yards town centre. Good food, comfortable rooms. Ideal for walkers, close to Chatsworth and other attractions.

🐄🚲🖥🖵💧🗝ULⓈ🍴🖫🖫🍽🌸🚲SPⓉ

◆◆◆ **RIVER WALK BED AND BREAKFAST**

River Walk, 3 New Lumford,
Bakewell, DE45 1GH
T: (01629) 812459 (Answerphone)

Bedrooms: 2 single,
1 double
Bathrooms: 2 public

Parking for 4

B&B per night:
S £16.00–£18.00
D £36.00–£40.00

OPEN All year round

A bed and breakfast overlooking the river, close to the town centre and local tourist attractions, Chatsworth House, Haddon Hall and local walks.

🐄🚭💧ULⓈ🍴🐾📺🖥🍽🌸🚲Ⓣ

◆◆◆◆◆ **TANNERY HOUSE**

Silver
Award

Matlock Street, Bakewell, DE45 1EE
T: (01629) 815011
F: (01629) 815327

Bedrooms: 2 double,
1 twin
Bathrooms: 3 en suite

Parking for 8

B&B per night:
S £30.00–£35.00
D £45.00–£55.00

HB per person:
DY £22.50–£27.50

OPEN Feb–Nov

Central Bakewell: Grade II Listed building, with guest wing, set in secluded gardens. Bedrooms en suite, opening onto garden. Private dining room overlooks swimming pool.

🅰🐄🚲🖁🖥🖵💧🗝ULⓈ🍴🐾🖫🍽🍽10🔴🏹🌸🎿🚲Ⓣ🌐

BALSALL COMMON, West Midlands Map ref 4B3

◆◆◆ **BLYTHE PADDOCKS**

Barston Lane, Balsall Common,
Coventry, CV7 7BT
T: (01676) 533050
F: (01676) 533050

Bedrooms: 2 single,
1 double, 1 twin
Bathrooms: 1 en suite,
1 public

Parking for 10

B&B per night:
S £18.00–£22.00
D £40.00–£44.00

OPEN All year round

Family home standing in 5 acres. Ten minutes from Birmingham Airport and National Exhibition Centre. NAC Stoneleigh 8 miles. Countryside location. Find us in Birmingham A–Z page 168 square 1D.

🐄🖁🖥🖵💧🗝ULⓈ📺🖫🍽🌸🚲Ⓣ

AT-A-GLANCE SYMBOLS

Symbols at the end of each accommodation entry give useful information about services and facilities. A key to symbols can be found inside the back cover flap. Keep this open for easy reference.

BAMFORD, Derbyshire Map ref 4B2

PIONEER HOUSE

Station Road, Bamford, Hope Valley,
S33 0BN
T: (01433) 650638
E: pioneerhouse@yahoo.co.uk

B&B per night:
D £40.00–£44.00

OPEN All year round

Pioneer House is a comfortable Edwardian home with spacious en suite bedrooms, beautifully decorated in turn-of-the-century style but with all modern conveniences. Nestling in the Hope Valley, we are ideally placed for visiting the Peak District and the Derbyshire Dales. Hearty breakfasts in a warm and friendly atmosphere.

Bedrooms: 2 double, 1 twin
Bathrooms: 2 en suite, 1 private

Parking for 6

BANBURY, Oxfordshire

*Ashlea Guest House, The Lodge, Prospect House Guest House, Roxtones, St Martins House
See South of England region for full entry details*

BARLOW, Derbyshire Map ref 4B2

Silver Award

MILLBROOK

Furnace Lane, Monkwood, Barlow,
Dronfield, S18 7SY
T: (0114) 2890253 &
07831 398373 (mobile)
F: (0114) 2891365

B&B per night:
S £30.00–£30.00
D £50.00–£50.00

OPEN All year round

Situated down a quiet country lane surrounded by lovely countryside with many walks around. On the edge of the Peak District, with Chatsworth House and Haddon Hall nearby, yet within easy reach of Sheffield and Chesterfield. Millbrook is spacious and comfortably furnished with attention to detail to make your stay as enjoyable as possible.

Bedrooms: 1 double, 1 twin
Bathrooms: 2 en suite

Parking for 10

BARTON UNDER NEEDWOOD, Staffordshire Map ref 4B3

Silver Award

FAIRFIELD GUEST HOUSE
55 Main Street,
Barton under Needwood,
Burton upon Trent, DE13 8AB
T: (01283) 716396
F: (01283) 716396
E: hotel@fairfield-uk.fsnet.co.uk

Bedrooms: 2 double, 1 twin
Bathrooms: 3 en suite

EM 1830 (LO 2000)
Parking for 3
CC: Delta, Mastercard, Visa

B&B per night:
S £35.00–£40.00
D £45.00–£55.00

OPEN All year round

An early Victorian spacious residence carefully restored, retaining many original features with the addition of modern facilities. Residential licence. Beautiful dining room, guests' sitting room.

BELPER, Derbyshire Map ref 4B2

HILL TOP FARM
80 Ashbourne Road, Cowers Lane,
Belper, DE56 2LF
T: (01773) 550338

Bedrooms: 1 twin, 1 triple
Bathrooms: 2 public, 1 private shower

Parking for 6

B&B per night:
S £20.00–£20.00
D £40.00–£40.00

OPEN All year round

A non-working farm with superb panoramic views over the surrounding countryside. All accommodation on ground floor. Ideal base for walking and touring.

BELPER continued

THE OLD SHOP
◆◆

10 Bakers Hill, Heage, Belper,
DE56 2BL
T: (01773) 856796

Bedrooms: 1 single,
1 double
Bathrooms: 1 public

Parking for 1

B&B per night:
S £15.00–£17.00
D £28.00–£30.00

HB per person:
DY £21.00–£23.00

OPEN All year round

Old house in a small village. Two bedrooms, stairlift access. Able-bodied and disabled guests welcome. Outings arranged to concerts, theatres, tourist attractions.

🛇 📧 💻 ♿ ⓤⓛ Ⓢ ⚒ 📺 🏧 ✈ 🚗 SP T

BELTON IN RUTLAND, Rutland Map ref 4C3

◆◆

THE OLD RECTORY
4 New Road, Belton in Rutland, Oakham,
Rutland LE15 9LE
T: (01572) 717279
F: (01572) 717343
E: bb@stablemate.demon.co.uk.

B&B per night:
S £18.00–£30.00
D £36.00–£52.00

OPEN All year round

Victorian country house and guest annexe on 14-acre smallholding. Conservation village overlooking the EyeBrook Valley and rolling Rutland countryside. Cottage-style en suite rooms, quiet, friendly atmosphere. Families welcome. Continental or full farmhouse cooked breakfast. Excellent local pubs and restaurants for your evening meal.

Bedrooms: 1 single,
2 double, 4 twin, 1 triple,
1 family room
Bathrooms: 5 en suite,
2 public

Parking for 10
CC: Barclaycard, Delta,
Eurocard, JCB,
Mastercard, Visa

🅰 🛇 🐴 💻 ♿ Ⓢ ⚒ 🍴 💻 🛏 ⏻ ☀ 🚗 🚭 SP 🏨 T

BIBURY, Gloucestershire Map ref 2B1

◆◆◆◆
**Gold
Award**

COTTESWOLD HOUSE
Arlington, Bibury, Cirencester, GL7 5ND
T: (01285) 740609
F: (01285) 740609
E: cotteswold.house@btclick.com
I: home.btclick.com/cotteswold.house

B&B per night:
S Max £30.00
D Max £45.00

OPEN All year round

Situated in this picturesque village, Cotteswold House offers high quality accommodation in a relaxed, friendly atmosphere. Three tastefully furnished bedrooms with en suite facilities, colour TV and tea/coffee. Spacious guest lounge/dining room. Cotteswold House is an ideal centre for touring Cotswolds and surrounding area. No smoking/pets. Private parking.

Bedrooms: 2 double,
1 twin
Bathrooms: 3 en suite

Parking for 3
CC: Mastercard, Visa

🛇 📧 💻 ♿ 🍴 ⓤⓛ Ⓢ ⚒ 🍴 💻 ☀ ✈ 🚗 SP T

BIRDLIP, Gloucestershire Map ref 2B1

◆◆◆

BEECHMOUNT
Birdlip, Cirencester, GL4 8JH
T: (01452) 862262
F: (01452) 862262
E: thebeechmount@breathemail.
net

Bedrooms: 2 double,
1 twin, 1 triple, 2 family
rooms
Bathrooms: 2 en suite,
2 public

EM 1900 (LO 1000)
Parking for 7
CC: Barclaycard, Delta,
Mastercard, Switch, Visa

B&B per night:
S £17.00–£31.00
D £36.00–£44.00

OPEN All year round

Warm hospitality in family-run guesthouse, ideal centre for the Cotswolds. All rooms individually decorated. Choice of menu for breakfast. Evening meal by arrangement. Unrestricted access.

🅰 🛇 📧 💻 ♿ ⓤⓛ 📱 Ⓢ ⚒ 🍴 💻 💻 ☀ 🚗 T

RATING All accommodation in this guide has been rated, or is awaiting
a rating, by a trained English Tourism Council assessor.

BIRMINGHAM, West Midlands Map ref 4B3 *Tourist Information Centre Tel: (0121) 643 2514 (City Arcade) or 780 4321 (NEC) or 693 6300 (Colmore Row)*

♦♦♦ CENTRAL GUEST HOUSE

1637 Coventry Road, South Yardley, Birmingham, B26 1DD T: (0121) 706 7757 F: (0121) 706 7757 E: mmou826384@aol.com	Bedrooms: 1 single, 3 twin, 1 triple Bathrooms: 4 en suite, 1 private	Parking for 4 CC: Barclaycard, Mastercard, Solo, Visa, Visa Electron	B&B per night: **S £17.50–£20.00** **D £35.00–£40.00** OPEN All year round

Small, family-run guesthouse, close to all local amenities, airport, National Exhibition Centre. All rooms en suite, tea/coffee, intercom, colour TV, hairdryer. Home from home.

♦♦♦ ELMDON GUEST HOUSE

2369 Coventry Road, Sheldon, Birmingham, B26 3PN T: (0121) 742 1626 & 688 1720 F: (0121) 7421626	Bedrooms: 2 single, 4 twin, 1 triple Bathrooms: 7 en suite	Lunch available EM 1830 (LO 1930) Parking for 7 CC: Barclaycard, Delta, Eurocard, Mastercard, Switch, Visa	B&B per night: **S £28.00–£36.00** **D £45.00–£55.00** HB per person: **DY £36.50–£41.50** OPEN All year round

Family-run guesthouse with en suite facilities. TV in all rooms, including Sky. On main A45 close to the National Exhibition Centre, airport, railway and city centre.

♦♦♦ HOMELEA

2399 Coventry Road, Sheldon, Birmingham, B26 3PN T: (0121) 742 0017 F: (0121) 688 1879	Bedrooms: 1 single, 1 double, 1 twin Bathrooms: 2 en suite, 1 private	Parking for 4 CC: Delta, Eurocard, Mastercard, Visa	B&B per night: **S £22.00–£35.00** **D £44.00–£48.00** OPEN All year round

A friendly bed and breakfast close to National Exhibition Centre and airport. Comfortable rooms all with TV. Full English breakfast included. Pubs and restaurants within walking distance.

♦♦♦ LYNDHURST HOTEL

135 Kingsbury Road, Erdington, Birmingham, B24 8QT T: (0121) 373 5695 F: (0121) 373 5697 E: info@lyndhurst-hotel.co.uk I: www.lyndhurst-hotel.co.uk	Bedrooms: 10 single, 2 double, 2 twin Bathrooms: 13 en suite, 1 private	EM 1800 (LO 2000) Parking for 12 CC: Amex, Barclaycard, Delta, Mastercard, Visa	B&B per night: **S £30.00–£42.00** **D £42.00–£56.00** HB per person: **DY £42.00–£54.00** OPEN All year round

Within half a mile of M6 (junction 6) and within easy reach of city and National Exhibition Centre. Comfortable bedrooms, spacious restaurant. Personal service in a quiet, friendly atmosphere.

♦♦ ROLLASON WOOD HOTEL

130 Wood End Road, Erdington, Birmingham, B24 8BJ T: (0121) 373 1230 F: (0121) 382 2578 E: rollwood@globalnet.co.uk	Bedrooms: 19 single, 3 double, 8 twin, 5 triple Bathrooms: 11 en suite, 5 public, 6 private showers	EM 1800 (LO 2030) Parking for 43 CC: Amex, Barclaycard, Delta, Diners, Mastercard, Solo, Switch, Visa	B&B per night: **S £18.00–£38.00** **D £32.00–£49.50** OPEN All year round

Friendly, family-run hotel, 1 mile from M6, exit 6. Convenient for city centre, NEC and convention centre. A la carte restaurant and bar.

♦ WOODVILLE HOUSE

39 Portland Road, Edgbaston, Birmingham, B16 9HN T: (0121) 454 0274 F: (0121) 454 5965	Bedrooms: 4 single, 4 double, 2 twin, 1 triple Bathrooms: 4 en suite, 4 public	Parking for 12	B&B per night: **S Min £18.00** **D £30.00–£35.00** OPEN All year round

High standard accommodation, 1 mile from city centre. Full English breakfast. All rooms have colour TV and tea/coffee-making facilities. En suite bedrooms available.

BIRMINGHAM AIRPORT

See under Balsall Common, Birmingham, Coventry, Hampton in Arden, Meriden, Solihull

WHERE TO STAY
Please mention this guide when making your booking.

BISHOP'S CASTLE, Shropshire Map ref 4A3

◆◆◆

CASTLE HOTEL

The Square, Bishop's Castle, SY9 5DG
T: (01588) 638403
F: (01588) 638403
E: castleotel@aol.com
I: www.bishops-castle.co.uk/castlehotel

B&B per night:
S Max £38.00
D Max £65.00

OPEN All year round

Five very comfortable en suite bedrooms, oak-panelled no-smoking dining room, 3 bars, open fires, Good Beer Guide since 1990. Wonderful walking country (Shropshire Way, Offa's Dyke, Wild Edric's Way). Special breaks.

Bedrooms: 1 single, 3 double, 1 twin
Bathrooms: 5 en suite

Lunch available
EM 1830 (LO 2100)
Parking for 35
CC: Barclaycard, Delta, Eurocard, Mastercard, Switch, Visa

BLAKENEY, Gloucestershire Map ref 2B1

◆◆◆◆
**Gold
Award**

THE OLD TUMP HOUSE
New Road, Blakeney, GL15 4DG
T: (01594) 510608
F: (01594) 510608

Bedrooms: 1 double, 1 twin
Bathrooms: 2 en suite

Parking for 6

B&B per night:
S £20.00–£25.00
D £40.00–£50.00

OPEN All year round

Stone-built former inn, nestling at the end of a small valley on the edge of the forest. Large well furnished rooms. Cooking facilities available.

BLEDINGTON, Gloucestershire Map ref 2B1

◆◆◆◆

KINGS HEAD INN AND RESTAURANT

The Green, Bledington, Oxford, OX7 6XQ
T: (01608) 658365
F: (01608) 658902
E: kingshead@btinternet.com
I: www.btinternet.com/~kingshead

B&B per night:
S £45.00–£50.00
D £65.00–£90.00

OPEN All year round

A hot buttered experience can be expected at this quintessential 15thC inn located on village green with brook and attendant ducks. Much of medieval character remains, exposed stone walls, inglenook fireplace, trestles and pews. Delightful accommodation complemented by full facilities and thoughtful extras. Award-winning restaurant. Ideally situated for main tourist attractions.

Bedrooms: 10 double, 2 twin
Bathrooms: 12 en suite

Lunch available
EM 1900 (LO 2200)
Parking for 60
CC: Barclaycard, Delta, Eurocard, Mastercard, Switch, Visa

BLOCKLEY, Gloucestershire Map ref 2B1

◆◆◆

THE MALINS
21 Station Road, Blockley,
Moreton-in-Marsh, GL56 9ED
T: (01386) 700402
F: (01386) 700402
E: johnmalin@talk21.com

Bedrooms: 1 double, 2 twin
Bathrooms: 3 en suite

Parking for 9

B&B per night:
D £40.00–£42.00

OPEN All year round

Beautifully presented Cotswold-stone house on edge of delightful village. Ideal base for touring Cotswolds and Shakespeare Country. Tastefully decorated, comfortable, non-smoking accommodation. A warm welcome awaits.

IMPORTANT NOTE Information on accommodation listed in this guide has been supplied by the proprietors. As changes may occur you are advised to check details at the time of booking.

BOURTON-ON-THE-WATER, Gloucestershire Map ref 2B1 *Tourist Information Centre Tel: (01451) 820211*

♦♦♦ **THE COTSWOLD HOUSE**
Lansdowne, Bourton-on-the-Water, Cheltenham, GL54 2AR
T: (01451) 822373

Bedrooms: 2 double, 2 triple
Bathrooms: 2 en suite, 2 private

Parking for 5

B&B per night:
S £25.00–£40.00
D £40.00–£55.00

OPEN All year round

Lovely detached Cotswold-stone house. Elegant hall, curved stairs to galleried landing, spacious en suite rooms overlooking pretty garden. Homely atmosphere.

♦♦♦ **LAMB INN**
Great Rissington, Bourton-on-the-Water, Cheltenham, GL54 2LP
T: (01451) 820388
F: (01451) 820724

Bedrooms: 13 double, 1 twin; suites available
Bathrooms: 14 en suite

Lunch available
EM 1900 (LO 2130)
Parking for 10
CC: Amex, Barclaycard, Delta, Mastercard, Solo, Switch, Visa

B&B per night:
S £35.00–£65.00
D £50.00–£90.00

HB per person:
DY £50.00–£80.00

OPEN All year round

Country inn in rural setting, with home-cooked food, including steaks and local trout, served in attractive restaurant. Beer garden and real ale. Honeymoon suite also available.

♦♦♦♦

LANSDOWNE HOUSE
Lansdowne, Bourton-on-the-Water, Cheltenham, GL54 2AT
T: (01451) 820812
F: (01451) 822484
E: lansdowne-house@ukf.net
I: www.SmoothHound.co.uk/hotels/lansdn1.html

Large period stone family house. Tastefully furnished en suite accommodation with a combination of old and antique furniture. All rooms have tea/coffee trays and colour TV. There is parking and a garden for guests' use and a good selection of guide books to help you explore the area.

Bedrooms: 2 double, 1 triple
Bathrooms: 3 en suite

Parking for 4

B&B per night:
S £30.00–£40.00
D £35.00–£40.00

OPEN All year round

♦♦♦ **MOUSETRAP INN**
Lansdowne, Bourton-on-the-Water, Cheltenham, GL54 2AR
T: (01451) 820579
F: (01451) 822393
E: mtinn@waverider.co.uk
I: mousetrap-inn.co.uk

Bedrooms: 7 double, 2 twin
Bathrooms: 9 en suite

Lunch available
EM 1830 (LO 2100)
Parking for 12
CC: Barclaycard, Delta, Mastercard, Solo, Switch, Visa

B&B per night:
D £40.00–£60.00

HB per person:
DY £30.00–£40.00

OPEN All year round

Small homely inn. All rooms en suite with TV and tea/coffee facilities. Excellent food served in relaxed surroundings. Open fire in the winter.

♦♦♦ **POLLY PERKINS**
1 The Chestnuts, Bourton-on-the-Water, Cheltenham, GL54 2AN
T: (01451) 820244
F: (01451) 820558

Bedrooms: 5 double, 1 twin
Bathrooms: 6 en suite

Lunch available
Parking for 15
CC: Delta, JCB, Mastercard, Solo, Switch, Visa

B&B per night:
S £50.00–£50.00
D £50.00–£60.00

OPEN All year round

Situated above Polly Perkins restaurant in centre of village. Building is 300 years old and the establishment retains old world charm. 15 miles from Cheltenham.

♦♦♦♦ Silver Award **THE RIDGE**
Whiteshoots Hill, Bourton-on-the-Water, Cheltenham, GL54 2LE
T: (01451) 820660
F: (01451) 822448

Bedrooms: 3 double, 1 triple
Bathrooms: 3 en suite, 1 private, 1 public

Parking for 12

B&B per night:
S £30.00–£32.00
D £45.00–£50.00

OPEN All year round

Large country house surrounded by beautiful grounds. Central for visiting many places of interest and close to all amenities. Ground floor en suite bedrooms available.

BRACKLEY, Northamptonshire Map ref 2C1 *Tourist Information Centre Tel: (01280) 700111*

◆◆◆◆
Silver Award

BRACKLEY HOUSE PRIVATE HOTEL
Brackley House, 4 High Street,
Brackley, NN13 7DT
T: (01280) 701550
F: (01280) 704965

Bedrooms: 6 double,
1 triple, 1 family room
Bathrooms: 8 en suite

Parking for 10
CC: Barclaycard, Delta,
Mastercard, Solo, Switch,
Visa, Visa Electron

B&B per night:
S £34.00–£42.00
D £52.00–£60.00

OPEN All year round

Large stone-built Grade II Listed Victorian house set in own grounds with private parking. Tastefully restored throughout. Town centre location overlooking market square.

 100 ⚫ ✈ 🚲 ⌂

◆◆◆

THE THATCHES
Whitfield, Brackley, NN13 5TQ
T: (01280) 850358

Bedrooms: 1 double,
2 twin
Bathrooms: 1 public

Parking for 2

B&B per night:
S £20.00–£30.00
D £35.00–£60.00

OPEN Jan–Nov

200-year-old house, facing south, with lovely views, in a quiet village location. Close to Stowe gardens (NT), Silverstone, Oxford and other interesting places.

⚫5 ⌂ ⚫ ⚫ ⚫ ⚫ ✈ ⌂ T

BRAILES, Warwickshire Map ref 2C1

◆◆◆

AGDON FARM
Brailes, Banbury, Oxfordshire
OX15 5JJ
T: (01608) 685226 (phone &
answerphone) &
07850 847786 (mobile)
F: (01608) 685226
E: cripps@farmersweekly.com

Bedrooms: 2 double,
1 twin
Bathrooms: 1 public

Lunch available
EM 1800 (LO 2100)
Parking for 8

B&B per night:
S £25.00–£25.00
D £42.00–£42.00

HB per person:
DY £25.00–£25.00

OPEN All year round

520-acre mixed farm. Old Cotswold-stone farmhouse in a designated Area of Outstanding Natural Beauty. Well situated for touring the Cotswolds, Oxford, Warwick and Stratford-upon-Avon.

 ⚫ ⚫ ⚫ ⚫ ⚫ ⚫ ⚫ ⚫ ⚫ ⚫ ⚫ ⚫ 6 ⚫ ⚫ ⚫ ⚫

BRIDGNORTH, Shropshire Map ref 4A3 *Tourist Information Centre Tel: (01746) 763257*

◆◆◆◆

BULLS HEAD INN
Chelmarsh, Bridgnorth, WV16 6BA
T: (01746) 861469
F: (01746) 862646
E: stsales@stargate-uk.co.uk
I: www.stargate-uk.co.uk/bullshead

B&B per night:
S £30.00–£35.00
D £42.00–£52.00

OPEN All year round

17thC country inn offering excellent accommodation and country fare, approximately 4 miles from Bridgnorth. All bedrooms are en suite with tea/coffee-making facilities. Three ground floor bedrooms for people with disabilities. Choice of cottages/apartments for self-catering or bed & breakfast. Fishing parties welcome – lock-up store for tackle and bait.

Bedrooms: 1 single,
4 double, 1 twin, 2 triple
Bathrooms: 8 en suite

Lunch available
EM 1900 (LO 2130)
Parking for 50
CC: Barclaycard, Delta,
Mastercard, Solo, Switch,
Visa

 ⚫ ⚫ ⚫ ⚫ ⚫ S ⚫ ⚫ TV ◐ ⚫ ⚫ ⚫ ⚫ SP T

◆◆◆

SEVERN ARMS HOTEL
Underhill Street, Bridgnorth,
WV16 4BB
T: (01746) 764616
F: (01746) 761750
E: severnarmshotel@compuserve.com
I: www.virtual-shropshire.co.uk/
severn-arms-hotel

Bedrooms: 2 single,
2 double, 3 twin, 2 triple,
1 family room
Bathrooms: 6 en suite,
2 public

EM 1830 (LO 1900)
CC: Barclaycard, Delta,
Mastercard, Solo, Switch,
Visa

B&B per night:
S £26.00–£38.00
D £43.00–£52.00

HB per person:
DY £38.50–£50.50

OPEN Mar–Dec

Listed building overlooking the River Severn, within walking distance of Severn Valley Railway. Close to the famous Ironbridge Gorge Museums. New cafe courtyard at rear.

 ⚫ ⚫ ⚫ ⚫ ⚫ S ⚫ ⚫ TV ⚫ ⚫ ⚫ ⚫ ⚫ SP ⌂ T

HALF BOARD PRICES Half board prices are given per person, but in some cases these may be based on double/twin occupancy.

BROADWAY, Worcestershire Map ref 2B1

◆◆◆◆◆
Gold
Award

BURHILL FARM
Buckland, Broadway, WR12 7LY
T: (01386) 858171
F: (01386) 858171

B&B per night:
D £40.00–£50.00

OPEN All year round

A warm welcome awaits guests at this mainly grass farm lying in the folds of the Cotswolds, just 2 miles south of Broadway. Both guest rooms are en suite and have TV and tea/coffee facilities. The Cotswold Way runs through the middle of the farm providing many lovely walks.

Bedrooms: 2 double
Bathrooms: 2 en suite

Parking for 4

◆◆◆

CROWN AND TRUMPET INN
Church Street, Broadway, WR12 7AE
T: (01386) 853202
F: (01386) 834650
E: ascott@cotswoldholidays.co.uk
I: www.cotswoldholidays.co.uk

B&B per night:
D £50.00–£65.00

OPEN All year round

17thC Cotswold-stone inn in picturesque Broadway, gateway to the Cotswolds and an ideal touring base. Extensive menu of seasonal and local dishes, many home-made, and fine selection of traditional beers and seasonal drinks. Oak beams, log fires in winter. Special offers for off-season and extended stays – telephone for details.

Bedrooms: 4 double, 1 twin
Bathrooms: 5 en suite

Lunch available
EM 1800 (LO 2100)
Parking for 6
CC: Barclaycard, Delta, JCB, Mastercard, Switch, Visa, Visa Electron

---

◆◆◆

DOVE COTTAGE
Colletts Fields, Broadway, WR12 7AT
T: (01386) 859085

B&B per night:
S £30.00–£35.00
D £50.00–£60.00

HB per person:
DY £40.00–£45.00

OPEN All year round

A peaceful, 16thC cottage with beamed interior and inglenook fireplaces, situated off Broadway's famous and picturesque high street, and ideal base for exploring the beautiful Cotswold towns and villages. Rooms en suite. Home-cooked evening meals, using all local produce, available by arrangement.

Bedrooms: 1 double, 1 twin
Bathrooms: 2 en suite

Parking for 2

◆◆◆◆

EASTBANK
Station Drive, Broadway, WR12 7DF
T: (01386) 852659
F: (01386) 852891
E: eastbank@talk21.com
I: www.broadway-cotswolds.co.uk/ebank.html

Bedrooms: 1 single, 2 double, 2 twin, 1 family room
Bathrooms: 6 en suite

Parking for 6
CC: Barclaycard, Delta, JCB, Mastercard, Visa

B&B per night:
S £22.00–£30.00
D £40.00–£50.00

OPEN All year round

Welcoming and friendly. Quiet location, half a mile from village. All rooms fully en suite (bath/shower), with colour TV and beverage facilities. Homely atmosphere. Free brochure.

◆◆◆◆
Silver Award

LEASOW HOUSE

Laverton Meadow, Broadway, WR12 7NA
T: (01386) 584526
F: (01386) 584596
E: leasow@clara.net
I: www.leasow.co.uk

B&B per night:
S £40.00–£50.00
D £53.00–£63.00

OPEN All year round

Set in tranquil countryside with panoramic views, close to the village of Broadway. Leasow House is a 16thC farmhouse, ideally based for touring the Cotswolds and Shakespeare Country or a quiet weekend break. All rooms are individually decorated and have en suite facilities, hospitality tray, colour TV.

Bedrooms: 3 double, 2 twin, 2 triple
Bathrooms: 7 en suite

Parking for 10
CC: Amex, Barclaycard, Mastercard, Visa

◆◆◆◆

LOWERFIELD FARM

Lowerfield Farm, Willersey, Broadway, WR11 5HF
T: (01386) 858273 &
07703 343996 (mobile)
F: (01386) 854608
E: info@lowerfield-farm.co.uk
I: www.lowerfield-farm.co.uk

B&B per night:
S £35.00–£45.00
D £45.00–£60.00

HB per person:
DY Min £42.50

OPEN All year round

2000-acre mixed farm. Genuine farmhouse comfort and hospitality, in a late 17thC Cotswold-stone farmhouse. Delightful accommodation, all en suite, with panoramic views over hills. Peaceful location provides an ideal base from which to explore the Cotswolds, Shakespeare Country and Hidcote Gardens. Evening meals by arrangement, colour brochure available.

Bedrooms: 2 double, 1 twin
Bathrooms: 3 en suite

EM 1830 (LO 1930)
Parking for 6

◆◆◆◆

MOUNT PLEASANT FARM

Childswickham, Broadway, WR12 7HZ
T: (01386) 853424

Bedrooms: 2 double, 1 twin
Bathrooms: 3 en suite

Parking for 8
CC: Barclaycard, Mastercard, Solo, Switch, Visa

B&B per night:
S £30.00–£35.00
D £48.00–£50.00

OPEN All year round

850-acre mixed farm. Large Victorian farmhouse with excellent views. Very quiet accommodation with all modern amenities. Approximately 3 miles from Broadway.

QUALITY ASSURANCE SCHEME

For an explanation of the quality and facilities represented by the Diamonds please refer to the front of this guide. A more detailed explanation can be found in the information pages at the back.

BROADWAY continued

◆◆◆◆

SOUTHWOLD GUEST HOUSE
Station Road, Broadway, WR12 7DE
T: (01386) 853681 & 07711 539660
F: (01386) 854610
E: sueandnick.southwold@talk21.com

B&B per night:
S Min £26.00
D Min £48.00

OPEN All year round

Sue and Nick Smiles invite you to their spacious and tastefully decorated Edwardian house situated in one of the Cotswolds' most picturesque villages. We are 3 minutes' walk from pubs, restaurants and the Cotswolds Way. All types of rooms available, all with en suites (single with private facilities), hospitality tray and colour TV. Guest lounge.

Bedrooms: 1 single, 4 double, 2 twin, 1 family room
Bathrooms: 7 en suite, 1 private

Parking for 8
CC: Barclaycard, Eurocard, Mastercard, Solo, Switch, Visa

◆◆◆◆

WHITEACRES
Station Road, Broadway, WR12 7DE
T: (01386) 852320
E: whiteacres@btinternet.com
I: www.broadway-cotswolds.co.uk/whiteacres.html

B&B per night:
D £50.00–£55.00

OPEN All year round

This beautiful Edwardian property offers 5 en suite bedrooms, 2 with 4-poster beds, all with colour TV, tea/coffee-making facilities, hairdryer and many thoughtful extras. There is a guests' lounge and ample car parking space. The house is decorated to a high standard and our aim is to provide a comfortable, happy base for a perfect holiday.

Bedrooms: 4 double, 1 twin
Bathrooms: 5 en suite

Parking for 6

◆◆◆◆

WINDRUSH HOUSE
Station Road, Broadway, WR12 7DE
T: (01386) 853577 & 853790
F: (01386) 853790
E: richard@broadway-windrush.co.uk
I: www.broadway-windrush.co.uk

B&B per night:
S £30.00–£40.00
D £45.00–£60.00

HB per person:
DY £34.00–£45.00

OPEN All year round

Windrush House is an outstanding example of Edwardian elegance, located a few minutes' walk from the centre of Broadway – the "jewel" of the Cotswolds. The house provides spacious, relaxed and sophisticated surroundings combined with a homely and welcoming atmosphere to make your stay one of those unforgettable memories.

Bedrooms: 4 double, 1 twin, 1 triple
Bathrooms: 5 en suite, 1 public

Lunch available
EM 1800 (LO 2000)
Parking for 7

WELCOME HOST This is a nationally recognised customer care programme which aims to promote the highest standards of service and a warm welcome. Establishments taking part in this initiative are indicated by the ⊛ symbol.

BROMSGROVE, Worcestershire Map ref 4B3 *Tourist Information Centre Tel: (01527) 831809*

♦♦♦♦ **OVERWOOD BED AND BREAKFAST**

Woodcote Lane, Woodcote,	Bedrooms: 1 double,	Parking for 4
Bromsgrove, B61 9EE	2 twin	
T: (01562) 777193	Bathrooms: 2 en suite,	
F: (01562) 777689	1 private	
E: barbbrianpalmer.overwood@		
tesco.net		

B&B per night:
S £26.00–£29.00
D £46.00–£50.00

OPEN All year round

Pretty cottage in rural surroundings, but convenient for M5/M42. Very comfortable rooms and high quality breakfasts with eggs from our own free-range hens.

🐎8 ▤▯☕♨🔌 UL S ⤫ 🐾 🏛 ▦ 🛋 ❄ ✈ 🚗 T

BROMYARD, Herefordshire Map ref 2B1 *Tourist Information Centre Tel: (01684) 482341*

♦♦♦ **LINTON BROOK FARM**

Malvern Road, Bringsty, Bromyard,	Bedrooms: 2 double,	Parking for 20
Herefordshire WR6 5TR	1 twin	
T: (01885) 488875	Bathrooms: 2 en suite,	
F: (01885) 488875	1 private	

B&B per night:
D £40.00–£55.00

OPEN All year round

A warm welcome to our fascinating 17thC farmhouse with large en suite rooms, oak beams, log fires; flag and oak floors. Wonderful walks, views and wildlife.

🐎 ♨ UL 🛏 ☕ S ⤫ 🐾 TV ▦ 🛋 ✓ ❄ 🚗 🏠

BROUGHTON ASTLEY, Leicestershire Map ref 4C3

♦♦♦ **THE OLD FARM HOUSE**

Old Mill Road, Broughton Astley,	Bedrooms: 1 single,	Parking for 6
Leicester, LE9 6PQ	1 double, 2 twin	
T: (01455) 282254 (All day)	Bathrooms: 2 public	

B&B per night:
S £19.00–£23.00
D £38.00–£46.00

OPEN All year round

Recently converted Georgian farmhouse overlooking fields. Quietly situated near village centre. Near junctions 20/21 of M1, junction 1 of M69. French spoken. No smoking or dogs in the house. Home produce.

🗙▯☕♨ UL 🛏 ☕ S ⤫ 🐾 TV ▦ 🛋 🚶 U ⏵ ❄ ✈ 🚗 🏠

BUCKNELL, Shropshire Map ref 4A3

♦♦♦ **THE HALL**

Bucknell, SY7 0AA	Bedrooms: 2 double,	EM 1800 (LO 1200)
T: (01547) 530249	1 twin	Parking for 4
F: (01547) 530249	Bathrooms: 1 en suite,	
	1 public	

B&B per night:
S Min £22.00
D £40.00–£44.00

HB per person:
DY Min £34.00

OPEN Mar–Nov

200-acre mixed farm. Georgian farmhouse in the picturesque village of Bucknell, with a peaceful and relaxed atmosphere.

Ⓜ🐎7 ▯☕♨ UL ⤫ 🐾 TV ▦ ❄ ✈ 🚗 T

BUNNY, Nottinghamshire Map ref 4C3

♦♦♦ **THE RANCLIFFE ARMS**

Loughborough Road, Bunny,	Bedrooms: 1 single,	Lunch available
Nottingham, NG11 6QT	2 double, 1 twin,	EM 1830 (LO 2100)
T: (0115) 9844727	1 family room	Parking for 50
	Bathrooms: 5 en suite,	CC: Barclaycard, Delta,
	1 public	Maestro, Mastercard,
		Solo, Switch, Visa, Visa
		Electron

B&B per night:
S £30.00–£35.00
D £40.00–£45.00

OPEN All year round

The Rancliffe Arms, formerly a coaching inn built 17thC, still retains its old charm in restaurant, lounge, bar and snug. Beer garden and aviary.

▯☕♨ S ▦ U ⏵ ❄ 🚗 T

BURFORD, Oxfordshire

The Highway, Merryfield, St Winnow, Tudor Cottage
See South of England region for full entry details

CREDIT CARD BOOKINGS If you book by telephone and are asked for your credit card number it is advisable to check the proprietor's policy should you cancel your reservation.

BURTON DASSETT, Warwickshire Map ref 2C1

◆◆◆◆

THE WHITE HOUSE BED AND BREAKFAST

Burton Dassett, Southam, CV47 2AB
T: (01295) 770143 & 0476 458314
E: lisa@whitehouse10.freeserve.co.uk

B&B per night:
S £35.00–£35.00
D £45.00–£45.00

OPEN All year round

Large country house situated at the top of the Burton Dassett Hills, enjoying superb views over the Warwickshire and Oxfordshire countryside. Evening meal and packed lunch on request. The White House provides a high standard of accommodation throughout the year and is both homely and welcoming to all who stay there. Please phone for a brochure.

Bedrooms: 2 double, 1 twin
Bathrooms: 3 en suite

Parking for 6

BUXTON, Derbyshire Map ref 4B2 *Tourist Information Centre Tel: (01298) 25106*

◆◆◆◆

BUXTON VIEW

74 Corbar Road, Buxton, SK17 6RJ
T: (01298) 79222 & 07710 516846 (Mobile)
F: (01298) 79222

B&B per night:
S £21.00–£24.00
D £43.00–£46.00

HB per person:
DY £54.00–£57.00

OPEN All year round

Lovely stone house in a "classy" residential area. Comfortable en suite bedrooms, residents' lounge. Easy walking distance to Buxton's gracious town centre. Pretty gardens, with woodland and moorland walks leading from the front door. Your hosts are Val and Roger Broad, whose hospitality is renowned.

Bedrooms: 1 single, 2 double, 1 twin, 1 triple
Bathrooms: 4 en suite, 1 private

EM 1830 (LO 1930)
Parking for 7
CC: Barclaycard, Delta, JCB, Mastercard, Solo, Switch, Visa, Visa Electron

---

◆◆◆

DEVONSHIRE ARMS

Peak Forest, Buxton, SK17 8EJ
T: (01298) 23875 &
07831 707325 (mobile)

Bedrooms: 2 double, 1 triple
Bathrooms: 3 en suite

Lunch available
EM 1830 (LO 2145)
Parking for 40
CC: Amex, Barclaycard, Delta, Maestro, Mastercard, Solo, Switch, Visa

B&B per night:
S Min £28.50
D Min £42.00

OPEN All year round

Traditional Peak District inn. Rooms refurbished to high standard, en suite, TV and coffee facilities. Excellent food and traditional ales. Good walking country. Dogs and children free.

◆◆◆◆

GROSVENOR HOUSE

1 Broad Walk, Buxton, SK17 6JE
T: (01298) 72439
F: (01298) 72439
I: www.SmoothHound.co.uk/hotels/grosvenr.html

Bedrooms: 5 double, 1 twin, 2 triple
Bathrooms: 8 en suite

B&B per night:
S £45.00–£50.00
D £50.00–£75.00

OPEN All year round

Privately-run, Victorian residence enjoying splendid views of Pavilion Gardens/theatre. Homely and peaceful atmosphere. Bedrooms non-smoking. Home-cooked traditional English food. Comfort and hospitality assured.

IDEAS For ideas on places to visit refer to the introduction at the beginning of this section.

◆◆◆◆
Silver Award

HAREFIELD

15 Marlborough Road, Buxton, SK17 6RD
T: (01298) 24029
F: (01298) 24029
E: hardie@harefield1.freeserve.co.uk
I: www.harefield1.freeserve.co.uk

B&B per night:
S £23.00–£25.00
D £46.00–£50.00

HB per person:
DY £35.50–£37.50

OPEN All year round

Elegant Victorian property set in its own grounds overlooking Buxton. Quiet location just a few minutes' walk from the historic town centre and an ideal base for exploring the beautiful Peak District. Spacious and comfortable accommodation with most bedrooms en suite. Friendly atmosphere, delicious food and lovely gardens to enjoy.

Bedrooms: 1 single, 1 double, 1 twin, 1 family room
Bathrooms: 3 en suite, 1 public

EM 1800 (LO 1930)
Parking for 8

HAWTHORN FARM GUESTHOUSE
◆◆◆

Fairfield Road, Buxton, SK17 7ED
T: (01298) 23230

Bedrooms: 4 single, 2 double, 2 twin, 4 triple
Bathrooms: 5 en suite, 2 public

Parking for 15

B&B per night:
S £22.00–£24.00
D £46.00–£52.00

OPEN Apr–Oct

A 400-year-old former farmhouse which has been in the family for 10 generations. Full English breakfast. En suite rooms available. Tea/coffee facilities, colour TV.

LAKENHAM GUESTHOUSE
◆◆◆

11 Burlington Road, Buxton, SK17 9AL
T: (01298) 79209

Bedrooms: 2 double, 2 twin, 2 family rooms
Bathrooms: 6 en suite

Parking for 10

B&B per night:
D Min £54.00

OPEN All year round

Elegant Victorian house in own grounds overlooking Pavilion Gardens. Furnished in Victorian manner and offering personal service in a friendly, relaxed atmosphere.

NITHEN COTTAGE
◆◆◆◆

123 Park Road, Buxton, SK17 6SP
T: (01298) 24679 &
07703 717335 (Mobile)

Bedrooms: 2 double
Bathrooms: 1 en suite, 1 private

B&B per night:
S £32.00–£32.00
D £44.00–£44.00

OPEN All year round

Charming, restored Victorian house. Tasteful, quality decor and furnishings, central heating, ceiling fans, colour TV, beverage tray, hairdryer. Excellent residential area, close town centre.

THE OLD MANSE PRIVATE HOTEL
◆◆◆

6 Clifton Road, Silverlands, Buxton, SK17 6QL
T: (01298) 25638
E: old_manse@yahoo.co.uk

Bedrooms: 2 single, 4 double, 2 triple
Bathrooms: 4 en suite, 2 public

EM 1800 (LO 1600)
Parking for 4
CC: Barclaycard, Delta, Mastercard, Switch, Visa

B&B per night:
S £22.00–£25.00
D £44.00–£50.00

HB per person:
DY £31.00–£34.00

OPEN All year round

Spacious Victorian house built in natural stone, quietly situated within 10 minutes' walk of Buxton's amenities, offering good home-cooked food from varied menu.

STADEN GRANGE COUNTRY HOUSE
◆◆◆

Staden Lane, Staden, Buxton, SK17 9RZ
T: (01298) 24965
F: (01298) 72067
E: staden@grange100.fsbusiness.co.uk
I: www.stadengrange.co.uk

Bedrooms: 7 double, 4 twin
Bathrooms: 10 en suite, 1 public, 1 private shower

Parking for 30
CC: Amex, Barclaycard, Delta, Mastercard, Switch, Visa

B&B per night:
S £35.00–£42.50
D £50.00–£60.00

OPEN All year round

250-acre beef farm. Spacious residence 1.5 miles from Buxton, in a magnificent scenic area. Carefully extended, uninterrupted views over open farmland. Ground floor rooms available.

CASTLE DONINGTON, Leicestershire Map ref 4B3

CASTLETOWN HOUSE
4 High Street, Castle Donington, Derby, DE74 2PP
T: (01332) 812018 & 814550
F: (01332) 812018

Bedrooms: 2 single, 1 double, 1 twin
Bathrooms: 2 en suite, 1 public

Parking for 10
CC: JCB

B&B per night:
S Min £35.00
D Min £50.00

OPEN All year round

17thC Tudor wood-framed farmhouse in village centre, with wood beams in most rooms. Ample parking. New barn development includes self-catering apartments.

DONINGTON PARK FARMHOUSE HOTEL
Melbourne Road, Isley Walton, Castle Donington, Derby, DE74 2RN
T: (01332) 862409
F: (01332) 862364
E: info@parkfarmhouse.co.uk
I: www.parkfarmhouse.co.uk

Half-timbered 17thC farmhouse, in its own grounds adjacent Donington Park. Family-run house with spacious rooms and a warm, friendly atmosphere. Log fires in winter. Real ale, farmhouse suppers and bar meals. Local produce used where possible, including venison from own herd of deer.

Bedrooms: 2 single, 4 double, 5 twin, 2 triple, 1 family room
Bathrooms: 14 en suite

EM 1800 (LO 2030)
Parking for 15
CC: Amex, Barclaycard, Delta, Diners, JCB, Mastercard, Switch, Visa, Visa Electron

B&B per night:
S £50.00–£70.00
D £72.00–£90.00

OPEN All year round

CASTLETON, Derbyshire Map ref 4B2

ASHBROOK
Brookside, Bradwell, Hope Valley, S33 9HF
T: (01433) 620803

Bedrooms: 2 double, 1 twin
Bathrooms: 1 public

Parking for 3

B&B per night:
S £20.00–£25.00
D £38.00–£38.00

OPEN All year round

Superb accommodation with good facilities in the heart of the Peak District, just 3 miles from Castleton. Ideal for walking, cycling, climbing and all the other attractions of the Peak.

BARGATE COTTAGE
Bargate, Market Place, Castleton, Hope Valley, S33 8WG
T: (01433) 620201
F: (01433) 621739
I: www.peakland.com/bargate

Bedrooms: 2 double, 1 twin
Bathrooms: 3 en suite

Parking for 6

B&B per night:
S Min £37.00
D £43.00–£47.00

OPEN All year round

Charming, warm, friendly 17thC cottage, quietly situated below Peveril Castle, in picturesque village. Ideal for walking, touring or relaxing in beautiful Hope Valley. Sorry, no smoking.

MYRTLE COTTAGE
Market Place, Castleton, Hope Valley, S33 8WQ
T: (01433) 620787 (answerphone after 10pm)

A warm welcome awaits at Myrtle Cottage, an 18thC cottage in the heart of Castleton. A superb base to explore the many delights of the Peak District. Start your day with our "hearty" breakfast and then ponder by what means you will work it off, if at all.

Bedrooms: 2 double, 1 triple, 1 family room
Bathrooms: 3 en suite, 1 private

Parking for 3

B&B per night:
S £26.00–£36.00
D £40.00–£44.00

OPEN All year round

CHAPEL-EN-LE-FRITH, Derbyshire Map ref 4B2

◆◆◆◆◆
Silver
Award

RIDGE HALL
Chapel-en-le-Frith, Buxton, SK23 9UD
T: (01298) 813130 (day/evening) & 815862
F: (01298) 815863
E: Ridge-hall@Aol.com
I: www.ridge-hall.com

B&B per night:
S £40.00–£50.00
D £55.00–£65.00

HB per person:
DY £42.50–£52.50

OPEN Feb–Nov

Occupied since 1142, this welcoming house and grounds is set in the heart of the Peak District. Norman, Tudor, Georgian and Victorian architecture all add to the historic atmosphere. All en suite rooms are furnished and equipped to a very high standard. Visit once and we know you will come again.

Bedrooms: 2 double, 1 twin
Bathrooms: 3 en suite

Parking for 11
CC: Barclaycard, Switch, Visa

CHARLEBURY, Oxfordshire

Banbury Hill Farm
See South of England region for full entry details

CHELTENHAM, Gloucestershire Map ref 2B1 *Tourist Information Centre Tel: (01242) 522878*

◆◆◆
THE BATTLEDOWN
125 Hales Road, Cheltenham, GL52 6ST
T: (01242) 233881
F: (01242) 524198
E: smurth@fsbdial.co.uk

Bedrooms: 1 single, 3 double, 2 twin, 1 triple
Bathrooms: 6 en suite, 1 private, 2 public

Parking for 8
CC: Barclaycard, Delta, JCB, Mastercard, Solo, Switch, Visa, Visa Electron

B&B per night:
S £25.00–£33.00
D £47.00–£50.00

OPEN All year round

Family-run Grade II Listed, detached Victorian house in French Colonial style, within walking distance of town centre. Colour TV, parking. Cheltenham Spa award.

◆◆◆◆
Silver
Award
BEAUMONT HOUSE HOTEL
Shurdington Road, Cheltenham, GL53 0JE
T: (01242) 245986
F: (01242) 520044
E: rocking.horse@virgin.net
I: www.smoothhound.co.uk/hotels/beauchel.html

Bedrooms: 2 single, 11 double, 2 twin
Bathrooms: 14 en suite, 1 private, 1 public

Parking for 20
CC: Amex, Barclaycard, Delta, Eurocard, JCB, Mastercard, Solo, Switch, Visa, Visa Electron

B&B per night:
S £42.00–£52.00
D £62.00–£78.00

HB per person:
DY £47.00–£69.00

OPEN All year round

Ideally situated where Cheltenham meets the Cotswolds, close to town centre or hill walks. Relaxation, comfort and service are our hallmarks. Private parking, garden.

◆◆◆
IVYDENE GUEST HOUSE
145 Hewlett Road, Cheltenham, GL52 6TS
T: (01242) 521726 & 525694
E: jvhopwood@ivydenehouse.freeserve.co.uk

Bedrooms: 3 single, 2 double, 3 twin, 1 triple
Bathrooms: 7 en suite, 2 public

Parking for 6

B&B per night:
S £25.00–£30.00
D £55.00–£60.00

OPEN All year round

A stylish, yet good value, Victorian house close to city centre. "Themed" en suite rooms (e.g, Tuscan, Greek, Oriental).

◆◆◆
STEYNE CROSS BED AND BREAKFAST
Steyne Cross, Malvern Road, Cheltenham, GL50 2NU
T: (01242) 255289
F: (01242) 255289
E: sumiko@susumago.f9.co.uk

Bedrooms: 1 double, 1 twin
Bathrooms: 1 en suite, 1 public

Parking for 4

B&B per night:
S £23.00–£25.00
D £42.00–£45.00

HB per person:
DY £28.00–£32.00

OPEN All year round

A small and cosy bed and breakfast situated in an attractive location. Easy walking distance of Cheltenham town centre and railway station.

SYMBOLS The symbols in each entry give information about services and facilities. A key to these symbols appears at the back of this guide.

CHELTENHAM continued

◆◆◆◆

STRETTON LODGE HOTEL
Western Road, Cheltenham, GL50 3RN
T: (01242) 570771
F: (01242) 528724
E: info@strettonlodge.demon.co.uk
I: www.strettonlodge.demon.co.uk

B&B per night:
S £40.00–£60.00
D £65.00–£85.00

HB per person:
DY £53.00–£55.00

OPEN All year round

Family-managed hotel in the heart of Cheltenham. Elegant rooms, traditional home-cooked food and personal service ensure a relaxing stay. From M5 to town centre, through 2 roundabouts, after 2nd traffic lights turn from Lansdown Road into Christchurch Road. At end, left into Malvern Road and 2nd right into Western Road. HB price based on minimum 2-night stay.

Bedrooms: 1 single, 2 double, 1 twin, 1 triple
Bathrooms: 5 en suite

Parking for 6
CC: Amex, Barclaycard, Delta, Eurocard, JCB, Mastercard, Solo, Switch, Visa, Visa Electron

---

◆◆◆◆
Silver Award

WISHMOOR GUEST HOUSE
147 Hales Road, Cheltenham, GL52 6TD
T: (01242) 238504
F: (01242) 226090

Bedrooms: 4 single, 4 double, 2 twin, 1 family room
Bathrooms: 9 en suite, 1 public

EM 1800 (LO 1200)
Parking for 11
CC: Barclaycard, Delta, JCB, Maestro, Mastercard, Switch, Visa

B&B per night:
S £26.00–£37.00
D £55.00–£55.00

OPEN All year round

Comfortable Victorian house with spacious accommodation and ample off-road parking, convenient for the town centre, Pump Room, racecourse and touring the Cotswolds.

◆◆◆◆

THE WYNYARDS
Butts Lane, Woodmancote, Cheltenham, GL52 4QH
T: (01242) 673876
E: graham@wynyards1.freeserve.co.uk
I: www.SmoothHound.co.uk/hotels/wynyards.html

Bedrooms: 1 double, 2 twin
Bathrooms: 1 en suite, 1 private, 2 public

Parking for 6

B&B per night:
S £20.00–£25.00
D £38.00–£38.00

OPEN All year round

Secluded old Cotswold-stone house in elevated position with panoramic views. Set in open countryside on outskirts of small village, 4 miles from Cheltenham.

CHESTERFIELD, Derbyshire Map ref 4B2 *Tourist Information Centre Tel: (01246) 345777*

◆◆◆

ABIGAILS
62 Brockwell Lane, Chesterfield, S40 4EE
T: (01246) 279391 &
07970 777909 (mobile)
E: gail@abigails.fsnet.co.uk

Bedrooms: 2 single, 3 double, 2 twin
Bathrooms: 7 en suite

Parking for 7

B&B per night:
S £26.00–£26.00
D £42.00–£42.00

OPEN All year round

Relax taking breakfast in the conservatory overlooking Chesterfield and surrounding moorlands. Garden with pond and waterfall, private car park.

◆◆◆◆
Silver Award

BATEMANS MILL HOTEL
Mill Lane, Old Tupton, Chesterfield, S42 6AE
T: (01246) 862296
F: (01246) 865672

Bedrooms: 1 single, 4 double, 2 twin, 1 triple
Bathrooms: 8 en suite

Lunch available
EM 1900 (LO 2100)
Parking for 48
CC: Amex, Barclaycard, Delta, Eurocard, JCB, Maestro, Mastercard, Solo, Switch, Visa, Visa Electron

B&B per night:
S £35.00–£55.00
D £45.00–£65.00

OPEN All year round

Batemans Mill Hotel boasts all the character and charm that you would find in a converted 1831 floor mill.

CHESTERFIELD continued

◆◆◆◆
Silver Award

BROOK HOUSE
45 Westbrook Drive, Brookside, Chesterfield, S4D 3PQ
T: (01246) 568535

Bedrooms: 1 double, 1 triple
Bathrooms: 1 en suite, 1 public

Parking for 2

B&B per night:
S £30.00–£30.00
D £45.00–£45.00

HB per person:
DY Min £42.50

OPEN All year round

Welcoming, delightful luxury accommodation in lovely rural setting adjacent fields and footpaths edging Peak National Park. Chatsworth is 10 minutes away. Good home cooking/baking.

◆◆

CLARENDON GUESTHOUSE
32 Clarence Road, West Bars, Chesterfield, S40 1LN
T: (01246) 235004

Bedrooms: 2 single, 1 double, 2 twin
Bathrooms: 4 en suite, 1 public

EM 1800 (LO 2000)
Parking for 1

B&B per night:
S £15.00–£17.50
D £30.00–£34.00

HB per person:
DY £20.50–£23.00

OPEN All year round

Victorian town residence, near town centre, cricket ground, leisure facilities and Peak District National Park. Special diets catered for. Overnight laundry service.

CHIPPING CAMPDEN, Gloucestershire Map ref 2B1

◆◆◆◆
Silver Award

M'DINA COURTYARD
Park Road, Chipping Campden, GL55 6EA
T: (01386) 841752
F: (01386) 840942
E: chilver@globalnet.co.uk

B&B per night:
S £38.00–£45.00
D £50.00–£55.00

OPEN All year round

Character Cotswold-stone house, apartment and 200-year-old cottage, in idyllic courtyard setting. Located at the quieter end of Chipping Campden's historic High Street. Extensive breakfast menu using local produce wherever possible. All rooms en suite with colour TV, hairdryer and tea/coffee facilities. Off-road parking.

Bedrooms: 2 double, 1 triple
Bathrooms: 3 en suite

Parking for 4

◆◆◆◆

MANOR FARM
Weston Subedge, Chipping Campden, GL55 6QH
T: (01386) 840390 & 07889 108812
F: 08701 640 638
E: lucy@manorfarmbnb.demon.co.uk
I: www.manorfarmbnb.demon.co.uk

B&B per night:
S £30.00–£30.00
D £45.00–£50.00

OPEN All year round

A warm, friendly welcome and a hearty, full English breakfast are assured for all guests at Manor Farm, a traditional 17thC Cotswold-stone, oak-beamed farmhouse. Excellent base for exploring the Cotswolds and Shakespeare Country from our 800 acre working farm. Superb choice of eating houses. 1.5 miles from Chipping Campden.

Bedrooms: 2 double, 1 twin
Bathrooms: 3 en suite

Parking for 8

ACCESSIBILITY
Look for the ♿ ♿ ♿ symbols which indicate accessibility for wheelchair users. A list of establishments is at the front of this guide.

CHIPPING CAMPDEN continued

◆◆◆◆

NINEVEH FARM HOUSE

Campden Road, Mickleton,
Chipping Campden, GL55 6PS
T: (01386) 438923 (Answerphone) &
07880 737649 (mobile)
E: nineveh@easicom.com
I: www.stratford-upon-avon.co.uk/
nineveh.htm

B&B per night:
S £35.00–£40.00
D £45.00–£50.00

OPEN All year round

18thC farmhouse with oak beams, flagstone floors and a warm welcome. Gardens of 1.5 acres in open countryside just a quarter mile from village pubs. Ideal for exploring Cotswolds, Stratford-upon-Avon and Warwick. Locally cured bacon, butcher's sausages and farm eggs for breakfast, cooked on the Aga.

Bedrooms: 2 double,
2 twin, 1 family room
Bathrooms: 5 en suite

Parking for 6
CC: Barclaycard, Delta,
Mastercard, Visa

◆◆◆◆

WYLDLANDS

Broad Campden, Chipping Campden,
GL55 6UR
T: (01386) 840478
F: (01386) 849031

B&B per night:
S £28.00–£30.00
D Min £44.00

OPEN All year round

Situated in the small conservation village of Broad Campden, this Cotswold-stone house has beautiful views and a TV featured garden. The well maintained, comfortable bedrooms have their own bath/ shower rooms. Choice of breakfast menu. Private parking. Ideal area for famous gardens, National Trust properties, walks and Shakespeare Country.

Bedrooms: 1 single,
1 double, 1 twin
Bathrooms: 2 en suite,
1 private

Parking for 4

CHIPPING NORTON, Oxfordshire

Southcombe Lodge Guest House
See South of England region for full entry details

CHURCH STRETTON, Shropshire Map ref 4A3

◆◆◆◆

BELVEDERE GUEST HOUSE
Burway Road, Church Stretton,
SY6 6DP
T: (01694) 722232
F: (01694) 722232
E: belv@bigfoot.com

Bedrooms: 3 single,
3 double, 2 twin, 3 triple,
1 family room
Bathrooms: 6 en suite,
4 public

EM 1900 (LO 1800)
Parking for 8
CC: Barclaycard,
Mastercard, Visa

B&B per night:
S £25.00–£29.00
D £50.00–£56.00

HB per person:
DY £36.00–£40.00

OPEN All year round

Quiet detached house set in its own grounds, convenient for Church Stretton town centre and Longmynd Hills. Adequate parking.

USE YOUR *i*s

There are more than 550 Tourist Information Centres throughout England offering friendly help with accommodation and holiday ideas as well as suggestions of places to visit and things to do. You'll find TIC addresses in the local Phone Book.

CHURCH STRETTON continued

◆◆◆◆

SAYANG HOUSE
Hope Bowdler, Church Stretton, SY6 7DD
T: (01694) 723981
E: madegan@aol.com
I: www.sayanghouse.co.uk

B&B per night:
S £28.50–£30.00
D £50.00–£55.00

HB per person:
DY £39.50–£45.00

OPEN All year round

Our house is 1 mile from Church Stretton set in an acre of landscaped gardens, commanding views of the surrounding countryside. All bedrooms are en suite and furnished to the highest standard. Delicious home-prepared meals on request, served in our homely oak-beamed sitting room. We have a full residents' licence.

Bedrooms: 3 twin, 2 triple
Bathrooms: 5 en suite

EM 1900 (LO 1930)
Parking for 6

◆◆◆◆◆
Gold
Award

WILLOWFIELD COUNTRY GUESTHOUSE
Lower Wood, All Stretton, Church Stretton, SY6 6LF
T: (01694) 751471
F: (01694) 751471
I: www.willowfieldguesthouse.co.uk

B&B per night:
S £42.00–£45.00
D £56.00–£60.00

HB per person:
DY £45.50–£47.50

OPEN Mar–Oct

Quiet and idyllic, set in its own garden for guests to enjoy beautiful rural views of unspoilt countryside and hills. Traditional and highly commended home cooking using own and local produce. Elizabethan dining room, candlelit dinners. Licensed. Delightful en suite bedrooms full of character, lounge with open fire. Non-smoking.

Bedrooms: 3 double, 3 twin
Bathrooms: 6 en suite

EM 1830
Parking for 6

CIRENCESTER, Gloucestershire Map ref 2B1 *Tourist Information Centre Tel: (01285) 654180*

◆◆

BROOKLANDS FARM
Ewen, Cirencester, GL7 6BU
T: (01285) 770487 (Anytime)
I: www.glosfarmhols.co.uk

B&B per night:
S £25.00–£25.00
D £40.00–£40.00

OPEN All year round

150-acre mixed farm on the banks of infant River Thames, which flows through the farm just 100 yards from the house (see picture). Within 3 miles are Cirencester, the Cotswold Water Park (for all watersports), the magnificent Cirencester Park (for walking), polo in summer and the source of the Thames at Coates.

Bedrooms: 2 twin
Bathrooms: 2 public

Parking for 4

QUALITY ASSURANCE SCHEME
Diamond ratings and awards were correct at the time of going to press but are subject to change. Please check at the time of booking.

CIRENCESTER continued

♦♦♦ **THE MASONS ARMS**
High Street, Meysey Hampton,
Cirencester, GL7 5JT
T: (01285) 850164
F: (01285) 850164
E: jane@themasonarms.freeserve.
co.uk

Bedrooms: 6 double,
1 twin, 1 triple
Bathrooms: 8 en suite

Lunch available
EM 1900 (LO 2130)
Parking for 8
CC: Barclaycard, Delta,
JCB, Mastercard, Solo,
Switch, Visa, Visa Electron

B&B per night:
S £36.00–£42.00
D £56.00–£68.00

OPEN All year round

Seeking peace and tranquillity? Treat yourself to a break in this 17thC inn set beside the village green. Oak beams and log fire. A warm welcome awaits you.

COLEFORD, Gloucestershire Map ref 2A1 *Tourist Information Centre Tel: (01594) 812388*

♦♦♦ **GRAYGILL**
Duke of York Road, Staunton,
Coleford, GL16 8PD
T: (01600) 712536

Bedrooms: 1 double,
1 twin
Bathrooms: 2 en suite

Parking for 3

B&B per night:
S Min £17.50
D Min £35.00

OPEN All year round

Secluded country house set in 11 acres of pasture, offering en suite bed and breakfast accommodation. Ideal for walking, cycling and touring.

♦♦♦♦ **LOWER PERRYGROVE FARM**
Coleford, GL16 8QB
T: (01594) 833187

Bedrooms: 1 double,
1 twin, 1 triple
Bathrooms: 3 en suite

Parking for 10
CC: Delta, Mastercard,
Switch, Visa

B&B per night:
S £31.00–£35.00
D £36.00–£54.00

OPEN All year round

Attractive old farmhouse central to the Forest of Dean and Wye Valley. Farm includes the beautiful Puzzlewood and tea gardens.

CONINGSBY, Lincolnshire Map ref 4D2

♦♦♦♦

THE LEA GATE INN
Leagate Road, Coningsby, Lincoln, LN4 4RS
T: (01526) 342370
F: (01526) 345468
E: markdennison4@virgin.net
I: www.theleagateinn.co.uk

B&B per night:
S £47.50–£50.00
D £55.00–£85.00

HB per person:
DY £38.50–£59.50

OPEN All year round

If you are searching for "something special", the Lea Gate has it all. Built in the 16thC, it has the atmosphere and cosiness of a country inn with the facilities of a modern high class hotel. All our rooms are very highly appointed with all facilities and splendid furnishings. Good home cooking.

Bedrooms: 4 double,
4 twin
Bathrooms: 8 en suite

Lunch available
EM 1830 (LO 2130)
CC: Amex, Barclaycard,
Delta, Mastercard, Solo,
Switch, Visa, Visa Electron

CORBY GLEN, Lincolnshire Map ref 3A1

♦♦♦♦ **STONEPIT FARMHOUSE**
Swinstead Road, Corby Glen,
Grantham, NG33 4NU
T: (01476) 550614
F: (01476) 550614
E: beds@stonepit.u-net.com

Bedrooms: 1 single,
1 double, 1 twin
Bathrooms: 1 en suite,
1 public

Parking for 3

B&B per night:
S £20.00–£25.00
D £40.00–£45.00

OPEN All year round

A peaceful setting in green, gently rolling countryside. Ground floor guest wing with TV lounge. Full English breakfast. 2 minute walk to pub/restaurant.

COTSWOLDS

See under Bibury, Birdlip, Bledington, Blockley, Bourton-on-the-Water, Broadway, Cheltenham, Chipping Campden, Cirencester, Donnington, Fairford, Gloucester, Great Rissington, Guiting Power, Lechlade, Minchinhampton, Moreton-in-Marsh, Nailsworth, Naunton, Northleach, Stonehouse, Stow-on-the-Wold, Stroud, Teddington, Tetbury, Tewkesbury, Winchcombe
See also Cotswolds in South of England region

COVENTRY, West Midlands Map ref 4B3 *Tourist Information Centre Tel: (02476) 832303 or 832304*

◆◆◆ ABIGAIL GUESTHOUSE

39 St. Patrick's Road, Coventry, West Midlands CV1 2LP
T: (024) 7622 1378

Bedrooms: 3 single, 1 double, 1 twin, 1 triple
Bathrooms: 2 public

B&B per night:
S £18.50–£25.00
D £37.00–£45.00

Family-run establishment in centre of city, very clean and friendly. Convenient for station, cathedral and city centre shopping, also NEC and NAC.

OPEN All year round

◆◆◆ ASHDOWNS GUEST HOUSE

12 Regent Street, Earlsdon, Coventry, CV1 3EP
T: (024) 7622 9280 (Answerphone)

B&B per night:
S £20.00–£25.00
D £40.00–£45.00

HB per person:
DY £42.00–£45.00

OPEN All year round

Family-run guesthouse offering quality accommodation. Convenient for city centre, rail and bus services, NEC, NAC, university and Birmingham International Airport. A warm welcome awaits you in this relaxed, non-smoking family home. Private car park at rear.

Bedrooms: 2 single, 5 twin, 1 triple
Bathrooms: 6 en suite, 1 public, 1 private shower

Parking for 8

◆◆◆ ASHLEIGH HOUSE

17 Park Road, Coventry, CV1 2LH
T: (024) 7622 3804

Bedrooms: 3 single, 3 double, 2 twin, 2 triple
Bathrooms: 8 en suite, 1 public

Parking for 12

B&B per night:
S £23.50–£27.50
D £40.00–£44.00

OPEN All year round

Recently renovated guesthouse only 100 yards from the railway station. All city amenities within 5 minutes' walk.

◆◆◆◆ BROOKFIELDS

134 Butt Lane, Allesley, Coventry, CV5 9FE
T: (024) 7640 4866
F: (024) 7640 2022
E: brookfieldscoventry@easicom.com

Bedrooms: 2 single, 1 double, 1 twin
Bathrooms: 4 en suite

Parking for 6

B&B per night:
S £25.00–£30.00
D £45.00–£50.00

OPEN All year round

Small, friendly guesthouse offering quality accommodation and service. Convenient city centre, National Exhibition Centre, Birmingham International Airport, Jaguar Cars/museum, NAC Stoneleigh. Ample parking.

CRESSBROOK, Derbyshire Map ref 4B2

◆◆◆◆ CRESSBROOK HALL

Cressbrook, Buxton, SK17 8SY
T: (01298) 871289 & 0800 3583003
F: (01298) 871845
E: stay@cressbrookhall.co.uk
I: www.cressbrookhall.co.uk

Bedrooms: 2 double, 1 twin
Bathrooms: 3 en suite

EM 1830 (LO 1930)
Parking for 10
CC: Barclaycard, Delta, Eurocard, Maestro, Mastercard, Solo, Switch, Visa

B&B per night:
S £32.50–£47.50
D £65.00–£95.00

HB per person:
DY £51.00–£65.50

OPEN All year round

Accommodation with a difference. Enjoy this magnificent family home built in 1835, set in 23 acres, with spectacular views around the compass.

DEDDINGTON, Oxfordshire

Hill Barn, Stonecrop Guest House
See South of England region for full entry details

PRICES
Please check prices and other details at the time of booking.

♦♦♦

BONEHILL FARM

Etwall Road, Mickleover, Derby, DE3 5DN
T: (01332) 513553

B&B per night:
S £22.00–£25.00
D £40.00–£46.00

OPEN All year round

A 120-acre mixed farm with traditional Georgian house which is comfortably furnished. Set in peaceful rural countryside, yet only 3 miles from Derby. Alton Towers, Peak District, Potteries, Chatsworth and Calke Abbey all within easy reach. Good food nearby.

Bedrooms: 1 double,
1 twin, 1 triple
Bathrooms: 2 en suite,
1 public

Parking for 6

♦♦

HOLMLEIGH
Donnington, Moreton-in-Marsh,
GL56 0XX
T: (01451) 830792

Bedrooms: 2 twin
Bathrooms: 1 private,
1 public

Parking for 3

B&B per night:
S £14.00–£16.00
D £28.00–£30.00

OPEN Apr–Oct

15-acre dairy farm. Farmhouse with friendly welcome. In a peaceful setting with own private lane from the village of Donnington, 1 mile from Stow-on-the-Wold.

♦

RICHMOND GUEST HOUSE
3 Ombersley St. West, Droitwich,
WR9 8HZ
T: (01905) 775722
F: (01905) 794642
I: www.infotel.co.uk/hotels/36340.
htm

Bedrooms: 6 single,
1 double, 2 twin, 4 triple,
1 family room
Bathrooms: 3 public

Parking for 12

B&B per night:
S £18.00–£20.00
D £32.00–£34.00

OPEN All year round

Victorian-built guesthouse in the town centre, 5 minutes from railway station and bus route. English breakfast. 30 minutes from National Exhibition Centre via M5/M42.

♦♦♦♦

THE BELL INN

Main Street, East Langton,
Market Harborough, LE16 7TW
T: (01858) 545278
F: (01858) 545748
E: achapman@thebellinn.co.uk
I: www.thebellinn.co.uk

B&B per night:
S £39.50–£39.50
D £55.00–£55.00

HB per person:
DY Min £55.00

OPEN All year round

17thC village inn in the heart of the village, serving fine ales brewed on the premises, wines and food 7 days a week. Low beams and winter log fires. Beautifully appointed en suite rooms and the friendly hospitality only a fine traditional English inn can provide.

Bedrooms: 1 double,
1 family room
Bathrooms: 2 en suite

Lunch available
EM 1900 (LO 2200)
Parking for 20
CC: Barclaycard, Delta,
Eurocard, JCB,
Mastercard, Solo, Switch,
Visa, Visa Electron

♦♦♦♦

PRETORIA VILLA
Wells Road, Eastcombe, Stroud,
GL6 7EE
T: (01452) 770435

Bedrooms: 1 single,
1 double, 1 twin
Bathrooms: 1 en suite,
2 private, 1 public

EM 1830 (LO 2030)
Parking for 3

B&B per night:
S £24.00–£24.00
D £48.00–£48.00

HB per person:
DY £39.00–£39.00

OPEN All year round

Cotswold-stone double-fronted detached house, built c1900, with private gardens. In quiet village lane with beautiful views.

ELMESTHORPE, Leicestershire Map ref 4C3

◆◆◆◆

BADGERS MOUNT

6 Station Road, Elmesthorpe, Leicester,
LE9 7SG
T: (01455) 848161
F: (01455) 848161
E: badgersmount@lineone.net
I: www.badgersmount.com

B&B per night:
S £35.00–£42.00
D £47.00–£60.00

OPEN All year round

Set in countryside surroundings between M1 and M69 for easy travel to Leicester, Coventry, Birmingham and many Midlands tourist attractions. The atmosphere is relaxed and informal. Residential licence, bar room overlooking large patio and spacious gardens and outdoor heated swimming pool for summer use.

Bedrooms: 1 single,
3 double, 2 family rooms
Bathrooms: 6 en suite

Lunch available
EM 1800 (LO 1800)
Parking for 13
CC: Amex, Barclaycard,
Delta, Maestro,
Mastercard, Solo, Switch,
Visa, Visa Electron

◆

WATER MEADOWS FARM

22 Billington Road East,
Elmesthorpe, Leicester, LE9 7SB
T: (01455) 843417
E: june-peter@
watermeadowsfarm.fsnet.co.uk

Bedrooms: 2 double,
1 family room
Bathrooms: 1 public

Parking for 13

B&B per night:
S £25.00–£25.00
D £35.00–£35.00

OPEN All year round

Tudor-style, oak-beamed farmhouse with extensive gardens, including 15-acre private conservation area, woodland and stream. Own produce, home cooking. Central for many places of scenic and historic interest.

EPWELL, Oxfordshire

Yarnhill Farm
See South of England region for full entry details

EVESHAM, Worcestershire Map ref 2B1 *Tourist Information Centre Tel: (01386) 446944*

◆◆◆◆
Silver
Award

BREDON VIEW GUEST HOUSE

Village Street, Harvington, Evesham,
WR11 5NQ
T: (01386) 871484 (answerphone)
F: (01386) 871484
I: www.bredonview.heartuk.net

B&B per night:
S £30.00–£35.00
D £40.00–£50.00

OPEN All year round

Bredon View Guest House is a detached Victorian residence, recently completely refurbished in a style befitting the Victorian era. En suite rooms, guests' lounge, safe off-road parking and use of lovely little back garden. We are ideally situated for visiting Warwick, Stratford-upon-Avon and the Cotswolds.

Bedrooms: 2 double,
1 twin
Bathrooms: 3 en suite

Parking for 4

◆◆◆

PARK VIEW HOTEL

Waterside, Evesham, WR11 6BS
T: (01386) 442639
E: mike.spires@btinternet.com
I: www.parkview.hotel.btinternet.
co.uk

Bedrooms: 11 single,
4 double, 10 twin,
1 triple
Bathrooms: 7 public

Parking for 30
CC: Amex, Barclaycard,
Delta, JCB, Mastercard,
Solo, Switch, Visa, Visa
Electron

B&B per night:
S £21.50–£23.00
D £38.00–£43.00

OPEN All year round

Family-run hotel offering comfortable accommodation in a friendly atmosphere. Riverside situation, close to town centre. Ideal base for touring the Cotswolds and Shakespeare Country.

FAIRFORD, Gloucestershire Map ref 2B1

◆◆◆ KEMPSFORD MANOR

Fairford, GL7 4EQ
T: (01285) 810131
F: (01285) 810131
E: www.kempsfordmanor.free.
online.co.uk

Bedrooms: 2 double
Bathrooms: 1 private,
1 private shower

B&B per night:
S £30.00–£35.00
D £50.00–£60.00

HB per person:
DY £45.00–£50.00

OPEN All year round

17thC manor-house set in peaceful gardens. Spacious bedrooms, elegant reception rooms, excellent cuisine with organic home-grown vegetables.

◆◆ WAITEN HILL FARM

Fairford, GL7 4JG
T: (01285) 712652
F: (01285) 712652

Bedrooms: 2 double,
1 twin
Bathrooms: 2 en suite,
1 public

Parking for 8

B&B per night:
S £20.00–£25.00
D £35.00–£40.00

OPEN All year round

350-acre mixed farm. Imposing 19thC farmhouse, overlooking River Coln, old mill and famous church. Short walk to shops, pubs, restaurants. Ideal for touring Cotswolds and water parks.

FARTHINGHOE, Northamptonshire Map ref 2C1

◆◆◆◆ GREENFIELD

Baker Street, Farthinghoe, Brackley,
NN13 5PH
T: (01295) 712380
F: (01295) 712380
E: VivWebb@aol.com
I: www.webbS2.freeserve.co.uk

Bedrooms: 1 double,
1 twin
Bathrooms: 1 private,
1 public

Parking for 2

B&B per night:
S Min £20.00
D Min £40.00

OPEN All year round

Modern, detached property in a picturesque village, close to a 16thC public house which serves meals.

FLEET HARGATE, Lincolnshire Map ref 3A1

◆◆ THE BULL INN

Old Main Road,
Fleet Hargate, Holbeach, Spalding,
PE12 8LH
T: (01406) 426866

Bedrooms: 3 double
Bathrooms: 1 public

Lunch available
EM 1900 (LO 2200)
Parking for 20
CC: Mastercard, Switch,
Visa

B&B per night:
S £20.00–£20.00
D £35.00–£35.00

HB per person:
DY £28.00–£35.00

OPEN All year round

Ancient coaching inn on the road round The Wash. Grade II Listed building, site of archaeological interest. Bar, restaurant, rooms, car park and beer garden.

FOREST OF DEAN

See under Blakeney, Coleford, Newland, Westbury-on-Severn

FOWNHOPE, Herefordshire Map ref 2A1

◆◆◆◆

THE BOWENS COUNTRY HOUSE

Fownhope, Hereford, HRI 4PS
T: (01432) 860430 (answerphone)
F: (01432) 860430

B&B per night:
S £32.50–£32.50
D £50.00–£65.00

HB per person:
DY £40.00–£47.50

OPEN All year round

Delightful Georgian house set in peaceful Wye Valley village of Fownhope, midway between Hereford and Ross-on-Wye (B4224. Ten well appointed en suite rooms (4 ground floor) with TV, telephone and tea trays. All home-cooked meals using local produce. Vegetarians welcome. Fully licensed bar, good wine list. Large garden, putting green and grass tennis court.

Bedrooms: 1 single,
4 double, 2 twin, 1 triple,
2 family rooms
Bathrooms: 10 en suite

Lunch available
EM 1900 (LO 2100)
Parking for 16
CC: Barclaycard, Delta,
Mastercard, Switch, Visa

FOXTON, Leicestershire Map ref 4C3

Silver Award ◆◆◆◆

THE OLD MANSE
Swingbridge Street, Foxton,
Market Harborough, LE16 7RH
T: (01858) 545456
E: theoldmanse37@hotmail.com

Bedrooms: 1 double, 2 twin
Bathrooms: 2 en suite, 1 private

Parking for 6

B&B per night:
S £32.00–£32.00
D £45.00–£46.00

OPEN All year round

Period house in large gardens with warm and friendly atmosphere, on edge of conservation village, 3 miles north of Market Harborough. Good food at both local inns.

FRAMPTON-ON-SEVERN, Gloucestershire Map ref 2B1

◆◆◆◆

ARCHWAY HOUSE
The Green, Frampton-on-Severn,
Gloucester, GL2 7DY
T: (01452) 740752 (Answerphone)
F: (01452) 741629

Bedrooms: 1 double, 1 twin
Bathrooms: 1 public

B&B per night:
S £25.00–£35.00
D £40.00–£45.00

HB per person:
DY £35.00–£50.00

OPEN All year round

200-year-old Georgian house in a Gloucestershire village, fronting on to 'Rosamunds Green'. Set in good walking country near the River Severn. Non-smoking establishment.

GAINSBOROUGH, Lincolnshire Map ref 4C2

◆◆◆

THE BECKETT ARMS
25 High Street, Corringham,
Gainsborough, DN21 5QP
T: (01427) 838201

Bedrooms: 1 twin, 3 triple
Bathrooms: 4 en suite, 1 public

Lunch available
EM 1730 (LO 2200)
Parking for 30
CC: Barclaycard, Delta, Mastercard, Solo, Switch, Visa, Visa Electron

B&B per night:
S £20.00–£25.00
D £34.00–£40.00

OPEN All year round

A family-run pub with good all round facilities, 4 miles east of Gainsborough and approximately 20 miles from the historic city of Lincoln.

GLOSSOP, Derbyshire Map ref 4B2 *Tourist Information Centre Tel: (01457) 855920*

◆◆◆

PEELS ARMS
6-12 Temple Street, Padfield,
Glossop, SK13 1EX
T: (01457) 852719
F: (01457) 860536
E: peels@talk21.com

Bedrooms: 3 double, 2 twin
Bathrooms: 2 en suite, 1 public, 1 private shower

Lunch available
EM 1900 (LO 2130)
Parking for 18
CC: Mastercard, Visa

B&B per night:
S £25.00–£25.00
D £40.00–£40.00

OPEN All year round

Traditional 19thC country inn with log fires and oak beams. Hand-poured ales, fine food and a warm welcome await you.

GLOUCESTER, Gloucestershire Map ref 2B1 *Tourist Information Centre Tel: (01452) 421188*

◆◆◆

BROOKTHORPE LODGE
Stroud Road, Brookthorpe, Gloucester, GL4 0UQ
T: (01452) 812645
F: (01452) 812645
E: enq@brookthorpelodge.demon.co.uk
I: www.brookthorpelodge.demon.co.uk

B&B per night:
S £22.00–£23.50
D £45.00–£50.00

HB per person:
DY £30.00–£35.00

OPEN All year round

Licensed, family-run, spacious and comfortable Georgian detached house on the outskirts of Gloucester (4 miles). Set in lovely countryside at the foot of the Cotswold escarpment. Close to ski-slope and golfing facilities. Excellent walking country. Ideal base for visiting the Cotswolds, Cheltenham, Bath and nearby WWT reserve at Slimbridge.

Bedrooms: 3 single, 2 double, 3 twin, 2 family rooms
Bathrooms: 6 en suite, 1 private, 2 public

EM 1800 (LO 2000)
Parking for 15
CC: Delta, JCB, Mastercard, Solo, Switch, Visa, Visa Electron

REGIONAL TOURIST BOARD The ⋀ symbol in an establishment entry indicates that it is a Regional Tourist Board member.

GLOUCESTER continued

◆

GEORGIAN GUEST HOUSE
85 Bristol Road, Gloucester,
GL1 5SN
T: (01452) 413286
F: (01452) 413286

Bedrooms: 2 single,
3 double, 3 twin, 1 triple
Bathrooms: 2 en suite,
1 public, 2 private
showers

Parking for 3

B&B per night:
S £14.50–£15.50
D £29.00–£33.00

OPEN All year round

On the main Bristol Road, 15 minutes' walk from Gloucester city centre.

◆◆◆

PEMBURY GUEST HOUSE
9 Pembury Road, St. Barnabas, Gloucester,
GL4 6UE
T: (01452) 521856
F: (01452) 303418

B&B per night:
S £20.00–£26.00
D £34.00–£40.00

OPEN All year round

Licensed, family-run detached house, close to ski-slope and golfing facilities. Ideal base for Cotswolds, Gloucester Docks and cathedral. Near south and north M5 junctions. All bedrooms are attractively decorated. You have the choice of en suite rooms or rooms with showers. Come as guests, leave as friends.

Bedrooms: 1 single,
4 double, 3 twin, 2 triple
Bathrooms: 5 en suite,
1 public, 2 private
showers

EM 1900 (LO 1930)
Parking for 10
CC: Barclaycard, Delta,
Mastercard, Solo, Switch,
Visa

GOTHERINGTON, Gloucestershire Map ref 2B1

◆◆◆

PARDON HILL FARM
Prescott, Gotherington,
Cheltenham, GL52 4RD
T: (01242) 672468 &
07802 708814 (mobile)
F: (01242) 672468
E: janet@pardonhillfarm.freeserve.
co.uk
I: www.glosfarmhols.co.uk

Bedrooms: 1 single,
1 double, 1 twin
Bathrooms: 3 en suite

Parking for 10

B&B per night:
S Min £27.00
D Min £44.00

OPEN All year round

300-acre mixed farm. Family-run farm. Outstanding views from all rooms. Ideal centre for walking and touring.

GREAT RISSINGTON, Gloucestershire Map ref 2B1

◆◆◆

LOWER FARMHOUSE
Great Rissington, Cheltenham,
GL54 2LH
T: (01451) 810163 & 810187
F: (01451) 810187
E: kathryn@fleming4 clocks.
netscapeonline.co.uk

Bedrooms: 1 single,
1 double
Bathrooms: 1 public

Parking for 4

B&B per night:
S £18.00–£22.00
D £36.00–£44.00

OPEN All year round

Grade II Listed Georgian home with separate guest rooms in Cotswold barn conversion. On north-west edge of peaceful village, yet close to attractions.

TOWN INDEX
This can be found at the back of the guide. If you know where you want to stay, the index will give you the page number listing accommodation in your chosen town, city or village.

◆◆◆

STEPPING STONE

Rectory Lane, Great Rissington,
Cheltenham, GL54 2LL
T: (01451) 821385
E: stepping-stone-b-b@excite.com

B&B per night:
S £33.00–£37.00
D £55.00–£65.00

OPEN All year round

Set in large garden at the edge of a picturesque village, providing quiet and comfortable accommodation for B&B and longer stays (two self contained doubles). Located 3 miles from Bourton-on-the-Water and just 200 metres from The Lamb restaurant and bar. Open all year.

Bedrooms: 1 single,
3 double, 1 twin; suites
available
Bathrooms: 3 en suite,
1 public

Parking for 11
CC: Barclaycard, Delta,
Mastercard, Visa

◆◆◆

THE HOLLOW BOTTOM

Winchcombe Road, Guiting Power,
Cheltenham, GL54 5UX
T: (01451) 850392
F: (01451) 850392

B&B per night:
S £25.00–£25.00
D £50.00–£50.00

HB per person:
DY £40.00–£40.00

OPEN All year round

17thC Cotswold inn, with a horse racing theme, set in the pretty village of Guiting Power, a designated Area of Outstanding Natural Beauty. En suite accommodation, real ales, log fire, warm and welcoming. Ideal for walking and or touring in the North Cotswolds. Golf, fishing, riding nearby. HB price varies according to meal choice.

Bedrooms: 2 twin,
1 triple
Bathrooms: 2 en suite,
1 private

Lunch available
EM 1900 (LO 2130)
Parking for 10
CC: Barclaycard, Delta,
Mastercard, Solo, Switch,
Visa, Visa Electron

◆◆◆

HALL FARM HOUSE

Hadnall, Shrewsbury, SY4 4AQ
T: (01939) 210269 (answerphone) &
07989 235181 (mobile)

B&B per night:
S £15.00–£20.00
D £30.00–£40.00

OPEN Apr–Sep

Part timber-framed 17thC Listed farmhouse, set in a well-established garden. Large, comfortable en suite bedrooms with colour TV and tea-making facilities. Private parking. Friendly atmosphere, children welcome. Within easy reach of Chester, Ironbridge, industrial museums and North Wales.

Bedrooms: 2 twin
Bathrooms: 1 en suite,
1 private

Parking for 5

TOWN INDEX

This can be found at the back of this guide. If you know where you want to stay, the index will give you the page number listing accommodation in your chosen town, city or village.

HAGWORTHINGHAM, Lincolnshire Map ref 4D2

◆◆◆◆
Silver
Award

WHITE OAK GRANGE
Hagworthingham, Spilsby, PE23 4LX
T: (01507) 588376
F: (01507) 588377
I: whiteoakgrange.com

Bedrooms: 2 double,
1 twin
Bathrooms: 2 en suite,
1 public

Lunch available
EM 1900 (LO 2030)
Parking for 11

B&B per night:
S Min £25.00
D Max £50.00

HB per person:
DY Max £40.00

OPEN Jan–Nov

Fine house with extensive gardens and superb views, set in open countryside of Lincolnshire Wolds. Excellent home cooking, home-grown produce, licensed, private fishing.

HAMPTON IN ARDEN, West Midlands Map ref 4B3

◆◆◆◆

CHELSEA LODGE
48 Meriden Road,
Hampton in Arden, Solihull,
West Midlands B92 0BT
T: (01675) 442408
F: (01675) 442408

Bedrooms: 3 twin
Bathrooms: 2 en suite,
1 private

Parking for 4

B&B per night:
S Min £25.00
D £45.00–£52.00

OPEN All year round

Comfortable, refurbished detached property with delightful gardens. Walking distance to Hampton in Arden station (direct NEC/Birmingham Airport) and village pubs. Village location 3 miles NEC.

HAYFIELD, Derbyshire Map ref 4B2

◆◆◆◆

THE ROYAL HOTEL
Market Street, Hayfield, High Peak,
SK22 2EP
T: (01663) 742721
F: (01663) 742997
E: royal.hotel@virgin.net
I: freespace.virgin.net/royal.hotel

Bedrooms: 2 double,
1 twin
Bathrooms: 3 en suite

Lunch available
EM 1800 (LO 2145)
Parking for 100
CC: Amex, Barclaycard,
Delta, Diners, Eurocard,
JCB, Maestro, Mastercard,
Solo, Switch, Visa, Visa
Electron

B&B per night:
S £37.00–£40.00
D £54.00–£60.00

HB per person:
DY £47.00–£50.00

OPEN All year round

Centrally located in Hayfield at the foot of Kinder Scout in the High Peak district. Built in 1755, comprises oak panelled pub and restaurant with log fires, function room and accommodation.

HEREFORD, Herefordshire Map ref 2A1 *Tourist Information Centre Tel: (01432) 268430*

◆◆◆

CEDAR GUEST HOUSE
123 Whitecross Road, Whitecross,
Hereford, HR4 0LS
T: (01432) 267235
F: (01432) 267235

B&B per night:
S £25.00–£40.00
D £38.00–£48.00

HB per person:
DY £30.00–£50.00

OPEN All year round

Former Victorian gentleman's residence, retaining many of the original features. Family-run offering spacious accommodation, within easy walking distance of Hereford's historic city centre. Situated on major tourist route, also close to the excellent coarse angling on River Wye.

Bedrooms: 2 double,
1 twin, 2 triple, 1 family
room
Bathrooms: 1 en suite,
1 public, 3 private
showers

Parking for 10
CC: Barclaycard, Delta,
JCB, Mastercard, Solo,
Switch, Visa, Visa Electron

CHECK THE MAPS
The colour maps at the front of this guide show all the cities, towns and villages for which you will find accommodation entries. Refer to the town index to find the page on which they are listed.

HEREFORD continued

Silver Award ◆◆◆◆

FELTON HOUSE
Felton, Hereford, HR1 3PH
T: (01432) 820366
F: (01432) 820366
I: www.smoothhound.co.uk/hotels/felton.html

On arrival relax with complimentary refreshments in a country house of character set in beautiful, tranquil gardens. Taste excellent evening meals in three local inns. Sleep soundly in a 4-poster or brass bed; awake refreshed to enjoy a healthy large breakfast selected from a wide choice of traditional and vegetarian dishes.

Bedrooms: 1 single, 2 double, 1 twin
Bathrooms: 2 en suite, 2 private, 1 public

Parking for 6

B&B per night:
S £23.00–£23.00
D £46.00–£46.00

OPEN All year round

◆◆◆◆

HEDLEY LODGE
Belmont Abbey, Abergavenny Road, Hereford, HR2 9RZ
T: (01432) 277475
F: (01432) 277597
E: procoffice@aol.com
I: www.belmontabbey.org.uk/hedley.shtml

Set in lovely grounds of Belmont Abbey (above), this friendly, modern guesthouse offers 17 bedrooms comfortably appointed with en suite facilities, TV and telephone. Our licensed restaurant offers a wide selection of snacks or main meals. Located 2.5 miles from Hereford off A465, an ideal venue for visiting the Wye Valley.

Bedrooms: 6 double, 10 twin, 1 triple
Bathrooms: 17 en suite

Lunch available
EM 1800 (LO 2030)
Parking for 200
CC: Barclaycard, Delta, Mastercard, Switch, Visa

B&B per night:
S £29.50–£35.00
D £49.00–£55.00

OPEN All year round

◆◆◆

HERON HOUSE
Canon Pyon Road, Portway, Burghill, Hereford, Herefordshire HR4 8NG
T: (01432) 761111 (Answerphone)
F: (01432) 760603
E: bb.hereford@tesco.net
I: homepages.tesco.net/~bb.hereford/hesou.htm

Bedrooms: 1 double, 1 triple
Bathrooms: 1 en suite, 1 public

Parking for 4

B&B per night:
S £17.50–£17.50
D £42.00–£42.00

OPEN All year round

Country location with panoramic view, 4 miles north of Hereford city. Off-road parking. Excellent centre for country pursuits and places of historic interest. No smoking.

HINCKLEY, Leicestershire Map ref 4B3 *Tourist Information Centre Tel: (01455) 635106*

◆◆◆

WOODSIDE FARM GUESTHOUSE
Ashby Road, Stapleton, Leicester, LE9 8JE
T: (01455) 291929
F: (01455) 292626

Bedrooms: 4 single, 3 double, 1 twin, 1 triple, 1 family room
Bathrooms: 8 en suite, 2 public, 1 private shower

Lunch available
EM 1830 (LO 2100)
Parking for 17
CC: Amex, Barclaycard, Delta, Eurocard, Mastercard, Switch, Visa

B&B per night:
S £30.00–£30.00
D £40.00–£40.00

OPEN All year round

16-acre arable and mixed farm. Close to the Battle of Bosworth site and Kirkby Mallory race track. 3 miles north of Hinckley on A447.

QUALITY ASSURANCE SCHEME
Diamond ratings and awards are explained at the back of this guide.

HOLBEACH, Lincolnshire Map ref 3A1

◆◆◆◆

CACKLE HILL HOUSE

Cackle Hill Lane, Holbeach,
PE12 8BS
T: (01406) 426721 &
07930 228755 (Mobile)
F: (01406) 424659

Bedrooms: 1 double,
2 twin
Bathrooms: 2 en suite,
1 private

Parking for 4

B&B per night:
S £25.00–£25.00
D £40.00–£44.00

OPEN All year round

We welcome you to our farm situated in a rural position just off the A17. Spacious accommodation, tea/coffee facilities, excellent traditional breakfasts.

⋔ 🛏10 🖳 ⚬ 🖤 ⓤⓛ Ⓢ ⤬ 🖳 🖵 📺 🗔 💺 ☀ 🚲 ⓢⓟ Ⓣ ◉

HOPE, Derbyshire Map ref 4B2

◆◆◆◆◆

Silver Award

UNDERLEIGH HOUSE

Off Edale Road, Hope, Hope Valley, S33 6RF
T: (01433) 621372 &
621324 (Answerphone)
F: (01433) 621324
E: Underleigh.House@btinternet.com
I: www.underleighhouse.co.uk

B&B per night:
S £33.00–£46.00
D £60.00–£66.00

OPEN All year round

Secluded cottage and barn conversion near the village of Hope with magnificent countryside views. Ideal for walking and exploring the Peak District. Delicious breakfasts featuring local and home-made specialities, served in flagstoned dining hall. Welcoming and relaxing atmosphere with a log fire on chilly evenings in the charming, beamed lounge.

Bedrooms: 4 double,
2 twin; suite available
Bathrooms: 6 en suite

Parking for 10
CC: Barclaycard, Delta,
Maestro, Mastercard,
Solo, Switch, Visa

⋔ 🛏12 🖴 ☎ 🖳 🖥 ⚬ 🖤 Ⓢ ⤬ 🖳 📺 🗔 💺 ☀ ✗ 🚲 ⓢⓟ 🏠 Ⓣ ◉

HUSBANDS BOSWORTH, Leicestershire Map ref 4C3

◆◆

MRS ARMITAGE'S

31-33 High Street,
Husbands Bosworth, Lutterworth,
LE17 6LJ
T: (01858) 880066

Bedrooms: 1 single,
1 twin, 1 triple
Bathrooms: 1 public

Parking for 6
CC: Eurocard

B&B per night:
S £16.00–£17.00
D £32.00–£34.00

OPEN All year round

Village centre home of character on A4304/A427, with wholesome cooking and warm welcome. Good choice of reasonably-priced evening meals at local inns.

🛏 🖵 ⚬ ⓤⓛ Ⓢ 🖳 📺 🗔 ✗ 🚲 Ⓣ

IRONBRIDGE, Shropshire Map ref 4A3 *Tourist Information Centre Tel: (01952) 432166*

◆◆

LORD HILL GUEST HOUSE

Duke Street, Broseley, TF12 5LU
T: (01952) 884270 & 580792

Bedrooms: 2 single,
1 double, 4 twin
Bathrooms: 2 en suite,
1 private, 1 public,
1 private shower

Parking for 9

B&B per night:
S £17.00–£20.00
D £34.00–£40.00

OPEN All year round

Former public house. Friendly atmosphere, full English breakfast, parking. Easy access to Ironbridge, Bridgnorth, Shrewsbury and Telford.

🛏8 ⚬ 🖧 🖵 🔒 Ⓢ 🖳 📺 🗔 💺 ⓢⓒ ⓢⓟ Ⓣ

◆◆◆

WHARFAGE COTTAGE

17 The Wharfage, Ironbridge,
Telford, TF8 7AW
T: (01952) 432721
F: (01952) 432639

Bedrooms: 1 double,
1 twin, 1 triple
Bathrooms: 2 en suite,
1 private

Parking for 5
CC: Barclaycard, Delta,
Mastercard, Solo, Switch,
Visa, Visa Electron

B&B per night:
S £25.00–£35.00
D £40.00–£50.00

OPEN All year round

Grade II Listed building of charm and character overlooking the River Severn, within 100 yards of Ironbridge and museums, situated on the Wharfage in Ironbridge.

🛏 🖵 ⚬ ⓤⓛ Ⓢ ⤬ 🗔 💺 ☀ ✗ 🚲 Ⓣ

MAP REFERENCES
The map references refer to the colour maps at the front of this guide. The first figure is the map number; the letter and figure which follow indicate the grid reference on the map.

KENILWORTH, Warwickshire Map ref 4B3 *Tourist Information Centre Tel: (01926) 852595*

◆◆◆◆ ABBEY GUEST HOUSE

41 Station Road, Kenilworth,	Bedrooms: 2 single,	Parking for 2	B&B per night:
CV8 1JD	3 double, 2 twin		S Max £28.00
T: (01926) 512707	Bathrooms: 6 en suite,		D Max £45.00
F: (01926) 859148	1 private		
E: the-abbey@virgin.net			OPEN All year round

Cosy Victorian house, 10 minutes from National Agricultural Centre, 15 minutes from NEC. Ideally placed for Warwick, Stratford-upon-Avon, Coventry and the Cotswolds.

◆◆◆ ENDERLEY GUEST HOUSE

20 Queens Road, Kenilworth,	Bedrooms: 1 single,	Parking for 2	B&B per night:
CV8 1JQ	2 double, 1 twin, 1 triple,		S £27.00–£30.00
T: (01926) 855388	1 family room		D £44.00–£60.00
F: (01926) 850450	Bathrooms: 6 en suite		

Family-run guesthouse, quietly situated near town centre and convenient for Warwick, Stratford-upon-Avon, Stoneleigh, Warwick University and National Exhibition Centre.

OPEN All year round

◆◆◆◆ FERNDALE GUEST HOUSE

45 Priory Road, Kenilworth, CV8 1LL	Bedrooms: 1 single,	Parking for 7	B&B per night:
T: (01926) 853214 (Answerphone)	2 double, 3 twin, 1 triple	CC: Barclaycard, Delta,	S £26.00–£30.00
F: (01926) 858336	Bathrooms: 7 en suite	Diners, Mastercard,	D £40.00–£40.00
		Switch, Visa	

Delightfully modernised Victorian house. Attractive en suite bedrooms with colour TV, tea/coffee facilities. Ideal for NEC, NAC and Warwick University. Private parking.

OPEN All year round

◆◆◆◆ VICTORIA LODGE HOTEL

180 Warwick Road, Kenilworth,	Bedrooms: 1 single,	Lunch available	B&B per night:
CV8 1HU	7 double, 1 twin	Parking for 11	S £40.00–£46.00
T: (01926) 512020	Bathrooms: 9 en suite	CC: Amex, Barclaycard,	D £59.00–£59.00
F: (01926) 858703		Delta, Eurocard, JCB,	
		Mastercard, Switch, Visa	OPEN All year round

Prestigious small hotel with a warming ambience. Beautiful bedrooms, with individual appeal and character, are complemented by traditional hospitality. Non-smoking.

KETTERING, Northamptonshire Map ref 3A2 *Tourist Information Centre Tel: (01536) 410266*

◆◆◆◆ DAIRY FARM
Silver Award

Cranford St Andrew, Kettering,	Bedrooms: 2 double,	EM 1900 (LO 1200)	B&B per night:
NN14 4AQ	1 twin	Parking for 10	S £22.00–£30.00
T: (01536) 330273	Bathrooms: 2 en suite,		D £44.00–£60.00
	1 public		

350-acre mixed farm. 17thC thatched house with inglenook fireplaces and a garden with an ancient circular dovecote and mature trees. Good food.

HB per person:
DY £36.00–£44.00

OPEN All year round

KEXBY, Lincolnshire Map ref 4C2

◆◆◆ KEXBY GRANGE

Kexby, Gainsborough, DN21 5PJ	Bedrooms: 1 single,	Lunch available	B&B per night:
T: (01427) 788265	1 double	EM 1700 (LO 2100)	S £16.00–£17.00
	Bathrooms: 1 private,	Parking for 4	D £32.00–£34.00
	1 public		

650-acre mixed farm. Victorian farmhouse offering warm welcome. 4 miles from Gainsborough. Convenient for Lincoln, Hemswell Antique Centre and Wolds. Double room has private bathroom.

HB per person:
DY £28.00–£29.00

OPEN All year round

IMPORTANT NOTE Information on accommodation listed in this guide has been supplied by the proprietors. As changes may occur you are advised to check details at the time of booking.

KIDDERMINSTER, Worcestershire Map ref 4B3

♦♦♦ **VICTORIA HOTEL**

15 Comberton Road, Kidderminster, DY10 1UA
T: (01562) 67240

Bedrooms: 3 single, 2 double, 2 triple
Bathrooms: 5 en suite, 1 public

Parking for 5
CC: Barclaycard, Delta, Eurocard, Maestro, Mastercard, Solo, Switch, Visa, Visa Electron

B&B per night:
S £25.00–£28.00
D £45.00–£45.00

OPEN All year round

Select family-run hotel offering traditional bed and breakfast. Accommodation complete with service and hospitality.

KINETON, Warwickshire Map ref 2C1

♦♦♦ **THE CASTLE**

Edgehill, Kineton, Banbury, Oxfordshire OX15 6DJ
T: (01295) 670255
F: (01295) 670521
E: castleedgehill@msn.com.
I: www.smoothound.co.uk/hotels/castle2

Bedrooms: 1 twin, 2 family rooms
Bathrooms: 3 en suite

Lunch available
EM 1830 (LO 2100)
Parking for 25
CC: Amex, Barclaycard, Delta, Diners, JCB, Maestro, Mastercard, Solo, Switch, Visa, Visa Electron

B&B per night:
S £35.00–£45.00
D £55.00–£65.00

OPEN All year round

"Folly" built by Sanderson-Miller. Copy of Guy's Tower at Warwick Castle. Erected to commemorate 100th anniversary of Battle of Edgehill (1642) traditionally where King Charles I stood.

KING'S CLIFFE, Northamptonshire Map ref 3A1

♦♦♦♦

19 WEST STREET

King's Cliffe, Peterborough, PE8 6XB
T: (01780) 470365
F: (01780) 470623
E: 100537.156@compuserve.com

B&B per night:
S £25.00–£25.00
D £40.00–£40.00

HB per person:
DY £35.00–£40.00

OPEN All year round

Grade II Listed 500-year-old stone house, beautiful walled garden, reputedly one of King John's hunting lodges. Situated in centre of unspoilt stone village near Stamford. Rooms have private bathroom and colour TV. Dinner on request. Central location for many stately homes and many other attractions. Secure parking.

Bedrooms: 1 single, 1 double, 1 twin
Bathrooms: 3 private

Lunch available
EM 1900 (LO 2300)
Parking for 2

LEADENHAM, Lincolnshire Map ref 3A1

♦♦♦ **GEORGE HOTEL**

High Street, Leadenham, Lincoln, LN5 0PN
T: (01400) 272251
F: (01400) 272091

Bedrooms: 1 single, 2 double, 3 twin
Bathrooms: 4 en suite, 1 public

Lunch available
EM 1900 (LO 2145)
Parking for 150
CC: Amex, Barclaycard, Delta, Diners, Eurocard, Mastercard, Solo, Switch, Visa

B&B per night:
S £30.00–£30.00
D £35.00–£45.00

OPEN All year round

A 17thC coaching inn, where we pride ourselves on our wide international menu and our collection of over 500 whiskies from all over the world.

WELCOME HOST This is a nationally recognised customer care programme which aims to promote the highest standards of service and a warm welcome. Establishments taking part in this initiative are indicated by the ⊚ symbol.

◆◆◆◆
Silver
Award

8 CLARENDON CRESCENT

Leamington Spa, CV32 5NR
T: (01926) 429840
F: (01926) 429190

B&B per night:
S £35.00–£35.00
D £55.00–£55.00

OPEN All year round

Grade II Listed Regency house overlooking private dell, in quiet backwater of Leamington Spa with its many shops and restaurants. Elegantly furnished with antiques. Individually designed en suite bedrooms. Five minutes' walk town centre, convenient for Warwick, Stratford, Royal Agricultural Centre and NEC.

Bedrooms: 2 single, 1 double, 1 twin
Bathrooms: 3 en suite, 1 private

Parking for 1

◆◆◆◆
THE COACH HOUSE

Snowford Hall Farm, Hunningham, Leamington Spa, CV33 9ES
T: (01926) 632297 (If out answerphone)
F: (01926) 633599
E: the_coach_house@lineone.net
I: lineone.net/~the_coach_house

Bedrooms: 1 double, 2 twin
Bathrooms: 2 en suite, 1 private

Parking for 4

B&B per night:
S £30.00–£34.00
D £40.00–£44.00

OPEN All year round

200-acre arable farm. Converted barn farmhouse off the Fosse Way, on the edge of Hunningham village. On elevated ground overlooking quiet surrounding countryside.

◆◆◆
HEDLEY VILLA GUEST HOUSE

31 Russell Terrace, Leamington Spa, CV31 1EZ
T: (01926) 424504 &
07767 207707 (Mobile)
F: (01926) 424504

Bedrooms: 3 single, 1 double, 2 triple, 1 family room
Bathrooms: 1 en suite, 3 public

B&B per night:
S £19.00–£25.00
D £38.00–£40.00

OPEN All year round

Homely guesthouse close to town centre. Convenient for National Exhibition Centre, National Agricultural Centre, Stratford, Coventry, Kenilworth, M40 and Warwick.

◆◆◆◆
HILL FARM

Lewis Road, Radford Semele, Leamington Spa, CV31 1UX
T: (01926) 337571

Bedrooms: 3 double, 2 twin
Bathrooms: 3 en suite, 1 public

Parking for 10

B&B per night:
S £20.00–£28.00
D £40.00–£50.00

OPEN All year round

350-acre mixed farm. Farmhouse set in large attractive garden, 2 miles from Leamington town centre and close to Warwick Castle and Stratford-upon-Avon.

◆◆◆
4 LILLINGTON ROAD

Leamington Spa, CV32 5YR
T: (01926) 429244
I: paulineburton@ukonline.co.uk

Bedrooms: 1 double, 2 twin
Bathrooms: 2 public, 1 private shower

B&B per night:
S £19.00–£19.00
D £38.00–£38.00

OPEN All year round

Attractive Victorian house within 5 minutes' walk of the town centre. Within easy reach of the NAC, NEC, Stratford-upon-Avon, Warwick and the Cotswolds.

CREDIT CARD BOOKINGS If you book by telephone and are asked for your credit card number it is advisable to check the proprietor's policy should you cancel your reservation.

LEAMINGTON SPA continued

◆◆◆ TRENDWAY GUEST HOUSE
45 Avenue Road, Leamington Spa,
CV31 3PF
T: (01926) 316644
F: (01926) 337506

Bedrooms: 4 twin,
2 triple
Bathrooms: 5 en suite,
1 private

EM 1800 (LO 1930)
Parking for 5

B&B per night:
S £23.00–£28.00
D £33.00–£40.00

HB per person:
DY £33.00–£40.00

OPEN All year round

Three-storey Victorian house with 6 letting bedrooms, just off the town centre and 5 minutes from railway station.

◆◆◆ VICTORIA PARK HOTEL
12 Adelaide Road, Leamington Spa,
CV31 3PW
T: (01926) 424195
F: (01926) 421521
I: www.victoria-park-hotel-ispa.co.uk

Bedrooms: 6 single,
6 double, 1 twin, 7 triple
Bathrooms: 20 en suite

Lunch available
EM 1830 (LO 1920)
Parking for 16
CC: Amex, Barclaycard,
Delta, Eurocard, Maestro,
Mastercard, Switch, Visa,
Visa Electron

B&B per night:
S £36.00–£45.00
D £50.00–£55.00

HB per person:
DY £52.50–£61.50

OPEN All year round

Victorian house close to bus and railway stations and town centre. Park, Pump Room, gardens, bowls, tennis and river all 3 minutes' walk away. .

LECHLADE, Gloucestershire Map ref 2B1

◆◆◆◆ CAMBRAI LODGE
Silver Award
Oak Street, Lechlade, GL7 3AY
T: (01367) 253173 & 07860 150467

Bedrooms: 2 single,
2 double
Bathrooms: 2 en suite,
1 public

Parking for 11

B&B per night:
S £28.00–£40.00
D £42.00–£55.00

OPEN All year round

Friendly, family-run guesthouse, recently modernised, close to River Thames. Ideal base for touring the Cotswolds. Four-poster bedroom, garden and ample parking.

◆◆◆ NEW INN HOTEL
Market Square, Lechlade-on-
Thames, Lechlade, GL7 3AB
T: (01367) 252296
F: (01367) 252315
E: newinnlech@aol.com
I: www.newinnhotel.co.uk

Bedrooms: 2 single,
9 double, 8 twin
Bathrooms: 19 en suite

Lunch available
EM 1830 (LO 2130)
Parking for 50
CC: Amex, Barclaycard,
Delta, Diners, Eurocard,
Mastercard, Switch, Visa

B&B per night:
S £42.50–£49.00
D £49.00–£65.00

HB per person:
DY £32.50–£40.00

OPEN All year round

Situated in a tranquil riverside setting, offering a comfortable blend of traditional hospitality and all modern advantages. Private parking. Restaurant and freehouse with en suite bedrooms.

LEDBURY, Herefordshire Map ref 2B1 *Tourist Information Centre Tel: (01531) 636147*

◆◆◆ MAINSTONE HOUSE
Trumpet, Ledbury, Herefordshire
HR8 2RA
T: (01531) 670230

Bedrooms: 1 double,
1 family room
Bathrooms: 2 private

Parking for 8

B&B per night:
D Min £34.00

OPEN All year round

Large 17thC former farmhouse with wealth of exposed beams. Large guest lounge and games room. Four miles from Ledbury towards Hereford. Old world pub opposite.

LEEK, Staffordshire Map ref 4B2 *Tourist Information Centre Tel: (01538) 483741*

◆◆◆ ABBEY INN
Abbey Green Road, Leek, ST13 8SA
T: (01538) 382865
F: (01538) 398604
E: martin@abbeyinn.co.uk
I: www.abbeyinn.co.uk

Bedrooms: 2 single,
2 double, 1 twin
Bathrooms: 5 en suite

Lunch available
EM 1830 (LO 2100)
Parking for 40
CC: Amex, Barclaycard,
Delta, Diners, Eurocard,
JCB, Mastercard, Switch,
Visa

B&B per night:
S £35.00–£35.00
D £50.00–£50.00

OPEN All year round

17thC inn with accommodation in a separate annexe, set in beautiful countryside, 1 mile from the town and just off the main A523.

MAP REFERENCES
Map references apply to the colour maps at the front of this guide.

LEEK continued

◆◆◆◆

PROSPECT HOUSE
334 Cheadle Road, Cheddleton,
Leek, ST13 7BW
T: (01782) 550639 &
07973 179478 (Mobile)
F: (01782) 550639
E: prospect@talk21.com
I: www.touristnetuk.com/wm/
prospect/index.htm

Bedrooms: 1 single,
1 double, 1 twin, 2 triple
Bathrooms: 5 en suite

EM 1700 (LO 2000)
Parking for 6
CC: Barclaycard, Delta,
Eurocard, JCB,
Mastercard, Visa

B&B per night:
S £21.00–£27.50
D £42.00–£45.00

HB per person:
DY £33.50–£35.00

OPEN All year round

A 19thC converted coach house in a tranquil courtyard setting, offering superior accommodation and a personal service tailored to your individual needs.

♠♞♿📞📺📠💧☎️ UL S ✂🏑 TV ▥ ☎✿ 🐕 SC 🚭 SP T

LEICESTER, Leicestershire Map ref 4C3 *Tourist Information Centre Tel: (0116) 299 8888*

◆◆◆

BURLINGTON HOTEL
Elmfield Avenue, Stoneygate,
Leicester, LE2 1RB
T: (0116) 270 5112 (Answerphone
between 11pm-7am)
F: (0116) 270 4207
E: welcome@burlingtonhotel.co.uk

Bedrooms: 9 single,
4 double, 2 twin, 1 triple
Bathrooms: 11 en suite,
1 public, 4 private
showers

EM 1845 (LO 2015)
Parking for 18
CC: Amex, Barclaycard,
Delta, Mastercard, Visa

B&B per night:
S £35.00–£45.00
D £48.00–£55.00

OPEN All year round

A friendly welcome awaits you at this family-run hotel. Situated in a quiet residential area close to the city centre.

♠♞📺📠💧☎️ S 🏑 TV ▥ ☎🍴20 ✿ ✈ SP T

◆◆◆

SPINDLE LODGE HOTEL
2 West Walk, Leicester, LE1 7NA
T: (0116) 233 8801
F: (0116) 233 8804
E: spindlelodgeleicester@hotmail.com

B&B per night:
S £27.50–£50.00
D £46.00–£65.00

OPEN All year round

Victorian house with friendly atmosphere, within easy walking distance of city centre, university, station, civic and entertainment centres.

Bedrooms: 5 single,
3 double, 3 twin, 2 triple
Bathrooms: 7 en suite,
3 public

EM 1800 (LO 1930)
Parking for 6
CC: Barclaycard, Delta,
Eurocard, JCB,
Mastercard, Switch, Visa

♠♞📞🖥💧☎️ S TV ▥ ☎🍴22 ✈ 🚐 SP T

LEOMINSTER, Herefordshire Map ref 2A1 *Tourist Information Centre Tel: (01568) 616460*

◆◆◆◆
Gold Award

THE PADDOCK
Shobdon, Leominster, Herefordshire
HR6 9NQ
T: (01568) 708176
F: (01568) 708829
E: thepaddock@talk21.com

B&B per night:
S £30.00–£30.00
D £42.00–£46.00

HB per person:
DY £36.00–£38.00

OPEN Feb–Dec

Delightful ground floor accommodation set in beautiful countryside bordering Wales. All rooms well equipped and en suite. Large garden and patio, ample off-road parking. Guests' lounge and dining room. We offer delicious home-cooked food and a very warm welcome.

Bedrooms: 4 double,
1 twin
Bathrooms: 5 en suite

Parking for 10

♠♞♿📺📠💧☎️ UL S ✂🏑 TV ▥ ☎☍✿ ✈ 🚐 🚭 SP 🏠 T

ACCESSIBILITY
Look for the 🚹🚹🚹 symbols which indicate accessibility for wheelchair users. A list of establishments is at the front of this guide.

LEOMINSTER continued

♦♦♦ **TYN-Y-COED**
Shobdon, Leominster, Herefordshire
HR6 9NY
T: (01568) 708277
F: (01568) 708277
E: jandrews@shobdondesign.kc3.
co.uk

Bedrooms: 1 double,
1 twin
Bathrooms: 1 en suite,
1 private

Parking for 2

B&B per night:
S £22.00–£22.00
D £40.00–£44.00

OPEN Apr–Oct

Country house in large garden on Mortimer Trail, close to Croft Castle and Berrington Hall (NT). Convenient for Leominster, Ludlow and Presteigne.

LICHFIELD, Staffordshire Map ref 4B3 *Tourist Information Centre Tel: (01543) 308209*

♦♦♦♦

BROAD LANE GUEST HOUSE
35 Broad Lane, Lichfield, WS14 9SU
T: (01543) 262301

B&B per night:
S £20.00–£22.00
D £40.00–£42.00

HB per person:
DY £28.00–£30.00

OPEN All year round

Detached, modern house, situated 1 mile from city centre. Maintained to a very high standard. Guests' own bathroom and car space. Home cooking.

Bedrooms: 1 twin
Bathrooms: 1 private

EM 1800 (LO 1930)
Parking for 1

♦♦♦

COPPERS END GUEST HOUSE
Walsall Road, Muckley Corner, Lichfield, WS14 0BG
T: (01543) 372910
F: (01543) 360423

B&B per night:
S £25.00–£34.00
D £40.00–£48.00

OPEN All year round

Detached guesthouse of character and charm in its own grounds. Conservatory dining room, large walled garden with patio, guests' own lounge, residential licence. All bedrooms non-smoking. Off-road parking. Easy access to M6, M42 and M1, Lichfield, Walsall and Birmingham. 16 miles to NEC, 6 miles Whittington Barracks. Motorcyle friendly.

Bedrooms: 3 double,
3 twin
Bathrooms: 3 en suite,
1 public

Parking for 10
CC: Amex, Barclaycard,
Delta, Diners, Eurocard,
Mastercard, Visa

♦♦♦♦ **THE FARMHOUSE**
Lysway Lane, Longdon Green,
Rugeley, WS15 4PZ
T: (0121) 378 4552 (day) &
(01543) 490416 (evening)
F: (0121) 311 2915
E: retail@daviddrury.demon.co.uk
I: www.daviddrury.demon.co.uk

Bedrooms: 1 single,
1 double, 1 twin
Bathrooms: 1 en suite,
1 private, 2 public

Parking for 6

B&B per night:
S Min £25.00
D £50.00–£55.00

OPEN All year round

Country residence with elegant bedrooms, cosy lounge. Within easy reach of the National Exhibition Centre, Belfry sporting club, Shugborough Hall. Lichfield 2.5 miles. Evening meals by arrangement.

♦♦ **THE WHITE HOUSE**
Market Lane, Wall, Lichfield,
WS14 0AS
T: (01543) 480384

Bedrooms: 2 twin
Bathrooms: 1 public

Parking for 6
CC: Barclaycard

B&B per night:
S Min £18.00
D Min £36.00

OPEN All year round

House built on site of Roman Baths. Some old beams in the house. Very peaceful, good garden. Near to motorway, NEC etc.

LINCOLN, Lincolnshire Map ref 4C2 *Tourist Information Centre Tel: (01522) 529828 or 579056*

♦♦♦♦
Silver Award

D'ISNEY PLACE HOTEL

Eastgate, Lincoln, LN2 4AA
T: (01522) 538881
F: (01522) 511321
E: info@disneyplacehotel.co.uk
I: www.disneyplacehotel.co.uk

Bedrooms: 1 single,
11 double, 3 twin,
2 family rooms; suite
available
Bathrooms: 17 en suite

Parking for 5
CC: Amex, Barclaycard,
Delta, Diners, Eurocard,
Maestro, Mastercard,
Switch, Visa

B&B per night:
S Min £63.00
D £82.00–£102.00

OPEN All year round

Small family-run hotel near the cathedral, with individually styled bedrooms and an emphasis on comfort and privacy.

♦♦♦

NEWPORT GUEST HOUSE

26-28 Newport, Lincoln, LN1 3DF
T: (01522) 528590
F: (01522) 544502
E: info@newportguesthouse.co.uk
I: www.newportguesthouse.co.uk

Bedrooms: 1 single,
2 double, 5 twin
Bathrooms: 3 en suite,
2 public

Parking for 5
CC: Amex, Barclaycard,
Delta, Diners, JCB,
Maestro, Mastercard,
Solo, Switch, Visa, Visa
Electron

B&B per night:
S £16.00–£28.00
D £32.00–£50.00

OPEN All year round

A Victorian double-fronted property, walking distance from historic centre of Lincoln. Own off-street parking for guests.

♦♦♦

73 STATION ROAD

Branston, Lincoln, LN4 1LG
T: (01522) 828658 &
07932 162940 (Mobile)

Bedrooms: 1 double,
1 twin
Bathrooms: 1 en suite,
1 private

Parking for 3

B&B per night:
D £40.00–£40.00

OPEN All year round

Bed and breakfast 3 miles from the city of Lincoln. Two bedrooms on ground floor overlooking attractive gardens. Off-street parking.

LONG BUCKBY, Northamptonshire Map ref 4C3

♦♦♦

MURCOTT MILL

Murcott, Long Buckby,
Northampton, NN6 7QR
T: (01327) 842236
F: (01327) 844524
E: bhart6@compuserve.com

Bedrooms: 1 double,
2 twin
Bathrooms: 3 en suite,
1 public

EM 1900 (LO 2030)
Parking for 12

B&B per night:
S £25.00–£30.00
D £42.00–£45.00

HB per person:
DY £35.00–£35.00

OPEN All year round

100-acre livestock farm. Imposing Georgian mill house overlooking open countryside. Recently renovated to a high standard, with open fires and en suite bedrooms. Ideal stopover for M1 travellers.

LOUGHBOROUGH, Leicestershire Map ref 4C3 *Tourist Information Centre Tel: (01509) 218113*

♦♦♦

CHARNWOOD LODGE

136 Leicester Road, Loughborough,
LE11 2AQ
T: (01509) 211120
F: (01509) 211121
E: charnwoodlodge@charwat.freeserve.co.uk
I: www.charnwoodlodge.com

B&B per night:
S £30.00–£45.00
D £40.00–£55.00

HB per person:
DY £37.50–£45.00

OPEN All year round

Elegant Victorian licensed guesthouse in pretty gardens with private parking. Peaceful, yet close to town centre, steam railway, university and Charnwood Forest. Spacious, comfortable interior with very attractive en suite rooms including a 4-poster suite. Ideal base for Leicester, Nottingham, Derby, East Midlands Airport and Donington Racecourse. Warm, friendly service assured.

Bedrooms: 1 single,
4 double, 1 twin, 2 triple
Bathrooms: 7 en suite,
1 private shower

Lunch available
EM 1800 (LO 2000)
Parking for 9
CC: Barclaycard, Delta,
Diners, Eurocard, JCB,
Maestro, Mastercard,
Solo, Switch, Visa, Visa
Electron

COLOUR MAPS Colour maps at the front of this guide pinpoint all places under which you will find accommodation listed.

LOUGHBOROUGH continued

DEMONTFORT HOTEL

◆◆◆

88 Leicester Road, Loughborough,
LE11 2AQ
T: (01509) 216061
F: (01509) 233667

Bedrooms: 1 single,
3 double, 2 twin, 3 triple
Bathrooms: 6 en suite,
1 public

Lunch available
EM 1830 (LO 2000)
CC: Amex, Barclaycard,
Diners, Eurocard,
Mastercard, Switch, Visa

B&B per night:
S £28.00–£35.00
D £40.00–£50.00

HB per person:
DY £35.00–£38.00

OPEN All year round

Family-run Victorian house hotel, with beautifully decorated rooms and warm, friendly atmosphere. Close to town centre, Steam Trust, Bell Foundry, University.

🅰️🐎🖥️🖵♿🔌👜🛎️🅢🕮📺🛏️🛋️❄️🏹🚗 SP T

◆◆◆

FOREST RISE HOTEL

55-57 Forest Road, Loughborough,
LE11 3NW
T: (01509) 215928
F: (01509) 210506

B&B per night:
S £25.00–£50.00
D £45.00–£80.00

HB per person:
DY £35.00–£60.00

OPEN All year round

Family-run establishment, friendly personal service, excellent standards throughout. Short walking distance to the town centre, university. Easy access to M1, M42, airport, Donington Park, Prestwold and Beaumanour Halls. Ample secure car parking, large garden and patio to the rear. 23 en suite bedrooms including executive, bridal, family, 4-poster rooms. All prices include full English breakfast.

Bedrooms: 8 single,
10 double, 1 twin,
4 triple
Bathrooms: 19 en suite,
4 private showers

EM 1900 (LO 2100)
Parking for 25
CC: Barclaycard, Delta,
Diners, Eurocard, JCB,
Maestro, Mastercard,
Solo, Switch, Visa, Visa
Electron

🐎♿🖥️📞🖵♿🔌👜🅢🕮📺🛏️🛋️❄️ SP

GARENDON PARK HOTEL

◆◆◆

92 Leicester Road, Loughborough,
LE11 2AQ
T: (01509) 236557
F: (01509) 265559
E: info@garendonparkhotel.co.uk
I: www.garendonparkhotel.co.uk

Bedrooms: 3 single,
2 double, 3 twin, 1 triple
Bathrooms: 7 en suite,
1 public

EM 1830 (LO 2030)
CC: Barclaycard, Delta,
Diners, Eurocard, JCB,
Mastercard, Solo, Switch,
Visa, Visa Electron

B&B per night:
S £25.00–£35.00
D £40.00–£50.00

HB per person:
DY £31.00–£41.00

OPEN All year round

Warm, friendly welcome and high standards in bright, comfortable surroundings. Five minutes from town centre. Local attractions include Great Central Railway, bell foundry, surrounding countryside.

🅰️🐎🖥️🖵♿🔌👜🅢📺🛏️🛋️❄️ SP T

LOUTH, Lincolnshire Map ref 4D2 *Tourist Information Centre Tel: (01507) 609289*

MASONS ARMS

◆◆◆

Cornmarket, Louth, LN11 9PY
T: (01507) 609525 & 609526
F: 0870 7066450
E: justin@themasons.co.uk
I: www.themasons.co.uk

Bedrooms: 3 single,
5 double, 2 twin
Bathrooms: 5 en suite,
2 public

Lunch available
EM 1900 (LO 2130)
Parking for 42
CC: Barclaycard, Eurocard,
Mastercard, Switch, Visa

B&B per night:
S £21.00–£36.00
D £36.00–£50.00

HB per person:
DY £27.00–£42.00

OPEN All year round

Friendly, family-run former posting inn which has been comfortably refurbished, reflecting the period. Centrally located in market town in the heart of the Wolds.

🅰️🐎🖥️🖵♿👜🅢❄️🛋️🍽️70►🏹🚗 SP 🏨 T

LUDFORD, Lincolnshire Map ref 4D2

LONG ACRE

◆◆◆

Magna Mile, Ludford, Market Rasen,
LN8 6AD
T: (01507) 313335
E: nick.feit@btinternet.com

Bedrooms: 1 single,
1 twin
Bathrooms: 1 en suite,
1 private

Parking for 3

B&B per night:
S £17.50–£25.00
D £35.00–£50.00

HB per person:
DY £27.50–£38.00

OPEN All year round

Large attractive bungalow with wheelchair access to both house and gardens. Situated on beautiful Linconshire Wolds, 20 miles from coast. Home cooking by arrangement.

🅰️🐎♿🖵♿🔌UL🅢❄️📺🛋️🖵∪►❄️🏹🚗 T

CONFIRM YOUR BOOKING

You are advised to confirm your booking in writing.

◆◆◆ BULL HOTEL

14 The Bull Ring, Ludlow, SY8 1AD
T: (01584) 873611
F: (01584) 873666
E: bull.ludlow@btinternet.com
I: www.goz.co.uk

Bedrooms: 2 double, 1 twin, 1 triple	Lunch available	
Bathrooms: 4 en suite	Parking for 8	
	CC: Amex, Delta, Eurocard, Mastercard, Visa	

B&B per night:
S £30.00–£33.00
D £45.00–£50.00

OPEN All year round

Situated in town centre. Oldest pub in Ludlow, earliest mention c1343. Was known as Peter of Proctors House and probably dates back to c1199.

◆◆◆ CECIL GUEST HOUSE

Sheet Road, Ludlow, SY8 1LR
T: (01584) 872442
F: (01584) 872442

Bedrooms: 2 single, 2 double, 4 twin, 1 triple
Bathrooms: 4 en suite, 2 public

EM 1900 (LO 0900)
Parking for 11
CC: Barclaycard, Delta, Eurocard, Mastercard, Visa

B&B per night:
S £20.00–£35.00
D £42.00–£56.00

HB per person:
DY £34.50–£49.50

OPEN All year round

Attractive guesthouse 15 minutes' walk from town centre and station. Freshly cooked food from local produce. Residents' bar and lounge. Off-street parking.

◆◆◆◆

CROWN INN

Hopton Wafers, DY14 0NB
T: (01299) 270372
F: (01299) 271127
E: desk@crownathopton.co.uk
I: www.go2.co.uk/crownathopton

B&B per night:
S £44.00–£52.00
D £70.00–£78.00

HB per person:
DY £55.00–£69.00

OPEN All year round

16thC coaching inn of exceptional period character, set in magnificent rolling countryside and only 30 minutes from M5 and M42. The perfect place to relax and discover the history and beauty of South Shropshire. En suite bedrooms and wide choice of menus. On A4117, 6 miles east of Ludlow.

Bedrooms: 6 double, 1 twin
Bathrooms: 7 en suite

Lunch available
EM 1800 (LO 2130)
Parking for 40
CC: Amex, Barclaycard, Delta, Eurocard, JCB, Mastercard, Switch, Visa, Visa Electron

---

◆◆◆ LONGLANDS

Woodhouse Lane, Richards Castle, Ludlow, SY8 4EU
T: (01584) 831636
E: iankkemsley@aol.com

Bedrooms: 1 double, 1 twin; suite available
Bathrooms: 1 en suite, 1 private

EM 1830 (LO 1930)
Parking for 2

B&B per night:
S £25.00–£25.00
D £45.00–£45.00

HB per person:
DY £37.00–£39.50

OPEN All year round

35-acre livestock farm. Farmhouse set in lovely rural landscape. Home-grown produce. Convenient for Ludlow, Mortimer Forest and Croft Castle. Interesting 14thC church and remains of 11thC castle in village.

◆◆◆◆◆ Gold Award

NUMBER TWENTY EIGHT

28 Lower Broad Street, Ludlow, SY8 1PQ
T: (01584) 876996 &
0800 0815000 (Reservations)
F: (01584) 876860
E: ross@no28.co.uk
I: www.no28.co.uk

B&B per night:
S £65.00–£80.00
D £75.00–£90.00

OPEN All year round

Three period townhouses of great charm and character, situated in old Ludlow town. All rooms individually furnished, providing superb en suite accommodation. We have more Michelin restaurants within walking distance than anywhere else in Britain! Come to lovely Ludlow, to relax, to eat, but most of all – to enjoy.

Bedrooms: 4 double, 2 twin
Bathrooms: 6 en suite, 1 public

CC: Barclaycard, Delta, Mastercard, Switch, Visa

LUDLOW continued

◆◆◆◆ Gold Award

RAVENSCOURT MANOR
Woofferton, Ludlow, SY8 4AL
T: (01584) 711905

B&B per night:
S £30.00–£40.00
D £50.00–£65.00

HB per person:
DY £37.50–£40.00

OPEN All year round

Historic beamed manor-house, 3 miles from Ludlow with its famous restaurants, castle and festival. Excellent en suite accommodation, tastefully decorated and furnished with antiques. Central heating, TV, tea/coffee-making facilities. Beautiful area for walking and touring. Warm welcome assured. Half board prices based on minimum 2-night stay.

Bedrooms: 2 double, 1 twin
Bathrooms: 3 en suite

Parking for 10

◆◆◆◆

THE WHEATSHEAF INN
Lower Broad Street, Ludlow, SY8 1PQ
T: (01584) 872980
F: (01584) 877990
E: karen.wheatsheaf@tinyworld.co.uk

Bedrooms: 4 double, 1 twin
Bathrooms: 5 en suite

Lunch available
EM 1830 (LO 2100)
CC: Barclaycard, Delta, Eurocard, JCB, Mastercard, Switch, Visa, Visa Electron

B&B per night:
S £25.00–£45.00
D £40.00–£50.00

OPEN All year round

Family-run mid-17thC beamed inn, 100 yards from the town centre, nestling under Ludlow's historic 13thC Broad Gate, the last remaining of 7 town gates.

MALVERN, Worcestershire Map ref 2B1 *Tourist Information Centre Tel: (01684) 892289*

◆◆◆◆

PEMBRIDGE HOTEL
114 Graham Road, Malvern, WR14 2HX
T: (01684) 574813
F: (01684) 566885
E: pembridgehotel@aol.com

Bedrooms: 4 double, 4 twin
Bathrooms: 8 en suite

Lunch available
EM 1900 (LO 2000)
Parking for 10
CC: Amex, Barclaycard, Delta, Mastercard, Switch, Visa, Visa Electron

B&B per night:
S £40.00–£48.00
D £60.00–£68.00

HB per person:
DY £39.00–£47.00

OPEN All year round

Small, friendly, detached hotel, close to town centre and Malvern Hills. Ample car parking. Double en suite rooms, full English breakfast, light evening suppers.

MARKET DRAYTON, Shropshire Map ref 4A2 *Tourist Information Centre Tel: (01630) 652139*

◆◆

HEATH FARM BED AND BREAKFAST
Heath Farm, Hodnet, Market Drayton, TF9 3JJ
T: (01630) 685570
F: (01630) 685570
E: hugh@gallery81.freeserve.co.uk

Bedrooms: 1 double, 2 twin
Bathrooms: 1 public

Parking for 5

B&B per night:
S £16.00–£18.00
D £32.00–£36.00

OPEN All year round

60-acre mixed farm. Traditional farmhouse welcome. Situated 1.5 miles south of Hodnet off A442, approached by private drive. Hodnet Hall, Hawkstone, Potteries, Ironbridge, Shrewsbury.

MARKET HARBOROUGH, Leicestershire Map ref 4C3 *Tourist Information Centre Tel: (01858) 821270*

◆◆◆◆

THE GEORGE AT GREAT OXENDON
Great Oxendon, Market Harborough, LE16 8NA
T: (01858) 465205
F: (01858) 465205

Bedrooms: 2 double, 1 twin
Bathrooms: 3 en suite

Lunch available
EM 1900 (LO 2200)
Parking for 36
CC: Amex, Barclaycard, Delta, Eurocard, JCB, Mastercard, Solo, Switch, Visa

B&B per night:
S £52.00–£55.00
D £55.00–£65.00

OPEN All year round

Bedroom accommodation and restaurant with bars and conservatory, all with views of the garden. Ex-QE2 chef/proprietor. Established 1986.

MARKET HARBOROUGH continued

◆◆◆ THE OLD HOUSE

Church Street, Wilbarston, Market
Harborough, LE16 8QG
T: (01536) 771724 (answerphone)
F: (01536) 771622
E: oldhousebb@aol.com

Bedrooms: 1 single,
1 double, 1 twin
Bathrooms: 2 en suite,
1 private

Parking for 2

B&B per night:
S £30.00
D £40.00

OPEN All year round

Welcome to our Grade II Listed stone village house dating from the 15thC. Large garden overlooking open countryside. Log fires. Home-made bread.

MARKET RASEN, Lincolnshire Map ref 4D2

◆◆◆ WAVENEY COTTAGE GUESTHOUSE

Willingham Road, Market Rasen,
LN8 3DN
T: (01673) 843236
F: (01673) 843236

Bedrooms: 1 double,
2 twin
Bathrooms: 2 en suite,
1 private

EM
Parking for 4

B&B per night:
S Min £21.50
D Min £39.00

HB per person:
DY £28.00–£29.50

OPEN All year round

Charming cottage offering a warm welcome. Clean, comfortable en suite accommodation. Home cooking our speciality. Close to local amenities, Lincolnshire Wolds and National Cycle Route.

MATLOCK, Derbyshire Map ref 4B2 *Tourist Information Centre Tel: (01629) 583388*

◆◆◆◆◆
Silver
Award

ROBERTSWOOD GUESTHOUSE

Farley Hill, Matlock, DE4 3LL
T: (01629) 55642
F: (01629) 55642
E: robertswood@supanet.com
I: www.robertswood.com

B&B per night:
D £48.00–£56.00

OPEN All year round

Robertswood is an elegant Victorian stone house in its own large garden. Peaceful, yet walking distance from centre of Matlock. Spacious and attactive interior with panoramic views. All bedrooms are en suite. On the edge of the Peak District, an ideal base for Derbyshire's many interesting places.

Bedrooms: 6 double,
2 twin
Bathrooms: 8 en suite

EM 1900 (LO 1900)
Parking for 8
CC: Barclaycard, Delta,
JCB, Maestro, Mastercard,
Switch, Visa, Visa Electron

MEDBOURNE, Leicestershire Map ref 4C3

◆◆◆◆

HOMESTEAD HOUSE

5 Ashley Road, Medbourne,
Market Harborough, LE16 8DL
T: (01858) 565724
F: (01858) 565324

B&B per night:
S Min £25.00
D Min £39.50

OPEN All year round

In a elevated position overlooking the Welland Valley on the outskirts of Medbourne, a picturesque village dating back to Roman times. Surrounded by open countryside and within easy reach of many places of interest. Three tastefully decorated bedrooms with rural views. A warm wlecome awaits you.

Bedrooms: 3 twin
Bathrooms: 3 en suite

EM 1800 (LO 2000)
Parking for 6
CC: Barclaycard,
Mastercard, Visa

QUALITY ASSURANCE SCHEME

Diamond ratings and awards were correct at the time of going to press but are subject to change. Please check at the time of booking.

MELTON MOWBRAY, Leicestershire Map ref 4C3 *Tourist Information Centre Tel: (01664) 480992*

♦♦♦♦

AMBERLEY GARDENS

4 Church Lane, Asfordby, Melton Mowbray, LE14 3RU
T: (01664) 812314
F: (01664) 813740
E: bruce.amberleybnb@ukgateway.net
I: members.aol.com/MeltonWeb/amberley.htm

B&B per night:
S £20.00–£25.00
D £38.00–£44.00

OPEN All year round

Beautiful riverside bungalow in conservation area. Acre of idyllic floodlit lawns and gardens to the river's edge. Enjoy breakfast in the garden room with the interest of swans and bird life on the river bank. Watch for foxes. Comfortable beds, good breakfasts, ample parking. A warm welcome awaits you.

Bedrooms: 1 double, 1 twin, 1 triple
Bathrooms: 2 en suite, 1 private

Parking for 7

□ ♦ ⌐ UL S ⌙ Ⅲ ◨ ♪ ✳ ✕ 🚗 T

♦♦♦♦

TOLE COTTAGE

10 Main Street, Kirby Bellars, Melton Mowbray, LE14 2EA
T: (01664) 812932
E: michael@handjean.freeserve.co.uk

B&B per night:
S £20.00–£25.00
D £40.00–£42.00

HB per person:
DY £30.00–£35.00

OPEN All year round

Situated in the heart of the picturesque Wreake Valley, a warm welcome awaits you at Tole Cottage. This charming, early 19thC traditional home has a colourful garden and inspirational interior. Ideal for touring or weekend breaks, guests can enjoy the relaxed atmosphere and home-cooked food in quiet, comfortable surroundings. Three miles south Melton Mowbray.

Bedrooms: 1 single, 1 double, 1 triple; suite available
Bathrooms: 1 en suite, 1 public

Parking for 3

🐴7 ⚄ ♦ ⌐ UL S ⌙ ⍥ TV Ⅲ ◨ ∪ ▸ ✳ ✕ 🚗 🔌 🏠 T

MERIDEN, West Midlands Map ref 4B3

♦♦

BONNIFINGLAS GUEST HOUSE

3 Berkswell Road, Meriden, Coventry, CV7 7LB
T: (01676) 523193 (answerphone) & 07721 363987
F: (01676) 523193

Bedrooms: 2 single, 2 double, 3 twin, 1 triple
Bathrooms: 8 en suite

EM 1800 (LO 1900)
Parking for 12

B&B per night:
S Max £25.00
D Max £38.00

OPEN All year round

Country house, all rooms en suite with TV. Several pubs and restaurants within walking distance.

🐴 □ ♦ ⌐ UL ▮ S TV Ⅲ ◨ ✳ 🚗 SP T

CHECK THE MAPS

The colour maps at the front of this guide show all the cities, towns and villages for which you will find accommodation entries. Refer to the town index to find the page on which they are listed.

MINCHINHAMPTON, Gloucestershire Map ref 2B1

◆◆◆◆

VALE VIEW
Besbury, Minchinhampton, Stroud,
GL6 9EP
T: (01453) 882610
F: (01453) 882610
E: reservations@vale-view.co.uk
I: www.vale-view.co.uk

B&B per night:
D £45.00–£45.00

OPEN All year round

The neighbours are ponies, rabbits, badgers and foxes at our lovely family home in 2.5 acres, with stunning Cotswold views. Ten minutes' walk to historic Minchinhampton with restaurant, pubs and golf course. Gatcombe and Badminton are close by. Visit nearby Cheltenham, Bath, Bristol and pretty Cotswold villages. Both rooms en suite.

Bedrooms: 1 twin,
1 family room
Bathrooms: 2 en suite

Parking for 10

MINSTERLEY, Shropshire Map ref 4A3

◆◆◆◆

CRICKLEWOOD COTTAGE
Plox Green, Minsterley, Shrewsbury,
SY5 0HT
T: (01743) 791229
I: www.SmoothHound.co.uk/hotels/crickle.htm

B&B per night:
S £23.50–£39.00
D £47.00–£52.00

OPEN All year round

Delightful 18thC cottage at foot of Stiperstones Hills, retaining its original character with exposed beams, inglenook fireplace and traditional furnishings. Beautiful countryside views from bedrooms and sun room where breakfast is served. Inviting cottage garden and trout stream. Excellent restaurants/inns nearby. Close Shrewsbury and Ironbridge. Brochure available.

Bedrooms: 2 double,
1 twin
Bathrooms: 3 en suite

Parking for 4

MONSAL HEAD, Derbyshire Map ref 4B2

◆◆◆

CLIFFE HOUSE
Monsal Head, Bakewell, DE45 1NL
T: (01629) 640376
F: (01629) 640376
I: www.cliffhouse.co.uk

Bedrooms: 4 double,
2 twin
Bathrooms: 6 en suite

Parking for 12
CC: Barclaycard,
Mastercard, Visa

B&B per night:
S £25.00–£35.00
D £48.00–£50.00

OPEN All year round

Country house with splendid views of Monsal Dale and surrounding countryside. An ideal base for exploring the Peak District.

MORETON–IN–MARSH, Gloucestershire Map ref 2B1

◆◆◆

BLUE CEDAR HOUSE
Stow Road, Moreton-in-Marsh,
GL56 0DW
T: (01608) 650299
E: gandsib@dialstart.net

Bedrooms: 1 single,
1 double, 1 twin,
1 family room
Bathrooms: 2 en suite,
2 public

EM 1800 (LO 1800)
Parking for 7

B&B per night:
S £21.00–£28.00
D £41.00–£44.00

OPEN Feb–Nov

Attractive detached residence set in half-acre garden in the Cotswolds, with pleasantly decorated, well-equipped accommodation and garden room. Complimentary tea/coffee. Close to village centre.

RATING All accommodation in this guide has been rated, or is awaiting a rating, by a trained English Tourism Council assessor.

MORETON-IN-MARSH continued

♦♦♦ DITCHFORD FARMHOUSE

Stretton on Fosse, Moreton-in-Marsh, GL56 9RD T: (01608) 663307 E: r.b.ditchford@talk21.com I: www.warks.co.uk	Bedrooms: 3 double, 1 twin, 2 family rooms Bathrooms: 3 en suite, 3 private	Parking for 8

B&B per night:
S £27.00–£32.00
D £46.00–£52.00

OPEN All year round

1000-acre arable farm. Secluded Georgian farmhouse in lovely north Cotswold countryside. Large garden with children's corner. Home-grown produce and country cooking. Winter breaks with log fires.

ⓜ♞⌂▯♿♒ⓘⓢ✁♨Ⓣⓥ▥▤♪❋❋➳SP🏠Ⓣ

♦♦♦ FARRIERS ARMS

Todenham, Moreton-in-Marsh, GL56 9PF T: (01608) 650901 & 07771 540261 E: wmoore9701@aol.com I: www.farriersarms.com	Bedrooms: 1 double, 1 triple Bathrooms: 1 en suite, 1 private	Lunch available EM 1830 (LO 2130) Parking for 25 CC: Barclaycard, Delta, Mastercard, Switch, Visa

B&B per night:
S £18.00–£30.00
D Min £46.00

HB per person:
DY £28.00–£40.00

OPEN All year round

Family-run bar and restaurant with comfortable, quiet spacious rooms. Picturesque Cotswold village with views over valley.

ⓜ♞☐▯♿♒ⓘⓢ♠♪❋➳SPⓉ

♦♦♦♦ FOSSEWAY FARM

Fosseway, Moreton-in-Marsh, GL56 0DS T: (01608) 650503	Bedrooms: 2 double, 1 twin, 1 triple Bathrooms: 4 en suite	Parking for 4 CC: Barclaycard, Mastercard, Visa

B&B per night:
S £20.00–£30.00
D £40.00–£45.00

OPEN All year round

Fosseway Farm is just a 5 minute walk into Morton-in-Marsh town. All rooms have en suite, TV, hairdryer and refreshments. Camping facilities.

♞14▯♿♒ULⓈ✁♨Ⓣⓥ▥♟♒❋➳SP

♦♦♦ NEW FARM

Dorn, Moreton-in-Marsh, GL56 9NS
T: (01608) 650782

B&B per night:
S £20.00–£25.00
D £38.00–£44.00

OPEN All year round

Old Cotswold farmhouse in small hamlet. Guests can enjoy, at very competitive prices, well-appointed, spacious bedrooms with private facilities, colour TV, coffee/tea tray. Beautiful double 4-poster bedroom and very attractive twin room. All rooms furnished with antiques. Dining room has large, impressive fireplace. Breakfast menu with hot crispy bread served.

Bedrooms: 2 double, 1 twin Bathrooms: 2 en suite, 1 private	Parking for 6

ⓜ♞3🗄▯♿UL♨Ⓣⓥ▥♿❋➳SPⓉ

COUNTRY CODE Always follow the Country Code ⚘ Enjoy the countryside and respect its life and work ⚘ Guard against all risk of fire ⚘ Fasten all gates ⚘ Keep your dogs under close control ⚘ Keep to public paths across farmland ⚘ Use gates and stiles to cross fences, hedges and walls ⚘ Leave livestock, crops and machinery alone ⚘ Take your litter home ⚘ Help to keep all water clean ⚘ Protect wildlife, plants and trees ⚘ Take special care on country roads ⚘ Make no unnecessary noise

MORETON-IN-MARSH continued

♦♦♦

OLD FARM

Dorn, Moreton-in-Marsh, GL56 9NS
T: (01608) 650394
F: (01608) 650394
E: simon@righton.freeserve.co.uk

B&B per night:
S Min £20.00
D Min £36.00

OPEN Mar–Oct

Enjoy the delights of a 15thC farmhouse on a 250-acre mixed farm surrounded by beautiful Cotswold countryside. Spacious en suite double bedrooms including 4-poster, twin room available. Tennis and croquet on lawn. Children welcome. Peaceful setting for relaxing break, ideal base for visiting Cotswolds/Stratford and only 1 mile from Moreton.

Bedrooms: 2 double, 1 twin
Bathrooms: 2 en suite, 1 public

Parking for 8

♦♦♦

WARWICK HOUSE

London Road, Moreton-in-Marsh, GL56 0HH
T: (01608) 650773
F: (01608) 650773
E: charlie@warwickhousebnb.demon.co.uk
I: www.snoozeandsizzle.com

B&B per night:
S £15.00–£25.00
D £35.00–£40.00

OPEN All year round

A lovely detached house with on-site parking. Five minutes' walk to centre, bus and railway station. Will collect from station, call on arrival. Rooms are large and well equipped including telephone, hairdryer, video player and fridge. Member of next door leisure club: swimming, sauna, squash and gym. Price deals available.

Bedrooms: 2 double, 1 twin
Bathrooms: 2 en suite, 1 private, 3 public

Parking for 7

MUCH MARCLE, Herefordshire Map ref 2B1

♦♦♦♦

BODENHAM FARM

Much Marcle, Ledbury, Herefordshire HR8 2NJ
T: (01531) 660222

B&B per night:
S £18.00–£25.00
D £36.00–£50.00

HB per person:
DY £18.00–£25.00

OPEN All year round

18thC Listed farmhouse set in 5 acres within conservation area. Many original features including oak beams and polished elm floors. Two 4-poster bedrooms plus one twin room. En suite or private bathroom, drawing and dining rooms for sole use of guests. Equal distance Ledbury and Ross-on-Wye, M50 4 miles.

Bedrooms: 2 double, 1 twin
Bathrooms: 2 en suite, 1 private

Parking for 8

TOWN INDEX

This can be found at the back of this guide. If you know where you want to stay, the index will give you the page number listing accommodation in your chosen town, city or village.

MUCH WENLOCK, Shropshire Map ref 4A3

◆◆◆ **GASKELL ARMS HOTEL**

Much Wenlock, TF13 6AQ
T: (01952) 727212
F: (01952) 728505

Bedrooms: 7 double,
3 twin, 1 family room
Bathrooms: 6 en suite,
2 public

Lunch available
EM 1900 (LO 2200)
Parking for 31
CC: Amex, Barclaycard,
Delta, Mastercard, Switch,
Visa

B&B per night:
S £36.00–£46.00
D £56.00–£80.00

HB per person:
DY £45.00–£60.00

OPEN All year round

17thC coaching inn built of stone and brick, with beamed ceilings, log fires. Family-run freehouse. Outskirts of small medieval town and Wenlock Edge, close to Ironbridge.

◆◆◆ **WALTON HOUSE**

35 Barrow Street, Much Wenlock,
TF13 6EP
T: (01952) 727139

Bedrooms: 1 single,
2 twin
Bathrooms: 1 public

Parking for 2

B&B per night:
S £16.00–£16.00
D £32.00–£32.00

OPEN Apr–Oct

Two minutes' walk from town centre. 5 miles from Ironbridge Gorge, 13 miles from Shrewsbury, 8 miles from Bridgnorth and 10 miles from Telford town centre. Lawns and patio.

NAILSWORTH, Gloucestershire Map ref 2B1

◆◆◆◆ **AARON FARM**

Nympsfield Road, Nailsworth,
Stroud, GL6 0ET
T: (01453) 833598
F: (01453) 833626
E: aaronfarm@aol.com
I: www.aaronfarm-
bedandbreakfast.co.uk

Bedrooms: 1 double,
2 twin
Bathrooms: 3 en suite

EM 1800 (LO 2000)
Parking for 6

B&B per night:
S £28.00–£30.00
D £40.00–£42.00

HB per person:
DY £33.00–£35.00

OPEN All year round

Former farmhouse, with large en suite bedrooms and panoramic views of the Cotswolds. Ideal touring centre. Many walks and attractions. Home cooking. Brochure on request.

NAUNTON, Gloucestershire Map ref 2B1

◆◆◆

NAUNTON VIEW GUESTHOUSE

Naunton, Cheltenham, GL54 3AD
T: (01451) 850482 (Answerphone)
F: (01451) 850482

B&B per night:
S £30.00–£35.00
D £45.00–£50.00

OPEN All year round

Recently opened family-run guesthouse in picturesque village near Bourton-on-the-Water. Good base for touring the Cotswolds and within easy reach of Bath and Stratford as well as having excellent walks in the area. All rooms en suite with TV and tea-making facilities. Good views over the village and plenty of safe off-road parking.

Bedrooms: 3 double
Bathrooms: 3 en suite

CC: Barclaycard, Delta,
Maestro, Mastercard,
Solo, Switch, Visa

AT-A-GLANCE SYMBOLS

Symbols at the end of each accommodation entry give useful information about services and facilities. A key to symbols can be found inside the back cover flap. Keep this open for easy reference.

NEWARK, Nottinghamshire Map ref 4C2 *Tourist Information Centre Tel: (01636) 655765*

◆◆◆

THE BOOT AND SHOE INN

Main Street, Flintham, Newark, NG23 5LA
T: (01636) 525246

B&B per night:
S Min £32.00
D Min £48.00

OPEN All year round

A 17thC village pub recently renovated to a high standard. All rooms en suite. Situated in an unspoilt conservation area at the edge of the Vale of Belvoir, 6 miles from Newark. Easy access off A46 to Nottingham, Leicester and Lincoln.

Bedrooms: 1 twin, 3 family rooms
Bathrooms: 4 en suite

EM 1900 (LO 2200)
Parking for 20
CC: Barclaycard, Delta, JCB, Mastercard, Switch, Visa

NEWLAND, Gloucestershire Map ref 2A1

◆◆◆

TAN HOUSE FARM
Newland, Coleford, GL16 8NP
T: (015948) 32222

Bedrooms: 2 double, 1 family room
Bathrooms: 3 en suite

Parking for 20

B&B per night:
S £23.00–£23.00
D £46.00–£46.00

OPEN All year round

14-acre livestock farm. Post Restoration. Queen Anne house dating from 1670, situated in one of the most beautiful villages in the Forest of Dean. Walking distance of 16thC pub.

NEWPORT, Shropshire Map ref 4A3

◆◆◆◆

Silver Award

LANE END FARM
Chetwynd, Newport, Shropshire TF10 8BN
T: (01952) 550337 (answerphone) & 0777 1632255 (mobile)
F: (01952) 550337
E: lane1.endfarm@ondigital.com
I: www.virtual-shropshire.co.uk/lef

Bedrooms: 2 double, 1 twin
Bathrooms: 2 en suite, 1 private

EM 1800 (LO 2100)
Parking for 5

B&B per night:
S £25.00–£25.00
D £40.00–£40.00

HB per person:
DY £31.00–£36.00

OPEN All year round

Delightful period farmhouse in lovely countryside, on A41 near Newport. Ideal for business/leisure, with good local walks. Reductions for 3 nights or more.

◆◆◆◆

NORWOOD HOUSE HOTEL AND RESTAURANT
Pave Lane, Newport, Shropshire TF10 9LQ
T: (01952) 825896
F: (01952) 825896

Bedrooms: 1 single, 1 double, 1 twin, 1 triple
Bathrooms: 4 en suite

Lunch available
Parking for 26
CC: Barclaycard, Delta, Eurocard, Mastercard, Switch, Visa

B&B per night:
S £30.00–£35.00
D £40.00–£45.00

OPEN All year round

Family-run hotel of character, just off the A41 Wolverhampton to Whitchurch road. Close to Lilleshall National Sports Centre, RAF Cosford and Ironbridge Gorge.

NORTHAMPTON, Northamptonshire Map ref 2C1 *Tourist Information Centre Tel: (01604) 622677*

◆◆◆◆

POPLARS HOTEL
Cross Street, Moulton, Northampton, NN3 7RZ
T: (01604) 643983
F: (01604) 790233
E: poplars@btclick.com

Bedrooms: 2 single, 4 double, 1 twin, 6 triple, 1 family room
Bathrooms: 14 en suite, 2 public

EM 1830 (LO 2000)
Parking for 21
CC: Amex, Barclaycard, Delta, Mastercard, Visa

B&B per night:
S £42.50–£49.50
D £55.00–£65.00

HB per person:
DY £55.00–£85.00

OPEN All year round

Personal attention is given at this small country hotel in the heart of Northamptonshire. Within easy reach of many tourist attractions.

◆◆◆◆

QUINTON GREEN FARM
Quinton, Northampton, NN7 2EG
T: (01604) 863685
F: (01604) 862230

Bedrooms: 1 single, 1 double, 1 twin
Bathrooms: 3 en suite

B&B per night:
S £25.00–£27.50
D £45.00–£50.00

OPEN All year round

Comfortable, rambling 17thC farmhouse with lovely views over own farmland. Convenient for Northampton, M1 (junction 15), Milton Keynes, Silverstone, Althorpe, Castle Ashby. Ample parking.

NORTHLEACH, Gloucestershire Map ref 2B1

Silver
Award

Detached family house in the country with large gardens and home-grown produce. Evening meals available with a large menu to choose from to suit all tastes. All rooms en suite on the ground floor. Excellent centre for visiting the Cotswolds and close to local services. A warm welcome awaits you.

NORTHFIELD BED AND BREAKFAST
Cirencester Road (A429), Northleach,
Cheltenham, GL54 3JL
T: (01451) 860427 (before 6pm)
F: (01451) 860820
E: nrthfield0@aol.com

Bedrooms: 1 double,
1 twin, 1 family room
Bathrooms: 3 en suite

EM 1800 (LO 1900)
Parking for 10
CC: Barclaycard, Delta,
Eurocard, JCB, Maestro,
Mastercard, Solo, Switch,
Visa, Visa Electron

B&B per night:
S Min £30.00
D £48.00–£56.00

HB per person:
DY £37.75–£45.35

OPEN All year round

NOTTINGHAM, Nottinghamshire Map ref 4C2 *Tourist Information Centre Tel: (0115) 915 5330*

ACORN HOTEL
4 Radcliffe Road, West Bridgford,
Nottingham, Nottinghamshire
NG2 5FW
T: (0115) 981 1297
F: (0115) 981 7654
E: acornhotel2@radcliffe18.
freeserve.co.uk

Bedrooms: 2 single,
8 twin, 2 family rooms
Bathrooms: 12 en suite,
2 public

Parking for 10
CC: Amex, Barclaycard,
Delta, Diners, Eurocard,
Mastercard, Visa

B&B per night:
S £30.00–£32.00
D £45.00–£47.00

OPEN All year round

Comfortable family-run hotel, convenient for city centre and Nottingham's sporting attractions. Situated on main bus route, within walking distance of many varied local restaurants.

ADAMS CASTLE VIEW GUESTHOUSE
85 Castle Boulevard, Nottingham,
Nottinghamshire NG7 1FE
T: (0115) 950 0022

Bedrooms: 2 single,
1 double, 1 twin
Bathrooms: 3 en suite,
1 public

B&B per night:
S £20.00–£22.00
D £40.00–£44.00

OPEN All year round

Late-Victorian private dwelling, completely refurbished to accommodate guests. Close to city centre, railway and bus stations. Museums, theatres, concert venues within easy walking distance.

NUNEATON, Warwickshire Map ref 4B3 *Tourist Information Centre Tel: (024) 7634 7006*

LA TAVOLA CALDA
70 Midland Road, Abbey Green,
Nuneaton, CV11 5DY
T: (024) 7638 3195 &
07747 010702 (mobile)
F: (024) 7638 1816

Bedrooms: 1 single,
5 twin, 2 triple
Bathrooms: 8 en suite

EM 1900 (LO 2200)
Parking for 30
CC: Amex, Barclaycard,
Delta, Diners, Eurocard,
Mastercard, Switch, Visa

B&B per night:
S £20.00–£25.00
D £32.00–£35.00

HB per person:
DY £28.50–£55.00

OPEN All year round

Family-run Italian restaurant and hotel.

OAKAMOOR, Staffordshire Map ref 4B2

BEEHIVE GUEST HOUSE
Churnet View Road, Oakamoor,
Stoke-on-Trent, ST10 3AE
T: (01538) 702420

Bedrooms: 2 double,
1 twin, 2 family rooms
Bathrooms: 3 en suite,
2 public

Parking for 8
CC: Barclaycard, Delta,
Eurocard, JCB,
Mastercard, Solo, Switch,
Visa

B&B per night:
D £36.00–£40.00

OPEN Apr–Nov

Family-run guesthouse, overlooking river and parkland, in the beautiful Churnet Valley. Within walking distance of Alton Towers. Rooms comfortably furnished.

WHERE TO STAY
Please mention this guide when making your booking.

◆◆◆◆

RIBDEN FARM
Oakamoor, Stoke-on-Trent, ST10 3BW
T: (01538) 702830 & 702153
F: (01538) 702830
I: www.ribdenfarm.com

B&B per night:
D £40.00–£50.00

OPEN All year round

Ribden Farm is a mid 18thC Grade II Listed farmhouse. Sympathetically renovated, exposed oak beams and crooked floors. All rooms have TV, tea/coffee facilities and toiletries, some have 4-poster beds. Two miles from Alton Towers and ideal for visiting Peak District and Potteries. Large gardens with safe off-road parking.

Bedrooms: 2 double,
1 triple, 4 family rooms
Bathrooms: 6 en suite,
1 private

Parking for 8
CC: Barclaycard, Delta,
Mastercard, Solo, Switch,
Visa

OAKHAM, Rutland Map ref 4C3 *Tourist Information Centre Tel: (01572) 724329*

◆◆◆

HALL FARM
Cottesmore Road, Exton, Oakham, Rutland
LE15 8AN
T: (01572) 812271 &
07711 979628 (Mobile)

B&B per night:
S £20.00–£24.50
D £35.00–£44.00

OPEN All year round

25-acre arable and horses farm. Early 19thC Grade II Listed stone farmhouse in open countryside. Approximately 2 miles from Rutland Water north shore and 1 mile from Geoff Hamilton's TV gardens. TV, hairdryer and hot drinks in all rooms. Many of our guests are now making frequent return visits.

Bedrooms: 1 double,
1 twin, 1 triple
Bathrooms: 1 en suite,
1 public

Parking for 6

◆◆◆

THE TITHE BARN
Clatterpot Lane, Cottesmore, Oakham,
Leicestershire LE15 7DW
T: (01572) 813591
F: (01572) 812719
E: jpryke@thetithebarn.co.uk

B&B per night:
S £20.00–£35.00
D £40.00–£48.00

OPEN All year round

17thC converted tithe barn. Outstanding original dovecote. Spacious and comfortable en suite rooms with a wealth of original features. Panelled dining room and attractive garden. In the heart of unspoilt Rutland, 5 minutes from Rutland Water, Geoff Hamilton's Barnsdale Gardens, Stamford, Oakham and A1. Children and dogs welcome.

Bedrooms: 1 double,
2 twin, 1 family room
Bathrooms: 3 en suite,
1 private, 1 public

Parking for 6
CC: Barclaycard, Delta,
JCB, Mastercard, Switch,
Visa, Visa Electron

CHECK THE MAPS
The colour maps at the front of this guide show all the cities, towns and villages for which you will find accommodation entries.
Refer to the town index to find the page on which they are listed.

OSGATHORPE, Leicestershire Map ref 4B3

◆◆◆ **THE ROYAL OAK INN**
20 Main Street, Osgathorpe,
Loughborough, LE12 9TA
T: (01530) 222443 (24 hours) &
07885 377652 (mobile)

Bedrooms: 2 double,
2 twin
Bathrooms: 4 en suite

Parking for 50

B&B per night:
S £30.00–£35.00
D £40.00–£45.00

OPEN All year round

*High standard coaching inn with chalet accommodation, in picturesque countryside.
Award winning gardens. Secure parking. Close to M1, M42, East Midlands Airport and
Donington Park.*

🐎 🛏 📞 ☐ ⬇ 🗄 🖺 🖩 ➡ 🍴 ✳ ✈ 🚲 🎴 Ⓣ

OUNDLE, Northamptonshire Map ref 3A1 *Tourist Information Centre Tel: (01832) 274333*

Rating
Applied For

TANSOR LODGE
Elmington, Oundle, Peterborough, PE8 5JY
T: (01832) 226070
F: (01832) 226474

B&B per night:
S £29.00–£29.00
D £42.00–£42.00

HB per person:
DY £26.95–£41.95

OPEN All year round

*A warm welcome awaits you in our
large, comfortable Georgian
farmhouse set in 1.25 acres of
gardens. All bedrooms are en suite.
Lovely rural views. Impressive guests'
sitting room. Evening meals
available. Swimming pool open in
summer. Conveniently situated for
Oundle, Peterborough, Stamford and
Rutland Water.*

Bedrooms: 2 double,
1 twin
Bathrooms: 3 en suite,
1 public

Parking for 15

🐎 🖥 ☐ ⬇ 🗄 🖳 🖺 ⤢ 🕮 📺 🅾 🖩 ➡ ⚲ ∪ ✳ 🚲 ⚲ 🎴

PARWICH, Derbyshire Map ref 4B2

◆◆◆◆ **FLAXDALE HOUSE**
Parwich, Ashbourne, DE6 1QA
T: (01335) 390252 (answerphone)
F: (01335) 390644
E: mike@mikerad.demon.co.uk

Bedrooms: 1 double,
1 twin
Bathrooms: 2 en suite

Parking for 3

B&B per night:
S £27.50–£30.00
D £42.00–£47.00

OPEN All year round

*Three-storey Listed Georgian building, with barn attached, comprising 1 double and 1 twin
bedroom, both en suite. Residents' lounge, gardens and paddock.*

Ⓜ 🐎 🖥 ⬇ 🖳 🖺 ⤢ 🕮 📺 🖩 ➡ ✳ ✈ 🚲 🎴

PEAK DISTRICT

*See under Ashbourne, Ashford in the Water, Bakewell, Bamford, Barlow, Buxton, Castleton,
Chapel-en-le-Frith, Cressbrook, Glossop, Hayfield, Hope, Monsal Head, Winster*

PERSHORE, Worcestershire Map ref 2B1 *Tourist Information Centre Tel: (01386) 554262*

◆◆◆◆
Silver
Award

ALDBURY HOUSE
George Lane, Wyre Piddle, Pershore,
WR10 2HX
T: (01386) 553754 (Redirected to Mobile)
F: (01386) 553754
E: jim@oldbury.freeserve.co.uk

B&B per night:
S £25.00–£35.00
D £42.00–£44.00

OPEN All year round

*Charming, spacious, quietly situated
family home in a small village near
Pershore. En suite rooms, guests'
lounge, safe off-road parking. Use of
garden, summerhouse, patio and
barbecue. Friendly welcome assured.
Ideally situated for visits to
Stratford-upon-Avon, Worcester, the
Malverns and Cotswolds. Nearby
riverside inn serves meals.*

Bedrooms: 1 double,
2 twin
Bathrooms: 3 en suite

Parking for 4

Ⓜ 🐎 🛏 🖥 ☐ ⬇ 🗄 🖳 🖺 ⤢ 🕮 📺 🖩 ➡ ✳ ✈ 🚲 🆂 Ⓣ

REDMILE, Leicestershire Map ref 4C2

◆◆◆ PEACOCK FARM GUESTHOUSE AND THE FEATHERS RESTAURANT

Redmile, Nottingham, NG13 0GQ
T: (01949) 842475
F: (01949) 43127

Bedrooms: 1 single,
2 double, 2 twin, 3 triple,
2 family rooms
Bathrooms: 9 en suite,
2 public

Lunch available
EM 1900 (LO 2100)
Parking for 40
CC: Amex, Barclaycard,
Delta, Diners, Eurocard,
Mastercard, Switch, Visa

B&B per night:
S Max £38.00
D Max £52.00

HB per person:
DY £42.50–£53.50

OPEN All year round

Nicky Need welcomes you to an 18thC Belvoir Vale farmhouse where professional service is combined with old-fashioned hospitality. Art gallery and giftshop.

RETFORD, Nottinghamshire Map ref 4C2 *Tourist Information Centre Tel: (01777) 860780*

◆◆◆◆ THE BARNS COUNTRY GUESTHOUSE

Morton Farm, Babworth, Retford,
DN22 8HA
T: (01777) 706336
F: (01777) 709773
E: harry@thebarns.co.uk
I: www.Thebarns.co.uk

Bedrooms: 5 double,
1 twin
Bathrooms: 6 en suite

Parking for 7
CC: Barclaycard, Delta,
Eurocard, JCB,
Mastercard, Solo, Switch,
Visa, Visa Electron

B&B per night:
S £30.00–£33.00
D £44.00–£48.00

OPEN All year round

18thC house with oak beams. Open fires in the dining room and lounge. Beautiful rural setting on B6420 near A1, 2 miles from Retford. Aga cooked breakfast.

ROSS-ON-WYE, Herefordshire Map ref 2A1 *Tourist Information Centre Tel: (01989) 562768*

◆◆◆

BROOKFIELD HOUSE

Over Ross, Ross-on-Wye, Herefordshire
HR9 7AT
T: (01989) 562188
F: (01989) 564053
E: reception@brookfieldhouse.co.uk
I: www.brookfieldhouse.co.uk

B&B per night:
S £20.00–£27.00
D £38.00–£50.00

OPEN All year round

Queen Anne and Georgian Grade II Listed house close to town centre. Large private car park. All rooms have colour TV and tea and coffee-making facilities, some en suite. Central heating. Come and go as you please. Pets with well-behaved owners welcome. You are offered a warm and friendly welcome.

Bedrooms: 2 single,
3 double, 3 twin
Bathrooms: 3 en suite,
3 public

Parking for 11
CC: Amex, Barclaycard,
Mastercard, Visa

◆◆◆◆ THE OLD RECTORY

Hope Mansell, Ross-on-Wye,
Herefordshire HR9 5TL
T: (01989) 750382
F: (01989) 750382
E: rectory@mansell.wyenet.co.uk

Bedrooms: 2 double,
1 twin
Bathrooms: 1 private,
1 public

Parking for 4

B&B per night:
S £22.50–£27.50
D £45.00–£50.00

OPEN All year round

Georgian house in beautiful rural surroundings near Ross-on-Wye. Friendly atmosphere, comfortable rooms with period furniture. Lovely mature gardens, tennis court, children's play facilities.

QUALITY ASSURANCE SCHEME

For an explanation of the quality and facilities represented by the Diamonds please refer to the front of this guide. A more detailed explanation can be found in the information pages at the back.

ROSS-ON-WYE continued

◆◆◆

THATCH CLOSE

Llangrove, Ross-on-Wye, Herefordshire
HR9 6EL
T: (01989) 770300
E: edward.drzymalski@virgin.net

B&B per night:
S £25.00–£28.00
D £36.00–£40.00

HB per person:
DY £30.00–£32.00

OPEN All year round

13-acre mixed farm. Secluded, peaceful and homely Georgian country farmhouse midway between Ross-on-Wye and Monmouth. Home-produced vegetables and meat. Ideal for country lovers of any age. Guests welcome to help with animals. Map sent on request. Ordnance Survey: 51535196.

Bedrooms: 2 double,
1 twin
Bathrooms: 2 en suite,
1 private

Lunch available
EM 1830 (LO 1800)
Parking for 7

🐄 🌢 🎏 UL 🅰 ⓢ ⅍ 🏮 TV 🞐 ➡ ♣ ❋ 🐾 SP T

RUGBY, Warwickshire Map ref 4C3 *Tourist Information Centre Tel: (01788) 534970 or 534975*

◆◆◆◆

THE GOLDEN LION INN OF EASENHALL
Easenhall, Rugby, CV23 0JA
T: (01788) 832265
F: (01788) 832878
E: james.austin@btinternet.com
I: www.rugbytown.co.uk/goldlion.htm

Bedrooms: 2 single,
10 double
Bathrooms: 12 en suite

Lunch available
EM 1800 (LO 2200)
Parking for 60
CC: Amex, Barclaycard,
Delta, Eurocard, JCB,
Mastercard, Solo, Switch,
Visa

B&B per night:
S £49.00–£59.00
D £59.00–£70.00

OPEN All year round

Individually styled bedrooms, all en suite, luxurious 4-poster, an unusual Chinese day bed, bar and restaurant meals – all set in the beautiful Warwickshire village of Easenhall.

📶 🐄 🏤 📞 🖵 🌢 🎏 🅰 ⓢ ⅍ 🞐 ➡ ♨ 🍸 14 Ｕ ► ❋ 🐾 SC ⅍ SP 🎭 T ◉

◆◆◆◆

THE OLD RECTORY

Main Street, Harborough Magna, Rugby,
CV23 0HS
T: (01788) 833151 &
07803 054509 (Mobile)
F: (01788) 833151
E: oldrectory@cwcom.net
I: www.rugbytown.co.uk/hotels/harborough/the_old_rectory.htm

B&B per night:
S £30.00–£35.00
D £50.00–£60.00

OPEN All year round

Victorian country house in peaceful village. We offer a relaxed and friendly atmosphere, spacious public areas, bright, tastefully furnished bedrooms (non-smoking) with all modern facilities and views over the surrounding countryside. Conveniently placed for touring Cotswolds, Shakespeare Country, also easy access to Stanford Hall, motorway links and NEC Birmingham.

Bedrooms: 2 double,
1 twin
Bathrooms: 3 en suite,
1 public

Parking for 7

📶 🐄 10 🖵 🌢 🎏 UL 🅰 ⓢ ⅍ 🏮 TV 🞐 ➡ ❋ 🐾 🎭 T

◆◆◆

WHITE LION INN
Coventry Road, Pailton, Rugby,
CV23 0QD
T: (01788) 832359
F: (01788) 832359

Bedrooms: 9 twin
Bathrooms: 5 en suite,
2 public

Lunch available
EM 1830 (LO 2200)
Parking for 60
CC: Barclaycard, Delta,
Eurocard, JCB,
Mastercard, Solo, Switch,
Visa, Visa Electron

B&B per night:
S £21.00–£31.00
D £39.00–£49.00

HB per person:
DY £26.00–£36.00

OPEN All year round

17thC coaching inn, recently refurbished but retaining all old world features. Close to Rugby, Coventry and Stratford. Within 2 miles of motorways. Home-cooked food served daily.

📶 🐄 🏤 📞 🖵 🌢 🅰 ⓢ ⅍ 🏮 TV 🞐 ➡ 🍸 30 Ｕ ❋ T

RUGELEY, Staffordshire Map ref 4B3

◆◆◆ **PARK FARM**
Hawkesyard, Armitage Lane,
Rugeley, WS15 1ED
T: (01889) 583477

Bedrooms: 2 triple;
suites available
Bathrooms: 2 en suite

Parking for 23

B&B per night:
S £18.00–£20.00
D £36.00–£40.00

OPEN All year round

40-acre livestock farm. While convenient for towns and attractions in the area, Park Farm is quietly tucked away in scenic hills.

RUTLAND WATER Tourist Information Centre Tel: (01572) 653026

See under Belton in Rutland, Oakham

SHERWOOD FOREST

See under Newark, Retford, Southwell, Worksop

SHREWSBURY, Shropshire Map ref 4A3 *Tourist Information Centre Tel: (01743) 281200 or 281210*

◆◆◆◆
Silver
Award

ASHTON LEES
Dorrington, Shrewsbury, SY5 7JW
T: (01743) 718378

B&B per night:
S £21.00–£25.00
D £42.00–£50.00

HB per person:
DY £31.00–£35.00

OPEN All year round

For many years we have welcomed guests to our family home. On winter evenings, roaring fires entice you to curl up and read a book, with a drink purchased from our small licensed bar. In summer we serve teas in the tree-shaded garden. A place of relaxation and tranquillity.

Bedrooms: 2 double,
1 twin
Bathrooms: 2 en suite,
1 public

Parking for 6

◆◆ **AVONLEA**
33 Coton Crescent, Coton Hill,
Shrewsbury, SY1 2NZ
T: (01743) 359398

Bedrooms: 1 single,
2 twin
Bathrooms: 1 public,
1 private shower

B&B per night:
S £18.00–£20.00
D £34.00–£36.00

OPEN All year round

Built around 1900, an Edwardian house in a crescent of similar houses. Close to town centre and all public transport.

◆◆◆ **CHATFORD HOUSE**
Bayston Hill, Shrewsbury, SY3 0AY
T: (01743) 718301

Bedrooms: 3 twin
Bathrooms: 1 public

Parking for 4

B&B per night:
S £17.00–£18.00
D £34.00–£36.00

OPEN Apr–Oct

Comfortable farmhouse built in 1776, 5.5 miles south of Shrewsbury off A49. Through Bayston Hill, take third right (Stapleton) then right to Chatford.

◆◆◆◆
Silver
Award

THE OLD STATION
Leaton, Bomere Heath, Shrewsbury,
SY4 3AP
T: (01939) 290905 (Evenings only) &
07885 526307

B&B per night:
S £30.00–£35.00
D £45.00–£60.00

HB per person:
DY £32.50–£43.00

OPEN All year round

A Great Western Railway station built in 1847 converted to a home/ bed and breakfast. Large bedrooms with luxurious antique beds and bathrooms decorated in Victorian antique style. Sitting room, dining room, conservatory and garden. In a rural setting with private parking.

Bedrooms: 2 double,
1 twin; suite available
Bathrooms: 3 en suite,
1 public

Parking for 12

SANDFORD HOUSE HOTEL

♦♦♦

St Julian's Friars, Shrewsbury,
SY1 1XL
T: (01743) 343829
F: (01743) 343829
E: sandfordhouse@lineone.net
I: www.lineone.net/
~sandfordhouse/

Bedrooms: 1 single,
3 double, 3 twin, 2 triple,
1 family room
Bathrooms: 10 en suite

Parking for 3
CC: Barclaycard, Delta,
Eurocard, JCB, Maestro,
Mastercard, Solo, Switch,
Visa, Visa Electron

B&B per night:
S £37.50–£55.00
D £55.00–£55.00

OPEN All year round

Family-run Grade II Listed townhouse, close to the river, with pleasant walks and access to good fishing. Easy parking and within a few minutes of the town centre.

♦♦♦♦

Silver
Award

SHORTHILL LODGE

Shorthill, Lea Cross, Shrewsbury, SY5 8JE
T: (01743) 860864
I: www.go2.co.uk/shorthill

B&B per night:
D £42.00–£48.00

OPEN All year round

A warm welcome to this comfortable, attractive house in open countryside. Views across meadows to the Stiperstones and Welsh Hills. Golf club, pub and restaurant within walking distance. Easy access to Shrewsbury and mid-Wales. Centrally heated rooms with TV/radio, hospitality tray. Full size en suite bathrooms. Reduced rates 3+ nights.

Bedrooms: 1 double,
1 twin
Bathrooms: 2 en suite,
1 public

Parking for 3

CHATSWORTH HOTEL

♦♦♦

North Parade, Skegness, PE25 2UB
T: (01754) 764177
F: (01754) 761173
E: Altipper@aol.com
I: www.chatsworthskegness.co.uk

Bedrooms: 5 single,
10 double, 11 twin,
2 triple, 2 family rooms
Bathrooms: 30 en suite

Lunch available
EM 1800 (LO 1930)
Parking for 16
CC: Amex, Barclaycard,
Delta, Diners, Eurocard,
JCB, Mastercard, Solo,
Switch, Visa, Visa Electron

B&B per night:
S £28.00–£36.00
D £46.00–£58.00

HB per person:
DY £36.00–£40.00

OPEN All year round

Centrally situated seafront hotel, close to many amenities. Dinner, lunches and snacks available. Open year round including Christmas and New Year. All rooms en suite.

SAXBY HOTEL

♦♦♦

12 Saxby Avenue, Skegness,
PE25 3LG
T: (01754) 763905
F: (01754) 763905

Bedrooms: 1 single,
8 double, 1 twin, 1 triple,
2 family rooms
Bathrooms: 11 en suite,
2 private

Lunch available
EM 1800 (LO 1900)
Parking for 8
CC: Barclaycard, Delta,
JCB, Mastercard, Visa

B&B per night:
S Min £25.00
D Min £50.00

HB per person:
DY Min £32.00

OPEN Mar–Oct

A family-run hotel, on a corner in a quiet residential area of Skegness, 300 yards from the seafront.

ACORN GUEST HOUSE

♦♦♦♦

29 Links Drive, Solihull,
West Midlands B91 2DJ
T: (0121) 7055241
E: acorn.wood@btinternet.com

Bedrooms: 2 single,
1 double, 2 twin
Bathrooms: 1 en suite,
2 public

Parking for 6

B&B per night:
S £22.00–£28.00
D £44.00–£50.00

OPEN All year round

Comfortable, quiet family home with ample private facilities, overlooking golf course. Parking and easy access to NEC, airport, M42 and Solihull centre.

HALF BOARD PRICES Half board prices are given per person, but in some cases these may be based on double/twin occupancy.

SOLIHULL continued

◆◆◆

BOXTREES FARM

Stratford Road, Hockley Heath, Solihull,
West Midlands B94 6EA
T: (01564) 782039 & 07970 736156
(Mobile)
F: (01564) 784661
E: b&b@boxtrees.co.uk
I: boxtrees.co.uk

*Family-run 18thC farmhouse set in
50 acres, with its own craft centre.
Spacious rooms, recently renovated
to a high standard, with timbered
ceilings throughout. Ideally situated
1 mile from junction 4 M42. National
Exhibition Centre, Birmingham
Airport and railway station 10
minutes away and Shakespeare's
Stratford-upon-Avon 20 minutes.*

Bedrooms: 1 double,
2 twin, 1 triple
Bathrooms: 4 en suite

Parking for 100
CC: Barclaycard, Delta,
Eurocard, Mastercard,
Solo, Switch, Visa, Visa
Electron

B&B per night:
S £45.00–£50.00
D £55.00–£65.00

OPEN All year round

◆◆◆ **THE GATE HOUSE**

Barston Lane, Barston, Solihull,
West Midlands B92 0JN
T: (01675) 443274
F: (01675) 443274

Bedrooms: 1 single,
1 double, 1 twin
Bathrooms: 2 en suite,
1 public

Parking for 20

B&B per night:
S £25.00–£35.00
D £45.00–£55.00

OPEN All year round

*Early Victorian mansion house set in beautiful countryside. Close to National Exhibition
Centre, International Convention Centre, airport and motorway.*

SOULDERN, Oxfordshire

Tower Fields
See South of England region for full entry details

SOUTH WITHAM, Lincolnshire Map ref 3A1

◆◆◆ **THE BLUE COW INN AND BREWERY**

29 High Street, South Witham,
Grantham, NG33 5QB
T: (01572) 768432
F: (01572) 768432

Bedrooms: 2 double,
4 twin, 1 triple, 1 family
room
Bathrooms: 7 en suite,
1 private, 4 public

Lunch available
EM 1800 (LO 2130)
Parking for 47
CC: Delta, Eurocard,
Mastercard, Solo, Switch,
Visa

B&B per night:
S £35.00–£45.00
D £45.00–£55.00

HB per person:
DY £40.00–£45.00

OPEN All year round

*13thC beamed freehouse with log fires, real ales and home-cooked meals. Convenient for
A1, Grantham, Oakham, Stamford and Melton Mowbray. Brewery on premises, brewing
own beers.*

SOUTHWELL, Nottinghamshire Map ref 4C2

◆◆◆ **BARN LODGE**

Duckers Cottage, Brinkley,
Southwell, NG25 0TP
T: (01636) 813435
E: barnlodge@hotmail.com

Bedrooms: 1 double,
1 twin, 1 triple
Bathrooms: 3 en suite

Parking for 3

B&B per night:
S £25.00–£25.00
D £40.00–£40.00

OPEN All year round

*Smallholding with panoramic views, 1 mile from the centre of Southwell and close to the
racecourse, railway station and River Trent.*

USE YOUR *i*s

There are more than 550 Tourist Information
Centres throughout England offering friendly help
with accommodation and holiday ideas as well as
suggestions of places to visit and things to do.
You'll find TIC addresses in the local Phone Book.

STAFFORD, Staffordshire Map ref 4B3 *Tourist Information Centre Tel: (01785) 619619*

◆◆◆

LITTYWOOD HOUSE
Bradley, Stafford, ST18 9DW
T: (01785) 780234 & 780770
F: (01785) 780770

B&B per night:
S £25.00–£30.00
D £40.00–£45.00

OPEN All year round

Littywood House occupies the only moated site in Staffordshire, with 2 circular moats. It is a beautiful 14thC manor house set in its own grounds, secluded, yet easily accessible from the M6. Centrally heated. Ideally situated for Alton Towers, Shugborough Hall and the Potteries.

Bedrooms: 1 double, 1 twin
Bathrooms: 1 en suite, 1 public

Parking for 10

🅰🐾1 🖵 💧 ⛎ Ⓢ 🏛 🆃🆅 🏠 ☎ 🍴 14 ✻ 🐎 🚲 🏤

STAMFORD, Lincolnshire Map ref 3A1 *Tourist Information Centre Tel: (01780) 755611*

◆◆◆◆

ABBEY HOUSE AND COACH HOUSE
West End Road, Maxey, Peterborough, PE6 9EJ
T: (01778) 344642 & 347499
F: (01778) 342706
E: sales@abbeyhouse.co.uk
I: www.abbeyhouse.co.uk

B&B per night:
S £28.00–£39.00
D £46.00–£60.00

OPEN All year round

Formerly owned by Peterborough Abbey, the house, dating in part from 1190 AD, is in a conservation area in a quiet village on the Lincs/Cambs border, close to Stamford and Peterborough. It offers en suite bedrooms, an elegant dining room, comfortable guest lounge with many old features and spacious, well tended gardens. Telephone for brochure.

Bedrooms: 1 single, 5 double, 3 twin, 1 family room
Bathrooms: 10 en suite

Parking for 12

🅰🐾6 🧺 📞 🖵 💧 ⛎ 🛈 Ⓢ ✂ 🏛 🆃🆅 🏠 ☎ 🎣 ✻ 🐎 🚲 SP 🏤 🆃

◆◆

DOLPHIN GUESTHOUSE
12 East Street, Stamford, PE9 1QD
T: (01780) 757515 & 481567
F: (01780) 57515
E: mikdolphin@mikdolphin.demon.co.uk

Bedrooms: 4 double, 3 twin, 1 triple; suites available
Bathrooms: 6 en suite, 1 public

Parking for 5
CC: Barclaycard, Delta, Mastercard, Visa

B&B per night:
S £18.00–£30.00
D £40.00–£50.00

OPEN All year round

En suite hotel-style accommodation next to the Dolphin Inn, renowned for its cask ales, friendliness and food. Off-road secure car parking and only 100 yards from the town centre.

🅰🐾 🧺 📧 🖵 💧 🍳 ⛎ Ⓢ ✂ 🏛 🆃🆅 🏠 ☎ 🍴 10 ✻ 🚲 SP 🆃

TOWN INDEX
This can be found at the back of the guide. If you know where you want to stay, the index will give you the page number listing accommodation in your chosen town, city or village.

◆◆◆◆

THE MILL

Mill Lane, Tallington, Stamford, PE9 4RR
T: (01780) 740815 & 07802 373326
F: (01780) 740280

B&B per night:
S £35.00–£40.00
D £55.00–£60.00

OPEN All year round

A 17thC watermill 4 miles from Stamford, surrounded by open farmland and watermeadows. All the bedrooms are en suite and overlook the river or millpond. Many original features have been retained to give The Mill its tremendous character and charm, including all the mill workings in the dining room.

Bedrooms: 2 twin, 3 triple, 1 family room
Bathrooms: 6 en suite

EM
Parking for 8

◆◆◆

THE OAK INN

48 Stamford Road, Easton on the Hill, Stamford, PE9 3PA
T: (01780) 752286
F: (01780) 752286
E: peter@klippon.demon.co.uk

B&B per night:
S £30.00–£35.00
D £45.00–£50.00

HB per person:
DY £38.00–£50.00

OPEN All year round

Lovely stone 17thC inn, set in the beautiful village of Easton-on-the-Hill, just 2 miles from Stamford. Tasteful en suite bedrooms, with colour TV, tea and coffee. The beautiful Bower Conservatory restaurant serves an a la carte menu and the Pine bar has tasty snacks and real ales.

Bedrooms: 1 single, 3 double, 1 twin
Bathrooms: 5 en suite

Lunch available
EM 1900 (LO 2115)
Parking for 30
CC: Barclaycard, Delta, Mastercard, Switch, Visa

◆◆◆

LAUREL FARM

Browns Lane, Stanton-on-the-Wolds, Keyworth, Nottingham, NG12 5BL
T: (0115) 937 3488
F: (0115) 937 6490
E: laurelfarm@yahoo.com

B&B per night:
S £27.50–£30.00
D £41.00–£46.00

OPEN All year round

An old farmhouse in 4 acres including a National Gardens Scheme garden, which guests may use. Spacious, well furnished rooms all en suite/private facilities, hospitality tray, TV, hairdryer and bath robes. Only fresh local produce and own free-range eggs used for breakfast. Nearest roads M1, A46, A606. No smoking

Bedrooms: 2 double, 2 twin
Bathrooms: 1 en suite, 2 private

EM 1900 (LO 1900)
Parking for 8
CC: Barclaycard, Delta, Mastercard, Switch, Visa

MAP REFERENCES The map references refer to the colour maps at the front of this guide. The first figure is the map number; the letter and figure which follow indicate the grid reference on the map.

STAUNTON, Gloucestershire Map ref 2B1

KILMORIE SMALL HOLDING

Gloucester Road, Corse, Snigs End, Staunton, Gloucester, GL19 3RQ
T: (01452) 840224
F: (01452) 840224
I: www.SmoothHound.co.uk/hotels/kilmorie.html

All ground floor quality rural accommodation, within a conservation area. Colour TV, tea tray, radio all bedrooms. Most are en suite, Grade II Listed Chartist smallholding (C1848) keeping farm livestock and free-range hens which provide excellent eggs for breakfast. Ample parking. Ideally situated for touring Cotswolds, Forest of Dean, Malvern Hills.

Bedrooms: 1 single, 2 double, 1 twin, 1 family room
Bathrooms: 3 en suite, 2 private

Lunch available
EM 1800
Parking for 8

B&B per night:
S Min £18.00
D Min £34.00

HB per person:
DY Min £24.50

OPEN All year round

STEEPLE ASTON, Oxfordshire

Westfield Farm Hotel
See South of England region for full entry details

STIPERSTONES, Shropshire Map ref 4A3

THE OLD CHAPEL

Perkins Beach Dingle, Stiperstones, Shrewsbury, SY5 0PE
T: (01743) 791449 (Answerphone)
E: jean@a-lees.freeserve.co.uk
I: www.SmoothHound.co.uk/hotels/oldchapel.html

Bedrooms: 1 single, 1 twin
Bathrooms: 1 public

Parking for 2

B&B per night:
S £20.00–£25.00
D £36.00–£36.00

OPEN All year round

Set in stunning scenery, a walkers' paradise. The Old Chapel was built c1869 and is a comfortable and interesting home.

STOKE BRUERNE, Northamptonshire Map ref 2C1

3 ROOKERY BARNS

Rookery Lane, Stoke Bruerne, Towcester, NN12 7SJ
T: (01604) 862274

Bedrooms: 4 double
Bathrooms: 2 en suite, 1 private, 1 public, 1 private shower

Parking for 8

B&B per night:
S £25.00–£25.00
D £50.00–£50.00

OPEN All year round

A four-bedroomed barn conversion with gardens and paddock, in a canal/tourist centre village.

STOKE-ON-TRENT, Staffordshire Map ref 4B2 *Tourist Information Centre Tel: (01782) 236000*

SNEYD ARMS HOTEL

Tower Square, Tunstall, Stoke-on-Trent, ST6 5AA
T: (01782) 826722
F: (01782) 826722

Bedrooms: 4 single, 4 double, 4 twin, 2 triple
Bathrooms: 6 en suite, 1 private, 2 public

Lunch available
EM 1900 (LO 2100)
Parking for 2
CC: Amex, Barclaycard, Mastercard, Switch, Visa

B&B per night:
S £20.00–£32.50
D £38.00–£46.00

OPEN All year round

Residential town centre hotel, restaurant and public house with function suite, en suite and budget accommodation available. Ideal location for Alton Towers and Potteries' factory shops.

IMPORTANT NOTE Information on accommodation listed in this guide has been supplied by the proprietors. As changes may occur you are advised to check details at the time of booking.

STOKE-ON-TRENT continued

◆◆ VERDON GUEST HOUSE

44 Charles Street, Hanley, Stoke-on-Trent, ST1 3JY
T: (01782) 264244 &
07711 514682 (Mobile)
F: (01782) 264244
E: debbie@howlett18.freeserve.co.uk
I: business.thisisstaffordshire.co.uk/verdon

Bedrooms: 1 single, 3 double, 3 twin, 1 triple, 5 family rooms	Parking for 8 CC: Eurocard, Mastercard, Visa	B&B per night: S £22.00–£22.00 D £38.00–£40.00
Bathrooms: 4 en suite, 3 public		OPEN All year round

Large, friendly guesthouse in town centre close to bus station. Convenient for pottery visits, museum. Alton Towers 20 minutes, M6 10 minutes. All rooms cable TV, some 4-poster beds.

⚅🛏🚗🖥🖵🚰🆙Ⓢ🖩🚘🐾🅣

STONEHOUSE, Gloucestershire Map ref 2B1

◆◆ MERTON LODGE

8 Ebley Road, Stonehouse, GL10 2LQ
T: (01453) 822018

Bedrooms: 3 double Bathrooms: 1 en suite, 2 public	Parking for 6 B&B per night: S £19.00–£21.00 D £38.00–£42.00

Former gentleman's residence offering a warm welcome. Non-smoking. Three miles from M5 junction 13, over 4 roundabouts. Along Ebley Old Road, under footbridge.

OPEN All year round

🛏🆙Ⓢ✄🖵📺🖩🚘✳🏹🐾🏨

STOURBRIDGE, West Midlands Map ref 4B3

◆◆◆◆ ST. ELIZABETH'S COTTAGE

Woodman Lane, Clent, Stourbridge, West Midlands DY9 9PX
T: (01562) 883883
E: sc_elizabeth_cote@btconnect.com

Bedrooms: 2 double, 1 twin	Parking for 3	B&B per night: S £27.00–£30.00 D £54.00–£60.00
Bathrooms: 3 en suite		OPEN All year round

Beautiful country cottage with lovely gardens and interior professionally decorated throughout. 20 minutes from Birmingham and close to motorway links.

🛏📞🖳🖵🚰🆙🖩🚘⚲🏹✳🏹🐾 SP 🏨

STOW-ON-THE-WOLD, Gloucestershire Map ref 2B1 *Tourist Information Centre Tel: (01451) 831082*

◆◆◆◆

ASTON HOUSE

Broadwell, Moreton-in-Marsh, GL56 0TJ
T: (01451) 830475 &
07773 452037 (mobile)
E: fja@netcomuk.co.uk
I: www.netcomuk.co.uk/~nmfa/aston_house.html

B&B per night:
D £44.00–£48.00

OPEN Feb–Nov

Guests are welcomed to our home in the quiet village of Broadwell, 1.5 miles from Stow-on-the-Wold and centrally situated for touring the Cotswolds. Rooms are comfortably furnished and have TV, tea-making facilities, bedtime drinks and biscuits, electric blankets. Good English breakfast; pub in walking distance. Reduced rates for weekly bookings. No smoking.

Bedrooms: 2 double, 1 twin	Parking for 3
Bathrooms: 2 en suite, 1 private	

⚅🛏10🖳🖵🚰🖵Ⓢ✄🖩🚘🏹✳🏹🐾🅣

CHECK THE MAPS

The colour maps at the front of this guide show all the cities, towns and villages for which you will find accommodation entries. Refer to the town index to find the page on which they are listed.

♦♦♦ **CORSHAM FIELD FARMHOUSE**
Bledington Road, Stow-on-the-Wold, Cheltenham, GL54 1JH
T: (01451) 831750

Bedrooms: 2 double, 2 twin, 3 family rooms
Bathrooms: 5 en suite, 1 public

Parking for 10

B&B per night:
S £20.00–£25.00
D £35.00–£45.00

OPEN All year round

100-acre mixed farm. Homely farmhouse with breathtaking views, ideal for exploring Cotswolds. En suite and standard rooms. TVs, guest lounge, tea/coffee facilities. Good pub food 5 minutes' walk.

♦♦♦  # MAUGERSBURY MANOR
Stow-on-the-Wold, Cheltenham, GL54 1HP
T: (01451) 830581
F: (01451) 870902
E: themanor@wiseholidays.com

B&B per night:
S £30.00–£30.00
D £40.00–£45.00

OPEN Apr–Oct

A warm, friendly welcome awaits you at this Jacobean manor house, in the heart of the beautiful Cotswold countryside. Situated near Stow, this is an ideal place to visit picturesque villages and historic towns. Oxford, Cheltenham, Stratford all within easy reach. Quiet, comfortable accommodation. Ample parking and lovely views.

Bedrooms: 3 double; suites available
Bathrooms: 2 en suite, 1 public

♦♦♦♦  # WOODLANDS
Upper Swell, Stow-on-the-Wold, Cheltenham, GL54 1EW
T: (01451) 832346

B&B per night:
S Max £30.00
D Max £54.00

OPEN All year round

Small guesthouse in quaint Cotswold village, 1 mile from Stow-on-the-Wold. Set in half-acre gardens with breathtaking views of the Cotswolds. All rooms en suite. Guest lounge where light snacks can be served.

Bedrooms: 1 single, 3 double, 1 twin
Bathrooms: 5 en suite

Parking for 6
CC: Barclaycard, Mastercard, Visa

♦♦♦♦♦ **WYCK HILL LODGE**
Burford Road, Stow-on-the-Wold, Cheltenham, GL54 1HT
T: (01451) 830141
E: gkhwyck@compuserve.com

Bedrooms: 2 double, 1 twin
Bathrooms: 3 en suite

Parking for 3

B&B per night:
D £44.00–£50.00

OPEN Mar–Nov

Tastefully furnished Victorian lodge in peaceful rural surroundings. Renowned for comfort, fine breakfasts and hospitality. Extensive views. 1 mile from Stow-on-the-Wold. Ample parking. Non-smokers only, please.

STRATFORD-UPON-AVON, Warwickshire Map ref 2B1 *Tourist Information Centre Tel: (01789) 293127*

♦♦♦ **AMELIA LINHILL GUESTHOUSE**
35 Evesham Place, Stratford-upon-Avon, CV37 6HT
T: (01789) 292879
F: (01789) 299691
E: Linhill@free4all.co.uk

Bedrooms: 1 single, 1 double, 3 twin, 1 triple, 1 family room
Bathrooms: 2 en suite, 2 public

Lunch available
EM 1700 (LO 1930)
CC: Barclaycard, Delta, Mastercard, Switch, Visa

B&B per night:
S £16.00–£25.00
D £32.00–£50.00

OPEN All year round

Comfortable Victorian guesthouse offering warm welcome and good food. 5 minutes' walk from town centre and theatres and convenient for Cotswolds. Baby sitting service.

HEART OF ENGLAND

◆◆◆◆ AVONLEA

47 Shipston Road, Stratford-upon-Avon, CV37 7LN
T: (01789) 205940
F: (01789) 209115

Bedrooms: 1 single, 2 double, 2 twin, 1 triple
Bathrooms: 6 en suite

Parking for 4
CC: Barclaycard, Eurocard, Maestro, Mastercard, Solo, Switch, Visa, Visa Electron

B&B per night:
S £29.00–£45.00
D £46.00–£68.00

OPEN All year round

Stylish Victorian townhouse situated only 5 minutes' walk away from the theatre and town centre. All rooms are en suite and furnished to the highest quality.

◆◆◆◆ BRADBOURNE HOUSE

44 Shipston Road, Stratford-upon-Avon, CV37 7LP
T: (01789) 204178
F: (01789) 262335
E: brad-bourne@talk21.com

B&B per night:
S £25.00–£30.00
D £40.00–£60.00

OPEN All year round

Detached Tudor-style house with a beautiful garden, just 8 minutes' walk from the town and theatres. All rooms recently refurbished and with satellite TV. Ground floor bedrooms available. Ample parking for all guests.

Bedrooms: 1 single, 4 double, 1 twin, 2 triple, 1 family room
Bathrooms: 6 en suite, 2 public

Parking for 9

◆◆◆ BRONHILL HOUSE

260 Alcester Road, Stratford-upon-Avon, CV37 9JQ
T: (01789) 299169

Bedrooms: 2 double, 1 twin
Bathrooms: 2 en suite, 1 private

Parking for 5

B&B per night:
D £30.00–£36.00

OPEN All year round

Detached family house in elevated position, 1 mile from Stratford-upon-Avon. Family-run with relaxed friendly atmosphere. A non-smoking establishment.

◆◆◆ CHURCH FARM

Dorsington, Stratford-upon-Avon, CV37 8AX
T: (01789) 720471 &
07831 504194 (Mobile)
F: (01789) 720830
E: chfarmdorsington@aol.com
I: www.travel-uk.net/churchfarm

Bedrooms: 4 double, 1 twin, 2 family rooms
Bathrooms: 6 en suite, 1 private

Parking for 12

B&B per night:
S £24.00–£27.00
D £38.00–£40.00

OPEN All year round

127-acre mixed farm. Situated on Heart of England Way, in pretty village. Most rooms en-suite, TV, tea and coffee facilities. Close Stratford-upon-Avon, Warwick, Cotswolds, Evesham.

◆◆◆ CLOMENDY BED AND BREAKFAST

10 Broad Walk, Stratford-upon-Avon, CV37 6HS
T: (01789) 266957

B&B per night:
S £30.00–£30.00
D £40.00–£46.00

OPEN All year round

Small, family-run Victorian house in a quiet, central position. Close to theatres, New Place, Hall's Croft and Anne Hathaway's cottage. All rooms en suite. Colourful walled garden. Rail and coach guests met and returned. Non-smokers only, please.

Bedrooms: 1 single, 2 double
Bathrooms: 2 en suite, 1 private

Parking for 1

◆◆◆

CRAIG CLEEVE HOUSE HOTEL & RESTAURANT

67-69 Shipston Road, Stratford-upon-Avon, CV37 7LW
T: (01789) 296573
F: (01789) 299452
E: craigcleev@aol.com

B&B per night:
S £35.00–£54.00
D £45.00–£58.00

OPEN All year round

This recently refurbished and well-appointed family-run hotel is ideally located for those wishing to visit Stratford and the theatre, both being within easy walking distance. With ample private parking, residents' lounge and bar, it is perfect for individuals seeking a quiet break, business people and large groups.

Bedrooms: 8 double, 2 twin, 3 triple, 1 family room
Bathrooms: 14 private

Parking for 15
CC: Barclaycard, Delta, Maestro, Mastercard, Solo, Switch, Visa, Visa Electron

---

◆◆◆◆

EASTNOR HOUSE HOTEL
Shipston Road, Stratford-upon-Avon, CV37 7LN
T: (01789) 268115
F: (01789) 266516
E: eastnor.house@tesco.net

Bedrooms: 3 double, 2 twin, 2 triple, 2 family rooms
Bathrooms: 9 en suite

Parking for 9
CC: Barclaycard, Delta, Eurocard, Mastercard, Solo, Switch, Visa, Visa Electron

B&B per night:
S £40.00–£65.00
D £60.00–£75.00

OPEN All year round

Comfortable Victorian private hotel, oak panelled and tastefully furnished. Spacious bedrooms with private bathrooms. Centrally located by River Avon, theatre 350 metres.

◆◆◆

HIGHCROFT

Banbury Road, Stratford-upon-Avon, CV37 7NF
T: (01789) 296293
F: (01789) 415236

B&B per night:
S £25.00–£30.00
D £40.00–£44.00

OPEN All year round

Lovely country house and converted barns in 2 acres of landscaped gardens in the heart of rural Warwickshire but only 2 miles from Stratford-upon-Avon and close to Cotswolds and Warwick. We welcome you with tea and home-made cakes and then ask you to relax and enjoy our home. Both rooms en suite, sitting room with open fire.

Bedrooms: 1 double, 1 family room
Bathrooms: 2 en suite

Parking for 3

◆◆◆◆

MELITA PRIVATE HOTEL

37 Shipston Road, Stratford-upon-Avon, CV37 7LN
T: (01789) 292432
F: (01789) 204867
E: Melita37@email.msn.com
I: www.stratford-upon-avon.co.uk/melita.htm

B&B per night:
S £37.00–£59.00
D £52.00–£82.00

OPEN All year round

Once a Victorian home, the Melita is now a warm and friendly hotel managed by caring proprietors. Accommodation and service are of a high standard, and breakfasts are individually prepared to suit guests' requirements. The Melita is only 400 metres from the theatres and town centre and has free private on-site car parking.

Bedrooms: 3 single, 4 double, 3 twin, 1 triple, 1 family room
Bathrooms: 10 en suite, 2 private

Parking for 12
CC: Amex, Barclaycard, Delta, Eurocard, JCB, Maestro, Mastercard, Solo, Switch, Visa, Visa Electron

STRATFORD-UPON-AVON continued

◆◆◆ MOONLIGHT BED & BREAKFAST

144 Alcester Road, Stratford-upon-Avon, CV37 9DR	Bedrooms: 1 single, 1 double, 1 twin, 1 triple	Parking for 4
T: (01789) 298213	Bathrooms: 2 en suite, 1 public	

B&B per night:
S £16.00–£18.00
D £33.00–£36.00

OPEN All year round

Small family guesthouse near town centre and station, offering comfortable accommodation at reasonable prices. Tea/coffee-making facilities, colour TV. En suite rooms available.

📺🕻🖵 💧 🕯 UL S 🎄 TV ▥ SC SP

MOONRAKER HOUSE

40 Alcester Road, Stratford-upon-Avon, CV37 9DB	Bedrooms: 13 double, 2 twin, 4 triple	Parking for 24
T: (01789) 299346 & 267115	Bathrooms: 19 en suite	CC: Mastercard, Visa
F: (01789) 295504		
E: moonraker.spencer@virgin.net		
I: www.stratford-upon.avon.co.uk/moonraker.htm		

B&B per night:
S £40.00–£48.00
D £49.00–£80.00

OPEN All year round

Family-run, near town centre. Beautifully co-ordinated decor throughout. Some rooms with 4-poster beds and garden terrace available for non-smokers.

Ề📺5 🖼 TV 🖵 💧 🕯 UL S ✂ 🎄 ▥ 🖧 SC SP T

◆◆◆◆ MOSS COTTAGE

61 Evesham Road, Stratford-upon-Avon, CV37 9BA	Bedrooms: 2 double	Parking for 3
T: (01789) 294770	Bathrooms: 2 en suite	
F: (01789) 294770		
E: pauline_rush@onetel.net.uk		

B&B per night:
D £40.00–£44.00

OPEN All year round

Pauline and Jim Rush welcome you to their charming detached cottage. Walking distance theatre/town. Spacious en suite accommodation. Hospitality tray, TV. Parking.

Ề📺12 🖵 💧 🕯 UL S ✂ 🎄 TV ▥ 🖧 🚲 SP T

◆◆ NANDO'S

18-19 Evesham Place, Stratford-upon-Avon, CV37 6HT	Bedrooms: 6 single, 11 double, 7 twin, 3 triple	EM 1800 Parking for 8
T: (01789) 204907	Bathrooms: 23 en suite, 1 public	CC: Amex, Barclaycard, Delta, Diners, Eurocard,
F: (01789) 204907		JCB, Mastercard, Visa

B&B per night:
S £18.00–£40.00
D £36.00–£48.00

OPEN All year round

A warm welcome and high standards await you. Convenient for theatre, town centre and Shakespeare properties. Full English breakfast. Children welcome, pets by arrangement.

Ề📺🖼🖵 💧 UL 🔒 S ✂ 🎄 TV ▥ 🖧 SP T ⊛

◆◆◆◆ NEWLANDS

7 Broad Walk, Stratford-upon-Avon, CV37 6HS	Bedrooms: 1 single, 1 double, 1 twin, 1 triple	Parking for 2 CC: Barclaycard, Delta,
T: (01789) 298449	Bathrooms: 3 en suite, 1 private, 1 public	Eurocard, Mastercard,
F: (01789) 263541		Solo, Switch, Visa
E: newlandssueboston@onet.co.uk		
I: www.smoothhound.co.uk/hotels/newlands.html		

B&B per night:
S £20.00–£24.00
D £45.00–£50.00

OPEN All year round

Sue Boston's home is a short walk to the Royal Shakespeare Theatre, town centre and Shakespeare properties, and has some forecourt parking.

Ề📺10 🖼 🖵 💧 🕯 UL S ✂ 🎄 TV ▥ 🖧 ✗ 🚲 T

◆◆◆ RAVENHURST

2 Broad Walk, Stratford-upon-Avon, CV37 6HS	Bedrooms: 4 double, 1 twin	Parking for 4
T: (01789) 292515	Bathrooms: 5 en suite	CC: Amex, Barclaycard, Mastercard, Visa
E: ravaccom@waverider.co.uk		
I: www.stratford-upon-avon.co.uk/ravenhurst.htm		

B&B per night:
D £44.00–£50.00

OPEN All year round

Quietly situated, a few minutes' walk from the town centre and places of historic interest. Comfortable home, with substantial breakfast provided. Four-poster available.

Ề📺3 🖼 🖵 💧 🕯 UL S ✂ 🎄 ▥ 🖧 ✗ 🚲 T

IDEAS For ideas on places to visit refer to the introduction at the beginning of this section.

STRATFORD-UPON-AVON continued

◆◆◆ SALAMANDER GUEST HOUSE

40 Grove Road, Stratford-upon-Avon, CV37 6PB T: (01789) 205728 & 297843 F: (01789) 205728 E: sejget@nova88.freeserve.co.uk	Bedrooms: 1 single, 1 double, 4 triple, 1 family room Bathrooms: 5 en suite, 1 private, 2 public, 1 private shower	Parking for 5	B&B per night: **S £18.00–£25.00** **D £40.00–£50.00** OPEN All year round

5 minutes' walk from the town centre, the Royal Shakespeare Theatre and many historic houses. Close to railway and bus stations.

◆◆◆ STRATHEDEN HOTEL

5 Chapel Street, Stratford-upon-Avon, CV37 6EP T: (01789) 297119 F: (01789) 297119 E: richard@stratheden.fsnet.co.uk I: www.stratheden.co.uk	Bedrooms: 6 double, 2 twin, 1 triple Bathrooms: 9 en suite	Parking for 5 CC: Barclaycard, Delta, Eurocard, Mastercard, Switch, Visa	B&B per night: **S £41.00–£55.00** **D £64.00–£70.00** OPEN All year round

Built in 1673 and located in one of the most historic parts of Stratford-upon-Avon. 2 minutes' walk from the theatre and town centre.

◆◆◆◆

VIRGINIA LODGE GUEST HOUSE

12 Evesham Place, Stratford-upon-Avon, CV37 6HT
T: (01789) 292157

B&B per night:
S £18.00–£25.00
D £36.00–£50.00

OPEN All year round

Beautiful Victorian house in the centre of Stratford. All bedrooms beautifully designed to a very high standard, all en suite with TV, hairdryer, tea/coffee, etc. Four-poster rooms, Laura Ashley, Country Manor. Full English breakfast served with real coffee. Private car park. A non-smoking house.	Bedrooms: 2 single, 5 double, 1 triple Bathrooms: 6 en suite, 2 private	Parking for 8

◆◆◆ WHITCHURCH FARM

Wimpstone, Stratford-upon-Avon, CV37 8NS T: (01789) 450275 F: (01789) 450275	Bedrooms: 2 double, 1 twin Bathrooms: 3 en suite, 1 public	Parking for 3	B&B per night: **S £20.00–£22.00** **D £38.00–£40.00** OPEN All year round

260-acre mixed farm. Listed Georgian farmhouse set in park-like surroundings on edge of Cotswolds. Ideal for a touring holiday. Small village 4 miles south of Stratford-upon-Avon.

STROUD, Gloucestershire Map ref 2B1 *Tourist Information Centre Tel: (01453) 765768*

◆◆◆ THE CLOTHIER'S ARMS

1 Bath Road, Stroud, GL5 3JJ T: (01453) 763801 F: (01453) 757161 E: luciano@clothiersarms.demon.co.uk I: www.clothiersarms.co.uk	Bedrooms: 2 double, 2 twin, 1 triple Bathrooms: 3 en suite, 2 private	Lunch available EM (LO 2100) Parking for 55 CC: Barclaycard, Delta, Eurocard, JCB, Maestro, Mastercard, Solo, Switch, Visa, Visa Electron	B&B per night: **S £25.00–£33.00** **D £45.00–£55.00** HB per person: **DY £33.00–£37.00** OPEN All year round

Cotswold inn, en suite rooms, restaurant, real ales, beer garden, children's play area. For reservations telephone or visit our website.

SYMBOLS The symbols in each entry give information about services and facilities. A key to these symbols appears at the back of this guide.

STROUD continued

◆◆◆ **DOWNFIELD HOTEL**

134 Cainscross Road, Stroud, GL5 4HN
T: (01453) 764496
F: (01453) 753150
E: messenger@downfieldhotel.demon.co.uk
I: www.downfieldhotel.demon.co.uk

B&B per night:
S £28.00–£40.00
D £38.00–£50.00

OPEN All year round

Imposing, friendly hotel in quiet location. Home cooking. 1 mile from town centre, 5 miles from M5 motorway, junction 13, on main A419 road.

Bedrooms: 4 single, 9 double, 7 twin, 1 triple
Bathrooms: 11 en suite, 3 public

EM 1830 (LO 2015)
Parking for 23
CC: Amex, Barclaycard, Delta, Maestro, Mastercard, Solo, Switch, Visa, Visa Electron

---

TEDDINGTON, Gloucestershire Map ref 2B1

◆◆◆ **BENGROVE FARM**

Bengrove, Teddington, Tewkesbury, GL20 8JB
T: (01242) 620332
F: (01242) 620851

Bedrooms: 3 twin
Bathrooms: 1 en suite, 1 public

Parking for 10

B&B per night:
S £22.00–£26.00
D £38.00–£42.00

OPEN All year round

10-acre mixed farm. Large interesting 17thC farmhouse with attractive, timber-beamed rooms and 2 guest lounges. In Area of Outstanding Natural Beauty. Peaceful setting.

TELFORD, Shropshire Map ref 4A3 *Tourist Information Centre Tel: (01952) 238008*

◆◆ **ALLSCOTT INN**

Walcot, Wellington, Telford, Shropshire TF6 5EQ
T: (01952) 248484

Bedrooms: 1 double, 2 twin, 1 triple
Bathrooms: 2 en suite, 1 public

Lunch available
EM 1900 (LO 2200)
Parking for 50
CC: Amex, Barclaycard, Delta, Eurocard, Mastercard, Solo, Switch, Visa

B&B per night:
S £20.00–£30.00
D £35.00–£45.00

OPEN All year round

Homely country inn offering delicious food and comfortable accommodation. Beer garden. Easy access Shrewsbury, Ironbridge and Telford.

◆◆◆ **FALCON HOTEL**

Holyhead Road, Wellington, Telford, Shropshire TF1 2DD
T: (01952) 255011
E: jamespearson@cableinet.co.uk

Bedrooms: 2 single, 4 double, 4 twin, 1 family room
Bathrooms: 7 en suite, 2 public

Lunch available
EM 1900 (LO 2100)
Parking for 30
CC: Barclaycard, Delta, Mastercard, Visa

B&B per night:
S £34.00–£40.00
D £42.00–£49.00

OPEN All year round

Small, family-run 18thC coaching hotel, 10 miles from Shrewsbury, 4 miles from Ironbridge, 18 miles from M6 at the end of M54 (exit 7).

◆◆◆ **GROVE HOUSE GUESTHOUSE**

Grove Street, St Georges, Telford, Shropshire TF2 9JW
T: (01952) 616140

Bedrooms: 1 single, 3 double, 2 twin
Bathrooms: 6 en suite

Parking for 10

B&B per night:
S £22.00–£26.00
D Max £36.00

OPEN All year round

Originally built as a hunting lodge. Close to Telford town centre/Exhibition centre/Ironbridge. Accessed from junction 4, M54. Centrally situated for Shropshire attractions.

◆◆◆◆ **THE MILL HOUSE**

Shrewsbury Road, High Ercall, Telford, Shropshire TF6 6BE
T: (01952) 770394
F: (01952) 770394
E: mill-house@talk21.com

Bedrooms: 1 double, 1 family room
Bathrooms: 1 public

Parking for 5

B&B per night:
S £30.00–£35.00
D £40.00–£45.00

OPEN All year round

A Grade II Listed watermill (no machinery) incorporating a working smallholding and family home, beside River Roden.

TELFORD continued

♦♦♦♦

OLD RECTORY
Stirchley Village, Telford, Shropshire
TF3 1DY
T: (01952) 596308 & 596518
F: (01952) 596308

Bedrooms: 2 single,
1 double, 2 twin,
1 family room
Bathrooms: 5 en suite,
1 private

Parking for 6

B&B per night:
S Min £25.00
D Min £38.00

HB per person:
DY Min £34.00

OPEN All year round

Large, comfortable guesthouse dating from 1734. Set in an acre of secluded gardens, on edge of town park. Convenient for town centre and Ironbridge museums.

♦♦♦♦

THE OLD VICARAGE
Church Street, St George's, Telford,
Shropshire TF2 9LZ
T: (01952) 616437 &
07889 546215 (mobile)
F: (01952) 610775
E: oldvicarage.stgeorges@tesco.net
I: www.oldvicarage.uk.com

B&B per night:
S £25.00–£35.00
D £40.00–£50.00

OPEN All year round

Charming 1860 period vicarage set in extensive picturesque gardens and countryside location. Enjoy a warm welcome and a comfortable, relaxing stay with a breakfast never to be forgotten. Just minutes from Telford town centre and the M54. Witin easy reach of Ironbridge, Weston Park and many other tourist attractions.

Bedrooms: 2 single,
2 double, 2 twin; suite
available
Bathrooms: 2 en suite,
1 private, 1 public

Parking for 9
CC: Barclaycard, Delta,
Mastercard, Switch, Visa

TETBURY, Gloucestershire Map ref 2B2 *Tourist Information Centre Tel: (01666) 503552*

♦♦♦♦♦
Gold
Award

TAVERN HOUSE
Willesley, Tetbury, GL8 8QU
T: (01666) 880444
F: (01666) 880254
I: tavernhousehotel@ukbusiness.com

B&B per night:
S £39.95–£70.00
D £65.00–£72.00

OPEN All year round

Delightfully situated 17thC former coaching inn, 1 mile from Westonbirt Arboretum. Superb luxury bed and breakfast. All rooms en suite with excellent facilities. Secluded walled gardens. Ideal base from which to explore the Cotswolds, Bath, Bristol, Cheltenham, Gloucester. ETB England for Excellence silver award 1993.

Bedrooms: 3 double,
1 twin
Bathrooms: 4 en suite

Parking for 4
CC: Mastercard, Visa

TEWKESBURY, Gloucestershire Map ref 2B1 *Tourist Information Centre Tel: (01684) 295027*

♦♦♦

TOWN STREET FARM
Tirley, Gloucester, GL19 4HG
T: (01452) 780442
F: (01452) 780890
I: townstreetfarm@hotmail.com

B&B per night:
S £25.00–£26.00
D £42.00–£44.00

OPEN All year round

A friendly welcome awaits you at our 18thC farmhouse close to the River Severn. Unspoilt views of our 500 acres of grassland on which we farm mostly cattle with a few horses and sheep. The comfortable en suite bedrooms and full English breakfasts will complement your stay.

Bedrooms: 1 double,
1 triple
Bathrooms: 2 en suite,
1 public

Parking for 4

TOWCESTER, Northamptonshire Map ref 2C1

♦♦♦♦ GREEN'S PARK
Woodend, Towcester, NN12 8SD
T: (01327) 860386
F: (01327) 860386

Bedrooms: 1 single, 2 twin
Bathrooms: 2 en suite, 1 private

Parking for 6

B&B per night:
S Min £30.00
D Min £60.00

OPEN All year round

230-acre mixed farm. Country house, good garden, floodlit tennis court and lake.

UPPINGHAM, Rutland Map ref 4C3

♦♦♦♦ RUTLAND HOUSE
61 High Street East, Uppingham,
Leicestershire LE15 9PY
T: (01572) 822497
F: (01572) 820065
E: rutland.house@virgin.net

Bedrooms: 1 single, 2 double, 1 twin, 1 triple
Bathrooms: 5 en suite

Parking for 2
CC: Barclaycard, Delta, Mastercard, Visa

B&B per night:
S £34.00–£34.00
D £44.00–£44.00

OPEN All year round

Family-run B&B close to Rutland Water. Full English or continental breakfast. Well-placed for exploring Rutland's villages and countryside, including Geoff Hamilton's famous gardens.

♦♦♦ THE VAULTS
Market Place, Uppingham, Oakham,
Leicestershire LE15 9QH
T: (01572) 823259

Bedrooms: 3 twin, 1 triple
Bathrooms: 4 en suite

Lunch available
EM 1900 (LO 2130)
CC: Amex, Barclaycard, Mastercard, Switch, Visa

B&B per night:
S £30.00–£35.00
D £40.00–£50.00

OPEN All year round

In the market place of this delightful Rutland town in the heart of the East Midlands. Convenient for Leicester, Corby, Peterborough, Melton Mowbray and Rutland Water.

UPTON-UPON-SEVERN, Worcestershire Map ref 2B1 *Tourist Information Centre Tel: (01684) 594200*

♦♦♦♦ TILTRIDGE FARM AND VINEYARD
Upper Hook Road, Upton-upon-
Severn, Worcester, WR8 0SA
T: (01684) 592906
F: (01684) 594142
E: elgarwine@aol.com

Bedrooms: 1 double, 1 twin, 1 triple
Bathrooms: 3 en suite

Parking for 12

B&B per night:
S £28.00–£30.00
D £44.00–£48.00

OPEN All year round

Mellow farmhouse set in vineyard, close to Upton and Three Counties Showground. Warm welcome, bumper breakfast and free wine tasting!

♦♦♦♦ WELLAND COURT
Upton-upon-Severn, Worcester,
WR8 0ST
T: (01684) 594426
F: (01684) 594426
E: archer@wellandcourt.demon.co.uk
I: www.upton.enta.net

Bedrooms: 1 double, 2 twin
Bathrooms: 3 en suite

Parking for 13

B&B per night:
S Max £47.50
D Max £75.00

OPEN All year round

Built c1450 and enlarged in the 18thC. Rescued from a dilapidated state and modernised to a high standard. At the foot of the Malvern Hills, an ideal base for touring.

COUNTRY CODE Always follow the Country Code ✿ Enjoy the countryside and respect its life and work ✿ Guard against all risk of fire ✿ Fasten all gates ✿ Keep your dogs under close control ✿ Keep to public paths across farmland ✿ Use gates and stiles to cross fences, hedges and walls ✿ Leave livestock, crops and machinery alone ✿ Take your litter home ✿ Help to keep all water clean ✿ Protect wildlife, plants and trees ✿ Take special care on country roads ✿ Make no unnecessary noise

VOWCHURCH, Herefordshire Map ref 2A1

◆◆◆◆
Silver
Award

UPPER GILVACH FARM

St. Margarets, Vowchurch, Hereford,
HR2 0QY
T: (01981) 510618
F: (01981) 510618
E: ruth@uppergilvach.freeserve.co.uk
I: www.golden-valley.co.uk/gilvach

B&B per night:
S £23.00–£30.00
D £46.00–£55.00

HB per person:
DY Min £37.00

OPEN All year round

A warm welcome awaits you on this family farm between the Golden Valley and Black Mountains. The 300-year-old farmhouse offers 3 spacious, attractively furnished bedrooms, all en suite with colour TV and hospitality tray. Delicious evening meals and hearty farmhouse breakfasts using local wines and produce.

Bedrooms: 1 single,
1 double, 1 twin
Bathrooms: 2 en suite,
1 private

EM
Parking for 20
CC: Barclaycard,
Mastercard, Switch, Visa

WARWICK, Warwickshire Map ref 2B1 *Tourist Information Centre Tel: (01926) 492212*

◆◆◆
AUSTIN HOUSE
96 Emscote Road, Warwick,
CV34 5QJ
T: (01926) 493583
F: (01926) 493679
E: mike@austinhouse96.freeserve.
co.uk

Bedrooms: 1 single,
2 double, 2 twin,
2 family rooms; suites
available
Bathrooms: 5 en suite,
1 public

Parking for 6
CC: Barclaycard, Delta,
Eurocard, JCB,
Mastercard, Visa

B&B per night:
S £18.00–£21.00
D £36.00–£42.00

OPEN All year round

Black and white Victorian house 1 mile from Warwick Castle and Royal Leamington Spa, 8 miles from Stratford-upon-Avon.

◆◆◆◆◆
Gold
Award

AVONSIDE COTTAGE

1 High Street, Barford, Warwick, CV35 8BU
T: (01926) 624779

B&B per night:
D £46.00–£54.00

OPEN All year round

17thC property in a peaceful village location, beautifully positioned on the banks of the River Avon between Warwick and Stratford-upon-Avon. Luxurious, spacious and well-equipped guest rooms with en suite bathrooms and river views. Delightful riverside garden. Within walking distance of village pubs. Ample off-road parking.

Bedrooms: 1 double,
1 twin
Bathrooms: 2 en suite

Parking for 2

◆◆◆◆
Silver
Award

THE COACH HOUSE
Old Budbrooke Road, Budbrooke,
Warwick, CV35 7DU
T: (01926) 410893
F: (01926) 490453
E: johnmannion@hotmail.com

Bedrooms: 3 double
Bathrooms: 1 en suite,
1 private, 1 public

Parking for 8

B&B per night:
S £33.00–£40.00
D £46.00–£58.00

OPEN Jan–Nov

Elegant c1820 coach house conversion in rural setting, 1 mile from Warwick town centre, 8 miles from Stratford-upon-Avon. Convenient for NEC/NAC. Friendly atmosphere. French and German spoken.

PRICES
Please check prices and other details at the time of booking.

♦♦♦♦

THE CROFT GUESTHOUSE

Haseley Knob, Warwick, CV35 7NL
T: (01926) 484447
F: (01926) 484447
E: david@croftguesthouse.co.uk
I: www.croftguesthouse.co.uk

B&B per night:
S Min £34.00
D Min £48.00

OPEN All year round

A non-smoking, friendly family guesthouse providing high quality clean and comfortable en suite accommodation at reasonable prices. Centrally located (off A4177) for exploring Warwick, Stratford, Coventry and Kenilworth, or for visiting NEC (15 minutes), National Agricultural Centre (15 minutes). Sky TV, fax and e-mail facilities. More details on our website.

Bedrooms: 2 single,
2 double, 1 twin, 2 triple
Bathrooms: 6 en suite,
1 private

Parking for 10
CC: Amex, Barclaycard,
Delta, JCB, Mastercard,
Visa

♦♦♦♦
Silver
Award

FORTH HOUSE
44 High Street, Warwick, CV34 4AX
T: (01926) 401512
F: (01926) 490809
E: info@forthhouseuk.co.uk
I: www.forthhouseuk.co.uk

Bedrooms: 1 double,
1 twin; suite available
Bathrooms: 2 en suite

Parking for 2
CC: Barclaycard, Delta,
Eurocard, JCB, Maestro,
Mastercard, Solo, Switch,
Visa, Visa Electron

B&B per night:
S £40.00–£45.00
D £55.00–£65.00

OPEN All year round

Ground floor and first floor guest suites with private sitting rooms and bathrooms. At the back of the house, overlooking peaceful garden, in town centre.

♦♦♦♦

HIGH HOUSE
Old Warwick Road, Rowington,
Warwick, CV35 7AA
T: (01926) 843270 & 07785 748134
F: (01926) 843689

Bedrooms: 2 double,
1 twin
Bathrooms: 3 en suite

Parking for 20

B&B per night:
S £30.00–£40.00
D £60.00–£60.00

OPEN All year round

Country house built 1690, in beautiful secluded rural position with outstanding views, north of Warwick. Antique 4-poster beds. Convenient for NEC, Birmingham, NAC, Coventry.

♦♦♦

HITHER BARN
Star Lane, Claverdon, Warwick,
CV35 8LW
T: (01926) 842839

Bedrooms: 2 double,
1 twin
Bathrooms: 3 en suite

Parking for 5

B&B per night:
S £29.00
D £45.00

OPEN All year round

Peaceful en suite accommodation set in 5 acres. First-class food, home-made bread, open fires, good local pubs. Easy run to NEC, NAC, Coventry, Solihull, Birmingham, Warwick, Stratford, Cotswolds, Oxford.

♦♦♦♦

LOWER ROWLEY

Wasperton, Warwick, CV35 8EB
T: (01926) 624937
F: (01926) 620053
E: lowerowley@uk.packardbell.org

B&B per night:
S £25.00–£35.00
D £40.00–£45.00

OPEN All year round

Peace and quiet in luxurious non-smoking accommodation, 4 miles from Warwick and 6 miles from Stratford-upon-Avon. Beautiful rural surroundings, with River Avon at bottom of the garden. En suite accommodation with colour TV, Hostess tray, hairdryer and many more extras to make your stay enjoyable.

Bedrooms: 1 double,
1 twin
Bathrooms: 1 en suite,
1 private, 1 public

Parking for 3

WARWICK continued

♦♦♦♦
Silver
Award

NORTHLEIGH HOUSE

Five Ways Road, Hatton, Warwick,
CV35 7HZ
T: (01926) 484203 & 07774 101894
F: (01926) 484006
E: www.northleigh.co.uk

B&B per night:
S £35.00–£42.00
D £50.00–£60.00

OPEN Feb–Nov

Comfortable, peaceful country house where the elegant rooms are individually designed, each having an en suite bathroom, TV, fridge and kettle and many thoughtful extras. A full English breakfast is freshly cooked to suit each guest. Handy for Warwick, Stratford-upon-Avon and the exhibition centres.

Bedrooms: 1 single,
5 double, 1 twin
Bathrooms: 7 en suite

EM
Parking for 8
CC: Mastercard, Visa

♦♦♦♦
Silver
Award

SHREWLEY POOLS FARM
Haseley, Warwick, CV35 7HB
T: (01926) 484315
I: www.s-h-systems.co.uk/hotels/shrewley.html

Bedrooms: 1 twin,
1 triple
Bathrooms: 2 en suite

EM 1800 (LO 2000)
Parking for 10

B&B per night:
S £30.00–£40.00
D £45.00–£55.00

HB per person:
DY £40.00–£55.00

OPEN All year round

260-acre mixed farm. Traditional mid-17thC beamed farmhouse with 1 acre garden, 5 miles north of Warwick on the A4177.

♦♦♦♦

THE TILTED WIG
11 Market Place, Warwick,
CV34 4SA
T: (01926) 410466 & 411740
F: (01926) 495740

Bedrooms: 2 double,
2 twin
Bathrooms: 4 en suite

Lunch available
EM 1800 (LO 2050)
Parking for 4
CC: Amex, Barclaycard,
Delta, Diners, Mastercard,
Switch, Visa

B&B per night:
S £55.00–£55.00
D £55.00–£55.00

OPEN All year round

Grade II Listed building situated comfortably in the market place, blending in with the town's historic architecture. A cafe bar, brasserie, wine bar atmosphere.

WEEDON, Northamptonshire Map ref 2C1

♦♦♦♦

SWAN HOUSE–ANNEX
Swan House, Dodford, Weedon,
Northampton, NN7 4SX
T: (01327) 341847 (Day/evening)

Bedrooms: 2 double
Bathrooms: 1 public

Parking for 2

B&B per night:
S £25.00–£25.00
D £45.00–£45.00

OPEN All year round

An annexe to Swan House comprising 2 double bedrooms, with handbasins, shaver points and TV. Separate shower and WC. Rural location, off-road parking.

WEM, Shropshire Map ref 4A3

♦♦

FORNCET
Soulton Road, Wem, Shrewsbury,
SY4 5HR
T: (01939) 232996

Bedrooms: 1 single,
1 twin, 1 triple
Bathrooms: 2 public

EM 1830 (LO 1930)
Parking for 6

B&B per night:
S £17.50–£17.50
D £35.00–£35.00

HB per person:
DY £27.50–£27.50

OPEN Jan–Nov

Spacious, centrally heated Victorian house on the edge of this small market town, 200 yards from rail station.

WELCOME HOST This is a nationally recognised customer care programme which aims to promote the highest standards of service and a warm welcome. Establishments taking part in this initiative are indicated by the ⊛ symbol.

WENLOCK EDGE, Shropshire Map ref 4A3

♦♦♦♦
Silver
Award

THE WENLOCK EDGE INN
Hilltop, Wenlock Edge,
Much Wenlock, TF13 6DJ
T: (01746) 785678
F: (01746) 785285
E: info@wenlockedgeinn.co.uk
I: www.wenlockedgeinn.co.uk

Bedrooms: 2 double,
1 twin
Bathrooms: 3 en suite

Lunch available
EM 1900 (LO 2100)
Parking for 40
CC: Amex, Barclaycard,
Delta, JCB, Mastercard,
Solo, Switch, Visa, Visa
Electron

B&B per night:
S £41.00–£48.00
D £63.00–£75.00

OPEN All year round

Traditional, family-run country inn. Peaceful location, fine views and National Trust walks. Comfortable rooms and good home cooking. Highly recommended by leading guides.

WEOBLEY, Herefordshire Map ref 2A1

♦♦♦

GARNSTONE HOUSE
Weobley, Hereford, HR4 8QP
T: (01544) 318943
F: (01544) 318197

Bedrooms: 1 double,
1 twin
Bathrooms: 1 public

Parking for 6

B&B per night:
S £25.00–£25.00
D £40.00–£50.00

HB per person:
DY £33.00–£40.00

OPEN All year round

Comfortable and friendly accommodation in peaceful setting 1 mile from Weobley. Lovely garden. Good home cooking. Easy reach of golf clubs, riding and hill walking.

WESTBURY-ON-SEVERN, Gloucestershire Map ref 2B1

♦♦♦♦♦
Gold
Award

BOXBUSH BARN
Rodley, Westbury-on-Severn,
GL14 1QZ
T: (01452) 760949 (24 hours
answerphone)
F: (01452) 760949

Bedrooms: 1 double,
1 twin
Bathrooms: 1 en suite,
1 private

Parking for 4

B&B per night:
D £40.00–£45.00

OPEN Feb–Nov

Centuries old timber framed barn, sensitively converted to combine modern comfort with the best of traditional materials and design.

WESTON-ON-THE-GREEN, Oxfordshire

Weston Grounds Farm
See South of England region for full entry details

WINCHCOMBE, Gloucestershire Map ref 2B1

♦♦♦♦

PARKS FARM
Sudeley, Winchcombe, Cheltenham,
GL54 5JB
T: (01242) 603874 (Answerphone)
F: (01242) 603874
E: rogerwilson.freeserve.co.uk

Bedrooms: 2 twin,
2 triple
Bathrooms: 2 private

Parking for 2

B&B per night:
S £30.00–£30.00
D £40.00–£40.00

OPEN All year round

Listed Cotswold hill farm with glorious views. Very comfortable. Peaceful rural location with no traffic. Welcoming local town 8 minutes' drive away.

WINSTER, Derbyshire Map ref 4B2

♦♦♦♦

BRAE COTTAGE
East Bank, Winster, Matlock,
DE4 2DT
T: (01629) 650375

Bedrooms: 2 double
Bathrooms: 2 en suite

Parking for 3

B&B per night:
S £25.00–£30.00
D £40.00–£60.00

OPEN All year round

18thC cottage in tranquil surroundings. Picturesque village in Peak District National Park. En suite accommodation, separate from cottage, furnished to high standard. Private courtyard parking.

WISHAW, Warwickshire Map ref 4B3

♦♦♦

ASH HOUSE
The Gravel, Wishaw,
Sutton Coldfield, West Midlands
B76 9QB
T: (01675) 475782 & 07850 414000
E: kate@rectory80.co.uk

Bedrooms: 2 double
Bathrooms: 2 en suite

Parking for 6
CC: Delta, Mastercard,
Visa

B&B per night:
S £25.00–£30.00
D £40.00–£50.00

OPEN All year round

Former rectory with lovely views. Few minutes' walk from Belfry Golf and Leisure Hotel. Half a mile M42, 10 minutes' drive from Birmingham Airport/NEC.

WITNEY, Oxfordshire

The Court Inn, The Witney Hotel
See South of England region for full entry details

WOODHALL SPA, Lincolnshire Map ref 4D2

♦♦

CLAREMONT GUESTHOUSE

9-11 Witham Road, Woodhall Spa, LN10 6RW T: (01526) 352000	Bedrooms: 2 single, 2 double, 1 twin, 4 triple, 1 family room Bathrooms: 3 en suite, 2 public	EM 1800 Parking for 5

B&B per night:
S £15.00–£20.00
D £30.00–£40.00

OPEN All year round

Homely B&B in unspoilt Victorian guesthouse within easy reach of the town's sporting and leisure facilities. Off-street car parking. Good choice of food nearby.

♦♦♦

PITCHAWAY GUESTHOUSE

The Broadway, Woodhall Spa, LN10 6SQ T: (01526) 352969	Bedrooms: 2 single, 1 double, 2 twin, 1 triple, 1 family room Bathrooms: 2 en suite, 2 public	EM 1930 (LO 0900) Parking for 8

B&B per night:
S £20.00–£28.00
D £40.00–£44.00

OPEN Feb–Dec

Just a 'pitch away' from the championship golf course. This family-run guesthouse offers comfortable accommodation. Home-cooked meals are available.

WOODSTOCK, Oxfordshire

Gorselands Hall, The Laurels, Shepherds Hall Inn
See South of England region for full entry details

WORCESTER, Worcestershire Map ref 2B1 *Tourist Information Centre Tel: (01905) 726311*

♦♦♦♦

YEW TREE HOUSE

Norchard, Crossway Green, Hartlebury, Kidderminster, DY13 9SN T: (01299) 250921 (Answerphone) & 07703 112392 (Mobile) E: paula@knightp.swinternet.co.uk	Bedrooms: 3 double, 2 twin Bathrooms: 4 en suite, 1 private	Parking for 6

B&B per night:
S £30.00–£30.00
D £50.00–£55.00

OPEN All year round

Elegant Georgian farmhouse, 10 minutes from M5. Delightful atmosphere and surroundings. Splendid breakfasts. Rooms with TV and teatray. Within easy reach of historic towns.

WORKSOP, Nottinghamshire Map ref 4C2 *Tourist Information Centre Tel: (01909) 501148*

♦♦♦

SHERWOOD GUESTHOUSE

57 Carlton Road, Worksop, S80 1PP T: (01909) 474209 (Answerphone) & 478214	Bedrooms: 1 single, 4 twin, 2 triple Bathrooms: 2 en suite, 2 public

B&B per night:
S Min £21.00
D £42.00–£47.00

OPEN All year round

In Robin Hood Country, near M1 and A1 and close to station and town centre. Comfortable rooms with TV and tea/coffee facilities.

WYE VALLEY

See under Fownhope, Hereford, Ross-on-Wye

AT-A-GLANCE SYMBOLS

Symbols at the end of each accommodation entry give useful information about services and facilities. A key to symbols can be found inside the back cover flap. Keep this open for easy reference.

WYRE PIDDLE, Worcestershire Map ref 2B1

◆◆◆◆
Silver
Award

ARBOUR HOUSE

Main Road, Wyre Piddle, Pershore,
WR10 2HU
T: (01386) 555833
F: (01386) 555833
E: arbourhouse@faxvia.net

B&B per night:
S £25.00–£32.00
D £44.00–£50.00

OPEN All year round

A fine Grade II Listed home with oak beams and log fires, overlooking Bredon Hill and close to the River Avon. Comfortable accommodation and good food in a relaxed, friendly atmosphere. Excellent riverside pub opposite. An ideal base for visiting the Cotswolds, Stratford-upon-Avon, Worcester and Malvern.

Bedrooms: 1 double,
2 twin
Bathrooms: 3 en suite

Parking for 5

WYSALL, Nottinghamshire Map ref 4C3

◆◆◆◆

LORNE HOUSE BED & BREAKFAST

Lorne House, Bradmore Road,
Wysall, Nottingham, NG12 5QR
T: (01509) 881433 (Answerphone)
& 07974 710037 (Mobile)
F: (0115) 942 3350
E: haymin@ukonline.co.uk

Bedrooms: 1 double,
1 family room
Bathrooms: 1 public,
1 private shower

B&B per night:
S £20.00–£25.00
D £36.00–£40.00

OPEN All year round

Country house with large bedrooms, extensive views of the countryside, separate lounge and dining room and accommodation also for dogs and horses.

QUALITY ASSURANCE SCHEME

For an explanation of the quality and facilities represented by the Diamonds please refer to the front of this guide. A more detailed explanation can be found in the information pages at the back.

A brief guide to the main Towns and Villages offering accommodation in the HEART OF ENGLAND

A **ALTON, STAFFORDSHIRE** - Alton Castle, an impressive 19th C building, dominates the village which is set in spectacular scenery. Nearby is Alton Towers, a romantic 19th C ruin with innumerable tourist attractions within one of England's largest theme parks in its 800 acres of magnificent gardens.

• **ASHBOURNE, DERBYSHIRE** - Market town on the edge of the Peak District National Park and an excellent centre for walking. Its impressive church with 212-ft spire stands in an unspoilt old street. Ashbourne is well-known for gingerbread and its Shrovetide football match.

• **ASHBY-DE-LA-ZOUCH, LEICESTERSHIRE** - Lovely market town with late 15th C church, impressive ruined 15th C castle, an interesting small museum and a wide, sloping main street with Georgian buildings. Twycross Zoo is nearby.

• **ASHFORD IN THE WATER, DERBYSHIRE** - Limestone village in attractive surroundings of the Peak District approached by 3 bridges over the River Wye. There is an annual well-dressing ceremony and the village was well-known in the 18th C for its black marble quarries.

• **ATHERSTONE, WARWICKSHIRE** - Pleasant market town with some 18th C houses and interesting old inns. Every Shrove Tuesday a game of football is played in the streets, a tradition dating from the 13th C. Twycross Zoo is nearby with an extensive collection of reptiles and butterflies.

B **BAKEWELL, DERBYSHIRE** - Pleasant market town, famous for its pudding. It is set in beautiful countryside on the River Wye and is an excellent centre for exploring the Derbyshire Dales, the Peak District National Park, Chatsworth and Haddon Hall.

• **BALSALL COMMON, WEST MIDLANDS** - Close to Birmingham NEC and Kenilworth and within easy reach of Coventry.

• **BAMFORD, DERBYSHIRE** - Village in the Peak District near the Upper Derwent Reservoirs of Ladybower, Derwent and Howden. An excellent centre for walking.

• **BARLOW, DERBYSHIRE** - Lying 4 miles north-west of Chesterfield, its recorded history dates back to William the Conqueror. The major event is annual well-dressing week.

• **BELPER, DERBYSHIRE** - Pleasant old market town in the valley of the River Derwent. Attractive scenery and a wealth of industrial history.

• **BELTON IN RUTLAND, GLOUCESTERSHIRE** - Conservation village with the oldest church in Rutland. Close to Rutland Water and "Barnsdale" TV gardens.

• **BIBURY, GLOUCESTERSHIRE** - Village on the River Coln with stone houses and the famous 17th C Arlington Row, former weavers' cottages. Arlington Mill is now a folk museum. Trout farm and Barnsley House Gardens nearby are open to the public.

• **BIRDLIP, GLOUCESTERSHIRE** - Hamlet at the top of a very steep descent down to the Gloucester Vale with excellent viewpoint over Crickley Hill Country Park.

• **BIRMINGHAM, WEST MIDLANDS** - Britain's second city, whose attractions include Centenary Square and the ICC with Symphony Hall, the NEC, the City Art Gallery, Barber Institute of Fine Arts, 17th C Aston Hall, science and railway museums, Jewellery Quarter, Cadbury World, 2 cathedrals and Botanical Gardens.

• **BISHOP'S CASTLE, SHROPSHIRE** - A 12th C Planned Town with a castle site at the top of the hill and a church at the bottom of the main street. Many interesting buildings with original timber frames hidden behind present day houses. On the Welsh border close to the Clun Forest in quiet, unspoilt countryside.

• **BLAKENEY, GLOUCESTERSHIRE** - Village in wooded hills near the Forest of Dean and the Severn Estuary. It is close to Lydney where the Dean Forest Railway has full size railway engines, a museum and steam days.

• **BLEDINGTON, GLOUCESTERSHIRE** - Village close to the Oxfordshire border, with a pleasant green and a beautiful church.

• **BLOCKLEY, GLOUCESTERSHIRE** - This village's prosperity was founded in silk mills and other factories but now it is a quiet, unspoilt place. An excellent centre for exploring pretty Cotswold villages, especially Chipping Campden and Broadway.

• **BOURTON-ON-THE-WATER, GLOUCESTERSHIRE** - The River Windrush flows through this famous Cotswold village which has a green, and cottages and houses of Cotswold stone. Its many attractions include a model village, Birdland, a Motor Museum and the Cotswold Perfumery.

• **BRACKLEY, NORTHAMPTONSHIRE** - Historic market town of mellow stone, with many fine buildings lining the wide High Street and Market Place. Sulgrave Manor (George Washington's ancestral home) and Silverstone Circuit are nearby.

• **BRAILES, WARWICKSHIRE** - Convenient for Banbury, Royal Leamington Spa and the Vale of Evesham. St George's Church has a tower dating from the 13th C and was restored in the 19th C.

• **BRIDGNORTH, SHROPSHIRE** - Red sandstone riverside town in 2 parts - High and Low - linked by a cliff railway. Much of interest including a ruined Norman keep, half-timbered 16th C houses, Midland Motor Museum and Severn Valley Railway.

• **BROADWAY, WORCESTERSHIRE** - Beautiful Cotswold village called the "Show village of England", with 16th C stone houses and cottages. Near the village is Broadway Tower with magnificent views over 12 counties and a country park with nature trails and adventure playground.

• **BROMSGROVE, WORCESTERSHIRE** - This market town near the Lickey Hills has an interesting museum and craft centre and 14th C church with fine tombs and a Carillon tower. The Avoncroft Museum of Buildings is nearby where many old buildings have been re-assembled, having been saved from destruction.

• **BROMYARD, HEREFORDSHIRE** - Market town on the River Frome surrounded by orchards, with black and white houses and a Norman church. Nearby at Lower Brockhampton is a 14th C half-timbered moated manor house owned by the National Trust. Heritage Centre.

• **BROUGHTON ASTLEY, LEICESTERSHIRE** - First mentioned in the Domesday Book, when it was three separate villages, Broctone, Sutone and Torp.

AT-A-GLANCE SYMBOLS

Symbols at the end of each accommodation entry give useful information about services and facilities. A key to symbols can be found inside the back cover flap. Keep this open for easy reference.

- **BUCKNELL, SHROPSHIRE** - Village by the River Redlake with thatched black and white cottages, a Norman church and the remains of an Iron Age fort on a nearby hill. It is a designated Area of Outstanding Natural Beauty.

- **BURTON DASSETT, WARWICKSHIRE** - The church tower looks out over the site of the Battle of Edgehill and it is said that Cromwell himself climbed the tower to watch the fighting. Nearby is a 16th C beacon tower from which news of the battle was sent.

- **BUXTON, DERBYSHIRE** - The highest market town in England and one of the oldest spas, with an elegant Crescent, Poole's Cavern, Opera House and attractive Pavilion Gardens. An excellent centre for exploring the Peak District.

- **C** **CASTLE DONINGTON, LEICESTERSHIRE** - A Norman castle once stood here. The world's largest collection of single-seater racing cars is displayed at Donington Park alongside the racing circuit, and an Aeropark Visitor Centre can be seen at nearby East Midlands International Airport.

- **CASTLETON, DERBYSHIRE** - Large village in a spectacular Peak District setting with ruined Peveril Castle and 4 great show caverns, where the Blue John stone and lead were mined. One cavern offers a mile-long underground boat journey.

- **CHAPEL-EN-LE-FRITH, DERBYSHIRE** - Small market town and a good base for climbing and walking. Close to the show caverns at Castleton.

- **CHELTENHAM, GLOUCESTERSHIRE** - Cheltenham was developed as a spa town in the 18th C and has some beautiful Regency architecture, in particular the Pittville Pump Room. It holds international music and literature festivals and is also famous for its race meetings and cricket.

- **CHESTERFIELD, DERBYSHIRE** - Famous for the twisted spire of its parish church, Chesterfield has some fine modern buildings and excellent shopping facilities, including a large, traditional open-air market. Hardwick Hall and Bolsover Castle are nearby.

- **CHIPPING CAMPDEN, GLOUCESTERSHIRE** - Outstanding Cotswold wool town with many old stone gabled houses, a splendid church and 17th C almshouses. Nearby are Kiftsgate Court Gardens and Hidcote Manor Gardens (National Trust).

- **CHURCH STRETTON, SHROPSHIRE** - Church Stretton lies under the eastern slope of the Longmynd surrounded by hills. It is deal for walkers, with marvellous views, golf and gliding. Wenlock Edge is not far away.

- **CIRENCESTER, GLOUCESTERSHIRE** - "Capital of the Cotswolds", Cirencester was Britain's second most important Roman town with many finds housed in the Corinium Museum. It has a very fine Perpendicular church and old houses around the market place.

- **COLEFORD, GLOUCESTERSHIRE** - Small town in the Forest of Dean with the ancient iron mines at Clearwell Caves nearby, where mining equipment and geological samples are displayed. There are several forest trails in the area.

- **CONINGSBY, LINCOLNSHIRE** - Large thriving village on the edge of the Lincolnshire Fens. It is within easy reach of main towns and has a pleasing church with an unusual one-handed clock.

- **CORBY GLEN, LINCOLNSHIRE** - Located conveniently off the A1 and the famous castle, park and gardens at Grimsthorpe.

- **COVENTRY, WEST MIDLANDS** - Modern city with a long history. It has many places of interest including the post-war and ruined medieval cathedrals, art gallery and museums, some 16th C almshouses, St Mary's Guildhall, Lunt Roman fort and the Belgrade Theatre.

- **CRESSBROOK, DERBYSHIRE** - Delightful dale with stone hall and pleasant houses, steep wooded slopes and superb views.

- **D** **DERBY** - Modern industrial city but with ancient origins. There is a wide range of attractions including several museums (notably Royal Crown Derby), a theatre, a concert hall, and the cathedral with fine ironwork and Bess of Hardwick's tomb.

- **DONNINGTON, SHROPSHIRE** - Village with a pretty church, tucked away amid back lanes to the south of Ledbury.

- **DROITWICH, WORCESTERSHIRE** - Old town with natural brine springs, now incorporated into the Brine Baths Health Centre, developed as a spa at the beginning of the 19th C. Of particular interest is the Church of the Sacred Heart with splendid mosaics. Fine parks and a Heritage Centre.

- **E** **EASTCOMBE, GLOUCESTERSHIRE** - Situated in the hills 3 miles from Stroud, the quiet village in the South Cotswolds overlooks the Golden Valley.

- **ELMESTHORPE, LEICESTERSHIRE** - Silhouetted against the horizon, the picturesque church of St Mary has a 17th C tower and 12th or 13th C font and is set in a beautiful churchyard with lovely views.

- **EVESHAM, WORCESTERSHIRE** - Market town in the centre of a fruit-growing area. There are pleasant walks along the River Avon and many old houses and inns. A fine 16th C bell tower stands between 2 churches near the medieval Almonry Museum.

- **F** **FAIRFORD, GLOUCESTERSHIRE** - Small town with a 15th C wool church famous for its complete 15th C stained glass windows, interesting carvings and original wall paintings. It is an excellent touring centre and the Cotswolds Wildlife Park is nearby.

- **FOWNHOPE, HEREFORDSHIRE** - Attractive village close to the River Wye with black and white cottages and other interesting houses. It has a large church with a Norman tower and a 14th C spire.

- **FOXTON, LEICESTERSHIRE** - Attractive village established in the 8th C. The 13th C church contains part of a Saxon Cross and a "lepers window". The Grand Union Canal passes through the village. Within walking distance is historic Foxton Locks with its unique staircase flight of 10 locks, and Inclined Plane Museum.

- **FRAMPTON-ON-SEVERN, GLOUCESTERSHIRE** - Near the River Severn in the Berkeley Vale, the village has a remarkably large green with an interesting range of buildings, the most notable being Frampton Court built around 1733. Beside the Sharpness Canal, close by is Berkeley Castle and Slimbridge Wildfowl Trust.

- **G** **GAINSBOROUGH, LINCOLNSHIRE** - Britain's most inland port has strong connections with the Pilgrim Fathers. Gainsborough Old Hall, where they worshipped, boasts a 15th C manor house with complete kitchens.

- **GLOSSOP, DERBYSHIRE** - Town in dramatic moorland surroundings with views over the High Peak. The settlement can be traced back to Roman times but expanded during the Industiral Revolution.

QUALITY ASSURANCE SCHEME

For an explanation of the quality and facilities represented by the Diamonds please refer to the front of this guide. A more detailed explanation can be found in the information pages at the back.

- **GLOUCESTER, GLOUCESTERSHIRE -**
A Roman city and inland port, its cathedral is one of the most beautiful in Britain. Gloucester's many attractions include museums and the restored warehouses in the Victorian docks containing the National Waterways Museum, Robert Opie Packaging Collection and other attractions.

- **GOTHERINGTON, GLOUCESTERSHIRE -**
A small village 5 miles north of Cheltenham, at the edge of the Cotswolds, looking towards Langley Hill and Prescott Hill. Famous for the special classic car climbs, close to Tewkesbury and Sudeley Castle.

- **GREAT RISSINGTON, GLOUCESTERSHIRE**
- One of two villages overlooking the River Windrush near Bourton-on-the-Water.

- **GUITING POWER, GLOUCESTERSHIRE -**
Unspoilt village with stone cottages and a green. The Cotswold Farm Park, with a collection of rare breeds, an adventure playground and farm trail, is nearby.

- **H HAMPTON-IN-ARDEN, WEST MIDLANDS**
- Midway between Birmingham and Coventry and with the National Exhibition Centre on the doorstep.

- **HAYFIELD, DERBYSHIRE -** Village set in spectacular scenery at the highest point of the Peak District with the best approach to the Kinder Scout plateau via the Kinder Downfall. An excellent centre for walking. Three reservoirs close by.

- **HEREFORD, HEREFORDSHIRE -**
Agricultural county town, its cathedral containing much Norman work, a large chained library and the world-famous Mappa Mundi exhibition. Among the city's varied attractions are several museums including the Cider Museum and the Old House.

- **HINCKLEY, LEICESTERSHIRE -** The town has an excellent leisure centre, Bosworth Battlefield, with its Visitor Centre and Battle Trail, is 5 miles away.

- **HOLBEACH, LINCOLNSHIRE -** Small town, mentioned in the Domesday Book, has spendid 14th C church with a fine tower and spire. The surrounding villages also have interesting churches, and the area is well-known for its bulbfields.

- **HOPE, DERBYSHIRE -** Village in the Hope Valley which is an excellent base for walking in the Peak District and for fishing and shooting. There is a well-dressing ceremony each June and its August sheep dog trials are well-known. Castleton Caves are nearby.

- **HUSBANDS BOSWORTH, LEICESTERSHIRE -** This village is situated at the crossroads between Lutterworth and Market Harborough and the A50, Northampton/Leicester. Stanford Hall is within easy reach.

- **I IRONBRIDGE, SHROPSHIRE -** Small town on the Severn where the Industrial Revolution began. It has the world's first iron bridge built in 1779. The Ironbridge Gorge Museum, of exceptional interest, comprises a rebuilt turn-of-the-century town and sites spread over 6 square miles.

- **K KENILWORTH, WARWICKSHIRE -** The main feature of the town is the ruined 12th C castle. It has many royal associations but was damaged by Cromwell. A good base for visiting Coventry, Leamington Spa and Warwick.

- **KETTERING, NORTHAMPTONSHIRE -**
Ancient industrial town based on shoe-making. Wicksteed Park to the south has many children's amusements. The splendid 17th C ducal mansion of Boughton House is to the north.

- **KIDDERMINSTER, WORCESTERSHIRE -**
The town is the centre for carpet manufacturing. It has a medieval church with good monuments and a statue of Sir Rowland Hill, a native of the town and founder of the penny post. West Midlands Safari Park is nearby. Severn Valley Railway station.

- **KINETON, WARWICKSHIRE -** Attractive old village in rolling countryside. 1 mile from site of famous battle of Edgehill. Medieval church of St Peter.

- **L LEADENHAM, LINCOLNSHIRE -**
Village on the Lincoln Edge, noted for its fine church spire.

- **LEAMINGTON SPA, WARWICKSHIRE -**
18th C spa town with many fine Georgian and Regency houses. The refurbished 19th C Pump Rooms with Heritage Centre. The attractive Jephson Gardens are laid out alongside the river.

- **LECHLADE, GLOUCESTERSHIRE -**
Attractive village on the River Thames and a popular spot for boating. It has a number of fine Georgian houses and a 15th C church. Nearby is Kelmscott Manor, with its William Morris furnishings, and 18th C Buscot House (National Trust).

- **LEDBURY, HEREFORDSHIRE -** Town with cobbled streets and many black and white timbered houses, including the 17th C market house and old inns. In attractive countryside nearby is Eastnor Castle, a venue for many events, with an interesting collection of tapestries and armour.

- **LEEK, STAFFORDSHIRE -** Old silk and textile town, with some interesting buildings and a number of inns dating from the 17th C. Its art gallery has displays of embroidery. Brindley Mill, designed by James Brindley, has been restored as a museum.

- **LEICESTER -** Modern industrial city with a wide variety of attractions including Roman remains, ancient churches, Georgian houses and a Victorian clock tower. Excellent shopping precincts, arcades and market, museums, theatres, concert hall and sports and leisure centres.

- **LEOMINSTER, HEREFORDSHIRE -** The town owed its prosperity to wool and has many interesting buildings, notably the timber-framed Grange Court, a former town hall. The impressive Norman priory church has 3 naves and a ducking stool. Berrington Hall (National Trust) is nearby.

- **LICHFIELD, STAFFORDSHIRE -** Lichfield is Dr Samuel Johnson's birthplace and commemorates him with a museum and statue. The 13th C cathedral has 3 spires and the west front is full of statues. Among the attractive town buildings is the Heritage Centre. The Regimental Museum is in Whittington Barracks.

- **LINCOLN, LINCOLNSHIRE -** Ancient city dominated by the magnificent 11th C cathedral with its triple towers. A Roman gateway is still used and there are medieval houses lining narrow, cobbled streets. Other attractions include the Norman castle, several museums and the Usher Gallery.

- **LONG BUCKBY, NORTHAMPTONSHIRE -**
Stretching for one and a half miles, this is a village with individuality and character.

- **LOUGHBOROUGH, LEICESTERSHIRE -**
Industrial town famous for its bell foundry and 47-bell Carillon Tower. The Great Central Railway operates steam railway rides of over 8 miles through the attractive scenery of Charnwood Forest.

- **LOUTH, LINCOLNSHIRE -** Attractive old market town set on the eastern edge of the Lincolnshire Wolds. St James's Church has an impressive tower and spire and there are the remains of a Cistercian abbey. The museum contains an interesting collection of local material.

- **LUDFORD, LINCOLNSHIRE -** The hamlets of Ludford Magna and Ludford Parva combine to form Ludford, situated on the busy road from Market Rasen to Louth.

- **LUDLOW, SHROPSHIRE -** Outstandingly interesting border town with a magnificent castle high above the River Teme, 2 half-timbered old inns and an impressive 15th C church. The Reader's House, with its 3-storey Jacobean porch, should also be seen.

- **M MALVERN, WORCESTERSHIRE -**
Spa town in Victorian times, its water is today bottled and sold worldwide. 6 resorts, set on the slopes of the Hills, form part of Malvern. Great Malvern Priory has splendid 15th C windows. It is an excellent walking centre.

TOWN INDEX

This can be found at the back of this guide. If you know where you want to stay, the index will give you the page number listing accommodation in your chosen town, city or village.

- **MARKET DRAYTON, SHROPSHIRE** - Old market town with black and white buildings and 17th C houses, also acclaimed for its gingerbread. Hodnet Hall is in the vicinity with its beautiful landscaped gardens covering 60 acres.

- **MARKET HARBOROUGH, LEICESTERSHIRE** - There have been markets here since the early 13th C, and the town was also an important coaching centre, with several ancient hostelries. The early 17th C grammar school was once the butter market.

- **MARKET RASEN, LINCOLNSHIRE** - Market town on the edge of the Lincolnshire Wolds. The racecourse and the picnic site and forest walks at Willingham Woods are to the east of the town.

- **MATLOCK, DERBYSHIRE** - The town lies beside the narrow valley of the River Derwent surrounded by steep wooded hills. Good centre for exploring Derbyshire's best scenery.

- **MEDBOURNE, LEICESTERSHIRE** - Picturesque village with medieval bridge.

- **MELTON MOWBRAY, LEICESTERSHIRE** - Close to the attractive Vale of Belvoir and famous for its pork pies and Stilton cheese which are the subjects of special displays in the museum. It has a beautiful church with a tower 100 ft high.

- **MERIDEN, WEST MIDLANDS** - Village halfway between Coventry and Birmingham. Said to be the centre of England, marked by a cross on the green.

- **MINCHINHAMPTON, GLOUCESTERSHIRE** - Stone-built town, with many 17th/18th C buildings, owing its existence to the wool and cloth trades. A 17th C pillared market house may be found in the town square, near which is the Norman and 14th C church.

- **MINSTERLEY, SHROPSHIRE** - Village with a curious little church of 1692 and a fine old black and white hall. The lofty ridge known as the Stiperstones is 4 miles to the south.

- **MORETON-IN-MARSH, GLOUCESTERSHIRE** - Attractive town of Cotswold stone with 17th C houses, an ideal base for touring the Cotswolds. Some of the local attractions include Batsford Park Arboretum, the Jacobean Chastleton House and Sezincote Garden.

- **MUCH MARCLE, HEREFORDSHIRE** - Village among cider orchards with some old black and white cottages and the 13th C manor house of Hellens with many of the original furnishings. The 13th C church has some unusual tomb figures.

- **MUCH WENLOCK, SHROPSHIRE** - Small town close to Wenlock Edge in beautiful scenery and full of interest. In particular there are the remains of an 11th C priory with fine carving and the black and white 16th C Guildhall.

- **N NAILSWORTH, GLOUCESTERSHIRE** - Ancient wool town with several elegant Jacobean and Georgian houses, surrounded by wooded hillsides with fine views.

- **NAUNTON, GLOUCESTERSHIRE** - A high place on the Windrush, renowned for its wild flowers and with an attractive dovecote.

- **NEWARK, NOTTINGHAMSHIRE** - The town has many fine old houses and ancient inns near the large, cobbled market-place. Substantial ruins of the 12th C castle, where King John died, dominate the riverside walk and there are several interesting museums. Sherwood Forest is nearby.

- **NEWLAND, GLOUCESTERSHIRE** - Probably the most attractive of the villages of the Forest of Dean. The church is often referred to as "the Cathedral of the Forest"; it contains a number of interesting monuments and the Forest Miner's Brass. Almshouses nearby were endowed by William Jones, founder of Monmouth School.

- **NEWPORT, SHROPSHIRE** - Small market town on the Shropshire Union Canal has a wide High Street and a church with some interesting monuments. Newport is close to Aqualate Mere which is the largest lake in Staffordshire.

- **NORTHAMPTON, NORTHAMPTONSHIRE** - A bustling town and a shoe manufacturing centre, with excellent shopping facilities, several museums and parks, a theatre and a concert hall. Several old churches include 1 of only 4 round churches in Britain.

- **NORTHLEACH, GLOUCESTERSHIRE** - Village famous for its beautiful 15th C wool church with its lovely porch and interesting interior. There are also some fine houses including a 17th C wool merchant's house containing Keith Harding's World of Mechanical Music. The Cotswold Countryside Collection is in the former prison.

- **NOTTINGHAM** - Attractive modern city with a rich history. Outside its castle, now a museum, is Robin Hood's statue. Attractions include "The Tales of Robin Hood"; the Lace Hall; Wollaton Hall; museums and excellent facilities for shopping, sports and entertainment.

- **NUNEATON, WARWICKSHIRE** - Busy town with an art gallery and museum which has a permanent exhibition of the work of George Eliot. The library also has an interesting collection of material. Arbury Hall, a fine example of Gothic architecture, is nearby.

- **O OAKAMOOR, STAFFORDSHIRE** - Small village below a steep hill amid the glorious scenery of the Churnet Valley. Its industrial links have now gone, as the site of the factory which made 20,000 miles of copper wire for the first Atlantic cable has been transformed into an attractive picnic site on the riverside.

- **OAKHAM, LEICESTERSHIRE** - Pleasant former county town of Rutland. Fine 12th C Great Hall, part of its castle, with a historic collection of horseshoes. An octagonal Butter Cross stands in the market-place and Rutland County Museum, Rutland Farm Park and Rutland Water are of interest.

- **OUNDLE, NORTHAMPTONSHIRE** - Historic town situated on the River Nene with narrow alleys and courtyards and many stone buildings, including a fine church and historic inns.

- **P PERSHORE, WORCESTERSHIRE** - Attractive Georgian town on the River Avon close to the Vale of Evesham, with fine houses and old inns. The remains of the beautiful Pershore Abbey form the parish church.

- **R REDMILE, LEICESTERSHIRE** - Vale of Belvoir village, overlooked by the hilltop castle.

- **RETFORD, NOTTINGHAMSHIRE** - Market town on the River Idle with a pleasant market square and Georgian houses. The surrounding villages were the homes and meeting places of the early Pilgrim Fathers.

- **ROSS-ON-WYE, HEREFORDSHIRE** - Attractive market town with a 17th C market hall, set above the River Wye. There are lovely views over the surrounding countryside from the Prospect and the town is close to Goodrich Castle and the Welsh border.

- **RUGBY, WARWICKSHIRE** - Town famous for its public school which gave its name to Rugby Union football and which featured in "Tom Brown's Schooldays".

- **RUGELEY, STAFFORDSHIRE** - Town close to Cannock Chase which has over 2,000 acres of heath and woodlands with forest trails and picnic sites. Nearby is Shugborough Hall (National Trust) with a fine collection of 18th C furniture and interesting monuments in the grounds.

- **S SHREWSBURY, SHROPSHIRE** - Beautiful historic town on the River Severn retaining many fine old timber-framed houses. Its attractions include Rowley's Museum with Roman finds, remains of a castle, Clive House Museum, St Chad's 18th C round church, rowing on the river and the Shrewsbury Flower Show in August.

- **SKEGNESS, LINCOLNSHIRE** - Famous seaside resort with 6 miles of sandy beaches and bracing air. Attractions include swimming pools, bowling greens, gardens, Natureland Marine Zoo, golf-courses and a wide range of entertainment at the Embassy Centre. Nearby is Gibraltar Point Nature Reserve.

- **SOLIHULL, WEST MIDLANDS** - On the outskirts of Birmingham. Some Tudor houses and a 13th C church remain amongst the new public buildings and shopping centre. The 16th C Malvern Hall is now a school and the 15th C Chester House at Knowle is now a library.

- **SOUTH WITHAM, LINCOLNSHIRE** - Well placed for the A1 and easy access to the historic towns of Stamford and Grantham.

- **SOUTHWELL, NOTTINGHAMSHIRE** - Town dominated by the Norman minster which has some beautiful 13th C stone carvings in the Chapter House. Charles I spent his last night of freedom in one of the inns. The original Bramley apple tree can still be seen.

- **STAFFORD, STAFFORDSHIRE** - The town has a long history and some half-timbered buildings still remain, notably the 16th C High House. There are several museums in the town and Shugborough Hall and the famous angler Izaak Walton's cottage, now a museum, are nearby.

- **STAMFORD, LINCOLNSHIRE** - Exceptionally beautiful and historic town with many houses of architectural interest, several notable churches and other public buildings all in the local stone. Burghley House, built by William Cecil, is a magnificent Tudor mansion on the edge of the town.

● **STANTON-ON-THE-WOLDS, NOTTINGHAMSHIRE** - Quiet village with golf course, just off the main route between Nottingham and Melton Mowbray, giving easy access to nearby attractions.

● **STAUNTON, GLOUCESTERSHIRE** - Village in attractive countryside, midway between Gloucester, Ledbury and Tewkesbury.

● **STIPERSTONES, SHROPSHIRE** - Below the spectacular ridge of the same name, from which superb views over moorland, forest and hills may be enjoyed.

● **STOKE BRUERNE, NORTHAMPTONSHIRE** - Village on the Grand Union Canal at the southern end of the long Blisworth Tunnel. The Waterways Museum traces the history of the waterways and canals over the last 200 years and there are trips on the canal in the summer.

● **STOKE-ON-TRENT, STAFFORDSHIRE** - Famous for its pottery. Factories of several famous makers, including Josiah Wedgwood, can be visited. The City Museum has one of the finest pottery and porcelain collections in the world.

● **STONEHOUSE, GLOUCESTERSHIRE** - Village in the Stroud Valley with an Elizabethan Court, later restored and altered by Lutyens.

● **STOURBRIDGE, WEST MIDLANDS** - Town on the River Stour, famous for its glassworks. Several of the factories can be visited and glassware purchased at the factory shops.

● **STOW-ON-THE-WOLD, GLOUCESTERSHIRE** - Attractive Cotswold wool town with a large market-place and some fine houses, especially the old grammar school. There is an interesting church dating from Norman times. Stow-on-the-Wold is surrounded by lovely countryside and Cotswold villages.

● **STRATFORD-UPON-AVON, WARWICKSHIRE** - Famous as Shakespeare's home town, Stratford's many attractions include his birthplace, New Place where he died, the Royal Shakespeare Theatre and Gallery and Hall's Croft (his daughter's house).

● **STROUD, GLOUCESTERSHIRE** - This old town, surrounded by attractive hilly country, has been producing broadcloth for centuries and the local museum has an interesting display on the subject. Many of the mills have been converted into craft centres.

T **TEDDINGTON, GLOUCESTERSHIRE** - Village a few miles east of Tewkesbury and north of Cheltenham, with just a few farms and houses, but an interesting church.

● **TELFORD, SHROPSHIRE** - New Town named after Thomas Telford, the famous engineer who designed many of the country's canals, bridges and viaducts. It is close to Ironbridge with its monuments and museums to the Industrial Revolution, including restored 18th C buildings.

● **TETBURY, GLOUCESTERSHIRE** - Small market town with 18th C houses and an attractive 17th C Town Hall. It is a good touring centre with many places of interest nearby including Badminton House and Westonbirt Arboretum.

● **TEWKESBURY, GLOUCESTERSHIRE** - Tewkesbury's outstanding possession is its magnificent church, built as an abbey, with a great Norman tower and beautiful 14th C interior. The town stands at the confluence of the Severn and Avon and has many medieval houses, inns and several museums.

● **TOWCESTER, NORTHAMPTONSHIRE** - Town built on the site of a Roman settlement. It has some interesting old buildings, including an inn featured in one of Dickens' novels. The racecourse lies alongside the A5 Watling Street, and motor racing takes place at nearby Silverstone.

U **UPPINGHAM, RUTLAND** - Quiet market town dominated by its famous public school which was founded in 1584. It has many stone houses and is surrounded by attractive countryside.

● **UPTON-UPON-SEVERN, WORCESTERSHIRE** - Attractive country town on the banks of the Severn and a good river cruising centre. It has many pleasant old houses and inns, and the pepperpot landmark is now the Heritage Centre.

V **VOWCHURCH, HEREFORDSHIRE** - Close to the Welsh border, its church has 15 dedications which were all confirmed in one day in 1348.

W **WARWICK, WARWICKSHIRE** - Castle rising above the River Avon, 15th C Beauchamp Chapel attached to St Mary's Church, medieval Lord Leycester's Hospital almshouses and several museums. Nearby is Ashorne Hall Nickelodeon and the National Heritage museum at Gaydon.

● **WEEDON, NORTHAMPTONSHIRE** - Old village steeped in history, with thatched cottages and several antique shops.

● **WEM, SHROPSHIRE** - Small town connected with Judge Jeffreys who lived in Lowe Hall. Well known for its ales.

● **WENLOCK EDGE, SHROPSHIRE** - A hill running from Craven Arms north-east to Much Wenlock, with attractive views across the south Shropshire Hills.

● **WEOBLEY, HEREFORDSHIRE** - One of the most beautiful Herefordshire villages, full of framed houses, at the heart of the Black and White Trail. It is dominated by the church which has a fine spire.

● **WINCHCOMBE, GLOUCESTERSHIRE** - Ancient town with a folk museum and railway museum. To the south lies Sudeley Castle with its fine collection of paintings and toys and an Elizabethan garden.

● **WINSTER, DERBYSHIRE** - Village with some interesting old gritstone houses and cottages, including the 17th C stone market hall now owned by the National Trust. It is a former lead mining centre.

● **WISHAW, WARWICKSHIRE** - A village with interesting features in the small church, and is now well known as the location of the National Golf Centre within easy reach of jct. 9 of the M42, close to Sutton Coldfield.

● **WOODHALL SPA, LINCOLNSHIRE** - Attractive town which was formerly a spa. It has excellent sporting facilities with a championship golf-course and is surrounded by pine woods.

● **WORCESTER, WORCESTERSHIRE** - Lovely riverside city dominated by its Norman and Early English cathedral, King John's burial place. Many old buildings including the 15th C Commandery and the 18th C Guildhall. There are several museums and the Royal Worcester porcelain factory.

● **WORKSOP, NOTTINGHAMSHIRE** - Market town close to the Dukeries, where a number of Ducal families had their estates, some of which, like Clumber Park, may be visited. The upper room of the 14th C gatehouse of the priory housed the country's first elementary school in 1628.

● **WYRE PIDDLE, WORCESTERSHIRE** - A small village on the north bank of the River Avon in the Vale of Evesham, known for its Blossom Trail. ideal base for visiting the Cotswolds and the historic city of Worcester.

Where to Stay

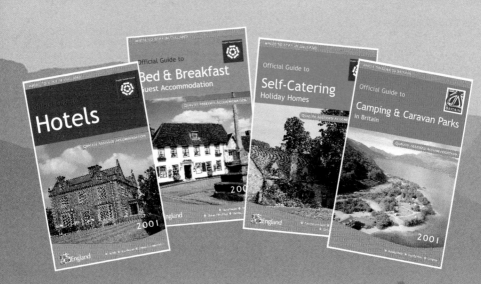

The official and best selling guides, offering the reassurance of quality assured accommodation

2001

Official Guide to **Hotels** | 2001 England

Official Guide to **Bed & Breakfast** Guest Accommodation | 200

Official Guide to **Self-Catering** Holiday Homes | England

Official Guide to **Camping & Caravan Parks** in Britain | 2001

Hotels, Townhouses
and Travel
Accommodation
in England 2001

£10.99

Guesthouses,
Bed & Breakfast,
Farmhouses and Inns
in England 2001

£10.99

Self Catering
Holiday Homes
in England 2001

£9.99

Camping
& Caravan Parks
in Britain 2001

£5.99

THE GUIDES INCLUDE

- Accommodation entries packed with information
- Full colour maps
- Places to visit
- Tourist Information Centres

Look out also for:

SOMEWHERE SPECIAL IN ENGLAND 2001

Accommodation achieving the highest standards in facilities and
quality of service - the perfect guide for the discerning traveller

INFORMATIVE   **EASY TO USE**   **GREAT VALUE FOR MONEY**

EAST OF ENGLAND

Open skies, rich Fenland, gorgeous villages and miles of sandy beaches - welcome to the East of England where life ticks slowly by.

Barge your way through the Norfolk Broads, punt along the River Cam, or walk over water on the pier at Southend.

Woburn Abbey, Sandringham and Kentwell Hall are just a few of the fabulous houses and gardens in the area. And if you fancy a day at the races, you can bet on Newmarket.

Graceful cathedrals pierce the skies at Ely, Norwich, Cambridge and Colchester. While beautiful Walsingham is dubbed 'England's Nazareth' and attracts an annual Pilgrimage in the remains of the Medieval Priory.

The counties of
Bedfordshire, Cambridgeshire,
Essex, Hertfordshire, Norfolk and Suffolk

FOR MORE INFORMATION CONTACT:
East of England Tourist Board
Toppesfield Hall, Hadleigh, Suffolk IP7 5DN
Tel: (01473) 822922
Fax: (01473) 823063
Email: eastofenglandtouristboard@compuserve.com
Internet: www.visitbritain.com/east-of-england/

Where to Go in the East of England - see pages 284-288
Where to Stay in the East of England - see pages 289-325

The Pictures:
1   Hunstanton, Norfolk;
2   King's College, Cambridge.

Whilst in the
EAST OF ENGLAND ...

You will find hundreds of interesting places to visit during your stay, just some of which are listed in these pages.

Contact any Tourist Information Centre in the region for more ideas on days out in the East of England.

Audley End House and Park
Audley End, Saffron Walden, Essex CB11 4JF
Tel: (01799) 522399
Palatial Jacobean house remodelled in the 18th-19thC. Magnificent Great Hall with 17thC plaster ceilings. Rooms and furniture by Robert Adam and park by 'Capability' Brown.

Banham Zoo
The Grove, Banham, Norwich, Norfolk NR16 2HE
Tel: (01953) 887771
Wildlife spectacular which will take you on a journey to experience at close quarters some of the world's most exotic, rare and endangered animals.

Barleylands Farm Museum and Visitor Centre
Billericay, Essex CM11 2UD
Tel: (01268) 532253
Visitor centre with a rural museum, animal centre, craft studios, blacksmith's shop, glass-blowing studio with viewing gallery, miniature steam railway. Restaurant.

Blickling Hall
Blickling, Norwich, Norfolk NR11 6NF
Tel: (01263) 738030
Jacobean redbrick mansion with garden, orangery, parkland and lake. Displays of fine tapestries and furniture. Picnic area, shop, restaurant and plant centre.

Bressingham Steam Museum and Gardens
Bressingham, Diss, Norfolk IP22 2AB
Tel: (01379) 687386
Steam rides through 8 km (5 miles) of woodland. Mainline locomotives, the Victorian Gallopers and over 50 steam engines. Plant centre.

Bure Valley Railway
Aylsham, Norwich, Norfolk NR11 6BW
Tel: (01263) 733858
A 15 inch narrow-gauge steam railway covering 14.4 km (9 miles) of track from Wroxham in the heart of the Norfolk Broads to Aylsham, a bustling market town.

Colchester Castle
Colchester, Essex CO1 1TJ
Tel: (01206) 282931
A Norman keep on the foundations of a Roman temple. The archaeological material includes much on Roman Colchester (Camulodunum).

Colchester Zoo
Stanway, Colchester, Essex CO3 5SL
Tel: (01206) 331292
Zoo with 200 species and some of the best cat collections in the UK, 40 acres of gardens and lakes, plus award-winning animal enclosures. Picnic areas, road train and four play areas.

Ely Cathedral
Ely, Cambridgeshire CB7 4DL
Tel: (01353) 667735
One of England's finest cathedrals. Monastic precinct, brass rubbing centre and stained glass museum. Guided tours.

284

Fritton Lake Country World

Fritton, Great Yarmouth, Norfolk NR31 9HA
Tel: (01493) 488208
A 250-acre centre with children's assault course, putting, an adventure playground, golf, fishing, boating, wildfowl, heavy horses, cart rides, falconry and flying displays.

The Gardens of the Rose

The Royal National Rose Society, Chiswell Green, St Albans, Hertfordshire AL2 3NR
Tel: (01727) 850461
The Royal National Rose Society's Garden with 27 acres of garden and trial grounds for new varieties of rose. Roses of all types displayed with 1,700 different varieties.

Hatfield House and Gardens

Hatfield, Hertfordshire AL9 5NQ
Tel: (01707) 262823
Magnificent Jacobean house, home of the Marquess of Salisbury. Exquisite gardens, model soldiers and park trails. Childhood home of Queen Elizabeth I.

Hedingham Castle

Castle Hedingham, Halstead, Essex CO9 3DJ
Tel: (01787) 460261
The finest Norman keep in England, built in 1140 by the deVeres, Earls of Oxford. Visited by Kings Henry VII and VIII and Queen Elizabeth I. Besieged by King John.

The Pictures:
1. Holkham Beach, Norfolk;
2. Globe Inn, Linslade, Bedfordshire;
3. Thorpeness, Suffolk;
4. Nene Valley Railway, Stibbington, Cambridgeshire;
5. Punting on the River Cam, Cambridge.

Holkham Hall

Wells-next-the-Sea, Norfolk NR23 1AB
Tel: (01328) 710227
A classic 18thC Palladian-style mansion. Part of a great agricultural estate and a living treasure-house of artistic and architectural history. Bygones collection.

Ickworth House, Park and Gardens

Horringer, Bury St Edmunds, Suffolk IP29 5QE
Tel: (01284) 735270
An extraordinary oval house with flanking wings, begun in 1795. Fine paintings, a beautiful collection of Georgian silver, an Italian garden and stunning parkland.

Imperial War Museum

Duxford, Cambridgeshire CB2 4QR
Tel: (01223) 835000
Over 150 aircraft on display with tanks, vehicles and guns. Simulator ride and an adventure playground. Shops and restaurant.

Kentwell Hall

Long Melford, Sudbury, Suffolk CO10 9BA
Tel: (01787) 310207
A mellow redbrick Tudor manor surrounded by a moat. This family home has been interestingly restored with Tudor costume displays, a 16thC house and mosaic Tudor rose maze.

Knebworth House, Gardens and Park

Knebworth, Stevenage, Hertfordshire SG3 6PY
Tel: (01438) 812661
Tudor manor house, re-fashioned in the 19thC, housing a collection of manuscripts. Portraits, Jacobean banquet hall. Formal gardens and adventure playground.

Leighton Buzzard Railway

Page's Park Station, Leighton Buzzard, Bedfordshire LU7 8TN
Tel: (01525) 373888
An authentic narrow-gauge light railway, built in 1919, offering a 65-minute return journey into the Bedfordshire countryside.

Marsh Farm Country Park

South Woodham, Ferrers, Chelmsford, Essex CM3 5WP
Tel: (01245) 321552
Farm centre with sheep, a pig unit, free-range chickens, milking demonstrations, indoor and outdoor adventure play areas, nature reserve, walks, picnic area and pets' corner.

Melford Hall

Long Melford, Sudbury, Suffolk CO10 9AA
Tel: (01787) 880286
Turreted brick Tudor mansion with 18thC and Regency interiors. Collection of Chinese porcelain, gardens and a walk in the grounds.

Minsmere Nature Reserve

Westleton, Saxmundham, Suffolk IP17 3BY
Tel: (01728) 648281
Purpose-built visitor centre situated on the Suffolk coast. Information areas, nature trails, bird-watching and wildlife. Shop and tearoom.

National Horseracing Museum and Tours

Newmarket, Suffolk CB8 8JL
Tel: (01638) 667333
A museum displaying the development of horse-racing. A display of sporting art includes loans from the Tate gallery. Also a hands-on gallery.

National Stud

Newmarket, Suffolk CB8 0XE
Tel: (01638) 663464
A visit to the National Stud consists of a conducted tour which includes top thoroughbred stallions, mares and foals.

Norfolk Lavender

Caley Mill, Heacham, King's Lynn, Norfolk PE31 7JE
Tel: (01485) 570384
Lavender is distilled from the flowers and the oil made into a wide range of gifts. There is a slide show when the distillery is not working.

Norwich Cathedral

The Close, Norwich, Norfolk NR1 4EH
Tel: (01603) 764385
A Norman cathedral from 1096 with 14thC roof bosses depicting bible scenes from Adam and Eve to the Day of Judgement. Cloisters, cathedral close, shop and restaurant.

Oliver Cromwell's House

St Marys Street, Ely, Cambridgeshire CB7 4HF
Tel: (01353) 662062
The family home of Oliver Cromwell with a 17thC kitchen, parlour and haunted bedroom. Tourist Information Centre, souvenirs and a craft shop.

Peter Beales Roses

Attleborough, Norfolk NR17 1AY
Tel: (01953) 454707
A large display garden featuring a world famous collection of classic roses. Mainly old-fashioned roses plus rare and those of historic value.

Pleasure Beach

Great Yarmouth, Norfolk NR30 3EH
Tel: (01493) 844585
Rollercoaster, Terminator, log flume, Twister, monorail, breakdance, galloping horses, caterpillar, go-karts, ghost train, fun house and sheer terror show.

Pleasurewood Hills Family Leisure Park

Corton, Lowestoft, Suffolk NR32 5DZ
Tel: (01502) 586000
Log flume, chairlift, Horror Dome, two railways, pirate ship, fort, Aladdin's cave, parrot, sealion shows, rollercoaster, waveswinger.

The Pictures:
1 St Alban's Cathedral;
2 South of Ipswich, Suffolk;
3 The Norfolk Broads;
4 'A day at the races', Newmarket;
5 Thurne, Norfolk Broads;
6 Cromer, Norfolk;
7 Imperial War Museum, Duxford.

Sainsbury Centre for Visual Arts

University of East Anglia, Norwich, Norfolk NR4 7TJ
Tel: (01603) 456060
Housing the Sainsbury collection of works by Picasso, Bacon and Henry Moore alongside many objects of pottery and art. Cafe and art bookshop with monthly activities.

Sandringham

Sandringham, King's Lynn, Norfolk PE35 6EN
Tel: (01553) 772675
The country retreat of HM The Queen. A delightful house and 60 acres of grounds and lakes, plus museum of royal vehicles and royal memorabilia.

Shuttleworth Collection

Old Warden Aerodrome, Biggleswade,
Bedfordshire SG18 9EP
Tel: (01767) 627288
A unique historical collection of aircraft from a 1909 Bleriot to a 1942 Spitfire in flying condition. Cars dating from an 1898 Panhard in running order.

Somerleyton Hall and Gardens

Somerleyton, Lowestoft, Suffolk NR32 5QQ
Tel: (01502) 730224
Anglo Italian-style mansion with state rooms, a maze, 12-acre garden with azaleas and rhododendrons. Miniature railway, shop and tearooms.

Stondon Museum

Lower Stondon, Henlow Camp, Bedfordshire SG16 6JN
Tel: (01462) 850339
The largest private collection in England of bygone vehicles from the beginning of the century. Transport exhibits from the early 1900s to the 1980s.

Thursford Collection

Thursford Green, Fakenham, Norfolk NR21 0AS
Tel: (01328) 878477
Musical evenings some Tuesdays from mid-July to the end of September. A live musical show with nine mechanical organs and a Wurlitzer show starring Robert Wolfe daily April to October.

Whipsnade Wild Animal Park

Dunstable, Bedfordshire LU6 2LF
Tel: (01582) 872171
Over 2,500 animals set in 600 acres of beautiful parkland. Free animal demonstrations, plus the Great Whipsnade Railway.

Wimpole Hall and Home Farm

Arrington, Royston, Hertfordshire SG8 0BW
Tel: (01223) 207257
An 18thC house in a landscaped park with a folly and Chinese bridge. Plunge bath and yellow drawing room in the house, the work of John Soane. Rare breeds centre at Home Farm.

Woburn Abbey

Woburn, Milton Keynes, Bedfordshire MK43 0TP
Tel: (01525) 290666
An 18thC Palladian mansion, altered by Henry Holland, the Prince Regent's architect. Contains a collection of English silver, French and English furniture and art.

Woburn Safari Park

Woburn, Milton Keynes, Bedfordshire MK17 9QN
Tel: (01525) 290407
Drive through the safari park with 30 species of animals in natural groups just a windscreen's width away. Action-packed Wild World Leisure Area with shows for all.

Find out more about the
EAST OF ENGLAND ...

Further information about holidays and attractions
in the East of England is available from:

EAST OF ENGLAND TOURIST BOARD
Toppesfield Hall, Hadleigh, Suffolk IP7 5DN.
Tel: (01473) 822922
Fax: (01473) 823063
Email: eastofenglandtouristboard@compuserve.com
Internet: www.visitbritain.com/east-of-england/

The following publications are available free from the East of England Tourist Board:

Bed & Breakfast Touring Map 2001
England's Cycling Country
Travel Trade Directory
Places to Stay

Also available (price includes postage and packaging):

East of England – The Official Guide 2001 – £4.99

The Pictures:
1 South Raynham,
   Norfolk;
2 Ely Cathedral,
   Cambridge;
3 Cromer, Norfolk;
4 Cley next the Sea,
   Norfolk.

Getting to the
EAST OF ENGLAND ...

BY ROAD: The region is easily accessible. From London and the south via the A1, M11,
M25, A10, M1, A46 and A12. From the north via the A17, A1, A15, A5, M1 and A6.
From the west via the A14, A47, A421, A428, A418, A41 and A427.

BY RAIL: Regular fast trains run to all major cities and towns in the region. London
stations which serve the region are Liverpool Street, Kings Cross, Fenchurch Street,
Moorgate, St Pancras, London Marylebone and London Euston. Bedford, Luton and
St Albans are on the Thameslink line which runs to Kings Cross and onto London
Gatwick Airport. There is also a direct link between London Stansted Airport and
Liverpool Street. Through the Channel Tunnel, there are trains direct from Paris and
Brussels to Waterloo Station, London. A short journey on the Underground will bring
passengers to those stations operating services into the East of England. Further
information on rail journeys in the East of England can be obtained on (0845) 748 4950.

Where to stay in the
EAST OF ENGLAND

Accommodation entries in this region are listed in alphabetical order of place name, and then in alphabetical order of establishment.

Map references refer to the colour location maps at the front of this guide. The first number indicates the map to use; the letter and number which follow refer to the grid reference on the map.

At-a-glance symbols at the end of each accommodation entry give useful information about services and facilities. A key to symbols can be found inside the back cover flap. Keep this open for easy reference.

A brief description of the towns and villages offering accommodation in the entries which follow, can be found at the end of this section.

A complete listing of all English Tourism Council assessed guest accommodation appears at the back of this guide.

ALDBOROUGH, Norfolk Map ref 3B1

◆◆◆ **BUTTERFLY COTTAGE**

The Green, Aldborough, Norwich, NR11 7AA
T: (01263) 768198
F: (01263) 768198

Bedrooms: 1 single, 1 double, 1 family room
Bathrooms: 2 en suite, 1 private

Parking for 3

B&B per night:
S £20.00–£20.00
D £40.00–£40.00

OPEN All year round

On the Weavers Way. Comfortable cottage-style, well-equipped, friendly atmosphere. Rooms overlook large garden or village green. Each has own entrance. Car parking.

ALDEBY, Norfolk Map ref 3C1

◆◆◆ **THE OLD VICARAGE**

Rectory Road, Aldeby, Beccles, Suffolk NR34 0BJ
T: (01502) 678229

Bedrooms: 2 twin, 1 triple
Bathrooms: 1 en suite, 2 private

Parking for 3

B&B per night:
S £17.00–£17.00
D £34.00–£34.00

OPEN All year round

Spacious old vicarage, quiet rural location. Convenient for Norfolk Broads, boating, wildlife and bird-watching. Non-smoking, no dogs. Ample parking for cars, bicycles and canoes.

ALDHAM, Essex Map ref 3B2

◆◆◆ **OLD HOUSE**

Ford Street, Aldham, Colchester, CO6 3PH
T: (01206) 240456
F: (01206) 240456

Bedrooms: 1 single, 1 twin, 1 triple
Bathrooms: 1 en suite, 2 private

Parking for 8
CC: Barclaycard, Delta, Eurocard, Mastercard, Visa

B&B per night:
S £25.00–£32.50
D £40.00–£50.00

OPEN All year round

Historic 14thC "old hall" house. Family home with friendly atmosphere, oak beams, log fires, large garden, ample parking. On A1124 5 miles west of Colchester.

BECCLES, Suffolk Map ref 3C1

◆◆◆◆

CATHERINE HOUSE
2 Ringsfield Road, Beccles,
NR34 9PQ
T: (01502) 716428
F: (01502) 716428

Bedrooms: 3 double
Bathrooms: 2 en suite,
1 public

Parking for 4

B&B per night:
S £20.00–£30.00
D £37.50–£40.00

OPEN All year round

Family home, tastefully decorated to high standard, in quiet position overlooking Waveney Valley. Five minutes' walk to town centre.

◆◆

COLVILLE ARMS MOTEL
Lowestoft Road, Worlingham,
Beccles, NR34 7EF
T: (01502) 712571
F: (01502) 712571
E: pat@thecolvillearms.freeserve.
co.uk

Bedrooms: 2 single,
4 double, 4 twin, 1 triple
Bathrooms: 11 en suite

Lunch available
EM 1900 (LO 2100)
Parking for 40
CC: Amex, Barclaycard,
Delta, Diners, Eurocard,
JCB, Maestro, Mastercard,
Solo, Switch, Visa, Visa
Electron

B&B per night:
S £30.00–£35.00
D £45.00–£55.00

HB per person:
DY £40.00–£45.00

OPEN All year round

Village setting half an hour Lowestoft, Norwich and Yarmouth, 5 minutes to Broads. Excellent fishing, golf, country walks. All rooms en suite, TV tea-making. Ample parking.

BEETLEY, Norfolk Map ref 3B1

◆◆◆◆
Gold
Award

PEACOCK HOUSE

Peacock Lane, Beetley, East Dereham,
NR20 4DG
T: (01362) 860371 &
0797 9013258 (mobile)
E: peackh@aol.com
I: www.smoothhound.co.uk/hotels/
peacockh.html/

Bedrooms: 2 double,
1 twin
Bathrooms: 3 en suite

Parking for 4

B&B per night:
S £20.00–£25.00
D £42.00–£45.00

OPEN All year round

Beautiful old farmhouse, peacefully situated in lovely garden and grounds. Offering excellent accommodation with all facilities, guests' lounge, open fires, beamed dining room, home cooking and a warm welcome. Centrally situated with Norwich, Sandringham, NT houses and the coast all within easy reach, and golf, fishing and swimming all close by.

◆◆◆

SHILLING STONE

Church Road, Beetley, Dereham, NR20 4AB
T: (01362) 861099 (Answerphone) &
07721 306190 (Mobile)
F: (01362) 869153
E: partridge@uk.gateway.net
I: www.visitbritain.com

Bedrooms: 1 double,
2 twin
Bathrooms: 3 en suite

Parking for 8

B&B per night:
S £20.00–£22.00
D £40.00–£42.00

OPEN All year round

A large country house on the edge of Beetley. Excellent accommodation with large double and twin rooms all en suite with colour TV. Full English breakfast. Guests' own lounge. Ideal base for touring Norfolk coast, Broads, Norwich, Sandringham and Gressenhall Rural Life Museum. A warm welcome awaits you. Children and pets welcome.

REGIONAL TOURIST BOARD The ♠ symbol in an establishment entry indicates that it is a Regional Tourist Board member.

BISHOP'S STORTFORD, Hertfordshire Map ref 2D1 *Tourist Information Centre Tel: (01279) 655831*

◆◆◆◆
Gold
Award

THE COTTAGE
71 Birchanger Lane, Birchanger,
Bishop's Stortford, CM23 5QA
T: (01279) 812349
F: (01279) 815045

B&B per night:
S £35.00–£50.00
D £55.00–£63.00

OPEN All year round

The Cottage is a 17thC Listed house with panelled rooms and wood-burning stove. Conservatory-style breakfast room overlooks large mature garden. Quiet and peaceful village setting yet near M11 junction 8, Stansted Airport and Bishop's Stortford. Guest rooms are furnished in a traditional cottage style, all with colour TV and tea/coffee facilities.

Bedrooms: 3 single,
7 double, 5 twin
Bathrooms: 11 en suite,
2 private, 1 public

Parking for 17
CC: Barclaycard, Delta,
Eurocard, JCB,
Mastercard, Solo, Switch,
Visa

BRADFIELD, Essex Map ref 3B2

◆◆◆
EMSWORTH HOUSE
Ship Hill, Bradfield, Manningtree,
CO11 2UP
T: (01255) 870860 & 07767 477771
F: (01255) 870869
E: emsworthhouse@hotmail.com

Formerly the vicarage. Spacious rooms with stunning views of the countryside and River Stour. Near Colchester and Harwich. On holiday, business or en route to the continent, it's perfect!

Bedrooms: 2 double,
1 twin
Bathrooms: 1 en suite,
2 public

Lunch available
EM 1830 (LO 2200)
Parking for 12

B&B per night:
S £28.00–£35.00
D £38.00–£48.00

HB per person:
DY £29.00–£45.00

OPEN All year round

BRAINTREE, Essex Map ref 3B2 *Tourist Information Centre Tel: (01376) 550066*

◆◆◆
BROOK FARM
Wethersfield, Braintree, CM7 4BX
T: (01371) 850284 (Answerphone)
& 07770 881966 (Mobile)
F: (01371) 850284

Beautiful Listed farmhouse, parts dating back to 13thC. On edge of picturesque village. Spacious, comfortable rooms, guest lounge. 30 minutes from Stansted. Camping available.

Bedrooms: 1 double,
1 twin, 1 family room
Bathrooms: 3 public

Parking for 10

B&B per night:
S £20.00–£25.00
D £37.00–£42.00

OPEN All year round

◆◆◆◆
SPICERS FARM
Rotten End, Wethersfield, Braintree,
CM7 4AL
T: (01371) 851021
F: (01371) 851021
E: spicers.farm@talk21.com

Attractive farmhouse set in delightful, peaceful position overlooking beautiful countryside. Comfortable and welcoming. All rooms en suite. Convenient for Harwich, Stansted and Cambridge.

Bedrooms: 1 double,
2 twin
Bathrooms: 3 en suite

Parking for 6

B&B per night:
S £26.00–£30.00
D £37.00–£39.00

OPEN All year round

BRANDON, Suffolk Map ref 3B2

◆◆
THE LAURELS
162 London Road, Brandon,
IP27 0LP
T: (01842) 812005

Built 1932, attractive bungalow and gardens on main road. Walking distance to town centre, forest and river. Excellent food and hospitality.

Bedrooms: 1 double,
1 twin
Bathrooms: 1 public

B&B per night:
S £16.50–£18.50
D £33.00–£37.00

OPEN All year round

CREDIT CARD BOOKINGS If you book by telephone and are asked for your credit card number it is advisable to check the proprietor's policy should you cancel your reservation.

BRENTWOOD, Essex Map ref 2D2 *Tourist Information Centre Tel: (01277) 200300*

◆◆◆ **BRENTWOOD GUESTHOUSE**
75/77 Rose Valley, Brentwood, CM14 4HJ
T: (01277) 262713 &
07710 523757 (Mobile)
F: (01277) 211146

Bedrooms: 2 single, 4 double, 2 twin, 2 triple
Bathrooms: 8 en suite, 2 public

Parking for 10
CC: Barclaycard, Delta, Maestro, Mastercard, Switch, Visa, Visa Electron

B&B per night:
S £35.00–£60.00
D £55.00–£65.00

OPEN All year round

Victorian house with spacious dining room, newly refurbished. Close to Brentwood centre, local station and parks (25 minutes by rail to London), M25, 1 mile.

BULPHAN, Essex Map ref 3B3

◆◆◆ **BONNY DOWNS FARM**
Doesgate Lane, Bulphan, Upminster, Essex RM14 3TB
T: (01268) 542129

Bedrooms: 2 twin, 1 triple
Bathrooms: 1 private, 2 public

Parking for 4

B&B per night:
S Min £23.00
D £40.00–£40.00

OPEN All year round

60-acre mixed farm. Large comfortable farmhouse offering home-cooked food. Conveniently placed for road links: M25, A13 and A127 to London and south-east England.

BUNGAY, Suffolk Map ref 3C1

◆◆◆◆ **SOUTH ELMHAM HALL**
St Cross, South Elmham, Harleston, Norfolk IP20 0PZ
T: (01986) 782526
F: (01986) 782203
E: jo@southelmham.co.uk
I: www.southelmham.co.uk

Bedrooms: 2 double, 1 twin
Bathrooms: 3 en suite

Parking for 4
CC: Barclaycard, Delta, Eurocard, JCB, Mastercard, Solo, Switch, Visa, Visa Electron

B&B per night:
S £30.00–£60.00
D £45.00–£80.00

OPEN Mar–Dec

Grade II Listed farmhouse within large moated grounds. Comfortable beds, modern en suite bathrooms, wonderful views, walks, wildlife and excellent breakfasts.

BUNTINGFORD, Hertfordshire Map ref 2D1

◆◆◆ **SOUTHFIELDS FARM**
Throcking, Buntingford, SG9 9RD
T: (01763) 281224 & 0777 551258
F: (01763) 281224
E: iamurchie@hotmail.com

Bedrooms: 1 single, 1 double, 1 twin
Bathrooms: 1 public

Parking for 5

B&B per night:
S Max £25.00
D Max £50.00

OPEN All year round

Warm, comfortable farmhouse 1.5 miles off A10 midway between London and Cambridge. TV, tea and coffee facilities. Closed at Christmas. No smoking in bedrooms.

ACCESSIBILITY
Look for the symbols which indicate accessibility for wheelchair users. A list of establishments is at the front of this guide.

BURY ST EDMUNDS, Suffolk Map ref 3B2 *Tourist Information Centre Tel: (01284) 764667*

♦♦♦♦

BRIGHTHOUSE FARM
Melford Road, Lawshall, Bury St Edmunds, IP29 4PX
T: (01284) 830385 &
07711 829546 (Mobile)
F: (01284) 830974
E: brighthousefarm@supanet.com

B&B per night:
S £22.00–£35.00
D £40.00–£50.00

OPEN All year round

A warm welcome awaits you at this 200-year-old Georgian farmhouse. Tastefully presented en suite rooms, outstanding breakfasts served in spacious conservatory. 3 acres of glorious gardens and farm trail to explore. Close to a wealth of interesting places to visit, good pubs and restaurants nearby. Send SAE for brochure.

Bedrooms: 2 single, 2 double, 1 twin
Bathrooms: 5 en suite, 1 public

Parking for 10

♦♦♦♦

SOUTH HILL HOUSE
43 Southgate Street,
Bury St Edmunds, IP33 2AZ
T: (01284) 755650
F: (01284) 752718
E: southill@cwcom.net
I: www.lineone.net/nsouthill/

Bedrooms: 1 double, 1 twin, 1 family room
Bathrooms: 3 en suite

Parking for 4
CC: Amex, Barclaycard, Delta, JCB, Mastercard, Switch, Visa

B&B per night:
S £32.00–£38.00
D £45.00–£54.00

OPEN All year round

Grade II* Listed townhouse, reputed to be the school mentioned in Charles Dickens' "Pickwick Papers". 10 minutes' walk town centre, 2 minutes' drive A14. Less 10% for 2+ nights.

CAMBRIDGE, Cambridgeshire Map ref 2D1 *Tourist Information Centre Tel: (01223) 322640*

♦♦♦

ALPHA MILTON GUESTHOUSE
61-63 Milton Road, Cambridge, CB4 1XA
T: (01223) 311625 & 565100
F: (01223) 565100

B&B per night:
S £25.00–£40.00
D £40.00–£60.00

OPEN All year round

Warm, welcoming family-run guesthouse. Most rooms are en suite with colour TV, coffee and tea. Very close to the town centre and within walking distance of colleges and the River Camb (for river cruises or punting). Parking available. Easy access to business and science park, M11, A14 and A10.

Bedrooms: 1 single, 1 double, 2 twin, 2 triple
Bathrooms: 4 en suite, 2 public

EM 1900 (LO 2100)
Parking for 8
CC: Mastercard, Visa

♦♦♦

ASHLEY HOTEL
74 Chesterton Road, Cambridge,
CB4 1ER
T: (01223) 350059
F: (01223) 350900

Bedrooms: 2 single, 3 double, 3 twin, 2 triple
Bathrooms: 8 en suite, 2 public

Parking for 10
CC: Barclaycard, Eurocard, Mastercard, Visa

B&B per night:
S £29.50–£49.50
D £49.50–£69.50

OPEN All year round

Well-appointed recently refurbished small hotel with modern facilities close to city centre. Nearby Arundel House Hotel's facilities available to Ashley residents (under same ownership).

QUALITY ASSURANCE SCHEME
Diamond ratings and awards were correct at the time of going to press but are subject to change. Please check at the time of booking.

ASHTREES GUESTHOUSE
◆◆◆

128 Perne Road, Cambridge, CB1 3RR
T: (01223) 411233
F: (01223) 411233
I: www.smoothhound.co.uk/hotels/ashtrees.html

Bedrooms: 2 single, 3 double, 1 twin, 1 triple
Bathrooms: 3 en suite, 1 public

EM 1830 (LO 1830)
Parking for 6
CC: JCB, Mastercard, Visa

B&B per night:
S £20.00–£38.00
D £38.00–£44.00

HB per person:
DY £29.00–£48.00

OPEN Feb–Dec

Comfort and an enjoyable stay are the priorities. Individually decorated rooms to a high standard. Home cooking. Garden and car park.

◆◆◆
Ad p292

ASSISI GUESTHOUSE
193 Cherry Hinton Road, Cambridge, CB1 7BX
T: (01223) 246648 & 211466
F: (01223) 412900

B&B per night:
S £34.00–£34.00
D £47.00–£47.00

OPEN All year round

Warm, welcoming, family-run guesthouse, ideally situated for the city, colleges and Addenbrookes Hospital. All modern facilities. Large car park.

Bedrooms: 4 single, 5 double, 7 twin, 1 triple
Bathrooms: 16 en suite, 1 private

Parking for 15
CC: Amex, Barclaycard, Eurocard, Mastercard, Visa

◆◆◆◆

AYLESBRAY LODGE GUESTHOUSE
5 Mowbray Road, Cambridge, CB1 7SR
T: (01223) 240089
F: (01223) 528678
I: www.cambridge-bedandbreakfast.co.uk/aylesbray.htm

B&B per night:
S £35.00–£40.00
D £45.00–£65.00

OPEN All year round

All rooms are en suite, tastefully decorated and have complimentary extras. Four-poster rooms, satellite TV, telephones, radio alarm, hairdryer. Car parking. Close to Addenbrookes Hospital and within easy reach of the city centre.

Bedrooms: 1 single, 1 double, 1 twin, 1 triple, 1 family room
Bathrooms: 5 en suite

Parking for 7
CC: Amex, Barclaycard, Delta, Eurocard, Maestro, Mastercard, Solo, Switch, Visa, Visa Electron

---

CAM GUESTHOUSE
◆◆◆

17 Elizabeth Way, Cambridge, CB4 1DD
T: (01223) 354512
F: (01223) 353164
E: camguesthouse@btinternet.com

Bedrooms: 3 single, 3 double, 2 triple, 1 family room
Bathrooms: 1 en suite, 3 public

Parking for 6

B&B per night:
S £32.00–£35.00
D £47.00–£58.00

OPEN All year round

Guesthouse close to the River Cam, within 15 minutes' walking distance of the city centre and 5 minutes from Grafton shopping centre. En suite jacuzzi bath. Parking.

CAMBRIDGE LODGE HOTEL
◆◆◆◆

139 Huntingdon Road, Cambridge, CB3 0DQ
T: (01223) 352833
F: (01223) 355166

Bedrooms: 1 single, 11 double, 3 twin
Bathrooms: 12 en suite, 1 public, 3 private showers

Lunch available
EM 1900 (LO 2115)
Parking for 23
CC: Amex, Barclaycard, Diners, Mastercard, Switch, Visa

B&B per night:
S £55.00–£67.00
D £65.00–£80.00

OPEN All year round

Tudor-style hotel with restaurant open to non-residents. Tastefully furnished. Oak-beamed dining room serving an array of freshly prepared foods.

QUALITY ASSURANCE SCHEME
Diamond ratings and awards are explained at the back of this guide.

◆◆◆

CAROLINA BED & BREAKFAST

148 Perne Road, Cambridge, CB1 3NX
T: (01223) 247015 &
07770 370914 (Mobile)
F: (01223) 247015
E: carolina.amabile@tesco.net
I: www.smoothhound.co.uk/hotels/carol.html

Comfortable home offering a warm and friendly service. Easy access from and to M11 and A14. Close to city centre, railway station, bus station, Addenbrookes Hospital and colleges. Excellent breakfast, parking, discount for long-term booking. Credit cards accepted, children welcome, non-smokers. We can cater for all your needs.

Bedrooms: 1 double, 1 twin
Bathrooms: 2 en suite

Parking for 3
CC: Barclaycard, Delta, Eurocard, JCB, Mastercard, Solo, Switch, Visa, Visa Electron

B&B per night:
S £22.00–£40.00
D £35.00–£60.00

OPEN All year round

◆◆◆

CRISTINAS

47 St Andrews Road, Cambridge, CB4 1DH
T: (01223) 365855 & 327700
F: (01223) 365855

Bedrooms: 5 double, 3 twin, 1 triple
Bathrooms: 7 en suite, 1 public

Parking for 8

B&B per night:
S £38.00–£49.00
D £49.00–£55.00

OPEN All year round

Small family-run business in quiet location, a short walk from city centre and colleges. Car park locked at night. A no-smoking house.

◆◆◆

DRESDEN VILLA GUESTHOUSE

34 Cherry Hinton Road, Cambridge, CB1 7AA
T: (01223) 247539
F: (01223) 410640

Bedrooms: 6 single, 3 double, 2 twin, 2 triple
Bathrooms: 13 en suite, 1 public

EM 1900 (LO 2000)
Parking for 8

B&B per night:
S £32.00–£36.00
D £46.00–£50.00

HB per person:
DY £44.00–£48.00

OPEN All year round

Family-run guesthouse offering friendly service. All rooms en suite, tea/coffee. Situated approximately 1 mile from city centre and Addenbrookes Hospital.

◆◆◆

DYKELANDS GUESTHOUSE

157 Mowbray Road, Cambridge, CB1 7SP
T: (01223) 244300
F: (01223) 566746
E: dykelands@fsbdial.co.uk
I: www.drakken.com/clientsites/dykelands

Bedrooms: 1 single, 2 double, 2 twin, 2 triple, 1 family room
Bathrooms: 6 en suite, 1 public

Parking for 7
CC: Barclaycard, Delta, Eurocard, JCB, Mastercard, Solo, Switch, Visa, Visa Electron

B&B per night:
S £27.00–£30.00
D £38.00–£45.00

OPEN All year round

Detached guesthouse offering modern accommodation, most rooms en suite. Ideally located for city centre and for touring. Two bedrooms on ground floor. Non-smoking establishment.

USE YOUR *i*s

There are more than 550 Tourist Information Centres throughout England offering friendly help with accommodation and holiday ideas as well as suggestions of places to visit and things to do. You'll find TIC addresses in the local Phone Book.

CAMBRIDGE continued

◆◆◆

FAIRWAYS GUESTHOUSE

141-143 Cherry Hinton Road, Cambridge, CB1 7BX
T: (01223) 246063
F: (01223) 212093
E: mike.slatter@btinternet.com

B&B per night:
S £23.00–£32.00
D £38.00–£50.00

OPEN All year round

Family-run Victorian guesthouse. En suite and standard rooms all with colour TV, tea and coffee facilities, telephone and central heating. English breakfast. TV Lounge. Large car park. City centre 1 mile. Railway station and Addenbrookes Hospital half a mile. Golf course 1.5 miles. Park and Ride bus service close by.

Bedrooms: 4 single, 4 double, 4 twin, 1 triple, 2 family rooms
Bathrooms: 8 en suite, 2 public

Parking for 20
CC: Barclaycard, Delta, JCB, Mastercard, Solo, Switch, Visa

◆◆◆◆

FINCHES
144 Thornton Road, Girton, Cambridge, CB3 0ND
T: (01223) 276653 &
07710 179214 (Mobile)
E: liz.green.b-b@talk21.com

Bedrooms: 1 double, 2 twin
Bathrooms: 3 en suite

Parking for 5

B&B per night:
D £40.00–£52.00

OPEN All year round

A 3 bedroom bed and breakfast establishment situated on the corner of Huntingdon Road, Cambridge. All en suite.

◆◆◆

FOXHOUNDS
71 Cambridge Road, Wimpole and Orwell, Royston, SG8 5QD
T: (01223) 207344
E: sjpalfinchf@freeserve.co.uk

Bedrooms: 1 single, 2 twin
Bathrooms: 2 public

EM 1930 (LO 1930)
Parking for 3

B&B per night:
S £19.00–£19.00
D £38.00–£38.00

HB per person:
DY £27.00–£27.00

OPEN All year round

Former pub, part 17thC, now a family home. On A603, 9 miles from Cambridge and within easy reach of Wimpole Hall (National Trust). Sitting room for guests, large garden.

◆◆◆

HAMILTON HOTEL

156 Chesterton Road, Cambridge, CB4 1DA
T: (01223) 365664
F: (01223) 314866

B&B per night:
S £25.00–£45.00
D £45.00–£69.00

HB per person:
DY £33.50–£53.50

OPEN All year round

Recently refurbished hotel less than 1 mile from centre of city. Easy access from A14 and M11. Most rooms have en suite shower and toilet. All rooms have colour TV, direct-dial telephone and hospitality tray.

Bedrooms: 5 single, 9 double, 7 twin, 4 triple
Bathrooms: 19 en suite, 2 public

EM 1830 (LO 2000)
Parking for 18
CC: Amex, Barclaycard, Delta, Eurocard, JCB, Mastercard, Switch, Visa

---

◆◆◆◆

56 HIGH STREET
Great Wilbraham, Cambridge, CB1 5JD
T: (01223) 880751 (answerphone) &
07711 845300 (mobile)
F: (01223) 880751
E: bcanning@dial.pipex.com
I: www.geocities.com/greatwilbraham

Bedrooms: 1 single, 2 double
Bathrooms: 1 public

Parking for 4

B&B per night:
S Min £22.00
D Min £44.00

OPEN Jan, Mar-Dec

Pleasantly situated detached house in small village with shop and pub. Five miles to Cambridge and Newmarket. Excellent for racing, cycling and touring.

CAMBRIDGE continued

◆◆◆◆ **HILLS GUESTHOUSE**
157 Hills Road, Cambridge, CB2 2RJ
T: (01223) 214216
F: (01223) 214216

Bedrooms: 1 double,
1 twin
Bathrooms: 2 en suite

Parking for 6
CC: Amex, Barclaycard,
Mastercard, Visa

B&B per night:
S £33.00–£33.00
D £46.00–£46.00

OPEN All year round

We are a friendly family-run guesthouse. Bedrooms are cosy and spacious. Situated in between Addenbrookes Hospital, railway station and city centre.

◆◆◆◆ **HOME FROM HOME**
39 Milton Road, Cambridge,
CB4 1XA
T: (01223) 323555 & 07889 990698
F: (01223) 323555
E: homefromhome@test.net
I: www.smoothound.co.uk/hotels/
homefromhome.html

Bedrooms: 1 double,
1 twin
Bathrooms: 2 private

Parking for 3
CC: Barclaycard, Delta,
JCB, Mastercard, Solo,
Switch, Visa, Visa Electron

B&B per night:
S £35.00–£45.00
D £48.00–£60.00

OPEN All year round

Comfortable, spacious family home, centrally located. All rooms with own facilities. Home-from-home hospitality and excellent breakfasts.

◆◆◆◆ **KING'S TITHE**
13a Comberton Road, Barton,
Cambridge, CB3 7BA
T: (01223) 263610
F: (01223) 263610
E: kingstithebarton@lineone.net

Bedrooms: 2 twin
Bathrooms: 1 public

Parking for 3

B&B per night:
S £34.00–£37.00
D £42.00–£55.00

OPEN All year round

Guests return to this up-market quiet home. Both rooms with countryside views. Excellent breakfasts. Good village pubs. Near M11 junction 12 (west A603 to B1046).

◆◆◆ **SEGOVIA LODGE**
2 Barton Road, Newnham,
Cambridge, CB3 9JZ
T: (01223) 354105
F: (01223) 323011

Bedrooms: 1 double,
1 twin
Bathrooms: 2 en suite,
1 public

Parking for 4

B&B per night:
D £50.00–£55.00

OPEN All year round

Within walking distance city centre and colleges. Next to cricket and tennis fields. Warm welcome, personal service, both rooms with private facilities. Non-smokers only, please.

◆◆◆◆

SORRENTO HOTEL
190-196 Cherry Hinton Road, Cambridge,
CB1 7AN
T: (01223) 243533
F: (01223) 213463
E: sorrento-hotel@cb17an.freeserve.co.uk
I: www.sorrentohotel.com

B&B per night:
S £59.50–£95.00
D £89.00–£129.50

HB per person:
DY £79.50–£79.50

OPEN All year round

Family-managed hotel in a quiet residential area, close to town centre, railway station, Addenbrookes Hospital. High standard of room facilities and service. Bridal suite with jacuzzi, sauna and 4-poster bed. Superb Italian restaurant in romantic setting. Special diets and children's meals available. Weddings, functions, conferences. Free private car park.

Bedrooms: 8 single,
12 double, 3 triple
Bathrooms: 23 en suite,
1 public

Lunch available
EM 1830 (LO 2130)
Parking for 25
CC: Amex, Barclaycard,
Delta, Diners, Eurocard,
Maestro, Mastercard,
Solo, Switch, Visa, Visa
Electron

◆◆◆ **SOUTHAMPTON GUEST HOUSE**
7 Elizabeth Way, Cambridge,
CB4 1DE
T: (01223) 357780
F: (01223) 314297

Bedrooms: 1 single,
1 double, 2 triple,
1 family room
Bathrooms: 5 en suite

Parking for 8

B&B per night:
S £30.00–£45.00
D £40.00–£52.00

OPEN All year round

Victorian property with friendly atmosphere, only 15 minutes' walk along riverside to city centre, colleges and new shopping mall.

CAMBRIDGE continued

◆◆◆

THE SUFFOLK HOUSE
69 Milton Road, Cambridge, CB4 1XA
T: (01223) 352016
F: (01223) 566816
I: suffolkhouse@yahoo.com

B&B per night:
S £58.00–£75.00
D £65.00–£80.00

OPEN All year round

Friendly, no smoking, family-run establishment, within easy walking distance of the city centre and colleges. All rooms are en suite with direct-dial telephone. Hearty breakfast served in our light and airy dining room overlooking the pleasant, secluded, garden. Private car park.

Bedrooms: 2 double, 2 twin, 4 triple
Bathrooms: 8 en suite

Parking for 10
CC: Amex, Barclaycard, Delta, Eurocard, JCB, Mastercard, Solo, Switch, Visa, Visa Electron

---

◆◆◆◆

VICTORIA
57 Arbury Road, Cambridge, CB4 2JB
T: (01223) 350086
F: (01223) 350086
E: vicmaria@globalnet.co.uk
I: www.touristnetuk.com/em/victoria

B&B per night:
S £20.00–£40.00
D £35.00–£55.00

OPEN All year round

Extremely comfortable Victorian house situated within easy reach of the colleges, river and city centre. Most rooms en suite. Decor is excellent and the housekeeping, like the rooms, is of a very good standard. Colour TV, radio, alarm clock, ironing facilities, payphone and tea/coffee-making facilities. Parking available.

Bedrooms: 2 double
Bathrooms: 1 en suite, 1 private

Parking for 3
CC: Barclaycard, Delta, Eurocard, Mastercard, Solo, Switch, Visa, Visa Electron

---

CHELMSFORD, Essex Map ref 3B3 *Tourist Information Centre Tel: (01245) 283400*

◆◆

AQUILA B & B
11 Daffodil Way, Springfield, Chelmsford, CM1 6XB
T: (01245) 465274

Bedrooms: 1 single, 1 double, 1 twin
Bathrooms: 1 public

Parking for 3

B&B per night:
S £17.50–£24.50
D £35.00–£49.00

OPEN All year round

Single/double/family rooms. Full English breakfast, special diets/evening meals by arrangement. Colour TV, tea-making, central heating all rooms. Twenty minutes' walk town centre, London 35 minutes by train.

◆◆◆

BEECHCROFT PRIVATE HOTEL
211 New London Road, Chelmsford, CM2 0AJ
T: (01245) 352462 (Office) & 250861 (Guests)
F: (01245) 347833
E: beechcroft.hotel@btinternet.com

Bedrooms: 11 single, 3 double, 3 twin, 2 family rooms
Bathrooms: 13 en suite, 3 public

Parking for 15
CC: Barclaycard, Delta, Diners, Eurocard, JCB, Mastercard, Solo, Switch, Visa, Visa Electron

B&B per night:
S £35.00–£44.00
D £52.00–£60.00

OPEN All year round

Central hotel offering clean and comfortable accommodation with friendly service. Under family ownership and management. Within walking distance of town centre.

TOWN INDEX
This can be found at the back of this guide. If you know where you want to stay, the index will give you the page number listing accommodation in your chosen town, city or village.

CHELMSFORD continued

◆◆◆◆ BOSWELL HOUSE HOTEL

118 Springfield Road, Chelmsford, CM2 6LF T: (01245) 287587 F: (01245) 287587	Bedrooms: 5 single, 6 double, 2 triple Bathrooms: 13 en suite	Lunch available EM 1900 (LO 2030) Parking for 15 CC: Amex, Barclaycard, Delta, Diners, Eurocard, Mastercard, Visa	B&B per night: S £45.00–£48.00 D £60.00–£65.00 HB per person: DY £47.00–£60.00

Victorian town house in central location, offering high-standard accommodation in friendly and informal surroundings. Family atmosphere and home cooking, lounge bar.

OPEN All year round

◆◆ NEPTUNE CAFE MOTEL

Burnham Road, Latchingdon, Chelmsford, CM3 6EX T: (01621) 740770 (answerphone)	Bedrooms: 4 double, 2 twin, 4 triple Bathrooms: 10 en suite	Lunch available EM Parking for 40	B&B per night: S £25.00–£25.00 D £35.00–£35.00 HB per person: DY Min £30.00

Cafe with adjoining chalet block, which includes 2 units suitable for physically disabled. Village location between Maldon and Burnham-on-Crouch.

OPEN All year round

◆◆◆◆ STUMP CROSS HOUSE

Silver Award

Moulsham Street, Chelmsford, CM2 9AQ T: (01245) 353804	Bedrooms: 1 twin Bathrooms: 1 private	Parking for 12	B&B per night: S £30.00–£38.00 D £45.00–£50.00

Comfortable, detached family house with high standard of accommodation. Easy reach of town centre and cricket ground. Warm and friendly atmosphere.

OPEN All year round

◆◆◆ TANUNDA HOTEL

217-219 New London Road, Chelmsford, CM2 0AJ T: (01245) 354295 F: (01245) 345503	Bedrooms: 8 single, 6 double, 6 twin Bathrooms: 11 en suite, 3 public	Parking for 20 CC: Amex, Barclaycard, Delta, Diners, JCB, Mastercard, Switch, Visa, Visa Electron	B&B per night: S £35.00–£60.00 D £52.00–£62.00 OPEN All year round

We are on the main road to London and Harwich and 5 minutes from the town centre.

CLACTON-ON-SEA, Essex Map ref 3B3 *Tourist Information Centre Tel: (01255) 423400*

◆◆◆ SANDROCK HOTEL

1 Penfold Road, Marine Parade West, Clacton-on-Sea, CO15 1JN T: (01255) 428215 F: (01255) 428215	Bedrooms: 5 double, 2 twin, 1 triple Bathrooms: 8 en suite	Lunch available EM 1830 (LO 1900) Parking for 6 CC: Amex, Barclaycard, Delta, Diners, Eurocard, JCB, Maestro, Mastercard, Solo, Switch, Visa, Visa Electron	B&B per night: S £26.50–£31.00 D £48.00–£53.00 HB per person: DY £38.50–£42.00 OPEN All year round

Private hotel in central position, just off seafront and close to town. Comfortable bedrooms with co-ordinated soft furnishings. Excellent, freshly cooked food. Licensed. Car park.

COLCHESTER, Essex Map ref 3B2 *Tourist Information Centre Tel: (01206) 282920*

◆◆◆◆ GLINSKA HOUSE

6 St Johns Green, Colchester, CO2 7HA T: (01206) 578961 & 07850 215598 F: (01206) 503406 E: rhawki@email.msn.com	Bedrooms: 3 double Bathrooms: 2 en suite, 1 private	EM 1800 (LO 2000)	B&B per night: S £25.00–£35.00 D £38.00–£45.00 OPEN All year round

Charming 1840 house, 2 minutes' walk from the town centre. Tranquil setting overlooking The Green and historic St John's Abbey Gate. Excellent shopping/theatre/leisure facilities.

MAP REFERENCES
Map references apply to the colour maps at the front of this guide.

COLCHESTER continued

◆◆◆ OLD COURTHOUSE INN (FORMERLY OLD BLACK BOY)

Harwich Road, Great Bromley,
Colchester, CO7 7JG
T: (01206) 250322 & 251906

Bedrooms: 2 double,
3 triple
Bathrooms: 5 en suite

Lunch available
EM 1800 (LO 2200)
Parking for 75
CC: Amex, Barclaycard,
Delta, Mastercard, Switch,
Visa

B&B per night:
S £25.00–£30.00
D £45.00–£50.00

HB per person:
DY £40.00–£55.00

OPEN All year round

A 17thC inn with separate non-smoking and smoking restaurants. Full a la carte menu and bar snacks available 7 days a week. Bed and breakfast accommodation, all en suite rooms.

◆ PEVERIL HOTEL

51 North Hill, Colchester, CO1 1PY
T: (01206) 574001
F: (01206) 574001

Bedrooms: 4 single,
7 double, 5 twin, 1 triple
Bathrooms: 7 en suite,
3 public

Lunch available
EM 1900 (LO 2145)
Parking for 24
CC: Amex, Barclaycard,
Delta, Diners, Eurocard,
Maestro, Mastercard,
Solo, Switch, Visa, Visa
Electron

B&B per night:
S £26.00–£42.00
D £38.00–£52.00

HB per person:
DY £30.00–£60.00

OPEN All year round

Friendly, family-run hotel with fine restaurant and bar. All rooms have colour TV and all facilities. Some en suite available.

◆◆ SCHEREGATE HOTEL

36 Osborne Street,
via St John's Street, Colchester,
CO2 7DB
T: (01206) 573034
F: (01206) 541561

Bedrooms: 11 single,
6 double, 8 twin, 1 triple,
1 family room
Bathrooms: 10 en suite,
5 public

Parking for 28
CC: Barclaycard,
Mastercard, Visa

B&B per night:
S £22.00–£35.00
D £37.00–£45.00

OPEN All year round

Interesting 15thC building, centrally situated, providing accommodation at moderate prices.

COLTISHALL, Norfolk Map ref 3C1

◆◆◆◆ TERRA NOVA LODGE

14 Westbourne Road, Coltishall,
Norwich, NR12 7HT
T: (01603) 736264

Bedrooms: 1 double,
1 twin
Bathrooms: 2 en suite

Parking for 5

B&B per night:
S £28.00–£32.00
D £40.00–£44.00

OPEN All year round

Accommodation within a large detached bungalow in this Broadland village, close to Norwich. Spacious rooms, both en suite, central heating, colour TV, pleasing decor and secluded gardens.

COTTENHAM, Cambridgeshire Map ref 3A2

◆◆◆◆ DENMARK HOUSE

58 Denmark Road, Cottenham,
Cambridge, CB4 8QS
T: (01954) 251060 & 250448
F: (01954) 251629
E: denmark.house@tesco.net

Bedrooms: 2 double,
1 twin
Bathrooms: 3 en suite,
1 public

Parking for 2

B&B per night:
S £20.00–£30.00
D £38.00–£48.00

OPEN All year round

Spacious and comfortable detached residence. 6 miles Cambridge, close to Ely and Newmarket. Relaxed, friendly atmosphere, en suite facilities.

TOWN INDEX

This can be found at the back of the guide. If you know where you want to stay, the index will give you the page number listing accommodation in your chosen town, city or village.

CRETINGHAM, Suffolk Map ref 3B2

◆◆◆◆
Silver
Award

THE CRETINGHAM BELL

The Street, Cretingham, Woodbridge,
IP13 7BJ
T: (01728) 685419

B&B per night:
S £39.95–£39.95
D £58.75–£58.75

OPEN All year round

In the quiet village of Cretingham. Its Tudor beams, log fires, luxury accommodation, old-world charm, traditional home-cooked food, locally brewed ales and a warm welcome make The Bell the ideal stop for travellers seeking peace and tranquillity.

Bedrooms: 1 double,
1 twin; suites available
Bathrooms: 2 en suite

Lunch available
EM 1900 (LO 2100)
Parking for 25
CC: Barclaycard, Delta, Eurocard, Mastercard, Solo, Switch, Visa, Visa Electron

◆◆◆◆
Silver
Award

SHRUBBERY FARMHOUSE

Chapel Hill, Cretingham, Woodbridge,
IP13 7DN
T: (01473) 737494 (day & evening) & 07860 352317 (Mobile)
F: (01473) 737312
E: sm@marmar.co.uk
I: www.shrubberyfarmhouse.co.uk

B&B per night:
S £22.00–£25.00
D £45.00–£50.00

OPEN All year round

Charming part 16thC listed Suffolk farmhouse set in some of the most quiet and beautiful countryside in East Anglia. Winter log fires. Al fresco summer breakfasts with fresh eggs from the farmhouse hens make this the ideal base for exploring Suffolk's Heritage Coast. Comfortable bedrooms, gymnasium and tennis court.

Bedrooms: 1 single,
1 double
Bathrooms: 1 en suite,
1 private, 2 public

EM
Parking for 12

CROMER, Norfolk Map ref 3C1 *Tourist Information Centre Tel: (01263) 512497*

◆◆◆

CAMBRIDGE HOUSE

Sea Front, Cromer, NR27 9HD
T: (01263) 512085
I: www.broadland.com/cambridgehouse

B&B per night:
S £18.00–£24.00
D £36.00–£48.00

HB per person:
DY £28.00–£34.00

OPEN All year round

Charming Victorian house (centre of picture) with uninterrupted sea views, sandy beach and pier. Central for all amenities and shops. Spacious sea-view bedrooms with colour TV, clock/radio, hospitality tray. Excellent home cooking. Private car parking. Non-smoking establishment. Short breaks available. Excellent base for touring. Closed Christmas and New Year.

Bedrooms: 1 single,
2 double, 3 triple
Bathrooms: 3 en suite,
2 public

EM 1900 (LO 1900)
Parking for 6

CHECK THE MAPS

The colour maps at the front of this guide show all the cities, towns and villages for which you will find accommodation entries.
Refer to the town index to find the page on which they are listed.

CROMER continued

◆◆◆

KNOLL GUESTHOUSE

23 Alfred Road, Cromer, NR27 9AN
T: (01263) 512753
E: ian@knollguesthouse.co.uk
I: www.knollguesthouse.co.uk

B&B per night:
S £18.00–£22.00
D £36.00–£44.00

HB per person:
DY £28.00–£32.00

OPEN All year round

Family-run guesthouse offering good, traditional home cooking and friendly customer service. Situated close to seafront, town centre and amenities. There are several golf courses nearby. Quiet lanes for priority walking, cycling and horse-riding, beach and cliff paths.

Bedrooms: 2 single,
1 double, 1 twin,
1 family room; suites available
Bathrooms: 4 en suite,
1 private, 3 public

EM 1800 (LO 2000)
Parking for 2

CUFFLEY, Hertfordshire Map ref 2D1

◆◆◆◆

WUTHERINGS

43 Colesdale, Cuffley, Potters Bar,
EN6 4LQ
T: (01707) 874545 & 0795 791 8548

Bedrooms: 1 single,
1 double
Bathrooms: 1 public

Parking for 2

B&B per night:
S £20.00–£20.00
D £40.00–£40.00

OPEN All year round

Unusual split-level bungalow. Although close to London, it has a fine panoramic view across open farmland.

DANBURY, Essex Map ref 3B3

◆◆◆

SOUTHWAYS

Copt Hill, Danbury, Chelmsford,
CM3 4NN
T: (01245) 223428

Bedrooms: 2 twin
Bathrooms: 1 public

Parking for 2

B&B per night:
S £20.20–£26.00
D £38.00–£38.00

OPEN All year round

Pleasant country house with large garden adjoining an area of National Trust common land.

DARSHAM, Suffolk Map ref 3C2

◆◆◆

WHITE HOUSE FARM

Main Road, Darsham,
Saxmundham, IP17 3PP
T: (01728) 668632

Bedrooms: 2 double,
1 twin
Bathrooms: 1 en suite,
1 public

Parking for 20

B&B per night:
S £25.00–£35.00
D £40.00–£55.00

OPEN All year round

Small, family-run, modernised farmhouse with pleasant gardens, on edge of village. Easy access to Aldeburgh, Southwold, Dunwich, Minsmere. Large gardens. Hearty farmhouse breakfasts.

DEBDEN GREEN, Essex Map ref 2D1

◆◆◆◆

WIGMORES FARM

Debden Green, Saffron Walden,
CB11 3LX
T: (01371) 830050 (Answerphone)
F: (01371) 830050
E: patrick.worth@tesco.net

Bedrooms: 2 double,
1 twin
Bathrooms: 2 public

Lunch available
EM 1900 (LO 2000)
Parking for 12

B&B per night:
S £25.00–£25.00
D £38.00–£38.00

HB per person:
DY £38.00–£38.00

OPEN All year round

1000-acre arable farm. 16thC thatched farmhouse in open countryside, 2.5 miles from Thaxted, just off the Thaxted to Debden road.

MAP REFERENCES
The map references refer to the colour maps at the front of this guide. The first figure is the map number; the letter and figure which follow indicate the grid reference on the map.

DEDHAM, Essex Map ref 3B2

◆◆◆◆ **MAY'S BARN FARM**

May's Lane, Off Long Road West,
Dedham, Colchester, CO7 6EW
T: (01206) 323191
E: maysbarn@talk21.com
I: www.mays-barn-btinternet.co.uk

Bedrooms: 1 double,
1 twin
Bathrooms: 1 en suite,
1 private

Parking for 5

B&B per night:
S £25.00–£27.00
D £40.00–£45.00

OPEN All year round

350-acre arable farm. Tranquil old farmhouse with outstanding views over Dedham Vale in Constable Country. Quarter mile down private lane. Comfortable, spacious rooms, with private facilities.

🐎10 ☐ 🔌 📺 🖵 § ↯ 🎵 📺 ▥ ☕ ✻ ✈ 🚗 Ⓣ

DERSINGHAM, Norfolk Map ref 3B1

◆◆◆ **ASHDENE HOUSE**

Dersingham, King's Lynn, PE31 6HQ
T: (01485) 540395

Bedrooms: 3 double,
2 twin
Bathrooms: 5 en suite

Lunch available
EM 1900 (LO 2130)
Parking for 10
CC: Delta, Maestro,
Mastercard, Solo, Switch,
Visa, Visa Electron

B&B per night:
S £20.00–£24.00
D £40.00–£45.00

HB per person:
DY Min £28.95

OPEN All year round

An elegant Victorian house in village centre, convenient for country walks and seaside activities. Pleasant garden and adequate car park.

🐎3 ☐ 🔌 § ↯ 🎵 ▥ ✻ ✈ 🚗

DISS, Norfolk Map ref 3B2 *Tourist Information Centre Tel: (01379) 650523*

◆◆◆◆ **OXFOOTSTONE GRANARY**

Low Common, South Lopham, Diss,
IP22 2JS
T: (01379) 687490

Bedrooms: 1 double,
1 twin
Bathrooms: 2 en suite

Parking for 4

B&B per night:
S £18.00–£25.00
D £38.00–£42.00

OPEN All year round

Converted barn in open countryside, erected in 1822. Guest rooms are situated in a single-storey wing, formerly cart-sheds, overlooking a large pond with waterfowl.

🐎5 ♿ 🖥 ☐ 🔌 📺 ↯ 🎵 ▥ ✻ 🚗 🏦

◆◆◆◆ **STRENNETH**

Airfield Road, Fersfield, Diss,
IP22 2BP
T: (01379) 688182
F: (01379) 688260
E: ken@strenneth.co.uk
I: www.strenneth.co.uk

Bedrooms: 1 single,
4 double, 2 twin
Bathrooms: 7 en suite,
1 public

Parking for 10
CC: Barclaycard, Delta,
Eurocard, JCB,
Mastercard, Solo, Switch,
Visa, Visa Electron

B&B per night:
S £28.00–£50.00
D £50.00–£70.00

OPEN All year round

Family-run, 17thC period property. Log fires, oak beams. Executive and 4-poster, all en suite, most on ground floor. Licensed. Pets welcome. Close to Bressingham Gardens.

🐎 ♿ 🖴 🖥 ☐ 🔌 § ↯ 🎵 ▥ ☕ ✻ 🚗 SP 🏦 Ⓣ

EARL SOHAM, Suffolk Map ref 3C2

◆◆◆◆

**Silver
Award**

BRIDGE HOUSE

Earl Soham, Woodbridge, IP13 7RT
T: (01728) 685473 & 685289

Bedrooms: 2 double,
1 twin
Bathrooms: 3 en suite

Lunch available
EM 1900 (LO 2030)
Parking for 6

B&B per night:
S £25.00–£28.00
D £45.00–£50.00

HB per person:
DY £37.00–£40.00

OPEN All year round

Bridge House is an attractive, 16thC property near Heritage Coast. A warm welcome and excellent food add charm to well-appointed, comfortable accommodation.

Ⓜ🐎10 🖥 ☐ 🔌 📺 🖵 🔒 § ↯ 🎵 ▥ ✻ 🚗 🏦

EARLS COLNE, Essex Map ref 3B2

◆◆◆

🚶

RIVERSIDE LODGE

40 Lower Holt Street, Earls Colne,
Colchester, CO6 2PH
T: (01787) 223487
F: (01787) 223487

Bedrooms: 2 double,
3 twin
Bathrooms: 5 en suite

Lunch available
EM 1930 (LO 2200)
Parking for 40
CC: Barclaycard,
Mastercard, Visa

B&B per night:
S £35.50–£37.50
D £45.00–£49.00

OPEN All year round

On the A1124 Colchester-Halstead road, single storey en suite chalets on the banks of the River Colne. Restaurants, pubs and village amenities within walking distance.

🐎 ♿ ☐ 🔌 § ▥ ☕ ☂ ✻ Ⓣ

REGIONAL TOURIST BOARD The Ⓜ symbol in an establishment entry indicates that it is a Regional Tourist Board member.

ELMSWELL, Suffolk Map ref 3B2

♦♦♦ **KILN FARM**
Kiln Lane, Elmswell,
Bury St Edmunds, IP30 9QR
T: (01359) 240442 & 242604
E: barry-sue@kilnfarm.fsnet.co.uk

Bedrooms: 1 single,
2 double, 1 twin
Bathrooms: 4 en suite

Parking for 7

B&B per night:
S £25.00–£30.00
D £40.00–£45.00

OPEN All year round

Victorian farmhouse and converted barns set in 3 acres. In quiet lane half a mile from A1088 roundabout off A14. Self-catering accommodation also available.

ELY, Cambridgeshire Map ref 3A2 *Tourist Information Centre Tel: (01353) 662062*

♦♦♦♦
Gold
Award

HILL HOUSE FARM
9 Main Street, Coveney, Ely, CB6 2DJ
T: (01353) 778369

B&B per night:
D £44.00–£50.00

OPEN All year round

Fine Victorian farmhouse on arable working farm 3 miles west of Ely. First class breakfast served in traditional dining room. Open views of surrounding countryside. No smoking, no pets, children over 12 welcome. Access from A142 or A10. Situated in the centre of quiet village. Convenient for Ely, Cambridge, Newmarket.

Bedrooms: 2 double,
1 twin
Bathrooms: 3 en suite

Parking for 4
CC: Barclaycard, Delta,
Eurocard, Mastercard,
Solo, Switch, Visa

♦♦♦♦♦
Silver
Award

ROSENDALE LODGE
223 Main Street, Witchford, Ely, CB6 2HT
T: (01353) 667700 (Answerphone)
F: (01353) 667799

B&B per night:
S £29.00–£39.00
D £44.00–£59.00

HB per person:
DY £34.00–£51.00

OPEN All year round

Elegant house with period furniture and secluded gardens. Spacious galleried dining and sitting room. Individually designed en suite bedrooms. Choice of breakfasts. Home-cooked evening meals by arrangement. Inns and restaurants nearby. Adjacent to Ely with its magnificent cathedral, museums and riverside amenities. Ideally situated for Cambridge, Newmarket and West Norfolk.

Bedrooms: 2 double,
2 twin
Bathrooms: 4 en suite

EM 1900 (LO 2100)
Parking for 6
CC: Barclaycard, Eurocard,
Mastercard, Switch, Visa

CHECK THE MAPS
The colour maps at the front of this guide show all the cities, towns and villages for which you will find accommodation entries. Refer to the town index to find the page on which they are listed.

◆◆◆◆

SPINNEY ABBEY

Stretham Road, Wicken, Ely, CB7 5XQ
T: (01353) 720971
E: spinney.abbey@tesco.net
I: www.smoothhound.co.uk/hotels/
spinneya.html

B&B per night:
D £44.00–£46.00

OPEN All year round

This attractive Georgian Grade II Listed farmhouse, surrounded by pasture fields, stands next to our dairy farm which borders the NT Nature Reserve "Wicken Fen", on the southern edge of the Fens. Guests are welcome to full use of spacious garden and all-weather tennis court. All rooms have private facilities.

Bedrooms: 1 double,
1 twin, 1 triple
Bathrooms: 2 en suite,
1 private

Parking for 4

◆◆◆◆

SYCAMORE HOUSE

91 Cambridge Road, Ely, CB7 4HX
T: (01353) 662139 (answerphone)

Bedrooms: 3 double,
1 twin
Bathrooms: 2 en suite,
1 private, 1 private
shower

Parking for 8

B&B per night:
S £30.00–£40.00
D £45.00–£50.00

OPEN All year round

Spacious Edwardian family home in acre of mature garden adjoining golf course. Ample private parking. Convenient for riverside and cathedral.

◆◆◆

ABBOTT FARM

Walsingham Road, Binham, Fakenham,
NR21 0AW
T: (01328) 830519 & 07850 731413
F: (01328) 830519
E: peabrown@aol.com.

B&B per night:
S £18.00–£22.00
D £36.00–£44.00

OPEN All year round

126-acre arable farm. A modern, brick-built farm bungalow with a loft conversion, an airy conservatory and rural views of north Norfolk including the historic Binham Priory.

Bedrooms: 1 double,
1 twin
Bathrooms: 2 private

EM 1900 (LO 2100)
Parking for 10

◆◆

DOLPHIN HOTEL

41 Beach Station Road, Felixstowe,
IP11 2EY
T: (01394) 282261 & 278319

Bedrooms: 3 single,
3 double, 2 twin, 1 triple
Bathrooms: 2 en suite,
2 public

Lunch available
EM 1900 (LO 2100)
Parking for 24
CC: Amex, Delta,
Eurocard, Mastercard,
Solo, Switch, Visa, Visa
Electron

B&B per night:
S £18.00–£36.00
D £32.00–£56.00

OPEN All year round

Private hotel, 5 minutes from beach and 10 minutes from town centre. Fully licensed bar, traditional bar menu. Family room.

◆◆◆

THE WHITE HART INN

White Hart Street, Foulden,
Thetford, IP26 5AW
T: (01366) 328638
E: sylvia.chisholm@virgin.net

Bedrooms: 1 single,
2 double
Bathrooms: 3 en suite

Lunch available
EM 1800 (LO 2100)
Parking for 25
CC: Barclaycard, Delta,
Mastercard, Solo, Switch,
Visa, Visa Electron

B&B per night:
S £30.00–£35.00
D £40.00–£45.00

OPEN All year round

Traditional country inn with beer garden, conservatory and car park. Home-cooked food and real ale. Accommodation in former barn.

FRAMLINGHAM, Suffolk Map ref 3C2

◆◆◆◆ FIELDWAY BED & BREAKFAST

Saxtead Road, Dennington,
Woodbridge, IP13 8AP
T: (01728) 638456
F: (01728) 638456
E: dianaturan@hotmail.com

Bedrooms: 1 single,
1 double, 1 twin
Bathrooms: 2 private,
1 public

EM 1900 (LO 2100)
Parking for 4

B&B per night:
S £25.00–£25.00
D £42.00–£45.00

HB per person:
DY £31.00–£31.00

OPEN All year round

Set in an attractive half-acre garden. Beautiful dining room overlooks the garden.
1 double room has private conservatory. Tea/coffee making facilities in all rooms.

◆◆◆ SHIMMENS PIGHTLE

Dennington Road, Framlingham,
Woodbridge, IP13 9JT
T: (01728) 724036

Bedrooms: 1 double,
2 twin
Bathrooms: 1 public

Parking for 5

B&B per night:
S Min £25.00
D £40.00–£45.00

OPEN Apr–Oct

Comfortable home in an acre of landscaped garden, overlooking fields on outskirts of
Framlingham. Ground floor accommodation. Home-made marmalade and locally cured
bacon.

GREAT DUNMOW, Essex Map ref 3B2

◆◆◆◆ HARWOOD GUEST HOUSE

52 Stortford Road, Great Dunmow,
CM6 1DN
T: (01371) 874627

Bedrooms: 2 twin,
1 family room
Bathrooms: 3 en suite

Parking for 8

B&B per night:
S Max £30.00
D Max £50.00

OPEN All year round

Family-run guesthouse in Great Dunmow, surrounded by beautiful countryside. Private
off-road car parking.

GREAT YARMOUTH, Norfolk Map ref 3C1

◆◆◆ TROTWOOD PRIVATE HOTEL

2 North Drive, Great Yarmouth,
NR30 1ED
T: (01493) 843971
E: richard@trotwood.fsbusiness.co.
uk

Bedrooms: 8 double,
1 twin
Bathrooms: 8 en suite,
1 private shower

Parking for 11
CC: Barclaycard, Delta,
Eurocard, Mastercard,
Visa

B&B per night:
S £27.50–£31.50
D £45.00–£55.00

OPEN All year round

Opposite bowling greens on seafront, giving unrivalled sea views. Close to Britannia Pier
and all amenities. En suite bedrooms, licensed bar, own car park.

HALESWORTH, Suffolk Map ref 3C2

◆◆◆ THE CROFT

Ubbeston Green, Halesworth,
IP19 0HB
T: (01986) 798502 (answerphone) &
0771 2414274 (mobile)

Bedrooms: 2 twin
Bathrooms: 1 public

B&B per night:
S £25.00–£25.00
D £38.00–£38.00

OPEN All year round

Delightful country house set in 5 acres of gardens and paddocks. Beautiful views and
excellent country inns. A hearty breakfast using local products. Warm welcome awaits.

HALSTEAD, Essex Map ref 3B2

◆◆◆ TIMBERS

Cross End, Pebmarsh, Halstead,
CO9 2NT
T: (01787) 269330 (Answer phone)

Bedrooms: 1 twin,
1 family room; suite
available
Bathrooms: 1 en suite,
1 private

EM 1800 (LO 1000)
Parking for 3

B&B per night:
S £20.00–£20.00
D £37.00–£40.00

HB per person:
DY £26.50–£28.00

OPEN Mar–Nov

"Timbers" is a spacious quiet bungalow near Halstead. Ideally situated for touring, with
easy access to the A131 and A12. Close to the Stour Valley.

IMPORTANT NOTE Information on accommodation listed
in this guide has been supplied by the proprietors. As changes may occur
you are advised to check details at the time of booking.

HARLESTON, Norfolk Map ref 3C2

◆◆◆

WESTON HOUSE FARM
Mendham, Harleston, IP20 0PB
T: (01986) 782206 &
07803 099203 (Mobile)
F: (01986) 782414
E: holden@farmline.com

B&B per night:
S £22.50–£27.00
D £36.00–£45.00

HB per person:
DY £28.00–£37.00

OPEN Mar–Nov

This peacefully located 17thC Grade II Listed farmhouse set in a one-acre garden offers comfortable, spacious accommodation on a 300-acre mixed farm on the Norfolk/Suffolk border. It is within easy reach of Suffolk Heritage Coast, Minsmere Nature Reserve, Norfolk Broads, the historic city of Norwich and nearby otter sanctuary.

Bedrooms: 2 double, 1 twin
Bathrooms: 3 en suite

EM (LO 1400)
Parking for 6
CC: Amex

HARPENDEN, Hertfordshire Map ref 2D1

◆◆◆

MILTON HOTEL
25 Milton Road, Harpenden, AL5 5LA
T: (01582) 762914

Bedrooms: 2 single, 3 double, 2 twin
Bathrooms: 5 en suite, 1 public

Parking for 9
CC: Mastercard, Visa

B&B per night:
S £27.00–£40.00
D Min £50.00

OPEN All year round

Family-run, comfortable hotel in residential area close to mainline station, junctions 9/10 of M1 and convenient for M25. Car park.

HARWICH, Essex Map ref 3C2 *Tourist Information Centre Tel: (01255) 506139*

◆◆◆

NEW FARM HOUSE
Spinnels Lane, Wix, Manningtree, CO11 2UJ
T: (01255) 870365
F: (01255) 870837
E: barrie.winch@which.net

Bedrooms: 2 single, 2 double, 2 twin, 3 triple, 2 family rooms
Bathrooms: 9 en suite, 1 public

EM 1900 (LO 2000)
Parking for 15
CC: Barclaycard, Delta, Eurocard, JCB, Mastercard, Solo, Switch, Visa, Visa Electron

B&B per night:
S £26.00–£33.00
D £44.00–£54.00

HB per person:
DY £35.00–£50.00

OPEN All year round

Large, non-working farmhouse in 4 acres of grounds, 10 minutes' drive from Harwich, convenient for Colchester and Constable Country. Spacious public rooms. Home cooking, licensed.

◆◆◆

PASTON LODGE
1 Una Road, Parkeston, Harwich, CO12 4PP
T: (01255) 551390 &
07867 888498 (Mobile)
F: (01255) 551390
E: dwright@globalnet.co.uk

Bedrooms: 1 single, 2 double, 1 twin
Bathrooms: 4 en suite

Parking for 3

B&B per night:
S £21.00–£26.00
D £42.00–£47.00

OPEN All year round

Edwardian house offering comfortable en suite bed and breakfast facilities, situated within walking distance of Harwich International port.

QUEENS HOTEL
119 High Street, Dovercourt, Harwich, CO12 3AP
T: (01255) 502634

Bedrooms: 2 single, 3 twin, 1 family room
Bathrooms: 2 public

Lunch available
EM 1900 (LO 2200)
Parking for 20
CC: Amex, Barclaycard, Delta, Maestro, Mastercard, Solo, Switch, Visa, Visa Electron

B&B per night:
S Min £20.00
D Min £40.00

HB per person:
DY Min £25.00

OPEN All year round

On the main road of the town, with 2 bars, a restaurant and beer garden.

CONFIRM YOUR BOOKING
You are advised to confirm your booking in writing.

HAUGHLEY, Suffolk Map ref 3B2

◆◆◆◆

RED HOUSE FARM
Station Road, Haughley,
Stowmarket, IP14 3QP
T: (01449) 673323
F: (01449) 675413
E: mary@noy1.fsnet.co.uk
I: www.farmstayanglia.co.uk

Bedrooms: 2 single,
1 double, 1 twin
Bathrooms: 4 en suite

Parking for 3

B&B per night:
S £25.00–£28.00
D £40.00–£44.00

OPEN All year round

*Attractive farmhouse in rural location on small grassland farm. First class breakfast.
Central heating and large garden.*

HELPSTON, Cambridgeshire Map ref 3A1

◆◆◆◆

HELPSTON HOUSE
Helpston, Peterborough, PE6 7DX
T: (01733) 252190
F: (01733) 253853
E: orton.helpstonhouse@btinternet.com
I: www.helpstonhouse.co.uk

B&B per night:
S £30.00–£30.00
D £40.00–£44.00

HB per person:
DY £40.00–£54.00

OPEN All year round

*Grade II Listed stone manor-house
dating back to 1090, between
Stamford and Peterborough in the
village where poet John Clare lived.
Spacious, comfortable
accommodation with heated
outdoor swimming pool. Rutland
Water, Tallington Lakes and Peakirk
Wildfowl Trust close by. A warm and
friendly welcome awaits you. Self-
catering accommodation also
available.*

Bedrooms: 1 single,
1 double, 1 family room;
suites available
Bathrooms: 1 en suite,
1 public

Parking for 6

HETHERSETT, Norfolk Map ref 3B1

◆◆◆

MAGNOLIA HOUSE
Cromwell Close, Hethersett,
NR9 3HD
T: (01603) 810749
F: (01603) 810749

Bedrooms: 2 single,
2 double, 1 twin
Bathrooms: 4 public

Parking for 7

B&B per night:
S £18.00–£24.00
D £36.00–£44.00

OPEN All year round

*Family-run B&B. All rooms centrally heated, colour TV, hot water, tea/coffee making
facilities. Laundry, public telephone and fax available. Weekend break discounts. Private
car park.*

HEVINGHAM, Norfolk Map ref 3B1

◆◆◆◆

MARSHAM ARMS INN
Holt Road, Hevingham, Norwich,
NR10 5NP
T: (01603) 754268
F: (01603) 754839
E: m.arms@paston.co.uk
I: www.marshamarms.co.uk

Bedrooms: 3 double,
5 twin
Bathrooms: 8 en suite

Lunch available
EM 1800 (LO 2200)
Parking for 100
CC: Amex, Barclaycard,
Delta, Eurocard, JCB,
Mastercard, Switch, Visa

B&B per night:
S £40.00–£45.00
D £60.00–£70.00

OPEN All year round

*Set in peaceful Norfolk countryside within reach of Norwich, the Broads and the coast.
Comfortable and spacious accommodation, good food and a fine selection of ales.*

HINTLESHAM, Suffolk Map ref 3B2

◆◆◆◆

COLLEGE FARM
Hintlesham, Ipswich, IP8 3NT
T: (01473) 652253
F: (01473) 652253
E: bryce1@agripro.co.uk

Bedrooms: 1 single,
1 double, 1 twin
Bathrooms: 1 en suite,
1 public

Parking for 6

B&B per night:
S £18.00–£28.00
D £38.00–£42.00

OPEN Feb–Nov

*600-acre arable farm. Peaceful 500-year-old beamed farmhouse offers a warm welcome,
hearty breakfasts and quality accommodation. Six miles west of Ipswich, close to
Constable Country and coast.*

◆◆◆

THE LORD LISTER HOTEL

1 Park Street, Hitchin, SG4 9AH
T: (01462) 432712 & 459451
F: (01462) 438506

B&B per night:
S £45.00–£60.00
D £55.00–£70.00

OPEN All year round

18thC country-style hotel on the edge of Hitchin town centre. Warm atmosphere with friendly and helpful staff. Individually furnished rooms, all en suite, some non-smoking. Lounge, cosy bar, free car park. Good choice of menu offered for breakfast. Special weekend rates.

Bedrooms: 4 single, 10 double, 3 twin, 3 triple
Bathrooms: 20 en suite

Parking for 11
CC: Amex, Barclaycard, Delta, Diners, Eurocard, JCB, Mastercard, Solo, Switch, Visa, Visa Electron

◆◆◆◆

LAWNS HOTEL

Station Road, Holt, NR25 6BS
T: (01263) 713390
E: lawnshotel.norfolk@btinternet.com
I: www.lawsnhotel.co.uk

B&B per night:
S £38.00–£45.00
D £56.00–£90.00

HB per person:
DY £39.00–£56.00

OPEN All year round

Situated in North Norfolk's historic town of Holt. Ideal for exploring both the enchanting coastline and scenic countryside, the Lawns is a charming Georgian hotel providing spacious accommodation with tranquil setting and delightful walled gardens. Car park. Much emphasis on hospitality and courteous service. The perfect retreat at any time.

Bedrooms: 1 single, 6 double, 3 twin
Bathrooms: 9 en suite, 1 private, 1 public

EM 1830 (LO 1930)
Parking for 11
CC: Barclaycard, JCB, Mastercard, Solo, Visa

◆◆

NORTH VIEW GUESTHOUSE

North View, Malting Row, Honington, Bury St Edmunds, IP31 1RE
T: (01359) 269423

Bedrooms: 1 single, 1 double, 1 triple
Bathrooms: 2 public

Parking for 6

B&B per night:
S £18.00–£20.00
D £36.00–£40.00

OPEN All year round

Situated opposite village church in a very quiet area, but within easy reach of shop, post office, garage and public house. Car park.

COUNTRY CODE
Always follow the Country Code ✤ Enjoy the countryside and respect its life and work ✤ Guard against all risk of fire ✤ Fasten all gates ✤ Keep your dogs under close control ✤ Keep to public paths across farmland ✤ Use gates and stiles to cross fences, hedges and walls ✤ Leave livestock, crops and machinery alone ✤ Take your litter home ✤ Help to keep all water clean ✤ Protect wildlife, plants and trees ✤ Take special care on country roads ✤ Make no unnecessary noise

HUNTINGTON, Norfolk Map ref 3B1 *Tourist Information Centre Tel: (01485) 532610*

◆◆◆

PEACOCK HOUSE

28 Park Road, Hunstanton, PE36 5BY
T: (01485) 534551

B&B per night:
D £35.00–£55.00

OPEN All year round

A large Victorian residence situated on the southern side of Hunstanton, just 300 metres to the Oasis Leisure Centre and beach, yet less than 3 minutes' walk to town centre. Thoughtful decor throughout, with many period features still remaining. Spacious rooms with modern en suite facilities and sea views.

Bedrooms: 1 twin,
1 triple
Bathrooms: 2 en suite

HUNTINGDON, Cambridgeshire Map ref 3A2 *Tourist Information Centre Tel: (01480) 388588*

◆◆◆◆

PRINCE OF WALES

Potton Road, Hilton, Huntingdon,
PE28 9NG
T: (01480) 830257
F: (01480) 830257
E: princeofwales.hilton@talk21.com

B&B per night:
S £45.00–£50.00
D £65.00–£65.00

OPEN All year round

Friendly, traditional village inn set in the heart of rural Cambridgeshire but only a short drive from Huntingdon, St Ives, Cambridge and Peterborough. Listed in the CAMRA Good Beer Guide for the past 13 years, you are assured of a quality pint of real ale to accompany good value, hearty meals.

Bedrooms: 2 single,
1 double, 1 twin
Bathrooms: 4 en suite

Lunch available
EM 1900 (LO 2115)
Parking for 9
CC: Amex, Barclaycard,
Delta, Eurocard, JCB,
Maestro, Mastercard,
Solo, Switch, Visa, Visa
Electron

KELVEDON, Essex Map ref 3B3

◆◆◆

HIGHFIELDS FARM

Kelvedon, Colchester, CO5 9BJ
T: (01376) 570334
F: (01376) 570334

Bedrooms: 1 double,
2 twin
Bathrooms: 2 en suite,
1 private

Parking for 6

B&B per night:
S Max £22.00
D Max £44.00

OPEN All year round

700-acre arable and horse farm. Timber-framed farmhouse in quiet location in open countryside. Easy access to A12. Heating in all rooms.

KERSEY, Suffolk Map ref 3B2

◆◆◆

RED HOUSE FARM

Wickerstreet Green, Kersey, Ipswich,
IP7 6EY
T: (01787) 210245

Bedrooms: 1 single,
1 double, 1 twin
Bathrooms: 3 en suite,
1 public

EM 1900 (LO 1000)
Parking for 5

B&B per night:
S £25.00–£25.00
D £40.00–£44.00

HB per person:
DY £29.00–£53.00

OPEN All year round

Comfortable, Listed farmhouse between Kersey and Boxford, central for Constable Country. Rooms have TV and tea-making facilities. Swimming pool.

WELCOME HOST This is a nationally recognised customer care programme which aims to promote the highest standards of service and a warm welcome. Establishments taking part in this initiative are indicated by the ⊛ symbol.

KING'S LYNN, Norfolk Map ref 3B1 *Tourist Information Centre Tel: (01553) 763044*

◆◆

THE BEECHES GUESTHOUSE
2 Guanock Terrace, King's Lynn,
PE30 5QT
T: (01553) 766577
F: (01553) 776664

Bedrooms: 1 single,
2 double, 3 twin, 1 triple
Bathrooms: 4 en suite,
1 public

EM 1830 (LO 1930)
Parking for 3
CC: Amex, Barclaycard,
Delta, Eurocard,
Mastercard, Switch, Visa

B&B per night:
S £22.00–£32.00
D £38.00–£48.00

HB per person:
DY £27.00–£42.00

OPEN All year round

Detached Victorian house, all rooms with TV, tea/coffee facilities and telephone. Most rooms en suite. Full English breakfast and 3-course evening meal with coffee.

◆◆◆◆

FAIRLIGHT LODGE
79 Goodwins Road, King's Lynn,
PE30 5PE
T: (01553) 762234
F: (01553) 770280
E: penny.rowe@lineone.net

Bedrooms: 2 single,
2 double, 3 twin
Bathrooms: 4 en suite,
2 public

Parking for 6

B&B per night:
S £18.00–£26.00
D £36.00–£42.00

OPEN All year round

Lovely owner-run Victorian house with friendly atmosphere and well appointed rooms. Ground floor en suite rooms available. Private parking. Closed Christmas.

◆◆◆

MARANATHA-HAVANA GUESTHOUSE
115-117 Gaywood Road,
King's Lynn, PE30 2PU
T: (01553) 774596 & 772331
F: (01553) 763747

Bedrooms: 2 single,
1 double, 5 twin, 4 triple
Bathrooms: 5 en suite,
2 public

Parking for 8

B&B per night:
S Min £20.00
D £30.00–£40.00

HB per person:
DY £20.00–£25.00

OPEN All year round

Large family-run guesthouse, 10 minutes' walk town centre, Lynnsport and Queen Elizabeth Hospital. Direct road to Sandringham and coast. Special rates for group bookings.

◆◆◆◆

MARSH FARM
Wolferton, King's Lynn, PE31 6HB
T: (01485) 540265
F: (01485) 543143
E: keith.larrington@farmline.com
I: www.members.farmline.com/
keith

Bedrooms: 2 double,
1 twin
Bathrooms: 1 en suite,
2 private

Parking for 5

B&B per night:
S £25.00–£30.00
D £40.00–£50.00

OPEN Feb–Dec

755-acre arable farm. Relaxing, comfortable farmhouse on working farm in quiet village of Wolferton, on the Norfolk coast, close to Sandringham. Coastal and countryside walks.

◆◆◆◆

THE OLD RECTORY
33 Goodwins Road, King's Lynn, PE30 5QX
T: (01553) 768544

B&B per night:
S £28.00–£32.00
D £38.00–£42.00

OPEN All year round

Elegant former rectory with high quality en suite accommodation. Complimentary tea, coffee and soft drinks. Guests have freedom of access at all times. Off-street parking with security lighting, secure storage for cycles. Non-smoking throughout but guests are welcome to use the terrace and garden areas. Quietly situated close to town centre.

Bedrooms: 2 double,
2 twin
Bathrooms: 4 en suite

Parking for 4

CREDIT CARD BOOKINGS If you book by telephone and are asked for your credit card number it is advisable to check the proprietor's policy should you cancel your reservation.

KINGS LANGLEY, Hertfordshire Map ref 2D1

♦♦♦

WOODCOTE HOUSE
7 The Grove, Whippendell,
Chipperfield, Kings Langley,
WD4 9JF
T: (01923) 262077
F: (01923) 266198
E: leveridge@btinternet.com

Bedrooms: 2 single,
1 double, 1 twin
Bathrooms: 4 en suite

EM 1800 (LO 2100)
Parking for 8

B&B per night:
S £24.00–£26.00
D £42.00–£46.00

OPEN All year round

Timber-framed house, sitting in 1 acre of landscaped gardens with quiet rural aspect. Convenient for M1 and M25 and close to Watford and Hemel Hempstead.

LAVENHAM, Suffolk Map ref 3B2

♦♦♦♦

HILL HOUSE FARM
Preston St Mary, Lavenham, Sudbury,
CO10 9LT
T: (01787) 247571
F: (01787) 247571

B&B per night:
S Min £35.00
D £50.00–£60.00

HB per person:
DY £40.00–£45.00

OPEN Mar–Nov

Beautiful Listed Tudor farmhouse in peaceful, rural setting close to historic Lavenham. Spacious accommodation with historic wall paintings and furnished with antiques. Private access, lovely gardens and small lake with black swans. Delicious home-cooked meals by prior arrangement. Very good restaurants and village pub nearby. A very warm welcome is assured.

Bedrooms: 1 single,
1 twin
Bathrooms: 2 private

EM
Parking for 7

♦♦♦♦
Silver
Award

LAVENHAM GREAT HOUSE HOTEL
Market Place, Lavenham, Sudbury,
CO10 9QZ
T: (01787) 247431
F: (01787) 248007
E: info@greathouse.co.uk
I: www.greathouse.co.uk

B&B per night:
S £65.00–£90.00
D £75.00–£125.00

HB per person:
DY £53.95–£63.95

OPEN Feb–Dec

Delightful 16thC house with award-winning restaurant, on magnificent Lavenham square. Beautifully decorated, individual bedooms, all furnished with antiques. Most have sitting areas and provide every comfort to modern travellers. Daily changing lunch and dinner (not Saturday) set menus offer excellent value. (One 4-poster bedroom).

Bedrooms: 3 double,
1 twin, 1 triple; suites
available
Bathrooms: 5 en suite

Lunch available
EM 1900 (LO 2130)
Parking for 10
CC: Amex, Barclaycard,
Delta, Eurocard, JCB,
Mastercard, Switch, Visa

LEIGH-ON-SEA, Essex Map ref 2B3

♦♦♦

52 UNDERCLIFF GARDENS
Leigh-on-Sea, Essex SS9 1EA
T: (01702) 474984 (answerphone) &
07967 788873

Bedrooms: 1 single,
1 double
Bathrooms: 1 public

Parking for 2

B&B per night:
S £20.00–£22.00
D £38.00–£38.00

OPEN Mar–Nov

Cosy accommodation with uninterrupted views of River Thames. Ideal for sightseeing in surrounding area, London 45 minutes by train. Off-street parking on Grand Parade.

ACCESSIBILITY
Look for the 🏠🏠🏠 symbols which indicate accessibility for wheelchair users. A list of establishments is at the front of this guide.

LEISTON, Suffolk Map ref 3C2

♦♦♦♦
Silver Award

FIELD END
1 Kings Road, Leiston, IP16 4DA
T: (01728) 833527
F: (01728) 833527
E: pwright@field-end.freeserve.co.uk
I: www.field-end.freeserve.co.uk

Bedrooms: 2 single, 1 double, 1 twin, 1 family room; suite available
Bathrooms: 1 en suite, 4 private

EM
Parking for 5

B&B per night:
S £25.00–£37.00
D £45.00–£50.00

HB per person:
DY £25.00–£37.00

OPEN All year round

A comfortable, newly refurbished Edwardian house with many original features; in ideal central position for touring the Suffolk Heritage Coast.

LITTLE WALSINGHAM, Norfolk Map ref 3B1

♦♦

ST DAVID'S HOUSE
Friday Market, Little Walsingham, Walsingham, NR22 6BY
T: (01328) 820633 & 07710 044452

Bedrooms: 1 double, 1 twin, 3 triple
Bathrooms: 1 en suite, 2 public

Lunch available
EM 1800 (LO 2100)

B&B per night:
D £42.00–£48.00

HB per person:
DY £32.00–£34.00

OPEN All year round

16thC brick house in a delightful medieval village. The village is fully signposted from Fakenham (A148). Four miles from the coast.

LONG MELFORD, Suffolk Map ref 3B2

♦♦

PERSEVERANCE HOTEL
Station Road, Long Melford, Sudbury, CO10 9HN
T: (01787) 375862 (Answerphone)

B&B per night:
S £30.00–£30.00
D £50.00–£50.00

HB per person:
DY £35.00–£70.00

OPEN All year round

Public house/motel with 1 family and 3 twin chalets. The family chalet sleeps 4 people at £60 per night, and can accommodate additional camp beds at £10 per night each. All chalets are en suite and have TV and tea/coffee facilities. Home-cooked meals are available at lunchtime and every evening.

Bedrooms: 1 single, 1 double, 4 twin, 1 triple
Bathrooms: 3 en suite, 1 public

Lunch available
EM 1900 (LO 2100)
Parking for 17

LOWESTOFT, Suffolk Map ref 3C1 *Tourist Information Centre Tel: (01502) 533600*

♦♦♦♦♦

CHURCH FARM
Corton, Lowestoft, NR32 5HX
T: (01502) 730359
F: (01502) 733426
E: medw149227@aol.com

B&B per night:
S Max £40.00
D £42.00–£45.00

OPEN Mar–Oct

Britain's most easterly farm near rural beach and cliff walks. Victorian farmhouse, attractive, high standard en suite double-bedded rooms. Generous traditional English breakfast. Non-smoking. German spoken. On A12 from Lowestoft to Great Yarmouth into Stirrups Lane, Church Farm opposite Corton Parish Church.

Bedrooms: 3 double
Bathrooms: 3 en suite

Parking for 4

QUALITY ASSURANCE SCHEME
Diamond ratings and awards were correct at the time of going to press but are subject to change. Please check at the time of booking.

LOWESTOFT continued

◆◆◆ FAIRWAYS GUESTHOUSE

398 London Road South, Lowestoft, NR33 0BQ
T: (01502) 572659
E: amontali@netmatters.co.uk

Bedrooms: 2 single, 1 twin, 2 triple, 2 family rooms
Bathrooms: 3 en suite, 1 private, 2 public

EM 1800 (LO 1850)
Parking for 2
CC: Amex, Barclaycard, Diners, Mastercard, Visa

B&B per night:
S £18.00–£24.00
D £32.00–£40.00

HB per person:
DY £28.00–£34.00

OPEN All year round

Spacious, well furnished and comfortable, with good food and a friendly atmosphere. Central position for town, sea and country. All rooms TV, tea/coffee and double glazing.

◆◆◆◆ HALL FARM

Jay Lane, Church Lane, Lound, Lowestoft, NR32 5LJ
T: (01502) 730415
E: josephashley@compuserve.com

Bedrooms: 1 single, 1 double, 1 triple
Bathrooms: 1 en suite, 1 public

Parking for 6

B&B per night:
S £18.00–£25.00
D £40.00–£45.00

OPEN Mar–Sep

101-acre arable farm. 16thC farmhouse within 2 miles of sea. Clean, comfortable accommodation with generous English breakfast. Farm down private lane, half mile from A12.

◆◆ ROYAL COURT HOTEL

146 London Road South, Lowestoft, NR33 0AZ
T: (01502) 568901 & 585400
F: (01502) 568901

Bedrooms: 2 single, 1 double, 8 twin, 2 triple, 4 family rooms
Bathrooms: 8 en suite, 9 private showers

EM 1800 (LO 2000)
Parking for 12
CC: Amex, Barclaycard, Delta, Eurocard, JCB, Mastercard, Solo, Switch, Visa, Visa Electron

B&B per night:
S £20.00–£25.00
D £40.00–£50.00

HB per person:
DY £27.50–£32.50

OPEN All year round

A family-run mainly commercial bed and breakfast hotel close to all amenities and award-winning beaches. Evening meals by arrangement.

LUTON, Bedfordshire Map ref 2D1 *Tourist Information Centre Tel: (01582) 401579*

◆◆◆ ADARA LODGE

539 Hitchin Road, Luton, LU2 7UL
T: (01582) 731361

Bedrooms: 1 twin
Bathrooms: 1 private, 1 public

EM 1830 (LO 2030)
Parking for 1

B&B per night:
S £22.00–£25.00
D £44.00–£50.00

HB per person:
DY £32.50–£40.00

OPEN All year round

Very comfortable, peaceful home with beautiful garden and off-road parking. Home cooking. Convenient M1, airport, station, town and sports centre.

◆◆ 44 SKELTON CLOSE

Barton Hills, Luton, LU3 4HF
T: (01582) 495205

Bedrooms: 1 single, 1 twin
Bathrooms: 2 private

Parking for 1

B&B per night:
S £20.00–£24.00
D £32.00–£36.00

OPEN All year round

Quiet, detached house 4 miles from Luton Airport (good taxi service). Easy reach of M1, A6 and trains to London.

MARGARET RODING, Essex Map ref 2D1

◆◆◆◆

GARNISH HALL

Margaret Roding, Dunmow, CM6 1QL
T: (01245) 231209 & 231224
F: (01708) 741172

B&B per night:
S £33.00–£33.00
D £55.00–£55.00

HB per person:
DY £48.00–£50.00

OPEN All year round

A 16thC manor-house which was once moated. Graceful curved staircase leading to bedrooms with lovely views of the island. On A1060 Chelmsford road, adjacent to a Norman church which boasts perhaps the most attractive doorway in Essex. Black swans, carp. Tennis court, walled garden, gentle walks.

Bedrooms: 2 double, 1 twin; suites available
Bathrooms: 2 en suite, 1 private, 1 public

Lunch available
EM 1830 (LO 2200)
Parking for 20

MARGARET RODING continued

◆◆◆ GREYS

Ongar Road, Margaret Roding, Dunmow, CM6 1QR	Bedrooms: 2 double, 1 twin	Parking for 6
T: (01245) 231509	Bathrooms: 1 public	

B&B per night:
S Min £22.50
D Min £44.00

OPEN All year round

B&B in old beamed cottage on family arable/sheep farm. A no smoking house. Turn off in village at sign to Berners Roding, half a mile along.

NORFOLK BROADS

See under Beccles, Bungay, Coltishall, Great Yarmouth, Hevingham, Lowestoft, Norwich, Potter Heigham, South Walsham, Sprowston, Wroxham

NORTH FAMBRIDGE, Essex Map ref 3B3

◆◆◆ FERRY BOAT INN

North Fambridge, Chelmsford, CM3 6LR	Bedrooms: 3 double, 3 twin	Lunch available EM 1900 (LO 2130)
T: (01621) 740208	Bathrooms: 6 en suite	Parking for 30
		CC: Barclaycard, Delta, Switch, Visa, Visa Electron

B&B per night:
S £32.00–£35.00
D £40.00–£45.00

OPEN All year round

A 500-year-old Essex weather-boarded inn located next to yachting centres on River Crouch and Essex Wildlife Trust 600-acre farm.

NORWICH, Norfolk Map ref 3C1 *Tourist Information Centre Tel: (01603) 666071*

◆◆◆◆ ARBOR LINDEN LODGE

Linden House, 557 Earlham Road, Norwich, NR4 7HW	Bedrooms: 1 single, 3 double, 1 twin	Parking for 8 CC: Barclaycard, Delta,
T: (01603) 451303 (2 lines)	1 family room	Eurocard, Mastercard,
F: (01603) 250641	Bathrooms: 6 en suite	Solo, Switch, Visa, Visa
E: linden@guesthouses.uk.com		Electron
I: www.linden.freeuk.com		

B&B per night:
S £25.00–£35.00
D £44.00–£50.00

OPEN All year round

Family-run, non-smoking, convenient for city (free parking), sports park, university, hospital. English breakfast, en suite rooms, family suite, TV, telephone, beverages, heating. Guest lounge, secure parking.

◆◆◆ BECKLANDS

105 Holt Road, Horsford, Norwich, NR10 3AB	Bedrooms: 4 single, 3 double, 2 twin	Parking for 30 CC: Barclaycard, Diners,
T: (01603) 898582	Bathrooms: 7 en suite,	Mastercard, Visa
F: (01603) 754223	1 private, 2 public	

B&B per night:
S £25.00–£30.00
D £35.00–£40.00

OPEN All year round

Quietly located modern house overlooking open countryside. 5 miles north of Norwich. Central for the Broads and coastal areas.

◆◆◆ CAVELL HOUSE

Swardeston, Norwich, NR14 8DZ	Bedrooms: 1 single, 1 double, 1 twin	Lunch available EM
T: (01508) 578195 (answerphone)	Bathrooms: 2 public	Parking for 10

B&B per night:
S £16.50–£18.50
D £35.00–£38.00

OPEN All year round

Birthplace of nurse Edith Cavell. Rural Georgian farmhouse on edge of Swardeston village. Off B1113 south of Norwich, 5 miles from centre. Near university, new hospital.

◆◆◆ CHURCH FARM GUESTHOUSE

Church Street, Horsford, Norwich, NR10 3DB	Bedrooms: 2 double, 2 twin, 1 triple, 1 family	Parking for 20 CC: Delta, Diners,
T: (01603) 898180 & 898582	room	Eurocard, Mastercard,
F: (01603) 891649	Bathrooms: 6 en suite	Visa

B&B per night:
S £25.00–£30.00
D £36.00–£40.00

OPEN All year round

Quiet, modernised 17thC farmhouse. Separate entrance, lounge and dining room for guests. Approximately 4 miles north of Norwich. All rooms en suite.

TOWN INDEX

This can be found at the back of this guide. If you know where you want to stay, the index will give you the page number listing accommodation in your chosen town, city or village.

NORWICH continued

◆◆◆

CONIFERS HOTEL
162 Dereham Road, Norwich,
NR2 3AH
T: (01603) 628737

Bedrooms: 4 single,
1 double, 3 twin
Bathrooms: 1 en suite,
3 public

Parking for 4

B&B per night:
S Min £20.00
D Min £40.00

OPEN All year round

Friendly hotel close to city centre, university, sports village and showground. All rooms have colour TV, tea/coffee, hairdryer.

◆◆◆◆

ELM FARM COUNTRY HOUSE
55 Norwich Road, St Faiths,
Norwich NR10 3HH
T: (01603) 898366
F: (01603) 897129

Bedrooms: 3 single,
4 double, 5 twin,
2 family rooms
Bathrooms: 14 en suite

Lunch available
Parking for 20
CC: Amex, Barclaycard,
Delta, Eurocard, JCB,
Mastercard, Solo, Switch,
Visa, Visa Electron

B&B per night:
S £32.00–£37.00
D £52.00–£58.00

OPEN All year round

Situated in quiet, pretty village 4 miles north of Norwich. Ideal base for touring Norfolk and Suffolk. En suite chalet bedrooms. Breakfast served in farmhouse dining room. Licensed.

◆◆◆◆

THE GABLES GUESTHOUSE
527 Earlham Road, Norwich, NR4 7HN
T: (01603) 456666
F: (01603) 250320

B&B per night:
S £40.00–£40.00
D £58.50–£63.50

OPEN All year round

Friendly, family-run, non-smoking guesthouse with very high quality accommodation, residents' lounge and full-size snooker table. Illuminated private car park at rear within secluded gardens. Situated within easy walking distance of university and close to Science Park and city centre.

Bedrooms: 6 double,
4 twin, 1 triple
Bathrooms: 11 en suite,
1 public

Parking for 14
CC: Barclaycard, Delta,
Eurocard, JCB,
Mastercard, Solo, Switch,
Visa, Visa Electron

◆◆◆

KINGSLEY LODGE
3 Kingsley Road, Norwich, NR1 3RB
T: (01603) 615819
F: (01603) 615819
E: kingsley@paston.co.uk

B&B per night:
S £28.00–£32.00
D £40.00–£44.00

OPEN Feb–Dec

Quiet, friendly, non-smoking Edwardian house in central Norwich. Close to the bus station and less than 10 minutes' walk to the Market Place, castle, shops and restaurants. All rooms have en suite bathroom, colour TV and tea/coffee making facilities. Full English breakfast, using organic food, cooked to order. Parking permits provided.

Bedrooms: 1 single,
1 double, 1 twin
Bathrooms: 3 en suite

◆◆

MARLBOROUGH HOUSE HOTEL
22 Stracey Road, Norwich, NR1 1EZ
T: (01603) 628005
F: (01603) 628005

Bedrooms: 9 single,
5 double, 4 twin, 2 triple
Bathrooms: 12 en suite,
2 public

EM 1730 (LO 1900)
Parking for 7

B&B per night:
S £25.00–£35.00
D £46.00–£52.00

HB per person:
DY £37.00–£47.00

OPEN All year round

Long established family hotel, close city centre, new Riverside development, Castle Mall, museum, cathedral. All double, twin and family rooms are en suite. Licensed bar, car park.

NORWICH continued

◆◆◆◆
Silver
Award

THE OLD RECTORY
Hall Road, Framingham Earl,
Norwich, NR14 7SB
T: (01508) 493590
E: brucewellings@drivedevice.
freeserve.co.uk

Bedrooms: 1 double,
1 twin
Bathrooms: 1 public

Parking for 6

B&B per night:
S £22.00–£26.00
D £42.00–£48.00

OPEN All year round

*Beautifully renovated and extended 17thC family house set in 2 acres of country garden.
Wealth of beams in lounge and dining room. Village 4.5 miles south-east of Norwich.*

◆◆

ROSEDALE
145 Earlham Road, Norwich,
NR2 3RG
T: (01603) 453743 &
07771 873089 (Mobile)
F: (01603) 259887
E: drcbac@aol.com.
I: members@aol.com/drcbac

Bedrooms: 2 single,
2 twin, 2 triple
Bathrooms: 2 public

CC: Barclaycard, Delta,
Maestro, Mastercard,
Solo, Switch, Visa

B&B per night:
S £18.00–£25.00
D £38.00–£45.00

OPEN All year round

*Friendly, family-run, non-smoking, Victorian guesthouse, on B1108, 1 mile from city
centre. Restaurants, shops and university nearby, convenient for coast and broads. Cards
taken.*

PETERBOROUGH, Cambridgeshire Map ref 3A1 *Tourist Information Centre Tel: (01733) 452336*

◆◆◆

THE ANCHOR LODGE
28 Percival Street, Peterborough, PE3 6AU
T: (01733) 312724 & 07767 611911

B&B per night:
S £20.00–£25.00
D £38.00–£42.00

OPEN All year round

*Friendly establishment, 7 minutes'
walk from shopping centre and
railway. Ten minutes' drive to East of
England Showground and A1.*

Bedrooms: 1 double,
3 twin
Bathrooms: 3 en suite,
1 private, 2 public

Parking for 5

◆◆◆

BLUE WISTERIA HOUSE
Church Lane, Helpston,
Peterborough, PE6 7DT
T: (01733) 252272

Bedrooms: 1 double,
2 twin
Bathrooms: 2 en suite,
1 private

Parking for 6

B&B per night:
S £25.00–£30.00
D £44.00–£44.00

OPEN All year round

*Old Listed cottage in pretty village , next to village pub with good food. Popular with
ramblers and cycling clubs.*

◆◆◆◆

HAWTHORN HOUSE
89 Thorpe Road, Peterborough,
PE3 6JQ
T: (01733) 340608 & 313470
F: (01733) 763800

Bedrooms: 3 single,
3 double, 2 twin
Bathrooms: 8 en suite

Parking for 5
CC: Amex, Barclaycard,
Delta, Diners, Mastercard,
Solo, Switch, Visa

B&B per night:
S £32.50–£40.00
D £52.00–£60.00

OPEN All year round

*City centre establishment. High standard of accommodation and service. All rooms are
tastefully furnished. En suite, TV and tea-making facilities.*

POTTER HEIGHAM, Norfolk Map ref 3C1

◆◆◆

FALGATE INN
Main Road, Potter Heigham,
Great Yarmouth, NR29 5HZ
T: (01692) 670003 & 07899 847262
E: cypress@euphony.net

Bedrooms: 1 single,
1 double, 2 twin, 1 triple
Bathrooms: 2 en suite,
1 public

Lunch available
EM 1900 (LO 2130)
Parking for 20
CC: Barclaycard, Delta,
JCB, Mastercard, Solo,
Switch, Visa

B&B per night:
S £17.00–£40.00
D £34.00–£42.00

OPEN All year round

*Bed and breakfast, with restaurant, bar snacks and beer garden. Open 7 days a week, full
on-licence.*

ROYSTON, Hertfordshire Map ref 2D1

◆◆◆◆ **HALL FARM**
Great Chishill, Royston, SG8 8SH
T: (01763) 838263
F: (01763) 838263
E: wisehall@farming.co.uk

Bedrooms: 2 double,
1 twin
Bathrooms: 1 en suite,
1 public

EM 1800 (LO 1930)
Parking for 8

B&B per night:
S £25.00–£30.00
D £40.00–£50.00

OPEN All year round

805-acre arable farm. Beautiful farmhouse accommodation on working farm, in secluded gardens on the highest point in Cambridgeshire. Royston 5 miles, Duxford Museum 4 miles, Cambridge 11 miles.

🐎 🖳 🖵 🕯 ⬚ 🛈 🖺 ✂ 🎨 🛍 🐾 ♻ ⛎ ⁑ 🚲 🏠 T ◉

SAFFRON WALDEN, Essex Map ref 2D1 *Tourist Information Centre Tel: (01799) 510444*

◆◆◆

THE PLOUGH INN AT RADWINTER
Sampford Road, Radwinter,
Saffron Walden, CB10 2TL
T: (01799) 599222 & 599161
F: (01799) 599161

B&B per night:
D £50.00–£75.00

HB per person:
DY £30.00–£50.00

OPEN All year round

Old travellers' inn with lovely gardens and views. Accommodation is in thatched cottages in grounds. Pub serves lunch and dinner daily and has a good selection of real ales and wines. Log fires in winter – al fresco dining on patio covered with clematis in summer. Five miles east of Saffron Walden.

Bedrooms: 1 double,
1 twin
Bathrooms: 2 en suite

Lunch available
EM 1900 (LO 2130)
Parking for 41
CC: Barclaycard, Delta,
Mastercard, Solo, Switch,
Visa, Visa Electron

🐎 ⛺ 🖳 🖵 🕯 ⬚ 🛈 ✂ 🐾 ⛎ 🍴 ♻ ⁑ 🚲 🏠 T

◆◆◆◆

ROWLEY HILL LODGE
Little Walden, Saffron Walden, CB10 1UZ
T: (01799) 525975
F: (01799) 516622
E: eh@clara.net

B&B per night:
S £24.00–£24.00
D £48.00–£48.00

OPEN All year round

Built originally in 1830, the house has a large secluded garden (with Dovecote) only minutes from the delightful old town of Saffron Walden – half an hour from Cambridge, Duxford Aircraft Museum and Stansted Airport. Each bedroom has a full-sized en suite bathroom with bath and powerful shower, colour TV and tea/coffee tray.

Bedrooms: 1 double,
1 twin
Bathrooms: 2 en suite

Parking for 4

🐎 🖳 🖵 🕯 ⬚ 🆄 🛈 TV 🐾 ⁑ 🍴 🚲 T

AT-A-GLANCE SYMBOLS
Symbols at the end of each accommodation entry give useful information about services and facilities. A key to symbols can be found inside the back cover flap. Keep this open for easy reference.

◆◆◆◆◆
Silver
Award

HIGHFIELD FARM

Great North Road, Sandy, SG19 2AQ
T: (01767) 682332
F: (01767) 692503

B&B per night:
S £28.00–£35.00
D £45.00–£55.00

OPEN All year round

Beautifully peaceful, welcoming farmhouse in own grounds on attractive arable farm. Wonderful location well back from A1. Bedford, Cambridge, Biggleswade, St Neots Hitchin and Stevenage all within easy reach. London just 50 minutes by train. Delightful sitting-room for guests' use. Hospitality tray in each bedroom. Safe parking. Most guest return.

Bedrooms: 2 double, 4 twin, 1 triple, 1 family room
Bathrooms: 6 en suite, 1 private, 1 public

Parking for 14
CC: Barclaycard, Delta, Eurocard, Mastercard, Solo, Switch, Visa

◆◆◆◆
KILN FARM
Kiln Lane, Benhall, Saxmundham, IP17 1HA
T: (01728) 603 166

Bedrooms: 1 single, 2 twin
Bathrooms: 2 public

Parking for 7
CC: Mastercard, Solo, Switch, Visa, Visa Electron

B&B per night:
S £25.00–£35.00
D £40.00–£50.00

OPEN All year round

Attractive Victorian farmhouse with mature enclosed garden. Three comfortable rooms. Secluded position but near Snape, Aldeburgh, Saxmundham and Minsmere.

◆◆◆
LIME TREE HOUSE B&B
Benhall Green, Saxmundham, IP17 1HU
T: (01728) 602149 (Answerphone)

Bedrooms: 1 double, 1 twin
Bathrooms: 1 public

Parking for 8

B&B per night:
S £15.00–£20.00
D £30.00–£40.00

OPEN Jan–Oct

Old village house behind ivy-covered walls. Large, airy rooms overlooking beautiful gardens in which to wander. Private parking. Good breakfasts. A warm welcome.

◆◆◆◆◆
Silver
Award

NORTH LODGE

6 North Entrance, Saxmundham, IP17 1AY
T: (01728) 603337
E: northlodgetoto@aol.com

B&B per night:
S £35.00–£45.00
D £50.00–£75.00

HB per person:
DY £37.50–£60.00

OPEN All year round

Explore Suffolk and its Heritage Coast from our beautifully renovated Grade II Listed guesthouse. Relax in our library. Unwind with a drink in our resident's lounge with its grand piano and open fire. Amble in our walled garden. Enjoy the delights of good home cooking from our kitchen.

Bedrooms: 3 double, 2 twin, 1 family room
Bathrooms: 6 en suite, 1 public

Lunch available
EM 1900 (LO 2030)
Parking for 9
CC: Barclaycard, Delta, JCB, Mastercard, Solo, Switch, Visa, Visa Electron

◆◆◆◆
SUN COTTAGE
Snape Road, Knodishall, Saxmundham, IP17 1UT
T: (01728) 833892
F: (01728) 833892
E: suncottage@supanet.com

Bedrooms: 1 double, 1 twin
Bathrooms: 1 en suite, 1 private, 1 public

Parking for 3

B&B per night:
D £40.00–£44.00

OPEN Mar–Oct

Modernised and extended 19thC cottage adjoining village common. Convenient for Aldeburgh, Snape Maltings and Minsmere. Ideal location for walking, cycling and bird-watching. Two miles from Saxmundham.

SHERINGHAM, Norfolk Map ref 3B1

♦♦♦

THE BAY LEAF GUEST HOUSE

10 St Peters Road, Sheringham,
NR26 8QY
T: (01263) 823779
F: (01263) 820041

Bedrooms: 3 double,
2 twin, 2 triple
Bathrooms: 7 en suite

Parking for 4

B&B per night:
D £38.00–£48.00

OPEN All year round

Charming Victorian guesthouse with licensed bar, open all year. Conveniently situated in the town. Near golf-course and woodlands, adjacent to steam railway and 5 minutes from sea.

♦♦♦

CAMBERLEY GUESTHOUSE

62 Cliff Road, Sheringham,
NR26 8BJ
T: (01263) 823101
F: (01263) 821433

Bedrooms: 2 double,
2 twin
Bathrooms: 4 en suite,
1 public

Parking for 6

B&B per night:
S £21.00–£27.00
D £42.00–£54.00

OPEN All year round

In its own grounds, overlooking sea, town and surrounding countryside. Slipway to beach directly opposite. Family-run.

♦♦♦♦

OLIVEDALE GUESTHOUSE

20 Augusta Street, Sheringham, NR26 8LA
T: (01263) 825871 (Answerphone) &
0794 1027170 (Mobile)
F: (01263) 821104
E: info@olivedale.co.uk
I: www.olivedale.co.uk

B&B per night:
S £25.00–£30.00
D £48.00–£53.00

HB per person:
DY £40.00–£43.00

OPEN All year round

Charming Victorian house with a pretty garden. Peaceful yet only 3 minutes from town and sea. Attractive en suite bedrooms with all modern comforts. Excellent home-cooked evening meals September-May. Ideal for exploring North Norfolk's coastline and wildlife. Four Diamonds ensure high standards – we guarantee a warm welcome.

Bedrooms: 4 double,
1 twin
Bathrooms: 4 en suite,
1 private

EM 1930
Parking for 3

SIBLE HEDINGHAM, Essex Map ref 3B2

Rating
Applied For

TOCAT HOUSE

9 Potter Street, Sible Hedingham,
Halstead, CO9 3RG
T: (01787) 461942 (Call minder)

Bedrooms: 2 double,
1 twin
Bathrooms: 3 private

EM (LO 2000)
Parking for 3

B&B per night:
S £30.00–£30.00
D £50.00–£50.00

OPEN All year round

Victorian Grade II Listed building. Comfortable, elegant family home with 3 tastefully furnished bedrooms. Mature, spacious garden with stunning views.

SIBTON, Suffolk Map ref 3C2

♦♦♦♦
Silver
Award

CHURCH FARM

Yoxford Road, Sibton, Saxmundham,
IP17 2LX
T: (01728) 660101 (answerphone)
F: (01728) 660102
E: dixons@church-farmhouse.demon.co.uk

B&B per night:
S £25.00–£35.00
D £48.00–£56.00

OPEN All year round

A warm welcome is assured at our period country house set in grounds of 3.5 acres amidst beautiful Suffolk countryside. A convenient location for the Heritage Coast. Relax in your elegant, light and exceptionally well appointed bedroom and unwind in the deep sofas of the spacious and comfortable lounge.

Bedrooms: 2 double,
1 twin
Bathrooms: 2 en suite,
1 private

Parking for 6

SOUTH WALSHAM, Norfolk Map ref 3C1

◆◆◆ **OLD HALL FARM**
Newport Road, South Walsham,
Norwich, NR13 6DT
T: (01603) 270271 & 270017
F: (01603) 270017

Bedrooms: 1 single,
1 double, 1 twin
Bathrooms: 3 en suite

Parking for 4

B&B per night:
S £21.00–£25.00
D £42.00–£50.00

OPEN All year round

Recently restored 17thC thatched farmhouse. Comfortable rooms, all en suite. Wide range of cooked breakfasts. Ideal centre for Norwich coast and Norfolk Broads. Non-smoking.

SOUTHWOLD, Suffolk Map ref 3C2 *Tourist Information Centre Tel: (01502) 523007*

◆◆◆ **AMBER HOUSE**
24 North Parade, Southwold,
IP18 6LT
T: (01502) 723303
E: spring@amberhouse.fsnet.co.uk
I: www.southwold.blythweb.co.uk/
amber_house/index.htm

Bedrooms: 3 double,
1 twin, 1 triple
Bathrooms: 5 en suite

B&B per night:
S £35.00–£45.00
D £50.00–£60.00

HB per person:
DY £50.00–£60.00

OPEN All year round

Elegantly furnished Victorian house on seafront offering a homely atmosphere. All bedrooms en suite with TV and tea-making facilities. Walking distance from town centre and restaurants.

◆◆◆◆ **NORTHCLIFFE GUESTHOUSE**
20 North Parade, Southwold,
IP18 6LT
T: (01502) 724074 & 07702 588554
F: (01502) 722218
E: northcliffe@southwold5.ffnet.
co.uk
I: www.s-h-systems.co.uk/hotels/
northcli.html

Bedrooms: 2 single,
4 double, 1 twin
Bathrooms: 5 en suite,
1 public

EM 1900 (LO 1900)

B&B per night:
S £25.00–£45.00
D £45.00–£65.00

HB per person:
DY £35.00–£45.00

OPEN All year round

Select en suite accommodation. Individually designed rooms of a high standard. Panoramic sea views. Next to beach, close to town centre. Lounge with log fire. Evening meal. Licensed.

◆◆◆◆ **THE OLD VICARAGE**
Wenhaston, Halesworth, IP19 9EG
T: (01502) 478339
F: (01502) 478068
E: theycock@aol.com

Bedrooms: 2 double,
1 twin
Bathrooms: 1 private

Parking for 6

B&B per night:
S £30.00–£35.00
D £50.00–£60.00

OPEN All year round

Period village house in peaceful surroundings close to Suffolk Heritage Coast, 4 miles from Southwold. Antique furnishings, comfortable surroundings, warm welcome assured.

SPROWSTON, Norfolk Map ref 3C1

◆◆◆◆

DRIFTWOOD LODGE
102 Wroxham Road, Sprowston, Norwich,
NR7 8EX
T: (01603) 444908 (answerphone)
E: johnniekate@driftwood16.freeserve.
co.uk

B&B per night:
S £18.00–£22.00
D £36.00–£44.00

HB per person:
DY £26.00–£32.00

OPEN All year round

Mid-1930s detached house surrounded by landscaped garden. Near Norwich Cathedral, city centre, easy reach of Broads. Tastefully decorated, comfortable rooms, bathroom/WC opposite. Warm, friendly welcome, relaxing atmosphere. Comfort, cleanliness and good home cooking our priority. Full English breakfast. Ideal base for exploring this beautiful city and surroundings.

Bedrooms: 1 single,
2 double
Bathrooms: 1 public

Parking for 3

321

STOKE-BY-NAYLAND, Suffolk Map ref 3B2

◆◆◆◆
Silver
Award

THE ANGEL INN
Polstead Street, Stoke-by-Nayland,
Colchester, CO6 4SA
T: (01206) 263245
F: (01206) 263373
I: www.angelhotel.com

Bedrooms: 5 double,
1 twin
Bathrooms: 6 en suite

Lunch available
EM 1830 (LO 2100)
Parking for 25
CC: Amex, Barclaycard,
Delta, Diners, Maestro,
Mastercard, Switch, Visa,
Visa Electron

B&B per night:
S £49.00–£49.00
D £65.00–£65.00

OPEN All year round

*Beautifully restored freehouse and restaurant in the historic village of Stoke-by-Nayland,
in the heart of Constable Country.*

◆◆◆◆
Gold
Award

RYEGATE HOUSE
Stoke-by-Nayland, Colchester,
CO6 4RA
T: (01206) 263679
E: ryegate@lineone.net
I: www.w-h-systems.co.uk/hotels/
ryegate.html

Bedrooms: 2 double,
1 twin
Bathrooms: 3 en suite

Parking for 6

B&B per night:
S £30.00–£35.00
D £42.50–£50.00

OPEN All year round

*Comfortable friendly house in Suffolk village within Dedham Vale. On the B1068, 5.5 miles
from A12 and 2.5 miles from A134. All rooms en suite. Non-smoking.*

STRETHAM, Cambridgeshire Map ref 3A2

◆◆◆

THE RED LION
High Street, Stretham, Ely, CB6 3JQ
T: (01353) 648132
F: (01353) 648327

B&B per night:
S £32.75–£32.75
D £43.75–£43.75

HB per person:
DY £39.50–£42.00

OPEN All year round

*A village inn, completely refurbished,
with 12 en suite bedrooms, ideally
situated for visiting the Fens and
other tourist attactions. Four miles
from Ely on A10. Cambridge 12 miles,
Newmarket 14 miles away. Pets
welcome, car park. Non-smoking
conservatory restaurant.*

Bedrooms: 2 single,
5 double, 2 twin, 3 triple
Bathrooms: 12 en suite

Lunch available
EM 1900 (LO 2100)
Parking for 20
CC: Amex, Barclaycard,
Delta, Mastercard, Switch,
Visa

SUDBURY, Suffolk Map ref 3B2 *Tourist Information Centre Tel: (01787) 881320*

◆◆◆

WEST HOUSE
59 Ballingdon Street, Sudbury,
CO10 2DA
T: (01787) 375033

Bedrooms: 1 double,
1 twin
Bathrooms: 1 public

EM
Parking for 2

B&B per night:
S £15.00–£17.50
D £25.00–£27.50

*Comfortable accommodation in Listed Georgian house in historic part of Sudbury, close to
water meadows. 10 minutes' walk from town centre, bus/rail stations, theatre, leisure
centre.*

HB per person:
DY £17.50–£22.50

OPEN All year round

SWAFFHAM, Norfolk Map ref 3B1

◆◆◆◆

LODGE FARM
Castle Acre, King's Lynn, PE32 2BS
T: (01760) 755506
F: (01760) 755103
E: coghill@messages.co.uk

Bedrooms: 3 twin
Bathrooms: 1 en suite,
1 public

Parking for 7

B&B per night:
S £24.00–£28.00
D £50.00–£56.00

OPEN All year round

*Spacious country farmhouse with garden and paddocks, 1 mile north of historic Castle
Acre. Peddars Way, Sandringham, walking country nearby.*

RATING All accommodation in this guide has been rated, or is awaiting
a rating, by a trained English Tourism Council assessor.

TERRINGTON ST JOHN, Norfolk Map ref 3A1

◆◆◆◆

SOMERVILLE HOUSE
Church Road, Terrington St John, Wisbech,
Cambridgeshire PE14 7RY
T: (01945) 880952
F: (01945) 880952

B&B per night:
S £25.00–£30.00
D £47.50–£50.00

HB per person:
DY £36.50–£42.50

OPEN All year round

Country house dating back 300 years, set in 2 acres of mature grounds with many trees and a crinkle crankle wall. Spacious en suite bedrooms, fine dining restaurant, comfortable lounges. Ideal location for exploring the Fens and North Norfolk. Small, friendly family-run business. Restaurant and residential licence.

Bedrooms: 1 single,
1 double, 1 twin
Bathrooms: 2 en suite

Lunch available
EM 1900 (LO 2200)
Parking for 10
CC: Barclaycard, Delta,
Mastercard, Solo, Switch,
Visa

THAXTED, Essex Map ref 3B2

◆◆◆◆

CROSSWAYS GUESTHOUSE
32 Town Street, Thaxted, Dunmow,
CM6 2LA
T: (01371) 830348

Bedrooms: 1 double,
1 twin
Bathrooms: 2 en suite

B&B per night:
S £33.00–£36.00
D £50.00–£55.00

OPEN All year round

Elegant 16thC house with Georgian additions, situated on B184 in centre of Thaxted opposite the 600-year-old Guildhall.

WANSFORD, Cambridgeshire Map ref 3A1

◆◆◆◆

CEDAR HOUSE BED & BREAKFAST
Cedar House, Riverside Spinney, Wansford,
Peterborough, Cambridgeshire PE8 6LF
T: (01780) 783062 & 07909 527304
F: (01780) 783062
E: cedarhousebandb@aol.com

B&B per night:
S £30.00–£38.00
D £45.00–£50.00

OPEN All year round

Conveniently close to Stamford, Peterborough and Oundle, situated on the banks of the River Nene. 2-3 minutes' walk from excellent pubs/ restaurants in Wansford village. Many local attractions close by and picturesque walks along the Nene Way. Seasonal private coarse fishing available. Business centre facilities available upon request.

Bedrooms: 1 single,
2 double
Bathrooms: 1 en suite,
1 public

Parking for 4

QUALITY ASSURANCE SCHEME

For an explanation of the quality and facilities represented by the Diamonds please refer to the front of this guide. A more detailed explanation can be found in the information pages at the back.

WINGFIELD, Suffolk Map ref 3C2

◆◆◆◆

GABLES FARM

Earsham Street, Wingfield, Diss, Norfolk
IP21 5RH
T: (01379) 586355 &
07808 448272 (Mobile)
F: (01379) 586355
E: sue.harvey@lineone.net
I: www.gablesfarm.co.uk

B&B per night:
S £22.00–£25.00
D £42.00–£45.00

OPEN All year round

*Gables Farm is a 16thC heavily
timbered farmhouse set in moated
gardens. The 3 en suite bedrooms
have colour TV, hairdryer, radio
alarm and hospitality tray. Wingfield
is a quiet village on the Suffolk/
Norfolk border ideally situated for
exploring East Anglia. Leaflet
available on request.*

Bedrooms: 2 double,
1 twin
Bathrooms: 2 en suite,
1 public

EM 1930 (LO 2030)
Parking for 6

WITHAM, Essex Map ref 3B3

◆◆◆◆

CHESTNUTS

8 Octavia Drive, Witham Lodge,
Witham, CM8 1HQ
T: (01376) 515990 & 07885 456803
F: (01376) 515990

Bedrooms: 1 single,
1 double, 1 twin
Bathrooms: 1 public

EM 1830 (LO 2000)
Parking for 6

B&B per night:
S Max £25.00
D Max £40.00

HB per person:
DY Max £32.00

OPEN All year round

*Spacious, detached, modern house with pretty gardens, in peaceful setting facing
greensward. Reached by small private road. Sports centre and golf course nearby. Healthy
home cooking.*

WOODBRIDGE, Suffolk Map ref 3C2 *Tourist Information Centre Tel: (01394) 382240*

◆◆◆

GROVE HOUSE

39 Grove Road, Woodbridge, IP12 4LG
T: (01394) 382202
F: (01394) 380652
E: grovehotel@btinternet.com
I: www.grovehousehotel.com

B&B per night:
S £37.50–£39.00
D £55.00–£58.00

HB per person:
DY £42.50–£54.00

OPEN All year round

*Comfortable, private hotel, recently
renovated and extended. Half mile
from market square. Superb
breakfast menu and choice of
evening meals. Bedrooms all with en
suite facilities and hairdryer, colour
TV, welcome tray, radio-alarm. Fully
adapted room suitable for
wheelchair users. Ideal area for
bird-watching, walking, golf and
painting.*

Bedrooms: 5 single,
4 double, 3 twin,
1 family room
Bathrooms: 10 en suite,
1 public

EM 1900 (LO 1945)
Parking for 14
CC: Barclaycard, Delta,
Mastercard, Solo, Switch,
Visa, Visa Electron

◆◆◆◆

LARK COTTAGE

Shingle Street, Woodbridge,
IP12 3BE
T: (01394) 411292

Bedrooms: 1 single,
1 double; suite available
Bathrooms: 1 private,
2 public

Lunch available
EM 1800 (LO 1930)
Parking for 5

B&B per night:
S Min £18.00
D Min £40.00

HB per person:
DY Min £30.00

OPEN Apr–Dec

*Beachside shingle bungalow with extended guest accommodation. Country setting, very
quiet. Good wildlife and plants. Village with shops 2.5 miles, Woodbridge 9 miles, Snape 14
miles.*

CHECK THE MAPS

The colour maps at the front of this guide show all the cities, towns
and villages for which you will find accommodation entries.
Refer to the town index to find the page on which they are listed.

WOOLPIT, Suffolk Map ref 3B2

♦♦♦ **THE BULL INN & RESTAURANT**
The Street, Woolpit,
Bury St Edmunds, IP30 9SA
T: (01359) 240393
E: trevor@howling.fsbusiness.co.uk

Bedrooms: 1 single,
2 double, 1 triple
Bathrooms: 4 en suite

Lunch available
EM 1800 (LO 2130)
Parking for 50
CC: Amex, Barclaycard,
Delta, JCB, Maestro,
Mastercard, Solo, Switch,
Visa, Visa Electron

B&B per night:
S £23.00–£26.00
D £42.00–£42.00

HB per person:
DY Min £28.00

OPEN All year round

Public house and restaurant offering good accommodation in centre of pretty village. Large garden, ample parking. Ideal base for touring Suffolk.

WORLINGTON, Suffolk Map ref 3B2

♦♦♦♦ **WORLINGTON HALL COUNTRY HOUSE HOTEL**
The Street, Worlington,
Bury St Edmunds, IP28 8RX
T: (01638) 712237
F: (01638) 712631

Bedrooms: 5 double,
3 twin, 1 triple
Bathrooms: 9 en suite

Lunch available
EM 1900 (LO 2145)
Parking for 150
CC: Amex, Barclaycard,
Delta, Diners, Mastercard,
Switch, Visa

B&B per night:
S Min £50.00
D £65.00–£90.00

HB per person:
DY Min £65.00

OPEN All year round

Grade II Listed former hall, dating back in parts to the 16thC. In 5 acres with frontage to the River Lark. Providing a full service and also a friendly "local".

WROXHAM, Norfolk Map ref 3C1

♦♦♦♦ **MANOR BARN HOUSE**
Back Lane, Rackheath, Norwich,
NR13 6NN
T: (01603) 783543

Bedrooms: 3 double,
2 twin
Bathrooms: 4 en suite,
1 private

Parking for 8

B&B per night:
S £21.00–£29.00
D £42.00–£48.00

OPEN All year round

Traditional Norfolk barn conversion with exposed beams, in quiet setting with pleasant gardens. Just off the A1151, 2 miles from Wroxham.

♦♦♦♦ **RIDGE HOUSE**
7 The Avenue, Wroxham, Norwich,
NR12 8TN
T: (01603) 782130

Bedrooms: 2 double
Bathrooms: 1 public

Parking for 2

B&B per night:
S £21.00–£21.00
D £36.00–£36.00

OPEN All year round

New house in quiet cul-de-sac. Walking distance to shops, restaurants. No children under 15 or pets. Private parking.

♦♦♦♦ **WROXHAM PARK LODGE**
142 Norwich Road, Wroxham,
Norwich, NR12 8SA
T: (01603) 782991

Bedrooms: 2 double,
1 twin
Bathrooms: 3 en suite

Parking for 6

B&B per night:
S £20.00–£27.00
D £40.00–£46.00

OPEN All year round

Warm welcome in comfortable Victorian house. All rooms en suite. In Broads capital of Wroxham, central for touring all Broads and North Norfolk amenities. Private parking.

WYMONDHAM, Norfolk Map ref 3B1

♦♦♦♦ **WITCH HAZEL**
Church Lane, Wicklewood,
Wymondham, NR18 9QH
T: (01953) 602247 & 0771 391
1853 (Mobile)
F: (01953) 602247

Bedrooms: 3 double;
suites available
Bathrooms: 3 en suite

EM 1900 (LO 2000)
Parking for 3

B&B per night:
S Max £26.00
D Max £42.00

HB per person:
DY Max £31.00

OPEN All year round

Spacious, detached house in quiet village. Large private garden and warm welcome. Well-appointed en suite bedrooms. Evening meals by arrangement. Children 15 and over welcome.

QUALITY ASSURANCE SCHEME

Diamond ratings and awards were correct at the time of going to press but are subject to change. Please check at the time of booking.

EAST OF ENGLAND

A brief guide to the main Towns and Villages offering accommodation in the EAST OF ENGLAND

A **ALDBOROUGH, NORFOLK** - Aldborough is a picturesque village with a large green and winner of Best Kept Village 1999. Situated on the "Weaver's Way". The location is ideal for visiting local National Trust properties, Norfolk Broads and the North Norfolk coastal area.

● **ALDHAM, ESSEX** - Small village in the Colne Valley convenient for Colchester.

B **BECCLES, SUFFOLK** - Fire destroyed the town in the 16th C and it was rebuilt in Georgian red brick. The River Waveney, on which the town stands, is popular with boating enthusiasts and has an annual regatta. Home of Beccles and District Museum.

● **BEETLEY, NORFOLK** - Rural village close to Dereham with its picturesque pargeted cottages.

● **BISHOP'S STORTFORD, HERTFORDSHIRE** Fine old town on the River Stort with many interesting buildings, particularly Victorian, and an imposing parish church. The vicarage where Cecil Rhodes was born is now a museum.

● **BRAINTREE, ESSEX** - The Heritage Centre in the Town Hall describes Braintree's former international importance in wool, silk and engineering. St Michael's parish church includes some Roman bricks. Braintree market was first chartered in 1199.

● **BRANDON, SUFFOLK** - Set on the edge of Thetford Forest in an area known as Breckland. Old stone 5-arched bridge links Suffolk with Norfolk. 3 miles north-east is Grime's Graves, the largest prehistoric flint mine in Europe.

● **BRENTWOOD, ESSEX** - The town grew up in the late 12th C and then developed as a staging post, being strategically placed close to the London to Chelmsford road. Deer roam by the lakes in the 428-acre park at South Weald, part of Brentwood's attractive Green Belt.

● **BULPHAN, ESSEX** - Small village, convenient for Brentwood, Basildon and Thurrock.

● **BUNGAY, SUFFOLK** - Market town and yachting centre on the River Waveney with the remains of a great 12th C castle. In the market-place stands the Butter Cross, rebuilt in 1689 after being largely destroyed by fire. Nearby at Earsham the Otter Trust.

● **BUNTINGFORD, HERTFORDSHIRE** - Situated on the River Rib, with parts of the Roman Ermine Street forming its High Street. Its famous clock tower is over 500 years old. Also of interest are the 17th C almshouses founded in 1684 by Bishop Seth Ward, a friend of Sir Christopher Wren.

● **BURY ST EDMUNDS, SUFFOLK** - Ancient market and cathedral town which takes its name from the martyred Saxon King, St Edmund. Bury St Edmunds has many fine buildings including the Athenaeum and Moyses Hall, reputed to be the oldest Norman house in the county.

C **CAMBRIDGE, CAMBRIDGESHIRE** - A most important and beautiful city on the River Cam with 31 colleges forming one of the oldest universities in the world. Numerous museums, good shopping centre, restaurants, theatres, cinema and fine bookshops.

● **CHELMSFORD, ESSEX** - The county town of Essex, originally a Roman settlement, Caesaromagus, thought to have been destroyed by Boudicca. Growth of the town's industry can be traced in the excellent museum in Oaklands Park. 15th C parish church has been Chelmsford Cathedral since 1914.

● **CLACTON-ON-SEA, ESSEX** - Developed in the 1870s into a popular holiday resort with pier, pavilion, funfair, theatres and traditional amusements. The Martello Towers on the seafront were built like many others in the early 19th C to defend Britain against Napoleon.

● **COLCHESTER, ESSEX** - Britain's oldest recorded town standing on the River Colne and famous for its oysters. Numerous historic buildings, ancient remains and museums. Plenty of parks and gardens, extensive shopping centre, theatre and zoo.

● **COLTISHALL, NORFOLK** - On the River Bure, with an RAF station nearby. The village is attractive with many pleasant 18th C brick houses and a thatched church.

● **CROMER, NORFOLK** - Once a small fishing village and now famous for its fishing boats that still work off the beach and offer freshly caught crabs. Excellent bathing on sandy beaches fringed by cliffs. The town boasts a fine pier, theatre, museum and a lifeboat station.

D **DANBURY, ESSEX** - Essex village set on a hill, 14th C church containing interesting oak effigies of Knights.

● **DARSHAM. SUFFOLK** - Well placed for touring North Suffolk and the coast. The nearby Otter Trust is fascinating to visit.

● **DEBDEN GREEN, ESSEX** - Small village set close to the pretty Essex town of Thaxted where the fine 16th C timbered Guildhall is a notable sight.

● **DEDHAM, ESSEX** - A former wool town. Dedham Vale is an Area of Outstanding Natural Beauty and there is a countryside centre in the village. This is John Constable country and Sir Alfred Munnings lived at Castle House which is open to the public.

● **DERSINGHAM, NORFOLK** - Large parish church, mostly of Perpendicular period, with 14th C font and Elizabethan barn dated 1672.

● **DISS, NORFOLK** - Old market town built around 3 sides of the Mere, a 6-acre stretch of water. Although modernised, some interesting Tudor, Georgian and Victorian buildings around the market-place remain. St Mary's church has a fine knapped flint chancel.

E **EARL SOHAM, SUFFOLK** - A good base for visiting Bury St Edmunds, Ipswich and the east of Suffolk. The church of St Mary is notable for its hammerbeam nave roof decorated with angels and its 17th C pulpit with hour-glasses.

● **EARLS COLNE, ESSEX** - In the Colne Valley. Large village with a fine 14th C church and some old houses with interesting pargeting.

● **ELMSWELL, SUFFOLK** - Close to Bury St Edmunds and a bird garden. The church of St John has a carved font and a monument to Sir Robert Gardener, Chief Justice of Ireland.

● **ELY, CAMBRIDGESHIRE** - Until the 17th C, when the Fens were drained, Ely was an island. The cathedral, completed in 1189, dominates the surrounding area. One particular feature is the central octagonal tower with a fan-vaulted timber roof and wooden lantern.

F **FAKENHAM, NORFOLK** - Attractive, small market town dates from Saxon times and was a Royal Manor until the 17th C. Its market place has 2 old coaching inns, both showing traces of earlier work behind Georgian facades, and the parish church has a commanding 15th C tower.

● **FELIXSTOWE, SUFFOLK** - Seaside resort that developed at the end of the 19th C. Lying in a gently curving bay with a 2-mile-long beach and backed by a wide promenade of lawns and floral gardens.

● **FRAMLINGHAM, SUFFOLK** - Pleasant old market town with an interesting church, impressive castle and some attractive houses round Market Hill. The town's history can be traced at the Lanman Museum.

G **GREAT DUNMOW, ESSEX** - On the main Roman road from Bishop's Stortford to Braintree. Doctor's Pond near the square was where the first lifeboat was tested in 1785. Home of the Dunmow Flitch trials held every 4 years on Whit Monday.

- **SAXMUNDHAM, SUFFOLK** - The church of St John the Baptist has a hammer-beam roof and contains a number of good monuments.

- **SHERINGHAM, NORFOLK** - Holiday resort with Victorian and Edwardian hotels and a sand and shingle beach where the fishing boats are hauled up. The North Norfolk Railway operates from Sheringham station during the summer. Other attractions include museums, theatre and Splash Fun Pool.

- **SOUTH WALSHAM, NORFOLK** - Village famous for having 2 churches in adjoining churchyards. South Walsham Broad consists of an inner and outer section, the former being private. Alongside, the Fairhaven Garden Trust has woodland and water-gardens open to the public.

- **SOUTHWOLD, SUFFOLK** - Pleasant and attractive seaside town with a triangular market square and spacious greens around which stand flint, brick and colour-washed cottages. The parish church of St Edmund is one of the greatest churches in Suffolk.

- **STOKE-BY-NAYLAND, SUFFOLK** - Picturesque village with a fine group of half-timbered cottages near the church of St Mary, the tower of which was one of Constable's favourite subjects. In School Street are the Guildhall and the Maltings, both 16th C timber-framed buildings.

- **STRETHAM, CAMBRIDGESHIRE** - On the edge of the Fens, Stretham is noted for its 20 ft high village cross from around 1400.

- **SUDBURY, SUFFOLK** - Former important cloth and market town on the River Stour. Birthplace of Thomas Gainsborough whose home is now an art gallery and museum. The Corn Exchange is an excellent example of early Victorian civic building.

- **SWAFFHAM, NORFOLK** - Busy market town with a triangular market place, a domed rotunda built in 1783 and a number of Georgian houses. The 15th C church possesses a large library of ancient books.

- **T THAXTED, ESSEX** - Small town rich in outstanding buildings and dominated by its hilltop medieval church. The magnificent Guildhall was built by the Cutlers' Guild in the late 14th C. A windmill built in 1804 has been restored and houses a rural museum.

- **W WANSFORD, CAMBRIDGESHIRE** - A terminus of the Nene Valley Railway with British and continental steam locomotives and rolling-stock.

- **WINGFIELD, SUFFOLK** - In rural Suffolk. Boasts a mainly Tudor castle, but with a 14th C south front, and Wingfield College, founded in 1361 and surrendered to Henry VIII at the Dissolution.

- **WITHAM, ESSEX** - Delightful town whose history goes back to the time of King Alfred. The High Street contains 16th C houses and the Spread Eagle, a famous Essex inn. The 14th C church is near the site of an ancient defensive mound.

- **WOODBRIDGE, SUFFOLK** - Once a busy seaport, the town is now a sailing centre on the River Deben. There are many buildings of architectural merit including the Bell and Angel Inns. The 18th C Tide Mill is now restored and open to the public.

- **WOOLPIT, SUFFOLK** - Village with a number of attractive timber-framed Tudor and Georgian houses. St Mary's Church is one of the most beautiful churches in Suffolk and has a fine porch. The brass eagle lectern is said to have been donated by Elizabeth I.

- **WORLINGTON, SUFFOLK** - Breckland village, within easy distance of Cromwell Country and West Stow Anglo-Saxon village. Close to Isleham Priory Church (English Heritage).

- **WROXHAM, NORFOLK** - Yachting centre on the River Bure which houses the headquarters of the Norfolk Broads Yacht Club. The church of St Mary has a famous doorway and the manor house nearby dates back to 1623.

- **WYMONDHAM, NORFOLK** - Thriving historic market town of charm and architectural interest. The octagonal market cross, 12th C abbey and 15th C Green Dragon inn blend with streetscapes spanning three centuries. An excellent touring base.

- **GREAT YARMOUTH, NORFOLK** - One of Britain's major seaside resorts with 5 miles of seafront and every possible amenity including an award winning leisure complex offering a huge variety of all-weather facilities. Busy harbour and fishing centre.

- **H HALESWORTH, SUFFOLK** - Small market town which grew firstly with navigation on the Blyth in the 18th C and then with the coming of the railways in the 19th C. Opposite the church in a beautiful 14th C building is the Halesworth Gallery.

- **HALSTEAD, ESSEX** - Situated close to the Roman city of Colchester and Braintree, Halstead is notable for the Blue Bridge House. A Queen Anne facade was built over the existing Tudor house between 1700 and 1712 and it contains collections of 17th C European furniture.

- **HARLESTON, NORFOLK** - Attractive small town on the River Waveney with 2 market-places and a museum. Candler's House is an outstanding example of an early Georgian town house. At Starston, 1 mile away, is a restored wind-pump.

- **HARPENDEN, HERTFORDSHIRE** -Delightful country town with many scenic walks through surrounding woods and fields. Harpenden train station provides a fast service into London.

- **HARWICH, ESSEX** - Port where the Rivers Orwell and Stour converge and enter the North Sea. The old town still has a medieval atmosphere with its narrow streets. To the south is the seaside resort of Dovercourt with long sandy beaches.

- **HAUGHLEY, SUFFOLK** - In the heart of Suffolk, very well placed for touring.

- **HELPSTON, CAMBRIDGESHIRE** - Situated very close to Peterborough and a good place for touring the Fens. There is a memorial to the poet John Clare standing on the cross roads in the village.

- **HETHERSETT, NORFOLK** - Conveniently located for Norwich.

- **HEVINGHAM, NORFOLK** - Located with easy access to Norwich, North Norfolk Coast, Broads and Blickling Hall.

- **HINTLESHAM, SUFFOLK** - Close to the county town of Ipswich. Hintlesham Hall is a fine example of a mid-Tudor mansion with additions in Queen Anne style made in 1842. Now a restaurant.

- **HITCHIN, HERTFORDSHIRE** - Once a flourishing wool town. Full of interest, with many old buildings around the market square. These include the 17th C almshouses, old inns and the Victorian Corn Exchange.

- **HOLT, NORFOLK** - Much of the town centre was destroyed by fire in 1708 but has since been restored. The famous Gresham's School founded by Sir Thomas Gresham is sited here.

- **HUNSTANTON, NORFOLK** - Seaside resort which faces the Wash. The shingle and sand beach is backed by striped cliffs and many unusual fossils can be found here. The town is predominantly Victorian. The Oasis family leisure centre has indoor and outdoor pools.

- **HUNTINGDON, CAMBRIDGESHIRE** - Attractive, interesting town which abounds in associations with the Cromwell family. The town is connected to Godmanchester by a beautiful 14th C bridge over the River Great Ouse.

- **K KELVEDON, ESSEX** - Village on the old Roman road from Colchester to London. Many of the buildings are 18th C but there is much of earlier date. The famous preacher Charles Spurgeon was born here in 1834.

- **KERSEY, SUFFOLK** - A most picturesque village, which was famous for cloth-making, set in a valley with a water-splash. The church of St Mary is an impressive building at the top of the hill.

- **KING'S LYNN, NORFOLK** - A busy town with many outstanding buildings. The Guildhall and Town Hall are both built of flint in a striking chequer design. Behind the Guildhall in the Old Gaol House the sounds and smells of prison life 2 centuries ago are recreated.

- **KINGS LANGLEY, HERTFORDSHIRE** - Between Hemel Hempstead and Watford. The Church of All Saints has parts which date from the 13th C.

- **L LAVENHAM, SUFFOLK** - A former prosperous wool town of timber-framed buildings with the cathedral-like church and its tall tower. The market-place is 13th C and the Guildhall now houses a museum.

- **LEIGH-ON-SEA, ESSEX** - A holiday resort at the mouth of the River Thames, close to Southend-on-Sea.

- **LEISTON, SUFFOLK** - Centrally placed for visiting the Suffolk Heritage Coast, Leiston is a bustling, working town in a rural setting famous for Leiston Abbey and the award winning Long Shop Museum.

- **LITTLE WALSINGHAM, NORFOLK** - Little Walsingham is larger than its neighbour Great Walsingham and more important because of its long history as a religious shrine to which many pilgrimages were made. The village has many picturesque buildings of the 16th C and later.

- **LONG MELFORD, SUFFOLK** - One of Suffolk's loveliest villages, remarkable for the length of its main street. Holy Trinity Church is considered to be the finest village church in England. The National Trust own the Eizabethan Melford Hall and nearby Kentwell Hall is also open to the public.

- **LOWESTOFT, SUFFOLK** - Seaside town with wide sandy beaches. Important fishing port with picturesque fishing quarter. Home of the famous Lowestoft porcelain and birthplace of Benjamin Britten. East Point Pavilion's exhibition describes the Lowestoft story.

- **LUTON, BEDFORDSHIRE** - Bedfordshire's largest town with its own airport, several industries and an excellent shopping centre. The town's history is depicted in the museum and art gallery in Wardown Park. Luton Hoo has a magnificent collection of treasures.

- **M MARGARET RODING, ESSEX** - One of the six Rodings, a group of old villages clustered in the rural Roding Valley. The church features some fine Norman work.

- **N NORWICH, NORFOLK** - Beautiful cathedral city and county town on the River Wensum with many fine museums and medieval churches. Norman castle, Guildhall and interesting medieval streets. Good shopping centre and market.

- **P PETERBOROUGH, CAMBRIDGESHIRE** - Prosperous and rapidly expanding cathedral city on the edge of the Fens on the River Nene. Catherine of Aragon is buried in the cathedral. City Museum and Art Gallery. Ferry Meadows Country Park has numerous leisure facilities.

- **POTTER HEIGHAM, NORFOLK** - On the River Thurne, the village is one of the most popular of the Broadland centres and is well known for its 13th C bridge and boatyard. The thatched church has a rare octagonal font made of brick.

- **R ROYSTON, HERTFORDSHIRE** - Old town lying at the crossing of the Roman road Ermine Street and the Icknield Way. It has many interesting old houses and inns.

- **S SAFFRON WALDEN, ESSEX** - Takes its name from the saffron crocus once grown around the town. The church of St Mary has superb carvings, magnificent roofs and brasses. A town maze can be seen on the common. Two miles south-west is Audley End, a magnificent Jacobean mansion owned by English Heritage.

- **SANDY, BEDFORDSHIRE** - Small town on the River Ivel on the site of a Roman settlement. Sandy is mentioned in Domesday.

MAP REFERENCES
The map references refer to the colour maps at the front of this guide. The first figure is the map number; the letter and figure which follow indicate the grid reference on the map.

SOUTH WEST

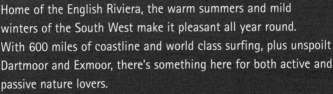

Home of the English Riviera, the warm summers and mild winters of the South West make it pleasant all year round. With 600 miles of coastline and world class surfing, plus unspoilt Dartmoor and Exmoor, there's something here for both active and passive nature lovers.

Step back 2000 year's in Bath's Roman Baths. Other great cities include Bristol, Plymouth and Wells. Clovelly, with its cobbled, car-free streets, and the little fishing village of Mousehole (which really is the cat's whiskers!) are just two of the many quaint places to visit.

The two-week Bath International Music Festival is on from mid May with something for everyone — from contemporary to classical, including jazz and more.

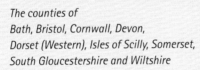

The counties of
Bath, Bristol, Cornwall, Devon,
Dorset (Western), Isles of Scilly, Somerset,
South Gloucestershire and Wiltshire

FOR MORE INFORMATION CONTACT:
South West Tourism
Admail 3186, Exeter EX2 7WH
Tel: (0870) 442 0880
Fax: (0870) 442 0881
Email: info@westcountryholidays.com
Internet: www.westcountryholidays.com

The Pictures:
1   Isles of Scilly;
2   Fingle Bridge, Dartmoor, Devon;
3   Cotehele, Cornwall.

Where to Go in the South West - see pages 330-334
Where to Stay in the South West - see pages 335-407

Whilst in the
SOUTH WEST ...

You will find hundreds of interesting places to visit during your stay, just some of which are listed in these pages.

Contact any Tourist Information Centre in the region for more ideas on days out in the South West.

At Bristol Harbourside

Bristol BS1 5DB

A new international, waterfront, leisure, education and entertainment complex. Including two visitor attractions – Wildscreen@Bristol, featuring wildlife and the environment, and Explore@Bristol, focusing on science and technology.

Atwell-Wilson Motor Museum Trust

Calne, Wiltshire SN11 0NF
Tel: (01249) 813119

Motor museum with vintage, post-vintage and classic cars, including American models. Classic motorbikes. A 17thC water meadow walk and play area.

Babbacombe Model Village

Babbacombe, Devon TQ1 3LA
Tel: (01803) 315315

Over 400 models many with sound and animation in four acres of award-winning gardens. See modern towns, villages and rural areas. Stunning illuminations.

Bristol City Museum & Art Gallery

Queen's Road, Bristol BS8 1RL
Tel: (0117) 922 3571

Collection representing applied, oriental and fine art, archaeology, geology, natural history, ethnography and Egyptology.

Bristol Zoo Gardens

Clifton, Bristol BS8 3HA
Tel: (0117) 973 8951

Enjoy an exciting real life experience and see over 300 species of wildlife in beautiful gardens.

Buckland Abbey

Yelverton, Devon PL20 6EY
Tel: (01822) 853607

Originally a Cistercian monastery, then home of Sir Francis Drake. Ancient buildings, exhibitions, herb garden, craft workshops and estate walks.

Cheddar Caves and Gorge

Cheddar, Somerset BS27 3QF
Tel: (01934) 742343

Beautiful caves located in Cheddar Gorge. Gough's Cave with cathedral-like caverns and Cox's Cave with stalagmites and stalactites. Also 'The Crystal Quest' fantasy adventure.

The Combe Martin Motor Cycle Collection

Combe Martin, Ilfracombe, Devon EX34 0DH
Tel: (01271) 882346

Collection of British motorcycles displayed against a background of old petrol pumps, signs and garage equipment. Motoring nostalgia in an old world atmosphere.

Combe Martin Wildlife and Dinosaur Park

Combe Martin, Ilfracombe, Devon EX34 0NG
Tel: (01271) 882486

Wildlife park and life-size models of dinosaurs.

Crealy Park

Clyst St Mary, Exeter, Devon EX5 1DR
Tel: (01395) 233200
One of Devon's largest animal farms. Milk a cow, feed a lamb and pick up a piglet. Adventure playgrounds. Dragonfly Lake and farm trails.

Dairyland Farm World

Tresillian, Barton, Newquay, Cornwall TR8 5AA
Tel: (01872) 510246
One hundred and seventy cows milked in a rotary parlour. Heritage centre. Farm nature trail. Farm park with animals, pets and wildfowl. Daily events.

Exmoor Falconry & Animal Farm

West Lynch Farm, Allerford, Somerset TA24 8HJ
Tel: (01643) 862816
Farm animals, rare breeds, pets' corner, birds of prey and owls. Flying displays daily. Historic farm buildings.

Flambards Village

Culdrose Manor, Helston, Cornwall TR13 0QA
Tel: (01326) 573404
Life-size Victorian village with fully stocked shops, carriages and fashions. 'Britain in the Blitz' life-size wartime street, historic aircraft. Exploratorium.

Heale Garden & Plant Centre

Middle Woodford, Salisbury, Wiltshire SP4 6NT
Tel: (01722) 782504
Mature, traditional garden with shrubs, musk and other roses, plus kitchen garden. Authentic Japanese teahouse in water garden. Magnolias. Snowdrops and aconites in winter.

International Animal Rescue Animal Tracks

Ash Mill, South Molton, Devon EX36 4QW
Tel: (01769) 550277
A 60-acre animal sanctuary with a wide range of rescued animals from monkeys to chinchillas. Shire horses and ponies. Also rare plant nursery.

Jamaica Inn Museums (Potters Museum of Curiosity)

Bolventor, Launceston, Cornwall PL15 7TS
Tel: (01566) 86838
Museums contain lifetime work of Walter Potter, a Victorian taxidermist. Exhibits include Kittens' Wedding, Death of Cock Robin and The Story of Smuggling.

Longleat

Warminster, Wiltshire BA12 7NW
Tel: (01985) 844400
Great Elizabethan house with lived-in atmosphere. Important libraries and Italian ceilings. 'Capability' Brown designed parkland. Safari Park.

The Lost Gardens of Heligan

Heligan, Pentewan, St Austell, Cornwall PL26 6EN
Tel: (01726) 845100
The largest garden restoration project undertaken since the war. New for 2000: The Lost Valley, covering 35 acres.

Lyme Regis Philpot Museum

Lyme Regis, Dorset DT7 3QA
Tel: (01297) 443370
Fossils, geology, local history and lace exhibitions. Museum shop.

The Pictures:
1 Selworthy, Somerset;
2 The interior of
  Salisbury Cathedral;
3 Land's End, Cornwall;
4 Wells Cathedral,
  Somerset;
5 Clifton Suspension
  Bridge, Bristol.

National Marine Aquarium

Plymouth, Devon PL4 0LF
Tel: (01752) 600301
The UK's only world-class aquarium. Visitor experiences include a mountain stream and Caribbean reef complete with sharks.

Paignton Zoo Environmental Park

Paignton, Devon TQ4 7EU
Tel: (01803) 557479
One of England's largest zoos with over 1200 animals in the beautiful setting of 75 acres of botanical gardens. A popular family day out.

Plant World

Newton Abbot, Devon TQ12 4SE
Tel: (01803) 872939
Four acres of gardens including the unique 'map of the world' gardens. Cottage garden. Panoramic views. Comprehensive nursery of rare and more unusual plants.

Plymouth Dome

The Hoe, Plymouth, Devon PL1 2NZ
Tel: (01752) 603300
Purpose-built visitor interpretation centre showing the history of Plymouth and its people from Stone Age beginnings to satellite technology.

Powderham Castle

Kenton, Exeter, Devon EX6 8JQ
Tel: (01626) 890243
Built in 1390 and restored in 18thC. Georgian interiors, china, furnishings and paintings. Family home of the Courtenays for over 600 years. Fine views across the deer park and River Exe.

Quaywest

Goodrington Sands, Paignton, Devon TQ4 6LN
Tel: (01803) 555550
Wettest and wildest fun at this outdoor waterpark. Eight flumes. Adult and children's swimming pool with water heated to 26°C. Grand-Prix go karts, amusement rides, bumper boats and crazy golf.

Railway Village Museum

Swindon, Wiltshire SN1 5BJ
Tel: (01793) 466555
Foreman's house in original Great Western Railway village. Furnished to re-create a Victorian working-class home.

Roman Baths Museum

Abbey Church Yard, Bath BA1 1LZ
Tel: (01225) 477785
Roman baths, hot springs and Roman temple. Jewellery, coins, curses and votive offerings from the sacred spring.

St Michael's Mount

Marazion, Cornwall TR17 0HT
Tel: (01736) 710507
Originally the site of a Benedictine chapel, the castle on its rock dates from 14thC. Fine views towards Land's End and the Lizard. Reached by foot, or ferry at high tide in the summer.

Steam - Museum of the Great Western Railway

Swindon, Wiltshire
Tel: (01793) 466646
Historic Great Western Railway locomotives, wide range of nameplates, models, illustrations, posters and tickets.

Stourhead House and Garden

Stourton, Warminster, Wiltshire BA12 6QH
Tel: (01747) 841152
Landscaped garden laid out in 1741-1780, with lakes, temples, rare trees and plants. The house, begun in 1721 by Colen Campbell, contains fine paintings and Chippendale furniture.

Tate Gallery St Ives

Porthmeor Beach, St Ives, Cornwall TR26 1TG
Tel: (01736) 796226
Opened in 1993 and offering a unique introduction to modern art. Changing displays focus on the modern movement St Ives is famous for.

Teignmouth Museum

French Street, Teignmouth, Devon TQ14 8ST
Tel: (01626) 777041
Exhibits include 16thC cannon and artefacts from Armada wreck and local history, 1920s pier machines and 1877 cannon.

The Time Machine

Weston-super-Mare, North Somerset BS23 1PR
Tel: (01934) 621028
Edwardian gaslight company building with central glazed courtyard. Seaside gallery, costume, Victorian cottage. Doll collection, local archaeology and natural history. Art gallery, people's collection.

Tintagel Castle

Tintagel, Cornwall PL34 0HE
Tel: (01840) 770328
Medieval ruined castle on wild, wind-swept coast. Famous for associations with Arthurian legend. Built largely in 13thC by Richard, Earl of Cornwall. Used as a prison in 14thC.

Tithe Barn Children's Farm

New Barn Road, Abbotsbury, Dorset DT3 4JF
Tel: (01305) 871817
Extensive children's farm for children under 11 years. Activities include hand-feeding milk to lambs and kids by bottle. Replicas of Terracotta Warriors on display in barn.

Totnes Costume Museum – Devonshire Collection of Period Costume

High Street, Totnes, Devon TQ9 5NP
Tel: (01803) 863821
New exhibition of costumes and accessories each season, displayed in one of the historic merchant's houses of Totnes.

Underground Passages

Exeter, Devon EX4 3PZ
Tel: (01392) 265887
Remarkable city passageways built during medieval times to carry water into the city centre. Now the only one's in Britain open to the public. Exhibition, video and guided tour.

West Somerset Railway

Minehead, Somerset TA24 5BG
Tel: (01643) 704996
Preserved steam railway operating between Minehead and Bishops Lydeard, near Taunton. Model railway and museums enroute. Longest independent railway in Britain, 32 km (20 miles).

Woodlands Leisure Park

Blackawton, Totnes, Devon TQ9 7DQ
Tel: (01803) 712598
A full day of variety set in 60 acres of countryside. Twelve venture playzones including 500-metre (1,640 ft) toboggan run, commando course, large indoor play area, toddlers' area and animals.

Wookey Hole Caves and Papermill

Wookey Hole, Wells, Somerset BA5 1BB
Tel: (01749) 672243
Spectacular caves and legendary home of the Witch of Wookey. Working Victorian papermill including Old Penny Arcade, Magical Mirror Maze and Cave Diving Museum.

The Pictures:
1 Dartmoor Ponies;
2 Torquay, Devon;
3 Bath;
4 Tarr Steps, Exmoor National Park;
5 Sunset at Stonehenge;
6 Shaftesbury Hill, Dorset;
7 Salisbury Cathedral, Wiltshire.

Find out more about the
SOUTH WEST ...

Further information about holidays and attractions in the South West is available from:

SOUTH WEST TOURISM
Admail 3186, Exeter EX2 7WH.

Tel: (0870) 442 0880

Fax: (0870) 442 0881

Email: info@westcountryholidays.com

Internet: www.westcountryholidays.com

The following publications are available free from South West Tourism:

Bed & Breakfast Touring Map

West Country Holiday Homes & Apartments

West Country Hotels and Guesthouses

Glorious Gardens of the West Country

Camping and Caravan Touring Map

Tourist Attractions Touring Map

Trencherman's West Country, Restaurant Guide

The Pictures:
1 Stonehenge;
2 Newquay, Cornwall.

Getting to the
SOUTH WEST ...

BY ROAD: Somerset, Devon and Cornwall are well served from the North and Midlands by the M6/M5 which extends just beyond Exeter, where it links in with the dual carriageways of the A38 to Plymouth, A380 to Torbay and the A30 into Cornwall. The North Devon Link Road A361 joins Junction 37 with the coast of north Devon and A39, which then becomes the Atlantic Highway into Cornwall.

BY RAIL: The main towns in the South West are served throughout the year by fast, direct and frequent rail services from all over the country. InterCity 125 trains operate from London (Paddington) to Chippenham, Swindon, Bath, Bristol, Weston-super-Mare, Taunton, Exeter, Plymouth and Penzance, and also from Scotland, the North East and the Midlands to the South West. A service runs from London (Waterloo) to Exeter, via Salisbury, Yeovil and Crewkerne. Sleeper services operate between Devon and Cornwall and London as well as between Bristol and Glasgow and Edinburgh. Motorail services operate from strategic points to key South West locations.

Where to stay in the

SOUTH WEST

Accommodation entries in this region are listed in alphabetical order of place name, and then in alphabetical order of establishment.

Map references refer to the colour location maps at the front of this guide. The first number indicates the map to use; the letter and number which follow refer to the grid reference on the map.

At-a-glance symbols at the end of each accommodation entry give useful information about services and facilities. A key to symbols can be found inside the back cover flap. Keep this open for easy reference.

A brief description of the towns and villages offering accommodation in the entries which follow, can be found at the end of this section.

A complete listing of all English Tourism Council assessed guest accommodation appears at the back of this guide.

ABBOTSBURY, Dorset Map ref 2A3

◆◆◆◆ **CORFE GATE HOUSE**

Coryates, Abbotsbury, Weymouth, DT3 4HW
T: (01305) 871483 & 07798 904602
F: (01305) 264024
E: maureenadams@corfegatehouse.co.uk
I: www.corfegatehouse.co.uk

Bedrooms: 1 single, 2 double, 1 twin
Bathrooms: 3 en suite

Parking for 3

B&B per night:
S £35.00–£35.00
D £40.00–£50.00

OPEN Apr–Oct

Three miles from the sea. Quietly situated Victorian house of character set in the beautiful Waddon Valley. Twenty minutes' drive from Dorchester, Weymouth and Bridport.

◆◆◆ **SWAN LODGE**

Rodden Row, Abbotsbury, Weymouth, DT3 4JL
T: (01305) 871249
F: (01305) 871249

Bedrooms: 3 double, 2 twin
Bathrooms: 2 en suite, 1 public

Lunch available
EM 1800 (LO 2200)
Parking for 10
CC: Barclaycard, Eurocard, Mastercard, Visa

B&B per night:
S £30.00–£40.00
D £44.00–£58.00

OPEN All year round

Situated on the B3157 coastal road between Weymouth and Bridport. Swan Inn public house opposite, where food is served all day in season, is under the same ownership.

IMPORTANT NOTE Information on accommodation listed in this guide has been supplied by the proprietors. As changes may occur you are advised to check details at the time of booking.

ALLERFORD, Somerset Map ref 1D1

◆◆◆◆

FERN COTTAGE

Allerford, Minehead, TA24 8HN
T: (01643) 862215
F: (01643) 862215

Comfortable, large, traditional Exmoor cottage, circa 16thC, set in a tiny National Trust village in a wood-fringed vale. Exhilarating walks in dramatic hill and coastal scenery start on doorstep. Noted for fine classic/bistro cooking and comprehensive cellar. A non-smoking house.

Bedrooms: 3 triple
Bathrooms: 3 en suite, 1 public

EM 1900 (LO 1800)
Parking for 8
CC: Barclaycard, Delta, Eurocard, JCB, Maestro, Mastercard, Solo, Switch, Visa, Visa Electron

B&B per night:
S £39.00–£39.00
D £58.00–£58.00

HB per person:
DY £42.90–£42.90

OPEN All year round

AMESBURY, Wiltshire Map ref 2B2 *Tourist Information Centre Tel: (01980) 622833*

◆◆◆

ENFORD HOUSE

Enford, Pewsey, SN9 6DJ
T: (01980) 670414

Bedrooms: 1 double, 2 twin
Bathrooms: 3 public

Parking for 8
CC: Amex

Listed country house with pretty garden. In attractive village 7 miles from Stonehenge. Good food at local village pub. Quiet and comfortable.

B&B per night:
S £20.00–£25.00
D £35.00–£40.00

OPEN All year round

◆◆◆◆

MANDALAY

15 Stonehenge Road, Amesbury, Salisbury, SP4 7BA
T: (01980) 623733
F: (01980) 626642

Bedrooms: 2 double, 2 twin, 1 triple
Bathrooms: 5 en suite

Parking for 5
CC: Amex, Barclaycard, Delta, Diners, Eurocard, JCB, Mastercard, Solo, Switch, Visa, Visa Electron

Beautiful bedrooms in house of great character. Fine breakfast served in classical breakfast room overlooking the garden temple. No-smoking policy.

B&B per night:
S £32.00–£38.00
D £42.00–£46.00

OPEN All year round

◆◆◆

SOLSTICE FARMHOUSE

39 Holders Road, Amesbury, Salisbury, SP4 7PH
T: (01980) 625052 &
07931 311778 (Mobile/voicemail)

Bedrooms: 1 double, 1 twin
Bathrooms: 2 private showers

Parking for 2

Grade II Listed farmhouse boasts a woodburning stove and large, attractive garden with pond and water feature. Comfortable rooms with private en suite showers.

B&B per night:
S £25.00–£28.00
D £40.00–£45.00

OPEN All year round

ASHBURTON, Devon Map ref 1C2

◆◆◆◆
Silver Award

GAGES MILL

Buckfastleigh Road, Ashburton, Newton Abbot, TQ13 7JW
T: (01364) 652391
F: (01364) 652391
E: moore@gagesmill.co.uk
I: www.gagesmill.co.uk

14thC former wool mill in over an acre of gardens. A friendly welcome and comfortable accommodation. High standard of cooking. Licensed. One mile from the ancient Stannary town of Ashburton. An ideal base for exploring South Devon, with its many National Trust properties, pretty villages and, of course, Dartmoor.

Bedrooms: 1 single, 6 double, 1 twin
Bathrooms: 7 en suite, 1 private shower

EM 1900 (LO 1900)
Parking for 10

B&B per night:
S £21.00–£30.00
D £42.00–£60.00

HB per person:
DY £35.00–£44.00

OPEN Mar–Nov

ASHBURTON continued

◆◆◆◆

NEW COTT FARM

Poundsgate, Ashburton, Newton Abbot,
TQ13 7PD
T: (01364) 631421
F: (01364) 631421

B&B per night:
D Min £40.00

HB per person:
DY Min £32.00

OPEN All year round

Enjoy freedom, peace and tranquillity of farm accommodation in Dartmoor National Park. Relax in the conservatory after enjoying the moors, valleys or one of the many attractions in Devon. Warm welcome, lovely food. Tea/coffee/ chocolate in your en suite bedroom. Suitable for less able guests. Special diets are not a problem.

Bedrooms: 2 double,
1 twin, 1 triple
Bathrooms: 4 en suite

EM 1800 (LO 1630)
Parking for 4

◆◆◆◆

SLADESDOWN FARM

Landscove, Ashburton, Newton Abbot,
TQ13 7ND
T: (01364) 653973

B&B per night:
S £25.00–£30.00
D £45.00–£50.00

OPEN Feb–Nov

A warm welcome awaits you at Sladesdown Farm. Set in the heart of the country, with peaceful, scenic walks. Close to the moors and coast yet only 2 miles off the A38. Two spacious, attractive bedrooms, en suite, with sitting area, TV and hot drinks facilities.

Bedrooms: 2 double,
1 triple
Bathrooms: 2 en suite,
1 private

Parking for 6

◆◆◆◆

WELLPRITTON FARM
Holne, Newton Abbot, TQ13 7RX
T: (01364) 631273

Bedrooms: 2 twin,
1 triple, 1 family room
Bathrooms: 3 en suite,
1 private

EM 1900 (LO 1200)
Parking for 6

B&B per night:
S £20.00–£20.00
D £40.00–£40.00

HB per person:
DY £30.00–£30.00

OPEN All year round

15-acre mixed farm. Plenty of mouth-watering farm-produced food in a tastefully modernised character farmhouse on edge of Dartmoor. Special diets by arrangement. Warm welcome, caring personal attention.

AVEBURY, Wiltshire Map ref 2B2

◆◆◆

THE NEW INN
Winterbourne Monkton, Swindon,
SN4 9NW
T: (01672) 539240
F: (01672) 539150

Bedrooms: 2 double,
3 twin
Bathrooms: 5 en suite

Lunch available
EM 1830 (LO 2130)
Parking for 20
CC: Barclaycard, Delta,
Eurocard, Mastercard,
Solo, Switch, Visa, Visa
Electron

B&B per night:
S £30.00–£40.00
D £45.00–£55.00

HB per person:
DY £40.00–£50.00

OPEN All year round

Small and friendly country pub only 1 mile from Avebury. Good, central touring position.

WELCOME HOST This is a nationally recognised customer care programme which aims to promote the highest standards of service and a warm welcome. Establishments taking part in this initiative are indicated by the ⊚ symbol.

BAMPTON, Devon Map ref 1D1

◆◆◆◆
Silver
Award

MANOR MILL HOUSE

Bampton, Tiverton, EX16 9LP
T: (01398) 332211
F: (01398) 332009
E: saty@manormill.demon.co.uk
I: www.manormill.demon.co.uk

B&B per night:
S £24.00–£24.00
D £42.00–£48.00

OPEN All year round

Relax in our 17thC miller's home with beams, inglenooks, log fires, 4-posters and delicious breakfasts using local produce. Rooms are en suite, non-smoking and have 24 hour access. One is on ground floor. Attractive riverside setting, close to the amenities of historic Bampton. Convenient for Exmoor, NT properties, walks.

Bedrooms: 2 double,
1 twin
Bathrooms: 3 en suite

Parking for 12
CC: Barclaycard,
Mastercard, Visa

BARNSTAPLE, Devon Map ref 1C1 *Tourist Information Centre Tel: (01271) 375000*

◆◆◆◆

BRADIFORD COTTAGE

Bradiford, Barnstaple, EX31 4DP
T: (01271) 345039
F: (01271) 345039
E: tony@humesfarm.co.uk
I: www.humesfarm.co.uk

B&B per night:
S £17.00–£20.00
D £34.00–£40.00

OPEN All year round

Family-run 17thC cottage set in the countryside just 1 mile from Barnstaple. Ideally situated for exploring the stunning Atlantic coast and the scenic beauty of Exmoor. Lovely, comfortable rooms, attractive garden and use of heated swimming pool. Excellent pub food within easy walking distance.

Bedrooms: 1 single,
2 double, 1 twin
Bathrooms: 2 public

Parking for 4

◆◆◆◆

THE RED HOUSE

Brynsworthy, Roundswell, Barnstaple,
EX31 3NP
T: (01271) 345966
F: (01271) 379966

B&B per night:
S £21.00–£23.00
D £36.00–£40.00

OPEN Feb–Nov

Period country house in an elevated position with panoramic views. Although within 2 miles of the historic market town of Barnstaple, the house is set in the countryside with its own half-acre garden. All rooms have colour TV, shower, hairdryer, tea/coffee-making facilities and central heating.

Bedrooms: 1 single,
1 double, 1 twin
Bathrooms: 1 public,
2 private showers

Parking for 6

CREDIT CARD BOOKINGS If you book by telephone and are asked for your credit card number it is advisable to check the proprietor's policy should you cancel your reservation.

♦♦♦♦

THE SPINNEY
Shirwell, Barnstaple, EX31 4JR
T: (01271) 850282

B&B per night:
S £18.50–£22.00
D £37.00–£44.00

HB per person:
DY £28.50–£32.00

OPEN All year round

Set in over an acre of grounds with views towards Exmoor, a former rectory. Spacious accommodation, en suite available. Centrally heated. Delicious meals cooked by chef/ proprietor, served during summer months in our restored Victorian conservatory under the ancient vine. Residential licence. The Spinney is non-smoking.

Bedrooms: 1 single, 1 double, 1 twin, 2 triple
Bathrooms: 2 en suite, 2 public

EM 1900 (LO 1700)
Parking for 7

BARTON ST. DAVID, Somerset Map 2A2

♦♦♦♦♦

MILL HOUSE
Mill House, Barton St. David, Somerton, TA11 6DF
T: (01458) 851215 (Answerphone)
F: (01458) 851372
E: knightsmillhouse@aol.com

B&B per night:
S £18.00–£20.00
D £44.00–£52.00

OPEN All year round

Beautifully restored Listed Georgian mill house in a peaceful garden with the mill stream still running through one end of the house. Set in lovely countryside but conveniently accessible from the A303. Spacious bedrooms all en suite. Close to Glastonbury and Wells. A warm welcome awaits you.

Bedrooms: 1 single, 1 double, 1 twin; suite available
Bathrooms: 3 en suite

Parking for 6

BATCOMBE, Somerset Map ref 2B2

♦♦♦

VALLEY VIEW FARM
Batcombe, Shepton Mallet, BA4 6AJ
T: (01749) 850302 & 07974 442284
F: (01749) 850302

Bedrooms: 1 double, 1 twin
Bathrooms: 1 private, 1 public

Parking for 6

B&B per night:
S Min £25.00
D £36.00–£42.00

OPEN Feb–Nov

200-acre mixed farm. A modern farm bungalow in 1 acre of garden, within walking distance of local pub. Peaceful location.

BATH, Bath and North East Somerset Map ref 2B2 *Tourist Information Centre Tel: (01225) 477101*

♦♦♦

ASTOR HOUSE
14 Oldfield Road, Bath, BA2 3ND
T: (01225) 429134
F: (01225) 429134
E: astorhouse.visitus@virgin.net

Bedrooms: 4 double, 2 twin, 2 triple
Bathrooms: 8 en suite

Parking for 6
CC: Barclaycard, Delta, Eurocard, JCB, Mastercard, Solo, Switch, Visa, Visa Electron

B&B per night:
S £25.00–£35.00
D £40.00–£50.00

OPEN Feb–Dec

Comfortable, spacious Victorian home with lovely views of the city and countryside yet only a short walk to the centre. Friendly welcome, varied delicious breakfasts.

ACCESSIBILITY
Look for the 🔲🔲🔲 symbols which indicate accessibility for wheelchair users. A list of establishments is at the front of this guide.

◆◆◆

BAILBROOK LODGE HOTEL

35/37 London Road West, Bath, Somerset
BA1 7HZ
T: (01225) 859090
F: (01225) 852299
E: hotel@bailbrooklodge.demon.co.uk
I: www.bailbrooklodge.demon.co.uk

Welcome to a fine Georgian house offering 12 bedrooms, all en suite (some 4-posters) with antiques and many original features. The lounge bar and dining room overlook the patio and lawns. Excellently located 1 mile from Bath's centre and close to junctions for M4 and beautiful surrounding countryside. Ample car parking.

Bedrooms: 4 double,
4 twin, 4 triple
Bathrooms: 12 en suite

EM 1830 (LO 2130)
Parking for 20
CC: Barclaycard, Diners,
Mastercard, Visa

B&B per night:
S £39.00–£60.00
D £60.00–£80.00

HB per person:
DY £44.00–£54.00

OPEN All year round

◆◆◆◆

BROMPTON HOUSE

St John's Road, Bath, BA2 6PT
T: (01225) 420972
F: (01225) 420505
E: bromptonhouse@btinternet.com
I: www.bromptonhouse.co.uk

Bedrooms: 1 single,
9 double, 5 twin,
1 family room
Bathrooms: 16 en suite

Parking for 18
CC: Amex, Barclaycard,
Delta, Eurocard, JCB,
Maestro, Mastercard,
Solo, Switch, Visa, Visa
Electron

B&B per night:
S £44.00–£76.00
D £60.00–£95.00

OPEN All year round

Charming Georgian rectory in beautiful secluded gardens. 5-6 minutes' level walk to city centre. Free private car park. No smoking, please.

◆◆◆◆

CARFAX HOTEL

Great Pulteney Street, Bath,
BA2 4BS
T: (01225) 462089
F: (01225) 443257
E: carfaxhotel@compuserve.com
I: www.carfaxhotel.co.uk

Bedrooms: 13 single,
13 double, 9 twin,
2 triple
Bathrooms: 36 en suite,
1 private

EM 1800 (LO 1830)
Parking for 17
CC: Amex, Barclaycard,
Delta, Eurocard,
Mastercard, Solo, Switch,
Visa, Visa Electron

B&B per night:
S £49.50–£62.50
D £75.00–£90.00

HB per person:
DY £55.50–£73.00

OPEN All year round

A trio of Georgian houses, overlooking Henrietta Park and surrounded by Bath's beautiful hills. A short stroll from Pump Rooms and Roman Baths.

◆◆◆

CHURCH FARM

Monkton Farleigh, Bradford-on-
Avon, Wiltshire BA15 2QJ
T: (01225) 858583 &
07889 596929 (Mobile)
F: (01225) 852474
E: rebecca@tuckerb.fsnet.co.uk
I: www.tuckerb.fsnet.co.uk

Bedrooms: 2 double,
1 twin
Bathrooms: 3 en suite,
1 public

Parking for 5

B&B per night:
D £45.00–£45.00

OPEN All year round

52-acre mixed farm. Sympathetically converted barn. Horses, golf and swimming. Ideal base for walking, or touring south-west England, 10 minutes from Bath.

◆◆◆

EDGAR HOTEL

64 Great Pulteney Street, Bath,
BA2 4DN
T: (01225) 420619
F: (01225) 466916

Bedrooms: 2 single,
9 double, 4 twin, 1 triple
Bathrooms: 16 en suite

CC: Barclaycard, Delta,
Maestro, Mastercard,
Switch, Visa

B&B per night:
S £30.00–£50.00
D £47.00–£75.00

OPEN All year round

Georgian townhouse hotel, close to city centre and Roman Baths. Privately run. All rooms with en suite facilities.

WHERE TO STAY

Please mention this guide when making your booking.

◆◆◆◆

THE GAINSBOROUGH
Weston Lane, Bath, BA1 4AB
T: (01225) 311380
F: (01225) 447411
E: gainsborough_hotel@compuserve.com
I: www.gainsboroughhotel.co.uk

B&B per night:
S £40.00–£59.00
D £58.00–£95.00

OPEN All year round

Spacious and comfortable country-house style bed and breakfast hotel. Situated in own grounds near the Botanical Gardens and within easy walking distance of the city. Large guests' lounge with books, magazines, also a small friendly bar. High ground, nice views, sun terraces, car park. Five-course breakfast, friendly staff. Warm welcome.

Bedrooms: 1 single, 10 double, 5 triple, 1 family room
Bathrooms: 17 en suite

Parking for 18
CC: Amex, Barclaycard, Delta, Eurocard, Mastercard, Switch, Visa

◆◆◆◆

HAUTE COMBE HOTEL
174/176 Newbridge Road, Bath, BA1 3LE
T: (01225) 420061 & 339064
F: (01225) 446077
E: enquiries@hautecombe.com
I: www.hautecombe.com

B&B per night:
S £45.00–£55.00
D £55.00–£85.00

OPEN All year round

Conveniently situated hotel with period character. Clean, no-smoking bedrooms with all the extras of a modern hotel alongside old charm. Satellite TV. Bar and smoking/no-smoking lounges. A la carte menu. Large monitored car park. Frequent shuttle or level walk to abbey. Free unlimited golf locally.

Bedrooms: 2 single, 3 double, 2 twin, 3 triple, 2 family rooms
Bathrooms: 11 en suite, 1 private

EM 1930 (LO 1800)
Parking for 12
CC: Amex, Barclaycard, Delta, Diners, Eurocard, JCB, Maestro, Mastercard, Solo, Switch, Visa, Visa Electron

◆◆◆

HENRIETTA HOTEL
32 Henrietta Street, Bath, BA2 6LR
T: (01225) 447779
F: (01225) 444150

Bedrooms: 7 double, 2 twin, 1 triple
Bathrooms: 10 en suite

CC: Barclaycard, Delta, Maestro, Mastercard, Switch, Visa

B&B per night:
S £30.00–£50.00
D £45.00–£75.00

OPEN All year round

Privately-run Georgian townhouse hotel, close to city centre and Roman Baths. All rooms with en suite facilities.

◆◆◆

HERMITAGE
Bath Road, Box, Corsham, Wiltshire SN13 8DT
T: (01225) 744187
F: (01225) 743447
E: hermitage@telecall.co.uk

Bedrooms: 4 double, 1 triple
Bathrooms: 5 en suite

Parking for 9

B&B per night:
S £35.00–£40.00
D £45.00–£55.00

OPEN All year round

Six miles from Bath on A4 to Chippenham, 1st drive on left by 30 mph sign. 16thC house with heated pool in summer. Dining room with vaulted ceiling.

◆◆◆◆◆
Silver Award

HOLLY LODGE
8 Upper Oldfield Park, Bath, BA2 3JZ
T: (01225) 424042 & (01255) 339187
F: (01225) 481138
E: George.H.Hall@btinternet.com
I: www.hollylodge.co.uk

Bedrooms: 1 single, 4 double, 2 twin
Bathrooms: 7 en suite

Parking for 8
CC: Amex, Barclaycard, Delta, Diners, Eurocard, JCB, Maestro, Mastercard, Solo, Switch, Visa, Visa Electron

B&B per night:
S £48.00–£60.00
D £79.00–£97.00

OPEN All year round

Elegant Victorian house set in its own grounds, enjoying magnificent views of the city. Visit my web site for further information.

BATH continued

◆◆◆◆ LAURA PLACE HOTEL

3 Laura Place,
Great Pulteney Street, Bath,
BA2 4BH
T: (01225) 463815
F: (01225) 310222

Bedrooms: 6 double,
1 twin, 1 family room
Bathrooms: 7 en suite,
1 public

Parking for 10
CC: Amex, Barclaycard,
Mastercard, Visa

B&B per night:
S £60.00–£65.00
D £70.00–£90.00

OPEN Mar–Dec

18thC townhouse, centrally located in Georgian square. 2 minutes from Roman Baths, Pump Rooms and abbey.

◆◆◆◆◆
Gold
Award

LEIGHTON HOUSE

139 Wells Road, Bath, BA2 3AL
T: (01225) 314769 & 420210
F: (01225) 443079
E: welcome@leighton-house.co.uk
I: www.leighton-house.co.uk

B&B per night:
S £45.00–£85.00
D £59.00–£99.00

OPEN All year round

An elegant, spotless, detached Victorian house where Gold Award-winning "Welcome Hosts" Marilyn and Colin offer total comfort. Spacious rooms – individual decoration – top-quality king, queen and twin beds – en suites with bath and shower – extensive-choice breakfasts – car park – and just a 10 minute walk to Bath city centre.

Bedrooms: 4 double,
3 twin, 1 family room
Bathrooms: 8 en suite

Parking for 8
CC: Barclaycard, Delta,
Eurocard, JCB, Maestro,
Mastercard, Solo, Switch,
Visa, Visa Electron

◆◆◆◆ MIDWAY COTTAGE

10 Farleigh Wick, Bradford-on-
Avon, Wiltshire BA15 2PU
T: (01225) 863932
F: (01225) 866836
E: midway_cottage@hotmail.com

Bedrooms: 2 double,
1 twin
Bathrooms: 3 en suite,
1 public

Parking for 5

B&B per night:
S £30.00–£30.00
D £40.00–£45.00

OPEN All year round

Friendly, relaxed cottage with high standards of comfort and service. On A363 between Bathford and Bradford-on-Avon, next door to a country inn serving excellent food.

◆◆ SAMPFORD

11 Oldfield Road, Bath, BA2 3ND
T: (01225) 310053

Bedrooms: 1 double,
1 twin, 1 family room
Bathrooms: 1 public,
3 private showers

Parking for 2

B&B per night:
D £42.00–£42.00

OPEN All year round

In a quiet residential area half a mile south of city centre off the A367 Exeter/Radstock/Shepton Mallet road. No commerical sign is displayed.

◆◆◆◆

SOMERSET HOUSE HOTEL

35 Bathwick Hill, Bath, BA2 6LD
T: (01225) 466451 & 463471
F: (01225) 317188
E: somersethouse@compuserve.com
I: www.somersethouse.co.uk

B&B per night:
S £27.00–£52.50
D £54.00–£71.00

OPEN All year round

An elegant Georgian house (1827), owned and run by the Seymour family. Large garden. Good views of city. Non-smoking house. 12 minutes' walk from Roman Baths and Abbey. Car park. Innovative buffet, continental and English breakfasts served each morning in the old Georgian kitchen. Restaurant available for family celebrations.

Bedrooms: 1 single,
2 double, 2 twin, 5 triple
Bathrooms: 10 en suite

Parking for 15
CC: Amex, Barclaycard,
Delta, Diners, Eurocard,
JCB, Maestro, Mastercard,
Solo, Switch, Visa, Visa
Electron

BATH continued

◆◆◆◆
Gold
Award

VILLA MAGDALA HOTEL

Henrietta Road, Bath, BA2 6LX
T: (01225) 466329
F: (01225) 483207
E: office@VillaMagdala.co.uk
I: www.VillaMagdala.co.uk

B&B per night:
S £65.00–£95.00
D £80.00–£110.00

OPEN All year round

Ideally situated, this charming Victorian townhouse hotel enjoys a peaceful location overlooking Henrietta Park, only 5 minutes' level walk to the city centre and Roman Baths. The spacious rooms, some with 4-poster beds, all have pleasant views. Private parking is available in the hotel grounds. The Villa Magdala is a non-smoking hotel.

Bedrooms: 2 single, 9 double, 6 twin, 1 triple
Bathrooms: 18 en suite

Parking for 18
CC: Amex, Barclaycard, Delta, Eurocard, Mastercard, Solo, Switch, Visa, Visa Electron

---

BEAMINSTER, Dorset Map ref 2A3

◆◆◆◆

BEAM COTTAGE

16 North Street, Beaminster, DT8 3DZ
T: (01308) 863639 (Ansaphone)
E: magie@beam-cottage.fsnt.co.uk

Bedrooms: 1 double, 1 twin, 1 family room; suites available
Bathrooms: 3 en suite

EM 1900 (LO 2100)
Parking for 3

B&B per night:
S £30.00–£30.00
D £50.00–£60.00

HB per person:
DY £37.00–£42.00

OPEN All year round

Attractive, Grade II Listed cottage in centre of Beaminster, with secluded and pretty garden. All rooms en suite with private sitting room.

BIDEFORD, Devon Map ref 1C1 *Tourist Information Centre Tel: (01237) 477676*

◆◆◆◆

THE MOUNT

Northdown Road, Bideford, EX39 3LP
T: (01237) 473748
I: www.5.50megs.com/themount

B&B per night:
S £25.00–£27.00
D £46.00–£50.00

OPEN All year round

Elegant Georgian licensed guesthouse, comfortably furnished. All rooms en suite. Peaceful garden for guests' use. Short walk to town centre. Convenient for trips to Lundy, Clovelly, Exmoor, Dartmoor and North Devon coast. No smoking.

Bedrooms: 1 single, 3 double, 1 twin, 1 triple
Bathrooms: 6 en suite

Parking for 4
CC: Barclaycard, Delta, Mastercard, Switch, Visa

USE YOUR *i*s

There are more than 550 Tourist Information Centres throughout England offering friendly help with accommodation and holiday ideas as well as suggestions of places to visit and things to do. You'll find TIC addresses in the local Phone Book.

BIDEFORD continued

SUNSET HOTEL

Landcross, Bideford, EX39 5JA
T: (01237) 472962
E: hazellamb@hotmail.com

B&B per night:
S £36.00–£46.00
D £54.00–£62.00

HB per person:
DY £39.00–£44.00

OPEN Apr–Oct

Small, elegant country hotel set in beautiful gardens in a quiet, peaceful location, overlooking spectacular scenery. 1.5 miles from town. Beautifully decorated and spotlessly clean. Highly recommended quality accommodation. All en suites with colour TV and beverages. Superb cooking, everything home-made. Special needs catered for. Licensed, private parking. Non-smoking establishment.

Bedrooms: 1 double,
1 twin, 2 triple
Bathrooms: 4 en suite

EM 1900 (LO 1900)
Parking for 10
CC: Barclaycard, Eurocard,
Mastercard, Visa, Visa
Electron

BISHOP SUTTON, Bath and North East Somerset Map ref 2A2

WITHYMEDE

The Street, Bishop Sutton, Bristol,
BS39 5UU
T: (01275) 332069

Bedrooms: 3 double
Bathrooms: 2 en suite,
3 public

Parking for 10

B&B per night:
D £35.00–£40.00

OPEN Feb–Nov

Detached house, ample parking. Chew Valley Lake half a mile. Bath/Wells/Bristol all approximately 20 minutes' drive. Bristol Airport/Farrington Golf Course 15 minutes' drive.

BISHOP'S LYDEARD, Somerset Map ref 1D1

WEST VIEW

Minehead Road, Bishop's Lydeard,
Taunton, TA4 3BS
T: (01823) 432223
F: (01823) 432223

Bedrooms: 1 double,
2 twin
Bathrooms: 1 en suite,
1 public

Parking for 4

B&B per night:
S £19.00–£26.00
D £38.00–£50.00

OPEN All year round

Attractive Victorian house in the village close to the privately-owned West Somerset Steam Railway. Your hosts were formerly at Slimbridge Station Farm.

BODMIN, Cornwall Map ref 1B2 Tourist Information Centre Tel: (01208) 76616

BOKIDDICK FARM

Gold
Award

Lanivet, Bodmin, PL30 5HP
T: (01208) 831481
F: (01208) 831481

Bedrooms: 2 double,
1 triple
Bathrooms: 3 en suite

Parking for 4

B&B per night:
S £25.00–£30.00
D £42.00–£46.00

OPEN All year round

Character Georgian farmhouse on dairy farm. Central for touring Cornwall. Close to National Trust Lanhydrock House and Eden Project. Enjoy magnificent views in peaceful location.

BOSCASTLE, Cornwall Map ref 1B2

THE OLD COACH HOUSE

Tintagel Road, Boscastle, PL35 0AS
T: (01840) 250398
F: (01840) 250346
E: parsons@old-coach.demon.co.uk
I: www.old-coach.co.uk

Bedrooms: 4 double,
1 twin, 2 triple, 1 family
room
Bathrooms: 8 en suite

Parking for 9
CC: Barclaycard, Delta,
Eurocard, JCB, Maestro,
Mastercard, Solo, Switch,
Visa, Visa Electron

B&B per night:
S £20.00–£40.00
D £38.00–£44.00

OPEN All year round

Relax in beautiful 300-year-old former coach house. All rooms en suite with colour TV, teamaker, hairdryer, etc. Friendly and helpful owners. Good parking.

HALF BOARD PRICES Half board prices are given per person, but in some cases these may be based on double/twin occupancy.

◆◆◆◆

TOLCARNE HOUSE HOTEL AND RESTAURANT

Tintagel Road, Boscastle, PL35 0AS

T: (01840) 250654
F: (01840) 250654
E: crowntolhouse@eclipse.co.uk
I: milford.co.uk/60/tolcarne

A charming Victorian residence, which provides all modern comforts in a peaceful and friendly environment. Our guest rooms are furnished to a high standard and all are en suite. Tolcarne stands in spacious gardens with splendid views of unspoilt countryside and National Trust owned coastline. Choice of menus. Lounge bar.

Bedrooms: 1 single, 5 double, 1 twin
Bathrooms: 7 en suite, 1 public

EM 1900 (LO 2100)
Parking for 15
CC: Delta, Eurocard, Mastercard, Visa

B&B per night:
S £28.00–£31.00
D £46.00–£62.00

HB per person:
DY £38.00–£46.00

OPEN Feb–Nov

◆◆◆◆
Silver
Award

BROOKFIELD HOUSE

Challabrook Lane, Bovey Tracey, Newton Abbot, TQ12 9DF

T: (01626) 836181
F: (01626) 836182
E: brookfieldh@tinyworld.co.uk

Spacious early Edwardian residence situated on the edge of Bovey Tracey and Dartmoor. Set in 2 acres with panoramic moor views and bounded by the gently flowing Pottery Leat. Secluded tranquillity yet within easy walking distance of town, local attractions and moorland. Individually decorated bedrooms, all with comfortable seating areas.

Bedrooms: 2 double, 1 twin
Bathrooms: 2 en suite, 1 private

EM 1930
Parking for 6

B&B per night:
D £50.00–£64.00

OPEN Feb–Nov

◆◆◆

LORNE HOUSE

London Road, Box, Corsham, SN13 8NA
T: (01225) 742597
F: (01225) 742597
E: gordontaylor@lornehouse100.freeserve.co.uk

Bedrooms: 1 double, 3 triple
Bathrooms: 4 en suite

Parking for 6
CC: Barclaycard, Mastercard, Visa

B&B per night:
S £25.00–£30.00
D £40.00–£45.00

OPEN All year round

Listed in guide books in Germany, Canada and America, this Victorian property boasts excellent service and accommodation to discerning travellers. Situated 6 miles from Bath.

TOWN INDEX

This can be found at the back of the guide. If you know where you want to stay, the index will give you the page number listing accommodation in your chosen town, city or village.

BRADFORD-ON-AVON, Wiltshire Map ref 2B2 *Tourist Information Centre Tel: (01225) 865797*

◆◆◆◆◆
Silver
Award

HILLSIDE LODGE BED & BREAKFAST

Hillside Lodge, Jones Hill, Bradford-on-Avon, Bath, BA15 2EE
T: (01225) 866312
F: (01225) 866312
E: barnes@hillsidelodge.fsnet.co.uk

A warm welcome greets you at this unique and spacious family home in tranquil setting. Located immediately above the canal, locks and Tithe Barn, yet only 5 minutes' walk to railway station, swimming pool, shops and restaurants. The beautiful Georgian city of Bath is 8 miles by car.

Bedrooms: 1 double, 1 family room; suite available
Bathrooms: 2 en suite

Parking for 4
CC: JCB, Maestro, Mastercard, Solo, Switch, Visa, Visa Electron

B&B per night:
S £30.00–£45.00
D £45.00–£55.00

OPEN All year round

BRIDESTOWE, Devon Map ref 1C2

◆◆◆◆
Silver
Award

THE KNOLE FARM

Bridestowe, Okehampton, EX20 4HA
T: (01837) 861241
F: (01837) 861241

Where guests return annually for the breathtaking views of Dartmoor, delicious food, warm welcome and a real countryside holiday. Walking, castles, golfing, pony-trekking are all on the doorstep of this working family farm. En suite rooms (2 doubles, family/twin, 1 single). Open all year.

Bedrooms: 2 double, 2 triple
Bathrooms: 4 en suite, 1 public

EM 1830 (LO 1500)
Parking for 4

B&B per night:
S £20.00–£25.00
D £40.00–£45.00

HB per person:
DY £30.00–£35.00

OPEN All year round

◆◆◆
WHITE HART INN
Fore Street, Bridestowe, Okehampton, EX20 4EL
T: (01837) 861318
F: (01837) 861318
E: whihartinn@aol.com
I: members.aol.com/whihartinn/bridestowe.html

Bedrooms: 2 double
Bathrooms: 2 en suite

Lunch available
EM 1900 (LO 2130)
Parking for 20
CC: Amex, Barclaycard, Delta, Diners, Maestro, Mastercard, Solo, Switch, Visa, Visa Electron

B&B per night:
S Min £30.00
D Min £47.00

OPEN All year round

17thC village inn, family-run for 38 years, primarily noted for good food. En suite accommodation. Close to Dartmoor National Park, Lydford Gorge and fishing at Roadford Lake.

BRIDGWATER, Somerset Map ref 1D1

◆◆◆
QUANTOCK VIEW HOUSE
Bridgwater Road, North Petherton, Bridgwater, TA6 6PR
T: (01278) 663309
E: wendy@quantockview.freeserve.co.uk
I: www.quantockview.freeserve.co.uk

Bedrooms: 1 double, 1 twin, 1 triple, 1 family room
Bathrooms: 3 en suite, 1 private shower

EM 1830
Parking for 5
CC: Barclaycard, Delta, Eurocard, Mastercard, Visa

B&B per night:
S £20.00–£25.00
D £32.00–£40.00

HB per person:
DY £28.00–£33.00

OPEN All year round

Comfortable, family-run guesthouse in central Somerset. En suite facilities available. Close to hills and coast, yet only minutes from M5, junction 24.

IDEAS For ideas on places to visit refer to the introduction at the beginning of this section.

BRIDPORT, Dorset Map ref 2A3 *Tourist Information Centre Tel: (01308) 424901*

♦♦♦ BRIDPORT ARMS HOTEL
West Bay, Bridport, DT6 4EN
T: (01308) 422994
F: (01308) 425141

Bedrooms: 3 single,
5 double, 2 twin, 1 triple,
2 family rooms
Bathrooms: 6 en suite,
3 public

Lunch available
EM 1900 (LO 2100)
Parking for 10
CC: Barclaycard, Delta,
Mastercard, Solo, Switch,
Visa, Visa Electron

B&B per night:
S £25.00–£32.00
D £46.00–£62.00

OPEN All year round

16thC thatched hotel on beach. Restaurant specialising in local sea food. 2 bars, real local ales and bar meals.

♦♦♦♦ BRITMEAD HOUSE
West Bay Road, Bridport, DT6 4EG
T: (01308) 422941
F: (01308) 422516
E: britmead@talk21.com

Bedrooms: 3 double,
2 twin, 2 family rooms
Bathrooms: 7 en suite

EM 1900 (LO 1700)
Parking for 8
CC: Barclaycard, Delta,
Eurocard, Mastercard,
Switch, Visa, Visa Electron

B&B per night:
S £25.00–£38.00
D £42.00–£62.00

HB per person:
DY £37.00–£48.00

OPEN All year round

Elegant, spacious, tastefully decorated house. Lounge and dining room overlooking garden. West Bay Harbour/Coastal Path, 10 minutes' walk away. Renowned for hospitality and comfort.

BRISTOL, Map ref 2A2 *Tourist Information Centre Tel: (0117) 926 0767 or (01275) 474444 (airport)*

♦♦♦ MAYFAIR HOTEL
5 Henleaze Road, Westbury-on-Trym, Bristol, BS9 4EX
T: (0117) 9622008 & 9493924

Bedrooms: 6 single,
1 double, 1 twin, 1 triple
Bathrooms: 3 en suite,
2 public

Parking for 9
CC: Barclaycard, Delta,
Mastercard, Switch, Visa

B&B per night:
S £26.00–£39.00
D £46.00–£50.00

OPEN All year round

Small hotel run by owners, situated close to the downs and within easy reach of both the city centre and motorway.

BRIXHAM, Devon Map ref 1D2 *Tourist Information Centre Tel: 0906 680 1268 (calls cost 25p per minute)*

♦♦♦

ANCHORAGE GUEST HOUSE
170 New Road, Brixham, Devon TQ5 8DA
T: (01803) 852960

B&B per night:
S £15.00–£23.00
D £30.00–£46.00

HB per person:
DY £24.50–£32.50

OPEN All year round

The chalet style bungalow, set in award-winning gardens, offers very comfortable, mostly en suite, accommodation. With good home cooking, a friendly atmosphere and ample parking. The Anchorage is a good base for exploring Dartmoor and the South Devon Coast. "Brixham's best kept secret" – Daily Telegraph, June 1999.

Bedrooms: 1 single,
3 double, 2 twin, 1 triple
Bathrooms: 3 en suite,
2 public

EM 1800
Parking for 13
CC: Delta, Mastercard,
Switch, Visa

♦♦♦ RICHMOND HOUSE HOTEL
Higher Manor Road, Brixham,
Devon TQ5 8HA
T: (01803) 882391
F: (01803) 882391

Bedrooms: 4 double,
1 triple, 1 family room
Bathrooms: 5 en suite,
1 private

Parking for 6
CC: Barclaycard, Delta,
Eurocard, Mastercard,
Visa

B&B per night:
D £36.00–£44.00

OPEN Mar–Dec

Detached Victorian house with well-appointed accommodation, sun-trap garden and adjacent car park. Convenient for shops and harbour, yet quiet location. First left after Golden Lion.

SYMBOLS The symbols in each entry give information about services and facilities. A key to these symbols appears at the back of this guide.

BUDE, Cornwall Map ref 1C2 *Tourist Information Centre Tel: (01288) 354240*

◆◆◆◆

HALLAGATHER FARMHOUSE

Crackington Haven, Bude, EX23 0LA
T: (01840) 230276
F: (01840) 230449

B&B per night:
S £18.00–£26.00
D £35.00–£49.00

OPEN Feb–Nov

Our farm and ancient house near the coast at Crackington Haven, are midway between Bude and Tintagel. We have awesome scenery, magnificent beaches and great walking country, together with a warm welcome, informality and individual attention. Our breakfasts are substantial, using the best locally produced food wherever possible.

Bedrooms: 1 single,
1 double, 1 triple
Bathrooms: 3 en suite,
1 public

Parking for 6

◆◆◆

LOWER NORTHCOTT FARM
Poughill, Bude, EX23 9EQ
T: (01288) 352350
F: (01288) 352712
E: sales@coast-countryside.co.uk
I: www.coast-countryside.co.uk

Bedrooms: 1 single,
1 twin, 3 family rooms
Bathrooms: 4 en suite,
1 private

EM 1830 (LO 1830)
Parking for 4

B&B per night:
S Min £20.00
D Min £40.00

HB per person:
DY Min £30.00

OPEN All year round

Georgian farmhouse in secluded valley with outstanding coastal views. Traditional farmhouse. Evening meals. All en suite. Walking holiday specialists. Ideal for walking and touring all seasons.

BUDLEIGH SALTERTON, Devon Map ref 1D2 *Tourist Information Centre Tel: (01395) 445275*

◆◆◆◆

Silver
Award

LUFFLANDS
Yettington, Budleigh Salterton,
EX9 7BP
T: (01395) 568422
F: (01395) 568810
E: Lufflands@compuserve.com
I: www.lufflands.co.uk

Bedrooms: 1 single,
1 double, 1 family room
Bathrooms: 2 en suite,
1 private

Parking for 10

B&B per night:
S £20.00–£22.00
D £40.00–£44.00

OPEN All year round

Comfortable old farmhouse. Guest dining room/lounge with inglenook. Children welcome. Country views, large garden, ample parking. Close beaches. Excellent walking.

BURNHAM-ON-SEA, Somerset Map ref 1D1 *Tourist Information Centre Tel: (01278) 787852*

◆◆◆

BOUNDRYS EDGE
40 Charlestone Road, Burnham-on-
Sea, TA8 2AP
T: (01278) 783128 &
0771 2737033 (Mobile)
F: (01278) 783128

Bedrooms: 1 double,
1 twin
Bathrooms: 2 en suite

Parking for 2

B&B per night:
D £30.00–£35.00

HB per person:
DY £23.00–£25.50

OPEN All year round

Small bed and breakfast situated in quiet cul-de-sac 5 minutes' walk from town centre and a few minutes' walk from beach. Close to tennis and golf courses.

CHECK THE MAPS

The colour maps at the front of this guide show all the cities, towns and villages for which you will find accommodation entries. Refer to the town index to find the page on which they are listed.

♦♦♦

PROSPECT FARM GUEST HOUSE

Strowlands, East Brent, Highbridge, TA9 4JH
T: (01278) 760507 (Ansaphone)

B&B per night:
S £19.00–£25.00
D £38.00–£50.00

OPEN All year round

17thC Somerset farmhouse with inglenook fireplaces, bread ovens, beamed ceilings and a colourful history. Surrounded by the natural West Country beauty of the Somerset Levels, near legendary Brent Knoll, with remains of Iron Age and Roman settlements. 2 miles junction 22 M5, 3 miles Burnham-on-Sea. Variety of small farm animals and pets. Children welcome.

Bedrooms: 1 double, 2 triple
Bathrooms: 1 en suite, 1 public

Parking for 12

♦♦♦♦

PEBBLE BEACH LODGE
Coast Road, Burton Bradstock, Bridport, DT6 4RJ
T: (01308) 897428
F: (01308) 897428

Bedrooms: 1 single, 5 double, 1 twin, 2 triple, 1 family room; suite available
Bathrooms: 10 en suite

Parking for 16

B&B per night:
S £22.00–£25.00
D £44.00–£50.00

OPEN Mar–Oct

Located on B3157 coast road, affording panoramic views of heritage coastline. Direct access to beach. Spacious and attractive accommodation, large conservatory.

♦♦♦♦

BUTCOMBE FARM

Aldwick Lane, Butcombe, Bristol, BS40 7UW
T: (01761) 462380
F: (01761) 462300
E: info@butcombe-farm.demon.co.uk
I: www.butcombe-farm.demon.co.uk

B&B per night:
S £30.00–£39.00
D £35.00–£49.00

OPEN All year round

Originally a 14thC medieval hall house, Butcombe Farm is now a beautiful manor-house with en suite bed and breakfast and individual self-catering accommodation. Set in several acres amid peaceful countryside. Close to Bristol, Bath, Cheddar, Wells, Mendips and Exmoor. For more information, please contact Barry and Josephine Harvey.

Bedrooms: 3 double, 2 triple
Bathrooms: 5 en suite

Parking for 20
CC: Barclaycard, Delta, Eurocard, Maestro, Mastercard, Solo, Switch, Visa, Visa Electron

♦♦♦

DOZMARY
Tors View Close, Tavistock Road, Callington, PL17 7DY
T: (01579) 383677
E: dozmarybb@aol.com

Bedrooms: 1 double, 1 twin, 1 family room
Bathrooms: 2 en suite, 1 private

Parking for 4

B&B per night:
S £19.00–£20.00
D £32.00–£34.00

OPEN Jan–Nov

Deceptively spacious dormer bungalow providing comfortable accommodation with good facilities, just a few minutes from Callington town centre.

PRICES
Please check prices and other details at the time of booking.

CALLINGTON continued

◆◆◆ **GREEN PASTURES**

Longhill, Callington, PL17 8AU
T: (01579) 382566
E: greenpast@aol.com

Bedrooms: 1 double,
1 twin, 1 family room;
suites available
Bathrooms: 2 en suite,
1 private

Parking for 8

B&B per night:
S Max £20.00
D Max £35.00

OPEN All year round

Spacious detached bungalow set within 5 acres of pastural land. Large car park. Extensive views towards Dartmoor, Tamar Valley. Cotehele, Morwellam Quay within easy reach.

CANNINGTON, Somerset Map ref 1D1

◆◆◆

THE FRIENDLY SPIRIT

Brook Street, Cannington, Bridgwater,
TA5 2HP
T: (01278) 652215
F: (01278) 653636

B&B per night:
S £25.00–£30.00
D £40.00–£50.00

OPEN All year round

A long established country inn (with resident ghost) lying within an attractive conservation area by the village green and brook. Ideal base for exploring the Quantocks and North Somerset coast. Cycle hire, golf and other attractions nearby. As featured on Carlton Television and winner of "Perfect Pint" award 1999-2000.

Bedrooms: 2 double,
7 twin, 1 family room
Bathrooms: 7 en suite,
1 public

Lunch available
EM 1900 (LO 2100)
Parking for 30
CC: Barclaycard, Delta,
Mastercard, Switch, Visa

CASTLE CARY, Somerset Map ref 2B2

◆◆◆◆

BOND'S

Ansford Hill, Castle Cary, BA7 7JL
T: (01963) 350464
F: (01963) 350464

B&B per night:
S £58.00–£58.00
D £68.00–£68.00

HB per person:
DY £45.00–£55.00

OPEN All year round

A lovely Georgian house of charm and character managed by the owners, Kevin and Yvonne Bond. Formerly known as Bond's Hotel and Restaurant, now with a little less formality than before, it continues to be featured in numerous leading hotel and food guides with delightful rooms and Yvonne still in the kitchen.

Bedrooms: 2 single,
3 double, 2 twin
Bathrooms: 6 en suite,
1 private

Lunch available
EM 1830 (LO 2130)
Parking for 16
CC: Barclaycard, Delta,
Eurocard, Mastercard,
Switch, Visa

◆◆◆ **THE HORSE POND INN AND MOTEL**

The Triangle, Castle Cary, BA7 7BD
T: (01963) 350318 & 351762
F: (01963) 351764
E: horsepondinn@aol.com

Bedrooms: 2 twin,
2 triple; suites available
Bathrooms: 4 en suite,
2 public

Lunch available
EM 1900 (LO 2100)
Parking for 24
CC: Amex, Diners, JCB,
Mastercard, Switch, Visa

B&B per night:
S £38.00–£42.00
D £50.00–£55.00

HB per person:
DY £50.00–£55.00

OPEN All year round

The inn and motel nestles at the foot of Castle Cary, Centrally located, making it an ideal base for travelling around Somerset, West Devon, Dorset and Wiltshire.

CHAGFORD, Devon Map ref 1C2

◆◆◆◆
Silver
Award

GLENDARAH HOUSE
Lower Street, Chagford,
Newton Abbot, TQ13 8BZ
T: (01647) 433270
F: (01647) 433483
E: enquiries@glendarah-house.co.uk
I: www.glendarah-house.co.uk

Bedrooms: 1 single,
3 double, 3 twin
Bathrooms: 7 en suite

Parking for 7
CC: Barclaycard, Delta,
Mastercard, Switch, Visa

B&B per night:
S £24.00–£28.00
D £48.00–£56.00

OPEN All year round

Non-smoking Victorian house with beautiful views in peaceful location, a short walk from village centre. Friendly service, en suite rooms with all facilities.

Ⓜ⌂10♨♫⟶♥🐾🖥Ⓢ⤢🅿🖥💷🍽🚗 SP Ⓣ

CHARD, Somerset Map ref 1D2 *Tourist Information Centre Tel: (01460) 67463*

◆◆◆

WAMBROOK FARM
Wambrook, Chard, TA20 3DF
T: (01460) 62371
F: (01460) 68827

B&B per night:
S £25.00–£25.00
D £40.00–£40.00

OPEN Apr–Nov

A listed farmhouse and buildings in the beautiful countryside of the Blackdown Hills, 2 miles from Chard in peaceful, rural village. An ideal base for visiting Devon, Dorset and Somerset, Forde Abbey and gardens, Lyme Regis, Honiton antiques and NT properties. Excellent pub food in village.

Bedrooms: 1 double,
1 family room
Bathrooms: 2 en suite,
1 public

Parking for 8

Ⓜ⌂♨Ⓤ🅿Ⓢ Ⓣ💷🖥🍽🚗🐾🏇

CHARMINSTER, Dorset Map ref 2B3

◆◆◆

THREE COMPASSES INN
Charminster, Dorchester, DT2 9QT
T: (01305) 263618

Bedrooms: 1 single,
1 double, 1 twin, 1 triple
Bathrooms: 2 en suite,
1 public

Lunch available
EM 1900 (LO 2200)
Parking for 50

B&B per night:
S £20.00–£25.00
D £40.00–£50.00

OPEN All year round

Traditional village public house/inn with skittle alley, set in village square.

⌂⟶♨🍽Ⓣ💷🖥🍽🏺15🅿🚗🐾Ⓣ

CHEDDAR, Somerset Map ref 1D1

◆◆◆

MARKET CROSS HOTEL
The Cross, Church Street, Cheddar,
BS27 3RA
T: (01934) 742264
F: (01934) 741411

Bedrooms: 2 single,
2 double, 1 triple,
1 family room
Bathrooms: 3 en suite,
1 public

Lunch available
EM 1900 (LO 2000)
Parking for 8
CC: Barclaycard, Delta,
Eurocard, Maestro,
Mastercard, Solo, Switch,
Visa, Visa Electron

B&B per night:
S £21.50–£30.00
D £43.50–£56.00

HB per person:
DY £31.50–£40.00

OPEN All year round

Delightful Regency hotel. Good walking area, 5 minutes' walk from Cheddar Gorge, caves and Mendip Hills. Wells, Glastonbury, Bristol, Bath, Weston-super-Mare within easy reach.

Ⓜ⌂📞⟶♨♥Ⓢ⤢🍽Ⓣ💷🖥🅿∪🐾🍽🚗 SP 🏺Ⓣ

◆◆◆◆

TOR FARM
Nyland, Cheddar, BS27 3UD
T: (01934) 743710
F: (01934) 743710
E: bcjbkj@aol.com

Bedrooms: 1 single,
3 double, 2 twin,
1 family room
Bathrooms: 5 en suite,
2 public

Parking for 10
CC: Barclaycard, Delta,
Eurocard, JCB,
Mastercard, Switch, Visa

B&B per night:
S £25.00–£30.00
D £35.00–£48.00

OPEN All year round

33-acre mixed farm. On A371 between Cheddar and Draycott. On Somerset Levels. Ideally situated for visiting Cheddar, Bath, Wookey Hole, Glastonbury, Wells and coast.

Ⓜ⌂♨🏛♥🍽Ⓣ💷🖥🏺20🔧∪🐾🍽 SP Ⓣ

REGIONAL TOURIST BOARD The Ⓜ symbol in an establishment entry indicates that it is a Regional Tourist Board member.

CHEW STOKE, Bath and North East Somerset Map ref 2A2

◆◆◆ **ORCHARD HOUSE**

Bristol Road, Chew Stoke, Bristol,
BS40 8UB
T: (01275) 333143
F: (01275) 333754

Bedrooms: 1 single,
2 double, 3 twin,
1 family room
Bathrooms: 5 en suite,
1 private, 2 public

EM 1830 (LO 1000)
Parking for 9
CC: Delta, Mastercard,
Solo, Switch, Visa, Visa
Electron

B&B per night:
S £20.00–£25.00
D £40.00–£50.00

HB per person:
DY £30.00–£35.00

OPEN All year round

Comfortable accommodation in a carefully modernised Georgian house and coach house annexe. Home cooking using local produce.

CHIDEOCK, Dorset Map ref 1D2

◆◆◆◆ **BETCHWORTH HOUSE**

Chideock, Bridport, DT6 6JW
T: (01297) 489478
F: (01297) 489932

Bedrooms: 2 double,
2 twin, 1 triple
Bathrooms: 3 en suite,
2 private

Parking for 6
CC: Amex, Barclaycard,
Delta, JCB, Maestro,
Mastercard, Switch, Visa,
Visa Electron

B&B per night:
S £27.00–£30.00
D £44.00–£50.00

OPEN All year round

Charming 17thC guesthouse offering a high standard of accommodation. Dorset cream teas served in attractive dining-room or pretty cottage garden.

CHIPPENHAM, Wiltshire Map ref 2B2 *Tourist Information Centre Tel: (01249) 706333*

◆◆◆◆

CHURCH FARM

Hartham Park, Corsham, SN13 0PU
T: (01249) 715180 &
07977 910775 (Mobile)
F: (01249) 715572
E: kmjbandb@aol.com.

B&B per night:
S £21.00–£25.00
D £42.00–£48.00

OPEN All year round

Cotswold farmhouse on working dairy and mixed farm, offering superb views over open countryside. Glorious walks nearby with plenty of wildlife. Garden available for guests' use. Local produce used wherever possible. Warm family welcome. Secure off-road parking. Good road/ rail links, easy access Bath, Castle Combe and Lacock.

Bedrooms: 1 single,
1 double, 1 triple
Bathrooms: 2 en suite,
1 private

Parking for 7

◆◆ **75 ROWDEN HILL**

Chippenham, SN15 2AL
T: (01249) 652981

Bedrooms: 2 double,
1 twin
Bathrooms: 1 public

Parking for 5

B&B per night:
S £20.00–£20.00
D £28.00–£28.00

OPEN All year round

Near National Trust village of Lacock and attractive Castle Combe. Corsham Court also nearby. Friendly welcome assured.

CHIPPING SODBURY, South Gloucestershire Map ref 2B2

◆◆◆◆ **THE SODBURY HOUSE HOTEL**

Badminton Road, Old Sodbury,
Bristol, BS37 6LU
T: (01454) 312847
F: (01454) 273105
E: sodhousehotel@tesco.net

Bedrooms: 6 single,
5 double, 4 twin,
2 family rooms
Bathrooms: 17 en suite

Parking for 30
CC: Amex, Barclaycard,
Eurocard, Mastercard,
Switch, Visa

B&B per night:
S £50.00–£54.00
D £78.00–£90.00

OPEN All year round

A warm welcome awaits you at this former farmhouse offering well-appointed en suite accommodation in attractive rural setting, within easy reach M4/M5, Bath, Bristol and Cotswolds.

TOWN INDEX

This can be found at the back of this guide. If you know where you want to stay, the index will give you the page number listing accommodation in your chosen town, city or village.

CLOVELLY, Devon Map ref 1C1

FUCHSIA COTTAGE

Burscott, Clovelly, Bideford,
EX39 5RR
T: (01237) 431398
E: tomsuecurtis.fuchsiacot@
currantbun.com

Bedrooms: 1 single,
1 double, 1 triple
Bathrooms: 2 en suite,
1 public

EM 1830
Parking for 3

B&B per night:
S Max £16.00
D Max £37.00

OPEN All year round

Fuchsia Cottage has comfortable ground and first floor en suite accommodation. Surrounded by beautiful views of sea and country. Good walking area. Ample parking.

COLYTON, Devon Map ref 1D2

SMALLICOMBE FARM

Northleigh, Colyton, EX24 6BU
T: (01404) 831310
F: (01404) 831431
E: maggie_todd@yahoo.com
I: www.smallicombe.com

B&B per night:
S £25.00–£30.00
D £40.00–£46.00

HB per person:
DY £31.50–£37.50

OPEN All year round

Idyllic setting with only the sights and sounds of the countryside yet close to the coast. Meet friendly farm animals including Berkshire pigs. Explore picturesque villages and historic houses and gardens. Return to enjoy a scrumptious farmhouse meal in our licensed restaurant.

Bedrooms: 1 double,
1 twin, 1 family room;
suite available
Bathrooms: 3 en suite

EM
Parking for 10

COMBE FLOREY, Somerset Map ref 1D1

REDLANDS

Trebles Holford, Combe Florey, Taunton,
TA4 3HA
T: (01823) 433159
E: redlandshouse@hotmail.com
I: www.escapetothecountry.co.uk

B&B per night:
S £28.00–£28.00
D £48.00–£53.00

OPEN All year round

Escape to the country to our peacefully located barn conversion set beside a stream adjacent to the Quantock Hills. Enjoy the outdoors or let off steam on the West Somerset Railway. Within easy reach are gardens, National Trust properties, the coast and Exmoor. Ground floor room suitable for disabled guests.

Bedrooms: 1 double,
1 twin
Bathrooms: 2 en suite

Parking for 4

CORSHAM, Wiltshire Map ref 2B2 *Tourist Information Centre Tel: (01249) 714660*

HEATHERLY COTTAGE

Ladbrook Lane, Gastard, Corsham,
SN13 9PE
T: (01249) 701402
F: (01249) 701412
E: ladbrook1@aol.com
I: www.smoothhound.co.uk/hotels/
heather3.html

Bedrooms: 2 double,
1 twin
Bathrooms: 3 en suite

Parking for 10

B&B per night:
S £26.00–£28.00
D £44.00–£47.00

OPEN All year round

Delightful 17thC cottage in 1.5 acres with views over open countryside. Rooms with TV and hospitality trays. Many pubs serving food nearby. Bath 9 miles. Ample parking.

CHECK THE MAPS

The colour maps at the front of this guide show all the cities, towns
and villages for which you will find accommodation entries.
Refer to the town index to find the page on which they are listed.

CRANTOCK, Cornwall Map ref 1B2

◆◆◆

HIGHFIELD LODGE HOTEL

Halwyn Road, Crantock, Newquay, TR8 5TR
T: (01637) 830744

B&B per night:
S £18.00–£23.00
D £36.00–£46.00

OPEN All year round

Highfield Lodge is a small, friendly, non-smoking hotel in the picturesque coastal village of Crantock. An ideal centre for touring Cornwall with nearby facilities for coarse and sea fishing, riding, surfing and golf, with Crantock beach a mere stroll away. Bar meals available in our cosy licensed bar.

Bedrooms: 2 single, 7 double, 1 twin, 1 family room
Bathrooms: 8 en suite, 1 public, 1 private shower

EM 1830 (LO 2100)
Parking for 14

CREWKERNE, Somerset Map ref 1D2

◆◆◆

THE GEORGE HOTEL & COURTYARD RESTAURANT

Market Square, Crewkerne, TA18 7LP
T: (01460) 73650
F: (01460) 72974
E: eddie@thegeorgehotel.sagehost.co.uk
I: www.crewkerne.co.uk/accommodation/george_hotel/indexhtml.

Bedrooms: 3 single, 6 double, 2 twin, 1 triple, 1 family room
Bathrooms: 7 en suite, 2 private, 1 public, 2 private showers

Lunch available
EM 1900 (LO 2130)
CC: Amex, Barclaycard, Delta, Diners, Eurocard, JCB, Maestro, Mastercard, Solo, Switch, Visa, Visa Electron

B&B per night:
S £25.00–£45.00
D £48.00–£80.00

HB per person:
DY £35.00–£65.00

OPEN All year round

Recently refurbished 17thC Grade II Listed coaching inn in the market square. Ideally located for touring. Fine food, real ales, warm welcome!

DARTMOOR

See under Ashburton, Bovey Tracey, Bridestowe, Chagford, Hexworthy, Moretonhampstead, Okehampton, Tavistock, Widecombe-in-the-Moor, Yelverton

DEVIZES, Wiltshire Map ref 2B2 *Tourist Information Centre Tel: (01380) 729408*

◆◆◆◆◆
Gold
Award

BLOUNTS COURT FARM

Coxhill Lane, Potterne, Devizes, SN10 5PH
T: (01380) 727180

B&B per night:
S £32.00–£37.00
D Min £50.00

OPEN All year round

Situated in a peaceful countryside setting of 150 acres with woodland backdrop. Traditional stone-built farmhouse with ground floor guest accommodation in recently converted stables adjoining house. Beautifully furnished rooms including 4-poster bed. Guests' own sitting room. Warm and homely atmosphere. Ideal base to explore this exciting part of Wiltshire.

Bedrooms: 1 double, 1 twin
Bathrooms: 2 en suite

MAP REFERENCES The map references refer to the colour maps at the front of this guide. The first figure is the map number; the letter and figure which follow indicate the grid reference on the map.

◆◆◆

EASTCOTT MANOR

Easterton, Devizes, SN10 4PL
T: (01380) 813313

B&B per night:
S £22.00–£23.00
D £48.00–£50.00

HB per person:
DY £44.00–£48.00

OPEN All year round

Very comfortable Grade II* Elizabethan manor house on north edge of Salisbury Plain. Wonderful walking, convenient for Kennet and Avon Canal, Bath, Salisbury, Stonehenge, Avebury, National Trust properties and other beautiful houses. Large garden, set in own 20-acre grounds. Tranquil setting, nearest road B3098.

Bedrooms: 2 single, 1 double, 1 twin
Bathrooms: 2 en suite, 2 private

EM 1930 (LO 1930)
Parking for 6

◆◆◆◆

LITTLETON LODGE

Littleton Panell (A360), West Lavington, Devizes, SN10 4ES
T: (01380) 813131
F: (01380) 816969
E: stay@littletonlodge.co.uk
I: www.littletonlodge.co.uk

B&B per night:
S £30.00–£40.00
D £45.00–£60.00

OPEN All year round

Comfortable Victorian house in conservation village. Own grounds, rural outlook. 3 good pubs within 5 minutes' walk. Private parking. Just 15 minutes north of Stonehenge, 10 minutes from White Horses. Excellent base for Avebury, Bath, Devizes, Lacock and Salisbury.

Bedrooms: 2 double, 1 twin
Bathrooms: 3 en suite

Parking for 5
CC: Amex, Barclaycard, Eurocard, Mastercard, Visa

◆

WHITEMOOR FARM

Doddiscombsleigh, Exeter, EX6 7PU
T: (01647) 252423
E: blaceystaffyrescue@easicom.com

B&B per night:
S £18.00–£19.00
D £35.00–£36.00

HB per person:
DY £25.50–£29.50

OPEN All year round

16thC thatched farmhouse surrounded by gardens and farmland in the picturesque Teign Valley, ideal for those appreciating peace and quiet. The house has oak beams, log fires in winter, central heating throughout. Home produce a speciality. Swimming pool available. Within easy reach of Exeter, forest walks, the sea and Dartmoor.

Bedrooms: 2 single, 1 double, 1 twin
Bathrooms: 1 public

EM 1900 (LO 2000)
Parking for 5

NB **IMPORTANT NOTE** Information on accommodation listed in this guide has been supplied by the proprietors. As changes may occur you are advised to check details at the time of booking.

DORCHESTER, Dorset Map ref 2B3 *Tourist Information Centre Tel: (01305) 267992*

◆◆◆

CHURCHVIEW GUEST HOUSE

Winterbourne Abbas, Dorchester, DT2 9LS
T: (01305) 889296
F: (01305) 889296

B&B per night:
S £22.00–£32.00
D £44.00–£58.00

HB per person:
DY £35.00–£44.00

OPEN All year round

Beautiful 17thC guesthouse set in a small village near Dorchester, offers a warm welcome and delicious home-cooked meals. Character bedrooms with hospitality trays, TV and radio. Two comfortable lounges and licensed bar. Your hosts will give every assistance with information to ensure a memorable stay.

Bedrooms: 6 double, 3 twin
Bathrooms: 7 en suite, 1 public

Parking for 10
CC: Barclaycard, Delta, Eurocard, Maestro, Mastercard, Solo, Switch, Visa, Visa Electron

---

◆◆◆◆

THE OLD RECTORY

Winterbourne Steepleton, Dorchester, DT2 9LG
T: (01305) 889468
F: (01305) 889737
E: trees@eurobell.co.uk.
I: www.trees.eurobell.co.uk

B&B per night:
D £45.00–£100.00

OPEN All year round (closed Christmas and New Year)

Built 1850 on one acre of private ground in a quiet hamlet, surrounded by spectacular walks, 6 miles from historic Dorchester, 8 miles from Weymouth's sandy beach. We offer a peaceful stay with a memorable breakfast including many home-made organic products. Excellent local pubs and restaurants. French spoken.

Bedrooms: 3 double, 1 twin
Bathrooms: 4 en suite, 1 public

Parking for 6

◆◆◆◆

WHITFIELD FARM COTTAGE

Poundbury Whitfield, Dorchester, DT2 9SL
T: (01305) 260233
F: (01305) 260233
E: dc.whitfield@clara.net
I: www.dc.whitfield.clara.net

B&B per night:
S £24.00–£27.00
D £48.00–£50.00

OPEN All year round

Comfortable, pretty, 200-year-old cottage of character and charm in peaceful countryside within 1 mile of Dorchester. Warm, friendly welcome assured. Safe parking within grounds. Pleasant walks nearby River Frome. Sea 8 miles. An ideal location from which to explore Dorset's stunning coastline and historic towns and villages.

Bedrooms: 1 single, 2 twin
Bathrooms: 1 en suite, 2 private

Parking for 6

WELCOME HOST This is a nationally recognised customer care programme which aims to promote the highest standards of service and a warm welcome. Establishments taking part in this initiative are indicated by the ⊛ symbol.

DORCHESTER continued

◆◆◆◆◆

YALBURY COTTAGE HOTEL AND RESTAURANT
Lower Bockhampton, Dorchester, DT2 8PZ
T: (01305) 262382
F: (01305) 266412
E: yalbury.cottage@virgin.net

Nestling amidst winding rivers and peaceful fields, Yalbury Cottage is the ideal place to relax and unwind. This friendly, 17thC thatched hotel is at the heart of Thomas Hardy's Wessex. Its pretty restaurant offers head chef Russell Brown's excellent award-winning food, in an atmosphere enhanced by oak beams and inglenooks.

Bedrooms: 6 double, 1 twin, 1 triple
Bathrooms: 8 en suite

EM 1900 (LO 2100)
Parking for 19
CC: Barclaycard, Delta, Eurocard, JCB, Mastercard, Solo, Switch, Visa

B&B per night:
S £53.00–£53.00
D £82.00–£82.00

HB per person:
DY £67.00–£79.00

OPEN Feb–Dec

◆◆◆◆
Silver
Award

YELLOWHAM FARM
Yellowham Wood, Dorchester, DT2 8RW
T: (01305) 262892
F: (01305) 257707
E: b&b@yellowham.freeserve.co.uk
I: www.yellowham.freeserve.co.uk

Bedrooms: 3 double, 1 twin
Bathrooms: 4 en suite

Parking for 8

B&B per night:
S £30.00–£40.00
D £45.00–£58.00

HB per person:
DY £40.00–£45.00

OPEN All year round

Situated in the heart of Hardy Country on the edge of the idyllic Yellowham Wood in 120 acres of farmland and 130 acres of woodland.

DULVERTON, Somerset Map ref 1D1

◆◆◆◆
Silver
Award

TOWN MILLS
High Street, Dulverton, TA22 9HB
T: (01398) 323124

B&B per night:
S £25.00–£42.00
D £38.00–£52.00

OPEN All year round

Escape for a while to enjoy comfort and peace in our secluded 19thC mill house situated in the centre of Dulverton. We serve full English breakfast in our attractive and spacious rooms, some having their own log fire. We are an ideal centre for exploring Exmoor.

Bedrooms: 3 double, 2 twin; suite available
Bathrooms: 3 en suite, 1 public

Parking for 5

DUNSTER, Somerset Map ref 1D1

◆◆◆◆
Silver
Award

CONYGAR HOUSE
2A The Ball, Dunster, Minehead, TA24 6SD
T: (01643) 821872
F: (01643) 821872
E: bale.dunster@virgin.net
I: www.homepage.virgin.net/bale_dunster

Bedrooms: 2 double, 1 twin
Bathrooms: 2 en suite, 1 private, 1 public

B&B per night:
D £44.00–£48.00

OPEN Feb–Oct

Well-appointed private house off main street of Dunster with country views from all bedrooms. Ideal for exploring Exmoor. Quiet location. Parking.

QUALITY ASSURANCE SCHEME
Diamond ratings and awards are explained at the back of this guide.

EXETER, Devon Map ref 1D2 *Tourist Information Centre Tel: (01392) 265700*

◆◆◆◆

BICKHAM FARMHOUSE
Kenn, Exeter, EX6 7XL
T: (01392) 832206 & 07773 456194
F: (01392) 832206

B&B per night:
S £20.00–£25.00
D Min £36.00

OPEN All year round

Medieval Devon longhouse in thatched village of Kenn near Exeter. Recently refurbished to high standard, retaining character oak beams and large open fireplaces. Ideal base to visit Dartmoor National Park and Devon's spectacular coastline. Adjacent 6 acres of gardens are open to public. Be sure of warm welcome and hearty breakfast.

Bedrooms: 1 double,
1 family room
Bathrooms: 1 en suite,
1 private

Parking for 10

◆◆◆◆

DANSON HOUSE
Marsh Green, Exeter, EX5 2ES
T: (01404) 823260
F: (01404) 823260
E: dk2789@eclipse.co.uk
I: www.eclipse.co.uk/danson/

B&B per night:
S £27.00–£30.00
D £46.00–£50.00

OPEN All year round

Large country house set in mature gardens, affording total peace and quiet. Ideal base for exploring the coast, moors and the beautiful cathedral city of Exeter. Excellent award-winning en suite accommodation in spacious, highly appointed rooms. Breakfast served in oak-furnished dining room. Friendly family atmosphere. No smoking in house.

Bedrooms: 1 double,
2 triple
Bathrooms: 2 en suite,
1 private

EM 1900 (LO 2000)
Parking for 4

◆◆◆◆

THE GRANGE
Stoke Hill, Exeter, EX4 7JH
T: (01392) 259723
E: dudleythegrange@aol.com

Bedrooms: 2 double,
2 twin
Bathrooms: 4 en suite

Parking for 11

B&B per night:
S £25.00–£28.00
D £35.00–£42.00

OPEN All year round

Country house set in 3 acres of woodlands, 1.5 miles from the city centre. Ideal for holidays and off-season breaks. En suite rooms.

COUNTRY CODE Always follow the Country Code 🐾
Enjoy the countryside and respect its life and work 🐾 Guard against all risk of fire 🐾 Fasten all gates 🐾 Keep your dogs under close control 🐾 Keep to public paths across farmland 🐾 Use gates and stiles to cross fences, hedges and walls 🐾 Leave livestock, crops and machinery alone 🐾 Take your litter home 🐾 Help to keep all water clean 🐾 Protect wildlife, plants and trees 🐾 Take special care on country roads 🐾 Make no unnecessary noise

◆◆◆

HAYNE BARTON
Whitestone, Exeter, EX4 2JN
T: (01392) 811268

B&B per night:
S £26.00–£30.00
D £44.00–£50.00

OPEN All year round

Listed Grade II farmhouse (Doomesday Book, 1086) with Saxon cellar, set in 16 acres of gardens, fields, streams and woods. Views to Dartmoor and Exe Estuary, 3 miles west of Exeter. Bed and breakfast. Both bedrooms en suite with colour TV. Ample parking. Dogs welcome. Stabling available. Bedding plant sales. Brochure available.

Bedrooms: 1 double, 1 twin
Bathrooms: 2 en suite

Parking for 10

◆◆◆ **HAYNE HOUSE**
Silverton, Exeter, EX5 4HE
T: (01392) 860725
F: (01392) 860725

Bedrooms: 1 single, 1 twin, 1 family room
Bathrooms: 3 private

Parking for 3
CC: Amex, Barclaycard, Delta, Eurocard, JCB, Mastercard, Solo, Switch, Visa, Visa Electron

B&B per night:
S £16.00–£20.00
D £32.00–£40.00

OPEN Mar–Oct

Detached Georgian farmhouse near National Trust property. Situated in the Culm Valley with views of Killerton, central for touring coast and moors. Traditional cooked breakfast.

◆◆◆ **PARK VIEW HOTEL**
8 Howell Road, Exeter, EX4 4LG
T: (01392) 271772
F: (01392) 253047
E: philbatho@parkviewhotel.freeserve.co.uk
I: www.parkviewhotel.freeserve.co.uk

Bedrooms: 3 single, 7 double, 3 twin, 2 triple
Bathrooms: 8 en suite, 2 private, 2 public

Parking for 6
CC: Amex, Barclaycard, Delta, Eurocard, Mastercard, Switch, Visa

B&B per night:
S £22.00–£34.00
D £40.00–£49.00

OPEN All year round

Charming family-run hotel, noted for peace and quiet and high standards, near city centre and stations. Tea/coffee, colour TV and telephone in all rooms.

See under Allerford, Dulverton, Dunster, Lynmouth, Lynton, West Anstey, Winsford

◆◆◆ **THE MEWS**
Knappe Cross, Brixington Lane, Exmouth, EX8 5DL
T: (01395) 272198

Bedrooms: 1 single, 1 double, 1 twin
Bathrooms: 1 public

Parking for 10

B&B per night:
S £18.00–£19.00
D £36.00–£38.00

OPEN All year round

Large part of a delightfully secluded mews building in a country setting. Midway between Exmouth and Woodbury Common. We ask that guests refrain from smoking.

◆◆◆◆ **THE SWALLOWS**
11 Carlton Hill, Exmouth, EX8 2AJ
T: (01395) 263937
F: (01395) 271040
E: firus@globalnet.co.uk
I: www.smoothhound.co.uk/hotels/swallows.html

Bedrooms: 1 single, 2 double, 1 twin, 1 family room
Bathrooms: 4 en suite, 1 private, 1 public

EM 1830 (LO 2000)
Parking for 3
CC: Delta, Eurocard, Mastercard, Solo, Switch, Visa, Visa Electron

B&B per night:
S £20.00–£20.00
D £40.00–£50.00

HB per person:
DY £28.00–£33.00

OPEN All year round

Late Georgian house, tastefully converted and modernised whilst retaining its comfortable and peaceful atmosphere. Close to seafront and town centre in attractive residential area.

MAP REFERENCES
Map references apply to the colour maps at the front of this guide.

◆◆◆◆

APPLE TREE COTTAGE

Laity Moor, Ponsanooth, Truro, TR3 7HR
T: (01872) 865047
E: raistlin@dial.pipex.com

B&B per night:
S £25.00–£27.50
D £45.00–£50.00

OPEN Feb–Nov

Set amid countryside between Falmouth and Truro with a river meandering through the gardens. Rooms are furnished in a country style and guests are offered traditional farmhouse fare cooked on the Aga. Close to superb Cornish gardens and beaches. No smoking. Member Falmouth Hotel Association. For brochure contact Mrs A Tremayne.

| Bedrooms: 2 double | Parking for 3 |
| Bathrooms: 1 public | |

◆◆◆◆

IVANHOE GUEST HOUSE
7 Melvill Road, Falmouth, TR11 4AS
T: (01326) 319083
F: (01326) 319083
E: berman.ivanhoe@talk21.com
I: www.smoothhound.co.uk/hotels/ivanhoe

Bedrooms: 2 single, 3 double, 2 twin
Bathrooms: 4 en suite, 2 public

Parking for 4
CC: Amex, Barclaycard, Diners, Eurocard, Mastercard, Visa

B&B per night:
S £18.00–£26.00
D £36.00–£52.00

OPEN All year round

A warm and comfortable guesthouse with particularly well equipped en suite rooms. Minutes from the beaches, harbour and town. Off-road parking.

◆◆◆

WICKHAM GUEST HOUSE

21 Gyllyngvase Terrace, Falmouth, TR11 4DL
T: (01326) 311140 (Ansaphone) & 07770 575381 (Mobile)
E: enquiries@wickhamhotel.freeserve.co.uk

B&B per night:
S £19.00–£19.00
D £38.00–£42.00

HB per person:
DY £28.00–£30.00

OPEN All year round

Small, friendly, no-smoking guesthouse. Situated between harbour and beach with views over Falmouth Bay, Wickham is the ideal base for exploring Falmouth and South Cornwall's gardens, castles, harbours, coastal footpath and much more. All rooms have TV and tea/coffee facilities, some have sea views.

Bedrooms: 2 single, 2 double, 1 triple, 1 family room
Bathrooms: 3 en suite, 1 public

EM 1845 (LO 1845)
Parking for 2
CC: Barclaycard, Mastercard, Visa

◆◆◆

VALE HOUSE
Figheldean, Salisbury, SP4 8JJ
T: (01980) 670713

Bedrooms: 1 single, 2 twin
Bathrooms: 1 en suite, 1 public

Parking for 2

B&B per night:
S £17.00–£19.00
D £35.00–£38.00

OPEN All year round

Secluded house in centre of picturesque village, 4 miles north of Amesbury on A345, 2 miles from Stonehenge.

CREDIT CARD BOOKINGS If you book by telephone and are asked for your credit card number it is advisable to check the proprietor's policy should you cancel your reservation.

FOWEY, Cornwall Map ref 1B3 *Tourist Information Centre Tel: (01726) 833616*

◆◆◆◆ **CARNETHIC HOUSE HOTEL**
Lambs Barn, Fowey, PL23 1HQ
T: (01726) 833336
F: (01726) 833296
E: carnethic@btinternet.com
I: www.crescom.co.uk/carnethic

Bedrooms: 1 single,
4 double, 1 twin, 1 triple,
1 family room
Bathrooms: 6 en suite,
2 private, 1 public

EM 1930 (LO 2030)
Parking for 20
CC: Amex, Barclaycard,
Delta, Diners, Eurocard,
Mastercard, Solo, Switch,
Visa, Visa Electron

B&B per night:
S £30.00–£40.00
D £50.00–£70.00

HB per person:
DY £40.00–£50.00

OPEN Feb–Nov

Regency house in 1.5 acres of mature gardens. Heated pool. Home cooking with local fish a speciality. Informal atmosphere.

FROME, Somerset Map ref 2B2 *Tourist Information Centre Tel: (01373) 467271*

◆◆◆◆

FOURWINDS GUEST HOUSE
19 Bath Road, Frome, BA11 2HJ
T: (01373) 462618
F: (01373) 453029

B&B per night:
S £30.00–£35.00
D £45.00–£55.00

OPEN All year round

Comfortable and friendly guesthouse with all the amenities of a small hotel. Half a mile north of town centre. Close to Longleat, Bath, Cheddar and Stourhead.

Bedrooms: 1 single,
2 double, 2 twin,
1 family room
Bathrooms: 4 en suite,
2 public

EM 1800 (LO 1900)
Parking for 12
CC: Barclaycard, Delta,
JCB, Maestro, Mastercard,
Solo, Switch, Visa, Visa
Electron

◆◆◆◆ **NORTH PARADE HOUSE**
7 North Parade, Frome, BA11 1AT
T: (01373) 474249
F: (01373) 467986

Bedrooms: 3 double;
suites available
Bathrooms: 3 en suite

B&B per night:
S Max £34.50
D Max £47.50

OPEN All year round

Newly renovated Grade II Listed Georgian town house with all en suite rooms. Stylishly decorated, well furnished, spacious and comfortable accommodation.

GLASTONBURY, Somerset Map ref 2A2 *Tourist Information Centre Tel: (01458) 832954*

◆◆◆ **LITTLE ORCHARD**
Ashwell Lane, Glastonbury,
BA6 8BG
T: (01458) 831620
I: www.smoothhound.co.uk/hotels/orchard.html

Bedrooms: 2 single,
1 double, 1 triple,
1 family room
Bathrooms: 2 public

Parking for 5

B&B per night:
S £17.50–£20.00
D £34.00–£40.00

OPEN All year round

On the A361 Glastonbury to Shepton Mallet road. Good central position for touring the West Country. At the foot of historic Glastonbury Tor, with views over the Vale of Avalon.

◆◆◆

MEADOW BARN
Middlewick Farm, Wick Lane, Glastonbury,
BA6 8JW
T: (01458) 832351
F: (01458) 832351

B&B per night:
S £27.00–£28.00
D £40.00–£44.00

HB per person:
DY £30.00–£38.00

OPEN All year round

Meadow Barn is ground floor en suite accommodation, in an old converted barn. It has country-style decor and old world charm, set in beautiful grounds, cottage gardens, meadows and apple orchards. Lovely walks and beautiful views of the Somerset Levels and the Mendip Hills beyond. Indoor heated swimming pool.

Bedrooms: 2 double,
1 twin
Bathrooms: 3 en suite

EM 1900 (LO 2030)
Parking for 20

GOONHAVERN, Cornwall Map ref 1B3

♦♦♦ **SEPTEMBER LODGE**

Wheal Hope, Goonhavern, Truro,
TR4 9QJ
T: (01872) 571435
F: (01872) 571435
E: jc.septlodge@virgin.net

Bedrooms: 1 double,
1 family room
Bathrooms: 2 en suite

Parking for 4

B&B per night:
S £25.00–£30.00
D £40.00–£40.00

OPEN All year round

Warm relaxed atmosphere. Spacious rooms in lovely setting, close to beautiful beaches, golf courses and coarse fishing lakes. Ideal touring base for Cornwall. Excellent breakfasts.

GRAMPOUND, Cornwall Map ref 1B3

♦♦♦ **PERRAN HOUSE**

Fore Street, Grampound, Truro,
TR2 4RS
T: (01726) 882066 & 884390

Bedrooms: 1 single,
3 double, 1 twin
Bathrooms: 3 en suite,
1 public

Parking for 10
CC: Barclaycard, Delta,
Mastercard, Visa

B&B per night:
S £16.00–£17.00
D £34.00–£38.00

OPEN All year round

Delightful Listed cottage in the pretty village of Grampound, between St Austell and Truro. Central for touring and visiting the many local gardens and Eden Project.

HARPFORD, Devon Map ref 1D2

♦♦♦♦

PEEKS HOUSE
Harpford, Sidmouth, EX10 0NH
T: (01395) 567664
F: (01395) 567664
E: peekshouse@fsbdial.co.uk

B&B per night:
S £33.00–£35.00
D £56.00–£60.00

OPEN Mar–Oct

Elegant Regency Grade II Listed house offering modern comforts in a warm and friendly atmosphere. All bedrooms are centrally heated, have an en suite bathroom and colour TV. Double and twin rooms are available. Off the beaten track in the beautiful hamlet of Harford with its 12thC church nestling between the River Otter and Harpford Woods

Bedrooms: 2 double,
2 twin
Bathrooms: 4 en suite,
1 public

EM 1800 (LO 1930)
Parking for 5

HARTLAND, Devon Map ref 1C1

♦♦♦♦

ELMSCOTT FARM
Hartland, Bideford, EX39 6ES
T: (01237) 441276
F: (01237) 441276

B&B per night:
S £20.00–£22.00
D £40.00–£44.00

OPEN Jan–Oct

Elmscott is a working farm on the beautiful South West Coast Path, close to the Devon/Cornwall border. The farmhouse offers spacious accommodation with every comfort and consideration for guests. Ideal for walking holidays with good local pubs and tourist attractions nearby. Signposted from the A39 approximately 4 miles away.

Bedrooms: 2 double,
1 twin
Bathrooms: 2 en suite,
1 private, 1 public

EM 1800 (LO 2000)
Parking for 8

ACCESSIBILITY

Look for the 🚾 symbols which indicate accessibility for wheelchair users. A list of establishments is at the front of this guide.

HARTLAND continued

◆◆◆ **HARTLAND QUAY HOTEL**
Hartland, Bideford, EX39 6DU
T: (01237) 441218
F: (01237) 441371

Bedrooms: 2 single,
4 double, 4 twin, 3 triple,
1 family room
Bathrooms: 10 en suite,
3 public

Lunch available
EM 1900 (LO 2000)
Parking for 100
CC: Barclaycard, Delta,
Mastercard, Solo, Switch,
Visa

B&B per night:
S £22.00–£24.00
D £44.00–£48.00

HB per person:
DY £32.00–£34.00

OPEN Mar–Oct

Small family-run hotel overlooking the rugged Atlantic coastline. Coastal walks. Important geological area.

HELSTON, Cornwall Map ref 1B3 *Tourist Information Centre Tel: (01326) 565431*

◆◆◆

LONGSTONE FARM
Coverack Bridges, Trenear, Helston,
TR13 0HG
T: (01326) 572483
F: (01326) 572483

B&B per night:
S Min £20.00
D Min £38.00

HB per person:
DY Min £30.00

OPEN Mar–Sep

Enjoy the warm and friendly atmosphere of our home, off the beaten track overlooking rolling fields and peaceful countryside. Central for sandy beaches and many attractions, particularly Flambards. Delicious meals using local produce attractively presented in our dining room overlooking the spacious garden. Relax and unwind in our TV lounge and sun-lounge.

Bedrooms: 1 double,
1 twin, 2 triple, 1 family
room
Bathrooms: 3 en suite,
2 private

EM 1800 (LO 0900)
Parking for 6

HENSTRIDGE, Somerset Map ref 2B3

◆◆

FOUNTAIN INN MOTEL
High Street, Henstridge,
Templecombe, BA8 0RA
T: (01963) 362722
F: (01963) 362722
I: www.fountaininn.fsnet.co.uk

Bedrooms: 6 double
Bathrooms: 6 en suite

Lunch available
EM 1800 (LO 2230)
Parking for 28
CC: Amex, Barclaycard,
Eurocard, Mastercard,
Visa

B&B per night:
S £21.00–£26.00
D £33.00–£40.00

OPEN All year round

Just off the A30 on the A357 Henstridge to Stalbridge road. Country inn (1700) with modern en suite motel-type accommodation.

HEXWORTHY, Devon Map ref 1C2

◆◆◆

THE FOREST INN
Hexworthy, Yelverton, PL20 6SD
T: (01364) 631211
F: (01364) 631515
E: forestinn@hotmail.com

B&B per night:
S £22.00–£35.00
D £44.00–£59.00

OPEN Feb–Dec

A haven for walkers, riders, fishermen, or anyone looking for an opportunity to enjoy the natural beauty of Dartmoor. The restaurant specialises in home-cooked foods and there is also an extensive range of snacks which can be enjoyed in the more informal Huccaby room. Dogs and muddy boots welcome!

Bedrooms: 2 single,
3 double, 3 twin, 2 triple
Bathrooms: 7 en suite,
3 private

Lunch available
EM 1900 (LO 2100)
Parking for 40
CC: Barclaycard, Delta,
Eurocard, Mastercard,
Solo, Switch, Visa, Visa
Electron

COLOUR MAPS Colour maps at the front of this guide pinpoint all places under which you will find accommodation listed.

HOLBETON, Devon Map ref 1C3

♦♦♦♦
Silver Award

BUGLE ROCKS

The Old School, Battisborough, Holbeton, Plymouth, PL8 1JX
T: (01752) 830422
F: (01752) 830558

B&B per night:
S £25.00–£25.00
D £50.00–£50.00

OPEN All year round

Located in an Area of Outstanding Natural Beauty, converted coach house and stable block. Formerly part of a gentleman's country residence, in a secluded valley overlooking the sea. Close to the spectacular coastal footpath, 5 minutes from the famous Mothecombe beach.

Bedrooms: 2 double
Bathrooms: 1 en suite, 1 private

Parking for 9

HOLCOMBE, Somerset Map ref 2B2

♦♦♦♦
RING O' ROSES
Stratton Road, Holcombe, Bath, BA3 5EB
T: (01761) 232478
F: (01761) 233737
E: ringorosesholcombe@tesco.net
I: www.ringoroses.co.uk

Bedrooms: 7 double, 1 twin
Bathrooms: 8 en suite

Lunch available
EM 1900 (LO 2100)
Parking for 30
CC: Barclaycard, Delta, Mastercard, Switch, Visa

B&B per night:
S £55.00–£58.00
D £69.00–£79.00

OPEN All year round

Revitalised 17thC inn nestling in the Mendip Hills. Renowned for excellent food, packed with atmosphere and antiques, it's a hidden treasure not to be missed.

HONITON, Devon Map ref 1D2 *Tourist Information Centre Tel: (01404) 43716*

♦♦♦♦
Silver Award

WESSINGTON FARM

Awliscombe, Honiton, EX14 0NU
T: (01404) 42280
E: b&b@eastdevon.com
I: www.eastdevon.com/bedandbreakfast

B&B per night:
S £20.00–£40.00
D £38.00–£46.00

OPEN All year round

140-acre dairy farm. Elegant Victorian stone farmhouse, situated in an Area of Outstanding Natural Beauty, with wonderful panoramic views over open countryside. On A373 2 miles from Honiton, picturesque East Devon coastline 20 minutes, historic Exeter 16 miles. High standard rooms, warm, friendly atmosphere, traditional Aga-cooked breakfast.

Bedrooms: 1 single, 1 double, 2 twin
Bathrooms: 3 en suite, 1 public

Parking for 6

ILFRACOMBE, Devon Map ref 1C1 *Tourist Information Centre Tel: (01271) 863001*

♦♦♦
CAPSTONE HOTEL AND RESTAURANT
St James Place, Ilfracombe, EX34 9BJ
T: (01271) 863540
F: (01271) 862277
I: www.ilfracombe2000.freeserve.co.uk

Bedrooms: 2 single, 6 double, 1 twin, 3 family rooms
Bathrooms: 12 en suite

Lunch available
EM 1800 (LO 2200)
Parking for 4
CC: Amex, Barclaycard, Delta, Mastercard, Switch, Visa

B&B per night:
S £17.50–£21.00
D £35.00–£42.00

HB per person:
DY £25.00–£28.50

OPEN Apr–Oct

Family-run hotel, with restaurant on ground floor. Close to harbour and all amenities. Local seafood a speciality.

CONFIRM YOUR BOOKING
You are advised to confirm your booking in writing.

ILFRACOMBE continued

◆◆◆ THE COLLINGDALE HOTEL

Larkstone Terrace, Ilfracombe,
EX34 9NU
T: (01271) 863770
F: (01271) 863770
E: collingdale@onet.co.uk
I: www.ilfracombe-guide.co.uk/
collingdale.htm

Bedrooms: 2 double,
3 twin, 1 triple, 3 family
rooms
Bathrooms: 8 en suite,
2 public, 1 private
shower

Lunch available
EM 1800 (LO 1900)
CC: Barclaycard, Delta,
Eurocard, JCB,
Mastercard, Solo, Switch,
Visa, Visa Electron

B&B per night:
S £19.00–£21.00
D £38.00–£42.00

HB per person:
DY £29.00–£31.00

OPEN Apr–Oct

Friendly hotel overlooking sea and harbour. Warm welcome. Cosy bar. Golf packages and other activities arranged. En suite rooms. Short walk to town centre.

◆◆◆◆ STRATHMORE HOTEL

57 St Brannocks Road, Ilfracombe,
EX34 8EQ
T: (01271) 862248 & 862243

Bedrooms: 2 single,
3 double, 1 twin, 2 triple,
1 family room
Bathrooms: 8 en suite,
1 public

EM 1900 (LO 2000)
Parking for 7
CC: Barclaycard, Eurocard,
JCB, Maestro, Mastercard,
Solo, Switch, Visa, Visa
Electron

B&B per night:
S £25.00–£31.00
D £44.00–£56.00

HB per person:
DY £32.95–£43.95

OPEN All year round

Quality hotel recommended for its superb home-cooked food, comfort and service. Licensed bar and parking. Close to beautiful beaches and Exmoor. Pets and children welcome.

ILMINSTER, Somerset Map ref 1D2

◆◆◆ GRADEN

Peasmarsh, Ilminster, TA19 0SG
T: (01460) 52371
F: (01460) 52371

Bedrooms: 2 double,
1 family room
Bathrooms: 2 public

EM
Parking for 5

B&B per night:
S £15.00–£16.00
D £30.00–£32.00

HB per person:
DY £25.00–£25.00

OPEN All year round

Friendly house, pretty garden in rural situation. Many local attractions, pubs serving good food. Taunton 13 miles, coast 18 miles. Log fire in comfortable lounge, central heating.

IPPLEPEN, Devon Map ref 1D2

◆◆◆ JUNE COTTAGE

Dornafield Road, Ipplepen,
Newton Abbot, TQ12 5SH
T: (01803) 813081

Bedrooms: 2 double,
1 twin
Bathrooms: 1 en suite,
1 public

EM 1800 (LO 1900)

B&B per night:
S £19.00–£22.00
D £38.00–£44.00

HB per person:
DY £31.50–£34.50

OPEN All year round

Very comfortable 250-year-old cottage, ideally situated for touring wider areas of South Hams, Teignbridge, Dartmoor and Torbay. Good home cooking.

ISLES OF SCILLY Map ref 1A3 Tourist Information Centre Tel: (01720) 4 22536

◆◆ HOTEL BEACHCOMBER

Thorofare, St Mary's, Isles of Scilly
TR21 0LN
T: (01720) 422682
F: (01720) 422532

Bedrooms: 2 single,
5 double, 3 twin, 2 triple
Bathrooms: 10 en suite,
2 private showers

EM 1830 (LO 1930)
CC: Barclaycard,
Mastercard, Switch, Visa

B&B per night:
S £34.00–£39.00
D £68.00–£88.00

HB per person:
DY £41.00–£45.00

OPEN Mar–Oct

Old, established, family hotel on the water's edge, close to the quay, main street, shops and boats. Outstanding sea views. All bedrooms have telephone, TV, private facilities, showers, tea-making facilities.

QUALITY ASSURANCE SCHEME

Diamond ratings and awards were correct at the time of going to press but are subject to change. Please check at the time of booking.

◆◆◆◆

HILLHEAD FARM
Ugborough, Ivybridge, PL21 0HQ
T: (01752) 892674 &
07785 915612 (Mobile)
F: (01752) 690111

B&B per night:
S £21.00–£23.00
D £42.00–£46.00

HB per person:
DY £33.50–£35.50

OPEN All year round

Antique furniture and light, sunny rooms combine to create a welcoming atmosphere in this peaceful, friendly farmhouse with lovely views over rolling Devon countryside. Turn off A38 at Wrangation, turn left, take 3rd right, continue over next crossroads, after three quarters of a mile, turn left at Hillhead, entrance 75 yards on left.

Bedrooms: 2 double,
1 twin
Bathrooms: 2 en suite,
1 private

EM 1900 (LO 2100)
Parking for 5

◆◆◆

VENN FARM
Ugborough, Ivybridge, PL21 0PE
T: (01364) 73240
F: (01364) 73240

Bedrooms: 1 triple,
2 family rooms
Bathrooms: 3 en suite,
1 public

EM 1830 (LO 1830)
Parking for 6

B&B per night:
S £22.00–£24.00
D £44.00–£48.00

HB per person:
DY £34.00–£36.00

OPEN Feb–Nov

Only 3 miles from A38. Large private gardens, streams, gypsy caravan, woodland glade, unlimited parking. You will want to return!

◆◆◆

DEVON ARMS
Fore Street, Kenton, Exeter, EX6 8LD
T: (01626) 890213
F: (01626) 891678

Bedrooms: 1 double,
1 twin, 1 triple, 3 family rooms
Bathrooms: 6 en suite

Lunch available
EM 1830 (LO 2130)
Parking for 20
CC: Barclaycard, Eurocard, JCB, Mastercard, Solo, Visa, Visa Electron

B&B per night:
S £30.00–£35.00
D £40.00–£50.00

OPEN All year round

Family-run inn on A379 between Exeter and Dawlish. Adjacent to Powderham Castle. Good base to explore Devon countryside: close to beach. All rooms en suite.

◆◆◆

ASHLEIGH HOUSE
Ashleigh Road, Kingsbridge,
TQ7 1HB
T: (01548) 852893 & 07967 737875
E: reception@ashleigh-house.co.uk
I: www.ashleigh-house.co.uk

Bedrooms: 4 double,
2 twin, 1 family room
Bathrooms: 4 en suite,
1 public

EM 1900 (LO 1700)
Parking for 4
CC: Barclaycard, Delta, Eurocard, JCB, Mastercard, Solo, Switch, Visa, Visa Electron

B&B per night:
S £20.00–£33.00
D £46.00–£52.00

HB per person:
DY £26.00–£45.00

OPEN Mar–Nov

Comfortable, informal licensed Victorian guesthouse. Edge of town, country views. All rooms colour TV and beverage tray. First floor en suite. Sun lounge, bar, parking.

AT-A-GLANCE SYMBOLS
Symbols at the end of each accommodation entry give useful information about services and facilities. A key to symbols can be found inside the back cover flap. Keep this open for easy reference.

KINGSBRIDGE continued

◆◆◆◆
Silver
Award

COMBE FARM B & B
Loddiswell, Kingsbridge, TQ7 4DT
T: (01548) 550560
F: (01548) 550560

B&B per night:
S £20.00–£30.00
D £45.00–£60.00

HB per person:
DY £35.00–£45.00

OPEN Mar–Oct

Beautiful Grade II Listed Georgian farmhouse completely renovated in 1994, nestling in small secluded valley down private drive. Good quality accommodation within a warm family atmosphere. Twelve peaceful acres with sheep, poultry, cats and dogs in residence. Heated outdoor swimming pool (May – September). Equidistant sandy beaches and picturesque moorland.

Bedrooms: 1 double, 2 twin
Bathrooms: 1 en suite, 1 public

EM 1730 (LO 2000)
Parking for 6

◆◆◆◆
Silver
Award

SOUTH ALLINGTON HOUSE
Chivelstone, Kingsbridge, TQ7 2NB
T: (01548) 511272
F: (01548) 511421
E: barbara@sthallingtonbnb.demon.co.uk
I: www.sthallingtonbnb.demon.co.uk

B&B per night:
S £22.75–£23.75
D £45.00–£63.50

OPEN Mar–Dec

Georgian country house in 4 acres of beautiful grounds, also 140 acres of mixed farm. Abundance of birds, wonderful coastline. Ideal for walking the coastal path. Between Start Point and Prawle Point. If you want peace and quiet, this is just the place for you. Croquet and coarse fishing.

Bedrooms: 1 single, 5 double, 2 twin, 1 triple
Bathrooms: 7 en suite, 2 private, 1 public

Parking for 20

LANGPORT, Somerset Map ref 1D1

◆◆◆

THE OLD POUND INN
Aller, Langport, TA10 0RA
T: (01458) 250469
F: (01458) 250469

B&B per night:
S £40.00–£40.00
D £50.00–£50.00

HB per person:
DY Min £50.00

OPEN All year round

Built in 1571 and upgraded to modern standards, with en suite bedrooms, 50-seat dining room and function room for 200. Log fires. Bar meals from £1.95. Ideal for country lovers, walking, fishing, bird watching. Winner of JPC national award of "Best Pub of the Year 1999".

Bedrooms: 1 single, 2 double, 1 twin, 1 family room
Bathrooms: 5 en suite

Lunch available
EM 1800 (LO 2200)
Parking for 30
CC: Barclaycard, Delta, Mastercard, Switch, Visa

TOWN INDEX
This can be found at the back of this guide. If you know where you want to stay, the index will give you the page number listing accommodation in your chosen town, city or village.

♦♦♦

HEALE FARMHOUSE

Liftondown, Launceston, PL15 9QX
T: (01566) 784869
F: (01566) 784869

B&B per night:
S £17.50–£18.50
D £35.00–£38.00

HB per person:
DY £27.50–£35.50

OPEN All year round

Gourmet organic vegetarian food amidst beautiful surroundings. Good books, serenity, a warm, relaxed atmosphere and no television. Heale, a 16thC Listed building, is set in a lovely river valley on Devon/Cornwall border, central for many famous houses and gardens. One mile from A30 trunk road. Children half rate. .

Bedrooms: 2 double,
1 family room
Bathrooms: 2 en suite,
1 private

Lunch available
EM 1800 (LO 2130)
Parking for 5

LEWDOWN, Devon Map ref 1C2

♦♦

STOWFORD GRANGE FARM

Lewdown, Okehampton, EX20 4BZ
T: (01566) 783298

Bedrooms: 2 double,
1 triple
Bathrooms: 2 public

Lunch available
EM 1900
Parking for 5

B&B per night:
S £16.00–£17.00
D £32.00–£34.00

HB per person:
DY £20.00–£22.00

OPEN Jan–Nov

220-acre mixed farm. Listed building in quiet village. Home-cooked food, fresh vegetables and poultry. Ten miles from Okehampton, 7 miles from Launceston. Half a mile from old A30, turn right at Royal Exchange.

LISKEARD, Cornwall Map ref 1C2

ELNOR GUEST HOUSE

1 Russell Street, Station Road,
Liskeard, PL14 4BP
T: (01579) 342472 (Answerphone)
F: (01579) 345673

Bedrooms: 4 single,
1 double, 1 twin, 3 triple
Bathrooms: 7 en suite,
1 public

EM 1800 (LO 1800)
Parking for 6

B&B per night:
S £19.00–£22.00
D £38.00–£44.00

OPEN All year round

Home-from-home with friendly family atmosphere in 100-year-old townhouse between the station and market town.

♦♦♦

HYVUE HOUSE

Barras Cross, Liskeard, PL14 6BN
T: (01579) 348175 (Ansaphone)

Bedrooms: 2 double,
1 twin
Bathrooms: 2 en suite,
1 private

B&B per night:
S £20.00–£20.00
D £35.00–£35.00

OPEN All year round

Family-run, exclusively for non-smokers, outskirts of town overlooking Bodmin Moor. Providing excellent food and comfort. En suite rooms with tea/coffee and TV. Car park.

♦♦♦♦
Silver
Award

TREGONDALE FARM

Menheniot, Liskeard, PL14 3RG
T: (01579) 342407
F: (01579) 342407

Bedrooms: 1 double,
1 twin, 1 triple
Bathrooms: 2 en suite,
1 private

EM 1900 (LO 1800)
Parking for 3

B&B per night:
S £25.00–£25.00
D £42.00–£46.00

HB per person:
DY £31.00–£35.00

OPEN All year round

200-acre mixed farm. Character farmhouse in beautiful countryside. Home-produced food our speciality. Log fires, tennis court. North east of Menheniot, between A38/A390.

THE LIZARD, Cornwall Map ref 1B3

♦♦♦

TRETHVAS FARMHOUSE

The Lizard, Helston, TR12 7AR
T: (01326) 290720
F: (01326) 290720

Bedrooms: 2 double,
1 triple
Bathrooms: 2 en suite,
1 public

Parking for 4

B&B per night:
D £38.00–£42.00

OPEN Mar–Oct

300-acre dairy farm. Sea views and coastal walks. Close to Kynance Cove and just a quarter mile from Lizard village. Central heating and tea/coffee-making facilities.

LOOE, Cornwall Map ref 1C2

◆◆◆◆
Silver
Award

BUCKLAWREN FARM

St Martin-by-Looe, Looe, PL13 1NZ
T: (01503) 240738
F: (01503) 240481
E: bucklawren@compuserve.com
I: www.cornwallexplore.co.uk/bucklawren

B&B per night:
S £22.00–£25.00
D £44.00–£46.00

HB per person:
DY £34.00–£35.00

OPEN Mar–Oct

Delightful farmhouse set in glorious countryside with spectacular sea views. Quiet location, situated one mile from the beach and three miles from the fishing village of Looe. An award-winning farm with all bedrooms en suite and a restaurant on site.

Bedrooms: 2 double, 2 twin, 1 triple, 1 family room
Bathrooms: 6 en suite, 1 public

Lunch available
EM 1800 (LO 2000)
Parking for 10
CC: Barclaycard, Eurocard, Mastercard, Visa

◆◆◆◆

LITTLE LARNICK FARM

Pelynt, Looe, PL13 2NB
T: (01503) 262837
F: (01503) 262837

B&B per night:
D £42.00–£46.00

OPEN Feb–Dec

200-acre dairy farm situated in the beautiful West Looe River valley. The farmhouse and newly converted barn offer peaceful and relaxing character en suite accommodation, including a barn suite and ground floor bedroom. Wonderful walks from the door. Drying room available. Special "Winter Warmer" breaks.

Bedrooms: 4 double, 1 twin, 1 triple
Bathrooms: 6 en suite

Parking for 3

◆◆◆◆

THE PANORAMA HOTEL

Hannafore Road, Looe, PL13 2DE
T: (01503) 262123
F: (01503) 265654
E: stay@looe.co.uk
I: www.looe.co.uk

Bedrooms: 2 single, 3 double, 1 twin, 2 triple, 1 family room
Bathrooms: 9 en suite, 1 public

EM 1830 (LO 1900)
Parking for 8
CC: Barclaycard, Delta, Eurocard, Maestro, Mastercard, Solo, Switch, Visa

B&B per night:
S £22.00–£38.00
D £44.00–£76.00

HB per person:
DY £36.00–£52.00

OPEN All year round

Family-run hotel, good food, friendly atmosphere. Magnificent setting overlooking harbour, beach and miles of beautiful coastline.

◆◆

STONEROCK COTTAGE

Portuan Road, Hannafore,
West Looe, PL13 2DN
T: (01503) 263651
F: (01503) 263414

Bedrooms: 1 single, 2 double, 1 triple
Bathrooms: 2 en suite, 1 private, 1 public

Parking for 4

B&B per night:
S £17.00–£18.00
D £38.00–£44.00

OPEN Jan–Oct

Modernised, old world cottage facing south to the Channel. Ample free parking. 2 minutes from the beach, shops, tennis and other amenities.

LYME REGIS, Dorset Map ref 1D2 *Tourist Information Centre Tel: (01297) 442138*

◆◆◆

LUCERNE

View Road, Lyme Regis, DT7 3AA
T: (01297) 443752

Bedrooms: 1 single, 3 double, 1 twin
Bathrooms: 4 en suite, 1 private

Parking for 7

B&B per night:
S £23.00–£28.00
D £36.00–£44.00

OPEN All year round

Private house in quiet residential area. Excellent sea and coastal views. Comfortably furnished, non-smoking. All rooms en suite or private with colour TV, tea/coffee.

LYME REGIS continued

LYDWELL HOUSE

♦♦♦

Lyme Road, Uplyme, Lyme Regis, DT7 3TJ
T: (01297) 443522
E: brittain16@fsbusiness.co.uk
I: www.smoothhound.co.uk/hotels/lydwell.
html

B&B per night:
S £22.00–£25.00
D £44.00–£50.00

HB per person:
DY £37.00–£40.00

OPEN All year round

Delightful pre-Victorian house in attractive gardens, ideally located for coast and country walks. One kilometre to beach and much less to centre of Lyme Regis along scenic footpath along the Lym Valley. All rooms are comfortable, spacious and well-equipped. Food is home-cooked and of very good quality.

Bedrooms: 1 single,
1 double, 1 twin,
2 family rooms
Bathrooms: 5 en suite

EM 1800 (LO 2000)
Parking for 7
CC: Delta, Mastercard,
Solo, Switch, Visa, Visa
Electron

♦♦♦

SOUTHERNHAYE
Pound Road, Lyme Regis, DT7 3HX
T: (01297) 443077
F: (01297) 443077

Bedrooms: 1 single,
1 double, 1 twin
Bathrooms: 1 public

Parking for 2

B&B per night:
S £19.00–£21.00
D £36.00–£38.00

OPEN All year round

Distinctive Edwardian house in quiet location with panoramic views over Lyme Bay, about 10 minutes' walk from town and beach. Off-road parking.

SPRINGFIELD

♦♦♦

Woodmead Road, Lyme Regis, DT7 3LJ
T: (01297) 443409
E: springfield@lymeregis.com
I: www.lymeregis.com/springfield

B&B per night:
S £19.00–£22.00
D £38.00–£44.00

OPEN Apr–Oct

Elegant Georgian house in partly walled garden with conservatory. Well proportioned rooms, all with far-reaching views over the sea and Dorset coastline. A short walk to the shops and seafront. Close to major footpaths. Concession at local golf course.

Bedrooms: 2 double,
1 twin, 2 family rooms
Bathrooms: 4 en suite,
1 private, 2 public

Parking for 9

THATCH LODGE HOTEL

♦♦♦♦♦
Gold
Award

The Street, Charmouth, Bridport, DT6 6PQ
T: (01297) 560407
F: (01297) 560407
E: thatchlodgehotel@cs.com
I: www.thatchlodgehotel.com

B&B per night:
D £78.00–£120.00

HB per person:
DY £66.50–£87.50

OPEN Mar–Dec

"Picture postcard" 14thC monks' retreat for nearby Forde Abbey. Four-poster and half tester bedrooms with many thoughtful extras. Antiques, grapes cascade from our 200-year-old vine, walled gardens. World famous fossil beach. We offer tranquillity, discerning quality and superb chef-inspired two rosette cuisine. Non-smoking throughout.

Bedrooms: 5 double,
1 twin; suite available
Bathrooms: 6 en suite

EM 1930 (LO 1930)
Parking for 10
CC: Barclaycard, Delta,
JCB, Mastercard, Solo,
Switch, Visa, Visa Electron

LYME REGIS continued

◆◆◆◆ **WHITE HOUSE**
47 Silver Street, Lyme Regis,
DT7 3HR
T: (01297) 443420

Bedrooms: 1 single,
4 double, 2 twin
Bathrooms: 7 en suite

Parking for 6

B&B per night:
D £42.00–£50.00

OPEN Apr–Sep

Fine views of Dorset coastline from rear of this 18thC guesthouse. A short walk from beach, gardens and shops.

LYNMOUTH, Devon Map ref 1C1

◆◆◆

Elegant, award-winning rock-built Victorian sea-captain's riverside home, amidst waterfalls, cascades, oak-wooded valleys, England's highest clifftops, enchanting harbourside in old world smugglers' village. Nature lovers' paradise. Devonshire cream teas served in our garden. Guests' drawing room, pretty bedrooms, blazing log fires (in cooler seasons). Dramatic views.

TREGONWELL RIVERSIDE GUESTHOUSE

1 Tors Road, Lynmouth, EX35 6ET
T: (01598) 753369
I: www.smoothhound.co.uk/hotels/
tregonwl.html

Bedrooms: 5 double
Bathrooms: 3 en suite,
2 private, 1 public

EM 1800 (LO 1815)
Parking for 9

B&B per night:
S £22.00–£25.00
D £44.00–£60.00

OPEN Jan–Nov

◆◆◆ **THE VILLAGE INN**
19 Lynmouth Street, Lynmouth,
EX35 6EH
T: (01598) 752354

Bedrooms: 6 double
Bathrooms: 6 en suite

Lunch available
EM 1830 (LO 2130)
CC: Barclaycard, Delta,
Eurocard, Mastercard,
Switch, Visa

B&B per night:
S £25.00–£25.00
D £50.00–£50.00

OPEN All year round

Refurbished without sacrificing the atmosphere of a traditional inn. Open stone fire, good home-cooked food, en suite rooms with facilities. Centrally located.

LYNTON, Devon Map ref 1C1 *Tourist Information Centre Tel: (01598) 752225*

◆◆◆

Homely, friendly guesthouse with spacious rooms, some having en suite facilities. Optional home-cooked evening meals and licensed for diners. The Denes has ample parking and offers baby sitting by arrangement. Situated at the entrance to the Valley of Rocks, it makes an ideal spot for walking, birdwatching and exploring Exmoor.

THE DENES GUEST HOUSE

15 Longmead, Lynton, EX35 6DQ
T: (01598) 753573 (Ansaphone)
F: (01598) 753573
E: j.e.mcgowan@btinternet.com
I: www.thedenes.com

Bedrooms: 2 double,
3 family rooms
Bathrooms: 2 en suite,
1 private, 1 public

EM 1900 (LO 1930)
Parking for 6
CC: Mastercard, Solo,
Switch, Visa

B&B per night:
S £19.00–£22.50
D £38.00–£45.00

HB per person:
DY £31.50–£35.00

OPEN All year round

CHECK THE MAPS

The colour maps at the front of this guide show all the cities, towns and villages for which you will find accommodation entries.
Refer to the town index to find the page on which they are listed.

◆◆◆

THE FERNERY

Lydiate Lane, Lynton, EX35 6AJ

T: (01598) 752440
F: (01598) 752396

B&B per night:
S £18.50–£22.50
D £35.00–£40.00

OPEN All year round
(closed Christmas and
New Year)

Victorian house, steeped in history and full of character, conveniently situated in the old village. Beautifully decorated, comfortable and spacious. Delicious food and homely atmosphere. Set in Exmoor National Park, in an area known as Little Switzerland – refresh yourself with spectacular scenery and coastal walks. A warm welcome awaits you.

Bedrooms: 2 double,
1 twin
Bathrooms: 1 en suite,
2 private

◆◆◆◆

INGLESIDE HOTEL

Lee Road, Lynton, EX35 6HW

T: (01598) 752223
E: johnpauldevon@aol.com

B&B per night:
S £35.00–£35.00
D £46.00–£50.00

OPEN All year round

Family-run hotel in premier position overlooking village. High standards of accommodation. All rooms en suite, colour TV, beverage facilities. Safe car park in hotel grounds. The perfect centre to enjoy the beauty of Exmoor's coast, cliffs, rivers and countryside, whether walking or motoring. Children and small dogs welcome.

Bedrooms: 5 double,
1 twin, 1 triple
Bathrooms: 7 en suite

EM
Parking for 10

◆◆◆◆

LONGMEAD HOUSE HOTEL

9 Longmead, Lynton, EX35 6DQ

T: (01598) 752523
F: (01598) 752523
E: info@longmeadhouse.co.uk
I: www.longmeadhouse.co.uk

B&B per night:
S £20.00–£22.00
D £40.00–£44.00

HB per person:
DY £33.00–£35.50

OPEN Mar–Oct

Delightful Victorian house set in a large garden, quietly situated towards the "Valley of Rocks" yet only 5 minutes' level walk to village centre. On coastal road/footpath. Private car park. Comfortable, pretty en suite bedrooms. Home cooking a speciality. "Special offer" half board breaks available. Relaxed, informal atmosphere with old fashioned hospitality.

Bedrooms: 5 double,
1 twin, 1 family room
Bathrooms: 6 en suite,
1 private

EM 1900 (LO 1530)
Parking for 7
CC: JCB, Maestro,
Mastercard, Solo, Switch,
Visa, Visa Electron

MAP REFERENCES
The map references refer to the colour maps at the front of this guide. The first figure is the map number; the letter and figure which follow indicate the grid reference on the map.

◆◆◆◆

ROCKVALE HOTEL
Lee Road, Lynton, EX35 6HW
T: (01598) 752279 & 753343
E: judithwoodland@rockvale.fsbusiness.co.uk

B&B per night:
S £24.00–£26.00
D £52.00–£56.00

HB per person:
DY £42.00–£44.00

OPEN Apr–Oct

Delightful Victorian property situated in its own grounds on the sunny south facing slopes of Hollerday Hill. Glorious panoramic views across the town towards Countisbury and Watersmeet Valley. Award-winning home cooking and hospitality. Peaceful and relaxing. Pretty bedrooms with many thoughtful extras. Large level car park. Totally non-smoking.

Bedrooms: 1 single,
5 double, 2 triple
Bathrooms: 6 en suite,
2 private

EM 1900 (LO 1600)
Parking for 10
CC: Barclaycard, Delta,
Eurocard, JCB, Maestro,
Mastercard, Solo, Switch,
Visa, Visa Electron

◆◆◆

SOUTH CHERITON FARM
Cheriton, Lynton, EX35 6LJ
T: (01598) 753280

Bedrooms: 2 double,
1 twin
Bathrooms: 3 en suite

Parking for 6

B&B per night:
S £21.00–£23.00
D £38.00–£42.00

OPEN Apr–Oct

10 acre mixed farm. 17thC farmhouse with inglenook fireplaces and extensive exposed beams. Set high up in the beautiful Exmoor countryside and offering a traditional welcome.

MARLBOROUGH, Wiltshire Map ref 2B2 *Tourist Information Centre Tel: (01672) 513989*

◆◆◆◆

FISHERMANS HOUSE
Mildenhall, Marlborough, SN8 2LZ
T: (01672) 515390 &
07785 225363 (Mobile)
F: (01672) 519009

B&B per night:
S £30.00–£30.00
D £50.00–£60.00

OPEN All year round

Set in the beautiful valley of the River Kennet is this exquisite Georgian house. Jeremy and Heather serve breakfast in the elegant conservatory which leads into the charming garden with the lawn sloping down to the river – the perfect place to sit and enjoy the wildlife and magnificent view.

Bedrooms: 1 single,
1 double; suite available
Bathrooms: 1 en suite,
1 private

Parking for 3

QUALITY ASSURANCE SCHEME

For an explanation of the quality and facilities represented by the Diamonds please refer to the front of this guide. A more detailed explanation can be found in the information pages at the back.

◆◆◆◆

WESTCOURT BOTTOM
165 Westcourt, Burbage, Marlborough,
SN8 3BW
T: (01672) 810924 & 811723

B&B per night:
S £26.00–£30.00
D £42.00–£50.00

OPEN All year round

Large 17thC thatched cottage 5 miles south of Marlborough. Half-timbered bedrooms, sitting room with TV, large garden with swimming pool offer a quiet, relaxed and informal atmosphere. Good local pubs. Ideal base for Ridgeway and Savernake Forest walks, Marlborough, Avebury and Stonehenge. Wonderful free-range breakfasts! Ample parking.

Bedrooms: 2 double,
1 twin
Bathrooms: 1 en suite,
1 public

Parking for 10

MARTOCK, Somerset Map ref 2A3

◆◆◆

THE WHITE HART HOTEL
East Street, Martock, TA12 6JQ
T: (01935) 822005
F: (01935) 822056

B&B per night:
S £30.00–£40.00
D £45.00–£70.00

OPEN All year round

Imposing Grade II Listed building (1735) in centre of Martock. Well-appointed bedrooms. Bar and restaurant menus available. Centrally situated to explore south Somerset and further afield. An area full of attractions: museums, historic sites, country parks, classic gardens, nature reserves, arts and crafts, shopping, entertainment and sporting facilities. Yeovil 7 miles.

Bedrooms: 2 single,
4 double, 3 triple
Bathrooms: 4 en suite,
3 public, 1 private
shower

Lunch available
EM 1900 (LO 2100)
Parking for 14
CC: Amex, Barclaycard,
Delta, Eurocard,
Mastercard, Switch, Visa,
Visa Electron

MELKSHAM, Wiltshire Map ref 2B2 *Tourist Information Centre Tel: (01225) 707424*

◆◆◆

LONGHOPE GUEST HOUSE
9 Beanacre Road, Melksham,
SN12 8AG
T: (01225) 706737
F: (01225) 706737

Bedrooms: 1 single,
1 double, 2 twin, 2 triple
Bathrooms: 6 en suite

Parking for 12

B&B per night:
S Max £28.00
D Max £45.00

OPEN All year round

Situated in its own grounds on the A350 Melksham-Chippenham road. Half a mile from Melksham town centre, 10 miles from M4 junction 17.

USE YOUR *i*s

There are more than 550 Tourist Information Centres throughout England offering friendly help with accommodation and holiday ideas as well as suggestions of places to visit and things to do. You'll find TIC addresses in the local Phone Book.

◆◆◆◆

POLGREEN FARM

London Apprentice, St Austell, PL26 7AP
T: (01726) 75151
F: (01726) 75151
E: polgreen.farm@btclick.com

B&B per night:
S £20.00–£25.00
D £36.00–£44.00

OPEN All year round

Situated in an Area of Outstanding Natural Beauty, 1 mile from the coast and 4 miles from the picturesque fishing village of Mevagissey. Centrally placed for touring Cornwall. Cornish Way leisure trail adjoining. Within a few miles' drive of the spectacular Eden Project and Heligan Gardens. All rooms with private facilities, colour TV, tea/coffee.

Bedrooms: 3 double, 1 twin, 1 family room
Bathrooms: 3 en suite, 1 public

Parking for 7

◆◆◆◆◆

THE OLD VICARAGE HOTEL

Sherborne Road, Milborne Port, Sherborne, Dorset DT9 5AT
T: (01963) 251117
F: (01963) 251515
I: www.milborneport.freeserve.co.uk

B&B per night:
S £27.00–£32.00
D £54.00–£95.00

HB per person:
DY £43.00–£65.00

OPEN Feb–Dec

Listed Victorian Gothic building, elegantly furnished with antiques, set in 3.5 acres of beautiful grounds. The spacious lounge and the dining room afford magnificent views of open country. On Fridays and Saturdays one of the partners, a highly acclaimed chef, prepares dinner. On other nights food can be provided by a pub restaurant 200 yards away.

Bedrooms: 1 single, 3 double, 2 twin, 1 triple
Bathrooms: 7 en suite

EM 1930 (LO 2100)
Parking for 15
CC: Amex, Barclaycard, Delta, JCB, Mastercard, Solo, Switch, Visa

◆◆◆

ALCOMBE COTE GUEST HOUSE

19 Manor Road, Alcombe, Minehead, TA24 6EH
T: (01643) 703309
F: (01643) 709901

B&B per night:
S £15.50–£15.50
D £29.00–£29.00

HB per person:
DY £22.50–£22.50

OPEN Mar–Oct

19thC residence in quiet location. Get away from the rat race and enjoy yourself in comfortable accommodation and friendly atmosphere. Home cooking in traditional, English manner. Located on the edge of Exmoor National Park close to moor and woods and delightful villages to explore. Minehead with sea and shops 1 mile.

Bedrooms: 1 single, 3 double, 2 twin
Bathrooms: 2 public

EM 1915
Parking for 6

RATING All accommodation in this guide has been rated, or is awaiting a rating, by a trained English Tourism Council assessor.

MINEHEAD continued

◆◆◆ FIELD HOUSE

The Parks, Minehead, TA24 8BU
T: (01643) 706958

Bedrooms: 1 double, 2 twin
Bathrooms: 2 en suite, 1 private, 1 public

Parking for 3

B&B per night:
S £19.00–£19.00
D £38.00–£38.00

OPEN All year round

Field House has fine views over the hills from the Quantocks to Exmoor, accessible to North Hill but yet a stroll into town.

◆◆◆◆ GASCONY HOTEL

The Avenue, Minehead, TA24 5BB
T: (01643) 705939

Bedrooms: 3 single, 4 double, 2 twin, 4 triple
Bathrooms: 13 en suite, 1 public

EM 1900 (LO 1800)
Parking for 15
CC: Barclaycard, Delta, Eurocard, JCB, Maestro, Mastercard, Solo, Switch, Visa

B&B per night:
S £25.00–£29.00
D £46.00–£52.00

HB per person:
DY £35.00–£37.00

OPEN Mar–Oct

Comfortable and well-appointed Victorian house hotel. Ideally positioned on the level, close to seafront. Home cooking. Large secure car park.

◆◆◆◆ MAYFAIR HOTEL

25 The Avenue, Minehead, TA24 5AY
T: (01643) 702719
F: (01643) 702719

Bedrooms: 2 single, 4 double, 2 twin, 5 triple
Bathrooms: 12 en suite, 1 private

EM 1830 (LO 1900)
Parking for 13
CC: Barclaycard, Delta, Mastercard, Visa

B&B per night:
S £25.00–£27.00
D £50.00–£54.00

HB per person:
DY £36.00–£38.00

OPEN Mar–Sep

Victorian house hotel. Lovely decor and furnishings. All rooms en suite with refrigerator. Family run, home cooking. On level, 3 minutes sea and shops. No smoking.

◆◆◆ OLD SHIP AGROUND

Quay Street, Minehead, TA24 5UL
T: (01643) 702087
F: (01643) 709066

Bedrooms: 1 single, 1 double, 2 twin, 1 triple, 2 family rooms; suites available
Bathrooms: 7 en suite, 1 public

Lunch available
EM 1800 (LO 2130)
Parking for 15
CC: Amex, Barclaycard, Delta, Mastercard, Switch, Visa

B&B per night:
S £20.00–£30.00
D £35.00–£45.00

OPEN All year round

Traditional family-run public house on harbour. Full en suite facilities. An ideal base for Exmoor, Minehead and all of Somerset.

MORETONHAMPSTEAD, Devon Map ref 1C2

◆◆◆◆ GREAT DOCCOMBE FARM

Doccombe, Moretonhampstead, Newton Abbot, TQ13 8SS
T: (01647) 440694

Bedrooms: 1 double, 1 triple
Bathrooms: 2 en suite

Parking for 6

B&B per night:
D £36.00–£40.00

OPEN Jan–Dec

In pretty Dartmoor hamlet, 300-year-old farmhouse in Dartmoor National Park. En suite rooms, farmhouse cooking. Ideal for exploring Dartmoor's delights.

◆◆◆◆ GREAT SLONCOMBE FARM
Silver Award

Moretonhampstead, Newton Abbot, TQ13 8QF
T: (01647) 440595
F: (01647) 440595
E: hmerchant@sloncombe.freeserve.co.uk

Bedrooms: 2 double, 1 twin
Bathrooms: 3 en suite

EM 1830 (LO 1000)
Parking for 3

B&B per night:
S £23.00–£24.00
D £46.00–£48.00

HB per person:
DY £35.00–£37.00

OPEN All year round

13thC farmhouse in a magical Dartmoor valley. Meadows, woodland, wildflowers, animals. Farmhouse breakfast with new baked bread. Everything provided for an enjoyable break.

NB IMPORTANT NOTE Information on accommodation listed in this guide has been supplied by the proprietors. As changes may occur you are advised to check details at the time of booking.

MORETONHAMPSTEAD continued

GREAT WOOSTON FARM BED & BREAKFAST

Moretonhampstead, Newton Abbot, TQ13 8QA
T: (01647) 440367 &
07798 670590 (Mobile)
F: (01647) 440367

Bedrooms: 2 double, 1 twin
Bathrooms: 2 en suite, 1 private

Parking for 3
CC: Mastercard, Switch, Visa

B&B per night:
S £22.00–£25.00
D £40.00–£46.00

OPEN All year round

Great Wooston is a peaceful haven with views across the moor and walks nearby. Two rooms en suite, one with 4-poster. Quality accommodation. Brochure available.

MULLION, Cornwall Map ref 1B3

Silver Award

TREGADDRA FARM
Cury, Helston, TR12 7BB
T: (01326) 240235
F: (01326) 240235
E: holidays@tregaddra.freeserve.co.uk
I: www.tregaddra.freeserve.co.uk

B&B per night:
S £23.00–£25.00
D £46.00–£50.00

HB per person:
DY £33.00–£37.00

OPEN All year round

For stress-free relaxation, join us at Tregaddra, a working farm. Set in an Area of Outstanding Natural Beauty, our views of rolling countryside are unrivalled. Exceptional en suite bedrooms, swimming pool, tennis court and peaceful garden. Open log fires, Aga cooking and a relaxed family atmosphere. Ideal area for walkers.

Bedrooms: 4 double, 2 family rooms
Bathrooms: 6 en suite

EM 1830
Parking for 8
CC: Amex, Barclaycard, Delta, Eurocard, Mastercard, Switch, Visa

NEWQUAY, Cornwall Map ref 1B2 *Tourist Information Centre Tel: (01637) 854020*

ALOHA HOTEL

122/124 Henver Road, Newquay, TR7 3EQ
T: (01637) 878366
E: Alohanewqu@aol.com
I: www.mjiggins.freeserve.co.uk/aloha/index.html

Bedrooms: 3 single, 6 double, 2 triple, 3 family rooms
Bathrooms: 8 en suite, 2 public, 2 private showers

Parking for 14
CC: Amex, Barclaycard, Diners, Eurocard, JCB, Mastercard, Visa

B&B per night:
S £13.00–£23.00
D £26.00–£46.00

OPEN All year round

Friendly licensed hotel with en suite rooms and home comforts. Well situated for beaches and touring Cornwall. Conservatory and garden overlooking Trencreek Valley. Ample parking.

CHICHESTER

14 Bay View Terrace, Newquay, TR7 2LR
T: (01637) 874216
F: (01637) 874216

Bedrooms: 2 single, 2 double, 2 twin, 1 triple
Bathrooms: 1 public, 5 private showers

EM 1830
Parking for 6

B&B per night:
S £16.00–£16.00
D £32.00–£32.00

HB per person:
DY £21.00–£21.00

OPEN All year round

Comfortable, licensed establishment convenient for shops, beaches and gardens. Showers in most bedrooms, many extras. Walking, mineral collecting, archaeology and Cornish heritage holidays in spring and autumn.

DEGEMBRIS FARMHOUSE

St Newlyn East, Newquay, TR8 5HY
T: (01872) 510555
F: (01872) 510230
E: kathy@tally-connect.co.uk
I: www.cornwall-farm-accommodation.co.uk

Bedrooms: 1 single, 1 double, 1 twin, 1 triple, 1 family room
Bathrooms: 3 en suite, 1 public

EM 1830
Parking for 8
CC: Barclaycard, Delta, Eurocard, JCB, Mastercard, Switch, Visa, Visa Electron

B&B per night:
S Max £22.00
D £46.00–£50.00

HB per person:
DY £35.50–£37.50

OPEN All year round

165-acre arable farm. Cosy south-facing farmhouse offering welcoming log fires in winter, comfortable en suite bedrooms and delicious home cooking. "A wonderful oasis from 23 million cars".

WHERE TO STAY
Please mention this guide when making your booking.

NEWQUAY continued

♦♦♦ THE HARBOUR HOTEL

North Quay Hill, Newquay, TR7 1HF
T: (01637) 873040
E: alan@harbournewquay.
freeserve.co.uk
I: www.harbourhotel.co.uk

Bedrooms: 1 single,
5 double, 1 twin, 1 triple
Bathrooms: 8 en suite

Lunch available
EM 1800 (LO 2100)
Parking for 7
CC: Amex, Mastercard,
Visa

B&B per night:
S £40.00–£40.00
D £62.00–£72.00

OPEN All year round

An outstandingly situated period building set on a cliff overlooking the harbour. Elegant en suite bedrooms with balconies. Near town centre and beaches.

OAKSEY, Wiltshire Map ref 2B2

♦♦♦♦ CHURCH FARM BARNS

Oaksey, Malmesbury, SN16 9TE
T: (01666) 577716

Bedrooms: 2 double
Bathrooms: 2 en suite

EM
Parking for 5

B&B per night:
S Max £25.00
D Max £50.00

HB per person:
DY £35.00–£40.00

OPEN All year round

A superb conversion of 18thC farm buildings in an exceptional garden with lovely views. Near village but total peace.

OKEHAMPTON, Devon Map ref 1C2

♦♦♦♦ HIGHER CADHAM FARM

Jacobstowe, Okehampton,
EX20 3RB
T: (01837) 851647
F: (01837) 851410

Bedrooms: 1 single,
2 double, 3 twin,
3 family rooms
Bathrooms: 5 en suite,
1 public

Lunch available
EM 1900 (LO 1500)
Parking for 16
CC: Barclaycard, Delta,
Eurocard, JCB,
Mastercard, Switch, Visa,
Visa Electron

B&B per night:
S £18.50–£25.00
D £37.00–£50.00

HB per person:
DY £30.50–£37.00

OPEN All year round

139-acre mixed farm. For a real Devonshire welcome come to our farm in the secluded Okement Valley near Dartmoor. Central heating, farmhouse food.

OTTERY ST MARY, Devon Map ref 1D2

♦♦♦♦ NORMANDY HOUSE HOTEL AND BISTRO

Silver Award

5 Cornhill, Ottery St Mary,
EX11 1DW
T: (01404) 811088
F: (01404) 811023

Bedrooms: 2 single,
2 double, 1 twin
Bathrooms: 5 en suite

EM 1900 (LO 2000)
CC: Barclaycard, Delta,
JCB, Mastercard, Solo,
Switch, Visa, Visa Electron

B&B per night:
S £29.95–£36.50
D £49.50–£55.00

OPEN Feb–Dec

Charming Georgian townhouse offering excellent cuisine and warm hospitality. Opposite beautiful 14thC church. Peaceful and relaxing. Selected home-grown produce. Licensed, with terraced patio garden.

♦♦♦♦ PITT FARM

Fairmile, Ottery St Mary, EX11 1NL
T: (01404) 812439
F: (01404) 812439

Bedrooms: 2 double,
2 twin, 2 family rooms;
suites available
Bathrooms: 2 en suite,
2 private, 2 public

Parking for 6
CC: Amex, Delta, Diners,
Eurocard, JCB, Maestro,
Mastercard, Solo, Switch,
Visa, Visa Electron

B&B per night:
S £19.00–£24.00
D £38.00–£48.00

OPEN All year round

190-acre mixed farm. 16thC thatched farmhouse. En suite rooms available, log fires in season. Half-a-mile off A30 on B3176.

TOWN INDEX

This can be found at the back of the guide. If you know where you want to stay, the index will give you the page number listing accommodation in your chosen town, city or village.

PADSTOW, Cornwall Map ref 1B2 *Tourist Information Centre Tel: (01841) 533449*

◆◆◆◆◆
Gold Award

TREGEA HOTEL
16-18 High Street, Padstow, PL28 8BB
T: (01841) 532455
F: (01841) 533542
E: reservations@tregea.co.uk
I: www.tregea.co.uk

B&B per night:
S £50.00–£68.00
D £64.00–£84.00

HB per person:
DY £48.95–£58.95

OPEN All year round

Beautiful 17thC house in quiet old part of Padstow, close to harbour, beaches and coastal walks. Superb food in our licensed restaurant. A small family-run hotel with personal, friendly service and comfortable accommodation of a very high standard. Off street parking.

Bedrooms: 6 double, 2 twin
Bathrooms: 8 en suite

EM 1930 (LO 2000)
Parking for 8
CC: Barclaycard, Delta, Maestro, Mastercard, Switch, Visa, Visa Electron

---

◆◆◆◆
TREVONE BAY HOTEL
Trevone Bay, Padstow, PL28 8QS
T: (01841) 520243
F: (01841) 521195
E: hamilton@trevonebay.demon.co.uk

Bedrooms: 3 single, 4 double, 3 twin, 2 family rooms
Bathrooms: 12 en suite

Lunch available
EM 1900 (LO 1930)
Parking for 12
CC: Delta, Mastercard, Visa

B&B per night:
S £25.00–£35.00
D £50.00–£70.00

HB per person:
DY £35.00–£50.00

OPEN Apr–Sep

Take a real break! Friendly, spotless, non-smoking hotel in beautiful, peaceful village location. Excellent cooking and personal service. Overlooking beautiful sandy beach and rugged coastline.

◆◆◆
TREVORRICK FARM
St Issey, Wadebridge, PL27 7QH
T: (01841) 540574
F: (01841) 540574
E: trevorrick.farm@talk21.com

Bedrooms: 2 double, 1 twin
Bathrooms: 3 en suite

EM 1800 (LO 1930)
Parking for 20
CC: Barclaycard, Delta, Eurocard, Mastercard, Visa

B&B per night:
S £19.00–£36.00
D £38.00–£50.00

OPEN All year round

12-acre mixed farm. Farmhouse by footpath to Camel Trail offers en suite rooms and welcomes families and pets. Indoor heated swimming pool. Near sandy beaches.

PAIGNTON, Devon Map ref 1D2 *Tourist Information Centre Tel: 0906 680 1268 (calls cost 25p per minute)*

◆◆◆◆
BERESFORD HOTEL
5 Adelphi Road, Paignton, Devon
TQ4 6AW
T: (01803) 551560
F: (01803) 407585
E: beresford@eurobell.co.uk

Bedrooms: 7 double, 1 twin
Bathrooms: 8 en suite

EM 1800 (LO 1400)
Parking for 5
CC: Barclaycard, Delta, Mastercard, Solo, Switch, Visa

B&B per night:
S £27.00–£42.00
D £36.00–£50.00

OPEN All year round

Small, quiet hotel, 100 level yards to sea/shops; close to stations. Short/long breaks; also 4-posters and "Romantic Breaks". Christmas, New Year packages.

◆◆◆◆◆
Silver Award

ROUNDHAM LODGE
16 Roundham Road, Paignton, Devon TQ4 6DN
T: (01803) 558485
F: (01803) 553090

Bedrooms: 1 single, 2 double, 1 twin, 2 triple
Bathrooms: 6 en suite

Parking for 9

B&B per night:
S £20.00–£23.00
D £40.00–£60.00

OPEN All year round

Family-run bed and breakfast. Three minutes' walk to beaches and harbour. Most rooms have sea views over Torbay, some have balconies. Non-smoking.

WELCOME HOST This is a nationally recognised customer care programme which aims to promote the highest standards of service and a warm welcome. Establishments taking part in this initiative are indicated by the ⊛ symbol.

PAIGNTON continued

♦♦♦ THE SANDS HOTEL

32 Sands Road, Paignton, Devon TQ4 6EJ T: (01803) 551282 F: (01803) 407269 E: sands.hotel@virgin.net	Bedrooms: 2 single, 9 double, 3 twin, 1 triple, 1 family room Bathrooms: 10 en suite, 2 public	EM 1830 (LO 1830) Parking for 12 CC: Amex, Barclaycard, Delta, Eurocard, Mastercard, Solo, Switch, Visa, Visa Electron	B&B per night: **S £16.00–£23.00** **D £32.00–£46.00** HB per person: **DY £24.00–£31.00** OPEN All year round

The hotel is situated on the seafront, close to level walk to harbour, pier, shops and all other amenities. Spectacular bay views.

♦♦♦ TORBAY COURT HOTEL

Steartfield Road, Paignton, Devon TQ3 2BJ T: (01803) 663332 F: (01803) 522680	Bedrooms: 10 single, 15 double, 27 twin, 3 triple, 1 family room Bathrooms: 56 en suite	Lunch available EM 1800 (LO 1830) Parking for 16	B&B per night: **S £15.36–£22.00** HB per person: **DY £20.36–£29.00** OPEN Mar–Dec

Situated in a quiet, secluded position. A few yards' level walk to the seafront. Close to park and amenities. Licensed, all rooms en suite.

♦♦♦ TWO BEACHES HOTEL

27 St Andrews Road, Paignton, Devon TQ4 6HA T: (01803) 522164	Bedrooms: 1 single, 3 double, 1 triple, 2 family rooms Bathrooms: 7 en suite	Parking for 8	B&B per night: **S £15.00–£20.00** **D £30.00–£44.00** OPEN All year round

Newly refurbished, family-run, friendly hotel with sea views. Spacious and modern rooms all en suite. Close to beaches, town harbour, waterpark and Paignton Zoo.

♦♦♦♦ WYNNCROFT HOTEL

2 Elmsleigh Park, Paignton, Devon TQ4 5AT
T: (01803) 525728
F: (01803) 526335
E: wynncroft@FSBDial.co.uk
I: www.wynncroft.co.uk

B&B per night:
S £20.00–£32.00
D £40.00–£64.00

HB per person:
DY £29.00–£41.00

OPEN Apr–Sep

Comfort, service and warm friendly welcome in our family-run Victorian hotel. Short level walk from the beach or town. Free transport to coach and railway station. Large free car park. A la carte menu using fresh local produce, including a range of special diets including gluten free. Licensed.	Bedrooms: 6 double, 2 twin, 2 triple Bathrooms: 9 en suite, 1 public	Lunch available EM 1800 (LO 1830) Parking for 8 CC: Barclaycard, Eurocard, JCB, Maestro, Mastercard, Solo, Switch, Visa, Visa Electron

PENSFORD, Bath and North East Somerset Map ref 2A2

♦♦♦ GREEN ACRES

Stanton Wick, Pensford, BS39 4BX T: (01761) 490397 F: (01761) 490397	Bedrooms: 2 single, 2 double, 1 twin Bathrooms: 1 en suite, 2 public	Parking for 22	B&B per night: **S £20.00–£25.00** **D £40.00–£50.00** OPEN All year round

A friendly welcome awaits you in peaceful setting, off A37/A368. Relax and enjoy panoramic views across Chew Valley to Dundry Hills.

CREDIT CARD BOOKINGS
If you book by telephone and are asked for your credit card number it is advisable to check the proprietor's policy should you cancel your reservation.

PENZANCE, Cornwall Map ref 1A3 *Tourist Information Centre Tel: (01736) 362207*

◆◆◆

LYNWOOD GUEST HOUSE

41 Morrab Road, Penzance, TR18 4EX
T: (01736) 365871
F: (01736) 365871
E: lynwoodpz@aol.com
I: www.penzance.co.uk/
lynwood-guesthouse

B&B per night:
S £13.50–£17.00
D £27.00–£34.00

OPEN All year round

Lynwood is a well established, family-run guesthouse. Over the years we have gained an international reputation for a warm welcome, cleanliness and good food. We are located between town centre and promenade. Ideally situated for touring Land's End, Lizard peninsula and nearby St Michael's Mount as well as the Isles of Scilly.

Bedrooms: 1 single, 2 double, 1 twin, 1 triple, 1 family room
Bathrooms: 4 en suite, 3 public

CC: Amex, Delta, Diners, Eurocard, Mastercard, Solo, Switch, Visa

◆◆◆

MENWIDDEN FARM

Ludgvan, Penzance, TR20 8BN
T: (01736) 740415

B&B per night:
S £17.00–£20.00
D £34.00–£40.00

HB per person:
DY Min £25.00

OPEN Mar–Oct

Small mixed farm, centrally situated in West Cornwall. Warm, family atmosphere with comfortable beds and good home cooking. Within easy reach of both coasts and Lands End. A warm welcome awaits you. Turn right at Crowlas crossroads on the A30 from Hayle, signpost Vellanoweth on right turn. Last farm on left.

Bedrooms: 1 single, 3 double, 1 twin
Bathrooms: 1 en suite, 2 public

EM 1800 (LO 1800)
Parking for 8

◆◆◆

PENMORVAH HOTEL
Alexandra Road, Penzance, TR18 4LZ
T: (01736) 363711
F: (01736) 363711

Bedrooms: 2 single, 1 double, 1 twin, 4 triple
Bathrooms: 8 en suite

EM 1830 (LO 1800)
CC: Amex, Barclaycard, Delta, Eurocard, Mastercard, Solo, Switch, Visa

B&B per night:
S £18.00–£25.00
D £36.00–£50.00

HB per person:
DY £32.00–£40.00

OPEN All year round

350 yards from promenade in tree-lined avenue. Easy reach of town centre and an ideal location for touring.

◆◆◆

RICHMOND LODGE
61 Morrab Road, Penzance, TR18 4EP
T: (01736) 365560
I: www.richmondlodge.fsnet.co.uk

Bedrooms: 1 single, 2 double, 2 twin, 2 family rooms
Bathrooms: 3 en suite, 2 public

B&B per night:
S £18.00–£20.00
D £36.00–£40.00

OPEN All year round

Victorian town house between St Michael's Mount and Land's End. Some rooms en suite, including a 4-poster room and a ground-floor twin. Licensed.

ACCESSIBILITY
Look for the symbols which indicate accessibility for wheelchair users. A list of establishments is at the front of this guide.

381

◆◆◆

TREVENTON GUEST HOUSE

Alexandra Place, Penzance, TR18 4NE
T: (01736) 363521
F: (01736) 361873
I: www.ukholidayaccommodation.com/
treventonguesthouse

This elegant Victorian house is situated at the foot of a tree-lined avenue, 200 metres from the sea. Constructed of Cornish granite, it has a restful, spacious atmosphere. Art galleries, antique shops, excellent restaurants nearby. The romantic Lamorna Cove must be visited on one's way to Lands End.

Bedrooms: 1 single,
3 double, 2 twin, 1 triple
Bathrooms: 4 en suite,
1 public

B&B per night:
S £15.00–£17.00
D £32.00–£36.00

OPEN All year round

◆◆◆ **WARWICK HOUSE HOTEL**
17 Regent Terrace, Penzance,
TR18 4DW
T: (01736) 363881
F: (01736) 331078

Bedrooms: 1 single,
3 double, 1 twin, 1 triple
Bathrooms: 4 en suite,
1 public

EM 1830 (LO 1900)
Parking for 10
CC: Amex, Barclaycard,
Delta, Eurocard, JCB,
Mastercard, Switch, Visa

B&B per night:
S £20.00–£23.00
D £40.00–£46.00

HB per person:
DY £34.00–£37.00

OPEN Feb–Nov

Family-run hotel near the sea, station and heliport. Tastefully decorated rooms, most en suite and with sea views. Car parking. No smoking.

◆◆◆◆

THE POACHERS INN

Piddletrenthide, Dorchester, DT2 7QX
T: (01300) 348358
F: (01300) 348153

B&B per night:
S £35.00–£35.00
D £60.00–£60.00

HB per person:
DY £42.00–£42.00

OPEN All year round

Country inn, with riverside garden and swimming pool, within easy reach of all Dorset's attractions. All rooms en suite, restaurant where half board guests choose from our a la carte menu at no extra cost. Short breaks: stay 2 nights DBB £84pp 3rd night DBB free, 2nd January – 30th April and 1st October – 31st December 2001, excluding Bank Holidays.

Bedrooms: 15 double,
2 twin, 1 family room
Bathrooms: 18 en suite

Lunch available
EM 1700 (LO 2130)
Parking for 30
CC: Barclaycard, Delta,
Eurocard, Mastercard,
Solo, Switch, Visa

◆◆◆◆ **BERKELEYS OF ST JAMES**
4 St James Place East, The Hoe,
Plymouth, Devon PL1 3AS
T: (01752) 221654
F: (01752) 221654
I: www.SmoothHound.Co.UK/
hotels/berkely2html.

Bedrooms: 1 single,
3 double, 1 triple
Bathrooms: 4 en suite,
1 private

Parking for 4
CC: Barclaycard, Delta,
Eurocard, JCB, Maestro,
Mastercard, Solo, Switch,
Visa, Visa Electron

B&B per night:
S £28.00–£32.00
D £40.00–£60.00

OPEN All year round

Non-smoking Victorian townhouse ideally situated for seafront, Barbican, theatre, ferry port and city centre. Flexible accommodation between double/twin/triple.

HALF BOARD PRICES
Half board prices are given per person, but in some cases these may be based on double/twin occupancy.

◆◆◆◆

BOWLING GREEN HOTEL
9-10 Osborne Place, Lockyer Street,
Plymouth, Devon PL1 2PU
T: (01752) 209090
F: (01752) 209092
I: www.smoothhound.co.uk/hotels/
bowling.html

B&B per night:
S £38.00–£42.00
D £50.00–£52.00

OPEN All year round

Opposite Drake's bowling green, this elegant Victorian hotel has superbly appointed bedrooms offering all modern facilities. Our friendly and efficient staff will make your stay a memorable one. Centrally situated for the Barbican Theatre Royal, leisure/conference centre, ferry port, National Marine Aquarium, with Dartmoor only a few minutes away.

Bedrooms: 1 single,
9 double, 1 twin, 1 triple
Bathrooms: 12 en suite

Parking for 4
CC: Amex, Barclaycard,
Delta, Diners, Eurocard,
Mastercard, Solo, Switch,
Visa, Visa Electron

◆◆◆

GABBER FARM
Down Thomas, Plymouth, Devon
PL9 0AW
T: (01752) 862269
F: (01752) 862269

Bedrooms: 1 single,
1 double, 1 twin, 1 triple,
1 family room
Bathrooms: 2 en suite,
1 public

EM 1900 (LO 1800)
Parking for 4

B&B per night:
S £17.00–£19.00
D £34.00–£38.00

HB per person:
DY £27.00–£29.00

OPEN All year round

Courteous welcome at this farm, near coast and Bovisand diving centre. Lovely walks. Special weekly rates, especially for senior citizens and children. Directions provided.

◆◆◆

LAMPLIGHTER HOTEL
103 Citadel Road, The Hoe,
Plymouth, Devon PL1 2RN
T: (01752) 663855
F: (01752) 228139
E: lampligherhotel@ukonline.co.uk

Bedrooms: 5 double,
3 twin, 1 family room
Bathrooms: 6 en suite,
2 private

Parking for 4
CC: Amex, Barclaycard,
Delta, Mastercard, Visa

B&B per night:
S £20.00–£28.00
D £32.00–£40.00

OPEN All year round

Small friendly hotel on Plymouth Hoe, 5 minutes' walk from the city centre and seafront.

◆◆◆◆

OSMOND GUEST HOUSE
42 Pier Street, Plymouth, PL1 3BT
T: (01752) 229705
F: (01752) 269655
E: mike@osmondgh.freeserve.co.uk
I: plymouth-explore.co.uk

Bedrooms: 1 single,
3 double, 2 twin
Bathrooms: 4 en suite,
2 public

Parking for 4
CC: Mastercard, Visa

B&B per night:
S £17.00–£25.00
D £36.00–£45.00

OPEN All year round

Elegant Edwardian house, converted to modern standards, 20 yards from seafront and within walking distance of main points of interest. Resident proprietors offer courtesy "pick-up" from stations.

◆◆◆◆

SQUIRES GUEST HOUSE
7 St James Place East, The Hoe,
Plymouth, Devon PL1 3AS
T: (01752) 261459
F: (01752) 261459

Bedrooms: 2 single,
4 double, 1 twin, 2 triple
Bathrooms: 6 en suite,
1 private, 1 public

Parking for 4
CC: Amex, Barclaycard,
Delta, Eurocard,
Mastercard, Switch, Visa

B&B per night:
S £18.00–£30.00
D £38.00–£42.00

OPEN All year round

Elegant Victorian establishment in a quiet secluded square on Plymouth Hoe, easy walking distance all amenities. Winner of Chairman's Cup for Excellence, awarded by Plymouth Marketing Bureau.

QUALITY ASSURANCE SCHEME
Diamond ratings and awards were correct at the time of going to press but are subject to change. Please check at the time of booking.

PLYMOUTH continued

◆◆◆ WESTWINDS HOTEL

99 Citadel Road, The Hoe,
Plymouth, Devon PL1 2RN
T: (01752) 601777 & 08007 315717
F: (01752) 662158
E: paul.colman@btinternet.com
I: business.thisisplymouth.co.uk/
westwindshotel

Bedrooms: 1 single,
5 double, 4 twin; suites
available
Bathrooms: 4 en suite,
2 public, 4 private
showers

CC: Amex, Barclaycard,
Mastercard, Visa

B&B per night:
S £18.00–£38.00
D £30.00–£42.00

OPEN All year round

A family-owned hotel which takes pride in looking after our guests in a professional, friendly and homely environment.

PORTHCURNO, Cornwall Map ref 1A3

◆◆◆◆ THE PORTHCURNO HOTEL

The Valley, Porthcurno, St Levan,
Penzance, TR19 6JX
T: (01736) 810119
F: (01736) 810711
E: PorthcurnoHotel@compuserve.
com

Bedrooms: 1 single,
4 double, 6 twin, 1 triple
Bathrooms: 5 en suite,
2 public

Parking for 12
CC: Amex, Barclaycard,
Mastercard, Switch, Visa

B&B per night:
S £18.00–£45.00
D £36.00–£60.00

HB per person:
DY £31.00–£45.00

OPEN All year round

Hotel set in large gardens 600 yards from beach, offering bed and breakfast accommodation in up-market surroundings. Close to Minack Theatre and Museum of Submarine Telegraphy.

PORTLAND, Dorset Map ref 2B3

◆◆◆ ALESSANDRIA HOTEL

71 Wakeham Easton, Portland,
Weymouth, DT5 1HW
T: (01305) 822270 & 820108
F: (01305) 820561
I: www.s-h-systems.co.uk/hotels/
alessand.html

Bedrooms: 6 single,
3 double, 3 twin, 2 triple,
1 family room; suite
available
Bathrooms: 10 en suite,
1 private, 3 public,
1 private shower

EM 1900 (LO 2000)
Parking for 17
CC: Amex, Barclaycard,
Delta, Eurocard,
Mastercard, Visa

B&B per night:
S £25.00–£45.00
D £45.00–£60.00

HB per person:
DY £45.00–£55.00

OPEN All year round

18thC Portland stone building in quiet location. Comfortable rooms, with new beds and all facilities, 2 on ground floor. Excellent fresh food and warm, friendly hospitality from Giovanni.

RADSTOCK, Bath and North East Somerset Map ref 2B2

◆◆◆

THE ROOKERY

Wells Road, Radstock, Bath, BA3 3RS
T: (01761) 432626
F: (01761) 432626
E: rookery@iname.com
I: www.smoothhound.co.uk/hotels/
rookery.html

B&B per night:
S £35.00–£40.00
D £49.00–£54.50

HB per person:
DY £43.25–£50.00

OPEN All year round

A 200-year-old family run property offering every comfort, situated centrally for Bath, Wells and the Mendips. We have a relaxing lounge, residents' bar and restaurant and offer the best in service coupled with an easy-going atmosphere. En suite rooms with tea/coffee facilities, TV, telephone. Large car park.

Bedrooms: 1 single,
6 double, 2 twin, 1 triple,
2 family rooms
Bathrooms: 12 en suite

EM 1900 (LO 2030)
Parking for 25
CC: Barclaycard, Delta,
Mastercard, Solo, Switch,
Visa, Visa Electron

TOWN INDEX

This can be found at the back of this guide. If you know where you want to stay, the index will give you the page number listing accommodation in your chosen town, city or village.

◆◆◆◆

HEMBAL MANOR

Hembal Lane, Trewoon, St Austell,
PL25 5TD
T: (01726) 72144
F: (01726) 72144
E: svhiggs@hembalmanor.freeserve.co.uk
I: www.hembalmanor.freeserve.co.uk

B&B per night:
S £27.50–£30.00
D £50.00–£55.00

OPEN Apr–Oct

Dating from the 16thC, Hembal Manor is set in 6 acres of gardens. Ideally situated for beaches and places of interest, including the Lost Gardens of Heligan, and easy travelling distance of main Cornish towns. All rooms tastefully decorated and furnished.

Bedrooms: 2 double, 1 twin
Bathrooms: 3 en suite, 1 public

Parking for 6

◆◆◆◆

POLTARROW FARM

St Mewan, St Austell, PL26 7DR
T: (01726) 67111
F: (01726) 67111
E: enquire@poltarrow.co.uk
I: www.poltarrow.co.uk

B&B per night:
S £28.00–£30.00
D £46.00–£50.00

OPEN All year round

The charming farmhouse at Poltarrow can be the perfect answer for your holiday. Secluded, yet centrally located for beaches, gardens and the exciting new Eden Project. The pretty en suite rooms, delicious breakfast and the all-year indoor swimming pool make it the perfect place to stay any time of year.

Bedrooms: 3 double, 1 twin, 1 family room
Bathrooms: 4 en suite, 1 private

Parking for 5
CC: Barclaycard, Eurocard, Mastercard, Visa

◆◆◆◆

THE ANCHORAGE GUEST HOUSE

5 Bunkers Hill, St Ives, TR26 1LJ
T: (01736) 797135
F: (01736) 797135
E: james@theanchoragebb.fsnet.co.uk
I: www.theanchoragebb.fsnet.co.uk

Bedrooms: 1 single, 4 double, 1 twin
Bathrooms: 4 en suite, 1 public

CC: Amex, Delta, Mastercard, Visa

B&B per night:
S £20.00–£24.00
D £30.00–£50.00

OPEN All year round

18thC fisherman's cottage, 30 yards from harbour front and beaches, full of old world charm. Two minutes from Tate Gallery.

◆◆◆◆

BLUE HAYES

Trelyon Avenue, St Ives, TR26 2AD
T: (01736) 797129
F: (01736) 797129
I: www.blue-hayes.com.uk

B&B per night:
S £32.00–£40.00
D £60.00–£90.00

OPEN Mar–Sep

A country house by the sea at St Ives, set in its own grounds on Porthminster Point, overlooking St Ives Bay and harbour, above one of the finest sandy beaches in the country – just a few minutes' walk from the bottom of the garden. Ample parking.

Bedrooms: 2 single, 5 double, 1 twin, 1 triple; suite available
Bathrooms: 5 en suite, 2 public

EM 1830 (LO 1830)
Parking for 9
CC: Barclaycard, Diners, Eurocard, Mastercard, Visa

385

ST IVES continued

◆◆◆◆
LONGSHIPS HOTEL
Talland Road, St Ives, TR26 2DF
T: (01736) 798180
F: (01736) 798180

Bedrooms: 3 single,	Lunch available	B&B per night:
9 double, 4 twin, 9 triple	EM 1800 (LO 1900)	**S £20.00–£27.00**
Bathrooms: 25 en suite	Parking for 18	**D £40.00–£54.00**
	CC: Barclaycard,	
	Mastercard, Switch, Visa	HB per person:
		DY £25.00–£33.00

Overlooking the harbour and town with beautiful views across the bay and North Cornish coastline. Only a brief walk from the town and Porthminster beach.

OPEN All year round

🐎♨️🖥️📺🛏️🍴☂️✴️🐕 SC 🔆 SP

◆◆◆◆

THE PONDAROSA
10 Porthminster Terrace, St Ives, TR26 2DQ
T: (01736) 795875
F: (01736) 797811
E: pondarosa.hotel@talk21.com
I: www.cornwall-online.co.uk

B&B per night:
S £20.00–£23.00
D £38.00–£46.00

HB per person:
DY £38.00–£46.00

OPEN All year round

Highly recommended guest	Bedrooms: 5 double,	Lunch available
accommodation. Licensed, warm and	2 triple, 2 family rooms	EM 1800 (LO 1930)
friendly atmosphere, excellent home-	Bathrooms: 8 en suite,	Parking for 12
cooked meals, all en suite rooms with	1 private	CC: Amex, Barclaycard,
tea/coffee-making facilities, central		Mastercard, Switch, Visa
heating. Conveniently situated for		
towns and beaches. Large private car		
park.		

📶🐎♨️🖥️📺🛏️🍴☂️✴️🐕 SC 🔆 SP T

◆◆◆
PRIMAVERA PRIVATE HOTEL
14 Draycott Terrace, St Ives,
TR26 2EF
T: (01736) 795595
F: (01736) 795595
E: clarkprima@aol.com
I: www.smoothhound.co.uk/hotels/
primaver.html

Bedrooms: 2 single,	Lunch available	B&B per night:
1 double, 1 triple,	EM 1830 (LO 2100)	**S £20.00–£25.00**
1 family room		**D £40.00–£50.00**
Bathrooms: 2 en suite,		
1 public		HB per person:
		DY £28.50–£33.50

Small, friendly hotel overlooking Porthminster Beach, with warm, personal and efficient service. Carefully prepared food – special dietary needs catered for. Bar meals served all day.

OPEN All year round

📶🐎♨️🖥️🛏️📺🍴☂️✴️🐕 SC SP ⊙

ST KEW, Cornwall Map ref 1B2

◆◆◆
TREGELLIST FARM
Tregellist, St Kew, Bodmin,
PL30 3HG
T: (01208) 880537
F: (01208) 881017

Bedrooms: 1 double,	EM 1800	B&B per night:
1 twin, 1 family room	Parking for 6	**S £24.00–£28.00**
Bathrooms: 3 en suite		**D Min £44.00**
		HB per person:
		DY Min £36.00

130-acre mixed farm set in pleasant countryside with lovely views. Central for coast and moors. Delicious home cooking and a warm welcome to all.

OPEN All year round

📶🐎♨️🖥️🛏️📺🛏️📺✴️🐕

ST NEOT, Cornwall Map ref 1C2

◆◆◆◆
THE LONDON INN
St Neot, Liskeard, PL14 6NG
T: (01579) 320263 & 07710 419527
F: (01579) 320263

Bedrooms: 2 double,	Lunch available	B&B per night:
1 twin	EM 1900 (LO 2100)	**S £30.00–£36.00**
Bathrooms: 3 en suite	Parking for 10	**D £40.00–£48.00**
	CC: Barclaycard, Delta,	
	JCB, Maestro, Mastercard,	HB per person:
	Solo, Switch, Visa, Visa	**DY £30.00–£48.00**
	Electron	

A 17thC inn, situated in the picturesque village of St Neot, offering fresh, home-cooked food in comfortable surroundings.

OPEN All year round

📶🐎♨️🖥️🛏️🍷🛏️🔍♪🍴✴️🐕

IDEAS For ideas on places to visit refer to the introduction at the beginning of this section.

SALCOMBE, Devon Map ref 1C3 *Tourist Information Centre Tel: (01548) 843927*

♦♦♦♦ **TORRE VIEW HOTEL**

Devon Road, Salcombe, TQ8 8HJ
T: (01548) 842633
F: (01548) 842633
E: torreview@eurobell.co.uk

Bedrooms: 5 double,
2 twin, 1 triple
Bathrooms: 5 en suite,
3 private

EM 1900 (LO 1800)
Parking for 5
CC: Delta, Eurocard,
Mastercard, Visa

B&B per night:
S £30.00–£33.00
D £54.00–£60.00

HB per person:
DY £39.00–£43.00

OPEN Mar–Oct

Detached Victorian residence with every modern comfort, commanding extensive views of the estuary and surrounding countryside yet within reach of the town. No smoking, please.

SALISBURY, Wiltshire Map ref 2B3 *Tourist Information Centre Tel: (01722) 334956*

♦♦♦ **BEULAH**

144 Britford Lane, Salisbury,
SP2 8AL
T: (01722) 333517

Bedrooms: 1 single,
1 twin
Bathrooms: 1 public

Parking for 4

B&B per night:
S £19.00–£20.00
D £38.00–£40.00

OPEN All year round

Bungalow in quiet road, 1.25 miles from city centre and overlooking meadows. Tea/coffee making and colour TV in bedrooms. No-smoking establishment.

♦♦♦

BYWAYS HOUSE

31 Fowlers Road, City Centre, Salisbury,
SP1 2QP
T: (01722) 328364
F: (01722) 322146
E: byways@stonehenge-uk.com
I: www.stonehenge-uk.com

B&B per night:
S Min £30.00
D £45.00–£60.00

OPEN All year round

Attractive family-run Victorian house close to cathedral in quiet area of city centre. Large car park. Bedrooms with private bathrooms and colour satellite TV, 4-poster beds. Traditional English and vegetarian breakfasts. From Byways you can walk all around Salisbury. Ideal for Stonehenge and Wilton House.

Bedrooms: 4 single,
7 double, 3 twin, 2 triple,
7 family rooms
Bathrooms: 19 en suite,
1 public

Parking for 15
CC: Barclaycard, Delta,
Eurocard, JCB, Maestro,
Mastercard, Solo, Switch,
Visa, Visa Electron

♦♦♦ **CASTLEWOOD**

45 Castle Road, Salisbury, SP1 3RH
T: (01722) 324809 &
07967 013897 (Mobile)
F: (01722) 421494

Bedrooms: 2 single,
1 twin, 2 triple, 1 family
room
Bathrooms: 3 en suite,
1 public

EM 1700 (LO 1900)
Parking for 4

B&B per night:
S £23.00–£26.00
D £42.00–£46.00

HB per person:
DY £29.00–£35.00

OPEN All year round

Large Edwardian house, tastefully restored throughout. Pleasant 10 minutes' riverside walk to city centre and cathedral.

♦♦♦ **LEENA'S GUEST HOUSE**

50 Castle Road, Salisbury, SP1 3RL
T: (01722) 335419
F: (01722) 335419

Bedrooms: 1 single,
2 double, 2 twin,
1 family room
Bathrooms: 5 en suite,
1 public

Parking for 7

B&B per night:
S £24.00–£39.00
D £38.00–£48.00

OPEN All year round

Friendly, family-run guesthouse with pretty bedrooms and delightful public areas. Close to riverside walk to city centre and cathedral.

CHECK THE MAPS

The colour maps at the front of this guide show all the cities, towns and villages for which you will find accommodation entries.
Refer to the town index to find the page on which they are listed.

◆◆◆◆

MANOR FARM
Burcombe, Salisbury, SP2 OEJ
T: (01722) 742177
F: (01722) 744600

B&B per night:
S £30.00–£35.00
D £44.00–£46.00

OPEN Mar–Nov

Comfortable farmhouse, warm and attractively furnished, on 960-acre mixed farm in a quiet, pretty village quarter of a mile off A30 west of Salisbury. Ideal base for touring this lovely area. Nearby attractions include Wilton House, Salisbury and Stonehenge. Wonderful walks, good riding. Pub with good food nearby. No smoking.

Bedrooms: 1 double, 1 twin
Bathrooms: 2 en suite

Parking for 6

◆◆◆◆
Silver
Award

NEWTON FARM HOUSE
Southampton Road, Whiteparish, Salisbury, SP5 2QL
T: (01794) 884416
F: (01794) 884416
E: reservations@newtonfarmhouse.co.uk
I: www.newtonfarmhouse.co.uk

B&B per night:
S £25.00–£30.00
D £40.00–£50.00

HB per person:
DY £41.00–£46.00

OPEN All year round

Historic 16thC farmhouse, once part of the Trafalgar Estate. Delightfully decorated en suite bedrooms, 5 with genuine 4-posters (see our website). Beamed dining room with flagstones, bread oven and Nelson memorabilia. Superb breakfasts include fresh fruits, home-made bread, preserves and free-range eggs. Extensive grounds with swimming pool.

Bedrooms: 3 double, 2 twin, 2 triple, 1 family room
Bathrooms: 8 en suite

EM 1900
Parking for 10

◆◆

THE OLD BAKERY
35 Bedwin Street, Salisbury, SP1 3UT
T: (01722) 320100

Bedrooms: 1 single, 2 double, 1 triple
Bathrooms: 2 en suite, 2 public

B&B per night:
S £18.00–£25.00
D £36.00–£50.00

OPEN All year round

15thC city centre cottage with interesting medieval features and cosy oak-beamed rooms. Careful smokers welcome. Room only rates available.

◆◆◆◆

THE OLD RECTORY BED & BREAKFAST
75 Belle Vue Road, Salisbury, SP1 3YE
T: (01722) 502702
F: (01722) 501135
E: stay@theoldrectory-bb.co.uk
I: www.theoldrectory-bb.co.uk

Bedrooms: 2 double, 1 twin
Bathrooms: 2 en suite, 1 private

Parking for 1

B&B per night:
D £36.00–£50.00

OPEN All year round

Victorian rectory in quiet street, a short walk from the heart of Salisbury and convenient for all attractions. Warm, welcoming atmosphere. Visit our web site.

MAP REFERENCES
The map references refer to the colour maps at the front of this guide. The first figure is the map number; the letter and figure which follow indicate the grid reference on the map.

♦♦♦♦

THE ROKEBY GUEST HOUSE

3 Wain-a-Long Road, Salisbury, SP1 1LJ
T: (01722) 329800
F: (01722) 329800
I: www.smoothhound.co.uk/hotels/rokeby.html

B&B per night:
S £35.00–£42.00
D £45.00–£50.00

HB per person:
DY £37.50–£50.00

OPEN All year round

Beautiful, nostalgic, Victorian guesthouse, quietly situated, 10 minutes' stroll city centre/cathedral. Large landscaped gardens, summerhouse, elegant 2-storey conservatory, satellite TV, licensed restaurant, gymnasium. Brochure available.

Bedrooms: 1 double, 3 twin, 1 triple, 2 family rooms; suite available
Bathrooms: 5 en suite, 2 private, 1 public

EM 1830 (LO 2100)
Parking for 6

♦♦♦

VICTORIA LODGE GUEST HOUSE

61 Castle Road, Salisbury, SP1 3RH
T: (01722) 320586
F: (01722) 414507
E: mail@viclodge.co.uk
I: www.viclodge.co.uk

Bedrooms: 4 single, 4 double, 4 twin, 3 triple
Bathrooms: 15 en suite

Lunch available
EM 1800 (LO 2000)
Parking for 15
CC: Barclaycard, Delta, Eurocard, JCB, Maestro, Mastercard, Solo, Switch, Visa, Visa Electron

B&B per night:
S £35.00–£37.50
D £48.00–£52.00

HB per person:
DY £44.00–£46.50

OPEN All year round

Victorian lodge, a short riverside walk to city centre, cathedral and Old Sarum. Home-cooked evening meals, good parking. Licensed bar. Stonehenge 15 minutes, Bath 45 minutes, Winchester 45 minutes.

See under Amesbury, Figheldean, Salisbury, Warminster, Winterbourne Stoke

---

♦♦♦

GLENSIDE HOUSE

Ringmore Road, Shaldon, Teignmouth, TQ14 0EP
T: (01626) 872448
I: www.smoothhound.co.uk/hotels/glensideho.html

B&B per night:
S £22.00–£28.00
D £44.00–£56.00

HB per person:
DY £34.00–£43.00

OPEN All year round

Old world cottage-style hotel overlooking river. Licensed and family-run, home cooking. Level walk by river to sea, easy access to Dartmoor, Torquay. South Hams. Car park, sunny garden.

Bedrooms: 1 single, 4 double, 3 twin
Bathrooms: 7 en suite, 1 public

EM 1900 (LO 1900)
Parking for 10

♦♦♦♦

BOWLISH HOUSE

Coombe Lane, Shepton Mallet, BA4 5JD
T: (01749) 342022
F: (01749) 342022

Bedrooms: 3 double, 1 twin
Bathrooms: 4 en suite

EM 1900 (LO 2130)
Parking for 10
CC: Barclaycard, Delta, Eurocard, JCB, Maestro, Mastercard, Solo, Switch, Visa, Visa Electron

B&B per night:
S Max £55.00
D Max £65.00

OPEN All year round

Bowlish House is a restaurant with en suite bedrooms, in a Listed Georgian house on the Wells road, quarter of a mile outside Shepton Mallet.

SYMBOLS The symbols in each entry give information about services and facilities. A key to these symbols appears at the back of this guide.

SHEPTON MALLET continued

◆◆◆◆
Silver
Award

BURNT HOUSE FARM
Waterlip, West Cranmore, Shepton Mallet, BA4 4RN
T: (01749) 880280
F: (01749) 880004

B&B per night:
S £30.00–£30.00
D £50.00–£50.00

OPEN All year round

Relax in hot-hydro garden-spa, sip a cool drink in the summer house, play snooker/pool on full size table. Garage your car after visiting wealth of local attaractions. Enjoy complimentary refreshments in visitors' drawing room whilst savouring roaring log burner, pine floors/beams. Sleep well under traditional blankets. Feast on breakfast.

Bedrooms: 2 double, 1 twin
Bathrooms: 1 en suite, 2 private

Parking for 14

◆◆◆◆

TEMPLE HOUSE FARM
Doulting, Shepton Mallet, BA4 4RQ
T: (01749) 880294
F: (01749) 880688

Bedrooms: 1 twin, 1 triple
Bathrooms: 2 en suite

EM
Parking for 4

B&B per night:
S £25.00–£30.00
D £42.00–£44.00

HB per person:
DY Min £35.00

OPEN All year round

200-acre dairy farm. 400-year-old Listed farmhouse. In rural area within easy reach of Wells, Bath, Shepton Mallet, the Mendips and of tourist attractions.

SHERBORNE, Dorset Map ref 2B3 *Tourist Information Centre Tel: (01935) 815341*

◆◆◆◆
Silver
Award

THE ALDERS
Sandford Orcas, Sherborne, DT9 4SB
T: (01963) 220666
F: (01963) 220106
E: jonsue@btinternet.com

B&B per night:
D £45.00–£50.00

OPEN All year round

Secluded stone house set in old walled garden, in picturesque conservation village near Sherborne. House is tastefully furnished, with original watercolour paintings and hand-made pottery. There is a woodburning fire in lounge inglenook fireplace. Good breakfasts served around large farmhouse table. Excellent food available in traditional friendly village pub.

Bedrooms: 1 double, 1 twin
Bathrooms: 2 en suite

Parking for 6

◆◆

BAY TREES
Bristol Road, Sherborne, DT9 4HP
T: (01935) 816527

Bedrooms: 1 single, 1 twin
Bathrooms: 1 public

Parking for 2

B&B per night:
S £16.00–£17.00
D £32.00–£34.00

OPEN All year round

Beatutifully furnished bungalow with off-road parking, 100 yards north of A30 and 5 minutes' walk from town centre. Non-smokers only.

IMPORTANT NOTE Information on accommodation listed in this guide has been supplied by the proprietors. As changes may occur you are advised to check details at the time of booking.

CROWN INN

Green Hill, Sherborne, DT9 4EP
T: (01935) 812930
F: (01935) 812930

Bedrooms: 2 double,
1 twin, 1 family room
Bathrooms: 2 en suite,
1 public

Lunch available
EM 1830 (LO 2130)
Parking for 10
CC: Barclaycard, Delta,
Eurocard, JCB, Maestro,
Mastercard, Solo, Switch,
Visa, Visa Electron

B&B per night:
S £28.00–£38.00
D £40.00–£50.00

HB per person:
DY Min £26.00

OPEN All year round

Friendly and comfortable freehouse. Excellent English and French cuisine. Quality wines and real ales. In the heart of Sherborne on the A30.

🕭 ❑ ♿ 🛈 🖫 ⚡ ▥ ▮ ♈70 ♨ ✈ 🚗

SIDMOUTH, Devon Map ref 1D2 *Tourist Information Centre Tel: (01395) 516441*

LOWER PINN FARM

Pinn, Sidmouth, EX10 0NN
T: (01395) 513733
F: (01395) 513733

B&B per night:
S £25.00–£30.00
D £40.00–£45.00

OPEN All year round

220-acre mixed farm in scenic surroundings. Fields extend to coastal path. Two miles west coastal resort Sidmouth. A friendly welcome with comfortable accommodation. En suite bedrooms with colour TV, hot drink facilities, central heating, keys for access all times. Good hearty breakfast served in dining room on separate tables.

Bedrooms: 2 double,
1 triple
Bathrooms: 3 en suite,
1 public

Parking for 3

🕭 🖳 ❑ ♿ 🖳 UL S 🖳 ▥ 🖳 🚗 🛁 SP T ◉

SLAPTON, Devon Map ref 1D3

START HOUSE

Start, Slapton, Kingsbridge, TQ7 2QD
T: (01548) 580254 (Ansaphone)

B&B per night:
S £25.00–£27.00
D £44.00–£48.00

HB per person:
DY £36.00–£38.00

OPEN Jan–Nov

In quiet hamlet, 1 mile from Slapton, comfortable Georgian house with 2-acre partly-terraced garden. All bedrooms overlook beautiful valley, with Slapton Ley and the sea at the end. Traditional or vegetarian breakfast. Evening meal by arrangement. Ideal for wildlife and walking.

Bedrooms: 2 double,
1 twin
Bathrooms: 2 en suite,
1 public

EM 1830 (LO 1000)
Parking for 4

🕭 ♿ 🖳 UL S 🖫 ▥ TV ▥ 🚗 ✻ 🛁 🏠 T

CHECK THE MAPS

The colour maps at the front of this guide show all the cities, towns and villages for which you will find accommodation entries. Refer to the town index to find the page on which they are listed.

SPREYTON, Devon Map ref 1C2

◆◆◆

THE TOM COBLEY TAVERN

Spreyton, Crediton, EX17 5AL
T: (01647) 231314
F: (01647) 231506
E: fjwfilor@tomcobley.fsnet.co.uk

B&B per night:
S £20.00–£20.00
D £40.00–£40.00

OPEN All year round

A small village inn serving its isolated community and offering a warm welcome to all guests. Real ales are on draught and food is home cooked on the premises. Rooms are comfortable, quiet and well equipped, service is cheerful and friendly. Dartmoor is 2 miles to the south.

Bedrooms: 2 single, 1 double, 1 twin
Bathrooms: 1 public

Lunch available
EM 1900 (LO 2045)
Parking for 8

STOGUMBER, Somerset Map ref 1D1

◆◆◆

HALL FARM
Stogumber, Taunton, TA4 3TQ
T: (01984) 656321

Bedrooms: 1 single, 4 double, 1 triple
Bathrooms: 5 en suite, 1 public

EM 1830
Parking for 20

B&B per night:
S Min £18.50
D Min £37.00

HB per person:
DY Min £28.50

OPEN All year round

Hall Farm is situated in the centre of picturesque Stogumber, between the Brendon and Quantock Hills. Close to sea and quiant villages of Dunster and Porlock.

◆◆◆◆

Silver Award

NORTHAM MILL

Water Lane, Stogumber, Taunton, TA4 3TT
T: (01984) 656916 (Ansaphone) & 656146
F: (01984) 656144
E: bmsspicer@aol.com
I: www.northam-mill.co.uk

B&B per night:
D £51.00–£75.00

HB per person:
DY £44.00–£56.00

OPEN Jan, Mar–Dec

Hidden for 300 years. Nesting between the Quantocks and the Brendon Hills, in 5 acres of gardens with trout stream. Welcoming and comfortable, log fires and original beams. All rooms en suite including luxury garden suite. Daily menu from all home-cooked food. Own heated kennels and stables. Hunting, shooting, walking.

Bedrooms: 2 double, 1 twin; suite available
Bathrooms: 3 en suite

EM 1930 (LO 2000)
Parking for 12
CC: Amex, Barclaycard, Diners, Mastercard, Visa

STOKE SUB HAMDON, Somerset Map ref 2A3

◆◆◆◆

CASTLE FARM
Stoke sub Hamdon, TA14 6QS
T: (01935) 822231
F: (01935) 822057

Bedrooms: 1 double, 1 twin, 1 family room
Bathrooms: 3 en suite

B&B per night:
S £25.00–£25.00
D £39.00–£39.00

OPEN All year round

Castle farm is an 18thC farmhouse, part of the Duchy of Cornwall estate, next to the A303 and close to Montacute House.

WELCOME HOST This is a nationally recognised customer care programme which aims to promote the highest standards of service and a warm welcome. Establishments taking part in this initiative are indicated by the ⊛ symbol.

STREET, Somerset Map ref 2A2

◆◆◆◆ OLD ORCHARD HOUSE

Middle Brooks, Street, BA16 0TU
T: (01458) 442212 (Ansaphone)
E: oldorchardhouse@amserve.net

Bedrooms: 1 double,
1 twin
Bathrooms: 1 public

EM
Parking for 3

B&B per night:
S £20.00–£25.00
D £40.00–£45.00

Peaceful, modern, centrally heated family home; log fires in winter, eat outside in summer; no TV, no smoking, excellent food, candlelit dinners, very warm welcome.

HB per person:
DY £30.00–£42.00

OPEN All year round

SUTTON POYNTZ, Dorset Map ref 2B3

◆◆◆ SELWYNS

Puddledock Lane, Sutton Poyntz,
Weymouth, DT3 6LZ
T: (01305) 832239 (Ansaphone)
E: selwyns-b-and-b@hotmail.com

Bedrooms: 2 double,
1 twin
Bathrooms: 1 public

EM 1800 (LO 2000)
Parking for 4

B&B per night:
S Max £25.00
D £35.00–£40.00

Chalet bungalow in pretty village, 1 mile inland, near Weymouth and White Horse, Osmington. A353 to Preston, turn into Seven Acres Road, right at top of hill into Puddledock Lane.

HB per person:
DY £27.50–£35.00

OPEN Feb–Oct
& Christmas

SWINDON, Wiltshire Map ref 2B2 *Tourist Information Centre Tel: (01793) 530328 or 466454*

◆◆◆ COURTLEIGH HOUSE

40 Draycott Road, Chiseldon,
Swindon, SN4 0LS
T: (01793) 740246

Bedrooms: 2 twin
Bathrooms: 1 en suite,
1 private

Parking for 3

B&B per night:
S £22.00–£25.00
D £37.00–£42.00

Large detached village house with downland views, ample parking, tennis court and gardens. Easy access to Marlborough, Swindon and M4.

OPEN All year round

TAUNTON, Somerset Map ref 1D1 *Tourist Information Centre Tel: (01823) 336344*

◆◆◆◆ FORDE HOUSE

9 Upper High Street, Taunton,
TA1 3PX
T: (01823) 279042
F: (01823) 279042

Bedrooms: 1 single,
2 double, 2 twin
Bathrooms: 5 en suite

Parking for 5
CC: Barclaycard,
Mastercard, Visa

B&B per night:
S £30.00–£32.00
D £50.00–£55.00

Peaceful location in the centre of town, close to all amenities, including public park and golf-course. Warm welcome guaranteed.

OPEN All year round

◆◆◆◆

HIGHER YARDE FARM COUNTRY BED & BREAKFAST

Higher Yarde Farm, Staplegrove, Taunton,
TA2 6SW
T: (01823) 451553 (Ansaphone) &
07770 866848 (Mobile)

Relax and enjoy this comfortable and peaceful country house, with cottage garden, stream and meadow. Ideal situation – only 2 miles from Taunton and convenient M5 access. Good centre for touring Somerset and north and south coasts, Dartmoor and Exmoor. A warm welcome guaranteed.

Bedrooms: 1 double,
1 twin
Bathrooms: 1 public,
1 private shower

B&B per night:
S £20.00–£22.50
D £35.00–£40.00

OPEN Feb–Nov

CREDIT CARD BOOKINGS If you book by telephone and are asked for your credit card number it is advisable to check the proprietor's policy should you cancel your reservation.

TAUNTON continued

◆◆◆◆ THE SPINNEY
Curland, Taunton, TA3 5SE
T: (01460) 234362
F: (01460) 234362
E: bartlett.spinney@zetnet.co.uk
I: www.somerweb.co.uk/spinney-bb

Bedrooms: 1 twin,
2 triple
Bathrooms: 3 en suite,
1 public

EM 1900 (LO 2000)
Parking for 6

B&B per night:
S £30.00–£30.00
D £42.00–£45.00

HB per person:
DY £33.50–£35.00

OPEN All year round

Modern detached house in quiet countryside. Lovely garden with panoramic views from slopes of Blackdown Hills. Quality en suite accommodation. Evening meals recommended. No smoking throughout.

◆◆

STAPLEGROVE LODGE
Staplegrove, Taunton, TA2 6PX
T: (01823) 331153

B&B per night:
S £22.00–£27.00
D £40.00–£50.00

OPEN All year round

A lovely, Listed Georgian family home, set in 1.5 acres with views of the Quantocks and Blackdown hills. Although rural, we are only 1.5 miles from Taunton town centre. All rooms are individually decorated and invitingly spacious. Family room is en suite and multi-purpose. Breakfast is freshly cooked, with produce from local farms.

Bedrooms: 1 single,
2 double, 2 family rooms
Bathrooms: 1 en suite,
1 public

Parking for 5

TAVISTOCK, Devon Map ref 1C2 *Tourist Information Centre Tel: (01822) 612938*

◆◆◆◆ ACORN COTTAGE
Heathfield, Tavistock, PL19 0LQ
T: (01822) 810038
E: viv@acorncot.fsnet.co.uk
I: www.visitbritain.com

Bedrooms: 1 double,
2 twin
Bathrooms: 3 en suite

Parking for 20

B&B per night:
S £25.00–£30.00
D £30.00–£40.00

OPEN All year round

17thC Grade II Listed. Many original features, lovely views, peaceful location. Lydford Gorge 3.5 miles and near Brentor medieval church. Central to many activities – bordering Dartmoor. Send for brochure.

◆◆◆◆ APRIL COTTAGE
Mount Tavy Road, Tavistock,
PL19 9JB
T: (01822) 613280

Bedrooms: 2 double,
1 twin
Bathrooms: 3 en suite

Parking for 5

B&B per night:
S £30.00–£35.00
D £38.00–£42.00

HB per person:
DY £28.00–£32.00

OPEN All year round

19thC character cottage close to town centre and all amenities. Breakfast served in the Victorian conservatory overlooking the River Tavy. En suite bedrooms, beautifully decorated. Parking.

COUNTRY CODE Always follow the Country Code ✿ Enjoy the countryside and respect its life and work ✿ Guard against all risk of fire ✿ Fasten all gates ✿ Keep your dogs under close control ✿ Keep to public paths across farmland ✿ Use gates and stiles to cross fences, hedges and walls ✿ Leave livestock, crops and machinery alone ✿ Take your litter home ✿ Help to keep all water clean ✿ Protect wildlife, plants and trees ✿ Take special care on country roads ✿ Make no unnecessary noise

TAVISTOCK continued

◆◆◆◆
Silver
Award

BEERA FARMHOUSE
Milton Abbot, Tavistock, PL19 8PL
T: (01822) 870216
F: (01822) 870216
E: robert.tucker@farming.co.uk

B&B per night:
S £15.00–£25.00
D £34.00–£40.00

HB per person:
DY £27.50–£37.50

OPEN All year round

Take peaceful walks on our working beef and sheep farm, admire the beautiful scenery, relax in the garden, enjoy excellent food using local produce or visit many of the local attractions: the Dartmoor National Park, historic buildings, the rugged cliffs of the North Cornwall coast and quaint fishing villages on the south coast. Brochure available.

Bedrooms: 2 double, 1 twin
Bathrooms: 3 en suite, 1 public

EM 1830
Parking for 8

◆◆◆

KINGFISHER COTTAGE
Mount Tavy Road, Vigo Bridge, Tavistock, PL19 9JB
T: (01822) 613801 & 07721 772095

Bedrooms: 2 double, 1 twin
Bathrooms: 1 en suite, 1 public

Parking for 5

B&B per night:
S £16.00–£38.00
D £32.00–£46.00

OPEN All year round

Riverside accommodation in newly built stone cottage, comfortable and convenient. Close to town centre and Dartmoor. Ideal base for touring Devon and Cornwall. Weekly discounts.

TINTAGEL, Cornwall Map ref 1B2

◆◆◆◆

THE CORNISHMAN INN
Fore Street, Tintagel, PL34 0DB
T: (01840) 770238
F: (01840) 770078

Bedrooms: 4 double, 4 twin, 1 triple, 1 family room; suites available
Bathrooms: 10 en suite

Lunch available
EM 1800 (LO 2130)
Parking for 30
CC: Amex, Barclaycard, Delta, Diners, Eurocard, Mastercard, Switch

B&B per night:
S £27.50–£35.00
D £40.00–£60.00

OPEN All year round

Family-run old world inn, set in the heart of King Arthur's Country. 3 bars, fine food, ales and wines. Large gardens and car park.

◆◆◆

PENDRIN HOUSE
Atlantic Road, Tintagel, PL34 0DE
T: (01840) 770560
F: (01840) 770560
E: pendrin@tesco.net

Bedrooms: 1 single, 4 double, 2 twin, 2 triple
Bathrooms: 3 en suite, 3 public

EM 1830 (LO 1930)
Parking for 6

B&B per night:
S Min £16.00
D £32.00–£38.00

HB per person:
DY Min £26.00

OPEN Mar–Oct

Beautiful Victorian house. In historic village, overlooking the cliffs and Atlantic Ocean. Close to the castle, beaches, coastal path and many other amenities.

◆◆◆◆

PORT WILLIAM INN
Trebarwith Strand, Tintagel, PL34 0HB
T: (01840) 770230
F: (01840) 770936
E: william@eurobell.co.uk

B&B per night:
S £50.00–£57.00
D £65.00–£79.00

OPEN All year round

Probably the best located inn in Cornwall, overlooking sea and beach. All rooms en suite with TV and telephone. Extensive menu, including local seafood. Open all day, all year.

Bedrooms: 2 double, 1 twin, 1 triple, 2 family rooms
Bathrooms: 6 en suite

Lunch available
EM 1800 (LO 2130)
Parking for 50
CC: Amex, Barclaycard, Delta, Eurocard, Mastercard, Switch, Visa

TIVERTON, Devon Map ref 1D2 *Tourist Information Centre Tel: (01884) 255827*

♦♦♦ BRIDGE GUEST HOUSE

23 Angel Hill, Tiverton, EX16 6PE
T: (01884) 252804
F: (01884) 252804

Bedrooms: 5 single,
2 double, 1 twin, 2 triple
Bathrooms: 6 en suite,
2 public

EM 1830 (LO 1930)
Parking for 8

B&B per night:
S £19.50–£24.50
D £38.00–£49.00

HB per person:
DY £31.50–£36.50

OPEN All year round

Attractive Victorian townhouse situated on the bank of the River Exe, with pretty riverside tea garden. Ideal for touring the heart of Devon.

TORQUAY, Devon Map ref 1D2 *Tourist Information Centre Tel: 0906 680 1268 (calls cost 25p per minute)*

♦♦♦ BRANDIZE HOTEL

19 Avenue Road, Torquay, Devon
TQ2 5LB
T: (01803) 297798
F: (01803) 297798
E: ted@brandize.freeserve.co.uk
I: www.smoothhound.co.uk/hotels/
brandize.html

Bedrooms: 3 double,
1 twin, 2 triple, 2 family
rooms
Bathrooms: 8 en suite

Lunch available
EM 1830 (LO 1700)
Parking for 10
CC: Amex, Barclaycard,
Delta, Diners, JCB,
Maestro, Mastercard,
Solo, Switch, Visa, Visa
Electron

B&B per night:
S £17.50–£23.00
D £35.00–£46.00

HB per person:
DY £26.00–£31.50

OPEN All year round

Friendly family hotel where you will find a very warm welcome, 500 yards from seafront and near Torre Abbey. Licence, large car park.

♦♦♦♦ CEDAR COURT HOTEL

3 St Matthew's Road, Chelston,
Torquay, TQ2 6JA
T: (01803) 607851

Bedrooms: 3 single,
5 double, 2 triple
Bathrooms: 10 en suite

EM 1800
Parking for 6

B&B per night:
S £17.00–£22.00
D £34.00–£44.00

HB per person:
DY £26.00–£30.00

OPEN All year round

Situated in peaceful surroundings within easy walking distance of seafront, town centre and railway station. All rooms en suite. Quality accommodation and meals.

♦♦♦

CHESTER COURT HOTEL

30 Cleveland Road, Torquay, Devon
TQ2 5BE
T: (01803) 294565
F: (01803) 294565
E: kevin@kpmorris.freeserve.co.uk
I: www.kpmorris.freeserve.co.uk/cch.html

B&B per night:
S £16.00–£20.00
D £32.00–£40.00

HB per person:
DY £24.00–£26.00

OPEN All year round

Small, family-run unlicensed hotel. Ample parking. All rooms en suite with colour TV, tea-making and full central heating for your comfort out of season. No-smoking rooms available. Varied menu, home cooking, English breakfast in spacious dining room. Level walk to Riviera Centre and seafront.

Bedrooms: 1 single,
3 double, 1 twin, 4 triple,
1 family room
Bathrooms: 9 en suite,
1 public

EM 1800 (LO 1830)
Parking for 11
CC: Delta, Eurocard,
Mastercard, Visa

♦♦♦♦♦ CRANBORNE HOTEL

Silver
Award

58 Belgrave Road, Torquay, Devon
TQ2 5HY
T: (01803) 298046
F: (01803) 298046

Bedrooms: 3 single,
3 double, 3 twin, 1 triple
Bathrooms: 10 en suite,
1 public

EM 1800 (LO 1500)
Parking for 3
CC: Barclaycard, Delta,
Eurocard, Mastercard,
Solo, Switch, Visa

B&B per night:
S £25.00–£25.00
D £40.00–£50.00

HB per person:
DY £30.00–£35.00

OPEN All year round

Victorian terraced hotel in excellent situation, being close to seafront, town centre and Riviera Centre. Torquay's only 5 Diamond Silver award hotel.

ACCESSIBILITY

Look for the symbols which indicate accessibility for wheelchair users. A list of establishments is at the front of this guide.

TORQUAY continued

◆◆◆◆ Silver Award — KINGSTON HOUSE
75 Avenue Road, Torquay, TQ2 5LL
T: (01803) 212760

Bedrooms: 2 single, 2 double, 2 triple
Bathrooms: 6 en suite

Parking for 6
CC: Barclaycard, Eurocard, Mastercard, Visa

B&B per night:
S £20.00–£22.50
D £35.00–£45.00

OPEN All year round

Combines Victorian elegance with modern amenities, ensuring a fulfilling, relaxed holiday. Conveniently situated for seafront, harbour, town. Private car park. Favourable weekly terms available.

◆◆◆ MAPLE LODGE
36 Ash Hill Road, Torquay, TQ1 3JD
T: (01803) 297391

Bedrooms: 1 single, 3 double, 1 twin, 1 triple, 1 family room
Bathrooms: 6 en suite, 1 private

Parking for 5

B&B per night:
S £16.00–£22.00
D £32.00–£44.00

OPEN Feb–Dec

Detached guesthouse with beautiful views. Relaxed atmosphere, home cooking, en suite rooms. Centrally situated for town and beaches.

◆◆◆◆ ROBIN HILL HOTEL
74 Braddons Hill Road East, Torquay, Devon TQ1 1HF
T: (01803) 214518
F: (01803) 291410
E: jo@robinhillhotel.co.uk
I: www.robinhillhotel.co.uk

Bedrooms: 4 single, 10 double, 2 twin, 1 triple, 1 family room
Bathrooms: 17 en suite, 1 private

EM 1830 (LO 1200)
Parking for 12
CC: Barclaycard, Delta, Eurocard, JCB, Mastercard, Solo, Switch, Visa, Visa Electron

B&B per night:
S £24.00–£32.00
D £48.00–£64.00

OPEN Apr–Oct

Quiet location yet close to town centre and harbour. Refurbished throughout to high standard of comfort and elegance.

◆◆◆ SOUTHBANK HOTEL
15/17 Belgrave Road, Torquay, Torquay, Devon TQ2 5HU
T: (01803) 296701 & 07774 948850
F: (01803) 292026

Bedrooms: 5 single, 5 double, 3 twin, 2 triple, 2 family rooms
Bathrooms: 12 en suite, 2 public, 1 private shower

EM 1800
Parking for 11
CC: Barclaycard, Delta, Eurocard, JCB, Mastercard, Solo, Switch, Visa, Visa Electron

B&B per night:
S £18.50–£23.50
D £40.00–£47.00

HB per person:
DY £27.50–£33.00

OPEN All year round

A family-run hotel. Home-cooked food and well stocked bar. Centrally situated for beaches, town and conference centre. A real home from home.

TOTNES, Devon Map ref 1D2 *Tourist Information Centre Tel: (01803) 863168*

◆◆◆◆◆ Silver Award

"OLD FOLLATON"
Plymouth Road, Totnes, TQ9 5NA
T: (01803) 865441
F: (01803) 863597

B&B per night:
S £40.00–£45.00
D £50.00–£60.00

HB per person:
DY £45.00–£55.00

OPEN All year round

Delightful Georgian country house on the edge of the historic town of Totnes, offering accommodation of the highest standard in a friendly and informal atmosphere. It is the ideal location surrounded by a wealth of places to visit, superb coastal and countryside walks and the splendour of Dartmoor.

Bedrooms: 1 double, 2 twin; suites available
Bathrooms: 3 en suite

EM 1800 (LO 2000)
Parking for 6

QUALITY ASSURANCE SCHEME
Diamond ratings and awards were correct at the time of going to press but are subject to change. Please check at the time of booking.

♦♦♦♦
Silver
Award

THE OLD FORGE AT TOTNES

Seymour Place, Totnes, TQ9 5AY
T: (01803) 862174
F: (01803) 865385

B&B per night:
S £40.00–£48.00
D £54.00–£74.00

OPEN All year round

A warm and friendly welcome awaits you in this delightful 600-year-old stone building, with walled garden and working smithy. Cottage suite suitable for family or disabled guests. No smoking indoors. Extensive breakfast menu (traditional, vegetarian, fish and continental). Whirlpool spa. Speciality: golf breaks. Close to town centre and riverside.

Bedrooms: 1 single, 5 double, 2 twin, 2 family rooms; suites available
Bathrooms: 9 en suite, 1 private, 1 public

Parking for 10
CC: Barclaycard, Delta, Eurocard, Mastercard, Visa

TRURO, Cornwall Map ref 1B3 *Tourist Information Centre Tel: (01872) 274555*

♦♦♦♦

BISSICK OLD MILL

Ladock, Truro, TR2 4PG
T: (01726) 882557
F: (01726) 884057

B&B per night:
S £39.95–£39.95
D £54.40–£69.00

HB per person:
DY £44.70–£57.45

OPEN All year round

17thC water mill sympathetically converted to provide well-appointed accommodation with exceptional standards throughout and a relaxing, friendly atmosphere. All bedrooms en suite and well equipped. Candlelit dinners prepared with fresh, quality ingredients and served in a beamed dining room. Ideal base for exploring all areas of Cornwall.

Bedrooms: 1 single, 3 double, 1 twin
Bathrooms: 5 en suite

EM 1900 (LO 1700)
Parking for 9
CC: Barclaycard, Delta, Eurocard, JCB, Mastercard, Switch, Visa, Visa Electron

---

♦♦♦♦

MARCORRIE HOTEL

20 Falmouth Road, Truro, TR1 2HX
T: (01872) 277374
F: (01872) 241666
E: marcorrie@aol.com
I: www.cornwall.net/marcorrie

B&B per night:
S £37.50–£44.00
D £47.50–£52.00

HB per person:
DY Min £48.00

OPEN All year round

Victorian town house with en suite bedrooms, only 5 minutes' walk to city centre and cathedral. Centrally situated for visiting all of Cornwall by car or bus. Many country houses and gardens, coastal and river walks nearby. Ample parking. Traditional English cuisine served in period dining room.

Bedrooms: 3 single, 3 double, 2 twin, 1 triple, 3 family rooms
Bathrooms: 12 en suite, 1 public

EM 1900 (LO 1700)
Parking for 16
CC: Amex, Barclaycard, Delta, Diners, Eurocard, JCB, Maestro, Mastercard, Solo, Switch, Visa, Visa Electron

---

TOWN INDEX

This can be found at the back of this guide. If you know where you want to stay, the index will give you the page number listing accommodation in your chosen town, city or village.

TRURO continued

◆◆◆◆

ROCK COTTAGE
Blackwater, Truro, TR4 8EU
T: (01872) 560252 &
07971 941399 (Mobile)
F: (01872) 560252
E: rockcottage@yahoo.com

B&B per night:
S £26.00–£28.00
D £44.00–£48.00

OPEN All year round

18thC, beamed cob cottage, formerly the village schoolmaster's home. A haven for non-smokers. Centrally heated throughout, all bedrooms en suite. Guest sitting room with colour TV. Cosy dining room with antique Cornish range. Private parking. Gardens. Village location, 3 miles ocean and 6 miles Truro. No pets or children.

Bedrooms: 2 double, 1 twin
Bathrooms: 3 en suite

Parking for 4
CC: Delta, Eurocard, JCB, Mastercard, Solo, Switch, Visa

WARMINSTER, Wiltshire Map ref 2B2 *Tourist Information Centre Tel: (01985) 218548*

◆◆◆

LANE END COTTAGE
72 Lane End, Corsley, Warminster, BA12 7PG
T: (01373) 832592 (Ansaphone)
F: (01373) 832935
E: hugh-kay@moredent.fsnet.co.uk

Bedrooms: 1 double, 1 twin
Bathrooms: 1 en suite, 1 public

Parking for 2

B&B per night:
S £30.00–£40.00
D £35.00–£45.00

OPEN Mar–Nov

Charming 17thC cottage, overlooking Longleat Estate in village location. Off-road parking. Local inn/restaurant within easy walk. Convenient for Bath, Salisbury, Stourhead, Stonehenge, Avebury.

◆◆◆◆

STURFORD MEAD FARM
Corsley, Warminster, BA12 7QU
T: (01373) 832213
F: (01373) 832213
E: lynn_sturford.bed@virgin.net

Bedrooms: 1 double, 2 twin
Bathrooms: 2 en suite, 1 private, 1 public

Parking for 10

B&B per night:
S £30.00–£30.00
D £44.00–£44.00

OPEN All year round

On A362 halfway between Frome and Warminster, nestling under Cley Hill (National Trust) and opposite Longleat. Convenient for Bath Wells, Salisbury, Stourhead, Wookey Hole.

WATERGATE BAY, Cornwall Map ref 1B2

◆◆◆

THE WHITE HOUSE
Watergate Bay, Newquay, TR8 4AD
T: (01637) 860119
F: (01637) 860449
E: jenny.vallance@virgin.net

B&B per night:
S £25.00–£30.00
D £50.00–£50.00

OPEN May–Oct

Quiet, elegant, spacious, country house with large gardens, overlooking Watergate Bay and beach for sandcastles and surfing. Beautifully appointed bed and breakfast suites, large, well-equipped family apartments plus a converted chapel for romantic couples. Ideally situated between Padstow and Newquay for touring, walking and sports.

Bedrooms: 2 single, 2 double; suites available
Bathrooms: 4 en suite

Parking for 15

PRICES
Please check prices and other details at the time of booking.

WELLS, Somerset Map ref 2A2 *Tourist Information Centre Tel: (01749) 672552*

◆◆◆

THE CROWN AT WELLS

Market Place, Wells, BA5 2RP
T: (01749) 673457
F: (01749) 679792
E: reception@crownwells.demon.co.uk
I: www.plus44.com/crown/

B&B per night:
S £45.00–£50.00
D £65.00–£75.00

HB per person:
DY £47.50–£55.00

OPEN All year round

The 15thC Crown Inn is situated in the Market Place in the heart of Wells, within a stone's throw of Wells Cathedral and moated Bishop's Palace. The Crown serves a variety of delicious meals, snacks and refreshments in the Penn Bar and Anton's Bistrot throughout the day.

Bedrooms: 2 single, 9 double, 4 twin
Bathrooms: 15 en suite

Lunch available
EM 1800 (LO 2130)
Parking for 15
CC: Amex, Barclaycard, Delta, Eurocard, Mastercard, Switch, Visa, Visa Electron

---

◆◆◆

FRANKLYNS FARM
Chewton Mendip, Bath, BA3 4NB
T: (01761) 241372

Bedrooms: 1 double, 2 twin; suites available
Bathrooms: 2 en suite, 1 private

Parking for 5

B&B per night:
D £38.00–£40.00

OPEN All year round

Cosy farmhouse in heart of Mendip. Superb views, peaceful setting. Large garden with tennis court. Offering genuine hospitality and delicious breakfast. Ideal touring Bath, Wells, Cheddar.

◆◆◆◆

HIGHCROFT
Wells Road, Priddy, Wells, BA5 3AU
T: (01749) 673446

Bedrooms: 1 single, 1 double, 1 twin, 1 triple
Bathrooms: 2 en suite, 1 public

Parking for 5

B&B per night:
S £20.00–£20.00
D £38.00–£40.00

OPEN Mar–Oct

A natural stone country house with large lawns. From Wells take A39 to Bristol for 3 miles, turn left to Priddy and Highcroft is on right after about 2 miles.

◆◆◆◆

LITTLEWELL FARM GUEST HOUSE

Coxley, Wells, BA5 1QP
T: (01749) 677914

B&B per night:
S £21.00–£26.00
D £39.00–£48.00

HB per person:
DY £31.00–£43.50

OPEN Feb–Dec

Delightful 18thC farmhouse on non-working farm, set in pretty garden and enjoying extensive views over beautiful countryside. Charming en suite bedrooms with antique furniture offer comfort and high standards coupled with personal and thoughtful touches. Our candlelit dinner is skilfully prepared and beautifully presented, using only the best of local produce. One mile south-west of Wells.

Bedrooms: 1 single, 2 double, 2 twin
Bathrooms: 4 en suite, 1 private

EM 1900 (LO 2000)
Parking for 12

CHECK THE MAPS

The colour maps at the front of this guide show all the cities, towns and villages for which you will find accommodation entries. Refer to the town index to find the page on which they are listed.

WEST ANSTEY, Devon Map ref 1D1

♦♦♦♦ **JUBILEE HOUSE**
Highaton Farm, West Anstey,
South Molton, EX36 3PJ
T: (01398) 341312
F: (01398) 341323
E: denton@jubileehouse.
exmoor-holidays.co.uk
I: www.jubileehouse.
exmoor-holidays.co.uk

Bedrooms: 3 single,
2 double
Bathrooms: 2 public

EM 1900 (LO 2100)
Parking for 5

B&B per night:
S £19.50–£19.50
D £39.00–£45.00

HB per person:
DY £31.50–£34.50

OPEN All year round

Elegant house in peaceful surroundings on Two Moors walk, close to Exmoor. Scenic views. Therapeutic hot tub spa/patio area. DIY livery. Excellent cuisine. Vegetarians/special diets catered for.

WEST CAMEL, Somerset Map ref 2B2

♦♦♦♦ # THE WALNUT TREE
Fore Street, West Camel, Yeovil, BA22 7QW
T: (01935) 851292
F: (01935) 851292

B&B per night:
S £49.50–£55.00
D £80.00–£95.00

OPEN all year round

In a tranquil village setting, just off A303, lies this family-run inn. Beautiful en suite bedrooms, 6 on the ground floor. Sky TV in all rooms. Imaginative food served in the charming candlelit dining room. Four local golf courses, Leyland Trail. Central for coastal towns.

Bedrooms: 6 double,
1 twin
Bathrooms: 7 en suite

Lunch available
EM 1900 (LO 2130)
Parking for 40
CC: Amex, Barclaycard,
Delta, Eurocard, JCB,
Mastercard, Solo, Switch,
Visa, Visa Electron

WESTBURY, Wiltshire Map ref 2B2 *Tourist Information Centre Tel: (01373) 827158*

♦♦♦ **BLACK DOG FARM**
Chapmanslade, Westbury,
BA13 4AE
T: (01373) 832858
E: im.mills@virgin.net

Bedrooms: 1 double,
1 twin
Bathrooms: 2 en suite

B&B per night:
S Min £30.00
D Min £45.00

OPEN All year round

Listed Georgian farmhouse with smallholding, within easy reach of Longleat, Bath, Salisbury, Stonehenge. Comfortable en suite rooms, own TV and video, traditional English breakfast a speciality.

WESTON-SUPER-MARE, North Somerset Map ref 1D1 *Tourist Information Centre Tel: (01934) 888800*

♦♦♦♦ # BRAESIDE HOTEL
2 Victoria Park, Weston-super-Mare,
BS23 2HZ
T: (01934) 626642
F: (01934) 626642
E: braeside@tesco.net
I: www.smoothhound.co.uk/hotels/
braeside.html

B&B per night:
S £25.00–£25.00
D £50.00–£50.00

OPEN Jan–Sep, Nov–
Dec

Fabulous views over Weston Bay; two minutes' walk from sandy beach. Quiet location with unrestricted on-street parking. Single rooms always available. Directions: with sea on left, take first right after Winter Gardens, then first left into Lower Church Road. Victoria Park is on the right after the left hand bend.

Bedrooms: 2 single,
5 double, 1 twin, 1 triple
Bathrooms: 9 en suite

REGIONAL TOURIST BOARD The ♠ symbol in an establishment entry indicates that it is a Regional Tourist Board member.

WESTON-SUPER-MARE continued

MOORLANDS COUNTRY GUESTHOUSE

Hutton, Weston-super-Mare, Somerset
BS24 9QH
T: (01934) 812283 (Ansaphone)
F: (01934) 812283
E: margaret_holt@email.com

Family-run 18thC house in mature landscaped grounds. The Holts have been at Moorlands for the past 30 years. Hutton is a pretty village with a pub serving meals. Close to hill and country walks, many places of interest easily reached by car. Riding can be arranged for children.

Bedrooms: 1 single,
1 double, 1 twin, 1 triple,
2 family rooms
Bathrooms: 5 en suite,
1 public

Parking for 8
CC: Amex, Barclaycard,
Diners, Eurocard,
Mastercard, Visa

B&B per night:
S £19.00–£30.00
D £38.00–£50.00

OPEN All year round

WESTWARD HO!, Devon Map ref 1C1

EVERSLEY ◆◆◆◆

1 Youngaton Road, Westward Ho!,
Bideford, EX39 1HU
T: (01237) 471603
E: lsharrat@ndevon.co.uk

Bedrooms: 1 double,
1 twin, 1 family room
Bathrooms: 1 en suite,
1 public

B&B per night:
S £20.00–£30.00
D £36.00–£42.00

OPEN All year round

A Victorian gentleman's residence, full of character. Each bedroom is individually styled, with toiletries, hospitality tray and fluffy dressing gowns. Two minutes from the sea.

WEYMOUTH, Dorset Map ref 2B3 *Tourist Information Centre Tel: (01305) 785747*

CUMBERLAND HOTEL ◆◆◆◆
Silver Award

95 Esplanade, Weymouth, DT4 7BA
T: (01305) 785644
F: (01305) 785644
I: www.theaa.co.uk/hotels

Bedrooms: 7 double,
2 twin, 3 triple
Bathrooms: 12 en suite

EM 1800 (LO 1830)
Parking for 2
CC: Mastercard, Visa

B&B per night:
S £35.00–£45.00
D £50.00–£65.00

OPEN All year round

Centre of Weymouth Bay, close to all amenities, rail and bus stations. All rooms en suite with TV, tea tray, hairdryer.

KENORA PRIVATE HOTEL ◆◆◆◆

5 Stavordale Road, Weymouth,
DT4 0AB
T: (01305) 771215 &
07976 826067 (Mobile)
E: kenora.hotel@wdi.co.uk

Bedrooms: 3 single,
7 double, 2 twin, 2 triple,
1 family room
Bathrooms: 13 en suite,
1 public

EM (LO 1630)
Parking for 15
CC: Barclaycard, Delta,
Mastercard, Visa, Visa
Electron

B&B per night:
S £36.75–£39.00
D £60.00–£65.00

HB per person:
DY £47.75–£50.50

OPEN Apr–Sep

Family-run hotel offering good food, comfortable accommodation, easy parking, garden to relax in. 700 metres from town, harbour and sandy beach.

THE PEBBLES GUEST HOUSE ◆◆◆

18 Kirtleton Avenue, Weymouth,
DT4 7PT
T: (01305) 784331
F: (01305) 784695
E: blackwoodg@aol.com

Bedrooms: 1 single,
2 double, 2 twin, 3 triple
Bathrooms: 4 en suite,
1 public

EM 1800
Parking for 9
CC: Barclaycard,
Mastercard, Visa

B&B per night:
S £16.00–£18.00
D £34.00–£40.00

HB per person:
DY £23.00–£27.00

OPEN All year round

Family-run guesthouse, close to beach, town centre and railway station. Good home cooking. Clean, warm and comfortable. Ground floor en suite room. Parking. Pets welcome.

SEAHAM GUEST HOUSE ◆◆◆◆
Gold Award

3 Waterloo Place, Weymouth,
DT4 7NU
T: (01305) 782010

Bedrooms: 5 double
Bathrooms: 5 en suite

CC: Amex, Barclaycard,
Mastercard, Visa

B&B per night:
S £22.00–£50.00
D £40.00–£55.00

OPEN All year round

The Seaham offers a high standard in en suite accommodation. Situated across from Weymouth's sandy beach, all amenities are within easy walking distance. Non-smoking only.

WHITCHURCH CANONICORUM, Dorset Map ref 1D2

◆◆◆◆ **CANDIDA HOUSE**
Whitchurch Canonicorum, Bridport, · Bedrooms: 1 double,
DT6 6RQ   2 twin
T: (01297) 489629   Bathrooms: 3 en suite
F: (01297) 489629
E: candida@globalnet.co.uk
I: www.holidayaccom.com/
candida-house.htm

B&B per night:
S £20.00–£25.00
D £40.00–£50.00

OPEN All year round

Comfortable en suite rooms in beautiful spacious Georgian rectory. Peaceful village two miles from the sea. Special breakfasts.

WIDECOMBE-IN-THE-MOOR, Devon Map ref 1C2

◆◆ **HIGHER VENTON FARM**
Widecombe-in-the-Moor,   Bedrooms: 2 double,   EM 1830 (LO 1730)
Newton Abbot, TQ13 7TF   1 twin   Parking for 4
T: (01364) 621235   Bathrooms: 2 en suite,
F: (01364) 621382   1 public

B&B per night:
S £23.00–£23.00
D £40.00–£46.00

HB per person:
DY £30.00–£33.00

OPEN All year round

40-acre farm. 17thC thatched farmhouse with a homely atmosphere and farmhouse cooking. Ideal for touring Dartmoor. 16 miles from the coast.

WINKLEIGH, Devon Map ref 1C2

◆◆◆

THE OLD PARSONAGE
Court Walk, Winkleigh, EX19 8JA
T: (01837) 83772

B&B per night:
S £25.00–£25.00
D £40.00–£40.00

HB per person:
DY £35.00–£37.50

OPEN Mar–Dec

Typical Devon thatched and cob-walled house, once the residence of the local squire. Park-like gardens have many magnificent trees, rhododendrons and azaleas. Comfortable en suite bedrooms with lots of old world charm. Garden gate leads to village square and the Kings Arms where excellent food is served.

Bedrooms: 3 double;   EM 1900 (LO 2000)
suite available   Parking for 9
Bathrooms: 3 en suite

AT-A-GLANCE SYMBOLS
Symbols at the end of each accommodation entry give useful information about services and facilities. A key to symbols can be found inside the back cover flap. Keep this open for easy reference.

◆◆◆ **KEMPS FARM**
Winsford, Minehead, TA24 7HT
T: (01643) 851312

Bedrooms: 2 double,
1 twin
Bathrooms: 1 en suite,
1 public

EM 1900
Parking for 8

B&B per night:
S £15.50–£17.50
D £31.00–£35.00

HB per person:
DY £23.00–£25.00

OPEN All year round

Spacious farmhouse with stunning views over Exe Valley. Superb walking, delicious home cooking with local produce. Guests' comfort is paramount. Hostess trays in all rooms.

◆◆◆◆

LARCOMBE FOOT
Winsford, Minehead, TA24 7HS
T: (01643) 851306

B&B per night:
S Max £23.00
D Max £46.00

HB per person:
DY Max £35.50

OPEN Mar–Nov

Attractive period house in beautiful, tranquil Exe Valley. Guests' comfort within a warm, happy atmosphere is paramount. Footpath access to the moor and surrounding wild life make Larcombe Foot an idyllic rural retreat. Dogs welcome.

Bedrooms: 1 single,
1 double, 1 twin
Bathrooms: 1 en suite,
1 private, 1 public

EM (LO 1930)
Parking for 3

◆◆◆◆

SCOTLAND LODGE FARM
Winterbourne Stoke, Salisbury, SP3 4TF
T: (01980) 621199 (Ansaphone)
F: (01680) 621188
E: william.lockwood@bigwig.net
I: www.smoothhound.co.uk/hotels/scotlandl.html

B&B per night:
S £27.00–£30.00
D £44.00–£48.00

OPEN All year round

Warm welcome at family-run competition yard set in 46 acres of grassland. Lovely views and walks, Stonehenge/Salisbury nearby. Dogs, children and horses welcomed – stabling available on shavings. Conservatory for guests' use. French, German, Italian spoken. Easy access off A303 with entry through automatic gate. Excellent local pubs.

Bedrooms: 2 double,
1 twin
Bathrooms: 2 private

Parking for 6

◆◆◆

THELBRIDGE CROSS INN
Thelbridge, Witheridge, Crediton, EX17 4SQ
T: (01884) 860316
F: (01884) 861318
E: thelbridgexinn@cwcom.net

B&B per night:
S Max £35.00
D £50.00–£60.00

HB per person:
DY £33.00–£37.50

OPEN All year round

Picturesque, family-run inn famous for its peaceful surroundings, friendly staff, and superb home-cooked food. The 7 en suite bedrooms are extremely clean and comfortable, and the inn offers splendid country views. A good central base from which to explore the whole of Devon. Extensive menu amd wine list. Real log fires in winter.

Bedrooms: 7 double
Bathrooms: 7 en suite

Lunch available
EM 1900 (LO 2100)
Parking for 50
CC: Amex, Barclaycard,
Delta, Diners, JCB,
Mastercard, Solo, Switch,
Visa, Visa Electron

WOODBOROUGH, Wiltshire Map ref 2B2

PANTAWICK
Woodborough, Pewsey, SN9 5PG
T: (01672) 851662
F: (01672) 851662
E: pantawick@aol.com

Bedrooms: 1 double,
1 twin
Bathrooms: 2 en suite

Parking for 4

B&B per night:
S £25.00–£30.00
D £40.00–£45.00

OPEN All year round

Modern fully centrally-heated house. One double room en suite and 1 twin en suite. Tea/coffee trays. Colour TV. Ample parking. No smoking, please.

WOOKEY HOLE, Somerset Map ref 2A2

Gold Award

GLENCOT HOUSE

Glencot Lane, Wookey Hole, Wells, BA5 1BH
T: (01749) 677160
F: (01749) 670210
E: Glencot@ukonline.co.uk
I: web.ukonline.co.uk/glencot

B&B per night:
S £65.00–£85.00
D £87.00–£106.00

OPEN All year round

This elegantly furnished Victorian mansion, set in 18 acres of gardens and parkland with river frontage, offers high class accommodation, good food and friendly service. There is a small indoor jet stream pool, sauna, snooker, table tennis, croquet and private fishing. Well behaved children and dogs welcome. Special breaks available.

Bedrooms: 3 single,
8 double, 2 twin
Bathrooms: 13 en suite

EM 1830 (LO 2030)
Parking for 25
CC: Amex, Barclaycard,
Delta, Mastercard, Switch,
Visa

WOOTTON BASSETT, Wiltshire Map ref 2B2

THE HOLLIES
Greenhill, Hook, Wootton Bassett,
Swindon, SN4 8EH
T: (01793) 770795
F: (01793) 770795

Bedrooms: 2 single,
2 double
Bathrooms: 1 en suite,
2 public

Parking for 4

B&B per night:
S £18.00–£20.00
D £32.00–£40.00

OPEN All year round

In beautiful countryside looking across the valley to the Cotswolds. Large garden, ample parking, non-smoking. One room en suite. 4 miles west of Swindon, 8 miles Cotswold Water Park.

YELVERTON, Devon Map ref 1C2

THE ROSEMONT GUEST HOUSE

Greenbank Terrace, Yelverton, PL20 6DR
T: (01822) 852175
E: b&b@rosemontgh.fsnet.co.uk

B&B per night:
S £21.00–£23.00
D £42.00–£46.00

OPEN All year round

Sunny Victorian House overlooking moorland green in the centre of Yelverton village. Set within the glorious Dartmoor National Park with Plymouth, Tavistock, Buckland Abbey, Garden House and Lydford Gorge, among many others, nearby. Excellent free-range breakfast is served using local produce. Pubs, restaurants and other amenities in village.

Bedrooms: 1 single,
2 double, 2 twin, 2 triple
Bathrooms: 6 en suite,
1 private

Parking for 7
CC: Barclaycard, Delta,
Eurocard, JCB, Maestro,
Mastercard, Solo, Switch,
Visa, Visa Electron

QUALITY ASSURANCE SCHEME
Diamond ratings and awards are explained at the back of this guide.

YELVERTON continued

TORRFIELDS ◆◆◆◆

Sheepstor, Yelverton, PL20 6PF
T: (01822) 852161
E: torrfields@beeb.net

Bedrooms: 2 double
Bathrooms: 2 en suite

EM 1730 (LO 1930)
Parking for 5

B&B per night:
S £20.00–£20.00
D £40.00–£40.00

HB per person:
DY £27.50–£27.50

OPEN All year round

Detached property in own grounds, with good views and direct access on to moorland. Super setting in Dartmoor National Park – ideal for walkers.

ᴍ ⅄ ᵴ ℄ ◳ ▯ ◌ ◵ ⓊⓁ ⓐ Ⓢ ⊬ ⓜ ⓉⓋ ▥ ⏚ ◵ ⓤ ⌐ ✲ ❀

YEOVIL, Somerset Map ref 2A3 *Tourist Information Centre Tel: (01935) 471279*

THE SPARKFORD INN ◆◆◆

Sparkford, Yeovil, BA22 7JN
T: (01963) 440218
F: (01963) 440358

B&B per night:
S Min £30.00
D Min £45.00

OPEN All year round

A 15thC coaching inn, in traditional style, with restaurant, lounge bars, outdoor play areas, function suite and en suite accomodation. New motel style rooms with family facilities.

Bedrooms: 3 double, 4 twin, 1 triple
Bathrooms: 8 en suite

Lunch available
EM 1900 (LO 2200)
Parking for 40
CC: Amex, Barclaycard, Delta, Eurocard, Mastercard, Switch, Visa

⅄ ◳ ▯ ◌ ⓐ Ⓢ ⊬ ▥ ⏚ ⓣ360 ✲ ❀ ⚑

YEOVILTON, Somerset Map ref 2A3

CARY FITZPAINE ◆◆◆◆

Yeovilton, Yeovil, BA22 8JB
T: (01458) 223250 &
07932 657140 (Mobile)
F: (01458) 223372
E: acrang@aol.com

Bedrooms: 1 double, 1 twin, 1 triple
Bathrooms: 3 en suite

Parking for 8
CC: Amex, Barclaycard, Delta, Diners, Eurocard, JCB, Maestro, Mastercard, Solo, Switch, Visa, Visa Electron

B&B per night:
S £24.00–£28.00
D £40.00–£44.00

OPEN All year round

600-acre mixed farm. Elegant Georgian manor farmhouse in idyllic setting. Large gardens. High standard of accommodation, all bedrooms with en suite bath. Four-poster bed.

⅄ ⌂ ▯ ◌ ◵ ⓊⓁ ⓐ Ⓢ ⊬ ⓜ ⓉⓋ ▥ ⏚ ⓤ ✲ ✈ ❀ ⓢⓟ Ⓣ

COURTRY FARM ◆◆◆

Bridgehampton, Yeovil, BA22 8HF
T: (01935) 840327
F: (01935) 840964
I: www.countyfarm@hotmail.com

B&B per night:
S Min £22.00
D Min £38.00

OPEN Apr–Nov

600-acre mixed working farm. Warm welcome at farmhouse and annexed accommodation. Ground floor rooms, en suite, TV, tea-making facilities. Tennis court and garden. Just off A303 – three quarters of a mile. Fleet Air Arm Museum Museum half a mile. Local attractions include Stourhead, Tintinhull and Montacute gardens. Longleat 40 minutes. Leland Trail for walkers and cycle trails.

Bedrooms: 1 twin, 1 triple
Bathrooms: 2 en suite

Parking for 20

ᴍ ⅄ ᵴ ▯ ◌ ⓊⓁ ⊬ ▥ ⏚ ◵ ✲ ❀ ⚑ Ⓣ

MAP REFERENCES The map references refer to the colour maps at the front of this guide. The first figure is the map number; the letter and figure which follow indicate the grid reference on the map.

♦♦♦♦ **CORNERWAYS COTTAGE**
Longcross, Zeals, Warminster,
BA12 6LL
T: (01747) 840477
F: (01747) 840477
E: cornerways.cottage@btinternet.
com
I: www.smoothhound.co.uk/hotels/
cornerwa.html

Bedrooms: 2 double,
1 twin
Bathrooms: 2 en suite,
1 private

EM 1830 (LO 1930)
Parking for 8

B&B per night:
S £25.00–£30.00
D £38.00–£40.00

HB per person:
DY £30.00–£41.00

OPEN All year round

*18thC cottage with original beams, 2 miles Stourhead. Ideal for visits to Longleat,
Stonehenge, Salisbury and Bath. Close A303 and midway London to Devon.*

COUNTRY CODE
Always follow the Country Code ☘
Enjoy the countryside and respect
its life and work ☘ Guard against
all risk of fire ☘ Fasten all gates
☘ Keep your dogs under close control
☘ Keep to public paths across
farmland ☘ Use gates and stiles to
cross fences, hedges and walls ☘
Leave livestock, crops and machinery
alone ☘ Take your litter home ☘
Help to keep all water clean ☘
Protect wildlife, plants and trees ☘
Take special care on country roads ☘
Make no unnecessary noise ☘

A brief guide to the main Towns and Villages offering accommodation in the SOUTH WEST

A **ABBOTSBURY, DORSET** - Beautiful village near Chesil Beach, with a long main street of mellow stone and thatched cottages and the ruins of a Benedictine monastery. High above the village on a hill is a prominent 15th C chapel. Abbotsbury's famous swannery and sub-tropical gardens lie just outside the village.

● **ALLERFORD, SOMERSET** - Village with picturesque stone and thatch cottages and a packhorse bridge, set in the beautiful Vale of Porlock.

● **AMESBURY, WILTSHIRE** - Standing on the banks of the River Avon, this is the nearest town to Stonehenge on Salisbury Plain. The area is rich in prehistoric sites.

● **ASHBURTON, DEVON** - Formerly a thriving wool centre and important as one of Dartmoor's four stannary towns. Today's busy market town has many period buildings. Ancient tradition is maintained in the annual ale-tasting and bread-weighing ceremony. Good centre for exploring Dartmoor or the south Devon coast.

● **AVEBURY, WILTSHIRE** - Set in a landscape of earthworks and megalithic standing stones, Avebury has a fine church and an Elizabethan manor. Remains from excavations may be seen in the museum. The area abounds in important prehistoric sites, among them Silbury Hill. Stonehenge stands about 20 miles due south.

B **BAMPTON, DEVON** - Riverside market town, famous for its fair each October.

● **BARNSTAPLE, DEVON** - At the head of the Taw Estuary, once a ship-building and textile town, now an agricultural centre with attractive period buildings, a modern civic centre and leisure centre. Attractions include Queen Anne's Walk, a charming colonnaded arcade and Pannier Market.

● **BATH, BATH & NORTH EAST SOMERSET** - Georgian spa city beside the River Avon. Important Roman site with impressive reconstructed baths, uncovered in 19th C. Bath Abbey built on site of monastery where first king of England was crowned (AD 973). Fine architecture in mellow local stone. Pump Room and museums.

● **BEAMINSTER, DORSET** - Old country town of mellow local stone set amid hills and rural vales. Mainly Georgian buildings; attractive almshouses date from 1603. The 17th C church with its ornate, pinnacled tower was restored inside by the Victorians. Parnham, a Tudor manor house, lies 1 mile south.

● **BIDEFORD, DEVON** - The home port of Sir Richard Grenville, the town with its 17th C merchants' houses flourished as a shipbuilding and cloth town. The bridge of 24 arches was built about 1460. Charles Kingsley stayed here while writing Westward Ho!

● **BISHOP'S LYDEARD, SOMERSET** - Village 5 miles north-west of Taunton, the county town. Terminus for the West Somerset steam railway.

● **BODMIN, CORNWALL** - County town south-west of Bodmin Moor with a ruined priory and church dedicated to St Petroc. Nearby are Lanhydrock House and Pencarrow House.

● **BOSCASTLE, CORNWALL** - Small, unspoilt village in Valency Valley. Active as a port until onset of railway era, its natural harbour affords rare shelter on this wild coast. Attractions include spectacular blow-hole, Celtic field strips, part-Norman church. Nearby St Juliot Church was restored by Thomas Hardy.

● **BOVEY TRACEY, DEVON** - Standing by the river just east of Dartmoor National Park, this old town has good moorland views. Its church, with a 14th C tower, holds one of Devon's finest medieval rood screens.

● **BOX, WILTSHIRE** - Village in an Area of Outstanding Natural Beauty, 7 miles south-west of Chippenham. It is famed for Box ground stone, used for centuries on buildings of national importance.

● **BRADFORD-ON-AVON, WILTSHIRE** - Huddled beside the river, the buildings of this former cloth-weaving town reflect continuing prosperity from the Middle Ages. There is a tiny Anglo-Saxon church, part of a monastery. The part-14th C bridge carries a medieval chapel, later used as a gaol.

● **BRIDESTOWE, DEVON** - Small Dartmoor village with a much restored 15th C church, and Great Links Tor rising to the south-east.

● **BRIDGWATER, SOMERSET** - Former medieval port on the River Parrett, now small industrial town with mostly 19th C or modern architecture. Georgian Castle Street leads to West Quay and site of 13th C castle razed to the ground by Cromwell. Birthplace of Cromwellian Admiral Robert Blake is now museum. Arts centre.

● **BRIDPORT, DORSET** - Market town and chief producer of nets and ropes just inland of dramatic Dorset coast. Old, broad streets built for drying and twisting and long gardens for rope-walks. Grand arcaded Town Hall and Georgian buildings. Local history museum has Roman relics.

● **BRISTOL** - Famous for maritime links, historic harbour, Georgian terraces and Brunel's Clifton suspension bridge. Many attractions including SS Great Britain, Bristol Zoo, museums and art galleries and top name entertainments. Events include Balloon Fiesta and Regatta.

● **BRIXHAM, DEVON** - Famous for its trawling fleet in the 19th C, a steeply-built fishing port overlooking the harbour and fish market. A statue of William of Orange recalls his landing here before deposing James II. There is an aquarium and museum. Good cliff views and walks.

● **BUDE, CORNWALL** - Resort on dramatic Atlantic coast. High cliffs give spectacular sea and inland views. Golf-course, cricket pitch, folly, surfing, coarse-fishing and boating. Mother-town Stratton was base of Royalist Sir Bevil Grenville.

● **BUDLEIGH SALTERTON, DEVON** - Small resort with pebble beach on coast of red cliffs, setting for famous Victorian painting "The Boyhood of Raleigh". Sir Walter Raleigh was born at Hayes Barton. A salt-panning village in medieval times, today's resort has some Georgian houses.

● **BURNHAM-ON-SEA, SOMERSET** - Small Victorian resort famous for sunsets and sandy beaches, a few minutes from junction 22 of the M5. Ideal base for touring Somerset, Cheddar and Bath. Good sporting facilities, championship golf-course.

● **BURTON BRADSTOCK, DORSET** - Lying amid fields beside the River Bride, a village of old stone houses, a 14th C church and a village green. The beautiful coast road from Abbotsbury to Bridport passes by and Iron Age forts top the surrounding hills. The sheltered river valley makes a staging post for migrating birds.

C **CALLINGTON, CORNWALL** - A quiet market town standing on high ground above the River Lynher. The 15th C church of St Mary's has an alabaster monument to Lord Willoughby de Broke, Henry VII's marshal. A 15th C chapel, 1 mile east, houses Dupath Well, one of the Cornish Holy Wells.

● **CANNINGTON, SOMERSET** - Quantock Hills village with Brymore House, birthplace of John Pym, a leading statesman in the reign of Charles I, lying to the west. Three fine old 16th C houses are close by.

● **CASTLE CARY, SOMERSET** - One of south Somerset's most attractive market towns, with a picturesque winding high street of golden stone and thatch, market-house and famous round 18th C lock-up.

● **CHAGFORD, DEVON** - Handsome stone houses, some from the Middle Ages, grace this former stannary town on northern Dartmoor. Popular centre for walking in beautiful scenery and ideal base for exploring the West Country. There is a splendid 15th C granite church, said to be haunted by the poet Godolphin.

● **CHARD, SOMERSET** - Market town in hilly countryside. The wide main street has some handsome buildings, among them the Guildhall, court house and almshouses. Modern light industry and dairy produce have replaced 19th C lace making which came at decline of cloth trade.

● **CHARMINSTER, DORSET** - Village just north of the county town of Dorchester, with its museums and Maiden Castle Iron Age hillfort. Within easy reach of Thomas Hardy's Cottage and the Cerne Giant hillside figure.

- **CHEDDAR, SOMERSET** - Large village at foot of Mendips just south of the spectacular Cheddar Gorge. Close by are Roman and Saxon sites and famous show caves. Traditional Cheddar cheese is still made here.

- **CHEW STOKE, SOMERSET** - Attractive village in the Mendip Hills with an interesting Tudor rectory and the remains of a Roman villa. To the south is the Chew Valley reservoir with its extensive leisure facilities.

- **CHIDEOCK, DORSET** - Village of sandstone thatched cottages in a valley near the dramatic Dorset coast. The church holds an interesting processional cross in mother-of-pearl and the manor house close by is associated with the Victorian Roman Catholic church. Seatown has a pebble beach and limestone cliffs.

- **CHIPPENHAM, WILTSHIRE** - Ancient market town with modern industry. Notable early buildings include the medieval Town Hall and the gabled 15th C Yelde Hall, now a local history museum. On the outskirts Hardenhuish has a charming hilltop church by the Georgian architect John Wood of Bath.

- **CHIPPING SODBURY, SOUTH GLOUCESTERSHIRE** - Old market town, its buildings a mixture of Cotswold stone and mellowed brickwork. The 15th C church and the market cross are of interest. Horton Court (National Trust) stands 4 miles north-east and preserves a very rare Norman hall.

- **CLOVELLY, DEVON** - Clinging to wooded cliffs, fishing village with steep cobbled street zigzagging, or cut in steps, to harbour. Carrying sledges stand beside whitewashed flower-decked cottages. Charles Kingsley's father was rector of the church set high up near the Hamlyn family's Clovelly Court.

- **COLYTON, DEVON** - Surrounded by fertile farmland, this small riverside town was an early Saxon settlement. Medieval prosperity from the wool trade built the grand church tower with its octagonal lantern and the church's fine west window.

- **CORSHAM, WILTSHIRE** - Growing town with old centre showing Flemish influence, legacy of former prosperity from weaving. The church, restored last century, retains Norman features. The Elizabethan Corsham Court, with additions by Capability Brown, has fine furniture.

- **CRANTOCK, CORNWALL** - Pretty village of thatched cottages and seaside bungalows. Village stocks, once used against smugglers, are in the churchyard and the pub has a smugglers' hideout

- **CREWKERNE, SOMERSET** - This charming little market town on the Dorset border nestles in undulating farmland and orchards in a conservation area. Built of local sandstone with Roman and Saxon origins. The magnificent St Bartholomew's Church dates from 15th C; St Bartholomew's Fair is held in September.

- **D DEVIZES, WILTSHIRE** - Old market town standing on the Kennet and Avon Canal. Rebuilt Norman castle, good 18th C buildings. St John's church has 12th C work and Norman tower. Museum of Wiltshire's archaeology and natural history reflects wealth of prehistoric sites in the county.

- **DODDISCOMBSLEIGH, DEVON** - Riverside village amid hilly countryside just east of Dartmoor. Former manor house stands beside granite church. Spared from the Roundheads by its remoteness, the church's chief interest lies in glowing 15th C windows said to contain Devon's finest collection of medieval glass.

- **DORCHESTER, DORSET** - Busy medieval county town destroyed by fires in 17th and 18th C. Cromwellian stronghold and scene of Judge Jeffreys' Bloody Assize after Monmouth Rebellion of 1685. Tolpuddle Martyrs were tried in Shire Hall. Museum has Roman and earlier exhibits and Hardy relics.

- **DULVERTON, SOMERSET** - Set among woods and hills of south-west Exmoor, a busy riverside town with a 13th C church. The Rivers Barle and Exe are rich in salmon and trout. The information centre at the Exmoor National Park Headquarters at Dulverton is open throughout the year.

- **DUNSTER, SOMERSET** - Ancient town with views of Exmoor. The hilltop castle has been continuously occupied since 1070. Medieval prosperity from cloth built 16th C octagonal Yarn Market and the church. A riverside mill, packhorse bridge and 18th C hilltop folly occupy other interesting corners in the town.

- **E EXETER, DEVON** - University city rebuilt after the 1940s around its cathedral. Attractions include 13th C cathedral with fine west front; notable waterfront buildings; Guildhall; Royal Albert Memorial Museum; underground passages; Northcott Theatre.

- **EXMOUTH, DEVON** - Developed as a seaside resort in George III's reign, set against the woods of the Exe Estuary and red cliffs of Orcombe Point. Extensive sands, small harbour, chapel and almshouses, a model railway and A la Ronde, a 16-sided house.

- **F FALMOUTH, CORNWALL** - Busy port and fishing harbour, popular resort on the balmy Cornish Riviera. Henry VIII's Pendennis Castle faces St Mawes Castle across the broad natural harbour and yacht basin Carrick Roads, which receives 7 rivers.

- **FIGHELDEAN, WILTSHIRE** - Village on the River Avon, 4 miles north of Amesbury. Stonehenge 2 miles south west.

- **FOWEY, CORNWALL** - Set on steep slopes at the mouth of the Fowey River, important clayport and fishing town. Ruined forts guarding the shore recall days of "Fowey Gallants" who ruled local seas. The lofty church rises above the town. Ferries to Polruan and Bodinnick; August Regatta.

- **FROME, SOMERSET** - Old market town with modern light industry, its medieval centre watered by the River Frome. Above Cheap Street with its flagstones and watercourse is the church showing work of varying periods. Interesting buildings include 18th C wool merchants' houses.

- **G GLASTONBURY, SOMERSET** - Market town associated with Joseph of Arimathea and the birth of English Christianity. Built around its 7th C abbey said to be the site of King Arthur's burial. Glastonbury Tor with its ancient tower gives panoramic views over flat country and the Mendip Hills.

- **GOONHAVERN, CORNWALL** - Small village 5 miles south of Newquay, within easy reach of the coast and beaches at Perranporth.

- **GRAMPOUND, CORNWALL** - Village on the River Fal, 6 miles south-west of St Austell. Probus Gardens 3 miles south-west.

- **H HARTLAND, DEVON** - Hamlet on high, wild country near Hartland Point. Just west, the parish church tower makes a magnificent landmark; the light, unrestored interior holds one of Devon's finest rood screens. There are spectacular cliffs around Hartland Point and the lighthouse.

- **HELSTON, CORNWALL** - Handsome town with steep, main street and narrow alleys. In medieval times it was a major port and stannary town. Most buildings date from Regency and Victorian periods. The famous May dance, the Furry, is thought to have pre-Christian origins. A museum occupies the old Butter Market.

- **HENSTRIDGE, SOUTH SOMERSET** - Village with a rebuilt church containing the Tudor Carent tomb.

- **HONITON, DEVON** - Old coaching town in undulating farmland. Formerly famous for lace-making, it is now an antiques trade centre and market town. Small museum.

- **I ILFRACOMBE, DEVON** - Resort of Victorian grandeur set on hillside between cliffs with sandy coves. At the mouth of the harbour stands an 18th C lighthouse, built over a medieval chapel. There are fine formal gardens and a museum. Chambercombe Manor, an interesting old house, is nearby.

- **ILMINSTER, SOMERSET** - Former wool town with modern industry, set in undulating, pastoral country. Fine market square of mellow Ham stone and Elizabethan school house. The 15th C church has a handsome tower and lofty, light interior with notable brass memorials. Nearby is an art centre with theatre and gardens.

- **ISLES OF SCILLY** - Picturesque group of islands and granitic rocks south-west of Lands End. Peaceful and unspoilt, they are noted for natural beauty, romantic maritime history, silver sands, early flowers and sub-tropical gardens on Tresco. Main island is St. Mary's.

- **IVYBRIDGE, DEVON** - Town set in delightful woodlands on the River Erme. Brunel designed the local railway viaduct. South Dartmoor Leisure Centre.

K KENTON, DEVON - Village between Exeter and Dawlish, separated from the Exe estuary by the large estate of Powderham Castle. Fine 14th C church of red sandstone with a massive medieval rood screen and loft.

● KINGSBRIDGE, DEVON - Formerly important as a port, now a market town overlooking head of beautiful, wooded estuary winding deep into rural countryside. Summer art exhibitions; Cookworthy Museum.

L LANGPORT, SOMERSET - Small market town with Anglo-Saxon origins, sloping to River Parrett. Well-known for glove making and, formerly, for eels. Interesting old buildings include some fine local churches.

● LAUNCESTON, CORNWALL - Medieval "Gateway to Cornwall", county town until 1838, founded by the Normans under their hilltop castle near the original monastic settlement. This market town, overlooked by its castle ruin, has a square with Georgian houses and an elaborately-carved granite church.

● LEWDOWN, DEVON - Small village on the very edge of Dartmoor. Lydford Castle is 4 miles to the east.

● LISKEARD, CORNWALL - Former stannary town with a livestock market and light industry, at the head of a valley running to the coast. Handsome Georgian and Victorian residences and a Victorian Guildhall reflect the prosperity of the mining boom. The large church has an early 20th C tower and a Norman font.

● THE LIZARD, CORNWALL - Ending in England's most southerly point, a treeless peninsula with rugged, many-coloured cliffs and deep shaded valleys facing the Helford River. Kynance Cove, famous for serpentine cliffs and lovely sands.

● LOOE, CORNWALL - Small resort developed around former fishing and smuggling ports occupying the deep estuary of the East and West Looe Rivers. Narrow winding streets, with old inns; museum and art gallery are housed in interesting old buildings. Shark fishing centre, boat trips; busy harbour.

● LYME REGIS, DORSET - Pretty, historic fishing town and resort set against the fossil-rich cliffs of Lyme Bay. In medieval times it was an important port and cloth centre. The Cobb, a massive stone breakwater, shelters the ancient harbour which is still lively with boats.

● LYNMOUTH, DEVON - Resort set beneath bracken-covered cliffs and pinewood gorges where 2 rivers meet, and cascade between boulders to the town. Lynton, set on cliffs above, can be reached by water-operated cliff railway from the Victorian esplanade. Valley of the Rocks, to the west, gives dramatic walks.

● LYNTON, DEVON - Hilltop resort on Exmoor coast linked to its seaside twin, Lynmouth, by a water-operated cliff railway which descends from the town hall. Spectacular surroundings of moorland cliffs with steep chasms of conifer and rocks through which rivers cascade.

M MARLBOROUGH, WILTSHIRE - Important market town, in a river valley cutting through chalk downlands. The broad main street, with colonnaded shops on one side, shows a medley of building styles, mainly from the Georgian period. Lanes wind away on either side and a church stands at each end.

● MELKSHAM, WILTSHIRE - Small industrial town standing on the banks of the River Avon. Old weavers' cottages and Regency houses are grouped around the attractive church which has traces of Norman work. The 18th C Round House, once used for dyeing fleeces, is now a craft centre.

● MEVAGISSEY, CORNWALL - Small fishing town, a favourite with holidaymakers. Earlier prosperity came from pilchard fisheries, boat-building and smuggling. By the harbour are fish cellars, some converted, and a local history museum is housed in an old boat-building shed. Handsome Methodist chapel; shark fishing, sailing.

● MINEHEAD, SOMERSET - Victorian resort with spreading sands developed around old fishing port on the coast below Exmoor. Former fishermen's cottages stand beside the 17th C harbour; cobbled streets climb the hill in steps to the church. Boat trips, steam railway. Hobby Horse festival 1 May.

● MORETONHAMPSTEAD, DEVON - Small market town with a row of 17th C almshouses standing on the Exeter road. Surrounding moorland is scattered with ancient farmhouses, prehistoric sites.

● MULLION, CORNWALL - Small holiday village with a golf-course, set back from the coast. The church has a serpentine tower of 1500, carved roof and beautiful medieval bench-ends. Beyond Mullion Cove, with its tiny harbour, wild untouched cliffs stretch south-eastward toward Lizard Point.

N NEWQUAY, CORNWALL - Popular resort spread over dramatic cliffs around its old fishing port. Many beaches with abundant sands, caves and rock pools; excellent surf. Pilots' gigs are still raced from the harbour and on the headland stands the stone Huer's House from the pilchard-fishing days.

O OKEHAMPTON, DEVON - Busy market town near the high tors of northern Dartmoor. The Victorian church, with William Morris windows and a 15th C tower, stands on the site of a Saxon church. A Norman castle ruin overlooks the river to the west of the town. Museum of Dartmoor Life in a restored mill.

● OTTERY ST MARY, DEVON - Former wool town with modern light industry set in countryside on the River Otter. The Cromwellian commander, Fairfax, made his headquarters here briefly during the Civil War. The interesting church, dating from the 14th C, is built to cathedral plan.

P PADSTOW, CORNWALL - Old town encircling its harbour on the Camel Estuary. The 15th C church has notable bench-ends. There are fine houses on North Quay and Raleigh's Court House on South Quay. Tall cliffs and golden sands along the coast and ferry to Rock. Famous 'Obby 'Oss Festival on 1 May.

● PAIGNTON, DEVON - Lively seaside resort with a pretty harbour on Torbay. Bronze Age and Saxon sites are occupied by the 15th C church, which has a Norman door and font. The beautiful Chantry Chapel was built by local landowners, the Kirkhams.

● PENSFORD, NORTH SOMERSET - Village 6 miles south of Bristol and within easy reach of the City of Bath. Chew Valley and Blagdon Lakes close by.

● PENZANCE, CORNWALL - Resort and fishing port on Mount's Bay with mainly Victorian promenade and some fine Regency terraces. Former prosperity came from tin trade and pilchard fishing. Grand Georgian style church by harbour. Georgian Egyptian building at head of Chapel Street and Morrab Gardens.

● PIDDLETRENTHIDE, DORSET - Situated on the River Piddle, north of Puddletown and Dorchester. Norman church with 15th C towers.

● PLYMOUTH - Devon's largest city, major port and naval base. Old houses on the Barbican and ambitious architecture in modern centre, with new National Marine Aquarium, museum and art gallery, the Dome - a heritage centre on the Hoe. Superb coastal views over Plymouth Sound from the Hoe.

● PORTLAND, DORSET - Joined by a narrow isthmus to the coast, a stony promontory sloping from the lofty landward side to a lighthouse on Portland Bill at its southern tip. Villages are built of the white limestone for which the "isle" is famous.

R RADSTOCK, BATH & NORTH EAST SOMERSET - Thriving small town ideally situated for touring the Mendip Hills.

S ST AUSTELL, CORNWALL - Leading market town, the meeting point of old and new Cornwall. One mile from St Austell Bay with its sandy beaches, old fishing villages and attractive countryside. Ancient narrow streets, pedestrian shopping precincts. Fine church of Pentewan stone and Italianate Town Hall.

● ST IVES, CORNWALL - Old fishing port, artists' colony and holiday town with good surfing beach. Fishermen's cottages, granite fish cellars, a sandy harbour and magnificent headlands typify a charm that has survived since the 19th C pilchard boom. Tate Gallery opened in 1993.

● ST KEW, CORNWALL - Old village sheltered by trees standing beside a stream. The church is noted for its medieval glass showing the Passion and the remains of a scene of the Tree of Jesse.

ST NEOT, CORNWALL - Pretty village of great historic interest, on wooded slopes in the Vale of Lanherne. At its centre, an old stone bridge over the River Menahyl is overlooked by the church with its lofty buttressed tower. Among ancient stone crosses in the churchyard is a 15th C lantern cross with carved figures.

SALCOMBE, DEVON - Sheltered yachting resort of whitewashed houses and narrow streets in a balmy setting on the Salcombe Estuary. Palm, myrtle and other Mediterranean plants flourish. There are sandy bays and creeks for boating.

SALISBURY, WILTSHIRE - Beautiful city and ancient regional capital set amid water meadows. Buildings of all periods are dominated by the cathedral whose spire is the tallest in England. Built between 1220 and 1258, it is one of the purest examples of Early English architecture.

SHALDON, DEVON - Pretty resort facing Teignmouth from the south bank of the Teign Estuary. Regency houses harmonise with others of later periods; there are old cottages and narrow lanes. On the Ness, a sandstone promontory nearby, a tunnel built in the 19th C leads to a beach revealed at low tide.

SHEPTON MALLET, SOMERSET - Historic town in the Mendip foothills, important in Roman times and site of many significant archaeological finds. Cloth industry reached its peak in the 17th C, and many fine examples of cloth merchants' houses remain. Beautiful parish church, market cross, local history museum, Collett Park.

SHERBORNE, DORSET - Dorset's "Cathedral City" of medieval streets, golden hamstone buildings and great abbey church, resting place of Saxon kings. Formidable 12th C castle ruins and Sir Walter Raleigh's splendid Tudor mansion and deer park. Street markets, leisure centre, many cultural activities.

SIDMOUTH, DEVON - Charming resort set amid lofty red cliffs where the River Sid meets the sea. The wealth of ornate Regency and Victorian villas recalls the time when this was one of the south coast's most exclusive resorts. Museum; August International Festival of Folk Arts.

SPREYTON, DEVON - Village situated 6 miles east of Okehampton, just north of the Dartmoor National Park. In 1802, Tom Cobley and his friends travelled from the village to Widecombe Fair.

STREET, SOMERSET - Busy shoe-making town set beneath the Polden Hills. A museum at the factory, which was developed with the rest of the town in the 19th C, can be visited. Just south, the National Trust has care of woodland on Ivythorn Hill which gives wide views northward. Factory shopping village.

SUTTON POYNTZ, DORSET - On the eastern edge of Weymouth and adjoining the village of Preston. Remains of a Roman villa on Jordan Hill.

SWINDON, WILTSHIRE - Wiltshire's industrial and commercial centre, an important railway town in the 19th C, situated just north of the Marlborough Downs. The railway village created in the mid-19th C has been preserved. Railway museum, art gallery, theatre and leisure centre. Designer shopping village.

TAUNTON, SOMERSET - County town, well-known for its public schools, sheltered by gentle hill-ranges on the River Tone. Medieval prosperity from wool has continued in marketing and manufacturing and the town retains many fine period buildings. Museum.

TAVISTOCK, DEVON - Old market town beside the River Tavy on the western edge of Dartmoor. Developed around its 10th C abbey, of which some fragments remain, it became a stannary town in 1305 when tin-streaming thrived on the moors. Tavistock Goose Fair, October.

TINTAGEL, CORNWALL - Coastal village near the legendary home of King Arthur. There is a lofty headland with the ruin of a Norman castle and traces of a Celtic monastery are still visible in the turf.

TIVERTON, DEVON - Busy market and textile town, settled since the 9th C, at the meeting of 2 rivers. Town houses, Tudor almshouses and parts of the fine church were built by wealthy cloth merchants; a medieval castle is incorporated into a private house; Blundells School.

TORQUAY, TORBAY - Devon's grandest resort, developed from a fishing village. Smart apartments and terraces rise from the seafront and Marine Drive along the headland gives views of beaches and colourful cliffs.

TOTNES, DEVON - Old market town steeply built near the head of the Dart Estuary. Remains of motte and bailey castle, medieval gateways, a noble church, 16th C Guildhall and medley of period houses recall former wealth from cloth and shipping, continued in rural and water industries.

TRURO, CORNWALL - Cornwall's administrative centre and cathedral city, set at the head of Truro River on the Fal Estuary. A medieval stannary town, it handled mineral ore from west Cornwall; fine Georgian buildings recall its heyday as a society haunt in the second mining boom.

W WARMINSTER, WILTSHIRE - Attractive stone-built town high up to the west of Salisbury Plain. A market town, it originally thrived on cloth and wheat. Many prehistoric camps and barrows nearby, along with Longleat House and Safari Park.

WATERGATE BAY, CORNWALL - Beautiful long board-riders' beach backed by tall cliffs, north-west of Newquay. A small holiday village nestles in a steep river valley making a cleft in the cliffs.

WELLS, SOMERSET - Small city set beneath the southern slopes of the Mendips. Built between 1180 and 1424, the magnificent cathedral is preserved in much of its original glory and with its ancient precincts forms one of our loveliest and most unified groups of medieval buildings.

WEST ANSTEY, DEVON - Village on Somerset border, 6 miles from the country town of Dulverton. Exmoor National Park lies to the north.

WESTBURY, WILTSHIRE - Wiltshire's best-known white horse looks down on the town with its Georgian houses around the Market Place. Handsome Perpendicular church with fine carved chancel screen and stone reredos. Above the white horse are the prehistoric earthworks of Bratton Castle.

WESTON-SUPER-MARE, SOMERSET - Large, friendly resort developed in the 19th C. Traditional seaside attractions include theatres and a dance hall. The museum has a Victorian seaside gallery and Iron Age finds from a hill fort on Worlebury Hill in Weston Woods.

WESTWARD HO!, DEVON - Small resort, whose name comes from the title of Charles Kingsley's famous novel, on Barnstaple Bay, close to the Taw and Torridge Estuary. There are good sands and a notable golf-course - one of the oldest in Britain.

WEYMOUTH, DORSET - Ancient port and one of the south's earliest resorts. Curving beside a long, sandy beach, the elegant Georgian esplanade is graced with a statue of George III and a cheerful Victorian Jubilee clock tower. Museum, Sea-Life Centre.

WIDECOMBE-IN-THE-MOOR, DEVON - Old village in pastoral country under the high tors of East Dartmoor. The "Cathedral of the Moor" stands near a tiny square, once used for archery practice, which has a 16th C Church House among other old buildings.

WINSFORD, SOMERSET - Small village in Exmoor National Park, on the River Exe in splendid walking country under Winsford Hill. On the other side of the hill is a Celtic standing stone, the Caratacus Stone, and nearby across the River Barle stretches an ancient packhorse bridge, Tarr Steps.

WOOKEY HOLE, SOMERSET - A series of spectacular limestone caverns on the southern slopes of the Mendips, near the source of the River Axe. The river flows through elaborate formations of stalactites and stalagmites.

WOOTTON BASSETT, WILTSHIRE - Small hillside town with attractive old buildings and a 13th C church. The church and the half-timbered town hall were both restored in the 19th C and the stocks and ducking pool are preserved.

Y YELVERTON, DEVON - Village on the edge of Dartmoor, where ponies wander over the flat common. Buckland Abbey is 2 miles south-west, while Burrator Reservoir is 2 miles to the east.

YEOVIL, SOMERSET - Lively market town, famous for glove making, set in dairying country beside the River Yeo. Interesting parish church. Museum of South Somerset at Hendford Manor.

YEOVILTON, SOMERSET - Village just south of A303. Royal Naval Air Station and Fleet Air Arm Museum situated close by.

Z ZEALS, WILTSHIRE - Pretty village of thatched cottages set high over the Dorset border. Zeals House dates from the medieval period and has some 19th C work. The Palladian Stourhead House (National Trust), in its magnificent gardens, lies further north.

FINDING ACCOMMODATION IS AS EASY AS *1 2 3*

Where to Stay makes it quick and easy to find a place to stay. There are several ways to use this guide.

1 Town Index
The town index, starting on page 748, lists all the places with accommodation featured in the regional sections. The index gives a page number where you can find full accommodation and contact details.

2 Colour Maps
All the place names in black on the colour maps at the front have an entry in the regional sections. Refer to the town index for the page number where you will find one or more establishments offering accommodation in your chosen town or village.

3 Accommodation listing
Contact details for all English Tourism Council assessed accommodation throughout England, together with their national Star rating is given in the listing section of this guide. Establishments with a full entry in the regional sections are shown in blue. Look in the town index for the page number on which their full entry appears.

SOUTH OF ENGLAND

This beautiful region includes the Chilterns, the New Forest and many seaside resorts along the South Coast.

For cream teas and sightseeing, Windsor is an olde worlde delight. And nearby Runnymede, where the Magna Carta was signed, is a beautiful spot for a picnic. Oxford, Winchester and Salisbury offer shopping, nightlife and culture. While Southampton and Portsmouth are awash with maritime museums. But if you're mainly interested in sun, sea and sand, hire a deckchair in the seaside resorts of Bournemouth, Poole, Swanage or Weymouth.

The annual regatta at Cowes on the Isle of Wight, starting at the end of July, is something even land lubbers will enjoy.

The counties of
Berkshire, Buckinghamshire,
Dorset (Eastern), Hampshire,
Isle of Wight and Oxfordshire

FOR MORE INFORMATION CONTACT:

Southern Tourist Board
40 Chamberlayne Road, Eastleigh,
Hampshire SO50 5JH
Tel: (023) 8062 0555
Fax: (023) 8062 0010
Email: stbinfo@bta.org.uk
Internet: www.visitbritain.com

The Pictures:
1 HMS Victory, Portsmouth;
2 Deer at Bolderwood, New Forest;
3 Blenheim Palace, Oxfordshire.

Where to Go in the South of England - see pages 414-417
Where to Stay in the South of England - see pages 418-457

Whilst in the
SOUTH OF ENGLAND ...

You will find hundreds of interesting places to visit during your stay, just some of which are listed in these pages.

Contact any Tourist Information Centre in the region for more ideas on days out in the South of England.

Beale Park

Lower Basildon, Reading, Berkshire RG8 9NH
Tel: (0118) 9845172
An extraordinary collection of rare birds and animals. Narrow gauge railway, adventure playground, splash pools. Also nature trails and fishing on day tickets.

Beaulieu National Motor Museum

Beaulieu, Brockenhurst, Hampshire SO42 7ZN
Tel: (01590) 612345
Motor museum with over 250 exhibits showing the history of motoring from 1896. Also Palace House, Wheels Experience, Beaulieu Abbey ruins and a display of monastic life.

Bekonscot Model Village

Beaconsfield, Buckinghamshire HP9 2PL
Tel: (01494) 672919
The oldest model village in the world, Bekonscot depicts rural England in the 1930s where time has stood still for 70 years.

Blenheim Palace

Woodstock, Oxfordshire OX20 1PX
Tel: (01993) 811325
Home of the 11th Duke of Marlborough. Birthplace of Sir Winston Churchill. Designed by Vanbrugh in the English baroque style. Landscaped by 'Capability' Brown.

Breamore House

Breamore, Fordingbridge, Hampshire SP6 2DF
Tel: (01725) 512233
Elizabethan manor house of 1583 with fine collection of works of art. Furniture, tapestries, needlework, paintings mainly 17th and 18thC Dutch School.

Buckinghamshire County Museum

Aylesbury, Buckinghamshire HP20 2QP
Tel: (01296) 331441
Lively, hands-on, innovative museum complex consisting of county heritage displays, regional art gallery and Roald Dahl Children's Gallery in lovely garden setting.

Carisbrooke Castle

Newport, Isle of Wight PO30 1X
Tel: (01983) 522107
A splendid Norman castle where Charles I was imprisoned. The governor's lodge houses the county museum. Wheelhouse with wheel operated by donkeys.

Compton Acres

Canford Cliffs, Poole, Dorset BH13 7ES
Tel: (01202) 700778
Ten separate and distinct gardens of the world including Italian, Japanese, subtropical glen, rock and water gardens. Country crafts and 'Off the Beaten Track Trail'.

Cotswold Wild Life Park

Burford, Oxford, Oxfordshire OX18 4JW
Tel: (01993) 823006
Wildlife park in 200 acres of gardens and woodland. Includes a variety of animals from all over the world.

The D Day Museum and Overlord Embroidery

Clarence Esplanade, Portsmouth, Hampshire PO5 3NT
Tel: (023) 9282 7261
The magnificent 83 metre long 'Overlord Embroidery' depicts the allied invasion of Normandy on 6 June 1944. Soundguides available in three languages.

Didcot Railway Centre

Didcot, Oxfordshire OX11 7NJ
Tel: (01235) 817200
Living museum re-creating the golden age of the Great Western Railway. Steam locomotives and trains, engine shed and small relics museum.

Exbury Gardens

Exbury, Southampton SO45 1AZ
Tel: (023) 8089 1203
Over 200 acres of woodland garden, including the Rothschild collection of rhododendrons, azaleas, camellias and magnolias.

Flagship Portsmouth

HM Naval Base, Portsmouth, Hampshire PO1 3LJ
Tel: (023) 9283 9766
The world's greatest historic ships - Mary Rose, HMS Victory, HMS Warrior 1860, plus Royal Naval Museum, 'Warships by Water' tours, and Dockyard Apprentice exhibition.

Gilbert White's House and Garden and The Oates Museum

Selborne, Alton, Hampshire GU34 3JH
Tel: (01420) 511275
Historic house and garden, home of Gilbert White, author of 'The Natural History of Selborne'. Exhibition on Frank Oates, explorer and Captain Lawrence Oates of Antarctic fame.

The Hawk Conservancy

Andover, Hampshire SP11 8DY
Tel: (01264) 772252
Unique to Great Britain - 'Valley of the Eagles' held here daily at 1400.

Jane Austen's House

Chawton, Alton, Hampshire GU34 1SD
Tel: (01420) 83262
The 17thC house where Jane Austen lived from 1809-1817, and wrote or revised her six great novels. Letters, pictures, memorabilia, garden with old-fashioned flowers.

The Pictures:
1 Poole, Dorset;
2 Swan Green, New Forest;
3 Oxford;
4 Lulworth Cove, Dorset;
5 Windsor, Berkshire;
6 Winchester Cathedral, Hampshire;
7 Hertford and New College, Oxford.

Legoland Windsor

Windsor, Berkshire SL4 4AY
Tel: 0870 5040404
A family park with hands-on activities, rides, themed playscapes and more Lego bricks than you ever dreamed possible.

Manor Farm

Manor Farm Country Park, Bursledon, Hampshire SO30 2ER
Tel: (01489) 787055
Traditional Hampshire farmstead - buildings, farm animals, machinery and equipment, pre-1950's farmhouse and 13thC church set for 1900.

Newport Roman Villa

Newport, Isle of Wight PO36 1EY
Tel: (01983) 529720
Underfloor heated bath system, tessellated floors displayed in reconstructed rooms, corn-drying kiln plus small site museum of objects recovered.

Osborne House

East Cowes, Isle of Wight PO32 6JY
Tel: (01983) 200022
Queen Victoria and Prince Albert's seaside holiday home. Swiss Cottage where royal children learnt cooking and gardening. Victorian carriage service to Swiss Cottage.

The Oxford Story

Broad Street, Oxford, Oxfordshire OX1 3AJ
Tel: (01865) 728822
An excellent introduction to Oxford - experience 800 years of University history in one hour. From scientists to poets, astronomers to comedians.

River and Rowing Museum

Mill Meadows, Henley-on-Thames, Oxfordshire RG9 1BF
Tel: (01491) 415600
A spectacular journey through over 250,000 years of life on the river. Discover the river's role in feeding the nation, its navigation and wildlife.

Royal Marines Museum

Southsea, Hampshire PO4 9PX
Tel: (023) 9281 9385
History of the Royal Marines from 1664 to present day. Jungle and trench warfare sight and sound exhibitions. Supporting exhibitions and memorial gardens.

Royal Navy Submarine Museum

Jetty Road, Gosport PO12 2AS
Tel: (023) 9252 9217
HM Submarine Alliance, HM Submarine No 1 (Holland 1) under restoration. Midget submarines and models of every type from earliest days to present nuclear age submarines.

The Sir Harold Hillier Gardens and Arboretum

Ampfield, Romsey, Hampshire SO51 0QA
Tel: (01794) 368787
Established in 1953, The Sir Harold Hillier Gardens and Arboretum comprises the greatest collection of wild and cultivated woody plants in the world.

Staunton Country Park

Havant, Hampshire PO9 5HB
Tel: (023) 9245 3405
Restored Victorian glasshouses with displays of exotic plants in the charming setting of the historic walled gardens. Ornamental farm with a wide range of animals.

Swanage Railway

Swanage, Dorset BH19 1HB
Tel: (01929) 425800
Enjoy a nostalgic steam-train ride on the Purbeck line. Steam trains run every weekend throughout the year, and daily at peak times.

The Tank Museum

Bovington, Wareham, Dorset BH20 6JG
Tel: (01929) 405096
The world's finest display of armoured fighting vehicles. Experimental vehicles, interactive displays, disabled access and facilities.

Tudor House Museum

Bugle Street, Southampton SO14 2AD
Tel: (023) 8033 2513
Large half-timbered Tudor house with exhibitions on Tudor, Georgian and Victorian domestic and local history. Unique Tudor garden.

The Vyne

Sherborne St John, Hampshire RG24 9HL
Tel: (01256) 881337
Original house dating back to Henry VIII's time. Extensively altered in the mid 17thC. Tudor chapel, beautiful gardens and lake.

Waterperry Gardens

Waterperry, Oxford, Oxfordshire OX33 1JZ
Tel: (01844) 339254
Ornamental gardens covering six acres of the 83-acre estate. Saxon village church, garden shop, teashop, art and craft gallery.

Whitchurch Silk Mill

Whitchurch, Hampshire RG28 7AL
Tel: (01256) 892065
A unique Georgian silk-weaving watermill still producing fine silk fabrics on Victorian machinery. Riverside garden, tearoom for light meals, silk gift shop.

Winchester Cathedral

Winchester, Hampshire SO23 9LS
Tel: (01962) 857200
Originally Norman, with nave converted to perpendicular. 16thC additions. Old Saxon site adjacent. Tombs, library, medieval wall paintings and Close.

Windsor Castle

Windsor, Berkshire SL4 1NJ
Tel: (01753) 869898
Official residence of HM The Queen and royal residence for nine centuries. State apartments, Queen Mary's Doll's House.

Find out more about the
SOUTH OF ENGLAND ...

Further information about holidays and attractions in the
South of England is available from:

SOUTHERN TOURIST BOARD
40 Chamberlayne Road, Eastleigh, Hampshire SO50 5JH.

Tel: (023) 8062 0555
Fax: (023) 8062 0010
Email: stbinfo@bta.org.uk
Internet: www.visitbritain.com

The Pictures:
1 Alum Bay,
   Isle of Wight;
2 Beaulieu, Hampshire;
3 Bucklers Hard,
   New Forest;
4 Broughton Castle,
   Oxfordshire;
5 Corfe, Dorset;
6 Cheyney Court,
   Winchester;
7 Radcliffe Camera, Oxford;
8 Chawton Church,
   Hampshire;
9 New Forest, Hampshire.

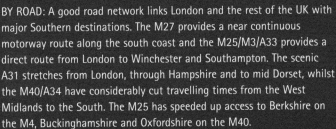

Getting to the
SOUTH OF ENGLAND ...

BY ROAD: A good road network links London and the rest of the UK with
major Southern destinations. The M27 provides a near continuous
motorway route along the south coast and the M25/M3/A33 provides a
direct route from London to Winchester and Southampton. The scenic
A31 stretches from London, through Hampshire and to mid Dorset, whilst
the M40/A34 have considerably cut travelling times from the West
Midlands to the South. The M25 has speeded up access to Berkshire on
the M4, Buckinghamshire and Oxfordshire on the M40.

BY RAIL: From London's Waterloo, trains travel to Portsmouth,
Southampton and Bournemouth approximately three times an hour. From
these stations, frequent trains go to Poole, Salisbury and Winchester.
Further information on rail journeys in the South of England can be
obtained from 08457 484950.

Where to stay in the
SOUTH OF ENGLAND

Accommodation entries in this region are listed in alphabetical order of place name, and then in alphabetical order of establishment.

Map references refer to the colour location maps at the front of this guide. The first number indicates the map to use; the letter and number which follow refer to the grid reference on the map.

At-a-glance symbols at the end of each accommodation entry give useful information about services and facilities. A key to symbols can be found inside the back cover flap. Keep this open for easy reference.

A brief description of the towns and villages offering accommodation in the entries which follow, can be found at the end of this section.

A complete listing of all English Tourism Council assessed guest accommodation appears at the back of this guide.

ALTON, Hampshire Map ref 2C2 *Tourist Information Centre Tel: (01420) 88448*

◆◆◆◆

Situated on the edge of the Meon Valley and on the boundary of the village of Lower Farringdon. Guests are assured of a warm welcome with comfortable accommodation in a relaxed atmosphere. Lovely garden; excellent breakfast. Ideal touring/ walking base. Many places of interest and good pubs/restaurants nearby. Parking.

BOUNDARY HOUSE
B & B
Gosport Road, Lower Farringdon, Alton, GU34 3DH
T: (01420) 587076
F: (01420) 587047
E: BoundaryS@Messages.co.uk

Bedrooms: 1 single, 1 double, 1 twin
Bathrooms: 1 en suite, 2 private

Parking for 4
CC: Barclaycard, Delta, JCB, Mastercard, Solo, Switch, Visa, Visa Electron

B&B per night:
S £25.00–£25.00
D £50.00–£50.00

OPEN Jan, Mar–Dec

◆◆◆

THE VICARAGE
East Worldham, Alton, GU34 3AS
T: (01420) 82392 &
07778 800804 (Mobile)
F: (01420) 82367
E: wenrose@bigfoot.com

Bedrooms: 1 single, 1 double, 1 twin, 1 triple
Bathrooms: 1 public

Parking for 5

B&B per night:
S £18.00–£20.00
D £34.00–£36.00

OPEN All year round

Warm, friendly, peaceful country hamlet, 2 miles from Alton on B3004. Good food daily in pub within walking distance. Worldham Park golf-course half a mile. Half-hour to Winchester and Portsmouth.

AMERSHAM, Buckinghamshire Map ref 2D1

◆◆◆◆

127 HIGH STREET
Amersham, HP7 0DY
T: (01494) 725352

Bedrooms: 1 twin
Bathrooms: 1 private

Parking for 1

B&B per night:
S Min £30.00
D Min £45.00

OPEN All year round

Georgian house with friendly, family atmosphere in the heart of Old Amersham, close to shops, restaurants and pubs.

◆◆◆◆

39 QUARRENDON ROAD
Amersham, HP7 9EF
T: (01494) 727959

Bedrooms: 1 single,
1 double
Bathrooms: 1 public

Parking for 3

B&B per night:
S £25.00–£25.00
D £48.00–£48.00

OPEN Mar–Nov

Detached house, comfortable, with friendly atmosphere. Residents' lounge, private parking, pleasant garden. One mile to London Underground station, easy reach of M25, M40 and A40.

AMPORT, Hampshire Map ref 2C2

◆◆◆◆

BROADWATER
Amport, Andover, SP11 8AY
T: (01264) 772240
F: (01264) 772240
E: carolyn@dmac.co.uk
I: www.dmac.co.uk/carolyn

B&B per night:
S £30.00–£35.00
D £50.00–£50.00

OPEN All year round

Listed thatched cottage in delightful secluded garden, providing relaxed and cosy atmosphere in peaceful village setting. Large bedrooms with en suite facilities. Sitting room with open log fire in winter. Excellent stopover for West Country and airport travellers (A303 half a mile). Stonehenge only 15 minutes' drive, Salisbury and Winchester 30 minutes.

Bedrooms: 2 twin
Bathrooms: 2 en suite,
1 public

Parking for 3
CC: Barclaycard, Delta,
Mastercard, Solo, Switch,
Visa

ANDOVER, Hampshire Map ref 2C2 *Tourist Information Centre Tel: (01264) 324320*

◆◆◆

AMBERLEY HOTEL
70 Weyhill Road, Andover,
SP10 3NP
T: (01264) 352224
F: (01264) 392555
E: amberleyand@fsbdial.co.uk.

Bedrooms: 3 single,
5 double, 4 twin, 3 triple
Bathrooms: 8 en suite,
2 public

Lunch available
EM 1845 (LO 2115)
Parking for 16
CC: Amex, Barclaycard,
Diners, Mastercard,
Switch, Visa

B&B per night:
S Min £44.00
D Min £54.00

HB per person:
DY Min £37.00

OPEN All year round

Small, comfortably furnished hotel, with attractive restaurant open to non-residents. Private meetings, luncheons and wedding receptions can be booked.

ASCOT, Berkshire Map ref 2C2

◆◆◆

ENNIS LODGE PRIVATE GUEST HOUSE
Winkfield Road, Ascot, Berkshire
SL5 7EX
T: (01344) 621009
F: (01344) 621009

Bedrooms: 1 single,
5 twin
Bathrooms: 6 en suite

Parking for 8
CC: Barclaycard, Eurocard,
Mastercard, Switch, Visa

B&B per night:
S Min £45.00
D £50.00–£60.00

OPEN All year round

Situated in central Ascot, Ennis Lodge offers top quality rooms, with en suite facilities. Close to M3, M4, Heathrow, main line station. Windsor and Legoland 10 minutes. German spoken.

IMPORTANT NOTE Information on accommodation listed in this guide has been supplied by the proprietors. As changes may occur you are advised to check details at the time of booking.

SOUTH OF ENGLAND

◆◆◆

FOREST GATE LODGE

161 Lyndhurst Road, Ashurst, Lyndhurst,
SO40 7AW
T: (023) 8029 3026

B&B per night:
S £18.00–£21.00
D £38.00–£44.00

OPEN All year round

Large Victorian house with direct access to New Forest and its attractions – walks, riding, cycling. Pubs and restaurants nearby, Lyndhurst – "capital of the New Forest" – 5 minutes' drive. Full English breakfast or vegetarian by prior arrangement. Special rates October–March: 3 nights for the price of 2.

Bedrooms: 1 single,
2 double
Bathrooms: 2 en suite,
1 public

Parking for 8

◆◆◆

THE OLD FORGE BARN

Ridings Way, Cublington,
Leighton Buzzard, Bedfordshire
LU7 0LW
T: (01296) 681194
F: (01296) 681194

Bedrooms: 1 twin
Bathrooms: 1 public

Parking for 4

B&B per night:
S £25.00–£25.00
D £38.00–£38.00

OPEN All year round

Converted barn in village location, close to Aylesbury, Leighton Buzzard, Milton Keynes. Restaurants and pubs nearby. Friendly welcome.

◆

ASHLEA GUEST HOUSE

58 Oxford Road, Banbury,
OX16 9AN
T: (01295) 250539
F: (01295) 250539
E: johnatashlea1@tinyworld.co.uk

Bedrooms: 3 double,
5 twin, 4 triple
Bathrooms: 8 en suite,
2 public

Parking for 6
CC: Mastercard, Visa

B&B per night:
S £20.00–£36.00
D £30.00–£46.00

OPEN All year round

A turn-of-the-century townhouse, set in its own large grounds and close to the town centre. Easy access to M40.

◆◆◆◆

THE LODGE

Main Road, Middleton Cheney,
Banbury, OX17 2PP
T: (01295) 710355

Bedrooms: 1 double,
1 twin
Bathrooms: 2 en suite

Parking for 5

B&B per night:
S £30.00–£30.00
D £52.00–£54.00

OPEN All year round

200-year-old lodge in lovely countryside, on outskirts of historic village, 2 miles east of Banbury on A422 and 1 mile from M40.

QUALITY ASSURANCE SCHEME

For an explanation of the quality and facilities represented by the Diamonds please refer to the front of this guide. A more detailed explanation can be found in the information pages at the back.

BANBURY continued

◆◆◆

PROSPECT HOUSE GUEST HOUSE

70 Oxford Road, Banbury, OX16 9AN
T: (01295) 268749 & 07798 772578
F: (01295) 268749

B&B per night:
S £32.00–£38.00
D £42.00–£48.00

OPEN All year round

Detached house standing in lovely gardens, situated on the A4260 only a few minutes' walk from Banbury Cross and Oxfordshire's newest regional shopping centre (Castle Quay). Modern en suite rooms, TV, tea and coffee, on-site parking. Conveniently situated for Blenheim Palace, Warwick Castle and Stratford-upon-Avon.

Bedrooms: 1 single, 4 double, 1 twin, 4 triple
Bathrooms: 10 en suite

Parking for 10
CC: Amex, Barclaycard, Mastercard, Visa

◆◆

ROXTONES

Malthouse Lane, Shutford, Banbury, OX15 6PB
T: (01295) 788240

Bedrooms: 2 single, 1 double
Bathrooms: 1 public

Parking for 3

B&B per night:
S Min £16.00
D Min £32.00

OPEN Apr–Sep

Stone-fronted semi-bungalow with garden surrounds, orchard and lawns. 6 miles from Banbury, 16 miles from Stratford-upon-Avon and 2 miles from Broughton Castle.

◆◆◆

ST MARTINS HOUSE

Warkworth, Banbury, OX17 2AG
T: (01295) 712684
F: (01295) 712838

Bedrooms: 2 double
Bathrooms: 1 en suite, 1 private, 1 public

Lunch available
EM 1900 (LO 2230)
Parking for 4

B&B per night:
S £25.00–£27.50
D £50.00–£55.00

HB per person:
DY £37.00–£39.50

OPEN All year round

600-year-old Listed converted barn with galleried dining room. Comfortable en suite rooms with TV. Safe parking, evening meals, French and English country cooking.

BARTLEY, Hampshire Map ref 2C3

◆◆◆◆

BARTLEY FARMHOUSE

Ringwood Road, Bartley, Southampton, SO40 7LD
T: (023) 8081 4194
F: (023) 80814117

Bedrooms: 3 double
Bathrooms: 3 private

Parking for 10

B&B per night:
S £40.00–£50.00
D £50.00–£60.00

OPEN All year round

Whether bringing your horse to ride in the forest, needing a mountain bike or simply a chair in the garden, a truly delightful place to stay.

BASINGSTOKE, Hampshire Map ref 2C2 *Tourist Information Centre Tel: (01256) 817618*

◆◆◆

CEDAR COURT

Reading Road, Hook, RG27 9DB
T: (01256) 762178
F: (01256) 762178

Bedrooms: 2 single, 3 double, 1 twin
Bathrooms: 5 en suite, 1 public

Parking for 6
CC: Barclaycard, Delta, Mastercard, Switch, Visa

B&B per night:
S £28.00–£37.00
D £45.00–£55.00

OPEN All year round

Comfortable ground floor accommodation with delightful gardens. On B3349 between the M3 and M4, 6 miles east of Basingstoke, 1 hour from London and the coast.

◆◆◆◆
Silver Award

FERNBANK HOTEL

4 Fairfields Road, Basingstoke, RG21 3DR
T: (01256) 321191
F: (01256) 321191
E: hotelfernbank@hernscott.net

Bedrooms: 8 single, 7 double, 1 twin
Bathrooms: 16 en suite

Parking for 18
CC: Amex, Barclaycard, Delta, Eurocard, Mastercard, Switch, Visa

B&B per night:
S £55.00–£67.00
D £69.00–£77.00

OPEN All year round

Extremely well-appointed family-run hotel, full of character. In residential area within a short walk of town's facilities. Charming conservatory/lounge. First class breakfast.

BEACONSFIELD, Buckinghamshire Map ref 2C2

◆◆◆ **BEACON HOUSE**

113 Maxwell Road, Beaconsfield, HP9 1RF	Bedrooms: 2 single, 1 double, 1 twin	Parking for 6
T: (01494) 672923	Bathrooms: 2 en suite,	
F: (01494) 672923	1 public	
E: Ben.dickinson@tesco.net		

B&B per night:
S £25.00–£35.00
D £36.00–£42.00

OPEN All year round

Extended, semi-detached house, with gardens front and back and use of patio. On Heathrow bus route and close to railway station. German/French spoken.

◆◆◆

HIGHCLERE FARM
Newbarn Lane, Seer Green, Beaconsfield, HP9 2QZ
T: (01494) 875665 & 874505
F: (01494) 875238

B&B per night:
S £42.00–£45.00
D £55.00–£58.00

OPEN Jan, Mar–Dec

Comfortable, family-run annexed farm accommodation with all rooms en suite. Two family rooms available (prices on request). Breakfast with our own eggs. Quiet location, yet within easy reach of Windsor (12 miles) and London, either from mainline station (1 mile) or lower cost underground station (5 miles).	Bedrooms: 1 single, 3 double, 3 twin, 2 triple Bathrooms: 9 en suite	Parking for 12 CC: Amex, Barclaycard, Delta, Diners, Eurocard, JCB, Mastercard, Solo, Switch, Visa

---

BEAULIEU, Hampshire Map ref 2C3

◆◆◆

DALE FARM HOUSE
Manor Road, Applemore Hill, Dibden, Southampton, SO45 5TJ
T: (023) 8084 9632
F: (023) 8084 0285
E: chris@dalefarmhouse.fsnet.co.uk

B&B per night:
S £23.50–£29.50
D £37.00–£47.00

HB per person:
DY £32.00–£42.00

OPEN All year round

Beautiful 18thC converted farmhouse in secluded wooded setting with direct access for walks or cycling. Peaceful garden in which to unwind and a bird-watcher's paradise. Excellent food to satisfy your appetite. Barbecues on request. Spoil yourself at this BBC holiday programme featured bed and breakfast.	Bedrooms: 1 single, 3 double, 1 twin, 1 triple Bathrooms: 2 en suite, 1 public	Parking for 20

◆◆◆ **LEYGREEN FARM HOUSE**

Lyndhurst Road, Beaulieu, Brockenhurst, SO42 7YP	Bedrooms: 2 double, 1 twin	Parking for 6
T: (01590) 612355	Bathrooms: 3 en suite	

B&B per night:
S £25.00–£27.00
D £42.00–£47.00

OPEN All year round

Comfortable Victorian farmhouse with large garden. Convenient for Beaulieu, Bucklers Hard museums and Exbury Gardens. Reductions for 3 days or more.

BLANDFORD FORUM, Dorset Map ref 2B3 *Tourist Information Centre Tel: (01258) 454770*

◆◆◆ **FARNHAM FARM HOUSE**

Farnham, Blandford Forum, DT11 8DG	Bedrooms: 2 double, 1 twin	Parking for 7
T: (01725) 516254	Bathrooms: 2 en suite,	
F: (01725) 516306	1 public	

B&B per night:
S £20.00–£25.00
D £40.00–£50.00

OPEN All year round

350-acre arable farm. 19thC farmhouse in the Cranborne Chase with extensive views to the south. Within easy reach of the coast.

BLANDFORD FORUM continued

◆◆◆◆
Silver Award

MEADOW HOUSE
Tarrant Hinton, Blandford Forum, DT11 8JG
T: (01258) 830498 (Answerphone)
F: (01258) 830498

Bedrooms: 1 single, 1 double, 1 triple
Bathrooms: 3 public

Parking for 6

B&B per night:
S £20.00–£25.00
D £40.00–£50.00

OPEN All year round

Farmhouse set in 4.5 acres. Warm welcome in peaceful, clean and comfortable family home. Noted for delicious home-produced English breakfast. Excellent base for touring.

BOLDRE, Hampshire Map ref 2C3

◆◆

PINECROFT
Coxhill, Boldre, Lymington, SO41 8PS
T: (01590) 624260
F: (01590) 624025
E: pinecroft@freeuk.com
I: www.smoothhound.co.uk/hotels/pinecrof.html

B&B per night:
S £20.00–£25.00
D £40.00–£55.00

OPEN All year round

Standing in approximately 2 acres, only the garden gate separates this charming and pretty Victorian cottage from the heart of the New Forest. An ideal base for exploring the forest and surrounding area. Within walking distance of the award-winning Hobler Inn. We even supply torches for your journey home.

Bedrooms: 1 double, 1 triple
Bathrooms: 2 en suite

Parking for 2

BONCHURCH, Isle of Wight Map ref 2C3

◆◆◆◆

THE LAKE HOTEL
Shore Road, Bonchurch, Ventnor, Isle of Wight PO38 1RF
T: (01983) 852613
F: (01983) 852613
E: Richard@lakehotel.co.uk
I: www.smoothhound.co.uk/hotels/lake.html

B&B per night:
S £25.00–£30.00
D £50.00–£60.00

HB per person:
DY £35.00–£38.00

OPEN Mar–Oct

Charming country house hotel in 2 acres of beautiful gardens. Located on the seaward side of Bonchurch pond in the old world village of Bonchurch. Run by the same family for over 35 years. We are confident of offering you the best value accommodation and food on our beautiful island.

Bedrooms: 1 single, 8 double, 4 twin, 4 triple, 3 family rooms
Bathrooms: 20 en suite, 3 public

EM 1830 (LO 1900)
Parking for 20

USE YOUR *i*s

There are more than 550 Tourist Information Centres throughout England offering friendly help with accommodation and holiday ideas as well as suggestions of places to visit and things to do. You'll find TIC addresses in the local Phone Book.

BOURNEMOUTH, Dorset Map ref 2B3 *Tourist Information Centre Tel: 0906 802 0234 (premium rate)*

◆◆◆◆

ALEXANDER LODGE HOTEL

21 Southern Road, Southbourne,
Bournemouth, Dorset BH6 3SR
T: (01202) 421662
F: (01202) 421662
E: alexanderlodge@yahoo.com
I: www.smoothhound.co.uk/a28852.html

Delightful, small hotel, offering a friendly welcome, in quiet Bournemouth suburb. 200 yards from Blue Flag sandy beach, cliff top and lift. Excelllent home-cooked meals, comfortable en suite rooms, licensed bar, parking. Low season specials! Ideal for holidays, short breaks and stopovers. Perfect for visiting Christchurch, New Forest, Bournemouth and Dorset.

Bedrooms: 3 double,
1 twin, 2 family rooms
Bathrooms: 5 en suite,
1 private, 1 public

EM 1800 (LO 1800)
Parking for 10

B&B per night:
S £19.00–£25.00
D £36.00–£42.00

HB per person:
DY £26.50–£29.50

OPEN All year round

◆◆◆

DORSET WESTBURY HOTEL
62 Lansdowne Road, Bournemouth,
Dorset BH1 1RS
T: (01202) 551811
F: (01202) 551811

Bedrooms: 2 single,
5 double, 4 twin, 1 triple,
2 family rooms
Bathrooms: 14 en suite,
2 public

EM 1800 (LO 1830)
Parking for 20

B&B per night:
S £23.00–£27.00
D £42.00–£52.00

HB per person:
DY £28.00–£35.00

OPEN All year round

Friendly, family-run hotel in own grounds with secluded garden and large car park. Easy access to town centre and sea.

◆◆◆◆

LANGDALE HOTEL
6 Earle Road, Alum Chine,
Bournemouth, Dorset BH4 8JQ
T: (01202) 761174
F: (01202) 761174

Bedrooms: 2 single,
6 double, 1 twin, 1 triple
Bathrooms: 10 en suite

EM 1800
Parking for 12
CC: Barclaycard, Delta,
Eurocard, Mastercard,
Switch, Visa

B&B per night:
S £28.00–£32.00
D £56.00–£64.00

HB per person:
DY £38.00–£42.00

OPEN All year round

Quietly located in pine-scented Alum Chine, close to seafront. All rooms en suite (bath or shower), with TV, radio/alarm. Trouble free parking.

◆◆◆◆

MAYFIELD PRIVATE HOTEL
46 Frances Road,
Knyveton Gardens, Bournemouth,
Dorset BH1 3SA
T: (01202) 551839
F: (01202) 551839
E: mayfield_98@yahoo.com
I: www.bizonline.co.uk/mayfield

Bedrooms: 1 single,
5 double, 1 twin,
1 family room
Bathrooms: 7 en suite,
1 private, 1 public

EM 1800
Parking for 5

B&B per night:
S £18.00–£22.00
D £36.00–£44.00

HB per person:
DY £25.00–£29.00

OPEN Jan–Nov

Ideally situated for all amenities, opposite Knyveton Gardens with bowling greens, sensory garden, tennis courts. Handy for rail/ coach stations, sea, shops and BIC.

◆

PINEWOOD
197 Holdenhurst Road,
Bournemouth, Dorset BH8 8DG
T: (01202) 292684
I: www.pinewoodguesthouse.co.uk

Bedrooms: 1 single,
2 double, 1 twin, 3 triple
Bathrooms: 2 public

Parking for 8
CC: Barclaycard,
Mastercard, Solo, Switch,
Visa

B&B per night:
S £18.00–£20.00
D £36.00–£40.00

OPEN All year round

Friendly guesthouse, close to rail, coach stations and all amenities. Satellite TV in all rooms. Traditional or vegetarian breakfast available.

WELCOME HOST This is a nationally recognised customer care programme which aims to promote the highest standards of service and a warm welcome. Establishments taking part in this initiative are indicated by the ⊛ symbol.

BOURNEMOUTH continued

◆◆◆ ROSEDENE COTTAGE HOTEL

St Peter's Road, Bournemouth,
Dorset BH1 2LA
T: (01202) 554102
F: (01202) 246995
E: enquiries@rosedalecottagehotel.
co.uk
I: www.rosedalecottagehotel.co.uk

Bedrooms: 3 single,
5 double, 1 twin, 1 triple
Bathrooms: 7 en suite,
1 public

Parking for 8
CC: Barclaycard, Delta,
Diners, Eurocard, JCB,
Maestro, Mastercard,
Solo, Switch, Visa, Visa
Electron

B&B per night:
S £26.00–£28.00
D £40.00–£50.00

OPEN Mar–Nov

Town centre location. Old world cottage hotel, quiet. A short stroll to pier, shops, gardens, Bournemouth International Centre, theatres and beaches. 20 minutes from airport.

◆◆◆ THE VINE HOTEL

22 Southern Road, Southbourne,
Bournemouth, Dorset BH6 3SR
T: (01202) 428309

Bedrooms: 5 double,
3 twin
Bathrooms: 8 en suite

EM
Parking for 6
CC: Barclaycard, Delta,
Eurocard, JCB,
Mastercard, Switch, Visa

B&B per night:
S £18.00–£25.00
D £36.00–£50.00

OPEN All year round

Small family hotel close to local amenities. Superb location twixt Bournemouth and Christchurch. Beaches and Hengistbury Head nearby. Residential licence. Parking. Dogs welcome. No smoking.

◆◆◆ WRENWOOD HOTEL

11 Florence Road, Boscombe,
Bournemouth, Dorset BH5 1HH
T: (01202) 395086 (Answerphone)
F: (01202) 396511
E: bookings@wrenwood.co.uk
I: www.wrenwood.co.uk

Bedrooms: 5 double,
4 triple, 1 family room
Bathrooms: 10 en suite,
1 public

EM 1800 (LO 0900)
Parking for 7
CC: Barclaycard, Delta,
Mastercard, Switch, Visa

B&B per night:
S £21.50–£32.50
D £35.00–£45.00

HB per person:
DY £26.00–£31.00

OPEN All year round

Licensed, family hotel, 5 minutes' walk to pier, shopping centre and entertainments. Convenient for tennis, bowling, golf and New Forest area. Close to buses/coaches.

◆◆◆◆ WYCHCOTE HOTEL

2 Somerville Road, West Cliff,
Bournemouth, Dorset BH2 5LH
T: (01202) 557898
F: (01202) 557898

Bedrooms: 3 single,
5 double, 3 twin, 1 triple
Bathrooms: 11 en suite,
1 private

EM 1815 (LO 2000)
Parking for 15
CC: Barclaycard, Delta,
Eurocard, Mastercard,
Visa

B&B per night:
S Min £22.00
D Min £44.00

HB per person:
DY £30.00–£39.50

OPEN Feb–Nov
& Christmas

Small, well-appointed Victorian house hotel standing in its own tree-lined grounds. Quiet but near all facilities. Home cooking. Two lounges overlooking the garden.

BURFORD, Oxfordshire Map ref 2B1 *Tourist Information Centre Tel: (01993) 823558*

◆◆◆ THE HIGHWAY

117 High Street, Burford, Oxford,
OX18 4RG
T: (01993) 822136
F: (01993) 824740
E: rbx20@dial.pipex.com
I: www.oxlink.co.uk/burford

Bedrooms: 9 double,
2 triple
Bathrooms: 9 en suite,
1 public

CC: Amex, Barclaycard,
Delta, Eurocard, JCB,
Mastercard, Switch, Visa,
Visa Electron

B&B per night:
S £36.00–£50.00
D £45.00–£60.00

OPEN All year round

Beamed medieval Cotswold guesthouse offering en suite rooms with TV. Ideal touring base for Cotswolds. Incorporates established needlecraft centre.

◆◆◆ MERRYFIELD

High Street, Fifield, Oxford, OX7 6HL
T: (01993) 830517
E: jpmgtd@freeuk.com
I: www.home.freeuk.com/jpmgtd

Bedrooms: 2 twin
Bathrooms: 1 en suite,
1 private

Parking for 4

B&B per night:
S £25.00–£30.00
D £45.00–£50.00

OPEN All year round

Stone chalet bungalow with magnificent views and access to the Cotswolds. Midway between Burford and Stow-on-the-Wold. Quiet and peaceful. Ample parking.

MAP REFERENCES

Map references apply to the colour maps at the front of this guide.

BURFORD continued

♦♦♦ ST WINNOW

160 The Hill, Burford, OX18 4QY
T: (01993) 823843 (Answerphone)
(24 hour)

Bedrooms: 1 single,
1 double, 1 twin
Bathrooms: 1 public

Parking for 3

B&B per night:
S £25.00–£35.00
D £40.00–£50.00

OPEN All year round

Comfortable 16thC Cotswold house above the historic high street. Close to restaurants and shops. Garden, garage and parking at rear. Organic and special diets provided.

♦♦♦ TUDOR COTTAGE

40 Witney Street, Burford, Oxford,
OX8 4SN
T: (01993) 823251 (Answerphone)
F: (01993) 823251
E: tudorcottage@supanet.com

Bedrooms: 2 double
Bathrooms: 2 private

B&B per night:
S £25.00–£30.00
D £48.00–£50.00

OPEN All year round

Elegant and very beautiful old Cotswold cottage in central Burford. Lovely garden and extremely comfortable en suite rooms.

BURLEY, Hampshire Map ref 2B3

♦♦♦♦♦ BURBUSH FARM
Gold Award

Pound Lane, Burley, Ringwood,
BH24 4EF
T: (01425) 403238 &
07711 381924 (Mobile)
F: (01425) 403238
E: burbush-farmexcite.com
I: www.burbush-farm

Bedrooms: 3 double
Bathrooms: 3 en suite

Parking for 150
CC: Barclaycard, Delta,
Mastercard, Switch, Visa,
Visa Electron

B&B per night:
D £50.00–£70.00

OPEN All year round

12-acre mixed farm. Secluded country house offering peace and tranquillity, nestling in 12 acres of scenic beauty, adjoining and with direct access to forest. Warm, welcoming atmosphere.

CHALFONT ST GILES, Buckinghamshire Map ref 2C2

♦♦♦ PICKWICKS

Nightingales Lane,
Chalfont St Giles, HP8 4SH
T: (01494) 874123
F: (01494) 870442

Bedrooms: 1 single,
1 double, 1 twin
Bathrooms: 1 en suite,
1 public

EM 1900 (LO 2000)
Parking for 20
CC: Eurocard, Mastercard,
Switch, Visa

B&B per night:
S £45.00–£45.00
D £60.00–£75.00

HB per person:
DY £65.00–£65.00

OPEN All year round

Large, old Tudor-style house in 1.25 acres of beautiful, peaceful gardens. Convenient for London, Heathrow, M40, M25, underground station and Bekonscot Model Village. Newlands College close by.

CHARLBURY, Oxfordshire Map ref 2C1

♦♦♦♦ BANBURY HILL FARM

Enstone Road, Charlbury, Oxford,
OX7 3JH
T: (01608) 810314
F: (01608) 811891

Bedrooms: 1 single,
4 double, 4 twin, 4 triple
Bathrooms: 10 en suite,
1 public

Parking for 16
CC: Barclaycard,
Mastercard, Switch, Visa

B&B per night:
S £20.00–£35.00
D £36.00–£45.00

OPEN Mar–Oct

54-acre mixed farm. Cotswold-stone farmhouse with extensive views across Evenlode Valley. Ideal touring centre for Blenheim Palace, Oxford and the Cotswolds.

CHILBOLTON, Hampshire Map ref 2C2

Rating Applied For UPLANDS

Drove Road, Chilbolton,
Stockbridge, SO20 6AD
T: (01264) 860650
F: (01264) 860650
E: june@haymanjoyce.freeserve.co.uk

Bedrooms: 1 single,
1 twin
Bathrooms: 1 private,
2 public

B&B per night:
S £22.50–£26.00
D £40.00–£45.00

OPEN Jan–Oct

Uplands is a quiet spacious bungalow with large driveway set in a sunny garden. The rooms to let face south west. Photo available.

COLOUR MAPS Colour maps at the front of this guide pinpoint all places under which you will find accommodation listed.

CHIPPING NORTON, Oxfordshire Map ref 2C1 *Tourist Information Centre Tel: (01608) 644379*

◆◆◆

SOUTHCOMBE LODGE GUEST HOUSE

Southcombe, Chipping Norton,
OX7 5QH
T: (01608) 643068
F: (01608) 642948
E: georgefinlysouthcombelodge@
tinyworld.co.uk

Bedrooms: 3 double,
2 twin, 1 triple
Bathrooms: 4 en suite,
2 public

Lunch available
EM 1900 (LO 1800)
Parking for 10

B&B per night:
S £30.00–£35.00
D £46.00–£54.00

OPEN All year round

Well-decorated pebbledash guesthouse set in 3.5 acres, at the junction of the A44/A3400, close to Chipping Norton.

CHOLDERTON, Hampshire Map ref 2B2

◆◆◆◆

PARKHOUSE MOTEL

Cholderton, Salisbury, Wiltshire SP4 0EG
T: (01980) 629256
F: (01980) 629256

B&B per night:
S £29.00–£42.00
D £50.00–£54.00

HB per person:
DY £36.00–£49.00

OPEN All year round

This attractive family-run 17thC former coaching inn, built of brick and flint with slate roof, is 5 miles east of Stonehenge, 10 miles north of Salisbury and 7 miles west of Andover, on the Wiltshire/Hampshire border. We offer a warm welcome to all our guests.

Bedrooms: 6 single,
18 double, 6 twin,
3 triple; suites available
Bathrooms: 23 en suite,
10 private, 3 public

EM 1900 (LO 2030)
Parking for 30
CC: Barclaycard, Delta,
Eurocard, Mastercard,
Switch, Visa, Visa Electron

CHRISTCHURCH, Dorset Map ref 2B3 *Tourist Information Centre Tel: (01202) 471780*

◆◆◆◆

THE WHITE HOUSE

428 Lymington Road, Highcliffe,
Christchurch, BH23 5HF
T: (01425) 271279
F: (01425) 276900
E: thewhitehouse@themail.co.uk
I: www.thewhite-house.co.uk

B&B per night:
S £25.00–£35.00
D £42.00–£46.00

OPEN All year round

Eileen and Fred welcome you to their beautiful Victorian house, furnished and decorated to high standards. Award-winning Highcliffe beach, shops and restaurants are just a short walk away. The New Forest, local golf course are also nearby. Rooms are equipped with hairdryer, clock/radio, colour TV and tea/coffee-making facilities. Private car park.

Bedrooms: 1 single,
5 double
Bathrooms: 5 en suite,
1 public

Parking for 7

COMPTON, Hampshire Map ref 2C3

◆◆

MANOR HOUSE

Place Lane, Compton, Winchester,
SO21 2BA
T: (01962) 712162

Bedrooms: 1 double
Bathrooms: 1 public

Parking for 1

B&B per night:
S £16.00–£16.00
D £32.00–£32.00

OPEN All year round

Comfortable country house in a large garden, 8 minutes from Shawford railway station and 2 miles from city of Winchester. Non-smokers preferred.

CREDIT CARD BOOKINGS
If you book by telephone and are asked for your credit card number it is advisable to check the proprietor's policy should you cancel your reservation.

CORFE CASTLE, Dorset Map ref 2B3

◆◆◆◆

BRADLE FARMHOUSE

Bradle Farm, Church Knowle, Wareham, BH20 5NU
T: (01929) 480712
F: (01929) 481144
E: hole.bradle@farmersweekly.net
I: www.smoothhound.co.uk/hotels/bradle.html

Relax and unwind in our period farmhouse in the heart of Purbeck on 550-acre farm. Spacious, attractively furnished rooms with superb views. We guarantee a breakfast to set you up for the day using home-made produce. A warm, friendly atmosphere is assured, come and sample what we have to offer. Local pub 1 mile.

Bedrooms: 2 double, 1 twin
Bathrooms: 2 en suite, 1 private

Parking for 3

B&B per night:
S £25.00–£34.00
D £44.00–£48.00

OPEN All year round

COTSWOLDS

See under Burford, Charlbury, Chipping Norton, Deddington, Steeple Aston, Witney, Woodstock
See also Cotswolds in Heart of England region

CRANBORNE, Dorset Map ref 2B3

◆◆◆

LA FOSSE AT CRANBORNE

London House, The Square, Cranborne, Wimborne Minster, BH21 5PR
T: (01725) 517604
F: (01725) 517778

Bedrooms: 2 double, 1 twin
Bathrooms: 3 en suite

Lunch available
EM 1845 (LO 2200)
CC: Amex, Barclaycard, Delta, Eurocard, JCB, Mastercard, Solo, Switch, Visa, Visa Electron

B&B per night:
S £32.50–£37.50
D £65.00–£75.00

HB per person:
DY £44.50–£55.00

OPEN All year round

Charming "restaurant with rooms" in idyllic Dorset village on Cranborne Chase. Family-run with excellent value. Individually furnished bedrooms. 20 minutes Bournemouth.

DEDDINGTON, Oxfordshire Map ref 2C1

◆◆

HILL BARN

Milton Gated Road, Deddington, Banbury, OX15 0TS
T: (01869) 338631 (Answerphone)
F: (01869) 338631

Bedrooms: 1 double, 2 twin
Bathrooms: 1 public

Parking for 6

B&B per night:
S £22.00–£27.50
D £40.00–£48.00

OPEN All year round

Converted barn set in open countryside. Banbury-Oxford road, half a mile before Deddington, turn right to Milton Gated Road. Hill Barn is 100 yards on right.

◆◆

STONECROP GUEST HOUSE

Hempton Road, Deddington, Banbury, OX15 0QH
T: (01869) 338335 & 338496
F: (01869) 338505

Bedrooms: 1 single, 1 double, 1 twin, 1 triple
Bathrooms: 1 public

Parking for 6

B&B per night:
S £16.00–£20.00
D £32.00–£40.00

OPEN All year round

Modern, detached accommodation, close to major roads, shops and places of interest.

EDGCOTT, Buckinghamshire Map ref 2C1

◆◆

PERRY MANOR FARM

Buckingham Road, Edgcott, Aylesbury, HP18 0TR
T: (01296) 770257

Bedrooms: 1 single, 1 double, 1 twin
Bathrooms: 1 public

Parking for 10

B&B per night:
S £20.00–£20.00
D £34.00–£34.00

OPEN All year round

200-acre working sheep farm, offering peaceful and comfortable accommodation, with en suite toilet and basin. Extensive views over Aylesbury Vale. Walkers welcome. Non-smokers only, please.

CONFIRM YOUR BOOKING

You are advised to confirm your booking in writing.

EPWELL, Oxfordshire Map ref 2C1

♦♦♦ **YARNHILL FARM**
Epwell, Banbury, OX15 6JA
T: (01295) 780250

Bedrooms: 1 single,
1 double, 1 twin, 1 triple
Bathrooms: 1 en suite,
1 private, 1 public

Parking for 6

B&B per night:
S £20.00–£25.00
D £38.00–£50.00

OPEN All year round

Warm welcome on family farm set in peaceful countryside of outstanding natural beauty. Ideally situated for the Cotswolds, Stratford-upon-Avon, Oxford. Many local sporting facilities.

FAREHAM, Hampshire Map ref 2C3 *Tourist Information Centre Tel: (01329) 221342*

♦♦♦ **AVENUE HOUSE HOTEL**
22 The Avenue, Fareham, PO14 1NS
T: (01329) 232175
F: (01329) 232196

Bedrooms: 2 single,
11 double, 3 twin,
3 triple
Bathrooms: 19 en suite

Parking for 17
CC: Amex, Barclaycard,
Diners, Eurocard,
Mastercard, Visa

B&B per night:
S £48.50–£48.50
D £57.00–£85.00

OPEN All year round

Comfortable, small hotel, with charm and character, set in mature gardens. 5 minutes' walk to town centre, railway station and restaurants.

FORDINGBRIDGE, Hampshire Map ref 2B3

♦♦♦♦ **THE AUGUSTUS JOHN**
116 Station Road, Fordingbridge,
SP6 1DG
T: (01425) 652098
E: peter@augustusjohn.
fordingbridge.com
I: www.augustusjohn.
fordingbridge.com

Bedrooms: 3 double,
1 twin
Bathrooms: 4 en suite

Lunch available
EM 1900 (LO 2100)
Parking for 40
CC: Barclaycard, Delta,
Mastercard, Switch, Visa

B&B per night:
S £25.00–£35.00
D £50.00–£60.00

OPEN All year round

Situated on B3078 approximately three quarters of a mile from Fordingbridge town centre. Large car park. Busy restaurant and bar.

♦♦♦♦ **BROOMY**
Ogdens, Fordingbridge, SP6 2PY
T: (01425) 653264

Bedrooms: 2 double,
1 twin
Bathrooms: 3 en suite

Parking for 6

B&B per night:
S £25.00–£35.00
D £45.00–£55.00

OPEN All year round

Originally built in 1930s. Secluded, peaceful location with direct access on to forest. Ideally situated for walks, riding and touring. Good base for the south.

♦♦♦♦ **NOARLUNGA**
16 Broomfield Drive, Alderholt,
Fordingbridge, SP6 3HY
T: (01425) 650491

Bedrooms: 1 single,
1 double
Bathrooms: 1 public

Parking for 2

B&B per night:
S £19.50–£21.50
D £39.00–£43.00

OPEN Mar–Oct

Comfortable accommodation and superb breakfasts combine with a friendly welcome to provide an enjoyable stay at our bungalow in a quiet village setting.

♦♦♦♦♦ **THE THREE LIONS**
Gold Award
Stuckton, Fordingbridge, SP6 2HF
T: (01425) 652489
F: (01425) 656144

Bedrooms: 2 double,
1 twin
Bathrooms: 3 en suite

Lunch available
EM 1900 (LO 2100)
Parking for 40
CC: Amex, Barclaycard,
Delta, JCB, Maestro,
Mastercard, Switch, Visa

B&B per night:
S £59.00–£75.00
D £65.00–£85.00

OPEN All year round

Quiet, rural restaurant with rooms, all individually decorated. Ground floor room. Wheelchair access. Whirlpool jaccuzi. English/French cuisine.

ACCESSIBILITY
Look for the symbols which indicate accessibility for wheelchair users. A list of establishments is at the front of this guide.

FRESHWATER, Isle of Wight Map ref 2C3

♦♦♦♦ **SEAHORSES**

Victoria Road, Freshwater,
Isle of Wight PO40 9PP
T: (01983) 752574
F: (01983) 752574
E: lanterncom@aol.com

Bedrooms: 1 double,
3 family rooms
Bathrooms: 4 en suite

Parking for 12

B&B per night:
S £21.00–£28.00
D £42.00–£56.00

OPEN All year round

Peaceful restored 18thC country house, standing in secluded gardens, retaining its original charm and character. Near beaches, nature reserve and the Tennyson Downs.

GODSHILL, Hampshire Map ref 2C3

♦♦♦ **VENNARDS COTTAGE**

Newgrounds, Godshill,
Fordingbridge, SP6 2LJ
T: (01425) 652644
F: (01425) 656646
E: gillian.bridgeman@virgin.net

Bedrooms: 1 twin
Bathrooms: 1 private

Parking for 2

B&B per night:
S £22.00–£28.00
D £44.00–£56.00

OPEN Feb–Nov

Friendly family home in glorious setting of New Forest. Ideal for walking, riding and all country pursuits. Private bathroom, TV and tea-making facilities.

GORING, Oxfordshire Map ref 2C2

♦♦♦ **MILLER OF MANSFIELD**

High Street, Goring, Reading,
Berkshire RG8 9AW
T: (01491) 872829
F: (01491) 874200

Bedrooms: 2 single,
5 double, 3 twin
Bathrooms: 10 en suite

Lunch available
EM 1900 (LO 2200)
Parking for 10
CC: Barclaycard, Delta,
Eurocard, Mastercard,
Solo, Switch, Visa

B&B per night:
S £49.50–£52.50
D £65.00–£69.50

OPEN All year round

Ivy-covered inn with Tudor-style exterior. Interior has original beams, open fires and comfortable bedrooms.

HAMBLEDON, Hampshire Map ref 2C3

♦♦♦ **CAMS**

Hambledon, Waterlooville, PO7 4SP
T: (023) 9263 2865
F: (023) 9263 2691

Bedrooms: 1 double,
2 twin
Bathrooms: 1 en suite,
1 private, 1 public

EM 1900
Parking for 6

B&B per night:
S £22.00–£24.00
D £42.00–£48.00

OPEN All year round

Comfortable, Grade II family house with large garden in beautiful setting on the edge of Hambledon village. Pub with good food within walking distance. Tennis court.*

HAYLING ISLAND, Hampshire Map ref 2C3

♦♦♦ **WHITE HOUSE**

250 Havant Road, Hayling Island,
PO11 0LN
T: (023) 9246 3464

Bedrooms: 2 double,
1 twin
Bathrooms: 2 en suite,
1 private

EM 1830
Parking for 6

B&B per night:
S £22.00–£30.00
D £45.00–£50.00

OPEN All year round

Family-run establishment, with warm, friendly atmosphere, no hidden extra costs and no restrictions. Ideal base for exploring south Hampshire.

TOWN INDEX

This can be found at the back of the guide. If you know where you want to stay, the index will give you the page number listing accommodation in your chosen town, city or village.

HENLEY-ON-THAMES, Oxfordshire Map ref 2C2 *Tourist Information Centre Tel: (01491) 578034*

◆◆◆◆

ALFTRUDIS

8 Norman Avenue, Henley-on-Thames, RG9 1SG
T: (01491) 573099 & 07802 408643
F: (01491) 411747
E: b&b@alftrudis.fsnet.co.uk

B&B per night:
S £40.00–£55.00
D £50.00–£55.00

OPEN All year round

Sue Lambert invites you to stay in her friendly, comfortable, Grade II Listed Victorian home. Centrally situated in a quiet, private, tree-lined cul-de-sac only 3 minutes' walk from the town centre, railway station and scenic River Thames. Easy parking, either in the driveway or private avenue.

Bedrooms: 2 double, 1 twin
Bathrooms: 2 en suite, 1 private

Parking for 2

◆◆◆◆

COLDHARBOUR HOUSE

3 Coldharbour Close, Henley-on-Thames, RG9 1QF
T: (01491) 575229
F: (01491) 575229
E: coldharbourhouse@compuserve.com

Bedrooms: 1 single, 1 double, 1 twin
Bathrooms: 1 en suite, 1 public

Parking for 2

B&B per night:
S £30.00–£40.00
D £50.00–£60.00

OPEN All year round

Old farmhouse-style home with walled garden, in a quiet close, 15 minutes' walk from town centre and river. Ample parking.

◆◆◆◆

HOLMWOOD

Shiplake Row, Binfield Heath, Henley-on-Thames, RG9 4DP
T: (0118) 947 8747
F: (0118) 947 8637

B&B per night:
S £40.00–£50.00
D £60.00–£60.00

OPEN All year round

Large, elegant, peaceful Georgian country house with very beautiful gardens and views over the Thames Valley. All bedrooms are large and en suite and furnished with period and antique furnishings. Holmwood is in Binfield Heath, which is signposted off the A4155, equidistant from Henley-on-Thames and Reading.

Bedrooms: 1 single, 2 double, 2 twin
Bathrooms: 5 en suite

Parking for 8
CC: Barclaycard, Delta, Mastercard, Switch, Visa

◆◆◆◆

THE KNOLL

Crowsley Road, Shiplake, Henley-on-Thames, RG9 3JT
T: (01189) 402705 (Answerphone) & 07885 755437 (Mobile)
F: (01189) 402705
E: milpops2@aol.com
I: www.saqnet.co.uk/users/the-knoll

Bedrooms: 1 double, 1 twin
Bathrooms: 2 en suite

Parking for 4

B&B per night:
S £48.00–£48.00
D £53.00–£55.00

OPEN All year round

Beautifully restored home with every modern convenience, riverside walks and landscaped garden. Good base for Cotswolds, Oxford, Windsor, London and Heathrow.

QUALITY ASSURANCE SCHEME

Diamond ratings and awards were correct at the time of going to press but are subject to change. Please check at the time of booking.

HENLEY-ON-THAMES continued

◆◆◆◆◆

LENWADE

3 Western Road, Henley-on-Thames, RG9 1JL
T: (01491) 573468 & 07774 941629
F: (01491) 573468
E: lenwadeuk@compuserve.com
I: www.w3b-ink.com/lenwade

Bedrooms: 2 double, 1 twin
Bathrooms: 2 en suite, 1 private

Parking for 2

B&B per night:
S £25.00–£45.00
D £50.00–£60.00

OPEN All year round

Delightful Victorian home in quiet surroundings within walking distance of town, river and station. Lovely walks and golf nearby. Convenient for Heathrow, Oxford and Windsor.

◆◆

PARK VIEW FARM

Lower Assendon, Henley-on-Thames, RG9 6AN
T: (01491) 414232 & 0786 766 0814 (Mobile)
F: (01491) 577515
E: info@thomasmartin.co.uk
I: www.thomasmartin.co.uk

Bedrooms: 1 double, 1 twin
Bathrooms: 1 public

Parking for 3

B&B per night:
S £20.00–£25.00
D £40.00–£50.00

OPEN All year round

An equestrian property with stunning Chiltern views. On bridle/footpath yet only 1 mile outside Henley. X39 bus stop nearby. Horses welcome.

◆◆◆

SLATERS FARM

Peppard Common, Henley-on-Thames, RG9 5JL
T: (01491) 628675
F: (01491) 628675

Bedrooms: 1 double, 2 twin
Bathrooms: 2 private, 2 public

EM 1900 (LO 2030)
Parking for 8

B&B per night:
S Min £28.00
D Min £48.00

OPEN All year round

A quiet and welcoming country house set in a lovely garden. Short walk to good traditional pubs.

HIGH WYCOMBE, Buckinghamshire Map ref 2C2 *Tourist Information Centre Tel: (01494) 421892*

◆◆◆

AYAM MANOR

Hammersley Lane, High Wycombe, HP10 8HS
T: (01494) 816932
F: (01494) 816932
E: jeansenior@ayammanor.freeserve.co.uk
I: www.ayammanorguesthouse.co.uk

B&B per night:
S Max £67.00
D Max £95.00

OPEN All year round

Very large Georgian house, decorated to a high standard, with spacious bedrooms, games room, swimming pool and sitting room. Secure off-road parking. A warm, friendly welcome awaits guests.

Bedrooms: 7 single, 1 twin, 2 family rooms
Bathrooms: 9 en suite, 1 private

Lunch available
EM 1800 (LO 2000)
Parking for 40
CC: Amex, Barclaycard, Delta, Diners, Mastercard, Solo, Switch, Visa

HUNGERFORD, Berkshire Map ref 2C2

◆◆◆◆

FISHERS FARM

Ermin Street, Shefford Woodlands, Hungerford, Berkshire RG17 7AB
T: (01488) 648466 & 07973 691901 (Mobile)
F: (01488) 648706
E: mail@fishersfarm.co.uk
I: www.fishersfarm.co.uk

B&B per night:
S £35.00–£45.00
D £52.00–£56.00

OPEN All year round

Historic farmhouse with all modern comforts on working farm. Peaceful rural setting, surrounded by large garden and fields, but within 1 mile of junction 14 of M4. Heated indoor swimming pool. Ideal touring base. Hungerford 3 miles, Heathrow Airport 45 miles. Dinner by arrangement. Spanish, German and French spoken.

Bedrooms: 1 double, 2 twin
Bathrooms: 2 en suite, 1 private

EM
Parking for 8

◆◆◆◆

MARSHGATE COTTAGE HOTEL
Marsh Lane, Hungerford, Berkshire
RG17 0QX
T: (01488) 682307
F: (01488) 685475
E: reservations@marshgate.co.uk
I: www.marshgate.co.uk

Bedrooms: 1 single,
6 double, 3 triple
Bathrooms: 10 en suite

Parking for 9
CC: Barclaycard, Delta,
Mastercard, Switch, Visa

B&B per night:
S £36.50–£45.00
D £52.00–£55.00

OPEN All year round

Family-run canalside hotel, linked to 350-year-old thatched cottage at end of quiet country lane. Overlooks marshland and trout streams. 1 hour from Heathrow and 5 minutes from M4.

◆◆◆◆
Silver
Award

WILTON HOUSE
83 High Street, Hungerford, Berkshire
RG17 0NF
T: (01488) 684228
F: (01488) 685037
E: welfares@hotmail.com

B&B per night:
D £54.00–£58.00

OPEN All year round

Classic English townhouse with documented history pre-dating 1470. Pevsner describes it as "the most ambitious house in Hungerford". Extremely attractive bedroom suites and dining room in elegant 18thC part with wood panelling, open fireplaces, period features. Delicious breakfasts. M4 3 miles. Oxford, Cotswolds close by. Heathrow 1 hour. Many antique shops.

Bedrooms: 2 double
Bathrooms: 2 en suite

Parking for 6

◆◆◆◆

CHANGRI-LA
12 Ashleigh Close, Hythe, Southampton,
SO45 3QP
T: (023) 8084 6664

B&B per night:
S Min £18.00
D Min £36.00

OPEN All year round

Comfortable home in unique position on edge of New Forest, a few minutes' drive from Beaulieu National Motor Museum, Bucklers Hard, Exbury Gardens, Calshot Activities Centre, for sailing, windsurfing etc, and many other places of interest.

Bedrooms: 1 double,
1 twin
Bathrooms: 2 private,
1 public

Parking for 3

CHECK THE MAPS
The colour maps at the front of this guide show all the cities, towns and villages for which you will find accommodation entries. Refer to the town index to find the page on which they are listed.

INKPEN, Berkshire Map ref 2C2

Rating
Applied For

THE SWAN INN

Inkpen, Hungerford, Berkshire RG17 9DX
T: (01488) 668326
F: (01488) 668306
E: enquiries@theswaninn-organics.co.uk
I: www.theswaninn-organics.co.uk

B&B per night:
S £40.00–£40.00
D £75.00–£90.00

HB per person:
DY £45.00–£55.00

OPEN All year round

17thC inn located in an Area of Outstanding Natural Beauty, one mile from Coombe Gibbet, the highest point in Southern England (965ft). En suite bedrooms. Owned by local organic beef farmers, the bar food and restaurant use the best, fresh organic ingredients. Featured in the Camra "Good Beer Guide".

Bedrooms: 1 single, 6 double, 3 twin
Bathrooms: 10 en suite

Lunch available
EM 1900 (LO 2130)
CC: Barclaycard, Delta, Eurocard, JCB, Maestro, Mastercard, Solo, Switch, Visa, Visa Electron

ISLE OF WIGHT

See under Bonchurch, Freshwater, Ryde, Sandown, Shanklin, Wroxall

KINGSCLERE, Hampshire Map ref 2C2

♦♦♦

11 HOOK ROAD

Kingsclere, Newbury, Berkshire RG20 5PD
T: (01635) 298861 (Answerphone)
& 07774 259917 (Mobile phone)
F: (01635) 298861
E: johnaphilips@compuserve.com

Bedrooms: 1 single, 2 twin
Bathrooms: 1 public

Lunch available
EM 1900 (LO 2100)
Parking for 6

B&B per night:
S £21.00–£22.00
D £34.00–£35.00

HB per person:
DY £29.00–£34.00

OPEN All year round

Comfortable, modern house in historic Kingsclere at the foot of the beautiful Hampshire Downs. Convenient for M3, M4, A34 and good local amenities.

KINGTON MAGNA, Dorset Map ref 2B3

♦♦♦♦

KINGTON MANOR FARM

Church Hill, Kington Magna, Gillingham, SP8 5EG
T: (01747) 838371 (Answerphone)
F: (01747) 838371

B&B per night:
S £24.00–£24.00
D £44.00–£44.00

OPEN Jan–Nov

100-acre mixed farm. Attractive farmhouse in quiet, pretty village. Views over Blackmore Vale. Ideal area for walking, cycling and fishing in the River Stour. Stourhead House/ Gardens and Longleat Safari Park nearby. Friendly village pubs serving excellent food and ales. Heated outdoor pool, hearty breakfasts. One mile off A30.

Bedrooms: 2 double, 1 triple
Bathrooms: 1 en suite, 2 private

Parking for 4

COUNTRY CODE Always follow the Country Code ✿ Enjoy the countryside and respect its life and work ✿ Guard against all risk of fire ✿ Fasten all gates ✿ Keep your dogs under close control ✿ Keep to public paths across farmland ✿ Use gates and stiles to cross fences, hedges and walls ✿ Leave livestock, crops and machinery alone ✿ Take your litter home ✿ Help to keep all water clean ✿ Protect wildlife, plants and trees ✿ Take special care on country roads ✿ Make no unnecessary noise

LYMINGTON, Hampshire Map ref 2C3

◆◆◆◆◆
Gold
Award

EFFORD COTTAGE

Everton, Lymington, SO41 0JD
T: (01590) 642315
F: (01590) 641030
E: effcottage@aol.com

B&B per night:
D £48.00–£65.00

OPEN All year round

Friendly, spacious Georgian cottage in an acre of garden. Award-winning guesthouse. Elegant bedrooms, luxury facilities. Delicious, 4-course breakfast from a wide and varied menu. Home-made bread/preserves. Patricia, a qualified chef, uses home-grown produce for traditional country cooking. Special midweek winter breaks. "Your comfort is our concern".

Bedrooms: 1 double, 1 twin, 1 triple; suite available
Bathrooms: 3 en suite

Lunch available
EM
Parking for 4

 14 📞 🖨 ▢ ♿ ⚲ UL ⓘ Ⓢ ☒ ▦ ▱ ∪ ✿ 🚲 🕸 SP T ⊚

◆◆◆
Ad on this page

GORSE MEADOW GUEST HOUSE

Gorse Meadow, Sway Road, Lymington, SO41 8LR
T: (01590) 673354 (3 lines)
F: (01590) 673336
E: gorsemeadow.guesthouse@wildmushrooms.co.uk
I: www.@wildmushrooms.co.uk

B&B per night:
S £45.00–£45.00
D £50.00–£70.00

HB per person:
DY £45.00–£55.00

OPEN All year round

Beautiful Edwardian residence in 14 acres, close to New Forest. Period furniture, modern utilities. Splendid galleried hall, impressive dining room (evening dinners) seating 12. Licensed. Residents'/visitors' lounge. Landscaped grounds with fishpond. Cookery courses, professional golf/tennis coach on staff. Bike and boat hire, beaches, riding and good pubs nearby.

Bedrooms: 4 double, 1 twin, 1 triple, 2 family rooms; suite available
Bathrooms: 7 en suite, 1 private

Lunch available
EM 1830 (LO 2030)
Parking for 12
CC: Barclaycard, Delta, Mastercard, Switch, Visa, Visa Electron

▲▲ 🦮 ⚲ ▢ ♿ ⚲ ⓘ Ⓢ ✂ ☒ ▦ ▱ 🍴 14 ∪ ✿ 🚲 🕸 SP T

TOWN INDEX

This can be found at the back of this guide. If you know where you want to stay, the index will give you the page number listing accommodation in your chosen town, city or village.

◆◆

JACK IN THE BASKET RESTAURANT

7 St Thomas Street, Lymington,
SO41 9NA
T: (01590) 673447 & 673812
I: www.newforest.demon.co.uk.
jackbasket.htm

Bedrooms: 1 double,
1 twin, 1 family room
Bathrooms: 2 public

Lunch available

B&B per night:
S Min £25.00
D Min £40.00

OPEN All year round

Family-owned business. 17thC building, with tasteful accommodation, friendly service and home cooking. Ideal centre for forest and ferries.

◆◆◆◆

THE MAYFLOWER INN

Kings Saltern Road, Lymington, SO41 3QD
T: (01590) 672160
E: mayflower@lymington.fsbusiness.co.uk

B&B per night:
S £35.00–£45.00
D £59.50–£79.50

OPEN All year round

Family-run inn overlooking the river and marina. Ideal base for touring the Solent coast and New Forest. Newly refurbished interior with very attractive bedrooms, all en suite, some with river views. Four-poster suite now available. Excellent home-cooked food, log fire, well stocked bar and always a warm welcome.

Bedrooms: 4 double,
1 twin, 1 triple
Bathrooms: 6 en suite

Lunch available
EM 1830 (LO 2100)
CC: Amex, Barclaycard,
Delta, Mastercard, Solo,
Switch, Visa, Visa Electron

◆◆◆◆

40 SOUTHAMPTON ROAD

Lymington, SO41 9GG
T: (01590) 672237
F: (01590) 673592

Bedrooms: 1 double,
1 twin
Bathrooms: 2 private,
1 public

Parking for 2

B&B per night:
S £28.00–£30.00
D £50.00–£54.00

OPEN All year round

Spacious Edwardian townhouse, elegantly furnished. Convenient position for New Forest and ferry to Isle of Wight. Private bathrooms, Stannah chairlift, garden, parking.

◆◆◆◆

BURWOOD LODGE

27 Romsey Road, Lyndhurst, SO43 7AA
T: (023) 8028 2445
F: (023) 8028 4104

B&B per night:
S £24.00–£30.00
D £42.00–£50.00

OPEN All year round

Lovely Edwardian house in half-acre grounds, located just 3 minutes' walk to village high street, 5 minutes from open forest. Guest lounge and separate dining room overlook the gardens, enhancing a relaxing environment. Bedrooms tastefully decorated: family, twin, single and a 4-poster room for those special, romantic occasions.

Bedrooms: 1 single,
3 double, 1 twin, 1 triple
Bathrooms: 6 en suite

Parking for 8

◆◆◆◆

ENGLEFIELD

Chapel Lane, Lyndhurst, SO43 7FG
T: (023) 8028 2685

Bedrooms: 1 double,
1 twin
Bathrooms: 2 private

B&B per night:
S £22.00–£25.00
D £40.00–£42.00

OPEN All year round

Elegant and peaceful house with beautiful garden which can be enjoyed from balcony of double bedroom. Very comfortable, convenient for forest and village. Come and relax!

◆◆◆◆
Silver
Award

FOREST COTTAGE
High Street, Lyndhurst, SO43 7BH
T: (023) 8028 3461
I: www.forestcottage.i12.com

B&B per night:
S £20.00–£22.00
D £40.00–£44.00

OPEN All year round

Charming 300-year-old cottage, in the village yet close to the forest. Guest lounge with TV, library of natural history books, maps and local literature. Tea/coffee always available. Warm, pretty bedrooms. The garden contains an interesting collection of plants. Private parking. Riding and bicycle hire available locally.

Bedrooms: 1 single, 1 double, 1 twin
Bathrooms: 2 public

Parking for 3

🛏14 UL S ≮ TV Ⅲ ♨ ✿ 犬 🐾 SP T

◆◆◆◆
Silver
Award

LYNDHURST HOUSE
35 Romsey Road, Lyndhurst, SO43 7AR
T: (023) 8028 2230 (Answerphone)
F: (023) 8028 2230
E: bcjwood@lyndhouse.freeserve.co.uk
I: www.newforest.demon.co.uk/lynho.html

Bedrooms: 4 double, 1 family room
Bathrooms: 5 en suite

Parking for 5
CC: Barclaycard, Mastercard, Visa

B&B per night:
D £44.00–£52.00

OPEN All year round

Tastefully furnished, comfortable accommodation with en suite facilities and some 4-poster beds. English/vegetarian breakfast. Locked cycle store. Two minutes' walk from village and forest. Warm welcome awaits.

Λ 🛏5 🗄 ⬜ ♿ ♨ 🍴 UL S ≮ Ⅲ ♨ ✿ 犬 🐾

◆◆◆◆

THE PENNY FARTHING HOTEL
Romsey Road, Lyndhurst, SO43 7AA
T: (023) 8028 4422
F: (023) 8028 4488
I: www.smoothhound.co.uk/hotels/pennyf.html

B&B per night:
S £35.00–£45.00
D £55.00–£79.00

OPEN All year round

Welcome to our cheerful hotel, conveniently situated a moment's walk from the village centre. Our cosy centrally heated bedrooms have en-suite shower or bath and WC, colour TV, clock, radio and tea/coffee making facilities. We also provide a residents' bar/lounge, lock up bicycle store and large private car park.

Bedrooms: 4 single, 6 double, 3 twin, 1 triple, 1 family room
Bathrooms: 11 en suite, 1 private, 2 public

Parking for 15
CC: Amex, Barclaycard, Delta, Diners, Eurocard, JCB, Mastercard, Solo, Switch, Visa, Visa Electron

Λ 🛏 🔔 🗄 📞 🖥 ⬜ ♿ 🍴 S ≮ ¤ TV Ⅲ ∪ ✿ 🐾 SP T

◆◆◆

ROSEDALE BED & BREAKFAST
24 Shaggs Meadow, Lyndhurst, SO43 7BN
T: (023) 8028 3793
E: jenny@theangels.freeserve.co.uk

Bedrooms: 1 twin, 1 family room
Bathrooms: 1 en suite, 1 public

Parking for 4

B&B per night:
S £18.00–£24.50
D £36.00–£49.00

HB per person:
DY £24.00–£30.59

OPEN All year round

Family-run bed and breakfast in the centre of Lyndhurst. We cater for families. Colour TV, tea/coffee facilities. Breakfast served at your convenience. Evening meals by arrangement.

🛏 ⬜ ♿ 🍴 UL S ≮ TV Ⅲ ♨ ✿ 犬 🐾

RATING All accommodation in this guide has been rated, or is awaiting a rating, by a trained English Tourism Council assessor.

LYNDHURST continued

◆◆◆◆
Silver
Award

RUFUS HOUSE HOTEL

Southampton Road, Lyndhurst, SO43 7BQ
T: (023) 8028 2930 & 8028 2200
F: (023) 8028 2930
E: rufushouse@talk21.com

B&B per night:
S £30.00–£40.00
D £55.00–£75.00

OPEN All year round

A family-run hotel, where all our attractive and comfortable bedrooms have views of either forest or fields. Turret bedrooms available for that "special occasion". An ideal base for exploring the New Forest. We offer traditional comforts with today's convenience. Visit us to experience our warm, friendly hospitality for yourself.

| Bedrooms: 1 single, 9 double, 1 twin | Parking for 15 |
| Bathrooms: 11 en suite | CC: Barclaycard, Delta, JCB, Mastercard, Solo, Switch, Visa, Visa Electron |

MAIDENHEAD, Berkshire Map ref 2C2 *Tourist Information Centre Tel: (01628) 781110*

◆

CARTLANDS COTTAGE

Kings Lane,
Cookham Dean, Cookham,
Maidenhead, Berkshire SL6 9AY
T: (01628) 482196

| Bedrooms: 1 triple | Parking for 4 |
| Bathrooms: 1 en suite, 1 public | |

B&B per night:
S £20.00–£27.50
D £40.00–£50.00

OPEN All year round

Family room in self-contained garden studio. Meals in delightful timbered character cottage with exposed beams. Traditional cottage garden. National Trust common land. Very quiet.

MARLOW, Buckinghamshire Map ref 2C2

◆◆◆

ACORN LODGE

79 Marlow Bottom Road, Marlow Bottom, Marlow, SL7 3NA
T: (01628) 472197 (Ansaphone) &
07710 974329 (Mobile)
F: (01628) 472197

B&B per night:
S £40.00–£60.00
D £55.00–£69.00

OPEN All year round

Backing on to woodland. Outdoor swimming pool (16ft x 32ft), guest gazebo. En suite rooms, comfortable beds, Victorian brass 4-poster plus twin or 6ft double, ceiling fans, remote TV. Suite has separate sitting room, whirlpool bath. Warm welcome, super breakfast, 2 small, happy dogs. Easy reach Heathrow, Windsor, Legoland, 1.5 miles Marlow centre.

| Bedrooms: 2 double, 1 twin | Parking for 6 |
| Bathrooms: 3 en suite | CC: Barclaycard, Delta, JCB, Mastercard, Solo, Switch, Visa |

◆◆◆◆

THE INN ON THE GREEN

The Old Cricket Common,
Cookham Dean, Cookham,
Maidenhead, Berkshire SL6 9NZ
T: (01628) 482638
F: (01628) 487474
E: chris@theinnonthegreen.com
I: www.theinnonthegreen.com

Bedrooms: 1 single, 5 double, 2 twin	Lunch available
Bathrooms: 8 en suite	EM 1930 (LO 2200)
	Parking for 40
	CC: Amex, Barclaycard, Delta, Eurocard, JCB, Mastercard, Solo, Switch, Visa

B&B per night:
S £65.00–£75.00
D £85.00–£110.00

HB per person:
DY £50.00–£60.00

OPEN All year round

An extensive restaurant menu is available, offering freshly cooked dishes for all meals. Residents' menu available from midday until midnight.

WHERE TO STAY

Please mention this guide when making your booking.

MARLOW continued

◆◆◆◆ SNEPPEN HOUSE

Henley Road, Marlow, SL7 2DF
T: (01628) 485227

Bedrooms: 1 double, 1 twin
Bathrooms: 1 public

Parking for 3

B&B per night:
S £25.00–£30.00
D £45.00–£45.00

OPEN All year round

Large modern house within level walking distance of town centre. Convenient for Thames Walk. Off-street parking. Good pub food nearby. Breakfast menu choice.

MARNHULL, Dorset Map ref 2B3

◆◆◆ THE OLD BANK

Burton Street, Marnhull,
Sturminster Newton, DT10 1PH
T: (01258) 821019
F: (01258) 821019

Bedrooms: 2 double
Bathrooms: 2 public

Parking for 5

B&B per night:
S £20.00–£20.00
D £40.00–£40.00

OPEN All year round

Stone-built (1730) house in quiet Dorset country village. Attractive courtyard bordered by barns, leading to pretty garden. Pub approximately 100 yards away. Friendly, family-run home.

MILFORD-ON-SEA, Hampshire Map ref 2C3

◆◆◆◆ ALMA MATER

4 Knowland Drive, Milford-on-Sea,
Lymington, SO41 0RH
T: (01590) 642811
E: bandbalmamater@aol.com
I: www.newforest.demon.co.uk/
almamater.htm

Bedrooms: 2 double, 1 twin
Bathrooms: 2 en suite, 1 private, 1 public

EM 1830 (LO 2000)
Parking for 4

B&B per night:
S £30.00–£35.00
D £40.00–£45.00

HB per person:
DY £30.00–£40.00

OPEN All year round

Detached, quiet, spacious, non-smoking chalet bunglow with en suite bedrooms overlooking lovely garden. Close to village, beaches, New Forest and IoW. Evening meals by request.

MILTON KEYNES, Buckinghamshire Map ref 2C1 *Tourist Information Centre Tel: (01908) 558300*

◆◆◆ CHANTRY FARM

Pindon End, Hanslope,
Milton Keynes, Buckinghamshire
MK19 7HL
T: (01908) 510269 & 07850 166122
F: (01908) 510269

Bedrooms: 1 double, 2 twin
Bathrooms: 1 en suite, 1 public

Parking for 7

B&B per night:
S £20.00–£25.00
D £40.00–£50.00

OPEN All year round

500-acre farm. Stone farmhouse, 1650, with inglenook. Surrounded by beautiful countryside. Swimming pool, trout lake, table tennis, croquet, clay pigeon shooting. 15 minutes from centre.

◆◆◆◆ HAVERSHAM GRANGE

Haversham, Milton Keynes,
Buckinghamshire MK19 7DX
T: (01908) 312389
F: (01908) 312389
E: havershamgrange.fsnet.co.uk

Bedrooms: 3 twin
Bathrooms: 2 en suite, 1 private, 1 public

Parking for 4

B&B per night:
S £25.00–£30.00
D £46.00–£50.00

OPEN All year round

Large 14thC stone house with en suite facilities. Set in own gardens backing on to lakes.

◆◆◆ KINGFISHERS

9 Rylstone Close, Heelands,
Milton Keynes, Buckinghamshire
MK13 7QT
T: (01908) 310231 & 318601
F: (01908) 318601
E: sheila-derek@m-keynes.
freeserve.co.uk
I: www.smoothhound.co.uk/hotels/
kingfishers.html

Bedrooms: 1 single, 1 double, 1 triple
Bathrooms: 2 en suite, 1 private

EM 1800 (LO 2000)
Parking for 6

B&B per night:
S £23.00–£25.00
D £40.00–£50.00

HB per person:
DY £27.00–£35.00

OPEN All year round

Large private home in quarter of an acre of grounds, convenient for city centre, shopping, theatre and railway station. Very comfortable, warm welcome assured.

MILTON KEYNES continued

◆◆◆ MILL FARM

Gayhurst, Newport Pagnell,
Buckinghamshire MK16 8LT
T: (01908) 611489
F: (01908) 611489

Bedrooms: 1 single,
1 double, 1 twin,
1 family room
Bathrooms: 1 en suite,
2 private, 1 public

Parking for 12

B&B per night:
S £20.00–£25.00
D £40.00–£45.00

OPEN All year round

500-acre mixed farm. 17thC farmhouse with hard tennis court, fishing on River Ouse, which flows through farm. Good touring centre. Easy reach of Oxford, Cambridge, Woburn Abbey and Whipsnade.

◆◆◆ VIGNOBLE

2 Medland, Woughton Park,
Milton Keynes, Buckinghamshire
MK6 3BH
T: (01908) 666804
F: (01908) 666626
E: 101532.627@compuserve.com

Bedrooms: 1 single,
1 double, 1 twin
Bathrooms: 2 public

Parking for 3

B&B per night:
S £26.00–£28.00
D £45.00–£47.00

OPEN All year round

In a quiet cul-de-sac within walking distance of the Open University and 2.5 miles from the city centre. A warm welcome home from home in 3 languages.

MOULSFORD ON THAMES, Oxfordshire Map ref 2C2

◆◆◆◆◆ WHITE HOUSE

Moulsford on Thames, Wallingford,
OX10 9JD
T: (01491) 651397 &
07831 372243 (Mobile)
F: (01491) 652560

Bedrooms: 1 single,
1 double, 1 twin
Bathrooms: 1 public

EM 1900 (LO 2030)
Parking for 6

B&B per night:
S £25.00–£30.00
D £45.00–£45.00

OPEN All year round

Beautifully appointed ground floor accommodation in a detached family home surrounded by large garden. Picturesque Thameside village, convenient for Oxford, Henley and Reading.

NEW FOREST

See under Ashurst, Bartley, Beaulieu, Boldre, Burley, Fordingbridge, Godshill, Hythe, Lymington, Lyndhurst, Milford-on-Sea, New Milton, Ringwood, Sway

NEW MILTON, Hampshire Map ref 2B3

◆◆◆ TAVERNERS COTTAGE

Bashley Cross Road, Bashley,
New Milton, BH25 5SZ
T: (01425) 615403 &
07966 463466 (Mobile)
F: (01425) 615403
E: jbaines@supanet.com
I: www.taverners.cottage.bandb.
baines.com

Bedrooms: 1 double,
1 triple
Bathrooms: 2 en suite

Parking for 3

B&B per night:
S £21.00–£23.00
D £39.00–£42.00

OPEN All year round

Pretty white painted cob cottage, dating back some 300 years, overlooking open farmland. Warm welcome in quality accommodation. Close to both sea and forest.

AT-A-GLANCE SYMBOLS

Symbols at the end of each accommodation entry give useful information about services and facilities. A key to symbols can be found inside the back cover flap. Keep this open for easy reference.

♦♦♦

THE OLD FARMHOUSE

Downend Lane, Chieveley, Newbury,
Berkshire RG20 8TN

T: (01635) 248361 &
07770 590844 (Mobile)
F: (01635) 528195
E: palletts@aol.com
I: www.smoothhound.co.uk/hotels/
oldfarmhouse.html

*Period farmhouse on edge of village
within 2 miles of M4/A34 (junction
13), 5 miles north of Newbury.
Accommodation in ground-floor
annexe comprising hall, kitchenette,
sitting room (with bed-settee),
double bedroom, bathroom. Large
gardens overlooking countryside.
Oxford, Bath, Windsor and Heathrow
Airport within easy reach. London
approximately one hour.*

Bedrooms: 2 single,   Parking for 5
1 double
Bathrooms: 3 en suite

B&B per night:
S £30.00–£35.00
D £50.00–£55.00

OPEN All year round

♦♦♦♦♦
Silver
Award

THE LIMES

North Square, Newport Pagnell,
Buckinghamshire MK16 8EP

T: (01908) 617041 (Answerphone (24
hour)) & 07860 908925 (Mobile)
F: (01908) 217292
E: royandruth@8thelimes.freeserve.co.uk

*Georgian townhouse with river
frontage, off-road parking, private
fishing and established gardens.
Comfortable and beautifully
furnished with antiques. All
bedrooms have en suite facilities and
one has a 4-poster bed. Good home
cooking. Meeting/conference room
available. Three miles from M1
junction 14.*

Bedrooms: 2 double,   EM 1930
1 twin   Parking for 5
Bathrooms: 3 en suite   CC: Amex, Barclaycard,
                             Delta, Eurocard, JCB,
                             Mastercard, Switch, Visa

B&B per night:
S Min £45.00
D £55.00–£65.00

HB per person:
DY £60.00–£65.00

OPEN All year round

♦♦

ACORN GUEST HOUSE

260-262 Iffley Road, Oxford,
OX4 1SE
T: (01865) 247998
F: (01865) 247998

Bedrooms: 4 single,   Parking for 11
2 double, 2 twin, 5 triple   CC: Amex, Barclaycard,
Bathrooms: 1 en suite,   JCB, Mastercard, Switch,
4 public   Visa

B&B per night:
S £26.00–£29.00
D £44.00–£56.00

OPEN All year round

*Victorian house situated midway between the city centre and the ring-road. Convenient
for all local attractions including the river, and more distant places.*

QUALITY ASSURANCE SCHEME

For an explanation of the quality and facilities
represented by the Diamonds please refer to the
front of this guide. A more detailed explanation
can be found in the information pages at the back.

◆◆◆

Comfortable family-run guesthouse, informal atmosphere, bright and airy rooms with TV, welcome tray, toiletries and towels. Completely non-smoking. No children under 6. Vegetarians catered for. Secure parking. Located in Headington, 2 miles from the city centre, and convenient for Brookes University. 24-hour coach links to Heathrow/Gatwick airports and London close by.

ALL SEASONS GUEST HOUSE

63 Windmill Road, Headington, Oxford, OX3 7BP
T: (01865) 742215
F: (01865) 432691
E: info@allseasons-oxford.com
I: www.allseasons-oxford.com

Bedrooms: 2 single, 3 double, 1 twin
Bathrooms: 4 en suite, 1 public

Parking for 6
CC: Barclaycard, Delta, Eurocard, Mastercard, Solo, Switch, Visa, Visa Electron

B&B per night:
S £28.00–£42.00
D £45.00–£62.00

OPEN All year round

 12

◆◆

BECKET HOUSE

5 Becket Street, Oxford, OX1 7PP
T: (01865) 724675 & 513045
F: (01865) 724675

Bedrooms: 2 single, 2 double, 1 twin, 4 triple, 1 family room
Bathrooms: 5 en suite, 1 public

CC: Barclaycard, Delta, Eurocard, JCB, Mastercard, Solo, Switch, Visa, Visa Electron

B&B per night:
S £30.00–£50.00
D £40.00–£70.00

OPEN All year round

Friendly guesthouse convenient for rail and bus station, within walking distance of city centre and colleges. Good, clean accommodation, en suite rooms.

◆◆◆

THE BUNGALOW

Cherwell Farm, Mill Lane, Old Marston, Oxford, OX3 0QF
T: (01865) 557171

Bedrooms: 2 double, 1 twin
Bathrooms: 1 en suite, 1 public

Parking for 4

B&B per night:
S £25.00–£35.00
D £42.00–£48.00

OPEN Apr–Oct

Modern bungalow set in 5 acres, in quiet location with views over open countryside, 3 miles from city centre. No smoking. No bus route – car essential.

 6

◆◆

CONIFER LODGE

159 Eynsham Road, Botley, Oxford, OX2 9NE
T: (01865) 862280

Bedrooms: 1 single, 1 double, 1 triple
Bathrooms: 3 en suite

Parking for 8

B&B per night:
S £32.00–£40.00
D £56.00–£62.00

OPEN All year round

Quiet house on the outskirts of Oxford city, overlooking farmland and offering a warm, friendly welcome. On frequent bus route. Plenty of off-street parking.

◆◆◆

FIVE MILE VIEW GUEST HOUSE

528 Banbury Road, Oxford, OX2 8EG
T: (01865) 558747 & 07802 758366
F: (01865) 558747
E: fivemileview@cableinet.co.uk
I: www.oxfordpages.co.uk/fivemileview

Bedrooms: 2 double, 2 twin, 1 triple
Bathrooms: 5 en suite

Parking for 6
CC: Barclaycard, Delta, Eurocard, Mastercard, Solo, Switch, Visa

B&B per night:
S Min £40.00
D Min £50.00

OPEN All year round

Well appointed, family-run guesthouse offering friendly service.

◆◆◆◆

HIGH HEDGES

8 Cumnor Hill, Oxford, OX2 9HA
T: (01865) 863395
F: (01865) 437351
E: tompkins@btinternet.com

Bedrooms: 1 single, 2 double, 2 triple
Bathrooms: 3 en suite, 1 public

Parking for 6
CC: Barclaycard, Eurocard, Mastercard, Visa

B&B per night:
S £24.00–£27.00
D £46.00–£50.00

OPEN All year round

Close to city centre. High standard of accommodation, including en suite rooms with TV/Sky and tea/coffee facilities, making your stay a comfortable one.

OXFORD continued

◆◆◆ **HIGHFIELD WEST**
188 Cumnor Hill, Oxford, OX2 9PJ
T: (01865) 863007
E: highfieldwest@email.msn.com

Bedrooms: 2 single,
1 double, 1 twin,
1 family room
Bathrooms: 3 en suite,
1 public

Parking for 6

B&B per night:
S £25.00–£29.00
D £45.00–£56.00

OPEN All year round

Non-smoking. Comfortable accommodation with good access to city centre and ring road. Large outdoor, heated swimming pool (summer season only). Vegetarians welcome.

◆◆ **ISIS GUEST HOUSE**
45-53 Iffley Road, Oxford, OX4 1ED
T: (01865) 248894 & 242466
F: (01865) 243492

Bedrooms: 12 single,
6 double, 17 twin,
2 triple
Bathrooms: 14 en suite,
10 public

Parking for 18
CC: Barclaycard, Eurocard,
Mastercard, Visa

B&B per night:
S £24.00–£30.00
D £48.00–£52.00

OPEN Jul–Sep

Modernised, Victorian, city centre guesthouse within walking distance of colleges and shops. Easy access to ring road.

◆◆◆◆

Immaculate, spacious, privately owned hotel located in attractive leafy area of Victorian houses, 1.5 miles city centre. Bedrooms equipped with a kitchenette containing fridge, microwave, tea and coffee making facilities, telephone and TV, comfortable chairs, dining table and desk. Restaurants and shops are located within 10 minutes' walk.

MARLBOROUGH HOUSE HOTEL

321 Woodstock Road, Oxford, OX2 7NY
T: (01865) 311321
F: (01865) 515329
E: enquiries@marlbhouse.win-uk.net
I: www.oxfordcity.co.uk/hotels/marlborough

Bedrooms: 2 single,
8 double, 4 twin, 2 triple
Bathrooms: 16 en suite,
1 public

Parking for 6
CC: Amex, Delta, Diners,
Eurocard, JCB,
Mastercard, Solo, Switch,
Visa

B&B per night:
S £70.00–£70.00
D £81.00–£81.00

OPEN All year round

◆◆◆ **MILKA'S GUEST HOUSE**
379 Iffley Road, Oxford, OX4 4DP
T: (01865) 778458
F: (01865) 776477
E: reservations@milkas.co.uk
I: www.milkas.co.uk

Bedrooms: 3 double
Bathrooms: 1 en suite,
1 public

Parking for 3
CC: Amex, Barclaycard,
Delta, Eurocard,
Mastercard, Solo, Switch,
Visa, Visa Electron

B&B per night:
S £25.00–£35.00
D £45.00–£55.00

OPEN All year round

Pleasant semi-detached house on main road, 1 mile from city centre.

◆◆◆ **MULBERRY GUEST HOUSE**
265 London Road, Headington,
Oxford, OX3 9EH
T: (01865) 767114
F: (01865) 767114
E: mulberryguesthouse@hotmail.com

Bedrooms: 3 double,
2 twin
Bathrooms: 4 en suite,
1 private

Parking for 5
CC: Barclaycard, Eurocard,
Mastercard, Visa

B&B per night:
S £38.00–£50.00
D £50.00–£60.00

OPEN All year round

Detached house with parking, close to Brookes University and local hospitals. Bus stops outside for Oxford colleges, London Heathrow and Gatwick. Good base for touring.

CHECK THE MAPS

The colour maps at the front of this guide show all the cities, towns and villages for which you will find accommodation entries.
Refer to the town index to find the page on which they are listed.

◆◆◆

NEWTON HOUSE

82-84 Abingdon Road, Oxford, OX1 4PL
T: (01865) 240561
F: (01865) 244647
E: newton.house@btinternet.com
I: www.guesthouse-oxford.com

B&B per night:
S £30.00–£54.00
D £38.00–£62.00

OPEN All year round

Centrally situated. Two handsome Victorian townhouses linked to form a sizable guesthouse, retaining many original features and period furniture. Conveniently located close to the city's restaurants, pubs and shops, university and River Thames (with punting).

Bedrooms: 5 double, 1 twin, 7 triple
Bathrooms: 10 en suite, 3 public

Parking for 8
CC: Amex, Barclaycard, Delta, Eurocard, JCB, Maestro, Mastercard, Solo, Switch, Visa, Visa Electron

---

◆◆◆

THE OLD BLACK HORSE HOTEL

102 St Clements, Oxford, OX4 1AR
T: (01865) 244691
F: (01865) 242771

B&B per night:
S £50.00–£50.00
D £85.00–£85.00

OPEN All year round

Former coaching inn, c1650, privately owned. Large, secure car park. Close to the historic High Magdalen Bridge, colleges, riverside walks and the city centre. The area has a wide variety of restaurants. Easy access M40 north and south. London and airport coaches stop close by.

Bedrooms: 1 single, 4 double, 3 twin, 2 triple
Bathrooms: 10 en suite, 1 public

Lunch available
EM 1830 (LO 2030)
Parking for 25
CC: Amex, Barclaycard, Delta, Mastercard, Switch, Visa

◆◆◆

PICKWICKS GUEST HOUSE

15-17 London Road, Headington, Oxford, OX3 7SP
T: (01865) 750487
F: (01865) 742208
E: pickwicks@x-stream.co.uk
I: www.oxfordcity.co.uk/accom/pickwicks/

B&B per night:
S £28.00–£38.00
D £48.00–£58.00

OPEN All year round

Comfortable, friendly, family-run guesthouse within five minutes' drive of Oxford ring road and M40 motorway. Nearby coach stop for 24-hour service to central London, Heathrow and Gatwick airports. Close to Oxford Brookes university, John Radcliffe, Nuffield and Churchill hospitals. Translation service available.

Bedrooms: 3 single, 5 double, 3 twin, 4 triple
Bathrooms: 9 en suite, 2 public

Parking for 10
CC: Amex, Barclaycard, Delta, Diners, Eurocard, Mastercard, Solo, Switch, Visa, Visa Electron

---

◆◆◆◆

PINE CASTLE HOTEL
290 Iffley Road, Oxford, OX4 4AE
T: (01865) 241497 & 728887
F: (01865) 727230
E: stay@pinecastle.co.uk
I: www.oxfordcity.co.uk/accommodation/pinecastle

Bedrooms: 5 double, 2 twin, 1 family room
Bathrooms: 8 en suite

Parking for 4
CC: Amex, Barclaycard, Delta, Eurocard, JCB, Maestro, Mastercard, Solo, Switch, Visa, Visa Electron

B&B per night:
D Min £65.00

OPEN All year round

Midway between ringroad and city centre, with excellent bus service. Breakfasts tailored to suit all tastes include home-made yoghurt and muesli. River walks.

OXFORD continued

♦♦♦ **RIVER HOTEL**

17 Botley Road, Oxford, OX2 0AA	Bedrooms: 5 single,	Parking for 25
T: (01865) 243475	8 double, 2 twin, 5 triple	CC: Barclaycard, Eurocard,
F: (01865) 724306	Bathrooms: 17 en suite,	Mastercard, Visa
	1 private, 2 private	
	showers	

B&B per night:
S £50.00–£65.00
D £70.00–£81.00

OPEN All year round

Excellent location on River Thames walk. Residents' bar, car park. Walking distance to city colleges, bus/rail stations. "Large enough to be comfortable, small enough to be friendly."

🅰️🐕♿🕯️📧🖥️💧🛗§♨️📺🛏️🛌☎️🍴50 🎿❄️✈️🚜

♦♦♦ **SPORTSVIEW GUEST HOUSE**

106-110 Abingdon Road, Oxford,	Bedrooms: 6 single,	Parking for 8
OX1 4PX	3 double, 6 twin, 4 triple,	CC: Delta, Eurocard,
T: (01865) 244268 & 07798 818190	1 family room	Mastercard, Solo, Switch,
F: (01865) 249270	Bathrooms: 12 en suite,	Visa, Visa Electron
E: stay@sportsview.guest-house.	3 public, 1 private	
freeserve.co.uk	shower	

B&B per night:
S £25.00–£35.00
D £40.00–£59.00

OPEN All year round

Guesthouse with garden, located near university and city centre. Views over tennis and cricket grounds and the River Thames. Open air swimming pool nearby.

🅰️🐕♿🕯️🗂️💧🛗UL§✂️♨️📺🛏️🛌☀️✈️🚜🏨SP🚽T

PANGBOURNE, Berkshire Map ref 2C2

♦♦♦ **WEIR VIEW HOUSE**

9 Shooters Hill, Pangbourne,	Bedrooms: 1 double,	Parking for 10
Reading, Berkshire RG8 7DZ	1 twin, 1 triple	CC: Barclaycard, Delta,
T: (01189) 842120	Bathrooms: 3 en suite,	Eurocard, Mastercard,
F: (01189) 842120	1 public	Switch, Visa, Visa Electron

B&B per night:
S Max £28.00
D Max £55.00

OPEN All year round

House with superb views overlooking falling waters of weir and river. Adjacent to excellent village shops, restaurants and rail-link.

🐕3🗂️💧🏆UL§✂️♨️📺🛏️🛌☀️🚜🏨🔕SPT

PETERSFIELD, Hampshire Map ref 2C3 *Tourist Information Centre Tel: (01730) 268829*

♦♦♦ **HEATH FARMHOUSE**

Heath Road East, Petersfield,	Bedrooms: 1 double,	Parking for 5
GU31 4HU	1 twin, 1 family room	
T: (01730) 264709	Bathrooms: 2 en suite,	
E: prue@scurfield.co.uk	1 private, 1 public	

B&B per night:
S £20.00–£25.00
D £36.00–£38.00

OPEN All year round

Georgian farmhouse with lovely views, large garden. Surrounded by quiet farmland only three-quarters of a mile from town centre. Within easy reach of Portsmouth, Chichester, Winchester.

🅰️🐕🗂️💧🏆UL🍴§✂️♨️🛌☀️🚜🏨T◉

♦♦♦ **1 THE SPAIN**

Petersfield, GU32 3JZ	Bedrooms: 1 double,	
T: (01730) 263261 & 261678	2 twin	
E: allantarver@cw.co.net	Bathrooms: 1 en suite,	
	1 public	

B&B per night:
S £20.00–£25.00
D £40.00–£45.00

OPEN All year round

18thC house with charming walled garden, in conservation area of Petersfield. Good eating places nearby, lovely walks, plenty to see and do.

🐕🗂️💧UL§✂️♨️📺🛌☀️🚜🏨

POOLE, Dorset Map ref 2B3 *Tourist Information Centre Tel: (01202) 253253*

♦♦♦♦ **HARLEQUINS B & B**

134 Ringwood Road, Poole, Dorset	Bedrooms: 1 double,	Parking for 5
BH14 0RP	1 triple	
T: (01202) 677624 (Answerphone)	Bathrooms: 2 en suite	
& 07887 888074 (Mobile)		
E: harlequins@tinyworld.co		

B&B per night:
S £28.00–£30.00
D £46.00–£50.00

OPEN All year round

Recently refurbished to extremely high standard offering individually designed luxury rooms, en suites and a warm welcome. Colour TV, tea/coffee, hairdryers, varied menu. Access all day.

🐕🗂️💧🏆UL§✂️🛌☀️✈️🚜T

HALF BOARD PRICES Half board prices are given per person, but in some cases these may be based on double/twin occupancy.

PORTSMOUTH & SOUTHSEA Hampshire Map ref 2C3 Tourist Information Centre Tel: (023) 9282 6722

◆◆◆ BEMBELL COURT HOTEL

69 Festing Road, Southsea,
Portsmouth, Hampshire PO4 0NQ
T: (023) 9273 5915 & 9275 0497
F: (023) 9275 6497
E: keith@bembell.freeserve.co.uk

Bedrooms: 2 single,
4 double, 3 twin, 1 triple,
2 family rooms
Bathrooms: 10 en suite,
3 public

EM 1800 (LO 1900)
Parking for 12
CC: Amex, Barclaycard,
Delta, Diners, Mastercard,
Visa

B&B per night:
S £35.00–£39.50
D £46.00–£49.50

OPEN All year round

Friendly, family-run hotel ideally situated in Portsmouth's prime holiday area. A short stroll from shops, restaurants, pubs, boating lake, Rose Gardens. Close to ferries.

◆◆◆ THE ELMS GUEST HOUSE

48 Victoria Road South, Southsea,
Hampshire PO5 2BT
T: (023) 9282 3924
F: (023) 9282 3924
E: TheElmsGH@aol.com

Bedrooms: 1 double,
3 triple, 1 family room
Bathrooms: 5 en suite

Parking for 2
CC: Barclaycard, Delta,
Eurocard, JCB,
Mastercard, Solo, Switch,
Visa

B&B per night:
S £19.00–£45.00
D £38.00–£45.00

OPEN All year round

Warm, friendly guesthouse within 8 minutes' walk of the seafront and restaurants. Close to the maritime attractions and ferry ports.

◆◆◆◆ HAMILTON HOUSE

95 Victoria Road North, Southsea,
Portsmouth, Hampshire PO5 1PS
T: (023) 9282 3502
F: (023) 9282 3502
E: sandra@hamiltonhouse.co.uk.
I: www.resort-guide.co.uk/
portsmouth/hamilton

Bedrooms: 1 single,
2 double, 3 twin, 1 triple,
2 family rooms
Bathrooms: 5 en suite,
2 public

CC: Barclaycard, Delta,
Mastercard, Switch, Visa

B&B per night:
S £20.00–£24.00
D £40.00–£48.00

OPEN All year round

Delightful Victorian townhouse B&B. Five minutes continental/IOW ferry ports, centres, stations, university, historic ships/museums. Ideal touring base. Breakfast served from 6.15am. Proprietors – Graham and Sandra Tubb.

◆◆◆◆ OAKDALE

71 St Ronans Road, Southsea,
Hampshire PO4 0PP
T: (023) 9273 7358
F: (023) 9273 7358
E: oakdale@btinternet.com

Bedrooms: 2 single,
2 double, 2 twin
Bathrooms: 6 en suite

EM 1800 (LO 1900)
CC: Amex, Barclaycard,
Eurocard, JCB,
Mastercard, Visa

B&B per night:
S £24.00–£34.00
D £41.00–£47.00

OPEN Feb–Dec

Elegant, comfortable Edwardian house, 5 minutes from flower-filled seafront. Handy for historic ships, shops, restaurants, and continental ferries. Experience the Oakdale welcome!

QUAINTON, Buckinghamshire Map ref 2C1

◆◆◆ WOODLANDS FARMHOUSE

Doddershall, Quainton, Aylesbury,
HP22 4DE
T: (01296) 770225

Bedrooms: 1 double,
2 twin, 1 family room
Bathrooms: 4 en suite

Parking for 8

B&B per night:
S Min £25.00
D Min £50.00

OPEN All year round

18thC farmhouse offering peaceful accommodation in 11 acres of grounds. Large en suite rooms with individual entrances in barn conversion.

READING, Berkshire Map ref 2C2 *Tourist Information Centre Tel: (0118) 956 6226*

◆◆◆ DITTISHAM GUEST HOUSE

63 Tilehurst Road, Reading,
Berkshire RG30 2JL
T: (0118) 956 9483 &
07889 605193

Bedrooms: 4 single,
1 twin
Bathrooms: 3 en suite,
1 public

Parking for 7
CC: Barclaycard, Delta,
Mastercard, Switch, Visa

B&B per night:
S £27.00–£35.00
D £40.00–£55.00

OPEN All year round

Renovated Edwardian property with garden, in a quiet but central location. Good value and quality. On bus routes for centre of town. Car park.

IDEAS   For ideas on places to visit refer to the introduction at the beginning of this section.

READING continued

◆◆◆◆ 10 GREYSTOKE ROAD
Caversham, Reading, Berkshire
RG4 5EL
T: (01189) 475784

Bedrooms: 2 single,
1 double
Bathrooms: 1 public

Parking for 2

B&B per night:
S £30.00–£35.00
D £50.00–£55.00

OPEN All year round

Private home in quiet, residential area. TV lounge, tea and coffee-making facilities. Non-smokers only, please.

◆◆◆ THE SIX BELLS
Beenham Village, Beenham,
Reading, Berkshire RG7 5NX
T: (0118) 971 3368

Bedrooms: 1 single,
2 double, 1 twin
Bathrooms: 4 en suite

Lunch available
EM 1830 (LO 2130)
Parking for 35
CC: Barclaycard, Delta,
Eurocard, Mastercard,
Switch, Visa

B&B per night:
S Min £42.00
D Min £49.00

HB per person:
DY Min £52.00

OPEN All year round

Village pub, overlooking farmland. Four miles from Theale M4 junction 12, 1 mile off A4. Newly-built bedrooms. Home cooking always available – varied menu.

RINGWOOD, Hampshire Map ref 2B3

◆◆◆

FRASER HOUSE
Salisbury Road, Blashford, Ringwood,
BH24 3PB
T: (01425) 473958

B&B per night:
S Min £30.00
D Min £45.00

OPEN All year round

Overlooking the Avon Valley, on edge of the New Forest, famous for its ponies, deer and picturesque scenery. Short walk to the market town of Ringwood. Convenient for visiting Stonehenge and the cathedral city of Salisbury. A short drive to Southampton and Poole, or to Christchurch, Bournemouth and the South Coast beaches.

Bedrooms: 2 double,
2 twin
Bathrooms: 4 en suite

Parking for 6
CC: Barclaycard, Delta,
JCB, Mastercard, Switch,
Visa

ROMSEY, Hampshire Map ref 2C3 *Tourist Information Centre Tel: (01794) 512987*

◆◆◆ 4 NEWTON LANE
Romsey, SO51 8GZ
T: (01794) 514150

Bedrooms: 1 single,
1 twin
Bathrooms: 1 public

Parking for 5

B&B per night:
S £20.00–£20.00
D £40.00–£40.00

OPEN All year round

Pretty town cottage ringing quiet square behind historic Norman abbey. Public car parking facilities. Restaurants, inns walking distance. Hampshire, Wiltshire, New Forest at your fingertips!

RYDE, Isle of Wight Map ref 2C3 *Tourist Information Centre Tel: (01983) 562905*

◆◆◆◆ SILLWOOD ACRE
Church Road, Binstead, Ryde,
Isle of Wight PO33 3TB
T: (01983) 563553
E: sillwood.acre@virginnet.co.uk

Bedrooms: 2 double,
1 triple
Bathrooms: 3 en suite

Parking for 3

B&B per night:
S £17.00–£19.00
D £34.00–£38.00

OPEN All year round

Large Victorian house near Ryde, convenient for the ferry and hovercraft terminals. Three spacious en suite rooms. Non-smoking.

MAP REFERENCES The map references refer to the colour maps at the front of this guide. The first figure is the map number; the letter and figure which follow indicate the grid reference on the map.

SANDOWN, Isle of Wight Map ref 2C3 *Tourist Information Centre Tel: (01983) 403886*

♦♦♦

IONA GUEST HOUSE
44 Sandown Road, Lake, Sandown,
Isle of Wight PO36 9JT
T: (01983) 402741
F: (01983) 402741
E: ionahotel@netscapeonline.co.uk

Bedrooms: 3 single,
2 double, 1 twin,
3 family rooms
Bathrooms: 4 en suite,
2 public

Parking for 6
CC: Amex, Barclaycard,
Mastercard, Visa

B&B per night:
S £15.00–£19.00
D £30.00–£38.00

HB per person:
DY £20.00–£24.00

OPEN All year round

Family-run guesthouse situated between Sandown and Shanklin, 5 minutes' walk from local station and cliff path, 10 minutes' walk from beautiful Lake beach.

SELBORNE, Hampshire Map ref 2C2

♦♦♦♦

8 GOSLINGS CROFT
Selborne, Alton, GU34 3HZ
T: (01420) 511285
F: (01420) 587451

Bedrooms: 1 twin
Bathrooms: 1 en suite

Parking for 1

B&B per night:
S £20.00–£20.00
D £40.00–£40.00

OPEN All year round

Family home, set on edge of historic village, adjacent to National Trust land. Ideal base for walking and touring. Non-smokers only, please.

♦♦♦♦

IVANHOE
Oakhanger, Selborne, Alton,
GU35 9JG
T: (01420) 473464

Bedrooms: 1 twin
Bathrooms: 1 private

Parking for 1

B&B per night:
S Max £25.00
D Max £36.00

OPEN All year round

Comfortable, homely accommodation in a small hamlet, with views to open countryside. Central base for tourists and business people. Good pub nearby.

SHAFTESBURY, Dorset Map ref 2B3 *Tourist Information Centre Tel: (01747) 853514*

♦♦♦♦

THE GROVE ARMS INN
Ludwell, Shaftesbury, SP7 9ND
T: (01747) 828328
F: (01747) 828960
I: www.wiltshireacommodation.com

B&B per night:
S £40.00–£45.00
D £50.00–£55.00

OPEN Jan–Nov
& Christmas

Grade II Listed 17thC inn, completely refurbished. Very attractive en suite bedrooms. Good position for walking in beautiful countryside. We pride ourselves on the quality of our food and service.

Bedrooms: 2 single,
2 double, 2 twin
Bathrooms: 6 en suite

Lunch available
EM 1800 (LO 2130)
Parking for 40
CC: Barclaycard, Delta,
Mastercard, Switch, Visa

SHANKLIN, Isle of Wight Map ref 2C3 *Tourist Information Centre Tel: (01983) 862942*

♦♦♦♦

CULHAM LODGE HOTEL
31 Landguard Manor Road, Shanklin,
Isle of Wight PO37 7HZ
T: (01983) 862880
F: (01983) 862880
E: metcalf@culham99.freeserve.co.uk
I: www.isleofwighthotel.co.uk

B&B per night:
S £23.00–£24.00
D £46.00–£48.00

HB per person:
DY £30.00–£31.00

OPEN Jan–Nov

Charming hotel in beautiful tree-lined road. Heated swimming pool in secluded garden, conservatory, home cooking and personal service. All rooms have TV with satellite channels, tea-maker and hairdryer. Culham Lodge is well placed for country walks and cycle trails. We can book your ferry crossing and save you money!

Bedrooms: 1 single,
4 double, 5 twin
Bathrooms: 10 en suite,
1 public

EM 1800 (LO 1800)
Parking for 8
CC: Barclaycard,
Mastercard, Visa

SHANKLIN continued

◆◆◆ HAZELWOOD HOTEL

14 Clarence Road, Shanklin, Isle of Wight PO37 7BH T: (01983) 862824 F: (01983) 862824 E: barbara.tubbs@thehazelwood.free-online.co.uk I: www.thehazelwood.free-online.co.uk	Bedrooms: 1 single, 3 double, 2 twin, 2 family rooms; suites available Bathrooms: 8 en suite, 1 public	EM 1800 (LO 1600) Parking for 5 CC: Amex, Barclaycard, Diners, Eurocard, Mastercard, Visa	B&B per night: **S £19.00–£21.00** **D £38.00–£42.00** HB per person: **DY £26.00–£28.00** OPEN All year round

Detached, friendly, comfortable hotel in a quiet tree-lined road, close to all amenities. Daily bookings taken. Parking available. All rooms en suite, family suites available.

◆◆◆ RYEDALE PRIVATE HOTEL

3 Atherley Road, Shanklin, Isle of Wight PO37 7AT T: (01983) 862375 & 07831 413233 F: (01983) 862375 E: ryedale@isleofwight5.fsnet.co.uk I: www.smoothhound.co.uk/hotels/ryedalep.html	Bedrooms: 2 single, 2 double, 1 triple, 3 family rooms Bathrooms: 5 en suite, 2 public	CC: Amex, Barclaycard, Delta, Eurocard, JCB, Maestro, Mastercard, Solo, Switch, Visa, Visa Electron	B&B per night: **S £17.50–£20.50** **D £35.00–£41.00** OPEN Apr–Oct

Small and friendly, close to all amenities. Child stays free until late July and from early September. Discounts in selected local restaurants. Free parking available.

SOULDERN, Oxfordshire Map ref 2C1

◆◆◆ TOWER FIELDS

Tusmore Road, Souldern, Bicester, OX6 9HY T: (01869) 346554 F: (01869) 345157 E: hgould@souldern.powernet.co.uk	Bedrooms: 1 single, 1 twin, 1 family room Bathrooms: 3 en suite	Parking for 22	B&B per night: **S £28.00–£30.00** **D £50.00–£50.00** OPEN All year round

Converted 18thC cottages and 14-acre smallholding with rare breeds of poultry, sheep and cattle. Small collection of vintage cars.

SOUTHAMPTON, Hampshire Map ref 2C3 *Tourist Information Centre Tel: (023) 8022 1106*

◆◆◆ ASHELEE LODGE

36 Atherley Road, Shirley, Southampton, Hampshire SO15 5DQ T: (023) 8022 2095 F: (023) 8022 2095	Bedrooms: 1 single, 1 double, 1 twin, 1 triple Bathrooms: 1 public	EM Parking for 2 CC: Barclaycard, Eurocard, Mastercard, Visa	B&B per night: **S £18.00–£20.00** **D £36.00–£40.00** OPEN All year round

Homely guesthouse, garden with pool. Half a mile from city centre, near station, M27 and Red Funnel ferryport. Good touring base for New Forest, Salisbury and Winchester. Near university.

◆◆◆ EATON COURT HOTEL

32 Hill Lane, Southampton, Hampshire SO15 5AY T: (023) 8022 3081 F: (023) 8032 2006 E: ecourthot@aol.com	Bedrooms: 8 single, 3 double, 3 twin Bathrooms: 7 en suite, 2 public, 1 private shower	EM 1830 (LO 2000) Parking for 12 CC: Amex, Barclaycard, Delta, Diners, JCB, Mastercard, Solo, Switch, Visa, Visa Electron	B&B per night: **S £27.00–£31.50** **D £42.00–£46.00** HB per person: **DY £38.00–£42.00** OPEN All year round

Comfortable, small, owner-run hotel for business or leisure stays. Bedrooms have all amenities and a generous traditional breakfast is served.

NB **IMPORTANT NOTE** Information on accommodation listed in this guide has been supplied by the proprietors. As changes may occur you are advised to check details at the time of booking.

SOUTHAMPTON continued

♦♦♦

VILLA CAPRI GUEST HOUSE

50-52 Archers Road, Southampton,
Hampshire SO15 2LU
T: (023) 8063 2800
F: (023) 8063 0100

B&B per night:
S £22.00–£27.00
D £44.00–£54.00

HB per person:
DY £28.50–£33.50

OPEN All year round

A well established guesthouse in city centre. All modern comforts. Hearty English breakfast, home-made evening meals. Ample parking.

Bedrooms: 7 single, 4 double, 6 twin, 1 family room
Bathrooms: 17 en suite, 2 public

EM 1800 (LO 2000)
Parking for 21
CC: Barclaycard, Mastercard, Visa

SOUTHSEA

See under Portsmouth & Southsea

STEEPLE ASTON, Oxfordshire Map ref 2C1

♦♦♦♦

WESTFIELD FARM MOTEL

Fenway, Steeple Aston, Bicester,
OX6 3SS
T: (01869) 340591
F: (01869) 347594
E: info@westfieldmotel.u-net.com

Bedrooms: 3 double, 2 twin, 1 family room
Bathrooms: 6 en suite

EM 1900 (LO 2030)
Parking for 24
CC: Amex, Barclaycard, Delta, Diners, Eurocard, Mastercard, Switch, Visa

B&B per night:
S £50.00–£55.00
D £65.00–£75.00

OPEN All year round

Converted stable block with comfortable bedroom units. Combined lounge, dining room and bar. Good touring centre. Fringe of Cotswolds, off A4260, 9 miles Banbury, 5 miles Woodstock.

STOCKBRIDGE, Hampshire Map ref 2C2

♦♦♦

CARBERY GUEST HOUSE

Salisbury Hill, Stockbridge, SO20 6EZ
T: (01264) 810771
F: (01264) 811022

B&B per night:
S £28.00–£35.00
D £50.00–£54.00

HB per person:
DY £42.50–£49.50

OPEN All year round

Fine old Georgian house in an acre of landscaped gardens and lawns, overlooking the River Test. Games and swimming facilities, riding and fishing can be arranged. Ideal for touring the South Coast and the New Forest.

Bedrooms: 4 single, 4 double, 2 twin, 1 triple
Bathrooms: 8 en suite, 1 public

EM 1900 (LO 1800)
Parking for 12

STREATLEY, Berkshire Map ref 2C2

♦♦♦♦

PENNYFIELD

The Coombe, Streatley, Reading,
Berkshire RG8 9QT
T: (01491) 872048 &
07774 946182 (Mobile)
F: (01491) 872048
E: mandrvanstone@hotmail.com

Bedrooms: 2 double
Bathrooms: 2 en suite

Parking for 4

B&B per night:
S £49.00–£49.00
D £49.00–£49.00

OPEN All year round

Charming house with terraced garden. Beautiful Thames-Path and Ridgeway routes. Easy access to London, Oxford, Windsor, Reading. Four-poster bed, heated covered spa pool.

WELCOME HOST This is a nationally recognised customer care programme which aims to promote the highest standards of service and a warm welcome. Establishments taking part in this initiative are indicated by the symbol.

STURMINSTER NEWTON, Dorset Map ref 2B3

♦♦♦

THE HOMESTEAD
Hole House Lane,
Sturminster Newton, DT10 2AA
T: (01258) 471390
F: (01258) 471090
E: townsend@dircon.co.uk
I: www.townsend@dircon.co.uk/

Bedrooms: 1 triple,
1 family room
Bathrooms: 2 en suite

Parking for 4

B&B per night:
S £25.00–£25.00
D £40.00–£40.00

OPEN All year round

Spacious bungalow. Views across Dorset hills. Peaceful location, few minutes from pretty town. Ideal touring base for Dorset, Somerset, countryside and coast.

SULHAMSTEAD, Berkshire Map ref 2C2

♦♦♦♦♦
Silver
Award

THE OLD MANOR
Whitehouse Green, Sulhamstead,
Reading, Berkshire RG7 4EA
T: (0118) 983 2423
F: (0118) 983 2423

Bedrooms: 2 double
Bathrooms: 2 en suite

EM
Parking for 6

B&B per night:
S £50.00–£50.00
D £70.00–£70.00

HB per person:
DY £47.50–£62.50

OPEN All year round

A 17thC manor house in rural situation, 2 miles from M4 junction 12. Two suites available, one with dressing room.

SWAY, Hampshire Map ref 2C3

♦♦♦

MANOR FARM
Coombe Lane, Sway, Lymington,
SO41 6BP
T: (01590) 683542

Bedrooms: 1 double,
1 family room
Bathrooms: 2 en suite,
1 public

Parking for 20

B&B per night:
S £20.00–£22.00
D £40.00–£44.00

OPEN All year round

Small working farm. 18thC, Grade II Listed farmhouse, surrounded by open fields and forest. Off B3055 Sway-Brockenhurst road.

♦♦♦♦♦
Gold
Award

THE NURSE'S COTTAGE
Station Road, Sway, Lymington, SO41 6BA
T: (01590) 683402
F: (01590) 683402
E: nurses.cottage@lineone.net
I: www.hantsgov.uk/tourist/hotels

B&B per night:
S £55.00–£65.00
D £95.00–£95.00

HB per person:
DY £50.00–£85.00

OPEN All year round

This popular New Forest restaurant and guest accommodation enjoys an enviable reputation for comfort and good food. Formerly home to Sway village's successive District Nurses, the cottage has been lovingly refurbished in recent years and now boasts an impressive array of awards. Half board bargain breaks for stays of 2+ nights.

Bedrooms: 1 single,
1 double, 1 twin
Bathrooms: 3 en suite

Lunch available
EM 1830 (LO 2030)
Parking for 4
CC: Amex, Barclaycard,
Delta, Eurocard, JCB,
Maestro, Mastercard,
Solo, Switch, Visa, Visa
Electron

USE YOUR *i*s
There are more than 550 Tourist Information Centres throughout England offering friendly help with accommodation and holiday ideas as well as suggestions of places to visit and things to do. You'll find TIC addresses in the local Phone Book.

THRUXTON, Hampshire Map ref 2B2

Silver
Award

◆◆◆◆

MAY COTTAGE

Thruxton, Andover, SP11 8LZ
T: (01264) 771241 & 07768 242166
F: (01264) 771770
E: may.cottage@talk21.com

B&B per night:
S £30.00–£35.00
D £50.00–£60.00

OPEN All year round

May Cottage dates back to 1740 and is situated in the heart of this picturesque tranquil village. All rooms have en suite/private bathrooms, TV, radio and beverage trays. Guests' own sitting room/ dining room. Pretty, secluded garden with stream. Many National Trust and stately homes/gardens within easy reach. Ample private parking. A non-smoking establishment.

Bedrooms: 1 double, 2 twin
Bathrooms: 2 en suite, 1 private

Parking for 4

TWYFORD, Berkshire Map ref 2C2

◆◆◆

CHESHAM HOUSE

79 Wargrave Road, Twyford, Reading, Berkshire RG40 9PE
T: (0118) 932 0428

Bedrooms: 1 double, 1 twin
Bathrooms: 2 en suite

Parking for 6

B&B per night:
S £32.00–£35.00
D £50.00–£55.00

OPEN All year round

In triangle formed by Reading, Maidenhead and Henley-on-Thames. Each room has en suite bathroom, colour TV, refrigerator, tea and coffee facilities. Parking in grounds.

WALLINGFORD, Oxfordshire Map ref 2C2 *Tourist Information Centre Tel: (01491) 826972*

◆◆◆

LITTLE GABLES

166 Crowmarsh Hill, Crowmarsh Gifford, Wallingford, OX10 8BG
T: (01491) 837834 & 07860 148882
F: (01491) 837834
E: jfreeves@globalnet.co.uk
I: www.users.globalnet.co.uk/ ~jfreeves

Bedrooms: 1 double, 1 twin, 1 triple
Bathrooms: 1 en suite, 2 private

Parking for 6

B&B per night:
S £30.00–£35.00
D £55.00–£55.00

OPEN All year round

Detached house, close to Ridgeway and Wallingford. Includes single and family room (cot), or twin, double or triple en suite. Tea/coffee making, colour TV.

WARSASH, Hampshire Map ref 2C3

◆◆◆◆

DORMY HOUSE HOTEL

21 Barnes Lane, Sarisbury Green, Southampton, SO31 7DA
T: (01489) 572626
F: (01489) 573370
E: dormyhousehotel@warsash. globalnet.co.uk
I: www.silverblue.co.uk/dormy

Bedrooms: 3 single, 4 double, 1 twin, 3 triple, 1 family room
Bathrooms: 12 en suite

EM 1830 (LO 1900)
Parking for 14
CC: Barclaycard, Mastercard, Switch, Visa

B&B per night:
S £41.00–£50.00
D £51.00–£60.00

OPEN All year round

Picturesque Victorian house near Hamble River marinas between Southampton and Portsmouth. Professionally run, offering en suite rooms, charming dining room, comfortable lounge and ample parking.

CREDIT CARD BOOKINGS
If you book by telephone and are asked for your credit card number it is advisable to check the proprietor's policy should you cancel your reservation.

◆◆◆◆
Silver
Award

FIELD COTTAGE
St Leonards, Tring, Hertfordshire HP23 6NS
T: (01494) 837602 &
07803 295337 (Mobile)

B&B per night:
S £30.00–£35.00
D £55.00–£60.00

OPEN All year round

Set in the heart of the Chilterns, close to Amersham, Wendover and The Ridgeway, Field Cottage is situated down a bridle path and is surrounded by open fields and woodland. Guests have the use of own large sitting room with doors into the pretty cottage garden. Breakfast is served in the conservatory overlooking the fields.

Bedrooms: 1 single, 1 double, 1 twin
Bathrooms: 2 en suite, 1 private, 1 public

Parking for 4

🛇12 🖫 🖵 ⬇ 🆄 🆂 ✕ 🗚 📺 🕮 🖪 ☼ ✕ 🚗 🆃 ⦿

◆◆◆

MILL FARM HOUSE
Westbury, Brackley,
Northamptonshire NN13 5JS
T: (01280) 704843

Bedrooms: 1 single, 1 double, 1 triple
Bathrooms: 1 en suite, 2 private, 1 public

Parking for 6

B&B per night:
S £20.00–£25.00
D £40.00–£45.00

OPEN All year round

1000-acre mixed farm. Grade II Listed farmhouse, overlooking a colourful garden including a covered heated swimming pool. Situated in the centre of Westbury village.

🛇 🖫 🖵 ⬇ 🆄 🆂 ✕ 🗚 📺 🕮 🖪 ⟲ ▷ ✎ 🚗 🆂🅲 🆂🅿 🏠 🆃

◆◆◆

WESTON GROUNDS FARM
Weston-on-the-Green, Bicester, OX6 8QX
T: (01869) 351168
F: (01869) 350887

B&B per night:
S £30.00–£35.00
D £45.00–£50.00

OPEN All year round

Large stone-built farmhouse situated in pretty countryside on outskirts of village with country pubs and village shop. Convenient for Oxford, Bicester village and Cotswolds.

Bedrooms: 1 single, 2 twin, 1 triple
Bathrooms: 3 en suite, 1 private

Parking for 10

Ⓜ 🛇 🖵 ⬇ 🖳 🆄 🆂 ✕ 🗚 📺 🕮 🖪 ☼ ✕ 🚗 🆃

◆◆◆◆
Silver
Award

ASHTON LODGE
10 Oakley Hill, Wimborne Minster,
BH21 1QH
T: (01202) 883423
F: (01202) 886180
E: ashtonlodge@ukgateway.net
I: www.ashtonlodge.ukgateway.net

B&B per night:
S Min £22.00
D £46.00–£50.00

OPEN All year round

Spacious, detached family house with ample off-street parking. Relaxed friendly atmosphere with all the comforts of home on offer, including a full English breakfast served in the dining room overlooking the attractively laid garden. All bedrooms are centrally heated, tastefully decorated and furnished to a high standard.

Bedrooms: 1 single, 1 twin, 2 triple
Bathrooms: 2 en suite, 2 private

Parking for 4

Ⓜ 🛇 🖫 🖵 ⬇ 🖳 🆄 🛈 🆂 ✕ 🗚 📺 🕮 🖪 ☼ ✕ 🚗

WIMBORNE MINSTER continued

◆◆◆◆

HENBURY FARM

Dorchester Road, Sturminster Marshall,
Wimborne Minster, BH21 3RN
T: (01258) 857306
F: (01258) 857928

B&B per night:
S Min £21.00
D £42.00–£48.00

OPEN All year round

Farmhouse dating back 300 years, with orignal exposed beams in the main reception rooms. The spacious, modernised, centrally-heated home provides a comfortable atmosphere where guests will enjoy the friendly relaxed surroundings during their stay. Sandy beaches and the New Forest are only a 30-minute drive away.

Bedrooms: 1 single, 3 double, 1 twin
Bathrooms: 2 en suite, 1 public

Parking for 10

◆◆◆

TWYNHAM
67 Poole Road, Wimborne Minster, BH21 1QB
T: (01202) 887310

Bedrooms: 2 double, 1 twin
Bathrooms: 2 public

Parking for 2

B&B per night:
S £15.00–£18.00
D £30.00–£36.00

OPEN All year round

Friendly family home, recently refurbished, with vanity unit, TV and beverages in rooms. Within walking distance of town centre.

WINCHESTER, Hampshire Map ref 2C3 *Tourist Information Centre Tel: (01962) 840500*

SANDY LODGE
47 Christchurch Road, Winchester, SO23 9TE
T: (01962) 853385

Bedrooms: 1 single, 3 double, 2 triple, 1 family room
Bathrooms: 6 en suite, 1 private

EM 1900 (LO 2100)
Parking for 6

B&B per night:
S £35.00–£40.00
D £50.00–£60.00

HB per person:
DY £50.00–£65.00

OPEN All year round

Warm, comfortable red brick and stone house, 6 minutes' walk from the city centre and overlooking St Catherine's Hill.

◆◆◆◆

SHAWLANDS

46 Kilham Lane, Winchester, SO22 5QD
T: (01962) 861166
F: (01962) 861166
E: kathy@pollshaw.u-net.com

B&B per night:
S £27.00–£30.00
D £40.00–£46.00

OPEN All year round

Attractive modern house in a quiet, elevated position overlooking open countryside, 1.5 miles from city centre. Bedrooms are spotlessly clean, bright and attractively decorated. Extra comforts include colour TV, hairdryer and welcome tray with tea and coffee. The inviting breakfast includes home-made bread and preserves with fruit from the garden.

Bedrooms: 2 double, 2 twin, 1 triple
Bathrooms: 1 private, 3 public

Parking for 4
CC: Barclaycard, Delta, Eurocard, Mastercard, Visa

ACCESSIBILITY

Look for the symbols which indicate accessibility for wheelchair users. A list of establishments is at the front of this guide.

WINDSOR, Berkshire Map ref 2D2 *Tourist Information Centre Tel: (01753) 743900*

◆◆◆◆ BEAUMONT LODGE

1 Beaumont Road, Windsor,
Berkshire SL4 1HY
T: (01753) 863436 &
07774 841273 (Mobile)
F: (01753) 863436
E: bhamshere@beaumontlodge.
demon.co.uk
I: www.smoothound.co.uk./hotels/
beaulos.html

Bedrooms: 1 double,
2 twin
Bathrooms: 3 en suite

CC: Barclaycard, Delta,
Mastercard, Switch, Visa

B&B per night:
S £50.00–£58.00
D £58.00–£66.00

OPEN All year round

All rooms have colour TV, video, clock/radio alarm, tea/coffee facilities and trouser press. Double has spa bath.

◆◆ CLARENCE HOTEL

9 Clarence Road, Windsor, Berkshire
SL4 5AE
T: (01753) 864436
F: (01753) 857060

Bedrooms: 4 single,
4 double, 6 twin, 4 triple,
2 family rooms
Bathrooms: 20 en suite,
1 public

Parking for 4
CC: Amex, Barclaycard,
Delta, Diners, Eurocard,
JCB, Mastercard, Solo,
Switch, Visa, Visa Electron

B&B per night:
S £35.00–£49.00
D £40.00–£60.00

OPEN All year round

Comfortable hotel with licensed bar and steam room, near town centre, castle and Eton. All rooms en suite, TV, hairdryer, radio and tea-maker. Convenient for Heathrow Airport and Legoland.

◆◆◆ MELROSE HOUSE

53 Frances Road, Windsor,
Berkshire SL4 3AQ
T: (01753) 865328
F: (01753) 865328

Bedrooms: 1 single,
3 double, 2 twin, 1 triple,
2 family rooms
Bathrooms: 9 en suite

Parking for 9
CC: Delta, Mastercard,
Solo, Switch, Visa

B&B per night:
S £50.00–£60.00
D £60.00–£70.00

OPEN All year round

Elegant, detached Victorian residence in the heart of Windsor. Car park at the rear. Only 5 minutes' walk to Windsor Castle. Telephone, clock and radio in all rooms.

◆◆◆ OSCAR HOTEL

65 Vansittart Road, Windsor,
Berkshire SL4 5DB
T: (01753) 830613
F: (01753) 833744

Bedrooms: 4 single,
3 double, 2 twin, 2 triple,
2 family rooms
Bathrooms: 13 en suite

EM 1800 (LO 1930)
Parking for 10
CC: Amex, Barclaycard,
Delta, Diners, Eurocard,
JCB, Maestro, Mastercard,
Solo, Switch, Visa, Visa
Electron

B&B per night:
S £50.00–£60.00
D £60.00–£75.00

HB per person:
DY £35.00–£45.00

OPEN All year round

Fully licensed bar. All rooms en suite with direct-dial telephone, colour TV, tea/coffee facilities. Own car park. Minutes' drive to Legoland and Heathrow.

WITNEY, Oxfordshire Map ref 2C1 *Tourist Information Centre Tel: (01993) 775802*

◆◆◆ THE COURT INN

43 Bridge Street, Witney, OX8 6DA
T: (01993) 703228
I: www.infocourtinn.uk

Bedrooms: 2 single,
3 double, 5 twin
Bathrooms: 7 en suite,
1 public

Lunch available
EM 1900 (LO 2100)
Parking for 12
CC: Barclaycard, Delta,
Eurocard, Mastercard,
Solo, Switch, Visa, Visa
Electron

B&B per night:
S £26.00–£40.00
D £42.00–£55.00

OPEN All year round

Historic inn with dining room and 2 bars. TV and telephone in all bedrooms. Car park. Friendly service.

◆◆ THE WITNEY HOTEL

7 Church Green, Witney, OX8 6AZ
T: (01993) 702137
F: (01993) 705337
E: bookings@thewitneyhotel.co.uk

Bedrooms: 1 single,
5 double, 2 twin,
2 family rooms
Bathrooms: 10 en suite

B&B per night:
S £30.00–£35.00
D £50.00–£80.00

OPEN All year round

A Listed building on historic Church Green.

WOODCOTE, Oxfordshire Map ref 2C2

HEDGES

◆◆◆

South Stoke Road, Woodcote,
Reading, Berkshire RG8 0PL
T: (01491) 680461

Bedrooms: 2 single,
2 twin
Bathrooms: 1 private,
2 public

Parking for 4

B&B per night:
S £17.00–£19.00
D £34.00–£38.00

OPEN All year round

Peaceful, rural situation on edge of village. Historic Area of Outstanding Natural Beauty. Good access Henley, Oxford, Reading (Heathrow link), M4, M40.

WOODSTOCK, Oxfordshire Map ref 2C1 *Tourist Information Centre Tel: (01993) 813276*

◆◆◆

GORSELANDS HALL
Boddington Lane, North Leigh, Witney,
OX8 6PU
T: (01993) 882292
F: (01993) 883629
E: hamilton@gorselandshall.com
I: www.gorselandshall.com

B&B per night:
S £35.00–£40.00
D £45.00–£55.00

OPEN All year round

Old Cotswold-stone farmhouse with oak beams and flagstone floors. All rooms en suite with colour TV. Large secluded garden. Croquet lawn. Tennis court. Snooker, table-tennis. Quiet rural location. Convenient for Oxford, Blenheim Palace and Cotswolds. Stratford 32 miles, Heathrow 1.25 hours by car and London (Paddington) 1.25 by train.

Bedrooms: 1 single,
2 double, 2 family rooms
Bathrooms: 5 en suite

EM 1900 (LO 2100)
Parking for 7
CC: Amex, Barclaycard,
Delta, Diners, Eurocard,
JCB, Maestro, Mastercard,
Solo, Switch, Visa, Visa
Electron

THE LAURELS

◆◆◆◆
Silver
Award

Hensington Road, Woodstock,
OX20 1JL
T: (01993) 812583
F: (01993) 812583
I: www.smoothhound.co.uk/hotels/
thelaur.html

Bedrooms: 2 double,
1 twin
Bathrooms: 2 en suite,
1 private

Parking for 3
CC: Barclaycard, Delta,
Mastercard, Solo, Switch,
Visa, Visa Electron

B&B per night:
S £40.00–£45.00
D £50.00–£55.00

OPEN All year round

Fine Victorian house, charmingly furnished with an emphasis on comfort and quality. Just off town centre and a short walk from Blenheim Palace.

SHEPHERDS HALL INN

◆◆◆

Witney Road, Freeland, Witney,
OX8 8HQ
T: (01993) 881256
F: (01993) 883455

Bedrooms: 1 single,
1 double, 2 twin, 1 triple
Bathrooms: 5 en suite

Lunch available
EM 1830 (LO 2100)
Parking for 50
CC: Barclaycard, Delta,
JCB, Mastercard, Solo,
Switch, Visa

B&B per night:
S £25.00–£35.00
D £45.00–£50.00

OPEN All year round

Well-appointed inn offering good accommodation. All rooms en suite. Ideally situated for Oxford, Woodstock and the Cotswolds, on the A4095 Woodstock to Witney road.

TOWN INDEX
This can be found at the back of the guide. If you know where you want to stay, the index will give you the page number listing accommodation in your chosen town, city or village.

WROXALL, Isle of Wight Map ref 2C3

Rating
Applied For

LITTLE SPAN FARM

Rew Lane, Wroxall, Ventnor, Isle of Wight
PO38 3AU
T: (01983) 852419
E: info@spanfarm.co.uk
I: www.spanfarm.co.uk

B&B per night:
S £16.00–£38.00
D £32.00–£38.00

OPEN All year round

17thC stone farmhouse on working sheep and arble farm in Area of Outstanding Natural Beauty. Three double bedrooms with en suite bathrooms, 1 twin with private bathroom. Colour TV and coffee/tea-making facilities in rooms. Reduced rates for children, dogs welcome by arrangement. Garden, off-road car parking. Non-smoking.

Bedrooms: 3 double,
1 twin
Bathrooms: 3 en suite,
1 private

Parking for 4

USE YOUR *i*s

There are more than 550 Tourist Information Centres throughout England offering friendly help with accommodation and holiday ideas as well as suggestions of places to visit and things to do. There may well be a centre in your home town which can help you before you set out. You'll find addresses in the local Phone Book.

A brief guide to the main Towns and Villages offering accommodation in the SOUTH OF ENGLAND

A ALTON, HAMPSHIRE - Pleasant old market town standing on the Pilgrim's Way, with some attractive Georgian buildings. The parish church still bears the scars of bullet marks, evidence of a bitter struggle between the Roundheads and the Royalists.

• **AMERSHAM, BUCKINGHAMSHIRE** - Old town with many fine buildings, particularly in the High Street. There are several interesting old inns.

• **ANDOVER, HAMPSHIRE** - Town that achieved importance from the wool trade and now has much modern development. A good centre for visiting places of interest.

• **ASCOT, BERKSHIRE** - Small country town famous for its racecourse which was founded by Queen Anne. The race meeting each June is attended by the Royal Family.

• **ASHURST, HAMPSHIRE** - Small village on the A35, on the edge of the New Forest and three miles north-east of Lyndhurst. Easy access to beautiful forest lawns.

• **AYLESBURY, BUCKINGHAMSHIRE** - Historic county town in the Vale of Aylesbury. The cobbled market square has a Victorian clock tower and the 15th C King's Head Inn (National Trust). Interesting county museum and 13th C parish church.

B BANBURY, OXFORDSHIRE - Famous for its cattle market, cakes, nursery rhyme and Cross. Founded in Saxon times, it has some fine houses and interesting old inns. A good centre for touring Warwickshire and the Cotswolds.

• **BASINGSTOKE, HAMPSHIRE** - Rapidly developing commercial and industrial centre. The town is surrounded by charming villages and places to visit.

• **BEACONSFIELD, BUCKINGHAMSHIRE** - Former coaching town with several inns still surviving. The old town has many fine houses and an interesting church. Beautiful countryside and beech woods nearby.

• **BEAULIEU, HAMPSHIRE** - Beautifully situated among woods and hills on the Beaulieu river, the village is both charming and unspoilt. The 13th C ruined Cistercian abbey and 14th C Palace House stand close to the National Motor Museum. There is a maritime museum at Bucklers Hard.

• **BLANDFORD FORUM, DORSET** - Almost completely destroyed by fire in 1731, the town was rebuilt in a handsome Georgian style. The church is large and grand and the town is the hub of a rich farming area.

• **BOLDRE, HAMPSHIRE** - An attractive village with pretty views of the village from the bridge. The white plastered church sits on top of a hill.

• **BONCHURCH, ISLE OF WIGHT** - Sheltered suburb at the foot of St Boniface Down.

• **BOURNEMOUTH, DORSET** - Seaside town set among the pines with a mild climate, sandy beaches and fine coastal views. The town has wide streets with excellent shops, a pier, a pavilion, museums and conference centre.

• **BURFORD, OXFORDSHIRE** - One of the most beautiful Cotswold wool towns with Georgian and Tudor houses, many antique shops and a picturesque High Street sloping to the River Windrush.

• **BURLEY, HAMPSHIRE** - Attractive centre from which to explore the south-west part of the New Forest. There is an ancient earthwork on Castle Hill nearby, which also offers good views.

C CHALFONT ST GILES, BUCKINGHAMSHIRE - Pretty, old village in wooded Chiltern Hills yet only 20 miles from London and a good base for visiting the city. Excellent base for Windsor, Henley, the Thames Valley, Oxford and the Cotswolds.

• **CHARLBURY, OXFORDSHIRE** - Large Cotswold village with beautiful views of the Evenlode Valley just outside the village and close to the ancient Forest of Wychwood.

• **CHIPPING NORTON, OXFORDSHIRE** - Old market town set high in the Cotswolds and an ideal touring centre. The wide market-place contains many 16th C and 17th C stone houses and the Town Hall and Tudor Guildhall.

• **CHRISTCHURCH, DORSET** - Tranquil town lying between the Avon and Stour just before they converge and flow into Christchurch Harbour. A fine 11th C church and the remains of a Norman castle and house can be seen.

• **CORFE CASTLE, DORSET** - One of the most spectacular ruined castles in Britain. Norman in origin, the castle was a Royalist stronghold during the Civil War and held out until 1645. The village had a considerable marble-carving industry in the Middle Ages.

• **CRANBORNE, DORSET** - Village with an interesting Jacobean manor house. Lies south-east of Cranborne Chase, formerly a forest and hunting preserve.

D DEDDINGTON, OXFORDSHIRE - On the edge of the Cotswolds and settled since the Stone Age, this is the only village in England to have been granted a full Coat of Arms, displayed on the 16th C Town Hall in the picturesque market square. Many places of interest include the Church of St Peter and St Paul.

E EDGCOTT, BUCKINGHAMSHIRE - Small village within easy reach of Aylesbury, Milton Keynes and Bicester.

F FAREHAM, HAMPSHIRE - Lies on a quiet backwater of Portsmouth Harbour. The High Street is lined with fine Georgian buildings.

• **FORDINGBRIDGE, HAMPSHIRE** - On the north-west edge of the New Forest. A medieval bridge crosses the Avon at this point and gave the town its name. A good centre for walking, exploring and fishing.

• **FRESHWATER, ISLE OF WIGHT** - This part of the island is associated with Tennyson, who lived in the village for 30 years. A monument on Tennyson's Down commemorates the poet.

G GODSHILL, ISLE OF WIGHT - Noted for its conspicuous church on its hill top site. There is a fine 15th C wall painting of Jesus crucified on a lily cross in the south transept.

• **GORING, OXFORDSHIRE** - Riverside town on the Oxfordshire/Berkshire border, linked by an attractive bridge to Streatley with views to the Goring Gap.

H HAMBLEDON, HAMPSHIRE - In a valley, surrounded by wooded downland and marked by an air of Georgian prosperity. It was here that cricket was given its first proper rules. The Bat and Ball Inn at Broadhalfpenny Down is the cradle of cricket.

• **HAYLING ISLAND, HAMPSHIRE** - Small island of historic interest, surrounded by natural harbours and with fine sandy beaches, linked to the mainland by an attractive bridge under which boats sail. Birthplace of windsurfing and home to many international sailing events.

• **HENLEY-ON-THAMES, OXFORDSHIRE** - The famous Thames Regatta is held in this prosperous and attractive town at the beginning of July each year. The town has many Georgian buildings and old coaching inns and the parish church has some fine monuments.

TOWN INDEX

This can be found at the back of this guide. If you know where you want to stay, the index will give you the page number listing accommodation in your chosen town, city or village.

- **HIGH WYCOMBE, BUCKINGHAMSHIRE** - Famous for furniture-making, historic examples of which feature in the museum. The 18th C Guildhall and the octagonal market house were designed by the Adam brothers. West Wycombe Park and Hughenden Manor (National Trust) are nearby.

- **HUNGERFORD, BERKSHIRE** - Attractive town on the Avon Canal and the River Kennet, famous for its fishing. It has a wide High Street and many antique shops. Nearby is the Tudor manor of Littlecote with its large Roman mosaic.

- **HYTHE, HAMPSHIRE** - Waterside village with spectacular views over Southampton Water. Marina with distinctive "fishing village" style development, 117-year-old pier, wide range of interesting shops.

- **K KINGSCLERE, HAMPSHIRE** - Small town, until the late 19th C the largest parish in Hampshire. Within easy reach of Basingstoke.

- **L LYMINGTON, HAMPSHIRE** - Small, pleasant town with bright cottages and attractive Georgian houses, lying on the edge of the New Forest with a ferry service to the Isle of Wight. A sheltered harbour makes it a busy yachting centre.

- **LYNDHURST, HAMPSHIRE** - The "capital" of the New Forest, surrounded by attractive woodland scenery and delightful villages. The town is dominated by the Victorian Gothic-style church where the original Alice in Wonderland is buried.

- **M MAIDENHEAD, BERKSHIRE** - Attractive town on the River Thames which is crossed by an elegant 18th C bridge and by Brunel's well-known railway bridge. It is a popular place for boating with delightful riverside walks. The Courage Shire Horse Centre is nearby.

- **MARLOW, BUCKINGHAMSHIRE** - Attractive Georgian town on the River Thames, famous for its 19th C suspension bridge. The High Street contains many old houses and there are connections with writers including Shelley and T S Eliot.

- **MARNHULL, DORSET** - Has a fine church and numerous attractive houses.

- **MILFORD-ON-SEA, HAMPSHIRE** - Victorian seaside resort with shingle beach and good bathing, set in pleasant countryside and looking out over the Isle of Wight. Nearby is Hurst Castle, built by Henry VIII. The school chapel, former abbey church, can be visited.

- **MILTON KEYNES, BUCKINGHAMSHIRE** - Designated a New Town in 1967, Milton Keynes offers a wide range of housing and is abundantly planted with trees. It has excellent shopping facilities and 3 centres for leisure and sporting activities. The Open University is based here.

- **MOULSFORD ON THAMES, OXFORDSHIRE** - Small village close to Wallingford and Goring and within easy reach of Abingdon.

- **N NEW MILTON, HAMPSHIRE** - New Forest residential town on the mainline railway.

- **NEWBURY** - Ancient town surrounded by the Downs and on the Kennet and Avon Canal. It has many buildings of interest, including the 17th C Cloth Hall, which is now a museum. The famous racecourse is nearby.

- **NEWPORT PAGNELL, BUCKINGHAMSHIRE** - Busy town situated on 2 rivers with some Georgian as well as modern buildings.

- **O OXFORD, OXFORDSHIRE** - Beautiful university town with many ancient colleges, some dating from the 13th C, and numerous buildings of historic and architectural interest. The Ashmolean Museum has outstanding collections. Lovely gardens and meadows with punting on the Cherwell.

- **P PANGBOURNE, WEST BERKSHIRE** - A pretty stretch of river where the Pang joins the Thames with views of the lock, weir and toll bridge. Once the home of Kenneth Grahame, author of "Wind in the Willows".

- **PETERSFIELD, HAMPSHIRE** - Grew prosperous from the wool trade and was famous as a coaching centre. Its attractive market square is dominated by a statue of William III. Close by are Petersfield Heath with numerous ancient barrows and Butser Hill with magnificent views.

- **POOLE, DORSET** - Tremendous natural harbour makes Poole a superb boating centre. The harbour area is crowded with historic buildings including the 15th C Town Cellars housing a maritime museum.

- **PORTSMOUTH & SOUTHSEA** - There have been connections with the Navy since early times and the first dock was built in 1194. HMS Victory, Nelson's flagship, is here and Charles Dickens' former home is open to the public. Neighbouring Southsea has a promenade with magnificent views of Spithead.

- **Q QUAINTON, BUCKINGHAMSHIRE** - Rural village with many 17th and 18th C monuments, including a large monument which is unsigned. Some Georgian buildings.

- **R READING, BERKSHIRE** - Busy, modern county town with large shopping centre and many leisure and recreation facilities. There are several interesting museums and the Duke of Wellington's Stratfield Saye is nearby.

- **RINGWOOD, HAMPSHIRE** - Market town by the River Avon comprising old cottages, many of them thatched. Although just outside the New Forest, there is heath and woodland nearby and it is a good centre for horse-riding and walking.

- **ROMSEY, HAMPSHIRE** - Town grew up around the important abbey and lies on the banks of the River Test, famous for trout and salmon. Broadlands House, home of the late Lord Mountbatten, is open to the public.

- **RYDE, ISLE OF WIGHT** - The island's chief entry port, connected to Portsmouth by ferries and hovercraft. 7 miles of sandy beaches with a half-mile pier, esplanade and gardens.

- **S SANDOWN, ISLE OF WIGHT** - The 6-mile sweep of Sandown Bay is one of the island's finest stretches, with excellent sands. The pier has a pavilion and sun terrace; the esplanade has amusements, bars, eating-places and gardens.

- **SELBORNE, HAMPSHIRE** - Village made famous by Gilbert White, who was a curate here and is remembered for his classic book "The Natural History of Selborne", published in 1788. His house is now a museum.

- **SHAFTESBURY, DORSET** - Hilltop town with a long history. The ancient and cobbled Gold Hill is one of the most attractive in Dorset. There is an excellent small museum containing a collection of buttons for which the town is famous.

- **SHANKLIN, ISLE OF WIGHT** - Set on a cliff with gentle slopes leading down to the beach, esplanade and marine gardens. The picturesque, old thatched village nestles at the end of the wooded chine.

- **SOUTHAMPTON** - One of Britain's leading seaports with a long history, now a major container port. In the 18th C it became a fashionable resort with the assembly rooms and theatre. The old Guildhall and the Wool House are now museums. Sections of the medieval wall can still be seen.

CONFIRM YOUR BOOKING
You are advised to confirm your booking in writing.

- **STEEPLE ASTON, OXFORDSHIRE** - Oxfordshire village whose church has one of the finest examples of church embroidery in the world. Nearby is the Jacobean Rousham House which stands in William Kent's only surviving landscaped garden.

- **STOCKBRIDGE, HAMPSHIRE** - Set in the Test Valley which has some of the best fishing in England. The wide main street has houses of all styles, mainly Tudor and Georgian.

- **STREATLEY, OXFORDSHIRE** - Pretty village on the River Thames, linked to Goring by an attractive bridge. It has Georgian houses and cottages and beautiful views over the countryside and the Goring Gap.

- **STURMINSTER NEWTON, DORSET** - Every Monday this small town holds a livestock market. One of the bridges over the River Stour is a fine medieval example and bears a plaque declaring that anyone "injuring" it will be deported.

- **SWAY, HAMPSHIRE** - Small village on the south-western edge of the New Forest. It is noted for its 220-ft tower, Peterson's Folly, built in the 1870s by a retired Indian judge to demonstrate the value of concrete as a building material.

- **TWYFORD, HAMPSHIRE** - Stands on the edge of the Loddon water meadows. There is a pleasant group of almshouses built by Sir Richard Harrison in 1640. The 19th C church is notable for the coloured marble on the floor of the baptistry.

- **WALLINGFORD, OXFORDSHIRE** - Site of an ancient ford over the River Thames, now crossed by a 900-ft-long bridge. The town has many timber-framed and Georgian buildings, Gainsborough portraits in the 17th C Town Hall and a few remains of a Norman Castle.

- **WARSASH, HAMPSHIRE** - On the edge of Southampton Water. Warships were built here in Napoleonic times.

- **WENDOVER, BUCKINGHAMSHIRE** - Historic town on the Icknield Way set amid beautiful scenery and spectacular views of the Chilterns. There are many old timbered cottages and inns, one visited by Oliver Cromwell. The church has some interesting carving.

- **WESTBURY, BUCKINGHAMSHIRE** - Village close to Buckingham and within easy reach of Milton Keynes and Banbury.

- **WESTON-ON-THE-GREEN, OXFORDSHIRE** - Pretty village with stocks on the village green and thatched cottages. The church of St Mary's has an attractive setting and a fine tower dating from the 12th C.

- **WIMBORNE MINSTER, DORSET** - Market town centred on the twin-towered Minster Church of St Cuthberga which gave the town the second part of its name. Good touring base for the surrounding countryside, depicted in the writings of Thomas Hardy.

- **WINCHESTER, HAMPSHIRE** - King Alfred the Great made Winchester the capital of Saxon England. A magnificent Norman cathedral, with one of the longest naves in Europe, dominates the city. Home of Winchester College founded in 1382.

- **WINDSOR, BERKSHIRE** - Town dominated by the spectacular castle, home of the Royal Family for over 900 years. Parts are open to the public. There are many attractions including the Great Park, Eton and trips on the river.

- **WITNEY, OXFORDSHIRE** - Town famous for its blanket-making and mentioned in the Domesday Book. The market-place contains the Butter Cross, a medieval meeting place, and there is a green with merchants' houses.

- **WOODCOTE, OXFORDSHIRE** - Town in the Chilterns close to Goring and Henley-on-Thames.

- **WOODSTOCK, OXFORDSHIRE** - Small country town clustered around the park gates of Blenheim Palace, the superb 18th C home of the Duke of Marlborough. The town has well-known inns and an interesting museum. Sir Winston Churchill was born and buried nearby.

- **WROXALL, ISLE OF WIGHT** - Good centre for exploring the downs. Nearby is Appuldurcombe House, set in gardens originally laid out by Capability Brown.

USE YOUR *i*'s

There are more than 550 Tourist Information Centres throughout England offering friendly help with accommodation and holiday ideas as well as suggestions of places to visit and things to do.

You'll find TIC addresses in the local Phone Book.

SOUTH EAST ENGLAND

The North and South Downs straddle the South East in a roller coaster of countryside delight. You'll also find over 270 miles of coastline with dramatic chalk cliffs and traditional seaside fun.

Whether you're a shopper or a bopper, Brighton is full of designer stores and nightclubs. While more sedate pleasures such as a Sussex cream tea can be enjoyed in the many picturesque villages.

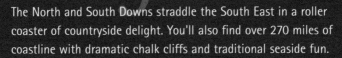

Kent of course is famous for its hops, but the south east is also a mecca for winegrowers, including Denbies Wine Estate in Surrey, which is the largest in England.

Oyez! Oyez! If you're in Hastings in August, listen out for the National Town Criers Championship.

The counties of
East Sussex, Kent, Surrey
and West Sussex

FOR MORE INFORMATION CONTACT:
South East England Tourist Board,
The Old Brew House, Warwick Park,
Tunbridge Wells, Kent TN2 5TU
Tel: (01892) 540766
Fax: (01892) 511008
Email: enquiries@seetb.org.uk
Internet: www.SouthEastEngland.uk.com

The Pictures:
1 Chiddingfold Village, Surrey;
2 Broadstairs Harbour, Kent;
3 Arundel Castle, West Sussex.

Where to Go in South East England - see pages 462-465
Where to Stay in South East England - see pages 466-501

Whilst in
SOUTH EAST ENGLAND ...

You will find hundreds of interesting places to visit during your stay, just some of which are listed in these pages.

Contact any Tourist Information Centre in the region for more ideas on days out in South East England.

A Smugglers Adventure at St Clements Caves

West Hill, Hastings, East Sussex TN34 3HY
Tel: (01424) 422964
An extensive exhibition of 18thC smuggling, housed in 2,000 sq m (6,562 sq ft) of caves. Exhibition, museum, video theatre, extensive Adventure Walk incorporating dramatic special effects.

Bateman's

Burwash, East Sussex TN19 7DS
Tel: (01435) 882302
A 17thC Ironmaster's house which was the home of Rudyard Kipling between 1902-1935. His study and Rolls Royce can be seen. Garden with working watermill.

The Bluebell Railway

Sheffield Park, Uckfield, East Sussex TN22 3QL
Tel: (01825) 722370
The Bluebell Railway runs standard-gauge steam trains through 14 km (9 miles) of Sussex countryside and has the largest collection of engines in the South.

Bodiam Castle

Bodiam, East Sussex TN32 5UA
Tel: (01580) 830436
A well-preserved ruin of a castle built in 1385. Exterior walls almost complete. Good views of surrounding area. Wide moat. Museum. Audio visual display on medieval life.

The Body Shop Tour

Watersmead, Littlehampton, West Sussex BN17 6LS
Tel: (01903) 844044
A guided tour of the Body Shop's headquarters. Discover how natural ingredients are used in products and how it campaigns for social and environmental change.

Clandon Park

West Clandon, Guildford, Surrey GU4 7RQ
Tel: (01483) 222482
A Palladian-style house built for Lord Onslow circa 1730. Marble Hall, Gubbay collection of furniture, needlework and porcelain. Royal Surrey Regiment Museum. Parterre in garden.

Claremont Landscape Garden

Esher, Surrey KT10 9JG
Tel: (01372) 467806
One of the earliest surviving English landscape gardens by Vanbrough and Bridgeman. Lake, island, view points and avenues with pavilion grotto and turf amphitheatre.

Denbies Wine Estate

Dorking, Surrey RH5 6AA
Tel: (01306) 876616
England's largest wine estate, 250 acres in beautiful countryside plus winery and visitor centre featuring 3-D time lapse film of vine growing. Viewing and picture galleries.

Hever Castle and Gardens

Hever, Kent TN8 7NG
Tel: (01732) 865224
Moated castle once the childhood home of Anne Boleyn. Restored by the Astor family, it contains furniture, paintings and panelling. Set in award-winning gardens.

Howletts Wild Animal Park

Bekesbourne, Canterbury, Kent CT4 5EL
Tel: (01303) 264647
Mature parkland containing John Aspinall's animals, famous for its gorilla and tiger collections. Many other animals including elephants, deer and cats.

Knockhatch Adventure Park

Hailsham, East Sussex BN27 3PR
Tel: (01323) 442051
Birds of prey centre, laser adventure game, off-road go-karting, paintball, children's farm and crazy golf.

Leonardslee Gardens

Lower Beeding, Horsham, West Sussex RH13 6PP
Tel: (01403) 891212
Rhododendrons and azaleas in a romantic 240-acre valley with seven lakes. Rock garden, bonsai, wallabies and wildfowl. Victorian motorcars and doll's house exhibition.

Marle Place Gardens

Brenchley, Tonbridge, Kent TN12 7HS
Tel: (01892) 722304
Romantic, peaceful gardens with topiary, unusual shrubs and plants, ponds, Edwardian rockery and Victorian gazebo. Walled scented garden and sculptures.

Michelham Priory

Upper Dicker, Hailsham, East Sussex BN27 3QS
Tel: (01323) 844224
An Augustinian priory incorporated into a Tudor mansion. Seven acres of gardens, a working watermill, an Elizabethan Great Barn, smithy and a rope museum.

Dover Castle and Secret Wartime Tunnels

Dover, Kent CT16 1HU
Tel: (01304) 201628
One of the most powerful medieval fortresses in Western Europe. St Mary-in-Castro Saxon church. Roman lighthouse, secret wartime tunnels, Henry II Great Keep.

Fishbourne Roman Palace and Museum

Fishbourne, West Sussex PO19 3QR
Tel: (01243) 785859
The remains of the largest Roman residence in Britain. Many beautiful mosaics, now under cover. Hypocaust and restored formal garden. Museum of finds. Model.

The Gardens of Gaia

Cranbrook, Kent TN17 3NS
Tel: (01580) 715289
Twenty-two acres of gardens and woodland in the spirit of 'Eden'. The historic and magical Lake Chad lies at its heart complimented by enviro-sculptures.

Great Dixter House and Gardens

Northiam, Kent TN31 6PH
Tel: (01797) 252878
An example of a 15thC manor house with antique furniture and needlework. Home of gardening writer Christopher Lloyd. The house is restored and the gardens were designed by Lutyens.

Guildford Boat House

Millbrook, Guildford, Surrey GU1 3XJ
Tel: (01483) 504494
Regular trips from Guildford to St Catherine's Lock and Godalming along the River Wey. Also 'Alfred Leroy' cruising restaurant. Rowing boats, canoes and holiday narrow boats.

The Pictures:
1 Southover Grange Gardens, Lewes, East Sussex;
2 Leeds Castle, Kent;
3 Chichester Cathedral, West Sussex;
4 Smallhythe Place, Kent;
5 Brighton Marina, East Sussex;
6 Guildford Castle, Surrey;
7 Sheffield Park, East Sussex.

Paddle Steamer Kingswear Castle

The Historic Dockyard, Chatham, Kent ME4 4TQ
Tel: (01634) 827648
A part of Britain's maritime heritage, the award-winning coal-fired paddle steamer, Kingswear Castle, offers morning, afternoon, evening and full day excursions on the Medway.

Penshurst Place and Gardens

Penshurst, Tonbridge, Kent TN11 8DG
Tel: (01892) 870307
A medieval manor house with Baron's Hall, portraits, tapestries, armour, park, lake, venture playground and toy museum. Tudor gardens. Visitor and plant centres.

Petworth House and Park

Petworth, West Sussex GU28 0AE
Tel: (01798) 342207
A late 17thC mansion set in 'Capability' Brown landscaped deer park. The house is noted for its paintings, Gibbons carvings and fine collection of furniture and sculpture.

Polesden Lacey

Great Bookham, Dorking, Surrey RH5 6BD
Tel: (01372) 458203
A Regency villa, re-modelled after 1906 with collections of paintings, porcelain, tapestries and furniture. Walled rose garden and extensive grounds with fine trees and views.

The RHS Garden, Wisley

Wisley, Woking, Surrey GU23 6QB
Tel: (01483) 224234
Stretching over 240 acres of glorious garden, Wisley demonstrates the best in British gardening practices, whatever the season. Plant centre, gift shop and restaurant.

Romney, Hythe and Dymchurch Railway

New Romney, Kent TN28 8PL
Tel: (01797) 362353
The world's only main line in miniature. Fourteen miles (22.5kms) of 15 inch gauge across Romney Marsh. Steam and diesel locomotives, engine sheds and a Toy and Model Museum.

St Mary's House and Gardens

Bramber, Steyning, West Sussex BN44 3WE
Tel: (01903) 816205
A medieval timber-framed Grade I house with rare 16thC wall-leather, fine panelled rooms and a unique painted room. Topiary gardens.

Sheffield Park Garden

Sheffield Park, Uckfield, East Sussex TN22 3QX
Tel: (01825) 790231
One-hundred acres of 'Capability' Brown designed landscaped gardens and woodland with four lakes on different levels. Noted for its rhododendrons, rare trees and azaleas.

Sussex Falconry Centre

Birdham, Chichester, West Sussex PO20 7BS
Tel: (01243) 512472
Aviaries containing birds of prey including hawks, falcons, and owls. Flying displays of birds throughout the day, weather permitting.

Wakehurst Place Gardens

Ardingly, Haywards Heath, West Sussex RH17 6TN
Tel: (01444) 894000
Extensive 202-hectare estate gardens administered by Royal Botanic Gardens, Kew with lakes, ponds and an important collection of exotic trees, plants and shrubs.

The Whitstable Oyster and Fishery Exhibition

The Harbour, Whitstable, Kent CT5 1AB
Tel: (01227) 280753
An exhibition of unique artefacts, memorabilia and photographs depicting oyster fishing. Live fish display and 'hands-on' seashore experience.

Find out more about
SOUTH EAST ENGLAND ...

Further information about holidays and attractions in
South East England is available from:

SOUTH EAST ENGLAND TOURIST BOARD
The Old Brew House, Warwick Park,
Tunbridge Wells, Kent TN2 5TU.
Tel: (01892) 540766
Fax: (01892) 511008
Email: enquiries@seetb.org.uk
Internet: www.SouthEastEngland.uk.com

The following publications are available free from the South East England Tourist Board:

Guide to the Guides

Bed and Breakfast Touring Map

Relaxation
*featuring the green, rural areas of the region. For those
seeking rest and relaxation in a rural setting*

Lively
*for those seeking heritage and history combined with
the entertainment possibilities of a city or coastal break*

Walk South East England

Glorious Gardens of South East England

Camping and Caravanning in the South of England

Outstanding Churches and Cathedrals

Golfing in the South East

Eating and Drinking in the South East

The Pictures:
1 Bateman's,
   East Sussex;
2 The Pantiles, Royal
   Tunbridge Wells, Kent;
3 Port Lympne Wild
   Animal Park, Kent;
4 Great Dixter House &
   Gardens, Northiam,
   East Sussex;
5 Bodiam Castle,
   East Sussex;
6 Chichester Cathedral
   Gardens, West Sussex.

Getting to
SOUTH EAST ENGLAND ...

BY ROAD: From the north of England - M1/M25; the west and Wales - M4/M25; the
east of England - M25; the south of England M3/M25; London - M20 or M2.

BY RAIL: Regular services from London's Charing Cross, Victoria and Waterloo East
stations to all parts of South East England.

Where to stay in

SOUTH EAST ENGLAND

Accommodation entries in this region are listed in alphabetical order of place name, and then in alphabetical order of establishment.

Map references refer to the colour location maps at the front of this guide. The first number indicates the map to use; the letter and number which follow refer to the grid reference on the map.

At-a-glance symbols at the end of each accommodation entry give useful information about services and facilities. A key to symbols can be found inside the back cover flap. Keep this open for easy reference.

A brief description of the towns and villages offering accommodation in the entries which follow, can be found at the end of this section.

A complete listing of all English Tourism Council assessed guest accommodation appears at the back of this guide.

ALFRISTON, East Sussex Map ref 2D3

◆◆◆◆ **RIVERDALE HOUSE**

Seaford Road, Alfriston, Polegate, East Sussex BN26 5TR T: (01323) 871038 I: www.cuckmere-valley.co.uk/riverdale/	Bedrooms: 3 double, 2 twin, 1 family room Bathrooms: 4 en suite, 2 private	Parking for 7 CC: Barclaycard, Eurocard, Mastercard, Visa	B&B per night: S £40.00–£50.00 D £50.00–£60.00 OPEN All year round

Lovely Victorian home, peacefully located on the edge of famous village. Wonderful views of the South Downs. Minimum stay of two nights on summer weekends.

🛇 ♿ 🖵 🌤 UL S ℳ IIII. 🖴 ✳ 🐾 SP T

ARUNDEL, West Sussex Map ref 2D3 *Tourist Information Centre Tel: (01903) 882268*

◆◆◆◆

HOUGHTON FARM
Arundel, West Sussex BN18 9LW
T: (01798) 831327 & 831100
F: (01798) 831183

B&B per night:
D £40.00–£48.00

OPEN Mar–Oct

In a small hamlet, 4 miles north of Arundel, Houghton Farm is set in a beautiful garden with superb views over the Arun Valley. It is very close to the South Downs Way. Two well-appointed bedrooms, with use of sitting-room. Full English breakfast. Bars and restaurants within walking distance.

Bedrooms: 1 double, 1 twin Bathrooms: 2 private	Parking for 4	

🛇 10 🗙 🖃 🖵 🌤 🖳 UL S ✁ ℳ TV IIII. 🖴 ✳ 🐾 🎋 🎐

ARUNDEL continued

◆◆◆

MILL LANE HOUSE
Slindon, Arundel, West Sussex
BN18 0RP
T: (01243) 814440
F: (01243) 814436

Bedrooms: 1 single,
3 double, 2 twin, 1 triple;
suite available
Bathrooms: 7 en suite,
1 public

EM 1900 (LO 1000)
Parking for 7

B&B per night:
S £28.50–£28.50
D £45.00–£45.00

OPEN All year round

17thC house in beautiful National Trust village. Magnificent views to coast. Pubs within easy walking distance. One mile from A29/A27 junction.

ASHFORD, Kent Map ref 3B4 *Tourist Information Centre Tel: (01233) 629165*

◆◆◆

CROFT HOTEL
Canterbury Road, Kennington,
Ashford, TN25 4DU
T: (01233) 622140
F: (01233) 635271
E: crofthotel@btconnect.com

Bedrooms: 6 single,
8 double, 9 twin, 4 triple,
1 family room
Bathrooms: 28 en suite

EM 1900 (LO 2030)
Parking for 32
CC: Amex, Barclaycard,
Delta, Eurocard, JCB,
Mastercard, Solo, Switch,
Visa

B&B per night:
S £47.00–£57.00
D £60.00–£70.00

HB per person:
DY £58.00–£68.00

OPEN All year round

Country house in 2 acres of gardens. Channel Tunnel 10 miles, Canterbury 12 miles, Dover 22 miles. Ideal for business people and tourists alike.

◆◆◆

17thC former coaching inn with oak beams and gleaming brasses. Ideal for touring and walking the Kent countryside and coast, and as stop-over for the Shuttle or ferries. Half board daily price is based on a minimum 2-night stay for two people.

NEW FLYING HORSE INN

Upper Bridge Street, Wye, Ashford,
TN25 5AN
T: (01233) 812297
F: (01233) 813487
E: newflyhorse@shepherd-neame.co.uk
I: www.shepherd-neame.co.uk

Bedrooms: 4 single,
4 double, 1 twin,
1 family room
Bathrooms: 10 en suite

Lunch available
EM 1830 (LO 2130)
Parking for 30
CC: Amex, Barclaycard,
Delta, Eurocard, JCB,
Maestro, Mastercard,
Solo, Switch, Visa, Visa
Electron

B&B per night:
S Min £45.00
D Min £56.50

HB per person:
DY Min £47.50

OPEN All year round

◆◆◆

17thC hotel and restaurant, set in 2.5 acres, where a cosy atmosphere awaits. All rooms en suite with colour TV. Large car park. M20 junction 10 and minutes from Ashford International Station, Channel Tunnel, Dover and Folkestone.

WARREN COTTAGE HOTEL AND RESTAURANT

136 The Street, Willesborough, Ashford,
TN24 0NB
T: (01233) 621905 & 632929
F: (01233) 623400
E: general@warrencottage.co.uk
I: www.warrencottage.co.uk

Bedrooms: 1 single,
3 double, 1 twin,
1 family room
Bathrooms: 6 en suite,
1 public

Lunch available
EM 1830 (LO 2130)
Parking for 33
CC: Barclaycard, Delta,
Mastercard, Switch, Visa

B&B per night:
S £34.90–£39.90
D £50.00–£69.90

HB per person:
DY £36.00–£46.00

OPEN All year round

QUALITY ASSURANCE SCHEME

Diamond ratings and awards were correct at the time of going to press but are subject to change. Please check at the time of booking.

BATTLE, East Sussex Map ref 3B4 *Tourist Information Centre Tel: (01424) 773721*

◆◆◆ **MOONS HILL FARM**
The Green, Ninfield, Battle,
East Sussex TN33 9LH
T: (01424) 892645
F: (01424) 892645

Bedrooms: 1 double,
2 twin
Bathrooms: 3 en suite

Parking for 12

B&B per night:
S £17.50–£20.00
D £35.00–£40.00

OPEN Mar–Nov

10-acre mixed farm. Modernised farmhouse in Ninfield village centre, in the heart of "1066" Country. A warm welcome and Sussex home cooking. Pub opposite. Large car park.

BERWICK, East Sussex Map ref 2D3

◆◆◆

LOWER CLAVERHAM FARM
Berwick, Polegate, East Sussex BN26 6TJ
T: (01323) 811267
F: (01323) 811267

B&B per night:
S £22.00–£25.00
D £44.00–£50.00

OPEN All year round

16thC farmhouse on working dairy farm, half a mile from the main road. Close to South Downs, Glyndebourne and the Sussex Coast. One mile from from train station.

Bedrooms: 1 double,
1 twin
Bathrooms: 2 private,
1 public

Parking for 2

BETHERSDEN, Kent Map ref 3B4

◆◆◆

THE COACH HOUSE
Oakmead Farm, Bethersden, Ashford,
TN26 3DU
T: (01233) 820583
F: (01233) 820583

B&B per night:
S £25.00–£25.00
D £38.00–£38.00

OPEN Mar–Oct

Comfortable family home, set well back from road, in 5 acres of garden and paddocks. Breakfast of your choice served in the dining room or conservatory, also used as a sitting room for guests. One mile from village – central for ferries, Channel Tunnel, Eurostar, Canterbury, Leeds Castle, Sissinghurst and many tourist attractions. Dutch spoken.

Bedrooms: 1 double,
1 twin, 1 family room
Bathrooms: 2 en suite,
1 private

Parking for 8

BEXHILL, East Sussex Map ref 3B4 *Tourist Information Centre Tel: (01424) 732208*

◆◆◆ **PARK LODGE HOTEL**
16 Egerton Road, Bexhill,
East Sussex TN39 3HH
T: (01424) 216547 & 215041
F: (01424) 217460

Bedrooms: 4 double,
4 twin, 2 triple
Bathrooms: 8 en suite,
1 public, 2 private
showers

EM 1800 (LO 1500)
Parking for 4
CC: Amex, Barclaycard,
Diners, Eurocard,
Mastercard, Visa

B&B per night:
S £23.00–£23.00
D £46.00–£50.00

HB per person:
DY £33.00–£35.00

OPEN All year round

Informal family-run hotel with home-from-home feel, renowned for high standards and fresh home cooking. Seafront shops and theatre 50 yards.

TOWN INDEX
This can be found at the back of this guide. If you know where you want to stay, the index will give you the page number listing accommodation in your chosen town, city or village.

BIDDENDEN, Kent Map ref 3B4

◆◆◆◆
Silver Award

BETTMANS OAST

Hareplain Road, Biddenden, Ashford, TN27 8LJ
T: (01580) 291463
F: (01580) 291463

B&B per night:
S £40.00–£45.00
D £50.00–£56.00

OPEN All year round

Attractive Grade II Listed oast house and converted barn set in 10 acres. Lovely garden. Large oak-beamed bedrooms, comfortable guests' lounge with log fires in winter. Close to Sissinghurst Castle Gardens and convenient for Leeds Castle, Great Dixter and Scotney Castle. Within walking distance of Three Chimneys country inn.

Bedrooms: 2 double
Bathrooms: 2 en suite

Parking for 4
CC: Barclaycard, Delta, Eurocard, JCB, Mastercard, Solo, Switch, Visa, Visa Electron

BOGNOR REGIS, West Sussex Map ref 2D3 *Tourist Information Centre Tel: (01243) 823140*

◆◆◆
JUBILEE GUEST HOUSE
5 Gloucester Road, Bognor Regis, West Sussex PO21 1NU
T: (01243) 863016 &
07702 275967 (Mobile)
F: (01243) 868017
E: jubileeguesthouse@breathemail.net
I: www.scoot.co.uk/jubilee_guesthouse/

Bedrooms: 2 single, 1 double, 2 triple, 1 family room
Bathrooms: 1 en suite, 1 private, 1 public, 2 private showers

Parking for 4
CC: Barclaycard, Delta, Mastercard, Visa

B&B per night:
S £18.00–£30.00
D £36.00–£60.00

OPEN All year round

Family-run business, 75 yards from seafront and beach. Ideal for visiting "Butlin's family entertainment resort", Chichester, Goodwood, Fontwell, Arundel, Portsmouth and IOW.

◆◆◆
REGIS LODGE
3 Gloucester Road, Bognor Regis, West Sussex PO21 1NU
T: (01243) 827110 & 07768 117770
F: (01243) 827110
E: frank@regislodge.fsbusiness.co.uk
I: www.regislodge.tripod.com

Bedrooms: 2 single, 2 double, 6 triple, 2 family rooms
Bathrooms: 10 en suite, 1 public

Parking for 9

B&B per night:
S £20.00–£25.00
D £40.00–£50.00

OPEN All year round

Family-run guesthouse, friendly atmosphere, comfortable, clean rooms. 30 yards from beach, opposite South Coast World. Close to town centre, shops, restaurants, park, leisure centre and Goodwood.

BOLNEY, West Sussex Map ref 2D3

◆◆◆◆

BUTCHERS BED & BREAKFAST

Butchers, Ryecroft Road, Bolney, Haywards Heath, West Sussex RH17 5PS
T: (01444) 881503
E: mark.darby@deloitte.co.uk

B&B per night:
S £30.00–£35.00
D £50.00–£55.00

OPEN All year round

A warm welcome awaits you at our attractive, period village house, set in 1 acre of landscaped gardens. Spacious, beamed, twin-bedded room with en suite bathroom. Bolney is an excellent base for many gardens and places of interest in Sussex. Gatwick Airport 15 miles, South Coast 10 miles.

Bedrooms: 1 twin
Bathrooms: 1 en suite

Parking for 4

BOROUGH GREEN, Kent Map ref 3B3

◆◆◆◆

YEW TREE BARN
Long Mill Lane, Crouch, Borough Green,
Sevenoaks, TN15 8QB
T: (01732) 883107
F: (01732) 883107

B&B per night:
S Max £40.00
D Max £55.00

OPEN Feb–Oct

Converted barn in peaceful hamlet, convenient for M20, M26/M25, National Trust properties and Brands Hatch. 40 minutes to Eurotunnel, 1 hour Dover, mainline rail to London 45 minutes. 1 double en suite with dressing room, 1 twin en suite. Parking.

Bedrooms: 1 double, 2 triple
Bathrooms: 2 en suite, 1 private

BRENCHLEY, Kent Map ref 3B4

◆◆◆

THE BULL OF BRENCHLEY
High Street, Brenchley, Tonbridge,
TN12 7NQ
T: (01892) 722701
F: (01892) 722760

B&B per night:
S £35.00–£40.00
D £40.00–£60.00

HB per person:
DY Min £40.00

OPEN All year round

The Bull Inn is situated in the centre of Brenchley, one of the most beautiful villages of Kent. This Listed Victorian inn provides an excellent range of facilities for tourist and business visitors alike. Listed by CAMRA. All rooms are spacious and elegant with en suite facilities. Excellent range of tourist attractions and golf courses.

Bedrooms: 2 single, 4 double, 1 triple
Bathrooms: 7 en suite

Lunch available
EM 1830 (LO 2130)
Parking for 10

BRIDGE, Kent Map ref 3B3

◆◆◆

HARROW COTTAGE
2 Brewery Lane, Bridge, Canterbury,
CT4 5LD
T: (01227) 830218
F: (01227) 830218
E: pamela@phooker.fsbusiness.co.uk

Bedrooms: 1 double, 1 twin
Bathrooms: 2 en suite

Parking for 2

B&B per night:
S £25.00–£25.00
D £40.00–£40.00

OPEN All year round

Situated in quiet cul-de-sac, in village setting. Three miles from Canterbury and 12 miles from Dover, off the A2.

BRIGHTON & HOVE East Sussex Map ref 2D3 Tourist Information Centre Tel: 0906 711 2255 (calls cost 50p per minute)

◆◆◆◆

AINSLEY HOUSE HOTEL
28 New Steine, Brighton,
East Sussex BN2 1PD
T: (01273) 605310
F: (01273) 688604
E: ahhotel@fastnet.co.uk.
I: www.search1.co.uk/ainsley house

Bedrooms: 3 single, 3 double, 4 twin
Bathrooms: 8 en suite, 1 public

EM
CC: Amex, Barclaycard, Delta, Diners, Eurocard, JCB, Maestro, Mastercard, Switch, Visa

B&B per night:
S £25.00–£32.00
D £48.00–£78.00

OPEN All year round

Comfortable, popular hotel on quiet garden square overlooking the sea. Close to all amenities. Extensive breakfast menu. Warm welcome guaranteed.

SYMBOLS The symbols in each entry give information about services and facilities. A key to these symbols appears at the back of this guide.

◆◆◆◆

AMBASSADOR HOTEL
22 New Steine, Marine Parade, Brighton,
East Sussex BN2 1PD
T: (01273) 676869
F: (01273) 689988

B&B per night:
S £26.00–£38.00
D £48.00–£70.00

OPEN All year round

Family-run, licensed hotel in a seafront garden square, overlooking the sea and Palace Pier. Close to Royal Pavilion, shops, conference halls and entertainments. All rooms en suite with colour TV, direct-dial telephone, radio, hospitality tray. Ground floor rooms available, bar.

Bedrooms: 6 single, 7 double, 6 triple, 1 family room
Bathrooms: 20 en suite

EM
CC: Amex, Barclaycard, JCB, Mastercard, Solo, Switch, Visa

◆◆◆◆
Silver
Award

ARLANDA HOTEL
20 New Steine, Brighton,
East Sussex BN2 1PD
T: (01273) 699300
F: (01273) 600930
E: arlanda@brighton.co.uk
I: www.brighton.co.uk/hotels/arlanda/welome.htm

Bedrooms: 4 single, 3 double, 4 twin, 1 triple
Bathrooms: 12 en suite

CC: Amex, Barclaycard, Delta, Diners, Eurocard, JCB, Maestro, Mastercard, Solo, Switch, Visa, Visa Electron

B&B per night:
S £30.00–£40.00
D £54.00–£80.00

OPEN All year round

Enjoy good food and company in a licensed, family-run hotel. Our warm rooms have full en suite facilities. Quiet 200-year-old Regency square, yet close to Brighton's attractions.

◆◆◆

ATLANTIC HOTEL
16 Marine Parade, Brighton,
East Sussex BN2 1TL
T: (01273) 695944
F: (01273) 695944

Bedrooms: 1 single, 6 double, 3 twin
Bathrooms: 9 en suite, 1 public

Lunch available
EM 1700 (LO 2000)
CC: Amex, Barclaycard, Diners, JCB, Mastercard, Visa

B&B per night:
S £20.00–£40.00
D £40.00–£60.00

HB per person:
DY £28.00–£30.00

OPEN All year round

Attractive family-run hotel facing seafront. Sea Life Centre, Palace Pier, historic Royal Pavilion and famous Lanes are just down the road. Brighton Centre nearby.

◆◆◆

THE BEACH HOTEL
2-4 Regency Square, Brighton,
East Sussex BN1 2GP
T: (01273) 323776
F: (01273) 747028
I: www.beachotel.co.uk

Bedrooms: 1 single, 15 double, 8 twin, 4 triple, 3 family rooms
Bathrooms: 31 en suite

CC: Amex, Barclaycard, Delta, Diners, Eurocard, JCB, Maestro, Mastercard, Solo, Switch, Visa, Visa

B&B per night:
S £40.00–£65.00
D £55.00–£80.00

OPEN All year round

In Regency Square, by seafront, few minutes' walk from major tourist attractions, conference centre, main shopping centre and the "Lanes". All rooms face the sea.

◆◆◆◆

BRIGHTON HOUSE HOTEL
52 Regency Square, Brighton,
East Sussex BN1 2FF
T: (01273) 323282
E: enquiries@brightonhousehotel.co.uk
I: www.brightonhousehotel.co.uk

Bedrooms: 6 single, 8 double/family rooms
Bathrooms: 14 en suite

B&B per night:
S £39.50–£59.50
D £44.50–£94.00

OPEN All year round

*Top quality *Listed hotel, in main seafront square in heart of town. Extensively refurbished, many original features. Luxury en suites. Healthy breakfast, excellent value. Non-smoking.*

CHECK THE MAPS
The colour maps at the front of this guide show all the cities, towns
and villages for which you will find accommodation entries.
Refer to the town index to find the page on which they are listed.

BRIGHTON & HOVE East Sussex continued

◆◆◆

BRIGHTON MARINA HOUSE HOTEL

8 Charlotte Street, Marine Parade,
Brighton, East Sussex BN2 1AG
T: (01273) 605349 & 819806
F: (01273) 679484
E: rooms@jungs.co.uk
I: www.s-h-systems.co.uk/hotels/brighton

Premier bed and breakfast located just off the seafront and within walking distance of all major attractions. Elegant rooms with en suite facility and hospitality tray, well-equipped for leisure and business guests. We are committed to creating the ultimate breakfast experience offering English, vegan, vegetarian and continental breakfast.

Bedrooms: 3 single,
3 double, 1 twin, 3 triple
Bathrooms: 7 en suite,
1 public

Lunch available
EM 1630 (LO 1500)
CC: Amex, Barclaycard,
Diners, JCB, Mastercard,
Visa

B&B per night:
S £19.00–£39.00
D £39.00–£95.00

HB per person:
DY £28.00–£79.00

OPEN All year round

◆◆

DIANA HOUSE

25 St Georges Terrace, Brighton,
East Sussex BN2 1JJ
T: (01273) 605797
F: (01273) 600533
E: diana@enterprise.co.net
I: www.dianahouse.co.uk

Bedrooms: 4 double,
5 twin, 1 triple
Bathrooms: 6 en suite,
1 public, 4 private
showers

CC: Barclaycard,
Mastercard, Visa

B&B per night:
S £22.00–£50.00
D £44.00–£50.00

OPEN All year round

Large, friendly guesthouse close to sea, town and conference centre. All rooms have TV, hospitality tray, clock/radio, shaver point. Some rooms en suite. 24-hour access.

◆◆◆◆

FYFIELD HOUSE

26 New Steine, Brighton, East Sussex
BN2 1PD
T: (01273) 602770
F: (01273) 602770
E: fyfield@aol.com
I: www.brighton.co.uk/hotels/fyfield

Excellent, clean, home-from-home private hotel, where Anna and Peter have welcomed their guests for the last 30 years. Central to all attractions in and out of town. All rooms are tastefully decorated and most have en suite facilities. Superb breakfast menu, from the traditional to the home-made vegetarian sausage.

Bedrooms: 4 single,
5 double
Bathrooms: 6 en suite,
1 public

EM 1800
CC: Amex, Barclaycard,
Delta, Diners, Eurocard,
JCB, Maestro, Mastercard,
Solo, Switch, Visa, Visa
Electron

B&B per night:
S £20.00–£37.00
D £45.00–£74.00

OPEN All year round

◆◆◆

KIMBERLEY HOTEL

17 Atlingworth Street, Brighton,
East Sussex BN2 1PL
T: (01273) 603504 (Office)
F: (01273) 603504
E: kimberley.hotel@iname.com
I: www.roland01.freeserve.co.uk/

Bedrooms: 3 single,
4 double, 5 twin, 1 triple,
2 family rooms
Bathrooms: 7 en suite,
1 public, 8 private
showers

CC: Amex, Barclaycard,
Delta, Diners, JCB,
Mastercard, Solo, Switch,
Visa, Visa Electron

B&B per night:
S £25.00–£28.00
D £46.00–£55.00

OPEN All year round

Family-run hotel, 2 minutes from seafront and central for amusements, shopping, marina and conference centre. Licensed residents' bar.

PRICES

Please check prices and other details at the time of booking.

◆◆◆

RUSSELL GUEST HOUSE

19 Russell Square, Brighton,
East Sussex BN1 2EE
T: (01273) 327969
F: (01273) 821535
E: russell.brighton@btinternet.com

Bedrooms: 1 double,
2 twin, 4 triple
Bathrooms: 7 en suite,
1 public

CC: Amex, Barclaycard,
Delta, Eurocard, JCB,
Maestro, Mastercard,
Solo, Switch, Visa, Visa
Electron

B&B per night:
S £35.00–£42.00
D £42.00–£60.00

OPEN All year round

Five-storey townhouse in pleasant garden square. Close Brighton centre, seafront, main shopping area. Unrestricted access. Theatres, cinemas, nightclubs all within easy walking distance.

◆

SANDPIPER GUEST HOUSE

11 Russell Square, Brighton,
East Sussex BN1 2EE
T: (01273) 328202
F: (01273) 329974
E: sandpiper@brighton.co.uk

Bedrooms: 3 single,
1 double, 1 twin, 1
family room
Bathrooms: 3 public

EM
CC: Amex, Delta,
Eurocards, Mastercard,
Solo, Switch, Visa

B&B per night:
S £15.00–£28.00
D £30.00–£56.00

OPEN All year round

Newly refurbished guesthouse, 2 minutes from conference centre, shopping area, leisure centres and seafront. All rooms have central heating, colour TV, tea/coffee. Unrestricted access.

◆◆◆

HOTEL SEAFIELD

23 Seafield Road, Hove, East Sussex
BN3 2TP
T: (01273) 735912
F: (01273) 323525
I: www.brighton.co.uk/hotels/
seafield/

Bedrooms: 2 single,
5 double, 2 twin, 2 triple,
3 family rooms
Bathrooms: 12 en suite,
3 public

Lunch available
EM 1900 (LO 1700)
Parking for 14
CC: Barclaycard, Delta,
Eurocard, Mastercard,
Solo, Switch, Visa, Visa
Electron

B&B per night:
S £30.00–£45.00
D £65.00–£90.00

OPEN All year round

Family-run hotel with home-cooked food, close to seafront and main shopping centre. Free street and private parking. Most rooms en suite with shower/toilet.

◆◆◆

BAY TREE HOTEL

12 Eastern Esplanade, Broadstairs,
CT10 1DR
T: (01843) 862502
F: (01843) 860589

B&B per night:
S £26.00–£26.00
D £52.00–£58.00

HB per person:
DY £38.00–£41.00

OPEN All year round

Situated on the lovely Eastern Esplanade overlooking Stone Bay, the hotel enjoys panoramic sea views across the English Channel. Minutes from the town centre and sandy beaches. A warm welcome awaits you at this family-run hotel.

Bedrooms: 1 single,
5 double, 5 twin
Bathrooms: 11 en suite

EM 1800 (LO 1800)
Parking for 12
CC: Barclaycard, Delta,
Eurocard, JCB,
Mastercard, Solo, Switch,
Visa, Visa Electron

CHECK THE MAPS

The colour maps at the front of this guide show all the cities, towns and villages for which you will find accommodation entries. Refer to the town index to find the page on which they are listed.

SOUTH EAST ENGLAND

BURGESS HILL, West Sussex Map ref 2D3 *Tourist Information Centre Tel: (01444) 247726*

◆◆◆◆

THE HOMESTEAD

Homestead Lane, Valebridge Road,
Burgess Hill, West Sussex RH15 0RQ
T: (01444) 246899
F: (01444) 246899
E: mike@burgess-hill.co.uk
I: www.burgess-hill.co.uk

B&B per night:
S £22.50–£25.00
D £45.00–£50.00

OPEN All year round

Quiet, comfortable, friendly home in peaceful setting of 7.5 acres at end of private lane. All rooms en suite with refreshment facilities and TV. Two ground-floor bedrooms have wheelchair access. Glyndebourne, numerous gardens, National Trust locations and Bluebell steam railway nearby. Wivelsfield railway station 1 km – Brighton/Gatwick/Lewes 15 minutes, London 50 minutes. Parking. Strictly no smoking.

Bedrooms: 1 single,
3 double
Bathrooms: 4 en suite

Parking for 2
CC: Barclaycard, Delta,
Mastercard, Visa

CANTERBURY, Kent Map ref 3B3 *Tourist Information Centre Tel: (01227) 766567*

◆◆◆

ABBERLEY HOUSE
115 Whitstable Road, Canterbury,
CT2 8EF
T: (01227) 450265
F: (01227) 478626

Bedrooms: 2 double,
1 twin
Bathrooms: 1 en suite,
1 public

Parking for 3

B&B per night:
S £22.00–£25.00
D £40.00–£48.00

OPEN All year round

Comfortable family-run guesthouse in a residential area. Parking. Easy walk to centre. Tea/coffee making. One double en-suite. English breakfast. Non-smokers, please.

◆◆◆

ALICANTE GUEST HOUSE
4 Roper Road, Canterbury, CT2 7EH
T: (01227) 766277
F: (01227) 766277

Bedrooms: 1 single,
3 double, 2 twin
Bathrooms: 6 en suite

B&B per night:
S £22.00–£28.00
D £40.00–£48.00

OPEN All year round

Attractive Victorian house with comfortable en suite rooms. Hearty breakfast. Close to all tourist attractions and other amenities.

◆◆◆◆
Silver
Award

BOWER FARM HOUSE
Stelling Minnis, Canterbury,
CT4 6BB
T: (01227) 709430
E: anne@bowerbb.freeserve.co.uk
I: www.kentac.co.uk/bowerfm

Bedrooms: 1 double,
1 twin
Bathrooms: 1 en suite,
1 private

Parking for 8

B&B per night:
S £25.00–£28.00
D £42.00–£45.00

OPEN All year round

Delightful heavily beamed 17thC farmhouse between the villages of Stelling Minnis and Bossingham. Canterbury and Hythe are approximately 7 miles away.

COUNTRY CODE Always follow the Country Code 🌾 Enjoy the countryside and respect its life and work 🌾 Guard against all risk of fire 🌾 Fasten all gates 🌾 Keep your dogs under close control 🌾 Keep to public paths across farmland 🌾 Use gates and stiles to cross fences, hedges and walls 🌾 Leave livestock, crops and machinery alone 🌾 Take your litter home 🌾 Help to keep all water clean 🌾 Protect wildlife, plants and trees 🌾 Take special care on country roads 🌾 Make no unnecessary noise

CANTERBURY continued

♦♦♦

CATHEDRAL GATE HOTEL

36 Burgate, Canterbury, CT1 2HA
T: (01227) 464381
F: (01227) 462800
E: cgate@cgate.demon.co.uk

B&B per night:
S £23.00–£54.00
D £44.00–£81.00

OPEN All year round

Pilgrims slept here! This 1438 building with massive beams, sloping floors and low doorways, offers modern comfort and is centrally situated at the main cathedral gateway. Our rooms have telephone, TV and welcome tray. Quiet lounge, bar and home-cooked meals in our bow-window dining room. English breakfast extra.

Bedrooms: 4 single, 8 double, 7 twin, 3 triple, 2 family rooms
Bathrooms: 12 en suite, 3 public

EM 1900 (LO 2100)
CC: Amex, Barclaycard, Delta, Diners, Eurocard, JCB, Mastercard, Solo, Switch, Visa, Visa Electron

---

♦♦♦♦

CHAUCER LODGE

62 New Dover Road, Canterbury, CT1 3DT
T: (01227) 459141
F: (01227) 459141
I: www.smoothhound.co.uk/hotels/chaucldg.html

Bedrooms: 2 double, 2 twin, 1 triple, 1 family room
Bathrooms: 5 en suite, 1 private, 1 public

EM 1800 (LO 2000)
Parking for 12
CC: Barclaycard, Delta, JCB, Mastercard, Visa, Visa Electron

B&B per night:
S £23.00–£35.00
D £38.00–£50.00

HB per person:
DY £28.00–£38.00

OPEN All year round

Maria and Alistair Wilson extend a warm welcome to their comfortable guesthouse. City 10 minutes' walk, cricket ground 5 minutes. High standard of cleanliness and furnishings.

♦♦♦♦
Silver
Award

A warm welcome and bed and breakfast in style. Large, quiet, elegant en suite rooms all with colour TV, clock/radio, hairdryer and tea/coffee-making facilities. Full English breakfast. Vegetarian and special diets on request. Six minutes' walk to city centre, 5 minutes' to Canterbury East train station. Car park/garage available.

CLARE-ELLEN GUEST HOUSE

9 Victoria Road, Wincheap, Canterbury, CT1 3SG
T: (01227) 760205
F: (01227) 784482
E: loraine.williams@virgin.net
I: www.clareellenguesthouse.co.uk

Bedrooms: 1 single, 1 double, 1 twin, 1 triple, 1 family room
Bathrooms: 5 en suite, 1 public

Parking for 9
CC: Barclaycard, Delta, JCB, Mastercard, Switch, Visa

B&B per night:
S £26.00–£30.00
D £46.00–£52.00

OPEN All year round

♦♦♦♦

HOMEWOOD FARM

Agester Lane, Denton, Canterbury, CT4 6NR
T: (01227) 832611
F: (01227) 832611

Bedrooms: 1 double, 1 twin
Bathrooms: 2 private, 1 public

Parking for 3

B&B per night:
S £18.00–£20.00
D £35.00–£40.00

OPEN All year round

Friendly, welcoming, non-smoking quiet countryside farm. Central for walks, Channel crossings and Canterbury city. Choice of fresh home-cooked food. Ample parking.

MAP REFERENCES The map references refer to the colour maps at the front of this guide. The first figure is the map number; the letter and figure which follow indicate the grid reference on the map.

♦♦♦♦♦
Gold
Award

MAGNOLIA HOUSE

36 St Dunstans Terrace, Canterbury, CT2 8AX
T: (01227) 765121 & 07885 595970
F: (01227) 765121
E: magnolia_house_canterbury@yahoo.com
I: www.freespace.virgin.net/magnolia.canterbury

Charming late Georgian house in quiet residential street, a 10-minute stroll from the city centre. Bedrooms, individually co-ordinated, have every facility for an enjoyable stay. Varied breakfasts are served overlooking the attractive walled garden, where you are welcome to relax after a busy day's sightseeing.

Bedrooms: 1 single, 4 double, 2 twin
Bathrooms: 7 en suite

EM 1800 (LO 1900)
Parking for 5
CC: Amex, Barclaycard, Delta, Diners, Eurocard, Mastercard, Solo, Switch, Visa

B&B per night:
S £40.00–£55.00
D £78.00–£110.00

OPEN All year round

♦♦♦♦
Silver
Award

ORIEL LODGE

3 Queens Avenue, Canterbury, CT2 8AY
T: (01227) 462845
F: (01227) 462845
E: info@oriel-lodge.co.uk
I: www.oriel-lodge.co.uk

In a tree-lined residential avenue, very near the city centre and restaurants, an attractive Edwardian house with 6 well-furnished bedrooms and clean, up-to-date facilities. Afternoon tea served in the garden or lounge with log fire. Restricted smoking. Private parking.

Bedrooms: 1 single, 3 double, 1 twin, 1 triple
Bathrooms: 2 en suite, 2 public

Parking for 6
CC: Barclaycard, Diners, Eurocard, JCB, Mastercard, Switch, Visa

B&B per night:
S £26.00–£32.00
D £43.00–£62.00

OPEN All year round

♦

RAEMORE HOUSE

33 New Dover Road, Canterbury, CT1 3AS
T: (01227) 769740 & 07836 786020
F: (01227) 769432
E: tom@raemore.demon.co.uk

Bedrooms: 1 single, 2 double, 2 twin, 1 triple, 1 family room
Bathrooms: 4 en suite, 2 public

Parking for 9
CC: Amex, Barclaycard, Eurocard, Mastercard, Visa

B&B per night:
S £22.00–£28.00
D £35.00–£48.00

OPEN All year round

Family-run guesthouse close to city centre. Four-poster and en suite rooms with TV and tea/coffee facilities. Private car park.

♦♦♦

RENVILLE OAST

Bridge, Canterbury, CT4 5AD
T: (01227) 830215
F: (01227) 830215
E: renville.oast@virgin.net
I: freespace.virgin.net/joan.hill/index.html

The 150-year-old Oast was once used for drying hops for the brewery trade. Enjoy a stay in beautiful Kentish countryside as well as experiencing the history of a magnificent cathedral city. Many interesting castles, historic houses and gardens within easy reach. All rooms comfortably furnished. Warm welcome awaits you.

Bedrooms: 1 double, 1 twin, 1 triple
Bathrooms: 2 en suite, 1 private

Parking for 6

B&B per night:
S £25.00–£35.00
D £45.00–£55.00

OPEN All year round

CANTERBURY continued

◆◆◆◆◆
Gold
Award

THANINGTON HOTEL
140 Wincheap, Canterbury, CT1 3RY
T: (01227) 453227
F: (01227) 453225
E: thanington@lineone.net
I: www.thanington-hotel.co.uk

B&B per night:
S £50.00–£55.00
D £68.00–£90.00

OPEN All year round

Enjoy the comfort and facilities of this special Georgian bed and breakfast hotel, just a short stroll from the city centre. Beautiful bedrooms, king size beds and 4-posters for added luxury. Indoor heated swimming pool. Walled garden. Secure car park. Convenient for Channel Tunnel, ports, and historic castles and gardens of Kent.

Bedrooms: 10 double, 3 twin, 2 family rooms
Bathrooms: 15 en suite, 3 public

Parking for 12
CC: Amex, Barclaycard, Delta, Diners, Eurocard, JCB, Mastercard, Solo, Switch, Visa, Visa Electron

◆◆◆

WHITE HORSE INN
Boughton, Faversham, ME13 9AX
T: (01227) 751700 & 751343
F: (01227) 751090
E: ihopkins@shepherd-neame.co.uk
I: www.shepherd-neame.co.uk

B&B per night:
S Min £45.00
D Min £56.50

HB per person:
DY Min £47.50

OPEN All year round

15thC coaching inn with oak beams and inglenook fireplaces. Freshly prepared regional specialities, locally brewed Shepherd Neame award-winning ales. Half board daily price is based on a minimum 2-night stay.

Bedrooms: 7 double, 4 twin, 2 triple
Bathrooms: 13 en suite

Lunch available
EM 1900 (LO 2130)
Parking for 50
CC: Amex, Barclaycard, Delta, Eurocard, Mastercard, Switch, Visa

◆◆◆◆

THE WHITE HOUSE
6 St Peters Lane, Canterbury, CT1 2BP
T: (01227) 761836
E: whwelcome@aol.com

Bedrooms: 1 single, 4 double, 1 triple, 1 family room
Bathrooms: 7 en suite

B&B per night:
S £30.00–£35.00
D £45.00–£55.00

OPEN All year round

Regency house situated within the city walls next to the Marlowe Theatre. Superior accommodation with all rooms en suite. Family run.

◆◆◆

THE WOOLPACK INN
High Street, Chilham, Canterbury, CT4 8DL
T: (01227) 730208 & 730351
F: (01227) 731053
E: ihopkins@shepherd-neame.co.uk
I: www.shepherd-neame.co.uk

B&B per night:
S Min £45.00
D Min £56.50

HB per person:
DY Min £47.50

OPEN All year round

Ancient inn, C1422, with inglenook fireplaces and oak-beamed restaurant, in picturesque Chilham. Regional specialities, locally brewed ales. Locally renowned restaurant serving fresh local produce. Half-board daily price is based on a minimum 2-night stay.

Bedrooms: 7 double, 3 twin, 1 triple, 2 family rooms
Bathrooms: 13 en suite

Lunch available
EM 1900 (LO 2130)
Parking for 30
CC: Amex, Barclaycard, Delta, Eurocard, JCB, Maestro, Mastercard, Solo, Switch, Visa

REGIONAL TOURIST BOARD The ⋀ symbol in an establishment entry indicates that it is a Regional Tourist Board member.

CHICHESTER, West Sussex Map ref 2C3 *Tourist Information Centre Tel: (01243) 775888*

◆◆◆◆

THE COACH HOUSE

Binderton, Chichester, West Sussex
PO18 0JS
T: (01243) 539624 &
07710 536085 (Mobile)
F: (01243) 539624
E: spightling@aol.com

B&B per night:
S £22.00–£25.00
D £36.00–£50.00

OPEN All year round

Converted flint and brick coach house of 17thC origin, peacefully set in 2 acres of walled gardens overlooking the unspoilt Lavant Valley on the slopes of the South Downs. Ten minutes' drive Chichester, Goodwood, West Dean Gardens. Convenient for country walks, local pub. Recently updated, spacious accommodation, delicious English breakfast.

Bedrooms: 1 twin,
1 family room
Bathrooms: 1 private,
1 public

Parking for 10

◆◆◆

HEDGEHOGS

45 Whyke Lane, Chichester,
West Sussex PO19 2JT
T: (01243) 780022

Bedrooms: 1 single,
2 double
Bathrooms: 2 public

Parking for 4

B&B per night:
S £23.00–£24.00
D £36.00–£40.00

OPEN All year round

Non-smokers are offered a friendly welcome at our peaceful family home and secluded garden – just a short walk from city centre, stations and theatre.

COLDRED, Kent Map ref 3C4

◆◆◆◆

COLRET HOUSE

The Green, Coldred, Dover, CT15 5AP
T: (01304) 830388 (24 hours)
F: (01304) 830348

B&B per night:
S £25.00–£30.00
D £50.00–£60.00

OPEN All year round

An early Edwardian property with modern, purpose-built, en suite garden rooms, standing in extensive well maintained grounds. Situated beside the village green in a conservation area on downs above Dover. Ideally situated for overnight stays when travelling by ferries or shuttle. Close to Canterbury and Sandwich. Ample secure parking.

Bedrooms: 1 double,
1 twin
Bathrooms: 2 en suite

EM 1930 (LO 2100)
Parking for 6

AT-A-GLANCE SYMBOLS

Symbols at the end of each accommodation entry give useful information about services and facilities. A key to symbols can be found inside the back cover flap. Keep this open for easy reference.

CRAWLEY, West Sussex Map ref 2D2

◆◆◆

Attractive country house set in beautiful countryside, only 5 minutes from Gatwick. The house is decorated and furnished to a high standard and we provide a warm and friendly welcome. All rooms are en suite and have colour TV and tea/coffee making facilities. Holiday parking available. Guest lounge/ conservatory.

WATERHALL COUNTRY HOUSE

Prestwood Lane, Ifield Wood, Crawley, West Sussex RH11 0LA
T: (01293) 520002
F: (01293) 539905
E: info@waterhall.co.uk
I: www.smoothhound/hotels/waterhall

Bedrooms: 1 single, 3 double, 3 twin, 1 family room
Bathrooms: 8 en suite, 1 public

Parking for 25
CC: Barclaycard, Delta, Mastercard, Switch, Visa

B&B per night:
S £35.00–£35.00
D £45.00–£45.00

OPEN All year round

DANEHILL, East Sussex Map ref 2D3

◆◆◆◆

New Glenmore is a spacious bungalow set in 6 acres of grounds in a rural location close to the Bluebell Steam Railway and Sheffield Park National Trust property. We have a large family en suite room, a double and a twin room. Breakfast comes with our own eggs and honey.

NEW GLENMORE

Sliders Lane, Furners Green, Uckfield, East Sussex TN22 3RU
T: (01825) 790783
E: alan.robinson@bigfoot.com

Bedrooms: 1 double, 1 twin, 1 family room
Bathrooms: 1 en suite, 1 public

B&B per night:
S £35.00–£45.00
D £35.00–£45.00

OPEN All year round

DEAL, Kent Map ref 3C4 *Tourist Information Centre Tel: (01304) 369576*

◆◆◆◆

Large, quiet, detached Victorian house with Channel views and secluded garden, situated 100 yards from the beach. Guests have unrestricted access to rooms. Close to 3 championship golf courses, ferries, and the Channel Tunnel. Ideal centre for cliff walks and exploring Canterbury and the castles and gardens of East Kent.

HARDICOT GUEST HOUSE

Kingsdown Road, Walmer, Deal, CT14 8AW
T: (01304) 389234
F: (01304) 389234
E: guestboss@talk21.com

Bedrooms: 1 double, 2 twin
Bathrooms: 1 en suite, 2 private

Parking for 4

B&B per night:
S £20.00–£20.00
D £40.00–£46.00

OPEN All year round

NB **IMPORTANT NOTE** Information on accommodation listed in this guide has been supplied by the proprietors. As changes may occur you are advised to check details at the time of booking.

DORKING, Surrey Map ref 2D2

♦♦♦♦

BULMER FARM

Holmbury St Mary, Dorking,
RH5 6LG
T: (01306) 730210

Bedrooms: 3 double,
5 twin
Bathrooms: 5 en suite,
2 public

Parking for 12

B&B per night:
S £22.00–£35.00
D £44.00–£48.00

OPEN All year round

30-acre beef farm. 17thC character farmhouse with beams, in Surrey hills. Choice of twin rooms in the house or double/twin rooms in adjoining converted barn.

🐎12 🛁 ♿ ℞ UL S ⚡ TV 📖 ♨ 🍴12 ✿ 🚲 🏧 T

♦♦♦

FAIRDENE GUEST HOUSE

Moores Road, Dorking, RH4 2BG
T: (01306) 888337
E: zoe@fairdene5.freeserve.co.uk

Bedrooms: 2 double,
2 twin, 1 triple
Bathrooms: 2 public

Parking for 7

B&B per night:
S £25.00–£30.00
D £40.00–£50.00

OPEN All year round

Late-Victorian house in convenient location, close to town centre, Gatwick Airport and North Downs Way. Friendly and homely atmosphere. Off-street parking.

🐎 ❏ ♿ UL ⚡ ♨ TV 📖 ♨ 🚲 T

DOVER, Kent Map ref 3C4 *Tourist Information Centre Tel: (01304) 205108*

♦♦♦

CHRISLYN'S GUEST HOUSE

15 Park Avenue, Dover, CT16 1ES
T: (01304) 202302
F: (01304) 203317

Bedrooms: 1 double,
2 twin, 1 triple, 1 family
room
Bathrooms: 1 public,
4 private showers

B&B per night:
S £19.00–£25.00
D £38.00–£50.00

OPEN All year round

Warm, friendly and clean establishment – excellent breakfast. Five minutes' drive to the docks, ten minutes' walk to town centre, parks, station and castle.

🅰 🐎 📧 ❏ ♿ ℞ UL ✈ 🚲 T

♦♦♦

DOVER HOTEL

122-124 Folkestone Road, Dover,
CT17 9SP
T: (01304) 206559
F: (01304) 203936

Bedrooms: 3 single,
7 double, 2 twin, 3 triple
Bathrooms: 12 en suite,
1 public

Lunch available
EM (LO 2030)
Parking for 61
CC: Amex, Barclaycard,
Delta, Eurocard,
Mastercard, Switch, Visa

B&B per night:
S £30.00–£35.00
D £50.00–£55.00

HB per person:
DY £30.00–£35.00

OPEN All year round

Family-run business, 200 yards from the railway station and minutes away from the docks. Bar, restaurant and pool table facilities.

🅰 🐎 🛁 📧 ❏ ♿ ℞ 🍴 ♨ TV ◐ 📖 ♨ 🔍 ✿ T

♦♦

LONGFIELD GUEST HOUSE

203 Folkestone Road, Dover, CT17 9SL
T: (01304) 204716

B&B per night:
S £18.00–£25.00
D £30.00–£45.00

OPEN All year round

A clean and highly recommended guesthouse, 2 minutes from Dover Priory station, Hoverport and town centre, 10 minutes from Channel Tunnel. Single, double, twin and family rooms, some en suite, with colour TV, tea/coffee facilities, washbasins and central heating. Large car park and lock-up garage.

Bedrooms: 4 single,
2 double, 1 triple
Bathrooms: 1 en suite,
1 private, 2 public

EM 1900 (LO 2100)
Parking for 10
CC: Delta, JCB,
Mastercard, Solo, Switch,
Visa

🐎2 ❏ ♿ UL 📖 ♨ ✈ 🚲 T

WELCOME HOST This is a nationally recognised customer care programme which aims to promote the highest standards of service and a warm welcome. Establishments taking part in this initiative are indicated by the 🌸 symbol.

◆◆◆◆
Silver
Award

OWLER LODGE

Alkham Valley Road, Alkham, Dover, CT15 7DF
T: (01304) 826375
F: (01304) 826375
E: owlerlodge@aol.com
I: www.smoothhound.co.uk/hotels/owlerlodge.html

B&B per night:
S £36.00–£38.00
D £44.00–£50.00

OPEN All year round

Small guesthouse situated in the beautiful Alkham Valley between Dover and Folkestone, 3 miles from Channel Tunnel, 4 miles from Dover Docks. An ideal base for touring East Kent. All rooms have en suite shower, toilet, colour TV, clock/radio, hairdryer and tea-making facilities. Relax in our beautiful garden with our Koi ponds. Off-street parking. A non-smoking residence.

Bedrooms: 2 double, 1 family room	Lunch available EM 1800 (LO 1930)
Bathrooms: 3 en suite	Parking for 5

◆◆◆◆
Silver
Award

THE PARK INN

1-2 Park Place, Ladywell, Dover, CT6 1DQ
T: (01304) 203300
F: (01304) 203324
E: theparkinn@c.s.com

B&B per night:
S £35.00–£45.00
D £54.00–£64.00

OPEN All year round

The feel of Victorian England immediately embraces guests on arrival at the Park Inn. An extremely high standard of finish in decor, furnishings and fittings prevails in our en suite rooms which complement our successful inn and restaurant. All our rooms are cosy and comfortable and contain many facilities.

Bedrooms: 1 single, 1 double, 2 twin, 1 family room	Lunch available EM (LO 2200)
Bathrooms: 5 en suite	Parking for 2
	CC: Amex, Barclaycard, Delta, Diners, Eurocard, JCB, Mastercard, Solo, Switch, Visa, Visa Electron

---

◆◆◆◆

WATERSIDE GUEST HOUSE

15 Hythe Road, Dymchurch, Romney Marsh, TN29 0LN
T: (01303) 872253
F: (01303) 872253
E: water.side@cwcom.net
I: www.smoothhound.co.uk/hotels/watersid.html

B&B per night:
S £20.00–£25.00
D £32.00–£40.00

HB per person:
DY £27.00–£32.00

OPEN All year round

Cottage-style house offering comfortable rooms and attractive gardens, ideally situated for Channel crossings and touring historic Romney Marsh countryside by foot or transport. Experience the RH&D railway, visit Port Lympne Wild Animal Park or stroll along nearby sandy beaches, finally enjoying a drink or meal from our varied menu.

Bedrooms: 2 double, 2 twin, 1 family room	Lunch available EM 1730 (LO 2000)
Bathrooms: 3 en suite, 2 public	Parking for 7
	CC: Barclaycard, Delta, Eurocard, JCB, Mastercard, Solo, Switch, Visa, Visa Electron

QUALITY ASSURANCE SCHEME
Diamond ratings and awards are explained at the back of this guide.

EAST GRINSTEAD, West Sussex Map ref 2D2

♦♦♦ **CRANSTON HOUSE**

Cranston Road, East Grinstead,
West Sussex RH19 3HW
T: (01342) 323609
F: (01342) 323609
E: accommodation@
cranstonhouse.screaming.net

Bedrooms: 1 double,
2 twin
Bathrooms: 1 en suite,
1 public

Parking for 4

B&B per night:
S £25.00–£28.00
D £38.00–£40.00

OPEN All year round

Detached house in quiet location near town centre, 15 minutes' drive from Gatwick. Spacious high quality accommodation. Ample parking off-road.

EASTBOURNE, East Sussex Map ref 3B4 *Tourist Information Centre Tel: (01323) 411400*

♦♦♦ **BAY LODGE HOTEL**

61-62 Royal Parade, Eastbourne,
East Sussex BN22 7AQ
T: (01323) 732515
F: (01323) 735009
E: Beryl@mnewson.freeserve.co.uk

Bedrooms: 3 single,
5 double, 4 twin
Bathrooms: 4 en suite,
5 private, 2 public

EM 1800 (LO 1800)
Parking for 2
CC: Barclaycard, Delta,
Mastercard, Switch, Visa

B&B per night:
S £22.00–£28.00
D £44.00–£56.00

HB per person:
DY £30.00–£36.00

OPEN All year round

Family-run seafront hotel, close to bowling greens and marina. Large sun-lounge. All double/twin bedrooms are en suite. Non-smokers' lounge, licensed bar.

◆◆◆◆
Silver Award

BRAYSCROFT HOTEL

13 South Cliff Avenue, Eastbourne,
East Sussex BN20 7AH
T: (01323) 647005
F: (01323) 720705
E: brayscroft@hotmail.com
I: www.brayscrofthotel.co.uk

B&B per night:
S £27.00–£34.00
D £52.00–£68.00

HB per person:
DY £39.00–£48.00

OPEN All year round

Elegant award-winning small hotel, one of only a handful in Eastbourne with coveted ETC 4 Diamonds – Silver Award for "outstanding accommodation and hospitality". Superb position less than a minute from seafront in fashionable Meads district and ideally situated for South Downs, theatres, restaurants and town centre. Totally non-smoking.

Bedrooms: 1 single,
3 double, 2 twin
Bathrooms: 6 en suite

EM 1800 (LO 1900)
CC: Barclaycard, Delta,
Eurocard, JCB,
Mastercard, Solo, Switch,
Visa, Visa Electron

◆◆◆◆ **CAMBRIDGE HOUSE**

6 Cambridge Road, Eastbourne,
East Sussex BN22 7BS
T: (01323) 721100

Bedrooms: 1 single,
3 double, 1 twin, 2 triple
Bathrooms: 4 en suite,
1 public

EM 1800 (LO 1800)

B&B per night:
S £15.00–£20.00
D £30.00–£40.00

HB per person:
DY £21.00–£26.00

OPEN All year round

Small, friendly guesthouse, 50 yards from the seafront near Redoubt Gardens. Home cooking and personal attention of resident proprietors.

QUALITY ASSURANCE SCHEME

For an explanation of the quality and facilities represented by the Diamonds please refer to the front of this guide. A more detailed explanation can be found in the information pages at the back.

◆◆◆◆
Silver
Award

CHERRY TREE HOTEL

15 Silverdale Road, Eastbourne, East Sussex
BN20 7AJ
T: (01323) 722406
F: (01323) 648838
E: anncherrytree@aol.com
I: www.eastbourne.org/cherrytree-hotel

B&B per night:
S £26.00–£33.00
D £52.00–£66.00

HB per person:
DY £38.50–£45.50

OPEN All year round

Tastefully converted Edwardian
residence, this award-winning
family-run licensed hotel retains its
original charm, elegance and
character yet offers all the comfort
and convenience expected by today's
discerning guest. Quiet location close
to seafront, downlands and theatres,
the hotel is noted for its excellent
traditional English cuisine. Non-
smoking.

Bedrooms: 2 single,
3 double, 4 twin, 1 triple
Bathrooms: 10 en suite

EM 1800 (LO 1830)
CC: Amex, Barclaycard,
Delta, Diners, Eurocard,
Maestro, Mastercard,
Switch, Visa, Visa Electron

◆◆◆

EDELWEISS PRIVATE HOTEL

10-12 Elms Avenue, Eastbourne,
East Sussex BN21 3DN
T: (01323) 732071
F: (01323) 732071
E: peterbutler@fsbdial.co.uk

B&B per night:
S £16.00–£18.00
D £32.00–£40.00

HB per person:
DY £22.00–£26.00

OPEN All year round

Set in an attractive avenue 50 yards
from the sea, the Edelweiss is a
14-bedroom family-run hotel with
licensed bar and lounge. Bedrooms
have colour TV and tea-making
facilities. We offer full English
breakfast with optional evening
dinners. An ideal base for touring the
Sussex Downs and 1066 Country.

Bedrooms: 2 single,
6 double, 5 twin,
1 family room
Bathrooms: 3 en suite,
4 public

EM 1800 (LO 1500)
CC: Barclaycard, Delta,
Eurocard, Mastercard,
Visa

◆◆◆◆

LITTLE FOXES

24 Wannock Road, Eastbourne,
East Sussex BN22 7JU
T: (01323) 640670
F: (01323) 640670
E: chris@foxholes55.freeserve.co.
uk

Bedrooms: 1 single,
1 twin; suites available
Bathrooms: 2 en suite

B&B per night:
S £19.00–£22.00
D £38.00–£44.00

OPEN All year round

Personally run B&B. Close to beach and 1 kilometre town centre. En suite facilities. Guests'
lounge with Sky TV. All ages welcome. No smoking.

◆◆◆◆◆
Gold
Award

PINNACLE POINT

Foyle Way, Eastbourne, East Sussex
BN20 7XL
T: (01323) 726666 &
0796 7209958 (Mobile)
F: (01323) 643946

B&B per night:
S £50.00–£100.00
D £60.00–£120.00

OPEN All year round

Not a B&B – an experience. Luxury
house with unrivalled views
overlooking the English Channel.
Unique position on the cliffs near the
foot of the South Downs. Used by
stars of theatre, TV and international
sport. The host encourages guests to
take an early morning Downland
walk. A must for bird lovers.

Bedrooms: 2 double,
1 twin
Bathrooms: 3 en suite

Parking for 4
CC: Visa

EASTBOURNE continued

♦♦ STRATFORD HOTEL & RESTAURANT

59 Cavendish Place, Eastbourne,	Bedrooms: 2 single,	Lunch available	B&B per night:
East Sussex BN21 3RL	5 double, 4 twin, 2 triple	EM 1800 (LO 2300)	**S £22.00–£24.00**
T: (01323) 724051 & 726391	Bathrooms: 11 en suite,	CC: Barclaycard, Delta,	**D £40.00–£44.00**
F: (01323) 726391	1 public	Mastercard, Visa	

Ideally situated near promenade, coaches and shopping centre. Licensed, centrally heated throughout. Ground floor and family rooms available. Most rooms with modern en suite.

HB per person:
DY £25.00–£28.00

OPEN All year round

EPSOM, Surrey Map ref 2D2

♦♦♦♦

WHITE HOUSE HOTEL
Downs Hill Road, Epsom, KT18 5HW
T: (01372) 722472
F: (01372) 744447

B&B per night:
S £45.00–£57.50
D £57.50–£75.50

HB per person:
DY £65.00–£100.00

OPEN All year round

Charming, spacious, traditional mansion converted into a modern hotel. Epsom town and station are only minutes away, with regular train services to London. Convenient for Gatwick and Heathrow airports and London via A23 and M25.	Bedrooms: 7 single, 2 double, 3 twin, 1 family room Bathrooms: 7 en suite, 6 private showers	Lunch available EM 1800 (LO 2030) Parking for 15 CC: Amex, Barclaycard, Delta, Diners, Eurocard, Mastercard, Switch, Visa

---

EWHURST, Surrey Map ref 2D2

♦♦♦ YARD FARM

Ewhurst, Cranleigh, GU6 7SN	Bedrooms: 1 single,	EM 1900 (LO 2030)	B&B per night:
T: (01483) 276649	1 double, 2 twin,	Parking for 6	**S £22.50–£25.00**
F: (01483) 276649	Bathrooms: 2 en suite,		**D £45.00–£50.00**
	1 public		

350-acre mixed farm. A 16thC farmhouse surrounded by countryside. Working farm, mainly grass with sheep and horses.

HB per person:
DY £37.50–£45.00

OPEN All year round

FAVERSHAM, Kent Map ref 3B3 *Tourist Information Centre Tel: (01795) 534542*

♦♦♦ BARNSFIELD

Fostall, Hernhill, Faversham,	Bedrooms: 2 double,	EM 1830 (LO 2100)	B&B per night:
ME13 9JH	1 twin	Parking for 10	**S £14.00–£24.00**
T: (01227) 750973 & 07889 836259	Bathrooms: 1 en suite,		**D £28.00–£48.00**
F: (01227) 273098	1 public		
E: barnsfield@yahoo.com			OPEN All year round
I: www.barnsfield.co.uk			

Listed Grade II country cottage accommodation, just off A299, set in 3 acres of orchards. 6 miles from Canterbury. Convenient for ports and touring.

USE YOUR *i*s

There are more than 550 Tourist Information Centres throughout England offering friendly help with accommodation and holiday ideas as well as suggestions of places to visit and things to do. You'll find TIC addresses in the local Phone Book.

FAVERSHAM continued

◆◆◆◆
Silver
Award

PRESTON LEA

Canterbury Road, Faversham, ME13 8XA
T: (01795) 535266
F: (01795) 533388
E: preston.lea@which.net
I: www.homepages.which.net/~alan.
turner10

B&B per night:
S £35.00–£35.00
D £48.00–£55.00

OPEN All year round

A unique and elegant Victorian Gothic house with turrets, set in large secluded gardens. Spacious, sunny bedrooms with garden views and antique furniture. Beautiful guest drawing room, panelled dining room and delicious breakfasts. Only 15 minutes from Canterbury, 35 minutes from ports, Eurotunnel, 70 minutes train to London.

Bedrooms: 2 double, 1 twin
Bathrooms: 2 en suite, 1 private

Parking for 11
CC: Barclaycard, Delta, Eurocard, JCB, Maestro, Mastercard, Solo, Switch, Visa, Visa Electron

FITTLEWORTH, West Sussex Map ref 2D3

◆◆◆◆
Silver
Award

SWAN INN
Lower Street, Fittleworth, Pulborough, West Sussex RH20 1EN
T: (01798) 865429
F: (01798) 865721
I: ww.swaninn.com

Bedrooms: 3 single, 6 double, 2 twin
Bathrooms: 11 en suite

Lunch available
EM 1830 (LO 2130)
Parking for 22
CC: Amex, Barclaycard, Delta, Eurocard, JCB, Mastercard, Solo, Switch, Visa, Visa Electron

B&B per night:
S £30.00–£35.00
D £60.00–£70.00

HB per person:
DY £38.00–£45.00

OPEN All year round

Listed 14thC building in centre of village, well placed for visiting many of the historic houses and places of interest in the area.

GATWICK AIRPORT, West Sussex

See under Crawley, East Grinstead, Horley, Redhill

GODALMING, Surrey Map ref 2D2

◆◆◆
HEATH HALL FARM
Bowlhead Green, Godalming, GU8 6NW
T: (01428) 682808
F: (01428) 684025

Bedrooms: 1 single, 1 double, 1 twin
Bathrooms: 2 en suite, 1 private

Parking for 10

B&B per night:
S £25.00–£30.00
D £45.00–£50.00

OPEN All year round

Farmhouse on the edge of hamlet. Converted stable courtyard. Free-range fowl, sheep and horse. Tennis court. Farmhouse atmosphere. Pets welcome if under control.

GOUDHURST, Kent Map ref 3B4

◆◆◆◆

MOUNT HOUSE

Ranters Lane, Goudhurst, Cranbrook, TN17 1HN
T: (01580) 211230 (answerphone) &
07808 170944 (mobile)
E: DavidMargaretSargent@compuserve.
com

B&B per night:
D £50.00–£50.00

OPEN Apr–Sep

18thC Grade II Listed country house set in delightful gardens of 2 acres and surrounded by countryside. Originally part of the Scotney Estate, the house has been fully restored and decorated in keeping with its period character. Many well-known gardens nearby, including Scotney Castle, Sissinghurst and Great Dixter.

Bedrooms: 1 double, 1 twin
Bathrooms: 1 en suite, 1 private

GUILDFORD, Surrey Map ref 2D2 *Tourist Information Centre Tel: (01483) 444333*

◆◆◆ CHALKLANDS

Beech Avenue, Effingham,
Leatherhead, KT24 5PJ
T: (01372) 454936
F: (01372) 459569
E: reilly@tecres.net

Bedrooms: 1 double,
2 twin
Bathrooms: 2 en suite,
1 private

EM
Parking for 10

B&B per night:
S £30.00–£35.00
D £42.00–£50.00

OPEN All year round

Detached house backing on to Effingham golf course. 30 minutes from Heathrow/Gatwick airports, 35 minutes from London Waterloo station. Excellent pub food nearby.

◆◆◆ HIGH EDSER

Shere Road, Ewhurst, Cranleigh,
Guildford, GU6 7PQ
T: (01483) 278214 (Answerphone)
& 0777 5865125 (Mobile)
F: (01483) 278200

Bedrooms: 2 double
Bathrooms: 1 public

Parking for 7

B&B per night:
S £25.00–£30.00
D £50.00–£55.00

OPEN All year round

Early 16thC family home in Area of Outstanding Natural Beauty. 6 miles from Guildford and Dorking, easy reach airports and many tourist attractions. Non-smokers only, please.

◆◆◆ LITTLEFIELD MANOR

Littlefield Common, Guildford,
GU3 3HJ
T: (01483) 233068 & 232687
F: (01483) 233686

Bedrooms: 2 double,
1 twin
Bathrooms: 3 en suite

EM 1900 (LO 2130)
Parking for 10
CC: Amex, Barclaycard,
Mastercard, Visa

B&B per night:
S £37.50–£40.00
D £55.00–£60.00

OPEN All year round

120-acre mixed farm. 17thC Listed manor house with Tudor origins. Enjoy the walled rose garden in summer or the blazing log fire in winter.

HALLAND, East Sussex Map ref 2D3

◆◆◆◆

TAMBERRY HALL

Eastbourne Road, Halland, Lewes,
East Sussex BN8 6PS
T: (01825) 880090
F: (01825) 880090

B&B per night:
S £30.00–£35.00
D £45.00–£60.00

OPEN All year round

Delightful country house in 3 acres. Comfortable friendly atmosphere, exposed beams and inglenook fireplace in guests' lounge. Central for touring this Area of Outstanding Natural Beauty, the coast, gardens, National Trust. Glyndebourne and golf nearby, restaurant and pub within walking distance. Self-catering annexe. Vegetarian a speciality. Midweek special breaks.

Bedrooms: 2 double,
1 triple
Bathrooms: 3 en suite

Parking for 6

HASLEMERE, Surrey Map ref 2C2

◆◆◆ SHEPS HOLLOW

Henley Common, Haslemere,
GU27 3HB
T: (01428) 653120

Bedrooms: 3 single,
1 double
Bathrooms: 1 en suite,
2 public

Lunch available
EM 1800 (LO 2200)
Parking for 5

B&B per night:
S £25.00–£30.00
D £50.00–£60.00

HB per person:
DY £30.00–£40.00

OPEN All year round

Charming 500-year-old cottage in a rural setting. Newly renovated. Sky TV in rooms, 4 ft movie screen.

CREDIT CARD BOOKINGS If you book by telephone and are asked for your credit card number it is advisable to check the proprietor's policy should you cancel your reservation.

HASTINGS, East Sussex Map ref 3B4 *Tourist Information Centre Tel: (01424) 781111*

◆◆◆◆

EAGLE HOUSE HOTEL

12 Pevensey Road, St Leonards-on-Sea,
Hastings, East Sussex TN38 0JZ
T: (01424) 430535 & 441273
F: (01424) 437771
E: info@eaglehousehotel.com
I: www.eaglehousehotel.com

B&B per night:
S £30.00–£33.00
D £48.00–£52.00

HB per person:
DY £45.00–£50.00

OPEN All year round

You are assured of a warm welcome at the Eagle House Hotel. The charm and style of a bygone age is reflected in the spacious Victorian reception rooms. Our competitive rates include full English breakfast and free parking. Few minutes' walk from Warrior Square railway station.

Bedrooms: 14 double,
2 twin, 2 triple
Bathrooms: 18 en suite,
2 public

Lunch available
EM 1830 (LO 2030)
Parking for 14
CC: Amex, Barclaycard,
Delta, Diners, Eurocard,
JCB, Maestro, Mastercard,
Solo, Switch, Visa, Visa
Electron

◆◆◆◆

THE GALLERY

24 Elphinstone Road, Hastings,
East Sussex TN34 2EQ
T: (01424) 718110 &
07703 255530 (Mobile)
E: freeserve.co.uk
I: www.thegallerybnb.freeserve.co.uk

Bedrooms: 2 double,
2 twin
Bathrooms: 2 en suite,
2 private, 1 public

Parking for 2

B&B per night:
D £34.00–£38.00

OPEN All year round

Well decorated and maintained. Some en suite rooms. All rooms have hot and cold water and beverage-making facilities. Full English breakfast, some parking on site.

◆◆

MAYFAIR HOTEL

9 Eversfield Place, St Leonards-on-Sea, Hastings, East Sussex
TN37 6BY
T: (01424) 434061

Bedrooms: 3 single,
2 double, 3 twin, 3 triple
Bathrooms: 6 en suite,
1 public, 2 private
showers

EM 1800 (LO 1900)
CC: Barclaycard, Delta,
Mastercard, Visa

B&B per night:
S £18.00–£30.00
D £35.00–£60.00

HB per person:
DY £25.00–£75.00

OPEN All year round

Family-owned and run hotel on the seafront. Several rooms are en suite and face the sea. Close to town centre.

◆◆◆

SOUTH RIDING GUEST HOUSE

96 Milward Road, Hastings,
East Sussex TN34 3RT
T: (01424) 420805

Bedrooms: 1 double,
2 twin
Bathrooms: 2 public

EM 1800

B&B per night:
S £15.00–£16.00
D £36.00–£40.00

HB per person:
DY £26.00–£28.00

OPEN All year round

Comfortable 10 minutes from the sea, the castle, old town and new shopping centre. Bus stop and parking outside. Home cooking. No smoking throughout.

HEATHFIELD, East Sussex Map ref 2D3

◆◆◆◆

SPICERS BED & BREAKFAST

21 Spicers Cottages, Cade Street,
Heathfield, East Sussex TN21 9BS
T: (01435) 866363 (Answerphone)
& 07973 188138 (Mobile)
F: (01435) 866363
E: spicersbb@cs.co.uk
I: www.spicers-bed-breakfast.com

Bedrooms: 1 single,
1 double, 1 twin
Bathrooms: 1 en suite,
2 private

Parking for 3
CC: Barclaycard, Delta,
JCB, Mastercard, Solo,
Switch, Visa, Visa Electron

B&B per night:
S £20.00–£25.00
D £40.00–£45.00

HB per person:
DY £35.00–£40.00

OPEN Jan–Oct
& Christmas

Beamed cottage in hamlet of Cade Street near Heathfield on the High Weald, between Eastbourne and Tunbridge Wells. Convenient for many places of interest.

MAP REFERENCES
Map references apply to the colour maps at the front of this guide.

HERSTMONCEUX, East Sussex Map ref 3B4

◆◆◆ **THE STUD FARM**

Bodle Street Green, Herstmonceux,
Hailsham, East Sussex BN27 4RJ
T: (01323) 833201
F: (01323) 833201

Bedrooms: 1 double,
2 twin
Bathrooms: 1 en suite,
1 public

EM 1830
Parking for 3

B&B per night:
S £23.00–£25.00
D £40.00–£42.00

OPEN All year round

70-acre mixed farm. Upstairs, 2 bedrooms and bathroom let as one unit to party of 2, 3 or 4. Downstairs, twin-bedded en suite room. Guests' sitting room and sunroom.

HIGHAM, Kent Map ref 3B3

◆◆◆ **THE GARDENERS ARMS**

Forge Lane, Higham, Rochester,
ME3 7AS
T: (01474) 822721
F: (01474) 823258
E: gardenersarms@barclays.net
I: www.gardenersarms.com

Bedrooms: 1 single,
3 double, 2 twin
Bathrooms: 4 en suite,
1 public

Lunch available
EM 1830 (LO 2130)
Parking for 10
CC: Barclaycard, Delta,
JCB, Mastercard, Solo,
Switch, Visa

B&B per night:
S £25.00–£35.00
D £40.00–£60.00

OPEN All year round

Award-winning inn and restaurant close to Rochester. Well appointed accommodation. Walking distance Dickens' home and Knowle Country House.

HORLEY, Surrey Map ref 2D2

◆◆◆ **GAINSBOROUGH LODGE**

39 Massetts Road, Horley, RH6 7DT
T: (01293) 783982
F: (01293) 785365
E: gainsbor@eurobell.co.uk
I: www.gainsboroughlodge.co.uk

Bedrooms: 7 single,
6 double, 9 twin, 1 triple,
2 family rooms
Bathrooms: 23 en suite,
1 public

Parking for 16
CC: Barclaycard, Diners,
JCB, Mastercard, Solo,
Switch, Visa

B&B per night:
S Min £39.50
D Min £52.00

OPEN All year round

Extended Edwardian house set in attractive garden. Five minutes' walk from Horley station and town centre. Five minutes' drive from Gatwick Airport.

◆◆◆◆

ROSEMEAD GUEST HOUSE

19 Church Road, Horley, RH6 7EY
T: (01293) 430546 & 784965
F: (01293) 430547
E: rosemead@globalnet.co.uk
I: www.rosemeadguesthouse.co.uk

B&B per night:
S £33.00–£37.00
D Min £50.00

OPEN All year round

Non-smoking guesthouse 5 minutes from Gatwick. Families welcome. Shops, restaurants and pubs nearby. All rooms have private bathroom, colour TV, beverage tray, full central heating. Full English breakfast included. Continental breakfast available for early departures. Holiday parking available.

Bedrooms: 2 single,
1 double, 1 twin,
2 family rooms
Bathrooms: 5 en suite,
1 private

Parking for 8
CC: Barclaycard, Delta,
JCB, Mastercard, Solo,
Switch, Visa

HOVE

See under Brighton & Hove

TOWN INDEX

This can be found at the back of the guide. If you know where you want to stay, the index will give you the page number listing accommodation in your chosen town, city or village.

◆◆◆◆

WICKHAM PLACE

Wickham Drive, Hurstpierpoint, Hassocks,
West Sussex BN6 9AP
T: (01273) 832172
F: (01273) 832172
E: stay@wickham-place.co.uk

B&B per night:
S Min £30.00
D Min £45.00

OPEN All year round

*Wickham Place is a large 1920s
character house in a lovely, quiet,
Sussex village. Within easy reach of
Brighton and Gatwick, it is ideally
situated for touring or just having a
relaxing break. Golf, walking, horse
riding, sightseeing and gardens all
within easy distance. Telephone, fax
or e-mail for brochure.*

Bedrooms: 1 single,
1 double, 1 twin
Bathrooms: 2 public

EM 1800 (LO 1900)
Parking for 6

◆◆◆

THE DOG & BEAR HOTEL

The Square, Lenham, Maidstone, ME17 2PG
T: (01622) 858219
F: (01622) 859415
E: dogbear@shepherd-neame.co.uk
I: www.shepherd-neame.co.uk

B&B per night:
S Min £45.00
D Min £56.50

HB per person:
DY Min £47.50

OPEN All year round

*15thC coaching inn retaining its old
world character and serving good
Kent ale, lagers and fine wines with
home cooking. En suite rooms. 5
minutes' drive from Leeds Castle.
Half board daily price is based on a
minimum 2-night stay.*

Bedrooms: 3 single,
13 double, 5 twin,
2 triple, 1 family room
Bathrooms: 24 en suite

Lunch available
EM 1900 (LO 2130)
Parking for 26
CC: Amex, Barclaycard,
Delta, Eurocard, Maestro,
Mastercard, Solo, Switch,
Visa, Visa Electron

◆◆◆◆

ECKINGTON HOUSE

Ripe, Lewes, East Sussex BN8 6AV
T: (01323) 811274 (Preferably pm/evening)
& (01825) 712864 (Part-time work)
F: (01323) 811140
E: suetj@mistral.co.uk
I: www3.mistral.co.uk/suetj

B&B per night:
S £25.00–£35.00
D £45.00–£55.00

OPEN Mar–Oct

*Historic 16thC Listed property with a
wealth of oak beams and inglenook
fireplaces, set in mature, peaceful
gardens. Clients can enjoy total
relaxation, yet still be close to the
interesting and ancient town of
Lewes, the South Downs,
Glyndebourne Opera House and the
lively coastal resorts of Eastbourne
and Brighton.*

Bedrooms: 3 double
Bathrooms: 3 en suite

ACCESSIBILITY

Look for the 🚻 symbols which indicate accessibility for
wheelchair users. A list of establishments is at the front of this guide.

LYMINSTER, West Sussex Map ref 2D3

◆◆◆◆

SANDFIELD HOUSE

Lyminster, Littlehampton,
West Sussex BN17 7PG
T: (01903) 724129 (BT
Answerphone)
F: (01903) 715041
E: thefbs@aol.com

Bedrooms: 1 double,
1 twin
Bathrooms: 1 public

Parking for 4

B&B per night:
D £36.00–£40.00

OPEN All year round

Spacious country-style family house in 2 acres. Between Arundel and sea, near area of Outstanding Natural Beauty.

MAIDSTONE, Kent Map ref 3B3 *Tourist Information Centre Tel: (01622) 602169 or 739029 (M20, jct 8)*

◆◆◆◆◆
Gold
Award

On the tranquil North Downs, just 10 minutes from Leeds Castle, this character Kentish farmhouse is luxuriously furnished in rustic oak throughout, including a canopied 4-poster bed. Opposite, the famous 16thC Ringlestone Inn is recommended for interesting Kentish fare incorporating English fruit wines in the traditional recipes.

THE RINGLESTONE INN & FARMHOUSE HOTEL

Ringlestone Hamlet, Harrietsham,
Maidstone, ME17 1NX
T: (01622) 859900 &
07973 612261 (Mobile)
F: (01622) 859966
E: bookings@ringlestone.com
I: www.ringlestone.com

B&B per night:
S £90.00–£100.00
D £111.00–£111.00

OPEN All year round

Bedrooms: 2 double,
1 family room; suites
available
Bathrooms: 3 en suite

Lunch available
EM 1900 (LO 2130)
Parking for 74
CC: Amex, Barclaycard,
Delta, Diners, Eurocard,
Mastercard, Switch, Visa

◆◆◆

SYLVIA HADDOW

51 Bower Mount Road, Maidstone,
ME16 8AX
T: (01622) 762948
E: sylviabnb@compuserve.com

Bedrooms: 1 double,
1 twin
Bathrooms: 1 public

B&B per night:
D £35.00–£38.00

OPEN All year round

Comfortable Edwardian semi-detached house. TV and tea and coffee making facilities in all rooms. Within walking distance of the town and easy access to the M20.

Rating
Applied For

WILLINGTON COURT

Willington Street, Maidstone,
ME15 8JW
T: (01622) 738885
F: (01622) 631790
E: willington@maidstone.prestel.
co.uk
I: www.bbchannel.com/bbc/
p604332.aspwww.hotelkent.com

Bedrooms: 2 double,
1 twin
Bathrooms: 3 en suite

Lunch available
EM 1900 (LO 2000)
Parking for 6
CC: Amex, Barclaycard,
Delta, Eurocard, JCB,
Maestro, Mastercard,
Solo, Switch, Visa, Visa
Electron

B&B per night:
S £27.00–£37.00
D £48.00–£68.00

OPEN All year round

Charming Grade II Listed building. Friendly and relaxed atmosphere. Adjacent to Mote Park and near Leeds Castle. Dinners, wines, 4-poster bed.

MARDEN, Kent Map ref 3B4

◆◆◆◆

TANNER HOUSE

Tanner Farm, Goudhurst Road,
Marden, Tonbridge, TN12 9ND
T: (01622) 831214
F: (01622) 832472
E: tannerfarm@compuserve.com

Bedrooms: 1 double,
2 twin
Bathrooms: 3 en suite,
1 public

EM
Parking for 3
CC: Barclaycard, Delta,
Maestro, Mastercard,
Solo, Switch, Visa, Visa
Electron

B&B per night:
S Max £30.00
D £40.00–£45.00

HB per person:
DY £34.00–£44.00

OPEN All year round

150-acre arable farm. Tudor farmhouse in centre of attractive family farm. Inglenook dining room. Off B2079. Car essential. Shire horses bred on farm.

COLOUR MAPS Colour maps at the front of this guide pinpoint all places under which you will find accommodation listed.

MIDHURST, West Sussex Map ref 2C3 *Tourist Information Centre Tel: (01730) 817322*

◆◆◆ **MOONLIGHT COTTAGE & TEA ROOMS**

Chichester Road, Cocking,	Bedrooms: 2 double	Parking for 10
Midhurst, West Sussex GU29 0HN	Bathrooms: 1 public	CC: Amex, Barclaycard,
T: (01730) 813336		Delta, Diners, Eurocard,
F: (01730) 813362		JCB, Maestro, Mastercard,
E: enquiries@moonlightcottage.net		Solo, Switch, Visa, Visa
I: www.moonlightcottage.net		Electron

B&B per night:
S £23.00–£30.00
D £46.00–£46.00

OPEN Feb–Dec

Grade II Listed period cottage with elegant tea rooms, pretty garden, art gallery with collectables. Attractive bedrooms, excellent breakfast. Convenient Goodwood, South Downs, Chichester Theatre.

OXTED, Surrey Map ref 2D2

◆◆◆ **ARAWA**

58 Granville Road, Limpsfield,	Bedrooms: 2 twin,	Parking for 4
Oxted, RH8 0BZ	1 family room	
T: (01883) 714104 & 0800 298	Bathrooms: 1 en suite,	
5732	1 public	
F: (01883) 714104		
E: david@davidgibbs.co.uk		

B&B per night:
S £20.00–£30.00
D £40.00–£50.00

OPEN All year round

Family home near North Downs Way, Chartwell and Hever. Near rail service to London and 30 minutes to Gatwick by car. Friendly and comfortable.

◆◆◆◆ **MEADS**

23 Granville Road, Oxted, RH8 0BX	Bedrooms: 1 single,
T: (01883) 730115	1 twin
	Bathrooms: 1 public

B&B per night:
S Min £28.00
D £45.00–£50.00

OPEN All year round

Tudor-style family house on Kent/Surrey border. Town centre and station to London within walking distance. Easy drive to Gatwick. Non-smoking room.

◆◆◆ **THE NEW BUNGALOW**

Old Hall Farm, Tandridge Lane,	Bedrooms: 2 double,	Parking for 5
Oxted, RH8 9NS	1 twin	
T: (01342) 892508	Bathrooms: 1 en suite,	
F: (01342) 892508	1 public	
E: donnunn@compuserve.com		

B&B per night:
S £24.00–£30.00
D £38.00–£42.00

OPEN All year round

40-acre livestock farm. Spacious, modern bungalow set in green fields and reached by a private drive. 5 minutes' drive from M25.

PARTRIDGE GREEN, West Sussex Map ref 2D3

◆◆◆ **POUND COTTAGE BED & BREAKFAST**

Mill Lane, Littleworth,	Bedrooms: 1 single,	Parking for 8
Partridge Green, Horsham,	1 double, 1 twin	
West Sussex RH13 8JU	Bathrooms: 1 public	
T: (01403) 710218 & 711285		
F: (01403) 711337		
E: poundcottagebb@amserve.net		
I: www.horsham.co.uk/		
poundcottage.html		

B&B per night:
S £18.00–£20.00
D £36.00–£40.00

OPEN All year round

Pleasant country house in quiet surroundings. 8 miles from Horsham, 25 minutes from Gatwick. Just off the B2135 West Grinstead to Steyning road.

PETWORTH, West Sussex Map ref 2D3 *Tourist Information Centre Tel: (01798) 343523*

◆◆◆ **BURTON PARK FARM**

Petworth, West Sussex GU28 0JT	Bedrooms: 1 double,	Parking for 4
T: (01798) 342431	1 twin	
	Bathrooms: 2 en suite	

B&B per night:
S £23.00–£25.00
D £46.00–£50.00

OPEN All year round

250-acre arable farm. Relax here with comfort, good food, off-road parking. Excellent pubs nearby.

CONFIRM YOUR BOOKING
You are advised to confirm your booking in writing.

PETWORTH continued

◆◆◆◆ EEDES COTTAGE

Bignor Park Road, Bury Gate, Pulborough, West Sussex RH20 1EZ T: (01798) 831438 F: (01798) 831942	Bedrooms: 1 double, 2 twin Bathrooms: 1 en suite, 1 public	Parking for 15

B&B per night:
S £30.00–£30.00
D £45.00–£50.00

OPEN All year round

Quiet country house surrounded by farmland. Convenient main roads to Arundel, Chichester and Brighton. Dogs, horses accommodated. TV in all rooms.

◆◆◆◆ THE HORSE GUARDS INN
Silver Award

Tillington, Petworth, West Sussex GU28 9AF T: (01798) 342332 F: (01798) 344351 E: mail@horseguardsinn.co.uk I: www.horseguardsinn.co.uk	Bedrooms: 2 double, 1 twin Bathrooms: 3 en suite	Lunch available EM 1900 (LO 2200) Parking for 5 CC: Amex, Barclaycard, Delta, Diners, Eurocard, Mastercard, Solo, Switch, Visa, Visa Electron

B&B per night:
D £73.00–£82.00

OPEN All year round

Charming 300-year-old inn, with lots of low beams, inglenook area, 3 open fires, secluded garden and magnificent views over South Downs.

PULBOROUGH, West Sussex Map ref 2D3

◆◆◆◆
Silver Award

MOSELEYS BARN
Hardham, Pulborough, West Sussex
RH20 1LB
T: (01798) 872912
F: (01798) 872912

B&B per night:
S £30.00–£35.00
D £44.00–£55.00

OPEN All year round

Converted 17thC barn with galleried beamed hall and light, south-facing bedrooms with panoramic views of South Downs. Accommodation consists of 2 ground floor en suite double bedrooms in the courtyard and a further double/twin bedroom, all with TV and tea/coffee facilities.	Bedrooms: 2 double, 2 twin Bathrooms: 2 en suite, 1 public	Parking for 5

RAMSGATE, Kent Map ref 3C3 *Tourist Information Centre Tel: (01843) 583333*

◆◆◆ GLENDEVON GUEST HOUSE

8 Truro Road, Ramsgate, CT1 8DB T: (01843) 570909 F: (01843) 570909 E: glendevon@currantbun.com	Bedrooms: 3 double, 1 twin, 1 triple, 1 family room Bathrooms: 6 en suite	CC: JCB, Maestro, Mastercard, Solo, Switch, Visa, Visa Electron

B&B per night:
S £20.00–£24.00
D £34.00–£40.00

OPEN All year round

Delightful converted Victorian house near beach, harbour and town. Very comfortable rooms, all en suite and each containing attractive feature of modern kitchen/dining area.

REDHILL, Surrey Map ref 2D2

◆◆◆◆ ASHLEIGH HOUSE HOTEL

39 Redstone Hill, Redhill, RH1 4BG T: (01737) 764763 F: (01737) 780308	Bedrooms: 1 single, 2 double, 3 twin, 1 triple, 1 family room Bathrooms: 6 en suite, 1 public	Parking for 9 CC: Barclaycard, Eurocard, Mastercard, Visa

B&B per night:
S £35.00–£50.00
D £50.00–£55.00

OPEN All year round

Friendly, family-run early Edwardian house with most rooms en suite. 500 yards from railway station, London 30 minutes, Gatwick Airport 15 minutes.

QUALITY ASSURANCE SCHEME
Diamond ratings and awards were correct at the time of going to press but are subject to change. Please check at the time of booking.

ROGATE, West Sussex Map ref 2C3

◆◆◆ **TROTTON FARM**

Trotton, Petersfield, Hampshire
GU31 5EN
T: (01730) 813618
F: (01730) 816093

Bedrooms: 1 double,
2 twin
Bathrooms: 3 en suite

B&B per night:
S £25.00–£30.00
D £35.00–£40.00

OPEN All year round

Farmhouse just off the A272, access through yard. Accommodation and lounge/games room in a converted cartshed adjoining farmhouse. All rooms with en suite shower.

ROTTINGDEAN, East Sussex Map ref 2D3

◆◆◆ **BRAEMAR GUEST HOUSE**

Steyning Road, Rottingdean,
Brighton, East Sussex BN2 7GA
T: (01273) 304263

Bedrooms: 6 single,
5 double, 2 twin, 2 triple
Bathrooms: 3 public

B&B per night:
S £16.00–£18.50
D £32.00–£37.00

OPEN All year round

Family-run guesthouse, proud of its cheerful atmosphere, in an old world village where Rudyard Kipling once lived.

ROYAL TUNBRIDGE WELLS, Kent Map ref 2D2 *Tourist Information Centre Tel: (01892) 515675*

◆◆◆◆ **CHEQUERS**

Camden Park,
Royal Tunbridge Wells, TN2 5AD
T: (01892) 532299
F: (01892) 526448
E: stubbs.mcd@talk21.com

Bedrooms: 1 single,
1 twin
Bathrooms: 1 en suite,
1 private

Parking for 5

B&B per night:
S £25.00–£25.00
D £50.00–£55.00

OPEN All year round

Friendly family house, origins 1840. Part-walled garden. Private location, 10 minutes from Pantiles, high street, railway station. Peaceful, comfortable, central base. Non-smokers only, please.

◆◆◆◆ **HAWKENBURY FARM**

Hawkenbury Road,
Royal Tunbridge Wells, TN3 9AD
T: (01892) 536977
F: (01892) 536200

Bedrooms: 1 double,
1 family room
Bathrooms: 2 en suite

Parking for 7

B&B per night:
D £40.00–£46.00

OPEN All year round

Comfortable accommodation on small working farm in quiet location 1.5 miles south-east of Tunbridge Wells. Ample parking, views and walks. Many National Trust properties nearby. No smoking.

◆◆◆

MANOR COURT FARM
Ashurst, Royal Tunbridge Wells, TN3 9TB
T: (01892) 740279
E: jsoyke@jsoyke.freeserve.co.uk

B&B per night:
S £22.00–£28.00
D £44.00–£46.00

OPEN All year round

Georgian farmhouse with friendly atmosphere, spacious rooms and lovely views of Medway Valley. 350-acre mixed farm, good base for walking. Penshurst Place, Hever Castle, Chartwell, Sissinghurst, etc, all within easy reach by car. London 50 minutes by train from Tonbridge. Guest lounge, cream teas at weekends. Camping. On A264 half a mile east of Ashurst village.

Bedrooms: 1 double,
2 twin
Bathrooms: 2 public

Parking for 19

TOWN INDEX

This can be found at the back of this guide. If you know where you want to stay, the index will give you the page number listing accommodation in your chosen town, city or village.

ROYAL TUNBRIDGE WELLS continued

◆◆ ROSNAREE

189 Upper Grosvenor Road,
Royal Tunbridge Wells, TN1 2EF
T: (01892) 524017 (Answerphone)
E: david@rosnaree.freeserve.co.uk

Bedrooms: 3 twin
Bathrooms: 1 public

Parking for 4

B&B per night:
S £22.00–£24.00
D £34.00–£36.00

OPEN All year round

Comfortable Victorian home with parking, pleasant gardens. Five minutes Tunbridge Wells centre, 90 minutes Channel ports. Ideal for visiting historic Kent, Sussex and London.

◆◆◆ VALE ROYAL HOTEL

54-57 London Road,
Royal Tunbridge Wells, TN1 1DS
T: (01892) 525580
F: (01892) 526022

Bedrooms: 12 single,
9 double, 8 twin, 1 triple,
1 family room
Bathrooms: 25 cn suite,
5 public

Lunch available
EM 1845 (LO 1930)
CC: Barclaycard, Diners,
Eurocard, Mastercard,
Visa

B&B per night:
S £38.00–£50.00
D £68.00–£75.00

HB per person:
DY £48.00–£60.00

OPEN All year round

Family hotel, overlooking the common, set in beautiful secluded rose garden. All rooms have telephone, TV, tea and coffee-making facilities. Victorian conservatory leading on to the patio.

RUSTINGTON, West Sussex Map ref 2D3

◆◆◆◆

Silver
Award

KENMORE

Claigmar Road, Rustington, West Sussex
BN16 2NL
T: (01903) 784634
F: (01903) 784634

B&B per night:
S £23.50–£26.00
D £47.00–£52.00

OPEN All year round

Secluded Edwardian house in a garden setting in the heart of the village and close to sea. Attractive en suite rooms, individually decorated and comfortably furnished. Private parking. Ideal for touring historic towns, castles, cathedrals and stately homes. Sylvia and Ray Dobbs offer a warm and friendly welcome.

Bedrooms: 1 single,
1 double, 1 twin, 3 triple,
1 family room
Bathrooms: 7 en suite,
1 public

Parking for 7
CC: Amex, Barclaycard,
Mastercard, Visa

RYE, East Sussex Map ref 3B4 *Tourist Information Centre Tel: (01797) 226696*

◆◆◆

AVIEMORE GUEST HOUSE

28-30 Fishmarket Road, Rye, East Sussex
TN31 7LP
T: (01797) 223052
F: (01797) 223052
E: aviemore@lineone.net
I: www.SmoothHound.co.uk/hotels/
aviemore.html

B&B per night:
S £20.00–£22.00
D £36.00–£45.00

HB per person:
DY £28.00–£32.00

OPEN All year round

Owner-run, friendly guesthouse offering a genuinely warm welcome and excellent breakfast, percolated Kenya tea and coffee and home-made preserves a speciality. Overlooking the park and River Rother. For that special occasion – a champagne breakfast (prior arrangement). Two minutes' walk from town centre, 45 minutes from Channel Tunnel.

Bedrooms: 1 single,
4 double, 3 twin
Bathrooms: 4 en suite,
2 public

EM 1930
CC: Amex, Barclaycard,
Eurocard, JCB,
Mastercard, Visa

RATING All accommodation in this guide has been rated, or is awaiting a rating, by a trained English Tourism Council assessor.

RYE continued

◆◆◆◆◆
Silver Award

JEAKE'S HOUSE
Mermaid Street, Rye, East Sussex
TN31 7ET
T: (01797) 222828
F: (01797) 222623
E: jeakeshouse@btinternet.com
I: www.s-h-systems.co.uk/hotels/jeakes.html

Bedrooms: 1 single, 7 double, 1 twin, 2 triple, 1 family room
Bathrooms: 9 en suite, 1 private, 2 public

CC: Barclaycard, Delta, Eurocard, Mastercard, Visa

B&B per night:
S £27.50–£61.00
D £52.00–£68.00

OPEN All year round

Award-winning, stylishly restored townhouse in cobbled centre. Traditional elegance combined with modern comfort. Book-lined bar and sitting room. Private car park.

◆◆◆◆◆
Silver Award

LITTLE ORCHARD HOUSE
West Street, Rye, East Sussex
TN31 7ES
T: (01797) 223831
F: (01797) 223831

Bedrooms: 2 double
Bathrooms: 2 en suite

CC: Barclaycard, Delta, Eurocard, JCB, Maestro, Mastercard, Solo, Switch, Visa, Visa Electron

B&B per night:
S £45.00–£65.00
D £64.00–£90.00

OPEN All year round

Georgian townhouse in centre of Rye. Antique furnishings and large walled garden give country-house atmosphere. Four-poster beds, generous free-range/organic breakfast. Parking available.

◆◆◆

THE OLD VICARAGE
Rye Harbour, Rye, East Sussex
TN31 7TT
T: (01797) 222088

Bedrooms: 1 double, 1 twin
Bathrooms: 1 public

Parking for 4

B&B per night:
S £27.00–£45.00
D £39.00–£52.00

OPEN All year round

Imposing Victorian former vicarage, quietly situated close to sea and nature reserve. Antique furniture and open fires. Magnificent English breakfast. Classic excellence and old fashioned hospitality.

◆◆◆◆◆
Silver Award

PLAYDEN COTTAGE GUESTHOUSE
Military Road, Rye, East Sussex TN31 7NY
T: (01797) 222234
I: www.SmoothHound.co.uk/hotels/playden.html

B&B per night:
D £56.00–£64.00

HB per person:
DY £68.00–£79.00

OPEN All year round

Large character cottage, said to be "Grebe" from E.F. Benson's Mapp and Lucia novels. Personal service in a comfortable family home. Pretty gardens, rural aspect, peaceful – and a very warm welcome. Every third night free during winter period.

Bedrooms: 1 double, 2 twin
Bathrooms: 3 en suite, 1 public

EM
Parking for 7
CC: Barclaycard, JCB, Mastercard, Visa

◆◆◆◆

THE STRAND HOUSE
Tanyard's Lane, Winchelsea, Rye, East Sussex TN36 4JT
T: (01797) 226276
F: (01797) 224806
I: www.s-h-systems.co.uk/hotels/strand.html

B&B per night:
D £48.00–£65.00

OPEN All year round

A warm welcome awaits in the old-world charm of one of Winchelsea's oldest houses, dating from the 15thC, with oak beams and inglenooks. Overlooking National Trust pastureland. Four-poster bedroom. Residents' bar. Traditional English breakfasts utilising local produce served in the heavily beamed dining room. Log fires in season. Pretty gardens.

Bedrooms: 8 double, 1 twin, 1 triple
Bathrooms: 9 en suite, 1 private

EM 1900 (LO 1930)
Parking for 15
CC: Barclaycard, Delta, JCB, Maestro, Mastercard, Switch, Visa

◆◆◆

CROWN INN (THE FAMOUS CHERRY BRANDY HOUSE)

Ramsgate Road, Sarre, Birchington, CT7 OLF
T: (01843) 847808
F: (01843) 847914
E: crown@shepherd-neame.co.uk
I: www.shepherd-neame.co.uk

B&B per night:
S Min £45.00
D Min £56.50

HB per person:
DY Min £47.50

OPEN All year round

Ancient traditional inn, convenient for Canterbury. Inglenook fireplaces, gleaming brasses, freshly prepared regional specialities. Excellent locally brewed ales. Internationally known as the Cherry Brandy House, this secret recipe is sold exclusively here at the Crown Inn. Half board daily price is based on a minimum 2-night stay.

Bedrooms: 9 double, 2 twin, 1 triple
Bathrooms: 12 en suite

Lunch available
EM 1900 (LO 2200)
Parking for 40
CC: Amex, Barclaycard, Delta, Eurocard, Mastercard, Solo, Switch, Visa

 10

◆◆◆◆

THE SILVERDALE

21 Sutton Park Road, Seaford, East Sussex BN25 1RH
T: (01323) 491849
F: (01323) 891131
E: silverdale@mistral.co.uk
I: www.mistral.co.uk/silverdale/silver.htm

B&B per night:
S £25.00–£45.00
D £28.00–£60.00

HB per person:
DY £26.00–£57.00

OPEN All year round

Small, expertly run house-hotel in the centre of peaceful Edwardian seaside town. Beautifully prepared food and a host of English wines. Over 120 single malt whiskies. Only a few minutes' walk from the seaside, the antique shops and the friendly local pubs. We'd love to meet you.

Bedrooms: 1 single, 5 double, 1 triple, 1 family room
Bathrooms: 6 en suite, 1 public

Lunch available
EM 1800 (LO 2000)
Parking for 6
CC: Amex, Barclaycard, Delta, Diners, Eurocard, Mastercard, Switch, Visa

◆◆◆

THE MOORINGS HOTEL

97 Hitchen Hatch Lane, Sevenoaks, TN13 3BE
T: (01732) 452589 & 742323
F: (01732) 456462
E: theryans@mooringshotel.co.uk
I: www.mooringshotel.co.uk

Bedrooms: 5 single, 7 double, 9 twin, 2 triple
Bathrooms: 23 en suite

Lunch available
EM 1800 (LO 2030)
Parking for 24
CC: Amex, Barclaycard, Delta, Diners, Eurocard, JCB, Mastercard, Solo, Switch, Visa, Visa Electron

B&B per night:
S £40.00–£50.00
D £60.00–£70.00

HB per person:
DY £55.00–£65.00

OPEN All year round

Friendly family hotel offering high standard accommodation for tourists and business travellers. 30 minutes from London. Close to BR station.

30

CHECK THE MAPS

The colour maps at the front of this guide show all the cities, towns and villages for which you will find accommodation entries. Refer to the town index to find the page on which they are listed.

◆◆◆◆

ROSEWOOD

Ismays Road, Ivy Hatch, Sevenoaks,
TN15 0PA
T: (01732) 810496
E: rosewood@covenantblessings.co.uk

B&B per night:
**S £30.00–£35.00
D £45.00–£50.00**

OPEN All year round

Lovely old tile-hung Kentish ragstone family home C,1750. Warm, friendly, peaceful setting, beautiful gardens with stream/pond. Close local pubs serving excellent food. Ideal for Ightham Mote and Knole Park. Excellent area for walkers, convenient for M20/M25/M26, Sevenoaks and main line station (31 minutes to London).

Bedrooms: 1 double,
1 twin
Bathrooms: 1 en suite,
1 private

Parking for 4

◆◆◆

STAR HOUSE

Star Hill, Sevenoaks, TN14 6HA
T: (01959) 533109 &
07774 281558 (Mobile)

B&B per night:
**S £20.00–£22.50
D £36.00–£41.00**

OPEN All year round

Near Sevenoaks and M25, half a mile from roundabout near Star Hill. Entrance marked with black star on white post. 2 twin, 1 double, 2 bathrooms. Children welcome. Spacious grounds, stunning views, heated swimming pool. Ironing facilities, drying room. Phone Mrs Viner for directions.

Bedrooms: 1 double,
2 twin
Bathrooms: 2 public

Parking for 6

◆◆◆◆◆

HEMPSTEAD HOUSE

London Road, Bapchild, Sittingbourne,
ME9 9PP
T: (01795) 428020
F: (01795) 436362
E: info@hempsteadhouse.co.uk
I: www.hempsteadhouse.co.uk

B&B per night:
**S £65.00–£65.00
D £75.00–£75.00**

OPEN All year round

Exclusive privately owned country house hotel and restaurant situated in rural location, but on the main A2 between Canterbury and Sittingbourne. Set in 3 acres of beautifully landscaped gardens, we offer beautifully appointed accommodation, fine cuisine, prepared solely from fresh, local produce by our French chef, and friendly hospitality.

Bedrooms: 10 double,
2 twin, 2 triple
Bathrooms: 14 en suite

Lunch available
EM 1800 (LO 2200)
Parking for 22
CC: Amex, Barclaycard,
Delta, Diners, Eurocard,
Mastercard, Switch, Visa

ACCESSIBILITY

Look for the symbols which indicate accessibility for wheelchair users. A list of establishments is at the front of this guide.

SMARDEN, Kent Map ref 3B4

◆◆◆

CHEQUERS INN
The Street, Smarden, Ashford, TN27 8QA
T: (01233) 770217
F: (01233) 770623

B&B per night:
S £35.00–£45.00
D £50.00–£65.00

OPEN All year round

Listed 14thC inn, in heart of the Weald. Wealth of oak beams, beautifully landscaped gardens with duck pond. All rooms individually decorated. Ideal for touring and visiting many places of historic interest, including Leeds Castle and Sissinghurst Gardens. Many interesting walks, 5 golf courses nearby. Good food always available.

Bedrooms: 1 single, 2 double, 2 twin
Bathrooms: 3 en suite, 2 private, 1 public

Lunch available
EM 1800 (LO 2200)
Parking for 18
CC: Amex, Barclaycard, Delta, Eurocard, Mastercard, Solo, Switch, Visa

STELLING MINNIS, Kent Map ref 3B4

◆◆◆◆
Silver Award

GREAT FIELD FARM
Misling Lane, Stelling Minnis, Canterbury, CT4 6DE
T: (01227) 709223
F: (01227) 709223

Bedrooms: 2 double, 1 twin; suites available
Bathrooms: 3 en suite

Parking for 6
CC: Delta, JCB, Mastercard, Solo, Switch, Visa, Visa Electron

B&B per night:
S £25.00–£40.00
D £40.00–£45.00

OPEN All year round

Delightful farmhouse amidst beautiful countryside, gardens and paddocks. Enjoy peace and privacy in our suites, B&B or self catering. 10 minutes Canterbury/Channel Tunnel.

TENTERDEN, Kent Map ref 3B4

◆◆◆

COLLINA HOUSE HOTEL
East Hill, Tenterden, TN30 6RL
T: (01580) 764852 & 764004
F: (01580) 762224
E: Collina.house@dial.pipex.com
I: dspace.dial.pipex.com/collina.house

Bedrooms: 1 single, 5 double, 1 twin, 4 triple, 3 family rooms
Bathrooms: 14 en suite

Lunch available
EM 1900 (LO 2130)
Parking for 16
CC: Amex, Barclaycard, Delta, Mastercard, Solo, Switch, Visa

B&B per night:
S £40.00–£55.00
D £50.00–£75.00

HB per person:
DY £56.50–£70.00

OPEN All year round

Edwardian house overlooking orchards and garden, within walking distance of picturesque town. Swiss-trained proprietors offering both English and continental cooking.

TICEHURST, East Sussex Map ref 3B4

◆◆◆

CHERRY TREE INN
Dale Hill, Ticehurst, Wadhurst, East Sussex TN5 7DG
T: (01580) 201229
F: (01580) 201325
E: leondiane@aol.com

B&B per night:
S £40.00–£50.00
D £45.00–£55.00

OPEN All year round

Delightful country pub on the edge of the village of Ticehurst. Bewl Water is within walking distance as is Dalehill Golf Course. All rooms are en suite. The beamed bar offers a wide range of meals lunchtime and evenings, together with wines and cask beers. Charming patio and gardens.

Bedrooms: 2 double, 1 twin
Bathrooms: 3 en suite

Lunch available
EM 1830 (LO 2130)
Parking for 35
CC: Barclaycard, Delta, Eurocard, JCB, Maestro, Mastercard, Solo, Switch, Visa, Visa Electron

TUNBRIDGE WELLS

See under Royal Tunbridge Wells

UCKFIELD, East Sussex Map ref 2D3

Gold Award ◆◆◆◆◆

HOOKE HALL
250 High Street, Uckfield,
East Sussex TN22 1EN
T: (01825) 761578
F: (01825) 768025
E: a.percy@virgin.net

Bedrooms: 6 double, 4 twin
Bathrooms: 10 en suite

Parking for 7
CC: Barclaycard, Eurocard, Mastercard, Visa

B&B per night:
S £55.00–£75.00
D £75.00–£135.00

OPEN All year round

Elegant Queen Anne townhouse, recently completely refurbished, with individual comfortably designed rooms equipped to a high standard. Friendly and informal atmosphere.

◆◆◆◆

OLD MILL FARM
High Hurstwood, Uckfield,
East Sussex TN22 4AD
T: (01825) 732279
F: (01825) 732279

Bedrooms: 1 single, 1 twin, 1 triple
Bathrooms: 2 en suite, 1 private

Parking for 6

B&B per night:
S £20.00–£24.00
D £40.00–£45.00

OPEN All year round

Sussex barn and buildings converted to a comfortable home, situated in the quiet village of High Hurstwood, off A26. Ashdown Forest nearby.

◆◆◆◆

ROBINS WOOD
Fairhazel, Piltdown, Uckfield,
East Sussex TN22 3XB
T: (01825) 763555 (Anytime)

Bedrooms: 1 single, 1 twin
Bathrooms: 1 public

Parking for 3

B&B per night:
S Min £28.00
D Min £50.00

OPEN Jan–Nov

Beautifully furnished house, comfortable rooms, attractive rural surroundings, lovely garden, good walks, close to Piltdown Golf Course and many National Trust houses and gardens.

WEST CLANDON, Surrey Map ref 2D2

◆◆◆◆

WAYS COTTAGE
Lime Grove, West Clandon,
Guildford, GU4 7UT
T: (01483) 222454 (Answerphone)

Bedrooms: 2 twin
Bathrooms: 1 en suite, 1 public

EM 1900 (LO 2100)
Parking for 3

B&B per night:
S £22.00–£24.00
D £34.00–£38.00

HB per person:
DY £32.00–£34.00

OPEN All year round

Rural detached house in quiet location, 5 miles from Guildford. Easy reach of A3 and M25. Close to station on Waterloo/Guildford line.

WEST MALLING, Kent Map ref 3B3

◆◆◆

WESTFIELDS FARM
St Vincents Lane, Addington,
West Malling, ME19 5BW
T: (01732) 843209

Bedrooms: 3 twin
Bathrooms: 2 public

Parking for 8

B&B per night:
S Min £25.00
D Min £50.00

OPEN All year round

Farmhouse of character, approximately 500 years old, in rural setting. Within easy reach of London, Canterbury, Tunbridge Wells and the coast. Tennis court. Golf nearby.

WEST WITTERING, West Sussex Map ref 2C3

◆◆◆

THE BEACH HOUSE
Rookwood Road, West Wittering,
Chichester, West Sussex PO20 8LT
T: (01243) 514800
F: (01243) 514798

Bedrooms: 1 double, 1 twin, 1 triple, 3 family rooms
Bathrooms: 6 en suite

Lunch available
EM 1800 (LO 2100)
Parking for 15
CC: Barclaycard, Delta, Eurocard, Mastercard, Solo, Switch, Visa, Visa Electron

B&B per night:
S £25.00–£32.50
D £50.00–£75.00

HB per person:
DY £40.00–£52.50

OPEN All year round

Bright, modern, twin, double, family rooms all en suite. Licensed restaurant serving fresh food prepared by our chef. Close to beaches, harbour and walks. Private parties catered for.

WHERE TO STAY
Please mention this guide when making your booking.

SOUTH EAST ENGLAND

WHITSTABLE, Kent Map ref 3B3 *Tourist Information Centre Tel: (01227) 275482*

◆◆◆

MARINE
Marine Parade, Tankerton, Whitstable, CT5 2BE
T: (01227) 272672
F: (01227) 264721
E: marine@shepherd-neame.co.uk
I: www.shepherd-neame.co.uk

B&B per night:
S £44.00–£46.75
D £59.50–£65.50

HB per person:
DY £47.75–£59.00

OPEN All year round

A hotel of original character refurbished with every modern facility. Good food, Kentish beers, comfortable en suite accommodation, sea-facing premium bedrooms. Next to delightful Whitstable, famous for its oysters.

Bedrooms: 2 single, 7 double, 5 twin, 1 triple, 1 family room
Bathrooms: 16 en suite

Lunch available
EM 1900 (LO 2100)
Parking for 20
CC: Amex, Barclaycard, Delta, Diners, Eurocard, Mastercard, Switch, Visa

WOKING, Surrey Map ref 2D2

◆◆◆

GRANTCHESTER
Boughton Hall Avenue, Send, Woking, GU23 7DF
T: (01483) 225383
F: (01483) 211594
E: gwinterbor@aol.com

Bedrooms: 3 twin
Bathrooms: 1 public

Parking for 8

B&B per night:
S £20.00–£20.00
D £40.00–£40.00

OPEN All year round

Attractive family house with large garden. Four minutes from Guildford, close to M25 and A3. Parking available. Long stays welcome.

WORTHING, West Sussex Map ref 2D3 *Tourist Information Centre Tel: (01903) 210022*

◆◆◆

MANOR GUEST HOUSE
100 Broadwater Road, Worthing, West Sussex BN14 8AN
T: (01903) 236028 &
07880 557615 (mobile)
F: (01903) 230404
E: stay@manorguesthouse.fsnet.co.uk

Bedrooms: 1 single, 3 double, 2 triple
Bathrooms: 3 en suite, 2 public

EM 1800 (LO 1900)
Parking for 6
CC: Barclaycard, Delta, JCB, Mastercard, Switch, Visa, Visa Electron

B&B per night:
S £20.00–£25.00
D £40.00–£70.00

OPEN All year round

Delightful, detached cottage-style townhouse conveniently located for station and all local amenities. Secure car park, gardens and lovely rooms await you.

◆◆◆◆

ROSEDALE GUEST HOUSE
12 Bath Road, Worthing, West Sussex BN11 3NU
T: (01903) 233181

Bedrooms: 2 single, 1 double, 1 twin
Bathrooms: 2 en suite, 1 public

B&B per night:
S £21.00–£23.50
D £42.00–£47.00

OPEN All year round

Delightful Victorian house run by the friendly Nightingale family. Quality, comfortable en suite accommodation, ideally situated for enjoying coast and countryside. Full English breakfast.

◆◆◆

TUDOR GUEST HOUSE
5 Windsor Road, Worthing, West Sussex BN11 2LU
T: (01903) 210265 & 202042

Bedrooms: 3 single, 5 double, 2 twin
Bathrooms: 6 en suite, 1 public

Parking for 5

B&B per night:
S £17.50–£22.00
D £40.00–£50.00

OPEN All year round

Ideally situated! 1 minute from seafront, restaurants, pubs, entertainment, etc. Friendly atmosphere, comfortable bedrooms with free trays tea/coffee/chocolate. All double rooms en suite. English or continental breakfast.

MAP REFERENCES The map references refer to the colour maps at the front of this guide. The first figure is the map number; the letter and figure which follow indicate the grid reference on the map.

♦♦♦

Family-run Edwardian guesthouse providing excellent home-cooked food and friendly service. Comfortable and well- appointed bedrooms. Honeymoon suite with jacuzzi bath. Situated in a quiet conservation area close to the town centre and seafront. Ideal touring base for West Sussex. Free parking.

WOODLANDS GUEST HOUSE

20-22 Warwick Gardens, Worthing, West Sussex BN11 1PF
T: (01903) 233557 & 231957
F: (01903) 536925
E: woodlandsghse@cwcom.net
I: www.woodlands20-22.freeserve.co.uk

Bedrooms: 3 single, 4 double, 4 twin, 3 triple	EM 1800 (LO 1700)
Bathrooms: 11 en suite, 1 private, 1 public	Parking for 8
	CC: Barclaycard, Delta, Eurocard, JCB, Mastercard, Solo, Switch, Visa, Visa Electron

B&B per night:
S £25.00–£32.00
D £44.00–£54.00

HB per person:
DY £30.00–£38.00

OPEN All year round

COUNTRY CODE
Always follow the Country Code ⚜
Enjoy the countryside and respect its life and work ⚜ Guard against all risk of fire ⚜ Fasten all gates ⚜ Keep your dogs under close control ⚜ Keep to public paths across farmland ⚜ Use gates and stiles to cross fences, hedges and walls ⚜ Leave livestock, crops and machinery alone ⚜ Take your litter home ⚜ Help to keep all water clean ⚜ Protect wildlife, plants and trees ⚜ Take special care on country roads ⚜ Make no unnecessary noise ⚜

SOUTH EAST ENGLAND

A brief guide to the main Towns and Villages offering accommodation in **SOUTH EAST ENGLAND**

A ALFRISTON, EAST SUSSEX - Old village in the Cuckmere Valley and a former smugglers' haunt. The 14th C Clergy House was the first building to be bought by the National Trust. Spacious 14th C St Andrew's church is known as the "Cathedral of the South Downs" and the 13th C Star Inn is one of the oldest in England.

● **ARUNDEL, WEST SUSSEX** - Picturesque, historic town on the River Arun, dominated by Arundel Castle, home of the Dukes of Norfolk. There are many 18th C houses, the Wildfowl and Wetlands Centre and Museum and Heritage Centre.

● **ASHFORD, KENT** - Once a market centre for the farmers of the Weald of Kent and Romney Marsh. The town centre has a number of Tudor and Georgian houses and a museum. Eurostar trains stop at Ashford International station.

B BATTLE, EAST SUSSEX - The Abbey at Battle was built on the site of the Battle of Hastings, when William defeated Harold II and so became the Conqueror in 1066. The museum has a fine collection relating to the Sussex iron industry and there is a social history museum - Buckleys Yesterday's World.

● **BERWICK, EAST SUSSEX** - Situated with good access to the South Downs Way and the Long Man of Wilmington. Church has a collection of murals painted in 1942 by the Bloomsbury Group artists, Duncan Grant, Vanessa Bell and her son Quentin.

● **BETHERSDEN, KENT** - Typical Wealden village with plenty of weatherboarded houses. Famous in the Middle Ages for its marble, used in Canterbury and Rochester Cathedrals.

● **BEXHILL-ON-SEA, EAST SUSSEX** - Popular resort with beach of shingle and firm sand at low tide. The impressive 1930s designed De la Warr Pavilion has good entertainment facilities. Costume Museum in Manor Gardens.

● **BIDDENDEN, KENT** - Perfect village with black and white houses, a tithe barn and a pond. Part of the village is grouped around a green with a village sign depicting the famous Biddenden Maids. It was an important centre of the Flemish weaving industry, hence the beautiful Old Cloth Hall. Vineyard nearby.

● **BOGNOR REGIS, WEST SUSSEX** - Five miles of firm, flat sand have made the town a popular family resort. Well supplied with gardens.

● **BRENCHLEY, KENT** - In the centre of this village is a small green, around which stand half-timbered, tile hung and weatherboard houses.

● **BRIDGE, KENT** - Village in a valley, with an 18th C brick-built bridge carrying the main road over the river. Canterbury and the North Downs Way are within easy reach.

● **BRIGHTON & HOVE**- Brighton's attractions include the Royal Pavilion, Volks Electric Railway, Sea Life Centre and Marina Village, Conference Centre, "The Lanes" and several theatres.

● **BROADSTAIRS, KENT** - Popular seaside resort with numerous sandy bays. Charles Dickens spent his summers at Bleak House where he wrote parts of "David Copperfield". The Dickens Festival is held in June, when many people wear Dickensian costume.

C CANTERBURY, KENT - Place of pilgrimage since the martyrdom of Becket in 1170 and the site of Canterbury Cathedral. Visit St Augustine's Abbey, St Martin's (the oldest church in England), Royal Museum and Art Gallery and the Canterbury Tales. Nearby is Howletts Wild Animal Park. Good shopping centre.

● **CHICHESTER, WEST SUSSEX** - The county town of West Sussex with a beautiful Norman cathedral. Noted for its Georgian architecture but also has modern buildings like the Festival Theatre. Surrounded by places of interest, including Fishbourne Roman Palace, Weald and Downland Open-Air Museum and West Dean Gardens.

● **COLDRED, KENT** - Village 5 miles north-west of Dover.

● **CRAWLEY, WEST SUSSEX** - One of the first New Towns built after World War II, but it also has some old buildings. Set in magnificent wooded countryside.

D DEAL, KENT - Coastal town and popular holiday resort. Deal Castle was built by Henry VIII as a fort and the museum is devoted to finds excavated in the area. Also the Time-Ball Tower museum. Angling available from both beach and pier.

● **DORKING, SURREY** - Ancient market town and a good centre for walking, delightfully set between Box Hill and the Downs. Denbies Wine Estate - England's largest vineyard - is situated here.

● **DOVER, KENT** - A Cinque Port and busiest passenger port in the world. Still a historic town and seaside resort beside the famous White Cliffs. The White Cliffs Experience attraction traces the town's history through the Roman, Saxon, Norman and Victorian periods.

● **DYMCHURCH, KENT** - For centuries the headquarters of the Lords of the Level, the local government of this area. Probably best known today because of the fame of its fictional parson, the notorious Dr Syn, who has inspired a regular festival.

E EAST GRINSTEAD, WEST SUSSEX - A number of fine old houses stand in the High Street, one of which is Sackville College, founded in 1609.

● **EASTBOURNE, EAST SUSSEX** - One of the finest, most elegant resorts on the south-east coast situated beside Beachy Head. Long promenade, well known Carpet Gardens on the seafront, Devonshire Park tennis and indoor leisure complex, theatres, Towner Art Gallery, "How We Lived Then" Museum of Shops and Social History.

● **EPSOM, SURREY** - Horse races have been held on the slopes of Epsom Downs for centuries. The racecourse is the home of the world-famous Derby. Many famous old homes are here, among them the 17th C Waterloo House.

● **EWHURST, SURREY** - Once a prosperous centre of the woollen trade. Nearby is Elstead Moat, a national nature reserve.

F FAVERSHAM, KENT - Historic town, once a port, dating back to prehistoric times. Abbey Street has more than 50 listed buildings. Roman and Anglo-Saxon finds and other exhibits can be seen in a museum in the Maison Dieu at Ospringe. Fleur de Lys Heritage Centre.

● **FITTLEWORTH, WEST SUSSEX** - Quiet village that attracts artists and anglers. Groups of cottages can be found beside the narrow lanes and paths in the woodlands near the River Rother.

G GODALMING, SURREY - Several old coaching inns are reminders that the town was once a staging point. The old Town Hall is now the local history museum. Charterhouse School moved here in 1872 and is dominated by the 150-ft Founder's Tower.

● **GOUDHURST, KENT** - Village on a hill surmounted by a square-towered church with fine views of orchards and hopfields. Achieved prosperity through weaving in the Middle Ages. Finchcocks houses a living museum of historic early keyboard instruments.

● **GUILDFORD, SURREY** - Bustling town with Lewis Carroll connections and many historic monuments, one of which is the Guildhall clock jutting out over the old High Street. The modern cathedral occupies a commanding position on Stag Hill.

H HALLAND, EAST SUSSEX - Village between Uckfield and Hailsham. Nearby is the Bentley Wildfowl and Motor Museum.

● **HASLEMERE, SURREY** - Town set in hilly, wooded countryside, much of it in the care of the National Trust. Its attractions include the educational museum and the annual music festival.

● **HASTINGS, EAST SUSSEX** - Ancient town which became famous as the base from which William the Conqueror set out to fight the Battle of Hastings. Later became one of the Cinque Ports, now a leading resort. Castle, Hastings Embroidery inspired by the Bayeux Tapestry and Sea Life Centre.

- **HEATHFIELD, EAST SUSSEX** - Old Heathfield is a pretty village which was one of the major centres of the Sussex iron industry.

- **HERSTMONCEUX, EAST SUSSEX** - Pleasant village noted for its woodcrafts and the beautiful 15th C moated Herstmonceux Castle with its Science Centre and gardens open to the public. The only village where traditional Sussex trug baskets are still made.

- **HORLEY, SURREY** - Town on the London to Brighton road, just north of Gatwick Airport, with an ancient parish church and 15th C inn.

L **LENHAM, KENT** - Shops, inns and houses, many displaying timber-work of the late Middle Ages, surround a square which is the centre of the village. The 14th C parish church has one of the best examples of a Kentish tower.

- **LEWES, EAST SUSSEX** - Historic county town with Norman castle. The steep High Street has many interesting features. There is a folk museum at Anne of Cleves House and the archaeological museum is in Barbican House.

- **LYMINSTER, WEST SUSSEX** - Links up with Littlehampton looking inland, and across the watermeadows to the churches and towers of Arundel. There is a vineyard here.

M **MAIDSTONE, KENT** - Busy county town of Kent on the River Medway has many interesting features and is an excellent centre for excursions. Museum of Carriages, Museum and Art Gallery, Mote Park.

- **MARDEN, KENT** - The village is believed to date back to Saxon times, though today more modern homes surround the 13th C church.

- **MIDHURST, WEST SUSSEX** - Historic, picturesque town just north of the South Downs, with the ruins of Cowdray House, medieval castle and 15th C parish church. Polo at Cowdray Park. Excellent base for Chichester, Petworth, Glorious Goodwood and the South Downs Way.

O **OXTED, SURREY** - Pleasant town on the edge of National Trust woodland and at the foot of the North Downs. Chartwell (National Trust), the former home of Sir Winston Churchill, is close by.

P **PARTRIDGE GREEN, WEST SUSSEX** - Small village between Henfield and Billingshurst.

- **PETWORTH, WEST SUSSEX** - Town known as an antique centre and dominated by Petworth House (National Trust), the great 17th C mansion, set in 2,000 acres of parkland laid out by Capability Brown. The house contains wood-carvings by Grinling Gibbons.

- **PULBOROUGH, WEST SUSSEX** - Here is Parham, an Elizabethan mansion with unusually tall, mullioned windows and a long gallery measuring 158ft. The house and the surrounding park and garden can be visited. In the grounds stands the church of St Peter.

R **RAMSGATE, KENT** - Popular holiday resort with good sandy beaches. At Pegwell Bay is a replica of a Viking longship.

- **REDHILL, SURREY** - Part of the borough of Reigate and now the commercial centre with good shopping facilities. Gatwick Airport is 3 miles to the south.

- **ROGATE, WEST SUSSEX** - On the main road between Midhurst and Petersfield, Rogate probably gets its name from its position as gateway to wooded hill slopes, the habitat of deer.

- **ROTTINGDEAN, EAST SUSSEX** - The quiet High Street contains a number of fine old buildings and the village pond and green are close by.

- **ROYAL TUNBRIDGE WELLS, KENT** - This "Royal" town became famous as a spa in the 17th C and much of its charm is retained, as in the Pantiles, a shaded walk lined with elegant shops. Heritage attraction "A Day at the Wells". Excellent shopping centre.

- **RUSTINGTON, WEST SUSSEX** - Village with thatched cottages and a medieval church.

- **RYE, EAST SUSSEX** - Cobbled, hilly streets and fine old buildings make Rye, once a Cinque Port, a most picturesque town. Noted for its church with ancient clock, potteries and antique shops. Town Model Sound and Light Show gives a good introduction to the town.

S **SARRE, KENT** - Attractive Dutch-gabled houses can be seen in this Thanet village. Names of many famous people are inscribed on the walls of the 16th C Crown Inn, noted for the manufacture of cherry brandy.

- **SEAFORD, EAST SUSSEX** - The town was a bustling port until 1579 when the course of the River Ouse was diverted. The downlands around the town make good walking country, with fine views of the Seven Sisters cliffs.

- **SEVENOAKS, KENT** - Set in pleasant wooded country, with a distinctive character and charm. Nearby is Knole (National Trust), home of the Sackville family and one of the largest houses in England, set in a vast deer park.

- **SITTINGBOURNE, KENT** - The town's position and its ample supply of water make it an ideal site for the paper-making industry. Delightful villages and orchards lie round about.

- **SMARDEN, KENT** - Pretty village with a number of old, well-presented buildings. The 14th C St Michael's Church is sometimes known as the "Barn of Kent" because of its 36-ft roof span.

- **STELLING MINNIS, KENT** - Off the Roman Stone Street, this quiet, picturesque village lies deep in the Lyminge Forest, south of Canterbury.

T **TENTERDEN, KENT** - Most attractive market town with a broad main street full of 16th C houses and shops. The tower of the 15th C parish church is the finest in Kent. Fine antiques centre.

U **UCKFIELD, EAST SUSSEX** - Once a medieval market town and centre of the iron industry, Uckfield is now a busy country town on the edge of the Ashdown Forest.

W **WEST CLANDON, SURREY** - Home of the Clandon Park (National Trust), the Palladian mansion built in the early 1730s and home of the Queen's Royal Surrey Regiment Museum.

- **WEST MALLING, KENT** - Became prominent in Norman times when an abbey was established here.

- **WHITSTABLE, KENT** - Seaside resort and yachting centre on Kent's north shore. The beach is shingle and there are the usual seaside amenities and entertainments and a museum.

- **WOKING, SURREY** - One of the largest towns in Surrey, which developed with the coming of the railway in the 1830s. Old Woking was a market town in the 17th C and still retains several interesting buildings. Large arts and entertainment centre.

- **WORTHING, WEST SUSSEX** - Town in the West Sussex countryside and by the South Coast, with excellent shopping and many pavement cafes and restaurants. Attractions include the award-winning Museum and Art Gallery, beautiful gardens, pier, elegant town houses, Cissbury Ring hill fort and the South Downs.

USE YOUR *i*s

There are more than 550 Tourist Information Centres throughout England offering friendly help with accommodation and holiday ideas as well as suggestions of places to visit and things to do. You'll find TIC addresses in the local Phone Book.

Ratings you can trust

English Tourism Council

GUEST
ACCOMMODATION

When you're looking for a place to stay, you need a rating system you can trust. The **English Tourism Council's** ratings are your clear guide to what to expect, in an easy-to-understand form. Properties are visited annually by our trained impartial assessors, so you can have confidence that your accommodation has been thoroughly checked and rated for quality before you make a booking.

Using a simple One to Five Diamond rating, the system puts great emphasis on quality and is based on research which shows exactly what consumers are looking for when choosing accommodation.

"Guest Accommodation" covers a wide variety of serviced accommodation for which England is renowned, including guesthouses, bed and breakfasts, inns and farmhouses. Establishments are rated from One to Five Diamonds. The same minimum requirement for facilities and services applies to all Guest Accommodation from One to Five Diamonds. Progressively higher levels of quality and customer care must be provided for each of the One to Five Diamond ratings. The rating reflects the unique character of Guest Accommodation, and covers areas such as cleanliness, service and hospitality, bedrooms, bathrooms and food quality.

Look out, too, for the English Tourism Council's Gold and Silver Awards, which are awarded to those establishments which not only achieve the overall quality required for their Diamond rating, but also reach the highest levels of quality in those specific areas which guests identify as being really important for them. They will reflect the quality of comfort and cleanliness you'll find in the bedrooms and bathrooms and the quality of service you'll enjoy throughout your stay.

The ratings are your sign of quality assurance, giving you the confidence to book the accommodation that meets your expectations.

English Tourism Council
Assessed Accommodation

English Tourism Council

♦ ♦ ♦

GUEST
ACCOMMODATION

On the following pages you will find an exclusive listing of *all guest accommodation in England that has been assessed for quality by the English Tourism Council.*

The information includes brief contact details for each place to stay, together with its Diamond rating, and quality award if appropriate. The listing also shows if an establishment is taking part in the Welcome Host scheme ⊛, and if it has a National Accessible rating (see the front of the guide for further information).

More detailed information on all the places shown in blue can be found in the regional sections (where establishments have paid to have their details included). To find these entries please refer to the appropriate regional section, or look in the town index at the back of this guide.

The list which follows was compiled slightly later than the regional sections. For this reason you may find that, in a few instances, a Diamond rating and quality award may differ between the two sections. This list contains the most up-to-date information and was correct at the time of going to press.

LONDON

INNER LONDON
E4

Aucklands
◆◆◆◆ SILVER AWARD
25 Eglington Road, North
Chingford, London E4 7AN
T: (020) 8529 1140
F: (020) 8529 9288

E7

Forest View Hotel ◆
227 Romford Road, Forest Gate,
London E7 9HL
T: (020) 8534 4844
F: (020) 8534 8959

Grangewood Lodge Hotel ◆
104 Clova Road, Forest Gate,
London E7 9AF
T: (020) 8534 0637 & 8503 0941
F: (020) 8503 0941

N1

Kandara Guest House ◆◆◆
68 Ockendon Road, London
N1 3NW
T: (020) 7226 5721 & 7226 3379
F: (020) 7226 3379
E: admin@kandara.co.uk
I: www.kandara.co.uk

N4

Costello Palace Hotel ◆◆
374 Seven Sisters Road, Finsbury
Park, London N4 2PG
T: (020) 8802 6551
F: (020) 8802 9461

N7

Europa Hotel ◆◆◆
60-62 Anson Road, London
N7 0AA
T: (020) 7607 5935
F: (020) 7607 5909

Five Kings Guest House ◆◆
59 Anson Road, Tufnell Park,
London N7 0AR
T: (020) 7607 3996 & 7607 6466
F: (020) 7609 5554

Queens Hotel ◆◆
33 Anson Road, Tufnell Park,
London N7 0RB
T: (020) 7607 4725
F: (020) 7697 9725
E: queens@stavrouhotels.co.uk

N8

Homestead ◆◆
141 Ferme Park Road, Crouch
End, London N8 9SG
T: (020) 8347 8768
F: (020) 8348 2256

White Lodge Hotel ◆◆◆
1 Church Lane, Hornsey, London
N8 7BU
T: (020) 8348 9765
F: (020) 8340 7851

N14

Cheeky Squirrels
Rating Applied For
57 Selborne Road, London
N14 7DE
T: (020) 8886 1853

N16

Rose Hotel ◆◆
69-71 Stoke Newington Road,
London N16 8AD
T: (020) 7254 5990 & 7923 0483
F: (020) 7923 0483
E: rosehotel@easicom.com

N20

The Corner Lodge ◆◆◆◆
9 Athenaeum Road, Whetstone,
London N20 9AA
T: (020) 8446 3720
F: (020) 8446 3720

N22

Pane Residence ◆◆
154 Boundary Road, Wood
Green, London N22 6AE
T: (020) 8889 3735

NW1

Americana Hotel ◆◆◆
172 Gloucester Place, Regent's
Park, London NW1 6DS
T: (020) 7723 1452
F: (020) 7723 4641
E: manager@americanahotel.
demon.co.uk

Four Seasons Hotel
◆◆◆◆ SILVER AWARD
173 Gloucester Place, London
NW1 6DX
T: (020) 7724 3461 & 7723 9471
F: (020) 7402 5594
E: fourseasons@dial.pipex.com

NW3

Comfort Inn Hampstead ◆◆◆
5 Frognal, Hampstead, London
NW3 6AL
T: (020) 7794 0101
F: (020) 7794 0100

Dillons Hotel ◆
21 Belsize Park, Hampstead,
London NW3 4DU
T: (020) 7794 3360
F: (020) 7431 7900
E: desk@dillonshotel.demon.co.
uk
I: www.dillonshotel.demon.co.uk

NW6

Cavendish Guest House
◆◆◆◆
24 Cavendish Road, London
NW6 7XP
T: (020) 8451 3249
F: (020) 8451 3249

Dawson House Hotel ◆◆◆◆
72 Canfield Gardens, London
NW6 3ED
T: (020) 7624 0079 & 7624 6525
F: (020) 7644 6321
E: dawsonhtl@aol.com
I: www.dawsonhouse.com

NW10

30 All Souls Avenue ◆◆
Willesden, London NW10 5AR
T: (020) 8965 6051
F: (020) 8965 6051

Aran Guest House ◆◆
21 Holland Road, Kensal Green,
London NW10 5AH
T: (020) 8968 6402 & 8968 2153

J and T Guest House ◆◆◆
98 Park Avenue North, Willesden
Green, London NW10 1JY
T: (020) 8452 4085
F: (020) 8450 2503
E: jandthome@aol.com
I: www.jandtguesthouses.com

NW11

Anchor–Nova Hotel ◆◆◆
10 West Heath Drive, Golders
Green, London NW11 7QH
T: (020) 8458 8764 & 8458 4311
F: (020) 8455 3204
E: enquir@anchor-hotel.co.uk
I: www.anchor-hotel.co.uk

SE3

64 Beaconsfield Road ◆◆
Blackheath, London SE3 7LG
T: (020) 8858 1685

49 Foxes Dale ◆◆◆
Blackheath, London SE3 9BH
T: (020) 8852 1076 &
07770 583487
F: (020) 8852 1076

The Grovers ◆◆◆
96 Merriman Road, London
SE3 8RZ
T: (020) 8488 7719 &
07713 226393
@
F: (020) 8488 7719

Hill Crest Guesthouse
Rating Applied For
2 Hardy Road, Blackheath,
London SE3 7NR
T: (020) 8305 0120 & 8305 2203
E: hillcrest@dial.pipex.com
I: ds.dial.pipex.
com/town/drive/xsd11/

59a Lee Road ◆◆
Blackheath, London SE3 9EN
T: (020) 8318 7244

59 Lee Terrace ◆◆
Blackheath, London SE3 9TA
T: (020) 8852 6334
E: susan.bedbreakfast@virgin.
net

Magpie Lodge ◆◆◆◆
26 Shooters Hill Road,
Blackheath, London SE3 7BD
T: (020) 8858 3953 & 8858 3908
F: (020) 8858 3968
I: www.maglodge.ukf.net

**Number Nine Blackheath
Limited** ◆◆◆◆
9 Charlton Road, Blackheath,
London SE3 7EU
T: (020) 8858 4175 &
07957 361997
F: (020) 8858 4175
E: no9limited@hotmail.com
I: www.numbernineblackheath.
com
@

3 Tilbrook Road ◆◆
3 Tilbrook Road, Kidbrooke,
London SE3 9QD
T: (020) 8319 8843

68 Wricklemarsh Road ◆◆
Blackheath, London SE3 8DS
T: (020) 8856 1331
E: emlynch@cwcom.net

SE4

66 Geoffrey Road ◆◆
London SE4 1NT
T: (020) 8691 3887 &
07790 467061
F: (020) 8691 3887
E: b&bgeoffrey@woodin.u-net.
com

SE6

Highfield Guest House
◆◆◆◆ SILVER AWARD
12 Dowanhill Road, London
SE6 1HJ
T: (020) 8698 8038
F: (020) 8698 8039
E: michel@highfieldbb.co.uk
I: www.highfieldbb.co.uk

Thornsbeach ◆◆◆
122 Bargery Road, Catford,
London SE6 2LR
T: (020) 8695 6544 & 8244 5554
F: (020) 8695 9577
E: helen@thornsbeach.co.uk
I: www.thornsbeach.co.uk

Tulip Tree House ◆◆◆
41 Minard Road, Catford,
London SE6 1NP
T: (020) 8697 2596
F: (020) 8698 2020

SE7

Old Rectory Guest House
Rating Applied For
80 Maryon Road, London
SE7 8DL
T: (020) 8317 9694
@

SE8

46 Rolt Street ◆◆
Deptford, London SE8 5NL
T: (020) 8691 7491

SE9

Abigail House ◆◆◆
68 Dunvegan Road, Eltham,
London SE9 1SB
T: (020) 8859 3924

Benvenuti ◆◆◆◆
217 Court Road, Eltham, London
SE9 4TG
T: (020) 8857 4855
F: (020) 8265 5635
E: val.smith.benvenuti@cwcom.
net
I: www.benvenuti.cwc.net

100 Dumbreck Road ◆◆◆
London SE9 1XD
T: (020) 8859 1927

70 Dunvegan Road ◆◆
Eltham, London SE9 1SB
T: (020) 8850 0584

33 Glenshiel Road ◆◆◆
33 Glenshiel Road, Eltham,
London SE9 1AQ
T: (020) 8850 4958

Meadow Croft Lodge ◆◆
96-98 Southwood Road, New
Eltham, London SE9 3QS
T: (020) 8859 1488
F: (020) 8850 8054

Pat and Charlies B&B ◆◆◆◆
40 Gourock Road, Eltham,
London SE9 1JA
T: (020) 8265 0949 &
0798 9229568
E: ellioreed@clara.cd.uk

80 Rennets Wood Road ◆◆◆
Eltham, London SE9 2NH
T: (020) 8850 1829

Westmount ♦♦♦
62 Westmount Road, Eltham,
London SE9 1JE
T: (020) 8850 4114
F: (020) 8850 4114
E: westmount@kaylott.fsnet.co.
uk

Weston House ♦♦
8 Eltham Green, Eltham, London
SE9 5LB
T: (020) 8850 5191
F: (020) 8850 0030

Yardley Court Private Hotel
♦♦♦
18 Court Yard, Eltham, London
SE9 5PZ
T: (020) 8850 1850
F: (020) 8488 0421
E: dcyardley@aol.com

SE10

69 Ashburnham Place ♦♦
Greenwich, London SE10 8UG
T: (020) 8692 9065

Greenwich Parkhouse Hotel
♦♦
1-2 Nevada Street, Greenwich,
London SE10 9JL
T: (020) 8305 1478

81 Greenwich South Street
♦♦♦♦ SILVER AWARD
London SE10 8NT
T: (020) 8293 3121

Mitre Inn ♦♦♦
291 Greenwich High Road,
London SE10 8NA
T: (020) 8355 6760 & 8293 0037
F: (020) 8355 6761

Trinity Cottage ♦♦
5 Trinity Grove, Greenwich,
London SE10 8TE
T: (020) 8469 2017
◉

SE12

Kingsland House ♦♦
45 Southbrook Road, Lee,
London SE12 8LJ
T: (020) 8318 4788

81 Micheldever Road ♦♦♦
London SE12 8LU
T: (020) 8852 2604 &
0786 7887888
E: tomcourtney@emailmoore.
com

SE13

Blue Danube Guest House
♦♦♦
54 Albacore Crescent, Lewisham,
London SE13 7HP
T: (020) 8244 3019 &
07941 286183
F: (020) 8690 4147
E: ma2.anita@lc24.net

Manna House ♦♦♦
320 Hither Green Lane,
Lewisham, London SE13 6TS
T: (020) 8461 5984 & 8695 5316
F: (020) 8695 5316
E: mannahouse@aol.com
I: members.aol.
com/mannahouse

13 Wellmeadow Road ♦
Hither Green, London SE13 6SY
T: (020) 8697 1398
◉

8 Yeats Close ♦♦
Eliot Park, London SE13 7ET
T: (020) 8318 3421 & 8694 3495
F: (020) 8318 3421
E: patu@tesco.net
◉

SE17

Hampton Court Palace Hotel
♦♦♦♦
Hampton Street, London
SE17 3AN
T: (020) 7703 0011
F: (020) 7703 6464
E: hcpal@aol.co.uk
I: www.hampton-hotel.com/

SE18

Dover House
Rating Applied For
155 Shooters Hill, London
SE18 3HP
T: (020) 8856 9892
F: (020) 8856 9892

Home from Home ♦♦
29 Tellson Avenue, Shooters Hill
Road, London SE18 4PD
T: (020) 8856 9213
F: (020) 8856 9213
E: 106440,2211@compuserve.
com

268 Shooters Hill Road ♦
Blackheath, London SE18 4LX
T: (020) 8319 2699 &
07713 422912

SE20

Melrose House ♦♦♦
89 Lennard Road, London
SE20 7LY
T: (020) 8776 8884 &
07956 357714
F: (020) 8776 8480
E: melrose.hotel@virgin.net
I: www.
guesthouseaccommodation.co.
uk

Sundance
Rating Applied For
186 Anerley Road, London
SE20 8BL
T: (020) 8289 2252

SE22

Dragon House ♦♦♦♦
39 Marmora Road, London
SE22 0RX
T: (020) 8693 4355 &
07956 645894
F: (020) 8693 7954
E: dragonbb@dialstart.co.uk
I: www.fsvo.com/dragonbb

SE27

The White House ♦
242 Norwood Road, West
Norwood, London SE27 9AW
T: (020) 8670 4149 & 8761 8892
F: (020) 8670 6440
E: dmark@globalnet.co.uk
I: memberstripod/twhgh

SW1

Airways Hotel Nationlodge Ltd
♦♦
29-31 St George's Drive,
Victoria, London SW1V 4DG
T: (020) 7834 0205 & 7834 3567
F: (020) 7932 0007
E: sales@airways-hotel.com
I: www.airways-hotel.com
◉

Carlton Hotel ♦♦
90 Belgrave Road, Victoria,
London SW1V 2BJ
T: (020) 7976 6634 & 7932 0913
F: (020) 7821 8020
E: cityhotelcarlton@btconnect.
com
I: home.btconnect.
com/cityhotelcarlton

Caswell Hotel ♦♦
25 Gloucester Street, London
SW1V 2DB
T: (020) 7834 6345
E: manager@hotellondon.co.uk
I: www.hotellondon.co.uk

Collin House ♦♦♦
104 Ebury Street, London
SW1W 9QD
T: (020) 7730 8031
F: (020) 7730 8031

Dover Hotel ♦♦
44 Belgrave Road, London
SW1V 1RG
T: (020) 7821 9085
F: (020) 7834 6425
E: dover@rooms.demon.co.uk
I: www.rooms.demon.co.uk
◉

Georgian House Hotel ♦♦
35-39 St George's Drive, London
SW1V 4DG
T: (020) 7834 1438
F: (020) 7976 6085
E: georgian@wildnet.co.uk
I: www.georgianhousehotel.co.
uk

Hamilton House Hotel ♦♦
60 Warwick Way, London
SW1V 1SA
T: (020) 7821 7113
F: (020) 7630 0806
E: reception@hamiltonhhotel.
demon.co.uk

Hanover Hotel ♦♦
30-32 St George's Drive, London
SW1V 4BN
T: (020) 7834 0367 & 7834 7617
F: (020) 7976 5587
E: reservations@hanoverhotel.
co.uk
I: www.hanoverhotel.co.uk

Huttons Hotel ♦
55 Belgrave Road, London
SW1V 2BB
T: (020) 7834 3726
F: (020) 7834 3389
E: reservations@huttons-hotel.
co.uk

Knightsbridge Green Hotel
♦♦♦♦
159 Knightsbridge, London
SW1X 7PD
T: (020) 7584 6274
F: (020) 7225 1635
E: thekghotel@aol.com

Luna-Simone Hotel ♦♦
47 Belgrave Road, London
SW1V 2BB
T: (020) 7834 5897
F: (020) 7828 2474
E: lunasimone@talk21.com

Melita House Hotel ♦♦♦
35 Charlwood Street, Victoria,
London SW1V 2DU
T: (020) 7828 0471 & 7834 1387
F: (020) 7932 0988
E: reserve@melita.co.uk
I: www.melita.co.uk

Oxford House Hotel ♦
92 Cambridge Street, Victoria,
London SW1V 4QG
T: (020) 7834 6467
F: (020) 7834 0225
E: oxfordhouse@breathemail.
net

Stanley House Hotel ♦
19-21 Belgrave Road, London
SW1V 1RB
T: (020) 7834 5042 & 7834 7292
F: (020) 7834 8439
E: cmahotel@aol.com
I: www.affordablehotel.com

Victor Hotel ♦♦♦
51 Belgrave Road, London
SW1V 2BB
T: (020) 7592 9853
F: (020) 7592 9854

The Victoria Inn ♦♦
65-67 Belgrave Road, London
SW1V 2BG
T: (020) 7834 6721 & 7834 0182
F: (020) 7931 0201
E: info@victoriainn.co.uk
I: www.victoriainn.co.uk

Windermere Hotel
♦♦♦♦ SILVER AWARD
142-144 Warwick Way, Victoria,
London SW1V 4JE
T: (020) 7834 5163 & 7834 5480
F: (020) 7630 8831
E: windermere@compuserve.
com
I: www.windermere-hotel.co.uk

SW2

Brixton Bed And Breakfast
Rating Applied For
12 Lambert Road, London
SW2 5BD
T: (020) 7274 6402
E: denis.naughton@ukgateway.
net

SW5

The Albany Hotel ♦♦♦
4-12 Barkston Gardens, London
SW5 0EN
T: (020) 7370 6116
F: (020) 7244 8024
E: albany@realco.co.uk
I: www.realco.co.uk

Amsterdam Hotel ♦♦♦
7 Trebovir Road, London
SW5 9LS
T: (020) 7370 5084
F: (020) 7244 7608
E: reservations@
amsterdam-hotel.com
I: www.amsterdam-hotel.com

Beaver Hotel ♦♦♦
57-59 Philbeach Gardens,
London SW5 9ED
T: (020) 7373 4553
F: (020) 7373 4555
I: www.smoothhound.co.
uk/hotels/beaver.html

Buosi Hotel ♦♦
50 Nevern Square, London
SW5 9PF
T: (020) 7370 3325
F: (020) 7370 3103
E: 6088@mjbart.demon.co.uk
I: www.hotelbuosi.com

Comfort Inn Earl's Court ♦♦
11-13 Penywern Road, Earl's
Court, London SW5 9TT
T: (020) 7373 6514
F: (020) 7370 3639
E: comfortinn@kenotel.co.uk

Hotel Earls Court ◆◆
28 Warwick Road, Earls Court,
London SW5 9UD
T: (020) 7373 7079 & 7373 0302
F: (020) 7912 0582
E: hotel.earlscourt@virgin.net
I: freespace.virgin.net
/hotel.earlscourt/index.htm

Enterprise Hotel ◆◆◆
15-25 Hogarth Road, London
SW5 0QJ
T: (020) 7373 4502 & 7373 4503
F: (020) 7373 5115
E: ehotel@aol.com
I: www.enterprisehotel.com

Half Moon Hotel ◆◆
10 Earl's Court Square, London
SW5 9DP
T: (020) 7373 9956
F: (020) 7373 8456

Henley House Hotel ◆◆◆
30 Barkston Gardens, Earl's
Court, London SW5 0EN
T: (020) 7370 4111
F: (020) 7370 0026
E: henleyhse@aol.com

Kensington Court Hotel ◆◆◆
33-35 Nevern Place, Earl's Court,
London SW5 9NP
T: (020) 7370 5151
F: (020) 7370 3499
E: kensington.court.hotel@visit.
uk.com

**Kensington International
Hotel** ◆◆◆
4 Templeton Place, London
SW5 9LZ
T: (020) 7370 4333
F: (020) 7244 7873
E: hotel@
kensington-international-hotel.
co.uk
I: www.
kensington-international-hotel.
co.uk

London Town Hotel ◆◆◆
15 Penywern Road, Earl's Court,
London SW5 9TT
T: (020) 7370 4356
F: (020) 7370 7923
E: townhotel@compuserve.com
I: www.londontownhotel.com

Lord Jim Hotel ◆◆
23-25 Penywern Road, London
SW5 9TT
T: (020) 7370 6071 &
07957 167081
F: (020) 7373 8919
E: taher_tayeb@compuserve.
com
I: www.lord-jim-hotel.co.uk

Manor Hotel ◆◆
23 Nevern Place, London
SW5 9NR
T: (020) 7370 6018
F: (020) 7244 6610
⊕

Maranton House Hotel ◆◆◆
14 Barkston Gardens, Earls
Court, London SW5 0EN
T: (020) 7373 5782
F: (020) 7244 9543
E: marantonhotel@hotmail.com

Mayflower Hotel ◆◆
26-28 Trebovir Road, Earls
Court, London SW5 9NJ
T: (020) 7370 0991
F: (020) 7370 0994
E: mayfhotel@aol.com
I: members.aol.
com/mayfhotel/private/may.htm

Merlyn Court Hotel ◆◆
2 Barkston Gardens, London
SW5 0EN
T: (020) 7370 1640
F: (020) 7370 4986
E: london@merlyncourt.demon.
co.uk
I: www.smoothhound.co.
uk/hotels/merlyn.html

Mowbray Court Hotel ◆◆
28-32 Penywern Road, Earl's
Court, London SW5 9SU
T: (020) 7370 2316 & 7370 3690
F: (020) 7370 5693
E: mowbraycrthot@hotmail.
com
I: www.m-c-hotel.mcmail.com

Nevern Hotel ◆
29-31 Nevern Place, London
SW5 9NP
T: (020) 7244 8366 & 7370 4827
F: (020) 7370 1541

Hotel Oliver ◆◆
198 Cromwell Road, London
SW5 0SN
T: (020) 7370 6881
F: (020) 7370 6556
E: reservations@hoteloliver.
freeserve.co.uk
⊕

Oliver Plaza Hotel ◆◆
33 Trebovir Road, Earl's Court,
London SW5 9NF
T: (020) 7373 7183
F: (020) 7244 6021
E: oliverplaza@capricornhotels.
co.uk
I: www.capricornhotels.co.uk

Hotel Plaza Continental ◆◆
9 Knaresborough Place, London
SW5 0TP
T: (020) 7370 3246
F: (020) 7373 9571

Ramsees Hotel ◆◆
32-36 Hogarth Road, Earl's
Court, London SW5 0PU
T: (020) 7370 1445
F: (020) 7244 6835
E: ramsees@rasool.demon.co.uk
I: www.ramseeshotel.com
⊕

Rasool Court Hotel ◆◆
19-21 Penywern Road, Earl's
Court, London SW5 9TT
T: (020) 7373 8900 & 7373 4893
F: (020) 7244 6835
E: rasool@rasool.demon.co.uk
I: www.rasoolcourthotel.com

Swiss House Hotel ◆◆◆
171 Old Brompton Road, London
SW5 0AN
T: (020) 7373 2769 & 7373 9383
F: (020) 7373 4983
E: recep@swiss-hh.demon.co.uk
I: www.swiss-hh.demon.co.uk

Windsor House ◆
12 Penywern Road, London
SW5 9ST
T: (020) 7373 9087
F: (020) 7385 2417

York House Hotel ◆◆
27-28 Philbeach Gardens,
London SW5 9EA
T: (020) 7373 7519 & 7373 7579
F: (020) 7370 4641
E: yorkhh@aol.com

Five Sumner Place Hotel ◆◆◆◆
5 Sumner Place, South
Kensington, London SW7 3EE
T: (020) 7584 7586
F: (020) 7823 9962
E: reservations@sumnerplace.
com
I: www.sumnerplace.com

Hotel Number Sixteen
◆◆◆◆◆ GOLD AWARD
16 Sumner Place, London
SW7 3EG
T: (020) 7589 5232
F: (020) 7584 8615
E: reservations@
numbersixteenhotel.co.uk
I: www.numbersixteenhotel.co.
uk

Lavender Guest House ◆◆◆
18 Lavender Sweep, London
SW11 1HA
T: (020) 7585 2767 & 7223 1973
F: (020) 7924 6274

106 ◆◆◆
106 East Sheen Avenue, London
SW14 8AU
T: (020) 8255 1900
F: (020) 8876 8084
E: rpratt@easynet.co.uk

The Plough Inn ◆◆◆
42 Christchurch Road, East
Sheen, London SW14 7AF
T: (020) 8876 7833 & 8876 4533
F: (020) 8392 8801
E: ploughthe@hotmail.com

The Konyots ◆
95 Pollards Hill South, London
SW16 4LS
T: (020) 8764 0075

The Brewers Inn ◆◆◆
147 East Hill, Wandsworth,
London SW18 2QB
T: (020) 8874 4128
F: (020) 8877 1953
I: www.youngs.co.uk

Grosvenor Arms ◆◆◆
204 Garratt Lane, Wandsworth,
London SW18 4ED
T: (020) 8874 2709
F: (020) 8874 0813

2 Melrose Road ◆◆◆
London SW18 1NE
T: (020) 8871 3259

Trochee Hotel ◆
21 Malcolm Road, Wimbledon,
London SW19 4AS
T: (020) 8946 1579 & 8946 3924
F: (020) 8785 4058

Trochee Hotel Annexe ◆◆
52 Ridgway Place, Wimbledon,
London SW19 4SW
T: (020) 8946 9425 & 8946 9400
F: (020) 8785 4058

Worcester House Hotel ◆◆◆
38 Alwyne Road, Wimbledon,
London SW19 7AE
T: (020) 8946 1300
F: (020) 8946 9120
E: janet@worcesterhousehotel.
demon.co.uk
I: www.worcesterhousehotel.
co.uk

Bentinck House Hotel ◆◆
20 Bentinck Street, London
W1M 5RL
T: (020) 7935 9141
F: (020) 7224 5903

Berkeley Court Hotel ◆◆
22 Upper Berkeley Street,
London W1H 7PF
T: (020) 7262 3091
F: (020) 7258 0290

The Edward Lear Hotel ◆◆
30 Seymour Street, Marble Arch,
London W1H 5WD
T: (020) 7402 5401
F: (020) 7706 3766
E: edwardlear@aol.com
I: www.edlear.com

Glynne Court Hotel ◆◆
41 Great Cumberland Place,
Marble Arch, London W1H 7LG
T: (020) 7262 4344
F: (020) 7724 2071
I: www.smoothhound.co.
uk/hotels/glynnec.html

Hallam Hotel ◆◆◆
12 Hallam Street, Portland Place,
London W1N 5LF
T: (020) 7580 1166
F: (020) 7323 4527

Kenwood House Hotel ◆
114 Gloucester Place, London
W1H 3DB
T: (020) 7935 3473 & 7935 9455
F: (020) 7224 0582
E: kenwoodhouse@yahoo.co.uk
I: www.hotelconnectionsuk.com
⊕

Lincoln House Hotel ◆◆
33 Gloucester Place, London
W1H 3PD
T: (020) 7486 7630
F: (020) 7486 0166
E: reservations@
lincoln-house-hotel.co.uk
I: www.lincoln-house-hotel.co.
uk

Marble Arch Inn ◆◆
49-50 Upper Berkeley Street,
Marble Arch, London W1H 7PN
T: (020) 7723 7888
F: (020) 7723 6060
E: marble@rooms.demon.co.uk
I: www.rooms.demon.co.uk
⊕

Mermaid Suites ◆◆◆
4 Blenheim Street, London
W1Y 9LB
T: (020) 7629 1875
F: (020) 7499 9475
⊕

Prince Regent Hotel ◆◆
37 Nottingham Place, London
W1M 3FE
T: (020) 7935 4276 & 7487 5153
F: (020) 7224 1582
I: www.accomodata.co.uk

Ten Manchester Street ♦♦♦♦
10 Manchester Street, London
W1M 5PG
T: (020) 7486 6669
F: (020) 7224 0348

Wigmore Court Hotel ♦♦♦
23 Gloucester Place, Portman
Square, London W1H 3PB
T: (020) 7935 0928
F: (020) 7487 4254
E: info@wigmore-court-hotel.
co.uk
I: www.wigmore-court-hotel.co.
uk

Wyndham Hotel ♦♦♦
30 Wyndham Street, London
W1H 1DD
T: (020) 7723 7204 & 7723 9400
F: (020) 7724 2893
E: wyndhamhotel@talk21.com

W2

**Abbey Court & Westpoint
Hotel ♦♦**
170-174 Sussex Gardens,
London W2 1TP
T: (020) 7402 0281 & 7402 0704
F: (020) 7224 9114
E: info@abbeycourt.com
I: www.abbeycourt.com

Admiral Hotel ♦♦
143 Sussex Gardens, Hyde Park,
London W2 2RY
T: (020) 7723 7309
F: (020) 7723 8731
E: frank@admiral143.demon.co.
uk
I: www.admiral-hotel.com

Albro House Hotel ♦♦
155 Sussex Gardens, London
W2 2RY
T: (020) 7724 2931 & 7706 8153
F: (020) 7262 2278

Allandale Hotel ♦♦♦
3 Devonshire Terrace, Lancaster
Gate, London W2 3DN
T: (020) 7723 8311 & 7723 7807
F: (020) 7723 8311
E: info@allandalehotel.co.uk
I: www.allandalehotel.co.uk
◉

Apollo Hotel ♦♦♦
64 Queensborough Terrace,
London W2 3SH
T: (020) 7727 3066
F: (020) 7727 2800
E: apollohotel@aol.com
I: www.hotelapollo.com

Ashley Hotel ♦♦
15 Norfolk Square, London
W2 1RU
T: (020) 7723 3375 & 7723 9966
F: (020) 7723 0173
E: ashot@btinternet.com

Barry House Hotel ♦♦
12 Sussex Place, London W2 2TP
T: (020) 7723 7340 & 7723 0994
F: (020) 7723 9775
E: bh-hotel@bigfoot.com
I: www.hotel.uk.com/barryhouse

Beverley House Hotel ♦♦♦
142 Sussex Gardens, London
W2 1UB
T: (020) 7723 3380
F: (020) 7262 0324
E: beverleyhousehotel@easynet.
co.uk
I: www.beverleyhousehotel.com

Caring Hotel ♦♦
24 Craven Hill Gardens, London
W2 3EA
T: (020) 7262 8708
F: (020) 7262 8590
E: caring@lineone.net
I: www.caringhotel.co.uk

Classic Hotel ♦♦
92 Sussex Gardens, Hyde Park,
London W2 1UH
T: (020) 7706 7776
F: (020) 7706 8136
E: bookings@classic-hotel.com
I: www.classic-hotel.com

Duke of Leinster ♦♦
34 Queen's Gardens, London
W2 3AA
T: (020) 7258 0079 & 7258 1839
F: (020) 7262 0741
E: dukeshotel@aol.com
I: www.booking.
org/uk/hotels/dukeofleinster

Dylan Hotel ♦♦
14 Devonshire Terrace, Lancaster
Gate, London W2 3DW
T: (020) 7723 3280
F: (020) 7402 2443

Europa House Hotel ♦♦
151 Sussex Gardens, London
W2 2RY
T: (020) 7723 7343 & 7402 1923
F: (020) 7224 9331
E: europahouse@enterprise.net
I: www.europahousehotel.com

Garden Court Hotel ♦♦
30-31 Kensington Gardens
Square, London W2 4BG
T: (020) 7229 2553
F: (020) 7727 2749
E: info@gardencourthotel.co.uk
I: www.gardencourthotel.co.uk

Gower Hotel ♦♦
129 Sussex Gardens, Hyde Park,
London W2 2RX
T: (020) 7262 2262
F: (020) 7262 2006
E: gower@stavrouhotels.co.uk
I: www.stavrouhotels.co.uk

Hyde Park House ♦
48 St Petersburgh Place,
Queensway, London W2 4LD
T: (020) 7229 9652 & 7229 1687

Hyde Park Rooms Hotel ♦
137 Sussex Gardens, Hyde Park,
London W2 2RX
T: (020) 7723 0225 & 7723 0965

**Kensington Gardens Hotel
♦♦♦**
9 Kensington Gardens Square,
London W2 4BH
T: (020) 7221 7790
F: (020) 7792 8612
E: kensingtongardenshotel@
phoenixhotel.co.uk
I: www.kensingtongardenshotel.
co.uk

Kings Arms Hotel ♦♦
254 Edgware Road, Paddington,
London W2 1DS
T: (020) 7262 8441
F: (020) 7258 0556
E: kingsarmshotel@
compuserve.com
◉

Kingsway Hotel ♦♦
27 Norfolk Square, Hyde Park,
London W2 1RX
T: (020) 7723 5569 & 7723 7784
F: (020) 7723 7317
E: kingsway.hotel@btinternet.
com
I: www.btinternet.
com/~Kingsway.hotel/index.
html

Lancaster Court Hotel ♦♦
202-204 Sussex Gardens, Hyde
Park, London W2 3UA
T: (020) 7402 8438 & 7402 6369
F: (020) 7706 3794
E: lch300999@compuserve.com
I: www.lancaster-court-hotel.co.
uk/

Linden House Hotel ♦♦
4-6 Sussex Place, London
W2 2TP
T: (020) 7723 9853 & 7262 0804
F: (020) 7724 1454
E: lindenhse@
sussexplacelondon.freeserve.co.
uk
I: www.smoothhound.co.
uk/hotels/lindenho.html

London Guards Hotel ♦♦♦
36-37 Lancaster Gate, London
W2 3NA
T: (020) 7402 1101
F: (020) 7262 2551
E: info@londonguardshotel.co.
uk

Manor Court Hotel ♦
7 Clanricarde Gardens, London
W2 4JJ
T: (020) 7727 5407 & 7792 3361
F: (020) 7229 2875

Nayland Hotel ♦♦♦
132-134 Sussex Gardens,
London W2 1UB
T: (020) 7723 4615
F: (020) 7402 3292
E: naylandhotel@easynet.co.uk
I: www.naylandhotel.com

Olympic House Hotel ♦♦
138-140 Sussex Gardens,
London W2 1UB
T: (020) 7723 5935
F: (020) 7224 8144
E: olympichousehotel@
btinternet.com

Oxford Hotel ♦♦
13-14 Craven Terrace,
Paddington, London W2 3QD
T: (020) 7402 6860 &
0800 318798
F: (020) 7262 7574
E: royalcourt@dial.pipex.com
I: dspace.dial.pipex.
com/royalcourt

Park Lodge Hotel ♦♦♦
73 Queensborough Terrace,
Bayswater, London W2 3SU
T: (020) 7229 6424
F: (020) 7221 4772
E: smegroup.kfc@cwcom.net

Parkwood Hotel ♦♦
4 Stanhope Place, London
W2 2HB
T: (020) 7402 2241
F: (020) 7402 1574
E: pkwdhotel@aol.com
I: www.parkwoodhotel.com

Rhodes House Hotel ♦♦♦
195 Sussex Gardens, London
W2 2RJ
T: (020) 7262 5617 & 7262 0537
F: (020) 7723 4054
E: chris@rhodeshotel.com
I: www.rhodeshotel.com

Ruddimans Hotel
160-162 Sussex Gardens,
London W2 1UD
T: (020) 7723 1026
F: (020) 7262 2983
E: reserve@ruddimanshotel.co.
uk
I: www.ruddimanshotel.co.uk

**St David's and Norfolk Court
Hotel**
16 Norfolk Square, Hyde Park,
London W2 1RS
T: (020) 7723 3856 & 7723 4963
F: (020) 7402 9061

Sass Hotel ♦♦
10-11 Craven Terrace, London
W2 3QD
T: (020) 7262 2325
F: (020) 7262 0889
E: Info@SassHotel.Com
I: www.SassHotel.Com

W4

Chiswick Lodge ♦♦♦
104 Turnham Green Terrace,
London W4 1QN
T: (020) 8994 9926 & 8994 1712
F: (020) 8742 8238
E: chishot@clara.net

Foubert's Hotel ♦♦
162-166 Chiswick High Road,
London W4 1PR
T: (020) 8994 5202 & 8995 6743

W5

Abbey Lodge Hotel ♦♦
51 Grange Park, Ealing, London
W5 3PR
T: (020) 8567 7914
F: (020) 8579 5350
E: enquiries@
londonlodgehotels.com
I: www.smoothhound.co.
uk/hotels/abbeylo1.html

Creffield Lodge ♦♦
2-4 Creffield Road, Ealing,
London W5 3HN
T: (020) 8993 2284
F: (020) 8992 7082

Grange Lodge Hotel ♦♦♦
48-50 Grange Road, Ealing,
London W5 5BX
T: (020) 8567 1049
F: (020) 8579 5350
E: enquiries@
londonlodgehotels.com
I: www.smoothhound.co.
uk/hotels/gran.html

**230 Meadvale Road
Rating Applied For**
London W5 1LT
T: (020) 8997 5597

W6

Hotel Orlando ♦♦
83 Shepherds Bush Road,
Hammersmith, London W6 7LR
T: (020) 7603 4890
F: (020) 7603 4890

St Peters Hotel ♦♦♦
407-411 Goldhawk Road,
London W6 0SA
T: (020) 8741 4239
F: (020) 8748 3845

W7

Boston Manor Hotel ◆◆◆
146-152 Boston Road, Hanwell,
London W7 2HJ
T: (020) 8566 1534
F: (020) 8567 9510
E: bmh@bostonmanor.com
I: www.bostonmanor.com

W8

Hotel Atlas-Apollo ◆◆◆
18-30 Lexham Gardens, London
W8 5JE
T: (020) 7835 1155 & 7835 1133
F: (020) 7370 4853
E: reservations@atlas-apollo.
com
I: www.atlas-apollo.com

Clearlake Hotel ◆◆
18-19 Prince of Wales Terrace,
Kensington, London W8 5PQ
T: (020) 7937 3274
F: (020) 7376 0604
E: clearlake@talk21.com

Vicarage Private Hotel ◆
10 Vicarage Gate, Kensington,
London W8 4AG
T: (020) 7229 4030
F: (020) 7792 5989
E: reception@
londonvicaragehotel.com
I: londonvicaragehotel.com/

W11

Kensington Guest House ◆◆
72 Holland Park Avenue, London
W11 3QZ
T: (020) 7229 9233
F: (020) 7221 1077
E: HotelLondon@aol.com

W14

Avonmore Hotel ◆◆◆◆
66 Avonmore Road, Kensington,
London W14 8RS
T: (020) 7603 3121 & 7603 4296
F: (020) 7603 4035
E: avonmore.hotel@dial.pipex.
com
I: www.avonmore.hotel.dial.
pipex.com

WC1

Arran House Hotel ◆
77 Gower Street, London
WC1E 6HJ
T: (020) 7636 2186 & 7637 1140
F: (020) 7436 5328
E: arran@dircon.co.uk
I: www.proteusweb.com/arran

Country Inn & Suites ◆◆◆◆
110 Great Russell Street, London
WC1B 3NA
T: (020) 7637 7777
F: (020) 7436 1142

Crescent Hotel ◆◆◆
49-50 Cartwright Gardens,
Bloomsbury, London WC1H 9EL
T: (020) 7387 1515
F: (020) 7383 2054
E: general.enquiries@
crescenthoteloflondon.com
I: www.crescenthoteloflondon.
com

Euro Hotel ◆◆◆
53 Cartwright Gardens, London
WC1H 9EL
T: (020) 7387 4321
F: (020) 7383 5044
E: Reception@eurohotel.co.uk
I: www.eurohotel.co.uk

Garth Hotel ◆
69 Gower Street, London
WC1E 6HJ
T: (020) 7636 5761
F: (020) 7637 4854
E: garth.hotel@virgin.net

George Hotel ◆◆◆
58-60 Cartwright Gardens,
London WC1H 9EL
T: (020) 7387 8777
F: (020) 7387 8666
E: ghotel@aol.com
I: www.georgehotel.com

Gower House Hotel ◆
57 Gower Street, London
WC1E 6HJ
T: (020) 7636 4685
F: (020) 7636 4685

Guilford House Hotel ◆◆
6 Guilford Street, London
WC1N 1DR
T: (020) 7430 2504
F: (020) 7430 0721
E: guilford-hotel@lineone.net
I: www.guilfordhotel.co.uk

St Athans Hotel ◆
20 Tavistock Place, Russell
Square, London WC1H 9RE
T: (020) 7837 9140 & 7837 9627
F: (020) 7833 8352

Thanet Hotel ◆◆
8 Bedford Place, London
WC1B 5JA
T: (020) 7580 3377 & 7636 2869
F: (020) 7323 6676
E: thanetlon@aol.com
I: www.freepages.co.
uk/thanet_hotel/

WC2

Royal Adelphi Hotel ◆◆
21 Villiers Street, London
WC2N 6ND
T: (020) 7930 8764
F: (020) 7930 8735
E: info@royaladelphi.co.uk
I: www.royaladelphi.co.uk

OUTER LONDON

BECKENHAM

Amberlea ◆◆
1 Lodge Gardens, Eden Park,
Beckenham, Kent BR3 3DP
T: (020) 8663 3638
F: (020) 8663 3638

BEXLEY

66 Arcadian Avenue
Rating Applied For
Bexley, Kent DA5 1JW
T: (020) 8303 5732

Buxted Lodge Guest House
Rating Applied For
40 Parkhurst Road, Bexley, Kent
DA5 1AS
T: (01322) 554010 &
07956 483289
E: buxted.lodge@cwcom.net

BRENTFORD

Kings Arms ◆◆◆
19 Boston Manor Road,
Brentford, Middlesex TW8 8EA
T: (020) 8560 5860
F: (020) 8847 4416

BROMLEY

Avondale House
Rating Applied For
56 Avondale Road, Bromley,
BR1 4EP
T: (020) 8402 0844
E: family@afortis.freeserve.co.
uk

Glendevon House Hotel ◆◆
80 Southborough Road, Bickley,
Bromley, BR1 2EN
T: (020) 8467 2183
F: (020) 8295 0701

CROYDON

63 Addington Road ◆◆◆
Sanderstead, South Croydon,
Surrey CR2 8RD
T: (020) 8657 8776
F: (020) 8657 8776

Alpha Guest House ◆◆
99 Brigstock Road, Thornton
Heath, Surrey CR7 7JL
T: (020) 8684 4811 & 8665 0032
F: (020) 8405 0302

Bramley
Rating Applied For
7 Green Court Avenue, Shirley
Park, Croydon, CR0 7LD
T: (020) 8654 6776

Croydon Hotel ◆◆
112 Lower Addiscombe Road,
Croydon, CR0 6AD
T: (020) 8656 7233
F: (020) 8655 0211

Stocks ◆◆◆
51 Selcroft Road, Purley, Surrey
CR8 1AJ
T: (020) 8660 3054
F: (020) 8660 3054

ENFIELD

1 Chinnery Close
Rating Applied For
Enfield, Middlesex EN1 4AX
T: (020) 8363 3887
F: (020) 8366 5496

HAMPTON

Friars Cottage ◆◆◆
2B Priory Road, Hampton,
Middlesex TW12 2WR
T: (020) 8287 4699

14 Nightingale Road ◆◆◆
Hampton, Middlesex TW12 3HX
T: (020) 8979 8074

HARROW

Central Hotel ◆◆
6 Hindes Road, Harrow,
Middlesex HA1 1SJ
T: (020) 8427 0893
F: (020) 8427 0893

Hindes Hotel ◆◆◆
8 Hindes Road, Harrow,
Middlesex HA1 1SJ
T: (020) 8427 7468
F: (020) 8424 0673

HAYES

Shepiston Lodge ◆◆◆
31 Shepiston Lane, Hayes,
Middlesex UB3 1LJ
T: (020) 8573 0266 & 8569 2536
F: (020) 8569 2536
E: shepiston@aol.com

HOUNSLOW

Ashdowne House ◆◆◆◆
9 Pownall Gardens, Hounslow,
Middlesex TW3 1YW
T: (020) 8572 0008
F: (020) 8570 1939
E: mail@ashdownehouse.com
I: www.ashdownehouse.com

Civic Guest House ◆◆
87-89 Lampton Road,
Hounslow, Middlesex TW3 4DP
T: (020) 8572 5107 & 8570 1851
F: (020) 8814 0203
E: enquiries@civicguesthouse.
freeserve.co.uk
I: www.civicguesthouse.
freeserve.co.uk

Shalimar Hotel ◆◆◆
215-221 Staines Road,
Hounslow, Middlesex TW3 3JJ
T: (020) 8572 2816 &
0500 238239
F: (020) 8569 6789

Skylark Bed & Breakfast ◆◆
297 Bath Road, Hounslow,
Middlesex TW3 3DB
T: (020) 8577 8455
F: (020) 8577 8741

ILFORD

Cranbrook Hotel ◆◆
24 Coventry Road, Ilford, Essex
IG1 4QR
T: (020) 8554 6544 & 8554 4765
F: (020) 8518 1463

Park Hotel ◆◆◆
327 Cranbrook Road, Ilford,
Essex IG1 4UE
T: (020) 8554 9616 & 8554 7187
F: (020) 8518 2700
E: parkhotelilford@
netscapeonline.co.uk
I: www.the-park-hotel.co.uk

KENLEY

Appledore ◆◆◆
6 Betula Close, Kenley, Surrey
CR8 5ET
T: (020) 8668 4631
F: (020) 8668 4631

KEW

35 Beechwood Avenue ◆◆◆◆
Kew, Richmond, Surrey
TW9 4DD
T: (020) 8878 0049 &
07768 551488
F: (020) 8878 0049

1 Chelwood Gardens ◆◆◆
Kew, Richmond, Surrey TW9 4JG
T: (020) 8876 8733 &
07860 811998
F: (020) 8255 0171
E: mrsljgray@aol.com

11 Leyborne Park ◆◆◆◆
Kew, Richmond, Surrey
TW9 3HB
T: (020) 8948 1615 &
07778 123736
F: (020) 8255 1141
E: garrigan@globalnet.co.uk

40 Marksbury Avenue ◆◆
Kew, Richmond, Surrey TW9 4JF
T: (020) 8878 9572

Melbury ◆◆
33 Marksbury Avenue, Kew,
Richmond, Surrey TW9 4JE
T: (020) 8876 3930 &
07712 472607
F: (020) 8876 3930

95 Mortlake Road ◆◆◆
Kew, Richmond, Surrey TW9 4AA
T: (020) 8876 3830

West Lodge ◆◆◆
179 Mortlake Road, Kew,
Richmond, Surrey TW9 4AW
T: (020) 8876 0584 & 8876 5375
F: (020) 8876 0584
E: westlodge@thakria.demon.
co.uk

29 West Park Road ◆◆◆
Kew, Richmond, Surrey
TW9 4DA
T: (020) 8878 0505 &
07958 538666
E: Alanbrooklands@aol.uk

MORDEN
28 Monkleigh Road
Rating Applied For
Morden, Surrey SM4 4EW
T: (020) 8542 5595 & 8287 7494

NORTHOLT
Brenda & Bertie Woosters Guesthouse ◆◆
5 Doncaster Drive, Northolt,
Middlesex UB5 4AS
T: (020) 8423 5072

PINNER
Delcon ◆◆
468 Pinner Road, Pinner,
Middlesex HA5 5RR
T: (020) 8863 1054
F: (020) 8863 1054

PURLEY
Arcadia ◆◆
212 Brighton Road, Purley,
Surrey CR8 4HB
T: (020) 8668 2486

Foxley Mount ◆◆◆
44 Foxley Lane, Purley, Surrey
CR8 3EE
T: (020) 8660 9751
F: (020) 8660 9751

The Maple House
Rating Applied For
174 Foxley Lane, Purley, Surrey
CR8 3NF
T: (020) 8407 5123

Purley Cross Guest House
Rating Applied For
50 Brighton Road, Purley, Surrey
CR8 2LG
T: (020) 8668 4964
F: (020) 8407 2133
E: purleycross@hotmail.com

Woodlands
Rating Applied For
2 Green Lane, Purley, Surrey
CR8 3PG
T: (020) 8660 3103

RICHMOND
Anna Guest House ◆
37 Church Road, Richmond,
Surrey TW9 1UA
T: (020) 8940 5237

8 Cardigan Mansions
Rating Applied For
19 Richmond Hill, Richmond,
Surrey TW10 6RD
T: (020) 8940 1654 &
07885 405420

Chalon House
◆◆◆◆◆ GOLD AWARD
8 Spring Terrace, Paradise Road,
Richmond, Surrey TW9 1LW
T: (020) 8332 1121
F: (020) 8332 1131
E: virgilioz@aol.com

Doughty Cottage
◆◆◆◆◆ GOLD AWARD
142a Richmond Hill, Richmond,
Surrey TW10 6RN
T: (020) 8332 9434
F: (020) 8332 9434
I: www.smoothhound.co.
uk/hotels/doughtycott

Dukes Head Inn ◆◆◆
42 The Vineyards, Richmond,
Surrey TW10 6AW
T: (020) 8948 4557
F: (020) 8948 4557
E: thedukeshead@yahoo.com
I: www.dukeshead.com

Farm Lodge
Rating Applied For
Petersham Road, Richmond,
Surrey TW10 7AD
T: (020) 8332 1974
E: paulineharman@hotmail.com

Hobart Hall Hotel ◆◆◆
43-47 Petersham Road,
Richmond, Surrey TW10 6UL
T: (020) 8940 0435 & 8940 1702
F: (020) 8332 2996
E: hobarthall@aol.com

Ivy Cottage ◆◆
Upper Ham Road, Ham
Common, Richmond, Surrey
TW10 5LA
T: (020) 8940 8601
F: (020) 8940 3865
E: taylor@dbt1.freeserve.co.uk
I: www.dbtl.freeserve.co.uk

54 Mount Ararat Road
Rating Applied For
Richmond, Surrey TW10 6PJ
T: (020) 8940 4538

147 Petersham Road
◆◆◆◆ SILVER AWARD
Richmond, Surrey TW10 7AH
T: (020) 8940 3424
E: sylviapeile@peile.force9.co.uk

Pro Kew Gardens B & B ◆◆◆
15 Pensford Avenue, Kew
Gardens, Richmond, Surrey
TW9 4HR
T: (020) 8876 3354

Quinns Hotel ◆◆◆
48 Sheen Road, Richmond,
Surrey TW9 1AW
T: (020) 8940 5444
F: (020) 8940 1828
I: www.quinnshotel.com

Richmond Park Hotel ◆◆◆
3 Petersham Road, Richmond,
Surrey TW10 6UH
T: (020) 8948 4666
F: (020) 8940 7376
E: richmdpk@globalnet.co.uk

Riverside Hotel ◆◆◆
23 Petersham Road, Richmond,
Surrey TW10 6UH
T: (020) 8940 1339
F: (020) 8948 0967
E: riversidehotel@yahoo.com
I: www.smoothhound.co.
uk/hotels/riversid.html

31 Rothesay Avenue ◆◆◆
Richmond, Surrey TW10 5EB
T: (020) 8876 2331

248 Sandycombe Road ◆◆◆
Kew, Richmond, Surrey TW9 3NP
T: (020) 8940 5970

9 Selwyn Court ◆◆
Church Road, Richmond, Surrey
TW10 6LR
T: (020) 8940 3309

Taylor Avenue ◆
Richmond, Surrey TW9 4EB
T: (020) 8876 1231 &
07885 690004
E: mrspa.thomas@virgin.net

3 Townshend Road ◆◆
Richmond, Surrey TW9 1XH
T: (020) 8948 2470

454 Upper Richmond Road West ◆◆◆
Richmond, Surrey TW10 5DY
T: (020) 8876 0327

ROMFORD
The Orchard Guest House
Rating Applied For
81 Eastern Road, Romford,
RM1 3PB
T: (01708) 744099
F: (01708) 768881
E: johnrt@globalnet.co.uk

SIDCUP
The Chimneys ◆◆◆
6 Clarence Road, Sidcup, Kent
DA14 4DL
T: (020) 8309 1460
F: (020) 8304 6978

SOUTH CROYDON
Dereen ◆◆
14 St Augustine's Avenue, South
Croydon, Surrey CR2 6BS
T: (020) 8686 2075

Owlets ◆◆
112 Arundel Avenue, South
Croydon, Surrey CR2 8BH
T: (020) 8657 5213
F: (020) 8657 5213

Waldenbury ◆◆◆
33 Crossways, Selsdon, South
Croydon, Surrey CR2 8JQ
T: (020) 8657 7791
F: (020) 8657 7791

SOUTH HARROW
4 Shaftesbury Avenue ◆◆
South Harrow, Harrow,
Middlesex HA2 0PH
T: (020) 8357 2548
⊚

TEDDINGTON
93 Clarence Road ◆◆◆◆
Teddington, Middlesex
TW11 0BN
T: (020) 8977 3459
F: (020) 8943 1560

Glenhurst
Rating Applied For
93 Langham Road, Teddington,
Middlesex TW11 9HG
T: (020) 8977 6962 &
07836 782132
F: (020) 8977 6962

6 Grove Gardens ◆◆◆
Teddington, Middlesex
TW11 8AP
T: (020) 8977 6066

Hazeldene ◆◆◆◆
58 Hampton Road, Teddington,
Middlesex TW11 0JX
T: (020) 8286 8500
E: lisa_smith@hotmail.com

King Edwards Grove ◆◆◆
Teddington, Middlesex
TW11 9LY
T: (020) 8977 7251

126 Kingston Road ◆◆◆
Teddington, Middlesex
TW11 9JA
T: (020) 8943 9302

Polly's Bed and Breakfast
◆◆◆
166 High Street, Teddington,
Middlesex TW11 8HU
T: (020) 8287 1188 &
07767 402231
E: polly31.fznet.co.uk

THORNTON HEATH
The Lloyd's House
Rating Applied For
41 Moffatt Road, Thornton
Heath, Surrey CR7 8PY
T: (020) 8768 1827

TWICKENHAM
Abigails Guest House ◆◆◆
7 Haggard Road, Twickenham,
TW1 3AL
T: (020) 8892 6223 & 8892 1301

Avalon Cottage ◆◆◆
50 Moor Mead Road, St
Margarets, Twickenham,
TW1 1JS
T: (020) 8744 2178
F: (020) 8891 2444
E: avalon@mead99.freeserve.co.
uk

59 Court Way
Rating Applied For
Twickenham, TW2 7SA
T: (020) 8892 4254 & 8744 0959
F: (020) 8891 0115

22 Ellesmere Road ◆◆
East Twickenham, Middlesex
TW1 2DL
T: (020) 8892 1188

136 London Road ◆◆◆
Twickenham, TW1 1HD
T: (020) 8892 3158 &
07956 499819

St George's Lodge
Rating Applied For
27 The Avenue, St Margaret's,
Twickenham, TW1 1QP
T: (020) 8892 7679 &
07703 355793

St Margarets Guest House ◆◆
53-55 Crown Road, St
Margarets, Twickenham,
TW1 3EJ
T: (020) 8744 2990 &
07836 763872
F: (020) 8744 2953

11 Spencer Road ◆◆◆
11 Spencer Road, Strawberry
Hill, Twickenham, TW2 5TH
T: (020) 8894 5271
F: (020) 8994 4751
E: bruceduff@hotmail.com

3 Waldegrave Gardens ◆◆◆
Strawberry Hill, Twickenham,
TW1 4PQ
T: (020) 8892 3523

UPMINSTER

Corner Farm ◆◆◆
Corner Farm, Fen Lane, North
Ockendon, Upminster, Essex
RM14 3RB
T: (01708) 851310
F: (01708) 852025
E: corner.farm@virgin.net

WELLING

De + Dees B & B ◆◆◆◆
91 Welling Way, Welling, Kent
DA16 2RW
T: (020) 8319 1592
F: (020) 8319 1592

WEMBLEY

**Aaron (Wembley Park) Hotel
Ltd** ◆
8 Forty Lane, Wembley,
Middlesex HA9 9EB
T: (020) 8904 6329 & 8908 5711
F: (020) 8385 0472
E: susmil@susmil.freeserve.co.
uk
I: aaronhotel.com

Adelphi Hotel ◆◆◆
4 Forty Lane, Wembley,
Middlesex HA9 9EB
T: (020) 8904 5629
F: (020) 8908 5314
E: adel@dial.pipex.com
I: www.hoteladelphi.co.uk

Arena Hotel ◆◆◆
6 Forty Lane, Wembley,
Middlesex HA9 9EB
T: (020) 8908 0670 & 8904 0019
F: (020) 8908 2007
E: enquiry@arenahotel.fsnet.co.
uk
I: www.arena-hotel.co.uk

Elm Hotel ◆◆◆
1-7 Elm Road, Wembley,
Middlesex HA9 7JA
T: (020) 8902 1764
F: (020) 8903 8365
E: elm.hotel@virgin.net
I: www.elmhotel.co.uk

WEST DRAYTON

The Alice House ◆◆
9 Hollycroft Close, Sipson, West
Drayton, Middlesex UB7 0JJ
T: (020) 8897 9032

WORCESTER PARK

The Graye House ◆◆◆
24 The Glebe, Worcester Park,
Surrey KT4 7PF
T: (020) 8330 1277 &
07710 376494
E: graye.house@virgin.net
I: www.smoothhound.co.uk

CUMBRIA

AINSTABLE
Cumbria

Bell House ◆◆◆◆
Ainstable, Carlisle, Cumbria
CA4 9RE
T: (01768) 896255 &
07767 888636
F: (01768) 896255
E: mrobinson@bellhouse.
fsbusiness.co.uk
⊕

Heather Glen Country Hotel
◆◆◆
Ainstable, Carlisle CA4 9QQ
T: (01768) 896219
F: (01768) 896219
E: sales@heather-glen-hotel.
com
I: www.heather-glen-hotel.co.uk

ALLONBY
Cumbria

Ship Hotel ◆◆◆
Main Street, Allonby, Maryport,
Cumbria CA15 6PD
T: (01900) 881017 & 881115
F: (01900) 881017
⊕

ALSTON
Cumbria

Albert House Guest House
◆◆◆
Townhead, Alston, Cumbria
CA9 3SL
T: (01434) 381793 &
07887 848790

Brownside House ◆◆◆
Leadgate, Alston, Cumbria
CA9 3EL
T: (01434) 382169 & 382100
F: (01434) 382169
E: brownside_hse@hotmail.com
I: www.cumbria1st.
com/brown_side/index.htm

Chapel House ◆◆◆
Overburn, Alston, Cumbria
CA9 3SH
T: (01434) 381112

Greycroft
◆◆◆◆ SILVER AWARD
Middle Park, The Raise, Alston,
Cumbria CA9 3AR
T: (01434) 381383
⊕

AMBLESIDE
Cumbria

Ambleside Lodge ◆◆◆◆
Rothay Road, Ambleside,
Cumbria LA22 0EJ
T: (015394) 31681
F: (015394) 34547
E: cherryho@globalnet.co.uk
I: www.ambleside-lodge.com

Amboseli Lodge ◆◆◆◆
Rothay Road, Ambleside,
Cumbria LA22 0EE
T: (015394) 31110
F: (015394) 31111
E: 101703.3723@compuserve.
com
I: www.fryamboseli@aol.com

The Anchorage ◆◆◆
Rydal Road, Ambleside, Cumbria
LA22 9AY
T: (015394) 32046
E: robanj@yahooo.com

Barnes Fell Guest House
◆◆◆◆ SILVER AWARD
Low Gale, Ambleside, Cumbria
LA22 0BB
T: (015394) 33311
F: (015394) 31919

Borrans Park Hotel
◆◆◆◆ SILVER AWARD
Borrans Road, Ambleside,
Cumbria LA22 0EN
T: (015394) 33454
F: (015394) 33003
E: info@borranspark.co.uk
I: www.borranspark.co.uk
♿

Brantfell House ◆◆◆
Rothay Road, Ambleside,
Cumbria LA22 0EE
T: (015394) 32239 & 34124
F: (015394) 32239
E: brantfell@kencomp.net

Broadview ◆◆◆
Low Fold, Lake Road, Ambleside,
Cumbria LA22 0DN
T: (015394) 32431
E: enquiries@
broadview-guesthouse.co.uk
I: broadview-guesthouse.co.uk

3 Cambridge Villas
Rating Applied For
Church Street, Ambleside,
Cumbria LA22 9DL
T: (015394) 32307

Cherry Garth Hotel ◆◆◆
Old Lake Road, Ambleside,
Cumbria LA22 0DH
T: (015394) 33128
F: (015394) 33885

Claremont House ◆◆◆
Compston Road, Ambleside,
Cumbria LA22 9DJ
T: (015394) 33448
F: (015394) 33448
E: olwenm@supanet.com

Compston House Hotel ◆◆◆◆
Compston Road, Ambleside,
Cumbria LA22 9DJ
T: (015394) 32305
F: (015394) 32652
E: compston@globalnet.co.uk
I: www.compstonhouse.co.uk

The Dower House ◆◆◆◆
Wray Castle, Ambleside, Cumbria
LA22 0JA
T: (015394) 33211

Easedale Guest House ◆◆◆◆
Compston Road, Ambleside,
Cumbria LA22 9DJ
T: (015394) 32112
F: (015394) 32112
I: www.
soar@easedaleguesthouse.
freeserve.uk

Elder Grove ◆◆◆◆
Lake Road, Ambleside, Cumbria
LA22 0DB
T: (015394) 32504
F: (015394) 32504
⊕

Fern Cottage ◆◆◆
6 Waterhead Terrace, Ambleside,
Cumbria LA22 0HA
T: (015394) 33007

Ferndale Hotel ◆◆◆
Lake Road, Ambleside, Cumbria
LA22 0DB
T: (015394) 32207

Fisherbeck Garden ◆◆◆
Old Lake Road, Ambleside,
Cumbria LA22 0DH
T: (015394) 33088
E: janice@fisherbeck.net1.co.uk

Foxghyll ◆◆◆◆
Under Loughrigg, Ambleside,
Cumbria LA22 9LL
T: (015394) 33292
E: foxghyll@hotmail.com
I: www.smoothhound.co.
uk/hotels/foxghyll.html

Freshfields ◆◆◆◆
Wansfell Road, Ambleside,
Cumbria LA22 0EG
T: (015394) 34469
F: (015394) 34469
⊕

The Gables ◆◆◆
Church Walk, Ambleside,
Cumbria LA22 9DJ
T: (015394) 33272
F: (015394) 34734
E: the.old.vicarage@kencomp.
net
⊕

Ghyll Head Hotel ◆◆◆
Waterhead, Ambleside, Cumbria
LA22 0HD
T: (015394) 32360 &
0500 200148

Glenside ◆◆◆◆
Old Lake Road, Ambleside,
Cumbria LA22 0DP
T: (015394) 32635

Greenbank
◆◆◆◆ SILVER AWARD
Skelwith Bridge, Ambleside,
Cumbria LA22 9NW
T: (015394) 33236
E: grenbank@bigwig.net
I: www.visitgreenbank.co.uk

**Grey Friar Lodge Country
House Hotel**
◆◆◆◆ SILVER AWARD
Clappersgate, Ambleside,
Cumbria LA22 9NE
T: (015394) 33158
F: (015394) 33158
E: greyfriar@veen.freeserve.co.
uk
I: www.cumbria-hotels.co.uk

High Wray Farm ◆◆◆◆
High Wray, Ambleside, Cumbria
LA22 0JE
T: (015394) 32280
E: high.wray.farm@bigwig.net
I: www.highwrayfarm.co.uk

Hillsdale ◆◆◆
Church Street, Ambleside,
Cumbria LA22 0BT
T: (015394) 33174
E: gstaley@hillsdale.freeserve.
co.uk
I: www.hillsdale.freeserve.co.uk

Holmeshead Farm ◆◆◆◆
Skelwith Fold, Ambleside,
Cumbria LA22 0HU
T: (015394) 33048

Howe Farm ◆◆ SILVER AWARD
Hawkshead, Ambleside, Cumbria
LA22 0QB
T: (015394) 36345
E: howefarm@nascr.net

Kent House ◆◆◆◆
Lake Road, Ambleside, Cumbria
LA22 0AD
T: (015394) 33279
F: (015394) 33279
E: info@kent-house.com
I: www.kent-house.com

**Kirkstone Foot Country House
Hotel**◆◆◆◆
Kirkstone Pass Road, Ambleside,
Cumbria LA22 9EH
T: (015394) 32232
F: (015394) 32805
E: kirkstone@breathemail.net

Lattendales ◆◆◆
Compston Road, Ambleside,
Cumbria LA22 9DJ
T: (015394) 32368
E: admin@latts.freeserve.co.uk
I: www.latts.freeserve.co.uk

Lyndale ◆◆◆
Low Fold, Lake Road, Ambleside,
Cumbria LA22 0DN
T: (015394) 34244
E: gavinlobb@lyndale.
totalserve.co.uk
I: www.lyndale.totalserve.co.uk

Lyndhurst Hotel ◆◆◆
Wansfell Road, Ambleside,
Cumbria LA22 0EG
T: (015394) 32421
F: (015394) 32421
E: lyndhurst@amblesidehotels.
co.uk
I: www.amblesidehotels.co.uk

Meadowbank ◆◆◆
Rydal Road, Ambleside, Cumbria
LA22 9BA
T: (015394) 32710 &
07989 623450
F: (015394) 32710
E: catherine@meadowbank10.
freeserve.co.uk

Melrose Hotel ◆◆◆
Church Street, Ambleside,
Cumbria LA22 0BT
T: (015394) 32500

The Old Vicarage ◆◆◆◆
Vicarage Road, Ambleside,
Cumbria LA22 9DH
T: (015394) 33364
F: (015394) 34734
E: theoldvicarage@kencomp.net

Park House Guest House ◆◆◆
3 Compston Villas, Compston
Road, Ambleside, Cumbria
LA22 9DJ
T: (015394) 31692

Red Bank Guesthouse ◆◆◆◆
SILVER AWARD
Wansfell Road, Ambleside,
Cumbria LA22 0EG
T: (015394) 34637
F: (015394) 34637
E: info@red-bank.co.uk
I: www.red-bank.co.uk

Riverside Hotel ◆◆◆◆
Under Loughrigg, Rothay Bridge,
Ambleside, Cumbria LA22 9LJ
T: (015394) 32395
F: (015394) 32395

Riverside Lodge ◆◆◆◆
Rothay Bridge, Ambleside,
Cumbria LA22 0EH
T: (015394) 34208
F: (015394) 31884
E: alanrhone@riversidelodge.co.
uk
I: www.riversidelodge.co.uk

**Rowanfield Country
Guesthouse** ◆◆◆◆◆
SILVER AWARD
Kirkstone Road, Ambleside,
Cumbria LA22 9ET
T: (015394) 33686
F: (015394) 31569
E: email@rowanfield.com
I: www.rowanfield.com

The Rysdale Hotel ◆◆◆
Rothay Road, Ambleside,
Cumbria LA22 0EE
T: (015394) 32140 & 33999
F: (015394) 33999

Scandale Brow ◆◆◆◆
Rydal Road, Ambleside, Cumbria
LA22 9PL
T: (015394) 34528
F: (015394) 34528
E: scandale.brow@virgin.net

Thorneyfield Guest House
◆◆◆◆
Compston Road, Ambleside,
Cumbria LA22 9DJ
T: (015394) 32464
F: (015394) 32464
E: info@thorneyfield.co.uk
I: www.thorneyfield.co.uk

Tock How Farm ◆◆◆
High Wray, Ambleside, Cumbria
LA22 0JF
T: (015394) 36106
F: (015394) 36106

Walmar Hotel ◆◆◆
Lake Road, Ambleside, Cumbria
LA22 0DB
T: (015394) 32454

Wanslea Guest House ◆◆◆◆
Lake Road, Ambleside, Cumbria
LA22 0DN
T: (015394) 33884
F: (015394) 33884
E: wanslea.guesthouse@virgin.
net

APPLEBY-IN-WESTMORLAND
Cumbria

Asby Grange Farm ◆◆◆
Great Asby, Appleby-in-
Westmorland, Cumbria
CA16 6HF
T: (017683) 52881

Bongate House ◆◆◆◆
Appleby-in-Westmorland,
Cumbria CA16 6UE
T: (017683) 51245 & 51423
E: bongatehse@aol.com

Brampton Tower ◆◆◆◆
Croft Ends, Appleby-in-
Westmorland, Cumbria
CA16 6JN
T: (017683) 53447
F: (017683) 53447

Bridge End Farm
◆◆◆◆◆ SILVER AWARD
Kirkby Thore, Penrith, Cumbria
CA10 1UZ
T: (017683) 61362

Dufton Hall Farm ◆◆◆
Dufton, Appleby-in-
Westmorland, Cumbria
CA16 6DD
T: (017683) 51573
F: (017683) 51573
E: howemargaret@hotmail.com

ARNSIDE
Cumbria

Willowfield Hotel ◆◆◆◆
The Promenade, Arnside,
Carnforth, Lancashire LA5 0AD
T: (01524) 761354
E: kerr@willowfield.net1.co.uk
I: www.smoothhound.co.
uk/hotels/willowfi.html

BARROW-IN-FURNESS
Cumbria

**Arlington House Hotel and
Restaurant**◆◆◆◆
200-202 Abbey Road, Barrow-
in-Furness, Cumbria LA14 5LD
T: (01229) 831976
F: (01229) 870990

BASSENTHWAITE
Cumbria

Herdwick Croft Guest House
◆◆◆
Bassenthwaite, Keswick,
Cumbria CA12 4RD
T: (017687) 76241

Kiln Hill Barn ◆◆◆
Bassenthwaite, Keswick,
Cumbria CA12 4RG
T: (017687) 76454
F: (017687) 76454
E: ken@kilnhillbarn.freeserve.co.
uk

Ravenstone Lodge ◆◆◆◆
Bassenthwaite, Keswick,
Cumbria CA12 4QG
T: (017687) 76629 & 76638
F: (017687) 76629
E: ravenstone.lodge@talk21.
com

Robin Hood House ◆◆◆
Bassenthwaite, Keswick,
Cumbria CA12 4RJ
T: (017687) 76296

BASSENTHWAITE LAKE
Cumbria

Lakeside ◆◆◆◆
Dubwath, Bassenthwaite Lake,
Cockermouth, Cumbria
CA13 9YD
T: (017687) 76358

Link House ◆◆◆◆
Bassenthwaite Lake,
Cockermouth, Cumbria
CA13 9YD
T: (017687) 76291
F: (017687) 76670
E: gfkerr@globalnet.co.uk
I: www.link-house.co.uk

BEETHAM
Cumbria

Barn Close/North West Birds
◆◆◆
Beetham, Milnthorpe, Cumbria
LA7 7AL
T: (015395) 63191 &
07802 700830
F: (015395) 63191
E: nwbirds@compuserve.com
I: ourworld.compuserve.
com/homepages/nwbirds

BIRKBY
Cumbria

**The Retreat Hotel and
Restaurant** ◆◆◆◆
Birkby, Maryport, Cumbria
CA15 6RG
T: (01900) 814056

BOLTON
Cumbria

Eden Grove House
◆◆◆◆ SILVER AWARD
Bolton, Appleby-in-
Westmorland, Cumbria CA16
T: (017683) 62321

BOOT
Cumbria

The Burnmoor Inn ◆◆◆
Boot, Holmrook, Cumbria
CA19 1TG
T: (019467) 23224
F: (019467) 23337
E: enquiries@burnmoor.co.uk
I: www.burnmoor.co.uk

BORROWDALE
Cumbria

Derwent House ◆◆◆◆
Grange-in-Borrowdale,
Borrowdale, Keswick, Cumbria
CA12 5UY
T: (017687) 77658
F: (017687) 77217
E: derwenthse@aol.com

**Greenbank Country House
Hotel** ◆◆◆◆ SILVER AWARD
Borrowdale, Keswick, Cumbria
CA12 5UY
T: (017687) 77215
F: (017687) 77215

Hazel Bank Country House
◆◆◆◆◆ GOLD AWARD
Rosthwaite, Keswick, Cumbria
CA12 5XB
T: (017687) 77248
F: (017678) 77733
E: enquiries@hazelbankhotel.
demon.co.uk
I: www.hazelbankhotel.demon.
co.uk

BOWNESS-ON-SOLWAY
Cumbria

Maia Lodge ◆◆◆
Bowness-on-Solway, Carlisle,
Cumbria CA5 5BH
T: (016973) 51955

Wallsend ◆◆◆◆
The Old Rectory, Church Lane,
Bowness-on-Solway, Carlisle
CA7 5AF
T: (016973) 51055 & 614224
F: (016973) 52180
E: wallsend@btinternet.com

CUMBRIA

BOWNESS-ON-WINDERMERE
Cumbria

Aphrodites Themed Accommodation ◆◆◆◆
Longtail Hill, Bowness-on-Windermere, Windermere, Cumbria LA23 2EQ
T: (015394) 46702
E: enquires@dalegarthe.demon.co.uk
I: www.dalegarthe.demon./bordriggshtm.co.uk

Beechwood Private Hotel ◆◆◆◆ SILVER AWARD
South Craig, Beresford Road, Bowness-on-Windermere, Windermere, Cumbria LA23 2JG
T: (015394) 43403
F: (015394) 43403

Belsfield House ◆◆◆◆
4 Belsfield Terrace, Kendal Road, Bowness-on-Windermere, Windermere, Cumbria LA23 3EQ
T: (015394) 45823

Biskey Howe Villa Hotel ◆◆◆
Craig Walk, Bowness-on-Windermere, Windermere, Cumbria LA23 3AX
T: (015394) 43988
F: (015394) 88379
E: biskey-howe@lakes-pages.com
I: www.biskey-howe-hotel.co.uk

Craig Wood Guest House ◆◆◆
119 Craig Walk, Bowness-on-Windermere, Windermere, Cumbria LA23 3AX
T: (015394) 44914

Elim Lodge ◆◆◆
Biskey Howe Road, Bowness-on-Windermere, Windermere, Cumbria LA23 2JP.
T: (015394) 47299
F: (015394) 47299
E: elimlodge@mickelfield.freeserve.co.uk

Latimer House ◆◆◆
Lake Road, Bowness-on-Windermere, Windermere, Cumbria LA23 2JJ
T: (015394) 46888
F: (015394) 46888
E: latimerhouse@hotmail.com

Little Longtail ◆◆◆
Ferry view, Bowness-on-Windermere, Windermere, Cumbria LA23 3JB
T: (015394) 43884

The Lonsdale ◆◆◆
Lake Road, Bowness-on-Windermere, Windermere, Cumbria LA23 2JJ
T: (015394) 43348
F: (015394) 43348
E: lonsdale@fsbdial.co.uk

Lowfell ◆◆◆◆ SILVER AWARD
Ferney Green, Bowness-on-Windermere, Windermere, Cumbria LA23 3ES
T: (015394) 45612 & 48411
F: (015394) 48411
E: louise@lakes-pages.co.uk
I: www.low-fell.co.uk

White Foss ◆◆◆◆
Longtail Hill, Bowness-on-Windermere, Windermere, Cumbria LA23 3JD
T: (015394) 46593
E: nicholson@whitefoss.freeserve.co.uk

BRAITHWAITE
Cumbria

Coledale Inn ◆◆◆
Braithwaite, Keswick, Cumbria CA12 5TN
T: (017687) 78272

Maple Bank ◆◆◆◆
Braithwaite, Keswick, Cumbria CA12 5RY
T: (017687) 78229
F: (017687) 78000
E: maplebank@aol.com
I: www.maplebank.co.uk

BRAMPTON
Cumbria

Blacksmiths Arms Hotel ◆◆◆
Talkin Village, Brampton, Cumbria CA8 1LE
T: (016977) 3452
F: (016977) 3396

Howard House Farm ◆◆◆◆
Gilsland, Carlisle CA6 7AN
T: (016977) 47285

Langthwaite ◆◆◆
Lanercost Road, Brampton, Cumbria CA8 1EN
T: (016977) 2883

Low Rigg Farm ◆◆◆
Walton, Brampton, Cumbria CA8 2DX
T: (016977) 3233
E: lowrigg@lineone.net

New Mills House ◆◆◆
Brampton, Cumbria CA8 2QS
T: (016977) 3376
E: boons@newmills.force9.net
I: www.newmills.force9.co.uk

Oakwood Park Hotel ◆◆◆
Longtown Road, Brampton, Cumbria CA8 2AP
T: (016977) 2436
F: (016977) 2436

South View ◆◆◆
Rating Applied For
Banks, Brampton, Cumbria CA8 2JH
T: (016977) 2309
E: sandrahodgson@southviewbanks.f9.co.uk

Walton High Rigg ◆◆◆
Walton, Brampton, Cumbria CA8 2AZ
T: (016977) 2117

BRISCO
Cumbria

Staggs Cottage ◆◆◆◆
Brisco, Carlisle CA4 0QS
T: (01228) 547419

BROUGH
Cumbria

River View ◆◆◆
Brough, Kirkby Stephen, Cumbria CA17 4BZ
T: (017683) 41894
F: (017683) 41894
E: riverviewbb@talk21.com

BROUGHAM
Cumbria

Keepers Cottage ◆◆◆
Brougham, Penrith, Cumbria CA10 2DE
T: (01768) 865280 & 07790 660427
F: (01768) 865280
E: keeperscottage@keeperscottage.screaming.net
I: stay.at/keeperscottage

BROUGHTON-IN-FURNESS
Cumbria

Broom Hill ◆◆◆
New Street, Broughton-in-Furness, Cumbria LA20 6JD
T: (01229) 716358 & 07966 129439
F: (01229) 716358

The Dower House ◆◆◆
High Duddon, Broughton-in-Furness, Cumbria LA20 6ET
T: (01229) 716279
F: (01229) 716279

Manor Arms ◆◆◆
The Square, Broughton-in-Furness, Cumbria LA20 6HY
T: (01229) 716286

Middlesyke ◆◆◆◆
Church Street, Broughton-in-Furness, Cumbria LA20 6ER
T: (01229) 716549

Oak Bank ◆◆
Ulpha, Broughton-in-Furness, Cumbria LA20 6DZ
T: (01229) 716393

CALDBECK
Cumbria

The Briars ◆◆◆
Friar Row, Caldbeck, Wigton, Cumbria CA7 8DS
T: (016974) 78633

Swaledale Watch ◆◆◆◆
Whelpo, Caldbeck, Wigton, Cumbria CA7 8HQ
T: (016974) 78409
F: (016974) 78409
I: nan.savage@talk21.com

CARLETON
Cumbria

River Forge Bed and Breakfast ◆◆◆◆
River Forge, Carleton, Carlisle CA4 0AA
T: (01228) 523569

CARLISLE
Cumbria

Abbey Court ◆◆◆◆
24 London Road, Carlisle, CA1 2EL
T: (01228) 528696
F: (01228) 528696

Ashleigh House ◆◆◆◆
46 Victoria Place, Carlisle, CA1 1EX
T: (01228) 521631 & 07710 604694

Avondale ◆◆◆◆
3 St Aidan's Road, Carlisle, Cumbria CA1 1LT
T: (01228) 523012
F: (01228) 523012
I: www.beeanbee@hotmail.com

Caldew View ◆◆◆
Metcalfe Street, Denton Holme, Carlisle, CA2 5EU
T: (01228) 595837

Calreena Guest House ◆◆
123 Warwick Road, Carlisle, CA1 1JZ
T: (01228) 525020 & 598260

Chatsworth Guesthouse ◆◆◆
22 Chatsworth Square, Carlisle, Cumbria CA1 1HF
T: (01228) 524023
F: (01228) 524023
E: chatsworth@interakt.net
I: www.interakt.net/chatsworth

Claremont Guest House ◆◆◆
30 London Road, Carlisle, Cumbria CA1 2EL
T: (01228) 524691
F: (01228) 527691

Corner House Hotel and Bar ◆◆◆
4 Grey Street, Off London Road, Carlisle, Cumbria CA1 2JP
T: (01228) 533239
F: (01228) 546628

Cornerways Guest House ◆◆◆◆
107 Warwick Road, Carlisle, Cumbria CA1 1EA
T: (01228) 521733

Courtfield House ◆◆◆◆ SILVER AWARD
169 Warwick Road, Carlisle, Cumbria CA1 1LP
T: (01228) 522767

Croft End ◆◆◆
Hurst, Ivegill, Carlisle CA4 0NL
T: (017684) 84362 & 07889 728400

Dalroc ◆◆◆
411 Warwick Road, Carlisle, CA1 2RZ
T: (01228) 542805

East View Guest House ◆◆◆
110 Warwick Road, Carlisle, CA1 1JU
T: (01228) 522112
F: (01228) 522112
I: www.guesthousecarlisle.co.uk

1 Etterby Street ◆◆◆
Stanwix, Carlisle, Cumbria CA3 9JB
T: (01228) 547285 & 0789 994 8711

Fern Lee Guest House ◆◆◆◆
9 St Aidans Road, Carlisle, CA1 1LT
T: (01228) 511930
F: (01228) 511930

Hazeldene Guest House ◆◆◆
Orton Grange, Wigton Road, Carlisle, Cumbria CA5 6LA
T: (01228) 711953

7 Hether Drive ◆◆◆
Lowry Hill, Carlisle, CA3 0ED
T: (01228) 527242
E: liljonmeg@aol.com

Howard Lodge Guesthouse ◆◆◆◆
90 Warwick Road, Carlisle, CA1 1JU
T: (01228) 529842

Langleigh House ◆◆◆
6 Howard Place, Carlisle,
CA1 1HR
T: (01228) 530440
F: (01228) 530440
E: james@langleigh.f9.co.uk
I: www.langleigh.f9.co.uk

Lynebank Guest House ◆◆◆◆
Westlinton, Carlisle CA6 6AA
T: (01228) 792820
F: (01228) 792820
E: jan@lynebank.co.uk
I: www.lynebank.co.uk

Marchmain Guest House ◆◆◆
151 Warwick Road, Carlisle,
CA1 1LU
T: (01228) 529551
F: (01228) 529551

Metal Bridge House ◆◆◆
Metal Bridge, Rockcliffe, Carlisle
CA6 4HG
T: (01228) 674695
☺

Naworth Guest House ◆◆◆◆
33 Victoria Place, Carlisle,
CA1 1HP
T: (01228) 521645
E: stay@naworth.com
I: www.naworth.com

New Pallyards ◆◆◆◆
Hethersgill, Carlisle CA6 6HZ
T: (01228) 577308
F: (01228) 577308
E: info@newpallyards.freeserve.
co.uk
I: www.newpallyards.freeserve.
co.uk
☺

Newfield Grange Hotel ◆◆◆
Newfield Drive, Kingstown,
Carlisle CA3 0AF
T: (01228) 819926 &
07930 278214
F: (01228) 546323
E: bb@newfield53.freeserve.co.
uk
I: www.newfield53.freeserve.co.
uk
🚶

Number Thirty One
◆◆◆◆◆ GOLD AWARD
31 Howard Place, Carlisle,
Cumbria CA1 1HR
T: (01228) 597080
F: (01228) 597080
E: bestpep@aol.com
I: number31.freeservers.com

Parkland Guest House ◆◆◆
136 Petteril Street, Carlisle,
CA1 2AW
T: (01228) 548331
F: (01228) 548331

Stratheden ◆◆◆◆
93 Warwick Road, Carlisle,
CA1 1EB
T: (01228) 520192

**Vallum House Garden Hotel
◆◆◆**
Burgh Road, Carlisle, CA2 7NB
T: (01228) 521860

Warren Guesthouse ◆◆◆
368 Warwick Road, Carlisle,
Cumbria CA1 2RU
T: (01228) 33663 & 512916
F: (01228) 33663
☺

Warwick Lodge ◆◆◆◆
112 Warwick Road, Carlisle,
CA1 1LF
T: (01228) 523796
F: (01228) 546789
E: warwick112@aol.com

White Lea Guest House ◆◆◆
191 Warwick Road, Carlisle,
CA1 1LP
T: (01228) 533139

Bank Court Cottage ◆◆◆
The Square, Cartmel, Grange-
over-Sands, Cumbria LA11 6QB
T: (015395) 36593 &
07798 790710
F: (015395) 36593

Lightwood Farmhouse ◆◆◆
Bowland Bridge, Cartmel Fell,
Grange-over-Sands, Cumbria
LA11 6NP
T: (015395) 31454
F: (01595) 31454

**Gelt Hall Bed and Breakfast
◆◆◆**
Castle Carrock, Carlisle CA4 9LT
T: (01228) 670261 &
07768 937977
F: (01228) 670610
E: melanie.j.brown@talk21.com

Rose Cottage ◆◆◆
Lorton Road, Cockermouth,
Cumbria CA13 9DX
T: (01900) 822189
F: (01900) 822189

**Arrowfield Country Guest
House ◆◆◆◆**
Little Arrow, Coniston, Cumbria
LA21 8AU
T: (015394) 41741

Bank Ground Farm ◆◆◆◆
East of Lake, Coniston, Cumbria
LA21 8AA
T: (015394) 41264
F: (015394) 41900
E: info@bankground.co.uk
I: bankground.co.uk

**Beech Tree Guest House
◆◆◆◆**
Yewdale Road, Coniston,
Cumbria LA21 8DX
T: (015394) 41717

**Brigg House
◆◆◆◆ SILVER AWARD**
Torver, Coniston, Cumbria
LA21 8AY
T: (015394) 41592
F: (015394) 41092
E: brigg.house@virgin.net
I: www.brigghouse.co.uk

**Coniston Lodge
◆◆◆◆◆ GOLD AWARD**
Station Road, Coniston, Cumbria
LA21 8HH
T: (015394) 41201
F: (015394) 41201
E: robinson@conistonlodge.
freeserve.co.uk

Crook Farm ◆
Torver, Coniston, Cumbria
LA21 8BP
T: (015394) 41453

Crown Hotel ◆◆
Coniston, Cumbria LA21 8EA
T: (015394) 41243
F: (015394) 41804
E: enntiidus@crownhotel
☺

Cruachan ◆◆◆◆
Collingwood Close, Coniston,
Cumbria LA21 8DZ
T: (015394) 41628

How Head Cottage ◆◆◆
East of Lake, Coniston, Cumbria
LA21 8AA
T: (015394) 41594
E: howhead@lineone.net
I: www.howheadcottages.co.uk

Lakeland House ◆◆◆
Tilberthwaite Avenue, Coniston,
Cumbria LA21 8ED
T: (015394) 41303
E: lakelandhouse_coniston@
hotmail.com

Oaklands ◆◆◆
Yewdale Road, Coniston,
Cumbria LA21 8DX
T: (015394) 41245

Orchard Cottage ◆◆◆◆
18 Yewdale Road, Coniston,
Cumbria LA21 8DU
T: (015394) 41373

Shepherds Villa ◆◆
Tilberthwaite Avenue, Coniston,
Cumbria LA21 8EE
T: (015394) 41337

Thwaite Cottage ◆◆◆
Waterhead, Coniston, Cumbria
LA21 8AJ
T: (015394) 41367
E: m@thwaitcot.freeserve.co.uk
I: www.thwaitcot.freeserve.co.uk

Townson Ground ◆◆◆◆
East of Lake Road, Coniston,
Cumbria LA21 8AA
T: (015394) 41272
F: (015394) 41110
E: nelson@tentlodge.fsnet.co.uk
I: www.townsonground.co.uk

**Wheelgate Country
Guesthouse
◆◆◆◆◆ SILVER AWARD**
Little Arrow, Coniston, Cumbria
LA21 8AU
T: (015394) 41418
F: (015394) 41114
E: wheelgate@
conistoncottages.co.uk
I: www.wheelgate.co.uk

Wilson Arms ◆◆◆
Torver, Coniston, Cumbria
LA21 8BB
T: (015394) 41237
F: (015394) 41590

**The Hillfarm
Rating Applied For**
Cowgill, Sedbergh, Cumbria
LA10 5RF
T: (015396) 25144
F: (015396) 25144

Mitchelland House ◆◆◆◆
Steeles Lane, Crook, Kendal,
Cumbria LA8 8LL
T: (015394) 48589
E: marie.mitchelland@talk21.
com

Crosby House ◆◆◆◆
Crosby-on-Eden, Carlisle
CA6 4QZ
T: (01228) 573239
F: (01228) 573338
E: enquiries@norbyways.
demon.co.uk
I: www/northumbria-byways.
com/crosby

Wickerslack Farm ◆◆◆
Crosby Ravensworth, Penrith,
Cumbria CA10 3LN
T: (01931) 715236

Crosthwaite House ◆◆◆◆
Crosthwaite, Kendal, Cumbria
LA8 8BP
T: (015395) 68264
F: (015395) 68264
E: crosthwaite.house@
kencomp.net

The Punch Bowl Inn ◆◆◆
Crosthwaite, Kendal, Cumbria
LA8 8HR
T: (015395) 68237
F: (015395) 68875
E: enquiries@punchbowl.fsnet.
co.uk
I: www.punchbowl.fsnet.co.uk

The Black Swan Inn ◆◆◆◆
Culgaith, Penrith, Cumbria
CA10 1QW
T: (01768) 88223
F: (01768) 88223

Park House Farm ◆◆◆
Dalemain, Penrith, Cumbria
CA11 0HB
T: (017684) 86212
F: (017684) 86212
☺

Black Dog Inn ◆◆
Holmes Green, Broughton Road,
Dalton-in-Furness, Cumbria
LA15 8JP
T: (01229) 462561 &
07931 751282
F: (01229) 468036
E: jack@blackdoginn.freeserve.
co.uk

**George and Dragon Hotel
◆◆◆**
Main Street, Dent, Sedbergh,
Cumbria LA10 5QL
T: (01539) 625256

Smithy Fold ◆◆◆
Whernside, Dent, Sedbergh,
Cumbria LA10 5RE
T: (015396) 25368

Stone Close Tea Shop ◆◆◆
Main Street, Dent, Sedbergh,
Cumbria LA10 5QL
T: (015396) 25231
F: (01539) 726567
E: accommodation@stoneclose.
co.uk
I: www.stoneclose.co.uk

Sun Inn ◆◆◆
Main Street, Dent, Sedbergh,
Cumbria LA10 5QL
T: (01539) 625208

Syke Fold ◆◆◆◆
Dent, Sedbergh, Cumbria
LA10 5RE
T: (015396) 25486

EGREMONT
Cumbria

Old Vicarage Guest House
◆◆◆
Oaklands, Egremont, Cumbria
CA22 2NX
T: (01946) 841577

ELTERWATER
Cumbria

Elterwater Park ◆◆◆◆
Skelwith Bridge, Ambleside,
Cumbria LA22 9NP
T: (015394) 32227
F: (015394) 31768
E: enquiries@elterwater.com
I: www.elterwater.com

EMBLETON
Cumbria

High Side Farm ◆◆◆◆
Embleton, Cockermouth,
Cumbria CA13 9TN
T: (017687) 76893
E: marshall@highsidehols.co.
freeserve.co.uk

ESKDALE
Cumbria

Forest How ◆◆◆
Eskdale Green, Holmrook,
Cumbria CA19 1TR
T: (019467) 23201
F: (019467) 23190
E: fcarter@easynet.co.uk
I: www.
foresthow-eskdale-cumbria.co.
uk/

The Gatehouse Outward Bound
◆◆◆
Eskdale, Holmrook, Cumbria
CA19 1TE
T: (019467) 23281
F: (019467) 23393
E: professional@
outwardbound-uk.org
I: www.outwardbound-uk.org

Woolpack Inn ◆◆◆
Boot, Eskdale, Cumbria
CA19 1TH
T: (01946) 723230
F: (01946) 723230
E: woolpack@eskdale.dial.
lakesnet.co.uk
I: www.insites.co.
uk/guide//cumbria/accom/
woolpack

FLOOKBURGH
Cumbria

The Late Kings Arms ◆◆◆
21 Market Street, Flookburgh,
Grange-over-Sands, Cumbria
LA11 7JU
T: (015395) 58991 &
07768 682817
E: thelatekingsarms@
southcumbria.freeserve.co.uk

GARRIGILL
Cumbria

**High Windy Hall Country
House Hotel and Restaurant**
◆◆◆◆
Middleton-in-Teesdale Road,
Garrigill, Alston, Cumbria
CA9 3EZ
T: (01434) 381547
F: (01434) 382477
E: sales@hwh.u-net.com
I: www.hwh.u-net.com

GARSDALE
Cumbria

Garsdale Foot Farm ◆◆◆
Garsdale, Sedbergh, Cumbria
LA10 5NU
T: (015396) 21329
F: (015396) 21399

GILSLAND
Cumbria

The Hill on the Wall ◆◆◆◆
Gilsland, Carlisle CA6 7DA
T: (01697) 747214
F: (01697) 747214
E: thehill@hadrians-wall.
demon.co.uk
I: www.
hadrians-wallbedandbreakfast.
com

Slack House Farm ◆◆◆
Gilsland, Carlisle, Cumbria
CA6 7DB
T: (016977) 47351

GRANGE-OVER-SANDS
Cumbria

Birchleigh Guest House ◆◆◆
Kents Bank Road, Grange-over-
Sands, Cumbria LA11 7EY
T: (015395) 32592

Corner Beech ◆◆◆
Kents Bank Road, Grange-over-
Sands, Cumbria LA11 7DP
T: (015395) 33088
F: (015395) 35288
E: freda.lightfoot@cornerbeech.
ndirect.co.uk
I: www.cornerbeech.ndirect.co.
uk

Elton Hotel ◆◆◆◆
Windermere Road, Grange-over-
Sands, Cumbria LA11 6EQ
T: (015395) 32838

The Laurels Bed and Breakfast
◆◆◆◆
Berriedale Terrace, Lindale Road,
Grange-over-Sands, Cumbria
LA11 6ER
T: (015395) 35919
F: (015395) 35919
E: gml@thelaurels71.freeserve.
co.uk

Mayfields ◆◆◆◆
3 Mayfield Terrace, Kents Bank
Road, Grange-over-Sands,
Cumbria LA11 7DW
T: (015395) 34730
I: www.accommodata.co.
uk/010699.htm

Methven Hotel ◆◆◆◆
Kents Bank Road, Grange-over-
Sands, Cumbria LA11 7DU
T: (015395) 32031

Somerset House ◆◆◆
Kents Bank Road, Grange-over-
Sands, Cumbria LA11 7EY
T: (015395) 32631

GRASMERE
Cumbria

Ash Cottage Guest House
◆◆◆◆
Red Lion Square, Grasmere,
Ambleside, Cumbria LA22 9SP
T: (015394) 35224

Beck Allans ◆◆◆◆
College Street, Grasmere,
Cumbria LA22 9SZ
T: (015394) 35563
F: (015394) 35563
E: mail@beckallans.com
I: www.beckallans.com

Chestnut Villa ◆◆◆
Keswick Road, Grasmere,
Ambleside, Cumbria LA22 9RE
T: (015394) 35218

Craigside House ◆◆◆◆
Grasmere, Ambleside, Cumbria
LA22 9SG
T: (015394) 35292

Dunmail House ◆◆◆◆
Keswick Road, Grasmere,
Ambleside, Cumbria LA22 9RE
T: (015394) 35256
E: enquiries@dunmailhouse.
freeserve.co.uk
I: www.dunmailhouse.com

Forest Side Hotel ◆◆◆
Grasmere, Ambleside, Cumbria
LA22 9RN
T: (015394) 35250
F: (015394) 35947
E: hotel@netcomuk.co.uk

How Foot Lodge ◆◆◆
Town End, Grasmere, Cumbria
LA22 9SQ
T: (015394) 35366

Lake View Country House
◆◆◆
Lake View Drive, Grasmere,
Ambleside, Cumbria LA22 9TD
T: (015394) 35384
E: info@lakeview-grasmere.com
I: www.lakeview-grasmere.com

Raise View Guest House ◆◆◆
White Bridge, Grasmere,
Cumbria LA22 9RQ
T: (015394) 35215
F: (015394) 35126
E: john@raisevw.demon.co.uk
I: www.raisevw.demon.co.uk

Redmayne Cottage ◆◆◆◆
Grasmere, Ambleside, Cumbria
LA22 9QY
T: (015394) 35635 &
07977 596133

Titteringdales Guest House
◆◆◆
Pye Lane, Grasmere, Cumbria
LA22 9RQ
T: (015394) 35439
E: titteringdales@grasmere.net
I: www.grasmere.net

Travellers Rest ◆◆◆
Grasmere, Ambleside, Cumbria
LA22 9RR
T: (015394) 35604 &
0500 600725
I: www.lakelandsheart.demon.
co.uk

Woodland Crag Guest House
◆◆◆◆
How Head Lane, Grasmere,
Ambleside, Cumbria LA22 9SG
T: (015394) 35351
F: (015394) 35351

GRAYRIGG
Cumbria

Grayrigg Hall Farm ◆◆
Grayrigg, Kendal, Cumbria
LA8 9BU
T: (01539) 824689

Punchbowl House
◆◆◆◆ SILVER AWARD
Grayrigg, Kendal, Cumbria
LA8 9BU
T: (01539) 824345
F: (01539) 824345
E: punchbowl.house@kencomp.
net

GREENHEAD
Cumbria

Greenhead Hotel ◆◆◆
Greenhead, Carlisle CA6 7HB
T: (01697) 747411

Wallend Farm ◆◆◆◆
Greenhead, Carlisle, Cumbria
CA6 7HN
T: (016977) 47339

GRIZEDALE
Cumbria

Grizedale Lodge Hotel
◆◆◆◆ SILVER AWARD
Grizedale, Ambleside, Cumbria
LA22 0QL
T: (015394) 36532
F: (015394) 36572
E: enquiries@grizedale-lodge.
com
I: www.grizedale-lodge.com

HAWKSHEAD
Cumbria

Betty Fold Country House
◆◆◆◆ SILVER AWARD
Hawkshead Hill, Ambleside,
Cumbria LA22 0PS
T: (015394) 36611

Borwick Lodge
◆◆◆◆ SILVER AWARD
Outgate, Ambleside, Cumbria
LA22 0PU
T: (015394) 36332
F: (015394) 36332
E: borwicklodge@talk21.com
I: www.smoothhound.co.
uk/hotels/borwickl.html

The Drunken Duck Inn
◆◆◆◆ SILVER AWARD
Barngates, Ambleside, Cumbria
LA22 0NG
T: (015394) 36347
F: (015394) 36781
E: info@drunkenduckinn.co.uk
I: www.drunkenduckinn.co.uk

High Grassings ◆◆◆◆
Sunny Brow, Outgate,
Hawkshead, Ambleside, Cumbria
LA22 0PU
T: (015394) 36484
F: (015394) 36140

Ivy House Hotel ◆◆◆◆
Main Street, Hawkshead,
Ambleside, Cumbria LA22 0NS
T: (015394) 36204 & 0800 056
3533
F: (015394) 36171
E: ivyhousehotel@btinternet.
com
I: www.ivyhousehotel.com

Red Lion Inn ◆◆◆
The Square, Hawkshead,
Ambleside, Cumbria LA22 0NS
T: (015394) 36213
F: (015394) 36747

The Sun Inn ◆◆◆◆
Main Street, Hawkshead,
Ambleside, Cumbria LA22 0NT
T: (015394) 36236 & 36353
F: (015394) 36155
E: thesuninn@hawkshead98.
freeserve.co.uk
I: www.suninn.co.uk

**Yewfield Vegetarian Guest
House ◆◆◆◆**
Yewfield, Hawkshead,
Ambleside, Cumbria LA22 0PR
T: (015394) 36765
F: (015394) 36765
E: derek.yewfield@btinternet.
com
I: www.yewfield.co.uk

HIGH LORTON
Cumbria

Swinside End Farm ◆◆◆
Scales, High Lorton,
Cockermouth, Cumbria
CA13 9UA
T: (01900) 85134

Terrace Farm ◆◆◆
Lorton, Cockermouth, Cumbria
CA13 9TX
T: (01900) 85278

HOLME
Cumbria

Marwin House ◆◆
Duke Street, Holme, Carnforth,
Lancashire LA6 1PY
T: (01524) 781144 & 0774 782
0435
F: (01524) 781144

HOUGHTON
Cumbria

The Steadings ◆◆◆
Townhead Farm, Houghton,
Carlisle CA6 4JB
T: (01228) 523019
F: (01228) 590178

IREBY
Cumbria

Daleside Farm ◆◆◆◆
Ireby, Carlisle CA5 1EW
T: (016973) 71268

**Woodlands Country House
◆◆◆◆**
Ireby, Cumbria CA5 1EX
T: (016973) 71791
F: (016973) 71482
E: wj@woodlnd.u-net.com
I: www.woodlnd.u-net.com

IRTHINGTON
Cumbria

**Vallum Barn
Rating Applied For**
Irthington, Carlisle CA6 4NN
T: (016977) 42478

KENDAL
Cumbria

Burrow Hall ◆◆◆◆
Plantation Bridge, Kendal,
Cumbria LA8 9JR
T: (01539) 821711
E: burrowhall@supanet.com

Cragg Farm ◆
New Hutton, Kendal, Cumbria
LA8 0BA
T: (01539) 721760
E: knowles.cragg@ukgateway.
net
I: www.stayfarmnorth.co.
uk/homedetailcfm?id=83

Fairways Guest House ◆◆◆
102 Windermere Road, Kendal,
Cumbria LA9 5EZ
T: (01539) 725564
E: mp@fairways1.fsnet.co.uk

Fell View ◆◆◆
100 Windermere Road, Kendal,
Cumbria LA9 5EZ
T: (01539) 728431

Gateside Farm ◆◆◆
Windermere Road, Kendal,
Cumbria LA9 5SE
T: (01539) 722036
F: (01539) 722036
E: gatesidefarm@aol.com

The Glen ◆◆◆
Oxenholme, Kendal, Cumbria
LA9 7RF
T: (01539) 726386
E: greeninthglen@easicom.
com
I: www.smoothhound.co.
uk/hotels/glen2.html

**Higher House Farm
◆◆◆◆ SILVER AWARD**
Oxenholme Lane, Natland,
Kendal, Cumbria LA9 7QH
T: (015395) 61177
F: (015395) 61520

Hillside Guest House ◆◆◆
4 Beast Banks, Kendal, Cumbria
LA9 4JW
T: (01539) 722836

Hollin Root Farm ◆◆◆
Garth Row, Kendal, Cumbria
LA8 9AW
T: (01539) 823638
E: b-and-b@hollin-root-farm.
freeserve.co.uk
I: www.s-h-systems.co.
uk/hotels/hollin.html

Kendal Arms and Hotel ◆◆
72 Milnthorpe Road, Kendal,
Cumbria LA9 5HG
T: (01539) 720956
F: (01539) 724851

**Lakeland Natural Vegetarian
Guesthouse◆◆◆**
Low Slack, Queens Road, Kendal,
Cumbria LA9 4PH
T: (01539) 733011
F: (01539) 733011
E: relax@lakelandnatural.co.uk
I: www.lakelandnatural.co.uk

Millers Beck ◆◆◆
Stainton, Kendal, Cumbria
LA8 0DU
T: (01539) 60877

**Newalls Country House
◆◆◆◆**
Skelsmergh, Kendal, Cumbria
LA9 6NU
T: (01539) 723202

Riversleigh ◆◆◆
49 Milnthorpe Road, Kendal,
Cumbria LA9 5QG
T: (01539) 726392

Sonata ◆◆◆
19 Burneside Road, Kendal,
Cumbria LA9 4RL
T: (01539) 732290
F: (01539) 732290
E: chriswilkinson@
sonataguesthouse.freeserve.co.
uk.
I: www.sonataguesthouse.co.uk

7 Thorny Hills ◆◆◆
Kendal, Cumbria LA9 7AL
T: (01539) 720207
E: martyn.jowett@btinternet.
com

Union Tavern ◆◆◆
159 Stricklandgate, Kendal,
Cumbria LA9 4RF
T: (01539) 724004
E: uniontavern@edirectory.co.
uk
I: www.edirectory.co.
uk/uniontavern

West Mount ◆◆◆
39 Milnthorpe Road, Kendal,
Cumbria LA9 5QG
T: (01539) 724621
F: (01539) 725282

KENTMERE
Cumbria

Maggs Howe ◆◆◆
Kentmere, Kendal, Cumbria
LA8 9JP
T: (01539) 821689

KESWICK
Cumbria

Abacourt House ◆◆◆◆
26 Stanger Street, Keswick,
Cumbria CA12 5JU
T: (017687) 72967
E: abacourt@aol.com
I: members.aol.com/abacourt

**Acorn House Hotel
◆◆◆◆ SILVER AWARD**
Ambleside Road, Keswick,
Cumbria CA12 4DL
T: (017687) 72553
F: (017687) 75332
E: enq@acornhouse.demon.co.
uk
I: www.smoothound.co.
uk/hotels/acornhse.html

The Anchorage ◆◆◆
14 Ambleside Road, Keswick,
Cumbria CA12 4DL
T: (017687) 72813

Anworth House ◆◆◆◆
27 Eskin Street, Keswick,
Cumbria CA12 4DQ
T: (017687) 72923

Avondale Guest House ◆◆◆◆
20 Southey Street, Keswick,
Cumbria CA12 4EF
T: (017687) 72735
F: (017687) 75431
I: www.smoothhound.co.
uk/hotels/available/html

Badgers Wood ◆◆◆◆
30 Stanger Street, Keswick,
Cumbria CA12 5JU
T: (017687) 72621
F: (017687) 72621
E: enquiries@badgers-wood.co.
uk
I: www.badgers-wood.co.uk

**Beckstones Farm Guest House
◆◆◆**
Thornthwaite, Keswick, Cumbria
CA12 5SQ
T: (017687) 78510
E: beckstones@lineone.net
I: website.lineone.
net/§beckstones

Berkeley Guest House ◆◆◆◆
The Heads, Keswick, Cumbria
CA12 5ER
T: (017687) 74222
E: berkeley@tesco.net
I: wwwhomepages.tesco.
net/§berkeley/mainpage.html

Birkrigg Farm ◆◆
Newlands, Keswick, Cumbria
CA12 5TS
T: (017687) 78278

Bonshaw Guest House ◆◆◆
20 Eskin Street, Keswick,
Cumbria CA12 4DG
T: (017687) 73084

Bowfell House ◆◆◆
Chestnut Hill, Keswick, Cumbria
CA12 4LR
T: (017687) 74859
E: bowfell.keswick@easicom.
com
I: www.
cumbria-the-lake-district.co.uk

Braemar ◆◆◆◆
21 Eskin Street, Keswick,
Cumbria CA12 4DQ
T: (017687) 73743
E: enquires@
braemar-guesthouse.co.uk
I: www.braemar-guesthouse.co.
uk

Brierholme Guest House ◆◆◆
21 Bank Street, Keswick,
Cumbria CA12 5JZ
T: (017687) 72938
E: brierholme@keswick72938.
freeserve.co.uk
I: www.keswick72938.freeserve.
co.uk

The Cartwheel ◆◆◆
5 Blencathra Street, Keswick,
Cumbria CA12 4HW
T: (017687) 73182
E: info@thecartwheel.co.uk
I: www.thecartwheel.co.uk

**Charnwood Guest House
◆◆◆◆**
6 Eskin Street, Keswick, Cumbria
CA12 4DH
T: (017687) 74111 &
07711 773925

Charnwood Lodge ◆◆◆
Thrushwood, Keswick, Cumbria
CA12 4PG
T: (017687) 71318

Cherry Trees ◆◆◆
16 Eskin Street, Keswick,
Cumbria CA12 4DQ
T: (017687) 71048
E: cherry.trees@virgin.net
I: www.
cumbria-the-lake-district.co.uk

Clarence House ◆◆◆◆
14 Eskin Street, Keswick,
Cumbria CA12 4DQ
T: (017687) 73186
F: (017687) 72317
E: clarenceho@aol.com
I: users.aol.
com/clarenceho/index.html

Cottage in the Wood ◆◆◆◆
Whinlatter Pass, Keswick,
Cumbria CA12 5TW
T: (017687) 78409
F: (017687) 78064
E: cottage@lake-district.net
I: www.lake-district.net/cottage

Craglands ◆◆◆◆
Penrith Road, Keswick, Cumbria
CA12 4LJ
T: (017687) 74406
E: keswick@craglands.freeserve.
co.uk

Cumbria House ◆◆◆◆
1 Derwentwater Place,
Ambleside Road, Keswick,
Cumbria CA12 4DR
T: (017687) 73171
F: (017687) 73171
E: enquiries.ctb@cumbriahouse.
co.uk
I: www.cumbriahouse.co.uk

Derwentdale Guesthouse ◆◆◆
8 Blencathra Street, Keswick,
Cumbria CA12 4HP
T: (017687) 74187

Dolly Waggon ◆◆◆
17 Helvellyn Street, Keswick,
Cumbria CA12 4EN
T: (017687) 73593
F: (017687) 73593
E: gjosborn@aol.com

Dunsford Guest House ◆◆◆◆
16 Stanger Street, Keswick,
Cumbria CA12 5JU
T: (017687) 75059
E: dunsford@clara.net
I: www.dunsford.clara.net

The Easedale Hotel ◆◆◆
Southey Street, Keswick,
Cumbria CA12 4EG
T: (017687) 72710 & 71127
F: (017687) 71127
E: easedaleH@aol.com
I: www.milford.co.
uk/go/easedale.html

Edwardene Hotel ◆◆◆◆
26 Southey Street, Keswick,
Cumbria CA12 4EF
T: (017687) 73586
F: (017687) 73824
E: haveabreak@
edwardenehotel.fsnet.co.uk
I: www.edwardenehotel.co.uk

Ellergill Guest House ◆◆◆◆
22 Stanger Street, Keswick,
Cumbria CA12 5JU
T: (017687) 73347 & 0780 889
9202
E: ellergill@yahoo.co.uk

Foye House Guest House ◆◆◆
23 Eskin Street, Keswick,
Cumbria CA12 4DQ
T: (017687) 73288
F: (017687) 80220
E: foye_house@keswick98.
freeserve.co.uk

Glencoe Guest House ◆◆◆◆
21 Helvellyn Street, Keswick,
Cumbria CA12 4EN
T: (017687) 71016 &
07711 376407
E: enquiriesglencoeguesthouse.
co.uk
I: www.glencoeguesthouse.co.uk

**The Grange Country House
Hotel** ◆◆◆◆ SILVER AWARD
Manor Brow, Ambleside Road,
Keswick, Cumbria CA12 4BA
T: (017687) 72500
E: sagem02458@talk21.com

Greystones Hotel ◆◆◆◆
Ambleside Road, Keswick,
Cumbria CA12 4DP
T: (017687) 73108
E: greystones@keslakes.
freeserve.co.uk

Hazeldene Hotel ◆◆◆
The Heads, Keswick, Cumbria
CA12 5ER
T: (017687) 72106
F: (017687) 754
E: helen8@netlineuk.net
I: www.hazeldene-hotel.co.uk

Hedgehog Hill Guesthouse
◆◆◆
18 Blencathra Street, Keswick,
Cumbria CA12 4HP
T: (017687) 74386
E: hedhil@fsbdial.co.uk

Howe Keld Lakeland Hotel
◆◆◆◆
5-7 The Heads, Keswick,
Cumbria CA12 5ES
T: (017687) 72417
F: (017687) 72417
E: david@howekeld.co.uk
I: www.howekeld.co.uk

Hunters Way Guest House
◆◆◆◆
4 Eskin Street, Keswick, Cumbria
CA12 4DH
T: (017687) 72324 &
07971 542284

Kalgurli Guest House ◆◆◆
33 Helvellyn Street, Keswick,
Cumbria CA12 4EP
T: (017687) 72935

Keskadale Farm ◆◆◆◆
Newlands Valley, Keswick,
Cumbria CA12 5TS
T: (017687) 78544
E: keskadale.bb.kencomp.net

Latrigg House ◆◆◆◆
St Herbert Street, Keswick,
Cumbria CA12 4DF
T: (017687) 73068
F: (017687) 72801
E: latrigghse@aol.com
I: members.aol.
com/latrigghse/index.html

Lindisfarne ◆◆◆
21 Church Street, Keswick,
Cumbria CA12 4DX
T: (017687) 73218 & 73261

Linnett Hill ◆◆◆
4 Penrith Road, Keswick,
Cumbria CA12 4HF
T: (017687) 73109

Littletown Farm ◆◆◆
Newlands, Keswick, Cumbria
CA12 5TU
T: (017687) 78353

Lynwood Hotel ◆◆◆
12 Ambleside Road, Keswick,
Cumbria CA12 4DL
T: (017687) 72081
F: (017687) 75021
E: lynwood.keswick@virgin.net
I: www.smoothhound.co.
uk/hotels/lynwoodh.html

Lynwood House ◆◆◆◆
35 Helvellyn Street, Keswick,
Cumbria CA12 4EP
T: (017687) 72398
F: (017687) 74090
E: lynwoodho@aol.com

Melbreak House ◆◆◆
29 Church Street, Keswick,
Cumbria CA12 4DX
T: (017687) 73398
F: (017687) 73398
E: melbreakhouse@btinternet.
com
I: www.melbreakhouse.co.uk

The Paddock ◆◆◆◆
Wordsworth Street, Keswick,
Cumbria CA12 4HU
T: (017687) 72510

Parkfield Guesthouse
◆◆◆◆ SILVER AWARD
The Heads, Keswick, Cumbria
CA12 5ES
T: (017687) 72328
E: parkfield@kencomp.net
I: www.kencomp.net/parkfield

Portland House ◆◆◆
19 Leonard Street, Keswick,
Cumbria CA12 4EL
T: (017687) 74230
E: portland.house@virgin.net
I: www.
welcometo/portlandhouse

Priorholme ◆◆◆◆
Borrowdale Road, Keswick,
Cumbria CA12 5DD
T: (017687) 72745
F: (017687) 75690
E: priorholme.fowler@virginnet

Ravensworth Hotel ◆◆◆◆
29 Station Street, Keswick,
Cumbria CA12 5HH
T: (017687) 72476
F: (017687) 75287
E: info@ravensworth-hotel.co.
uk
I: www.ravensworth-hotel.co.uk

Richmond House ◆◆◆
37-39 Eskin Street, Keswick,
Cumbria CA12 4DG
T: (017687) 73965
E: richmondhouse@easycom.
com

Rickerby Grange ◆◆◆◆
Portinscale, Keswick, Cumbria
CA12 5RH
T: (017687) 72344
F: (017687) 75588
E: val@ricor.demon.co.uk
I: www.ricor.demon.co.uk

Sandon Guesthouse ◆◆◆
13 Southey Street, Keswick,
Cumbria CA12 4EG
T: (017687) 73648

Seymour House ◆◆◆
36 Lake Road, Keswick, Cumbria
CA12 5DQ
T: (017687) 72764 &
0800 0566401
F: (017687) 71289
E: andy042195@aol.com
I: www.seymour-house.com

Shemara Guest House ◆◆◆◆
27 Bank Street, Keswick,
Cumbria CA12 5JZ
T: (017687) 73936

The Silverdale Hotel ◆◆◆
Blencathra Street, Keswick,
Cumbria CA12 4HT
T: (017687) 72294
F: (017687) 73122
E: silvhot@lineone.net

**Skiddaw Grove Country Guest
House** ◆◆◆
Vicarage Hill, Keswick, Cumbria
CA12 5QB
T: (017687) 73324
F: (017687) 73324

Stonegarth ◆◆◆◆
2 Eskin Street, Keswick, Cumbria
CA12 4DH
T: (017687) 72436

Strathmore Guest House
◆◆◆◆
8 St John's Terrace, Ambleside
Road, Keswick, Cumbria
CA12 4DP
T: (017687) 72584
F: (017687) 72584
E: pbrown@strathmore-lakes.
demon.co.uk
I: www.keswick-info.co.uk

Sunnyside Guest House
◆◆◆◆
25 Southey Street, Keswick,
Cumbria CA12 4EF
T: (017687) 72446
F: (017687) 74447
E: raynewton@survey.u-net.
com
I: www.survey.u-net.com

Swinside Inn ◆◆◆
Newlands, Keswick, Cumbria
CA12 5UE
T: (017687) 78253 & 78285
F: (017687) 78253
E: theswinsideinn@btinternet.
com
I: www.kesnet.co.uk

Swiss Court Guest House ◆◆◆
25 Bank Road, Keswick, Cumbria
CA12 5JZ
T: (017687) 72637
E: info@swisscourt.co.uk
I: www.swisscourt.co.uk

Tarn Hows ◆◆◆◆
3-5 Eskin Street, Keswick,
Cumbria CA12 4DH
T: (017687) 73217
F: (017687) 73217
E: david@tarnhows40.freeserve.
co.uk
I: www.smoothhound.co.
uk/hotels/tarnhows.html

Watendlath Guest House
◆◆◆
15 Acorn Street, Keswick,
Cumbria CA12 4EA
T: (017687) 74165

West View Guest House
◆◆◆◆
The Heads, Keswick, Cumbria
CA12 5ES
T: (017687) 73638

Whitehouse Guest House
◆◆◆◆
15 Ambleside Road, Keswick,
Cumbria CA12 4DL
T: (017687) 73176
F: (017687) 73176

KIRKBY-IN-FURNESS
Cumbria
Commercial Inn ◆◆◆
Askew Gate Brow, Kirkby-in-
Furness, Cumbria LA17 7TE
T: (01229) 889039

KIRKBY LONSDALE
Cumbria
Capernwray House
◆◆◆◆ SILVER AWARD
Borrans Lane, Capernwray,
Carnforth, Lancashire LA6 1AE
T: (01524) 732363
F: (01524) 732363
E: thesmiths@
capernwrayhouse.com
I: www.village2000.co.uk

The Copper Kettle ◆◆
3-5 Market Street, Kirkby
Lonsdale, Carnforth, Lancashire
LA6 2AU
T: (015242) 71714
F: (015242) 71714

Lupton Tower ◆◆◆◆
Lupton, Kirkby Lonsdale,
Carnforth, Lancashire LA6 2PR
T: (015395) 67400

KIRKBY STEPHEN
Cumbria
Ing Hill Lodge ◆◆◆◆
Mallerstang Dale, Kirkby
Stephen, Cumbria CA17 4JT
T: (017683) 71153
F: (017683) 71153
E: inghill@fsbdial.co.uk

Jolly Farmers Guest House
◆◆◆◆
63 High Street, Kirkby Stephen,
Cumbria CA17 4SH
T: (017683) 71063
F: (017683) 71063
E: jollyf@cumbria.com
I: www.cumbria.com/jollyf/

The Old Court House ◆◆◆◆
High Street, Kirkby Stephen,
Cumbria CA17 4SH
T: (017683) 71061
F: (017683) 71061
E: hilary-claxton@hotmail.com

KIRKLINTON
Cumbria
Clift House Farm ◆◆◆
Kirklinton, Carlisle CA6 6DE
T: (01228) 675237 &
07790 758272
F: (01228) 675237

LANGWATHBY
Cumbria
Langstanes ◆◆◆◆
Culgaith Road, Langwathby,
Penrith, Cumbria CA10 1NA
T: (01768) 881004
F: (01768) 881004

LAZONBY
Cumbria
Banktop House ◆◆◆
Lazonby, Penrith, Cumbria
CA10 1AQ
T: (01768) 898268
F: (01768) 898851
E: hartsop@globalnet.co.uk

Harlea ◆◆◆◆
Lazonby, Penrith, Cumbria
CA10 1BX
T: (01768) 897055
E: harlea.eden@ukgateway.net

LINDALE
Cumbria
**Greenacres Country
Guesthouse** ◆◆◆◆
Lindale, Grange-over-Sands,
Cumbria LA11 6LP
T: (015395) 34578
F: (015395) 34578

LITTLE CLIFTON
Cumbria
The Melbreak Hotel ◆◆◆
Winscales Road, Little Clifton,
Workington, Cumbria CA14 1XS
T: (01900) 61443
F: (01900) 606589

LONGTOWN
Cumbria
Bessiestown ◆◆◆◆◆
SILVER AWARD
Catlowdy, Longtown, Carlisle,
Cumbria CA6 5QP
T: (01228) 577219 & 577019
F: (01228) 577219
E: bestbb2000@cs.com
I: www.smoothhound.co.
uk/hotels/bessies

Briar Lea House ◆◆◆◆
Brampton Road, Longtown,
Carlisle CA6 5TN
T: (01228) 791538
F: (01228) 791538

Craigburn ◆◆◆
Catlowdy, Longtown, Carlisle
CA6 5QP
T: (01228) 577214
F: (01228) 577014
E: louiselawson@hotmail.com

Orchard House ◆◆◆◆
Blackbank, Longtown, Carlisle
CA6 5LQ
T: (01461) 338596
E: orchard.gretna
I: www.gretnaweddings.
com/orchardhouse.html

LOWESWATER
Cumbria
Askhill Farm ◆◆
Loweswater, Cockermouth,
Cumbria CA13 0SU
T: (01946) 861640

Kirkstile Inn ◆◆
Loweswater, Cockermouth,
Cumbria CA13 0RU
T: (0190085) 219
T: (01900) 85219
E: kirkstileinn@aol.com

LOWICK
Cumbria
Everard Lodge ◆◆◆
Lowick, Ulverston, Cumbria
LA12 8ER
T: (01229) 885245
F: (01229) 885245

LOWICK GREEN
Cumbria
Garth Row ◆◆◆
Lowick Green, Ulverston,
Cumbria LA12 8EB
T: (01229) 885633
E: jon@garthrow.freeserve.co.
uk

MARTINDALE
Cumbria
Winter Crag ◆◆◆◆
Martindale, Penrith, Cumbria
CA10 2NF
T: (017684) 86524

MAULDS MEABURN
Cumbria
Trainlands Bed & Breakfast
◆◆
Maulds Meaburn, Penrith,
Cumbria CA10 3HX
T: (017683) 51249
F: (017683) 53983
E: bousfield@trainlands.u-net.
com

MIDDLETON
Cumbria
Swan Inn ◆◆◆
Middleton, Sedbergh, Cumbria
LA6 2NB
T: (015242) 76223 &
07831 279972
F: (015242) 76223

MILBURN
Cumbria
Slakes Farm ◆◆◆
Milburn, Appleby-in-
Westmorland, Cumbria
CA16 6DP
T: (017683) 61385

MILLOM
Cumbria
The Duddon Pilot Hotel
◆◆◆◆
Devonshire Road, Millom,
Cumbria LA18 4JT
T: (01229) 774116
F: (01229) 774116

MOSEDALE
Cumbria
Mosedale House ◆◆◆◆
Mosedale, Mungrisdale, Cumbria
CA11 0XQ
T: (017687) 79371
E: colin.smith2@ukonline.co.uk

MUNGRISDALE
Cumbria
The Mill Inn ◆◆◆
Mungrisdale, Penrith, Cumbria
CA11 0XR
T: (017687) 79632
F: (017687) 79632
E: the_mill_inn@compuserve.
com

Mosedale End Farm ◆◆◆
Mungrisdale, Penrith, Cumbria
CA11 0XQ
T: (017687) 79605
E: armstrong@awmcmanus.
screaming.net
I: www.smoothhound.co.
uk/hotels/mosedale.html

Near Howe Hotel ◆◆◆
Mungrisdale, Penrith, Cumbria
CA11 0SH
T: (017687) 79678
F: (017687) 79678

NEAR SAWREY
Cumbria
Beechmount Country House
◆◆◆
Near Sawrey, Ambleside,
Cumbria LA22 0JZ
T: (015394) 36356
I: www.
beechmountcountryhouse.co.uk

The Garth Country House
◆◆◆◆ SILVER AWARD
Near Sawrey, Ambleside,
Cumbria LA22 0JZ
T: (015394) 36373
F: (015394) 36373
E: thegarthcountryhouse@
compuserve.com
I: www.smoothhound.co.
uk/hotels/thegarth

High Green Gate Guest House
◆◆◆
Near Sawrey, Ambleside,
Cumbria LA22 0LF
T: (015394) 36296

Lakefield ◆◆◆◆
Near Sawrey, Ambleside,
Cumbria LA22 0JZ
T: (015394) 36635
F: (015394) 36635

Tower Bank Arms ◆◆◆
Near Sawrey, Ambleside,
Cumbria LA22 0LF
T: (015394) 36334
F: (015394) 36334

NEWBIGGIN-ON-LUNE
Cumbria
Tranna Hill ◆◆◆
Newbiggin-on-Lune, Kirkby
Stephen, Cumbria CA17 4NY
T: (015396) 23227 &
07989 892368
E: trannahill@hotmail.com

NEWBY BRIDGE
Cumbria

The Knoll ◆◆◆◆
Lakeside, Newby Bridge,
Cumbria LA12 8AU
T: (015395) 31347
F: (015395) 31347
E: info@theknoll.co.uk
I: www.theknoll.co.uk

Low Graythwaite Hall ◆◆◆◆
Graythwaite, Newby Bridge,
Cumbria LA12 8AZ
T: (015395) 31676
F: (015395) 31948

Old Barn Farm ◆◆◆◆
Fiddler Hall, Newby Bridge,
Cumbria LA12 8NQ
T: (015395) 31842
F: (015395) 31842
E: barch@btinternet.com

NEWLANDS
Cumbria

Low Skelgill ◆◆
Newlands, Keswick, Cumbria
CA12 5UE
T: (017687) 78453

Uzzicar Farm ◆◆◆
Newlands, Keswick, Cumbria
CA12 5TS
T: (017687) 78367

OUTGATE
Cumbria

Bracken Fell ◆◆◆
Outgate, Ambleside, Cumbria
LA22 0NH
T: (015394) 36289
F: (015394) 36142
E: hart.brackenfell@virgin.net

OXENHOLME
Cumbria

Station Inn ◆◆◆
Oxenholme, Kendal, Cumbria
LA9 7RF
T: (01539) 724094

PARDSHAW
Cumbria

Sunny Corner ◆◆◆◆
Pardshaw, Cockermouth,
Cumbria CA13 0SP
T: (01900) 826380
F: (01900) 826380

PATTERDALE
Cumbria

Deepdale Hall ◆◆◆◆
Patterdale, Penrith, Cumbria
CA11 0NR
T: (017684) 82369 & 82608
E: brown@deepdalehall.
freeserve.co.uk

**Ullswater View Bed and
Breakfast** ◆◆◆◆
Ullswater View, Patterdale,
Penrith, Cumbria CA11 0NW
T: (017684) 82175
F: (017684) 82181
E: ext@btinternet.com
I: www.btinternet.com/§ext/

PENRITH
Cumbria

Albany House ◆◆◆
5 Portland Place, Penrith,
Cumbria CA11 7QN
T: (01768) 863072
F: (01768) 863072
I: www.albanyhouse.com.uk

Beacon Bank Hotel ◆◆◆◆
Beacon Edge, Penrith, Cumbria
CA11 7BD
T: (01768) 862633
F: (01768) 899055
E: beaconbank.hotel@virgin.net
I: www.beaconbankkhotel.co.uk

Blue Swallow Guesthouse
◆◆◆
11 Victoria Road, Penrith,
Cumbria CA11 8HR
T: (01768) 866335

Brandelhow Guest House
◆◆◆
1 Portland Place, Penrith,
Cumbria CA11 7QN
T: (01768) 864470

Cumrew ◆◆◆◆
Graham Street, Penrith, Cumbria
CA11 9LG
T: (01768) 867923
F: (01768) 867923

The Friarage ◆◆◆◆
Friargate, Penrith, Cumbria
CA11 7XR
T: (01768) 863635
F: (01768) 863635

Glendale ◆◆◆
4 Portland Place, Penrith,
Cumbria CA11 7QN
T: (01768) 862579
F: (01768) 895080
E: glendale@lineone.net

Greenfields
◆◆◆◆ SILVER AWARD
Ellonby, Penrith, Cumbria
CA11 9SJ
T: (017684) 84671
F: (017684) 84671
E: greenfields@gofornet.co.uk
I: www.smoothhound.co.
uk/hotels/grenfields.html

**Hornby Hall Country Guest
House** ◆◆◆◆
Hornby Hall, Brougham, Penrith,
Cumbria CA10 2AR
T: (01768) 891114
F: (01768) 891114

Limes Country Hotel ◆◆◆
Redhills, Penrith, Cumbria
CA11 0DT
T: (01768) 863343
F: (01768) 867190
E: jdhanton@aol.com
I: www.member.aol.
com/jdhanton/index.htm

Little Blencowe Farm ◆◆◆
Blencowe, Penrith, Cumbria
CA11 0DG
T: (017684) 83338
F: (017684) 83054
E: bart.fawcett@ukgateway.net

Newvic ◆◆
46 Castlegate, Penrith, Cumbria
CA11 7HY
T: (01768) 862467
F: (01768) 890438

Norcroft Guesthouse ◆◆◆
Graham Street, Penrith, Cumbria
CA11 9LQ
T: (01768) 862365
F: (01768) 862365
&

Queen's Head Inn ◆◆
Tirril, Penrith, Cumbria CA10 2JF
T: (01768) 863219
F: (01768) 863243
E: bookings@queensheadinn.co.
uk
I: www.queensheadinn.co.uk

Roundthorn Country House
◆◆◆◆ SILVER AWARD
Beacon Edge, Penrith, Cumbria
CA11 8SJ
T: (01768) 863952
F: (01768) 864100
E: enquiries@roundthorn.co.uk
I: www.roundthorn.co.uk

The White House ◆◆◆◆
Clifton, Penrith, Cumbria
CA10 2EL
T: (01768) 865115

Woodland House Hotel ◆◆◆
Wordsworth Street, Penrith,
Cumbria CA11 7QY
T: (01768) 864177
F: (01768) 890152
E: ivordavies@woodlandhouse.
co.uk
I: www.woodlandhouse.co.uk

POOLEY BRIDGE
Cumbria

Sun Inn ◆◆◆
Pooley Bridge, Penrith, Cumbria
CA10 2NN
T: (017684) 86205
F: (017684) 86913

PORTINSCALE
Cumbria

**Dalegarth House Country
Hotel** ◆◆◆◆
Portinscale, Keswick, Cumbria
CA12 5RQ
T: (017687) 72817
F: (017687) 72817
E: john@dalegarthhousehotel.
freeserve.co.uk

Derwent Cottage
◆◆◆◆◆ GOLD AWARD
Portinscale, Keswick, Cumbria
CA12 5RF
T: (017687) 74838
E: dercott@btinternet.com

RYDAL
Cumbria

Nab Cottage Guest House ◆
Nab Cottage, Rydal, Ambleside,
Cumbria LA22 9SD
T: (01539) 435311
F: (01539) 435493
E: ell@nab.dial.lakesnet.co.uk
I: www.lakesnet.
net/homepages/ell/nab

Rydal Lodge Hotel ◆◆◆
Rydal, Ambleside, Cumbria
LA22 9LR
T: (015394) 33208

ST BEES
Cumbria

Stonehouse Farm ◆◆◆
Main Street, St Bees, Cumbria
CA27 0DE
T: (01946) 822224

SANDFORD
Cumbria

Sandford Arms ◆◆◆◆
Sandford, Appleby-in-
Westmorland, Cumbria
CA16 6NR
T: (017683) 51121
F: (017683) 53200
E: jsddl@aol.com

SANDSIDE
Cumbria

**Kingfisher House and
Restaurant** ◆◆◆
Sandside, Milnthorpe, Cumbria
LA7 7HW
T: (015395) 63909
F: (015395) 64022
E: kingfisherest@tinyworld.co.
uk

Plantation Cottage ◆◆◆◆
Arnside Road, Sandside,
Milnthorpe, Cumbria LA7 7JU
T: (01524) 762069 &
07768 353202

SATTERTHWAITE
Cumbria

Town End ◆◆◆◆
Satterthwaite, Ulverston,
Cumbria LA12 8LN
T: (01229) 860936 &
07967 879452

SAWREY
Cumbria

Buckle Yeat Guest House
◆◆◆◆
Sawrey, Ambleside, Cumbria
LA22 0LF
T: (015394) 36446 & 36538
F: (015394) 36446
E: info@buckle-yeat.co.uk
I: www.buckle-yeat.co.uk

Sawrey House Country Hotel
◆◆◆◆◆ SILVER AWARD
Near Sawrey, Ambleside,
Cumbria LA22 0LF
T: (015394) 36387
F: (015394) 36010
E: enquiries@sawrey-house.
com
I: www.sawrey-house.com

West Vale Country House
◆◆◆◆
Far Sawrey, Hawkshead,
Ambleside, Cumbria LA22 0LQ
T: (015394) 42817
F: (015394) 88214

SEBERGHAM
Cumbria

Stockwell Hall ◆◆◆◆
Sebergham, Carlisle, Cumbria
CA5 7DY
T: (016974) 76364
F: (01694) 76364

SEDBERGH
Cumbria

Ash Hining Farm ◆◆◆
Howgill, Sedbergh, Cumbria
LA10 5HU
T: (015396) 20957
F: (015396) 20957

Bridge House ◆◆◆◆
Brigflatts, Sedbergh, Cumbria
LA10 5HN
T: (015396) 21820
F: (015396) 21820

Bull Hotel ♦♦♦♦
Main Street, Sedbergh, Cumbria
LA10 5BL
T: (015396) 20264

Dalesman Country Inn ♦♦♦
Main Street, Sedbergh, Cumbria
LA10 5BN
T: (015396) 21183
F: (015396) 21311
I: www.infotel.co.uk

The Lodge ♦♦♦
10 Loftus Manor, Sedbergh,
Cumbria LA10 5SQ
T: (015396) 21855
I: www.thedalesway.co.
uk/thelodge

Marshall House ♦♦♦♦
Main Street, Sedbergh, Cumbria
LA10 5BL
T: (015396) 21053

Randall Hill ♦♦♦
Station Road, Sedbergh,
Cumbria LA10 5HJ
T: (015396) 20633
F: (015396) 21944
E: julia.gerzon@randall-hill.
demon.co.uk
I: www.randall-hill.demon.co.uk/

St Mark's ♦♦♦♦
Cautley, Sedbergh, Cumbria
LA10 5LZ
T: (015396) 20287 & 21585
F: (015396) 21585
E: 100540.1376@compuserve.
com

Stable Antiques ♦♦
15 Back Lane, Sedbergh,
Cumbria LA10 5AQ
T: (015396) 20251
I: ourworld.compuserve.
com/homepages/sedbergh

Hollowgate Farm ♦♦♦
Hollowgate, Selside, Kendal,
Cumbria LA8 9LG
T: (01539) 823258

STAVELEY
Cumbria

Eagle & Child Hotel ♦
Kendal Road, Staveley, Kendal,
Cumbria LA8 9LP
T: (01539) 821320
E: eagleandc@g-wizz.net

Tarn House ♦♦♦♦
18 Danes Road, Staveley, Kendal,
Cumbria LA8 9PW
T: (01539) 821656 &
07771 516156

Watermill Inn ♦♦♦
Ings, Staveley, Kendal, Cumbria
LA8 9PY
T: (01539) 821309
F: (01539) 822309
E: all@watermill-inn.demon.co.
uk
I: www.watermill-inn.demon.co.
uk

TALKIN
Cumbria

Hullerbank ♦♦♦
Talkin, Brampton, Cumbria
CA8 1LB
T: (016977) 46668
F: (016977) 46668
E: info@hullerbank.freeserve.co.
uk
I: www.smoothhound.co.
uk/hotels/huller.html
⊛

TEBAY
Cumbria

Primrose Cottage ♦♦♦♦
Orton Road, Tebay, Penrith,
Cumbria CA10 3TL
T: (015396) 24791 &
07778 520930

THORNTHWAITE
Cumbria

Jenkin Hill Cottage
♦♦♦ SILVER AWARD
Thornthwaite, Keswick, Cumbria
CA12 5SG
T: (017687) 78443 & 0777 594
2861
F: (017687) 78445
E: quality@jenkinhill.co.uk
I: www.jenkinhill.co.uk

Thornthwaite Hall ♦♦♦♦
Thornthwaite, Keswick, Cumbria
CA12 5SA
T: (017687) 78424
F: (017687) 78122
E: thornthwaite@msn.com

THRELKELD
Cumbria

**Scales Farm Country
Guesthouse** ♦♦♦♦
Scales, Threlkeld, Keswick,
Cumbria CA12 4SY
T: (017687) 79660
F: (017687) 79660
E: scales@scalesfarm.com.
I: www.scalesfarm.com
⊛ 🏃

TORVER
Cumbria

Old Rectory Hotel ♦♦♦♦
Torver, Coniston, Cumbria
LA21 8AX
T: (015394) 41353
F: (015394) 41156
E: enquiries@
theoldrectoryhotel.com
⊛

TROUTBECK, PENRITH
Cumbria

Gill Head Farm ♦♦♦
Troutbeck, Penrith, Cumbria
CA11 0ST
T: (01768) 779652
F: (01768) 779130
E: gillhead@talk21.com
I: www.gillheadfarm.co.uk

Lane Head Farm Guest House
♦♦♦♦
Troutbeck, Penrith, Cumbria
CA11 0SY
T: (017687) 79220
F: (017687) 79220
E: liz@laneheadfarm.freeserve.
co.uk

Troutbeck Inn ♦♦♦♦
Troutbeck, Penrith, Cumbria
CA11 0SJ
T: (017684) 83635
F: (017684) 83928
E: troutbeckinn@supanet.com
I: www.troutbeckinn.sagenet.co.
uk

TROUTBECK, WINDERMERE
Cumbria

High Fold Farm ♦♦♦♦
Troutbeck, Windermere, Cumbria
LA23 1PG
T: (015394) 32200
F: (015394) 34970

High Green Lodge ♦♦♦♦
High Green, Troutbeck,
Windermere, Cumbria LA23 1PN
T: (015394) 33005

TROUTBECK BRIDGE
Cumbria

**High View
Rating Applied For**
Troutbeck Bridge, Windermere,
Cumbria LA23 1HJ
T: (015394) 44618
F: (015394) 44618
⊛

ULLSWATER
Cumbria

Elm House ♦♦♦♦
Pooley Bridge, Penrith, Cumbria
CA10 2NH
T: (017684) 86334
E: b&b@elmhouse.demon.co.uk
I: www.elmhouse.demon.co.uk

Knotts Mill Country Lodge
♦♦♦
Watermillock, Penrith, Cumbria
CA11 0JN
T: (017684) 86699
E: knottsmill@cwcom.net
I: www.knottsmill.cwc.net

Land Ends ♦♦♦
Ullswater, Penrith, Cumbria
CA11 0NB
T: (017684) 86438
F: (017684) 86959

Moss Crag ♦♦♦
Eagle Road, Glenridding, Penrith,
Cumbria CA11 0PA
T: (017684) 82500 &
0789 9777419
F: (017684) 82500
E: mosscrag@talk21.com

Netherdene Guest House ♦♦♦
Troutbeck, Penrith, Cumbria
CA11 0SJ
T: (017684) 83475 & 83475
F: (017684) 83475
⊛

Tymparon Hall ♦♦♦
Newbiggin, Stainton, Penrith,
Cumbria CA11 0HS
T: (017684) 83236
F: (017684) 83236
E: margaret@peeearson.
freeserve.co.uk
I: www.peeearson.freeserve.co.
uk

Ullswater House ♦♦♦
Pooley Bridge, Penrith, Cumbria
CA10 2NN
T: (017684) 86259

Whitbarrow Farm ♦♦♦
Berrier, Penrith, Cumbria
CA11 0XB
T: (017684) 83366
F: (017684) 83179
E: gmharris@farmersweekly.net

White Lion Inn ♦♦♦
Patterdale, Penrith, Cumbria
CA11 0NW
T: (017684) 82214

ULVERSTON
Cumbria

Trinity House Hotel ♦♦♦♦
Prince's Street, Ulverston,
Cumbria LA12 7NB
T: (01229) 587639 &
07802 226273
F: (01229) 588552
E: hotel@trinityhouse.furness.
co.uk.

Virginia House Hotel ♦♦♦♦
24 Queen Street, Ulverston,
Cumbria LA12 7AF
T: (01229) 584844
F: (01229) 588565
E: virginia@ulverstonhotels.co.
uk
I: www.ulverstonhotels.co.uk

UNDERBARROW
Cumbria

High Gregg Hall Farm ♦♦
Underbarrow, Kendal, Cumbria
LA8 8BL
T: (015395) 68318

Tranthwaite Hall ♦♦♦♦
Underbarrow, Kendal, Cumbria
LA8 8HG
T: (015395) 68285
E: b&b@tranthwaitehall.
freeserve.co.uk

Tullythwaite House ♦♦♦♦
Underbarrow, Kendal, Cumbria
LA8 8BB
T: (015395) 68397

WALTON
Cumbria

Town Head Farm ♦♦♦
Walton, Brampton, Cumbria
CA8 2DJ
T: (016977) 2730

WARWICK BRIDGE
Cumbria

Brookside Bed and Breakfast
♦♦♦♦
Warwick Bridge, Carlisle,
Cumbria CA4 8RE
T: (01228) 560250

WHITEHAVEN
Cumbria

Corkickle Guest House ♦♦♦♦
1 Corkickle, Whitehaven,
Cumbria CA28 8AA
T: (01946) 692073
F: (01946) 692073
E: corkickle@tinyworld.co.uk
⊛

The Cottage Bed and Breakfast
♦♦
The Cottage, Mirehouse Road,
Whitehaven, Cumbria CA28 9UD
T: (01946) 695820

WINDERMERE
Cumbria

Acton House ♦♦♦
41 Craig Walk, Windermere,
Cumbria LA23 2HB
T: (015394) 45340

Almaria House ◆◆◆
17 Broad Street, Windermere,
Cumbria LA23 2AB
T: (015394) 43026

Applegarth Hotel ◆◆◆
College Road, Windermere,
Cumbria LA23 1BU
T: (015394) 43206
F: (015394) 46636
E: applegarthhotel@zoom.co.uk
I: www.smoothhound.co.
uk/hotels/apple.html

The Archway ◆◆◆◆
13 College Road, Windermere,
Cumbria LA23 1BU
T: (015394) 45613 & 45328
F: (015394) 45328
E: archway@btinternet.com
I: www.lakedistrictguesthouses.
co.uk

Ashleigh Guest House ◆◆◆◆
11 College Road, Windermere,
Cumbria LA23 1BU
T: (015394) 42292 &
07940 598634
F: (015394) 42292
⊚

Aspen Cottage ◆◆
6 Havelock Road, Windermere,
Cumbria LA23 1EH
T: (015394) 43946 &
07930 959110

Autumn Leaves Guest House
◆◆◆
29 Broad Street, Windermere,
Cumbria LA23 2AB
T: (015394) 48410 &
07703 752246
F: (015394) 47396
E: res@autumnleavesgh.demon.
co.uk

The Beaumont
◆◆◆◆◆ SILVER AWARD
Holly Road, Windermere,
Cumbria LA23 2AF
T: (015394) 47075
F: (015394) 47075
E: thebeaumonthotel@
btinternet.com
I: www.lakesbeaumont.co.uk
⊚

Beaumont ◆◆◆◆
Thornbarrow Road, Windermere,
Cumbria LA23 2DG
T: (015394) 45521
F: (015394) 46267
E: etc@beaumont-holidays.co.
uk
I: www.beaumont-holidays.co.
uk
⛄

Beckmead House ◆◆◆
5 Park Avenue, Windermere,
Cumbria LA23 2AR
T: (015394) 42757
F: (015394) 42757

Beckside Cottage ◆◆◆
4 Park Road, Windermere,
Cumbria LA23 2AW
T: (015394) 42069 & 88105

Boston House ◆◆◆◆
4 The Terrace, Windermere,
Cumbria LA23 1AJ
T: (015394) 43654
E: info@bostonhouse.co.uk
I: www.bostonhouse.co.uk

Bowfell Cottage ◆◆
Middle Entrance Drive, Storrs
Park, Bowness-on-Windermere,
Windermere, Cumbria LA23 3JY
T: (015394) 44835

Braemount House ◆◆◆◆
Sunny Bank Road, Windermere,
Cumbria LA23 2EN
T: (015394) 45967 & 47737
F: (015394) 47737
E: braemount.house@virgin.net
I: freespace.virgin.
net/braemount.house

Brook House ◆◆◆
30 Ellerthwaite Road,
Windermere, Cumbria LA23 2AH
T: (015394) 44932

Brooklands ◆◆◆
Ferry View, Bowness-on-
Windermere, Windermere,
Cumbria LA23 3JB
T: (015394) 42344

Cambridge House ◆◆◆
9 Oak Street, Windermere,
Cumbria LA23 1EN
T: (015394) 43846
F: (015394) 46662
E: reservations@
cambridge-house.fsbusiness.co.
uk
I: www.cambridge-house.
fsbusiness.co.uk

The Chestnuts ◆◆◆◆
Prince's Road, Windermere,
Cumbria LA23 2EF
T: (015394) 46999
E: chestnuts@chestnuts92.
freeserve.co.uk
I: www.chestnuts92.freeserve.
co.uk

Clifton House ◆◆◆
28 Ellerthwaite Road,
Windermere, Cumbria LA23 2AH
T: (015394) 44968

College House ◆◆◆
15 College Road, Windermere,
Cumbria LA23 1BU
T: (015394) 45767
E: clghse@aol.com
I: www.college-house.com
⊚

The Common Farm ◆◆◆
Windermere, Cumbria LA23 1JQ
T: (015394) 43433

The Cottage ◆◆◆
Elleray Road, Windermere,
Cumbria LA23 1AG
T: (015394) 44796
F: (015394) 44796

Dene Crest ◆◆◆
Woodland Road, Windermere,
Cumbria LA23 2AE
T: (015394) 44979
E: denecrest@tinyworld.co.uk

Denehurst Guest House ◆◆◆
40 Queens Drive, Windermere,
Cumbria LA23 2EL
T: (015394) 44710 & 0771 297
5987
F: (015394) 44710
E: quinn@denehurst.netlineuk.
net
I: www.smoothhound.co.
uk/hotels/dene.html

Eastbourne ◆◆◆◆
Biskey Howe Road, Bowness-
on-Windermere, Windermere,
Cumbria LA23 2JR
T: (015394) 43525
F: (015394) 43525
E: eastbourne@lakes-pages.co.
uk
I: www.lakes-pages.co.uk

The Fairfield ◆◆◆◆
Brantfell Road, Bowness-on-
Windermere, Windermere,
Cumbria LA23 3AE
T: (015394) 46565
F: (015394) 46565
E: Ray&tbarb@the-fairfield.co.uk
I: www.the-fairfield.co.uk
⊚

Fir Trees ◆◆◆◆
Lake Road, Windermere,
Cumbria LA23 2EQ
T: (015394) 42272
F: (015394) 42272
E: firtreeshotel@email.msn.com
I: www.fir-trees.com

Firgarth ◆◆◆
Ambleside Road, Windermere,
Cumbria LA23 1EU
T: (015394) 46974
F: (015394) 42384

Glenville Hotel ◆◆◆
Lake Road, Windermere,
Cumbria LA23 2EQ
T: (015394) 43371
F: (015394) 43371
E: glenville@talk21.com
I: www.smoothhound.co.
uk/hotels/glenville.html

Haisthorpe Guest House
◆◆◆◆ SILVER AWARD
Holly Road, Windermere,
Cumbria LA23 2AF
T: (015394) 43445
F: (015394) 48875
E: haisthorpe@clara.net
I: www.haisthorpe-house.co.uk

Hawksmoor ◆◆◆◆
Lake Road, Windermere,
Cumbria LA23 2EQ
T: (015394) 42110
F: (015394) 42110
E: tyson@hawksmoor.netl.co.uk
I: www.six-of-the-best.
com/hawksmoor.htm
⛄

Hazel Bank ◆◆◆◆
Hazel Street, Windermere,
Cumbria LA23 1EL
T: (015394) 45486
F: (015394) 45486

Heatherbank Guest House
◆◆◆
13 Birch Street, Windermere,
Cumbria LA23 1EG
T: (015394) 46503 &
07970 634050
F: (015394) 46503
E: heatherbank@btinternet.com

Hilton House ◆◆◆◆
New Road, Windermere,
Cumbria LA23 2EE
T: (015394) 43934
F: (015394) 43934
⊚

Holly Lodge ◆◆◆
6 College Road, Windermere,
Cumbria LA23 1BX
T: (015394) 43873
F: (015394) 43873

Holly Park House ◆◆◆◆
1 Park Road, Windermere,
Cumbria LA23 2AW
T: (015394) 42107
F: (015394) 48997
I: www.s-h-systems.co.
uk/hotels/hollypk.html

Holly-Wood ◆◆◆◆
Holly Road, Windermere,
Cumbria LA23 2AF
T: (015394) 42219

Holmlea ◆◆◆
Kendal Road, Bowness-on-
Windermere, Windermere,
Cumbria LA23 3EW
T: (015394) 42597

Ivy Bank ◆◆◆◆
Holly Road, Windermere,
Cumbria LA23 2AF
T: (015394) 42601 &
07808 516245
E: ivybank@clara.co.uk
I: www.ivybank.clara.co.uk

Kays Cottage ◆◆◆
7 Broad Street, Windermere,
Cumbria LA23 2AB
T: (015394) 44146
F: (015394) 44146
E: kayscottage@freenetname.
co.uk
I: www.kayscottage.co.uk

Kirkwood Guest House ◆◆◆◆
Prince's Road, Windermere,
Cumbria LA23 2DD
T: (015394) 43907
F: (015394) 43907
E: neil.cox@kirkwood51.
freeserve.co.uk
I: www.kirkwood51.freeserve.co.
uk

Lakes Hotel ◆◆◆
1 High Street, Windermere,
Cumbria LA23 1AF
T: (015394) 42751
F: (015394) 46026
E: admin@lakes-hotel.com
I: www.lakes-hotel.com

Lakeshore House
◆◆◆◆◆ SILVER AWARD
Ecclerigg, Windermere, Cumbria
LA23 1LJ
T: (015394) 33202
F: (015394) 33213
E: lakeshore@lakedistrict.uk.
com
I: www.lakedistrict.uk.com

Langdale View Guest House
◆◆◆
114 Craig Walk, Off Helm Road,
Bowness-on-Windermere,
Windermere, Cumbria LA23 3AX
T: (015394) 44076

Laurel Cottage ◆◆◆◆
St Martin's Square, Kendal Road,
Bowness-on-Windermere,
Windermere, Cumbria LA23 3EF
T: (015394) 45594
F: (015394) 45594
E: enquiries@laurelcottage-bnb.
co.uk
I: laurelcottage-bnb.co.uk

Laurel Cottage ◆◆◆◆
8 Park Road, Windermere,
Cumbria LA23 2BJ
T: (015394) 43053
E: wendy@laurelcottage8.
freeserve.co.uk

Lindisfarne ◆◆◆
Sunny Bank Road, Windermere,
Cumbria LA23 2EN
T: (015394) 46295 &
07711 329540
F: (015394) 45310
E: lindisfarne@zoom.co.uk

Lingwood ◆◆◆
Birkett Hill, Bowness-on-
Windermere, Cumbria LA23 3EZ
T: (015394) 44680
F: (015394) 48154
E: enquiries@
lingwood-guesthouse.co.uk
I: www.lingwood-guesthouse.
co.uk

Lynwood Guest House ◆◆◆
Broad Street, Windermere,
Cumbria LA23 2AB
T: (015394) 42550
F: (015394) 42550

Meadfoot Guest House ◆◆◆◆
New Road, Windermere,
Cumbria LA23 2LA
T: (015394) 42610
F: (015394) 45280
E: enquiries@
meadfoot-guesthouse.co.uk
I: www.meadfoot-guesthouse.
co.uk

Melbourne Guest House ◆◆◆
2-3 Biskey Howe Road,
Bowness-on-Windermere,
Windermere, Cumbria LA23 2JP
T: (015394) 43475
F: (015394) 42475

Mount View Guest House
◆◆◆
New Road, Windermere,
Cumbria LA23 2LA
T: (015394) 45548

Mylne Bridge House ◆◆◆
Brookside, Lake Road,
Windermere, Cumbria LA23 2BX
T: (015394) 43314
F: (015394) 48052
E: mylnebridgehouse@talk21.
com
I: www.s-h-systems.co.
uk/hotels/mylne.html

Oakbank House
◆◆◆◆◆ SILVER AWARD
Helm Road, Bowness-on-
Windermere, Cumbria LA23 3BU
T: (015394) 43386
F: (015394) 47965
E: enquiries@
oakbarnkhousehotel.co.uk
I: www.oakbankhousehotel.co.
uk

Oakworth ◆◆◆
11 Upper Oak Street,
Windermere, Cumbria LA23 2LB
T: (015394) 42782
F: (015394) 42265

Oldfield House ◆◆◆◆
Oldfield Road, Windermere,
Cumbria LA23 2BY
T: (015394) 88445
F: (015394) 43250
E: pat.reeves@virgin.net

Orrest Cottage ◆◆◆
17 Church Street, Windermere,
Cumbria LA23 1AQ
T: (015394) 88722

Park Beck ◆◆◆
3 Park Road, Windermere,
Cumbria LA23 2AW
T: (015394) 44025

Rayrigg Villa Guest House
◆◆◆◆
Ellerthwaite Square,
Windermere, Cumbria LA23 1DP
T: (015394) 88342
E: rayriggvilla@nascr.net
I: www.smoothhound.co.
uk/hotels/rayrigg.html

Rocklea ◆◆◆
Brookside, Lake Road,
Windermere, Cumbria LA23 2BX
T: (015394) 45326
F: (015394) 45326
I: www.rocklea.co.uk

Royal Hotel ◆◆◆
Queens Square, Bowness-on-
Windermere, Windermere,
Cumbria LA23 3DB
T: (015394) 43045
F: (015394) 44990
E: royal@elh.co.uk
I: www.elh.co.uk

St John's Lodge ◆◆◆
Lake Road, Windermere,
Cumbria LA23 2EQ
T: (015394) 43078
F: (015394) 88054
E: mail@st-johns-lodge.co.uk
I: www.st-johns-lodge.co.uk

Sandown ◆◆◆
Lake Road, Bowness-on-
Windermere, Windermere,
Cumbria LA23 2JF
T: (015394) 45275
F: (015394) 45275

Storrs Gate House ◆◆◆◆
Longtail Hill, Bowness-on-
Windermere, Windermere,
Cumbria LA23 3JD
T: (015394) 43272
E: enquiries@storrsgatehouse.
co.uk
I: www.storrsgatehouse.co.uk

Sunny-Bec ◆◆◆
Thornbarrow Road, Windermere,
Cumbria LA23 2EN
T: (015394) 42103

Tarn Rigg ◆◆◆
Thornbarrow Road, Windermere,
Cumbria LA23 2DG
T: (015394) 43690
E: stay@tarn-rigg.co.uk
I: www.tarn-rigg.co.uk

Thornbank House ◆◆◆
4 Thornbarrow Road,
Windermere, Cumbria LA23 2EW
T: (015394) 43724
F: (015394) 43724

Thornleigh Guest House ◆◆◆
Thornbarrow Road, Windermere,
Cumbria LA23 2EW
T: (015394) 44203

Upper Oakmere ◆◆
3 Upper Oak Street, Windermere,
Cumbria LA23 2LB
T: (015394) 45649 &
07798 806732

Villa Lodge Guest House
◆◆◆◆
25 Cross Street, Windermere,
Cumbria LA23 1AE
T: (015394) 43318
F: (015394) 43318
E: rooneym@btconnect.com
I: www.villa-lodge.co.uk

Virginia Cottage ◆◆◆
1 and 2 Crown Villas, Kendal
Road, Bowness-on-Windermere,
Windermere, Cumbria LA23 3EJ
T: (015394) 44891 & 44855
F: (015394) 44891
E: paul-des@virginia-cottage.
freeserve.co.uk

Westbourne Hotel ◆◆◆◆
Biskey Howe Road, Bowness-
on-Windermere, Cumbria
LA23 2JR
T: (015394) 43625 &
07702 025305
F: (015394) 43625
E: westbourne@btinternet.com
I: www.milford.co.uk

Westbury House ◆◆◆
27 Broad Street, Windermere,
Cumbria LA23 2AB
T: (015394) 46839
F: (015394) 44575
E: westhouse@comundo.net
I: www.westhouse@comundo.
net

Westwood House ◆◆◆◆
4 Ellerthwaite Road,
Windermere, Cumbria LA23 2AH
T: (015394) 43514

White Lodge Hotel ◆◆◆◆
Lake Road, Windermere,
Cumbria LA23 2JJ
T: (015394) 43624
F: (015394) 44749
E: enquiries@whitelodgehotel.
com
I: www.whitelodgehotel.com

White Rose ◆◆◆
Broad Street, Windermere,
Cumbria LA23 2AB
T: (015394) 45180

Yorkshire House ◆◆◆
1 Upper Oak Street, Windermere,
Cumbria LA23 2LB
T: (015394) 44689
E: applethwaitehouse@
btinternet.com
I: www.btinternet.
com/§applethwaitehouse

Morven Guest House ◆◆◆
Siddick Road, Siddick,
Workington, Cumbria CA14 1LE
T: (01900) 602118 & 602002
F: (01900) 602118

NORTHUMBRIA

The Sun Inn ◆◆◆◆
Main Street, Acomb, Hexham,
Northumberland NE46 4PW
T: (01434) 602934
F: (01434) 606635
E: sun_inn@hotmail.com

Allendale Tea Rooms ◆◆◆
Market Square, Allendale,
Hexham, Northumberland
NE47 9BD
T: (01434) 683575

Kings Head Hotel ◆◆
Market Place, Allendale,
Hexham, Northumberland
NE47 9BD
T: (01434) 683681

Oakey Dene ◆◆◆◆
Allendale, Hexham,
Northumberland NE47 9EL
T: (01434) 683572

Plane Trees ◆◆◆◆
Allendale, Hexham,
Northumberland NE47 9NT
T: (01434) 345236

Struthers Farm ◆◆◆
Catton, Allendale, Hexham,
Northumberland NE47 9LP
T: (01434) 683580

Thornley House ◆◆◆◆
Allendale, Hexham,
Northumberland NE47 9NH
T: (01434) 683255
E: e.finn@ukonline.co.uk

Bilton Barns Farmhouse
◆◆◆◆ SILVER AWARD
Alnmouth, Alnwick,
Northumberland NE66 2TB
T: (01665) 830427
F: (01665) 830063
E: dorothy@biltonbarns.co.uk
I: www.biltonbarns.co.uk

The Famous Schooner Hotel and Restaurant ◆◆◆
Northumberland Street,
Alnmouth, Alnwick,
Northumberland NE66 2RS
T: (01665) 830216
F: (01665) 830287
E: ghost@schooner.sagehost.co.uk
I: www.schooner.sagehost.co.uk

The Grange
◆◆◆◆ SILVER AWARD
Northumberland Street,
Alnmouth, Alnwick,
Northumberland NE66 2RJ
T: (01665) 830401
F: (01665) 830401
E: thegrange.alnmouth@virgin.net

High Buston Hall
◆◆◆◆ GOLD AWARD
High Buston, Alnmouth,
Alnwick, Northumberland
NE66 3QH
T: (01665) 830606 &
07050 041774
F: (01665) 830707
E: highbuston@aol.com
I: members.aol.com/highbuston

Hipsburn Farm ◆◆◆◆
Alnmouth, Alnwick,
Northumberland NE66 3PY
T: (01665) 830206 &
07710 896430

Hope and Anchor Hotel ◆◆◆
44 Northumberland Street,
Alnmouth, Alnwick,
Northumberland NE66 2RA
T: (01665) 830363
E: alan@hope-and-anchor.demon.co.uk

Marine House Private Hotel (Alnmouth) Ltd ◆◆◆◆
1 Marine Road, Alnmouth,
Alnwick, Northumberland
NE66 2RW
T: (01665) 830349
F: (01665) 830394
E: tanney@marinehouse.freeserve.co.uk
I: www.northumberland-hotel.co.uk

Sefton House ◆◆◆
15 Argyle Street, Alnmouth,
Alnwick, Northumberland
NE66 2SB
T: (01665) 830002

Westlea Guest House ◆◆◆
29 Riverside Road, Alnmouth,
Alnwick, Northumberland
NE66 2SD
T: (01665) 830730

Aln House ◆◆◆◆
South Road, Alnwick,
Northumberland NE66 2NZ
T: (01665) 602265
E: alyn@alnhouse.freeserve.co.uk

Aydon House ◆◆◆
South Road, Alnwick,
Northumberland NE66 2NT
T: (01665) 602218

Bondgate House Hotel ◆◆◆
20 Bondgate Without, Alnwick,
Northumberland NE66 1PN
T: (01665) 602025
F: (01665) 602025
E: kenforbes@lineone.net
I: www.bondgatehotel.ntb.org.uk

21 Boulmer Village ◆◆◆◆
Alnwick, Northumberland
NE66 3BS
T: (01665) 577262

Charlton House ◆◆◆◆
2 Aydon Gardens, Alnwick,
Northumberland NE66 2NT
T: (01665) 605185
E: charltonhouse@talk21.com

Crosshills House ◆◆◆◆
40 Blakelaw Road, Alnwick,
Northumberland NE66 1BA
T: (01665) 602518

East Cawledge Park Farm
◆◆◆
Alnwick, Northumberland
NE66 2HB
T: (01665) 606670 & 605705
F: (01665) 605963

The Georgian Guest House ◆◆
3 Hotspur Street, Alnwick,
Northumberland NE66 1QE
T: (01665) 602 398
F: (01665) 602 398
E: georgianguesthouse@eggconnect.net

Hawkhill Farmhouse
◆◆◆◆ SILVER AWARD
Lesbury, Alnwick,
Northumberland NE66 3PG
T: (01665) 830380
F: (01665) 830380

Ingleside ◆◆◆◆
23 Stott Street, Alnwick,
Northumberland NE66 1QA
T: (01665) 602229

Lilburn Grange ◆◆◆
West Lilburn, Alnwick,
Northumberland NE66 4PP
T: (01668) 217274

Limetree Cottage ◆◆◆◆
38 Eglingham Village, Alnwick,
Northumberland NE66 2TX
T: (01665) 578322

Market Tavern ◆◆
7 Fenkle Street, Alnwick,
Northumberland NE66 1HW
T: (01665) 602759

Masons Arms ◆◆◆◆
Stamford, Rennington, Alnwick,
Northumberland NE66 3RX
T: (01665) 577275
F: (01665) 577894
E: masonsarms@lineone.net

Norfolk ◆◆◆◆ SILVER AWARD
41 Blakelaw Road, Alnwick,
Northumberland NE66 1BA
T: (01665) 602892
I: www.norfolk.ntb.org.uk

Oronsay Guest House
Rating Applied For
18 Bondgate Without, Alnwick,
Northumberland NE66 1PP
T: (01665) 603559

Reighamsyde ◆◆◆◆
The Moor, Alnwick,
Northumberland NE66 2AJ
T: (01665) 602535

Rock Midstead Farm House
◆◆◆
Rock Midstead, Rock, Alnwick,
Northumberland NE66 2TH
T: (01665) 579225
E: ian@rockmidstead.freeserve.co.uk

Rooftops
◆◆◆◆ SILVER AWARD
14 Blakelaw Road, Alnwick,
Northumberland NE66 1AZ
T: (01665) 604201

Tower Guest Rooms ◆◆◆◆
10 Bondgate Within, Alnwick,
Northumberland NE66 1TD
T: (01665) 603888 & 0797 102 3692
F: (01665) 603692
E: hopeatalnwick@aol.com

Bisley Place ◆◆◆
37 Bisley Road, Amble-by-the-Sea, Morpeth, Northumberland
NE65 0NP
T: (01665) 710473 &
07773 162545

Coquetside ◆◆◆◆
16 Broomhill Street, Amble-by-the-Sea, Morpeth,
Northumberland NE65 0AN
T: (01665) 710352 &
07970 967757
I: coquetside.future.easyspace.com

The Hollies ◆◆◆◆
3 Riverside Park, Amble-by-the-Sea, Morpeth, Northumberland
NE65 0YR
T: (01665) 712323 & 712708
E: terrihollies@clara.co.uk
I: www.baldeagle50.demon.co.uk/holliesmain.htm.

Togston Hall Farmhouse ◆◆◆
North Togston, Morpeth,
Northumberland NE65 0HR
T: (01665) 712699 &
07971 541365
F: (01665) 712699

Broome ◆◆◆◆
22 Ingram Road, Bamburgh,
Northumberland NE69 7BT
T: (01668) 214287 &
07971 248230
E: MDixon4394@aol.com
I: www.member.xoom.com/bamburgh

Burton Hall ◆◆◆
East Burton, Bamburgh,
Northumberland NE69 7AR
T: (01668) 214213 & 214458
F: (01668) 214538

Glenander Guest House
◆◆◆◆ SILVER AWARD
27 Lucker Road, Bamburgh,
Northumberland NE69 7BS
T: (01668) 214336
F: (01668) 214100

Green Gates ◆◆◆
34 Front Street, Bamburgh,
Northumberland NE69 7BJ
T: (01668) 214535

Squirrel Cottage ◆◆◆◆
1 Friars Court, Bamburgh,
Northumberland NE69 7AE
T: (01668) 214494 & 214572

Carrsgate East ◆◆◆◆
Bardon Mill, Hexham,
Northumberland NE47 7EX
T: (01434) 344376 &
07710 981533
F: (01434) 344011
E: lesley@armstrongrl.freeserve.co.uk

Craws Nest ◆◆
East Twice Brewed, Bardon Mill,
Hexham, Northumberland
NE47 7AL
T: (01434) 344348

Crindledykes Farm ◆◆◆◆
Nr Housesteads, Bardon Mill,
Hexham, Northumberland
NE47 7AF
T: (01434) 344316

Strand Cottage Bed and Breakfast ◆◆◆
Main Road, Bardon Mill,
Hexham, Northumberland NE47
T: (01434) 344643 &
07833 986655
E: strandcottage@aol.com

Vallum Lodge Hotel ◆◆◆◆
Military Road, Twice Brewed,
Bardon Mill, Hexham,
Northumberland NE47 7AN
T: (01434) 344248
F: (01434) 344488
E: vallum.lodge@ukonline.co.uk

Whitegates ◆◆
Henshaw, Bardon Mill, Hexham,
Northumberland NE47 7EP
T: (01434) 344557 &
07703 810059

Bowes Moor Hotel ◆◆◆
Bowes Moor, Barnard Castle,
County Durham DL12 9RH
T: (01833) 628331
F: (01833) 628333
E: bowesmoorhotel@barnard-castle.co.uk
I: www.barnard-castle.co.uk

Bowfield Farm ◆◆
Scargill, Barnard Castle, County
Durham DL12 9SU
T: (01833) 638636

Cloud High
◆◆◆◆ GOLD AWARD
Eggleston, Barnard Castle,
County Durham DL12 0AU
T: (01833) 650644
F: (01833) 650644

Demesnes Mill
◆◆◆◆◆ GOLD AWARD
Barnard Castle, County Durham
DL12 8PE
T: (01833) 637929
F: (01833) 637974
E: millbb@msn.com
I: www.webproze.com/millbb

East Mellwaters Farm ◆◆◆
Bowes, Barnard Castle, County
Durham DL12 9RH
T: (01833) 628269 & 628022
F: (01833) 628269

George & Dragon Inn ♦♦♦
Boldron, Barnard Castle, County
Durham DL12 9RF
T: (01833) 638215

Greta House
♦♦♦♦ SILVER AWARD
89 Galgate, Barnard Castle,
County Durham DL12 8ES
T: (01833) 631193
F: (01833) 631193

The Homelands
♦♦♦♦ SILVER AWARD
85 Galgate, Barnard Castle,
County Durham DL12 8ES
T: (01833) 638757

Marwood House ♦♦♦♦
98 Galgate, Barnard Castle,
County Durham DL12 8BJ
T: (01833) 637493
F: (01833) 637493
E: john&sheila@kilgarriff.
demon.co.uk

Montalbo Hotel ♦♦♦
Montalbo Road, Barnard Castle,
County Durham DL12 8BP
T: (01833) 637342
F: (01833) 637342

33 Newgate ♦♦♦
Barnard Castle, County Durham
DL12 8NJ
T: (01833) 690208
E: peterwhittaker@ndirect.co.uk
I: www.barnard-castle.co.
uk/accommodation/whittaker.
html
⊛

Old Well Inn ♦♦♦
21 The Bank, Barnard Castle,
County Durham DL12 8PH
T: (01833) 690130
F: (01833) 690140
E: reservations@oldwellinn.co.
uk
I: www.oldwellinn.co.uk
⊛

Raygill Farm ♦♦♦
Lartington, Barnard Castle,
County Durham DL12 9DG
T: (01833) 690118
F: (01833) 690118

Spring Lodge ♦♦♦
Newgate, Barnard Castle,
County Durham DL12 8NW
T: (01833) 638110
F: (01833) 638110
⊛

Strathmore Lawn East ♦♦
81 Galgate, Barnard Castle,
County Durham DL12 8ES
T: (01833) 637061

Wilson House ♦♦♦♦
Barningham, Richmond, North
Yorkshire DL11 7EB
T: (01833) 621218

Barrasford Arms ♦♦♦
Barrasford, Hexham,
Northumberland NE48 4AA
T: (01434) 681237
F: (01434) 681237

Beach Court
♦♦♦♦♦ SILVER AWARD
Harbour Road, Beadnell,
Chathill, Northumberland
NE67 5BJ
T: (01665) 720225 &
07703 555125
F: (01665) 721499
E: info@beachcourt.com
I: www.beachcourt.com
⊛

Beadnell House ♦♦
Beadnell, Chathill,
Northumberland NE67 5AT
T: (01665) 721380
F: (01665) 720848
⊛

Beadnell Towers Hotel ♦♦♦
Beadnell, Chathill,
Northumberland NE67 5AU
T: (01665) 721211
F: (01665) 720424
E: beadnell@towers.fsnet.co.uk

Low Dover Beadnell Bay
♦♦♦♦
Harbour Road, Beadnell,
Chathill, Northumberland
NE67 5BJ
T: (01665) 720291 &
07971 444070
F: (01665) 720291
E: kathandbob@lowdover.
demon.co.uk
I: www.lowdover.demon.co.uk

Shepherds Cottage ♦♦♦♦
Beadnell, Chathill,
Northumberland NE67 5AD
T: (01665) 720497 &
07703 455131
F: (01665) 720497
I: www.shepherdscottage.ntb.
org.uk

Brock Mill Farmhouse ♦♦♦
Brock Mill, Beal, Berwick-upon-
Tweed TD15 2PB
T: (01289) 381283 &
07889 099517
F: (01289) 381283

West Mains House ♦♦♦
Beal, Berwick-upon-Tweed
TD15 2PD
T: (01289) 381227

The Beamish Mary Inn ♦♦♦
No Place, Beamish, Stanley,
County Durham DH9 0QH
T: (0191) 370 0237
F: (0191) 370 0091

The Coach House ♦♦♦♦
High Urpeth, Beamish, Stanley,
County Durham DH9 0SE
T: (0191) 370 0309
F: (0191) 370 0046
E: coachhouse@foreman25.
freeserve.co.uk
I: www.coachhousebeamish.ntb.
org.uk

Malling House ♦♦♦
1 Oakdale Terrace, Newfield,
Chester-le-Street, County
Durham DH2 2SU
T: (0191) 370 2571 & 0750 856
5967
F: (0191) 370 1391
E: heather@mallingguesthouse.
co.uk
I: www.mallinghouse.com
⊛

**No Place House Bed &
Breakfast♦♦**
Beamish, Stanley, County
Durham DH9 0QH
T: (0191) 370 0891
E: colin@no-place.freeserve.co.
uk
I: www.noplace.co.uk

Easington Farm ♦♦♦♦
Belford, Northumberland
NE70 7EG
T: (01668) 213298

The Farmhouse Guest House
♦♦♦
24 West Street, Belford,
Northumberland NE70 7QE
T: (01668) 213083

Fenham-le-Moor ♦♦♦♦
Belford, Northumberland
NE70 7PN
T: (01668) 213247
F: (01668) 213247

Oakwood House
♦♦♦♦ SILVER AWARD
3 Cragside Avenue, Belford,
Northumberland NE70 7NA
T: (01668) 213303

Rosebank ♦♦♦
5 Cragside Avenue, Belford,
Northumberland NE70 7NA
T: (01668) 213762
F: (01668) 213762

11 West Street ♦
Belford, Northumberland
NE70 7QA
T: (01668) 213480

The Cheviot Hotel ♦♦♦
Bellingham, Hexham,
Northumberland NE48 2AU
T: (01434) 220696
F: (01434) 220696
⊛

Ivy Cottage ♦♦♦
Lanehead, Tarset, Hexham,
Northumberland NE48 1NT
T: (01434) 240337
F: (01434) 240073

**Lyndale Guest House and
Holiday Cottage♦♦♦♦**
Off The Square, Bellingham,
Hexham, Northumberland
NE48 2AW
T: (01434) 220361 &
03778 925479
F: (01434) 220361
E: lyndale.SmoothHound@
chelsolfdemon.co.uk
I: www.SmoothHound.co.
uk/hotels/lyndale.html
⊛

Westfield House ♦♦♦♦
Bellingham, Hexham,
Northumberland NE48 2DP
T: (01434) 220340
F: (01434) 220694
E: westfield.house@virgin.net
I: freespace.virgin.net/westfield.
house/index.htm

**Moor End House Bed and
Breakfast♦♦**
7-8 Moor End Terrace, Belmont,
Durham DH1 1BJ
T: (0191) 384 2796 &
07702 896562

Alannah House ♦♦♦♦
84 Church Street, Berwick-
upon-Tweed, Northumberland
TD15 1DU
T: (01289) 307252
E: eileenandian@alannahouse.
freeserve.co.uk

Ben More Guest House ♦♦♦
51 Church Street, Berwick-
upon-Tweed, Northumberland
TD15 1EE
T: (01289) 306666

Bridge View ♦♦♦♦
14 Tweed Street, Berwick-upon-
Tweed, TD15 1NG
T: (01289) 308098

The Castle ♦♦♦
Castlegate, Berwick-upon-
Tweed, Northumberland
TD15 1LF
T: (01289) 307900
F: (01289) 307900

Castle Hills House ♦♦♦
Berwick-upon-Tweed,
Northumberland TD15 1PB
T: (01289) 302496 &
07803 904264
F: (01289) 302496
E: guersthouse.berwick.co.uk
I: www.guesthouse.berwick.co.
uk

The Cat Inn ♦♦♦
Great North Road, Cheswick,
Berwick-upon-Tweed, TD15 2RL
T: (01289) 387251
F: (01289) 387251

Cear Urfa ♦♦♦♦
15 Springfield Park, East Ord,
Berwick-upon-Tweed,
Northumberland TD15 2FD
T: (01289) 303528

Clovelly House
♦♦♦♦ SILVER AWARD
58 West Street, Berwick-upon-
Tweed, Northumberland
TD15 1AS
T: (01289) 302337
F: (01289) 302052
E: vivroc@clovelly53.freeserve.
co.uk
I: www.clovelly53.freeserve.co.
uk
⊛

Dervaig Guest House ♦♦♦♦
1 North Road, Berwick-upon-
Tweed, Northumberland
TD15 1PW
T: (01289) 307378
E: dervaig@btinternet.com

Drousha Guest House ♦♦
11 Sandgate, Berwick-upon-Tweed, TD15 1EP
T: (01289) 306659

Fairholm ♦♦♦♦
East Ord, Berwick-upon-Tweed, TD15 2NS
T: (01289) 305370

The Friendly Hound ♦♦♦♦
Ford Common, Berwick-upon-Tweed, Northumberland TD15 2QD
T: (01289) 388554

Harberton Guest House ♦♦
181 Main Street, Spittal, Berwick-upon-Tweed, Northumberland TD15 1RP
T: (01289) 308813 & 305056
E: maurw@zetnet.co.uk
I: www.harberton.com
◎

High Letham Farmhouse ♦♦♦♦ SILVER AWARD
High Letham, Berwick-upon-Tweed, Northumberland TD15 1UX
T: (01289) 306585
F: (01289) 304194
E: hlf-b@fantasyprints.co.uk
I: www.secretkingdom.com/high/letham.htm

Ladythorne House ♦♦♦
Cheswick, Berwick-upon-Tweed, Northumberland TD15 2RW
T: (01289) 387382
F: (01289) 387073
E: parkerbankb@ladythorne.freeserve.co.uk

Meadow Hill Guest House ♦♦♦♦
Duns Road, Berwick-upon-Tweed, Northumberland TD15 1UB
T: (01289) 306325
F: (01289) 306325
E: barryandhazel@meadow-hill.co.uk
I: www.meadowhill.ntb.org.uk
♿

Middle Ord Manor House ♦♦♦♦♦ GOLD AWARD
Middle Ord Farm, Berwick-upon-Tweed, Northumberland TD15 2XQ
T: (01289) 306323
F: (01289) 308423
E: joan@middleord.freeserve.co.uk
I: www.middleord.ntb.org.uk
◎

No 1 Sallyport ♦♦♦♦ SILVER AWARD
Berwick-upon-Tweed, Northumberland TD15 1EZ
T: (01289) 308827 &
07703 116796
F: (01289) 308827

4 North Road ♦♦♦♦ SILVER AWARD
Berwick-upon-Tweed, Northumberland TD15 1PL
T: (01289) 306146 & 0771 242 6145
F: (01289) 306146
E: sandra@thorntonfour.freeserve.co.uk

6 North Road ♦♦♦♦
Berwick-upon-Tweed, TD15 1PL
T: (01289) 308949

The Old Vicarage Guest House ♦♦♦♦
24 Church Road, Tweedmouth, Berwick-upon-Tweed, Northumberland TD15 2AN
T: (01289) 306909
◎

Orkney House ♦♦
37 Woolmarket, Berwick-upon-Tweed, Northumberland TD15 1BH
T: (01289) 331710

6 Parade ♦♦♦
Berwick-upon-Tweed, TD15 1DF
T: (01289) 308454

40 Ravensdowne ♦♦♦♦
Berwick-upon-Tweed, Northumberland TD15 1DQ
T: (01289) 306992
◎

The Ravensholme Hotel ♦♦♦
34-36 Ravensdowne, Berwick-upon-Tweed, Northumberland TD15 1DQ
T: (01289) 330770
E: john@thewalls79.freeserve.co.uk

Rob Roy ♦♦♦♦
Dock Road, Tweedmouth, Berwick-upon-Tweed TD15 2BQ
T: (01289) 306428
I: www.secretkingdom.com/rob/roy.htm

Westsunnyside House ♦♦♦
Tweedmouth, Berwick-upon-Tweed TD15 2QH
T: (01289) 305387
F: (01289) 305387
I: www.tweeddalepress.co.uk/westsunnysideb+b

Whyteside House ♦♦♦♦ SILVER AWARD
46 Castlegate, Berwick-upon-Tweed, Northumberland TD15 1JT
T: (01289) 331019
F: (01289) 331419
E: albert@whyteside100.freeserve.co.uk
I: www.secretkingdom.com/whyte/side.htm
◎

BISHOP AUCKLAND
Durham

Albion Cottage Guest House ♦♦♦
Albion Terrace, Bishop Auckland, County Durham DL14 6EL
T: (01388) 602217

Five Gables Guest House ♦♦♦
Five Gables, Binchester, Bishop Auckland, County Durham DL14 8AT
T: (01388) 608204
F: (01388) 663092
E: book.in@fivegables.co.uk
I: www.fivegables.co.uk
◎

The Old Farmhouse ♦♦♦
Grange Hill, Bishop Auckland, County Durham DL14 8EG
T: (01388) 602123 & 0780 864 7134
F: (01388) 602123
◎

BLYTH
Northumberland

The Anchor Hotel ♦♦
36 Beaconsfield Street, Blyth, Northumberland NE24 2DP
T: (01670) 352688

BOWBURN
Durham

Prince Bishop Guest House ♦♦♦
1 Oxford Terrace, Bowburn, Durham DH6 5AX
T: (0191) 377 8703 &
07710 964200
F: (0191) 377 3483

BRIGNALL
Durham

Lily Hill Farm ♦♦♦
Brignall, Barnard Castle, County Durham DL12 9SF
T: (01833) 627254

BROOMPARK
Durham

The Loves ♦♦♦
17 Front Street, Broompark, Durham DH7 7QT
T: (0191) 384 9283

BURNHOPE
Durham

**Burnhope Lodge Bed and Breakfast
Rating Applied For**
1 Wrightsway, Burnhope, Durham DH7 0DL
T: (01207) 529351 & 529546
F: (01207) 529546

CAMBO
Northumberland

Shieldhall ♦♦♦♦
Wallington, Cambo, Morpeth, Northumberland NE61 4AQ
T: (01830) 540387
F: (01830) 540490
E: robinson.gay@btinternet.com

CARTERWAY HEADS
Northumberland

Manor Motel ♦♦♦
Carterway Heads, Consett, County Durham DH8 9LX
T: (01207) 255269

CASTLESIDE
Durham

Castleneuk Guest House ♦♦
18-20 Front Street, Castleside, Consett, County Durham DH8 9AR
T: (01207) 506634
E: jan@castleneuk.freeserve.co.uk
I: www.castleneuk.freeserve.co.uk

Deneview ♦♦♦
15 Front Street, Castleside, Consett, County Durham DH8 9AR
T: (01207) 502925 &
07957 948498
E: cyndyglancy@lineone.net

CHATHILL
Northumberland

North Charlton Farm ♦♦♦♦♦ SILVER AWARD
Chathill, Alnwick, Northumberland NE67 5HP
T: (01665) 579443 &
07831 518061
F: (01665) 579443
E: glenc99@aol.com

West Link Hall Farmhouse ♦♦♦♦
Chathill, Alnwick, Northumberland NE67 5HU
T: (01665) 579306 &
(01655) 577262

CHATTON
Northumberland

South Hazelrigg Farmhouse ♦♦♦♦
South Hazelrigg, Chatton, Alnwick, Northumberland NE66
T: (01668) 215216 &
07710 346076
E: sdodds@farmhousebandb.co.uk
I: www.farmhousebandb.co.uk

CHESTER-LE-STREET
Durham

Hollycroft ♦♦♦♦
11 The Parade, Chester-le-Street, County Durham DH3 3LR
T: (0191) 388 7088 &
07932 675069
E: cutter@hollycroft11.freeserve.co.uk

Low Urpeth Farm House ♦♦♦♦
Ouston, Chester-le-Street, County Durham DH2 1BD
T: (0191) 410 2901
F: (0191) 410 0081
E: treesplease@btinternet.com
I: www.btinternet.com/§treesplease
◎

Waldridge Fell House ♦♦♦♦
Waldridge Lane, Waldridge, Chester-le-Street, County Durham DH2 3RY
T: (0191) 389 1908

CHOLLERFORD
Northumberland

Brunton Water Mill ♦♦♦♦
Chollerford, Hexham, Northumberland NE46 4EL
T: (01434) 681002
E: pesarra@brunton-mill.freeserve.co.uk

CLEASBY
Durham

Cleasby House ♦♦♦
Cleasby, Darlington, County Durham DL2 2QY
T: (01325) 350160 &
(01642) 226886
F: (01642) 213659

CONSETT
Durham

Bee Cottage Farm ♦♦♦
Castleside, Consett, County Durham DH8 9HW
T: (01207) 508224
◎

Low Brooms Farm ♦♦
Leadgate, Consett, County Durham DH8 7SR
T: (01207) 500594
F: (01207) 500594

CORBRIDGE
Northumberland

Clive House ♦♦♦♦
Appletree Lane, Corbridge, Northumberland NE45 5DN
T: (01434) 632617

Dilston Mill ◆◆◆◆
Corbridge, Northumberland
NE45 5QZ
T: (01434) 633493
F: (01434) 633513
E: jan.ketelaar@virgin.net

Dilston Plains ◆◆
Corbridge, Northumberland
NE45 5RE
T: (01434) 602785 & 632586

Fellcroft ◆◆◆◆
Station Road, Corbridge,
Northumberland NE45 5AY
T: (01434) 632384

Firtrees ◆◆◆◆
Cow Lane, Corbridge,
Northumberland NE45 5HX
T: (01434) 632257

The Hayes Guest House ◆
Newcastle Road, Corbridge,
Northumberland NE45 5LP
T: (01434) 632010

Holmlea ◆◆◆
Station Road, Corbridge,
Northumberland NE45 5AY
T: (01434) 632486

Priorfield ◆◆◆◆
Hippingstones Lane, Corbridge,
Northumberland NE45 5JA
T: (01434) 633179 &
07860 962448
F: (01434) 633179
E: nsteenberg@lineone.net

Riverside Guest House ◆◆◆◆
Main Street, Corbridge,
Northumberland NE45 5LE
T: (01434) 632942
F: (01434) 633883
E: riverside@ukonline.co.uk
I: web.ukonline.co.uk/riverside/

Town Barns ◆◆◆◆
Off Trinity Terrace, Corbridge,
Northumberland NE45 5HP
T: (01434) 633345

COTHERSTONE
Durham

Fox and Hounds ◆◆◆
Cotherstone, Barnard Castle,
County Durham DL12 9PF
T: (01833) 650241 &
07710 351822
F: (01833) 650241
E: mcarlisle@foxcothe.
freenetname.com
I: foxcotherstone.co.uk

Glendale ◆◆◆
Cotherstone, Barnard Castle,
County Durham DL12 9UH
T: (01833) 650384
I: www.barnard-castle.co.uk

COXHOE
Durham

The Black Horse ◆◆
Station Road East, Coxhoe,
Durham DH6 4AT
T: (0191) 377 9574
F: (0191) 377 9555
E: ian@blackhorse11.co.uk

CRAGHEAD
Durham

The Punch Bowl ◆◆
Craghead, Stanley, County
Durham DH9 6EF
T: (01207) 232917

CRASTER
Northumberland

Cottage Inn ◆◆◆
Dunstan Village, Craster,
Alnwick, Northumberland
NE66 3SZ
T: (01665) 576658
F: (01665) 576788
◉

Howick Scar Farmhouse ◆◆◆
Craster, Alnwick,
Northumberland NE66 3SU
T: (01665) 576665
F: (01665) 576665

Stonecroft
◆◆◆◆ SILVER AWARD
Dunstan, Craster, Alnwick,
Northumberland NE66 3SZ
T: (01665) 576433
F: (01665) 576311
E: sally@stonestaff.freeserve.co.
uk
I: www.stonecroft.ntb.org.uk

CRESSWELL
Northumberland

Cresswell House ◆◆◆◆
Cresswell, Morpeth,
Northumberland NE61 5LA
T: (01670) 861302

CROOK
Durham

Watergate Lane Farm ◆◆◆
Rumby Hill, Crook, County
Durham DL15 8EN
T: (01388) 766913
F: (01388) 764727
◉

CROOKHAM
Northumberland

The Coach House at Crookham
◆◆◆◆
Cornhill-on-Tweed,
Northumberland TD12 4TD
T: (01890) 820293
F: (01890) 820284
E: thecoachouse@englandmail.
com
I: www.secretkingdom.
com/coach/house.htm
♿

CROXDALE
Durham

Croxdale Inn ◆◆◆
Front Street, Croxdale, Durham
DH6 5HX
T: (01388) 815727 & 420294
F: (01388) 815368
E: croxdale@talk21.com

DARLINGTON
Durham

Aberlady Guest House ◆
51 Corporation Road,
Darlington, County Durham
DL3 6AD
T: (01325) 461449 &
07970 379939

Balmoral Guest House ◆◆◆
63 Woodland Road, Darlington,
County Durham DL3 7BQ
T: (01325) 461908
F: (01325) 461908

The Chequers Inn ◆◆
Darlington, County Durham
DL2 2NT
T: (01325) 721213 & 722307
F: (01325) 721213

Clow–Beck House
◆◆◆◆◆ GOLD AWARD
Monk End Farm, Croft,
Darlington, County Durham
DL2 2SW
T: (01325) 721075 & 0779 908
4526
F: (01325) 720419
E: david@clowbeckhouse.co.uk
I: www.clowbeckhouse.co.uk
◉

The Dalesman Hotel ◆◆
96-100 Victoria Road,
Darlington, County Durham
DL1 5JW
T: (01325) 466695 & 357654
F: (01325) 467855

Greenbank Guest House ◆◆◆
90 Greenbank Road, Darlington,
County Durham DL3 6EL
T: (01325) 462624
F: (01325) 250233

Harewood Lodge ◆◆◆
40 Grange Road, Darlington,
County Durham DL1 5NP
T: (01325) 358152
E: heenan@hlbb.freeserve.co.uk

The Nook ◆◆◆
31 Southend Avenue,
Darlington, County Durham
DL3 7HT
T: (01325) 460613 &
07710 445419
F: (01325) 284396

DURHAM
Durham

60 Albert Street ◆◆◆
Western Hill, Durham, DH1 4RJ
T: (0191) 386 0608 &
07930 369429
E: laura@sixtyalbertstreet.co.uk
I: www.sixtyalbertstreet.co.uk

The Anchorage ◆◆◆
25 Langley Road, Newton Hall,
Durham, DH1 5LR
T: (0191) 386 2323
F: (0191) 384 1842
E: anchorageb@aol.com

12 The Avenue ◆◆◆
Durham, DH1 4ED
T: (0191) 384 1020
E: janhanim@aol.com

The Avenue Inn ◆
Avenue Street, High Shincliffe,
Durham DH1 2PT
T: (0191) 386 5954
E: wenmah@aol.com

Bay Horse Inn ◆◆◆
Brandon Village, Durham,
DH7 8ST
T: (0191) 378 0498

Belle Vue Guest House ◆◆
4 Belle Vue Terrace, Gilesgate
Moor, Durham, DH1 2HR
T: (0191) 386 4800

Broom Farm Guest House
◆◆◆
Broom Farm, Broom Park Village,
Durham, DH7 7QX
T: (0191) 386 4755

Castle View Guest House ◆◆◆
4 Crossgate, Durham, DH1 4PS
T: (0191) 386 8852
F: (0191) 386 8852
E: castle_view@hotmail.com

Castledene ◆◆◆
37 Nevilledale Terrace, Durham,
DH1 4QG
T: (0191) 384 8386 &
07710 425921
F: (0191) 384 8386
E: lornabyrne@tinyworld.co.uk

**Cathedral View Guest House
Rating Applied For**
212 Gilesgate, Durham, Co
Durham DH1 1QN
T: (0191) 386 9566
F: (0191) 386 9566
E: cathedralview@hotmail.com

**College of Saint Hild and Saint
Bede (Guest Rooms & Gables)**
◆
Durham, DH1 1SZ
T: (0191) 374 3069 & 374 3064
F: (0191) 374 4740
E: l.c.hugill@durham.ac.uk
I: www.dur.ac.uk/HildBede

**Collingwood College Cumbrian
Wing** ◆◆◆
South Road, Durham, DH1 3LT
T: (0191) 374 4568
F: (0191) 374 4595
E: collingwood_college.
conference@durham.ac.uk
◉

Elmgarth ◆◆◆
Mainsforth, Ferryhill, County
Durham DL17 9AA
T: (01740) 652676
F: (01740) 652676
E: elmgarth_bedandbreakfast@
yahoo.com
I: www.elmgarth.ntb.org.uk

Farnley Tower ◆◆◆◆
The Avenue, Durham, DH1 4DX
T: (0191) 375 0011
F: (0191) 383 9694
E: enquiries@farnleytower.
freeservenet.co.uk

The Georgian Town House
◆◆◆◆
10 Crossgate, Durham, DH1 4PS
T: (0191) 386 8070
F: (0191) 386 8070

10 Gilesgate ◆◆
Durham, DH1 1QW
T: (0191) 386 2026 &
07711 956476
F: (0191) 386 2026

14 Gilesgate ◆◆
Top of Claypath, Durham,
County Durham DH1 1QW
T: (0191) 384 6485
F: (0191) 386 5173
E: bb@nimmins.co.uk
I: www.nimmins.co.uk

The Gilesgate Moor Hotel
◆◆◆
Teasdale Terrace, Gilesgate,
Durham, Co Durham DH1 2RN
T: (0191) 386 6453
F: (0191) 386 6453

Grey College (Holgate) ◆◆
South Road, Durham, DH1 3LG
T: (0191) 374 2968 & 374 2965
F: (0191) 374 2992
E: t.j.s.heath@durham.ac.uk
I: www.dur.ac.uk/GreyCollege
◉

Hatfield College, Jevons Rating Applied For
North Bailey, Durham, DH1 3RQ
T: (0191) 374 3165
F: (0191) 374 7472
E: a.m.ankers@durham.ac.uk
I: www.hatfield.ntb.org.uk

Hill Rise Guest House ◆◆◆◆
13 Durham Road West,
Bowburn, Durham DH6 5AU
T: (0191) 377 0302
F: (0191) 377 0302

Knights Rest ◆◆◆
1 Anchorage Terrace, Durham,
DH1 3DL
T: (0191) 386 6229 & 0780 170 0896
F: (0191) 386 6229

Paddock Cottage ◆◆◆
70 Hallgarth Street, Durham,
DH1 3AY
T: (0191) 386 3845

Pelaw Rise
◆◆◆◆ SILVER AWARD
Leazes Road, Durham, DH1 1TS
T: (0191) 386 5778 &
07802 697965
F: (0191) 386 5778
E: hospitality@pelawrise.
freeserve.co.uk

5 Pickwick Close ◆◆◆
Elvet Moor, Durham, DH1 3QU
T: (0191) 386 8910 & 0780 113 8494
E: dennis@wilcock81.freeserve.co.uk
I: www.wilcock81.freeserve.co.uk/accommodation.htm

Redhills Hotel ◆◆
Redhills Lane, Crossgate Moor,
Durham DH1 4AW
T: (0191) 386 4331
F: (0191) 386 9612

St Aidan's College ◆◆◆
University of Durham, Windmill Hill, Durham, DH1 3LJ
T: (0191) 374 3269
F: (0191) 374 4749
E: a.davis.conf@durham.ac.uk
I: www.st-aidans.org.uk

St Chad's College ◆◆
18 North Bailey, Durham,
DH1 3RH
T: (0191) 374 3364
F: (0191) 374 3309
E: St-Chads.www@durham.ac.uk
I: www.dur.ac.uk/StChads

Saint Cuthberts Society ◆◆
12 South Bailey, Durham,
DH1 3EE
T: (0191) 374 3464 & 374 3400
F: (0191) 374 4753
E: i.d.barton@durham.ac.uk

Saint Johns College (Cruddas) ◆◆
3 South Bailey, Durham,
DH1 3RJ
T: (0191) 374 3579
F: (0191) 374 3569
E: s.l.hobson@durham.ac.uk
I: www.dur.ac.uk/§dsj0www

Seven Stars Inn ◆◆◆
Shincliffe Village, Durham,
DH1 2NU
T: (0191) 384 8454
F: (0191) 386 0640

Trevelyan College (Macaulay Wing) ◆◆
Elvet Hill Road, Durham,
DH1 3LN
T: (0191) 374 3765 & 374 3768
F: (0191) 374 3789
E: trev.coll@durham.ac.uk
I: www.dur.ac.uk/§dtr0www

Triermayne ◆◆◆◆
Nevilles Cross Bank, Durham,
DH1 4JP
T: (0191) 384 6036

Van Mildert College (Tunstall Stairs) ◆◆◆
Mill Hill Lane, Durham, DH1 3LH
T: (0191) 374 3900
F: (0191) 374 3974
E: van-mildert.college@durham.ac.uk
I: www.dur.ac.uk/VanMildert/Conferences

Victoria Inn ◆◆◆
86 Hallgarth Street, Durham,
DH1 3AS
T: (0191) 386 5269 & 386 0465
F: (0191) 386 0465

Waterside
◆◆◆◆ SILVER AWARD
Elvet Waterside, Durham,
DH1 3BW
T: (0191) 384 6660 & 384 6996
F: (0191) 384 6996

EASINGTON
Tees Valley

The Grapes ◆◆◆
Scaling Dam, Easington,
Saltburn-by-the-Sea, Cleveland
TS13 4TP
T: (01287) 640461
E: mark79@kenny7997.freeserve.co.uk
I: www.touristnetuk.com/ne/grapes/

EAST ORD
Northumberland

Inverleacainn ◆◆◆◆
4 Springfield Park, East Ord,
Berwick-upon-Tweed TD15 2FD
T: (01289) 304627

Tweed View House ◆◆◆
East Ord, Berwick-upon-Tweed
TD15 2NS
T: (01289) 332378
F: (01289) 332378
E: khdobson@aol.com

EASTGATE-IN-WEARDALE
Durham

Rose Hill Farm Bed and Breakfast ◆◆◆◆
Rose Hill Farm, Eastgate-in-Weardale, Bishop Auckland,
County Durham DL13 2LB
T: (01388) 517209 &
07808 402425

EGGLESTON
Durham

Moorcock Inn ◆◆◆
Hill Top, Gordon Bank,
Eggleston, Barnard Castle,
County Durham DL12 0AU
T: (01833) 650395
F: (01833) 650052

EGLINGHAM
Northumberland

Ash Tree House ◆◆◆◆
The Terrace, Eglingham, Alnwick,
Northumberland NE66 2UA
T: (01665) 578533
I: www.secretkingdom.com/ashtree/house.htm

ELLINGHAM
Northumberland

Pack Horse Inn ◆◆◆
Ellingham, Chathill,
Northumberland NE67 5HA
T: (01665) 589292 &
07050 189333
F: (01665) 589053
E: graham.simpson@farmline.com
I: www.thepackhorseinn.co.uk

EMBLETON
Northumberland

Blue Bell Inn ◆◆◆
Embleton, Alnwick,
Northumberland NE66 3UP
T: (01665) 576573 & 576639

Dunstanburgh Castle Hotel ◆◆◆◆
Embleton, Alnwick,
Northumberland NE66 3UN
T: (01665) 576111
E: duncashot@compuserve.com
I: www.dunstanburghcastlehotel.co.uk

Rock Farmhouse ◆◆◆
Rock Village, Alnwick,
Northumberland NE66 3SB
T: (01665) 579235
F: (01665) 579215
E: rockfarmbb@cs.com
I: www.rockfarmhouse.freeserve.co.uk

The Sportsman ◆◆◆
Sea Lane, Embleton, Alnwick,
Northumberland NE66 3XF
T: (01665) 576588
F: (01665) 576524

ESCOMB
Durham

The Gables ◆◆
3 Lane Ends, Escomb, Bishop
Auckland, County Durham
DL14 7SR
T: (01388) 604745

FALSTONE
Northumberland

The Blackcock Inn ◆◆◆
Falstone, Hexham,
Northumberland NE48 1AA
T: (01434) 240200
F: (01434) 240200
E: blackcock@falstone.fsbusiness.co.uk
I: www.smoothhound.co.uk/hotels/black.html

High Yarrow Farm ◆◆◆
Falstone, Hexham,
Northumberland NE48 1BG
T: (01434) 240264

Woodside ◆◆◆◆
Yarrow, Falstone, Hexham,
Northumberland NE48 1BG
T: (01434) 240443

FELTON
Northumberland

Cook and Barker Inn
◆◆◆◆ SILVER AWARD
Newton-on-the-Moor, Felton,
Morpeth, Northumberland
NE65 9JY
T: (01665) 575234

FENHAM
Tyne and Wear

The Brighton ◆◆
47-49 Brighton Grove, Fenham,
Newcastle upon Tyne NE4 5NS
T: (0191) 273 3600
F: (0191) 226 0563

FIR TREE
Durham

Duke of York Inn
◆◆◆◆ SILVER AWARD
Fir Tree, Crook, County Durham
DL15 8DG
T: (01388) 762848

FORD
Northumberland

The Estate House ◆◆◆◆
Ford, Berwick-upon-Tweed,
Northumberland TD15 2PX
T: (01890) 820668 &
07715 313989
F: (01890) 82000672
E: theestatehouse@supanet.com

Hay Farm Farmhouse ◆◆◆◆
Ford, Berwick-upon-Tweed
TD12 4TR
T: (01890) 820647 & 820659
F: (01890) 820659

The Old Post Office ◆◆◆
2 Old Post Office Cottages, Ford,
Berwick-upon-Tweed,
Northumberland TD15 2QA
T: (01890) 820286 &
07803 819452

FOREST-IN-TEESDALE
Durham

High Force Hotel ◆◆◆
Forest-in-Teesdale, Barnard
Castle, County Durham
DL12 0XH
T: (01833) 622222

FOURSTONES
Northumberland

8 St Aidans Park ◆◆◆◆
Fourstones, Hexham,
Northumberland NE47 5EB
T: (01434) 674073
F: (01434) 674073
E: janet@hadrians-wall.co.uk
I: www.hadrians-wall.co.uk

FOXTON
Northumberland

Out of Bounds ◆◆◆
Foxton, Alnwick,
Northumberland NE66 3BE
T: (01665) 830150
F: (01665) 830150

FROSTERLEY
Durham

High Laithe ♦♦♦
10A Hill End, Frosterley, Bishop
Auckland, County Durham
DL13 2SX
T: (01388) 526421

GATESHEAD
Tyne and Wear

The Bewick Hotel ♦♦
145 Prince Consort Road,
Gateshead, Tyne and Wear
NE8 4DS
T: (0191) 477 1809 & 477 3401
F: (0191) 477 6146
E: bewickenquiries@145bewick.
fsnet.co.uk
I: www.bewickhotel.co.uk

Gilbert Guest House ♦♦♦
1 Gladstone Terrace, Gateshead,
Tyne and Wear NE8 4DY
T: (0191) 478 6061

**Shaftesbury Guest House
♦♦♦**
245 Prince Consort Road,
Gateshead, Tyne and Wear
NE8 4DT
T: (0191) 478 2544
F: (0191) 478 2544

GILSLAND
Northumberland

**North View Bed & Breakfast
♦♦♦**
Gilsland, Carlisle, Cumbria
CA6 7DX
T: (016977) 47696

GREAT TOSSON
Northumberland

**Tosson Tower Farm
♦♦♦♦ SILVER AWARD**
Great Tosson, Morpeth,
Northumberland NE65 7NW
T: (01669) 620228
F: (01669) 620228
E: sgkett@aol.com
I: www.tossontowerfarm.ntb.
org.uk

GREENHAUGH
Northumberland

Hollybush Inn ♦♦♦
Greenhaugh, Hexham,
Northumberland NE48 1PW
T: (01434) 240391 & 240228

GREENHEAD
Northumberland

**Holmhead Guest House
♦♦♦♦**
Thirlwall Castle Farm, Hadrian's
Wall, Greenhead, Carlisle
CA8 7HY
T: (016977) 47402
F: (016977) 47402
E: holmhead@hadrianswall.
freeserve.co.uk
I: www.bankbhadrianswall.com

GRETA BRIDGE
Durham

**The Coach House
♦♦♦♦ SILVER AWARD**
Greta Bridge, Barnard Castle,
County Durham DL12 9SD
T: (01833) 627201
F: (01833) 627201
E: info@coachhousegreta.co.uk
I: www.coachhousegreta.co.uk

HALTWHISTLE
Northumberland

Ald White Craig Farm ♦♦♦♦
Near Hadrian's Wall, Haltwhistle,
Northumberland NE49 9NW
T: (01434) 320565
F: (01434) 320565
E: isobel@ald-white-craig-farm.
co.uk
I: www.ald-white-craig-farm.co.
uk

**Ashcroft
♦♦♦♦ SILVER AWARD**
Lantys Lonnen, Haltwhistle,
Northumberland NE49 0DA
T: (01434) 320213
F: (01434) 320213

**Brookside House Vegetarian
Bed and Breakfast♦♦♦♦**
Brookside House, Town Foot,
Haltwhistle, Northumberland
NE49 0ER
T: (01434) 322481
E: brooksideveg-b-and-b@
lineone.net
I: www.lineone.net&billstapleton

**Broomshaw Hill Farm
♦♦♦♦♦ GOLD AWARD**
Willia Road, Haltwhistle,
Northumberland NE49 9NP
T: (01434) 320866 & 0771 483
5828
F: (01434) 320866
E: broomshaw@msn.com
I: www.broomshawhill.ntb.org.
uk

**Centre of Britain Hotel and
Restaurant
♦♦♦♦ SILVER AWARD**
Haltwhistle, Northumberland
NE49 0BH
T: (01434) 322422
F: (01434) 322655
I: www.centre-of-britain.org.uk

**Doors Cottage Bed and
Breakfast ♦♦♦**
Shield Hill, Haltwhistle,
Northumberland NE49 9NW
T: (01434) 322556 &
07867 668574

The Grey Bull Hotel ♦♦♦
Main Street, Haltwhistle,
Northumberland NE49 0DL
T: (01434) 321991
F: (01434) 320770

Hall Meadows ♦♦♦
Main Street, Haltwhistle,
Northumberland NE49 0AZ
T: (01434) 321021

Kirkholmedale ♦♦♦
Lantys Lonnen, Haltwhistle,
Northumberland NE49 0HQ
T: (01434) 322948

Oaky Knowe Farm ♦♦♦
Haltwhistle, Northumberland
NE49 0NB
T: (01434) 320648
F: (01434) 320648

The Old School House ♦♦♦♦
Fair Hill, Haltwhistle,
Northumberland NE49 9EE
T: (01434) 322595
F: (01434) 322595
E: vera@oshouse.freeserve.co.
uk
I: www.oshouse.freeserve.co.uk

Saughy Rigg Farm ♦♦♦
Twice Brewed, Haltwhistle,
Northumberland NE49 9PT
T: (01434) 344120
E: kathandbrad@
northumberland
accommodation.co.uk
I: www.northumberland
accommodation.co.uk

Spring House ♦♦♦♦
Comb Hill, Haltwhistle,
Northumberland NE49 9NS
T: (01434) 320334

HAMSTERLEY
Durham

Dryderdale Hall ♦♦♦♦
Hamsterley, Bishop Auckland,
County Durham DL13 3NR
T: (01388) 488494 & 0780 328
3222
F: (01388) 488195

HARBOTTLE
Northumberland

The Byre ♦♦♦♦
Harbottle, Morpeth,
Northumberland NE65 7DG
T: (01669) 650476
E: rosemary@the-byre.co.uk
I: www.the-byre.co.uk

HARTFORD BRIDGE
Northumberland

Woodside ♦♦♦
Hartford Bridge Farm, Hartford
Bridge, Bedlington,
Northumberland NE22 6AL
T: (01670) 822035

HARTLEPOOL
Tees Valley

Hillcarter Hotel ♦♦♦♦
31-32 Church Street, Hartlepool,
Cleveland TS24 7DH
T: (01429) 855800 & 855826
T: (01429) 855829
E: hillcarter@btinternet.com

The York Hotel ♦♦
185 York Road, Hartlepool,
Cleveland TS26 9EE
T: (01429) 867373
F: (01429) 867220
E: info@theyorkhotel.co.uk
I: www.theyorkhotel.co.uk

HAYDON BRIDGE
Northumberland

Anchor Hotel ♦♦♦
John Martin Street, Haydon
Bridge, Hexham,
Northumberland NE47 6AB
T: (01434) 684227
F: (01434) 684586
E: anchor.hotel@virgin.net
I: www.freespace.virgin.net/alan.
mcjannet4/index.html

Hadrian Lodge ♦♦♦
Hindshield Moss, North Road,
Haydon Bridge, Hexham,
Northumberland NE47 6NF
T: (01434) 688688
F: (01434) 684867
E: hadrianlodge@hadrianswall.
co.uk
I: www.hadrianswall.co.uk

Railway Hotel ♦♦♦
Church Street, Haydon Bridge,
Hexham, Northumberland
NE47 6JG
T: (01434) 684254

West Mill Hills ♦♦♦
Haydon Bridge, Hexham,
Northumberland NE47 6JR
T: (01434) 684387

HEIGHINGTON
Durham

**Eldon House
Rating Applied For**
East Green, Heighington,
Darlington, County Durham
DL5 6PP
T: (01325) 312270
F: (01325) 315580
E: kbartram@btinternet.com

HEXHAM
Northumberland

10 Alexandra Terrace ♦♦
Hexham, Northumberland
NE46 3JQ
T: (01434) 601954

Anick Grange ♦♦♦
Hexham, Northumberland
NE46 4LP
T: (01434) 603807

The Beeches ♦♦♦
40 Leazes Park, Hexham,
Northumberland NE46 3AY
T: (01434) 605900

The Coach and Horses ♦♦♦
Priestpopple, Hexham,
Northumberland NE46 1PQ
T: (01434) 601004 & 600492

Corio House ♦♦♦
3 Woodlands, Corbridge Road,
Hexham, Northumberland
NE46 1HT
T: (01434) 603370 &
07790 397161

**Dene House
♦♦♦♦ SILVER AWARD**
Juniper, Hexham,
Northumberland NE46 1SJ
T: (01434) 673413
F: (01434) 673413
E: margaret@dene-house.
freeserve.co.uk
I: www.smoothhound.co.
uk/hotels/denehse.html

Dukesfield Hall Farm ♦♦♦
Steel, Hexham, Northumberland
NE46 1SH
T: (01434) 673634
E: cath@dukesfield.netlineuk.
net

Dukeslea ♦♦♦♦
32 Shaws Park, Hexham,
Northumberland NE46 3BJ
T: (01434) 602947
F: (01434) 602947
E: kukeslea@hotmail.com
I: www.angelfire.
com/id/dukeslea

The Fairway ♦♦♦♦
4 Shaws Park, Hexham,
Northumberland NE46 3BJ
T: (01434) 604846
E: gailcowley@aol.com

**Gairshield Farm
♦♦♦♦ SILVER AWARD**
Whitley Chapel, Hexham,
Northumberland NE47 0HS
T: (01434) 673562

Hetherington ♦♦♦♦
Wark-on-Tyne, Hexham,
Northumberland NE48 3DR
T: (01434) 230260
F: (01434) 230260
E: a_nichol@hotmail.com

529

The Hexham Royal Hotel ◆◆◆
Priestpopple, Hexham,
Northumberland NE46 1PQ
T: (01434) 602270
F: (01434) 604084
E: service@hexham-royal-hotel.
co.uk
I: www.hexham-royal-hotel.co.
uk

High Dalton Farm ◆◆◆
Hexham, Northumberland
NE46 2LB
T: (01434) 673320

High Reins ◆◆◆◆
Leazes Lane, Hexham,
Northumberland NE46 3AT
T: (01434) 603590

Ingarth ◆◆◆◆
Leazes Lane, Hexham,
Northumberland NE46 3AE
T: (01434) 603625 &
07710 419638
E: mattinson@clara.co.uk

Kitty Frisk House
◆◆◆◆ SILVER AWARD
Corbridge Road, Hexham,
Northumberland NE46 1UN
T: (01434) 601533
F: (01434) 601533
E: alan@kittyfriskhouse.co.uk

Laburnum House ◆◆◆◆
23 Leazes Crescent, Hexham,
Northumberland NE46 3JZ
T: (01434) 601828

Number 18 Hextol Terrace
◆◆◆
Hexham, Northumberland
NE46 2DF
T: (01434) 602265

Old Redhouse Farm ◆◆◆◆
Dipton Mill, Hexham,
Northumberland NE46 1XY
T: (01434) 604463
E: susanbradley@ukonline.co.uk

Peth Head Cottage ◆◆◆◆
Juniper, Steel, Hexham,
Northumberland NE47 0LA
T: (01434) 673286
F: (01434) 673038
E: 113736.1113@compuserve.
com
I: pethheadcottage.ntb.org.uk

Queensgate House ◆◆◆
Cockshaw, Hexham,
Northumberland NE46 3QU
T: (01434) 605592
F: (01434) 608940
E: njareed@aol.com

Rose and Crown Inn ◆◆◆
Main Street, Slaley, Hexham,
Northumberland NE47 0AA
T: (01434) 673263
F: (01434) 673305

Rye Hill Farm ◆◆◆◆
Slaley, Hexham,
Northumberland NE47 0AH
T: (01434) 673259
F: (01434) 673259
E: enquiries@consult-courage.
co.uk
I: www.smoothhound.co.
uk/hotels/ryehill.html
◉

4 St Cuthberts Terrace ◆◆◆
Hexham, Northumberland
NE46 2EL
T: (01434) 604151
F: (01434) 604151

Thistlerigg Farm ◆◆◆
High Warden, Hexham,
Northumberland NE46 4SR
T: (01434) 602041 &
07790 384675
F: (01434) 602041

Topsy Turvy ◆◆◆◆
9 Leazes Lane, Hexham,
Northumberland NE46 3BA
T: (01434) 603152
E: topsy.turvy@ukonline.co.uk

Ventnor House ◆◆◆
23 Elvaston Road, Hexham,
Northumberland NE46 2HA
T: (01434) 607814

West Close House
◆◆◆◆ GOLD AWARD
Hextol Terrace, Hexham,
Northumberland NE46 2AD
T: (01434) 603307 &
07971 529949

West Wharmley ◆◆◆◆
Hexham, Northumberland
NE46 2PL
T: (01434) 674227 &
07788 711112

Westbrooke Hotel ◆◆◆
Allendale Road, Hexham,
Northumberland NE46 2DE
T: (01434) 603818

Woodley Field ◆◆◆
Allendale Road, Hexham,
Northumberland NE46 2NB
T: (01434) 601600 &
07801 057407

HIGH SHINCLIFFE
Durham
Shincliffe Station House ◆◆◆
High Shincliffe, Durham
DH1 2TE
T: (0191) 384 6906
E: joan@shincliffe.demon.co.uk
I: www.shincliffe.demon.co.uk

HOLY ISLAND
Northumberland
Britannia ◆◆◆
Britannia House, Holy Island,
Berwick-upon-Tweed,
Northumberland TD15 2RX
T: (01289) 389218

The Bungalow ◆◆◆◆
Holy Island, Berwick-upon-
Tweed, Northumberland
TD15 2SE
T: (01289) 389308
E: bungalow@celtic121.demon.
co.uk
I: www.lindisfarne.org.
uk/bungalow

Crown & Anchor Hotel ◆◆◆
Market Place, Holy Island,
Berwick-upon-Tweed,
Northumberland TD15 2RX
T: (01289) 389215
F: (01289) 389215

Open Gate ◆◆◆◆
Marygate, Holy Island, Berwick-
upon-Tweed, Northumberland
TD15 2SD
T: (01289) 389222
E: theopengateatheopengate.
mdo.co.uk
I: www.theopengate.org.uk

The Ship ◆◆◆
Marygate, Holy Island, Berwick-
upon-Tweed, Northumberland
TD15 2SJ
T: (01289) 389311
F: (01289) 389316
E: theship@holyissland7.
freeserve.co.uk
I: www.
lindisfarneaccommodate.com

HORSLEY
Northumberland
Belvedere ◆◆◆◆
Harlow Hill, Horsley, Newcastle
upon Tyne NE15 0QD
T: (01661) 853689

HOUSESTEADS
Northumberland
Moss Kennels Farm ◆◆◆◆
Housesteads, Hexham,
Northumberland NE47 9NL
T: (01434) 344016 &
07889 111885
F: (01434) 344016
◉

HUMSHAUGH
Northumberland
**Haughton Strother Bed and
Breakfast** ◆◆◆◆
Haughton Strother House,
Humshaugh, Hexham,
Northumberland NE46 4BX
T: (01434) 681438
F: (01434) 681438
E: joycehhunt@hotmail.com

HUTTON MAGNA
Durham
Rokeby Close Farm ◆◆◆◆
Hutton Magna, Richmond,
North Yorkshire DL11 7HN
T: (01833) 627171 &
07710 745961
F: (01833) 627662
E: don.wilkinson@farmline.com
◉

KIELDER
Northumberland
Deadwater Farm ◆◆◆◆
Kielder, Hexham,
Northumberland NE48 1EW
T: (01434) 250216

Gowanburn ◆◆
Kielder, Hexham,
Northumberland NE48 1HL
T: (01434) 250254

KIELDER WATER
Northumberland
**The Pheasant Inn (by Kielder
Water)** ◆◆◆◆
Stannersburn, Falstone, Hexham,
Northumberland NE48 1DD
T: (01434) 240382
F: (01434) 240382
E: thepheasantinn@
kielderwater.demon.co.uk
◉

Ridge End Farm ◆◆◆◆
Falstone, Hexham,
Northumberland NE48 1DE
T: (01434) 240395
E: ridge_end_farm@talk21.com

KIRKWHELPINGTON
Northumberland
Cornhills Farmhouse
◆◆◆◆ SILVER AWARD
Cornhills, Kirkwhelpington,
Newcastle upon Tyne NE19 2RE
T: (01830) 540232
F: (01830) 540538
E: cornhills@farming.co.uk
I: www.cornhillsfarmhouse.ntb.
org.com

LANCHESTER
Durham
**Maiden Hall Farmhouse Bed
and Breakfast** ◆◆◆
Maiden Law, Lanchester,
Durham, Co Durham DH7 0QX
T: (01207) 520796 &
07932 973686

LONGFRAMLINGTON
Northumberland
The Angler's Arms ◆◆◆◆
Weldon Bridge,
Longframlington,
Northumberland NE65 8AX
T: (01665) 570655 & 570271
F: (01665) 570041

Besom Byre ◆◆◆◆
Longframlington, Morpeth,
Northumberland NE65 8EN
T: (01665) 570136
F: (01665) 570136

Lee Farm
◆◆◆◆ SILVER AWARD
Longframlington, Morpeth,
Northumberland NE65 8JQ
T: (01665) 570257
E: susanleefarm@talk21.com

LONGHORSLEY
Northumberland
The Baronial ◆◆◆
Cross Cottage, Longhorsley,
Morpeth, Northumberland
NE65 8TD
T: (01670) 788379
F: (01670) 788378

Kington ◆◆◆
East Linden, Longhorsley,
Morpeth, Northumberland
NE65 8TH
T: (01670) 788554
F: (01670) 788747
E: clive@taylor-services.
freeserve.co.uk

Thistleyhaugh Farm ◆◆◆◆◆
Longhorsley, Morpeth,
Northumberland NE65 8RG
T: (01665) 570629
F: (01665) 570629

LOWICK
Northumberland
Black Bull Inn ◆◆◆◆
Main Street, Lowick, Berwick-
upon-Tweed TD15 2UA
T: (01289) 388228
F: (01289) 388395
E: tom@blackbullowick.
freeserve.co.uk

High Steads ◆◆◆◆
Lowick, Berwick-upon-Tweed
TD15 2QE
T: (01289) 388689 &
07850 108305
F: (01289) 388689
E: highstead@aol.com
I: www.lindisfarne.org.
uk/accommodation

The Old Manse ♦♦♦♦
5 Cheviot View, Lowick, Berwick-upon-Tweed, Northumberland
TD15 2TY
T: (01289) 388264
F: (01289) 388264
E: glenc99@aol.com

Southwood ♦♦♦♦
75 Main Street, Lowick, Berwick-upon-Tweed, Northumberland
TD15 2UD
T: (01289) 388619
F: (01289) 388619
E: anne.waite@virgin.net
I: www.freespace.virgin.net/anne.waite

MARLEY HILL
Tyne and Wear

Hedley Hall
♦♦♦♦ SILVER AWARD
Hedley Lane, Marley Hill,
Newcastle upon Tyne NE16 5EH
T: (01207) 231835
I: sfr1008452@aol.com

MATFEN
Northumberland

Matfen High House ♦♦♦♦
Matfen, Newcastle upon Tyne
NE20 0RG
T: (01661) 886592
F: (01661) 886592
E: struan@struan.enterprise-plc.com

MICKLETON
Durham

Pine Grove ♦♦♦
Lowside, Mickleton, Barnard
Castle, County Durham
DL12 0JR
T: (01833) 640886
E: chris@cgillings.freeserve.co.uk
I: www.barnardcastleindex.i12.com

MIDDLETON
Northumberland

East Shaftoe Hall ♦♦♦♦
Middleton, Morpeth,
Northumberland NE61 4EA
T: (01830) 530249
F: (01830) 530249
E: shaftoe.fsbusiness.co.uk
I: www.s-h-systems.co.uk/hotels/eastshaf.html

MIDDLETON-IN-TEESDALE
Durham

Belvedere House ♦♦♦
54 Market Place, Middleton-in-Teesdale, Barnard Castle, County
Durham DL12 0QH
T: (01833) 640884
F: (01833) 640884
E: infobelvedere@thecoachhouse.net
I: www.thecoachhouse.net

Bluebell House ♦♦♦
Market Place, Middleton-in-Teesdale, Barnard Castle, County
Durham DL12 0QG
T: (01833) 640584

Brunswick House ♦♦♦♦
55 Market Place, Middleton-in-Teesdale, Barnard Castle, County
Durham DL12 0QH
T: (01833) 640393
F: (01833) 640393
E: brunswick@teesdaleonline.co.uk
I: www.brunswickhouse.net

Grove Lodge ♦♦♦♦
Hude, Middleton-in-Teesdale,
Barnard Castle, County Durham
DL12 0QW
T: (01833) 640798

Ivy House ♦♦♦
Stanhope Road, Middleton-in-Teesdale, Barnard Castle, County
Durham DL12 0RT
T: (01833) 640603

Lonton South Farm ♦♦♦
Middleton-in-Teesdale, Barnard
Castle, County Durham
DL12 0PL
T: (01833) 640409

Marketplace Guest House ♦♦♦
16 Market Place, Middleton-in-Teesdale, Barnard Castle, County
Durham DL12 0QG
T: (01833) 640300

Snaisgill Farm ♦♦
Middleton-in-Teesdale, Barnard
Castle, County Durham
DL12 0RP
T: (01833) 640343

Wemmergill Hall Farm ♦♦♦
Lunedale, Middleton-in-Teesdale, Barnard Castle, County
Durham DL12 0PA
T: (01833) 640379
F: (01833) 640379

MORPETH
Northumberland

Allendale House ♦♦♦
7 Howard Terrace, Morpeth,
Northumberland NE61 1HU
T: (01670) 504763

The Baker's Chest ♦♦♦
Hartburn, Morpeth,
Northumberland NE61 4JB
T: (01670) 772214
F: (01670) 772363
E: swsfilt@dial.pipex.com

Cottage View Guest House ♦♦♦
6 Staithes Lane, Morpeth,
Northumberland NE61 1TD
T: (01670) 518550
F: (01670) 510840
E: cottageview.morpeth@virgin.net
I: www.cottageview.co.uk

Elder Cottage ♦♦♦♦
High Church, Morpeth,
Northumberland NE61 2QT
T: (01670) 517664
F: (01670) 517644
E: cook@eldercot.freeserve.co.uk

Newminster Cottage ♦♦♦♦
Auburn Place, Morpeth,
Northumberland NE61 1QL
T: (01670) 503124

Riverside Bed and Breakfast ♦♦♦
77 Newgate Street, Morpeth,
Northumberland NE61 1BX
T: (01670) 515026
F: (01670) 514647
I: www.morpethnet.co.uk/accommodation/riverside

NEW BRANCEPETH
Durham

Alum Waters Guest House ♦♦♦
Unthank Farmhouse, Alum
Waters, New Brancepeth,
Durham DH7 7JJ
T: (0191) 373 0628
F: (0191) 373 0628
E: tony@alumwaters.freeserve.co.uk

NEWBIGGIN-BY-THE-SEA
Northumberland

Seaton House ♦♦♦
20 Seaton Avenue, Newbiggin-by-the-Sea, Northumberland
NE64 6UX
T: (01670) 816057

NEWBROUGH
Northumberland

Allerwash Farmhouse ♦♦♦♦♦ SILVER AWARD
Newbrough, Hexham,
Northumberland NE47 5AB
T: (01434) 674574
F: (01434) 674574

Newbrough Park ♦♦♦♦ GOLD AWARD
Newbrough, Hexham,
Northumberland NE47 5AR
T: (01434) 674545
F: (01434) 674544

NEWCASTLE UPON TYNE
Tyne and Wear

Avenue Hotel ♦♦♦
2 Manor House Road, Jesmond,
Newcastle upon Tyne NE2 2LU
T: (0191) 281 1396
F: (0191) 281 6588

Chirton House Hotel ♦♦♦
46 Clifton Road, Off Grainger
Park Road, Newcastle upon
Tyne, NE4 6XH
T: (0191) 273 0407 & 273 3454
F: (0191) 273 0407

Dene Hotel ♦♦♦
38-42 Grosvenor Road,
Jesmond, Newcastle upon Tyne
NE2 2RP
T: (0191) 281 1502
F: (0191) 281 8110

Eldon Hotel ♦♦
24 Akenside Terrace, Jesmond,
Newcastle upon Tyne NE2 1TN
T: (0191) 281 2562
F: (0191) 213 0546
E: enquiries@acornproperties.freeserve.co.uk

Jesmond Park Hotel ♦♦♦
74-76 Queens Road, Jesmond,
Newcastle upon Tyne NE2 2PR
T: (0191) 281 2821 & 281 1913
F: (0191) 281 0515
E: vh@dilston11.freeserve.co.uk
I: www.jesmondpark.freeserve.co.uk

The Keelman's Lodge ♦♦♦♦
Grange Road, Newburn,
Newcastle upon Tyne NE15 8NL
T: (0191) 267 1689 & 267 0772
F: (0191) 499 0041
E: admin@petersen-stainless.co.uk
I: www.petersen-stainless.co.uk

The Lynnwood ♦♦♦
1 Lynwood Terrace, Newcastle
upon Tyne, NE4 6UL
T: (0191) 273 3497
F: (0191) 273 3497

University of Northumbria Claude Gibb Hall's of Residence ♦♦
Ellison Place, Newcastle upon
Tyne, NE1 8ST
T: (0191) 227 4024
F: (0191) 227 3197
E: carmel.wright@unn.ac.uk
I: www.unn.ac.uk/samu6

Westland Hotel ♦♦♦
27 Osborne Avenue, Jesmond,
Newcastle upon Tyne, Tyne and
Wear NE2 1JR
T: (0191) 281 0412
F: (0191) 281 5005

NEWFIELD
Durham

The Newfield Inn ♦♦♦
New Field Road, Newfield,
Chester-le-Street, County
Durham DH2 2SP
T: (0191) 370 0565 & 370 3988

NEWTON
Northumberland

Crookhill Farm ♦♦♦
Newton, Stocksfield,
Northumberland NE43 7UX
T: (01661) 843117
F: (01661) 844702

NINEBANKS
Northumberland

Manor House Farm ♦♦♦
Ninebanks, Hexham,
Northumberland NE47 8DA
T: (01434) 345068
F: (01434) 345068
E: manorhouse@ukonline.co.uk
I: www.manorhouse.ntb.org.uk

NORHAM
Northumberland

Dromore House ♦♦♦
12 Pedwell Way, Norham,
Berwick-upon-Tweed,
Northumberland TD15 2LD
T: (01289) 382313

Threeways ♦♦♦♦
Norham, Berwick-upon-Tweed,
Northumberland TD15 2JZ
T: (01289) 382795

NORTH HYLTON
Tyne and Wear

The Shipwrights Hotel ♦♦♦
Ferry Boat Lane, North Hylton,
Sunderland, Tyne & Wear
SR5 3HW
T: (0191) 549 5139
F: (0191) 549 7464

NORTH SUNDERLAND
Northumberland

132 Main Street
♦♦♦♦ SILVER AWARD
North Sunderland, Seahouses,
Northumberland NE68 7TZ
T: (01665) 720729

NORTON
Tees Valley

Grange Guest House ♦♦♦
33 Grange Road, Norton,
Stockton-on-Tees TS20 2NS
T: (01642) 552541
I: www.shlwell.co.uk

OTTERBURN
Northumberland

Butterchurn Guest House ♦♦♦
Main Street, Otterburn,
Northumberland NE19 1NP
T: (01830) 520585
F: (01830) 520874
E: keith@butterchurn.freeserve.
co.uk
I: www.butterchurn.freeserve.co.
uk

**Dunns Houses Farmhouse Bed
and Breakfast ♦♦♦♦**
Dunns Houses, Otterburn,
Newcastle upon Tyne NE19 1LB
T: (01830) 520677 Et 0780 859
2701
F: (01830) 520677
E: dunnshouses@hotmail.com
I: www.dunnshouse.ntb.org.uk

Field House Guesthouse ♦♦♦
Main Street, Otterburn,
Newcastle upon Tyne NE19 1NP
T: (01830) 520532
F: (01830) 520532

Low Byrness ♦♦♦♦
Rochester, Newcastle upon Tyne
NE19 1TF
T: (01830) 520648
F: (01830) 520733
E: pdq@globalnet.co.uk

Redesdale Arms Hotel ♦♦♦♦
Rochester, Otterburn, Newcastle
upon Tyne NE19 1TA
T: (01830) 520668
F: (01830) 520063

OVINGTON
Northumberland

Ovington House ♦♦♦♦
Ovington, Prudhoe,
Northumberland NE42 6DH
T: (01661) 832442
F: (01661) 832442
E: ovhouse@talk21.com

Southcroft ♦♦♦♦
Ovington, Prudhoe,
Northumberland NE42 6EE
T: (01661) 830651 Et 832515
F: (01661) 834312

PIERCEBRIDGE
Durham

The Bridge House ♦♦♦
Piercebridge, Darlington, County
Durham DL2 3SG
T: (01325) 374727

Holme House ♦♦♦
Piercebridge, Darlington, County
Durham DL2 3SY
T: (01325) 374280
F: (01325) 374280
E: graham@holmehouse22.
freeserve.co.uk
I: www.destinationengland.co.
uk/holmehousse.html

PITY ME
Durham

**The Lambton Hounds Inn
♦♦♦**
Front Street, Pity Me, Durham,
County Durham DH1 5DE
T: (0191) 386 4742
F: (0191) 375 0805

PLAWSWORTH
Durham

Lilac Cottage ♦♦
Wheatley Well Lane,
Plawsworth, Chester-le-Street,
County Durham DH2 3LD
T: (0191) 371 2969

PONTELAND
Northumberland

Hazel Cottage ♦♦♦♦
Eachwick, Dalton, Newcastle
upon Tyne, Northumberland
NE18 0BE
T: (01661) 852415
F: (01661) 854797
E: hazelcottage@eachwick.
fsbusiness.co.uk

Stone Cottage ♦♦♦
Prestwick Road End, Ponteland,
Newcastle upon Tyne NE20 9BX
T: (01661) 823957 Et 823947
E: klee@euphony.net

QUEBEC
Durham

Hamsteels Inn ♦♦
Front Street, Quebec, Durham,
County Durham DH7 9DF
T: (0191) 373 7604
F: (0191) 373 7604

REDBURN
Northumberland

The Willows ♦♦♦
Redburn, Hexham,
Northumberland NE47 7EA
T: (01434) 344665

REDCAR
Tees Valley

Claxton Hotel ♦♦♦
196 High Street, Redcar,
Cleveland TS10 3AW
T: (01642) 486745
F: (01642) 486522

Falcon Hotel ♦♦♦
13 Station Road, Redcar,
Cleveland TS10 1AH
T: (01642) 484300

RIDING MILL
Northumberland

Broomley Fell Farm ♦♦♦
Riding Mill, Northumberland
NE44 6AY
T: (01434) 682682 Et
07802 676143
E: broomley@aol.com

**Low Fotherley Farmhouse Bed
and Breakfast ♦♦♦♦**
Riding Mill, Northumberland
NE44 6BB
T: (01434) 682277
F: (01434) 682277
E: hugh@lowfotherley.fsnet.co.
uk
I: www.westfarm.freeserve.co.uk

Woodside House ♦♦♦
Sandy Bank, Riding Mill,
Northumberland NE44 6HS
T: (01434) 682306

ROMALDKIRK
Durham

Mill Riggs Cottage ♦♦♦
Romaldkirk, Barnard Castle,
County Durham DL12 9EW
T: (01833) 650392

ROOKHOPE
Durham

High Brandon ♦♦♦♦
Rookhope, Bishop Auckland,
County Durham DL13 2AF
T: (01388) 517673
E: highbrandonbt@aol.com
I: members.aol.
com/highbrandonbb

ROTHBURY
Northumberland

Alexandra House ♦♦♦♦
High Street, Rothbury, Morpeth,
Northumberland NE65 7TE
T: (01669) 621463

The Haven ♦♦♦
Backcroft, Rothbury, Morpeth,
Northumberland NE65 7YA
T: (01669) 620577 Et
07885 431814
F: (01669) 620577
E: dogmikec@aol.com

**Katerina's Guest House
♦♦♦♦**
Sun Buildings, High Street,
Rothbury, Morpeth,
Northumberland NE65 7TQ
T: (01669) 620691 Et
07977 555692

Lorbottle West Steads ♦♦♦
Thropton, Morpeth,
Northumberland NE65 7JT
T: (01665) 574672
F: (01665) 574672
E: helen.farr@farming.co.uk
I: www.destination-england.co.
uk/lorbottle.html

Newcastle Hotel ♦♦♦
Rothbury, Morpeth,
Northumberland NE65 7UT
T: (01669) 620334
F: (01669) 620334

Orchard Guest House ♦♦♦♦
High Street, Rothbury, Morpeth,
Northumberland NE65 7TL
T: (01669) 620684
E: jpickard@orchardguesthouse.
co.uk
I: www.orchardguesthouse.co.uk

Silverton House ♦♦♦♦
Silverton Lane, Rothbury,
Morpeth, Northumberland
NE65 7RJ
T: (01669) 621395
E: maggie.wallacel@virgin.net

Silverton Lodge
♦♦♦♦ SILVER AWARD
Silverton Lane, Rothbury,
Morpeth, Northumberland
NE65 7RJ
T: (01669) 620144
F: (01669) 621920
E: silverton.lodge@btinternet.
com
I: www.silvertonlodge.ntb.org.uk

Wagtail Farm ♦♦♦
Rothbury, Morpeth,
Northumberland NE65 7PL
T: (01669) 620367

**Whitton Farmhouse Hotel
♦♦♦**
Whitton, Rothbury, Morpeth,
Northumberland NE65 7RL
T: (01669) 620811
F: (01669) 620811

RUNSWICK
Tees Valley

Newholme ♦♦♦
8 Hinderwell Lane, Runswick,
Saltburn-by-the-Sea, Cleveland
TS13 5HR
T: (01947) 840358

RUSHYFORD
Durham

Garden House ♦♦♦♦
Windlestone Park, Windlestone,
Rushyford, Ferryhill, County
Durham DL17 0LZ
T: (01388) 720217 Et 0797 929
7374

RYTON
Tyne and Wear

Hedgefield House ♦♦♦
Stella Road, Ryton, Newcastle
upon Tyne, Tyne and Wear
NE21 4LR
T: (0191) 413 7373 Et
07958 304942
F: (0191) 413 7373

The Old Manse ♦♦♦
Barmoor, Ryton, Tyne and Wear
NE40 3BD
T: (0191) 413 2438

ST JOHN'S CHAPEL
Durham

**Low Chesters Guesthouse
Rating Applied For**
St John's Chapel, Bishop
Auckland, County Durham
DL13 1QP
T: (01388) 537406

SALTBURN-BY-THE-SEA
Tees Valley

The Rose Garden ♦♦♦♦
20 Hilda Place, Saltburn-by-the-
Sea, Cleveland TS12 1BP
T: (01287) 622947
F: (01287) 622947
I: www.therosegarden.co.uk

SEAHOUSES
Northumberland

Elford Farmhouse ♦♦♦♦
Elford, Seahouses,
Northumberland NE68 7UT
T: (01665) 720244 Et
07703 582126
F: (01665) 720244
E: bill@elford.totalserve.co.uk

Kingsway ♦♦♦
19 Kings Street, Seahouses,
Northumberland NE68 7XW
T: (01665) 720449
F: (01665) 720449

Leeholme ♦♦♦
93 Main Street, Seahouses,
Northumberland NE68 7TS
T: (01665) 720230 Et 0780 838
1590

Railston House
♦♦♦♦ SILVER AWARD
133 Main Street, North
Sunderland, Seahouses,
Northumberland NE68 7TS
T: (01665) 720912
F: (01665) 721978

Rowena ♦♦♦
99 Main Street, Seahouses,
Northumberland NE68 7TS
T: (01665) 721309

St Aidan Hotel ◆◆◆
1 St Aidans, Seafield Road,
Seahouses, Northumberland
NE68 7SR
T: (01665) 720355
F: (01665) 721989
E: staidan@globalnet.co.uk
I: www.users.globalnet.co.
uk/§staidan/

**Slate Hall Riding Centre
◆◆◆◆**
174 Main Street, Seahouses,
Northumberland NE68 7UA
T: (01665) 720320
F: (01665) 720199
E: ian@slatehall.freeserve.co.uk
I: www.slatehall.ntb.org.uk

Stoneridge ◆◆
15 Quarry Field, Seahouses,
Northumberland NE68 7TB
T: (01665) 720835

**Union Cottage Guest House
◆◆◆◆**
11 Union Street, Seahouses,
Northumberland NE68 7RT
T: (01665) 720521
F: (01665) 720521

Wyndgrove House ◆◆◆
156 Main Street, North
Sunderland, Seahouses,
Northumberland NE68 7UA
T: (01665) 720658

SEATON CAREW
Tees Valley

**Altonlea Lodge Guest House
◆◆◆**
19 The Green, Seaton Carew,
Hartlepool, Cleveland TS25 1AT
T: (01429) 271289
E: enquiries@altonlea.co.uk
I: www.altonlea.co.uk

Durham Hotel ◆
38-39 The Front, Seaton Carew,
Hartlepool, Cleveland TS25 1DA
T: (01429) 236502

Norton Hotel ◆
The Green, Seaton Carew,
Hartlepool, Cleveland TS25 1AR
T: (01429) 268317
F: (01429) 268317
E: steve@leeholme.1.freeserve.
co.uk

SEDGEFIELD
Durham

Forge Cottage ◆◆◆
2 West End, Sedgefield,
Stockton-on-Tees TS21 2BS
T: (01740) 622831 & 620031

Todds House Farm ◆◆◆
Sedgefield, Stockton-on-Tees,
Cleveland TS21 3EL
T: (01740) 620244
F: (01740) 620244
E: edgoosej@aol.com

SHERBURN HOUSE
Durham

Three Horse Shoes Inn ◆◆◆
Running Waters, Sherburn
House, Durham, County Durham
DH1 2SR
T: (0191) 372 0286 & 372 3386
F: (0191) 372 3386
E: m.s.parkinson@
threehorseshoes.fsbosiness.co.
uk
I: www.smoothhounds.co.uk/

SHINCLIFFE
Durham

**The Bracken Hotel
◆◆◆◆ SILVER AWARD**
Bank Foot, Shincliffe, Durham
DH1 2PD
T: (0191) 386 2966
F: (0191) 384 5423

SHOTLEY BRIDGE
Durham

**The Manor House Inn
◆◆◆◆ SILVER AWARD**
Carterway Heads, Shotley
Bridge, Consett, County Durham
DH8 9LX
T: (01207) 255268 & 255332
F: (01207) 255268
I: www.scoot.co.uk/manor.
house/

SIMONBURN
Northumberland

Simonburn Guest House ◆◆◆
1 The Mains, Simonburn,
Hexham, Northumberland
NE48 3AW
T: (01434) 681321 &
07801 229866

SKELTON
Cleveland

The Wharton Arms ◆◆
133 High Street, Skelton,
Saltburn-by-the-Sea, Cleveland
TS12 2DY
T: (01287) 650618

SLALEY
Northumberland

Flothers Farm ◆◆◆
Slaley, Hexham,
Northumberland NE47 0BJ
T: (01434) 673240 & 673587
F: (01434) 673240

Rosyth Bed & Breakfast ◆◆◆
Slaley, Hexham,
Northumberland NE47 0AA
T: (01434) 673042

**The Strothers
◆◆◆◆ SILVER AWARD**
Slaley, Hexham,
Northumberland NE47 0AA
T: (01434) 673417 &
007803 280379
F: (01434) 673417
E: edna.hardy@talk21.com

**Travellers Rest
◆◆◆◆ SILVER AWARD**
Slaley, Hexham,
Northumberland NE47 1TT
T: (01434) 673231
F: (01434) 673906
E: enq@travellersrest.sagehost.
co.uk
I: www.travellersrest.sagesite.co.
uk

SOUTH SHIELDS
Tyne and Wear

Ainsley Guest House ◆◆◆
59 Ocean Road, South Shields,
Tyne and Wear NE33 2JJ
T: (0191) 454 3399 &
07879 461492
F: (0191) 454 3399

**Algarve Guest House
Rating Applied For**
77 Ocean Road, South Shields,
Tyne and Wear NE33 2JJ
T: (0191) 455 3783

Dunlin Guest House ◆◆◆
11 Urfa Terrace, South Shields,
Tyne and Wear NE33 2ES
T: (0191) 456 7442
F: (0191) 456 7442

Forest Guest House ◆◆◆◆
117 Ocean Road, South Shields,
Tyne and Wear NE33 2JL
T: (0191) 454 8160
F: (0191) 454 8160
E: audrey@forestguesthouse.
freeserve.co.uk

The Kingsmere ◆◆◆
9 Urfa Terrace, South Shields,
Tyne and Wear NE33 2ES
T: (0191) 456 0234
F: (0191) 425 5026

Marina Guest House ◆◆◆
32 Seaview Terrace, South
Shields, Tyne and Wear
NE33 2NW
T: (0191) 456 1998
F: (0191) 456 1998

North View ◆◆◆
12 Urfa Terrace, South Shields,
Tyne and Wear NE33 2ES
T: (0191) 454 4950
F: (0191) 454 4950

**Ravensbourne Guest House
Rating Applied For**
106 Beach Road, South Shields,
Tyne and Wear NE33 2NE
T: (0191) 456 5849

River's End Guest House ◆◆◆
41 Lawe Road, South Shields,
Tyne and Wear NE33 2EU
T: (0191) 456 4229
F: (0191) 456 4229

Royale Guest House ◆◆◆
13 Urfa Terrace, South Shields,
Tyne and Wear NE33 2ES
T: (0191) 4559 085

Saraville Guest House ◆◆◆
103 Ocean Road, South Shields,
Tyne and Wear NE33 2JL
T: (0191) 454 1169 &
07961 907435
F: (0191) 454 1169
E: emma@saravillefreeserve.co.
uk

South Shore ◆◆◆
115 Ocean Road, South Shields,
Tyne and Wear NE33 2JL
T: (0191) 454 4049 &
07711 567053
F: (0191) 454 4049

SPENNYMOOR
Durham

The Gables ◆◆◆
10 South View, Middlestone
Moor, Spennymoor, County
Durham DL16 7DF
T: (01388) 817544
E: thegablesghouse@aol.com

Highview Country House ◆◆◆
Kirkmerrington, Spennymoor,
County Durham DL16 7JT
T: (01388) 811006

Idsley House ◆◆◆◆
4 Green Lane, Spennymoor,
Bishop Auckland, County
Durham DL16 6HD
T: (01388) 814237

The Old Vicarage ◆◆◆
7 North Road, Spennymoor,
County Durham DL16 6EW
T: (01388) 420550

SPITTAL
Northumberland

The Roxburgh ◆◆
117 Main Street, Spittal,
Berwick-upon-Tweed,
Northumberland TD15 1RP
T: (01289) 306266

STAMFORDHAM
Northumberland

**The Stamfordham Bay Horse
Inn ◆◆◆◆**
Southside, Stamfordham,
Newcastle upon Tyne NE18 0PB
T: (01661) 886244
E: eric@stamfordham_bay.
freeserve.co.uk

STANHOPE
Durham

**Horsley Hall
◆◆◆◆ SILVER AWARD**
Eastgate, Stanhope, Bishop
Auckland, County Durham
DL13 2LJ
T: (01388) 517239 &
07850 425615
E: hotel@horsleyhall.co.uk
I: www.horsleyhall.co.uk

STANLEY
Durham

Bushblades Farm ◆◆◆
Harperley, Stanley, County
Durham DH9 9UA
T: (01207) 232722

Harperley Hotel ◆◆◆
Harperley, Stanley, County
Durham DH9 9TY
T: (01207) 234011
F: (01207) 232325
E: harperley-hotel@supernet.
com

STANNERSBURN
Northumberland

Spring Cottage ◆◆◆◆
Stannersburn, Hexham,
Northumberland NE48 1DD
T: (01434) 240388

STANNINGTON
Northumberland

**Cheviot View Farmhouse Bed
& Breakfast◆◆◆◆**
North Shotton Farm,
Stannington, Morpeth,
Northumberland NE61 6EU
T: (01670) 789231 &
07711 479035

STARTFORTH
Durham

Royal Star Inn ◆◆
Deerbolt Bank, Startforth,
Barnard Castle, County Durham
DL12 8AG
T: (01833) 637216 &
07711 755176
F: (0191) 259 9099

STOCKSFIELD
Northumberland

Old Ridley Hall ◆◆◆
Stocksfield, Northumberland
NE43 7RU
T: (01661) 842816
E: oldridleyhall@talk21.com

Wheelbirks Farm ◆◆◆
Stocksfield, Northumberland
NE43 7HY
T: (01661) 843378
F: (01661) 844605
E: richardsonsatwheelbirks.ndo.
co.uk
I: www.wheelbirks.ndo.co.uk

**Abingdon and Belmont Guest
House ◆◆◆**
5 St George's Terrace, Roker,
Sunderland, SR6 9LX
T: (0191) 567 2438 &
07973 318210
E: belmontguesthouse@
hotmail.com

Acorn Guest House ◆◆
10 Mowbray Road, Hendon,
Sunderland SR2 8EN
T: (0191) 514 2170

**Anchor Lodge Guest House
◆◆◆**
16 Roker Terrace, Roker
Seafront, Sunderland, Tyne and
Wear SR6 9NB
T: (0191) 567 4154

April Guest House ◆◆◆
12 Saint Georges Terrace, Roker,
Sunderland, Tyne & Wear
SR6 9LX
T: (0191) 565 9550
F: (0191) 565 9550
E: ghunter@aprilguesthouse.
freeserve.co.uk

Areldee Guest House ◆◆◆
18 Roker Terrace, Sunderland,
Tyne and Wear SR6 9NB
T: (0191) 514 1971 &
07775 856335
F: (0191) 514 0678
E: peter@areldeeguesthouse.
freeserve.co.uk

The Ashborne ◆◆◆
7 St George's Terrace, Roker,
Sunderland, Tyne and Wear
SR6 9LX
T: (0191) 565 3997
F: (0191) 565 3997

Beach View ◆◆◆
15 Roker Terrace, Sunderland,
Tyne and Wear SR6 9NB
T: (0191) 567 0719

Braeside Guest House ◆◆
26 Western Hill, Sunderland,
Tyne and Wear SR2 7PH
T: (0191) 565 4801 & 0771 282
8723
F: (0191) 552 4198
I: www.braeside.ntb.org.uk

Brendon House ◆◆◆
49 Roker Park Road, Roker,
Sunderland, Tyne & Wear
SR6 9PL
T: (0191) 548 9303 & 529 2365
E: brendonhouse@hotmail.com

**Brookside Bed and Breakfast
◆◆◆**
6 Brookside Terrace, Tunstall
Road, Sunderland, Tyne & Wear
SR2 7RN
T: (0191) 565 6739

The Chaise Guest House ◆◆
5 Roker Terrace, Roker Seafront,
Sunderland, Tyne & Wear
SR6 9NB
T: (0191) 565 9218
F: (0191) 565 9218
E: thechaise@aol.com

Felicitations ◆◆◆
94 Ewesley Road, High Barnes,
Sunderland, Tyne & Wear
SR4 7RJ
T: (0191) 522 0960
F: (0191) 551 8915

Lemonfield Hotel ◆◆◆
Sea Lane, Seaburn, Sunderland,
Tyne & Wear SR6 8FE
I: (0191) 529 3018 & 529 5735
F: (0191) 529 5952
E: ian@lemonfield.fsnet.co.uk

Mayfield Hotel ◆◆◆
Sea Lane, Seaburn, Sunderland,
Tyne & Wear SR6 8EE
T: (0191) 529 3345
F: (0191) 529 3345

Terrace Guest House ◆◆◆
2 Roker Terrace, Sunderland,
SR6 9NB
T: (0191) 565 0132

The Angel Guest House ◆◆◆
6 Front Street, Swalwell,
Gateshead, Tyne and Wear
NE16 3DW
T: (0191) 496 0186
F: (0191) 496 0186
E: angel@swalwell6.freeserve.
com

Swarland Old Hall ◆◆◆◆
Swarland, Morpeth,
Northumberland NE65 9HU
T: (01670) 787642 &
07801 688153
E: procter@swarlandoldhall.
fsnet.co.uk

Tanfield Garden Lodge ◆◆◆
Tanfield Lane, Tanfield, Stanley,
County Durham DH9 9QF
T: (01207) 282821 & 0797 039
8890
F: (01207) 282821

Tanfield Lane Farm ◆◆◆
Tanfield, Stanley, County
Durham DH9 9QE
T: (01207) 232739

Oak Tree Inn ◆◆
Tantobie, Stanley, County
Durham DH9 9RF
T: (01207) 235445
F: (01207) 230438

Demense Farmhouse ◆◆◆
Thropton, Morpeth,
Northumberland NE65 7LT
T: (01669) 620196

Bracken Hill Weardale ◆◆◆◆
Thornley, Tow Law, Bishop
Auckland, County Durham
DL13 4PQ
T: (01388) 731329

**Martineau Guest House
◆◆◆◆**
57 Front Street, Tynemouth,
North Shields, Tyne and Wear
NE30 4BX
T: (0191) 296 0746
E: martineau.house@
ukgateway.net
I: www.martineau-house.co.uk

Hadrian Hotel ◆◆◆
Wall, Hexham, Northumberland
NE46 4EE
T: (01434) 681232
F: (01434) 681232

St Oswalds Farm ◆◆
Wall, Hexham, Northumberland
NE46 4HB
T: (01434) 681307

Battlesteads Hotel ◆◆◆
Wark, Hexham, Northumberland
NE48 3LS
T: (01434) 230209
F: (01434) 230730
E: info@battlesteads-hotel.co.
uk
I: www.Battlesteads-Hotel.co.uk

Beck 'N' Call ◆◆◆◆
Birling West Cottage,
Warkworth, Morpeth,
Northumberland NE65 0XS
T: (01665) 711653
E: beck-n-call@lineone.net
I: website.lineone.
net/§beck-n-call/

Bide A While ◆◆◆
4 Beal Croft, Warkworth,
Morpeth, Northumberland
NE65 0XL
T: (01665) 711753
F: (01665) 510267

North Cottage ◆◆◆◆
Birling, Warkworth, Morpeth,
Northumberland NE65 0XS
T: (01665) 711263

The Old Manse ◆◆◆◆
20 The Butts, Warkworth,
Morpeth, Northumberland
NE65 0SS
T: (01665) 710850

Willow Lodge ◆◆◆◆
12 The Willows, Washington,
Tyne and Wear NE38 8JE
T: (0191) 419 4363
F: (0191) 419 4363
E: glover@nobrad.demon.co.uk

Ye Olde Cop Shop ◆◆◆◆
6 The Green, Washington
Village, Washington, Tyne and
Wear NE38 7AB
T: (0191) 416 5333
E: yeoldecopshop@btinternet.
com

Ivesley ◆◆◆◆
Waterhouses, Durham DH7 9HB
T: (0191) 373 4324
F: (0191) 373 4757
E: ivesley@msn.com

Wheatside Hotel ◆
Bildershaw Bank, West
Auckland, Bishop Auckland,
County Durham DL14 9PL
T: (01388) 832725
F: (01388) 832485

Bay Horse Inn ◆◆◆◆
West Woodburn, Hexham,
Northumberland NE48 2RX
T: (01434) 270218
F: (01434) 270118

Plevna House ◆◆◆◆
West Woodburn, Hexham,
Northumberland NE48 2RA
T: (01434) 270369 &
07703 778323
F: (01434) 270369
E: plevnaho@aol.com
I: www.plevnahouse.ntb.org.uk

**Toad Hall
◆◆◆◆◆ SILVER AWARD**
Woodburn Park, West
Woodburn, Hexham,
Northumberland NE48 2RA
T: (01434) 270013

Yellow House Farm ◆◆◆◆
Yellow House, West Woodburn,
Hexham, Northumberland
NE48 2RA
T: (01434) 270070

**Lands Farm
◆◆◆◆ SILVER AWARD**
Westgate-in-Weardale, Bishop
Auckland, County Durham
DL13 1SN
T: (01388) 517210

**East Byermoor Guest House
◆◆◆◆**
Fellside Road, Whickham,
Newcastle upon Tyne NE16 5BD
T: (01207) 272687
F: (01207) 272145
E: eastbyermoor-gh.arbon@
virgin.net

The Cara ◆◆
9 The Links, Whitley Bay, Tyne
and Wear NE26 1PS
T: (0191) 253 0172

Chedburgh Hotel ◆◆◆
12 The Esplanade, Whitley Bay,
Tyne and Wear NE26 1AH
T: (0191) 253 0415 & 0780 128
6606
F: (0191) 253 0415
E: scottcarlucci@freenetname.
co.uk

The Glen Esk Guest House
◆◆◆
8 South Parade, Whitley Bay,
Tyne and Wear NE26 2RG
T: (0191) 253 0103 & 291 0128
F: (0191) 252 6017

Marlborough Hotel ◆◆◆◆
20-21 East Parade, The
Promenade, Whitley Bay, Tyne
and Wear NE26 1AP
T: (0191) 251 3628
F: (0191) 252 5033
E: marlborough.hotel@virgin.
net
I: freespace.virgin.
net/marlborough.hotel/

Shan-Gri-La ◆◆◆
29 Esplanade, Whitley Bay, Tyne
and Wear NE26 2AL
T: (0191) 253 0230

The Waterford Arms ◆◆
Collywell Bay Road, Whitley Bay,
Tyne and Wear NE26 4QZ
T: (0191) 237 0450
F: (0191) 237 0450

York House Hotel ◆◆◆◆
30 Park Parade, Whitley Bay,
Tyne and Wear NE26 1DX
T: (0191) 252 8313
F: (0191) 251 3953
E: reservations@
yorkhousehotel.com
I: www.yorkhousehotel.com

WHITTINGHAM
Northumberland

**Callaly Cottage Bed and
Breakfast** ◆◆◆◆
Callaly, Alnwick,
Northumberland NE66 4TA
T: 07712 502284
E: callaly@alnwick.org.uk
I: www.callaly.alnwick.org.uk

WITTON GILBERT
Durham

The Coach House
Rating Applied For
Stobbilee House, Witton Gilbert,
Durham DH7 6TW
T: (0191) 373 6132 &
07802 320439
F: (0191) 373 6711
E: suzanne.cronin@genie.co.uk
I: www.stobbilee.com

Prospect House ◆◆
5 Dene Terrace, Front Street,
Witton Gilbert, Durham, Co
Durham DH7 6SS
T: (0191) 371 0760 &
07932 959238

WOLSINGHAM
Durham

Bay Horse Hotel ◆◆
59 Uppertown, Wolsingham,
Bishop Auckland, County
Durham DL13 3EX
T: (01388) 527220
F: (01388) 528721

Holywell Farm ◆◆◆
Wolsingham, Bishop Auckland,
County Durham DL13 3HB
T: (01388) 527249

The Mill Race Hotel ◆◆◆
8B West End, Wolsingham,
Bishop Auckland, County
Durham DL13 3AP
T: (01388) 526551
F: (01388) 526551

WOOLER
Northumberland

Loreto Guest House ◆◆
1 Ryecroft Way, Wooler,
Northumberland NE71 6BW
T: (01668) 281 350

The Old Manse
◆◆◆◆◆ GOLD AWARD
New Road, Chatton, Alnwick,
Northumberland NE66 5PU
T: (01668) 215343 &
07885 540567
E: chattonbb@aol.com
I: www.oldmansechatton.ntb.
org.uk

Ryecroft Hotel ◆◆◆
28 Ryecroft Way, Wooler,
Northumberland NE71 6AB
T: (01668) 281459 & 281233
F: (01668) 282214
E: dhogg91344@aol.com

Sheileen ◆◆◆◆
Rating Applied For
17 Victoria Road, Wooler,
Northumberland NE71 6DX
T: (01668) 281924
F: (01668) 281026
E: billyates@wjyates.freeserve.
co.uk

Southgate ◆◆◆
20 High Street, Wooler,
Northumberland NE71 6BY
T: (01668) 282004

Tilldale House ◆◆◆◆
34-40 High Street, Wooler,
Northumberland NE71 6BG
T: (01668) 281450
F: (01668) 281450
E: tilldalehouse@freezone.co.uk

West Weetwood Farmhouse
Rating Applied For
West Weetwood, Wooler,
Northumberland NE71 6AQ
T: (01668) 281497
F: (01668) 281497

Winton House ◆◆◆
39 Glendale Road, Wooler,
Northumberland NE71 6DL
T: (01668) 281362
F: (01668) 281362
E: winton.house@virgin.net
I: www.secretkingdom.
com/winton/house.htm

WYLAM
Northumberland

Wormald House ◆◆◆◆
Main Street, Wylam,
Northumberland NE41 8DN
T: (01661) 852529 & 852552
F: (01661) 852529

NORTH WEST

ABBEYSTEAD
Lancashire

Greenbank Farmhouse ◆◆◆
Abbeystead, Lancaster LA2 9BA
T: (01524) 792063
E: tait@greenbankfarmhouse.
freeserve.co.uk
I: www.greenbankfarmhouse.co.
uk

ACCRINGTON
Lancashire

**Horizons Hotel and Restaurant
Traders Brasserie** ◆◆◆
The Globe Centre, St James
Square, Accrington, Lancashire
BB5 0RE
T: (01254) 602020 & 602022
F: (01254) 602021
E: horizonshotel@hotmail.com

ACTON BRIDGE
Cheshire

Manor Farm ◆◆◆◆
Cliff Road, Acton Bridge,
Northwich, Cheshire CW8 3QP
T: (01606) 853181
F: (01606) 853181

AINTREE
Merseyside

Church View Guest House ◆◆
7 Church Avenue, Aintree,
Liverpool L9 4SG
T: (0151) 525 8166

ALLGREAVE
Cheshire

Rose and Crown ◆◆◆
Allgreave, Macclesfield, Cheshire
SK11 0BJ
T: (01260) 227232
F: (01260) 227232

ALPRAHAM
Cheshire

Tollemache Arms ◆◆◆
Chester Road, Alpraham,
Tarporley, Cheshire CW6 9JE
T: (01829) 260030
F: (01829) 260030

ALSAGER
Cheshire

Sappho Cottage ◆◆◆◆
118 Crewe Road, Alsager, Stoke-
on-Trent ST7 2JA
T: (01270) 882033
F: (01270) 883556
E: reception@sappho-cottage.
demon.co.uk
I: www.sappho-cottage.demon.
co.uk

ALTRINCHAM
Greater Manchester

The Lodge at The Bulls Head
◆◆◆◆
Wicker Lane, Hale Barns,
Altrincham, Cheshire WA15 0HG
T: (0161) 903 1300
F: (0161) 903 1301
E: lodge@bullshead.co.uk
I: www.bullshead.co.uk

ANFIELD
Merseyside

Fitzgeralds ◆◆◆
29 Priory Road, Anfield,
Liverpool L4 2RT
T: (0151) 285 9110
F: (0151) 285 9110

APPLETON
Cheshire

Birchdale Hotel ◆◆◆
Birchdale Road, Appleton,
Warrington WA4 5AW
T: (01925) 263662
F: (01925) 860607
E: rfw@birchdalehotel.co.uk
I: www.birchdalehotel.co.uk

ARKHOLME
Lancashire

Redwell Inn ◆◆◆
Kirkby Lonsdale Road, Arkholme,
Carnforth, Lancashire LA6 1BQ
T: (015242) 21240
F: (015242) 21107
E: julie@redwellinn.freeserve.co.
uk

The Tithe Barn ◆◆◆◆
Arkholme, Carnforth, Lancashire
LA6 1AU
T: (015242) 22236
F: (015242) 22207
E: enquiries@tithe-barn.com
I: www.mailerassoc.co.uk

ASHLEY
Greater Manchester

Birtles Farm ◆◆◆◆
Ashley, Altrincham, Cheshire
WA14 3QH
T: (0161) 928 0458

ASHTON-UNDER-LYNE
Greater Manchester

Lynwood Hotel ◆◆◆
3 Richmond Street, Ashton-
under-Lyne, Lancashire OL6 7TX
T: (0161) 330 5358
F: (0161) 330 5358

BACUP
Lancashire
Irwell Inn ◆◆
71 Burnley Road, Bacup,
Lancashire OL13 8DB
T: (01706) 873346

Oakenclough Farm ◆◆◆
Oakenclough Road, Bacup,
Lancashire OL13 9ET
T: (01706) 879319 & 879794
F: (01706) 879319

Pasture Bottom Farm ◆◆◆
Bacup, Lancashire OL13 9UZ
T: (01706) 873790
F: (01706) 873790
E: ha.isherwood@zen.co.uk
I: www.zen.co.uk/home/page/ha.
isherwood

BARLEY
Lancashire
The Pendle Inn ◆◆◆
Barley, Burnley, Lancashire
BB12 9JX
T: (01282) 614808
F: (01282) 614808
E: john@pendleinn.freeserve.co.
uk
I: www.pendleinn.freeserve.co.
uk

BASHALL EAVES
Lancashire
Hodder House B&B ◆◆◆
Hodder House Farm, Mitton
Road, Bashall Eaves, Clitheroe,
Lancashire BB7 3LZ
T: (01254) 826328
F: (01254) 826328
E: heather@hodderhousebb.
freeserve.co.uk
I: www.hodderhousebb.
freeserve.co.uk

BAY HORSE
Lancashire
Stanley Lodge Farmhouse
◆◆◆
Cockerham Road, Bay Horse,
Lancaster LA2 0HE
T: (01524) 791863

BILLINGTON
Lancashire
Rosebury ◆◆◆
51 Pasturelands Drive,
Billington, Clitheroe, Lancashire
BB7 9LW
T: (01254) 822658 & 780 927
4910

BIRKDALE
Merseyside
Belgravia Hotel ◆◆◆
11 Trafalgar Road, Birkdale,
Southport, Merseyside PR8 2EA
T: (01704) 565298
F: (01704) 562728
E: belgravias@aol.com
I: www.hotelsouthport.com

BIRKENHEAD
Merseyside
Shrewsbury Lodge Hotel ◆◆◆
31 Shrewsbury Road, Oxton,
Birkenhead, Merseyside
CH43 2JB
T: (0151) 652 4029 &
07973 776694
F: (0151) 653 4079
E: info@shrewsbury-hotel.com
I: www.shrewsbury-hotel.com

Treetops Guest House ◆◆◆
506 Old Chester Road, Rock
Ferry, Birkenhead, Merseyside
CH42 4PE
T: (0151) 645 0740

Victoria House ◆◆
12 Shrewsbury Road, Oxton,
Birkenhead, Merseyside
CH41 1UX
T: (0151) 652 8379 &
07771 618778

Villa Venezia ◆◆◆
14-16 Prenton Road West,
Birkenhead, Merseyside
CH42 9PN
T: (0151) 608 9212
F: (0151) 608 6671

BLACKBURN
Lancashire
Shalom
Rating Applied For
Livesey Branch Road, Blackburn,
Lancashire BB2 5DF
T: (01254) 209032
F: (01254) 209032
E: paul@shalomblackburn.co.uk

BLACKPOOL
Lancashire
Abbey Hotel ◆◆◆
31 Palatine Road, Blackpool,
FY1 4BX
T: (01253) 624721
F: (01253) 624721
E: abbeybpool@aol.com
I: abbeyhotel-blackpool.co.uk

Adelaide House Hotel ◆◆◆
66-68 Adelaide Street,
Blackpool, FY1 4LA
T: (01253) 625172
F: (01253) 625172

Alderley House ◆◆◆
581 South Promenade,
Blackpool, FY4 1NG
T: (01253) 342173

Arncliffe Hotel ◆◆◆
24 Osborne Road, Blackpool,
FY4 1HJ
T: (01253) 345209 &
07802 438907
F: (01253) 345209
E: arncliffehotel@talk21.com

Ashcroft Hotel ◆◆◆
42 King Edward Avenue,
Blackpool, FY2 9TA
T: (01253) 351538
F: (01253) 351538

Baricia ◆◆◆
40-42 Egerton Road, Blackpool,
FY1 2NW
T: (01253) 623130

Beachcomber Hotel ◆◆◆
78 Reads Avenue, Blackpool,
Lancashire FY1 4DE
T: (01253) 621622
F: (01253) 299254

Beauchief Hotel ◆◆◆
48 King Edward Avenue,
Blackpool, FY2 9TA
T: (01253) 353314
F: (01253) 353314
E: beauchiefhotel@blackpool.
net
I: www.fyldecoast.co.
uk/beauchief

The Beaucliffe Hotel ◆◆◆
20-22 Holmfield Road,
Blackpool, FY2 9TB
T: (01253) 351663
E: info@beaucliffe.
netscapeonline.co.uk
I: www.members.
netscapeonline.co.uk/beaucliffe

Belmont Hotel ◆◆
299 Promenade, Blackpool,
FY1 6AL
T: (01253) 345815
F: (01253) 346102

Berwick Hotel ◆◆◆
23 King Edward Avenue, North
Shore, Blackpool, FY2 9TA
T: (01253) 351496
F: (01253) 351496
E: info@berwickhotel.freeserve.
co.uk
I: www.berwickhotel.freeserve.
co.uk

Berwyn Hotel ◆◆◆◆
1 Finchley Road, Gynn Square,
Blackpool, FY1 2LP
T: (01253) 352896
F: (01253) 594391
I: www.blackpool-holidays.com

Beverley Hotel ◆◆◆
25 Dean Street, Blackpool,
Lancashire FY1 4AU
T: (01253) 344426

Blakely Hotel ◆◆◆
37 Rawcliffe Street, Blackpool,
FY4 1BY
T: (01253) 343044
F: (01253) 343044

Bona Vista Hotel ◆◆◆
104-106 Queens Promenade,
Blackpool, FY2 9NX
T: (01253) 351396
F: (01253) 594985

The Bourne Private Hotel ◆◆
2 Wimbourne Place, New South
Promenade, Blackpool,
Lancashire FY4 1NN
T: (01253) 342930 & 341517
F: (01253) 342930

The Brayton ◆◆◆
7-8 Finchley Road, Gynn Square,
Blackpool, Lancashire FY1 2LP
T: (01253) 351645
F: (01253) 351645
E: brayton@globalnet.co.uk
I: www.users.globalnet.co.
uk/$brayton

Briny View ◆◆
2 Woodfield Road, Blackpool,
FY1 6AX
T: (01253) 346584

Hotel Camelot ◆◆◆
487 Promenade, Blackpool,
FY4 1AZ
T: (01253) 404597 & 341948
F: (01253) 341948

Canasta Hotel ◆◆◆
288 North Promenade,
Blackpool, FY1 2EY
T: (01253) 290501 & 752518
F: (01253) 290501
E: canasta@blackpool.net
I: www.blackpool.
net/canastahotel

Cardoh Lodge ◆◆◆
21 Hull Road, Blackpool,
FY1 4QB
T: (01253) 627755
F: (01253) 292624
E: dougie.hall@virgin.net
I: www.blackpoolhotels.og.
uk/cardohlodge.html

The Cheslyn ◆◆◆
21 Moore Street, Blackpool,
FY4 1DA
T: (01253) 349672

Clifton Court Hotel ◆◆
12 Clifton Drive, Blackpool,
FY4 1NX
T: (01253) 342385
F: (01253) 342358

Cliftonville Hotel ◆◆◆
14 Empress Drive, Blackpool,
Lancashire FY2 9SE
T: (01253) 351052
F: (01253) 590052
I: www.cliftonville-blackpool.co.
uk

Collingwood Hotel ◆◆◆◆
8-10 Holmfield Road, North
Shore, Blackpool, Lancashire
FY2 9SL
T: (01253) 352929
F: (01253) 352929
E: enquiries@collingwoodhotel.
co.uk
I: www.collingwoodhotel.co.uk

Colris Hotel ◆◆◆
209 Central Promenade,
Blackpool, FY1 5DL
T: (01253) 625461

Courtneys of Gynn Square
◆◆◆
1 Warbreck Hill Road, Blackpool,
Lancashire FY2 9SP
T: (01253) 352179 &
07802 786117

Croydon Hotel ◆◆◆◆
12 Empress Drive, Blackpool,
FY2 9SE
T: (01253) 352497

Denely Private Hotel ◆◆
15 King Edward Avenue,
Blackpool, FY2 9TA
T: (01253) 352757

Derwent Hotel ◆◆◆
Rating Applied For
8 Gynn Avenue, North Shore,
Blackpool, Lancashire FY1 2LD
T: (01253) 355194
F: (01253) 355194

Dudley Hotel ◆◆
67 Dickson Road, Blackpool,
FY1 2BX
T: (01253) 620281

Elgin Hotel ◆◆◆
40-42 Queens Promenade,
Blackpool, FY2 9RW
T: (01253) 351433
F: (01253) 353535
I: www.elginhotel.com

Fairway Hotel ◆◆◆
34-36 Hull Road, Blackpool,
Lancashire FY1 4QB
T: (01253) 623777
F: (01253) 753455
E: fair.way@virgin.net
I: www.come.to/fairway

Fern Villa ◆◆
51 Chapel Street, Blackpool,
FY1 5HF
T: (01253) 620984

Fortuna House Hotel ◆◆
32 Rawcliffe Street, Blackpool,
FY4 1BZ
T: (01253) 344604
E: fortunhh@clobalnet.co.uk

Fylde Hotel ◆◆◆
93 Palatine Road, Blackpool,
FY1 4BX
T: (01253) 623735
F: (01253) 622801
E: fyldehotel@talk21.com

The Grand Hotel ◆◆◆
Station Road, Blackpool,
FY4 1EU
T: (01253) 343741
F: (01253) 408228
E: max.smith@lineone.net
I: www.grandholidayflats.co.uk
◎

Granville Hotel ◆◆◆
12 Station Road, Blackpool,
FY4 1BE
T: (01253) 343012
F: (01253) 408594

Happy Return Hotel ◆◆◆
17-19 Hull Road, Blackpool,
FY1 4QB
T: (01253) 622596
F: (01253) 290024

Hartshead Private Hotel ◆◆◆
17 King Edward Avenue,
Blackpool, FY2 9TA
T: (01253) 353133 & 357111

Hertford Hotel ◆◆◆
18 Lord Street, North Shore,
Blackpool, FY1 2BD
T: (01253) 622793
F: (01253) 622793
E: ceges@dircon.co.uk
I: www.ceges.dircon.co.uk

Holmsdale Hotel ◆◆◆
6-8 Pleasant Street, North
Shore, Blackpool, Lancashire
FY1 2JA
T: (01253) 621008
F: 0870 133 1487
E: holmsdale@talk21.com
I: www.hotelblackpool.glo.cc

Homecliffe Hotel ◆◆◆
5-6 Wilton Parade, North
Promenade, Blackpool, FY1 2HE
T: (01253) 625147
F: (01253) 292667
E: douglas@
homecliffe56freeserve.co.uk

Hornby Villa ◆◆◆
130 Hornby Road, Blackpool,
FY1 4QS
T: (01253) 624959
E: hornby.villa@virgin.net

The Hotel Bambi ◆◆◆
27 Bright Street, Blackpool,
FY4 1BS
T: (01253) 343756
F: (01253) 343756

Hurstmere Hotel ◆◆
5 Alexandra Road, Blackpool,
FY1 6BU
T: (01253) 345843
F: (01253) 347188

Inglewood Hotel ◆◆◆
18 Holmfield Road, Blackpool,
FY2 9TB
T: (01253) 351668
F: (01253) 351668
E: elaine_hodgin@talk21.com
I: www.blackpool-hotels.co.
uk/inglewood.html
◎

Jay-Mar Guesthouse ◆◆◆
36 Egerton Road, North Shore,
Blackpool, FY1 2NW
T: (01253) 297626
◎

Jeanne Hotel ◆◆
45 Station Road, Blackpool,
FY4 1EU
T: (01253) 343430

The Kimberley ◆◆◆
25 Gynn Avenue, Blackpool,
FY1 2LD
T: (01253) 352264
◎

Langwith Hotel ◆◆
73 Dickson Road, North Shore,
Blackpool, Lancashire FY1 2BX
T: (01253) 299202

Lynmoore Guest House ◆◆◆
25 Moore Street, Blackpool,
FY4 1DA
T: (01253) 349888

Manor Private Hotel ◆◆◆
32 Queens Promenade,
Blackpool, FY2 9RN
T: (01253) 351446
E: jlm@kmanorhotel.fsnet.co.uk

Marlow Lodge Hotel ◆◆◆
76 Station Road, Blackpool,
Lancashire FY4 1EU
T: (01253) 341580
F: (01253) 408330
E: ofice@blackpool-hotel.co.uk
I: www.blackpool-hotel.co.uk
◎

May-Dene Licensed Hotel
◆◆◆
10 Dean Street, Blackpool,
FY4 1AU
T: (01253) 343464
F: (01253) 401424
◎

Hotel Montclair ◆◆◆
95 Albert Road, Blackpool,
FY1 4PW
T: (01253) 625860

The Moores Hotel ◆◆◆
42 Banks Street, Blackpool,
FY1 2BE
T: (01253) 623638

Motel Mimosa ◆◆
24A Lonsdale Road, Blackpool,
FY1 6EE
T: (01253) 341906

New Bolingbroke Hotel ◆◆◆
36-38 Queens Promenade,
Blackpool, FY2 9RW
T: (01253) 351109
F: (01253) 351109

New Bond Hotel ◆◆◆
72 Lord Street, Blackpool,
FY1 2DG
T: (01253) 628123 & 0771 298
1328

Newholme Private Hotel ◆◆◆
2 Wilton Parade, Blackpool,
FY1 2HE
T: (01253) 624010
I: www.fyldecoast.co.
uk/newholme.

Nordelph Hotel ◆◆◆
9 Empress Drive, Blackpool,
FY2 9SE
T: (01253) 351925
◎

North Crest Hotel ◆◆◆
22 King Edward Avenue,
Blackpool, FY2 9TD
T: (01253) 355937

Northlands Hotel ◆◆◆
31-33 Hornby Road, Blackpool,
FY1 4QG
T: (01253) 625795
F: (01253) 625795
E: northlands.hotel@virgin.net
I: www.freespace.virgin.
nee/northlands.hotel

The Old Coach House
◆◆◆◆◆ SILVER AWARD
50 Dean Street, Blackpool,
FY4 1BP
T: (01253) 349195
F: (01253) 344330
E: blackpool@
theoldcoachhouse.freeserve.co.
uk
I: www.theoldcoachhouse.
freeserve.co.uk

Pembroke Private Hotel
◆◆◆◆
11 King Edward Avenue,
Blackpool, FY2 9TD
T: (01253) 351306
F: (01253) 351306
E: stay@pembroke-blackpool.
freeserve.co.uk
I: www.fyldecoast.co.
uk/pembroke/

Penrhyn Hotel ◆◆◆
38 King Edward Avenue,
Blackpool, Lancashire FY2 9TA
T: (01253) 352762
E: ericpenrhyn@talk21.com

Pickwick Hotel ◆◆◆
93 Albert Road, Blackpool,
FY1 4PW
T: (01253) 624229
F: (01253) 624229

Raffles Hotel ◆◆◆
73-75 Hornby Road, Blackpool,
FY1 4QJ
T: (01253) 294713
F: (01253) 294713

The Robin Hood Hotel ◆◆◆
100 Queens Promenade,
Blackpool, FY2 9NS
T: (01253) 351599

Rosedale Private Hotel ◆◆◆
9 Chatsworth Avenue, Bispham,
Blackpool, Lancashire FY2 9AN
T: (01253) 352661
F: (01253) 352661
I: www.blackpool_internet.co.
uk/homerosedale.html
◎

The Royal Seabank Hotel ◆◆◆
219-221 Central Promenade,
Blackpool, FY1 5DL
T: (01253) 622717 & 622173
F: (01253) 295148
E: seabank@blackpool.net.
I: www.blackpool.
net/wwwroyalseabank
◎

Rutlands Hotel ◆◆◆
13 Hornby Road, Blackpool,
Lancashire FY1 4QG
T: (01253) 623067

Seaforth Hotel ◆◆◆
18 Lonsdale Road, Blackpool,
FY1 6EE
T: (01253) 345820 & 405079
F: (01253) 345820
E: enquiries@seaforthhotel.co.
uk
I: www.seaforthhotel.co.uk

Sheron House ◆◆◆
21 Gynn Avenue, Blackpool
North Shore, Blackpool,
Lancashire FY1 2LD
T: (01253) 354614
I: www.hotels.fg.co.uk/sheron

South Lea Hotel ◆◆◆
4 Willshaw Road, Blackpool,
FY2 9SH
T: (01253) 351940 & 595758
F: (01253) 595758
E: southlea@hotmail.com
I: www.blackpool-holidays.
com/southlea.htm.

Stuart Hotel ◆◆
27-29 Clifton Drive, Blackpool,
Lancashire FY4 1NT
T: (01253) 345485
F: (01253) 406239
◎

Sunnyside Hotel ◆◆◆
36 King Edward Avenue, North
Shore, Blackpool, Lancashire
FY2 9TA
T: (01253) 352031
E: stuart@sunnysidehotel.com
I: www.sunnysidehotel.com
◎

Tiffany's Hotel ◆◆
254-262 North Promenade,
Blackpool, Lancashire FY1 1SA
T: (01253) 313414
F: (01253) 313415
E: enquiries@tiffanys.uk.com
I: www.tiffanys.uk.com

Tudor Rose Original ◆◆◆◆
5 Withnell Road, Blackpool,
FY4 1HF
T: (01253) 343485

Victoria House ◆◆◆
14 Regent Road, Blackpool,
FY1 4LY
T: (01253) 626967
F: (01253) 626967

Vidella Hotel ◆◆◆
80-82 Dickson Road, Blackpool,
FY1 2BU
T: (01253) 624947 & 621201

Waverley Hotel ◆◆◆
95 Reads Avenue, Blackpool,
FY1 4DG
T: (01253) 621633
F: (01253) 753581
E: wavehotel@aol.com
I: blackpool.internet.co.
uk/homewaverleyhote.html
◎

Wescoe Private Hotel ◆◆
14 Dean Street, Blackpool,
Lancashire FY4 1AU
T: (01253) 342772 &
07833 732946
F: (01253) 342772

Westdean Hotel ◆◆◆
59 Dean Street, Blackpool,
FY4 1BP
T: (01253) 342904
F: (01253) 342926
E: mikeball@westdeanhotel.
freeserve.co.uk
I: www.westdeanhotel.com

Wilmar ◆◆◆
42 Osborne Road, Blackpool,
FY4 1HQ
T: (01253) 346229
◎

Wilton Hotel ◆◆◆
108-112 Dickson Road,
Blackpool, FY1 2HF
T: (01253) 627763
F: (01253) 295379
◎

The Windsor Hotel ◆◆◆
21 King Edward Avenue, North
Shore, Blackpool, FY2 9TA
T: (01253) 353735
◎

Windsor Hotel ◆◆◆
53 Dean Street, Blackpool,
FY4 1BP
T: (01253) 400232
F: (01253) 346886
E: reservations@windsorhotel.
co.uk
I: www.windsorhotel.co.uk

Windsor Park Hotel ◆◆◆
96 Queens Promenade,
Blackpool, FY2 9NS
T: (01253) 357025

Wingate Hotel ◆◆
8 Dean Street, Blackpool,
FY4 1AU
T: (01253) 342672
F: (01253) 405085

Yealm Guest House ◆◆
32 Reads Avenue, Blackpool,
FY1 4BP
T: (01253) 625398 & 0800 074
3453
◎

BLUNDELLSANDS
Merseyside
Blundellsands Bed & Breakfast
◆◆◆◆
9 Elton Avenue, Blundellsands,
Liverpool L23 8UN
T: (0151) 924 6947
F: (0151) 924 6947
E: liz@bsbb.freeserve.co.uk

BOLTON
Greater Manchester
Fourways Hotel ◆◆◆
13-15 Bolton Road, Moses Gate,
Farnworth, Bolton BL4 7JN
T: (01204) 573661
F: (01204) 862488
E: fourwayshotel@pureapshalt.
co.uk

Heron Lodge ◆◆◆
8 Bolton Road, Edgworth,
Bolton, BL7 0DS
T: (01204) 852262
F: (01204) 852262
E: heronlodge@hotmail.com

Pelton Fold Farm ◆◆◆◆
Bury Road, Turton, Bolton,
BL7 0BS
T: (01204) 852207

BOLTON-BY-BOWLAND
Lancashire
Copy Nook Hotel ◆◆◆
Bolton-by-Bowland, Clitheroe,
Lancashire BB7 4NL
T: (01200) 447205
F: (01200) 447004
E: copynookhotel@btinternet.
com
I: www.copynookhotel.com

Middle Flass Lodge ◆◆◆◆
Forest Becks Brow, Settle Road,
Bolton-by-Bowland, Clitheroe,
Lancashire BB7 4NY
T: (01200) 447259
F: (01200) 447300
I: www.mflodge.freeservers.
com/

BOLTON-LE-SANDS
Lancashire
Blue Anchor Hotel ◆◆◆
68 Main Road, Bolton-le-Sands,
Carnforth, Lancashire LA5 8DN
T: (01524) 823241 & 824745
F: (01524) 824745

Row Bar ◆◆◆
4 Whin Grove, Bolton-le-Sands,
Carnforth, Lancashire LA5 8DD
T: (01524) 735369

Thwaite End Farm ◆◆◆◆
A6 Road, Bolton-le-Sands,
Carnforth, Lancashire LA5 9TN
T: (01524) 732551
F: (01524) 732551

BOOTLE
Merseyside
Regent Hotel ◆◆
58-62 Regent Road, Bootle,
Merseyside L20 8DG
T: (0151) 922 4090
F: (0151) 922 6308

Rimrose House ◆◆
234 Rimrose Road, Bootle,
Merseyside L20 4QT
T: (0151) 922 4445

BROADHEATH
Greater Manchester
Old Packet House ◆◆◆
Navigation Road, Broadheath,
Altrincham, Cheshire WA14 1LW
T: (0161) 929 1331
F: (0161) 233 0048
E: theoldpackethouse@
cheshireinns.co.uk
I: www.cheshireinns.co.uk

BROMBOROUGH
Merseyside
Dibbinsdale Inn ◆◆
Dibbinsdale Road,
Bromborough, Wirral,
Merseyside CH63 0HJ
T: (0151) 334 5171
F: (0151) 334 0097

Woodlands Guest House ◆◆◆
66 Woodyear Road,
Bromborough, Wirral,
Merseyside CH62 6AZ
T: (0151) 327 3735

BURNLEY
Lancashire
Ormerod Hotel ◆◆◆
121-123 Ormerod Road,
Burnley, Lancashire BB11 3QW
T: (01282) 423255

BURSCOUGH
Lancashire
**Brandreth Barn Brandreth
Farm** ◆◆◆
Tarlscough Lane, Burscough,
Ormskirk, Lancashire L40 0RJ
T: (01704) 893510

Martin Inn ◆◆
Martin Lane, Burscough,
Ormskirk, Lancashire L40 0RT
T: (01704) 892302 &
07768 352216
F: (01704) 895735

BURY
Greater Manchester
Rostrevor Hotel and Bistro
◆◆◆
148 Manchester Road, Bury,
Lancashire BL9 0TL
T: (0161) 764 3944
F: (0161) 764 8266
E: enquiries@rostrevor.co.uk
I: www.rostrevorhotel.co.uk

CALDY
Merseyside
Berrington Guest House ◆◆
Telegraph Road, Caldy, Wirral,
Merseyside CH48 1NZ
T: (0151) 625 2663

Cheriton ◆◆◆◆
151 Caldy Road, Caldy, Wirral,
Merseyside CH48 1LP
T: (0151) 625 5271
F: (0151) 625 5271
E: cheriton151@hotmail.com

CAPERNWRAY
Lancashire
New Capernwray Farm
◆◆◆◆◆ SILVER AWARD
Capernwray, Carnforth,
Lancashire LA6 1AD
T: (01524) 734284
F: (01524) 734284
E: info@newcapfarm.co.uk
I: www.newcapfarm.co.uk

CARNFORTH
Lancashire
Dale Grove ◆◆◆
162 Lancaster Road, Carnforth,
Lancashire LA5 9EF
T: (01524) 733382 &
07974 125426
E: craigie@clara.co.uk
I: home.clara.net/craigie

Galley Hall Farm ◆◆◆◆
Shore Road, Carnforth,
Lancashire LA5 9HZ
T: (01524) 732544

The George Washington ◆◆◆
Main Street, Warton, Carnforth,
Lancashire LA5 9PJ
T: (01524) 732865

Grisedale Farm ◆◆◆◆
Leighton, Carnforth, Lancashire
LA5 9ST
T: (01524) 734360

High Bank ◆◆◆◆
Hawk Street, Carnforth,
Lancashire LA5 9LA
T: (01524) 733827

Longlands Hotel ◆◆◆
Tewitfield, Carnforth, Lancashire
LA6 1JH
T: (01524) 781256
F: (01524) 69393

The Manse Bed and Breakfast
◆◆
74 Kellet Road, Carnforth,
Lancashire LA5 9LP
T: (01524) 732623
F: (01524) 732623

CATON
Lancashire
Ellerdene ◆◆◆◆
85 Horby Road, Caton,
Lancaster, Lancashire LA2 9QR
T: (01524) 770625

Kilcredan ◆
14 Brookhouse Road, Caton,
Lancaster LA2 9QT
T: (01524) 770271

CHEADLE
Greater Manchester
Curzon House ◆◆◆
3 Curzon Road, Heald Green,
Cheadle, Cheshire SK8 3LN
T: (0161) 436 2804

CHEADLE HULME
Greater Manchester
The Governor's House ◆◆◆◆
43 Ravenoak Road, Cheadle
Hulme, Stockport, Cheshire
SK8 7EQ
T: (0161) 488 4222
F: (0161) 486 1850
E: governors.house@yates-bros.
co.uk

Rydal Court Guest House
Rating Applied For
147 Stanley Road, Cheadle
Hulme, Cheadle, Cheshire
SK8 6RF
T: (0161) 436 4454
F: (0161) 498 8316
E: rydalcourt@btinternet.com
I: www.smoothhounds.co.uk

Spring Cottage Guest House
◆◆◆
60 Hulme Hall Road, Cheadle
Hulme, Stockport, Cheshire
SK8 6JZ
T: (0161) 485 1037

CHELFORD
Cheshire
Astle Farm East ◆◆
Chelford, Macclesfield, Cheshire
SK10 4TA
T: (01625) 861270

CHESTER
Cheshire
Abbotsford Court Hotel ◆◆
17 Victoria Road, Chester,
CH2 2AX
T: (01244) 390898
F: (01244) 390898
E: abbotsford_court_hotel@
hotmail.com

Alton Lodge Hotel ◆◆◆
78 Hoole Road, Chester,
CH2 3NT
T: (01244) 310213
F: (01244) 319206
E: enquiries@altonlodge.co.uk
I: www.altonlodge.co.uk
◎

Belgrave Hotel ◆◆
City Road, Chester, CH1 3AE
T: (01244) 312138
F: (01244) 324951
E: satishsharma82@hotmail.
com
I: www.belgravehotel.com

Bowman Lodge ♦♦♦
52 Hoole Road, Chester,
CH2 3NL
T: (01244) 342208
E: cig.davies@virgin.net
I: freespace.virgin.net/cig.
davies/bowman.htm

Buckingham House ♦♦♦
38 Hough Green, Chester,
CH4 8JQ
T: (01244) 678885
F: (01244) 678885

Castle House ♦♦♦
23 Castle Street, Chester,
Cheshire CH1 2DS
T: (01244) 350354
F: (01244) 350354

Cheyney Lodge Hotel ♦♦♦
77-79 Cheyney Road, Chester,
CH1 4BS
T: (01244) 381925

Comfort Inn ♦♦♦♦
74 Hoole Road, Chester,
CH2 3NL
T: (01244) 327542
F: (01244) 344889
E: comfortinn@chestergb.u-net.
com
🏃

The Commercial Hotel ♦♦
St Peters Churchyard, Chester,
Cheshire CH1 2HG
T: (01244) 320749
F: (01244) 348318
I: www.stayhereuk.com

Dee Hills Lodge
Rating Applied For
7 Dee Hills, Boughton, Chester,
CH3 5AR
T: (01244) 325719

Derry Raghan Guest House
♦♦♦
54 Hoole Road, Chester,
CH2 3NL
T: (01244) 318740

Donegal House ♦♦♦
73 Whitchurch Road, Boughton,
Chester, CH3 5QB
T: (01244) 311342 &
07711 586859

Eaton House
Rating Applied For
36 Eaton Road, Handbridge,
Chester, Cheshire CH4 7EN
T: (01244) 680349 & 659021
F: (01244) 659021
E: graham@aol.com

Edwards House Hotel ♦♦♦♦
61-63 Hoole Road, Chester,
CH2 3NJ
T: (01244) 318055
F: (01244) 310948
E: steanerob@sypanet.com
I: www.smoothhound.co.
uk/hotels/edwardhou.html

Golborne Manor ♦♦♦♦
Platts Lane, Hatton Heath,
Chester CH3 9AN
T: (01829) 770310 &
07774 695268
F: (01829) 770370
E: ann.ikin@golbornemanor.co.
uk

Grove House ♦♦♦♦
Holme Street, Tarvin, Chester
CH3 8EQ
T: (01829) 740893
F: (01829) 741769

Grove Villa
Rating Applied For
18 The Groves, Chester, CH1 1SD
T: (01244) 349713
E: grovevilla@tesco.net

**The Guesthouse at Old Hall
Country Club**
Rating Applied For
Aldford Road, Chester, CH3 6EA
T: (01244) 311593 & 311593
F: (01244) 313785
I: www.oldhallcountryclub.com

Hameldaeus
Rating Applied For
9 Lorne Street, Chester, Cheshire
CH1 4AE
T: (01244) 374913
E: joyce33@brunton81.
freeserve.co.uk

Homeleigh Guest House ♦♦♦
14 Hough Green, Chester,
Cheshire CH4 8JG
T: (01244) 676761
F: (01244) 679977
I: www.scoot.co.
uk/homeleigh_guest_house/

Kent House ♦♦
147 Boughton, Chester, Cheshire
CH3 5BH
T: (01244) 324171
F: (01244) 319758
I: kent-house@turner10101.
freeserve.co.uk

Laburnum House
Rating Applied For
2 St Anne Street, Chester,
CH1 3HS
T: (01244) 380313
F: (01244) 380313

Latymer Swiss Hotel
Rating Applied For
82 Hough Green, Chester,
CH4 8JW
T: (01244) 675074
F: (01244) 683413
E: markus@latymerhotel.fsnet
I: www.latymerhotel.com

Laurels ♦♦♦♦
14 Selkirk Road, Curzon Park,
Chester, Cheshire CH4 8AH
T: (01244) 697682
E: howell@ellisroberts.freeserve.
co.uk

Malvern Guest House ♦
21 Victoria Road, Chester,
CH2 2AX
T: (01244) 380865

**Mitchells of Chester Guest
House** ♦♦♦♦ SILVER AWARD
28 Hough Green, Chester,
Cheshire CH4 8JQ
T: (01244) 679004
F: (01244) 659567
E: mitoches@dialstart.net

Newton Hall ♦♦♦♦
Tattenhall, Chester CH3 9AY
T: (01829) 770153
F: (01829) 770655

Recorder Hotel ♦♦♦
19 City Walls, Chester, CH1 1SB
T: (01244) 326580
F: (01244) 401674
E: ebbs@compuserve.com
I: www.ourworld.compuserve.
com/homepages/ebbs

Rowland House ♦♦♦
No 2 Chichester Street, Chester,
Cheshire CH1 4AD
T: (01244) 390967
F: (01244) 390967

Strathearn Guest House
Rating Applied For
38 Hoole Road, Chester,
Cheshire CH2 3NL
T: (01244) 321522
F: (01244) 321522
E: strathearn@breathemail.net

Ten The Groves ♦♦♦
10 The Groves, Chester, Cheshire
CH1 1SD
T: (01244) 317907

Walpole House
Rating Applied For
26 Walpole Street, Chester,
CH1 4HG
T: (01244) 373373
F: (01244) 373373
E: walphse@aol.com

CHILDWALL
Merseyside

The Real McCoy ♦♦
126 Childwall Park Avenue,
Childwall, Liverpool L16 0JH
T: (0151) 722 7116 &
97971 161542

CHORLEY
Lancashire

Conifers Guest House ♦♦♦
121 Wigan Road, Euxton,
Chorley, Lancashire PR7 6JH
T: (01257) 260904

The Original Farmers Arms
♦♦♦
Towngate, Eccleston, Chorley,
Lancashire PR7 5QS
T: (01257) 451594
F: (01257) 453329

Parr Hall Farm ♦♦♦♦
Parr Lane, Eccleston, Chorley,
Lancashire PR7 5SL
T: (01257) 451917
F: (01257) 453749
E: parrhall@talk21.com

CLAUGHTON
Lancashire

The Old Rectory ♦♦♦♦
Claughton, Lancaster LA2 9LA
T: (015242) 21150
F: (015242) 21098
E: info@rectorylancs.co.uk
I: www.rectorylancs.co.uk

CLAYTON-LE-MOORS
Lancashire

Maple Lodge Hotel ♦♦♦
70 Blackburn Road, Clayton-le-
Moors, Accrington, Lancashire
BB5 5JH
T: (01254) 301284
F: (01254) 388152
E: maplelod@aol.com

CLEVELEYS
Lancashire

Briardene Hotel ♦♦♦♦
56 Kelso Avenue, Cleveleys,
Blackpool FY5 3JG
T: (01253) 852312 & 852379
F: (01253) 851190

CLITHEROE
Lancashire

Brooklands ♦♦♦♦
9 Pendle Road, Clitheroe,
Lancashire BB7 1JQ
T: (01200) 422797 & 422797
F: (01200) 422797
E: kenandjean@tesco.net
I: www.ribblevalley.gov.
uk/hotel/brooklan/index.htm
🌐

Don Dino ♦♦♦♦
78-82 Whalley Road, Clitheroe,
Lancashire BB7 1EE
T: (01200) 424450

Mitton Hall Lodgings ♦♦♦
Mitton Road, Mitton, Clitheroe,
Lancashire BB7 9PQ
T: (01254) 826544
F: (01254) 826386

Rakefoot Farm ♦♦♦♦
Chaigley, Clitheroe, Lancashire
BB7 3LY
T: (01995) 61332 &
07889 279063
🌐

Selborne Guest House ♦♦♦
Back Commons, Kirkmoor Road,
Clitheroe, Lancashire BB7 2DX
T: (01200) 423571 & 422236
F: (01200) 423571
E: judithv.barnes@lineone.net

Timothy Cottage ♦♦
Whalley Road, Hurst Green,
Clitheroe, Lancashire BB7 9QJ
T: (01254) 826337 &
07889 194507
F: 07070 600902

COLNE
Lancashire

Blakey Hall Farm ♦♦♦
Red Lane, Colne, Lancashire
BB8 9TD
T: (01282) 863121

Higher Wanless Farm ♦♦♦♦
Red Lane, Barrowford, Nelson,
Lancashire BB8 7JP
T: (01282) 865301
F: (01282) 865823
E: wanlessfarm@bun.com

Hullown Farm ♦♦
Emmott House, School Lane,
Laneshawbridge, Colne,
Lancashire BB8 7EQ
T: (01282) 869789
E: julie@hullown-farm.
in2home.co.uk

Middle Beardshaw Head Farm
♦♦♦
Burnley Road, Trawden, Colne,
Lancashire BB8 8PP
T: (01282) 865257
🌐

Reedymoor Farm ♦♦♦♦
Reedymoor Lane, Foulridge,
Colne, Lancashire BB8 7LJ
T: (01282) 865074

Wickets ♦♦♦♦
148 Keighley Road, Colne,
Lancashire BB8 0PJ
T: (01282) 862002
F: (01282) 859675
E: wickets@colne148.fsnet.co.
uk
🌐

CONDER GREEN
Lancashire
Stork Hotel ◆◆◆
Conder Green, Lancaster
LA2 0AN
T: (01524) 751234
F: (01524) 752660

CONGLETON
Cheshire
Sandhole Farm ◆◆◆◆
Hulme Walfield, Congleton,
Cheshire CW12 2JH
T: (01260) 224419
F: (01260) 224766
E: veronica@sandholefarm.co.uk
I: www.sandholefarm.co.uk
◉ 👣

Yew Tree Farm ◆◆◆◆
North Rode, Congleton, Cheshire
CW12 2PF
T: (01260) 223569
◉

COTTON EDMUNDS
Cheshire
Cotton Farmhouse ◆◆◆◆
Cotton Edmunds, Chester
CH3 7PT
T: (01244) 336699 & 336616
F: (01244) 336699
E: nigelhill@
cottonhmt-freeserve.co.uk

CREWE
Cheshire
Balterley Green Farm ◆◆◆◆
Deans Lane, Balterley Green,
Crewe, Cheshire CW2 5QJ
T: (01270) 820214
E: greenfarm@balterley.fsnet.co.uk

Coole Hall Farm ◆◆◆◆
Hankelow, Crewe, CW3 0JD
T: (01270) 811232

CULCHETH
Cheshire
99 Hob Hey Lane ◆◆◆◆
Culcheth, Warrington WA3 4NS
T: (01925) 763448
F: (01925) 763448

DISLEY
Cheshire
The Grey Cottage ◆◆◆◆
20 Jacksons Edge Road, Disley,
Stockport, Cheshire SK12 2JE
T: (01663) 763286

Waterside Cottage Guest House ◆◆◆◆
Waterside, Disley, Stockport,
Cheshire SK12 2HJ
T: (01663) 764756
T: (01663) 763428
E: waterside@mainlm.freeserve.co.uk
I: www.mainlm.freeserve.co.uk

DUKINFIELD
Greater Manchester
Barton Villa Guest House ◆◆◆
Crescent Road, Dukinfield,
Cheshire SK16 4EY
T: (0161) 330 3952
F: (0161) 285 8488
E: bartonvillas.fsnet.co.uk
◉

DUNSOP BRIDGE
Lancashire
Wood End Farm ◆◆◆◆
Dunsop Bridge, Clitheroe,
Lancashire BB7 3BE
T: (01200) 448223
E: spencers@beatrix-freeserve.co.uk
I: www.members.tripod.co.uk/Woodend

EATON
Cheshire
The Cottage at The Waggon and Horses◆◆◆◆
Manchester Road, Eaton,
Congleton, Cheshire CW12 2JD
T: (01260) 224229
F: (01260) 224238
I: www.waggonandhorses.com

EGERTON
Cheshire
Manor Farm ◆◆◆◆
Egerton, Malpas, Cheshire
SY14 8AW
T: (01829) 720261

GARSTANG
Lancashire
Ashdene ◆◆
Parkside Lane, Nateby, Garstang,
Preston PR3 0JA
T: (01995) 602676 &
07957 745624
E: ashdene@supanet.com

Guy's Thatched Hamlet ◆◆◆
Canalside, St Michael's Road,
Bilsborrow, Garstang, Preston,
Lancashire PR3 0RS
T: (01995) 640010 & 640020
F: (01995) 640141
E: guyshamlet@aol.com
I: www.guysthatchedhamlet.co.uk
◉

Tudor Farm ◆◆◆
Sowerby Road, St Michaels,
Garstang, Preston PR3 0TT
T: (01995) 679717
◉

Woodacre Hall Farm ◆◆◆
Scorton, Preston, Lancashire
PR3 1BN
T: (01995) 602253
F: (01995) 602253

GARSTON
Merseyside
Aplin House Hotel ◆◆
35 Clarendon Road, Garston,
Liverpool L19 6PJ
T: (0151) 427 5047
◉

GAWSWORTH
Cheshire
Rough Hey Farm ◆◆◆◆
Leek Road, Gawsworth,
Macclesfield, Cheshire SK11 0JQ
T: (01260) 252296

GOODSHAW
Lancashire
The Old White Horse ◆◆◆◆
211 Goodshaw Lane, Goodshaw,
Rossendale, Lancashire BB4 8DD
T: (01706) 215474 &
07703 763448

GOOSNARGH
Lancashire
Isles Field Barn ◆◆◆
Syke, Goosnargh, Preston
PR3 2EN
T: (01995) 640398

GREAT ECCLESTON
Lancashire
Cartford Hotel ◆◆◆
Cartford Lane, Little Eccleston,
Preston PR3 0YP
T: (01995) 670166
F: (01995) 671785

GREAT HARWOOD
Lancashire
Royal Hotel ◆◆◆
Station Road, Great Harwood,
Blackburn BB6 7BA
T: (01254) 883541

HAPTON
Lancashire
Eaves Barn Farm ◆◆◆◆
Hapton, Burnley, Lancashire
BB12 7LP
T: (01282) 771591 & 770478
F: (01282) 771591
◉

HESKIN
Lancashire
Farmers Arms ◆◆◆
85 Wood Lane, Heskin, Chorley,
Lancashire PR7 5NP
T: (01257) 451276 & 453562
E: andy@farmersarms.co.uk
I: www.farmersarms.co.uk

HEYSHAM
Lancashire
It'l Do ◆◆◆
15 Oxcliffe Road, Heysham
T: (01524) 850763

HEYWOOD
Greater Manchester
Albany Hotel ◆◆◆
87-89 Rochdale Road East,
Heywood, Lancashire OL10 1PX
T: (01706) 369606
F: (01706) 627914
E: mike@thealbanyhotel.co.uk
I: www.thealbanyhotel.co.uk

HOLMES CHAPEL
Cheshire
Bridge Farm Bed and Breakfast ◆◆◆
Blackden, Jodrell Bank, Holmes
Chapel, Crewe, Cheshire
CW4 8BX
T: (01477) 571202
E: stay@bridgefarm.com
◉

Padgate Guest House ◆◆◆◆
Twemlow Lane, Cranage,
Middlewich, Cheshire CW4 8EX
T: (01477) 534291
F: (01477) 544726

HOOLE
Cheshire
Glann Hotel ◆◆◆
2 Stone Place, Hoole, Chester
CH2 3NR
T: (01244) 344800

Hamilton Court Hotel ◆◆◆◆
5-7 Hamilton Street, Hoole,
Chester CH2 3JG
T: (01244) 345387
F: (01244) 317404
E: hamiltoncourth@aol.com

Holly House Guest House ◆◆◆
1 Stone Place, Hoole, Chester,
Cheshire CH2 3NR
T: (01244) 328967

Oaklea Guest House ◆◆
63 Oaklea Avenue, Hoole,
Chester CH2 3RG
T: (01244) 340516

HORNBY
Lancashire
Castle Hotel
Main Street, Hornby, Lancaster
LA2 8JT
T: (015242) 21204
F: (015242) 22258

HOYLAKE
Merseyside
Crestwood ◆◆◆
25 Drummond Road, Hoylake,
Wirral, Merseyside CH47 4AU
T: (0151) 632 2937

HUXLEY
Cheshire
Higher Huxley Hall ◆◆◆◆
Huxley, Chester CH3 9BZ
T: (01829) 781484
F: (01829) 781142
E: info@huxleyhall.co.uk
I: www.huxleyhall.co.uk

HYDE
Greater Manchester
White House Farm ◆◆◆
Padfield Main Road, Hyde,
Cheshire SK13 1ET
T: (01457) 854695

KIRKBY
Merseyside
Greenbank ◆◆
193 Rowan Drive, Westvale,
Kirkby, Liverpool L32 0SG
T: (0151) 546 9971

KNUTSFORD
Cheshire
Cross Keys Hotel and Restaurant ◆◆◆◆
52 King Street, Knutsford,
Cheshire WA16 6DT
T: (01565) 750404
F: (01565) 750510
E: jburke_1066@aol
I: www.thisischeshire

Laburnum Cottage Guest House ◆◆◆◆
Knutsford Road, Mobberley,
Knutsford, Cheshire WA16 7PU
T: (01565) 872464
F: (01565) 872464
◉

Wash Lane Farm ◆◆
Allostock, Knutsford, Cheshire
WA16
T: (01565) 722215

LANCASTER
Lancashire
Castle Hill Bed and Breakfast ◆◆◆
27 St Mary's Parade, Castle Hill,
Lancaster, LA1 1YX
T: (01524) 849137
F: (01524) 849137
E: gsutclif@aol.com.uk
◉

Edenbreck House ◆◆◆◆
Sunnyside Lane, Lancaster,
LA1 5ED
T: (01524) 32464

Farmers Arms Hotel ◆◆
Penny Street, Lancaster, LA1 1XT
T: (01524) 36368

Grey Court ◆◆
Hasty Brow Road, Hest Bank,
Lancaster, Lancashire LA2 6AF
T: (01524) 822309 & 822309
F: (01524) 825007
E: office@grey-court.freeserve.
co.uk

The Horse and Farrier
Rating Applied For
16 Brock Street, Lancaster,
LA1 1WW
T: (01524) 63491

Lancaster Town House ◆◆◆
11-12 Newton Terrace, Caton
Road, Lancaster, Lancashire
LA1 3PB
T: (01524) 65527
F: (01524) 65527

Low House Farm ◆◆◆
Claughton, Lancaster, LA2 9LA
T: (015242) 21260
E: shirley@lunevalley.freeserve.
co.uk
⊕

Manesty ◆◆◆
36 Scotforth Road, Lancaster,
LA1 4SB
T: (01524) 60611

Middle Holly Cottage ◆◆◆
Middle Holly Lane, Forton,
Preston PR3 1AH
T: (01524) 792399

Priory Bed and Breakfast
◆◆◆◆
15 St Mary's Parade, Castle Hill,
Lancaster, Lancashire LA1 1YX
T: (01524) 845711

Scale Hall Farmhouse Tavern
◆◆◆
Morecambe Road, Lancaster,
LA1 5JB
T: (01524) 69255
F: (01524) 69255

Shakespeare Hotel ◆◆◆◆
96 St Leonardgate, Lancaster,
LA1 1NN
T: (01524) 841041

Station House Bed and
Breakfast ◆◆◆
25 Meeting House Lane,
Lancaster, LA1 1NN
T: (01524) 381060

Wagon and Horses ◆◆◆
St Georges Quay, Lancaster,
LA1 1RD
T: (01524) 382949 & 846094

LANGHO
Lancashire

Petre Lodge Country Hotel
◆◆◆◆
Northcote Road, Langho,
Blackburn BB6 8BG
T: (01254) 245506
F: (01254) 245506
E: aslambert@fsbdial.co.uk
⊕

LEYLAND
Lancashire

Oxen House Farm ◆◆◆
204 Longmeanygate, Leyland,
Preston, Lancashire PR5 3TB
T: (01772) 423749

LITHERLAND
Merseyside

Litherland Park Bed and
Breakfast ◆◆◆
34 Litherland Park, Litherland,
Bootle, Merseyside L21 9HP
T: (0151) 928 1085 & 0794 217
2357

LITTLEBOROUGH
Greater Manchester

Hollingworth Lake Bed and
Breakfast ◆◆◆◆
164 Smithy Bridge Road,
Hollingworth Lake,
Littleborough, Lancashire
OL15 0DB
T: (01706) 376583 &
07714 341078
E: hollingworth@zoom.co.uk

Swing Cottage ◆◆◆◆
31 Lakebank, Hollingworth Lake
Country Park, Littleborough,
Lancashire OL15 0DQ
T: (01706) 379094
F: (01706) 379091
E: swingcottage@compuserve.
com
I: www.hollingworthlake.com

LIVERPOOL
Merseyside

Aachen Hotel ◆◆◆
89-91 Mount Pleasant,
Liverpool, Merseyside L3 5TB
T: (0151) 709 3477 & 709 3633
F: (0151) 709 1126
I: www.merseyworld.
com/aachen
⊕

Antrim Hotel ◆◆
73 Mount Pleasant, Liverpool,
L3 5TB
T: (0151) 709 5239 & 709 9212
F: (0151) 709 7169
E: antrimhotel@ukbusiness.com

Blenheim Lodge ◆◆◆
37 Aigburth Drive, Liverpool,
L17 4JE
T: (0151) 727 7380
F: (0151) 727 5833
E: blenheimlodge@btinternet.
com

The Feathers Inn ◆◆
1 Paul Street, Vauxhall Road,
Liverpool, L3 6DX
T: (0151) 236 1203
F: (0151) 236 0081

Holme Leigh Guest House ◆◆
93 Woodcroft Road, Wavertree,
Liverpool, L15 2HG
T: (0151) 734 2216 & 427 9806
F: (0151) 291 9877
E: bridges01@cableinetco.uk
⊕

Lord Nelson ◆
Lord Nelson Street, Liverpool,
L3 5PD
T: (0151) 709 4362
F: (0151) 707 1321

Parkland ◆◆◆
38 Coachmans Drive, Croxteth
Park, Liverpool, L12 0HX
T: (0151) 259 1417

Somersby Guest House ◆◆◆
57 Green Lane, off Menlove
Avenue, Liverpool, L18 2EP
T: (0151) 722 7549
F: (0151) 722 7549

Woolton Redbourne Hotel
◆◆◆◆ SILVER AWARD
Acrefield Road, Woolton,
Liverpool, L25 5JN
T: (0151) 421 1500
F: (0151) 421 1501
E: wooltonredbourne@cwcom.
net

LONGRIDGE
Lancashire

Oak Lea ◆◆◆◆
Clitheroe Road, Knowle Green,
Longridge, Preston PR3 2YS
T: (01254) 878486
F: (01254) 878486
⊕

LONGTON
Lancashire

Moorside Villa ◆◆◆◆
Drumacre Lane West, Longton,
Preston PR4 4SB
T: (01772) 616612

Willow Cottage ◆◆◆◆
Longton Bypass, Longton,
Preston PR4 4RA
T: (01772) 617570
⊕

LOWER WHITLEY
Cheshire

Tall Trees Lodge ◆◆◆
Tarporley Road, Lower Whitley,
Warrington WA4 4EZ
T: (01928) 790824 & 715117
F: (01928) 791330
E: booking@talltreeslodge.co.uk
I: www.talltreeslodge.co.uk
⊕ ♿

LYTHAM ST ANNES
Lancashire

Clifton Park Hotel ◆◆◆
299-301 Clifton Drive South,
Lytham St Annes, Lancashire
FY8 1HN
T: (01253) 725801
F: (01253) 721135
E: reservations@
cliftonparkhotel.freeserve.co.uk
I: www.cliftonpark.co.uk
⊕

Cullerne Hotel ◆
55 Lightburne Avenue, Lytham
St Annes, Lancashire FY8 1JE
T: (01253) 721753

Fairmile Hotel ◆◆◆
9 St Annes Road East, Lytham St
Annes, Lancashire FY8 1TA
T: (01253) 728375
F: (01253) 728375

Monarch Hotel ◆◆◆
29 St Annes Road East, Lytham
St Annes, Lancashire FY8 1TA
T: (01253) 720464 &
07778 422523
F: (01253) 720464
E: churchill@monarch91.
freeserve.co.uk

Strathmore Hotel ◆◆◆
305 Clifton Drive South, Lytham
St Annes, Lancashire FY8 1HN
T: (01253) 725478

MACCLESFIELD
Cheshire

Carr House Farm ◆◆◆
Mill Lane, Adlington,
Macclesfield, Cheshire SK10 4LG
T: (01625) 828337
F: (01625) 828337

Chadwick House Hotel ◆◆◆
55 Beech Lane, Macclesfield,
Cheshire SK10 2DS
T: (01625) 615558 &
07803 031911
F: (01625) 610265

Moorhayes House Hotel ◆◆◆
27 Manchester Road,
Tytherington, Macclesfield,
Cheshire SK10 2JJ
T: (01625) 433228
F: (01625) 429878
E: helen@moorhayeshouse.
freeserve.co.uk

Oldhams Hollow Farm ◆◆◆
Manchester Road, Tytherington,
Macclesfield, Cheshire SK10 2JW
T: (01625) 424128
⊕

Sandpit Farm ◆◆◆
Messuage Lane, Marton,
Macclesfield, Cheshire SK11 9HS
T: (01260) 224254

MAGHULL
Merseyside

Rosedene ◆◆◆
175 Liverpool Road South,
Maghull, Liverpool L31 8AA
T: (0151) 527 1897

MALPAS
Cheshire

Millmoor Farm ◆◆◆
No Mans Heath, Malpas,
Cheshire SY14 8ED
T: (01948) 820304
E: dave-sal@millmoor_farm.
fsnet.co.uk
⊕

MANCHESTER
Greater Manchester

Anbermar ◆◆◆
32 Gibwood Road, Northenden,
Manchester, M22 4BS
T: (0161) 998 2375

Bentley Guest House ◆◆◆
64 Hill Lane, Blackley,
Manchester M9 6PF
T: (0161) 795 1115

Luther King House ◆◆◆
Brighton Grove, Wilmslow Road,
Manchester, M14 5JP
T: (0161) 224 6404
F: (0161) 248 9201
E: reception@lkh.co.uk
I: www.lkh.co.uk
♿

Monroe's ◆
38 London Road, Piccadilly,
Manchester, M1 1PE
T: (0161) 236 0564

Palatine Hotel ◆◆◆
88 Palatine Road, West
Didsbury, Manchester, M20 3JW
T: (0161) 446 2222
F: (0161) 446 2233

Rembrandt Hotel ◆◆◆
33 Sackville Street, Manchester,
M1 3LZ
T: (0161) 236 1311 & 236 2435
F: (0161) 236 4257
E: rembrandthotel@aol.com
I: www.therembrandthotel.co.uk

MARPLE
Greater Manchester

Sinclair Lodge ◆◆◆
84 Strines Road, Marple,
Stockport, Cheshire SK6 7DU
T: (0161) 449 9435
F: (0161) 449 9435
E: mscott144@aol.com
I: www.members.aol.
com/mscott144

MARTHALL
Cheshire

Moat Hall Motel ◆◆◆
Chelford Road, Marthall,
Knutsford, Cheshire WA16 8SU
T: (01625) 861214 & 860367
F: (01625) 861136
E: val@moathall.fsnet.co.uk
I: moathallmotel.co.uk

MINSHULL VERNON
Cheshire

Higher Elms Farm ◆◆
Minshull Vernon, Crewe
CW1 4RG
T: (01270) 522252
F: (01270) 522252

MOBBERLEY
Cheshire

The Hinton
◆◆◆ SILVER AWARD
Town Lane, Mobberley,
Knutsford, Cheshire WA16 7HH
T: (01565) 873484
F: (01565) 873484

MORECAMBE
Lancashire

Ashley Private Hotel ◆◆◆
371 Marine Road, Morecambe,
Lancashire LA4 5AH
T: (01524) 412034
F: (01524) 421390
E: info@ashleyhotel.co.uk
I: www.ashleyhotel.co.uk
⊛

Belle Vue Hotel ◆◆
330 Marine Road, Morecambe,
Lancashire LA4 5AA
T: (01524) 411375
F: (01524) 411375

Berkeley Private Hotel ◆◆◆
39 Marine Road West,
Promenade West, Morecambe,
Lancashire LA3 1BZ
T: (01524) 418201
⊛

The Broadwater Private Hotel
◆◆
356 Marine Road, Morecambe,
Lancashire LA4 5AQ
T: (01524) 411333
⊛

Caledonian Hotel ◆
60 Marine Road West,
Morecambe, Lancashire LA4 4ET
T: (01524) 418503
F: (01524) 401710

The Clifton Hotel ◆◆
43-46 Marine Road West,
Morecambe, Lancashire LA3 1BZ
T: (01524) 411573
F: (01524) 420839

Craigwell Hotel ◆◆◆
372 Marine Road East,
Morecambe, Lancashire LA4 5AH
T: (01524) 410095
F: (01524) 410095
⊛

The Devonia ◆◆◆
11 Skipton Street, Morecambe,
Lancashire LA4 4AR
T: (01524) 418506
F: (01524) 418506
E: thedevoniah@
netscapeonline.co.uk

The Durham Guest House ◆◆
73 Albert Road, Morecambe,
Lancashire LA4 4HY
T: (01524) 424790

Eidsforth Hotel ◆◆◆
317-318 Marine Road Central,
Promenade, Morecambe,
Lancashire LA4 5AA
T: (01524) 411691 & 420960
F: (01524) 832334

Jacaranda Guest House ◆◆
68 Clarendon Road, Morecambe,
Lancashire LA3 1QZ
T: (01524) 416915

Lakeland View Guest House
◆◆
130 Clarendon Road,
Morecambe, Lancashire LA3 1SD
T: (01524) 415873
⊛

The Marina Hotel ◆◆◆
324 Marine Road Central,
Morecambe, Lancashire LA4 5AA
T: (01524) 423979
F: (01524) 426699
E: marina@marina-hotel.
demon.co.uk
I: www.marina-hotel.demon.co.
uk
⊛

New Hazelmere Hotel ◆◆◆
391 Marine Road East,
Morecambe, Lancashire LA4 5AN
T: (01524) 417876
F: (01524) 414488

Roxbury Private Hotel ◆◆
78 Thornton Road, Morecambe,
Lancashire LA4 5PJ
T: (01524) 410561
F: (01524) 420286
E: ritall@bigfoot.com

St Winifred's Hotel ◆◆◆
Marine Road East, Morecambe,
Lancashire LA4 5AR
T: (01524) 412322 & 417903
F: (01524) 412322

Seashelt Private Hotel ◆◆
85 Regent Road, Morecambe,
Lancashire LA3 1AD
T: (01524) 410265
⊛

Sunnyside Hotel ◆◆
8 Thornton Road, Morecambe,
Lancashire LA4 5PB
T: (01524) 418363

Tern Bay Hotel ◆◆◆
43 Heysham Road, Morecambe,
Lancashire LA3 1DA
T: (01524) 421209 &
07880 582544
F: (01524) 421209
E: info@ternbayhotel.co.uk
I: www.ternbayhotel.co.uk

Trevelyan Private Hotel ◆◆
27 West End Road, Morecambe,
Lancashire LA4 4DJ
T: (01524) 412013
E: thetrevelyan@supanet.com
I: www.thetrevelyan.freeserve.
co.uk

Warwick Hotel ◆◆◆◆
394 Marine Road East,
Morecambe, Lancashire LA4 5AN
T: (01524) 418151
F: (01524) 418151

Westleigh Hotel ◆◆◆
9 Marine Road, Morecambe,
Lancashire LA3 1BS
T: (01524) 418352
F: (01524) 418352

The Wycollar Hotel ◆◆◆
28 Seaview Parade, West End
Road, Morecambe, Lancashire
LA4 4DL
T: (01524) 412335

Yacht Bay View Hotel ◆◆◆
359 Marine Road, Morecambe,
Lancashire LA4 5AQ
T: (01524) 414481
E: yachtbayview@
nationwideisp.net
I: www.morecambe.co.
uk/yachtbayview

MOTTRAM ST ANDREW
Cheshire

Goose Green Farm ◆◆◆
Oak Road, Mottram St Andrew,
Macclesfield, Cheshire SK10 4RA
T: (01625) 828814
F: (01625) 828814
E: goosegreenfarm@talk21.com
⊛

MUCH HOOLE
Lancashire

The Barn Guest House ◆◆◆
204 Liverpool Old Road, Much
Hoole, Preston PR4 4QB
T: (01772) 612654 &
07932 735681

NANTWICH
Cheshire

Henhull Hall ◆◆◆◆
Welshmans Lane, Nantwich,
Cheshire CW5 6AD
T: (01270) 624158 &
07774 885305
F: (01270) 624158
E: philip.percival@virgin.net
⊛

Poole Bank Farm ◆◆◆
Wettenhall Road, Poole,
Nantwich, Cheshire CW5 6AL
T: (01270) 625169

Stoke Grange Farm ◆◆◆
Chester Road, Nantwich,
Cheshire CW5 6BT
T: (01270) 625525
F: (01270) 625525

NATEBY
Lancashire

Bowers Hotel and Brasserie
◆◆◆
Bowers Lane, Nateby, Preston
PR3 0JD
T: (01995) 601500
F: (01995) 603770

NELSON
Lancashire

Lovett House ◆◆◆
6 Howard Street, Off Carr Road,
Nelson, Lancashire BB9 7SZ
T: (01282) 697352 &
07710 600186
F: (01282) 700186
E: lovetthouse@cwcom.net
⊛

NETHER ALDERLEY
Cheshire

**Millbrook Cottage Guest
House** ◆◆◆◆
Congleton Road, Nether
Alderley, Macclesfield, Cheshire
SK10 4TW
T: (01625) 583567 &
0780 3207567
F: (01625) 583567
E: millbrookcottage@hotmail.
com
I: www.millbrookcottage.co.uk

NEW BRIGHTON
Merseyside

Sea Level Hotel ◆◆
126 Victoria Road, New
Brighton, Wallasey, Merseyside
CH45 9LD
T: (0151) 639 3408
F: (0151) 639 3408

Sherwood Guest House ◆◆◆
55 Wellington Road, New
Brighton, Wirral, Merseyside
CH45 2ND
T: (0151) 639 5198

Wellington House Hotel ◆◆◆
65 Wellington Road, New
Brighton, Wirral, Merseyside
CH45 2NE
T: (0151) 639 6594
F: (0151) 639 6594

NORTHWICH
Cheshire

Ash House Farm ◆◆◆
Chapel Lane, Acton Bridge,
Northwich, Cheshire CW8 3QS
T: (01606) 852717
⊛

Park Dale Guest House ◆◆◆
140 Middlewich Road,
Rudheath, Northwich, Cheshire
CW9 7DS
T: (01606) 45228
F: (01606) 331770

Springfield Guest House ◆◆◆
Chester Road, Delamere,
Oakmere, Northwich, Cheshire
CW8 2HB
T: (01606) 882538

OFFERTON
Greater Manchester

Hallfield House ◆◆◆
50 Hall Street, Offerton,
Stockport, Cheshire SK1 4DA
T: (0161) 429 8977 & 429 6153
F: (0161) 429 9017
E: hallfieldhouse@btconnect.
com

OLDHAM
Greater Manchester

Boothstead Farm ◆◆◆
Rochdale Road, Denshaw,
Oldham OL3 5UE
T: (01457) 878622

Globe Farm Guest House ◆◆◆
Huddersfield Road, Standedge,
Delph, Oldham OL3 5LU
T: (01457) 873040
F: (01457) 873040
I: www.smoothhound.co.
uk/hotels/globef.html

ORMSKIRK
Lancashire
The Meadows ◆◆◆◆
New Sutch Farm, Sutch Lane,
Ormskirk, Lancashire L40 4BU
T: (01704) 894048

OVER ALDERLEY
Cheshire
Lower Harebarrow Farm ◆◆
Over Alderley, Macclesfield,
Cheshire SK10 4SW
T: (01625) 829882

OVERTON
Lancashire
The Globe Hotel ◆◆◆
40 Main Street, Overton,
Morecambe, Lancashire LA3 3HD
T: (01524) 858228 & 858073
F: (015424) 858228
E: theglobe@talk21.com

PADIHAM
Lancashire
Windsor House ◆◆
71 Church Street, Padiham,
Burnley, Lancashire BB12 8JH
T: (01282) 773271

PRESTON
Lancashire
County Hotel ◆◆
1 Fishergate Hill, Preston,
Lancashire PR1 8UL
T: (01772) 253188
F: (01772) 253188

Derby Court Hotel ◆◆
1 Pole Street, Preston, PR1 1DX
T: (01772) 202077
F: (01772) 252277

Olde Duncombe House ◆◆◆
Garstang Road, Bilsborrow,
Preston PR3 0RE
T: (01995) 640336
F: (01995) 640336
E: bolton3@netline.uk.net

Tulketh Hotel ◆◆◆
209 Tulketh Road, Ashton,
Preston, PR2 1ES
T: (01772) 728096 & 726250
F: (01772) 723743
I: www.smoothhound.co.
uk/hotels/tulketh.html

Ye Horns Inn ◆◆◆◆
Horns Lane, Goosnargh, Preston,
PR3 2FJ
T: (01772) 865230
F: (01772) 864299
E: enquiries@yehornsinn.co.uk
I: www.yehornsinn.co.uk

PRESTWICH
Greater Manchester
Church Inn ◆◆◆
Church Lane, Prestwich,
Manchester M25 1AJ
T: (0161) 798 6727
F: (0161) 773 6281
E: tom.gribben@virgin.net

ROSSENDALE
Lancashire
The Willows ◆◆◆◆
41 Cherry Tree Way, Helmshore,
Rossendale, Lancashire BB4 4JZ
T: (01706) 212698
I: www.btinternet.com/§fred.
mitchell1/

RUSHTON
Cheshire
**Hill House Farm Bed and
Breakfast** ◆◆◆
The Hall Lane, Rushton,
Tarporley, Cheshire CW6 9AU
T: (01829) 732238 &
07973 284863
F: (01829) 733929

SADDLEWORTH
Greater Manchester
Farrars Arms ◆◆
56 Oldham Road, Grasscroft,
Oldham OL4 4HL
T: (01457) 872124
F: (01457) 820351

ST ANNES
Lancashire
Elsinghurst Hotel ◆◆◆
34 Derbe Road, St Annes,
Lytham St Annes, Lancashire
FY8 1NJ
T: (01253) 724629
F: (01253) 7244629

ST MICHAEL'S ON WYRE
Lancashire
Compton House ◆◆◆
Garstang Road, St Michael's on
Wyre, Preston PR3 0TE
T: (01995) 679378
F: (01995) 679378
E: djones@compton-hs.
freeserve.co.uk
I: www.in-uk.com/compton

SALE
Greater Manchester
Cornerstones ◆◆◆◆
230 Washway Road, Sale,
Cheshire M33 4RA
T: (0161) 283 6909
F: (0161) 283 6909
E: tcasey@cwcom.net

SALFORD
Greater Manchester
Hazeldean Hotel ◆◆◆
467 Bury New Road, Kersal Bar,
Salford, Lancashire M7 3NE
T: (0161) 792 6667 & 792 2079
F: (0161) 792 6668

White Lodge Private Hotel ◆
87-89 Great Cheetham Street
West, Broughton, Salford,
Greater Manchester M7 2JA
T: (0161) 792 3047

SALTNEY
Cheshire
The Garden Gate Guest House ◆◆◆
8 Chester Street, Saltney,
Chester, Cheshire CH4 8BJ
T: (01244) 682306 &
07711 698361

SANDBACH
Cheshire
Canal Centre and Village Store ◆◆◆
Hassall Green, Sandbach,
Cheshire CW11 4YB
T: (01270) 762266
F: (01270) 762266
E: canalhassall@btconnect.com
I: www.canal-centre.co.uk

Moss Cottage Farm ◆◆◆◆
Hassall Road, Winterley,
Sandbach, Cheshire CW11 4RU
T: (01270) 583018

SCORTON
Lancashire
Tuft Cottage ◆◆◆
Scorton, Preston PR3 1BT
T: (01524) 791955
E: tuftcottage@quista.net

SCOTFORTH
Lancashire
West View Farm ◆◆◆
Langthwaite Road, Scotforth,
Lancaster LA1 3JJ
T: (01524) 841 336

SIDDINGTON
Cheshire
Golden Cross Farm ◆◆◆
Siddington, Macclesfield,
Cheshire SK11 9JP
T: (01260) 224358

SILVERDALE
Lancashire
Silverdale Hotel ◆◆◆
Shore Road, Silverdale,
Carnforth, Lancashire LA5 0TP
T: (01524) 701206

SINGLETON
Lancashire
Old Castle Farm ◆◆◆
Garstang Road, Singleton,
Blackpool FY6 8ND
T: (01253) 883839
F: (01253) 883839

SLAIDBURN
Lancashire
Hark to Bounty Inn ◆◆◆
Slaidburn, Clitheroe, Lancashire
BB7 3EP
T: (01200) 446246
F: (01200) 446361
E: isobel@hark-to-ounty.co.uk
I: www.yell.co.
uk/sites/harktobounty

Pages Farm ◆◆
Woodhouse Lane, Slaidburn,
Clitheroe, Lancashire BB7 3AH
T: (01200) 446205

SOUTHPORT
Merseyside
Adelphi Hotel ◆◆
39 Bold Street, Southport,
Merseyside PR9 0ED
T: (01704) 544947
F: (01704) 544947
E: gromad@aol.com
I: www.merseyworld.
com/adelphi-hotel.

Alhambra Hotel ◆◆◆
41 Bold Street, Southport,
Merseyside PR9 0ED
T: (01704) 534853
E: info@alhambrahotel.co.uk
I: www.alhambrahotel.co.uk

Allenby ◆◆
56 Bath Street, Southport,
Merseyside PR9 0DH
T: (01704) 532953

Ambassador Private Hotel ◆◆◆◆
13 Bath Street, Southport,
Merseyside PR9 0DP
T: (01704) 543998
F: (01704) 536269

Carleton House Hotel ◆◆◆
17 Alexandra Road, Southport,
Merseyside PR9 0NB
T: (01704) 538035
F: (01704) 538035
E: bookings@carleton-house.co.
uk
I: www.carleton-house.co.uk

Carlton Lodge Hotel ◆◆◆◆
43 Bath Street, Southport,
Merseyside PR9 0DP
T: (01704) 542290 &
0500 400413
F: (01704) 542290
E: benvale@which.net
I: www.smoothhound.co.
uk/hotels/carlton

Cora Hotel ◆◆
29 Bath Street, Southport,
Merseyside PR9 0DP
T: (01704) 530204
F: (01704) 530204

Crescent House Hotel ◆◆◆
27 Bath Street, Southport,
Merseyside PR9 0DP
T: (01704) 530339
F: (01704) 530339
E: glynor@creshohotel.
freeserve.co.uk
I: www.smoothhound.co.
uk/hotels/crescnt.html

Fairfield Private Hotel ◆◆◆
83 Promenade, Southport,
Merseyside PR9 0JN
T: (01704) 530137

Le Maitre Hotel ◆◆◆◆
69 Bath Street, Southport,
Merseyside PR9 0DN
T: (01704) 530394 &
07889 399357
F: (01704) 548755
E: enquiries@hotel-lemaitre.co.
uk
I: www.hotel-lemaitre.co.uk

Leicester Hotel ◆◆◆
24 Leicester Street, Southport,
Merseyside PR9 0EZ
T: (01704) 530049
F: (01704) 530049
E: leicester.hotel@mail.cybase.
co.uk

Lynwood Private Hotel ◆◆◆◆
11a Leicester Street, Southport,
Merseyside PR9 0ER
T: (01704) 540794
F: (01704) 500724
I: www.smoothound.co.
uk/lynwood.html.

Oakwood Private Hotel ◆◆◆◆
7 Portland Street, Southport,
Merseyside PR8 1LJ
T: (01704) 531858
E: oakwoodhotel@tinyworld.co.
uk
I: www.merseyworld.
com/oakwood
◎

Penkelie Hotel ◆◆◆
34 Bold Street, Southport,
Merseyside PR9 0ED
T: (01704) 538510
F: (01704) 538510
E: info@penkelie.co.uk
I: www.penkelie.co.uk

Richmond House Hotel ◆◆◆
28 Bold Street, Southport,
Merseyside PR9 0ED
T: (01704) 535265
F: (01704) 547708
E: info@richmond-house.co.uk
I: www.richmond-house.co.uk
◎

Rosedale Hotel ◆◆◆
11 Talbot Street, Southport,
Merseyside PR8 1HP
T: (01704) 530604
F: (01704) 530604
E: rosedale.hotel@rapid.co.uk
I: www.merseyworld.
com/rosedale

Sandy Brook Farm ◆◆◆
52 Wyke Cop Road, Scarisbrick,
Southport, Merseyside PR8 5LR
T: (01704) 880337
F: (01704) 880337
▲

Sidbrook Hotel ◆◆◆
14 Talbot Street, Southport,
Merseyside PR8 1HP
T: (01704) 530608
F: (01704) 530608
E: sidbrookhotel@tesco.net

Silverdale Hotel ◆◆◆◆
10 Victoria Street, Southport,
Merseyside PR9 0DU
T: (01704) 536479
F: (01704) 536479

Squires Hotel ◆◆◆
78/80 King Street, Southport,
Merseyside PR8 1LG
T: (01704) 544462 & 07957 747
4031
F: (01704) 544462
E: mail@squireshotel.co.uk
I: www.squireshotel.co.uk

Sunnyside Hotel ◆◆◆
47 Bath Street, Southport,
Merseyside PR9 0DP
T: (01704) 536521
F: (01704) 539237
E: sunnysidehotel@rapid.co.uk
I: www.sunny-lisa.co.uk

Waterford ◆◆◆◆
37 Leicester Street, Southport,
Merseyside PR9 0EX
T: (01704) 530559
F: (01704) 530559
E: waterfordhotel@rapidnet
I: www.waterford-hotel.co.uk

Whitworth Falls Hotel ◆◆◆
16 Lathom Road, Southport,
Merseyside PR9 0JH
T: (01704) 530074 & 534505
F: (01704) 530074
E: whitworthfalls@rapid.co.uk
I: www.whitworthfallshotel.co.
uk

Windsor Lodge Hotel ◆◆◆
37 Saunders Street, Southport,
Merseyside PR9 0HJ
T: (01704) 530070

York Villa Hotel ◆◆◆
18 Bath Street, Southport,
Merseyside PR9 0DA
T: (01704) 530283
F: (01704) 501055
E: info@yorkvilla.co.uk
I: www.yorkvilla.co.uk

STOCKPORT
Greater Manchester

Moss Deeping
Rating Applied For
7 Robins Lane, Bramhall,
Stockport, Cheshire SK7 2PE
T: (0161) 439 1969

Needhams Farm ◆◆◆
Uplands Road, Werneth Low,
Gee Cross, Hyde, Cheshire
SK14 3AG
T: (0161) 368 4610
F: (0161) 367 9106
E: charlotte@needhamsfarm.
demon.co.uk
I: www.needhamsfarm.co.uk

Red Lion Inn ◆◆◆◆
112 Buxton Road, High Lane,
Stockport, Cheshire SK6 8ED
T: (01663) 765227
F: (01663) 762170

Shire Cottage Farmhouse
◆◆◆
Benches Lane, Marple Bridge,
Stockport, Cheshire SK6 5RY
T: (01457) 866536

Southlands Hotel ◆◆◆
Adswood Lane West, Cale Green,
Stockport, Cheshire SK3 8HF
T: (0161) 480 8701 & 480 5681
F: (0161) 476 2143

STONYHURST
Lancashire

Alden Cottage
◆◆◆◆ SILVER AWARD
Kemple End, Birdy Brow,
Stonyhurst, Clitheroe,
Lancashire BB7 9QY
T: (01254) 826468
E: carpenter@aldencottage.f9.
co.uk
◎

TARPORLEY
Cheshire

Foresters Arms ◆◆◆
92 High Street, Tarporley,
Cheshire CW6 0AX
T: (01829) 733151
F: (01829) 730020

Roughlow Farm
◆◆◆◆ SILVER AWARD
Willington, Tarporley, Cheshire
CW6 0PG
T: (01829) 751199
F: (01829) 751199
E: sutcliffe@roughlow.
freeserve.co.uk
I: www.roughlow.freeserve.co.uk

TATTENHALL
Cheshire

Ford Farm ◆◆◆
Newton Lane, Tattenhall,
Chester CH3 9NE
T: (01829) 770307

TIMPERLEY
Greater Manchester

Acorn of Oakmere ◆◆◆
Oakmere, 6 Wingate Drive,
Timperley, Altrincham, Cheshire
WA15 7PX
T: (0161) 980 8391
F: (0161) 980 8391
E: oakmere6@ewetv.net

TORSIDE
Greater Manchester

The Old House
Rating Applied For
Woodhead Road, Torside,
Glossop, Derbyshire SK13
T: (01457) 857527

TURTON
Greater Manchester

Quarlton Manor Farm ◆◆◆◆
Plantation Road, Turton, Bolton
BL7 0DD
T: (01204) 852277 &
07976 535540
F: (01204) 852286

WADDINGTON
Lancashire

Peter Barn Country House
◆◆◆◆
Cross Lane, Waddington,
Clitheroe, Lancashire BB7 3JH
T: (01200) 428585 &
09790 826370
◎

WALLASEY
Merseyside

Dean Lodge Guest House ◆
8 Dean Avenue, Wallasey,
Merseyside CH45 3HT
T: (0151) 630 2320
F: (0151) 630 2320

The Russell Hotel ◆◆◆
44 Church Road, Seacombe,
Wallasey, Merseyside CH44 7BA
T: (0151) 639 5723 & 639 5728
F: (0151) 639 5723

WARMINGHAM
Cheshire

The Bears Paw ◆◆◆
School Lane, Warmingham,
Crewe CW11 3QN
T: (01270) 526317 & 526342
F: (01270) 526465

WARRINGTON
Cheshire

Imperial Hotel ◆◆
145 Bewsey Road, Warrington,
Cheshire WA5 5L9
T: (01925) 637255 & 634915

WARTON
Lancashire

Cotestones Farm ◆◆◆
Sand Lane, Warton, Carnforth,
Lancashire LA5 9NH
T: (01524) 732418
F: (01524) 732418

WATERLOO
Merseyside

Woodlands Guest House ◆◆◆
10 Haigh Road, Waterloo,
Liverpool L22 3XP
T: (0151) 920 5373

WEST DERBY
Merseyside

Blackmoor ◆◆◆
160 Blackmoor Drive, West
Derby, Liverpool, Merseyside
L12 9EF
T: (0151) 291 1407 & 228 4886

WEST KIRBY
Merseyside

Maconachie Guest House
◆◆◆
1 Victoria Road, West Kirby,
Wirral, Merseyside CH48 3HL
T: (0151) 625 1915

WESTHOUGHTON
Greater Manchester

Daisy Hill Hotel ◆◆◆
3 Lower Leigh Road, Daisy Hill,
Westhoughton, Bolton BL5 2JP
T: (01942) 812096 & 797180
F: (01942) 797180
◎

WESTON
Cheshire

Snape Farm ◆◆◆
Snape Lane, Weston, Crewe,
Cheshire CW2 5NB
T: (01270) 820208
F: (01270) 820208
◎

WHALLEY
Lancashire

Bayley Arms Hotel ◆◆◆
Avenue Road, Hurst Green,
Whalley, Clitheroe, Lancashire
BB7 9QB
T: (01254) 826478
F: (01254) 826797

WHALLEY RANGE
Greater Manchester

The Beechwood Hotel ◆◆◆
193 Withington Road, Whalley
Range, Manchester M16 8HF
T: (0161) 226 9015 &
07973 185902
F: (0161) 226 9015
I: www.scoot.co.
uk/beechwood_hotel/

WHITEWELL
Lancashire

The Inn at Whitewell ◆◆◆◆
Whitewell, Clitheroe, Lancashire
BB7 3AT
T: (01200) 448222 & 448640
F: (01200) 448298

WIGAN
Greater Manchester

Wilden ◆◆◆
11a Miles Lane, Shevington,
Wigan, Lancashire WN6 8EB
T: (01257) 251516 &
07798 935373
F: (01257) 255622
E: wildenass@aol.com
◎

WILMSLOW
Cheshire

Dean Bank Hotel ◆◆◆
Adlington Road, Wilmslow,
Cheshire SK9 2BT
T: (01625) 524268
F: (01625) 549715
▲

Fern Bank Guest House ◆◆◆◆
188 Wilmslow Road, Handforth,
Wilmslow, Cheshire SK9 3JX
T: (01625) 523729
F: (01625) 539515

Finney Green Cottage ♦♦♦♦
134 Manchester Road,
Wilmslow, Cheshire SK9 2JW
T: (01625) 533343

Hollow Bridge Guest House
♦♦♦♦
90 Manchester Road, Wilmslow,
Cheshire SK9 2JY
T: (01625) 537303
F: (01625) 528718

Marigold House ♦♦♦♦
132 Knutsford Road, Wilmslow,
Cheshire SK9 6JH
T: (01625) 584414 &
07778 509565

Oversley House ♦♦♦♦
Altrincham Road, Morley Green,
Wilmslow, Cheshire SK9 4LT
T: (01625) 535551
F: (01625) 531510

Rylands Farm Guest House
♦♦♦
Altrincham Road, Wilmslow,
Cheshire SK9 4LT
T: (01625) 535646 & 548041
F: (01625) 535646

WINTERLEY
Cheshire
Field Mews ♦♦♦♦
The Fields, 36 Hassall Road,
Winterley, Sandbach, Cheshire
CW11 4RL
T: (01270) 761858 &
07973 867609

WISWELL
Lancashire
Pepper Hill ♦♦♦♦
Pendleton Road, Wiswell,
Clitheroe, Lancashire BB7 9BZ
T: (01254) 825098

WYCOLLER
Lancashire
Parson Lee Farm ♦♦♦
Wycoller, Colne, Lancashire
BB8 8SU
T: (01282) 864747
E: pathodgson@hotmail.com
I: www.parsonleefarm.co.uk

YORKSHIRE

ACKLAM
North Yorkshire
Trout Pond Barn ♦♦♦♦
Acklam, Malton, North Yorkshire
YO17 9RG
T: (01653) 658468 & 693088
F: (01653) 693088

ADDINGHAM
West Yorkshire
Ghyll House Farm ♦♦♦
Straight Lane, Addingham, Ilkley,
West Yorkshire LS29 9JX
T: (01943) 830370

Lumb Beck Farmhouse Bed and Breakfast
♦♦♦♦ SILVER AWARD
Moorside Lane, Addingham,
Ilkley, West Yorkshire LS29 9JX
T: (01943) 830400

AINTHORPE
North Yorkshire
The Fox & Hounds Inn ♦♦♦♦
45 Brook Lane, Ainthorpe,
Whitby, North Yorkshire
YO21 2LD
T: (01287) 660218
F: (01287) 660030
E: ajbfox@globalnet.co.uk

AIRTON
North Yorkshire
Lindon House ♦♦♦
Malhamdale, Airton, Skipton,
North Yorkshire BD23 4BE
T: (01729) 830418

AISLABY
North Yorkshire
Blacksmiths Arms Restaurant
♦♦♦
Aislaby, Pickering, North
Yorkshire YO18 8PE
T: (01751) 472182 &
07885 573808

ALDBROUGH
East Riding of Yorkshire
West Carlton ♦♦♦♦
Carlton Lane, Aldbrough, Hull,
East Yorkshire HU11 4RB
T: (01964) 527724 &
07767 830868
F: (01964) 527505
E: caroline_maltas@hotmail.com

ALDFIELD
North Yorkshire
Bay Tree Farm
♦♦♦♦ SILVER AWARD
Aldfield, Ripon, North Yorkshire
HG4 3BE
T: (01765) 620394
F: (01765) 620394
E: baytree@wotz.freeserve.co.uk

ALLERTON
West Yorkshire
Victoria Hotel ♦♦♦
10 Cottingley Road, Sandy Lane,
Allerton, Bradford, West
Yorkshire BD15 9JP
T: (01274) 823820
F: (01274) 823820

AMOTHERBY
North Yorkshire
Old Station Farm Country Guest House♦♦♦♦
High Street, Amotherby, Malton,
North Yorkshire YO17 6TL
T: (01653) 693683
F: (01653) 693683
E: info@oldstationfarm.co.uk
I: www.oldstationfarm.co.uk

AMPLEFORTH
North Yorkshire
Carr House Farm ♦♦♦
Shallowdale, Ampleforth, York
YO62 4ED
T: (01347) 868526 &
07977 113197

Shallowdale House
♦♦♦♦♦ SILVER AWARD
West End, Ampleforth, York
YO62 4DY
T: (01439) 788325
F: (01439) 788885

Spring Cottage ♦♦♦
Ampleforth, York YO62 4DA
T: (01439) 788579

The White Horse Inn ♦♦♦
West End, Ampleforth, York,
North Yorkshire YO62 4DX
T: (01439) 788378 & 788120

APPERSETT
North Yorkshire
Thorney Mire House ♦♦♦♦
Appersett, Hawes, North
Yorkshire DL8 3LU
T: (01969) 667159
E: sylvia@thorneymire.yorks.net
I: www.thorneymire.yorks.net

APPLETON-LE-MOORS
North Yorkshire
Appleton Mill Farm ♦♦♦
Appleton-le-Moors, York
YO62 6TG
T: (01751) 417212

APPLETREEWICK
North Yorkshire
Knowles Lodge ♦♦♦♦
Appletreewick, Skipton, North
Yorkshire BD23 6DQ
T: (01756) 720228
F: (01756) 720381

ARKENGARTHDALE
North Yorkshire
Chapel Farmhouse ♦♦♦♦
Whaw, Arkengarthdale,
Richmond, North Yorkshire
DL11 6RT
T: (01748) 884062
F: (01748) 884062
E: chapelfarmbb@aol.com

The Charles Bathurst Inn ♦♦♦
Arkengarthdale, Richmond,
North Yorkshire DL11 6EN
T: (01748) 884567 & 884058
F: (01748) 884062
E: cb-inn@msn.com

The Ghyll ♦♦
Arkle Town, Arkengarthdale,
Richmond, North Yorkshire
DL11 6EU
T: (01748) 884353
F: (01748) 884015
E: bookings@theghyll.co.uk
I: www.theghyll.co.uk

The White House ♦♦♦
Arkle Town, Arkengarthdale,
Richmond, North Yorkshire
DL11 6RB
T: (01748) 884203
F: (01748) 884088
I: www.yorkshirenet.co.uk/stayat/thewhitehouse

ASKRIGG
North Yorkshire
The Apothecary's House
♦♦♦♦
Market Place, Askrigg, Leyburn,
North Yorkshire DL8 3HT
T: (01969) 650626

Helm ♦♦♦♦ GOLD AWARD
Askrigg, Leyburn, North
Yorkshire DL8 3JF
T: (01969) 650443
F: (01969) 650443
E: holiday@helmyorkshire.com
I: www.helmyorkshire.com

Home Farm ♦♦♦
Stalling Busk, Askrigg, Leyburn,
North Yorkshire DL8 3DH
T: (01969) 650360

Lucy's House ♦♦♦
Askrigg, Leyburn, North
Yorkshire DL8 3HT
T: (01969) 650586

Milton House ♦♦♦
Askrigg, Leyburn, North
Yorkshire DL8 3HJ
T: (01969) 650217

Stoney End
♦♦♦♦ SILVER AWARD
Worton, Leyburn, North
Yorkshire DL8 3ET
T: (01969) 650652
F: (01969) 650077
E: stoneyendholidays@btinternet.com
I: www.wensleydale.org/links/stoneyendfrm.htm

Thornsgill Guest House ♦♦♦♦
Moor Road, Askrigg, Leyburn,
North Yorkshire DL8 3HH
T: (01969) 650617

AUSTWICK
North Yorkshire
Dalesbridge House ♦♦♦
Austwick, Settle, North Yorkshire
LA2 8AZ
T: (015242) 51021 & 0800 458 1021
F: (015242) 51051
E: info@dalesbridge.co.uk
I: www.dalesbridge.co.uk

Woodview Guest House
♦♦♦♦
The Green, Austwick, Lancaster
LA2 8BB
T: (015242) 51268

AYSGARTH
North Yorkshire

Cornlee ♦♦♦
Aysgarth, Leyburn, North
Yorkshire DL8 3AE
T: (01969) 663779 & 663053
F: (01969) 663779
E: cornlee@tesco.net

Field House ♦♦♦
East End, Aysgarth, Leyburn,
North Yorkshire DL8 3AB
T: (01969) 663556

Low Gill Farm ♦♦♦
Aysgarth, Leyburn, North
Yorkshire DL8 3AL
T: (01969) 663554

Palmer Flatt Hotel ♦♦♦
Aysgarth, Leyburn, North
Yorkshire DL8 3SR
T: (01969) 663228
F: (01969) 663182

Stow House Hotel ♦♦♦♦
Aysgarth Falls, Aysgarth,
Leyburn, North Yorkshire
DL8 3SR
T: (01969) 663635

BAILDON
West Yorkshire

**Ford House Farm Bed and
Breakfast ♦♦♦♦**
Buck Lane, Baildon, Shipley,
West Yorkshire BD177 7R
T: (01274) 584489 &
07747 002626
F: (01274) 584489
E: mick@mpadley.fsnet.co.uk

BAINBRIDGE
North Yorkshire

Hazel's Roost ♦♦♦
Bainbridge, Leyburn, North
Yorkshire DL8 3EH
T: (01969) 650400

High Force Farm ♦♦♦
Bainbridge, Leyburn, North
Yorkshire DL8 3DL
T: (01969) 650379

BAINTON
East Riding of Yorkshire

Bainton Burrows Farm ♦♦♦
Bainton, Driffield, East Yorkshire
YO25 9BS
T: (01377) 217202

BALDERSBY
North Yorkshire

The Barn ♦♦♦
Nemur, Baldersby, Thirsk, North
Yorkshire YO7 4PE
T: (01765) 640561 & 604666
F: (01765) 609399

BARLOW
North Yorkshire

**Berewick House ♦♦♦♦
Rating Applied For**
Park Lane, Barlow, Selby, North
Yorkshire YO8 8EW
T: (01757) 617051 &
07961 919678
F: (01751) 617051

BARNBY DUN
South Yorkshire

**Gateway Inn & Restaurant
♦♦♦**
Station Road, Barnby Dun,
Doncaster, South Yorkshire
DN3 1HA
T: (01302) 882849 & 880641
F: (01302) 891434
E: brnsmit@aol.com
I: www.gatewayinn.co.uk

BARNETBY
North Lincolnshire

Reginald House ♦♦♦♦
27 Queens Road, Barnetby,
North Lincolnshire DN38 6JH
T: (01652) 688566
F: (01652) 688510

BARNSLEY
South Yorkshire

Travellers Inn ♦♦♦
23 Green Road, Dodworth,
Barnsley, South Yorkshire
S75 3RR
T: (01226) 284173
F: (01226) 284173
E: jeremy@travellersinn.
freeserve.co.uk

BARROW HAVEN
North Lincolnshire

Haven Inn ♦♦♦
Ferry Road, Barrow Haven,
Barrow upon Humber, North
Lincolnshire DN19 7EX
T: (01469) 530247
F: (01469) 530625
E: dmhav123@aol.com

BARROW UPON HUMBER
North Lincolnshire

Glebe Farm ♦♦♦
Cross Street, Barrow upon
Humber, North Lincolnshire
DN19 7AL
T: (01469) 531548
F: (01469) 530034
E: glebe_farm@lineone.net

BARTON-LE-STREET
North Yorkshire

Laurel Barn Cottage ♦♦♦
Barton-le-Street, Malton, North
Yorkshire YO17 6QB
T: (01653) 628329

BEADLAM, NAWTON
North Yorkshire

White Horse Inn ♦♦
Main Road, Beadlam, Nawton,
York YO62 7SU
T: (01439) 770627

BECKWITHSHAW
North Yorkshire

Garden Cottage ♦♦♦♦
Moor Park, Norwood Lane,
Beckwithshaw, Harrogate, North
Yorkshire HG3 1QN
T: (01423) 530197

BEDALE
North Yorkshire

The Castle Arms Inn ♦♦♦♦
Snape, Bedale, North Yorkshire
DL8 2TB
T: (01677) 470270
F: (01677) 470837
E: castlearms@aol.com

**Elmfield Country House
♦♦♦♦♦**
Arrathorne, Bedale, North
Yorkshire DL8 1NE
T: (01677) 450558
F: (01677) 450557
E: stay@elmfieldhouse.
freeserve.co.uk
○

**Georgian Bed and Breakfast
♦♦♦♦**
16 North End, Stabann, Bedale,
North Yorkshire DL8 1AB
T: (01677) 424454

Hyperion House ♦♦♦♦
88 South End, Bedale, North
Yorkshire DL8 2DS
T: (01677) 422334
○

**The Lodge at Leeming Bar
Rating Applied For**
A1/A684 Intersection, Great
North Road, Bedale, North
Yorkshire DL8 1DT
T: (01677) 422122
F: (01677) 424507
E: thelodgeatleemingbar@
btinternet.com

Low Leases Farm ♦♦
Low Street, Scruton, Bedale,
North Yorkshire DL7 9LU
T: (01609) 748177 &
07808 592539
E: rjm@tutor.open.ac.uk
I: www.lowleases.free-online.co.
uk

**Milton House
♦♦♦♦♦ SILVER AWARD**
Londonderry, Northallerton,
North Yorkshire DL7 9NE
T: (01677) 423142
F: (01677) 423142
E: rachel@miltonhouse79.co.uk

BEESTON
West Yorkshire

Crescent Hotel ♦♦
274 Dewsbury Road, Beeston,
Leeds LS11 6JT
T: (0113) 270 1819
F: (0113) 270 1819

BELL BUSK
North Yorkshire

Tudor House ♦♦♦♦
Bell Busk, Skipton, North
Yorkshire BD23 4DT
T: (01729) 830301
F: (01729) 830037
E: bellbusk.hitch@virgin.net

BEN RHYDDING
West Yorkshire

Gracefield ♦♦♦
133 Bolling Road, Ben Rhydding,
Ilkley, West Yorkshire LS29 8PN
T: (01943) 600960

BEVERLEY
East Riding of Yorkshire

Eastgate Guest House ♦♦♦
7 Eastgate, Beverley, East Riding
of Yorkshire HU17 0DR
T: (01482) 868464
F: (01482) 871899
○

Market Cross Hotel ♦♦♦
14 Lairgate, Beverley, North
Humberside HU17 8EE
T: (01482) 882573 & 679029
○

The Pipe and Glass Inn ♦♦♦
West End, South Dalton,
Beverley, North Humberside
HU17 7PN
T: (01430) 810246
F: (01430) 810246

**Springdale Bed and Breakfast
♦♦♦**
Springdale Stud, Long Lane,
Beverley, East Yorkshire
HU17 0RN
T: (01482) 888264

BILSDALE WEST, HELMSLEY
North Yorkshire

Hill End Farm ♦♦♦
Chop Gate, Middlesbrough,
Cleveland TS9 7JR
T: (01439) 798278

BILTON-IN-AINSTY
North Yorkshire

The Chequers Inn ♦♦♦
Bilton-in-Ainsty, York YO26 7NN
T: (01423) 359066
F: (01423) 359066

BINGLEY
West Yorkshire

Ashley End ♦♦♦
22 Ashley Road, Bingley, West
Yorkshire BD16 1DZ
T: (01274) 569679

**Five Rise Locks Hotel
♦♦♦♦ SILVER AWARD**
Beck Lane, Bingley, West
Yorkshire BD16 4DD
T: (01274) 565296
F: (01274) 568828
E: 101731.2134@compuserve.
com

March Cote Farm ♦♦♦♦
Off Woodside Avenue,
Cottingley, Bingley, West
Yorkshire BD16 1UB
T: (01274) 487433 &
07889 162257
F: (01274) 488153
E: jean.warin@nevisuk.net.
I: www.yorkshirenet.co.
uk/accqde/marchcote

BIRKBY
West Yorkshire

**Cherry Tree Bed and Breakfast
♦♦♦**
Stanwell Royd, Birkby Road,
Birkby, Huddersfield, West
Yorkshire HD2 2BX
T: (01484) 546628
F: (01484) 546628
E: hyatt@royd2.fsnet.co.uk
○

BISHOP THORNTON
North Yorkshire

Bowes Green Farm ♦♦♦♦
Colber Lane, Bishop Thornton,
Harrogate, North Yorkshire
HG3 3JX
T: (01423) 770114
F: (01423) 770114

BISHOP WILTON
North Yorkshire

High Belthorpe ♦♦♦
High Belthorpe, Bishop Wilton,
York YO42 1SB
T: (01759) 368238 &
07802 270970

BOLTBY
North Yorkshire

High Paradise Farm
Rating Applied For
Boltby, Thirsk, North Yorkshire
YO7 2HT
T: (01845) 537235
F: (01845) 537033
E: info@highparadise.co.uk
I: www.highparadise.co.uk

BOLTON ABBEY
North Yorkshire

Holme House Farm ♦♦♦
Barden, Bolton Abbey, Skipton,
North Yorkshire BD23 6AT
T: (01756) 720661

BOLTON PERCY
North Yorkshire

Glebe Farm ♦♦♦♦
Bolton Percy, York, North
Yorkshire YO23 7AL
T: (01904) 744228

BOROUGHBRIDGE
North Yorkshire

Primrose Cottage ♦♦♦♦
Lime Bar Lane, Grafton, York
YO51 9QJ
T: (01423) 322835 & 322711
F: (01423) 323985
E: primrosecottage@btinternet.
com

BOSTON SPA
West Yorkshire

Crown Hotel ♦♦♦
128 High Street, Boston Spa,
Wetherby, West Yorkshire
LS23 6BW
T: (01937) 842608
F: (01937) 541373

Four Gables
♦♦♦♦ SILVER AWARD
Oaks Lane, Boston Spa,
Wetherby, West Yorkshire
LS23 6DS
T: (01937) 849031 &
07721 055497
F: (01937) 845592
E: info@fourgables.co.uk
I: www.fourgables.co.uk

Little Orchard
♦♦♦♦ SILVER AWARD
Lime Tree Avenue, Boston Spa,
Wetherby, West Yorkshire
LS23 6DP
T: (01937) 843356
F: (01937) 841193
E: littleorchard@emphony.net

BOUTHWAITE
North Yorkshire

Covill Barn ♦♦♦♦
Bouthwaite, Harrogate, North
Yorkshire HG3 5RW
T: (01423) 755306
F: (01423) 755322

BRADFORD
West Yorkshire

35 Bierley Lanc ♦♦
Bierley, Bradford, West Yorkshire
BD4 6AD
T: (01274) 682929

Brow Top Farm ♦♦♦♦
Baldwin Lane, Clayton, Bradford,
West Yorkshire BD14 6PS
T: (01274) 882178
F: (01274) 882178

Carnoustie ♦♦♦
8 Park Grove, Frizinghall,
Bradford, West Yorkshire
BD9 4JY
T: (01274) 490561
F: (01274) 490561

Hillside House ♦♦♦
10 Hazelhurst Road, Daisy Hill,
Bradford, West Yorkshire
BD9 6BJ
T: (01274) 542621 & 830396

Ivy Guest House ♦♦
3 Melbourne Place, Bradford,
West Yorkshire BD5 0HZ
T: (01274) 727060 &
07721 509207
F: (01274) 306347
E: 101524,3725@compuserve.
com

Norland Guest House ♦♦♦
695 Great Horton Road,
Bradford, West Yorkshire
BD7 4DU
T: (01274) 571698
F: (01274) 503290
E: pipin@ic24.net

Westleigh Hotel ♦♦
30 Easby Road, Bradford, West
Yorkshire BD7 1QX
T: (01274) 727089
F: (01274) 394658
E: westleigh@hotel27.freeserve.
co.uk
I: www.come.
to/the_westleigh_hotel

Woodlands Guest House
♦♦♦♦
2 The Grove, Shelf, Halifax, West
Yorkshire HX3 7PD
T: (01274) 677533 &
07710 760994

BRAMHOPE
West Yorkshire

The Cottages
♦♦♦♦ SILVER AWARD
Moor Road, Bramhope, Leeds
LS16 9HH
T: (0113) 284 2754
F: (0113) 203 7496

BRAMLEY
South Yorkshire

Express By Holiday Inn ♦♦♦♦
Moorhead Way, Bramley,
Rotherham, South Yorkshire
S66 1YY
T: (01709) 730333
F: (01709) 730444
E: rotherham@
premierhotels-30.demon.co.uk

BRAYTON
North Yorkshire

Beric ♦♦♦♦
West Cottage, Mill Lane,
Brayton, Selby, North Yorkshire
YO8 9LB
T: (01757) 213318
F: (01757) 213318

BRETTON
West Yorkshire

Birch Laithes Farm ♦♦
Bretton Lane, Bretton,
Wakefield, West Yorkshire
WF4 4LF
T: (01924) 252129

BRIDLINGTON
East Riding of Yorkshire

Bay Court Hotel ♦♦♦♦
35a Sands Lane, Bridlington,
East Riding of Yorkshire
YO15 2JG
T: (01262) 676288

Bay Ridge Hotel ♦♦♦
11 Summerfield Road,
Bridlington, East Riding of
Yorkshire YO15 3LF
T: (01262) 673425
I: bridlington.
net/accommodation.
hotels/bayridge

Blantyre House Hotel ♦♦♦
21 Pembroke Terrace,
Bridlington, East Yorkshire
YO15 3BX
T: (01262) 400660
E: baker.blantyre@cwcom.net

Bosville Arms Country Hotel
♦♦♦
High Street, Rudston, Driffield,
East Yorkshire YO25 4UB
T: (01262) 420259
F: (01262) 420259
E: hogan@bosville.freeserve.co.
uk

The Ferns Hotel
Rating Applied For
Main Street, Carnaby,
Bridlington, North Humberside
YO16 4UJ
T: (01262) 678961
F: (01262) 400712
E: theferns.hotel@virgin.net

Glen Alan Hotel ♦♦♦
21 Flamborough Road,
Bridlington, East Yorkshire
YO15 2HU
T: (01262) 674650

Longcroft Hotel ♦♦♦
100 Trinity Road, Bridlington,
East Riding of Yorkshire
YO15 2HF
T: (01262) 672180
F: (01262) 672180

Newcliffe Hotel ♦♦♦
6 Belgrave Road, Bridlington,
East Riding Of Yorkshire
YO15 3JR
T: (01262) 674244

Rags Restaurant & Dyl's Hotel
♦♦♦
South Pier, Southcliff Road,
Bridlington, East Riding of
Yorkshire YO15 3AN
T: (01262) 400355 & 674791

Rosebery House ♦♦♦
1 Belle Vue, Tennyson Ave,
Bridlington, East Riding of
Yorkshire YO15 2ET
T: (01262) 670336
F: (01262) 608381

St Aubyn's Hotel ♦♦♦
111-113 Cardigan Road,
Bridlington, East Riding of
Yorkshire YO15 3LP
T: (01262) 673002

Spinnaker House Hotel ♦♦♦
19 Pembroke Terrace,
Bridlington, East Riding of
Yorkshire YO15 3BX
T: (01262) 678440
F: (01262) 678440

The Tennyson Hotel ♦♦♦
19 Tennyson Avenue,
Bridlington, North Humberside
YO15 2EU
T: (01262) 604382
I: www.bridlington.
net/accommodation/hotels/
tennyson

Victoria Hotel ♦♦♦
25/27 Victoria Road, Bridlington,
East Yorkshire YO15 2AT
T: (01262) 673871 &
07808 650600
F: (01262) 609431
E: victoria.hotel@virgin.net

The White Rose ♦♦♦
123 Cardigan Road, Bridlington,
East Riding of Yorkshire
YO15 3LP
T: (01262) 673245 &
07860 159208

Winston House Private Hotel
♦♦♦
5-6 South Street, Bridlington,
East Riding of Yorkshire
YO15 3BY
T: (01262) 670216
F: (01262) 670216
E: david@dbotham.demon.co.uk
I: www.winston@dbotham.
demon.co.uk

BRIGG
North Lincolnshire

Arties Mill ♦♦♦
Wressle Road, Castlethorpe,
Brigg, North Lincolnshire
DN20 9LF
T: (01652) 652094 & 657107
F: (01652) 657107

Holcombe Guest House ♦♦♦
34 Victoria Road, Barnetby,
North Lincolnshire DN38 6JR
T: 07850 764002
F: (01652) 680841
E: holcombe.house@virgin.net
I: holcombeguesthouse.co.uk

The Woolpack Hotel ♦♦
4 Market Place, Brigg, North
Lincolnshire DN20 8HA
T: (01652) 655649 &
07971 965826
F: (01652) 655649
E: harry@woolpack488.
freeserve.co.uk

BRIGHOUSE
West Yorkshire

The Black Bull ♦♦♦
46 Briggate, Thornton Square,
Brighouse, West Yorkshire
HD6 1EF
T: (01484) 714816
F: (01484) 721711
E: blackbullhotel@barclay.net
I: www.westel.co.uk/blackbull.
htmlwww.dukeofyork.co.uk

BRIGSLEY
North East Lincolnshire

Prospect Farm ♦♦♦♦
Waltham Road, Brigsley,
Grimsby, North East Lincolnshire
DN37 0RQ
T: (01472) 826491
F: (01472) 826491

BROUGH
East Riding of Yorkshire
Woldway ◆◆◆
10 Elloughton Road, Brough,
East Yorkshire HU15 1AE
T: (01482) 667666
I: www.spacecorp.demon.co.
uk/brough.htm

BUCKDEN
North Yorkshire
Low Raisgill ◆◆◆◆
Buckden, Skipton, North
Yorkshire BD23 5JQ
T: (01756) 760351

Redmire Farm
◆◆◆◆ SILVER AWARD
Upper Wharfedale, Buckden,
Skipton, North Yorkshire
BD23 5JD
T: (01756) 760253

BULMER
North Yorkshire
Grange Farm ◆◆◆
Bulmer, York YO60 7BN
T: (01653) 618376
F: (01653) 618600
E: foster@grangefarm35.fsnet.
co.uk

Lower Barn ◆◆◆◆
Wandales Lane, Castle Howard,
Bulmer, York YO60 7ES
T: (01653) 618575 &
07930 756289
F: (01653) 618183
E: isabelhall@lowerbarn@fsnet.
co.uk

BURNSALL
North Yorkshire
Valley View ◆◆◆◆
Burnsall, Skipton, North
Yorkshire BD23 6BN
T: (01756) 720314
F: (01756) 720314
E: fitton_valley_view@lineone.
net

BURNT YATES
North Yorkshire
High Winsley Farm ◆◆◆
Burnt Yates, Harrogate, North
Yorkshire HG3 3EP
T: (01423) 770376
E: highwinsley@got.com

The New Inn ◆◆◆◆
Burnt Yates, Harrogate, North
Yorkshire HG3 3EG
T: (01423) 771070 &
07710 513182
F: (01423) 771070
E: newinn@chrisgnaylor.force9.
co.uk
I: www.chrisgnaylor.force9.co.uk

CARLTON
North Yorkshire
Abbots Thorn ◆◆◆◆
Carlton, Leyburn, North
Yorkshire DL8 4AY
T: (01969) 640620
F: (01969) 640304
E: abbots.thorn@virgin.net
I: www.business.virgin.
net/patricia.lashmar

The Foresters Arms ◆◆◆◆
Carlton, Leyburn, North
Yorkshire DL8 4BB
T: (01969) 640272
F: (01969) 640272

Foxwood ◆◆◆
Carr Lane, Carlton, Wakefield,
West Yorkshire WF3 3RT
T: (0113) 282 4786 &
07710 830645
F: (0113) 282 4786

Middleham House ◆◆◆
Carlton, Leyburn, North
Yorkshire DL8 4BB
T: (01969) 640645

CARLTON MINIOTT
North Yorkshire
The Chesters ◆◆
Carlton Miniott, Thirsk, North
Yorkshire YO7 4NJ
T: (01845) 525505 &
17931 931422
E: holme@fasbdial.co.uk
I: members.aol.com/chestersbb

Old Red House ◆◆
Station Road, Carlton Miniott,
Thirsk, North Yorkshire YO7 4LT
T: (01845) 524383
F: (01845) 525902
E: anthony@oldredhouse.
demon.co.uk
I: www.oldredhouse.demon.co.
uk

The Poplars ◆◆◆
Carlton Miniott, Thirsk, North
Yorkshire YO7 4LX
T: (01845) 522712
F: (01845) 522712
E: chrischilton.thepoplars@
virginnet
I: www.yorkshirebandb.co.uk

CARPERBY
North Yorkshire
Cross House ◆◆
Carperby, Leyburn, North
Yorkshire DL8 4DQ
T: (01969) 663457

CASTLETON
North Yorkshire
Crown End ◆◆◆◆
Castleton, Whitby, North
Yorkshire YO21 2HP
T: (01287) 660267

The Eskdale Inn ◆◆◆
Station Road, Castleton, Whitby,
North Yorkshire YO21 2EU
T: (01287) 660234

Greystones ◆◆◆
30 High Street, Castleton,
Whitby, North Yorkshire
YO21 2DA
T: (01287) 660744

CATTERICK
North Yorkshire
Rose Cottage Guest House
◆◆◆
26 High Street, Catterick,
Richmond, North Yorkshire
DL10 7LJ
T: (01748) 811164

CHAPEL ALLERTON
West Yorkshire
Green House ◆◆◆
5 Bank View, Chapel Allerton,
Leeds LS7 2EX
T: (0113) 268 1380
E: anniegreen11@hotmail.com

CLAPHAM
North Yorkshire
Brook House Guest House
◆◆◆
Station Road, Clapham,
Lancaster LA2 8ER
T: (015242) 51580

CLEETHORPES
North East Lincolnshire
Abbeydale Guest House ◆◆◆
39 Isaacs Hill, Cleethorpes,
North East Lincolnshire
DN35 8JT
T: (01472) 692248 & 311088
F: (01472) 311088
E: abbeydale@tinyworld.co.uk
I: www.SmoothHound.co.
uk/hotels/abbeydale.html

Adelaide Hotel ◆◆◆◆
41 Isaacs Hill, Cleethorpes,
North East Lincolnshire
DN35 8JT
T: (01472) 693594
F: (01472) 329717

Alpine Guest House ◆◆◆
55 Clee Road, Cleethorpes,
South Humberside DN35 8AD
T: (01472) 690804

Ascot Lodge Guest House
◆◆◆
11 Princes Road, Cleethorpes,
North East Lincolnshire
DN35 8AW
T: (01472) 290129
F: (01472) 290129
E: ascotclee@aol.com

Brentwood Guest House ◆◆◆
9 Princes Road, Cleethorpes,
North East Lincolnshire
DN35 8AW
T: (01472) 693982

Carlton Lodge
Rating Applied For
14 Isaacs Hill, Cleethorpes,
South Humberside DN35 8JS
T: (01472) 691844

Clee House ◆◆◆◆
31-33 Clee Road, Cleethorpes,
North East Lincolnshire
DN35 8AD
T: (01472) 200850 & 200130
F: (01472) 200850
E: david@cleehouse.com
I: www.cleehouse.com

Comat Guest House ◆◆◆◆
26 Yarra Road, Cleethorpes,
North East Lincolnshire
DN35 8LS
T: (01472) 694791 & 591861
F: (01472) 592823
E: comat.guesthouse@dtn.ntl.
com

Ginnies ◆◆◆
27 Queens Parade, Cleethorpes,
North East Lincolnshire
DN35 0DF
T: (01472) 694997

Sandside Guest House ◆◆◆
17 Kingsway, Cleethorpes, North
East Lincolnshire DN35 8QU
T: (01472) 694039

Tudor Terrace Guest House
◆◆◆◆
11 Bradford Avenue,
Cleethorpes, North East
Lincolnshire DN35 0BB
T: (01472) 600800
F: (01472) 501395
E: tudor.terrace@btinternet.
com
I: web-marketing.co.
uk/tudor-terrace

White Rose Guest House ◆◆◆
13 Princes Road, Cleethorpes,
North East Lincolnshire
DN35 8AW
T: (01472) 695060

CLIFTON
North Yorkshire
Avenue Guest House ◆◆◆
6 The Avenue, Clifton, York
YO30 6AS
T: (01904) 620575

CLOUGHTON
North Yorkshire
Blacksmiths Arms ◆◆◆
High Street, Cloughton,
Scarborough, North Yorkshire
YO13 0AE
T: (01723) 870244

Cober Hill ◆◆◆
Newlands Road, Cloughton,
Scarborough, North Yorkshire
YO13 0AR
T: (01723) 870310
F: (01723) 870271
E: enquireis@coberhill.demon.
co.uk
I: www.coberhill.demon.co.uk

Wayside Farm ◆◆◆
Whitby Road, Cloughton,
Scarborough, North Yorkshire
YO13 0DX
T: (01723) 870519

CONISTONE
North Yorkshire
Ebony House ◆◆◆◆
Conistone, Skipton, North
Yorkshire BD23 5HS
T: (01756) 753139

COTTINGHAM
East Riding of Yorkshire
Kenwood House ◆◆◆
7 Newgate Street, Cottingham,
North Humberside HU16 4DY
T: (01482) 847558

COUNTERSETT
North Yorkshire
Carr End House ◆◆◆◆
Countersett, Askrigg, Leyburn,
North Yorkshire DL8 3DE
T: (01969) 650346

COXWOLD
North Yorkshire

Oldstead Grange
♦♦♦♦♦ GOLD AWARD
Oldstead, Coxwold, York
YO61 4BJ
T: (01347) 868634
F: (01347) 868634
E: oldsteadgrange@yorkshireuk.com
I: www.yorkshireuk.com

Sunley Woods Farm ♦♦♦
Husthwaite, York YO61 4QQ
T: (01347) 868418
F: (01347) 868418

CRACOE
North Yorkshire

The Corncrake ♦♦♦
Main Street, Cracoe, Skipton,
North Yorkshire BD23 6LA
T: (01756) 730205 & 730175
F: (01756) 730174
I: www.yorkshirenet.co.uk/accgde/corncrake

Devonshire Arms ♦♦♦
Grassington Road, Cracoe,
Skipton, North Yorkshire
BD23 6LA
T: (01756) 730237
F: (01756) 730142
I: www.jennings

CRAGG VALE
West Yorkshire

Hinchliffe Arms ♦♦♦♦
Cragg Vale, Hebden Bridge, West
Yorkshire HX7 5TA
T: (01422) 883256
F: (01422) 886216
E: phil.chaplin@ultonline.co.uk
I: www.hinchliffearms.com

CRAYKE
North Yorkshire

The Hermitage ♦♦♦
Mill Lane, Crayke, York YO61 4TB
T: (01347) 821635

CROPTON
North Yorkshire

Burr Bank
♦♦♦♦♦ GOLD AWARD
Cropton, Pickering, North
Yorkshire YO18 8HL
T: (01751) 417777 & 0776 884 2233
F: (01751) 417789
E: bandb@burrbank.com
I: www.burrbank.com

High Farm
♦♦♦♦ SILVER AWARD
Cropton, Pickering, North
Yorkshire YO18 8HL
T: (01751) 417461

New Inn and Cropton Brewery
♦♦♦
Cropton, Pickering, North
Yorkshire YO18 8HH
T: (01751) 417330 & 417310
F: (01751) 417310

Rose Cottage Farm Bed and Breakfast ♦♦♦♦
Rose Cottage Farm, Cropton,
Pickering, North Yorkshire
YO18 8HL
T: (01751) 417302

CROWLE
North Lincolnshire

Seven Lakes Motel ♦♦♦
Seven Lakes Leisure Park, Ealand,
Crowle, Scunthorpe, South
Humberside DN17 4JS
T: (01724) 710245
F: (01724) 711814

CROXTON
North Lincolnshire

Croxton House ♦♦♦
Croxton, Ulceby, South
Humberside DN39 6YD
T: (01652) 688306 &
07879 935343
F: (01652) 680967
E: kgallimore@supanet.com

CUNDALL
North Yorkshire

Cundall Lodge Farm ♦♦♦♦
Cundall, York YO61 2RN
T: (01423) 360203
F: (01423) 360805

DACRE BANKS
North Yorkshire

Dalriada ♦♦
Cabin Lane, Dacre Banks,
Harrogate, North Yorkshire
HG3 4EE
T: (01423) 780512 & 0771 280 5383

Gate Eel Farm ♦♦♦♦
Dacre Banks, Harrogate, North
Yorkshire HG3 4ED
T: (01423) 781707

The Royal Oak Inn ♦♦♦♦
Oak Lane, Dacre Banks,
Harrogate, North Yorkshire
HG3 4EN
T: (01423) 780200
F: (01423) 781748
E: royaloakdacre@scock@virgin.net

DALTON
North Yorkshire

Dalton Hall ♦♦♦♦
Dalton, Richmond, North
Yorkshire DL11 7HU
T: (01833) 621339

The Gables Guest House
Rating Applied For
25-27 Broad Lane, Dalton,
Huddersfield HD5 9BX
T: (01484) 540409 & 345500
F: (01484) 540409

Stonesthrow ♦♦♦
Dalton, Richmond, North
Yorkshire DL11 7HS
T: (01833) 621493 &
07970 655726

Throstle Gill Farm ♦♦♦♦
Dalton, Richmond, North
Yorkshire DL11 7HZ
T: (01833) 621363
F: (01833) 621363

Ye Jolly Farmers of Olden Times ♦♦♦
Dalton, Thirsk, North Yorkshire
YO7 3HY
T: (01845) 577359
F: (01845) 577359

DANBY
North Yorkshire

Botton Grove Farm ♦♦♦
Danby Head, Danby, Whitby,
North Yorkshire YO21 2NH
T: (01287) 660284
E: judytait@bottongrove.freeserve.co.uk

Crag Farm ♦♦♦♦
Danby, Whitby, North Yorkshire
YO21 2LQ
T: (01287) 660279
F: (01287) 660279
E: sal.b.b.cragfarm.n.y.@ukgateway.net

Crossley Gate Farm House
♦♦♦♦ SILVER AWARD
Crossley Gate Farm, Little Fryup,
Danby, Whitby, North Yorkshire
YO21 2NR
T: (01287) 660165 &
07710 263149

Duke of Wellington ♦♦♦
Danby, Whitby, North Yorkshire
YO21 2LY
T: (01287) 660351

Rowantree Farm ♦♦♦
Ainthorpe, Whitby, North
Yorkshire YO21 2LE
T: (01287) 660396
E: krbsatindall@aol.com

Stonebeck Gate Farm ♦♦♦
Little Fryup, Danby, Whitby,
North Yorkshire YO21 2NS
T: (01287) 660363
F: (01287) 660363
I: www.stonebeckgatefarm.co.uk

Sycamore House ♦♦♦
Danby Dale, Danby, Whitby,
North Yorkshire YO21 2NW
T: (01287) 660125 &
07403 714676
F: (01287) 669122
E: sycamore.danby@btinternet.com

DARLEY
North Yorkshire

Brimham Guest house ♦♦♦♦
Brookfield, Silverdale Close,
Darley, Harrogate, North
Yorkshire HG3 2PQ
T: (01423) 780948

Greenbanks ♦♦♦♦
Nidd Side, Station Road, Darley,
Harrogate, North Yorkshire
HG3 2PW
T: (01423) 780883
E: terryn'doris@nidd-side.fsnet.co.uk

DEEPDALE
North Lincolnshire

West Wold Farmhouse
Rating Applied For
West Wold Farm, Deepdale,
Barton-upon-Humber, North
Lincolnshire DN18 6ED
T: (01652) 633293
F: (01652) 633293

DEIGHTON
North Yorkshire

Grimston House ♦♦♦
Deighton, York YO19 6HB
T: (01904) 728328

Rush Farm ♦♦
Deighton, York YO19 6HQ
T: (01904) 728459

DENBY DALE
West Yorkshire

Eastfield Cottage ♦♦♦
248 Wakefield Road, Denby
Dale, Huddersfield, West
Yorkshire HD8 8SU
T: (01484) 861562

DONCASTER
South Yorkshire

Almel Hotel ♦♦
20 Christchurch Road,
Doncaster, South Yorkshire
DN1 2QL
T: (01302) 365230
F: (01302) 341434

Ashlea Hotel ♦♦♦
81 Thorne Road, Doncaster,
South Yorkshire DN1 2ES
T: (01302) 363303 & 363374
F: (01302) 760215
E: brigby@ashlea25.freeserve.co.uk

The Balmoral Hotel ♦♦♦
129 Thorne Road, Doncaster,
South Yorkshire DN2 5BH
T: (01302) 364385 &
07702 399326
F: (01302) 364385

Hamilton's Restaurant and Hotel ♦♦♦♦
Carr House Road, Doncaster,
South Yorkshire DN4 5HP
T: (01302) 760770
F: (01302) 768101
E: ham760770@aol.com

Low Farm ♦♦♦♦
The Green, Clayton, Doncaster,
South Yorkshire DN5 7DB
T: (01977) 648433 & 640472
F: (01977) 640472
E: bar@lowfarm.freeserve.co.uk
I: www.lowfarm.freeserve.co.uk

Lyntone Hotel ♦♦♦
24 Avenue Road, Wheatley,
Doncaster, South Yorkshire
DN2 4AQ
T: (01302) 361586
F: (01302) 361079

DOWNHOLME
North Yorkshire

Walburn Hall
♦♦♦♦ SILVER AWARD
Downholme, Richmond, North
Yorkshire DL11 6AF
T: (01748) 822152
F: (01748) 822152

DRIFFIELD
East Riding of Yorkshire

Kelleythorpe Farm ♦♦♦
Driffield, East Yorkshire
YO25 9DW
T: (01377) 252297
E: kelleythorpe@mcmail.com

The White Horse Inn ♦♦♦
Main Street, Hutton Cranswick,
Driffield, East Riding of
Yorkshire YO25 9QN
T: (01377) 270383 & 270136
F: (01377) 270383

EASINGWOLD
North Yorkshire

Dimple Wells ♦♦♦♦
Thormanby, York YO61 4NL
T: (01845) 501068
F: (01845) 501068

The Old Vicarage
◆◆◆◆ SILVER AWARD
Market Place, Easingwold, York
YO61 3AL
T: (01347) 821015
F: (01347) 823465
E: kirman@oldvic-easingwold.
freeserve.co.uk

Yeoman's Course House ◆◆
Thornton Hill, Easingwold, York
YO61 3PY
T: (01347) 868126
F: (01347) 868129
E: chris@yeomanscourse.fsnet.
co.uk

EAST HESLERTON
North Yorkshire

Manor Farm ◆◆◆
East Heslerton, Malton, North
Yorkshire YO17 8RN
T: (01944) 728268 &
07977 934550
F: (01944) 728268
E: dclumley@netscapeonline.co.
uk
I: members.netscapeonline.co.
uk/dclumley/

EAST MARTON
North Yorkshire

Drumlins ◆◆◆◆
Heber Drive, East Marton,
Skipton, North Yorkshire
BD23 3LS
T: (01282) 843521

EBBERSTON
North Yorkshire

Foxholm Hotel ◆◆◆
Ebberston, Scarborough, North
Yorkshire YO13 9NJ
T: (01723) 859550 &
07977 141656
F: (01723) 859550
E: kay@foxholm.freeserve.co.uk
I: www.foxholm.freeserve.co.uk

Givendale Head Farm ◆◆◆
Ebberston, Scarborough, North
Yorkshire YO13 9PU
T: (01723) 859383
F: (01723) 859383
E: Sue.gwilliam@talk21.com
I: www.visityorkshire.com
◉

Littlegarth ◆◆◆◆
High Street, Ebberston,
Scarborough, North Yorkshire
YO13 9PA
T: (01723) 850045 & 850151
F: (01723) 850151

Studley House ◆◆◆
67 Main Street, Ebberston,
Scarborough, North Yorkshire
YO13 9NR
T: (01723) 859285
F: (01723) 859285
E: ernie@jhodgson.fsnet.co.uk
I: www.studley-house.co.uk
◉

EGTON
North Yorkshire

Flushing Meadow ◆◆◆
Egton, Whitby, North Yorkshire
YO21 1UA
T: (01947) 895395
F: (01947) 895395
E: flushing_meadow_egton@
yahoo.co.uk

EGTON BRIDGE
North Yorkshire

Broom House ◆◆◆◆
Broom House Lane, Egton
Bridge, Whitby, North Yorkshire
YO21 1XD
T: (01947) 895279
F: (01947) 895657
E: welcome@
broomhouseegtonbridge.
freeserve.co.uk

The Postgate ◆◆◆
Egton Bridge, Whitby, North
Yorkshire YO21 1UX
T: (01947) 895241 & 895111
F: (01947) 895111
I: www.touristnetuk.
com/ne/postgate

ELLERKER
East Riding of Yorkshire

Littleover Lodge ◆◆◆
Hill Top, Howden Croft Hill,
Ellerker, Brough, East Yorkshire
HU15 2DE
T: (01430) 421821

ELLERTON ABBEY
North Yorkshire

Ellerton Abbey ◆◆◆
Ellerton Abbey, Richmond, North
Yorkshire DL11 6AN
T: (01748) 884067
F: (01748) 884909

ELSLACK
North Yorkshire

Tempest Arms ◆◆◆
Elslack, Skipton, North Yorkshire
BD23 3AY
T: (01282) 842450
F: (01282) 843331

EMBSAY
North Yorkshire

Bondcroft Farm ◆◆◆◆
Embsay, Skipton, North
Yorkshire BD23 6SF
T: (01756) 793371
F: (01756) 793371
E: bondcroft@yorksnet.co.uk
I: www.yorkshirenet.co.
uk/accgde/farms.htm

Rockwood House ◆◆◆
14 Main Street, Embsay, Skipton,
North Yorkshire BD23 6RE
T: (01756) 799755 &
07976 314980
F: (01756) 799755
E: jstead@btclick.com
I: home.btclick.com/jstead

EMLEY
West Yorkshire

Thorncliffe Farmhouse ◆◆◆
Thorncliffe Lane, Emley,
Huddersfield, West Yorkshire
HD8 9RS
T: (01924) 848277
F: (01924) 849041

EPPLEBY
North Yorkshire

Holly House ◆◆◆
Eppleby, Richmond, North
Yorkshire DL11 7AR
T: (01325) 718526

FACEBY
North Yorkshire

Four Wynds Bed and Breakfast
◆◆◆
Whorl Hill, Faceby,
Middlesbrough, Cleveland
TS9 7BZ
T: (01642) 701315

FADMOOR
North Yorkshire

Mount Pleasant ◆◆◆
Rudland, Fadmoor, York, North
Yorkshire YO62 7JJ
T: (01751) 431579
E: mary@rudland59.freeserve.
co.uk
I: www.rudland59.freeserve.co.
uk
◉

FEATHERSTONE
West Yorkshire

Rolands Croft Guest House ◆◆
Waldenhowe Close, Ackton Lane,
Featherstone, Pontefract, West
Yorkshire WF7 6ED
T: (01977) 790802 &
07711 915330
F: (01977) 790802

FILEY
North Yorkshire

Abbot's Leigh Hotel ◆◆◆
7 Rutland Street, Filey, North
Yorkshire YO14 9JA
T: (01723) 513334
◉

Athol Guest House ◆◆◆◆
67 West Avenue, Filey, North
Yorkshire YO14 9AX
T: (01723) 515189
E: baker@athol67.co.uk

Binton Guest House ◆◆◆
25 West Avenue, Filey, North
Yorkshire YO14 9AX
T: (01723) 513260 &
07712 657535
E: davies@bintonfiley.freeserve.
uk
◉

Cherries ◆◆◆◆
59 West Avenue, Filey, North
Yorkshire YO14 9AX
T: (01723) 513299
E: janetcherries@cs.com

Gables Guest House ◆◆◆
Rutland Street, Filey, North
Yorkshire YO14 9JB
T: (01723) 514750

Seafield Hotel ◆◆◆
9-11 Rutland Street, Filey, North
Yorkshire YO14 9JA
T: (01723) 513715
◉

FREMINGTON
North Yorkshire

Broadlands Bed & Breakfast ◆
Fremington, Richmond, North
Yorkshire DL11 6AW
T: (01748) 884297
F: (01748) 884297

FRIDAYTHORPE
East Riding of Yorkshire

**Manor House Inn and
Restaurant** ◆◆◆
Fridaythorpe, Driffield, North
Humberside YO25 9RT
T: (01377) 288221
F: (01377) 288402

FRYUP, DANBY
North Yorkshire

Crossley Side Farm ◆◆◆◆
Fryup, Danby, Whitby, North
Yorkshire YO21 2NR
T: (01287) 660313

Furnace Farm ◆◆◆
Fryup, Danby, Whitby, North
Yorkshire YO21 2AP
T: (01947) 897271

FULFORD
North Yorkshire

Adams House Hotel ◆◆◆
5 Main Street, Fulford, York
YO10 4HJ
T: (01904) 655413
F: (01904) 643203
E: bob.cook@virgin.net

FYLINGTHORPE
North Yorkshire

Croft Farm ◆◆◆◆
Church Lane, Fylingthorpe,
Whitby, North Yorkshire
YO22 4PW
T: (01947) 880231
F: (01947) 880231
◉

GANTON
North Yorkshire

Cherry Tree Cottage ◆◆◆
23 Main Street, Ganton,
Scarborough, North Yorkshire
YO12 4NR
T: (01944) 710507

Key Cottage ◆◆◆◆
10 Main Street, Ganton,
Scarborough, North Yorkshire
YO12 4NR
T: (01944) 710807 & 710062

GARFORTH
West Yorkshire

Myrtle House ◆◆◆
31 Wakefield Road, Garforth,
Leeds LS25 1AN
T: (0113) 286 6445

GARGRAVE
North Yorkshire

Old Hall Cottage ◆◆◆
41 West Street, Gargrave,
Skipton, North Yorkshire
BD23 3RJ
T: (01756) 749412
F: (01756) 748123
E: oldhallcot@aol.com

GAYLE
North Yorkshire

Blackburn Farm/Trout Fishery
◆◆◆
Blackburn Farm, Gayle, Hawes,
North Yorkshire DL8 3NX
T: (01969) 667524

Force Head Farm ◆◆◆
Gayle, Hawes, North Yorkshire
DL8 3RZ
T: (01969) 667518
F: (01969) 667518

**Rookhurst Country House
Hotel** ◆◆◆◆
West End, Gayle, Hawes, North
Yorkshire DL8 3RT
T: (01969) 667454
F: (01969) 667128
E: rookhurst@lineone.net
I: www.smoothhound.co.
uk/hotels/rookhurst

GIGGLESWICK
North Yorkshire

Black Horse Hotel ◆◆◆
Church Street, Giggleswick,
Settle, North Yorkshire
BD24 0BE
T: (01729) 822506
◉

The Harts Head Hotel ◆◆◆
Belle Hill, Giggleswick, Settle,
North Yorkshire BD24 0BA
T: (01729) 822086
F: (01729) 824992
E: hartshead@hotel52.
freeserve.co.uk

The Old Station ◆◆◆
Brackenber Lane, Giggleswick,
Settle, North Yorkshire
BD24 0EA
T: (01729) 823623 & 823623
F: (01729) 825710
E: oldstatn@dailstart.net

GILDERSOME
West Yorkshire

End Lea ◆◆◆◆
39 Town Street, Gildersome,
Morley, Leeds, West Yorkshire
LS27 7AX
T: (0113) 252 1661 &
07702 223653

GILLAMOOR
North Yorkshire

Manor Farm ◆◆◆
Gillamoor, York, North Yorkshire
YO62 7HX
T: (01751) 432695
F: (01751) 432695

GILLING EAST
North Yorkshire

Hall Farm ◆◆◆
Gilling East, York YO62 4JW
T: (01439) 788314 & 0771 328
3492
E: virginia@collinson2.fsnet.co.
uk
I: www.collinson2.fsnet.co.uk

GLAISDALE
North Yorkshire

Egton Banks Farm ◆◆◆◆
Glaisdale, Whitby, North
Yorkshire YO21 2QP
T: (01947) 897289

Hollins Farm ◆◆◆
Glaisdale, Whitby, North
Yorkshire YO21 2PZ
T: (01947) 897516

GOATHLAND
North Yorkshire

Barnet House Guest House
◆◆◆
Goathland, Whitby, North
Yorkshire YO22 5NG
T: (01947) 896201
F: (01947) 896201
E: barnethouse@gofornet.co.uk

The Beacon Guest House
◆◆◆◆
The Beacon, Goathland, Whitby,
North Yorkshire YO22 5AN
T: (01947) 896409
F: (01947) 896431
E: stewartkatz@compuserve.
com
I: www.touristnetuk.
com/ne/beacon.

Dale End Farm ◆◆
Green End, Goathland, Whitby,
North Yorkshire YO22 5LJ
T: (01947) 895371

Fairhaven Country Hotel ◆◆◆
The Common, Goathland,
Whitby, North Yorkshire
YO22 5AN
T: (01947) 896361

Heatherdene Hotel ◆◆◆
The Common, Goathland,
Whitby, North Yorkshire
YO22 5AN
T: (01947) 896334
F: (01947) 896334
E: smtco@globalnet.co.uk
I: www.touristnetuk.
com/ne/heatherdene

Heatherlands ◆◆◆
Darnholm, Goathland, Whitby,
North Yorkshire YO22 5LA
T: (01947) 896311

Prudom Guest House ◆◆◆◆
Goathland, Whitby, North
Yorkshire YO22 5AN
T: (01947) 896368
F: (01947) 896030
E: prudomhouse@free4all.co.uk
I: www.prudomhouse.free4all.
co.uk

GOLDSBOROUGH
North Yorkshire

Goldsborough House Barn Flat
◆◆◆
Goldsborough House,
Goldsborough, Knaresborough,
North Yorkshire HG5 8PS
T: (01423) 860300
F: (01423) 860301
E: camillab@travelcounsellors.
com

GOXHILL
North Lincolnshire

Glengarth ◆◆◆
South End, Goxhill, Barrow upon
Humber, North Lincolnshire
DN19 7LZ
T: (01469) 530991 &
07977 946957
F: (01469) 530991

King's Well ◆◆
Howe Lane, Goxhill, Barrow
upon Humber, North
Lincolnshire DN19 7HU
T: (01469) 532471
F: (01469) 532471

GRASSINGTON
North Yorkshire

Clarendon Hotel ◆◆◆
Hebden, Grassington, Skipton,
North Yorkshire BD23 5DE
T: (01756) 752446
E: clarhotel@aol.com
I: www.
daelnet/information/
clarendonhotel.

Craiglands Guest House
◆◆◆◆
1 Brooklyn, Threshfield,
Grassington, Skipton, North
Yorkshire BD23 5ER
T: (01756) 752093
E: craiglands@talk21.com
I: www.craiglands.yorks.net

Foresters Arms Hotel ◆◆◆
20 Main Street, Grassington,
Skipton, North Yorkshire
BD23 5AA
T: (01756) 752349
F: (01756) 753633
E: phil&rita@theforesters.
freeserve.co.uk!

Grange Cottage ◆◆◆
Linton, Skipton, North Yorkshire
BD23 5HH
T: (01756) 752527

**Grassington Lodge Guest
House** ◆◆◆◆ SILVER AWARD
8 Wood Lane, Grassington,
Skipton, North Yorkshire
BD23 5LU
T: (01756) 752518
F: (01756) 752518

Long Ashes Inn ◆◆◆◆
Long Ashes Park, Threshfield,
Skipton, North Yorkshire
BD23 5PN
T: (01756) 752434
F: (01756) 752937
E: info@longashesinn.co.uk
I: www.longashesinn.co.uk

New Laithe House ◆◆◆
Wood Lane, Grassington,
Skipton, North Yorkshire
BD23 5LU
T: (01756) 752764
E: enquiries@newlaithehouse.
co.uk
I: www.newlaithehouse.co.uk

Raines Close Guest House
◆◆◆◆
Station Road, Grassington,
Skipton, North Yorkshire
BD23 5LS
T: (01756) 752678
E: rainesclose@yorks.net
I: www.yorkshirenet.co.uk

Springroyd House ◆◆◆
8A Station Road, Grassington,
Skipton, North Yorkshire
BD23 5NQ
T: (01756) 752473 &
07703 203607
F: (01756) 7522473
E: springroyd.house@
btinternet.com

GREAT AYTON
North Yorkshire

Pinchinthorpe Hall ◆◆◆◆
Pinchinthorpe, Great Ayton,
Middlesbrough, Cleveland
TS14 8HG
T: (01287) 630200 & 632000
F: (01287) 630200

Royal Oak Hotel ◆◆◆
High Green, Great Ayton,
Middlesbrough, Cleveland
TS9 6BW
T: (01642) 722361
F: (01642) 724047

GREAT BARUGH
North Yorkshire

Hill Brow ◆◆◆
Great Barugh, Malton, North
Yorkshire YO17 0UZ
T: (01653) 668426

Old Church House ◆◆◆◆
Great Barugh, Malton, North
Yorkshire YO17 6UZ
T: (01653) 668110

White House Farm ◆◆◆◆
Great Barugh, Malton, North
Yorkshire YO17 6XB
T: (01653) 668317

GREAT EDSTONE
North Yorkshire

Cowldyke Farm ◆◆◆
Great Edstone, York YO62 6PE
T: (01751) 431242

GREAT LANGTON
North Yorkshire

Wishing Well Inn ◆◆
Great Langton, Northallerton,
North Yorkshire DL7 0TE
T: (01609) 748233

GREEN HAMMERTON
North Yorkshire

Bay Horse Inn ◆◆◆
York Road, Green Hammerton,
York YO26 8BN
T: (01423) 330338 & 331113
F: (01423) 331279
E: bayhorsepc@ao.com
I: www.thebayhorse.com

GREETLAND
West Yorkshire

Winchester ◆◆◆
4 Minster Close, Greetland,
Halifax, West Yorkshire
HX4 8QW
T: (01422) 377005

GRIMSBY
North East Lincolnshire

The Danish Lodge ◆◆◆◆
2-4 Cleethorpes Road, Grimsby,
North East Lincolnshire
DN31 3LQ
T: (01472) 342257
F: (01472) 344156

GROSMONT
North Yorkshire

Eskdale ◆◆◆
Grosmont, Whitby, North
Yorkshire YO22 5PT
T: (01947) 895385
E: d_and_s_counsell@yahoo.co.
uk

GUISELEY
West Yorkshire

Bowood ◆◆◆
Carlton Lane, Guiseley, Leeds
LS20 9NL
T: (01943) 874556

GUNNERSIDE
North Yorkshire

Dalegarth House ◆◆◆
Gunnerside, Richmond, North
Yorkshire DL11 6LD
T: (01748) 886275

Oxnop Hall ◆◆◆
Low Oxnop, Gunnerside,
Richmond, North Yorkshire
DL11 6JJ
T: (01748) 886253
F: (01748) 886253

HABROUGH
North East Lincolnshire

Church Farm ◆◆◆◆
Immingham Road, Habrough,
Immingham, North East
Lincolnshire DN40 3BD
T: (01469) 576190

HACKFORTH
North Yorkshire

Ainderby Myers Farm ◆◆
Hackforth, Bedale, North
Yorkshire DL8 1PF
T: (01609) 748668 & 748424
F: (01609) 748424

HALIFAX
West Yorkshire

Beech Court ◆◆◆
40 Prescott Street, Halifax, West
Yorkshire HX1 2QW
T: (01422) 366004

551

35 Cheltenham Gardens ◆◆
Huddersfield Road, Halifax, West
Yorkshire HX3 0AN
T: (01422) 364696

Claytons ◆◆◆
146 Pye Nest Road, Halifax,
West Yorkshire HX2 7HS
T: (01422) 835053

The Elms ◆◆◆
Keighley Road, Illingworth,
Halifax, West Yorkshire HX2 8HT
T: (01422) 244430
I: sylvia@theelms.f9.co.uk

Field House ◆◆◆◆
Staups Lane, Stump Cross,
Halifax, West Yorkshire
HX3 6XW
T: (01422) 355457 &
0772 066580
E: stayatfieldhouse@yahoo.co.
uk

Halifax Guest House ◆◆◆◆
130 Skircoat Road, Halifax, West
Yorkshire HX1 2RE
T: (01422) 355912
F: (01422) 344924
◎

Heathleigh ◆◆◆
124 Skircoat Road, Halifax, West
Yorkshire HX1 2RE
T: (01422) 323957

Joan's Guest House ◆◆
13 Heath Park Avenue, Halifax,
West Yorkshire HX1 2PP
T: (01422) 369290

Mozart House ◆◆◆
34 Prescott Street, Halifax, West
Yorkshire HX1 2QW
T: (01422) 340319 & 256419
F: (01422) 340319

Shibden Mill Inn ◆◆◆
Shibden Mill Fold, Halifax, West
Yorkshire HX3 7UL
T: (01422) 365840 & 365840
F: (01422) 362971
E: shibdenmillinn@zoom.co.uk

Victoria Hotel ◆◆
31-35 Horton Street, Halifax,
West Yorkshire HX1 1QE
T: (01422) 351209 & 358392
F: (01422) 351209
E: greg@victoriahotelltd.

HAMPSTHWAITE
North Yorkshire
Graystone View Farm ◆◆◆◆
Grayston Plain Lane,
Hampsthwaite, Harrogate, North
Yorkshire HG3 2LY
T: (01423) 770324
F: (01423) 772536
E: graystonefm.freeserve.co.uk
◎

HARDRAW
North Yorkshire
Bushby Garth ◆◆◆
Hardraw, Hawes, North
Yorkshire DL8 3LZ
T: (01969) 667644

HARMBY
North Yorkshire
Sunnyridge ◆
Argill Farm, Harmby, Leyburn,
North Yorkshire DL8 5HQ
T: (01969) 622478
◎

HARPHAM
East Riding of Yorkshire
St Quintin Arms Inn ◆◆◆◆
Main Street, Harpham, Driffield,
East Riding of Yorkshire
YO25 4QY
T: (01262) 490329

HARROGATE
North Yorkshire
Abbatt & Young's Hotel ◆◆◆
15 York Road, Off Swan Road,
Harrogate, North Yorkshire
HG1 2QL
T: (01423) 567336 & 521231
F: (01423) 500042
E: abbatt@aol.com
I: www.members.aol.
com/abbatt/hotel.htm

Abbey Lodge ◆◆◆
29-31 Ripon Road, Harrogate,
North Yorkshire HG1 2JL
T: (01423) 569712
F: (01423) 530570
E: abbey@hotels.harrogate.com

Acomb Lodge ◆◆◆
6 Franklin Road, Harrogate,
North Yorkshire HG1 5EE
T: (01423) 563599

Acorn Lodge Hotel ◆◆◆
1 Studley Road, Harrogate,
North Yorkshire HG1 5JU
T: (01423) 525630
F: (01423) 564413

Alamah ◆◆◆
88 Kings Road, Harrogate, North
Yorkshire HG1 5JX
T: (01423) 502187
F: (01423) 566175

Albany Hotel ◆◆◆
22-23 Harlow Moor Drive,
Harrogate, North Yorkshire
HG2 0JY
T: (01423) 565890
F: (01423) 565890

Alderside Guest House ◆◆
11 Belmont Road, Harrogate,
North Yorkshire HG2 0LR
T: (01423) 529400 &
10142 527531

The Alexander ◆◆◆◆
88 Franklin Road, Harrogate,
North Yorkshire HG1 5EN
T: (01423) 503348
F: (01423) 540230
◎

Alexandra Court Hotel
◆◆◆◆ SILVER AWARD
8 Alexandra Road, Harrogate,
North Yorkshire HG1 5JS
T: (01423) 502764
F: (01423) 523151
E: alexandracourt@zoom.co.uk

Alvera Court Hotel ◆◆◆◆
76 Kings Road, Harrogate, North
Yorkshire HG1 5JX
T: (01423) 505735
F: (01423) 507996

Amadeus Hotel ◆◆◆◆
115 Franklin Road, Harrogate,
North Yorkshire HG1 5EN
T: (01423) 505151
F: (01423) 505151
E: frankland@theamadeushotel.
totalserve.co.uk
I: www.acartha.
com/amadeushotel

Anro ◆◆◆
90 Kings Road, Harrogate, North
Yorkshire HG1 5JX
T: (01423) 503087
F: (01423) 561719
E: anro@joyner.fsnet.co.uk
I: www.smoothhound.co.
uk/hotels/anro.html

Arden House Hotel ◆◆◆◆
69-71 Franklin Road, Harrogate,
North Yorkshire HG1 5EH
T: (01423) 509224
F: (01423) 561170
E: prop@ardenhousehotel.
free-online.co.uk

Argyll House ◆◆◆
80 King's Road, Harrogate,
North Yorkshire HG1 5JX
T: (01423) 562408
F: (01423) 567166

Ashbrooke House Hotel
◆◆◆◆
140 Valley Drive, Harrogate,
North Yorkshire HG2 0JS
T: (01423) 564478
F: (01423) 564478
E: ashbrooke@harogate.com
I: www.harrogate.
com/ashbrooke

Ashley House Hotel ◆◆◆◆
36-40 Franklin Road, Harrogate,
North Yorkshire HG1 5EE
T: (01423) 507474
F: (01423) 560858
E: ron@ashleyhousehotel.com
I: www.ashleyhousehotel.com
◎

Ashwood House ◆◆◆◆
7 Spring Grove, Harrogate,
North Yorkshire HG1 2HS
T: (01423) 560081
F: (01423) 527928
E: ashwoodhouse@excite.com
I: www.ashwoodhouse.co.uk

Askern Guest House ◆◆◆
3 Dragon Parade, Harrogate,
North Yorkshire HG1 5BZ
T: (01423) 523057
F: (01423) 523057
E: john.coughtrey@virgin.net

Aston House ◆◆◆
7-9 Franklin Mount, Harrogate,
North Yorkshire HG1 5EJ
T: (01423) 564262
F: (01423) 505542
E: astonhotel@btinternet.com

Azalea Court Hotel ◆◆◆
56-58 Kings Road, Harrogate,
North Yorkshire HG1 5JR
T: (01423) 560424
F: (01423) 505662
🚶

Barkers Guest House ◆◆◆
202-204 King's Road, Harrogate,
North Yorkshire HG1 5JG
T: (01423) 568494

The Beeches Hotel ◆◆◆
103-105 Valley Drive, Harrogate,
North Yorkshire HG2 0JP
T: (01423) 522246
F: (01423) 531940
E: beeches@harrogate.com
I: www.beecheshotel.com

Britannia Lodge Hotel ◆◆◆◆
16 Swan Road, Harrogate, North
Yorkshire HG1 2SA
T: (01423) 508482
F: (01423) 526840
E: britlodge3@aol.com
I: www.hotelregister.co.uk
◎

Brookfield House ◆◆◆◆
5 Alexandra Road, Harrogate,
North Yorkshire HG1 5JS
T: (01423) 506646
F: (01423) 566470
◎

Brooklands ◆◆◆
5 Valley Drive, Harrogate, North
Yorkshire HG2 0JJ
T: (01423) 564609

Camberley Hotel ◆◆◆◆
52-54 Kings Road, Harrogate,
North Yorkshire HG1 5JR
T: (01423) 561618
F: (01423) 536360

Cavendish Hotel ◆◆◆◆
3 Valley Drive, Harrogate, North
Yorkshire HG2 0JJ
T: (01423) 509637

Claremont House ◆◆◆
8 Westcliffe Grove, Harrogate,
North Yorkshire HG2 0PL
T: (01423) 502738 &
07966 174785

Conference View Guest House
◆◆◆
74 Kings Road, Harrogate, North
Yorkshire HG1 5JR
T: (01423) 563075 &
07778 143160
F: (01423) 563075
E: admin@conferenceview.f9.
co.uk
I: www.conferenceview.f9.co.uk

The Coppice ◆◆◆
9 Studley Road, Harrogate,
North Yorkshire HG1 5JU
T: (01423) 569626
F: (01423) 569005
E: coppice@harrogate.com
I: www.harrogate.com/coppice

Craigmoor Manor Hotel ◆◆◆
10 Harlow Moor Drive,
Harrogate, North Yorkshire
HG2 0JX
T: (01423) 523562
F: (01423) 523562

Crescent Lodge ◆◆◆◆
20 Swan Road, Harrogate, North
Yorkshire HG1 2SA
T: (01423) 503688
F: (01423) 503688
E: peter.humphris@dial.pipex.
com

The Dales Hotel ◆◆◆◆
101 Valley Drive, Harrogate,
North Yorkshire HG2 0JP
T: (01423) 507248
F: (01423) 507248
E: dales.hotel@virgin.net
I: www.4tourism.
com/uk/hotels/dales.html

Daryl House Hotel ◆◆◆◆
42 Dragon Parade, Harrogate,
North Yorkshire HG1 5DA
T: (01423) 502775
F: (01423) 502775

Delaine Hotel
♦♦♦♦ SILVER AWARD
17 Ripon Road, Harrogate,
North Yorkshire HG1 2JL
T: (01423) 567974
F: (01423) 561723

Dragon House ♦♦♦
6 Dragon Parade, Harrogate,
North Yorkshire HG1 5DA
T: (01423) 569888 &
07808 416576

Eton House ♦♦♦
3 Eton Terrace, Knaresborough
Road, Harrogate, North
Yorkshire HG2 7SU
T: (01423) 886850
F: (01423) 886850

Franklin Hotel ♦♦♦
25 Franklin Road, Harrogate,
North Yorkshire HG1 5ED
T: (01423) 569028
E: flack@frantel74.freeserve.co.
uk
I: www.thefranklinhotel.com

Franklin View ♦♦♦♦
19 Grove Road, Harrogate,
North Yorkshire HG1 5EW
T: (01423) 541388
F: (01423) 547872
E: frnkview@dialstart.net

The Gables Hotel ♦♦♦
2 West Grove Road, Harrogate,
North Yorkshire HG1 2AD
T: (01423) 505625
F: (01423) 561312

Garden House Hotel ♦♦♦♦
14 Harlow Moor Drive,
Harrogate, North Yorkshire
HG2 0JX
T: (01423) 503059
F: (01423) 503059
E: gardenhouse@hotels.
harrogate.com
I: www.harrogate.
com/gardenhouse
🌐

Geminian Guest House ♦♦♦
11-13 Franklin Road, Harrogate,
North Yorkshire HG1 5ED
T: (01423) 523347 & 561768
F: (01423) 523347

Gillmore Hotel ♦♦♦
98 Kings Road, Harrogate, North
Yorkshire HG1 5HH
T: (01423) 503699 & 507122
F: (01423) 563223
E: gillmoregh@aol.com

Glynhaven ♦♦♦
72 Kings Road, Harrogate, North
Yorkshire HG1 5JR
T: (01423) 569970
F: (01423) 569970

Grafton Hotel ♦♦♦♦
1-3 Franklin Mount, Harrogate,
North Yorkshire HG1 5EJ
T: (01423) 508491
F: (01423) 523168
E: enquiries@graftonhotel.co.uk
I: www.graftonhotel.co.uk

Half Moon Inn ♦♦
Main Street, Pool in Wharfedale,
Otley, West Yorkshire LS21 1LH
T: (0113) 284 2878

Hatton House Farm ♦♦♦♦
Colber Lane, Bishop Thornton,
Harrogate, North Yorkshire
HG3 3JA
T: (01423) 770315
F: (01423) 771438

Hollins House ♦♦♦
17 Hollins Road, Harrogate,
North Yorkshire HG1 2JF
T: (01423) 503646
F: (01423) 503646

Imbercourt Hotel ♦♦
57 Valley Drive, Harrogate,
North Yorkshire HG2 0JW
T: (01423) 502513
F: (01423) 562696

Kimberley Hotel ♦♦♦♦
11-19 Kings Road, Harrogate,
North Yorkshire HG1 5JY
T: (01423) 505613
F: (01423) 530276
E: info@kimberley.scotnet

Kingsway Hotel ♦♦♦
36 Kings Road, Harrogate, North
Yorkshire HG1 5JW
T: (01423) 562179
F: (01423) 562179
E: baznoble@aol.com

Knabbs Ash
♦♦♦♦ GOLD AWARD
Skipton Road, Felliscliffe,
Harrogate, North Yorkshire
HG3 2LT
T: (01423) 771040
F: (01423) 771515
E: colin&tsheila@knabbsash.
freeserve.co.uk
🌐

Lamont House ♦♦♦
12 St Mary's Walk, Harrogate,
North Yorkshire HG2 0LW
T: (01423) 567143
F: (01423) 567143

Mrs Murray's Guest House
♦♦♦
67 Franklin Road, Harrogate,
North Yorkshire HG1 5EH
T: (01423) 505857
F: (01423) 530027

Oakbrae Guest House ♦♦♦♦
3 Springfield Avenue, Harrogate,
North Yorkshire HG1 2HR
T: (01423) 567682
F: (01423) 567682

Park Gate Hotel ♦♦♦
61-63 Valley Drive, Harrogate,
North Yorkshire HG2 0JW
T: (01423) 567010
F: (01423) 504045

Parnas Hotel ♦♦♦♦
98 Franklin Road, Harrogate,
North Yorkshire HG1 5EN
T: (01423) 564493
F: (01423) 564493
E: robert@parho.freeserve.co.uk
I: www.scoot.co.
uk/parnas_hotel/

17 Peckfield Close ♦♦♦
Hampsthwaite, Harrogate, North
Yorkshire HG3 2ES
T: (01423) 770765

Rosedale Hotel ♦♦♦
86 Kings Road, Harrogate, North
Yorkshire HG1 5JX
T: (01423) 566630
F: (01423) 505082
E: larryweatherill@aol.com
I: www.smoothhound.co.
uk/hotels/rosedali.html

Royd Mount ♦♦♦♦
4 Grove Road, Harrogate, North
Yorkshire HG1 5EW
T: (01423) 529525

Ruskin Hotel
♦♦♦♦♦ SILVER AWARD
1 Swan Road, Harrogate, North
Yorkshire HG1 2SS
T: (01423) 502045
F: (01423) 506131
E: ruskin.hotel@virgin.net
I: www.smoothhound.co.
uk/hotels/ruskin.html

Scotia House Hotel ♦♦♦
66-68 Kings Road, Harrogate,
North Yorkshire HG1 5JR
T: (01423) 504361
F: (01423) 526578
E: info@scotiahotel.harrogate.
net
I: www.scotiahotel.harrogate.net

Shannon Court Hotel ♦♦♦♦
65 Dragon Avenue, Harrogate,
North Yorkshire HG1 5DS
T: (01423) 509858
F: (01423) 530606
E: shannon@hotel.harrogate.
com
I: courthotel.freeserve.co.uk

Sherwood ♦♦♦
7 Studley Road, Harrogate,
North Yorkshire HG1 5JU
T: (01423) 503033
F: (01423) 564659
E: sherwood@hotels.harrogate.
com
I: www.sherwood-hotel.com

Spring Lodge Guest House
♦♦♦
22 Spring Mount, Harrogate,
North Yorkshire HG1 2HX
T: (01423) 506036
F: (01423) 506036

Staveleigh
♦♦♦♦ SILVER AWARD
20 Ripon Road, Harrogate,
North Yorkshire HG1 2JJ
T: (01423) 524175
F: (01423) 524178
E: staveleigh.uk@virgin.net

Sunflower House ♦♦♦
61 Grantley Drive, Harrogate,
North Yorkshire HG3 2XU
T: (01423) 503261

Valley Hotel ♦♦♦♦
93-95 Valley Drive, Harrogate,
North Yorkshire HG2 0JP
T: (01423) 504868
F: (01423) 531940
E: valley@harrogate.com
I: www.harrogate.com/valley

The Welford ♦♦♦
27 Franklin Road, Harrogate,
North Yorkshire HG1 5ED
T: (01423) 566041 & 525344
F: (01423) 566041

Wharfedale House ♦♦♦
28 Harlow Moor Drive,
Harrogate, North Yorkshire
HG2 0JY
T: (01423) 522233

Windmill House ♦♦
9 Belmont Road, Harrogate,
North Yorkshire HG2 0LR
T: (01423) 565382

HARTWITH
North Yorkshire

Brimham Lodge ♦♦♦
Hartwith, Harrogate, North
Yorkshire HG3 3HE
T: (01423) 771770
F: (01423) 770370

HARWOOD DALE
North Yorkshire

Burgate Farm ♦♦♦
Harwood Dale, Scarborough,
North Yorkshire YO13 0DS
T: (01723) 870333

The Grainary ♦♦♦♦
Keasbeck Hill Farm, Harwood
Dale, Scarborough, North
Yorkshire YO13 0DT
T: (01723) 870026 &
07712 652633
F: (01723) 870026
E: thesimpsons@grainary.
freeserve.co.uk
🌐 ♿

Hardwick House
♦♦♦♦ SILVER AWARD
Harwood Dale, Scarborough,
North Yorkshire YO13 0LA
T: (01723) 870682
F: (01723) 871416
E: hardwick@globalnet.co.uk

HAWES
North Yorkshire

Beech House ♦♦
Burtersett Road, Hawes, North
Yorkshire DL8 3NP
T: (01969) 667486

Bulls Head Hotel ♦♦♦♦
Market Place, Hawes, North
Yorkshire DL8 3RD
T: (01969) 667437
F: (01969) 667048
I: www.bullsheadhotel.com

The Bungalow ♦♦♦
Spring Bank, Hawes, North
Yorkshire DL8 3NW
T: (01969) 667209

Cocketts Hotel and Restaurant
♦♦♦♦
Market Place, Hawes, North
Yorkshire DL8 3RD
T: (01969) 667312
F: (01969) 667162
E: cocketss@callnetuk.com
I: www.yell.co.
uk/sites/cocketts-hotel/

East House ♦♦♦♦
Gayle, Hawes, North Yorkshire
DL8 3RZ
T: (01969) 667405
E: lorna@lineone.net

Ebor Guest House ♦♦♦
Burtersett Road, Hawes, North
Yorkshire DL8 3NT
T: (01969) 667337
F: (01969) 667337
E: eborhouse@freeserve.co.uk
🌐

Fairview House ◆◆◆◆
Burtersett Road, Hawes, North
Yorkshire DL8 3NP
T: (01969) 667348
F: (01969) 6677348
E: joan.bill.fairview@tinyonline.
co.uk
I: www.wensleydale.org

Herriots Hotel & Restaurant
◆◆◆◆
Main Street, Hawes, North
Yorkshire DL8 3QW
T: (01969) 667536
F: (01969) 667810
E: herriotshotel@aol.com
I: www.herriots.com

Old Station House ◆◆◆◆
Hardraw Road, Hawes, North
Yorkshire DL8 3NL
T: (01969) 667785
E: alan@watkinson@virgin.net
🌐 👣

Pry House ◆◆◆
Hawes, North Yorkshire DL8 3LP
T: (01969) 667241
🌐

South View ◆◆◆
Gayle Lane, Hawes, North
Yorkshire DL8 3RW
T: (01969) 667447

Springbank House ◆◆◆
Springbank, Townfoot, Hawes,
North Yorkshire DL8 3NW
T: (01969) 667376

White Hart Inn ◆◆◆
Main Street, Hawes, North
Yorkshire DL8 3QL
T: (01969) 667259
F: (01969) 667259
E: gordon@white-hart.
totalserve.com
I: www.wensleydale.org
🌐

Widdale Foot ◆◆◆
Hawes, North Yorkshire DL8 3LX
T: (01969) 667383
F: (01969) 667383
🌐

HAWNBY
North Yorkshire

Easterside Farm ◆◆◆
Hawnby, York YO62 5QT
T: (01439) 798277
F: (01439) 798277

The Hawnby Hotel ◆◆◆
Hawnby, York YO62 5QS
T: (01439) 798202
F: (01439) 798344
E: info@hawnbyhotel.co.uk
I: www.hawnbyhotel.co.uk

HAWORTH
West Yorkshire

Aiches Guest House
Rating Applied For
11 West Lane, Haworth,
Keighley, West Yorkshire
BD22 8OU
T: (01535) 642501

The Apothecary Guest House
◆◆◆
86 Main Street, Haworth,
Keighley, West Yorkshire
BD22 8DA
T: (01535) 643642
F: (01535) 643642
E: apot@sisley86.freeserve.co.
uk
I: www.sisley86.freeserve.co.uk

Ashmount
◆◆◆◆ SILVER AWARD
Mytholmes Lane, Haworth,
Keighley, West Yorkshire
BD22 8EZ
T: (01535) 645726
F: (01535) 645726
E: ashmounthaworth@aol.com
I: members.aol.
com/ashmounthaworth

Bronte Hotel ◆◆
Lees Lane, Haworth, Keighley,
West Yorkshire BD22 8RA
T: (01535) 644112
F: (01535) 646725

Ebor House ◆◆◆
Lees Lane, Haworth, Keighley,
West Yorkshire BD22 8RA
T: (01535) 645869

**Haworth Tea Rooms and Guest
House** ◆◆◆
68 Main Street, Haworth,
Keighley, West Yorkshire
BD22 8DP
T: (01535) 644278 &
(01780) 751799

Heather Cottage Guest House
◆◆◆
25-27 Main Street, Haworth,
Keighley, West Yorkshire
BD22 8DA
T: (01535) 644511 &
07702 552076
E: heathercott@
haworthmsfreeserve.co.uk

Hole Farm ◆◆◆◆
Dimples Lane, Haworth,
Keighley, West Yorkshire
BD22 8QT
T: (01535) 644755
F: (01535) 644755
E: holefarm@bronteholidays.co.
uk
I: www.bronteholidays.co.uk
🌐

Jennrita Cottage ◆◆◆◆
3 Oldfield Gate, Haworth,
Keighley, West Yorkshire
BD22 0EW
T: (01535) 647121

Kershaw House ◆◆◆◆
90 West Lane, Haworth,
Keighley, West Yorkshire
BD22 8EN
T: (01535) 642074 &
07973 734758
F: (01535) 642074

Meltham House ◆◆
3 Belle Isle Road, Haworth,
Keighley, West Yorkshire
BD22 8QQ
T: (01535) 645282

Moorfield Guest House ◆◆◆
80 West Lane, Haworth,
Keighley, West Yorkshire
BD22 8EN
T: (01535) 643689
F: (01535) 643689
E: daveandann@moorfieldgh.
demon.co.uk

The Old Registry ◆◆◆
2-4 Main Street, Haworth,
Keighley, West Yorkshire
BD22 8DA
T: (01535) 646503
F: (01535) 646503
E: oldregistry.haworth@virgin.
net
I: www.old-registry.co.uk

Park Top House ◆◆◆◆
1 Rawdon Road, Haworth,
Keighley, West Yorkshire
BD22 8DX
T: (01535) 646102

6 Penistone Mews ◆◆◆◆
Rawdon Road, Haworth,
Keighley, West Yorkshire
BD22 8DF
T: (01535) 647412
E: philip@haworth3.freeserve.
co.uk

**Woodlands Grange Private
Hotel** ◆◆◆
Woodlands Grange, Belle Isle,
Haworth, Keighley, West
Yorkshire BD22 8PB
T: (01535) 646814

Ye Sleeping House ◆
8 Main Street, Haworth,
Keighley, West Yorkshire
BD22 8DA
T: (01535) 645992 & 644102
F: (01535) 645992
E: mike@sleepyhouse.freeserve.
co.uk
I: www.smoothhound.co.uk

HAXEY
South Yorkshire

Duke William ◆◆◆
Church Street, Haxey, Doncaster,
South Yorkshire DN9 2HY
T: (01427) 752210
F: (01427) 752210

HEADINGLEY
West Yorkshire

Boundary Hotel Express ◆◆
42 Cardigan Road, Headingley,
Leeds LS6 3AG
T: (0113) 275 7700
F: (0113) 275 7700

Cardigan Private Hotel ◆◆◆
36 Cardigan Road, Headingley,
Leeds LS6 3AG
T: (0113) 278 4301
F: (0113) 230 7792

17 Cottage Road ◆◆
Headingley, Leeds, West
Yorkshire LS6 4DD
T: (0113) 275 5575

Oak Villa Hotel ◆◆◆
55/57 Cardigan Road,
Headingley, Leeds LS6 1DW
T: (0113) 275 8439
F: (0113) 275 8439

HEATON
West Yorkshire

49 Haslingden Drive
Rating Applied For
Heaton, Bradford, West
Yorkshire BD9 5HT
T: (01274) 545164
E: johndickson@49haslingden.
freeserve.co.uk

HEBDEN
North Yorkshire

Court Croft ◆◆◆
Church Lane, Hebden, Skipton,
North Yorkshire BD23 5DX
T: (01756) 753406

HEBDEN BRIDGE
West Yorkshire

Angeldale Guest House ◆◆◆
Hanging Royd Lane, Hebden
Bridge, West Yorkshire HX7 7DD
T: (01422) 847321

Badger Fields Farm ◆◆◆
Badger Lane, Blackshaw Head,
Hebden Bridge, West Yorkshire
HX7 7JX
T: (01422) 845161

8 Birchcliffe ◆◆◆
Off Sandy Gate, Hebden Bridge,
West Yorkshire HX7 8JA
T: (01422) 844777

The Grove Inn ◆◆◆
Burnley Road, Brearley,
Luddendenfoot, Halifax, West
Yorkshire HX2 6HS
T: (01422) 883235
F: (01422) 883905

Myrtle Grove ◆◆◆◆
Old Lees Road, Hebden Bridge,
West Yorkshire HX7 8HL
T: (01422) 846078 &
07946 478360
🌐

Nutclough House Hotel ◆◆◆
Keighley Road, Hebden Bridge,
West Yorkshire HX7 8EZ
T: (01422) 844361

1 Primrose Terrace ◆◆
Hebden Bridge, West Yorkshire
HX7 6HN
T: (01422) 844747

Prospect End ◆◆◆
8 Prospect Terrace, Savile Road,
Hebden Bridge, West Yorkshire
HX7 6NA
T: (01422) 843586
🌐

Robin Hood Inn ◆◆◆
Pecket Well, Hebden Bridge,
West Yorkshire HX7 8QR
T: (01422) 842593 &
07979 854338
F: (01422) 844938
E: enquires@therobinhoodinn.
co.uk
🌐

Royd Well ◆◆◆
35 Royd Terrace, Hebden Bridge,
West Yorkshire HX7 7BT
T: (01422) 845304
🌐

1 St John's Close ◆◆◆
Rating Applied For
Hebden Bridge, West Yorkshire
HX7 8PD
T: (01422) 843321
E: angela.barrs@lineone.net

White Lion Hotel ◆◆◆
Bridge Gate, Hebden Bridge,
West Yorkshire HX7 8EX
T: (01422) 842197
F: (01422) 846619

HELMSLEY
North Yorkshire

Argyle House ◆◆◆◆
Ashdale Road, Helmsley, York
YO62 5DD
T: (01439) 770590

Carlton Grange ◆◆◆
Helmsley, York YO62 5HH
T: (01439) 770259

Griff Farm Bed & Breakfast
◆◆◆◆
Griff Farm, Helmsley, York
YO62 5EN
T: (01439) 771600 &
07801 145049
F: (01439) 770462
E: j.fairburn@farmline.com

High House Farm ◆◆◆
Sutton Bank, Thirsk, North
Yorkshire YO7 2HA
T: (01845) 597557

Laskill Farm ◆◆◆◆
Hawnby, York YO62 5NB
T: (01439) 798268
F: (01439) 798268
E: suesmith@laskillfarm.fsnet.
co.uk

Lemm's ◆◆◆
19 Bridge Street, Helmsley, York
YO62 5BG
T: (01439) 771555 & 771515
F: (01439) 771515
E: cuisine-eclairee@
compuserve.com

Mount Grace Farm ◆◆◆◆
Cold Kirby, Thirsk, North
Yorkshire YO7 2HL
T: (01845) 597389 & 597389
F: (01845) 579389
E: joyce@mountgracefarm.com
I: www.mountgracefarm.com

**Plumpton Court
Rating Applied For**
High Street, Nawton, York
YO62 7TT
T: (01439) 771223 &
07943 712048
F: (01439) 771223
E: plumptoncourt@ukgateway.
net
I: www.swiftlink.pnc-uk.
net/gh/1020.htm

Sproxton Hall ◆◆◆◆
Sproxton, York YO62 5EQ
T: (01439) 770225
F: (01439) 771373
E: info@sproxtonhall.demon.co.
uk
I: www.yorkshirenet.co.
uk/stayat/sproxtonhall

Stilworth House ◆◆◆◆
1 Church Street, Helmsley, York,
North Yorkshire YO62 5AD
T: (01439) 771072
E: carol@stilworth.co.uk
I: www.stilworth.co.uk

HEPTONSTALL
West Yorkshire

Poppyfields House ◆◆◆
29 Slack Top, Heptonstall,
Hebden Bridge, West Yorkshire
HX7 7HA
T: (01422) 843636
F: (01422) 845621

HEPWORTH, HOLMFIRTH
West Yorkshire

Uppergate Farm ◆◆◆◆
Hepworth, Holmfirth,
Huddersfield HD7 1TG
T: (01484) 681369
F: (01484) 687343

HESSLE
East Riding of Yorkshire

Weir Lodge Guest House
◆◆◆◆
Tower Hill, Hessle, Hull
HU13 0SG
T: (01482) 648564
I: www.weirlodge.co.uk

HEWORTH
North Yorkshire

The Nags Head ◆◆◆
56 Heworth Road, Heworth,
York YO3 0AD
T: (01904) 422989

HIBALDSTOW
North East Lincolnshire

Thornfield Guest House ◆
23 Station Road, Hibaldstow,
Brigg, North Lincolnshire
DN20 9EA
T: (01652) 655555 &
07885 497149

HIGH BENTHAM
North Yorkshire

Fowgill Park ◆◆◆◆
High Bentham, Lancaster
LA2 7AH
T: (015242) 61630

Lane House Farm ◆◆◆◆
High Bentham, Lancaster
LA2 7DJ
T: (015242) 61479

HIGH STITTENHAM
North Yorkshire

Hall Farm ◆◆◆◆
High Stittenham, York
YO60 7TW
T: (01347) 878461 & 0798 928
1897
F: (01347) 878461
E: hallfarm@btinternet.com

HOLMBRIDGE, HOLMFIRTH
West Yorkshire

Corn Loft House ◆◆◆
146 Woodhead Road,
Holmbridge, Holmfirth,
Huddersfield HD7 1NL
T: (01484) 683147

HOLMFIRTH
West Yorkshire

**The Chapel
Rating Applied For**
Low Gate (off Well Hill Road),
Underbank, Holmfirth,
Huddersfield, West Yorkshire
HD7 1AY
T: (01484) 681962
I: soo@jellygreen.freeserve.co.
uk

Holme Valley Guest House ◆◆
97 Huddersfield Road,
Holmfirth, Huddersfield HD7 1JA
T: (01484) 681361
I: www.smoothhound.co.
uk/hotels/valley2.htmlwww.
s-hsystems.co.
uk/hotels/valley2-html

**Linden Grove Bed and
Breakfast** ◆◆
39 Huddersfield Road,
Holmfirth, Huddersfield, West
Yorkshire HD7 1JH
T: (01484) 683718

The Old Bridge Bakery ◆
15 Victoria Street, Holmfirth,
Huddersfield HD7 1DF
T: (01484) 685807

Red Lion Inn ◆◆◆
Sheffield Road, Jackson Bridge,
Holmfirth, Huddersfield
HD7 7HS
T: (01484) 683499 &
07979 968655
E: soscroft@compuserve.com

Spring Head House ◆◆
15 Holmfirth Road, Shepley,
Huddersfield HD8 8BB
T: (01484) 606300
F: (01484) 608030

Springfield House ◆◆◆
95 Huddersfield Road,
Holmfirth, Huddersfield HD7 1JA
T: (01484) 683031
E: ann_brook@hotmail.com

29 Woodhead Road ◆◆◆
Holmfirth, Huddersfield
HD7 1JU
T: (01484) 683962

HOLTBY
North Yorkshire

Sycamore House ◆◆◆◆
Holtby, York YO19 5UD
T: (01904) 488089
F: (01904) 488089

HOOTON PAGNELL
South Yorkshire

Rock Farm ◆◆◆
Hooton Pagnell, Doncaster,
South Yorkshire DN5 7BT
T: (01977) 642200 &
07785 916186

HORNSEA
East Riding of Yorkshire

Merlstead Private Hotel ◆◆◆
59 Eastgate, Hornsea, East
Riding of Yorkshire HU18 1NB
T: (01964) 533068
F: (01964) 536975

HORTON–IN–RIBBLESDALE
North Yorkshire

Crown Hotel ◆◆◆
Horton-in-Ribblesdale, Settle,
North Yorkshire BD24 0HF
T: (01729) 860209
F: (01729) 860444
E: crown.hotel@dalenet.co.uk
I: www.crown-hotel.co.uk

Middle Studfold Farm ◆◆◆
Horton-in-Ribblesdale, Settle,
North Yorkshire BD24 0ER
T: (01729) 860236 &
07774 918908

The Rowe House ◆◆◆
Horton-in-Ribblesdale, Settle,
North Yorkshire BD24 0HT
T: (01729) 860212
E: therowehouse@lineone.net
I: www.therowehouse.co.uk

HUBBERHOLME
North Yorkshire

Church Farm ◆◆◆◆
Hubberholme, Skipton, North
Yorkshire BD23 5JE
T: (01756) 760240

HUDDERSFIELD
West Yorkshire

Ashfield Hotel ◆◆◆
93 New North Road,
Huddersfield, HD1 5ND
T: (01484) 425916
F: (01484) 425916
E: ashfieldhotel@excite.co.uk
I: www.smoothhound.co.
uk/hotels/ashfieldhotel.html

Cambridge Lodge ◆◆◆
4 Clare Hill, Huddersfield,
HD1 5BS
T: (01484) 519892
F: (01484) 534534

Croppers Arms ◆◆◆
136 Westbourne Road, Marsh,
Huddersfield, HD1 4LF
T: (01484) 421522
F: (01484) 301300

Ellasley Guest House ◆◆
86 New North Road,
Huddersfield, HD1 5NE
T: (01484) 423995

Holmcliffe Guest House ◆◆◆
16 Mountjoy Road, Edgerton,
Huddersfield, HD1 5PZ
T: (01484) 429598
F: (01484) 429598
E: jwilso@mwfree.net

Laurel Cottage Guest House
◆◆◆
34 Far Dene, Kirkburton,
Huddersfield, West Yorkshire
HD8 0QU
T: (01484) 607907

The Mallows Guest House
◆◆◆
55 Spring Street, Springwood,
Huddersfield, West Yorkshire
HD1 4AZ
T: (01484) 544684

Manor Mill Cottage ◆◆◆
21 Linfit Lane, Kirkburton,
Huddersfield HD8 0TY
T: (01484) 604109
E: manormill@paskham.
freeserve.co.uk

The White House ◆◆◆
Holthead, Slaithwaite,
Huddersfield HD7 5TY
T: (01484) 842245
F: (01484) 842245
E: whthouse@globalnet.co.uk
I: www.users.globalnet.co.
uk/§whthouse/

Woods End ◆◆◆◆
46 Inglewood Ave, Birkby,
Huddersfield HD2 2DS
T: (01484) 513580 &
07710 691151
F: (01484) 513580

HUGGATE
North Yorkshire
Greenwick Farm ♦♦♦
Huggate, York YO42 1YR
T: (01377) 288122
E: wf@talk21.com

HULL
Humberside
Acorn Guest House ♦♦♦
719 Beverley High Road, Hull,
HU6 7JN
T: (01482) 853248 & 853148

The Admiral Guest House ♦♦
234 The Boulevard, Hull,
HU3 3ED
T: (01482) 329664
F: (01482) 329664
⊛

Allandra Hotel ♦♦
5 Park Avenue, Hull, HU5 3EN
T: (01482) 493349 & 492680
⊛

The Arches ♦♦♦
38 Saner Street, Hull, HU3 2TR
T: (01482) 211558

Clyde House Hotel ♦♦♦
13 John Street, Hull, East
Yorkshire HU2 8DH
T: (01482) 214981 & 214981

**Conway–Roseberry Hotel
♦♦♦♦**
86 Marlborough Avenue, Hull,
HU5 3JT
T: (01482) 445256 &
07909 517328
F: (01482) 445256

The Earlsmere Hotel ♦♦♦
76-78 Sunnybank, Off Spring
Bank West, Hull, HU3 1LQ
T: (01482) 341977
F: (01482) 473714
E: hotel7678.freeserve.co.uk
⊛

**The Old English Gentleman
♦♦♦**
22 Worship Street, Hull,
HU2 8BG
T: (01482) 324659

Hotel Tennyson ♦♦♦
Fountain Road, Hull, East
Yorkshire HU2 0LL
T: (01482) 328844
F: 04182 323345
E: stevetradewell@
hoteltennyson.freeserve.co.uk

West Park Hotel ♦♦♦
405-411 Anlaby Road, Hull,
HU3 6AB
T: (01482) 571888 & 351215
F: (01482) 351215

HUMBERSTON
North East Lincolnshire
South Sea Lane Farm ♦♦♦
Humberston, Grimsby, South
Humberside DN36 4JY
T: (01472) 812144

HUNMANBY
North Yorkshire
Saxdale House Farm ♦♦♦♦
The Row, Hunmanby, Filey,
North Yorkshire YO14 0JD
T: (01723) 892346
F: (01723) 892400
E: saxdale.house@virgin.net
I: www.saxdale.co.uk

HUSTHWAITE
North Yorkshire
Flower of May ♦♦♦
Husthwaite, York, North
Yorkshire YO61 4PG
T: (01347) 868317

HUTTON-LE-HOLE
North Yorkshire
**Barn Hotel and Tea Room
♦♦♦**
Hutton-le-Hole, York YO62 6UA
T: (01751) 417311
E: fairhurst@lineone.net

**Hammer & Hand Country
Guest House♦♦♦♦**
Hutton-le-Hole, York YO62 6UA
T: (01751) 417300
F: (01751) 417711

Westfield Lodge ♦♦♦
Hutton-le-Hole, York YO62 6UG
T: (01751) 417261
F: (01751) 417876
E: sticklandrw@farmersweekly.
net

HUTTON SESSAY
North Yorkshire
Burtree Country House ♦♦♦♦
Burtree House, York Road,
Hutton Sessay, Thirsk, North
Yorkshire YO7 3AY
T: (01845) 501333 & 501562
F: (01845) 501596
⊛

HUTTONS AMBO
North Yorkshire
Bar Farm ♦
Huttons Ambo, York YO60 7HZ
T: (01653) 693267

High Gaterley Farm ♦♦♦♦
Castle Howard Estate, Huttons
Ambo, York YO60 7HT
T: (01653) 694636 &
07703 188086
F: (01653) 694636
E: relax@highgaterley.com
I: www.highgaterley.com

ILKLEY
West Yorkshire
Archway Cottage ♦♦♦
24 Skipton Road, Ilkley, West
Yorkshire LS29 9EP
T: (01943) 603399
F: (01943) 603399
⊛

Cow & Calf ♦♦♦♦
Hangingstone Road, Ilkley, West
Yorkshire LS29 8BT
T: (01943) 607335
F: (01943) 604712
I: www.cowandcalf.co.uk

Grove Hotel ♦♦♦♦
66 The Grove, Ilkley, West
Yorkshire LS29 9PA
T: (01943) 600298
F: 0870 706 5587
E: info@grovehotel.org
I: www.grovehotel.org

**Ilkley Vicarage Bed and
Breakfast ♦♦**
58 Curly Hill, Ilkley, West
Yorkshire LS29 0BA
T: (01943) 607537 & 607058
F: (01943) 607058
E: paultudge@mcmail.com

One Tivoli Place ♦♦♦♦
Ilkley, West Yorkshire LS29 8SU
T: (01943) 600328 &
07860 293193
F: (01943) 600320
E: tivolipl@aol.com

**Robert's Family Bed and
Breakfast ♦♦**
63 Skipton Road, Ilkley, West
Yorkshire LS29 9HF
T: (01943) 817542
E: roberts.petra@tauc21.com

Summerhill Guest House ♦♦♦
24 Crossbeck Road, Ilkley, West
Yorkshire LS29 9JN
T: (01943) 607067

Summerhouse ♦♦♦♦
Hangingtone Road, Ilkley, West
Yorkshire LS29 8RS
T: (01943) 601612
F: (01943) 601612

**Westwood Lodge
♦♦♦♦ SILVER AWARD**
Wells Road, Ilkley, West
Yorkshire LS29 9JF
T: (01943) 433430
F: (01943) 433431
E: welcome@westwoodlodge.
demon.co.uk
I: www.westwoodlodge.demon.
co.uk

ILLINGWORTH
West Yorkshire
Beechwood House ♦♦♦
Beechwood Road, Illingworth,
Halifax, West Yorkshire HX2 9BU
T: (01422) 241325
F: (01422) 241325

Whitehill Lodge ♦♦♦
102 Keighley Road, Illingworth,
Halifax, West Yorkshire HX2 8HF
T: (01422) 240813 &
07889 750757

IMMINGHAM
North East Lincolnshire
**The Poplars Guest House
Rating Applied For**
30 Church Lane, Immingham,
DN40 2EU
T: (01469) 573067

INGBIRCHWORTH
South Yorkshire
**The Fountain Inn & Rooms
♦♦♦♦**
Wellthorne Lane, Ingbirchworth,
Penistone, Sheffield S36 7GJ
T: (01226) 763125
F: (01226) 761336
E: reservations@fountain-inn.
co.uk
I: www.fountain-inn.co.uk

INGLEBY CROSS
North Yorkshire
Blue Bell Inn ♦
Ingleby Cross, Northallerton,
North Yorkshire DL6 3NF
T: (01609) 882272
E: david.kinsella@tesco.net

INGLEBY GREENHOW
North Yorkshire
Manor House Farm ♦♦♦♦
Ingleby Greenhow,
Middlesbrough, Cleveland
TS9 6RB
T: (01642) 722384
E: mbloom@globalnet.co.uk

INGLETON
North Yorkshire
Bridge End Guest House ♦♦♦
Mill Lane, Ingleton, Carnforth,
Lancashire LA6 3EP
T: (015242) 41413
E: garner01@tinyworld.co.uk

The Dales Guest House ♦♦♦
Main Street, Ingleton, Carnforth,
Lancashire LA6 3HH
T: (015242) 41401
E: dalesgh@hotmail.com

**Ferncliffe Country Guest
House ♦♦♦♦**
55 Main Street, Ingleton,
Carnforth, North Yorkshire
LA6 3HJ
T: (015242) 42405
E: ferncliffe@hotmail.com

Gatehouse Farm ♦♦♦♦
Far Westhouse, Ingleton, North
Yorkshire LA6 3NR
T: (015242) 41458 & 41307
⊛

Ingleborough View ♦♦♦♦
Main Street, Ingleton, Carnforth,
North Yorkshire LA6 3HH
T: (015242) 41523
I: www.ingleton.co.
uk/stayat/ingleboroughview/
index.htm

Inglenook Guest House ♦♦♦
20 Main Street, Ingleton,
Carnforth, Lancashire LA6 3HJ
T: (015242) 41270
E: phillsmith@
inglenookguesthouse.fsbusiness.
co.uk

**Langber Country Guest House
♦♦♦**
Tatterthorne Road, Ingleton,
Carnforth, North Yorkshire
LA6 3DT
T: (015242) 41587
⊛

New Butts Farm ♦♦♦
High Bentham, Lancaster
LA2 7AN
T: (015242) 41238

Pines Country House ♦♦♦♦
Ingleton, Carnforth, Lancashire
LA6 3HN
T: (015242) 41252
F: (015242) 41252
E: pineshotel@aol.com
I: www.yorkshirenet.co.
uk/stayat/thepines

Riverside Lodge ♦♦♦
24 Main Street, Ingleton,
Carnforth, Lancashire LA6 3HJ
T: (015242) 41359
E: manuel@telinco.co.uk
I: www.telinco.
uk/riversidelodge
⬆

**Springfield Country House
Hotel ♦♦♦**
Main Street, Ingleton, Carnforth,
Lancashire LA6 3HJ
T: (015242) 41280
F: (015242) 41280
I: www.destination-england.co.
uk.springfield
⊛

Station Inn ♦♦♦
Ribblehead, Ingleton, Carnforth, Lancashire LA6 3AS
T: (015242) 41274
I: www.smoothhound.co.uk/hotelsstation2.html

Wheatsheaf Inn & Hotel ♦♦♦♦
22 High Street, Ingleton, Carnforth, Lancashire LA6 3AD
T: (015242) 41275
F: (015242) 41275
E: randall.d@ingleton01.freeserve.co.uk
I: www.yorkshirenet.co.uk/stayat/thewheatsheaf

KETTLESING
North Yorkshire

Green Acres
♦♦♦♦ SILVER AWARD
Sleights Lane, Kettlesing, Harrogate, North Yorkshire HG3 2LE
T: (01423) 771524
E: a.smith@virgin.net.co.uk

The Queen's Head ♦♦♦♦
Kettlesing, Harrogate, North Yorkshire HG3 2LB
T: (01423) 770263
E: glengarb@aol.com
I: www.harrogate.com/queenshead

KETTLEWELL
North Yorkshire

Chestnut Cottage ♦♦♦
Kettlewell, Skipton, North Yorkshire BD23 5RL
T: (01756) 760804

The Elms ♦♦♦♦
Middle Lane, Kettlewell, Skipton, North Yorkshire BD23 5QX
T: (01756) 760224
T: (01756) 760380
E: cuthbert@kettlewell.yorks.net
I: www.yorkshirenet.co.uk/stayat/theelms/index.html

High Fold
♦♦♦♦ SILVER AWARD
Kettlewell, Skipton, North Yorkshire BD23 5RJ
T: (01756) 760390
F: (01756) 760390
E: deborah@highfold.fsnet.co.uk
I: www.highfold.co.uk

Littlebeck ♦♦♦♦
The Green, Kettlewell, Skipton, North Yorkshire BD23 5RD
T: (01756) 760378
I: www.little-beckatbarclays.net

Lynburn ♦♦♦
Kettlewell, Skipton, North Yorkshire BD23 5RF
T: (01756) 760803

KILBURN
North Yorkshire

Church Farm ♦♦
Kilburn, York YO61 4AH
T: (01347) 868318

The Forresters Arms Hotel ♦♦♦
Kilburn, North Yorkshire YO61 4AH
T: (01347) 868550 & 868386
F: (01347) 868386
E: forresters@destination-england-co.uk
I: wwwdestination-england.co.uk/forresters

KIRBY HILL
North Yorkshire

Shoulder of Mutton Inn ♦♦♦
Kirby Hill, Richmond, North Yorkshire DL11 7JH
T: (01748) 822772
E: john@homledale.com
I: www.holmedale.com

KIRKBY
North Yorkshire

Dromonby Hall Farm ♦♦♦
Busby Lane, Kirkby, Stokesley, Middlesbrough, Cleveland TS9 7AP
T: (01642) 712312
F: (01642) 712312
E: B&B@dromonby.swinternet.co.uk
I: www.touristnetuk.com/ne/dromonby

KIRKBYMOORSIDE
North Yorkshire

Cartoft Lodge ♦♦♦♦
Keldholme, Kirkbymoorside, York, North Yorkshire YO62 6NU
T: (01751) 431566

The Cornmill ♦♦♦♦
Kirby Mills, Kirkbymoorside, York, North Yorkshire YO62 6NP
T: (01751) 432000
T: (01751) 432300
E: cornmill@kirbymills.demon.co.uk
I: www.kirbymills.demon.co.uk

Dale End ♦♦♦
25 Dale End, Kirkbymoorside, York YO62 6EE
T: (01751) 431689

High Blakey House ♦♦♦♦
Blakey Ridge, Kirkbymoorside, York YO62 7LQ
T: (01751) 417186
E: highblakey.house@virgin.net
I: www.freespace.virgin.net/highblakey.house

The Lion Inn ♦♦♦
Blakey Ridge, Kirkbymoorside, York YO62 7LQ
T: (01751) 417320
F: (01751) 417717
I: www.lionblakey.co.uk

Oaklands Bed and Breakfast ♦♦
Oaklands, Keldholme, Kirkbymoorside, York YO62 6ND
T: (01751) 431495

Red Lion House ♦♦♦♦
Crown Square, Kirkbymoorside, York YO62 6AY
T: (01751) 431815
E: angela.thomson@red-lion-house.freeserve.co.uk

Sinnington Common Farm ♦♦♦♦
Kirkbymoorside, York YO62 6NX
T: (01751) 431719
E: Felicity@scfarm.demon.co.uk
I: www.scfarmdemon.co.uk

White Horse Hotel ♦♦♦
5 Market Place, Kirkbymoorside, York YO62 6AB
T: (01751) 431296

KIRKLINGTON
North Yorkshire

Upsland Farm ♦♦♦♦
Kirklington, Bedale, North Yorkshire DL8 2PA
T: (01845) 567709
F: (01845) 567709

KIRKSTALL
West Yorkshire

Abbey Guest House ♦♦♦♦
44 Vesper Road, Kirkstall, Leeds LS5 3NX
T: (0113) 278 5580

KIRTON IN LINDSEY
North Lincolnshire

Kirton Lodge Hotel ♦♦♦
13 Dunstan Hill, Kirton in Lindsey, Gainsborough, North Lincolnshire DN21 4DU
T: (01652) 648994
F: (01652) 648994

KNARESBOROUGH
North Yorkshire

Ebor Mount ♦♦♦
18 York Place, Knaresborough, North Yorkshire HG5 0AA
T: (01423) 863315
F: (01423) 863315

Hermitage Guest House & Tea Garden♦♦♦
10 Waterside, Knaresborough, North Yorkshire HG5 9AZ
T: (01423) 863349
I: www.smoothhound.co.uk/hotels/hermitage1.html

Holly Corner ♦♦♦♦
3 Coverdale Drive, High Bond End, Knaresborough, North Yorkshire HG5 9BW
T: (01423) 864204
F: (01423) 864204
I: www.knaresborough.co.uk/guest-accom/

Kirkgate House ♦♦♦♦
17 Kirkgate, Knaresborough, North Yorkshire HG5 8AD
T: (01423) 862704
F: (01423) 862704

Newton House Hotel ♦♦♦♦
5-7 York Place, Knaresborough, North Yorkshire HG5 0AD
T: (01423) 863539
F: (01423) 869748
E: newton@knaresborough.co.uk
I: www.harrogate.com/newton

Rosedale ♦♦♦
11 Aspin Way, Knaresborough, North Yorkshire HG5 8HL
T: (01423) 867210
F: (01423) 860675
I: www.knaresborough.co.uk/placestostay/guest-accommodation

Watergate Lodge ♦♦♦
Watergate Haven, Ripley Road, Knaresborough, North Yorkshire HG5 9BU
T: (01423) 864627
F: (01423) 861087
E: watergate.haven@virgin.net
I: business.virgin.net/watergate.haven

Windsor House ♦♦♦♦
16b Windsor Lane, Knaresborough, North Yorkshire HG5 8DX
T: (01423) 865398

Yorkshire Lass ♦♦♦
High Bridge, Harrogate Road, Knaresborough, North Yorkshire HG5 8DA
T: (01423) 862962
F: (01423) 869091
E: yorkshirelass@knaresborough.co.uk
I: www.knaresborough.co.uk/yorkshirelass

KNOTTINGLEY
West Yorkshire

Wentvale ♦♦♦♦
Knottingley, West Yorkshire WF11 8PF
T: (01977) 676714
F: (01977) 676714
E: wentvale@aol.com
I: www.wentvale.co.uk

LANGCLIFFE
North Yorkshire

Langcliffe Lodge Bed and Breakfast Accommodation♦♦
Langcliffe Road, Langcliffe, Settle, North Yorkshire BD24 9LT
T: (01729) 823362

LANGSETT, STOCKSBRIDGE
South Yorkshire

Waggon and Horses ♦♦♦
Langsett, Stocksbridge, Sheffield S36 4GY
T: (01226) 763147
F: (01226) 763147
E: langsett@empty.co.uk

LANGTOFT
East Riding of Yorkshire

The Ship Inn ♦♦♦
Scarborough Road, Langtoft, Driffield, North Humberside YO25 3TH
T: (01377) 267243

LAYCOCK
West Yorkshire

Far Laithe Farm
♦♦♦♦ SILVER AWARD
Laycock, Keighley, West Yorkshire BD22 0PP
T: (01535) 661993

LEALHOLM
North Yorkshire

High Park Farm ♦♦♦
Lealholm, Whitby, North Yorkshire YO21 2AQ
T: (01947) 897416

LEEDS
West Yorkshire

Adriatic Hotel ♦♦♦
87 Harehills Avenue, Leeds, West Yorkshire LS8 4ET
T: (0113) 262 0115 & 262 3606
F: (0113) 262 6071

Aintree Hotel ◆◆◆
38 Cardigan Road, Headingley,
Leeds LS6 3AG
T: (0113) 275 8290 & 275 7053
F: (0113) 275 8290

Ash Mount Hotel ◆◆◆
22 Wetherby Road, Oakwood,
Leeds, LS8 2QD
T: (0113) 265 8164 & 265 4263
F: (0113) 265 8164
I: www.leeds.gov.uk

Avalon Guest House ◆◆◆
132 Woodsley Road, Leeds,
LS2 9LZ
T: (0113) 243 2545
◉

Beechwood Hotel ◆◆◆
32-34 Street Lane, Roundhay,
Leeds, West Yorkshire LS8 2ET
T: (0113) 266 2578
F: (0113) 266 2578

Broomhurst Hotel ◆◆◆
12 Chapel Lane, Off Cardigan
Road, Headingley, Leeds
LS6 3BW
T: (0113) 278 6836 & 278 5764
F: (0113) 230 7099
◉

Central Hotel ◆◆
35 - 47 New Briggate, Leeds,
LS2 8JD
T: (0113) 294 1456
F: (0113) 294 1551
E: reception@central-hotel.
freeserve.com.uk

Eagle Tavern ◆
North Street, Leeds, LS7 1AF
T: (0113) 245 7146
F: (0113) 244 4882

Fairbairn House ◆◆◆
71-75 Clarendon Road, Leeds,
LS2 9PL
T: (0113) 233 6633 & 233 6913
F: (0113) 233 6914
E: m.a.timm@leeds.ac.uk

7 Glebelands Drive ◆◆
Leeds, LS6 4AG
T: (0113) 275 6621
E: jeanbel7@aol.com

Glengarth Hotel ◆◆◆
162 Woodsley Road, Leeds,
LS2 9LZ
T: (0113) 245 7940
F: (0113) 216 8033

Hanover Court Hotel ◆◆
16 Hanover Square, Leeds, West
Yorkshire LS3 1AP
T: (0113) 295 7381 & 0771 324
4279
F: (0113) 295 5781
E: hanovercourthotel@
gofornet.co.uk

**Highbank Hotel & Restauarnt
◆◆**
83 Harehills Lane, Leeds, West
Yorkshire LS7 4HA
T: 0870 741 9227 & 741 4230
F: 0870 741 4225
E: highbank.hotel@hotmail.com
I: www.leedshotel.com
◉

Hilldene Hotel ◆◆
99 Harehills Lane, Leeds,
LS8 4DN
T: (0113) 262 1292
F: (0113) 262 1292
◉

Hinsley Hall ◆◆◆
62 Headingley Lane, Leeds,
LS6 2BX
T: (0113) 261 8000
F: (0113) 224 2406
E: info@hinsley-hall.co.uk

**Kirkstall Hall, Trinity and All
Saints College ◆◆◆**
Brownberrie Lane, Horsforth,
Leeds LS18 5HD
T: (0113) 283 7240 & 283 7100
F: (0113) 283 7239
E: j.cressey@tasc.ac.uk
I: www.tasc.ac.uk

Manxdene Private Hotel ◆◆
154 Woodsley Road, Leeds,
LS2 9LZ
T: (0113) 243 2586

Moorlea Hotel ◆◆
146 Woodsley Road, Leeds,
LS2 9LZ
T: (0113) 243 2653
F: (0113) 246 8096

Nordic Hotel ◆
18 Kelso Road, Leeds, LS2 9PR
T: (0113) 245 2357 & 244 8261
F: (0113) 243 3009

Number 23 ◆◆◆
23 St Chad's Rise, Far
Headingley, Leeds, LS6 3QE
T: (0113) 275 7825 & 226 9575

Pinewood Hotel ◆◆◆◆
78 Potternewton Lane, Leeds,
LS7 3LW
T: (0113) 262 2561 & 0800 096
7463

Rydal Bank Hotel ◆◆
20 Street Lane, Roundhay, Leeds
LS8 2ET
T: (0113) 266 1178 & 00113 266
8690
F: (0113) 266 1178

St Michael's Tower Hotel ◆◆◆
5 St Michael's Villas, Cardigan
Road, Headingley, Leeds LS6 3AF
T: (0113) 275 5557 & 275 6039
F: (0113) 230 7491

Sandylands ◆◆◆
44 Lidgett Lane, Leeds, LS8 1PQ
T: (0113) 266 1666
E: spackman@cwnet.com.net

Temple Manor ◆◆◆◆
2 Field End Garth, Temple
Newsam, Leeds, West Yorkshire
LS15 0QQ
T: (0113) 264 1384
◉

Wheelgate Guest House ◆◆◆
7 Kirkgate, Sherburn-In-Elmet,
Leeds, West Yorkshire LS25 6BH
T: (01977) 682231
F: (01977) 682231

LEEMING BAR
North Yorkshire

Little Holtby ◆◆◆◆
Leeming Bar, Northallerton,
North Yorkshire DL7 9LH
T: (01609) 748762
F: (01609) 748822
E: dothodgson@claranet.co.uk

LEVISHAM
North Yorkshire

Horseshoe Inn ◆◆◆
Levisham, Pickering, North
Yorkshire YO18 7NL
T: (01751) 460240
F: (01751) 460240

The Moorlands ◆◆◆◆◆
Levisham, Pickering, North
Yorkshire YO18 7NL
T: (01751) 460229
F: (01751) 460470
E: ronaldoleonardo@aol.com
I: www.smoothhound.co.
uk/hotels/moorlands.html

Rectory Farm House ◆◆◆◆
Levisham, Pickering, North
Yorkshire YO18 7NL
T: (01751) 460304
E: rectoryfarmhouse@barclays.
net
I: www.members.tripod.co.
uk/rectoryfarmhouse/index.
html/

LEYBURN
North Yorkshire

Clyde House ◆◆◆
5 Railway Street, Leyburn, North
Yorkshire DL8 5AY
T: (01969) 623941
F: (01969) 623941
I: www.yorkshirenet.co.
uk/accgde/clydehouse
◉

**Eastfield Lodge Private Hotel
◆◆◆**
St Matthews Terrace, Leyburn,
North Yorkshire DL8 5EL
T: (01969) 623196
F: (01969) 624599
&

**Greenhills
◆◆◆◆◆ SILVER AWARD**
5 Middleham Road, Leyburn,
North Yorkshire DL8 5EY
T: (01969) 623859
E: val.pringle@freenet.co.uk
I: www.yorkshirenet.co.uk

Grove Hotel ◆◆◆
8 Grove Square, Leyburn, North
Yorkshire DL8 5AE
T: (01969) 622569
E: grove@bensonk.freeserve.co.
uk
I: www.yorkshirenet.co.
uk/stayat/grovehotel

Hayloft Suite ◆◆◆
Foal Barn, Spennithorne,
Leyburn, North Yorkshire
DL8 5PR
T: (01969) 622580

**Park Gate House
◆◆◆◆◆ SILVER AWARD**
Constable Burton, Leyburn,
North Yorkshire DL8 2RG
T: (01677) 450466
E: parkgatehouse@freenet.co.uk

Secret Garden House ◆◆◆
Grove Square, Leyburn, North
Yorkshire DL8 5AE
T: (01969) 623589

Walk Mill ◆◆◆◆
Leyburn, North Yorkshire
DL8 5HF
T: (01969) 624829
◉

LINTON
West Yorkshire

Glendales ◆◆◆
Muddy Lane, Linton, Wetherby,
West Yorkshire LS22 4HW
T: (01937) 585915

LITTLE RIBSTON
North Yorkshire

Beck House ◆◆◆
Wetherby Road, Little Ribston,
Wetherby, West Yorkshire
LS22 4EP
T: (01937) 583362

LOCKTON
North Yorkshire

Farfields Farmhouse ◆◆◆◆
Farfields Farm, Lockton,
Pickering, North Yorkshire
YO18 7NQ
T: (01751) 460239
&

LONDONDERRY
North Yorkshire

Tatton Lodge ◆◆◆
Londonderry, Northallerton,
North Yorkshire DL7 9NF
T: (01677) 422222
F: (01677) 422222
E: enquiries@tattonlodge.co.uk
I: www.tattonlodge.co.uk

LONG PRESTON
North Yorkshire

Boar's Head Hotel ◆◆◆
Main Street, Long Preston,
Skipton, North Yorkshire
BD23 4ND
T: (01729) 840217

LOW ROW
North Yorkshire

Park End ◆◆◆
Kearton, Low Row, Richmond,
North Yorkshire DL11 6PL
T: (01748) 886287
◉

Summer Lodge Farm ◆◆◆
Summer Lodge, Low Row,
Richmond, North Yorkshire
DL11 6NP
T: (01748) 886504
◉

LUDDENDENFOOT
West Yorkshire

**Bankfield Bed and Breakfast
◆◆◆◆**
Danny Lane, Luddendenfoot,
Halifax, West Yorkshire
HX2 6AW
T: (01422) 883147

2 Lane Ends ◆◆◆◆
Luddendenfoot, Halifax, West
Yorkshire HX2 6TU
T: (01422) 883388 &
07775 904474

Rockcliffe West ◆◆◆◆
Burnley Road, Luddendenfoot,
Halifax, West Yorkshire HX2 6HL
T: (01422) 882151
F: (01422) 881421
E: rockcliffe.b.b@virgin.net

LUND
East Riding of Yorkshire

**Clematis House, Farmhouse
Bed and Breakfast◆◆◆◆**
1 Eastgate, Lund, Driffield, East
Riding of Yorkshire YO25 9TQ
T: (01377) 217204
F: (01377) 217204
◉

MALHAM
North Yorkshire

Beck Hall Guest House ◆◆◆
Malham, Skipton, North
Yorkshire BD23 4DJ
T: (01729) 830332

Miresfield Farm ◆◆◆
Malham, Skipton, North
Yorkshire BD23 4DA
T: (01729) 830414
E: chris@miresfield.freeserve.co.
uk

River House Hotel ◆◆◆
Malham, Skipton, North
Yorkshire BD23 4DA
T: (01729) 830315
F: (01729) 830672
E: info@riverhousehotel.co.uk
I: www.riverhousehotel.co.uk
⊕ ⚹

MALTBY
South Yorkshire
The Cottages Guest House ◆◆
1, 3 & 5 Blyth Road, Maltby,
Rotherham, South Yorkshire
S66 8HX
T: (01709) 813382

MALTON
North Yorkshire
The George Hotel ◆◆◆
19 Yorkersgate, Malton, North
Yorkshire YO17 7AA
T: (01653) 692884 &
07768 344337
F: (01653) 698674

Leonard House ◆◆◆◆
45 Old Maltongate, Malton,
North Yorkshire YO17 7EH
T: (01653) 695711

**Murray's Coffee Shop and
Restaurant ◆◆◆**
2 Market Place, Malton, North
Yorkshire YO17 7LX
T: (01653) 692979

The Old Rectory ◆◆◆◆
West Heslerton, Malton, North
Yorkshire YO17 8RE
T: (01944) 728285 &
07778 064580
E: bhillas@netlineuk.net
I: www.oldrectoryny.fsnet.co.uk/
⊕

MANKINHOLES
West Yorkshire
Cross Farm ◆◆◆◆
Mankinholes, Todmorden,
Lancashire OL14 6HB
T: (01706) 813481

MANNINGHAM
West Yorkshire
The Park Hotel ◆◆
6 Oak Avenue, Manningham,
Bradford, West Yorkshire
BD8 7AQ
T: (01274) 546262
F: (01274) 482207

MAPPLEWELL
South Yorkshire
The Grange ◆◆◆
29 Spark Lane, Mapplewell,
Barnsley, South Yorkshire
S75 6AA
T: (01226) 380078 &
07971 239974
E: the.grange@telineo.com

MARKET WEIGHTON
East Riding of Yorkshire
Arras Farmhouse ◆◆◆
Arras Farm, Market Weighton,
York YO43 4RN
T: (01430) 872404
F: (01430) 872404

MARSDEN
West Yorkshire
Coach & Horses ◆◆◆
Manchester Road, Marsden,
Huddersfield HD7 6NL
T: (01484) 844241
F: (01484) 844241

**Olive Branch Restaurant with
Rooms and Bar
◆◆◆◆ SILVER AWARD**
Manchester Road, Marsden,
Huddersfield HD7 6LU
T: (01484) 844487
E: olivebranch@supanet.com

Throstle Nest Cottage ◆◆◆
3 Old Mount Road, Marsden,
Huddersfield HD7 6DU
T: (01484) 846371 &
07710 727513
E: d.l.j.nest@cwctv.net

MARTON
North Yorkshire
Orchard House ◆◆◆◆
Main Street, Marton, Sinnington,
York YO61 6RD
T: (01751) 432904

Wildsmith House ◆◆◆◆
Marton, Sinnington, York
YO62 6RD
T: (01751) 432702
E: pgrms@easynet.co.uk

MASHAM
North Yorkshire
Garden House ◆◆◆
1 Park Street, Masham, Ripon,
North Yorkshire HG4 4HN
T: (01765) 689989

Haregill Lodge ◆◆◆
Ellingstring, Masham, Ripon,
North Yorkshire HG4 4PW
T: (01677) 460272
F: (01677) 460272
E: haregilllodge@freenet.co.uk
⊕

Limetree Farm ◆◆◆◆
Hutts Lane, Grewelthorpe,
Ripon, North Yorkshire HG4 3DA
T: (01765) 658450

Pasture House ◆◆◆
Healey, Ripon, North Yorkshire
HG4 4LJ
T: (01765) 689149
F: (01765) 689990

Warren House Farm ◆◆◆
High Ellington, Masham, Ripon,
North Yorkshire HG4 4PP
T: (01677) 460244
F: (01677) 460244

MENSTON
West Yorkshire
Chevin End Guest House ◆◆◆
West Chevin Road, Menston,
Ilkley, West Yorkshire LS29 6DU
T: (01943) 876845
E: chevinendguest@virgin.net
I: www.members.xoom.
com/chevinguest/

MIDDLEHAM
North Yorkshire
The Black Bull Inn ◆◆◆◆
Market Place, Middleham,
Leyburn, North Yorkshire
DL8 4NX
T: (01969) 623669
E: blackbull@tinyworld.co.uk

Black Swan Hotel ◆◆◆
Market Place, Middleham, North
Yorkshire DL8 4NP
T: (01969) 622221
F: (01969) 622221

Domus ◆◆◆◆
Market Place, Middleham,
Leyburn, North Yorkshire
DL8 4NR
T: (01969) 623497
E: domus_2000@yahoo.co.uk

**Jasmine House
◆◆◆◆◆ SILVER AWARD**
Market Place, Middleham,
Leyburn, North Yorkshire
DL8 4NU
T: (01969) 622858
E: enquiries@jasminehouse.net
I: jasminehouse.net

The Priory ◆◆◆
West End, Middleham, Leyburn,
North Yorkshire DL8 4QG
T: (01969) 623279

Richard III Hotel ◆◆◆
Market Place, Middleham,
Leyburn, North Yorkshire
DL8 4NP
T: (01969) 623240

**Seventeenth-Century Castle
Keep ◆◆◆◆**
Castle Hill, Middleham, Leyburn,
North Yorkshire DL8 4QR
T: (01969) 623665

Yore View ◆◆◆◆
Leyburn Road, Middleham,
Leyburn, North Yorkshire
DL8 4PL
T: (01969) 622987
⊕

MIDDLESMOOR
North Yorkshire
**Dovenor House Bed and
Breakfast ◆◆**
Middlesmoor, Harrogate, North
Yorkshire HG3 5ST
T: (01423) 755697
F: (01423) 755697
I: www.nidderdale.co.uk

MUKER
North Yorkshire
**Hylands
Rating Applied For**
Muker, Richmond, North
Yorkshire DL11 6QQ
T: (01748) 886003 &
07802 758198
E: jonesr3@btinternet.com

MYTHOLMROYD
West Yorkshire
Redacre Mill ◆◆◆◆
Redacre, Mytholmroyd, Hebden
Bridge, West Yorkshire HX7 5DQ
T: (01422) 885563 & 0771 340
3563
F: (01422) 885563
E: peters@redacremill.freeserve.
co.uk
I: www.redacremill.freeserve.co.
uk
⊕

Southfield ◆◆◆◆
Burnley Road, Mytholmroyd,
Hebden Bridge, West Yorkshire
HX7 5PD
T: (01422) 883007
E: philip@fieldsouth.freeserve.
co.uk

NAWTON
North Yorkshire
Little Manor Farm ◆◆◆
Highfield Lane, Nawton, York
YO62 7TU
T: (01439) 771672

Nawton Grange ◆◆◆
Gale Lane, Nawton, York, North
Yorkshire YO62 7SD
T: (01439) 771146
⊕

NETHERTON
West Yorkshire
The Conifers ◆◆◆
3 Strands Court, Netherton,
Wakefield, West Yorkshire
WF4 4JB
T: (01924) 277370

NEW WALTHAM
North East Lincolnshire
Peaks Top Farm ◆◆◆
Hewitts Avenue, New Waltham,
Grimsby, North East Lincolnshire
DN36 4RS
T: (01472) 812941
F: (01472) 812941
E: lmclayton@tinyworld.co.uk

NEWBY WISKE
North Yorkshire
Well House ◆◆◆◆
Newby Wiske, Northallerton,
North Yorkshire DL7 9EX
T: (01609) 772253

NEWTON-ON-OUSE
North Yorkshire
Village Farm Holidays ◆◆◆◆
Cherry Tree Avenue, Newton-
on-Ouse, York YO30 2BN
T: (01347) 848064
F: (01347) 848065
E: vfholidays@cs.com
I: www.yorkshire.co.
uk/stayat/villagefarm

NEWTON-ON-RAWCLIFFE
North Yorkshire
Elm House Farm ◆◆◆◆
Newton-on-Rawcliffe, Pickering,
North Yorkshire YO18 8QA
T: (01751) 473223

Swan Cottage ◆◆◆
Newton-on-Rawcliffe, Pickering,
North Yorkshire YO18 8QA
T: (01751) 472502

NORTH CAVE
East Riding of Yorkshire
Albion House ◆◆
18 Westgate, North Cave,
Brough, North Humberside
HU15 2NJ
T: (01430) 422958 &
07703 896094

NORTH FERRIBY
East Riding of Yorkshire
B & B @103 ◆◆◆
103 Ferriby High Road, North
Ferriby, East Riding of Yorkshire
HU14 3LA
T: (01482) 633637 &
07808 387651
E: simpson.103@usa.net
I: www.bnb103.co.uk

YORKSHIRE

NORTH KILLINGHOLME
North East Lincolnshire
Giovanni's Hotel and Restaurant
Rating Applied For
Vicarage Lane, North Killingholme, Immingham, North Lincolnshire DN40 3JQ
T: (01469) 541010
F: (01469) 541020

NORTH NEWBALD
East Riding of Yorkshire
The Gnu Inn ♦♦♦
The Green, North Newbald, York YO43 4SA
T: (01430) 827799

NORTHALLERTON
North Yorkshire
Alverton Guest House ♦♦♦
26 South Parade, Northallerton, North Yorkshire DL7 8SG
T: (01609) 776207
F: (01609) 776207

Elmscott ♦♦♦♦
10 Hatfield Road, Northallerton, North Yorkshire DL7 8QX
T: (01609) 760575

Lovesome Hill Farm ♦♦♦♦
Lovesome Hill, Northallerton, North Yorkshire DL6 2PB
T: (01609) 772311

Porch House
♦♦♦♦ SILVER AWARD
68 High Street, Northallerton, North Yorkshire DL7 8EG
T: (01609) 779831
F: (01609) 778603

Windsor Guest House ♦♦♦
56 South Parade, Northallerton, North Yorkshire DL7 8SL
T: (01609) 774100 &
07713 274491

NORTON
North Yorkshire
Lynden ♦♦♦
165 Welham Road, Norton, Malton, North Yorkshire YO17 9DU
T: (01653) 694236

NORWOOD
North Yorkshire
The Old Primary ♦♦♦♦
Bland Hill, Norwood, Harrogate, North Yorkshire HG3 1TB
T: (01943) 880472

NUNNINGTON
North Yorkshire
Sunley Court ♦♦♦
Nunnington, York YO62 5XQ
T: (01439) 748233
F: (01439) 748233

OAKWORTH
West Yorkshire
Railway Cottage ♦♦♦
59 Station Road, Oakworth, Keighley, West Yorkshire BD22 0DZ
T: (01535) 642693

OLD EARSWICK
North Yorkshire
The Gables ♦♦♦
344 Strensall Road, Old Earswick, York YO32 9SW
T: (01904) 768235 &
07801 843746

OSMOTHERLEY
North Yorkshire
Oak Garth Farm ♦♦
North End, Osmotherley, Northallerton, North Yorkshire DL6 3BH
T: (01609) 883314

Osmotherley Post Office ♦♦♦
4 West End, Osmotherley, Northallerton, North Yorkshire DL6 3AA
T: (01609) 883818
E: walkingshop@osmotherley.fsbusiness.co.uk
I: www.coast2coast.co.uk

OSSETT
West Yorkshire
The Mill ♦♦
194-198 Dewsbury Road, Ossett, West Yorkshire WF5 9QG
T: (01924) 277851 &
(01624) 267322
F: (01924) 277851

OSWALDKIRK
North Yorkshire
The Red House Bed and Breakfast
Rating Applied For
The Red Hosue, Oswaldkirk, York YO62 5XY
T: (01439) 788063
F: (01439) 788063
E: dmatthias@themutual.net

OTLEY
West Yorkshire
11 Newall Mount ♦♦♦
Otley, West Yorkshire LS21 2DY
T: (01943) 462898

Paddock Hill ♦♦
Norwood, Otley, West Yorkshire LS21 2QU
T: (01943) 465977

Scaife Hall Farm
♦♦♦♦ SILVER AWARD
Blubberhouses, Otley, West Yorkshire LS21 2PL
T: (01943) 880354
F: (01943) 880374
E: christine.a.ryder@btinternet.com

Wood Top Farm ♦♦♦♦
Off Norwood Edge, Lindley, Otley, West Yorkshire LS21 2QS
T: (01943) 464010
F: (01943) 464010
E: mailwoodtop@aol.com

OUGHTERSHAW
North Yorkshire
Camm Farm ♦♦♦♦
Cam Houses, Oughtershaw, Skipton, North Yorkshire BD23 2JT
T: 07860 648045 & (0113) 271 1339
F: (0113) 277 9750

PATELEY BRIDGE
North Yorkshire
Bewerley Hall Farm ♦♦♦
Bewerley, Harrogate, North Yorkshire HG3 5JA
T: (01423) 711636 & 0780 848 0417

Bruce House Farm ♦♦♦
Top Wath Road, Pateley Bridge, Harrogate, North Yorkshire HG3 5PG
T: (01423) 711813
F: (01423) 712843
E: brucehse@aol.com
I: members.aol.com/brucehse

Dale View ♦♦♦
Old Church Lane, Pateley Bridge, Harrogate, North Yorkshire HG3 5LY
T: (01423) 711506
F: (01423) 711506
E: kenjsimpson@yahoo.co.uk

Greengarth ♦♦♦
Greenwood Road, Pateley Bridge, Harrogate, North Yorkshire HG3 5LR
T: (01423) 711688

Knottside Farm
♦♦♦♦♦ GOLD AWARD
The Knott, Pateley Bridge, Harrogate, North Yorkshire HG3 5DQ
T: (01423) 712927
F: (01423) 712927

Nidderdale Lodge Farm ♦♦♦
Felbeck, Pateley Bridge, Harrogate, North Yorkshire HG3 5DR
T: (01423) 711677

North Pasture Farm
♦♦♦♦ SILVER AWARD
Brimham Rocks, Summer Bridge, Harrogate, North Yorkshire HG3 4DW
T: (01423) 711470

Prospect House ♦♦
1 Millfield Street, Pateley Bridge, Harrogate, North Yorkshire HG3 5AX
T: (01423) 711167
F: (01423) 711591
E: writessc@supanet.com

The Talbot Hotel ♦♦♦
High Street, Pateley Bridge, Harrogate, North Yorkshire HG3 5AL
T: (01423) 711597

The Watermill Inn ♦♦♦
Foster Beck, Pateley Bridge, Harrogate, North Yorkshire HG3 5AX
T: (01423) 711484 &
07889 142793
F: (01423) 712788
E: watermillinn@btinternet.com

PATRICK BROMPTON
North Yorkshire
Mill Close Farm
♦♦♦♦ SILVER AWARD
Patrick Brompton, Bedale, North Yorkshire DL8 1JY
T: (01677) 450257
F: (01677) 450585

PENISTONE
South Yorkshire
Cubley Hall Freehouse Pub-Restaurant-Hotel♦♦♦♦
Mortimer Road, Penistone, Sheffield S36 9DF
T: (01226) 766086
F: (01226) 767335
E: cubley.hall@ukonline.co.uk

PICKERING
North Yorkshire
Barker Stakes Farm ♦♦♦
Lendales Lane, Pickering, North Yorkshire YO18 8EE
T: (01751) 476759

Beech Cottage ♦♦♦
Saintoft, Pickering, North Yorkshire YO18 8QQ
T: (01751) 417625
F: (01751) 417625

Black Bull Inn ♦♦♦
Malton Road, Pickering, North Yorkshire YO18 8EA
T: (01751) 475258 & 475824
F: (01751) 475824

Black Swan Hotel ♦♦♦
18 Birdgate, Pickering, North Yorkshire YO18 7AL
T: (01751) 472286
F: (01751) 472928

Bramwood Guest House ♦♦♦♦
19 Hallgarth, Pickering, North Yorkshire YO18 7AW
T: (01751) 474066

Bridge House ♦♦♦♦
8 Bridge Street, Pickering, North Yorkshire YO18 8DT
T: (01751) 477234

Burgate House Hotel & Restaurant♦♦♦♦
17 Burgate, Pickering, North Yorkshire YO18 7AU
T: (01751) 473463
F: (01751) 473463
E: burgate.house@btinternet.com
I: www.burgatehouse.btinternet.co.uk

Clent House ♦♦♦
15 Burgate, Pickering, North Yorkshire YO18 7AU
T: (01751) 477928

Cottage Leas Country Hotel ♦♦♦♦
Nova Lane, Middleton, Pickering, North Yorkshire YO18 8PN
T: (01751) 472129
F: (01751) 474930

Eden House
♦♦♦♦ SILVER AWARD
120 Eastgate, Pickering, North Yorkshire YO18 7DW
T: (01751) 472289 & 476066
F: (01751) 476066
E: edenhouse@breathemail.net
I: www.edenhousebandb.co.uk

Fox and Hounds Country Inn ♦♦♦♦
Sinnington, York YO62 6SQ
T: (01751) 431577
F: (01751) 432791
E: foxhoundsinn@easynet.co.uk

560

Establishments printed in blue have a detailed entry in this guide

Grindale House ◆◆◆◆
123 Eastgate, Pickering, North
Yorkshire YO18 7DW
T: (01751) 476636
F: (01751) 475727

Heathcote House ◆◆◆◆
100 Eastgate, Pickering, North
Yorkshire YO18 7DW
T: (01751) 476991
F: (01751) 476991
E: joanlovejooy@lineone.net

Munda Wanga ◆
14 Garden Way, Pickering, North
Yorkshire YO18 8BG
T: (01751) 473310

The Old Manse Guest House
◆◆◆◆
Middleton Road, Pickering,
North Yorkshire YO18 8AL
T: (01751) 476484
F: (01751) 477124
E: valerie-a-gardner@talk21.
com

Rains Farm ◆◆◆◆
Allerston, Pickering, North
Yorkshire YO18 7PQ
T: (01723) 859333
F: (01723) 859333
E: allan@rainsfarm.freeserve.co.
uk
I: www.rains-farm-holidays.co.
uk

Rose Folly ◆◆◆◆
112 Eastgate, Pickering, North
Yorkshire YO18 7DW
T: (01751) 457057
E: gail@rosefolly.freeserve.co.uk

Rosebank Bed & Breakfast
◆◆◆◆
61 Ruffa Lane, Pickering, North
Yorkshire YO18 7HN
T: (01751) 472531

Sunnyside ◆◆◆◆
Carr Lane, Middleton, Pickering,
North Yorkshire YO18 8PD
T: (01751) 476104
F: (01751) 476104

Vivers Mill ◆◆◆
Mill Lane, Pickering, North
Yorkshire YO18 8DJ
T: (01751) 473640
E: viversmill@talk21.com

POCKLEY
North Yorkshire

West View Cottage ◆◆◆◆
Pockley, York YO62 7TE
T: (01439) 770526

POCKLINGTON
East Riding of Yorkshire

Star Inn ◆◆◆
North Dalton, Driffield, East
Riding of Yorkshire YO25 9UX
T: (01377) 217688
F: (01377) 217791

POOL IN WHARFEDALE
West Yorkshire

Rawson Garth ◆◆◆
Pool Bank Farm, Pool in
Wharfedale, Otley, West
Yorkshire LS21 1EU
T: (0113) 284 3221
F: (0113) 284 3221

PRESTON
East Riding of Yorkshire

Little Weghill Farm ◆◆◆◆
Weghill Road, Preston, Hull, East
Yorkshire HU12 8SX
T: (01482) 897650 &
0731 777823
F: (01482) 897650

PUDSEY
West Yorkshire

Heatherlea House ◆◆◆
105 Littlemoor Road, Pudsey,
West Yorkshire LS28 8AP
T: (0113) 257 4397
E: heatherlea_pudsey.leeds@
excite.co.uk

Lynnwood House ◆◆◆
18 Alexandra Road, Uppermoor,
Pudsey, Leeds LS28 8BY
T: (0113) 257 1117

RASKELF
North Yorkshire

Old Black Bull Inn ◆◆◆
Raskelf, York, North Yorkshire
YO61 3LF
T: (01347) 821431
E: pjacksobbull@bizonline.co.uk

RASTRICK
West Yorkshire

Elder Lea House
◆◆◆◆◆ SILVER AWARD
Clough Lane, Rastrick,
Brighouse, West Yorkshire
HD6 3QH
T: (01484) 717832 &
07721 046131
F: (01484) 717832
E: pinetrees@gallery 2a.
freeserve.co.uk

RATHMELL
North Yorkshire

The Stables ◆◆◆◆
Field House, Rathmell, Settle,
North Yorkshire BD24 0LA
T: (01729) 840234
F: (01729) 840775
E: rosehyslop@easynet.co.uk

RAVENSCAR
North Yorkshire

Bide-a-While ◆◆◆
3 Loring Road, Ravenscar,
Scarborough, North Yorkshire
YO13 0LY
T: (01723) 870643

Cliff House ◆◆◆◆
Ravenscar, Scarborough, North
Yorkshire YO13 0LX
T: (01723) 870889
E: hodgson@cliffhouse.
fsbusiness.co.uk
I: www.smoothhound.co.
uk/hotels/cliffhouse.html

Crag Hill ◆◆◆
Ravenhall Road, Ravenscar,
Scarborough, North Yorkshire
YO13 0NA
T: (01723) 870925

**Smugglers Rock Country
House** ◆◆◆
Ravenscar, Scarborough, North
Yorkshire YO13 0ER
T: (01723) 870044
F: (01723) 870044
E: info@smugglersrock.co.uk
I: www.smugglersrock.co.uk

RAVENSWORTH
North Yorkshire

The Bay Horse Inn ◆◆◆
Ravensworth, Richmond, North
Yorkshire DL11 7ET
T: (01325) 718328

REDBOURNE
North Lincolnshire

The Red Lion Hotel
Rating Applied For
Main Street, Redbourne,
Gainsborough, Lincolnshire
DN21 4QR
T: (01652) 648302
F: (01652) 648302
E: enquiries@redlion.org
I: www.redlion.org

REETH
North Yorkshire

Arkle House ◆◆◆◆
Mill Lane, Reeth, Richmond,
North Yorkshire DL11 6SJ
T: (01748) 884815
E: arkle.house@breathemail.net

Arkleside Hotel
◆◆◆◆ SILVER AWARD
Reeth, Richmond, North
Yorkshire DL11 6SG
T: (01748) 884200
F: (01748) 884200

Black Bull Hotel ◆◆◆
Reeth, Richmond, North
Yorkshire DL11 6SZ
T: (01748) 884213
F: (01748) 884213
I: www.blackbull.co.uk

2 Bridge Terrace ◆
Reeth, Richmond, North
Yorkshire DL11 6TP
T: (01748) 884572

Buck Hotel ◆◆◆
Reeth, Richmond, North
Yorkshire DL11 6SW
T: (01748) 884210
F: (01748) 884802
E: buck.htl@aol.com
I: www.yorkshirenet.co.uk.
accgde.buckhotel

Elder Peak ◆◆◆
Arkengarthdale Road, Reeth,
Richmond, North Yorkshire
DL11 6QX
T: (01748) 884770

Hackney House ◆◆◆
Reeth, Richmond, North
Yorkshire DL11 6TW
T: (01748) 884302

Kernot Court ◆◆
Reeth, Richmond, North
Yorkshire DL11 6SF
T: (01748) 884662

Springfield House ◆◆
Quaker Close, Reeth, Richmond,
North Yorkshire DL11 6UY
T: (01748) 884634 &
(01794) 104 4048
E: springfield.house@
breathemail.net

RICCALL
North Yorkshire

South Newlands Farm ◆◆◆
Selby Road, Riccall, York
YO19 6QR
T: (01757) 248203
F: (01757) 248203

RICHMOND
North Yorkshire

The Buck Inn ◆◆
27-29 Newbiggin, Richmond,
North Yorkshire DL10 4DX
T: (01748) 822259 & 850141

Emmanuel Guest House ◆◆◆
41 Maison Dieu, Richmond,
North Yorkshire DL10 7AU
T: (01748) 823584 &
0585 2722361
F: (01748) 821554

66 Frenchgate ◆◆◆
Richmond, North Yorkshire
DL10 7AG
T: (01748) 823421
E: paul@66french.freeserve.co.
uk

Greencroft ◆◆◆
Middleton Tyas, Richmond,
North Yorkshire DL10 6PE
T: (01325) 377392
F: (01833) 621423

Holmedale ◆◆◆
Dalton, Richmond, North
Yorkshire DL11 7HX
T: (01833) 621236
F: (01833) 621236

27 Hurgill Road ◆◆
Richmond, North Yorkshire
DL10 4AR
T: (01748) 824092
F: (01748) 824092

Mount Pleasant Farm ◆◆◆◆
Whashton, Richmond, North
Yorkshire DL11 7JP
T: (01748) 822784
F: (01748) 822784

Nunns Cottage ◆◆◆◆
5 Hurgill Road, Richmond, North
Yorkshire DL10 4AR
T: (01748) 822809
F: (01748) 822809
E: nunscottage@tinternet.com
I: richmond.org.
uk/business/nunscottage

Old Brewery Guest House
◆◆◆◆
29 The Green, Richmond, North
Yorkshire DL10 4RG
T: (01748) 822460
F: (01748) 825561

Pottergate Guest House ◆◆
4 Pottergate, Richmond, North
Yorkshire DL10 4AB
T: (01748) 823826

The Restaurant on the Green
◆◆◆
5-7 Bridge Street, Richmond,
North Yorkshire DL10 4RW
T: (01748) 826229
F: (01748) 826229
E: accom.bennett@talk21.com
I: www.ytb.org.uk

Victoria House ◆◆◆◆
49 Maison Dieu, Richmond,
North Yorkshire DL10 7AU
T: (01748) 824830 &
07803 367276
◎

West End Guest House ◆◆◆◆
45 Reeth Road, Richmond,
North Yorkshire DL10 4EX
T: (01748) 824783
E: alex@cranson.freeserve.co.uk
I: www.geocities.
com/westendgh.

Whashton Springs Farm
◆◆◆◆ SILVER AWARD
Richmond, North Yorkshire
DL11 7JS
T: (01748) 822884
F: (01748) 826285
◎

Willance House Guesthouse
◆◆◆
24 Frenchgate, Richmond, North
Yorkshire DL10 7AG
T: (01748) 824467
F: (01748) 824467

RIEVAULX
North Yorkshire
Barn Close Farm ◆◆◆
Rievaulx, York YO62 5LH
T: (01439) 798321

RILLINGTON
North Yorkshire
Little Beck ◆◆◆◆
22 Low Moorgate, Rillington,
Malton, North Yorkshire
YO17 8JW
T: (01944) 758655
E: flinton@tinyworld.co.uk

RIPLEY
North Yorkshire
Slate Rigg Farm ◆◆◆
Birthwaite Lane, Ripley,
Harrogate, North Yorkshire
HG3 3JQ
T: (01423) 770135

RIPON
North Yorkshire
Abbey Nordale Hotel ◆◆◆
1 & 2 North Parade, North Road,
Ripon, North Yorkshire HG4 1ES
T: (01765) 603557
F: (01765) 603557
E: skerridge@callnetuk.com

Beech House ◆◆◆
7 South Crescent, Ripon, North
Yorkshire HG4 1SW
T: (01765) 603294 &
07932 651055
F: (01765) 603294

Bishopton Grove House ◆◆◆
Bishopton, Ripon, North
Yorkshire HG4 2QL
T: (01765) 600888
E: wimpress@bronco.co.uk

The Coopers ◆◆◆
36 College Road, Ripon, North
Yorkshire HG4 2HA
T: (01765) 603708
E: joe_cooper74@hotmail.com

Fremantle House ◆◆◆
35 North Road, Ripon, North
Yorkshire HG4 1JR
T: (01765) 605819
F: (01765) 601313
E: jcar105462@aol.com

Graywel ◆◆◆◆
Marlborough Grove, Ripon,
North Yorkshire HG4 2EZ
T: (01765) 692693 &
07808 209130
F: (01765) 600112
E: sallyrobinson@excite.co.uk

Mallard Grange
◆◆◆◆ SILVER AWARD
Aldfield, Ripon, North Yorkshire
HG4 3BE
T: (01765) 620242

Middle Ridge ◆◆◆◆
42 Mallorie Park Drive, Ripon,
North Yorkshire HG4 2QF
T: (01765) 690558
F: (01765) 690558
E: john@midrig.demon.co.uk

Moor End Farm ◆◆◆
Knaresborough Road,
Littlethorpe, Ripon, North
Yorkshire HG4 3LU
T: (01765) 677419
E: pspensley@ukonline.co.uk
I: www.yorkshirebandb.co.uk

River Side Guest House ◆◆◆
20-21 Iddesleigh Terrace,
Boroughbridge Road, Ripon,
North Yorkshire HG4 1QW
T: (01765) 603864 & 602707
F: (01765) 602707
E: christopher-pearson3@
virgin-net

St George's Court ◆◆◆◆
Old Home Farm, Grantley, Ripon,
North Yorkshire HG4 3EU
T: (01765) 620618
◎

Yew Tree Farm ◆◆◆◆
Main Street, Kirkby Malzeard,
Ripon, North Yorkshire HG4 3SE
T: (01765) 658474
F: (01765) 658474
E: barbara@carol.rapidial.co.uk

ROBIN HOOD'S BAY
North Yorkshire
Boathouse Bistro ◆◆◆
The Dock, Robin Hood's Bay,
Whitby, North Yorkshire
YO22 4SJ
T: (01947) 880099

Flask Inn ◆◆◆◆
Robin Hood's Bay, Whitby, North
Yorkshire YO22 4QH
T: (01947) 880305
F: (01947) 880592
E: flaskinn@aol.com
I: www.flaskinn.com

Flask Inn Travel Lodge ◆◆◆◆
Robin Hoods Bay, Fylingdales,
Whitby, North Yorkshire
YO22 4QH
T: (01947) 880692 & 880592
F: (01947) 880592
E: flaskinn@aol.com

Lee-Side ◆◆◆◆
Mount Pleasant South, Robin
Hood's Bay, Whitby, North
Yorkshire YO22 4RQ
T: (01947) 881143

Ravenswood Bed and Breakfast
◆◆◆
Ravenswood, Mount Pleasant
North, Robin Hood's Bay,
Whitby, North Yorkshire
YO22 4RE
T: (01947) 880690

Victoria Hotel ◆◆◆
Station Road, Robin Hood's Bay,
Whitby, North Yorkshire
YO22 4RL
T: (01947) 880205
F: (01947) 881170

ROECLIFFE
North Yorkshire
The Crown at Roecliffe ◆◆◆
Roecliffe, York YO51 9LY
T: (01423) 322578
F: (01423) 324060
E: crownroecliffe@btclick.com

ROSEDALE ABBEY
North Yorkshire
Sevenford House ◆◆◆◆
Rosedale Abbey, Pickering,
North Yorkshire YO18 8SE
T: (01751) 417283
F: (01751) 417505
E: sevenford@aol.com
◎

ROSEDALE EAST
North Yorkshire
Moordale House ◆◆◆
Rosedale East, Pickering, North
Yorkshire YO18 8RH
T: (01751) 417219

ROTHERHAM
South Yorkshire
Fernlea Hotel ◆◆◆
74 Gerard Road, Moorgate,
Rotherham, South Yorkshire
S60 2PW
T: (01709) 830884
F: (01709) 305951

Phoenix Hotel ◆◆
1 College Road, Rotherham,
South Yorkshire S60 1EY
T: (01709) 364611 & 511121
F: (01709) 511121

RUDSTON
East Riding of Yorkshire
Eastgate Farm Cottage ◆◆◆
Rudston, Driffield, East Riding of
Yorkshire YO25 0UX
T: (01262) 420150 &
07710 161897
F: (01262) 420150
E: ebrudston@aol.com
I: www.eastgatefarmcottage.
com

RUNSWICK BAY
North Yorkshire
Cliffemount Hotel
◆◆◆◆ SILVER AWARD
Runswick Bay, Saltburn-by-the-
Sea, Cleveland TS13 5HU
T: (01947) 840103
F: (01947) 841025
E: cliffemount@runswickbay.
fsnet.co.uk
I: www.cliffemounthotel.co.uk

Cockpit House ◆◆
The Old Village, Runswick Bay,
Saltburn-by-the-Sea, Cleveland
TS13 5HU
T: (01947) 840504 & 603047

Ellerby Hotel
◆◆◆◆ SILVER AWARD
Ellerby, Saltburn-by-the-Sea,
Cleveland TS13 5LP
T: (01947) 840342
F: (01947) 841221
E: ellerbyhotel@yahooo.co.uk
I: www.smoothhound.co.
uk/hotels/ellerby.html
🏠

SALTERSGATE
North Yorkshire
Newgate Foot Farm ◆◆◆◆
Newgate Foot, Saltersgate,
Pickering, North Yorkshire
YO18 7NR
T: (01751) 460215
F: (01751) 460215
◎

SCACKLETON
North Yorkshire
Church Farm ◆◆◆
Scackleton, York YO62 4NB
T: (01653) 628403
F: (01653) 628403

SCAGGLETHORPE
North Yorkshire
Scagglethorpe Manor
◆◆◆◆ SILVER AWARD
Main Street, Scagglethorpe,
Malton, North Yorkshire
YO17 8DT
T: (01944) 758909
F: (01944) 758909

SCALBY
North Yorkshire
Holly Croft ◆◆◆◆◆
28 Station Road, Scalby,
Scarborough, North Yorkshire
YO13 0QA
T: (01723) 375376
F: (01723) 360563

SCARBOROUGH
North Yorkshire
Aldon Hotel ◆◆◆◆
120-122 Columbus Ravine,
Scarborough, North Yorkshire
YO12 7QZ
T: (01723) 372198

Arlington Private Hotel ◆◆◆
42 West Street, South Cliff,
Scarborough, North Yorkshire
YO11 2QP
T: (01723) 503600
I: www.s-h.a.dipcon.co.uk./

Arran Licensed Hotel ◆◆◆
114 North Marine Road,
Scarborough, North Yorkshire
YO12 7JA
T: (01723) 364692

Ash-Lea Private Hotel ◆◆◆◆
119 Columbus Ravine,
Scarborough, North Yorkshire
YO12 7QU
T: (01723) 361874
F: (01723) 361874

Avenwood Hotel ◆◆◆
129 Castle Road, Scarborough,
North Yorkshire YO11 1HX
T: (01723) 374640

Avoncroft Hotel ◆◆◆
5-7 Crown Terrace, South Cliff,
Scarborough, North Yorkshire
YO11 2BL
T: (01723) 372737
F: (01723) 372737

Beaches Private Hotel ◆◆◆
167 Columbus Ravine,
Scarborough, North Yorkshire
YO12 7QZ
T: (01723) 374587

Boston Hotel ◆◆◆
1-2 Blenheim Terrace, North Bay, Scarborough, North Yorkshire YO12 7HF
T: (01723) 360296 & 362226
F: (01723) 360296
E: suzanne@whitton@ bostonhotel.freeserve.co.uk
I: www.200k. com/ta/bostonhotel

Chessington Hotel ◆◆◆
The Crescent, Scarborough, North Yorkshire YO11 2PP
T: (01723) 365207

Earlsmere Hotel ◆◆◆◆
5 Belvedere Road, South Cliff, Scarborough, North Yorkshire YO11 2UU
T: (01723) 361340 & 07721 925188
F: (01723) 350924

Excelsior Private Hotel ◆◆◆
1 Marlborough Street, Scarborough, North Yorkshire YO12 7HG
T: (01723) 360716

Falcon Inn ◆◆◆
Whitby Road, Cloughton, Scarborough, North Yorkshire YO13 0DY
T: (01723) 870717

Givendale Hotel ◆◆◆◆
33 Burniston Road, Scarborough, North Yorkshire YO12 6PG
T: (01723) 363178
F: (01723) 354821
E: djhelms@dial.pipex.com
I: www.spiderweb.co. uk/givendalehotel/

Glenderry Non-smoking Guest House ◆◆◆
26 The Dene, Scarborough, North Yorkshire YO12 7NJ
T: (01723) 362546
E: glenderry@aol.com.uk
I: www.s-h-n.dircon.co. uk/glenderrynonsmoking guesthouse.htm

Greno Seafront Hotel ◆◆
25 Blenheim Terrace, Queens Parade, Scarborough, North Yorkshire YO12 7HD
T: (01723) 375705
F: (01723) 355512

The Gresham Hotel ◆◆◆
18 Lowdale Avenue, Northstead, Scarborough, North Yorkshire YO12 6JW
T: (01723) 372117
F: (01723) 372117
E: karen.robinson3@tesco.net

Harcourt Hotel ◆◆◆
45 Esplanade, Scarborough, North Yorkshire YO11 2AY
T: (01723) 373930
E: harcourthotel@ netscapeonline.co.uk

Harmony Country Lodge ◆◆◆◆
80 Limestone Road, Burniston, Scarborough, North Yorkshire YO13 0DG
T: (01723) 870276 & 07967 157689
F: (01723) 8700276
E: harmonylodge@cwcom.net
I: www.spiderweb.co. uk/Harmony

Headlands Hotel ◆◆◆
Weydale Avenue, Scarborough, North Yorkshire YO12 6AX
T: (01723) 373717
F: (01723) 373717

Hotel Helaina ◆◆◆
14 Blenheim Terrace, Scarborough, North Yorkshire YO12 7HF
T: (01723) 375191

Hillcrest Private Hotel ◆◆◆◆
2 Peasholm Avenue, Scarborough, North Yorkshire YO12 7NE
T: (01723) 361981
E: hillcresthotel.fsnet.co.uk
I: www.hillcresthotel.fs.net.co.uk

Killerby Cottage Farm ◆◆◆◆
Killerby Lane, Cayton, Scarborough, North Yorkshire YO11 3TP
T: (01723) 581236
F: (01723) 585465
E: val@green-glass.demon.co.uk
I: www.yorkshire.co.uk/valgreen

Lonsdale Villa Hotel ◆◆◆
Lonsdale Road, Scarborough, North Yorkshire YO11 2QY
T: (01723) 363383
E: lonsdale@scarborough.co.uk
I: www.lonsdale.co.uk

Lysander Hotel ◆◆◆
22 Weydale Avenue, Scarborough, North Yorkshire YO12 6AX
T: (01723) 373369 & 07957 251428
E: joy-harry@lysanderhotel. freeserve.com.uk
I: www.lysanderhotel.freeserve. com.uk

Moseley Lodge Private Hotel ◆◆◆◆
26 Avenue Victoria, South Cliff, Scarborough, North Yorkshire YO11 2QT
T: (01723) 360564
F: (01723) 363088
I: www.yorkshirenet.co. uk/moseleylodge

Mount House Hotel ◆◆◆◆
33 Trinity Road, South Cliff, Scarborough, North Yorkshire YO11 2TD
T: (01723) 362967

Mountview Private Hotel (Non-Smoking) ◆◆◆
32 West Street, South Cliff, Scarborough, North Yorkshire YO11 2QP
T: (01723) 500608
F: (01723) 501385
E: stay@mountview-hotel.co.uk
I: www.mountview-hotel.co.uk

The Old Mill Hotel ◆◆◆
Mill Street, Scarborough, North Yorkshire YO11 1SZ
T: (01723) 372735
F: (01723) 377190
E: info@windmill-hotel.co.uk
I: www.windmill-hotel.co.uk

Parmelia Hotel ◆◆◆
17 West Street, Southcliff, Scarborough, North Yorkshire YO11 2QN
T: (01723) 361914
E: parmeliahotel@btinternet. com

Peasholm Park Hotel ◆◆◆
21-23 Victoria Park, Columbus Ravine, Scarborough, North Yorkshire YO12 7TS
T: (01723) 375580 & 500954
E: peasholmpark@tesco.net

Perry's Court ◆◆◆
1 & 2 Rutland Terrace, Queen's Parade, Scarborough, North Yorkshire YO12 7JB
T: (01723) 373768
F: (01723) 353274

Philamon ◆◆◆
108 North Marine Road, Scarborough, North Yorkshire YO12 7JA
T: (01723) 373107 & 0771 320 6194

Philmore Hotel ◆◆◆◆
126 Columbus Ravine, Scarborough, North Yorkshire YO12 7QZ
T: (01723) 361516

The Phoenix ◆◆◆
157 Columbus Ravine, Scarborough, North Yorkshire YO12 7QZ
T: (01723) 368319
F: (01723) 368319

Powy's Lodge ◆◆◆◆
2 Westbourne Road, Scarborough, North Yorkshire YO12 2SP
T: (01723) 374019

Princess Court Guest House ◆◆◆
11 Princess Royal Terrace, Scarborough, North Yorkshire YO11 2RP
T: (01723) 501922
E: anoy@princesscourt. co.uk
I: www.princesscourt.co.uk

Raincliffe Hotel ◆◆◆◆
21 Valley Road, Scarborough, North Yorkshire YO11 2LY
T: (01723) 373541
E: enquiries@rainccliffehotel.co. uk
I: www.rainccliffehotel.co.uk

Rex Hotel ◆◆
9 Crown Crescent, Scarborough, North Yorkshire YO11 2BJ
T: (01723) 373297

Rivelyn Hotel ◆◆
1-4 Crown Crescent, South Cliff, Scarborough, North Yorkshire YO11 2BJ
T: (01723) 361248
F: (01723) 361248

Rose Dene ◆◆◆
106 Columbus Ravine, Scarborough, North Yorkshire YO12 7QZ
T: (01723) 374252
F: (01723) 507356
E: janice@@rosedenehotel.co. uk
I: www.rosedenehotel.co.uk

St Michael's Hotel ◆◆◆
27 Blenheim Terrace, Scarborough, North Yorkshire YO12 7HD
T: (01723) 374631
E: v.rennie@stmichaels27. freeserve.co.uk

Selomar Hotel ◆◆◆◆
23 Blenheim Terrace, Scarborough, North Yorkshire YO12 7HD
T: (01723) 364964

Victoria Seaview Hotel ◆◆◆◆
125 Queen's Parade, Scarborough, North Yorkshire YO12 7HY
T: (01723) 362164
E: victoria-seaview-hotel@ tinyworld.co.uk

Villa Marina ◆◆◆◆
59 Northstead Manor Drive, Scarborough, North Yorkshire YO12 6AF
T: (01723) 361088

Wharncliffe Hotel ◆◆◆◆
26 Blenheim Terrace, Scarborough, North Yorkshire YO12 7HD
T: (01723) 374635
E: wharncliffe.hotel@virginnet. co.uk
I: www.freespace.virginnet.co. uk.wharncliffe.hotel

SCAWBY
North Lincolnshire
The Old School ◆◆◆◆
Church Street, Scawby, Brigg, North Lincolnshire DN20 9AH
T: (01652) 654239

Olivers ◆◆◆
Church Street, Scawby, Brigg, North Lincolnshire DN20 9AM
T: (01652) 650446
E: eileen_harrison@lineone.net

SCHOLES
West Yorkshire
24 The Avenue ◆◆◆
Arthursdale, Scholes, Leeds LS15 4AS
T: (0113) 273 0289
E: ian.mann@virgin.net

SCHOLES, HOLMFIRTH
West Yorkshire
The Willows ◆◆
Scholes Moor Road, Scholes, Holmfirth, Huddersfield, West Yorkshire HD7 1SN
T: (01484) 684231

SCOTCH CORNER
North Yorkshire
Vintage Hotel ◆◆◆
Scotch Corner, Richmond, North Yorkshire DL10 6NP
T: (01748) 824424 & 822961
F: (01748) 826272

SCOTTON
North Yorkshire
Moorcock Hall Farm ◆◆◆
Scotton, Knaresborough, North
Yorkshire HG5 9HN
T: (01423) 863338

SCUNTHORPE
North Lincolnshire
Beverley Hotel ◆◆◆
55 Old Brumby Street,
Scunthorpe, North Lincolnshire
DN16 2AJ
T: (01724) 282212
F: (01724) 270422

The Downs Guest House ◆◆◆
33 Deyne Avenue, Scunthorpe,
North Lincolnshire DN15 7PZ
T: (01724) 850710
F: (01724) 330928

Elm Field ◆◆
22 Deyne Avenue, Scunthorpe,
North Lincolnshire DN15 7PZ
T: (01724) 869306

Kirks Korner ◆◆
12 Scotter Road, Scunthorpe,
North Lincolncshire DN15 8DR
T: (01724) 855344 & 281637
E: pkirk12@aol.com

Larchwood Hotel ◆◆
1-5 Shelford Street, off Mary
Street, Scunthorpe, North
Lincolnshire DN15 6NU
T: (01724) 864712
F: (01724) 864712

Normanby Hotel ◆◆◆
9-11 Normanby Road,
Scunthorpe, North Lincolnshire
DN15 6AR
T: (01724) 289982 & 341421

SELBY
North Yorkshire
Barff Lodge ◆◆◆◆
Mill Lane, Brayton, Selby, North
Yorkshire YO8 9LB
T: (01757) 213030
F: (01757) 212313
E: barfflodge@aol.com

Hazeldene Guest House ◆◆
34 Brook Street, Doncaster
Road, Selby, North Yorkshire
YO8 4AR
T: (01757) 704809
F: (01757) 709300
E: hazeldene@breathemail.net
I: www.smoothhound.co.
uk/hotels/hazel.html

SETTLE
North Yorkshire
Arbutus Guest House ◆◆◆◆
Riverside, Clapham, North
Yorkshire LA2 8DS
T: (015242) 51240
F: (015242) 51197
E: david@arbutus.co.uk
I: www.arbutus.co.uk

Golden Lion Hotel ◆◆◆
Duke Street, Settle, North
Yorkshire BD24 9DU
T: (01729) 822203
F: (01729) 824103
E: bookings@goldenlion.yorks.
net
I: www.yorkshirenet.co.
uk/stayat/goldenlion

Husbands Barn ◆◆◆◆
Stainforth, Settle, North
Yorkshire BD24 9PB
T: (01729) 822240
F: (01729) 822240
I: www.husbands.force9.co.uk

Maypole Inn ◆◆◆
Maypole Green, Main Street,
Long Preston, Skipton, North
Yorkshire BD23 4PH
T: (01729) 840219
E: landlord@maypole.co.uk
I: www.maypole.co.uk

Oast Guest House ◆◆◆
5 Pen-Y-Ghent View, Settle,
North Yorkshire BD24 9JJ
T: (01729) 822989
F: (01729) 822989
E: king@oast2000.freeserve.co.
uk
I: www.yorkshirenet.co.
uk/stayat/theoast

Ottawa ◆◆◆
Station Road, Giggleswick,
Settle, North Yorkshire
BD24 0AE
T: (01729) 822757

Scar Close Farm ◆◆◆◆
Feizor, Austwick, Lancaster
LA2 8DF
T: (01729) 823496

Station House ◆◆◆
Settle, North Yorkshire
BD24 9AA
T: (01729) 822533
E: stationhouse@zoom.co.uk
I: stationhouse_settle.co.uk

**Whitefriars Country Guest
House** ◆◆◆
Church Street, Settle, North
Yorkshire BD24 9JD
T: (01729) 823753
I: www.whitefriars-settle.co.uk

Yorkshire Rose Guest House
◆◆◆
Duke Street, Settle, North
Yorkshire BD24 9AW
T: (01729) 822032
E: yorkshirerose@tinyonline.co.
uk

SHAROW
North Yorkshire
Half Moon Inn ◆◆◆
Sharow Lane, Sharow, Ripon,
North Yorkshire HG4 5BP
T: (01765) 600291

SHEFFIELD
South Yorkshire
Anna's Bed and Breakfast ◆
981 Penistone Road,
Hillsborough, Sheffield, S6 2DH
T: (0114) 234 0108
F: (0114) 234 0108

Ashford ◆◆◆
44 Westwick Crescent,
Beauchief, Sheffield, South
Yorkshire S8 7DH
T: (0114) 237 5900 & 0787 940
5335

Coniston Guest House ◆◆◆
90 Beechwood Road,
Hillsborough, Sheffield, S6 4LQ
T: (0114) 233 9680
F: (0114) 233 9680
E: conistonguest.freeuk.co.uk
I: www.conistonguest@freeuk.
co.uk

Etruria House Hotel ◆◆◆
91 Crookes Road, Broomhill,
Sheffield, South Yorkshire
S10 5BD
T: (0114) 266 2241 & 267 0853
F: (0114) 267 0853
E: etruria@waitrose.com

Holme Lane Farm Private Hotel
◆◆◆◆
38 Halifax Road, Grenoside,
Sheffield S35 8PB
T: (0114) 246 8858
F: (0114) 246 8858

Ivory House Hotel ◆◆◆
34 Wostenholm Road, Sheffield,
S7 1LJ
T: (0114) 255 1853
F: (0114) 255 1578
E: ivoryhouse@fsmail.net

Lindrick Hotel ◆◆◆
226-230 Chippinghouse Road,
Sheffield, S7 1DR
T: (0114) 258 5041
F: (0114) 255 4758
E: reception@thelindrick.co.uk
I: www.thelindrick.co.uk

Peace Guest House ◆◆
92 Brocco Bank, Sheffield,
S11 8RS
T: (0114) 268 5110 & 267 0760

Priory Lodge Hotel ◆◆
40 Wostenholm Road,
Netheredge, Sheffield, S7 1LJ
T: (0114) 258 4670 & 258 4030
F: (0114) 255 6672
I: www.priorylodgehotel.co.uk

Riverside Court Hotel ◆◆◆
4 Nursery Street, Sheffield,
S3 8EG
T: (0114) 273 1962
F: (0114) 273 1962

The Rock Inn Hotel ◆◆◆◆
Cranemoor Road, Cranemoor,
Sheffield, South Yorkshire
S35 7AT
T: (0114) 288 3427 &
07778 386508
F: (0114) 288 3726
E: rmk@rockinn.co.uk
I: www.rockinn.co.uk

St Pellegrino ◆◆
2 Oak Park, Off Manchester
Road, Sheffield, S10 5DE
T: (0114) 268 1953 & 266 0151
F: (0114) 2666 0151

Thornsett House ◆◆
2 Thornsett Road, Sheffield,
South Yorkshire S7 1NA
T: (0114) 255 0157
F: (0114) 258 5223
E: deshague@2thornsett-house.
freeserve.co.uk
I: www.smothhound.co.uk/shs.
html

Tyndale ◆◆
164 Millhouses Lane, Sheffield,
South Yorkshire S7 2HE
T: (0114) 236 1660

SHELF
West Yorkshire
Duke of York Inn ◆◆◆
West Street, Shelf, Halifax, West
Yorkshire HL7 7LN
T: (01422) 202056
F: (01422) 206618
E: dukeofyork@england.com
I: www.dukeofyork.co.uk/

SHELLEY
West Yorkshire
Three Acres Inn and Restaurant
◆◆
Roydhouse, Shelley,
Huddersfield HD8 8LR
T: (01484) 602606
F: (01484) 608411
E: 3acres@globalnet.co.uk

SHERBURN
North Yorkshire
Cherry Tree Cottage ◆◆◆
37 St Hilda's Street, Sherburn,
Malton, North Yorkshire
YO17 8PG
T: (01944) 710851

SHIPLEY
West Yorkshire
Beeties With Rooms ◆◆◆◆
7 Victoria Road, Saltaire Village,
Shipley, West Yorkshire
BD18 3LA
T: (01274) 581718 & 595988
F: (01274) 582118
E: maureen@beeties.co.uk
I: www.beeties.co.uk

Clifton Lodge ◆◆◆
75 Kirkgate, Shipley, West
Yorkshire BD18 3LU
T: (01274) 580509
F: (01274) 580343
E: j.e.foster@lineone.net

SILSDEN
West Yorkshire
Dalesbank Holiday Park ◆◆◆
Low Lane, Silsden, Keighley,
West Yorkshire BD20 9JH
T: (01535) 653321 & 656523

SINNINGTON
North Yorkshire
Green Lea ◆◆◆
Sinnington, York YO62 6SH
T: (01751) 432008

Sinnington Manor ◆◆◆◆
Sinnington, York YO62 6SN
T: (01751) 433296
F: (01751) 433296

SKEEBY
North Yorkshire
The Old Chapel ◆◆◆◆
Richmond Road, Skeeby,
Richmond, North Yorkshire
DL10 5DR
T: (01748) 824170 & 0780 310
3871
I: hazel@theoldchapel.fsnet.co.
uk

SKIPSEA
East Riding of Yorkshire
The Grainary ◆◆◆
Skipsea Grange, Hornsea Road,
Skipsea, Driffield, East Riding of
Yorkshire YO25 8SY
T: (01262) 468745
F: (01262) 468840
E: francesdavies@btconnect.
com
I: www.the-grainary.co.uk

SKIPTON
North Yorkshire
Bourne House ◆◆◆
22 Upper Sackville Street,
Skipton, North Yorkshire
BD23 2EB
T: (01756) 792633
F: (01756) 701609

Craven Heifer Inn ◆◆◆
Grassington Road, Skipton,
North Yorkshire BD23 3LA
T: (01756) 792521 &
07767 476077
F: (01756) 794442
E: philandlynn@cravenheifer.co.
uk
I: www.cravenheifer.co.uk
🧗

Cravendale ◆◆◆
57 Keighley Road, Skipton,
North Yorkshire BD23 2LX
T: (01756) 795129 & 793866
F: (01756) 795129
I: www.yorkshirenet.co.
uk/stayat/cravendale/indexhtml
🌐

Dalesgate Lodge ◆◆◆◆
69 Gargrave Road, Skipton,
North Yorkshire BD23 1QN
T: (01756) 790672
E: dalesgatelodge@talk21.com

Devonshire Hotel ◆◆
Newmarket Street, Skipton,
North Yorkshire BD23 2HR
T: (01756) 793078 & 793625
F: (01756) 793078

Napier's Restaurant ◆◆◆◆
Chapel Hill, Skipton, North
Yorkshire BD23 1NL
T: (01756) 799688
F: (01756) 798111
I: www.restaurant-skipton.co.uk

Skipton Park Guest'otel ◆◆◆
2 Salisbury Street, Skipton,
North Yorkshire BD23 1NQ
T: (01756) 700640
F: (01756) 700641
E: derekchurch@skiptonpark.
freeserve.co.uk
I: www.milford.co.
uk/go/skiptonpark.html

Westby Lodge ◆◆◆◆
46 Keighley Road, Skipton,
North Yorkshire BD23 2NB
T: (01756) 700921

SLAITHWAITE
West Yorkshire
Hey Leys Farm ◆◆◆◆
Marsden Lane, Cop Hill,
Slaithwaite, Huddersfield
HD7 5XA
T: (01484) 845404 &
07803 744499
F: (01484) 843188

SLEDMERE
East Riding of Yorkshire
The Triton Inn ◆◆◆
Sledmere, Driffield, East
Yorkshire YO25 3XQ
T: (01377) 236644
E: thetritoninn@sledmere.
fsbusiness.co.uk

SLEIGHTS
North Yorkshire
The Lawns
◆◆◆◆◆ GOLD AWARD
73 Carr Hill Lane, Sleights,
Whitby, North Yorkshire
YO21 1RS
T: (01947) 810310
F: (01947) 810310
E: thelortons@tesco.net

Netherby House ◆◆◆◆
90 Coach Road, Sleights,
Whitby, North Yorkshire
YO22 5EQ
T: (01947) 810211
F: (01947) 810211

SLINGSBY
North Yorkshire
Beech Tree House Farm ◆◆◆
South Holme, Slingsby, York
YO62 4BA
T: (01653) 628257
F: (01653) 628973

**Lowry's Restaurant and Guest
House** ◆◆
Malton Road, Slingsby, York,
North Yorkshire YO62 4AF
T: (01653) 628417
F: (01653) 628417

SNAITH
East Riding of Yorkshire
Brewers Arms Hotel ◆◆◆
10 Pontefract Road, Snaith,
Goole, East Riding of Yorkshire
DN14 9JS
T: (01405) 862404
F: (01405) 862397

SOUTH CAVE
East Riding of Yorkshire
**Rudstone Walk Country
Accommodation and Cottages**
◆◆◆◆
South Cave, Brough, East
Yorkshire HU15 2AH
T: (01430) 422230
F: (01430) 424552
E: office@rudstone-walk.co.uk
I: www.rudstone-walk.co.uk
🌐 🧗

SOWERBY
North Yorkshire
Long Acre Bed and Breakfast
◆◆
Long Acre, 86A Topcliffe Road,
Sowerby, Thirsk, North Yorkshire
YO7 1RY
T: (01845) 522360

SOWERBY BRIDGE
West Yorkshire
Rishworth Hall ◆◆◆◆
Rishworth New Road, Sowerby
Bridge, West Yorkshire HX6 4QN
T: (01422) 822948

SPAUNTON, APPLETON-LE-MOORS
Holywell House ◆◆◆◆
Spaunton Bank Foot, Spaunton,
Appleton-le-Moors, York
YO62 6TR
T: (01751) 417624

STAINFORTH
North Yorkshire
2 Bridge End Cottage ◆◆◆
Stainforth, Settle, North
Yorkshire BD24 9PG
T: (01729) 822149

STAINTONDALE
North Yorkshire
Island Farm ◆◆◆◆
Staintondale, Scarborough,
North Yorkshire YO13 0EB
T: (01723) 870249
🌐

Plane Tree Cottage Farm ◆◆◆
Down Dale Road, Staintondale,
Scarborough, North Yorkshire
YO13 0EY
T: (01723) 870796

Wellington Lodge ◆◆◆◆
Staintondale, Scarborough,
North Yorkshire YO13 0EL
T: (01723) 871234
F: (01723) 871234
E: info@llamatreks.co.uk
I: www.llamatreks.co.uk

STAITHES
North Yorkshire
Springfields ◆◆◆
42 Staithes Lane, Staithes,
Saltburn-by-the-Sea, Cleveland
TS13 5AD
T: (01947) 841011

STAMFORD BRIDGE
East Riding of Yorkshire
High Catton Grange ◆◆◆◆
Stamford Bridge, York YO41 1EP
T: (01759) 371374
F: (01759) 371374

STANBURY
West Yorkshire
Ponden House ◆◆◆◆
Stanbury, Keighley, West
Yorkshire BD22 0HR
T: (01535) 644154
E: ponden@whitehofm.nildram.
co.uk
I: www.homepages.nildram.co.
uk/§gpsout/ponden

STAPE
North Yorkshire
Grange Farm ◆◆◆◆
Stape, Pickering, North Yorkshire
YO18 8HZ
T: (01751) 473805
F: (01751) 477805
I: www.smoothhound.co.
uk/hotels/grange.html

Rawcliffe House Farm ◆◆◆◆
Stape, Pickering, North Yorkshire
YO18 8JA
T: (01751) 473292
F: (01751) 473766
E: sheila@
yorkshireaccommodation.com
I: www.
yorkshireaccommodation.com

Seavy Slack ◆◆◆
Stape, Pickering, North Yorkshire
YO18 8HZ
T: (01751) 473131
🌐

STARBOTTON
North Yorkshire
Bushey Lodge Farm
◆◆◆◆ SILVER AWARD
Starbotton, Skipton, North
Yorkshire BD23 5HY
T: (01756) 760424
🌐

STEARSBY
North Yorkshire
The Granary ◆◆◆◆
Stearsby, York, North Yorkshire
YO61 4SA
T: (01347) 888652
F: (01347) 888652

STOKESLEY
North Yorkshire
The Buck Inn Hotel ◆◆◆
Chopgate, Stokesley,
Middlesbrough, Cleveland
TS9 7JL
T: (01642) 778334 & 778205
F: (01642) 778205
E: buckinn@aol.com
🌐

Harker Hill Farm ◆◆◆
Harker Hill, Seamer, Stokesley,
Middlesbrough TS9 5NF
T: (01642) 710431
F: (01642) 710431
E: harkerhill@freeuk.com
I: www.destination-england.co.
uk/harkerhill.html

STONEGRAVE
North Yorkshire
**Manor Cottage Bed and
Breakfast** ◆◆◆◆
Manor Cottage, Stonegrave,
York YO62 4LJ
T: (01653) 628599
E: gideon.v@virgin.net
I: business.virgin.net/gideon.
v/index.html

STUDLEY ROGER
North Yorkshire
Downing House Farm ◆◆◆◆
Studley Roger, Ripon, North
Yorkshire HG4 3AY
T: (01765) 601014
F: (01765) 601014
E: dickhelen@supanet.com
I: www.yorkshiredalesholidays.
co.uk

SUTTON-ON-THE-FOREST
North Yorkshire
Goose Farm ◆◆◆
Eastmoor, Sutton-on-the-
Forest, York YO61 1ET
T: (01347) 810577
F: (01347) 810577
E: stay@goosefarm.fsnet.co.uk
I: www.yorkshirenet.co.
uk/stayat/goosefarm

SWILLINGTON
West Yorkshire
Bridge Farm Hotel ◆◆◆
Wakefield Road, Swillington,
Leeds LS26 8PZ
T: (0113) 282 3718
F: (0113) 282 5135

TERRINGTON
North Yorkshire
Gate Farm ♦♦♦
Ganthorpe, Terrington, York
YO60 6QD
T: (01653) 648269
E: millgate001@aol.com

THIMBLEBY
North Yorkshire
Stonehaven ♦♦♦
Thimbleby, Northallerton, North
Yorkshire DL6 3PY
T: (01609) 883689

THIRSK
North Yorkshire
Fourways Guest House ♦♦
Town End, Thirsk, North
Yorkshire YO7 1PY
T: (01845) 522601
F: (01845) 522131
E: fairways@nyorks.fsbusiness.
co.uk

Kirkgate House Hotel ♦♦♦
35 Kirkgate, Thirsk, North
Yorkshire YO7 1PL
T: (01845) 525015
F: (01845) 522181
E: kirkgate_hotel@hotmail.com

Laburnum House ♦♦♦♦
31 Topcliffe Road, Thirsk, North
Yorkshire YO7 1RX
T: (01845) 524120

Lavender House ♦♦♦
27 Kirkgate, Thirsk, North
Yorkshire YO7 1PL
T: (01845) 522224

Lord Nelson Inn ♦♦♦
40/41 St James Green, Thirsk,
North Yorkshire YO7 1AQ
T: (01845) 522845
F: (01845) 522845
E: dmoore8813@aol.comm.

Plump Bank ♦♦♦♦
Felixkirk Road, Thirsk, North
Yorkshire YO7 2EW
T: (01845) 522406

Town Pasture Farm ♦♦♦
Boltby, Thirsk, North Yorkshire
YO7 2DY
T: (01845) 537298

THORALBY
North Yorkshire
Pen View ♦♦♦
Thoralby, Leyburn, North
Yorkshire DL8 3SU
T: (01969) 663319
F: (01969) 663319
E: penview@wensleydale.org
I: www.wensleydale.
org/links/penviewfrm.htm

THORNER
West Yorkshire
Carr Farm ♦
Carr Lane, Thorner, Leeds
LS14 3HE
T: (0113) 289 2278

THORNHILL EDGE
West Yorkshire
**Daleside Holidays
♦♦♦♦♦ SILVER AWARD**
Sundar, 16 Daleside, Thornhill
Edge, Dewsbury, West Yorkshire
WF12 0PJ
T: (01924) 438740
F: (01924) 438740
E: cross@sundar16.freeserve.co.
uk
I: www.dalesideholidays.com

THORNTON
West Yorkshire
Ann's Farmhouse ♦♦♦
New Farm, Thornton Road,
Thornton, Bradford, West
Yorkshire BD13 3QE
T: (01274) 833214

THORNTON DALE
North Yorkshire
Banavie ♦♦♦♦
Roxby Road, Thornton Dale,
Pickering, North Yorkshire
YO18 7SX
T: (01751) 474616 &
07803 098604

Bridgefoot Guest House ♦♦♦
Thornton Dale, Pickering, North
Yorkshire YO18 7RR
T: (01751) 474749

The Buck Hotel ♦♦♦
Chestnut Avenue, Thornton
Dale, Pickering, North Yorkshire
YO18 7RW
T: (01751) 474212
F: (01751) 474212

Hall Farm ♦♦♦
Maltongate, Thornton Dale,
Pickering, North Yorkshire
YO18 7SD
T: (01751) 475526

Nabgate ♦♦♦♦
Wilton Road, Thornton Dale,
Pickering, North Yorkshire
YO18 7QP
T: (01751) 474279 &
07703 804859

New Inn ♦♦♦♦
Maltongate, Thornton Dale,
Pickering, North Yorkshire
YO18 7LF
T: (01751) 474226
F: (01751) 477715
E: Newinntld@aol.com

**The Old Granary Bed and
Breakfast ♦♦♦♦**
Top Bridge Farm, Thornton Dale,
Pickering, North Yorkshire
YO18 7RA
T: (01751) 477217 &
07775 617107

Prospect Farm Bungalow ♦♦♦
Prospect Place, Thornton Dale,
Pickering, North Yorkshire
YO18 7LQ
T: (01751) 474451

Tangalwood ♦♦♦
Roxby Road, Thornton Dale,
Pickering, North Yorkshire
YO18 7SX
T: (01751) 474688

THORNTON RUST
North Yorkshire
Fellside ♦♦♦♦
Thornton Rust, Leyburn, North
Yorkshire DL8 3AP
T: (01969) 663504
F: (01969) 663965
E: harvey@plwmp.freeserve.co.
uk

THORPE
North Yorkshire
Langerton House Farm ♦♦♦
Cracoe, Thorpe Lane, Thorpe,
Skipton, North Yorkshire
BD23 5HN
T: (01756) 730260

THRESHFIELD
North Yorkshire
Greenways House ♦♦♦♦
Wharfeside Avenue, Threshfield,
Skipton, North Yorkshire
BD23 5BS
T: (01756) 752598
E: soxby@tinyonline.co.uk

Station House ♦♦♦
Station Road, Threshfield,
Skipton, North Yorkshire
BD23 5ES
T: (01756) 752667
E: peter@station-ouse.
freeserve.co.uk
I: www.yorkshirenet.co.
uk/stayat/stationhouse

THWAITE
North Yorkshire
Kearton Country Hotel ♦♦♦
Thwaite, Richmond, North
Yorkshire DL11 6DR
T: (01748) 886277
F: (01748) 886590
E: jdanton@aol.com

TODMORDEN
West Yorkshire
**The Berghof Brandstatter
♦♦♦**
Cross Stone Road, Todmorden,
Lancashire OL14 8RQ
T: (01706) 812966
F: (01706) 812966
E: berghof@tinyworld.co.uk

Cherry Tree Cottage ♦♦♦♦
Woodhouse Road, Todmorden,
Lancashire OL14 5RJ
T: (01706) 817492

Watty Farm ♦♦
Watty Lane, Todmorden,
Lancashire OL14 7JQ
T: (01706) 818531
F: (01706) 818531

Woodleigh Hall ♦♦♦♦
Ewood Lane, Todmorden,
Lancashire OL14 7DF
T: (01706) 814664 & 810788
F: (01706) 810673
E: maurinceheath@lineone.net

TOLLERTON
North Yorkshire
Bungalow Farm ♦♦♦
Warehills Lane, Tollerton, York
YO61 1RG
T: (01347) 838732

TRIANGLE
West Yorkshire
The Dene ♦♦♦♦
Triangle, Sowerby Bridge, West
Yorkshire HX6 3EA
T: (01422) 823562
E: noble@thedene-triangle.
freeserve.co.uk

ULCEBY
North Lincolnshire
**Gillingham Rest Guest House
♦♦♦♦**
Spruce Lane, Ulceby, North
Lincolnshire DN39 6UL
T: (01469) 588427

UPPER GREETLAND
West Yorkshire
Crawstone Knowl Farm ♦♦♦
Rochdale Road, Upper
Greetland, Halifax, West
Yorkshire HX4 8PX
T: (01422) 370470

WADSWORTH
West Yorkshire
Hare & Hounds ♦♦♦
Billy Lane, Wadsworth, Hebden
Bridge, West Yorkshire HX7 8TN
T: (01422) 842671
I: www.hare.and.hounds.
connectfree.co.uk

WAKEFIELD
West Yorkshire
Heath House ♦♦♦
Chancery Road, Ossett, West
Yorkshire WF5 9RZ
T: (01924) 260654 & 273098
F: (01924) 260654
E: bookings@heath-house.co.uk
I: www.heath-house.co.uk

WALSDEN
West Yorkshire
Birks Clough ♦♦♦
Hollingworth Lane, Walsden,
Todmorden, Lancashire
OL14 6QX
T: (01706) 814438
F: (01706) 819002
E: mstorah@mwfree.net

Highstones Guest House ♦♦
Lane Bottom, Walsden,
Todmorden, Lancashire
OL14 6TY
T: (01706) 816534

WEAVERTHORPE
North Yorkshire
The Star Country Inn ♦♦♦
Weaverthorpe, Malton, North
Yorkshire YO17 8EY
T: (01944) 738273 &
07977 472221
E: starinn@qunta.net
I: www.starinnweaverthorpe.
com

WEETON
North Yorkshire
Arthington Lodge ♦♦♦♦
Jubilee Farm, Wescoe Hill Lane,
Weeton, Leeds LS17 0EZ
T: (01423) 734102

WEST BRETTON
West Yorkshire
The Old Manor House ♦♦♦
19 Sycamore Lane, West
Bretton, Wakefield, West
Yorkshire WF4 4JR
T: (01924) 830324 &
07979 750590

The Poppies ◆◆
8 Cobbler Hall, West Bretton,
Wakefield, West Yorkshire
WF4 4LJ
T: (01924) 830317

WEST BURTON
North Yorkshire

The Grange ◆◆◆◆◆
West Burton, Leyburn, North
Yorkshire DL8 4JR
T: (01969) 663348

Grange House ◆◆◆◆
Waldenhead, West Burton,
Leyburn, North Yorkshire
DL8 4LF
T: (01969) 663641

WEST WITTON
North Yorkshire

Ivy Dene Country Guesthouse
◆◆◆
West Witton, Leyburn, North
Yorkshire DL8 4LP
T: (01969) 622785
F: (01969) 622785

The Old Star ◆◆◆
West Witton, Leyburn, North
Yorkshire DL8 4LU
T: (01969) 622949
E: martins@the-old-star.
freeserve.co.uk

The Old Vicarage ◆◆◆
Main Street, West Witton,
Leyburn, North Yorkshire
DL8 4LX
T: (01969) 622108
I: smoothhound.co.
uk/hotels/oldvicar1.html

WESTOW
North Yorkshire

Blacksmiths Arms Inn ◆◆◆
Westow, York, North Yorkshire
YO60 7NE
T: (01653) 618365 & 618343
🚶

WETHERBY
West Yorkshire

Bush House Guest House ◆◆◆
4 Caxton Street, Wetherby, West
Yorkshire LS22 6RU
T: (01937) 582104

**The Coach House Garden
Studio** ◆◆◆◆
North Grove Approach,
Wetherby, West Yorkshire
LS22 7GA
T: (01937) 586100
F: (01937) 586100
◎

Highfield
◆◆◆◆ SILVER AWARD
6 Prospect Villas, Wetherby,
West Yorkshire LS22 6PL
T: (01937) 583351
F: (01937) 583351
E: robertrolfe@compuserve.com

Lindum Fields ◆◆◆◆
48a Spofforth Hill, Wetherby,
West Yorkshire LS22 6SE
T: (01937) 520389
F: (01937) 520389
E: peter@pstretton.freeserve.co.
uk

Linton Close ◆◆◆◆
2 Wharfe Grove, Wetherby, West
Yorkshire LS22 6HA
T: (01937) 582711
F: (01937) 588499
◎

Prospect House ◆◆
8 Caxton Street, Wetherby, West
Yorkshire LS22 6RU
T: (01937) 582428

The Red House ◆◆◆
12 The Spinney, Wetherby, West
Yorkshire LS22 6SH
T: (01937) 585497
F: (01937) 580712

Swan Guest House ◆◆
38 North Street, Wetherby, West
Yorkshire LS22 6NN
T: (01937) 582381 & 0771 204
3931
F: (01937) 584908

14 Woodhill View ◆◆
Wetherby, West Yorkshire
LS22 6PP
T: (01937) 581200 &
07967 152091

WHITBY
North Yorkshire

**Bramblewick Bed and
Breakfast** ◆◆◆◆
3 Havelock Place, Whitby, North
Yorkshire YO21 3ER
T: (01947) 604504

Chiltern Guest House ◆◆◆◆
13 Normanby Terrace, West
Cliff, Whitby, North Yorkshire
YO21 3ES
T: (01947) 604981
F: (01947) 604981
◎

Corner Guest House ◆◆◆◆
3-4 Crescent Place, Whitby,
North Yorkshire YO21 3HE
T: (01947) 602444

Esklet Guest House ◆◆◆
22 Crescent Avenue, West Cliff,
Whitby, North Yorkshire
YO21 3ED
T: (01947) 605663

Glendale Guest House ◆◆◆◆
16 Crescent Avenue, Whitby,
North Yorkshire YO21 3ED
T: (01947) 604242

Grantley House ◆◆◆◆
26 Hudson Street, Whitby, North
Yorkshire YO21 3EP
T: (01947) 600895
F: (01947) 600895
E: kevin@thegrantley.freeserve.
co.uk

Grove Hotel ◆◆◆◆
36 Bagdale, Whitby, North
Yorkshire YO21 1QL
T: (01947) 603551
I: www.smoothhound.co.
uk/hotels/grove2.html

Jaydee Guest House ◆◆◆
15 John Street, Whitby, North
Yorkshire YO21 3ET
T: (01947) 605422
F: (01947) 605422
I: www.smoothhound.co.uk.
hotels/jaydee.html

Kom Binne Guest House ◆◆◆
5 Broomfield Terrace, Whitby,
North Yorkshire YO21 1QP
T: (01947) 602752

Lansbury Guest House ◆◆◆
29 Hudson Street, Whitby, North
Yorkshire YO21 3EP
T: (01947) 604821
F: (01947) 604821
E: anne-tom.wheeler@virgin.
net
I: www.whitby-uk.
com/lansburyhse.html

Leeway Guest House ◆◆◆
1 Havelock Place, Whitby, North
Yorkshire YO21 3ER
T: (01947) 602604

The Middleham ◆◆
3 Church Square, Whitby, North
Yorkshire YO21 3EG
T: (01947) 603423 & 0777 3199
2934
F: (01947) 603423

Morningside Hotel ◆◆◆
10 North Promenade, West Cliff,
Whitby, North Yorkshire
YO21 3JX
T: (01947) 602643 & 604030

Number Five ◆◆◆
5 Havelock Place, Whitby, North
Yorkshire YO21 3ER
T: (01947) 606361
F: (01947) 606361
E: kevin.butler2@btinternet.
com

Number Seven Guest House
◆◆◆◆
7 East Cresent, Whitby, North
Yorkshire YO21 3HD
T: (01947) 606019
F: (01947) 606019

The Olde Ford ◆◆◆◆
1 Briggswath, Whitby, North
Yorkshire YO21 1RU
T: (01947) 810704 & 0798 989
8833
E: grey@theoldeford.fsnet.co.uk

Partridge Nest Farm ◆◆◆
Sleights, Whitby, North
Yorkshire YO22 5ES
T: (01947) 810450 & 811412
F: (01947) 811413
E: pnfarm@aol.com
I: www.tmis.
com/partridge-nest/

Postgate Farm ◆◆◆◆
Glaisdale, Whitby, North
Yorkshire YO21 2PZ
T: (01947) 897353
F: (01947) 897353
E: j-m.thompson.bandb@talk21.
com

Prospect Villa Hotel ◆◆◆
13 Prospect Hill, Whitby, North
Yorkshire YO21 1QE
T: (01947) 603118 &
07778 782638
F: (01947) 825445

Rosewood Bed & Breakfast
◆◆◆◆ SILVER AWARD
3 Ocean Road, Whitby, North
Yorkshire YO21 3HY
T: (01947) 820534
E: rose.wood@virgin.net
◎

Rosslyn House ◆◆◆
11 Abbey Terrace, Whitby, North
Yorkshire YO21 3HQ
T: (01947) 604086 &
07768 963589
F: (01947) 604086
I: www.whitby-uk.com

Rothbury ◆◆◆◆
2 Ocean Road, Whitby, North
Yorkshire YO21 3HY
T: (01974) 606282 &
07713 784574

Ryedale House ◆◆◆◆
156 Coach Road, Sleights,
Whitby, North Yorkshire
YO22 5EQ
T: (01947) 810534
F: (01947) 810534

Seacliffe Hotel ◆◆◆◆
12 North Promenade, West Cliff,
Whitby, North Yorkshire
YO21 3JX
T: (01947) 603139 &
08000 191747
F: (01947) 603139
E: julie@seacliffe.fsnet.co.uk
I: www.seacliffe.co.uk

Seaview ◆◆◆
5 East Crescent, Whitby, North
Yorkshire YO21 3HD
T: (01947) 604462

Storrbeck ◆◆◆
9 Crescent Avenue, Whitby,
North Yorkshire YO21 3ED
T: (01947) 605468

Weardale Guest House ◆◆◆
12 Normanby Terrace, Whitby,
North Yorkshire YO21 3ES
T: (01947) 820389 &
07710 701047
F: (01947) 820389
I: infotel.co.uk/hotels/17281.htm

Wentworth House ◆◆◆
27 Hudson Street, West Cliff,
Whitby, North Yorkshire
YO21 3EP
T: (01947) 602433

Wheeldale Hotel ◆◆◆◆
11 North Promenade, Whitby,
North Yorkshire YO21 3JX
T: (01947) 602365 &
07710 994277

York House Private Hotel
◆◆◆◆ SILVER AWARD
3 Back Lane, High Hawsker,
Whitby, North Yorkshire
YO22 4LW
T: (01947) 880314
F: (01947) 880314
E: yorkhouse@
destination-england.co.uk
I: www.destination-england.co.
uk/yorkhouse.html

WICKERSLEY
South Yorkshire

Millstone Farm ◆◆◆
Wickersley, Rotherham, South
Yorkshire S66 1EA
I: (01709) 542382

WIKE
West Yorkshire

Wike Ridge Farm ◆◆◆◆
Wike Ridge Lane, Wike, Leeds,
West Yorkshire LS17 9JF
T: (0113) 266 1190
E: wikeridge@aol.com

YORKSHIRE

WILBERFOSS
East Riding of Yorkshire
Cuckoo Nest Farm ♦♦♦
Wilberfoss, York YO41 5NL
T: (01759) 380365

WILSDEN
West Yorkshire
Springhill Bed and Breakfast ♦♦
2 Spring Hill, Wilsden, Bradford,
West Yorkshire BD15 0AW
T: (01535) 275211 &
07974 959197

WILTON
North Yorkshire
The Old Forge ♦♦♦♦
Wilton, Pickering, North
Yorkshire YO18 7JY
T: (01751) 477399
F: (01751) 477464
E: theoldforge@themutual.net
I: www.forgecottages.
themutual.net/fc.html

WOLD NEWTON
East Riding of Yorkshire
The Wold Cottage
♦♦♦♦♦ SILVER AWARD
Wold Newton, Driffield, East
Riding of Yorkshire YO25 3HL
T: (01262) 470696
F: (01262) 470696

WOMBLETON
North Yorkshire
Rockery Cottage
♦♦♦♦ SILVER AWARD
Main Street, Wombleton, York
YO62 7RX
T: (01751) 432257 &
07771 657222

WORTLEY
South Yorkshire
Wortley Hall Ltd ♦♦
Wortley, Sheffield, South
Yorkshire S35 7DB
T: (0114) 288 2100 & 288 5750
F: (0114) 283 0695
E: wortley.hall@virgin.net

WRAWBY
North Lincolnshire
The Jolly Miller ♦♦♦
Brigg Road, Wrawby, Brigg,
North Lincolnshire DN20 8RH
T: (01652) 655658
F: (01652) 652048
E: john@jollymiller.co.uk
I: www.jollymiller.co.uk

Wish 'u' Well Guest House ♦♦♦
Brigg Road, Wrawby, Brigg,
North Lincolnshire DN20 8RH
T: (01652) 652301

WRELTON
North Yorkshire
Huntsman Restaurant ♦♦♦
Main Street, Wrelton, Pickering,
North Yorkshire YO18 8PG
T: (01751) 472530
E: howard@thehuntsman.
freeserve.co.uk
I: www.europage.co.
uk/huntsman

WROOT
South Yorkshire
Green Garth Country Guest House ♦♦♦♦
High Street, Wroot, Doncaster,
South Yorkshire DN9 2BU
T: (01302) 770416 &
07711 734128
F: (01302) 770416

YORK
North Yorkshire
Aaron Guest House ♦♦♦
42 Bootham Crescent, Bootham,
York, YO30 7AH
T: (01904) 625927

Abbey Guest House ♦♦♦
14 Earlsborough Terrace,
Marygate, York, YO30 7BQ
T: (01904) 627782
F: (01904) 671743
E: abbey@rsummers.cix.co.uk
I: www.cix.co.
uk/§munin/sworld/abbey.htm

Abbeyfields ♦♦♦
19 Bootham Terrace, York,
YO30 7DH
T: (01904) 636471 & 624197
F: (01904) 636471
E: info@abbeyfields.co.uk
I: www.abbeyfields.co.uk

The Abbingdon ♦♦
60 Bootham Crescent, Bootham,
York, YO30 7AH
T: (01904) 621761
F: (01904) 610002
E: paula@abbingdon.freeserve.
co.uk

The Acer Hotel
♦♦♦♦ SILVER AWARD
52 Scarcroft Hill, York, YO24 1DE
T: (01904) 653839
F: (01904) 677017
E: info@acerhotel.co.uk
I: www.acerhotel.co.uk

Acorn Guest House
Rating Applied For
1 Southlands Road, York, North
Yorkshire YO23 1NP
T: (01904) 620081 &
07710 507536
F: (01904) 613331
E: acorn.gh@btinternet.com

Acres Dene Guesthouse ♦♦♦
87 Fulford Road, York, YO10 4BD
T: (01904) 625280 & 623126
F: (01904) 637330
E: acresdene@bigwig.net

Airden House ♦♦♦
1 St Mary's, Bootham, York,
YO30 7DD
T: (01904) 638915

Alcuin Lodge ♦♦♦
15 Sycamore Place, Bootham,
York, YO30 7DW
T: (01904) 632222
F: (01904) 626630
E: alcuinlodg@aol.com

Aldwark Bridge House ♦♦
Ouseburn, York, YO26 9SJ
T: (01423) 331097
F: (01423) 331097
E: bbabh@netscapeonline.co.uk

Aldwark Guest House ♦♦♦
30 St Saviourgate, Aldwark,
York, YO1 8NN
T: (01904) 627781

Alfreda Guest House ♦♦♦
61 Heslington Lane, Fulford,
York YO10 4HN
T: (01904) 631698
F: (01904) 411215

Ambleside Guest House ♦♦♦
62 Bootham Crescent, Bootham,
York, YO30 7AH
T: (01904) 637165
F: (01904) 637165
E: ambles@globalnet.co.uk

Arndale Hotel ♦♦♦♦
290 Tadcaster Road, York,
YO24 1ET
T: (01904) 702424
F: (01904) 709800

Arnot House
♦♦♦♦ SILVER AWARD
17 Grosvenor Terrace, Bootham,
York, YO30 7AG
T: (01904) 641966
F: (01904) 641966

Ascot House ♦♦♦♦
80 East Parade, York, YO31 7YH
T: (01904) 426826
F: (01904) 431077
E: j&tk@ascot-house-york.
demon.co.uk
I: www.smoothhound.co.
uk/hotels/ascothou.html

Ashbourne House ♦♦♦♦
139 Fulford Road, York,
YO10 4HG
T: (01904) 639912
F: (01904) 631332
E: ashbourneh@aol.com

Ashbury Hotel ♦♦♦
103 The Mount, York, YO24 1AX
T: (01904) 647339
F: (01904) 647339
E: ashbury@talk21.com

Ashwood Guest House ♦♦♦
19 Nunthorpe Avenue, Scarcroft
Road, York, YO23 1PF
T: (01904) 623412
F: (01904) 623412

Astley House ♦♦♦
123 Clifton, York, YO30 6BL
T: (01904) 634745 & 621327
F: (01904) 621327
E: astley123@aol.com
I: members@aol.
com/astley1223/astley.html

Avimore House Hotel ♦♦♦
78 Stockton Lane, York,
YO31 1BS
T: (01904) 425556
F: (01904) 426264
E: avimore.house@tinyonline.
co.uk

Avondale ♦♦♦
61 Bishopthorpe Road, York,
YO23 1NX
T: (01904) 633989

The Bar Convent Enterprises Ltd ♦♦♦
17 Blossom Street, York,
YO24 1AQ
T: (01904) 643238 & 629359
F: (01904) 631792
E: info@bar-convent.org.uk
I: www.bar-convent.org.uk

Barbican House ♦♦♦♦
20 Barbican Road, York,
YO10 5AA
T: (01904) 627617
F: (01904) 647140
E: info@barbicanhouse.com
I: www.barbicanhouse.com

Barrington House ♦♦♦
15 Nunthorpe Avenue, Scarcroft
Road, York, YO23 1PF
T: (01904) 634539

Bay Tree Guest House ♦♦♦
92 Bishopthorpe Road, York,
YO23 1JS
T: (01904) 659462
F: (01904) 659462

The Beckett ♦♦♦
58 Bootham Crescent, Bootham,
York, YO30 7AH
T: (01904) 644728
E: abrownyork@aol.com
I: www.mywebpage.
net/thebeckett

Bedford Hotel ♦♦♦
108-110 Bootham, York,
YO30 7DG
T: (01904) 624412
F: (01904) 632851

Beech House ♦♦♦
6-7 Longfield Terrace, Bootham,
York, YO30 7DJ
T: (01904) 634581

Bentley Guest House ♦♦♦♦
25 Grosvenor Terrace, Bootham,
York, YO30 7AG
T: (01904) 644313 &
07860 199440
F: (01904) 644313
E: p.a.lefebve@tesco.net

Birchfield Guest House ♦♦♦
2 Nunthorpe Avenue, Scarcroft
Road, York, YO23 1PF
T: (01904) 636395

Bishopgarth Guest House ♦♦♦
3 Southlands Road,
Bishopthorpe Road, York,
YO23 1NP
T: (01904) 635220 &
07050 383711
I: web.ukonline.co.
uk/spreckley/index.html

Bishops Hotel
♦♦♦♦ SILVER AWARD
135 Holgate Road, Holgate,
York, YO24 4DF
T: (01904) 628000
F: (01904) 628181
E: bishops@ukonline.co.uk

Black Bull Inn ♦♦♦
91 Main Street, Escrick, York
YO19 6JP
T: (01904) 728245
F: (01904) 728154

Blakeney Hotel ♦♦♦
180 Stockton Lane, York,
YO31 1ES
T: (01904) 422786
F: (01904) 422786
E: reception@blakeneyhtlyork.
abelgratis.co.uk
I: www.blakeneyhtlyork.
abelgratis.co.uk

Blue Bridge Hotel ◆◆◆
Fishergate, York, YO10 4AP
T: (01904) 621193
F: (01904) 671571
E: book@bluebridgehotel.co.uk
I: www.bluebridgehotel.co.uk

Bootham Guest House ◆◆◆
56 Bootham Crescent, York,
North Yorkshire YO30 7AH
T: (01904) 672123
F: (01904) 672123
E: boothamguesthouse@
btinternet.com

Bootham Park ◆◆◆◆
9 Grosvenor Terrace, Bootham,
York, YO30 7AG
T: (01904) 644262
F: (01904) 645647
I: www.
hotelboothampark@easicom.
com

Bowen House ◆◆◆
4 Gladstone Street, Huntington
Road, York, YO31 8RF
T: (01904) 636881
F: (01904) 338700
E: info@bowenhouse.co.uk
I: www.bowenhouse.co.uk

Brentwood Guest House ◆◆◆
54 Bootham Crescent, Bootham,
York, YO30 7AH
T: (01904) 636419
F: (01904) 636419
I: www.visitus.co.uk

Briar Lea Guest House ◆◆◆
8 Longfield Terrace, Bootham,
York, YO30 7DJ
T: (01904) 635061 &
07703 344302
F: (01904) 330356
E: briargh8l@aol.com

Bridge House ◆◆
181 Haxby Road, York, YO31 8JL
T: (01904) 636161
F: (01904) 636161

Bronte Guesthouse ◆◆◆◆
22 Grosvenor Terrace, Bootham,
York, YO30 7AG
T: (01904) 621066
F: (01904) 653434
E: enquires@
bronte-guesthouse.com
I: www.bronte-guesthouse.com/

Bull Lodge Guest House ◆◆◆
37 Bull Lane, Lawrence Street,
York, YO10 3EN
T: (01904) 415522
F: (01904) 415522
E: bullodge@nationwideisp.net

Burton Villa ◆◆◆
24 Haxby Road, York, YO31 8JX
T: (01904) 626364
F: (01904) 671743
I: burton@rsummers.cix.co.uk

Butterworth Welgarth House ◆◆◆
Wetherby Road, Rufforth, York
YO23 3QB
T: (01904) 738592 & 738595
F: (01904) 738595

Carlton House Hotel ◆◆◆
134 The Mount, York, YO24 1AS
T: (01904) 622265
F: (01904) 637157
E: etb@carltonhouse.co.uk
I: www.carltonhouse.co.uk

Carousel Guest House ◆◆◆
83 Eldon Street, off Stanley
Street, Haxby Road, York,
YO31 7NH
T: (01904) 646709

Cavalier Hotel ◆◆◆
39 Monkgate, York, YO31 7PB
T: (01904) 636615
F: (01904) 636615
E: julia@cavalierhotel.fsnet.co.
uk
I: www.cavalierhotel.co.uk

Chelmsford Place Guest House ◆◆◆
85 Fulford Road, York, YO10 4BD
T: (01904) 624491 &
07802 339681
F: (01904) 624491

Chilton Guest House ◆◆◆
1 Claremont Terrace, Gillygate,
York, YO31 7EJ
T: (01904) 612465

Chimneys ◆◆◆
18 Bootham Crescent, York,
North Yorkshire YO30 7AH
T: (01904) 644334

City Guest House ◆◆◆◆
68 Monkgate, York, YO31 7PF
T: (01904) 622483
E: info@cityguesthouse.co.uk
I: www.cityguesthouse.co.uk

Claremont Guest House ◆◆◆◆
18 Claremont Terrace, Gillygate,
York, YO31 7EJ
T: (01904) 625158
E: claremont.york@dial.pipex.
com
I: www.claremont.york.dial.
pipex.com

Clarence Gardens Hotel ◆◆◆
Haxby Road, York, YO31 8JS
T: (01904) 624252
F: (01904) 671293

Claxton Hall Cottage ◆◆◆◆
Malton Road, York, YO60 7RE
T: (01904) 468697
E: claxcott@aol.com
I: www.members.aol.
com/claxcott

Clifton View Guest House ◆◆◆
118/120 Clifton, York, YO30 6BQ
T: (01904) 625047
F: (01904) 625047
I: www.smoothhound.co.
uk/hotels/cliftonview.html

Cook's Guest House ◆◆◆
120 Bishopthorpe Road, York,
YO23 1JX
T: (01904) 652519 &
07946 577247
F: (01904) 652519

Cornmill Lodge, Vegetarian Bed and Breakfast ◆◆◆
120 Haxby Road, York, YO31 8JP
T: (01904) 620566
E: cornmill@aol.com
I: members.aol.com/cornmil/hi.
htm

Crescent Guest House ◆◆
77 Bootham, York, YO30 7DQ
T: (01904) 623216
F: (01904) 623216

Crook Lodge ◆◆◆◆
26 St Mary's, Bootham, York,
YO30 7DD
T: (01904) 655614
F: (01904) 655614

Crossways Guest House ◆◆◆
23 Wigginton Road, York,
YO31 8HJ
T: (01904) 637250 &
07801 436267
E: crossways@tineyonline.co.uk

Cumbria House ◆◆◆
2 Vyner Street, Haxby Road,
York, YO31 8HS
T: (01904) 636817 & 0771 278
0004
E: reservation@cumbriahouse.
freeserve.co.uk
I: www.cumbriahouse.freeserve.
co.uk

Curzon Lodge and Stable Cottages ◆◆◆◆
23 Tadcaster Road, Dringhouses,
York, North Yorkshire YO24 1QG
T: (01904) 703157
F: (01904) 703157
I: www.smoothhound.co.
uk/hotels/curzon.html

Dairy Guest House ◆◆◆
3 Scarcroft Road, York,
YO23 1ND
T: (01904) 639367
E: kikis@globelnet.co.uk

Dalescroft Guest House ◆◆◆
10 Southlands Road,
Bishopthorpe Road, York,
YO23 1NP
T: (01904) 626801

Eastons ◆◆◆◆
90 Bishopthorpe Road, York,
YO23 1JS
T: (01904) 626646
F: (01904) 626165
E: eastonsbbyork@aol.com
I: members.aol.
com/eastonsbbyork/home.htm

Fairthorne ◆◆◆
356 Strensall Road, Earswick,
York YO32 9SW
T: (01904) 768609
F: (01904) 768609

Farthings Hotel ◆◆◆
5 Nunthorpe Avenue, York,
YO23 1PF
T: (01904) 653545
F: (01904) 628355
E: farthings@york181.
fsbusiness.co.uk

Ferns ◆◆
5 Claremont Terrace, off
Gillygate, York, North Yorkshire
YO31 7EJ
T: (01904) 636335
E: jferguson@supanet.com

Feversham Lodge International Guest House ◆◆◆
No 1 Feversham Crescent, Off
Wigginton Road, York,
YO31 8HQ
T: (01904) 623882
F: (01904) 623882
E: feversham@lutyens.
freeserve.co.uk
I: www.s-h-systems.co.
uk/hotels/feversha.html

Foss Bank Guest House ◆◆◆
16 Huntington Road, York,
YO31 8RB
T: (01904) 635548

Four Seasons Hotel
◆◆◆◆ SILVER AWARD
7 St Peter's Grove, Bootham,
York, North Yorkshire YO30 6AQ
T: (01904) 622621
F: (01904) 620976
E: roe@fourseasons.netlineuk.
net
I: www.fourseasons_hotel.co.uk

Fourposter Lodge Hotel ◆◆◆
68-70 Heslington Road,
Barbican Road, York, YO10 5AU
T: (01904) 651170
F: (01904) 651170
E: fourposter.lodge@virgin.net
I: www.smoothhound.co.
uk/hotels/fourposter.html

Friars Rest Guest House ◆◆◆
81 Fulford Road, York, YO10 4BD
T: (01904) 629823 & 0771 536
5931
E: k.coman@bun.com
I: www.smoothhound.co.
uk/hotels/friars.html

Gables Guest House ◆◆
50 Bootham Crescent, Bootham,
York, YO30 7AH
T: (01904) 624381
F: (01904) 624381

Galtres Lodge Hotel ◆
54 Low Petergate, York, YO1 7HZ
T: (01904) 622478
F: (01904) 627804

George Hotel ◆◆◆
6 St George's Place, Tadcaster
Road, York, YO24 1DR
T: (01904) 625056
F: (01904) 625009
E: sixstgeorg@aol.com
I: www.members.aol.
com/sixstgeorg/

Georgian Guest House ◆◆◆
35 Bootham, York, YO30 7BT
T: (01904) 622874
F: (01904) 635379
E: georgian.house@virgin.net
I: www.georgianhouse.co.uk

Grange Lodge ◆◆◆
52 Bootham Crescent, Bootham,
York, YO30 7AH
T: (01904) 621137
E: grangeldg@aol.com

Grasmead House Hotel ◆◆◆◆
1 Scarcroft Hill, The Mount,
York, YO24 1DF
T: (01904) 629996
F: (01904) 629996
E: stansue@grasmeadhouse.
freeserve.co.uk
I: www.uktourism.
com/yk-grasmead

Greenside ◆◆◆
124 Clifton, York, YO30 6BQ
T: (01904) 623631
F: (01904) 623631

The Hazelwood ◆◆◆◆
24-25 Portland Street, York,
YO31 7EH
T: (01904) 626548
F: (01904) 628032
E: Reservations@
thehazelwoodyork.com
I: www.thehazelwoodyork.com

Heworth Guest House ◆◆◆
126 East Parade, Heworth, York
YO31 7YG
T: (01904) 426384
F: (01904) 426384
E: chris.thompson1@virgin.net
I: www.yorkcity.co.uk

Hillcrest Guest House ◆◆◆
110 Bishopthorpe Road, York,
YO23 1JX
T: (01904) 653160
F: (01904) 656168
E: hillcrest@accommodation.
gbr.fm
I: www.accommodation.gbr.fm

Hobbits Hotel ◆◆◆
9 St Peter's Grove, York,
YO30 6AQ
T: (01904) 624538 & 642926
F: (01904) 651765
E: admin@ecsyork.co.uk
I: www.ecsyork.co.
uk/hobbitshotel/hobbits.html
⊛

Holgate Bridge Hotel ◆◆◆
106-108 Holgate Road, York,
YO24 4BB
T: (01904) 635971 & 647288
F: (01904) 670049
⊛

The Hollies Guest House ◆◆◆
141 Fulford Road, York,
YO10 4HG
T: (01904) 634279
F: (01904) 625435
E: enquiries@
hollies-guesthouse.co.uk
I: www.hollies-guesthouse.co.uk
⊛

Holly Lodge ◆◆◆
206 Fulford Road, York,
YO10 4DD
T: (01904) 646005
I: www.thehollylodge.co.uk

Holme Lea Manor Guest House
◆◆◆
18 St Peter's Grove, Bootham,
York, YO30 6AQ
T: (01904) 623529
F: (01904) 653584
E: holmeleamanor@aol.com

Holmlea Guest House ◆◆
6-7 Southlands Road,
Bishopthorpe Road, York,
YO23 1NP
T: (01904) 621010 &
07971 400991
F: (01904) 659566
E: steve@holmelea.co.uk
I: www.holmlea.co.uk

Holmwood House Hotel
◆◆◆◆
114 Holgate Road, York,
YO24 4BB
T: (01904) 626183
F: (01904) 670899
E: holmwood.house@dial.pipex.
com
I: www.holmwoodhousehotel.
co.uk

Keys House ◆◆◆
137 Fulford Road, York,
YO10 4HG
T: (01904) 658488
F: (01904) 658488

Linden Lodge ◆◆◆
6 Nunthorpe Avenue, Scarcroft
Road, York, YO23 1PF
T: (01904) 620107
F: (01904) 620985

The Lodge ◆◆◆
302 Strensall Road, Old
Earswick, York YO32 9SW
T: (01904) 761387
F: (01904) 761387
E: the.lodge@talk21.com
⊛

The Manor Country House
◆◆◆◆
Acaster Malbis, York YO23 2UL
T: (01904) 706723
F: (01904) 706723
E: manorhouse@selcom.co.uk
I: www.manorhse.co.uk

Martin's Guest House ◆◆
5 Longfield Terrace, York,
YO30 7DJ
T: (01904) 634551
F: (01904) 634551
I: www.smoothhound.co.uk.
hotels/martins.html

Midway House ◆◆◆
145 Fulford Road, York,
YO10 4HG
T: (01904) 659272
F: (01904) 659272
E: midwayhouse@btinternet.
com
I: www.s-h-systems.co.
uk/hotels/midway.html
⊛

Millfield Lodge ◆◆
34 Millfield Road, Scarcroft
Road, York, YO23 1NQ
T: (01904) 653731
F: (01904) 643281

Minster View Guest House
◆◆◆
2 Grosvenor Terrace, Bootham,
York, YO30 7AG
T: (01904) 655034 & 643410

Monkgate Guest House ◆◆◆
65 Monkgate, York, YO31 7PA
T: (01904) 655947
E: jmb@monkgate.swinternet.
co.uk

Mont Clare Guest House ◆◆◆
32 Claremont Terrace, Gillygate,
York, YO31 7EJ
T: (01904) 627054 & 651011
F: (01904) 627054
E: montclarey@aol.com
I: www.mont-clare.co.uk/index.
htm
⊛

Moorgarth Guest House ◆◆◆
158 Fulford Road, York,
YO10 4DA
T: (01904) 636768
F: (01904) 636768
E: moorgarth@fsbdial.co.uk
I: www.avaweb.co.
uk/moorgarth.york.html

Moorland House ◆◆
1A Moorland Road, Fulford
Road, York, YO10 4HF
T: (01904) 629354
F: (01904) 629354

Mowbray House ◆◆◆
34 Haxby Road, York, YO31 8JX
T: (01904) 637710

Newton Guest House ◆◆◆
Neville Street, Haxby Road, York,
YO31 8NP
T: (01904) 635627

Northolme Guest House ◆◆◆
114 Shipton Road, Rawcliffe,
York, North Yorkshire YO30 5RN
T: (01904) 639132
E: g.liddle@tesco.net

Number 37 ◆◆◆
37 East Mount Road, York,
YO24 1BD
T: (01904) 610384
F: (01904) 610384
⊛

Nunmill House ◆◆◆◆
85 Bishopthorpe Road, York,
YO23 1NX
T: (01904) 634047
F: (01904) 655879
E: info@nunmill.co.uk
I: www.nunmill.co.uk

Oaklands Guest House ◆◆◆
351 Strensall Road, Old
Earswick, York YO32 9SW
T: (01904) 768443
E: mavmo@oaklands5.fsnet.co.
uk
I: www.business.thisisyork.
co.uk/oaklands/

The Old Registry ◆◆◆
12 Main Street, Fulford, York,
North Yorkshire YO10 4PQ
T: (01904) 628136

Olga's Licensed Guest House
◆◆
12 Wenlock Terrace, Fulford
Road, York, YO10 4DU
T: (01904) 641456 &
07850 225682
F: (01904) 641456
I: www.scoot.co.
uk/olgas_guest_house/

Orillia House ◆◆◆
89 The Village, Stockton-on-the-
Forest, York YO32 9UP
T: (01904) 400600
F: (01904) 400101
E: orillia@globalnet.co.uk

Palm Court Hotel ◆◆◆◆
17 Huntington Road, York,
YO31 8RB
T: (01904) 639387

Papillon Hotel ◆◆
43 Gillygate, York, YO31 7EA
T: (01904) 636505
F: (01904) 611968
E: papillonhotel@btinternet.
com
I: www.btinternet.
com/§papillonhotel

Park View Guest House ◆◆◆
34 Grosvenor Terrace, Bootham,
York, YO30 7AG
T: (01904) 620437
F: (01904) 620437
E: park_view@talk21.com

Primrose Lodge ◆◆◆
Hull Road, Dunnington, York
YO19 5LP
T: (01904) 489140

**Priory Hotel & Garth
Restaurant** ◆◆◆
126-128 Fulford Road, York,
YO10 4BE
T: (01904) 625280
F: (01904) 637330
E: reservations@
priory-hotelyork.co.uk
I: www.priory-hotelyork.co.uk

Queen Anne's Guest House
◆◆◆
24 Queen Anne's Road,
Bootham, York, YO30 7AA
T: (01904) 629389
F: (01904) 619529
F: info@queenannes.fsnet.co.uk
I: www.s-h-systems.co.
uk/hotels/queenann

**Red Lion Motel and Country
Inn** ◆◆◆
Boroughbridge Road, Upper
Poppleton, York, North Yorkshire
YO26 6PR
T: (01904) 781141
F: (01904) 785143
E: reservations@redlion-motel.
demon.co.uk
I: www.redlion-motel.demon.co.
uk

Regency House ◆◆◆◆
7 South Parade, Blossom Street,
York, North Yorkshire YO23 1BF
T: (01904) 633053

**Riverside Walk Bed and
Breakfast** ◆◆◆
9 Earlsborough Terrace,
Marygate, York, YO30 7BQ
T: (01904) 620769 & 646249
F: (01904) 646249
E: julie@riversidewalkbb.demon.
co.uk
I: www.riversidewalkbb.demon.
co.uk

Romley Guest House ◆◆◆
2 Millfield Road, Scarcroft Road,
York, YO23 1NQ
T: (01904) 652822
E: info@romleyhouse.co.uk
I: www.romleyhouse.co.uk
⊛

St Deny's Hotel ◆◆◆
51 St Denys Road, York,
YO1 9QD
T: (01904) 622207 & 646776
F: (01904) 624800
E: info@stdenyshotel.co.uk
I: www.stdenyshotel.co.uk

St Mary's Hotel ◆◆◆
17 Longfield Terrace, Bootham,
York, YO30 7DJ
T: (01904) 626972
F: (01904) 626972
I: www.stayhereuk.
com/wp/14012/index.html

St Paul's Hotel ◆◆◆
120 Holgate Road, York,
YO24 4BB
T: (01904) 611514
E: normfran@supernet.com

St Raphael Guest House ◆
44 Queen Anne's Road,
Bootham, York, YO30 7AF
T: (01904) 645028 & 658788
F: (01904) 658788
E: straphael2000@yahoo.co.uk

Saxon House Hotel ◆◆◆
Fishergate, 71-73 Fulford Road,
York, YO10 4BD
T: (01904) 622106
F: (01904) 633764
E: saxon@househotel.freeserve.
co.uk
I: www.saxonhousehotel.co.uk

Skelton Grange Farmhouse
◆◆◆
Orchard View, Skelton, York
YO30 1XQ
T: (01904) 470780
F: (01904) 470229
E: info@skelton-farm.co.uk
I: www.skelton-farm.co.uk

Southlands Bed and Breakfast
◆◆◆◆
Huntington Road, Huntington,
York YO32 9PX
T: (01904) 766796
F: (01904) 764536
E: southlandsbandb.york@
btinternet.com
I: www.southlandsbandb.
freeserve.co.uk

Southland's Guest House
◆◆◆
69 Nunmill Street, South Bank,
York, YO23 1NT
T: (01904) 631203
I: www.southlandsguesthouse.
freeserve.co.uk/

23 St Marys ◆◆◆◆
Bootham, York, YO30 7DD
T: (01904) 622738
F: (01904) 628802

Stanley House ◆◆◆
Stanley Street, Haxby Road,
York, YO31 8NW
T: (01904) 637111
F: (01904) 659599
E: enquiry@stanleyhouse.uk.
com
I: www.stanleyhouse.uk.com

Staymor Guest House ◆◆◆
2 Southlands Road, York,
YO23 1NP
T: (01904) 626935
E: kathwilson@lineone.net

Sycamore Guest House ◆◆◆
19 Sycamore Place, Bootham,
York, YO30 7DW
T: (01904) 624712
F: (01904) 624712
E: thesycamore@talk21.com
I: www.guesthousesyork.co.uk

Tower Guest House ◆◆◆
2 Feversham Crescent,
Wigginton Road, York,
YO31 8HQ
T: (01904) 655571 & 635924
F: (01904) 655571
E: toweryork@aol.com

Tree Tops ◆◆◆
21 St Mary's, Bootham, York,
YO30 7DD
T: (01904) 658053
F: (01904) 658053
E: treetops.guesthouse@
virgin.net

Turnberry House ◆◆◆
143 Fulford Road, York,
YO10 4HG
T: (01904) 658435
F: (01904) 658435

Tyburn House ◆◆◆
11 Albemarle Road, The Mount,
York, YO23 1EN
T: (01904) 655069
F: (01904) 655069
E: york@tyburnhotel.freeserve.
co.uk

Vegetarian Guest House ◆◆◆
21 Park Grove, York, North
Yorkshire YO31 7LG
T: (01904) 644790

The Victoria Hotel ◆◆◆
1 Heslington Road, York,
YO10 5AR
T: (01904) 622295
F: (01904) 677860

Victoria Villa ◆◆
72 Heslington Road, York,
YO10 5AU
T: (01904) 631647

Warrens Guest House ◆◆◆
30 Scarcroft Road, York,
YO23 1NF
T: (01904) 643139
F: (01904) 658297
I: www.warrens.ndo.co.uk

Westgate Hotel ◆◆◆
132 The Mount, York, YO24 1AS
T: (01904) 653303
F: (01904) 635717
E: westgateyork@gofornet.co.
uk
I: www.smoothhound.co.
uk/hotels/westgate.html

White Doves ◆◆◆
20 Claremont Terrace, Gillygate,
York, YO31 7EJ
T: (01904) 625957

York Lodge Guest House ◆◆◆
64 Bootham Crescent, Bootham,
York, YO30 7AH
T: (01904) 654289 &
07860 449460
F: (01904) 488803
E: moore.york@virgin.net

HEART OF ENGLAND

AB KETTLEBY
Leicestershire
White Lodge Farm ◆◆◆◆
Nottingham Road, Ab Kettleby,
Melton Mowbray, Leicestershire
LE14 3JB
T: (01664) 822286 & 823729

ABBEY DORE
Herefordshire
The Mynd ◆◆◆
Abbey Dore, Hereford,
Herefordshire HR2 0AE
T: (01981) 570440
F: (01981) 570440
E: roselloyd@themynd.co.uk
I: www.golden-valley.co.
uk/mynd

ABBOTS BROMLEY
Staffordshire
Crown Inn ◆◆
Market Place, Abbots Bromley,
Rugeley, Staffordshire
WS15 3BS
T: (01283) 840227
F: (01283) 840016
E: f.j.crown@aol.com

ABBOTS MORTON
Worcestershire
The Cottage Apartment
◆◆◆◆
The Cottage, Gooms Hill, Abbots
Morton Manor, Abbots Morton,
Worcester WR7 4LT
T: (01386) 792783
F: (01386) 792783

ABINGTON
Northamptonshire
Abington Park Guesthouse
Rating Applied For
407 Wellingborough Road,
Abington, Northampton
NN1 4EY
T: (01604) 635072

ABTHORPE
Northamptonshire
Rignall Farm Barns
Rating Applied For
Handley Park, Abthorpe,
Towcester, Northamptonshire
NN12 8PA
T: (01327) 350766
F: (01327) 350766

ACOCKS GREEN
West Midlands
Bridge House Hotel ◆◆◆◆
49 Sherbourne Road, Acocks
Green, Birmingham B27 6DX
T: (0121) 706 5900 & 706 5395
F: (0121) 624 5900
E: bridgehousehotel.co.uk
I: www.bridgehousehotel.co.uk

Elmdon Lodge Hotel ◆◆◆
20/24 Elmdon Road, Acocks
Green, Birmingham B27 6LH
T: (0121) 706 6968
F: (0121) 628 5566

ACTON BURNELL
Shropshire
Acton Pigot ◆◆◆◆
SILVER AWARD
Acton Burnell, Shrewsbury,
Shropshire SY5 7PH
T: (01694) 731209 &
0797 1974643
E: acton@farmline.com

ADSTONE
Northamptonshire
Manor Farm ◆◆◆
Adstone, Towcester,
Northamptonshire NN12 8DT
T: (01327) 860284
F: (01327) 860685

ALBRIGHTON
Shropshire
Parkside Farm ◆◆◆◆
Holyhead Road, Albrighton,
Wolverhampton WV7 3DA
T: (01902) 372310
F: (01902) 375013
E: jmshanks@farming

ALCESTER
Warwickshire
Orchard Lawns
◆◆◆◆ SILVER AWARD
Wixford, Alcester, Warwickshire
B49 6DA
T: (01789) 772668

Sambourne Hall Farm ◆◆◆◆
Wike Lane, Sambourne,
Redditch, Worcestershire
B96 6NZ
T: (01527) 852151

ALDERTON
Gloucestershire
Corner Cottage ◆◆◆
Stow Road, Alderton,
Tewkesbury, Gloucestershire
GL20 8NH
T: (01242) 620630 &
07770 225548
F: (01242) 620630

Moors Farm House
◆◆◆◆◆ GOLD AWARD
32 Beckford Road, Alderton,
Tewkesbury, Gloucestershire
GL20 8NL
T: (01242) 620523

ALDSWORTH
Gloucestershire
The Old Chapel ◆◆◆◆
Aldsworth, Cheltenham,
Gloucestershire GL54 3QZ
T: (01451) 844547

ALDWARK
Derbyshire
Lydgate Farm ◆◆◆◆
Aldwark, Matlock, Derbyshire
DE4 4HW
T: (01629) 540250
E: joy.lomas@btinternet.com
I: www.cressbrook.co.uk/path

ALDWINCLE
Northamptonshire
Pear Tree Farm ◆◆◆◆
Aldwincle, Kettering,
Northamptonshire NN14 3EL
T: (01832) 720614
F: (01832) 720559

ALFRETON
Derbyshire
Crown Inn ◆◆
73 Sleetmoor Lane, Somercotes,
Alfreton, Derbyshire DE55 1RE
T: (01773) 602537

The Spinney Cottage ◆◆◆
Derby Road, Swanwick, Alfreton,
Derbyshire DE55 1BG
T: (01773) 609020

HEART OF ENGLAND

ALKMONTON
Derbyshire
The Courtyard ♦♦♦♦
Dairy House Farm, Alkmonton,
Ashbourne, Derbyshire DE6 3DG
T: (01335) 330187
F: (01335) 330187
I: www.digitalpages.co.uk.
/courtyard

ALTON
Staffordshire
Admirals House ♦♦♦
Mill Road, Oakamoor, Stoke-on-
Trent, Staffordshire ST10 3AG
T: (01538) 702187
F: (01538) 702957
E: adhouse@ew.com

Alverton Motel ♦♦♦
Denstone Lane, Alton, Stoke-on-
Trent, Staffordshire ST10 4AX
T: (01538) 702265
F: (01538) 703284

Bee Cottage ♦♦♦
Saltersford Lane, Alton, Stoke-
on-Trent, Staffordshire
ST10 4AU
T: (01538) 702802

Bradley Elms Farm ♦♦♦♦
Threapwood, Cheadle, Stoke-on-
Trent, Staffordshire ST10 4RA
T: (01538) 750202
F: (01538) 753135

Bulls Head Inn ♦♦♦
High Street, Alton, Staffordshire
ST10 4AQ
T: (01538) 702307
F: (01538) 702065
E: janet@alton.freeserve.co.uk
I: www.thebullsheadinn.co.uk

Church Grange ♦♦♦♦
Bradley in the Moors, Alton,
Stoke-on-Trent, Staffs ST10 4DF
T: (01889) 507525 &
0780 3530655
F: (01889) 507282
E: ddeb@lineone.net
I: www.staffordshire.gov.
uk/tourism/chgrange.htm

The Cross Inn ♦♦♦
Cauldon Low, Waterhouses,
Stoke-on-Trent, Staffs ST10 3EX
T: (01538) 308338 & 308767
F: (01538) 308767
E: 106245.3615@compuserve.
com
I: www.crossinn.co.uk

The Dale ♦♦♦♦
Off Battlesteads, Alton, Stoke-
on-Trent, Staffordshire
ST10 4BG
T: (01538) 702394 &
07711 891655
E: thedalealton@talk21.com

Fairview Guesthouse ♦♦♦
1 Vicarage Row, Alton, Stoke-
on-Trent ST10 4BL
T: (01538) 702086

Fernlea Guest House ♦♦♦
Cedar Hill, Alton, Stoke-on-Trent
ST10 4BH
T: (01538) 702327

Fields Farm ♦♦♦♦
Chapel Lane, Threapwood, Alton,
Stoke-on-Trent, Staffs ST10 4QZ
T: (01538) 752721 &
07850 310381
F: (01538) 757404

Hansley Cross Cottage ♦♦♦
Cheadle Road, Alton, Stoke-on-
Trent ST10 4DH
T: (01538) 702189
F: (01538) 702189

The Hawthorns ♦♦♦
8 Tythe Barn, Alton, Stoke-on-
Trent ST10 4AZ
T: (01538) 702197
E: altonbb@aol.com
I: www.members.aol.
com/altonbb

Hillside Farm ♦♦♦
Alton Road, Denstone, Uttoxeter,
Staffordshire ST14 5HG
T: (01889) 590760

The Malthouse ♦♦♦
Malthouse Road, Alton, Stoke-
on-Trent ST10 4AG
T: (01538) 703273

The Old School House ♦♦♦♦♦ SILVER AWARD
Castle Hill Road, Alton, Stoke-
on-Trent ST10 4AJ
T: (01538) 702151
F: (01538) 702151
E: 100721.762@compuserve.
com
I: members.tripod.co.
uk/old_school_house/

The Peakstones Inn ♦♦
Cheadle Road, Alton, Stoke-on-
Trent ST10 4DH
T: (01538) 755776

Rockhaven ♦♦♦
Smithy Bank, Alton, Stoke-on-
Trent ST10 4AA
T: (01538) 702066

Royal Oak ♦♦
Alton, Stoke-on-Trent ST10 4BH
T: (01538) 702625

Trough Ivy House ♦♦♦♦
1 Hay Lane, Farley, Alton, Stoke-
on-Trent, Staffordshire
ST10 3BQ
T: (01538) 702683
F: (01538) 702683
E: bookings@trough-ivy-house.
demon.co.uk
I: www.trough-ivy-house.
demon.co.uk

Tythe Barn House ♦♦♦
Denstone Lane, Alton, Stoke-on-
Trent ST10 4AX
T: (01538) 702852

The Warren
Rating Applied For
The Dale, Battlesteads, Alton,
Stoke-on-Trent ST10 4BG
T: (01538) 702493
F: (01538) 702493

Yoxall Cottage ♦♦♦
Malt House Road, Alton, Stoke-
on-Trent ST10 4AG
T: (01538) 702537

ALVASTON
Derbyshire
Grace Guesthouse ♦♦
1063 London Road, Alvaston,
Derby DE24 8PZ
T: (01332) 571051

ALVECHURCH
Worcestershire
Alcott Farm ♦♦♦
Weatheroak, Alvechurch,
Birmingham, Worcestershire
B48 7EH
T: (01564) 824051 &
07774 163253
F: (01564) 824051

AMBERGATE
Derbyshire
Lord Nelson ♦♦♦
Bullbridge, Ambergate, Belper,
Derbyshire DE56 2EW
T: (01773) 852037

AMBERLEY
Gloucestershire
High Tumps ♦♦♦♦
St Chloe Green, Amberley,
Stroud, Gloucestershire GL5 5AR
T: (01453) 873584
F: (01453) 873587

AMINGTON
Staffordshire
Gongolfin ♦♦♦
21 Carnoustie, Amington,
Tamworth, Staffordshire
B77 4NN
T: (01827) 59060
F: (01827) 59060
E: joe@gongolfin.fsnet.co.uk

APPLEBY MAGNA
Leicestershire
Elms Farm ♦♦♦
Appleby Magna, Swadlincote,
Derbyshire DE12 7AP
T: (01530) 270450
F: (01530) 272718

ARLEY
Worcestershire
Tudor Barn
♦♦♦♦ SILVER AWARD
Arley, Bewdley, Worcestershire
DY2 3LY
T: (01299) 400129 &
0797 4817092
E: tudorbarn@aol.com

ARLINGHAM
Gloucestershire
Horseshoe View ♦♦
Overton Lane, Arlingham,
Gloucester GL2 7JJ
T: (01452) 740293

ARMSCOTE
Warwickshire
Willow Corner
♦♦♦♦ SILVER AWARD
Armscote, Stratford-upon-Avon,
Warwickshire CV37 8DE
T: (01608) 682391 & 0780 371
0149
E: 113610.3511@compuserve.
com
I: www.shakespeare-country.co.
uk

ARNOLD
Nottinghamshire
Rufford Guesthouse ♦♦♦♦
117 Redhill Road, Arnold,
Nottingham NG5 8GZ
T: (0115) 926 1759

ASFORDBY VALLEY
Leicestershire
Valley End ♦♦♦♦
17 North Street, Asfordby Valley,
Melton Mowbray, Leicestershire
LE14 3SQ
T: (01664) 812003

ASH MAGNA
Shropshire
Ash Hall ♦♦♦
Ash Magna, Whitchurch,
Shropshire SY13 4DL
T: (01948) 663151

ASHBOURNE
Derbyshire
The Black Horse Inn ♦♦♦
Main Road, Hulland Ward,
Ashbourne, Derbyshire DE6 3EE
T: (01335) 370206
F: (01335) 370206

Bramble Lodge ♦♦♦♦
8 Spencer Close, Ashbourne,
Derbyshire DE6 1BU
T: (01335) 344256

Calton Moor House
♦♦♦♦ SILVER AWARD
Calton Moor House, Calton,
Ashbourne, Derbyshire DE6 2BU
T: (01538) 308328

Compton House ♦♦♦
27-31 Compton, Ashbourne,
Derbyshire DE6 1BX
T: (01335) 343100
F: (01335) 348100
E: JANE@COMPTONHOUSE.CO.
UK
I: WWW.COMPTONHOUSE.CO.
UK

Cross Farm ♦♦♦♦
Main Road, Ellastone,
Ashbourne, Derbyshire DE6 2GZ
T: (01335) 324668

Cubley Common Farm ♦♦♦♦
Cubley, Ashbourne, Derbyshire
DE6 2EX
T: (01335) 330041 &
07710 591407

Dove House ♦♦♦♦
Bridge Hill, Mayfield, Ashbourne,
Derbyshire DE6 2HN
T: (01335) 343329

Foxgloves ♦♦♦♦
Calwich Rise, Ellastone,
Ashbourne, Derbyshire DE6 2HE
T: (01335) 324664

Green Gables ♦♦♦♦
107 The Green Road, Ashbourne,
Derbyshire DE6 1EE
T: (01335) 342431

Henmore Cottage ♦♦♦♦
Clifton, Ashbourne, Derbyshire
DE6 2GL
T: (01335) 344492 &
0786 7334835
F: (01335) 348094
E: mclarke@henmorecottagebb.
fsnet.co.uk
I: www.henmorecottagebb.fsnet.
co.uk

Hurtswood ◆◆◆
Buxton Road, Sandybrook,
Ashbourne, Derbyshire DE6 2AQ
T: (01335) 342031 & 347467
F: (01335) 347467
E: gl.hurtswood@virgin.net
I: www.hurtswood.co.uk
◉

Jinglers Inn ◆◆
Fox and Hounds, Belper Road
(A517), Bradley, Ashbourne,
Derbyshire DE6 3EN
T: (01335) 370855
F: (01335) 370855
E: jinglers@gdc.globalnet.co.uk

Lichfield Guest House
◆◆◆◆ GOLD AWARD
Bridge View, Mayfield,
Ashbourne, Derbyshire DE6 2HN
T: (01335) 344422
F: (01335) 344422

The Lilacs ◆◆◆◆
Mayfield Road, Ashbourne,
Derbyshire DE6 2BJ
T: (01335) 343749
F: (01335) 343749

Little Park Farm ◆◆◆
Mappleton, Ashbourne,
Derbyshire DE6 2BR
T: (01335) 350341

Meadow Bank
◆◆◆◆ SILVER AWARD
Belle Vue Road, Ashbourne,
Derbyshire DE6 1AT
T: (01335) 346034

Omnia Somnia
◆◆◆◆◆ GOLD AWARD
The Coach House, The Firs,
Ashbourne, Derbyshire DE6 1HF
T: (01335) 300145
F: (01335) 300958
E: omnia.somnia@talk21.com
◉

Overfield Farm ◆◆◆
Tissington, Ashbourne,
Derbyshire DE6 1RA
T: (01335) 390285

Shirley Hall Farm
◆◆◆◆ SILVER AWARD
Shirley, Ashbourne, Derbyshire
DE6 3AS
T: (01335) 360346 & 360820
F: (01335) 360346
E: sylviafoster@shirleyhallfarm.
com
I: www.shirleyhallfarm.com
◉

Stanshope Hall ◆◆◆◆
Stanshope, Ashbourne,
Derbyshire DE6 2AD
T: (01335) 310278
F: (01335) 310470
E: naomi@stanshope.demon.co.
uk
I: www.stanshope.demon.co.uk
◉

Tan Mill Farm ◆◆◆◆
Mappleton Road, Ashbourne,
Derbyshire DE6 2AA
T: (01335) 342387
F: (01335) 342387

Thorpe Cottage ◆◆◆◆
Thorpe, Ashbourne, Derbyshire
DE6 2AW
T: (01335) 350466 &
04411 217475
F: (01335) 350217

The Wheelhouse ◆◆◆◆
Belper Road, Hulland Ward,
Ashbourne, Derbyshire DE6 3EE
T: (01335) 370953

White Cottage ◆◆◆◆
Wyaston, Ashbourne, Derbyshire
DE6 2DR
T: (01335) 345503

ASHBY-DE-LA-ZOUCH
Leicestershire

Church Lane Farm House
◆◆◆◆
Ravenstone, Leicestershire
LE67 2AE
T: (01530) 810536 &
07973 772341
F: (01530) 810536
E: aa.bnb.coalville@talk21
◉

Holywell House Hotel ◆◆
58 Burton Road, Ashby-de-la-
Zouch, Leicestershire LE65 2LN
T: (01530) 412005

The Laurels Bed and Breakfast
◆◆◆
17 Ashby Road, Measham,
Burton upon Trent, Staffordshire
DE12 7JR
T: (01530) 272567
F: (01530) 272567
E: thelaurelguesthouse@
totalise.co.uk

Measham House Farm ◆◆◆◆
Gallows Lane, Measham,
Swadlincote, Derbyshire
DE12 7HD
T: (01530) 270465
F: (01530) 270465

Smisby Manor ◆◆◆
Annwell Lane, Ashby-de-la-
Zouch, Leicestershire LE65 2TA
T: (01530) 415881
F: (01530) 411914
E: cbill@smisbymanor.freeserve.
co.uk

ASHFORD IN THE WATER
Derbyshire

Arncliffe House
Rating Applied For
Greaves Lane, Ashford in the
Water, Bakewell, Derbyshire
DE45 1QH
T: (01629) 813121

Chy-an-Dour ◆◆◆◆
Vicarage Lane, Ashford in the
Water, Bakewell, Derbyshire
DE45 1QN
T: (0162981) 3162
◉

Gritstone House
◆◆◆◆ SILVER AWARD
Greaves Lane, Ashford in the
Water, Bakewell, Derbyshire
DE45 1QH
T: (01629) 813563
F: (01629) 813563

Marble Cottage
◆◆◆◆ SILVER AWARD
The Dukes Drive, Ashford in the
Water, Bakewell, Derbyshire
DE45 1QP
T: (01629) 813624
F: (01629) 813832
E: MARBLECOTTAGE@AOL.COM
I: WWW.CRESSBROOK.CO.
UK/BAKEWELL/
MARBLECOTTAGE/INDEX.HTM

Warlands ◆◆◆
Hill Cross, Ashford in the Water,
Bakewell, Derbyshire DE45 1QL
T: (01629) 813736

Woodland View ◆◆◆
John Bank Lane, Ashford in the
Water, Bakewell, Derbyshire
DE45 1PY
T: (01629) 813008
F: (01629) 813008
E: wwodview@neilellis.
free-online.co.uk
I: www.neilellis.free-online.co.uk

ASHLEWORTH
Gloucestershire

Ashleworth Court ◆◆◆
Ashleworth, Gloucester
GL19 4JA
T: (01452) 700241
F: (01452) 700411
E: chamberlayne@farmline.com

ASHOVER
Derbyshire

Hardwick View ◆◆◆◆
Ashover Road, Littlemoor,
Ashover, Chesterfield,
Derbyshire S45 0BL
T: (01246) 590876

Old School Farm ◆◆◆◆
Uppertown, Ashover,
Chesterfield, Derbyshire S45 0JF
T: (01246) 590813

ASHPERTON
Herefordshire

Pridewood ◆◆◆
Ashperton, Ledbury,
Herefordshire HR8 2SF
T: (01531) 670416
F: (01531) 670416

ASTLEY
Worcestershire

Woodhampton House ◆◆◆
Weather Lane, Astley, Stourport-
on-Severn, Worcestershire
DY13 0SF
T: (01299) 826510
E: pete-@sally-.freeserve.co.uk

ASTON MUNSLOW
Shropshire

Chadstone
◆◆◆◆ SILVER AWARD
Aston Munslow, Craven Arms,
Shropshire SY7 9ER
T: (01584) 841675
E: chadstone.lee@btinternet.
com

ASTON-ON-CLUN
Shropshire

Mill Stream Cottage ◆◆◆
Aston-on-Clun, Craven Arms,
Shropshire SY7 8EP
T: (01588) 660699 &
07977 922572

ATHERSTONE
Warwickshire

Manor Farm Bed and Breakfast
◆◆◆
Manor Farm, Ratcliffe Culey,
Atherstone, Warwickshire
CV9 3NY
T: (01827) 712269 & 716947
E: user880243@aol.com

Mythe Farm Bed & Breakfast
Rating Applied For
Pinwall Lane, Sheepy Magna,
Atherstone, Warwickshire
CV9 3PF
T: (01827) 712367 &
07710 643143
E: bosworth/
advertising@connectfree.co.uk
◉

AUDLEY
Staffordshire

The Domvilles Farm ◆◆◆◆
Barthomley Road, Audley,
Stoke-on-Trent ST7 8HT
T: (01782) 720378 &
07831 268045
F: (01782) 720883

AVON DASSETT
Warwickshire

Crandon House
◆◆◆◆◆ SILVER AWARD
Avon Dassett, Leamington Spa,
Warwickshire CV47 2AA
T: (01295) 770632
F: (01295) 770652
E: crandonhouse@talk21.com

AWSWORTH
Nottinghamshire

Hog's Head Hotel ◆◆◆
Main Street, Awsworth,
Nottinghamshire NG16 2RN
T: (0115) 938 4095
F: (0115) 945 9718

AYLBURTON
Gloucestershire

Bridge Cottage ◆◆
High Street, Aylburton, Lydney,
Gloucestershire GL15 6BX
T: (01594) 843527

AYNHO
Northamptonshire

**Cartwright Arms Hotel and
Restaurant** ◆◆
Aynho, Banbury, Oxfordshire
OX17 3BE
T: (01869) 811111
F: (01869) 811110
E: eric@hotel25.freeserve.co.UK

BACTON
Herefordshire

Pentwyn Cottage Gardens
◆◆◆
Pentwyn Cottage, Bacton,
Hereford HR2 0AP
T: (01981) 240508
F: (01981) 240508
E: f.w.pentwyn@tinyworld.co.uk
I: www.golden-valley.co.
uk/pentwyn

BADBY
Northamptonshire

Meadows Farm
◆◆◆◆◆ GOLD AWARD
Newnham Lane, Badby,
Daventry, Northamptonshire
NN11 3AA
T: (01327) 703302
F: (01327) 703085

The Old House
◆◆◆◆ SILVER AWARD
Church Hill, Badby, Daventry,
Northamptonshire NN11 3AR
T: (01327) 879053
F: (01327) 310967
E: rose.susan@talk21.com

BADSEY
Worcestershire
Orchard House ♦♦♦
99 Bretforton Road, Badsey,
Evesham, Worcestershire
WR11 5UQ
T: (01386) 831245

BAKEWELL
Derbyshire
Castle Cliffe ♦♦♦
Monsal Head, Bakewell,
Derbyshire DE45 1NL
T: (01629) 640258
F: (01629) 640258

Castle Inn ♦♦♦♦
Castle Street, Bakewell,
Derbyshire DE45 1DU
T: (01629) 812103
F: (01629) 814830

Easthorpe ♦♦♦♦
Buxton Road, Bakewell,
Derbyshire DE45 1DA
T: (01629) 814929

Ferndale Mews ♦♦♦♦
Buxton Road, Bakewell,
Derbyshire DE45 1DA
T: (01629) 814339

The Garden Room ♦♦♦♦
1 Park Road, Bakewell,
Derbyshire DE45 1AX
T: (01629) 814299

Haddon House Farm
♦♦♦♦♦ GOLD AWARD
Haddon Road, Bakewell,
Derbyshire DE45 1BN
T: (01629) 814024
F: (01629) 812759
E: bb@haddon-house.co.uk
I: www.haddon-house.co.uk

The Haven ♦♦♦♦
Haddon Road, Bakewell,
Derbyshire DE45 1AW
T: (01629) 812113 &
07790 790664
E: rosearmstg@aol.com
I: members.aol.com/RoseArmstg

**Long Meadow House Bed and
Breakfast Long Meadow House
♦♦♦♦ GOLD AWARD**
Coombs Road, Bakewell,
Derbyshire DE45 1AQ
T: (01629) 812500
F: (01629) 815505
E: AMSHowarth@compuserve.
com

Loughrigg
♦♦♦♦ SILVER AWARD
Burton Close Drive, Bakewell,
Derbyshire DE45 1BG
T: (01629) 813173
E: john@bakewell55.freeserve.
co.uk
I: www.bakewell55.freeserve.co.
uk

2 Lumford Cottages ♦♦♦
Off Holme Lane, Bakewell,
Derbyshire DE45 1GG
T: (01629) 813273
F: (01629) 813273

Mandale House ♦♦♦♦
Haddon Grove, Bakewell,
Derbyshire DE45 1JF
T: (01629) 812416
F: (01629) 812416

Melbourne House ♦♦♦
Buxton Road, Bakewell,
Derbyshire DE45 1DA
T: (01629) 815357

**River Walk Bed and Breakfast
♦♦♦**
River Walk, 3 New Lumford,
Bakewell, Derbyshire DE45 1GH
T: (01629) 812459

30 Riverside Crescent
♦♦♦♦♦ SILVER AWARD
30 Riverside Crescent, Bakewell,
Derbyshire DE45 1HF
T: (01629) 815722

Sheldon House ♦♦♦♦
Chapel Street, Monyash,
Bakewell, Derbyshire DE45 1JJ
T: (01629) 813067
F: (01629) 813067
E: sheldonhouse@lineone.net

Tannery House
♦♦♦♦ SILVER AWARD
Matlock Street, Bakewell,
Derbyshire DE45 1EE
T: (01629) 815011
F: (01629) 815327

**West Lawn Bed and Breakfast
♦♦♦♦**
2 Aldern Way, Bakewell,
Derbyshire DE45 1AJ
T: (01629) 812243

BALSALL COMMON
West Midlands
Avonlea ♦♦
135 Kenilworth Road, Balsall
Common, Coventry, West
Midlands CV7 7EU
T: (01676) 533003 &
07768 663892
F: (01676) 533003

Blythe Paddocks ♦♦♦
Barston Lane, Balsall Common,
Coventry CV7 7BT
T: (01676) 533050
F: (01676) 533050

Camp Farm ♦♦♦
Hob Lane, Balsall Common,
Coventry CV7 7GX
T: (01676) 533804

BALTERLEY
Staffordshire
Balterley Hall Farm ♦♦♦♦
Balterley, Crewe, Staffordshire
CW2 5QG
T: (01270) 820206 &
07831 248496

Pear Tree Lake Farm ♦♦♦♦
Balterley, Crewe CW2 5QE
T: (01270) 820307 &
07970 158658
F: (01270) 820868

BAMFORD
Derbyshire
Pioneer House ♦♦♦♦
Station Road, Bamford, Hope
Valley S33 0BN
T: (01433) 650638
E: pioneerhouse@yahoo.co.uk

Ye Derwent Hotel ♦♦♦
Main Road, Bamford, Hope
Valley, Derbyshire S33 0AY
T: (01433) 651395
F: (01433) 651943
E: thederwent@aol.com

BARBER BOOTH, EDALE
Derbyshire
Brookfield Guesthouse ♦♦
Brookfield, Barber Booth, Edale,
Hope Valley S33 7ZL
T: (01433) 670227

BARLASTON
Staffordshire
Hurden Hall Farm ♦♦♦
Barlaston, Stoke-on-Trent,
Staffordshire ST12 9AZ
T: (01782) 372378

**Wedgwood Memorial College
♦♦♦**
Station Road, Barlaston, Stoke-
on-Trent ST12 9DG
T: (01782) 372105 & 373427
F: (01782) 372393
E: wedgwood.college@
staffordshire.gov.uk.
I: www.aredu.demon.co.
uk/wedgwoodcollege

BARLBOROUGH
Derbyshire
**Stone Croft Bed and Breakfast
♦♦♦**
15 Church Street, Barlborough,
Chesterfield, Derbyshire S43 4ER
T: (01246) 810974 &
0771 8080904

BARLOW
Derbyshire
Millbrook
♦♦♦♦ SILVER AWARD
Furnace Lane, Monkwood,
Barlow, Dronfield S18 7SY
T: (0114) 2890253 &
07831 398373
F: (0114) 2891365

Woodview Cottage ♦♦♦♦
Millcross Lane, Barlow, Dronfield
S18 7TA
T: (0114) 289 0724
F: (0114) 289 0724

BARNBY MOOR
Nottinghamshire
**White Horse Inn and
Restaurant♦♦♦**
Great North Road, Barnby Moor,
Retford, Nottinghamshire
DN22 8QS
T: (01777) 707721
F: (01777) 869445

BARNSTONE
Nottinghamshire
Barnstone Olde House ♦♦♦
Barnstone, Nottingham,
Nottinghamshire NG13 9JP
T: (01949) 860456
F: (01949) 860456

BARROW-ON-TRENT
Derbyshire
5 Nook Cottages ♦♦♦♦
The Nook, Barrow-on-Trent,
Derby DE73 1NA
T: (01332) 703390
F: (01332) 703390
E: nookcottage@nookcottage.
com
I: www.nookcottage.com

BARTON UNDER NEEDWOOD
Staffordshire
Fairfield Guest House
♦♦♦♦ SILVER AWARD
55 Main Street, Barton under
Needwood, Burton upon Trent,
Staffordshire DE13 8AB
T: (01283) 716396
F: (01283) 716396
E: hotel@fairfield-uk.fsnet.co.uk

Three Way Cottage ♦♦♦
2 Wales Lane, Barton under
Needwood, Burton upon Trent,
Staffordshire DE13 8JF
T: (01283) 713572
E: marion@threewaycottage.
fsnet.co.uk
I: communities.msn.co.
uk/
threewayscottagebedbreakfast

BASLOW
Derbyshire
Bubnell Cliff Farm ♦♦♦
Wheatlands Lane, Baslow,
Bakewell, Derbyshire DE45 1RF
T: (01246) 582454
E: C.K.MILLS@UKGATEWAY.NET

Nether Croft ♦♦♦♦
Eaton Place, Baslow, Bakewell,
Derbyshire DE45 1RW
T: (01246) 583564

The Old School House
♦♦♦♦ SILVER AWARD
School Lane, Baslow, Bakewell,
Derbyshire DE45 1RZ
T: (01246) 582488
F: (01246) 583323
E: yvonnewright@talk21.com

Rose Hill Farm ♦♦♦
Over End, Baslow, Bakewell,
Derbyshire DE45 1SG
T: (01246) 583280

BASSINGTHORPE
Lincolnshire
Sycamore Farm
♦♦♦♦ SILVER AWARD
Bassingthorpe, Grantham,
Lincolnshire NG33 4EB
T: (01476) 585274

BAUMBER
Lincolnshire
Baumber Park ♦♦♦♦
Baumber, Horncastle,
Lincolnshire LN9 5NE
T: (01507) 578235
F: (01507) 578417

BAYSTON HILL
Shropshire
**Lythwood Hall Bed and
Breakfast ♦♦♦**
2 Lythwood Hall, Lythwood,
Bayston Hill, Shrewsbury,
Shropshire SY3 0AD
T: (01743) 874747 &
07074 874747
F: (01743) 874747

BEESTON
Nottinghamshire
Andrews Private Hotel ♦♦♦
310 Queens Road, Beeston,
Nottingham, Nottinghamshire
NG9 1JA
T: (0115) 925 4902
F: (0115) 925 4902

The Grove Guesthouse ♦♦
8 Grove Street, Beeston,
Nottingham NG9 1JL
T: (0115) 9259854

Hylands Hotel ♦♦♦
307 Queens Road, Beeston,
Nottingham NG9 1JB
T: (0115) 925 5472 & 9225678
F: (0115) 922 5574
E: hylands.hotel@telinco.co.uk
I: www.s-h-systmes.co.
uk/hotels/hylands.html

BELPER
Derbyshire

Amber Hills ♦♦♦♦
Whitehouse Farm, Belper Lane,
Belper, Derbyshire DE56 2UJ
T: (01773) 824080 &
07808 393687
F: (01773) 824080
E: scooke@connectfree.co.uk

Broadhurst Bed and Breakfast
♦♦♦♦ SILVER AWARD
West Lodge, Bridge Hill, Belper,
DE56 2BY
T: (01773) 823596
F: (01773) 880810

The Cedars ♦♦♦♦
Field Lane, Belper, Derbyshire
DE56 1DD
T: (01773) 824157 &
07802 708389
F: (01773) 825573
E: neil_wayne@freedmus.
demon.co.uk
I: www.come.to/derbyshire

Chevin Green Farm ♦♦♦♦
Chevin Road, Belper, Derby
DE56 2UN
T: (01773) 822328
F: (01773) 822328
E: spostles@globalnet.co.uk
I: www.chevingreenfarm.co.uk

Hill Top Farm ♦♦♦♦
80 Ashbourne Road, Cowers
Lane, Belper, DE56 2LF
T: (01773) 550338

The Old Shop ♦♦
10 Bakers Hill, Heage, Belper,
Derbyshire DE56 2BL
T: (01773) 856796

32 Spencer Road ♦♦♦♦
Belper, Derbyshire DE56 1JY
T: (01773) 823877

BELTON IN RUTLAND
Rutland

The Old Rectory ♦♦
4 New Road, Belton in Rutland,
Oakham, Rutland LE15 9LE
T: (01572) 717279
F: (01572) 717343
E: bb@stablemate.demon.co.uk.

BENNIWORTH
Lincolnshire

Glebe Farm ♦♦♦♦
Benniworth, Market Rasen,
Lincolnshire LN8 6JP
T: (01507) 313231
F: (01507) 313231

BENTHALL
Shropshire

Hilltop House ♦♦♦♦
Bridge Road, Benthall, Broseley,
Shropshire TF12 5RB
T: (01952) 884821

BEOLEY
Worcestershire

Windmill Hill ♦♦♦♦
Cherry Pit Lane, Beoley,
Redditch, Worcestershire
B98 9DH
T: (01527) 62284

BERKELEY
Gloucestershire

Pickwick Farm ♦♦♦
A38, Berkeley, Gloucestershire
GL13 9EU
T: (01453) 810241
E: piclwick@supanet.com

BERKSWELL
West Midlands

Elmcroft Country Guesthouse
♦♦♦♦
Elmcroft, Hodgetts Lane,
Berkswell, Coventry CV7 7DW
T: (01676) 535204
F: (01676) 535204

BERROW
Worcestershire

Berewe Court ♦♦♦♦
Whiting Lane, Berrow, Malvern,
Worcestershire WR13 6AY
T: (01531) 650250 &
07702 303810

BESTHORPE
Nottinghamshire

Lord Nelson Inn ♦♦♦
Besthorpe, Newark,
Nottinghamshire NG23 7HR
T: (01636) 892265

BETLEY
Staffordshire

Adderley Green Farm ♦♦♦♦
Heighley Lane, Betley, Crewe
CW3 9BA
T: (01270) 820203 & 820542
F: (01270) 820542
E: betley.fsbusiness.co.uk

BEWDLEY
Worcestershire

Clay Farm ♦♦♦♦
Clows Top, Kidderminster,
Worcestershire DY14 9NN
T: (01299) 832421
F: (01299) 832421

42 High Street ♦♦
Bewdley, Worcestershire
DY12 2DJ
T: (01299) 405941

Lightmarsh Farm ♦♦♦♦
Crundalls Lane, Bewdley,
Worcestershire DY12 1NE
T: (01299) 404027

Sydney Place ♦♦♦
7 Kidderminster Road, Bewdley,
Worcestershire DY12 1AQ
T: (01299) 404832

BIBURY
Gloucestershire

Coln Cottage ♦♦♦♦
Coln Court, Bibury, Cirencester,
Gloucestershire GL7 5NL
T: (01285) 740314
F: (01285) 740314

Cotteswold House
♦♦♦♦ GOLD AWARD
Arlington, Bibury, Cirencester,
Gloucestershire GL7 5ND
T: (01285) 740609
F: (01285) 740609
E: cotteswold.house@btclick.
com
I: home.btclick.com/cotteswold.
house

The William Morris Brasserie,
Tearoom and Bed & Breakfast
♦♦♦♦
11 The Street, Bibury,
Cirencester, Gloucestershire
GL7 5NP
T: (01285) 740555
F: (01285) 850648
E: alex@ndra2000.freeserve.co.
uk

BICKENHILL
West Midlands

Church Farm Accommodation
Ltd ♦♦
Church Farm, Church Lane,
Bickenhill, Solihull, West
Midlands B92 0DN
T: (01675) 442641 &
07775 835799
F: (01675) 442905

BIDDULPH
Staffordshire

Chapel Croft Bed and
Breakfast♦♦♦
Newtown Road, Biddulph Park,
Biddulph, Stoke-on-Trent,
Staffordshire ST8 7SW
T: (01782) 511013 &
07970 022217

BIDFORD–ON–AVON
Warwickshire

Bidford Grange Golf and
Country Club♦♦
Stratford Road, Bidford-on-
Avon, Alcester, Warwickshire
B50 4LY
T: (01789) 490319
F: (01789) 778184

Brook Leys Bed and Breakfast
♦♦♦♦
Honeybourne Road, Bidford-on-
Avon, Alcester, Warwickshire
B50 4PD
T: (01789) 772785

Broom Hall Inn ♦♦♦
Bidford Road, Broom, Alcester,
Warwickshire B50 4HE
T: (01789) 773757

Fosbroke House ♦♦♦♦
4 High Street, Bidford-on-Avon,
Alcester, Warwickshire B50 4BU
T: (01789) 772327

The Harbour ♦♦♦
Salford Road, Bidford-on-Avon,
Alcester, Warwickshire B50 4EN
T: (01789) 772975
E: pwarwick@globalnet.co.uk

BIGGIN–BY–HARTINGTON
Derbyshire

The Kings at Ivy House
♦♦♦♦ SILVER AWARD
Biggin-by-Hartington, Buxton,
Derbyshire SK17 0DT
T: (01298) 84709
F: (01298) 84710
E: kings.ivyhouse@lineone.net
I: www.SmoothHound.co.
uk/hotels/kingsivy.html

BIRCH VALE
Derbyshire

Spinney Cottage ♦♦♦♦
Spinnerbottom, Hayfield, High
Peak SK22 1BL
T: (01663) 743230

BIRCHOVER
Derbyshire

Uppertown Farmhouse
♦♦♦♦ SILVER AWARD
Uppertown Lane, Birchover,
Matlock, Derbyshire DE4 2BH
T: (01629) 650112
F: (01629) 650112
E: upperb&b@hudrow.
enterprise-plc.com
I: www.holiday-rentals.co.
uk/upperb&bfarm

BIRDLIP
Gloucestershire

Beechmount ♦♦♦
Birdlip, Cirencester,
Gloucestershire GL4 8JH
T: (01452) 862262
F: (01452) 862262
E: thebeechmount@
breathemail.net

BIRMINGHAM
West Midlands

Alden ♦♦♦
7 Elmdon Road, Marston Green,
Birmingham, B37 7BS
T: (0121) 779 2063
F: (0121) 788 0898

Ashley House ♦♦♦
18 Alcott Lane, Marston Green,
Birmingham, B37 7AT
T: (0121) 779 5368
F: (0121) 779 5368

Atholl Lodge ♦♦♦
16 Elmdon Road, Acocks Green,
Birmingham, B27 6LH
T: (0121) 707 4417
F: (0121) 707 4417

Central Guest House ♦♦♦
1637 Coventry Road, South
Yardley, Birmingham, B26 1DD
T: (0121) 706 7757
F: (0121) 706 7757
E: mmou826384@aol.com

Cook House Hotel ♦♦♦
425 Hagley Road, Edgbaston,
Birmingham, B17 8BL
T: (0121) 429 1916

Elmdon Guest House ♦♦♦
2369 Coventry Road, Sheldon,
Birmingham, B26 3PN
T: (0121) 742 1626 & 688 1720
F: (0121) 7421626

Gables Nest ♦♦♦
1639 Coventry Road, South
Yardley, Birmingham, West
Midlands B26 1DD
T: (0121) 708 2712
F: (0121) 707 3396
E: mal-bb.gables@virgin.net

The Glades Guest House ◆◆◆
2469 Coventry Road, Sheldon,
Birmingham, B26 3PP
T: (0121) 742 1871
F: (0121) 743 6827

Grants Guest House ◆◆◆
643 Walsall Road, Great Barr,
Birmingham, B42 1EH
T: (0121) 357 4826
F: (0121) 604 5910
E: wendygrant@
guesthouse643.fsnet.co.uk

Grasmere Guesthouse ◆◆
37 Serpentine Road, Harborne,
Birmingham, B17 9RD
T: (0121) 427 4546
F: (0121) 427 4546

Greenway House Hotel ◆◆
978 Warwick Road, Acocks
Green, Birmingham B27 6QG
T: (0121) 706 1361 & 624 8356
F: (0121) 706 1361

Homelea ◆◆◆
2399 Coventry Road, Sheldon,
Birmingham B26 3PN
T: (0121) 742 0017
F: (0121) 688 1879

Kensington Guest House Hotel
◆◆◆
785 Pershore Road, Selly Park,
Birmingham, B29 7LR
T: (0121) 472 7086 & 414 1874
F: (0121) 472 5520

Knowle Lodge Hotel ◆◆
423 Hagley Road, Edgbaston,
Birmingham B17 8BL
T: (0121) 429 8366 & 429 3150

Lyndhurst Hotel ◆◆◆
135 Kingsbury Road, Erdington,
Birmingham B24 8QT
T: (0121) 373 5695
F: (0121) 373 5697
E: info@lyndhurst-hotel.co.uk
I: www.lyndhurst-hotel.co.uk

Rollason Wood Hotel ◆◆
130 Wood End Road, Erdington,
Birmingham B24 8BJ
T: (0121) 373 1230
F: (0121) 382 2578
E: rollwood@globalnet.co.uk

Royce Land ◆◆◆
33 Elmdon Road, Marston
Green, Birmingham, B37 7BU
T: (0121) 779 4343 &
07973 479122
F: (0121) 779 4343
I: www.roycelandguesthouse.co.
uk
⊛

Villanova Hotel ◆◆
2 Grove Hill Road, Handsworth
Wood, Birmingham, B21 9PA
T: (0121) 523 7787 & 551 1139
F: (0121) 523 7787

Wentworth Hotel ◆◆
103 Wentworth Road, Harborne,
Birmingham, B17 9SU
T: (0121) 427 2839 & 427 6818
F: (0121) 427 2839
E: wentworthhotel@freeuk.com
I: www.hotelbirmingham.com

Woodville House ◆
39 Portland Road, Edgbaston,
Birmingham B16 9HN
T: (0121) 454 0274
F: (0121) 454 5965

BIRTSMORTON
Worcestershire

Brook House
Rating Applied For
Birtsmorton, Malvern,
Worcestershire WR13 6AF
T: (01531) 650664
F: (01531) 650664
E: maryd@lineone.net
I: website.lineone.net/§maryd

BISHOP'S CASTLE
Shropshire

The Boars Head Hotel ◆◆◆
Church Street, Bishop's Castle,
Shropshire SY9 5AE
T: (01588) 638521 &
07990 971042
F: (01588) 630126
E: sales@boarsheadhotel.co.uk
I: www.boarsheadhotel.co.uk

Castle Hotel ◆◆◆
The Square, Bishop's Castle,
Shropshire SY9 5DG
T: (01588) 638403
F: (01588) 638403
E: castleotel@aol.com
I: www.bishops-castle.co.
uk/castlehotel

Lower Broughton Farm ◆◆◆
Bishop's Castle, Montgomery,
Powys SY15 6SZ
T: (01588) 638393

Old Time ◆◆
29 High Street, Bishop's Castle,
Shropshire SY9 5BE
T: (01588) 638467

BISHOP'S CLEEVE
Gloucestershire

Manor Cottage ◆◆
41 Station Road, Bishop's
Cleeve, Cheltenham,
Gloucestershire GL52 4HH
T: (01242) 673537

BLAKENEY
Gloucestershire

Brook House ◆◆◆
Bridge Street, Blakeney,
Gloucestershire GL15 4DY
T: (01594) 517101

The Old Tump House
◆◆◆◆ GOLD AWARD
New Road, Blakeney,
Gloucestershire GL15 4DG
T: (01594) 510608
F: (01594) 510608

BLEDINGTON
Gloucestershire

Kings Head Inn and Restaurant
◆◆◆◆
The Green, Bledington, Oxford
OX7 6XQ
T: (01608) 658365
F: (01608) 658902
E: kingshead@btinternet.com
I: www.btinternet.
com/§kingshead

BLOCKLEY
Gloucestershire

Arreton Guest House ◆◆◆◆
Station Road, Blockley,
Moreton-in-Marsh,
Gloucestershire GL56 9DT
T: (01386) 701077
F: (01386) 701077
E: bandb@arreton.demon.uk
I: www.arreton.demon.co.uk

The Malins ◆◆◆
21 Station Road, Blockley,
Moreton-in-Marsh,
Gloucestershire GL56 9ED
T: (01386) 700402
F: (01386) 700402
E: johnmalin@talk21.com

Mill Dene ◆◆◆
Mill Dene, Blockley, Moreton-in-
Marsh, Gloucestershire
GL56 9HU
T: (01386) 700457
F: (01386) 700526
E: wdare@
visitgarden-cotswold.
I: www.smoothhound.co.uk.
hotels/milldene.html

The Old Bakery
◆◆◆◆◆ GOLD AWARD
High Street, Blockley, Moreton-
in-Marsh, Gloucestershire
GL56 9EU
T: (01386) 700408
F: (01386) 700408

BLYTH
Nottinghamshire

Priory Farm Guesthouse ◆◆◆
Hodsock Priory Estate, Blyth,
Worksop, Nottinghamshire
S81 0TY
T: (01909) 591515
E: vera@guesthse.force9.co.uk.
I: www.guesthse.force9.co.uk.

White Gates Farm ◆◆◆◆
Blyth Road, Ranskill, Retford,
Nottinghamshire DN22 8LT
T: (01777) 818954

BOBBINGTON
Staffordshire

**Blakelands Country Guest
House and Restaurant** ◆◆◆◆
Halfpenny Green, Bobbington,
Stourbridge, West Midlands
DY7 5DP
T: (01384) 221464 & 221000
F: (01384) 221585
E: enquiries@blakeland.
freeserve.co.uk
I: www.blakelands.co.uk

BODENHAM
Herefordshire

The Forge
◆◆◆◆ SILVER AWARD
Bodenham, Hereford HR1 3JZ
T: (01568) 797144
E: bodenham.freeserve.co.uk
I: www.fsvo.
com/bodenhamforge

BONSALL
Derbyshire

Townhead Farmhouse
◆◆◆◆ SILVER AWARD
70 High Street, Bonsall, Matlock,
Derbyshire DE4 2AR
T: (01629) 823762
E: townhead70@hotmail.com

BOSTON
Lincolnshire

Bramley House ◆◆◆
267 Sleaford Road, Boston,
Lincolnshire PE21 7PQ
T: (01205) 354538
F: (01205) 354538
⊛

Ye Olde Magnet Tavern ◆◆
South Square, Boston,
Lincolnshire PE21 6HX
T: (01205) 369186

BOURNE
Lincolnshire

Angel Hotel ◆◆◆
Market Place, Bourne,
Lincolnshire PE10 9AE
T: (01778) 422346
F: (01778) 426113

Mill House
Rating Applied For
64 North Road, Bourne,
Lincolnshire PE10 9BU
T: (01778) 422278 & 422546
F: (01778) 422546

BOURTON-ON-THE-WATER
Gloucestershire

Berkeley Guesthouse ◆◆◆◆
Moore Road, Bourton-on-the-
Water, Cheltenham,
Gloucestershire GL54 2AZ
T: (01451) 810388
F: (01451) 810388

Broadlands Guest House
◆◆◆◆
Clapton Row, Bourton-on-the-
Water, Cheltenham,
Gloucestershire GL54 2DN
T: (01451) 822002
F: (01451) 821776

Coombe House
◆◆◆◆ SILVER AWARD
Rissington Road, Bourton-on-
the-Water, Cheltenham,
Gloucestershire GL54 2DT
T: (01451) 821966 & 822367
F: (01451) 810477
E: stephie.etherington@virgin.
net
I: www.smoouthound.co.
uk/hotels/coombeho.html

Cotswold Carp Farm ◆◆◆◆
Bury Barn Lane, Bourton-on-
the-Water, Cheltenham,
Gloucestershire GL54 2HB
T: (01451) 821795

The Cotswold House ◆◆◆
Lansdowne, Bourton-on-the-
Water, Cheltenham,
Gloucestershire GL54 2AR
T: (01451) 822373

Elvington Bed and Breakfast
◆◆◆
Elvington, Rissington Road,
Bourton-on-the-Water,
Cheltenham, Gloucestershire
GL54 2DX
T: (01451) 822026

Fairlie ◆◆◆
Riverside, Bourton-on-the-
Water, Cheltenham,
Gloucestershire GL54 2DP
T: (01451) 821842

Farncombe ◆◆◆◆
Clapton, Bourton-on-the-Water,
Cheltenham, Gloucestershire
GL54 2LG
T: (01451) 820120 &
07714 703142
F: (01451) 820120
E: jwrightbb@aol.com
I: www.SmoothHound.co.
uk/hotels/farncomb.html

Fosseside House
◆◆◆◆ GOLD AWARD
Lansdowne, Bourton-on-the-
Water, Cheltenham,
Gloucestershire GL54 2AT
T: (01451) 820574

Holly House ◆◆◆◆
Station Road, Bourton-on-the-
Water, Cheltenham,
Gloucestershire GL54 2ER
T: (01451) 821302

The Kingsbridge Inn ◆◆◆◆
Riverside, Bourton-on-the-
Water, Cheltenham,
Gloucestershire GL54 2BS
T: (01451) 820371
F: (01451) 810179
E: book@lionheartinns.co.uk
I: www.lionheartinns.co.uk

Lamb Inn ◆◆◆
Great Rissington, Bourton-on-
the-Water, Cheltenham,
Gloucestershire GL54 2LP
T: (01451) 820388
F: (01451) 820724

Lansdowne House ◆◆◆◆
Lansdowne, Bourton-on-the-
Water, Cheltenham,
Gloucestershire GL54 2AT
T: (01451) 820812
F: (01451) 822484
E: lansdowne-house@ukf.net
I: www.SmoothHound.co.
uk/hotels/lansdn1.html

Lansdowne Villa Guest House
◆◆◆◆
Lansdowne, Bourton-on-the-
Water, Cheltenham,
Gloucestershire GL54 2AR
T: (01451) 820673
F: (01451) 822099
E: lansdowne@star.co.uk
I: www.lansdownevilla.co.uk

Larch House
◆◆◆◆◆ GOLD AWARD
Station Road, Bourton-on-the-
Water, Cheltenham,
Gloucestershire GL54 2AA
T: (01451) 821172
I: www.s-n-systems.co.
uk/hotels/larcnnse.nm

The Lawns ◆◆◆◆
Station Road, Bourton-on-the-
Water, Cheltenham,
Gloucestershire GL54 2ER
T: (01451) 821195
F: (01451) 821195

Manor Close
◆◆◆◆ GOLD AWARD
High Street, Bourton-on-the-
Water, Cheltenham,
Gloucestershire GL54 2AP
T: (01451) 820339

Mousetrap Inn ◆◆◆
Lansdowne, Bourton-on-the-
Water, Cheltenham,
Gloucestershire GL54 2AR
T: (01451) 820579
F: (01451) 822393
E: mtinn@waverider.co.uk
I: mousetrap-inn.co.uk

Old New Inn ◆◆◆
Bourton-on-the-Water,
Cheltenham, Gloucestershire
GL54 2AF
T: (01451) 820467
F: (01451) 810236
E: old_new_inn@compuserve.
com
I: ourworld.compuserve.
com/homepages/old_new_inn

Polly Perkins ◆◆◆
1 The Chestnuts, Bourton-on-
the-Water, Cheltenham,
Gloucestershire GL54 2AN
T: (01451) 820244
F: (01451) 820558

**The Red House Bed and
Breakfast** ◆◆◆
Station Road, Bourton-on-the-
Water, Cheltenham,
Gloucestershire GL54 2EN
T: (01451) 810201

The Ridge
◆◆◆◆ SILVER AWARD
Whiteshoots Hill, Bourton-on-
the-Water, Cheltenham,
Gloucestershire GL54 2LE
T: (01451) 820660
F: (01451) 822448

Rooftrees ◆◆◆◆
Rissington Road, Bourton-on-
the-Water, Cheltenham,
Gloucestershire GL54 2DX
T: (01451) 821943
F: (01451) 810614

Strathspey ◆◆
Lansdown, Bourton-on-the-
Water, Cheltenham,
Gloucestershire GL54 2AR
T: (01451) 820694
F: (01451) 820694

Sycamore House ◆◆◆
Lansdowne, Bourton-on-the-
Water, Cheltenham,
Gloucestershire GL54 2AR
T: (01451) 821647

Touchstone
◆◆◆◆ SILVER AWARD
Little Rissington, Bourton-on-
the-Water, Cheltenham,
Gloucestershire GL54 2ND
T: (01451) 822481
F: (01451) 822481
E: touchstone.bb@lineone.net

Upper Farm ◆◆◆◆◆
Clapton on the Hill, Bourton-on-
the-Water, Cheltenham,
Gloucestershire GL54 2LG
T: (01451) 820453
F: (01451) 810185

Willow Crest ◆◆◆◆
Rissington Road, Bourton-on-
the-Water, Cheltenham,
Gloucestershire GL54 2DZ
T: (01451) 822073

BOYLESTONE
Derbyshire

Lees Hall Farm ◆◆◆
Boylestone, Ashbourne,
Derbyshire DE6 5AA
T: (01335) 330259
F: (01335) 330259

BRACKLEY
Northamptonshire

Astwell Mill ◆◆◆◆
Helmdon, Brackley,
Northamptonshire NN13 5QU
T: (01295) 760507
F: (01295) 768602
E: astwell01@aol.com

Brackley House Private Hotel
◆◆◆◆ SILVER AWARD
Brackley House, 4 High Street,
Brackley, Northamptonshire
NN13 7DT
T: (01280) 701550
F: (01280) 704965

The Thatches ◆◆◆
Whitfield, Brackley,
Northamptonshire NN13 5TQ
T: (01280) 850358

Walltree House Farm ◆◆◆◆
Steane, Brackley,
Northamptonshire NN13 5NS
T: (01295) 811235 &
07860 913399
F: (01295) 811147

Welbeck House ◆◆
Pebble Lane, Brackley,
Northamptonshire NN13 7DA
T: (01280) 702364
F: (01280) 702364

BRADLEY
Derbyshire

Yeldersley Old Hall Farm
◆◆◆◆
Yeldersley Lane, Bradley,
Ashbourne, Derbyshire DE6 1PH
T: (01335) 344504
F: (01335) 344504
E: janethindsfarm@yahoo.co.uk

BRADNOP
Staffordshire

Middle Farm Guest House
◆◆◆
Apesford, Bradnop, Leek,
Staffordshire ST13 7EX
T: (01538) 382839 & 399571
F: (01538) 382839

BRADWELL
Derbyshire

Stoney Ridge
◆◆◆◆ SILVER AWARD
Granby Road, Bradwell, Hope
Valley, Derbyshire S33 9HU
T: (01433) 620538
F: (01433) 623154
E: toneyridge@aol.com
I: www.cressbrook.co.
uk/hopev/stoneyridge

Stoneycroft Bed & Breakfast
◆◆◆
Smalldale, Bradwell, Hope Valley
S33 9JQ
T: (01433) 620599 &
07831 520474

BRAILES
Warwickshire

Agdon Farm ◆◆◆
Brailes, Banbury, Oxfordshire
OX15 5JJ
T: (01608) 685226 &
07850 847786
F: (01608) 685226
E: cripps@farmersweekly.com

BRAMPTON ABBOTTS
Herefordshire

Netherton House ◆◆◆◆
Netherton, Brampton Abbotts,
Ross-on-Wye, Herefordshire
HR9 7HZ
T: (01989) 562060

BREDENBURY
Herefordshire

Redhill Farm ◆◆
Bredenbury, Bromyard,
Herefordshire HR7 4SY
T: (01885) 483255 & 483535
F: (01885) 483535

BREDON
Worcestershire

Royal Oak Inn ◆◆◆◆
Main Road, Bredon, Tewkesbury,
Gloucestershire GL20 7LW
T: (01689) 772393

BREDON'S NORTON
Worcestershire

Round Bank House ◆◆◆
Lampitt Lane, Bredon's Norton,
Tewkesbury, Gloucestershire
GL20 7HB
T: (01684) 772983 & 772142
F: (01684) 773035

BREDWARDINE
Herefordshire

Old Court Farm ◆◆◆
Bredwardine, Hereford HR3 6BT
T: (01981) 500375

BRETFORTON
Worcestershire

**Bretforton House Farm Bed
and Breakfast**◆◆◆◆
Bretforton House Farm,
Bretforton, Evesham,
Worcestershire WR11 5JH
T: (01386) 830831
F: (01386) 830831
E: japplebya@aol.com

The Pond House
◆◆◆◆◆ GOLD AWARD
Lower Fields, Weston Road,
Bretforton, Evesham,
Worcestershire WR11 5QA
T: (01386) 831687
F: (01386) 831558
E: anne@pondhousebnb.
freeserve.co.uk
I: www.smoothhound.co.
uk/hotels/pondhous.html.

BREWOOD
Staffordshire

The Blackladies
◆◆◆◆◆ GOLD AWARD
Kiddemore Green Road,
Brewood, Stafford ST19 9BH
T: (01902) 850210
F: (01902) 851782

BRIDGNORTH
Shropshire

The Albynes
◆◆◆◆◆ SILVER AWARD
Nordley, Bridgnorth, Shropshire
WV16 4SX
T: (01746) 762261

Bassa Villa Bar and Grill ◆◆◆
48 Cartway, Bridgnorth,
Shropshire WV16 4BG
T: (01746) 763977 &
(01952) 691184
F: (01952) 691604
E: sugarloaf@globalnet.co.uk

Bear Inn ◆◆◆
Northgate, Bridgnorth,
Shropshire WV16 4ET
T: (01746) 763250

Bridgnorth Guest House ◆◆◆
45 Victoria Road, Bridgnorth,
Shropshire WV16 4LD
T: (01746) 766251 &
07958 561619
F: (01746) 762279
E: derekbartlett@bridgnorth76.
freeserve.co.uk

Bulls Head Inn ◆◆◆◆
Chelmarsh, Bridgnorth,
Shropshire WV16 6BA
T: (01746) 861469
F: (01746) 862646
E: stsales@stargate-uk.co.uk
I: www.stargate-uk.co.
uk/bullshead
🅰

Cherry's ◆◆◆◆
22 Saint Mary's Street,
Bridgnorth, Shropshire
WV16 4DW
T: (01746) 764976
F: (01746) 764976
E: pandcsell@aol.com

Dinney Farm ◆◆
Chelmarsh, Bridgnorth,
Shropshire WV16 6AU
T: (01746) 861070
F: (01746) 861070

Friar's Inn ◆◆◆
3 St. Mary's Street, Bridgnorth,
Shropshire WV16 4DW
T: (01746) 762396

The Golden Lion Inn ◆◆◆
83 High Street, Bridgnorth,
Shropshire WV16 4DS
T: (01746) 762016
F: (01746) 762016

Haven Pasture ◆◆◆◆
Underton, Bridgnorth,
Shropshire WV16 6TY
T: (01746) 789632
F: (01746) 789333
E: havenpasture@underton.co.
uk
I: www.underton.co.uk/haven
🅰

Highfields ◆◆◆◆
44 Ludlow Road, Bridgnorth,
Shropshire WV16 5AF
T: (01746) 763110 &
07974 501228

Hillside House ◆◆◆
St. Mary's Steps, Bridgnorth,
Shropshire WV16 4AQ
T: (01746) 762205
F: (01746) 762205

Linley Crest
◆◆◆◆ SILVER AWARD
Linley Brook, Bridgnorth,
Shropshire WV16 4SZ
T: (01746) 765527 &
07889 227875
F: (01746) 765527
E: linleycrest@easicome.com

Pen-y-Ghent ◆◆◆
7 Sabrina Road, Bridgnorth,
Shropshire WV15 6DQ
T: (01746) 762880
E: firman.margret@freeuk.com
I: pen-y-ghent.8m.com

Saint Leonards Gate ◆◆
6 Church Street, Bridgnorth,
Shropshire WV16 4EQ
T: (01746) 766647
E: stewboch@aol.uk

Sandward Guesthouse ◆◆◆
47 Cartway, Bridgnorth,
Shropshire WV16 4BG
T: (01746) 765913

Severn Arms Hotel ◆◆◆
Underhill Street, Bridgnorth,
Shropshire WV16 4BB
T: (01746) 764616
F: (01746) 761750
E: severnarmshotel@
compuserve.com
I: www.virtual-shropshire.co.
uk/severn-arms-hotel

Severn Hall ◆◆◆◆
Stanley Lane, Bridgnorth,
Shropshire WV16 4SR
T: (01746) 763241

Severn House
◆◆◆◆ GOLD AWARD
38 Underhill Street, Bridgnorth,
Shropshire WV16 4BB
T: (01746) 766976
F: (01746) 766976

BRIMPSFIELD
Gloucestershire
Highcroft
◆◆◆◆ GOLD AWARD
Brimpsfield, Gloucester GL4 8LF
T: (01452) 862405

BRINKLOW
Warwickshire
White Lion ◆◆◆
32 Broad Street, Brinklow,
Rugby, Warwickshire CV23 0LN
T: (01788) 832579
T: (01788) 833844
E: brinklowlion@supanet.com
I: www.aceserve.co.
uk/whitelioninn

BRIXWORTH
Northamptonshire
The Rookery
◆◆◆◆ SILVER AWARD
36 Church Street, Brixworth,
Northampton NN6 9BZ
T: (01604) 883699
F: (01604) 880886
E: cherryliell@
rookeryb-bfreeserve.co.uk
I: www.rookeryb-b.freeserve.co.
uk

BROAD CAMPDEN
Gloucestershire
Marnic ◆◆◆◆ GOLD AWARD
Broad Campden, Chipping
Campden, Gloucestershire
GL55 6UR
T: (01386) 840014 & 841473
F: (01386) 840441
E: MARNIC@ZOOM.CO.UK

BROADWAY
Worcestershire
Barn House
◆◆◆◆ SILVER AWARD
152 High Street, Broadway,
Worcestershire WR12 7AJ
T: (01386) 858633
F: (01386) 858633

Bourne House
◆◆◆◆ SILVER AWARD
Leamington Road, Broadway,
Worcestershire WR12 7DZ
T: (01386) 853486
F: (01386) 853793
E: maria@
bournehousebroadway.
freeserve.co.uk

Burhill Farm
◆◆◆◆◆ GOLD AWARD
Buckland, Broadway,
Worcestershire WR12 7LY
T: (01386) 858171
F: (01386) 858171
🌐

Crown and Trumpet Inn ◆◆◆
Church Street, Broadway,
Worcestershire WR12 7AE
T: (01386) 853202
F: (01386) 834650
E: ascott@cotswoldholidays.co.
uk
I: www.cotswoldholidays.co.uk

Dove Cottage ◆◆◆
Colletts Fields, Broadway,
Worcestershire WR12 7AT
T: (01386) 859085

Eastbank ◆◆◆◆
Station Drive, Broadway,
Worcestershire WR12 7DF
T: (01386) 852659
F: (01386) 852891
E: eastbank@talk21.com
I: www.broadway-cotswolds.co.
uk/ebank.html

**Highlands Country House Bed
and Breakfast**◆◆◆◆
Highlands, Fish Hill, Broadway,
Worcestershire WR12 7LD
T: (01386) 858015
F: (01386) 852584
E: adames@demon.co.uk

**Knoll Bed and Breakfast
Rating Applied For**
The Knoll, Springfield Lane,
Broadway, Worcestershire
WR12 7BT
T: (01386) 858702

Leasow House
◆◆◆◆ SILVER AWARD
Laverton Meadow, Broadway,
Worcestershire WR12 7NA
T: (01386) 584526
F: (01386) 584596
E: leasow@clara.net
I: www.leasow.co.uk

Lowerfield Farm ◆◆◆◆
Lowerfield Farm, Willersey,
Broadway, Worcestershire
WR11 5HF
T: (01386) 858273 &
07703 343996
F: (01386) 854608
E: info@lowerfield-farm.co.uk
I: www.lowerfield-farm.co.uk

Mount Pleasant Farm ◆◆◆◆
Childswickham, Broadway,
Worcestershire WR12 7HZ
T: (01386) 853424

The Old Rectory
◆◆◆◆ GOLD AWARD
Church Street, Willersey,
Broadway, Worcestershire
WR12 7PN
T: (01386) 853729
F: (01386) 858061
E: beauvoisin@btinternet.com
I: homepages.tesco.net/§j.
walker/

Olive Branch Guest House
◆◆◆
78 High Street, Broadway,
Worcestershire WR12 7AJ
T: (01386) 853440
F: (01386) 859070
E: clive@theolivebranch.u-net.
com
I: www.theoilvebranch.u-net.
com

Pathlow House ◆◆◆
82 High Street, Broadway,
Worcestershire WR12 7AJ
T: (01386) 853444 &
(01527) 65861
F: (01386) 853444
E: pathlow@aol.com
I: www.pathlowguesthouse.co.
uk

Shenberrow Hill ◆◆◆◆
Stanton, Broadway,
Worcestershire WR12 7NE
T: (01386) 584468

Small Talk Lodge ◆◆◆
32 High Street, Broadway,
Worcestershire WR12 7DP
T: (01386) 858953 & 854611
I: www.broadway-cotswolds.co.
uk

Southwold Guest House
◆◆◆◆
Station Road, Broadway,
Worcestershire WR12 7DE
T: (01386) 853681 &
07711 539660
F: (01386) 854610
E: sueandnick.southwold@
talk21.com

Whiteacres ◆◆◆◆
Station Road, Broadway,
Worcestershire WR12 7DE
T: (01386) 852320
E: whiteacres@btinternet.com
I: www.broadway-cotswolds.co.
uk/whiteacres.html

Windrush House ◆◆◆◆
Station Road, Broadway,
Worcestershire WR12 7DE
T: (01386) 853577 & 853790
F: (01386) 853790
E: richard@
broadway-windrush.co.uk
I: www.broadway-windrush.co.
uk

BROADWELL
Gloucestershire
The White House ◆◆◆
2 South Road, Broadwell,
Coleford, Gloucestershire
GL16 7BH
T: (01594) 837069 &
07074 837069
F: (01594) 833130
I: www.ukworld-int.co.uk

BROMSGROVE
Worcestershire
Bea's Lodge ◆◆
245 Pennine Road, Bromsgrove,
Worcestershire B61 0TN
T: (01527) 877613

Bromsgrove Country Hotel
◆◆◆◆
249 Worcester Road, Stoke
Heath, Bromsgrove,
Worcestershire B61 7JA
T: (01527) 835522
F: (01527) 871257
E: bchotel@talk21.com
🌐

The Durrance ◆◆◆◆
Berry Lane, Upton Warren,
Bromsgrove, Worcestershire
B61 9EL
T: (01562) 777533
F: (01562) 777533
E: helenhirons@thedurrance.
fsnet.co.uk

The Grahams
Rating Applied For
95 Old Station Road,
Bromsgrove, Worcestershire
B60 2AF
T: (01527) 874463

Honeypot ◆◆◆◆
305 Old Birmingham Road,
Lickey, Bromsgrove,
Worcestershire B60 1HQ
T: (0121) 445 2580 &
07803 473737

Merrivale ◆◆◆◆
309 Old Birmingham Road,
Lickey, Bromsgrove,
Worcestershire B60 1HQ
T: (0121) 445 1694 &
07721 641268
F: (0121) 445 1694

Overwood Bed and Breakfast
◆◆◆◆
Woodcote Lane, Woodcote,
Bromsgrove, Worcestershire
B61 9EE
T: (01562) 777193
F: (01562) 777689
E: barbbrianpalmer.overwood@
tesco.net

Sprite House ◆◆
58 Stratford Road, Bromsgrove,
Worcestershire B60 1AU
T: (01527) 874565 & 870935
F: (01527) 870935

BROMYARD
Herefordshire

The Granary Restaurant ◆◆◆
Church House Farm, Collington,
Bromyard, Herefordshire
HR7 4NA
T: (01885) 410345
F: (01885) 410555

Linton Brook Farm ◆◆◆
Malvern Road, Bringsty,
Bromyard, Herefordshire
WR6 5TR
T: (01885) 488875
F: (01885) 488875

The Old Cowshed
◆◆◆◆ SILVER AWARD
Avenbury Court Farm, Bromyard,
Herefordshire HR7 4LA
T: (01885) 482384
F: (01885) 482367
E: ruralb.b@clara.co.uk
I: www.ruralb.b.clara.co.uk

Park House Hotel ◆◆◆
28 Sherford Street, Bromyard,
Herefordshire HR7 4DL
T: (01885) 482294
E: parkhouse@cellnet.com
I: www.bromyard.co.
uk/parkhouse

BROOM
Warwickshire

The Arrows
◆◆◆◆ SILVER AWARD
Broom, Alcester, Warwickshire
B50 4HR
T: (01789) 772260 &
07788 140182
F: (01789) 772260
E: softly@compuserve.com
I: www.SmoothHound.co.
uk/hotels/arrows.html

BROSELEY
Shropshire

Rock Dell
◆◆◆◆ SILVER AWARD
30 Ironbridge Road, Broseley,
Shropshire TF12 5AJ
T: (01952) 883054
F: (01952) 883054

BROUGHTON ASTLEY
Leicestershire

The Old Farm House ◆◆◆
Old Mill Road, Broughton Astley,
Leicester LE9 6PQ
T: (01455) 282254

BROXWOOD
Herefordshire

Broxwood Court
◆◆◆◆ SILVER AWARD
Broxwood, Leominster,
Herefordshire HR6 9JJ
T: (01544) 340245
F: (01544) 340573
E: mikeanne@broxwood.kc3.co.
uk

BUCKNELL
Shropshire

The Hall ◆◆◆
Bucknell, Shropshire SY7 0AA
T: (01547) 530249
F: (01547) 530249

BUGBROOKE
Northamptonshire

The Byre ◆◆◆◆
2 Church Lane, Bugbrooke,
Northampton NN7 3PB
T: (01604) 830319

Cherry Tree Cottage ◆◆◆◆
26a Camphill, Bugbrooke,
Northampton NN7 3PH
T: (01604) 830929

BUNNY
Nottinghamshire

The Rancliffe Arms ◆◆◆
Loughborough Road, Bunny,
Nottingham NG11 6QT
T: (0115) 9844727

BURLTON
Shropshire

Petton Hall Farm
◆◆◆◆ SILVER AWARD
Petton, Burlton, Shrewsbury
SY4 5TH
T: (01939) 270601
F: (01939) 270601
I: www.go2.co.uk/pettonhall

BURSTON
Staffordshire

Yew Tree House ◆◆◆
Burston, Staffordshire ST18 0DR
T: (01889) 508063
F: (01889) 508063
E: hazel@yewtreeburston.
freeserve.co.uk

BURTON DASSETT
Warwickshire

**The White House Bed and
Breakfast** ◆◆◆◆
Burton Dassett, Southam,
Warwickshire CV47 2AB
T: (01295) 770143 &
0476 458314
E: lisa@whitehouse10.freeserve.
co.uk

BURTON LAZARS
Leicestershire

The Grange ◆◆◆◆
New Road, Burton Lazars,
Melton Mowbray, Leicestershire
LE14 2UU
T: (01664) 560775
F: (01664) 560775

BURTON UPON TRENT
Staffordshire

The Delter Hotel ◆◆◆
5 Derby Road, Burton upon
Trent, Staffordshire DE14 1RU
T: (01283) 535115
F: (01283) 845261
E: delterhotel@hotmail.com

Meadowview ◆◆◆
203 Newton Road, Winshill,
Burton upon Trent, Staffordshire
DE15 0TU
T: (01283) 564046

The New Inn ◆◆◆
Five Lanes End, Burton Road,
Needwood, Burton upon Trent,
Staffordshire DE13 9PB
T: (01283) 575392
F: (01283) 575708
E: barry@newinn.co.uk
I: www.newinn.co.uk

New Inn Farm ◆◆◆
Burton Road, Needwood, Burton
upon Trent, Staffordshire
DE13 9PB
T: (01283) 575435 &
07801 491482

Primrose Bank House ◆◆
194A Newton Road, Burton
upon Trent, Staffordshire
DE15 0TU
T: (01283) 532569

BUSHLEY
Worcestershire

Shiloh House ◆◆◆
Church End, Bushley,
Tewkesbury, Gloucestershire
GL20 6HT
T: (01684) 293435

BUTTERTON
Staffordshire

Black Lion Inn ◆◆◆
Butterton, Leek, Staffordshire
ST13 7SP
T: (01538) 304232
E: the blacklion@clara.net
I: www.theblacklion.clara.net

Butterton House ◆◆◆
Park Road, Butterton,
Newcastle-under-Lyme,
Staffordshire ST5 4DZ
T: (01782) 619085
E: sjtoast@aol.com

Butterton Moor House
◆◆◆◆ SILVER AWARD
Parsons Lane, Butterton, Leek,
Staffordshire ST13 7PD
T: (01538) 304506
F: (01538) 304506

Coxon Green Farm ◆◆◆◆
Butterton, Leek, Staffordshire
ST13 7TA
T: (01538) 304221

Heathy Roods Farm ◆◆◆◆
Butterton, Leek, Staffordshire
ST13 7SR
T: (01538) 304397

New Hayes Farm ◆◆◆
Trentham Road, Butterton,
Newcastle-under-Lyme,
Staffordshire ST5 4DX
T: (01782) 680889 &
07703 882593

BUXTON
Derbyshire

Abbey Guesthouse ◆◆◆
43 South Avenue, Buxton,
Derbyshire SK17 6NQ
T: (01298) 26419

Alpine Guesthouse ◆◆◆◆
1 Thornsett, Hardwick Mount,
Buxton, Derbyshire SK17 6PS
T: (01298) 26155 &
07970 652238
E: exclusively.psandqs@talk21.
com
I: www.exclusivelypsandqs.com

Barn House ◆◆◆◆
Litton Mill, Buxton, Derbyshire
SK17 8SW
T: (01298) 872751
F: (01298) 872751

Braemar ◆◆◆◆
10 Compton Road, Buxton,
Derbyshire SK17 9DN
T: (01298) 78050

Buxton View ◆◆◆◆
74 Corbar Road, Buxton,
Derbyshire SK17 6RJ
T: (01298) 79222 &
07710 516846
F: (01298) 79222
⊚

Buxton Wheelhouse Hotel
◆◆◆◆
19 College Road, Buxton,
Derbyshire SK17 9DZ
T: (01298) 24869 & 26040
F: (01298) 24869
E: lyndsie@buxton-wheelhouse.
com
I: www.buxton-wheelhouse.com
⊚

Buxton's Victorian Guesthouse
◆◆◆◆◆ GOLD AWARD
3A Broad Walk, Buxton,
Derbyshire SK17 6JE
T: (01298) 78759 &
07801 361228
E: buxtonsvictorian@x-stream.
co.uk
I: www.smoothhound.co.uk

Compton House Guesthouse
◆◆◆
4 Compton Road, Buxton,
Derbyshire SK17 9DN
T: (01298) 26926
F: (01298) 26926

Coningsby
◆◆◆◆◆ GOLD AWARD
6 Macclesfield Road, Buxton,
Derbyshire SK17 9AH
T: (01298) 26735
F: (01298) 26735
E: coningsby@btinternet.com
⊚

Cotesfield Farm ◆◆
Parsley Hay, Buxton, Derbyshire
SK17 0BD
T: (01298) 83256 &
07850 451148
F: (01298) 83256

Devonshire Arms ◆◆◆
Peak Forest, Buxton, Derbyshire
SK17 8EJ
T: (01298) 23875 &
07831 707325

Devonshire Lodge Guesthouse
◆◆◆◆
2 Manchester Road, Buxton,
Derbyshire SK17 6SB
T: (01298) 71487

Fairhaven ◆◆
1 Dale Terrace, Buxton,
Derbyshire SK17 6LU
T: (01298) 24481
F: (01298) 24481

Ford Side House
◆◆◆◆ SILVER AWARD
125 Lightwood Road, Buxton,
Derbyshire SK17 6RW
T: (01298) 72842

Grendon Guesthouse
◆◆◆◆ SILVER AWARD
Bishops Lane, Buxton,
Derbyshire SK17 6UN
T: (01298) 78831 &
07711 380143
I: www.cressbrook.co.uk/buxton

Griff Guesthouse ◆◆
2 Compton Road, Buxton,
Derbyshire SK17 9DN
T: (01298) 23628 & 71778

Grosvenor House ◆◆◆◆
1 Broad Walk, Buxton,
Derbyshire SK17 6JE
T: (01298) 72439
F: (01298) 72439
I: www.SmoothHound.co.
uk/hotels/grosvenr.html

Harefield
◆◆◆◆ SILVER AWARD
15 Marlborough Road, Buxton,
Derbyshire SK17 6RD
T: (01298) 24029
F: (01298) 24029
E: hardie@harefield1.freeserve.
co.uk
I: www.harefield1.freeserve.co.
uk

Hawthorn Farm Guesthouse
◆◆◆
Fairfield Road, Buxton,
Derbyshire SK17 7ED
T: (01298) 23230

Kingscroft ◆◆◆◆
10 Green Lane, Buxton,
Derbyshire SK17 9DP
T: (01298) 22757 &
07889 977971
F: (01298) 27858

Lakenham Guesthouse ◆◆◆
11 Burlington Road, Buxton,
Derbyshire SK17 9AL
T: (01298) 79209

Lowther Guesthouse ◆◆◆◆
7 Hardwick Square West,
Buxton, Derbyshire SK17 6PX
T: (01298) 71479

Netherdale Guesthouse
◆◆◆◆
16 Green Lane, Buxton,
Derbyshire SK17 9DP
T: (01298) 23896
F: (01298) 23896
E: netherdale@btn-ltdfreeserve.
co.uk

Nithen Cottage ◆◆◆◆
123 Park Road, Buxton,
Derbyshire SK17 6SP
T: (01298) 24679 &
07703 717335

The Old Manse Private Hotel
◆◆◆
6 Clifton Road, Silverlands,
Buxton, Derbyshire SK17 6QL
T: (01298) 25638
E: old_manse@yahoo.co.uk

Oldfield House ◆◆◆◆
8 Macclesfield Road, Buxton,
Derbyshire SK17 9AH
T: (01298) 24371
E: bbookings@oldfieldhouses.
freeserve.co.uk
I: www.oldfieldhouses.freeserve.
co.uk

The Queens Head Hotel ◆◆◆
High Street, Buxton, Derbyshire
SK17 6EU
T: (01298) 23841
F: (01298) 71238

Roseleigh Hotel ◆◆◆
19 Broad Walk, Buxton,
Derbyshire SK17 6JR
T: (01298) 24904
F: (01298) 24904
E: enquiries@roseleighhotel.co.
uk
I: www.roseleighhotel.co.uk

Sevenways Guesthouse
◆◆◆◆
1 College Road, Buxton,
Derbyshire SK17 9DZ
T: (01298) 77809 &
07966 436262
E: mick@sevenways.fsnet.co.uk

Staden Grange Country House
◆◆◆
Staden Lane, Staden, Buxton,
Derbyshire SK17 9RZ
T: (01298) 24965
F: (01298) 72067
E: staden@grange100.
fsbusiness.co.uk
I: www.stadengrange.co.uk

Stoneridge
◆◆◆◆ SILVER AWARD
9 Park Road, Buxton, Derbyshire
SK17 6SG
T: (01298) 26120
E: hoskin@stoneridge.demon.
co.uk
I: www.stoneridge.co.uk

Westlands ◆◆◆◆
Bishops Lane, St Johns Road,
Buxton, Derbyshire SK17 6UN
T: (01298) 23242

Westminster Hotel ◆◆◆
21 Broad Walk, Buxton,
Derbyshire SK17 6JR
T: (01298) 23929 &
07770 503629
F: (01298) 71121

CALDECOTE
Warwickshire

Hill House Country Guest
House◆◆◆◆
Off Mancetter Road, Caldecote,
Nuneaton, Warwickshire
CV10 0RS
T: (024) 7639 6685
F: (024) 7639 6685

CALLOW
Herefordshire

Knockerhill Farm ◆◆◆◆
Callow, Hereford HR2 8BP
T: (01432) 268460
F: (01432) 268460

CALMSDEN
Gloucestershire

The Old House ◆◆◆◆
Calmsden, Cirencester,
Gloucestershire GL7 5ET
T: (01285) 831240 &
07720 779456
F: (01285) 831240
E: baxter@calmsden.freeserve.
co.uk

CALVER
Derbyshire

Old Orchard
Rating Applied For
The Green, Froggatt, Calver,
Hope Valley S32 3ZA
T: (01433) 630659

The Old Village Store ◆◆◆
High Street, Calver, Hope Valley
S32 3XP
T: (01433) 630523
I: www.oldvillagestore.com

Rose Cottage ◆◆◆◆
Main Street, Calver, Hope Valley
S32 3XR
T: (01433) 630769

Valley View ◆◆◆◆
Smithy Knoll Road, Calver, Hope
Valley S32 3XW
T: (01433) 631407
F: (01433) 631407
E: david@stone25.freeserve.co.
uk
I: www.a-place-2-stay

CANON PYON
Herefordshire

Nags Head ◆◆◆
Canon Pyon, Hereford HR4 8NY
T: (01432) 830252

CARDINGTON
Shropshire

Woodside Farm ◆◆◆◆
Cardington, Church Stretton,
Shropshire SY6 7LB
T: (01694) 771314

CARRINGTON
Nottinghamshire

Paramount Hotel and Tandoori
Restaurant◆◆
328 Mansfield Road, Carrington,
Nottingham NG5 2EF
T: (0115) 962 1621
F: (0115) 956 1561

CARSINGTON
Derbyshire

Breach Farm
Rating Applied For
Carsington, Matlock, Derbyshire
DE4 4DD
T: (01629) 540265

CASTLE DONINGTON
Leicestershire

Castletown House ◆◆◆
4 High Street, Castle Donington,
Derby DE74 2PP
T: (01332) 812018 & 814550
F: (01332) 812018

Donington Park Farmhouse
Hotel ◆◆◆
Melbourne Road, Isley Walton,
Castle Donington, Derby
DE74 2RN
T: (01332) 862409
F: (01332) 862364
E: info@parkfarmhouse.co.uk
I: www.parkfarmhouse.co.uk

Little Chimneys Guesthouse
◆◆◆
19 The Green, Diseworth, Castle
Donington, Derby DE74 2QN
T: (01332) 812458 &
07889 338828
F: (01332) 853336
E: kay@little-chimneys.demon.
co.uk
I: www.little-chimneys.demon.
co.uk

Scot's Corner Guesthouse Bed
and Breakfast◆◆◆
82 Park Lane, Castle Donington,
Derby DE74 2JG
T: (01332) 811226 &
0771 2084119

CASTLETON
Derbyshire

Ashbrook ◆◆◆
Brookside, Bradwell, Hope
Valley, Derbyshire S33 9HF
T: (01433) 620803

Bargate Cottage ◆◆◆◆
Bargate, Market Place, Castleton,
Hope Valley, Derbyshire
S33 8WG
T: (01433) 620201
F: (01433) 621739
I: www.peakland.com/bargate

Causeway House ◆◆◆
Back Street, Castleton, Hope
Valley, Derbyshire S33 8WE
T: (01433) 623291 & (0114) 236
8574

Cryer House ◆◆◆
Castle Street, Castleton, Hope
Valley S33 8WG
T: (01433) 620244
F: (01433) 620244
E: FleeSkel@aol.com

Dunscar Farm Bed & Breakfast
◆◆◆◆
Dunscar Farm, Castleton, Hope
Valley S33 8WA
T: (01433) 620483

Hillside House ◆◆◆◆
Pindale Road, Castleton, Hope
Valley S33 8WU
T: (01433) 620312
F: (01433) 620312

Myrtle Cottage ◆◆◆
Market Place, Castleton, Hope
Valley S33 8WQ
T: (01433) 620787

Ramblers Rest ◆◆
Mill Bridge, Back Street,
Castleton, Hope Valley S33 8WR
T: (01433) 620125
F: (01433) 621677

Swiss House Hotel and Restaurant ♦♦♦
How Lane, Castleton, Hope Valley S33 8WJ
T: (01433) 621098

Ye Olde Cheshire Cheese Inn
Rating Applied For
How Lane, Castleton, Hope Valley S33 8WJ
T: (01433) 620330 &
07836 369636
F: (01433) 621847
I: www.peakland.com.
cheshirecheese

CAUNTON
Nottinghamshire

Knapthorpe Lodge ♦♦♦
Hockerton Road, Caunton, Newark, Nottinghamshire
NG23 6AZ
T: (01636) 636262
F: (01636) 636415

CHALFORD
Gloucestershire

The Ragged Cot Inn ♦♦♦♦
Hyde, Chalford, Stroud, Gloucestershire GL6 8PE
T: (01453) 884643 & 731333
F: (01453) 731166

CHAPEL-EN-LE-FRITH
Derbyshire

The Potting Shed ♦♦♦♦
Bank Hall, Chapel-en-le-Frith, High Peak SK23 9UB
T: (01298) 812656 & (0161) 338 8134
E: 106541,3166@compuserve.com.

Ridge Hall
♦♦♦♦♦ SILVER AWARD
Chapel-en-le-Frith, Buxton, Derbyshire SK23 9UD
T: (01298) 813130 & 815862
F: (01298) 815863
E: Ridge-hall@Aol.com
I: www.ridge-hall.com

Slack Hall Farm ♦♦♦
Castleton Road, Chapel-en-le-Frith, High Peak SK23 0QS
T: (01298) 812845

CHARLECOTE
Warwickshire

Kingsmead Farm ♦♦♦♦
Stratford Road, Charlecote, Warwick CV35 9ES
T: (01789) 840254 &
07976 243893

CHARLTON KINGS
Gloucestershire

Orion House ♦♦♦
220 London Road, Charlton Kings, Cheltenham, Gloucestershire GL52 6HW
T: (01242) 233309
F: (01242) 233309
E: ena@orionhouse.fs.net.co.uk

CHEADLE
Staffordshire

Caverswall Castle
♦♦♦♦♦ GOLD AWARD
Caverswall, Staffordshire
ST11 9EA
T: (01782) 393239
F: (01782) 394590
E: YARSARGENT@HOTMAIL.COM

The Church Farm ♦♦♦♦
Holt Lane, Kingsley, Stoke-on-Trent ST10 2BA
T: (01538) 754759
F: (01538) 754759

Ley Fields Farm
♦♦♦♦ SILVER AWARD
Leek Road, Cheadle, Stoke-on-Trent, Staffordshire ST10 2EF
T: (01538) 752875

Park Lodge Guest House ♦♦♦
1 Tean Road, Cheadle, Staffordshire ST10 1LG
T: (01538) 753562

Park View Guest House ♦♦♦
15 Mill Road, Cheadle, Stoke-on-Trent, Staffordshire ST10 1NG
T: (01538) 755412

Woodhouse Farm Country Guesthouse ♦♦♦
Lockwood Road, Near Kingsley Holt, Cheadle, Stoke-on-Trent, Staffordshire ST10 4QU
T: (01538) 754250
F: (01538) 754470
E: woodhousefarm@btinternet.com

CHEDDLETON
Staffordshire

Brook House Farm ♦♦♦
Cheddleton, Leek, Staffordshire ST13 7DF
T: (01538) 360296

Choir Cottage and Choir House
♦♦♦♦♦ GOLD AWARD
Ostlers Lane, Cheddleton, Leek, Staffordshire ST13 7HS
T: (01538) 360561 &
07703 622328
E: ELAINE.SUTCLIFFEdic24.net

Hillcrest ♦♦♦♦
74 Folly Lane, Cheddleton, Leek, Staffordshire ST13 7DA
T: (01782) 550483

CHELMARSH
Shropshire

Hampton House ♦♦♦♦
Hampton Loade, Chelmarsh, Bridgnorth, Shropshire
WV16 6BN
T: (01746) 861436

CHELMORTON
Derbyshire

Ditch House ♦♦♦♦
Chelmorton, Buxton, Derbyshire SK17 9SG
T: (01298) 85719
F: (01298) 85719

Shallow Grange
♦♦♦♦♦ GOLD AWARD
Chelmorton, Buxton, Derbyshire SK17 9SG
T: (01298) 23578
F: (01298) 78242
E: holland@shallowgrangefarm.freeserve.co.uk

CHELTENHAM
Gloucestershire

The Abbey Hotel ♦♦♦♦
14-16 Bath Parade, Cheltenham, Gloucestershire GL53 7HN
T: (01242) 516053
F: (01242) 513034
E: Manager@AbbeyHotel.demon.co.uk

Acanthus Court Hotel
♦♦♦♦♦ GOLD AWARD
59 Leckhampton Road, Cheltenham, Gloucestershire GL53 0BS
T: (01242) 576083
F: (01242) 224579
E: R&S@acanthus-court.co.uk
I: www.acanthus-court.co.uk

Barn End ♦♦♦♦
23 Cheltenham Road, Bishop's Cleeve, Cheltenham, Gloucestershire GL52 4LU
T: (01242) 672404

The Battledown ♦♦♦
125 Hales Road, Cheltenham, Gloucestershire GL52 6ST
T: (01242) 233881
F: (01242) 524198
E: SMURTH@FSBDIAL.CO.UK

Beaumont House Hotel
♦♦♦♦ SILVER AWARD
Shurdington Road, Cheltenham, Gloucestershire GL53 0JE
T: (01242) 245986
F: (01242) 520044
E: rocking.horse@virgin.net
I: www.smoothhound.co.uk/hotels/beauchel.html

Beechworth Lawn Hotel
♦♦♦♦
133 Hales Road, Cheltenham, Gloucestershire GL52 6ST
T: (01242) 522583
F: (01242) 574800
E: xpjtl@dial.pipex.com
I: www.beechworthlawnhotel@dial.pipex.com

Bentons ♦♦♦
71 Bath Road, Cheltenham, Gloucestershire GL53 7LH
T: (01242) 517417 & 527772
F: (01242) 527772

Bibury House ♦♦♦
Priory Place, Cheltenham, Gloucestershire GL52 6HG
T: (01242) 525014

Bridge House ♦♦♦♦
88 Lansdown Road, Cheltenham, Gloucestershire GL51 6QR
T: (01242) 583559
F: (01242) 255920
E: bridgehouse@freeuk.com

Central Hotel ♦♦♦
7-9 Portland Street, Cheltenham, Gloucestershire GL52 2NZ
T: (01242) 582172 & 524789

Charlton House
♦♦♦♦ SILVER AWARD
18 Greenhills Road, Charlton Kings, Cheltenham, Gloucestershire GL53 9EB
T: (01242) 238997
F: (01242) 238997

Crossways Guest House ♦♦♦
Oriel Place, 57 Bath Road, Cheltenham, Gloucestershire GL53 7LH
T: (01242) 527683
F: (01242) 577226
E: croww.ways@btinternet.com

Detmore House ♦♦♦
London Road, Charlton Kings, Cheltenham, Gloucestershire GL52 6UT
T: (01242) 582868
F: (01242) 582868

Elm Villa ♦♦
49 London Road, Cheltenham, Gloucestershire GL52 6HE
T: (01242) 231909

Elmington Bed and Breakfast
♦♦♦♦
44 Leckhampton Road, Cheltenham, Gloucestershire GL53 0BB
T: (01242) 573357
F: (01242) 263201

Evington Hill Farm
♦♦♦ GOLD AWARD
Tewkesbury Road, The Leigh, Gloucester, GL19 4AQ
T: (01242) 680255

Fromefield ♦♦
127 St. George's Road, Cheltenham, Gloucestershire GL50 3EQ
T: (01242) 514391

Georgian House
♦♦♦♦♦ SILVER AWARD
77 Montpellier Terrace, Cheltenham, Gloucestershire GL50 1XA
T: (01242) 515577
F: (01242) 545929
E: georgian_house@yahoo.com

Glencree ♦♦♦
80 Lansdown Road, Cheltenham, Gloucestershire GL51 6QW
T: (01242) 260242
F: (01242) 260242

Ham Hill Farm
♦♦♦♦ SILVER AWARD
Whittington, Cheltenham, Gloucestershire GL54 4EZ
T: (01242) 584415 &
07711 832041
F: (01242) 222535

Hamilton House ♦♦♦
65 Bath Road, Cheltenham, Gloucestershire GL53 7LH
T: (01242) 527772

Hannaford's ♦♦♦♦
20 Evesham Road, Cheltenham, Gloucestershire GL52 2AB
T: (01242) 515181 & 524190
F: (01242) 257571
E: dc@hannafords-hotel.demon.co.uk
I: www.hannafords-hotel.demon.co.uk

Hollington House Hotel
♦♦♦♦
115 Hales Road, Cheltenham, Gloucestershire GL52 6ST
T: (01242) 256652
F: (01242) 570280

Home Cottage ♦♦♦
1 Priors Road, Cheltenham, Gloucestershire GL52 5AB
T: (01242) 518144

Ivydene Guest House ◆◆◆
145 Hewlett Road, Cheltenham,
Gloucestershire GL52 6TS
T: (01242) 521726 & 525694
E: jvhopwood@ivydenehouse.
freeserve.co.uk

Lawn Hotel ◆◆◆
5 Pittville Lawn, Cheltenham,
Gloucestershire GL52 2BE
T: (01242) 526638
F: (01242) 526638

Lawn House ◆◆◆◆
11 London Road, Cheltenham,
Gloucestershire GL52 6EX
T: (01242) 578486 &
07768 457403
F: (01242) 578486

Leeswood ◆◆
14 Montpellier Drive,
Cheltenham, Gloucestershire
GL50 1TX
T: (01242) 524813
F: (01242) 524813
E: leeswood@hotmail.com

Lonsdale House ◆◆◆
Montpellier Drive, Cheltenham,
Gloucestershire GL50 1TX
T: (01242) 232379
F: (01242) 232379
E: lonsdalehouse@hotmail.com

Milton House
◆◆◆◆◆ GOLD AWARD
12 Bayshill Rod, Royal Parade,
Cheltenham, Gloucestershire
GL50 3AY
T: (01242) 582601
F: (01242) 222326
E: info@miltonhousehotel.co.uk
I: www.miltonhousehotel.co.uk

Montpellier Hotel ◆◆◆
33 Montpellier Terrace,
Cheltenham, Gloucestershire
GL50 1UX
T: (01242) 526009

Number 91 ◆◆◆◆
91 Montpellier Terrace,
Cheltenham, Gloucestershire
GL50 1XA
T: (01242) 579441
F: (01242) 579441

Old Rectory ◆◆◆
Woolstone, Cheltenham,
Gloucestershire GL52 4RG
T: (01242) 673766
E: fesey@aol.com
I: www.theoldrectory.com

Parkview ◆◆◆
4 Pittville Crescent, Cheltenham,
Gloucestershire GL52 2QZ
T: (01242) 575567
E: jospa@tr250.freeserve.co.uk

Pittville Gate Hotel ◆◆◆
12/14 Pittville Lawn,
Cheltenham, Gloucestershire
GL52 2BD
T: (01242) 221922
F: (01242) 244687

Saint Cloud ◆◆◆
97 Leckhampton Road,
Cheltenham, Gloucestershire
GL53 0BZ
T: (01242) 575245

St Michaels ◆◆◆◆
4 Montpellier Drive,
Cheltenham, Gloucestershire
GL50 1TX
T: (01242) 513587
F: (01242) 513587
E: st_michaels_guesthouse@
yahoo.com
I: st_michaels.future.easyspace.
com

Segrave ◆◆◆
7 Park Place, Cheltenham,
Gloucestershire GL50 2QS
T: (01242) 523606

**Steyne Cross Bed and
Breakfast** ◆◆◆
Steyne Cross, Malvern Road,
Cheltenham, Gloucestershire
GL50 2NU
T: (01242) 255289
F: (01242) 255289
E: sumiko@susumago.f9.co.uk

Stray Leaves ◆◆◆
282 Gloucester Road,
Cheltenham, Gloucestershire
GL51 7AG
T: (01242) 572303
F: (01242) 708382

Stretton Lodge Hotel ◆◆◆◆
Western Road, Cheltenham,
Gloucestershire GL50 3RN
T: (01242) 570771
F: (01242) 528724
E: info@strettonlodge.demon.
co.uk
I: www.strettonlodge.demon.co.
uk

Westcourt ◆◆◆◆
14 Old Bath Road, Cheltenham,
Gloucestershire GL53 7QD
T: (01242) 241777 & 228555
F: (01242) 228666
E: michael.seston@which.net

Whittington Lodge Farm
◆◆◆◆
Whittington, Cheltenham,
Gloucestershire GL54 4HB
T: (01242) 820603 &
07976 691589
F: (01242) 820603

Wishmoor Guest House
◆◆◆◆ SILVER AWARD
147 Hales Road, Cheltenham,
Gloucestershire GL52 6TD
T: (01242) 238504
F: (01242) 226090

The Wynyards ◆◆◆◆
Butts Lane, Woodmancote,
Cheltenham, Gloucestershire
GL52 4QH
T: (01242) 673876
E: graham@wynyards1.
freeserve.co.uk
I: www.SmoothHound.co.
uk/hotels/wynyards.html

Abigails ◆◆◆
62 Brockwell Lane, Chesterfield,
Derbyshire S40 4EE
T: (01246) 279391 &
07970 777909
E: gail@abigails.fsnet.co.uk

Anis Louise Guesthouse ◆◆◆
34 Clarence Road, Chesterfield,
Derbyshire S40 1LN
T: (01246) 235412
E: neil@anislouise.freeserve.co.
uk
I: www.anislouise.co.uk

Batemans Mill Hotel
◆◆◆◆ SILVER AWARD
Mill Lane, Old Tupton,
Chesterfield, Derbyshire S42 6AE
T: (01246) 862296
F: (01246) 865672

Brook House
◆◆◆◆ SILVER AWARD
45 Westbrook Drive, Brookside,
Chesterfield, Derbyshire
S4D 3PQ
T: (01246) 568535

Clarendon Guesthouse ◆◆
32 Clarence Road, West Bars,
Chesterfield, Derbyshire S40 1LN
T: (01246) 235004

Fairfield House ◆◆◆
3 Fairfield Road, Chesterfield,
Derbyshire S40 4TR
T: (01246) 204905
F: (01246) 230155

Little Lonsdale Guesthouse
◆◆
187 Ashgate Road, Chesterfield,
Derbyshire S40 4AP
T: (01246) 272950
F: (01246) 271062

Locksley ◆◆
21 Tennyson Avenue,
Chesterfield, Derbyshire S40 4SN
T: (01246) 273332

The Maylands ◆◆◆
56 Sheffield Road, Chesterfield,
Derbyshire S41 7LS
T: (01246) 233602

Shakespeare Villa ◆◆◆
3 Saint Margarets Drive,
Saltergate, Chesterfield,
Derbyshire S40 4SY
T: (01246) 200704

Springbank Guesthouse ◆
35 Springbank Road,
Chesterfield, Derbyshire S40 1NL
T: (01246) 279232

Mossley House Farm ◆◆◆
Maynestone Road, Chinley, High
Peak SK23 6AH
T: (01663) 750240
F: (01663) 750240

Badgers Hall Tearooms
◆◆◆◆ SILVER AWARD
High Street, Chipping Campden,
Gloucestershire GL55 6HB
T: (01386) 840839
E: badgershall@talk21.com
I: www.stratford.upon.avon.co.
uk/badgershall.htm

Brymbo ◆◆◆◆
Honeybourne Lane, Mickleton,
Chipping Campden,
Gloucestershire GL55 6PU
T: (01386) 438890
F: (01386) 438113
E: enquries@brymbo.com

Dragon House ◆◆◆◆
High Street, Chipping Campden,
Gloucestershire GL55 6AG
T: (01386) 840734
F: (01386) 840734

The Eight Bells ◆◆◆
Church Street, Chipping
Campden, Gloucestershire
GL55 6JG
T: (01386) 840371
F: (01386) 841669

The Kettle House ◆◆◆
Leysbourne, Chipping Campden,
Gloucestershire GL55 6HN
T: (01386) 840328
F: (01386) 841740
E: info@kettlehouse.co.uk
I: www.kettlehouse.co.uk

Lower High Street
Rating Applied For
Chipping Campden,
Gloucestershire GL55 6DZ
T: (01386) 840163

Manor Farm ◆◆◆◆
Weston Subedge, Chipping
Campden, Gloucestershire
GL55 6QH
T: (01386) 840390 &
07889 108812
F: 08701 640 638
E: lucy@manorfarmbnb.demon.
co.uk
I: www.manorfarmbnb.demon.
co.uk

M'Dina Courtyard
◆◆◆◆ SILVER AWARD
Park Road, Chipping Campden,
Gloucestershire GL55 6EA
T: (01386) 841752
F: (01386) 840942
E: chilver@globalnet.co.uk

Nineveh Farm House ◆◆◆◆
Campden Road, Mickleton,
Chipping Campden,
Gloucestershire GL55 6PS
T: (01386) 438923 &
07880 737649
E: nineveh@easicom.com
I: www.stratford-upon-avon.co.
uk/nineveh.htm

Sandalwood House ◆◆◆◆
Back-Ends, Chipping Campden,
Gloucestershire GL55 6AU
T: (01386) 840091
F: (01386) 840091

Weston Park Farm ◆◆◆
Dovers Hill, Chipping Campden,
Gloucestershire GL55 6UW
T: (01386) 840835

Wyldlands ◆◆◆◆
Broad Campden, Chipping
Campden, Gloucestershire
GL55 6UR
T: (01386) 840478
F: (01386) 840931

Windrush House ◆◆◆
Hillersland Lane, Christchurch,
Coleford, Gloucestershire
GL16 7NU
T: (01594) 810350

Slab Bridge Cottage ◆◆◆
Little Onn, Church Eaton,
Stafford, Staffordshire ST20 0AY
T: (01785) 840220
F: (01785) 840220

CHURCH STRETTON
Shropshire

Acton Scott Farm ♦♦♦
Acton Scott, Church Stretton,
Shropshire SY6 6QN
T: (01694) 781260
E: edandm@clara.co.uk
I: www.SmoothHound.co.
uk/hotels/actonscot.html
⊚

Belvedere Guest House ♦♦♦♦
Burway Road, Church Stretton,
Shropshire SY6 6DP
T: (01694) 722232
F: (01694) 722232
E: BELV@BIGFOOT.COM
⊚

Brook House Farm ♦♦♦
Wall-under-Heywood, Church
Stretton, Shropshire SY6 7DS
T: (01694) 771308

Brookfields Guesthouse ♦♦♦
Watling St. North, Church
Stretton, Shropshire SY6 7AR
T: (01694) 722314

The Coates ♦♦
Rushbury, Church Stretton,
Shropshire SY6 7DZ
T: (01694) 771330
F: (01694) 771330

Gilberries Cottage ♦♦♦♦
Wall-under-Heywood, Church
Stretton, Shropshire SY6 7HZ
T: (01694) 771400
F: (01694) 771663

Gilberries Hall Farm ♦♦♦♦
Gilberries Lane, Wall-under-
Heywood, Church Stretton,
Shropshire SY6 7HZ
T: (01694) 771253
⚘

Grove Farm ♦♦
Cardington, Church Stretton,
Shropshire SY6 7JZ
T: (01694) 771451

Highcliffe ♦♦
Madeira Walk, Church Stretton,
Shropshire SY6 6JQ
T: (01694) 722908

Jinlye ♦♦♦♦♦ GOLD AWARD
Castle Hill, All Stretton, Church
Stretton, Shropshire SY6 6JP
T: (01694) 723243
F: (01694) 723243
E: info@jinlye.co.uk
I: www.jinlye.co.uk
⚘

Juniper Cottage ♦♦♦♦
All Stretton, Church Stretton,
Shropshire SY6 6HG
T: (01694) 723427
F: (01694) 723427

Lawley House ♦♦♦♦
Smethcott, Church Stretton,
Shropshire SY6 6NX
T: (01694) 751236 & 751396
F: (01694) 751396
E: lawleyhouse@easicom.com

The Old Rectory ♦♦♦
Burway Road, Church Stretton,
Shropshire SY6 6DW
T: (01694) 724462
F: (01694) 724799

Rheingold ♦♦
9 The Bridleways, Church
Stretton, Shropshire SY6 7AN
T: (01694) 723969

Sayang House ♦♦♦♦
Hope Bowdler, Church Stretton,
Shropshire SY6 7DD
T: (01694) 723981
E: madegan@aol.com
I: www.sayanghouse.co.uk

Travellers Rest Inn ♦♦♦
Upper Affcot, Church Stretton,
Shropshire SY6 6RL
T: (01694) 781275
F: (01694) 781555
E: reception@travellersrestinn.
co.uk
I: www.travellersrestinn.co.uk

**Willowfield Country
Guesthouse
♦♦♦♦♦ GOLD AWARD**
Lower Wood, All Stretton,
Church Stretton, Shropshire
SY6 6LF
T: (01694) 751471
F: (01694) 751471
I: www.willowfieldguesthouse.
co.uk

Woolston Farm ♦♦♦
Church Stretton, Shropshire
SY6 6QD
T: (01694) 781201
F: (01694) 781201

CHURCHAM
Gloucestershire

Woodgreen Farm ♦♦♦♦
Bulley, Churcham, Gloucester
GL2 8BJ
T: (01452) 790292

CHURCHDOWN
Gloucestershire

Sherwood House ♦♦♦♦
Green Lane, Churchdown,
Gloucester GL3 2LA
T: (01452) 855652

CINDERFORD
Gloucestershire

**Latimer Bungalow
Rating Applied For**
Littledean Hill Road, Cinderford,
Gloucestershire GL14 2BT
T: (01594) 822065

CIRENCESTER
Gloucestershire

Abbeymead ♦♦♦
39a Victoria Road, Cirencester,
Gloucestershire GL7 1ES
T: (01285) 653740
F: (01285) 720770

Apsley Villa ♦♦♦
16 Victoria Road, Cirencester,
Gloucestershire GL7 1ES
T: (01285) 653489

The Black Horse ♦♦
17 Castle Street, Cirencester,
Gloucestershire GL7 1QD
T: (01285) 653187
F: (01285) 659772

Brooklands Farm ♦♦
Ewen, Cirencester,
Gloucestershire GL7 6BU
T: (01285) 770487
I: www.glosfarmhols.co.uk

The Bungalow ♦♦♦
93 Victoria Road, Cirencester,
Gloucestershire GL7 1ES
T: (01285) 654179 &
07778 985975
F: (01285) 656159
E: CBEARD7@compuserve.com

Catherine Wheel ♦♦♦
Arlington Bibury, Cirencester,
Gloucestershire GL7 5ND
T: (01285) 740250
F: (01285) 740779
⊚

Chesil Rocks ♦♦♦
Baunton Lane, Stratton,
Cirencester, Gloucestershire
GL7 2LL
T: (01285) 655031

**Claremont Villa Bed and
Breakfast ♦♦♦**
131 Cheltenham Road, Stratton,
Cirencester, Gloucestershire
GL7 2JF
T: (01285) 654759

**Coleen Bed and Breakfast
♦♦♦♦**
Ashton Road, Siddington,
Cirencester, Gloucestershire
GL7 6HR
T: (01285) 642203
E: bookings@coleen.co.uk or
josephine@coleen.co.uk
I: www.coleen.co.uk

Coltsmoor Farm ♦♦♦♦
Coln St Aldwyns, Cirencester,
Gloucestershire GL7 5AX
T: (01285) 750527
F: (01285) 750246

**Eliot Arms Hotel Free House
♦♦♦♦**
Clarks Hay, South Cerney,
Cirencester, Gloucestershire
GL7 5UA
T: (01285) 860215
F: (01285) 861121
E: eliotarm.aol.uk

**11 Gosditch Street
Rating Applied For**
Cirencester, Gloucestershire
GL7 2AG
T: (01285) 640808
F: (01285) 640808
E: andrew_moore_ward@
compuserve.com

Hunters New House ♦♦♦♦♦
Cherry Tree Lane, Cirencester,
Gloucestershire GL7 5DT
T: (01285) 640790 &
07974 387385
F: (01285) 652275

The Ivy House ♦♦♦
2 Victoria Road, Cirencester,
Gloucestershire GL7 1EN
T: (01285) 656626

Landage House ♦♦♦
Rendcomb, Cirencester,
Gloucestershire GL7 7HB
T: (01285) 831250

The Leauses ♦♦♦
101 Victoria Road, Cirencester,
Gloucestershire GL7 1EU
T: (01285) 653643

Manby's Farm ♦♦♦♦
Oaksey, Malmesbury, Wiltshire
SN16 9SA
T: (01666) 577399 & 577241
F: (01666) 577241
E: DJHackle@compuserve.com

The Masons Arms ♦♦♦
High Street, Meysey Hampton,
Cirencester, Gloucestershire
GL7 5JT
T: (01285) 850164
F: (01285) 850164
E: jane@themasonarms.
freeserve.co.uk

Millstone ♦♦♦♦
Down Ampney, Cirencester,
Gloucestershire GL7 5QR
T: (01793) 750475

The Old Rectory ♦♦♦♦
Rodmarton, Cirencester,
Gloucestershire GL7 6PE
T: (01285) 841246 &
07970 434302
F: (01285) 841488
E: jfitz@globalnet.co.uk

Raydon House Hotel ♦♦♦
3 The Avenue, Cirencester,
Gloucestershire GL7 1EH
T: (01285) 653485
F: (01285) 653485

**Smerrill Barns
♦♦♦♦ SILVER AWARD**
Kemble, Cirencester,
Gloucestershire GL7 6BW
T: (01285) 770907
F: (01285) 770706
E: gsopher@smerrillbarns.com
I: www.smerrillbarns.com

Sunset ♦♦♦
Baunton Lane, Cirencester,
Gloucestershire GL7 2NQ
T: (01285) 654822

The White Lion Inn ♦♦
8 Gloucester Street, Cirencester,
Gloucestershire GL7 2DU
T: (01285) 654053
F: (01285) 641316
E: roylion@aol.com.
I: MEMBERS.AOL.COM/ROYLION

Willows ♦♦♦
2 Glebe Lane, Kemble,
Cirencester, Gloucestershire
GL7 6BD
T: (01285) 770667

**Windrush
Rating Applied For**
The Whiteway, Baunton,
Cirencester, Gloucestershire
GL7 7BA
T: (01285) 655942
F: (01285) 655942

CLAVERDON
Warwickshire

Oaktree Farm ♦♦♦♦
Buttermilk Lane, Yarningale
Common, Claverdon, Warwick
CV35 8HP
T: (01926) 842413
F: (01926) 842413

CLEEVE HILL
Gloucestershire

Malvern View ♦♦♦
Cleeve Hill, Cheltenham,
Gloucestershire GL52 3PR
T: (01242) 672017
F: (01242) 676207

CLEOBURY MORTIMER
Shropshire

Clod Hall ♦♦
Milson, Kidderminster,
Worcestershire DY14 0BJ
T: (01584) 781421

Cox's Barn ◆◆◆◆
Bagginswood, Cleobury
Mortimer, Kidderminster,
Worcestershire DY14 8LS
T: (01746) 718415 & 718277

The Old Bake House ◆◆◆◆
46/47 High Street, Cleobury
Mortimer, Kidderminster,
Worcestershire DY14 8DQ
T: (01299) 270193
⊛

The Old Cider House ◆◆◆◆
1 Lion Lane, Cleobury Mortimer,
Kidderminster, Worcestershire
DY14 8BT
T: (01299) 270304
F: (01299) 270304

Woodview ◆◆◆◆
Mawley Oak, Cleobury Mortimer,
Kidderminster, Worcestershire
DY14 9BA
T: (01299) 271422

CLIFFORD
Herefordshire

Cottage Farm ◆◆◆
Middlewood, Clifford, Hereford,
Herefordshire HR3 5SX
T: (01497) 831496
F: (01497) 831496

CLIFFORDS MESNE
Gloucestershire

The Yew Tree Inn ◆◆◆
Mayhill, Cliffords Mesne,
Newent, Gloucestershire
GL18 1JS
T: (01531) 820719

CLIFTON
Derbyshire

Stone Cottage ◆◆◆
Green Lane, Clifton, Ashbourne,
Derbyshire DE6 2BL
T: (01335) 343377
F: (01335) 343117
E: info@stone-cottage.fsnet.co.
uk
I: www.stone-cottage.fsnet.co.
uk

CLUN
Shropshire

Cockford Hall
◆◆◆◆◆ GOLD AWARD
Cockford Bank, Clun, Craven
Arms, Shropshire SY7 8LR
T: (01588) 640327
F: (01588) 640881
E: cockford.hall@virgin.net
I: www.go2.co.uk/cockfordhall

Crown House ◆◆◆◆
Church Street, Clun, Craven
Arms, Shropshire SY7 8JW
T: (01588) 640780

Hill House Farm ◆
Church Bank, Clun, Craven Arms,
Shropshire SY7 8LP
T: (01588) 640325 & 640729

Hurst Mill Farm ◆◆◆
Clun, Craven Arms, Shropshire
SY7 0JA
T: (01588) 640224

Llanhedric Farm ◆◆◆
Clun, Craven Arms, Shropshire
SY7 8NG
T: (01588) 640203
F: (01588) 640203
⊛

New House Farm
◆◆◆◆◆ GOLD AWARD
Clun, Shropshire SY7 8NJ
T: (01588) 638314

The Old Farmhouse ◆◆◆
Woodside, Clun, Craven Arms,
Shropshire SY7 0JB
T: (01588) 640695

Springhill Farm ◆◆◆
Clun, Craven Arms, Shropshire
SY7 8PE
T: (01588) 640337
F: (01588) 640337

The Sun Inn ◆◆
High Street, Clun, Craven Arms,
Shropshire SY7 8JB
T: (01588) 640277 & 640559

CLUNGUNFORD
Shropshire

Knock Hundred Cottage
◆◆◆◆ GOLD AWARD
Abcott, Clungunford, Craven
Arms, Shropshire SY7 0PX
T: (01588) 660594
F: (01588) 660594

COALBROOKDALE
Shropshire

The Grove Inn ◆◆◆
10 Wellington Road,
Coalbrookdale, Telford,
Shropshire TF8 7DX
T: (01952) 433269 & 432240
F: (01952) 433269
E: frogat@fat-frog.co.uk
I: www.fat-frog.co.uk

The Lodge ◆◆◆
Sunniside, Coalbrookdale,
Telford, Shropshire TF8 7EX
T: (01952) 432423
E: thelodge.cbds.fsnet.co.uk

The Old Vicarage ◆◆◆◆
Church Road, Coalbrookdale,
Telford, Shropshire TF11 8DT
T: (01952) 432525 &
07831 348343
F: (01952) 433169
E: theoldvicarage@tf87nt.
freeserve.co.uk

COALEY
Gloucestershire

Silver Street Farmhouse
◆◆◆◆
Silver Street, Coaley, Dursley,
Gloucestershire GL11 5AX
T: (01453) 860514

COALPORT
Shropshire

Thorpe House ◆◆◆
High Street, Coalport, Telford,
Shropshire TF8 7HP
T: (01952) 586789
F: (01952) 586789

COALVILLE
Leicestershire

Applegate Frame Cottages
◆◆◆
4 Parsonwood Hill, Whitwick,
Coalville, Leicester LE67 5AT
T: (01530) 812260 &
07970 161905
F: (01530) 812260

Broadlawns ◆◆◆
98 London Road, Coalville,
Leicester LE67 3JD
T: (01530) 836724 &
07702 056586

COLD ASTON
Gloucestershire

Bangup Cottage ◆◆◆
Bangup Lane, Cold Aston,
Cheltenham, Gloucestershire
GL54 3BQ
T: (01451) 810127

COLEFORD
Gloucestershire

Allary House ◆◆◆
14 Boxbush Road, Coleford,
Gloucestershire GL16 8DN
T: (01594) 835206
F: (01594) 835206

Forest House Hotel ◆◆
Cinder Hill, Coleford,
Gloucestershire GL16 8HQ
T: (01594) 832424

Graygill ◆◆◆
Duke of York Road, Staunton,
Coleford, Gloucestershire
GL16 8PD
T: (01600) 712536

Lower Perrygrove Farm ◆◆◆◆
Coleford, Gloucestershire
GL16 8QB
T: (01594) 833187

Meadow Cottage ◆◆◆
59 Coalway Road, Coleford,
Gloucestershire GL16 7HL
T: (01594) 833444
F: (01594) 833444

Millend House and Garden
◆◆◆◆
Newland, Coleford,
Gloucestershire GL16 8NF
T: (01594) 832128
F: (01594) 832128
E: APRILJOHNT

Oak Farm ◆◆◆
Ross Road, English Bicknor,
Coleford, Gloucestershire
GL16 7PA
T: (01594) 860606

Perouges ◆◆◆
31 Newland Street, Coleford,
Gloucestershire GL16 8AJ
T: (01594) 834287

Symonds Yat Rock Lodge ◆◆◆
Hillersland, Coleford,
Gloucestershire GL16 7NY
T: (01594) 836191

COLEORTON
Leicestershire

Zion Cottage ◆◆◆
93 Zion Hill, Peggs Green,
Coleorton, Leicester,
Leicestershire LE67 8JP
T: (01530) 223914 &
07973 422668
F: (01530) 222483
E: zionbnb@aol.com

COLESHILL
Warwickshire

The Old Rectory ◆◆◆◆
Church Lane, Maxstoke,
Coleshill, Birmingham B46 2QW
T: (01675) 462248
F: (01675) 481615

Packington Lane Farm ◆◆◆◆
Packington Lane, Coleshill,
Birmingham B46 3JJ
T: (01675) 462228
F: (01675) 462228

COLLINGHAM
Nottinghamshire

Lime Tree Farm ◆◆◆◆
Lunn Lane, Collingham, Newark,
Nottinghamshire NG23 7LP
T: (01636) 892044 &
07976 902814

COLSTERWORTH
Lincolnshire

The Stables ◆◆◆◆
Stainby Road, Colsterworth,
Grantham, Lincolnshire
NG33 5JB
T: (01476) 861057

COLWALL
Worcestershire

Brook House
◆◆◆◆◆ SILVER AWARD
Walwyn Road, Colwall, Malvern,
Worcestershire WR13 6PZ
T: (01684) 540604 &
07803 061023
F: (01684) 540604

COLWALL GREEN
Worcestershire

Oakley House ◆◆◆
Colwall Green, Malvern,
Worcestershire WR13 6DX
T: (01684) 540215

CONINGSBY
Lincolnshire

The Lea Gate Inn ◆◆◆◆
Leagate Road, Coningsby,
Lincoln LN4 4RS
T: (01526) 342370
F: (01526) 345468
E: markdennison4@virgin.net
I: www.theleagateinn.co.uk

White Bull Inn ◆
55 High Street, Coningsby,
Lincoln LN4 4RB
T: (01526) 342439
E: ANN-GORDON@SKYNOW.
NET
I: WWW.THEWHITEBULL.
freeserve.co.uk

CONISHOLME
Lincolnshire

Wickham House ◆◆◆◆◆
Church Lane, Conisholme, Louth,
Lincolnshire LN11 7LX
T: (01507) 358465
F: (01507) 358465

CORBY GLEN
Lincolnshire

Stonepit Farmhouse ◆◆◆◆
Swinstead Road, Corby Glen,
Grantham, Lincolnshire
NG33 4NG
T: (01476) 550614
F: (01476) 550614
E: beds@stonepit.u-net.com

The Woodhouse Inn ◆◆◆◆
2 Bourne Road, Corby Glen,
Grantham, Lincolnshire
NG33 4NS
T: (01476) 550316 & 550006
F: (01476) 550096
E: papajay@btinternet.com
⊛

CORELEY
Shropshire

Brookfield House ◆◆◆◆
Coreley, Ludlow, Shropshire
SY8 3AS
T: (01584) 890059

COTGRAVE
Nottinghamshire

Heronbrook ◆◆◆◆
Peashill Lane, Cotgrave,
Nottingham NG12 3HD
T: (0115) 9899285

Jerico Farm ◆◆◆◆
Fosse Way, Cotgrave,
Nottingham NG12 3HG
T: (01949) 81733
F: (01949) 81733
E: herrick@jerico.swinternet.co.uk
⊛

COTON IN THE ELMS
Staffordshire

Hill Rise ◆◆◆◆
42 Church Street, Coton in the
Elms, Derbyshire DE12 8EZ
T: (01283) 761405

COUGHTON
Herefordshire

Coughton House ◆◆◆◆
Coughton, Ross-on-Wye,
Herefordshire HR9 5SF
T: (01989) 562612 & 567322
F: (01989) 567322

COVENTRY
West Midlands

Abigail Guesthouse ◆◆◆
39 St. Patrick's Road, Coventry,
West Midlands CV1 2LP
T: (024) 7622 1378

Aburley ◆◆◆
23 St Patricks Road,
Cheylesmore, Coventry, CV1 2LP
T: (024) 76251348 &
07957 925596
F: (024) 76251348

Acacia Guest House ◆◆◆◆
11 Park Road, Coventry,
Warwickshire CV1 2LE
T: (02476) 633622 &
07970 966016
F: (02476) 221808

Albany Guest House ◆◆◆
121 Holyhead Road, Coundon,
Coventry, CV1 3AD
T: (024) 7622 3601
F: (024) 7622 3601

Arlon Guest House ◆◆◆
25 St Patricks Road, Coventry,
CV1 2LP
T: (024) 7622 5942

Ashdowns Guest House ◆◆◆
12 Regent Street, Earlsdon,
Coventry, CV1 3EP
T: (024) 7622 9280

Ashleigh House ◆◆◆
17 Park Road, Coventry, CV1 2LH
T: (024) 7622 3804

Brookfields ◆◆◆◆
134 Butt Lane, Allesley,
Coventry, CV5 9FE
T: (024) 7640 4866
F: (024) 7640 2022
F: brookfieldscoventry@
easicom.com

Chester House ◆◆◆
Rating Applied For
3 Chester Street, Coventry,
CV1 4DH
T: (024) 7622 3857

Crest Guest House
◆◆◆◆ SILVER AWARD
39 Friars Road, Coventry,
CV1 2LJ
T: (024) 7622 7822
F: (024) 7622 7244
E: AlanHarve@aol.com
I: www.SmoothHound.co.uk/hotels/crestgue.html

Croft Hotel ◆◆◆
23 Stoke Green, Coventry,
CV3 1FP
T: (024) 7645 7846
F: (024) 7645 7846

Fairlight Guest House ◆◆◆
14 Regent Street, Off Queen's
Road, Coventry, CV1 3EP
T: (024) 7622 4215

Falcon Hotel ◆◆◆
13-19 Manor Road, Coventry,
CV1 2LH
T: (024) 7625 8615
F: (024) 7652 0680
E: falcon.hotel@talk21.co.uk

Hearsall Lodge Hotel
Rating Applied For
1 Broad Lane, Coventry,
CV5 7AA
T: (024) 7667 4543

Highcroft Guest House ◆◆◆
65 Barras Lane, Coundon,
Coventry, CV1 4AQ
T: (02476) 7622 8157
F: (02476) 7663 1609

**Lodge Farm House Bed and
Breakfast** ◆◆◆◆
Westwood Heath Road,
Coventry, CV4 8AA
T: (024) 7646 6786
F: (024) 7646 6786
E: davidjohnhall@msn.com

Mill Farmhouse ◆◆◆◆
Mill Lane, Fillongley, Coventry
CV7 8EE
T: (01676) 541898
F: (01676) 541898

Mount Guest House ◆◆◆
9 Coundon Road, Coventry,
CV1 4AR
T: (024) 7622 5998 &
07703 218238
F: (024) 7622 5998

Northanger House ◆◆
35 Westminster Road, Coventry,
CV1 3GB
T: (024) 7622 6780
F: (024) 7622 6780

St Mary's Cottage ◆◆◆
107 Kingsbury Road, Coventry,
CV6 1PT
T: (024) 7659 1557
F: (024) 7659 1557
E: afoster543@aol.com

Spire View Guest House
◆◆◆◆
36 Park Road(Near Railway
Station), Coventry, CV1 2LD
T: (024) 7625 1602
E: j-m@spireviewcov.freeserve.co.uk

Vardre ◆◆
68 Spencer Avenue, Earlsdon,
Coventry, CV5 6NP
T: (024) 7671 5154
F: (024) 76715748
E: valvardre@aol.com
I: www.s-h.systems.co.uk

Westwood Cottage ◆◆◆
79 Westwood Heath Road,
Westwood Heath, Coventry,
CV4 8GN
T: (024) 7647 1084
F: (024) 7647 1084
⊛

COWLEY
Gloucestershire

Butlers Hill Farm ◆◆◆
Cockleford, Cowley, Cheltenham,
Gloucestershire GL53 9NW
T: (01242) 870455

The Green Dragon Inn ◆◆◆◆
Cockleford, Cowley, Cheltenham,
Gloucestershire GL53 9NW
T: (01242) 870271
F: (01242) 870171

CRADLEY
Worcestershire

Hollings Hill Farm
Rating Applied For
Bosbury Road, Cradley, Malvern,
Worcestershire WR13 5LY
T: (01886) 880203 &
07966 184278
E: ajgkhollingshill@
farmersweekly.net

CRANWELL
Lincolnshire

Byards Leap Cottage ◆◆
Cranwell, Sleaford, Lincolnshire
NG34 8EY
T: (01400) 261537 & 272779
F: (01400) 261537
⊛

CRAVEN ARMS
Shropshire

Blacksmith's Cottage ◆◆◆◆
Rating Applied For
9 Lower Corfton, Craven Arms,
Shropshire SY7 9LD
T: (01584) 861 241
F: (01584) 861 241
E: Beryl@corfton.freeserve.co.uk

Castle View
◆◆◆◆ SILVER AWARD
148 Stokesay, Craven Arms,
Shropshire SY7 9AL
T: (01588) 673712

Earnstrey Hill House ◆◆◆◆
Rating Applied For
Abdon, Craven Arms, Shropshire
SY7 9HU
T: (01746) 712579
F: (01746) 712631
E: hugh.scurfield@smwh.org.uk

The Firs ◆◆◆◆
Norton, Craven Arms, Shropshire
SY7 9LS
T: (01588) 672511 &
07977 697903
F: (01588) 672511
I: www.go2.co.uk/firs

Glebelands ◆◆◆
25 Kington Road, Clun, Craven
Arms, Shropshire SY7 8JH
T: (01588) 640442
F: (01588) 640442
E: Tourism@clun25.freeserve.co.uk
I: www.clun25.freeserve.co.uk

Groveside ◆◆◆
Shrewsbury Road, Craven Arms,
Shropshire SY7 8BX
T: (01588) 672948
⊛

Hill View ◆◆◆
Clun Road, Craven Arms,
Shropshire SY7 9QW
T: (01588) 672619
E: topazw@aol.com

Strefford Hall ◆◆◆◆
Strefford, Craven Arms,
Shropshire SY7 8DE
T: (01588) 672383
F: (01588) 672383

CRESSBROOK
Derbyshire

Cressbrook Hall ◆◆◆◆
Cressbrook, Buxton, Derbyshire
SK17 8SY
T: (01298) 871289 &
0800 3583003
F: (01298) 871845
E: stay@cressbrookhall.co.uk
I: www.cressbrookhall.co.uk
⊛ ⬱

The Old Toll House ◆◆◆◆
Cressbrook, Buxton, Derbyshire
SK17 8SY
T: (01298) 872547

CRICH
Derbyshire

Avista B&B at Penrose
◆◆◆◆ SILVER AWARD
Penrose, Sandy Lane, Crich,
Derbyshire DE4 5DE
T: (01773) 852625 &
07889 297608
E: keith@avista.freeserve.co.uk
I: www.s-h-systems.co.uk/hotels/avista.html

Clovelly ◆◆◆
Roe's Lane, Crich, Matlock,
Derbyshire DE4 5DH
T: (01773) 852295 &
07932 694025

Mount Tabor House ◆◆◆◆
Bowns Hill, Crich, Matlock,
Derbyshire DE4 5DG
T: (01773) 857008 &
07768 438890
F: (01773) 852040
E: mountabor@email.msn.com
⊛

Upper Rosskeen Guesthouse
◆◆◆
Surgery Lane, Crich, Matlock,
Derbyshire DE4 5BP
T: (01773) 857186
E: elaine@stay-crich.co.uk
I: www.stay-crich.co.uk

CROWLAND
Lincolnshire

Abbey Hotel ◆◆◆
21 East Street, Crowland,
Peterborough PE6 0EN
T: (01733) 210200
F: (01733) 210938
E: AbbeyHotel@hotmail.com
I: www.peterborough-net/abbeyhotel/

CROXDEN
Staffordshire

Farriers Cottage and Mews
◆◆◆◆
Woodhouse Farm, Nabb Lane,
Croxden, Uttoxeter,
Staffordshire ST14 5JB
T: (01889) 507507
F: (01889) 507282
E: ddeb@lineone.net
I: www.alton-towers.glo.uk
⬱
◆◆◆◆

CUBBINGTON
Warwickshire

Bakers Cottage ◆◆◆◆
52/54 Queen Street, Cubbington,
Leamington Spa, Warwickshire
CV32 7NA
T: (01926) 772146

**Staddlestones Bed and
Breakfast** ◆◆◆
67 Rugby Road, Cubbington,
Leamington Spa, Warwickshire
CV32 7HY
T: (01926) 336 958

CULWORTH
Northamptonshire

Ivy Cottage ◆◆◆
Sulgrave Road, Culworth,
Banbury, Oxfordshire OX17 2AP
T: (01295) 768131
F: (01295) 768131

CURBAR
Derbyshire

Bridgend ◆◆◆
Rating Applied For
Dukes Drive, Curbar, Calver,
Hope Valley S32 3YP
T: (01433) 630226

CUTTHORPE
Derbyshire

Cow Close Farm ◆◆◆
Overgreen, Cutthorpe,
Chesterfield, Derbyshire S42 7BA
T: (01246) 232055

DAGLINGWORTH
Gloucestershire

Windrush Cottage ◆◆◆
Itlay, Daglingworth, Cirencester,
Gloucestershire GL7 7HZ
T: (01285) 652917

DARLEY ABBEY
Derbyshire

The Coach House ◆◆◆
185A Duffield Road, Darley
Abbey, Derby DE22 1JB
T: (01332) 551795

DARLEY BRIDGE
Derbyshire

Square and Compass ◆◆◆◆
Station Road, Darley Bridge,
Matlock, Derbyshire DE4 2EQ
T: (01629) 733255

DAVENTRY
Northamptonshire

Drayton Lodge ◆◆◆
Staverton Road, Daventry,
Northamptonshire NN11 4NL
T: (01327) 702449 & 876365
F: (01327) 872110
E: annspicer@farming.co.uk

Kingsthorpe Guesthouse
Rating Applied For
18 Badby Road, Daventry,
Northamptonshire NN11 4AW
T: (01327) 702752
F: (01327) 301854

Threeways House
◆◆◆◆ SILVER AWARD
Everdon, Daventry,
Northamptonshire NN11 6BL
T: (01327) 361631 &
07774 428242
F: (01327) 361359

DEFFORD
Worcestershire

**Brook Cottages Bed &
Breakfast** ◆◆◆
Upton Road, Defford, Pershore,
Worcestershire WR8 9BA
T: (01386) 750229 &
07768 384761
F: (01386) 750229
E: brook_cottages@tesco.net
I: www.homepages.tesco.
net/&brook_cottages

DENSTONE
Staffordshire

Denstone Hall Farm ◆◆◆
Denstone, Uttoxeter,
Staffordshire ST14 5HF
T: (01889) 590253 &
07970 808151
F: (01889) 590930
E: denstonehallfarm@talk21.
com

Manor House Farm ◆◆◆◆
Prestwood, Denstone, Uttoxeter,
Staffordshire ST14 5DD
T: (01889) 590415 &
07976 767629
F: (01335) 342198
E: cm_ball@yahoo.co.uk
I: towers.above.the.rest.com

Rowan Lodge ◆◆◆◆
Stubwood, Denstone, Uttoxeter,
Staffordshire ST14 5HU
T: (01889) 590913

DERBY
Derbyshire

Alambie ◆◆◆
189 Main Road, Morley, Derby,
Derbyshire DE7 6DG
T: (01332) 780349 &
0780 3636130
F: (01332) 780349
E: alambie@beeb.net

Bonehill Farm ◆◆◆
Etwall Road, Mickleover, Derby
DE3 5DN
T: (01332) 513553

Chambers House ◆◆
110 Green Lane, Derby, DE1 1RY
T: (01332) 746412

Chuckles Guesthouse ◆◆◆
48 Crompton Street, Derby,
DE1 1NX
T: (01332) 367193 &
07711 379490
E: IanFraser@
Chucklesguesthouse.freeserve.
co.uk

European Inn ◆◆◆
Midland Road, Derby, DE1 2SL
T: (01332) 292000
F: (01332) 293940
E: admin@euro-derby.co.uk
I: www.euro-derby.co.uk

The Hill House Hotel ◆◆◆
294 Burton Road, Derby,
DE23 6AD
T: (01332) 361523
F: (01332) 361523

Red Setters Guesthouse ◆◆
85 Curzon Street, Derby,
DE1 1LN
T: (01332) 362770
E: yvonne@derbycity.com
I: www.derbycity.
com/michael/redset.html

Rose & Thistle ◆◆◆
21 Charnwood Street, Derby,
DE1 2GU
T: (01332) 344103
F: (01332) 294006

Victoria Park Hotel ◆◆◆
312 Burton Road, Derby,
DE23 6AD
T: (01332) 341551

DIGBETH
West Midlands

The Works Guesthouse ◆◆◆
29-30 Warner Street, Digbeth,
Birmingham B12 0JG
T: (0121) 7723326
F: (0121) 7723326

DILHORNE
Staffordshire

The Beeches
◆◆◆◆ SILVER AWARD
Dilhorne, Stoke-on-Trent
ST10 2PQ
T: (01782) 397104
F: (01782) 397104

DONNINGTON
Gloucestershire

Holmleigh ◆◆
Donnington, Moreton-in-Marsh,
Gloucestershire GL56 0XX
T: (01451) 830792

DORRINGTON
Shropshire

Meadowlands ◆◆◆
Lodge Lane, Frodesley,
Dorrington, Shrewsbury
SY5 7HD
T: (01694) 731350
F: (01694) 731350

DORSTONE
Herefordshire

Haie Barn ◆◆◆◆
The Bage, Dorstone, Hereford,
Herefordshire HR3 5SU
T: (01497) 831729

**Westbrook Manor Bed and
Breakfast** ◆◆◆
Westbrook Manor, Dorstone,
Hereford, Herefordshire
HR3 5SY
T: (01497) 831431
F: (01497) 831431
I: www.golden-valley.co.
uk/wmamor

DOVERIDGE
Derbyshire

The Beeches Farmhouse
◆◆◆◆
The Beeches, Waldley,
Doveridge, Ashbourne,
Derbyshire DE6 5LR
T: (01889) 590288
F: (01889) 590559
E: beechesfa@aol.com

DROITWICH
Worcestershire

Foxbrook ◆◆◆
238A Worcester Road,
Droitwich, Worcestershire
WR9 8AY
T: (01905) 772414

Larches Guest House
Rating Applied For
46 Worcester Road, Droitwich,
Worcestershire WR9 8AJ
T: (01905) 773441

Middleton Grange ◆◆◆◆
Ladywood Road, Salwarpe,
Droitwich, Worcestershire
WR9 0AH
T: (01905) 451678
F: (01905) 453978
E: harrison@middletongrange.
demon.co.uk
I: www.middletongrange.demon.
co.uk

The Old Farmhouse
◆◆◆◆◆ SILVER AWARD
Hadley Heath, Droitwich,
Worcestershire WR9 0AR
T: (01905) 620837
F: (01905) 621722
E: judylambe@ombersley.
demon.co.uk
I: www.SmoothHound.co.
uk/hotels/farmhous.html

Richmond Guest House ◆
3 Ombersley St. West, Droitwich,
Worcestershire WR9 8HZ
T: (01905) 775722
F: (01905) 794642
I: www.infotel.co.
uk/hotels/36340.htm

South Hall Farm ◆◆◆
Doverdale, Droitwich,
Worcestershire WR9 0QB
T: (01299) 851236
F: (01299) 851531
E: admin@dbsystems.demon.co.
uk

Temple Broughton Farm
◆◆◆◆ GOLD AWARD
Broughton Green, Droitwich,
Worcestershire WR9 7EF
T: (01905) 391456 &
07803 737501
F: (01905) 391515

DRONFIELD
Derbyshire

Cassita ◆◆◆◆
Off Snape Hill Lane, Dronfield,
S18 2GL
T: (01246) 417303
F: (01246) 417303

DUNCHURCH
Warwickshire

Toft Hill ◆◆◆◆
Dunchurch, Rugby,
Warwickshire CV22 6NR
T: (01788) 810342

DUNTISBOURNE ABBOTS
Gloucestershire

Dixs Barn ◆◆◆
Duntisbourne Abbots,
Cirencester, Gloucestershire
GL7 7JN
T: (01285) 821249

DURSLEY
Gloucestershire

Foresters ◆◆◆◆
Chapel Street, Upper Cam
Village, Dursley, Gloucestershire
GL5 5NX
T: (01453) 549996 &
07973 890477
F: (01453) 549996

**Stanthill House Bed and
Breakfast** ◆◆◆◆
Uley Road, Dursley,
Gloucestershire GL11 4PF
T: (01453) 549037
F: (01453) 549174
I: www.smoothhound.co.
uk/hotels/stant.html

DYKE
Lincolnshire
The Wishing Well Inn and Restaurants♦♦♦
Main Street, Dyke, Bourne,
Lincolnshire PE10 0AF
T: (01778) 422970 & 423626
F: (01778) 394508

DYMOCK
Gloucestershire
Lower House Farm ♦♦♦
Kempley, Dymock,
Gloucestershire GL18 2BS
T: (01531) 890301
F: (01531) 890301

The White House ♦♦♦
Dymock, Gloucestershire
GL18 2AQ
T: (01531) 890516

EARDISLAND
Herefordshire
Eardisland Tea Room ♦♦
Church Lane, Eardisland,
Leominster, Herefordshire
HR6 9BP
T: (01544) 388226

The Manor House ♦♦♦♦
Eardisland, Leominster,
Herefordshire HR6 9BN
T: (01544) 388138
E: www.magicalat.demon.co.
uk/manor/manorhouse

EARL STERNDALE
Derbyshire
Chrome Cottage ♦♦♦
Earl Sterndale, Buxton,
Derbyshire SK17 0BS
T: (01298) 83360
F: (01298) 83360
E: adgregg@bigwig.net

Fernydale Farm ♦♦♦♦
Earl Sterndale, Buxton,
Derbyshire SK17 0BS
T: (01298) 83236
F: (01298) 83605
E: william.nadin@virgin.net

EAST BARKWITH
Lincolnshire
Bodkin Lodge
♦♦♦♦♦ GOLD AWARD
Grange Farm, Torrington Lane,
East Barkwith, Market Rasen,
Lincolnshire LN8 5RY
T: (01673) 858249

The Grange
♦♦♦♦ SILVER AWARD
Torrington Lane, East Barkwith,
Market Rasen, Lincolnshire
LN8 5RY
T: (01673) 858670
E: jonathanstamp@
farmersweekly.net

EAST HADDON
Northamptonshire
East Haddon Lodge ♦♦♦
East Haddon, Northampton
NN6 8BU
T: (01604) 770240

Ryehills ♦♦♦♦ SILVER AWARD
Holdenby Road, East Haddon,
Northampton NN6 8DH
T: (01604) 770990
F: (01604) 770237
E: ryehills@compuserve.com

EAST LANGTON
Leicestershire
The Bell Inn ♦♦♦♦
Main Street, East Langton,
Market Harborough,
Leicestershire LE16 7TW
T: (01858) 545278
F: (01858) 545748
E: achapman@thebellinn.co.uk
I: www.thebellinn.co.uk

EASTCOMBE
Gloucestershire
Pretoria Villa ♦♦♦♦
Wells Road, Eastcombe, Stroud,
Gloucestershire GL6 7EE
T: (01452) 770435

EASTCOTE
Northamptonshire
West Farm
♦♦♦♦ SILVER AWARD
Gayton Road, Eastcote,
Towcester, Northamptonshire
NN12 8NS
T: (01327) 830310
F: (01327) 830310

EASTHOPE
Shropshire
Madam's Hill Bed and Breakfast♦♦♦
Hilltop, Easthope, Much
Wenlock, Shropshire TF13 6DJ
T: (01746) 785269 &
07712 255310
F: (01746) 785269

EASTNOR
Herefordshire
Hill Farmhouse Bed and Breakfast ♦♦
Eastnor, Ledbury, Herefordshire
HR8 1EF
T: (01531) 632827

Woodside Country House
Rating Applied For
Woodside, Ledbury Road,
Eastnor, Ledbury, Herefordshire
HR8 1EL
T: (01531) 633831
F: (01531) 633831

EASTON ON THE HILL
Northamptonshire
Hillcroft House
Rating Applied For
25 High Street, Easton on the
Hill, Stamford, Lincolnshire
PE9 3LN
T: (01780) 755598

EASTWOOD
Nottinghamshire
Horseshoe Cottage ♦♦♦♦
25 Babbington Village,
Eastwood, Nottingham
NG16 2SS
T: (0115) 930 4769 &
0786 7507870
F: (0115) 930 4769
E: janet@jtserve.force9.co.uk

ECCLESHALL
Staffordshire
Cobblers Cottage ♦♦♦♦
Kerry Lane, Eccleshall, Stafford
ST21 6EJ
T: (01785) 850116
F: (01785) 850116
E: cobblerscottage@tinyonline.
co.uk

ECKINGTON
Worcestershire
The Anchor Inn and Restaurant
♦♦♦
Cotheridge Lane, Eckington,
Pershore, Worcestershire
WR10 3BA
T: (01386) 750356
F: (01386) 750356
E: anchoreck@aol.com
I: www.anchoreckington.co.uk

The Bell Inn ♦♦♦
Church Street, Eckington,
Pershore, Worcestershire
WR10 3AN
T: (01386) 750205 & 751073
F: (01386) 750205
E: the_bell_uk@hotmail.com
I: www.jks.org/bell.html

Lantern House ♦♦♦
Boon Street, Eckington,
Pershore, Worcestershire
WR10 3BL
T: (01386) 750003 &
0771 3160402

Nafford House ♦♦♦♦
Eckington, Pershore,
Worcestershire WR10 3DJ
T: (01386) 750233

EDALE
Derbyshire
Stonecroft
♦♦♦♦ SILVER AWARD
Grindsbrook, Edale, Hope Valley
S33 7ZA
T: (01433) 670262 &
07879 427937

EDGBASTON
West Midlands
Asquith House Hotel and Restaurant ♦♦♦
19 Portland Road, Edgbaston,
Birmingham B16 9HN
T: (0121) 454 5282 & 454 6699
F: (0121) 456 4668
I: www.smoothhound.co.uk/

Swiss Cottage Hotel ♦♦
475 Gillott Road, Edgbaston,
Birmingham B16 9LJ
T: (0121) 454 0371
F: (0121) 454 0371

EDGE
Gloucestershire
Wild Acre ♦♦♦
Back Edge Lane, Edge, Stroud,
Gloucestershire GL6 6PE
T: (01452) 813077

EDWINSTOWE
Nottinghamshire
Black Swan ♦♦♦
High Street, Edwinstowe,
Mansfield, Nottinghamshire
NG21 9QR
T: (01623) 822598
E: blackswan.fsbusiness.co.uk

ELLESMERE
Shropshire
The Grange ♦♦♦
Rating Applied For
Grange Road, Ellesmere,
Shropshire SY12 9DE
T: (01691) 623495

Hordley Hall ♦♦♦
Hordley, Ellesmere, Shropshire
SY12 9BB
T: (01691) 622772

Mereside Farm ♦♦♦♦
Ellesmere, Shropshire SY12 0PA
T: (01691) 622404
F: (01691) 622404
E: nicky@mereside.free-online.
co.uk
I: www.ellesmere.co.uk/mereside

Oakhill ♦♦♦♦
Dudleston, Ellesmere, Shropshire
SY12 9LL
T: (01691) 690548

ELMESTHORPE
Leicestershire
Badgers Mount ♦♦♦♦
6 Station Road, Elmesthorpe,
Leicester LE9 7SG
T: (01455) 848161
F: (01455) 848161
E: badgersmount@lineone.net
I: www.badgersmount.com

Water Meadows Farm ♦
22 Billington Road East,
Elmesthorpe, Leicester LE9 7SB
T: (01455) 843417
E: june-peter@
watermeadowsfarm.fsnet.co.uk

ELTON
Derbyshire
Homestead Farm ♦♦♦
Main Street, Elton, Matlock,
Derbyshire DE4 2BW
T: (01629) 650359

ENDON
Staffordshire
Hollinhurst Farm ♦♦♦
Park Lane, Endon, Stoke-on-
Trent ST9 9JB
T: (01782) 502633 &
07967 7784340
E: hjball@ukf.net

ENGLISH BICKNOR
Gloucestershire
Dryslade Farm ♦♦♦♦
English Bicknor, Coleford,
Gloucestershire GL16 7PA
T: (01594) 860259 &
0780 1732778
F: (01594) 860259
I: www.fweb.org.uk/dryslade

Lower Tump Farm
Rating Applied For
Eastbach, English Bicknor,
Coleford, Gloucestershire
GL16 7EU
T: (01594) 860253 &
07836 536674

ETTINGTON
Warwickshire
White Horse Inn
Rating Applied For
Banbury Road, Ettington,
Stratford-upon-Avon,
Warwickshire CV37 7SU
T: (01789) 740641
F: (01789) 740641

ETWALL
Derbyshire
The Blenheim Inn ◆◆◆◆
Main Street, Etwall, Derby
DE65 6LP
T: (01283) 732254
F: (01283) 733860

EVESHAM
Worcestershire
Bredon View Guest House
◆◆◆ SILVER AWARD
Village Street, Harvington,
Evesham, Worcestershire
WR11 5NQ
T: (01386) 871484
F: (01386) 871484
I: www.bredonview.heartuk.net

Fircroft ◆◆◆
84 Greenhill, Evesham,
Worcestershire WR11 4NH
T: (01386) 45828

Park View Hotel ◆◆◆
Waterside, Evesham,
Worcestershire WR11 6BS
T: (01386) 442639
E: mike.spires@btinternet.com
I: www.parkview.hotel.
btinternet.co.uk

EWYAS HAROLD
Herefordshire
Kingstreet Farmhouse ◆◆◆
Ewyas Harold, Hereford,
Herefordshire HR2 0HB
T: (01981) 240208

The Old Rectory ◆◆◆◆
Ewyas Harold, Hereford,
Herefordshire HR2 0EY
T: (01981) 240498
F: (01981) 240498

The Poplars
Rating Applied For
Ewyas Harold, Hereford,
Herefordshire HR2 0HU
T: (01981) 240516
F: (01981) 240516
E: chrispye@woodcarver.force9.
co.uk

EYAM
Derbyshire
The Old Rose and Crown
◆◆◆◆
Main Road, Eyam, Hope Valley
S32 5QW
T: (01433) 630858 &
07710 344688
E: mdriver@free.uk.com
I: www.smoothhound.co.
uk/hotels/oldrose.html

EYDON
Northamptonshire
Crockwell Farm
◆◆◆◆ SILVER AWARD
Eydon, Daventry,
Northamptonshire NN11 3QA
T: (01327) 361358 &
07850 050716
F: (01327) 361573
E: crockwellfarm@supanet.com

FAIRFIELD
Derbyshire
Barms Farm ◆◆◆◆
Fairfield, Buxton, Derbyshire
SK17 7HW
T: (01298) 77723 &
07957 863963
F: (01298) 78692
E: info@peakpracticegolf.co.uk

FAIRFORD
Gloucestershire
East End House
◆◆◆◆◆ GOLD AWARD
Fairford, Gloucestershire
GL7 4AP
T: (01285) 713715
F: (01285) 713505
E: eastendho@cs.com

Kempsford Manor ◆◆◆
Fairford, Gloucestershire
GL7 4EQ
T: (01285) 810131
F: (01285) 810131
E: www.kempsfordmanor.free.
online.co.uk

Milton Farm ◆◆◆
Fairford, Gloucestershire
GL7 4HZ
T: (01285) 712205
F: (01285) 712205

Waiten Hill Farm ◆◆
Fairford, Gloucestershire
GL7 4JG
T: (01285) 712652
F: (01285) 712652

FARTHINGHOE
Northamptonshire
Grafton House ◆◆◆◆
Baker Street, Farthinghoe,
Brackley, Northamptonshire
NN13 5PH
T: (01295) 710741
F: (01295) 712249
E: ACAddison@aol.com

Greenfield ◆◆◆◆
Baker Street, Farthinghoe,
Brackley, Northamptonshire
NN13 5PH
T: (01295) 712380
F: (01295) 712380
E: VivWebb@aol.com
I: www.webbS2.freeserve.co.uk

FARTHINGSTONE
Northamptonshire
Glebe Farm ◆◆◆◆
Maidford Road, Farthingstone,
Towcester, Northamptonshire
NN12 8HE
T: (01327) 361558
F: (01327) 361558
E: gbryce@glebefarm34.
freeserve.co.uk

FECKENHAM
Worcestershire
Orchard House ◆◆◆◆
Berrow Hill Lane, Feckenham,
Redditch, Worcestershire
B96 6QJ
T: (01527) 821497
F: (01527) 821497

The Steps ◆◆
6 High Street, Feckenham,
Redditch, Worcestershire
B96 6HS
T: (01527) 892678
E: thestepsgh@aol.com

FENNY BENTLEY
Derbyshire
Cairn Grove ◆◆◆◆
Ashes Lane, Fenny Bentley,
Ashbourne, Derbyshire DE6 1LD
T: (01335) 350538 &
07973 859992
E: keith.wheeldon@virgin.net

FENNY COMPTON
Warwickshire
Willow Cottage ◆◆
Brook Street, Fenny Compton,
Southam, Warwickshire
CV47 2YH
T: (01295) 770429

FENNY DRAYTON
Leicestershire
White Wings
◆◆◆◆◆ SILVER AWARD
Quaker Close, Fenny Drayton,
Nuneaton CV13 6BS
T: (01827) 716100 &
07767 266215
F: (01827) 717191

FERNHILL HEATH
Worcestershire
Dilmore House Hotel ◆◆◆
Droitwich Road, Fernhill Heath,
Worcester WR3 7UL
T: (01905) 451543
F: (01905) 452015
E: dilmorehouse@ukgateway.
net

Heathside ◆◆◆
Droitwich Road, Fernhill Heath,
Worcester WR3 7UA
T: (01905) 458245
F: (01905) 458245

FILLINGHAM
Lincolnshire
Church Farm ◆◆◆◆
Fillingham, Gainsborough,
Lincolnshire DN21 5BS
T: (01427) 668279
F: (01427) 668025

FILLONGLEY
Warwickshire
Manor House Farm
◆◆◆◆ SILVER AWARD
Fillongley, Coventry,
Warwickshire CV7 8DS
T: (01676) 540256

FINSTALL
Worcestershire
Stoke Cross Farm ◆◆◆
Dusthouse Lane, Finstall,
Bromsgrove, Worcestershire
B60 3AE
T: (01527) 876676
F: (01527) 874729

FISHMORE
Shropshire
Acorn Place ◆◆◆◆
Fishmore, Ludlow, Shropshire
SY8 3DP
T: (01584) 875295

FLEET HARGATE
Lincolnshire
The Bull Inn ◆◆
Old Main Road, Fleet Hargate,
Holbeach, Spalding, Lincolnshire
PE12 8LH
T: (01406) 426866

FOWNHOPE
Herefordshire
The Bowens Country House
◆◆◆◆
Fownhope, Hereford HRI 4PS
T: (01432) 860430
F: (01432) 860430

The Tan House ◆◆◆
Fownhope, Hereford HR1 4NJ
T: (01432) 860549

FOXTON
Leicestershire
The Old Manse
◆◆◆◆ SILVER AWARD
Swingbridge Street, Foxton,
Market Harborough,
Leicestershire LE16 7RH
T: (01858) 545456
E: theoldmanse37@hotmail.
com

FRAMPTON MANSELL
Gloucestershire
The Crown Inn ◆◆◆◆
Frampton Mansell, Stroud,
Gloucestershire GL6 8JG
T: (01285) 760601
F: (01285) 760681
E: book@lionheartinns.co.uk OR
hs@lionheartinns.co.uk
I: www.lionheartinn.co.uk

FRAMPTON-ON-SEVERN
Gloucestershire
Archway House ◆◆◆◆
The Green, Frampton-on-Severn,
Gloucester GL2 7DY
T: (01452) 740752
F: (01452) 741629

FRANKTON
Warwickshire
Frankton Grounds ◆◆◆
Frankton Grounds Farm,
Frankton, Rugby, Warwickshire
CV23 9PD
T: (01926) 632391
F: (01926) 632391

FRODESLEY
Shropshire
The Haven ◆◆◆◆
Frodesley, Dorrington,
Shrewsbury SY5 7EY
T: (01694) 731672

FULBECK
Lincolnshire
**The Hare and Hounds Country
Inn** ◆◆◆
The Green, Fulbeck, Lincolnshire
NG32 3JJ
T: (01400) 272090
F: (01400) 273663

GAINSBOROUGH
Lincolnshire
The Beckett Arms ◆◆◆
25 High Street, Corringham,
Gainsborough, Lincolnshire
DN21 5QP
T: (01427) 838201

Swallow Barn ◆◆◆◆
Sturgate, Gainsborough,
Lincolnshire DN21 5PX
T: (01427) 839042 &
07714 183858
F: (01427) 839043
E: gwen.anselm@ntlworld.com

GARWAY
Herefordshire
The Old Rectory ◆◆◆◆
Garway, Hereford HR2 8RH
T: (01600) 750363 &
07860 366679
F: (01600) 750364

GAYTON LE MARSH
Lincolnshire
Westbrook House ◆◆◆◆
Gayton le Marsh, Alford,
Lincolnshire LN13 0NW
T: (01507) 450624

Establishments printed in blue have a detailed entry in this guide

GILMORTON
Leicestershire
Orchard House ◆◆◆◆
Church Drive, Gilmorton,
Lutterworth, Leicestershire
LE17 5LR
T: (01455) 559487
E: 01455
I: 559487

GLOOSTON
Leicestershire
**The Old Barn Inn and
Restaurant** ◆◆◆
Glooston, Market Harborough,
Leicestershire LE16 7ST
T: (01858) 545215
F: (01858) 545215

GLOSSOP
Derbyshire
Avondale ◆◆◆◆
28 Woodhead Road, Glossop,
Derbyshire SK13 7RH
T: (01457) 853132
F: (01457) 853132

Peels Arms ◆◆◆
6-12 Temple Street, Padfield,
Glossop, Derbyshire SK13 1EX
T: (01457) 852719
F: (01457) 860536
E: peels@talk21.com

GLOUCESTER
Gloucestershire
Albert Hotel ◆◆◆
56-58 Worcester Street,
Gloucester, GL1 3AG
T: (01452) 502081 & 300832
F: (01452) 311738
I: WWW.SMOOTHHOUND.CO.
UK/

Alston Field Guest House ◆◆
88 Stroud Road, Gloucester,
GL1 5AJ
T: (01452) 529170

Brookthorpe Lodge ◆◆◆
Stroud Road, Brookthorpe,
Gloucester GL4 0UQ
T: (01452) 812645
F: (01452) 812645
E: enq@brookthorpelodge.
demon.co.uk
I: www.brookthorpelodge.
demon.co.uk

The Chestnuts ◆◆◆◆
9 Brunswick Square, Gloucester,
GL1 1UG
T: (01452) 330356 &
07887 650231
F: (01452) 330356
E: davidchampion1@
compurserve.com

The Coppins ◆◆◆◆
11c Kenilworth Avenue,
Gloucester, GL2 0QN
T: (01452) 302777

Cyder Press Farm ◆◆◆◆
The Leigh, Gloucester, GL19 4AG
T: (01242) 680661
F: (01242) 680023
E: Archers@CyderPressFarm.
Freeserve.co.uk

Georgian Guest House ◆
85 Bristol Road, Gloucester,
GL1 5SN
T: (01452) 413286
F: (01452) 413286

Gilbert's ◆◆◆◆
Brookthorpe, Gloucester,
GL4 0UH
T: (01452) 812364 & 813224
F: (01452) 812364
E: jenny@gilbertsbb.demon.co.
uk
I: www.SmoothHound.co.uk

Lulworth ◆◆◆
12 Midland Road, Gloucester,
GL1 4UF
T: (01452) 521881
F: (01452) 521881
E: peterdickinson1@
compuserve.com
I: www.lulworth.swinternet.co.
uk

**Notley House and The Coach
House** ◆◆◆
93 Hucclecote Road, Hucclecote,
Gloucester GL3 3TR
T: (01452) 611584
F: (01452) 371229
E: notleyhouse@compuserve.
com
I: ourworld.compuserve.
com/homepages/notleyhouse

Pembury Guest House ◆◆◆
9 Pembury Road, St. Barnabas,
Gloucester, GL4 6UE
T: (01452) 521856
F: (01452) 303418

**Spalite Hotel
Rating Applied For**
121 Southgate Street,
Gloucester, GL1 1XQ
T: (01452) 380828

GNOSALL
Staffordshire
The Leys House ◆◆◆◆
Gnosall, Stafford, Staffordshire
ST20 0BZ
T: (01785) 822532
F: (01785) 822060

GOADBY
Leicestershire
The Hollies ◆◆◆
Goadby, Leicester LE7 9EE
T: (0116) 259 8301
F: (0116) 2598491
E: holliesbb@aol.com

GOODRICH
Herefordshire
**New Barn House Bed and
Breakfast** ◆◆◆
Goodrich, Ross-on-Wye,
Herefordshire HR9 6JB
T: (01600) 890572
F: (01600) 890572
E: newbarnhouse@themail.co.
uk

GOTHERINGTON
Gloucestershire
Pardon Hill Farm ◆◆◆
Prescott, Gotherington,
Cheltenham, Gloucestershire
GL52 4RD
T: (01242) 672468 &
07802 708814
F: (01242) 672468
E: janet@pardonhillfarm.
freeserve.co.uk
I: www.glosfarmhols.co.uk

GRANGEMILL
Derbyshire
Middle Hills Farm ◆◆◆◆
Grangemill, Derby DE4 4HY
T: (01629) 650368
F: (01629) 650368
E: l.lomas@btinternet.com

GRANTHAM
Lincolnshire
Beechleigh Town House Hotel
◆◆◆◆
55 North Parade, Grantham,
Lincolnshire NG31 8AT
T: (01476) 572213
F: (01476) 572213
E: info@beechleigh.com
I: www.beechleigh.com

GREAT DALBY
Leicestershire
Dairy Farm ◆◆◆
8 Burrough End, Great Dalby,
Melton Mowbray, Leicestershire
LE14 2EW
T: (01664) 562783

GREAT HUCKLOW
Derbyshire
Holly House ◆◆◆◆
Windmill, Great Hucklow,
Buxton, Derbyshire SK17 8RE
T: (01298) 871568
E: holly.house@which.net

GREAT LONGSTONE
Derbyshire
Fieldview ◆◆◆◆
Station Road, Great Longstone,
Bakewell, Derbyshire DE45 1TS
T: (01629) 640593
E: mikes@ga-memik.demon.co.
uk
I: www.ga-memik.demon.co.uk

GREAT RISSINGTON
Gloucestershire
Lower Farmhouse ◆◆◆
Great Rissington, Cheltenham,
Gloucestershire GL54 2LH
T: (01451) 810163 & 810187
F: (01451) 810187
E: kathryn@fleming4 clocks.
netscapeonline.co.uk

Stepping Stone ◆◆◆
Rectory Lane, Great Rissington,
Cheltenham, Gloucestershire
GL54 2LL
T: (01451) 821385
E: stepping-stone-b-b@excite.
com

GREAT WITLEY
Worcestershire
Home Farm
◆◆◆◆ SILVER AWARD
Great Witley, Worcester WR6 6JJ
T: (01299) 896825
F: (01299) 896176

GRETTON
Gloucestershire
Elms Farm ◆◆◆
Gretton, Cheltenham,
Gloucestershire GL54 5HQ
T: (01242) 620150 &
07774 461107
E: rose@elmfarm.demon.co.uk.
I: www.elmfarm.demon.co.uk.

Gretton Court
◆◆◆◆ SILVER AWARD
Gretton, SY6 7HU
T: (01694) 771630

GRIMSTON
Leicestershire
Gorse House ◆◆◆◆
33 Main Street, Grimston,
Melton Mowbray, Leicestershire
LE14 3BZ
T: (01664) 813537 &
07785 297411
F: (01664) 813537

GRINDLEFORD
Derbyshire
Woodlands ◆◆◆◆
Sir William Hill Road,
Grindleford, Hope Valley
S32 2HS
T: (01433) 631593

GRINDON
Staffordshire
Summerhill Farm ◆◆◆◆
Grindon, Leek, Staffordshire
ST13 7TT
T: (01538) 304264

GUITING POWER
Gloucestershire
Castlett Bank ◆◆◆◆
Castlett Street, Guiting Power,
Cheltenham, Gloucestershire
GL54 5US
T: (01451) 850300
F: (01451) 850300

Cobnutt Cottage ◆◆◆
Winchcombe Road, Guiting
Power, Cheltenham,
Gloucestershire GL54 5UX
T: (01451) 850658

Farmers Arms ◆◆◆
Guiting Power, Cheltenham,
Gloucestershire GL54 5TZ
T: (01451) 850358

Guiting Guesthouse
◆◆◆◆◆ GOLD AWARD
Post Office Lane, Guiting Power,
Cheltenham, Gloucestershire
GL54 5TZ
T: (01451) 850470
F: (01451) 850034
E: guiting.guest_house@virgin.
net
I: freespace.virgin.net/guiting.
guest_house/

Halfway House ◆◆◆
Kineton, Guiting Power,
Cheltenham, Gloucestershire
GL54 5UG
T: (01451) 850344 &
07880 552118
F: (01451) 850344
E: halfwayhouse1@cs.com
I: members.aol.
com/halfwayhs/pubpage.htm

The Hollow Bottom ◆◆◆
Winchcombe Road, Guiting
Power, Cheltenham,
Gloucestershire GL54 5UX
T: (01451) 850392
F: (01451) 850392

Tally Ho Guesthouse ◆◆◆◆
1 Tally Ho Lane, Guiting Power,
Cheltenham, Gloucestershire
GL54 5TY
T: (01451) 850186
E: tallyhobb@aol.com

HACKNEY
Derbyshire
The Orchard ♦♦♦
12 Greenaway Lane, Hackney,
Matlock, Derbyshire DE4 2QB
T: (01629) 734140
E: AA-GN@foster56.fsnet.co.uk

HACKTHORN
Lincolnshire
Honeyholes ♦♦♦♦
South Farm, Hackthorn, Lincoln
LN2 3PW
T: (01673) 861838
F: (01673) 861868

HADDINGTON
Lincolnshire
Wheelwrights Cottage ♦♦♦♦
Haddington, Lincoln LN5 9EF
T: (01522) 788154

HADNALL
Shropshire
Hall Farm House ♦♦♦
Hadnall, Shrewsbury SY4 4AQ
T: (01939) 210269 &
07989 235181

HAGWORTHINGHAM
Lincolnshire
White Oak Grange
♦♦♦♦ SILVER AWARD
Hagworthingham, Spilsby,
Lincolnshire PE23 4LX
T: (01507) 588376
F: (01507) 588377
I: whiteoakgrange.com

HALFORD
Warwickshire
Halford Bridge Inn ♦♦♦
Fosseway, Halford, Shipston-on-
Stour, Warwickshire CV36 5BN
T: (01789) 740382
F: (01789) 740935
E: halfordbridgeinn@easicom.
com

HAMPTON IN ARDEN
West Midlands
Chelsea Lodge ♦♦♦♦
48 Meriden Road, Hampton in
Arden, Solihull, West Midlands
B92 0BT
T: (01675) 442408
F: (01675) 442408

**The Cottage Guest House
♦♦♦**
Kenilworth Road, On A452 to
Balsall Common, Hampton in
Arden, Solihull, West Midlands
B92 0LW
T: (01675) 442323
F: (01675) 442323
I: www.smoothhound.co.uk/
hotels/cottage.html

The Hollies ♦♦♦
Kenilworth Road, Hampton in
Arden, Solihull, West Midlands
B92 0LW
T: (01675) 442941 & 442681
F: (01675) 442941

White Lion ♦♦♦
High Street, Hampton in Arden,
Solihull, West Midlands B92 0AA
T: (01675) 442833
F: (01675) 443168

HANLEY
Staffordshire
**Northwood Hotel Limited
♦♦♦**
146 Keelings Road, Northwood,
Hanley, Stoke-on-Trent ST1 6QA
T: (01782) 279729 &
07971 222130
F: (01782) 207507

Star Hotel ♦♦♦
92 Marsh Street North, Hanley,
Stoke-on-Trent ST1 5HH
T: (01782) 207507 & 289989
F: (01782) 289989

HANLEY SWAN
Worcestershire
Meadowbank
♦♦♦♦ SILVER AWARD
Picken End, Hanley Swan,
Worcester WR8 0DQ
T: (01684) 310917 &
07976 749866
E: dave@meadowbank.
freeserve.co.uk

**Pyndar Lodge Bed and
Breakfast**
♦♦♦♦ SILVER AWARD
Roberts End, Hanley Swan,
Worcester WR8 0DN
T: (01684) 310716
F: (01684) 311402
E: info@pyndarlodge.co.uk
I: www.pyndarlodge.co.uk

**Yew Tree House Bed and
Breakfast**
♦♦♦♦♦ SILVER AWARD
Yew Tree House, Hanley Swan,
Worcester WR8 0DN
T: (01684) 310736 &
07498 753543
F: (01684) 311709
E: yewtreehs@aol.com
I: www.yewtreehouse.co.uk

HARDWICK
Herefordshire
The Haven ♦♦♦♦
Hardwick, Hay on Wye, Hereford
HR3 5TA
T: (01497) 831254 & 831407
F: (01497) 831254
E: robinson@havenhay.demon.
co.uk
I: www.golden-valley.co.
uk/haven

HARESFIELD
Gloucestershire
Lower Green Farmhouse ♦♦♦
Haresfield, Stonehouse,
Gloucestershire GL10 3DS
T: (01452) 728264
F: (01452) 728264
E: lowergreen@lineone.net

HARLASTON
Staffordshire
The Old Rectory ♦♦♦♦
Churchside, Harlaston,
Tamworth, Staffordshire
B79 9HE
T: (01827) 383583 &
07973 756367
F: (01827) 383583

HARLEY
Shropshire
Rowley Farm Hospitality ♦♦♦
Harley, Shrewsbury SY5 6LX
T: (01952) 727348

HARTINGTON
Derbyshire
Bank Top Farm ♦♦♦
Pilsbury Road, Hartington,
Buxton, Derbyshire SK17 0AD
T: (01298) 84205 &
07885 021474

Manifold Inn ♦♦♦
Hulme End, Hartington, Buxton,
Derbyshire SK17 0EX
T: (01298) 84537

Wolfscote Grange Farm ♦♦♦
Wolfscote Grange, Hartington,
Buxton, Derbyshire SK17 0AX
T: (01298) 84342
E: wolfscote@btinternet.com
I: www.peakdistrictfarmhols.co.
uk

HARTLEBURY
Worcestershire
Garden Cottages
♦♦♦♦ SILVER AWARD
Crossway Green, Hartlebury,
Kidderminster, Worcestershire
DY13 9SJ
T: (01299) 250626
F: (01299) 250626
E: mamod@btinternet.com

HASELOR
Warwickshire
Walcote Farm ♦♦♦♦
Walcote, Haselor, Alcester,
Warwickshire B49 6LY
T: (01789) 488264
F: (01789) 488264
E: john@walcotefarm.co.uk
I: www.walcotefarm.co.uk

HASSOP
Derbyshire
Flatts Farm ♦♦♦♦
Hassop, Bakewell, Derbyshire
DE45 1NU
T: (01629) 812983

HATHERSAGE
Derbyshire
Cannon Croft
♦♦♦♦ SILVER AWARD
Cannonfields, Hathersage, Hope
Valley S32 1AG
T: (01433) 650005 &
0771 3352327
F: (01433) 650005
I: www.cannoncroft.fsbusiness.
co.uk

Hillfoot Farm ♦♦♦♦
Castleton Road, Hathersage,
Hope Valley, Derbyshire S32 1EG
T: (01433) 651673

The Plough Inn ♦♦♦♦
Leadmill Bridge, Hathersage,
Hope Valley S32 1BA
T: (01433) 650319 & 650180
F: (01433) 651049

Sladen ♦♦♦
Jaggers Lane, Hathersage, Hope
Valley S32 1AZ
T: (01433) 650706
F: (01433) 650315

HAYFIELD
Derbyshire
The Royal Hotel ♦♦♦♦
Market Street, Hayfield, High
Peak, Derbyshire SK22 2EP
T: (01663) 742721
F: (01663) 742997
E: royal.hotel@virgin.net
I: freespace.virgin.net/royal.hotel

HENLEY-IN-ARDEN
Warwickshire
Holland Park Farm ♦♦♦
Buckley Green, Henley-in-Arden,
Solihull, West Midlands B95 5QF
T: (01564) 792625
F: (01564) 792625

HEREFORD
Herefordshire
Alberta ♦
7-11 Newtown Road, Hereford,
Herefordshire HR4 9LH
T: (01432) 270313
F: (01432) 270313

Ancroft ♦♦♦
10 Cheviot Close, Kings Acre,
Hereford, HR4 0TF
T: (01432) 274394 &
07803 430888

Ashgrove House ♦♦♦♦
Wellington Marsh, Hereford,
Herefordshire HR4 8DU
T: (01432) 830608

Aylestone Court Hotel
♦♦♦♦ SILVER AWARD
Aylestone Hill, Hereford,
Herefordshire HR1 1HS
T: (01432) 341891 & 359342
F: (01432) 267691

Bouvrie Guest House ♦
26 Victoria Street, Hereford,
HR4 0AA
T: (01432) 266265

Brandon Lodge
♦♦♦♦ SILVER AWARD
Ross Road, Grafton, Hereford,
HR2 8BL
T: (01432) 355621
F: (01432) 355621

Breinton Court Lodge ♦♦♦♦
Lower Breinton, Hereford,
Herefordshire HR4 7PG
T: (01432) 274523 & 760534

Cedar Guest House ♦♦♦
123 Whitecross Road,
Whitecross, Hereford, HR4 0LS
T: (01432) 267235
F: (01432) 267235

Charades ♦♦♦
34 Southbank Road, Hereford,
HR1 2TJ
T: (01432) 269444

Felton House
♦♦♦♦ SILVER AWARD
Felton, Hereford HR1 3PH
T: (01432) 820366
F: (01432) 820366
I: www.smoothhound.co.
uk/hotels/felton.html

Grafton Villa Farm House
♦♦♦♦ SILVER AWARD
Grafton, Hereford HR2 8ED
T: (01432) 268689
F: (01432) 268689

Hedley Lodge ♦♦♦♦
Belmont Abbey, Abergavenny
Road, Hereford, HR2 9RZ
T: (01432) 277475
F: (01432) 277597
E: procoffice@aol.com
I: www.belmontabbey.org.
uk/hedley.shtml

Heron House ♦♦♦
Canon Pyon Road, Portway,
Burghill, Hereford, Herefordshire
HR4 8NG
T: (01432) 761111
F: (01432) 760603
E: bb.hereford@tesco.net
I: homepages.tesco.net/§bb.
hereford/hesou.htm

Holly Tree Guest House ♦♦♦
21 Barton Road, Hereford,
HR4 0AY
T: (01432) 357845

Sink Green Farm ♦♦♦♦
Rotherwas, Hereford HR2 6LE
T: (01432) 870223
E: sinkgreenfarm@classic.msn.
com

The Somerville ♦♦♦
12 Bodenham Road, Hereford,
HR1 2TS
T: (01432) 273991
F: (01432) 268719

HILCOTE
Derbyshire

Hilcote Hall ♦♦
Hilcote Lane, Hilcote, Alfreton,
Derbyshire DE55 5HR
T: (01773) 812608
F: (01773) 812608

HIMBLETON
Worcestershire

Phepson Farm ♦♦♦♦
Himbleton, Droitwich,
Worcestershire WR9 7JZ
T: (01905) 391205
F: (01905) 391205
I: www.webscape.co.
uk/farmaccom/worcestershire/
phepson/
⊚

HINCKLEY
Leicestershire

**Woodside Farm Guesthouse
♦♦♦**
Ashby Road, Stapleton, Leicester
LE9 8JE
T: (01455) 291929
F: (01455) 292626
⊚ ⬧

HINTON IN THE HEDGES
Northamptonshire

The Old Rectory ♦♦♦
Hinton in the Hedges, Brackley,
Northamptonshire NN13 5NG
T: (01280) 706807
F: (01280) 706809
E: sam@lavinia.demon.co.uk

HOARWITHY
Herefordshire

Aspen House ♦♦♦♦
Hoarwithy, Hereford,
Herefordshire HR2 6QP
T: (01432) 840353 &
00860 709924
F: (01432) 840353
E: hoarwithy@a.o.l.com

Old Mill
♦♦♦♦ SILVER AWARD
Hoarwithy, Hereford HR2 6QH
T: (01432) 840602
F: (01432) 840602
⊚

HOCKLEY HEATH
West Midlands

Illshaw Heath Farm ♦♦♦♦
Kineton Lane, Hockley Heath,
Solihull, West Midlands B94 6RX
T: (01564) 782214

HOGNASTON
Derbyshire

Ye Olde Forge ♦♦♦♦
Hognaston, Ashbourne,
Derbyshire DE6 1PU
T: (01335) 370404

HOLBEACH
Lincolnshire

Cackle Hill House ♦♦♦♦
Cackle Hill Lane, Holbeach,
Lincolnshire PE12 8BS
T: (01406) 426721 &
07930 228755
F: (01406) 424659
⊚

Pipwell Manor ♦♦♦♦
Washway Road, Saracens Head,
Holbeach, Spalding, Lincolnshire
PE12 8AL
T: (01406) 423119
F: (01406) 423119

HOLBECK
Nottinghamshire

Browns
♦♦♦♦♦ SILVER AWARD
The Old Orchard Cottage,
Holbeck, Worksop,
Nottinghamshire S80 3NF
T: (01909) 720659
F: (01909) 720659
E: Browns@holbeck.sfnet.co.uk

HOLLINGTON
Derbyshire

Reevsmoor ♦♦♦♦
Hoargate Lane, Hollington,
Ashbourne, Derbyshire DE6 3AG
T: (01335) 330318

HOLMESFIELD
Derbyshire

Carpenter House ♦♦♦
Millthorpe, Holmesfield,
Dronfield S18 7WH
T: (0114) 289 0307

HOLYMOORSIDE
Derbyshire

Burnell ♦♦♦♦
Baslow Road, Holymoorside,
Chesterfield, Derbyshire S42 7HJ
T: (01246) 567570

HOPE
Derbyshire

Mill Farm ♦♦♦
Edale Road, Hope, Hope Valley
S33 6ZF
T: (01433) 621181

The Poachers Arms ♦♦♦
95 Castleton Road, Hope, Hope
Valley S33 6SB
T: (01433) 620380
F: (01433) 621915

Underleigh House
♦♦♦♦♦ SILVER AWARD
Off Edale Road, Hope, Hope
Valley S33 6RF
T: (01433) 621372 & 621324
F: (01433) 621324
E: Underleigh.House@
btinternet.com
I: www.underleighhouse.co.uk

Woodroffe Arms ♦♦♦
1 Castleton Road, Hope, Hope
Valley S33 6SB
T: (01433) 620351

HOPE BAGOT
Shropshire

Croft Cottage ♦♦♦
Cumberley Lane, Hope Bagot,
Ludlow, Shropshire SY8 3LJ
T: (01584) 890664
F: (01584) 890664
E: croft.cottage@virgin.net
I: freespace.virgin.
net/david-elizabeth.hatchell

HOPE MANSELL
Herefordshire

Sutton House ♦♦♦♦
Hope Mansell, Ross-on-Wye,
Herefordshire HR9 5TJ
T: (01989) 750351 &
0771 2230320
F: (01989) 750351
E: sutton.house@virgin.net

HOPTON CASTLE
Shropshire

Upper House Farm ♦♦♦♦
Hopton Castle, Craven Arms,
Shropshire SY7 0QF
T: (01547) 530319
I: www.go2.co.uk/upperhouse

HORTON
Staffordshire

Croft Meadows Farm ♦♦♦
Horton, Leek, Staffordshire
ST13 8QE
T: (01782) 513039
⬧

HULLAND
Derbyshire

Hulland Nurseries ♦♦♦
The Green, Hulland, Ashbourne,
Derbyshire DE6 3EP
T: (01335) 370052

HULME END
Staffordshire

Raikes Farm ♦♦♦
Raikes, Hulme End, Buxton,
Derbyshire SK17 0HJ
T: (01298) 84344
F: (01298) 84344

HUNTLEY
Gloucestershire

Birdwood Villa Farm ♦♦
Main Road, Birdwood, Huntley,
Gloucester GL19 3EQ
T: (01452) 750451

Forest Gate ♦♦♦
Huntley, Gloucester GL19 3EU
T: (01452) 831192 &
(01836) 632415
F: (01452) 831192
E: forest.gate@huntley-glos.
demon.co.uk
I: www.huntley-glos.demon.co.
uk
⊚

The Kings Head Inn ♦♦♦
Birdwood, Huntley, Gloucester
GL19 3EF
T: (01452) 750348
F: (01452) 750348

HUSBANDS BOSWORTH
Leicestershire

Mrs Armitage's ♦♦
31-33 High Street, Husbands
Bosworth, Lutterworth,
Leicestershire LE17 6LJ
T: (01858) 880066

IDRIDGEHAY
Derbyshire

**Millbank Cottage Bed and
Breakfast ♦♦♦**
Idridgehay, Belper, Derbyshire
DE56 2SH
T: (01629) 823 161 & 822 318

ILAM
Staffordshire

Beechenhill Farm ♦♦♦♦
Ilam, Ashbourne, Derbyshire
DE6 2BD
T: (01335) 310274
F: (01335) 310274
E: beechenhill@btinternet.com
I: www.beechenhill.co.uk
⊚

Throwley Hall ♦♦♦♦
Ilam, Ashbourne, Derbyshire
DE6 2BB
T: (01538) 308202 & 308243
F: (01538) 308243
E: throwleyhgall@talk21.com
⊚

ILMINGTON
Warwickshire

Howard Arms ♦♦♦♦
Lower Green, Ilmington,
Shipston-on-Stour,
Warwickshire CV36 4LT
T: (01608) 682226
F: (01608) 682226
E: howard.arms@virgin.net
I: www.howardarms.com

INCHBROOK
Gloucestershire

The Crown Inn ♦♦♦
Bath Road, Inchbrook, Stroud,
Gloucestershire GL5 5HA
T: (01453) 832914 &
07977 096224
F: (01453) 832914
E: www.inchbrook.cwc.net

INKBERROW
Worcestershire

Bulls Head Inn ♦♦♦
The Village Green, Inkberrow,
Worcester WR7 4DY
T: (01386) 792233
F: (01386) 793090

IRONBRIDGE
Shropshire

Bird in Hand Inn ♦♦♦
Waterloo Street, Ironbridge,
Telford, Shropshire TF8 7HG
T: (01952) 432226
⊚

591

Bridge House
◆◆◆◆◆ SILVER AWARD
Buildwas, Telford, Shropshire
TF8 7BN
T: (01952) 432105
F: (01952) 432105
I: www.smoothhound.co.uk/

Broseley Guest House ◆◆◆
The Square, Broseley, Shropshire
TF12 5EW
T: (01952) 882043
F: (01952) 882043
E: laurie@broseley-guesthouse.
co.uk
I: www.broseley-guesthouse.co.
uk

The Calcutts House ◆◆◆
Jackfield, Ironbridge, Telford,
Shropshire TF8 7LH
T: (01952) 882631
F: (01952) 882951

Coalbrookdale Villa
◆◆◆◆ GOLD AWARD
Paradise, Coalbrookdale,
Ironbridge, Telford, Shropshire
TF8 7NR
T: (01952) 433450
E: june@ashdown5.freeserve.co.
uk

Eleys of Ironbridge ◆◆◆
10 Tontine Hill, Ironbridge,
Telford, Shropshire TF8 7AL
T: (01952) 432541 & 433914
F: (01952) 433405
◎

The Golden Ball Inn ◆◆◆◆
1 Newbridge Road, Ironbridge,
Telford, Shropshire TF8 7BA
T: (01952) 432179
F: (01952) 433123

Greenways Guest House ◆◆◆
57 High Street, Madeley, Telford,
Shropshire TF7 5AT
T: (01952) 583118

Hill View Farm ◆◆◆
Buildwas, Ironbridge, Telford,
Shropshire TF8 7BP
T: (01952) 432228

The Library House
◆◆◆◆ GOLD AWARD
11 Severn Bank, Ironbridge,
Telford, Shropshire TF8 7AN
T: (01952) 432299
F: (01952) 433967
E: libhouse@enta.net
I: www.libhouse@enta.net

Lord Hill Guest House ◆◆
Duke Street, Broseley,
Shropshire TF12 5LU
T: (01952) 884270 & 580792

The Malthouse ◆◆◆◆
The Wharfage, Ironbridge,
Telford, Shropshire TF8 7NH
T: (01952) 433712
F: (01952) 433298
E: malthse@globalnet.co.uk
I: malthousepubs.co.uk

The Old Church Guest House
◆◆◆◆ SILVER AWARD
Park Avenue, Madeley, Telford,
Shropshire TF7 5AB
T: (01952) 583745
F: (01952) 583745

Orchard House ◆◆◆
40 King Street, Broseley,
Shropshire TF12 5NA
T: (01952) 882684

Post Office House ◆◆◆
6 The Square, Ironbridge,
Telford, Shropshire TF8 7AQ
T: (01952) 433201
F: (01952) 433582
E: Hunter@pohouse-ironbridge.
fsnet.co.uk
I: www.pohouse-ironbridge.
fsnet.co.uk

Tontine Hotel ◆◆◆
The Square, Ironbridge, Telford,
Shropshire TF8 7AL
T: (01952) 432127
F: (01952) 432094
E: tontinehotel@
netscapeonline.co.uk
I: www.tontine-ironbridge.co.uk

Wharfage Cottage ◆◆◆
17 The Wharfage, Ironbridge,
Telford, Shropshire TF8 7AW
T: (01952) 432721
F: (01952) 432639

Woodlands Farm ◆◆
Beech Road, Ironbridge, Telford,
Shropshire TF8 7PA
T: (01952) 432741

KEMBERTON
Shropshire
West Ridge Bed and Breakfast
◆◆◆◆ SILVER AWARD
Kemberton, Shifnal, Shropshire
TF11 9LB
T: (01952) 580992
F: (01952) 580992
E: peter@westridgebb.freeserve.
co.uk

KEMERTON
Worcestershire
Wings Cottage
◆◆◆◆ GOLD AWARD
Wing Lane, Kemerton,
Tewkesbury, Gloucestershire
GL20 7JG
T: (01386) 725273
F: (01386) 725273
E: jway@wingscottage.demon.
co.uk
I: www.wingscottage.demon.co.
uk/index.html

KEMPSEY
Worcestershire
Malbre Hotel ◆◆
Baynhall, Kempsey, Worcester
WR5 3PA
T: (01905) 820412

KENILWORTH
Warwickshire
Abbey Guest House ◆◆◆◆
41 Station Road, Kenilworth,
Warwickshire CV8 1JD
T: (01926) 512707
F: (01926) 859148
E: the-abbey@virgin.net
◎

Bridgend ◆◆◆
15 Farmer Ward Road,
Kenilworth, Warwickshire
CV8 2DJ
T: (01926) 511995 &
07713 141396

Castle Laurels Hotel
◆◆◆◆ SILVER AWARD
22 Castle Road, Kenilworth,
Warwickshire CV8 1NG
T: (01926) 856179
F: (01926) 854954
E: moores22@aol
I: www.castlelaurelshotel.co.uk

The Cottage Inn ◆◆◆
36 Stoneleigh Road, Kenilworth,
Warwickshire CV8 2GD
T: (01926) 853900
F: (01926) 856032

Enderley Guest House ◆◆◆
20 Queens Road, Kenilworth,
Warwickshire CV8 1JQ
T: (01926) 855388
F: (01926) 850450

Ferndale Guest House ◆◆◆◆
45 Priory Road, Kenilworth,
Warwickshire CV8 1LL
T: (01926) 853214
F: (01926) 858336

Howden House ◆◆
170 Warwick Road, Kenilworth,
Warwickshire CV8 1HS
T: (01926) 850310

Oldwych House Farm
Rating Applied For
Oldwych Lane, Fen End,
Kenilworth, Warwickshire
CV8 1NR
T: (01676) 533552
F: (01676) 530177

The Priory Guesthouse ◆◆◆
58 Priory Road, Kenilworth,
Warwickshire CV8 1LQ
T: (01926) 856173

The Quince House ◆◆◆◆
29 Moseley Road, Kenilworth,
Warwickshire CV8 2AR
T: (01926) 858652
E: gomers@supanet.com
I: www.balldesi.demon.co.
uk/b_b.html

Victoria Lodge Hotel ◆◆◆◆
180 Warwick Road, Kenilworth,
Warwickshire CV8 1HU
T: (01926) 512020
F: (01926) 858703

KETTERING
Northamptonshire
Dairy Farm
◆◆◆◆ SILVER AWARD
Cranford St Andrew, Kettering,
Northamptonshire NN14 4AQ
T: (01536) 330273

**Hawthorn House (Private)
Hotel** ◆◆◆
2 Hawthorn Road, Kettering,
Northamptonshire NN15 7HS
T: (01536) 482513
F: (01536) 513121

Headlands Hotel ◆◆◆◆
49 Headlands, Kettering,
Northamptonshire NN15 7ET
T: (01536) 524624 &
07710 434224
F: (01536) 483367

Pennels Guesthouse ◆◆◆
175 Beatrice Road, Kettering,
Northamptonshire NN16 9QR
T: (01536) 481940 &
07713 899508
F: (01536) 410798
E: pennelsgh@aol.com
I: www.members.aol.
com/pennelsgh
◎

KEXBY
Lincolnshire
Kexby Grange ◆◆◆
Kexby, Gainsborough,
Lincolnshire DN21 5PJ
T: (01427) 788265
◎

KEYWORTH
Nottinghamshire
Flinders Farm Bed & Breakfast
◆◆◆◆
33 Main Street, Keyworth,
Nottingham NG12 5HA
T: (0115) 937 2352

KIDDERMINSTER
Worcestershire
Bewdley Hill House ◆◆◆
8 Bewdley Hill, Kidderminster,
Worcestershire DY11 6BS
T: (01562) 60473
F: (01562) 60473
◎

Collingdale Private Hotel ◆◆◆
197 Comberton Road,
Kidderminster, Worcestershire
DY10 1UE
T: (01562) 515460 & 862839
F: (01562) 863937

Hollies Farm Cottage ◆◆◆◆
Hollies Lane, Franche,
Kidderminster, Worcestershire
DY11 5RW
T: (01562) 745677 &
0777 5645183

Victoria Hotel ◆◆◆
15 Comberton Road,
Kidderminster, Worcestershire
DY10 1UA
T: (01562) 67240

KILCOT
Gloucestershire
**Withyland Heights Bed and
Breakfast** ◆◆◆
Withyland Heights, Beavans Hill,
Kilcot, Newent, Gloucestershire
GL18 1PG
T: (01989) 720582
F: (01989) 720238
E: withyland@farming.co.uk

KILSBY
Northamptonshire
The Hollies Farm ◆◆◆
Main Road, Kilsby, Rugby,
Warwickshire CV23 8XR
T: (01788) 822629

KIMBOLTON
Herefordshire
The Fieldhouse Farm ◆◆◆
Bache Hill, Kimbolton,
Leominster, Herefordshire
HR6 0EP
T: (01568) 614789
◎

KINETON
Warwickshire
The Castle ◆◆◆
Edgehill, Kineton, Banbury,
Oxfordshire OX15 6DJ
T: (01295) 670255
F: (01295) 670521
E: castleedgehill@msn.com.
I: www.smoothhound.co.
uk/hotels/castle2

KING'S CLIFFE
Northamptonshire
19 West Street ◆◆◆◆
King's Cliffe, Peterborough
PE8 6XB
T: (01780) 470365
F: (01780) 470623
E: 100537.156@compuserve.
com
◎

KINGS CAPLE
Herefordshire
Ruxton Farm ◆◆◆◆
Kings Caple, Hereford HR1 4TX
T: (01432) 840493
F: (01432) 840493

KINGSLAND
Herefordshire
The Buzzards ◆◆◆
Kingsland, Leominster,
Herefordshire HR6 9QE
T: (01568) 708941
E: booking@bakerpovey.co.uk
I: www.bakerpovey.co.uk

The Corners Inn
◆◆◆ SILVER AWARD
Kingsland, Leominster,
Herefordshire HR6 9RY
T: (01568) 708385
F: (01568) 709033
E: info@cornerinn.co.uk
I: www.cornerinn.co.uk
◉

Holgate Farm ◆◆◆◆
Kingsland, Leominster,
Herefordshire HR6 9QS
T: (01568) 708275

KINGSTONE
Herefordshire
Mill Orchard
◆◆◆ GOLD AWARD
Kingstone, Hereford HR2 9ES
T: (01981) 250326
F: (01981) 250520
E: cleveland@millorchard.co.uk
I: www.millorchard.co.uk
◉

Webton Court Farmhouse ◆◆
Kingstone, Hereford HR2 9NF
T: (01981) 250220
F: (01981) 250220
E: juliet@pudgefsnet.co.uk

KINGTON
Herefordshire
Tumbledown ◆◆◆
Headbrook, Kington,
Herefordshire HR5 3DZ
T: (01544) 231380

KINLET
Worcestershire
Catsley Farm ◆◆
Kinlet, Bewdley, Worcestershire
DY12 3AP
T: (01299) 841323

KINVER
Staffordshire
Anchor Hotel ◆◆◆
Dark Lane, Kinver, Stourbridge,
West Midlands DY7 6NR
T: (01384) 872085 & 873291
F: (01384) 878824
E: anchorhotel@kinver2000.
freeserve.co.uk

KIRTON
Nottinghamshire
The Fox at Kirton ◆◆◆
Main Street, Kirton, Newark,
Nottinghamshire NG22 9LP
T: (01623) 860502 & 861909
F: (01623) 861909
E: foxkirton@aol.com

KISLINGBURY
Northamptonshire
The Elms ◆◆◆
Kislingbury, Northampton,
Northamptonshire NN7 4AH
T: (01604) 830326

KNIPTON
Leicestershire
Red House Inn ◆◆◆
Knipton, Grantham, Lincolnshire
NG32 1RH
T: (01476) 870352
F: (01476) 870429

KNOCKDOWN
Gloucestershire
Avenue Farm ◆◆◆
Knockdown, Tetbury,
Gloucestershire GL8 8QY
T: (01454) 238207
F: (01454) 238033
I: www.glosfarmhols.co.uk

KNOWLE
West Midlands
Ivy House Guest House ◆◆◆
Warwick Road, Heronfield,
Knowle, Solihull, West Midlands
B93 0EB
T: (01564) 770247
F: (01564) 778063

LAMBLEY
Nottinghamshire
Magnolia Guest House ◆◆◆◆
22 Spring Lane, Lambley,
Nottingham NG4 4PH
T: (0115) 9314404
F: 07977 991978

LAXTON
Nottinghamshire
Lilac Farm ◆◆
Laxton, Newark,
Nottinghamshire NG22 0NX
T: (01777) 870376
F: (01777) 870376

Manor Farm ◆◆
Moorhouse Road, Laxton,
Newark, Nottinghamshire
NG22 0NU
T: (01777) 870417

Spanhoe Lodge
Rating Applied For
Harringworth Road, Laxton,
Corby, Northamptonshire
NN17 3AT
T: (01780) 450328 &
07867 520917
F: (01780) 450328

LEA
Herefordshire
Forest Edge ◆◆◆◆
4 Noden Drive, Lea, Ross-on-
Wye, Herefordshire HR9 7NB
T: (01989) 750682 &
07974 770358
E: don@wood11.freeserve.co.uk
I: www.wood11.freeserve.co.uk

Warren Farm ◆◆◆◆
Warren Lane, Lea, Ross-on-Wye,
Herefordshire HR9 7LT
T: (01989) 750272 &
07802 167395
F: (01989) 750272

LEADENHAM
Lincolnshire
George Hotel ◆◆◆
High Street, Leadenham, Lincoln
LN5 0PN
T: (01400) 272251
F: (01400) 272091

LEAMINGTON SPA
Warwickshire
Adams Hotel ◆◆◆◆
22 Avenue Road, Leamington
Spa, Warwickshire CV31 3PQ
T: (01926) 450742
F: (01926) 313110
◉

Adelaide ◆◆◆
15 Adelaide Road, Leamington
Spa, Warwickshire CV31 3PN
T: (01926) 450633
F: (01926) 450633

Almond House ◆◆◆◆
8 Parklands, Lillington,
Leamington Spa, Warwickshire
CV32 7BA
T: (01926) 424052 &
07931 286945

Avenue Lodge Guest House
◆◆◆
61 Avenue Road, Leamington
Spa, Warwickshire CV31 3PF
T: (01926) 338555 &
07932 652521

Buckland Lodge Hotel ◆◆
35 Avenue Road, Leamington
Spa, Warwickshire CV31 3PG
T: (01926) 423843
F: (01926) 423843
E: buckland.lodge1@btinternet.
com
I: www.Buckland-Lodge.co.uk.

Bungalow Farm ◆◆◆◆
Windmill Hill, Cubbington,
Leamington Spa, Warwickshire
CV32 7LW
T: (01926) 423276 &
07970 818305
F: (01926) 887357
◉

Charnwood Guest House ◆◆◆
47 Avenue Road, Leamington
Spa, Warwickshire CV31 3PF
T: (01926) 831074
F: (01926) 831074

8 Clarendon Crescent
◆◆◆ SILVER AWARD
Leamington Spa, Warwickshire
CV32 5NR
T: (01926) 429840
F: (01926) 429190

The Coach House ◆◆◆◆
Snowford Hall Farm,
Hunningham, Leamington Spa,
Warwickshire CV33 9ES
T: (01926) 632297
F: (01926) 633599
E: the_coach_house@lineone.
net
I: lineone.net/§the_coach_house

Corkill Bed and Breakfast
◆◆◆
27 Newbold Street, Leamington
Spa, Warwickshire CV32 4HN
T: (01926) 336303
F: (01926) 336303
E: mrscorkill@aol.com
◉

The Dell Guesthouse ◆◆◆
8 Warwick Place, Leamington
Spa, Warwickshire CV32 5BJ
T: (01926) 422784
F: (01926) 422784
E: dellguesthouse@virgin.net
I: www.dellguesthouse.co.uk

Fountain House ◆◆◆
4 Willes Road, Leamington Spa,
Warwickshire CV32 4PY
T: (01926) 424822
E: fountain@apswabey.demon.
co.uk

5 The Grange ◆◆◆
Cubbington, Leamington Spa,
Warwickshire CV32 7LE
T: (01926) 744762

Grove Farm ◆◆◆
Burton Dassett, Leamington Spa,
Warwickshire CV47 2AB
T: (01295) 770204

Hedley Villa Guest House
◆◆◆
31 Russell Terrace, Leamington
Spa, Warwickshire CV31 1EZ
T: (01926) 424504 &
07767 207707
F: (01926) 424504

Hill Farm ◆◆◆◆
Lewis Road, Radford Semele,
Leamington Spa, Warwickshire
CV31 1UX
T: (01926) 337571

4 Lillington Road ◆◆◆
Leamington Spa, Warwickshire
CV32 5YR
T: (01926) 429244
I: PAULINEBURTON@UKONLINE.
CO.UK

Milverton House Hotel ◆◆◆◆
1 Milverton Terrace, Leamington
Spa, Warwickshire CV32 5BE
T: (01926) 428335
F: (01926) 428335
◉

Trendway Guest House ◆◆◆
45 Avenue Road, Leamington
Spa, Warwickshire CV31 3PF
T: (01926) 316644
F: (01926) 337506

Victoria Park Hotel ◆◆◆
12 Adelaide Road, Leamington
Spa, Warwickshire CV31 3PW
T: (01926) 424195
F: (01926) 421521
I: www.victoria-park-hotel-ispa.
co.uk

The Willis ◆◆◆
11 Eastnor Grove, Leamington
Spa, Warwickshire CV31 1LD
T: (01926) 425820

York House Hotel ◆◆◆
9 York Road, Leamington Spa,
Warwickshire CV31 3PR
T: (01926) 424671
F: (01926) 832272
E: yorkhouse@leamington.
freeserve-co-uk

LEASINGHAM
Lincolnshire
Manor Farm ◆◆
Leasingham, Sleaford,
Lincolnshire NG34 8JN
T: (01529) 302671
F: (01529) 414946

LECHLADE
Gloucestershire
Apple Tree House ◆◆◆
Buscot, Faringdon, Oxfordshire
SN7 8DA
T: (01367) 252592
E: emreay@aol.com

Cambrai Lodge
◆◆◆◆ SILVER AWARD
Oak Street, Lechlade,
Gloucestershire GL7 3AY
T: (01367) 253173 &
07860 150467

New Inn Hotel ◆◆◆
Market Square, Lechlade-on-
Thames, Lechlade,
Gloucestershire GL7 3AB
T: (01367) 252296
F: (01367) 252315
E: newinnlech@aol.com
I: www.newinnhotel.co.uk

LEDBURY
Herefordshire
Foley House Bed and Breakfast
◆◆◆
39 Bye Street, Ledbury,
Herefordshire HR8 2AA
T: (01531) 632471
F: (01531) 632471

The Hopton Arms
Rating Applied For
Ashperton, Ledbury,
Herefordshire HR8 2SE
T: (01531) 670520

Kilmory
◆◆◆◆◆ SILVER AWARD
Bradlow, Ledbury, Herefordshire
HR8 1JF
T: (01531) 631951
E: seymour@clara.co.uk

Little Marcle Court ◆◆◆◆
Little Marcle, Ledbury,
Herefordshire HR8 2LB
T: (01531) 670936

Mainstone House ◆◆◆
Trumpet, Ledbury, Herefordshire
HR8 2RA
T: (01531) 670230

The Oasthouse ◆◆◆◆
Hereford Road, Ledbury,
Herefordshire HR8 2PZ
T: (01531) 670631
F: (01531) 670631

**Wall Hills Country Guest
House** ◆◆◆◆
Hereford Road, Ledbury,
Herefordshire HR8 2PR
T: (01531) 632833
I: www.smoothhound.co.
uk/hotels/wallhill.html

White House ◆◆◆
Aylton, Ledbury, Herefordshire
HR8 2RQ
T: (01531) 670349
F: (01531) 670349

LEEK
Staffordshire
Abbey Inn ◆◆◆
Abbey Green Road, Leek,
Staffordshire ST13 8SA
T: (01538) 382865
F: (01538) 398604
E: martin@abbeyinn.co.uk
I: www.abbeyinn.co.uk

Bank End Farm Motel ◆◆◆
Leek Old Road, Longsdon, Stoke-
on-Trent ST9 9QJ
T: (01538) 383638

Beechfields ◆◆◆◆
Park Road, Leek, Staffordshire
ST13 8JS
T: (01538) 372825
E: jrider@fenetre.co.uk
I: www.cressbrook.co.
uk/leek/beechfields

The Green Man ◆◆◆
38 Compton, Leek, Staffordshire
ST13 5NH
T: (01538) 388084

The Hatcheries ◆◆
Church Lane, Leek, Staffordshire
ST13 5EX
T: (01538) 399552 & 383544
I: www.smoothhound.co.
uk/hotels/hatcheri.html

Little Brookhouse Farm
◆◆◆◆
Cheddleton, Leek, Staffordshire
ST13 7DF
T: (01538) 360350

New House Farm ◆◆◆
Bottomhouse, Leek,
Staffordshire ST13 7PA
T: (01538) 304350 &
(01850) 183208
F: (01538) 304338
E: newhousefarm@btinternet.
com

Peak Weavers Hotel ◆◆◆
21 King Street, Leek,
Staffordshire ST13 5NW
T: (01538) 383729 & 387475
F: (01538) 387475
E: peak.weavers@virgin.net

Prospect House ◆◆◆◆
334 Cheadle Road, Cheddleton,
Leek, Staffordshire ST13 7BW
T: (01782) 550639 &
07973 179478
F: (01782) 550639
E: prospect@talk21.com
I: www.touristnetuk.
com/wm/prospect/index.htm

LEICESTER
Leicestershire
Beaumaris Guesthouse ◆◆
18 Westcotes Drive, Leicester,
LE3 0QR
T: (0116) 254 0261 &
07957 763922

Burlington Hotel ◆◆◆
Elmfield Avenue, Stoneygate,
Leicester, LE2 1RB
T: (0116) 270 5112
F: (0116) 270 4207
E: welcome@burlingtonhotel.
co.uk

Glenfield Lodge Hotel
Rating Applied For
4 Glenfield Road, Leicester,
LE3 6AP
T: (0116) 262 7554

Spindle Lodge Hotel ◆◆◆
2 West Walk, Leicester, LE1 7NA
T: (0116) 233 8801
F: (0116) 233 8804
E: spindlelodgeleicester@
hotmail.com

Waltham House ◆◆
500 Narborough Road, Leicester,
LE3 2FU
T: (0116) 289 1129

LEIGH SINTON
Worcestershire
Chirkenhill ◆◆◆◆
Leigh Sinton, Malvern,
Worcestershire WR13 5DE
T: (01886) 832205
E: wenden@eidosnet.co.uk

LEINTWARDINE
Shropshire
Lower House ◆◆◆◆
Adforton, Leintwardine, Craven
Arms, Shropshire SY7 0NF
T: (01568) 770223
F: (01568) 770592
E: cutler@sy7.com
I: www.sy7.com/lower-house

LEOMINSTER
Herefordshire
Bedford House ◆◆◆
Dilwyn, Hereford HR4 8JJ
T: (01544) 388260

Bramlea ◆◆◆
Barons Cross Road, Leominster,
Herefordshire HR6 8RW
T: (01568) 613406
F: (01568) 613406
E: lesbramlea@netlineUK.net

Chesfield ◆◆◆
112 South Street, Leominster,
Herefordshire HR6 8JF
T: (01568) 613204

Copper Hall ◆◆◆◆
South Street, Leominster,
Herefordshire HR6 8JN
T: (01568) 611622
E: sccrick@copperhall.freeserve.
co.uk

Heath House ◆◆◆◆
Stoke Prior, Leominster,
Herefordshire HR6 0NF
T: (01568) 760385
F: (01568) 760385

Highfield ◆◆◆◆
Ivington Road, Newtown,
Leominster, Herefordshire
HR6 8QD
T: (01568) 613216
E: highfieldgh@talk21.com

Highgate House ◆◆◆◆
29 Hereford Road, Leominster,
Herefordshire HR6 8JS
T: (01568) 614562
F: (01568) 614562
E: highgatehouse@easicom.
com

Home Farm ◆◆◆◆
Bircher, Leominster,
Herefordshire HR6 0AX
T: (01568) 780525

Little Bury Farm ◆◆◆
Luston, Leominster,
Herefordshire HR6 0EB
T: (01568) 611575

Lower Bache House ◆◆◆◆
Kimbolton, Leominster,
Herefordshire HR6 0ER
T: (01568) 750304
E: lesliewiles@care4free.net

The Paddock
◆◆◆◆ GOLD AWARD
Shobdon, Leominster,
Herefordshire HR6 9NQ
T: (01568) 708176
F: (01568) 708829
E: thepaddock@talk21.com

Peel Villa ◆◆◆
Baron's Cross Road, Leominster,
Herefordshire HR6 8QX
T: (01568) 611273

Rossendale Guesthouse ◆◆◆
46 Broad Street, Leominster,
Herefordshire HR6 8BS
T: (01568) 612464

Tyn-Y-Coed ◆◆◆
Shobdon, Leominster,
Herefordshire HR6 9NY
T: (01568) 708277
F: (01568) 708277
E: jandrews@shobdondesign.
kc3.co.uk

LICHFIELD
Staffordshire
Abnalls Cottage ◆◆◆◆
Abnalls Lane, Lichfield,
Staffordshire WS13 8BN
T: (01543) 263500

32 Beacon Street ◆◆◆◆
Lichfield, Staffordshire
WS13 7AJ
T: (01543) 262378

Broad Lane Guest House
◆◆◆◆
35 Broad Lane, Lichfield,
Staffordshire WS14 9SU
T: (01543) 262301

8 The Close ◆◆◆
Lichfield, Staffordshire
WS13 7LD
T: (01543) 418483
F: (01543) 418483

Coppers End Guest House
◆◆◆
Walsall Road, Muckley Corner,
Lichfield, Staffordshire
WS14 0BG
T: (01543) 372910
F: (01543) 360423

Davolls Cottage ◆◆◆
156 Woodhouses Road,
Burntwood, Lichfield,
Staffordshire WS7 9EL
T: (01543) 671250

16 Dimbles Lane ◆◆◆
Lichfield, Staffordshire
WS13 7HW
T: (01543) 251107

The Farmhouse ◆◆◆◆
Lysway Lane, Longdon Green,
Rugeley, Staffordshire
WS15 4PZ
T: (0121) 378 4552 &
(01543) 490416
F: (0121) 311 2915
E: retall@daviddrury.demon.co.
uk
I: www.daviddrury.demon.co.uk

4 Hayes View ◆◆◆
Lichfield, Staffordshire
WS13 7BT
T: (01543) 253725

Holly House Bed and Breakfast
◆◆◆
198 Upper St John Street,
Lichfield, Staffordshire
WS14 9EF
T: (01543) 263078

Netherstowe House North ◆◆
Netherstowe Lane, Lichfield,
Staffordshire WS13 6AY
T: (01543) 254631

Pauline Duvals Bed and Breakfast ◆◆◆
21-23 Dam Street, The Bogey Hole, Lichfield, Staffordshire WS13 6AE
T: (01543) 264303

The Swan ◆◆◆
Bird Street, Lichfield, Staffordshire WS13 6PT
T: (01543) 414777 & 301235
F: (01543) 411277

Twenty Three The Close ◆◆◆◆
23 The Close, Lichfield, Staffordshire WS13 7LD
T: (01543) 306140 &
0780 3689897
E: charles.taylor@
lichfield-cathedral.org

The White House ◆◆
Market Lane, Wall, Lichfield, Staffordshire WS14 0AS
T: (01543) 480384

LINCOLN
Lincolnshire

AA and M Guesthouse ◆◆◆
79 Carholme Road, Lincoln, Lincolnshire LN1 1RT
T: (01522) 543736
F: (01522) 543736
◉

Aaron Whisby Guest House
Rating Applied For
262 West Parade, Lincoln, LN1 1LY
T: (01522) 526930

Damon's Motel ◆◆◆◆
997 Doddington Road, Lincoln, LN6 3ES
T: (01522) 887733
F: (01522) 887734
🧍

D'isney Place Hotel
◆◆◆◆ SILVER AWARD
Eastgate, Lincoln, Lincolnshire LN2 4AA
T: (01522) 538881
F: (01522) 511321
E: info@disneyplacehotel.co.uk
I: www.disneyplacehotel.co.uk
◉

Hamilton Hotel ◆◆
2 Hamilton Road, Lincoln, LN5 8ED
T: (01522) 528243
F: (01522) 528243

Hollies Hotel ◆◆
65 Carholme Road, Lincoln, LN1 1RT
T: (01522) 522419
F: (01522) 522419
E: holhotel@aol.com
I: www.4-front.co.
uk/hollies-hotel

Jaymar
Rating Applied For
31 Newland St West, Lincoln, LN1 1QQ
T: (01522) 532934
◉

Manor House ◆◆◆◆
Bracebridge Heath, Lincoln LN4 2HW
T: (01522) 520825
F: (01522) 542418
E: mikescoley@farming.co.uk

Mayfield Guesthouse ◆◆◆
213 Yarborough Road, Lincoln, LN1 3NQ
T: (01522) 533732 &
07771 744121
F: (01522) 533732

New Farm ◆◆◆
Burton, Lincoln LN1 2RD
T: (01522) 527326
◉

Newport Cottage ◆◆◆◆
21 Newport, Lincoln, LN1 3DQ
T: (01522) 534470
◉

Newport Guest House ◆◆◆
26-28 Newport, Lincoln, LN1 3DF
T: (01522) 528590
F: (01522) 544502
E: info@newportguesthouse.co.uk
I: www.newportguesthouse.co.uk

73 Station Road ◆◆◆
Branston, Lincoln, LN4 1LG
T: (01522) 828658 &
07932 162940

Tennyson Hotel ◆◆◆◆
7 South Park Avenue, Lincoln, LN5 8EN
T: (01522) 521624
F: (01522) 521624
E: tennyson.hotel@virgin.net
I: freespace.virgin.net/tennyson.hotel

Truro House
Rating Applied For
421 Newark Road, North Hykeham, Lincoln, LN6 9SP
T: (01522) 882073 &
07798 791484

LINTON
Derbyshire

The Manor
◆◆◆◆ SILVER AWARD
Hillside Road, Linton, Swadlincote, Staffordshire DE12 6RA
T: (01283) 761177

LITTLE BYTHAM
Lincolnshire

The Mallard Inn ◆◆◆◆
1 High Street, Little Bytham, Stamford, Lincolnshire NG33 4PP
T: (01780) 410470
F: (01780) 410245
E: john@mallard-inn.freeserve.co.uk
I: www.mallard-inn.co.uk

LITTLE COWARNE
Herefordshire

Three Horseshoes Inn ◆◆◆
Little Cowarne, Bromyard, Herefordshire HR7 4RQ
T: (01885) 400276 & 40035
F: (01885) 400276
◉

LITTLE HAYFIELD
Derbyshire

Lantern Pike Inn ◆◆◆
Glossop Road, Little Hayfield, High Peak SK22 2NG
T: (01663) 747590

LITTLE INKBERROW
Worcestershire

Perrymill Farm ◆◆◆
Little Inkberrow, Worcester WR7 4JQ
T: (01386) 792177
F: (01386) 793449
E: alexander@estatergazette.net

LITTLE RISSINGTON
Gloucestershire

Weaveley Cottage ◆◆◆◆
Little Rissington, Cheltenham, Gloucestershire GL54 2ND
T: (01451) 822482 & 821091
F: (01451) 822482
E: bourtonb@aol.com

LITTLE WENLOCK
Shropshire

Wenboro Cottage ◆◆◆
Church Lane, Little Wenlock, Telford, Shropshire TF6 5BB
T: (01952) 505573
E: rcarter@wenboro.freeserve.co.uk

LITTLEDEAN
Gloucestershire

Brayne Court ◆◆
High Street, Littledean, Cinderford, Gloucestershire GL14 3JY
T: (01594) 822163 &
07887 524991
F: (01594) 822163
E: jgreen4021@aol.com

LITTON
Derbyshire

Beacon House ◆◆◆
Litton, Buxton, Derbyshire SK17 8QP
T: (01298) 871752

Hall Farm House ◆◆◆◆
Litton, Buxton, Derbyshire SK17 8QP
T: (01298) 872172

LONG BUCKBY
Northamptonshire

Murcott Mill ◆◆◆
Murcott, Long Buckby, Northampton NN6 7QR
T: (01327) 842236
F: (01327) 844524
E: bhart6@commpuserve.com
◉

LONG CLAWSON
Leicestershire

Elms Farm
Rating Applied For
East End, Long Clawson, Melton Mowbray, Leicestershire LE14 4NG
T: (01664) 822395
F: (01664) 823399
E: elmsfarm@whittard.net
I: www.whittard.net

LONG COMPTON
Warwickshire

Ashby House Bed and Breakfast ◆◆◆◆
Ashby House, Clarks Lane, Long Compton, Shipston-on-Stour, Warwickshire CV36 5LB
T: (01608) 684286 &
07976 700763
F: (01608) 684286
E: epfield@fieldashby.demon.co.uk
I: www.travel-uk.com/country/stratford.htm

Butlers Road Farm ◆◆◆
Long Compton, Shipston-on-Stour, Warwickshire CV36 5JZ
T: (01608) 684262
F: (01608) 684262
E: eileenwhittaker@easicom.com

Manor House Hotel & Restaurant ◆◆◆◆
Long Compton, Shipston-on-Stour, Warwickshire CV36 5JJ
T: (01608) 684218 &
07885 621177
F: (01608) 684218

LONG MARSTON
Warwickshire

The Grange
◆◆◆◆ GOLD AWARD
The Grange, Long Marston, Stratford-upon-Avon, Warwickshire CV37 8RH
T: (01789) 721800 &
07785 577048
F: (01789) 721901
E: grangeline@msn.com
I: www.stratford-upon-avon.co.uk/grange.htm
◉

LONGBOROUGH
Gloucestershire

The Long House
Rating Applied For
Old Rectory Gardens, Longborough, Moreton-in-Marsh, Gloucestershire GL56 0QF
T: (01451) 830577
F: (01451) 830577

Luckley Farm Bed and Breakfast ◆◆◆
Luckley Farm, Longborough, Moreton-in-Marsh, Gloucestershire GL56 0RD
T: (01451) 870885
F: (01451) 831481
E: luckleyholidays@talk21.com
I: www.luckley-holidays.co.uk

LONGDON
Staffordshire

Grand Lodge ◆◆◆◆
Horsey Lane, Longdon, Rugeley, Staffordshire WS15 4LW
T: (01543) 686103
F: (01543) 676266
E: grandlodge@edbroemt.demon.co.uk

LONGHOPE
Gloucestershire

New House Farm ◆◆◆
Barrel Lane, Aston Ingham, Longhope, Gloucestershire GL17 0LS
T: (01452) 830484
F: (01452) 830484
E: scaldbrain@aol.com
I: www.newhousefarm-accommodation.co.uk

The Old Farm ◆◆◆◆
Barrel Lane, Longhope, Gloucestershire GL17 0LR
T: (01452) 830252 &
0789 9831998
F: (01452) 830252
E: lucyr@avnet.co.uk
I: ww.avnet.co.uk/theoldfarm

Royal Spring Farm ◆◆◆◆
(A4136), Longhope,
Gloucestershire GL17 0PY
T: (01452) 830550

LONGLEVENS
Gloucestershire

Gemini Guest House ◆◆
83a Innsworth Lane, Longlevens,
Gloucester GL2 0TT
T: (01452) 415849

LONGNOR
Staffordshire

Crewe and Harpur Arms Hotel
◆◆◆
Longnor, Buxton, Derbyshire
SK17 0NC
T: (01298) 83205

LONGTOWN
Herefordshire

Olchon Cottage Farm ◆◆◆
Longtown, Hereford,
Herefordshire HR2 0NS
T: (01873) 860233
F: (01873) 860233
I: www.golden-valley.co.
uk/Olchon

LOUGHBOROUGH
Leicestershire

Charnwood Lodge ◆◆◆
136 Leicester Road,
Loughborough, Leicestershire
LE11 2AQ
T: (01509) 211120
F: (01509) 211121
E: charnwoodlodge@charwat.
freeserve.com
I: www.charnwoodlodge.com

Demontfort Hotel ◆◆◆
88 Leicester Road,
Loughborough, Leicestershire
LE11 2AQ
T: (01509) 216061
F: (01509) 233667

Forest Rise Hotel Ltd ◆◆◆
55-57 Forest Road,
Loughborough, Leicestershire
LE11 3NW
T: (01509) 215928
F: (01509) 210506

Garendon Park Hotel ◆◆◆
92 Leicester Road,
Loughborough, Leicestershire
LE11 2AQ
T: (01509) 236557
F: (01509) 265559
E: info@garendonparkhotel.co.
uk
I: www.garendonparkhotel.co.uk

The Highbury Guesthouse
◆◆◆
146 Leicester Road,
Loughborough, Leicestershire
LE11 2AQ
T: (01509) 230545
F: (01509) 233086

Holywell House ◆◆◆
40 Leicester Road,
Loughborough, Leicestershire
LE11 2AG
T: (01509) 267891 &
07899 755556
F: (01509) 267891

Lane End Cottage ◆◆◆◆
45 School Lane, Old Woodhouse,
Loughborough, Leicestershire
LE12 8UJ
T: (01509) 890706
E: maryhudson@talk21.com

New Life Guesthouse
Rating Applied For
121 Ashby Road, Loughborough,
Leicestershire LE11 3AB
T: (01509) 216699
F: (01509) 210020
E: john_of_newlife@assureweb.
com

Peachnook ◆◆
154 Ashby Road, Loughborough,
Leicestershire LE11 3AG
T: (01509) 264390 & 217525
I: www.SmoothHound.co.
uk/hotels/peachnohtml

LOUTH
Lincolnshire

Masons Arms ◆◆◆
Cornmarket, Louth, Lincolnshire
LN11 9PY
T: (01507) 609525 & 609526
F: 0870 7066450
E: justin@themasons.co.uk
I: www.themasons.co.uk

LOWER BODDINGTON
Northamptonshire

Sears Cottage
◆◆◆◆ SILVER AWARD
Owl End Lane, Lower
Boddington, Daventry,
Northamptonshire NN11 6XZ
T: (01327) 260271 & 262476
F: (01327) 262476
E: Lynne.Sydenham@mcmail.
com
I: www.searscottage.freeserve.
co.uk

LOWER SLAUGHTER
Gloucestershire

Church Farm House ◆◆◆
Lower Slaughter, Cheltenham,
Gloucestershire GL54 2HR
T: (01451) 810725 &
07801 069631
F: (01451) 810725

Greenfingers ◆◆◆◆
Wyck Rissington Lane, Lower
Slaughter, Cheltenham,
Gloucestershire GL54 2EX
T: (01451) 821217 &
07710 798985

Lakeside ◆◆◆
Fosseway, Lower Slaughter,
Cheltenham, Gloucestershire
GL54 2EY
T: (01451) 821206

The Old Mill Lodge
Rating Applied For
Lower Slaughter, Cheltenham,
Gloucestershire GL54 2HX
T: (01451) 822127 & 0790 1972
820
F: (01451) 822127

LOXLEY
Warwickshire

Elm Cottage ◆◆◆◆
Stratford Road, Loxley, Warwick
CV35 9JW
T: (01789) 840609

Loxley Farm ◆◆◆◆
Loxley, Warwick CV35 9JN
T: (01789) 840265
F: (01789) 840265

Oldborough Farmhouse
◆◆◆◆
Loxley Road, Loxley, Warwick
CV35 9JW
T: (01789) 840938
F: (01789) 840938

LUBENHAM
Leicestershire

The Old Bakehouse ◆◆◆◆
9 The Green, Lubenham, Market
Harborough, Leicestershire
LE16 9TD
T: (01858) 463401

LUDFORD
Lincolnshire

Long Acre ◆◆◆
Magna Mile, Ludford, Market
Rasen, Lincolnshire LN8 6AD
T: (01507) 313335
E: nick.feit@btinternet.com

LUDLOW
Shropshire

Arran House ◆◆◆
42 Gravel Hill, Ludlow,
Shropshire SY8 1QR
T: (01584) 873764

The Brakes ◆◆◆◆
Downton, Ludlow, Shropshire
SY8 2LF
T: (01584) 856485
F: (01584) 856485
E: thebrakes@cwcom.net

Broadgate Cottage ◆◆◆
Silkmill Lane, Ludlow, Shropshire
SY8 1BJ
T: (01584) 876009 &
07976 535527

Bromfield Manor ◆◆◆◆
Bromfield, Ludlow, Shropshire
SY8 2JU
T: (01584) 856536 &
07850 713340
F: (01584) 856536
E: john.mason9@virgin.net
I: www.go2.co.uk/bromfield

Bull Hotel ◆◆◆
14 The Bull Ring, Ludlow,
Shropshire SY8 1AD
T: (01584) 873611
F: (01584) 873666
E: bull.ludlow@btinternet.com
I: www.goz.co.uk

Castle View ◆◆◆
7 Castle View Terrace, Ludlow,
Shropshire SY8 2NG
T: (01584) 875592
F: (01584) 875592

Cecil Guest House ◆◆◆
Sheet Road, Ludlow, Shropshire
SY8 1LR
T: (01584) 872442
F: (01584) 872442

Crown Inn ◆◆◆◆
Hopton Wafers, Shropshire
DY14 0NB
T: (01299) 270372
F: (01299) 271127
E: desk@crownathopton.co.uk
I: www.go2.co.
uk/crownathopton

Eight Dinham ◆◆◆
Dinham, Ludlow, Shropshire
SY8 1EJ
T: (01584) 875661

Elsich Manor Cottage ◆◆◆
Seifton, Ludlow, Shropshire
SY8 2DL
T: (01584) 861406 &
07989 623813
F: (01584) 861406

Fernleigh ◆◆◆
Saint Julians Avenue, Ludlow,
Shropshire SY8 1ET
T: (01584) 873248

**The Hen and Chickens
Guesthouse** ◆◆◆
103 Old Street, Ludlow,
Shropshire SY8 1NU
T: (01584) 874318 &
07977 140473
E: sally@hen-and-chickens.co.
uk
I: www.hen-and-chickens.co.uk

Henwick House ◆◆◆
Gravel Hill, Ludlow, Shropshire
SY8 1QU
T: (01584) 873338

Longlands ◆◆◆
Woodhouse Lane, Richards
Castle, Ludlow, Shropshire
SY8 4EU
T: (01584) 831636
E: IANKKEMSLEY@aol.com

Lower House Farm Guesthouse
◆◆◆◆
Cleedownton, Ludlow,
Shropshire SY8 3EH
T: (01584) 823648
I: www.go2.co.
uk/lowerhousefarm

The Moor Hall ◆◆◆
Cleedownton, Ludlow,
Shropshire SY8 3EG
T: (01584) 823209 & 823333
F: (01584) 823387

Mr Underhills
◆◆◆◆◆ SILVER AWARD
Dinham Weir, Dinham, Ludlow,
Shropshire SY8 1EH
T: (01584) 874431

Nelson Cottage ◆◆◆
Rocks Green, Ludlow, Shropshire
SY8 2DS
T: (01584) 878108
F: (01584) 878108
E: hotmail@nelsoncottage.com

Number Twenty Eight
◆◆◆◆◆ GOLD AWARD
28 Lower Broad Street, Ludlow,
Shropshire SY8 1PQ
T: (01584) 876996 &
0800 0815000
F: (01584) 876860
E: ross@no28.co.uk
I: www.no28.co.uk

Old Downton House
◆◆◆◆◆ SILVER AWARD
Donnton on the Rock, Ludlow,
Shropshire SY8 2HU
T: (01568) 770389 &
07976 579006
F: (01568) 770776

Ravenscourt Manor
◆◆◆◆ GOLD AWARD
Woofferton, Ludlow, Shropshire
SY8 4AL
T: (01584) 711905

Spring Cottage
◆◆◆◆◆ GOLD AWARD
Abdon, Craven Arms, Shropshire
SY7 9HU
T: (01746) 712551
F: (01746) 712001

The Wheatsheaf Inn ◆◆◆◆
Lower Broad Street, Ludlow,
Shropshire SY8 1PQ
T: (01584) 872980
F: (01584) 877990
E: karen.wheatsheaf@tinyworld.
co.uk

LUSTON
Herefordshire

Knapp House ◆◆◆
Luston, Leominster,
Herefordshire HR6 0EB
T: (01568) 615705

Ladymeadow Farm ◆◆◆
Luston, Leominster,
Herefordshire HR6 0AS
T: (01568) 780262

LUTTERWORTH
Leicestershire

The Greyhound Coaching Inn
◆◆◆
9 Market Street, Lutterworth,
Leicestershire LE17 4EJ
T: (01455) 553307
F: (01455) 554558
E: bookings@greyhoundinn.
fsnet.co.uk
I: www.greyhoundinn.co.uk

Highcross House ◆◆
Highcross, Lutterworth,
Leicestershire LE17 5AT
T: (01455) 220840 & 220060
F: (01455) 220840
E: highcrosshse@lineone.net
I: www.highcrosshouse.co.uk

LYDBURY NORTH
Shropshire

Brunslow ◆
Lydbury North, Shropshire
SY7 8AD
T: (01588) 680244
F: (01588) 680244

The Powis Arms ◆◆◆
Lydbury North, Shropshire
SY7 8AU
T: (01588) 680254

Walcot Farm ◆◆◆◆
Lydbury North, Shropshire
SY7 8AA
T: (01588) 680243
F: (01588) 680243

LYONSHALL
Herefordshire

Penrhos Farm ◆◆◆
Lyonshall, Kington,
Herefordshire HR5 3LH
T: (01544) 231467
F: (01544) 340273

Royal George Inn ◆◆◆◆
Lyonshall, Kington,
Herefordshire HR5 3JN
T: (01544) 340210
E: rtae.b@virgin.net
⊚

The Woodlands ◆◆◆
Lyonshall, Kington,
Herefordshire HR5 3LJ
T: (01544) 340394
⊚

MACKWORTH
Derbyshire

Thames House ◆◆◆◆
6 Thames Close, Mackworth,
Derby DE22 4HT
T: (01332) 513526
F: (01332) 513526

MADELEY
Staffordshire

Bar Hill House ◆◆◆◆
Bar Hill, Madeley, Crewe
CW3 9QE
T: (01782) 752199
F: (01782) 750981
E: barhillbb@hotmail.com
I: www.touristnet.com

MALTBY LE MARSH
Lincolnshire

Farmhouse Bed and Breakfast
◆◆◆
Grange Farm, Maltby le Marsh,
Alford, Lincolnshire LN13 0JP
T: (01507) 450267
F: (01507) 450180

MALVERN
Worcestershire

Clevelands ◆◆◆
41 Alexandra Road, Malvern,
Worcestershire WR14 1HE
T: (01684) 572164
F: (01684) 576691
E: jonmargstocks@aol.com.

Como House ◆◆◆
Como Road, Malvern,
Worcestershire WR14 2TH
T: (01684) 561486
E: mary@como-house.
freeserve.co.uk

Cowleigh Park Farm ◆◆◆◆
Cowleigh Road, Malvern,
Worcestershire WR13 5HJ
T: (01684) 566750
F: (01684) 566750

Danemoor Farm ◆◆◆
Welland, Malvern,
Worcestershire WR13 6NL
T: (01684) 310905
F: (01684) 310905

Edgeworth ◆◆◆
4 Carlton Road, Malvern,
Worcestershire WR14 1HH
T: (01684) 572565 &
0771 285914

Fair View Cottage ◆◆◆
77 Old Wyche Road, Malvern,
Worcestershire WR14 4EP
T: (01684) 560908
E: fairviewcottage@
netscapeonline.co.uk
I: www.geocities.
com/fairviewcottageuk/

The Firs ◆◆◆
243 West Malvern Road,
Malvern, Worcestershire
WR14 4BE
T: (01684) 564016 &
07885 789609
F: (01684) 564016
E: valshearerthefirs@hotmail.
com
I: www.smoothhound.co

Grove House Farm ◆◆◆
Guarlford, Malvern,
Worcestershire WR14 3QZ
T: (01684) 574256
F: (01684) 574256

Guarlford Grange
◆◆◆◆ SILVER AWARD
11 Guarlford Road, Malvern,
Worcestershire WR14 3QW
T: (01684) 575996
F: (01684) 575996

Harcourt Cottage ◆◆◆
252 West Malvern Road, West
Malvern, Malvern,
Worcestershire WR14 4DQ
T: (01684) 574561
E: harcourtcottage@lineone.net

Homestead Lodge ◆◆◆
25 Somers Park Avenue,
Malvern, Worcestershire
WR14 1SE
T: (01684) 573094 &
07880 874537
F: (01684) 573094
E: trant@homesteadlodge.
freeserve.co.uk
I: www.homestead.lodge.
freeserve.co.uk

Kylemore ◆◆
30 Avenue Road, Malvern,
Worcestershire WR14 3BJ
T: (01684) 563753
E: ftbell@kylemore30.fsnet.co.
uk

Mellor Heights
Rating Applied For
46A West Malvern Road,
Malvern, Worcestershire
WR14 4NA
T: (01684) 565105
F: (01684) 565105
E: mary@malvern_worcs.
prestel.co.uk

Montrose Hotel ◆◆◆
23 Graham Road, Malvern,
Worcestershire WR14 2HU
T: (01684) 572335

Pembridge Hotel ◆◆◆◆
114 Graham Road, Malvern,
Worcestershire WR14 2HX
T: (01684) 574813
F: (01684) 566885
E: pembridgehotel@aol.com

Priory Holme ◆◆◆◆
18 Avenue Road, Malvern,
Worcestershire WR14 3AR
T: (01684) 568455

Rathlin ◆◆◆◆
1 Carlton Road, Malvern,
Worcestershire WR14 1HH
T: (01684) 572491

The Red Gate
◆◆◆◆ SILVER AWARD
32 Avenue Road, Malvern,
Worcestershire WR14 3BJ
T: (01684) 565013
F: (01684) 565013
E: red_gate@lineone.net
I: www.SmoothHound.co.uk/shs.
html

Robin's Orchard ◆◆◆
New Road, Castlemorton,
Malvern, Worcestershire
WR13 6BT
T: (01684) 833251

Sunnydale
◆◆◆◆ SILVER AWARD
69 Tanhouse Lane, Malvern,
Worcestershire WR14 1LQ
T: (01886) 832066

The White Cottage ◆◆◆◆
260 Wells Road, Malvern,
Worcestershire WR14 4HD
T: (01684) 576426 &
07703 525862
F: (01684) 561881
E: fiona@
finonacowleylanguageservices.
co.uk

Wyche Keep Country House
◆◆◆◆ SILVER AWARD
22 Wyche Road, Malvern,
Worcestershire WR14 4EG
T: (01684) 567018
F: (01684) 892304
E: wyche-keep-tours@england.
com
I: www.jks.org/wychekeep

York House
◆◆◆◆ SILVER AWARD
Walwyn Road, Colwall, Malvern,
Worcestershire WR13 6QG
T: (01684) 540449 &
0797 4961470
E: yorkhousecolwall@
netscapeonline.co.uk

MANSFIELD
Nottinghamshire

Blue Barn Farm ◆◆◆
Nether Langwith, Mansfield,
Nottinghamshire NG20 9JD
T: (01623) 742248 &
07885 485346
F: (01623) 742248
E: IbbotsonBluebarn@
Netscape-online.co.uk
⊚

Clifton Hotel ◆◆
Terrace Road, Mansfield,
Nottinghamshire NG18 2BP
T: (01623) 623876

MARCHINGTON
Staffordshire

Forest Hills ◆◆◆
Moisty Lane, Marchington,
Uttoxeter, Staffordshire
ST14 8JY
T: (01283) 820447

MARDEN
Herefordshire

Vauld House Farm ◆◆◆◆
Marden, Hereford HR1 3HA
T: (01568) 797347
F: (01568) 797366
E: wellthevauld@talk21.com

MARKET DRAYTON
Shropshire

Crofton ◆◆◆◆
80 Rowan Road, Market
Drayton, Shropshire TF9 1RR
T: (01630) 655484
⊚

Heath Farm Bed and Breakfast
◆◆
Heath Farm, Hodnet, Market
Drayton, Shropshire TF9 3JJ
T: (01630) 685570
F: (01630) 685570
E: hugh@gallery81.freeserve.co.
uk

Marton ◆◆
7 Broom Hollow, Loggerheads,
Market Drayton, Shropshire
TF9 4NT
T: (01630) 673329

Milford ◆◆
Adderley Road, Market Drayton,
Shropshire TF9 3SW
T: (01630) 655249

Millstone ◆◆◆
Adderley Road, Market Drayton, Shropshire TF9 3SW
T: (01630) 657584

Red House Cottage ◆◆◆
31 Shropshire Street, Market Drayton, Shropshire TF9 3DA
T: (01630) 655206

The Tudor House Hotel and Restaurant ◆◆◆
1 Cheshire Street, Market Drayton, Shropshire TF9 1PD
T: (01630) 657523 &
(01952) 691184
F: (01630) 657806
E: sugarloaf@globalnet.co.uk

Willow House ◆◆◆◆
Shrewsbury Road, Tern Hill, Market Drayton, Shropshire TF9 3PX
T: (01630) 638326
⊛

MARKET HARBOROUGH
Leicestershire

Farndon Grange ◆◆◆◆
Marston Lane, East Farndon, Market Harborough, Leicestershire LE16 9SL
T: (01858) 434492 &
07801 880859
F: (01858) 434181

The Fox Inn ◆◆◆
Church Street, Wilbarston, Market Harborough, Leicestershire LE16 8QG
T: (01536) 771270
F: (01536) 771270

The George at Great Oxendon ◆◆◆◆
Great Oxendon, Market Harborough, Leicestershire LE16 8NA
T: (01858) 465205
F: (01858) 465205
⊛

MARKET RASEN
Lincolnshire

Beechwood Guesthouse ◆◆◆◆
54 Willingham Road, Market Rasen, Lincolnshire LN8 3DX
T: (01673) 844043
F: (01673) 844043
⊛

East Farmhouse ◆◆◆◆
Middle Rasen Road, Buslingthorpe, Market Rasen, Lincolnshire LN3 5AQ
T: (01673) 842283

Waveney Cottage Guesthouse ◆◆◆
Willingham Road, Market Rasen, Lincolnshire LN8 3DN
T: (01673) 843236
F: (01673) 843236

MARSTON
Lincolnshire

Gelston Grange Farm ◆◆◆◆
Marston, Grantham, Lincolnshire NG32 2AQ
T: (01400) 250281
F: (01400) 250281

Thorold Arms ◆◆◆
Main Street, Marston, Grantham, Lincolnshire NG32 2HH
T: (01400) 250899 &
07831 340018
F: (01400) 251030

MARSTON MONTGOMERY
Derbyshire

The Old Barn ◆◆◆◆
Marston Montgomery, Ashbourne, Derbyshire DE6 2FF
T: (01889) 590848
F: (01889) 590698

MARTIN
Lincolnshire

Beechwood Barn ◆◆◆◆
North Moor Lane, Linwood Road, Martin, Lincoln LN4 3RA
T: (01526) 378339

MARTLEY
Worcestershire

The Chandlery ◆◆◆◆
Worcester Road, Martley, Worcester, Worcestershire WR6 6QA
T: (01886) 888318
F: (01886) 889047
E: john.nicklin@virgin.net
I: freespace.virgin.net/john.nicklin

MATLOCK
Derbyshire

Bank House
◆◆◆◆◆ SILVER AWARD
12 Snitterton Road, Matlock, Derbyshire DE4 3LZ
T: (01629) 56101
F: (01629) 56101

Derwent House ◆◆◆
Knowleston Place, Matlock, Derbyshire DE4 3BU
T: (01629) 584681

Dimple House ◆◆◆◆
Dimple Road, Matlock, Derbyshire DE4 3JX
T: (01629) 583228

Edgemount ◆◆
16 Edge Road, Matlock, Derbyshire DE4 3NH
T: (01629) 584787

Ellen House ◆◆◆◆
37 Snitterton Road, Matlock, Derbyshire DE4 3LZ
T: (01629) 55584 &
0777 5588562

Henmore Grange ◆◆◆◆
Hopton, Wirksworth, Derby DE4 4DF
T: (01629) 540420
F: (01629) 540720
E: marycollins@henmoregrange.freeserve.co.uk
I: www.henmoregrange.freeserve.co.uk

Home Farm ◆◆◆
Ible, Grange Mill, Matlock, Derbyshire DE4 4HS
T: (01629) 650349

Jackson Tor House Hotel ◆◆◆
76 Jackson Road, Matlock, Derbyshire DE4 3JQ
T: (01629) 582348
F: (01629) 582348

Riverbank House ◆◆◆◆
Derwent Avenue, (Off Old English Road), Matlock, Derbyshire DE4 3LX
T: (01629) 582593
I: www.riverbankhouse.co.uk

Robertswood Guesthouse
◆◆◆◆◆ SILVER AWARD
Farley Hill, Matlock, Derbyshire DE4 3LL
T: (01629) 55642
F: (01629) 55642
E: robertswood@supanet.com

Springfield House ◆◆◆
268 Bakewell Road, Matlock, Derbyshire DE4 3BN
T: (01629) 55820
F: (01629) 581310
I: marguerite@talk21.com

Warren Carr Barn ◆◆◆◆
Warren Carr, Matlock, Derbyshire DE4 2LN
T: (01629) 733856
E: cherry@warrencarrbarn.freeserve.co.uk
I: www.SmoothHound.co.uk/hotels/warrenca.html

Wayside Farm ◆◆◆
Matlock Moor, Matlock, Derbyshire DE4 5LZ
T: (01629) 582967 &
0797 1415510

The White Lion Inn ◆◆◆◆
195 Starkholmes Road, Matlock, Derbyshire DE4 5JA
T: (01629) 582511

MATLOCK BATH
Derbyshire

Ashdale ◆◆◆
92 North Parade, Matlock Bath, Matlock, Derbyshire DE4 3NS
T: (01629) 57826 &
07714 106402
E: ashdale@matlockbath.fsnet.co.uk

The Firs ◆◆◆
180 Dale Road, Matlock Bath, Matlock, Derbyshire DE4 3PS
T: (01629) 582426 & 581235
F: (01629) 582426
E: moira@thefirs180.demon.co.uk

Fountain Villa ◆◆◆◆
86 North Parade, Matlock Bath, Matlock, Derbyshire DE4 3NS
T: (01629) 56195
F: (01629) 581057
E: enquiries@fountainvilla.co.uk
I: www.fountainvilla.co.uk

Hodgkinsons Hotel ◆◆◆◆
150 South Parade, Matlock Bath, Matlock, Derbyshire DE4 3NR
T: (01629) 582170
F: (01629) 584891

Old Museum Guesthouse ◆◆◆
170-172 South Parade, Matlock Bath, Matlock, Derbyshire DE4 3NR
T: (01629) 57783
E: lindsayandstewartbailey@tinyworld.co.uk

Sunnybank Guesthouse
◆◆◆◆ SILVER AWARD
37 Clifton Road, Matlock Bath, Matlock, Derbyshire DE4 3PW
T: (01629) 584621
E: sunward@lineone.net
⊛

Temple Hotel ◆◆◆◆
Temple Walk, Matlock Bath, Matlock, Derbyshire DE4 3PG
T: (01629) 583911
F: (01629) 580851
I: www.temple.co.uk

MAVESYN RIDWARE
Staffordshire

The Old Rectory
Rating Applied For
Mavesyn Ridware, Rugeley, Staffordshire WS15 3QE
T: (01543) 490792

MAYFIELD
Staffordshire

The Old Kennels ◆◆◆
Birdsgrove Lane, Mayfield, Ashbourne, Derbyshire DE6 2BP
T: (01335) 344418
E: carole@zenith55.demon.co-uk and bandb@zenith55.demon.co.uk
I: www.zenith55.demon.co.uk

MEDBOURNE
Leicestershire

Homestead House ◆◆◆◆
5 Ashley Road, Medbourne, Market Harborough, Leicestershire LE16 8DL
T: (01858) 565724
F: (01858) 565324

MELBOURNE
Derbyshire

Sir Francis Burdett Inn ◆◆
Derby Road, Melbourne, Derby DE73 1DE
T: (01332) 862105

MELTON MOWBRAY
Leicestershire

Amberley Gardens ◆◆◆◆
4 Church Lane, Asfordby, Melton Mowbray, Leicestershire LE14 3RU
T: (01664) 812314
F: (01664) 813740
E: bruce.amberleybnb@ukgateway.net
I: members.aol.com/MeltonWeb/amberley.htm

Hillside House ◆◆◆◆
27 Melton Road, Burton Lazars, Melton Mowbray, Leicestershire LE14 2UR
T: (01664) 566312
F: (01664) 501819
E: Hillshs27@aol.com.uk

Tole Cottage ◆◆◆◆
10 Main Street, Kirby Bellars, Melton Mowbray, Leicestershire LE14 2EA
T: (01664) 812932
E: michael@handjean.freeserve.co.uk

MELVERLEY
Shropshire

Church House ◆◆◆
Melverley, Oswestry, Shropshire SY10 8PJ
T: (01691) 682754 &
07711 132852
E: melverley@aol.com

MERIDEN
West Midlands

Barnacle Farm ◆◆◆
Back Lane, Meriden, Coventry, West Midlands CV7 7LD
T: (024) 7646 8875
F: (024) 7646 8875

Bonnifinglas Guest House ◆◆
3 Berkswell Road, Meriden,
Coventry CV7 7LB
T: (01676) 523193 &
07721 363987
F: (01676) 523193

Cooperage Farm Bed and Breakfast ◆◆
Old Road, Meriden, Coventry
CV7 7JP
T: (01676) 523493
F: (01676) 523876
E: lucy@cooperagefarm.co.uk
I: www.cooperagefarm.co.uk

Innellan House ◆◆◆
Eaves Green Lane, Meriden,
Coventry CV7 7JL
T: (01676) 523005 & 522548
⊚

MICKLETON
Gloucestershire

Bank House ◆◆◆
Mickleton, Chipping Campden,
Gloucestershire GL55 6RX
T: (01386) 438302

Myrtle House ◆◆◆◆
High Street, Mickleton, Chipping
Campden, Gloucestershire
GL55 6SA
T: (01386) 430032 &
07971 938085
F: (01386) 438965
E: myrtlehouse@lineone.net
I: website.lineone.
net/§myrtlehouse

Old Barn House ◆◆◆◆
Mill Lane, Mickleton, Chipping
Campden, Gloucestershire
GL55 6RT
T: (01386) 438668
F: (01386) 438668

MIDDLE DUNTISBOURNE
Gloucestershire

Manor Farm ◆◆◆
Middle Duntisbourne,
Cirencester, Gloucestershire
GL7 7AR
T: (01285) 658145 &
07971 236474
F: (01285) 641504
E: tina.barton@farming.co.uk
I: www.smoothhound.co.
uk/hotels/manorfar.html

MIDDLETON
Derbyshire

Eastas Gate ◆◆◆◆
18 Main Street, Middleton,
Matlock, Derbyshire DE4 4LQ
T: (01629) 822707

Valley View ◆◆◆
3 Camsdale Walk, Middleton,
Market Harborough,
Leicestershire LE16 8YR
T: (01536) 770874

MIDDLETON-BY-YOULGREAVE
Derbyshire

Castle Farm ◆◆◆
Middleton-by-Youlgreave,
Bakewell, Derbyshire DE45 1LS
T: (01629) 636746

MILLTHORPE
Derbyshire

Cordwell House ◆◆◆◆
Cordwell Lane, Millthorpe,
Holmesfield, Dronfield S18 7WH
T: (0114) 289 0271

MINCHINHAMPTON
Gloucestershire

Foresters House
Rating Applied For
Chapel Lane, Minchinhampton,
Stroud, Gloucestershire GL6 9DL
T: (01453) 882106
F: (01453) 882106
E: ssma249701@aol.com

Hyde Crest ◆◆◆◆
Cirencester Road,
Minchinhampton, Stroud,
Gloucestershire GL6 8PE
T: (01453) 731631
E: 100621,3266@compuserve;

The Old Ram Bed and Breakfast
◆◆◆◆
Market Square,
Minchinhampton, Stroud,
Gloucestershire GL6 9BW
T: (01453) 882287
E: awheeler@btinternet.com

Vale View ◆◆◆◆
Besbury, Minchinhampton,
Stroud, Gloucestershire GL6 9EP
T: (01453) 882610
F: (01453) 882610
E: reservations@vale-view.co.uk
I: www.vale-view.co.uk

MINSTERLEY
Shropshire

The Callow Inn ◆◆◆
Bromlow, Minsterley,
Shrewsbury SY5 0EA
T: (01743) 891933
F: (01743) 891933
E: del@callowinn.freeserve.co.
uk
I: www.callowinn.freeserve.co.uk
⊚

Cricklewood Cottage ◆◆◆◆
Plox Green, Minsterley,
Shrewsbury, Shropshire SY5 0HT
T: (01743) 791229
I: www.SmoothHound.co.
uk/hotels/crickle.htm

Mandalay Bed and Breakfast
◆◆◆◆
The Grove, Minsterley,
Shrewsbury SY5 0AG
T: (01743) 791758 &
07980 135888

Village Farm
◆◆◆◆ SILVER AWARD
Bromlow, Minsterley,
Shrewsbury SY5 0DX
T: (01743) 891398
E: village-farm@fsmail.net

MITCHELDEAN
Gloucestershire

Gunn Mill House
◆◆◆◆ SILVER AWARD
Lower Spout Lane, Mitcheldean,
Gloucestershire GL17 0EA
T: (01594) 827577
F: (01594) 827577
E: info@gunnmillhouse.co.uk
I: www.gunnmillhouse.co.uk

MONSAL DALE
Derbyshire

Upperdale House ◆◆◆
Monsal Dale, Buxton, Derbyshire
SK17 8SZ
T: (01629) 640536
F: (01629) 640536
E: bookings@upperdale.fsnet.
co.uk
I: www.monsaldale.com

MONSAL HEAD
Derbyshire

Cliffe House ◆◆◆
Monsal Head, Bakewell,
Derbyshire DE45 1NL
T: (01629) 640376
F: (01629) 640376
I: www.cliffhouse.co.uk
⊚

Monsal Head Hotel ◆◆◆
Monsal Head, Bakewell,
Derbyshire DE45 1NL
T: (01629) 640250
F: (01629) 640455
E: chris@monsalhead.com
I: www.monsalhead.com

MONYASH
Derbyshire

Chapel View Farm ◆◆◆◆
Chapel Street, Monyash,
Bakewell, Derbyshire DE45 1JJ
T: (01629) 814317

High Rakes Farm
◆◆◆◆ SILVER AWARD
Rakes Road, Monyash, Bakewell,
Derbyshire DE45 1JL
T: (01298) 84692 &
07850 453986

MORETON-IN-MARSH
Gloucestershire

Acacia ◆◆
2 New Road, Moreton-in-Marsh,
Gloucestershire GL56 0AS
T: (01608) 650130

The Bell Inn ◆◆◆
High Street, Moreton-in-Marsh,
Gloucestershire GL56 0AF
T: (01608) 651688
F: (01608) 652195
I: www.Accofind.com
⊚

Blue Cedar House ◆◆◆
Stow Road, Moreton-in-Marsh,
Gloucestershire GL56 0DW
T: (01608) 650299
E: gandsib@dialstart.net

Bran Mill Cottage ◆◆◆
Moreton-in-Marsh,
Gloucestershire GL56 9QP
T: (01386) 593517 &
07971 253544

Ditchford Farmhouse ◆◆◆
Stretton on Fosse, Moreton-in-
Marsh, Gloucestershire
GL56 9RD
T: (01608) 663307
E: r.b.ditchford@talk21.com
I: www.warks.co.uk

Farriers Arms ◆◆◆
Todenham, Moreton-in-Marsh,
Gloucestershire GL56 9PF
T: (01608) 650901 &
07771 540261
E: wmoore9701@aol.com
I: www.farriersarms.com

Fosseway Farm ◆◆◆◆
Fosseway, Moreton-in-Marsh,
Gloucestershire GL56 0DS
T: (01608) 650503

Four Gables ◆◆◆
Little Compton, Moreton-in-
Marsh, Gloucestershire
GL56 0SQ
T: (01608) 674233

Fourshires Bed and Breakfast
◆◆◆◆
Fourshires House, Great Wolford
Road, Moreton-in-Marsh,
Gloucestershire GL56 0PE
T: (01608) 651412 & 652069
F: (01608) 651412

Moreton House ◆◆
High Street, Moreton-in-Marsh,
Gloucestershire GL56 0LQ
T: (01608) 650747
F: (01608) 652747
E: moreton_house@msn.com

New Farm ◆◆◆
Dorn, Moreton-in-Marsh,
Gloucestershire GL56 9NS
T: (01608) 650782

The Old Chequer
◆◆◆◆ SILVER AWARD
Draycott, Moreton-in-Marsh,
Gloucestershire GL56 9LB
T: (01386) 700647 &
07885 560228
F: (01386) 700647
E: g.f.linley@tesco.net
⊚

Old Farm ◆◆◆
Dorn, Moreton-in-Marsh,
Gloucestershire GL56 9NS
T: (01608) 650394
F: (01608) 650394
E: simon@righton.freeserve.co.
uk

Rest Harrow ◆◆◆
Evenlode Road, Moreton-in-
Marsh, Gloucestershire
GL56 0NJ
T: (01608) 650653

Roosters ◆◆◆◆
Todenham, Moreton-in-Marsh,
Gloucestershire GL56 9PA
T: (01608) 650645
F: (01608) 650645
I: www.touristnet.uk.
com/wm/roosters/indexhtm

Staddle Stones Guest House
◆◆
Rowborough, Stretton-on-
Fosse, Moreton-in-Marsh,
Gloucestershire GL56 9RE
T: (01608) 662774

**Townend Cottage and Coach
House** ◆◆◆
High Street, Moreton-in-Marsh,
Gloucestershire GL56 0AD
T: (01608) 650846
E: chris.gant@talk21.com
I: www.townend-cottage.co.uk

Treetops ◆◆◆
London Road, Moreton-in-
Marsh, Gloucestershire
GL56 0HE
T: (01608) 651036
F: (01608) 651036
E: dean@treetops1.freeserve.co.
uk
(🏃)

Warwick House ◆◆◆
London Road, Moreton-in-
Marsh, Gloucestershire
GL56 0HH
T: (01608) 650773
F: (01608) 650773
E: charlie@warwickhousebnb.
demon.co.uk
I: www.snoozeandsizzle.com

MORETON PINKNEY
Northamptonshire

The Old Vicarage
◆◆◆◆ SILVER AWARD
Moreton Pinkney, Daventry,
Northamptonshire NN11 3SQ
T: (01295) 760057
F: (01295) 760057
E: tim@tandjeastwood.fsnet.co.uk

MORVILLE
Shropshire

Hannigans Farm ◆◆◆◆
Morville, Bridgnorth, Shropshire
WV16 4RN
T: (01746) 714332
F: (01746) 714332
E: AMNFET@hotmail.com

MOUNTSORREL
Leicestershire

The Mountsorrel Hotel ◆◆◆
217 Loughborough Road,
Mountsorrel, Loughborough,
Leicestershire LE12 7AR
T: (01509) 412627 & 416105
F: (01509) 416105
E: mountsorrelhotel@route56.co.uk
I: www.uktourism.com/le-mountsorrel

The Swan Inn ◆◆◆
10 Loughborough Road,
Mountsorrel, Loughborough,
Leicestershire LE12 7AT
T: (0116) 230 2340
F: (0116) 237 6115
E: dmw@jvf.co.uk
I: www.jvf.co.uk/swan

MUCH BIRCH
Herefordshire

The Old School ◆◆◆
Much Birch, Hereford HR2 8HJ
T: (01981) 540006
F: (01981) 540006

MUCH MARCLE
Herefordshire

Bodenham Farm ◆◆◆◆
Much Marcle, Ledbury,
Herefordshire HR8 2NJ
T: (01531) 660222

New House Farm ◆◆◆
Much Marcle, Ledbury,
Herefordshire HR8 2PH
T: (01531) 660674 & 660604

MUCH WENLOCK
Shropshire

Broadstone Mill
◆◆◆◆◆ GOLD AWARD
Broadstone, Much Wenlock,
Shropshire TF13 6LE
T: (01584) 841494
F: (01584) 841515
E: hargreaves@broadstones.fsnet.co.uk
I: www.virtual-shropshire.co.uk/broadstone

Danywenallt ◆◆◆
Farley Road, Much Wenlock,
Shropshire TF13 6NB
T: (01952) 727892

Gaskell Arms Hotel ◆◆◆
Much Wenlock, Shropshire
TF13 6AQ
T: (01952) 727212
F: (01952) 728505

The Manor House ◆◆◆◆
Sheinton Street, Much Wenlock,
Shropshire TF13 6HT
T: (01952) 728046

31 Oakfield Park ◆◆
Much Wenlock, Shropshire
TF13 6HH
T: (01952) 727473

The Old Police Station ◆◆◆◆
Sheinton Street, Much Wenlock,
Shropshire TF13 6HU
T: (01952) 727056

Old Quarry Cottage ◆◆◆◆
Brockton, Much Wenlock,
Shropshire TF13 6JR
T: (01746) 785596

Talbot Inn ◆◆◆
Much Wenlock, Shropshire
TF13 6AA
T: (01952) 727077
F: (01952) 728436

Walton House ◆◆◆
35 Barrow Street, Much
Wenlock, Shropshire TF13 6EP
T: (01952) 727139

MUNSLOW
Shropshire

The Old Laundry
◆◆◆◆◆ GOLD AWARD
Beambridge, Munslow, Craven
Arms, Shropshire SY7 9HA
T: (01584) 841520
E: diana@theoldlaundry.free-online.co.uk

MUXTON
Shropshire

Muxton House
◆◆◆◆◆ SILVER AWARD
Muxton Lane, Muxton, Telford,
Shropshire TF2 8PF
T: (01952) 603312
F: (01952) 603312
E: sarahcarlton@compuserve.com

MYDDLE
Shropshire

Oakfields ◆◆◆
Oakfields, Baschurch Road,
Myddle, Shrewsbury, Shropshire
SY4 3RX
T: (01939) 290823

NAILSWORTH
Gloucestershire

Aaron Farm ◆◆◆◆
Nympsfield Road, Nailsworth,
Stroud, Gloucestershire GL6 0ET
T: (01453) 833598
F: (01453) 833626
E: aaronfarm@aol.com
I: www.aaronfarm-bedandbreakfast.co.uk

Highlands ◆◆◆◆
Shortwood, Nailsworth, Stroud,
Gloucestershire GL6 0SJ
T: (01453) 832591
F: (01453) 833590

1 Orchard Mead ◆◆
Chestnut Hill, Nailsworth,
Stroud, Gloucestershire GL6 0RE
T: (01453) 833581

The Upper House ◆◆◆◆
Spring Hill, Nailsworth, Stroud,
Gloucestershire GL6 0LX
T: (01453) 836606
F: (01453) 836769

The Vicarage ◆
Avening Road, Nailsworth,
Stroud, Gloucestershire GL6 0BS
T: (01453) 832181

NANTMAWR
Shropshire

Four Gables ◆◆◆
Nantmawr, Oswestry, Shropshire
SY10 9HH
T: (01691) 828708

NASSINGTON
Northamptonshire

Sunnyside ◆◆◆
62 Church Street, Nassington,
Peterborough PE8 6QG
T: (01780) 782864

NAUNTON
Gloucestershire

Fox Hill ◆◆◆
Stow Road, Naunton,
Cheltenham, Gloucestershire
GL54 5RL
T: (01451) 850496 &
07774 785690
F: (01451) 850602

Naunton View Guesthouse
◆◆◆
Naunton, Cheltenham,
Gloucestershire GL54 3AD
T: (01451) 850482
F: (01451) 850482

NAVENBY
Lincolnshire

The Barn
◆◆◆◆ SILVER AWARD
North Lane, Navenby, Lincoln
LN5 0EH
T: (01522) 810318
F: (01522) 810318
E: peter.sheila@thebarnnavenby.freeserve.uk

NETHER HEYFORD
Northamptonshire

Heyford Bed and Breakfast ◆◆
27 Church Street, Nether
Heyford, Northampton NN7 3LH
T: (01327) 340872

NETHER WESTCOTE
Gloucestershire

Cotswold View Guesthouse
◆◆◆
Nether Westcote, Chipping
Norton, Oxfordshire OX7 6SD
T: (01993) 830699
F: (01993) 830699

NEW DUSTON
Northamptonshire

Rowena ◆◆◆◆
569 Harlestone Road, New
Duston, Northampton NN5 6NX
T: (01604) 755889
F: 0870 1376484
E: info@rowenaBB.co.uk
I: www.rowenaBB.co.uk

NEW YORK
Lincolnshire

Westgate House ◆◆◆◆
Sandy Bank, New York, Lincoln,
Lincolnshire LN4 4YG
T: (01526) 342658

NEWARK
Nottinghamshire

The Boot and Shoe Inn ◆◆◆
Main Street, Flintham, Newark,
Nottinghamshire NG23 5LA
T: (01636) 525246

St Clares ◆◆◆◆
1 Elm Close, Elm Avenue,
Newark, Nottinghamshire
NG24 1SG
T: (01636) 685347
F: (01636) 685347

Willow Tree Inn ◆◆◆
Front Street, Barnby-in-the-
Willows, Newark,
Nottinghamshire NG24 2SA
T: (01636) 626613
F: (01636) 626060
E: www@willowtreeinn.co.uk
I: www.info@willowtreeinn.co.uk

NEWCASTLE-UNDER-LYME
Staffordshire

Graythwaite Guest House
◆◆◆
106 Lancaster Road, Newcastle-
under-Lyme, Staffordshire
ST5 1DS
T: (01782) 612875 &
07977 541422

NEWENT
Gloucestershire

George Hotel ◆◆◆
Church Street, Newent,
Gloucestershire GL18 1PU
T: (01531) 820203
F: (01531) 822899

Newent Golf and Lodges ◆◆◆
Newent Golf Course,
Coldharbour Lane, Newent,
Gloucestershire GL18 1DJ
T: (01531) 820478
F: (01531) 820478
E: tomnewentgolf@aol.com
I: www.short-golf-break.com

The Old Winery
◆◆◆◆◆ GOLD AWARD
Welsh House Lane, Dymock,
Newent, Gloucestershire
GL18 1LR
T: (01531) 890824

Orchard House
◆◆◆◆ SILVER AWARD
Aston Ingham Road, Kilcot,
Newent, Gloucestershire
GL18 1NP
T: (01989) 720417 &
07703 657348
F: (01989) 720770

**Sandyway Nurseries
Countryside B & B** ◆◆◆
Redmarley Road, Newent,
Gloucestershire GL18 1DR
T: (01531) 820693

Three Choirs Vineyards
◆◆◆◆◆
Newent, Gloucestershire
GL18 1LS
T: (01531) 890223
F: (01531) 890877
E: ts@threechoirs.freeserve.co.uk
I: www.three-choirs-vineyards.co.uk

NEWLAND
Gloucestershire

Birchamp House ◆◆◆
Newland, Coleford,
Gloucestershire GL16 8NP
T: (01594) 833143
F: (01594) 836775
E: birchamp.1@virgin.net
I: www.fweb.org.uk/birchamp/

Rookery Farm ◆◆◆
Newland, Coleford,
Gloucestershire GL16 8NJ
T: (01594) 832432

Scatterford Farm ◆◆◆◆
Newland, Coleford,
Gloucestershire GL16 8NG
T: (01594) 836562
F: (01594) 836323

Tan House Farm ◆◆◆
Newland, Coleford,
Gloucestershire GL16 8NP
T: (015948) 32222

Hayden Lea ◆◆◆
Dean Road, Newnham-on-
Severn, Gloucestershire
GL14 1AB
T: (01594) 516626

Swan House ◆◆◆◆
High Street, Newnham-on-
Severn, Gloucestershire
GL14 1BY
T: (01594) 516504
F: (01594) 516177
E: joanne@
swanhouse-newnham.freeserve.
co.uk
I: www.swanhouse-newnham.
freeserve.co.uk

The White House World ◆◆◆
Popes Hill, Newnham-on-
Severn, Gloucestershire
GL14 1LE
T: (01452) 760463
F: (01452) 760776
E: whitehouseworld@talk21.
com
I: www.fweb.org.uk/whitehouse

Lane End Farm
◆◆◆◆ SILVER AWARD
Chetwynd, Newport, Shropshire
TF10 8BN
T: (01952) 550337 &
0777 1632255
F: (01952) 550337
E: lane1.endfarm@ondigital.
com
I: www.virtual-shropshire.co.
uk/lef

**Norwood House Hotel and
Restaurant** ◆◆◆◆
Pave Lane, Newport, Shropshire
TF10 9LQ
T: (01952) 825896
F: (01952) 825896

Pear Tree Farmhouse ◆◆◆◆
Rating Applied For
Farm Grove, Newport,
Shropshire TF10 7PX
T: (01952) 811193
F: (01952) 812115
E: patgreen@peakfarmhouse.co.
uk
I: www.peartreefarmhouse.co.uk

Sambrook Manor ◆◆◆
Sambrook, Newport, Shropshire
TF10 8AL
T: (01952) 550256

The Unicorn Inn ◆◆◆◆
Repton Road, Newton Solney,
Burton upon Trent, Staffordshire
DE15 0SG
T: (01283) 703324
F: (01283) 703324

Oulton House Farm ◆◆◆◆
Norbury, Stafford ST20 0PG
T: (01785) 284264
F: (01785) 284264

Shuttocks Wood ◆◆◆◆
Norbury, Bishop's Castle,
Shropshire SY9 5EA
T: (01588) 650433
F: (01588) 650492
E: shuttockswood@barclays.net
I: www.go2.co.
uk/shuttockswood/

Fleece Inn ◆
Lock Road, North Cotes,
Grimsby, North East Lincolnshire
DN36 5UP
T: (01472) 388233

Lakeview Guesthouse ◆◆◆◆
50 Station Road, North
Hykeham, Lincoln LN6 9AQ
T: (01522) 680455

**Old Coach House Tea Rooms &
Cafe** ◆◆◆◆
Church Lane, North Kyme,
Lincolnshire LN4 4DJ
T: (01526) 861465
F: (01526) 861658

**Pigeon Cottage Bed &
Breakfast & LLA Summer
Camps** ◆◆
Conisholme Road, North
Somercotes, Louth, Lincolnshire
LN11 7PS
T: (01507) 359063
F: (01507) 359063

South View ◆◆
95 Church Lane, North
Wingfield, Chesterfield,
Derbyshire S42 5HR
T: (01246) 850091

**Aarandale Regent Hotel and
Guesthouse** ◆
6-8 Royal Terrace, Barrack Road
(A508), Northampton,
Northamptonshire NN1 3RF
T: (01604) 631096
F: (01604) 621035
E: aarandale@aol.com

**Paddock Cottage Bed and
Breakfast** ◆◆◆◆
Paddock Cottage, The Gated
Road, Nr Crick, Northampton,
NN6 7UE
T: (01788) 823615

Poplars Hotel ◆◆◆◆
Cross Street, Moulton,
Northampton NN3 7RZ
T: (01604) 643983
F: (01604) 790233
E: poplars@btclick.com

Quinton Green Farm ◆◆◆◆
Quinton, Northampton NN7 2EG
T: (01604) 863685
F: (01604) 862230

Saint Georges Private Hotel
◆◆◆
128 Saint Georges Avenue,
Northampton, NN2 6JF
T: (01604) 792755
E: stgeorgeshotel@email.msn.
com
I: stgeorgeshotel.co.uk

Upton Mill ◆◆◆
Northampton, NN5 4UY
T: (01604) 753277
F: (01604) 753277

Cotteswold House
◆◆◆◆ SILVER AWARD
Market Place, Northleach,
Cheltenham, Gloucestershire
GL54 3EG
T: (01451) 860493
F: (01451) 860493
E: cotteswoldhouse@talk21.
com

The Eastington Suite
◆◆◆◆◆ GOLD AWARD
Japonica, Upper End Eastington,
Northleach, Cheltenham,
Gloucestershire GL54 3PJ
T: (01451) 861117 &
07774 680091
F: (01451) 861117

Long Barrow ◆◆◆◆
Farmington, Northleach,
Cheltenham, Gloucestershire
GL54 3NQ
T: (01451) 860428
F: (01451) 860166
E: ghowson@longbarrow.fsnet.
co.uk

The Mead House ◆◆◆
Sherborne, Cheltenham,
Gloucestershire GL54 3DR
T: (01451) 844239

Northfield Bed and Breakfast
◆◆◆◆ SILVER AWARD
Cirencester Road (A429),
Northleach, Cheltenham,
Gloucestershire GL54 3JL
T: (01451) 860427
F: (01451) 860820
E: nrthfield0@aol.com

The Sherborne Arms ◆◆
Market Place, Northleach,
Cheltenham, Gloucestershire
GL54 3EE
T: (01451) 860241

Norton Grange Farm ◆◆
Norton, Mansfield,
Nottinghamshire NG20 9LP
T: (01623) 842666

Norton Farm ◆◆◆◆
Norton in Hales, Market
Drayton, Shropshire TF9 4AT
T: (01630) 653003
F: (01630) 653003
I: www.interactive/info.co.
uk/farmholls/norton./home.htm

Acorn Hotel ◆◆◆
4 Radcliffe Road, West
Bridgford, Nottingham,
Nottinghamshire NG2 5FW
T: (0115) 981 1297
F: (0115) 981 7654
E: acornhotel2@radcliffe18.
freeserve.co.uk

Adams Castle View Guesthouse
◆◆◆
85 Castle Boulevard,
Nottingham, Nottinghamshire
NG7 1FE
T: (0115) 950 0022

Calerin House ◆◆◆◆
21 Redcliffe Road, Mapperley
Park, Nottingham, NG3 5BW
T: (0115) 9605366
F: (0115) 9605366

Cotswold Hotel ◆◆◆
330-332 Mansfield Road,
Nottingham, NG5 2EF
T: (0115) 955 1070
F: (0115) 955 1071
E: colswold.hotel@virgin.net
I: www.information.Brittan.co.
uk

Fairhaven Private Hotel ◆◆◆
19 Meadow Road, Beeston
Rylands, Nottingham, NG9 1JP
T: (0115) 922 7509
F: (0115) 943 6217
E: bookings@fairhaven.fsnet.co.
uk
I: www.smoothhound.co.
uk/hotels/fairhave.html

Grantham Hotel ◆◆◆
24-26 Radcliffe Road, West
Bridgford, Nottingham
NG2 5FW
T: (0115) 981 1373
F: (0115) 981 8567
E: granthamhotel@netlineuk.
net

**Greenwood Lodge City
Guesthouse**
◆◆◆◆◆ GOLD AWARD
Third Avenue, Sherwood Rise,
Nottingham NG7 6JH
T: (0115) 962 1206
F: (0115) 962 1206
E: coolspratt@aol.com
I: www.SmoothHound.co.
uk/hotels/greenwo.html

Lindum House ◆◆◆
1 Burn Street, Nottingham,
Notthinghamshire NG7 4DS
T: (0115) 847 1089
F: (0115) 847 1089
E: john_s_hugh@hotmail.com

Milford Hotel ◆◆
Pavilion Road, West Bridgford,
Nottingham NG2 5FG
T: (0115) 981 1464 & 9811044
F: (0115) 982 2204

Nelson and Railway Inn ◆◆
Station Road, Kimberley,
Nottingham, NG16 2NR
T: (0115) 938 2177

Yew Tree Grange ◆◆◆◆
2 Nethergate, Clifton Village,
Nottingham, NG11 8NL
T: (0115) 984 7562 & 9142886
F: (0115) 984 7562
E: yewtreel@nascr.net
I: www.yewtreegrange.co.uk

NUNEATON
Warwickshire
La Tavola Calda ◆◆
70 Midland Road, Abbey Green,
Nuneaton, Warwickshire
CV11 5DY
T: (024) 7638 3195 &
07747 010702
F: (024) 7638 1816

OAKAMOOR
Staffordshire
Bank House
◆◆◆◆◆ GOLD AWARD
Farley Road, Oakamoor, Stoke-
on-Trent, Staffordshire
ST10 3BD
T: (01538) 702810
F: (01538) 702810
E: john.orme@dial.pipex.com
I: www.smoothhound.co.
uk/hotels/bank.html

Beehive Guest House ◆◆◆
Churnet View Road, Oakamoor,
Stoke-on-Trent, Staffordshire
ST10 3AE
T: (01538) 702420

Crowtrees Farm ◆◆◆◆
Oakamoor, Stoke-on-Trent
ST10 3DY
T: (01538) 702260
F: (01538) 702260
E: crowtrees@fenetre.co.uk.
I: www.touristnetuk.
com/wm/crowtrees

The Laurels ◆◆◆◆
Star Bank, Oakamoor, Stoke-on-
Trent ST10 3BN
T: (01538) 702629 &
0771 2008802
F: (01538) 702796
E: The Laurels@compuserve.
com
I: www.TOURISTNETUK.
COM/WM/LAURELS

Ribden Farm ◆◆◆◆
Oakamoor, Stoke-on-Trent
ST10 3BW
T: (01538) 702830 & 702153
F: (01538) 702830
I: www.ribdenfarm.com

Tenement Farm ◆◆◆◆
Three Lows, Ribden, Oakamoor,
Stoke-on-Trent ST10 3BW
T: (01538) 702333 & 703603
F: (01538) 703603
E: stanleese@aol.com
I: www.touristnetuk.
com/wm/tenement-farm

OAKENGATES
Shropshire
Chellow Dene ◆◆
Park Road, Malinslee, Dawley,
Telford, Shropshire TF3 1LA
T: (01952) 505917

OAKHAM
Rutland
Hall Farm ◆◆◆
Cottesmore Road, Exton,
Oakham, Rutland LE15 8AN
T: (01572) 812271 &
07711 979628

The Tithe Barn ◆◆◆
Clatterpot Lane, Cottesmore,
Oakham, Leicestershire
LE15 7DW
T: (01572) 813591
T: (01572) 812719
E: jpryke@thetithebarn.co.uk

Westgate Lodge ◆◆◆◆
9 Westgate, Oakham,
Leicestershire LE15 6BH
T: (01572) 757370
F: (01572) 757370
E: westgatelodge@gofornet.co.
uk

OAKRIDGE LYNCH
Gloucestershire
Lower Weir Farm ◆◆◆◆
Oakridge Lynch, Stroud,
Gloucestershire GL6 7NS
T: (01285) 760701
F: (01285) 760690

OLD
Northamptonshire
Wold Farm
◆◆◆◆ SILVER AWARD
Old, Northamptonshire NN6 9RJ
T: (01604) 781258

OMBERSLEY
Worcestershire
Eden Farm ◆◆◆◆
Ombersley, Droitwich,
Worcestershire WR9 0JX
T: (01905) 620244

Greenlands ◆◆◆◆
Uphampton, Ombersley,
Droitwich, Worcestershire
WR9 0JP
T: (01905) 620873

ORLETON
Worcestershire
**Hope Cottage Bed and
Breakfast ◆◆◆**
Hope Cottage, Orleton, Ludlow,
Shropshire SY8 4JB
T: (01584) 831674
F: (01584) 831124
E: hopecott@aol.com

Line Farm
◆◆◆◆◆ GOLD AWARD
Tunnel Lane, Orleton, Ludlow,
Shropshire SY8 4HY
T: (01568) 780400

OSGATHORPE
Leicestershire
The Royal Oak Inn ◆◆◆
20 Main Street, Osgathorpe,
Loughborough, Leicestershire
LE12 9TA
T: (01530) 222443 &
07885 377652

OSWESTRY
Shropshire
Ash Court ◆◆◆◆
Weston Lane, Oswestry,
Shropshire SY11 2BB
T: (01691) 662921

Ashfield Farmhouse
◆◆◆◆ SILVER AWARD
Maesbury, Oswestry, Shropshire
SY10 8JH
T: (01691) 653589 &
07712 406413
F: (01691) 653589
I: www.smoothhound.co.
uk/hotel/ashfield.html

Bridge House ◆◆◆◆
Llynclys, Oswestry, Shropshire
SY10 8AE
T: (01691) 830496
F: (01691) 830496
E: jenny@llynclys.freeserve.co.
uk

Elgar House ◆◆◆◆
16 Elgar Close, Oswestry,
Shropshire SY11 2LZ
T: (01691) 661323 &
07802 690098

Foel Guesthouse ◆◆◆
18 Hampton Road, Oswestry,
Shropshire SY11 1SJ
T: (01691) 652184 &
07702 232252

Frankton House
◆◆◆◆ GOLD AWARD
Welsh Frankton, Oswestry,
Shropshire SY11 4PA
T: (01691) 623422 &
07803 955823

Greyhound Inn ◆◆
Willow Street, Oswestry,
Shropshire SY11 1AJ
T: (01691) 653392

Llwyn Guesthouse ◆◆◆
5 Llwyn Terrace, Oswestry,
Shropshire SY11 1HR
T: (01691) 670746
E: llwyn@virtual-shropshire.co.
uk
I: www.virtual-shropshire.co.
uk/llwyn

Montrose ◆◆◆
Weston Lane, Oswestry,
Shropshire SY11 2BG
T: (01691) 652063

35 Oak Drive ◆◆◆
Oswestry, Shropshire SY11 2RX
T: (01691) 655286

The Old Rectory ◆◆◆
Selattyn, Oswestry, Shropshire
SY10 7DH
T: (01691) 659708

Top Farm House
◆◆◆◆ SILVER AWARD
Knockin, Oswestry, Shropshire
SY10 8HN
T: (01691) 682582

Westbourne House
◆◆◆◆ SILVER AWARD
11 Top Street, Whittington,
Oswestry, Shropshire SY11 4DR
T: (01691) 661824

OUNDLE
Northamptonshire
Ashworth House ◆◆◆
75 West Street, Oundle,
Peterborough PE8 4EJ
T: (01832) 275312

2 Benefield Road ◆◆◆◆
Oundle, Peterborough,
Northamptonshire PE8 4ET
T: (01832) 273953

**Castle Farm Guesthouse
◆◆◆◆**
Castle Farm, Fotheringhay,
Peterborough PE8 5HZ
T: (01832) 226200
F: (01832) 226200

Lilford Lodge Farm ◆◆◆◆
Barnwell, Oundle, Peterborough
PE8 5SA
T: (01832) 272230
T: (01832) 272230
E: trudy@lilford-lodge.demon.
co.uk
I: www.lilford-lodge.demon.co.
uk

Tansor Lodge
Rating Applied For
Elmington, Oundle,
Peterborough PE8 5JY
T: (01832) 226070
F: (01832) 226474

OVER HADDON
Derbyshire
Lathkill Cottage ◆◆◆◆
Over Haddon, Bakewell,
Derbyshire DE45 1JE
T: (01629) 814518
F: (01629) 814518
E: judithparker@talk21.com

OXLYNCH
Gloucestershire
Tiled House Farm ◆◆◆◆
Oxlynch, Stonehouse,
Gloucestershire GL10 3DF
T: (01453) 822363 &
07778 841853
F: (01453) 822363
E: nigel.jeffery@ukgateway.net

OXTON
Nottinghamshire
Far Baulker Farm ◆◆◆
Oxton, Southwell,
Nottinghamshire NG25 0RQ
T: (01623) 882375 &
0797 1087605
F: (01623) 882375
E: j.esam@virgin.net

PAINSWICK
Gloucestershire
Cardynham House ◆◆◆◆
The Cross, Painswick, Stroud,
Gloucestershire GL6 6XX
T: (01452) 814006
F: (01452) 812321
E: info@cardynham.co.uk
I: www.cardynham.co.uk

Castle Lodge ◆◆◆◆
The Beacon, Painswick, Stroud,
Gloucestershire GL6 6TU
T: (01452) 813603

Culvert Cottage ◆◆◆
Kingsmill Lane, Painswick,
Stroud, Gloucestershire GL6 6RT
T: (01452) 812293

Hambutts Mynd ◆◆◆
Edge Road, Painswick, Stroud,
Gloucestershire GL6 6UP
T: (01452) 812352
F: (01452) 813862
E: ewarland@aol.com
I: www.s-h-systems.co.
uk/hotels/hambutts.html

Meadowcote ◆◆◆◆
Stroud Road, Painswick, Stroud,
Gloucestershire GL6 6UT
T: (01452) 813565

St Michael's Cottage
◆◆◆ SILVER AWARD
Victoria Street, Painswick,
Stroud, Gloucestershire GL6 6QA
T: (01452) 812998
F: (01452) 812998

Skyrack ◆◆◆
The Highlands, Painswick,
Stroud, Gloucestershire GL6 6SL
T: (01452) 812029 &
07971 264041
F: (01452) 813846
E: wendyskyrack@hotmail.com

Thorne ◆◆◆
Friday Street, Painswick, Stroud,
Gloucestershire GL6 6QJ
T: (01452) 812476
I: www.painswick.co.uk.
forward/thorne.

Upper Doreys Mill ◆◆◆
Edge, Painswick, Stroud,
Gloucestershire GL6 6NF
T: (01452) 812459 &
07971 300563
E: sylvia@painswick.co.uk
I: www.painswick.co.uk/doreys

Wheatleys
◆◆◆◆ GOLD AWARD
Cotswold Mead, Painswick,
Stroud, Gloucestershire GL6 6XB
T: (01452) 812167
F: (01452) 814270
E: jean.burgess@dial.pipex.com

Wickridge Farm ◆◆◆
Folly Lane, Stroud,
Gloucestershire GL6 7JT
T: (01453) 764357

PANT
Shropshire

The Palms ◆◆◆
Pant, Oswestry, Shropshire
SY10 8JZ
T: (01691) 830813

PAPPLEWICK
Nottinghamshire

Forest Farm ◆◆◆
Mansfield Road, Papplewick,
NG15 8FL
T: (0115) 963 2310

PARKEND
Gloucestershire

Edale House ◆◆◆
Folly Road, Parkend, Lydney,
Gloucestershire GL15 4JF
T: (01594) 562835
F: (01594) 564488
E: edale@lineone.net
I: www.edalehouse.co.uk

The Fountain Inn ◆◆◆
Fountain Way, Parkend, Lydney,
Gloucestershire GL15 4JD
T: (01594) 562189
F: (01594) 564438
🚶

PARWICH
Derbyshire

Flaxdale House ◆◆◆◆
Parwich, Ashbourne, Derbyshire
DE6 1QA
T: (01335) 390252
F: (01335) 390644
E: mike@mikerad.demon.co.uk

PEMBRIDGE
Herefordshire

Lowe Farm Bed and Breakfast
◆◆◆◆ SILVER AWARD
Lowe Farm, Pembridge,
Leominster, Herefordshire
HR6 9JD
T: (01544) 388395 &
07711 374599
E: williams-family@lineone.net
🔵

PENTRICH
Derbyshire

Coney Grey Farm ◆
Chesterfield Road, Pentrich,
Ripley, Derbyshire DE5 3RF
T: (01773) 833179

PERSHORE
Worcestershire

Aldbury House
◆◆◆ SILVER AWARD
George Lane, Wyre Piddle,
Pershore, Worcestershire
WR10 2HX
T: (01386) 553754
F: (01386) 553754
E: jim@oldbury.freeserve.co.uk

The Barn
◆◆◆◆ GOLD AWARD
Pensham Hill House, Pensham,
Pershore, Worcestershire
WR10 3HA
T: (01386) 555270
F: (01386) 552894
🔵

Byeways ◆◆◆
Pershore Road, Little
Comberton, Pershore,
Worcestershire WR10 3EW
T: (01386) 710203
F: (01386) 710203

PILLERTON HERSEY
Warwickshire

The Old Vicarage ◆◆◆◆
Pillerton Hersey, Warwick
CV35 0QJ
T: (01789) 740185 &
07836 796674
E: oldvicarage98@hotmail.com

PILSLEY
Derbyshire

**The Stud Farm Countryside
Bed and Breakfast**
◆◆◆ SILVER AWARD
Hardstoft, Pilsley, Chesterfield,
Derbyshire S45 8AE
T: (01773) 875994

PITCHCOMBE
Gloucestershire

Gable End ◆◆◆
Pitchcombe, Stroud,
Gloucestershire GL6 6LN
T: (01452) 812166
F: (01452) 812719

PITSFORD
Northamptonshire

Ashley House ◆◆◆◆
19 Broadlands, Pitsford,
Northampton NN6 9AZ
T: (01604) 880691
F: (01604) 880691

PONTESBURY
Shropshire

Jasmine Cottage
◆◆◆ SILVER AWARD
Pontesford, Pontesbury,
Shrewsbury SY5 0UA
T: (01743) 792771

PONTRILAS
Herefordshire

Station House ◆◆
Pontrilas, Hereford,
Herefordshire HR2 0EH
T: (01981) 240564
F: (01981) 240564
I: www.golden-valley.co.
uk/stationhouse
🔵

PONTSHILL
Herefordshire

Rowan Lea ◆◆
Pontshill, Ross-on-Wye,
Herefordshire HR9 5SY
T: (01989) 750693

POULTON
Gloucestershire

Sprucewood ◆◆◆◆
Elf Meadow, Poulton,
Cirencester, Gloucestershire
GL7 5HQ
T: (01285) 851351
F: (01285) 851351

PRIORS HARDWICK
Warwickshire

Hill Farm ◆◆◆
Priors Hardwick, Southam,
Warwickshire CV47 7SP
T: (01327) 260338 &
07710 457262

PULVERBATCH
Shropshire

Lane Farm ◆◆◆
Wilderley, Pulverbatch,
Shrewsbury, Shropshire SY5 8DF
T: (01743) 718935
F: (01743) 728448
E: bgreig@enterprise.net
I: www.homepages.enterprise.
net/bgreig

QUENIBOROUGH
Leicestershire

Three Ways Farm ◆◆◆
Melton Road, Queniborough,
Leicester LE7 3FN
T: (0116) 260 0472
🔵

RAGNALL
Nottinghamshire

Ragnall House ◆◆◆
Main Street, Ragnall, Newark,
Nottinghamshire NG22 0UR
T: (01777) 228575 &
07774 455792

REDDITCH
Worcestershire

Avonhill Lodge Guest House
◆◆◆
Alcester Road, Beoley, Redditch,
Worcestershire B98 9EP
T: (01564) 742413
F: (01564) 741873

REDMILE
Leicestershire

**Peacock Farm Guesthouse and
The Feathers Restaurant** ◆◆◆
Redmile, Nottingham NG13 0GQ
T: (01949) 842475
F: (01949) 43127

RETFORD
Nottinghamshire

The Barns Country Guesthouse
◆◆◆◆
Morton Farm, Babworth,
Retford, Nottinghamshire
DN22 8HA
T: (01777) 706336
F: (01777) 709773
E: harry@thebarns.co.uk
I: www.Thebarns.co.uk
🔵

**The Brick and Tile
Rating Applied For**
81 Moorgate, Retford,
Nottinghamshire DN22 6RR
T: (01777) 703681

RICHARDS CASTLE
Shropshire

**The Barn
Rating Applied For**
Ryecroft, Richards Castle,
Ludlow, Shropshire SY8 4EU
T: (01584) 831224
F: (01584) 831224
I: www.ludlow.org.uk/ryecroft

RIPLEY
Derbyshire

Spinney Lodge Guesthouse
◆◆◆
Coach Road, Butterley Park,
Ripley, Derbyshire DE5 3QU
T: (01773) 740168

RIPPLE
Worcestershire

Green Gables ◆◆◆
Ripple, Tewkesbury,
Gloucestershire GL20 6EX
T: (01684) 592740
F: (01684) 592740

RISLEY
Derbyshire

Braeside Guest House ◆◆◆◆
113 Derby Road, Risley,
Draycott, Derby DE72 3SS
T: (0115) 939 5885

ROADE
Northamptonshire

Chapter House ◆◆◆◆
High Street, Roade,
Northampton NN7 2NW
T: (01604) 862523
F: (01604) 864117

**Roade House Restaurant and
Hotel** ◆◆◆ SILVER AWARD
16 High Street, Roade,
Northampton NN7 2NW
T: (01604) 863372
F: (01604) 862421

ROCESTER
Staffordshire

The Leeze Guest House ◆◆◆
63 High Street, Rocester,
Uttoxeter, Staffordshire
ST14 5JU
T: (01889) 591146
F: (01889) 591146

ROCK
Worcestershire

The Old Forge ◆◆◆
Gorst Hill, Rock, Kidderminster,
Worcestershire DY14 9YG
T: (01299) 266745

ROSS-ON-WYE
Herefordshire

The Arches ◆◆◆
Walford Road, Ross-on-Wye,
Herefordshire HR9 5PT
T: (01989) 563348
F: (01989) 563348
E: the.arches@which.net

Ashe Leigh ◆◆◆
Bridstow, Ross-on-Wye,
Herefordshire HR9 6QB
T: (01989) 565020

Brookfield House ◆◆◆
Over Ross, Ross-on-Wye,
Herefordshire HR9 7AT
T: (01989) 562188
F: (01989) 564053
E: reception@brookfieldhouse.
co.uk
I: www.brookfieldhouse.co.uk

63 Duxmere Drive ◆◆
Lincoln Green, Ross-on-Wye,
Herefordshire HR9 5UD
T: (01989) 767674

The Falcon Guest House ◆◆
How Caple, Hereford HR1 4TF
T: (01989) 740223
F: (01989) 740223
E: botterill@rbbm.co.uk

Fernside ◆◆◆
Archenfield Road, Ross-on-Wye,
Herefordshire HR9 5AY
T: (01989) 562054

Four Seasons ◆◆◆◆
Coughton, Walford, Ross-on-
Wye, Herefordshire HR9 5SE
T: (01989) 567884

Lavender Cottage ◆◆◆
Bridstow, Ross-on-Wye,
Herefordshire HR9 6QB
T: (01989) 562836 &
07790 729131
F: (01989) 762129
E: barbara_lavender@yahoo.co.
uk

**Lea House Bed and Breakfast
◆◆◆◆**
Lea House, The Lea, Ross-on-
Wye, Herefordshire HR9 7JZ
T: (01989) 750652 &
07889 521797
F: (01989) 750652
E: leahouse@wyenet.co.uk
I: www.leahouse.wyenet.co.uk/

Linden House ◆◆◆◆
14 Church Street, Ross-on-Wye,
Herefordshire HR9 5HN
T: (01989) 565373
F: (01989) 565575
I: WWW.LINDENHOUSE.WYENET.
CO.UK

Lumleys
◆◆◆◆ SILVER AWARD
Kerne Bridge, Bishopswood,
Ross-on-Wye, Herefordshire
HR9 5QT
T: (01600) 890040
F: (01600) 891095
E: helen@lumleys.force9.co.uk
I: www.lumleys.force9.co.uk

**Lyndor Bed and Breakfast
◆◆◆**
Lyndor, Hole-in-the-Wall, Ross-
on-Wye, Herefordshire HR9 7JW
T: (01989) 563833

Norton House
◆◆◆◆ GOLD AWARD
Whitchurch, Ross-on-Wye,
Herefordshire HR9 6DJ
T: (01600) 890046
F: (01600) 890045
E: jackson@osconwhi.source.co.
uk
⊛

The Old Rectory ◆◆◆◆
Hope Mansell, Ross-on-Wye,
Herefordshire HR9 5TL
T: (01989) 750382
F: (01989) 750382
E: rectory@mansell.wyenet.co.
uk

Radcliffe Guest House ◆◆◆
Wye Street, Ross-on-Wye,
Herefordshire HR9 7BS
T: (01989) 563895

Rudhall Farm ◆◆◆◆
Ross-on-Wye, Herefordshire
HR9 7TL
T: (01989) 780240

Sunnymount Hotel ◆◆◆◆
Ryefield Road, Ross-on-Wye,
Herefordshire HR9 5LU
T: (01989) 563880
F: (01989) 566251

Thatch Close ◆◆◆
Llangrove, Ross-on-Wye,
Herefordshire HR9 6EL
T: (01989) 770300
E: edward.drzymalski@virgin.
net

Vaga House ◆◆
Wye Street, Ross-on-Wye,
Herefordshire HR9 7BS
T: (01989) 563024
E: vagahouse@hotmail.comm

Welland House ◆◆◆
Archenfield Road, Ross-on-Wye,
Herefordshire HR9 5BA
T: (01989) 566500
F: (01989) 566500
E: wellandhouse@hotmail.com

ROWSLEY
Derbyshire

The Old Station House ◆◆◆◆
4 Chatsworth Road, Rowsley,
Matlock, Derbyshire DE4 2EJ
T: (01629) 732987

Vernon House ◆◆◆◆
Bakewell Road, Rowsley,
Matlock, Derbyshire DE4 2EB
T: (01629) 734294

1 Vicarage Croft ◆◆◆
Church Lane, Rowsley, Matlock,
Derbyshire DE4 2EA
T: (01629) 735429

ROWTON
Shropshire

Church Farm ◆◆◆
Rowton, Telford, Shropshire
TF6 6QY
T: (01952) 770381
F: (01952) 770381
E: church.farm@pipemedia.co.
uk

RUARDEAN
Gloucestershire

The Malt Shovel Inn ◆◆◆
Ruardean, Gloucestershire
GL17 9TW
T: (01594) 543028
E: MARK@MALTSHOVEL.U-NET.
COM
I: MALTHSHOVEL.U-NET.COM

Oakleigh Farm House ◆◆
Crooked End, Ruardean,
Gloucestershire GL17 9XF
T: (01594) 542284
F: (01594) 543610
E: christine@iconmodel2.
demon.co.uk

RUDYARD
Staffordshire

Hotel Rudyard ◆◆
Lake Road, Rudyard, Leek,
Staffordshire ST13 8RN
T: (01538) 306208
F: (01538) 306208

Wits End ◆◆◆
Horton Road, Rudyard, Leek,
Staffordshire ST13 8RU
T: (01538) 306243
F: (01782) 502934

RUGBY
Warwickshire

Diamond House Hotel ◆◆◆
30 Hillmorton Road, Rugby,
Warwickshire CV22 5AA
T: (01788) 572701
F: (01788) 572701

**The Golden Lion Inn of
Easenhall ◆◆◆◆**
Easenhall, Rugby, Warwickshire
CV23 0JA
T: (01788) 832265
F: (01788) 832878
E: james.austin@btinternet.com
I: www.rugbytown.co.
uk/goldlion.htm

Lawford Hill Farm ◆◆◆◆
Lawford Heath Lane, Rugby,
Warwickshire CV23 9HG
T: (01788) 542001
F: (01788) 537880
E: lawford.hill@talk21.com

Marston House ◆◆◆◆
Priors Marston, Rugby,
Southam, Warwickshire
CV47 7RP
T: (01327) 260297
F: (01327) 262846
E: john.mahon@coltel.co.uk

The Old Rectory ◆◆◆◆
Main Street, Harborough
Magna, Rugby, Warwickshire
CV23 0HS
T: (01788) 833151 &
07803 054509
F: (01788) 833151
E: oldrectory@cwcom.net
I: www.rugbytown.co.
uk/hotels/harborough/
the_old_rectory.htm

Village Green Hotel ◆◆◆◆
The Green, Dunchurch, Rugby,
Warwickshire CV22 6NX
T: (01788) 813434 &
07710 576867
F: (01788) 814714
E: villagegreenhotel.rugby@
btinternet.com
I: www.villagegreenhotelrugby.
com

White Lion Inn ◆◆◆
Coventry Road, Pailton, Rugby,
Warwickshire CV23 0QD
T: (01788) 832359
F: (01788) 832359

RUGELEY
Staffordshire

Park Farm ◆◆◆
Hawkesyard, Armitage Lane,
Rugeley, Staffordshire
WS15 1ED
T: (01889) 583477

ST BRIAVELS
Gloucestershire

Cinderhill House ◆◆◆◆
St Briavels, Lydney,
Gloucestershire GL15 6RH
T: (01594) 530393
F: (01594) 530098
E: cinderhill.house@virgin.net

ST OWENS CROSS
Herefordshire

Amberley
◆◆◆◆ SILVER AWARD
Aberhall Farm, St Owens Cross,
Hereford HR2 8LL
T: (01989) 730256
F: (01989) 730256
E: freda-davies@ereal.net
I: www.travel.uk.com

SANDHURST
Gloucestershire

Brawn Farm ◆◆◆
Sandhurst, Gloucester GL2 9NR
T: (01452) 731010 &
07989 779440
F: (01452) 731102
E: williams.sally@excite.com
⊛

SAXILBY
Lincolnshire

Orchard Cottage ◆◆◆◆
3 Orchard Lane, Saxilby, Lincoln
LN1 2HT
T: (01522) 703192
F: (01522) 703192
E: margaretallen@
orchardcottage.org.uk
I: www.orchardcottage.org.uk

SCALDWELL
Northamptonshire

The Old House ◆◆◆◆
East End, Scaldwell,
Northampton NN6 9LB
T: (01604) 880359 & 882287
F: (01604) 882287
I: www.northampton-index.co.
uk

SCOPWICK
Lincolnshire

The Mill House ◆◆◆◆
Heath Road, Scopwick, Lincoln
LN4 3JB
T: (01526) 321716
F: (01526) 321716

SCOTTER
Lincolnshire

Ivy Lodge Hotel ◆◆◆◆
4 Messingham Road, Scotter,
Gainsborough, Lincolnshire
DN21 3UQ
T: (01724) 763723
F: (01724) 763770
I: www.SmoothHound.co.
uk/hotels/ivylodge.html
⊛

SHAWBURY
Shropshire
Unity Lodge ♦♦
Moreton Mill, Shawbury,
Shrewsbury SY4 4ES
T: (01939) 250831

SHEEPSCOMBE
Gloucestershire
Sen Sook ♦♦♦
Far End Lane, Sheepscombe,
Stroud, Gloucestershire GL6 7RL
T: (01452) 812047

SHELDON
West Midlands
La Caverna Hotel & Restaurant ♦♦♦
2327 Coventry Road, Sheldon,
Birmingham B26 3PG
T: (0121) 743 7917
F: (0121) 722 3307

SHEPSHED
Leicestershire
Croft Guesthouse ♦♦♦
19-21 Hall Croft, Shepshed,
Loughborough, Leicestershire
LE12 9AN
T: (01509) 505657
F: 0870 0522266
E: jeremy@croftguesthouse.
demon.co.uk
I: www.croftguesthouse.demon.
co.uk

SHERBORNE
Gloucestershire
**Prescott House
Rating Applied For**
Sherborne, Cheltenham,
Gloucestershire GL54 3DU
T: (01451) 844255
F: (01451) 844434
E: RandSRichards@care4free.
net

SHERWOOD RISE
Nottinghamshire
Pelham House ♦♦
6-8 Vivian Avenue, Sherwood
Rise, Nottingham NG5 1AP
T: (0115) 960 4829 & 962 5881

SHIFNAL
Shropshire
Brookwood ♦♦
Haughton Lane, Shifnal,
Shropshire TF11 8HW
T: (01952) 460239

Cross Keys Guest House ♦♦♦
62 Broadway, Shifnal,
Shropshire TF11 8AZ
T: (01952) 460173

Naughty Nell's Limited ♦♦♦
1 Park Street, Shifnal, Shropshire
TF11 9BA
T: (01952) 411412
F: (01952) 463336

Odfellows – The Wine Bar ♦♦♦
Market Place, Shifnal,
Shropshire TF11 9AU
T: (01952) 461517
F: (01952) 463855
E: matt@odfellows.freeserve.co.
uk

Village Farm Lodge ♦♦
Sheriffhales, Shifnal, Shropshire
TF11 8RD
T: (01952) 462763 &
07976 977212
F: (01952) 201310

SHILTON
Warwickshire
**Barnacle Hall
♦♦♦♦♦ SILVER AWARD**
Shilton Lane, Shilton, Coventry,
Warwickshire CV7 9LH
T: (024) 76612629

SHIPSTON-ON-STOUR
Warwickshire
Tallet Barn Bed and Breakfast ♦♦♦♦
Yerdley Farm, Long Compton,
Shipston-on-Stour,
Warwickshire CV36 5LH
T: (01608) 684248
I: www.country-accom.co.uk

White Bear Hotel ♦♦♦
High Street, Shipston-on-Stour,
Warwickshire CV36 4AJ
T: (01608) 661558
F: (01608) 661558
E: inisfallen@aol.com

SHIREBROOK
Derbyshire
The Old School Guesthouse ♦♦♦
80 Main Street, Shirebrook,
Mansfield, Nottinghamshire
NG20 8DL
T: (01623) 744610 &
07889 726098
F: (01623) 744610

SHIRLAND
Derbyshire
Park Lane Farm ♦♦♦♦
Park Lane, Shirland, Alfreton,
Derbyshire DE55 6AX
T: (01773) 831880

SHIRLEY
West Midlands
Chale Guest House ♦♦♦
967 Stratford Road, Shirley,
Solihull, West Midlands B90 4BG
T: (0121) 744 2846 &
07956 429154
F: (0121) 7442846
E: chale.guesthouse@iname.
com
I: www.welcome.to/chale

The Old Byre Guesthouse ♦♦♦♦
Hollington Lane, Shirley,
Ashbourne, Derbyshire DE6 3AS
T: (01335) 360054
F: (01335) 360054

SHOBY
Leicestershire
Shoby Lodge Farm ♦♦♦♦
Shoby, Melton Mowbray,
Leicestershire LE14 3PF
T: (01664) 812156 &
07802 961300

SHREWSBURY
Shropshire
Abbey Court House ♦♦♦
134 Abbey Foregate,
Shrewsbury, SY2 6AU
T: (01743) 364416
F: (01743) 358559

Abbey Lodge Guest House ♦♦♦
68 Abbey Foregate, Shrewsbury,
Shropshire SY2 6BG
T: (01743) 235832 &
07860 335225
F: (01743) 235832
E: Lindsay.Abbeylodge@Virgin.
Net

Anton Guest House ♦♦♦♦
1 Canon Street, Monkmoor,
Shrewsbury, SY2 5HG
T: (01743) 359275
E: antonhouse@supanet.com
I: www.antonhouse.supanet.
com

**Ashton Lees
♦♦♦♦ SILVER AWARD**
Dorrington, Shrewsbury,
Shropshire SY5 7JW
T: (01743) 718378

Avonlea ♦♦
33 Coton Crescent, Coton Hill,
Shrewsbury, Shropshire SY1 2NZ
T: (01743) 359398

Bancroft ♦♦♦♦
17 Coton Crescent, Shrewsbury,
Shropshire SY1 2NY
T: (01743) 231746
F: (01743) 231746
E: Bancroft01@aol.com

The Boars Head ♦
18 Belle Vue Road, Shrewsbury,
SY3 7LL
T: (01743) 350590

Brambleberry ♦♦♦♦
Halfway House, Shrewsbury,
Shropshire SY5 9DD
T: (01743) 884762

Cardeston Park Farm ♦♦♦
Ford, Shrewsbury SY5 9NH
T: (01743) 884265
F: (01743) 886265

Castlecote ♦♦♦
77 Monkmoor Road,
Shrewsbury, SY2 5AT
T: (01743) 245473
E: btench@castlecote.
fsbusiness.co.uk

Chatford House ♦♦♦
Bayston Hill, Shrewsbury,
SY3 0AY
T: (01743) 718301

Cromwells Hotel & Wine Bar ♦♦
11 Dogpole, Shrewsbury,
SY1 1EN
T: (01743) 361440
F: (01743) 341121

Eye Manor ♦♦♦♦
Leighton, Shrewsbury, SY5 6SQ
T: (01952) 510066 & 200061
F: (01952) 200061

Golden Cross Hotel ♦♦♦
14 Princess Street, Shrewsbury,
SY1 1LP
T: (01743) 362507

Hillsboro ♦♦♦
1 Port Hill Gardens, Shrewsbury,
SY3 8SH
T: (01743) 231033

Jasmine House ♦♦
102 Copthorne Road,
Shrewsbury, SY3 8NA
T: (01743) 232208

Lyth Hill House ♦♦♦♦
28 Old Coppice, Lyth Hill,
Shrewsbury, SY3 0BP
T: (01743) 874660
F: (01743) 874660
E: B&B@lythhill.globalnet.co.uk
I: www.lythhillhouse.co.uk

Noneley Hall ♦♦♦♦
Noneley, Near Wem,
Shrewsbury, SY4 5SL
T: (01939) 233271
F: (01939) 233271
E: cpbirch@callnetuk.com

North Farm ♦♦♦
Eaton Mascot, Shrewsbury,
Shropshire SY5 6HF
T: (01743) 761031
F: (01743) 761854
E: northfarm@talk21.com
I: www.virtual-shropshire.co.
uk/northfarm

**The Old Station
♦♦♦♦ SILVER AWARD**
Leaton, Bomere Heath,
Shrewsbury, Shropshire SY4 3AP
T: (01939) 290905 &
07885 526307

The Old Vicarage ♦♦♦♦
Leaton, Shrewsbury, SY4 3AP
T: (01939) 290989
F: (01939) 290989
E: m-j@oldvicleaton.freeserve.
co.uk
I: www.visitorlinks.com

**Pinewood House
♦♦♦♦♦ GOLD AWARD**
Shelton Park, The Mount,
Shrewsbury, SY3 8BL
T: (01743) 364200

Prynce's Villa ♦♦
15 Monkmoor Road,
Shrewsbury, Shropshire SY2 5AG
T: (01743) 356217

Restawhile ♦♦♦
36 Coton Crescent, Coton Hill,
Shrewsbury, SY1 2NZ
T: (01743) 240969
F: (01743) 231841
E: restawhile@breathemail.net
I: www.virtual-shropshire.co.
uk/restawhile

Sandford House Hotel ♦♦♦
St Julian's Friars, Shrewsbury,
SY1 1XL
T: (01743) 343829
F: (01743) 343829
E: sandfordhouse@lineone.net
I: www.lineone.
net/§sandfordhouse/

**Severn Cottage ♦♦♦♦
Rating Applied For**
4 Coton Hill, Shrewsbury,
SY1 2DZ
T: (01743) 358467 &
07971 569339
F: (01743) 340254
E: davidtudor1@virgin.net
I: www.shrewsbury.net.com

**Shorthill Lodge
♦♦♦♦ SILVER AWARD**
Shorthill, Lea Cross, Shrewsbury,
SY5 8JE
T: (01743) 860864
I: www.go2.co.uk/shorthill

The Stiperstones Guest House
♦♦♦
18 Coton Crescent, Coton Hill,
Shrewsbury, SY1 2NZ
T: (01743) 246720 & 350303
F: (01743) 350303
E: stiperston@aol.com
I: www.go2.co.uk/stiperstones

Sydney House Hotel ♦♦♦
Coton Crescent, Coton Hill,
Shrewsbury, SY1 2LJ
T: (01743) 354681 &
0800 2981243
F: (01743) 354681

Trevellion House ♦♦♦
1 Bradford Street, Monkmoor,
Shrewsbury, SY1 5DP
T: (01743) 249582
F: (01743) 232096
E: marktaplin@
bradfordstreetjunglelink.co.uk

Upper Brompton Farm
♦♦♦♦♦ GOLD AWARD
Brompton, Cross Houses,
Shrewsbury SY5 6LE
T: (01743) 761629
F: (01743) 761679
E: upper-brompton.farm@dial.
pipex.com
I: www.smoothound.co.
uk/hotels/upperbro.html

SKEGNESS
Lincolnshire

Chatsworth Hotel ♦♦♦
North Parade, Skegness,
Lincolnshire PE25 2UB
T: (01754) 764177
F: (01754) 761173
E: Altipper@aol.com
I: www.chatsworthskegness.co.
uk

Clarence House Hotel
Rating Applied For
32 South Parade, Skegness,
Lincolnshire PE25 3HW
T: (01754) 765588
E: hartley34@skeg3.freeserve.
co.uk

Crawford Hotel ♦♦♦
104 South Parade, Skegness,
Lincolnshire PE25 3HR
T: (01754) 764215
F: (01754) 764215

Merton Hotel ♦♦♦
14 Firbeck Avenue, Skegness,
Lincolnshire PE25 3JY
T: (01754) 764423
F: (01754) 766627

North Parade Hotel ♦♦♦
20 North Parade, Skegness,
Lincolnshire PE25 2UB
T: (01754) 762309 & 765235
F: (01754) 762309
E: sthomson@btclick.com

Palm Court Hotel ♦♦♦
74 South Parade, Skegness,
Lincolnshire PE25 3HP
T: (01754) 767711
F: (01754) 767711

Rufford Hotel ♦♦♦
5 Saxby Avenue, Skegness,
Lincolnshire PE25 3JZ
T: (01754) 763428 &
0500 657841

Saxby Hotel ♦♦♦
12 Saxby Avenue, Skegness,
Lincolnshire PE25 3LG
T: (01754) 763905
F: (01754) 763905

Seacroft Hotel ♦♦
South Parade, Skegness,
Lincolnshire PE25 3EH
T: (01754) 762301
F: (01754) 761037

Stoneleigh Private Hotel ♦♦♦
67 Sandbeck Avenue, Skegness,
Lincolnshire PE25 3JS
T: (01754) 769138
E: enquiries@stoneleigh-hotel.
freeserve.co.uk
I: www.stoneleigh-hotel.
freeserve.co.uk

Woodthorpe Private Hotel ♦♦
64 South Parade, Skegness,
Lincolnshire PE25 3HP
T: (01754) 763452

SKILLINGTON
Lincolnshire

Sproxton Lodge Farm ♦♦
Sproxton Lodge, Skillington,
Grantham, Lincolnshire
NG33 5HJ
T: (01476) 860307

SLEAFORD
Lincolnshire

The Tally Ho Inn ♦♦♦
Aswarby, Sleaford, Lincolnshire
NG34 8SA
T: (01529) 455205
F: (01529) 455205

SNELSTON
Derbyshire

Sidesmill Farm ♦♦♦♦
Snelston, Ashbourne, Derbyshire
DE6 2GQ
T: (01335) 342710

SOLIHULL
West Midlands

Acorn Guest House ♦♦♦♦
29 Links Drive, Solihull, West
Midlands B91 2DJ
T: (0121) 7055241
E: acorn.wood@btinternet.com

Boxtrees Farm ♦♦♦
Stratford Road, Hockley Heath,
Solihull, West Midlands B94 6EA
T: (01564) 782039 &
07970 736156
F: (01564) 784661
E: b&b@boxtrees.co.uk
I: boxtrees.co.uk

Cedarwood House ♦♦♦
347 Lyndon Road, Solihull, West
Midlands B92 7QT
T: (0121) 743 5844
F: (0121) 743 5844
E: mail@cedarwooduk.co.uk
I: www.cedarwooduk.co.uk

Clovelly Guest House ♦♦♦
Coleshill Heath Road, Marston
Green, Solihull, West Midlands
B37 7HY
T: (0121) 779 2886 &
07885 412780

The Edwardian Guest House
♦♦♦♦
7 St Bernards Road, Olton,
Solihull, West Midlands B92 7AU
T: (0121) 706 2138

The Gate House ♦♦♦
Barston Lane, Barston, Solihull,
West Midlands B92 0JN
T: (01675) 443274
F: (01675) 443274

Ravenhurst ♦♦♦
56 Lode Lane, Solihull, West
Midlands B91 2AW
T: (0121) 7055754 &
07973 954930
F: (0121) 704 0717

Triangle Guest House ♦♦
512-514 Stratford Road, Shirley,
Solihull, West Midlands B90 4AY
T: (0121) 744 4182 &
0797 7666489
F: (0121) 744 4182

SOUTH HYKEHAM
Lincolnshire

The Hall Farm Farmhouse
♦♦♦
Meadow Lane, South Hykeham,
Lincoln LN6 9PF
T: (01522) 686432
F: (01522) 686432
E: raymondphillips@nkdcuucp.
dircon.co.uk

SOUTH WINGFIELD
Derbyshire

Platts Farm Guesthouse ♦♦♦
High Road, South Wingfield,
Alfreton, Derbyshire DE55 7LX
T: (01773) 832280

SOUTH WITHAM
Lincolnshire

The Blue Cow Inn and Brewery
♦♦♦
29 High Street, South Witham,
Grantham, Lincolnshire
NG33 5QB
T: (01572) 768432
F: (01572) 768432

SOUTHAM
Warwickshire

Briarwood ♦♦♦
34 Warwick Road, Southam,
Leamington Spa, Warwickshire
CV47 0HN
T: (01926) 814756

SOUTHWELL
Nottinghamshire

Barn Lodge ♦♦♦
Duckers Cottage, Brinkley,
Southwell, Nottinghamshire
NG25 0TP
T: (01636) 813435
E: barnlodge@hotmail.com

SPALDING
Lincolnshire

Guy Wells Farm ♦♦♦♦
East Gate, Whaplode, Spalding,
Lincolnshire PE12 6TZ
T: (01406) 422239
F: (01406) 422239

Travel Stop RAC Lodge ♦♦
Locks Mill Farm, 50 Cowbit
Road, Spalding, Lincolnshire
PE11 2RJ
T: (01775) 767290 & 767716
F: (01775) 767716
E: TRAVELSTOPRACLODGE

STAFFORD
Staffordshire

Cedarwood
♦♦♦♦ SILVER AWARD
46 Weeping Cross, Stafford,
ST17 0DS
T: (01785) 662981

Furtherhill Guest House ♦♦
55 Lichfield Road, Stafford,
ST17 4LL
T: (01785) 258723

Littywood House ♦♦♦
Bradley, Stafford, ST18 9DW
T: (01785) 780234 & 780770
F: (01785) 780770

Park Farm ♦♦♦
Weston Road, Stafford,
ST18 0BD
T: (01785) 240257
F: (01785) 240257

Woodhouse Farm ♦♦♦♦
Woodhouse Lane, Haughton,
Stafford, ST18 9JJ
T: (01785) 822259

Wyndale Guest House ♦♦
199 Corporation Street,
Stafford, ST16 3LQ
T: (01785) 223069

STAMFORD
Lincolnshire

Birch House ♦♦♦
4 Lonsdale Road, Stamford,
Lincolnshire PE9 2RW
T: (01780) 754876

Chestnut View Bed & Breakfast
♦♦♦
Chestnut View, 94 Casterton
Road, Stamford, Lincolnshire
PE9 2UB
T: (01780) 763648

Dolphin Guesthouse ♦♦
12 East Street, Stamford,
Lincolnshire PE9 1QD
T: (01780) 757515 & 481567
F: (01780) 57515
E: mikdolphin@mikdolphin.
demon.co.uk

Martins ♦♦♦♦
20 High Street, Saint Martin's,
Stamford, Lincolnshire PE9 2LF
T: (01780) 752106
F: (01780) 482691
E: marie@martins-b-b.demon.
co.uk

Midstone Farmhouse
♦♦♦♦ SILVER AWARD
Southorpe, Stamford,
Lincolnshire PE9 3BX
T: (01780) 740136
F: (01780) 740136

The Mill ♦♦♦♦
Mill Lane, Tallington, Stamford,
Lincolnshire PE9 4RR
T: (01780) 740815 &
07802 373326
F: (01780) 740280

The Oak Inn ♦♦♦
48 Stamford Road, Easton on
the Hill, Stamford, Lincolnshire
PE9 3PA
T: (01780) 752286
F: (01780) 752286
E: peter@klippon.demon.co.uk

5 Rock Terrace ♦♦♦♦
Scotgate, Stamford, Lincolnshire
PE9 2YJ
T: (01780) 755475

STANDISH
Gloucestershire
Oaktree Farm ♦♦♦♦
Little Haresfield, Standish,
Stonehouse, Gloucestershire
GL10 3DS
T: (01452) 883323
E: Jackie@oaktreefarm.fsnet.co.
uk

STANTON-BY-BRIDGE
Derbyshire
Ivy House Farm ♦♦♦♦
Ivy House Farm, Stanton-by-
Bridge, Derby DE73 1HT
T: (01332) 863152 &
07774 112292
F: (01332) 863152

St Brides Farmhouse ♦♦♦♦
Stanton-by-Bridge, Derby,
South Derbyshire DE73 1JQ
T: (01332) 865255
E: stbrides.bb@talk21.com

STANTON IN PEAK
Derbyshire
Congreave Farm
♦♦♦♦ SILVER AWARD
Congreave, Stanton in Peak,
Matlock, Derbyshire DE4 2NF
T: (01629) 732063
E: deborahbettney@congreave.
junglelink.co.uk
I: www.matsam16.freeserve.co.
uk/congreave/

STANTON-ON-THE-WOLDS, KEYWORTH
Laurel Farm ♦♦♦
Browns Lane, Stanton-on-the-
Wolds, Keyworth, Nottingham
NG12 5BL
T: (0115) 937 3488
F: (0115) 9376490
E: laurelfarm@yahoo.com

STAPLOW
Worcestershire
Woodleigh ♦♦♦♦
Staplow, Ledbury, Herefordshire
HR8 1NP
T: (01531) 640204
F: (01531) 640767

STAUNTON
Gloucestershire
Kilmorie Small Holding ♦♦♦
Gloucester Road, Corse, Snigs
End, Staunton, Gloucester,
Gloucestershire GL19 3RQ
T: (01452) 840224
F: (01452) 840224
I: www.SmoothHound.co.
uk/hotels/kilmorie.html

STAVELEY
Derbyshire
Foresters Arms ♦♦
Market Street, Staveley,
Chesterfield, Derbyshire S43 3UT
T: (01246) 477455
E: john.amer@virgin.net
I: www.forestersarms.ukcom.cx

STIPERSTONES
Shropshire
The Old Chapel ♦♦♦♦
Perkins Beach Dingle,
Stiperstones, Shrewsbury,
Shropshire SY5 0PE
T: (01743) 791449
E: jean@a-lees.freeserve.co.uk
I: www.SmoothHound.co.
uk/hotels/oldchapel.html

STOCKINGFORD
Warwickshire
Aberglynmarch Guest House ♦♦♦
198 Church Road, Stockingford,
Nuneaton, Warwickshire
CV10 8LH
T: (024) 7634 2793

STOCKTON ON TEME
Worcestershire
Wharf Farm ♦♦♦
Pensax Lane, Stockton on Teme,
Worcester WR6 6XF
T: (01584) 881341

STOKE BRUERNE
Northamptonshire
Beam End
♦♦♦♦ SILVER AWARD
Stoke Park, Stoke Bruerne,
Towcester, Northamptonshire
NN12 7RZ
T: (01604) 864802 & 864638
F: (01604) 864637
E: beamend@bun.com

3 Rookery Barns ♦♦♦♦
Rookery Lane, Stoke Bruerne,
Towcester, Northamptonshire
NN12 7SJ
T: (01604) 862274

STOKE DOYLE
Northamptonshire
Shuckburgh Arms ♦♦♦♦
Stoke Doyle, Peterborough
PE8 5TG
T: (01832) 272339
F: (01832) 275230
E: paulkirkby@shuckburgharms.
co.uk
I: www.shuckburgharms.co.uk

STOKE-ON-TRENT
Staffordshire
Chestnut Grange
♦♦♦♦ SILVER AWARD
Windmill Hill, Rough Close,
Stoke-on-Trent, Staffordshire
ST3 7PJ
T: (01782) 396084 &
07885 847832
F: (01782) 396084

Flower Pot Hotel ♦
44-46 Snow Hill, Shelton, Stoke-
on-Trent, ST1 4LY
T: (01782) 207204

Holly Trees ♦♦♦♦
Crewe Road, Alsager, Stoke-on-
Trent, ST7 2JL
T: (01270) 876847
F: (01270) 883301

The Limes ♦♦♦
Cheadle Road, Blythe Bridge,
Stoke-on-Trent ST11 9PW
T: (01782) 393278

The Old Dairy House
♦♦♦♦♦ SILVER AWARD
Trentham Park, Stoke-on-Trent,
ST4 8AE
T: (01782) 641209
F: (01782) 712904

The Old Vicarage ♦♦♦
6 The Close, Endon, Stoke-on-
Trent, Staffordshire ST9 9JH
T: (01782) 503686

Old Vicarage Guesthouse ♦♦♦♦
Birchenwood Road, Newchapel,
Stoke-on-Trent ST7 4QT
T: (01782) 785270
E: kentbaguley@hotmail.co.uk

The Olde House on the Green ♦♦♦♦
Fulford, Stoke-on-Trent,
ST11 9QS
T: (01782) 394555

Reynolds Hey ♦♦♦
Park Lane, Endon, Stoke-on-
Trent ST9 9JB
T: (01782) 502717

Shaw Gate Farm ♦♦♦
Shay Lane, Foxt, Stoke-on-Trent,
ST10 2HN
T: (01538) 266590
F: (01538) 266590

Sneyd Arms Hotel ♦♦
Tower Square, Tunstall, Stoke-
on-Trent ST6 5AA
T: (01782) 826722
F: (01782) 826722

Verdon Guest House ♦♦
44 Charles Street, Hanley, Stoke-
on-Trent ST1 3JY
T: (01782) 264244 &
07711 514682
F: (01782) 264244
E: debbie@howlett18.freeserve.
co.uk
I: business.thisisstaffordshire.co.
uk/verdon

STONE
Staffordshire
Couldreys ♦♦♦♦
8 Airdale Road, Stone,
Staffordshire ST15 8DW
T: (01785) 812500
F: (01785) 811761
E: bcouldrey@aol.com

Lock House ♦♦♦♦
74 Newcastle Road, Stone,
Staffordshire ST15 8LB
T: (01785) 811551 & 814822
F: (01785) 286587
E: mbd@fsbdial.co.uk

Mayfield House ♦♦♦
112 Newcastle Road, Stone,
Staffordshire ST15 8LG
T: (01785) 811446

STONEHOUSE
Gloucestershire
Beacon Inn Hotel ♦♦♦
Haresfield, Stonehouse,
Gloucestershire GL10 3DX
T: (01452) 728884
F: (01452) 728884
E: beaconinn@aol.com

The Grey Cottage
♦♦♦♦♦ GOLD AWARD
Bath Road, Leonard Stanley,
Stonehouse, Gloucestershire
GL10 3LU
T: (01453) 822515
F: (01453) 822515

Merton Lodge ♦♦
8 Ebley Road, Stonehouse,
Gloucestershire GL10 2LQ
T: (01453) 822018

STOTTESDON
Worcestershire
Hardwicke Farm ♦♦♦♦
Stottesdon, Kidderminster,
Worcestershire DY14 8TN
T: (01746) 718220

STOULTON
Worcestershire
Caldewell ♦♦♦
Pershore Road, Stoulton,
Worcester WR7 4RL
T: (01905) 840894
F: (01905) 840894
E: sheila@demon.co.uk
I: www.caldewell.demon.co.
uk/indexhtml

STOURBRIDGE
West Midlands
St. Elizabeth's Cottage ♦♦♦♦
Woodman Lane, Clent,
Stourbridge, West Midlands
DY9 9PX
T: (01562) 883883
E: sc_elizabeth_cotebtconnect.
com

STOURPORT-ON-SEVERN
Worcestershire
Baldwin House ♦♦♦
8 Lichfield Street, Stourport-on-
Severn, Worcestershire
DY13 9EU
T: (01299) 877221 & 824613
F: (01299) 877221
E: BALDWINHOUSEBB@A.O.L.
COM

STOW-ON-THE-WOLD
Gloucestershire
Aston House ♦♦♦♦
Broadwell, Moreton-in-Marsh,
Gloucestershire GL56 0TJ
T: (01451) 830475 &
07773 452037
E: fja@netcomuk.co.uk
I: www.netcomuk.co.
uk/§nmfa/aston_house.html

The Beeches ♦♦♦
Fosse Lane, Stow-on-the-Wold,
Cheltenham, Gloucestershire
GL54 1EH
T: (01451) 870836

Corsham Field Farmhouse ♦♦♦
Bledington Road, Stow-on-the-
Wold, Cheltenham,
Gloucestershire GL54 1JH
T: (01451) 831750

The Cotswold Garden Tea Room & B&B. ♦♦♦
Wells Cottage, Digbeth Street,
Stow-on-the-Wold,
Cheltenham, Gloucestershire
GL54 1BN
T: (01451) 870999

Crestow House ♦♦♦♦
Stow-on-the-Wold,
Cheltenham, Gloucestershire
GL54 1JX
T: (01451) 830969
F: (01451) 832129
E: fjsimon@compuserve.com
I: ourworld.compuserve.
com/homespaces/fjsimon

Cross Keys Cottage ♦♦♦
Park Street, Stow-on-the-Wold,
Cheltenham, Gloucestershire
GL54 1AQ
T: (01451) 831128
F: (01451) 831128

Fairview Farmhouse
◆◆◆◆ SILVER AWARD
Bledington Road, Stow-on-the-Wold, Gloucestershire GL54 1JH
T: (01451) 830279 &
07711 979944
F: (01451) 830279

The Gate Lodge ◆◆◆◆
Stow Hill, Stow-on-the-Wold, Cheltenham, Gloucestershire GL54 1JZ
T: (01451) 832103

22 Glebe Close ◆◆◆
Stow-on-the-Wold, Cheltenham, Gloucestershire GL54 1DJ
T: (01451) 830042

Horse and Groom Inn ◆◆
Upper Oddington, Moreton-in-Marsh, Gloucestershire GL56 0XH
T: (01451) 830584
F: (01451) 831496

Littlebroom ◆◆◆◆
Maugersbury, Stow-on-the-Wold, Cheltenham, Gloucestershire GL54 1HP
T: (01451) 830510
I: www.accofind.com/

Maugersbury Manor ◆◆◆
Stow-on-the-Wold, Cheltenham, Gloucestershire GL54 1HP
T: (01451) 830581
F: (01451) 870902
E: themanor@wiseholidays.com

Number Nine
◆◆◆◆ SILVER AWARD
9 Park Street, Stow-on-the-Wold, Cheltenham, Gloucestershire GL54 1AQ
T: (01451) 870333 &
07836 205431
F: (01451) 870445
E: numbernine@talk21.com

Pear Tree Cottage ◆◆◆
High Street, Stow-on-the-Wold, Cheltenham, Gloucestershire GL54 1DL
T: (01451) 831210
E: peartreecottage@btinternet.com

South Hill Farmhouse ◆◆◆
Fosseway, Stow-on-the-Wold, Cheltenham, Gloucestershire GL54 1JU
T: (01451) 831219
F: (01451) 831554

South Hill Lodge ◆◆◆◆
Fosseway, Stow-on-the-Wold, Cheltenham, Gloucestershire GL54 1JU
T: (01451) 831083 & 870694
F: (01451) 870694
E: digby@southilllodge.freeserve.co.uk

Talbot Rooms ◆◆
Talbot Hotel, The Square, Stow-on-the-Wold, Cheltenham, Gloucestershire GL54 1AF
T: (01451) 830631

Tall Trees ◆◆◆
Rating Applied For
Oddington Road, Stow-on-the-Wold, Cheltenham, Gloucestershire GL54 1AL
T: (01451) 831296
F: (01451) 870049
E: TallTrees.Stow/@Virgin.Net

Top of the Wold
Rating Applied For
The Manor House, The Square, Stow-on-the-Wold, Cheltenham, Gloucestershire GL54 1AF
T: (01451) 870364
F: (01451) 870717
E: topofthewold@btinternet.com

White Hart Inn ◆◆
The Square, Stow-on-the-Wold, Cheltenham, Gloucestershire GL54 1AF
T: (01451) 830674
F: (01451) 830090

Woodlands ◆◆◆◆
Upper Swell, Stow-on-the-Wold, Cheltenham, Gloucestershire GL54 1EW
T: (01451) 832346

Wyck Hill Lodge ◆◆◆◆◆
Burford Road, Stow-on-the-Wold, Cheltenham, Gloucestershire GL54 1HT
T: (01451) 830141
E: gkhwyck@compuserve.com

STOWE-BY-CHARTLEY
Staffordshire

Mill Cottage Bed & Breakfast ◆
Chartley, Stowe-by-Chartley, Stafford ST18 0LH
T: (01889) 271109 &
07711 381669

STRAGGLETHORPE
Lincolnshire

Stragglethorpe Hall
◆◆◆◆ SILVER AWARD
Stragglethorpe, Lincoln LN5 0QZ
T: (01400) 272308
F: (01400) 273816
E: stragglethorpe@compuserve.com
I: www.stragglethorpe.com

STRATFORD-UPON-AVON
Warwickshire

Aberfoyle Guest House ◆◆◆
3 Evesham Place, Stratford-upon-Avon, Warwickshire CV37 6HT
T: (01789) 295703
F: (01789) 295703

Aidan Guest House ◆◆◆
11 Evesham Place, Stratford-upon-Avon, Warwickshire CV37 6HT
T: (01789) 292824 &
0709 1000445
F: (01789) 292824
E: john2aidan@aol.com
I: www.aidanhouse.co.uk

Alderminster Farm
◆◆◆◆ SILVER AWARD
Alderminster, Stratford-upon-Avon, Warwickshire CV37 8BP
T: (01789) 450774 &
07785 915777
F: (01789) 450774
E: christopher-denley.wright@virgin.net
I: www.tpointmc.demon.co.uk/alderminster/.

All Seasons ◆◆
51 Grove Road, Stratford-upon-Avon, Warwickshire CV37 6PB
T: (01789) 293404
F: (01789) 293404

Amelia Linhill Guesthouse ◆◆◆
35 Evesham Place, Stratford-upon-Avon, Warwickshire CV37 6HT
T: (01789) 292879
F: (01789) 299691
E: Linhill@free4all.co.uk

The Applegarth ◆◆◆
Warwick Road, Stratford-upon-Avon, Warwickshire CV37 6YW
T: (01789) 267388
F: (01789) 267388
E: applegarth@supanet.com

Arden Park Hotel ◆◆◆
6 Arden Street, Stratford-upon-Avon, Warwickshire CV37 6PA
T: (01789) 296072
F: (01789) 296072

Arrandale Guesthouse ◆◆◆
208 Evesham Road, Stratford-upon-Avon, Warwickshire CV37 9AS
T: (01789) 267112

Ashley Court Hotel ◆◆◆
55 Shipston Road, Stratford-upon-Avon, Warwickshire CV37 7LN
T: (01789) 297278
F: (01789) 204453
E: info@ashleycourthotel.co.uk
I: www.ashleycourthotel.co.uk

Avon View Hotel ◆◆◆
121 Shipston Road, Stratford-upon-Avon, Warwickshire CV37 7LW
T: (01789) 297542
F: (01789) 292936
E: avon.view@lineone.net

Avonlea ◆◆◆◆
47 Shipston Road, Stratford-upon-Avon, Warwickshire CV37 7LN
T: (01789) 205940
F: (01789) 209115

34 Banbury Road ◆◆◆
Stratford-upon-Avon, Warwickshire CV37 7HY
T: (01789) 269714
E: clodagh@compuserve.com
I: www.smoothhound.co.uk/hotels/34banbur.html

Barbette ◆◆◆
165 Evesham Road, Stratford-upon-Avon, Warwickshire CV37 9BP
T: (01789) 297822

Bradbourne House ◆◆◆◆
44 Shipston Road, Stratford-upon-Avon, Warwickshire CV37 7LP
T: (01789) 204178
F: (01789) 262335
E: brad-bourne@talk21.com

Brett House ◆◆◆
8 Broad Walk, Stratford-upon-Avon, Warwickshire CV37 6HS
T: (01789) 266374
F: (01789) 414027

Broadlands Guest House ◆◆◆
23 Evesham Place, Stratford-upon-Avon, Warwickshire CV37 6HT
T: (01789) 299181
F: (01789) 551382

Broadmead ◆◆◆◆
Broadmead, Luddington, Stratford-upon-Avon, Warwickshire CV37 9SD
T: (01789) 750644
F: (01789) 750644
E: simmons@Free4all.co.uk
I: www.Stratford-upon-Avon.co.uk/broadmead.htm

Bronhill House ◆◆◆
260 Alcester Road, Stratford-upon-Avon, Warwickshire CV37 9JQ
T: (01789) 299169

Brook Lodge Guest House ◆◆◆◆
192 Alcester Road, Stratford-upon-Avon, Warwickshire CV37 9DR
T: (01789) 295988
F: (01789) 295988
E: brooklodge@free4all.co.uk
I: www.smoothhound.co.uk/hotels/brooklod.html

Burton Farm ◆◆◆◆
Bishopton, Stratford-upon-Avon, Warwickshire CV37 0RW
T: (01789) 293338
F: (01789) 262877

Carlton Guest House ◆◆◆
22 Evesham Place, Stratford-upon-Avon, Warwickshire CV37 6HT
T: (01789) 293548
F: (01789) 293548

Chadwyns Guest House ◆◆◆◆
6 Broad Walk, Stratford-upon-Avon, Warwickshire CV37 6HS
T: (01789) 269077
F: (01789) 298855
E: reservations@chadwyns.freeserve.co.uk
I: www.chadwyns.freeserve.co.uk

Church Farm ◆◆◆
Dorsington, Stratford-upon-Avon, Warwickshire CV37 8AX
T: (01789) 720471 &
07831 504194
F: (01789) 720830
E: chfarmdorsington@aol.com
I: www.travel-uk.net/churchfarm

Clomendy Bed and Breakfast ◆◆◆
10 Broad Walk, Stratford-upon-Avon, Warwickshire CV37 6HS
T: (01789) 266957

Courtland Hotel ◆◆
12 Guild Street, Stratford-upon-Avon, Warwickshire CV37 6RE
T: (01789) 292401
F: (01789) 292401
E: bridget.johnson4@virgin.net
I: www.courtlands@uk-vacation.comwww.courtlands@travel-uk.com

**Craig Cleeve House Hotel &
Restaurant**◆◆◆
67-69 Shipston Road, Stratford-
upon-Avon, Warwickshire
CV37 7LW
T: (01789) 296573
F: (01789) 299452
E: craigcleev@aol.com

The Croft ◆◆
49 Shipston Road, Stratford-
upon-Avon, Warwickshire
CV37 7LN
T: (01789) 293419
F: (01789) 293419
E: Croft.stratford-uk@virgin.net
I: WWW.THECROFT.HEARTUK.
NET

Curtain Call ◆◆◆
142 Alcester Road, Stratford-
upon-Avon, Warwickshire
CV37 9DR
T: (01789) 267734
F: (01789) 267734
E: curtaincall@btinternet.com

Cymbeline ◆◆◆
24 Evesham Place, Stratford-
upon-Avon, Warwickshire
CV37 6HT
T: (01789) 292958
F: (01789) 292958
@

Dylan Guesthouse ◆◆◆
10 Evesham Place, Stratford-
upon-Avon, Warwickshire
CV37 6HT
T: (01789) 204819

East Bank House ◆◆◆◆
19 Warwick Road, Stratford-
upon-Avon, Warwickshire
CV37 6YW
T: (01789) 292758
F: (01789) 292758
E: eastbank.house@virgin.net or
andrewmarsh@btconnect.com
I: www.east-bank-house.co.uk
🏃

Eastnor House Hotel ◆◆◆◆
Shipston Road, Stratford-upon-
Avon, Warwickshire CV37 7LN
T: (01789) 268115
F: (01789) 266516
E: eastnor.house@tesco.net

Emsley ◆◆◆
4 Arden Street, Stratford-upon-
Avon, Warwickshire CV37 6PA
T: (01789) 299557
E: pennydis@msn.com

**Ettington Chase Conference
Centre**◆◆◆◆◆ SILVER AWARD
Banbury Road, Ettington,
Stratford-upon-Avon,
Warwickshire CV37 7NZ
T: (01789) 740000
F: (01789) 740909
E: ettconf@hayleycc.co.uk
I: www.hayley-conf.co.uk

Eversley Bears' Guest House
◆◆◆◆
37 Grove Road, Stratford-upon-
Avon, Warwickshire CV37 6PB
T: (01789) 292334
F: (01789) 292334
E: eversleybears@btinternet.
com
I: www.stratford-upon-avon.co.
uk/eversleybears.htm

Faviere ◆◆◆◆
127 Shipston Road, Stratford-
upon-Avon, Warwickshire
CV37 7LW
T: (01789) 293764
F: (01789) 269365
E: guestsfaviere@cwcom.net
I: www.SmoothHound.co.
uk/hotels/faviere.html

Folly Farm Cottage
◆◆◆◆ GOLD AWARD
Back Street, Ilmington,
Shipston-on-Stour,
Warwickshire CV36 4LJ
T: (01608) 682425
F: (01608) 682425
E: slowe@cwcom.net
I: www.follypages.mcmail.com

Glebe Farm House
◆◆◆◆◆ GOLD AWARD
Loxley, Stratford-upon-Avon,
Stratford-upon-Avon CV35 9JW
T: (01789) 842501
F: (01789) 842501
E: scorpiolimited@msn.com
I: www.glebefarmhouse.com
@

Graveslide Barn
◆◆◆◆◆ GOLD AWARD
Binton, Stratford-upon-Avon,
Warwickshire CV37 9TU
T: (01789) 750502 & 297000
F: (01789) 298056
E: denise@gravelside.fsnet.co.
uk

Green Gables ◆◆◆
47 Banbury Road, Stratford-
upon-Avon, Warwickshire
CV37 7HW
T: (01789) 205557
E: jeankerr@talk21.com
I: www.stratford-upon-avon.co.
uk/greengables.htm

Green Haven ◆◆◆◆
217 Evesham Road, Stratford-
upon-Avon, Warwickshire
CV37 9AS
T: (01789) 297874
E: greenhaven@travel-uk.com

Grosvenor Villa ◆◆◆
9 Evesham Place, Stratford-
upon-Avon, Warwickshire
CV37 6HT
T: (01789) 266192
F: (01789) 297353

Hampton Lodge Guest House
◆◆◆
38 Shipston Road, Stratford-
upon-Avon, Warwickshire
CV37 7LP
T: (01789) 299374 &
07778 251128
F: (01789) 299374
E: reedbrew@aol.com
I: www.hamptonlodge.co.uk

Harvard Private Hotel ◆◆◆
89 Shipston Road, Stratford-
upon-Avon, Warwickshire
CV37 7LW
T: (01789) 262623 & 261354
F: (01789) 261354

Highcroft ◆◆◆
Banbury Road, Stratford-upon-
Avon, Warwickshire CV37 7NF
T: (01789) 296293
F: (01789) 415236

Houndshill House ◆◆◆
Banbury Road, Ettington,
Stratford-upon-Avon,
Warwickshire CV37 7NS
T: (01789) 740267
F: (01789) 740075

Ingon Bank Farm ◆◆◆
Warwick Road, Stratford-upon-
Avon, Warwickshire CV37 0NY
T: (01789) 292642
F: (01789) 292642

**Ingon Grange
Rating Applied For**
Ingon Lane, Snitterfield,
Stratford-upon-Avon,
Warwickshire CV37 0QF
T: (01789) 731122

Kawartha House ◆◆◆
39 Grove Road, Stratford-upon-
Avon, Warwickshire CV37 6PB
T: (01789) 204469
F: (01789) 292837

Marlyn Hotel ◆◆◆
3 Chestnut Walk, Stratford-
upon-Avon, Warwickshire
CV37 6HG
T: (01789) 293752 &
07973 492673
F: (01789) 293752
E: TTEvans@talk21.com

Melita Private Hotel ◆◆◆◆
37 Shipston Road, Stratford-
upon-Avon, Warwickshire
CV37 7LN
T: (01789) 292432
F: (01789) 204867
E: Melita37@email.msn.com
I: www.stratford-upon-avon.co.
uk/melita.htm

Meridian Guest House ◆◆◆
3 St. Gregory's Road, Stratford-
upon-Avon, Warwickshire
CV37 6UH
T: (01789) 292356

Midway ◆◆◆◆
182 Evesham Road, Stratford-
upon-Avon, Warwickshire
CV37 9BS
T: (01789) 204154

Mil-Mar ◆◆◆◆
96 Alcester Road, Stratford-
upon-Avon, Warwickshire
CV37 9DP
T: (01789) 267095
F: (01789) 262205
E: milmar@btinternet.com

Minola Guest House ◆◆◆
25 Evesham Place, Stratford-
upon-Avon, Warwickshire
CV37 6HT
T: (01789) 293573
F: (01789) 551625

Moonlight Bed & Breakfast
◆◆◆
144 Alcester Road, Stratford-
upon-Avon, Warwickshire
CV37 9DR
T: (01789) 298213

Moonraker House
40 Alcester Road, Stratford-
upon-Avon, Warwickshire
CV37 9DB
T: (01789) 299346 & 267115
F: (01789) 295504
E: moonraker.spencer@virgin.
net
I: www.stratford-upon.avon.co.
uk/moonraker.htm

Moss Cottage ◆◆◆◆
61 Evesham Road, Stratford-
upon-Avon, Warwickshire
CV37 9BA
T: (01789) 294770
F: (01789) 294770
E: pauline_rush@onetel.net.uk

The Myrtles Bed and Breakfast
◆◆◆
6 Rother Street, Stratford-upon-
Avon, Warwickshire CV37 6LU
T: (01789) 295511

Naini Tal Guest House ◆◆◆
63A Evesham Road, Stratford-
upon-Avon, Warwickshire
CV37 9BA
T: (01789) 204956

Nando's ◆◆
18-19 Evesham Place, Stratford-
upon-Avon, Warwickshire
CV37 6HT
T: (01789) 204907
F: (01789) 204907
@

Newlands ◆◆◆◆
7 Broad Walk, Stratford-upon-
Avon, Warwickshire CV37 6HS
T: (01789) 298449
F: (01789) 263541
E: newlandsueboston@onet.co.
uk
I: www.smoothhound.co.
uk/hotels/newlands.html

One Acre Guest House
◆◆◆◆ SILVER AWARD
One Acre, Barton Road, Welford-
on-Avon, Stratford-upon-Avon,
Warwickshire CV37 8EZ
T: (01789) 750477 &
07771 540590
@

Oxstalls Farm ◆◆◆
Warwick Road, Stratford-upon-
Avon, Warwickshire CV37 0NS
T: (01789) 205277

Park View ◆◆◆◆
57 Rother Street, Stratford-
upon-Avon, Warwickshire
CV37 6LT
T: (01789) 266839
F: (01789) 266839

Parkfield ◆◆◆
3 Broad Walk, Stratford-upon-
Avon, Warwickshire CV37 6HS
T: (01789) 293313
F: (01789) 293313
E: parkfield@btinternet.com
I: www.btinternet.com/§parkfiel
@

Payton Hotel ◆◆◆◆
6 John Street, Stratford-upon-
Avon, Warwickshire CV37 6UB
T: (01789) 266442
F: (01789) 294410
E: payton@waverider.co.uk
I: www.payton.co.uk
@

Peartree Cottage
◆◆◆◆ SILVER AWARD
7 Church Road, Wilmcote,
Stratford-upon-Avon,
Warwickshire CV37 9UX
T: (01789) 205889
F: (01789) 262862

Penryn Guesthouse ◆◆◆◆
126 Alcester Road, Stratford-
upon-Avon, Warwickshire
CV37 9DP
T: (01789) 293718 &
07889 486345
F: (01789) 266077
E: penrynhouse@btinternet.
com
I: www.stratford-upon-avon.co.
uk/penryn.htm

Penshurst Guesthouse ◆◆◆
34 Evesham Place, Stratford-
upon-Avon, Warwickshire
CV37 6HT
T: (01789) 205259 & 295322
F: (01789) 295322
E: penshurst@cwcom.net
I: www.smoothhound.co.
uk/hotels/penshurs/html
◎ ▦

The Poplars ◆◆◆
Mansell Farm, Newbold-on-
Stour, Stratford-upon-Avon,
Warwickshire CV37 8BZ
T: (01789) 450540
F: (01789) 450540
E: RSPENCER@farming.co.uk
I: www.SmoothHound.co.
uk/hotel/poplars2html

Quilt and Croissants ◆◆◆
33 Evesham Place, Stratford-
upon-Avon, Warwickshire
CV37 6HT
T: (01789) 267629
F: (01789) 551661
E: rooms@quilt-croissants.
demon.co.uk
I: www.smoothhound.co.
uk/hotels/quilt.html

Ravenhurst ◆◆◆
2 Broad Walk, Stratford-upon-
Avon, Warwickshire CV37 6HS
T: (01789) 292515
E: ravaccom@waverider.co.uk
I: www.stratford-upon-avon.co.
uk/ravenhurst.htm

Salamander Guest House ◆◆◆
40 Grove Road, Stratford-upon-
Avon, Warwickshire CV37 6PB
T: (01789) 205728 & 297843
F: (01789) 205728
E: sejget@nova88.freeserve.co.
uk

Shakespeare's View Uporchard
◆◆◆◆◆ SILVER AWARD
Kings Lane, Snitterfield,
Stratford-upon-Avon,
Warwickshire CV37 0QB
T: (01789) 731824 &
07973 144151
F: (01789) 731824

Stratheden Hotel ◆◆◆
5 Chapel Street, Stratford-upon-
Avon, Warwickshire CV37 6EP
T: (01789) 297119
F: (01789) 297119
E: richard@stratheden.fsnet.co.
uk
I: www.stratheden.co.uk

Sunnydale Guest House
Rating Applied For
64 Shipston Road, Stratford-
upon-Avon, Warwickshire
CV37 7LP
T: (01789) 295166
◎

Victoria Spa Lodge
◆◆◆◆ SILVER AWARD
Bishopton Lane, Bishopton,
Stratford-upon-Avon,
Warwickshire CV37 9QY
T: (01789) 267985
F: (01789) 204728
E: ptozer@victoriaspalodge.
demon.co.uk
I: www.stratford-upon-avon.co.
uk/victoriaspa.htm
◎

Virginia Lodge Guest House
◆◆◆◆
12 Evesham Place, Stratford-
upon-Avon, Warwickshire
CV37 6HT
T: (01789) 292157

Whitchurch Farm ◆◆◆
Wimpstone, Stratford-upon-
Avon, Warwickshire CV37 8NS
T: (01789) 450275
F: (01789) 450275
◎

Woodstock Guest House
◆◆◆◆ SILVER AWARD
30 Grove Road, Stratford-upon-
Avon, Warwickshire CV37 6PB
T: (01789) 299881

Dovecliff Hall
◆◆◆◆◆ SILVER AWARD
Dovecliff Road, Stretton, Burton
upon Trent, Staffordshire
DE13 0DJ
T: (01283) 531818
F: (01283) 516546

Jasmine Cottage ◆◆◆
Stretton on Fosse, Moreton-in-
Marsh, Gloucestershire
GL56 9SA
T: (01608) 661972 &
07701 002990

Ashleigh House ◆◆◆◆
Bussage, Stroud, Gloucestershire
GL6 8AZ
T: (01453) 883944
F: (01453) 886931

Beechcroft ◆◆◆
Brownshill, Stroud,
Gloucestershire GL6 8AG
T: (01453) 883422 &
07976 657797

Bidfield Farmhouse ◆◆◆
Bidfield Farm, Camp, Stroud,
Gloucestershire GL6 7ET
T: (01285) 821263 &
07831 239767
F: (01285) 821263
E: DavidBaird@Bidfield.
freeserve.co.uk

Burleigh Farm
◆◆◆◆ SILVER AWARD
Minchinhampton, Stroud,
Gloucestershire GL5 2PF
T: (01453) 883112
F: (01453) 883112

Cairngall ◆◆◆
65 Bisley Old Road, Stroud,
Gloucestershire GL5 1NF
T: (01453) 766689 & 758063
F: (01453) 758063
E: mike.fabb@virgin.net

The Clothier's Arms ◆◆◆
1 Bath Road, Stroud,
Gloucestershire GL5 3JJ
T: (01453) 763801
F: (01453) 757161
E: luciano@clothiersarms.
demon.co.uk
I: www.clothiersarms.co.uk

Downfield Hotel ◆◆◆
134 Cainscross Road, Stroud,
Gloucestershire GL5 4HN
T: (01453) 764496
F: (01453) 753150
E: messenger@downfieldhotel.
demon.co.uk
I: www.downfieldhotel.demon.
co.uk

Edendale Guesthouse ◆◆◆
92 Westward Road, Cainscross,
Stroud, Gloucestershire GL5 4JA
T: (01453) 751490
F: (01453) 751490

The Firs Bed and Breakfast
◆◆◆◆◆
Selsley Road, North
Woodchester, Stroud,
Gloucestershire GL5 5NQ
T: (01453) 873088 &
07932 172653
F: (01453) 873053
E: cwalsh3088@aol.com

Glenlyn House ◆◆◆
Frome Avenue, Bath Road,
Stroud, Gloucestershire GL5 3JZ
T: (01453) 765053

Grove Cottage ◆◆◆◆
Browns Hill, Stroud,
Gloucestershire GL6 8AJ
T: (01453) 882561

Home Farm Bed and Breakfast
◆◆
Home Farm, South
Woodchester, Stroud,
Gloucestershire GL5 5EL
T: (01453) 872470

The Laye-Bye ◆◆◆◆
7 Castlemead Road,
Rodborough, Stroud,
Gloucestershire GL5 3SF
T: (01453) 751514
F: (01453) 751514

Threeways ◆◆◆
Bisley Road, Lypiatt Hill, Stroud,
Gloucestershire GL6 7LQ
T: (01453) 756001
F: (01453) 764819
E: threewaysbedandbreakfast@
tinyworld.co.uk

**The Yew Tree Bed and
Breakfast** ◆◆◆◆
Walls Quarry, Brimscombe,
Stroud, Gloucestershire GL5 2PA
T: (01453) 883428 & 887594
F: (01453) 883428
E: elizabeth.peters@tesco.net

Rectory Farm ◆◆◆
Little Street, Sulgrave, Banbury,
Oxfordshire OX17 2SG
T: (01295) 760261
F: (01295) 760089
E: rectoryfarm@talk21.com

Georgian House ◆◆◆◆
Station Road, Sutterton, Boston,
Lincolnshire PE20 2JH
T: (01205) 460048
F: (01205) 460048

The Almshouse ◆◆◆
Sutton Cheney, Nuneaton,
Warwickshire CV13 0AH
T: (01455) 291050
F: (01455) 290601

Athelstone Lodge Hotel ◆◆◆
25 Trusthorpe Road, Sutton-on-
Sea, Mablethorpe, Lincolnshire
LN12 2LR
T: (01507) 441521
◎

Fiveways ◆◆◆
Barrel Hill Road, Sutton-on-
Trent, Newark, Nottinghamshire
NG23 6PT
T: (01636) 822086

Ferne Cottage ◆◆◆
5 Black Horse Hill, Appleby
Magna, Swadlincote, Derby
DE12 7AQ
T: (01530) 271772
F: (01503) 270652

Hurst Farm Guesthouse
◆◆◆◆
Chilcote, Swadlincote, Burton
upon Trent, Staffordshire
DE12 8DQ
T: (01827) 373853

Hillfield House
Rating Applied For
52 Station Hill, Swannington,
Leicester LE67 8RH
T: (01530) 837 414
F: (01530) 458 233

October House ◆◆◆◆
The Water Meadows,
Swarkestone, Derby DE73 1JA
T: (01332) 705849
E: longsons@hotmail.com

The Royal Oak Inn ◆◆◆
High Street, Swayfield,
Grantham, Lincolnshire
NG33 4LL
T: (01476) 550247
F: (01476) 550996

SWINSCOE
Staffordshire
Common End Farm ◆◆◆◆
Swinscoe, Ashbourne,
Derbyshire DE6 2BW
T: (01335) 342342 & 342342

SWYNNERTON
Staffordshire
Home Farm ◆◆
Swynnerton, Stone,
Staffordshire ST15 0RA
T: (01782) 796241

SYMONDS YAT EAST
Herefordshire
Garth Cottage
◆◆◆◆ SILVER AWARD
Symonds Yat East, Ross-on-
Wye, Herefordshire HR9 6JL
T: (01600) 890364
F: (01600) 890364

Rose Cottage Tea Gardens
◆◆◆
Symonds Yat East, Ross-on-
Wye, Herefordshire HR9 6JL
T: (01600) 890514 &
07721 423890
F: (01600) 890498

SYMONDS YAT ROCK
Gloucestershire
River View ◆◆◆
Symonds Yat Rock, Coleford,
Gloucestershire GL16 7NZ
T: (01600) 891000 &
0771 5618697
E: kiernan@symondsyatrock.
fsnet.co.uk
I: www.symondsyat.co.uk

SYMONDS YAT WEST
Herefordshire
Riversdale Lodge Hotel ◆◆◆
Symonds Yat West, Ross-on-
Wye, Herefordshire HR9 6BL
T: (01600) 890445
F: (01600) 890443
E: info@riversdale.uk.com
I: www.riversdale.uk.com

SYRESHAM
Northamptonshire
The Priory ◆◆
36 Wappenham Road,
Syresham, Brackley,
Northamptonshire NN13 5HH
T: (01280) 850218 & 850603
F: (01280) 850576
E: info@signpost.co.uk

TADDINGTON
Derbyshire
Ade House ◆◆◆◆
Taddington, Buxton, Derbyshire
SK17 9TY
T: (01298) 85203

The Old Bake and Brewhouse
◆◆◆
Blackwell Hall, Blackwell in the
Peak, Taddington, Buxton,
Derbyshire SK17 9TQ
T: (01298) 85271
F: (01298) 85271
E: christine.gregory@btinternet.
com
I: www.cressbrook.co.uk/pdfh
◉

TAMWORTH
Staffordshire
Bonehill Farm House ◆◆◆
Bonehill Road, Tamworth,
Staffordshire B78 3HP
T: (01827) 310797
E: JAMES@BONEHILL.
JUNGLELINK.CO.UK

Oak Tree Farm
◆◆◆◆ GOLD AWARD
Hints Road, Hopwas, Tamworth,
Staffordshire B78 3AA
T: (01827) 56807 &
07836 387887
F: (01827) 56807
◉

TANSLEY
Derbyshire
Packhorse Farm ◆◆◆◆
Tansley, Matlock, Derbyshire
DE4 5LF
T: (01629) 580950
F: (01629) 580950

Packhorse Farm Bungalow
◆◆◆◆
Tansley, Matlock, Derbyshire
DE4 5LF
T: (01629) 582781

TEDDINGTON
Gloucestershire
Bengrove Farm ◆◆◆
Bengrove, Teddington,
Tewkesbury, Gloucestershire
GL20 8JB
T: (01242) 620332
F: (01242) 620851

TELFORD
Shropshire
Albion Inn ◆◆◆
West Street, St Georges, Telford,
Shropshire TF2 9AD
T: (01952) 614193

Allscott Inn ◆◆
Walcot, Wellington, Telford,
Shropshire TF6 5EQ
T: (01952) 248484

Church Farm ◆◆◆◆
Wrockwardine, Wellington,
Telford, Shropshire TF6 5DG
T: (01952) 244917
F: (01952) 244917
◉

Coppice Heights ◆◆◆
Spout Lane, Little Wenlock,
Telford, Shropshire TF6 5BL
T: (01952) 505655

Falcon Hotel ◆◆◆
Holyhead Road, Wellington,
Telford, Shropshire TF1 2DD
T: (01952) 255011
E: jamespearson@cableinet.co.
uk

Grove House Guesthouse
Grove House◆◆◆
Grove Street, St Georges,
Telford, Shropshire TF2 9JW
T: (01952) 616140

Grove Farm House
◆◆◆ SILVER AWARD
Leighton Road, Buildwas,
Telford, Shropshire TF8 7DF
T: (01952) 433572
F: (01952) 433650

The Mill House ◆◆◆◆
Shrewsbury Road, High Ercall,
Telford, Shropshire TF6 6BE
T: (01952) 770394
F: (01952) 770394
E: mill-house@talk21.com

Old Rectory ◆◆◆◆
Stirchley Village, Telford,
Shropshire TF3 1DY
T: (01952) 596308 & 596518
F: (01952) 596308
◉ ♿

The Old Vicarage ◆◆◆◆
Church Street, St George's,
Telford, Shropshire TF2 9LZ
T: (01952) 616437 &
07889 546215
F: (01952) 610775
E: oldvicarage.stgeorges@tesco.
net
I: www.oldvicarage.uk.com

Stone House ◆◆◆◆
Shifnal Road, Priorslee, Telford,
Shropshire TF2 9NN
T: (01952) 290119 &
07976 847278
F: (01952) 290119
E: dave@
stonehouseguesthouse.
freeserve.co.uk
I: www.smoothhound.co.
uk/hotels/stonehou.html

Westbrook House ◆◆
78a Holy Head Road, Ketly,
Telford, Shropshire TF1 4DJ
T: (01952) 615535
F: (01952) 615535

Willow House ◆◆◆
137 Holyhead Road, Wellington,
Telford, Shropshire TF1 2DH
T: (01952) 223817
F: (01952) 223817

TEMPLE GRAFTON
Warwickshire
The Blue Boar Inn ◆◆◆
Temple Grafton, Alcester,
Warwickshire B49 6NR
T: (01789) 750010
F: (01789) 750635
E: blueboar@covlink.co.uk
I: www.stratford.upon.avon.co.
uk/blueboar

TENBURY WELLS
Worcestershire
Court Farm ◆◆◆◆
Hanley Childe, Tenbury Wells,
Worcestershire WR15 8QY
T: (01885) 410265

Peacock Inn ◆◆◆◆
Worcester Road, Boraston,
Tenbury Wells, Worcestershire
WR15 8LL
T: (01584) 810506 & 811236
F: (01584) 811236
E: juidler@fsbdial.co.uk
I: www.smoothhound.co.
uk/hotels/peacockinn.html

TETBURY
Gloucestershire
Folly Farm Cottages ◆◆
Long Newnton, Tetbury,
Gloucestershire GL8 8XA
T: (01666) 502475
F: (01666) 502358
E: info@gtb.co.uk
I: www.gtb.co.uk

The Old Rectory
◆◆◆◆ GOLD AWARD
Didmarton, Gloucestershire
GL9 1DS
T: (01454) 238233
◉

Tavern House
◆◆◆◆ GOLD AWARD
Willesley, Tetbury,
Gloucestershire GL8 8QU
T: (01666) 880444
F: (01666) 880254
I: tavernhousehotel@
ukbusiness.com

TEWKESBURY
Gloucestershire
The Abbey Hotel ◆◆
67 Church Street, Tewkesbury,
Gloucestershire GL20 5RX
T: (01684) 294247
F: (01684) 297208

Abbots Court Farm ◆◆◆
Church End, Twyning,
Tewkesbury, Gloucestershire
GL20 6DA
T: (01684) 292515
F: (01684) 292515

Alstone Fields Farm
◆◆◆◆ SILVER AWARD
Teddington Hands, Stow Road,
Tewkesbury, Gloucestershire
GL20 8NG
T: (01242) 620592

Carrant Brook House ◆◆◆
3 Rope Walk, Tewkesbury,
Gloucestershire GL20 5DS
T: (01684) 290355 & 0771 808
5136
E: anna@shail.freesave.com

Jessop House Hotel ◆◆◆◆
65 Church Street, Tewkesbury,
Gloucestershire GL20 5RZ
T: (01684) 292017
F: (01684) 273076

Malvern View Guest House ◆◆
1 St. Mary's Road, Tewkesbury,
Gloucestershire GL20 5SF
T: (01684) 292776

Town Street Farm ◆◆◆
Tirley, Gloucester GL19 4HG
T: (01452) 780442
F: (01452) 780890
I: townstreetfarm@hotmail.com

Two Back of Avon ◆◆
2 Back of Avon, Riverside Walk,
Tewkesbury, Gloucestershire
GL20 5BA
T: (01684) 298935 &
07711 947016

THORPE
Derbyshire
Hillcrest House ◆◆◆
Dovedale, Thorpe, Ashbourne,
Derbyshire DE6 2AW
T: (01335) 350436
F: (01335) 350436
E: hillcresthouse@freenet.co.uk
I: www.
ashbourne-towncom/accom/
hillcrest

The Old Orchard ◆◆◆
Stoney Lane, Thorpe, Ashbourne,
Derbyshire DE6 2AW
T: (01335) 350410
F: (01335) 350410

THRAPSTON
Northamptonshire
The Poplars ◆◆◆◆
50 Oundle Road, Thrapston,
Kettering, Northamptonshire
NN14 4PD
T: (01832) 732499

THURLBY
Lincolnshire
6 The Pingles ◆◆◆◆
Thurlby, Bourne, Lincolnshire
PE10 0EX
T: (01778) 394517

TIBSHELF
Derbyshire
**Rosvern House Bed and
Breakfast** ◆◆◆◆
High Street, Tibshelf, Alfreton,
Derbyshire DE55 5NY
T: (01773) 874800
F: (01773) 874800

TICKNALL
Derbyshire
Limeyards Stables
◆◆◆◆ SILVER AWARD
136 Main Street, Ticknall, Derby
DE73 1JZ
T: (01332) 864802
E: stay@limeyard.demon.co.uk
I: www.limeyard.demon.co.uk

TIDESWELL
Derbyshire
Laurel House ◆◆◆◆
The Green, Litton, Buxton,
Derbyshire SK17 8QP
T: (01298) 871971

Poppies ◆◆◆
Bank Square, Tideswell, Buxton,
Derbyshire SK17 8LA
T: (01298) 871083
E: poptidza@dialstart.net.a.s.a.p

TISSINGTON
Derbyshire
**Bassett Wood Farmhouse Bed
and Breakfast** ◆◆◆◆
Bassett Wood Farm, Tissington,
Ashbourne, Derbyshire DE6 1RD
T: (01335) 350254
E: janet@bassettwood.
freeserve.co.uk
I: www.peakdistrictfarmhols.co.
uk

TOTON
Nottinghamshire
Brookfield Cottage ◆◆◆
108 Carrfield Avenue, Toton,
Beeston, Nottingham NG9 6FB
T: (0115) 9178046 &
07974 968917

TOWCESTER
Northamptonshire
Cutchems End
◆◆◆◆ SILVER AWARD
Yorks Farm, Watling Street,
Towcester, Northamptonshire
NN12 8EU
T: (01327) 830640 & 830645
F: (01327) 830645

Green's Park ◆◆◆◆
Woodend, Towcester,
Northamptonshire NN12 8SD
T: (01327) 860386
F: (01327) 860386

The Leys
◆◆◆◆ SILVER AWARD
Field Burcote, Towcester,
Northamptonshire NN12 8AL
T: (01327) 350431
F: (01327) 350431

Rose Cottage ◆◆◆◆
Plumpton Road, Woodend,
Towcester, Northampton
NN12 8RZ
T: (01327) 860968
F: (01327) 860004

TROWELL
Nottinghamshire
Orchard Cottage ◆◆◆◆
The Old Workhouse, Trowell,
Nottingham NG9 3PQ
T: (0115) 9280933 &
07790 817597
F: (0115) 9280933

TRUSTHORPE
Lincolnshire
The Ramblers Hotel ◆◆◆
Sutton Road, Trusthorpe,
Mablethorpe, Lincolnshire
LN12 2PY
T: (01507) 441171

TUNSTALL
Staffordshire
Victoria Hotel ◆◆◆
4 Roundwell Street, Tunstall,
Stoke-on-Trent ST6 5JJ
T: (01782) 835964
F: (01782) 835964
E: victoria-hotel@tunstall51.
fsnet.co.uk

TUTBURY
Staffordshire
**Woodhouse Farm Bed and
Breakfast** ◆◆◆
Woodhouse Farm, Tutbury,
Burton upon Trent, Staffordshire
DE13 9HR
T: (01283) 812185 & 814046
F: (01283) 815743
E: enquiries@tutbury.co.uk
I: www.tutbury.co.
uk/woodhouse

TWO DALES
Derbyshire
Norden House ◆◆◆◆
Chesterfield Road, Two Dales,
Matlock, Derbyshire DE4 2EZ
T: (01629) 732074 &
07710 839985
F: (01629) 735805

UPPER BENEFIELD
Northamptonshire
**The Benefield Wheatsheaf
Hotel** ◆◆◆
Upper Benefield, Peterborough
PE8 5AN
T: (01832) 205254
F: (01832) 205245

UPPER COBERLEY
Gloucestershire
Upper Coberley Farm
◆◆◆◆ SILVER AWARD
Upper Coberley, Cheltenham,
Gloucestershire GL53 9RB
T: (01242) 870306

UPPER HULME
Staffordshire
**Paddock Farm Bed and
Breakfast** ◆◆◆◆
Paddock Farm, Upper Hulme,
Leek, Staffordshire ST13 8TY
T: (01538) 300345 & 300145

Roaches Hall ◆◆◆◆
Upper Hulme, Leek,
Staffordshire ST13 8UB
T: (01538) 300115

UPPER QUINTON
Warwickshire
Winton House
◆◆◆◆ SILVER AWARD
The Green, Upper Quinton,
Stratford-upon-Avon,
Warwickshire CV37 8SX
T: (01789) 720500 &
07831 485483
E: lyong@attglobal.net
I: www.stratford-upon-avon.co.
uk/winton.htm

UPPINGHAM
Rutland
Boundary Farm ◆◆◆◆
Glaston Road, Uppingham,
Oakham, Leicestershire LE15 9PX
T: (01572) 822354
E: suescott58.

Garden Hotel ◆◆◆◆
High Street West, Uppingham,
Rutland LE15 9QD
T: (01572) 822352
F: (01572) 821156
E: gardenhotel@btinternet.com

Rutland House ◆◆◆◆
61 High Street East, Uppingham,
Leicestershire LE15 9PY
T: (01572) 822497
F: (01572) 820065
E: rutland.house@virgin.net

The Vaults ◆◆◆
Market Place, Uppingham,
Oakham, Leicestershire
LE15 9QH
T: (01572) 823259

UPPINGTON
Shropshire
**Avenue Farm Bed and
Breakfast** ◆◆◆
Uppington, Telford, Shropshire
TF6 5HW
T: (01952) 740253
F: (01952) 740401
E: jones@avenuefarm.fsnet.co.
uk

UPTON ST LEONARDS
Gloucestershire
Bullens Manor Farm ◆◆◆◆
Portway, Upton St Leonards,
Gloucester GL4 8DL
T: (01452) 616463

UPTON-UPON-SEVERN
Worcestershire
Bridge House
◆◆◆◆ SILVER AWARD
Welland Stone, Upton-upon-
Severn, Worcester WR8 0RW
T: (01684) 593046
F: (01684) 593046
E: merrymichael@clara.net
I: www.malvern.
net/commerce/bridge-house.
htm

Cobbetts Retreat ◆◆◆
Ryall, Upton-upon-Severn,
Worcester WR8 0PL
T: (01684) 592013 &
07973 385183
F: (01684) 592013

**The Courtyard
Rating Applied For**
5 Old Street, Upton-upon-
Severn, Worcester,
Worcestershire WR8 0HN
T: (01684) 592120 &
07966 370340
F: (01684) 593353
E: paul@hanley-castle.
freeserve.co.uk
I: hanley-castle.freeserve.co.uk

Kimberlee ◆◆◆
The Beeches, Ryall, Upton-upon-
Severn, Worcester WR8 0QQ
T: (01684) 591234 &
07702 307207
F: (01684) 591234

Tiltridge Farm and Vineyard
◆◆◆◆
Upper Hook Road, Upton-upon-
Severn, Worcester WR8 0SA
T: (01684) 592906
F: (01684) 594142
E: elgarwine@aol.com

Welland Court ◆◆◆◆
Upton-upon-Severn, Worcester
WR8 0ST
T: (01684) 594426
F: (01684) 594426
E: archer@wellandcourt.demon.
co.uk
I: www.upton.enta.net

UTTOXETER
Staffordshire
Oldroyd Guest House & Motel
◆◆◆
18-22 Bridge Street, Uttoxeter,
Staffordshire ST14 8AP
T: (01889) 562763
F: (01889) 568916
I: www.scool

VOWCHURCH
Herefordshire
The Old Vicarage
◆◆◆◆ SILVER AWARD
Vowchurch, Hereford,
Herefordshire HR2 0QD
T: (01981) 550357
F: (01981) 550357
I: golden-valley.co.uk/vicarage

Upper Gilvach Farm
◆◆◆◆ SILVER AWARD
St. Margarets, Vowchurch,
Hereford HR2 0QY
T: (01981) 510618
F: (01981) 510618
E: ruth@uppergilvach.freeserve.
co.uk
I: www.golden-valley.co.
uk/gilvach

WADDINGTON
Lincolnshire
Horse and Jockey ◆◆◆◆
High Street, Waddington,
Lincoln LN5 9RF
T: (01522) 720224
F: (01527) 722551
E: ltott@globelnet.com
I: www.vanguardpubs.
com/horseandjockey

WADENHOE
Northamptonshire
The Kings Head ◆◆◆◆
Church Street, Wadenhoe,
Peterborough PE8 5ST
T: (01832) 720024
F: (01832) 720024

WADSHELF
Derbyshire
Temperance House Farm
◆◆◆◆ SILVER AWARD
Bradshaw Lane, Wadshelf,
Chesterfield, Derbyshire S42 7BT
T: (01246) 566416

WALTERSTONE
Herefordshire
Coed Y Grafel ◆◆
Coed Y Grafel, Walterstone,
Hereford, Herefordshire HR2 0DJ
T: (01873) 890675
F: (01873) 890675
⊕

Lodge Farm Cottage ◆◆◆
Walterstone Common,
Walterstone, Hereford,
Herefordshire HR2 0DT
T: (01873) 890263
⊕

WARWICK
Warwickshire
Agincourt Lodge Hotel ◆◆◆
36 Coten End, Warwick,
Warwickshire CV34 4NP
T: (01926) 499399 & 497252
F: (01926) 499399

Apothecary's ◆◆◆◆
The Old Dispensary, Stratford
Road, Wellesbourne, Warwick
CV35 9RN
T: (01789) 470060

Ashburton Guest House ◆◆◆
74 Emscote Road, Warwick,
Warwickshire CV34 5QG
T: (01926) 401082 &
07977 973780
F: (01926) 419237
E: 100534.444@compuserve.
com

Austin House ◆◆◆
96 Emscote Road, Warwick,
Warwickshire CV34 5QJ
T: (01926) 493583
F: (01926) 493679
E: mike@austinhouse96.
freeserve.co.uk
⊕

Avon Guest House ◆◆◆
7 Emscote Road, Warwick,
Warwickshire CV34 4PH
T: (01926) 491367

Avonside Cottage
◆◆◆◆◆ GOLD AWARD
1 High Street, Barford, Warwick
CV35 8BU
T: (01926) 624779
⊕

Brome House
◆◆◆◆ SILVER AWARD
35 Bridge End, Warwick,
CV34 6PB
T: (01926) 491069
F: (01926) 491069

Cambridge Villa Hotel ◆◆
20A Emscote Road, Warwick,
CV34 4PP
T: (01926) 491169
F: (01926) 491169

Charter House
◆◆◆◆◆ GOLD AWARD
87-91 West Street, Warwick,
CV34 6AH
T: (01926) 496965
F: (01926) 411910
E: penon@charterhouse8.
freeserve.co.uk
⊕

**Cliffe Hill House Bed and
Breakfast** ◆◆◆◆
37 Coventry Road, Warwick,
CV34 5HW
T: (01926) 496431 &
07771 630006
E: quirke@cliffehillhouse.
freeserve.co.uk

The Coach House
◆◆◆◆ SILVER AWARD
Old Budbrooke Road, Budbrooke,
Warwick, CV35 7DU
T: (01926) 410893
F: (01926) 490453
E: johnmannion@hotmail.com

The Croft Guesthouse ◆◆◆◆
Haseley Knob, Warwick
CV35 7NL
T: (01926) 484447
F: (01926) 484447
E: david@croftguesthouse.co.uk
I: www.croftguesthouse.co.uk

Dinas ◆◆◆◆ SILVER AWARD
30 Eastley Crescent, Warwick,
CV34 5RX
T: (01926) 496480
⊕

Forth House
◆◆◆◆ SILVER AWARD
44 High Street, Warwick,
CV34 4AX
T: (01926) 401512
F: (01926) 490809
E: info@forthhouseuk.co.uk
I: www.forthhouseuk.co.uk

High House ◆◆◆◆
Old Warwick Road, Rowington,
Warwick CV35 7AA
T: (01926) 843270 &
07785 748134
F: (01926) 843689

Hill House ◆◆◆◆
Hampton Lucy, Warwick,
CV35 8AU
T: (01789) 840329
E: eliz-hunter@hotmail.com
I: www.stratford-upon-avon.co.
uk/hillhouse.htm

Hillcrest ◆◆◆
Sherbourne Hill, Stratford Road,
Warwick, Warwickshire
CV35 8AG
T: (01926) 624386
F: (01926) 624386
E: hillcrestguesthouse@
btinternet.com

Hither Barn ◆◆◆
Star Lane, Claverdon, Warwick
CV35 8LW
T: (01926) 842839

Jersey Villa Guest House ◆◆◆
69 Emscote Road, Warwick,
CV34 5QR
T: (01926) 774607
F: (01926) 774607
E: jerseyvillaguesthouse@
emscote.freeserve.co.uk

Longbridge Farm
Rating Applied For
Stratford Road, Warwick,
CV34 6RB
T: (01926) 401857

Lower Rowley ◆◆◆◆
Wasperton, Warwick, CV35 8EB
T: (01926) 624937
F: (01926) 620053
E: lowerowley@uk.packardbell.
org

Lower Watchbury Farm
◆◆◆◆
Wasperton Lane, Barford,
Warwick CV35 8DH
T: (01926) 624772 &
07880 557668
F: (01926) 624772
E: eykyn@barford.
spacomputers.com

Northleigh House
◆◆◆◆ SILVER AWARD
Five Ways Road, Hatton,
Warwick CV35 7HZ
T: (01926) 484203 &
07774 101894
F: (01926) 484006
E: www.northleigh.co.uk

Park Cottage
◆◆◆◆ SILVER AWARD
113 West Street, Warwick,
CV34 6AH
T: (01926) 410319
F: (01926) 410319
E: parkcott@aol.com

Park House Guest House ◆◆◆
17 Emscote Road, Warwick,
CV34 4PH
T: (01926) 494359
F: (01926) 494359

Peacock Lodge ◆◆◆
97 West Street, Warwick,
CV34 6AH
T: (01926) 775221
F: (01926) 776268
E: paul.farley7@virgin.net

The Seven Stars Public House
◆◆◆◆
Friars Street, Warwick,
CV34 6HD
T: (01926) 492658

Shrewley Pools Farm
◆◆◆◆ SILVER AWARD
Haseley, Warwick CV35 7HB
T: (01926) 484315
I: www.s-h-systems.co.
uk/hotels/shrewley.html

The Tilted Wig ◆◆◆◆
11 Market Place, Warwick,
CV34 4SA
T: (01926) 410466 & 411740
F: (01926) 495740

Tudor House Inn ◆◆◆
90-92 West Street, Warwick,
CV34 6AW
T: (01926) 495447
F: (01926) 492948
I: www.oldenglish.co.uk

Warwick Lodge Guest House
◆◆◆
82 Emscote Road, Warwick,
CV34 5QJ
T: (01926) 492927

Westham Guest House ◆◆◆
76 Emscote Road, Warwick,
CV34 5QG
T: (01926) 491756
F: (01926) 491756

Woodside ◆◆◆
Langley Road, Claverdon,
Warwick CV35 8PJ
T: (01926) 842446
F: (01926) 843697
🕆

WATERHOUSES
Staffordshire
Broadhurst Farm ◆◆◆
Waterhouses, Stoke-on-Trent
ST10 3LQ
T: (01538) 308261

Croft House Farm ◆◆◆
Waterfall, Waterhouses,
Staffordshire ST10 3HZ
T: (01538) 308626 &
0778 7352792
F: (01538) 308626
E: enquiries@junglelink.co.uk
⊕

Lee House Farm
◆◆◆◆ SILVER AWARD
Leek Road, Waterhouses, Stoke-
on-Trent ST10 3HW
T: (01538) 308439

Ye Olde Crown ◆◆
Leek Road, Waterhouses, Stoke-
on-Trent ST10 3HL
T: (01538) 308204

WEEDON
Northamptonshire
Mullions ◆◆◆◆
9 Oak Street, Upper Weedon,
Weedon, Northampton
NN7 4RQ
T: (01327) 341439
F: (01327) 341439

Swan House – Annex ◆◆◆◆
Swan House, Dodford, Weedon,
Northampton,
Northamptonshire NN7 4SX
T: (01327) 341847

WEEDON LOIS
Northamptonshire
Green Farm ◆◆◆
Green Farm, Weedon Lois,
Towcester, Northamptonshire
NN12 8PL
T: (01327) 860249
F: (01327) 860249
⊕

WELDON
Northamptonshire
Laundimer House
◆◆◆◆ SILVER AWARD
Bears Lane, Weldon, Corby,
Northamptonshire NN17 3LH
T: (01536) 206770
F: (01536) 206770
E: pauline@aol.com
I: www.laundimerhouse.co.uk

Thatches on the Green ◆◆◆◆
9 School Lane, Weldon, Corby,
Northamptonshire NN17 3JN
T: (01536) 266681
F: (01536) 266659
⊕

WELFORD
Northamptonshire

West End Farm ♦♦♦♦
5 West End, Welford,
Northampton NN6 6HJ
T: (01858) 575226
E: bevin@uklynx.net

WELFORD-ON-AVON
Warwickshire

Bridgend ♦♦♦
Binton Road, Welford-on-Avon,
Stratford-upon-Avon,
Warwickshire CV37 8PW
T: (01789) 750900
F: (01789) 750900
E: BRIDGEND@PRIORY50.
FREESERVE.CO.UK

WELLESBOURNE
Warwickshire

Brook House
♦♦♦♦ SILVER AWARD
9 Chestnut Square,
Wellesbourne, Warwick
CV35 9QS
T: (01789) 840922

WELLINGTON
Shropshire

Barnfield House ♦♦
5 Barnfield Court, Wellington,
Telford, Shropshire TF1 2ET
T: (01952) 223406

Birtley House ♦♦
285 Holyhead Road, Wellington,
Telford, Shropshire TF1 2EW
T: (01952) 240483

The Paddock ♦♦♦♦
Arleston Manor, Arleston Lane,
Wellington, Telford, Shropshire
TF1 2LT
T: (01952) 243311 &
07836 329568
F: (01952) 243311

Wilvers Guesthouse ♦♦♦
250 Holyhead Road, Wellington,
Telford, Shropshire TF1 2EB
T: (01952) 243444 &
07930 917087

WEM
Shropshire

Chez Michael ♦♦♦
23 Roden Grove, Wem,
Shrewsbury SY4 5HJ
T: (01939) 232947
F: (01939) 232947

Forncet ♦♦
Soulton Road, Wem, Shrewsbury
SY4 5HR
T: (01939) 232996

Lowe Hall Farm
♦♦♦♦ SILVER AWARD
Wem, Shrewsbury SY4 5UE
T: (01939) 232236
F: (01939) 232236
E: bandb@lowehallfarm.demon.
co.uk
I: www.lowehallfarm.demon.co.
uk

Polstead House ♦♦♦
Shawbury Road, Wem,
Shrewsbury SY4 5PF
T: (01939) 233530

WENLOCK EDGE
Shropshire

The Wenlock Edge Inn
♦♦♦♦ SILVER AWARD
Hilltop, Wenlock Edge, Much
Wenlock, Shropshire TF13 6DJ
T: (01746) 785678
F: (01746) 785285
E: info@wenlockedgeinn.co.uk
I: www.wenlockedgeinn.co.uk

WENTNOR
Shropshire

Crown Inn ♦♦♦♦
Wentnor, Bishop's Castle,
Shropshire SY9 5EE
T: (01588) 650613
F: (01588) 650436
E: crown.inn@talk21.com

Inn on the Green ♦♦
Wentnor, Bishop's Castle,
Shropshire SY9 5EF
T: (01588) 650105 &
07974 670691

WEOBLEY
Herefordshire

Garnstone House ♦♦♦
Weobley, Hereford HR4 8QP
T: (01544) 318943
F: (01544) 318197

The Marshpools Country Inn
♦♦♦
Ledgemoor, Weobley, Hereford
HR4 8RN
T: (01544) 318215 & 318847
F: (01544) 318847
E: marshpools@fsnet.co.uk

WESSINGTON
Derbyshire

Crich Lane Farm ♦♦♦♦
Moorwood Moor Lane,
Wessington, Alfreton,
Derbyshire DE55 6DU
T: (01773) 835186 &
07775 881423
⊚

WEST BARKWITH
Lincolnshire

The Manor House
♦♦♦♦ SILVER AWARD
Louth Road, West Barkwith,
Market Rasen, Lincolnshire
LN8 5LF
T: (01673) 858253
F: (01673) 858253

WEST BRIDGFORD
Nottinghamshire

The Croft Hotel ♦♦
6-8 North Road, West Bridgford,
Nottingham NG2 7NH
T: (0115) 981 2744
F: (0115) 9812744
E: CROFT.HOTEL.WB@TALK21.
COM
I: WWW.SMOOTHHOUND.CO.UK

The Gallery Hotel ♦♦♦
8-10 Radcliffe Road, West
Bridgford, Nottingham
NG2 5FW
T: (0115) 981 3651 & 981 1346
F: (0115) 981 3732
I: www.yell.co.
uk/sites/galleryhotel/

Number 56 ♦♦
56 Melton Road, West Bridgford,
Nottingham NG2 7NF
T: (0115) 9821965

WEST HADDON
Northamptonshire

Pear Trees ♦♦♦♦
31 Station Road, West Haddon,
Northampton NN6 7AU
T: (01788) 510389

WESTBURY-ON-SEVERN
Gloucestershire

Boxbush Barn
♦♦♦♦♦ GOLD AWARD
Rodley, Westbury-on-Severn,
Gloucestershire GL14 1QZ
T: (01452) 760949
F: (01452) 760949

WESTON
Staffordshire

Canalside Bed and Breakfast
♦♦♦
Bridge Cottage, Green Road,
Weston, Stafford ST18 0HZ
T: (01889) 271403

WESTON UNDER PENYARD
Herefordshire

The Hill ♦♦♦
Weston under Penyard, Ross-
on-Wye, Herefordshire HR9 7PZ
T: (01989) 750225
F: (01989) 750225

Wharton Farm Bed and
Breakfast ♦♦♦
Wharton Farm, Weston under
Penyard, Ross-on-Wye,
Herefordshire HR9 5SX
T: (01989) 750255
F: (01989) 750255
⊚

WESTON-UNDER-REDCASTLE
Shropshire

Windmill Cottage Guesthouse
♦♦♦
Weston-under-Redcastle,
Shrewsbury SY4 5UX
T: (01939) 200219
E: GLT@windmillcottage.fsnet.
co.uk
I: www.windmillcottage.fsnet.co.
uk

WETTON
Staffordshire

Croft Cottage ♦♦♦♦
Wetton, Ashbourne, Derbyshire
DE6 2AF
T: (01335) 310402

The Old Chapel ♦♦♦♦
Wetton, Ashbourne, Derbyshire
DE6 2AF
T: (01335) 310450
F: (01335) 310448

WHALEY BRIDGE
Derbyshire

Cote Bank Farm
♦♦♦♦ SILVER AWARD
Buxworth, Whaley Bridge, High
Peak SK23 7NP
T: (01663) 750566
F: (01663) 750566
E: cotebank@btinternet.com
I: www.peakdistrictfarmhols.co.
uk
⊚

WHAPLODE
Lincolnshire

Westgate House ♦♦♦♦
Little Lane, Whaplode, Spalding,
Lincolnshire PE12 6RU
T: (01406) 370546
E: bandb@westgate.f9.co.uk
I: www.westgatehouse.f9.co.uk
⊚

WHATSTANDWELL
Derbyshire

Meerbrook Farm ♦♦♦
Wirksworth Road,
Whatstandwell, Matlock,
Derbyshire DE4 5HU
T: (01629) 824180 &
07850 103927
⊚

Riverdale ♦♦♦♦
Middle Lane, Whatstandwell,
Matlock, Derbyshire DE4 5EG
T: (01773) 853905
F: (01773) 853905

WHATTON
Nottinghamshire

The Dell ♦♦♦♦
Church Street, Whatton,
Nottingham NG13 9EL
T: (01949) 850832

WHISTON
Staffordshire

Heath House Farm ♦♦♦
Ross Road, Whiston, Stoke-on-
Trent ST10 2JF
T: (01538) 266497

WHITCHURCH
Herefordshire

The Old Pound Bed and
Breakfast ♦♦♦
The Old Pound House,
Whitchurch, Ross-on-Wye,
Herefordshire HR9 6DW
T: (01600) 890637 &
07711 283328
F: (01600) 890508
E: tilfykabir@aol.com

WHITCHURCH
Shropshire

Barmere House Bed and
Breakfast ♦♦♦
Barmere House, Bickley,
Whitchurch, Shropshire
SY13 4HH
T: (01943) 663748

Bridge House ♦♦♦♦
Wrexham Road, Whitchurch,
Shropshire SY13 3AA
T: (01948) 664664
F: (01948) 664664
E: bhgh@madasafish.com
I: www.madasafish.com/§bhgh

The Laurels ♦♦♦
Tushingham, Cum Grindley
Brook, Whitchurch, Shropshire
SY13 4QL
T: (01948) 664203
F: (01948) 664203

Pheasant Walk ♦♦♦
Terrick Road, Whitchurch,
Shropshire SY13 4JZ
T: (01948) 667118
⊚

Roden View ♦♦♦♦
Dobsons Bridge, Whixall,
Whitchurch, Shropshire
SY13 2QL
T: (01948) 710320 &
07974 785318
F: (01948) 710320
⊚

Wood Farm ♦♦♦♦
Old Woodhouses, Whitchurch,
Shropshire SY13 4EJ
T: (01948) 871224 &
07977 920429
⊚

WHITFIELD
Northamptonshire
Chestnut View ♦♦
Mill Lane, Whitfield, Brackley,
Northamptonshire NN13 5TQ
T: (01280) 850246

WHITTINGTON
Staffordshire
**The Dog Inn and Restaurant
♦♦♦**
Main Street, Whittington,
Lichfield, Staffordshire
WS14 9JU
T: (01543) 432252
F: (01543) 433748
E: THEDOGINN@leighnadi.
freeserve.co.uk

WICKHAMFORD
Worcestershire
**Avonwood
♦♦♦♦ SILVER AWARD**
30 Pitchers Hill, Wickhamford,
Evesham, Worcestershire
WR11 6RT
T: (01386) 834271 &
07790 672004
F: (01386) 834271

WIGMORE
Herefordshire
Compasses Hotel ♦♦
Ford Street, Wigmore,
Leominster, Herefordshire
HR6 9UN
T: (01568) 770203
F: (01568) 770705

Gotherment Farmhouse ♦♦♦
Wigmore, Leominster,
Herefordshire HR6 9UF
T: (01568) 770547
E: blair@gotherment.freeserve.
co.uk

Pear Tree Farm ♦♦♦♦
Wigmore, Leominster,
Herefordshire HR6 9UR
T: (01568) 770140
F: (01568) 770140
E: steveandjill@peartreefarmco.
freeserve.co.uk
I: www.peartreefarmco.
freeserve.co.uk

WILBARSTON
Northamptonshire
**The Old House
Rating Applied For**
Church Street, Wilbarston,
Market Harborough,
Leicestershire LE16 8QG
T: (01536) 771724
F: (01536) 771622
E: oldhousebb@aol.com.uk

WILLERSEY
Gloucestershire
Bowers Hill Farm ♦♦♦♦
Bowers Hill, Willersey,
Broadway, Worcestershire
WR11 5HG
T: (01386) 834585 &
07966 171861
F: (01386) 830234
E: sarah@bowershillfarm.com
I: www.bowershillfarm.com

Garnons Chase ♦♦♦♦
Collin Close, Willersey,
Broadway, Worcestershire
WR12 7PP
T: (01386) 853718
F: (01386) 853795
E: jgooding@clara.co.uk

WILMCOTE
Warwickshire
**Mary Arden Inn
Rating Applied For**
The Green, Wilmcote, Stratford-
upon-Avon, Warwickshire
CV37 9XJ
T: (01789) 267030
F: (01789) 204875

WILTON
Herefordshire
Benhall Farm ♦♦♦
Wilton, Ross-on-Wye,
Herefordshire HR9 6AG
T: (01989) 563900

**Benhall House Bed and
Breakfast ♦♦♦**
Wilton, Ross-on-Wye,
Herefordshire HR9 6AG
T: (01989) 567420
F: (01989) 567420

Copperfield House ♦♦♦♦
Wilton Lane, Wilton, Ross-on-
Wye, Herefordshire HR9 6AH
T: (01989) 764379 &
07710 282878
E: fran_brown@talk21.com
I: ourworld.compuserve.
com/homepages/fran_brown

WINCHCOMBE
Gloucestershire
Blair House ♦♦♦
41 Gretton Road, Winchcombe,
Cheltenham, Gloucestershire
GL54 5EG
T: (01242) 603626
F: (01242) 604214

Cleveley ♦♦♦
Wadfield Farm, Corndean Lane,
Winchcombe, Cheltenham,
Gloucestershire GL54 5AL
T: (01242) 602059

Gower House ♦♦♦
16 North Street, Winchcombe,
Cheltenham, Gloucestershire
GL54 5LH
T: (01242) 602616

Greenhyde ♦♦♦♦
Langley Road, Winchcombe,
Cheltenham, Gloucestershire
GL54 5QP
T: (01242) 602569

The Homestead ♦♦♦
Footbridge, Broadway Road,
Winchcombe, Cheltenham,
Gloucestershire GL54 5JG
T: (01242) 602536
E: homesteadbandb@virgin.net

Ireley Grounds ♦♦♦♦
Broadway Road, Winchcombe,
Cheltenham, Gloucestershire
GL54 5NY
T: (01242) 603736 &
07836 322230

**Isbourne Manor House
♦♦♦♦♦ GOLD AWARD**
Castle Street, Winchcombe,
Cheltenham, Gloucestershire
GL54 5JA
T: (01242) 602281
F: (01242) 602281

Manor Farm ♦♦♦♦
Greet, Winchcombe,
Cheltenham, Gloucestershire
GL54 5BJ
T: (01242) 602423 &
0777 1732307
F: (01242) 602423
E: JANET@
DICKANDJANET/FSNET.CO.UK

Mercia ♦♦♦♦ SILVER AWARD
Hailes Street, Winchcombe,
Cheltenham, Gloucestershire
GL54 5HU
T: (01242) 602251
E: JONATHANUPTON@
HOTMAIL.COM

The Old Bakehouse ♦♦♦♦
Castle Street, Winchcombe,
Cheltenham, Gloucestershire
GL54 5JA
T: (01242) 602441
F: (01242) 602441
E: deniseparker@onetel.net.uk

Old Station House ♦♦♦
Greet Road, Winchcombe,
Cheltenham, Gloucestershire
GL54 5LB
T: (01242) 602283
F: (01242) 602283

Parks Farm ♦♦♦♦
Sudeley, Winchcombe,
Cheltenham, Gloucestershire
GL54 5JB
T: (01242) 603874
F: (01242) 603874
E: rogerwilson.freeserve.co.uk

**Postlip Hall Farm
♦♦♦♦ GOLD AWARD**
Winchcombe, Cheltenham,
Gloucestershire GL54 5AQ
T: (01242) 603351
F: (01242) 603351
E: val@postliphallfarm.
free-online.co.uk

Rutland Court ♦♦
Cowl Lane, Winchcombe,
Cheltenham, Gloucestershire
GL54 5RA
T: (01242) 603101 &
07957 728706

1 Stancombe View ♦♦♦
Winchcombe, Cheltenham,
Gloucestershire GL54 5LE
T: (01242) 603654

Sudeley Hill Farm ♦♦♦♦
Winchcombe, Cheltenham,
Gloucestershire GL54 5JB
T: (01242) 602344
F: (01242) 602344
E: scudamore4@aol.com

Sudeley Lawn Barn ♦♦♦♦
Sudeley Hill, Winchcombe,
Cheltenham, Gloucestershire
GL54 5JB
T: (01242) 604762 & 604709
F: (01242) 604710

WINFORTON
Herefordshire
**Well Farm
Rating Applied For**
Winforton, Hereford HR3 6EA
T: (01544) 327278
F: (01544) 327278

WING
Rutland
Kings Arms Inn ♦♦♦♦
Top Street, Wing, Oakham,
Rutland LE15 8SE
T: (01572) 737634
F: (01572) 737255

WINKHILL
Staffordshire
Country Cottage ♦♦♦♦
Back Lane Farm, Winkhill, Leek,
Staffordshire ST13 7XZ
T: (01538) 308273
F: (01538) 308098
E: mjb6435@netscapeonline.co.
uk
I: www.biophysics.umn.
edu/$bent/

WINSLOW
Worcestershire
Munderfield Harold ♦♦
Winslow, Bromyard,
Herefordshire HR7 4SZ
T: (01885) 483231

WINSTER
Derbyshire
Brae Cottage ♦♦♦♦
East Bank, Winster, Matlock,
Derbyshire DE4 2DT
T: (01629) 650375

**The Dower House
♦♦♦♦ GOLD AWARD**
Main Street, Winster, Matlock,
Derbyshire DE4 2DH
T: (01629) 650931
F: (01629) 650932
E: fosterbig@aol.com

**Old Shoulder of Mutton
♦♦♦♦**
West Bank, Winster, Matlock,
Derbyshire DE4 2DQ
T: (01629) 650778

WIRKSWORTH
Derbyshire
**Avondale Farm
♦♦♦♦ SILVER AWARD**
Grangemill, Matlock, Derbyshire
DE4 4HT
T: (01629) 650820
F: (01629) 650233

**Old Lock Up
♦♦♦♦ GOLD AWARD**
North End, Wirksworth, Derby
DE4 4FG
T: (01629) 826272 & 826929
F: (01629) 826272

Saw Mill Cottage ♦♦♦♦
36 Wash Green, Wirksworth,
Derby DE4 4FD
T: (01629) 822723

WISHAW
Warwickshire
Ash House ♦♦♦
The Gravel, Wishaw, Sutton
Coldfield, West Midlands
B76 9QB
T: (01675) 475782 &
07850 414000
E: kate@rectory80.co.uk

WITCOMBE
Gloucestershire
Springfields Farm ♦♦
Little Witcombe, Witcombe,
Gloucester GL3 4TU
T: (01452) 863532

WITHINGTON
Shropshire

Garden Cottage ◆◆◆
Withington, Shrewsbury
SY4 4QA
T: (01743) 709511 &
(01771) 3818743
F: (01743) 709511
E: silvia-hopper@
garden-cottage.fsnet.co.uk

Willowside Farm ◆◆◆
Withington, Cheltenham,
Gloucestershire GL54 4DA
T: (01242) 890362
F: (01242) 890556

WOLLASTON
Northamptonshire

Duckmire ◆◆◆◆
1 Duck End, Wollaston,
Wellingborough,
Northamptonshire NN29 7SH
T: (01933) 664249
F: (01933) 664249
E: kerry@foreverengland.
freeserve.co.uk

WOLSTANTON
Staffordshire

Whispering Pines
◆◆◆◆ GOLD AWARD
11A Milehouse Lane,
Wolstanton, Newcastle-under-
Lyme, Staffordshire ST5 9JR
T: (01782) 639376
F: (01782) 639376
E: timpriestman@
whisperingpinesbb45.freeserve.
co.uk
I: whisperingpinesbb45.
freeserve.co.uk

WOLSTON
Warwickshire

The Byre
◆◆◆◆ SILVER AWARD
Lords Hill Farm, Coalpit Lane,
Wolston, Coventry CV8 3GB
T: (024) 7654 2098

WOODCHESTER
Gloucestershire

Southfield Mill ◆◆◆◆
Southfield Road, Woodchester,
Stroud, Gloucestershire GL5 5PA
T: (01453) 872896
F: (01453) 872896
E: judtsntch@hotmail.com

WOODHALL SPA
Lincolnshire

Claremont Guesthouse ◆◆
9-11 Witham Road, Woodhall
Spa, Lincolnshire LN10 6RW
T: (01526) 352000

Newlands ◆◆◆◆
56 Woodland Drive, Woodhall
Spa, Lincolnshire LN10 6YG
T: (01526) 352881

Pitchaway Guesthouse ◆◆◆
The Broadway, Woodhall Spa,
Lincolnshire LN10 6SQ
T: (01526) 352969

WOONTON
Herefordshire

Rose Cottage
◆◆◆◆ SILVER AWARD
Woonton, Hereford HR3 6QW
T: (01544) 340459
F: (01544) 340459

WORCESTER
Worcestershire

Barbourne ◆◆◆
42 Barbourne Road, Worcester,
Worcestershire WR1 1HU
T: (01905) 27505
F: (01905) 27505

The Boot Inn ◆◆◆◆
Radford Road, Flyford Flavell,
Worcester WR7 4BS
T: (01386) 462658 & 792931
F: (01386) 462547
E: thebootinn@yahoo.com

The Croft
Rating Applied For
25 Station Road, Fernhill Heath,
Worcester, Worcestershire
WR3 7UJ
T: (01905) 773174 & 453482

Foresters Arms ◆◆◆
2 Chestnut Walk, Worcester,
Worcestershire WR1 1PP
T: (01905) 20348

Green Farm ◆◆◆◆
Crowle Green, Crowle,
Worcester, Worcestershire
WR7 4AB
T: (01905) 381807 &
07421 029023
F: (01905) 381807
E: lupa@beeb.net

Hidelow House
◆◆◆◆ SILVER AWARD
Acton Green, Acton Beauchamp,
Worcester, WR6 5AH
T: (01886) 884547
F: (01886) 884060
E: accommodation@hidelow.co.
uk
I: www.hidelow.co.uk

Ivy Cottage ◆◆◆◆
Sinton Green, Hallow, Worcester
WR2 6NP
T: (01905) 641123
E: rendle@ukgateway.net

Little Lightwood Farm ◆◆◆◆
Lightwood Lane, Cotheridge,
Worcester WR6 5LT
T: (01905) 333236
F: (01905) 333236
E: lightwood.holidays@virgin.
net

The Manor Arms Country Inn
◆◆◆
Abberley Village, Worcester,
WR6 6BN
T: (01299) 896507
F: (01299) 896723
E: themanorarms@btconnect.
com
I: themanorarms.co.uk

Oaklands ◆◆◆◆
Claines, Worcester WR3 7RR
T: (01905) 458871 &
07885 378771
F: (01905) 759362
E: oaklands@easicom.com

The Old Smithy ◆◆◆◆
Pirton, Worcester WR8 9EJ
T: (01905) 820482
E: wyivn_the_smithy@
compuserve.com
I: www.smoothound.co.
uk/hotels/oldsmith.html

Osborne House ◆◆◆
17 Chestnut Walk, Worcester,
Worcestershire WR1 1PR
T: (01905) 22296
F: (01905) 22296
E: enquiries@osborne-house.
freeserve.co.uk
I: www.a1tourism.
com/uk/hotels/osborneh.html

**Park House Guest
Accommodation** ◆◆◆
12 Droitwich Road, Worcester,
WR3 7LJ
T: (01905) 21816 & 612029

Retreat Farm ◆◆◆◆
Camp Lane, Grimley, Worcester,
WR2 6LX
T: (01905) 640266
F: (01905) 641397

Shrubbery Guest House ◆◆◆
38 Barbourne Road, Worcester,
WR1 1HU
T: (01905) 24871
F: (01905) 23620

Yew Tree House ◆◆◆◆
Norchard, Crossway Green,
Hartlebury, Kidderminster,
Worcestershire DY13 9SN
T: (01299) 250921 &
07703 112392
E: paula@knightp.swinternet.co.
uk

WORKSOP
Nottinghamshire

Carlton Road Guesthouse
◆◆◆
67 Carlton Road, Worksop,
Nottinghamshire S80 1PP
T: (01909) 483084

The Old Blue Bell ◆◆◆
30 Park Street, Worksop,
Nottinghamshire S80 1HF
T: (01909) 500304
F: (01909) 500304

Sherwood Guesthouse ◆◆◆
57 Carlton Road, Worksop,
Nottinghamshire S80 1PP
T: (01909) 474209 & 478214

WORMELOW
Herefordshire

Lyston Villa ◆◆◆
Wormelow, Hereford HR2 8EL
T: (01981) 540130
F: (01981) 540130

WORMHILL
Derbyshire

Wellhead Farm
Rating Applied For
Wormhill, Buxton, Derbyshire
SK17 8SL
T: (01298) 871023

WOTTON-UNDER-EDGE
Gloucestershire

Falcon Cottage ◆◆◆◆
15 Station Road, Charfield,
Wotton-under-Edge,
Gloucestershire GL12 8SY
T: (01453) 843528

Hillesley Mill ◆◆◆
Alderley, Wotton-under-Edge,
Gloucestershire GL12 7QT
T: (01453) 843258

WYMONDHAM
Leicestershire

The Old Rectory ◆◆◆
Sycamore Lane, Wymondham,
Melton Mowbray, Leicestershire
LE14 2AZ
T: (01572) 787583
F: (01572) 787347
I: www.rutnet.co.uk/oldrectory

WYRE PIDDLE
Worcestershire

Arbour House
◆◆◆◆ SILVER AWARD
Main Road, Wyre Piddle,
Pershore, Worcestershire
WR10 2HU
T: (01386) 555833
F: (01386) 555833
E: arbourhouse@faxvia.net

Avonbank House ◆◆◆
Main Road, Wyre Piddle,
Pershore, Worcestershire
WR10 2JB
T: (01386) 553334

Avonside Hotel ◆◆◆
Main Road, Wyre Piddle,
Pershore, Worcestershire
WR10 2JB
T: (01386) 552654

WYSALL
Nottinghamshire

Lorne House Bed & Breakfast
◆◆◆◆
Lorne House, Bradmore Road,
Wysall, Nottingham NG12 5QR
T: (01509) 881433 &
07974 710037
F: (0115) 942 3350
E: haymin@ukonline.co.uk

YARDLEY
West Midlands

Olton Cottage Guest House
◆◆◆◆
School Lane, Yardley,
Birmingham B33 8PD
T: (0121) 783 9249 &
07885 163291
F: (0121) 789 6545
E: olton.cottage@virgin.net
I: www.olton-cottage.com

Yardley Guesthouse ◆◆◆
330 Church Road, Yardley,
Birmingham B25 8XT
T: (0121) 783 6634
F: (0121) 7836634

YARKHILL
Herefordshire

Garford Farm ◆◆◆
Yarkhill, Hereford HR1 3ST
T: (01432) 890226
F: (01432) 890707
E: garfordfarm@lineone.net

YOULGREAVE
Derbyshire

Bankside Cottage ◆◆◆
Bankside, Youlgreave, Bakewell,
Derbyshire DE45 1WD
T: (01629) 636689

Fairview
Rating Applied For
Bradford Road, Youlgreave,
Bakewell, Derbyshire DE45 1WG
T: (01629) 636043

The Farmyard Inn ♦♦♦
Main Street, Youlgreave,
Bakewell, Derbyshire DE45 1UW
T: (01629) 636221

The Old Bakery ♦♦♦
Church Street, Youlgreave,
Bakewell, Derbyshire DE45 1UR
T: (01629) 636887
E: croasdell@
oldbakeryyoulgrave.freeserve.co.
uk

YOXALL
Staffordshire

Thimble Hall ♦♦♦
School Green, Yoxall, Burton
upon Trent, Staffordshire
DE13 8NB
T: (01543) 472226
F: (01543) 472226
E: jo@thimble.fsbusiness.co.uk

EAST OF ENGLAND

ACTON
Suffolk

Barbie's ♦♦
25 Clayhall Place, Acton,
Sudbury CO10 0BT
T: (01787) 373702

Lime Tree House ♦♦♦♦
Lime Tree Green, Acton,
Sudbury, Suffolk CO10 0UU
T: (01787) 373551 & 312413

ALBURY
Hertfordshire

Tudor Cottage ♦♦♦♦
Upwick Green, Albury, Ware,
Hertfordshire SG11 2JX
T: (01279) 771440 &
07770 898424

ALDBOROUGH
Norfolk

Butterfly Cottage ♦♦♦
The Green, Aldborough, Norwich
NR11 7AA
T: (01263) 768198
F: (01263) 768198

ALDBURY
Hertfordshire

Livingston's Bed & Breakfast
♦♦♦
Chimanimani, Toms Hill Road,
Aldbury, Tring, Hertfordshire
HP23 5SA
T: (01442) 851527

ALDEBURGH
Suffolk

East Cottage ♦♦
55 King Street, Aldeburgh,
Suffolk IP15 5BZ
T: (01728) 453010
F: (01728) 453010
E: anglian55@hotmail.com

Faraway ♦♦♦
28 Linden Close, Aldeburgh,
Suffolk IP15 5JL
T: (01728) 452571

Margaret's ♦♦♦
50 Victoria Road, Aldeburgh,
Suffolk IP15 5EJ
T: (01728) 453239

Sanviv ♦♦♦
59 Fairfield Road, Aldeburgh,
Suffolk IP1 5JN
T: (01728) 453107

ALDEBY
Norfolk

The Old Vicarage ♦♦♦
Rectory Road, Aldeby, Beccles,
Suffolk NR34 0BJ
T: (01502) 678229

ALDHAM
Essex

Old House ♦♦♦
Ford Street, Aldham, Colchester,
Essex CO6 3PH
T: (01206) 240456
F: (01206) 240456

ALDRINGHAM
Suffolk

Fern House ♦♦♦
6 The Follies, Aldringham,
Leiston, Suffolk IP16 4LU
T: (01728) 830759
E: gallowaymd@aol.com

ALPHETON
Suffolk

Amicus ♦♦♦ SILVER AWARD
Old Bury Road, Alpheton,
Sudbury CO10 9BT
T: (01284) 828579 &
07702 961151

ARDLEIGH
Essex

Old Shields Farm
Rating Applied For
Waterhouse Lane, Ardleigh,
Colchester CO7 7NE
T: (01206) 230251
F: (01206) 231825

ARKESDEN
Essex

Parsonage Farm ♦♦♦♦
Arkesden, Saffron Walden, Essex
CB11 4HB
T: (01799) 550306

ASHDON
Essex

Cobblers
♦♦♦♦ SILVER AWARD
Bartlow Road, Ashdon, Saffron
Walden, Essex CB10 2HR
T: (01799) 584666
E: cobblers@ashdon2000.
freeserve.co.uk

ASPLEY GUISE
Bedfordshire

Chain Guest House
♦♦♦♦ SILVER AWARD
Church Street, Aspley Guise,
Milton Keynes MK17 8HQ
T: (01908) 586511
F: (01908) 586511
E: chainhouse@ukgateway.net
I: www.chainhouse.ukgateway.
net

The Strawberry Farm ♦♦♦♦
Salford Road, Aspley Guise,
Milton Keynes MK17 8HZ
T: (01908) 587070 &
07788 514967
E: liz@strawberryfarm.co.uk

ATTLEBOROUGH
Norfolk

Scales Farm ♦♦♦♦
Old Buckenham, Attleborough,
Norfolk NR17 1PE
T: (01953) 860324

AYLMERTON
Norfolk

Felbrigg Lodge
♦♦♦♦♦ GOLD AWARD
Aylmerton, Holt, Norfolk
NR11 8RA
T: (01263) 837588
F: (01263) 838012
E: info@felbrigglodge.co.uk
I: www.felbrigglodge.co.uk

AYLSHAM
Norfolk

The Old Manse ♦♦♦
43 Burgh Road, Aylsham,
Norwich NR11 6AT
T: (01263) 731283

The Old Pump House ♦♦♦♦
Holman Road, Aylsham,
Norwich, Norfolk NR11 6BY
T: (01263) 733789

AYOT ST LAWRENCE
Hertfordshire

The Brocket Arms
Rating Applied For
Ayot St Lawrence, Welwyn,
Hertfordshire AL6 9BT
T: (01438) 820250
F: (01438) 820068
I: www.brocketarms.com

BACTON-ON-SEA
Norfolk

Keswick Hotel ♦♦♦
Walcott Road, Bacton-on-Sea,
Norwich NR12 0LS
T: (01692) 650468

BADINGHAM
Suffolk

Colston Hall ♦♦♦
Badingham, Woodbridge,
Suffolk IP13 8LB
T: (01728) 638375 &
07850 869744
F: (01728) 638084

BANNINGHAM
Norfolk

Wheelers Meadow ♦♦♦
Colby Road, Briggs Loke,
Banningham, Norwich
NR11 7DY
T: (01263) 733325 &
07703 434219
F: (01263) 731896
E: bridgetarchibald@hotmail.
com

BARHAM
Suffolk

The Sorrel Horse Inn♦♦♦
Old Norwich Road, Barham,
Ipswich IP6 0PG
T: (01473) 830327
F: (01473) 833149
E: matt@sorrelhorse.freeserve.
co.uk
I: www.sorrelhouse.freeserve.co.
uk

Tamarisk House ♦♦♦♦
Sandy Lane, Barham, Ipswich
IP6 0PB
T: (01473) 831825

BASILDON
Essex

38 Kelly Road ♦♦♦
Bowers Gifford, Basildon, Essex
SS13 2HL
T: (01268) 726701 & 246195
F: (01268) 246060
E: patricia.jenkinson@tesco.net

BATTLESBRIDGE
Essex

The Cottages Guest House ♦♦
The Cottages, Beeches Road,
Battlesbridge, Wickford, Essex
SS11 8TJ
T: (01702) 232105 &
07885 489419
E: cottage2000@totalise.co.uk

BECCLES
Suffolk

Catherine House ♦♦♦♦
2 Ringsfield Road, Beccles,
Suffolk NR34 9PQ
T: (01502) 716428
F: (01502) 716428

Colville Arms Motel ♦♦
Lowestoft Road, Worlingham,
Beccles, Suffolk NR34 7EF
T: (01502) 712571
F: (01502) 712571
E: pat@thecolvillearms.
freeserve.co.uk

The Kings Head ♦♦♦
New Market, Beccles, Suffolk
NR34 9HA
T: (01502) 712147
F: (01502) 715386

BEDFORD
Bedfordshire

1 Ravensden Grange ♦♦♦
Sunderland Hill, Ravensden,
Bedford, Bedfordshire
MK44 2SH
T: (01234) 771771

BEESTON
Norfolk

Holmdene Farm ♦♦♦
Beeston, King's Lynn, Norfolk
PE32 2NJ
T: (01328) 701284

EAST OF ENGLAND

BEETLEY
Norfolk
Peacock House
◆◆◆◆ GOLD AWARD
Peacock Lane, Beetley, East
Dereham, Norfolk NR20 4DG
T: (01362) 860371 &
0797 9013258
E: peackh@aol.com
I: www.smoothhound.co.
uk/hotels/peacockh.html/

Shilling Stone ◆◆◆
Church Road, Beetley, Dereham,
Norfolk NR20 4AB
T: (01362) 861099 &
07721 306190
F: (01362) 869153
E: partridge@uk.gateway.net
I: www.visitbritain.com

BELCHAMP ST PAUL
Essex
The Plough
◆◆◆◆ SILVER AWARD
Gages Road, Belchamp St Paul,
Sudbury, Suffolk CO10 7BT
T: (01787) 278882
E: chris.stormont@virgin.net

BERKHAMSTED
Hertfordshire
Broadway Farm
◆◆◆◆ SILVER AWARD
Berkhamsted, Hertfordshire
HP4 2RR
T: (01442) 866541
F: (01442) 866541
E: a.knowles@broadway.
nildram.co.uk

BEYTON
Suffolk
Brook Farm ◆◆◆◆
Drinkstone Road, Beyton, Bury
St Edmunds, Suffolk IP30 9AQ
T: (01359) 270733

BIGGLESWADE
Bedfordshire
The Crown Hotel ◆◆◆
23 High Street, Biggleswade,
Bedfordshire SG18 0JE
T: (01767) 312228
F: (01767) 312567

Old Warden Guesthouse ◆◆◆
Shop and Post Office, Old
Warden, Biggleswade,
Bedfordshire SG18 9HQ
T: (01767) 627201

BILDESTON
Suffolk
Christmas Hall ◆◆◆◆
Market Square, Bildeston,
Ipswich IP7 7EN
T: (01449) 741428

BILLERICAY
Essex
Badgers Rest ◆◆◆◆
2 Mount View, Billericay, Essex
CM11 1HB
T: (01277) 625384 &
07778 444169
F: (01277) 633912

Oakwood House ◆◆◆◆
126 Norsey Road, Billericay,
Essex CM11 1BH
T: (01277) 655865
F: (01277) 655865

BINHAM
Norfolk
Field House ◆◆◆◆
Field House, Walsingham Road,
Binham, Fakenham, Norfolk
NR21 0BU
T: (01328) 830639

BIRCHAM
Norfolk
Country Stores ◆◆◆
Lynn Road, Bircham, King's
Lynn, Norfolk PE31 6RJ
T: (01485) 578502

BISHOP'S STORTFORD
Hertfordshire
The Cottage
◆◆◆◆ GOLD AWARD
71 Birchanger Lane, Birchanger,
Bishop's Stortford, Hertfordshire
CM23 5QA
T: (01279) 812349
F: (01279) 815045

Gowar Cottage ◆◆◆◆
10 Half Acres, Bishop's
Stortford, Hertfordshire
CM23 2QP
T: (01279) 503019 &
07801 478688

Pleasant Cottage ◆◆◆◆
Woodend Green, Henham,
Bishop's Stortford, Hertfordshire
CM22 6AZ
T: (01279) 850792

47 Southmill Road
Rating Applied For
Bishop's Stortford, Hertfordshire
CM23 3DH
T: (01279) 755536 &
07966 490748

52 Thorley Hill
Rating Applied For
Bishop's Stortford, Hertfordshire
CM23 3NA
T: (01279) 658311

Woodlands Lodge ◆◆◆
Dunmow Road, Bishop's
Stortford, CM23 5QX
T: (01279) 504784
F: (01279) 461474

BLAKENEY
Norfolk
Ryecroft ◆◆◆◆
Back Lane, Blakeney, Holt,
Norfolk NR25 7NP
T: (01263) 740701
F: (01263) 740701

BLAXHALL
Suffolk
The Ship Inn ◆◆◆
Blaxhall, Woodbridge, Suffolk
IP12 2DY
T: (01728) 688316
F: (01728) 688316
E: theshipinnblaxhallatalk21.
com

BLETSOE
Bedfordshire
North End Barns
◆◆◆◆ SILVER AWARD
North End Farm, Risley Road,
Bletsoe, Bedford MK44 1QT
T: (01234) 781320
F: (01234) 781320

BLICKLING
Norfolk
The Buckinghamshire Arms
◆◆◆
Blickling, Norwich NR11 6NF
T: (01263) 732133

BLYTHBURGH
Suffolk
Little Thorbyns ◆◆◆
The Street, Blythburgh,
Halesworth, Suffolk IP19 9LS
T: (01502) 478664

BOCKING
Essex
Greengages Bed & Breakfast
◆◆◆◆
268 Broad Road, Bocking,
Braintree, Essex CM7 5NJ
T: (01376) 345868 &
0780 3752210

BOTESDALE
Suffolk
Virginia Cottage ◆◆◆◆
The Street, Botesdale, Diss,
Norfolk IP22 1BZ
T: (01379) 890128

BOXFORD
Suffolk
Hurrells Farmhouse
◆◆◆◆ SILVER AWARD
Boxford Lane, Boxford, Sudbury,
Suffolk CO10 5JY
T: (01787) 210215
F: (01787) 211806
E: hurrellsf@a.o.l.com
I: members.a.o.l.
com/hurrellsf/index.htm

BOXTED
Essex
Round Hill House ◆◆◆◆
Parsonage Hill, Boxted,
Colchester, Essex CO4 5ST
T: (01206) 272392
F: (01206) 272392
E: jermar@appleonline.net
I: www.information-britain.co.
uk

BRADFIELD
Essex
Emsworth House ◆◆◆
Ship Hill, Bradfield,
Manningtree, Essex CO11 2UP
T: (01255) 870860 &
07767 477771
F: (01255) 870869
E: emsworthhouse@hotmail.
com

BRADFIELD COMBUST
Suffolk
Church Farm ◆◆◆◆
Bradfield Combust, Bury St
Edmunds, Suffolk IP30 0LW
T: (01284) 386333
F: (01284) 386155
E: paul@williamsonff.freeserve.
co.uk

BRADFIELD ST GEORGE
Suffolk
Freewood Lodge ◆◆◆
Freewood Street, Bradfield St
George, Bury St Edmunds,
Suffolk IP30 0AY
T: (01284) 386809

BRADWELL
Essex
Park Farmhouse ◆◆◆
Church Road, Bradwell,
Braintree, Essex CM7 8EP
T: (01376) 563584

BRAINTREE
Essex
16 Acorn Avenue ◆◆
Braintree, Essex CM7 2LR
T: (01376) 320155

Brook Farm ◆◆◆
Wethersfield, Braintree, Essex
CM7 4BX
T: (01371) 850284 &
07770 881966
F: (01371) 850284

70 High Garrett ◆◆
Braintree, Essex CM7 5NT
T: (01376) 345330

The Old House ◆◆◆
11 Bradford Street, Braintree,
Essex CM7 9AS
T: (01376) 550457
F: (01376) 343863
E: old_house@talk21.com

Spicers Farm ◆◆◆◆
Rotten End, Wethersfield,
Braintree, Essex CM7 4AL
T: (01371) 851021
F: (01371) 851021
E: spicers.farm@talk21.com

BRAMFIELD
Suffolk
Broad Oak Farm ◆◆◆◆
Bramfield, Halesworth, Suffolk
IP19 9AB
T: (01986) 784232

BRAMPTON
Cambridgeshire
Grange Hotel ◆◆◆
115 High Street, Brampton,
Huntingdon, Cambridgeshire
PE18 8RA
T: (01480) 459516
F: (01480) 459391

BRANDON
Suffolk
The Laurels ◆◆
162 London Road, Brandon,
Suffolk IP27 0LP
T: (01842) 812005

BRENT ELEIGH
Suffolk
Wroughton Lodge
◆◆◆◆ SILVER AWARD
Brent Eleigh, Sudbury, Suffolk
CO10 9PB
T: (01787) 247495

BRENTWOOD
Essex
Brentwood Guesthouse ◆◆◆
75/77 Rose Valley, Brentwood,
Essex CM14 4HJ
T: (01277) 262713 &
07710 523757
F: (01277) 211146

Chestnut Tree Cottage ◆◆◆
Great Warley Street, Great
Warley Village Green,
Brentwood, Essex CM13 3JF
T: (01277) 221727 &
0780 3131731

618

Establishments printed in blue have a detailed entry in this guide

BRESSINGHAM
Norfolk

Hazel Barn ◆◆◆
Lodge Lane, Bressingham, Diss,
Norfolk IP22 2BE
T: (01379) 644396
E: hazelbarn@net-traders.co.uk

BRETTON
Cambridgeshire

The Oaks ◆◆◆
27 Westhawe, Bretton,
Peterborough PE3 8BA
T: (01733) 268742

BRICKET WOOD
Hertfordshire

Little Oaks
Rating Applied For
Lye Lane, Bricket Wood, St
Albans, Hertfordshire AL2 3TE
T: (01923) 681299
F: (01923) 681299

BRIGHTLINGSEA
Essex

Paxton Dene ◆◆◆◆
Church Road, Brightlingsea,
Colchester CO7 0QT
T: (01206) 304560
F: (01206) 302877

BRISLEY
Norfolk

Pond Farm ◆◆◆◆
Brisley, East Dereham, Norfolk
NR20 5LL
T: (01362) 668332 &
07747 877375
F: (01362) 668332

BROCKDISH
Norfolk

Grove Thorpe
◆◆◆◆◆ GOLD AWARD
Grove Road, Brockdish, Diss,
Norfolk IP21 4JE
T: (01379) 668305
F: (01379) 668305

BROMESWELL
Suffolk

Meadow View ◆◆◆
School Lane, Bromeswell,
Woodbridge, Suffolk IP12 2PY
T: (01394) 460635

BROOKE
Norfolk

Hillside Farm ◆◆◆◆
Welbeck Road, Brooke, Norwich
NR15 1AU
T: (01508) 550260
F: (01508) 550260

The Old Vicarage ◆◆◆◆
48 The Street, Brooke, Norwich
NR15 1JU
T: (01508) 558329

BROOME
Norfolk

Outlaws Cottage ◆◆◆◆
Lugs Lane, Broome, Bungay,
Suffolk NR35 2HT
T: (01508) 518559
F: (01508) 518559

BRUNDALL
Norfolk

Braydeston House ◆◆◆
The Street, Brundall, Norwich,
Norfolk NR13 5JY
T: (01603) 713123

3 Oak Hill ◆◆◆
Brundall, Norwich NR13 5AQ
T: (01603) 717903

BULPHAN
Essex

Bonny Downs Farm ◆◆◆
Doesgate Lane, Bulphan,
Upminster, Essex RM14 3TB
T: (01268) 542129

BUNGAY
Suffolk

Castles ◆◆◆◆
35 Earsham Street, Bungay,
Suffolk NR35 1AF
T: (01986) 892283

Dove Restaurant ◆◆◆
Wortwell, Harleston, Norfolk
IP20 0EN
T: (01986) 788315

Earsham Park Farm
◆◆◆◆ SILVER AWARD
Harleston Road, Earsham,
Bungay, Suffolk NR35 2AQ
T: (01986) 892180 &
07798 728936
F: (01986) 892180
I: watchorn_s@freenet.co.uk

South Elmham Hall ◆◆◆◆
St Cross, South Elmham,
Harleston, Norfolk IP20 0PZ
T: (01986) 782526
F: (01986) 782203
E: jo@southelmham.co.uk
I: www.southelmham.co.uk

BUNTINGFORD
Hertfordshire

Buckland Bury Farm ◆◆◆◆
Buckland Bury, Buntingford,
Hertfordshire SG9 0PY
T: (01763) 272958 &
07710 992938
F: (01763) 274722
E: buckbury@farming.co.uk

Southfields Farm ◆◆◆
Throcking, Buntingford,
Hertfordshire SG9 9RD
T: (01763) 281224 &
0777 551258
F: (01763) 281224
E: iamurchie@hotmail.com

**Wyddial Bury Farm Bed &
Breakfast ◆◆◆**
Wyddial Bury, Buntingford,
Hertfordshire SG9 0EL
T: (01763) 272249 & 271770
F: (01763) 273276
E: dahodge@lineone.net

BURES
Suffolk

Queen's House ◆◆◆
Church Square, Bures, Suffolk
CO8 5AB
T: (01787) 227760 &
07802 841448
F: (01787) 227082
E: rogerarnold1@compuserve.
com

BURGH ST PETER
Norfolk

Shrublands Farm ◆◆◆◆
Burgh St Peter, Beccles, Suffolk
NR34 0BB
T: (01502) 677241
F: (01502) 677241

BURNHAM MARKET
Norfolk

Wood Lodge
◆◆◆◆ SILVER AWARD
Millwood, Burnham Market,
King's Lynn, Norfolk PE31 8DP
T: (01328) 730152
F: (01328) 730158

BURNHAM OVERY STAITHE
Norfolk

Domville Guesthouse ◆◆◆
Glebe Lane, Burnham Overy
Staithe, King's Lynn, Norfolk
PE31 8JQ
T: (01328) 738298

BURNHAM THORPE
Norfolk

Whitehall Farm ◆◆◆
Burnham Thorpe, King's Lynn,
Norfolk PE31 8HN
T: (01328) 738416 &
07831 794029
F: (01328) 738416
E: www.farmstayanglia.co.uk

BURWELL
Cambridgeshire

The Meadow House ◆◆◆◆
2A High Street, Burwell,
Cambridge, Cambridgeshire
CB5 0HB
T: (01638) 741926 & 741354
F: (01638) 743424

BURY ST EDMUNDS
Suffolk

**Abbotts House Bed &
Breakfast◆◆◆**
2 Grove Road, Bury St Edmunds,
Suffolk IP33 3BE
T: (01284) 749660
F: (01284) 749660
I: www.abbottshouse.co.uk

Brighthouse Farm ◆◆◆◆
Melford Road, Lawshall, Bury St
Edmunds, Suffolk IP29 4PX
T: (01284) 830385 &
07711 829546
F: (01284) 830974
E: brighthousefarm@supanet.
com

Craufurd House ◆◆◆
Howe Lane, Cockfield, Bury St
Edmunds, Suffolk IP30 0HA
T: (01284) 828216

**Dunston Guesthouse/Hotel
◆◆◆**
8 Springfield Road, Bury St
Edmunds, Suffolk IP33 3AN
T: (01284) 767981

Hilltop ◆◆
22 Bronyon Close, Bury St
Edmunds, Suffolk IP33 3XB
T: (01284) 767066
E: bandb@hilltop.22br.
freeserve.co.uk
I: www.smoothhound.co.
uk/hotels/

The Leys ◆◆◆◆
113 Fornham Road, Bury St
Edmunds, Suffolk IP32 6AT
T: (01284) 760225

Manorhouse
◆◆◆◆◆ GOLD AWARD
The Green, Beyton, Bury St
Edmunds, Suffolk IP30 9AF
T: (01359) 270960
F: (01359) 271425
E: manorhouse@beyton1.
freeserve.co.uk
I: www.beyton1.freeserve.co.uk

The Old Bakery ◆◆◆◆
Farley Green, Wickhambrook,
Newmarket, Suffolk CB8 8PX
T: (01440) 820852 &
07778 380538
F: (01440) 820852

Regency House Hotel
Rating Applied For
3 Looms Lane, Bury St Edmunds,
Suffolk IP33 1HE
T: (01284) 764676
F: (01284) 725444

**82 Risbygate Street Bed &
Breakfast◆◆◆**
Bury St Edmunds, Suffolk
IP33 3AQ
T: (01284) 760594
E: harold@par4.fsnet.co.uk

South Hill House ◆◆◆◆
43 Southgate Street, Bury St
Edmunds, Suffolk IP33 2AZ
T: (01284) 755650
F: (01284) 752718
E: southill@cwcom.net
I: www.lineone.net/nsouthill/

Toad Hall ◆◆◆◆
Gedding, Bury St Edmunds,
Suffolk IP30 0QA
T: (01449) 736488 &
07747 621096
F: (01449) 736706
E: selucy@compuserve.com

BUXTON
Norfolk

Belair ◆◆◆
Crown Road, Buxton, Norwich
NR10 5EN
T: (01603) 279637 &
0790 1655348
F: (01603) 279637
E: johnblake1234@aol.com

Birds Place Farm ◆◆◆◆
Back Lane, Buxton, Norwich
NR10 5HD
T: (01603) 279585

CAMBRIDGE
Cambridgeshire

Acer House ◆◆◆
3 Dean Drive, Holbrook Road,
Cambridge, CB1 7SW
T: (01223) 210404
E: carol.dennett@btinternet.
com
I: www.smoothhound.co.
uk/hotels/acerhous.html

Acorn Guesthouse ◆◆◆
154 Chesterton Road,
Cambridge, CB4 1DA
T: (01223) 353888
F: (01223) 350527

**Alpha Milton Guesthouse
◆◆◆**
61-63 Milton Road, Cambridge,
CB4 1XA
T: (01223) 311625 & 565100
F: (01223) 565100

Arbury Lodge Guesthouse ♦♦♦
82 Arbury Road, Cambridge,
CB4 2JE
T: (01223) 364319 & 566988
F: (01223) 566988
E: arburylodge@dtn.ntl.com

Ashley Hotel ♦♦♦
74 Chesterton Road, Cambridge,
CB4 1ER
T: (01223) 350059
F: (01223) 350900

Ashtrees Guesthouse ♦♦♦
128 Perne Road, Cambridge,
CB1 3RR
T: (01223) 411233
F: (01223) 411233
I: www.smoothhound.co.
uk/hotels/ashtrees.html

Assisi Guesthouse ♦♦♦
193 Cherry Hinton Road,
Cambridge, CB1 7BX
T: (01223) 246648 & 211466
F: (01223) 412900

Aylesbray Lodge Guesthouse ♦♦♦♦
5 Mowbray Road, Cambridge,
CB1 7SR
T: (01223) 240089
F: (01223) 528678
I: www.
cambridge-bedandbreakfast.co.
uk/aylesbray.htm

Brooklands Guesthouse ♦♦♦
95 Cherry Hinton Road,
Cambridge, CB1 7BS
T: (01223) 242035
F: (01223) 242035

Cam Guesthouse ♦♦♦
17 Elizabeth Way, Cambridge,
CB4 1DD
T: (01223) 354512
F: (01223) 353164
E: camguesthouse@btinternet.
com

Cambridge Lodge Hotel ♦♦♦♦
139 Huntingdon Road,
Cambridge, CB3 0DQ
T: (01223) 352833
F: (01223) 355166

Carolina Bed & Breakfast ♦♦♦
148 Perne Road, Cambridge,
CB1 3NX
T: (01223) 247015 &
07770 370914
F: (01223) 247015
E: carolina.amabile@tesco.net
I: www.smoothhound.co.
uk/hotels/carol.html

City Haven Guesthouse ♦♦♦
20 St Margarets Square,
Cambridge, CB1 8AP
T: (01223) 411188
E: bon.accord.house@dial.pipex.
com

Cristinas ♦♦♦
47 St Andrews Road, Cambridge,
CB4 1DH
T: (01223) 365855 & 327700
F: (01223) 365855

Dresden Villa Guesthouse ♦♦♦
34 Cherry Hinton Road,
Cambridge, CB1 7AA
T: (01223) 247539
F: (01223) 410640

Dykelands Guesthouse ♦♦♦
157 Mowbray Road, Cambridge,
CB1 7SP
T: (01223) 244300
F: (01223) 566746
E: dykelands@fsbdial.co.uk
I: www.drakken.
com/clientsites/dykelands

Fairways Guesthouse ♦♦♦
141-143 Cherry Hinton Road,
Cambridge, CB1 7BX
T: (01223) 246063
F: (01223) 212093
E: mike.slatter@btinternet.com

Finches ♦♦♦♦
144 Thornton Road, Girton,
Cambridge CB3 0ND
T: (01223) 276653 &
07710 179214
E: liz.green.b-b@talk21.com

Foxhounds ♦♦♦
71 Cambridge Road, Wimpole
and Orwell, Royston, SG8 5QD
T: (01223) 207344
E: sjpalfinch@freeserve.co.uk

Gransden Lodge Farm ♦♦♦♦
Little Gransden, Longstowe,
Cambridge SG19 3EB
T: (01767) 677365
F: (01767) 677647

Hamilton Hotel ♦♦♦
156 Chesterton Road,
Cambridge, CB4 1DA
T: (01223) 365664
F: (01223) 314866

Helen Hotel ♦♦♦♦
167-169 Hills Road, Cambridge,
CB2 2RJ
T: (01223) 246465
F: (01223) 214406

56 High Street ♦♦♦♦
Great Wilbraham, Cambridge
CB1 5JD
T: (01223) 880751 &
07711 845300
F: (01223) 880751
E: bcanning@dial.pipex.com
I: www.geocities.
com/greatwilbraham

Hills Guesthouse ♦♦♦♦
157 Hills Road, Cambridge,
CB2 2RJ
T: (01223) 214216
F: (01223) 214216

Home From Home ♦♦♦♦
39 Milton Road, Cambridge,
CB4 1XA
T: (01223) 323555 &
07889 990698
F: (01223) 323555
E: homefromhome@test.net
I: www.smoothhound.co.
uk/hotels/homefromhome.html

King's Tithe ♦♦♦♦
13a Comberton Road, Barton,
Cambridge CB3 7BA
T: (01223) 263610
F: (01223) 263610
E: kingstithebarton@lineone.net

Lensfield Hotel ♦♦♦
53 Lensfield Road, Cambridge,
CB2 1EN
T: (01223) 355017
F: (01223) 312022

Lovell Lodge Hotel ♦♦
365 Milton Road, Cambridge,
CB4 1SR
T: (01223) 425478
F: (01223) 426581

Romanhurst House ♦♦♦♦
3 Grange Road, Cambridge,
CB3 9AS
T: (01223) 352344

Segovia Lodge ♦♦♦
2 Barton Road, Newnham,
Cambridge, Cambridgeshire
CB3 9JZ
T: (01223) 354105
F: (01223) 323011

Sorrento Hotel ♦♦♦♦
190-196 Cherry Hinton Road,
Cambridge, CB1 7AN
T: (01223) 243533
F: (01223) 213463
E: sorrento-hotel@cb17an.
freeserve.co.uk
I: www.sorrentohotel.com

Southampton Guest House ♦♦♦
7 Elizabeth Way, Cambridge,
CB4 1DE
T: (01223) 357780
F: (01223) 314297

The Suffolk House ♦♦♦
69 Milton Road, Cambridge,
CB4 1XA
T: (01223) 352016
F: (01223) 566816
I: suffolkhouse@yahoo.com

Victoria ♦♦♦♦
57 Arbury Road, Cambridge,
CB4 2JB
T: (01223) 350086
F: (01223) 350086
E: vicmaria@globalnet.co.uk
I: www.touristnetuk.
com/em/victoria

Woodfield House ♦♦♦♦
Madingley Road, Coton,
Cambridge CB3 7PH
T: (01954) 210265
F: (01954) 212650
E: wendy-johncwsadler_
freeserve.co.uk

CAMPSEA ASHE
Suffolk
The Old Rectory
♦♦♦♦♦ GOLD AWARD
Campsea Ashe, Woodbridge,
Suffolk IP13 0PU
T: (01728) 746524
F: (01728) 746524

CAPEL ST MARY
Suffolk
Grove Farmhouse
♦♦♦♦ SILVER AWARD
Little Wenham, Colchester
CO7 6QB
T: (01473) 310341
F: (01473) 310341
@

CARBROOKE
Norfolk
White Hall
♦♦♦♦ GOLD AWARD
Carbrooke, Thetford, Norfolk
IP25 6SG
T: (01953) 885950
F: (01953) 884420

CARLETON RODE
Norfolk
Upgate Farm ♦♦♦
Carleton Rode, Norwich
NR16 1NJ
T: (01953) 860300
F: (01953) 860300

CASTLE ACRE
Norfolk
Pilgrims Cottage ♦♦
3 Stocks Green, Castle Acre,
King's Lynn, Norfolk PE32 2AE
T: (01328) 820044 &
07889 902818
F: (01328) 821006

CASTLE HEDINGHAM
Essex
Fishers
Rating Applied For
St James Street, Castle
Hedingham, Halstead, Essex
CO9 3EW
T: (01787) 460382
F: (01787) 460382

The Old School House ♦♦♦
St James Street, Castle
Hedingham, Halstead, Essex
CO9 3EW
T: (01787) 461629

CASTOR
Cambridgeshire
Old Smithy ♦♦♦♦
47 Peterborough Road, Castor,
Peterborough PE5 7AX
T: (01733) 380186
F: (01733) 380186

CATFIELD
Norfolk
Summer House Farm ♦♦♦
Sharp Street, Catfield, Great
Yarmouth, Norfolk NR29 5AF
T: (01692) 670122
F: (01692) 670122
E: stuffie@lineone.net
I: www.broadland.
com/summerhousefarm

CAVENDISH
Suffolk
The Red House
♦♦♦♦ SILVER AWARD
Stour Street, Cavendish,
Sudbury, Suffolk CO10 8BH
T: (01787) 280611
F: (01787) 280611

CAWSTON
Norfolk
The Walnuts ♦♦♦♦
8-12 New Street, Cawston,
Norwich NR10 4AL
T: (01603) 871357
F: (01603) 871357

CHELMSFORD
Essex
Aarandale ♦♦♦
9 Roxwell Road, Chelmsford,
CM1 2LY
T: (01245) 251713
F: (01245) 251713
E: aarandale@btclick.com

Almond Lodge ♦♦♦
The Bringey, Great Baddow,
Chelmsford CM2 7JW
T: (01245) 471564

Aquila B & B ♦♦
11 Daffodil Way, Springfield,
Chelmsford, CM1 6XB
T: (01245) 465274

Beechcroft Private Hotel ♦♦♦
211 New London Road,
Chelmsford, Essex CM2 0AJ
T: (01245) 352462 & 250861
F: (01245) 347833
E: beechcroft.hotel@btinternet.com

66 Beehive Lane ♦♦♦
Chelmsford, Essex CM2 9RX
T: (01245) 355919 &
07867 520407

Boswell House Hotel ♦♦♦♦
118 Springfield Road,
Chelmsford, CM2 6LF
T: (01245) 287587
F: (01245) 287587

Brook House
♦♦♦♦ SILVER AWARD
Chelmsford Road, Great
Waltham, Chelmsford, Essex
CM3 1AQ
T: (01245) 360776 &
07723 006154

The Chelmer Hotel ♦♦
2-4 Hamlet Road, Chelmsford,
CM2 0EU
T: (01245) 353360 & 609055
F: (01245) 609055

Four Oaks ♦♦♦
33a White Elm Road, Bicknacre,
Chelmsford, Essex CM3 4LU
T: (01245) 226329
E: woodentops@tesco.net

Neptune Cafe Motel ♦♦
Burnham Road, Latchingdon,
Chelmsford CM3 6EX
T: (01621) 740770

Old Bakery ♦♦♦♦
Waltham Road, Terling,
Chelmsford, Essex CM3 2QR
T: (01245) 233363

Pemajero ♦♦♦
Cedar Avenue West, Chelmsford,
Essex CM1 2XA
T: (01245) 264679
F: (01245) 264679

Sherwood ♦♦♦
Cedar Avenue West, Chelmsford,
Essex CM1 2XA
T: (01245) 257981
F: (01245) 257981

Silvertrees ♦♦
565 Galleywood Road,
Chelmsford, CM2 8AA
T: (01245) 268767

Springford ♦♦♦
8 Well Lane, Galleywood,
Chelmsford, Essex CM2 8QY
T: (01245) 257821
🌐

Stump Cross House
♦♦♦♦ SILVER AWARD
Moulsham Street, Chelmsford,
Essex CM2 9AQ
T: (01245) 353804

Tanunda Hotel ♦♦♦
217-219 New London Road,
Chelmsford, CM2 0AJ
T: (01245) 354295
F: (01245) 345503

CHRISHALL
Essex

Whitebeams
Rating Applied For
Crawley End, Chrishall, Royston,
Hertfordshire SG8 8QN
T: (01763) 837169

CLACTON-ON-SEA
Essex

Le'Vere House Hotel ♦♦♦
15 Agate Road, Clacton-on-Sea,
Essex CO15 1RA
T: (01255) 423044
F: (01255) 423044

Sandrock Hotel ♦♦♦
1 Penfold Road, Marine Parade
West, Clacton-on-Sea, Essex
CO15 1JN
T: (01255) 428215
F: (01255) 428215

Stonar Hotel ♦♦♦
19 Agate Road, Clacton-on-Sea,
Essex CO15 1RA
T: (01255) 221011 &
07802 387778
F: (01255) 221011

CLAPHAM
Bedfordshire

Narly Oak Lodge Narly Oak
♦♦♦♦
The Baulk, Green Lane, Clapham,
Bedford MK41 6AA
T: (01234) 350353
F: (01234) 350353
E: fostert@csdbedfordshire.gov.uk

CLARE
Suffolk

The Clare Hotel ♦♦♦
19 Nethergate Street, Clare,
Sudbury, Suffolk CO10 8NP
T: (01787) 277449
F: (01787) 277161
E: clarehotel.qtalk21.com

Cobwebs ♦♦♦
26 Nethergate Street, Clare,
Sudbury, Suffolk CO10 8NP
T: (01787) 277539
F: (01787) 278252

Ship Stores ♦♦♦
22 Callis Street, Clare, Sudbury,
Suffolk CO10 8PX
T: (01787) 277834
E: shipclare@aol.co.uk
I: www.s-h-systems.co.uk/hotels/shipstor.html

CLAYDON
Suffolk

**Mockbeggars Hall Bed &
Breakfast**
♦♦♦♦ SILVER AWARD
Paper Mill Lane, Claydon,
Ipswich IP6 0AH
T: (01473) 830239 &
0770 2627770
F: (01473) 830239
E: priscillagibson@england.com
I: www.mockbeggars.co.uk

CLEY NEXT THE SEA
Norfolk

George and Dragon Hotel
♦♦♦
High Street, Cley next the Sea,
Holt, Norfolk NR25 7RN
T: (01263) 740652
F: (01263) 741275

CLOPHILL
Bedfordshire

Shallmarose Bed & Breakfast
♦♦♦
32 Bedford Road, Clophill,
Bedford MK45 4AE
T: (01525) 861565

COCKFIELD
Suffolk

Holly Cottage ♦♦♦♦
Great Green, Cockfield, Bury St
Edmunds, Suffolk IP30 0HQ
T: (01284) 828682

COLCHESTER
Essex

Appleblossoms ♦♦♦
8 Guildford Road, Colchester,
CO1 2YL
T: (01206) 512303
F: (01206) 840260
🌐

Athelstan House ♦♦♦♦
201 Maldon Road, Colchester,
Essex CO3 3BQ
T: (01206) 548652
E: mackman@mcmail.com
🌐

8 Broadmead Road ♦♦♦
Parsons Heath, Colchester,
CO4 3HB
T: (01206) 861818
F: (01206) 861818
🌐

Darcy House ♦♦♦♦
3-5 Culver Street East,
Colchester, CO1 1LD
T: (01206) 768111
F: (01206) 763938
E: jacquelineedgar@dtn.ntl.com

Four Sevens Guesthouse ♦♦♦
28 Inglis Road, Colchester,
CO3 3HU
T: (01206) 546093
F: (01206) 546093
E: calypsod@hotmail.com
I: www.cdemetri.freeserve.com.uk

Fridaywood Farm ♦♦♦♦
Bounstead Road, Colchester,
CO2 0DF
T: (01206) 573595 &
07970 836285
F: (01206) 547011

Glinska House ♦♦♦♦
6 St Johns Green, Colchester,
CO2 7HA
T: (01206) 578961 &
07850 215598
F: (01206) 503406
E: rhawki@email.msn.com

The Globe Hotel ♦♦
71 North Station Road,
Colchester, CO1 1RQ
T: (01206) 502502
F: (01206) 506506
I: www.theglobehotel.co.uk

Hampton House ♦♦♦
224 Maldon Road, Colchester,
CO3 3BD
T: (01206) 579291

11 Harvest End ♦♦♦
Stanway, Colchester, Essex
CO3 5YX
T: (01206) 543202

Lemoine ♦♦♦
2 Whitefriars Way, Colchester,
Essex CO3 4EL
T: (01206) 574710

11a Lincoln Way ♦♦♦
Colchester, CO1 2RL
T: (01206) 867192 &
07710 208168
F: (01206) 799993
E: j.medwards@easicom.com
🌐

Nutcrackers ♦♦♦
6 Mayberry Walk, Colchester,
Essex CO2 8PS
T: (01206) 543085
F: (01206) 543085
E: jean@aflex.net.

**Old Courthouse Inn Formerly
Old Black Boy** ♦♦♦
Harwich Road, Great Bromley,
Colchester, CO7 7JG
T: (01206) 250322 & 251906

The Old Manse ♦♦♦
15 Roman Road, Colchester,
CO1 1UR
T: (01206) 545154
F: (01206) 545153
I: www.doveuk.com/oldmanse
🌐

Pescara House ♦♦♦
88 Manor Road, Colchester,
CO3 3LY
T: (01206) 520055
F: (01206) 512127
E: dave@pescarahouse.co.uk
I: www.pescarahouse.co.uk

Peveril Hotel ♦
51 North Hill, Colchester, Essex
CO1 1PY
T: (01206) 574001
F: (01206) 574001

The Red House ♦♦♦
29 Wimpole Road, Colchester,
CO1 2DL
T: (01206) 509005
F: (01206) 500311
🌐

76 Roman Road ♦♦♦
Colchester, CO1 1UP
T: (01206) 514949

Saint Johns Guesthouse ♦♦♦
330 Ipswich Road, Colchester,
CO4 4ET
T: (01206) 852288

Scheregate Hotel ♦♦
36 Osborne Street, via St John's
Street, Colchester, CO2 7DB
T: (01206) 573034
F: (01206) 541561

Seven Arches Farm ♦♦
Chitts Hill, Lexden, Colchester,
CO3 5SX
T: (01206) 574896
F: (01206) 574896

Sevilla ♦♦♦♦
74 Roman Road, Colchester,
CO1 1UP
T: (01206) 544453 &
07721 014843
F: (01206) 764473
E: sherill@zest-leisure.com
I: www.sevillabedandbreakfast.co.uk

Silver Springs ♦♦
Restaurant and Lodge, Tenpenny
Hill, Thorrington, Colchester,
Essex CO7 8JG
T: (01206) 250366
F: (01206) 250700

Tall Trees ◆◆◆◆
25 Irvine Road, Colchester,
CO3 3TP
T: (01206) 576650 & 0794 122
3688
E: whiteheads.talltrees@
barclays.net

Telstar ◆◆◆
Layer Breton, Colchester,
CO2 0PS
T: (01206) 331642

4 Wavell Avenue ◆◆
Colchester, CO2 7HP
T: (01206) 571736

COLTISHALL
Norfolk

The Hedges Guesthouse
◆◆◆◆
Tunstead Road, Coltishall,
Norwich NR12 7AL
T: (01603) 738361
F: (01603) 738983
E: thehedges@msn.com
⊕

Kings Head ◆◆◆
26 Wroxham Road, Coltishall,
Norwich NR12 7EA
T: (01603) 737426
F: (01603) 736542

Station Bed & Breakfast ◆◆
Station House, Coltishall,
Norwich NR12 7JG
T: (01603) 737069

Terra Nova Lodge ◆◆◆◆
14 Westbourne Road, Coltishall,
Norwich NR12 7HT
T: (01603) 736264

COPDOCK
Suffolk

Westhill ◆◆◆
Elm Lane, Copdock, Ipswich
IP8 3ET
T: (01473) 730934
F: (01473) 730259
E: alpheco@anglianet.co.uk.

CORTON
Suffolk

Holly Cottage ◆◆◆◆
11 Mill Lane, Corton, Lowestoft,
Suffolk NR32 5HZ
T: (01502) 731224

COTTENHAM
Cambridgeshire

Denmark House ◆◆◆◆
58 Denmark Road, Cottenham,
Cambridge CB4 8QS
T: (01954) 251060 & 250448
F: (01954) 251629
E: denmark.house@tesco.net
⊕

CRANFIELD
Bedfordshire

The Swan ◆◆
2 Court Road, Cranfield, Bedford
MK43 0DR
T: (01234) 750332
F: (01234) 750332

CREETING ST MARY
Suffolk

Grange Farm Bed & Breakfast
◆◆◆◆
Grange Farm, Creeting St Mary,
Ipswich IP6 8NG
T: (01449) 722711 &
07801 252612
F: (01449) 723039

CRETINGHAM
Suffolk

The Cretingham Bell
◆◆◆◆ SILVER AWARD
The Street, Cretingham,
Woodbridge, Suffolk IP13 7BJ
T: (01728) 685419

Shrubbery Farmhouse
◆◆◆◆ SILVER AWARD
Chapel Hill, Cretingham,
Woodbridge, Suffolk IP13 7DN
T: (01473) 737494 &
07860 352317
F: (01473) 737312
E: sm@marmar.co.uk
I: www.shrubberyfarmhouse.co.
uk

CROMER
Norfolk

Beachcomber ◆◆◆
17 Macdonald Road, Cromer,
Norfolk NR27 9AP
T: (01263) 513398
I: www.broadland.
com/beachcomber

Birch House ◆◆◆
34 Cabbell Road, Cromer,
Norfolk NR27 9HX
T: (01263) 512521

Cambridge House ◆◆◆
Sea Front, Cromer, Norfolk
NR27 9HD
T: (01263) 512085
I: www.broadland.
com/cambridgehouse
⊕

The Grove Guesthouse ◆◆◆
95 Overstrand Road, Cromer,
Norfolk NR27 0DJ
T: (01263) 512412
F: (01263) 513416
E: thegrove@barclays.net
I: www.broadland.
com/thegrovewww.
smoothhound.co.uk/hotels

Knoll Guesthouse ◆◆◆
23 Alfred Road, Cromer, Norfolk
NR27 9AN
T: (01263) 512753
E: ian@knollguesthouse.co.uk
I: www.knollguesthouse.co.uk

Morden House ◆◆◆◆
20 Cliff Avenue, Cromer, Norfolk
NR27 0AN
T: (01263) 513396
E: rosemary@broadland.com
I: www.broadland.
com/mordenhouse
⊕

Seaspray ◆◆◆◆
1 Cliff Drive, Cromer, Norfolk
NR27 0AW
T: (01263) 512116

Shrublands Farm
◆◆◆◆ SILVER AWARD
Northrepps, Cromer, Norfolk
NR27 0AA
T: (01263) 579297
F: (01263) 579297
E: youngman@farming.co.uk
I: www.broadland.
com/shrublands
⊕

Stenson ◆◆◆◆
32 Overstrand Road, Cromer,
Norfolk NR27 0AJ
T: (01263) 511308
⊕

CUFFLEY
Hertfordshire

Wutherings ◆◆◆◆
43 Colesdale, Cuffley, Potters
Bar, Hertfordshire EN6 4LQ
T: (01707) 874545 & 0795 791
8548

DALLINGHOO
Suffolk

Old Rectory ◆◆◆
Dallinghoo, Woodbridge, Suffolk
IP13 0LA
T: (01473) 737700

DANBURY
Essex

Southways ◆◆◆
Copt Hill, Danbury, Chelmsford,
Essex CM3 4NN
T: (01245) 223428

DARSHAM
Suffolk

Priory Farm ◆◆◆
Darsham, Saxmundham, Suffolk
IP17 3QD
T: (01728) 668459
⊕

White House Farm ◆◆◆
Main Road, Darsham,
Saxmundham, Suffolk IP17 3PP
T: (01728) 668632

DEBDEN
Essex

Redbrick House
Rating Applied For
Deynes Road, Debden, Saffron
Walden, Essex CB11 3LG
T: (01799) 540221
E: bandb@redbrick-house.fsnet.
co.uk

DEBDEN GREEN
Essex

The Granary ◆◆◆◆
The Old Bakehouse, Debden
Green, Saffron Walden, Essex
CB11 3LX
T: (01371) 830687
F: (01371) 830687

Wigmores Farm ◆◆◆◆
Debden Green, Saffron Walden,
Essex CB11 3LX
T: (01371) 830050
F: (01371) 830050
E: patrick.worth@tesco.net

DEDHAM
Essex

Good Hall
◆◆◆◆ SILVER AWARD
Coggeshall Road, Dedham,
Colchester CO7 7LR
T: (01206) 322100

The Marlborough ◆◆◆
Mill Lane, Dedham, Colchester
CO7 6DH
T: (01206) 323250
F: (01206) 322331
E: themarlborough@fsmail.net
I: www.oldenglish.co.uk

May's Barn Farm ◆◆◆
May's Lane, Off Long Road West,
Dedham, Colchester, Essex
CO7 6EW
T: (01206) 323191
E: maysbarn@talk21.com
I: www.mays-barn-btinternet.
co.uk

Sun Hotel ◆◆◆
Dedham, Colchester CO7
T:

DENNINGTON
Suffolk

Grange Farm Bed & Breakfast
◆◆◆
Grange Farm, Dennington,
Woodbridge, Suffolk IP13 8BT
T: (01986) 798388 &
07774 182835
⊕

DENVER
Norfolk

Westhall Cottage ◆◆◆
20-22 Sluice Road, Denver,
Downham Market, Norfolk
PE38 0DY
T: (01366) 382987
F: (01366) 385553

DEPDEN
Suffolk

Elms Farm Bed & Breakfast
◆◆◆◆
Elms Farm, Depden, Bury St
Edmunds, Suffolk IP29 4BS
T: (01284) 850289 &
07887 875943
F: (01284) 851085

DEREHAM
Norfolk

Greenbanks Country Hotel
◆◆◆◆
Swaffham Road, Wendling,
Dereham, Norfolk NR19 2AR
T: (01362) 687742
⛷

Lynn Hill Guesthouse ◆◆◆
Lynn Hill, Yaxham Road,
Dereham, Norfolk NR19 1HA
T: (01362) 696142

Park Farm ◆◆◆◆
Bylaugh, East Dereham, Norfolk
NR20 4QE
T: (01362) 688584
E: lakeparkfm@aol.com
⊕

DERSINGHAM
Norfolk

Ashdene House ◆◆◆
Dersingham, King's Lynn,
Norfolk PE31 6HQ
T: (01485) 540395

The Corner House
◆◆◆◆ SILVER AWARD
2 Sandringham Road,
Dersingham, King's Lynn,
Norfolk PE31 6LL
T: (01485) 543532

Dove Lodge ◆◆◆◆
21 Woodside Avenue,
Dersingham, King's Lynn,
Norfolk PE31 6QB
T: (01485) 540053 &
07703 790789

Spring Cottage
Rating Applied For
11 Fern Hill, Dersingham, King's
Lynn, Norfolk PE31 6HT
T: (01485) 541012

Tall Trees ◆◆◆
7 Centre Vale, Dersingham,
King's Lynn, Norfolk PE31 6JR
T: (01485) 542638
F: (01485) 542638

The White House ◆◆◆
44 Hunstanton Road,
Dersingham, King's Lynn,
Norfolk PE31 6HQ
T: (01485) 541895 & 544880
F: (01485) 544880

Woodroyal ◆◆◆◆
Manor Road, Dersingham, King's Lynn, Norfolk PE31 6LD
T: (01485) 543156

DISS
Norfolk

Abbey Farm ◆◆◆
Great Green, Thrandeston, Diss, Norfolk IP21 4BN
T: (01379) 783422
I: wwwdiss.co.uk

Dickleburgh Hall
◆◆◆◆◆ GOLD AWARD
Diss, Norfolk IP21 4NT
T: (01379) 741259 &
07702 273497

Ducksfoot Farm
◆◆◆◆ SILVER AWARD
Bush Green, Pulham Market, Diss, Norfolk IP21 4YB
T: (01379) 608561 &
07711 528469
F: (01379) 608562
E: mvenables@duckfoot.fsnet.co.uk
I: www.diss.co.uk

Koliba ◆◆◆
8 Louie's Lane, Diss, Norfolk IP22 4LR
T: (01379) 650046 &
07788 400040
F: (01379) 650046
E: olgakoliba@aol.com

Oxfootstone Granary ◆◆◆◆
Low Common, South Lopham, Diss, Norfolk IP22 2JS
T: (01379) 687490

Rose Cottage ◆◆◆
Diss Road, Burston, Diss, Norfolk IP22 5TP
T: (01379) 740602 &
07770 410534
F: (01379) 740602
E: cyrilbrom@aol.com

South View ◆◆◆
High Road, Roydon, Diss, Norfolk IP22 5RU
T: (01379) 651620

Strenneth ◆◆◆◆
Airfield Road, Fersfield, Diss, Norfolk IP22 2BP
T: (01379) 688182
F: (01379) 688260
E: ken@strenneth.co.uk
I: www.strenneth.co.uk

DOCKING
Norfolk

Bakers Cottage ◆◆◆
Station Road, Docking, King's Lynn, Norfolk PE31 8LR
T: (01485) 518710

Jubilee Lodge ◆◆◆
Station Road, Docking, King's Lynn, Norfolk PE31 8LS
T: (01485) 518473
F: (01485) 518473
E: edwardhoward3@ntl.dtn.com

DOVERCOURT
Essex

Dudley Guesthouse ◆◆
34 Cliff Road, Dovercourt, Harwich, Essex CO12 3PP
T: (01255) 504927

Homebay ◆◆◆
9 Bay Road, Dovercourt, Harwich, Essex CO12 3JZ
T: (01255) 504428
E: sydie@dialstart.net

Tudor Rose ◆◆◆
124 Fronks Road, Dovercourt, Harwich, Essex CO12 4EQ
T: (01255) 552398
E: jane@morgan-co12.freeserve.co.uk

DOWNHAM MARKET
Norfolk

Lion House Licensed Restaurant and Guest House
Rating Applied For
Lion House, 140 Lynn Road, Downham Market, Norfolk PE38 9QF
T: (01366) 382017
E: lionhouse@supanot.com
I: www.lionhouse.supanot.com

EARL SOHAM
Suffolk

Bridge House
◆◆◆◆ SILVER AWARD
Earl Soham, Woodbridge, Suffolk IP13 7RT
T: (01728) 685473 & 685289

EARLS COLNE
Essex

Chalkney Wood Cottage
◆◆◆◆
Tey Road, Earls Colne, Colchester, Essex CO6 2LD
T: (01787) 223522
F: (01787) 224267

Riverside Lodge ◆◆◆
40 Lower Holt Street, Earls Colne, Colchester, Essex CO6 2PH
T: (01787) 223487
F: (01787) 223487
🏃

EAST BARSHAM
Norfolk

White Horse Inn ◆◆◆
Fakenham Road, East Barsham, Fakenham, Norfolk NR21 0LH
T: (01328) 820645
F: (01328) 820645

EAST BERGHOLT
Suffolk

Rosemary ◆◆◆
Rectory Hill, East Bergholt, Colchester CO7 6TH
T: (01206) 298241
E: s.finch@bcs.org.uk

EAST MERSEA
Essex

Bromans Farm ◆◆◆◆
Mersea Island, East Mersea, Colchester CO5 8UE
T: (01206) 383235
F: (01206) 383235

The Thatched Cottage ◆◆◆
East Road, East Mersea, Colchester CO5 8UJ
T: (01206) 384683 &
07976 829763

ELMSWELL
Suffolk

Elmswell Hall Bed & Breakfast
◆◆◆◆
Elmswell Hall, Elmswell, Bury St Edmunds, Suffolk IP30 9EN
T: (01359) 240215
F: (01359) 240215

Kiln Farm ◆◆◆
Kiln Lane, Elmswell, Bury St Edmunds, Suffolk IP30 9QR
T: (01359) 240442 & 242604
E: barry-sue@kilnfarm.fsnet.co.uk

Mulberry Farm ◆◆◆◆
Ashfield Road, Elmswell, Bury St Edmunds, Suffolk IP30 9HG
T: (01359) 244244 &
07885 934309
F: (01359) 244244

ELY
Cambridgeshire

Cambridge House ◆◆◆
2 Ship Lane, Ely, Cambridgeshire CB7 4BB
T: (01353) 662088
E: info@ukdomains.net
I: www.ukdomains.net

Cathedral House
◆◆◆◆ SILVER AWARD
17 St Mary's Street, Ely, Cambridgeshire CB7 4ER
T: (01353) 662124
F: (01353) 662124
E: farndale@cathedralhouse.co.uk
I: www.cathedralhouse.co.uk
🌐

The Grove ◆◆◆◆
Bury Lane, Sutton Gault, Ely, Cambridgeshire CB6 2BD
T: (01353) 777196
F: (01353) 777196

The High Flyer Restaurant, Public House & Hotel ◆◆◆
69 Newnham Street, Ely, Cambridgeshire CB7 4PQ
T: (01353) 669200
F: (01353) 669100

Hill House Farm
◆◆◆◆ GOLD AWARD
9 Main Street, Coveney, Ely, Cambridgeshire CB6 2DJ
T: (01353) 778369
🌐

Lamb Hotel ◆◆◆
2 Lynn Road, Ely, Cambridgeshire CB7 4EJ
T: (01353) 663574
F: (01353) 662023

Rosendale Lodge
◆◆◆◆◆ SILVER AWARD
223 Main Street, Witchford, Ely, Cambridgeshire CB6 2HT
T: (01353) 667700
F: (01353) 667799
🌐 ♿

Spinney Abbey ◆◆◆◆
Stretham Road, Wicken, Ely, Cambridgeshire CB7 5XQ
T: (01353) 720971
E: spinney.abbey@tesco.net
I: www.smoothhound.co.uk/hotels/spinneya.html
🌐

Springfields ◆◆◆◆◆
Ely Road, Little Thetford, Ely, Cambridgeshire CB6 3HJ
T: (01353) 663637
F: (01353) 663130

Sycamore House ◆◆◆◆
91 Cambridge Road, Ely, Cambridgeshire CB7 4HX
T: (01353) 662139

Waterside Bed & Breakfast
◆◆◆◆ SILVER AWARD
52 Waterside, Ely, Cambridgeshire CB7 4AZ
T: (01353) 667570
E: jane.latimer@classicfm.net
I: www.waterside-ely.co.uk

EPPING
Essex

Brooklands ◆◆◆
1 Chapel Road, Epping, Essex CM16 5DS
T: (01992) 575424
I: www.abrookland@aol.com

ERPINGHAM
Norfolk

Saracens Head Inn ◆◆◆
Wolterton, Erpingham, Norwich NR11 7LX
T: (01263) 768909
F: (01263) 768993
I: www/broadland.com/saracenshead

EYE
Suffolk

The White Horse Inn ◆◆◆
Stoke Ash, Eye, Suffolk IP23 7ET
T: (01379) 678222
F: (01379) 678557

EYKE
Suffolk

The Old House ◆◆◆◆
Eyke, Woodbridge, Suffolk IP12 2QW
T: (01394) 460213

FAKENHAM
Norfolk

Abbott Farm ◆◆◆
Walsingham Road, Binham, Fakenham, Norfolk NR21 0AW
T: (01328) 830519 &
07850 731413
F: (01328) 830519
E: peabrown@aol.com.

Erika's Bed and Breakfast
◆◆◆
3 Gladstone Road, Fakenham, Norfolk NR21 9BZ
T: (01328) 863058
🌐

Hardlands ◆◆◆◆
East Raynham, Fakenham, Norfolk NR21 7EQ
T: (01328) 862567 &
07710 232441
F: (01328) 856005
E: harlands@waitrose.com
I: harlands@waitrose.com

Highfield Farm ◆◆◆◆
Great Ryburgh, Fakenham, Norfolk NR21 7AL
T: (01328) 829249
F: (01328) 829422
E: jegshighfield@onet.co.uk
I: www.broadland.com/highfield
🌐

Hillside Bed & Breakfast
◆◆◆◆ SILVER AWARD
47 Wells Road, Fakenham, Norfolk NR21 9HQ
T: (01328) 855128
E: hillsideb_b@compuserve.com
🌐

Holly Lodge
Rating Applied For
The Street, Thursford Green, Fakenham, Norfolk NR21 0AS
T: (01328) 878465
F: (01328) 878465

Mulberry Cottage ◆◆◆◆
Green Farm Lane, Thursford
Green, Fakenham, Norfolk
NR21 0RX
T: (01328) 878968
♨

The Old Brick Kilns Guesthouse ◆◆◆◆
Little Barney Lane, Little Barney,
Fakenham, Norfolk NR21 0NL
T: (01328) 878305
F: (01328) 878948
E: enquire@old-brick-kilns.co.
uk
I: www.old-brick-kilns.co.uk
♨

FARCET
Cambridgeshire

Red House Farm ◆◆◆
Broadway, Farcet, Peterborough
PE7 3AZ
T: (01733) 243129 &
07711 612239
F: (01733) 243129

FEERING
Essex

Old Wills Farm
Rating Applied For
Feering, Colchester CO5 9RP
T: (01376) 570259
E: janecrayston@barclays.net

FELIXSTOWE
Suffolk

Castle Lodge Private Hotel ◆◆◆
Chevalier Road, Felixstowe,
Suffolk IP11 7EY
T: (01394) 282149

Dolphin Hotel ◆◆
41 Beach Station Road,
Felixstowe, Suffolk IP11 2EY
T: (01394) 282261 & 278319

Dorincourt Guesthouse ◆◆◆
41 Undercliff Road West,
Felixstowe, Suffolk IP11 2AH
T: (01394) 270447 & 270577
F: (01394) 270447
🏂

Fludyer Arms Hotel ◆◆
Undercliff Road East, Felixstowe,
Suffolk IP11 7LU
T: (01394) 283279
F: (01394) 670754
E: FLUDYERS@BTINTERNET.
COM

The Grafton Guesthouse ◆◆◆◆
13 Sea Road, Felixstowe, Suffolk
IP11 2BB
T: (01394) 284881

The Jays ◆◆◆◆
16 Estuary Drive, Felixstowe,
Suffolk IP11 9TL
T: (01394) 283194

Mansard Cottage
◆◆◆◆ SILVER AWARD
Golf Road, Felixstowe, Suffolk
IP11 7NB
T: (01394) 282817
E: richard.thomas@easynet.co.
uk

Primrose Gate Bed & Breakfast ◆◆◆◆
263 Ferry Road, Felixstowe,
Suffolk IP11 9RX
T: (01394) 271699
F: (01394) 283614
E: lesley_berry@hotmail.com

FELMINGHAM
Norfolk

Larks Rise ◆◆
North Walsham Road,
Felmingham, North Walsham,
Norfolk NR28 0JU
T: (01692) 403173

FELSTED
Essex

Potash Farm ◆◆◆◆
Cobblers Green, Causeway End
Road, Felsted, Dunmow, Essex
CM6 3LX
T: (01371) 820510
F: (01371) 820510
E: richardsmith«106160.
14467@compuserve.com»

FENSTANTON
Cambridgeshire

Orchard House ◆◆◆
Hilton Road, Fenstanton,
Huntingdon, Cambridgeshire
PE18 9LH
T: (01480) 469208
F: (01480) 497487
E: ascarrow@aol.com

FINCHAM
Norfolk

Rose Cottage Bed and Breakfast ◆◆◆
Downham Road, Fincham, King's
Lynn, Norfolk PE33 9HF
T: (01366) 347426
F: (01366) 347426

FINCHINGFIELD
Essex

The Red Lion Inn ◆◆◆
6 Church Hill, Finchingfield,
Braintree, Essex CM7 4NN
T: (01371) 810400
F: (01371) 851062

FLATFORD MILL, EAST
BERGHOLT

The Granary
Rating Applied For
Granary Museum, Flatford Mill,
East Bergholt, Colchester
CO7 6UL
T: (01206) 298111

FOULDEN
Norfolk

The White Hart Inn ◆◆◆
White Hart Street, Foulden,
Thetford, Norfolk IP26 5AW
T: (01366) 328638
E: sylvia.chisholm@virgin.net

FRAMLINGHAM
Suffolk

Fieldway Bed & Breakfast ◆◆◆◆
Saxtead Road, Dennington,
Woodbridge, Suffolk IP13 8AP
T: (01728) 638456
F: (01728) 638456
E: dianaturan@hotmail.com

High House Farm ◆◆◆
Cransford, Framlingham,
Woodbridge, Suffolk IP13 9PD
T: (01728) 663461
F: (01728) 663409
♨

Shimmens Pightle ◆◆◆
Dennington Road, Framlingham,
Woodbridge, Suffolk IP13 9JT
T: (01728) 724036

FRESSINGFIELD
Suffolk

Chippenhall Hall
◆◆◆◆◆ SILVER AWARD
Fressingfield, Eye, Suffolk
IP21 5TD
T: (01379) 588180 & 586733
F: (01379) 586272
E: info@chippenhall.co.uk
I: www.chippenhall.co.uk

Elm Lodge ◆◆◆◆
Chippenhall Green, Fressingfield,
Eye, Suffolk IP21 5SL
T: (01379) 586249
♨

FRINTON-ON-SEA
Essex

Uplands Guesthouse ◆◆◆
41 Hadleigh Road, Frinton-on-
Sea, Essex CO13 9HQ
T: (01255) 674889

FRISTON
Suffolk

The Flint House ◆◆◆◆
Aldeburgh Road, Friston,
Saxmundham, Suffolk IP17 1PD
T: (01728) 689123
E: handsel@eidosnet.co.uk

The Old School ◆◆◆
Aldeburgh Road, Friston,
Saxmundham, Suffolk IP17 1NP
T: (01728) 688173
E: oldschool@fristonoldschool.
freeserve.co.uk

GISLINGHAM
Suffolk

The Old Guildhall ◆◆◆◆
Mill Street, Gislingham, Eye,
Suffolk IP23 8JT
T: (01379) 783361

GREAT BADDOW
Essex

Homecroft ◆◆◆
Southend Road, Great Baddow,
Chelmsford CM2 7AD
T: (01245) 475070 & 0788 181
6560
F: (01245) 475070

Little Sir Hughes
◆◆◆◆ SILVER AWARD
West Hanningfield Road, Great
Baddow, Chelmsford, Essex
CM2 7SZ
T: (01245) 471701
F: (01245) 478023
E: accom@englishlive.co.uk

Orchard House ◆◆◆
The Bringey, Church Street,
Great Baddow, Chelmsford
CM2 7JW
T: (01245) 474333

Rothmans ◆◆◆
22 High Street, Great Baddow,
Chelmsford CM2 7HQ
T: (01245) 473837 & 477144
F: (01245) 476833
E: jcbarron@excite.co.uk
I: www.city2000.
com/h/rothmans-b&b.
essex-html

GREAT BRICETT
Suffolk

Riverside Cottage ◆◆◆◆
The Street, Great Bricett, Ipswich
IP7 7DH
T: (01473) 658266
E: chasmhorne@aol.com

GREAT CANFIELD
Essex

The Grange ◆◆◆◆
Great Canfield, Dunmow, Essex
CM6 1JZ
T: (01279) 870341
F: (01279) 871648
E: asainthill@channel-express.
co.uk

GREAT CHESTERFORD
Essex

July Cottage ◆◆◆
Carmel Street, Great
Chesterford, Saffron Walden,
Essex CB10 1PH
T: (01799) 530315

White Gates ◆◆◆◆
School Street, Great
Chesterford, Saffron Walden,
Essex CB10 1NN
T: (01799) 530249

GREAT CORNARD
Suffolk

Richmond Lodge ◆◆◆
Kings Hill, Great Cornard,
Sudbury, Suffolk CO10 0EH
T: (01787) 373728 & 379232
F: (01787) 373728
E: jenny@digitalfinecut.co.uk
I: digitalfinecut.co.uk

GREAT CRESSINGHAM
Norfolk

The Vines ◆◆◆
The Street, Great Cressingham,
Thetford, Norfolk IP25 6NL
T: (01760) 756303
E: the.vines@eidosnet.co.uk

GREAT DUNMOW
Essex

Harwood Guest House ◆◆◆◆
52 Stortford Road, Great
Dunmow, CM6 1DN
T: (01371) 874627

Homelye Farm ◆◆◆◆
Homelye Chase, Braintree Road,
Dunmow, Essex CM6 3AW
T: (01371) 872127 & 0771 825
9076
F: (01371) 876428
E: homelye@netlineuk.net
I: www.netlineuk.net/§homelye

Mallards ◆◆◆◆
Star Lane, Great Dunmow,
CM6 1AY
T: (01371) 872641

Rose Cottage ◆◆◆
Pharisee Green, Great Dunmow,
CM6 1JN
T: (01371) 872254

Starr Restaurant with Rooms
◆◆◆◆ SILVER AWARD
Market Place, Great Dunmow,
CM6 1AX
T: (01371) 874321
F: (01371) 876337
E: terry@starrdunmow.co.uk
I: www.zynet.co.uk/menu/starr

GREAT ELLINGHAM
Norfolk

Cannells Farm ◆◆◆
Bow Street, Great Ellingham,
Attleborough, Norfolk NR17 1JA
T: (01953) 454133 &
07836 695303
F: (01953) 454133

Manor Farm
♦♦♦♦ SILVER AWARD
Hingham Road, Great Ellingham,
Attleborough, Norfolk NR17 1JE
T: (01953) 453388
F: (01953) 453388
🌐

GREAT FINBOROUGH
Suffolk

Dairy Farmhouse
♦♦♦♦ SILVER AWARD
Valley Lane, Great Finborough,
Stowmarket, Suffolk IP14 3BE
T: (01449) 615730
F: (01449) 615730

GREAT HOCKHAM
Norfolk

Manor Farm Bed & Breakfast
♦♦♦
Manor Farm, Vicarage Road,
Great Hockham, Thetford,
Norfolk IP24 1PE
T: (01953) 498204

GREAT MAPLESTEAD
Essex

Kent House ♦♦♦♦
Church Street, Great
Maplestead, Halstead, Essex
CO9 2RQ
T: (01787) 460787
F: (01787) 463515

GREAT RYBURGH
Norfolk

The Boar Inn ♦♦♦
Great Ryburgh, Fakenham,
Norfolk NR21 0DX
T: (01328) 829212
E: boarinn@aol.com
I: ourworld.compuserve.
com/homepages/boar_inn

The Meadows ♦♦♦♦
Station Road, Great Ryburgh,
Fakenham, Norfolk NR21 0DX
T: (01328) 829774

GREAT SNORING
Norfolk

Unicorn House
♦♦♦♦ SILVER AWARD
Norwich Road, Great Snoring,
Fakenham, Norfolk NR21 0HR
T: (01328) 820407
🌐

GREAT WALDINGFIELD
Suffolk

Jasmine Cottage ♦♦♦♦
The Heath, Lavenham Road,
Great Waldingfield, Sudbury,
Suffolk CO10 0RN
T: (01787) 374665

Virginia Cottage ♦♦♦
The Heath, Great Waldingfield,
Sudbury, Suffolk CO10 0SA
T: (01787) 370878
F: (01787) 370878
E: virginia-cottage@yahoo.co.
uk

GREAT YARMOUTH
Norfolk

Alexandra Private Hotel ♦♦♦
9 Kent Square, Great Yarmouth,
Norfolk NR30 2EX
T: (01493) 853115

Barnard House
♦♦♦♦ SILVER AWARD
2 Barnard Crescent, Great
Yarmouth, Norfolk NR30 4DR
T: (01493) 855139
F: (01493) 843143
E: barnardhouse@btinternet.
com
I: wwwbtinternet.
com/§barnardhouse/

Chatsworth Hotel ♦♦
32 Wellesley Road, Great
Yarmouth, Norfolk NR30 1EU
T: (01493) 842890
F: (01493) 843284

Cleaswood Private Hotel ♦
55 Wellesley Road, Great
Yarmouth, Norfolk NR30 1EX
T: (01493) 843960

The Edwardian Hotel ♦♦
18-20 Crown Road, Great
Yarmouth, Norfolk NR30 2JN
T: (01493) 856482
E: sandy@eaglemont.freeserve.
co.uk
I: www.edwardianhotel.co.uk

Fjaerland Hotel ♦♦
24-25 Trafalgar Road, Great
Yarmouth, Norfolk NR30 2LD
T: (01493) 856339 &
0780 3859951
F: (01493) 856339
🌐

Kingsley House Hotel ♦♦
68 King Street, Great Yarmouth,
Norfolk NR30 2PP
T: (01493) 850948

Midland Hotel ♦♦♦
7-9 Wellesley Road, Great
Yarmouth, Norfolk NR30 2AP
T: (01493) 330046 &
07850 047999
F: (01493) 330046

New Beach Hotel ♦♦♦
Marine Parade, Great Yarmouth,
Norfolk NR30 2EJ
T: (01493) 332300
F: (01493) 331880

Oasis Hotel ♦♦
Tower Building, Marine Parade,
Great Yarmouth, Norfolk
NR30 2EW
T: (01493) 855281
F: (01493) 330697

Royston House ♦♦
11 Euston Road, Great
Yarmouth, Norfolk NR30 1DY
T: (01493) 844680
F: (01493) 844680

Ryecroft Licensed Guesthouse
♦♦♦
91 North Denes Road, Great
Yarmouth, Norfolk NR30 4LW
T: (01493) 844015 &
07713 815569
F: (01493) 856096
E: lee-van-kassel@compuserve.
com

Shadingfield Lodge
♦♦♦♦ SILVER AWARD
Marine Parade, Great Yarmouth,
Norfolk NR30 3JG
T: (01493) 843915 & 847200
F: (01493) 847206
E: shadlodge@aol.com
I: www.shadingfieldlodge.co.uk

Southern Hotel ♦♦♦
46 Queens Road, Great
Yarmouth, Norfolk NR30 3JR
T: (01493) 843313
F: (01493) 853047
E: southern.hotel@tinyonline.
co.uk

Sunnydene Hotel ♦♦♦
83 North Denes Road, Great
Yarmouth, Norfolk NR30 4LW
T: (01493) 843554 & 332391
F: (01493) 332391
E: davidatsunnydene@aol.com
I: www.s-h.systems.co.
uk/hotels/sunnyden.htm/

Taunton House Hotel ♦♦♦
9 Nelson Road South, Great
Yarmouth, Norfolk NR30 3JL
T: (01493) 850043
E: taunton@wilkinsonb.
fsbusiness.co.uk
🌐

Trotwood Private Hotel ♦♦♦
2 North Drive, Great Yarmouth,
Norfolk NR30 1ED
T: (01493) 843971
E: richard@trotwood.fsbusiness.
co.uk

The Waverley Hotel
Rating Applied For
32-37 Princes Road, Great
Yarmouth, Norfolk NR30 2DG
T: (01493) 842508
F: (01493) 842508
E: malcolm@waverley-hotel.co.
uk
I: www.waverley-hotel.co.uk

GRISTON
Norfolk

Park Farm Bed & Breakfast
Rating Applied For
Park Farm, Caston Road, Griston,
Thetford, Norfolk IP25 6QD
T: (01953) 483020 &
07974 772485
F: (01953) 483056
🌐

HADDISCOE
Norfolk

Brook House ♦♦♦♦
Aldeby Road, Haddiscoe,
Norwich NR14 6PQ
T: (01502) 677772

Plantation House ♦♦♦♦
Rectory Road, Haddiscoe,
Norwich NR14 6PG
T: (01502) 677778

HADLEIGH
Suffolk

Edgehall Hotel ♦♦♦♦
2 High Street, Hadleigh, Ipswich
IP7 5AP
T: (01473) 822458
F: (01473) 827751

Mount Pleasant Farm ♦♦♦
Offton, Ipswich IP8 4RP
T: (01473) 658896 &
(01282) 445444

Odds and Ends House ♦♦♦
131 High Street, Hadleigh,
Ipswich, Suffolk IP7 5EG
T: (01473) 822032 & 829825
F: (01473) 829816
E: gordonranson@aol.com
🚶

Weavers ♦♦♦♦
25 High Street, Hadleigh,
Ipswich IP7 5AG
T: (01473) 827247 & 823185
F: (01473) 822802
E: cyndymiles@aol.com
I: www.weaversrestaurant.co.uk

The White Hart ♦♦♦
46 Bridge Street, Hadleigh,
Ipswich IP7 6DB
T: (01473) 822206
I: www.whiteharthadleigh.co.uk

HALESWORTH
Suffolk

The Croft ♦♦♦
Ubbeston Green, Halesworth,
Suffolk IP19 0HB
T: (01986) 798502 &
0771 2414274

Stradbroke Town Farm ♦♦♦♦
Westhall, Halesworth, Suffolk
IP19 8NY
T: (01502) 575204

HALSTEAD
Essex

The Dog Inn ♦♦♦
37 Hedingham Road, Halstead,
Essex CO9 2DB
T: (01787) 477774
F: (01787) 474754

Hedingham Antiques Bed &
Breakfast ♦♦♦
100 Swan Street, Sible
Hedingham, Halstead, Essex
CO9 3HP
T: (01787) 460360
F: (01787) 460360
E: patriciapatterson@totalise

Timbers ♦♦♦
Cross End, Pebmarsh, Halstead,
Essex CO9 2NT
T: (01787) 269330

Townsford Mill ♦♦♦♦
Mill House, The Causeway,
Halstead, Essex CO9 1ET
T: (01787) 474451
F: (01787) 473893
E: stukey@freeserve.co.uk
I: townsford.freeserve.co.uk.

HALVERGATE
Norfolk

School Lodge Country
Guesthouse ♦♦♦♦
Marsh Road, Halvergate,
Norwich, Norfolk NR13 3QB
T: (01493) 700111 & 700808
F: (01493) 700808

HAPPISBURGH
Norfolk

Cliff House Guesthouse
Teashop and Restaurant ♦♦♦
Beach Road, Happisburgh,
Norwich, Norfolk NR12 0PP
T: (01692) 650775

Manor Farmhouse ♦♦♦
Happisburgh, Norwich
NR12 0SA
T: (01692) 651262 & 650220
I: www.broadland.
com/manorfarmhouse

HARDWICK
Cambridgeshire

Wallis Farm ♦♦♦♦
98 Main Street, Hardwick,
Cambridge CB3 7QU
T: (01954) 210347
F: (01954) 210988
E: wallisfarm@mcmail.com

625

HARLESTON
Suffolk

Green Farmhouse ◆◆◆◆
Harleston, Stowmarket, Suffolk
IP14 3HW
T: (01449) 736841
F: (01449) 736894
E: grnfarm@globalnet.co.uk

Weston House Farm ◆◆◆
Mendham, Harleston, Norfolk
IP20 0PB
T: (01986) 782206 &
07803 099203
F: (01986) 782414
E: holden@farmline.com
◎

HARPENDEN
Hertfordshire

Acacia House ◆◆◆
81 Luton Road, Harpenden,
Hertfordshire AL5 3BA
T: (01582) 460402 & 0797 116
2226
F: (01582) 461174
E: elaine@rowsell04.freeserve.
co.uk

Hall Barn ◆◆◆◆
20 Sun Lane, Harpenden,
Hertfordshire AL5 4EU
T: (01582) 769700

**The Laurels Guest House
◆◆◆◆**
22 Leyton Road, Harpenden,
Hertfordshire AL5 2HU
T: (01582) 712226
F: (01727) 712226

Milton Hotel ◆◆◆
25 Milton Road, Harpenden,
Hertfordshire AL5 5LA
T: (01582) 762914

HARSTON
Cambridgeshire

Hoffers Brook Farm ◆◆◆
Royston Road, Harston,
Cambridge CB2 5NJ
T: (01223) 870065
E: smcgr62117@yahoo.co.uk

HARTEST
Suffolk

Giffords Hall ◆◆◆
Hartest, Bury St Edmunds,
Suffolk IP29 4EX
T: (01284) 830464
F: (01284) 830964
E: inquiries@giffordshall.co.uk
I: www.giffordshall.co.uk

**The Hatch
◆◆◆◆◆ SILVER AWARD**
Pilgrims Lane, Cross Green,
Hartest, Bury St Edmunds,
Suffolk IP29 4ED
T: (01284) 830226
F: (01284) 830226

HARWICH
Essex

New Farm House ◆◆◆
Spinnels Lane, Wix,
Manningtree, Essex CO11 2UJ
T: (01255) 870365
F: (01255) 870837
E: barrie.winch@which.net

**Oceanview
Rating Applied For**
86 Main Road, Dovercourt,
Harwich, Essex CO13 1LH
T: (01255) 554078 &
07801 689002
F: (01255) 554519
E: oceanview@dovercourt.org.
uk
I: www.oceanview.fsbusiness.co.
uk

Paston Lodge ◆◆◆
1 Una Road, Parkeston, Harwich,
Essex CO12 4PP
T: (01255) 551390 &
07867 888498
F: (01255) 551390
E: dwright@globalnet.co.uk

Queens Hotel
119 High Street, Dovercourt,
Harwich, Essex CO12 3AP
T: (01255) 502634

HATFIELD BROAD OAK
Essex

**The Cottage
Rating Applied For**
Dunmow Road, Hatfield Broad
Oak, Hertfordshire CM22 7JJ
T: (01279) 718230

HATFIELD HEATH
Essex

**Hunters' Meet Restaurant and
Hotel
Rating Applied For**
Chelmsford Road, Hatfield
Heath, Bishop's Stortford,
Hertfordshire CM22 7BQ
T: (01279) 730549
F: (01279) 731587
E: info@huntersmeet.co.uk
I: www.huntersmeet.co.uk

HAUGHLEY
Suffolk

Red House Farm ◆◆◆◆
Station Road, Haughley,
Stowmarket, Suffolk IP14 3QP
T: (01449) 673323
F: (01449) 675413
E: mary@noy1.fsnet.co.uk
I: www.farmstayanglia.co.uk
◎

HEACHAM
Norfolk

**Allington Bed and Breakfast
◆◆◆◆**
10 Neville Road, Heacham,
King's Lynn, Norfolk PE31 7HB
T: (01485) 571148

Ash Tree House ◆◆◆
20a Lords Lane, Heacham, King's
Lynn, Norfolk PE31 7DJ
T: (01485) 571540

Holly House ◆◆◆
3 Broadway, Heacham, King's
Lynn, Norfolk PE31 7DF
T: (01485) 572935

Saint Annes Guesthouse ◆◆◆
53 Neville Road, Heacham,
King's Lynn, Norfolk PE31 7HB
T: (01485) 570021
F: (01485) 570021
I: www.smoothhound.co.uk/

HELLESDON
Norfolk

**The Old Corner Shop
Guesthouse ◆◆◆**
26 Cromer Road, Hellesdon,
Norwich, Norfolk NR6 6LZ
T: (01603) 419000
F: (01603) 419000

HELPSTON
Cambridgeshire

Helpston House ◆◆◆◆
Helpston, Peterborough PE6 7DX
T: (01733) 252190
F: (01733) 253853
E: orton.helpstonhouse@
btinternet.com
I: www.helpstonhouse.co.uk

HEMEL HEMPSTEAD
Hertfordshire

Alexandra Guesthouse ◆◆
40/42 Alexandra Road, Hemel
Hempstead, Hertfordshire
HP2 5BP
T: (01442) 242897
F: (01442) 211829
E: alexhous@aol.com

HENGRAVE
Suffolk

Minstrels ◆◆◆
Bury Road, Hengrave, Bury St
Edmunds, Suffolk IP28 6LT
T: (01284) 703677 &
07788 148337
F: (01284) 703677

HETHEL
Norfolk

Old Thorn Barn ◆◆◆◆
Corporation Farm, Wymondham
Road, Hethel, Norwich
NR14 8EU
T: (01953) 607785
F: (01953) 607785
E: oldthornbarn@tinyonline.co.
uk
I: www.oldthornbarn.co.uk

HETHERSETT
Norfolk

Magnolia House ◆◆◆
Cromwell Close, Hethersett,
Norfolk NR9 3HD
T: (01603) 810749
F: (01603) 810749

HEVINGHAM
Norfolk

Marsham Arms Inn ◆◆◆◆
Holt Road, Hevingham, Norwich
NR10 5NP
T: (01603) 754268
F: (01603) 754839
E: m.arms@paston.co.uk
I: www.marshamarms.co.uk
◎

HILGAY
Norfolk

**Crosskeys Riverside Hotel
◆◆◆**
Bridge Street, Hilgay, Downham
Market, Norfolk PE38 0LD
T: (01366) 387777

HINTLESHAM
Suffolk

College Farm ◆◆◆◆
Hintlesham, Ipswich IP8 3NT
T: (01473) 652253
F: (01473) 652253
E: bryce1@agripro.co.uk
◎

HITCHAM
Suffolk

Pansy Cottage ◆◆◆
The Causeway, Hitcham, Ipswich
IP7 7NE
T: (01449) 740858

HITCHIN
Hertfordshire

The Greyhound ◆◆◆
London Road, St Ippolyts,
Hitchin, Hertfordshire SG4 7NL
T: (01462) 440989

The Lord Lister Hotel ◆◆◆
1 Park Street, Hitchin,
Hertfordshire SG4 9AH
T: (01462) 432712 & 459451
F: (01462) 438506

HOLBROOK
Suffolk

**Highfield
◆◆◆ GOLD AWARD**
Harkstead Road, Holbrook,
Ipswich IP9 2RA
T: (01473) 328250
F: (01473) 328250

HOLT
Norfolk

Hempstead Hall ◆◆◆◆
Holt, Norfolk NR25 6TN
T: (01263) 712224 &
07721 827246
F: (01263) 710137
I: www.broadland.
com/hempsteadhall

Lawns Hotel ◆◆◆◆
Station Road, Holt, Norfolk
NR25 6BS
T: (01263) 713390
E: lawnshotel.norfolk@
btinternet.com
I: www.lawnshotel.co.uk

HOLTON
Suffolk

Blythwood House ◆◆◆
Beccles Road, Holton,
Halesworth, Suffolk IP19 8NQ
T: (01986) 873379 &
07967 143618

HOLTON ST MARY
Suffolk

Stratford House ◆◆◆◆
Holton St Mary, Colchester
CO7 6NT
T: (01206) 298246
F: (01206) 298246
E: fjs.stratho@quista.net

HONINGTON
Suffolk

North View Guesthouse ◆◆
North View, Malting Row,
Honington, Bury St Edmunds,
Suffolk IP31 1RE
T: (01359) 269423

HORSEY
Norfolk

The Old Chapel ◆◆◆◆
Horsey Corner, Horsey, Norfolk
NR29 4EH
T: (01493) 393498
F: (01493) 393444
E: rectoryh@aol.com
I: www.hitelregister.co.
uk/hotel/oldrectory.asp
⚘

HORSFORD
Norfolk
Lower Farm B&B
◆◆◆◆ SILVER AWARD
Lower Farm, Horsford, Norwich
NR10 3AW
T: (01603) 891291

HORSTEAD
Norfolk
Beverley Farm ◆◆◆
Norwich Road, Horstead,
Norwich NR12 7EH
T: (01603) 737279

HOVETON
Norfolk
The Beehive ◆◆◆
Riverside Road, Hoveton,
Wroxham, Norwich NR12 8UD
T: (01603) 784107
F: (01603) 784107

HUNSTANTON
Norfolk
Avocet House ◆◆◆
44 Greevegate, Hunstanton,
Norfolk PE36 6AG
T: (01485) 533118

Burleigh Hotel ◆◆◆◆
7 Cliff Terrace, Hunstanton,
Norfolk PE36 6DY
T: (01485) 533080

Cobblers Cottage ◆◆◆
3 Wodehouse Road, Old
Hunstanton, Hunstanton,
Norfolk PE36 6JD
T: (01485) 534036

Eccles Cottage ◆◆◆
Heacham Road, Sedgeford,
Hunstanton, Norfolk PE36 5LU
T: (01485) 572688
E: mike99.barker@virgin.net
I: www.mike99.barker@virgin.
net

Fieldsend House ◆◆◆◆
Homefields Road, Hunstanton,
Norfolk PE36 5HL
T: (01485) 532593
F: (01485) 532593
◎

The Gables ◆◆◆◆
28 Austin Street, Hunstanton,
Norfolk PE36 6AW
T: (01485) 532514

Garganey House ◆◆◆
46 Northgate, Hunstanton,
Norfolk PE36 6DR
T: (01485) 533269

Gate Lodge ◆◆◆
2 Westgate, Hunstanton,
Norfolk PE36 5AL
T: (01485) 533549
F: (01485) 533579
E: sagemo2206@talk21.com

Gemini Lodge ◆◆◆
5 Alexandra Road, Hunstanton,
Norfolk PE36 5BT
T: (01485) 533902
F: (01485) 533902

Glenberis ◆◆◆◆
6 St Edmunds Avenue,
Hunstanton, Norfolk PE36 6AY
T: (01485) 533663

Kiama Cottage Guesthouse
◆◆◆
23 Austin Street, Hunstanton,
Norfolk PE36 6AN
T: (01485) 533615

Lakeside ◆◆◆
Waterworks Road, Old
Hunstanton, Hunstanton,
Norfolk PE36 6JE
T: (01485) 533763

Miramar Guesthouse ◆◆◆
7 Boston Square, Hunstanton,
Norfolk PE36 6DT
T: (01485) 532902 & 0771 202
3134

Oriel Lodge
◆◆◆◆ SILVER AWARD
24 Homefields Road,
Hunstanton, Norfolk PE36 5HJ
T: (01485) 532368
F: (01485) 535737
E: info@oriellodge.co.uk
I: www.oriellodge.co.uk

Peacock House ◆◆◆
28 Park Road, Hunstanton,
Norfolk PE36 5BY
T: (01485) 534551

Queensbury House ◆◆◆
18 Glebe Avenue, Hunstanton,
Norfolk PE36 6BS
T: (01485) 534320

Rosamaly Guesthouse ◆◆◆
14 Glebe Avenue, Hunstanton,
Norfolk PE36 6BS
T: (01485) 534187

The Shelbrooke Hotel ◆◆◆
9 Cliff Terrace, Hunstanton,
Norfolk PE36 6DY
T: (01485) 532289
F: (01485) 535385
I: www.shelbrooke.force9.co.uk

Sunningdale Hotel ◆◆◆
3-5 Avenue Road, Hunstanton,
Norfolk PE36 5BW
T: (01485) 532562
F: (01485) 534915
E: reception@sunningdalehotel.
com

**Troon Cottage Bed and
Breakfast** ◆◆
4 Victoria Avenue, Hunstanton,
Norfolk PE36 6BX
T: (01485) 533290 &
0800 654321

HUNTINGDON
Cambridgeshire
Prince of Wales ◆◆◆◆
Potton Road, Hilton,
Huntingdon, Cambridgeshire
PE28 9NG
T: (01480) 830257
F: (01480) 830257
E: princeof wales.hilton@talk21.
com

ICKLETON
Cambridgeshire
Hessett Grange ◆◆◆◆
60 Frogge Street, Ickleton,
Saffron Walden, Essex CB10 1SH
T: (01799) 530300

IKEN
Suffolk
The Studio ◆◆◆
Fazeboons, Iken, Woodbridge,
Suffolk IP12 2AY
T: (01728) 689095

INGOLDISTHORPE
Norfolk
Goldcrest
Rating Applied For
4 Sandy Lane, Ingoldisthorpe,
King's Lynn, Norfolk PE31 6NN
T: (01485) 544681

IPSWICH
Suffolk
Anglesea Hotel ◆◆
10 Oban Street, Ipswich, IP1 3PH
T: (01473) 255630 & 254278
F: (01473) 255630

Carlton Hotel ◆◆
41-43 Berners Street, Ipswich,
Suffolk IP1 3LN
T: (01473) 254955
F: (01473) 211145
E: carlton@hotmail.com

The Gatehouse Hotel Ltd
◆◆◆◆◆ SILVER AWARD
799 Old Norwich Road, Ipswich,
IP1 6LH
T: (01473) 741897
F: (01473) 744236
E: info@gatehousehotel.co.uk
I: www.gatehousehotel.co.uk

231 Humber Doucy Lane ◆◆◆
Ipswich, Suffolk IP4 3PE
T: (01473) 402664

Lattice Lodge Guest House
◆◆◆◆ SILVER AWARD
499 Woodbridge Road, Ipswich,
IP4 4EP
T: (01473) 712474 &
07931 737663
F: (01473) 272239
E: lattice.lodge@btinternet.com
I: www.netcomuk.co.
uk/§dcbright/lattice.lodge.html

Redholme ◆◆◆◆
52 Ivry Street, Ipswich, IP1 3QP
T: (01473) 250018 & 233174
E: johnmcneilredholmeipswich.
freeserve.co.uk

Sidegate Guesthouse
◆◆◆◆ SILVER AWARD
121 Sidegate Lane, Ipswich,
IP4 4JB
T: (01473) 728714
F: (01473) 728714

Stebbings ◆◆◆◆
Back Lane, Washbrook, Ipswich,
Suffolk IP8 3JA
T: (01473) 730216 &
0780 3642040
E: carolinefox@netscapeline.co.
uk

KEDINGTON
Suffolk
The White House
◆◆◆◆◆ GOLD AWARD
Silver Street, Kedington,
Haverhill, Suffolk CB9 7QG
T: (01440) 707731 &
07778 986693
F: (01440) 707731

KELSALE
Suffolk
Fir Tree Farm ◆◆
Kelsale, Saxmundham, Suffolk
IP17 2RH
T: (01728) 668356

Mile Hill Barn
◆◆◆◆◆ SILVER AWARD
Main Road, Kelsale,
Saxmundham, Suffolk IP17 2RG
T: (01728) 668519
E: richard@milehillbarn.
freeserve.co.uk
I: www.milehillbarn.freeserve.co.
uk

KELVEDON
Essex
Highfields Farm ◆◆◆
Kelvedon, Colchester CO5 9BJ
T: (01376) 570334
F: (01376) 570334
◎

KERSEY
Suffolk
Fair View
◆◆◆◆ SILVER AWARD
Priory Hill, Kersey, Ipswich,
Suffolk IP7 6DU
T: (01473) 828606 &
07798 841707
F: (01473) 828602
E: f.view.kersey@lineone.net

Red House Farm ◆◆◆
Wickerstreet Green, Kersey,
Ipswich IP7 6EY
T: (01787) 210245

KETTLEBASTON
Suffolk
Box Tree Farm ◆◆◆
Kettlebaston, Ipswich IP7 7PZ
T: (01449) 741318
F: (01449) 741318

KETTLEBURGH
Suffolk
Rookery Farm ◆◆◆
Framlingham Road, Kettleburgh,
Woodbridge, Suffolk IP13 7LL
T: (01728) 723248
I: bazin@btinternet.com

KING'S LYNN
Suffolk
The Beeches Guesthouse ◆◆
2 Guanock Terrace, King's Lynn,
Norfolk PE30 5QT
T: (01553) 766577
F: (01553) 776664

Fairlight Lodge ◆◆◆◆
79 Goodwins Road, King's Lynn,
Norfolk PE30 5PE
T: (01553) 762234
F: (01553) 770280
E: penny.rowe@lineone.net
◎

Flint's Hotel ◆◆
73 Norfolk Street, King's Lynn,
Norfolk PE30 1AD
T: (01553) 769400 & 0780 100
4870

Hall Farm Bed & Breakfast ◆
Shouldham Thorpe, King's Lynn,
Norfolk PE33 0DP
T: (01366) 347940 &
07768 208673
F: (01366) 347946
E: hallfarm@freenetname.co.uk
I: www.
hall-farmbedandbreakfast.co.uk

**Maranatha-Havana
Guesthouse** ◆◆◆
115-117 Gaywood Road, King's
Lynn, Norfolk PE30 2PU
T: (01553) 774596 & 772331
F: (01553) 763747

Marsh Farm ◆◆◆◆
Wolferton, King's Lynn, Norfolk
PE31 6HB
T: (01485) 540265
F: (01485) 543143
E: keith.larrington@farmline.
com
I: www.members.farmline.
com/keith

The Old Rectory ◆◆◆◆
33 Goodwins Road, King's Lynn,
Norfolk PE30 5QX
T: (01553) 768544

KINGS LANGLEY
Hertfordshire
Woodcote House ◆◆◆
7 The Grove, Whippendell,
Chipperfield, Kings Langley,
Hertfordshire WD4 9JF
T: (01923) 262077
F: (01923) 266198
E: leveridge@btinternet.com

KIRBY CANE
Norfolk
Butterley House ◆◆◆
Leet Hill Farm, Kirby Cane,
Bungay, Suffolk NR35 2HJ
T: (01508) 518301
F: (01508) 518224

LANGHAM
Essex
Oak Apple Farm ◆◆◆◆
Greyhound Hill, Langham,
Colchester CO4 5QF
T: (01206) 272234
E: rosie@helliwell@excite.com.
uk
I: www.smoothhound.co.
uk/hotels/oak.html

LAVENHAM
Suffolk
Anchor House
◆◆◆◆ SILVER AWARD
27 Prentice Street, Lavenham,
Sudbury, Suffolk CO10 9RD
T: 01787) 249018 &
07974 212629
E: suewade@tinyworld.co.uk

Angel Gallery ◆◆◆◆
17 Market Place, Lavenham,
Sudbury, Suffolk CO10 9QZ
T: (01787) 248417
F: (01787) 248417
E: angel-gallery@gofornet.co.uk
I: www.angel-gallery@gofornet.
co.uk

Angel Hotel ◆◆◆◆
Market Place, Lavenham,
Sudbury, Suffolk CO10 9QZ
T: (01787) 247388
F: (01787) 248344
E: angellav@aol.com
I: www.lavenham.co.uk/angel

Brett Farm ◆◆◆◆
The Common, Lavenham,
Sudbury, Suffolk CO10 9PG
T: (01787) 248533

Greenview ◆◆◆
48 The Glebe, Lavenham,
Sudbury, Suffolk CO10 9SN
T: (01787) 248587

Hill House Farm ◆◆◆◆
Preston St Mary, Lavenham,
Sudbury, Suffolk CO10 9LT
T: (01787) 247571
F: (01787) 247571

The Island House ◆◆◆◆
Lower Road, Lavenham,
Sudbury, Suffolk CO10 9QJ
T: (01787) 248181
E: islandhouse@dial.pipex.com
I: lavenham.co.uk/islandhouse/

Lavenham Great House Hotel
◆◆◆◆ SILVER AWARD
Market Place, Lavenham,
Sudbury, Suffolk CO10 9QZ
T: (01787) 247431
F: (01787) 248007
E: info@greathouse.co.uk
I: www.greathouse.co.uk

Lavenham Priory
◆◆◆◆◆ GOLD AWARD
Water Street, Lavenham,
Sudbury, Suffolk CO10 9RW
T: (01787) 247404
F: (01787) 248472
E: mail@lavenhampriory.co.uk
I: www.lavenhampriory.co.uk

Mortimer's Barn
◆◆◆◆ SILVER AWARD
Preston St Mary, Lavenham,
Sudbury, Suffolk CO10 9ND
T: (01787) 248231 & 248075
F: (01787) 248075
E: mervyn@mortimers.
freeserve.co.uk
I: www.diggins.co.uk/mortimers/

The Red House ◆◆◆◆
29 Bolton Street, Lavenham,
Sudbury, Suffolk CO10 9RG
T: (01787) 248074 &
07885 536148
I: www.lavenham.co.
uk/redhouse

Sunrise Cottage ◆◆◆
32 The Glebe, Sudbury Road,
Lavenham, Sudbury, Suffolk
CO10 9SN
T: (01787) 248439 &
07778 709964
E: deallen@talk21.com

Sunset House ◆◆◆
3 The Glebe, Lavenham, Sudbury,
Suffolk CO10 9SN
T: (01787) 247979
E: ctreve,cyrtus@talk21.com

Wood Hall ◆◆◆◆
Little Waldingfield, Lavenham,
Sudbury, Suffolk CO10 0SY
T: (01787) 247362
F: (01787) 248326
E: nisbett@nisbett.enta.net
I: www.nisbett.enta.net

LAXFIELD
Suffolk
The Villa Stables ◆◆◆◆
The Villa, High Street, Laxfield,
Woodbridge, Suffolk IP13 8DU
T: (01986) 798019
F: (01986) 798019
E: laxfieldleisure@talk21.com

Watersmeet ◆◆◆◆
Chestnut Tree Farm,
Framlingham Road, Laxfield,
Woodbridge, Suffolk IP13 8DH
T: (01986) 798880
F: (01986) 798880
E: info@watersmeet.co.uk
I: www.watersmeet.co.uk

LEAVENHEATH
Suffolk
**The Stoke by Nayland Club
Hotel**
Rating Applied For
Keepers Lane, Leavenheath,
Colchester, Essex CO6 4PZ
T: (01206) 262836
F: (01206) 263356
E: info@golf-club.co.uk
I: www.stokebynaylandclub.co.
uk

LEIGH-ON-SEA
Essex
The Grand Hotel ◆◆◆
The Broadway, Leigh-on-Sea,
Essex SS9 1PJ
T: (01702) 710768
F: (01702) 710709

52 Undercliff Gardens ◆◆◆
Leigh-on-Sea, Essex SS9 1EA
T: (01702) 474984 &
07967 788873

LEISTON
Suffolk
Field End
◆◆◆◆ SILVER AWARD
1 Kings Road, Leiston, Suffolk
IP16 4DA
T: (01728) 833527
F: (01728) 833527
E: pwright@field-end.freeserve.
co.uk
I: www.field-end.freeserve.co.uk

LESSINGHAM
Norfolk
The Seafarers ◆◆◆◆
North Gap Eccles Beach,
Lessingham, Norwich NR12 0SW
T: (01692) 598218 &
07798 900061

LEVINGTON
Suffolk
Lilac Cottage ◆◆◆◆
Levington Green, Levington,
Ipswich, Suffolk IP10 0LE
T: (01473) 659509

LINTON
Cambridgeshire
Springfield House ◆◆◆◆
16 Horn Lane, Linton, Cambridge
CB1 6HT
T: (01223) 891383
F: (01223) 890335
I: www.smoothhound.co.
uk/hotels/springf2.html

LITTLE BADDOW
Essex
Chestnuts ◆◆◆
Chestnut Walk, Little Baddow,
Chelmsford CM3 4SP
T: (01245) 223905

LITTLE BEALINGS
Suffolk
10 Michaels Mount ◆◆◆
Little Bealings, Woodbridge,
Suffolk IP13 6LS
T: (01473) 610466

Timbers ◆◆◆
Martlesham Road, Little
Bealings, Woodbridge, Suffolk
IP13 6LY
T: (01473) 622713

LITTLE CANFIELD
Essex
Canfield Moat
◆◆◆◆◆ SILVER AWARD
High Cross Lane West, Little
Canfield, Dunmow, Essex
CM6 1TD
T: (01371) 872565 &
07785 384648
F: (01371) 876264
E: vfalk@compuserve.com

LITTLE HALLINGBURY
Hertfordshire
Little Hallingbury Mill
Rating Applied For
Old Mill Lane, Gaston Green,
Little Hallingbury, Bishop's
Stortford, Hertfordshire
CM22 7QT
T: (01279) 726554
F: (01279) 724162
I: www.littlehallingburymill.net

LITTLE SAMPFORD
Essex
Bush Farm
Rating Applied For
Little Sampford, Saffron Walden,
Essex CB10 2RY
T: (01799) 586636 &
07702 955290
E: aimreso@iname.com

Woodlands
◆◆◆◆ SILVER AWARD
Hawkins Hill, Little Sampford,
Saffron Walden, Essex
CB10 2QW
T: (01371) 810862 &
07885 637283

LITTLE WALSINGHAM
Norfolk
The Old Bakehouse
◆◆◆◆ SILVER AWARD
33 High Street, Little
Walsingham, Walsingham,
Norfolk NR22 6BZ
T: (01328) 820454
F: (01328) 820454
E: chris@cpadley.freeserve.co.uk

St David's House ◆◆
Friday Market, Little
Walsingham, Walsingham,
Norfolk NR22 6BY
T: (01328) 820633 &
07710 044452

LITTLE WALTHAM
Essex
Little Belsteads ◆◆◆◆
Back Lane, Little Waltham,
Chelmsford CM3 3PP
T: (01245) 360249
F: (01245) 360996

Windmill Motor Inn
Rating Applied For
Chatham Green, Little Waltham,
Chelmsford CM3 3LE
T: (01245) 361188
F: (01245) 362992
E: chris@a131windmill.essex@
virginnet

LITTLEBURY
Essex
Queens Head Inn ◆◆◆
High Street, Littlebury, Saffron
Walden, Essex CB11 4TD
T: (01799) 522251
F: (01799) 522251

LODDON
Norfolk
Poplar Farm ◆◆◆
Sisland, Loddon, Norwich,
Norfolk NR14 6EF
T: (01508) 520706
E: milly@hemmant.myhome.
org.uk
I: www.hemmant.myhome.org.
uk

LONDON COLNEY
Hertfordshire
The Conifers ◆◆◆
42 Thamesdale, London Colney,
St Albans, Hertfordshire AL2 1TL
T: (01727) 823622

LONG MELFORD
Suffolk
The Crown Hotel ◆◆◆
Hall Street, Long Melford,
Sudbury, Suffolk CO10 9JL
T: (01787) 377666
F: (01787) 379005

The George & Dragon ◆◆◆◆
Long Melford, Sudbury, Suffolk
CO10 9JB
T: (01787) 371285
F: (01787) 312428
E: geodrg.@ mail.globalnet.co.
uk

High Street Farmhouse ◆◆◆◆
Long Melford, Sudbury, Suffolk
CO10 9BD
T: (01787) 375765 &
07710 893116
F: (01787) 375765
E: anroy@lineone.net
I: www.longmelford.co.uk/index.
html

Perseverance Hotel ◆◆
Station Road, Long Melford,
Sudbury, Suffolk CO10 9HN
T: (01787) 375862

LONG STRATTON
Norfolk
Greenacres Farm ◆◆◆◆
Woodgreen, Long Stratton,
Norwich NR15 2RR
T: (01508) 530261
F: (01508) 530261

LOUGHTON
Essex
Forest Edge ◆◆◆
61 York Hill, Loughton, Essex
IG10 1HZ
T: (020) 8508 9834
F: (020) 8281 1894

9 Garden Way ◆◆◆
Loughton, Essex IG10 2SF
T: (020) 8508 6134

LOWER LAYHAM
Suffolk
Badgers ◆◆◆◆
Rands Road, Lower Layham,
Ipswich IP7 5RW
T: (01473) 823396 &
07774 184613
E: catbadgers@aol.com

LOWESTOFT
Suffolk
Albany Hotel ◆◆◆
400 London Road South,
Lowestoft, Suffolk NR33 0BQ
T: (01502) 574394
F: (01502) 581198
E: geoffrey.ward@btclick.com
I: www.albany.lowestoft.org.uk

Church Farm ◆◆◆◆◆
Corton, Lowestoft, Suffolk
NR32 5HX
T: (01502) 730359
F: (01502) 733426
E: medw149227@aol.com

Fairways Guesthouse ◆◆◆
398 London Road South,
Lowestoft, Suffolk NR33 0BQ
T: (01502) 572659
E: amontali@netmatters.co.uk

Hall Farm ◆◆◆◆
Jay Lane, Church Lane, Lound,
Lowestoft, Suffolk NR32 5LJ
T: (01502) 730415
E: josephashley@compuserve.
com

Longshore Guesthouse ◆◆◆
7 Wellington Esplanade,
Lowestoft, Suffolk NR33 0QQ
T: (01502) 565037
F: (01502) 582032
E: longshore@7wellington.
fsnet.co.uk

Oak Farm ◆◆◆
Market Lane, Blundeston,
Lowestoft, Suffolk NR32 5AP
T: (01502) 731622

Royal Court Hotel ◆◆
146 London Road South,
Lowestoft, Suffolk NR33 0AZ
T: (01502) 568901 & 585400
F: (01502) 568901

Somerton House ◆◆◆
7 Kirkley Cliff, Lowestoft, Suffolk
NR33 0BY
T: (01502) 565665
F: (01502) 501176
E: reception@somerton.
screaming.net
I: www.members.tripod.co.
uk/somerton/somerton.html

LUDHAM
Norfolk
Malthouse Farmhouse ◆◆◆
Malthouse Lane, Ludham, Great
Yarmouth, Norfolk NR29 5QL
T: (01692) 678747
F: (01692) 678747
E: lynn@demon.co.uk
I: www.whiteswan.u-net.
com/malthouse

LUTON
Bedfordshire
Adara Lodge ◆◆◆
539 Hitchin Road, Luton,
LU2 7UL
T: (01582) 731361

The Pines Hotel ◆◆◆
10 Marsh Road, Luton,
Bedfordshire LU3 3NH
T: (01582) 651130 & 651140
F: (01582) 615182
E: pineshotelluton@aol.com
I: www.pineshotel.com

44 Skelton Close ◆◆
Barton Hills, Luton, LU3 4HF
T: (01582) 495205

MALDON
Essex
Anchor Guesthouse
Rating Applied For
7 Church Street, Maldon, Essex
CM9 5HW
T: (01621) 855706
F: (01621) 850405

Barges Galore ◆◆◆
28 The Hythe, Maldon, Essex
CM9 5HN
T: (01621) 853520

Hilly Pool House ◆◆◆◆
14 North Street, Maldon, Essex
CM9 5HL
T: (01621) 853885
F: (01621) 853885

Jolly Sailor ◆◆
Hythe Quay, Maldon, Essex
CM9 5HP
T: (01621) 853463
F: (01621) 840253

The Limes
Rating Applied For
21 Market Hill, Maldon, Essex
CM9 4PZ
T: (01621) 850350 &
07714 551227

4 Lodge Road ◆◆◆
Maldon, Essex CM9 6HW
T: (01621) 858736

The Swan Hotel ◆◆
73 High Street, Maldon, Essex
CM9 5EP
T: (01621) 853170
F: (01621) 854490
E: john@swanhotel.freeserve.
co.uk
I: swanhotel_maldon.co.uk

**Wilsons Motel & Bed and
Breakfast** ◆◆
154 High Street, Maldon, Essex
CM9 5BX
T: (01621) 853667 & 851850
F: (01621) 851850

MANNINGTREE
Essex
Aldhams ◆◆◆◆
Bromley Road, Lawford,
Manningtree, Essex CO11 2NE
T: (01206) 393210 &
07626 299136
F: (01206) 393210
E: coral.mcewen3@which.net

MARCH
Cambridgeshire
Woodpecker Cottage ◆◆◆
20 Kingswood Road, March,
Cambridgeshire PE15 9RT
T: (01354) 660188
E: johnliz.spencer@talk21.com
I: www.smoothhound.co.
uk/hotel/woodpecker.html

MARGARET RODING
Essex
Garnish Hall ◆◆◆◆
Margaret Roding, Dunmow,
Essex CM6 1QL
T: (01245) 231209 & 231224
F: (01708) 741172

Greys ◆◆◆
Ongar Road, Margaret Roding,
Dunmow, Essex CM6 1QR
T: (01245) 231509

MARKYATE
Hertfordshire
Beechwood Home Farm ◆◆◆
Markyate, St Albans,
Hertfordshire AL3 8AJ
T: (01582) 840209

MARSHAM
Norfolk
Plough Inn ◆◆◆
Old Norwich Road, Marsham,
Norwich, Norfolk NR10 5PS
T: (01263) 735000

MARSTON MORETAINE
Bedfordshire
The White Cottage ◆◆◆◆
Marston Hill, Marston
Moretaine, Bedford MK43 0QJ
T: (01234) 751766 &
0830 554778
F: (01234) 751766

MESSING
Essex
Crispin's Restaurant ◆◆◆◆
The Street, Messing, Colchester
CO5 9TR
T: (01621) 815868
E: crispins@messing77.
freeserve.co.uk
I: www.crispinsrestaurant.co.uk

MIDDLETON
Suffolk
Rose Farm ◆◆◆◆
Middleton, Saxmundham,
Suffolk IP17 3NG
T: (01728) 648456 &
07885 194945

MILDENHALL
Suffolk
Oakland House
Rating Applied For
9 Mill Street, Mildenhall, Bury St
Edmunds, Suffolk IP28 7DP
T: (01638) 717099
F: (01638) 714852
E: lardnerjk@eggconnect.net
I: www.oaklandhouse.co.uk

Pear Tree House
◆◆◆◆ SILVER AWARD
Chapel Road, West Row,
Mildenhall, Bury St Edmunds,
Suffolk IP28 8PA
T: (01638) 711112
F: (01638) 711112
E: peartree@hello.to
I: www.peartree.hello.to.

MILTON BRYAN
Bedfordshire
Town Farm ◆◆◆◆
Milton Bryan, Milton Keynes
MK17 9HS
T: (01525) 210001
F: (01525) 210001

MISTLEY
Essex
Thorn Hotel ◆◆◆
High Street, Mistley,
Manningtree, Essex CO11 1HE
T: (01206) 392821
F: (01206) 392133

MUCH HADHAM
Hertfordshire
Sidehill House ◆◆◆◆
Much Hadham, SG10 6DS
T: (01279) 843167

MUNDESLEY
Norfolk

Newlands ♦♦♦♦
31 Trunch Road, Mundesley,
Norwich NR11 8JU
T: (01263) 720205
F: (01263) 720205
E: newlands@mcmail.com

Overcliff Lodge ♦♦♦
46 Cromer Road, Mundesley,
Norwich NR11 8DB
T: (01263) 720016
I: www.broadland.
com/overclifflodge/

MUNDFORD
Norfolk

Colveston Manor ♦♦♦♦
Mundford, Thetford, Norfolk
IP26 5HU
T: (01842) 878218
F: (01842) 878218
I: www.farmstayanglia.co.uk

NARBOROUGH
Norfolk

Park Cottage ♦
Narford Road, Narborough,
King's Lynn, Norfolk PE32 1HZ
T: (01760) 337220

NAYLAND
Suffolk

Gladwins Farm ♦♦♦♦
Harpers Hill, Nayland,
Colchester, Suffolk CO6 4NU
T: (01206) 262261
F: (01206) 263001
E: gladwinsfarm@compuserve.
com
I: www/gladwinsfarm.co.uk

Hill House ♦♦♦♦
Gravel Hill, Nayland, Colchester
CO6 4JB
T: (01206) 262782
E: heigham.hillhouse@ie-mail.
co.uk

The White Hart Inn
♦♦♦♦ SILVER AWARD
High Street, Nayland, Colchester,
Essex CO6 4JF
T: (01206) 263382
F: (01206) 263638
E: nayhart@aol.com
I: www.whitehart-nayland.co.uk

NEATISHEAD
Norfolk

Allens Farmhouse ♦
Three Hammer Common,
Neatishead, Norwich NR12 8XW
T: (01692) 630080

The Barton Angler Country Inn
♦♦♦
Irstead Road, Neatishead,
Norwich NR12 8XP
T: (01692) 630740
F: (01692) 631122

Ramblers ♦♦♦
School Lane, Neatishead,
Norwich NR12 8XW
T: (01692) 630864

Regency Guesthouse ♦♦♦♦
The Street, Neatishead, Norwich
NR12 8AD
T: (01692) 630233
F: (01692) 630233

NEEDHAM MARKET
Suffolk

The Annex ♦♦♦
17 High Street, Needham
Market, Ipswich IP6 8AL
T: (01449) 720687
F: (01449) 722230

St Eia ♦♦♦♦
All Saints Road, Creeting St
Mary, Needham Market, Ipswich
IP6 8PP
T: (01449) 721977

NEWMARKET
Suffolk

2 Birdcage Walk
♦♦♦♦ GOLD AWARD
Newmarket, Suffolk CB8 0NE
T: (01638) 669456
F: (01638) 669456

NORTH FAMBRIDGE
Essex

Ferry Boat Inn ♦♦♦
North Fambridge, Chelmsford,
Essex CM3 6LR
T: (01621) 740208

NORTH LOPHAM
Norfolk

Church Farm House
♦♦♦♦ SILVER AWARD
North Lopham, Diss, Norfolk
IP22 2LP
T: (01379) 687270
F: (01379) 687270
E: b&tb@bassetts.demon.co.uk
I: www.bassetts.demon.co.
uk/cfhmain.htm

NORTH WALSHAM
Norfolk

Pinetrees ♦♦♦♦
45 Happisburgh Road, North
Walsham, Norfolk NR28 9HB
T: (01692) 404213
F: (01692) 404213

Tollgate Farmhouse ♦♦♦
Off Norwich Road, North
Walsham, Norfolk NR28 0JB
T: (01692) 406572
F: (01692) 406582
E: jrc-ltd@freenet.co.uk

NORTH WOOTTON
Norfolk

Red Cat Hotel ♦♦♦
Station Road, North Wootton,
King's Lynn, Norfolk PE30 3QH
T: (01553) 631244 & 631574
F: (01553) 631574
E: enquiries@redcathotel.
demon.co.uk
I: www.redcathotel.demon.co.uk

NORWICH
Norfolk

The Abbey Hotel ♦♦♦
16 Stracey Road, Thorpe Road,
Norwich, NR1 1EZ
T: (01603) 612915
F: (01603) 612915

Arbor Linden Lodge ♦♦♦♦
Linden House, 557 Earlham
Road, Norwich, Norfolk
NR4 7HW
T: (01603) 451303
F: (01603) 250641
E: linden@guesthouses.uk.com
I: www.linden.freeuk.com

Arrow Guest House ♦♦
2 Britannia Road, Norwich,
NR1 4HP
T: (01603) 628051

Aylwyne House ♦♦♦
59 Aylsham Road, Norwich,
NR3 2HF
T: (01603) 665798

Becklands ♦♦♦
105 Holt Road, Horsford,
Norwich NR10 3AB
T: (01603) 898582
F: (01603) 754223

**Hotel Belmonte and Belmonte
Restaurant♦♦♦**
60-62 Prince of Wales Road,
Norwich, NR1 1LT
T: (01603) 622533
F: (01603) 760805
E: bar7seven@yahoo.com
I: www.geocities.
com/bar7seven/

**Blue Cedar Lodge Guesthouse
♦♦♦**
391 Earlham Road, Norwich,
NR2 3RQ
T: (01603) 458331 &
07836 792659

Cavell House ♦♦♦
Swardeston, Norwich NR14 8DZ
T: (01508) 578195

**Church Farm Guesthouse
♦♦♦**
Church Street, Horsford,
Norwich NR10 3DB
T: (01603) 898020 & 898582
F: (01603) 891649

Conifers Hotel ♦♦♦
162 Dereham Road, Norwich,
NR2 3AH
T: (01603) 628737

Earlham Guesthouse ♦♦♦♦
147 Earlham Road, Norwich,
NR2 3RG
T: (01603) 454169
F: (01603) 454169
E: earlhamgh@hotmail.com

Eaton Bower ♦♦♦
20 Mile End Road, Norwich,
NR4 7QY
T: (01603) 462204
F: (01603) 462204
E: eaton-bower@hotmail.com

Edmar Lodge ♦♦♦
64 Earlham Road, Norwich,
NR2 3DF
T: (01603) 615599
F: (01603) 495599

Elm Farm Country House
♦♦♦♦
55 Norwich Road, St Faiths,
Norwich NR10 3HH
T: (01603) 898366
F: (01603) 897129

Fuchsias Guesthouse ♦♦♦
139 Earlham Road, Norwich,
NR2 3RG
T: (01603) 451410
F: (01603) 259696

The Gables Guesthouse ♦♦♦♦
527 Earlham Road, Norwich,
NR4 7HN
T: (01603) 456666
F: (01603) 250320

Grange Hotel ♦♦
230 Thorpe Road, Norwich,
NR1 1TJ
T: (01603) 434734
F: (01603) 434734

**Harvey House Guesthouse
♦♦♦**
50 Harvey Lane, Norwich,
NR7 0AQ
T: (01603) 436575
F: (01603) 436575
E: harveyhouse@which.net

Kingsley Lodge ♦♦♦
3 Kingsley Road, Norwich,
NR1 3RB
T: (01603) 615819
F: (01603) 615819
E: kingsley@paston.co.uk

The Limes ♦♦
188 Unthank Road, Norwich,
NR2 2AH
T: (01603) 454282 &
0771 3026517

Marlborough House Hotel ♦♦
22 Stracey Road, Norwich,
NR1 1EZ
T: (01603) 628005
F: (01603) 628005

**Mousehold Lodge Guesthouse
♦♦♦**
53 Mousehold Lane, Norwich,
Norfolk NR7 8HL
T: (01603) 426026 & 413009
F: (01603) 413009
E: mousehold.lodge
I: www.mousehold-lodge.co.uk

The Old Rectory
♦♦♦♦ SILVER AWARD
Hall Road, Framingham Earl,
Norwich NR14 7SB
T: (01508) 493590
E: brucewellings@drivedevice.
freeserve.co.uk

Rosedale ♦♦
145 Earlham Road, Norwich,
NR2 3RG
T: (01603) 453743 &
07771 873089
F: (01603) 259887
E: drcbac@aol.com.
I: members@aol.com/drcbac

Wedgewood House ♦♦♦
42 St Stephens Road, Norwich,
NR1 3RE
T: (01603) 625730
F: (01603) 615035

Witton Hall Farm ♦♦♦
Witton, North Walsham, Norfolk
NR13 5DN
T: (01603) 714580
I: www.wittonhall@cwcom.net

OCCOLD
Suffolk

The Cedars Guesthouse ♦♦♦♦
Church Street, Occold, Eye,
Suffolk IP23 7PS
T: (01379) 678439

OLD CATTON
Norfolk

Catton Old Hall
♦♦♦♦♦ SILVER AWARD
Lodge Lane, Old Catton, Norwich
NR6 7HG
T: (01603) 419379
F: (01603) 400339
E: enquiries@catton-hall.co.uk
I: catton-hall.co.uk

ORSETT
Essex

The Larches ◆◆◆
Rectory Road, Orsett, Grays,
Essex RM16 3EH
T: (01375) 891217 &
07778 873612
F: (01375) 891747

ORTON LONGUEVILLE
Cambridgeshire

Orton Mere Guest House ◆◆◆
547 Oundle Road, Orton
Longueville, Peterborough
PE2 7DH
T: (01733) 708432
F: (01733) 708425

OULTON
Suffolk

Laurel Farm ◆◆◆◆
Hall Lane, Oulton, Lowestoft,
Suffolk NR32 5DL
T: (01502) 568724 &
(01788) 147758
F: (01502) 568724
E: laurelfarm@hodgkin.
screaming.net

OVERSTRAND
Norfolk

Danum House ◆◆◆
22 Pauls Lane, Overstrand,
Cromer, Norfolk NR27 0PE
T: (01263) 579327
F: (01263) 579327

PAKEFIELD
Suffolk

Pipers Lodge Hotel & Motel
◆◆◆
41 London Road, Pakefield,
Lowestoft, Suffolk NR33 7AA
T: (01502) 569805
F: (01502) 565383

PALGRAVE
Suffolk

Brambley House ◆◆◆
Lion Road, Palgrave, Diss,
Norfolk IP22 1AL
T: (01379) 641666

The Paddocks B & B ◆◆◆
3 The Paddocks, Palgrave, Diss,
Norfolk IP22 1AG
T: (01379) 642098 & 640518
F: (01379) 642098
E: rod@rodjones.force9.co.uk
I: www.rodjones.force9.co.uk

PAMPISFORD
Cambridgeshire

**South Cambridgeshire
Guesthouse** ◆◆◆
2 and 4 London Road,
Pampisford, Cambridge, CB2 4EF
T: (01223) 834523 &
07971 073758
F: (01223) 570379
E: south.cambs@lineone.net

PEASENHALL
Suffolk

Sibton White Horse ◆◆
Halesworth Road, Sibton,
Peasenhall, Saxmundham,
Suffolk IP17 2JJ
T: (01728) 660337 &
07889 393097

PELDON
Essex

**Sampsons Farm & Country
House** ◆◆◆◆ SILVER AWARD
Sampsons Lane, Peldon,
Colchester, Essex CO5 7QS
T: (01206) 735100
F: (01206) 735027

PETERBOROUGH
Cambridgeshire

Aaron Park Hotel ◆◆◆
109 Park Road, Peterborough,
PE1 2TR
T: (01733) 564849 & 752491
F: (01733) 564849

The Anchor Lodge ◆◆◆
28 Percival Street, Peterborough,
PE3 6AU
T: (01733) 312724 &
07767 611911

Aragon House ◆◆◆
75-77 London Road,
Peterborough, PE2 9BS
T: (01733) 563718
F: (01733) 563718
I: ww.aragonhouse.co.uk

Blue Wisteria House ◆◆◆
Church Lane, Helpston,
Peterborough PE6 7DT
T: (01733) 252272

The Brandon ◆◆◆
161 Lincoln Road, Peterborough,
PE1 2PW
T: (01733) 568631
F: (01733) 568631
I: www.
peterboroughaccommodation.
co.uk

The Charlotte House Hotel ◆◆
78 London Road, Peterborough,
Cambridgeshire PE2 9BP
T: (01733) 315870 &
07979 776201
F: (01733) 315870

Clarks
Rating Applied For
19 Oundle Road, Peterborough,
PE2 9PB
T: (01733) 342482

Courtyard Cottage ◆◆◆◆
2 West End, Langtoft,
Peterborough, PE6 9LS
T: (01778) 348354
F: (01778) 348354
E: david_tinegate@ic24.net
I: www.courtyardcottage.8m.
com/

The Graham Guesthouse ◆◆◆
296 Oundle Road, Peterborough,
Cambridgeshire PE2 9QA
T: (01733) 567824
F: (01733) 567824

Hawthorn House ◆◆◆◆
89 Thorpe Road, Peterborough,
PE3 6JQ
T: (01733) 340608 & 313470
F: (01733) 763800

Longueville Guesthouse
◆◆◆◆
411 Oundle Road, Orton
Longueville, Peterborough,
PE2 7DA
T: (01733) 233442 &
07703 540059
F: (01733) 233442

Montana ◆◆◆
15 Fletton Avenue,
Peterborough, PE2 8AX
T: (01733) 567917
F: (01733) 567917
I: www.stilwell.co.uk

Park Road Guesthouse ◆◆◆
67 Park Road, Peterborough,
Cambridgeshire PE1 2TN
T: (01733) 562220

Stoneacre ◆◆◆◆
Elton Road, Wansford,
Peterborough PE8 6JT
T: (01780) 783283 &
07802 720379
F: (01780) 783283

PETTISTREE
Suffolk

The Three Tuns Coaching Inn
Rating Applied For
Main Road, Pettistree,
Woodbridge, Suffolk IP13 0HW
T: (01728) 747979 & 746244
F: (01728) 746244
E: jon@threetuns-coachinginn.
co.uk
I: www.threetuns-coachinginn.
co.uk

PLAYFORD
Suffolk

Glenham ◆◆◆
Hill Farm Road, Playford,
Ipswich, Suffolk IP6 9DU
T: (01473) 624939 & 410115
E: glenham@tesco.net
I: www.glenham.hypermart.net

POLSTEAD
Suffolk

Polstead Lodge ◆◆◆◆
Mill Street, Polstead, Suffolk
CO6 5AD
T: (01206) 262196

POTTER HEIGHAM
Norfolk

Falgate Inn ◆◆◆
Main Road, Potter Heigham,
Great Yarmouth, Norfolk
NR29 5HZ
T: (01692) 670003 &
07899 847262
E: cypress@euphony.net

POTTERS BAR
Hertfordshire

Bruggen Lodge ◆◆◆◆
13 The Drive, Potters Bar,
Hertfordshire EN6 2AP
T: (01707) 655904 & 665070
F: (01707) 857287
E: xtraguard@lineone.uk.

PULHAM MARKET
Norfolk

The Old Bakery
◆◆◆◆ GOLD AWARD
Church Walk, Pulham Market,
Diss, Norfolk IP21 4SJ
T: (01379) 676492
F: (01379) 676492

QUIDENHAM
Norfolk

Manor Farm ◆◆◆
Quidenham, Norwich, Norfolk
NR16 2NY
T: (01953) 887540
F: (01953) 887540
E: jennypilgrim@supanet.com

RACKHEATH
Norfolk

Barn Court ◆◆◆
6 Back Lane, Rackheath,
Norwich, Norfolk NR13 6NN
T: (01603) 782536
F: (01603) 782536

RAMSHOLT
Suffolk

The Ramsholt Arms ◆◆◆
Dock Road, Ramsholt,
Woodbridge, Suffolk IP12 3AB
T: (01394) 411229
F: (01394) 411818

RAVENSDEN
Bedfordshire

Tree Garth ◆◆◆
Church End, Ravensden, Bedford
MK44 2RP
T: (01234) 771745
F: (01234) 771745

REEDHAM
Norfolk

Briars ◆◆◆◆
10 Riverside, Reedham, Norwich
NR13 3TF
T: (01493) 700054
F: (01493) 700054

RENDHAM
Suffolk

Rendham Hall ◆◆◆
Rendham, Saxmundham, Suffolk
IP17 2AW
T: (01728) 663440
F: (01728) 663245
E: strachan@anglianet.co.uk

RETTENDON
Essex

Crossways ◆◆◆
Main Road, Rettendon Common,
Chelmsford CM3 8DY
T: (01245) 400539
F: (01245) 400127
E: crossways@somnific.
freeserve.co.uk

RICKINGHALL
Suffolk

The Bell Inn ◆◆◆◆
The Street, Rickinghall, Diss,
Norfolk IP22 1BN
T: (01379) 898445

RIDLINGTON
Norfolk

Mill Common House ◆◆◆◆
Mill Common Road, Ridlington,
North Walsham, Norfolk
NR28 9TY
T: (01692) 650792
F: (01692) 651480
E: johnpugh@millcommon.
freeserve.co.uk
I: www.broadland.
com/millcommon

RIVENHALL
Essex

**Rickstones Farmhouse Bed &
Breakfast ♦♦♦♦**
Rickstones Farmhouse,
Rickstones Road, Rivenhall,
Witham, Essex CM8 3HQ
T: (01376) 514351
F: (01376) 514351

ROXTON
Bedfordshire

**Church Farm
♦♦♦♦ SILVER AWARD**
41 High Street, Roxton, Bedford
MK44 3EB
T: (01234) 870234
F: (01234) 870234

ROYDON
Essex

**Roydon Motel
Rating Applied For**
Roydon Mill Leisure Park,
Roydon, Harlow, Essex CM19 5EJ
T: (01279) 792777 & 792695
E: motel@roydonpark.com
I: www.roydonpark.com

ROYSTON
Hertfordshire

Hall Farm ♦♦♦♦
Great Chishill, Royston,
Hertfordshire SG8 8SH
T: (01763) 838263
F: (01763) 838263
E: wisehall@farming.co.uk

RUMBURGH
Suffolk

Rumburgh Farm ♦♦♦
Rumburgh, Halesworth, Suffolk
IP19 0RU
T: (01986) 781351
F: (01986) 781351
E: binder@rumburghfarm.
freedserve.co.uk
I: www.rumburghfarm.freeserve.
co.uk

SAFFRON WALDEN
Essex

Archway Guesthouse ♦♦♦♦
Archway House, Church Street,
Saffron Walden, Essex CB10 1JW
T: (01799) 501500 &
0780 1555435
F: (01799) 501500

Ashleigh House ♦♦♦
7 Farmadine Grove, Saffron
Walden, Essex CB11 3DR
T: (01799) 513611
E: deborah@anngilder.fsnet.co.
uk

The Bell House ♦♦♦♦
53-55 Castle Street, Saffron
Walden, Essex CB10 1BD
T: (01799) 527857

**Bridge End Orchard
♦♦♦♦♦ GOLD AWARD**
Bridge Street, Saffron Walden,
Essex CB10 1BT
T: (01799) 522001
F: (01799) 524576
E: beo@btinternet.com

The Cricketers ♦♦♦♦
Clavering, Saffron Walden, Essex
CB11 4QT
T: (01799) 550442
F: (01799) 550882
E: cricketers@lineone.net
I: www.thecricketers.co.uk

11 Dawson Close ♦♦♦
Saffron Walden, Essex CB10 2AR
T: (01799) 528491

1 Gunters Cottages ♦♦♦♦
Thaxted Road, Saffron Walden,
Essex CB10 2UT
T: (01799) 522091

30 Lambert Cross ♦♦
Saffron Walden, Essex CB10 2DP
T: (01799) 527287

Oak House ♦♦♦
40 Audley Road, Saffron
Walden, Essex CB11 3HD
T: (01799) 523290 &
07802 705555
E: anthony@awaj.freeserve.co.
uk

**The Plough Inn at Radwinter
♦♦♦**
Sampford Road, Radwinter,
Saffron Walden, Essex CB10 2TL
T: (01799) 599222 & 599161
F: (01799) 599161

Pudding House ♦♦♦
9a Museum Street, Saffron
Walden, Essex CB10 1JL
T: (01799) 522089

Redgates Farmhouse ♦♦♦♦
Redgate Lane, Sewards End,
Saffron Walden, Essex CB10 2LP
T: (01799) 516166

Rockells Farm ♦♦♦♦
Duddenhoe End, Saffron
Walden, Essex CB11 4UY
T: (01763) 838053

Rowley Hill Lodge ♦♦♦♦
Little Walden, Saffron Walden,
Essex CB10 1UZ
T: (01799) 525975
F: (01799) 516622
E: eh@clara.net

Saffron Lodge ♦♦♦♦
11 Mount Pleasant Road,
Saffron Walden, Essex CB11 3EA
T: (01799) 522179

10 Victoria Avenue ♦♦
Saffron Walden, Essex CB11 3AE
T: (01799) 525923

Yardley's ♦♦♦♦
Orchard Pightle, Hadstock,
Cambridge, Essex CB1 6PQ
T: (01223) 891822
F: (01223) 891822

SAHAM TONEY
Norfolk

Cranford House ♦♦♦♦
Ovington Road, Saham Toney,
Thetford, Norfolk IP25 7HF
T: (01953) 885292
F: (01953) 885611
E: dsf@anstruthers.com
I: www.anstruthers.
com/cranfordhouse

ST ALBANS
Hertfordshire

5 Approach Road ♦♦
St Albans, Hertfordshire AL1 1SP
T: (01727) 852471 & 858571
E: nigelcocks@compuserve.com

22 Ardens Way ♦♦♦
St Albans, Hertfordshire AL4 9UJ
T: (01727) 861986

Avona ♦♦♦
478 Hatfield Road, St Albans,
Hertfordshire AL4 0SX
T: (01727) 842216 &
07956 857353

Black Lion Inn ♦♦♦
198 Fishpool Street, St Albans,
Hertfordshire AL3 4SB
T: (01727) 851786
F: (01727) 859243

Braemar House ♦♦♦♦
89 Salisbury Avenue, St Albans,
Hertfordshire AL1 4TY
T: (01727) 839641
F: (01727) 839641

55 Charmouth Road ♦♦♦
St Albans, Hertfordshire AL1 4SE
T: (01727) 860002
E: terry@charmouthfsnet.co.uk

**35 Chestnut Drive
Rating Applied For**
St Albans, Hertfordshire AL4 0ER
T: (01727) 833401

5 Cunningham Avenue ♦♦♦
St Albans, Hertfordshire AL1 1JJ
T: (01727) 857388

Fern Cottage ♦♦♦♦
116 Old London Road, St Albans,
Hertfordshire AL1 1PU
T: (01727) 834200 &
07957 484349
F: (01727) 834200
I: www.ferncottage.cjb.net

Fleuchary House ♦♦♦♦
3 Upper Lattimore Road, St
Albans, Hertfordshire AL1 3UD
T: (01727) 766764

4 Green Lane ♦♦♦
St Albans, Hertfordshire
AL3 6HA
T: (01727) 830538 & 0777 551
1130

32 Gurney Court Road ♦♦♦
St Albans, AL1 4RL
T: (01727) 835819 & 760250
E: the-salisburys@cwcom.net

8 Hall Place Gardens ♦♦♦
St Albans, Hertfordshire AL1 3SP
T: (01727) 858939

2 The Limes ♦♦♦
Spencer Gate, St Albans,
Hertfordshire AL1 4AT
T: (01727) 831080
E: hunter.mitchell@virgin.net

178 London Road ♦♦♦
St Albans, Hertfordshire AL1 1PL
T: (01727) 846726 & 831267
F: (01727) 843898

7 Marlborough Gate ♦♦♦
St Albans, Hertfordshire AL1 3TX
T: (01727) 865498 &
07767 236122
F: (01727) 812965
E: michael.johnson@btinternet.
com

Park House ♦♦♦
30 The Park, St Albans,
Hertfordshire AL1 4RY
T: (01727) 832054

**36 Potters Field
Rating Applied For**
St Albans, Hertfordshire AL3 6LJ
T: (01727) 766840 &
07790 452920
F: (01727) 766840
E: manners-smith@compuserve

56 Sandpit Lane ♦♦♦♦
St Albans, Hertfordshire
AL1 4BW
T: (01727) 856799
F: (01727) 856799

Tresco ♦♦♦♦
76 Clarence Road, St Albans,
AL1 4NG
T: (01727) 864880
F: (01727) 864880
E: pat.leggatt@talk21.com

The White House ♦♦
28 Salisbury Avenue, St Albans,
Hertfordshire AL1 4TU
T: (01727) 861017

Wren Lodge ♦♦♦
24 Beaconsfield Road, St Albans,
Hertfordshire AL1 3RB
T: (01727) 855540 &
07836 285196
F: (01727) 766674
E: wreb.lodge@ukonline.co.uk
I: www.destination-england.co.
uk/wrenlodge.html

16 York Road ♦♦♦
St Albans, Hertfordshire AL1 4PL
T: (01727) 853647

ST NEOTS
Cambridgeshire

The Nags Head Hotel ♦♦♦
2 Berkley Street, Eynesbury, St
Neots, Huntingdon,
Cambridgeshire PE19 2NA
T: (01480) 476812
F: (01480) 391881

SALHOUSE
Norfolk

Oldfield ♦♦♦♦
Vicarage Road, Salhouse,
Norwich NR13 6HA
T: (01603) 781080
F: (01603) 781083

SANDY
Bedfordshire

**Highfield Farm
♦♦♦♦♦ SILVER AWARD**
Great North Road, Sandy,
Bedfordshire SG19 2AQ
T: (01767) 682332
F: (01767) 692503

Village Farm ♦♦
Thorncote Green, Sandy,
Bedfordshire SG19 1PU
T: (01767) 627345

SAWTRY
Cambridgeshire

A1 Bed & Breakfast ♦
5 High Street, Sawtry,
Peterborough PE17 5SR
T: (01487) 830201
F: (01487) 830201

SAXLINGHAM
Norfolk

**The Map House
♦♦♦♦ GOLD AWARD**
The Map House, Smokers Hole,
Saxlingham, Holt, Norfolk
NR25 7JU
T: (01263) 741304
F: (01263) 741304
E: the.maphouse@virgin.net

SAXLINGHAM THORPE
Norfolk

Foxhole Farm ♦♦♦♦
Windy Lane, Foxhole,
Saxlingham Thorpe, Norwich
NR15 1UG
T: (01508) 499226
F: (01508) 499226
E: foxholefarm@hotmail.com

SAXMUNDHAM
Suffolk

Kiln Farm ♦♦♦♦
Kiln Lane, Benhall,
Saxmundham, Suffolk IP17 1HA
T: (01728) 603166

Lime Tree House B&B ♦♦♦
Benhall Green, Saxmundham,
Suffolk IP17 1HU
T: (01728) 602149

North Lodge
♦♦♦♦♦ SILVER AWARD
6 North Entrance, Saxmundham,
Suffolk IP17 1AY
T: (01728) 603337
E: northlodgetoto@aol.com

Stratford Hall
♦♦♦♦ SILVER AWARD
Stratford St Andrew,
Saxmundham, Suffolk IP17 1LH
T: (01728) 602025

Sun Cottage ♦♦♦♦
Snape Road, Knodishall,
Saxmundham, Suffolk IP17 1UT
T: (01728) 833892
F: (01728) 833892
E: suncottage@supanet.com

SAXTEAD
Suffolk

Ivy Farm ♦♦♦♦
The Green, Saxtead, Woodbridge,
Suffolk IP13 9QG
T: (01728) 685621 &
07957 690544
F: (01728) 685621
E: sarahiggins@skynow.net
I: www.ukworld.net/ivyfarm.htm

Ivy Forge ♦♦♦♦
The Green, Saxtead, Woodbridge,
Suffolk IP13 9QG
T: (01728) 685054
F: (01728) 6865054
E: george@ivyforge.freeserve.
co.uk

SCOTTOW
Norfolk

Holmwood House ♦♦♦♦
Tunstead Road, Scottow,
Norwich NR10 5DA
T: (01692) 538386
F: (01692) 538386
E: enquiries@norfolkbroads.
com
I: www.norfolkbroads.
com/holmwood

SCULTHORPE
Norfolk

**Manor Farm Bed & Breakfast
♦♦♦♦**
Manor Farm, Sculthorpe,
Fakenham, Norfolk NR21 9NJ
T: (01328) 862185
F: (01328) 862033

SHERINGHAM
Norfolk

Achimota ♦♦♦
31 North Street, Sheringham,
Norfolk NR26 8LW
T: (01263) 822379
I: www.broadland.com/achimota
☺

Alverstone
Rating Applied For
33 The Avenue, Sheringham,
Norfolk NR26 8DG
T: (01263) 825527

**The Bay Leaf Guest House
♦♦♦**
10 St Peters Road, Sheringham,
Norfolk NR26 8QY
T: (01263) 823779
F: (01263) 820041

Camberley Guesthouse ♦♦♦
62 Cliff Road, Sheringham,
Norfolk NR26 8BJ
T: (01263) 823101
F: (01263) 821433

Holly Cottage ♦♦♦♦
14a The Rise, Sheringham,
Norfolk NR26 8QB
T: (01263) 822807
F: (01263) 824822
E: hollyperks@aol.com

Knollside Lodge ♦♦♦♦
43 Cliff Road, Sheringham,
Norfolk NR26 8BJ
T: (01263) 823320 &
07771 631980
F: (01263) 823320
E: millar@knollside.
free-1online.co.uk
I: www.broadland.
com/knollsidelodge

The Melrose ♦♦♦
9 Holway Road, Sheringham,
Norfolk NR26 8HN
T: (01263) 823299
E: jparsonage@btconnect.com
I: www.themelrsosesheringham.
co.uk

Olivedale Guesthouse ♦♦♦♦
20 Augusta Street, Sheringham,
Norfolk NR26 8LA
T: (01263) 825871 &
0794 1027170
F: (01263) 821104
E: info@olivedale.co.uk
I: www.olivedale.co.uk

Pentland Lodge ♦♦
51 The Avenue, Sheringham,
Norfolk NR26 8DQ
T: (01263) 823533
F: (01263) 823533

Pinecones ♦♦♦♦
70 Cromer Road, Sheringham,
Norfolk NR26 8RT
T: (01263) 824955
F: (01263) 824955

Sheringham Lodge ♦♦♦
50 Cromer Road, Sheringham,
Norfolk NR26 8RS
T: (01263) 821954
F: (01263) 824783
☺

The Two Lifeboats Hotel ♦♦♦
2 The High Street, Sheringham,
Norfolk NR26 8JR
T: (01263) 822401
F: (01263) 823130
E: info@twolifeboats.co.uk
I: www.twolifeboats.co.uk

Westwater Guest House ♦♦
28 Norfolk Road, Sheringham,
Norfolk NR26 8HJ
T: (01263) 822321
F: (01263) 822321
E: westwater@x-stream.co.uk
I: smoothhound.co.uk

SHIMPLING
Suffolk

Gannocks House ♦♦♦♦
Old Rectory Lane, Shimpling,
Bury St Edmunds, Suffolk
IP29 4HG
T: (01284) 830499 &
07702 833240
F: (01284) 830499
E: gannocks-house@lineone.net
I: www.countrybreak.co.uk

SHUDY CAMPS
Cambridgeshire

Old Well Cottage
Rating Applied For
Main Street, Shudy Camps,
Cambridge CB1 6RA
T: (01799) 584387 & 584486
F: (01799) 584486

SIBLE HEDINGHAM
Essex

Brickwall Farm ♦♦♦♦
Queen Street, Sible Hedingham,
Halstead, Essex CO9 3RH
T: (01787) 460329
F: (01787) 460329

Tocat House
Rating Applied For
9 Potter Street, Sible
Hedingham, Halstead, Essex
CO9 3RG
T: (01787) 461942

SIBTON
Suffolk

Church Farm
♦♦♦♦ SILVER AWARD
Yoxford Road, Sibton,
Saxmundham, Suffolk IP17 2LX
T: (01728) 660101
F: (01728) 660102
E: dixons@church-farmhouse.
demon.co.uk

Park Farm ♦♦♦♦
Sibton, Saxmundham, Suffolk
IP17 2LZ
T: (01728) 668324
F: (01728) 668564
E: margaret.gray@btinternet.
com
☺

SLOLEY
Norfolk

Sloley Farm ♦♦♦♦
Sloley, Norwich, Norfolk
NR12 8HJ
T: (01692) 536281
F: (01692) 535162
E: sloley@farmhotel.u-net.com
I: http://www.smoothhound.co.
uk/hotels/sloley/html
☺

SNAPE
Suffolk

Chimneys ♦♦♦
7 Church Road, Snape,
Saxmundham, Suffolk IP17 1SZ
T: (01728) 688453
F: (01728) 688453

Flemings Lodge ♦♦♦♦
Gromford Lane, Snape,
Saxmundham, Suffolk IP17 1RG
T: (01728) 688502
F: (01728) 688502

Keva ♦♦♦
School Hill, Blaxhall,
Woodbridge, Suffolk IP12 2HN
T: (01728) 688036 &
07703 436073

SNETTISHAM
Norfolk

The Rose & Crown ♦♦♦♦
Old Church Road, Snettisham,
King's Lynn, Norfolk PE31 7LX
T: (01485) 541382
F: (01485) 543172

The Round House ♦♦♦♦
131 Lynn Road, Snettisham,
King's Lynn, Norfolk PE31 7QG
T: (01485) 540580
E: ziphy@aol.com

SOUTH LOPHAM
Norfolk

Malting Farm ♦♦♦
Blo' Norton Road, South
Lopham, Diss, Norfolk IP22 2HT
T: (01379) 687201
I: www.farmstayanglia.co.uk

SOUTH WALSHAM
Norfolk

Old Hall Farm ♦♦♦
Newport Road, South Walsham,
Norwich NR13 6DT
T: (01603) 270271 & 270017
F: (01603) 270017
☺

SOUTHEND-ON-SEA
Essex

Atlantis Guest House ♦♦♦♦
63 Alexandra Road, Southend-
on-Sea, SS1 1EY
T: (01702) 332538
F: (01702) 392736

The Bay Guesthouse ♦♦♦♦
187 Eastern Esplanade, Thorpe
Bay, Southend-on-Sea, Essex
SS1 3AA
T: (01702) 588415
E: thebayguesthouse@hotmail.
com

Beaches ♦♦♦♦
192 Eastern Esplanade, Thorpe
Bay, Southend-on-Sea, SS1 3AA
T: (01702) 586124
F: (01702) 588377

Cliffview Guesthouse ♦
8 Clifftown Parade, Southend-
on-Sea, SS1 1DP
T: (01702) 331645

Gladstone Guesthouse
Rating Applied For
40 Hartington Road, Southend-
on-Sea, Essex SS1 2HS
T: (01702) 462776

Haven House Hotel ♦♦
47 Heygate Avenue, Southend-
on-Sea, SS1 2AN
T: (01702) 619246

Lee Villas Guesthouse ◆
1 & 2 Hartington Place,
Southend-on-Sea, Essex
SS1 2HP
T: (01702) 613768 & 317214
E: leevillas@aol.com

The Norman Guesthouse ◆◆
191 Eastern Esplanade, Thorpe
Bay, Southend-on-Sea, SS1 3AA
T: (01702) 585212

Pebbles Guesthouse ◆◆◆◆
190 Eastern Esplanade, Thorpe
Bay, Southend-on-Sea, SS1 3AA
T: (01702) 582329
F: (01702) 582329

Strand Guesthouse ◆◆
165 Eastern Esplanade, Thorpe
Bay, Southend-on-Sea, SS1 2YB
T: (01702) 586611

SOUTHMINSTER
Essex

New Moor Farm ◆◆◆◆
Tillingham Road, Southminster,
Essex CM0 7DS
T: (01621) 772840
F: (01621) 774087

Saxegate Guesthouse ◆◆◆
44 North Street, Southminster,
Essex CM0 7DG
T: (01621) 773180
F: (01621) 774116

SOUTHREPPS
Norfolk

Avalon ◆◆◆◆
Lower Southrepps, Southrepps,
Norwich NR11 8UJ
T: (01263) 834461 &
07833 563005
F: (01263) 834461
E: mokies@msn.com

SOUTHWOLD
Suffolk

Amber House ◆◆◆
24 North Parade, Southwold,
Suffolk IP18 6LT
T: (01502) 723303
E: spring@amberhouse.fsnet.co.
uk
I: www.southwold.blythweb.co.
uk/amber_house/index.htm

The Angel Inn ◆◆◆
39 High Street, Wangford,
Southwold, Suffolk NR34 8RL
T: (01502) 578636
F: (01502) 578535
E: inn@wangford.freeserve.co.
uk
I: www.angel-wangford.co.uk

Avocet House ◆◆◆◆
1 Strickland Place, Southwold,
Suffolk IP18 6HN
T: (01502) 725073
E: barnett@beeb.net
I: www.southwold.blythweb.co.
uk/avocet-house/index.htm

Dunburgh Guesthouse ◆◆◆◆
28 North Parade, Southwold,
Suffolk IP18 6LT
T: (01502) 723253
I: www.southwold.blythweb.co.
uk/dunburgh/index.htm

Lighthouse View ◆◆◆
14 Chester Road, Southwold,
Suffolk IP18 6LN
T: (01502) 724321

Northcliffe Guesthouse
◆◆◆◆
20 North Parade, Southwold,
Suffolk IP18 6LT
T: (01502) 724074 &
07702 588554
F: (01502) 722218
E: northcliffe@southwold5.
ffnet.co.uk
I: www.s-h-systems.co.
uk/hotels/northcli.html

Number Three ◆◆◆◆
3 Cautley Road, Southwold,
Suffolk IP18 6DD
T: (01502) 723611

The Old Vicarage ◆◆◆◆
Wenhaston, Halesworth, Suffolk
IP19 9EG
T: (01502) 478339
F: (01502) 478068
E: theycock@aol.COM

Prospect Place ◆◆◆
33 Station Road, Southwold,
Suffolk IP18 6AX
T: (01502) 722757
E: sally@prospect-place.demon.
co.uk
I: www.prospect-place.demon.
co.uk

Saxon House ◆◆◆
86 Pier Avenue, Southwold,
Suffolk IP18 6BL
T: (01502) 723651

Victoria House ◆◆◆◆
9 Dunwich Road, Southwold,
Suffolk IP18 6LJ
T: (01502) 722317

'No 21' North Parade ◆◆◆
Southwold, Suffolk IP18 6LT
T: (01502) 722573
F: (01502) 724326
E: richard.comrie@cwcom.net

SPORLE
Norfolk

Corfield House
◆◆◆◆ SILVER AWARD
Sporle, Swaffham, Norfolk
PE32 2EA
T: (01760) 723636
E: corfield.house@virgin.net

SPROUGHTON
Suffolk

Express By Holiday Inn Ipswich
◆◆◆◆
Old Hadleigh Road, Sproughton,
Ipswich IP8 3AR
T: (01473) 222279
F: (01473) 222297

Finjaro ◆◆◆◆
Valley Farm Drive, Hadleigh
Road, Sproughton, Ipswich,
Suffolk IP8 3EL
T: 0705 0065465 &
(01473) 652581
F: (01473) 652139
E: jan@finjaro.freeserve.co.uk
I: www.s-h-systems.co.
uk/hotels/finjaro.html

SPROWSTON
Norfolk

Driftwood Lodge ◆◆◆◆
102 Wroxham Road, Sprowston,
Norwich NR7 8EX
T: (01603) 444908
E: johnniekate@driftwood16.
freeserve.co.uk

STALHAM
Norfolk

Bramble House
◆◆◆◆ SILVER AWARD
Cat's Common, Norwich Road,
Smallburgh, Norwich NR12 9NS
T: (01692) 535069
F: (01692) 535069
E: bramblehouse@tesco.net
I: www.norfolkbroads.
com/bramblehouse

Chapelfield Cottage ◆◆◆
Chapelfield, Stalham, Norwich
NR12 9EN
T: (01692) 582173 &
07775 650656
F: (01692) 583009
E: gary@cinqueportsmarine.
freeserve.co.uk
I: www.whiteswan.u-net.com

STAMFORD
Lincolnshire

Abbey House and Coach House
◆◆◆◆
West End Road, Maxey,
Peterborough PE6 9EJ
T: (01778) 344642 & 347499
F: (01778) 342706
E: sales@abbeyhouse.co.uk
I: www.abbeyhouse.co.uk

STANDON
Hertfordshire

Leamington House ◆◆◆
1 Churchfields, Standon, Ware,
Hertfordshire SG11 1QR
T: (01920) 821926

STANSTEAD
Suffolk

The White Hart Inn ◆◆◆
Lower Street, Stanstead,
Sudbury, Suffolk CO10 9AH
T: (01787) 280902 & 280417

STANSTED
Essex

High Trees ◆◆◆
Parsonage Road, Takeley,
Bishop's Stortford, Hertfordshire
CM22 6QX
T: (01279) 871306 &
07767 431491

STANSTED MOUNTFITCHET
Essex

The Laurels Guesthouse ◆◆◆
84 St Johns Road, Stansted
Mountfitchet, Stansted, Essex
CM24 8JS
T: (01279) 813023
F: (01279) 813023

Norman House ◆◆◆
Alsa Street, Stansted
Mountfitchet, Stansted, Essex
CM24 8SX
T: (01279) 812343
F: (01279) 816876
E: david.shepherd@tesco.net

STEBBING
Essex

Motts Cottage
Rating Applied For
High Street, Stebbing, Dunmow,
Essex CM6 3SE
T: (01371) 856633

STEEPLE BUMPSTEAD
Essex

Yew Tree House ◆◆◆
15 Chapel Street, Steeple
Bumpstead, Haverhill, Suffolk
CB9 7DQ
T: (01440) 730364
F: (01440) 730364
E: yewtreehouse@talk21.com

STIBBINGTON
Cambridgeshire

The Sibson Inn
Rating Applied For
A1 Great North Road,
Stibbington, Peterborough
PE8 6ND
T: (01780) 782227
F: (01780) 783071
I: www.oldenglish.co.uk

STOKE-BY-NAYLAND
Suffolk

The Angel Inn
◆◆◆◆ SILVER AWARD
Polstead Street, Stoke-by-
Nayland, Colchester CO6 4SA
T: (01206) 263245
F: (01206) 263373
I: www.angelhotel.com

Ryegate House
◆◆◆◆ GOLD AWARD
Stoke-by-Nayland, Colchester,
Suffolk CO6 4RA
T: (01206) 263679
E: ryegate@lineone.net
I: www.w-h-systems.co.
uk/hotels/ryegate.html

Thorington Hall ◆◆◆
Stoke-by-Nayland, Colchester
CO6 4SS
T: (01206) 337329

STOKE HOLY CROSS
Norfolk

Salamanca Farm ◆◆◆
116-118 Norwich Road, Stoke
Holy Cross, Norwich, Norfolk
NR14 8QJ
T: (01508) 492322
I: www.smoothhound.co.
uk/salamanc.html

STONHAM ASPAL
Suffolk

Morgans ◆◆◆
East End Lane, Stonham Aspal,
Stowmarket, Suffolk IP14 6AS
T: (01449) 711419
E: joanna.hase@btinternet.com
I: www.btinternet.com§joanna.
hase/morgans

STOWMARKET
Suffolk

Gipping Heights Hotel ◆◆◆◆
Creeting Road, Stowmarket,
Suffolk IP14 5BT
T: (01449) 675264

The Three Bears House
Mulberrytree Farm ◆◆◆
Blacksmiths Lane, Middlewood
Green, Stowmarket, Suffolk
IP14 5ET
T: (01449) 711707 &
07711 112114
F: (01449) 711707

Verandah House ♦♦♦
29 Ipswich Road, Stowmarket,
Suffolk IP14 1BD
T: (01449) 676104
F: (01449) 616127
E: verandahs@aol.com
I: www.verandah-house.co.uk

STRETHAM
Cambridgeshire

The Red Lion ♦♦♦
High Street, Stretham, Ely,
Cambridgeshire CB6 3JQ
T: (01353) 648132
F: (01353) 648327

SUDBOURNE
Suffolk

Long Meadows ♦♦♦
Gorse Lane, Sudbourne,
Woodbridge, Suffolk IP12 2BD
T: (01394) 450269

SUDBURY
Suffolk

The Boathouse Hotel ♦♦♦
Ballingdon Bridge, Sudbury,
Suffolk CO10 2DL
T: (01787) 379090
F: (01787) 379090
E: boathousesudbury@
netscapeonline.co

Durham Cottage ♦♦♦♦
Melford Road, Acton, Sudbury,
Suffolk CO10 0BA
T: (01787) 370142

The Hall ♦♦♦♦
Milden, Lavenham, Sudbury,
Suffolk CO10 9NY
T: (01787) 247235
F: (01787) 247235
E: gjb53@dial.pipex.com
I: www.farmstayanglia.co.uk

Lychgate ♦♦♦
45 Clarence Road, Sudbury,
Suffolk CO10 1NJ
T: (01787) 373429
F: (01787) 880494

Old Bull Hotel and Restaurant
♦♦♦
Church Street, Ballingdon,
Sudbury, Suffolk CO10 6BL
T: (01787) 374120
F: (01787) 379044

West House ♦♦♦
59 Ballingdon Street, Sudbury,
Suffolk CO10 2DA
T: (01787) 375033

SUTTON
Cambridgeshire

Anchor Inn ♦♦♦♦
Sutton Gault, Sutton, Ely,
Cambridgeshire CB6 2BD
T: (01353) 778537
F: (01353) 776180
E: anchor_sutton_gault@
compuserve.com

SWAFFHAM
Norfolk

Glebe Bungalow ♦♦♦♦
8a Princes Street, Swaffham,
Norfolk PE37 7BP
T: (01760) 722764 &
07778 163706

Lodge Farm ♦♦♦♦
Castle Acre, King's Lynn, Norfolk
PE32 2BS
T: (01760) 755506
F: (01760) 755103
E: coghill@messages.co.uk

Strattons
♦♦♦♦♦ SILVER AWARD
Strattons, 4 Ash Close,
Swaffham, Norfolk PE37 7NH
T: (01760) 723845
F: (01760) 720458

SWAFFHAM BULBECK
Cambridgeshire

**Black Horse Motel, Public
House and Restaurant** ♦♦♦
High Street, Swaffham Bulbeck,
Cambridge CB5 0HP
T: (01223) 811366

SWAFFHAM PRIOR
Cambridgeshire

Sterling Farm ♦♦♦
Heath Road, Swaffham Prior,
Cambridge CB5 0LA
T: (01638) 741431

SWANTON MORLEY
Norfolk

Park Farm ♦♦♦
Park Farm, Swanton Morley, East
Dereham, Norfolk NR20 4JU
T: (01362) 637457 & 637841
F: (01362) 637987

SWEFFLING
Suffolk

Wayside Bed and Breakfast
♦♦♦♦
Glemham Road, Sweffling,
Saxmundham, Suffolk IP17 2BQ
T: (01728) 663256

TAKELEY
Essex

Jan Smiths B&B ♦♦♦
The Cottage, Jacks Lane, Takeley,
Bishop's Stortford, Hertfordshire
CM22 6NT
T: (01279) 870603
F: (01279) 870603

Joseph's Drive ♦♦
2 Joseph's Drive, The Street,
Takeley, Bishop's Stortford,
Hertfordshire CM22 6QT
T: (01279) 870652 &
07990 671824

Joyners
Rating Applied For
The Street, Takeley, Bishop's
Stortford, Hertfordshire
CM22 6QU
T: (01279) 870944
I: andersonsi.@joyners99.
freeserve.co.uk

Pippins ♦♦
Smiths Green, Takeley, Essex
CM22 6NR
T: (01279) 870369
F: (01279) 871216

TANNINGTON
Suffolk

Tannington Hall ♦♦♦
Tannington, Woodbridge,
Suffolk IP13 7NH
T: (01728) 628226
F: (01728) 628646
E: info@tannington-hall.co.uk
I: www.tannington-hall.co.uk

TERRINGTON ST JOHN
Norfolk

Somerville House ♦♦♦♦
Church Road, Terrington St
John, Wisbech, Cambridgeshire
PE14 7RY
T: (01945) 880952
F: (01945) 880952

THAXTED
Essex

Crossways Guesthouse ♦♦♦♦
32 Town Street, Thaxted,
Dunmow, Essex CM6 2LA
T: (01371) 830348

The Farmhouse Inn ♦♦♦
Monk Street, Thaxted, Great
Dunmow, Essex CM6 2NR
T: (01371) 830864
F: (01371) 831196

Piggots Mill
♦♦♦♦ SILVER AWARD
Watling Lane, Thaxted, Dunmow,
Essex CM6 2QY
T: (01371) 830379
F: (01371) 831309
E: richard.hingston@virgin.net

Recorders House Restaurant
♦♦♦♦
17 Town Street, Thaxted,
Dunmow, Essex CM6 2LD
T: (01371) 830438
F: (01371) 831645
E: recordershouse.co.uk
I: www.recordershouse.co.uk

THEBERTON
Suffolk

The Alders ♦♦♦
Potters Street, Theberton,
Leiston, Suffolk IP16 4RL
T: (01728) 831790
F: (01728) 831790

The Granary ♦♦♦♦
Theberton, Leiston, Suffolk
IP16 4RR
T: (01728) 831633 &
07703 219259
F: (01728) 831633
E: assistant@aldeburghfestivals.
org

THETFORD
Norfolk

East Farm ♦♦♦♦
Euston Road, Barnham,
Thetford, Norfolk IP24 2PB
T: (01842) 890231
F: (01842) 890457

THORNDON
Suffolk

Moat Farm ♦♦♦♦
Thorndon, Eye, Suffolk IP23 7LX
T: (01379) 678437 &
07775 761318
E: gerald@clara.co.uk
I: www.moatfarm.co.uk

THORNHAM
Norfolk

Orchard House ♦♦♦♦
High Street, Thornham,
Hunstanton, Norfolk PE36 6LY
T: (01485) 512259

Rushmeadow ♦♦♦♦
Main Road, Thornham,
Hunstanton, Norfolk PE36 6LZ
T: (01485) 512372

THORNHAM MAGNA
Suffolk

**The Four Horseshoes Country
Inn and Hotel** ♦♦♦
Wickham Road, Thornham
Magna, Eye IP23 7HD
T: (01379) 678777
F: (01379) 678134

THORPE MARKET
Norfolk

Manorwood ♦♦♦
Church Road, Thorpe Market,
Norwich NR11 8UA
T: (01263) 834938

THORPE MORIEUX
Suffolk

Mount Farm House
♦♦♦♦ GOLD AWARD
Thorpe Morieux, Lavenham,
Sudbury, Suffolk IP30 0NQ
T: (01787) 248428
F: (01787) 248428
E: mntfarm@waitrose.com

TIPTREE
Essex

Linden ♦♦♦♦
8 Clarkesmead, Maldon Road,
Tiptree, Colchester, Essex
CO5 0BX
T: (01621) 819737 &
07885 243425
F: (01621) 819737
E: linden.tiptree@aspects.net
I: www.aspects.net/§linden/

TITCHWELL
Norfolk

The Three Horseshoes Inn
♦♦♦
Main Road, Titchwell, Norfolk
PE31 8BB
T: (01485) 210202

TOFT
Cambridgeshire

Orchard Farmhouse ♦♦♦♦
56 Comberton Road, Toft,
Cambridge CB3 7RY
T: (01223) 262309
F: (01223) 263979
E: tebbit.bxb.toft@talk21.com

West View ♦♦♦
6 Hardwick Road, Toft,
Cambridge CB3 7RQ
T: (01223) 263287 & 264202

TOLLESBURY
Essex

Fernleigh ♦♦♦
16 Woodrolfe Farm Lane,
Tollesbury, Maldon, Essex
CM9 8SX
T: (01621) 868245
F: (01621) 868245
E: gill.willson@ntlworld.com
I: homepage.ntlworld.com/gill.
willson

TOLLESHUNT MAJOR
Essex

Mill Lodge ♦♦♦
Mill Lane, Tolleshunt Major,
Maldon, Essex CM9 8YF
T: (01621) 860311

Wicks Manor Farm ♦♦♦♦
Witham Road, Tolleshunt Major,
Maldon, Essex CM9 8JU
T: (01621) 860629
F: (01621) 860629

TRIMLEY ST MARY
Suffolk
Roseberry Cottage ♦♦♦
6 Church Lane, Trimley St Mary,
Felixstowe, Suffolk IP11 0SW
T: (01394) 275794
F: (01394) 284361

UFFORD
Suffolk
Strawberry Hill ♦♦♦♦
Loudham Lane, Ufford,
Woodbridge, Suffolk IP13 6ED
T: (01394) 460252
E: strawberry.hill@ukgateway.
net
I: www.smoothound.co.
uk/hotels/strawber.html

UGGESHALL
Suffolk
Uggeshall Manor Farm ♦♦♦♦
Uggeshall, Southwold, Suffolk
NR34 8BD
T: (01502) 578546
F: (01502) 578560

UPPER SHERINGHAM
Norfolk
Lodge Cottage ♦♦♦♦
Lodge Hill, Upper Sheringham,
Sheringham, Norfolk NR26 8TJ
T: (01263) 821445

UPWELL
Cambridgeshire
The Olde Mill Hotel ♦♦♦♦
Town Street, Upwell, Wisbech,
Cambridgeshire PE14 9AF
T: (01945) 772614
F: (01945) 772614
E: oldemill@lineone

WALBERSWICK
Suffolk
Dickon ♦♦
Main Street, Walberswick,
Southwold, Suffolk IP18 6UX
T: (01502) 724446

WALSHAM-LE-WILLOWS
Suffolk
Wagner Cottage ♦♦
Walsham-le-Willows, Bury St
Edmunds, Suffolk IP31 3AA
T: (01359) 259380

WALTON-ON-THE-NAZE
Essex
The Regency Hotel ♦♦♦
45 The Parade, Walton-on-the-
Naze, Essex CO14 8AS
T: (01255) 676300
F: (01255) 676300

WANGFORD
Suffolk
Poplar Hall ♦♦♦♦
Frostenden Corner, Frostenden,
Wangford, Beccles, Suffolk
NR34 7JA
T: (01502) 578549
I: www.southwold.demon.co.
uk/poplar-hall/index.html

WANSFORD
Cambridgeshire
Cedar House Bed & Breakfast
♦♦♦♦
Cedar House, Riverside Spinney,
Wansford, Peterborough,
Cambridgeshire PE8 6LF
T: (01780) 783062 &
07909 527304
F: (01780) 783062
E: cedarhousebandb@aol.com

The Cross Keys ♦♦♦
21 Elton Road, Wansford,
Peterborough, Cambridgeshire
PE8 6JD
T: (01780) 782266
F: (01780) 782266

WASHBROOK
Suffolk
High View ♦♦♦♦
Back Lane, Washbrook, Ipswich
IP8 3JA
T: (01473) 730494
E: graham.steward@pmail.net

WELLINGHAM
Norfolk
Manor House Farm
♦♦♦♦ SILVER AWARD
Wellingham, King's Lynn,
Norfolk PE32 2TH
T: (01328) 838227
F: (01328) 838348
E: robinellis@farming.co.uk

WELLS-NEXT-THE-SEA
Norfolk
The Artist's House
♦♦♦♦ SILVER AWARD
Wingate, Two Furlong Hill,
Wells-next-the-Sea, Norfolk
NR23 1HQ
T: (01328) 711814

Blenheim House ♦♦♦♦
Theatre Road, Wells-next-the-
Sea, Norfolk NR23 1DJ
T: (01328) 711368
F: (01328) 711368
E: marjorams@lineone.net

The Cobblers Guesthouse
Rating Applied For
Standard Road, Wells-next-the-
Sea, Norfolk NR23 1JU
T: (01328) 710155 & 710155
F: (01328) 710355
E: ina@cobblers.co.uk
I: www.cobblers.co.uk

Corner House
Rating Applied For
Staithe Street, Wells-next-the-
Sea, Norfolk NR23 1AF
T: (01328) 710701
E: lmoney@ukonline.co.uk

Glebe Barn ♦♦♦♦
7a Glebe Road, Wells-next-the-
Sea, Norfolk NR23 1AZ
T: (01328) 711809
E: derek@glebebarn.netlineuk.
net

Hideaway ♦♦♦
Red Lion Yard, Wells-next-the-
Sea, Norfolk NR23 1AX
T: (01328) 710524

Ilex House ♦♦♦
Bases Lane, Wells-next-the-Sea,
Norfolk NR23 1DH
T: (01328) 710556
F: (01328) 710556
E: tommcjay@aol.com
I: www.broadland.com/ilexhouse

Machrimore ♦♦♦♦
Burn Street, Wells-next-the-Sea,
Norfolk NR23 1HS
T: (01328) 711653 &
0771 3225990

Mill House Guesthouse ♦♦♦
Mill House, Northfield Lane,
Wells-next-the-Sea, Norfolk
NR23 1JZ
T: (01328) 710739
I: www.broadlands.
com/millhouse

The Normans ♦♦♦♦
Invaders Court, Standard Road,
Wells-next-the-Sea, Norfolk
NR23 1JW
T: (01328) 710657
F: (01328) 710468

Old Police House ♦♦♦
Polka Road, Wells-next-the-Sea,
Norfolk NR23 1ED
T: (01328) 710630 &
07767 660213
F: (01328) 710630
E: d-jwhitaker@yahoo.com

The Warren ♦♦♦♦
Warham Road, Wells-next-the-
Sea, Norfolk R23 1NE
T: (01328) 710273

WEST BERGHOLT
Essex
The Old Post House ♦♦♦
10 Colchester Road, West
Bergholt, Colchester, Essex
CO6 3JG
T: (01206) 240379
F: (01206) 243301

WEST DEREHAM
Norfolk
Bell Barn ♦♦♦♦
Lime Kiln Road, West Dereham,
King's Lynn, Norfolk PE33 9RT
T: (01366) 500762
F: (01366) 500762
E: chris@woodbarn.freeserve.
co.uk

WEST MERSEA
Essex
Hazel Oak ♦♦♦
28 Seaview Avenue, West
Mersea, Colchester CO5 8HE
T: (01206) 383030
E: ann.blackmore@btinternet.
com
I: www.btinternet.
com/§daveblackmore/

WEST RUNTON
Norfolk
The Old Barn ♦♦♦♦
Cromer Road, West Runton,
Cromer, Norfolk NR27 9QT
T: (01263) 838285

Village Inn ♦♦♦
Rating Applied For
Water Lane, West Runton,
Sheringham, Norfolk NR27 9QP.
T: (01263) 838000
F: (01263) 837877

WEST SOMERTON
Norfolk
The White House Farm ♦♦♦♦
The Street, West Somerton,
Great Yarmouth, Norfolk
NR29 4EA
T: (01493) 393991

WESTCLIFF-ON-SEA
Essex
Chilton House ♦♦♦
3 Trinity Avenue, Westcliff-on-
Sea, Essex SS0 7PU
T: (01702) 342282
F: (01702) 342282

Pavilion Hotel ♦♦
1 Trinity Avenue, Westcliff-on-
Sea, Essex SS0 7PU
T: (01702) 332767
F: (01702) 332767

Retreat Guesthouse ♦♦♦
12 Canewdon Road, Westcliff-
on-Sea, Essex SS0 7NE
T: (01702) 348217 & 337413
F: (01702) 391179

Welbeck Hotel ♦♦♦
27 Palmerston Road, Westcliff-
on-Sea, Essex SS0 7TA
T: (01702) 347736
F: (01702) 339140
E: welbeck@tinyworld.co.uk

WESTLETON
Suffolk
Pond House ♦♦♦♦
The Hill, Westleton,
Saxmundham, Suffolk IP17 3AN
T: (01728) 648773

WHITE COLNE
Essex
Larkswood ♦♦♦
32 Colchester Road, White
Colne, Colchester CO6 2PN
T: (01787) 224362

WHITE RODING
Essex
Marks Hall Farmhouse ♦♦♦♦
Marks Hall, White Roding,
Dunmow, Essex CM6 1RT
T: (01279) 876438 & 876236
F: (01279) 876236
E: jane@markshall.fsnet.co.uk

WHITTLESEY
Cambridgeshire
Whitmore House ♦♦♦♦
31 Whitmore Street, Whittlesey,
Peterborough PE7 1HE
T: (01733) 203088

WICKHAM BISHOPS
Essex
Wickham Hall
♦♦♦♦ SILVER AWARD
Langford Road, Wickham
Bishops, Witham, Maldon, Essex
CM8 3JQ
T: (01621) 891049

WIGHTON
Norfolk
Shrublands ♦♦♦♦
Wells Road, Wighton, Wells-
next-the-Sea, Norfolk NR23 1PR
T: (01328) 820743
F: (01328) 820088
E: shrublands@shrub-lands.
freeserve.co.uk

WIMBISH
Essex
Blossom Cottage ♦♦♦
Rowney Corner, Wimbish,
Saffron Walden, Essex CB10 2UZ
T: (01799) 599430

Newdegate House
♦♦♦♦ SILVER AWARD
Howlett End, Wimbish, Saffron
Walden, Essex CB10 2XW
T: (01799) 599748
F: (01799) 599748

WINGFIELD
Suffolk

Gables Farm ♦♦♦♦
Earsham Street, Wingfield, Diss,
Norfolk IP21 5RH
T: (01379) 586355 &
07808 448272
F: (01379) 586355
E: sue.harvey@lineone.net
I: www.gablesfarm.co.uk

WISBECH
Cambridgeshire

Marmion House Hotel ♦♦♦
11 Lynn Road, Wisbech,
Cambridgeshire PE13 3DD
T: (01945) 582822
F: (01945) 475889

Stratton Farm ♦♦♦♦
West Drove North, Walton
Highway, Norfolk PE14 7DP
T: (01945) 880162

WITHAM
Essex

Abbotts ♦♦♦
45 Collingwood Road, Witham,
Essex CM8 2DZ
T: (01376) 512586

Chestnuts ♦♦♦♦
8 Octavia Drive, Witham Lodge,
Witham, Essex CM8 1HQ
T: (01376) 515990 &
07885 456803
F: (01376) 515990

WITHERSFIELD
Suffolk

**White Horse Inn
♦♦♦♦ SILVER AWARD**
Hollow Hill, Withersfield,
Haverhill, Suffolk CB9 7SH
T: (01440) 706081

WIX
Essex

**Dairy House Farm
♦♦♦♦ GOLD AWARD**
Bradfield Road, Wix,
Manningtree, Essex CO11 2SR
T: (01255) 870322
F: (01255) 870186

WOOD DALLING
Norfolk

Westwood Barn ♦♦♦♦
Crabgate Lane South, Wood
Dalling, Norwich NR11 6SW
T: (01263) 584108 &
07990 760124

WOOD NORTON
Norfolk

**Manor Farm Bed and Breakfast
♦♦♦♦**
Manor Farm, Hall Lane, Wood
Norton, Dereham, Norfolk
NR20 5BE
T: (01362) 683231

WOODBRIDGE
Suffolk

Deben Lodge ♦♦♦
Melton Road, Woodbridge,
Suffolk IP12 1NH
T: (01394) 382740

Grove House ♦♦♦
39 Grove Road, Woodbridge,
Suffolk IP12 4LG
T: (01394) 382202
F: (01394) 380652
E: grovehotel@btinternet.com
I: www.grovehousehotel.com

Lark Cottage ♦♦♦♦
Shingle Street, Woodbridge,
Suffolk IP12 3BE
T: (01394) 411292

Moat Barn ♦♦♦
Bredfield, Woodbridge, Suffolk
IP13 6BD
T: (01473) 737520
F: (01473) 737520

Moat Farmhouse ♦♦♦
Dallinghoo Road, Bredfield,
Woodbridge, Suffolk IP13 6BD
T: (01473) 737475

The Station Hotel ♦♦
Station Road, Woodbridge,
Suffolk IP12 4AU
T: (01394) 384831

Willow House ♦♦♦
20 Woolnough Road,
Woodbridge, Suffolk IP12 1HJ
T: (01394) 385798
F: (01394) 385798

WOODHAM MORTIMER
Essex

**Chase Farm Bed & Breakfast
Rating Applied For**
Chase Farm, Hyde Chase,
Woodham Mortimer, Maldon,
Essex CM9
T: (01245) 223268 &
07703 409444

Little Owls ♦♦♦
Post Office Road, Woodham
Mortimer, Maldon, Essex
CM9 6ST
T: (01245) 224355 &
07889 964584
F: (01245) 224355
E: the.bushes@virgin.net

WOODSTON
Cambridgeshire

White House Guesthouse ♦♦
White House, 318 Oundle Road,
Woodston, Peterborough
PE2 9QP
T: (01733) 566650

WOOLPIT
Suffolk

**The Bull Inn & Restaurant
♦♦♦**
The Street, Woolpit, Bury St
Edmunds, Suffolk IP30 9SA
T: (01359) 240393
E: trevor@howling.fsbusiness.
co.uk

Grange Farm ♦♦♦♦
Woolpit, Bury St Edmunds,
Suffolk IP30 9RG
T: (01359) 241143
F: (01359) 244296
E: grangefarm@btinternet.com
I: www.farmstayanglia.co.
uk/grangefarm/

WOOTTON
Bedfordshire

Maple Tree Cottage ♦♦♦♦
Wootton Green, Wootton,
Bedford MK43 9EE
T: (01234) 768631
F: (01234) 768631
E: francy.mtc@cwcom.net

WORLINGTON
Suffolk

**Worlington Hall Country
House Hotel ♦♦♦♦**
The Street, Worlington, Bury St
Edmunds, Suffolk IP28 8RX
T: (01638) 712237
F: (01638) 712631

WORSTEAD
Norfolk

Hall Farm Guesthouse ♦♦♦♦
Hall Farm, Sloley Road,
Worstead, North Walsham,
Norfolk NR28 9RS
T: (01692) 536124
E: jon.lowe@btclick.com

The Ollands ♦♦♦♦
Swanns Loke, Worstead, North
Walsham, Norfolk NR28 9RP
T: (01692) 535150
F: (01692) 535150

WOTHORPE
Cambridgeshire

Firwood ♦♦♦♦
First Drift, Wothorpe, Stamford,
Lincolnshire PE9 3JL
T: (01780) 765654
F: (01780) 765654

WRESTLINGWORTH
Bedfordshire

Orchard Cottage ♦♦♦
1 High Street, Wrestlingworth,
Sandy, Bedfordshire SG19 2EW
T: (01767) 631355
F: (01767) 631355

WRITTLE
Essex

**Moor Hall
♦♦♦♦ SILVER AWARD**
Newney Green, Writtle,
Chelmsford CM1 3SE
T: (01245) 420814 &
07946 584636
E: moorhall@talk21.com

WROXHAM
Norfolk

**The Dragon Flies
♦♦♦♦ SILVER AWARD**
5 The Avenue, Wroxham,
Norwich NR12 8TN
T: (01603) 783822
F: (01603) 783822
E: geoff.g.kimberley@talk21.
com

Garden Cottage ♦♦♦♦
The Limes, 96 Norwich Road,
Wroxham, Norwich, Norfolk
NR12 8RY
T: (01603) 784376 & 0771 224
2388
F: (01603) 783734

Manor Barn House ♦♦♦♦
Back Lane, Rackheath, Norwich
NR13 6NN
T: (01603) 783543

Ridge House ♦♦♦♦
7 The Avenue, Wroxham,
Norwich, Norfolk NR12 8TN
T: (01603) 782130

Wroxham Park Lodge ♦♦♦♦
142 Norwich Road, Wroxham,
Norwich NR12 8SA
T: (01603) 782991

WYMONDHAM
Norfolk

Witch Hazel ♦♦♦♦
Church Lane, Wicklewood,
Wymondham, Norfolk
NR18 9QH
T: (01953) 602247 & 0771 391
1853
F: (01953) 602247

YOXFORD
Suffolk

The Griffin ♦♦♦
High Street, Yoxford,
Saxmundham, Suffolk IP17 3EP
T: (01728) 668229 & 668749
E: i.terry@thegriffin.co.uk
I: www.thegriffin.co.uk

**The Old Methodist Chapel
♦♦♦♦**
High Street, Yoxford,
Saxmundham, Suffolk IP17 3EU
T: (01728) 668333 &
07931 668681
F: (01728) 668333
E: dfabrown@waitrose.com
I: www.chapelsuffolk.co.uk

SOUTH WEST

SOUTH WEST

ABBOTSBURY
Dorset

Corfe Gate House ♦♦♦♦
Coryates, Abbotsbury,
Weymouth, Dorset DT3 4HW
T: (01305) 871483 &
07798 904602
F: (01305) 264024
E: maureenadams@
corfegatehouse.co.uk
I: www.corfegatehouse.co.uk

Linton Cottage
♦♦♦♦ SILVER AWARD
Abbotsbury, Weymouth, Dorset
DT3 4JL
T: (01305) 871339
F: (01305) 871339
E: queenbee@abbotsbury.co.uk
I: www.abbotsbury.co.
uk/lintoncottage

Swan Lodge ♦♦♦
Rodden Row, Abbotsbury,
Weymouth, Dorset DT3 4JL
T: (01305) 871249
F: (01305) 871249

ALCOMBE
Somerset

Pennyhill Farm ♦♦♦
Combeland Road, Alcombe,
Minehead, Somerset TA24 6BT
T: (01643) 707806
E: pennyhill.farm@care4free.net

ALDBOURNE
Wiltshire

The Crown Hotel ♦♦
2 The Square, Aldbourne,
Marlborough, Wiltshire SN8 2DU
T: (01672) 540214
F: (01672) 540214

ALDERBURY
Wiltshire

Wisteria Cottage ♦♦♦
Silver Street, Alderbury,
Salisbury, Wiltshire SP5 3AN
T: (01722) 710274

ALHAMPTON
Somerset

**The Barn at Yew Tree Cottage
♦♦♦**
No Through Road, Alhampton,
Shepton Mallet, Somerset
BA4 6PZ
T: (01749) 860615
F: (01749) 860512
E: hhassoc@lineone.net

ALLERFORD
Somerset

**Exmoor Falconry & Animal
Farm ♦♦♦**
West Lynch Farm, Allerford,
Minehead, Somerset TA24 8HJ
T: (01643) 862816
F: (01643) 862816
E: exmoorfalcon@freenet.co.uk
I: www.exmoor-holidays.co.
uk/bossington

Fern Cottage ♦♦♦♦
Allerford, Minehead, Somerset
TA24 8HN
T: (01643) 862215
F: (01643) 862215

AMESBURY
Wiltshire

Enford House ♦♦♦
Enford, Pewsey, Wiltshire
SN9 6DJ
T: (01980) 670414

**Epworth House Bed and
Breakfast ♦♦♦♦**
21 Edwards Road, Amesbury,
Salisbury, Wiltshire SP4 7LT
T: (01980) 624242
F: (01980) 590419

Fairlawn Hotel ♦♦
42 High Street, Amesbury,
Salisbury, Wiltshire SP4 7DJ
T: (01980) 622103

Mandalay ♦♦♦♦
15 Stonehenge Road, Amesbury,
Salisbury, Wiltshire SP4 7BA
T: (01980) 623733
F: (01980) 626642

The Old Bakery ♦♦♦
Netton, Salisbury, Wiltshire
SP4 6AW
T: (01722) 782351
E: valahen@aol.com
I: members.aol.com/valahen

Solstice Farmhouse ♦♦♦
39 Holders Road, Amesbury,
Salisbury SP4 7PH
T: (01980) 625052 &
07931 311778

Westavon ♦♦♦
76 Countess Road, Amesbury,
Salisbury, Wiltshire SP4 7AT
T: (01980) 623698

ASHBRITTLE
Somerset

Lower Westcott Farm ♦♦♦
Ashbrittle, Wellington, Somerset
TA21 0HZ
T: (01398) 361296

ASHBURTON
Devon

Gages Mill
♦♦♦♦ SILVER AWARD
Buckfastleigh Road, Ashburton,
Newton Abbot, Devon TQ13 7JW
T: (01364) 652391
F: (01364) 652391
E: moore@gagesmill.co.uk
I: www.gagesmill.co.uk

New Cott Farm ♦♦♦♦
Poundsgate, Ashburton, Newton
Abbot, Devon TQ13 7PD
T: (01364) 631421
F: (01364) 631421

Sladesdown Farm ♦♦♦♦
Landscove, Ashburton, Newton
Abbot, Devon TQ13 7ND
T: (01364) 653973

Wellpritton Farm ♦♦♦♦
Holne, Newton Abbot, Devon
TQ13 7RX
T: (01364) 631273

ASHTON
Somerset

Ashton Road Farm ♦♦♦
Ashton, Wedmore, Somerset
BS28 4QE
T: (01934) 713462
F: (01934) 713462

**Cumberland Guest House
♦♦♦**
6 Clift House Road, Ashton,
Bristol BS3 1RY
T: (0117) 966 0810
F: (0117) 966 0810

ASHTON KEYNES
Wiltshire

Corner Cottage ♦♦♦
Fore Street, Ashton Keynes,
Swindon, Wiltshire SN6 6NP
T: (01285) 861454

ASHWICKE
Wiltshire

Pixtons Green ♦♦♦♦
Ashwicke, Chippenham,
Wiltshire SN14 8AL
T: (01225) 859959
T: (01225) 812202
E: office@gldbalins.demon.co.
uk

ASKERSWELL
Dorset

Hembury House ♦♦♦
Askerswell, Dorchester, Dorset
DT2 9EN
T: (01308) 485297 & 485032
F: (01308) 485032
E: askers@askers.free-online.co.
uk
I: www.freeyellow.
com/members5/hembury/page1.
html

ATWORTH
Wiltshire

Church Farm ♦♦♦
Atworth, Melksham, Wiltshire
SN12 8JA
T: (01225) 702215 &
07974 786387
F: (01225) 702215
E: chrchfarm@tinyonline.co.uk
I: www.churchfarm-atworth.
freeserve.co.uk

AVEBURY
Wiltshire

The New Inn ♦♦♦
Winterbourne Monkton,
Swindon, Wiltshire SN4 9NW
T: (01672) 539240
F: (01672) 539150

AVEBURY TRUSLOE
Wiltshire

Manor Farm ♦♦♦
Avebury Trusloe, Marlborough,
Wiltshire SN8 1QY
T: (01672) 539243
F: (01672) 539230

AVETON GIFFORD
Devon

Helliers Farm ♦♦♦♦
Ashford, Aveton Gifford,
Kingsbridge, Devon TQ7 4ND
T: (01548) 550689
F: (01548) 550689

AWLISCOMBE
Devon

Godford Farm ♦♦♦♦
Awliscombe, Honiton, Devon
EX14 3PW
T: (01404) 42825
F: (01404) 42825
E: lawrencesally@hotmail.com
I: www.smoothhound.co.
uk/hotels/godford.html

AXBRIDGE
Somerset

Waterside
Rating Applied For
Cheddar Road, Axbridge,
Somerset BS26 2DP
T: (01934) 743182

AXMINSTER
Devon

Chalfont House ♦♦♦♦
Crewkerne Road, Raymonds Hill,
Axminster, Devon EX13 5SX
T: (01297) 33852

Coaxdon Farm ♦♦♦♦
Axminster, Devon EX13 7LP
T: (01297) 35540

BABBACOMBE
Devon

Seabury Hotel ♦♦♦♦
Manor Road, Babbacombe,
Torquay TQ1 3JX
T: (01803) 327255
F: (01803) 315321

BACKWELL
North Somerset

**Ambassadors Health Farm
♦♦♦**
Backwell Hill House, Backwell,
Bristol BS48 3DA
T: (01275) 464462
F: (01275) 462951

Moorlands ♦♦♦♦
Backwell Hill, Backwell, Bristol
BS48 3EJ
T: (01275) 462755

BAMPTON
Devon

Bampton Gallery ♦♦♦♦
2-4 Brook Street, Bampton,
Tiverton, Devon EX16 9LY
T: (01398) 331354
F: (01398) 331119
E: bampgall@aol.com
I: www.exmoortourism.
org/bamptongallery.htm

Exeter Arms ♦♦
Rating Applied For
Tiverton Road, Bampton,
Tiverton, Devon EX16 9DY
T: (01398) 331345
F: (01398) 331345

**Lodfin Farm Bed & Breakfast
♦♦♦♦**
Morebath, Bampton, Tiverton,
Devon EX16 9DD
T: (01398) 331400
F: (01398) 331400
E: lodfin.farm@eclipse.co.uk
I: www.exmoor-holidays.co.uk

Manor Mill House
◆◆◆◆ SILVER AWARD
Bampton, Tiverton, Devon
EX16 9LP
T: (01398) 332211
F: (01398) 332009
E: saty@manormill.demon.co.uk
I: www.manormill.demon.co.uk

The Old Mill Guest House
◆◆◆◆ SILVER AWARD
Shillingford, Tiverton, Devon
EX16 9BW
T: (01398) 331064
F: (01398) 331064

BANWELL
North Somerset
Banwell Castle ◆◆◆
Banwell, Somerset BS29 6NX
T: (01934) 822263
F: (01934) 823946
I: www.smoothhound.co.uk

BARBROOK
Devon
Manor Hotel and Beggars Roost Inn ◆◆◆
Barbrook, Lynton, Devon
EX35 6LD
T: (01598) 752404
F: (01598) 753636

Old Sawmills ◆◆◆
Stockhill, Barbrook, Lynton,
Devon EX35 6PF
T: (01598) 753660

BARFORD ST MARTIN
Wiltshire
The Barford Inn ◆◆◆◆
Barford St Martin, Salisbury
SP3 4AB
T: (01722) 742242 & 743606
E: ido@barfordinn.co.uk
I: www.barfordinn.co.uk

Briden House ◆◆◆◆
West Street, Barford St Martin,
Salisbury SP3 4AH
T: (01722) 743471
F: (01722) 743471
E: bridenhouse@barford25.
freeserve.net
I: www.smoothhound.co.
uk/hotels/bridenho.html

BARNSTAPLE
Devon
Bradiford Cottage ◆◆◆◆
Bradiford, Barnstaple, Devon
EX31 4DP
T: (01271) 345039
F: (01271) 345039
E: tony@humesfarm.co.uk
I: www.humesfarm.co.uk

Home Park Farm Accommodation ◆◆◆◆
Lower Blakewell, Muddiford,
Barnstaple, Devon EX31 4ET
T: (01271) 342955
F: (01271) 342955
I: www.smoothhound.co.
uk/hotels/homepark.html

The Red House ◆◆◆◆
Brynsworthy, Roundswell,
Barnstaple, Devon EX31 3NP
T: (01271) 345966
F: (01271) 379966

The Spinney ◆◆◆◆
Shirwell, Barnstaple, Devon
EX31 4JR
T: (01271) 850282

Waytown Farm ◆◆◆◆
Shirwell, Barnstaple, Devon
EX31 4JN
T: (01271) 850396
F: (01271) 850396
E: hazel@waytown.
enterprise-plc.com

BARTON ST. DAVID
Somerset
Mill House ◆◆◆◆◆
Mill House, Barton St. David,
Somerton, Somerset TA11 6DF
T: (01458) 851215
F: (01458) 851372
E: knightsmillhouse@aol.com

BASONBRIDGE
Somerset
Merry Farm ◆◆◆◆
Merry Lane, Basonbridge,
Highbridge, Somerset TA9 3PS
T: (01278) 783655

BATCOMBE
Somerset
Home Farm ◆◆◆
Batcombe, Shepton Mallet,
Somerset BA4 6HF
T: (01749) 850303
F: (01749) 850540
E: christopher.frederick@virgin.
net

Valley View Farm ◆◆◆
Batcombe, Shepton Mallet,
Somerset BA4 6AJ
T: (01749) 850302 &
07974 442284
F: (01749) 850302

BATH
Bath & North East Somerset
Abode ◆◆◆
7 Widcombe Crescent,
Widcombe Hill, Bath, BA2 6AH
T: (01225) 422726

The Albany Guest House ◆◆◆◆
24 Crescent Gardens, Upper
Bristol Road, Bath, BA1 2NB
T: (01225) 313339
E: the_albany@lineone.net
I: www.bath.org/hotel/albany.
htm

Apartment 1 ◆◆◆
60 Great Pulteney Street, Bath,
BA2 4DN
T: (01225) 464134 & 483663
F: (01225) 483663

Ashgrove Guest House ◆◆◆
39 Bathwick Street, Bath,
BA2 6PA
T: (01225) 421911
F: (01225) 461287

Ashley House ◆◆◆
8 Pulteney Gardens, Bath,
BA2 4HG
T: (01225) 425027

Astor House ◆◆◆
14 Oldfield Road, Bath, BA2 3ND
T: (01225) 429134
F: (01225) 429134
E: astorhouse.visitus@virgin.net

Athelney Guest House ◆◆◆
5 Marlborough Lane, Bath,
BA1 2NQ
T: (01225) 312031
F: (01225) 312031

Avoca ◆◆
16 Newbridge Road, Bath,
BA1 3JX
T: (01225) 333665

Avon Guest House ◆◆
1 Pulteney Gardens, Bath,
BA2 4HG
T: (01225) 313009

Ayrlington Hotel ◆◆◆◆◆
24/25 Pulteney Road, Bath,
BA2 4EZ
T: (01225) 425495
F: (01225) 469029
E: mail@ayrlington.com
I: www.ayrlington.com

Badminton Villa
◆◆◆◆ SILVER AWARD
10 Upper Oldfield Park, Bath,
BA2 3JZ
T: (01225) 426347
F: (01225) 420393
E: badmintonvilla@cableinet.co.
uk
I: www.smoothhound.co.
uk/hotels/badmintn.html

Bailbrook Lodge Hotel ◆◆◆
35/37 London Road West, Bath,
Somerset BA1 7HZ
T: (01225) 859090
F: (01225) 852299
E: hotel@bailbrooklodge.
demon.co.uk
I: www.bailbrooklodge.demon.
co.uk

Bloomfield House
◆◆◆◆◆ SILVER AWARD
146 Bloomfield Road, Bath,
BA2 2AS
T: (01225) 420105
F: (01225) 481958
E: bloomfieldhouse@
compuserve.com
I: www.bloomfield.house.co.uk

16 Bloomfield Road ◆◆◆
Bear Flat, Bath, BA2 2AB
T: (01225) 337804

Bridgnorth Guest House ◆◆◆
2 Crescent Gardens, Bath,
BA1 2NA
T: (01225) 331186

Brinsley Sheridan Guest House
◆◆◆◆
95 Wellsway, Bear Flat, Bath,
BA2 4RU
T: (01225) 429562
F: (01225) 429616
E: post@bsgh.freeserve.co.uk
I: www.bsgh.freeserve.co.uk

Brompton House ◆◆◆◆
Rating Applied For
St John's Road, Bath, BA2 6PT
T: (01225) 420972
F: (01225) 420505
E: bromptonhouse@btinternet.
com
I: www.bromptonhouse.co.uk

Carfax Hotel ◆◆◆◆
Great Pulteney Street, Bath,
BA2 4BS
T: (01225) 462089
F: (01225) 443257
E: carfaxhotel@compuserve.
com
I: www.carfaxhotel.co.uk

Cherry Tree Villa ◆◆◆
7 Newbridge Hill, Bath, BA1 3PW
T: (01225) 331671

Church Farm ◆◆◆
Monkton Farleigh, Bradford-on-
Avon, Wiltshire BA15 2QJ
T: (01225) 858583 &
07889 596929
F: (01225) 852474
E: rebecca@tuckerb.fsnet.co.uk
I: www.tuckerb.fsnet.co.uk

Corston Fields Farm ◆◆◆◆
Corston, Bath BA2 9EZ
T: (01225) 873305 &
07721 379294
F: (01225) 873305
E: corston.fields@3wa.co.uk

County Hotel ◆◆◆◆◆
18-19 Pulteney Road, Bath,
BA2 4EZ
T: (01225) 425003
F: (01225) 466493
E: reservations@county-hotel.
co.uk
I: www.county-hotel.co.uk

Crescent Guest House ◆◆◆
21 Crescent Gardens, Bath,
BA1 2NA
T: (01225) 425945

Dorset Villa ◆◆◆
14 Newbridge Road, Bath,
BA1 3JZ
T: (01225) 425975
F: (01225) 425975
E: itsgreat@btinternet.com
I: www.btinternet.
com/mitsgreat

Dunsford Place Bed & Breakfast ◆◆◆◆
4 Dunsford Place, Bathwick Hill,
Bath, BA2 6HF
T: (01225) 460662 &
0797 4440018
E: wanir@aol.com

Edgar Hotel ◆◆◆
64 Great Pulteney Street, Bath,
BA2 4DN
T: (01225) 420619
F: (01225) 466916

Elgin Villa ◆◆◆
6 Marlborough Lane, Bath,
BA1 2NQ
T: (01225) 424557
F: (01225) 424557
E: stay@elginvilla.co.uk
I: www.elginvilla.co.uk

Fairhaven Guest House ◆◆◆
21 Newbridge Road, Bath,
BA1 3HE
T: (01225) 314694

Flaxley Villa ◆◆◆
9 Newbridge Hill, Bath, BA1 3PW
T: (01225) 313237 & 480574

Forres House ◆◆◆
172 Newbridge Road, Bath,
BA1 3LE
T: (01225) 427698
E: clive.sampson@eke.co.uk

The Gainsborough ♦♦♦♦
Weston Lane, Bath, BA1 4AB
T: (01225) 311380
F: (01225) 447411
E: gainsborough_hotel@
compuserve.com
I: www.gainsboroughhotel.co.uk

Georgian Guest House ♦♦♦
34 Henrietta Street, Bath,
BA2 6LR
T: (01225) 424103
F: (01225) 425279
E: georgian@georgian-house.
co.uk
I: www.georgian-house.co.uk

Glan Y Dwr ♦♦♦
14 Newbridge Hill, Bath,
BA1 3PU
T: (01225) 317521 &
07968 263343
F: (01225) 317521
E: glanydwr@batheng.freeserve.
co.uk

Glen View ♦♦♦♦
162 Newbridge Road, Bath,
BA1 3LE
T: (01225) 421376
F: (01225) 310271
E: info@glenviewbath.co.uk
I: www.glenviewbath.co.uk

Glentworth
♦♦♦♦ SILVER AWARD
12 Marlborough Lane, Bath,
BA1 2NQ
T: (01225) 334554
F: (01225) 334554
E: stay@glentworthbath.co.uk
I: www.glentworthbath.co.uk

Hatt Farm ♦♦♦♦
Old Jockey, Box, Corsham,
Wiltshire SN13 8DJ
T: (01225) 742989
F: (01225) 742779
E: hattfarm@netlineuk.net

Haute Combe Hotel ♦♦♦♦
174/176 Newbridge Road, Bath,
BA1 3LE
T: (01225) 420061 & 339064
F: (01225) 446077
E: enquiries@hautecombe.com
I: www.hautecombe.com

Haydon House
♦♦♦♦♦ SILVER AWARD
9 Bloomfield Park, Bath,
BA2 2BY
T: (01225) 444919 & 427351
F: (01225) 444919
E: stay@haydonhouse.co.uk
I: www.haydonhouse.co.uk

Henrietta Hotel ♦♦♦
32 Henrietta Street, Bath,
BA2 6LR
T: (01225) 447779
F: (01225) 444150

Henry Guest House ♦
6 Henry Street, Bath, BA1 1JT
T: (01225) 424052
E: cox@thehenrybath.freeserve.
co.uk

Hermitage ♦♦♦
Bath Road, Box, Corsham,
Wiltshire SN13 8DT
T: (01225) 744187
F: (01225) 743447
E: hermitage@telecall.co.uk

Highways House ♦♦♦♦
143 Wells Road, Bath, BA2 3AL
T: (01225) 421238 &
0800 0749250
F: (01225) 481169
E: highways@toscar.clara.co.uk
I: www.visitus.co.
uk/bath/hotel/highways.htm

The Hollies ♦♦♦♦
Hatfield Road, Wellsway, Bath,
BA2 2BD
T: (01255) 313366
F: (01255) 313366
I: www.visitus.co.uk/bath/hotel.
hollies.html

Holly Lodge
♦♦♦♦♦ SILVER AWARD
8 Upper Oldfield Park, Bath,
BA2 3JZ
T: (01225) 424042 &
(01255) 339187
F: (01225) 481138
E: George.H.Hall@btinternet.
com
I: www.hollylodge.co.uk

Kennard Hotel
♦♦♦♦ SILVER AWARD
11 Henrietta Street, Bath,
BA2 6LL
T: (01225) 310472
F: (01225) 460054
E: kennard@dircon.co.uk
I: www.kennard.co.uk

Kinlet Villa Guest House ♦♦♦
99 Wellsway, Bath, BA2 4RX
T: (01225) 420268
F: (01225) 420268
E: kinlet@inbath.freeserve.co.uk
I: www.visitus.co.
uk/bath/hotel/kinlet.htm

Lamp Post Villa ♦♦♦
3 Crescent Gardens, Upper
Bristol Road, Bath, BA1 2NA
T: (01225) 331221
F: (01225) 426783

Laura Place Hotel ♦♦♦♦
3 Laura Place, Great Pulteney
Street, Bath, BA2 4BH
T: (01225) 463815
F: (01225) 310222

Lavender House
♦♦♦♦♦ SILVER AWARD
17 Bloomfield Park, Bath,
BA2 2BY
T: (01225) 314500
F: (01225) 448564
E: lavenderhouse@btintenet.
com
I: www.bath.co.
uk/lavenderhouse/

Leighton House
♦♦♦♦ GOLD AWARD
139 Wells Road, Bath, BA2 3AL
T: (01225) 314769 & 420210
F: (01225) 443079
E: welcome@leighton-house.co.
uk
I: www.leighton-house.co.uk

Lindisfarne ♦♦♦♦
41a Warminster Road,
Bathampton, Bath BA2 6XJ
T: (01225) 466342
F: (01225) 444062
E: brian.youngs@virgin.net
I: www.visitus.co.uk

The Manor House ♦♦♦
Mill Lane, Monkton Combe, Bath
BA2 7HD
T: (01225) 723128
F: (01225) 722972
E: beth@manorhousebath.co.uk
I: www.manorhousebath.co.uk

Marisha's Guest House ♦♦♦
68 Newbridge Hill, Bath,
BA1 3QA
T: (01225) 446881

Marlborough House ♦♦♦♦
1 Marlborough Lane, Bath,
BA1 2NQ
T: (01225) 318175
F: (01225) 466127
E: mars@manque.dircon.co.uk
I: www.s-h-systems.co.
uk/hotels/marlbor1.html

Meadowland
♦♦♦♦♦ GOLD AWARD
36 Bloomfield Park, Bath,
BA2 2BX
T: (01225) 311079
F: (01225) 311079
E: meadowland@bath92.
freeserve.co.uk
I: www.bath.
org/hotel/meadowland.html

Melody Guest House ♦♦♦
12 Hensley Road, Bath, BA2 2DR
T: (01225) 420169

Membland Guest House ♦
7 Pulteney Terrace, Pulteney
Road, Bath, BA2 4HJ
T: (01225) 336712 &
07958 599572

Midway Cottage ♦♦♦♦
10 Farleigh Wick, Bradford-on-
Avon, Wiltshire BA15 2PU
T: (01225) 863932
F: (01225) 866836
E: midway_cottage@hotmail.
com

Milton Guest House ♦♦♦♦
75 Wellsway, Bear Flat, Bath,
BA2 4RU
T: (01225) 335632

Monkshill
♦♦♦♦♦ GOLD AWARD
Shaft Road, Monkton Combe,
Bath BA2 7HL
T: (01225) 833028
F: (01225) 833028
E: monks.hill@virgin.net

Number 30 Crescent Gardens
♦♦♦♦
Bath, BA1 2NB
T: (01225) 337393
F: (01225) 337393
E: david.greenwood@
nationwideisp.co.uk
I: www.stay@numberthirty.co.
uk

Parkside ♦♦♦♦
11 Marlborough Lane, Bath,
BA1 2NQ
T: (01225) 429444
F: (01225) 429444
E: parkside@lynall.freeserve.co.
uk
I: www.visitus.co.
uk/bath/hotel/parkside.html

Pine Bank ♦♦♦
2 Audley Park Road, Bath,
BA1 2XJ
T: (01225) 334283
F: (01225) 446389

Poplar Farm ♦♦♦
Stanton Prior, Bath BA2 9HX
T: (01761) 470382
F: (01761) 470382
E: poplarfarm@Talk21.com

Pulteney Hotel ♦♦♦
14 Pulteney Road, Bath,
BA2 4HA
T: (01225) 460991 & 421261
F: (01225) 460991
E: pulteneyhotel@currantbun

The Quarrymans Arms
Rating Applied For
Box Hill, Box, Corsham, Wiltshire
SN13 8HN
T: (01225) 743569 & 742610

14 Raby Place ♦♦♦♦
Bathwick Hill, Bath, BA2 4EH
T: (01225) 465120

Radnor Guesthouse ♦♦♦♦
9 Pulteney Terrace, Pulteney
Road, Bath, BA2 4HJ
T: (01225) 316159
F: (01225) 319199

Rainbow Wood Farm ♦♦
Claverton Down Road, Bath,
BA2 7AR
T: (01225) 466366
F: (01225) 466366

Ravenscroft
♦♦♦♦ SILVER AWARD
Sydney Road, Bath, BA2 6NT
T: (01225) 469267 &
0790 9680885
F: (01225) 448722
E: chmbaker@gatewayuk.net

Rosemary House ♦♦♦
63 Wellsway, Bath, BA2 4RT
T: (01225) 425667
F: (01225) 425667
E: rosemary.house@which.net
I: www.visitus.co.uk

Royal Park Guest House ♦
16 Crescent Gardens, Upper
Bristol Road, Bath, BA1 2NA
T: (01225) 317651
E: royal@parkb-b.freeserve.co.
uk

Hotel Saint Clair ♦♦♦
1 Crescent Gardens, Upper
Bristol Road, Bath, BA1 2NA
T: (01225) 425543
F: (01225) 425543
E: hotel-st-clair@ukonline.co.uk
I: web.ukonline.co.
uk/hotel-st-clair

St Leonards
♦♦♦♦ SILVER AWARD
Warminster Road, Bathampton,
Bath BA2 6SQ
T: (01225) 465838
F: (01225) 442800
I: www.bath.org/hotel/stleon.
htm

Sampford ♦♦
11 Oldfield Road, Bath, BA2 3ND
T: (01225) 310053

Somerset House Hotel ♦♦♦♦
35 Bathwick Hill, Bath, BA2 6LD
T: (01225) 466451 & 463471
F: (01225) 317188
E: somersethouse@compuserve.
com
I: www.somersethouse.co.uk

Stoke Bottom Farm ◆◆
Stoke St Michael, Bath,
BA3 5HW
T: (01761) 232273

Sydney Gardens Hotel ◆◆◆◆
Sydney Road, Bath, BA2 6NT
T: (01225) 464818 & 445362
F: (01225) 484347
E: pete@sydneygardens.co.uk
I: www.sydneygardens.co.uk

3 Thomas Street ◆◆◆
Bath, BA1 5NW
T: (01225) 789540

Toad Hall Guest House ◆◆◆
6 Lime Grove, Widcombe, Bath,
BA2 4HF
T: (01225) 423254
F: (01225) 423254

Toghill House Farm ◆◆◆
Wick, Bristol BS30 5RT
T: (01225) 891261
F: (01225) 892128

The Town House
◆◆◆◆ SILVER AWARD
7 Bennett Street, Bath, BA1 2QJ
T: (01225) 422505

Villa Magdala Hotel
◆◆◆◆ GOLD AWARD
Henrietta Road, Bath, BA2 6LX
T: (01225) 466329
F: (01225) 483207
E: office@VillaMagdala.co.uk
I: www.VillaMagdala.co.uk

Walton Villa ◆◆◆◆
3 Newbridge Hill, Bath, BA1 3PW
T: (01225) 482792
F: (01225) 313093

Wellsway Guest House ◆◆
Rating Applied For
51 Wellsway, Bath, BA2 4RS
T: (01225) 423434

The Wheatsheaf Inn ◆◆◆◆
Combe Hay, Bath BA2 7EG
T: (01225) 833504
F: (01225) 833504
I: www.the-wheatsheaf.
freeserve.co.uk

Wheelwrights Arms ◆◆
Monkton Combe, Bath BA2 7HD
T: (01225) 722287
F: (01225) 723029
I: www.yell.co.
uk/sites/the-wheelwright-arms/

Redwood House ◆◆◆
Trossachs Drive, Bathampton,
Bath BA2 6RP
T: (01225) 464930 &
07778 648209

Dolphin House ◆◆◆
8 Northend, Batheaston, Bath
BA1 7EH
T: (01225) 858915 &
07801 444521
F: (01225) 858915

Garston Cottage ◆◆◆
28 Ashley Road, Bathford, Bath
BA1 7TT
T: (01225) 852510 &
07771 998120
F: (01225) 852793
E: garstoncot@aol.com

The Lodge Hotel ◆◆◆◆
Bathford Hill, Bathford, Bath
BA1 7SL
T: (01225) 858467 & 858575
F: (01225) 858172
E: lodgethe@aol.com
I: www.lodgehotelbath.co.uk

Ravenscroft
◆◆◆◆ GOLD AWARD
North Road, Bathwick, Bath
BA2 6HZ
T: (01225) 461919
F: (01225) 461919
E: ravenscroft@compuserve.
com
I: www.ravenscroftbandb.co.uk

Kings Farm ◆◆◆
10 Eastside Lane, Bawdrip,
Bridgwater, Somerset TA7 8QB
T: (01278) 683233 &
07801 079138

Beam Cottage ◆◆◆◆
16 North Street, Beaminster,
Dorset DT8 3DZ
T: (01308) 863639
E: magie@beam-cottage.fsnt.
co.uk

Brook Cottage ◆◆◆◆
Rating Applied For
7 Bridport Road, Beaminster,
Dorset DT8 3LU
T: (01308) 863007

Higher Langdon ◆◆◆
Beaminster, Dorset DT8 3NN
T: (01308) 862537
F: (01308) 863532
E: a.j.thompson@farming.co.uk

Jenny Wrens ◆◆◆
1 Hogshill Street, Beaminster,
Dorset DT8 3AE
T: (01308) 862814
F: (01308) 861191

Kitwhistle Farm ◆◆◆
Beaminster Down, Beaminster,
Dorset DT8 3SG
T: (01308) 862458

North Buckham Farm ◆◆◆
Beaminster, Dorset DT8 3SH
T: (01308) 863054 &
07967 499720
F: (01308) 863054
E: andrew@northbuckham.
fsnet.co.uk

The Walnuts
◆◆◆◆ SILVER AWARD
2 Prout Bridge, Beaminster,
Dorset DT8 3AY
T: (01308) 862211

Water Meadow House
◆◆◆◆ SILVER AWARD
Bridge Farm, Hooke, Beaminster,
Dorset DT8 3PD
T: (01308) 862619
F: (01308) 862619

Longcross House ◆◆◆
Black Torrington, Beaworthy,
Devon EX21 5QG
T: (01409) 231219

Three Oaks ◆◆◆
Henford Barton, Ashwater,
Beaworthy, Devon EX21 5DA
T: (01409) 211417

Eden Vale Farm ◆◆◆
Mill Lane, Beckington, Bath,
Somerset BA3 6SN
T: (01373) 830371

Berrow Links House ◆◆◆◆
Coast Road, Berrow, Burnham-
on-Sea, Somerset TA8 2QS
T: (01278) 751422
F: (01278) 751822

Martins Hill Farmhouse ◆◆◆
Red Road, Berrow, Burnham-
on-Sea, Somerset TA8 2RW
T: (01278) 751726
F: (01278) 751230
I: www.marinshillfarm.co.uk

Yew Tree House
◆◆◆◆ SILVER AWARD
Hurn Lane, Berrow, Burnham-
on-Sea, Somerset TA8 2QT
T: (01278) 751382
F: (01278) 751382

Berry Farm ◆◆◆
Berry Pomeroy, Totnes, Devon
TQ9 6LG
T: (01803) 863231

Bessemer Thatch Hotel
◆◆◆◆ SILVER AWARD
Berrynarbor, Ilfracombe, Devon
EX34 9SE
T: (01271) 882296
F: (01271) 882296

Langleigh House ◆◆◆
The Village, Berrynarbor,
Ilfracombe, Devon EX34 9SG
T: (01271) 883410
F: (01271) 882396
E: langleigh@hotmail.com

The Lodge ◆◆◆◆
Pitt Hill, Berrynarbor, Ilfracombe,
Devon EX34 9SG
T: (01271) 883246
F: (01271) 883246
E: teem.mabin@virgin.nets

Mill Park House ◆◆◆◆
Mill Lane, Berrynarbor,
Ilfracombe, Devon EX34 9SH
T: (01271) 882990

Marshwood Manor ◆◆◆◆
Bettiscombe, Bridport, Dorset
DT6 5NS
T: (01308) 868442 & 868825

Elm Farmhouse ◆◆◆◆
The Green, Biddestone,
Chippenham, Wiltshire
SN14 7DG
T: (01249) 713354
F: (01249) 713354
E: r_g_sexton@hotmail.com

The Granary ◆◆◆
Cuttle Lane, Biddestone,
Chippenham, Wiltshire
SN14 7DA
T: (01249) 715077

Home Farm ◆◆◆◆
Harts Lane, Biddestone,
Chippenham, Wiltshire
SN14 7DQ
T: (01249) 714475 &
07966 549759
F: (01249) 701488
E: smith@homefarmb-b.
freeserve.co.uk

Home Place ◆◆
The Green, Biddestone,
Chippenham, Wiltshire
SN14 7DG
T: (01249) 712928

The Mount ◆◆◆◆
Northdown Road, Bideford,
Devon EX39 3LP
T: (01237) 473748
I: www5.50megs.com/themount

Sunset Hotel ◆◆◆
Landcross, Bideford, Devon
EX39 5JA
T: (01237) 472962
E: hazellamb@hotmail.com

Steps Farmhouse ◆◆◆◆
Bilbrook, Minehead, Somerset
TA24 6HE
T: (01984) 640974
E: stepsfarmhouse@fsbdial.co.
uk

Mansfield House
◆◆◆◆ SILVER AWARD
Binegar, Shepton Mallet,
Somerset BA3 4UG
T: (01749) 840568 &
07976 705157
F: (01749) 840572
E: mansfieldhouse@aolcomm

Centaur ◆◆◆
Ham Lane, Bishop Sutton, Bristol
BS39 5TZ
T: (01275) 332321

Withymede ◆◆◆
The Street, Bishop Sutton,
Bristol BS39 5UU
T: (01275) 332069

The Lethbridge Arms ◆◆◆
Gore Square, Bishop's Lydeard,
Taunton, Somerset TA4 3BW
T: (01823) 432234
F: (01823) 433982

The Mount ◆◆◆◆
32 Mount Street, Bishop's
Lydeard, Taunton, Somerset
TA4 3AN
T: (01823) 432208
E: d.hinton@talk21.com

West View ◆◆◆◆
Minehead Road, Bishop's
Lydeard, Taunton, Somerset
TA4 3BS
T: (01823) 432223
F: (01823) 432223

BISHOPS HULL
Somerset

Hillview Guest House ◆◆◆
Bishops Hull Road, Bishops Hull,
Taunton, Somerset TA1 5EG
T: (01823) 275510
F: (01823) 275510

The Old Mill
Rating Applied For
Roughmoor, Bishops Hull,
Taunton, Somerset TA1 5AB
T: (01823) 289732
F: (01823) 289732

BISHOPSTON
Bristol

Basca Guest House ◆◆◆
19 Broadway Road, Bishopston,
Bristol BS7 8ES
T: (0117) 9422182

BISHOPSWOOD
Somerset

Hawthorne House ◆◆◆
Bishopswood, Chard, Somerset
TA20 3RS
T: (01460) 234482 &
07710 250059
F: (01460) 234482

BLACK DOG
Devon

Hele Barton Farm Guest House
◆◆◆
Black Dog, Crediton, Devon
EX17 4QJ
T: (01884) 860278
F: (01884) 860278
E: gillbard@eclipse.co.uk
I: www.eclipse.co.uk/helebarton

BLACKAWTON
Devon

The Normandy Arms ◆◆◆◆
Chapel Street, Blackawton,
Totnes, Devon TQ9 7BN
T: (01803) 712316
F: (01803) 712316
E: su2230@eclipse.co.uk

BLUE ANCHOR
Somerset

Camelot ◆◆◆
Carhampton Road, Blue Anchor,
Minehead, Somerset TA24 6LB
T: (01643) 821348
E: d.thrush@btinternet.com

The Langbury ◆◆◆
Blue Anchor, Minehead,
Somerset TA24 6LB
T: (01643) 821375
F: (01643) 821375
E: langbury@globalnet.co.uk
I: www.users.globalnet.co.
uk/$langbury

BODMIN
Cornwall

Bokiddick Farm
◆◆◆◆◆ GOLD AWARD
Lanivet, Bodmin, Cornwall
PL30 5HP
T: (01208) 831481
F: (01208) 831481

Castle Canyke Farmhouse
◆◆◆◆
Bodmin, Cornwall PL31 1HG
T: (01208) 79109
F: (01208) 79109

Colliford Tavern ◆◆◆◆
Colliford Lake, St Neot, Liskeard,
Cornwall PL14 6PZ
T: (01208) 821335
F: (01208) 821335
E: colliford@hotmail.com
I: www.cornwall-online.co.
uk/colliford-tavern

Mount Pleasant Farmhouse
◆◆◆◆ SILVER AWARD
Mount, Bodmin, Cornwall
PL30 4EX
T: (01208) 821342
E: colettecapper@hotmail.com
I: www.capperbl.freeserve.co.uk

BOLVENTOR
Cornwall

Jamaica Inn ◆◆◆
Bolventor, Launceston, Cornwall
PL15 7TS
T: (01566) 86250
F: (01566) 86177
I: jamaicainn@eclipse.co.uk

BOSCASTLE
Cornwall

The Old Coach House ◆◆◆◆
Tintagel Road, Boscastle,
Cornwall PL35 0AS
T: (01840) 250398
F: (01840) 250346
E: parsons@old-coach.demon.
co.uk
I: www.old-coach.co.uk

Rivendell Court ◆◆◆◆
Boscastle, Cornwall PL35 0BN
T: (01840) 250130
F: (01840) 250130

**Tolcarne House Hotel and
Restaurant** ◆◆◆◆
Tintagel Road, Boscastle,
Cornwall PL35 0AS
T: (01840) 250654
F: (01840) 250654
E: crowntolhouse@eclipse.co.uk
I: milford.co.uk/60/tolcarne

Trerosewill Farmhouse
◆◆◆◆ SILVER AWARD
Paradise, Boscastle, Cornwall
PL35 0DL
T: (01840) 250545
F: (01840) 250545
E: Nicholls@trerosewill.telme.
com
I: www.ipl.co.uk/trerosewill

BOSSINGTON
Somerset

Buckley Lodge ◆◆◆◆
Bossington, Minehead, Somerset
TA24 8HQ
T: (01643) 862521

Orchard Guest House ◆◆◆
Bossington, Minehead, Somerset
TA24 8HQ
T: (01643) 862336
F: (01643) 862002
E: denis@sewell.u-net.com
I: www.vli.co.uk/orchard/default.
htm

BOVEY TRACEY
Devon

Brookfield House ◆◆◆◆
SILVER AWARD
Challabrook Lane, Bovey Tracey,
Newton Abbot, Devon TQ12 9DF
T: (01626) 836181
F: (01626) 836182
E: brookfieldh@tinyworld.co.uk

The Cromwell Arms Hotel
◆◆◆◆
Fore Street, Bovey Tracey,
Newton Abbot, Devon TQ13 9AE
T: (01626) 833473
F: (01626) 836873

Frost Farmhouse ◆◆◆
Frost Farm, Hennock Road,
Bovey Tracey, Newton Abbot,
Devon TQ13 9PP
T: (01626) 833266
F: (01626) 833266

BOWERHILL
Wiltshire

32 Duxford Close ◆◆◆
Bowerhill, Melksham, Wiltshire
SN12 6XN
T: (01225) 704679

BOX
Wiltshire

Baylys Ale House ◆◆
High Street, Box, Corsham,
Wiltshire SN13 8NJ
T: (01225) 743622

Cheney Cottage ◆◆◆◆
Ditteridge, Box, Corsham,
Wiltshire SN13 8QF
T: (01225) 742346
F: (01225) 742346
E: cheneycottage@btinternet.
com
I: www.visitus.co.
uk/bath/hotel/cheney.htm

Highfield House ◆◆◆
London Road, Box, Corsham,
Wiltshire SN13 8LU
T: (01225) 743030
F: (01225) 743030
E: lizmillward@dknet.co.uk

Lorne House ◆◆◆
London Road, Box, Corsham,
Wiltshire SN13 8NA
T: (01225) 742597
F: (01225) 742597
E: gordontaylor@
lornehouse100.freeserve.co.uk

Manor Farm ◆◆◆◆
Wadswick, Box, Corsham,
Wiltshire SN13 8JB
T: (01225) 810700
F: (01225) 810307

BRADFORD ABBAS
Dorset

Purbeck House ◆◆
North Street, Bradford Abbas,
Sherborne, Dorset DT9 6SA
T: (01935) 474817

BRADFORD-ON-AVON
Wiltshire

Applegates ◆◆◆◆
32 Winsley Village, Bradford-on-
Avon, Wiltshire BA15 2LU
T: (01225) 723803
F: (01225) 722174
E: stay@applegatesbandb.co.uk
I: www.applegatesbandb.co.uk

The Beeches Farmhouse
◆◆◆◆◆
Holt Road, Bradford-on-Avon,
Wiltshire BA15 1TS
T: (01225) 863475 &
07774 607417
F: (01225) 863475
E: beeches-farmhouse@1way.
co.uk
I: www.bath.co.
uk/beeches-farmhouse

Brookfield House ◆◆◆◆
Vaggs Hill, Southwick,
Trowbridge, Wiltshire BA14 9NA
T: (01373) 830615 & 0777 160
3842
F: (01373) 830615

The Georgian Lodge ◆◆◆◆
25 Bridge Street, Bradford-on-
Avon, Wiltshire BA15 1BY
T: (01225) 862268
F: (01225) 862218
E: georgianlodge.hotel@
btinternet.com

Great Ashley Farm
◆◆◆◆ SILVER AWARD
Ashley Lane, Bradford-on-Avon,
Wiltshire BA15 2PP
T: (01225) 864563 &
07774 861858
F: (01225) 864563
E: greatashleyfarm@
farmersweekly.net

Hillside Lodge Bed & Breakfast
◆◆◆◆ SILVER AWARD
Hillside Lodge, Jones Hill,
Bradford-on-Avon, Bath
BA15 2EE
T: (01225) 866312
F: (01225) 866312
E: barnes@hillsidelodge.fsnet.
co.uk

Springfields ◆◆◆
182a Great Ashley, Bradford-
on-Avon, Wiltshire BA15 2PP
T: (01225) 866125

BRADPOLE
Dorset

Spray Copse Farm
◆◆◆◆ SILVER AWARD
Lee Lane, Bradpole, Bridport,
Dorset DT6 4AP
T: (01308) 458510 &
07850 300044
F: (01308) 421015
E: spraycopse@lineone.net

BRADWORTHY
Devon

Lake House Holiday Cottages
◆◆◆
Lake Villa, Bradworthy,
Holsworthy, Devon EX22 7SQ
T: (01409) 241962

BRANSCOMBE
Devon

The Bulstone Hotel
Rating Applied For
Higher Bulstone, Branscombe,
Sidmouth, Devon EX12 3BL
T: (01297) 680446
F: (01297) 680446
E: kevinmon@aol.com
I: www.best-hotel.co.
uk/bulstone/index.html

BRATTON FLEMING
Devon

Bracken House Country Hotel
◆◆◆◆◆ GOLD AWARD
Bratton Fleming, Barnstaple,
Devon EX31 4TG
T: (01598) 710320
🏃

Haxton Down Farm ◆◆◆
Bratton Fleming, Barnstaple,
Devon EX32 7JL
T: (01598) 710275
F: (01598) 710275
⊚

BRAUNTON
Devon

Poyers Hotel ◆◆◆
Wrafton, Braunton, North Devon
EX33 2DN
T: (01271) 812149
I: www.poyers.co.uk

BRAYFORD
Devon

Rockley Farmhouse
◆◆◆◆ SILVER AWARD
Brayford, Barnstaple, Devon
EX32 7QR
T: (01598) 710429
F: (01598) 710429
E: rockley@hicon.co.uk
I: www.hicon.co.uk/rockley
⊚

BREAN
Somerset

Brean Farm ◆◆◆
Brean Down, Brean, Burnham-
on-Sea, Somerset TA8 2RR
T: (01278) 751055
F: (01278) 751055

The Old Rectory ◆◆◆
Church Road, Brean, Burnham-
on-Sea, Somerset TA8 2SF
T: (01278) 751447
F: (01278) 751447
I: www.old-rectory.fsbusiness.
co.uk

BREMHILL
Wiltshire

Hilltop Farm ◆◆◆
Bremhill, Calne, Wiltshire
SN11 9HQ
T: (01249) 740620

BRENDON
Devon

Brendon House Hotel ◆◆◆
Brendon, Lynton, Devon
EX35 6PS
T: (01598) 741206
E: dave@brendonhouse.
freeserve.co.uk
I: www.brendonvalley.co.uk

Millslade Country House Hotel
◆◆◆
Brendon, Lynton, Devon
EX35 6PS
T: (01598) 741322
F: (01598) 741355

Shilstone Farm ◆◆◆
Brendon, Lynton, Devon
EX35 6PU
T: (01598) 741262

Southernwood Farm ◆◆◆
Brendon, Lynton, Devon
EX35 6NU
T: (01598) 741277 &
07710 299504
E: 113726.65@compuserve.com
I: www.brendonvalley.co.uk

BRENT KNOLL
Somerset

Yonder Hill Bed and Breakfast
◆◆◆
Yonder Hill, Crooked Lane, Brent
Knoll, Highbridge, Somerset
TA9 4BQ
T: (01278) 760181
F: (01278) 760181

BRIDESTOWE
Devon

The Knole Farm
◆◆◆◆ SILVER AWARD
Bridestowe, Okehampton, Devon
EX20 4HA
T: (01837) 861241
F: (01837) 861241

Little Bidlake Farm ◆◆◆
Dartmoor Horse Trails,
Bridestowe, Okehampton, Devon
EX20 4NS
T: (01837) 861233
F: (01837) 861233
E: bidlakefrm@aol.com
I: www.littlebidlakefarm.co.uk

Way Barton Barn ◆◆◆
Bridestowe, Okehampton, Devon
EX20 4QH
T: (01837) 861513

White Hart Inn ◆◆◆
Fore Street, Bridestowe,
Okehampton, Devon EX20 4EL
T: (01837) 861318
F: (01837) 861318
E: whihartinn@aol.com
I: members.aol.
com/whihartinn/bridestowe.
html

BRIDGWATER
Somerset

Admirals Rest ◆◆◆
5 Taunton Road, Bridgwater,
Somerset TA6 3LW
T: (01278) 458580
F: (01278) 458580
E: sueparker@admiralsrest.
freeserve.co.uk

Ash–Wembdon Farm
◆◆◆◆ SILVER AWARD
Hollow Lane, Wembdon,
Bridgwater, Somerset TA5 2BD
T: (01278) 453097 &
07702 272755
F: (01278) 445856
E: mary.rowe@btinternet.com
I: www.farmaccommodation.co.
uk
⊚

Bower Green Pub Restaurant
◆◆◆
Bower Lane, Bridgwater,
Somerset TA6 4TY
T: (01278) 422926
F: (01278) 434426

Brookland Hotel ◆
56 North Street, Bridgwater,
Somerset TA6 3PN
T: (01278) 423263
F: (01278) 452988

Cokerhurst Farm ◆◆◆◆
87 Wembdon Hill, Bridgwater,
Somerset TA6 7QA
T: (01278) 422330 &
07850 692065
F: (01278) 422330
E: cokerhurst@clara.net
I: www.cokerhurst.clara.net
⊚

Manor Farmhouse ◆◆◆
Wembdon, Bridgwater,
Somerset TA5 2BB
T: (01278) 427913

Quantock View House ◆◆◆
Bridgwater Road, North
Petherton, Bridgwater, Somerset
TA6 6PR
T: (01278) 663309
E: wendy@quantockview.
freeserve.co.uk
I: www.quantockview.freeserve.
co.uk

BRIDPORT
Dorset

Bridge House Hotel ◆◆◆
115 East Street, Bridport, Dorset
DT6 3LB
T: (01308) 423371
F: (01308) 423371

Bridport Arms Hotel ◆◆◆
West Bay, Bridport, Dorset
DT6 4EN
T: (01308) 422994
F: (01308) 425141

Britmead House ◆◆◆◆
West Bay Road, Bridport, Dorset
DT6 4EG
T: (01308) 422941
F: (01308) 422516
E: britmead@talk21.com

The Bull Hotel ◆◆
34 East Street, Bridport, Dorset
DT6 3LF
T: (01308) 422878
F: (01308) 422878

Durbeyfield Guest House ◆◆◆
10 West Bay, West Bay, Bridport,
Dorset DT6 4EL
T: (01308) 423307 &
07976 420867
F: (01308) 423307
E: durbeyfield@morency.
freeserve.co.uk
I: www.morency.freeserve.co.uk

Neptune Cottage ◆◆◆
107 South Street, Bridport,
Dorset DT6 3PA
T: (01308) 420907
E: winniedog@talk21.com

New House Farm ◆◆◆
Mangerton Lane, Bradpole,
Bridport, Dorset DT6 3SF
T: (01308) 422884
F: (01308) 422884
E: jane@mangertonlake.
freeserve.co.uk
I: www.mangertonlake.co.uk

Polly's ◆◆◆◆
22 West Allington, Bridport,
Dorset DT6 5BG
T: (01308) 458095 &
07957 856112
F: (01308) 421834
E: mail@hume.org.uk

Rudge Farm
◆◆◆◆ SILVER AWARD
Chilcombe, Bridport, Dorset
DT6 4NF
T: (01308) 482630
F: (01308) 482635
E: sue@rudge-farm.co.uk
I: www.rudge-farm.co.uk

Southcroft
◆◆◆◆ SILVER AWARD
Park Road, Bridport, Dorset
DT6 5DA
T: (01308) 423335
F: (01308) 423335

Southview ◆◆◆
Whitecross, Netherbury,
Bridport, Dorset DT6 5NH
T: (01308) 488471

Urella ◆◆◆◆
65 Burton Road, Bridport, Dorset
DT6 4JE
T: (01308) 422450

The Well ◆◆◆
St Andrews Well, Bridport,
Dorset DT6 3DL
T: (01308) 424156

BRISLINGTON
Bristol

A4 Hotel ◆◆◆
511 Bath Road, Brislington,
Bristol BS4 3LA
T: (0117) 9715492
T: (0117) 9711791
E: a4hotel@lineone.net

The Beeches ◆◆◆◆
Broomhill Road, Brislington,
Bristol BS4 5RG
T: (0117) 972 8778
F: (0117) 971 1968

Kingston House ◆◆
101 Hardenhuish Road,
Brislington, Bristol BS4 3SR
T: (0117) 9712456

Woodstock ◆◆◆
534 Bath Road, Brislington,
Bristol BS4 3JZ
T: (0117) 987 1613
F: (0117) 987 1613
E: woodstock@cableinet.co.uk
I: www.homestead.com/wstock/

BRISTOL

Arches Hotel ◆◆◆
132 Cotham Brow, Cotham,
Bristol BS6 6AE
T: (0117) 9247398
F: (0117) 9247398
E: ml@arches-hotel.co.uk
I: www.arches-hotel.co.uk
⊚

Downlands House ◆◆◆◆
33 Henleaze Gardens, Bristol,
BS9 4HH
T: (0117) 9621639
F: (0117) 9621639
E: mjdownlands@compuserve.
com
I: www.s-h-systems.co.
uk/hotels/downland.html

Ferndale Guest House ◆◆◆
37 Deanery Road, Warmley,
Bristol, BS15 9JB
T: (01179) 858247

Gala Guest House ◆◆
479 Fishponds Road, Fishponds,
Bristol BS16 3AL
T: (0117) 965 3938
F: (0117) 965 3938
E: anngala@aol.com

Harpenden ◆◆◆◆
149 Richmond Road,
Montpelier, Bristol, BS6 5ES
T: (0117) 924 0016 & 0788 763
7176
F: (0117) 924 0016
E: harpenden@compuserve.com

The Hunters Rest
Rating Applied For
King Lane, Clutton Hill, Bristol,
BS39 5QL
T: (01761) 452303
F: (01761) 453308
E: paul.r.thomas@lineone.net

Mayfair Hotel ◆◆◆
5 Henleaze Road, Westbury-on-
Trym, Bristol BS9 4EX
T: (0117) 9622008 & 9493924

Norfolk House ◆◆◆
577 Gloucester Road, Horfield,
Bristol, BS7 0BW
T: (0117) 9513191
F: (0117) 9513191

Oakfield Hotel ◆◆◆
52 Oakfield Road, Clifton, Bristol
BS8 2BG
T: (0117) 973 5556 & 973 3643
F: (0117) 974 4141

The Old Court ◆◆◆◆
Main Road, Temple Cloud,
Bristol BS39 5DA
T: (01761) 451101
F: (01761) 451224
E: oldcourt@gifford.co.uk
I: www.theoldcourt.com

The Old Inn
◆◆◆◆ SILVER AWARD
1 The Old Inn, Kingsweston
Road, Bristol, BS11 0IIW
T: (0117) 962 6811 &
07831 614499
F: (0117) 962 6856
E: guy.littlemore@virgin.net

Rockleaze House ◆◆◆
91 Gloucester Road North,
Filton, Bristol BS34 7PT
T: (0117) 9692536

Rowan Lodge Hotel ◆◆◆
41 Gloucester Road North, Filton
Park, Bristol, BS7 0SN
T: (0117) 931 2170
F: (0117) 975 3601

Thornbury House
◆◆◆◆ GOLD AWARD
80 Chesterfield Road, St
Andrews, Bristol BS6 5DR
T: (0117) 924 5654
F: (0117) 944 1620
E: kaysmith@thornburyhouse.
fsbusiness.co.uk

Anchorage Guest House ◆◆◆
170 New Road, Brixham, Devon
TQ5 8DA
T: (01803) 852960

Melville Hotel ◆◆◆
45 New Road, Brixham, Devon
TQ5 8NL
T: (01803) 852033
E: melvillehotel@brixham45.co.
uk

Raddicombe Lodge ◆◆◆
Kingswear Road, Brixham,
Devon TQ5 0EX
T: (01803) 882125
F: (01803) 882125
E: judy@raddlodge.freeserve.co.
uk

Ranscombe House Hotel
◆◆◆◆
Ranscombe Road, Brixham,
Devon TQ5 9UP
T: (01803) 882337
F: (01803) 882337
E: ranscombe@lineone.net
@

Richmond House Hotel ◆◆◆
Higher Manor Road, Brixham,
Devon TQ5 8HA
T: (01803) 882391
F: (01803) 882391

Sea Tang Guest House ◆◆◆
67 Berry Head Road, Brixham,
Devon TQ5 9AA
T: (01803) 854651
F: (01803) 854651
E: b&b@seatang.freeserve.co.uk

The Shoalstone Hotel ◆◆◆
105 Berry Head Road, Brixham,
Devon TQ5 9AG
T: (01803) 857919 & 850550
F: (01803) 850540

Tor Haven Hotel ◆◆◆
97 King Street, Brixham, Devon
TQ5 9TH
T: (01803) 882281

Venn Farm ◆
Brixton, Plymouth, Devon
PL8 2AX
T: (01752) 880378
F: (01752) 880378

The Queens Head Inn ◆◆◆◆
1 North Street, Broad Chalke,
Salisbury, Wiltshire SP5 5EN
T: (01722) 780344
F: (01722) 780344

Huntersley ◆◆◆
Post Office Lane, Broad Hinton,
Swindon SN4 9PB
T: (01793) 731115
F: (01793) 731115

Lane End Farm ◆◆◆
Broadhembury, Honiton, Devon
EX14 0LU
T: (01404) 841563
@

Stafford Barton
◆◆◆◆◆ GOLD AWARD
Broadhembury, Honiton, Devon
EX14 3LU
T: (01404) 841403
F: (01404) 841403
E: anne@staffordbawton.
devonfarms.co.uk

Dunster Farm ◆◆◆
Broadoak, Bridport, Dorset
DT6 5NR
T: (01308) 424626
@

Crosskeys House
Rating Applied For
Broadwindsor, Beaminster,
Dorset DT8 3QP
T: (01308) 868063

Frankaborough Farm ◆◆◆
Broadwoodwidger, Lifton, Devon
PL16 0JS
T: (01409) 211308 &
07971 525550

The Cottage ◆◆◆
Westbrook, Bromham,
Chippenham, Wiltshire
SN15 2EE
T: (01380) 850255
E: RJSteed@cottage16.
freeserve.co.uk

Sandycroft ◆◆◆◆
Chittoe Heath, Bromham,
Chippenham, Wiltshire
SN15 2EQ
T: (01380) 850030 &
07702 364324

Westleigh Farm ◆◆◆
Broomfield, Bridgwater,
Somerset TA5 2EH
T: (01823) 451773
F: (01823) 451772

Frying Pan Farm ◆◆◆
Broughton Gifford, Melksham,
Wiltshire SN12 8LL
T: (01225) 702343
F: (01225) 793652
E: fr65@dial.pipex.com

Gants Mill ◆◆◆
Gants Mill Lane, Bruton,
Somerset BA10 0DB
T: (01749) 812393
E: shingler@gantsmill.ndo.co.uk
I: www.gantsmill.co.uk

Bank Cottage Guest House
◆◆◆◆
Bryher, Isles of Scilly TR23 0PR
T: (01720) 422612
F: (01720) 422612
E: macmace@patrol.i-way.co.uk

Soleil D'or ◆◆◆◆
Bryher, Isles of Scilly TR23 0PR
T: (01720) 422003

Furzeleigh Mill Country Hotel
◆◆◆
Dartbridge, Buckfast, Devon
TQ11 0JP
T: (01364) 643476 & 642245
F: (01364) 643476

Dartbridge Inn ◆◆◆◆
Totnes Road, Buckfastleigh,
Devon TQ11 0JR
T: (01364) 642214
F: (01364) 643977

Wellpark Farm ◆◆◆◆
Dean Prior, Buckfastleigh, Devon
TQ11 0LY
T: (01364) 643775
F: (01364) 643775

Uppaton Country Guest House
◆◆◆◆
Coppicetown Road, Buckland
Monachorum, Yelverton, Devon
PL20 7LL
T: (01822) 855511
F: (01822) 855511

Holyleas House
◆◆◆◆ SILVER AWARD
Buckland Newton, Dorchester,
Dorset DT2 7DP
T: (01300) 345214
F: (01305) 264488
E: tiabunkall@holyleas.co.uk

Rew Cottage ◆◆◆◆
Buckland Newton, Dorchester,
Dorset DT2 7DN
T: (01300) 345467
F: (01300) 345467

Whiteways Farmhouse
Accommodation ◆◆◆◆
Bookham Farm, Buckland
Newton, Dorchester, Dorset
DT2 7RP
T: (01300) 345511
F: (01300) 345511
E: bookhamfarm@
netscapeonline.co.uk

Atlantic Calm ◆◆◆◆
30 Downs View, Bude, Cornwall
EX23 8RG
T: (01288) 359165
E: mike@talk21.com
I: www.atlantic-calm.
bude-cornwall.co.uk

Cliff Hotel ◆◆◆◆
Crooklets Beach, Bude, Cornwall
EX23 8NG
T: (01288) 353110
F: (01288) 353110

Clovelly House ◆◆◆
Rating Applied For
4 Burn View, Bude, Cornwall
EX23 8BY
T: (01288) 352761
F: (01288) 352761

Corisande Hotel ◆◆◆
24 Downs View, Bude, Cornwall
EX23 8RG
T: (01288) 353474
F: (01288) 353474
E: janerouse@compuserve.com
I: www.bude-cornwall.co.
uk/corisande

The Elms ◆◆◆
37 Lynstone Road, Bude,
Cornwall EX23 8LR
T: (01288) 353429

Hallagather Farmhouse
◆◆◆◆
Crackington Haven, Bude,
Cornwall EX23 0LA
T: (01840) 230276
F: (01840) 230449
@

Link's Side ♦♦♦♦
7 Burn View, Bude, Cornwall
EX23 8BY
T: (01288) 352410 & 352561
E: linksidebude@
north-cornwall.co.uk
I: www.north-cornwall.co.
uk/bude/client/linkside

Lower Northcott Farm ♦♦♦
Poughill, Bude, Cornwall
EX23 9EQ
T: (01288) 352350
T: (01288) 352712
E: sales@coast-countryside.co.
uk
I: www.coast-countryside.co.uk
🌐

Lower Tresmorn
♦♦♦♦ SILVER AWARD
Lower Tresmorn Farm,
Crackington Haven, Bude,
Cornwall EX23 0LQ
T: (01840) 230667
F: (01840) 230667

Seagulls Guest House
Rating Applied For
11 Downs View, Bude, Cornwall
EX23 8RF
T: (01288) 352059
F: (01288) 359259
E: seagullgh@aol.com

Sunrise Guest House ♦♦♦♦
6 Burn View, Bude, Cornwall
EX23 8BY
T: (01288) 353214

Teeside Guest House ♦♦♦
2 Burn View, Bude, Cornwall
EX23 8BY
T: (01288) 352351

BUDLEIGH SALTERTON
Devon
Clyst Hayes Farm ♦♦♦♦
Knowle Road, Budleigh
Salterton, Devon EX9 6AR
T: (01395) 444033
F: (01395) 444033
E: sheila.downs@usa.net
I: wol.ra.phy.cam.ac.
uk/obd20/CHFBB.htm

Lufflands
♦♦♦♦ SILVER AWARD
Yettington, Budleigh Salterton,
Devon EX9 7BP
T: (01395) 568422
F: (01395) 568810
E: Lufflands@compuserve.com
I: www.lufflands.co.uk

BUDOCK WATER
Cornwall
Higher Kergilliack Farm ♦♦♦
Budock Water, Falmouth,
Cornwall TR11 5PB
T: (01326) 372271

**The Home Country House
Hotel** ♦♦♦
Penjerrick, Budock Water,
Falmouth, Cornwall TR11 5EE
T: (01326) 250427 & 250143
F: (01326) 250143

BURLAWN
Cornwall
Pengelly Farmhouse ♦♦♦
Burlawn, Wadebridge, Cornwall
PL27 7LA
T: (01208) 814217

BURNHAM-ON-SEA
Somerset
Ar Dhachaedh ♦♦♦
36 Abingdon Street, Burnham-
on-Sea, Somerset TA8 1PJ
T: (01278) 783652

Boundrys Edge ♦♦♦
40 Charlestone Road, Burnham-
on-Sea, Somerset TA8 2AP
T: (01278) 783128 &
0771 2737033
F: (01278) 783128

Cresta B&B ♦♦
230 Berrow Road, Burnham-on-
Sea, Somerset TA8 2JG
T: (01278) 795626

Dunstan House Inn ♦♦♦
Love Lane, Burnham-on-Sea,
Somerset TA8 1EU
T: (01278) 784343

Emahruo Guest House ♦♦
34 Abingdon Street, Burnham-
on-Sea, Somerset TA8 1PH
T: (01278) 788816

Knights Rest ♦
9 Dunstan Road, Knights Rest,
Burnham-on-Sea, Somerset
TA8 1ER
T: (01278) 782318

Priors Mead ♦♦♦
23 Rectory Road, Burnham-on-
Sea, Somerset TA8 2BZ
T: (01278) 782116 &
07860 573018
F: (01278) 782116
I: www.smoothhound.co.
uk/hotels/priors.html

Prospect Farm Guest House
♦♦♦
Strowlands, East Brent,
Highbridge, Somerset TA9 4JH
T: (01278) 760507
🌐

Sandhills Guest House ♦
3 Poplar Road, Burnham-on-
Sea, Somerset TA8 2HD
T: (01278) 781208

Shalimar Guest House ♦♦
174 Berrow Road, Burnham-on-
Sea, Somerset TA8 2JE
T: (01278) 785898

Somewhere House ♦♦♦
68 Berrow Road, Burnham-on-
Sea, Somerset TA8 2EZ
T: (01278) 795236
E: somewhere@ukonline.co.uk
I: www.somewherehouse.co.uk

Thornbury
Rating Applied For
4 Manor Road, Burnham-on-
Sea, Somerset TA8 2AS
T: (01278) 784882

The Warren Guest House ♦♦♦
29 Berrow Road, Burnham-on-
Sea, Somerset TA8 2EZ
T: (01278) 786726 & 788204

BURTLE
Somerset
The Tom Mogg Inn ♦♦♦
Station Road, Burtle, Bridgwater,
Somerset TA7 8NU
T: (01278) 722399
F: (01278) 722724

BURTON BRADSTOCK
Dorset
Bridge Cottage Stores ♦♦♦
87 High Street, Burton
Bradstock, Bridport, Dorset
DT6 4RA
T: (01308) 897222

Burton Cliff Hotel ♦♦♦
Cliff Road, Burton Bradstock,
Bridport, Dorset DT6 4RB
T: (01308) 897205
F: (01308) 898111
♿

Pebble Beach Lodge ♦♦♦♦
Coast Road, Burton Bradstock,
Bridport, Dorset DT6 4RJ
T: (01308) 897428
F: (01308) 897428
🌐

BUTCOMBE
North Somerset
Butcombe Farm ♦♦♦♦
Aldwick Lane, Butcombe, Bristol
BS40 7UW
T: (01761) 462380
F: (01761) 462300
E: info@butcombe-farm.
demon.co.uk
I: www.butcombe-farm.demon.
co.uk
🌐

CADLEY
Wiltshire
Kingstones Farm ♦♦♦♦
Cadley, Marlborough, Wiltshire
SN8 4NE
T: (01672) 512039
F: (01672) 515947

CALLINGTON
Cornwall
Dozmary ♦♦♦
Tors View Close, Tavistock Road,
Callington, Cornwall PL17 7DY
T: (01579) 383677
E: dozmarybb@aol.com

Green Pastures ♦♦♦
Longhill, Callington, Cornwall
PL17 8AU
T: (01579) 382566
E: greenpast@aol.com

Higher Manaton ♦♦♦
Callington, Cornwall PL17 8PX
T: (01579) 370460
F: (01579) 370460

CALNE
Wiltshire
Chilvester Hill House
♦♦♦♦♦ SILVER AWARD
Calne, Wiltshire SN11 0LP
T: (01249) 813981 & 815785
F: (01249) 814217
E: gill.dilley@talk21.com
I: www.wolsey-lodges.co.uk

**Hayle Farm Hotel and
Restaurant** ♦♦♦
Quemerford, Calne, Wiltshire
SN11 8UJ
T: (01249) 813275
F: (01249) 813275
E: hayle-farm@eclipse.co.uk
I: www.eclipse.co.uk/hayle-farm

Lower Sands Farm ♦
Calne, Wiltshire SN11 8TR
T: (01249) 812402

Manor Farm (Calstone)
♦♦♦♦ SILVER AWARD
Calstone Wellington, Calne,
Calne, Wiltshire SN11 8PY
T: (01249) 816804 &
07050 208886
F: (01249) 817966
E: calstonebandb@
farmersweekly.net
I: www.calstone.co.uk

Maundrell House ♦♦♦♦
Horsebrook, The Green, Calne,
Wiltshire SN11 8DL
T: (01249) 821267
F: (01249) 821267
I: www.maundrell.bigwig.net

Queenwood Golf Lodge
Rating Applied For
Bowood Golf & Country Club,
Calne, Wiltshire SN11
T: (01249) 822228
F: (01249) 822218

White Hart Hotel ♦♦
2 London Road, Calne, Wiltshire
SN11 0AB
T: (01249) 812413 & 812467
F: (01249) 812467

CANNINGTON
Somerset
Blackmore Farm ♦♦♦♦♦
Cannington, Bridgwater,
Somerset TA5 2NE
T: (01278) 653442
F: (01278) 653427
E: Dyerfarm@aol.com
I: www.dyerfarm.co.uk
🌐 ♿

The Friendly Spirit ♦♦♦
Brook Street, Cannington,
Bridgwater, Somerset TA5 2HP
T: (01278) 652215
F: (01278) 653636

Gurney Manor Mill ♦♦♦♦
Gurney Street, Cannington,
Bridgwater, Somerset TA5 2HW
T: (01278) 653582
F: (01278) 653993
E: gurneymill@yahoo.co.uk
I: www.gurneymill.freeserve.co.
uk

Kings Head Inn ♦♦♦
12-14 High Street, Cannington,
Bridgwater, Somerset TA5 2HE
T: (01278) 652293

CARBIS BAY
Cornwall
Howards Hotel ♦♦♦
St Ives Road, Carbis Bay, St Ives,
Cornwall TR26 2SB
T: (01736) 795651
F: (01736) 795535
E: dmg1how@btclick.com
I: www.cornwall-online.co.
uk/howardshotel

Tregorran Hotel ♦♦♦♦
Headland Road, Carbis Bay, St
Ives, Cornwall TR26 2NU
T: (01736) 795889

Trelowena Guest House ♦♦♦
27 Richmond Way, Carbis Bay,
St Ives, Cornwall TR26 2JY
I: (01736) 798276

**The White House Hotel &
Restaurant** ♦♦♦
The Valley, Carbis Bay, St Ives,
Cornwall TR26 2QY
T: (01736) 797405 & 797426

CARLYON BAY
Cornwall
Horizon House ◆◆◆◆
Sea Road, Carlyon Bay, St
Austell, Cornwall PL25 3SG
T: (01726) 817221
F: (01726) 817221

CASTLE CARY
Somerset
Bond's ◆◆◆◆
Ansford Hill, Castle Cary,
Somerset BA7 7JL
T: (01963) 350464
F: (01963) 350464

Clanville Manor
◆◆◆◆ SILVER AWARD
Castle Cary, Somerset BA7 7PJ
T: (01963) 350124 &
07966 512732
F: (01963) 350313
E: clanville@aol.com
I: www.clanville@aol.com

The Horse Pond Inn and Motel
◆◆◆
The Triangle, Castle Cary,
Somerset BA7 7BD
T: (01963) 350318 & 351762
F: (01963) 351764
E: horsepondinn@aol.com

Orchard Farm ◆◆◆
Cockhill, Castle Cary, Somerset
BA7 7NY
T: (01963) 350418
F: (01963) 350418
E: http/wwwleisurehuntcom/
adhtml/cockhillfarm

CASTLE COMBE
Wiltshire
Goulters Mill Farm ◆◆◆
Goulters Mill, Nettleton,
Chippenham, Wiltshire SN14 7LL
T: (01249) 782555

Thorngrove Cottage ◆◆◆
Summer Lane, Castle Combe,
Chippenham, Wiltshire
SN14 7LG
T: (01249) 782607 &
0780 1304676

CATTISTOCK
Dorset
Greystones ◆◆◆
Cattistock, Dorchester, Dorset
DT2 OJB
T: (01300) 320477
E: j_f.fletcher@virgin.net

Sandhills Cottage ◆◆◆◆
Sandhills, Cattistock, Dorchester,
Dorset DT2 OHQ
T: (01300) 321146
F: (01300) 321146
E: m.roca@lineone.net

CAUNDLE MARSH
Dorset
Caphays House ◆◆
Caundle Marsh, Sherborne,
Dorset DT9 5LX
T: (01963) 23325
F: (01963) 23325

CERNE ABBAS
Dorset
Badger Hill ◆◆◆◆
11 Springfield, Cerne Abbas,
Dorchester, Dorset DT2 7JZ
T: (01300) 341698
F: (01300) 341698

Cerne River Cottage ◆◆◆◆
8 The Folly, Cerne Abbas,
Dorchester, Dorset DT2 7JR
T: (01300) 341355
E: B&B@W-ellis.freeserve.co.uk

CHAGFORD
Devon
Glendarah House
◆◆◆◆ SILVER AWARD
Lower Street, Chagford, Newton
Abbot, Devon TQ13 8BZ
T: (01647) 433270
F: (01647) 433483
E: enquiries@glendarah-house.
co.uk
I: www.glendarah-house.co.uk

Throwleigh Manor ◆◆◆◆
Throwleigh, Okehampton, Devon
EX20 2JF
T: (01647) 231630
F: (01647) 231630

CHALLACOMBE
Devon
Home Place Farm ◆◆◆
Challacombe, Barnstaple, Devon
EX31 4TS
T: (01598) 763283
F: (01598) 763283

Twitchen Farm ◆◆◆
Challacombe, Barnstaple, Devon
EX31 4TT
T: (01598) 763568
F: (01598) 763310
E: holidays@twitchen.co.uk
I: www.twitchen.co.uk

CHAPMANSLADE
Wiltshire
Spinney Farmhouse
Rating Applied For
Thoulstone, Chapmanslade,
Westbury, Wiltshire BA13 4AQ
T: (01373) 832412

CHARD
Somerset
Bellplot House ◆◆◆◆◆
High Street, Chard, Somerset
TA20 1QB
T: (01460) 62600
F: (01460) 62600

Home Farm ◆◆◆
Hornsbury Hill, Chard, Somerset
TA20 3DB
T: (01460) 63731

Wambrook Farm ◆◆◆
Wambrook, Chard, Somerset
TA20 3DF
T: (01460) 62371
F: (01460) 68827

CHARLESTOWN
Cornwall
Rashleigh Arms ◆◆◆
Charlestown Road, Charlestown,
St Austell, Cornwall PL25 3NJ
T: (01726) 73635
F: (01726) 73635

T'Gallants ◆◆◆
6 Charlestown Road,
Charlestown, St Austell,
Cornwall PL25 3NJ
T: (01726) 70203

CHARLTON HORETHORNE
Somerset
Ashclose Farm ◆◆◆
Blackford Road, Charlton
Horethorne, Sherborne, Dorset
DT9 4PG
T: (01963) 220360 &
07710 235494
E: gooding@ashclosefarm.
freeserve.co.uk

CHARMINSTER
Dorset
Slades Farm ◆◆◆◆
North Street, Charminster,
Dorchester, Dorset DT2 9QZ
T: (01305) 265614
F: (01305) 265614

Three Compasses Inn ◆◆◆
Charminster, Dorchester, Dorset
DT2 9QT
T: (01305) 263618

CHARMOUTH
Dorset
Cardsmill Farm ◆◆◆
Whitchurch Canonicorum,
Bridport, Dorset DT6 6RP
T: (01297) 489375
F: (01297) 489375
E: cardsmill@aol.com
I: www.farmhousedorest.com

Fernhill Hotel ◆◆◆
Charmouth, Bridport, Dorset
DT6 6BX
T: (01297) 560492
F: (01297) 560492

CHEDDAR
Somerset
Chedwell Cottage ◆◆◆◆
59 Redcliffe Street, Cheddar,
Somerset BS27 3PF
T: (01934) 743268

Constantine ◆◆◆
Lower New Road, Cheddar,
Somerset BS27 3DY
T: (01934) 741339 &
07710 966695

Gordons Hotel ◆◆◆
Cliff Street, Cheddar, Somerset
BS27 3PT
T: (01934) 742497
F: (01934) 744965
I: gordons.hotel@virgin.net

Innisbeg ◆◆◆
West Lynne, Cheddar, Somerset
BS27 3JL
T: (01934) 743494
F: (01934) 743494
E: innishbeg@btinternet.com
I: www.innishbeg.btinternet.co.
uk

Market Cross Hotel ◆◆◆
The Cross, Church Street,
Cheddar, Somerset BS27 3RA
T: (01934) 742264
F: (01934) 741411

Neuholme ◆◆◆◆
The Barrows, Cheddar, Somerset
BS27 3BG
T: (01934) 742841 &
07977 644712

South Barn B & B ◆◆
The Hayes, Cheddar, Somerset
BS27 3AN
T: (01934) 743146 &
0471 579593
F: (01934) 743146

Tor Farm ◆◆◆◆
Nyland, Cheddar, Somerset
BS27 3UD
T: (01934) 743710
F: (01934) 743710
E: bcjbkj@aol.com

Wassells House ◆◆◆◆
Upper New Road, Cheddar,
Somerset BS27 3DN
T: (01934) 744317 &
07977 580453
E: afinders@wassells99.
freeserve.co.uk

CHEDZOY
Somerset
Apple View ◆◆◆◆
Temple Farm, Chedzoy,
Bridgwater, Somerset TA7 8QR
T: (01278) 423201 &
07710 594063
E: templefarm@netscapeonline.
co.uk

CHELSTON
Devon
Colindale Hotel ◆◆◆
20 Rathmore Road, Chelston,
Torquay, Devon TQ2 6NY
T: (01803) 293947

Elmdene Hotel ◆◆◆◆
Rathmore Road, Chelston,
Torquay TQ2 6NZ
T: (01803) 294940
F: (01803) 294940
E: elmdenehotel@torquay5563.
freeserve.co.uk
I: www.s-h-systems.co.
uk/hotels/elmdene.html

Millbrook House Hotel
◆◆◆◆◆
Old Mill Road, Chelston,
Torquay, Devon TQ2 6AP
T: (01803) 297394
F: (01803) 297394
E: millbrookhotel@virgin.net

Parks Hotel ◆◆◆◆
Rathmore Road, Chelston,
Torquay TQ2 6NZ
T: (01803) 292420 &
08000 191799
F: (01803) 405267

Strathnaver Hotel ◆◆◆
Rawlyn Road, Chelston, Torquay
TQ2 6PQ
T: (01803) 605523
F: (01803) 605529

White Gables Hotel ◆◆◆
Rawlyn Road, Chelston, Torquay,
Devon TQ2 6PQ
T: (01803) 605233
F: (01803) 606634

Windsurfer Hotel ◆◆◆
St Agnes' Lane, Chelston,
Torquay TQ2 6QD
T: (01803) 606550

CHERHILL
Wiltshire
Poachers Croft ◆◆◆
Yatesbury Hill, Cherhill, Calne,
Wiltshire SN11 8XY
T: (01249) 812587

CHERITON FITZPAINE
Devon

Hayne Farm ◆
Cheriton Fitzpaine, Crediton,
Devon EX17 4HR
T: (01363) 866392

CHEW MAGNA
Bath & North East Somerset

Valley Farm ◆◆◆◆
Sandy Lane, Stanton Drew,
Bristol BS39 4EL
T: (01275) 332723
T: (01275) 332723

Woodbarn Farm ◆◆◆
Denny Lane, Chew Magna,
Bristol BS40 8SZ
T: (01275) 332599
F: (01275) 332599

CHEW STOKE
Bath & North East Somerset

Dewdown Cottage ◆◆◆
Nempnett Thrubwell, Chew
Stoke, Bristol BS40 8YF
T: (01761) 462917
E: dewdown@hotmail.com

Orchard House ◆◆◆
Bristol Road, Chew Stoke, Bristol
BS40 8UB
T: (01275) 333143
F: (01275) 333754

CHEWTON MENDIP
Somerset

The Pantiles ◆◆◆◆
Bathway, Chewton Mendip,
Bath BA3 4NS
T: (01761) 241519

CHICKERELL
Dorset

Stonebank
◆◆◆◆◆ GOLD AWARD
14 West Street, Chickerell,
Weymouth, Dorset DT3 4DY
T: (01305) 760120
F: (01305) 760871
E: reservations@
stonebank-chickerell.co.uk

CHICKLADE, HINDON
Wiltshire

The Old Rectory ◆◆◆◆
Chicklade, Hindon, Salisbury,
Wiltshire SP3 5SU
T: (01747) 820226
F: (01747) 820783
E: vbronson@old-rectory.co.uk
I: www.old-rectory.co.uk

CHIDEOCK
Dorset

Betchworth House ◆◆◆◆
Chideock, Bridport, Dorset
DT6 6JW
T: (01297) 489478
F: (01297) 489932

**Warren House Bed and
Breakfast**
◆◆◆◆ SILVER AWARD
Warren House, Chideock,
Bridport, Dorset DT6 6JW
T: (01297) 489704
F: (01297) 489704

CHILSWORTHY
Devon

Ugworthy Barton ◆◆◆◆
Chilsworthy, Holsworthy, Devon
EX22 7JH
T: (01409) 254435
F: (01409) 254435

CHILTON CANTELO
Somerset

Higher Farm ◆◆◆◆
Chilton Cantelo, Yeovil,
Somerset BA22 8BE
T: (01935) 850213

CHIPPENHAM
Wiltshire

The Bramleys ◆
73 Marshfield Road,
Chippenham, Wiltshire
SN15 1JR
T: (01249) 653770

Church Farm ◆◆◆◆
Hartham Park, Corsham,
Wiltshire SN13 0PU
T: (01249) 715180 &
07977 910775
F: (01249) 715572
E: kmjbandb@aol.com.

Fairfield Farm ◆◆◆◆
Upper Wraxall, Chippenham,
Wiltshire SN14 7AG
T: (01225) 891750
F: (01225) 891050
E: mcdonoug@globalnet.co.uk

Frogwell House ◆◆◆◆
132 Hungerdown Lane,
Chippenham, Wiltshire
SN14 0BD
T: (01249) 650328
F: (01249) 650328

London Road Guest House
◆◆◆
122 London Road, Chippenham,
Wiltshire SN15 3BA
T: (01249) 660027 &
07976 740060

New Road Guest House ◆◆◆
31 New Road, Chippenham,
Wiltshire SN15 1HP
T: (01249) 657259
F: (01249) 657259

Oakfield Farm ◆◆◆◆
Easton Piercy Lane, Yatton
Keynell, Chippenham, Wiltshire
SN14 6JU
T: (01249) 782355
F: (01249) 783458

75 Rowden Hill ◆◆
Chippenham, Wiltshire
SN15 2AL
T: (01249) 652981

Teresa Lodge (Glen Avon)
◆◆◆
43 Bristol Road, Chippenham,
Wiltshire SN15 1NT
T: (01249) 653350

CHIPPING SODBURY
South Gloucestershire

The Sodbury House Hotel
◆◆◆◆
Badminton Road, Old Sodbury,
Bristol BS37 6LU
T: (01454) 312847
F: (01454) 273105
E: sodhousehotel@tesco.net

CHISELDON
Wiltshire

Norton House ◆◆◆◆
46 Draycott Road, Chiseldon,
Swindon, Wiltshire SN4 0LS
T: (01793) 741210 &
07976 750767
E: sharian@nortonhouse.wilts.
clara.co.uk
I: www.nortonhousewilts.clara.
co.uk

CHITTLEHAMPTON
Devon

Higher Biddacott Farm ◆◆◆
Chittlehampton, Umberleigh,
Devon EX37 9PY
T: (01769) 540222
F: (01769) 540222

CHRISTIAN MALFORD
Wiltshire

Beanhill Farm ◆◆◆
Main Road, Christian Malford,
Chippenham, Wiltshire
SN15 4BS
T: (01249) 720672 &
07775 660000

The Ferns ◆◆◆
Church Road, Christian Malford,
Chippenham, Wiltshire
SN15 4BW
T: (01249) 720371

Friday Street Farm ◆◆◆◆
Christian Malford, Chippenham,
Wiltshire SN15 4BU
T: (01249) 720146
F: (01249) 720146

CHRISTOW
Devon

Weir Park Farm ◆◆◆
Waterwell Lane, Christow, Exeter
EX6 7PB
T: (01647) 252549 &
0797 4752734
F: (01647) 252549
E: louise@baber.co.uk
I: www.devonfarms.co.uk

CHUDLEIGH
Devon

Farmborough House
◆◆◆◆ SILVER AWARD
Old Exeter Road, Chudleigh,
Newton Abbot, Devon TQ13 0DR
T: (01626) 853258
F: (01626) 853258
E: holidays@
farmborough-house.com
I: www.farmborough-house.
com

CHUDLEIGH KNIGHTON
Devon

Church House ◆◆◆◆
Chudleigh Knighton, Newton
Abbot, Devon TQ13 0HE
T: (01626) 852123
F: (01626) 852123
E: brandon@churchhouse100.
freeserve.co.uk
I: www.smoothhound.co.
uk/hotels/churchho.html

CHURCHILL
Bath & North East Somerset

Clumber Lodge ◆◆◆
New Road, Churchill,
Winscombe BS25 5NW
T: (01934) 852078

**Hillslee House
Rating Applied For**
New Road, Churchill,
Winscombe BS25 5NP
T: (01934) 853035

CHURCHINFORD
Somerset

The York Inn ◆◆◆◆
Honiton Road, Churchinford,
Taunton, Somerset TA3 7RF
T: (01823) 601333

CLEVEDON
Bath & North East Somerset

Highcliffe Hotel ◆◆◆
Wellington Terrace, Clevedon,
Somerset BS21 7PU
T: (01275) 873250
F: (01275) 873572

Maybank Guest House ◆
4 Jesmond Road, Clevedon,
Somerset BS21 7SA
T: (01275) 876387

CLIFTON
Bristol

14 Camden Terrace ◆◆◆
Clifton, Bristol BS8 4PU
T: (0117) 9149508 &
0777 1871251
F: (0117) 9149508
E: anne@amalindine.freeserve.
co.uk

Downs View Guest House
◆◆◆
38 Upper Belgrave Road, Clifton,
Bristol BS8 2XN
T: (0117) 973 7046 &
07976 432430
F: (0117) 973 8169

Naseby House Hotel ◆◆◆
105 Pembroke Road, Clifton,
Bristol BS8 3EF
T: (0117) 9737859 & 9080011
F: (0117) 9737859

Number 31 ◆◆◆◆
31 York Crescent, Clifton, Bristol
BS8 4JU
T: (0117) 9735330

Westbourne Hotel ◆◆◆
40-44 St Paul's Road, Clifton,
Bristol BS8 1LR
T: (0117) 973 4214
F: (0117) 974 3552
E: westbourne@clemshaws.
freeserve.co.uk

CLOVELLY
Devon

Dyke Green Farm ◆◆◆◆
Clovelly, Bideford, Devon
EX39 5RU
T: (01237) 431699 & 431279
E: edward@ecjohns.freeserve.
co.uk

Fuchsia Cottage ◆◆◆
Burscott, Clovelly, Bideford,
Devon EX39 5RR
T: (01237) 431398
E: tomsuecurtis.fuchsiacot@
currantbun.com

Holloford Farm ◆◆◆◆
Higher Clovelly, Bideford, Devon
EX39 5SD
T: (01237) 441275
I: www.wade@holloford.
freeserve.co.uk

CLUTTON
Bath & North East Somerset
Cholwell Hall
Rating Applied For
Clutton, Bristol BS39 5TE
T: (01761) 452380

CODFORD ST MARY
Wiltshire
Glebe Cottage
♦♦♦♦ SILVER AWARD
Church Lane, Codford St Mary,
Warminster, Wiltshire BA12 0PJ
T: (01985) 850565
F: (01985) 850666

COLEFORD
Somerset
Brook Cottage ♦♦
Highbury Street, Coleford, Bath
BA3 5NW
T: (01373) 812633

COLLINGBOURNE KINGSTON
Wiltshire
Cum-Bye ♦♦♦
Aughton, Collingbourne
Kingston, Marlborough,
Wiltshire SN8 3RZ
T: (01264) 850256

COLYTON
Devon
Smallicombe Farm ♦♦♦♦
Northleigh, Colyton, Devon
EX24 6BU
T: (01404) 831310
F: (01404) 831431
E: maggie_todd@yahoo.com
I: www.smallicombe.com
⊚ ⚐

COMBE DOWN
Bath & North East Somerset
The Glade ♦♦♦
Shaft Road, Combe Down, Bath
BA2 7HP
T: (01225) 833172

Grey Lodge
♦♦♦♦ SILVER AWARD
Summer Lane, Combe Down,
Bath, BA2 7EU
T: (01225) 832069
F: (01225) 830161
E: greylodge@freenet.co.uk
I: www.visitus.co.uk

COMBE FLOREY
Somerset
Combe Down Lodge ♦♦♦♦
Combe Florey, Taunton,
Somerset TA4 3JG
T: (01984) 667379

Redlands ♦♦♦♦
Trebles Holford, Combe Florey,
Taunton, Somerset TA4 3HA
T: (01823) 433159
E: redlandshouse@hotmail.com
I: www.escapetothecountry.co.
uk
⊚

COMBE MARTIN
Devon
Channel Vista ♦♦♦
Woodlands, Combe Martin,
Devon EX34 0AT
T: (01271) 883514

The London Inn ♦♦
Lynton Road, Combe Martin,
Ilfracombe, Devon EX34 0NA
T: (01271) 883409
F: (01271) 883409

Saffron House Hotel ♦♦♦
King Street, Combe Martin,
Ilfracombe, Devon EX34 0BX
T: (01271) 883521

COMBPYNE
Devon
1 Granary Cottage ♦♦♦
Combpyne, Axminster, Devon
EX13 8SX
T: (01297) 442856

COMPTON BASSETT
Wiltshire
The White Horse ♦♦♦♦
Compton Bassett, Calne,
Wiltshire SN11 8RG
T: (01249) 813118
F: (01249) 811595

COMPTON DUNDON
Somerset
Rickham House ♦♦♦
Compton Dundon, Somerton,
Somerset TA11 6QA
T: (01458) 445056
F: (01458) 445056
E: rickham.house@talk21.com

COOMBE BISSETT
Wiltshire
Evening Hill ♦♦♦
Blandford Road, Coombe Bissett,
Salisbury SP5 4LH
T: (01722) 718561 &
07831 765615
E: henrys@tresco.net

COOMBE DINGLE
Bristol
Treborough ♦♦
3 Grove Road, Coombe Dingle,
Bristol BS9 2RQ
T: (0117) 968 2712

CORSHAM
Wiltshire
Boyds Farm
♦♦♦♦♦ SILVER AWARD
Gastard, Corsham, Wiltshire
SN13 9PT
T: (01249) 713146
F: (01249) 713146
E: dorothyrobinson@
boydsfarm.freeserve.co.uk
I: www.webscape.co.
uk/farmaccom/england/wilts/
index.nt

Heatherly Cottage ♦♦♦♦
Ladbrook Lane, Gastard,
Corsham, Wiltshire SN13 9PE
T: (01249) 701402
F: (01249) 701412
E: ladbrook1@aol.com
I: www.smoothhound.co.
uk/hotels/heather3.html

Pickwick Lodge Farm ♦♦♦♦
Guyers Lane, Corsham, Wiltshire
SN13 0PS
T: (01249) 712207 &
07710 287263
F: (01249) 701904
⊚

Saltbox Farm ♦♦♦
Drewetts Mill, Box, Corsham,
Wiltshire SN13 8PT
T: (01225) 742608
⊚

Thingley Court Farm ♦♦♦
Corsham, Wiltshire SN13 9QQ
T: (01249) 713617 &
070501 28466

CORSLEY
Wiltshire
Sturford Mead ♦♦♦♦
Corsley, Warminster, Wiltshire
BA12 7QT
T: (01373) 832039
F: (01373) 832104
E: bradshaw@sturford.co.uk
I: www.sturford.co.uk

CORTON
Wiltshire
The Dove Inn ♦♦♦♦
Corton, Warminster, Wiltshire
BA12 0SZ
T: (01985) 850109
F: (01985) 851041

COSSINGTON
Somerset
Brookhayes Farm ♦♦♦♦
Bell Lane, Cossington,
Bridgwater, Somerset TA7 8LR
T: (01278) 722559
F: (01278) 722559

COTHAM
Bristol
Tricomo House B & B ♦♦♦
183 Cheltenham Road, Cotham,
Bristol BS6 5RH
T: (0117) 9248082

COVERACK
Cornwall
The Paris Hotel ♦♦♦
Coverack, Helston, Cornwall
TR12 6SX
T: (01326) 280258
F: (01326) 280774

Tregwenyn ♦♦♦
School Hill, Coverack, Helston,
Cornwall TR12 6SA
T: (01326) 280774
F: (01326) 280774

COXLEY
Somerset
The Pound Inn ♦♦♦
Burcott Lane, Coxley, Wells,
Somerset BA5 1QZ
T: (01749) 672785
F: (01749) 677220
E: wsscram@aol.com

CRACKINGTON HAVEN
Cornwall
Coombe Barton Inn ♦♦♦
Crackington Haven, Cornwall
EX23 0JG
T: (01840) 230345
F: (01840) 230788

CRANMORE
Somerset
Lynfield ♦♦♦
Frome Road, Cranmore, Shepton
Mallet, Somerset BA4 4QQ
T: (01749) 880600

CRANTOCK
Cornwall
Highfield Lodge Hotel ♦♦♦
Halwyn Road, Crantock,
Newquay, Cornwall TR8 5TR
T: (01637) 830744

Tregenna House
Rating Applied For
West Pentire Road, Crantock,
Newquay, Cornwall TR8 5RZ
T: (01637) 830222
F: (01637) 831267

Treringey Farm
Rating Applied For
Crantock, Newquay, Cornwall
TR8 5EN
T: (01637) 830265

CREDITON
Devon
Great Park Farm ♦♦
Crediton, Devon EX17 3PR
T: (01363) 772050

CREWKERNE
Somerset
Calendar Cottage ♦♦♦♦
Silver Street, Misterton,
Crewkerne, Somerset TA18 8NB
T: (01460) 75680

**The George Hotel & Courtyard
Restaurant** ♦♦♦
Market Square, Crewkerne,
Somerset TA18 7LP
T: (01460) 73650
F: (01460) 72974
E: eddie@thegeorgehotel.
sagehost.co.uk
I: www.crewkerne.co.
uk/accommodation/
george_hotel/indexhtml.
⊚

The Manor Arms ♦♦♦
North Perrott, Crewkerne,
Somerset TA18 7SG
T: (01460) 72901
F: (01460) 72901

CRICKLADE
Wiltshire
Waterhay Farm ♦♦♦
Leigh, Leigh, Swindon SN6 6QY
T: (01285) 861253

CROCKERTON
Wiltshire
Stoneyside ♦♦♦
Potters Hill, Crockerton,
Warminster, Wiltshire BA12 8AS
T: (01985) 218149

CROWCOMBE HEATHFIELD
Somerset
Meadowsweet ♦♦♦♦
3 Bakers Orchard, Crowcombe
Heathfield, Taunton, Somerset
TA4 4PA
T: (01984) 618305

CROYDE
Devon
Combas Farm ♦♦♦
Putsborough, Croyde, Devon
EX33 1PH
T: (01271) 890398
⊚

**Denham Farm and Country
House** ♦♦♦♦ SILVER AWARD
North Buckland, Braunton,
Devon EX33 1HY
T: (01271) 890297
F: (01271) 890297
⊚

CROYDE BAY
Devon
West Winds ♦♦♦♦
Moor Lane, Croyde Bay,
Braunton, Devon EX33 1PA
T: (01271) 890489 &
07831 211247
F: (01271) 890489
E: chris@croydewestwinds.
freeserve.co.uk
I: www.westwindsguesthouse.
co.uk
⊚

CULLOMPTON
Devon

Aller Barton Farm ◆◆◆
Cullompton, Devon EX15 1QQ
T: (01884) 32275
F: (01884) 35837
◉

Rullands ◆◆◆◆
Rull Lane, Cullompton, Devon
EX15 1NQ
T: (01884) 33356
F: (01884) 35890

Upton ◆◆◆◆◆ GOLD AWARD
Cullompton, Devon EX15 1RA
T: (01884) 33097
F: (01884) 33097

Weir Mill Farm
◆◆◆ SILVER AWARD
Jaycroft, Willand, Cullompton,
Devon EX15 2RE
T: (01884) 820803
F: (01884) 820973
E: parish@weirmillfarm.
freeserve.co.uk
I: www.smoothound.co.
uk/hotels/weirmill.html
◉

Wishay ◆◆◆
Trinity, Cullompton, Devon
EX15 1PE
T: (01884) 33223
F: (01884) 33223
◉

CURRY RIVEL
Somerset
Orchard Cottage ◆◆◆◆
Townsend, Curry Rivel, Langport,
Somerset TA10 0HT
T: (01458) 251511
F: (01458) 251511

CURY
Cornwall
Cobblers Cottage
◆◆◆◆ SILVER AWARD
Nantithet, Cury, Helston,
Cornwall TR12 7RB
T: (01326) 241342
F: (01326) 241342

DARTMOUTH
Devon
BARRINGTON HOUSE
◆◆◆◆ SILVER AWARD
Mount Boone, Dartmouth,
Devon TQ6 9HZ
T: (01803) 835545 &
07968 080410
F: (01803) 835545
E: enquiries@barringtonhse.co.
uk
I: www.barringtonhse.co.uk

Campbells
◆◆◆◆ SILVER AWARD
5 Mount Boone, Dartmouth,
Devon TQ6 9PB
T: (01803) 833438
F: (01803) 833438
I: www.webmachine.co.
uk/campbells

Nonsuch House ◆◆◆◆◆
Church Hill, Kingswear,
Dartmouth, Devon TQ6 0BX
T: (01803) 752829 & 752297
F: (01803) 752357
E: enquiries@nonsuch-house.
co.uk
I: www.nonsuch-house.co.uk

Sunnybanks ◆◆◆
1 Vicarage Hill, Dartmouth,
Devon TQ6 9EW
T: (01803) 832766
F: (01803) 832766
E: sue@sunnybanks@talk21.
com

Woodside Cottage Bed &
Breakfast ◆◆◆◆
Blackawton, Dartmouth, Devon
TQ9 7BL
T: (01803) 712375
F: (01803) 712605
E: b&b@woodside-cottage.
demon.co.uk
I: www.woodside-cottage.
demon.co.uk

DAUNTSEY
Wiltshire
Olivemead Farm ◆◆
Olivemead Lane, Dauntsey,
Chippenham, Wiltshire
SN15 4JQ
T: (01666) 510205
F: (01666) 510205
E: olivemead@farming.co.uk
◉

DAWLISH
Devon
Smallacombe Farm ◆◆◆
Dawlish, Devon EX7 0PS
T: (01626) 862536

West Hatch Hotel ◆◆◆◆
34 West Cliff, Dawlish, Devon
EX7 9DN
T: (01626) 864211
F: (01626) 864211
I: www.smoothound.co.
uk/hotels/westhatc.html

DENBURY
Devon
Tornewton ◆◆◆◆
Denbury, Newton Abbot, Devon
TQ12 6EF
T: (01803) 812257
F: (01803) 812257

DEVIZES
Wiltshire
Asta ◆◆
66 Downlands Road, Devizes,
Wiltshire SN10 5EF
T: (01380) 722546

Blounts Court Farm
◆◆◆◆◆ GOLD AWARD
Coxhill Lane, Potterne, Devizes,
Wiltshire SN10 5PH
T: (01380) 727180

The Chestnuts ◆◆◆◆
Potterne Road, Devizes,
Wiltshire SN10 5DD
T: (01380) 724532

Eastcott Manor ◆◆◆
Easterton, Devizes, Wiltshire
SN10 4PL
T: (01380) 813313

Eastfield House ◆◆◆
London Road, Devizes, Wiltshire
SN10 2DW
T: (01380) 721562
F: (01380) 721562
E: david@devizes.force9.co.uk

The Gate House ◆◆◆
Wick Lane, Devizes, Wiltshire
SN10 5DW
T: (01380) 725283 &
07889 637047
F: (01380) 722382

Glenholme Guest House ◆◆
77 Nursteed Road, Devizes,
Wiltshire SN10 3AJ
T: (01380) 723187

Heathcote House ◆◆◆
The Green, Devizes, Wiltshire
SN10 2JG
T: (01380) 725080

Littleton Lodge ◆◆◆◆
Littleton Panell (A360), West
Lavington, Devizes, Wiltshire
SN10 4ES
T: (01380) 813131
F: (01380) 816969
E: stay@littletonlodge.co.uk
I: www.littletonlodge.co.uk

Longwater ◆◆◆
Lower Road, Erlestoke, Devizes,
Wiltshire SN10 5UE
T: (01380) 830095
F: (01380) 830095
E: pam.hampton@talk21.com
◉ 🐾

DILTON MARSH
Wiltshire
The Old George
◆◆◆◆ SILVER AWARD
St Mary's Lane, Dilton Marsh,
Westbury, Wiltshire BA13 4BL
T: (01373) 822466
F: (01373) 824381
E: tony@rose114.freeserve.co.
uk

DINTON
Wiltshire
Morris' Farm House ◆◆◆
Baverstock, Dinton, Salisbury
SP3 5EL
T: (01722) 716874
F: (01722) 716874
E: marriott@dircon.co.uk
I: www.kgp-publishing.co.uk

The Penruddocke Arms ◆◆◆
Hindon Road, Dinton, Salisbury,
Wiltshire SP3 5EL
T: (01722) 716253
F: (01722) 716253

DITTISHAM
Devon
The Red Lion Inn ◆◆◆
Dittisham, Dartmouth, Devon
TQ6 0ES
T: (01803) 722235

DODDISCOMBSLEIGH
Devon
Whitemoor Farm ◆
Doddiscombsleigh, Exeter,
Devon EX6 7PU
T: (01647) 252423
E: blaceystaffyrescue@easicom.
com

DORCHESTER
Dorset
The Beagles ◆◆
37 London Road, Dorchester,
Dorset DT1 1NF
T: (01305) 267338
E: joycegraham@talk21.com

The Casterbridge Hotel
◆◆◆◆ SILVER AWARD
49 High East Street, Dorchester,
Dorset DT1 1HU
T: (01305) 264043
F: (01305) 260884
E: reception@casterbridgehotel.
co.uk
I: www.casterbridgehotel.co.uk
◉

Churchview Guest House ◆◆◆
Winterbourne Abbas,
Dorchester, Dorset DT2 9LS
T: (01305) 889296
F: (01305) 889296

Higher Came Farmhouse ◆◆◆
Rating Applied For
Higher Came, Dorchester, Dorset
DT2
T: (01305) 268908

Hillfort View ◆◆
10 Hillfort Close, Dorchester,
Dorset DT1 2QT
T: (01305) 268476

Joan's Bed and Breakfast ◆◆◆
119 Bridport Road, Dorchester,
Dorset DT1 2NH
T: (01305) 267145
E: b-and-b@joancox.freeserve.
co.uk

Junction Hotel Dorchester
◆◆◆◆
42 Great Western Road,
Dorchester, Dorset DT1 1UF
T: (01305) 263094
F: (01305) 751949
I: www.stayhereuk.com

5 Little Britain Farmhouse
◆◆◆
Fordington, Dorchester, Dorset
DT1 1NN
T: (01305) 263431

Maiden Castle Farm
◆◆◆◆ SILVER AWARD
Dorchester, Dorset DT2 9PR
T: (01305) 262356
F: (01305) 251085
◉

Mountain Ash ◆◆◆
30 Mountain Ash Road,
Dorchester, Dorset DT1 2PB
T: (01305) 264811

The Old Manor
◆◆◆◆◆ GOLD AWARD
Kingston Maurward, Dorchester,
Dorset DT2 8PX
T: (01305) 261110
F: (01305) 263734
E: thomson@
kingston-maurward.co.uk
I: www.kingston-maurward.co.
uk

The Old Rectory ◆◆◆◆
Winterbourne Steepleton,
Dorchester, Dorset DT2 9LG
T: (01305) 889468
F: (01305) 889737
E: trees@eurobell.co.uk.
I: www.trees.eurobell.co.uk

Port Bredy ◆◆◆◆
107 Bridport Road, Dorchester,
Dorset DT1 2NH
T: (01305) 265778
F: (01305) 265778
E: B&Benquires@portbredy.
fsnet.co.uk

Sunrise Guest House ◆◆◆
34 London Road, Dorchester,
Dorset DT1 1NE
T: (01305) 262425

Tarkaville ◆◆◆◆
30 Shaston Crescent, Manor
Park, Dorchester, Dorset DT1 2EB
T: (01305) 266253 &
07802 509084
⊚

**Westwood House Hotel
◆◆◆◆**
29 High West Street, Dorchester,
Dorset DT1 1UP
T: (01305) 268018
F: (01305) 250282
E: reservations@
westwoodhouse.co.uk
I: www.westwoodhouse.co.uk

The White House ◆◆◆
9 Queens Avenue, Dorchester,
Dorset DT1 2EW
T: (01305) 266714
E: lees.twh@tinyonline.co.uk

**Whitfield Farm Cottage
◆◆◆◆**
Poundbury Whitfield,
Dorchester, Dorset DT2 9SL
T: (01305) 260233
F: (01305) 260233
E: dc.whitfield@clara.net
I: www.dc.whitfield.clara.net

**Yalbury Cottage Hotel and
Restaurant◆◆◆◆◆**
Lower Bockhampton,
Dorchester, Dorset DT2 8PZ
T: (01305) 262382
F: (01305) 266412
E: yalbury.cottage@virgin.net
⊚

Yalbury Park ◆◆◆◆
Frome Whitfield Farm, Frome
Whitfield, Dorchester, Dorset
DT2 7SE
T: (01305) 250336
F: (01305) 260070
E: yalburypark@tesco.net

**Yellowham Farm
◆◆◆◆ SILVER AWARD**
Yellowham Wood, Dorchester,
Dorset DT2 8RW
T: (01305) 262892
F: (01305) 257707
E: b&b@yellowham.freeserve.
co.uk
I: www.yellowham.freeserve.co.
uk

Witherington Farm ◆◆◆◆◆
Downton, Salisbury SP5 3QT
T: (01722) 710222
F: (01722) 710405

The Drewe Arms ◆◆◆◆
Drewsteignton, Exeter EX6 6QN
T: (01647) 281224

Carglonnon Farm ◆◆◆◆
Duloe, Liskeard, Cornwall
PL14 4QA
T: (01579) 320210
F: (01579) 320210

Dassels Country House ◆◆◆◆
Dassels, Dulverton, Somerset
TA22 9RZ
T: (01398) 341203
F: (01398) 341561
E: margaret.spencer@dassels.
demon.co.uk

Exton House Hotel ◆◆◆◆
Exton, Dulverton, Somerset
TA22 9JT
T: (01643) 851365
F: (01643) 851213

**Highercombe Farm
◆◆◆◆ SILVER AWARD**
Dulverton, Somerset TA22 9PT
T: (01398) 323616
F: (01398) 323616
E: abigal@highercombe.demon.
co.uk
I: www.highercombe.demon.co.
uk

Penlee ◆◆◆
31 Battleton, Dulverton,
Somerset TA22 9HU
T: (01398) 323798
F: (01398) 323780
E: paula@pointproms.co.uk
I: www.sbes.com/penlee.htm
⊚

Springfield Farm ◆◆◆◆
Ashwick Lane, Dulverton,
Somerset TA22 9QD
T: (01398) 323722
F: (01398) 323722

**Town Mills
◆◆◆◆ SILVER AWARD**
High Street, Dulverton, Somerset
TA22 9HB
T: (01398) 323124

Winsbere House ◆◆◆
64 Battleton, Dulverton,
Somerset TA22 9HU
T: (01398) 323278

**Admiral's Table
Rating Applied For**
Bristol Road, Dunball,
Bridgwater, Somerset TA6 4TW
T: (01278) 685671
F: (01278) 685672

Moor Farm ◆
Dunsford, Exeter EX6 7DP
T: (01647) 24292

**Oak Lodge
◆◆◆◆ SILVER AWARD**
The Court, Dunsford, Exeter
EX6 7DD
T: (01647) 252829

**Cobbles Bed & Breakfast
◆◆◆◆**
14-16 Church Street, Dunster,
Minehead, Somerset TA24 6SH
T: (01643) 821305

**Conygar House
◆◆◆◆ SILVER AWARD**
2A The Ball, Dunster, Minehead,
Somerset TA24 6SD
T: (01643) 821872
F: (01643) 821872
E: bale.dunster@virgin.net
I: www.homepage.virgin.
net/bale_dunster

**Dollons House
◆◆◆◆◆ SILVER AWARD**
10 Church Street, Dunster,
Minehead, Somerset TA24 6SH
T: (01643) 821880
F: (01643) 822016
E: hannah.bradshaw@virgin.net

Higher Orchard ◆◆◆◆
30 St Georges Street, Dunster,
Minehead, Somerset TA24 6RS
T: (01643) 821915

Spears Cross Hotel ◆◆◆◆
1 West Street, Dunster,
Minehead, Somerset TA24 6SN
T: (01643) 821439
F: (01643) 821439
E: john.rathbone@ndirect.co.uk
I: www.s-h-systems.co.
uk/hotels/spearsx.html

Durrington House ◆◆◆
Church Street, Durrington,
Salisbury SP4 8AL
T: (01980) 652270

**Higher Torr Farm
Rating Applied For**
East Allington, Totnes, Devon
TQ9 7QH
T: (01548) 521248

**Chesells Guest House
◆◆◆◆ SILVER AWARD**
Yeovil Road, East Coker, Yeovil,
Somerset BA22 9HD
T: (01935) 428581

Granary House ◆◆◆◆
East Coker, Yeovil, Somerset
BA22 9LY
T: (01935) 862738
E: granary.house@virgin.net
⊚

Penryn ◆◆◆◆
Southay, East Lambrook, South
Petherton, Somerset TA13 5HQ
T: (01460) 241358
E: pjandea@tesco.net

**Hyghdowne House
Rating Applied For**
East Prawle, Kingsbridge, Devon
TQ7 2NL
T: (01548) 511210
F: (01548) 511210

Caduscott ◆◆◆
East Taphouse, Liskeard,
Cornwall PL14 4NG
T: (01579) 320262
F: (01579) 320262
E: caduscott@farmline.com
⊚

Barnbridge ◆
East Tytherton, Chippenham,
Wiltshire SN15 4LT
T: (01249) 740280
E: bgiffard@aol.com

**The Pines at Eastleigh
◆◆◆◆ SILVER AWARD**
Old Barnstaple Road, Eastleigh,
Bideford, Devon EX39 4PA
T: (01271) 860561
F: (01271) 861248
E: barry@thepinesateastleigh.
co.uk
I: www.thepinesateastleigh.co.
uk
⊚

Follets B & B ◆◆◆◆
Easton Royal, Pewsey, Wiltshire
SN9 5LZ
T: (01672) 810619 &
07768 560302
F: (01672) 810619
E: margaretlandless@talk21.
com

**Tudor House
Rating Applied For**
Easton Royal, Pewsey, Wiltshire
SN9 5LS
T: (01672) 811611
F: (01672) 811611

**Goosey Cottage ◆◆◆
Rating Applied For**
Clapper, Egloshayle,
Wadebridge, Cornwall PL27 6HZ
T: (01208) 814997

The Bell Inn ◆◆◆
Bruton Road, Evercreech,
Shepton Mallet, Somerset
BA4 6HY
T: (01749) 830287
F: (01749) 831296

Crossdale Cottage ◆◆◆
Pecking Mill, Evercreech,
Shepton Mallet, Somerset
BA4 6PQ
T: (01749) 830293
F: (01749) 830293

The Acorn Inn ◆◆◆◆
Fore Street, Evershot,
Dorchester, Dorset DT2 0JW
T: (01935) 83228
F: (01935) 83707
E: stay@acorn-inn.co.uk
I: www.acorn-inn.co.uk

Westwood Farm B&B ◆◆◆◆
Evershot, Dorchester, Dorset
DT2 0PG
T: (01935) 83351 &
0797 0052785

Bickham Farmhouse ◆◆◆◆
Kenn, Exeter, Devon EX6 7XL
T: (01392) 832206 &
07773 456194
F: (01392) 832206

Danson House ◆◆◆◆
Marsh Green, Exeter, Devon
EX5 2ES
T: (01404) 823260
F: (01404) 823260
E: dk2789@eclipse.co.uk
I: www.eclipse.co.uk/danson/

Globe Hotel ◆◆◆
Fore Street, Topsham, Exeter,
Devon EX3 0HR
T: (01392) 873471
F: (01392) 873879
E: sales@globehotel.com
I: www.globehotel.com

The Grange ◆◆◆◆
Stoke Hill, Exeter, Devon EX4 7JH
T: (01392) 259723
E: dudleythegrange@aol.com

Hayne Barton ◆◆◆
Whitestone, Exeter, Devon
EX4 2JN
T: (01392) 811268

Hayne House ◆◆◆
Silverton, Exeter, Devon EX5 4HE
T: (01392) 860725
F: (01392) 860725

Lochinvar ◆◆◆
Shepherds Park Farm,
Woodbury, Exeter, Devon
EX5 1LA
T: (01395) 232185 & 232284
F: (01395) 232284
E: jglanuil@devon-cc-gov.uk

Park View Hotel ◆◆◆
8 Howell Road, Exeter, EX4 4LG
T: (01392) 271772
F: (01392) 253047
E: philbatho@parkviewhotel.
freeserve.co.uk
I: www.parkviewhotel.freeserve.
co.uk

Raffles Hotel ◆◆◆
11 Blackall Road, Exeter,
EX4 4HD
T: (01392) 270200
F: (01392) 270200
E: raffleshtl@btinternet.com

Rydon Farm ◆◆◆◆
Woodbury, Exeter EX5 1LB
T: (01395) 232341
F: (01395) 232341

Silversprings
◆◆◆◆◆ SILVER AWARD
12 Richmond Road, St Davids,
Exeter, DEVON EX4 4JA
T: (01392) 494040 &
07768 637103
F: 0870 0561615
E: juliet@silversprings.co.uk
I: www.silversprings.co.uk

The Weir Guest House
◆◆◆◆ SILVER AWARD
8 Weirfield Road, Exeter,
EX2 4DN
T:

Edgcott House ◆◆◆
Exford, Minehead, Somerset
TA24 7QG
T: (01643) 831495
F: (01643) 831495

The Imperial
Rating Applied For
The Esplanade, Exmouth, Devon
EX8 2SW
T: (01395) 274761
F: (01395) 265161

The Mews ◆◆◆
Knappe Cross, Brixington Lane,
Exmouth, Devon EX8 5DL
T: (01395) 272198

Noble House ◆◆◆◆
1 Stevenstone Road, Exmouth,
Devon EX8 2EP
T: (01395) 264803 & 272501

The Swallows ◆◆◆◆
11 Carlton Hill, Exmouth, Devon
EX8 2AJ
T: (01395) 263937
F: (01395) 271040
E: firus@globalnet.co.uk
I: www.smoothhound.co.
uk/hotels/swallows.html

Apple Tree Cottage ◆◆◆◆
Laity Moor, Ponsanooth, Truro,
Cornwall TR3 7HR
T: (01872) 865047
E: raistlin@dial.pipex.com

Ivanhoe Guest House ◆◆◆◆
7 Melvill Road, Falmouth,
Cornwall TR11 4AS
T: (01326) 319083
F: (01326) 319083
E: berman.ivanhoe@talk21.com
I: www.smoothhound.co.
uk/hotels/ivanhoe

Tresillian House Hotel ◆◆◆
3 Stracey Road, Falmouth,
Cornwall TR11 4DW
T: (01326) 312425 & 311139
F: (01326) 312425
E: tresillianhouse@connexions.
co.uk
I: www.connexions.co.
uk/treshouse/index.htm

The Trevelyan ◆◆
6 Avenue Road, Falmouth,
Cornwall TR11 4AZ
T: (01326) 311545 &
07974 732366
F: (01326) 311545
E: gaunt@tre6.freeserve.co.uk

Wickham Guest House ◆◆◆
21 Gyllyngvase Terrace,
Falmouth, Cornwall TR11 4DL
T: (01326) 311140 &
07770 575381
E: enquiries@wickhamhotel.
freeserve.co.uk

Barrow Vale Farm ◆◆◆◆
Farmborough, Bath BA3 1BL
T: (01761) 470300

Home Farm ◆◆◆◆
Farrington Gurney, Bristol
BS39 6UB
T: (01761) 452287 & 0797 153
8971
F: (01761) 452287
E: tish_andy@tish-andy.
freeserve.co.uk
I: www.firstspace.
com/msn&r/smallpages/
homefarm.htm

Skinners Ash Farm ◆◆◆
Fenny Bridges, Honiton, Devon
EX14 0BH
T: (01404) 850231
F: (01404) 850231
I: www.cottageguide.co.
uk/skinnersash/

Vale House ◆◆◆
Figheldean, Salisbury, Wiltshire
SP4 4JJ
T: (01980) 670713

Highfield
◆◆◆◆ SILVER AWARD
Fleet, Weymouth, Dorset
DT3 4EB
T: (01305) 776822

Riverbarn ◆◆◆
Fonthill Bishop, Salisbury,
Wiltshire SP3 5SF
T: (01747) 820232
F: (01747) 820232
E: rbarn@globalnet.co.uk

The White Hart
Rating Applied For
Ford, Chippenham, Wiltshire
SN14 8RP
T: (01249) 782213
F: (01249) 783075
E: booked@lionheatinns.co.uk
I: www.lionheartinns.co.uk

The Pembroke Arms ◆◆◆
Fovant, Salisbury, Wiltshire
SP3 5JH
T: (01722) 714201
F: (01722) 714201
E: mwillo@aol.com

Carnethic House Hotel ◆◆◆◆
Lambs Barn, Fowey, Cornwall
PL23 1HQ
T: (01726) 833336
F: (01726) 833296
E: carnethic@btinternet.com
I: www.crescom.co.uk/carnethic

The Old Ferry Inn ◆◆◆
Bodinnick, Fowey, Cornwall
PL23 1LX
T: (01726) 870237
F: (01726) 870116

Seahorses
Rating Applied For
14 Fimbarrus Road, Fowey,
Cornwall PL23 1JJ
T: (01726) 833148

The Stables ◆◆◆
Hyde Crook, Frampton,
Dorchester, Dorset DT2 9NW
T: (01300) 320075

Longacre ◆◆◆
17 Staples Hill, Freshford, Bath
BA3 6EL
T: (01225) 723254
F: (01225) 723254

Abergele Guest House ◆◆◆◆
2 Fromefield, Frome, Somerset
BA11 2HA
T: (01373) 463998

**Fourwinds Guest House
◆◆◆◆**
19 Bath Road, Frome, Somerset
BA11 2HJ
T: (01373) 462618
F: (01373) 453029

North Parade House ◆◆◆◆
7 North Parade, Frome,
Somerset BA11 1AT
T: (01373) 474249
F: (01373) 467986

Number Four
Rating Applied For
Catherine Street, Frome,
Somerset BA11 1DA
T: (01373) 455690
F: (01373) 455992

Stonewall Manor ◆◆◆
Culver Hill, Frome, Somerset
BA11 4AS
T: (01373) 462131

The Sun Inn
Rating Applied For
6 Catherine Street, Frome,
Somerset BA11 1DA
T: (01373) 471913

Wadbury House ◆◆◆
Mells, Frome, Somerset
BA11 3PA
T: (01373) 812359
E: sally.brinkmann@talk21.com

Rose Cottage ◆◆◆◆
Galmpton, Hope Cove,
Kingsbridge, Devon TQ7 3EU
T: (01548) 561953
F: (01548) 561953
I: www.wsfb.co.uk/rosecottage

Catshayes Farm ◆◆
Gittisham, Honiton, Devon
EX14 3AE
T: (01404) 850302 & 850267
F: (01404) 850302
E: christine@bapt.org.uk
I: www.devonfarms.co.uk

GLASTONBURY
Somerset

Abbey Garth ◆◆
5 Bere Lane, Glastonbury,
Somerset BA6 8BD
T: (01458) 832675
E: ann.matkins@freeserve.co.uk
I: www.glastonbury.co.uk.
accommodation

Avalon Barn ◆◆◆◆
Lower Godney, Glastonbury,
Somerset BA5 1RZ
T: (01458) 835005
F: (01458) 835005
E: william.n@virgin.net

Bellhay Orchard
Rating Applied For
7 Lambrook Street, Glastonbury,
Somerset BA6 8BY
T: (01458) 832432

The Bolthole ◆◆◆
32 Chilkwell Street, Glastonbury,
Somerset BA6 8DA
T: (01458) 832800

46 Bove Town ◆◆◆
Glastonbury, Somerset BA6 8JE
T: (01458) 833684

Coig Deug ◆◆
15 Helyar Close, Glastonbury,
Somerset BA6 9LQ
T: (01458) 835945 & 830498

The Hangmans House ◆◆◆
8 High Street, Glastonbury,
Somerset BA6 9DU
T: (01458) 834163
E: joel@hangmanshouse.co.uk
I: www.hangmanshouse.co.uk

**The Heart Centred Bed &
Breakfast with Morning
Meditation**◆◆◆
24 Bove Town, Glastonbury,
Somerset BA6 8JE
T: (01458) 833467
I: www.glastonbury.co.
uk/users/mitchell-a.html

46a High Street ◆◆
Glastonbury, Somerset BA6 9DX
T: (01458) 832214

Highlands Guest House
◆◆◆◆ SILVER AWARD
21 Rowley Road, Glastonbury,
Somerset BA6 8HU
T: (01458) 834587
F: (01458) 834587
E: highlands@eclipse.co.uk
I: www.travel-uk.net/highlands

The Lightship ◆◆◆
82 Bove Town, Glastonbury,
Somerset BA6 8JG
T: (01458) 833698
E: roselightship@
netscapeonline.co.uk

Little Orchard ◆◆◆
Ashwell Lane, Glastonbury,
Somerset BA6 8BG
T: (01458) 831620
I: www.smoothhound.co.
uk/hotels/orchard.html

Mafeking
◆◆◆◆ SILVER AWARD
67 Wells Road, Glastonbury,
Somerset BA6 9BY
T: (01458) 833379
E: mafeking@wellsroad.
freeserve.co.uk

Meadow Barn ◆◆◆
Middlewick Farm, Wick Lane,
Glastonbury, Somerset BA6 8JW
T: (01458) 832351
F: (01458) 832351

Melrose ◆◆◆
Coursing Batch, Glastonbury,
Somerset BA6 8BH
T: (01458) 834706
I: www.nick&sarahmelrose
glastonbury.uk

Merryall House
Rating Applied For
50 Roman Way, Glastonbury,
Somerset BA6 8AD
T: (01458) 834511 & 830208
E: francider@hotmail.com

Middle Farm ◆◆◆
West Pennard, Glastonbury,
Somerset BA6 8NQ
T: (01749) 890753

Number Three ◆◆◆◆
3 Magdalene Street,
Glastonbury, Somerset BA6 9EW
T: (01458) 832129
F: (01458) 834227
E: patredmond@numberthree.
co.uk
I: www.numberthree.co.uk

The Old Bakery ◆◆◆
84A Bove Town, Glastonbury,
Somerset BA6 8JG
T: (01458) 833400
E: oldbakery@talk21.com

1 Park Terrace ◆◆◆
Street Road, Glastonbury,
Somerset BA6 9EA
T: (01458) 835845 & 833296
F: (01458) 833296
E: no1parkterrace@iname.com

Perks Croft ◆◆◆
95 The Roman Way,
Glastonbury, Somerset BA6 8AD
T: (01458) 832326

Pilgrims ◆◆◆
12/13 Norbins Road,
Glastonbury, Somerset BA6 9JE
T: (01458) 834650 & 834606
E: pbrown0848@aol.com
I: www.glastonbury.co.
uk/users/brown-alison.html

Pippin ◆◆◆
4 Ridgeway Gardens,
Glastonbury, Somerset BA6 8ER
T: (01458) 834262
E: daphneslaterpippinbb@
talk21.com
I: www.smoothhound.co.
uk/hotels/pippin.html

15 Saint Brides Close ◆◆
Glastonbury, Somerset BA6 9JU
T: (01458) 835909

Sheffern ◆◆
38 Hamlyn Road, Glastonbury,
Somerset BA6 8HT
T: (01458) 832587

Tordown Guest House ◆◆◆
5 Ashwell Lane, Glastonbury,
Somerset BA6 8BG
T: (01458) 832287
F: (01458) 831100
E: torangel@aol.com
I: www.tordown.com

The Who'd A Thought It Inn
Rating Applied For
17 Northload Street,
Glastonbury, Somerset BA6 9JJ
T: (01458) 834460
F: (01458) 831039

Wyrrall House
◆◆◆◆◆ SILVER AWARD
78 The Roman Way,
Glastonbury, Somerset BA6 8AD
T: (01458) 835510 &
07976 978060
F: 0870 0568111
E: djw@wyrrallhouse.demon.co.
uk
I: www.wyrrallhouse.demon.co.
uk

GOATHURST
Somerset

Willowburn ◆◆◆
Goathurst, Bridgwater, Somerset
TA5 2DJ
T: (01278) 662398

GODNEY
Somerset

Double-Gate Farm
◆◆◆◆ GOLD AWARD
Godney, Wells, Somerset
BA5 1RX
T: (01458) 832217
F: (01458) 835612
E: hilary@doublegate.demon.co.
uk
I: www.somerset-farm-holiday.
co.uk/double_gate_farm_
home_page.htm
&

GOONHAVERN
Cornwall

September Lodge ◆◆◆
Wheal Hope, Goonhavern, Truro,
Cornwall TR4 9QJ
T: (01872) 571435
F: (01872) 571435
E: jc.septlodge@virgin.net

GRAMPOUND
Cornwall

Perran House ◆◆◆
Fore Street, Grampound, Truro,
Cornwall TR2 4RS
T: (01726) 882066 & 884390

GREAT BEDWYN
Wiltshire

The Cross Keys Inn ◆◆◆
High Street, Great Bedwyn,
Marlborough, Wiltshire
SN8 3NU
T: (01672) 870678

GREAT DURNFORD
Wiltshire

Meadow Croft ◆◆◆◆
Great Durnford, Salisbury
SP4 6AY
T: (01722) 782643

GREENHAM
Somerset

Bishops Barton ◆◆◆◆
Greenham, Wellington,
Somerset TA21 0JJ
T: (01823) 672969

Greenham Hall ◆◆
Greenham, Wellington,
Somerset TA21 0JJ
T: (01823) 672603
F: (01823) 672307
E: peterjayre@cs.com

GREINTON
Somerset

The Greylake Inn ◆◆
Greinton, Bridgwater, Somerset
TA7 9BP
T: (01458) 210383
F: (01458) 210383

West Town Farm ◆◆◆◆
Greinton, Bridgwater, Somerset
TA7 9BW
T: (01458) 210277

GRITTLETON
Wiltshire

Garden House ◆◆◆◆
Grittleton, Chippenham,
Wiltshire SN14 6AJ
T: (01249) 782507

The Neeld Arms Inn ◆◆◆
The Street, Grittleton,
Chippenham, Wiltshire
SN14 6AP
T: (01249) 782470
F: (01249) 782470
E: neeldarms@genie.co.uk
I: www.neeldarms.co.uk

GULWORTHY
Devon

Colcharton Farm ◆◆◆◆
Gulworthy, Tavistock, Devon
PL19 8HU
T: (01822) 616435 &
07970 863974
F: (01822) 616435

Hele Farm ◆◆◆
Gulworthy, Tavistock, Devon
PL19 8PA
T: (01822) 833084
F: (01822) 833084

GURNEY SLADE
Somerset

The Old Mendip Coaching Inn
Rating Applied For
Gurney Slade, Bath BA3 4UU
T: (01749) 841234
E: gsymonds@compuserve.com

HALSE
Somerset

New Inn ◆◆◆
Halse, Taunton, Somerset
TA4 3AF
T: (01823) 432352

HALWELL
Devon

Orchard House
◆◆◆◆◆ SILVER AWARD
Horner, Halwell, Totnes, Devon
TQ9 7LB
T: (01548) 821448

HAM
Wiltshire

Crown & Anchor ◆◆◆
Ham, Marlborough, Wiltshire
SN8 3RB
T: (01488) 668242
&

HARBERTONFORD
Devon

The Hungry Horse Restaurant
◆◆◆◆
Old Road, Harbertonford, Totnes,
Devon TQ9 7TA
T: (01803) 732441
F: (01803) 732780

HARLYN BAY
Cornwall
The Harlyn Inn ◆◆◆
Harlyn Bay, Padstow, Cornwall
PL28 8SB
T: (01841) 520207
F: (01841) 520722
E: harlyninn@aol.com
⊕

Polmark Hotel ◆◆◆
Harlyn Bay, Padstow, Cornwall
PL28 8SB
T: (01841) 520206
F: (01841) 520206

HARPFORD
Devon
Peeks House ◆◆◆◆
Harpford, Sidmouth, Devon
EX10 0NH
T: (01395) 567664
F: (01395) 567664
E: peekshouse@fsbdial.co.uk

HARTLAKE
Somerset
Hartlake Farm ◆◆◆◆
Hartlake, Glastonbury, Somerset
BA6 9AB
T: (01458) 835406
F: (01749) 670373
I: www.hartlakebandb.co.uk

HARTLAND
Devon
Elmscott Farm ◆◆◆◆
Hartland, Bideford, Devon
EX39 6ES
T: (01237) 441276
F: (01237) 441276

Golden Park
◆◆◆◆ SILVER AWARD
Hartland, Bideford, Devon
EX39 6EP
T: (01237) 441254
⊕

Hartland Quay Hotel ◆◆◆
Hartland, Bideford, Devon
EX39 6DU
T: (01237) 441218
F: (01237) 441371

Trutrese ◆◆◆
Harton Cross, Hartland,
Bideford, Devon EX39 6AE
T: (01237) 441274

HASELBURY PLUCKNETT
Somerset
Oak House ◆◆◆
North Street, Haselbury
Plucknett, Crewkerne, Somerset
TA18 7RB
T: (01460) 73625
F: (01460) 73625

HATCH BEAUCHAMP
Somerset
The Hatch Inn ◆
Village Road, Hatch Beauchamp,
Taunton, Somerset TA3 6SG
T: (01823) 480245
F: (01823) 480245
⊕

HATHERLEIGH
Devon
George Hotel ◆◆◆
Market Street, Hatherleigh,
Okehampton, Devon EX20 3JN
T: (01837) 810454
F: (01837) 810901
E: davidljeffries@msn.com

Orchard House ◆◆◆◆
Hatherleigh, Okehampton,
Devon EX20 3LE
T: (01837) 810911
E: jden@euphony.net
I: www.devonarms.co.uk

Seldon Farm ◆◆
Monkokehampton, Winkleigh,
Devon EX19 8RY
T: (01837) 810312

HAYLE
Cornwall
Penellen Hotel ◆◆◆
Riviere Towans, Hayle, Cornwall
TR27 5AF
T: (01736) 753777
F: (01736) 753777

Treglisson ◆◆◆◆◆
11 Wheal Alfred Road, Hayle,
Cornwall TR27 5JT
T: (01736) 753141
F: (01736) 753141
⊕

HELSTON
Cornwall
Longstone Farm ◆◆◆
Coverack Bridges, Trenear,
Helston, Cornwall TR13 0HG
T: (01326) 572483
F: (01326) 572483

Lyndale Guest House ◆◆◆
4 Greenbank, Meneage Road,
Helston, Cornwall TR13 8JA
T: (01326) 561082
F: (01326) 565813
E: enquiries@lyndale1.freeserve.
co.uk
I: www.lyndale1.freeserve.co.uk
⊕

Mandeley Guest House ◆◆◆
Clodgey Lane, Helston, Cornwall
TR13 8PJ
T: (01326) 572550

Strathallan ◆◆◆◆
6 Monument Road, Helston,
Cornwall TR13 8HF
T: (01326) 573683
F: (01326) 565777
E: strathallan@compuserve.com
I: www.connexions.co.
uk/strathallan

HENLADE
Somerset
Barn Close Nurseries ◆◆◆
Henlade, Taunton, Somerset
TA3 5DH
T: (01823) 443507

HENSTRIDGE
Somerset
Fountain Inn Motel ◆◆
High Street, Henstridge,
Templecombe, Somerset
BA8 0RA
T: (01963) 362722
F: (01963) 362722
I: www.fountaininn.fsnet.co.uk
⊕

Quiet Corner Farm ◆◆◆◆
Henstridge, Somerset BA8 0RA
T: (01963) 363045
F: (01963) 363045
E: quietcorner.thompson@
virgin.net
⊕

HERMITAGE
Dorset
Almshouse Farm
◆◆◆◆ SILVER AWARD
Hermitage, Holnest, Sherborne,
Dorset DT9 6HA
T: (01963) 210296
F: (01963) 210296
E: almshousefarm@lineone.net
⊕

HEXWORTHY
Devon
The Forest Inn ◆◆◆
Hexworthy, Yelverton, Devon
PL20 6SD
T: (01364) 631211
F: (01364) 631515
E: forestinn@hotmail.com

HEYTESBURY
Wiltshire
Red Lion Hotel
Rating Applied For
42a High Street, Heytesbury,
Warminster, Wiltshire BA12 0EA
T: (01985) 840315

HIGHBRIDGE
Somerset
46 Church Street ◆◆◆
Highbridge, Somerset TA9 3AQ
T: (01278) 788365

Sandacre ◆◆
75 Old Burnham Road,
Highbridge, Somerset TA9 3JG
T: (01278) 781221
F: (01278) 781221

HIGHWORTH
Wiltshire
Roves Farm ◆◆◆
Sevenhampton, Highworth,
Swindon, Wiltshire SN6 7QG
T: (01793) 763939
F: (01793) 763939

HILMARTON
Wiltshire
Burfoots ◆◆◆◆
The Close, Hilmarton, Calne,
Wiltshire SN11 8TH
T: (01249) 760492 & 760493
F: (01249) 760609
E: anncooke@burfoots.co.uk
I: www.burfoots.co.uk

HILPERTON
Wiltshire
62b Paxcroft Cottages ◆◆◆
Devizes Road, Hilperton,
Trowbridge, Wiltshire BA14 6JB
T: (01225) 765838

HOLBETON
Devon
Bugle Rocks
◆◆◆◆ SILVER AWARD
The Old School, Battisborough,
Holbeton, Plymouth PL8 1JX
T: (01752) 830422
F: (01752) 830558

HOLCOMBE
Somerset
Ring O' Roses ◆◆◆◆
Stratton Road, Holcombe, Bath,
Somerset BA3 5EB
T: (01761) 232478
F: (01761) 233737
E: ringorosesholcombe@tesco.
net
I: www.ringoroses.co.uk

HOLNE
Devon
Mill Leat Farm ◆◆◆
Holne, Newton Abbot, Devon
TQ13 7RZ
T: (01364) 631283
F: (01364) 631283
⊕

HOLNEST
Dorset
Berkley Farm ◆◆◆
Holnest, Sherborne, Dorset
DT9 5PJ
T: (01963) 210269

Common Gate Farm ◆◆◆
Holnest, Sherborne, Dorset
DT9 6HY
T: (01963) 210411
F: (01963) 210411

HOLSWORTHY
Devon
Bason Farm ◆◆◆◆
Bradford, Holsworthy, Devon
EX22 7AW
T: (01409) 281277

Whitecroft Farm
◆◆◆◆ SILVER AWARD
Clawton, Holsworthy, Devon
EX22 6PW
T: (01409) 254623
F: (01409) 254623
E: ddmorris@talk21.com
I: www.atlantic-heritage-coast.
co.uk
⊕

HONITON
Devon
The Bliss Centre ◆◆◆◆
Snodwell Farm, Stockland Hill,
Honiton, Devon EX14 9HZ
T: (01404) 861696
F: (01404) 861696
E: blisscentre@hotmail.com

Lelamarie ◆◆◆
Awliscombe, Honiton, Devon
EX14 3PP
T: (01404) 44646 & 42308
F: (01404) 42131

The New Dolphin Hotel ◆◆◆
115 High Street, Honiton, Devon
EX14 1LS
T: (01404) 42377
F: (01404) 47662

The Old Vicarage ◆◆◆◆
Yarcombe, Honiton, Devon
EX14 9BD
T: (01404) 861594
F: (01404) 861594
E: jonannstockwell@aol.com

Wessington Farm ◆◆◆◆
SILVER AWARD
Awliscombe, Honiton, Devon
EX14 0NU
T: (01404) 42280
E: asummers@farming.co.uk

HORNINGSHAM
Wiltshire
Mill Farm ◆◆◆◆
Horningsham, Warminster,
Wiltshire BA12 7LL
I: (01985) 844333

Woodlands ◆◆◆
White Street, Horningsham,
Warminster, Wiltshire BA12 7LH
T: (01985) 844335
F: (01985) 844335

HORSINGTON
Somerset

Half Moon Inn ♦♦
Horsington, Templecombe,
Somerset BA8 0EF
T: (01963) 370140
E: halfmoon@horsington.co.uk
I: www.halfmoon.horsington.co.
uk

HORTON
Somerset

Lympool House ♦♦♦
Forest Mill Lane, Horton,
Ilminster, Somerset TA19 9QU
T: (01460) 57924

Partacre ♦♦
Horton, Devizes, Wiltshire
SN10 3NB
T: (01380) 860261

HUISH EPISCOPI
Somerset

Spring View ♦♦♦
Wagg Drove, Huish Episcopi,
Langport, Somerset TA10 9ER
T: (01458) 251215
⊛

Wagg Bridge Cottage ♦♦♦♦
Ducks Hill, Huish Episcopi,
Langport, Somerset TA10 9EN
T: (01458) 251488 &
07939 374234

IDDESLEIGH
Devon

Parsonage Farm ♦♦♦♦
Iddesleigh, Winkleigh, Devon
EX19 8SN
T: (01837) 810318

ILCHESTER
Somerset

Liongate House ♦♦♦
Northover, Ilchester, Yeovil,
Somerset BA22 8NG
T: (01935) 841193
F: (01935) 841037

ILFRACOMBE
Devon

Avalon Hotel ♦♦♦
6 Capstone Crescent, Ilfracombe,
Devon EX34 9BT
T: (01271) 863325
F: (01271) 866543
E: christine@ avalon hotel.
force9.co.uk
I: www.avalon-hotel.co.uk

Avoncourt Hotel ♦♦♦
6 Torrs Walk Avenue, Ilfracombe,
Devon EX34 8AU
T: (01271) 862543

The Bath House Hotel ♦♦♦
Runnacleave Road, Ilfracombe,
Devon EX34 8AR
T: (01271) 866859
F: (01271) 866879
E: enquiries@bathhousehotel.
co.uk
I: www.bathhousehotel.co.uk

Belvedere
♦♦♦♦ SILVER AWARD
12 Broad Park Avenue,
Ilfracombe, Devon EX34 8DZ
T: (01271) 862710
⊛

Capstone Hotel and Restaurant
♦♦♦
St James Place, Ilfracombe,
Devon EX34 9BJ
T: (01271) 863540
F: (01271) 862277
I: www.ilfracombe2000.
freeserve.co.uk

The Collingdale Hotel ♦♦♦
Larkstone Terrace, Ilfracombe,
Devon EX34 9NU
T: (01271) 863770
F: (01271) 863770
E: collingdale@onet.co.uk
I: www.ilfracombe-guide.co.
uk/collingdale.htm

Dedes Hotel ♦♦♦
1-4 The Promenade, Ilfracombe,
Devon EX34 9BD
T: (01271) 862545
F: (01271) 862234
E: jackie@dedes.fsbusiness.co.
uk
I: www.dedesshootingholidays.
co.uk

Dilkhusa Grand Hotel ♦♦♦
Wilder Road, Ilfracombe, Devon
EX34 9AH
T: (01271) 863505
F: (01271) 864739

The Epchris Hotel ♦♦♦
Torrs Park, Ilfracombe, Devon
EX34 8AZ
T: (01271) 862751
F: (01271) 862751

Glen Tor Hotel ♦♦♦♦
Torrs Park, Ilfracombe, Devon
EX34 8AZ
T: (01271) 862403
F: (01271) 862403
E: wenjoto@madasafish.com
I: www.ilfracombe_guide.co.uk

Grosvenor Hotel ♦♦♦
Wilder Road, Ilfracombe, Devon
EX34 9AF
T: (01271) 863426
F: (01271) 863714

Kelvin Guest House ♦♦♦
28 St Brannocks Road,
Ilfracombe, Devon EX34 8EQ
T: (01271) 866852
⊛

Laston House Hotel ♦♦♦
Hillsborough Road, Ilfracombe,
Devon EX34 9NT
T: (01271) 866557
F: (01271) 864440
E: robinlasto@msn.com
I: www.s-h-systems.co.
uk/hotels/laston.html

Norbury House Hotel ♦♦♦
Torrs Park, Ilfracombe, Devon
EX34 8AZ
T: (01271) 863888

St Brannocks House Hotel
♦♦♦
61 St Brannocks Road,
Ilfracombe, Devon EX34 8EQ
T: (01271) 863873
F: (01271) 863873
E: stbrannocks@aol.com
⊛

Sherborne Lodge Hotel ♦♦♦
Torrs Park, Ilfracombe, Devon
EX34 8AY
T: (01271) 862297
F: (01271) 865520
E: 113121.222@compuserve.
com
I: www.smoothhound.co.
uk/hotels/sherborne.html

Southcliffe Hotel ♦♦♦♦
Torrs Park, Ilfracombe, Devon
EX34 8AZ
T: (01271) 862958

Strathmore Hotel ♦♦♦♦
57 St Brannocks Road,
Ilfracombe, Devon EX34 8EQ
T: (01271) 862248 & 862243

**Sunnymeade Country House
Hotel** ♦♦♦
Dean Cross, West Down,
Ilfracombe, Devon EX34 8NT
T: (01271) 863668
F: (01271) 863668
E: sunnymeade@btinternet.com
I: www.btinternet.
com/$sunnymeade
⊛ ⚹

The Towers Hotel ♦♦♦
Chambercombe Park Road,
Ilfracombe, Devon EX34 9QN
T: (01271) 862809
F: (01271) 879442
E: info@thetowers.co.uk
I: www.thetowers.co.uk

Varley House ♦♦♦♦
Chambercombe Park,
Ilfracombe, Devon EX34 9QW
T: (01271) 863927
F: (01271) 879299
E: info@varleyhouse.freeserve.
co.uk
⊛

ILMINSTER
Somerset

Dillington House
♦♦♦♦ SILVER AWARD
Ilminster, Somerset TA19 9DT
T: (01460) 52427
F: (01460) 52433
E: dillington@somerset.gov.uk
I: www.dillington.co.uk

Graden ♦♦♦
Peasmarsh, Ilminster, Somerset
TA19 0SG
T: (01460) 52371
F: (01460) 52371

Hermitage ♦♦♦
29 Station Road, Ilminster,
Somerset TA19 9BE
T: (01460) 53028
⊛

IPPLEPEN
Devon

June Cottage ♦♦♦
Dornafield Road, Ipplepen,
Newton Abbot, Devon TQ12 5SH
T: (01803) 813081

ISLES OF SCILLY

Covean Cottage ♦♦♦♦
St Agnes, Isles of Scilly TR22 0PL
T: (01720) 422620

Hotel Beachcomber ♦♦
Thorofare, St Mary's, Isles of
Scilly TR21 0LN
T: (01720) 422682
F: (01720) 422532

Seaview Moorings
♦♦♦♦♦ SILVER AWARD
The Strand, St Mary's, Isles of
Scilly TR21 0PT
T: (01720) 422327

IVYBRIDGE
Devon

Hillhead Farm ♦♦♦♦
Ugborough, Ivybridge, Devon
PL21 0HQ
T: (01752) 892674 &
07785 915612
F: (01752) 690111
⊛

Venn Farm ♦♦♦
Ugborough, Ivybridge, Devon
PL21 0PE
T: (01364) 73240
F: (01364) 73240

KEINTON MANDEVILLE
Somerset

Stangray House ♦♦♦♦
Church Street, Keinton
Mandeville, Somerton, Somerset
TA11 6ER
T: (01458) 223984
F: (01458) 223992
E: dpm@euphony.net

KELLATON
Devon

Higher Kellaton Farm ♦♦♦
Kellaton, Kingsbridge, Devon
TQ7 2ES
T: (01548) 511514
F: (01548) 511514

KELSTON
Bath & North East Somerset

Old Crown ♦♦♦
Kelston, Bath BA1 9AQ
T: (01225) 423032
F: (01225) 480115

KENN
Devon

Lower Thornton Farm ♦♦♦♦
Kenn, Exeter, Devon EX6 7XH
T: (01392) 833434 &
07970 972012
F: (01392) 833434

KENNFORD
Devon

**Kerswell Grange Country
House** ♦♦♦♦
Old Dawlish Road, Kennford,
Exeter EX6 7LR
T: (01392) 833660
F: (01392) 833601
E: forrest@kerswellgrange.
telme.com
I: communities.msn.co.
uk/kerswellgrangebedbreakfast

KENTON
Devon

Devon Arms ♦♦♦
Fore Street, Kenton, Exeter,
Devon EX6 8LD
T: (01626) 890213
F: (01626) 891678

KEPNAL
Wiltshire

Eastfield House ♦♦♦
Kepnal, Pewsey, Wiltshire
SN9 5JL
T: (01672) 562489

KEYNSHAM
Bath & North East Somerset
Chewton Place ♦♦
Chewton Road, Keynsham,
Bristol BS31 2SX
T: (0117) 986 3105
F: (0117) 986 5948
E: conferenceoffice@
chewton-place.co.uk

Old Manor House ♦♦♦
5 Bristol Road, Keynsham,
Bristol BS31 2BA
T: (0117) 986 3107
F: (0117) 986 5940
E: oldmanorhouse@
compuserve.com

KILVE
Somerset
The Old Mill ♦♦♦♦
Kilve, Bridgwater, Somerset
TA5 1EB
T: (01278) 741571

KINGSAND
Cornwall
Halfway House Inn ♦♦♦
Fore Street, Kingsand, Torpoint,
Cornwall PL10 1NA
T: (01752) 822279
F: (01752) 823146
E: halfway@eggconnect.net
I: www.crappot.co.uk

KINGSBRIDGE
Devon
The Ashburton Arms ♦♦♦
West Charleton, Kingsbridge,
Devon TQ7 2AH
T: (01548) 531242

Ashleigh House ♦♦♦
Ashleigh Road, Kingsbridge,
Devon TQ7 1HB
T: (01548) 852893 &
07967 737875
E: reception@ashleigh-house.
co.uk
I: www.ashleigh-house.co.uk

Combe Farm B & B
♦♦♦ SILVER AWARD
Loddiswell, Kingsbridge, Devon
TQ7 4DT
T: (01548) 550560
F: (01548) 550560

Coombe Farm ♦♦♦♦
Kingsbridge, Devon TQ7 4AB
T: (01548) 852038
F: (01548) 852038

Crannacombe Farm ♦♦♦
Hazelwood, Loddiswell,
Kingsbridge, Devon TQ7 4DX
T: (01548) 550256

Globe Inn ♦♦
Frogmore, Kingsbridge, Devon
TQ7 2NR
T: (01548) 531351
F: (01548) 531351

Sloop Inn ♦♦♦
Bantham, Kingsbridge, Devon
TQ7 3AJ
T: (01548) 560489 & 560215
F: (01548) 561940

South Allington House
♦♦♦♦ SILVER AWARD
Chivelstone, Kingsbridge, Devon
TQ7 2NB
T: (01548) 511272
F: (01548) 511421
E: barbara@sthallingtonbnb.
demon.co.uk
I: www.sthallingtonbnb.demon.
co.uk

KINGSBURY EPISCOPI
Somerset
The Retreat ♦♦♦♦
Kingsbury Episcopi, Martock,
Somerset TA12
T: (01935) 823500

KINGSKERSWELL
Devon
The Barn Owl ♦♦♦♦
Aller Mills, Kingskerswell,
Newton Abbot, Devon TQ12 5AN
T: (01803) 872130 & 872968
F: (01803) 875279
E: book@lionheartinns.co.uk
I: www.lionheartinns.co.uk

Harewood Guest House ♦♦
17 Torquay Road, Kingskerswell,
Newton Abbot, Devon TQ12 5HH
T: (01803) 872228

KINGTON LANGLEY
Wiltshire
The Moors ♦♦♦
Malmesbury Road, Kington
Langley, Chippenham, Wiltshire
SN14 6HT
T: (01249) 750288
F: (01249) 7508814

KINGWESTON
Somerset
Lower Farm ♦♦♦♦
Kingweston, Somerton,
Somerset TA11 6BA
T: (01458) 223237 &
07860 350426
F: (01458) 223276
E: lowerfarm@kingweston.
demon.co.uk
I: www.lowerfarm.net

KNOWSTONE
Devon
West Bowden Farm ♦♦♦
Knowstone, South Molton,
Devon EX36 4RP
T: (01398) 341224

LACOCK
Wiltshire
King John's Hunting Lodge ♦♦♦
21 Church Street, Lacock,
Chippenham, Wiltshire
SN15 2LB
T: (01249) 730313
F: (01249) 730313

**Lacock Pottery Bed &
Breakfast** ♦♦♦♦
1 The Tanyard, Church Street,
Lacock, Chippenham, Wiltshire
SN15 2LB
T: (01249) 730266
F: (01249) 730946
E: simonmcdowell@
lacockbedandbreakfast.com
I: www.lacockbedandbreakfast.
com

Lower Lodge ♦♦♦
35 Bowden Hill, Lacock,
Chippenham, Wiltshire
SN15 2PP
T: (01249) 730711
F: (01249) 730955

The Old Rectory ♦♦♦♦
Cantax Hill, Lacock,
Chippenham, Wiltshire SN15 2JZ
T: (01249) 730335
F: (01249) 730166
E: elaine@oldrectorylacock.
freeserve.co.uk
I: www.oldrectorylacock.
freeserve.co.uk

Pen-Y-Brook ♦♦
Notton, Lacock, Chippenham,
Wiltshire SN15 2NF
T: (01249) 730376 &
07711 111643

Videl ♦♦♦
6A Bewley Lane, Lacock,
Chippenham, Wiltshire
SN15 2PG
T: (01249) 730279

LADOCK
Cornwall
Swallows Court ♦♦♦
Treworyan, Ladock, Truro,
Cornwall TR2 4QD
T: (01726) 883488

LAMERTON
Devon
New Court Farm ♦♦♦
Lamerton, Tavistock, Devon
PL19 8RR
T: (01822) 614319

LANDFORD
Wiltshire
New Forest Lodge
♦♦♦♦ SILVER AWARD
Southampton Road, Landford,
Salisbury SP5 2ED
T: (01794) 390999
F: (01794) 390066
E: reservations@
newforestlodge.co.uk
I: www.newforestlodge.co.uk

LANDSCOVE, ASHBURTON
Devon
Thornecroft ♦♦♦♦
Landscove, Ashburton, Newton
Abbot, Devon TQ13 7LX
T: (01803) 762500
E: tony@thornecroft.demon.co.
uk

LANGFORD
Miltons ♦♦♦
Stock Lane, Lower Langford,
Langford, Bristol BS40 5EU
T: (01934) 852352
F: (01934) 852302

Newcourt Barton ♦♦♦
Langford, Cullompton, Devon
EX15 1SE
T: (01884) 277326
F: (01884) 277326

LANGPORT
Somerset
Amberley ♦♦♦♦
Long Load, Langport, Somerset
TA10 9LD
T: (01458) 241542
E: jeanatamberley@talk21.com

Gothic House ♦♦♦♦
Muchelney, Langport, Somerset
TA10 0DW
T: (01458) 250626
E: joy_thorne@gothic-house.
totalserve.co.uk

The Old Pound Inn ♦♦♦
Aller, Langport, Somerset
TA10 0RA
T: (01458) 250469
F: (01458) 250469

Tuckers Hill ♦♦♦♦
Frog Lane, Langport, Somerset
TA10 0NE
T: (01458) 250413

LANGTON HERRING
Dorset
Fox Barrow House
♦♦♦♦ SILVER AWARD
The Square, Langton Herring,
Weymouth, Dorset DT3 4HT
T: (01305) 871463
F: (01305) 871995
E: austen@foxbarrow.co.uk
I: www.foxbarrow.co.uk

LANIVET
Cornwall
Willowbrook ♦♦♦♦
Old Coach Road, Lamorick,
Lanivet, Bodmin, Cornwall
PL30 5HB
T: (01208) 831670 &
07788 925865
F: (01208) 831670
E: miles.willowbrook@talk21.
com

LANSALLOS
Cornwall
Lesquite
♦♦♦♦ SILVER AWARD
Lansallos, Looe, Cornwall
PL13 2QE
T: (01503) 220315

LATTON
Wiltshire
Dolls House ♦♦♦
55 The Street, Latton, Swindon,
Wiltshire SN6 6DJ
T: (01793) 750384
E: gemma-maraffi@
bbdollshouse.freeserve.co.uk

LAUNCESTON
Cornwall
Berrio Bridge House ♦♦♦
Berrio Bridge, North Hill,
Launceston, Cornwall PL15 7NL
T: (01566) 782714
F: (01566) 782714

Heale Farmhouse ♦♦♦
Liftondown, Launceston,
Cornwall PL15 9QX
T: (01566) 784869
F: (01566) 784869

Hurdon Farm ♦♦♦♦
Launceston, Cornwall PL15 9LS
T: (01566) 772955

Middle Tremollett Farm ♦♦♦
Coad's Green, Launceston,
Cornwall PL15 7NA
T: (01566) 782416 &
07974 682603
F: (01566) 782416

The Old Vicarage
♦♦♦♦ SILVER AWARD
Treneglos, Launceston, Cornwall
PL15 8UQ
T: (01566) 781351
F: (01566) 781351
E: maggie@fancourt.freeserve.
co.uk
I: www.fancourt.freeserve.co.uk

Trethorne Leisure Farm ♦♦♦
Kennards House, Launceston,
Cornwall PL15 8QE
T: (01566) 86324 & 86992
F: (01566) 86981
E: trethorneleisure@eclipse.co.
uk

Trevadlock Farm
♦♦♦♦ SILVER AWARD
Trevadlock, Congdon Shop,
Launceston, Cornwall PL15 7PW
T: (01566) 782239
F: (01566) 782239

Wheatley Farm
♦♦♦♦ SILVER AWARD
Maxworthy, Launceston,
Cornwall PL15 8LY
T: (01566) 781232
F; (01566) 781232
E: wheatleyfrm@compuserve.
com
I: www.chycor.co.
uk/cottages/wheatley

White Hart Hotel ♦♦♦
15 Broad Street, Launceston,
Cornwall PL15 8AA
T: (01566) 772013 & 773567
F: (01566) 773668

LAVERSTOCK
Wiltshire

20 Potters Way ♦♦♦
Laverstock, Salisbury, Wiltshire
SP1 1PY
T: (01722) 335031
F: (01722) 335031

1 Riverside Close ♦♦♦♦
Laverstock, Salisbury, Wiltshire
SP1 1QW
T: (01722) 320287
F: (01722) 320287
E: marytucker@fdn.co.uk

The Twitterings ♦♦♦
73 Church Road, Laverstock,
Salisbury, Wiltshire SP1 1QZ
T: (01722) 321760

LAVERTON
Somerset

**Hollytree Cottage
Rating Applied For**
Laverton, Bath BA3 6QZ
T: (01373) 830786 & 0790 186
7694
F: (01373) 830786

LEIGH
Wiltshire

Leighfield Lodge Farm ♦♦♦♦
Malmesbury Road, Leigh,
Swindon SN6 6RH
T: (01666) 860241
F: (01666) 860241

LEWANNICK
Cornwall

Trevadlock Manor ♦♦♦
Lewannick, Launceston,
Cornwall PL15 7PW
T: (01566) 782227

LEWDOWN
Devon

Old Cottage ♦♦♦♦
Dippertown, Lewdown,
Okehampton, Devon EX20 4PT
T: (01566) 783250

Stowford Grange Farm ♦♦
Lewdown, Okehampton, Devon
EX20 4BZ
T: (01566) 783298

Stowford House Hotel ♦♦♦♦
Lewdown, Okehampton, Devon
EX20 4BZ
T: (01566) 783415
F: (01566) 783489

LISKEARD
Cornwall

Elnor Guest House
1 Russell Street, Station Road,
Liskeard, Cornwall PL14 4BP
T: (01579) 342472
F: (01579) 345673

Hyvue House ♦♦♦
Barras Cross, Liskeard, Cornwall
PL14 6BN
T: (01579) 348175

Tregondale Farm
♦♦♦♦ SILVER AWARD
Menheniot, Liskeard, Cornwall
PL14 3RG
T: (01579) 342407
F: (01579) 342407

Trewint Farm ♦♦♦♦
Menheniot, Liskeard, Cornwall
PL14 3RE
T: (01579) 347155
F: (01579) 347155

LITTLE BEDWYN
Wiltshire

Bridge Cottage ♦♦♦
Little Bedwyn, Marlborough,
Wiltshire SN8 3JS
T: (01672) 870795
F: (01672) 870795
E: rwdaniel@bridgecott.fsnet.
co.uk

LITTLE LANGFORD
Wiltshire

Little Langford Farmhouse
♦♦♦♦ SILVER AWARD
Little Langford, Salisbury,
Wiltshire SP3 4NR
T: (01722) 790205
F: (01722) 790086
E: bandb@littlelangford.co.uk
I: www.dmac.co.uk/llf

LITTLEHEMPSTON
Devon

Court Farm ♦♦♦♦
Littlehempston, Totnes, Devon
TQ9 6LU
T: (01803) 840255
F: (01803) 840266

THE LIZARD
Cornwall

Trethvas Farmhouse ♦♦♦
The Lizard, Helston, Cornwall
TR12 7AR
T: (01326) 290720
F: (01326) 290720

LODDISWELL
Devon

Blackwell Park ♦♦
Loddiswell, Kingsbridge, Devon
TQ7 4EA
T: (01548) 821230

The Shippen ♦♦♦♦
Rake Farm, Loddiswell,
Kingsbridge, Devon TQ7 4DA
T: (01548) 550016
E: theshippen@barclays.net
I: james.dircon.co.uk /
theshippen.html

LODERS
Dorset

Highacres House ♦♦♦
Highacres, Loders, Bridport,
Dorset DT6 3UJ
T: (01308) 421335 &
(01305) 889502
F: (01308) 421335

LONG BREDY
Dorset

Middle Farm ♦♦♦
Long Bredy, Dorchester, Dorset
DT2 9HW
T: (01308) 482215

LONG LOAD
Somerset

Fairlight ♦♦♦
Martock Road, Long Load,
Langport, Somerset TA10 9LG
T: (01458) 241323

LONG SUTTON
Somerset

The Old Mill ♦♦♦♦
Knole, Long Sutton, Langport,
Somerset TA10 9HY
T: (01458) 241599
F: (01458) 241710

LONGLEAT
Wiltshire

Post Office Farm ♦♦♦
Corsley Heath, Longleat,
Warminster, Wiltshire BA12 7PR
T: (01373) 832734 &
(01409) 19130
F: (01373) 832734
E: kevin.youdan@lineone.net

LOOE
Cornwall

Bucklawren Farm
♦♦♦♦ SILVER AWARD
St Martin-by-Looe, Looe,
Cornwall PL13 1NZ
T: (01503) 240738
F: (01503) 240481
E: bucklawren@compuserve.
com
I: www.cornwallexplore.co.
uk/bucklawren

Coombe Farm ♦♦♦♦
Widegates, Looe, Cornwall
PL13 1QN
T: (01503) 240223 & 240329
F: (01503) 240895
E: coombe-farm@hotmail.com
I: www.coombefarmhotel.co.uk

Hall Barton Farm ♦♦♦
Pelynt, Looe, Cornwall PL13 2LG
T: (01503) 220203
F: (01503) 220203

Little Larnick Farm ♦♦♦♦
Pelynt, Looe, Cornwall PL13 2NB
T: (01503) 262837
F: (01503) 262837

The Panorama Hotel ♦♦♦♦
Hannafore Road, Looe, Cornwall
PL13 2DE
T: (01503) 262123
F: (01503) 265654
E: stay@looe.co.uk
I: www.looe.co.uk

Stonerock Cottage ♦♦
Portuan Road, Hannafore, West
Looe, Cornwall PL13 2DN
T: (01503) 263651
F: (01503) 263414

Trehaven Manor
♦♦♦♦ SILVER AWARD
Station Road, Looe, Cornwall
PL13 1HN
T: (01503) 262028

Trevanion Hotel ♦♦♦
Hannafore Road, Looe, Cornwall
PL13 2DE
T: (01503) 262003 &
07802 447544
F: (01503) 265408
E: hotel@looecornwall.co.uk
I: www.looecornwall.co.uk

LOWER WOODFORD
Wiltshire

**Swallow Cottage Bed &
Breakfast ♦♦♦**
Swallow Cottage, Lower
Woodford, Salisbury SP4
T: (01722) 782393 &
07973 265419
F: (01722) 782739
E: swallow.cottage@amserve.
net

LOXTON
Somerset

Church Farm ♦♦♦♦
Christon Road, Loxton, Axbridge,
Somerset BS26 2XH
T: (01934) 750886 &
07702 273296

LUCCOMBE
Somerset

Luccombe Knap ♦♦♦♦
Luccombe, Minehead, Somerset
TA24 8TE
T: (01643) 862378

LUDGERSHALL
Wiltshire

Heysgarth ♦♦
34 Astor Crescent, Ludgershall,
Andover, Hampshire SP11 9RF
T: (01264) 790372

White Marley B & B ♦♦♦♦
5 Graspan Road, Faberstown,
Ludgershall, Andover,
Hampshire SP11 9NY
T: (01264) 790641

LUXBOROUGH
Somerset

Nurcott Farm ♦♦
Luxborough, Watchet, Somerset
TA23 0SG
T: (01984) 641388
F: (01984) 641388
E: nelar@epulse.net

LYDFORD
Devon

Hall Farm
Rating Applied For
Lydford, Okehampton, Devon
EX20 4BJ
T: (01822) 820252

LYDIARD TREGOZE
Wiltshire

Park Farm ♦♦♦
Hook Street, Lydiard Tregoze,
Swindon, Wiltshire SN5 3NY
T: (01793) 853608

LYME REGIS
Dorset

Charnwood Guest House ♦♦♦
21 Woodmead Road, Lyme
Regis, Dorset DT7 3AD
T: (01297) 445281
E: charnwood@lymeregis62.
freeserve.co.uk
I: lymeregis.com/charnwood

Clappentail House
♦♦♦♦ SILVER AWARD
Uplyme Road, Lyme Regis,
Dorset DT7 3LP
T: (01297) 445739
F: (01297) 444794
E: pountain@clappentail.
freeserve.co.uk

Cliff Cottage ♦♦♦
Cobb Road, Lyme Regis, Dorset
DT7 3JE
T: (01297) 443334

Coombe House ♦♦♦
41 Coombe Street, Lyme Regis,
Dorset DT7 3PY
T: (01297) 443849

Devonia Guest House ♦♦♦
2 Woodmead Road, Lyme Regis,
Dorset DT7 3AB
T: (01297) 442869
F: (01297) 442869

Higher Spence ♦♦♦
Wootton Fitzpaine, Bridport,
Dorset DT6 6DF
T: (01297) 560556

**The London Bed and Breakfast
♦♦♦**
40 Church Street, Lyme Regis,
Dorset DT7 3DA
T: (01297) 442083

Lucerne ♦♦♦
View Road, Lyme Regis, Dorset
DT7 3AA
T: (01297) 443752

Lydwell House ♦♦♦
Lyme Road, Uplyme, Lyme Regis,
Dorset DT7 3TJ
T: (01297) 443522
E: brittain16@fsbusiness.co.uk
I: www.smoothhound.co.
uk/hotels/lydwell.html

Manaton Guest House ♦♦♦♦
Hill Road, Lyme Regis, Dorset
DT7 3PE
T: (01297) 445138

Mermaid House ♦♦♦♦
32 Coombe Street, Lyme Regis,
Dorset DT7 3PP
T: (01297) 445351
E: mermaidhouse@talk21.com
I: www.smoothhound.co.uk

Ocean View ♦♦♦♦
2 Hadleigh Villas, Silver Street,
Lyme Regis, Dorset DT7 3HR
T: (01297) 442567

Old Lyme Guest House
♦♦♦♦ GOLD AWARD
29 Coombe Street, Lyme Regis,
Dorset DT7 3PP
T: (01297) 442929
F: (01297) 444652
E: oldlyme.guesthouse@virgin.
net
I: www.oldlymeguesthouse.co.
uk

The Red House ♦♦♦♦
Sidmouth Road, Lyme Regis,
Dorset DT7 3ES
T: (01297) 442055
F: (01297) 442055
E: red.house@virgin.net
I: smooth.hound.co.uk/hotels.
redhous2.html

Rotherfield ♦♦♦
View Road, Lyme Regis, Dorset
DT7 3AA
T: (01297) 445585
E: rotherfieldatlymeregis.com
I: lymeregis.com/rotherfield/

Southernhaye ♦♦♦
Pound Road, Lyme Regis, Dorset
DT7 3HX
T: (01297) 443077
F: (01297) 443077

Springfield ♦♦♦
Woodmead Road, Lyme Regis,
Dorset DT7 3LJ
T: (01297) 443409
E: springfield@lymeregis.com
I: www.lymeregis.
com/springfield

Thatch ♦♦♦♦
Uplyme Road, Lyme Regis,
Dorset DT7 3LP
T: (01297) 442212
F: (01297) 443485

Thatch Lodge Hotel
♦♦♦♦♦ GOLD AWARD
The Street, Charmouth, Bridport,
Dorset DT6 6PQ
T: (01297) 560407
F: (01297) 560407
E: thatchlodgehotel@cs.com
I: www.thatchlodgehotel.com

Victoria Hotel ♦♦♦
Uplyme Road, Lyme Regis,
Dorset DT7 3LP
T: (01297) 444801
F: (01297) 442949
E: info@vichotel.co.uk
I: www.vichotel.co.uk

Westwood Guest House ♦♦♦
1 Woodmead Road, Lyme Regis,
Dorset DT7 3LJ
T: (01297) 442376

White House ♦♦♦♦
47 Silver Street, Lyme Regis,
Dorset DT7 3HR
T: (01297) 443420

Woodberry Down ♦♦
Colway Lane, Lyme Regis, Dorset
DT7 3HF
T: (01297) 444655
F: (01297) 444655

LYNMOUTH
Devon

**Bonnicott House Hotel
♦♦♦♦♦**
Watersmeet Road, Lynmouth,
Devon EX35 6EP
T: (01598) 753346

Coombe Farm ♦♦♦
Countisbury, Lynton, Devon
EX35 6NF
T: (01598) 741236 & 741227
F: (01598) 741236

East Lyn House ♦♦♦♦
17 Watersmeet Road, Lynmouth,
Devon EX35 6EP
T: (01598) 752540
F: (01598) 752540

Ferndale House ♦♦♦
Summerhouse Path,
Watersmeet Road, Lynmouth,
Devon EX35 6EP
T: (01598) 753431

Orchard House Hotel ♦♦♦♦
12 Watersmeet Road, Lynmouth,
Devon EX35 6EP
T: (01598) 753247
F: (01598) 753855
E: orchardhouse@lynmouth.
fsnet.co.uk
I: www.welcome.
to/orchardhouse

Seaview Villa ♦♦♦
6 Summerhouse Path,
Lynmouth, Devon EX35 6ES
T: (01598) 753460
F: (01598) 752399

**Tregonwell Riverside
Guesthouse ♦♦♦**
1 Tors Road, Lynmouth, Devon
EX35 6ET
T: (01598) 753369
I: www.smoothhound.co.
uk/hotels/tregonwl.html

The Village Inn ♦♦♦
19 Lynmouth Street, Lynmouth,
Devon EX35 6EH
T: (01598) 752354

LYNTON
Devon

Alford House Hotel ♦♦♦
3 Alford Terrace, Lynton, Devon
EX35 6AT
T: (01598) 752359
F: (01598) 752359
E: bookings@alfordhouse.
freeserve.co.uk
I: www.smoothhound.co.
uk/hotels/alford.html

Caffyns Heanton Farm ♦♦♦♦
Lynton, Devon EX35 6JW
T: (01598) 753770
F: (01598) 753770

Croft House Hotel ♦♦♦♦
Lydiate Lane, Lynton, Devon
EX35 6HE
T: (01598) 752391
E: jane.woolnough@lineone.net
I: www.smoothhound.co.
uk/hotels/croftnow.html

The Denes Guest House ♦♦♦
Rating Applied For
15 Longmead, Lynton, Devon
EX35 6DQ
T: (01598) 753573
F: (01598) 753573
E: j.e.mcgowan@btinternet.com
I: www.thedenes.com

Fairholme Hotel ♦♦♦
North Walk, Lynton, Devon
EX35 6ED
T: (01598) 752263
F: (01598) 752263

The Fernery ♦♦♦
Lydiate Lane, Lynton, Devon
EX35 6AJ
T: (01598) 752440
F: (01598) 752396

Fernleigh Guest House ♦♦♦♦
Park Street, Lynton, Devon
EX35 6BY
T: (01598) 753575
F: (01598) 753575
E: hugh_mcdonnell@hotmail.
com

Ingleside Hotel ♦♦♦♦
Lee Road, Lynton, Devon
EX35 6HW
T: (01598) 752223
E: johnpauldevon@aol.com

Kingford House ♦♦♦♦
Longmead, Lynton, Devon
EX35 6DQ
T: (01598) 752361

Lauraleigh ♦♦♦
14 Park Street, Lynton, Devon
EX35 6BY
T: (01598) 752613

Lee House ♦♦♦
27 Lee Road, Lynton, Devon
EX35 6BP
T: (01598) 752364
F: (01598) 752364

**Longmead House Hotel
♦♦♦♦**
9 Longmead, Lynton, Devon
EX35 6DQ
T: (01598) 752523
F: (01598) 752523
E: info@longmeadhouse.co.uk
I: www.longmeadhouse.co.uk

Meadhaven ♦♦
12 Crossmead, Lynton, Devon
EX35 6DG
T: (01598) 753288

North Walk House ♦♦♦♦
North Walk, Lynton, Devon
EX35 6HJ
T: (01598) 753372

Pine Lodge ♦♦♦♦
Lynway, Lynton, Devon
EX35 6AX
T: (01598) 753230
E: pine1lodge@aol.com

Rockvale Hotel ♦♦♦♦
Lee Road, Lynton, Devon
EX35 6HW
T: (01598) 752279 & 753343
E: judithwoodland@rockvale.
fsbusiness.co.uk

Rodwell House ♦♦♦
21 Lee Road, Lynton, Devon
EX35 6BP
T: (01598) 753324

St Vincent House ♦♦♦♦
Castle Hill, Lynton, Devon
EX35 6JA
T: (01598) 752244
F: (01598) 753971
E: keentvins@lineone.net
I: www.hotelsaccommodation.
co.uk/devon/vincent.htm

South Cheriton Farm ♦♦♦
Barbrook, Lynton, Devon
EX35 6LJ
T: (01598) 753280

South View Guest House ♦♦♦
23 Lee Road, Lynton, Devon
EX35 6BP
T: (01598) 752289 & 752289

Southcliffe ♦♦♦♦
34 Lee Road, Lynton, Devon
EX35 6BS
T: (01598) 753328
F: (01598) 753328

The Turret ♦♦♦
33 Lee Road, Lynton, Devon
EX35 6BS
T: (01598) 753284
F: (01598) 753284
I: www.smoothhound.co.
uk/hotels/theturre.html

Valley House Hotel ♦♦♦
Lynbridge Road, Lynton, Devon
EX35 6BD
T: (01598) 752285
E: valleyhouse@westcountry.
net
I: www.westcountry.net

Woodlands ♦♦♦♦
Lynbridge Road, Lynton, Devon
EX35 6AX
T: (01598) 752324
F: (01598) 753828

MAIDENCOMBE
Devon

Bowden Close Hotel ♦♦♦
Teignmouth Road,
Maidencombe, Torquay, Devon
TQ1 4TJ
T: (01803) 328029
F: (01803) 327331
I: www.SmoothHound.co.
uk/BowdenClose

MALBOROUGH
Devon

The Lodge
♦♦♦♦ SILVER AWARD
Higher Town, Malborough,
Kingsbridge, Devon TQ7 3RN
T: (01548) 561405
F: (01548) 561111
E: accom@compuserve.com
I: ourworld.compuserve.
com/homepages/accom

MALMESBURY
Wiltshire

Bremilham House ♦♦♦
Bremilham Road, Malmesbury,
Wiltshire SN16 0DQ
T: (01666) 822680

Flisteridge Cottage ♦♦♦♦
Flisteridge Road, Upper Minety,
Malmesbury, Wiltshire SN16 9PS
T: (01666) 860343

Honeysuckle ♦♦♦
Foxley Road, Malmesbury,
Wiltshire SN16 0JQ
T: (01666) 825267

Ivy House ♦♦♦
Burton Hill, Malmesbury,
Wiltshire SN16 0EW
T: (01666) 823452
F: (01666) 823452

The Kings Arms Hotel ♦♦♦
High Street, Malmesbury,
Wiltshire SN16 9AA
T: (01666) 823383
F: (01666) 825327

Lovett Farm ♦♦♦♦
Little Somerford, Chippenham,
Wiltshire SN15 5BP
T: (01666) 823268 &
07808 858612
F: (01666) 823268
E: lovetts_farm@hotmail.com
⊚

Manor Farm ♦♦♦♦
Corston, Malmesbury, Wiltshire
SN16 0HF
T: (01666) 822148
F: (01666) 826565
E: ross@manorfarmbandb.fsnet.
co.uk
I: www.manorfarmbandb.co.uk
⊚

Marsh Farmhouse ♦♦♦
Crudwell Road, Malmesbury,
Wiltshire SN16 9JL
T: (01666) 822208 &
07785 535944

Oakwood Farm ♦♦♦
Upper Minety, Malmesbury,
Wiltshire SN16 9PY
T: (01666) 860286 &
07785 916039
F: (01666) 860286
⊚

The Old Manor House ♦♦
6 Oxford Street, Malmesbury,
Wiltshire SN16 9AX
T: (01666) 823494

Rothay ♦♦♦♦
Milbourne Lane, Malmesbury,
Wiltshire SN16 9JQ
T: (01666) 823509

Stonehill Farm ♦♦♦♦
Charlton, Malmesbury, Wiltshire
SN16 9DY
T: (01666) 823310
F: (01666) 823310

Trucklebridge ♦♦♦
Foxley Road, Malmesbury,
Wiltshire SN16 0JE
T: (01666) 826027
F: (01666) 824805

Whychurch Farm ♦♦♦♦
Whychurch Hill, Malmesbury,
Wiltshire SN16 9JL
T: (01666) 822156
E: c_eweaver@talk21.com

Winkworth Farm ♦♦♦♦
Lea, Malmesbury, Wiltshire
SN16 9NH
T: (01666) 823267

MANNAMEAD
Devon

Devonshire Guest House ♦♦♦
22 Lockyer Road, Mannamead,
Plymouth, Devon PL3 4RL
T: (01752) 220726
F: (01752) 220766
E: phil@devshire.demon.co.uk
I: www.devshire.demon.co.uk

MANNINGFORD ABBOTS
Wiltshire

Huntlys ♦♦♦
Manningford Abbots, Pewsey,
Wiltshire SN9 6HZ
T: (01672) 563663
F: (01672) 851249

MANTON
Wiltshire

Sunrise Farm ♦♦♦
Manton, Marlborough, Wiltshire
SN8 4HL
T: (01672) 512878
F: (01672) 512878

MARAZION
Cornwall

**Chymorvah Private Hotel
♦♦♦**
Marazion, Cornwall TR17 0DQ
T: (01736) 710497 & 710508
F: (01736) 710508

MARK
Somerset

Burnt House Farm ♦♦♦
Yarrow Road, Mark, Highbridge,
Somerset TA9 4LR
T: (01278) 641280 &
07909 888692
F: (01278) 641119
E: burnthousefarm@hotmail.
com

Laurel Farm ♦♦♦
The Causeway, Mark,
Highbridge, Somerset TA9 4PZ
T: (01278) 641216
F: (01278) 641447

MARLBOROUGH
Wiltshire

Ash Lodge ♦♦♦♦
Choppingknife Lane,
Marlborough, Wiltshire SN8 2AT
T: (01672) 516745

Beam End ♦♦♦
67 George Lane, Marlborough,
Wiltshire SN8 4BY
T: (01672) 515048
F: (01672) 515048
E: tony@drew67.freeserve.co.uk

Cartref ♦♦♦
63 George Lane, Marlborough,
Wiltshire SN8 4BY
T: (01672) 512771

Fishermans House ♦♦♦♦
Mildenhall, Marlborough,
Wiltshire SN8 2LZ
T: (01672) 515390 &
07785 225363
F: (01672) 519009

13 Hyde Lane ♦♦
Marlborough, Wiltshire SN8 1JL
T: (01672) 514415
F: (01672) 514415

Kennet Beeches ♦♦
54 George Lane, Marlborough,
Wiltshire SN8 4BY
T: (01672) 512579

The Lamb Inn ♦♦♦
The Parade, Marlborough,
Wiltshire SN8 1NE
T: (01672) 512668
F: (01672) 512668

Manton Weir ♦♦♦♦
Marlborough, Wiltshire SN8 4HR
T: (01672) 511398

Merlin Hotel ♦♦♦
36/39 High Street, Marlborough,
Wiltshire SN8 1LW
T: (01672) 512151
F: (01672) 514656

5 Reeds Ground ♦♦♦
London Road, Marlborough,
Wiltshire SN8 2AW
T: (01672) 513926

Wernham Farm ♦♦♦
Clench Common, Marlborough,
Wiltshire SN8 4DR
T: (01672) 512236 &
07880 728980
F: (01672) 515001
E: margglvsf@aol.com

West View ♦♦♦
Barnfield, Marlborough,
Wiltshire SN8 2AX
T: (01672) 515583 &
0771 2165258
F: (01672) 519014
E: maggiestewart@euphony.net
I: www.westviewb-b.co.uk

Westcourt Bottom ♦♦♦♦
165 Westcourt, Burbage,
Marlborough, Wiltshire
SN8 3BW
T: (01672) 810924 & 811723

MARSTON
Wiltshire

Home Farm ♦♦♦
Close Lane, Marston, Devizes,
Wiltshire SN10 5SN
T: (01380) 725484

MARTINSTOWN
Dorset

Old Post Office ♦♦
Martinstown, Dorchester, Dorset
DT2 9LF
T: (01305) 889254

MARTOCK
Somerset

Madey Mills ♦
Martock, Somerset TA12 6NN
T: (01935) 823268

The Nags Head ♦♦♦
East Street, Martock, Somerset
TA12 6NF
T: (01935) 823432
E: chris@nagsheadinn.fsnet.co.
uk

The White Hart Hotel ♦♦♦
East Street, Martock, Somerset
TA12 6JQ
T: (01935) 822005
F: (01935) 822056

Wychwood ♦♦♦♦
7 Bearley Road, Martock,
Somerset TA12 6PG
T: (01935) 825601
F: (01935) 825601
E: wychwoodmartock@yahoo.
co.uk
I: www.theaa.co.
uk/region8/76883.html
⊚

MAWGAN PORTH
Cornwall

Bre-Pen Farm ♦♦♦♦
Mawgan Porth, Newquay,
Cornwall TR8 4AL
T: (01637) 860420

MEAVY
Devon
Callisham Farm ♦♦♦
Meavy, Yelverton, Devon
PL20 6PS
T: (01822) 853901
F: (01822) 853901
E: wills@callishamfarm.fsnet.co.
uk

MELKSHAM
Wiltshire
Honeysuckle Cottage ♦♦♦♦
Rating Applied For
95 the Common, Broughton
Gifford, Melksham, Wiltshire
SN12 8ND
T: (01225) 782463 &
07747 754157
E: jmehta@globalnet.co.uk
I: www.users.globalnet.co.
uk/$jmehta/index.htm

Longhope Guest House ♦♦♦
9 Beanacre Road, Melksham,
Wiltshire SN12 8AG
T: (01225) 706737
F: (01225) 706737

The Old Manor
Rating Applied For
Spa Road, Melksham, Wiltshire
SN12 7NY
T: (01225) 793803
F: (01225) 793803

The Regency Hotel ♦♦
10-12 Spa Road, Melksham,
Wiltshire SN12 7NS
T: (01225) 702971
F: (01225) 790745
E: regency.hotel@btinternet.
com
I: www.regencyhotel.co.uk

The Spa Bed & Breakfast
Rating Applied For
402 The Spa, Melksham,
Wiltshire SN12 6QL
T: (01225) 707984

Springfield B & B ♦♦♦
403 The Spa, Melksham,
Wiltshire SN12 6QL
T: (01225) 703694
F: (01225) 703694

MELLS
Somerset
Talbot Inn
Rating Applied For
High Street, Mells, Frome,
Somerset BA11 3PN
T: (01373) 812254
F: (01373) 813599
E: talbot.inn@lineone.net

MELPLASH
Dorset
Mount Meadow Farm ♦♦♦
The Mount, Melplash, Bridport,
Dorset DT6 3TV
T: (01308) 488524
E: rosie@mountmeadow
I: www.mountmeadow.co.uk

MERE
Wiltshire
The Beeches ♦♦♦
Chetcombe Road, Mere,
Warminster, Wiltshire BA12 6AU
T: (01747) 860687

**Chetcombe House Hotel
♦♦♦♦**
Chetcombe Road, Mere,
Warminster, Wiltshire BA12 6AZ
T: (01747) 860219
F: (01747) 860111

Downleaze ♦♦
North Street, Mere, Warminster,
Wiltshire BA12 6HH
T: (01747) 860876

Talbot Hotel ♦♦♦♦
The Square, Mere, Wiltshire
BA12 6DR
T: (01747) 860427

Willowdown House ♦♦♦♦
Wet Lane, Mere, Warminster,
Wiltshire BA12 6BA
T: (01747) 860218

MEVAGISSEY
Cornwall
**Kerry Anna Country House
♦♦♦♦**
Treleaven Farm, Mevagissey, St
Austell, Cornwall PL26 6RZ
T: (01726) 843558
F: (01726) 843558

Polgreen Farm ♦♦♦♦
London Apprentice, St Austell,
Cornwall PL26 7AP
T: (01726) 75151
F: (01726) 75151
E: polgreen.farm@btclick.com

Polrudden Farm ♦♦♦♦
Pentewan, St Austell, Cornwall
PL26 6BJ
T: (01726) 843213 & 842051

MIDDLEMARSH
Dorset
White Horse Farm
Rating Applied For
Middlemarsh, Sherborne, Dorset
DT9 5QN
T: (01963) 210222
E: enquiries@whitehorsefarm.
co.uk
I: www.whitehorsefarm.co.uk

MILBORNE PORT
Somerset
**The Old Vicarage Hotel
♦♦♦♦♦**
Sherborne Road, Milborne Port,
Sherborne, Dorset DT9 5AT
T: (01963) 251117
F: (01963) 251515
I: www.milborneport.freeserve.
co.uk

MILDENHALL
Wiltshire
Watersedge ♦♦♦
Mildenhall, Marlborough,
Wiltshire SN8 2LY
T: (01672) 511590

MILLBROOK
Cornwall
**Stone Farm Bed and Breakfast
♦♦♦♦**
Whitsand Bay, Millbrook,
Torpoint, Cornwall PL10 1JJ
T: (01752) 822267
F: (01752) 822267

MILVERTON
Somerset
Cullendown ♦♦
Springrove, Milverton, Taunton,
Somerset TA4 1NL
T: (01823) 400731

MINEHEAD
Somerset
**Alcombe Cote Guest House
♦♦♦**
19 Manor Road, Alcombe,
Minehead, Somerset TA24 6EH
T: (01643) 703309
F: (01643) 709901

Allington House ♦♦♦♦
30 Ponsford Road, Minehead,
Somerset TA24 5DY
T: (01643) 703898

Avill House ♦♦♦
Townsend Road, Minehead,
Somerset TA24 5RG
T: (01643) 704370

Avondale ♦♦♦♦
Martlet Road, Minehead,
Somerset TA24 5QD
T: (01643) 706931

Bactonleigh Hotel ♦♦
20 Tregonwell Road, Minehead,
Somerset TA24 5DU
T: (01643) 702147

**The Beacon Country House
Hotel ♦♦♦♦**
Beacon Road, Minehead,
Somerset TA24 5SD
T: (01643) 703476
F: (01643) 707007
E: beacon@globalnet.co.uk

Dorchester Hotel ♦♦♦
38 The Avenue, Minehead,
Somerset TA24 5AZ
T: (01643) 702052

Fernside ♦♦♦
The Holloway, Minehead,
Somerset TA24 5PB
T: (01643) 707594 & 708995
E: colin.cjs@btinternet.com

Field House ♦♦♦
The Parks, Minehead, Somerset
TA24 8BU
T: (01643) 706958

Finial ♦♦♦♦
24 Ponsford Road, Minehead,
Somerset TA24 5DY
T: (01643) 703945

Foxes Hotel ♦♦♦
The Esplanade, Minehead,
Somerset TA24 5PQ
T: (01643) 704450
F: (01643) 708249
E: Foxeshotel@aol.com

Gascony Hotel ♦♦♦♦
The Avenue, Minehead,
Somerset TA24 5BB
T: (01643) 705939

Higher Rodhuish Farm ♦♦♦
Rodhuish, Minehead, Somerset
TA24 6QL
T: (01984) 640253
F: (01984) 640253

Hillside ♦♦♦♦ SILVER AWARD
Higher Allerford, Allerford,
Minehead, Somerset TA24 8HS
T: (01643) 862831
F: (01643) 862279
E: michael.prideaux@virgin.net

Hindon Farm ♦♦♦
Minehead, Somerset TA24 8SH
T: (01643) 705244
F: (01643) 705244
E: rogpenweb@farmersweekly.
net
I: www.exmoortourism.org

The Kildare Lodge ♦♦♦
Townsend Road, Minehead,
Somerset TA24 5RQ
T: (01643) 702009
F: (01643) 706516

Kingsway Hotel ♦♦♦♦
36 Ponsford Road, Minehead,
Somerset TA24 5DY
T: (01643) 702313

Lorna Doone ♦♦♦
26 Tregonwell Road, Minehead,
Somerset TA24 5DU
T: (01643) 702540

Lyn Valley Guest House ♦♦♦
3 Tregonwell Road, Minehead,
Somerset TA24 5DT
T: (01643) 703748
F: (01643) 703748

Marshfield Hotel ♦♦♦♦
18 Tregonwell Road, Minehead,
Somerset TA24 5DU
T: (01643) 702517 &
0500 600734
F: (01643) 702517
E: marshfield.hotel@
minehead18.freeserve.co.uk
I: www.marshfield-hotel.co.uk

Mayfair Hotel ♦♦♦♦
25 The Avenue, Minehead,
Somerset TA24 5AY
T: (01643) 702719
F: (01643) 702719

1 Moorlands ♦♦♦
Moor Road, Minehead, Somerset
TA24 5RT
T: (01643) 703453

Old Ship Aground ♦♦♦
Quay Street, Minehead,
Somerset TA24 5UL
T: (01643) 702087
F: (01643) 709066

The Parks Guest House
Rating Applied For
26 The Parks, Minehead,
Somerset TA24 8BT
T: (01643) 703547
F: (01643) 708088

Promenade Hotel ♦♦♦
The Esplanade, Minehead,
Somerset TA24 5QS
T: (01643) 702572
F: (01643) 702572
E: jgph@globalnet.co.uk
I: www.johngroons.org.uk

Sunfield Private Hotel ♦♦♦
83 Summerland Avenue,
Minehead, Somerset TA24 5BW
T: (01643) 703565 &
0800 0566601
F: (01643) 703565
E: sunfield@primex.co.uk
I: www.placestostay.com

Tranmere House ♦♦♦
24 Tregonwell Road, Minehead,
Somerset TA24 5DU
T: (01643) 702647

Tregonwell House ♦
1 Tregonwell Road, Minehead,
Somerset TA24 5DT
T: (01643) 703595

Wanneroo Farm ◆◆◆
Timberscombe, Minehead,
Somerset TA24 7TU
T: (01643) 841493
F: (01643) 841693
E: bambwanneroo@cs.com

MINSTER
Cornwall
Branarth ◆◆◆◆
Minster, Boscastle, Cornwall
PL35 0BN
T: (01840) 250102
F: (01840) 250102
E: arthur.bradleyl@which.net

Home Farm ◆◆◆
Minster, Boscastle, Cornwall
PL35 0BN
T: (01840) 250195
F: (01840) 250195
E: jackie.haddy@btclick.com
⊛

MODBURY
Devon
Goutsford ◆◆◆◆
Ermington, Modbury, Ivybridge,
Devon PL21 9NY
T: (01548) 831299 &
07977 200324
F: (01752) 601728

Weeke Farm ◆◆◆
Modbury, Ivybridge, Devon
PL21 0TT
T: (01548) 830219
F: (01548) 830219

MOLLAND
Devon
Great Woods Farm ◆
Molland, South Molton, Devon
EX36 3NL
T: (01769) 550203

MONKLEIGH
Devon
Annery Barton ◆◆◆
Monkleigh, Bideford, Devon
EX39 5JL
T: (01237) 473629
F: (01237) 424468

MONTACUTE
Somerset
Mad Hatters Tearooms ◆◆◆
1 South Street, Montacute,
Somerset TA15 6XD
T: (01935) 823024

Slipper Cottage ◆◆◆
41 Bishopston, Montacute,
Somerset TA15 6UX
T: (01935) 823073 &
07966 368544
E: patandsue@41slippercottage.
freeserve.co.uk

MORCOMBELAKE
Dorset
Wisteria Cottage ◆◆◆
Taylors Lane, Morcombelake,
Bridport, Dorset DT6 6ED
T: (01297) 489019

MORELEIGH
Devon
Higher Barton ◆◆◆◆
Moreleigh, Totnes, Devon
TQ9 7JN
T: (01548) 821475 &
07721 068181

MORETONHAMPSTEAD
Devon
**Cookshayes Country Guest
House** ◆◆◆
33 Court Street,
Moretonhampstead, Newton
Abbot, Devon TQ13 8LG
T: (01647) 440374
F: (01647) 440374

Great Doccombe Farm ◆◆◆◆
Doccombe, Moretonhampstead,
Newton Abbot, Devon TQ13 8SS
T: (01647) 440694

Great Sloncombe Farm
◆◆◆◆ SILVER AWARD
Moretonhampstead, Newton
Abbot, Devon TQ13 8QF
T: (01647) 440595
F: (01647) 440595
E: hmerchant@sloncombe.
freeserve.co.uk
⊛

**Great Wooston Farm Bed &
Breakfast** ◆◆◆◆
Moretonhampstead, Newton
Abbot, Devon TQ13 8QA
T: (01647) 440367 &
07798 670590
F: (01647) 440367
⊛

Little Wooston Farm ◆◆◆
Moretonhampstead, Newton
Abbot, Devon TQ13 8QA
T: (01647) 440551 &
07850 098789
F: (01647) 440551
⊛

Midfields ◆◆◆◆
North Bovey Road,
Moretonhampstead, Newton
Abbot, Devon TQ13 8PB
T: (01647) 440462 &
07901 562778
F: (01647) 440039
E: davies@ridgetor.softnet.co.uk
I: www.guestbeds.com

Moorcote Guest House ◆◆◆◆
Chagford Cross,
Moretonhampstead, Newton
Abbot, Devon TQ13 8LS
T: (01647) 440966

Yarningale ◆◆◆
Exeter Road,
Moretonhampstead, Newton
Abbot, Devon TQ13 8SW
T: (01647) 440560
F: (01647) 440560
E: sally-radcliffe@virgin.net

MORTEHOE
Devon
Baycliffe Hotel ◆◆◆◆
Chapel Hill, Mortehoe,
Woolacombe, Devon EX34 7DZ
T: (01271) 870393
F: (01271) 870393

The Cleeve House
◆◆◆◆ SILVER AWARD
North Morte Road, Mortehoe,
Woolacombe, Devon EX34 7ED
T: (01271) 870719
F: (01271) 870719
E: cleevehouse@mcmail.com
⊛ ⊛

Gull Rock Hotel ◆◆◆◆
Mortehoe, Woolacombe, Devon
EX34 7EA
T: (01271) 870534

MORWENSTOW
Cornwall
Cornakey Farm ◆◆◆
Morwenstow, Bude, Cornwall
EX23 9SS
T: (01288) 331260

MOSTERTON
Dorset
Yeabridge Farm ◆◆◆◆
Whetley Cross, Mosterton,
Beaminster, Dorset DT8 3HE
T: (01308) 868944 &
07836 515843
F: (01308) 868944

MUCHELNEY HAM
Somerset
Muchelney Ham Farm
◆◆◆◆◆ GOLD AWARD
Muchelney, Langport, Somerset
TA10 0DJ
T: (01458) 250737
I: www.muchelneyhamfarm.co.
uk

MUDFORD
Somerset
The Old Kiln ◆
Higher Brickyard, Main Street,
Mudford, Yeovil, Somerset
BA21 5TG
T: (01935) 850958

MULLION
Cornwall
Meaver Farm
◆◆◆◆ SILVER AWARD
Mullion, Helston, Cornwall
TR12 7DN
T: (01326) 240128
F: (01326) 240011
E: meaverfarm@nationwideisp.
net
I: www.meaverfarm.freeserve.co.
uk
⊛

Polhormon Farm ◆◆◆
Polhormon Lane, Mullion,
Helston, Cornwall TR12 7JE
T: (01326) 240304
F: (01326) 240304
E: polhormonfarm@
farmersweekly.net
⊛

Tregaddra Farm
◆◆◆◆ SILVER AWARD
Cury, Helston, Cornwall
TR12 7BB
T: (01326) 240235
F: (01326) 240235
E: holidays@tregaddra.
freeserve.co.uk
I: www.tregaddra.freeserve.co.uk
⊛

Trenance Farmhouse ◆◆◆◆
Mullion, Helston, Cornwall
TR12 7HB
T: (01326) 240639
F: (01326) 240639
E: trenancefarm@cwcom.net

MUSBURY
Devon
Kate's Farm Bed & Breakfast ◆
Lower Bruckland Farm, Musbury,
Axminster, Devon EX13 8ST
T: (01297) 552861

Sellers Wood Farm ◆◆◆
Combpyne Road, Musbury,
Axminster, Devon EX13 8SR
T: (01297) 552944 &
07836 345198
F: (01297) 552944

MUTLEY
Devon
The Dudley ◆◆◆◆
42 Sutherland Road, Mutley,
Plymouth, Devon PL4 6BN
T: (01752) 668322
F: (01752) 673763
E: butler@dudleyhotels.fsnet.co.
uk

NANCEGOLLAN
Cornwall
Little Pengwedna Farm ◆◆◆◆
Nancegollan, Helston, Cornwall
TR13 0AY
T: (01736) 850649
F: (01736) 850649
E: ray@good-holidays.demon.
co.uk
I: www.good-holidays.demon.
co.uk
⊛

NETHER STOWEY
Somerset
Rose and Crown ◆◆
St Mary Street, Nether Stowey,
Somerset TA5 1LJ
T: (01278) 732265

NETHERAVON
Wiltshire
**Paddock House Bed and
Breakfast** ◆◆◆
Paddock House, High Street,
Netheravon, Salisbury SP4 9QP
T: (01980) 670401
F: (01980) 670401

NETHERBURY
Dorset
Jasmine Cottage
◆◆◆◆ SILVER AWARD
St James Road, Netherbury,
Bridport, Dorset DT6 5LP
T: (01308) 488767

NETTLETON
Wiltshire
Fosse Farmhouse ◆◆◆◆
Nettleton Shrub, Nettleton,
Chippenham, Wiltshire
SN14 7NJ
T: (01249) 782286 &
0771 3686516
F: (01249) 783066
E: caroncooper@compuserve.
com
I: fossefarmhouse.uk.com
⊛

NETTON
Wiltshire
Avonbank ◆◆◆
Netton, Salisbury, Wiltshire
SP4 6AW
T: (01722) 782331

NEWBRIDGE
Cornwall
Wheal Buller ◆◆◆◆
North Road, Newbridge,
Penzance, Cornwall TR20 8PS
T: (01736) 787999
E: rwrgibson@supanet.com

NEWQUAY
Cornwall
Aloha Hotel ◆◆◆
122/124 Henver Road, Newquay,
Cornwall TR7 3EQ
T: (01637) 878366
E: Alohanewqu@aol.com
I: www.mjiggins.freeserve.co.
uk/aloha/index.html
⊛

Beresford Hotel ◆◆◆
Narrowcliff, Newquay, Cornwall
TR7 2PR
T: (01637) 873238
F: (01637) 851874

Chichester ◆◆◆
14 Bay View Terrace, Newquay,
Cornwall TR7 2LR
T: (01637) 874216
F: (01637) 874216
●

Degembris Farmhouse ◆◆◆◆
St Newlyn East, Newquay,
Cornwall TR8 5HY
T: (01872) 510555
F: (01872) 510230
E: kathy@tally-connect.co.uk
I: www.
cornwall-farm-accommodation.
co.uk
●

Golden Bay Hotel ◆◆◆
59 Pentire Avenue, Pentire,
Newquay, Cornwall TR7 1PD
T: (01637) 873318

The Harbour Hotel ◆◆◆
North Quay Hill, Newquay,
Cornwall TR7 1HF
T: (01637) 873040
E: alan@harbournewquay.
freeserve.co.uk
I: www.harbourhotel.co.uk

Manuels Farm ◆◆◆◆
Quintrell Downs, Newquay,
Cornwall TR8 4NY
T: (01637) 873577
F: (01637) 873577
●

Marina Hotel ◆◆◆◆
Narrowcliff, Newquay, Cornwall
TR7 2PL
T: (01637) 873012
F: (01637) 851273

Pendeen Hotel ◆◆◆◆
Alexandra Road, Porth,
Newquay, Cornwall TR7 3ND
T: (01637) 873521
F: (01637) 873521
E: pendeen@cornwall.net
I: www.cornwall.net/pendeen/

Rose Cottage ◆◆◆◆
Shepherds Farm, St Newlyn East,
Newquay, Cornwall TR8 5NW
T: (01872) 540502

Tir Chonaill Lodge Hotel ◆◆◆
106 Mount Wise, Newquay,
Cornwall TR7 1QP
T: (01637) 876492
F: (01637) 852676

Towan Beach Hotel ◆◆◆
7 Trebarwith Crescent,
Newquay, Cornwall TR7 1DX
T: (01637) 872093

Tregarn Hotel ◆◆◆
Pentire Crescent, Newquay,
Cornwall TR7 1PX
T: (01637) 874292
F: (01637) 850116

**Trenance Lodge Hotel and
Restaurant◆◆◆◆**
83 Trenance Road, Newquay,
Cornwall TR7 2HW
T: (01637) 876702
F: (01637) 878772

Trevilla ◆◆◆
18 Berry Road, Newquay,
Cornwall TR7 1AR
T: (01637) 871504

Wenden Guest House ◆◆◆
11 Berry Road, Newquay,
Cornwall TR7 1AU
T: (01637) 872604
F: (01637) 872604

Westward Ho! Hotel ◆◆◆
26 Headland Road, Newquay,
Cornwall TR7 1HN
T: (01637) 873069
F: (01637) 851611

Windward Hotel ◆◆◆◆
Alexandra Road, Porth,
Newquay, Cornwall TR7 3NB
T: (01637) 873185 & 852436
F: (01637) 852436
E: caswind@aol.com

NEWTON ABBOT
Devon

The Rowans ◆◆◆
85 Highweek Village, Highweek,
Newton Abbot, Devon TQ12 1QQ
T: (01626) 365584

NEWTON FERRERS
Devon

Broadmoor Farm ◆◆◆
Newton Ferrers, Plymouth
PL8 2NE
T: (01752) 880407

NEWTON ST LOE
Bath & North East Somerset

Pennsylvania Farm ◆◆◆◆
Newton St Loe, Bath BA2 9JD
T: (01225) 314912
F: (01225) 314912
E: info@pennsylvaniafarm.co.uk
I: ww.pennsylvaniafarm.co.uk

NORTH BRADLEY
Wiltshire

49a Church Lane ◆◆◆
North Bradley, Trowbridge,
Wiltshire BA14 0TA
T: (01225) 762558

NORTH CADBURY
Somerset

Ashlea House ◆◆◆◆
High Street, North Cadbury,
Yeovil, Somerset BA22 7DP
T: (01963) 440891
E: ashlea@btinternet.com
I: www.btinternet.com/§ashlea/
●

The Catash Inn ◆◆
North Cadbury, Yeovil, Somerset
BA22 7DH
T: (01963) 440248
F: (01963) 440248
E: clive&sandra@catash.demon.
co.uk
I: www.catash.demon.co.uk

**Hill Ash Farm
◆◆◆◆ SILVER AWARD**
Woolston, North Cadbury,
Yeovil, Somerset BA22 7BL
T: (01963) 440332 &
07798 835173
F: (01963) 440332
●

NORTH CHIDEOCK
Dorset

Champs Land ◆◆◆◆
North Chideock, Bridport, Dorset
DT6
T: (01297) 489314

NORTH TAWTON
Devon

Kayden House Hotel ◆◆◆
High Street, North Tawton,
Devon EX20 2HF
T: (01837) 82242

**Lower Nichols Nymet Farm
◆◆◆◆ SILVER AWARD**
Lower Nichols Nymet, North
Tawton, Devon EX20 2BW
T: (01363) 82510
F: (01363) 82510

Oaklands Farm ◆◆◆
North Tawton, Okehampton,
Devon EX20 2BQ
T: (01837) 82340

NORTH WOOTTON
Dorset

**Stoneleigh Barn
◆◆◆◆ SILVER AWARD**
North Wootton, Sherborne,
Dorset DT9 5JW
T: (01935) 815964
E: stoneleigh@ic24.net

NORTH WRAXALL
Wiltshire

Court Close House ◆◆◆◆
North Wraxall, Chippenham,
Wiltshire SN14 7AD
T: (01225) 891930
E: vedeco@aol.com

NORTON FITZWARREN
Somerset

**Allerford Farm
◆◆◆◆◆ GOLD AWARD**
Norton Fitzwarren, Taunton,
Somerset TA4 1AL
T: (01823) 461210
F: (01823) 461210

NORTON ST PHILIP
Somerset

**George Inn ◆◆◆◆
Rating Applied For**
High Street, Norton St Philip,
Bath BA3 6LH
T: (01373) 834224
F: (01373) 834861

The Old Police House ◆◆◆
Town Barton, Norton St Philip,
Bath BA3 6LN
T: (01373) 834308
F: (01373) 834145
E: grahamjenkinson@
compuserve.com

NORTON SUB HAMDON
Somerset

**Brook House
◆◆◆◆ SILVER AWARD**
Little Street, Norton Sub
Hamdon, Stoke sub Hamdon,
Somerset TA14 6SR
T: (01935) 881789
F: (01935) 881789

NOSS MAYO
Devon

**Netton Farmhouse
◆◆◆◆◆ SILVER AWARD**
Noss Mayo, Plymouth, Devon
PL8 1HB
T: (01752) 873080 &
07899 923444
F: (01752) 873107
E: lesley@brunning-host.co.uk
I: www.brunning-host.co.uk

OAKFORD
Devon

Harton Farm ◆◆◆
Oakford, Tiverton, Devon
EX16 9HH
T: (01398) 351209
F: (01398) 351209
E: harton@eclipse.co.uk
●

**The Old Rectory
Rating Applied For**
Holme Place, Oakford, Tiverton,
Devon EX16 9EW
T: (01398) 351486
F: (01398) 351486
E: prot@oakfordst.fsnet.co.uk

OAKHILL
Somerset

Blakes Farm ◆◆
Oakhill, Bath BA3 5HY
T: (01749) 840301

The Boltons ◆◆◆
Sumach House, Neighbourne,
Oakhill, Bath, Somerset BA3 5BQ
T: (01749) 840366
F: (01749) 840366
E: billjill@theboltons-f.s.
business.co.uk

OAKSEY
Wiltshire

Church Farm Barns ◆◆◆◆
Oaksey, Malmesbury, Wiltshire
SN16 9TE
T: (01666) 577716

OBORNE
Dorset

**The Grange Restaurant and
Hotel ◆◆◆◆◆ SILVER AWARD**
Oborne, Sherborne, Dorset
DT9 4LA
T: (01935) 813463
F: (01935) 817464

OKEHAMPTON
Devon

Higher Cadham Farm ◆◆◆◆
Jacobstowe, Okehampton,
Devon EX20 3RB
T: (01837) 851647
F: (01837) 851410

Staddlestones ◆◆◆◆
Thorndon, Thorndon Cross,
Okehampton, Devon EX20 4NG
T: (01837) 861389

OLD SODBURY
South Gloucestershire

Dornden Guest House ◆◆◆◆
Church Lane, Old Sodbury,
Bristol BS37 6NB
T: (01454) 313325
F: (01454) 312263

ORCHESTON
Wiltshire

The Crown Inn ◆◆◆
Stonehenge Park, Orcheston,
Salisbury, Wiltshire SP3 4SH
T: (01980) 620304
F: (01980) 621121
E: stp@orcheston.freeserve.co.
uk
I: www.orcheston.freeserve.co.
uk

OSMINGTON
Dorset

Rosedale ◆◆
Lower Church Lane, Osmington,
Weymouth, Dorset DT3 6EW
T: (01305) 832056

OTTERY ST MARY
Devon

Normandy House Hotel and Bistro ◆◆◆◆ SILVER AWARD
5 Cornhill, Ottery St Mary, Devon EX11 1DW
T: (01404) 811088
F: (01404) 811023

Pitt Farm ◆◆◆◆
Fairmile, Ottery St Mary, Devon EX11 1NL
T: (01404) 812439
F: (01404) 812439

OWERMOIGNE
Dorset

Chilbury Lodge ◆◆◆◆
5 Wareham Road, Owermoigne, Dorchester, Dorset DT2 8HL
T: (01305) 854773
E: susan/@euphony.net

PADSTOW
Cornwall

Althea Library Bed and Breakfast ◆◆◆◆ SILVER AWARD
27 High Street, Padstow, Cornwall PL28 8BB
T: (01841) 532717 & 532679
F: (01841) 532717

Beau Vista ◆◆◆◆
Sarah's Lane, Padstow, Cornwall PL28 8EL
T: (01841) 533270 &
07767 405550
F: (01841) 533270

The Dower House Hotel ◆◆◆◆◆ GOLD AWARD
Fentonluna Lane, Padstow, Cornwall PL28 8BA
T: (01841) 532317
F: (01841) 532667
E: dower@btinternet.com

Trealaw ◆◆◆
22 Duke Street, Padstow, Cornwall PL28 8AB
T: (01841) 533161
F: (01841) 533161

Tregea Hotel ◆◆◆◆◆ GOLD AWARD
16-18 High Street, Padstow, Cornwall PL28 8BB
T: (01841) 532455
F: (01841) 533542
E: reservations@tregea.co.uk
I: www.tregea.co.uk

Treverbyn House ◆◆◆◆
Station Road, Padstow, Cornwall PL28 8AD
T: (01841) 532855

Trevone Bay Hotel ◆◆◆◆
Trevone Bay, Padstow, Cornwall PL28 8QS
T: (01841) 520243
F: (01841) 521195
E: hamilton@trevonebay.demon.co.uk

Trevorrick Farm ◆◆◆
St Issey, Wadebridge, Cornwall PL27 7QH
T: (01841) 540574
F: (01841) 540574
E: trevorrick.farm@talk21.com

The White Hart ◆◆◆◆
1 New Street, Padstow, Cornwall PL28 8EA
T: (01841) 532350
E: whthartpad@aol.com

Woodlands Country House ◆◆◆
Treator, Padstow, Cornwall PL28 8RU
T: (01841) 532426 & 533353
F: (01841) 532426

PAIGNTON
Devon

Arden House Hotel ◆◆◆
10 Youngs Park Road, Paignton, Devon TQ4 6BU
T: (01803) 558443
F: (01803) 558443

Bay Sands Hotel ◆◆◆
14 Colin Road, Paignton, Devon TQ3 2NR
T: (01803) 524877
F: (01803) 557827
E: baysandshotel@excite.co.uk
I: www.english.riveria.co.uk/baysands

Beach House ◆◆◆
39 Garfield Road, Paignton, Devon TQ4 6AX
T: (01803) 525742

Beresford Hotel ◆◆◆◆
5 Adelphi Road, Paignton, Devon TQ4 6AW
T: (01803) 551560
F: (01803) 407585
E: beresford@eurobell.co.uk

Birchwood House Hotel ◆◆◆◆
33 St Andrews Road, Paignton, Devon TQ4 6HA
T: (01803) 551323
F: (01803) 401301
E: yates3048@aol.com
I: www.hotelpaignton.com

Birklands Guest House ◆◆◆
33 Garfield Road, Paignton, Devon TQ4 6AX
T: (01803) 556970

Bou-Saada House ◆◆◆◆
62a Osney Crescent, Paignton, Devon TQ4 5EZ
T: (01803) 551158
F: (01803) 551158
E: bousaada@eurobell.co.uk

Bronte Hotel ◆◆◆
7 Colin Road, Paignton, Devon TQ3 2NR
T: (01803) 550254

Bruce Lodge Guest House ◆◆◆
2 Elmsleigh Road, Paignton, Devon TQ4 5AU
T: (01803) 550972
F: (01803) 550972
E: rogerkingdon@barclays.net

Cherwood Hotel ◆◆◆◆
26 Garfield Road, Paignton, Devon TQ4 6AX
T: (01803) 556515
F: (01803) 555126
E: james-pauline.cherwood-hotel.co.uk
I: www.cherwood-hotel.co.uk

Cliveden ◆◆◆
27 Garfield Road, Paignton, Devon TQ4 6AX
T: (01803) 557461
E: cliveden@lineone.net
I: www.clivedenguesthouse.co.uk

Colin House ◆◆◆
2 Colin Road, Paignton, Devon TQ3 2NR
T: (01803) 550609
F: (01803) 550609
E: colin-house@talk21.com
I: www.paigntondevon.co.uk/colinhouse.htm

Crofton Guest House ◆◆◆
67 Dartmouth Road, Paignton, Devon TQ4 5AF
T: (01803) 525723

Danethorpe Hotel ◆◆◆◆
23 St Andrews Road, Roundham, Paignton, Devon TQ4 6HA
T: (01803) 551251
F: (01803) 557075

Hotel Fiesta ◆◆◆
2 Kernou Road, Paignton, Devon TQ4 6BA
T: (01803) 521862 &
07802 427401
F: (01803) 521862

Harbour Lodge ◆◆◆
4 Cleveland Road, Paignton, Devon TQ4 6EN
T: (01803) 556932

Lyncourt Hotel ◆◆◆
14 Elmsleigh Park, Paignton, Devon TQ4 5AT
T: (01803) 557124

Mayfield Hotel ◆◆◆
8 Queens Road, Paignton, Devon TQ4 6AT
T: (01803) 556802

Middlepark Hotel ◆◆
3 Marine Drive, Paignton, Devon TQ3 2NJ
T: (01803) 559025
F: (01803) 559025

Roscrea Hotel ◆◆◆◆
2 Alta Vista Road, Paignton, Devon TQ4 6BZ
T: (01803) 558706
F: (01803) 558706
E: roscrea@globalnet.co.uk
I: www.paigntonhotels.com

Rougemont Private Hotel ◆◆◆
23 Roundham Road, Paignton, Devon TQ4 6DN
T: (01803) 556570
F: (01803) 556570
E: beds@rougemonthotel.co.uk
I: www.rougemonthotel.co.uk

Roundham Lodge ◆◆◆◆ SILVER AWARD
16 Roundham Road, Paignton, Devon TQ4 6DN
T: (01803) 558485
F: (01803) 553090

St Petrox Hotel ◆◆◆
6 Adelphi Road, Paignton, Devon TQ4 6AW
T: (01803) 551572
F: (01803) 557648
I: www.paigntonhotel.com

St Weonards Private Hotel ◆◆◆
12 Kernou Road, Paignton, Devon TQ4 6BA
T: (01803) 558842

The Sands Hotel ◆◆◆
32 Sands Road, Paignton, Devon TQ4 6EJ
T: (01803) 551282
F: (01803) 407269
E: sands.hotel@virgin.net

Sealawn Hotel ◆◆◆
Sea Front, 20 Esplanade Road, Paignton, Devon TQ4 6BE
T: (01803) 559031

Southberry Hotel ◆
6 Berry Square, Kernou Road, Paignton, Devon TQ4 6AZ
T: (01803) 551335
F: (01803) 551335

Summerhill Hotel ◆◆◆◆
Braeside Road, Goodrington Sands, Goodrington, Paignton, Devon TQ4 6BX
T: (01803) 558101
F: (01803) 558101

Torbay Court Hotel ◆◆◆
Steartfield Road, Paignton, Devon TQ3 2BJ
T: (01803) 663332
F: (01803) 522680

Two Beaches Hotel ◆◆◆
27 St Andrews Road, Paignton, Devon TQ4 6HA
T: (01803) 522164

Wulfruna Hotel ◆◆◆◆
8 Esplanade, Paignton, Devon TQ4 6EB
T: (01803) 555567

Wynncroft Hotel ◆◆◆◆
2 Elmsleigh Park, Paignton, Devon TQ4 5AT
T: (01803) 525728
F: (01803) 526335
E: wynncroft@FSBDial.co.uk
I: www.wynncroft.co.uk

PANBOROUGH
Somerset

Garden End Farm ◆◆◆
Panborough, Wells, Somerset BA5 1PN
T: (01934) 712414
E: sheila@gardenendfar.freeserve.co.uk
I: www.gardenendfarm.freeserve.co.uk

PATCHWAY
Bristol

Willow Hotel ◆◆◆
209 Gloucester Road, Patchway, Bristol BS34 6ND
T: (01454) 612276
F: (01454) 201107
E: colinm@gifford.co.uk.
I: www.gifford.co.uk.willowhotel

PATTERDOWN
Wiltshire

Bennetts ◆◆◆
Holywell House, Patterdown, Chippenham, Wiltshire SN15 2NP
T: (01249) 652922
E: holywell-house@btinternet.com
I: www.smoothhound.co.uk

PAYHEMBURY
Devon
Yellingham Farm ◆◆◆
Payhembury, Honiton, Devon
EX14 3HE
T: (01404) 850272
F: (01404) 850873
E: JanetEast@compuserve.com

PEASEDOWN ST JOHN
Bath & North East Somerset
Eastfield Farm Guest House ◆◆◆
Eastfield, Dunkerton Hill,
Peasedown St John, Bath
BA2 8PF
T: (01761) 432161

PEDWELL
Somerset
Barncroft ◆◆◆
20a Taunton Road, Pedwell,
Bridgwater, Somerset TA7 9BG
T: (01458) 211011

Sunnyside ◆◆◆◆
34 Taunton Road, Pedwell,
Bridgwater, Somerset TA7 9BG
T: (01458) 210097 &
07971 527771

PELYNT
Cornwall
Bake Farm ◆◆◆
Pelynt, Looe, Cornwall PL13 2QQ
T: (01503) 220244
F: (01503) 220244

Trenderway Farm
◆◆◆◆◆ SILVER AWARD
Pelynt, Polperro, Looe, Cornwall
PL13 2LY
T: (01503) 272214
F: (01503) 272991

PENDEEN
Cornwall
Field House ◆◆◆
8 Trewellard Road, Pendeen,
Penzance, Cornwall TR19 7ST
T: (01736) 788097

Trewellard Manor Farm ◆◆◆◆
Pendeen, Penzance, Cornwall
TR19 7SU
T: (01736) 788526

PENSFORD
Bath & North East Somerset
Green Acres ◆◆◆
Stanton Wick, Pensford,
BS39 4BX
T: (01761) 490397
F: (01761) 490397

Leigh Farm ◆◆
Old Road, Pensford, BS39 4BA
T: (01761) 490281 &
07860 914600
F: (01761) 490281

The Model Farm ◆◆◆
Norton Hawkfield, Pensford,
BS39 4HA
T: (01275) 832144
F: (01275) 832144

PENZANCE
Cornwall
Carnson House Hotel ◆
2 East Terrace, Penzance,
Cornwall TR18 2TD
T: (01736) 365589
F: (01736) 365594
E: carnson@netcomuk.co.uk
I: www.chycor.co.
uk/carnson-house

Con Amore ◆◆◆
38 Morrab Road, Penzance,
Cornwall TR18 4EX
T: (01736) 363423
F: (01736) 363423

Glencree Private Hotel ◆◆◆
2 Mennaye Road, Penzance,
Cornwall TR18 4NG
T: (01736) 362026
F: (01736) 362026

Halcyon Guest House ◆◆◆
6 Chyandour Square, Penzance,
Cornwall TR18 3LW
T: (01736) 366302

Lombard House ◆◆◆◆
16 Regent Terrace, Penzance,
Cornwall TR18 4DW
T: (01736) 364897
F: (01736) 364897
E: rita.kruge@talk21.com
I: www.cornwall-online.co.
uk/lombard-house

Lynwood Guest House ◆◆◆
41 Morrab Road, Penzance,
Cornwall TR18 4EX
T: (01736) 365871
F: (01736) 365871
E: lynwoodpz@aol.com
I: www.penzance.co.
uk/lynwood-guesthouse

Maldens Private Hotel ◆◆◆◆
1 Regent Terrace, Penzance,
Cornwall TR18 4DW
T: (01736) 362042
F: (01736) 362042

Menwidden Farm ◆◆◆
Ludgvan, Penzance, Cornwall
TR20 8BN
T: (01736) 740415

Penmorvah Hotel ◆◆◆
Alexandra Road, Penzance,
Cornwall TR18 4LZ
T: (01736) 363711
F: (01736) 363711

Richmond Lodge ◆◆◆
61 Morrab Road, Penzance,
Cornwall TR18 4EP
T: (01736) 365560
I: www.richmondlodge.fsnet.co.
uk

Rose Farm ◆◆◆◆
Chyanhal, Buryas Bridge,
Penzance, Cornwall TR19 6AN
T: (01736) 731808
F: (01736) 731808

Roseudian ◆◆◆◆
Crippas Hill, Kelynack, St. Just,
Penzance, Cornwall TR19 7RE
T: (01736) 788556

The Summer House
◆◆◆◆◆ SILVER AWARD
Cornwall Terrace, Penzance,
Cornwall TR18 4HL
T: (01736) 363744
F: (01736) 360959
E: summerhouse@dial.pipex.
com
I: www.cornwall-online.co.
uk/summer-house/

Treventon Guest House ◆◆◆
Alexandra Place, Penzance,
Cornwall TR18 4NE
T: (01736) 363521
F: (01736) 361873
I: www.
ukholidayaccommodation.
com/treventonguesthouse

Warwick House Hotel ◆◆◆
17 Regent Terrace, Penzance,
Cornwall TR18 4DW
T: (01736) 363881
F: (01736) 331078

Woodstock House ◆◆◆
29 Morrab Road, Penzance,
Cornwall TR18 4AZ
T: (01736) 369049
F: (01736) 369049
E: woodstocp@aol.com
I: www.members@aol.
com/woodstock

PERRANPORTH
Cornwall
Chy-an-Kerensa Guest House ◆◆◆
Cliff Road, Perranporth,
Cornwall TR6 0DR
T: (01872) 572470

Ponsmere Hotel ◆◆◆
Ponsmere Road, Perranporth,
Cornwall TR6 0BW
T: (01872) 572225
F: (01872) 572225
E: info@ponsmere.co.uk
I: www.ponsmere.co.uk

Trevie Guest House ◆◆◆
Mill Road, Bolingey,
Perranporth, Cornwall TR6 0AP
T: (01872) 573475
F: (01872) 573475

PIDDLEHINTON
Dorset
Muston Manor ◆◆◆◆
Piddlehinton, Dorchester, Dorset
DT2 7SY
T: (01305) 848242

PIDDLETRENTHIDE
Dorset
Fern Cottage ◆◆
Piddletrenthide, Dorchester,
Dorset DT2 7QF
T: (01300) 348277
F: (01300) 348277

Kingsmead ◆◆◆◆
Piddletrenthide, Dorchester,
Dorset DT2
T: (01300) 348234
F: (01300) 348234

The Poachers Inn ◆◆◆◆
Piddletrenthide, Dorchester,
Dorset DT2 7QX
T: (01300) 348358
F: (01300) 348153

PILLATON
Cornwall
The Weary Friar Inn ◆◆◆
Pillaton, Saltash, Cornwall
PL12 6QS
T: (01579) 350238
F: (01579) 350238

PINKNEY
Wiltshire
Home Farm House ◆◆◆
Pinkney, Malmesbury, Wiltshire
SN16 0NX
T: (01666) 840772

PLUSH
Dorset
The Old Barn House ◆◆◆
Plush, Dorchester, Dorset
DT2 7RQ
T: (01300) 348730

PLYMOUTH
Devon
Athenaeum Lodge ◆◆◆◆
4 Athenaeum Street, The Hoe,
Plymouth, Devon PL1 2RQ
T: (01752) 665005
F: (01752) 665005

Berkeleys of St James ◆◆◆◆
4 St James Place East, The Hoe,
Plymouth, Devon PL1 3AS
T: (01752) 221654
F: (01752) 221654
I: www.SmoothHound.Co.
UK/hotels/berkely2html.

Blackhall Lodge ◆◆◆◆
Old Staddiscombe Road,
Plymouth, Devon PL9 9NA
T: (01752) 482482
F: (01752) 482482
E: JohnM@jboocock.freeserve.
co.uk
I: www.jboocock.freeserve.co.uk

Bowling Green Hotel ◆◆◆◆
9-10 Osborne Place, Lockyer
Street, Plymouth, Devon
PL1 2PU
T: (01752) 209090
F: (01752) 209092
I: www.smoothhound.co.
uk/hotels/bowling.html

Cranbourne Hotel ◆◆◆
278-282 Citadel Road, The Hoe,
Plymouth, Devon PL1 2PZ
T: (01752) 263858 & 661400
F: (01752) 263858

Gabber Farm ◆◆◆
Down Thomas, Plymouth, Devon
PL9 0AW
T: (01752) 862269
F: (01752) 862269

Hotspur Guest House ◆◆
108 North Road East, Plymouth,
PL4 6AW
T: (01752) 663928
F: (01752) 261493
E: info@hotspur.co.uk

Jewells ◆◆◆
220 Citadel Road, The Hoe,
Plymouth, Devon PL1 3BB
T: (01752) 254760

Lamplighter Hotel ◆◆◆
103 Citadel Road, The Hoe,
Plymouth, Devon PL1 2RN
T: (01752) 663855
F: (01752) 228139
E: lamplighterhotel@ukonline.
co.uk

Mayflower Guest House ♦♦♦
209 Citadel Road East, The Hoe,
Plymouth, Devon PL1 2JF
T: (01752) 202727 & 667496
F: (01752) 202727
E: info@mayflowerguesthouse.
co.uk
I: www.mayflowerguesthouse.
co.uk

The Old Pier Guest House
♦♦♦
20 Radford Road, West Hoe,
Plymouth, Devon PL1 3BY
T: (01752) 268468
E: enquiries@oldpier.freeserve.
co.uk
I: www.oldpier.freeserve.co.
uk/oldpier

Osmond Guest House ♦♦♦♦
42 Pier Street, Plymouth,
PL1 3BT
T: (01752) 229705
F: (01752) 269655
E: mike@osmondgh.freeserve.
co.uk
I: plymouth-explore.co.uk

Rosaland Hotel ♦♦♦♦
32 Houndiscombe Road,
Plymouth, PL4 6HQ
T: (01752) 664749
F: (01752) 256984
E: manager@rosalandhotel.com
I: www.rosalandhotel.com

The Roscoff Guest House ♦♦♦
32 Grand Parade, West Hoe,
Plymouth, PL1 3DJ
T: (01752) 257900
F: (01803) 213606

Smeatons Tower Hotel
Rating Applied For
40-42 Grand Parade, The Hoe,
Plymouth, Devon PL1 3DJ
T: (01752) 221007
F: (01752) 221664
E: info@smeatonstowerhotel.
co.uk
I: www.smeatonstowerhotel.co.
uk

Squires Guest House ♦♦♦♦
7 St James Place East, The Hoe,
Plymouth, Devon PL1 3AS
T: (01752) 261459
F: (01752) 261459

The Teviot Guest House
♦♦♦♦ SILVER AWARD
20 North Road East, Plymouth,
Devon PL4 6AS
T: (01752) 262656
F: (01752) 251660
E: teviotgh@btinternet.com
I: www.btinternet.com/$teviotgh

Westwinds Hotel ♦♦♦
99 Citadel Road, The Hoe,
Plymouth, Devon PL1 2RN
T: (01752) 601777 &
08007 315717
F: (01752) 662158
E: paul.colman@btinternet.com
I: business.thisisplymouth.co.
uk/westwindshotel

POLBATHIC
Cornwall

Hendra Farm ♦♦♦♦
Polbathic, Torpoint, Cornwall
PL11 3DT
T: (01503) 250225
F: (01503) 250225

POLPERRO
Cornwall

Brent House ♦♦
1 Brent House, Talland Hill,
Polperro, Looe, Cornwall
PL13 2RY
T: (01503) 272495

Natal House ♦♦♦
The Coombes, Polperro, Looe,
Cornwall PL13 2RH
T: (01503) 272532

Penryn House ♦♦♦
The Coombes, Polperro, Looe,
Cornwall PL13 2RQ
T: (01503) 272157
F: (01503) 273055

POLZEATH
Cornwall

The White Heron ♦♦♦
Polzeath, Cornwall PL27 6TJ
T: (01208) 863623
E: info@whiteheronhotel.co.uk
I: www.whiteheronhotel.co.uk

PORLOCK
Somerset

The Lorna Doone Hotel ♦♦♦
High Street, Porlock, Minehead,
Somerset TA24 8PS
T: (01643) 862404
F: (01643) 863018
E: lorna@doone99.freeserve.co.
uk

Myrtle Cottage ♦♦♦
High Street, Porlock, Minehead,
Somerset TA24 8PU
T: (01643) 862978
F: (01243) 862978
E: Bob.steer@talk21.com
I: smoothhound@chelsoft.
demon.com

Overstream Hotel ♦♦♦
Parson's Street, Porlock,
Minehead, Somerset TA24 8QJ
T: (01643) 862421
F: (01643) 862421

Sanctuary Cottage ♦♦♦♦
High Street, Porlock, Minehead,
Somerset TA24 8PS
T: (01643) 862409
I: www.exmoortourism.org

Seapoint ♦♦♦♦
Upway, Porlock, Minehead,
Somerset TA24 8QE
T: (01643) 862289
F: (01643) 862289

PORTESHAM
Dorset

The Old Fountain ♦♦♦
36 Front Street, Portesham,
Weymouth, Dorset DT3 4ET
T: (01305) 871278
F: (01305) 871278

PORTHCURNO
Cornwall

The Porthcurno Hotel ♦♦♦♦
The Valley, Porthcurno, St Levan,
Penzance, Cornwall TR19 6JX
T: (01736) 810119
F: (01736) 810711
E: PorthcurnoHotel@
compuserve.com

PORTHLEVEN
Cornwall

Seefar ♦♦♦
Peverell Terrace, Porthleven,
Helston, Cornwall TR13 9DZ
T: (01326) 573778
E: seefar@talk21.com
I: www.cornwall-online.co.uk

Tye Rock Country House Hotel
♦♦♦♦♦ SILVER AWARD
Loe Bar Road, Porthleven,
Helston, Cornwall TR13 9EW
T: (01326) 572695
F: (01326) 572695

PORTLAND
Dorset

Alessandria Hotel ♦♦♦
71 Wakeham Easton, Portland,
Weymouth, Dorset DT5 1HW
T: (01305) 822270 & 820108
F: (01305) 820561
I: www.s-h-systems.co.
uk/hotels/alessand.html

PORTMELLON
Cornwall

Bodrugan Barton ♦♦♦♦
Portmellon, Mevagissey, St
Austell, Cornwall PL26 6PT
T: (01726) 842094
F: (01726) 844378

POULSHOT
Wiltshire

Higher Green Farm ♦♦
Poulshot, Devizes, Wiltshire
SN10 1RW
T: (01380) 828355
F: (01380) 828355

Middle Green Farm ♦♦♦
The Green, Poulshot, Devizes,
Wiltshire SN10 1RT
T: (01380) 828413
F: (01380) 828826

Poulshot Lodge Farm ♦♦
Poulshot, Devizes, Wiltshire
SN10 1RQ
T: (01380) 828255
F: (01380) 827008

POYNTINGTON
Dorset

Welgoer ♦♦♦
Poyntington, Sherborne, Dorset
DT9 4LF
T: (01963) 220737

PUNCKNOWLE
Dorset

The Crown Inn ♦♦♦
Church Street, Puncknowle,
Dorchester, Dorset DT2 9BN
T: (01308) 897711
F: (01308) 898282
E: thecrowninn@puncknowle.
fsnet.co.uk

PURITON
Somerset

Canns Farm ♦♦♦
Canns Lane, Puriton, Bridgwater,
Somerset TA7 8AY
T: (01278) 684773 & 0797 143
2483
F: (01278) 684773
E: cannsfarm@minim.com
I: www.minim.com/cannsfarm

RADSTOCK
Bath & North East Somerset

The Rookery ♦♦♦
Wells Road, Radstock, Bath
BA3 3RS
T: (01761) 432626
F: (01761) 432626
E: rookery@iname.com
I: www.smoothhound.co.
ukhotels/rookery.html

RAMPISHAM
Dorset

Holly Cottage ♦♦♦
Rampisham, Dorchester, Dorset
DT2 0PP
T: (01935) 83515

RAMSBURY
Wiltshire

Marridge Hill Cottage ♦♦♦
Marridge Hill, Ramsbury,
Marlborough, Wiltshire
SN8 2HG
T: (01672) 520486

Marridge Hill House ♦♦♦♦
Ramsbury, Marlborough,
Wiltshire SN8 2HG
T: (01672) 520237
F: (01672) 520053
E: dando@impedaci.demon.co.
uk

RATTERY
Devon

Knowle Farm
♦♦♦♦ SILVER AWARD
Rattery, Totnes, Devon TQ10 9JY
T: (01364) 73914
F: (01364) 73914

REDLYNCH
Wiltshire

**Orchards Country House Bed &
Breakfast**♦♦♦♦
Kiln Road, Redlynch, Salisbury,
Wiltshire SP5 2HT
T: (01725) 510372
F: (01725) 510372
E: alanjj1@hotmail.com
I: www.hompepages.tesco.
net/$alanjj

Templeman's Old Farmhouse
♦♦♦♦
Redlynch, Salisbury, Wiltshire
SP5 2JS
T: (01725) 510331
F: (01752) 510331

ROADWATER
Somerset

Briar Cottage ♦♦♦♦
The Old Mineral Line, Roadwater,
Watchet, Somerset TA23 0RJ
T: (01984) 640020

Stamborough Farm
♦♦♦♦ SILVER AWARD
Roadwater, Watchet, Somerset
TA23 0RW
T: (01984) 640258
F: (01984) 641051
E: rileystamco@compuserve.
com

ROCK
Cornwall

Silvermead ♦♦♦
Rock, Wadebridge, Cornwall
PL27 6LB
T: (01208) 862425
F: (01208) 862919
E: barbara@silvermead.
freeserve.co.uk

ROCKBEARE
Devon

Lower Marsh Farm ♦♦♦
Marsh Green, Rockbeare, Exeter
EX5 2EX
T: (01404) 822432

RODE
Somerset

Rode Farm ♦♦♦
Rode, Bath BA3 6QQ
T: (01373) 831479 &
07971 929398

ROWDE
Wiltshire

Lower Foxhangers Farm ♦♦♦
Rowde, Devizes, Wiltshire
SN10 1SS
T: (01380) 828254
F: (01380) 828254

RUISHTON
Somerset

Taunton Premier Lodge ♦♦♦
Ilminster Road, Ruishton,
Taunton, Somerset TA3 5LU
T: (01823) 443121 & 0870 700
1558
F: 0870 700 1559
I: www.premierlodge.com

RUSHALL
Wiltshire

Little Thatch ♦♦♦
Rushall, Pewsey, Wiltshire
SN9 6EN
T: (01980) 635282

ST AGNES
Cornwall

Penkerris ♦♦
Penwinnick Road, St Agnes,
Cornwall TR5 0PA
T: (01872) 552262
F: (01872) 552262
@

ST ANNS CHAPEL
Cornwall

The Rifle Volunteer Inn ♦♦♦
St Anns Chapel, Gunnislake,
Cornwall PL18 9HL
T: (01822) 832508

ST AUSTELL
Cornwall

Hembal Manor ♦♦♦♦
Hembal Lane, Trewoon, St
Austell, Cornwall PL25 5TD
T: (01726) 72144
F: (01726) 72144
E: svhiggs@hembalmanor.
freeserve.co.uk
I: www.hembalmanor.freeserve.
co.uk

Poltarrow Farm ♦♦♦♦
St Mewan, St Austell, Cornwall
PL26 7DR
T: (01726) 67111
F: (01726) 67111
E: enquire@poltarrow.co.uk
I: www.poltarrow.co.uk
@

ST BREWARD
Cornwall

Tarny Guesthouse
♦♦♦ SILVER AWARD
Row, St Breward, Bodmin,
Cornwall PL30 4LW
T: (01208) 850583

Treswallock Farm ♦♦♦
St Breward, Bodmin, Cornwall
PL30 4PL
T: (01208) 850255
F: (01208) 850255

ST BURYAN
Cornwall

Boskenna Home Farm ♦♦♦♦
St Buryan, Penzance, Cornwall
TR19 6DQ
T: (01736) 810705
F: (01736) 810705

Higher Leah Farm ♦♦
St Buryan, Penzance, Cornwall
TR19 6EJ
T: (01736) 810424

Tregurnow Farm ♦♦♦♦
St Buryan, Penzance, Cornwall
TR19 6BL
T: (01736) 810255
F: (01736) 810255
E: tregurno@eurobell.co.uk
I: homepage.eurobell.co.
uk/tregurnol

ST COLUMB MAJOR
Cornwall

Twas-A-Barn ♦♦♦♦
Tregaswith, Newquay, Cornwall
TR8 4HY
T: (01637) 880907
E: pbduc888@aol.com
I: www.cornwall-online.co.
uk/twas-a-barn

ST DAY
Cornwall

**Lower Poldice Cottage
Accommodation** ♦♦♦
Lower Poldice, St Day, Redruth,
Cornwall TR16 5PP
T: (01209) 820438 &
07887 881752

ST EWE
Cornwall

Higher Kestle Farm
♦♦♦♦ SILVER AWARD
St Ewe, Mevagissey, St Austell,
Cornwall PL26 6EP
T: (01726) 842001
F: (01726) 842001
E: vicky@higherkestle.freeserve.
co.uk

ST ISSEY
Cornwall

Ring O'Bells ♦♦♦
Church Town, St Issey,
Wadebridge, Cornwall PL27 7QA
T: (01841) 540251
E: ringersstissey-freeserve.co.uk

ST IVES
Cornwall

The Anchorage Guest House
♦♦♦♦
5 Bunkers Hill, St Ives,
TR26 1LJ
T: (01736) 797135
F: (01736) 797135
E: james@theanchoragebb.
fsnet.co.uk
I: www.theanchoragebb.fsnet.
co.uk

Blue Hayes ♦♦♦♦
Trelyon Avenue, St Ives,
Cornwall TR26 2AD
T: (01736) 797129
F: (01736) 797129
I: www.blue-hayes.com.uk

Channings Hotel ♦♦♦
3 Talland Road, St Ives, Cornwall
TR26 2EF
T: (01736) 799500
F: (01736) 799500
E: channings@tinyworld.co.uk
I: www.cornwall-online.
uk/channings

Chy-an-Creet Hotel ♦♦♦
Higher Stennack, St Ives,
Cornwall TR26 2HA
T: (01736) 796559
F: (01736) 796559
E: relax@chy.co.uk
I: www.chy.co.uk

Cornerways ♦♦♦
Bethesda Place, St Ives, Cornwall
TR26 1PA
T: (01736) 796706 &
07070 800577
E: bryan.pyecroft@lineone.net
I: www.tregenna.
com/cornerways

The Countryman at Trink
♦♦♦♦
Old Coach Road, St Ives,
Cornwall TR26 3JQ
T: (01736) 797571
F: (01736) 797571

Dean Court Hotel ♦♦♦♦
Trelyon Avenue, St Ives,
Cornwall TR26 2AD
T: (01736) 796023
F: (01736) 796233

The Grey Mullet Guest House
♦♦♦
2 Bunkers Hill, St Ives, Cornwall
TR26 1LJ
T: (01736) 796635

Longships Hotel ♦♦♦♦
Talland Road, St Ives, Cornwall
TR26 2DF
T: (01736) 798180
F: (01736) 798180

Pierview Guesthouse ♦♦♦
32-34 Back Road East, St Ives,
Cornwall TR26 1PD
T: (01736) 794268
F: (01736) 794268

The Pondarosa ♦♦♦♦
10 Porthminster Terrace, St Ives,
Cornwall TR26 2DQ
T: (01736) 795875
F: (01736) 797811
E: pondarosa.hotel@talk21.com
I: www.cornwall-online.co.uk

Porthmeor Hotel ♦♦♦
Godrevy Terrace, St Ives,
Cornwall TR26 1JA
T: (01736) 796712

Primavera Private Hotel ♦♦♦
14 Draycott Terrace, St Ives,
Cornwall TR26 2EF
T: (01736) 795595
F: (01736) 795595
E: clarkprima@aol.com
I: www.smoothhound.co.
uk/hotels/primaver.html
@

Tregony Guest House ♦♦♦♦
1 Clodgy View, St Ives, Cornwall
TR26 1JG
T: (01736) 795884
F: (01736) 798942
E: info@tregony.com
I: www.tregony.com

ST JULIOT
Cornwall

Higher Pennycrocker Farm
♦♦♦♦
St Juliot, Boscastle, Cornwall
PL35 0BY
T: (01840) 250488
F: (01840) 250488
E: Jackiefarm@aol.com
@

The Old Rectory
♦♦♦♦♦ GOLD AWARD
St Juliot, Boscastle, Cornwall
PL25 0BT
T: (01840) 250225
F: (01840) 250225
E: sally@stjuliot.com
I: www.stjuliot.com

ST JUST-IN-PENWITH
Cornwall

Bosavern House ♦♦♦
St Just-in-Penwith, Penzance,
Cornwall TR19 7RD
T: (01736) 788301
F: (01736) 788301
E: Marcol@bosavern.u-net.com
I: www.bosavern.u-net.com

Boscean Country Hotel ♦♦♦
Boswedden Road, St Just-in-
Penwith, Cornwall TR19 7QP
T: (01736) 788748
F: (01736) 788748
E: boscean@aol.com
I: www.connexions.co.
uk/boscean/index.htm

Boswedden House ♦♦♦
Cape Cornwall, St Just-in-
Penwith, Cornwall TR19 7NJ
T: (01736) 788733
F: (01736) 788733
E: relax@boswedden.org.uk
I: www.smoothhound.co.
uk/hotels/boswedd.html

ST KEVERNE
Cornwall

Eden House ♦♦♦♦
Lemon Street, St Keverne,
Helston, Cornwall TR12 6NE
T: (01326) 280005

Gallen-Treath Guest House
♦♦♦
Porthallow, St Keverne, Helston,
Cornwall TR12 6PL
T: (01326) 280400
E: gallen-treathguesthouse@
porthallow.fsnet.co.uk

ST KEW
Cornwall

Tregellist Farm ♦♦♦
Tregellist, St Kew, Bodmin,
Cornwall PL30 3HG
T: (01208) 880537
F: (01208) 881017

ST MABYN
Cornwall

Treglown House ♦♦♦
Haywood Farm, St Mabyn,
Bodmin, Cornwall PL30 3BU
T: (01208) 841896
F: (01208) 841896
E: treglownhouse@stmabyn.
fsnet.co.uk
@

ST MARTIN'S
Isles of Scilly

Polreath
Rating Applied For
Highertown, St Martin's, Isles of Scilly TR25 0QL
T: (01720) 422046
F: (01720) 422046
E: polreath.scilly@virginnet.co.uk
I: www.polreath.scilly@virginnet.co.uk
🖂

ST MARY'S
Isles of Scilly

Anjeric Guest House ◆◆◆
The Strand, St Mary's, Isles of Scilly TR21 0PS
T: (01720) 422700
F: (01720) 422700
I: www.scillyonline.co.uk/accomm/anjeric.html

Annet ◆◆◆◆
Porthlow, St Mary's, Isles of Scilly TR21 0NF
T: (01720) 422441 &
07771 663772
🖂

April Cottage
◆◆◆◆ SILVER AWARD
Church Road, St Mary's, Isles of Scilly TR21 0NA
T: (01720) 422279
F: (01720) 423247

Armeria ◆◆
1 Porthloo Terrace, St Mary's, Isles of Scilly TR21 0NF
T: (01720) 422961

Beachfield House ◆◆◆◆
Porthloo, St Mary's, Isles of Scilly TR21 0NE
T: (01720) 422463
F: (01720) 422463

Belmont ◆◆◆◆
Church Road, St Mary's, Isles of Scilly TR21 0NA
T: (01720) 423154
F: (01720) 423357
E: enquiries@the-belmont.freeserve.co.uk

Blue Carn Cottage ◆◆◆
Old Town, St Mary's, Isles of Scilly TR21 0NH
T: (01720) 422309

The Boathouse ◆◆◆
Thorofare Hugh Town, St Mary's, Isles of Scilly TR21 0LN
T: (01720) 422688

Buckingham House ◆◆
The Bank, St Mary's, Isles of Scilly TR21 0HY
T: (01720) 422543

The Bylet ◆◆◆
Church Road, St Mary's, Isles of Scilly TR21 0NA
T: (01720) 422479
F: (01720) 422479

Carn Vean Guest House ◆◆◆
Pelistry, St Mary's, Isles of Scilly TR21 0NX
T: (01720) 422462
🖂

Cornerways ◆◆◆◆
Jackson's Hill, St Mary's, Isles of Scilly TR21 0JZ
T: (01720) 422757
F: (01720) 422757

Crebinick House
◆◆◆◆ SILVER AWARD
Church Street, St Mary's, Isles of Scilly TR21 0JT
T: (01720) 422968
F: (01720) 422968

Evergreen Cottage Guest House ◆◆◆◆
The Parade, Hugh Town, St Mary's, Isles of Scilly TR21 0LP
T: (01720) 422711

Garrison House ◆◆◆◆
St Mary's, Isles of Scilly TR21 0LS
T: (01720) 422972

Hazeldene ◆◆◆◆
Church Street, St Mary's, Isles of Scilly TR21 0JT
T: (01720) 422864

High Lanes Farm ◆◆◆
Atlantic View, St Mary's, Isles of Scilly TR21 0NW
T: (01720) 422684

Higher Trenoweth ◆◆◆◆
St Mary's, Isles of Scilly TR21 0NS
T: (01720) 422419

Innisidgen Guest House ◆◆◆
Church Street, St Mary's, Isles of Scilly TR21 0JT
T: (01720) 422899 & 422736
F: (01720) 422899
E: innisidgen@yahoo.co.uk
I: www.isles-of-scilly.co.uk

Kistvaen ◆◆◆◆
St Mary's, Isles of Scilly TR21 0JE
T: (01720) 422002
F: (01720) 422002
E: chivy002@aol.com

Lamorna ◆◆
Rams Valley, St Mary's, Isles of Scilly TR21 0JX
T: (01720) 422333

Lynwood ◆◆◆◆
Church Street, St Mary's, Isles of Scilly TR21 0JT
T: (01720) 423313
F: (01720) 423313

Lyonnesse Guest House ◆◆◆
The Strand, St Mary's, Isles of Scilly TR21 0PS
T: (01720) 422458

Marine House ◆◆◆
Church Street, Hugh Town, St Mary's, Isles of Scilly TR21 0JT
T: (01720) 422966
E: peggy@rowe55.freeserve.co.uk

Men-a-Vaur ◆◆◆
Church Road, St Mary's, Isles of Scilly TR21 0NA
T: (01720) 422245

Morgelyn ◆◆◆
McFarlands Down, St Mary's, Isles of Scilly TR21 0NS
T: (01720) 422897
E: morgelyn@scillyonline.co.uk
I: www.scillyonline.co.uk/accomm/morgelyn.html

Nundeeps ◆◆◆
Rams Valley, St Mary's, Isles of Scilly TR21 0JX
T: (01720) 422517

Pieces of Eight ◆◆◆
11 Porthcressa Road, St Mary's, Isles of Scilly TR21 0JL
T: (01720) 422163

Pier House
Rating Applied For
The Bank, St Mary's, Isles of Scilly TR21 0HY
T: (01720) 423061

Rose Cottage
◆◆◆◆ SILVER AWARD
The Strand, St Mary's, Isles of Scilly TR21 0PT
T: (01720) 422078
F: (01720) 422078
E: rosecottage@infinnet.co.uk

St Hellena ◆◆◆
13 Garrison Lane, St Mary's, Isles of Scilly TR21 0JD
T: (01720) 423231 & 422536
🖂

Santa Maria ◆◆◆◆
Sallyport, St Mary's, Isles of Scilly TR21 0JE
T: (01720) 422687
F: (01720) 422687

Scillonia ◆◆
Bank, St Mary's, Isles of Scilly TR21 0HY
T: (01720) 422101 & 422798

Shearwater Guest House ◆◆◆
The Parade, Hugh Town, St Mary's, Isles of Scilly TR21 0LP
T: (01720) 422402
F: (01720) 422351
E: ianhopkin@aol.com

Strand House ◆◆◆
The Strand, St Mary's, Isles of Scilly TR21 0PS
T: (01720) 422808
F: (01720) 422808

Sylina ◆◆◆
McFarlands Downs, St Mary's, Isles of Scilly TR21 0NS
T: (01720) 422129
F: (01720) 422129

Tolman House ◆◆◆◆
Old Town, St Mary's, Isles of Scilly TR21 0NH
T: (01720) 422967
F: (01720) 422967

The Town House
◆◆◆◆ SILVER AWARD
Little Porth, St Mary's, Isles of Scilly TR21 0JG
T: (01720) 422793

Trelawney Guest House ◆◆◆
Church Street, St Mary's, Isles of Scilly TR21 0JT
T: (01720) 422377 &
07721 622624
F: (01720) 422377
E: dtownend@netcomuk.co.uk

Veronica Lodge ◆◆◆◆
The Garrison, St Mary's, Isles of Scilly TR21 0LS
T: (01720) 422585

Westford House ◆◆◆
Church Street, St Mary's, Isles of Scilly TR21 0JT
T: (01720) 422510
F: (01720) 422510

The Wheelhouse ◆◆◆◆
Porthcressa, St Mary's, Isles of Scilly TR21 0JG
T: (01720) 422719 & 423043
F: (01720) 422719

Wingletang Guest House ◆◆◆
The Parade, St Mary's, Isles of Scilly TR21 0LP
T: (01720) 422381

The Withies ◆◆◆◆
Trench Lane, Old Town, St Mary's, Isles of Scilly TR21 0PA
T: (01720) 422986

ST MAWES
Cornwall

The Ship and Castle ◆◆◆
The Waterfront, St Mawes, Truro, Cornwall TR2 5DG
T: (01326) 270401
F: (01326) 270152

ST MAWGAN
Cornwall

The Falcon Inn ◆◆◆
St Mawgan, Newquay, Cornwall TR8 4EP
T: (01637) 860225
F: (01637) 860884
E: abanks@cwcom.net

ST MERRYN
Cornwall

Trewithen Farm ◆◆◆
St Merryn, Padstow, Cornwall PL28 8JZ
T: (01841) 520420

ST NEOT
Cornwall

The London Inn ◆◆◆◆
St Neot, Liskeard, Cornwall PL14 6NG
T: (01579) 320263 &
07710 419527
F: (01579) 320263

ST TUDY
Cornwall

Polrode Mill Cottage ◆◆◆◆
Allen Valley, St Tudy, Bodmin, Cornwall PL30 3NS
T: (01208) 850203

ST WENN
Cornwall

Tregolls Farm ◆◆◆
St Wenn, Bodmin, Cornwall PL30 5PG
T: (01208) 812154

SALCOMBE
Devon

Burton Farm ◆◆◆◆
Galmpton, Kingsbridge, Devon TQ7 3EY
T: (01548) 561210
F: (01548) 561210
🖂

Torre View Hotel ◆◆◆◆
Devon Road, Salcombe, Devon TQ8 8HJ
T: (01548) 842633
F: (01548) 842633
E: torreview@eurobell.co.uk

SALISBURY
Wiltshire

Avalon ◆◆
10 Belle Vue Road, Salisbury, Wiltshire SP1 3YF
T: (01722) 324799

Avila ◆◆◆
130 Exeter Street, Salisbury, Wiltshire SP1 2SG
T: (01722) 421093

Avonlee ◆◆
231 Castle Road, Salisbury, Wiltshire SP1 3RY
T: (01722) 338351

Barlings ◆◆◆◆
41 Gravel Close, Downton, Salisbury, Wiltshire SP5 3JQ
T: (01725) 510310

The Beadles
♦♦♦♦ SILVER AWARD
Middleton, Middle Winterslow,
Salisbury, Wiltshire SP5 1QS
T: (01980) 862922
F: (01980) 862922
E: winterlead@aol.com
winterbead@aol.com
I: www.guestaccom.co.uk/754.
htm

The Bell Inn ♦♦♦
Warminster Road, South
Newton, Salisbury, Wiltshire
SP2 0QD
T: (01722) 743336
F: (01722) 744202

40 Belle Vue Road ♦♦
Salisbury, Wiltshire SP1 3YD
T: (01722) 325773

78 Belle Vue Road ♦♦♦
Salisbury, Wiltshire SP1 3YD
T: (01722) 329477

Beulah ♦♦♦
144 Britford Lane, Salisbury,
Wiltshire SP2 8AL
T: (01722) 333517

Bridge Farm
♦♦♦ GOLD AWARD
Lower Road, Britford, Salisbury,
Wiltshire SP5 4DY
T: (01722) 332376
F: (01722) 332376
E: mail@bridgefarmbb.co.uk
I: www.bridgefarmbb.co.uk

Byways House ♦♦♦
31 Fowlers Road, City Centre,
Salisbury, Wiltshire SP1 2QP
T: (01722) 328364
F: (01722) 322146
E: byways@stonehenge-uk.com
I: www.stonehenge-uk.com

Castlewood ♦♦♦
45 Castle Road, Salisbury,
Wiltshire SP1 3RH
T: (01722) 324809 &
07967 013897
F: (01722) 421494

Cathedral Close ♦♦♦
19A The Close, Salisbury,
Wiltshire SP1 2EB
T: (01722) 324525
F: (01722) 324525
E: salisbury@cathedralclose.
freeserve.co.uk
I: www.smoothhound.co.
uk/hotels/cathedl.html

Clovelly Hotel ♦♦♦♦
Mill Road, Salisbury, Wiltshire
SP2 7RT
T: (01722) 322055
F: (01722) 327677
E: clovelly.hotel@virgin.net
I: www.virgin.net/clovelly.hotel

132 Coombe Road ♦♦♦♦
Salisbury, Wiltshire SP2 8BL
T: (01722) 320275
E: jim.izzard@ukonline.co.uk

The Devizes Inn ♦♦♦
53 Devizes Road, Salisbury,
Wiltshire SP2 7LQ
T: (01722) 327842

The Edwardian Lodge ♦♦♦♦
59 Castle Road, Salisbury,
Wiltshire SP1 3RH
T: (01722) 413329 & 410500
F: (01722) 503105
E: richardwhite@edlodge.
freeserve.co.uk

Farthings ♦♦♦
9 Swaynes Close, Salisbury,
Wiltshire SP1 3AE
T: (01722) 330749
F: (01722) 330749
E: farthings@shammer.
freeserve.co.uk
I: www.shammer.freeserve.co.uk

Five Bells Inn ♦♦♦
Salt Lane, Salisbury, Wiltshire
SP1 1EG
T: (01722) 327022
I: www.fivebellsinn.co.uk

The Gallery ♦♦♦♦
36 Wyndham Road, Salisbury,
Wiltshire SP1 3AB
T: (01722) 324586
F: (01722) 324586
I: www.smoothhound.co.
uk/hotels/gallery.html

Gerrans House
♦♦♦♦ SILVER AWARD
91 Castle Road, Salisbury,
Wiltshire SP1 3RW
T: (01722) 334394
F: (01722) 332508

Glenshee ♦♦ SILVER AWARD
3 Montague Road, West
Harnham, Salisbury, Wiltshire
SP2 8NJ
T: (01722) 322620 &
07971 827804
F: (01722) 322620
E: glenshee@breathemil.net
I: www.dmac.co.uk/glemshee

Griffin Cottage ♦♦♦♦
10 St Edmunds Church Street,
Salisbury, Wiltshire SP1 1EF
T: (01722) 328259 &
07767 395898
F: (01722) 416928
E: mark@brandonasoc.demon.
co.uk
I: www.smoothhound.co.
uk/hotels/griffinc.htmlwww.
net2000.co.
uk/salisbury/xoo1/default.html

Harvest Moon ♦
31 Hillside Drive, Gomeldon,
Salisbury, Wiltshire SP4 6LF
T: (01980) 610126 &
07767 896278
F: (01980) 610126

High Bank ♦♦♦
4 St John's Close, Milford,
Salisbury, Wiltshire SP1 1NW
T: (01722) 505386 &
07710 484340
F: (01722) 505386
E: derek.jean@tesco.net
I: homepages.tesco.net/§derek.
jean

Highveld 44 Hulse Road ♦♦♦
Salisbury, Salisbury, Wiltshire
SP1 3LY
T: (01722) 338172

Holly Tree House ♦♦
53 Wyndham Road, Salisbury,
Wiltshire SP1 3AH
T: (01722) 322955

Holmhurst Guest House ♦♦
Downton Road, Salisbury,
SP2 8AR
T: (01722) 410407
F: (01722) 323164
E: holmhurt@talk21.com

Leena's Guest House ♦♦♦
50 Castle Road, Salisbury,
SP1 3RL
T: (01722) 335419
F: (01722) 335419

The Little House ♦♦
38 Fairview Road, Salisbury,
Wiltshire SP1 1JX
T: (01722) 320381 &
07885 100918

Malvern
♦♦♦♦ SILVER AWARD
31 Hulse Road, Salisbury,
Wiltshire SP1 3LU
T: (01722) 327995

Manor Farm ♦♦♦♦
Burcombe, Salisbury, Wiltshire
SP2 0EJ
T: (01722) 742177
F: (01722) 744600

94 Milford Hill ♦♦♦
Salisbury, Wiltshire SP1 2QL
T: (01722) 322454

Newton Farm House
♦♦♦♦ SILVER AWARD
Southampton Road,
Whiteparish, Salisbury, Wiltshire
SP5 2QU
T: (01794) 884416
F: (01794) 884416
E: reservations@
newtonfarmhouse.co.uk
I: www.newtonfarmhouse.co.uk

Number Eighty Eight ♦♦♦♦
88 Exeter Street, Salisbury,
SP1 2SE
T: (01722) 330139 &
07971 561349
I: www.no88.co.uk

The Old Bakery ♦♦
35 Bedwin Street, Salisbury,
SP1 3UT
T: (01722) 320100

Old Chequers Cottage ♦♦
17 Guilder Lane, Salisbury,
Wiltshire SP1 1HW
T: (01722) 325335
F: (01722) 325335

**The Old Rectory Bed &
Breakfast** ♦♦♦♦
75 Belle Vue Road, Salisbury,
Wiltshire SP1 3YE
T: (01722) 502702
F: (01722) 501135
E: stay@theoldrectory-bb.co.uk
I: www.theoldrectory-bb.co.uk

Pasket House ♦♦♦
57 Church Road, Laverstock,
Salisbury, Wiltshire SP1 1QY
T: (01722) 327651
E: abelbs@aol.com

Pathways ♦♦
41 Shady Bower, Salisbury,
Wiltshire SP1 2RG
T: (01722) 324252

Richburn Guest House ♦♦♦
25 Estcourt Road, Salisbury,
Wiltshire SP1 3AP
T: (01722) 325189 & 411551
F: (01722) 325189

The Rokeby Guest House
♦♦♦♦
3 Wain-a-Long Road, Salisbury,
Wiltshire SP1 1LJ
T: (01722) 329800
F: (01722) 329800
I: www.smoothhound.co.
uk/hotels/rokeby.html

Saddlers ♦♦♦♦
Princes Hill, Redlynch, Salisbury
SP5 2HF
T: (01725) 510571
F: (01725) 510571
E: sadd.lers@virgin.net
I: www.s-h-systems.co.
uk/hotels/saddlers.html

34 Salt Lane ♦♦♦
Salisbury, Wiltshire SP1 1EG
T: (01722) 326141

Spire House ♦♦♦♦
84 Exeter Street, Salisbury,
Wiltshire SP1 2SE
T: (01722) 339213
F: (01722) 339213
E: lois.faulkner@talk21.com
I: www.smoothhound.co.
uk/hotels/spirt.html

Stratford Lodge ♦♦♦♦
4 Park Lane, Castle Road,
Salisbury, SP1 3NP
T: (01722) 325177
F: (01722) 325177
E: enquiries@stratfordlodge.co.
uk
I: www.stratfordlodge.co.uk

Swaynes Firs Farm ♦♦♦
Grimsdyke, Coombe Bissett,
Salisbury, Wiltshire SP5 5RF
T: (01725) 519240
E: swaynes.firs@virgin.net
I: freespace.virgin.net/swaynes.
firs/index.htm

Tamar House ♦♦♦
237 Castle Road, Salisbury,
Wiltshire SP1 3RY
T: (01722) 502254 &
07710 297053
E: wenda.rampton@ukgateway.
net
I: www.smoothhound.co.
uk/hotels/tamar.html

Tiffany ♦♦♦
2 Bourne Villas, off College
Street, Salisbury, Wiltshire
SP1 3AW
T: (01722) 332367

Torrisholme ♦♦♦
Stratford Sub Castle, Salisbury
SP1 3LQ
T: (01722) 329089
E: torrisholme@hotmail.com

Vale View Farm ♦♦♦
Slab Lane, Woodfalls, Salisbury,
Wiltshire SP5 2NE
T: (01725) 512116

Victoria Lodge Guest House
♦♦♦
61 Castle Road, Salisbury,
Wiltshire SP1 3RH
T: (01722) 320586
F: (01722) 414507
E: mail@viclodge.co.uk
I: www.viclodge.co.uk

Websters
◆◆◆◆ SILVER AWARD
11 Hartington Road, Salisbury,
Wiltshire SP2 7LG
T: (01722) 339779
F: (01722) 339779
E: websters.salis@eclipse.co.uk
I: www.smoothhound.co.
uk/hotels.websters.html
◉ ⚐

White Horse Inn ◆◆
38 Castle Street, Salisbury,
Wiltshire SP1 1BN
T: (01722) 327844
F: (01722) 336226

Wyndham Park Lodge ◆◆◆◆
51 Wyndham Road, Salisbury,
SP1 3AB
T: (01722) 416517
F: (01722) 328851
E: Wyndham@wyndam51.
freeserve.co.uk
◉

48 Wyndham Road ◆◆◆◆
Salisbury, Wiltshire SP1 3AB
T: (01722) 327757

SALTASH
Cornwall

Haye Farm ◆◆◆◆
Landulph, Saltash, Cornwall
PL12 6QQ
T: (01752) 842786
F: (01752) 842786

SALTFORD
Bath & North East Somerset

Brunels Tunnel House Hotel
◆◆◆
High Street, Saltford, Bristol
BS31 3BQ
T: (01225) 873873
F: (01225) 874875
E: info@brunelstunnelhouse.
com
I: www.brunelstunnelhouse.com

SAMPFORD COURTENAY
Devon

Langdale ◆◆
Sampford Courtenay,
Okehampton, Devon EX20 2SY
T: (01837) 82433

SAND
Somerset

Townsend Farm ◆◆◆◆
Sand, Wedmore, Somerset
BS28 4XH
T: (01934) 712342
F: (01934) 712405
E: smewillcox0@farmersweekly.
net

SANDYWAY
Devon

Barkham ◆◆◆◆
Sandyway, South Molton, Devon
EX36 3LU
T: (01643) 831370
F: (01643) 831370
I: www.exmoor-vacations.co.uk

SEATON
Cornwall

Blue Haven Hotel ◆◆◆
Looe Hill, Seaton, Torpoint,
Cornwall PL11 3JQ
T: (01503) 250310
F: (01503) 250310
E: bluehaven@btinternet.com
I: www.smoothhound.co.
uk/hotels.bluehave.html

SEATON
Devon

Beach End Guest House
◆◆◆◆ SILVER AWARD
8 Trevelyan Road, Seaton, Devon
EX12 2NL
T: (01297) 23388
F: (01297) 625604

Beaumont ◆◆◆
Castle Hill, Seaton, Devon
EX12 2QW
T: (01297) 20832
F: 0870 0554708
E: tony@lymebay.demon.co.uk
I: www.smoothhound.co.
uk/hotels/beaumont.html

Gatcombe Farm ◆◆◆
Seaton, Devon EX12 3AA
T: (01297) 21235
F: (01297) 23010
E: gatcombefarm@
farmersweekly.net

Hill House ◆◆◆◆
Highcliffe Crescent, Seaton,
Devon EX12 2PS
T: (01297) 20377
E: jphil.beard@lineone.net
◉

Mariners Hotel
◆◆◆◆ SILVER AWARD
The Esplanade, Seaton, Devon
EX12 2NP
T: (01297) 20560

SEEND CLEEVE
Wiltshire

Rew Farm ◆◆◆
Seend Cleeve, Melksham,
Wiltshire SN12 6PS
T: (01380) 828289

SEMINGTON
Wiltshire

Newhouse Farm ◆◆◆
Littleton, Semington,
Trowbridge, Wiltshire BA14 6LF
T: (01380) 870349

The Old Manor House
Rating Applied For
73 High Street, Semington,
Trowbridge, Wiltshire BA14 6JR
T: (01380) 870450

SHALDON
Devon

Glenside House ◆◆◆
Ringmore Road, Shaldon,
Teignmouth, Devon TQ14 0EP
T: (01626) 872448
I: www.smoothhound.co.
uk/hotels/glensideho.html

SHARCOTT
Wiltshire

The Old Dairy House ◆◆◆◆
Sharcott, Pewsey, Wiltshire
SN9 5PA
T: (01672) 562287
E: old.dairy@virgin.net
I: business.virgin.net/neville.
burrell/sharcott.htm

SHEPTON MALLET
Somerset

Belfield Guest House ◆◆◆
34 Charlton Road, Shepton
Mallet, Somerset BA4 5PA
T: (01749) 344353 & 343050
F: (01749) 344353
E: andrea@bellfield-house.co.uk

Bowlish House ◆◆◆◆
Coombe Lane, Shepton Mallet,
Somerset BA4 5JD
T: (01749) 342022
F: (01749) 342022

Burnt House Farm
◆◆◆◆ SILVER AWARD
Waterlip, West Cranmore,
Shepton Mallet, Somerset
BA4 4RN
T: (01749) 880280
F: (01749) 880004

Hillbury House ◆◆◆
65 Compton Road, Shepton
Mallet, Somerset BA4 5QT
T: (01749) 345473

Hurlingpot Farm ◆◆◆
Chelynch, Shepton Mallet,
Somerset BA4 4PY
T: (01749) 880256

Leamount ◆◆◆
60 Compton Road, Shepton
Mallet, Somerset BA4 5QT
T: (01749) 344278 &
07970 947068

Pecking Mill Inn and Hotel
◆◆◆
A371 Evercreech, Evercreech,
Shepton Mallet, Somerset
BA4 6PG
T: (01749) 830336 & 830006
F: (01749) 831316

Temple House Farm ◆◆◆◆
Doulting, Shepton Mallet,
Somerset BA4 4RQ
T: (01749) 880294
F: (01749) 880688

SHERBORNE
Dorset

The Alders
◆◆◆◆ SILVER AWARD
Sandford Orcas, Sherborne,
Dorset DT9 4SB
T: (01963) 220666
F: (01963) 220106
E: jonsue@btinternet.com

Bay Trees ◆◆
Bristol Road, Sherborne, Dorset
DT9 4HP
T: (01935) 816527

Bridleways ◆◆◆
Oborne Road, Sherborne, Dorset
DT9 3RX
T: (01935) 814716
F: (01935) 814716

The Britannia Inn ◆◆◆
Westbury, Sherborne, Dorset
DT9 3EH
T: (01935) 813300

Clatcombe Grange ◆◆◆◆
Bristol Road, Sherborne, Dorset
DT9 4RH
T: (01935) 814355

Cromwell House
◆◆◆◆ SILVER AWARD
Long Street, Sherborne, Dorset
DT9 3BS
T: (01935) 813352

Crown Inn ◆◆◆
Green Hill, Sherborne, Dorset
DT9 4EP
T: (01935) 812930
F: (01935) 812930

Half Moon Hotel
◆◆◆◆ SILVER AWARD
Half Moon Street, Sherborne,
Dorset DT9 3LN
T: (01935) 812017
F: (01935) 815295
E: book@lionheartinns.co.uk
I: lionheartinns.co.uk

Heartsease Cottage
◆◆◆◆ SILVER AWARD
North Street, Bradford Abbas,
Sherborne, Dorset DT9 6SA
T: (01935) 475480
F: (01935) 475480
E: heartsease@talk21.com

Huntsbridge Farm
◆◆◆◆ SILVER AWARD
Batcombe Road, Leigh,
Sherborne, Dorset DT9 6JA
T: (01935) 872150
F: (01935) 872150
E: huntsbridge@lineone.net
◉

Village Vacations ◆◆◆
Brookmead, Rimpton, Yeovil,
Somerset BA22 8AQ
T: (01935) 850241
F: (01935) 850241
E: villagevac@aol.com
I: www.villagevacations.co.uk
◉

SHERFORD
Devon

Higher Stancombe Farm
◆◆◆◆
Sherford, Kingsbridge, Devon
TQ7 2BG
T: (01548) 531013 &
07767 398053
F: (01548) 531013
E: jentuc@globalnet.co.uk
I: www.higher-stancombe.co.uk

SHERSTON
Wiltshire

Widleys Farm
Rating Applied For
Sherston, Malmesbury, Wiltshire
SN16 0PY
T: (01666) 840213
F: (01666) 840156

SHIPHAM
Somerset

Herongates ◆◆◆
Horseleaze Lane, Shipham,
Winscombe BS25 1UQ
T: (01934) 843280
F: (01934) 843280
◉

Penscot Farmhouse Hotel
◆◆◆
The Square, Shipham,
Winscombe BS25 1TW
T: (01934) 842659
F: (01934) 842576

SHIPTON GORGE
Dorset

Cairnhill
◆◆◆◆◆ GOLD AWARD
Shipton Gorge, Bridport, Dorset
DT6 4LL
T: (01308) 898203
F: (01308) 898203
E: cairnhill@talk21.com

SHREWTON
Wiltshire

Maddington House ◆◆◆◆
Maddington Street, Shrewton,
Salisbury, Wiltshire SP3 4JD
T: (01980) 620406
F: (01980) 620406
E: rsrobatham@freenet.co.uk

Tuscans ◆◆◆
Tanners Lane, Shrewton,
Salisbury SP3 4JT
T: (01980) 621038

SIDBURY
Devon

Bovett's Farm
◆◆◆ SILVER AWARD
Roncombe Lane, Sidbury,
Sidmouth, Devon EX10 0QN
T: (01395) 597456
E: brian-bridget@bovetts.
demon.co.uk
I: www.smoothhound.co.uk/

**Cotfordbridge Hotel and
Restaurant** ◆◆◆◆
Cotford Road, Sidbury,
Sidmouth, Devon EX10 0SQ
T: (01395) 597351

SIDFORD
Devon

**The Salty Monk Hotel and
Restaurant** ◆◆◆◆
Church Street, Sidford,
Sidmouth, Devon EX10 9QP
T: (01395) 513174
F: (01395) 514722
I: www.
saltymonkhotelsidmouth.co.uk

SIDMOUTH
Devon

Berwick Guest House ◆◆◆◆
Salcombe Road, Sidmouth,
Devon EX10 8PX
T: (01395) 513621

Canterbury Guest House ◆◆◆
Salcombe Road, Sidmouth,
Devon EX10 8PR
T: (01395) 513373 & 0800 328
1775
E: cgh@eclipse.co.uk

Coombe Bank Guest House
◆◆◆◆ SILVER AWARD
86 Alexandria Road, Sidmouth,
Devon EX10 9HG
T: (01395) 514843 & 515181
F: (01395) 515181
E: info@coombebank.com
I: www.coombebank.com

Cranmere House ◆◆◆
2 Fortfield Place, Station Road,
Sidmouth, Devon EX10 8NX
T: (01395) 513933

Ferndale ◆◆◆◆
92 Winslade Road, Sidmouth,
Devon EX10 9EZ
T: (01395) 515495 &
07889 332492
F: (01395) 515495

Higher Coombe Farm ◆◆◆
Tipton St John, Sidmouth, Devon
EX10 0AX
T: (01404) 813385
F: (01404) 813385
E: KerstinFarmer@farming.co.uk
I: www.smoothhound.co.
uk/hotels/higherco.html

Kyneton Cottage
◆◆◆◆ SILVER AWARD
87 Alexandria Road, Sidmouth,
Devon EX10 9HG
T: (01395) 513213 &
07803 921688
E: june@kyneton.freeserve.co.uk

Lower Pinn Farm ◆◆◆◆
Pinn, Sidmouth, Devon
EX10 0NN
T: (01395) 513733
F: (01395) 513733

Lynstead ◆◆◆◆
Vicarage Road, Sidmouth, Devon
EX10 8UQ
T: (01395) 514635
F: (01395) 578954
E: lynstead@aol.com

Mariners ◆◆◆◆
69 Sidford High Street, Sidford,
Sidmouth, Devon EX10 9SH
T: (01395) 515876

Pinn Barton Farm ◆◆◆◆
Peak Hill, Pinn Lane, Sidmouth,
Devon EX10 0NN
T: (01395) 514004
F: (01395) 514004
I: www.smoothhound.co.
uk/hotels/pinn.html

Willow Bridge Private Hotel
◆◆◆◆
Millford Road, Sidmouth, Devon
EX10 8DR
T: (01395) 513599 &
07966 531132
F: (01395) 513599

Wiscombe Linhaye Farm
◆◆◆◆
Southleigh, Colyton, Devon
EX24 6JF
T: (01404) 871342
E: rabjohns@btinternet.com

SILVERTON
Devon

Three Tuns Inn ◆◆◆
14 Exeter Road, Silverton, Exeter,
Devon EX5 4HX
T: (01392) 860352
F: (01392) 860636

SITHNEY
Cornwall

Parc–An–Ithan House Hotel
◆◆◆
Sithney, Helston, Cornwall
TR13 0RN
T: (01326) 572565
F: (01326) 572565
E: parc@dircon.co.uk
I: visitweb.com

SKILGATE
Somerset

Chapple Farm ◆
Skilgate, Taunton, Somerset
TA4 2DP
T: (01398) 331364

SLAPTON
Devon

Little Pittaford
◆◆◆◆◆ SILVER AWARD
Slapton, Kingsbridge, Devon
TQ7 2QG
T: (01548) 580418
F: (01548) 580406
E: LittlePittaford@compuserve.
com
I: www.ourworld.compuserve.
com/hompages/littlepittaford

Start House ◆◆◆
Start, Slapton, Kingsbridge,
Devon TQ7 2QD
T: (01548) 580254

SOMERTON
Somerset

Littleton House ◆◆◆
New Street, Somerton, Somerset
TA11 7NU
T: (01458) 273072

Still Cottage ◆◆◆◆
North Street, Somerton,
Somerset TA11 7NY
T: (01458) 272323

SOURTON
Devon

Sleekers Farm ◆◆◆◆
Sourton, Okehampton, Devon
EX20 4HN
T: (01837) 861381

SOUTH MILTON
Devon

Shute Farm ◆◆◆
South Milton, Kingsbridge,
Devon TQ7 3JL
T: (01548) 560680

SOUTH MOLTON
Devon

Huxtable Farm ◆◆◆◆
West Buckland, Barnstaple,
Devon EX32 0SR
T: (01598) 760254
F: (01598) 760254
E: jpayne@huxhilton.
enterprise-plc.com
I: www.huxtablefarm.co.uk

Kerscott Farm
◆◆◆◆◆ GOLD AWARD
Ash Mill, South Molton, Devon
EX36 4QG
T: (01769) 550262
I: www.greencountry.co.
uk/kerscott

Old Coaching Inn ◆◆
Queen Street, South Molton,
Devon EX36 3BJ
T: (01769) 572526 & 572397

SOUTH NEWTON
Wiltshire

Salisbury Old Mill House
◆◆◆◆ SILVER AWARD
Warminster Road, South
Newton, Salisbury, Wiltshire
SP2 0QD
T: (01722) 742458 &
07860 542475
F: (01722) 742458

SOUTH PERROTT
Dorset

Shepherds Farmhouse ◆◆◆
South Perrott, Beaminster,
Dorset DT8 3HU
T: (01935) 891599 &
07977 422916
E: shepherds@eclipse.co.uk

SOUTH PETHERTON
Somerset

Kings Pleasure
◆◆◆◆ SILVER AWARD
24 Silver Street, South
Petherton, Somerset TA13 5BZ
T: (01460) 241747

SOUTHVILLE
Bristol

Walmer House ◆◆◆
94 Stackpool Road, Southville,
Bristol BS3 1NW
T: (0117) 966 8253
F: (0117) 966 8253

SPREYTON
Devon

The Tom Cobley Tavern ◆◆◆
Spreyton, Crediton, Devon
EX17 5AL
T: (01647) 231314
F: (01647) 231506
E: fjwfilor@tomcobley.fsnet.co.
uk

STANTON DREW
Bath & North East Somerset

Greenlands ◆◆◆◆
Stanton Drew, Bristol BS39 4ES
T: (01275) 333487
F: (01275) 331211

STANTON WICK, PENSFORD
Bath & North East Somerset

The Carpenters Arms ◆◆◆◆
Stanton Wick, Pensford, Bristol
BS39 4BX
T: (01761) 490202
F: (01761) 490763
E: carpenters@dialpipex.com

STAPLEFORD
Wiltshire

The Parsonage ◆◆◆◆
Stapleford, Salisbury, Wiltshire
SP3 4LJ
T: (01722) 790334

STARCROSS
Devon

The Croft Guest House ◆◆◆
Cockwood Harbour, Starcross,
Exeter, Devon EX6 8QY
T: (01626) 890282
F: (01626) 891768

The Old Vicarage ◆◆◆
Starcross, Exeter EX6 8PX
T: (01626) 890206
F: (01626) 890206
E: maggie@theoldvicarage.
clara.co.uk
I: www.theoldvicarage.clara.net

STATHE
Somerset

Black Smock Inn ◆◆◆
Stathe Road, Stathe, Bridgwater,
Somerset TA7 0JN
T: (01823) 698352
F: (01823) 698352
E: blacksmock@aol.com
I: www.blacksmock.co.uk

STAVERTON
Devon

Kingston House
◆◆◆◆◆ SILVER AWARD
Staverton, Totnes, Devon
TQ9 6AR
T: (01803) 762235 &
07976 728794
F: (01803) 762444
E: info@kingston-estate.net
I: www.kingston-estate.net

STEEPLE ASHTON
Wiltshire

Church Farm ◆◆◆◆
Steeple Ashton, Trowbridge,
Wiltshire BA14 6EL
T: (01380) 870518

Longs Arms Inn ◆◆◆
High Street, Steeple Ashton,
Trowbridge, Wiltshire BA14 6EU
T: (01380) 870245
F: (01380) 870245
E: chantal@stayatthepub.
freeserve.co.uk
I: www.stayatthepub.freeserve.
co.uk

STERT
Wiltshire

Hill House
Rating Applied For
Stert, Devizes, Wiltshire
SN10 3JB
T: (01380) 722356
F: (01380) 722356

Orchard Cottage ◆◆
Stert, Devizes, Wiltshire
SN10 3JD
T: (01380) 723103

STICKLEPATH
Devon

Higher Coombe Head House
◆◆◆◆
Sticklepath, Okehampton, Devon
EX20 1QL
T: (01837) 840240

STOCKWOOD
Dorset

Church Farm ◆◆◆◆
Stockwood, Dorchester, Dorset
DT2 0NG
T: (01935) 83221
F: (01935) 83771
E: ruth@churchfarm.co.uk
I: www.churchfarm.co.uk

STOGUMBER
Somerset

Hall Farm ◆◆◆
Stogumber, Taunton, Somerset
TA4 3TQ
T: (01984) 656321

Northam Mill
◆◆◆◆ SILVER AWARD
Water Lane, Stogumber,
Taunton, Somerset TA4 3TT
T: (01984) 656916 & 656146
F: (01984) 656144
E: bmsspicer@aol.com
I: www.northam-mill.co.uk

STOKE
Devon

Mountbatten Hotel ◆◆◆
52 Exmouth Road, Stoke,
Plymouth PL1 4QH
T: (01752) 563843
F: (01752) 606014

STOKE BISHOP
Bristol

Downs Edge ◆◆◆◆
Saville Road, Stoke Bishop,
Bristol BS9 1JA
T: (0117) 9683264 &
07885 866463
F: (0117) 9683264

STOKE-IN-TEIGNHEAD
Devon

Deane Thatch Accommodation
◆◆◆
Deane Road, Stoke-in-
Teignhead, Newton Abbot,
Devon TQ12 4QU
T: (01626) 873724 &
07971 939364
F: (01626) 873724
E: deanethatch@hotmail.com
I: www.ukchoice.
net/17/deanethatch.htm

STOKE ST GREGORY
Somerset

Ashgrove
◆◆◆◆ SILVER AWARD
Meare Green, Stoke St Gregory,
Taunton, Somerset TA3 6HZ
T: (01823) 490209
E: sue.perowne@talk21.com

Meare Green Farm ◆◆◆◆
Meare Green, Stoke St Gregory,
Taunton, Somerset TA3 6HT
T: (01823) 490759
F: (01823) 490759

STOKE SUB HAMDON
Somerset

Castle Farm ◆◆◆◆
Stoke sub Hamdon, Somerset
TA14 6QS
T: (01935) 822231
F: (01935) 822057

STOKENHAM
Devon

Brookfield ◆◆◆
Stokenham, Kingsbridge, Devon
TQ7 2SL
T: (01548) 580615

STONEY STRATTON
Somerset

Stratton Farm ◆◆◆◆
Stoney Stratton, Shepton Mallet,
Somerset BA4 6DY
T: (01749) 830830
F: (01749) 831080

STRATFORD SUB CASTLE
Wiltshire

Carp Cottage ◆◆◆◆
Stratford Sub Castle, Salisbury,
Wiltshire SP1 3LH
T: (01722) 327219 &
07967 153298

STRATTON
Cornwall

Cann Orchard ◆◆◆◆
Howard Lane, Stratton, Bude,
Cornwall EX23 9TD
T: (01288) 352098
F: (01288) 352098

Stamford Hill Hotel ◆◆◆◆
Stamford Hill, Stratton, Bude,
Cornwall EX23 9AY
T: (01288) 352709
F: (01288) 352709
I: www.stamfordhillhotel.co.uk

Stratton Gardens Hotel
◆◆◆◆
Cot Hill, Stratton, Bude,
Cornwall EX23 9DN
T: (01288) 352500
F: (01288) 352256
E: stratton.gardens@which.net
I: www.cornwall-online.co.
uk/stratton-gardens

STRATTON-ON-THE-FOSSE
Somerset

Oval House ◆◆◆
Stratton-on-the-Fosse, Near
Bath, Stratton-on-the-Fosse,
BA3 4RB
T: (01761) 232183
F: (01761) 232183
E: mellotte@clara.co.uk
I: www.mellotte.clara.co.uk

STREET
Somerset

Chimbles ◆◆◆
27 Underhill Road, Street,
Somerset BA16 0NS
T: (01458) 442527
E: bool@chimbles.freeserve.co.
uk

Francis House
Rating Applied For
197-199 High Street, Street,
Somerset BA16 0NE
T: (01458) 445308

Leigh Nook ◆◆◆◆
Marshalls Elm, Somerton Road,
Street, Somerset BA16 0TZ
T: (01458) 443511 &
07971 430278

Old Orchard House ◆◆◆◆
Middle Brooks, Street, Somerset
BA16 0TU
T: (01458) 442212
E: oldorchardhouse@amserve.
net

SUTTON BENGER
Wiltshire

Gate Cottage ◆◆◆◆
Sutton Benger, Chippenham,
Wiltshire SN15 4RE
T: (01249) 720121 &
07710 990201

SUTTON POYNTZ
Dorset

Brookfield ◆◆◆
White Horse Lane, Sutton
Poyntz, Weymouth, Dorset
DT3 6LU
T: (01305) 833674

Selwyns ◆◆◆
Puddledock Lane, Sutton Poyntz,
Weymouth, Dorset DT3 6LZ
T: (01305) 832239
E: selwyns-b-and-b@hotmail.
com

SWINDON
Wiltshire

Courtleigh House ◆◆◆
40 Draycott Road, Chiseldon,
Swindon SN4 0LS
T: (01793) 740246

Internos ◆◆◆
3 Turnpike Road, Blunsdon,
Swindon, Wilshire SN2 4EA
T: (01793) 721496
F: (01793) 721496

SYDLING ST NICHOLAS
Dorset

Lamperts Farmhouse ◆◆◆
11 Dorchester Road, Sydling St
Nicholas, Dorset DT2 9NU
T: (013003) 41790

Magiston Farm ◆◆◆
Sydling St Nicholas, Dorchester,
Dorset DT2 9NR
T: (01300) 320295

Upper Mill ◆◆◆◆
Sydling St Nicholas, Dorchester,
Dorset DT2 9PD
T: (01300) 341230
F: (01300) 341230

TAUNTON
Somerset

Acorn Lodge ◆
22 Wellington Road, Taunton,
Somerset TA1 4EQ
T: (01823) 337613

Bryngwyn ◆◆
15 Wellington Road, Taunton,
Somerset TA1 5AN
T: (01823) 254953
E: john@evansjh.freeserve.co.uk

Forde House ◆◆◆◆
9 Upper High Street, Taunton,
Somerset TA1 3PX
T: (01823) 279042
F: (01823) 279042

Fursdon House ◆◆◆
88-90 Greenway Road, Taunton,
Somerset TA2 6LE
T: (01823) 331955

Gatchells ◆◆◆◆
Angersleigh, Taunton, Somerset
TA3 7SY
T: (01823) 421580 &
07808 164276
E: gatchells@somerweb.co.uk
I: www.somerweb.co.
uk/gatchells

Heathercroft ◆◆◆
118 Wellington Road, Taunton,
Somerset TA1 5LA
T: (01823) 275516

**Higher Yarde Farm Country
Bed & Breakfast** ◆◆◆◆
Higher Yarde Farm, Staplegrove,
Taunton, Somerset TA2 6SW
T: (01823) 451553 &
07770 866848

Lowdens House ◆◆◆
26 Wellington Road, Taunton,
Somerset TA1 4EQ
T: (01823) 334500

**North Down Farm Bed &
Breakfast** ◆◆◆
Pyncombe Lane, Wiveliscombe,
Taunton, Somerset TA4 2BL
T: (01984) 623730 & 077
90 858450
F: (01984) 623730

Orchard House
◆◆◆◆ SILVER AWARD
Fons George, Middleway,
Taunton, Somerset TA1 3JS
T: (01823) 351783
F: (01823) 351785
E: orch-hse@dircon.co.uk
I: www.smoothhound.co.
uk/hotels/orchard2.html

Prockters Farm ♦♦♦
West Monkton, Taunton,
Somerset TA2 8QN
T: (01823) 412269
F: (01823) 412269
◉

Southview ♦
2 St Andrew's Road, Taunton,
Somerset TA2 7BW
T: (01823) 284639
E: southstyle@easicom.com

The Spinney ♦♦♦♦
Curland, Taunton, Somerset
TA3 5SE
T: (01460) 234362
F: (01460) 234362
E: bartlett.spinney@zetnet.co.uk
I: www.somerweb.co.
uk/spinney-bb

Staplegrove Lodge ♦♦
Staplegrove, Taunton, Somerset
TA2 6PX
T: (01823) 331153

Yallands Farmhouse ♦♦♦♦
Staplegrove, Taunton, Somerset
TA2 6PZ
T: (01823) 278979
F: (01823) 278983
E: mail@yallands.co.uk
I: www.yallands.co.uk

TAVISTOCK
Devon

Acorn Cottage ♦♦♦♦
Heathfield, Tavistock, Devon
PL19 0LQ
T: (01822) 810038
E: viv@acorncot.fsnet.co.uk
I: www.visitbritain.com

April Cottage ♦♦♦♦
Mount Tavy Road, Tavistock,
Devon PL19 9JB
T: (01822) 613280

Beera Farmhouse
♦♦♦♦ SILVER AWARD
Milton Abbot, Tavistock, Devon
PL19 8PL
T: (01822) 870216
F: (01822) 870216
E: robert.tucker@farming.co.uk

Eko Brae Guest House ♦♦♦♦
4 Bedford Villas, Spring Hill,
Tavistock, Devon PL19 8LA
T: (01822) 614028
F: (01822) 613693
E: ekobrae@aol.com.

Kingfisher Cottage ♦♦♦
Mount Tavy Road, Vigo Bridge,
Tavistock, Devon PL19 9JB
T: (01822) 613801 &
07721 772095
◉

Mallards ♦♦♦♦
48 Plymouth Road, Tavistock,
Devon PL19 8BU
T: (01822) 615171

Rubbytown Farm ♦♦♦♦
Gulworthy, Tavistock, Devon
PL19 8PA
T: (01822) 832493

Tor Cottage
♦♦♦♦♦ GOLD AWARD
Chillaton, Tavistock, Devon
PL16 0JE
T: (01822) 860248
F: (01822) 860126
E: info@torcottage.co.uk
I: www.torcottage.co.uk
◉

Westward ♦♦♦
15 Plymouth Road, Tavistock,
Devon PL19 8AU
T: (01822) 612094
◉

TEIGNMOUTH
Devon

Hill Rise Hotel ♦♦♦
1 Winterbourne Road,
Teignmouth, Devon TQ14 8JT
T: (01626) 773108
F: (01626) 773108

**Leicester House
Rating Applied For**
2 Winterbourne Road,
Teignmouth, Devon TQ14 8JT
T: (01626) 773043 &
07710 772097
◉

Rathlin House ♦♦♦
Upper Hermosa Road,
Teignmouth, Devon TQ14 9JW
T: (01626) 774473

Thomas Luny House
♦♦♦♦♦ SILVER AWARD
Teign Street, Teignmouth, Devon
TQ14 8EG
T: (01626) 772976
E: thos-lung@freeuk.com

THORNBURY
Devon

Forda Farm ♦♦♦
Thornbury, Holsworthy, Devon
EX22 7BS
T: (01409) 261369
◉

THORNE
Somerset

Thorne Cottage ♦♦
Thorne, Yeovil, Somerset
BA21 3PZ
T: (01935) 421735

THORNE ST MARGARET
Somerset

**Thorne Manor
Rating Applied For**
Thorne St Margaret, Wellington,
Somerset TA21 0EQ
T: (01823) 672264

TILSHEAD
Wiltshire

Black Horse Inn ♦♦♦
High Street, Tilshead, Salisbury,
Wiltshire SP3 4RY
T: (01980) 620104
F: (01980) 620104

TIMBERSCOMBE
Somerset

The Dell ♦♦♦
Cowbridge, Timberscombe,
Minehead, Somerset TA24 7TD
T: (01643) 841564
E: hcrawford@zetnet.co.uk

**Knowle Manor and Riding
Centre** ♦♦♦
Timberscombe, Minehead,
Somerset TA24 6TZ
T: (01643) 841342
F: (01643) 841644
E: http://www.wctb.co.
uk/knowle OR knowlemnr@aol.
com
I: welcome.to/knowle

TINTAGEL
Cornwall

Camelot Hotel ♦♦
Atlanta Road, Tintagel, Cornwall
PL34 0DQ
T: (01840) 770202
F: (01840) 770978

The Cornishman Inn ♦♦♦♦
Fore Street, Tintagel, Cornwall
PL34 0DB
T: (01840) 770238
F: (01840) 770078

Pendrin House ♦♦♦
Atlantic Road, Tintagel, Cornwall
PL34 0DE
T: (01840) 770560
F: (01840) 770560
E: pendrin@tesco.net

Polkerr Guest House ♦♦♦♦
Tintagel, Cornwall PL34 0BY
T: (01840) 770382 & 770132

Port William Inn ♦♦♦♦
Trebarwith Strand, Tintagel,
Cornwall PL34 0HB
T: (01840) 770230
F: (01840) 770936
E: william@eurobell.co.uk

**Trewarmett Lodge Hotel and
Restaurant** ♦♦
Trewarmett, Tintagel, Cornwall
PL34 0ET
T: (01840) 770460

Ye Olde Malthouse ♦♦♦♦
Fore Street, Tintagel, Cornwall
PL34 0DA
T: (01840) 770461
F: (01840) 770461
E: info@yeoldemalthouse.
demon.co.uk
I: www.cornwall-online.co.
uk/olde-malthouse

TIVERTON
Devon

Bridge Guest House ♦♦♦
23 Angel Hill, Tiverton, Devon
EX16 6PE
T: (01884) 252804
F: (01884) 252804

The Fishermans Cot ♦♦♦♦
Bickleigh, Tiverton, Devon
EX16 8RW
T: (01884) 855237
F: (01884) 855241
E: book@lionheartinns.co.uk
I: www.lionheartinns.co.uk

Great Bradley Farm ♦♦♦♦
Withleigh, Tiverton, Devon
EX16 8JL
T: (01884) 256946
F: (01884) 256946

Lodgehill Farm Hotel ♦♦♦
Tiverton, Devon EX16 5PA
T: (01884) 252907
F: (01884) 242090
E: Lodgehill@dial.pipex.com
I: www.lodgehill.co.uk
◉

Lower Collipriest Farm
♦♦♦♦ SILVER AWARD
Tiverton, Devon EX16 4PT
T: (01884) 252321
F: (01884) 252321
E: linda@lowercollipriest.co.uk

Quoit-at-Cross Farm ♦♦♦
Stoodleigh, Tiverton, Devon
EX16 9PJ
T: (01398) 351280
F: (01398) 351351
E: quiot-at-cross@talk21.com
◉

TOLLER PORCORUM
Dorset

Barrowlands ♦♦♦
Toller Porcorum, Dorchester,
Dorset DT2 0DW
T: (01300) 320281
E: jrdovey@ukgateway.net

Colesmoor Farm ♦♦♦♦
Toller Porcorum, Dorchester,
Dorset DT2 0DU
T: (01300) 320812
F: (01300) 321402
E: geddes.colesmoor@eclipse.
co.uk
◉ 🏃

The Kingcombe Centre ♦♦
Lower Kingcombe, Toller
Porcorum, Dorchester, Dorset
DT2 0EQ
T: (01300) 320684
F: (01300) 321409
E: nspring@kingcombe-centre.
demon.co.uk
I: www.kingcombe-cente.
demon.co.uk

The Manor
♦♦♦♦ SILVER AWARD
5 Kingcombe Road, Toller
Porcorum, Dorchester, Dorset
DT2 0DG
T: (01300) 320010 &
0797 1956120

TORCROSS
Devon

Cove Guest House ♦♦♦
Torcross, Kingsbridge, Devon
TQ7 2TH
T: (01548) 580350
F: (01548) 580350

TORQUAY
Devon

**Alstone Hotel
Rating Applied For**
22 Bridge Road, Torquay,
TQ2 5BA
T: (01803) 293243
E: alstonehotel@hotmail.com

**Ascot House Hotel
Rating Applied For**
7 Tor Church Road, Torquay,
Devon TQ2 5UR
T: (01803) 295142

Ashleigh House ♦♦♦
61 Meadfoot Lane, Torquay,
Devon TQ1 2BP
T: (01803) 294660

Avenue Park Guest House
♦♦♦
3 Avenue Road, Torquay, Devon
TQ2 5LA
T: (01803) 293902
F: (01803) 293902
E: avepark@aol.com
I: www.torbay.gov.
uk/tourism/t-hotels/avepark.htm

Avron Hotel ♦♦♦
70 Windsor Road, Torquay,
Devon TQ1 1SZ
T: (01803) 294182
F: (01803) 294182

Bahamas Hotel ♦♦♦
17 Avenue Road, Torquay,
Devon TQ2 5LB
T: (01803) 296005 &
0500 526022
⊚

Barclay Court Hotel ♦♦♦
29 Castle Road, Torquay, Devon
TQ1 3BB
T: (01803) 292791
F: (01803) 215715
E: reservations@barclaycourt.
co.uk
I: www.barclaycourt.co.uk

Beverley House Hotel ♦♦♦
9 Clifton Grove, Old Torwood
Road, Torquay, Devon TQ1 1PR
T: (01803) 294626

Blue Haze Hotel
♦♦♦♦ SILVER AWARD
Seaway Lane, Torquay, Devon
TQ2 6PS
T: (01803) 607186 & 606205
F: (01803) 607186
E: mail@bluehazehotel.co.uk
I: www.bluehazehotel.co.uk
⊚

Braddon Hall Hotel ♦♦♦
70 Braddons Hill Road East,
Torquay, Devon TQ1 1HF
T: (01803) 293908
F: (01803) 293908
⊚

Brampton Court Hotel ♦♦♦♦
St Luke's Road South, Torquay,
Devon TQ2 5NZ
T: (01803) 294237
F: (01803) 294237
E: stay@bramptoncourt.co.uk
I: www.bramptoncourt.co.uk

Brandize Hotel ♦♦♦
19 Avenue Road, Torquay,
Devon TQ2 5LB
T: (01803) 297798
F: (01803) 297798
E: ted@brandize.freeserve.co.uk
I: www.
smoothhound.co.uk/hotels/
brandize.html

Brocklehurst Hotel ♦♦♦
Rathmore Road, Torquay, Devon
TQ2 6NZ
T: (01803) 292735 &
0500 505450
F: (01803) 403204
E: enquiries@brocklehursthotel.
co.uk
I: www.brocklehursthotel.co.uk

Burleigh House ♦♦♦
25 Newton Road, Torquay,
Devon TQ2 5DB
T: (01803) 291557

Capri Hotel ♦♦♦♦
12 Torbay Road, Livermead,
Torquay, Devon TQ2 6RG
T: (01803) 293158

Cedar Court Hotel ♦♦♦♦
3 St Matthew's Road, Chelston,
Torquay, TQ2 6JA
T: (01803) 607851
⊚

The Chelston Manor Hotel
♦♦♦
Old Mill Road, Torquay, Devon
TQ2 6HW
T: (01803) 605142
F: (01803) 605267

Chester Court Hotel ♦♦♦
30 Cleveland Road, Torquay,
Devon TQ2 5BE
T: (01803) 294565
F: (01803) 294565
E: kevin@kpmorris.freeserve.co.
uk
I: www.kpmorris.freeserve.co.
uk/cch.html

Chesterfield Hotel ♦♦♦♦
62 Belgrave Road, Torquay,
Devon TQ2 5HY
T: (01803) 292318
F: (01803) 293676

Clovelly Guest House ♦♦♦
91 Avenue Road, Chelston,
Torquay, Devon TQ2 5LH
T: (01803) 292286
F: (01803) 242286
E: clovelly@supanet.com
I: www.hotelstorquayuk.com

Coombe Court Hotel ♦♦♦♦
Babbacombe Downs Road,
Torquay, Devon TQ1 3LP
T: (01803) 327097 & 344840
F: (01803) 327097
E: Phil&Jackie@
Coombecourthotel
I: www.coombecourthotel.co.uk
⊚

Cranborne Hotel
♦♦♦♦♦ SILVER AWARD
58 Belgrave Road, Torquay,
Devon TQ2 5HY
T: (01803) 298046
F: (01803) 298046

The Cranmore ♦♦♦
89 Avenue Road, Torquay,
Devon TQ2 5LH
T: (01803) 298488
F: (01803) 298488
E: dave@thecranmore.fsnet.co.
uk
⊚

Crowndale Hotel ♦♦♦
18 Bridge Road, Torquay, Devon
TQ2 5BA
T: (01803) 293068
F: (01803) 293068

Everglades Hotel ♦♦♦
32 St Marychurch Road,
Torquay, Devon TQ1 3HY
T: (01803) 295389
F: (01803) 214357

Fairmount House Hotel
♦♦♦♦
Herbert Road, Chelston, Torquay,
Devon TQ2 6RW
T: (01803) 605446
F: (01803) 605446
⊼

Fairways ♦♦♦♦
72 Avenue Road, Torquay,
Devon TQ2 5LF
T: (01803) 298471
F: (01803) 298471

Ferndale Hotel ♦♦♦♦
22 St Marychurch Road,
Torquay, Devon TQ1 3HY
T: (01803) 295311
F: (01803) 299888

Gainsboro Hotel ♦♦♦
22 Rathmore Road, Torquay,
Devon TQ2 6NY
T: (01803) 292032
F: (01803) 292032

The Garlieston Hotel ♦♦♦
Bridge Road, Torquay, Devon
TQ2 5BA
T: (01803) 294050
E: garliestonhotel@jridewood.
fsnet.co.uk

Glenross Hotel ♦♦♦♦
25 Avenue Road, Torquay,
Devon TQ2 5LB
T: (01803) 297517
F: (01803) 299033
E: holiday@glenross-hotel.co.uk
I: www.glenross-hotel.co.uk

The Green Park Hotel ♦♦♦
25 Morgan Avenue, Torquay,
Devon TQ2 5RR
T: (01803) 293618
E: greenpark.torquay@cwcom.
net
I: greenpark@eclipse.co.uk

Grosvenor House Hotel ♦♦♦
Falkland Road, Torquay, TQ2 5JP
T: (01803) 294110
⊚

Haytor Hotel ♦♦♦
Meadfoot Road, Torquay,
TQ1 2JP
T: (01803) 294708 & 380184

Heritage Hotel ♦♦♦
Shedden Hill, Torquay, Devon
TQ2 5TY
T: (01803) 299332
F: (01803) 293060
E: pk@viewcircle.fsnet.co.uk
I: www.english-riviera.co.
uk/hotels/heritage

Hillcroft Hotel ♦♦♦
9 St Luke's Road, Torquay,
TQ2 5NY
T: (01803) 297247

Hylton Court Hotel ♦♦♦
109 Abbey Road, Torquay,
TQ2 5NP
T: (01803) 298643 & 264464
F: (01803) 298643

Ingoldsby Hotel ♦♦♦♦
1 Chelston Road, Torquay,
TQ2 6PT
T: (01803) 607497
F: (01803) 607497

Jesmond Dene Hotel ♦♦
85 Abbey Road, Torquay,
TQ2 5NN
T: (01803) 293062

Kings Hotel ♦♦♦♦
44 Bampfylde Road, Torquay,
TQ2 5AY
T: (01803) 293108
F: (01803) 292482
E: kingshotel@bigfoot.com
I: www.eggconnect.
net/kingshotel/

Kingston House
♦♦♦♦ SILVER AWARD
75 Avenue Road, Torquay,
TQ2 5LL
T: (01803) 212760

Kingsway Lodge Guest House
♦♦♦
95 Avenue Road, Torquay,
TQ2 5LH
T: (01803) 295288
I: www.smoothhoundco.
uk/hotels/kingsway.html

Lindum Hotel ♦♦♦
105 Abbey Road, Torquay, Devon
TQ2 5NP
T: (01803) 292795
F: (01803) 299358
E: lindum@eurobell.co.uk

Maple Lodge ♦♦♦
36 Ash Hill Road, Torquay,
TQ1 3JD
T: (01803) 297391

Marstan Hotel ♦♦♦♦
Meadfoot Sea Road, Torquay,
TQ1 2LQ
T: (01803) 292837
F: (01803) 299202
E: enquiries@
marstan-hotel-torquay.co.uk
I: www.marstan-hotel-torquay.
co.uk

Melbourne Tower Hotel ♦♦♦
Solsbro Road, Torquay, TQ2 6PF
T: (01803) 607252
F: (01803) 607252

Mount Edgcombe Hotel
♦♦♦♦
23 Avenue Road, Torquay,
TQ2 5LB
T: (01803) 292310
F: (01803) 292310

Mount Nessing Hotel ♦♦♦
St Luke's Road North, Torquay,
TQ2 5PD
T: (01803) 294259
F: (01803) 294259
E: mount_nessing@hotmail.
com
I: www.smoothhound.co.uk

Newlyn Hotel ♦♦♦♦
62 Braddons Hill Road East,
Torquay, Devon TQ1 1HF
T: (01803) 295100
E: Barbara@newlyn-hotel.co.uk
I: www.newlyn-hotel.co.uk
⊚

Norwood Hotel ♦♦♦♦
60 Belgrave Road, Torquay,
TQ2 5HY
T: (01803) 294236
F: (01803) 294236
E: enquires@norwood-hotel.co.
uk
I: www.norwood-hotel.co.uk
⊚

Richwood Hotel ♦♦♦
20 Newton Road, Torquay,
Devon TQ2 5BZ
T: (01803) 293729
F: (01803) 213632
E: enq@
richwood-hotel-torquay.co.uk
I: www.richwood-hotel-torquay.
co.uk

Robin Hill Hotel ♦♦♦♦
74 Braddons Hill Road East,
Torquay, Devon TQ1 1HF
T: (01803) 214518
F: (01803) 291410
E: jo@robinhillhotel.co.uk
I: www.robinhillhotel.co.uk
⊚

Sandpiper Hotel ◆◆◆
Rowdens Road, Torquay,
TQ2 5AZ
T: (01803) 292779

Silverlands ◆◆◆
27 Newton Road, Torquay,
Devon TQ2 5DB
T: (01803) 292013

Southbank Hotel ◆◆◆
15/17 Belgrave Road, Torquay,
Torquay, Devon TQ2 5HU
T: (01803) 296701 &
07774 948850
F: (01803) 292026

Stover Lodge Hotel ◆◆
29 Newton Road, Torquay,
TQ2 5DB
T: (01803) 297287
F: (01803) 297287

Suite Dreams Hotel ◆◆◆◆
Steep Hill, Maidencombe,
Torquay TQ1 4TS
T: (01803) 313900
F: (01803) 313841
E: suitedreams@suitedreams.co.
uk
I: www.suitedreams.co.uk

Torbay Hotel ◆◆◆
Torbay Road, Torquay, Devon
TQ2 5EY
T: (01803) 295218
F: (01803) 291127

Torbay Rise Hotel ◆◆◆
Old Mill Road, Torquay, TQ2 6HL
T: (01803) 605541
E: vivienne.plewes@IC24.net
I: www.torbayrisehotel.
freeservers.com

Torbay Star Guesthouse ◆◆◆
73 Avenue Road, Torquay,
TQ2 5LL
T: (01803) 293998
F: (01803) 293998
E: christian@torbaystar.
freeserve.co.uk
I: www.torbay-star.co.uk

Villa Marina ◆◆◆
Tor Park Road, Torquay, Devon
TQ2 5BQ
T: (01803) 292187 & 389483

Westbourne Hotel ◆◆◆◆
106 Avenue Road, Torquay,
TQ2 5LQ
T: (01803) 292927

Wilsbrook Guest House ◆◆◆
77 Avenue Road, Torquay,
TQ2 5LL
T: (01803) 298413

TORRINGTON
Devon

Beaford House Hotel ◆◆◆
Beaford, Winkleigh, Devon
EX19 8AB
T: (01805) 603305 & 603330
F: (01805) 603305

Locksbeam Farm ◆◆◆◆
Torrington, Devon EX38 7EZ
T: (01805) 623213
F: (01805) 623213

TOTNES
Devon

Buckyette Farm ◆◆◆
Buckyette, Totnes, Devon
TQ9 6ND
T: (01803) 762638
F: (01803) 762638

The Elbow Room ◆◆◆◆◆
North Street, Totnes, Devon
TQ9 5NZ
T: (01803) 863480 &
0797 1516824

Foales Leigh
◆◆◆◆ SILVER AWARD
Harberton, Totnes, Devon
TQ9 7SS
T: (01803) 862365
F: (01803) 862365

Four Seasons Guest House
◆◆◆
13 Bridgetown, Totnes, Devon
TQ9 5AB
T: (01803) 862146

Great Court Farm
◆◆◆◆ SILVER AWARD
Weston Lane, Totnes, Devon
TQ9 6LB
T: (01803) 862326
F: (01803) 862326

The Old Forge at Totnes
◆◆◆◆ SILVER AWARD
Seymour Place, Totnes, Devon
TQ9 5AY
T: (01803) 862174
F: (01803) 865385

The Watermans Arms
◆◆◆◆◆
Bow Bridge, Ashprington,
Totnes, Devon TQ9 7EG
T: (01803) 732214
F: (01803) 732314
E: book@lionheartinns.co.uk
I: www.lionheartinns.co.uk

"Old Follaton"
◆◆◆◆◆ SILVER AWARD
Plymouth Road, Totnes, Devon
TQ9 5NA
T: (01803) 865441
F: (01803) 863597

TREATOR
Cornwall

Woodlands Close ◆◆◆
Treator, Padstow, Cornwall
PL28 8RU
T: (01841) 533109
E: john@stock65.freeserve.co.uk
I: www.cornwall-online.co.
uk/woodlands-close

TREGASWITH
Cornwall

Tregaswith Farmhouse ◆◆◆◆
Tregaswith, Newquay, Cornwall
TR8 4HY
T: (01637) 881181
F: (01637) 881181

TREGONY
Cornwall

Tregonan ◆◆◆◆
Tregony, Truro, Cornwall
TR2 5SN
T: (01872) 530249
F: (01872) 530249

TRELIGHTS
Cornwall

**Long Cross Hotel and Victorian
Garden** ◆◆◆
Trelights, Port Isaac, Cornwall
PL29 3TF
T: (01208) 880243
F: (01208) 880243

TRENEGLOS
Cornwall

Trescar Bed & Breakfast
◆◆◆◆
Lower Scarsick, Treneglos,
Launceston, Cornwall PL15 8UH
T: (01566) 781282
F: (01566) 781282

TRESILLIAN
Cornwall

Polsue Manor Farm ◆◆◆
Tresillian, Truro, Cornwall
TR2 4BP
T: (01872) 520234
F: (01872) 520616

TREVALGA
Cornwall

Trehane Farm ◆◆◆
Trevalga, Boscastle, Cornwall
PL35 0EB
T: (01840) 250510

TREVAUNANCE COVE
Cornwall

Driftwood Spars Hotel ◆◆◆
Trevaunance Cove, St Agnes,
Cornwall TR5 0RT
T: (01872) 552428 & 553323
F: (01872) 553701

TREVONE
Cornwall

Tarka's Rest ◆◆◆◆
Sandy Lane, Trevone, Padstow,
Cornwall PL28 8RE
T: (01841) 520007

TROWBRIDGE
Wiltshire

26 The Beeches ◆◆◆
Trowbridge, Wiltshire BA14 7HG
T: (01225) 760760

Herons Knoll ◆◆
18 Middle Lane, Trowbridge,
Wiltshire BA14 7LG
T: (01225) 752593

Lion and Fiddle ◆◆◆
Devizes Road, Hilperton,
Trowbridge, Wiltshire BA14 7QS
T: (01225) 776392
F: (01225) 774501

Old Manor Hotel ◆◆◆◆◆
Trowle, Trowbridge, Wiltshire
BA14 9BL
T: (01225) 777393
F: (01225) 765443
E: oldbeams@ddmanorhotel.
com
I: www.oldmanorhotel.
comwww.bradfordonavon

Sue's B & B ◆◆◆
25 Blair Road, Trowbridge,
Wiltshire BA14 9JZ
T: (01225) 764559 &
07977 655017
E: sue_b_n_b@yahoo.com
I: www.visitbritain.com

Welam House ◆◆◆
Bratton Road, West Ashton,
Trowbridge, Wiltshire BA14 6AZ
T: (01225) 755908

TRURO
Cornwall

Bissick Old Mill ◆◆◆◆
Ladock, Truro, Cornwall TR2 4PG
T: (01726) 882557
F: (01726) 884057

Great Hewas Farm ◆◆◆
Grampound Road, Truro,
Cornwall TR2 4EP
T: (01726) 882218 &
07860 117572

Marcorrie Hotel ◆◆◆◆
20 Falmouth Road, Truro,
Cornwall TR1 2HX
T: (01872) 277374
F: (01872) 241666
E: marcorrie@aol.com
I: www.cornwall.net/marcorrie

Rock Cottage ◆◆◆◆
Blackwater, Truro, Cornwall
TR4 8EU
T: (01872) 560252 &
07971 941399
F: (01872) 560252
E: rockcottage@yahoo.com

**Trevispian–Vean Farm Guest
House** ◆◆◆◆
St Erme, Truro, Cornwall TR4 9AT
T: (01872) 279514
F: (01872) 263730

UFFCULME
Devon

Waterloo Cross Inn ◆◆
Waterloo Cross, Uffculme,
Cullompton, Devon EX15 3ES
T: (01884) 840328
F: (01884) 840908

UPLODERS
Dorset

Uploders Farm ◆◆◆
Dorchester Road, Uploders,
Bridport, Dorset DT6 4NZ
T: (01308) 423380

UPLYME
Devon

Elton ◆◆◆◆
Lyme Road, Uplyme, Lyme Regis,
Dorset DT7 3TH
T: (01297) 445986
E: mikecawte@aol.com

Hill Barn ◆◆◆◆
Gore Lane, Uplyme, Lyme Regis,
Dorset DT7 3RJ
T: (01297) 445185
F: (01297) 445185

UPTON LOVELL
Wiltshire

Prince Leopold ◆◆◆
Upton Lovell, Warminster,
Wiltshire BA12 0JP
T: (01985) 850460
F: (01985) 850737

UPTON NOBLE
Somerset

Kingston House ◆◆◆◆
Upton Noble, Shepton Mallet,
Somerset BA4 6BA
T: (01749) 850805
E: tim.r.stroud@rexam.co.uk

UPWEY
Dorset

Bankside Cottage ◆◆◆
Church Street, Upwey,
Weymouth, Dorset DT3 5QE
T: (01305) 812320

Friars Way
◆◆◆◆ SILVER AWARD
Church Street, Upwey,
Weymouth, Dorset DT3 5QE
T: (01305) 813243
F: (01305) 813243

URCHFONT
Wiltshire

The Nags Head ◆
High Street, Urchfont, Devizes,
Wiltshire SN10 4QH
T: (01380) 840346

VIRGINSTOW
Devon

**Percy's Country Hotel &
Restaurant**
◆◆◆◆◆ GOLD AWARD
Virginstow, Beaworthy, Devon
EX21 5EA
T: (01409) 211236
F: (01409) 211275
E: info@percys.co.uk
I: www.percys.co.uk

WARMINSTER
Wiltshire

Angel Cottage B & B ◆◆◆
34B Upton Scudamore,
Warminster, Wiltshire BA12 0AQ
T: (01985) 218504
F: (01985) 218504

Bugley Barton
◆◆◆◆◆ SILVER AWARD
Victoria Road, Warminster,
Wiltshire BA12 7RB
T: (01985) 213389
F: (01985) 300450
E: bugleybarton@aol.com

Croft House Farm ◆◆◆◆
147a Bath Road, Warminster,
Wiltshire BA12 7RZ
T: (01985) 213460
F: (01985) 213460

Lane End Cottage
Rating Applied For
72 Lane End, Corsley,
Warminster, Wiltshire BA12 7PG
T: (01373) 832592
F: (01373) 832935
E: hugh-kay@moredent.fsnet.
co.uk

Sturford Mead Farm ◆◆◆◆
Corsley, Warminster, Wiltshire
BA12 7QU
T: (01373) 832213
F: (01373) 832213
E: lynn_sturford.bed@virgin.net

WASHBOURNE
Devon

Penny Rowden ◆◆◆◆
Washbourne, Totnes, Devon
TQ9 7DN
T: (01803) 712485
F: (01803) 712485
E: ap@pennyrowden.freeserve.
co.uk

WASHFORD
Somerset

Green Bay ◆◆◆
Washford, Watchet, Somerset
TA23 0NN
T: (01984) 640303
E: greenbay@tinyonline.co.uk

WATCHET
Somerset

Esplanade House ◆◆◆
The Esplanade, Watchet,
Somerset TA23 0AJ
T: (01984) 633444

Wood Advent Farm
Rating Applied For
Roadwater, Somerset TA23 0RR
T: (01984) 640920
F: (01984) 640920
E: info@woodaventfarm.co.uk

WATERGATE BAY
Cornwall

The White House ◆◆◆
Watergate Bay, Newquay,
Cornwall TR8 4AD
T: (01637) 860119
F: (01637) 860449
E: jenny.vallance@virgin.net

WAYTOWN
Dorset

Slape Hill Barn ◆◆◆
Waytown, Bridport, Dorset
DT6 5LQ
T: (01308) 488429

**Springfield House Bed &
Breakfast**
Rating Applied For
Springfield House, Waytown,
Bridport, Dorset DT6 5LF
T: (01308) 488425 & 488022
F: (01308) 488040
E: sales@mrhchemicals.co.uk

WEARE GIFFARD
Devon

Cleave Farm House ◆◆
Weare Giffard, Bideford, Devon
EX39 4QX
T: (01805) 623671
F: (01805) 623235

WELLS
Somerset

Beaconsfield Farm
◆◆◆◆ GOLD AWARD
Easton, Wells, Somerset
BA5 1DU
T: (01749) 870308
E: beaconsfield@dial.pipex.com
I: www.beaconsfield.dial.pipex.
com

Beryl ◆◆◆◆ SILVER AWARD
Wells, Somerset BA5 3JP
T: (01749) 678738
F: (01749) 670508
E: stay@beryl.co.uk
I: www.smoothhound.co.uk

**Burcott Mill Guest House
◆◆◆**
Burcott, Wells, Somerset
BA5 1NJ
T: (01749) 673118
F: (01749) 673118
E: burcottmillwells@
compuserve.com
I: www.smoothhound.co.
uk/hotels/burcott.html

Cadgwith ◆◆◆◆
Hawkers Lane, Wells, Somerset
BA5 3JH
T: (01749) 677799

Canon Grange ◆◆◆◆
Cathedral Green, Wells,
Somerset BA5 2UB
T: (01749) 671800
E: canongrange@email.com
I: www.canongrange.co.uk

Carmen B & B
◆◆◆◆ SILVER AWARD
Bath Road, Wells, Somerset
BA5 3LQ
T: (01749) 677331 &
07977 098607

The Crown at Wells ◆◆◆
Market Place, Wells, Somerset
BA5 2RP
T: (01749) 673457
F: (01749) 679792
E: reception@crownwells.
demon.co.uk
I: www.plus44.com/crown/

Franklyns Farm ◆◆◆
Chewton Mendip, Bath,
Somerset BA3 4NB
T: (01761) 241372

Glengarth ◆◆◆
7 Glastonbury Road, Wells,
Somerset BA5 1TW
T: (01749) 673087

Highcroft ◆◆◆◆
Wells Road, Priddy, Wells,
Somerset BA5 3AU
T: (01749) 673446

Highfield ◆◆◆◆
93 Portway, Wells, Somerset
BA5 2BR
T: (01749) 675330

Highgate Cottage ◆◆◆
Worth, Wells, Somerset
BA5 1LW
T: (01749) 674201
F: (01749) 674201

Hillside Cottage ◆◆◆
5-6 Keward, Glastonbury Road,
Wells, Somerset BA5 1TR
T: (01749) 673770
E: hillsidecott@compuserve.
com

Hillview Cottage
◆◆◆◆ SILVER AWARD
Paradise Lane, Croscombe, Wells,
Somerset BA5 3RL
T: (01749) 343526
E: wells@alderking.co.uk
I: www.smoothhound.co.uk

**Littlewell Farm Guest House
◆◆◆◆**
Coxley, Wells, Somerset BA5 1QP
T: (01749) 677914

30 Mary Road ◆◆◆
Wells, Somerset BA5 2NF
T: (01749) 674031
F: (01749) 674031
E: triciabailey30@hotmail.com

Southway Farm ◆◆◆◆
Polsham, Wells, Somerset
BA5 1RW
T: (01749) 673396
F: (01749) 670373

Worth House Hotel ◆◆◆◆
Worth, Wookey, Wells, Somerset
BA5 1LW
T: (01749) 672041
F: (01749) 672041

WEMBDON
Somerset

Model Farm ◆◆◆◆
Perry Green, Wembdon,
Bridgwater, Somerset TA5 2BA
T: (01278) 433999
E: rmodelfarm@aol.com

WEMBURY
Devon

Bay Cottage ◆◆◆
150 Church Road, Wembury,
Plymouth PL9 0HR
T: (01752) 862559
F: (01752) 862559
E: TheFairies@aol.com

WEST ANSTEY
Devon

Greenhills Farm
◆◆◆◆ SILVER AWARD
Yeo Mill, West Anstey, South
Molton, Devon EX36 3NU
T: (01398) 341300

Jubilee House ◆◆◆◆
Highaton Farm, West Anstey,
South Molton, Devon EX36 3PJ
T: (01398) 341312
F: (01398) 341323
E: denton@jubileehouse.
exmoor-holidays.co.uk
I: www.jubileehouse.
exmoor-holidays.co.uk

Partridge Arms Farm ◆◆◆
Yeo Mill, West Anstey, South
Molton, Devon EX36 3NU
T: (01398) 341217
F: (01398) 341569

WEST BAY
Dorset

Egdon ◆
Third Cliff Walk, West Bay,
Bridport, Dorset DT6 4HX
T: (01308) 422542

The George Hotel ◆◆◆
West Bay, Bridport, Dorset
DT6 4EY
T: (01308) 423191

Heatherbell Cottage ◆◆◆
Hills Close, West Bay, Bridport,
Dorset DT6 4HW
T: (01308) 422998 &
07967 859896

WEST BUCKLAND
Somerset

Causeway Cottage ◆◆◆◆
West Buckland, Wellington,
Somerset TA21 9JZ
T: (01823) 663458
F: (01823) 663458
E: orrs@westbuckland.freeserve.
co.uk
I: welcome.to/causeway-cottage

WEST CAMEL
Somerset

The Walnut Tree ◆◆◆◆
Fore Street, West Camel, Yeovil,
Somerset BA22 7QW
T: (01935) 851292
F: (01935) 851292

WEST DOWN
Devon

The Long House ◆◆◆◆
The Square, West Down,
Ilfracombe, Devon EX34 8NF
T: (01271) 863242

WEST KNIGHTON
Dorset

Church Cottage
♦♦♦♦ SILVER AWARD
West Knighton, Dorchester,
Dorset DT2 8PF
T: (01305) 852243

WEST MONKTON
Somerset

Springfield House ♦♦♦♦
Walford Cross, West Monkton,
Taunton, Somerset TA2 8QW
T: (01823) 412116
F: (01823) 412116

WEST OVERTON
Wiltshire

Cairncot ♦♦♦
West Overton, Marlborough,
Wiltshire SN8 4ER
T: (01672) 861617 &
07798 603455

WEST PENNARD
Somerset

The Lion At Pennard ♦♦♦
Glastonbury Road, West
Pennard, Glastonbury, Somerset
BA6 8NH
T: (01458) 832941
F: (01458) 832941

Middle East Street Farm ♦♦♦
West Pennard, Glastonbury,
Somerset BA6 8NS
T: (01458) 832981

WEST PORLOCK
Somerset

West Porlock House ♦♦♦♦
West Porlock, Minehead,
Somerset TA24 8NX
T: (01643) 862880

WEST STAFFORD
Dorset

Church Cottages ♦♦♦
2 Church Cottages, West
Stafford, Dorchester, Dorset
DT2 8AB
T: (01305) 269287
F: (01305) 269287
E: bill.newton@talk21.com

Keepers Cottage
♦♦♦♦ SILVER AWARD
West Stafford, Dorchester,
Dorset DT2 8AA
T: (01305) 264389 &
07979 316046
F: (01305) 264389

Long Barn House ♦♦♦♦
1 Barton Mews, West Stafford,
Dorchester, Dorset DT2 8UB
T: (01305) 266899

WESTBURY
Wiltshire

Black Dog Farm ♦♦♦
Chapmanslade, Westbury,
Wiltshire BA13 4AE
T: (01373) 832858
E: im.mills@virgin.net

Sherbourne House ♦♦♦
47 Station Road, Westbury,
Wiltshire BA13 3JW
T: (01373) 864865

WESTBURY-SUB-MENDIP
Somerset

The Old Stores ♦♦♦♦
Westbury-sub-Mendip, Wells,
Somerset BA5 1HA
T: (01749) 870817 &
07721 514306
F: (01749) 870980
E: moglin980@aol.com

WESTHAY
Somerset

New House Farm
♦♦♦♦ SILVER AWARD
Burtle Road, Westhay,
Glastonbury, Somerset BA6 9TT
T: (01458) 860238 &
07944 828819
F: (01458) 860568
E: newhousefarm@
farmersweekly.net

WESTON
Devon

Higher Weston Farm ♦♦♦♦
Weston, Sidmouth, Devon
EX10 0PH
T: (01395) 513741

WESTON-SUPER-MARE
North Somerset

Algarve Guest House ♦♦♦
24 Quantock Road, Weston-
super-Mare, BS23 4DT
T: (01934) 626128

Ashcombe Court ♦♦♦♦
17 Milton Road, Weston-super-
Mare, BS23 2SH
T: (01934) 625104
F: (01934) 625104

Baymead Hotel ♦♦♦
19/23 Longton Grove Road,
Weston-super-Mare, BS23 1LS
T: (01934) 622951
F: (01934) 628110

Braeside Hotel ♦♦♦♦
2 Victoria Park, Weston-super-
Mare, BS23 2HZ
T: (01934) 626642
F: (01934) 626642
E: braeside@tesco.net
I: www.smoothhound.co.
uk/hotels/braeside.html

Conifers ♦♦♦
63 Milton Road, Weston-super-
Mare, BS23 2SP
T: (01934) 624404
F: (01934) 624404

Cornerways ♦♦♦
14 Whitecross Road, Weston-
super-Mare, BS23 1EW
T: (01934) 623708

Four Seasons Guest House ♦
103 Locking Road, Weston-
super-Mare, BS23 3EW
T: (01934) 631124

The Grand Atlantic ♦♦♦
Beach Road, Weston-super-
Mare, BS23 1BA
T: (01934) 626543
F: (01934) 415048
I: www.skypages.com

L'Arrivee Licensed Hotel ♦♦♦
75/77 Locking Road, Weston-
super-Mare, North Somerset
BS23 3DW
T: (01934) 625328
F: (01934) 625328
E: carolinetr@bun.com

The Milton Lodge Hotel
♦♦♦♦
15 Milton Road, Weston-super-
Mare, BS23 2SH
T: (01934) 623161
F: (01934) 623210
E: vallen@miltonlodge.
freeserve.co.uk
I: www.miltonlodge.com

**Moorlands Country
Guesthouse** ♦♦♦
Hutton, Weston-super-Mare,
Somerset BS24 9QH
T: (01934) 812283
F: (01934) 812283
E: margaret_holt@email.comm

Orchard House
♦♦♦♦ SILVER AWARD
Summer Lane, West Wick,
Weston-super-Mare, BS24 7TF
T: (01934) 520948
F: (01934) 520948

Savoy Hotel ♦♦♦
Madiera Cove, Weston-super-
Mare, BS23 2BX
T: (01934) 629559 & 621145

Saxonia ♦♦♦
95 Locking Road, Weston-super-
Mare, BS23 3EW
T: (01934) 633856
F: (01934) 623141
E: saxonia@lineone.net
I: www.smoothhound.co.
uk/hotels/saxonia.html

Shire Elms Guest House ♦♦♦
71 Locking Road, Weston-super-
Mare, BS23 3DQ
T: (01934) 628605

Spreyton Guest House ♦♦♦
72 Locking Road, Weston-super-
Mare, BS23 3EN
T: (01934) 416887

Welbeck Hotel ♦♦♦
Knightstone Road, Marine
Parade, Weston-super-Mare,
BS23 2BB
T: (01934) 621258
F: (01934) 643585

Wychwood Private Hotel
♦♦♦♦
148 Milton Road, Weston-
super-Mare, BS23 2UZ
T: (01934) 627793

WESTONZOYLAND
Somerset

Staddlestones Guest House
♦♦♦♦ SILVER AWARD
3 Standards Road,
Westonzoyland, Bridgwater,
Somerset TA7 0EL
T: (01278) 691179
F: (01278) 691333
E: staddlestones@euphony.net
I: www.guide2britain.co.
uk/where2stay/staddlestones

WESTROP
Wiltshire

Park Farm Barn ♦♦♦♦
Westrop, Corsham, Wiltshire
SN13 9QF
T: (01249) 715911
F: (01249) 715911

WESTWARD HO!
Devon

Brockenhurst ♦♦♦
11 Atlantic Way, Westward Ho!,
Bideford, Devon EX39 1HX
T: (01237) 423346
F: (01237) 423346
E: snowball@brockenhurst1.
freeserve.co.uk

Eversley ♦♦♦♦
1 Youngaton Road, Westward
Ho!, Bideford, Devon EX39 1HU
T: (01237) 471603
E: lsharrat@ndevon.co.uk

WEYMOUTH
Dorset

Albatross Hotel ♦♦♦
96 The Esplanade, Weymouth,
Dorset DT4 7AT
T: (01305) 785191
F: (01305) 785191

Bay Lodge
♦♦♦♦♦ GOLD AWARD
27 Greenhill, Weymouth, Dorset
DT4 7SW
T: (01305) 782419
F: (01305) 782828
E: barbara@baylodge.co.uk
I: www.baylodge.co.uk

Bay View Hotel ♦♦♦♦
35 The Esplanade, Weymouth,
Dorset DT4 8DH
T: (01305) 782083
F: (01305) 782083

Chadwood House ♦♦♦♦
77 Preston Road, Weymouth,
Dorset DT3 6PY
T: (01305) 834887

The Channel Hotel ♦♦♦
93 The Esplanade, Weymouth,
Dorset DT4 7AY
T: (01305) 785405
F: (01305) 785405
E: lee@thechannel.freeserve.co.
uk
I: www.resort-guide.co.
uk/channel

The Chatsworth
♦♦♦♦ SILVER AWARD
14 The Esplanade, Weymouth,
Dorset DT4 8EB
T: (01305) 785012
F: (01305) 766342
E: david@chatsworth.freeserve.
co.uk

Crofton Guest House ♦♦♦
36 Lennox Street, Weymouth,
Dorset DT4 7ND
T: (01305) 785903 &
0777 5905149
F: (01305) 750165
E: stevemerrill1@excite.com

Cumberland Hotel
◆ ◆ ◆ ◆ SILVER AWARD
95 Esplanade, Weymouth,
Dorset DT4 7BA
T: (01305) 785644
F: (01305) 785644
I: www.theaa.co.uk/hotels

Eastney ◆ ◆ ◆ ◆
15 Longfield Road, Weymouth,
Dorset DT4 8RQ
T: (01305) 771682
F: (01305) 771682
E: eastneyhot@aol.com
I: www.resort-guide.co.
uk/eastney

Florian ◆ ◆ ◆
59 Abbotsbury Road,
Weymouth, Dorset DT4 0AQ
T: (01305) 773836 &
07970 873770
F: (01305) 750160

Kenora Private Hotel ◆ ◆ ◆ ◆
5 Stavordale Road, Weymouth,
Dorset DT4 0AB
T: (01305) 771215 &
07976 826067
E: kenora.hotel@wdi.co.uk

Kimberley Family Run Guest House ◆ ◆ ◆
16 Kirtleton Avenue, Weymouth,
Dorset DT4 7PT
T: (01305) 783333

Kings Acre Hotel ◆ ◆ ◆ ◆
140 The Esplanade, Weymouth,
Dorset DT4 7NH
T: (01305) 782534
F: (01305) 782534

The Kingsley Hotel ◆ ◆ ◆ ◆
10 Kirtleton Avenue, Weymouth,
Dorset DT4 7PT
T: (01305) 777715
E: thekingsleyhotel@fs.mail
I: www.thekingsleyhotel.com

The Pebbles Guest House ◆ ◆ ◆
18 Kirtleton Avenue, Weymouth,
Dorset DT4 7PT
T: (01305) 784331
F: (01305) 784695
E: blackwoodg@aol.com
⊕

Province of Natal Hotel ◆ ◆ ◆
5 Greenhill, Weymouth, Dorset
DT4 7SR
T: (01305) 784108
F: (01305) 770575

Seaham Guest House
◆ ◆ ◆ ◆ GOLD AWARD
3 Waterloo Place, Weymouth,
Dorset DT4 7NU
T: (01305) 782010

Southbrook ◆ ◆ ◆
13 Preston Road, Weymouth,
Dorset DT3 6PU
T: (01305) 832208

Hotel Sunnywey ◆ ◆ ◆
23 Kirtleton Avenue, Weymouth,
Dorset DT4 7PS
T: (01305) 786911
F: (01305) 767084

Weyside Guest House ◆ ◆ ◆
1a Abbotsbury Road,
Weymouth, Dorset DT4 0AD
T: (01305) 772685
E: weyside@globalnet.co.uk
I: www.weyside@globalnet.co.
uk
⊕

Cutthorne Farm
◆ ◆ ◆ ◆ GOLD AWARD
Luckwell Bridge, Wheddon
Cross, Minehead, Somerset
TA24 7EW
T: (01643) 831255
F: (01643) 831255
E: durbin@cutthorne.co.uk
I: www.cutthorne.co.uk

Exmoor House ◆ ◆ ◆ ◆
Rating Applied For
Wheddon Cross, Somerset
TA24 7DU
T: (01643) 841432
F: (01643) 841811
E: exmoorhouse@hotmail.com
⊕

Little Brendon Hill Farm
◆ ◆ ◆ ◆ ◆ GOLD AWARD
Wheddon Cross, Minehead,
Somerset TA24 7BG
T: (01643) 841556
F: (01643) 841556
E: Larry.Maxwell@btinternet.
com
⊕

Little Quarme Farm
◆ ◆ ◆ ◆ SILVER AWARD
Wheddon Cross, Minehead,
Somerset TA24 7EA
T: (01643) 841249
F: (01643) 841249
E: 106425743@compuserve.
com
I: www.traveluk.netlittlequarme
⊕

The Rest And Be Thankful Inn
◆ ◆ ◆ ◆ SILVER AWARD
Wheddon Cross, Minehead,
Somerset TA24 7DR
T: (01643) 841222
F: (01643) 841222
E: enquiries@
restandbethankful.co.uk
I: www.restandbethankful.co.uk

Sundial House
◆ ◆ ◆ ◆ SILVER AWARD
Wheddon Cross, Minehead,
Somerset TA24 7DP
T: (01643) 841188
F: (01643) 841188
E: sundialhouse@lineone.net

Triscombe Farm ◆ ◆ ◆ ◆
Wheddon Cross, Minehead,
Somerset TA24 7HA
T: (01643) 851227
F: (01643) 851227

Fairhaven Farm ◆ ◆ ◆
Gooseford, Whiddon Down,
Okehampton, Devon EX20 2QH
T: (01647) 231261

Down House
◆ ◆ ◆ ◆ SILVER AWARD
Woodhayes Lane, Whimple,
Exeter, Devon EX5 2QR
T: (01404) 822860
E: downhouse@talk21.com
I: www.whimple.swest.co.uk

Saundercroft ◆
Whimple, Exeter, Devon EX5 2PF
T: (01404) 822380

Candida House ◆ ◆ ◆ ◆
Whitchurch Canonicorum,
Bridport, Dorset DT6 6RQ
T: (01297) 489629
F: (01297) 489629
E: candida@globalnet.co.uk
I: www.holidayaccom.
com/candida-house.htm

Icelton Farm ◆ ◆ ◆
Wick St Lawrence, Weston-
super-Mare BS22 7YJ
T: (01934) 515704

Higher Venton Farm ◆ ◆
Widecombe-in-the-Moor,
Newton Abbot, Devon TQ13 7TF
T: (01364) 621235
F: (01364) 621382

Sheena Tower ◆ ◆ ◆
Widecombe-in-the-Moor,
Newton Abbot, Devon TQ13 7TE
T: (01364) 621308
E: sheenatower@compuserve.
com

Brocksmoor Hotel ◆ ◆ ◆
Widemouth Bay, Bude, Cornwall
EX23 0DF
T: (01288) 361207 & 361589

Wilcot Lodge ◆ ◆ ◆ ◆
Wilcot, Pewsey, Wiltshire
SN9 5NS
T: (01672) 563465 &
07974 700735
F: (01672) 569040
E: gmikegswimdells@hotmail.
com
I: www.bed-breakfast-uk.
com/66-uk-wt04.htm

The Old Stable
Rating Applied For
Orchard Cottage, 11 Lower
Vellow, Williton, Taunton,
Somerset TA4 4LS
T: (01984) 656640
F: (01984) 656858
E: jhbrigden@compuserve.com

The Pembroke Arms Hotel
◆ ◆ ◆ ◆
Minster Street, Wilton, Salisbury,
Wiltshire SP2 0BH
T: (01722) 743328
F: (01722) 744886
⊕

Pit Folly
◆ ◆ ◆ ◆ SILVER AWARD
The Avenue, Wilton, Salisbury
SP2 0BU
T: (01722) 742108

The Old Parsonage ◆ ◆ ◆
Court Walk, Winkleigh, Devon
EX19 8JA
T: (01837) 83772

Home Farm
◆ ◆ ◆ ◆ SILVER AWARD
Barton, Winscombe, Cheddar,
Somerset BS25 1DX
T: (01934) 842078
E: chris@homefarmcottages.co.
uk
I: www.homefarmcottages.co.uk

Karslake House Hotel
◆ ◆ ◆ ◆ SILVER AWARD
Halse Lane, Winsford, Minehead,
Somerset TA24 7JE
T: (01643) 851242
F: (01643) 851242

Kemps Farm ◆ ◆ ◆
Winsford, Minehead, Somerset
TA24 7HT
T: (01643) 851312

Larcombe Foot ◆ ◆ ◆ ◆
Winsford, Minehead, Somerset
TA24 7HS
T: (01643) 851306

The Conifers ◆ ◆
4 King Alfred Way, Winsley,
Bradford-on-Avon, Wiltshire
BA15 2NG
T: (01225) 722482

Stillmeadow
◆ ◆ ◆ ◆ SILVER AWARD
18 Bradford Road, Winsley,
Bradford-on-Avon, Wiltshire
BA15 2HW
T: (01225) 722119
F: (01225) 722633
E: sue.gilby@btinternet.com

Scotland Lodge ◆ ◆ ◆ ◆
Winterbourne Stoke, Salisbury,
Wiltshire SP3 4TF
T: (01980) 620943 &
07957 856302
F: (01980) 621403
E: scotland.lodge@virginnet.co.
uk
I: www.scotland-lodge.co.uk
⊕

Scotland Lodge Farm ◆ ◆ ◆ ◆
Winterbourne Stoke, Salisbury
SP3 4TF
T: (01980) 621199
F: (01680) 621188
E: william.lockwood@bigwig.
net
I: www.smoothhound.co.
uk/hotels/scotlandl.html

Shiralee Bed & Breakfast
Rating Applied For
Tytherley Road, Winterslow,
Salisbury SP5 1PY
T: (01980) 862004 &
07818 415354
F: (01980) 862004
E: anything@faisa.co.uk
I: www.faisa.co.uk

WITHAM FRIARY
Somerset
Higher West Barn Farm
♦♦♦♦ SILVER AWARD
Witham Friary, Frome, Somerset
BA11 5HH
T: (01749) 850819 &
07976 162207

WITHERIDGE
Devon
Thelbridge Cross Inn ♦♦♦
Thelbridge, Witheridge, Crediton,
Devon EX17 4SQ
T: (01884) 860316
F: (01884) 861318
E: thelbridgeinn@cwcom.net

WIVELISCOMBE
Somerset
Greenway Farm ♦♦♦
Wiveliscombe, Taunton,
Somerset TA4 2UA
T: (01984) 623359
F: (01984) 624051

Mill Barn ♦♦♦♦
Jews Farm, Maundown,
Wiveliscombe, Taunton,
Somerset TA4 2HL
T: (01984) 624739

WOODBOROUGH
Wiltshire
Pantawick ♦♦♦♦
Woodborough, Pewsey,
Wiltshire SN9 5PG
T: (01672) 851662
F: (01672) 851662
E: pantawick@aol.com

Well Cottage ♦♦♦
Honey Street, Woodborough,
Pewsey, Wiltshire SN9 5PS
T: (01672) 851577 &
07966 298863

WOODLAND
Devon
The Rising Sun ♦♦♦♦
Woodland, Ashburton, Newton
Abbot, Devon TQ13 7JT
T: (01364) 652544
F: (01364) 654202

WOODY BAY
Devon
Moorlands ♦♦♦
Woody Bay, Parracombe,
Barnstaple, Devon EX31 4RA
T: (01598) 763224

WOOKEY HOLE
Somerset
Broadleys
♦♦♦♦ SILVER AWARD
21 Wells Road, Wookey Hole,
Wells, Somerset BA5 1DN
T: (01749) 674746
F: (01749) 674746
E: broadleys@bobmilton.
totalserve.co.uk

Glencot House
♦♦♦♦♦ GOLD AWARD
Glencot Lane, Wookey Hole,
Wells, Somerset BA5 1BH
T: (01749) 677160
F: (01749) 670210
E: Glencot@ukonline.co.uk
I: web.ukonline.co.uk/glencot

Whitegate Cottage ♦♦♦
Milton Lane, Wookey Hole,
Wells, Somerset BA5 1DG
T: (01749) 675326
E: sueandnic@whitegate.
freeserve.co.uk

WOOLACOMBE
Devon
Camberley ♦♦♦
Beach Road, Woolacombe,
Devon EX34 7AA
T: (01271) 870231
E: camberley@tesco.net

Castle Hotel ♦♦♦♦
The Esplanade, Woolacombe,
Devon EX34 7DJ
T: (01271) 870788
F: (01271) 870788

Ossaborough House ♦♦♦
Ossaborough Lane,
Woolacombe, Devon EX34 7HJ
T: (01271) 870297

Sunnyside House ♦♦♦
Sunnyside Road, Woolacombe,
Devon EX34 7DG
T: (01271) 870267

WOOLAVINGTON
Somerset
Chestnut House ♦♦♦♦♦
Hectors Stone, Lower Road,
Woolavington, Bridgwater,
Somerset TA7 8EF
T: (01278) 683658
F: (01278) 684333
I: www.chestnuthouse.freeserve.
co.uk

The Willows ♦♦♦
45 Woolavington Hill,
Woolavington, Bridgwater,
Somerset TA7 8HQ
T: (01278) 683494

WOOLLEY
Cornwall
East Woolley Farm ♦♦♦
Woolley, Bude, Cornwall
EX23 9PP
T: (01288) 331525

WOOLVERTON
Somerset
The Old School House
Rating Applied For
Woolverton, Bath BA3 6RH
T: (01373) 830200
F: (01373) 830200

WOOTTON BASSETT
Wiltshire
1 Highgate Cottages ♦♦
Brinkworth Road, Wootton
Bassett, Swindon, Wiltshire
SN4 8DU
T: (01793) 848054

The Hollies ♦♦♦
Greenhill, Hook, Wootton
Bassett, Swindon, Wiltshire
SN4 8EH
T: (01793) 770795
F: (01793) 770795

Tockenham Court Farm
♦♦♦♦
Tockenham, Swindon SN4 7PH
T: (01793) 852315 &
07836 241686
F: (01793) 852315

WOOTTON COURTENAY
Somerset
Robin How ♦♦♦
Brockwell Lane, Wootton
Courtenay, Minehead, Somerset
TA24 0RN
T: (01643) 841247
F: (01643) 841247
E: robinhow.rolfe@virgin.net

WRAXALL
Somerset
Rose's Farm ♦♦♦♦
Wraxall, Shepton Mallet,
Somerset BA4 6RQ
T: (01749) 860261

WRINGTON
North Somerset
Bracken Hill ♦♦♦♦
Wrington Hill, Wrington, Bristol
BS40 5PN
T: (01934) 862261
F: (01934) 862875
E: brackenhill@btinternet.com

YARCOMBE
Devon
Crawley Farm ♦♦♦
Yarcombe, Honiton, Devon
EX14 9AX
T: (01460) 64760
F: (01460) 64760

YATTON KEYNELL
Wiltshire
The Crown Inn ♦♦♦♦
Giddea Hall, Yatton Keynell,
Chippenham, Wiltshire
SN14 7ER
T: (01249) 782229
F: (01249) 782337

YELVERTON
Devon
Eggworthy Farm ♦♦♦
Sampford Spiney, Yelverton,
Devon PL20 6LJ
T: (01822) 852142

Greenwell Farm ♦♦♦♦
Meavy, Yelverton, Devon
PL20 6PY
T: (01822) 853563
F: (01822) 853563
E: greenwellfarm@btconnect.
com

**Harrabeer Country House
Hotel** ♦♦♦♦
Harrowbeer Lane, Yelverton,
Devon PL20 6EA
T: (01822) 853302
F: (01822) 853302
E: reception@harrabeer.
freeserve.co.uk
I: www.harrabeer.freeserve.co.uk

**Knightstone Tearooms and
Restaurant** ♦♦
Crapstone Road, Yelverton,
Devon PL20 6BT
T: (01822) 853679

The Old Orchard ♦♦♦♦
Harrowbeer Lane, Yelverton,
Devon PL20 6DZ
T: (01822) 854310
F: (01822) 854310
E: babs@baross.demon.co.uk
I: www.baross.demon.co.
uk/theoldorchard

Peek Hill Farm ♦♦♦
Dousland, Yelverton, Devon
PL20 6PD
T: (01822) 854808 & 852908
F: (01822) 854808
E: colton@peekhill.freeserve.co.
uk & peekhill@freeserve.co.uk

The Rosemont Guest House
♦♦♦
Greenbank Terrace, Yelverton,
Devon PL20 6DR
T: (01822) 852175
E: b&b@rosemontgh.fsnet.co.uk

Torrfields ♦♦♦♦
Sheepstor, Yelverton, Devon
PL20 6PF
T: (01822) 852161
E: torrfields@beeb.net

Waverley Guest House ♦♦♦
5 Greenbank Terrace, Yelverton,
Devon PL20 6DR
T: (01822) 854617
F: (01822) 854617

YEOVIL
Somerset
Cartref ♦♦♦
10 Home Drive, Yeovil, Somerset
BA21 3AP
T: (01935) 421607
E: tere@lattanzio.freeserve.co.
uk

**Globetrotters Cafe, Bar,
Restaurant and Lodge** ♦♦♦
73-74 South Street, Yeovil,
Somerset BA20 1QF
T: (01935) 423328
F: (01935) 411701
E: Reception@
globetrotters-lodge.co.uk
I: www.theglobetrotters.co.uk

Greystones Court ♦♦♦♦
152 Hendford Hill, Yeovil,
Somerset BA20 2RG
T: (01935) 426124 &
07970 897580
F: (01935) 426124
E: rich&isobel@greystones.
freeserve.co.uk
I: www.greystones.freeserve.co.
uk

The Sparkford Inn ♦♦♦
Sparkford, Yeovil, Somerset
BA22 7JN
T: (01963) 440218
F: (01963) 440358

Sunnymede
♦♦♦♦ SILVER AWARD
26 Lower Wraxhill Road, Yeovil,
Somerset BA20 2JU
T: (01935) 425786

White Horse Inn
Rating Applied For
10 St Michaels Avenue, Yeovil,
Somerset BA21 4LB
T: (01935) 476471 &
0771 2827305
F: (01935) 476480

YEOVILTON
Somerset
Cary Fitzpaine ♦♦♦♦
Yeovilton, Yeovil, Somerset
BA22 8JB
T: (01458) 223250 &
07932 657140
F: (01458) 223372
E: ACRANG@AOL.COM

SOUTH WEST

Courtry Farm ◆◆◆
Bridgehampton, Yeovil,
Somerset BA22 8HF
T: (01935) 840327
F: (01935) 840964
I: www.countyfarm@hotmail.
com

Bingers Farm ◆◆◆◆
Ryme Road, Yetminster,
Sherborne, Dorset DT9 6JY
T: (01935) 872555
F: (01935) 872555

Cornerways Cottage ◆◆◆◆
Longcross, Zeals, Warminster,
Wiltshire BA12 6LL
T: (01747) 840477
F: (01747) 840477
E: cornerways.cottage@
btinternet.com
I: www.smoothhound.co.
uk/hotels/cornerwa.html

SOUTH OF ENGLAND

Carinya Farm ◆◆◆
Cattle Lane, Abbotts Ann,
Andover, Hampshire SP11 7DR
T: (01264) 710269
E: carinya.fram@virginnet.co.uk

East Manor House
◆◆◆◆◆ SILVER AWARD
Abbotts Ann, Andover,
Hampshire SP11 7BH
T: (01264) 710031

Virginia Lodge ◆◆◆
Salisbury Road, Abbotts Ann,
Andover, Hampshire SP11 7NX
T: (01264) 710713

Dinckley Court ◆◆◆◆
Burcot, Abingdon, Oxfordshire
OX14 3DP
T: (01865) 407763 &
07976 883925
F: (01865) 407010
E: annette@dinckleycourt.co.uk
I: www.dinckleycourt.co.uk

8 Melrose Gardens ◆◆
Aborfield Cross, Reading,
Berkshire RG2 9PZ
T: (01189) 760287 &
07774 455971
E: roking@henforyd.freeserve.
com

The Bell Inn ◆◆◆
High Street, Adderbury, Banbury,
Oxfordshire OX17 3LS
T: (01295) 810338
F: (01295) 812221
I: www.banbury-cross.co.
uk/bellinn.ntm

**Le Restaurant Francais at
Morgans Orchard** ◆◆◆
9 Twyford Gardens, Adderbury,
Banbury, Oxfordshire OX17 3JA
T: (01295) 812047
F: (01295) 812047
E: morgarest@aol.co.uk
I: www.banbury-cross.co.
uk/morgans.htm

The Folly Inn ◆◆
Buckingham Road, Adstock,
Buckingham, Buckinghamshire
MK18 2HS
T: (01296) 712671
F: (01296) 712671

46 Manor Road ◆◆◆
Akeley, Buckingham,
Buckinghamshire MK18 5HQ
T: (01280) 860009
F: (01280) 860331

Blackwater House ◆◆◆◆
Blackwater Grove, Alderholt,
Fordingbridge, Hampshire
SP6 3AD
T: (01425) 653443
E: bandb@blackwater47.fsnet.
co.uk

Merrimead
◆◆◆◆ SILVER AWARD
12 Station Road, Alderholt,
Fordingbridge, Hampshire
SP6 3RB
T: (01425) 657544
F: (01425) 650400
E: merrimead@ic24.net

Boundary House B & B ◆◆◆◆
Gosport Road, Lower
Farringdon, Alton, Hampshire
GU34 3DH
T: (01420) 587076
F: (01420) 587047
E: BoundaryS@Messages.co.uk

The Vicarage ◆◆◆
East Worldham, Alton,
Hampshire GU34 3AS
T: (01420) 82392 &
07778 800804
F: (01420) 82367
E: wenrose@bigfoot.com

**The Grange Country House
Hotel** ◆◆◆
Alverstone, Sandown, Isle of
Wight PO36 0EZ
T: (01983) 403729
F: (01983) 403729
E: grange_alverstone@
compuserve.com

Kern Farm ◆◆◆◆
Alverstone, Sandown, Isle of
Wight PO36 0EY
T: (01983) 403721

Coldmoreham House ◆◆◆◆
172 High Street, Amersham,
Buckinghamshire HP7 0EG
T: (01494) 725245

The Dacha ◆◆◆
118 Chestnut Lane, Amersham,
Buckinghamshire HP6 6DZ
T: (01494) 433063
F: (01895) 843307

127 High Street ◆◆◆◆
Amersham, Buckinghamshire
HP7 0DY
T: (01494) 725352

63 Hundred Acres Lane ◆◆◆
Amersham, Buckinghamshire
HP7 9BX
T: (01494) 433095

39 Quarrendon Road ◆◆◆◆
Amersham, Buckinghamshire
HP7 9EF
T: (01494) 727959

St Catherins ◆◆
9 Parkfield Avenue, Amersham,
Buckinghamshire HP6 6BE
T: (01494) 728125
E: jelliott@callnetuk.com

The White House ◆◆◆◆
20 Church Street, Amersham,
Buckinghamshire HP7 0DB
T: (01494) 433015
F: (01494) 433015

The Taj ◆◆◆◆
2 Hook Crescent, Ampfield,
Romsey, Hampshire SO51 9DE
T: (023) 8027 0810 &
07702 227366
I: christine@jeaves.freeserve.co.
uk

Broadwater ◆◆◆◆
Amport, Andover, Hampshire
SP11 8AY
T: (01264) 772240
F: (01264) 772240
E: carolyn@dmac.co.uk
I: www.dmac.co.uk/carolyn

Tilehurst ◆◆◆◆
Furzedown Lane, Amport,
Andover, Hampshire SP11 8BW
T: (01264) 771437
F: (01264) 773651
E: tilehurst@compuserve.com

18 Altona Gardens ◆◆◆
Andover, Hampshire SP10 4LG
T: (01264) 351932

Amberley Hotel ◆◆◆
70 Weyhill Road, Andover,
Hampshire SP10 3NP
T: (01264) 352224
F: (01264) 392555
E: amberleyand@fsbdial.co.uk.

Amport Inn ◆◆◆
Amport, Andover, Hampshire
SP11 8AE
T: (01264) 710371
F: (01264) 710112

Fernihurst ◆◆
1 Strathfield Road, Andover,
Hampshire SP10 2HH
T: (01264) 361936

Holmdene Guest House ◆◆
1 Winchester Road, Andover,
Hampshire SP10 2EG
T: (01264) 365414
F: (01264) 365414

Malt Cottage ◆◆◆◆
Upper Clatford, Andover,
Hampshire SP11 7QL
T: (01264) 323469
F: (01264) 334100
E: info@maltcottage.co.uk
I: www.maltcottage.co.uk

Old Grange ◆◆◆
86 Winchester Road, Andover,
Hampshire SP10 2ER
T: (01264) 352784

**Salisbury Road Bed &
Breakfast** ◆◆◆
99 Salisbury Road, Andover,
Hampshire SP10 2LN
T: (01264) 362638

Shangri–La Guest House ◆◆◆
Walworth Road, Picket Piece,
Andover, Hampshire SP11 6LU
T: (01264) 354399

78 Springfield Close ◆◆
Andover, Hampshire SP10 2QT
T: (01264) 350489

Sutherland Guest House
◆◆◆◆
Micheldever Road, Andover,
Hampshire SP10 2BH
T: (01264) 365307

The Old Post Office ◆◆◆
Church Road, Ardley, Bicester,
Oxfordshire OX6 9NP
T: (01869) 345958
F: (01869) 345958

Ascot Corner ◆◆◆◆
Wells Lane, Ascot, Berkshire
SL5 7DY
T: (01344) 627722
F: (01344) 873965
E: susan.powell@easynet.co.uk

Ennis Lodge Private Guest House ♦♦♦
Winkfield Road, Ascot, Berkshire
SL5 7EX
T: (01344) 621009
F: (01344) 621009

Tanglewood ♦♦♦
Birch Lane, off Longhill Road,
Chavey Down, Ascot, Berkshire
SL5 8RF
T: (01344) 882528

ASCOTT-UNDER-WYCHWOOD
Oxfordshire

College Farm
Rating Applied For
Ascott-under-Wychwood,
Chipping Norton, Oxfordshire
OX7 6AL
T: (01993) 831900
F: (01993) 831900
E: walkers@collegefarmbandb.
fsnet.co.uk

Crown Farm Bed & Breakfast ♦♦♦♦
Crown Farm, 13 The Green,
Ascott-under-Wychwood,
Oxford, Oxfordshire OX7 6AB
T: (01993) 832083 & 830045
I: www.crown-farm.co.uk

The Mill ♦♦♦
Ascott-under-Wychwood,
Chipping Norton, Oxfordshire
OX7 6AP
T: (01993) 831282
E: Mill@auwoxon32.freeserve.
co.uk

ASHENDON
Buckinghamshire

The Gatehangers ♦♦♦
Lower End, Ashendon, Aylesbury,
Buckinghamshire HP18 0HE
T: (01296) 651296
F: (01296) 651340

ASHEY
Isle of Wight

Little Upton Farmhouse ♦♦♦♦♦ SILVER AWARD
Little Upton Farm, Gatehouse
Road, Ashey, Ryde, Isle of Wight
PO33 4BS
T: (01983) 563236

ASHLEY HEATH
Dorset

Fir Tree Cottage ♦♦♦
4 Forest Edge Drive, Ashley
Heath, Ringwood, Hampshire
BH24 2ER
T: (01425) 477977

Lions Hill Farm ♦♦
Horton Road, Ashley Heath,
Ringwood, Hampshire BH24 2EX
T: (01425) 472115
F: (01425) 472115
I: www.internetonline.co.
uk/holidays/49375246html

ASHMORE
Dorset

Glebe Cottage Farm ♦♦♦♦
Ashmore, Shaftesbury, Dorset
DT5 5AE
T: (01747) 811974
F: (01747) 811104
E: all@glebe.force9.co.uk

ASHURST
Hampshire

Forest Gate Lodge ♦♦♦
161 Lyndhurst Road, Ashurst,
Lyndhurst, Hampshire
SO40 7AW
T: (023) 8029 3026

Kingswood Cottage ♦♦♦♦ SILVER AWARD
10 Woodlands Road, Ashurst,
Southampton, Hampshire
SO40 7AD
T: (023) 8029 2582
F: (023) 8029 3435

ASTON ABBOTTS
Buckinghamshire

The Royal Oak Inn ♦♦
Wingrave Road, Aston Abbotts,
Aylesbury, Buckinghamshire
HP22 4LT
T: (01296) 681262

Windmill Hill Barns ♦♦♦♦
Moat Lane, Aston Abbotts,
Aylesbury, Buckinghamshire
HP22 4NF
T: (01296) 681714

ASTON CLINTON
Buckinghamshire

Baywood Guest House ♦♦
98 Weston Road, Aston Clinton,
Aylesbury, Buckinghamshire
HP22 5EJ
T: (01296) 630612

ASTON UPTHORPE
Oxfordshire

Middle Fell ♦♦♦♦
Moreton Road, Aston Upthorpe,
Didcot, Oxfordshire OX11 9ER
T: (01235) 850207 &
07889 489870
F: (01235) 850207

AWBRIDGE
Hampshire

Crofton Country Accommodation
Rating Applied For
Kents Oak, Awbridge, Romsey,
Hampshire SO51 0HH
T: (01794) 340333
F: (01794) 340333

AYLESBURY
Buckinghamshire

Amber Court ♦
116 Bierton Road, Aylesbury,
Buckinghamshire HP20 1EN
T: (01296) 432184 &
07801 958116

Cherrycroft ♦♦♦♦
11 Church Farm Close, Bierton,
Aylesbury, Buckinghamshire
HP22 5EL
T: (01296) 334834 &
07737 041751
E: linda@cherrycroft.nildram.co.
uk

Crystal Hill Guest House ♦
32 Bicester Road, Aylesbury,
Buckinghamshire HP19 3AD
T: (01296) 426313

Dovedale Court Guest House
Rating Applied For
46 Wendover Road, Aylesbury,
Buckinghamshire HP21 9LB
T: (01296) 339400

The Old Forge Barn ♦♦♦
Ridings Way, Cublington,
Leighton Buzzard, Bedfordshire
LU7 0LW
T: (01296) 681194
F: (01296) 681194

The Town House ♦
35 Tring Road, Aylesbury,
Buckinghamshire HP20 1LD
T: (01296) 395295

331 Tring Road ♦♦♦♦
Aylesbury, Buckinghamshire
HP20 1PJ
T: (01296) 424012

Wallace Farm ♦♦♦
Dinton, Aylesbury,
Buckinghamshire HP17 8UF
T: (01296) 748660
F: (01296) 748851
E: jackiecook@wallacefarm.
freeserve.co.uk
I: www.country-accom.co.uk

BAMPTON
Oxfordshire

Cedars ♦♦♦♦
Mill Lane, Black Bourton,
Bampton, Oxfordshire OX18 2PJ
T: (01993) 841368
F: (01993) 841368

Chimney Farm House ♦♦♦♦
Chimney-on-Thames, Aston,
Bampton, Oxfordshire OX18 2EH
T: (01367) 870279
F: (01367) 870279

The Granary ♦♦♦
Main Street, Clanfield, Bampton,
Oxfordshire OX18 2SH
T: (01367) 810266

Morar ♦♦♦
Weald Street, Bampton, Oxford,
Oxfordshire OX18 2HL
T: (01993) 850162
F: (01993) 851738
E: morar@cwcom.net
I: www.farm-holidays.co.
uk/morar/

BANBURY
Oxfordshire

Amberley Guest House ♦♦
151 Middleton Road, Banbury,
Oxfordshire OX16 8QS
T: (01295) 255797

Ashlea Guest House ♦
58 Oxford Road, Banbury,
Oxfordshire OX16 9AN
T: (01295) 250539
F: (01295) 250539
E: johnatashlea1@tinyworld.co.
uk

Avonlea Guest House ♦♦
41 Southam Road, Banbury,
Oxfordshire OX16 7EP
T: (01295) 267837

Banbury Cross Bed & Breakfast ♦♦♦♦
1 Broughton Road, Banbury,
Oxfordshire OX16 9QB
T: (01295) 266048
F: (01295) 266698

College Farmhouse ♦♦♦♦
Kings Sutton, Banbury,
Oxfordshire OX17 3PS
T: (01295) 811473
F: (01295) 812505
E: sallday@compuserve.com
I: www.banburytown.co.
uk/accom/collegefarmhouse

Cotefields Bed & Breakfast ♦
Opposite Bodicote Park,
Banbury, Oxfordshire OX15 4AQ
T: (01295) 264977 &
07899 901743
F: (01295) 264977
E: tony.stockford@ic24.net

Fernleigh Guest House ♦♦♦
67 Oxford Road, Banbury,
Oxfordshire OX16 9AJ
T: (01295) 250853
F: (01295) 269349
E: mark-gill@bidwell.fsbusiness.
co.uk

George & Dragon
Rating Applied For
Silver Street, Chacombe,
Banbury, Oxfordshire OX15 2JR
T: (01295) 711500

The Glebe House ♦♦♦♦
Village Road, Warmington,
Banbury, Oxfordshire OX17 1BT
T: (01295) 690642

Grafton Lodge ♦♦♦
63 Oxford Road, Banbury,
Oxfordshire OX16 9AJ
T: (01295) 257000
F: (01295) 258545

The Lodge ♦♦♦♦
Main Road, Middleton Cheney,
Banbury, Oxfordshire OX17 2PP
T: (01295) 710355

119 Middleton Road ♦♦♦
Banbury, Oxfordshire OX16 8QS
T: (01295) 253236

Prospect House Guest House ♦♦♦
70 Oxford Road, Banbury,
Oxfordshire OX16 9AN
T: (01295) 268749 &
07798 772578
F: (01295) 268749

Roxtones ♦♦
Malthouse Lane, Shutford,
Banbury, Oxfordshire OX15 6PB
T: (01295) 788240

St Martins House ♦♦♦
Warkworth, Banbury,
Oxfordshire OX17 2AG
T: (01295) 712684
F: (01295) 712838

Treetops Guest House ♦♦
28 Dashwood Road, Banbury,
Oxfordshire OX16 8HD
T: (01295) 254444

Winstons ♦♦♦
65 Oxford Road, Banbury,
Oxfordshire OX16 9AJ
T: (01295) 270790

BARKHAM
Berkshire

Columbine ♦♦♦
12 Almond Close, Barkham,
Wokingham, Berkshire
RG41 4UU
T: (0118) 978 8356

SOUTH OF ENGLAND

BARTLEY
Hampshire
Bartley Farmhouse ♦♦♦♦
Ringwood Road, Bartley,
Southampton, Hampshire
SO40 7LD
T: (023) 8081 4194
F: (023) 8081 4117

BARTON ON SEA
Hampshire
Cleeve House ♦♦♦♦
58 Barton Court Avenue, Barton
on Sea, New Milton, Hampshire
BH25 7HG
T: (01425) 615211
F: (01425) 615211

Eureka Guest House ♦♦♦
Christchurch Road, Barton on
Sea, New Milton, Hampshire
BH25 6QQ
T: (01425) 610289

Hotel Gainsborough ♦♦♦♦
Marine Drive East, Barton on
Sea, New Milton, Hampshire
BH25 7DX
T: (01425) 610541

Laurel Lodge ♦♦♦
48 Western Avenue, Barton on
Sea, New Milton, Hampshire
BH25 7PZ
T: (01425) 618309

The Old Coastguard Hotel
♦♦♦
53 Marine Drive East, Barton on
Sea, New Milton, Hampshire
BH25 7DX
T: (01425) 612987
F: (01425) 612987
E: dp@theoldcoastguardfsnet.
co.uk
I: www.theoldcoastguardfsnet.
co.uk

Westbury House ♦♦♦
12 Greenacre, Barton on Sea,
New Milton, Hampshire
BH25 7BS
T: (01425) 620935 &
07976 871756
E: les@westbury-house.
freeserve.co.uk
I: www.westbury-house.
freeserve.co.uk

The Wight House ♦♦♦♦
41 Marine Drive East, Barton on
Sea, New Milton, Hampshire
BH25 7DX
T: (01425) 614008

BARTON STACEY
Hampshire
The Meadows B & B ♦♦♦♦
Greenacres, Barton Stacey,
Winchester, Hampshire
SO21 3RH
T: (01962) 760123 &
07850 934309
F: (01962) 761023

Swan Inn ♦♦♦
Barton Stacey, Winchester,
Hampshire SO21 3RL
T: (01962) 760470

BASINGSTOKE
Hampshire
Cedar Court ♦♦♦
Reading Road, Hook, Hampshire
RG27 9DB
T: (01256) 762178
F: (01256) 762178

Fernbank Hotel
♦♦♦♦ SILVER AWARD
4 Fairfields Road, Basingstoke,
Hampshire RG21 3DR
T: (01256) 321191
F: (01256) 321191
E: hotelfernbank@hernscott.net

Street Farm House ♦♦♦♦
The Street, South Warnborough,
Hook, Hampshire RG29 1RS
T: (01256) 862225
F: (01256) 862225

BEACONSFIELD
Buckinghamshire
Beacon House ♦♦♦
113 Maxwell Road, Beaconsfield,
Buckinghamshire HP9 1RF
T: (01494) 672923
F: (01494) 672923
E: Ben.dickinson@tesco.net

Highclere Farm ♦♦♦
Newbarn Lane, Seer Green,
Beaconsfield, Buckinghamshire
HP9 2QZ
T: (01494) 875665 & 874505
F: (01494) 875238

BEAULIEU
Hampshire
2-3 Northern Cottages ♦♦♦♦
Lyndhurst Road, Beaulieu,
Brockenhurst, Hampshire
SO42 7YE
T: (01590) 612127
F: (01590) 612127
E: christine.hills@btinternet

Dale Farm House ♦♦♦
Manor Road, Applemore Hill,
Dibden, Southampton,
Hampshire SO45 5TJ
T: (023) 8084 9632
F: (023) 8084 0285
E: chris@dalefarnhouse.fsnet.
co.uk

Leygreen Farm House ♦♦♦
Lyndhurst Road, Beaulieu,
Brockenhurst, Hampshire
SO42 7YP
T: (01590) 612355

Old School House ♦♦♦♦
High Street, Beaulieu,
Brockenhurst, Hampshire
SO42 7YD
T: (01590) 612062
F: (01590) 612062

The Rectory ♦♦♦
Palace Lane, Beaulieu,
Hampshire SO42 7YG
T: (01590) 612242
F: (01590) 612242

BEMBRIDGE
Isle of Wight
Harbour Farm ♦♦♦♦
Embankment Road, Bembridge,
Isle of Wight PO35 5NS
T: (01983) 872610 & 874080
F: (01983) 874080

BERE REGIS
Dorset
The Dorsetshire Golf Lodge
♦♦♦♦
East Dorset Golf Club, Bere
Regis, Wareham, Dorset
BH20 7NT
T: (01929) 472244
F: (01929) 471294
E: edgc@golf.co.uk

The Royal Oak ♦♦♦♦
West Street, Bere Regis,
Wareham, Dorset BH20 7HQ
T: (01929) 471203
F: (01929) 472636

BICESTER
Oxfordshire
Manor Farm Bed & Breakfast
♦♦♦
Poundon, Bicester, Oxfordshire
OX6 0BB
T: (01869) 277212 & 277166
F: (01869) 277166

BINSTEAD
Isle of Wight
Elm Close Cottage ♦♦♦♦
Elm Close, Ladies Walk, Binstead,
Ryde, Isle of Wight PO33 3SY
T: (01983) 567161 &
0771 3540134
E: elm_cottage@hotmail.com

**Newnham Farm Bed &
Breakfast**
♦♦♦♦♦ GOLD AWARD
Newnham Lane, Binstead, Ryde,
Isle of Wight PO33 4ED
T: (01983) 882423
F: (01983) 882423

BLACKTHORN
Oxfordshire
Limetrees Farm
Rating Applied For
Lower Road, Blackthorn,
Bicester, Oxfordshire OX6 9TG
T: (01869) 248435
F: (01869) 248435
E: limetreesfarm@freeserve.co.
uk

BLANDFORD FORUM
Dorset
Farnham Farm House ♦♦♦
Farnham, Blandford Forum,
Dorset DT11 8DG
T: (01725) 516254
F: (01725) 516306

Meadow House
♦♦♦♦ SILVER AWARD
Tarrant Hinton, Blandford
Forum, Dorset DT11 8JG
T: (01258) 830498
F: (01258) 830498

BLEDLOW
Buckinghamshire
Cross Lanes Guest House
♦♦♦♦
Cross Lanes Cottage, Bledlow,
Aylesbury, Buckinghamshire
HP27 9PF
T: (01844) 345139
F: (01844) 274165

BLEWBURY
Oxfordshire
The Barley Mow
Rating Applied For
London Road, Blewbury, Didcot,
Oxfordshire OX11 9NU
T: (01235) 850296
F: (01235) 850296

BLOXHAM
Oxfordshire
Brook Cottage ♦♦
Little Bridge Road, Bloxham,
Banbury, Oxfordshire OX15 4PU
T: (01295) 721089

Virginia House ♦♦♦
1 High Street, Bloxham,
Banbury, Oxfordshire OX15 4LX
T: (01295) 720596
F: (01295) 720596

BOLDRE
Hampshire
Fernbrake ♦♦
Coxhill, Boldre, Lymington,
Hampshire SO41 8PS
T: (01590) 622257
F: (01590) 624256

Kingston Cottage ♦♦♦
Lower Sandy Down, Boldre,
Lymington, Hampshire
SO41 8PP
T: (01590) 623051

Passford Farm ♦♦♦
Southampton Road, Boldre,
Lymington, Hampshire
SO41 8ND
T: (01590) 674103

Pinecroft ♦♦
Coxhill, Boldre, Lymington,
Hampshire SO41 8PS
T: (01590) 624260
F: (01590) 624025
E: pinecroft@freeuk.com
I: www.smoothhound.co.
uk/hotels/pinecrof.html

The Well House ♦♦♦♦
Southampton Road, Boldre,
Lymington, Hampshire SO41 8PT
T: (01590) 689055
F: (01590) 688993
E: darver@msn.com
I: www.thewellhouse.bnb.com

BONCHURCH
Isle of Wight
The Lake Hotel ♦♦♦♦
Shore Road, Bonchurch,
Ventnor, Isle of Wight PO38 1RF
T: (01983) 852613
F: (01983) 852613
E: Richard@lakehotel.co.uk
I: www.smoothhound.co.
uk/hotels/lake.html

**Under Rock Country House Bed
& Breakfast** ♦♦♦
Shore Road, Bonchurch,
Ventnor, Isle of Wight PO38 1RF
T: (01983) 855274
E: www.underock@btinternet.
com

BOSCOMBE
Dorset
Au-Levant Hotel ♦♦
15 Westby Road, Boscombe,
Bournemouth, Dorset BH5 1HA
T: (01202) 394884

Audmore Hotel ♦♦♦
3 Cecil Road, Boscombe,
Bournemouth, Dorset BH5 1DU
T: (01202) 395166

Bramcote Hall Hotel ♦♦♦
1 Glen Road, Boscombe,
Bournemouth, Dorset BH5 1HR
T: (01202) 395555 & 398623
F: (01202) 398623
E: bramcoteh@aol.com

Denewood Hotel ◆◆◆
1 Percy Road, Boscombe,
Bournemouth, Dorset BH5 1JE
T: (01202) 394493
F: (01202) 391155
E: peteer@denewood.co.uk
I: www.denewood.co.uk

Knightlow Hotel ◆◆◆
5 Percy Road, Boscombe,
Bournemouth, Dorset BH5 1JE
T: (01202) 396415 & 255973
F: (01202) 387871
E: ros@knightlow-hotel.co.uk
I: www.knightlow-hotel.co.uk

The Marven Hotel ◆◆◆
5 Watkin Road, Boscombe,
Bournemouth, Dorset BH5 1HP
T: (01202) 397099
⊛

Siena Private Hotel ◆◆◆◆
17 Cecil Road, Boscombe,
Bournemouth, Dorset BH5 1DU
T: (01202) 394159
F: (01202) 309798

Hotel Sorrento ◆◆◆◆
16 Owls Road, Boscombe,
Bournemouth, Dorset BH5 1AG
T: (01202) 394019
F: (01202) 394019

Southlands Private Hotel
◆◆◆◆
11 Crabton Close Road,
Boscombe, Bournemouth,
Dorset BH5 1HN
T: (01202) 394887
F: (01202) 397882
E: southlandshotel@ukonline.
co.uk

BOTLEY
Hampshire

Steeple Court Farm ◆◆◆
Church Lane, Botley,
Southampton, Hampshire
SO30 2EQ
T: (01489) 798824
E: theblue.room@btinternet.
com

BOTOLPH CLAYDON
Buckinghamshire

Hickwell House ◆◆◆
40 Botyl Road, Botolph Claydon,
Buckingham, Buckinghamshire
MK18 2LR
T: (01296) 712217 &
07703 115972
F: (01296) 712217
⊛

BOURNE END
Buckinghamshire

Hollands Farm ◆◆◆◆
Hedsor Road, Bourne End,
Buckinghamshire SL8 5EE
T: (01628) 520423
F: (01628) 531602

BOURNEMOUTH
Dorset

Alexander Lodge Hotel ◆◆◆◆
21 Southern Road, Southbourne,
Bournemouth, Dorset BH6 3SR
T: (01202) 421662
F: (01202) 421662
E: alexanderlodge@yahoo.com
I: www.smoothhound.co.
uk/a28852.html

Ardene Hotel ◆◆◆
12 Glen Road, Boscombe,
Bournemouth, Dorset BH5 1HR
T: (01202) 394928 & 393856
F: (01202) 394928

Avonwood Hotel ◆◆◆
20 Owls Road, Boscombe,
Bournemouth, Dorset BH5 1AF
T: (01202) 394704
F: (01202) 309906
E: avonwood.hotel@virgin.net

Bay View Hotel ◆◆◆
Southbourne Overcliff Drive,
Bournemouth, Dorset BH6 3QB
T: (01202) 429315
F: (01202) 429689
⊛

Cairnsmore Hotel ◆◆◆
37 Beaulieu Road, Alum Chine,
Bournemouth, Dorset BH4 8HY
T: (01202) 763705
E: ritacoombs@hotmail.com

Carisbrooke Hotel ◆◆◆
42 Tregonwell Road,
Bournemouth, Dorset BH2 5NT
T: (01202) 290432
F: (01202) 310499
E: all@carisbrooke58.freeserve.
co.uk
I: www.carisbrooke.co.uk

Chase Lodge ◆◆◆
4 Herbert Road, Alum Chine,
Bournemouth, Dorset BH4 8HD
T: (01202) 768515
F: (01202) 757847
E: chaselodge@hotmail.com

Chine Cote Hotel ◆◆
25 Studland Road, Alum Chine,
Bournemouth, Dorset BH4 8HZ
T: (01202) 761208
E: t.f.sanford@skynow.net
I: www.smoothhound.co.
uk/hotels/chine2.html

Coniston Hotel ◆◆◆
27 Studland Road, Alum Chine,
Bournemouth, Dorset BH4 8HZ
T: (01202) 765386

Cransley Hotel ◆◆◆
11 Knyveton Road, East Cliff,
Bournemouth, Dorset BH1 3QG
T: (01202) 290067
F: (01202) 294368
E: reservations@cransley.co.uk
I: www.cransley.co.uk

Crosbie Hall Hotel ◆◆◆
21 Florence Road, Boscombe,
Bournemouth, Dorset BH5 1HJ
T: (01202) 394714
F: (01202) 394714
E: david@crosbiehall.fsnet.co.uk

Dene Court Hotel
Rating Applied For
19 Boscombe Spa Road,
Bournemouth, Dorset BH5 1AR
T: (01202) 394874
F: (01202) 394874

Dorset Westbury Hotel ◆◆◆
62 Lansdowne Road,
Bournemouth, Dorset BH1 1RS
T: (01202) 551811
F: (01202) 551811
⊛

Earlham Lodge ◆◆◆◆
91 Alumhurst Road, Alum Chine,
Bournemouth, Dorset BH4 8HR
T: (01202) 761943
F: (01202) 768223

East Cliff Cottage Hotel ◆◆◆
57 Grove Road, Bournemouth,
Dorset BH1 3AT
T: (01202) 552788
F: (01202) 556400
E: len@wallen.freeserve.co.uk

Fairmount Hotel ◆◆◆◆
15 Priory Road, West Cliff,
Bournemouth, Dorset BH2 5DF
T: (01202) 551105
F: (01202) 551105
E: reservations@
fairmount-hotel.co.uk
I: www.fairmount-hotels.co.uk

Glenbourne Hotel ◆◆◆
81 Alumhurst Road, Alum Chine,
Bournemouth, Dorset BH4 8HR
T: (01202) 761607

Hawthorns Hotel ◆◆◆
40 Alumhurst Road,
Westbourne, Bournemouth,
Dorset BH4 8EY
T: (01202) 760220
E: liz-mcdonald@yahoo.co.uk

Highclere Private Hotel ◆◆◆
15 Burnaby Road, Alum Chine,
Bournemouth, Dorset BH4 8JF
T: (01202) 761350 &
07711 562886
F: (01202) 767110
I: www.bournemouth.co.uk

Holmcroft Hotel ◆◆◆
Earle Road, Alum Chine,
Bournemouth, Dorset BH4 8JQ
T: (01202) 761289 & 761395
F: (01202) 761289

The Inverness Hotel ◆◆◆◆
26 Tregonwell Road,
Bournemouth, Dorset BH2 5NS
T: (01202) 554968
F: (01202) 554968
I: www.hotelsbournemouth.uk.
com

Kings Langley Hotel ◆◆◆
1 West Cliff Road,
Bournemouth, Dorset BH2 5ES
T: (01202) 557349 & 553736
F: (01202) 789739
E: john@kingslangley.fsnet.co.
uk
I: www.kingslangleyhotel.co.uk

Langdale Hotel ◆◆◆◆
6 Earle Road, Alum Chine,
Bournemouth, Dorset BH4 8JQ
T: (01202) 761174
F: (01202) 761174

Lawnswood Hotel ◆◆◆
22A Studland Road, Alum Chine,
Bournemouth, Dorset BH4 8JA
T: (01202) 761170
F: 4401202 761170
E: lawnswood_hotel_uk@
yahoo.com

Mayfield Private Hotel ◆◆◆◆
46 Frances Road, Knyveton
Gardens, Bournemouth, Dorset
BH1 3SA
T: (01202) 551839
F: (01202) 551839
E: mayfield_98@yahoo.com
I: www.bizonline.co.uk/mayfield

Hotel Mon Bijou ◆◆◆
47 Manor Road, East Cliff,
Bournemouth, Dorset BH1 3EU
T: (01202) 551389
F: (01202) 316081

Mount Lodge Hotel ◆◆◆
19 Beaulieu Road, Alum Chine,
Bournemouth, Dorset BH4 8HY
T: (01202) 761173

Oxford Hall Hotel
Rating Applied For
6 Sandbourne Road,
Bournemouth, Dorset BH4 8JH
T: (01202) 761016

Parklands Hotel ◆◆◆
4 Rushton Crescent,
Bournemouth, Dorset BH3 7AF
T: (01202) 552529 &
07768 716217
F: (01202) 552529
E: alan@parklandshotel.
freeserve.co.uk
I: www.parklandshotel.aol

Pinewood ◆
197 Holdenhurst Road,
Bournemouth, Dorset BH8 8DG
T: (01202) 292684
I: www.pinewoodguesthouse.co.
uk

Rosedene Cottage Hotel ◆◆◆
St Peter's Road, Bournemouth,
Dorset BH1 2LA
T: (01202) 554102
F: (01202) 246995
E: enquiries@
rosedalecottagehotel.co.uk
I: www.rosedalecottagehotel.co.
uk

Silver How Hotel ◆◆◆
5 West Cliff Gardens,
Bournemouth, Dorset BH2 5HL
T: (01202) 551537
F: (01202) 551456
E: reservations@silverhowhotel.
co.uk
I: www.silverhowhotel.co.uk

Southern Comfort Hotel ◆◆◆
10 Earle Road, Alum Chine,
Bournemouth, Dorset BH4 8JQ
T: (01202) 767349
F: (01202) 752504
E: southerncomfort
bournemouth@hotmail.com

Southernhay Hotel ◆◆◆
42 Alum Chine Road,
Westbourne, Bournemouth,
Dorset BH4 8DX
T: (01202) 761251
F: (01202) 761251

Tiffanys ◆◆◆◆
31 Chine Crescent, West Cliff,
Bournemouth, Dorset BH2 5LB
T: (01202) 551424
F: (01202) 318559

Tralee Lodge ◆◆◆◆
95 St Michael's Road, West Cliff,
Bournemouth, Dorset BH2 5DS
T: (01202) 556246
F: (01202) 295229
E: hotel@tralee.co.uk
⊛

The Ventura Hotel ◆◆◆
1 Herbert Road, Bournemouth,
Dorset BH4 8HD
T: (01202) 761265
E: nancy@venturahotel.co.uk
I: www.venturahotel.co.uk

The Vine Hotel ◆◆◆
22 Southern Road, Southbourne,
Bournemouth, Dorset BH6 3SR
T: (01202) 428309

Whitley Court Hotel ◆◆◆
West Cliff Gardens,
Bournemouth, Dorset BH2 5HL
T: (01202) 551302
F: (01202) 551302

Willowdene Hotel
◆◆◆◆ SILVER AWARD
43 Grand Avenue, Southbourne,
Bournemouth, Dorset BH6 3SY
T: (01202) 425370
E: willowdenehotel@aol.com

Winter Dene Hotel ◆◆◆
11 Durley Road South, West
Cliff, Bournemouth, Dorset
BH2 5JH
T: (01202) 554150
F: (01202) 555426
I: www.bournemouth-hotels.co.
uk/winterdene

Wood Lodge Hotel ◆◆◆◆
10 Manor Road, East Cliff,
Bournemouth, Dorset BH1 3EY
T: (01202) 290891
F: (01202) 290892

Woodside Private Hotel ◆◆◆
29 Southern Road, Southbourne,
Bournemouth, Dorset BH6 3SR
T: (01202) 427213
F: (01202) 417609

Wrenwood Hotel ◆◆◆
11 Florence Road, Boscombe,
Bournemouth, Dorset BH5 1HH
T: (01202) 395086
F: (01202) 396511
E: bookings@wrenwood.co.uk
I: www.wrenwood.co.uk

Wychcote Hotel ◆◆◆◆
2 Somerville Road, West Cliff,
Bournemouth, Dorset BH2 5LH
T: (01202) 557898
F: (01202) 557898

BRACKNELL
Berkshire

Elizabeth House ◆◆◆
Wokingham Road, Bracknell,
Berkshire RG42 1PB
T: (01344) 868480

22 Evedon ◆◆
Birch Hill, Bracknell, Berkshire
RG12 7NF
T: (01344) 450637

BRAISHFIELD
Hampshire

Tregoyd House ◆◆
Crook Hill, Braishfield, Romsey,
Hampshire SO51 0QB
T: (01794) 368307
F: (01794) 368307
E: gill@tregoyd.fsnet.co.uk
I: www.geocities.
com/eureka/park/2485

BRAMSHAW
Hampshire

Forge Cottage ◆◆◆
Stocks Cross, Bramshaw,
Lyndhurst, Hampshire SO43 7JB
T: (023) 8081 3873 &
07850 305606
F: (023) 8081 3873
E: idavies1@compuserve.com
I: www.leisurehunt.com

BRANSGORE
Hampshire

The Corner House ◆◆◆◆
Betsy Lane, Bransgore,
Christchurch, Dorset BH23 8AQ
T: (01425) 673201

Wiltshire House
◆◆◆◆ SILVER AWARD
West Road, Bransgore,
Christchurch, Dorset BH23 8BD
T: (01425) 672450
F: (01425) 672450
E: hooper@wiltshirehouse.
freeserve.co.uk
I: www.newforest.demon.co.
uk/wiltshire.html

BRIGHSTONE
Isle of Wight

Buddlebrook Guest House
◆◆◆
Moortown Lane, Brighstone, Isle
of Wight PO30 4AN
T: (01983) 740381
F: (01983) 740381

The Bunnery ◆◆◆
Moortown Cottage, Moortown
Lane, Brighstone, Newport, Isle
of Wight PO30 4AN
T: (01983) 740820
E: carol@moortowncottage.
freeserve.co.uk
I: www.wightweb.cd.uk/bunnery

Chilton Farm ◆◆◆
Chilton Lane, Brighstone,
Newport, Isle of Wight
PO30 4DS
T: (01983) 740338
F: (01983) 741370
E: chfarm@globalnet.co.uk

The Lodge ◆◆◆◆
Main Road, Brighstone,
Newport, Isle of Wight PO30 4DJ
T: (01983) 741272
F: (01983) 741144
E: thelodge@yawmail.com
I: www.isle-of-wight.com/lodge/

BRILL
Buckinghamshire

Laplands Farm ◆◆◆◆
Ludgershall Road, Brill,
Aylesbury, Buckinghamshire
HP18 9TZ
T: (01844) 237888

Poletrees Farm ◆◆◆
Ludgershall Road, Brill,
Aylesbury, Buckinghamshire
HP18 9TZ
T: (01844) 238276
F: (01844) 238276

BRIZE NORTON
Oxfordshire

Anvil Croft ◆◆◆
64 Station Road, Brize Norton,
Oxfordshire OX18 3QA
T: (01993) 843655
F: (01993) 843655
E: judyleckyt@aol.com

Carpenters ◆◆◆
96 Station Road, Brize Norton,
Carterton, Oxfordshire
OX18 3QA
T: (01993) 844222 &
07889 246500

Foxbury Farmhouse ◆◆◆
Burford Road, Brize Norton,
Oxfordshire OX18 3NX
T: (01993) 844141
F: (01993) 844141

Kithicks Cottage ◆◆◆
50 Station Road, Brize Norton,
Oxfordshire OX18 3QA
T: (01993) 842472

The Long Barn ◆◆◆◆
26 Carterton Road, Brize Norton,
Oxfordshire OX18 3LY
T: (01993) 843309
F: (01993) 843309

The Manor House ◆◆◆◆
Manor Road, Brize Norton,
Oxford, Oxfordshire OX18 3NA
T: (01993) 846232

BROADSTONE
Dorset

Honey Lodge ◆◆◆◆
41 Dunyeats Road, Broadstone,
Dorset BH18 8AB
T: (01202) 694247

Tarven ◆◆◆
Corfe Lodge Road, Broadstone,
Dorset BH18 9NF
T: (01202) 694338

Weston Cottage ◆◆◆
6 Macaulay Road, Broadstone,
Dorset BH18 8AR
T: (01202) 699638
F: (01202) 699638
E: westoncot@aol.com

54A York Road ◆◆◆
Broadstone, Dorset BH18 8ET
T: (01202) 696938 & 257160
F: (01202) 604543

BROCKENHURST
Hampshire

Briardale ◆◆◆
11 Noel Close, Brockenhurst,
Hampshire SO42 7RP
T: (01590) 623946
F: (01590) 623946
E: briardale@brockenhurst.
fsbusiness.co.uk
I: www.brockenhurst.fsbusiness.
co.uk

Broad Oak
◆◆◆◆ SILVER AWARD
Broadlands, Brockenhurst,
Hampshire SO42 7SX
T: (01590) 622208 & (023) 8032
1198
F: (01590) 622208

Brookside Cottage ◆◆◆
Collyers Road, Brockenhurst,
Hampshire SO42 7SE
T: (01590) 623973

Caters Cottage ◆◆◆
Latchmoor, Brockenhurst,
Hampshire SO42 7UP
T: (01590) 623225

Evergreen ◆◆◆◆
Sway Road, Brockenhurst,
Hampshire SO42 7RX
T: (01590) 623411

The Filly Inn ◆◆◆
Lymington Road, Setley,
Brockenhurst, Hampshire
SO42 7UF
T: (01590) 623449
F: (01590) 622915
E: pub@fillyinn.co.uk
I: www.fillyinn.co.uk

Garlands Cottage
◆◆◆◆ SILVER AWARD
2 Garlands Cottage, Lyndhurst
Road, Brockenhurst, Hampshire
SO42 7RH
T: (01590) 623250
F: (01590) 623250
E: rkdalley@t.c.pco.uk

Goldenhayes ◆◆
9 Chestnut Road, Brockenhurst,
Hampshire SO42 7RF
T: (01590) 623743

Hilden Bed & Breakfast ◆◆◆
Southampton Road, Boldre,
Lymington, Hampshire SO41 8PT
T: (01590) 623682 &
07802 668658
F: (01590) 624444
E: aliab@totalise
I: www.newforestbandb-hilden.
co.uk

Jacmar Cottage ◆◆◆
Mill Lane, Brockenhurst,
Hampshire SO42 7UA
T: (01590) 622019

Little Heathers
◆◆◆◆ SILVER AWARD
Whitemoor Road, Brockenhurst,
Hampshire SO42 7QG
T: (01590) 623512 &
07889 141523
F: (01590) 624255
E: little_heathers@hotmail.com
I: www.newforest.demon.co.
uk/littleheathers.htm

Mansfield ◆◆◆◆
Partridge Road, Brockenhurst,
Hampshire SO42 7RZ
T: (01590) 623877
E: chippie.lorri@virgin.net

Old Oak ◆◆◆
Meerut Road, Brockenhurst,
Hampshire SO42 7TD
T: (01590) 623735
F: (01590) 623735

Porthilly ◆◆◆◆
Armstrong Road, Brockenhurst,
Hampshire SO42 7TA
T: (01590) 623182
F: (01590) 622178

Rose & Crown ◆◆◆◆
Lyndhurst Road, Brockenhurst,
Hampshire SO42 7RH
T: (01590) 622225
F: (01590) 623056

BUCKINGHAM
Buckinghamshire

5 Bristle Hill ◆◆◆
Buckingham, Buckinghamshire
MK18 1EZ
T: (01280) 814426 &
0780 1258455

Churchwell ◆◆
23 Church Street, Buckingham,
Buckinghamshire MK18 1BY
T: (01280) 815415 & 822223
F: (01280) 815415

Folly Farm ◆◆◆
Padbury, Buckingham,
Buckinghamshire MK18 2HS
T: (01296) 712413
F: (01296) 714923

White Hart Hotel ◆◆◆
Market Square, Buckingham,
Buckinghamshire MK18 1NL
T: (01280) 815151
F: (01280) 823165

BURFORD
Oxfordshire

Bee Cottage ◆◆◆
Fulbrook, Burford, Oxfordshire
OX18 4BZ
T: (01993) 822070
F: (01993) 822070
I: www.oxlink.co.uk/travel/

The Bird in Hand
◆◆◆◆ SILVER AWARD
Whiteoak Green, Hailey,
Oxfordshire OX8 5XP
T: (01993) 868321 & 868811
F: (01993) 868702
I: www.oxfordpages.co.
uk/birdinhand

Burford House Hotel
◆◆◆◆◆ SILVER AWARD
99 High Street, Burford, Oxford,
Oxfordshire OX18 4QA
T: (01993) 823151
F: (01993) 823240
E: stay@burfordhouse.co.uk
I: www.burford-house.co.uk.

Chevrons
Rating Applied For
Swan Lane, Burford, Oxford,
Oxfordshire OX18 4SH
T: (01993) 823416

The Fox Inn ◆◆◆
Great Barrington, Burford,
Oxfordshire OX18 4TB
T: (01451) 844385

The Highway ◆◆◆
117 High Street, Burford,
Oxford, Oxfordshire OX18 4RG
T: (01993) 822136
F: (01993) 824740
E: rbx20@dial.pipex.com
I: www.oxlink.co.uk/burford

Jonathan's at The Angel
◆◆◆◆◆ GOLD AWARD
14 Witney Street, Burford,
Oxford, Oxfordshire OX18 4SN
T: (01993) 822714
F: (01993) 822069
E: jo@theangel.uk.com

Manor Lodge ◆◆◆◆
Shilton, Burford, Oxfordshire
OX18 4AS
T: (01993) 841444
F: (01993) 841446
E: enquiries@manorlodgebnb.
co.uk
I: www.manorlodgebnb.co.uk

Merryfield ◆◆◆
High Street, Fifield, Oxford,
Oxfordshire OX7 6HL
T: (01993) 830517
E: jpmgtd@freeuk.com
I: www.home.freeuk.
com/jpmgtd

The Old Bell Foundry ◆◆◆◆
45 Witney Street, Burford,
Oxford, Oxfordshire OX18 4RX
T: (01993) 822234
F: (01993) 822234

Potters Hill Farm ◆◆◆
Leafield, Burford, Oxford,
Oxfordshire OX8 5QB
T: (01993) 878018 &
07711 045207
F: (01993) 878018
E: k.stanley@virgin.net
I: www.country-accom.co.
uk/potters-hill-farm

St Winnow ◆◆◆
160 The Hill, Burford,
Oxfordshire OX18 4QY
T: (01993) 823843

Tudor Cottage ◆◆◆
40 Witney Street, Burford,
Oxford, Oxfordshire OX8 4SN
T: (01993) 823251
F: (01993) 823251
E: tudorcottage@supanet.com

BURGHFIELD COMMON
Berkshire

Firlands ◆
Burghfield Common, Reading,
Berkshire RG7 3JN
T: (0118) 983 2414
F: (0118) 983 2414

BURLEY
Hampshire

Bay Tree House ◆◆◆
1 Clough Lane, Burley,
Ringwood, Hampshire BH24 4AE
T: (01425) 403215
F: (01425) 403215

Burbush Farm
◆◆◆◆◆ GOLD AWARD
Pound Lane, Burley, Ringwood,
Hampshire BH24 4EF
T: (01425) 403238 &
07711 381924
F: (01425) 403238
E: burbush-farm@excite.com
I: www.burbush-farm

Charlwood ◆◆◆◆
Longmead Road, Burley,
Ringwood, Hampshire BH24 4BY
T: (01425) 403242

Great Wells House
◆◆◆◆◆ GOLD AWARD
Beechwood Lane, Burley,
Ringwood, Hampshire BH24 4AS
T: (01425) 402302
F: (01425) 402302
E: chrisstewart@compuserve.
com

Holmans
◆◆◆◆ SILVER AWARD
Bisterne Close, Burley,
Ringwood, Hampshire BH24 4AZ
T: (01425) 402307
F: (01425) 402307

Little Deeracres ◆◆◆
Bisterne Close, Burley,
Ringwood, Hampshire BH24 4BA
T: (01425) 402477

BURSLEDON
Hampshire

Dodwell Cottage
◆◆◆◆ SILVER AWARD
Dodwell Lane, Bursledon,
Southampton, Hampshire
SO31 1AD
T: (023) 8040 6074
F: (023) 8040 6074

BUSCOT WICK
Oxfordshire

Weston Farm ◆◆◆◆
Buscot Wick, Faringdon,
Oxfordshire SN7 8DJ
T: (01367) 252222
F: (01367) 252222

CADMORE END
Buckinghamshire

South Fields ◆◆◆
Cadmore End, High Wycombe,
Buckinghamshire HP14 3PJ
T: (01494) 881976 &
07968 214389
F: (01494) 883765
E: crichtons@crichtonville.
freeserve.co.uk
I: www.crichtonville.freeserve.
co.uk

CADNAM
Hampshire

**The Old Well Hotel &
Restaurant ◆◆◆**
Romsey Road, Copythorne,
Southampton, Hampshire
SO40 2PE
T: (023) 8081 2321 & 8081 2700
F: (023) 8081 2158
I: www.yell.co.
uk/sites/old-well-restaurant/

The Willows ◆◆◆
Holly Farm, Pound Lane,
Copythorne, Cadnam,
Southampton, Hampshire
SO40 2PD
T: (023) 8081 3168

CANFORD CLIFFS
Dorset

Canford Haven ◆◆◆◆
97 Canford Cliffs Road, Canford
Cliffs, Poole, Dorset BH13 7EP
T: (01202) 701474 &
07710 694225
F: (01202) 706920
E: creasy@mcmail.com

Sea Witch Hotel ◆◆◆
47 Haven Road, Canford Cliffs,
Poole, Dorset BH13 7LH
T: (01202) 707697
F: (01202) 707666

CARISBROOKE
Isle of Wight

Alvington Manor Farm ◆◆◆
Carisbrooke, Newport, Isle of
Wight PO30 5SP
T: (01983) 523463
F: (01983) 523463

CARTERTON
Oxfordshire

The Priory Manor Farm
Rating Applied For
Manor Road, Brize Norton,
Carterton, Oxfordshire
OX18 3NA
T: (01993) 843062 & 0771 838
6264

CASHMOOR
Dorset

Cashmoor House ◆◆◆
Cashmoor, Blandford Forum,
Dorset DT11 8DN
T: (01725) 552339
E: spencer.jones@ukonline.co.
uk
I: www.cashmoorhouse.cjb.net

CASSINGTON
Oxfordshire

St Margaret's Lodge
Rating Applied For
The Green, Cassington, Oxford,
Oxfordshire OX8 1DN
T: (01865) 880361
F: (01993) 882799

CAVERSHAM
Berkshire

127 Upper Woodcote Road
Rating Applied For
Caversham, Reading, Berkshire
RG4 7LB
T: (0118) 947 3786
F: (0118) 947 3786

CHADLINGTON
Oxfordshire

Stone Croft ◆◆◆
East End, Chadlington, Oxford,
Oxfordshire OX7 3LX
T: (01608) 676551 &
07860 472605

CHALE
Isle of Wight

Chale Bay Farm ◆◆◆◆◆
Military Road, Chale, Ventnor,
Isle of Wight PO38 2JF
T: (01983) 730950
F: (01983) 730395
E: wightmouse@aol.com
I: www.trad-inns.co.
uk/clarendon

Cortina ◆◆◆
Gotten Lane, Chale, Ventnor, Isle
of Wight PO38 2HQ
T: (01983) 551292

Gotten Manor ◆◆◆
Gotten Lane, Chale, Ventnor, Isle
of Wight PO38 2HQ
T: (01983) 551368
F: (01983) 551368
E: caroline.smith6@virgin.net

Little Atherfield Farm ◆◆◆
Chale, Ventnor, Isle of Wight
PO38 2LQ
T: (01983) 551363
F: (01983) 551033
E: david's.farm@virgin.net

CHALFONT ST GILES
Buckinghamshire

Gorelands Corner ◆◆◆
Gorelands Lane, Chalfont St
Giles, Buckinghamshire
HP8 4HQ
T: (01494) 872689
F: (01494) 872689
E: bickfordcsg@compuserve.
com

Holmdale ◆◆◆◆
Cokes Lane, Little Chalfont,
Amersham, Chalfont St Giles,
Buckinghamshire HP8 4TX
T: (01494) 762527
F: (01494) 764701
E: judy@holmdalebb.freeserve.
co.uk
I: www.smoothhand.co.
uk/hotels/holmdale.html

Pickwicks ◆◆◆
Nightingales Lane, Chalfont St
Giles, Buckinghamshire HP8 4SH
T: (01494) 874123
F: (01494) 870442

The White Hart Inn ♦♦♦
Three Households, Chalfont St
Giles, Buckinghamshire HP8 4LP
T: (01494) 872441

CHALFONT ST PETER
Buckinghamshire

Whitewebbs ♦♦♦♦
Grange Road, Off Lower Road,
Chalfont St Peter, Gerrards
Cross, Buckinghamshire SL9 9AQ
T: (01753) 884105
F: (01753) 884105
E: marsh@argonet.co.uk

CHALGROVE
Oxfordshire

Cornerstones ♦♦♦
1 Cromwell Close, Chalgrove,
Oxfordshire OX44 7SE
T: (01865) 890298

CHANDLERS FORD
Hampshire

Blackbird Hill ♦♦♦
24 Ashbridge Rise, Chandlers
Ford, Eastleigh, Hampshire
SO53 1SA
T: (023) 8026 0398

Landfall ♦♦♦
133 Bournemouth Road,
Chandlers Ford, Eastleigh,
Hampshire SO53 3HA
T: (023) 8025 4801
F: (023) 8025 4801

Little Oak ♦♦♦
176 Hiltingbury Road, Chandlers
Ford, Eastleigh, Hampshire
SO53 5NS
T: (023) 8090 3063

Rawa ♦♦♦♦
24 Baddesley Road, Chandlers
Ford, Eastleigh, Hampshire
SO53 5NG
T: (023) 8026 3043 &
07703 137387
E: forshaw1@tinyonline.co.uk

Thornbury ♦♦♦♦
243 Winchester Road, Chandlers
Ford, Eastleigh, Hampshire
SO53 2DX
T: (023) 8026 0703 &
07775 862133
F: (023) 8061 3100

CHARLBURY
Oxfordshire

Banbury Hill Farm ♦♦♦♦
Enstone Road, Charlbury,
Oxford, Oxfordshire OX7 3JH
T: (01608) 810314
F: (01608) 811891

Tanyer's House ♦♦♦♦
Hundley Way, Charlbury, Oxford
OX7 3QX
T: (01608) 811711 &
0780 3867424
E: jskelton@charlbury56.
freeserve.co.uk
I: www.charlbury56.freeserve.co.
uk

CHARLTON MARSHALL
Dorset

Keston House
♦♦♦♦ SILVER AWARD
314 Bournemouth Road,
Charlton Marshall, Blandford
Forum, Dorset DT11 9NQ
T: (01258) 451973
F: (01258) 451973

CHARTRIDGE
Buckinghamshire

Qastina
Rating Applied For
Cogdells Lane, Chartridge,
Chesham, Buckinghamshire
HP5 2TW
T: (01494) 837776
F: (01494) 837949

CHESHAM
Buckinghamshire

49 Lowndes Avenue ♦♦
Chesham, Buckinghamshire
HP5 2HH
T: (01494) 792647

Wychelm Farm ♦♦
Pednor Vale, Chesham,
Buckinghamshire HP5 2ST
T: (01494) 782309

CHESTERTON
Oxfordshire

Larchmont ♦♦♦
Alchester Road, Chesterton,
Bicester, Oxfordshire OX6 8UN
T: (01869) 245033
F: (01869) 245033

CHIEVELEY
Berkshire

19 Heathfields ♦♦♦
Chieveley, Newbury, Berkshire
RG20 8TW
T: (01635) 248179
F: (01635) 248799

CHILBOLTON
Hampshire

Sycamores B & B
Rating Applied For
Meadow View, Chilbolton,
Stockbridge, Hampshire
SO20 6AZ
T: (01264) 860380
E: maureen@sycamoreresbb.
freeserve.co.uk
I: www.sycamoresbb.freeserve.
co.uk/sycamores2

Uplands
Rating Applied For
Drove Road, Chilbolton,
Stockbridge, Hampshire
SO20 6AD
T: (01264) 860650
F: (01264) 860650
E: june@haymanjoyce.freeserve.
co.uk

CHILDREY
Oxfordshire

Ridgeway House
♦♦♦♦ SILVER AWARD
West Street, Childrey, Wantage,
Oxfordshire OX12 9UL
T: (01235) 751538 &
07774 182154
F: (01235) 751538
E: ROBERTSFAMILY@
COMPUSERVE.COM

CHIPPING NORTON
Oxfordshire

Kings Arms Hotel ♦♦♦
18 West Street, Chipping
Norton, Oxfordshire OX7 5AA
T: (01608) 642668
F: (01608) 646673

Leckford ♦♦♦
10 Cooper Close, Chipping
Norton, Oxfordshire OX7 5BQ
T: (01608) 644571

**Southcombe Lodge Guest
House** ♦♦♦
Southcombe, Chipping Norton,
Oxfordshire OX7 5QH
T: (01608) 643068
F: (01608) 642948
E: georgefinlysouth
combelodge@tinyworld.co.uk

CHOLDERTON
Hampshire

Parkhouse Motel ♦♦♦♦
Cholderton, Salisbury, Wiltshire
SP4 0EG
T: (01980) 629256
F: (01980) 629256

CHRISTCHURCH
Dorset

The Beech Tree ♦♦♦♦
2 Stuart Road, Highcliffe,
Christchurch, Dorset BH23 5JS
T: (01425) 272038

Belvedere Guest House ♦♦
3 Twynham Avenue,
Christchurch, Dorset BH23 1QU
T: (01202) 485978
F: (01202) 485978
⊚

Beverly Glen Guest House
♦♦♦♦
1 Stuart Road, Highcliffe,
Christchurch, Dorset BH23 5JS
T: (01425) 273811

Bure Farm House ♦♦♦
107 Bure Lane, Friars Cliff,
Christchurch, Dorset BH23 4DN
T: (01425) 275498

Cafe 39 – The Pines Hotel
♦♦♦
39 Mudeford, Christchurch,
Dorset BH23 3NQ
T: (01202) 475121 & 482393
F: (01202) 487666
E: pineshotelcafe39@ic24.net
I: www.mudeford.com

Druid House ♦♦♦♦♦
26 Sopers Lane, Christchurch,
Dorset BH23 1JE
T: (01202) 485615
F: (01202) 473484
E: druid_house@yahoo.com
⊚

Grosvenor Lodge ♦♦♦♦
53 Stour Road, Christchurch,
Dorset BH23 1LN
T: (01202) 499008 &
07970 979881
F: (01202) 486041
E: grosvenorlodge@bigfoot.com
I: www/grosvenorlodge.co.uk

Rothesay Hotel ♦♦♦♦
175 Lymington Road,
Christchurch, Dorset BH23 4JS
T: (01425) 274172
F: (01425) 270780
E: rothesay.hotel@virgin.net
⊚

Salmons Reach Guest House
♦♦
28 Stanpit, Christchurch, Dorset
BH23 3LZ
T: (01202) 477315
F: (01202) 477315

Seapoint
Rating Applied For
121 Mudeford, Christchurch,
Dorset BH23 4AF
T: (01425) 279541
F: (01425) 279541

Stour Lodge Guest House
♦♦♦
54 Stour Road, Christchurch,
Dorset BH23 1LW
T: (01202) 486902
E: kcat@stourbridge.fsnet.co.uk

Stour Villa ♦♦♦
67 Stour Road, Christchurch,
Dorset BH23 1LN
T: (01202) 483379
F: (01202) 483379

Three Gables ♦♦♦
11 Wickfield Avenue,
Christchurch, Dorset BH23 1JB
T: (01202) 481166

The White House ♦♦♦♦
428 Lymington Road, Highcliffe,
Christchurch, Dorset BH23 5HF
T: (01425) 271279
F: (01425) 276900
E: thewhitehouse@themail.co.
uk
I: www.thewhite-house.co.uk

CHURCHILL
Oxfordshire

The Forge ♦♦♦♦
Churchill, Chipping Norton,
Oxfordshire OX7 6NJ
T: (01608) 658173
F: (01608) 659262
E: jon.price1@virgin.net
I: www.theforge.co.uk

COLE HENLEY
Hampshire

Long Barrow House ♦♦♦♦
Cole Henley, Whitchurch,
Hampshire RG28 7QJ
T: (01256) 895980
⊚

COLEHILL
Dorset

Long Lane Farmhouse ♦♦♦♦
Long Lane, Colehill, Wimborne
Minster, Dorset BH21 7AQ
T: (01202) 887829
E: paddysmyth@aol.com
I: www.eastdorsetdc.gov.
uk/tourism

COLESHILL
Buckinghamshire

Pond Cottage ♦♦♦♦
Village Road, Coleshill,
Amersham, Buckinghamshire
HP7 0LH
T: (01494) 728177
F: (01494) 729168
E: pondcott@msn.com

COLWELL BAY
Isle of Wight

Chine Cottage ♦♦♦
Colwell Chine Road, Colwell Bay,
Freshwater, Isle of Wight
PO40 9NP
T: (01983) 752808
E: enq1999@hotmail.com

Rockstone Cottage ♦♦♦♦
Colwell Chine Road, Colwell Bay,
Freshwater, Isle of Wight
PO40 9NR
T: (01983) 753723
F: (01983) 753721
E: rockstonecottage.co.uk
I: www.rockstonecottage.co.uk

Shorefield House
♦♦♦♦ SILVER AWARD
Madeira Lane, Colwell Bay, Isle
of Wight PO40 9SP
T: (01983) 752232

COMPTON
Hampshire
Manor House ◆◆
Place Lane, Compton,
Winchester, Hampshire
SO21 2BA
T: (01962) 712162

COMPTON ABBAS
Dorset
The Old Forge ◆◆◆◆
Fanners Yard, Compton Abbas,
Shaftesbury, Dorset SP7 0NQ
T: (01747) 811881
F: (01747) 811881
⊛

CONNIBURROW
Buckinghamshire
Wistaria Guest House ◆◆
12 Yarrow Place, Conniburrow,
Milton Keynes, Buckinghamshire
MK14 7AX
T: (01908) 607613

COOKHAM
Berkshire
Wylie Cottage ◆◆◆
School Lane, Cookham,
Maidenhead, Berkshire SL6 9QJ
T: (01628) 520106
F: (01628) 520106
E: crowegc@cwcom.net

COOMBE KEYNES
Dorset
Highfield ◆◆◆
Coombe Keynes, Wareham,
Dorset BH20 5PS
T: (01929) 463208
F: (01929) 463208
⊛

West Coombe Farmhouse
◆◆◆◆ GOLD AWARD
Coombe Keynes, Wareham,
Dorset BH20 5PS
T: (01929) 462889
F: (01929) 405863
E: WEST.COOMBE.
FARMHOUSE@BARCLAYS.NET
I: WWW.
WESTCOOMBEFARMHOUSE.CO.
UK
⊛

CORFE CASTLE
Dorset
Bradle Farmhouse ◆◆◆◆
Bradle Farm, Church Knowle,
Wareham, Dorset BH20 5NU
T: (01929) 480712
F: (01929) 481144
E: hole.bradle@farmersweekly.
net
I: www.smoothhound.co.
uk/hotels/bradle.html

COWES
Isle of Wight
Comforts Gate
Rating Applied For
108 Pallance Road, Northwood,
Cowes, Isle of Wight PO31 8LS
T: (01983) 290342 & 299436
F: (01983) 297810

Furzyhurst Farmhouse ◆◆◆
69 Oxford Street, Northwood,
Cowes, Isle of Wight PO31 8PT
T: (01983) 292513
F: (01983) 292513
E: mary.mcbride@pemail.net

Halcyone Villa ◆◆◆
Grove Road, Cowes, Isle of
Wight PO31 7JP
T: (01983) 291334
E: sandra@halcyone.freeserve.
co.uk
I: www.halcyonevills.freeuk.com

Noss Mayo ◆◆◆◆
66a Baring Road, Cowes, Isle of
Wight PO31 8DW
T: (01983) 200266
E: nossmayo.one@freeuk.com

Skye Villa Guest House ◆◆
11 Newport Road, Cowes, Isle of
Wight PO31 7PA
T: (01983) 292803 &
07768 960732
F: (01983) 292803
E: sharonounsworth@hotmail.
com

CRANBORNE
Dorset
Acorns ◆◆◆◆
55a The Green, Woodlands,
Wimborne Minster, Dorset
BH21 8LN
T: (01202) 823991
E: wgac.@tesco.net

The Fleur de Lys ◆◆◆◆
5 Wimborne Street, Cranborne,
Wimborne Minster, Dorset
BH21 5PP
T: (01725) 517282 & 517765
F: (01725) 517631
E: fleurdelys@btinternet.com
I: www.btinternet.
com/fleurdelys/

La Fosse at Cranborne ◆◆◆
London House, The Square,
Cranborne, Wimborne Minster,
Dorset BH21 5PR
T: (01725) 517604
F: (01725) 517778
⊛

CUBLINGTON
Buckinghamshire
Homeground Farm ◆◆◆
Ridings Way, Cublington,
Leighton Buzzard, Bedfordshire
LU7 0LW
T: (01296) 681107 &
07968 264769
F: (01296) 681107

DAMERHAM
Hampshire
The Compasses Inn ◆◆◆
Damerham, Fordingbridge,
Hampshire SP6 3HQ
T: (01725) 518231
F: (01725) 518880

DEDDINGTON
Oxfordshire
Hill Barn ◆◆
Milton Gated Road, Deddington,
Banbury, Oxfordshire OX15 0TS
T: (01869) 338631
F: (01869) 338631

The Leadenporch House
Rating Applied For
New Street, Deddington,
Banbury, Oxfordshire OX15 0SP
T: (01869) 338791 &
0789 9865359
E: phethean@clara.co.uk
⊛

The Little House ◆◆◆◆
Clifton Road, Deddington,
Banbury, Oxfordshire OX15 0TP
T: (01869) 337319
F: (01869) 337355
E: clarkejs@msn.com

Stonecrop Guest House ◆◆
Hempton Road, Deddington,
Banbury, Oxfordshire OX15 0QH
T: (01869) 338335 & 338496
F: (01869) 338505

DINTON
Buckinghamshire
Perryfield ◆◆◆◆
New Road, Dinton, Aylesbury,
Buckinghamshire HP17 8UT
T: (01296) 748265 &
07885 273574
F: (01296) 747765
E: 106402.270@compuserve.
com

DORCHESTER ON THAMES
Oxfordshire
Harley's Lodge ◆◆◆◆
14 Bridge End, Dorchester on
Thames, Wallingford,
Oxfordshire OX10 7JP
T: (01865) 340830 &
07850 394090
F: (01865) 340248
E: tsawtell@harleys-lodge.
freeserve.co.uk
I: www.scoot.co.
uk/harleys_lodge/

DOWNLEY
Buckinghamshire
Avon Guest House ◆◆
2 Grays Lane, Downley, High
Wycombe, Buckinghamshire
HP13 5TZ
T: (01494) 523014

DRAYTON PARSLOW
Buckinghamshire
The Three Horseshoes ◆◆◆
10 Main Road, Drayton Parslow,
Milton Keynes, Buckinghamshire
MK17 0JS
T: (01296) 720296
F: (01296) 720841
E: 3shoes@threehorseshoes.
idps.co.uk
I: www.threehorseshoes.
free-online.co.uk

DUMMER
Hampshire
Oakdown Farm Bungalow
◆◆◆
Oakdown Farm, Dummer,
Basingstoke, Hampshire
RG23 7LR
T: (01256) 397218
⊛

DUNBRIDGE
Hampshire
The Mill Arms ◆◆◆◆
Barley Hill, Dunbridge, Romsey,
Hampshire SO51 0LF
T: (01794) 340401
F: (01794) 340401
E: the-mill-arms@river-dun.
demon.co.uk
I: www.river-dun.demon.co.uk/

EARLEY
Berkshire
Elmhurst Hotel ◆◆
51 Church Road, Earley,
Reading, Berkshire RG6 1EY
T: (01189) 661588 & 265273
F: (01189) 352180

EAST COWES
Isle of Wight
Crossways House ◆◆◆
Crossways Road, East Cowes,
Isle of Wight PO32 6LJ
T: (01983) 298282 &
07771 623129
F: (01983) 298282

The Doghouse ◆◆◆◆
Crossways Road, East Cowes,
Isle of Wight PO32 6LJ
T: (01983) 293677

EAST END
Oxfordshire
The Leather Bottel Guest
House ◆◆◆
East End, North Leigh, Witney,
Oxfordshire OX8 6PX
T: (01993) 882174 &
07711 782302

EAST HOLME
Dorset
Priory Farm ◆◆◆◆
East Holme, Wareham, Dorset
BH20 6AG
T: (01929) 553832
F: (01929) 553832
E: goldpriory@aol.com
I: www.members.aol.
com/goldpriory/
⊛

EAST MEON
Hampshire
Coombe Cross House & Stables
◆◆◆
Coombe Road, East Meon,
Petersfield, Hampshire
GU32 1HQ
T: (01730) 823298
F: (01730) 823515

Drayton Cottage
◆◆◆◆ SILVER AWARD
East Meon, Petersfield,
Hampshire GU32 1PW
T: (01730) 823472 &
07703 642085

Dunvegan Cottage ◆◆◆
Frogmore Lane, East Meon,
Petersfield, Hampshire
GU32 1QJ
T: (01730) 823213
F: (01730) 823858
E: dunvegan@btinternet.com
🛉

EAST STOUR
Dorset
Aysgarth ◆◆◆◆
Back Street, East Stour,
Gillingham, Dorset SP8 5JY
T: (01747) 838351
E: aysgarth@lineone.net

EAST WELLOW
Hampshire
Country Views B & B
Rating Applied For
Willowbend, Dunwood Hill, East
Wellow, Romsey, Hampshire
SO51 6FD
T: (01794) 514735 & 521867
F: (01794) 521867

Roselea ◆◆◆◆
Hamdown Crescent, East
Wellow, Romsey, Hampshire
SO51 6BJ
T: (01794) 323262
F: (01794) 323262
E: pennyc@tcp.co.uk

EDGCOTT
Buckinghamshire
Perry Manor Farm ♦♦
Buckingham Road, Edgcott,
Aylesbury, Buckinghamshire
HP18 0TR
T: (01296) 770257

EMBERTON
Buckinghamshire
Ekeney House ♦♦♦
Wood Farm, Emberton, Olney,
Buckinghamshire MK46 5JH
T: (01234) 711133
F: (01234) 711133

EMSWORTH
Hampshire
Apple Blossom ♦♦♦
19A Bosmere Gardens,
Emsworth, Hampshire PO10 7NP
T: (01243) 372201

Bunbury Lodge ♦♦♦
10 West Road, Emsworth,
Hampshire PO10 4JT
T: (01243) 432030
F: (01243) 432030

Jingles Hotel ♦♦♦
77 Horndean Road, Emsworth,
Hampshire PO10 7PU
T: (01243) 373755
F: (01243) 373755
E: info@jingleshotel.freeserve.
co.uk

The Merry Hall Hotel ♦♦♦
73 Horndean Road, Emsworth,
Hampshire PO10 7PU
T: (01243) 431377
F: (01243) 431411

EPWELL
Oxfordshire
Yarnhill Farm ♦♦♦
Epwell, Banbury, Oxfordshire
OX15 6JA
T: (01295) 780250

EWELME
Oxfordshire
Mays Farm ♦♦♦♦
Ewelme, Wallingford,
Oxfordshire OX10 6QF
T: (01491) 641294 & 642056
F: (01491) 641697

EYNSHAM
Oxfordshire
Baker's Restaurant & Hotel Ltd
♦♦♦♦
4 Lombard Street, Eynsham,
Witney, Oxfordshire OX8 1HT
T: (01865) 881888
F: (01865) 883537

Grange House ♦♦♦
Station Road, Eynsham, Witney,
Oxfordshire OX8 1HX
T: (01865) 880326 &
07803 012805
F: (01865) 880326
E: jh4lhgd@aol.com
I: www.oxfordcity.co.
uk/accom/grangehouse

The White Hart Inn ♦♦♦♦
31 Newland Street, Eynsham,
Oxford, Oxfordshire OX8 1LB
T: (01865) 880711
F: (01865) 880169

FAREHAM
Hampshire
Avenue House Hotel ♦♦♦
22 The Avenue, Fareham,
Hampshire PO14 1NS
T: (01329) 232175
F: (01329) 232196

Catisfield Cottage Guest House
♦♦
1 Catisfield Lane, Catisfield,
Fareham, Hampshire PO15 5NW
T: (01329) 843301
F: (01329) 841652

Seven Sevens Guest House
♦♦♦
56 Hill Head Road, Hill Head,
Fareham, Hampshire PO14 3JL
T: (01329) 662408

Springfield Hotel ♦♦♦
67 The Avenue, Fareham,
Hampshire PO14 1PE
T: (01329) 828325

FARINGDON
Oxfordshire
Ashen Copse Farm ♦♦♦
Coleshill, Faringdon, Oxfordshire
SN6 7PU
T: (01367) 240175
F: (01367) 241418
E: pat@hodd.demon.co.uk
I: www.hodd.demon.co.uk

Bowling Green Farm ♦♦♦
Stanford Road, Faringdon,
Oxfordshire SN7 8EZ
T: (01367) 240229
F: (01367) 242568
E: data@bowling-green-farm.
co.uk
I: www.leading.co.uk/bgfarm

FARNBOROUGH
Hampshire
Colebrook Guest House ♦♦
56 Netley Street, Farnborough,
Hampshire GU14 6AT
T: (01252) 542269
F: (01252) 542269

**The White Residence Town
House Hotel**
♦♦♦♦ GOLD AWARD
Farnborough Park, 76 Avenue
Road, Farnborough, Hampshire
GU14 7BG
T: (01252) 375510 & 371817
F: (01252) 655567
E: info@countyapartments.com
I: www.countryapartment.co.uk

FAWLEY
Hampshire
Walcot House ♦♦
Blackfield Road, Fawley,
Southampton, Hampshire
SO45 1ED
T: (023) 8089 1344
F: (023) 8089 0748

FIFEHEAD ST QUINTON
Dorset
Lower Fifehead Farm ♦♦♦♦
Fifehead St Quinton,
Sturminster Newton, Dorset
DT10 2AP
T: (01258) 817335

FIFIELD
Oxfordshire
The Merrymouth Inn ♦♦♦
Stow Road, Fifield, Oxford,
Oxfordshire OX7 6HR
T: (01993) 831652
F: (01993) 830840
E: alan.flaherty@btclick.com

FORDINGBRIDGE
Hampshire
A Green Patch ♦♦♦♦
Furze Hill, Fordingbridge,
Hampshire SP6 2PS
T: (01425) 652387
F: (01425) 656594

Appletree ♦♦♦♦
159 Station Road, Alderholt,
Fordingbridge, Hampshire
SP6 3AZ
T: (01425) 652154

The Augustus John ♦♦♦♦
116 Station Road,
Fordingbridge, Hampshire
SP6 1DG
T: (01425) 652098
E: peter@augustusjohn.
fordingbridge.com
I: www.augustusjohn.
fordingbridge.com

Broomy ♦♦♦♦
Ogdens, Fordingbridge,
Hampshire SP6 2PY
T: (01425) 653264

Drummond House ♦♦♦♦
Bowerwood Road,
Fordingbridge, Hampshire
SP6 1BL
T: (01425) 653165
E: drumbb@btinternet.com

Hillbury ♦♦♦♦
2 Fir Tree Hill, Camel Green
Road, Alderholt, Fordingbridge,
Hampshire SP6 3AY
T: (01425) 652582
F: (01425) 657587
I: www.smoothhound.co.
uk/hotels/hillbury.html

Noarlunga ♦♦♦♦
16 Broomfield Drive, Alderholt,
Fordingbridge, Hampshire
SP6 3HY
T: (01425) 650491

Primrose Cottage ♦♦♦♦
Newgrounds, Godshill,
Fordingbridge, Hampshire
SP6 2LJ
T: (01425) 650447 &
07712 469394
F: (01425) 650447
E: ann@blake98.freeserve.co.uk

The Three Lions
♦♦♦♦♦ GOLD AWARD
Stuckton, Fordingbridge,
Hampshire SP6 2HF
T: (01425) 652489
F: (01425) 656144

FREELAND
Oxfordshire
Three Oaks ♦♦♦
26 Wroslyn Road, Freeland,
Witney, Oxfordshire OX8 8HH
T: (01993) 881473
E: gayle_cook@talk21.com

Wintersbrook
♦♦♦♦ SILVER AWARD
15 Broadmarsh Lane, Freeland,
Witney, Oxfordshire OX8 8QP
T: (01993) 883602

FRESHWATER
Isle of Wight
Brookside Forge Hotel ♦♦♦
Brookside Road, Freshwater, Isle
of Wight PO40 9ER
T: (01983) 754644

Royal Standard Hotel ♦♦♦
School Green Road, Freshwater,
Isle of Wight PO40 9AJ
T: (01983) 753227
E: sue.stephenson84@freeserve.
co.uk

Ruskin Lodge ♦♦
Guyers Road, Freshwater Bay,
Isle of Wight PO40 9QA
T: 07071 225313 &
(01983) 756604
F: (01983) 756604
E: ruskiniow@aol.com
I: www.isle-of-wight.uk.
com/ruskin-lodge

Seahorses ♦♦♦♦
Victoria Road, Freshwater, Isle of
Wight PO40 9PP
T: (01983) 752574
F: (01983) 752574
E: lanterncom@aol.com

2 Tollgate Cottages ♦♦♦
Wilmingham Lane, Freshwater,
Isle of Wight PO40 9UX
T: (01983) 756535 &
07770 774870
E: mark@tollgateiow.fsnet.co.uk
I: www.iow.uk.
com/tollgate-cottages

Traidcraft ♦♦
119 School Green Road,
Freshwater, Isle of Wight
PO40 9AZ
T: (01983) 752451

FRESHWATER BAY
Isle of Wight
Rosemary Cottage
Rating Applied For
Gate Lane, Freshwater Bay, Isle
of Wight PO40 9RD
T: (01983) 756184

Wighthaven ♦♦♦♦
Afton Road, Freshwater Bay, Isle
of Wight PO40 9TT
T: (01983) 753184 & 755957

FRIETH
Buckinghamshire
St Katharines ♦♦♦
Parmoor, Frieth, Henley-on-
Thames, Oxfordshire RG9 6NN
T: (01494) 881037
F: (01494) 881037

FRITHAM
Hampshire
Amberwood Cottage ♦♦♦
Fritham, Lyndhurst, Hampshire
SO43 7HL
T: (023) 8081 2359

Fritham Farm ♦♦♦♦
Fritham, Lyndhurst, Hampshire
SO43 7HH
T: (023) 8081 2333
F: (023) 8081 2333

Primrose Cottage ◆◆◆
Fritham, Lyndhurst, Hampshire
SO43 7HH
T: (023) 8081 2272
I: www.s-h-systems.co.
uk/hotels/primrose.html

GARSINGTON
Oxfordshire
Hill Copse Cottage ◆◆◆
Wheatley Road, Garsington,
Oxford, Oxfordshire OX44 9DT
T: (01865) 361478
F: (01865) 361478

GATCOMBE
Isle of Wight
Freewaters ◆◆◆◆
New Barn Lane, Gatcombe,
Newport, Isle of Wight
PO30 3EQ
T: (01983) 721439
F: (01983) 294173
E: john@pitstopmodels.demon.
co.uk

Little Gatcombe Farm ◆◆◆◆
New Barn Lane, Gatcombe,
Newport, Isle of Wight
PO30 3EG
T: (01983) 721580
I: www.visitbritain.com

GAWCOTT
Buckinghamshire
Radclive Dairy Farm
Rating Applied For
Radclive Road, Gawcott,
Buckingham, Buckinghamshire
MK18 4AA
T: (01280) 813433
F: (01280) 813433

GERRARDS CROSS
Buckinghamshire
15 Howards Wood Drive ◆◆◆
Gerrards Cross,
Buckinghamshire SL9 7HR
T: (01753) 884911
F: (01753) 884911
E: james.crosby@tesco.net

GIFFARD PARK
Buckinghamshire
Giffard House ◆◆◆
10 Broadway Avenue, Giffard
Park, Milton Keynes,
Buckinghamshire MK14 5QF
T: (01908) 618868
F: (01908) 618868
E: phil.mason@lineone.net

GODSHILL
Hampshire
Croft Cottage ◆◆◆
Southampton Road, Godshill,
Fordingbridge, Hampshire
SP6 2LE
T: (01425) 657955 &
07977 142745

Vennards Cottage ◆◆◆
Newgrounds, Godshill,
Fordingbridge, Hampshire
SP6 2LJ
T: (01425) 652644
F: (01425) 656646
E: gillian.bridgeman@virgin.net

GORING
Oxfordshire
The John Barleycorn ◆
Manor Road, Goring, Reading,
Berkshire RG8 9DP
T: (01491) 872509

Miller of Mansfield ◆◆◆
High Street, Goring, Reading,
Berkshire RG8 9AW
T: (01491) 872829
F: (01491) 874200

14 Mountfield ◆◆
Wallingford Road, Goring,
Reading, Berkshire RG8 0BE
T: (01491) 872029

GOSPORT
Hampshire
Spring Garden Guest House ◆
Spring Garden Lane, Gosport,
Hampshire PO12 1LP
T: (023) 9251 0336
F: (023) 9251 0336

West Wind Guest House
◆◆◆◆
197 Portsmouth Road, Lee on
the Solent, Gosport, Hampshire
PO13 9AA
T: (023) 9255 2550
F: (023) 9255 4657
E: maggie@west-wind.co.uk
I: www.west-wind.co.uk

GREAT KINGSHILL
Buckinghamshire
Hatches Farm ◆◆
Hatches Lane, Great Kingshill,
High Wycombe,
Buckinghamshire HP15 6DS
T: (01494) 713125
F: (01494) 714666

GREAT TEW
Oxfordshire
The Falkland Arms ◆◆◆◆
Great Tew, Chipping Norton,
Oxfordshire OX7 4DB
T: (01608) 683653
E: sjcourage@btconnect.com
I: www.banbury-cross.co.
uk/falklandsarms/

GURNARD
Isle of Wight
Hillbrow Private Hotel ◆◆◆◆
Tuttons Hill, Gurnard, Cowes,
Isle of Wight PO31 8JA
T: (01983) 297240
F: (01983) 297240

The Woodvale Hotel ◆◆◆
1 Princes Esplanade, Gurnard,
Cowes, Isle of Wight PO31 8LE
T: (01983) 292037
F: (01983) 292037

HADDENHAM
Buckinghamshire
The Majors ◆◆◆◆
19-21 Townside, Haddenham,
Aylesbury, Buckinghamshire
HP17 8BQ
T: (01844) 292654
F: (01844) 299050

HAMBLE
Hampshire
Farthings Bed & Breakfast
◆◆◆◆
Farthings, School Lane, Hamble,
Southampton, Hampshire
SO31 4JD
T: (023) 8045 2009 &
07979 746717
F: (023) 8045 2009
E: straker@hamble2.fsnet.co.uk
I: www.hamble-le-rice.co.uk

HAMBLEDON
Hampshire
Cams ◆◆◆
Hambledon, Waterlooville,
Hampshire PO7 4SP
T: (023) 9263 2865
F: (023) 9263 2691

Mornington House ◆◆◆
Speltham Hill, Hambledon,
Waterlooville, Hampshire
PO7 4RU
T: (023) 9263 2704
F: (023) 9263 2704

Nightingale Cottage
◆◆◆◆ SILVER AWARD
Hoegate, Hambledon,
Waterlooville, Hampshire
PO7 4RD
T: (023) 9263 2447
F: (023) 9263 2027
E: johnfitt@business.ntl.com

HAMWORTHY
Dorset
Harbourside Guest House
◆◆◆
195 Blandford Road,
Hamworthy, Poole, Dorset
BH15 4AX
T: (01202) 673053

Holes Bay B & B ◆◆◆
365 Blandford Road,
Hamworthy, Poole, Dorset
BH15 4JL
T: (01202) 672069

ITP Lodge ◆◆◆◆
53 Branksea Avenue,
Hamworthy, Poole, Dorset
BH15 4DP
T: (01202) 673419 &
07710 725301
F: (01202) 667260
E: johnrenate@lineone.net

San-Michele Guest House
◆◆◆
237 Blandford Road,
Hamworthy, Poole, Dorset
BH15 4AZ
T: (01202) 675442

Seashells ◆◆◆
4 Lake Road, Hamworthy, Poole,
Dorset BH15 4LH
T: (01202) 671921
F: (01202) 671921

HANSLOPE
Buckinghamshire
Woad Farm ◆◆◆
Tathall End, Hanslope, Milton
Keynes, Buckinghamshire
MK19 7NE
T: (01908) 510985
F: (01908) 510985
E: mail@sarahstacey.freeserve.
co.uk

HAVANT
Hampshire
High Towers ◆◆◆
14 Portsdown Hill Road,
Bedhampton, Havant,
Hampshire PO9 3JY
T: (023) 9247 1748

HAYLING ISLAND
Hampshire
Broad Oak Hotel ◆◆◆
Copse Lane, Hayling Island,
Hampshire PO11 0QB
T: (023) 9246 2333 & 9246 4205
E: broadoak@hay-isle.demon.
co.uk

The Rook Hollow Hotel ◆◆◆
84 Church Road, Hayling Island,
Hampshire PO11 0NX
T: (023) 9246 7080
F: (023) 9246 1078

Tide Reach ◆◆◆
214 Southwood Road, Hayling
Island, Hampshire PO11 9QQ
T: (023) 9246 7828 &
07798 921236
F: (023) 9246 7828

White House ◆◆◆
250 Havant Road, Hayling
Island, Hampshire PO11 0LN
T: (023) 9246 3464

HAZLEMERE
Buckinghamshire
Vardar
Rating Applied For
321 Amersham Road,
Hazlemere, High Wycombe,
Buckinghamshire HP15 7PX
T: (01494) 718333

HEADINGTON
Oxfordshire
Conifers Guest House ◆◆◆
116 The Slade, Headington,
Oxford, Oxfordshire OX3 7DX
T: (01865) 763055
F: (01865) 742232

HEDGE END
Hampshire
Copper Beeches House Hotel ◆
72 Lower Northam Road, Hedge
End, Southampton, Hampshire
SO30 4FT
T: (01489) 787447

Montana Guest House ◆◆◆
90 Lower Northam Road, Hedge
End, Southampton, Hampshire
SO30 4FT
T: (01489) 782797
F: (01489) 782797

HEELANDS
Buckinghamshire
Rovers Return
Rating Applied For
49 Langcliffe Drive, Heelands,
Milton Keynes, Buckinghamshire
MK13 7LA
T: (01908) 310465

HENLEY-ON-THAMES
Oxfordshire
Alftrudis ◆◆◆◆
8 Norman Avenue, Henley-on-
Thames, Oxfordshire RG9 1SG
T: (01491) 573099 &
07802 408643
F: (01491) 411747
E: b&b@alftrudis.fsnet.co.uk

Avalon ◆◆◆
36 Queen Street, Henley-on-
Thames, Oxfordshire RG9 1AP
T: (01491) 577829
E: avalon@henleybb.fsnet.co.uk
I: www.henleybb.fsnet.co.uk

Azalea House ♦♦♦
55 Deanfield Road, Henley-on-Thames, Oxfordshire RG9 1UU
T: (01491) 576407
F: (01491) 411123
I: masseyp@globalnet.co.uk

4 Coldharbour Close ♦♦♦
Henley-on-Thames, Oxfordshire RG9 1QF
T: (01491) 575297
F: (01491) 575297
E: jennybower@email.com
I: www.henley-bb.freeserve.co.uk

Coldharbour House ♦♦♦♦
3 Coldharbour Close, Henley-on-Thames, Oxfordshire RG9 1QF
T: (01491) 575229
F: (01491) 575229
E: coldharbourhouse@compuserve.com

Henley House ♦♦♦
School Lane, Medmenham, Marlow, Buckinghamshire SL7 2HJ
T: (01491) 576100
F: (01491) 571764
E: dres@henleyhouse.co.uk
I: www.crownandanchor.co.uk

Holmwood ♦♦♦♦
Shiplake Row, Binfield Heath, Henley-on-Thames, Oxfordshire RG9 4DP
T: (0118) 947 8747
F: (0118) 947 8637
🛉

The Knoll ♦♦♦♦
Crowsley Road, Shiplake, Henley-on-Thames, Oxfordshire RG9 3JT
T: (01189) 402705 &
07885 755437
F: (01189) 402705
E: milpops2@aol.com
I: www.saqnet.co.uk/users/the-knoll

Lenwade ♦♦♦♦♦
3 Western Road, Henley-on-Thames, Oxfordshire RG9 1JL
T: (01491) 573468 &
07774 941629
F: (01491) 573468
E: lenwadeuk@compuserve.com
I: www.w3b-ink.com/lenwade

Little Parmoor Farm ♦♦♦♦
Frieth, Henley-on-Thames, Oxfordshire RG9 6NL
T: (01494) 881600
F: (01494) 883634
♿

New Lodge ♦♦♦
Henley Park, Henley-on-Thames, Oxfordshire RG9 6HU
T: (01491) 576340
F: (01491) 576340
E: newlodge@mail.com

5 New Street
Rating Applied For
Henley-on-Thames, Oxfordshire RG9 2BP
T: (01491) 411711
E: fivenewstreet@aol.com

Park View Farm ♦♦
Lower Assendon, Henley-on-Thames, Oxfordshire RG9 6AN
T: (01491) 414232 & 0786 766 0814
F: (01491) 577515
E: info@thomasmartin.co.uk
I: www.thomasmartin.co.uk

Pennyford House ♦♦♦
Peppard Common, Henley-on-Thames, Oxfordshire RG9 5JE
T: (01491) 628272
F: (01491) 628779

12 Rupert Place ♦♦♦♦
Rupert Lane, Henley-on-Thames, Oxfordshire RG9 2JE
T: (01491) 573810 &
07932 312889
E: jo.bausor@virgin.net
I: www.12rupertplace.com

Shepherds ♦♦♦
Shepherds Green, Rotherfield Greys, Henley-on-Thames, Oxfordshire RG9 4QL
T: (01491) 628413
F: (01491) 628413

Slaters Farm ♦♦♦
Peppard Common, Henley-on-Thames, Oxfordshire RG9 5JL
T: (01491) 628675
F: (01491) 628675

Stag Hall ♦♦♦
Peppard, Henley-on-Thames, Oxfordshire RG9 5NX
T: (01491) 680338
F: (01491) 680338

Watermans
Rating Applied For
Harpsden Way, Henley-on-Thames, Oxfordshire RG9 1NX
T: (01491) 578741
F: (01491) 578741

Windy Brow ♦♦♦♦
204 Victoria Road, Wargrave, Reading, Berkshire RG40 8AJ
T: (0118) 940 3336
F: (0118) 940 1260
E: heathcar@aol.com

Manor Farm ♦♦♦♦
Hethe, Bicester, Oxfordshire OX6 9ES
T: (01869) 277602
F: (01869) 278376

Ayam Manor ♦♦♦
Hammersley Lane, High Wycombe, Buckinghamshire HP10 8HS
T: (01494) 816932
F: (01494) 816932
E: jeansenior@ayammanor.freeserve.co.uk
I: www.ayammanorguesthouse.co.uk

The Birches ♦♦
30 Lucas Road, High Wycombe, Buckinghamshire HP13 6QG
T: (01494) 533547

Bird in Hand ♦♦♦
81 West Wycombe Road, High Wycombe, Buckinghamshire HP11 2LR
T: (01494) 523502
F: (01494) 459449

Mull Cottage ♦♦
219 West Wycombe Road, High Wycombe, Buckinghamshire HP12 3AS
T: (01494) 449850
F: (01494) 449850

P A Smails Guest Accommodation ♦♦♦
106 Green Hill, High Wycombe, Buckinghamshire HP13 5QE
T: (01494) 524310
E: pauline.smails@talk21.com

Sunnydale ♦♦♦
425 Amersham Road, Hazlemere, High Wycombe, Buckinghamshire HP15 7JG
T: (01494) 711439

10 Brook Way
Rating Applied For
Friars Cliff, Highcliffe, Christchurch, Dorset BH23 4HA
T: (01425) 276738

Castle Lodge ♦♦♦♦
173 Lymington Road, Highcliffe, Christchurch, Dorset BH23 4JS
T: (01425) 275170
F: (01425) 275170

The Close ♦♦♦
12 Shelley Close, Highcliffe, Christchurch, Dorset BH23 4HW
T: (01425) 273559

Field Cottage ♦♦♦
Hillesden Hamlet, Hillesden, Buckinghamshire MK18 4BX
T: (01280) 815360
F: (01280) 815360
E: martin.tessa@virgin.net

The Old Post Office Guest House ♦♦♦♦
Hinton St Mary, Sturminster Newton, Dorset DT10 1NG
T: (01258) 472366
F: (01258) 472173
E: sofields@aol.com

Bridge House Bed & Breakfast
Rating Applied For
Bridge House, Ipers Bridge, Holbury, Southampton, Hampshire SO45 2HD
T: (023) 8089 4302
F: (023) 8089 4071

Cherry Lodge Guest House ♦♦♦
Reading Road, Hook, Hampshire RG27 9DB
T: (01256) 762532
F: (01256) 762532

Oaklea Guest House ♦♦♦
London Road, Hook, Hampshire RG27 9LA
T: (01256) 762673
F: (01256) 762150
♿

Manor Farm ♦♦♦
Hook Norton, Banbury, Oxfordshire OX15 6NL
T: (01608) 737204

Symnel ♦♦
High Street, Hook Norton, Oxfordshire OX15 5NH
T: (01608) 737547
E: cornelius@hooky13.freeserve.co.uk

Long Acre Farm ♦♦♦
Vaggs Lane, Hordle, Lymington, Hampshire SO41 0FP
T: (01425) 610443
F: (01425) 613026

Miranda ♦♦♦
Vaggs Lane, Hordle, Lymington, Hampshire SO41 0FP
T: (01425) 621561

Spinney Cottage ♦♦♦♦ SILVER AWARD
219 Everton Road, Hordle, Lymington, Hampshire SO41 0HE
T: (01590) 644555 &
07711 138555
F: (01590) 644555
E: pbb001@aol.com or spinneycottage@ad.com
I: www.newforest.demon.co.uk/spinneycottage.htm

Sor Brook House Farm ♦♦♦♦
Horley, Banbury, Oxfordshire OX15 6BL
T: (01295) 738121
♿

Rosedene ♦♦♦♦
63 Rosemary Way, Horndean, Waterlooville, Hampshire PO8 9DQ
T: (023) 9261 5804
F: (023) 9242 3948
E: PBBATT@AOL.COM

The Ship & Bell Hotel ♦♦♦
6 London Road, Horndean, Waterlooville, Hampshire PO8 0BZ
T: (023) 9259 2107
F: (023) 9257 1644
♿

The Horton Inn ♦♦♦♦
Cranborne Road, Horton, Wimborne Minster, Dorset BH21 5AD
T: (01258) 840252
F: (01258) 841400
E: thehorton@btinternet.com
I: www.welcome.to/thehortoninn

Rowans ♦♦♦♦
Houghton, Stockbridge, Hampshire SO20 6LT
T: (01794) 388551

HUNGERFORD
Berkshire
Fishers Farm ◆◆◆◆
Ermin Street, Shefford
Woodlands, Hungerford,
Berkshire RG17 7AB
T: (01488) 648466 &
07973 691901
F: (01488) 648706
E: mail@fishersfarm.co.uk
I: www.fishersfarm.co.uk

Honeybones
Rating Applied For
33 Bourne Vale, Hungerford,
Berkshire RG17 0LL
T: (01488) 683228

Marshgate Cottage Hotel
◆◆◆◆
Marsh Lane, Hungerford,
Berkshire RG17 0QX
T: (01488) 682307
F: (01488) 685475
E: reservations@marshgate.co.
uk
I: www.marshgate.co.uk

Wilton House
Rating Applied For
83 High Street, Hungerford,
Berkshire RG17 0NF
T: (01488) 684228
F: (01488) 685037
E: welfares@hotmail.com

HUNTINGFORD
Dorset
Huntingford Oak ◆◆◆◆
Huntingford, Gillingham, Dorset
SP8 5QH
T: (01747) 860574

HURN
Dorset
Avon Causeway Inn ◆◆◆
Hurn, Christchurch, Dorset
BH23 6AS
T: (01202) 482714
F: (01202) 477416
E: avoncauseway@wadworth.
co.uk
I: www.avoncausewayhotel.co.
uk

HYTHE
Hampshire
Changri-La ◆◆◆◆
12 Ashleigh Close, Hythe,
Southampton, Hampshire
SO45 3QP
T: (023) 8084 6664

IBTHORPE
Hampshire
Staggs Cottage ◆◆
Windmill Hill, Ibthorpe, Andover,
Hampshire SP11 0BP
T: (01264) 736235
F: (01264) 736597

IFFLEY
Oxfordshire
Bramley House
Rating Applied For
76 Iffley Turn, Iffley, Oxford,
Oxfordshire OX4 4HN
T: (01865) 770824
E: joyce.stephen@talk21

INKPEN
Berkshire
The Swan Inn
Rating Applied For
Inkpen, Hungerford, Berkshire
RG17 9DX
T: (01488) 668326
F: (01488) 668306
E: enquiries@
theswaninn-organics.co.uk
I: www.theswaninn-organics.co.
uk

IVINGHOE
Buckinghamshire
The Old Forge ◆◆◆◆
5 High Street, Ivinghoe, Leighton
Buzzard, Bedfordshire LU7 9EP
T: (01296) 668122
F: (01296) 668122
E: hotelsainfotel.co.uk.h25076

IWERNE MINSTER
Dorset
Cleff House
Rating Applied For
Brookmans Valley, Iwerne
Minster, Blandford Forum,
Dorset DT11 8NG
T: (01747) 811129 & 811112
F: (01747) 811112

KENNINGTON
Oxfordshire
The Lawns ◆◆◆
10 Jackson Drive, Kennington,
Oxford, Oxfordshire OX1 5LL
T: (01865) 739595

The Poplars ◆◆
204 Poplar Grove, Kennington,
Oxford, Oxfordshire OX1 5QT
T: (01865) 326443
F: (01865) 739133

KIDLINGTON
Oxfordshire
Breffni House ◆◆
9 Lovelace Drive, Kidlington,
Oxfordshire OX5 2LY
T: (01865) 372569

55 Nethercote Road
Rating Applied For
Tackley, Kidlington, Oxfordshire
OX5 3AT
T: (01869) 331255 &
07790 338225
F: (01869) 331670

Wise Alderman Inn ◆◆◆
249 Banbury Road, Kidlington,
Oxford, Oxfordshire OX5 1BF
T: (01865) 372281
F: (01865) 370153

KIMMERIDGE
Dorset
Kimmeridge Farmhouse
◆◆◆◆ GOLD AWARD
Kimmeridge, Wareham, Dorset
BH20 5PE
T: (01929) 480990

KINGHAM
Oxfordshire
The Plough Inn
Rating Applied For
17 The Green, Kingham, Oxford,
Oxfordshire OX7 6YD
T: (01608) 658327

The Tollgate Inn & Restaurant
◆◆◆◆ SILVER AWARD
Church Street, Kingham, Oxford,
Oxfordshire OX7 6YA
T: (01608) 658389
F: (01608) 659467

KINGSCLERE
Hampshire
Cleremede ◆◆◆◆
Fox's Lane, Kingsclere, Newbury,
Berkshire RG20 5SL
T: (01635) 297298 &
07774 280716
F: (01635) 299934
E: salm@cleremede.demon.co.
uk
I: www.cleremede.demon.co.uk

11 Hook Road ◆◆◆
Kingsclere, Newbury, Berkshire
RG20 5PD
T: (01635) 298861 &
07774 259917
F: (01635) 298861
E: johnaphilips@compuserve.
com

KINGSTON
Hampshire
Greenacres Farmhouse ◆◆◆◆
Christchurch Road, Kingston,
Ringwood, Hampshire BH24 3BJ
T: (01425) 480945
E: paddy@strongarm.freeserve.
co.uk

KINGSTON, CORFE CASTLE
Dorset
Kingston Country Courtyard
◆◆◆◆
Kingston Road, Corfe Castle,
Wareham, Dorset BH20 5LR
T: (01929) 481066
F: (01929) 481256
E: kingstoncountrycourt@
talk21.com

KINGTON MAGNA
Dorset
Kington Manor Farm ◆◆◆◆
Church Hill, Kington Magna,
Gillingham, Dorset SP8 5EG
T: (01747) 838371
F: (01747) 838371

KINTBURY
Berkshire
Holt Lodge ◆◆◆
Kintbury, Hungerford, Berkshire
RG17 9SX
T: (01488) 668244
F: (01488) 668244
E: johnfreeland@holtlodge.
freeserve.co.uk

KIRTLINGTON
Oxfordshire
Vicarage Farm ◆◆◆◆
Kirtlington, Oxford, Oxfordshire
OX5 3JY
T: (01869) 350254
F: (01869) 350254
E: jahunter@freenet.co.uk
I: www.country-accom.co.
uk/vicaragefarm

LAKE
Isle of Wight
Ashleigh House Hotel ◆◆◆◆
81 Sandown Road, Lake,
Sandown, Isle of Wight
PO36 9LE
T: (01983) 402340 & 403835

Cliff Lodge ◆◆◆
13 Cliff Path, Lake, Sandown,
Isle of Wight PO36 8PL
T: (01983) 402963

Haytor Lodge ◆◆◆◆
16 Cliff Path, Lake, Sandown,
Isle of Wight PO36 8PL
T: (01983) 402969
F: (01983) 402969

Osterley Lodge ◆◆◆
62 Sandown Road, Lake,
Sandown, Isle of Wight
PO36 9JX
T: (01983) 402017
F: (01983) 402017
E: osterleylodge@netguides.co.
uk
I: www.netguides.co.
uk/wight/basic/osterley.html

Pebblecombe Guest House ◆◆
48 Sandown Road, Lake,
Sandown, Isle of Wight
PO36 9JT
T: (01983) 402609
F: (01983) 402609

Piers View Guest House ◆◆◆
20 Cliff Path, Lake, Sandown,
Isle of Wight PO36 8PL
T: (01983) 404646

LANGFORD
Oxfordshire
Dovecote House ◆◆◆
Filkins Road, Langford, Lechlade,
Gloucestershire GL7 3LW
T: (01367) 860289 & 860711
F: (01367) 860711
E: dovecote@hotmail.com

LANGTON LONG
Dorset
The Old Brew House
◆◆◆◆◆ SILVER AWARD
Langton Long, Blandford Forum,
Dorset DT11 9HR
T: (01258) 452861
F: (01258) 450718

LEAFIELD
Oxfordshire
Greenside Cottage ◆◆◆
The Ridings, Leafield, Oxford,
Oxfordshire OX8 5NN
T: (01993) 878368
F: (01993) 878368

Langley Farm ◆◆◆
Leafield, Oxford, Oxfordshire
OX8 5QD
T: (01993) 878686 &
0797 0955924

Pond View ◆◆◆
Fairspear Road, Leafield, Witney,
Oxfordshire OX8 5NT
T: (01993) 878133

LEE ON THE SOLENT
Hampshire
Avon Manor Guest House
◆◆◆
12 South Place, Lee on the
Solent, Hampshire PO13 9AS
T: (023) 9255 2773

Chester Lodge ◆◆◆
20 Chester Crescent, Lee on the
Solent, Gosport, Hampshire
PO13 9BH
T: (02392) 550894

Kings Lodge Guest House ◆
16 Kings Road, Lee on the
Solent, Hampshire PO13 9NU
T: (023) 9255 2118

LIPHOOK
Hampshire
The Bailiff's Cottage ◆◆◆
Hollycombe, Liphook, Hampshire
GU30 7LR
T: (01428) 722171
F: (01428) 722171
◎

LISS
Hampshire
Greywalls House ◆◆◆
London Road, Hillbrow, Liss,
Hampshire GU33 7QR
T: (01730) 894246 & 895596
F: (01730) 894865
E: hillbrow.la@lineone.net
I: www.bidbury.co.uk
◎

LITTLE CHESTERTON
Oxfordshire
Cover Point ◆◆◆◆
Little Chesterton, Bicester,
Oxfordshire OX6 8PD
T: (01869) 252500
F: (01869) 252500
E: lamb@coverpoint100.co.uk

LITTLE COXWELL
Oxfordshire
The Eagle Tavern ◆◆◆
Little Coxwell, Faringdon,
Oxfordshire SN7 7LW
T: (01367) 240120

LOCKERLEY
Hampshire
Dunmeads ◆◆◆◆
Butts Green, Lockerley, Romsey,
Hampshire SO51 0JG
T: (01794) 340568
E: alecraymond@thew99.co.uk

St Brelade ◆◆
Top Green, Lockerley, Romsey,
Hampshire SO51 0JP
T: (01794) 340603
E: goodrg@waitrose.com

LONG HANBOROUGH
Oxfordshire
The Close Guest House ◆◆◆
Witney Road, Long Hanborough,
Oxford, Oxfordshire OX8 8HF
T: (01993) 882485 & 883819
F: (01993) 883819

Old Farmhouse ◆◆◆◆
Station Hill, Long Hanborough,
Oxford, Oxfordshire OX8 8JZ
T: (01993) 882097
E: old.farm@virgin.net

LONGPARISH
Hampshire
Yew Cottage Bed & Breakfast
◆◆◆
Yew Cottage, Longparish,
Andover, Hampshire SP11 6QE
T: (01264) 720325 &
0777 1675341
E: yewcottage@ukgateway.net

LYMINGTON
Hampshire
Albany House ◆◆◆◆◆
Highfield, Lymington, Hampshire
SO41 9GB
T: (01590) 671900

Angel Inn ◆◆◆
108 High Street, Lymington,
Hampshire SO41 9AP
T: (01590) 672050
F: (01590) 671661
I: www.stayhere.uk.com

Birchcroft ◆◆◆
Westfield Road, Lymington,
Hampshire SO41 3QB
T: (01590) 688844
F: (01590) 688766

Cedars ◆◆◆
2 Linden Way, Highfield,
Lymington, Hampshire SO41 9JU
T: (01590) 676468

Dolphins ◆◆◆◆
6 Emsworth Road, Lymington,
Hampshire SO41 9BL
T: (01590) 676108 &
07958 727536
F: (01590) 688275
E: dolphins@easynet.co.uk

Durlston Guest House ◆◆◆◆
Durlston House, Gosport Street,
Lymington, Hampshire
SO41 9EG
T: (01590) 676908 & 677364

Efford Cottage
◆◆◆◆◆ GOLD AWARD
Everton, Lymington, Hampshire
SO41 0JD
T: (01590) 642315
F: (01590) 641030
E: effcottage@aol.com

Gleneagles ◆◆◆◆
34 Belmore Road, Lymington,
Hampshire SO41 3NT
T: (01590) 675958
F: (01590) 675958
E: gleneagles34@hotmail.com

Gorse Meadow Guest House
◆◆◆
Gorse Meadow, Sway Road,
Lymington, Hampshire SO41 8LR
T: (01590) 673354
F: (01590) 673336
E: gorsemeadow.guesthouse@
wildmushrooms.co.uk
I: www.@wildmushrooms.co.uk

Hideaway ◆◆◆
Middle Common Road,
Pennington, Lymington,
Hampshire SO41 8LE
T: (01590) 676974 &
07956 520802
F: (01590) 676974

The Hillsman House
◆◆◆◆◆ SILVER AWARD
74 Milford Road, Lymington,
Hampshire SO41 8DP
T: (01590) 674737
E: reservations@hillsmanhouse.
co.uk
I: www.newforest.demon.co.
uk/hillsman.htm

Jack in the Basket Restaurant
◆◆
7 St Thomas Street, Lymington,
Hampshire SO41 9NA
T: (01590) 673447 & 673812
I: www.newforest.demon.co.uk.
jackbasket.htm

The Mayflower Inn ◆◆◆◆
Kings Saltern Road, Lymington,
Hampshire SO41 3QD
T: (01590) 672160
E: mayflower@lymington.
fsbusiness.co.uk

Monks Pool ◆◆◆
Waterford Lane, Lymington,
Hampshire SO41 3PS
T: (01590) 678850
E: cam@monkspool.junglelink.
co.uk

Moonraker Cottage ◆◆◆◆
62 Milford Road, Lymington,
Hampshire SO41 8DU
T: (01590) 678677

Our Bench ◆◆◆◆
9 Lodge Road, Pennington,
Lymington, Hampshire
SO41 8HH
T: (01590) 673141
F: (01590) 673141
E: ourbench@newforest.demon.
co.uk
I: www.newforest.demon.co.
uk/bench.htm
◎ ♿

Pennavon House
◆◆◆◆ SILVER AWARD
Lower Pennington Lane,
Lymington, Hampshire SO41 8AL
T: (01590) 673984

Rosefield House
◆◆◆◆◆ GOLD AWARD
Sway Road, Lymington,
Hampshire SO41 8LR
T: (01590) 671526
F: (01590) 689007

The Rowans ◆◆◆◆
76 Southampton Road,
Lymington, Hampshire
SO41 9GZ
T: (01590) 672276 &
07860 630361
F: (01590) 688610
E: the.rowans@totalise.co.uk

40 Southampton Road ◆◆◆◆
Lymington, Hampshire
SO41 9GG
T: (01590) 672237
F: (01590) 673592

Tranmere House ◆◆◆◆
Tranmere Close, Lymington,
Hampshire SO41 3QQ
T: (01590) 671983
E: tranmere.house@tesco.net
◎

The Vicarage ◆◆◆
Grove Road, Lymington,
Hampshire SO41 3RF
T: (01590) 673847
F: (01590) 673847
E: junovicarage@hotmail.com

Woodslee ◆◆◆◆
Sway Road, Lymington,
Hampshire SO41 8LR
T: (01590) 676572
F: (01590) 676572
◎

LYNDHURST
Hampshire
Beechen House ◆◆◆
Clay Hill, Lyndhurst, Hampshire
SO43 7DN
T: (023) 8028 3584

Burwood Lodge ◆◆◆◆
27 Romsey Road, Lyndhurst,
Hampshire SO43 7AA
T: (023) 8028 2445
F: (023) 8028 4104

Clayhill House ◆◆◆◆
Clayhill, Lyndhurst, Hampshire
SO43 7DE
T: (023) 8028 2304 &
(01585) 578656
F: (023) 8028 2093
E: bookings@clayhillhouse.
demon.co.uk
I: http://clayhillhouse.demon.co.
uk

Englefield ◆◆◆◆
Chapel Lane, Lyndhurst,
Hampshire SO43 7FG
T: (023) 8028 2685

Forest Cottage
◆◆◆◆ SILVER AWARD
High Street, Lyndhurst,
Hampshire SO43 7BH
T: (023) 8028 3461
I: www.forestcottage.i12.com

Little Hayes ◆◆◆◆
43 Romsey Road, Lyndhurst,
Hampshire SO43 7AR
T: (023) 8028 3816

Lyndhurst House
◆◆◆◆ SILVER AWARD
35 Romsey Road, Lyndhurst,
Hampshire SO43 7AR
T: (023) 8028 2230
F: (023) 8028 2230
E: bcjwood@lyndhouse.
freeserve.co.uk
I: www.newforest.demon.co.
uk/lynho.html

Pen Cottage ◆◆◆
Bournemouth Road, Swan
Green, Lyndhurst, Hampshire
SO43 7DP
T: (023) 8028 2075
◎

The Penny Farthing Hotel
◆◆◆◆
Romsey Road, Lyndhurst,
Hampshire SO43 7AA
T: (023) 8028 4422
F: (023) 8028 4488
I: www.smoothhound.co.
uk/hotels/pennyf.html

Reepham House
◆◆◆◆ SILVER AWARD
12 Romsey Road, Lyndhurst,
Hampshire SO43 7AA
T: (023) 8028 3091
F: (023) 8028 3091

Rose Cottage ◆◆◆◆
Chapel Lane, Lyndhurst,
Hampshire SO43 7FG
T: (023) 8028 3413
F: (023) 8028 3413
E: cindy@rosecottageb-b.
freeserve
I: www.rosecottageb-b.
freeserve.co.uk/
◎

Rosedale Bed & Breakfast
◆◆◆
24 Shaggs Meadow, Lyndhurst,
Hampshire SO43 7BN
T: (023) 8028 3793
E: jenny@theangels.freeserve.
co.uk

Rufus House Hotel
◆◆◆◆ SILVER AWARD
Southampton Road, Lyndhurst,
Hampshire SO43 7BQ
T: (023) 8028 2930 & 8028 2200
F: (023) 8028 2930
E: rufushouse@talk21.com

Southview ◆◆◆
Gosport Lane, Lyndhurst,
Hampshire SO43 7BL
T: (023) 8028 2224
E: gburbidge@virgin.net

LYTCHETT MATRAVERS
Dorset

Sonora ◆◆◆
Flowers Drove, Lytchett
Matravers, Poole, Dorset
BH16 6BX
T: (01202) 632337
F: (01202) 632337
E: ashsonora@aol.com

MAIDENHEAD
Berkshire

Cartlands Cottage ◆
Kings Lane, Cookham Dean,
Cookham, Maidenhead,
Berkshire SL6 9AY
T: (01628) 482196

Clifton Guest House
Rating Applied For
21 Crauford Rise, Maidenhead,
Berkshire SL6 7LR
T: (01628) 623572 & 620086
F: (01628) 623572
E: clifton@aroram.freeserve.co.
uk
I: www.cliftonguestonhouse.
com
◎

Moor Farm
◆◆◆◆ SILVER AWARD
Ascot Road, Holyport,
Maidenhead, Berkshire SL6 2HY
T: (01628) 633761
F: (01628) 636167
E: moorfm@aol.com

Ray Corner Guest House ◆◆◆
141 Bridge Road, Maidenhead,
Berkshire SL6 8NQ
T: (01628) 632784
F: (01628) 789029

Sheephouse Manor ◆◆◆
Sheephouse Road, Maidenhead,
Berkshire SL6 8HJ
T: (01628) 776902
F: (01628) 625138
E: info@sheephousemanor.co.
uk
I: www.sheephousemanor.co.uk

MARLOW
Buckinghamshire

Acha Pani ◆◆
Bovingdon Green, Marlow,
Buckinghamshire SL7 2JL
T: (01628) 483435
F: (01628) 483435

Acorn Lodge ◆◆◆
79 Marlow Bottom Road,
Marlow Bottom, Marlow,
Buckinghamshire SL7 3NA
T: (01628) 472197 &
07710 974329
F: (01628) 472197

16 Claremont Road ◆◆
Marlow, Buckinghamshire
SL7 1BW
T: (01628) 471334
E: tony-peperell@hotmail.com

The Country House ◆◆◆◆
Bisham, Marlow,
Buckinghamshire SL7 1RP
T: (01628) 890606
F: (01628) 890983

Fisherman's Reach ◆◆◆
Gossmore Lane, Marlow,
Buckinghamshire SL7 1QF
T: (01628) 482290
F: (01628) 482290

Four Winds ◆◆◆
18 Bovingdon Heights, Marlow,
Buckinghamshire SL7 2JS
T: (01628) 476567 & 481710
F: (01628) 481711
E: gooding@globalnet.co.uk

Holly Tree House ◆◆◆◆
Burford Close, Marlow Bottom,
Marlow, Buckinghamshire
SL7 3NE
T: (01628) 891110
F: (01628) 481278

Huxley ◆◆◆◆
18 Lock Road, Marlow,
Buckinghamshire SL7 1QW
T: (01628) 487741
F: (01628) 890777
E: 101732.2025@compuserve.
com

The Inn on the Green Limited
◆◆◆◆
The Old Cricket Common,
Cookham Dean, Cookham,
Maidenhead, Berkshire SL6 9NZ
T: (01628) 482638
F: (01628) 487474
E: chris@theinnonthegreen.com
I: www.theinnonthegreen.com

31 Institute Road ◆◆
Marlow, Buckinghamshire
SL7 1BJ
T: (01628) 485662

10 Lock Road ◆◆
Marlow, Buckinghamshire
SL7 1QP
T: (01628) 473875 &
07899 913805

3 Lodge Close ◆◆
Marlow, Buckinghamshire
SL7 1RB
T: (01628) 473704 &
07887 950504

Merrie Hollow ◆◆◆
Seymour Court Hill, Marlow
Road, Marlow, Buckinghamshire
SL7 3DE
T: (01628) 485663

Oak Lodge ◆◆◆
29 Oaktree Road, Marlow,
Buckinghamshire SL7 3ED
T: (01628) 472145 &
07973 842616

The Puffins ◆◆◆
83 Wycombe Road, Marlow,
Buckinghamshire SL7 3HZ
T: (01628) 440674 & 440619

Red Barn Farm ◆◆◆
Marlow Road, Marlow,
Buckinghamshire SL7 3DQ
T: (01494) 882820
F: (01494) 883545

Riverdale ◆◆◆
Marlow Bridge Lane, Marlow,
Buckinghamshire SL7 1RH
T: (01628) 485206

18 Rookery Court ◆◆◆
Marlow, Buckinghamshire
SL7 3HR
T: (01628) 486451 &
07970 555814
F: (01628) 486451
E: gillbullen@compuserve.com

Sneppen House ◆◆◆◆
Henley Road, Marlow,
Buckinghamshire SL7 2DF
T: (01628) 485227

Sunnyside ◆◆
Munday Dean Lane, Marlow,
Buckinghamshire SL7 3BU
T: (01628) 485701
E: ruthandtom@tinyworld.co.uk

The White House ◆◆◆
194 Little Marlow Road, Marlow,
Buckinghamshire SL7 1HX
T: (01628) 485765
F: (01628) 485765

"Nia Roo" ◆◆
4 Pound Crescent, Marlow,
Buckinghamshire SL7 2BG
T: (01628) 486679
F: (01628) 486679

MARLOW BOTTOM
Buckinghamshire

61 Hill Farm Road ◆◆
Marlow Bottom, Marlow,
Buckinghamshire SL7 3LX
T: (01628) 475145 &
07768 923331
F: (01628) 475775
E: p.simmons@ukonline.co.uk

63 Hill Farm Road ◆◆
Marlow Bottom, Marlow,
Buckinghamshire SL7 3LX
T: (01628) 472970 &
07958 524438

50A New Road ◆◆◆
Marlow Bottom, Marlow,
Buckinghamshire SL7 3NW
T: (01628) 472666

Number One B & B ◆◆◆
1 Meadow View, Marlow
Bottom, Buckinghamshire
SL7 3PA
T: (01628) 483426
E: number.one.bed.and.
breakfast@dial.pipex.com

T J O'Reillys ◆◆◆
61 Marlow Bottom Road,
Marlow Bottom, Marlow,
Buckinghamshire SL7 3NA
T: (01628) 891187
F: (01628) 484926

MARNHULL
Dorset

The Old Bank ◆◆◆
Burton Street, Marnhull,
Sturminster Newton, Dorset
DT10 1PH
T: (01258) 821019
F: (01258) 821019

Yew House Farm
◆◆◆◆ SILVER AWARD
Marnhull, Sturminster Newton,
Dorset DT10 1PD
T: (01258) 820412
F: (01258) 821044
◎

MARSH GIBBON
Buckinghamshire

Furze Grounds Farm
Rating Applied For
Blackthorn Road, Marsh Gibbon,
Bicester, Oxfordshire OX6 0AQ
T: (01869) 252048
E: jendot@furze47.freeserve.co.
uk

Judges Close ◆◆◆
West Edge, Marsh Gibbon,
Bicester, Oxfordshire OX6 0HA
T: (01869) 278508 & 277528
F: (01869) 278508
E: royllambourne1@
farmersweekly.net

MENTMORE
Buckinghamshire

The Orchard ◆◆◆
Mentmore, Leighton Buzzard,
Bedfordshire LU7 0QF
T: (01296) 662189 & 668976
F: (01296) 662459

MEONSTOKE
Hampshire

The Bucks Head ◆◆◆◆
Bucks Head Hill, Meonstoke,
Southampton, Hampshire
SO32 3NA
T: (01489) 877313

MERSTONE
Isle of Wight

Redway Farm ◆◆◆◆
Merstone, Newport, Isle of
Wight PO30 3DJ
T: (01983) 865228
F: (01983) 865228

MIDDLE ASTON
Oxfordshire

Home Farm House ◆◆◆
Middle Aston, Bicester,
Oxfordshire OX6 3PX
T: (01869) 340666
F: (01869) 347789
E: cparsons@telinco.co.uk
I: www.country-accom.co.
uk/home-farm-house
◎

MIDDLE WALLOP
Hampshire

The George Inn ◆◆◆◆
The Crossroads, Middle Wallop,
Stockbridge, Hampshire
SO20 8EG
T: (01264) 781224
E: joanne.george@virgin.net

MILFORD-ON-SEA
Hampshire

Alma Mater ◆◆◆◆
4 Knowland Drive, Milford-on-
Sea, Lymington, Hampshire
SO41 0RH
T: (01590) 642811
E: bandbalmamater@aol.com
I: www.newforest.demon.co.
uk/almamater.htm

The Bay Trees
◆◆◆◆◆ SILVER AWARD
8 High Street, Milford-on-Sea,
Lymington, Hampshire
SO41 0QD
T: (01590) 642186
F: (01590) 645461
E: thebaytrees@netscapeonline.
co.uk
I: www.newforestbandb.com

Compton Hotel ◆◆◆
59 Keyhaven Road, Milford-on-
Sea, Lymington, Hampshire
SO41 0QX
T: (01590) 643117
F: (01590) 643117
E: dbembo@talk21.com

Ha'Penny House ◆◆◆◆
16 Whitby Road, Milford-on-
Sea, Lymington, Hampshire
SO41 0ND
T: (01590) 641210
F: (01590) 641227
E: info@hapennyhouse.co.uk
◎

Laburnum Cottage ◆◆◆
19 Carrington Lane, Milford-on-Sea, Lymington, Hampshire
SO41 0RA
T: (01590) 644225

Southerly House
◆◆◆◆◆ SILVER AWARD
15 Hurst Road, Milford-on-Sea, Lymington, Hampshire
SO41 0PY
T: (01590) 642918

MILTON ABBAS
Dorset

Dunbury Heights ◆◆◆◆
Milton Abbas, Blandford Forum, Dorset DT11 0DH
T: (01258) 880445

Park Farm ◆◆◆
Milton Abbas, Blandford Forum, Dorset DT11 0AX
T: (01258) 880828
T: (01258) 880828
E: burch@parkfarmcottages.co.uk
I: www.parkfarmcottages.co.uk

MILTON COMMON
Oxfordshire

Byways ◆◆◆
Old London Road, Milton Common, Thame, Oxfordshire
OX9 2JR
T: (01844) 279386

MILTON KEYNES
Buckinghamshire

B Line Guest House ◆◆
72 Watling Street, Fenny Stratford, Milton Keynes, Buckinghamshire MK2 2BY
T: (01908) 378283

Chantry Farm ◆◆◆
Pindon End, Hanslope, Milton Keynes, Buckinghamshire
MK19 7HL
T: (01908) 510269 &
07850 166122
F: (01908) 510269

Conifers Bed & Breakfast ◆◆
29 William Smith Close, Woolstone, Milton Keynes, Buckinghamshire MK15 0AN
T: (01908) 674506

The Croft ◆◆◆
Little Crawley, Newport Pagnell, Buckinghamshire MK16 9LT
T: (01234) 391296

Furtho Manor Farm ◆◆◆
Old Stratford, Milton Keynes, Buckinghamshire MK19 6BA
T: (01908) 542139
F: (01908) 542139
E: dsansome@farming.co.uk

The Grange Stables ◆◆◆
Winslow Road, Great Horwood, Milton Keynes, Buckinghamshire
MK18 0QN
T: (01296) 712051
F: (01296) 714991

Haversham Grange ◆◆◆◆
Haversham, Milton Keynes, Buckinghamshire MK19 7DX
T: (01908) 312389
F: (01908) 312389
E: havershamgrange.fsnet.co.uk

Kingfishers ◆◆◆
9 Rylstone Close, Heelands, Milton Keynes, Buckinghamshire
MK13 7QT
T: (01908) 310231 & 318601
F: (01908) 318601
E: sheila-derek@m-keynes.freeserve.co.uk
I: www.smoothhound.co.uk/hotels/kingfishers.html

Milford Leys Farm ◆◆
Castlethorpe, Milton Keynes, Buckinghamshire MK19 7HH
T: (01908) 510153

Mill Farm ◆◆◆
Gayhurst, Newport Pagnell, Buckinghamshire MK16 8LT
T: (01908) 611489
F: (01908) 611489

The Old Bakery Hotel ◆◆◆◆
Main Street, Cosgrove, Milton Keynes MK19 7JL
T: (01908) 263103 & 262255
F: (01908) 263620

The Old Rectory ◆◆◆
Drayton Road, Newton Longville, Milton Keynes, Buckinghamshire
MK17 0BH
T: (01908) 375794

Rose Cottage Guest Accommodation
◆◆◆◆ SILVER AWARD
Broughton Road, Salford, Milton Keynes, Buckinghamshire
MK17 8BQ
T: (01908) 582239 &
07702 587648
F: (01908) 282029
E: jbassc@globalnet.co.uk

Spinney Lodge Farm ◆◆◆
Forest Road, Hanslope, Milton Keynes, Buckinghamshire
MK19 7DE
T: (01908) 510267

Vignoble ◆◆◆
2 Medland, Woughton Park, Milton Keynes, Buckinghamshire
MK6 3BH
T: (01908) 666804
F: (01908) 666626
E: 101532.627@compuserve.com

MINSTEAD
Hampshire

Eugenie Cottage ◆◆◆
Seamans Corner, Minstead, Lyndhurst, Hampshire
SO43 7FW
T: (023) 8081 3325
F: (023) 8081 3325
E: eugeniemcc@ad.uk

Grove House ◆◆
Newtown, Minstead, Lyndhurst, Hampshire SO43 7GG
T: (023) 8081 3211

The Trusty Servant ◆◆◆
Minstead, Lyndhurst, Hampshire
SO43 7FY
T: (023) 8081 2137

MINSTER LOVELL
Oxfordshire

Hill Grove Farm ◆◆◆◆
Crawley Road, Minster Lovell, Oxford, Oxfordshire OX8 5NA
T: (01993) 703120
F: (01993) 700528

MOLLINGTON
Oxfordshire

Point to Point House ◆◆◆◆
Claydon Road, Mollington, Banbury, Oxfordshire OX17 1AU
T: (01295) 690346

MOTCOMBE
Dorset

The Coppleridge Inn ◆◆◆◆
Elm Hill, Motcombe, Shaftesbury, Dorset SP7 9HW
T: (01747) 851980
T: (01747) 851858
E: thecoppleridgeinn@btinternet.com

Manor Farm
◆◆◆◆ SILVER AWARD
Motcombe, Shaftesbury, Dorset
SP7 9PL
T: (01747) 853811
T: (01747) 853811
E: manor.motcombe@talk21

Shorts Green Farm
◆◆◆◆ SILVER AWARD
Motcombe, Shaftesbury, Dorset
SP7 9PA
T: (01747) 852260
F: (01747) 852260

MOTTISTONE
Isle of Wight

Mottistone Manor Farm
◆◆◆◆
Mottistone, Newport, Isle of Wight PO30 4ED
T: (01983) 740232

MOULSFORD ON THAMES
Oxfordshire

White House ◆◆◆◆◆
Moulsford on Thames, Wallingford, Oxfordshire
OX10 9JD
T: (01491) 651397 &
07831 372243
F: (01491) 652560

MUDEFORD
Dorset

Seahaze
◆◆◆◆ SILVER AWARD
4 Rook Hill Road, Friars Cliff, Mudeford, Christchurch, Dorset
BH23 4DZ
T: (01425) 270866
F: (01425) 278285
E: seahaze@mudeford04.freeserve.co.uk

MURSLEY
Buckinghamshire

Fourpenny Cottage ◆◆◆
Main Street, Mursley, Milton Keynes, Buckinghamshire
MK17 0RT
T: (01296) 720544
F: (01296) 720906

Richmond Hill Farm ◆◆◆
Stewkley Lane, Mursley, Milton Keynes, Buckinghamshire
MK17 0JD
T: (01296) 720385
F: (01296) 730385

NAPHILL
Buckinghamshire

Woodpeckers ◆◆◆
244 Main Road, Naphill, High Wycombe, Buckinghamshire
HP14 4RX
T: (01494) 563728
E: brandroillard@btinternet.com

NETHER WALLOP
Hampshire

Halcyon ◆◆◆
Church Hill, Nether Wallop, Stockbridge, Hampshire
SO20 8EY
T: (01264) 781348

NETLEY ABBEY
Hampshire

The Prince Consort ◆◆◆
71 Victoria Road, Netley Abbey, Southampton, Hampshire
SO31 5DQ
T: (023) 8045 2676
F: (023) 8045 6334

NEW MILTON
Hampshire

Canada Cottage ◆◆◆◆
New Lane, Bashley, New Milton, Hamphire BH25 5TE
T: (01425) 627446

Fairways ◆◆◆
Sway Road, New Milton, Hampshire BH25 5QP
T: (01425) 619001
E: fairways@swayroad.co.uk

St Ursula ◆◆◆
30 Hobart Road, New Milton, Hampshire BH25 6EG
T: (01425) 613515

Taverners Cottage ◆◆◆
Bashley Cross Road, Bashley, New Milton, Hampshire
BH25 5SZ
T: (01425) 615403 &
07966 463466
F: (01425) 615403
E: jbaines@supanet.com
I: www.taverners.cottage.bandb.baines.com

NEWBRIDGE
Isle of Wight

Homestead Farmhouse ◆◆◆
Newbridge, Yarmouth, Isle of Wight PO41 0TZ
T: (01983) 531270 &
07836 583982
F: (01983) 531270

NEWBURY
Berkshire

The Bacon Arms ◆◆◆
10 Oxford Street, Newbury, Berkshire RG14 1JB
T: (01635) 31822
F: (01635) 552496

10 Cheviot Close
Rating Applied For
Wash Common, Newbury, Berkshire RG14 6SQ
T: (01635) 48887
E: taciliaok@aol.com

15 Dalby Crescent ◆◆◆
Newbury, Berkshire RG14 7JR
T: (01635) 522405 &
07768 038206

Little Paddocks ◆◆◆
Woolhampton Hill,
Woolhampton, Reading,
Berkshire RG7 5SY
T: (0118) 9713451
F: (0118) 9713451
E: annie_pat@gardner38.
freeserve.co.uk

Livingstone House ◆◆◆
48 Queens Road, Newbury,
Berkshire RG14 7PA
T: (01635) 45444

The Old Farmhouse ◆◆◆
Downend Lane, Chieveley,
Newbury, Berkshire RG20 8TN
T: (01635) 248361 &
07770 590844
F: (01635) 528195
E: palletts@aol.com
I: www.smoothhound.co.
uk/hotels/oldfarmhouse.html

Rookwood Farmhouse ◆◆◆◆
Stockcross, Newbury, Berkshire
RG20 8JX
T: (01488) 608676
F: (01488) 608676

White Cottage ◆◆◆
Newtown, Newbury, Berkshire
RG20 9AP
T: (01635) 43097 &
07721 613224
F: (01635) 43097

NEWPORT
Isle of Wight

Litten Park Guest House ◆◆◆
48 Medina Avenue, Newport,
Isle of Wight PO30 1EL
T: (01983) 526836

Magnolia House ◆◆◆◆
6 Cypress Road, Newport, Isle of
Wight PO30 1EY
T: (01983) 529489
E: magnolia@aol.com

Newclose House East ◆◆◆◆
134 Watergate Road, Newport,
Isle of Wight PO30 1YP
T: (01983) 826290

Newport Quay Hotel ◆◆◆
41 Quay Street, Newport, Isle of
Wight PO30 5BA
T: (01983) 528544
F: (01983) 527143
I: keith@newportquayhotel.
freeserve.co.uk

Wheatsheaf Hotel ◆◆◆
St Thomas Square, Newport, Isle
of Wight PO30 1SG
T: (01983) 523865
F: (01983) 528255

NEWPORT PAGNELL
Buckinghamshire

The Limes
◆◆◆◆◆ SILVER AWARD
North Square, Newport Pagnell,
Buckinghamshire MK16 8EP
T: (01908) 617041 &
07860 908925
F: (01908) 217292
E: royandruth@8thelimes.
freeserve.co.uk

5 Walnut Close ◆◆
Newport Pagnell,
Buckinghamshire MK16 8JH
T: (01908) 611643
F: (01908) 611643

NORTH CRAWLEY
Buckinghamshire

Rectory Farm ◆◆◆
North Crawley, Newport Pagnell,
Buckinghamshire MK16 9HH
T: (01234) 391213

NORTH LEIGH
Oxfordshire

Elbie House ◆◆◆◆
East End, North Leigh, Witney,
Oxfordshire OX8 6PZ
T: (01993) 880166 &
07712 462405
E: buck@elbiehouse.freeserve.
co.uk
I: www.smoothhound.co.
uk/hotels/elbiehouse.htm/

Forge Cottage ◆◆
East End, North Leigh,
Woodstock, Oxfordshire
OX8 6PZ
T: (01993) 881120
E: jill.french@talk21.com

The Woodman Inn ◆◆◆
New Yatt Road, North Leigh,
Witney, Oxfordshire OX8 6TT
T: (01993) 881790
F: (01993) 881790

NORTH NEWINGTON
Oxfordshire

**The Blinking Owl Country Inn
◆◆◆**
Main Street, North Newington,
Banbury, Oxfordshire OX15 6AE
T: (01295) 730650

**La Madonette Country Guest
House ◆◆◆◆**
North Newington, Banbury,
Oxfordshire OX15 6AA
T: (01295) 730212
F: (01295) 730363
E: camadonett@aol.com

NORTHMOOR
Oxfordshire

Rectory Farm ◆◆◆◆
Northmoor, Oxford, Oxfordshire
OX8 1SX
T: (01865) 300207 &
07974 102198
F: (01865) 300559
E: PJ.Florey@farmline.com

NURSLING
Hampshire

Conifers ◆◆◆
6 Nursling Street Cottages,
Nursling, Southampton,
Hampshire SO16 0XH
T: (023) 8034 9491 &
07775 830539
F: (023) 8034 9491

OAKDALE
Dorset

**Heathwood Guest House
◆◆◆◆**
266 Wimborne Road, Oakdale,
Poole, Dorset BH15 3EF
T: (01202) 679176 & 679746
F: (01202) 679176

OAKLEY
Buckinghamshire

New Farm ◆◆◆
Oxford Road, Oakley, Aylesbury,
Buckinghamshire HP18 9UR
T: (01844) 237360

OLNEY
Buckinghamshire

The Lindens ◆◆◆
30A High Street, Olney,
Buckinghamshire MK46 4BB
T: (01234) 712891

OVER NORTON
Oxfordshire

Cleeves Farm ◆◆
Over Norton, Chipping Norton,
Oxfordshire OX7 5RB
T: (01608) 645019
F: (01608) 645021

OXFORD
Oxfordshire

Acorn Guest House ◆◆
260-262 Iffley Road, Oxford,
Oxfordshire OX4 1SE
T: (01865) 247998
F: (01865) 247998

Adams Guest House ◆◆
302 Banbury Road, Oxford,
Oxfordshire OX2 7ED
T: (01865) 556118
F: (01865) 514066

All Seasons Guest House ◆◆◆
63 Windmill Road, Headington,
Oxford, Oxfordshire OX3 7BP
T: (01865) 742215
F: (01865) 432691
E: info@allseasons-oxford.com
I: www.allseasons-oxford.com

Arden Lodge ◆◆◆
34 Sunderland Avenue, off
Banbury Road, Oxford,
Oxfordshire OX2 8DX
T: (01865) 552076 & 512265

Beaumont Guest House ◆◆
234 Abingdon Road, Oxford,
Oxfordshire OX1 4SP
T: (01865) 241767
F: (01865) 241767
E: info@beaumont.sagehost.co.
uk
I: www.beaumont.sagehost.co.
uk

Becket House ◆◆
5 Becket Street, Oxford,
Oxfordshire OX1 7PP
T: (01865) 724675 & 513045
F: (01865) 724675

Bravalla Guest House ◆◆
242 Iffley Road, Oxford,
Oxfordshire OX4 1SE
T: (01865) 241326 & 250511
F: (01865) 250511
E: bravalla.guesthouse@virgin.
net
I: oxfordcity.co.
uk/accom/bravalla

Bronte Guest House ◆◆◆
282 Iffley Road, Oxford,
Oxfordshire OX4 4AA
T: (01865) 244594
F: (01865) 244772

Brown's Guest House ◆◆◆
281 Iffley Road, Oxford,
Oxfordshire OX4 4AQ
T: (01865) 246822
F: (01865) 246822

The Bungalow ◆◆◆
Cherwell Farm, Mill Lane, Old
Marston, Oxford, Oxfordshire
OX3 0QF
T: (01865) 557171

Casa Villa Guest House ◆◆
388 Banbury Road,
Summertown, Oxford,
Oxfordshire OX2 7PW
T: (01865) 512642
F: (01865) 512642
E: casavilla@compuserve.com
I: www.oxfordcity.co.
uk/accom/casavilla/

Chestnuts ◆◆◆
72 Cumnor Hill, Oxford,
Oxfordshire OX2 9HU
T: (01865) 863602 & 865070

**Chestnuts Guest House
◆◆◆◆◆ SILVER AWARD**
45 Davenant Road, Off
Woodstock Road, Oxford,
Oxfordshire OX2 8BU
T: (01865) 553375
F: (01865) 553375

The Coach & Horses Inn ◆◆◆
Watlington Road,
Chiselhampton, Oxford,
Oxfordshire OX44 7UX
T: (01865) 890255
F: (01865) 891995
I: david-mcphillips@lineone.net

Cock and Camel ◆◆◆◆
24-26 George Street, Oxford,
Oxfordshire OX1 2AE
T: (01865) 203705
F: (01865) 792130

College Guest House ◆◆
103-105 Woodstock Road,
Oxford, Oxfordshire OX2 6HL
T: (01865) 552579
F: (01865) 311244
E: rpal@ukonline.co.uk

Conifer Lodge ◆◆
159 Eynsham Road, Botley,
Oxford, Oxfordshire OX2 9NE
T: (01865) 862280

Cornerways Guest House ◆◆◆
282 Abingdon Road, Oxford,
Oxfordshire OX1 4TA
T: (01865) 240135
F: (01865) 247652
E: jeakings@btinternet.com

Cotswold House ◆◆◆◆◆
363 Banbury Road, Oxford,
Oxfordshire OX2 7PL
T: (01865) 310558
F: (01865) 310558

Earlmont Guest House ◆◆◆
322-324 Cowley Road, Oxford,
Oxfordshire OX4 2AF
T: (01865) 240236
F: (01865) 434903
E: beds@earlmont.prestel.co.uk
I: www.oxfordcity.co.
uk/accom/earlmont.html

**Euro Bar and Hotel Oxford
◆◆◆**
48 George Street, Oxford,
Oxfordshire OX1 2AQ
T: (01865) 725087 & 242998
E: eurobarox@aol.com
I: www.oxfordcity.co.
uk/accom/eurobar/

Falcon Private Hotel ◆◆◆
88-90 Abingdon Road, Oxford,
Oxfordshire OX1 4PX
T: (01865) 511122
F: (01865) 246642
I: www.oxfordcity.co.
uk/hotels/falcon

Five Mile View Guest House ♦♦♦
528 Banbury Road, Oxford,
Oxfordshire OX2 8EG
T: (01865) 558747 &
07802 758366
F: (01865) 558747
E: fivemileview@cableinet.co.uk
I: www.oxfordpages.co.
uk/fivemileview

Gables ♦♦♦♦
6 Cumnor Hill, Oxford,
Oxfordshire OX2 9HA
T: (01865) 862153
F: (01865) 864054
E: stay@gables-oxford.co.uk
I: www.oxfordcity.co.
uk/accom/gables/

Green Gables ♦♦♦
326 Abingdon Road, Oxford,
Oxfordshire OX1 4TE
T: (01865) 725870
F: (01865) 723115
E: green.gables@virgin.net

Head of the River ♦♦♦♦
Folly Bridge, St Aldates, Oxford,
Oxfordshire OX1 4LB
T: (01865) 721600
F: (01865) 726158

Heather House B & B ♦♦
192 Iffley Road, Oxford,
Oxfordshire OX4 1SD
T: (01865) 249757
F: (01865) 249757

High Hedges ♦♦♦♦
8 Cumnor Hill, Oxford,
Oxfordshire OX2 9HA
T: (01865) 863395
F: (01865) 437351
E: tompkins@btinternet.com

Highfield West ♦♦♦
188 Cumnor Hill, Oxford,
Oxfordshire OX2 9PJ
T: (01865) 863007
E: highfieldwest@email.msn.
com

Hollybush Guest House ♦♦♦
530 Banbury Road, Oxford,
Oxfordshire OX2 8EG
T: (01865) 554886
F: (01865) 554886
E: heather@hollybush.
fsbusiness.co.uk
I: www.angelfire.com

Homelea Guest House ♦♦♦♦
356 Abingdon Road, Oxford,
Oxfordshire OX1 4TQ
T: (01865) 245150
F: (01865) 245150
E: homelea@talk21.com
I: www.guesthouseoxford.com

Isis Guest House ♦♦
45-53 Iffley Road, Oxford,
Oxfordshire OX4 1ED
T: (01865) 248894 & 242466
F: (01865) 243492

Lakeside Guest House ♦♦♦
118 Abingdon Road, Oxford,
Oxfordshire OX1 4PZ
T: (01865) 244725
F: (01865) 244725

21 Lincoln Road ♦♦♦♦
Oxford, Oxfordshire OX1 4TB
T: (01865) 246944
E: lbaleham@cwcom.net

Lonsdale Guest House ♦♦♦
312 Banbury Road, Oxford,
Oxfordshire OX2 7ED
T: (01865) 554872
F: (01865) 554872

Marlborough House Hotel ♦♦♦♦
321 Woodstock Road, Oxford,
Oxfordshire OX2 7NY
T: (01865) 311321
F: (01865) 515329
E: enquiries@marlbhouse.
win-uk.net
I: www.oxfordcity.co.
uk/hotels/marlborough

Milka's Guest House ♦♦♦
379 Iffley Road, Oxford,
Oxfordshire OX4 4DP
T: (01865) 778458
F: (01865) 776477
E: reservations@milkas.co.uk
I: www.milkas.co.uk

Mulberry Guest House ♦♦♦
265 London Road, Headington,
Oxford, Oxfordshire OX3 9EH
T: (01865) 767114
F: (01865) 767114
E: mulberryguesthouse@
hotmail.com

Newton House ♦♦♦
82-84 Abingdon Road, Oxford,
Oxfordshire OX1 4PL
T: (01865) 240561
F: (01865) 244647
E: newton.house@btinternet.
com
I: www.guesthouse-oxford.com

The Old Black Horse Hotel ♦♦♦
102 St Clements, Oxford,
Oxfordshire OX4 1AR
T: (01865) 244691
F: (01865) 242771

Oxford Guest House ♦♦♦
107 Botley Road, Oxford,
Oxfordshire OX2 0HB
T: (01865) 243620

Parklands Hotel ♦♦♦
100 Banbury Road, Oxford,
Oxfordshire OX2 6JU
T: (01865) 554374
F: (01865) 559860
E: theparklands@freenet.co.uk
I: www.oxfordcity.co.
uk/hotels/parklands

Pembroke House ♦♦♦♦
379 Woodstock Road, Oxford,
Oxfordshire OX2 8AA
T: (01865) 310782
F: (01865) 310649
E: john@g.c.pipkins.freeserve.
co.uk

Pickwicks Guest House ♦♦♦
15-17 London Road,
Headington, Oxford, Oxfordshire
OX3 7SP
T: (01865) 750487
F: (01865) 742208
E: pickwicks@x-stream.co.uk
I: www.oxfordcity.
co.uk/accom/pickwicks/

Pine Castle Hotel ♦♦♦♦
290 Iffley Road, Oxford,
Oxfordshire OX4 4AE
T: (01865) 241497 & 728887
F: (01865) 727230
E: stay@pinecastle.co.uk
I: www.oxfordcity.co.
uk/accommodation/pinecastle

The Ridings ♦♦♦
280 Abingdon Road, Oxford,
Oxfordshire OX1 4TA
T: (01865) 248364
F: (01865) 251348
E: ringsoxi@aol.com
I: www.members@aol.
com/ridingsoxi

River Hotel ♦♦♦
17 Botley Road, Oxford,
Oxfordshire OX2 0AA
T: (01865) 243475
F: (01865) 724306

Ryan's Guest House ♦♦♦
164 Banbury Road,
Summertown, Oxford,
Oxfordshire OX2 7BU
T: (01865) 558876
F: (01865) 558876

Sandfield House ♦♦♦♦
19 London Road, Headington,
Oxford, Oxfordshire OX3 7RE
T: (01865) 762406
F: (01865) 762406
E: stay@sandfield-guesthouse.
co.uk
I: www.sandfield-guesthouse.co.
uk

Sportsview Guest House ♦♦♦
106-110 Abingdon Road,
Oxford, Oxfordshire OX1 4PX
T: (01865) 244268 &
07798 818190
F: (01865) 249270
E: stay@sportsview.
guest-house.freeserve.co.uk

The Tower House ♦♦♦♦
15 Ship Street, Oxford,
Oxfordshire OX1 3DA
T: (01865) 246828
F: (01865) 246828

West Farm
Rating Applied For
Eaton, Appleton, Abingdon,
Oxfordshire OX13 5PR
T: (01865) 862908
F: (01865) 865512

The Westgate Hotel ♦♦
1 Botley Road, Oxford,
Oxfordshire OX2 0AA
T: (01865) 726721
F: (01865) 722078

Whitehouse View ♦♦
9 Whitehouse Road, Oxford,
Oxfordshire OX1 4PA
T: (01865) 721626 &
07702 816050

Lanteglos House ♦♦
Rectory Road, Padworth
Common, Reading, Berkshire
RG7 4JD
T: (01189) 700333

PANGBOURNE
Berkshire

Weir View House ♦♦♦
9 Shooters Hill, Pangbourne,
Reading, Berkshire RG8 7DZ
T: (01189) 842120
F: (01189) 842120

PARK GATE
Hampshire

Four Winds Guest House ♦♦♦
17 Station Road, Park Gate,
Southampton, Hampshire
SO31 7GJ
T: (01489) 584433 & 570965
F: (01489) 570965

60 Southampton Road ♦♦♦
Park Gate, Southampton,
Hampshire SO31 6AF
T: (01489) 573994

PARKSTONE
Dorset

Casa Ana Guest House ♦
93 North Road, Parkstone, Poole,
Dorset BH14 0LT
T: (01202) 741367

Danecourt Lodge ♦♦♦♦
58 Danecourt Road, Parkstone,
Poole, Dorset BH14 0PQ
T: (01202) 730957

Marrick Guest House ♦♦♦
151 Bournemouth Road,
Parkstone, Poole, Dorset
BH14 9HT
T: (01202) 721576
F: (01202) 747255

Toad Hall ♦♦♦♦
30 Church Road, Parkstone,
Poole, Dorset BH14 0NS
T: (01202) 733900 &
07885 242132
F: (01202) 733900

**Viewpoint Guest House
♦♦♦♦ SILVER AWARD**
11 Constitution Hill Road,
Parkstone, Poole, Dorset
BH14 0QB
T: (01202) 733586 &
07850 164934
F: (01202) 733586
E: viewpointgh@viewpoint-gh
I: www.viewpoint-gh.co.uk

PENN
Buckinghamshire

Little Penn Farmhouse ♦♦♦♦
Penn Bottom, Penn,
Buckinghamshire HP10 8PJ
T: (01494) 813439
F: (01494) 817740
E: sally@saundersharris.co.uk

PENNINGTON
Hampshire

**Restormel Bed & Breakfast
♦♦♦♦**
Restormel, Sway Road,
Pennington, Lymington,
Hampshire SO41 8LJ
T: (01590) 673875 &
07703 918188
F: (01590) 673875

PETERSFIELD
Hampshire

Beaumont ♦♦♦
22 Stafford Road, Petersfield,
Hampshire GU32 2JG
T: (01730) 264744
F: (01730) 264744

Heath Farmhouse ◆◆◆
Heath Road East, Petersfield,
Hampshire GU31 4HU
T: (01730) 264709
E: prue@scurfield.co.uk

Heathside ◆◆◆
36 Heath Road East, Petersfield,
Hampshire GU31 4HR
T: (01730) 262337
F: (01730) 262337

The Holt ◆◆◆
60 Heath Road, Petersfield,
Hampshire GU31 4EJ
T: (01730) 262836

Ridgefield ◆◆
Station Road, Petersfield,
Hampshire GU32 3DE
T: (01730) 261402
E: ymcokw@hants.gov.uk

Rose Cottage ◆◆◆
1 The Mead, Liss, Hampshire
GU33 7DU
T: (01730) 892378

South Gardens Cottage ◆◆◆
South Harting, Petersfield,
Hampshire GU31 5QJ
T: (01730) 825040
F: (01730) 825040
E: rogerandjulia@beeb.net

1 The Spain ◆◆◆
Petersfield, Hampshire GU32 3JZ
T: (01730) 263261 & 261678
E: allantarver@cw.co.net

Ye Olde George ◆◆◆
Church Street, East Meon,
Petersfield, Hampshire
GU32 1NH
T: (01730) 823481
F: (01730) 823759

PICKET PIECE
Hampshire

Cherry Trees ◆◆◆
Picket Piece, Andover,
Hampshire SP11 6LY
T: (01264) 334891

PILLEY
Hampshire

Mistletoe Cottage ◆◆◆◆
3 Jordans Lane, Pilley Bailey,
Pilley, Lymington, Hampshire
SO41 5QW
T: (01590) 676361

PISHILL
Oxfordshire

Bank Farm ◆◆
Pishill, Henley-on-Thames,
Oxfordshire RG9 6HJ
T: (01491) 638601
F: (01491) 638601
E: bankfarm@compuserve.com

Orchard House ◆◆◆
Pishill, Henley-on-Thames,
Oxfordshire RG9 6HJ
T: (01491) 638351
F: (01491) 638351

POOLE
Dorset

Annelise ◆◆◆
41 Danecourt Road, Lower
Parkstone, Poole, Dorset
BH14 0PG
T: (01202) 744833 &
07702 025442
F: (01202) 744833
E: vincent41.fsnet.co.uk

Ashdell ◆◆
85 Dunyeats Road, Broadstone,
Dorset BH18 8AF
T: (01202) 692032
E: ashdell@excite.com

B & B on the Quay ◆◆◆
23 Barbers Wharf, Poole, Dorset
BH15 1ZB
T: (01202) 669214 &
07802 410520
F: (01202) 669214

Corkers ◆◆◆◆ SILVER AWARD
1 High Street, The Quay, Poole,
Dorset BH15 1AB
T: (01202) 681393 & 674184
F: (01202) 667393
E: corkers@corkers.co.uk
I: www.corkers.co.uk/corkers

Fernway ◆◆◆
56 Fernside Road, Poole, Dorset
BH15 2JJ
T: (01202) 252044 &
07802 351033
F: (01202) 666587
E: g0wtg@demon.co.uk

Fleetwater Guest House ◆◆◆
161 Longfleet Road, Poole,
Dorset BH15 2HS
T: (01202) 682509

The Golden Sovereign Hotel ◆◆◆
97 Alumhurst Road, Alum Chine,
Bournemouth, Dorset BH4 8HR
T: (01202) 762088 &
07850 808140
F: (01202) 762088
E: goldensov@aol.com

The Grange Guest House ◆◆
1 Linthorpe Road, Poole, Dorset
BH15 2JS
T: (01202) 671336

Harbour Lea ◆◆◆
1 Whitecliff Road, Poole, Dorset
BH14 8DU
T: (01202) 744346
F: (01202) 268930
E: harbourlea@easicom.com
@

Harlequins B & B ◆◆◆◆
134 Ringwood Road, Poole,
Dorset BH14 0RP
T: (01202) 677624 &
07887 888074
E: harlequins@tinyworld.co

Highways ◆◆◆
29 Fernside Road, Poole, Dorset
BH15 2QU
T: (01202) 677060
@

Laurel Cottages ◆◆◆
41 Foxholes Road, Poole, Dorset
BH15 3NA
T: (01202) 730894
F: (01202) 730894
E: anne.howarth@cwcom.net

Lytchett Mere ◆◆◆◆
191 Sandy Lane, Upton, Poole,
Dorset BH16 5LU
T: (01202) 622854

The Mariners Guest House ◆◆◆
26 Sandbanks Road, Poole,
Dorset BH14 8AQ
T: (01202) 247218

26 Porter Road ◆◆
Creekmoor, Poole, Dorset
BH17 7AW
T: (01202) 678835

Quay House ◆◆◆
3A Thames Street, Poole, Dorset
BH15 1JN
T: (01202) 686335
F: (01202) 686335

The Saltings ◆◆◆◆
5 Salterns Way, Lilliput, Poole,
Dorset BH14 8JR
T: (01202) 707349
E: saltingsbridle@compuserve.
com.

Sarnia Cherie ◆◆◆◆
375 Blandford Road,
Hamworthy, Poole, Dorset
BH15 4JL
T: (01202) 679470 &
07885 319931
F: (01202) 679470
E: criscollier@aol.com

Sea Haven ◆
39 Hunt Road, Poole, Dorset
BH15 3QD
T: (01202) 671770 &
07977 698670

The Shah of Persia
◆◆◆◆ SILVER AWARD
173 Longfleet Road, Poole,
Dorset BH15 2HS
T: (01202) 676587 & 685346
F: (01202) 679327

South Rising ◆◆◆
86 Parkstone Road, Poole,
Dorset BH15 2QE
T: (01202) 240766
F: (01202) 565193
E: normanundercroft@
netscapeonline.co.uk

The Squirrels ◆◆◆
431 Ringwood Road, Alderney,
Poole, Dorset BH12 4LX
T: (01202) 734529

Tatnam Farm ◆◆◆◆
82 Tatnam Road, Poole, Dorset
BH15 2DS
T: (01202) 672969
F: (01202) 682732
E: helenbishop@jrb.netkonect.
co.uk

Upper House ◆◆◆
19 Church Street, Poole, Dorset
BH15 1JP
T: (01202) 670491

Vernon ◆◆
96 Blandford Road North,
Beacon Hill, Poole, Dorset
BH16 6AD
T: (01202) 625185

PORCHFIELD
Isle of Wight

Youngwoods Farm ◆◆◆
Whitehouse Road, Porchfield,
Newport, Isle of Wight PO30 4LJ
T: (01983) 522170
F: (01983) 522170

PORTCHESTER
Hampshire

Harbour View ◆◆
85 Windmill Grove, Portchester,
Fareham, Hampshire PO16 9HH
T: (023) 9237 6740

PORTMORE
Hampshire

A Thatched House ◆◆◆
Hundred Lane, Portmore,
Lymington, Hampshire
SO41 5RG
T: (01590) 679977
F: (01590) 679977

Cherry Tree ◆◆◆◆
Hundred Lane, Portmore,
Lymington, Hampshire
SO41 5RG
T: (01590) 672990

PORTSMOUTH & SOUTHSEA
Hampshire

Abbey Lodge ◆◆◆
30 Waverley Road, Southsea,
Hampshire PO5 2PW
T: (023) 9282 8285
F: (023) 9287 2943
E: linda@abbeylodge.co.uk
I: www.abbeylodge.co.uk

The Albatross Guest House
◆◆◆
51 Waverley Road, Southsea,
Hampshire PO5 2PJ
T: (023) 9282 8325

Amberley Court ◆◆◆
97 Waverley Road, Southsea,
Portsmouth, Hampshire PO5 2PL
T: (023) 9273 7473 &
07801 379514
F: (023) 9235 6911
E: nigelward@compuserve.com
I: www.amberley-court.co.uk

Anne Boleyn Guest House ◆
33 Granada Road, Southsea,
Hampshire PO4 0RD
T: (023) 9273 1043
F: (023) 9243 6229
E: annieandlyndon@ukonline.
co.uk

April House ◆
7 Malvern Road, Southsea,
Portsmouth, Hampshire PO5 2LZ
T: (023) 9281 4824 &
07850 547551
F: (023) 9273 2555
E: acpropertys@newnet.com
I: www.portsnet.
com/acpropertys

Aquarius Court Hotel ◆◆◆
34 St Ronans Road, Southsea,
Hampshire PO4 0PT
T: (023) 9282 2872 & 9282 0148
F: (023) 9261 9065

Arden Guest House ◆◆◆
14 Herbert Road, Southsea,
Hampshire PO4 0QA
T: (023) 9282 6409

Ashwood Guest House ◆◆◆
10 St Davids Road, Southsea,
Hampshire PO5 1QN
T: (023) 9281 6228
F: (023) 9275 3955

Avarest Guest House ◆
10 Waverley Grove, Southsea,
Hampshire PO4 0PZ
T: (023) 9282 9444

Bembell Court Hotel ◆◆◆
69 Festing Road, Southsea,
Portsmouth, Hampshire
PO4 0NQ
T: (023) 9273 5915 & 9275 0497
F: (023) 9275 6497
E: keith@bembell.freeserve.co.
uk
@

Birchwood Guest House ♦♦♦
44 Waverley Road, Southsea,
Portsmouth, Hampshire
PO5 2PP
T: (023) 9281 1337 &
07711 897789
E: ged@birchwoodguesthouse.
freeserve.co.uk
I: www.smoothound.co.
uk/hotels/birchwood/hmtl

Britannia Guest House ♦♦♦
8 Outram Road, Southsea,
Hampshire PO5 1QU
T: (023) 9281 4234
F: (023) 9281 4234

Corran Guest House ♦♦♦
25 Herbert Road, Southsea,
Hampshire PO4 0QA
T: (023) 9273 3006

The Dorcliffe ♦♦♦
42 Waverley Road, Southsea,
Hampshire PO5 2PP
T: (023) 9282 8283

The Elms Guest House ♦♦♦
48 Victoria Road South,
Southsea, Hampshire PO5 2BT
T: (023) 9282 3924
F: (023) 9282 3924
E: TheElmsGH@aol.com

Esk Vale Guest House ♦♦♦
39 Granada Road, Southsea,
Hampshire PO4 0RD
T: (023) 9286 2639
F: (023) 9235 5589

Everley Guest House ♦♦♦
33 Festing Road, Southsea,
Hampshire PO4 0NG
T: (023) 9273 1001
F: (023) 9278 0995

Fairlea Guest House ♦♦
19 Beach Road, Southsea,
Hampshire PO5 2JH
T: (023) 9273 3090

The Festing Grove Guest House
♦♦♦
8 Festing Grove, Southsea,
Portsmouth, Hampshire
PO4 9QA
T: (023) 9273 5239
E: festinggrove@talk21.com

Fortitude Cottage ♦♦♦
51 Broad Street, Portsmouth,
Hampshire PO1 2JD
T: (023) 9282 3748
F: (023) 9282 3748
E: fortcott@aol.com
I: www.visitus.co.uk

Gainsborough House ♦
9 Malvern Road, Southsea,
Hampshire PO5 2LZ
T: (023) 9282 2604

Glenroy Guest House ♦♦
28 Waverley Road, Southsea,
Hampshire PO5 2PW
T: (023) 9281 4922

Granada House Hotel
Rating Applied For
29 Granada Road, Southsea,
Hampshire PO4 0RD
T: (023) 9286 1575
F: (023) 9271 8343

Greenacres Guest House ♦♦♦
12 Marion Road, Southsea,
Portsmouth, Hampshire
PO4 0QX
T: (023) 9235 3137 & 9275 1312
E: katad@greenacres80.
freeserve.co.uk

Hamilton House ♦♦♦♦
95 Victoria Road North,
Southsea, Portsmouth,
Hampshire PO5 1PS
T: (023) 9282 3502
F: (023) 9282 3502
E: sandra@hamiltonhouse.co.
uk.
I: www.resort-guide.co.
uk/portsmouth/hamilton
@

Hillside Lodge
Rating Applied For
1 Blake Road, Farlington,
Portsmouth, Hampshire PO6 1ET
T: (023) 9237 2687

Homestead Guest House ♦♦♦
11 Bembridge Crescent,
Southsea, Hampshire PO4 0QT
T: (023) 9273 2362

Kilbenny Guest House ♦♦♦
2 Malvern Road, Southsea,
Hampshire PO5 2NA
T: (023) 9286 1347

Kingsley Guest House ♦♦♦
16 Craneswater Avenue,
Southsea, Hampshire PO4 0PB
T: (023) 9273 9113

Lamorna Guest House ♦♦
23 Victoria Road South,
Southsea, Hampshire PO5 2BX
T: (023) 9281 1157

Langdale Guest House ♦♦♦
13 St Edwards Road, Southsea,
Hampshire PO5 3DH
T: (023) 9282 2146
F: (023) 9235 3303
E: langdale@btinternet.com
I: www.smoothhound.co.
uk/hotels/langdal.html

Mandalay ♦
31 St Andrews Road, Southsea,
Hampshire PO5 1EP
T: (023) 9282 9600
F: (023) 9282 9600

Marmion Lodge Guest House
♦♦♦♦
71 Marmion Road, Southsea,
Hampshire PO5 2AX
T: (023) 9282 2150
F: (023) 9282 2150
E: marmionlodge@btinternet.
com

Oakdale ♦♦♦♦
71 St Ronans Road, Southsea,
Hampshire PO4 0PP
T: (023) 9273 7358
F: (023) 9273 7358
E: oakdale@btinternet.com

Oakleigh Guest House ♦♦♦
48 Festing Grove, Southsea,
Hampshire PO4 9QD
T: (023) 9281 2276

The Pembroke Park Hotel
♦♦♦
1 Bellevue Terrace, Southsea,
Portsmouth, Hampshire PO5 3AT
T: (023) 9229 6817
F: (023) 9229 6817
E: pembrokeparkhotel@
compuserve.com
I: www.visit.
com/pembrokeparkhotel

**Rees Hall University of
Portsmouth**♦♦♦
Southsea Terrace, Southsea,
Hampshire PO5 3AP
T: (023) 9284 3884
F: (023) 9284 3888

The Rowans ♦♦♦♦
43 Festing Grove, Southsea,
Hampshire PO4 9QB
T: (023) 9273 6614
F: (023) 9282 3711

Sailmaker's Loft ♦
5 Bath Square, Spice Island,
Portsmouth, Hampshire PO1 2JL
T: (023) 9282 3045 & 9229 5961
F: (023) 9229 5961

Sally Port Inn ♦♦
57-58 High Street, Portsmouth,
Hampshire PO1 2LU
T: (023) 9282 1860
F: (023) 9282 1293

Stacey Court Hotel ♦♦
42 Clarence Parade, Southsea,
Hampshire PO5 2EU
T: (023) 92826827
F: (023) 92361365
E: garry.small@virgin.net

Strand Court Guest House ♦♦
28 Granada Road, Southsea,
Hampshire PO4 0RH
T: (023) 9273 2535
@

Uplands Hotel ♦♦♦
34 Granada Road, Southsea,
Hampshire PO4 0RH
T: (023) 9282 1508
F: (023) 9287 0126
@

Upper Mount House Hotel
♦♦♦♦
The Vale, Clarendon Road,
Southsea, Hampshire PO5 2EQ
T: (023) 9282 0456
F: (023) 9282 0456

Victoria Court ♦♦♦
29 Victoria Road North,
Southsea, Hampshire PO5 1PL
T: (023) 9282 0305
F: (023) 9283 8277
E: stay@victoriacourt.co.uk
I: www.victoriacourt.co.uk

Walsingham Guest House
♦♦♦
18 Festing Road, Southsea,
Hampshire PO4 0NG
T: (023) 9283 2818
F: (023) 9283 2818

Waveney Hotel ♦♦♦
54 Granada Road, Southsea,
Portsmouth, Hampshire PO4 0RJ
T: (023) 9282 5805
F: (023) 9275 4263
E: wavhot@btinternet.com

**Waverley Park Lodge Guest
House**♦♦♦
99 Waverley Road, Southsea,
Hampshire PO5 2PL
T: (023) 9273 0402 & 9278 1094

The White House Hotel ♦♦
26 South Parade, Southsea,
Hampshire PO5 2JF
T: (023) 9282 3709 & 9273 2759
F: (023) 9273 2759

Wolverton Guest House ♦♦♦
22 Granada Road, Southsea,
Hampshire PO4 0RH
T: (023) 9273 2819 & 9234 5474

Woodville Hotel ♦♦♦
6 Florence Road, Southsea,
Hampshire PO5 2NE
T: (023) 9282 3409
F: (023) 9234 6089
I: woodvillehotel@cwcom.net

POULNER
Hampshire

A Secret Garden ♦♦♦
132 Kingfisher Way, Poulner,
Ringwood, Hampshire
BH24 3LW
T: (01425) 477563 &
079577 356748
F: (01425) 477563
E: jennybandb@aol.com

PRINCES RISBOROUGH
Buckinghamshire

Grahurst ♦♦♦
6 Abbotswood, Speen, Princes
Risborough, Buckinghamshire
HP27 0SR
T: (01494) 488544

Solis Ortu ♦♦♦
Aylesbury Road, Askett, Princes
Risborough, Buckinghamshire
HP27 9LY
T: (01844) 344175
F: (01844) 343509

PRIVETT
Hampshire

Thatched Cottage Farm
Rating Applied For
Filmore Hill, Privett, Alton,
Hampshire GU34 3NX
T: (01730) 828278

QUAINTON
Buckinghamshire

The White Hart ♦♦
4 The Strand, Quainton,
Aylesbury, Buckinghamshire
HP22 4AS
T: (01296) 655234

Woodlands Farmhouse ♦♦♦
Doddershall, Quainton,
Aylesbury, Buckinghamshire
HP22 4DE
T: (01296) 770225

QUARLEY
Hampshire

Lains Cottage ♦♦♦♦
Quarley, Andover, Hampshire
SP11 8PX
T: (01264) 889697
F: (01264) 889227
E: lains-cott-hols@dial.pipex.
com
I: dspace.dial.pipex.
com/lains-cott-hols/

RAMSDEN
Oxfordshire

Akeman Cottage
Rating Applied For
Ramsden, Chipping Norton,
Oxfordshire OX7 3AU
T: (01993) 868383
F: (01993) 868075

Ann's Cottage ♦♦
Lower End, Ramsden, Chipping
Norton, Oxfordshire OX7 3AZ
T: (01993) 868592

READING
Berkshire

Abadair House ♦♦
46 Redlands Road, Reading,
Berkshire RG1 5HE
T: (0118) 986 3792
F: (0118) 986 3792
E: abadair@globalnet.co.uk
I: www.smoothhound.co.
uk/hotels/abadair/.html

Bath Hotel ♦♦♦
54 Bath Road, Reading,
Berkshire RG1 6PG
T: (0118) 957 2019
F: (0118) 950 3203

Belstone ♦♦♦♦
36 Upper Warren Avenue,
Caversham, Reading, Berkshire
RG4 7EB
T: (0118) 947 7435
F: (0118) 946 1465

61 Bulmershe Road
Rating Applied For
Reading, Berkshire RG1 5RH
T: (0118) 926 7595

Caversham Lodge ♦♦
133a Caversham Road, Reading,
Berkshire RG1 8AS
T: (01189) 573529 & 612110

Crescent Hotel ♦
35 Coley Avenue, Reading,
Berkshire RG1 6LL
T: (01189) 507980
F: (01189) 507980

Dittisham Guest House ♦♦♦
63 Tilehurst Road, Reading,
Berkshire RG30 2JL
T: (0118) 956 9483 &
07889 605193

The Elms ♦♦
Gallowstree Road, Rotherfield
Peppard, Henley-on-Thames,
Oxfordshire RG9 5HT
T: (0118) 972 3164
F: (0118) 972 4594

10 Greystoke Road ♦♦♦♦
Caversham, Reading, Berkshire
RG4 5EL
T: (01189) 475784

The Old Forge ♦
109 Grovelands Road, Reading,
Berkshire RG30 2PB
T: (0118) 958 2928
F: (0118) 958 2408
E: john.reesl@virgin.net

Orchid Guest House ♦♦♦
1 Micklands Road, Caversham,
Reading, Berkshire RG4 6LT
T: (0118) 947 9635 &
07958 953582
E: orchid@netcomuk.co.uk
I: www.netcomuk.co.
uk/Sorchid/main.html

The Six Bells ♦♦♦
Beenham Village, Beenham,
Reading, Berkshire RG7 5NX
T: (0118) 971 3368

Warren Dene Hotel ♦♦♦
1017 Oxford Road, Tilehurst,
Reading, Berkshire RG31 6TL
T: (0118) 942 2556
F: (0118) 945 1096
E: wdh@globalnet.co.uk

REMENHAM
Oxfordshire

Thamesmead House Hotel
♦♦♦♦♦ SILVER AWARD
Remenham Lane, Remenham,
Henley-on-Thames, Oxfordshire
RG9 2LR
T: (01491) 574745
I: www.thamesmeadhousehotel.
co.uk

RINGWOOD
Hampshire

Amberwood ♦♦♦♦
3-5 Top Lane, Mansfield,
Ringwood, Hampshire BH24 1LF
T: (01425) 476615
E: maynsing@aol.com
I: www.amberwoodbandb.co.uk

The Auld Kennels ♦♦♦
215 Christchurch Road,
Moortown, Ringwood,
Hampshire BH24 3AN
T: (01425) 475170
F: (01425) 461577

Beau Cottage ♦♦♦
1 Hiltom Road, Ringwood,
Hampshire BH24 1PW
T: (01425) 461274
E: sagemo5734@talk21.com
⊛

Fraser House ♦♦♦
Salisbury Road, Blashford,
Ringwood, Hampshire BH24 3PB
T: (01425) 473958

Lochend ♦♦♦
Hurst Corner, Salisbury Road,
Ringwood, Hampshire BH24 1AX
T: (01425) 473836
F: (01425) 475624
E: kenbbrown@kbblochend.
demon.co.uk

Old Stacks ♦♦♦♦
154 Hightown Road, Ringwood,
Hampshire BH24 1NP
T: (01425) 473840
F: (01425) 473840
E: oldstacksbandb@aol.com
⊛

Original White Hart ♦♦♦
Market Place, Ringwood,
Hampshire BH24 1AW
T: (01425) 472702
F: (01425) 471993

Picket Hill House
♦♦♦♦ SILVER AWARD
Picket Hill, Ringwood,
Hampshire BH24 3HH
T: (01425) 476173
F: (01425) 470022
E: b&b@pickethill.freeserve.co.
uk

Torre Avon
♦♦♦♦ SILVER AWARD
21 Salisbury Road, Ringwood,
Hampshire BH24 1AS
T: (01425) 472769 &
07967 972770
F: (01425) 472769
E: b&b@torreavon.freeserve.co.
uk
I: www.torreavon.freeserve.co.uk
⊛

ROMSEY
Hampshire

Abbey Hotel ♦♦♦
11 Church Street, Romsey,
Hampshire SO51 8BT
T: (01794) 513360
F: (01794) 524318
E: di@abbeyhotelromsey.co.uk
I: www.abbeyhotelromsey.co.uk

The Chalet Guest House ♦♦♦
Botley Road, Whitenap, Romsey,
Hampshire SO51 5RQ
T: (01794) 517299 &
07703 638550

79 Mercer Way ♦♦
Romsey, Hampshire SO51 7PH
T: (01794) 502009
F: (01794) 503009

4 Newton Lane ♦♦♦
Romsey, Hampshire SO51 8GZ
T: (01794) 514150
⊛

Pauncefoot House ♦♦♦
Pauncefoot Hill, Romsey,
Hampshire SO51 6AA
T: (01794) 513139
F: (01794) 513139
E: lendupont@netscapeonline.
co.uk

Pillar Box Cottage
Rating Applied For
Toothill, Romsey, Hampshire
SO51 9LN
T: (023) 8073 2390 &
07774 460970

Pyesmead Farm ♦♦♦
Plaitford, Romsey, Hampshire
SO51 6EE
T: (01794) 323386
F: (01794) 323386
E: pysemead@talk21.com

Stoneymarsh Cottage ♦♦♦
Stoneymarsh, Romsey,
Hampshire SO51 0LB
T: (01794) 368867
F: (01794) 368867
E: m.m.moran@btinternet.com

Wessex Guest House ♦
5 Palmerston Street, Romsey,
Hampshire SO51 8GF
T: (01794) 512038

RYDE
Isle of Wight

Arlyn ♦♦
59 West Hill Road, Ryde, Isle of
Wight PO33 1LG
T: (01983) 567743
E: arlyn@supanet.com

Claverton ♦♦♦♦
12 The Strand, Ryde, Isle of
Wight PO33 1JE
T: (01983) 613015
F: (01983) 613015

The Dorset Hotel ♦♦♦
31 Dover Street, Ryde, Isle of
Wight PO33 2BW
T: (01983) 564327 & 563892
F: (01983) 614635
E: hoteldorset@aol.com
I: www.thedorsethotel.co.uk

Elmfield Lodge ♦♦♦♦
35 Marlborough Road, Elmfield,
Ryde, Isle of Wight PO33 1AB
T: (01983) 614131

Fern Cottage ♦♦♦♦
8 West Street, Ryde, Isle of
Wight PO33 2NW
T: (01983) 565856
F: (01983) 565856

Havencroft Farm ♦♦
Havenstreet, Ryde, Isle of Wight
PO33 4DJ
T: (01983) 883974

Kemphill Farm ♦♦♦♦
Stroudwood Road, Upton, Ryde,
Isle of Wight PO33 4BZ
T: (01983) 563880
F: (01983) 563880
E: ron.holland@farming.co.uk

Rodborough ♦♦♦
25 Queens Road, Ryde, Isle of
Wight PO33 3BG
T: (01983) 565370

Seaward Guest House ♦♦
14-16 George Street, Ryde, Isle
of Wight PO33 2EW
T: (01983) 563168
F: (01983) 563168
E: seaward@fsbdial.co.uk

Sillwood Acre ♦♦♦♦
Church Road, Binstead, Ryde,
Isle of Wight PO33 3TB
T: (01983) 563553
E: sillwood.acre@virginnet.co.uk

Stonelands ♦♦♦♦
Binstead Road, Binstead, Ryde,
Isle of Wight PO33 3NJ
T: (01983) 616947
F: (01983) 812857

Trentham Guest House ♦♦
38 The Strand, Ryde, Isle of
Wight PO33 1JF
T: (01983) 563418
F: (01983) 563418

The Vine Guest House ♦♦♦
16 Castle Street, Ryde, Isle of
Wight PO33 2EG
T: (01983) 566633

RYDE-WOOTTON
Isle of Wight

Bridge House
♦♦♦♦ SILVER AWARD
Kite Hill, Wootton Bridge, Ryde,
Isle of Wight PO33 4LA
T: (01983) 884163

ST LAWRENCE
Isle of Wight

Lisle Combe (Bank End Farm)
♦♦
Undercliff Drive, St Lawrence,
Ventnor, Isle of Wight
PO38 1UW
T: (01983) 852582

Little Orchard ♦♦♦♦
Undercliff Drive, St Lawrence,
Ventnor, Isle of Wight PO38 1YA
T: (01983) 731106

ST MARY BOURNE
Hampshire

Trestan Cottage ♦♦♦
Church Street, St Mary Bourne,
Andover, Hampshire SP11 6BL
T: (01264) 738380

SANDFORD
Isle of Wight

The Barn ♦♦♦♦
Pound Farm, Shanklin Road,
Sandford, Ventnor, Isle of Wight
PO38 3AW
T: (01983) 840047
F: (01983) 840047

SANDFORD-ON-THAMES
Oxfordshire
The Old Post Office
Rating Applied For
11 Church Road, Sandford-on-
Thames, Oxford, Oxfordshire
OX4 4XZ
T: (01865) 777213

SANDLEHEATH
Hampshire
Sandleheath Post Office &
Stores ◆◆◆
Sandleheath, Fordingbridge,
Hampshire SP6 1PP
T: (01425) 652230
F: (01425) 652230
E: david@cordelle.co.uk
I: www.cordelle.co.
uk/sandleheath

SANDOWN
Isle of Wight
Alendel Hotel ◆◆
1 Leed Street, Sandown, Isle of
Wight PO36 9DA
T: (01983) 402967

Belmore Private Hotel ◆◆◆
101 Station Avenue, Sandown,
Isle of Wight PO36 8HD
T: (01983) 404189 & 404169
F: (01983) 405942
⊛

Bernay Hotel ◆◆◆
24 Victoria Road, Sandown, Isle
of Wight PO36 8AL
T: (01983) 402205
F: (01983) 402205
E: david.john9@virgin.net

Bertram Lodge ◆◆◆
3 Leed Street, Sandown, Isle of
Wight PO36 9DA
T: (01983) 402551
F: (01983) 402551

Carisbrooke House Hotel ◆◆
11 Beachfield Road, Sandown,
Isle of Wight PO36 8NA
T: (01983) 402257

The Danebury ◆◆◆
26 Victoria Road, Sandown, Isle
of Wight PO36 8AL
T: (01983) 403795
E: danebury@madasafish.com

Denewood Hotel ◆◆◆
7 Victoria Road, Sandown, Isle of
Wight PO36 8AL
T: (01983) 402980 & 403517
F: (01983) 402980

Homeland Private Hotel ◆◆
38 Grove Road, Sandown, Isle of
Wight PO36 8HH
T: (01983) 404305

Inglewood Guest House ◆◆◆
15 Avenue Road, Sandown, Isle
of Wight PO36 8BN
T: (01983) 403485

Iona Guest House ◆◆◆
44 Sandown Road, Lake,
Sandown, Isle of Wight
PO36 9JT
T: (01983) 402741
F: (01983) 402741
E: ionahotel@netscapeonline.
co.uk

Kingswood Hotel ◆◆
15 Melville Street, Sandown, Isle
of Wight PO36 9DP
T: (01983) 402685
F: (01983) 402685

Lanowlee ◆◆◆
99 Station Avenue, Sandown,
Isle of Wight PO36 8ND
T: (01983) 403577

The Lawns Hotel ◆◆◆
72 The Broadway, Sandown, Isle
of Wight PO36 9AA
T: (01983) 402549
F: (01983) 402549
E: kdlawns@ukgateway.net

Lyndhurst Hotel ◆◆◆
8 Royal Crescent, Sandown, Isle
of Wight PO36 8LZ
T: (01983) 403663

Montague House Hotel ◆◆
109 Station Avenue, Sandown,
Isle of Wight PO36 8HD
T: (01983) 404295
F: (01983) 403322
E: chosefil@aol.com
I: www.netguides.co.
uk/wight/motague.html
⊛

Montpelier Hotel ◆◆◆
Pier Street, Sandown, Isle of
Wight PO36 8JR
T: (01983) 403964
F: (01983) 403074
E: enquiries@montoelier-hotel.
co.uk
I: www.montpelier-hotel.co.uk

Oakfields ◆
26 Melville Street, Sandown, Isle
of Wight PO36 8HX
T: (01983) 405410

Philomel Hotel ◆
21 Carter Street, Sandown, Isle
of Wight PO36 8BL
T: (01983) 406413

Rooftree Hotel ◆◆◆◆
26 Broadway, Sandown, Isle of
Wight PO36 9BY
T: (01983) 403175
F: (01983) 407354
E: rooftree@netguides.co.uk

St Catherines Hotel ◆◆◆◆
1 Winchester Park Road,
Sandown, Isle of Wight
PO36 8HJ
T: (01983) 402392
F: (01983) 402392
E: stcathhotel@hotmail.com
I: www.isleofwight-holidays.co.
uk

St Michaels Hotel ◆◆◆◆
33 Leed Street, Sandown, Isle of
Wight PO36 8JE
T: (01983) 403636

St Ninians Guest House ◆◆◆
19 Avenue Road, Sandown, Isle
of Wight PO36 8BN
T: (01983) 402755

Sandhill Hotel ◆◆◆
6 Hill Street, Sandown, Isle of
Wight PO36 9DB
T: (01983) 403635 & 403695
F: (01983) 403635
E: sandhill@ukgateway.net
I: www.sandhill-hotel.com

Shachri ◆◆◆
31 Avenue Road, Sandown, Isle
of Wight PO36 8BN
T: (01983) 405718

Shangri-La Hotel ◆◆
30 Broadway, Sandown, Isle of
Wight PO36 9BY
T: (01983) 403672 & 403415
F: (01983) 403672

Victoria Lodge ◆◆◆
4-6 Victoria Road, Sandown, Isle
of Wight PO36 8AP
T: (01983) 403209

Westfield Hotel ◆◆◆◆
17 Broadway, Sandown, Isle of
Wight PO36 9BY
T: (01983) 403802 & 408225
F: (01983) 408225

SEAVIEW
Isle of Wight
1 Cluniac Cottages ◆◆◆◆
Priory Road, Seaview, Isle of
Wight PO34 5BU
T: (01983) 812119
I: www.cluniaccottages.fsnet.co.
uk/

Maple Villa ◆◆◆◆
Oakhill Road, Seaview, Isle of
Wight PO34 5AP
T: (01983) 614826
E: dveccles@free4all.co.uk

SELBORNE
Hampshire
8 Goslings Croft ◆◆◆◆
Selborne, Alton, Hampshire
GU34 3HZ
T: (01420) 511285
F: (01420) 587451

Ivanhoe ◆◆◆◆
Oakhanger, Selborne, Alton,
Hampshire GU35 9JG
T: (01420) 473464

The Queen's & The Limes ◆◆◆
High Street, Selborne, Alton,
Hampshire GU34 3JJ
T: (01420) 511454
F: (01420) 511272
E: enquiries@queens-selborne.
co.uk
I: www.queens-selborne.co.uk
⊛

Seale Cottage ◆◆◆
Gracious Street, Selborne,
Hampshire GU34 3JE
T: (01420) 511396 &
07771 736925

Thatched Barn House ◆◆◆◆
Grange Farm, Gracious Street,
Selborne, Alton, Hampshire
GU34 3JG
T: (01420) 511007
F: (01420) 511008
E: bandb@bobt.dircon.co.uk
I: www.bobt.dircon.co.uk

SHAFTESBURY
Dorset
Cliff House
◆◆◆◆◆ SILVER AWARD
Breach Lane, Shaftesbury,
Dorset SP7 8LF
T: (01747) 852548 &
07710 380948
F: (01747) 852548
E: dianaepow@aol.com
I: www.cliff-house.co.uk

The Grove Arms Inn ◆◆◆◆
Ludwell, Shaftesbury, Dorset
SP7 9ND
T: (01747) 828328
F: (01747) 828960
I: www.wiltshireaccommodation.
com

The Kings Arms Inn ◆◆◆◆
East Stour Common, East Stour,
Gillingham, Dorset SP8 5NB
T: (01747) 838325
E: jenny@kings-arms.fsnet.co.
uk

The Knoll
◆◆◆◆ SILVER AWARD
Bleke Street, Shaftesbury, Dorset
SP7 8AH
T: (01747) 855243
E: pickshaftesbury@
compuserve.com
⊛

Paynes Place Barn
◆◆◆◆ SILVER AWARD
New Road, Shaftesbury, Dorset
SP7 8QL
T: (01747) 855016
F: (01747) 855016
E: xstal@globalnet.co.uk
I: www.accomodata.co.
uk/140498.htm

The Retreat ◆◆◆◆
47 Bell Street, Shaftesbury,
Dorset SP7 8AE
T: (01747) 850372
F: (01747) 854198

SHALFLEET
Isle of Wight
The Old Malthouse ◆◆◆◆
1 Mill Road, Shalfleet, Newport,
Isle of Wight PO30 4NE
T: (01983) 531329

Orchard Cottage ◆◆◆◆
2 Mill Road, Shalfleet, Newport,
Isle of Wight PO30 4NE
T: (01983) 531589

SHALSTONE
Buckinghamshire
Barnita ◆◆◆
Wood Green, Shalstone,
Buckingham, Buckinghamshire
MK18 5DZ
T: (01280) 850639

SHANKLIN
Isle of Wight
Atholl Court Guest House
◆◆◆
1 Atherley Road, Shanklin, Isle of
Wight PO37 7AT
T: (01983) 862414 &
07889 731227
F: (01983) 862414
E: infro@atholl-court.co.uk
I: www.atholl-court.co.uk

Bay House Hotel ◆◆◆
Chine Avenue, Keats Green,
Shanklin, Isle of Wight
PO37 6AG
T: (01983) 863180
F: (01983) 866604
E: bay_house@netguides.co.uk
I: www.netguides.co.
uk/wight/super/bayhouse.html

Bedford Lodge Hotel ◆◆◆
4 Chine Avenue, Old Village,
Shanklin, Isle of Wight
PO37 6AQ
T: (01983) 862416
F: (01983) 868704
E: mail@bedfordlodge.co.uk
I: www.bedfordlodge.co.uk

Broadwater Private Hotel
◆◆◆
6 Northcliff Gardens, Shanklin,
Isle of Wight PO37 6ES
T: (01983) 862194

Brooke House Hotel ◆◆◆
2 St Pauls Avenue, Shanklin, Isle
of Wight PO37 7AL
T: (01983) 863162

The Burlington Hotel ◆◆◆
6 Chine Avenue, Shanklin, Isle of
Wight PO37 6AG
T: (01983) 862090
F: (01983) 862191
E: mtulett@zoom.uk

Cedar Lodge Hotel ◆◆◆
28 Arthurs Hill, Shanklin, Isle of
Wight PO37 6EX
T: (01983) 863268
F: (01983) 863268

Celebration Hotel ◆◆◆◆
6 Avenue Road, Shanklin, Isle of
Wight PO37 7BG
T: (01983) 862746

Chestnuts Hotel ◆◆◆
Hope Road, Shanklin, Isle of
Wight PO37 6EA
T: (01983) 862162

Claremont Guest House ◆◆◆
4 Eastmount Road, Shanklin, Isle
of Wight PO37 6DN
T: (01983) 862083

Cliftonville Hotel ◆◆◆
6 Hope Road, Shanklin, Isle of
Wight PO37 6EA
T: (01983) 862197
F: (01983) 862197

Courtlands Hotel ◆◆◆
Paddock Road, Shanklin, Isle of
Wight PO37 6PA
T: (01983) 862167
F: (01983) 863308
E: simon@courtlandshotel.co.uk
I: www.courtlandshotel.co.uk

Culham Lodge Hotel ◆◆◆◆
31 Landguard Manor Road,
Shanklin, Isle of Wight
PO37 7HZ
T: (01983) 862880
F: (01983) 862880
E: metcalf@culham99.freeserve.
co.uk
I: www.isleofwighthotel.co.uk

Duncroft Hotel ◆◆◆
2 Wilton Park Road, Shanklin,
Isle of Wight PO37 7BT
T: (01983) 862427
F: (01983) 862963
E: angela@duncrofthotel.
freeserve.co.uk
I: www.duncrofthotel.freeserve.
co.uk

The Edgecliffe Hotel ◆◆◆◆
7 Clarence Gardens, Shanklin,
Isle of Wight PO37 6HA
T: (01983) 866199 & 862137
F: (01983) 868841
E: edgecliffe.hotel@
nationwideisp.net
I: www.wightonline.co.
uk/edgecliffehotel

**The Empress of the Sea Hotel
◆◆◆◆**
Luccombe Road, Shanklin, Isle of
Wight PO37 6RQ
T: (01983) 862178
E: empress.sea@virgin.net

Farringford Hotel ◆◆◆
19 Hope Road, Shanklin, Isle of
Wight PO37 6EA
T: (01983) 862176
E: crrome@excite.com
I: www.smoothound.co.
uk/hotels/farringford.html

Fawley Guest House ◆◆◆
12 Hope Road, Shanklin, Isle of
Wight PO37 6EA
T: (01983) 868898 & 868828

Foxhills
◆◆◆◆ GOLD AWARD
30 Victoria Avenue, Shanklin,
Isle of Wight PO37 6LS
T: (01983) 862329
F: (01983) 866666
E: info@foxhillshotel.co.uk
I: www.foxhillshotel.co.uk

The Glen Hotel ◆◆◆
4 Avenue Road, Shanklin, Isle of
Wight PO37 7BG
T: (01983) 862154

Grange Bank Hotel ◆◆◆◆
Grange Road, Shanklin, Isle of
Wight PO37 6NN
T: (01983) 862337
F: (01983) 862737
E: grangebank@netguides.co.uk
I: www.netguides.co.
uk/wight/standard/
grange_bank.html

Hazelwood Hotel ◆◆◆
14 Clarence Road, Shanklin, Isle
of Wight PO37 7BH
T: (01983) 862824
F: (01983) 862824
E: barbara.tubbs@
thehazelwood.free-online.co.uk
I: www.thehazelwood.
free-online.co.uk

**Holly Lodge
Rating Applied For**
29 Queens Road, Shanklin, Isle
of Wight PO37 6DQ
T: (01983) 863604

Hope Lodge Hotel ◆◆◆◆
21 Hope Road, Shanklin, Isle of
Wight PO37 6EA
T: (01983) 863140
F: (01983) 863140
E: janetwf@aol.com
I: placestostay.com

Ingress ◆◆◆
29 St Pauls Crescent, Shanklin,
Isle of Wight PO37 7AN
T: (01983) 862623

Jasmine Lodge ◆◆
156 Sandown Road, Shanklin,
Isle of Wight PO37 6HF
T: (01983) 863296
F: (01983) 863296

Kenbury Hotel ◆◆◆
Clarence Road, Shanklin, Isle of
Wight PO37 7BH
T: (01983) 862085
E: kenbury@isleofwighthotel.co.
uk
I: www.isleofwighthotel.co.uk

Kings Lodge Hotel ◆◆◆
Acacia House, 20 Queens Road,
Shanklin, Isle of Wight
PO37 6AW
T: (01983) 862990
F: (01983) 868685

Meyrick Cliffs Hotel ◆◆
Esplanade, Shanklin, Isle of
Wight PO37 6BH
T: (01983) 862691
F: (01983) 862648

Miclaran Hotel ◆◆◆
37 Littlestairs Road, Shanklin,
Isle of Wight PO37 6HS
T: (01983) 862726
F: (01983) 862726

Mount House Hotel ◆◆◆
20 Arthurs Hill, Shanklin, Isle of
Wight PO37 6EE
T: (01983) 862556
F: (01983) 867551
E: mounthouse@netguides.co.
uk
I: www.netguides.co.uk

**The Norfolk House Hotel
◆◆◆◆**
The Esplanade, Shanklin, Isle of
Wight PO37 6BN
T: (01983) 863023
E: thenorfolkhousehotel@
tinywould.co.uk
I: www.nebsweb.co.
uk/thenorfolkhousehotel

**Palmerston Hotel
Rating Applied For**
Palmerston Road, Shanklin, Isle
of Wight PO37 6AS
T: (01983) 865547
F: (01983) 868008

The Richmond Hotel ◆◆◆
23 Palmerston Road, Shanklin,
Isle of Wight PO37 6AS
T: (01983) 862874
F: (01983) 862874
E: richmondhotel.shanklin@
virgin.net

The Roseglen Hotel ◆◆◆
12 Palmerston Road, Shanklin,
Isle of Wight PO37 6AS
T: (01983) 863164
F: (01983) 862271
E: david@roseglen.co.uk

**Rowborough Private Hotel
◆◆◆**
32 Arthurs Hill, Shanklin, Isle of
Wight PO37 6EX
T: (01983) 866072
F: (01983) 867703

The Royson ◆◆◆
26 Littlestairs Road, Shanklin,
Isle of Wight PO37 6HS
T: (01983) 862163
F: (01983) 865403
I: www.theroyson.co.uk

Rozelle Hotel ◆◆
Atherley Road, Shanklin, Isle of
Wight PO37 7AT
T: (01983) 862745

Ryedale Private Hotel ◆◆◆
3 Atherley Road, Shanklin, Isle of
Wight PO37 7AT
T: (01983) 862375 &
07831 413233
F: (01983) 862375
E: ryedale@isleofwight5.fsnet.
co.uk
I: www.smoothhound.co.
uk/hotels/ryedalep.html

St Brelades Hotel ◆◆◆
15 Hope Road, Shanklin, Isle of
Wight PO37 6EA
T: (01983) 862967
E: julie@st-brelades-hotel.co.uk
I: www.st-brelades-hotel.co.uk

St Leonards Hotel ◆◆◆◆
22 Queens Road, Shanklin, Isle
of Wight PO37 6AW
T: (01983) 862121
F: (01983) 868895
E: les@stleonardsiw.freeserve.
co.uk
I: www.wight-breaks.co.uk

Seamer House ◆◆◆◆
30 Atherley Road, Shanklin, Isle
of Wight PO37 7AT
T: (01983) 864926
F: (01983) 864926
E: seamerhouse@tinyworld.co.
uk

Shoreside Hotel ◆◆◆
39 The Esplanade, Shanklin, Isle
of Wight PO37 6BG
T: (01983) 863169 & 864786

Somerville Hotel ◆◆◆
14 St Georges Road, Shanklin,
Isle of Wight PO37 6BA
T: (01983) 862821

The Steamer Inn ◆◆◆◆
18 The Esplanade, Shanklin, Isle
of Wight PO37 6BS
T: (01983) 862641

Suncliffe Private Hotel ◆◆◆
8 Hope Road, Shanklin, Isle of
Wight PO37 6EA
T: (01983) 863009
F: (01983) 864868
E: suncliffe@pmorter.tcp.co.uk
I: www.homepages.tcp.co.
uk/§pmorter

Swiss Cottage Hotel ◆◆◆
10 St Georges Road, Shanklin,
Isle of Wight PO37 6BA
T: (01983) 862333
F: (01983) 862333
E: mail@swiss-cottage.co.uk
I: www.swiss-cottage.co.uk

The Triton Hotel ◆
23 Atherley Road, Shanklin, Isle
of Wight PO37 7AU
T: (01983) 862494

**Westbourne Guest House
◆◆◆**
23 Queens Road, Shanklin, Isle
of Wight PO37 6AW
T: (01983) 862360

Whitegates Guest House ◆◆◆
18 Wilton Park Road, Shanklin,
Isle of Wight PO37 7BT
T: (01983) 866126

Willow Bank Hotel ◆◆◆
36 Atherley Road, Shanklin, Isle
of Wight PO37 7AU
T: (01983) 862482

SHENINGTON
Oxfordshire

Sugarswell Farm ◆◆◆◆
Shenington, Banbury,
Oxfordshire OX15 6HW
T: (01295) 680512
F: (01295) 688149

Top Farm House ◆◆◆
Shenington, Banbury,
Oxfordshire OX15 6LZ
T: (01295) 670226
F: (01295) 678170
E: cc.services@virgin.net

SHENLEY CHURCH END
Buckinghamshire
3 Selby Grove
Rating Applied For
Shenley Church End, Milton
Keynes, Buckinghamshire
MK5 6BN
T: (01908) 504663
E: chris@ceyes.freeserve.co.uk

SHILLINGFORD
Oxfordshire
Marsh House ◆◆◆
7 Court Drive, Shillingford,
Wallingford, Oxfordshire
OX10 7ER
T: (01865) 858496
F: (01865) 858496
E: chippynickson@hotmail.com

SHIPTON BELLINGER
Hampshire
Parsonage Farm ◆◆◆◆
Shipton Bellinger, Tidworth,
Hampshire SP9 7UF
T: (01980) 842404
F: (01980) 842404

SHIPTON-UNDER-WYCHWOOD
Oxfordshire
Court Farm
◆◆◆◆ SILVER AWARD
Mawles Lane, Shipton-under-
Wychwood, Oxford, Oxfordshire
OX7 6DA
T: (01993) 831515
F: (01993) 831813
E: belinda@courtfarmbb.fsnet.
co.uk

Courtlands ◆◆◆◆
6 Courtlands Road, Shipton-
under-Wychwood, Oxford,
Oxfordshire OX7 6DF
T: (01993) 830551
E: j-jfletcher@which.net
I: www.homepages.which.
net/9j-jfletcher/j-jfletcher/index.
html

Garden Cottage ◆◆◆
Fiddlers Hill, Shipton-under-
Wychwood, Chipping Norton,
Oxfordshire OX7 6DR
T: (01993) 830640 &
07803 399697
E: charmain@ukgateway.net

Lodge Cottage ◆◆◆
Shipton-under-Wychwood,
Oxford, Oxfordshire OX7 6DG
T: (01993) 830811

SHOOTASH
Hampshire
Kintail ◆◆◆
Salisbury Road, Shootash,
Romsey, Hampshire SO51 6GA
T: (01794) 513849

Lower Frenchwood Farm ◆◆◆
The Frenches, Shootash,
Romsey, Hampshire SO51 6FE
T: (01794) 322939

SHORWELL
Isle of Wight
Bucks Farm ◆◆◆◆
Shorwell, Newport, Isle of Wight
PO30 3LP
T: (01983) 551206
F: (01983) 551206

Northcourt ◆◆◆◆
Main Road, Shorwell, Newport,
Isle of Wight PO30 3JG
T: (01983) 740415
F: (01983) 740409
E: john@north-court.demon.co.
uk

Westcourt Farm ◆◆◆
Limerstone Road, Shorwell,
Newport, Isle of Wight PO30 3LA
T: (01983) 740233

SIXPENNY HANDLEY
Dorset
The Barleycorn House ◆◆◆◆
Deanland, Sixpenny Handley,
Salisbury, Wiltshire SP5 5PD
T: (01725) 552583
F: (01725) 552090

SONNING COMMON
Oxfordshire
The Spinney ◆◆◆
40 Woodlands Road, Sonning
Common, Reading, Berkshire
RG4 9TE
T: (0118) 9723248

SOULDERN
Oxfordshire
The Fox Inn ◆◆◆
Fox Lane, Souldern, Bicester,
Oxfordshire OX6 9JW
T: (01869) 345284
F: (01869) 345667

Tower Fields ◆◆◆
Tusmore Road, Souldern,
Bicester, Oxfordshire OX6 9HY
T: (01869) 346554
F: (01869) 345157
E: hgould@souldern.powernet.
co.uk

SOUTH GORLEY
Hampshire
Hucklesbrook Farm
◆◆◆◆ SILVER AWARD
South Gorley, Fordingbridge,
Hampshire SP6 2PN
T: (01425) 653180
E: dh.sampson@virgin.net

SOUTH LEIGH
Oxfordshire
Stow Cottage ◆◆◆
Station Road, South Leigh,
Witney, Oxfordshire OX8 6XN
T: (01993) 704005 &
07703 681920
F: (01993) 704005

SOUTHAMPTON
Hampshire
Abbey Lodge Guest House
Rating Applied For
37 The Polygon, Southampton,
Hampshire SO15 2BP
T: (023) 8022 1466

Acorn Lodge Guest House ◆◆
75 Morris Road, Polygon,
Southampton, Hampshire
SO15 2QB
T: (023) 8022 4837

Addenro House Hotel ◆◆
40-42 Howard Road, Shirley,
Southampton, Hampshire
SO15 5BL
T: (023) 8022 7144

Alcantara Guest House ◆◆◆
20 Howard Road, Shirley,
Southampton, Hampshire
SO15 5BN
T: (023) 8033 2966 & 8049 6163
F: (023) 8049 6163

Argyle Lodge ◆◆◆
13 Landguard Road, Shirley,
Southampton, Hampshire
SO15 5DL
T: (023) 8022 4063
F: (023) 8033 3688

Ashelee Lodge ◆◆◆
36 Atherley Road, Shirley,
Southampton, Hampshire
SO15 5DQ
T: (023) 8022 2095
F: (023) 8022 2095

Banister House Hotel ◆◆
Banister Road, Southampton,
Hampshire SO15 2JJ
T: (023) 8022 1279 & 8022 5753
F: (023) 8022 1279
E: banisterhouse@lineone.net

Carmel Guest House ◆◆◆
306 Winchester Road, Shirley,
Southampton, Hampshire
SO16 6TU
T: (023) 8077 3579

Eaton Court Hotel ◆◆◆
32 Hill Lane, Southampton,
Hampshire SO15 5AY
T: (023) 8022 3081
F: (023) 8032 2006
E: ecourthot@aol.com

Ellenborough House ◆◆◆
172 Hill Lane, Shirley,
Southampton, Hampshire
SO15 5DB
T: (023) 8022 1716
F: (023) 8034 8486

Fenland Guest House ◆◆◆
79 Hill Lane, Southampton,
Hampshire SO15 5AD
T: (023) 8022 0360
F: (023) 8022 6574
E: sde5999756@aol.com

Hunters Lodge Hotel
◆◆◆◆ SILVER AWARD
25 Landguard Road, Shirley,
Southampton, Hampshire
SO15 5DL
T: (023) 8022 7919
F: (023) 8023 0913
E: traceydugdale@virgin.net

Linden Guest House ◆◆◆
51-53 The Polygon,
Southampton, Hampshire
SO15 2BP
T: (023) 8022 5653
F: (023) 8063 0808

The Lodge ◆◆◆
No 1 Winn Road, The Avenue,
Southampton, Hampshire
SO17 1EH
T: (023) 8055 7537
F: (023) 8055 3586
I: www.yell.co.uk/siteslodgeso17

Madeleine Guest House
Rating Applied For
55 The Polygon, Southampton,
Hampshire SO15 2BP
T: (023) 8033 3331
F: (023) 8033 3331

Madison House
Rating Applied For
137 Hill Lane, Southampton,
Hampshire SO15 5AF
T: (023) 8033 3374
F: (023) 8033 1209
E: foley@madisonhouse.co.uk
I: www.madisonhouse.co.uk

The Mayfair Guest House
◆◆◆◆
11 Landguard Road, Shirley,
Southampton, Hampshire
SO15 5DL
T: (023) 8022 9861
F: (023) 8021 1552

Mayview Guest House ◆◆◆
30 The Polygon, Southampton,
Hampshire SO15 2BN
T: (023) 8022 0907
E: j_cole_new.qexcite.co.uk

Rivendell ◆◆◆
19 Landguard Road, Shirley,
Southampton, Hampshire
SO15 5DL
T: (02380) 223240
E: rivendell@alice16.freeserve.
co.uk

The Spinnaker ◆◆◆
Bridge Road, Lower Swanwick,
Southampton, Hampshire
SO31 7EB
T: (01489) 572123
F: (01489) 577394

Villa Capri Guest House ◆◆◆
50-52 Archers Road,
Southampton, Hampshire
SO15 2LU
T: (023) 8063 2800
F: (023) 8063 0100

The Winston Hotel ◆◆
51 Archers Road, Southampton,
Hampshire SO14 2NF
T: (023) 8022 4404
F: (023) 8022 3824

SOUTHBOURNE
Dorset
Acorns Hotel ◆◆◆◆
14 Southwood Avenue,
Southbourne, Bournemouth,
Dorset BH6 3QA
T: (01202) 422438
F: (01202) 778119

Hawkesmore Hotel ◆◆◆
3 Beech Avenue, Southbourne,
Bournemouth, Dorset BH6 3ST
T: (01202) 426787

Pennington Hotel ◆◆◆◆
26 Southern Road, Southbourne,
Bournemouth, Dorset BH6 3SS
T: (01202) 428653

Shearwater Hotel ◆◆◆
61 Grand Avenue, Southbourne,
Bournemouth, Dorset BH6 3TA
T: (01202) 423396
F: (01202) 423396
E: shearwaterbb@hotmail.com
I: www.theshearwater.freeserve.
co.uk

Sherbourne House Hotel
◆◆◆◆
14 Southern Road, Southbourne,
Bournemouth, Dorset BH6 3SR
T: (01202) 425680
F: (01202) 257423
E: ian@sherbournehousehotel.
co.uk
I: www.sherbournehousehotel.
co.uk

Shoreline Hotel ◆◆◆◆
7 Pinecliffe Avenue,
Southbourne, Bournemouth,
Dorset BH6 3PY
T: (01202) 429654
F: (01202) 429654

SPENCERS WOOD
Berkshire
Meadow View ◆◆
Basingstoke Road, Spencers
Wood, Reading, Berkshire
RG7 1AL
T: (0118) 988 3270

STANDLAKE
Oxfordshire
Pinkhill Cottage
◆◆◆◆ SILVER AWARD
45 Rack End, Standlake, Witney,
Oxfordshire OX8 7SA
T: (01865) 300544

STANFORD IN THE VALE
Oxfordshire
Stanford Park House
Rating Applied For
Park Lane, Stanford in the Vale,
Faringdon, Oxfordshire SN7 8PF
T: (01367) 710702 &
07831 242694
F: (01367) 710329

STEEPLE ASTON
Oxfordshire
Westfield Farm Motel ◆◆◆◆
Fenway, Steeple Aston, Bicester,
Oxfordshire OX6 3SS
T: (01869) 340591
T: (01869) 347594
E: info@westfieldmotel.u-net.
com

STOCKBRIDGE
Hampshire
Carbery Guest House ◆◆◆
Salisbury Hill, Stockbridge,
Hampshire SO20 6EZ
T: (01264) 810771
F: (01264) 811022

The Greyhound ◆◆◆
High Street, Stockbridge,
Hampshire SO20 6EY
T: (01264) 810833
F: (01264) 810833

STOKE POGES
Berkshire
Wexham Park Hall ◆◆◆◆
Wexham Street, Wexham, Stoke
Poges, Slough, Berkshire
SL3 6NB
T: (01753) 663254 & 663666
F: (01753) 663587

STONE
Buckinghamshire
Vicarage Farmhouse ◆◆◆◆
Churchway, Stone, Aylesbury,
Buckinghamshire HP17 8RG
T: (01296) 748182 &
07885 181435

STRATTON AUDLEY
Oxfordshire
The Old School ◆◆
Mill Road, Stratton Audley,
Bicester, Oxfordshire OX6 9BJ
T: (01869) 277371
E: sawertheimer@hotmail.com
I: www.old-school.co.uk

West Farm ◆◆◆◆
Launton Road, Stratton Audley,
Bicester, Oxfordshire OX6 9BW
T: (01869) 278344
F: (01869) 278344
E: sara.westfarmbb@virgin.net
I: www.westfarm.supaweb.co.uk
◉

STREATLEY
Berkshire
Pennyfield ◆◆◆◆
The Coombe, Streatley, Reading,
Berkshire RG8 9QT
T: (01491) 872048 &
07774 946182
F: (01491) 872048
E: mandrvanstone@hotmail.
com

STUDLAND
Dorset
Fairfields Hotel ◆◆◆◆
Swanage Road, Studland,
Swanage, Dorset BH19 3AE
T: (01929) 450224
F: (01929) 450224

STURMINSTER NEWTON
Dorset
The Homestead ◆◆◆
Hole House Lane, Sturminster
Newton, Dorset DT10 2AA
T: (01258) 471390
F: (01258) 471090
E: townsend@dircon.co.uk
I: www.townsend@dircon.co.
uk/

Swan Inn ◆◆◆◆
Market Place, Sturminster
Newton, Dorset DT10 1AR
T: (01258) 472208
F: (01258) 473767

SULHAMSTEAD
Berkshire
The Old Manor
◆◆◆◆◆ SILVER AWARD
Whitehouse Green,
Sulhamstead, Reading, Berkshire
RG7 4EA
T: (0118) 983 2423
F: (0118) 983 2423

SWALCLIFFE
Oxfordshire
Partway House ◆◆◆◆
Swalcliffe, Banbury, Oxfordshire
OX15 5HA
T: (01295) 780246
F: (01295) 780988

SWANAGE
Dorset
Amberlea Hotel ◆◆◆◆
36 Victoria Avenue, Swanage,
Dorset BH19 1AP
T: (01929) 426213
◉

Bella Vista Hotel ◆◆◆◆
Burlington Road, Swanage,
Dorset BH19 1LS
T: (01929) 422873
F: (01929) 426220
E: bella.vista@cwcom.net
I: www.bella.vista.mcmail.com

Easter Cottage
Rating Applied For
9 Eldon Terrace, Swanage,
Dorset BH19 1HA
T: (01929) 427782

Firswood Hotel ◆◆◆
29 Kings Road West, Swanage,
Dorset BH19 1HF
T: (01929) 422306 &
07957 181652
◉

Glenlee Hotel ◆◆◆
6 Cauldon Avenue, Swanage,
Dorset BH19 1PQ
T: (01929) 425794
F: (01929) 421530
E: martin@glenleehotel.
freeserve.co.uk

The Limes Hotel ◆◆◆
48 Park Road, Swanage, Dorset
BH19 2AE
T: (01929) 422664 &
0870 0548794
E: info@limeshotel.demon.co.uk
I: www.limeshotel.demon.co.uk

Millbrook Guest House ◆◆◆
56 Kings Road West, Swanage,
Dorset BH19 1HR
T: (01929) 423443
F: (01929) 423443
E: bob.millbrook@virgin.net
I: freespace.virgin.net/bob.
millbrook

St Michael ◆◆◆◆
31 Kings Road, Swanage, Dorset
BH19 1HF
T: (01929) 422064

Sandringham Hotel ◆◆◆
20 Durlston Road, Swanage,
Dorset BH19 2HX
T: (01929) 423076
F: (01929) 423076
E: silk@sandhot.fsnet.co.uk

White Lodge Hotel ◆◆◆◆
Grosvenor Road, Swanage,
Dorset BH19 2DD
T: (01929) 422696
F: (01929) 425510
E: whitelodge.hotel@virgin.net
I: www.whitelodgehotel.co.uk
◉

SWANMORE
Hampshire
Hill Top ◆◆◆
Upper Swanmore, Swanmore,
Southampton, Hampshire
SO32 2QQ
T: (01489) 892653
F: (01489) 892653

SWAY
Hampshire
Forest Heath Hotel ◆◆◆
Station Road, Sway, Lymington,
Hampshire SO41 6BA
T: (01590) 682287
F: (01590) 682626

Little Purley Farm ◆◆◆
Chapel Lane, Sway, Lymington,
Hampshire SO41 6BS
T: (01590) 682707
F: (01590) 682707

Manor Farm ◆◆◆
Coombe Lane, Sway, Lymington,
Hampshire SO41 6BP
T: (01590) 683542

The Nurse's Cottage
◆◆◆◆ GOLD AWARD
Station Road, Sway, Lymington,
Hampshire SO41 6BA
T: (01590) 683402
F: (01590) 683402
E: nurses.cottage@lineone.net
I: www.hantsgov.
uk/tourist/hotels
◉ 👤

The Old Chapel ◆◆◆◆
Chapel House, Coombe Lane,
Sway, Lymington, Hampshire
SO41 6BP
T: (01590) 683382
F: (01590) 682979

Squirrels ◆◆◆
Broadmead, (off Silver Street),
Sway, Lymington, Hampshire
SO41 6DH
T: (01590) 683163
◉

Tiverton ◆◆◆
9 Cruse Close, Sway, Lymington,
Hampshire SO41 6AY
T: (01590) 683092
F: (01590) 683092
E: r&ttrowe@talk21.com

TAPLOW
Buckinghamshire
Bridge Cottage Guest House
◆◆◆◆
Bath Road, Taplow, Maidenhead,
Berkshire SL6 0AR
T: (01628) 626805
F: (01628) 788785

TARRANT LAUNCESTON
Dorset
Ramblers Cottage ◆◆◆◆
Tarrant Launceston, Blandford
Forum, Dorset DT11 8BY
T: (01258) 830528
E: sworrall@ramblerscottage.
fsnet.co.uk
I: www.ramblerscottage.fsnet.
co.uk

THAME
Oxfordshire
The Dairy
◆◆◆◆◆ GOLD AWARD
Moreton, Thame, Oxfordshire
OX9 2HX
T: (01844) 214075
F: (01844) 214075
E: thedairy@freeuk.com
I: www.thedairy.freeuk.com

Field Farm ◆◆◆
Rycote Lane, North Weston,
Thame, Oxfordshire OX9 2HQ
T: (01844) 215428
◉

Oakfield ◆◆◆◆
Thame Park Road, Thame,
Oxfordshire OX9 3PL
T: (01844) 213709 &
07785 764447

THREE LEGGED CROSS
Dorset
Thatch Cottage ◆◆◆◆
Ringwood Road, Three Legged
Cross, Wimborne Minster,
Dorset BH21 6QY
T: (01202) 822042
F: (01202) 822042
E: dthatchcottage@aol.com

THRUXTON
Hampshire

May Cottage
♦♦♦♦ SILVER AWARD
Thruxton, Andover, Hampshire
SP11 8LZ
T: (01264) 771241 &
07768 242166
F: (01264) 771770
E: may.cottage@talk21.com

TILEHURST
Berkshire

Beethovens Hotel ♦♦
De Hillier Taverns plc, Oxford
Road, Tilehurst, Reading,
Berkshire RG31 6TG
T: (0118) 942 7517
F: (0118) 941 7629

2 Cotswold Way ♦♦
Tilehurst, Reading, Berkshire
RG31 6SH
T: (01189) 413286

The Oaks ♦♦
14 Clevedon Road, Tilehurst,
Reading, Berkshire RG31 6R;
T: (01189) 424595

TIPTOE
Hampshire

Acorn Stud ♦♦♦
Brockhills Farm, Sway Road,
Tiptoe, Lymington, Hampshire
SO41 6FQ
T: (01425) 611280
F: (01425) 611280

TITCHFIELD
Hampshire

**Westcote Bed & Breakfast
♦♦♦♦**
325 Southampton Road,
Titchfield, Fareham, Hampshire
PO14 4AY
T: (01329) 846297 &
07711 293421
F: (01329) 846297

TOTLAND BAY
Isle of Wight

Chart House ♦♦♦♦
Madeira Road, Totland Bay, Isle
of Wight PO39 0BJ
T: (01983) 755091

**Frenchman's Cove Country
Hotel ♦♦♦**
Alum Bay Old Road, Totland Bay,
Isle of Wight PO39 0HZ
T: (01983) 752227
F: (01983) 755125
E: boatfield@which.net
⊛

**The Highdown Inn
Rating Applied For**
Highdown Lane, Totland Bay,
Isle of Wight PO39 0HY
T: (01983) 752450

Littledene Lodge ♦♦♦
Granville Road, Totland Bay, Isle
of Wight PO39 0AX
T: (01983) 752411
F: (01983) 752411
⊛

Lomarick ♦♦♦
Church Hill, Totland Bay, Isle of
Wight PO39 0EU
T: (01983) 753364

The Mount ♦♦♦
Cliff Road, Totland Bay, Isle of
Wight PO39 0EW
T: (01983) 753486
F: (01983) 755530

Norton Lodge ♦♦
Granville Road, Totland Bay, Isle
of Wight PO39 0AZ
T: (01983) 752772 &
07971 815460
E: jacquie.simmons@talk21.com

Sandford Lodge ♦♦♦♦
61 The Avenue, Totland Bay, Isle
of Wight PO39 0DN
T: (01983) 753478
F: (01983) 753478
E: sandfordlodge@cwcom.net

Sandy Lane Guest House ♦♦♦
Colwell Common Road, Totland
Bay, Isle of Wight PO39 0DD
T: (01983) 752240
F: (01983) 752240

TOTTON
Hampshire

Colbury Manor
♦♦♦♦ SILVER AWARD
Jacobs Gutter Lane, Eling,
Totton, Southampton,
Hampshire SO40 9FY
T: (023) 8086 2283
F: (023) 8086 5545
⊛

**The Dormers Guest House
♦♦♦**
308 Salisbury Road, Totton,
Southampton, Hampshire
SO40 3ND
T: (023) 8086 5316 &
07703 969141
F: (023) 8066 3218

Ivy Lawn ♦♦♦
Eling Hill, Totton, Southampton,
Hampshire SO40 9HE
T: (023) 8066 0925 &
07803 246202

TWYFORD
Berkshire

Chesham House ♦♦♦
79 Wargrave Road, Twyford,
Reading, Berkshire RG40 9PE
T: (0118) 932 0428

Somewhere to Stay ♦♦♦
c/o Loddon Acres, Bath Road,
Twyford, Reading, Berkshire
RG10 9RU
T: (0118) 934 5880 &
07798 801088
F: (0118) 934 5880

VENTNOR
Isle of Wight

Bermuda Guest House ♦♦♦
3 Alexandra Gardens, Ventnor,
Isle of Wight PO38 1EE
T: (01983) 852349

Brunswick House ♦♦♦
Victoria Street, Ventnor, Isle of
Wight PO38 1ET
T: (01983) 852656

Chalet Hotel ♦♦♦
Esplanade, Ventnor, Isle of
Wight PO38 1TA
T: (01983) 852285
F: (01983) 856630
⊛

Cornerways Hotel ♦♦♦
39 Madeira Road, Ventnor, Isle
of Wight PO38 1QS
T: (01983) 852323
I: www.bandbisleofwight.com

Delamere Guest House ♦♦♦♦
Bellevue Road, Ventnor, Isle of
Wight PO38 1DB
T: (01983) 852322
F: (01983) 852322

Sterlings ♦♦♦♦
11 Altofts Gardens, Ventnor, Isle
of Wight PO38 1DT
T: (01983) 853479
F: (01983) 853479

VERNEY JUNCTION
Buckinghamshire

The White Cottage ♦♦
Verney Junction, Buckingham,
Buckinghamshire MK18 2JZ
T: (01296) 714416 &
07836 642191

VERNHAM DEAN
Hampshire

Upton Cottage ♦♦♦
Vernham Dean, Andover,
Hampshire SP11 0JY
T: (01264) 737640

VERWOOD
Dorset

Verwood Farmhouse ♦♦♦♦
Margards Lane, Verwood,
Wimborne Minster, Dorset
BH31 6JQ
T: (01202) 822083
F: (01202) 820077

WADDESDON
Buckinghamshire

**The Georgian Doll's Cottage
♦♦♦♦**
High Street, Waddesdon,
Aylesbury, Buckinghamshire
HP18 0NE
T: (01296) 655553 &
07956 941820

WALLINGFORD
Oxfordshire

Fords Farm ♦♦♦♦
Ewelme, Wallingford,
Oxfordshire OX10 6HU
T: (01491) 839272
E: fordsfarm@callnetuk.com

Little Gables ♦♦♦
166 Crowmarsh Hill, Crowmarsh
Gifford, Wallingford,
Oxfordshire OX10 8BG
T: (01491) 837834 &
07860 148882
F: (01491) 837834
E: jfreeves@globalnet.co.uk
I: www.users.globalnet.co.
uk/§jfreeves
⊛

North Farm
♦♦♦♦ SILVER AWARD
Shillingford Hill, Wallingford,
Oxfordshire OX10 8NB
T: (01865) 858406
F: (01865) 858519
E: northfarm@compuserve.com
I: www.country-accom.co.
uk/north-farm/

WAREHAM
Dorset

The Old Granary
♦♦♦♦ SILVER AWARD
West Holme Farm, Wareham,
Dorset BH20 6AQ
T: (01929) 552972
F: (01929) 551616
E: venngoldsack@lineone.net
⊛ 🔥

WARGRAVE
Berkshire

Appletree Cottage ♦♦♦♦
Backsideans, Wargrave, Reading,
Berkshire RG10 8JS
T: (0118) 940 4306
E: trishlangham@
appletreecottage.co.uk
I: www.appletreecottage.co.uk

WARNFORD
Hampshire

Paper Mill ♦♦♦
Peake Lane, Warnford,
Southampton, Hampshire
SO32 3LA
T: (01730) 829387

WARRINGTON
Buckinghamshire

Home Farm ♦♦♦♦
Warrington, Olney,
Buckinghamshire MK46 4HN
T: (01234) 711655
F: (01234) 711855
E: ruth@oldstonebarn.co.uk
I: www.oldstonebarn.co.uk

WARSASH
Hampshire

Dormy House Hotel ♦♦♦♦
21 Barnes Lane, Sarisbury Green,
Southampton, Hampshire
SO31 7DA
T: (01489) 572626
F: (01489) 573370
E: dormyhousehotel@warsash.
globalnet.co.uk
I: www.silverblue.co.uk/dormy

Solent View Hotel ♦♦♦♦
33 Newtown Road, Warsash,
Southampton, Hampshire
SO31 9FY
T: (01489) 572300
F: (01489) 572300

WATER STRATFORD
Buckinghamshire

The Rolling Acres ♦♦♦
Water Stratford, Buckingham,
Buckinghamshire MK18 5DX
T: (01280) 847302 &
07770 608366

WATERPERRY
Oxfordshire

Common Leys Farm ♦♦♦♦
Waterperry Common,
Waterperry, Oxfordshire
OX33 1LQ
T: (01865) 351266 &
07802 960651
F: (01865) 358005
⊛

WENDOVER
Buckinghamshire

Belton House ♦
26 Chiltern Road, Wendover,
Aylesbury, Buckinghamshire
HP22 6DB
T: (01296) 622351

Dunsmore Edge ♦♦♦
London Road, Wendover,
Aylesbury, Buckinghamshire
HP22 6PN
T: (01296) 623080
E: ron_drachford@lineone.net.
uk

Field Cottage
◆◆◆◆ SILVER AWARD
St Leonards, Tring, Hertfordshire
HP23 6NS
T: (01494) 837602 &
07803 295337

17 Icknield Close ◆◆◆
Wendover, Aylesbury,
Buckinghamshire HP22 6HG
T: (01296) 583312
E: grbr@cwcom.net
I: www.visitbritain.com

46 Lionel Avenue ◆◆◆
Wendover, Aylesbury,
Buckinghamshire HP22 6LP
T: (01296) 623426

WENDOVER DEAN
Buckinghamshire

Wisteria Cottage ◆◆◆◆
Bowood Lane, Wendover Dean,
Aylesbury, Buckinghamshire
HP22 6PY
T: (01296) 625509 &
07711 062288
F: (01296) 622141
E: wisteria.cottage@virgin.net
I: freespace.virgin.net/wisteria.
cottage

WEST END
Hampshire

Oakmount House ◆◆◆
11 Larch Close, West End,
Southampton, Hampshire
SO30 3RB
T: (023) 8047 1240
E: oakmount@hotmail.com

WEST LULWORTH
Dorset

Gatton House ◆◆◆◆
West Lulworth, Wareham,
Dorset BH20 5RU
T: (01929) 400252
F: (01929) 400252
E: mikedale@gattonhouse.co.uk
I: gattonhouse.co.uk

Graybank Guest House ◆◆◆
Main Road, West Lulworth,
Wareham, Dorset BH20 5RL
T: (01929) 400256

Lulworth Cove Hotel ◆◆◆
Main Road, West Lulworth,
Wareham, Dorset BH20 5RQ
T: (01929) 400333
F: (01929) 400534
E: lulworthcove@saqnet.co.uk
I: www.saqnet.co.
uk/users/lulworthcove/

WEST MEON
Hampshire

Brocklands Farm ◆◆◆
West Meon, Petersfield,
Hampshire GU32 1JN
T: (01730) 829325
E: hf.morris@virgin.net

WEST WELLOW
Hampshire

Lukes Barn ◆◆◆
Maury's Lane, West Wellow,
Romsey, Hampshire SO51 6DA
T: (01794) 324431
F: (01794) 324431

WESTBURY
Buckinghamshire

Mill Farm House ◆◆◆
Westbury, Brackley,
Northamptonshire NN13 5JS
T: (01280) 704843

WESTON-ON-THE-GREEN
Oxfordshire

Weston Grounds Farm ◆◆◆
Weston-on-the-Green, Bicester,
Oxfordshire OX6 8QX
T: (01869) 351168
F: (01869) 350887

WESTON TURVILLE
Buckinghamshire

The Hideaway
Rating Applied For
Main Street, Weston Turville,
Aylesbury, Buckinghamshire
HP22 5RR
T: (01296) 612604
F: (01296) 615705

Loosley House ◆◆◆◆
87 New Road, Weston Turville,
Aylesbury, Buckinghamshire
HP22 5QT
T: (01296) 428285 & 484157
F: (01296) 428285

WEYHILL
Hampshire

Juglans ◆◆
Red Post Lane, Weyhill, Andover,
Hampshire SP11 0PY
T: (01264) 772651 &
07802 664540

WHERWELL
Hampshire

New House Bed & Breakfast
◆◆◆
New House, Fullerton Road,
Wherwell, Andover, Hampshire
SP11 7JS
T: (01264) 860817
E: dwoodipsa@aol.com

WHITCHURCH
Hampshire

Peak House Farm ◆◆◆
Cole Henley, Whitchurch,
Hampshire RG28 7QJ
T: (01256) 892052

White Hart Hotel ◆◆
Newbury Street, Whitchurch,
Hampshire RG28 7DN
T: (01256) 892900
F: (01256) 896628

WICKHAM
Hampshire

Chiphall Acre ◆◆◆
Droxford Road (A32), Wickham,
Fareham, Hampshire PO17 5AY
T: (01329) 833188
F: (01329) 833188
I: www.smoothhound.co.uk

Montrose ◆◆◆◆
Solomons Lane, Shirrell Heath,
Southampton, Hampshire
SO32 2HU
T: (01329) 833345
F: (01329) 833345
E: bb@montrose78.fsnet.co.uk

WIDMER END
Buckinghamshire

The White House ◆◆◆
North Road, Widmer End, High
Wycombe, Buckinghamshire
HP15 6ND
T: (01494) 712221
F: (01494) 712221

WIMBORNE MINSTER
Dorset

Ashton Lodge
◆◆◆◆ SILVER AWARD
10 Oakley Hill, Wimborne
Minster, Dorset BH21 1QH
T: (01202) 883423
F: (01202) 886180
E: ashtonlodge@ukgateway.net
I: www.ashtonlodge.ukgateway.
net

Henbury Farm ◆◆◆◆
Dorchester Road, Sturminster
Marshall, Wimborne Minster,
Dorset BH21 3RN
T: (01258) 857306
F: (01258) 857928

Hopewell
◆◆◆◆◆ SILVER AWARD
Little Lonnen, Colehill,
Wimborne Minster, Dorset
BH21 7BB
T: (01202) 880311
E: hopewell@cwcom.net

Lantern Lodge
◆◆◆◆ GOLD AWARD
47 Gravel Hill, Merley,
Wimborne Minster, Dorset
BH21 1RW
T: (01202) 884183

No 2 Stoneleaze ◆◆◆◆
Stone Lane, Wimborne Minster,
Dorset BH21 1HD
T: (01202) 842739

Old Merchant's House ◆◆◆◆
44 West Borough, Wimborne
Minster, Dorset BH21 1NQ
T: (01202) 841955

Peacehaven B & B ◆◆
282 Sopwith Crescent, Merley,
Wimborne Minster, Dorset
BH21 1XL
T: (01202) 880281

Pear Tree Cottage ◆◆
248 Wimborne Road West,
Stapehill, Wimborne Minster,
Dorset BH21 2DZ
T: (01202) 890174
E: caro-peartreeco@hotmail.
com

Twynham ◆◆◆
67 Poole Road, Wimborne
Minster, Dorset BH21 1QB
T: (01202) 887310

WINCHESTER
Hampshire

Acacia ◆◆◆◆ SILVER AWARD
44 Kilham Lane, Winchester,
Hampshire SO22 5PT
T: (01962) 852259 &
04801 537703
F: (01962) 852259
E: eric.buchanan@mcmail.com

Cathedral View ◆◆◆
9A Magdalen Hill, Winchester,
Hampshire SO23 0HJ
T: (01962) 863802

12 Christchurch Road
Rating Applied For
Winchester, Hampshire
SO23 9SR
T: (01962) 854272

85 Christchurch Road ◆◆◆◆
Winchester, Hampshire
SO23 9QY
T: (01962) 868661
F: (01962) 868661
E: fetherstondilke@x-stream.co.
uk

Dawn Cottage
◆◆◆◆ SILVER AWARD
Romsey Road, Winchester,
Hampshire SO22 5PQ
T: (01962) 869956
F: (01962) 869956

Dellbrook ◆◆◆
Hubert Road, St Cross,
Winchester, Hampshire
SO23 9RG
T: (01962) 865093
F: (01962) 865093
E: dellbrook2@aol.com

East View
◆◆◆◆ SILVER AWARD
16 Clifton Hill, Winchester,
Hampshire SO22 5BL
T: (01962) 862986

The Farrells ◆◆◆
5 Ranelagh Road, St Cross,
Winchester, Hampshire
SO23 9TA
T: (01962) 869555
F: (01962) 869555
E: thefarrells@easicom.com

Portland House ◆◆◆
63 Tower Street, Winchester,
Hampshire SO23 8TA
T: (01962) 865195 &
07710 425577
F: (01962) 865195

St Margaret's ◆◆
3 St Michael's Road, Winchester,
Hampshire SO23 9JE
T: (01962) 861450 &
07802 478926

Sandy Lodge
47 Christchurch Road,
Winchester, Hampshire
SO23 9TE
T: (01962) 853385

Shawlands ◆◆◆◆
46 Kilham Lane, Winchester,
Hampshire SO22 5QD
T: (01962) 861166
F: (01962) 861166
E: kathy@pollshaw.u-net.com

54 St Cross Road ◆◆◆
Winchester, Hampshire
SO23 9PS
T: (01962) 852073
F: (01962) 852073

67 St Cross Road ◆◆
Winchester, Hampshire
SO23 9RE
T: (01962) 863002
F: (01962) 863002

Stanmore Hotel ◆◆◆
Stanmore Lane, Stanmore,
Winchester, Hampshire
SO22 4BL
T: (01962) 852720
F: (01962) 850467

Stratton House ◆◆◆
Stratton Road, St Giles Hill,
Winchester, Hampshire
SO23 0JQ
T: (01962) 863919 & 864529
F: (01962) 842095
E: Strattongroup@btinternet.
com
I: www.winchester.gov.
uk/tourism

Sullivan's ◆◆
29 Stockbridge Road,
Winchester, Hampshire
SO22 6RW
T: (01962) 862027

Sycamores ◆◆◆
4 Bereweeke Close, Winchester,
Hampshire SO22 6AR
T: (01962) 867242
F: (01962) 620300

WINDRUSH
Oxfordshire

Dellwood ◆◆◆
Quarry Lane, Windrush, Oxford,
Oxfordshire OX18 4TR
T: (01451) 844268
F: (01451) 844400

WINDSOR
Berkshire

Alma House ◆◆◆
56 Alma Road, Windsor,
Berkshire SL4 3HA
T: (01753) 862983
F: (01753) 833742
E: harpoonlouies@compuserve.
com

Beaumont Lodge ◆◆◆◆
1 Beaumont Road, Windsor,
Berkshire SL4 1HY
T: (01753) 863436 &
07774 841273
F: (01753) 863436
E: bhamshere@beaumontlodge.
demon.co.uk
I: www.smoothound.co.uk.
/hotels/beaulos.html

Clarence Hotel ◆◆
9 Clarence Road, Windsor,
Berkshire SL4 5AE
T: (01753) 864436
F: (01753) 857060
◉

The Crown & Cushion Inn ◆
84 High Street, Eton, Windsor,
Berkshire SL4 6AF
T: (01753) 861531
E: sylvieghmister@yahoo.com

Halcyon House ◆◆◆
131 Clarence Road, Windsor,
Berkshire SL4 5AR
T: (01753) 863262 &
07768 034128
F: (01753) 863262
E: halcyonhouse@hotmail.com

Honeysuckle Cottage ◆◆◆◆
61 Fairfield Approach,
Wraysbury, Windsor, Berkshire
TW19 5DR
T: (01784) 482519
F: (01784) 482305
E: B&B@berks.force9.co.uk
I: www.berks.force9.co.uk

Jeans ◆◆
1 Stovell Road, Windsor,
Berkshire SL4 5JB
T: (01753) 852055
F: (01753) 852055

Melrose House ◆◆◆
53 Frances Road, Windsor,
Berkshire SL4 3AQ
T: (01753) 865328
F: (01753) 865328

Oscar Hotel ◆◆◆
65 Vansittart Road, Windsor,
Berkshire SL4 5DB
T: (01753) 830613
F: (01753) 833744

22 York Avenue ◆◆
Windsor, Berkshire SL4 3PD
T: (01753) 865775

WINGRAVE
Buckinghamshire

The Old Vicarage ◆◆◆◆
Leighton Road, Wingrave,
Aylesbury, Buckinghamshire
HP22 4PA
T: (01296) 681235
E: thekeighleys@talk21.com

WINSLOW
Buckinghamshire

The Congregational Church
◆◆◆
15 Horn Street, Winslow,
Buckingham, Buckinghamshire
MK18 3AP
T: (01296) 715717
F: (01296) 715717

The Old Manse ◆◆◆
9 Horn Street, Winslow,
Aylesbury, Buckinghamshire
MK18 3AP
T: (01296) 712048 &
0859 313339

Puzzletree ◆◆◆◆
3 Buckingham Road, Winslow,
Buckingham, Buckinghamshire
MK18 3DT
T: (01296) 712437
F: (01296) 712437

'Witsend' ◆◆
9 Buckingham Road, Winslow,
Buckingham, Buckinghamshire
MK18 3DT
T: (01296) 712503 & 715499
E: sheila.spatcher@tesco.net
◉

WINSOR
Hampshire

Trees ◆◆◆
Tatchbury Lane, Winsor,
Southampton, Hampshire
SO40 2HA
T: (023) 8081 3128 &
07860 624462
F: (023) 8081 3128

WINTERBORNE STICKLAND
Dorset

Stickland Farmhouse ◆◆◆◆
Winterborne Stickland,
Blandford Forum, Dorset
DT11 0NT
T: (01258) 880119
F: (01258) 880119
E: stickland.farm@virginnet.co.
uk

WINTERBORNE ZELSTON
Dorset

Brook Farm ◆◆◆
Winterborne Zelston, Blandford
Forum, Dorset DT11 9EU
T: (01929) 459267

Rainbow View Farm ◆◆◆
Winterborne Zelston, Blandford
Forum, Dorset DT11 9EU
T: (01929) 459529 &
0797 0032278

WITCHAMPTON
Dorset

Hemsworth Manor Farm
◆◆◆◆
Witchampton, Wimborne
Minster, Dorset BH21 5BN
T: (01258) 840216
F: (01258) 841278

WITNEY
Oxfordshire

Cassidys ◆◆◆◆
Puck Lane, Witney, Oxfordshire
OX8 5LD
T: (01993) 779445
F: (01993) 779445
E: mc1351@aol.com

The Court Inn ◆◆◆
43 Bridge Street, Witney,
Oxfordshire OX8 6DA
T: (01993) 703228
I: www.infocourtinn.uk

Crofters Guest House ◆◆◆
29 Oxford Hill, Witney,
Oxfordshire OX8 6JU
T: (01993) 778165
F: (01993) 778165

Ducklington Farm ◆◆◆
Coursehill Lane, Ducklington,
Witney, Oxfordshire OX8 7YG
T: (01993) 772175
I: www.country-accom.co.uk
◉

Field View
◆◆◆◆ SILVER AWARD
Wood Green, Witney,
Oxfordshire OX8 6DE
T: (01993) 705485 &
07768 614347
E: jsimpson@netcomuk.co.uk
I: www.netcomuk.co.
uk/§kearse/index.html

Hawthorn House ◆◆◆
79 Burford Road, Witney,
Oxfordshire OX8 5DR
T: (01993) 772768
E: roland@hawthorn79.
freeserve.co.uk
I: www.travel-uk.net/hawthorn

North Leigh Guest House
◆◆◆◆
28 Common Road, North Leigh,
Witney, Oxfordshire OX8 6RA
T: (01993) 881622

Quarrydene ◆◆
17 Dene Rise, Witney,
Oxfordshire OX8 5LU
T: (01993) 772152 &
07850 054786
F: (01993) 772152

**Springhill Farm Bed &
Breakfast** ◆◆◆
Cogges, Witney, Oxfordshire
OX8 6UL
T: (01993) 704919

Windrush House B & B ◆◆◆
55 Crawley Road, Witney,
Oxfordshire OX8 5HX
T: (01993) 774454 &
07778 181516
F: (01993) 709877
E: heraldic@compuserve.com

The Witney Hotel ◆◆
7 Church Green, Witney,
Oxfordshire OX8 6AZ
T: (01993) 702137
F: (01993) 705337
E: bookings@thewitneyhotel.co.
uk

WOBURN SANDS
Buckinghamshire

The Old Stables ◆◆◆◆
Woodleys Farm, Bow Brickhill
Road, Woburn Sands,
Buckinghamshire MK17 8DE
T: (01908) 281340 &
07778 313906
F: (01908) 584812

WOKINGHAM
Berkshire

South Lodge
◆◆◆◆ SILVER AWARD
1A South Drive, Wokingham,
Berkshire RG40 2DH
T: (01189) 789413
F: (01189) 789413

WOODCOTE
Oxfordshire

Hedges ◆◆◆
South Stoke Road, Woodcote,
Reading, Berkshire RG8 0PL
T: (01491) 680461

WOODFALLS
Hampshire

The Woodfalls Inn ◆◆◆◆
The Ridge, Woodfalls, Salisbury,
Wiltshire SP5 2LN
T: (01725) 513222
F: (01725) 513220
E: woodfallsi@aol.com

WOODLEY
Berkshire

72 Butts Hill Road
Rating Applied For
Woodley, Reading, Berkshire
RG5 4NP
T: (01189) 693295

26 Haddon Drive ◆◆
Woodley, Reading, Berkshire
RG5 4LU
T: (118) 969 3770

Woodville Guest House ◆◆◆
78 Reading Road, Woodley,
Reading, Berkshire RG5 3AD
T: (118) 961 8873
F: (118) 961 8873
E: mary@woodville-gh/shet.co.
uk

WOODSTOCK
Oxfordshire

**Blenheim Guest House & Tea
Rooms** ◆◆◆◆
17 Park Street, Woodstock,
Oxford, Oxfordshire OX20 1SJ
T: (01993) 813814
F: (01993) 813810
E: blenheimguesthouse@talk21.
com
I: www.oxlink.co.
uk/woodstock/blenheim.html

Burleigh Farm ◆◆◆
Bladon Road, Cassington,
Oxfordshire OX8 1EA
T: (01865) 881352
E: j.cook@farmline.com

The Crown Inn ◆◆◆
31 High Street, Woodstock,
Oxford, Oxfordshire OX20 1TE
T: (01993) 811117
F: (01993) 813339

Gorselands Hall ◆◆◆
Boddington Lane, North Leigh,
Witney, Oxfordshire OX8 6PU
T: (01993) 882292
F: (01993) 883629
E: hamilton@gorselandshall.
com
I: www.gorselandshall.com

The Kings Head Inn ◆◆◆◆
Chapel Hill, Wootton,
Woodstock, Oxford, Oxfordshire
OX20 1DX
T: (01993) 811340
F: (01993) 811340
E: t.fay@kings-head.co.uk
I: www.kings-head.co.uk

The Laurels
◆◆◆◆ SILVER AWARD
Hensington Road, Woodstock,
Oxfordshire OX20 1JL
T: (01993) 812583
F: (01993) 812583
I: www.smoothhound.co.
uk/hotels/thelaur.html

The Lawns ◆◆
2 Flemings Road, Woodstock,
Oxford, Oxfordshire OX20 1NA
T: (01993) 812599
F: (01993) 812599
I: www.touristnetuk.
com/wm/lawns

Pine Trees Bed & Breakfast
◆◆◆◆
44 Green Lane, Woodstock,
Oxford, Oxfordshire OX20 1JZ
T: (01993) 813300
F: (01608) 646658

Plane Tree House ◆◆◆
48 Oxford Street, Woodstock,
Oxford, Oxfordshire OX20 1TT
T: (01993) 813075

The Punchbowl Inn ◆◆◆
12 Oxford Street, Woodstock,
Oxford, Oxfordshire OX20 1TR
T: (01993) 811218
F: (01993) 811393
E: punchbowl@ox20.freeserve.
co.uk
I: www.oxlink.co.
uk/woodstock/punchbowl/

Shepherds Hall Inn ◆◆◆
Witney Road, Freeland, Witney,
Oxfordshire OX8 8HQ
T: (01993) 881256
F: (01993) 883455

Shipton Glebe
◆◆◆◆◆ GOLD AWARD
Woodstock, Oxford, Oxfordshire
OX20 1QQ
T: (01993) 812688
F: (01993) 813142
E: stay@shipton-glebe.com
I: www.shipton-glebe.com

The Townhouse
Rating Applied For
15 High Street, Woodstock,
Oxford, Oxfordshire OX20 1TE
T: (01993) 810843 & 0780 359
9001
F: (01993) 810843
E: info@woodstock-townhouse.
com
I: www.woodstock-townhouse.
com

River View House ◆◆◆◆
Station Road, Woolhampton,
Reading, Berkshire RG7 5SF
T: (0118) 971 3449
F: (0118) 971 3446

Grange Farm ◆◆◆◆
Staplers Road, Wootton Bridge,
Ryde, Isle of Wight PO33 4RW
T: (01983) 882147
F: (01983) 882147

Island Charters Sea Urchin ◆◆
26 Barge Lane, Wootton Creek,
Wootton Bridge, Ryde, Isle of
Wight PO33 4LB
T: (01983) 882315 &
07889 038877
F: (01983) 882315

Crabtree Barn ◆◆◆
Field Farm, Worminghall,
Aylesbury, Buckinghamshire
HP18 9JY
T: (01844) 339719
F: (01844) 339719
E: issymcguinness@talk21.com

Oaktree Copse
Rating Applied For
Wood Farm, Menmarsh Road,
Worminghall, Aylesbury,
Buckinghamshire HP18 9UP
T: (01865) 351695

Apple Tree House ◆◆◆◆
16 Verley Close, Woughton on
the Green, Milton Keynes,
Buckinghamshire MK6 3ER
T: (01908) 669681
F: (01908) 669681
E: apples@mrobinson5.fsnet.co.
uk

The Oast Barn ◆◆◆
Staines Road, Wraysbury,
Staines, Berkshire TW19 5BS
T: (01784) 481598 &
07867 504424
F: (01784) 483022
E: theoastbarn@netscapeonline.
com

Little Span Farm
Rating Applied For
Rew Lane, Wroxall, Ventnor, Isle
of Wight PO38 3AU
T: (01983) 852419
E: info@spanfarm.co.uk
I: www.spanfarm.co.uk

Medlars ◆◆◆
Halletts Shute, Yarmouth, Isle of
Wight PO41 0RH
T: (01983) 761541
F: (01983) 761541

Rosemead ◆◆
Tennyson Road, Yarmouth, Isle
of Wight PO41 0PX
T: (01983) 761078
E: barbara_boon@hotmail.com

Eltham Villa Guest House
◆◆◆◆
148 Woodstock Road, Yarnton,
Kidlington, Oxfordshire
OX5 1PW
T: (01865) 376037 &
07802 722595
F: (01865) 376037

King's Bridge Guest House
◆◆◆
Woodstock Road, Yarnton,
Kidlington, Oxfordshire OX5 1PH
T: (01865) 841748
F: (01865) 370215
E: kings.bridge@talk21.com
🖰

Holly Lodge ◆◆◆
24 Sandhurst Road, Yateley,
Hampshire GU46 7UU
T: (01252) 870716
F: (01252) 668471
E: eshanks@aol.com

Leylands Farm ◆◆◆◆
Leylands Lane, Abinger
Common, Dorking, Surrey
RH5 6JU
T: (01306) 730115 &
07702 488606
F: (01306) 731675

Park House Farm ◆◆◆◆
Hollow Lane, Abinger Common,
Dorking, Surrey RH5 6LW
T: (01306) 730101
F: (01306) 730643
E: Peterwallis@msn.com
I: www.smoothhound.co.
uk/hotels/parthous.html

Ladwood Farm ◆◆◆
Acrise, Folkestone, Kent
CT18 8LL
T: (01303) 891328 &
07778 498455
F: (01303) 891427
E: mail@ladwood.com
I: www.ladwood.com

Barn Cottage ◆◆◆◆
Brook Hill, Farley Green, Albury,
Guildford, Surrey GU5 9DN
T: (01483) 202571

Limmer Pond House ◆◆◆
Church Road, Aldingbourne,
Chichester, West Sussex
PO20 6TU
T: (01243) 543210

Hogben Farm ◆◆◆◆
Church Lane, Aldington,
Ashford, Kent TN25 7EH
T: (01233) 720219
F: (01233) 720285

Meadowbank ◆◆◆◆
Sloe Lane, Alfriston, Polegate,
East Sussex BN26 5UR
T: (01323) 870742

Riverdale House ◆◆◆◆
Seaford Road, Alfriston,
Polegate, East Sussex BN26 5TR
T: (01323) 871038
I: www.cuckmere-valley.co.
uk/riverdale/

Russets ◆◆◆◆ SILVER AWARD
14 Deans Road, Alfriston,
Polegate, East Sussex BN26 5XJ
T: (01323) 870626
F: (01323) 870626
E: russets@yahoo.co.uk

Simon's Lee ◆◆◆◆
Rackham Road, Amberley,
Arundel, West Sussex BN18 9NR
T: (01798) 831321
F: (01798) 831169
E: shirleybenn@simonslee.
freeserve.co.uk
I: www.sussexlive.com

Horne's Place ◆◆◆
Appledore, Ashford, Kent
TN26 2BS
T: (01233) 758305

Park Farm Barn ◆◆◆
School Lane, Appledore, Ashford,
Kent TN26 2AR
T: (01233) 758159
F: (01233) 758159

Coneybury
◆◆◆◆ SILVER AWARD
Hook Lane, West Hoathly, East
Grinstead, West Sussex
RH19 4PX
T: (01342) 810200
F: (01342) 810887

Jordans ◆◆◆◆
Church Lane, Ardingly,
Haywards Heath, West Sussex
RH17 6UP
T: (01444) 892681
F: (01444) 892710

SOUTH EAST ENGLAND

ARPINGE
Kent
Pigeonwood House ♦♦♦♦
Grove Farm, Arpinge, Folkestone,
Kent CT18 8AQ
T: (01303) 891111
F: (01303) 891019
E: samandmary@aol.com
I: www.arpinge.com

ARUNDEL
West Sussex
Arundel House ♦♦♦
11 High Street, Arundel, West
Sussex BN18 9AD
T: (01903) 882136
F: (01909) 882136
E: arundelhouse@btinternet.
com
I: btinternet.
com/§arundelhouse/

Bridge House ♦♦♦
18 Queen Street, Arundel, West
Sussex BN18 9JG
T: (01903) 882142 & 0800 056
0629
F: (01903) 883600

Castle View ♦♦♦
63 High Street, Arundel, West
Sussex BN18 9AJ
T: (01903) 883029
F: (01903) 883029
E: suse@lineone.net
I: www.lineone.net/§suse

Houghton Farm ♦♦♦♦
Arundel, West Sussex BN18 9LW
T: (01798) 831327 & 831100
F: (01798) 831183

Mill Lane House ♦♦♦
Slindon, Arundel, West Sussex
BN18 0RP
T: (01243) 814440
F: (01243) 814436

Pindars ♦♦♦♦
Lyminster, Arundel, West Sussex
BN17 7QF
T: (01903) 882628

St Mary's Gate Inn ♦♦♦
London Road, Arundel, West
Sussex BN18 9BA
T: (01903) 883145
F: (01903) 882256

Woodpeckers ♦♦♦♦
15 Dalloway Road, Arundel,
West Sussex BN18 9HJ
T: (01903) 883948 &
0411 4322281

ASH
Kent
Great Weddington ♦♦♦♦
Ash, Canterbury, Kent CT3 2AR
T: (01304) 813407 & 812531
F: (01304) 812531
E: traveltale@aol.com

ASHFORD
Kent
Ashford Guest House ♦♦♦♦
15 Canterbury Road, Ashford,
Kent TN24 8LE
T: (01233) 640460
F: (01233) 626504
E: srcnoel@netcomuk.co.uk
I: www.mounteverest.uk.com

Croft Hotel ♦♦♦
Canterbury Road, Kennington,
Ashford, Kent TN25 4DU
T: (01233) 622140
F: (01233) 635271
E: crofthotel@btconnect.com

Glenmoor ♦♦♦
Maidstone Road, Ashford, Kent
TN25 4NP
T: (01233) 634767

Goldwell Manor ♦♦♦
Great Chart, Ashford, Kent
TN23 3BY
T: (01233) 631495
F: (01233) 631495

Mayflower House ♦♦♦
61 Magazine Road, Ashford,
Kent TN24 8NR
T: (01233) 621959
F: (01233) 621959

New Flying Horse Inn ♦♦♦
Upper Bridge Street, Wye,
Ashford, Kent TN25 5AN
T: (01233) 812297
F: (01233) 813487
E: newflyhorse@
shepherd-neame.co.uk
I: www.shepherd-neame.co.uk

Quantock House ♦♦♦
Quantock Drive, Ashford, Kent
TN24 8QH
T: (01233) 638921

**Warren Cottage Hotel and
Restaurant♦♦♦**
136 The Street, Willesborough,
Ashford, Kent TN24 0NB
T: (01233) 621905 & 632929
F: (01233) 623400
E: general@warrencottage.co.
uk
I: www.warrencottage.co.uk

ASHTEAD
Surrey
**Silver Firs
♦♦♦♦ SILVER AWARD**
7A Leatherhead Road, Ashtead,
Leatherhead, Surrey KT21 2TW
T: (01372) 272122
F: (01372) 278600
E: silverfirs@lineone.net
I: www.smoothhound.co.
uk/silverfirs

AYLESFORD
Kent
Wickham Lodge ♦♦♦♦
The Quay, High Street, Aylesford,
Kent ME20 7AY
T: (01622) 717267
F: (01622) 717267
E: wickhamlodge@aol.com

BALCOMBE
West Sussex
Rocks Lane Cottage ♦♦♦
Rocks Lane, Balcombe,
Haywards Heath, West Sussex
RH17 6JG
T: (01444) 811245 &
07989 197348
E: kpa@fsbdial.co.uk

BALLS CROSS
West Sussex
The Stag Inn ♦♦♦
Balls Cross, Petworth, West
Sussex GU28 9JP
T: (01403) 820241

BARHAM
Kent
Heaseland House ♦♦♦♦
South Barham Road, Barham,
Canterbury, Kent CT4 6LA
T: (01227) 831643

BARNHAM
West Sussex
Todhurst Farm ♦♦♦
Lake Lane, Barnham, Bognor
Regis, West Sussex PO22 0AL
T: (01243) 551959
F: (01243) 554596
E: nigelsedg@aol.uk

BATTLE
East Sussex
**Abbey View Bed & Breakfast
♦♦♦♦**
Caldbec Hill, Battle, East Sussex
TN33 0JS
T: (01424) 775513
F: (01424) 775513

April Cottage ♦♦♦
46 North Trade Road, Battle,
East Sussex TN33 0HU
T: (01424) 775108

Clematis Cottage ♦♦♦
The Green, 3 The High Street,
Battle, East Sussex TN33 0TD
T: (01424) 774261

Farthings Farm ♦♦♦♦
Farthings Lane, Catsfield, Battle,
East Sussex TN33 9BA
T: (01424) 773107
E: farthings@dial.pipex.com
I: dspace.dial.pipex.
com/farthings-farm.

High Hedges ♦♦♦♦
28 North Trade Road, Battle,
East Sussex TN33 0HB
T: (01424) 774140 &
0780 8551064

Kelklands ♦♦♦
Off Chain Lane, Battle, East
Sussex TN33 0HG
T: (01424) 773013

Little Hemingfold Hotel ♦♦♦
Telham, Battle, East Sussex
TN33 0TT
T: (01424) 774338
F: (01424) 775351

Moons Hill Farm ♦♦♦
The Green, Ninfield, Battle, East
Sussex TN33 9LH
T: (01424) 892645
F: (01424) 892645

BEAN
Kent
**Black Horse Cottage
Rating Applied For**
High Street, Bean, Dartford, Kent
DA2 8AS
T: (01474) 704962

BEARSTED
Kent
88 Ashford Road ♦♦♦
Bearsted, Maidstone, Kent
ME14 4LT
T: (01622) 738278
F: (01622) 738278

**Hurstfield House
Rating Applied For**
24 Nursery Avenue, Bearsted,
Maidstone, Kent ME14 4JS
T: (01622) 737584
E: jacquiSV@globalnet.co.uk

Tollgate House ♦♦♦
Ashford Road, Bearsted,
Maidstone, Kent ME14 4NS
T: (01622) 738428

BELLS YEW GREEN
East Sussex
Rushlye Barn ♦♦♦
Bells Yew Green, Royal
Tunbridge Wells, Kent TN3 9AP
T: (01892) 750398

BEPTON
West Sussex
**Park House Hotel
♦♦♦♦♦ SILVER AWARD**
Bepton, Midhurst, West Sussex
GU29 0JB
T: (01730) 812880
F: (01730) 815643
I: www.Freepages.co.
uk/parkhouse_hotel/

BERWICK
East Sussex
Lower Claverham Farm ♦♦♦
Berwick, Polegate, East Sussex
BN26 6TJ
T: (01323) 811267
F: (01323) 811267

BETHERSDEN
Kent
Cloverlea ♦♦♦
Hothfield Road, Bethersden,
Ashford, Kent TN26 3DU
T: (01233) 820353 &
07711 739690
F: (01233) 820353

The Coach House ♦♦♦
Oakmead Farm, Bethersden,
Ashford, Kent TN26 3DU
T: (01233) 820583
F: (01233) 820583

Potters Farm ♦♦♦
Bethersden, Ashford, Kent
TN26 3JX
T: (01233) 820341
F: (01233) 820469

BEXHILL
East Sussex
Albany House ♦♦♦
30 Magdalen Road, Bexhill, East
Sussex TN40 1SB
T: (01424) 223012

**The Arosa Hotel
♦♦♦♦ SILVER AWARD**
6 Albert Road, Bexhill, East
Sussex TN40 1DG
T: (01424) 212574 &
08000 748041
F: (01424) 212574
E: www.arosehotel.co.uk

Barnoak ♦♦♦♦
22 Barnhorn Road, Little
Common, Bexhill, East Sussex
TN39 4QA
T: (01424) 843269

Barrington B & B ♦♦♦♦
14 Wilton Road, Bexhill, East
Sussex TN40 1HY
T: (01424) 210250
F: (01424) 211433
E: mick@barrington14.
freeserve.co.uk
I: www.barrington14.freeserve.
co.uk

Buenos Aires Guest House
◆◆◆
24 Albany Road, Bexhill, East
Sussex TN40 1BZ
T: (01424) 212269
F: (01424) 212269

Collington Lodge Guest House
◆◆◆
41 Collington Avenue, Bexhill,
East Sussex TN39 3PX
T: (01424) 210024
F: (01424) 210024
E: info@collington.co.uk
I: www.collington.co.uk

Dunselma ◆◆◆
25 Marina, Bexhill, East Sussex
TN40 1BP
T: (01424) 734144

Hartfield House
◆◆◆◆ SILVER AWARD
27 Hartfield Road, Cooden,
Bexhill, East Sussex TN39 3EA
T: (01424) 845715
F: (01424) 845715
E: mansi@hartfieldhouse.
free-online.co.uk

Henry House ◆◆◆
16 Linden Road, Bexhill, East
Sussex TN40 1DN
T: (01424) 225528
E: sylvia.laidlaw@henry.dialnet.
com
⊚

Linden Lodge ◆◆◆
31 Linden Road, Bexhill, East
Sussex TN40 1DN
T: (01424) 225005
F: (01424) 222895
E: lindenlodge@hotmail.com

Little Shelter ◆◆◆
5 Ashdown Road, Bexhill-on-
Sea, Bexhill, East Sussex
TN40 1SE
T: (01424) 225386

16 Magdalen Road ◆◆◆
Bexhill, East Sussex TN40 1SB
T: (01424) 218969

Manor Barn ◆◆◆
Lunsford Cross, Bexhill, East
Sussex TN39 5JJ
T: (01424) 893018
F: (01424) 893018

Marabou Mansions ◆◆
60 Devonshire Road, Bexhill,
East Sussex TN40 1AX
T: (01424) 212189
F: (01424) 212189

Messens Farmhouse ◆◆◆◆
Potmans Lane, Lunsford Cross,
Bexhill, East Sussex TN39 5JL
T: (01424) 893456 &
07976 644652
F: (01424) 893456

Mulberry ◆◆◆◆
31 Warwick Road, Bexhill, East
Sussex TN39 4HG
T: (01424) 219204

Park Lodge Hotel ◆◆◆
16 Egerton Road, Bexhill, East
Sussex TN39 3HH
T: (01424) 216547 & 215041
F: (01424) 217460

Sackville Hotel ◆◆◆◆
De La Warr Parade, Bexhill-on-
Sea, Bexhill, East Sussex
TN40 1LS
T: (01424) 224694
F: (01424) 734132

Southolme ◆◆◆
129 Cooden Drive, Cooden,
Bexhill, East Sussex TN39 3AJ
T: (01424) 843811 &
07889 912628
E: southolme@aol.com

Sunshine Guest House ◆◆◆
Sandhurst Lane, Little Common,
Bexhill, East Sussex TN39 4RH
T: (01424) 842009

Tamarind ◆◆◆
143 Cooden Drive, Bexhill, East
Sussex TN39 3AJ
T: (01424) 844146
E: tamarind@tesco.net

Treforfan Guest House ◆◆◆
33 Woodville Road, Bexhill, East
Sussex TN39 3ET
T: (01424) 223767
⊚

Westwood Farm ◆◆◆
Stonestile Lane, Hastings, East
Sussex TN35 4PG
T: (01424) 751038
F: (01424) 751038

BEXLEYHILL
West Sussex

Elidge Farm ◆◆◆
Bexleyhill, Petworth, West
Sussex GU28 9EA
T: (01798) 861617
F: (01798) 861617
E: aaw@comms-audit.co.uk

BIDDENDEN
Kent

Bettmans Oast
◆◆◆◆ SILVER AWARD
Hareplain Road, Biddenden,
Ashford, Kent TN27 8LJ
T: (01580) 291463
F: (01580) 291463
⊚

Birchley House West ◆◆◆◆
Fosten Green, Biddenden,
Ashford, Kent TN27 8DZ
T: (01580) 291124
F: (01580) 291416
E: birchley@globalnet.co.uk
I: www.birchleywest.co.uk

Bishopsdale Oast ◆◆◆◆
Biddenden, Ashford, Kent
TN27 8DR
T: (01580) 291027 & 292065
F: (01580) 292321
E: bishopsdale@pavilion.co.uk
I: www.bishopsdaleoast.co.uk

Heron Cottage ◆◆◆◆
Biddenden, Ashford, Kent
TN27 8HH
T: (01580) 291358

Tudor Cottage ◆◆◆◆
25 High Street, Biddenden,
Ashford, Kent TN27 8AL
T: (01580) 291913
E: suemorris.biddenden@virgin.
net
I: freespace.virgin.net/suemorris.
biddenden

Whitfield Farm
Rating Applied For
Dashmonden Lane, Biddenden,
Ashford, Kent TN27 8BZ
T: (01580) 291092
E: davidbarbour@whitfieldfarm.
freeserve.co.uk

BILSINGTON
Kent

Willow Farm ◆◆
Stone Cross, Bilsington, Ashford,
Kent TN25 7JJ
T: (01233) 720484 & 721700
F: (01233) 720484
E: renee@willow-farm.
freeserve.co.uk

BIRDHAM
West Sussex

Croftside Cottage
◆◆◆◆ GOLD AWARD
Main Road, Birdham, Chichester,
West Sussex PO20 7HS
T: (01243) 512864 &
07721 325755
F: (01243) 512864
E: connex@cwcom.net
I: www.travellingsouth.co.uk
⊚

BIRLING GAP
East Sussex

Birling Gap Hotel ◆◆◆
Birling Gap, Seven Sisters Cliffs,
East Dean, Eastbourne, East
Sussex BN20 0AB
T: (01323) 423197
F: (01323) 423030
⊚

BLACKHAM
East Sussex

Salehurst Farm ◆◆◆
Blackham, Royal Tunbridge
Wells, Kent TN3 9UB
T: (01892) 740357
F: (01892) 740158

BLADBEAN
Kent

Molehills ◆◆◆◆
Bladbean, Canterbury, Kent
CT4 6LU
T: (01303) 840051
E: molehills@hotmail.com

BOARS HEAD
East Sussex

Wareham Lodge ◆◆◆◆
Boars Head, Crowborough, East
Sussex TN6 3HE
T: (01892) 653444 &
07803 198420

BODIAM
East Sussex

Elms Farm ◆◆
Bodiam, Robertsbridge, East
Sussex TN32 5UT
T: (01580) 830494

Northlands House
Rating Applied For
Bodiam, Robertsbridge, East
Sussex TN32 5UX
T: (01580) 831849
F: (01580) 831949

BOGNOR REGIS
West Sussex

Alancourt Hotel ◆◆◆
Marine Drive West, Bognor
Regis, West Sussex PO21 2QA
T: (01243) 864844
F: (01243) 866443
I: www.m.hands@arunet.co.uk

Homestead Guest House ◆◆◆
90 Aldwick Road, Bognor Regis,
West Sussex PO21 2PD
T: (01243) 823443

Jubilee Guest House ◆◆◆
5 Gloucester Road, Bognor
Regis, West Sussex PO21 1NU
T: (01243) 863016 &
07702 275967
F: (01243) 868017
E: jubileeguesthouse@
breathemail.net
I: www.scoot.co.
uk/jubilee_guesthouse/

The Old Priory
◆◆◆◆ SILVER AWARD
80 North Bersted Street, Bognor
Regis, West Sussex PO22 9AQ
T: (01243) 863580
F: (01243) 826597
E: old.priory@btinternet.com
I: www.old-priory.com

Regis Lodge ◆◆◆
3 Gloucester Road, Bognor
Regis, West Sussex PO21 1NU
T: (01243) 827110 &
07768 117770
F: (01243) 827110
E: frank@regislodge.fsbusiness.
co.uk
I: www.regislodge.tripod.com

St Albans ◆◆◆◆
The Esplanade, Bognor Regis,
West Sussex PO21 1NY
T: (01243) 860516

Sea Crest Private Hotel ◆◆◆
19 Nyewood Lane, Bognor Regis,
West Sussex PO21 2QB
T: (01243) 821438

Swan Guest House ◆◆◆◆
17 Nyewood Lane, Bognor Regis,
West Sussex PO21 2QB
T: (01243) 826880
F: (01243) 826880
E: swanhse@globalnet.co.uk
I: www.users.globalnet.co.
uk/§swanhse

Tudor Cottage Guest House
◆◆◆
194 Chichester Road, North
Bersted, Bognor Regis, West
Sussex PO21 5BJ
T: (01243) 821826
F: (01243) 821826
E: tudorcottage@supernet.com

BOLNEY
West Sussex

Broxmead Paddock ◆◆◆◆
Broxmead Lane, Bolney,
Haywards Heath, West Sussex
RH17 5RG
T: (01444) 881458
F: (01444) 881491
E: bishop4goats@bishop4goats.
screaming.net

Butchers Bed & Breakfast
◆◆◆◆
Butchers, Ryecroft Road, Bolney,
Haywards Heath, West Sussex
RH17 5PS
T: (01444) 881503
E: mark.darby@deloitte.co.uk

Colwood Manor West
Rating Applied For
Spronketts Lane, Bolney,
Haywards Heath, West Sussex
RH17 5SA
T: (01444) 461331

New Farm House ◆◆◆◆
Nyes Hill, Wineham Lane,
Bolney, Haywards Heath, West
Sussex RH17 5SD
T: (01444) 881617 &
(01410) 710555
F: (01444) 881850
E: newfarmhouse@btinternet.
com
I: www.myrtle-cottage.co.
uk/haddrell.htm

BOROUGH GREEN
Kent

Yew Tree Barn ◆◆◆◆
Long Mill Lane, Crouch, Borough
Green, Sevenoaks, Kent
TN15 8QB
T: (01732) 883107
F: (01732) 883107

BOSHAM
West Sussex

Crede Farmhouse ◆◆◆◆
Crede Lane, Bosham, Chichester,
West Sussex PO18 8NX
T: (01243) 574929
E: lesley@credefarmhouse.
fsnet.co.uk

**Critchfield House
◆◆◆◆ GOLD AWARD**
Bosham Lane, Bosham,
Chichester, West Sussex
PO18 8HG
T: (01243) 572370
F: (01243) 572370

Good Hope ◆◆◆◆
Delling Lane, Bosham,
Chichester, West Sussex
PO18 8NR
T: (01243) 572487
F: (01243) 530760
♨

Govers ◆◆◆
Crede Lane, Bosham, Chichester,
West Sussex PO18 8NX
T: (01243) 573163

**Hatpins
◆◆◆◆◆ GOLD AWARD**
Bosham Lane, Old Bosham,
Chichester, West Sussex
PO18 8HG
T: (01243) 572644 & 575816
F: (01243) 572644

BOUGH BEECH
Kent

Bank View ◆◆◆
Chequers Hill, Bough Beech,
Edenbridge, Kent TN8 7PD
T: (01732) 700315
F: (01732) 700315

BOUGHTON
Kent

Brenley ◆◆◆
Brenley Lane, Boughton,
Faversham, Kent ME13 9LY
T: (01227) 751203
F: (01227) 751203
E: maggie@brenley.freeserve.co.
uk

10 Horselees Road ◆◆◆
Boughton under Blean,
Boughton, Faversham, Kent
ME13 9TG
T: (01227) 751332
F: (01227) 751332
E: keyway@bigfoot.com

BOUGHTON MONCHELSEA
Kent

Hideaway ◆◆
Heath Road, Boughton
Monchelsea, Maidstone, Kent
ME17 4JD
T: (01622) 747453
F: (01622) 747453

Wierton Hall Farm ◆◆◆
East Hall Hill, Boughton
Monchelsea, Maidstone, Kent
ME17 4JU
T: (01622) 743535
F: (01622) 743535

BOXGROVE
West Sussex

The Brufords ◆◆◆◆
66 The Street, Boxgrove,
Chichester, West Sussex
PO18 0EE
T: (01243) 774085
F: (01243) 781235
E: brendan@bjcoffey.freeserve.
co.uk

BOXLEY
Kent

**Barn Cottage
Rating Applied For**
Harbourland, Boxley, Maidstone,
Kent ME14 3DN
T: (01622) 675891
F: (01622) 675891

BRABOURNE LEES
Kent

Meadowsweet ◆◆◆
Manor Pound Lane, Brabourne
Lees, Ashford, Kent TN25 5LG
T: (01303) 814050
F: (01303) 813905
E: meadowsweet@onet.co.uk

BRAMLEY
Surrey

Highpoint ◆◆◆◆
Munstead View Road, Bramley,
Guildford, Surrey GU5 0DA
T: (01483) 893566
F: (01483) 894205
E: chriscard@compuserve.com

BRASTED
Kent

Lodge House ◆◆
High Street, Brasted,
Westerham, Kent TN16 1HS
T: (01959) 562195
F: (01959) 562195

The Mount House ◆◆◆
Brasted, Westerham, Kent
TN16 1JB
T: (01959) 563617
F: (01959) 561296
E: jpaulco@webspeed.net

The Orchard House ◆◆◆
Brasted Chart, Westerham, Kent
TN16 1LR
T: (01959) 563702
E: david.godsal@tesco.net

BREDE
East Sussex

**Brede Court Country House
Hotel ◆◆◆◆**
Brede Hill, Brede, Rye, East
Sussex TN31 6EJ
T: (01424) 883105
F: (01424) 883104
E: bredecrt@globalnet.co.uk
I: www.english-training.com

2 Stonelink Cottages ◆◆◆
Stubb Lane, Brede, Rye, East
Sussex TN31 6BL
T: (01424) 882943 &
07802 573612
F: (01424) 883052
E: stonelinkc@aol.com

BRENCHLEY
Kent

The Bull of Brenchley ◆◆◆
High Street, Brenchley,
Tonbridge, Kent TN12 7NQ
T: (01892) 722701
F: (01892) 722760

**Chillmill Manor
◆◆◆◆ GOLD AWARD**
Fairmans Road, Brenchley,
Tonbridge, Kent TN12 7AL
T: (01892) 722518 &
07721 586632
F: (01892) 722003

**Hononton Cottage
Rating Applied For**
Palmers Green Lane, Brenchley,
Tonbridge, Kent TN12 7BJ
T: (01892) 722483

BRIDGE
Kent

**East Bridge Country Hotel
◆◆◆◆**
Bridge Hill, Bridge, Canterbury,
Kent CT4 5AS
T: (01227) 830808
F: (01227) 832181

Harrow Cottage ◆◆◆
2 Brewery Lane, Bridge,
Canterbury, Kent CT4 5LD
T: (01227) 830218
F: (01227) 830218
E: pamela@phooker.fsbusiness.
co.uk

Skippers Restaurant ◆◆◆
73 High Street, Bridge,
Canterbury, Kent CT4 5LB
T: (01227) 830788

BRIGHTLING
East Sussex

Orchard Barn ◆◆◆
3 Twelve Oaks Cottages,
Brightling, Robertsbridge, East
Sussex TN32 5HS
T: (01424) 838263

BRIGHTON & HOVE
East Sussex

The Acropolis Hotel ◆◆
14–15 Burlington Street, Marine
Parade, Brighton, East Sussex
BN2 1AU
T: (01273) 698195
F: (01273) 698991

Adastral Hotel ◆◆◆
8 Westbourne Villas, Hove, East
Sussex BN3 4GQ
T: (01273) 888800
F: (01273) 883839
E: adastral@mistral.co.uk
I: www.adastralhotel.co.uk

**Adelaide Hotel
◆◆◆◆ SILVER AWARD**
51 Regency Square, Brighton,
East Sussex BN1 2FF
T: (01273) 205286
F: (01273) 220904
E: adelaide@pavilion.co.uk

Aegean Hotel ◆◆◆
5 New Steine, Brighton, East
Sussex BN2 1PB
T: (01273) 686547
F: (01273) 625613

Ainsley House Hotel ◆◆◆◆
28 New Steine, Brighton, East
Sussex BN2 1PD
T: (01273) 605310
F: (01273) 688604
E: ahhotel@fastnet.co.uk.
I: www.search1.co.uk/ainsley
house

Allendale Hotel ◆◆◆
3 New Steine, Brighton, East
Sussex BN2 1PB
T: (01273) 675436
F: (01273) 602603

Amalfi Hotel ◆◆
44 Marine Parade, Brighton, East
Sussex BN2 1PE
T: (01273) 607956

Ambassador Hotel ◆◆◆◆
22 New Steine, Marine Parade,
Brighton, East Sussex BN2 1PD
T: (01273) 676869
F: (01273) 689988

Andorra Hotel ◆◆◆
15-16 Oriental Place, Brighton,
East Sussex BN1 2LJ
T: (01273) 321787 & 725485
F: (01273) 721418

Aquarium Guest House ◆◆◆
13 Madeira Place, Brighton, East
Sussex BN2 1TN
T: (01273) 605761

**Arlanda Hotel
◆◆◆◆ SILVER AWARD**
20 New Steine, Brighton, East
Sussex BN2 1PD
T: (01273) 699300
F: (01273) 600930
E: arlanda@brighton.co.uk
I: www.brighton.co.
uk/hotels/arlanda/welome.htm

Atlantic Hotel ◆◆◆
16 Marine Parade, Brighton, East
Sussex BN2 1TL
T: (01273) 695944
F: (01273) 695944

Aymer ◆◆◆◆
13 Aymer Road, Hove, Brighton,
East Sussex BN3 4GB
T: (01273) 271165 &
07770 488764
F: (01273) 321653
I: WWW.sussexlive.com

The Beach Hotel ◆◆◆
2-4 Regency Square, Brighton,
East Sussex BN1 2GP
T: (01273) 323776
F: (01273) 747028
I: www.beachotel.co.uk

Beynon House ◆◆◆
24 St George's Terrace, Brighton,
East Sussex BN2 1JJ
T: (01273) 681014
E: beynonhouse@hotmail.com
I: www.brightonpages.co.
uk/beynonhouse

Brighton House Hotel ◆◆◆◆
52 Regency Square, Brighton,
East Sussex BN1 2FF
T: (01273) 323282
E: enquiries@brightonhouse
hotel.co.uk
I: www.brightonhousehotel.
co.uk

Brighton Marina House Hotel
♦♦♦
8 Charlotte Street, Marine
Parade, Brighton, East Sussex
BN2 1AG
T: (01273) 605349 & 819806
F: (01273) 679484
E: rooms@jungs.co.uk
I: www.s-h-systems.co.
uk/hotels/brighton

Brighton Twenty One Hotel
♦♦♦♦
21 Charlotte Street, Marine
Parade, Brighton, East Sussex
BN2 1AG
T: (01273) 686450 & 681617
F: (01273) 695560
E: rooms@the21.co.uk
I: www.s-h-systems.co.
uk/hotels/21

Brunswick Square Hotel ♦♦
11 Brunswick Square, Hove,
Brighton, East Sussex BN3 1EH
T: (01273) 205047
F: (01273) 205047
E: brunswick@brighton.co.uk
I: www.brighton.co.
uk/hotels/brunswick

Cavalaire Hotel ♦♦♦
34 Upper Rock Gardens,
Brighton, East Sussex BN2 1QF
T: (01273) 696899
F: (01273) 600504
E: Cavalaire.hotel@virgin.net
I: business.virgin.net/cava/aire.
hotel

Chatsworth Hotel ♦♦♦
9 Salisbury Road, Hove, East
Sussex BN3 3AB
T: (01273) 737360
F: (01273) 737360

Chester Court Hotel ♦♦♦
7 Charlotte Street, Brighton,
East Sussex BN2 1AG
T: (01273) 621750 & 621725
E: sanchez-crespo@lineone.net
I: www.brightonpages.co.
uk/brightonpavilions

Churchill Guest House ♦♦♦
44 Russell Square, Brighton, East
Sussex BN1 2EF
T: (01273) 700777
F: (01273) 700887

Cinderella Hotel ♦♦
48 St Aubyns, Hove, Brighton,
East Sussex BN3 2TE
T: (01273) 727827
F: (01273) 746272

Cosmopolitan Hotel ♦♦♦
31 New Steine, Marine Parade,
Brighton, East Sussex BN2 1PD
T: (01273) 682461
F: (01273) 622311
E: enquiries@
cosmopolitanhotel.co.uk
I: www.cosmopolitanhotel.co.uk

Diana House ♦♦
25 St Georges Terrace, Brighton,
East Sussex BN2 1JJ
T: (01273) 605797
F: (01273) 600533
E: diana@enterprise.co.net
I: www.dianahouse.co.uk

Dove Hotel ♦♦♦
18 Regency Square, Brighton,
East Sussex BN1 2FG
T: (01273) 779222
F: (01273) 746912
E: dovehotel@
dovehotelfree-online.co.uk

Dudley House ♦♦♦
10 Madeira Place, Brighton, East
Sussex BN2 1TN
T: (01273) 676794
E: boydys@msn.com

Funchal Guest House ♦♦♦
17 Madeira Place, Brighton, East
Sussex BN2 1TN
T: (01273) 603975
F: (01273) 603975

Fyfield House ♦♦♦♦
26 New Steine, Brighton, East
Sussex BN2 1PD
T: (01273) 602770
F: (01273) 602770
E: fyfield@aol.com
I: www.brighton.co.
uk/hotels/fyfield

Georjan Guest House ♦♦
27 Upper Rock Gardens,
Brighton, East Sussex BN2 1QE
T: (01273) 694951
F: (01273) 694951
E: georjan.gh@virgin.net

Granada House Hotel ♦♦♦
35 Walsingham Road, Hove,
Brighton, East Sussex BN3 4FE
T: (01273) 723855
F: (01273) 723855

Harveys ♦♦♦
1 Broad Street, Brighton, East
Sussex BN2 1TJ
T: (01273) 699227
F: (01273) 699227

Hudsons Guest House ♦♦♦
22 Devonshire Place, Brighton,
East Sussex BN2 1QA
T: (01273) 683642
F: (01273) 696088
E: hudsons@brighton.co.uk
I: brighton.co.uk/hotels/hudsons

Kimberley Hotel ♦♦♦
17 Atlingworth Street, Brighton,
East Sussex BN2 1PL
T: (01273) 603504
F: (01273) 603504
E: kimberley.hotel@iname.com
I: www.roland01.freeserve.co.uk/

Kingsway Hotel
♦♦♦♦ SILVER AWARD
2 St Aubyns, Hove, East Sussex
BN3 2TB
T: (01273) 722068
F: 0870 0554661
E: admin@kingswayent.demon.
co.uk

Leona House ♦♦
74 Middle Street, Brighton, East
Sussex BN1 1AL
T: (01273) 327309

Lichfield House ♦♦
30 Waterloo Street, Hove,
Brighton, East Sussex BN3 1AN
T: (01273) 777740 &
07970 945464
E: feelgood@lichfieldhouse@
freeserve.co.uk
I: www.lichfieldhouse.freeserve.
co.uk

Madeira Guest House ♦♦♦
14 Madeira Place, Brighton, East
Sussex BN2 1TN
T: (01273) 681115
F: (01273) 681115

Marina West Hotel ♦♦♦
26 Oriental Place, Brighton, East
Sussex BN1 2LL
T: (01273) 323087 & 207045
F: (01273) 206888
E: info@marinawest.co.uk
I: www.marinawest.co.uk

Miami Hotel ♦♦♦
22 Bedford Square, Brighton,
East Sussex BN1 2PL
T: (01273) 730169 &
07889 582797
F: (01273) 730169
E: themiami@pavilion.co.uk
I: www.brighton.co.
uk/hotels/miami

New Madeira Hotel ♦♦♦
19-23 Marine Parade, Brighton,
East Sussex BN2 1TL
T: (01273) 698331
F: (01273) 606193

Oriental Hotel ♦♦♦
9 Oriental Place, Brighton, East
Sussex BN1 2LJ
T: (01273) 205050 &
07973 334893
F: (01273) 821096
E: info@orientalhotel.co.uk
I: www.brighton.co.
uk/hotels/oriental

The Palace Hotel ♦♦♦
10-12 Grand Junction Road,
Brighton, East Sussex BN1 1PN
T: (01273) 202035 &
07711 987642
F: (01273) 202034

Pavilion Guest House ♦♦♦
12 Madeira Place, Brighton, East
Sussex BN2 1TN
T: (01273) 683195

Penny Lanes ♦♦♦
11 Charlotte Street, Brighton,
East Sussex BN2 1AG
T: (01273) 603197 & 684041
F: (01273) 689408
E: welcome@pennylanes.co.uk
I: www.pennylanes.co.uk

Russell Guest House ♦♦♦
19 Russell Square, Brighton, East
Sussex BN1 2EE
T: (01273) 327969
F: (01273) 821535
E: russell.brighton@btinternet.
com
@

Sandpiper Guest House ♦
11 Russell Square, Brighton, East
Sussex BN1 2EE
T: (01273) 328202
F: (01273) 329974
E: sandpiper@brighton.co.uk
@

Sea Spray ♦♦♦
25 New Steine, Marine Parade,
Brighton, East Sussex BN2 1PD
T: (01273) 680332

Hotel Seafield ♦♦♦
23 Seafield Road, Hove, East
Sussex BN3 2TP
T: (01273) 735912
F: (01273) 323525
I: www.brighton.co.
uk/hotels/seafield/

Shirley Guest House ♦♦
20 St George's Terrace, Brighton,
East Sussex BN2 1JH
T: (01273) 690862

Strawberry Fields Hotel ♦♦♦
6-7 New Steine, Brighton, East
Sussex BN2 1PB
T: (01273) 681576 & 693397
F: (01273) 693397
E: strawberryfields@pavilion.co.
uk
I: www.brighton.co.
uk/hotels/strawberryfields

BROAD OAK
East Sussex

Layces Bed & Breakfast
♦♦♦♦
Chitcombe Road, Broad Oak,
Rye, East Sussex TN31 6EU
T: (01424) 882836
F: (01424) 882281
E: stephens@layces.demon.co.
uk
I: www.layces.demon.co.uk

BROADSTAIRS
Kent

Bay Tree Hotel ♦♦♦
12 Eastern Esplanade,
Broadstairs, Kent CT10 1DR
T: (01843) 862502
F: (01843) 860589

Devonhurst Hotel ♦♦♦♦
Eastern Esplanade, Broadstairs,
Kent CT10 1DR
T: (01843) 863010
F: (01843) 868940
E: devhotel@aol.com
I: www.Smoothhound.co.
uk/hotels/devonhst.html.
@

Gull Cottage Hotel ♦♦♦♦
5 Eastern Esplanade,
Broadstairs, Kent CT10 1DP
T: (01843) 861936

North Goodwin House ♦♦♦♦
Cliff Promenade, Broadstairs,
Kent CT10 3QY
T: (01843) 864128
E: bandb@nblaw.co.uk
I: www.nblaw.co.uk/ngh/index.
html

Oakfield Private Hotel ♦♦♦♦
11 The Vale, Broadstairs, Kent
CT10 1RB
T: (01843) 862506 & 864021
F: (01843) 600659
E: oakfield.hotel@lineone.net
I: www.travelcheck.co.uk

The Queens Hotel ♦♦
31 Queens Road, Broadstairs,
Kent CT10 1PG
T: (01843) 861727
F: (01843) 600993
E: quehot@excite.com
I: www.qhotel.demon.co.uk

Sunnydene Hotel ♦♦♦♦
10 Chandos Road, Broadstairs,
Kent CT10 1QP
T: (01843) 863347
F: (01843) 863347

Velindre Hotel ♦♦♦
10 Western Esplanade,
Broadstairs, Kent CT10 1TG
T: (01843) 601081

BURGESS HILL
West Sussex

The Homestead ◆◆◆◆
Homestead Lane, Valebridge
Road, Burgess Hill, West Sussex
RH15 0RQ
T: (01444) 246899
F: (01444) 246899
E: mike@burgess-hill.co.uk
I: www.burgess-hill.co.uk

St Owens ◆◆◆
11 Silverdale Road, Burgess Hill,
West Sussex RH15 0ED
T: (01444) 236435

Wellhouse ◆◆◆◆
Wellhouse Lane, Burgess Hill,
West Sussex RH15 0BN
T: (01444) 233231
F: (01444) 233231

BURMARSH
Kent

Dolly Plum Cottage ◆◆◆◆
Burmarsh Road, Burmarsh,
Romney Marsh, Kent TN29 0JT
T: (01303) 874558

BURWASH
East Sussex

Glydwish Place
◆◆◆◆◆ SILVER AWARD
Fontridge Lane, Burwash,
Etchingham, East Sussex
TN19 7DG
T: (01435) 882869 &
07860 624197
F: (01435) 882749
E: collins@collinsdolores.
screaming.net
I: www.glydwish.co.uk

BURWASH WEALD
East Sussex

Church House ◆◆◆
Heathfield Road, Burwash
Weald, Etchingham, East Sussex
TN19 7LA
T: (01435) 882688

CAMBER
East Sussex

Glenrose ◆◆◆
127 Lydd Road, Camber, Rye,
East Sussex TN31 7RS
T: (01797) 224417

CANTERBURY
Kent

Abberley House ◆◆◆
115 Whitstable Road,
Canterbury, Kent CT2 8EF
T: (01227) 450265
F: (01227) 478626

Acacia Lodge ◆◆◆◆
39 London Road, Canterbury,
Kent CT2 8LF
T: (01227) 769955 &
0975 433486
F: (01227) 769955
E: michael.cain1@virgin.net

Alexandra House ◆◆◆◆
1 Roper Road, Canterbury, Kent
CT2 7EH
T: (01227) 767011
F: (01227) 786617

Alicante Guest House ◆◆◆
4 Roper Road, Canterbury, Kent
CT2 7EH
T: (01227) 766277
F: (01227) 766277

**Anchor House Restaurant &
Guest House** ◆◆◆
25 North Lane, Canterbury, Kent
CT2 7EE
T: (01227) 768105
F: (01227) 768105

Anns House ◆◆◆◆
63 London Road, Canterbury,
Kent CT2 8JZ
T: (01227) 768767
F: (01227) 768172
E: annshotel.canterbury@
btinternet.com

Ashley Guest House ◆◆
9 London Road, Canterbury,
Kent CT2 8LR
T: (01227) 455863

Bower Farm House
◆◆◆◆ SILVER AWARD
Stelling Minnis, Canterbury,
Kent CT4 6BB
T: (01227) 709430
E: anne@bowerbb.freeserve.co.
uk
I: www.kentac.co.uk/bowerfm

Carena Guest House ◆◆◆
250 Wincheap, Canterbury, Kent
CT1 3TY
T: (01227) 765630
F: (01227) 765630

Castle Court Guest House ◆◆
8 Castle Street, Canterbury, Kent
CT1 2QF
T: (01227) 463441
F: (01227) 463441

Cathedral Gate Hotel ◆◆◆
36 Burgate, Canterbury, Kent
CT1 2HA
T: (01227) 464381
F: (01227) 462800
E: cgate@cgate.demon.co.uk

Chaucer Lodge ◆◆◆◆
62 New Dover Road, Canterbury,
Kent CT1 3DT
T: (01227) 459141
F: (01227) 459141
I: www.smoothhound.co.
uk/hotels/chaucldg.html

Clare-Ellen Guest House
◆◆◆◆ SILVER AWARD
9 Victoria Road, Wincheap,
Canterbury, Kent CT1 3SG
T: (01227) 760205
F: (01227) 784482
E: loraine.williams@virgin.net
I: www.clareellenguesthouse.co.
uk

**The Coach House
Rating Applied For**
34 Watling Street, Canterbury,
Kent CT1 2UD
T: (01227) 784324

Corner House ◆◆◆
113 Whitstable Road,
Canterbury, Kent CT2 8EF
T: (01227) 761352
F: (01227) 761065
E: Jean@unispacekent.co.uk
I: WWW.forge.co.
uk/cornerhouse

Courtney Guest House ◆◆◆◆
4 London Road, Canterbury,
Kent CT2 8LR
T: (01227) 769668
F: (01227) 479989
E: b.broad@lineone.net

Four Seasons ◆◆◆
77 Sturry Road, Canterbury,
Kent CT1 1BU
T: (01227) 787078
F: (01227) 787078
E: cmoore2570@aol.com

The Green House ◆◆◆
86 Wincheap, Canterbury, Kent
CT1 3RS
T: (01227) 453338
E: chrismac@greenhouse48.
fsnet.co.uk
I: www.bednbreakfastkent.co.uk

Greyfriars House ◆◆◆
6 Stour Street, Canterbury, Kent
CT1 2NR
T: (01227) 456255 & 830931
F: (01227) 455233
E: christine@greyfriars-house.
co.uk
I: www.greyfriars-house.co.uk

Harriet House
◆◆◆◆ SILVER AWARD
3 Broad Oak Road, Canterbury,
Kent CT2 7PL
T: (01227) 457363
F: (01227) 788214

Homewood Farm ◆◆◆◆
Agester Lane, Denton,
Canterbury, Kent CT4 6NR
T: (01227) 832611
F: (01227) 832611

Iffin Farmhouse ◆◆◆◆
Iffin Lane, Canterbury, Kent
CT4 7BE
T: (01227) 462776
F: (01227) 462776

The Kings Head ◆◆◆
204 Wincheap, Canterbury, Kent
CT1 3RY
T: (01227) 462885
F: (01227) 459627

Kingsbridge Villas ◆◆◆
15 Best Lane, Canterbury, Kent
CT1 2JB
T: (01227) 766415

Kingsmead House ◆◆◆
68 St Stephen's Road,
Canterbury, Kent CT2 7JF
T: (01227) 760132
E: kingsmead@cwcom.net

Lindens Guest House ◆◆◆
38b St Dunstans Street,
Canterbury, Kent CT2 8BY
T: (01227) 462339
E: ellencommon@ukgateway.
net
I: www.canterbury.co.
uk/pages/linden.htm

London Guest House ◆◆◆
14 London Road, Canterbury,
Kent CT2 8LR
T: (01227) 765860
F: (01227) 456721
E: londonguesthousecabnkz@
supernet.com

Magnolia House
◆◆◆◆ GOLD AWARD
36 St Dunstans Terrace,
Canterbury, Kent CT2 8AX
T: (01227) 765121 &
07885 595970
F: (01227) 765121
E: magnolia_house_
canterbury@yahoo.com
I: www.freespace.virgin.
net/magnolia.canterbury

The Millers ◆◆◆
2 Mill Lane, Canterbury, Kent
CT1 2AW
T: (01227) 456057
F: (01227) 452421

Oriel Lodge
◆◆◆◆ SILVER AWARD
3 Queens Avenue, Canterbury,
Kent CT2 8AY
T: (01227) 462845
F: (01227) 462845
E: info@oriel-lodge.co.uk
I: www.oriel-lodge.co.uk

Peregrine House ◆◆
18 Hawks Lane, Canterbury,
Kent CT1 2NU
T: (01227) 472153 & 830931
F: (01227) 455233
E: christine@greyfriars-house.
co.uk
I: greyfriars-house.co.uk

The Plantation
◆◆◆◆ SILVER AWARD
Iffin Lane, Canterbury, Kent
CT4 7BD
T: (01227) 472104
E: plantation@excite.co.uk
I: www.media-p.co.
uk/plantation/

Raemore House ◆
33 New Dover Road, Canterbury,
Kent CT1 3AS
T: (01227) 769740 &
07836 786020
F: (01227) 769432
E: tom@raemore.demon.co.uk

Renville Oast ◆◆◆
Bridge, Canterbury, Kent
CT4 5AD
T: (01227) 830215
F: (01227) 830215
E: renville.oast@virgin.net
I: freespace.virgin.net/joan.
hill/index.html

St Johns Court Guest House ◆
St Johns Lane, Canterbury, Kent
CT1 2QG
T: (01227) 456425
F: (01227) 785933

St Lawrence Guest House
◆◆◆
183 Old Dover Road, Canterbury,
Kent CT1 3EP
T: (01227) 451336
F: (01227) 451148

St Stephens Guest House
◆◆◆
100 St Stephens Road,
Canterbury, Kent CT2 7JL
T: (01227) 767644
F: (01227) 767644
E: info@st-stephens.fsnet.co.uk
I: www.com.to/st-stephens

Tanglewood Cottage ◆◆◆
40 London Road, Canterbury,
Kent CT2 8LF
T: (01227) 786806

Thanington Hotel
◆◆◆◆◆ GOLD AWARD
140 Wincheap, Canterbury, Kent
CT1 3RY
T: (01227) 453227
F: (01227) 453225
E: thanington@lineone.net
I: www.thanington-hotel.co.uk
◎

Tudor House ◆◆◆
6 Best Lane, Canterbury, Kent
CT1 2JB
T: (01227) 765650

Waltham Court Hotel ◆◆◆◆
Kake Street, Petham, Canterbury,
Kent CT4 5SB
T: (01227) 700413
F: (01227) 700127
E: sgw.chives.waltham@dial.
pipex.com
I: www.s-h-systems.co.
uk/hotels/waltham.html
◎

White Horse Inn ◆◆◆
Boughton, Faversham, Kent
ME13 9AX
T: (01227) 751700 & 751343
F: (01227) 751090
E: ihopkins@shepherd-neame.
co.uk
I: www.shepherd-neame.co.uk

The White House ◆◆◆◆
6 St Peters Lane, Canterbury,
Kent CT1 2BP
T: (01227) 761836
E: whwelcome@aol.com

Wincheap Guest House ◆
94 Wincheap, Canterbury, Kent
CT1 3RS
T: (01227) 762309 &
07889 482487
F: (01227) 762309

The Woolpack Inn ◆◆◆
High Street, Chilham,
Canterbury, Kent CT4 8DL
T: (01227) 730208 & 730351
F: (01227) 731053
E: ihopkins@shepherd-neame.
co.uk
I: www.shepherd-neame.co.uk

Woolverton House ◆◆◆
39 St Stephens Road,
Canterbury, Kent CT2 7JD
T: (01227) 764357
F: (01227) 764357

Yorke Lodge ◆◆◆◆
50 London Road, Canterbury,
Kent CT2 8LF
T: (01227) 451243
F: (01227) 462006
E: yorke-lg@dircon.co.uk
I: www.users.dircon.co.
uk/§yorke-lg

Zan Stel Lodge
◆◆◆◆ SILVER AWARD
140 Old Dover Road, Canterbury,
Kent CT1 3NX
T: (01227) 453654

CATSFIELD
East Sussex
Ostlers Cottage Farm ◆◆◆
The Stream, Catsfield, Battle,
East Sussex TN33 9BB
T: (01424) 892406

CHARING
Kent
Barnfield ◆◆◆
Charing, Ashford, Kent
TN27 0BN
T: (01233) 712421 &
07798 686168
F: (01233) 712421

Royal Oak Inn ◆◆◆
5 High Street, Charing, Ashford,
Kent TN27 0HU
T: (01233) 712612
F: (01233) 713355

Timber Lodge ◆◆◆◆
Charing Hill, Charing, Kent
TN27 0NG
T: (01233) 712822
F: (01233) 712822

CHART SUTTON
Kent
White House Farm ◆◆◆
Green Lane, Chart Sutton,
Maidstone, Kent ME17 3ES
T: (01622) 842490
F: (01622) 842490

CHARTHAM
Kent
Stour Farm ◆◆◆◆
Riverside, Chartham,
Canterbury, Kent CT4 7NX
T: (01227) 731977
F: (01227) 731977
E: jjwilson@adept.co.uk
I: www.innt.com/stourfarm

CHATHAM
Kent
Officers Hill ◆◆◆◆
7 College Road, Historic
Dockyard, Chatham, Kent
ME4 4QW
T: (01634) 828436
F: (01634) 828735
◎

CHELWOOD GATE
East Sussex
Holly House ◆◆◆◆
Beaconsfield Road, Chelwood
Gate, Haywards Heath, East
Sussex RH17 7LF
T: (01825) 740484
F: (01825) 740172
E: deebirchell@hollyhousebnb.
demon.co.uk
I: hollyhousebnb.demon.co.uk

CHEVENING
Kent
Crossways House ◆◆◆◆
Chevening, Sevenoaks, Kent
TN14 6HF
T: (01732) 456334
F: (01732) 452312

CHICHESTER
West Sussex
Abelands Barn
◆◆◆◆ SILVER AWARD
Bognor Road, Merston,
Chichester, West Sussex
PO20 6DY
T: (01243) 533826 & 551234
F: (01243) 555533
I: www.accomodata.co.
uk/170998.htm

Annas ◆◆◆
27 Westhampnett Road,
Chichester, West Sussex
PO19 4HW
T: (01243) 788522 &
07885 446077
F: (01243) 788522
E: nick@annas.freeserve.co.uk
I: www.annasofchichester.co.uk

**Apuldram Manor Farm Bed &
Breakfast ◆◆◆◆**
Dell Quay, Apuldram Lane,
Chichester, West Sussex
PO20 7EF
T: (01243) 782522
F: (01243) 782052
E: ma.sawday@farmersweekly.
net

Barford ◆◆◆
Bosham Lane, Bosham,
Chichester, West Sussex
PO18 8HL
T: (01243) 573393
F: (01243) 573393
E: Tony@aflanagan.freeserve.co.
uk

Bayleaf ◆◆◆
16 Whyke Road, Chichester,
West Sussex PO19 2HN
T: (01243) 774330
◎

21 Brandy Hole Lane ◆◆◆
Chichester, West Sussex
PO19 4RL
T: (01243) 528201
F: (01243) 528201

The Chichester Inn ◆◆◆
38 West Street, Chichester, West
Sussex PO19 1RP
T: (01243) 783185
◎

The Coach House ◆◆◆◆
Binderton, Chichester, West
Sussex PO18 0JS
T: (01243) 539624 &
07710 536085
F: (01243) 539624
E: spightling@aol.com

The Cottage ◆◆◆
22B Westhampnett Road,
Chichester, West Sussex
PO19 4HW
T: (01243) 774979

Encore ◆◆◆◆
11 Clydesdale Avenue,
Chichester, West Sussex
PO19 2LW
T: (01243) 528271

Englewood ◆◆◆◆
East Ashling, Chichester, West
Sussex PO18 9AS
T: (01243) 575407 &
0777 1964769

Finisterre ◆◆◆◆
9 Albert Road, Chichester, West
Sussex PO19 3JE
T: (01243) 532680 &
07889 285407

Forge Hotel
◆◆◆◆ SILVER AWARD
High Street, Chilgrove,
Chichester, West Sussex
PO18 9HX
T: (01243) 535333
F: (01243) 535363
E: neil@forgehotel.com
I: www.forgehotel.com

Friary Close
◆◆◆◆ SILVER AWARD
Friary Lane, Chichester, West
Sussex PO19 1UF
T: (01243) 527294
F: (01243) 533876
E: friaryclose@argonet.co.uk

George and Dragon ◆◆
51 North Street, Chichester,
West Sussex PO19 1NQ
T: (01243) 775525 & 785660

Hedgehogs ◆◆◆
45 Whyke Lane, Chichester,
West Sussex PO19 2JT
T: (01243) 780022

Herons ◆◆
6 Orchard Gardens, Chichester,
West Sussex PO19 1DG
T: (01243) 531424

Home Farm House
◆◆◆◆ GOLD AWARD
Elms Lane, West Wittering,
Chichester, West Sussex
PO20 8LW
T: (01243) 514252

Kia-ora Nursery ◆◆◆
Main Road, Nutbourne,
Chichester, West Sussex
PO18 8RT
T: (01243) 572858
F: (01243) 572858

4 The Lane ◆◆◆◆
Summersdale, Chichester, West
Sussex PO19 4PY
T: (01243) 527293 &
07711 499685
E: ynyo5@dial.pipex.com

Leef Daal ◆◆◆
Warren Farm Lane, Chichester,
West Sussex PO19 4RU
T: (01243) 790692
F: (01243) 790535
E: leefdaal@elmac.demon.co.uk
I: www.elmac.co.uk/leefdaal

Litten House ◆◆◆
148 St Pancras, Chichester, West
Sussex PO19 1SH
T: (01243) 774503
F: (01243) 539187
E: victoria@littenho.demon.co.
uk
I: www.littenho.demon.co.uk

5A Little London ◆◆
Chichester, West Sussex
PO19 1PH
T: (01243) 788405

**Longmeadow Guest House
◆◆◆**
Pine Grove, Chichester, West
Sussex PO19 3PN
T: (01243) 782063
E: bbeeching@supanet.com

1 Maplehurst Road ◆◆◆◆
Chichester, West Sussex
PO19 4QL
T: (01243) 528467 &
07710 649300
F: (01243) 528467

Millstone Cottage ◆◆◆
Church Lane, Pagham, Bognor
Regis, West Sussex PO21 4NU
T: (01243) 262495
F: (01243) 262668
E: inglenook@btinternet.com
I: www.btinternet.
com/§inglenook/

The Old Store Guest House
♦♦♦♦
Stane Street, Halnaker,
Chichester, West Sussex
PO18 0QL
T: (01243) 531977
F: (01243) 531977

Palm Tree Cottage ♦♦♦♦
110 Fishbourne West,
Chichester, West Sussex
PO19 3JR
T: (01243) 782110

Primrose Cottage ♦♦♦
Old Broyle Road, West Broyle,
Chichester, West Sussex
PO19 3PR
T: (01243) 788873

Riverside Lodge ♦♦♦
7 Market Avenue, Chichester,
West Sussex PO19 1JU
T: (01243) 783164

112 St Pancras ♦♦♦
Chichester, West Sussex
PO19 4LH
T: (01243) 789872
F: (01243) 785474

Sycamores ♦♦♦♦
16 Hunters Way, Chichester,
West Sussex PO19 4RB
T: (01243) 528294
E: sally.bassett@sycamores16.
freeserve.co.uk

1 Tower Street ♦♦♦
Chichester, West Sussex
PO19 1QH
T: (01243) 782526

University College Chicester
♦♦♦
Bishop Otter Campus, College
Lane, Chichester, West Sussex
PO19 4PE
T: (01243) 816000
F: (01243) 816080
E: conference@chihe.ac.uk
I: www.chihe.ac.uk

Whyke Cottage ♦♦♦♦
17 Whyke Lane, Chichester,
West Sussex PO19 2JR
T: (01243) 788767

5 Willowbed Avenue ♦♦♦
Chichester, West Sussex
PO19 2JD
T: (01243) 786366

Xavier House ♦♦♦♦
Old Broyle Road, Chichester,
West Sussex PO19 3PR
T: (01243) 784930

CHIDDINGLY
East Sussex
Hale Farm House ♦♦♦
Chiddingly, Lewes, East Sussex
BN8 6HQ
T: (01825) 872619 &
07702 340631
F: (01825) 872619
E: s.burrough@virgin.net
I: www.cuckmere-valley.co.
uk/hale

CHIDDINGSTONE
Kent
Hoath Holidays ♦♦♦
Hoath House, Chiddingstone
Hoath, Edenbridge, Kent
TN8 7DB
T: (01342) 850362
E: jstreatfield@hoath-house.
freeserve.co.uk
I: www.hoath_house.freeserve.
co.uk

CHILHAM
Kent
Folly House ♦♦♦♦
Chilham, Canterbury, Kent
CT4 8DW
T: (01227) 738669 & 730425
F: (01227) 730425

The Old Alma ♦♦♦
Canterbury Road, Chilham,
Canterbury, Kent CT4 8DX
T: (01227) 731913 &
07785 775930
F: (01227) 731078
E: oldalma@aol.co.uk

Stour Valley House
♦♦♦♦ SILVER AWARD
Pilgrims Lane, Chilham,
Canterbury, Kent CT4 8AA
T: (01227) 738991 &
07768 074177
F: (01227) 738991
E: fionaely@stourvalleyhouse.
freeserve.co.uk

Woodchip House ♦♦♦
Maidstone Road, Chilham,
Canterbury, Kent CT4 8DD
T: (01227) 730386 &
07889 321978
E: woodchip@talk21.com

CHIPSTEAD
Kent
Chevers ♦♦♦♦
Moat Close, Homedean Road,
Chipstead, Sevenoaks, Kent
TN13 2HZ
T: (01732) 779144 &
07887 717429
E: japarish@supanet.com

29 Chipstead Park ♦♦♦
Chipstead, Sevenoaks, Kent
TN13 2SL
T: (01732) 457094

Windmill Farm ♦♦♦♦
Chevening Road, Chipstead,
Sevenoaks, Kent TN13 2SA
T: (01732) 452054

CHURT
Surrey
Anne's Cottage
Rating Applied For
Green Cross Lane, Churt,
Farnham, Surrey GU10 2ND
T: (01484) 714181

CLIFTONVILLE
Kent
Carnforth Hotel ♦♦♦
103 Norfolk Road, Cliftonville,
Margate, Kent CT9 2HX
T: (01843) 292127

Debenham Lodge Hotel ♦♦♦
25 Norfolk Road, Cliftonville,
Margate, Kent CT9 2HU
T: (01843) 292568

Ferndale Hotel ♦♦
26-30 Athelstan Road,
Cliftonville, Margate, Kent
CT9 2BA
T: (01843) 229192

Hotel Marina ♦♦♦
8 Dalby Square, Cliftonville,
Margate, Kent CT9 2ER
T: (01843) 230120
F: (01843) 230120

Mentone Lodge
Rating Applied For
5 Norfolk Road, Cliftonville,
Margate, Kent CT9 2HU
T: (01843) 292152 &
07775 515741
E: mentone@libertysurf.co.uk

CLIMPING
West Sussex
Amberley Court
♦♦♦♦ SILVER AWARD
Crookthorn Lane, Climping,
Littlehampton, West Sussex
BN17 5QU
T: (01903) 725131
F: (01903) 734555

COBHAM
Kent
Roxena
Rating Applied For
34 Manor Road, Sole Street,
Cobham, Gravesend, Kent
DA13 9BN
T: (01474) 814174

COLDRED
Kent
Colret House ♦♦♦♦
The Green, Coldred, Dover, Kent
CT15 5AP
T: (01304) 830388
F: (01304) 830348

COLEMANS HATCH
East Sussex
Gospel Oak ♦♦♦
Sandy Lane, Colemans Hatch,
Hartfield, East Sussex TN7 4ER
T: (01342) 823840

COMPTON
West Sussex
Apiary Cottage ♦♦♦
Compton, Chichester, West
Sussex PO18 9EX
T: (023) 9263 1306

Compton Farmhouse ♦♦
Church Lane, Compton,
Chichester, West Sussex
PO18 9HB
T: (023) 9263 1597

COOKSBRIDGE
East Sussex
Lower Tulleys Wells Farm
♦♦♦
Beechwood Lane, East
Chiltington Road, Cooksbridge,
Lewes, East Sussex BN7 3QG
T: (01273) 472622

COWBEECH
East Sussex
Batchelors ♦♦♦
Cowbeech Hill, Cowbeech,
Hailsham, East Sussex BN27 4JB
T: (01323) 832215

The Mill
♦♦♦♦ SILVER AWARD
Trolliloes Lane, Cowbeech,
Hailsham, East Sussex BN27 4JG
T: (01323) 833952

COWDEN
Kent
Becketts Bed & Breakfast
Rating Applied For
Pylegate Farm, Hartfield Road,
Cowden, Edenbridge, Kent
TN8 7HE
T: (01342) 850514 &
07884 427550
F: (01342) 850514

Saxbys ♦♦♦♦
Cowden, Royal Tunbridge Wells,
Kent TN8 7DU
T: (01342) 850581
F: (01342) 850830
I: www.saxbys@cowden.fsnet.
com.uk

Southernwood House ♦♦♦♦
(The Old Rectory), Church Street,
Cowden, Edenbridge, Kent
TN8 7JE
T: (01342) 850880

CRANBROOK
Kent
Bargate House ♦♦♦♦
Angley Road, Cranbrook, Kent
TN17 2PQ
T: (01580) 714254

Folly Hill Cottage ♦♦♦♦
Friezley Lane, Hocker Edge,
Cranbrook, Kent TN17 2LL
T: (01580) 714299
F: (01580) 714299
E: decarlej@aol.com
I: members.aol.com:/decarlej

Guernsey Cottage ♦♦♦
Wilsley Green, Cranbrook, Kent
TN17 2LG
T: (01580) 712542

Hallwood Farm House ♦♦♦
Hallwood Farm, Cranbrook, Kent
TN17 2SP
T: (01580) 713204
F: (01580) 713204

Millfields House ♦♦♦♦
The Hill, Cranbrook, Kent
TN17 3AJ
T: (01580) 714344 & 720045
F: (01580) 720045
E: janepugh@millfieldshouse.
freeserve.co.uk
I: www.millfieldshouse.
freeserve.co.uk

Old Rectory
♦♦♦♦ SILVER AWARD
Frittenden, Cranbrook, Kent
TN17 2DG
T: (01580) 852313
F: (01580) 852313

Sissinghurst Castle Farm
♦♦♦♦
Sissinghurst, Cranbrook, Kent
TN17 2AB
T: (01580) 712885
F: (01580) 712601

Swattenden Ridge ♦♦♦
Swattenden Lane, Cranbrook,
Kent TN17 3PR
T: (01580) 712327

Tolehurst Barn ◆◆◆◆
Cranbrook Road, Frittenden,
Cranbrook, Kent TN17 2BP
T: (01580) 714385
F: (01580) 714385

White Horse Inn ◆◆
High Street, Cranbrook, Kent
TN17 3EX
T: (01580) 712615

CRAWLEY
West Sussex

The Manor House ◆◆◆
Bonnetts Lane, Ifield, Crawley,
West Sussex RH11 0NY
T: (01293) 510000 & 512298
F: (01293) 518046
E: info@manorhouse.totalserve.
co.uk
I: www.manorhouse.totalserve.
co.uk

Three Bridges Lodge ◆◆◆
190 Three Bridges Road,
Crawley, West Sussex RH10 1LN
T: (01293) 612190
F: (01293) 553078
E: nisangah@yahoo.com

Waterhall Country House
◆◆◆
Prestwood Lane, Ifield Wood,
Crawley, West Sussex RH11 0LA
T: (01293) 520002
F: (01293) 539905
E: info@waterhall.co.uk
I: www.smoothhound/hotels/
waterhall

CROWBOROUGH
East Sussex

Alpina ◆◆◆◆
27 Beacon Close, Crowborough,
East Sussex TN6 1DX
T: (01892) 655743
F: (01892) 652545

Bathurst ◆◆◆◆
Fielden Road, Crowborough,
East Sussex TN6 1TR
T: (01892) 665476 & 654189

Braemore
◆◆◆◆ SILVER AWARD
Eridge Road, Steel Cross,
Crowborough, East Sussex
TN6 2SS
T: (01892) 665700

Bryher Patch ◆◆◆
18 Hydehurst Close,
Crowborough, East Sussex
TN6 1EN
T: (01892) 663038

Hope Court ◆◆◆◆
Rannoch Road, Crowborough,
East Sussex TN6 1RA
T: (01892) 654017 &
07710 289138

CUCKFIELD
West Sussex

The Wheatsheaf Inn ◆◆◆
Broad Street, Cuckfield,
Haywards Heath, West Sussex
RH17 5DW
T: (01444) 454078
F: (01444) 417265

DANEHILL
East Sussex

New Glenmore ◆◆◆◆
Sliders Lane, Furners Green,
Uckfield, East Sussex TN22 3RU
T: (01825) 790783
E: alan.robinson@bigfoot.com

DARGATE
Kent

Twin Mays ◆◆◆◆
Plumpudding Lane, Dargate,
Faversham, Kent ME13 9EX
T: (01227) 751346
E: janetm@harper128.freeserve.
co.uk

DARTFORD
Kent

Chashir ◆
3 Tynedale Close, Fleet Estate,
Dartford, Kent DA2 6LL
T: (01322) 227886

DEAL
Kent

Cannongate Guest House
◆◆◆
26 Gilford Road, Deal, Kent
CT14 7DJ
T: (01304) 375238

Hardicot Guest House ◆◆◆◆
Kingsdown Road, Walmer, Deal,
Kent CT14 8AW
T: (01304) 389234
F: (01304) 389234
E: guestboss@talk21.com

The Hole in the Roof Hotel
Rating Applied For
42-44 Queen Street, Deal, Kent
CT14 6EY
T: (01304) 374839 & 373768
F: (01304) 373768

Ilex Cottage ◆◆◆◆
Temple Way, Worth, Deal, Kent
CT14 0DA
T: (01304) 617026
F: (01304) 620890
E: info@ilexcottage
I: www.ilexcottage.com

Keep House ◆◆◆
1 Deal Castle Road, Deal, Kent
CT14 7BB
T: (01304) 368162
F: (01304) 368162
E: keehouse@talk21.com
I: www.keephouse.co.uk

Kings Head Public House ◆◆◆
9 Beach Street, Deal, Kent
CT14 7AH
T: (01304) 368194
F: (01304) 364182

The Malvern ◆◆◆
5-7 Ranelagh Road, Deal, Kent
CT14 7BG
T: (01304) 372944
F: (01304) 372944

Richmond Villa Guest House
Rating Applied For
1 Ranelagh Road, Deal, Kent
CT14 7BG
T: (01304) 366211

The Roast House Lodge ◆◆◆
224 London Road, Deal, Kent
CT14 9PW
T: (01304) 380824
F: (01304) 380824

Sondes Lodge Guesthouse
◆◆◆◆
14 Sondes Road, Deal, Kent
CT14 7BW
T: (01304) 368741

DENSOLE
Kent

Garden Lodge ◆◆◆◆
324 Canterbury Road, Densole,
Folkestone, Kent CT18 7BB
T: (01303) 893147 &
07885 933683
F: (01303) 893147
E: gardenlodge@tritontek.com
I: www.smoothhound.co.
uk/hotels/gardenlo.html

DETLING
Kent

East Lodge ◆◆◆◆
Harple Lane, Detling, Maidstone,
Kent ME14 3ET
T: (01622) 734205
F: (01622) 735500

DITCHLING
East Sussex

The White Barn ◆◆◆◆
Lodge Hill Lane, Ditchling,
Hassocks, West Sussex BN6 8SP
T: (01273) 842920

DODDINGTON
Kent

Palace Farmhouse ◆◆◆
Chequers Hill, Doddington,
Sittingbourne, Kent ME9 0AU
T: (01795) 886820

DORKING
Surrey

Bulmer Farm ◆◆◆◆
Holmbury St Mary, Dorking,
Surrey RH5 6LG
T: (01306) 730210

Fairdene Guest House ◆◆◆
Moores Road, Dorking, Surrey
RH4 2BG
T: (01306) 888337
E: zoe@fairdene5.freeserve.co.
uk

Kerne Hus ◆◆◆◆
Walliswood, Dorking, Surrey
RH5 5RD
T: (01306) 627548

Sturtwood Farm ◆◆◆
Partridge Lane, Newdigate,
Dorking, Surrey RH5 5EE
T: (01306) 631308
F: (01306) 631908

Torridon Guest House ◆◆◆
Longfield Road, Dorking, Surrey
RH4 3DF
T: (01306) 883724
F: (01306) 880759

DOVER
Kent

Amanda Guest House ◆◆◆
4 Harold Street, Dover, Kent
CT16 1SF
T: (01304) 201711
E: pageant@port-of-dover.com
I: www.port-of-dover.
com/pageant/bb.htm#amanda

Beulah House
Rating Applied For
94 Crabble Hill, Dover, Kent
CT17 0SA
T: (01304) 824615

Blakes of Dover ◆◆◆
52 Castle Street, Dover, Kent
CT16 1PJ
T: (01304) 202194 & 211263
F: (01304) 202194
E: jjt@btinternet.com

Byways Hotel ◆◆
245-249 Folkestone Road,
Dover, Kent CT17 9LL
T: (01304) 242221
F: (01304) 240681

Castle Guest House ◆◆◆
10 Castle Hill Road, Dover, Kent
CT16 1QW
T: (01304) 201656
F: (01304) 210197
E: dimechr@aol.com
I: www.doveraccommodation.
co.uk/castle.html

Chrislyn's Guest House ◆◆◆
15 Park Avenue, Dover, Kent
CT16 1ES
T: (01304) 202302
F: (01304) 203317

Clare Guest House ◆◆◆
167 Folkestone Road, Dover,
Kent CT17 9SJ
T: (01304) 204553

Cleveland Guest House ◆◆◆
2 Laureston Place, off Castle Hill
Road, Dover, Kent CT16 1QX
T: (01304) 204622
F: (01304) 211598
E: albetcleve@aol.com
I: www.home@aol.
com/albetcleve

The Dell Guest House ◆◆◆
233 Folkestone Road, Dover,
Kent CT17 9SL
T: (01304) 202422
F: (01304) 204816
E: dellneo@aol.com
I: www.smoothhound.co.
uk/hotels/dell.html

Dover Hotel ◆◆◆
122-124 Folkestone Road,
Dover, Kent CT17 9SP
T: (01304) 206559
F: (01304) 203936

**Dover's Restover Bed &
Breakfast** ◆◆◆
69 Folkestone Road, Dover, Kent
CT17 9RZ
T: (01304) 206031
E: restover69@hotmail.com

Elmo Guest House ◆◆◆
120 Folkestone Road, Dover,
Kent CT17 9SP
T: (01304) 206236

Esther House ◆◆◆
55 Barton Road, Dover, Kent
CT16 2NF
T: (01304) 241332
F: (01304) 241332

Frith Lodge ◆◆◆
14 Frith Road, Dover, Kent
CT16 2PY
T: (01304) 208139

Gladstone Guest House ◆◆◆
3 Laureston Place, Dover, Kent
CT16 1QX
T: (01304) 208457
F: (01304) 208457
E: kkd3gladstone@aol.com
I: www.doveraccommodation.
co.uk/gladstone.htm

Linden Guest House ◆◆◆◆
231 Folkestone Road, Dover,
Kent CT17 9SL
T: (01304) 205449 &
07785 987706
F: (01304) 212499
E: Lindenrog@aol.com
I: www.smoothhound.
uk/hotels/linden.html
⊕

Loddington House Hotel
◆◆◆◆
14 East Cliff, (Seafront - Marine
Parade), Dover, Kent CT16 1LX
T: (01304) 201947
F: (01304) 201947

Longfield Guest House ◆◆
203 Folkestone Road, Dover,
Kent CT17 9SL
T: (01304) 204716

Maison Dieu Guest House ◆
89 Maison Dieu Road, Dover,
Kent CT16 1RU
T: (01304) 204033
E: bookings@maisondieu.
freeserve.co.uk
I: www.maisondieu.freeserve.co.
uk
⊕

The Norman Guest House
◆◆◆
75 Folkestone Road, Dover, Kent
CT17 9RZ
T: (01304) 207803

Owler Lodge
◆◆◆ SILVER AWARD
Alkham Valley Road, Alkham,
Dover, Kent CT15 7DF
T: (01304) 826375
F: (01304) 826375
E: owlerlodge@aol.com
I: www.smoothhound.co.
uk/hotels/owlerlodge.html

The Park Inn
◆◆◆ SILVER AWARD
1-2 Park Place, Ladywell, Dover,
Kent CT6 1DQ
T: (01304) 203300
F: (01304) 203324
E: theparkinn@c.s.com

St Brelades Guest House
◆◆◆◆
80-82 Buckland Avenue, Dover,
Kent CT16 2NW
T: (01304) 206126
F: (01304) 211486
E: stbrelades@compuserve.com
I: www.stbrelades-dover.co.
ukwww.doveraccommodation.
co.uk

Talavera House ◆◆◆
275 Folkestone Road, Dover,
Kent CT17 9LL
T: (01304) 206794
F: (01304) 207067
E: john-jan@talavera-house.
freeserve.co.uk
I: www.smoothhound.co.
uk/hotels

Victoria Guest House ◆◆◆
1 Laureston Place, Dover, Kent
CT16 1QX
T: (01304) 205140 &
07885 686428
F: (01304) 205140

Westbank Guest House ◆◆◆◆
239-241 Folkestone Road,
Dover, Kent CT17 9LL
T: (01304) 201061 & 205609

Whitmore Guest House ◆◆◆
261 Folkestone Road, Dover,
Kent CT17 9LL
T: (01304) 203080 &
0771 2435294
F: (01304) 240110
E: whitmoredover@aol.com
I: www.smoothhound.co.
uk/hotels/whitmore.html.
⊕

DUDDLESWELL
East Sussex
Duddleswell Manor ◆◆◆◆
Duddleswell, Uckfield, East
Sussex TN22 3JL
T: (01825) 712701

DUNCTUN
West Sussex
Duncton Mill House
◆◆◆◆◆ SILVER AWARD
Dye House Lane, Dunctun,
Petworth, West Sussex
GU28 0LF
T: (01798) 342294
F: (01798) 344122
E: sheila@dunctonmill.com
I: www.dunctonmill.com

Wild Cherries ◆◆◆
Dyehouse Lane, Dunctun,
Petworth, West Sussex
GU28 0LF
T: (01798) 342313 &
07971 828020

DYMCHURCH
Kent
The Ship Inn ◆◆
118 High Street, Dymchurch,
Romney Marsh, Kent TN29 0LD
T: (01303) 872122
F: (01303) 872311
E: bookings@theshipinn.co.uk
I: www.theshipinn.co.uk

Waterside Guest House
◆◆◆◆
15 Hythe Road, Dymchurch,
Romney Marsh, Kent TN29 0LN
T: (01303) 872253
F: (01303) 872253
E: water.side@cwcom.net
I: www.smoothhound.co.
uk/hotels/watersid.html

EARNLEY
West Sussex
Millstone
◆◆◆◆ GOLD AWARD
Clappers Lane, Earnley,
Chichester, West Sussex
PO20 7JJ
T: (01243) 670116 &
07768 958223
F: (01243) 672280
E: michaelharrington@talk21.
com

EAST ASHLING
West Sussex
Horse & Groom ◆◆◆
East Ashling, Chichester, West
Sussex PO18 9AX
T: (01243) 575339
F: (01243) 575339

EAST GRINSTEAD
West Sussex
Cranston House ◆◆◆
Cranston Road, East Grinstead,
West Sussex RH19 3HW
T: (01342) 323609
F: (01342) 323609
E: accommodation@
cranstonhouse.screaming.net

EAST LAVANT
West Sussex
The Flint House
◆◆◆◆ SILVER AWARD
Pook Lane, East Lavant,
Chichester, West Sussex
PO18 0AS
T: (01243) 773482

EAST PECKHAM
Kent
Roydon Hall ◆◆◆
Seven Mile Lane, East Peckham,
Tonbridge, Kent TN12 5NH
T: (01622) 812121
F: (01622) 813959
E: roydonhall@btinternet.com

EAST PRESTON
West Sussex
Roselea Cottage ◆◆◆
2 Elm Avenue, East Preston,
Littlehampton, West Sussex
BN16 1HJ
T: (01903) 786787
F: (01903) 770220
E: bartam1@aol.com

EAST WITTERING
West Sussex
Apples & Pears ◆◆◆◆
65 Stocks Lane, East Wittering,
Chichester, West Sussex
PO20 8NH
T: (01243) 670551
F: (01243) 672069

Gig House ◆◆◆
Stubcroft Lane, East Wittering,
Chichester, West Sussex
PO20 8PJ
T: (01243) 670206 &
07831 224972
F: (01243) 670206
E: gighouse@waitrose.com

Stubcroft Farm ◆◆◆
Stubcroft Lane, East Wittering,
Chichester, West Sussex
PO20 8PJ
T: (01243) 671469
E: slgreen@ax.co.uk

EASTBOURNE
East Sussex
The Alfriston Hotel ◆◆◆
16 Lushington Road,
Eastbourne, East Sussex
BN21 4LL
T: (01323) 725640
⊕

Bay Lodge Hotel ◆◆◆
61-62 Royal Parade, Eastbourne,
East Sussex BN22 7AQ
T: (01323) 732515
F: (01323) 735009
E: Beryl@mnewson.freeserve.co.
uk
⊕

Bella Vista ◆◆◆◆
30 Redoubt Road, Eastbourne,
East Sussex BN22 7DH
T: (01323) 724222
⊕

Boyne House ◆◆◆
12 St Aubyns Road, Eastbourne,
East Sussex BN22 7AS
T: (01323) 430245
E: derek@derekandjoan.fsnet.
co.uk

Brayscroft Hotel
◆◆◆◆ SILVER AWARD
13 South Cliff Avenue,
Eastbourne, East Sussex
BN20 7AH
T: (01323) 647005
F: (01323) 720705
E: brayscroft@hotmail.com
I: www.brayscrofthotel.co.uk

Cambridge House ◆◆◆◆
6 Cambridge Road, Eastbourne,
East Sussex BN22 7BS
T: (01323) 721100

Cherry Tree Hotel
◆◆◆◆ SILVER AWARD
15 Silverdale Road, Eastbourne,
East Sussex BN20 7AJ
T: (01323) 722406
F: (01323) 648838
E: anncherrytree@aol.com
I: www.eastbourne.
org/cherrytree-hotel

Cornerways Hotel ◆◆◆
60 Royal Parade, Eastbourne,
East Sussex BN21 7AQ
T: (01323) 721899
F: (01323) 724422

Cromwell Private Hotel
◆◆◆◆
23 Cavendish Place, Eastbourne,
East Sussex BN21 3EJ
T: (01323) 725288
F: (01323) 725288
E: Cromwell.hotel@lineone.net
I: www.smoothhound.co.
uk/hotels/cromwell.html
⊕

Edelweiss Private Hotel ◆◆◆
10-12 Elms Avenue, Eastbourne,
East Sussex BN21 3DN
T: (01323) 732071
F: (01323) 732071
E: peterbutler@fsbdial.co.uk

Hanburies Hotel ◆◆◆
4 Hardwick Road, Eastbourne,
East Sussex BN21 4NY
T: (01323) 730698
⊕

Heatherdene Hotel ◆◆◆
26-28 Elms Avenue, Eastbourne,
East Sussex BN21 3DN
T: (01323) 723598
F: (01323) 723598
🛉

Jenric Guest House ◆◆◆
36 Ceylon Place, Eastbourne,
East Sussex BN21 3JF
T: (01323) 728857
E: jenric@lineone.net
⊕

Little Foxes ◆◆◆◆
24 Wannock Road, Eastbourne,
East Sussex BN22 7JU
T: (01323) 640670
F: (01323) 640670
E: chris@foxholes55.freeserve.
co.uk

Loriston Guest House ◆◆◆
17 St Aubyns Road, Eastbourne,
East Sussex BN22 7AS
T: (01323) 726193

Nirvana Private Hotel ◆◆◆
32 Redoubt Road, Eastbourne,
East Sussex BN22 7DL
T: (01323) 722603

Pinnacle Point
◆◆◆◆◆ GOLD AWARD
Foyle Way, Eastbourne, East
Sussex BN20 7XL
T: (01323) 726666 &
0796 7209958
F: (01323) 643946

St Omer Hotel ◆◆◆
13 Royal Parade, Eastbourne,
East Sussex BN22 7AR
T: (01323) 722152
F: (01323) 723400
E: derek.holdrop@lineone.net

Sea Beach House Hotel ◆◆◆◆
39-40 Marine Parade,
Eastbourne, East Sussex
BN22 7AY
T: (01323) 410458 & 410459
E: brian@seabeach.freeserve.co.
uk

Sherwood Hotel ◆◆◆
7 Lascelles Terrace, Eastbourne,
East Sussex BN21 4BJ
T: (01323) 724002

Southcroft Hotel ◆◆◆◆
15 South Cliff Avenue,
Eastbourne, East Sussex
BN20 7AH
T: (01323) 729071
E: southcroft@eastbourne34.
freeserve.co.uk
I: www.eastbourne34.freeserve.
co.uk

Stratford Hotel & Restaurant
◆◆
59 Cavendish Place, Eastbourne,
East Sussex BN21 3RL
T: (01323) 724051 & 726391
F: (01323) 726391

Trevinhurst Lodge
◆◆◆◆ SILVER AWARD
10 Baslow Road, Meads,
Eastbourne, East Sussex
BN20 7UJ
T: (01323) 410023
F: (01323) 643238

Tudor House ◆◆◆
5 Marine Road, Eastbourne, East
Sussex BN22 7AU
T: (01323) 721796

EASTCHURCH
Kent

Dunmow House ◆◆◆
9 Church Road, Eastchurch,
Sheerness, Kent ME12 4DG
T: (01795) 880576
E: meportage@msn.com

EASTERGATE
West Sussex

Dormy Lodge ◆◆◆◆
Fontwell Avenue, Eastergate,
Chichester, West Sussex
PO20 6RU
T: (01243) 544193
E: robinson.123kip@tesco.net

Highfield ◆◆◆
Cherry Tree Drive, Eastergate,
Chichester, West Sussex
PO20 6RR
T: (01243) 545194
F: (01243) 545194
E: jenny.price@talk21.com

EASTLING
Kent

Carpenters Arms ◆◆◆
The Street, Eastling, Faversham,
Kent ME13 0AZ
T: (01795) 890234
F: (01795) 890654
I: www.swale.gov.uk

EDENBRIDGE
Kent

Black Robins Farm ◆◆◆◆
Grants Lane, Edenbridge, Kent
TN8 6QP
T: (01732) 863212

Mowshurst Farm House
◆◆◆◆
Swan Lane, Edenbridge, Kent
TN8 6AH
T: (01732) 862064

Ye Old Crown Inn ◆◆◆◆
74-76 The High Street,
Edenbridge, Kent TN8 5AR
T: (01732) 867896
F: (01732) 868316

EGERTON
Kent

Coldharbour Farm
Rating Applied For
Egerton, Ashford, Kent
TN27 9DD
T: (01233) 756548

ELHAM
Kent

Abbot's Fireside Hotel ◆◆◆
High Street, Elham, Canterbury,
Kent CT4 6TD
T: (01303) 840265
F: (01303) 840852
E: info@abbotsfireside.freewire.
co.uk
I: www.abbotsfireside.freewire.
co.uk

ELSTED
West Sussex

Three Elsted ◆◆◆
Elsted, Midhurst, West Sussex
GU29 0JY
T: (01730) 825065
E: rh@rhill.ftech.co.uk

EPSOM
Surrey

White House Hotel ◆◆◆◆
Downs Hill Road, Epsom, Surrey
KT18 5HW
T: (01372) 722472
F: (01372) 744447

ERIDGE GREEN
East Sussex

The Goodwood Lodge ◆◆◆
Eridge Green, Royal Tunbridge
Wells, Kent TN3 9JB
T: (01892) 750470
F: (01892) 750470

ESHER
Surrey

The Bear Inn ◆◆◆
71 High Street, Esher, Surrey
KT10 9LQ
T: (01372) 469786
F: (01372) 468378

EWHURST
Surrey

Sixpenny Buckle
Rating Applied For
Gransden Close, Ewhurst,
Cranleigh, Surrey GU6 7RL
T: (01483) 273988

Yard Farm ◆◆◆
Ewhurst, Cranleigh, Surrey
GU6 7SN
T: (01483) 276649
F: (01483) 276649

FAIRLIGHT
East Sussex

Fairlight Cottage ◆◆◆◆
Warren Road, (Via Coastguard
Lane), Fairlight, Hastings, East
Sussex TN35 4AG
T: (01424) 812545
F: (01424) 812545
E: fairlightcottage@supanet.
com

FAIRWARP
East Sussex

Broom Cottage ◆◆◆◆
Browns Brook, Fairwarp,
Uckfield, East Sussex TN22 3BY
T: (01825) 712942

FARNHAM
Surrey

A to B&B ◆◆◆
The Wrens, 16 Aveley Lane,
Farnham, Surrey GU9 8PR
T: (01252) 715046
F: (01252) 715046
E: colin-barbara-wrens@talk21.
com

High Wray ◆◆◆
73 Lodge Hill Road, Farnham,
Surrey GU10 3RB
T: (01252) 715589
F: (01252) 715746
E: sd99@dial.pipex.com
&

Mala Strana ◆◆◆◆
66 Boundstone Road, Farnham,
Surrey GU9 4TR
T: (01252) 793262

FAVERSHAM
Kent

Barnsfield ◆◆◆
Fostall, Hernhill, Faversham,
Kent ME13 9JH
T: (01227) 750973 &
07889 836259
F: (01227) 273098
E: barnsfield@yahoo.com
I: www.barnsfield.co.uk

The Granary
◆◆◆◆ SILVER AWARD
Plumford Lane, Off Brogdale
Road, Ospringe, Faversham, Kent
ME13 0DS
T: (01795) 538416 &
07710 199177
F: (01795) 538416
E: annette@the-granary.co.uk
I: www.the-granary.co.uk

Leaveland Court ◆◆◆◆
Leaveland, Faversham, Kent
ME13 0NP
T: (01233) 740596

March Cottage ◆◆◆
5 Preston Avenue, Faversham,
Kent ME13 8NH
T: (01795) 536514

---

19 Nobel Court ◆◆◆
Faversham, Kent ME13 7SD
T: (01795) 536767
E: keith@griff16.freeserve.co.uk

Owens Court Farm ◆◆◆
Selling, Faversham, Kent
ME13 9QN
T: (01227) 752247
F: (01227) 752247

Preston Lea
◆◆◆◆ SILVER AWARD
Canterbury Road, Faversham,
Kent ME13 8XA
T: (01795) 535266
F: (01795) 533388
E: preston.lea@which.net
I: www.homepages.which.
net/5alan.turner10

Tanners Cottage ◆◆
37 Tanners Street, Faversham,
Kent ME13 7JP
T: (01795) 536698

FAYGATE
West Sussex

The Willows
◆◆◆◆ SILVER AWARD
Wimlands Lane, Faygate,
Horsham, West Sussex
RH12 4SP
T: (01293) 851030
F: (01293) 852466

FINDON
West Sussex

Findon Tower ◆◆◆◆
Cross Lane, Findon, Worthing,
West Sussex BN14 0UG
T: (01903) 873870

FIRLE
East Sussex

New House Farm ◆◆◆
Firle, Lewes, East Sussex
BN8 6ND
T: (01273) 858242
F: (01273) 858242

FISHBOURNE
West Sussex

Maycroft ◆◆◆◆
Clay Lane, Fishbourne,
Chichester, West Sussex
PO19 3PX
T: (01243) 778338
F: (01243) 778338
E: jbumfrey@aol.co

Whyke Ford ◆◆◆◆
Salthill Road, Fishbourne,
Chichester, West Sussex
PO19 3PZ
T: (01243) 784127

Wilbury House ◆◆◆◆
Main Road, Fishbourne,
Chichester, West Sussex
PO18 8AT
T: (01243) 572953
F: (01243) 574150
E: PUFFIN01@GLOBALNET.CO.
UK

FITTLEWORTH
West Sussex

The Old Post Office ◆◆◆◆
Lower Street, Fittleworth,
Pulborough, West Sussex
RH20 1JE
T: (01798) 865315
F: (01798) 865315

Street Farm B & B
◆◆◆◆ SILVER AWARD
Street Farm, Lower Street,
Fittleworth, Pulborough, West
Sussex RH20 1EN
T: (01798) 865885
F: (01798) 865870
◎

Swan Inn
◆◆◆◆ SILVER AWARD
Lower Street, Fittleworth,
Pulborough, West Sussex
RH20 1EN
T: (01798) 865429
F: (01798) 865721
I: ww.swaninn.com

FIVE OAK GREEN
Kent

Ivy House
Rating Applied For
Five Oak Green, Tonbridge, Kent
TN12 6RB
T: (01892) 832041
F: (01892) 832041

FOLKESTONE
Kent

Banque Hotel ◆◆◆
4 Castle Hill Avenue, Folkestone,
Kent CT20 2QT
T: (01303) 253797
F: (01303) 253797

Beachborough Park ◆◆◆
Newington, Folkestone, Kent
CT18 8BW
T: (01303) 275432
F: (01843) 845131
I: www.kentaccess.org.uk

Chandos Guest House ◆◆◆
77 Cheriton Road, Folkestone,
Kent CT20 1DG
T: (01303) 851202
F: (01303) 272073
E: froggydon@aol.com
I: www.smoothhound.co.
uk/hotels/chandos.html

Chilton House Hotel ◆◆◆
14-15 Marine Parade,
Folkestone, Kent CT20 1PX
T: (01303) 249786
F: (01303) 226520

**Harbourside Bed & Breakfast
Hotel** ◆◆◆◆◆ GOLD AWARD
13/14 Wear Bay Road,
Folkestone, Kent CT19 6AT
T: (01303) 256528 &
07768 123884
F: (01303) 241299
E: r.j.pye@dial.pipex.com
I: www.harboursidehotel.com

The Rob Roy Guest House ◆
227 Dover Road, Folkestone,
Kent CT19 6NH
T: (01303) 253341
F: (01303) 770060
E: alan&tsue@therobroy.
freeserve.co.uk
I: www.therobroy.freeserve.co.
uk

Sunny Lodge Guest House
◆◆◆
85 Cheriton Road, Folkestone,
Kent CT20 2QL
T: (01303) 251498
E: linda.dowsett@btclick.com
I: www.s-hsystems.
com/hotels/sunnyl
◎

Windsor Hotel ◆◆
5-6 Langhorne Gardens,
Folkestone, Kent CT20 2EA
T: (01303) 251348
E: Williams.Windsor@Virginnet.
co.uk

FONTWELL
West Sussex

Woodacre ◆◆◆◆
Arundel Road, Fontwell, Arundel,
West Sussex BN18 0SD
T: (01243) 814301
F: (01243) 814344
E: wacrebb@aol.com
I: www.hotelline.co.uk/woodacre
◎

FOUR ELMS
Kent

Oak House Barn
◆◆◆◆◆ SILVER AWARD
Mapleton Road, Four Elms,
Edenbridge, Kent TN8 6PL
T: (01732) 700725

FRAMFIELD
East Sussex

Beggars Barn
◆◆◆◆ SILVER AWARD
Barn Lane, Framfield, Uckfield,
East Sussex TN22 5RX
T: (01825) 890869 &
07770 687686
F: (01825) 890868
E: caroline@beggarsbarn.co.uk
I: www.beggarsbarn.co.uk

Gatehouse Green Farm ◆◆◆◆
Gatehouse Lane, Framfield,
Uckfield, East Sussex TN22 5RS
T: (01825) 890212
F: (01825) 890212

The Old Farmhouse
◆◆◆◆ SILVER AWARD
Honey's Green, Framfield,
Uckfield, East Sussex TN22 5RE
T: (01825) 841054
F: 0870 122 9055
E: stay@honeysgreen.com
I: www.honeysgreen.com

FRANT
East Sussex

Cornhill ◆◆◆◆
Manor Farm, Frant, Royal
Tunbridge Wells, Kent TN3 9BH
T: (01892) 750604
F: (01892) 750733

FRENSHAM
Surrey

The Mariners Hotel ◆◆◆
Millbridge, Frensham, Farnham,
Surrey GU10 3DJ
T: (01252) 792050 & 794745
F: (01252) 792649

GATWICK
West Sussex

Brooklyn Manor Hotel ◆◆◆
Bonnetts Lane, Ifield, Gatwick,
Crawley, West Sussex RH11 0NY
T: (01293) 546024
F: (01293) 510366

GILLINGHAM
Kent

Dalmeny ◆◆
84 Holmside, Gillingham, Kent
ME7 4BE
T: (01634) 572083

Mayfield Guest House ◆◆
34 Kingswood Road, Gillingham,
Kent ME7 1DZ
T: (01634) 852606

Ramsey House ◆◆◆
228A Barnsole Road, Gillingham,
Kent ME7 4JB
T: (01634) 854193

GODALMING
Surrey

Heath Hall Farm ◆◆◆
Bowlhead Green, Godalming,
Surrey GU8 6NW
T: (01428) 682808
F: (01428) 684025

GODMERSHAM
Kent

Waggoners Lodge ◆◆◆
Eggarton Lane, Godmersham,
Canterbury, Kent CT4 7DY
T: (01227) 731118 & 731221
F: (01227) 730292
E: maud@waggoners.freeserve.
co.uk

GOODWOOD
West Sussex

1 Pilleygreen Lodge ◆◆◆◆
Goodwood, Chichester, West
Sussex PO18 0QE
T: (01243) 811467
F: (01243) 811408
E: j.robinson@worthing.ac.uk
I: www.sussexlive@enta.net

GORING-BY-SEA
West Sussex

The Court House Guest House
◆◆◆
Sea Lane, Goring-by-Sea,
Worthing, West Sussex
BN12 4NY
T: (01903) 248473

GOUDHURST
Kent

Lidwell Lodge Nursery ◆◆
Lidwell Lane, Goudhurst,
Cranbrook, Kent TN17 1EJ
T: (01580) 211188

Mill House ◆◆◆◆
Church Road, Goudhurst,
Cranbrook, Kent TN17 1BN
T: (01580) 211703 &
07702 714195

Mount House ◆◆◆◆
Ranters Lane, Goudhurst,
Cranbrook, Kent TN17 1HN
T: (01580) 211230 &
07808 170944
E: DavidMargaretSargent@
compuserve.com

GRAFFHAM
West Sussex

Brook Barn ◆◆◆◆
Selham Road, Graffham,
Petworth, West Sussex
GU28 0PU
T: (01798) 867356
E: jollands@lineone.net

GRAFTY GREEN
Kent

Who'd A Thought It ◆◆◆
Headcorn Road, Grafty Green,
Maidstone, Kent ME17 2AR
T: (01622) 858951
F: (01622) 858078

GRAVESEND
Kent

48 Clipper Crescent
Rating Applied For
Riverview Park, Gravesend, Kent
DA12 4NN
T: (01474) 365360

Eastcourt Oast ◆◆◆◆
14 Church Lane, Chalk,
Gravesend, Kent DA12 2NL
T: (01474) 823937
F: (01474) 823937
E: mary.james@lineone.net

GREATSTONE
Kent

White Horses Cottage
Rating Applied For
180 The Parade, Greatstone,
New Romney, Kent TN28 8RS
T: (01797) 366626

GUESTLING
East Sussex

Mount Pleasant Farm ◆◆◆◆
White Hart Hill, Guestling,
Hastings, East Sussex TN35 4LR
T: (01424) 813108 &
07711 717695
F: (01424) 813818
◎

GUILDFORD
Surrey

Beevers Farm
Rating Applied For
Chinthurst Lane, Bramley,
Guildford, Surrey GU5 0DR
T: (01483) 898764

Chalklands ◆◆◆
Beech Avenue, Effingham,
Leatherhead, Surrey KT24 5PJ
T: (01372) 454936
F: (01372) 459569
E: reilly@tecres.net

High Edser ◆◆◆
Shere Road, Ewhurst, Cranleigh,
Guildford, Surrey GU6 7PQ
T: (01483) 278214 &
0777 5865125
F: (01483) 278200

Littlefield Manor ◆◆◆
Littlefield Common, Guildford,
Surrey GU3 3HJ
T: (01483) 233068 & 232687
F: (01483) 233686

The Old Malt House ◆◆◆
Bagshot Road, Worplesdon,
Guildford, Surrey GU3 3PT
T: (01483) 232152

HADLOW
Kent

Bourneside Farm
◆◆◆◆◆ SILVER AWARD
Blackmans Lane, Hadlow,
Tonbridge, Kent TN11 0AX
T: (01732) 850281

Leavers Oast ◆◆◆◆
Stanford Lane, Hadlow,
Tonbridge, Kent TN11 0JN
T: (01732) 850924
F: (01732) 850924
E: denis@leavers-oast.freeserve.
co.uk
I: www.tonbridge-kent.
com/commerce/leavers-
oast-b&b.htm

HAILSHAM
East Sussex

Longleys Farm Cottage ◆◆◆
Harebeating Lane, Hailsham,
East Sussex BN27 1ER
T: (01323) 841227
F: (01323) 841227
◎

Windesworth ◆◆◆
Carters Corner, Hailsham, East
Sussex BN27 4HT
T: (01323) 847178 & 440696
F: (01323) 440696

HALLAND
East Sussex

Shortgate Manor Farm
◆◆◆ SILVER AWARD
Halland, Lewes, East Sussex
BN8 6PJ
T: (01825) 840320
F: (01825) 840320
E: ewalt@shortgate.co.uk
I: www.shortgate.co.uk

Tamberry Hall ◆◆◆◆
Eastbourne Road, Halland,
Lewes, East Sussex BN8 6PS
T: (01825) 880090
F: (01825) 880090

HALNAKER
West Sussex

Veronica Cottage ◆◆◆
Halnaker, Chichester, West
Sussex PO18 0NG
T: (01243) 774929
F: (01243) 774929

HAMBROOK
West Sussex

Willowbrook Riding Centre
◆◆◆
Hambrook Hill South, Hambrook,
Chichester, West Sussex
PO18 8UJ
T: (01243) 572683

HARRIETSHAM
Kent

Homestay ◆◆◆
14 Chippendayle Drive,
Harrietsham, Maidstone, Kent
ME17 1AD
T: (01622) 858698
F: (01622) 858698
E: johnb@skybiz.com
I: www.skybusiness.com/jonba

HARTFIELD
East Sussex

Bolebroke Castle Ltd ◆◆◆
Edenbridge Road, Hartfield, East
Sussex TN7 4JJ
T: (01892) 770061
F: (01892) 771041
I: www.bolebrokecastle.co.uk

HASLEMERE
Surrey

Little Hoewyck ◆◆◆◆
Lickfold Road, Fernhurst,
Haslemere, Surrey GU27 3JH
T: (01428) 653059
E: suehodge@hoewyck.
freeserve.co.uk

Sheps Hollow ◆◆◆
Henley Common, Haslemere,
Surrey GU27 3HB
T: (01428) 653120

Strathire
◆◆◆◆ SILVER AWARD
Grayswood Road, Haslemere,
Surrey GU27 2BW
T: (01428) 642466
F: (01428) 656708
⊚

HASSOCKS
West Sussex

New Close Farm ◆◆◆
London Road, Hassocks, West
Sussex BN6 9ND
T: (01273) 843144
E: sharon.ballard@
newclosefarm.co.uk
I: www.newclosefarm.co.uk

HASTINGLEIGH
Kent

Crabtree Farm ◆◆◆
Tamley Lane, Hastingleigh,
Ashford, Kent TN25 5HW
T: (01233) 750327 & 750507

HASTINGS
East Sussex

Amberlene Guest House ◆◆◆
12 Cambridge Gardens,
Hastings, East Sussex TN34 1EH
T: (01424) 439447

Ashleigh Guest House ◆
4 Millward Crescent, Hastings,
East Sussex TN34 3RU
T: (01424) 439066

Badgers Run Guest House
◆◆◆
167 Old London Road, Hastings,
East Sussex TN35 5LU
T: (01424) 712082 &
07703 975755
E: badgers.run@talk21.com
I: www.badgersrun.thenetzone.
co.uk/

Beechwood Hotel ◆◆◆
59 Baldslow Road, Hastings,
East Sussex TN34 2EY
T: (01424) 420078
⊚

Bell Cottage ◆◆◆◆
Vinehall Road, Robertsbridge,
Hastings, East Sussex TN32 5JN
T: (01580) 881164
F: (01580) 880519
E: patricia.lowe@tesco.net
I: homepages.tesco.net/timothy.
lowe/bellcottage.html

Bryn-Y-Mor
◆◆◆◆◆ GOLD AWARD
12 Godwin Road, Hastings, East
Sussex TN35 5JR
T: (01424) 722744
F: (01424) 445933

Cambridge Guest House ◆◆◆
18 Cambridge Gardens,
Hastings, East Sussex TN34 1EH
T: (01424) 712995 &
07713 174025

Churchills Hotel ◆◆◆◆
3 St Helens Crescent, Hastings,
East Sussex TN34 2EN
T: (01424) 439359
F: (01424) 439359
E: churchills.hotel@btinternet.
com

Croft Place ◆◆◆◆
2 The Croft, Hastings, East
Sussex TN34 3HH
T: (01424) 433004

Eagle House Hotel ◆◆◆◆
12 Pevensey Road, St Leonards-
on-Sea, Hastings, East Sussex
TN38 0JZ
T: (01424) 430535 & 441273
F: (01424) 437771
E: info@eaglehousehotel.com
I: www.eaglehousehotel.com

Ecclesbourne Lodge ◆◆◆
Barley Lane, Hastings, East
Sussex TN35 5NT
T: (01424) 443172
F: (01424) 443172
E: ecclesbournelodge@supanet.
com
I: www.business-uk.com
⊚

The Elms ◆◆◆
9 St Helens Park Road, Hastings,
East Sussex TN34 2ER
T: (01424) 429979

Emerydale ◆◆◆◆
6 King Edward Avenue, Hastings,
East Sussex TN34 2NQ
T: (01424) 437915

Europa Hotel ◆◆◆
2 Carlisle Parade, Hastings, East
Sussex TN34 1JG
T: (01424) 717329

Fantail Cottage
◆◆◆◆ SILVER AWARD
Rosemary Lane, Fairlight,
Hastings, East Sussex TN35 4EB
T: (01424) 813637

The Gallery ◆◆◆◆
24 Elphinstone Road, Hastings,
East Sussex TN34 2EQ
T: (01424) 718110 &
07703 255530
E: freeserve.co.uk
I: www.thegallerybnb.freeserve.
co.uk

Glastonbury Guest House ◆◆
45 Eversfield Place, St Leonards
On Sea, Hastings, East Sussex
TN37 6DB
T: (01424) 422280 & 444711
E: hic-info@hastings.gov.uk
I: www.hastings.gov.uk

Grand Hotel ◆◆◆
Grand Parade, St Leonards,
Hastings, East Sussex TN38 0DD
T: (01424) 428510
F: (01424) 428510
🧍

Harbour View Guest House
◆◆◆
21 Priory Road, Hastings, East
Sussex TN34 3JL
T: (01424) 721435 &
07957 909521

64 High Street ◆◆◆
Old Town, Hastings, East Sussex
TN34 3EW
T: (01424) 712584

Highlands Inn ◆◆
Boscobel Road, St Leonards-on-
Sea, Hastings, East Sussex
TN38 0LU
T: (01424) 420299
F: (01424) 465065

Lavender & Lace Guest House
◆◆◆◆
106 All Saints Street, Old Town,
Hastings, East Sussex TN34 3BE
T: (01424) 716290

Lionsdown House ◆◆◆◆
116 High Street, Old Town,
Hastings, East Sussex TN34 3ET
T: (01424) 420802
F: (01424) 420802
⊚

Mayfair Hotel ◆◆
9 Eversfield Place, St Leonards-
on-Sea, Hastings, East Sussex
TN37 6BY
T: (01424) 434061

Millifont Guest House ◆◆◆
8-9 Cambridge Gardens,
Hastings, East Sussex TN34 1EH
T: (01424) 425645

The Pines ◆◆◆
50 Baldslow Road, Hastings,
East Sussex TN34 2EY
T: (01424) 435838
F: (01424) 435838
E: robert-jean@beeb.net

The Priory Guest House
Rating Applied For
13-15 Priory Avenue, Hastings,
East Sussex TN34 1UH
T: (01424) 443306
F: (01424) 439078

Seagull House ◆◆◆
96 High Street, Old Town,
Hastings, East Sussex TN34 3ES
T: (01424) 447789
⊚

Senlac Guest House ◆◆◆
47 Cambridge Gardens,
Hastings, East Sussex TN34 1EN
T: (01424) 430080 &
0780 8959694
F: 0870 0557636
E: senlac@1066-country.com
I: www.1066-country.
com/senlac

South Riding Guest House
◆◆◆
96 Milward Road, Hastings, East
Sussex TN34 3RT
T: (01424) 420805

Tower House
◆◆◆◆ GOLD AWARD
26-28 Tower Road West, St
Leonards, Hastings, East Sussex
TN38 0RG
T: (01424) 427217
F: (01424) 427217
E: towerhot@dial.pipex.com

West Hill Cottage ◆◆◆
Exmouth Place, Old Town,
Hastings, East Sussex TN34 3JA
T: (01424) 716021

Woodhurst Lodge ◆◆
Ivyhouse Lane, Hastings, East
Sussex TN35 4NN
T: (01424) 754147
F: (01424) 754147

HAWKHURST
Kent

Conghurst Farm
◆◆◆◆◆ SILVER AWARD
Conghurst Lane, Hawkhurst,
Cranbrook, Kent TN18 4RW
T: (01580) 753331
F: (01580) 754579
E: rosa@conghurst.co.uk

Patricks ◆◆◆◆
Horns Hill, Hawkhurst,
Cranbrook, Kent TN18 4XH
T: (01580) 752143
F: (01580) 754649
I: elliotpat@aol.com.

Springfield ◆◆◆◆
High Street, Hawkhurst,
Cranbrook, Kent TN18 4JS
T: (01580) 753377 & 753879
F: (01580) 753377

The Wren's Nest
◆◆◆◆◆ GOLD AWARD
Hastings Road, Hawkhurst,
Cranbrook, Kent TN18 4RT
T: (01580) 754919

HAYWARDS HEATH
West Sussex

**Copyhold Hollow Bed &
Breakfast**
◆◆◆◆ SILVER AWARD
Copyhold Lane, Borde Hill,
Haywards Heath, West Sussex
RH16 1XU
T: (01444) 413265
E: 2@copyholdhollow.freeserve.
co.uk
I: www.copyholdhollow.
freeserve.co.uk

HEADCORN
Kent

Bon Anse
Rating Applied For
2 Station Road, Headcorn,
Ashford, Kent TN27 9SA
T: (01622) 890627 &
07885 968076

Four Oaks ◆◆◆
Four Oaks Road, Headcorn,
Ashford, Kent TN27 9PB
T: (01622) 891224 &
07931 603104
F: (01622) 890630
E: fouroaks@compuserve.com
I: ourworld.compuserve.
com/homepages/fouroaks

Waterkant Guest House ◆◆◆
Moat Road, Headcorn, Ashford,
Kent TN27 9NT
T: (01622) 890154

HEATHFIELD
East Sussex

Great Ivy Mill ◆◆◆
Horebeech Lane, Marle Green,
Heathfield, East Sussex
TN21 9EA
T: (01435) 812393 &
07860 371422
F: (01435) 813486
E: greativymill@mistral.co.uk
I: www.mistral.co.
uk/greativymill

Iwood B & B ◆◆◆◆
Mutton Hall Lane, Heathfield,
East Sussex TN21 8NR
T: (01435) 863918 &
07768 917816

Spicers Bed & Breakfast
◆◆◆◆
21 Spicers Cottages, Cade Street,
Heathfield, East Sussex
TN21 9BS
T: (01435) 866363 &
07973 188138
F: (01435) 866363
E: spicersbb@cs.co.uk
I: www.spicers-bed-breakfast.
com

HENFIELD
West Sussex

1 The Laurels ◆◆◆◆
Martyns Close, Henfield, West
Sussex BN5 9QH
T: (01273) 493518 &
07788 713864

HERONS GHYLL
East Sussex

Tanglewood ◆◆◆◆
Oldlands Hall, Herons Ghyll,
Uckfield, East Sussex TN22 3DA
T: (01825) 712757

HERSHAM
Surrey

Bricklayers Arms ◆◆◆◆
6 Queens Road, Hersham,
Walton-on-Thames, Surrey
KT12 5LS
T: (01932) 220936
F: (01932) 230400

HERSTMONCEUX
East Sussex

Conquerors ◆◆◆◆
Stunts Green, Herstmonceux,
Hailsham, East Sussex BN27 4PR
T: (01323) 832446

Sandhurst ◆◆◆◆
Church Road, Herstmonceux,
Hailsham, East Sussex
BN27 1RG
T: (01323) 833088
F: (01323) 833088
E: janerussell@compuserve.com

The Stud Farm ◆◆◆
Bodle Street Green,
Herstmonceux, Hailsham, East
Sussex BN27 4RJ
T: (01323) 833201
F: (01323) 833201

HEYSHOTT
West Sussex

Amberfold ◆◆◆◆
Heyshott, Midhurst, West Sussex
GU29 0DA
T: (01730) 812385

Little Hoyle ◆◆◆◆
Hoyle Lane, Heyshott, Midhurst,
West Sussex GU29 0DX
T: (01798) 867359 & 871943
F: (01798) 867359

HIGH HALDEN
Kent

Bachelors Cottage ◆◆◆◆
Harbourne Lane, High Halden,
Ashford, Kent TN26 3JD
T: (01233) 850280

Badgers ◆◆◆◆
Ashford Road, High Halden,
Ashford, Kent TN26 3LY
T: (01233) 850158
E: wendy@wen.u.net.com
I: www.wen.u-net.
com/badgers/badgers.htm

Draylands ◆◆◆
Woodchurch Road, High Halden,
Ashford, Kent TN26 3JG
T: (01233) 850048 & 850830
F: (01233) 850048

11 The Martins ◆◆◆◆
High Halden, Ashford, Kent
TN26 3LD
T: (01233) 850013

Turks Head Farm ◆◆◆
High Halden, Ashford, Kent
TN26 3HT
T: (01233) 850279

HIGH HURSTWOOD
East Sussex

Chillies Granary ◆◆◆◆
Chillies Lane, High Hurstwood,
Crowborough, East Sussex
TN6 3TB
T: (01892) 655560
F: (01892) 655560

HIGHAM
Kent

The Gardeners Arms ◆◆◆
Forge Lane, Higham, Rochester,
Kent ME3 7AS
T: (01474) 822721
F: (01474) 823258
E: gardenersarms@barclays.net
I: www.gardenersarms.com

Kinsale ◆◆◆
1A School Lane, Mid Higham,
Higham, Rochester, Kent
ME3 7AT
T: (01474) 822106

HILDENBOROUGH
Kent

Froxfield ◆◆◆
98 Tonbridge Road,
Hildenborough, Tonbridge, Kent
TN11 9BT
T: (01732) 833759
F: (01732) 833759
E: dobson@tinyonine.co.uk

150 Tonbridge Road ◆◆
Hildenborough, Tonbridge, Kent
TN11 9HW
T: (01732) 838894

HOLLINGBOURNE
Kent

Eyhorne Manor ◆◆◆
Eyhorne Green, Hollingbourne,
Maidstone, Kent ME17 1UU
T: (01622) 880263
E: eyhorne.manor@virginnet.co.
uk

The Limes ◆◆◆◆
53 Eyhorne Street,
Hollingbourne, Maidstone, Kent
ME17 1TS
T: (01622) 880554
F: (01622) 880063
E: thelimes@btinternet.com

Woodhouses ◆◆◆◆
49 Eyhorne Street,
Hollingbourne, Maidstone, Kent
ME17 1TR
T: (01622) 880594
F: (01622) 880594

HOLT POUND
Surrey

South Lodge
Rating Applied For
Gravel Hill Road, Holt Pound,
Farnham, Surrey GU10 4LG
T: (01420) 520960
F: (01420) 520961
E: southlodge.farnham@
btinternet.com
I: www.southlodge.
farnham@btinternet.com

HORAM
East Sussex

Oak Mead Bed & Breakfast
◆◆◆
Oak Mead Nursery, Cowden Hall
Lane, Horam, Heathfield, East
Sussex TN21 9ED
T: (01435) 812962

Wimbles Farm ◆◆◆
Vines Cross, Horam, Heathfield,
East Sussex TN21 9HA
T: (01435) 812342
F: (01435) 812342
E: sue@ramsay-smith.freeserve.
com

HORLEY
Surrey

Belmont House ◆◆◆
46 Massetts Road, Horley,
Surrey RH6 7DS
T: (01293) 820500
F: (01293) 783812
E: stay@gatwickbelmont.com
I: www.gatwickbelmont.com

Berrens Guest House ◆◆
62 Massetts Road, Horley,
Surrey RH6 7DS
T: (01293) 786125 & 430800
F: (01293) 786125

Castle Lodge ◆◆
28 Massetts Road, Horley,
Surrey RH6 7DE
T: (01293) 783200
F: (01293) 782738

Copperwood Guest House
◆◆◆◆
Massetts Road, Horley, Gatwick,
West Sussex RH6 7DJ
T: (01293) 783388
F: (01293) 420156
E: copperwood@cableinet.co.uk
I: www.copperwood.co.uk

The Corner House ◆◆◆◆
72 Massetts Road, Horley,
Surrey RH6 7ED
T: (01293) 784574
F: (01293) 784620
E: info@thecornerhouse.co.uk
I: www.thecornerhouse.co.uk

Gables Guest House ◆
50 Bonehurst Road, Horley,
Surrey RH6 8QJ
T: (01293) 774553
F: (01293) 430006
I: www.thegables.com.ok

Gainsborough Lodge ◆◆◆
39 Massetts Road, Horley,
Surrey RH6 7DT
T: (01293) 783982 & 430830
F: (01293) 785365
E: gainsbor@eurobell.co.uk
I: www.gainsboroughlodge.co.uk

The Lawn Guest House
◆◆◆◆ SILVER AWARD
30 Massetts Road, Horley,
Surrey RH6 7DE
T: (01293) 775751 & 782795
F: (01293) 821803
E: info@lawnguesthouse.co.uk
I: www.lawnguesthouse.co.uk

Lenton Lodge ◆◆◆
36 Massetts Road, Horley,
Surrey RH6 7DS
T: (01293) 772571
F: (01293) 432391

Masslink House ◆◆◆
70 Massetts Road, Horley,
Surrey RH6 7ED
T: (01293) 785798
F: (01293) 783279

Melville Lodge Guest House
◆◆
15 Brighton Road, Horley,
Gatwick, Surrey RH6 7HH
T: (01293) 784951
F: (01293) 785669
E: melvillelodge.guesthouse@
tesco.net

Prinsted Guest House ◆◆◆
Oldfield Road, Horley, Surrey
RH6 7EP
T: (01293) 785233
F: (01293) 820624
I: www.networkclub.co.
uk/prinsted

Rosemead Guest House
◆◆◆◆
19 Church Road, Horley, Surrey
RH6 7EY
T: (01293) 430546 & 784965
F: (01293) 430547
E: rosemead@globalnet.co.uk
I: www.rosemeadguesthouse.co.
uk

Springwood Guest House
◆◆◆
58 Massetts Road, Horley,
Surrey RH6 7DS
T: (01293) 775998
F: (01293) 823103
E: ernest@springwood58.u-net.
com
I: www.networkclub.co.
uk/springwood

Trumbles Guest House
◆◆◆ SILVER AWARD
Stanhill, Charlwood, Horley,
Surrey RH6 0EP
T: (01293) 862925 & 863418
F: (01293) 862925
E: info@trumbles.co.uk
I: www.trumbles.co.uk

The Turret Guest House ◆◆◆
48 Massetts Road, Horley,
Surrey RH6 7DS
T: (01293) 782490 & 431491
F: (01293) 431492
E: theturret@tesco.net
I: www.theturret.com

Yew Tree ◆
31 Massetts Road, Horley,
Surrey RH6 7DQ
T: (01293) 785855
F: (01293) 785855
I: www.smoothhound.co.
uk/hotels/yewtree.html.

HORSHAM
West Sussex

Deans Bed & Breakfast ◆◆◆◆
8 Wimblehurst Road, Horsham,
West Sussex RH12 2ED
T: (01403) 268166 &
07802 843866
F: (01403) 268166
E: contact@thedeans.co.uk
I: www.thedeans.co.uk

163 Heathway
Rating Applied For
Horsham, West Sussex
RH12 5XX
T: (01403) 257066

The Wirrals
Rating Applied For
1 Downsview Road, Horsham,
West Sussex RH12 4PF
T: (01403) 269400 &
07774 745262
F: (01403) 269400
E: p.archibald@lineone.net
I: www.lineone.net/§p.
archibald/webba.htm

HOUGHAM
Kent

Old Vicarage
◆◆◆◆◆ GOLD AWARD
Chilverton Elms, Hougham,
Dover, Kent CT15 7AS
T: (01304) 210668
F: (01304) 225118

HUNSTON
West Sussex

2 Meadow Close ◆◆◆◆
Hunston, Chichester, West
Sussex PO20 6PB
T: (01243) 788504

HUNTON
Kent

Barn Hill Oast ◆◆◆◆
Barn Hill, Hunton, Maidstone,
Kent ME15 0QT
T: (01622) 820206 &
07778 266515
F: (01622) 820886

HURSTPIERPOINT
West Sussex

The Vinyard Lodge ◆◆◆◆
42 The High Street,
Hurstpierpoint, Hassocks, West
Sussex BN6 9RG
T: (01273) 835000
F: (01273) 835041
E: vinyards@btconnect.com
I: www.smoothhound.co.
uk/hotels/vinyard.html

Wickham Place ◆◆◆◆
Wickham Drive, Hurstpierpoint,
Hassocks, West Sussex BN6 9AP
T: (01273) 832172
F: (01273) 832172
E: stay@wickham-place.co.uk
◎

HYTHE
Kent

Seabrook House
◆◆◆◆ SILVER AWARD
81 Seabrook Road, Hythe, Kent
CT21 5QW
T: (01303) 269282
F: (01303) 237822
E: seabhouse@globalnet.co.uk
I: www.smoothhound.co.
uk/hotels/seabrook.html
◎

ICKHAM
Kent

Baye Oast ◆◆◆◆
1 Baye Oast, Baye Lane, Ickham,
Canterbury, Kent CT3 1RB
T: (01227) 720813
E: tracy@bayeoast.freeserve.co.
uk

ICKLESHAM
East Sussex

The Old Farmhouse ◆◆◆
Snaylham Farm, Icklesham,
Winchelsea, East Sussex
TN36 4AT
T: (01424) 814711 &
07966 282569
F: (01424) 814007
E: oldfrmhse@aol.com
I: www.members.aol.
com/oldfrmhse

IDEN
East Sussex

Conkers Guest House ◆◆◆
Main Street, Iden, Rye, East
Sussex TN31 7PT
T: (01797) 280437
F: (01797) 280437
E: keith.lovejoy@tinyonline.co.
uk

ISFIELD
East Sussex

Farm Place ◆◆◆◆
Lewes Road, Isfield, Uckfield,
East Sussex TN22 5TY
T: (01825) 750485
F: (01825) 750485

The Faulkners
◆◆◆◆ GOLD AWARD
Isfield, Uckfield, East Sussex
TN22 5XG
T: (01825) 750344
F: (01825) 750577

ITCHENOR
West Sussex

Itchenor Park House ◆◆◆◆
Itchenor, Chichester, West
Sussex PO20 7DN
T: (01243) 512221
E: susie.green@lineone.net

KENNINGTON
Kent

Heather House ◆◆◆
40 Burton Road, Kennington,
Ashford, Kent TN24 9DS
T: (01233) 661826 & 0793 11
50489

Stone House ◆◆◆
Faversham Road, Kennington,
Ashford, Kent TN25 4PQ
T: (01233) 623776

KINGSDOWN
Kent

**Blencathra Country Guest
House**
Rating Applied For
Kingsdown Hill, Kingsdown,
Deal, Kent CT14 8EA
T: (01304) 373725

Sparrow Court
Rating Applied For
Chalk Hill Road, Kingsdown,
Deal, Kent CT14 8DP
T: (01304) 389253
F: (01304) 389016

KINGSNORTH
Kent

Glenmore Lodge ◆◆◆
Millbank Road, Kingsnorth,
Ashford, Kent TN23 3JF
T: (01233) 641485
F: (01233) 642727

KINGSTON
East Sussex

Settlands ◆◆◆◆
Wellgreen Lane, Kingston,
Lewes, East Sussex BN7 3NP
T: (01273) 472295
F: (01273) 472295

KIRDFORD
West Sussex

Half Moon Inn ◆◆◆
Kirdford, Billingshurst, West
Sussex RH14 0LT
T: (01403) 820223
F: (01403) 820224

LADDINGFORD
Kent

The Chequers
Rating Applied For
The Street, Laddingford,
Maidstone, Kent ME18 6BP
T: (01622) 871266

LAMBERHURST
Kent

Chequers Oast ◆◆◆
The Broadway, Lamberhurst,
Royal Tunbridge Wells, Kent
TN3 8DB
T: (01892) 890579
F: (01892) 890579

LANCING
West Sussex

Edelweiss Guest House ◆◆◆
17 Kings Road, Lancing, West
Sussex BN15 8EB
T: (01903) 753412
F: (01903) 527424

LARKFIELD
Kent

Mead Cottage
Rating Applied For
433 Lunsford Lane, Larkfield,
Aylesford, Kent ME20 6JA
T: (01634) 241133

LAUGHTON
East Sussex

Holly Cottage ◆◆◆◆
Lewes Road, Laughton, Lewes,
East Sussex BN8 6BL
T: (01323) 811309 &
07711 660520
F: (01323) 811019

Spences Farm ◆◆◆
Laughton, Lewes, East Sussex
BN8 6BX
T: (01825) 840489

LAVANT
West Sussex

47 Mid Lavant ◆◆◆
Lavant, Chichester, West Sussex
PO18 0AA
T: (01243) 785883

LEEDS
Kent

West Forge ◆◆◆
Back Street, Leeds, Maidstone,
Kent ME17 1TF
T: (01622) 861428

LEIGH
Kent

Charcott B & B ◆◆◆◆
Charcott, Leigh, Tonbridge, Kent
TN11 8LG
T: (01892) 870024
F: (01892) 870158
E: nicholasmorris@charcott.
freeserve.co.uk
I: www.smoothhound.co.
uk/hotels/charcott.html

719

Herons Head Farm ♦♦♦♦
Mynthurst, Leigh, Reigate,
Gatwick, West Sussex RH2 8QD
T: (01293) 862475
F: (01293) 863350
E: heronshead@clara.net
I: seetb.org.uk/heronshead

LENHAM
Kent

Bramley Knowle Farm ♦♦♦
Eastwood Road, Ulcombe,
Maidstone, Kent ME17 1ET
T: (01622) 858878
F: (01622) 851121

The Dog & Bear Hotel ♦♦♦
The Square, Lenham, Maidstone,
Kent ME17 2PG
T: (01622) 858219
F: (01622) 859415
E: dogbear@shepherd-neame.
co.uk
I: www.shepherd-neame.co.uk

LEWES
East Sussex

Barn House ♦♦♦
Rodmell, Lewes, East Sussex
BN7 3HE
T: (01273) 477865
F: (01273) 476317
E: sharifindgn.apc.org
I: www.knowledge.co.
uk/barnhouse/

The Crown Inn ♦♦
High Street, Lewes, East Sussex
BN7 2NA
T: (01273) 480670
F: (01273) 480679
E: dahall@tesco.net

Downsview ♦♦♦
15 Montacute Road, Lewes, East
Sussex BN7 1EW
T: (01273) 472719

Eckington House ♦♦♦♦
Ripe, Lewes, East Sussex
BN8 6AV
T: (01323) 811274 &
(01825) 712864
F: (01323) 811140
E: suetj@mistral.co.uk
I: www3.mistral.co.uk/suetj

Racecourse House ♦♦♦♦
Old Lewes Racecourse, Lewes,
East Sussex BN7 1UR
T: (01273) 480804
F: (01273) 486478
E: a.heyes@btinternet.com

Studfarm House ♦♦♦
Telscombe Village, Lewes, East
Sussex BN7 3HZ
T: (01273) 302486
F: (01273) 302486

Whitesmith Barn
♦♦♦♦ SILVER AWARD
Whitesmith, Lewes, East Sussex
BN8 6HA
T: (01825) 872867

LEYSDOWN ON SEA
Kent

Muswell Manor ♦♦♦
Shellness Road, Leysdown on
Sea, Sheerness, Kent ME12 4RJ
T: (01795) 510245

LIGHTWATER
Surrey

Carlton Guest House ♦♦♦♦
63-65 Macdonald Road,
Lightwater, Camberley, Surrey
GU18 5XY
T: (01276) 473580 &
07703 868994
F: (01276) 453595
E: carltongh@aol.com

LINDFIELD
West Sussex

Little Lywood ♦♦♦
Ardingly Road, Lindfield,
Haywards Heath, West Sussex
RH16 2QX
T: (01444) 892571

LITTLEBOURNE
Kent

King William IV ♦♦♦
4 High Street, Littlebourne,
Canterbury, Kent CT3 1ST
T: (01227) 721244
F: (01227) 721244

LITTLEHAMPTON
West Sussex

Amberley Guest House ♦♦♦
74 Arundel Road, Littlehampton,
West Sussex BN17 7DF
T: (01903) 721627
F: (01903) 721627

Arun View Inn ♦♦
Wharf Road, Littlehampton,
West Sussex BN17 5DD
T: (01903) 722335
F: (01903) 722335

Sharoleen Guest House
♦♦♦♦
85 Bayford Road, Littlehampton,
West Sussex BN17 5HW
T: (01903) 713464

Tudor Lodge Guest House
♦♦♦
2 Horsham Road, Littlehampton,
West Sussex BN17 6BU
T: (01903) 716203

LONGFIELD
Kent

Kaye Cottage ♦♦♦♦
Old Downs, Hartley, Longfield,
Kent DA3 7AA
T: (01474) 702384 &
07778 250650
F: (01474) 702384

The Rising Sun Inn ♦♦♦
Fawkham Green, Longfield, Kent
DA3 8NL
T: (01474) 872291
F: (01474) 872291

LOOSE
Kent

Vale House ♦♦♦
Old Loose Hill, Loose, Maidstone,
Kent ME15 0BH
T: (01622) 743339 & 743400
F: (01622) 743103
E: valehouse@aventi

LOWER BEEDING
West Sussex

The Village Pantry ♦♦♦
Handcross Road, Plummers
Plain, Lower Beeding, Horsham,
West Sussex RH13 6NU
T: (01403) 891319

LYMINSTER
West Sussex

Sandfield House ♦♦♦♦
Lyminster, Littlehampton, West
Sussex BN17 7PG
T: (01903) 724129
F: (01903) 715041
E: thefbs@aol.com

MAIDSTONE
Kent

Aylesbury Hotel ♦♦♦
56-58 London Road, Maidstone,
Kent ME16 8QL
T: (01622) 762100

The Bower House
Rating Applied For
64 Tonbridge Road, Maidstone,
Kent ME16 8SE
T: (01622) 763448

Conway House ♦♦♦♦
12 Conway Road, Maidstone,
Kent ME16 0HD
T: (01622) 688287
F: (01622) 662589

Fairlawn ♦♦
White Rock Place, off Terrace
Road, Maidstone, Kent
ME16 8HX
T: (01622) 763642

The Flower Pot ♦♦
96 Sandling Road, Maidstone,
Kent ME14 2RJ
T: (01622) 757705
F: (01622) 833051
I: www.homleighgroup.co.uk

Grove House ♦♦♦♦
Grove Green Road, Weavering
Street, Maidstone, Kent
ME14 5JT
T: (01622) 738441

The Hazels ♦♦♦♦
13 Yeoman Way, Bearsted,
Maidstone, Kent ME15 8PQ
T: (01622) 737943
E: dbuse@totalise.co.uk
I: www.redrival.com/thehazels

Homestead ♦
Greenhill, Otham, Maidstone,
Kent ME15 8RR
T: (01622) 862234
F: (01622) 862234

King Street Hotel ♦♦♦
74 King Street, Maidstone, Kent
ME14 1BH
T: (01622) 663266
F: (01622) 663123

The Limes ♦♦♦♦
118 Boxley Road, Maidstone,
Kent ME14 2BD
T: (01622) 750629
F: (01622) 691266

514 Loose Road ♦♦♦
Maidstone, Kent ME15 9UF
T: (01622) 741001

54 Mote Avenue ♦♦
Maidstone, Kent ME15 7ST
T: (01622) 754016

Raigersfeld House
Rating Applied For
Mote Park, Ashford Road,
Maidstone, Kent ME14 4AE
T: (01622) 685211 & 687377
F: (01622) 691013
E: chipdbs@aol.com

**The Ringlestone Inn &
Farmhouse Hotel**
♦♦♦♦♦ GOLD AWARD
Ringlestone Hamlet,
Harrietsham, Maidstone, Kent
ME17 1NX
T: (01622) 859900 &
07973 612261
F: (01622) 859966
E: bookings@ringlestone.com
I: www.ringlestone.com

Rock House Hotel ♦♦♦
102 Tonbridge Road, Maidstone,
Kent ME16 8SL
T: (01622) 751616
F: (01622) 756119

Rose Cottage ♦♦♦
10 Fant Lane, Maidstone, Kent
ME16 8NL
T: (01622) 729883 &
07885 162566

Roslin Villa ♦♦♦
11 St Michael's Road,
Maidstone, Kent ME16 8BS
T: (01622) 758301
F: (01622) 695646

Sylvia Haddow ♦♦♦
51 Bower Mount Road,
Maidstone, Kent ME16 8AX
T: (01622) 762948
E: sylviabnb@compuserve.com

Wealden Hall House ♦♦♦♦
East Street, Hunton, Maidstone,
Kent ME15 0RB
T: (01622) 820246
I: www.smoothhound.co.
uk/hotels/wealden.html

West Belringham ♦♦♦
Chart Road, Sutton Valence,
Maidstone, Kent ME17 3AW
T: (01622) 843995
F: (01622) 843995
E: west.belringhametesco.net
I: www.travelengland.org.uk

4 White Rock Court ♦♦♦
White Rock Place, Maidstone,
Kent ME16 8HX
T: (01622) 753566 &
07809 015773

Willington Court
Rating Applied For
Willington Street, Maidstone,
Kent ME15 8JW
T: (01622) 738885
F: (01622) 631790
E: willington@maidstone.
prestel.co.uk
I: www.bbchannel.
com/bbc/p604332.aspwww.
hotelkent.com

Wits End Guest House ♦♦♦
78 Bower Mount Road,
Maidstone, Kent ME16 8AT
T: (01622) 752684 & 762696
F: (01622) 688943

63 Woolley Road ♦♦♦
Senacre Wood, Maidstone, Kent
ME15 8PZ
T: (01622) 761052

MARDEN
Kent

Tanner House ♦♦♦♦
Tanner Farm, Goudhurst Road,
Marden, Tonbridge, Kent
TN12 9ND
T: (01622) 831214
F: (01622) 832472
E: tannerfarm@compuserve.
com
🌐

MARESFIELD
East Sussex

The Chequers Inn ♦♦♦
London Road, Maresfield,
Uckfield, East Sussex TN22 3EB
T: (01825) 763843
F: (01825) 767504
E: chequers@
maresfielde-sussex.freeserve.co.
uk

MARK CROSS
East Sussex

Houndsell Cottage ♦♦♦
Mark Cross, Crowborough, East
Sussex TN6 3PF
T: (01892) 782292

Rose Cottage ♦♦♦
Mill Lane, Mark Cross,
Crowborough, East Sussex
TN6 3PJ
T: (01892) 852592
F: (01892) 853268

MARSHBOROUGH
Kent

Honey Pot Cottage ♦♦♦
Marshborough Road,
Marshborough, Sandwich, Kent
CT13 0PQ
T: (01304) 813374 &
07798 804920
F: (01304) 813374

MATFIELD
Kent

Maycotts
Rating Applied For
Matfield, Tonbridge, Kent
TN12 7JU
T: (01892) 723983
F: (01892) 722203
E: debbie.jolley@dial.pipex.com
I: www.bbgl.co.uk

MEOPHAM
Kent

Nurstead Court
Rating Applied For
Meopham, Gravesend, Kent
DA13 9AD
T: (01474) 812121
F: (01474) 815133

MERSTON
West Sussex

Abelands House ♦♦♦♦
Merston, Chichester, West
Sussex PO20 6DY
T: (01243) 532675
F: (01243) 788884

The White House ♦♦♦
Merston, Chichester, West
Sussex PO20 6EF
T: (01243) 783669

MIDHURST
West Sussex

Carron Dune ♦♦♦
Carron Lane, Midhurst, West
Sussex GU29 9LD
T: (01730) 813558

4 Close Walks ♦♦♦
Midhurst, West Sussex
GU29 0ET
T: (01730) 813801
F: (01730) 813801

Crown Inn ♦♦
Edinburgh Square, Midhurst,
West Sussex GU29 9NL
T: (01730) 813462

20 Guillards Oak ♦♦♦
Midhurst, West Sussex
GU29 9JZ
T: (01730) 812550
F: (01730) 816765

**Moonlight Cottage & Tea
Rooms ♦♦♦**
Chichester Road, Cocking,
Midhurst, West Sussex
GU29 0HN
T: (01730) 813336
F: (01730) 813362
E: enquiries@moonlightcottage.
net
I: www.moonlightcottage.net

Oakhurst Cottage ♦♦♦
Carron Lane, Midhurst, West
Sussex GU29 9LF
T: (01730) 813523

Pear Tree Cottage ♦♦♦
Lamberts Lane, Midhurst, West
Sussex GU29 9EF
T: (01730) 817216

Rumbolds House ♦♦♦
Rumbolds Hill, Midhurst, West
Sussex GU29 9BY
T: (01730) 816175 &
07970 015214
F: (01730) 816175
E: anngr@atd.net

MILSTEAD
Kent

The Cottage ♦♦♦♦
Frinsted Road, Milstead,
Sittingbourne, Kent ME9 0SA
T: (01795) 830367

MINSTER-IN-SHEPPEY
Kent

Abbots Gate ♦♦♦
Falcon Gardens, Minster-in-
Sheppey, Sheerness, Kent
ME12 3QE
T: (01795) 872882
E: b&tb@abbotsgate.demon.co.
uk

Glen Haven Farm ♦♦♦
Lower Road, Minster-in-
Sheppey, Sheerness, Kent
ME12 3ST
T: (01795) 877064

Mia Crieff ♦♦♦♦
Mill Hill, Chequers Road,
Minster-in-Sheppey, Sheerness,
Kent ME12 3QL
T: (01795) 870620

NETHERFIELD
East Sussex

**Upper Homestead Farm
♦♦♦♦**
Darwell Hill, Netherfield, Battle,
East Sussex TN33 9QH
T: (01424) 838457

NETTLESTEAD
Kent

Rock Farm House
Rating Applied For
Gibbs Hill, Nettlestead,
Maidstone, Kent ME18 5HT
T: (01622) 812244

NEW ROMNEY
Kent

Martinfield Manor ♦♦♦♦
Lydd Road, New Romney, Kent
TN28 8HB
T: (01797) 363802

Warren Lodge Motel
Rating Applied For
Dymchurch Road, New Romney,
Kent TN28 8UE
T: (01797) 362138
F: (01797) 367373

NEWHAVEN
East Sussex

Foxhole Farm ♦♦♦
Seaford Road, Newhaven, East
Sussex BN9 0EE
T: (01273) 515966
E: guesthouse@foxholefarm.
freeserve.co.uk

**Newhaven Lodge Guest House
♦**
12 Brighton Road, Newhaven,
East Sussex BN9 9NB
T: (01273) 513736 &
07776 293398
F: (01273) 734619
E: dcare-88201@aol.com
🌐

NEWICK
East Sussex

Firle Cottage ♦♦♦
High Street, Newick, Lewes, East
Sussex BN8 4LG
T: (01825) 722392

Holly Lodge ♦♦♦
Newick, Lewes, East Sussex
BN8 4RA
T: (01825) 722738
F: (01825) 723624

NINFIELD
East Sussex

Hollybank House ♦♦♦
Lower Street, Ninfield, Battle,
East Sussex TN33 9EA
T: (01424) 892052
F: (01424) 892052

London House ♦♦♦♦
Manchester Road, Ninfield,
Battle, East Sussex TN33 9JX
T: (01424) 893532
F: (01424) 893595

NORTH BERSTED
West Sussex

**Lorna Doone Bed & Breakfast
♦♦♦♦**
58 Sandymount Avenue, North
Bersted, Bognor Regis, West
Sussex PO22 9EP
T: (01243) 822203 & 0780 149
3678
F: (01243) 822203
E: joan@lornadoone.freeserve.
co.uk
I: www.lornadoone.freeserve.co.
uk

Willow Rise ♦
131 North Bersted Street, North
Bersted, Bognor Regis, West
Sussex PO22 9AG
T: (01243) 829544
F: (01243) 829544

NORTH MUNDHAM
West Sussex

The Cottage
♦♦♦♦ SILVER AWARD
Church Road, North Mundham,
Chichester, West Sussex
PO20 6JU
T: (01243) 784586

NORTHIAM
East Sussex

A Taste of Heritage
♦♦♦♦♦ GOLD AWARD
Tantalus, Main Street, Northiam,
Rye, East Sussex TN31 6NB
T: (01797) 252123
F: (01797) 252123
E: heritage@whd.net
I: www.heritage.whd.net

NUTFIELD
Surrey

Hillside Cottage ♦♦♦
Coopers Hill Road, Nutfield,
Redhill, Surrey RH1 4HX
T: (01737) 822916
F: (01737) 822916

NUTLEY
East Sussex

The Court House ♦♦♦♦
School Lane, Nutley, Uckfield,
East Sussex TN22 3PG
T: (01825) 713129
F: (01825) 712650
E: execrelocation@compuserve.
com

Funnells Farm ♦♦♦
Down Street, Nutley, Uckfield,
East Sussex TN22 3LG
T: (01825) 712034
F: (01825) 713511

OARE
Kent

Mount House
Rating Applied For
Mount Pleasant, Oare,
Faversham, Kent ME13 0PZ
T: (01795) 534735

OCKHAM
Surrey

The Hautboy
♦♦♦♦ SILVER AWARD
Ockham Lane, Ockham, Woking,
Surrey GU23 6NP
T: (01483) 225355
F: (01483) 211176

OCKLEY
Surrey

The Kings Arms Inn ♦♦♦♦
Stane Street, Ockley, Dorking,
Surrey RH5 5TP
T: (01306) 711224
F: (01306) 711224
🌐

OLD ROMNEY
Kent

Rose & Crown Inn ♦♦♦
Old Romney, Romney Marsh,
Kent TN29 9SQ
T: (01797) 367500
F: (01797) 361262

OTFORD
Kent

Darenth Dene ♦♦♦♦
Shoreham Road, Otford,
Sevenoaks, Kent TN14 5RP
T: (01959) 522293

The Hop Barn ◆◆◆
Park Farm, High Street, Otford,
Sevenoaks, Kent TN14 5PQ
T: (01959) 523509
F: (01959) 525326

9 Warham Road ◆◆
Otford, Sevenoaks, Kent
TN14 5PF
T: (01959) 523596

OTHAM
Kent
Valley View ◆◆◆
Greenhill, Otham, Maidstone,
Kent ME15 8RR
T: (01622) 862279
F: (01622) 862279

OUTWOOD
Surrey
The Coach House
◆◆◆◆ SILVER AWARD
Millers Lane, Outwood, Redhill,
Surrey RH1 5PZ
T: (01342) 843193
F: (01342) 843193

OXTED
Surrey
Arawa ◆◆◆
58 Granville Road, Limpsfield,
Oxted, Surrey RH8 0BZ
T: (01883) 714104 & 0800 298
5732
F: (01883) 714104
E: david@davidgibbs.co.uk

Meads ◆◆◆◆
23 Granville Road, Oxted, Surrey
RH8 0BX
T: (01883) 730115

The New Bungalow ◆◆◆
Old Hall Farm, Tandridge Lane,
Oxted, Surrey RH8 9NS
T: (01342) 892508
F: (01342) 892508
E: donnunn@compuserve.com

PADDOCK WOOD
Kent
Little Fowle Hall Oast ◆◆
Lucks Lane, Paddock Wood,
Tonbridge, Kent TN12 6PA
T: (01892) 832602

PARTRIDGE GREEN
West Sussex
**Pound Cottage Bed &
Breakfast** ◆◆◆
Mill lane, Littleworth, Partridge
Green, Horsham, West Sussex
RH13 8JU
T: (01403) 710218 & 711285
F: (01403) 711337
E: poundcottagebb@amserve.
net
I: www.horsham.co.
uk/poundcottage.html

PEASMARSH
East Sussex
Busti ◆◆◆
Barnetts Hill, Peasmarsh, Rye,
East Sussex TN31 6YJ
T: (01797) 230408

PEMBURY
Kent
Gates House ◆◆◆
5 Lower Green Road, Pembury,
Royal Tunbridge Wells, Kent
TN2 4DZ
T: (01892) 822866
F: (01892) 824626
E: simon@s.galway.freeserve.co.
uk

**Horse Pastures Bed &
Breakfast**
◆◆◆◆ SILVER AWARD
2 Horse Pasture Cottages, Little
Hawkwell Farm, Pembury, Royal
Tunbridge Wells, Kent TN2 4AQ
T: (01892) 824754
F: (01892) 824754
E: hobepastures@lineare.net

Meadowlands ◆◆◆◆
54 High Street, Pembury, Royal
Tunbridge Wells, Kent TN2 4NU
T: (01892) 823900

PENSHURST
Kent
Finch Green
◆◆◆◆ GOLD AWARD
Chiddingstone Hoath,
Edenbridge, Kent TN8 7DJ
T: (01892) 870648 &
07468 150698
F: (01892) 870648
E: finchgreen@compuserve.com

PETHAM
Kent
South Wootton House ◆◆
Capel Lane, Petham, Canterbury,
Kent CT4 5RG
T: (01227) 700643
F: (01227) 700613
E: mountfrances@farming.co.uk

PETT
East Sussex
Pendragon Lodge ◆◆◆◆◆
Watermill Lane, Pett, Rye, East
Sussex TN35 4HY
T: (01424) 814051

PETT LEVEL
East Sussex
Cliff End ◆◆◆◆
Pett Level Road, Pett Level,
Hastings, East Sussex TN35 4EE
T: (01424) 813135
F: (01424) 813135
E: roastbeef@zoom.co.uk
I: www.rye.org.uk

PETWORTH
West Sussex
Burton Park Farm ◆◆◆
Petworth, West Sussex GU28 0JT
T: (01798) 342431

Drifters ◆◆◆
Duncton, Petworth, West Sussex
GU28 0JZ
T: (01798) 342706

Eedes Cottage ◆◆◆◆
Bignor Park Road, Bury Gate,
Pulborough, West Sussex
RH20 1EZ
T: (01798) 831438
F: (01798) 831942

The Horse Guards Inn
◆◆◆◆ SILVER AWARD
Tillington, Petworth, West
Sussex GU28 9AF
T: (01798) 342332
F: (01798) 344351
E: mail@horseguardsinn.co.uk
I: www.horseguardsinn.co.uk

The Old Railway Station
◆◆◆◆◆ SILVER AWARD
Coultershaw Bridge, Petworth,
West Sussex GU28 0JF
T: (01798) 342346 &
07860 435370
F: (01798) 342346
E: mlr@old-station.co.uk
I: www.old-station.co.uk

Rectory Cottage ◆◆◆
Rectory Lane, Petworth, West
Sussex GU28 0DB
T: (01798) 342380
E: dcredd@aol.com

**Stonemasons Inn
Rating Applied For**
North Street, Petworth, West
Sussex GU28 9NL
T: (01798) 342510
F: (01798) 344111

White Horse Inn ◆◆◆◆
The Street, Sutton, Pulborough,
West Sussex RH20 1PS
T: (01798) 869221
F: (01798) 869291

PILTDOWN
East Sussex
Deerview Farm ◆◆◆
Down Street, Piltdown, Uckfield,
East Sussex TN22 3XX
T: (01825) 713139
F: (01825) 713139
E: b&tb@deerviewfarm.
freeserve.co.uk

The Piltdown Man Free House
◆◆◆
Piltdown, Uckfield, East Sussex
TN22 5XL
T: (01825) 723563
F: (01825) 721087
E: enquiries@thepiltdownman.
com
I: www.thepiltdownman.com

PLAYDEN
East Sussex
The Corner House ◆◆◆
Playden, Rye, East Sussex
TN31 7UL
T: (01797) 280439
E: richard.turner5@virgin.net
I: http://www.smoothHound.co.
uk/hotels/corner2.html

The Playden Oast Hotel ◆◆◆
Peasmarsh Road, Playden, Rye,
East Sussex TN31 7UL
T: (01797) 223502
F: (01797) 223502

PLUCKLEY
Kent
Elvey Farm Country Hotel
◆◆◆
Elvey Farm, Pluckley, Ashford,
Kent TN27 0SU
T: (01233) 840442
F: (01233) 840726

PLUMMERS PLAIN
West Sussex
Cinnamon Cottage ◆◆◆
Handcross Road, Plummers
Plain, Horsham, West Sussex
RH13 6NZ
T: (01444) 400539 &
07885 424579

POLEGATE
East Sussex
The Cottage ◆◆◆◆
Dittons Road, Polegate, East
Sussex BN26 6HS
T: (01323) 482011
F: (01323) 482011

POLING
West Sussex
Medlar Cottage ◆◆◆
Poling, Arundel, West Sussex
BN18 9PT
T: (01903) 883106
F: (01903) 883106

POYNINGS
West Sussex
Poynings Manor Farm ◆◆◆
Poynings, Brighton, East Sussex
BN45 7AG
T: (01273) 857371
F: (01273) 857371

PRESTON
Kent
The Windmill Inn ◆◆
Canterbury Road, Preston,
Faversham, Kent ME13 8LT
T: (01795) 536505

PULBOROUGH
West Sussex
Barn House Lodge ◆◆◆◆
Barn House Lane, Pulborough,
West Sussex RH20 2BS
T: (01798) 872682
F: (01798) 872682

Hurston Warren ◆◆◆
Golf Club Lane, Wiggonholt,
Pulborough, West Sussex
RH20 2EN
T: (01798) 875831
F: (01798) 874989
E: kglazier@btinternet.com
I: www.sussexlive.com

Moseleys Barn
◆◆◆◆ SILVER AWARD
Hardham, Pulborough, West
Sussex RH20 1LB
T: (01798) 872912
F: (01798) 872912

Sotchers ◆◆◆
Bury Gate, Pulborough, West
Sussex RH20 1EY
T: (01798) 865227

PUNNETTS TOWN
East Sussex
Ringwood ◆◆◆◆
Forest Lane, Punnetts Town,
Heathfield, East Sussex
TN21 9JA
T: (01435) 830630

RAINHAM
Kent
Sans Souci ◆◆◆
43 Wakeley Road, Rainham,
Gillingham, Kent ME8 8HD
T: (01634) 370847 &
0771 8551663

RAMSGATE
Kent
Abbeygail Guest House ◆◆◆
17 Penshurst Road, Ramsgate,
Kent CT11 8EG
T: (01843) 594154

The Crescent ◆◆◆
19 Wellington Crescent,
Ramsgate, Kent CT11 8JD
T: (01843) 591419
F: (01843) 591419

Eastwood Guest House ◆◆
28 Augusta Road, Ramsgate,
Kent CT11 8JS
T: (01843) 591505
F: (01843) 591505

Glendevon Guest House ◆◆◆
8 Truro Road, Ramsgate, Kent
CT1 8DB
T: (01843) 570909
F: (01843) 570909
E: glendevon@currantbun.com

Mortons Fork ◆◆◆◆
Station Road, Minster-in-
Thanet, Ramsgate, Kent
CT12 4BZ
T: (01843) 823000
F: (01843) 821224

The Royal Harbour Hotel ◆
8 Nelson Crescent, Ramsgate,
Kent CT11 9JF
T: (01843) 584198
F: (01843) 586759

The Royale Guest House ◆
7 Royal Road, Ramsgate, Kent
CT11 9LE
T: (01843) 594712
F: (01843) 594712

Spencer Court Hotel ◆◆◆
37 Spencer Square, Ramsgate,
Kent CT11 9LD
T: (01843) 594582
F: (01843) 594582

Sunnymede Hotel ◆◆◆
10 Truro Road, Ramsgate, Kent
CT11 8DP
T: (01843) 593974
F: (01843) 594327
◎

REDFORD
West Sussex

Redford Cottage ◆◆◆◆
Redford, Midhurst, West Sussex
GU29 0QF
T: (01428) 741242
F: (01428) 741242

REDHILL
Surrey

Ashleigh House Hotel ◆◆◆◆
39 Redstone Hill, Redhill, Surrey
RH1 4BG
T: (01737) 764763
F: (01737) 780308

REIGATE
Surrey

Highview ◆◆◆
78 Woodcrest Walk, Reigate,
Surrey RH2 0JL
T: (01737) 768294
F: (01737) 760433
E: highview@creative-eye.
demon.co.uk

RHODES MINNIS
Kent

Monsoon Lodge ◆◆◆
Rhodes Minnis, Canterbury, Kent
CT4 6XX
T: (01303) 863272 &
07712 580441
F: (01303) 863272

RINGMER
East Sussex

Bethany ◆◆◆
25 Ballard Drive, Ringmer,
Lewes, East Sussex BN8 5NU
T: (01273) 812025
F: (01273) 812025
E: dybethany@aol.com

Bryn-Clai ◆◆◆
Uckfield Road (A26), Ringmer,
Lewes, East Sussex BN8 5RU
T: (01273) 814042

Chamberlaines Barns ◆◆◆◆
Chamberlaines Lane, Ringmer,
Lewes, East Sussex BN8 5ND
T: (01273) 814932 &
07774 157095
F: (01273) 813302

Drove Park ◆◆◆◆
Half Mile Drove, Ringmer, Lewes,
East Sussex BN8 5NL
T: (01273) 814470
F: (01273) 814470
E: pru@drovepark.com
I: www.drovepark.com

Gote Farm ◆◆◆◆
Gote Lane, Ringmer, Lewes, East
Sussex BN8 5HX
T: (01273) 812303
F: (01273) 812303
E: janecraig@ukgateway.net

RIVER
Kent

Woodlands ◆◆◆
29 London Road, River, Dover,
Kent CT17 0SF
T: (01304) 823635

ROBERTSBRIDGE
East Sussex

Glenferness ◆◆◆◆
Brightling Road, Robertsbridge,
East Sussex TN32 5DP
T: (01580) 881841
E: dong.wriglt@pareuro.com

ROCHESTER
Kent

Ambleside Lodge ◆◆◆
12 Abbotts Close, Priestfields,
Rochester, Kent ME1 3AZ
T: (01634) 815926

14 Beech Road ◆◆
Rochester, Kent ME2 2LP
T: (01634) 724291
E: melzo@strood1950.freeserve.
co.uk

Glaisdale ◆◆◆
29 Langdon Road, Bishop
Square, Rochester, Kent
ME1 1UN
T: (01634) 409559
E: hlsinclair@supanet.com

Holly House ◆◆◆
144 Maidstone Road, Rochester,
Kent ME1 3ED
T: (01634) 815998

Linden House ◆◆◆
10 Nag's Head Lane, Rochester,
Kent ME1 1BB
T: (01634) 819438

Longley House ◆◆◆
Boley Hill, Rochester, Kent
ME1 1TE
T: (01634) 819108
F: (01634) 819108
E: marguerita@jtq.globalnet.co.
uk
I: www.users.globalnet.co.
uk/§jtq

The Old Priory ◆◆
4 Mill Road, Frindsbury,
Rochester, Kent ME2 3BT
T: (01634) 714053
F: (01634) 717716

Riverview Lodge
Rating Applied For
88 Borstal Road, Rochester, Kent
ME1 3BD
T: (01634) 842241 &
07956 279628
F: (01634) 843404

Wouldham Court Farmhouse
◆◆◆
246 High Street, Wouldham,
Rochester, Kent ME1 3TY
T: (01634) 683271
F: (01634) 683271

RODMERSHAM
Kent

Matsons House
◆◆◆ SILVER AWARD
Rodmersham, Sittingbourne,
Kent ME9 0QD
T: (01795) 475861

ROGATE
West Sussex

Trotton Farm ◆◆◆
Trotton, Petersfield, Hampshire
GU31 5EN
T: (01730) 813618
F: (01730) 816093

ROLVENDEN
Kent

Duck & Drake Cottage ◆◆◆
Sandhurst Lane, Rolvenden,
Cranbrook, Kent TN17 4PQ
T: (01580) 241533

ROTTINGDEAN
East Sussex

Braemar Guest House ◆◆◆
Steyning Road, Rottingdean,
Brighton, East Sussex BN2 7GA
T: (01273) 304263

ROWLEDGE
Surrey

Borderfield Farm ◆◆◆◆
Boundary Road, Rowledge,
Farnham, Surrey GU10 4EP
T: (01252) 793985 &
07885 581443

ROYAL TUNBRIDGE WELLS
Kent

Ash Tree Cottage ◆◆◆◆
7 Eden Road, Royal Tunbridge
Wells, Kent TN1 1TS
T: (01892) 541317 &
07050 160322
F: (01892) 541317
E: rogersashtree@excite.co.uk

Badgers End ◆◆
47 Thirlmere Road, Royal
Tunbridge Wells, Kent TN4 9SS
T: (01892) 533176

Bankside ◆◆◆
6 Scotts Way, Royal Tunbridge
Wells, Kent TN2 5RG
T: (01892) 531776

4 Bedford Terrace ◆◆◆
Royal Tunbridge Wells, Kent
TN1 1YJ
T: (01892) 532084

Blinkbonnie ◆◆
4 Beltring Road, Royal Tunbridge
Wells, Kent TN4 9UA
T: (01892) 527908

Blundeston ◆◆◆◆
Eden Road, Royal Tunbridge
Wells, Kent TN1 1TS
T: (01892) 513030
F: (01892) 540255

Braeside ◆◆◆
7 Rusthall Road, Royal
Tunbridge Wells, Kent TN4 8RA
T: (01892) 521786
F: (01892) 521786
E: itucker@eggconnect.net

Chequers ◆◆◆◆
Camden Park, Royal Tunbridge
Wells, Kent TN2 5AD
T: (01892) 532299
F: (01892) 526448
E: stubbs.mcd@talk21.com

Cheviots ◆◆◆
Cousley Wood, Wadhurst, East
Sussex TN5 6HD
T: (01892) 782952
F: (01892) 782952
E: b&tb@cheviots99.freeserve.
co.uk
I: www.cheviots99.freeserve.co.
uk

Clarken Guest House ◆◆◆
61 Frant Road, Royal Tunbridge
Wells, Kent TN2 5LH
T: (01892) 533397
F: (01892) 617121
E: barrykench@virgin.net

The Coach House ◆◆◆
51A Frant Road, Royal Tunbridge
Wells, Kent TN2 5LE
T: (01892) 530615
F: (01892) 530615

69 Culverden Park ◆◆◆
Royal Tunbridge Wells, Kent
TN4 9QS
T: (01892) 533314
E: peter@petergbell.demon.co.
uk

Danehurst ◆◆◆◆◆
41 Lower Green Road, Rusthall,
Royal Tunbridge Wells, Kent
TN4 8TW
T: (01892) 527739
F: (01892) 514804

Doughty Cottage
Rating Applied For
5 Little Mount Sion, Royal
Tunbridge Wells, Kent TN1 1YS
T: (01892) 519196
F: (020) 8332 9434
I: www.smoothhound.co.
uk/hotels/doughty cott.

Ephraim Lodge
◆◆◆◆◆ SILVER AWARD
The Common, Royal Tunbridge
Wells, Kent TN4 8BX
T: (01892) 523053
F: (01892) 523053

Ford Cottage ◆◆◆◆
Linden Park Road, Royal
Tunbridge Wells, Kent TN2 5QL
T: (01892) 531419
E: fordcottage@tinyworld.co.uk

The Grove Tavern ◆◆
19 Berkerley Road, Royal
Tunbridge Wells, Kent TN1 1YS
T: (01892) 526549
F: (01622) 761020
◎

Hadleigh ◆◆◆
69 Sandown Park, Royal
Tunbridge Wells, Kent TN2 4RT
T: (01892) 822760
F: (01892) 823170

Hamsell Wood Farm ◆◆◆
The Forstal, Eridge, Royal
Tunbridge Wells, Kent TN3 9JY
T: (01892) 864326

Hawkenbury Farm ◆◆◆◆
Hawkenbury Road, Royal
Tunbridge Wells, Kent TN3 9AD
T: (01892) 536977
F: (01892) 536200

Hazelwood House ◆◆◆
Bishop's Down Park Road, Royal
Tunbridge Wells, Kent TN4 8XS
T: (01892) 545924
E: judith02@globalnet.co.uk

Manor Court Farm ◆◆◆
Ashurst, Royal Tunbridge Wells,
Kent TN3 9TB
T: (01892) 740279
E: jsoyke@jsoyke.freeserve.co.uk
⊚

Nightingales ◆◆◆
London Road, Southborough,
Royal Tunbridge Wells, Kent
TN4 0UJ
T: (01892) 528443
F: (01892) 511376
E: the_nightingales@bigfoot.
com
I: www.bcity.
com/the_nightingales

Number Ten ◆◆◆
Modest Corner, Southborough,
Royal Tunbridge Wells, Kent
TN4 0LS
T: (01892) 522450
F: (01892) 522450
E: modestannekaco.lineone.net

Orchard House
Rating Applied For
Kingswood Road, Royal
Tunbridge Wells, Kent TN2 4UJ
T: (01892) 521549
F: (01892) 618637
E: bennettryanassociates@
btinternet.com

19 Ravenswood Avenue ◆
Royal Tunbridge Wells, Kent
TN2 3SG
T: (01892) 530167

80 Ravenswood Avenue ◆◆
Royal Tunbridge Wells, Kent
TN2 3SJ
T: (01892) 523069

Rosnaree ◆◆
189 Upper Grosvenor Road,
Royal Tunbridge Wells, Kent
TN1 2EF
T: (01892) 524017
E: david@rosnaree.freeserve.co.
uk

Southview House
Rating Applied For
21 Rusthall Road, Royal
Tunbridge Wells, Kent TN4 8RD
T: (01892) 518832

Studley Cottage ◆◆◆◆
Bishops Down Park Road, Royal
Tunbridge Wells, Kent TN4 8XX
T: (01892) 539854 &
0771 848333
⊚

Triton
Rating Applied For
46 Broadwater Down, Royal
Tunbridge Wells, Kent TN2 5PE
T: (01892) 530547

**191 Upper Grosvenor Road
◆◆◆**
Royal Tunbridge Wells, Kent
TN1 2EF
T: (01892) 537305

Vale Royal Hotel ◆◆◆
54-57 London Road, Royal
Tunbridge Wells, Kent TN1 1DS
T: (01892) 525580
F: (01892) 526022

40 York Road ◆◆◆
Royal Tunbridge Wells, Kent
TN1 1JY
T: (01892) 531342
F: (01892) 531342

RUDGWICK
West Sussex
The Mucky Duck ◆◆
Loxwood Road, Tismans
Common, Rudgwick, Horsham,
West Sussex RH12 3BW
T: (01403) 822300
F: (01403) 822300
E: mucky-duck-pub@msn.com
I: www.mucky-duck.co.uk

RUNCTON
West Sussex
Springdale Cottage
Rating Applied For
Runcton Lane, Runcton,
Chichester, West Sussex
PO20 6PS
T: (01243) 783912

RUSTINGTON
West Sussex
Kenmore
◆◆◆◆ SILVER AWARD
Claigmar Road, Rustington,
West Sussex BN16 2NL
T: (01903) 784634
F: (01903) 784634

Rustington House Hotel ◆◆◆
Broadmark Lane, Rustington,
Littlehampton, West Sussex
BN16 2HH
T: (01903) 771198
F: (01903) 850742
E: rustingtonhousehotel@
yahoo.co
I: www.rustingtonhotel.com

RYE
East Sussex
Arndale Cottage ◆◆◆◆
Northiam Road, Broad Oak
Brede, Rye, East Sussex
TN31 6EP
T: (01424) 882813 & 882852
F: (01424) 882813

Aviemore Guest House ◆◆◆
28-30 Fishmarket Road, Rye,
East Sussex TN31 7LP
T: (01797) 223052
F: (01797) 223052
E: aviemore@lineone.net
I: www.SmoothHound.co.
uk/hotels/aviemore.html

Benson Hotel ◆◆◆◆◆
15 East Street, Rye, East Sussex
TN31 7JY
T: (01797) 225131
F: (01797) 225512

Cinque Ports Hotel ◆◆◆
Cinque Ports Street, Rye, East
Sussex TN31 7AN
T: (01797) 222319
F: (01797) 224184
E: jane@fiveports.freeserve.co.
uk
I: www.rye.org.uk

The Clocks ◆◆◆
8 Rock Channel Quay, Rye, East
Sussex TN31 7DL
T: (01797) 226466

Culpeppers ◆◆◆◆
15 Love Lane, Rye, East Sussex
TN31 7NE
T: (01797) 224411
F: (01797) 224411
E: peppersrye@aol.com
I: www.rye-tourism.co.
uk/culpeppers

**Durrant House Hotel
◆◆◆◆ SILVER AWARD**
2 Market Street, Rye, East Sussex
TN31 7LA
T: (01797) 223182
F: (01797) 226639

Four Seasons ◆◆◆◆
96 Udimore Road, Rye, East
Sussex TN31 7DX
T: (01797) 224305
F: (01797) 224305

Furnace Lane Oast ◆◆◆◆
Broad Oak Brede, Rye, East
Sussex TN31 6ET
T: (01424) 882407
F: (01424) 882407
E: furnacelane@pavilion.co.uk
I: www.seetb.org.
uk/furnace-lane-oast/

Glencoe Farm ◆◆◆◆
West Undercliff, Rye, East
Sussex TN31 7DX
T: (01797) 224347 &
07774 683530

11 High Street ◆◆◆
Rye, East Sussex TN31 7JF
T: (01797) 223952

Jeake's House
◆◆◆◆◆ SILVER AWARD
Mermaid Street, Rye, East Sussex
TN31 7ET
T: (01797) 222828
F: (01797) 222623
E: jeakeshouse@btinternet.com
I: www.s-h-systems.co.
uk/hotels/jeakes.html
⊚

Kimbley Cottage ◆◆◆
Main Street, Peasmarsh, Rye,
East Sussex TN31 6UL
T: (01797) 230514
E: kimbley@clara.co.uk

Little Orchard House
◆◆◆◆◆ SILVER AWARD
West Street, Rye, East Sussex
TN31 7ES
T: (01797) 223831
F: (01797) 223831

Little Saltcote ◆◆◆
22 Military Road, Rye, East
Sussex TN31 7NY
T: (01797) 223210
F: (01797) 223210
E: littlesaltcote.rye@virgin.net

Llamedos ◆◆
11 Cadborough Cliff, Rye, East
Sussex TN31 7EB
T: (01797) 227220

Manor Farm Oast
◆◆◆◆◆ GOLD AWARD
Windmill Orchard, Workhouse
Lane, Icklesham, Winchelsea,
East Sussex TN36 4AJ
T: (01424) 813787
F: (01424) 813787

The Mint B & B ◆◆◆
Rye Fine Art, 39 The Mint, Rye,
East Sussex TN31 7EN
T: (01797) 224968

Mint Court Cottage ◆◆◆
The Mint, High Street, Rye, East
Sussex TN31 7EN
T: (01797) 227780
F: (01797) 223432

Mint Lodge ◆◆◆
38 The Mint, Rye, East Sussex
TN31 7EN
T: (01797) 223268

Mountsfield ◆◆◆◆
Rye Hill, Rye, East Sussex
TN31 7NH
T: (01797) 227105
F: (01797) 227106

The Old Vicarage ◆◆◆
Rye Harbour, Rye, East Sussex
TN31 7TT
T: (01797) 222088

Owlet ◆◆◆
37 New Road, Rye, East Sussex
TN31 7LS
T: (01797) 222544

**Playden Cottage Guesthouse
◆◆◆◆◆ SILVER AWARD**
Military Road, Rye, East Sussex
TN31 7NY
T: (01797) 222234
I: www.SmoothHound.co.
uk/hotels/playden.html
⊚

The Queens Head Hotel ◆◆◆
19 Landgate, Rye, East Sussex
TN31 7LH
T: (01797) 222181

The Rise
◆◆◆◆ SILVER AWARD
82 Udimore Road, Rye, East
Sussex TN31 7DY
T: (01797) 222285

St Margarets ◆◆◆
Dumbwomans Lane, Udimore,
Rye, East Sussex TN31 6AD
T: (01797) 222586

Ship Inn ◆◆◆
The Strand, Rye, East Sussex
TN31 7DS
T: (01797) 222233
F: (01797) 222715

The Strand House ◆◆◆◆
Tanyard's Lane, Winchelsea, Rye,
East Sussex TN36 4JT
T: (01797) 226276
F: (01797) 224806
I: www.s-h-systems.co.
uk/hotels/strand.html
⊚

Thacker House ◆◆◆
Old Brickyard, Rye, East Sussex
TN31 7EE
T: (01797) 226850
F: (01797) 226850
E: abb25@supanet.com

Tidings ◆◆◆◆
26A Military Road, Rye, East
Sussex TN31 7NY
T: (01797) 223760

Tillingham House ◆◆◆◆
75 Ferry Road, Rye, East Sussex
TN31 7DJ
T: (01797) 222225 & 223268

Top o'The Hill at Rye ◆◆◆
Rye Hill, Rye, East Sussex
TN31 7NH
T: (01797) 223284
F: (01797) 227030
⊚

Tower House ◆◆◆
(The Old Dormy), Hilders Cliff,
Rye, East Sussex TN31 7LD
T: (01797) 226865
F: (01797) 226865
@

Vine Cottage ◆◆◆
25a Udimore Road, Rye, East
Sussex TN31 7DS
T: (01797) 222822 &
0780 3431406
F: (01797) 222822

The Windmill Guest House
◆◆◆
Mill Lane, (off Ferry Road), Rye,
East Sussex TN31 7DW
T: (01797) 224027

Wish House ◆◆◆
Wish Ward, Rye, East Sussex
TN31 7DH
T: (01797) 223672

Woodpeckers ◆◆◆
West Undercliff, Rye, East
Sussex TN31 7DX
T: (01797) 223013 & 222264

RYE FOREIGN
East Sussex

The Hare & Hounds ◆◆◆
Main Road, Rye Foreign, Rye,
East Sussex TN31 7ST
T: (01797) 230483

ST LEONARDS
East Sussex

Ashton House ◆◆◆
381 Battle Road, St Leonards on
Sea, St Leonards, Hastings, East
Sussex TN37 7BE
T: (01424) 853624

Hollington Croft ◆◆◆
272 Battle Road, St Leonards-
on-Sea, St Leonards, Hastings,
East Sussex TN37 7BA
T: (01424) 851795

Marina Lodge ◆◆
123 Marina, St Leonards-on-
Sea, St Leonards, Hastings, East
Sussex TN38 0BN
T: (01424) 715067
E: marinalodge@lineone.net
I: www.marinalodgeguesthouse.
co.uk

May Tree House ◆◆◆
41 Albany Road, St Leonards,
Hastings, East Sussex TN38 0LJ
T: (01424) 421760 &
07973 283117
F: (01424) 421760
E: tricia.owen@tesco.net

Melrose Guest House ◆◆◆
18 De Cham Road, St Leonards,
Hastings, East Sussex TN37 6JP
T: (01424) 715163
F: (01424) 715163

Rutland Guest House ◆◆◆
17 Grosvenor Cres, St Leonards,
Hastings, East Sussex TN38 0AA
T: (01424) 432620 & 714720
F: (01424) 720379

Sherwood Guest House ◆◆◆
15 Grosvenor Crescent, St
Leonards-on-Sea, St Leonards,
East Sussex TN38 0AA
T: (01424) 433331
F: (01424) 433331

The Windsor Hotel ◆◆◆
9 Warrior Square, St Leonards-
on-Sea, St Leonards, Hastings,
East Sussex TN37 6BA
T: (01424) 422709
F: (01424) 422709

ST MICHAELS
Kent

Forge House ◆◆◆
Biddenden Road, St Michaels,
Tenterden, Kent TN30 6SX
T: (01233) 850779

Whitelands Farm ◆◆◆
Grange Road, St Michaels,
Tenterden, Kent TN30 6TJ
T: (01580) 765971 &
07770 796288
E: whitelandsfarm@tinyonline.
co.uk

SANDGATE
Kent

Royal Norfolk Hotel ◆◆
7 Sandgate High Street,
Sandgate, Folkestone, Kent
CT20 3BD
T: (01303) 248262
F: (01303) 238433

SANDHURST
Kent

Heronden Barn ◆◆◆◆
Rye Road, Sandhurst, Cranbrook,
Kent TN18 5PH
T: (01580) 850809
F: (01580) 850809
E: hdj@hdjohns.idps.co.uk

Hoads Farm ◆◆◆
Crouch Lane, Sandhurst,
Cranbrook, Kent TN18 5PA
T: (01580) 850296
F: (01580) 850296

Hope Barn ◆◆◆◆
Crouch Lane, Sandhurst,
Cranbrook, Kent TN18 5PD
T: (01580) 850689
F: (01580) 850689

Lamberden House ◆◆◆◆
Rye Road, Sandhurst, Cranbrook,
Kent TN18 5PH
T: (01580) 850968
T: (01580) 850121
E: croysdill@lamberden.
freeserve.co.uk
I: www.lamberden.freeserve.co.
uk

SANDWICH
Kent

**Fleur De Lis Hotel Inn &
Restaurant** ◆◆◆
6-8 Delf Street, Sandwich, Kent
CT13 9BZ
T: (01304) 611131
F: (01304) 611199

The St Crispin Inn ◆◆
The Street, Worth, Deal, Kent
CT14 0DF
T: (01304) 612081
F: (01304) 614838

57 St Georges Road ◆◆◆
Sandwich, Kent CT13 9LE
T: (01304) 612772

SARRE
Kent

**Crown Inn (The Famous Cherry
Brandy House)** ◆◆◆
Ramsgate Road, Sarre,
Birchington, Kent CT7 0LF
T: (01843) 847808
F: (01843) 847914
E: crown@shepherd-neame.co.
uk
I: www.shepherd-neame.co.uk
🏃

SEAFORD
East Sussex

Copperfields ◆◆◆◆
12 Connaught Road, Seaford,
East Sussex BN25 2PY
T: (01323) 492152 &
07775 700625
E: sally.green@btinternet.co.uk.

Cornerways ◆◆◆
10 The Covers, Seaford, East
Sussex BN25 1DF
T: (01323) 492400

Holmes Lodge ◆◆◆
72 Claremont Road, Seaford,
East Sussex BN25 2BJ
T: (01323) 898331
F: (01323) 491346
E: holmes.lodge@freemail.co.uk
I: www.seaford.co.
uk/holmes/holmes.htm

Malvern House ◆◆◆
Alfriston Road, Seaford, East
Sussex BN25 3QG
T: (01323) 492058 &
07860 262271
F: (01323) 492000
E: 106750.621@compuserve.
com
I: www.seaford.co.uk/malvern/

The Silverdale ◆◆◆◆
21 Sutton Park Road, Seaford,
East Sussex BN25 1RH
T: (01323) 491849
F: (01323) 891131
E: silverdale@mistral.co.uk
I: www.mistral.co.
uk/silverdale/silver.htm
@

Tudor Manor Hotel ◆◆◆◆
Eastbourne Road, Seaford, East
Sussex BN25 4DB
T: (01323) 896006

SELLING
Kent

Norham Grange ◆◆◆
Norham, Selling, Faversham,
Kent ME13 9RL
T: (01227) 752721
F: (01227) 752721

SELSEY
West Sussex

Greenacre ◆◆◆◆
5 Manor Farm Court, Selsey,
Chichester, West Sussex
PO20 0LY
T: (01243) 602912 &
07973 392629
I: www.greenacre@zoom.co.uk

The Homestead ◆◆◆
154 High Street, Selsey,
Chichester, West Sussex
PO20 0QE
T: (01243) 605878

42 Kingsway ◆◆◆
Selsey, Chichester, West Sussex
PO20 0SY
T: (01243) 604711 &
07860 109819
F: (01243) 604711
E: stephen.lucas2@virgin.net

Norton Lea ◆◆
Upper Norton, Selsey,
Chichester, West Sussex
PO20 9EA
T: (01243) 605454

St Andrews Lodge ◆◆◆◆
Chichester Road, Selsey,
Chichester, West Sussex
PO20 0LX
T: (01243) 606899
F: (01243) 607826
E: st.andrews@selsey.org.uk
I: www.smoothhound.co.
uk/hotels/standrlg.html
@ ♿

Windfall Cottage ◆◆
29 Woodland Road, Selsey,
Chichester, West Sussex
PO20 0AL
T: (01243) 602205

SEVENOAKS
Kent

Austens Cottage ◆◆◆
South Park, Sevenoaks, Kent
TN13 1EL
T: (01732) 452988
F: (01732) 451729
E: gcampac@aol.com

Beechcombe ◆◆◆◆
Vine Lodge Court, Holly Bush
Lane, Sevenoaks, Kent TN13 3XY
T: (01732) 741643
F: (01732) 741643
E: anthonytait@hotmail.com

Bramber ◆◆◆
45 Shoreham Lane, Riverhead,
Sevenoaks, Kent TN13 3DX
T: (01732) 457466
F: (01732) 457466

Candleford ◆
57 Chipstead Lane, Riverhead,
Sevenoaks, Kent TN13 2AJ
T: (01732) 452725

The Bull Inn Hotel ◆◆◆
Wrotham, Sevenoaks, Kent
TN15 7RF
T: (01732) 789800 & 789819
F: (01732) 886288
E: bookings@bullhotel.
freeserve.co.uk
@

1 Burley Lodge ◆◆◆
Rockdale Road, Sevenoaks, Kent
TN13 1JT
T: (01732) 455761
F: (01732) 458178

75 Clarendon Road ◆◆◆
Sevenoaks, Kent TN13 1ET
T: (01732) 456000
F: (01732) 456000
E: info@chocolateshop.uk.com
@

Crofters ◆◆◆◆
67 Oakhill Road, Sevenoaks,
Kent TN13 1NU
T: (01732) 460189
F: (01732) 460189

56 The Drive ◆◆◆
Sevenoaks, Kent TN13 3AF
T: (01732) 453236
E: jwlloydsks@aol.com

Garden House ◆◆◆◆
Solefields Road, Sevenoaks, Kent
TN13 1PJ
T: (01732) 457225

Hornshaw House ◆◆◆◆
47 Mount Harry Road,
Sevenoaks, Kent TN13 3JN
T: (01732) 465262
I: www.
hornshawhouse-sevenoaks.co.
uk

Legh House ◆◆◆◆
Woodland Rise, Sevenoaks, Kent
TN15 0HZ
T: (01732) 761587

The Moorings Hotel ◆◆◆
97 Hitchen Hatch Lane,
Sevenoaks, Kent TN13 3BE
T: (01732) 452589 & 742323
F: (01732) 456462
E: theryans@mooringshotel.co.
uk
I: www.mooringshotel.co.uk
◎

Oakwood ◆◆◆
White House Road, Bayley's Hill,
Sevenoaks, Kent TN14 6HS
T: (01732) 454993

The Old Police House ◆◆◆◆
18 Shenden Way, Sevenoaks,
Kent TN13 1SE
T: (01732) 457088

The Pightle ◆◆◆◆
21 White Hart Wood, Sevenoaks,
Kent TN13 1RS
T: (01732) 451678
F: (01732) 464905
E: miketessa@pightle21.fsnet.
co.uk
I: www.pightle21.fsnet.co.uk

40 Robyns Way ◆◆◆
Sevenoaks, Kent TN13 3EB
T: (01732) 452401
E: valerie.engram@centrent.co.
uk

Rosewood ◆◆◆◆
Ismays Road, Ivy Hatch,
Sevenoaks, Kent TN15 0PA
T: (01732) 810496
E: rosewood@
covenantblessings.co.uk

Star House ◆◆◆
Star Hill, Sevenoaks, Kent
TN14 6HA
T: (01959) 533109 &
07774 281558

Welford ◆◆◆
6 Crownfields, Sevenoaks, Kent
TN13 1EE
T: (01732) 452689
F: (01732) 455422
E: rcjollye@compuserve.com

Wendy Wood ◆◆◆◆
86 Childsbridge Lane, Seal,
Sevenoaks, Kent TN15 0BW
T: (01732) 763755
E: wendywood@freeuk.com
I: www.wendywood.co.
ukjgodber

SHARPTHORNE
West Sussex

Coach House ◆◆◆
Courtlands, Chilling Street,
Sharpthorne, East Grinstead,
West Sussex RH19 4JF
T: (01342) 810512 &
07930 977076
F: (01342) 810512
E: sussexlive@enta.net
I: www.sussexlive.com

SHEPHERDSWELL
Kent

Sunshine Cottage
◆◆◆◆ SILVER AWARD
The Green, Mill Lane,
Shepherdswell, Dover, Kent
CT15 7LQ
T: (01304) 831359 & 831218

SHIPLEY
West Sussex

Goffsland Farm ◆◆◆◆
Shipley, Horsham, West Sussex
RH13 7BQ
T: (01403) 730434
F: (01403) 730434

SHOLDEN
Kent

The Sportsman
◆◆◆◆ GOLD AWARD
23 The Street, Sholden, Deal,
Kent CT14 0AL
T: (01304) 374973
F: (01304) 374973
E: rgr1445880@aol.co

SHOREHAM
Kent

Church House
◆◆◆◆ SILVER AWARD
Church Street, Shoreham,
Sevenoaks, Kent TN14 7SB
T: (01959) 522241
F: (01959) 522241
E: katehowie@compuserve.com
I: www.intacom.co.
uk/shore/churchouse.htm

Preston Farmhouse ◆◆◆◆
Preston Farm, Shoreham,
Sevenoaks, Kent TN14 7UD
T: (01959) 522029

SIDLESHAM
West Sussex

Bird Pond Nursery ◆◆◆
Selsey Road, Sidlesham,
Chichester, West Sussex
PO20 7NF
T: (01243) 641212
F: (01243) 641212
E: roy.upstone@btinternet.com

SISSINGHURST
Kent

1 Hillview Cottage ◆◆◆
Starvenden Lane, Sissinghurst,
Cranbrook, Kent TN17 2AN
T: (01580) 712823 &
07850 909838

The Oast House ◆◆◆◆
Buckhurst Farm, Sissinghurst,
Cranbrook, Kent TN17 2AA
T: (01580) 720044
F: (01580) 720022

SITTINGBOURNE
Kent

Hempstead House ◆◆◆◆◆
London Road, Bapchild,
Sittingbourne, Kent ME9 9PP
T: (01795) 428020
F: (01795) 436362
E: info@hempsteadhouse.co.uk
I: www.hempsteadhouse.co.uk

**Scuttington Manor Guest
House** ◆◆◆
Dully Road, Dully, Sittingbourne,
Kent ME9 9PA
T: (01795) 521316
F: (01795) 521316

SMARDEN
Kent

Chequers Inn ◆◆◆
The Street, Smarden, Ashford,
Kent TN27 8QA
T: (01233) 770217
F: (01233) 770623

Dering Barn ◆◆◆◆
Pluckley Road, Smarden,
Ashford, Kent TN27 8ND
T: (01233) 770836

Hereford Oast ◆◆◆◆
Smarden, Ashford, Kent
TN27 8PA
T: (01233) 770541
F: (01233) 770045

SOUTHBOROUGH
Kent

The Croft ◆◆
Argyle Road, Southborough,
Royal Tunbridge Wells, Kent
TN4 0SU
T: (01892) 522671

SOUTHWATER
West Sussex

Meadow House ◆◆◆
Church Lane, Bonfire Hill,
Southwater, Horsham, West
Sussex RH13 7BT
T: (01403) 730324

ST-MARGARETS-AT-CLIFFE
Kent

Holm Oaks ◆◆◆◆
Dover Road, St-Margarets-at-
Cliffe, Dover, Kent CT15 6EP
T: (01304) 852990 & 853473
F: (01304) 853433
E: holmoaks852@icqmail.com

Merzenich Guest House ◆◆◆
Station Road, St-Margarets-at-
Cliffe, Dover, Kent CT15 6AY
T: (01304) 852260
F: (01304) 852167
E: robclaringbould@lineone.net
I: www.smoothhound.co.
uk/hotels/merzen.html

STANSTED
Kent

The Black Horse ◆◆◆◆
Tumblefield Road, Stansted,
Sevenoaks, Kent TN15 7PR
T: (01732) 822355
F: (01732) 824415

STAPLE
Kent

The Three Tuns Inn ◆◆◆
Staple, Canterbury, Kent
CT3 1LN
T: (01304) 812317
F: (01304) 812317
E: johngunner@totalise.co.uk
I: www.three-tuns-staple.
freeserve.co.uk

STAPLEHURST
Kent

Tudorhurst ◆◆◆◆
Pagehurst Road, Staplehurst,
Tonbridge, Kent TN12 0JA
T: (01580) 891564 &
07711 760677
E: laurie@bluey39.freeserve.co.
uk

The White Cottage ◆◆◆◆
Hawkenbury Road, Hawkenbury,
Staplehurst, Tonbridge, Kent
TN12 0DU
T: (01580) 891480 & 753573
F: (01580) 754066

STEDHAM
West Sussex

Meadowhills ◆◆
Stedham, Midhurst, West Sussex
GU29 0PT
T: (01730) 812609

STELLING MINNIS
Kent

Great Field Farm
◆◆◆◆ SILVER AWARD
Misling Lane, Stelling Minnis,
Canterbury, Kent CT4 6DE
T: (01227) 709223
F: (01227) 709223

STEYNING
West Sussex

Chequer Inn ◆◆◆
41 High Street, Steyning, West
Sussex BN44 3RE
T: (01903) 814437
F: (01903) 879707
E: chequerinn@btinternet.com

Wappingthorn Farmhouse
◆◆◆◆
Horsham Road, Steyning, West
Sussex BN44 3AA
T: (01903) 813236
F: (01903) 813236
E: arianne@wappingthorn.
demon.co.uk
I: www.wappingthorn.demon.co.
uk

STONEGATE
East Sussex

The Oast ◆◆◆
Battenhurst Farm, Stonegate,
Wadhurst, East Sussex TN5 7DU
T: (01435) 883728
F: (01435) 882521

STORRINGTON
West Sussex

Chardonnay ◆◆◆◆
Hampers Lane, Storrington,
Pulborough, West Sussex
RH20 3HZ
T: (01903) 746688
I: www.sussexlive.co.uk

Hampers End
◆◆◆◆ SILVER AWARD
Rock Road, Storrington,
Pulborough, West Sussex
RH20 3AF
T: (01903) 742777
F: (01903) 742776
◎

No 1 Lime Chase
♦♦♦♦♦ GOLD AWARD
(off Fryern Road), Storrington,
Pulborough, West Sussex
RH20 4LX
T: (01903) 740437 &
07721 042826
F: (01903) 740437
E: fionawarton@limechase.co.
uk
I: www.limechase.co.uk
@

STROOD
Kent
Squires Corner ♦♦♦
38 Sharfleet Drive, Strood,
Rochester, Kent ME2 2TY
T: (01634) 296898

SUTTON AT HONE
Kent
Hamilton ♦♦♦
Arnolds Lane, Sutton at Hone,
Dartford, Kent DA4 9HE
T: (01322) 272535
F: (01322) 284856

SUTTON VALENCE
Kent
Sparks Oast Farm ♦♦♦
Forsham lane, Sutton Valence,
Maidstone, Kent ME17 3EW
T: (01622) 842213

SWANLEY
Kent
The Dees ♦♦♦
56 Old Chapel Road, Crockenhill,
Swanley, Kent BR8 8LJ
T: (01322) 667645
@

TEMPLE EWELL
Kent
The Woodville Hall Hotel
♦♦♦♦♦ GOLD AWARD
London Road, Temple Ewell,
Dover, Kent CT16 3DJ
T: (01304) 825256
F: (01304) 825256

TENTERDEN
Kent
Collina House Hotel ♦♦♦
East Hill, Tenterden, Kent
TN30 6RL
T: (01580) 764852 & 764004
F: (01580) 762224
E: Collina.house@dial.pipex.com
I: dspace.dial.pipex.com/collina.
house

11 East Hill ♦♦♦
Tenterden, Kent TN30 6RL
T: (01580) 766805
F: (01580) 766805

Eight Bells Public House ♦♦♦
43 High Street, Tenterden, Kent
TN30 6BJ
T: (01580) 762788
F: (01580) 766070

**The Lemon Tree Restaurant
with Rooms**♦♦♦♦
52-56 High Street, Tenterden,
Kent TN30 6AU
T: (01580) 762060
F: (01580) 765146
E: nick.lemontree@talk21.com

Old Burren ♦♦♦
25 Ashford Road, Tenterden,
Kent TN30 6LL
T: (01580) 764442 & 764254
E: pool@tiny.co.uk

Two Willows
♦♦♦♦ SILVER AWARD
10 The Martins, High Halden,
Ashford, Kent TN26 3LD
T: (01233) 850859
F: (01233) 850859
E: bettyq@freenet.co.uk
I: www.smoothhound.co.
uk/twowillo.html

White Cottage ♦♦♦
London Beach, St Michaels,
Tenterden, Kent TN30 6SR
T: (01233) 850583

White Lion Hotel ♦♦♦♦
High Street, Tenterden, Kent
TN30 6BD
T: (01580) 765077
F: (01580) 764157

The Woolpack Hotel ♦♦
26 High Street, Tenterden, Kent
TN30 6AP
T: (01580) 762934

TICEHURST
East Sussex
Cherry Tree Inn ♦♦♦
Dale Hill, Ticehurst, Wadhurst,
East Sussex TN5 7DG
T: (01580) 201229
F: (01580) 201325
E: leondiane@aol.com

Pashley Farm ♦♦♦♦
Pashley Road, Ticehurst,
Wadhurst, East Sussex TN5 7HE
T: (01580) 200362
F: (01580) 200832
E: pashleyfarm@aol.com

TONBRIDGE
Kent
86 Hadlow Road ♦♦
Tonbridge, Kent TN9 1PA
T: (01732) 357332

Lodge Oast ♦♦♦♦
Horns Lodge Lane, Shipbourne
Road, Tonbridge, Kent TN11 9NJ
T: (01732) 833976
F: (01732) 838394
E: maryann@lodgeoast.
freeserve.co.uk
I: www.lodgeoast.electricfence.
co.uk

Marigolds ♦♦♦
19 Old Hadlow Road, Tonbridge,
Kent TN10 4EY
T: (01732) 356539 &
07885 450638
E: jmtn10@aol.com
I: www.tonbridge-kent.com

**Masters
Rating Applied For**
Matfield Green, Tonbridge, Kent
TN12 7LA
T: (01892) 722126
F: (01892) 722126

61 The Ridgeway ♦♦♦
Tonbridge, Kent TN10 4NL
T: (01732) 353530
@

30 Stacey Road ♦♦♦
Tonbridge, Kent TN10 3AR
T: (01732) 358027

UCKFIELD
East Sussex
Hooke Hall
♦♦♦♦♦ GOLD AWARD
250 High Street, Uckfield, East
Sussex TN22 1EN
T: (01825) 761578
F: (01825) 768025
E: a.percy@virgin.net

Old Mill Farm ♦♦♦♦
High Hurstwood, Uckfield, East
Sussex TN22 4AD
T: (01825) 732279
F: (01825) 732279

Robins Wood ♦♦♦♦
Fairhazel, Piltdown, Uckfield,
East Sussex TN22 3XB
T: (01825) 763555

South Paddock
♦♦♦♦ SILVER AWARD
Maresfield Park, Uckfield, East
Sussex TN22 2HA
T: (01825) 762335
@

UPCHURCH
Kent
Suffield House ♦♦♦♦
The Street, Upchurch,
Sittingbourne, Kent ME9 7EU
T: (01634) 230409
@

VINES CROSS
East Sussex
The Coach House ♦♦♦♦
Wellbrook Place, Hammer Lane,
Vines Cross, Heathfield, East
Sussex TN21 9HF
T: (01435) 812529
F: (01435) 812529
E: farrow@wellbrookplace.
freeserve.co.uk

WADHURST
East Sussex
Best Beech Inn ♦♦♦
Best Beech, Mayfield Lane,
Wadhurst, East Sussex TN5 6JH
T: (01892) 782046
F: (01892) 785092
I: www.bestbeechinn.com

Four Keys ♦♦♦
Station Road, Wadhurst, East
Sussex TN5 6RZ
T: (01892) 782252 & 784113

Little Tidebrook Farm ♦♦♦
Riseden Road, Wadhurst, East
Sussex TN5 6NY
T: (01892) 782688 &
07970 159988
E: sally-mike@marleyward.
freeserve.co.uk

Spring Cottage ♦♦♦
Best Beech Hill, Wadhurst, East
Sussex TN5 6JH
T: (01892) 783896
F: (01892) 784866

WALBERTON
West Sussex
Felsted Cottage ♦♦♦
Arundel Road, Walberton,
Arundel, West Sussex BN18 0QP
T: (01243) 814237 &
0788 7507122

**Oaks Lodge
Rating Applied For**
Yapton Lane, Walberton,
Arundel, West Sussex BN18 0LS
T: (01243) 552865
F: (01243) 553862

WALDRON
East Sussex
Barns Oak ♦♦♦♦
Firgrove Road, Waldron,
Heathfield, East Sussex
TN21 0RE
T: (01435) 864574
F: (01435) 864574

WALTHAM
Kent
Beech Bank
♦♦♦♦ GOLD AWARD
Duckpit Lane, Waltham,
Canterbury, Kent CT4 5QA
T: (01227) 700302
F: (01227) 700302

WALTON-ON-THAMES
Surrey
Beech Tree Lodge ♦♦♦
7 Rydens Avenue, Walton-on-
Thames, Surrey KT12 3JB
T: (01932) 242738 & 886667
E: fredspiteri@yahoo.co.uk

WARLINGHAM
Surrey
Glenmore ♦♦♦
Southview Road, Warlingham,
Surrey CR6 9JE
T: (01883) 624530
F: (01883) 624199

WARNINGLID
West Sussex
Gillhurst ♦♦♦♦
The Street, Warninglid,
Haywards Heath, West Sussex
RH17 5SZ
T: (01444) 461388

WATERSFIELD
West Sussex
Beacon Lodge B & B ♦♦♦
London Road, Watersfield,
Arundel, West Sussex RH20 1NH
T: (01798) 831026
F: (01798) 831026
E: beaconlodge@freeuk.com
I: www.beaconlodge.co.uk

WEALD
Kent
Church Cottage ♦♦
Glebe Road, Weald, Sevenoaks,
Kent TN14 6PB
T: (01732) 463583
F: (01732) 463583

WEST BRABOURNE
Kent
**Bulltown Farmhouse Bed &
Breakfast** ♦♦♦
Bulltown Lane, West Brabourne,
Ashford, Kent TN25 6NB
T: (01233) 813505
F: (01227) 709544

WEST BURTON
West Sussex
Cokes Barn ♦♦♦
West Burton, Pulborough, West
Sussex RH20 1HD
T: (01798) 831636 &
07885 060154
F: (01798) 831636

WEST CHILTINGTON
West Sussex
New Barn Cottage ♦♦♦♦
New Barn Lane, off Harborough
Hill, West Chiltington,
Pulborough, West Sussex
RH20 2PP
T: (01798) 813231

New House Farm ◆◆◆
Broadford Bridge Road, West
Chiltington, Pulborough, West
Sussex RH20 2LA
T: (01798) 812215
F: (01798) 813209
E: alma.steele@virgin.net

WEST CLANDON
Surrey

Ways Cottage ◆◆◆◆
Lime Grove, West Clandon,
Guildford, Surrey GU4 7UT
T: (01483) 222454

WEST DEAN
West Sussex

Lodge Hill Farm
Rating Applied For
West Dean, Chichester, West
Sussex PO18 0RT
T: (01243) 535245

WEST FARLEIGH
Kent

7 & 8 St Helens Cottages
Rating Applied For
St Helens Lane, West Farleigh,
Maidstone, Kent ME15
T: (01622) 720263 &
(01732) 770070

Wynngarth Farmhouse ◆◆◆
Lower Road, West Farleigh,
Maidstone, Kent ME15 0PF
T: (01622) 812616
F: (01622) 812616

WEST HARTING
West Sussex

Three Quebec ◆◆◆
West Harting, Petersfield,
Hampshire GU31 5PG
T: (01730) 825386
E: steve3quebec@sofarnet.co.uk

WEST HOATHLY
West Sussex

Stonelands West Lodge ◆◆◆
Ardingly Road, West Hoathly,
East Grinstead, West Sussex
RH19 4RA
T: (01342) 715372

WEST HORSLEY
Surrey

Silkmore
◆◆◆◆ SILVER AWARD
Silkmore Lane, West Horsley,
Guildford, Surrey KT24 6JQ
T: (01483) 282042 & 284109
F: (01483) 284109
E: ckimpton@btclick.com

WEST MALLING
Kent

Appledene ◆◆◆◆
164 Norman Road, West
Malling, Kent ME19 6RW
T: (01732) 842071
F: (01732) 842071

The Barn ◆◆◆◆
16 West Street, West Malling,
Kent ME19 6QX
T: (01732) 846512
F: (01732) 846512

Westfields Farm ◆◆◆
St Vincents Lane, Addington,
West Malling, Kent ME19 5BW
T: (01732) 843209

WEST PECKHAM
Kent

Adams Well Cottage ◆◆◆
Forge Lane, Gover Hill, West
Peckham, Maidstone, Kent
ME18 5JR
T: (01732) 851729 &
07790 969069
F: (01732) 851729
E: adamswell@msn.com

WEST WITTERING
West Sussex

The Beach House ◆◆◆
Rookwood Road, West
Wittering, Chichester, West
Sussex PO20 8LT
T: (01243) 514800
F: (01243) 514798

Thornton Cottage ◆◆◆◆
Chichester Road, West
Wittering, Chichester, West
Sussex PO20 8QA
T: (01243) 512470
F: (01243) 512470
E: thornton@b-andb.fsbusiness.
co.uk

WESTERHAM
Kent

Worples Field ◆◆◆◆
Farley Common, Westerham,
Kent TN16 1UB
T: (01959) 562869
E: marr@worplesfield.com
I: www.worplesfield.com

WESTWELL
Kent

Dean Court Farm ◆◆◆
Challock Lane, Westwell,
Ashford, Kent TN25 4NH
T: (01233) 712924

WHITSTABLE
Kent

Alliston House ◆◆◆
1 Joy Lane, Whitstable, Kent
CT5 4LS
T: (01227) 779066 &
07702 203188

The Cherry Garden ◆◆◆
62 Joy Lane, Whitstable, Kent
CT5 4LT
T: (01227) 266497

Hotel Continental ◆◆◆
29 Beach Walk, Whitstable, Kent
CT5 2BP
T: (01227) 280280
F: (01227) 280257
E: DEC2@UKC.AC.UK

Copeland House ◆◆◆
4 Island Wall, Whitstable, Kent
CT15 1EP
T: (01227) 266207
F: (01227) 266207

Marine ◆◆◆
Marine Parade, Tankerton,
Whitstable, Kent CT5 2BE
T: (01227) 272672
F: (01227) 264721
E: marine@shepherd-neame.co.
uk
I: www.shepherd-neame.co.uk

Marine Lodge ◆◆◆
82 Marine Parade, Tankerton,
Whitstable, Kent CT5 2BA
T: (01227) 273707
E: Christine.Tilley@Tesco.net

Windyridge Guest House
◆◆◆◆
Wraik Hill, Whitstable, Kent
CT5 3BY
T: (01227) 263506
F: (01227) 771191

WILLESBOROUGH
Kent

Rosemary House ◆◆◆
94 Church Road, Willesborough,
Ashford, Kent TN24 0JG
T: (01233) 625215

WINCHELSEA
East Sussex

Cleveland Place ◆◆◆
Friars Road, Winchelsea, East
Sussex TN36 4ED
T: (01797) 225358

The New Inn ◆◆◆
German Street, Winchelsea, East
Sussex TN36 4EN
T: (01797) 226252

St Anthonys ◆◆◆◆
Castle Street, Winchelsea, East
Sussex TN36 4EL
T: (01797) 226255

Wickham Manor ◆◆◆
Pannel Lane, Winchelsea, East
Sussex TN36 4AG
T: (01797) 226216
F: (01797) 226216

Winchelsea Lodge Motel &
Restaurant ◆◆◆◆
Hastings Road (A259),
Winchelsea, East Sussex
TN36 4AD
T: (01797) 226211
F: (01797) 226312

WINGHAM
Kent

Dambridge Oast ◆◆◆◆
Staple Road, Wingham,
Canterbury, Kent CT3 1LU
T: (01227) 720082 &
07889 707828
F: (01227) 720082
E: pagoast@primex.co.uk
I: homepages.primex.co.
uk/§pagoast

WISBOROUGH GREEN
West Sussex

Lower Sparr Farm ◆◆◆◆
Skiff Lane, Wisborough Green,
Billingshurst, West Sussex
RH14 0AA
T: (01403) 820465
F: (01403) 820678
E: sclater@lowersparrbb.f9.co.
uk

Meadowbank House ◆◆◆
Petworth Road, Wisborough
Green, Billingshurst, West
Sussex RH14 0BJ
T: (01403) 700482

WISTON
West Sussex

Farm House Bed & breakfast
◆◆◆
Buncton Manor Farm, Wiston,
Steyning, West Sussex
BN44 3DD
T: (01903) 812736
F: (01903) 814838
E: bandb@bunctonmanor.
prestel.co.uk

WITTERSHAM
Kent

Knoll House ◆◆◆
Acton Lane, Wittersham,
Tenterden, Kent TN30 7HN
T: (01797) 270258

Oxney Farm ◆◆◆◆◆
Moons Green, Wittersham,
Tenterden, Kent TN30 7PS
T: (01797) 270558 &
07850 219830
F: (01797) 270958
E: oxneyf@globalnet.co.uk
I: www.users.globalnet.co.
uk/§oxneyf

WOKING
Surrey

Amberhurst ◆◆◆
Hollybank Road, Hook Heath,
Woking, Surrey GU22 0JN
T: (01483) 762748
F: (01483) 762748

Grantchester ◆◆◆
Boughton Hall Avenue, Send,
Woking, Surrey GU23 7DF
T: (01483) 225383
F: (01483) 211594
E: gwinterbor@aol.com

Swallow Barn ◆◆◆
Milford Green, Chobham,
Woking, Surrey GU24 8AU
T: (01276) 856030 &
07768 972904
F: (01276) 856030
E: swallowbarn@compuserve.
com

WOODCHURCH
Kent

Little Tiffenden Farm ◆◆◆◆
Redbrook Street, Woodchurch,
Ashford, Kent TN26 3QU
T: (01233) 860238
F: (01233) 860238
E: accommodation@
lt-tiffendenfarm.ndirect.co.uk
I: www.lt-tiffendenfarm.ndirect.
co.uk

Shirkoak Farm
◆◆◆◆ SILVER AWARD
Bethersden Road, Woodchurch,
Ashford, Kent TN26 3PZ
T: (01233) 860056
F: (01233) 861402
E: shirkoakfarm@aol.com
I: www.shirkoakfarm.com

WORTH
Kent

The Blue Pigeons Inn ◆◆◆
The Street, Worth, Deal, Kent
CT14 0DE
T: (01304) 613245
F: (01304) 613245

WORTHING
West Sussex

Acacia Guest House ◆◆
5-7 Warwick Gardens, Worthing,
West Sussex BN11 1PE
T: (01903) 232995

The Beacons Hotel ◆◆◆◆
18 Shelley Road, Worthing, West
Sussex BN11 1TU
T: (01903) 230948
F: (01903) 230948

Blair House Hotel ◆◆◆◆
11 St Georges Road, Worthing,
West Sussex BN11 2DS
T: (01903) 234071
F: (01903) 234071
E: stay@blairhousehotel.
freeserve.co.uk

Bonchurch House ◆◆◆
1 Winchester Road, Worthing,
West Sussex BN11 4DJ
T: (01903) 202492
F: (01903) 202492
I: www.smoothhound.co.
uk/hotels/bonchurch.html

The Brunswick ◆◆
Thorn Road, Worthing, West
Sussex BN11 3ND
T: (01903) 202141
E: b&b@brunswick.freeserve.co.
uk
I: www.brunswick.fsnet.co.uk

Bute House ◆◆◆◆
325 Brighton Road, Worthing,
West Sussex BN11 2HP
T: (01903) 210247
F: (01903) 208109

Camelot House ◆◆
20 Gannon Road, Worthing,
West Sussex BN11 2DT
T: (01903) 204334

Delmar Hotel ◆◆◆
1-2 New Parade, Worthing,
West Sussex BN11 2BQ
T: (01903) 211834 &
07889 890393
F: (01903) 219052
I: www.SmoothHound.co.
uk/hotels/delmar.html

Haytor Guest House ◆◆◆
5 Salisbury Road, Worthing,
West Sussex BN11 1RB
T: (01903) 235287
F: (01903) 235287

High Beach
Rating Applied For
201 Brighton Road, Worthing,
West Sussex BN11 2EX
T: (01903) 236389

High Trees Guest House
◆◆◆◆
2 Warwick Gardens, Worthing,
West Sussex BN11 1PE
T: (01903) 236668

The Lantern Hotel ◆◆◆
54 Shelley Road, Worthing, West
Sussex BN11 4BX
T: (01903) 238476
F: (01903) 602429
♿

Manor Guest House ◆◆◆
100 Broadwater Road,
Worthing, West Sussex
BN14 8AN
T: (01903) 236028 &
07880 557615
F: (01903) 230404
E: stay@manorguesthouse.
fsnet.co.uk

Marcroft ◆◆◆◆
17 St Georges Road, Worthing,
West Sussex BN11 2DS
T: (01903) 233626
◎

Marina Guest House ◆◆◆◆
191 Brighton Road, Worthing,
West Sussex BN11 2EX
T: (01903) 207844
◎

Marine View Hotel ◆◆
111 Marine Parade, Worthing,
West Sussex BN11 3QG
T: (01903) 238413
F: (01903) 238630

Merton House ◆◆◆
96 Broadwater Road, Worthing,
West Sussex BN14 8AW
T: (01903) 238222
F: (01903) 238222
◎

The Moorings Hotel ◆◆◆◆
4 Selden Road, Worthing, West
Sussex BN11 2LL
T: (01903) 208882
F: (01903) 236878

Oakville Guest House ◆◆◆◆
13 Wyke Avenue, Worthing,
West Sussex BN11 1PB
T: (01903) 205026
F: (01903) 205026

Olinda Guest House ◆◆◆◆
199 Brighton Road, Worthing,
West Sussex BN11 2EX
T: (01903) 206114

Park House Guest House
◆◆◆◆
4 St Georges Road, Worthing,
West Sussex BN11 2DS
T: (01903) 525354 & 207939
F: (01903) 207939

Pebble Beach ◆◆◆
281 Brighton Road, Worthing,
West Sussex BN11 2HG
T: (01903) 210766
F: (01903) 210766

Queens Lodge ◆◆◆◆
2 Queens Road, Worthing, West
Sussex BN11 3LX
T: (01903) 205519

Rosedale Guest House ◆◆◆◆
12 Bath Road, Worthing, West
Sussex BN11 3NU
T: (01903) 233181

St Albans Guest House ◆◆◆◆
143 Brighton Road, Worthing,
West Sussex BN11 2EU
T: (01903) 206623
E: precipitator@aol.com
◎

School House ◆◆◆◆
11 Ambrose Place, Worthing,
West Sussex BN11 1PZ
T: (01903) 206823
F: (01903) 821902

Sea Lodge ◆◆◆
183 Brighton Road, Worthing,
West Sussex BN11 2EX
T: (01903) 201214
F: (01903) 201214

Seaward House ◆◆◆◆
30 Windsor Road, Worthing,
West Sussex BN11 2LX
T: (01903) 230484
F: (01903) 230484

Southdene Guest House
Rating Applied For
41 Warwick Gardens, Worthing,
West Sussex BN11 1PF
T: (01903) 232909

Tamara Guest House ◆◆◆
19 Alexandra Road, Worthing,
West Sussex BN11 2DX
T: (01903) 520332

Tudor Guest House ◆◆◆
5 Windsor Road, Worthing, West
Sussex BN11 2LU
T: (01903) 210265 & 202042

Vila Anjo Da Guarda
Rating Applied For
19 Malvern Close, Worthing,
West Sussex BN11 2HE
T: (01903) 233002 & 0777 921
7734

Woodlands Guest House ◆◆◆
20-22 Warwick Gardens,
Worthing, West Sussex
BN11 1PF
T: (01903) 233557 & 231957
F: (01903) 536925
E: woodlandsghse@cwcom.net
I: www.woodlands20-22.
freeserve.co.uk

| WROTHAM |
| Kent |

Hillside House ◆◆◆
Gravesend Road, Wrotham,
Sevenoaks, Kent TN15 7JH
T: (01732) 822564
E: clive@bxoteham.freeserve.co.
uk

| WYE |
| Kent |

Farriers ◆◆◆
Little Olantigh Road, Wye,
Ashford, Kent TN25 5DQ
T: (01233) 813105

Mistral ◆◆◆
3 Oxenturn Road, Wye, Ashford,
Kent TN25 5BH
T: (01233) 813011
F: (01233) 813011
E: geoff@chapman.invictanet.
co.uk
I: www.wye.org

| YAPTON |
| West Sussex |

Hawthorn Lodge
Rating Applied For
North End Road, Yapton,
Arundel, West Sussex BN18 0DU
T: (01243) 551526

FINDING ACCOMMODATION
IS AS EASY AS *1 2 3*

Where to Stay makes it quick and easy to find a place to stay.
There are several ways to use this guide.

1 Town Index

The town index, starting on page 748, lists all the places with
accommodation featured in the regional sections. The index
gives a page number where you can find full accommodation
and contact details.

2 Colour Maps

All the place names in black on the colour maps at the front
have an entry in the regional sections. Refer to the town index
for the page number where you will find one or more
establishments offering accommodation in your chosen
town or village.

3 Accommodation listing

Contact details for **all** English Tourism Council assessed
accommodation throughout England, together with their
national Diamond rating is given in the listing section of this guide.
Establishments with a full entry in the regional sections are
shown in blue. Look in the town index for the page number on
which their full entry appears.

Information

The
Quality Assurance Scheme

English Tourism Council

◆ ◆ ◆
GUEST ACCOMMODATION

A rating you can trust

When you're looking for a place to stay, you need a rating system you can trust. The English Tourism Council's ratings are your clear guide to what to expect, in an easy-to-understand form. Properties are visited annually by our trained impartial assessors, so you can have confidence that your accommodation has been thoroughly checked and rated for quality before you make a booking.

Using a simple One to Five Diamond rating, the system puts a much greater emphasis on quality and is based on research which shows exactly what consumers are looking for when choosing accommodation.

"Guest Accommodation" covers a wide variety of serviced accommodation for which England is renowned, including guesthouses, bed and breakfasts, inns and farmhouses. Establishments are rated from one to five Diamonds. The same minimum requirement for facilities and services applies to all Guest Accommodation from One to Five Diamonds. Progressively higher levels of quality and customer care must be provided for each of the One to Five Diamond ratings. The rating reflects the unique character of Guest Accommodation, and covers areas such as cleanliness, service and hospitality, bedrooms, bathrooms and food quality.

Look out, too, for the English Tourism Council's Gold and Silver Awards, which are awarded to those establishments which not only achieve the overall quality required for their Diamond rating, but also reach the highest levels of quality in those specific areas which guests identify as being really important for them. They will reflect the quality of comfort and cleanliness you'll find in the bedrooms and bathrooms and the quality of service you'll enjoy throughout your stay.

Diamond ratings are your sign of quality assurance, giving you the confidence to book the accommodation that meets your expectations.

What to expect at each rating level

The Diamond ratings for Guest Accommodation reflect visitor expectations of this sector. The quality of what is provided is more important to visitors than a wide range of facilities and services. Therefore, the same minimum requirement for facilities and services applies to all Guest Accommodation from One to Five Diamonds, while progressively higher levels of quality and customer care must be provided for each of the One to Five Diamond ratings.

- **At One Diamond Guest Accommodation, you will find:**

Clean and comfortable accommodation offering, as a minimum, a full cooked or continental breakfast. Other meals, where provided, will be freshly prepared. You will have a comfortable bed, with clean bed linen and towels and fresh soap. Adequate heating and hot water available at reasonable times for baths or showers at no extra charge. An acceptable overall level of quality and helpful service.

- **At Two Diamond Guest Accommodation, you will find** (in addition to what is provided at One Diamond)**:**

A higher level of quality and comfort, with a geater emphasis on guest care in all areas.

- **At Three Diamond Guest Accommodation, you will find** (in addition to what is provided at Two Diamond)**:**

A very good overall level of quality. For example, good quality, comfortable bedrooms; well maintained, practical décor; a good choice of quality items available for breakfast; other meals, where provided, will be freshly cooked from good quality ingredients. A greater degree of comfort provided for you, with good levels of customer care.

- **At Four Diamond Guest Accommodation, you will find** (in addition to what is provided at Three Diamond)**:**

A very good overall level of quality in all areas and customer care showing very good levels of attention to your needs.

- At Five Diamond Guest Accommodation, you will find (in addition to what is provided at Four Diamond):

An excellent overall level of quality. For example, ample space with a degree of luxury, an excellent quality bed, high quality furniture, excellent interior design. Breakfast offering a wide choice of high quality fresh ingredients; other meals, where provided, featuring fresh, seasonal, and often local ingredients. Excellent levels of customer care, anticipating your needs.

NB. Ensuite and private bathrooms contribute to the quality score at all Diamond levels. Please check when booking or see entry details.

Awaiting confirmation of rating

At the time of going to press some establishments featured in this guide had not yet been assessed for their rating for the year 2001 and so their new rating could not be included.

For your information, the most up-to-date information regarding these establishments' ratings is in the listings pages at the back of this guide.

General
Advice & Information

MAKING A BOOKING

When enquiring about accommodation, make sure you check prices and other important details. You will also need to state your requirements, clearly and precisely - for example:

- **Arrival and departure dates**, with acceptable alternatives if appropriate.
- **The type of accommodation you need;** for example, room with twin beds, private bathroom.
- **The terms you want;** for example, room only, bed and breakfast, half board, full board.
- **If you have children with you;** their ages, whether you want them to share your room or be next door, any other special requirements, such as a cot.
- **Particular requirements you may have,** such as a special diet.

Booking by letter

Misunderstandings can easily happen over the telephone, so we strongly advise you to confirm your booking in writing if there is time.

Please note that the English Tourism Council does not make reservations - you should write direct to the accommodation.

DEPOSITS

If you make your reservation weeks or months in advance, you will probably be asked for a deposit. The amount will vary according to the time of year, the number of people in your party and how long you plan to stay. The deposit will then be deducted from the final bill when you leave.

PAYMENT ON ARRIVAL

Some establishments may ask you to pay for your room on arrival if you have not booked it in advance. This is especially likely to happen if you arrive late and have little or no luggage.

If you are asked to pay on arrival, it is a good idea to see your room first, to make sure it meets your requirements.

CANCELLATIONS

Legal contract

When you accept accommodation that is offered to you, by telephone or in writing, you enter a legally binding contract with the proprietor.

This means that if you cancel your booking, fail to take up the accommodation or leave early, the proprietor may be entitled to compensation if he cannot re-let for all or a good part of the booked period. You will probably forfeit any deposit you have paid, and may well be asked for an additional payment.

The proprietor cannot make a claim until after the booked period, however, and during that time every effort should be made by the proprietor to re-let the accommodation.

If there is a dispute it is sensible for both sides to seek legal advice on the matter.

If you do have to change your travel plans, it is in your own interests to let the proprietors know in writing as soon as possible, to give them a chance to re-let your accommodation.

And remember, if you book by telephone and are asked for your credit card number, you should check whether the proprietor intends charging your credit card account should you later cancel your reservation. A proprietor should not be able to charge your credit card account with a cancellation unless he or she has made this clear at the time of your booking and you have agreed. However, to avoid later disputes, we suggest you check with the proprietor whether he or she intends to charge your credit card account if you cancel.

INSURANCE

A travel or holiday insurance policy will safeguard you if you have to cancel or change your holiday plans. You can arrange a policy quite cheaply through your insurance company or travel agent. Some hotels also offer their own insurance schemes.

ARRIVING LATE

If you know you will be arriving late in the evening, it is a good idea to say so when you book. If you are delayed on your way, a telephone call to say that you will be late will help prevent any problems when you arrive.

SERVICE CHARGES AND TIPPING

These days many places levy service charges automatically. If they do, they must clearly say so in their offer of accommodation, at the time of booking. Then the service charge becomes part of the legal contract when you accept the offer of accommodation.

If a service charge is levied automatically, there is no need to tip the staff, unless they provide some exceptional service. The usual tip for meals is ten per cent of the total bill.

TELEPHONE CHARGES

Guest accommodation establishments can set their own charges for telephone calls made through their switchboard or from direct-dial telephones in bedrooms. These charges are often much higher than telephone companies' standard charges (to defray the cost of providing the service).

Comparing costs

It is a condition of the quality assurance scheme, that unit charges for using the telephone are on display, by the phones or with the room information. But in practice it is not always easy to compare these charges with standard telephone rates. Before using the telephone for long-distance calls, you may decide to ask how the charges compare.

SECURITY OF VALUABLES

You can deposit your valuables with the proprietor or manager during your stay, and we recommend you do this as a sensible precaution. Make sure you obtain a receipt for them.

Some places do not accept articles for safe custody, and in that case it is wisest to keep your valuables with you.

Disclaimer

Some proprietors put up a notice which disclaims liability for property brought on to their premises by a guest. In fact, they can only restrict their liability to a minimum laid down by law (The Hotel Proprietors Act 1956).

Under that Act, a proprietor is liable for the value of the loss or damage to any property (except a motor car or its contents) of a guest who has engaged overnight accommodation, but if the proprietor has the notice on display as prescribed under that Act, liability is limited to £50 for one article and a total of £100 for any one guest. The notice must be prominently displayed in the reception area or main entrance. These limits do not apply to valuables you have deposited with the proprietor for safe-keeping, or to property lost through the default, neglect of wilful act of the proprietor or his staff.

BRINGING PETS TO ENGLAND

The quarantine laws have recently changed in England and a pilot Pet Travel Scheme (PETS) is currently in operation. Under this new scheme pet dogs are able to come into Britain from over 35 countries via certain sea, air and rail routes into England.

Dogs that have been resident in these countries for more than 6 months may enter the UK under the Pilot Scheme providing they are accompanied by the appropriate documentation.

For dogs to be able to enter the UK without quarantine under the PETS Pilot Scheme they will have to meet certain conditions and travel with the following documents: the Official PETS Certificate, a certificate of treatment against tapeworm and ticks and a declaration of residence.

For details of participating countries, routes, operators and further information about the PETS Pilot Scheme please contact the Ministry of Agriculture, Fisheries and Food, 1a Page Street, London SW1P 4PQ

Tel: +44 (0) 870 241 1710 Fax: +44 (0) 20 7904 6834
Email: pets@ahvg.maff.gsi.gov.uk, or visit their web
site at www.maff.gov.uk/animalh/quarantine

CODE OF CONDUCT

All the places featured in this guide have agreed to
observe the following Codes of Conduct:

1 To ensure high standards of courtesy and
   cleanliness, catering and service appropriate to
   the type of establishment.

2 To describe fairly to all visitors and prospective
   visitors the amenities, facilities and services
   provided by the establishment, whether by
   advertisement, brochure, word of mouth or
   any other means. To allow visitors to see
   accommodation, if requested, before booking.

3 To make clear to visitors exactly what is included
   in all prices quoted for accommodation, meals and
   refreshments, including service charges, taxes and
   other surcharges. Details of charges, if any, for
   heating or additional service of facilities should
   also be made clear.

4 To adhere to, and not to exceed, prices current at
   time of occupation for accommodation or other
   services.

5 To advise visitors at the time of booking, and
   subsequently of any change, if the accommodation
   offered is in an unconnected annexe, or similar, or
   by boarding out; and to indicate the location of
   such accommodation and any difference in comfort
   or amenities from accommodation in the main
   establishment.

6 To give each visitor, on request, details of payments
   due and a receipt if required.

7 To deal promptly and courteously with all enquiries,
   requests, reservations, correspondence and
   complaints from visitors.

8 To allow an English Tourism Council representative
   reasonable access to the establishment, on request,
   to confirm that the Code of Conduct is being
   observed.

COMMENTS AND COMPLAINTS

Guest accommodation and the law
Places that offer accommodation have legal and
statutory responsibilities to their customers, such as
providing information about prices, providing adequate
fire precautions and safeguarding valuables. Like other
businesses, they must also abide by the Trades
Description Acts 1968 and 1972 when they describe
their accommodation and facilities.

All the places featured in this guide have declared that
they do fulfil all applicable statutory obligations.

Information
The proprietors themselves supply the descriptions of
their establishments and other information for the
entries, and they pay to be included in the regional
sections of the guide. All the acommodation featured
in this guide has also been assessed or has applied for
assessment under the new quality assurance scheme.

The English Tourism Council cannot guarantee
accuracy of information in this guide, and accepts no
responsibility for any error or misrepresentation. All
liability for loss, disappointment, negligence or other
damage caused by reliance on the information
contained in this guide, or in the event of bankruptcy
or liquidation or cessation of trade of any company,
individual or firm mentioned, is hereby excluded.

We strongly recommend that you carefully check
prices and other details when you book your
accommodation.

Problems
Of course, we hope you will not have cause for
complaint, but problems do occur from time to time.

If you are dissatisfied with anything, make your
complaint to the management immediately. Then the
management can take action at once to investigate
the matter and put things right. The longer you leave a
complaint, the harder it is to deal with it effectively.

In certain circumstances, the English Tourism Council
may look into complaints. However, the Council has no
statutory control over establishments or their methods
of operating. The Council cannot become involved in
legal or contractual matters.

If you do have problems that have not been resolved
by the proprietor and which you would like to bring to
our attention, please write to: Quality Standards
Department, English Tourism Council, Thames Tower,
Black's Road, Hammersmith, London W6 9EL.

About the
Guide Entries

LOCATIONS

Places to stay are listed under the town, city or village where they are located. If a place is out in the countryside, you will find it listed under the nearest village or town.

Town names are listed alphabetically within each regional section of the guide, along with the name of the county or unitary authority they are in (see note on page 14), and their map reference.

Map references

These refer to the colour location maps at the front of the guide. The first figure shown is the map number, the following letter and figure indicate the grid reference on the map.

Some entries were included just before the guide went to press, so they do not appear on the maps.

Addresses

County names, which appear in the town headings, are not repeated in the entries. When you are writing, you should of course make sure you use the full address and postcode.

Telephone numbers

Telephone numbers are listed below the accommodation address for each entry. Area codes are shown in brackets.

PRICES

The prices shown in Where to Stay 2001 are only a general guide; they were supplied to us by proprietors in summer 2000. Remember, changes may occur after the guide goes to press, so we strongly advise you to check prices when you book your accommodation.

Prices are shown in pounds sterling and include VAT where applicable. Some places also include a service charge in their standard tariff so check this when you book.

Standardised method

There are many different ways of quoting prices for accommodation. We use a standardised method in the guide to allow you to compare prices. For example when we show:

Bed and breakfast, the prices shown are for overnight accommodation with breakfast, for single and double rooms.

The double-room price is for two people. If a double room is occupied by one person there is sometimes a reduction in price.

Halfboard, the prices shown are for room, breakfast and evening meal, per person per day.

Some places provide only a continental breakfast in the set price, and you may have to pay extra if you want a full English breakfast.

Checking prices

According to the law, hotels and guest accommodation with at least four bedrooms or eight beds must display their overnight accommodation charges in the reception area or entrance. In your own interests, do make sure you check prices and what they include.

Children's rates

You will find that many places charge a reduced rate for children especially if they share a room with their parents.

Some places charge the full rate, however, when a child occupies a room which might otherwise have been let to an adult.

The upper age limit for reductions for children varies from one hotel to another, so check this when you book.

Seasonal packages

Prices often vary through the year, and may be significantly lower outside peak holiday weeks. Many places offer special package rates - fully inclusive weekend breaks, for example - in the autumn, winter and spring.

You can get details of bargain packages from the establishment themselves, the Regional Tourist Boards or your local Tourist Information Centre (TIC).

Your local travel agent may also have information, and can help you make bookings.

BATHROOMS

Each accommodation entry shows you the number of en-suite and private bathrooms available, the number of private showers and the number of public bathrooms.

'En-suite bathroom' means the bath or shower and WC are contained behind the main door of the bedroom. 'Private bathroom' means a bath or shower and WC solely for the occupants of one bedroom, on the same floor, reasonably close and with a key provided. 'Private shower' means a shower en-suite with the bedroom but no WC.

Public bathrooms normally have a bath, sometimes with a shower attachment. If the availability of a bath is important to you, remember to check when you book.

MEALS

If an establishment serves evening meals, you will find the starting time and the last order times shown in the entry; some smaller places may ask you at breakfast or at midday whether you want an evening meal.

The prices shown in each entry are for bed and breakfast or half board, but many places also offer lunch, as you will see indicated in the entry.

OPENING PERIOD

All places are open for the months indicated in their entry.

SYMBOLS

The at-a-glance symbols included at the end of each entry show many of the services and facilities available at each place. You will find the key to these symbols on the back cover flap. Open out the flap and you can check the meanings of the symbols as you go.

ALCOHOLIC DRINKS

All the places listed in the guide are licensed to serve alcohol, unless the symbol ⬚ appears. The license may be restricted - to diners only, for example - so you may want to check this when you book.

SMOKING

Many places provide non-smoking areas - from no-smoking bedrooms and lounges to no-smoking sections of the restaurant. Some places prefer not to accommodate smokers, and in such cases the descriptions in each entry makes this clear.

PETS

Many places accept guests with dogs, but we do advise that you check this when you book, and ask if there are any extra charges or rules about exactly where your pet is allowed. The acceptance of dogs is not always extended to cats and it is strongly advised that cat owners contact the establishment well in advance. Some establishments do not accept pets at all. These places are indicated with the symbol ✗.

The quarantine laws have recently changed in England and pet dogs are able to come into Britain from selected European countries. For details of the Pet Travel Scheme (PETS) please turn to page 734.

CREDIT AND CHARGE CARDS

The credit and charge cards accepted by a place are listed in the entry following the letters CC.

If you do plan to pay by card, check that the establishment will take your card before you book.

Some proprietors will charge you a higher rate if you pay by credit card rather than cash or cheque. The difference is to cover the percentage paid by the proprietor to the credit card company.

If you are planning to pay by credit card, you may want to ask whether it would, in fact, be cheaper to pay by cheque or cash. When you book by telephone, you may be asked for your credit card number as 'confirmation'. But remember, the proprietor may then charge your credit card account if you cancel your booking. See under Cancellations on page 733.

CONFERENCES AND GROUPS

Places which cater for conferences and meetings are marked with the symbol ✠ (the number that follows the symbol shows the capacity). Rates are often negotiable, depending on the time of year, numbers of people involved and any special requirements you may have.

A selection of events for
2001

This is a selection of the many cultural, sporting and other events that will be taking place throughout England during 2001. Please note, as changes often occur after press date, it is advisable to confirm the date and location before travelling.

* Provisional at time of going to press.

January 2001

4-28 January
Holiday on Ice 2001: Xotica - A Journey to the Heart
Brighton Centre, Kings Road, Brighton, East Sussex
Contact: (0870) 900 9100

5-14 January
47th London International Boat Show
Earls Court Exhibition Centre, Warwick Road,
London SW5
Contact: (01784) 473377

6 January
Old Custom: Haxey Hood Game
The Village, Haxey, Doncaster, South Yorkshire
Contact: (01427) 752845

20-21 January
Motorbike 2001
Springfields Exhibition Centre, Camelgate,
Spalding, Lincolnshire
Contact: (01775) 724843

February 2001

1-3 February
Wakefield Rhubarb Trail and Festival of Rhubarb
Various venues, Wakefield, West Yorkshire
Contact: (01924) 305841

3-4 February
The 22nd Bristol Classic Car Show
The Royal Bath and West Showground,
Shepton Mallet, Somerset
Contact: (0117) 907 1000

15-17 February
Garrick Drama Festival
Civic Hall, Castle Dyke, Lichfield, Staffordshire
Contact: (01543) 308797

17-18 February*
Motorsport Day
Brooklands Museum, Brooklands Road,
Weybridge, Surrey
Contact: (01932) 857381

17-25 February
National Boat, Caravan and Leisure Show
National Exhibition Centre, Birmingham,
West Midlands
Contact: (024) 7622 1443

March 2001

1 March
Lancashire Food Festival
Accrington Town Hall, Accrington, Lancashire
Contact: (01254) 872595

8-11 March
Crufts 2001
National Exhibition Centre, Birmingham,
West Midlands

13-15 March
Cheltenham Gold Cup National Hunt Racing Festival
Cheltenham Racecourse, Cheltenham, Gloucestershire
Contact: (01242) 513014

25-28 March
Diesel Gala - GWR (Gloucestershire/Warwickshire)
The Railway Station, Toddington, Cheltenham,
Gloucestershire
Contact: (01242) 621405

April 2001

1 April-23 December*
Cornwall 2001 Festival of Steam and Invention
Various venues, Wakefield, West Yorkshire,
Contact: (01924) 305841

5-7 April
Grand National Festival
Aintree Racecourse, Ormskirk Road, Aintree,
Liverpool, Merseyside
Contact: (0151) 523 2600

8 April
World Dock Pudding Championship
Mytholmroyd Community Centre, Elphaborough,
Mytholmroyd, Hebden Bridge, West Yorkshire
Contact: (01422) 883023

13-20 April
Harrogate International Youth Music Festival
Various venues, Harrogate, North Yorkshire
Contact: (01306) 744360

15-16 April
Easter Egg Hunt
Crealy Park, Clyst St Mary, Exeter, Devon
Contact: (01395) 233200

28-29 April*
South West Custom and Classic Bike Show
The Royal Bath and West Showground,
Shepton Mallet, Somerset
Contact: (01749) 822222

May 2001

4-7 May
Hastings Traditional Jack in the Green Morris
Dance Festival
Various venues, Hastings, East Sussex
Contact: (01424) 716576

4-7 May*
Lincoln Folk Festival
The Lawn, Union Road, Lincoln, Lincolnshire
Contact: (01522) 523000

6-7 May
Bexhill 100 Festival of Motoring
Seafront, De La Warr Parade, Bexhill, East Sussex
Contact: (01424) 730564

9-13 May*
Royal Windsor Horse Show
Windsor Home Park, Datchet Road, Windsor, Berkshire
Contact: (01753) 860633

18 May-3 June
Bath International Music Festival
Various venues, Bath
Contact: (01225) 463362

26-28 May
Window on the World International Music Festival
North Shields Fishquay and Town, Tyne & Wear
Contact: (0191) 200 8909

28 May
Luton International Carnival
Town Centre and nearby, Luton, Bedfordshire
Contact: (01582) 877282

28 May
Northumberland County Show
Tynedale Park, Corbridge, Northumberland
Contact: (01697) 747848

June 2001

1 June
Robert Dover's Cotswold Olimpick Games
Dovers Hill, Weston Subedge, Chipping Campden,
Gloucestershire
Contact: (01384) 274041

1-30 June*
Royal Cornwall Show
Royal Cornwall Showground, Wadebridge, Cornwall
Contact: (01208) 812183

7-9 June
South of England Agricultural Show
South of England Showground, Ardingly,
Haywards Heath, West Sussex
Contact: (01444) 892700

8-10 June*
Wimborne Folk Festival 2001
Town Centre, Wimborne Minster, Dorset
Contact: (01202) 743465

9 June*
Trooping the Colour - The Queen's Birthday Parade
Horse Guards Parade, London, SW1
Contact: (020) 7414 2479

10 June
**Manchester to Blackpool Veteran Vintage
and Classic Car Run**
Granada Studios, Manchester, Greater Manchester
Contact: (01925) 791922

12-14 June*
Three Counties Show
Three Counties Showground, The Showground,
Malvern, Worcestershire
Contact: (01684) 584900

13-19 June*
Grosvenor House Art and Antiques Fair
Le Meridien Grosvenor House, Park Lane, London, W1A
Contact: (020) 7399 8100

22 June-1 July
Newcastle Hoppings
Town Moor, Newcastle upon Tyne, Tyne & Wear
Contact: (07831) 458774

24-30 June
Alnwick Medieval Fair
Market Square, Alnwick, Northumberland
Contact: (01665) 602552

25 June-8 July*
Wimbledon Lawn Tennis Championships
All England Lawn Tennis and Croquet Club,
Church Road, London, SW19
Contact: (020) 8946 2244

29 June-1 July*
Milton Keynes International Festival
Milton Keynes Theatre & Gallery,
Central Milton Keynes, Buckinghamshire
Contact: (01908) 610564

30 June
Toe Wrestling
Wetton, Staffordshire
Contact: (01782) 283377

July 2001

1-31 July*
The Balloon and Flower Festival
Southampton Common, Southampton, Hampshire
Contact: (023) 8083 2525

4-8 July
Henley Royal Regatta
Henley-on-Thames, Oxfordshire
Contact: (01491) 572153

7-8 July
Sunderland International Kite Festival
Northern Area Playing Fields, District 12, Washington,
Tyne & Wear
Contact: (0191) 514 1235

7 July-11 August*
Cookson Country Festival
Various venues, South Shields, Tyne & Wear
Contact: (0191) 427 1717

10-12 July
Great Yorkshire Show
Great Yorkshire Showground, Harrogate,
North Yorkshire
Contact: (01423) 541000

14 July
Tendring Hundred Show
Lawford House Park, Lawford, Manningtree, Essex
Contact: (01206) 571517

14-15 July
Tewkesbury Medieval Festival
The Gastons, Gloucester Road, Tewkesbury,
Gloucestershire
Contact: (01684) 297607

19-22 July
Golf: The Open Championship 2001
Royal Lytham St Annes Golf Club, Lytham St Annes,
Lancashire
Contact: (01253) 725610

20 July-15 September
Henry Wood Promenade Concerts
Royal Albert Hall, London, SW7
Contact: (020) 7765 5575

25 July
Sandringham Flower Show
Sandringham Park, Sandringham, Norfolk
Contact: (01485) 540860

27 July-5 August*
Stockton International Riverside Festival
Various venues, Stockton-on-Tees, Cleveland
Contact: (0191) 276 9911

28 July-4 August
Cowes Week
Cowes, Isle of Wight
Contact: (01703) 620006

August 2001

3-4 August
Living History Weekend
Northernhay Gardens, Exeter, Devon
Contact: (01392) 265118

4-11 August
Alnwick International Music and Dance Festival
Market Place, Alnwick, Northumberland
Contact: (01665) 606033

10-12 August
**Saltburn International Festival of Folk Music,
Dance and Song**
Various venues, Saltburn-by-the-Sea, Cleveland
Contact: (01947) 840928

11-18 August
Billingham International Folklore Festival
Town Centre, Queensway, Billingham, Cleveland
Contact: (01642) 553220

12-18 August*
Falmouth Regatta Week
Helford River, Carrick Roads and Falmouth Bay,
Cornwall
Contact: (01326) 211555

25-26 August
**Saddleworth Rushcart
Festival**
Various venues, Uppermill,
Saddleworth,
Greater Manchester
Contact: (01457) 834871

25-27 August
**Herstmonceux Castle
Medieval Festival**
Herstmonceux, Hailsham,
East Sussex
Contact: (0891) 172902

25-27 August*
The Chelmsford Spectacular
Hylands Park, Writtle, Chelmsford, Essex
Contact: (01245) 606985

26-27 August*
Notting Hill Carnival
Streets around Ladbroke Grove, London, W11
Contact: (020) 8964 0544

31 August-2 September
The Long Weekend – Clevedon's Annual Jazz Festival
Prince's Hall, Clevedon, North Somerset
Contact: (01275) 343210

September 2001

1-2 September
Berwick Military Tattoo
Berwick Barracks, Berwick-upon-Tweed,
Northumberland
Contact: (01289) 307426

1-30 September*
New Brighton Classic Car Show
Fort Perch Rock Car Park, off Kings Parade,
New Brighton, Wirral, Merseyside
Contact: (0151) 647 6780

EVENTS

*1-30 September**
Ocean Race – Round the World Yacht Race
Mayflower Park, Town Quay, Southampton, Hampshire
Contact: (023) 8083 2453

*14-23 September**
Southampton International Boat Show
Western Esplanade, Southampton, Hampshire
Contact: (01784) 473377

*26-30 September**
Horse of the Year Show
Wembley Arena, Middlesex
Contact: (020) 8900 9282

October 2001

*1-31 October**
Great North Run, The World's Biggest Half Marathon
Various venues throughout Tyne & Wear,
Newcastle upon Tyne, Tyne & Wear
Contact: (0191) 402 0016

13-27 October
Canterbury Festival
Various venues, Canterbury, Kent
Contact: (01227) 452853

*21 October**
Trafalgar Day Parade – The Sea Cadet Corps
Trafalgar Square, London, WC2
Contact: (020) 7928 8978

November 2001

*4 November**
London to Brighton Veteran Car Run
Hyde Park, London, W2
Contact: (01753) 681736

4 November
Old Custom: Rolling of the Tar Barrels
Town Centre, Ottery St Mary, Devon
Contact: (01404) 813964

*10 November**
Lord Mayor's Show
City of London, London
Contact: (020) 7606 3030

*11 November**
Remembrance Day Service and Parade
Cenotaph, Whitehall, London, SW1
Contact: (020) 7273 3498

16-25 November
International Guitar Festival of Great Britain
Various venues, Wirral, Merseyside
Contact: (0151) 666 5060

17 November-23 December
Thursford Christmas Spectacular
Thursford Green, Fakenham, Norfolk
Contact: (01328) 878477

21 November-2 December
Huddersfield Contemporary Music Festival
Various venues, Huddersfield
Contact: (01484) 425082

December 2001

6-13 December
Victorian Christmas in Maldon
High Street, Maldon, Essex

24 December
Old Custom: Tolling the Devil's Knell
All Saints Parish Church, Rishworth Road,
Dewsbury, West Yorkshire
Contact: (01484) 223200

31 December
The Snow Ball – New Years Eve Party
Sheffield Ski Village, Parkwood Springs,
Sheffield, South Yorkshire
Contact: (0114) 276 9459

USE YOUR *i*'s

There are more than 550 Tourist Information Centres throughout England offering friendly help with accommodation and holiday ideas as well as suggestions of places to visit and things to do.

You'll find TIC addresses in the local Phone Book.

www.travelengland.org.uk

Log on to travelengland.org.uk and discover something different around every corner. Meander through pages for ideas of places to visit and things to do. Spend time in each region and discover the diversity - from busy vibrant cities to rural village greens; rugged peaks to gentle rolling hills; dramatic coastline to idyllic sandy beaches. England might be a small country but it is brimming with choice and opportunity. Visit www.travelengland.org.uk and see for yourself.

 England

Distance Chart

The distances between towns on the chart below are given to the nearest mile, and are measured along routes based on the quickest travelling time, making maximum use of motorways or dual-carriageway roads. The chart is based upon information supplied by the Automobile Association.

To calculate the distance in kilometres multiply the mileage by 1.6

For example: Brighton to Dover
82 miles x 1.6
=131.2 kilometres

Distances (in miles) between towns. Each row lists the distances from the town named at the end of the row to every town listed above it, read left to right (Aberdeen, Aberystwyth, Barnstaple, Birmingham, Brighton, Bristol, Cambridge, Cardiff, Carlisle, Carmarthen, Colchester, Dorchester, Dover, Edinburgh, Exeter, Fort William, Glasgow, Gloucester, Guildford, Holyhead, Hull, Inverness, Kendal, Leeds, Lincoln, Liverpool, Maidstone, Manchester, Middlesbrough, Newcastle, Norwich, Nottingham, Oxford, Penzance, Perth, Plymouth, Sheffield, Southampton, Stranraer, Taunton, York, London).

```
468 — Aberystwyth
603 214 — Barnstaple
431 124 180 — Birmingham
605 288 208 171 — Brighton
513 128 99 90 169 — Bristol
462 215 267 97 120 170 — Cambridge
531 110 127 109 201 44 203 — Cardiff
231 236 372 199 375 282 257 300 — Carlisle
513 48 190 171 264 106 266 67 282 — Carmarthen
516 289 292 171 112 195 48 227 310 290 — Colchester
595 206 94 172 119 62 179 119 363 182 206 — Dorchester
587 325 273 207 82 206 124 238 400 301 116 200 — Dover
125 335 470 298 473 380 333 398 98 381 385 462 458 — Edinburgh
585 196 53 162 175 82 249 109 353 172 274 55 245 453 — Exeter
156 446 581 409 584 491 466 509 209 491 518 573 590 133 563 — Fort William
147 333 468 296 472 379 353 397 96 379 405 461 478 49 451 102 — Glasgow
479 111 125 56 155 35 150 61 247 124 171 117 192 347 107 456 343 — Gloucester
563 224 175 128 44 106 91 138 332 201 103 97 97 432 147 541 428 99 — Guildford
459 101 339 167 343 250 259 201 227 149 333 332 369 327 322 436 323 215 300 — Holyhead
375 228 321 140 258 231 138 249 170 312 191 313 262 247 303 379 266 196 239 219 — Hull
106 494 630 457 633 540 514 558 257 540 566 622 639 174 505 66 169 574 591 485 428 — Inverness
279 190 325 153 329 236 245 254 47 236 319 318 355 147 308 256 143 201 286 181 164 305 — Kendal
331 174 302 121 263 212 146 230 126 267 200 294 271 205 308 335 219 154 235 165 60 383 71 — Leeds
387 199 276 89 216 186 95 204 182 267 147 245 220 258 258 391 278 151 173 204 46 439 176 72 — Lincoln
357 110 274 102 277 184 193 202 126 163 268 266 304 225 256 335 222 150 235 101 128 383 79 74 140 — Liverpool
548 286 234 168 50 167 85 199 361 262 77 161 41 419 206 570 458 153 58 329 223 619 315 233 181 263 — Maidstone
356 134 261 89 264 171 160 189 123 180 212 253 291 223 243 332 219 137 222 125 97 381 77 44 85 35 251 — Manchester
276 245 357 177 318 268 198 286 95 291 251 350 322 147 340 280 191 233 276 236 89 308 84 63 123 145 283 115 — Middlesbrough
234 126 388 208 349 299 229 317 60 322 282 381 353 106 371 239 154 264 307 267 142 266 102 94 154 176 314 46 38 — Newcastle
488 277 329 159 171 233 63 264 282 327 61 241 175 359 311 491 379 212 162 320 150 540 276 173 104 241 135 186 223 254 — Norwich
393 162 234 54 195 144 86 163 188 226 139 226 218 265 216 397 284 110 153 178 92 446 164 74 38 112 179 71 129 160 119 — Nottingham
503 159 170 68 109 73 81 105 271 168 124 115 146 371 152 480 367 48 67 239 189 529 225 171 130 173 106 161 226 257 145 103 — Oxford
697 308 108 274 287 194 361 221 465 284 386 167 357 565 111 674 562 219 259 433 414 723 419 396 369 367 317 355 451 482 423 328 264 — Penzance
87 382 518 345 521 428 402 446 145 428 454 510 527 42 500 102 62 393 478 373 315 114 193 268 327 271 487 266 192 151 428 334 418 611 — Perth
628 239 67 205 218 125 292 152 396 215 316 98 288 496 45 605 492 150 190 364 345 654 350 326 300 298 248 286 382 413 354 259 195 77 542 — Plymouth
365 167 272 76 233 182 122 201 159 264 176 264 247 236 254 368 255 148 191 158 66 417 125 36 47 79 207 39 100 131 147 44 141 366 281 297 — Sheffield
570 225 142 135 66 106 131 138 339 201 159 53 152 439 109 548 435 100 49 307 257 596 292 238 197 241 112 228 293 324 193 171 67 221 484 152 208 — Southampton
232 342 478 305 481 388 363 406 106 388 415 470 487 133 460 188 86 344 445 405 333 276 258 288 231 448 226 201 163 388 294 378 572 146 503 265 446 — Stranraer
554 165 50 132 160 51 218 79 323 142 243 45 224 423 32 532 419 77 126 291 272 581 276 253 227 225 184 212 308 339 280 186 121 144 469 75 223 94 429 — Taunton
322 202 315 134 276 225 155 243 117 248 209 307 280 193 297 326 213 191 233 193 38 374 91 24 80 103 240 72 50 89 180 86 184 409 238 340 58 251 223 266 — York
544 238 216 120 59 120 60 152 313 215 61 128 79 413 198 522 409 102 30 281 186 571 266 198 143 215 39 202 253 284 115 131 56 310 458 241 168 80 419 167 211 — London
```

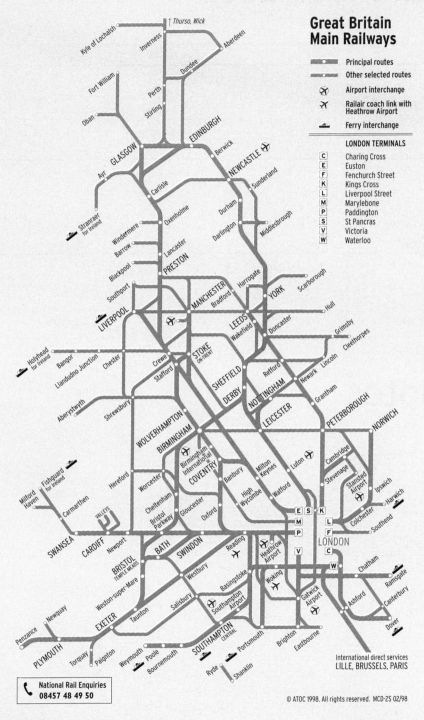

Great Britain Main Railways

Principal routes
Other selected routes
Airport interchange
Railair coach link with Heathrow Airport
Ferry interchange

LONDON TERMINALS

C	Charing Cross
E	Euston
F	Fenchurch Street
K	Kings Cross
L	Liverpool Street
M	Marylebone
P	Paddington
S	St Pancras
V	Victoria
W	Waterloo

International direct services
LILLE, BRUSSELS, PARIS

National Rail Enquiries
08457 48 49 50

© ATOC 1998. All rights reserved. MCD-2S 02/98

01/MRE/1134

Calendar 2001

JANUARY
M	T	W	T	F	S	S
1	2	3	4	5	6	7
8	9	10	11	12	13	14
15	16	17	18	19	20	21
22	23	24	25	26	27	28
29	30	31				

FEBRUARY
M	T	W	T	F	S	S
			1	2	3	4
5	6	7	8	9	10	11
12	13	14	15	16	17	18
19	20	21	22	23	24	25
26	27	28				

MARCH
M	T	W	T	F	S	S
			1	2	3	4
5	6	7	8	9	10	11
12	13	14	15	16	17	18
19	20	21	22	23	24	25
26	27	28	29	30	31	

APRIL
M	T	W	T	F	S	S
30						1
2	3	4	5	6	7	8
9	10	11	12	13	14	15
16	17	18	19	20	21	22
23	24	25	26	27	28	29

MAY
M	T	W	T	F	S	S
	1	2	3	4	5	6
7	8	9	10	11	12	13
14	15	16	17	18	19	20
21	22	23	24	25	26	27
28	29	30	31			

JUNE
M	T	W	T	F	S	S
				1	2	3
4	5	6	7	8	9	10
11	12	13	14	15	16	17
18	19	20	21	22	23	24
25	26	27	28	29	30	

JULY
M	T	W	T	F	S	S
30	31					1
2	3	4	5	6	7	8
9	10	11	12	13	14	15
16	17	18	19	20	21	22
23	24	25	26	27	28	29

AUGUST
M	T	W	T	F	S	S
		1	2	3	4	5
6	7	8	9	10	11	12
13	14	15	16	17	18	19
20	21	22	23	24	25	26
27	28	29	30	31		

SEPTEMBER
M	T	W	T	F	S	S
					1	2
3	4	5	6	7	8	9
10	11	12	13	14	15	16
17	18	19	20	21	22	23
24	25	26	27	28	29	30

OCTOBER
M	T	W	T	F	S	S
1	2	3	4	5	6	7
8	9	10	11	12	13	14
15	16	17	18	19	20	21
22	23	24	25	26	27	28
29	30	31				

NOVEMBER
M	T	W	T	F	S	S
			1	2	3	4
5	6	7	8	9	10	11
12	13	14	15	16	17	18
19	20	21	22	23	24	25
26	27	28	29	30		

DECEMBER
M	T	W	T	F	S	S
31					1	2
3	4	5	6	7	8	9
10	11	12	13	14	15	16
17	18	19	20	21	22	23
24	25	26	27	28	29	30

Notes

Calendar 2002

JANUARY								FEBRUARY								MARCH								APRIL						
M	T	W	T	F	S	S		M	T	W	T	F	S	S		M	T	W	T	F	S	S		M	T	W	T	F	S	S
	1	2	3	4	5	6						1	2	3						1	2	3		1	2	3	4	5	6	7
7	8	9	10	11	12	13		4	5	6	7	8	9	10		4	5	6	7	8	9	10		8	9	10	11	12	13	14
14	15	16	17	18	19	20		11	12	13	14	15	16	17		11	12	13	14	15	16	17		15	16	17	18	19	20	21
21	22	23	24	25	26	27		18	19	20	21	22	23	24		18	19	20	21	22	23	24		22	23	24	25	26	27	28
28	29	30	31					25	26	27	28					25	26	27	28	29	30	31		29	30					

MAY								JUNE								JULY								AUGUST						
M	T	W	T	F	S	S		M	T	W	T	F	S	S		M	T	W	T	F	S	S		M	T	W	T	F	S	S
		1	2	3	4	5							1	2		1	2	3	4	5	6	7					1	2	3	4
6	7	8	9	10	11	12		3	4	5	6	7	8	9		8	9	10	11	12	13	14		5	6	7	8	9	10	11
13	14	15	16	17	18	19		10	11	12	13	14	15	16		15	16	17	18	19	20	21		12	13	14	15	16	17	18
20	21	22	23	24	25	26		17	18	19	20	21	22	23		22	23	24	25	26	27	28		19	20	21	22	23	24	25
27	28	29	30	31				24	25	26	27	28	29	30		29	30	31						26	27	28	29	30	31	

SEPTEMBER								OCTOBER								NOVEMBER								DECEMBER						
M	T	W	T	F	S	S		M	T	W	T	F	S	S		M	T	W	T	F	S	S		M	T	W	T	F	S	S
30						1			1	2	3	4	5	6						1	2	3		30	31					1
2	3	4	5	6	7	8		7	8	9	10	11	12	13		4	5	6	7	8	9	10		2	3	4	5	6	7	8
9	10	11	12	13	14	15		14	15	16	17	18	19	20		11	12	13	14	15	16	17		9	10	11	12	13	14	15
16	17	18	19	20	21	22		21	22	23	24	25	26	27		18	19	20	21	22	23	24		16	17	18	19	20	21	22
23	24	25	26	27	28	29		28	29	30	31					25	26	27	28	29	30			23	24	25	26	27	28	29

Notes

TOWN INDEX

The following cities, towns and villages all have accommodation listed in this guide. If the place where you wish to stay is not shown, the location maps (starting on page 16) will help you to find somewhere suitable in the same area.

CHECK THE MAPS

The colour maps at the front of this guide show all the cities, towns and villages for which you will find accommodation entries. Refer to the town index to find the page on which it is listed.